Neu

Preiswert

Zuverlässig

Dieses neue Taschenbuch ist ein ganz außergewöhnliches Wörterbuch. Sein Inhalt basiert auf den zweisprachigen Wörterbüchern des Verlages Langenscheidt — des bedeutendsten Verlages auf diesem Gebiet. Es enthält über 40000 Stichwörter, gibt die Aussprache in beiden Teilen in Internationaler Lautschrift und besitzt besondere Anhänge für Eigennamen, Abkürzungen und Maße und Gewichte.

Neu und einzigartig ist die Fülle der grammatischen Informationen: Mehr als 15000 deutsche Substantive und Verben haben Angaben zur Deklination und Konjugation. Über die unregelmäßigen Verben in beiden Sprachen gibt der Hauptteil und der Anhang zuverlässig Auskunft.

Dieses Wörterbuch ist somit ein modernes und handliches Nachschlagewerk für jeden, der in seinem Beruf, beim Lernen oder Lehren mit der englischen und deutschen Sprache zu tun hat.

LANGENSCHEIDTS

DEUTSCH-ENGLISCHES
ENGLISCH-DEUTSCHES
WÖRTERBUCH

Beide Teile in einem Band

Bearbeitet und herausgegeben

von der

LANGENSCHEIDT-REDAKTION

PUBLISHED BY POCKET BOOKS NEW YORK

LANGENSCHEIDT'S
GERMAN-ENGLISH
ENGLISH-GERMAN
DICTIONARY

Two Volumes in One

Edited by
THE LANGENSCHEIDT
EDITORIAL STAFF

PUBLISHED BY POCKET BOOKS NEW YORK

POCKET BOOKS, a division of Simon & Schuster, Inc.
1230 Avenue of the Americas, New York, N.Y. 10020

This Pocket Books edition may not be sold in Germany, Switzerland or Austria.

Copyright 1952, © 1969, 1970 by Langenscheidt KG, Berlin and Munich, Germany.

Published by arrangement with Langenscheidt KG, Publishers, Berlin and Munich, Germany.

All rights reserved, including the right to reproduce this book or portions thereof in any form whatsoever. For information address Langenscheidt KG, Publishers, Berlin, Germany.

ISBN: 0-671-54107-2

First Pocket Books printing March, 1953

32 31 30 29 28 27 26 25

POCKET and colophon are registered trademarks of Simon & Schuster, Inc.

Printed in the U.S.A.

Preface

For over 100 years Langenscheidt's bilingual dictionaries have been an essential tool of the language student. For several decades Langenscheidt's German-English dictionaries have been used in all walks of life as well as in schools.

However, languages are in a constant process of change. To bring you abreast of these changes Langenscheidt has compiled this entirely new dictionary. Many new words which have entered the German and English languages in the last few years have been included in the vocabulary: e.g., Mondfähre, Mehrwertsteuer, Einwegflasche, Antirakete; lunar probe, heart transplant, non-violence.

Langenscheidt's German-English Dictionary contains another new and long desired feature for the English-speaking user: it provides clear answers to questions of declension and conjugation in over 15,000 German noun and verb entries (see pp. 7 to 8).

The phonetic transcription of the German and English headwords follows the principles laid down by the International Phonetic Association (IPA).

In addition to the vocabulary this Dictionary contains special quick-reference sections of proper names — up-to-date with names like Wankel, Mössbauer, Henze —, abbreviations and weights and measures.

Designed for the widest possible variety of uses, this Dictionary, with its more than 40,000 entries in all, will be of great value to students, teachers, and tourists as well as in home and office libraries.

Contents

Arrangement of the Dictionary and Guide for the User

1. Arrangement. Strict alphabetical order has been maintained throughout this Dictionary. The irregular plural forms of English nouns as well as the principal parts (infinitive, preterite, and past participle) of the irregular English and German verbs have also been given in their proper alphabetical order; e.g. *man - men; bite - bit - bitten; beißen - biß - gebissen.*

2. Pronunciation. Pronunciation is given in square brackets by means of the symbols of the International Phonetic Association. No transcription of compounds is given if the parts appear as separate headwords. The German suffixes as given on page 12 are not transcribed unless they are parts of catchwords.

3. Explanatory additions have been printed in italics; e.g. *abstract Inhalt kurz zs.-fassen; Abbau pulling down (of structure); abbauen pull down (structure); durchsichtig glass, etc.*: transparent.

4. Subject Labels. The field of knowledge from which a headword or some of its meanings are taken is, where possible, indicated by figurative or abbreviated labels or by other labels written out in full. A figurative or abbreviated label placed immediately after a headword applies to all translations. Any label preceding an individual translation refers to this only. In Part I, any abbreviated label with a colon applies to all following translations. An F placed before a German illustrative phrase or its English equivalent indicates that the phrase in question is colloquial usage. An F: placed before a German phrase applies to that phrase and its translation(s). Figurative labels have always, other labels sometimes, been placed between illustrative phrases and their translations.

5. Translations of similar meanings have been subdivided by **commas**, the various senses by **semicolons**.

6. American spelling has been given in the following ways: *theat|re, Am. -er, defen|ce, Am. -se; council(l)or, hono(u)r, judg(e)ment; plough, Am. plow.*

7. Grammatical References in Part I. Parts of speech (adjective, verb, etc.) have been indicated throughout. Entries have been subdivided by Arabic numerals to distinguish the various parts of speech.

I. Nouns. The inflectional forms (*genitive singular nominative plural*) follow immediately after the indication of gender No forms are given for compounds if the parts appear as separate headwords.

The horizontal stroke replaces that part of the word which remains unchanged in the inflexion: *Affe m (-n/-n); Affäre f (-/-n).*

The sign ˮ indicates that an Umlaut appears in the inflected form in question: *Blatt n (-[e]s/ˮer).*

II. Verbs. Verbs have been treated in the following ways:

a) *bändigen v/t. (ge-, h):* The past participle of this verb is formed by means of the prefix *ge-* and the auxiliary verb *haben: er hat gebändigt.*

b) *abfassen v/t. (sep., -ge-, h):* In conjugation the prefix *ab* must be separated from the primary verb *fassen: er faßt ab; er hat abgefaßt.*

c) *verderben v/i. (irr., no -ge-, sein): irr.* following the verb refers the reader to the list of irregular German verbs in the appendix (p. 573) for the principal parts of this particular verb: *es verdarb; es ist verdorben.*

d) *abfallen v/i. (irr. fallen, sep., -ge-, sein):* A reference such as *irr. fallen* indicates that the compound verb *abfallen* is conjugated exactly like the primary verb *fallen* as given in the list of irregular verbs: *er fiel ab; er ist abgefallen.*

e) *sieden v/t. and v/i. ([irr.,] ge-, h):* The square brackets indicate that *sieden* can be treated as a regular or irregular verb *er siedete or sott; er hat gesiedet or er hat gesotten.*

III. Prepositions. Prepositions governing a headword are given in both languages. The grammatical construction following a German preposition is indicated only if the preposition governs two different cases. If a German preposition applies to all translations it is given only with the first whereas its English equivalents are given after each translation: *schützen* ... protect (*gegen, vor dat.* against, from), defend (against, from), guard (against, from); shelter (from).

IV. Subdivision. Entries have been subdivided by Arabic numerals

a) to distinguish the various parts of speech: *laut 1. adj.* ...; *2. adv.* ...; *3. prp.* ...; *4. ♀ m* ...;

b) to distinguish between the transitive and intransitive meanings of a verb if these differ in their translations;

c) to show that in case of change of meaning a noun or verb may be differently inflected or conjugated: *Bau m 1.* (-[e]s/*no pl.*) ...; *2.* (-[e]s/-ten) ...; *3.* (-[e]s/-e) ...; *schwimmen v/i.* (*irr.*, ge-) *1.* (sein) ...; *2.* (h) ...

If grammatical indications come before the subdivision they refer to all translations following: *Alte* (-n/-n) *1. m* ...; *2. f* ...; *humpeln v/i.* (ge-) *1.* (sein) ...; *2.* (h) ...

8. Grammatical References in Part II. Parts of speech (adjective, verb, etc.) have been indicated only in cases of doubt. Entries have been subdivided by Arabic numerals to distinguish the various parts of speech.

a) (~*ally*) after an English adjective means that the adverb is formed by affixing ...ally: *automatic* (~*ally*) = *automatically.*

b) *irr.* following a verb refers the reader to the list of irregular English verbs in the appendix (p. 575) for the principal parts of this particular verb. A reference such as *irr. fall* indicates that the compound verb, e.g. *befall*, is conjugated exactly like the primary verb *fall.*

Symbols and Abbreviations Used in This Dictionary

1. Symbols

The swung dash or tilde (~ ♀, ~ ♀) serves as a mark of repetition within an entry. The tilde in bold type (~) represents either the complete word at the beginning of the entry or the unchanged part of that word which is followed by a vertical line (|). The simple tilde (~) represents: a) the headword immediately preceding, which itself may contain a tilde in bold type; b) in phonetic transcrip-tion, any part of the preceding transcription that remains unchanged.

When the initial letter changes from small to capital or vice versa, the usual tilde is replaced by ♀ or ♀.

Examples: *abandon* [ə'bændən], ~*ment* [~nmənt = ə'bændənmənt]; *certi*|*ficate*, ~*fication*, ~*fy*, ~*tude.* *Drama*, ~*tiker*, ♀*tisch*; *Haus*|*flur*, ~*frau*; *fassen: sich kurz* ~

□	after an English adjective means that an adverb may be formed regularly from it by adding ...ly, or by changing ...le into ...ly, or ...y into ...ily; e.g.: *rich* □ = *richly*; *acceptable* □ = *acceptably*; *happy* □ = *happily.*
F	*familiar*, familiär; *colloquial usage*, Umgangssprache.
P	*low colloquialism*, populär, Sprache des Volkes.
V	*vulgar*, vulgär.
†	*archaic*, veraltet.
✴	*rare, little used*, selten.
⊔	*scientific term*, wissenschaftlich.
♀	*botany*, Botanik.
⊕	*engineering*, Technik; *handicraft*, Handwerk.
⚒	*mining*, Bergbau.
⚔	*military term*, militärisch.
⚓	*nautical term*, Schiffahrt.
✝	*commercial term*, Handelswesen.
▦	*railway, railroad*, Eisenbahn.
✈	*aviation*, Flugwesen.
✉	*postal affairs*, Postwesen.

♪ musical term, Musik.
⚠ architecture, Architektur.
⚡ electrical engineering, Elektrotechnik.
⚖ legal term, Rechtswissenschaft.

♈ mathematics, Mathematik.
⚶ farming, Landwirtschaft.
🜍 chemistry, Chemie.
⚕ medicine, Medizin.

2. Abbreviations

a. also, auch.
abbr. abbreviation, Abkürzung.
acc. accusative (case), Akkusativ.
adj. adjective, Adjektiv.
adv. adverb, Adverb.
allg. commonly, allgemein.
Am. American English, amerikanisches Englisch.
anat. anatomy, Anatomie.
appr. approximately, etwa.
art. article, Artikel.
ast. astronomy, Astronomie.
attr. attributively, attributiv.

biol. biology, Biologie.
Brt. British English, britisches Englisch.
b.s. bad sense, in schlechtem Sinne.
bsd. especially, besonders.

cj. conjunction, Konjunktion.
co. comic(al), scherzhaft.
coll. collectively, als Sammelwort.
comp. comparative, Komparativ.
contp. contemptuously, verächtlich.

dat. dative (case), Dativ.
dem. demonstrative, Demonstrativ...

ea. one another, each other, einander.
eccl. ecclesiastical, kirchlich.
e-e, e-e, e-e a(n), eine.
e-m, e-m, e-m to a(n), einem.
e-n, e-n, e-n a(n), einen.
engS. more strictly taken, in engerem Sinne.
e-r, e-r, e-r of a(n), to a(n), einer.
e-s, e-s, e-s of a(n), eines.
esp. especially, besonders.
et., et., et. something, etwas.
etc. et cetera, and so on, und so weiter.

f feminine, weiblich.
fig. figuratively, bildlich.
frz. French, französisch.

gen. genitive (case), Genitiv.
geogr. geography, Geographie.
geol. geology, Geologie.
geom. geometry, Geometrie.
ger. gerund, Gerundium.
Ggs. antonym, Gegensatz.
gr. grammar, Grammatik.

h have, haben.
hist. history, Geschichte.
hunt. hunting, Jagdwesen.

ichth. ichthyology, Ichthyologie.
impers. impersonal, unpersönlich.
indef. indefinite, Indefinit...
inf. infinitive (mood), Infinitiv.
int. interjection, Interjektion.
interr. interrogative, Interrogativ...
iro. ironically, ironisch.
irr. irregular, unregelmäßig.

j., j., j. someone, jemand.
j-m, j-m, j-m to s.o. jemandem.
j-n, j-n, j-n someone, jemanden.
j-s, j-s, j-s someone's, jemandes.

konkr. concretely, konkret.

ling. linguistics, Linguistik.
lit. literary, nur in der Schriftsprache vorkommend.

m masculine, männlich.
m-e, m-e, m-e my, meine.
m-r of my, to my, meiner.
metall. metallurgy, Metallurgie.
meteor. meteorology, Meteorologie.
min. mineralogy, Mineralogie.
mot. motoring, Kraftfahrwesen.
mount. mountaineering, Bergsteigerei.
mst mostly, usually, meistens.
myth. mythology, Mythologie.

n neuter, sächlich.
nom. nominative (case), Nominativ.
npr. proper name, Eigenname.

od. or, oder.
opt. optics, Optik.

orn.	ornithology, Ornithologie.	sl.	slang, Slang.
o.s.	oneself, sich.	s-m, s-m, s-m to his, to one's, seinem.
			s-n, s-n, s-n his, one's, seinen.
P.,	person, Person.	s.o., s.o., s.o. someone, jemand(en).
p.	person, Person.	s-r, s-r, s-r of his, of one's, to his, to
paint.	painting, Malerei.		one's, seiner.
parl.	parliamentary term, parla-	s-s, s-s, s-s of his, of one's, seines.
	mentarischer Ausdruck.	s.th., s.th., s.th. something, etwas.
pass.	passive voice, Passiv.	subj.	subjunctive (mood), Kon-
pers.	personal, Personal...		junktiv.
pharm.	pharmacy, Pharmazie.	sup.	superlative, Superlativ.
phls.	philosophy, Philosophie.	surv.	surveying, Landvermessung.
phot.	photography, Photographie.		
phys.	physics, Physik.	tel.	telegraphy, Telegraphie.
physiol.	physiology, Physiologie.	teleph.	telephony, Fernsprechwesen.
pl.	plural, Plural.	thea.	theat|re, Am. -er, Theater.
poet.	poetry, Dichtung.	typ.	typography, Typographie.
pol.	politics, Politik.		
poss.	possessive, Possessiv...	u., u.	and, und.
p.p.	past participle, Partizip Per-	univ.	university, Hochschulwesen,
	fekt.		Studentensprache.
p.pr.	present participle, Partizip		
	Präsens.	v/aux.	auxiliary verb, Hilfsverb.
pred.	predicative, prädikativ.	vb.	verb, Verb.
pres.	present, Präsens.	vet.	veterinary medicine, Veteri-
pret.	preterit(e), Präteritum.		närmedizin.
pron.	pronoun, Pronomen.	vgl.	confer, vergleiche.
prov.	provincialism, Provinzialis-	v/i.	verb intransitive, intransiti-
	mus.		ves Verb.
prp.	preposition, Präposition.	v/refl.	verb reflexive, reflexives
psych.	psychology, Psychologie.		Verb.
		v/t.	verb transitive, transitives
refl.	reflexive, reflexiv.		Verb.
rel.	relative, Relativ...		
rhet.	rhetoric, Rhetorik.	weitS.	more widely taken, in weite-
			rem Sinne.
S., S.	thing, Sache.		
s.	see, refer to, siehe.	z.B.	for example, zum Beispiel.
schott.	Scotch, schottisch.	zo.	zoology, Zoologie.
s-e, s-e, s-e his, one's, seine.	zs.	together, zusammen.
sep.	separable, abtrennbar.	Zssg(n).	compound word(s), Zusam-
sg.	singular, Singular.		mensetzung(en).

Guide to Pronunciation
for the German-English Part

The length of vowels is indicated by [:] following the vowel symbol, the stress by ['] preceding the stressed syllable. The glottal stop [ʔ] is the forced stop between one word or syllable and a following one beginning with a vowel, as in *unentbehrlich* [unʔɛntˈbeːrliç].

A. Vowels

[a] as in French *carte*: Mann [man].

[ɑː] as in *father*: Wagen ['vɑːgən].

[e] as in *bed*: Edikt [eˈdikt].

[eː] resembles the sound in *day*: Weg [veːk].

[ə] unstressed e as in *ago*: Bitte ['bitə].

[ɛ] as in *fair*: männlich ['mɛnliç], Geld [gɛlt].

[ɛː] same sound but long: zählen ['tsɛːlən].

[i] as in *it*: Wind [vint].

[iː] as in *meet*: hier [hiːr].

[ɔ] as in *long*: Ort [ɔrt].

[ɔː] same sound but long as in *draw*: Komfort [kɔmˈfɔːr].

[o] as in *molest*: Moral [moˈrɑːl].

[oː] resembles the English sound in *go* [gou] but without the [u]: Boot [boːt].

[øː] as in French *feu*. The sound may be acquired by saying [e] through closely rounded lips: schön [ʃøːn].

[ø] same sound but short: Ökonomie [økonoˈmiː].

[œ] as in French *neuf*. The sound resembles the English vowel in *her*. Lips, however, must be well rounded as for [ɔ]: öffnen ['œfnən].

[u] as in *book*: Mutter ['mutər].

[uː] as in *boot*: Uhr [uːr].

[y] almost like the French u as in *sur*. It may be acquired by saying [i] through fairly closely rounded lips: Glück [glʏk].

[yː] same sound but long: führen ['fyːrən].

B. Diphthongs

[aɪ] as in *like*: Mai [maɪ].

[au] as in *mouse*: Maus [maus].

[ɔy] as in *boy*: Beute ['bɔytə], Läufer ['lɔyfər].

C. Consonants

[b] as in *better*: besser ['bɛsər].

[d] as in *dance*: du [duː].

[f] as in *find*: finden ['findən], Vater ['fɑːtər], Philosoph [filoˈzoːf].

[g] as in *gold*: Gold [gɔlt], Geld [gɛlt].

[ʒ] as in *measure*: Genie [ʒeˈniː], Journalist [ʒurnaˈlist].

[h] as in *house* but not aspirated: Haus [haus].

[ç] an approximation to this sound may be acquired by assuming the mouth-configuration for [i] and emitting a strong current of breath: Licht [liçt], Mönch [mœnç], lustig ['lustiç].

[x] as in Scotch *loch*. Whereas [ç] is pronounced at the front of the mouth, [x] is pronounced in the throat: Loch [lɔx].

[j] as in *year*: ja [jɑː].

[k] as in *kick*: keck [kɛk], Tag [tɑːk], Chronist [kroˈnist], Café [kaˈfeː].

[l] as in *lump*. Pronounced like English initial "clear l": lassen ['lasən].

[m] as in *mouse*: Maus [maus].

[n] as in *not*: nein [naɪn].

[ŋ] as in *sing*, *drink*: singen ['ziŋən], trinken ['triŋkən].

[p] as in *pass*: Paß [pas], Weib [vaɪp], obgleich [ɔpˈglaɪç].

[r] as in *rot*. There are two pronunciations: the frontal or lingual r and the uvular r (the latter unknown in England): *rot* [roːt].

[s] as in *miss*. Unvoiced when final, doubled, or next a voiceless consonant: *Glas* [glaːs], *Masse* ['masə], *Mast* [mast], *naß* [nas].

[z] as in *zero*. S voiced when initial in a word or syllable: *Sohn* [zoːn], *Rose* ['roːzə].

[ʃ] as in *ship*: *Schiff* [ʃif], *Charme* [ʃarm], *Spiel* [ʃpiːl], *Stein* [ʃtaɪn].

[t] as in *tea*: *Tee* [teː], *Thron* [troːn], *Stadt* [ʃtat], *Bad* [baːt], *Findling* ['fintliŋ], *Wind* [vint].

[v] as in *vast*: *Vase* ['vaːzə], *Winter* ['vintər].

[ã, ẽ, õ] are nasalized vowels. Examples: *Ensemble* [ã'sã:bəl], *Terrain* [tɛ'rɛ̃:], *Bonbon* [bõ'bõ:].

List of Suffixes

often given without phonetic transcription

-bar	[-baːr]	-ist	[-ist]
-chen	[-çən]	-keit	[-kaɪt]
-d	[-t]	-lich	[-liç]
-de	[-də]	-ling	[-liŋ]
-ei	[-aɪ]	-losigkeit	[-loːziçkaɪt]
-en	[-ən]	-nis	[-nis]
-end	[-ənt]	-sal	[-zaːl]
-er	[-ər]	-sam	[-zaːm]
-haft	[-haft]	-schaft	[-ʃaft]
-heit	[-haɪt]	-sieren	[-ziːrən]
-ie	[-iː]	-ste	[-stə]
-ieren	[-iːrən]	-tät	[-tɛːt]
-ig	[-iç]	-tum	[-tuːm]
-ik	[-ik]	-ung	[-uŋ]
-in	[-in]	-ungs-	[-uŋs-]
-isch	[-iʃ]		

Erläuterung der phonetischen Umschrift im englisch-deutschen Teil

A. Vokale und Diphthonge

[ɑː] reines langes a, wie in Vater, kam, Schwan: *far* [fɑː], *father* ['fɑːðə].

[ʌ] kommt im Deutschen nicht vor. Kurzes dunkles a, bei dem die Lippen nicht gerundet sind. Vorn und offen gebildet: *butter* ['bʌtə], *come* [kʌm], *colour* ['kʌlə], *blood* [blʌd], *flourish* ['flʌriʃ], *twopence* ['tʌpəns].

[æ] heller, ziemlich offener, nicht zu kurzer Laut. Raum zwischen Zunge und Gaumen noch größer als bei ä in Ähre: *fat* [fæt], *man* [mæn].

[ɛə] nicht zu offenes halblanges ä; im Englischen nur vor r, das als ein dem ä nachhallendes ə erscheint: *bare* [bɛə], *pair* [pɛə], *there* [ðɛə].

[ai] Bestandteile: helles, zwischen ɑː und æ liegendes a und schwächeres offenes i. Die Zunge hebt sich halbwegs zur i-Stellung: *I* [ai], *lie* [lai], *dry* [drai].

[au] Bestandteile: helles, zwischen ɑː und æ liegendes a und schwächeres offenes u: *house* [haus], *now* [nau].

[ei] halboffenes e, nach i auslautend, indem die Zunge sich halbwegs zur i-Stellung hebt: *date* [deit], *play* [plei], *obey* [ə'bei].

[e] halboffenes kurzes e, etwas geschlossener als das e in Bett: *bed* [bed], *less* [les].

[ə] flüchtiger Gleitlaut, ähnlich dem deutschen flüchtig gesprochenen e in Gelage: *about* [ə'baut], *butter* ['bʌtə], *nation* ['neiʃən], *connect* [kə'nekt].

[iː] langes i wie in lieb, Bibel, aber etwas offener einsetzend als im Deutschen; wird in Südengland doppellautig gesprochen, indem sich die Zunge allmählich zur i-Stellung hebt: *scene* [siːn], *sea* [siː], *feet* [fiːt], *ceiling* ['siːliŋ].

[i] kurzes offenes i wie in bin, mit: *big* [big], *city* ['siti].

[iə] halboffenes halblanges i mit nachhallendem ə: *here* [hiə], *hear* [hiə], *inferior* [in'fiəriə].

[ou] halboffenes langes o, in schwaches u auslautend; keine Rundung der Lippen, kein Heben der Zunge: *note* [nout], *boat* [bout], *below* [bi'lou].

[ɔː] offener langer, zwischen a und o schwebender Laut: *fall* [fɔːl], *nought* [nɔːt], *or* [ɔː], *before* [bi'fɔː].

[ɔ] offener kurzer, zwischen a und o schwebender Laut, offener als das o in Motto: *god* [gɔd], *not* [nɔt], *wash* [wɔʃ], *hobby* ['hɔbi].

[əː] im Deutschen fehlender Laut; offenes langes ö, etwa wie gedehnt gesprochenes ö in öffnen, Mörder; kein Vorstülpen oder Runden der Lippen, kein Heben der Zunge: *word* [wəːd], *girl* [gəːl], *learn* [ləːn], *murmur* ['məːmə].

[ɔi] Bestandteile: offenes o und schwächeres offenes i. Die Zunge hebt sich halbwegs zur i-Stellung: *voice* [vɔis], *boy* [bɔi], *annoy* [ə'nɔi].

[uː] langes u wie in Buch, doch ohne Lippenrundung; vielfach diphthongisch als halboffenes langes u mit nachhallendem geschlossenen u: *fool* [fuːl], *shoe* [ʃuː], *you* [juː], *rule* [ruːl], *canoe* [kə'nuː].

[uə] halboffenes halblanges u mit nachhallendem ə: *poor* [puə], *sure* [ʃuə], *allure* [ə'ljuə].

[u] flüchtiges u: *put* [put], *look* [luk], *full* [ful].

Die **Länge eines Vokals** wird durch [ː] bezeichnet, z.B. *ask* [ɑːsk], *astir* [ə'stəː].

Vereinzelt werden auch die folgenden französischen Nasallaute gebraucht: [ã] wie in frz. *blanc*, [õ] wie in frz. *bonbon* und [ɛ̃] wie in frz. *vin*.

B. Konsonanten

[r] nur vor Vokalen gesprochen. Völlig verschieden vom deutschen Zungenspitzen- oder Zäpfchen-r. Die Zungenspitze bildet mit der oberen Zahnwulst eine Enge, durch die der Ausatmungsstrom mit Stimmton hindurchgetrieben wird, ohne den Laut zu rollen. Am Ende eines Wortes wird r nur bei Bindung mit dem Anlautvokal des folgenden Wortes gesprochen: *rose* [rouz], *pride* [praid], *there is* [ðɛər'iz].

[ʒ] stimmhaftes sch, wie g in Genie, j in Journal: *azure* ['æʒə], *jazz* [dʒæz], *jeep* [dʒiːp], *large* [lɑːdʒ].

[ʃ] stimmloses sch, wie im Deutschen Schnee, rasch: *shake* [ʃeik], *washing* ['wɔʃiŋ], *lash* [læʃ].

[θ] im Deutschen nicht vorhandener stimmloser Lispellaut; durch Anlegen der Zunge an die oberen Schneidezähne hervorgebracht: *thin* [θin], *path* [pɑːθ], *method* ['meθəd].

[ð] derselbe Laut wie θ, nur stimmhaft, d.h. mit Stimmton: *there* [ðɛə], *breathe* [briːð], *father* ['fɑːðə].

[s] stimmloser Zischlaut, entsprechend dem deutschen ß in Spaß, reißen: *see* [siː], *hats* [hæts], *decide* [di'said].

[z] stimmhafter Zischlaut wie im Deutschen sausen: *zeal* [ziːl], *rise* [raiz], *horizon* [hə'raizn].

[ŋ] wird wie der deutsche Nasenlaut in fangen, singen gebildet: *ring* [riŋ], *singer* ['siŋə].

[ŋk] derselbe Laut mit nachfolgendem k wie im Deutschen senken, Wink: *ink* [iŋk], *tinker* ['tiŋkə].

[w] flüchtiges, mit Lippe an Lippe gesprochenes w, aus der Mundstellung für u: gebildet: *will* [wil], *swear* [swɛə], *queen* [kwiːn].

[f] stimmloser Lippenlaut wie im Deutschen flott, Pfeife: *fat* [fæt], *tough* [tʌf], *effort* ['efət].

[v] stimmhafter Lippenlaut wie im Deutschen Vase, Ventil: *vein* [vein], *velvet* ['velvit].

[j] flüchtiger zwischen j und i schwebender Laut: *onion* ['ʌnjən], *yes* [jes], *filial* ['filjəl].

Die Betonung der englischen Wörter wird durch das Zeichen ['] vor der zu betonenden Silbe angegeben, z.B. *onion* ['ʌnjən]. Sind zwei Silben eines Wortes mit Tonzeichen versehen, so sind beide gleichmäßig zu betonen, z.B. *unsound* ['ʌn'saund].

Um Raum zu sparen, werden die Endung -ed* und das Plural-s** der englischen Stichwörter hier im Vorwort einmal mit Lautschrift gegeben, erscheinen dann aber im Wörterverzeichnis ohne Lautschrift, sofern keine Ausnahmen vorliegen.

* [-d] nach Vokalen und stimmhaften Konsonanten; [-t] nach stimmlosen Konsonanten; [-id] nach auslautendem d und t.

** [-z] nach Vokalen und stimmhaften Konsonanten; [-s] nach stimmlosen Konsonanten.

Numerals

Cardinal Numbers

0 null *nought, zero, cipher*	51 einundfünfzig *fifty-one*
1 eins *one*	60 sechzig *sixty*
2 zwei *two*	61 einundsechzig *sixty-one*
3 drei *three*	70 siebzig *seventy*
4 vier *four*	71 einundsiebzig *seventy-one*
5 fünf *five*	80 achtzig *eighty*
6 sechs *six*	81 einundachtzig *eighty-one*
7 sieben *seven*	90 neunzig *ninety*
8 acht *eight*	91 einundneunzig *ninety-one*
9 neun *nine*	100 hundert *a or one hundred*
10 zehn *ten*	101 hundert(und)eins *a hundred*
11 elf *eleven*	*and one*
12 zwölf *twelve*	200 zweihundert *two hundred*
13 dreizehn *thirteen*	300 dreihundert *three hundred*
14 vierzehn *fourteen*	572 fünfhundert(und)zweiund-
15 fünfzehn *fifteen*	siebzig *five hundred and*
16 sechzehn *sixteen*	*seventy-two*
17 siebzehn *seventeen*	1000 tausend *a or one thousand*
18 achtzehn *eighteen*	1972 neunzehnhundertzweiund-
19 neunzehn *nineteen*	siebzig *nineteen hundred and*
20 zwanzig *twenty*	*seventy-two*
21 einundzwanzig *twenty-one*	500 000 fünfhunderttausend *five*
22 zweiundzwanzig *twenty-two*	*hundred thousand*
23 dreiundzwanzig *twenty-three*	1 000 000 eine Million *a or one*
30 dreißig *thirty*	*million*
31 einunddreißig *thirty-one*	2 000 000 zwei Millionen *two*
40 vierzig *forty*	*million*
41 einundvierzig *forty-one*	1 000 000 000 eine Milliarde *a or*
50 fünfzig *fifty*	*one milliard (Am. billion)*

Ordinal Numbers

1. erste *first (1st)*	16. sechzehnte *sixteenth*
2. zweite *second (2nd)*	17. siebzehnte *seventeenth*
3. dritte *third (3rd)*	18. achtzehnte *eighteenth*
4. vierte *fourth (4th)*	19. neunzehnte *nineteenth*
5. fünfte *fifth (5th), etc.*	20. zwanzigste *twentieth*
6. sechste *sixth*	21. einundzwanzigste *twenty-first*
7. siebente *seventh*	22. zweiundzwanzigste *twenty-*
8. achte *eighth*	*second*
9. neunte *ninth*	23. dreiundzwanzigste *twenty-*
10. zehnte *tenth*	*third*
11. elfte *eleventh*	30. dreißigste *thirtieth*
12. zwölfte *twelfth*	31. einunddreißigste *thirty-first*
13. dreizehnte *thirteenth*	40. vierzigste *fortieth*
14. vierzehnte *fourteenth*	41. einundvierzigste *forty-first*
15. fünfzehnte *fifteenth*	50. fünfzigste *fiftieth*

51. einundfünfzigste *fifty-first*
60. sechzigste *sixtieth*
61. einundsechzigste *sixty-first*
70. siebzigste *seventieth*
71. einundsiebzigste *seventy-first*
80. achtzigste *eightieth*
81. einundachtzigste *eighty-first*
90. neunzigste *ninetieth*
100. hundertste (*one*) *hundredth*
101. hundert(und)erste (*one*) *hundred and first*
200. zweihundertste *two hundredth*

300. dreihundertste *three hundredth*
572. fünfhundert(und)zweiund-siebzigste *five hundred and seventy-second*
1000. tausendste (*one*) *thousandth*
1970. neunzehnhundert(und)sieb-zigste *nineteen hundred and seventieth*
500000. fünfhunderttausendste *five hundred thousandth*
1000000. millionste (*one*) *millionth*
2000000. zweimillionste *two millionth*

Fractional Numbers and other Numerical Values

$1/_2$ halb *one* or *a half*
$1/_2$ eine halbe Meile *half a mile*
$1^1/_2$ anderthalb *or* eineinhalb *one and a half*
$2^1/_2$ zweieinhalb *two and a half*
$1/_3$ ein Drittel *one* or *a third*
$2/_3$ zwei Drittel *two thirds*
$1/_4$ ein Viertel *one fourth, one* or *a quarter*
$3/_4$ drei Viertel *three fourths, three quarters*
$1^1/_4$ ein und eine viertel Stunde *one hour and a quarter*
$1/_5$ ein Fünftel *one* or *a fifth*
$3^4/_5$ drei vier Fünftel *three and four fifths*
0,4 null Komma vier *point four* (.4)
2,5 zwei Komma fünf *two point five* (2.5)

einfach *single*
  zweifach *double, twofold*
  dreifach *threefold, treble, triple*
  vierfach *fourfold, quadruple*
  fünffach *fivefold, quintuple*

einmal *once*
  zweimal *twice*
  drei-, vier-, fünfmal *three* or *four* or *five times*
  zweimal soviel(e) *twice as much* or *many*

erstens, zweitens, drittens *first(ly), secondly, thirdly; in the first* or *second* or *third place*

$2 \times 3 = 6$ zwei mal drei ist sechs, zwei multipliziert mit drei ist sechs *twice three are* or *make six, two multiplied by three are* or *make six*

$7 + 8 = 15$ sieben plus acht ist fünf-zehn *seven plus eight are fifteen*

$10 - 3 = 7$ zehn minus drei ist sieben *ten minus three are seven*

$20 : 5 = 4$ zwanzig (dividiert) durch fünf ist vier *twenty divided by five make four*

PART I

GERMAN-ENGLISH DICTIONARY

A

'**Aal** *ichth.* [ɑ:l] *m* (-[e]s/-e) eel; '**~-glatt** *adj.* (as) slippery as an eel.

Aas [ɑ:s] *n* 1. (-es/~-e) carrion, carcass; 2. *fig.* (-es/Äser) beast; '**~geier** *orn. m* vulture.

ab [ap] 1. *prp.* (*dat.*): ~ *Brüssel* from Brussels onwards; ~ *Fabrik, Lager etc.* ✝ ex works, warehouse, *etc.*; 2. *prp.* (*dat.*, F *acc.*): ~ *erstem or ersten März* from March 1st, on and after March 1st; 3. ✝ *prp.* (*gen.*) less; ~ *Unkosten* less charges; 4. *adv. time: von jetzt* ~ from now on, in future; ~ *und zu* from time to time, now and then; *von da* ~ from that time forward; *space: thea.* exit, *pl.* exeunt; *von da* ~ from there (on).

abänder|n ['ap?-] *v/t.* (*sep.*, -ge-, h) alter, modify; *parl.* amend; '**~ung** *f* alteration, modification; *parl.* amendment (*to bill, etc.*); '**~ungs-antrag** *parl. m* amendment.

abarbeiten ['ap?-] *v/t.* (*sep.*, -ge-, h) work off (*debt*); *sich* ~ drudge, toil.

Abart ['ap?-] *f* variety.

'**Abbau** *m* 1. (-[e]s/*no pl.*) pulling down, demolition (*of structure*); dismantling (*of machine, etc.*); dismissal, discharge (*of personnel*); reduction (*of staff, prices, etc.*); cut (*of prices, etc.*); 2. ⚒ (-[e]s/-e) working, exploitation; '**2en** *v/t.* (*sep.*, -ge-, h) pull or take down, demolish (*structure*); dismantle (*machine, etc.*); dismiss, discharge (*personnel*); reduce (*staff, prices, etc.*); cut (*prices, etc.*); ⚒ work, exploit.

'**ab|beißen** *v/t.* (*irr.* beißen, *sep.*, -ge-, h) bite off; '**~bekommen** *v/t.* (*irr.* kommen, *sep.*, no -ge-, h) get off; *s-n Teil* or *et.* ~ get one's share; *et.* ~ be hurt, get hurt.

abberuf|en *v/t.* (*irr.* rufen, *sep.*, no -ge-, h) recall; '**2ung** *f* recall.

'**ab|bestellen** *v/t.* (*sep.*, no -ge-, h) countermand, cancel one's order for (*goods, etc.*); cancel one's subscription to, discontinue (*newspaper, etc.*); '**~biegen** *v/i.* (*irr.* biegen, *sep.*, -ge-, sein) p. turn off; *road:* turn off, bend; *nach rechts* (*links*) ~ turn right (left); *von e-r Straße* ~ turn off a road.

'**Abbild** *n* likeness; image; **2en** ['~dən] *v/t.* (*sep.*, -ge-, h) figure, represent; *sie ist auf der ersten Seite abgebildet* her picture is on the front page; **~ung** ['~dun] *f* picture, illustration.

'**abbinden** *v/t.* (*irr.* binden, *sep.*,

-ge-, h) untie, unbind, remove; ⚕ ligate, tie up.

'**Abbitte** *f* apology; ~ *leisten* or *tun* make one's apology (*bei j-m wegen et.* to s.o. for s.th.); '**2n** *v/t.* (*irr.* bitten, *sep.*, -ge-, h): *j-m et.* ~ apologize to s.o. for s.th.

'**ab|blasen** *v/t.* (*irr.* blasen, *sep.*, -ge-, h) blow off (*dust, etc.*); call off (*strike, etc.*), cancel; ⚔ break off (*attack*); '**~blättern** *v/i.* (*sep.*, -ge-, sein) paint, *etc.*: scale, peel (off); ⚘ *skin*: desquamate; ⚘ shed the leaves; '**~blenden** (*sep.*, -ge-, h) 1. *v/t.* screen (*light*); *mot.* dim, dip (*headlights*); 2. *v/i. mot.* dim or dip the headlights; *phot.* stop down; '**~blitzen** F *v/i.* (*sep.*, -ge-, sein) meet with a rebuff; ~ *lassen* snub; '**~brausen** (*sep.*, -ge-) 1. *v/refl.* (h) have a shower(-bath), douche; 2. F *v/i.* (sein) rush off; '**~brechen** *v/i. brechen, sep.*, -ge-) 1. *v/t.* (h) break off (*a. fig.*); pull down, demolish (*building, etc.*); strike (*tent*); *fig.* stop; *das Lager* ~ break up camp, strike tents; 2. *v/i.* (sein) break off; 3. *fig. v/i.* (h) stop; '**~bremsen** *v/t. and v/i.* (*sep.*, -ge-, h) slow down; brake; '**~brennen** *v/i. brennen, sep.*, -ge-) 1. *v/t.* (h) burn down (*building, etc.*); let or set off (*firework*); 2. *v/i.* (sein) burn away or down; *s. abgebrannt*; '**~bringen** *v/t.* (*irr.* bringen, *sep.*, -ge-, h) get off; *j-n* ~ *von* argue s.o. out of; dissuade s.o. from; '**~bröckeln** *v/i.* (*sep.*, -ge-, sein) crumble (*a.* ✝).

'**Abbruch** *m* pulling down, demolition (*of building, etc.*); rupture (*of relations*); breaking off (*of negotiations, etc.*); *fig.* damage, injury; *j-m* ~ *tun* damage s.o.

'**ab|brühen** *v/t.* (*sep.*, -ge-, h) scald; *s. abgebrüht*; '**~bürsten** *v/t.* (*sep.*, -ge-, h) brush off (*dirt, etc.*); brush (*coat, etc.*); '**~büßen** *v/t.* (*sep.*, -ge-, h) expiate, atone for (*sin, etc.*); serve (*sentence*). [bet.]

Abc [ɑ:be'tse:] *n* (-/-) ABC, alpha-]

'**abdank|en** *v/i.* (*sep.*, -ge-, h) resign; *ruler:* abdicate; '**2ung** *f* (-/-en) resignation; abdication.

'**ab|decken** *v/t.* (*sep.*, -ge-, h) uncover; untile (*roof*); unroof (*building*); clear (*table*); cover; '**~dichten** *v/t.* (*sep.*, -ge-, h) make tight; seal up (*window, etc.*); ⊕ pack (*gland, etc.*); '**~dienen** *v/t.* (*sep.*, -ge-, h): *s-e Zeit* ~ ⚔ serve one's time; '**~drängen** *v/t.* (*sep.*, -ge-, h) push aside; '**~drehen** (*sep.*, -ge-, h)

1. v/t. twist off (wire); turn off
(water, gas, etc.); ✂ switch off
(light); 2. ⏚, ✗ v/i. change one's
course; '**drosseln** mot. v/t. (sep.,
-ge-, h) throttle.

'**Abdruck** m (-[e]s/⁓e) impression,
print, mark; cast; '⁓**en** v/t. (sep.,
-ge-, h) print; publish (article).

'**abdrücken** (sep., -ge-, h) 1. v/t.
fire (gun, etc.); F hug or squeeze
affectionately; sich ⁓ leave an impression or a mark; 2. v/i. pull the
trigger.

Abend ['ɑːbənt] m (-s/-e) evening;
am ⁓ in the evening, at night; heute
abend tonight; morgen (gestern)
abend tomorrow (last) night; s.
essen; '⁓**anzug** m evening dress;
'⁓**blatt** n evening paper; '⁓**brot** n
supper, dinner; '⁓**dämmerung** f
(evening) twilight, dusk; '⁓**essen** n
s. Abendbrot; '⁓**gesellschaft** f
evening party; '⁓**kasse** thea. f box-
office; '⁓**kleid** n evening dress or
gown; '⁓**land** n (-[e]s/no pl.) the
Occident; 2**ländisch** adj. ['⁓lɛndiʃ]
western, occidental; '⁓**mahl** eccl. n
(-[e]s/-e) the (Holy) Communion,
the Lord's Supper; '⁓**rot** n evening
or sunset glow.   [evening.\

abends adv. ['ɑːbənts] in the
'**Abend**|**schule** f evening school,
night-school; '⁓**sonne** f setting
sun; '⁓**toilette** f evening dress;
'⁓**wind** m evening breeze; '⁓**zei**-
tung f evening paper.

Abenteu|**er** ['ɑːbəntɔʏər] n (-s/-)
adventure; 2**erlich** adj. adventur-
ous; fig.: strange; wild, fantastic;
'⁓**rer** ['⁓rər] m (-s/-) adventurer.

aber ['ɑːbər] 1. adv. again; Tausende
und ⁓ Tausende thousands upon
thousands; 2. cj. but; oder ⁓ otherwise, (or) else; 3. int.: ⁓! now
then!; ⁓, ⁓! come, come!; ⁓ nein!
no!, on the contrary!; 4. 2 n (-s/-)
but.

'**Aber**|**glaube** m superstition; 2-
gläubisch adj. ['⁓ɡlɔʏbiʃ] super-
stitious.

aberkenn|**en** ['ap⁹-] v/t. (irr. ken-
nen, sep., no -ge-, h): j-m et. ⁓ deprive s.o. of s.th. (a. ⟨⟩); dispossess
s.o. of s.th.; '2**ung** f (-/-en) deprivation (a. ⟨⟩); dispossession.

aber|**malig** adj. ['ɑːbərmɑːliç] re-
peated; ⁓**mals** adv. ['⁓s] again,
once more.

ab|**ernten** ['ap⁹-] v/t. (sep., -ge-, h)
reap, harvest; '⁓**essen** ['ap⁹-] (irr.
essen, sep., -ge-, h) 1. v/t. clear
(plate); 2. v/i. finish eating; '⁓**fah**-
ren (irr. fahren, sep., -ge-) 1. v/i.
(sein) leave (nach for), depart (for),
start (for); set out or off (for);
2. v/t. (h) carry or cart away (load).

'**Abfahrt** f departure (nach for),
start (for); setting out or off (for);
skiing: downhill run; '⁓**sbahnsteig**

m departure platform; '⁓**slauf** m
skiing: downhill race; '⁓**ssignal** n
starting-signal; '⁓**szeit** f time of
departure; ⏚ a. time of sailing.

'**Abfall** m defection (von from), falling away (from); esp. pol. secession
(from); eccl. apostasy (from); often
Abfälle pl. waste, refuse, rubbish,
Am. a. garbage; ⊕ clippings pl.,
shavings pl.; at butcher's: offal;
'⁓**eimer** m dust-bin, Am. ash can;
'2**en** v/i. (irr. fallen, sep., -ge-, sein)
leaves, etc.: fall (off); ground, etc.:
slope (down), fig. fall away (von
from); esp. pol. secede (from); eccl.
apostatize (from); ⁓ gegen come off
badly by comparison with, be inferior to; '⁓**erzeugnis** n waste product; by-product.

'**abfällig** adj. judgement, etc.: adverse, unfavo(u)rable; remark: dis-
paraging, depreciatory.

'**Abfallprodukt** n by-product;
waste product.

'**ab**|**fangen** v/t. (irr. fangen, sep.,
-ge-, h) catch; snatch (ball, etc.);
intercept (letter, etc.); ⏚, ✗ prop;
✗ check (attack); ✗ flatten out;
mot., ✗ right; '⁓**färben** v/i. (sep.,
-ge-, h): der Pullover färbt ab the
colo(u)r of the pull-over runs (auf
acc. on); ⁓ auf (acc.) influence, affect.

'**abfass**|**en** v/t. (sep., -ge-, h) com-
pose, write, pen; catch (thief, etc.);
'2**ung** f composition; wording.

'**ab**|**faulen** v/i. (sep., -ge-, sein) rot
off; '⁓**fegen** v/t. (sep., -ge-, h)
sweep off; '⁓**feilen** v/t. (sep., -ge-,
h) file off.

abfertig|**en** ['apfɛrtigən] v/t. (sep.,
-ge-, h) dispatch (a. ⟨⟩); customs:
clear; serve, attend to (customer);
j-n kurz ⁓ snub s.o.; '2**ung** f (-/-en)
dispatch; customs: clearance; schrof-
fe ⁓ snub.   [(off), discharge.\

'**abfeuern** v/t. (sep., -ge-, h) fire\

'**abfind**|**en** v/t. (irr. finden, sep.,
-ge-, h) satisfy, pay off (creditor);
compensate; sich mit et. ⁓ resign
o.s. to s.th.; put up with s.th.;
'2**ung** f (-/-en) settlement; satisfaction; compensation; '2**ung(ssum-
me)** f indemnity; compensation.

'**ab**|**flachen** v/t. and v/refl. (sep.,
-ge-, h) flatten; '⁓**flauen** v/i. (sep.,
-ge-, sein) wind, etc.: abate; interest,
etc.: flag; ✝ business: slacken; '⁓-
fliegen v/i. (irr. fliegen, sep., -ge-,
sein) leave by plane; ✗ take off,
start; '⁓**fließen** v/i. (irr. fließen,
sep., -ge-, sein) drain or flow off or
away.   [parture.\

'**Abflug** ✗ m take-off, start, de-\

'**Abfluß** m flowing or draining off
or away; discharge (a. ⚕); drain
(a. fig.); sink; outlet (of lake, etc.).

'**abfordern** v/t. (sep., -ge-, h): j-m
et. ⁓ demand s.th. of or from s.o.

Abfuhr ['apfuːr] *f* (-/-en) removal; *fig.* rebuff.

'abführ|en (*sep.*, -ge-, *h*) **1.** *v/t.* lead off *or* away; march (*prisoner*) off; pay over (*money*) (*an acc.* to); **2.** *v/i.* purge (the bowels), loosen the bowels; **'~end** *adj.* purgative, aperient, laxative; **'2mittel** *n* purgative, aperient, laxative.

'abfüllen *v/t.* (*sep.*, -ge-, *h*) decant; *in Flaschen* ~ bottle; *Bier in Fässer* ~ rack casks with beer.

'Abgabe *f sports:* pass; casting (*of one's vote*); sale (*of shares, etc.*); *mst* ~ *n pl.* taxes *pl.*; rates *pl.*, *Am.* local taxes *pl.*; duties *pl.*; **'2frei** *adj.* tax-free; duty-free; **'2npflichtig** *adj.* taxable; dutiable; liable to tax *or* duty.

'Abgang *m* departure; start; *thea.* exit (*a. fig.*); retirement (*from a job*); loss, wastage; deficiency (*in weight, etc.*); **3°** discharge; **3°** miscarriage; *nach* ~ *von der Schule* after leaving school.

'abgängig *adj.* missing.

'Abgangszeugnis *n* (school-)leaving certificate, *Am. a.* diploma.

'Abgas *n* waste gas; *esp. mot.* exhaust gas.   [toil-worn, worn-out.]

abgearbeitet *adj.* ['apgəˈʔarbaɪtət]

'abgeben *v/t.* (*irr. geben, sep.,* -ge-, *h*) leave (*bei, an dat.* at); hand in (*paper, etc.*); deposit, leave (*luggage*); cast (*one's vote*); *sports:* pass (*ball, etc.*); sell, dispose of (*goods*); give off (*heat, etc.*); *e-e Erklärung* ~ make a statement; *s-e Meinung* ~ express one's opinion (*über acc.* on); *j-m et.* ~ *von* et. give s.o. some of s.th.; *e-n guten Gelehrten* ~ make a good scholar; *sich* ~ *mit* occupy o.s. with *s.th.*; *sie gibt sich gern mit Kindern ab* she loves to be among children.

'abge|brannt *adj.* burnt down; *F fig.* hard up, *sl.* broke; **~brüht** *fig. adj.* ['~bryːt] hardened, callous; **~droschen** *adj.* trite, hackneyed; **~feimt** *adj.* ['~faɪmt] cunning, crafty; **~griffen** *adj.* worn; *book:* well-thumbed; **~härtet** *adj.* ['~hertet] hardened (*gegen* to), inured (to); **~härmt** *adj.* ['~hermt] careworn.

'abgehen (*irr. gehen, sep.,* -ge-) **1.** *v/i.* (sein) go off *or* away; leave, start, depart; *letter, etc.:* be dispatched; *post:* go; *thea.* make one's exit; *side-road:* branch off; *goods:* sell; *button, etc.:* come off; *stain, etc.:* come out; **3°** be discharged; (*von e-m Amt*) ~ give up a post; retire; *von der Schule* ~ leave school; ~ *von* digress from (*main subject*); deviate from (*rule*); alter, change (*one's opinion*); relinquish (*plan, etc.*); *diese Eigenschaft geht ihm ab* he lacks this quality; *gut* ~ end well, pass off well; *hiervon geht or gehen*

... *ab* ✝ less, minus; **2.** *v/t.* (*h*) measure by steps; patrol.

abge|hetzt *adj.* ['apgəhetst] harassed; exhausted; run down; breathless; **~kartet** *F adj.* ['~kartət]: *~e Sache* prearranged affair, put-up job; **'~legen** *adj.* remote, distant; secluded; out-of-the-way; **~macht** *adj.* ['~maxt]: *~l* it's a bargain *or* deal!; **~magert** *adj.* ['~maːgərt] emaciated; **~neigt** *adj.* ['~naɪkt] disinclined (*dat.* for *s.th.*; *zu tun* to do), averse (to; *from* doing), unwilling (*zu tun* to do); **~nutzt** *adj.* ['~nutst] worn-out.

Abgeordnete ['apgəˈʔɔrdnətə] *m, f* (-*n*/-*n*) deputy, delegate; *in Germany:* member of the Bundestag *or* Landtag; *Brt.* Member of Parliament, *Am.* Representative.

'abgerissen *fig. adj.* ragged; shabby; *style, speech:* abrupt, broken.

'Abgesandte *m, f* (-*n*/-*n*) envoy; emissary; ambassador.

'abgeschieden *fig. adj.* isolated, secluded, retired; **'2heit** *f* (-/-en) seclusion; retirement.

'abgeschlossen *adj.* *fig.:* self-contained; *training, etc.:* complete.

abgeschmackt *adj.* ['apgəʃmakt] tasteless; tactless; **'2heit** *f* (-/-en) tastelessness; tactlessness.

'abgesehen *adj.:* ~ *von* apart from, *Am. a.* aside from.

abge|spannt *fig. adj.* ['apgəʃpant] exhausted, tired, run down; **'~standen** *adj.* stale, flat; **'~storben** *adj.* numb; dead; **'~stumpft** *adj.* ['~ʃtumpft] blunt(ed); *fig.* indifferent (*gegen* to); **'~tragen** *adj.* worn-out; threadbare, shabby.

'abgewöhnen *v/t.* (*sep.*, -ge-, *h*): *j-m et.* ~ break *or* cure s.o. of s.th.; *sich das Rauchen* ~ give up smoking.

abgezehrt *adj.* ['apgətseːrt] emaciated, wasted.

'abgießen *v/t.* (*irr. gießen, sep.,* -ge-, *h*) pour off; **3°** decant; **⊕** cast.

'Abglanz *m* reflection (*a. fig.*).

'abgleiten *v/i.* (*irr. gleiten, sep.,* -ge-, *sein*) slip off; slide off; glide.

'Abgott *m* idol.   [off.]

abgöttisch *adv.* ['apgœtiʃ]: *j-n* ~ *lieben* idolize *or* worship s.o.; dote (up)on s.o.

'ab|grasen *v/t.* (*sep.*, -ge-, *h*) graze; *fig.* scour; **'~grenzen** *v/t.* (*sep.*, -ge-, *h*) mark off, delimit; demarcate (*a. fig.*); *fig.* define.

'Abgrund *m* abyss; precipice; chasm, gulf; *am Rande des* ~*s* on the brink of disaster.

'Abguß *m* cast.

'ab|hacken *v/t.* (*sep.*, -ge-, *h*) chop *or* cut off; **'~haken** *fig. v/t.* (*sep.*, -ge-, *h*) tick *or* check off; **'~halten** *v/t.* (*irr. halten, sep.,* -ge-, *h*) hold (*meeting, examination, etc.*); keep out (*rain*); *j-n von der Arbeit* ~ keep

s.o. from his work; *j-n davon* ~
et. *zu tun* keep *or* restrain s.o. from
doing s.th.; et. *von j-m* ~ keep s.th.
away from s.o.; '~**handeln** *v/t.*
(*sep., -ge-, h*) discuss, treat; *j-m*
et. ~ bargain s.th. out of s.o.

abhanden *adv.* [ap'handən]: ~ *kommen* get lost.

'**Abhandlung** *f* treatise (*über acc.*
[up]on), dissertation ([up]on, concerning); essay.

'**Abhang** *m* slope, incline; declivity.

'**abhängen** 1. *v/t.* (*sep., -ge-, h*) take
down (*picture, etc.*); 🐎 uncouple;
2. *v/i.* (*irr. hängen, sep., -ge-, h*):
~ *von* depend (up)on.

abhängig *adj.* ['aphɛniç]: ~ *von* dependent (up)on; '**2keit** *f* (-/*no pl.*)
dependence (*von* [up]on).

ab|härmen ['aphɛrmən] *v/refl.*
(*sep., -ge-, h*) pine away (*über acc.*
at); '~**härten** *v/t.* (*sep., -ge-, h*)
harden (*gegen* to), inure (to); *sich*
~ harden o.s. (*gegen* to), inure o.s.
(to); '~**hauen** (*irr. hauen, sep.,*
-ge-*) 1. *v/t.* (*h*) cut *or* chop off;
2. F *v/i.* (*sein*) be off; *hau ab! sl.*
beat it!, scram!; '~**häuten** *v/t.*
(*sep., -ge-, h*) skin, flay; '~**heben**
(*irr. heben, sep., -ge-, h*) 1. *v/t.* lift
or take off; *teleph.* lift (*receiver*);
(with)draw (*money*); *sich* ~ *von*
stand out against; *fig. a.* contrast
with; 2. *v/i.* cut (the cards); *teleph.*
lift the receiver; '~**heilen** *v/i.* (*sep.,*
-ge-*, sein*) heal (up); '~**helfen** *v/i.*
(*irr. helfen, sep., -ge-, h*): *e-m Übel*
~ cure *or* redress an evil; *dem ist
nicht abzuhelfen* there is nothing to
be done about it; '~**hetzen** *v/refl.*
(*sep., -ge-, h*) tire o.s. out; rush,
hurry.

'**Abhilfe** *f* remedy, redress, relief;
~ *schaffen* take remedial measures.

'**abhobeln** *v/t.* (*sep., -ge-, h*) plane
(away, down).

abhold *adj.* ['aphɔlt] averse (*dat.*
to *s.th.*); ill-disposed (towards
s.o.).

'**ab|holen** *v/t.* (*sep., -ge-, h*) fetch;
call for, come for; *j-n von der Bahn*
~ go to meet s.o. at the station;
'~**holzen** *v/t.* (*sep., -ge-, h*) fell,
cut down (*trees*); deforest; '~**horchen** 🐎 *v/t.* (*sep., -ge-, h*) auscultate, sound; '~**hören** *v/t.* (*sep.,*
-ge-*, h*) listen in to, intercept (*telephone conversation*); *e-n Schüler* ~
hear a pupil's lesson.

Abitur [abi'tuːr] *n* (-s/🐎-e) school-
leaving examination (*qualifying for
university entrance*).

'**ab|jagen** *v/t.* (*sep., -ge-, h*): *j-m* et.
~ recover s.th. from s.o.; '~**kanzeln**
F *v/t.* (*sep., -ge-, h*) reprimand, F
tell *s.o.* off; '~**kaufen** *v/t.* (*sep.,*
-ge-*, h*): *j-m* et. ~ buy *or* purchase
s.th. from s.o.

Abkehr *fig.* ['apkeːr] *f* (-/*no pl.*)
estrangement (*von* from); withdrawal (from); '**2en** *v/t.* (*sep., -ge-,*
h) sweep off; *sich* ~ *von* turn away
from; *fig.*: take no further interest
in; become estranged from; withdraw from.

'**ab|klingen** *v/i.* (*irr. klingen, sep.,*
-ge-*, sein*) fade away; *pain, etc.*: die
down; *pain, illness*: ease off; '~**klopfen** (*sep., -ge-, h*) 1. *v/t.* knock (*dust,*
etc.) off; dust (*coat, etc.*); 🐎 sound,
percuss; 2. *v/i. conductor*: stop the
orchestra; '~**knicken** *v/t.* (*sep.,*
-ge-*, h*) snap *or* break off; bend
off; '~**knöpfen** *v/t.* (*sep., -ge-, h*)
unbutton; F *j-m Geld* ~ get money
out of s.o.; '~**kochen** (*sep., -ge-, h*)
1. *v/t.* boil; scald (*milk*); 2. *v/i.*
cook in the open air (*a.* 🗙); '~**kommandieren** 🗙 *v/t.* (*sep., no -ge-, h*)
detach, detail; second (*officer*).

Abkomme ['apkɔmə] *m* (-n/-n)
descendant.

'**abkommen** 1. *v/i.* (*irr. kommen,*
sep., -ge-, sein) come away, get
away *or* off; *von e-r Ansicht* ~ change
one's opinion; *von e-m Thema* ~
digress from a topic; *vom Wege* ~
lose one's way; 2. 💲 *n* (-s/-) agreement.

abkömm|lich *adj.* ['apkœmliç] dis-
pensable; available; *er ist nicht* ~
he cannot be spared; **2ling** ['~liŋ]
m (-s/-e) descendant.

'**ab|koppeln** *v/t.* (*sep., -ge-, h*) un-
couple; '~**kratzen** (*sep., -ge-*) 1. *v/t.*
(*h*) scrape off; 2. *sl. v/i.* (*sein*) kick
the bucket; '~**kühlen** *v/t.* (*sep.,*
-ge-*, h*) cool; refrigerate; *sich* ~ cool
down (*a. fig.*).

Abkunft ['apkunft] *f* (-/🐎-e) descent; origin; extraction; birth.

'**abkürz|en** *v/t.* (*sep., -ge-, h*)
shorten; abbreviate (*word, story,*
etc.); *den Weg* ~ take a short cut;
'**2ung** *f* (-/-en) abridgement; abbreviation; short cut.

'**abladen** *v/t.* (*irr. laden, sep., -ge-, h*)
unload; dump (*rubbish, etc.*).

'**Ablage** *f* place of deposit; filing
tray; files *pl.*; cloak-room.

'**ab|lagern** (*sep., -ge-*) 1. *v/t.* (*h*)
season (*wood, wine*); age (*wine*);
sich ~ settle; be deposited; 2. *v/i.*
(*sein*) *wood, wine*: season; *wine*: age;
'~**lassen** (*irr. lassen, sep., -ge-, h*)
1. *v/t.* let (*liquid*) run off; let
off (*steam*); drain (*pond, etc.*);
2. *v/i.* leave off (*von* et. [*doing*]
s.th.).

'**Ablauf** *m* running off; outlet, drain;
sports: start; *fig.* expiration, end;
nach ~ *von* at the end of; '**2en** (*irr.*
laufen, sep., -ge-) 1. *v/i.* (*sein*) run
off; drain off; *period of time*: expire; ✝ *bill of exchange*: fall due;
clock, etc.: run down; *thread, film*:
unwind; *spool*: run out; *gut* ~ end

well; 2. *v/t.* (*h*) wear out (*shoes*); scour (*region, etc.*); *sich die Beine ~* run one's legs off; *s.* **Rang.**

'Ableben *n* (*-s/ no pl.*) death, decease (*esp.* 🐾, 🐾); 🐾 demise.

'ab|lecken *v/t.* (*sep., -ge-, h*) lick (off); **'~legen** (*sep., -ge-, h*) **1.** *v/t.* take off (*garments*); leave off (*garments*); give up, break o.s. of (*habit*); file (*documents, letters, etc.*); make (*confession, vow*); take (*oath, examination*); *Zeugnis ~* bear witness (*für* to; *von* of); *s.* **Rechenschaft;** **2.** *v/i.* take off one's (hat and) coat.

'Ableger ♀ *m* (*-s/-*) layer, shoot.

'ablehn|en (*sep., -ge-, h*) **1.** *v/t.* decline, refuse; reject (*doctrine, candidate, etc.*); turn down (*proposal, etc.*); **2.** *v/i.* decline; *dankend ~* decline with thanks; **'~end** *adj.* negative; **'2ung** *f* (*-/-en*) refusal; rejection.

ableit|en *v/t.* (*sep., -ge-, h*) divert (*river, etc.*); drain off or away (*water, etc.*); *gr.,* ♀, *fig.* derive (*aus, von* from); *fig.* infer (from); **'2ung** *f* diversion; drainage; *gr.,* ♀ derivation (*a. fig.*).

'ab|lenken *v/t.* (*sep., -ge-, h*) turn aside; divert (*suspicion, etc.*) (*von* from); *phys., etc.*: deflect (*rays, etc.*); *j-n von der Arbeit ~* distract s.o. from his work; **'~lesen** *v/t.* (*irr. lesen, sep., -ge-, h*) read (*speech, etc.*); read (off) (*values from instruments*); **'~leugnen** *v/t.* (*sep., -ge-, h*) deny, disavow, disown.

'abliefer|n *v/t.* (*sep., -ge-, h*) deliver; hand over; surrender; **'2ung** *f* delivery.

'ablösch|en *v/t.* (*sep., -ge-, h*) blot (up) (*ink*); ⊕ temper (*steel*).

'ablös|en *v/t.* (*sep., -ge-, h*) detach; take off; ✂, *etc.*: relieve; supersede (*predecessor in office*); discharge (*debt*); redeem (*obligation*); *sich ~* come off; *fig.* alternate, take turns; **'2ung** *f* detachment; ✂, *etc.*: relief; *fig.* supersession; discharge; redemption.

'abmach|en *v/t.* (*sep., -ge-, h*) remove, detach; *fig.* settle, arrange (*business, etc.*); agree (up)on (*price, etc.*); **'2ung** *f* (*-/-en*) arrangement; settlement; agreement.

'abmager|n *v/i.* (*sep., -ge-, sein*) lose flesh; grow lean or thin; **'2ung** *f* (*-/-en*) emaciation.

'ab|mähen *v/t.* (*sep., -ge-, h*) mow (off); **'~malen** *v/t.* (*sep., -ge-, h*) copy.

'Abmarsch *m* start; ✂ marching off; **'2ieren** *v/i.* (*sep., no -ge-, sein*) start; ✂ march off.

'abmeld|en *v/t.* (*sep., -ge-, h*): *j-n von der Schule ~* give notice of the withdrawal of a pupil (from school); *sich polizeilich ~* give notice to the police of one's departure (from town, *etc.*); **'2ung** *f* notice of withdrawal; notice of departure.

'abmess|en *v/t.* (*irr. messen, sep., -ge-, h*) measure; **'2ung** *f* (*-/-en*) measurement.

'ab|montieren *v/t.* (*sep., no -ge-, h*) disassemble; dismantle, strip (*machinery*); remove (*tyre, etc.*); **'~mühen** *v/refl.* (*sep., -ge-, h*) drudge, toil; **'~nagen** *v/t.* (*sep., -ge-, h*) gnaw off; pick (*bone*).

Abnahme ['apnɑːmə] *f* (*-/~-n*) taking off; removal; 🐾 amputation; ✝ taking delivery; ✝ purchase; ✝ sale; ⊕ acceptance (*of machine, etc.*); administering (*of oath*); decrease, diminution; loss (*of weight*).

'abnehm|en (*irr. nehmen, sep., -ge-, h*) **1.** *v/t.* take off; remove; *teleph.* lift (*receiver*); 🐾 amputate; gather (*fruit*); ⊕ accept (*machine, etc.*); *j-m et. ~* take s.th. from s.o.; ✝ *a.* buy or purchase s.th. from s.o.; *j-m zuviel ~* overcharge s.o.; **2.** *v/i.* decrease, diminish; decline; lose weight; *moon:* wane; *storm:* abate; *days:* grow shorter; **'2er** ✝ *m* (*-s/-*) buyer; customer; consumer.

'Abneigung *f* aversion (*gegen* to); disinclination (to); dislike (to, of, for); antipathy (against, to).

abnorm *adj.* [ap'nɔrm] abnormal; anomalous; exceptional; **2i'tät** *f* (*-/-en*) abnormality; anomaly.

'abnötigen *v/t.* (*sep., -ge-, h*): *j-m et. ~* extort s.th. from s.o.

'ab|nutzen *v/t. and v/refl.* (*sep., -ge-, h*), **'~nützen** *v/t. and v/refl.* (*sep., -ge-, h*) wear out; **'2nutzung** *f*, **'2nützung** *f* (*-/-en*) wear (and tear).

Abonn|ement [abɔn(ə)'mãː] *n* (*-s/-s*) subscription (*auf acc.* to); **~ent** [~'nɛnt] *m* (*-en/-en*) subscriber; **2ieren** [~'niːrən] *v/t.* (*no -ge-, h*) subscribe to (*newspaper*); **2iert** *adj.* [~'niːrt]: *~ sein auf* (*acc.*) take in (*newspaper, etc.*).

abordn|en ['apʔ-] *v/t.* (*sep., -ge-, h*) depute, delegate, *Am. a.* deputize; **'2ung** *f* delegation, deputation.

Abort [a'bɔrt] *m* (*-[e]s/-e*) lavatory, toilet.

'ab|passen *v/t.* (*sep., -ge-, h*) fit, adjust; watch for, wait for (*s.o., opportunity*); waylay *s.o.*; **'~pflükken** *v/t.* (*sep., -ge-, h*) pick, pluck (off), gather; **'~plagen** *v/refl.* (*sep., -ge-, h*) toil; **'~platzen** *v/i.* (*sep., -ge-, sein*) burst off; fly off; **'~prallen** *v/i.* (*sep., -ge-, sein*) rebound, bounce (off); ricochet; **'~putzen** *v/t.* (*sep., -ge-, h*) clean (off, up); wipe off; polish; **'~raten** *v/i.* (*irr. raten, sep., -ge-, h*): *j-m ~ von* dissuade s.o. from, advise s.o. against; **'~räumen** *v/t.* (*sep., -ge-, h*) clear (away); **'~reagieren** *v/t.* (*sep., no -ge-, h*) work off (*one's anger, etc.*); *sich ~* F *a.* let off steam.

'**abrechn|en** (*sep.*, -ge-, *h*) **1.** *v/t.* deduct; settle (*account*); **2.** *v/i.*: mit *j-m* ~ settle with s.o.; *fig.* settle (accounts) with s.o., F get even with s.o.; '**2ung** *f* settlement (of accounts); deduction, discount.

'**Abrede** *f*: in ~ stellen deny *or* question *s.th.*

'**abreib|en** *v/t.* (*irr. reiben*, *sep.*, -ge-, *h*) rub off; rub down (*body*); polish; '**2ung** *f* rub-down; F *fig.* beating.

'**Abreise** *f* departure (*nach* for); '**2n** *v/i.* (*sep.*, -ge-, *sein*) depart (*nach* for), leave (for), start (for), set out (for).

'**abreiß|en** (*irr. reißen*, *sep.*, -ge-) **1.** *v/t.* (*h*) tear *or* pull off; pull down (*building*); *s. abgerissen*; **2.** *v/i.* (*sein*) break off; button, etc.: come off; '**2kalender** *m* tear-off calendar.

'**ab|richten** *v/t.* (*sep.*, -ge-, *h*) train (*animal*), break (*horse*) (in); '**~riegeln** *v/t.* (*sep.*, -ge-, *h*) bolt, bar (*door*); block (*road*).

'**Abriß** *m* draft; summary, abstract; (brief) outlines *pl.*; brief survey.

'**ab|rollen** (*sep.*, -ge-) *v/t.* (*h*) *and* *v/i.* (*sein*) unroll; uncoil; unwind, unreel; roll off; '**~rücken** (*sep.*, -ge-) **1.** *v/t.* (*h*) move off *or* away (*von* from), remove; **2.** 🗙 *v/i.* (*sein*) march off, withdraw.

'**Abruf** *m* call; recall; *auf* ~ ✝ on call; '**2en** *v/t.* (*irr. rufen*, *sep.*, -ge-, *h*) call off (*a.* ✝), call away; recall; 📱 call out.

'**ab|runden** *v/t.* (*sep.*, -ge-, *h*) round (off); '**~rupfen** *v/t.* (*sep.*, -ge-, *h*) pluck off.

abrupt *adj.* [ap'rupt] abrupt.

'**abrüst|en** 🗙 *v/i.* (*sep.*, -ge-, *h*) disarm; '**2ung** 🗙 *f* disarmament.

'**abrutschen** *v/i.* (*sep.*, -ge-, *sein*) slip off, glide down; 🗲 skid.

'**Absage** *f* cancellation; refusal; '**2n** (*sep.*, -ge-, *h*) **1.** *v/t.* cancel, call off; refuse; recall (*invitation*); **2.** *v/i.* *guest*: decline; *j-m* ~ cancel one's appointment with s.o.

'**absägen** *v/t.* (*sep.*, -ge-, *h*) saw off; F *fig.* sack *s.o.*

'**Absatz** *m* stop, pause; *typ.* paragraph; ✝ sale; heel (*of shoe*); landing (*of stairs*); '**2fähig** ✝ *adj.* saleable, marketable; '**~markt** ✝ *m* market, outlet; '**~möglichkeit** ✝ *f* opening, outlet.

'**abschaben** *v/t.* (*sep.*, -ge-, *h*) scrape off.

'**abschaff|en** *v/t.* (*sep.*, -ge-, *h*) abolish; abrogate (*law*); dismiss (*servants*); '**2ung** *f* (-/-en) abolition; abrogation; dismissal.

'**ab|schälen** *v/t.* (*sep.*, -ge-, *h*) peel (off), pare; bark (*tree*); '**~schalten** *v/t.* (*sep.*, -ge-, *h*) switch off, turn off *or* out; 🗲 disconnect.

'**abschätz|en** *v/t.* (*sep.*, -ge-, *h*) esti-

mate; value; assess; '**2ung** *f* valuation; estimate; assessment.

'**Abschaum** *m* (-[e]s/*no pl.*) scum; *fig. a.* dregs *pl.*

'**Abscheu** *m* (-[e]s/*no pl.*) horror (*vor dat.* of), abhorrence (of); loathing (of); disgust (for).

abscheuern *v/t.* (*sep.*, -ge-, *h*) scour (off); wear out; chafe, abrade.

abscheulich *adj.* [ap'ʃɔʏlɪç] abominable, detestable, horrid; **2keit** *f* (-/-en) detestableness; atrocity.

'**ab|schicken** *v/t.* (*sep.*, -ge-, *h*) send off, dispatch; 📯 post, *esp. Am.* mail; '**~schieben** *v/t.* (*irr. schieben*, *sep.*, -ge-, *h*) push *or* shove off.

'**Abschied** ['apʃiːt] *m* (-[e]s/✝-e) departure; parting; leave-taking, farewell; dismissal, 🗙 discharge; ~ *nehmen* take leave (*von* of), bid farewell (to); *j-m den* ~ *geben* dismiss s.o., 🗙 discharge s.o.; *s-n* ~ *nehmen* resign, retire; '**~sfeier** *f* farewell party; '**~sgesuch** *n* resignation.

'**ab|schießen** *v/t.* (*irr. schießen*, *sep.*, -ge-, *h*) shoot off; shoot, discharge, fire (off) (*fire-arm*); launch (*rocket*); kill, shoot; (shoot *or* bring) down (*aircraft*); *s. Vogel*; '**~schinden** *v/refl.* (*irr. schinden*, *sep.*, -ge-, *h*) toil and moil, slave, drudge; '**~schirmen** *v/t.* (*sep.*, -ge-, *h*) shield (*gegen* from); screen (from), screen off (from); '**~schlachten** *v/t.* (*sep.*, -ge-, *h*) slaughter, butcher.

'**Abschlag** *m* reduction (*in price*); *auf* ~ on account; **2en** ['~gən] *v/t.* (*irr. schlagen*, *sep.*, -ge-, *h*) knock off, beat off, strike off; cut off (*head*); refuse (*request*); repel (*attack*).

abschlägig *adj.* ['apʃlɛːgɪç] negative; *~e Antwort* refusal, denial.

'**Abschlagszahlung** *f* payment on account; instal(l)ment.

'**abschleifen** *v/t.* (*irr. schleifen*, *sep.*, -ge-, *h*) grind off; *fig.* refine, polish.

'**Abschlepp|dienst** *mot. m* towing service, *Am. a.* wrecking service; '**2en** *v/t.* (*sep.*, -ge-, *h*) drag off; *mot.* tow off.

'**abschließen** (*irr. schließen*, *sep.*, -ge-, *h*) **1.** *v/t.* lock (up); ⊕ seal (up); conclude (*letter*, *etc.*); settle (*account*); balance (*the books*); effect (*insurance*); contract (*loan*); *fig.* seclude, isolate; *e-n Handel* ~ strike a bargain; *sich* ~ seclude o.s.; **2.** *v/i.* conclude; '**~d 1.** *adj.* concluding; final; **2.** *adv.* in conclusion.

'**Abschluß** *m* settlement; conclusion; ⊕ seal; '**~prüfung** *f* final examination, finals *pl.*, *Am. a.* graduation; '**~zeugnis** *n* leaving certificate; diploma.

'**ab|schmeicheln** *v/t.* (*sep.*, -ge-, *h*): *j-m et.* ~ coax s.th. out of s.o.; '**~schmelzen** (*irr. schmelzen*, *sep.*,

-ge-) v/t. (h) and v/i. (sein) melt (off); ⊕ fuse; '~schmieren ⊕ v/t. (sep., -ge-, h) lubricate, grease; '~schnallen v/t. (sep., -ge-, h) unbuckle; take off (ski, etc.); '~schneiden (irr. schneiden, sep., -ge-, h) 1. v/t. cut (off); slice off; den Weg ~ take a short cut; j-m das Wort ~ cut s.o. short; 2. v/i.: gut ~ come out or off well.

'Abschnitt m ⋏ segment; ✝ coupon; typ. section, paragraph; counterfoil, Am. a. stub (of cheque, etc.); stage (of journey); phase (of development); period (of time).

'ab|schöpfen v/t. (sep., -ge-, h) skim (off); '~schrauben v/t. (sep., -ge-, h) unscrew, screw off.

'abschrecken v/t. (sep., -ge-, h) deter (von from); scare away; '~d adj. deterrent; repulsive, forbidding.

'abschreib|en (irr. schreiben, sep., -ge-, h) 1. v/t. copy; write off (debt, etc.); plagiarize; in school: crib; 2. v/i. send a refusal; '2er m copyist; plagiarist; '2ung ✝ f (-/-en) depreciation.

'abschreiten v/t. (irr. schreiten, sep., -ge-, h) pace (off); e-e Ehrenwache ~ inspect a guard of hono(u)r.

'Abschrift f copy, duplicate.

'abschürf|en v/t. (sep., -ge-, h) graze, abrade (skin); '2ung f (-/-en) abrasion.

'Abschuß m discharge (of fire-arm); launching (of rocket); hunt. shooting; shooting down, downing (of aircraft); '~rampe f launching platform.

abschüssig adj. ['apʃysiç] sloping; steep.

'ab|schütteln v/t. (sep., -ge-, h) shake off (a. fig.); fig. get rid of; '~schwächen v/t. (sep., -ge-, h) weaken, lessen, diminish; '~schweifen v/i. (sep., -ge-, sein) deviate; fig. digress; '~schwenken v/i. (sep., -ge-, sein) swerve; ⚔ wheel; '~schwören v/i. (irr. schwören, sep., -ge-, h) abjure; forswear; '~segeln v/i. (sep., -ge-, sein) set sail, sail away.

abseh|bar adj. ['apze:ba:r]: in ~er Zeit in the not-too-distant future; '~en (irr. sehen, sep., -ge-, h) 1. v/t. (fore)see; j-m et. ~ learn s.th. by observing s.o.; es abgesehen haben auf (acc.) have an eye on, be aiming at; 2. v/i.: ~ von refrain from; disregard.

abseits ['apzaits] 1. adv. aside, apart; football, etc.: off side; 2. prp. (gen.) aside from; off (the road).

'absend|en v/t. ([irr. senden,] sep., -ge-, h) send off, dispatch; ✍ post, esp. Am. mail; '2er ✍ m sender.

'absengen v/t. (sep., -ge-, h) singe off.

'Absenker ⚘ m (-s/-) layer, shoot.

'absetz|en (sep., -ge-, h) 1. v/t. set or put down, deposit; deduct (sum); take off (hat); remove, dismiss (official); depose, dethrone (king); drop, put down (passenger); ✝ sell (goods); typ. set up (in type); thea.: ein Stück ~ take off a play; 2. v/i. break off, stop, pause; '2ung f (-/-en) deposition; removal, dismissal.

'Absicht f (-/-en) intention, purpose, design; '2lich 1. adj. intentional; 2. adv. on purpose.

'absitzen (irr. sitzen, sep., -ge-) 1. v/i. (sein) rider: dismount; 2. v/t. (h) serve (sentence), F do (time).

absolut adj. [apzo'lu:t] absolute.

absolvieren [apzɔl'vi:rən] v/t. (no -ge-, h) absolve; complete (studies); get through, graduate from (school).

'absonder|n v/t. (sep., -ge-, h) separate; ⚕ secrete; sich ~ withdraw; '2ung f (-/-en) separation; ⚕ secretion.

ab|sorbieren [apzɔr'bi:rən] v/t. (no -ge-, h) absorb; '~speisen fig. v/t. (sep., -ge-, h) put s.o. off.

abspenstig adj. ['apʃpɛnstiç]: ~ machen entice away (von from).

'absperr|en v/t. (sep., -ge-, h) lock; shut off; bar (way); block (road); turn off (gas, etc.); '2hahn m stopcock.

'ab|spielen v/t. (sep., -ge-, h) play (record, etc.); play back (tape recording); sich ~ happen, take place; '~sprechen v/t. (irr. sprechen, sep., -ge-, h) deny; arrange; agree; '~springen v/i. (irr. springen, sep., -ge-, sein) jump down or off; ⚔ jump, bale out, (Am. only) bail out; rebound.

'Absprung m jump; sports: take-off.

'abspülen v/t. (sep., -ge-, h) wash up; rinse.

'abstamm|en v/i. (sep., -ge-, sein) be descended; gr. be derived (both: von from); '2ung f (-/-en) descent; gr. derivation.

'Abstand m distance; interval; ✝ compensation, indemnification; ~ nehmen von desist from.

ab|statten ['apʃtatən] v/t. (sep., -ge-, h): e-n Besuch ~ pay a visit; Dank ~ return or render thanks; '~stauben v/t. (sep., -ge-, h) dust.

'abstech|en (irr. stechen, sep., -ge-, h) 1. v/t. cut (sods); stick (pig, sheep, etc.); stab (animal); 2. v/i. contrast (von with); '2er m (-s/-) excursion, trip; detour.

'ab|stecken v/t. (sep., -ge-, h) unpin, undo; fit, pin (dress); surv. mark out; '~stehen v/i. (irr. stehen, sep., -ge-, h) stand off; stick out, protrude; s. abgestanden; '~steigen v/i. (irr. steigen, sep., -ge-, sein) descend; alight (von from) (carriage); get off, dismount (from) (horse); put up (in dat. at) (hotel); **'~stellen** v/t. (sep., -ge-, h) put down; stop, turn off (gas, etc.); park (car); fig. put an end to s.th.; **'~stempeln** v/t. (sep., -ge-, h) stamp; **'~sterben** v/i. (irr. sterben, sep., -ge-, sein) die off; limb: mortify.

Abstieg ['apʃtiːk] m (-[e]s/-e) descent; fig. decline.

'abstimm|en (sep., -ge-, h) **1.** v/i. vote; **2.** v/t. tune in (radio); fig.: harmonize; time; ✝ balance (books); **'2ung** f voting; vote; tuning.

Abstinenzler [apstiˈnɛntslər] m (-s/-) teetotal(l)er.

'abstoppen (sep., -ge-, h) **1.** v/t. stop; slow down; sports: clock, time; **2.** v/i. stop.

'abstoßen v/t. (irr. stoßen, sep., -ge-, h) knock off; push off; clear off (goods); fig. repel; sich die Hörner ~ sow one's wild oats; **'~d** fig. adj. repulsive.

abstrakt adj. [apˈstrakt] abstract.

'ab|streichen v/t. (irr. streichen, sep., -ge-, h) take or wipe off; **'~streifen** v/t. (sep., -ge-, h) strip off; take or pull off (glove, etc.); slip off (dress); wipe (shoes); **'~streiten** v/t. (irr. streiten, sep., -ge-, h) contest, dispute; deny.

'Abstrich m deduction, cut; ✂ swab.

'ab|stufen v/t. (sep., -ge-, h) graduate; gradate; **'~stumpfen** (sep., -ge-) **1.** v/t. (h) blunt; fig. dull (mind); **2.** fig. v/i. (sein) become dull.

'Absturz m fall; ✈ crash.

'ab|stürzen v/i. (sep., -ge-, sein) fall down; ✈ crash; **'~suchen** v/t. (sep., -ge-, h) search (nach for); scour or comb (area) (for).

absurd adj. [apˈzurt] absurd, preposterous.

Abszeß ✗ [apsˈtsɛs] m (Abszesses/ Abszesse) abscess.

Abt [apt] m (-[e]s/=e) abbot.

'abtakeln ⚓ v/t. (sep., -ge-, h) unrig, dismantle, strip.

Abtei [apˈtai] f (-/-en) abbey.

Ab|'teil 🚃 n compartment; **'2teilen** v/t. (sep., -ge-, h) divide; ⚖ partition off; **'~teilung** f division; **'~teilung** f department; ward (of hospital); compartment; ✗ detachment; **'~teilungsleiter** m head of a department.

'abtelegraphieren v/i. (sep., no -ge-, h) cancel a visit, etc. by telegram.

Äbtissin [ɛpˈtisin] f (-/-nen) abbess.

'ab|töten v/t. (sep., -ge-, h) destroy, kill (bacteria, etc.); **'~tragen** v/t. (irr. tragen, sep., -ge-, h) carry off; pull down (building); wear out (garment); pay (debt).

abträglich adj. ['aptrɛːkliç] injurious, detrimental.

'abtreib|en (irr. treiben, sep., -ge-) **1.** v/t. (h) drive away or off; ein Kind ~ procure abortion; **2.** ⚓, ✈ v/i. (sein) drift off; **'2ung** f (-/-en) abortion.

'abtrennen v/t. (sep., -ge-, h) detach; separate; sever (limbs, etc.); take (trimmings) off (dress).

'abtret|en (irr. treten, sep., -ge-) **1.** v/t. (h) wear down (heels); wear out (steps, etc.); fig. cede, transfer; **2.** v/i. (sein) retire, withdraw; resign; thea. make one's exit; **'2er** m (-s/-) doormat; **'2ung** f (-/-en) cession, transfer.

'ab|trocknen (sep., -ge-) **1.** v/t. (h) dry (up); wipe (dry); sich ~ dry oneself, rub oneself down; **2.** v/i. (sein) dry up, become dry; **'~tropfen** v/i. (sep., -ge-, sein) liquid: drip; dishes, vegetables: drain.

abtrünnig adj. ['aptrynic] unfaithful, disloyal; eccl. apostate; **2e** ['~gə] m (-n/-n) deserter; eccl. apostate.

'ab|tun v/t. (irr. tun, sep., -ge-, h) take off; settle (matter); fig.: dispose of; dismiss; **'~urteilen** ['apʔ-] v/t. (sep., -ge-, h) pass sentence on s.o.; **'~wägen** v/t. (irr. wägen) sep., -ge-, h) weigh (out); fig. consider carefully; **'~wälzen** v/t. (sep., -ge-, h) roll away; fig. shift; **'~wandeln** v/t. (sep., -ge-, h) vary, modify; **'~wandern** v/i. (sep., -ge-, sein) wander away; migrate (von from).

'Abwandlung f modification, variation.

'abwarten (sep., -ge-, h) **1.** v/t. wait for, await; s-e Zeit ~ bide one's time; **2.** v/i. wait.

abwärts adv. ['apvɛrts] down, downward(s).

'abwaschen v/t. (irr. waschen, sep., -ge-, h) wash (off, away); bathe; sponge off; wash up (dishes, etc.).

'abwechseln (sep., -ge-, h) **1.** v/t. vary; alternate; **2.** v/i. vary; alternate; mit j-m ~ take turns; **'~d** adj. alternate.

'Abwechs(e)lung f (-/-en) change; alternation; variation; diversion; zur ~ for a change.

'Abweg m: auf ~e geraten go astray; **2ig** [-'giç] erroneous, wrong.

'Abwehr f defen|ce, Am. -se; warding off (of thrust, etc.); **'~dienst** ✗ m counter-espionage service; **'2en** v/t. (sep., -ge-, h) ward off; avert; repulse, repel, ward off (attack, enemy).

'abweich|en v/i. (irr. weichen, sep., -ge-, sein) deviate (von from), swerve (from); differ (from); compass-needle: deviate; **'2ung** f (-/-en) deviation; difference; deflexion, (Am. only) deflection.

'abweiden v/t. (sep., -ge-, h) graze.

'abweis|en v/t. (irr. weisen, sep., -ge-, h) refuse, reject; repel (a. ✗);

rebuff; '~end *adj.* unfriendly, cool; '2ung *f* refusal, rejection; repulse (*a.* ✕); rebuff.

'ab|wenden *v/t.* ([irr. wenden,] *sep.*, -ge-, *h*) turn away, avert (*disaster, etc.*); parry (*thrust*); sich ~ turn away (von from); '~werfen *v/t.* (*irr.* werfen, *sep.*, -ge-, *h*) throw off; ✕ drop (*bombs*); shed, cast (*skin, etc.*); shed (*leaves*); yield (*profit*).

'abwert|en *v/t.* (*sep.*, -ge-, *h*) devaluate; '2ung *f* devaluation.

abwesen|d *adj.* ['apve:zənt] absent; '2heit *f* (-/-en) absence.

'ab|wickeln *v/t.* (*sep.*, -ge-, *h*) unwind, unreel, wind off; transact (*business*); '~wiegen *v/t.* (*irr.* wiegen, *sep.*, -ge-, *h*) weigh (out) (*goods*); '~wischen *v/t.* (*sep.*, -ge-, *h*) wipe (off); '~würgen *v/t.* (*sep.*, -ge-, *h*) strangle, throttle, choke; *mot.* stall; '~zahlen *v/t.* (*sep.*, -ge-, *h*) pay off; pay by instal(l)ments; '~zählen *v/t.* (*sep.*, -ge-, *h*) count (out, over).

'Abzahlung *f* instal(l)ment, payment on account; '~sgeschäft *n* hire-purchase.

'abzapfen *v/t.* (*sep.*, -ge-, *h*) tap, draw off.

'Abzehrung *f* (-/-en) wasting away, emaciation; ✶ consumption.

'Abzeichen *n* badge; ✕ marking.

'ab|zeichnen *v/t.* (*sep.*, -ge-, *h*) copy, draw; mark off; initial; tick off; sich ~ gegen stand out against; '~ziehen (*irr.* ziehen, *sep.*, -ge-) 1. *v/t.* (*h*) take off, remove; ⅋ subtract; strip (*bed*); bottle (*wine*); *phot.* print (*film*); *typ.* pull (*proof*); take out (*key*); das Fell ~ skin (*animal*); 2. *v/i.* (sein) go away; ✕ march off; *smoke:* escape; *thunderstorm, clouds:* move on.

'Abzug *m* departure; ✕ withdrawal, retreat; ⊕ drain; outlet; deduction (*of sum*); *phot.* print; *typ.* proof (-sheet).

abzüglich *prp.* (*gen.*) ['aptsy:kliç] less, minus, deducting.

Abzugsrohr *n* waste-pipe.

abzweig|en ['aptsvaigən] (*sep.*, -ge-) 1. *v/t.* (*h*) branch; divert (*money*); sich ~ branch off; 2. *v/i.* (sein) branch off; '2ung *f* (-/-en) branch; road-junction.

ach *int.* [ax] oh!, ah!, alas!; ~ so! oh, I see!

Achse ['aksə] *f* (-/-n) axis; ⊕: axle; shaft; axle(-tree) (*of carriage*); auf der ~ on the move.

Achsel ['aksəl] *f* (-/-n) shoulder; die ~n zucken shrug one's shoulders; '~höhle *f* armpit.

acht[1] [axt] 1. *adj.* eight; in ~ Tagen today week, this day week; vor ~ Tagen a week ago; 2. 2 *f* (-/-en) (figure) eight.

Acht[2] [~] *f* (-/*no pl.*) ban, outlawry; attention; außer acht lassen disregard; sich in acht nehmen be careful; be on one's guard (vor j-m or et. against s.o. or s.th.); look out (for s.o. or s.th.).

'achtbar *adj.* respectable.

'achte *adj.* eighth; 21 ['~əl] *n* (-*s*/-) eighth (part).

'achten (ge-, *h*) 1. *v/t.* respect, esteem; regard; 2. *v/i.:* ~ auf (*acc.*) pay attention to; achte auf meine Worte mark or mind my words; darauf ~ daß see to it that, take care that.

ächten ['ɛçtən] *v/t.* (ge-, *h*) outlaw, proscribe; ban.

'Achter *m* (-*s*/-) *rowing:* eight.

achtfach *adj.* ['axtfax] eightfold.

'achtgeben *v/i.* (*irr.* geben, *sep.*, -ge-, *h*) be careful; pay attention (auf *acc.* to); take care (of); gib acht! look or watch out!, be careful!

'achtlos *adj.* inattentive, careless, heedless.

Acht'stundentag *m* eight-hour day.

'Achtung *f* (-/*no pl.*) attention; respect, esteem, regard; ~! look out!, ✕ attention!; ~ Stufe! mind the step!; 2svoll *adj.* respectful.

'achtzehn *adj.* eighteen; ~te *adj.* ['~tə] eighteenth.

achtzig *adj.* ['axtsiç] eighty; '~ste *adj.* eightieth.

ächzen ['ɛçtsən] *v/i.* (ge-, *h*) groan, moan.

Acker ['akər] *m* (-ɛ/⁼) field; '~bau *m* agriculture; farming; '2bautreibend *adj.* agricultural, farming; '~geräte *n/pl.* farm implements *pl.*; '2n arable land; '2n *v/t.* and *v/i.* (ge-, *h*) plough, till, *Am.* plow.

add|ieren [a'di:rən] *v/t.* (*no* -ge-, *h*) add (up); 2tion [adi'tsjo:n] *f* (-/-en) addition, adding up.

Adel ['a:dəl] *m* (-*s*/*no pl.*) nobility, aristocracy; '2ig *adj.* noble; '2n *v/t.* (ge-, *h*) ennoble (*a. fig.*); *Brt.* knight, raise to the peerage; '~sstand *m* nobility; aristocracy; *Brt.* peerage.

Ader ['a:dər] *f* (-/-n) ✗, *wood, etc.*: vein; *anat.*: vein; artery; zur ~ lassen bleed.

adieu *int.* [a'djø:] good-bye, farewell, adieu, F cheerio.

Adjektiv *gr.* ['atjekti:f] *n* (-*s*/-e) adjective.

Adler *orn.* ['a:dlər] *m* (-*s*/-) eagle; '~nase *f* aquiline nose.

adlig *adj.* ['a:dliç] noble; 2e ['~gə] *m* (-*n*/-*n*) nobleman, peer.

Admiral ⚓ [atmi'ra:l] *m* (-*s*/-e, ⁼e) admiral.

adopt|ieren [adɔp'ti:rən] *v/t.* (*no* -ge-, *h*) adopt; 2ivkind [~'ti:f-] *n* adopted child.

Adressat [adrɛ'sa:t] *m* (-en/-en) addressee; consignee (*of goods*).

Adreßbuch [a'drɛs-] *n* directory.

Adress|e [a'drɛsə] f (-/-n) address; direction; per ~ care of (abbr. c/o); **2ieren** [~'si:rən] v/t. (no -ge-, h) address, direct; † consign; falsch ~ misdirect.

adrett adj. [a'drɛt] smart, neat.

Adverb gr. [at'vɛrp] n (-s/-ien) adverb.

Affäre [a'fɛːrə] f (-/-n) (love) affair; matter, business, incident.

Affe zo. ['afə] m (-n/-n) ape; monkey.

Affekt [a'fɛkt] m (-[e]s/-e) emotion; passion; **2iert** adj. [~'ti:rt] affected. **'affig** F adj. foppish; affected; silly.

Afrikan|er [afri'ka:nər] m (-s/-) African; **2isch** adj. African.

After anat. ['aftər] m (-s/-) anus.

Agent [a'gɛnt] m (-en/-en) agent; broker; pol. (secret) agent; ~ur [~'tu:r] f (-/-en) agency.

aggressiv adj. [agrɛ'si:f] aggressive.

Agio † ['a:ʒio] n (-s/no pl.) agio, premium.

Agitator [agi'ta:tər] m (-s/-en) agitator. [brooch.]

Agraffe [a'grafə] f (-/-n) clasp;]

agrarisch adj. [a'gra:riʃ] agrarian.

Ägypt|er [ɛ:'gyptər] m (-s/-) Egyptian; **2isch** adj. Egyptian.

ah int. [a:] ah!

aha int. [a'ha] aha!, I see!

Ahle ['a:lə] f (-/-n) awl, pricker; punch.

Ahn [a:n] m (-[e]s, -en/-en) ancestor; ~en pl. a. forefathers pl.

ähneln ['ɛ:nəln] v/i. (ge-, h) be like, resemble.

ahnen ['a:nən] v/t. (ge-, h) have a presentiment of or that; suspect; divine.

ähnlich adj. ['ɛ:nliç] like, resembling; similar (dat. to); iro.: das sieht ihm ~ that's just like him; **2keit** f (-/-en) likeness, resemblance; similarity.

Ahnung ['a:nuŋ] f (-/-en) presentiment; foreboding; notion, idea; **2slos** adj. unsuspecting; **2svoll** adj. full of misgivings.

Ahorn ♀ ['a:hɔrn] m (-s/-e) maple (-tree).

Ähre ♀ ['ɛ:rə] f (-/-n) ear, head; spike; ~n lesen glean.

Akademi|e [akadɛ'mi:] f (-/-n) academy, society; ~ker [~'de:mikər] m (-s/-) university man, esp. Am. university graduate; **2sch** adj. [~'de:miʃ] academic.

Akazie ♀ [a'ka:tsjə] f (-/-n) acacia.

akklimatisieren [aklimati'zi:rən] v/t. and v/refl. (no -ge-, h) acclimatize, Am. acclimate.

Akkord [a'kɔrt] m (-[e]s/-e) ♪ chord; †: contract; agreement; composition; im ~ † by the piece or job; ~arbeit f piece-work; ~arbeiter m piece-worker; ~lohn m piece-wages pl.

akkredit|ieren [akredi'ti:rən] v/t. (no -ge-, h) accredit (bei to); **2iv** [~'ti:f] n (-s/-e) credentials pl.; † letter of credit.

Akku F ⊕ ['aku] m (-s/-s), ~mulator ⊕ [~mu'la:tɔr] m (-s/-en) accumulator, (storage-)battery.

Akkusativ gr. ['akuzati:f] m (-s/-e) accusative (case). [acrobat.]

Akrobat [akro'ba:t] m (-en/-en)]

Akt [akt] m (-[e]s/-e) act(ion), deed; thea. act; paint. nude.

Akte ['aktə] f (-/-n) document, deed; file; ~n pl. records pl., papers pl.; deeds pl., documents pl.; files pl.; zu den ~n to be filed; zu den ~n legen file; '~ndeckel m folder; '~nmappe f, '~ntasche f portfolio; briefcase; '~nzeichen n reference or file number.

Aktie † ['aktsjə] f (-/-n) share, Am. stock; ~n besitzen hold shares, Am. hold stock; '~nbesitz m shareholdings pl., Am. stockholdings pl.; '~ngesellschaft f appr. joint-stock company, Am. (stock) corporation; '~nkapital n share-capital, Am. capital stock.

Aktion [ak'tsjo:n] f (-/-en) action; activity; pol., etc.: campaign, drive; ✕ operation; ~är [~'nɛ:r] m (-s/-e) shareholder, Am. stockholder.

aktiv adj. [ak'ti:f] active.

Aktiv|a † [ak'ti:va] n/pl. assets pl.; ~posten [~'ti:f-] m asset (a. fig.).

aktuell adj. [aktu'ɛl] current, present-day, up-to-date, topical.

Akust|ik [a'kustik] f (-/no pl.) acoustics sg., pl.; **2isch** adj. acoustic.

akut adj. [a'ku:t] acute.

Akzent [ak'tsɛnt] m (-[e]s/-e) accent; stress; **2uieren** [~u'i:rən] v/t. (no -ge-, h) accent(uate); stress.

Akzept † [ak'tsɛpt] n (-[e]s/-e) acceptance; ~ant [~'tsant] m (-en/-en) acceptor; **2ieren** [~'ti:rən] v/t. (no -ge-, h) accept.

Alarm [a'larm] m (-[e]s/-e) alarm; ~ blasen or schlagen ✕ sound or give the alarm; ~bereitschaft f: in ~ sein stand by; **2ieren** [~'mi:rən] v/t. (no -ge-, h) alarm.

Alaun ♠ [a'laun] m (-[e]s/-e) alum.

albern adj. ['albərn] silly, foolish.

Album ['album] n (-s/Alben) album.

Alge ♀ [a'lgə] f (-/-n) alga, seaweed.

Algebra ♠ ['algebra] f (-/no pl.) algebra.

Alibi ⚖ ['a:libi] n (-s/-s) alibi.

Alimente ⚖ [ali'mɛntə] pl. alimony.

Alkohol ['alkohɔl] m (-s/-e) alcohol; **2frei** adj. non-alcoholic, esp. Am. soft; ~es Restaurant temperance restaurant; ~iker [~'ho:likər] m (-s/-) alcoholic; **2isch** adj. [~'ho:liʃ] alcoholic; '~schmuggler m liquorsmuggler, Am. bootlegger; '~verbot n prohibition; '~vergiftung f alcoholic poisoning.

all[1] [al] **1.** *pron.* all; ~e everybody; ~es in ~em on the whole; vor ~em first of all; **2.** *adj.* all; every, each; any; ~e beide both of them; auf ~e Fälle in any case, at all events; ~e Tage every day; ~e zwei Minuten every two minutes.

All[2] [..] *n* (-s/no *pl.*) the universe.

'**alle** F *adj.* all gone; ~ werden come to an end; *supplies, etc.*: run out.

Allee [a'le:] *f* (-/-n) avenue; (treelined) walk.

allein [a'lain] **1.** *adj.* alone; single; unassisted; **2.** *adv.* alone; only; **3.** *cj.* yet, only, but, however; **2berechtigung** *f* exclusive right; **2besitz** *m* exclusive possession; **2herrscher** *m* absolute monarch, autocrat; dictator; ~ig *adj.* only, exclusive, sole; **2sein** *n* loneliness, solitariness, solitude; **~stehend** *adj. p.*: alone in the world; single; *building, etc.*: isolated, detached; **2verkauf** *m* exclusive sale; monopoly; **2vertreter** *m* sole representative or agent; **2vertrieb** *m* sole distributors *pl.*

allemal *adv.* ['alə'ma:l] always; *ein für ~* once (and) for all.

'**allen**|'**falls** *adv.* if need be; possibly, perhaps; at best.

allenthalben † *adv.* ['alənt'halbən] everywhere.

'**aller**|'**best** *adj.* best ... of all, very best; ~**dings** *adv.* ['..'diŋs] indeed; to be sure; ~**l** certainly!, Am. F sure!; '~'**erst 1.** *adj.* first ... of all, very first; foremost; **2.** *adv.*: zu ~ first of all.

Allergie 🛪 [alɛr'gi:] *f* (-/-n) allergy.

'**aller**|'**hand** *adj.* of all kinds or sorts; F das ist ja ~! F I say!; *sl.* that's the limit!; '**2'heiligen** *n* (-/no *pl.*) All Saints' Day; ~**lei** *adj.* ['..'lai] of all kinds or sorts; '**2'lei** *n* (-s/-s) medley; '~'**letzt 1.** *adj.* last of all, very last; latest (*news, fashion, etc.*); **2.** *adv.*: zu ~ last of all; '~'**liebst 1.** *adj.* dearest of all; (most) lovely; **2.** *adv.*: am ~en best of all; '~'**meist 1.** *adj.* most; **2.** *adv.*: am ~en mostly; chiefly; '~'**nächst** *adj.* very next; '~'**neu(e)st** *adj.* the very latest; '**2'seelen** *n* (-/no *pl.*) All Souls' Day; '~'**seits** *adv.* on all sides; universally; '~'**wenigst** *adv.*: am ~en least of all.

'**alle**|'**samt** *adv.* one and all, all together; '~'**zeit** *adv.* always, at all times, for ever.

'**all**|'**gegenwärtig** *adj.* omnipresent, ubiquitous; ~'**ge'mein 1.** *adj.* general; common; universal; **2.** *adv.*: im ~en in general, generally; **2ge'meinheit** *f* (-/no *pl.*) generality; universality; general public; **2'heilmittel** *n* panacea, cure-all (both *a. fig.*).

Allianz [ali'ants] *f* (-/-en) alliance.

alli'**ier**|**en** *v/refl.* (no -ge-, h) ally o.s. (*mit* to, with); **2te** *m* (-n/-n) ally.

'**all**|'**jährlich 1.** *adj.* annual; **2.** *adv.* annually, every year; '**2macht** *f* (-/no *pl.*) omnipotence; ~'**mächtig** *adj.* omnipotent, almighty; ~**mählich** [..'mɛ:liç] **1.** *adj.* gradual; **2.** *adv.* gradually, by degrees.

Allopathie 🛪 [alopa'ti:] allopathy.

all|**seitig** *adj.* ['alzaitiç] universal; all-round; '**2strom** ⚡ *m* (-[e]s/no *pl.*) alternating current/direct current (*abbr.* A.C./D.C.); '**2tag** *m* workday; week-day; *fig.* everyday life, daily routine; ~'**täglich** *adj.* daily; *fig.* common, trivial; '**2tags-leben** *n* (-s/no *pl.*) everyday life; '~'**wissend** *adj.* omniscient; '**2'wissenheit** *f* (-/no *pl.*) omniscience; '~'**wöchentlich** *adj.* weekly; '~**zu** *adv.* (much) too; '~**zu'viel** *adv.* too much.

Alm [alm] *f* (-/-en) Alpine pasture, alp.

Almosen ['almo:zən] *n* (-s/-) alms; ~ *pl.* alms *pl.*, charity.

Alp|**druck** ['alp-] *m* (-[e]s/~e), '~**drücken** *n* (-s/no *pl.*) nightmare.

Alpen ['alpən] *pl.* Alps *pl.*

Alphabet [alfa'be:t] *n* (-[c]s/-e) alphabet; **2isch** *adj.* alphabetic(al).

'**Alptraum** *m* nightmare.

als *cj.* [als] than; as, like; (in one's capacity) as; but, except; *temporal*: after, when; as; ~ ob as if, as though; so viel ~ as much as; er ist zu dumm, ~ daß er es verstehen könnte he is too stupid to understand it; ~'**bald** *adv.* immediately; ~'**dann** *adv.* then.

also ['alzo:] **1.** *adv.* thus, so; **2.** *cj.* therefore, so, consequently; na ~! there you are!

alt[1] *adj.* [alt] old; aged; ancient, antique; stale; second-hand.

Alt[2] ♪ [..] *m* (-[e]s/-e) alto, contralto.

Altar [al'ta:r] *m* (-[e]s/~e) altar.

Alteisen ['alt?-] *n* scrap-iron.

'**Alte** (-n/-n) **1.** *m* old man; F: der ~ the governor; *hist.*: die ~n *pl.* the ancients *pl.*; **2.** *f* old woman.

'**Alter** *n* (-s/-) age; old age; seniority; er ist in meinem ~ he is my age; von mittlerem ~ middle-aged.

älter *adj.* ['ɛltər] older; senior; der ~e Bruder the elder brother.

altern ['altərn] *v/i.* (ge-, h, sein) grow old, age.

Alternative [altɛrna'ti:və] *f* (-/-n) alternative; keine ~ haben have no choice.

'**Alters**|**grenze** *f* age-limit; retirement age; '~**heim** *n* old people's home; '~**rente** *f* old-age pension; '**2schwach** *adj.* decrepit; senile; '~**schwäche** *f* decrepitude; '~**versorgung** *f* old-age pension.

Altertum ['altərtu:m] *n* **1.** (-s/*no pl.*) antiquity; **2.** (-s/=er) *mst* Altertümer *pl.* antiquities *pl.*

altertümlich *adj.* ['altərty:mliç] ancient, antique, archaic.

'Altertums|forscher *m* arch(a)eologist; **'~kunde** *f* arch(a)eology.

ältest *adj.* ['eltəst] oldest; eldest (*sister, etc.*); earliest (*recollections*); **'2e** *m* (-n/-n) elder; senior; mein ~r my eldest (son).

Altistin ♪ [al'tistin] *f* (-/-nen) altosinger, contralto-singer.

'altklug *adj.* precocious, forward.

ältlich *adj.* ['eltliç] elderly, oldish.

'Alt|material *n* junk, scrap; salvage; **'~meister** *m* doyen, dean, F Grand Old Man (*a. sports*); *sports*: ex-champion; **'2modisch** *adj.* oldfashioned; **'~papier** *n* waste paper; **'~philologe** *m* classical philologist *or* scholar; **'~stadt** *f* old town *or* city; **'~warenhändler** *m* second-hand dealer; **~'weibersommer** *m* Indian summer; gossamer.

Aluminium ♫ [alu'mi:njum] *n* (-s/*no pl.*) aluminium, *Am.* aluminum.

am *prp.* [am] = an dem.

Amateur [ama'tø:r] *m* (-s/-e) amateur.

Amboß ['ambɔs] *m* (Ambosses/Ambosse) anvil.

ambulan|t ♂ *adj.* [ambu'lant]: ~ Behandelte out-patient; **2z** [~ts] *f* (-/-en) ambulance.

Ameise *zo.* ['a:maizə] *f* (-/-n) ant; **'~nhaufen** *m* ant-hill.

Amerikan|er [ameri'ka:nər] *m* (-s/-), **~erin** *f* (-/-nen) American; **2isch** *adj.* American.

Amme ['amə] *f* (-/-n) (wet-)nurse.

Amnestie [amnes'ti:] *f* (-/-n) amnesty, general pardon.

Amor ['a:mɔr] *m* (-s/*no pl.*) Cupid.

Amortis|ation [amɔrtiza'tsjo:n] *f* (-/-en) amortization, redemption; **2ieren** [~'zi:rən] *v/t.* (*no* -ge-, *h*) amortize, redeem; pay off.

Ampel ['ampəl] *f* (-/-n) hanging lamp; traffic light.

Amphibie *zo.* [am'fi:bjə] *f* (-/-n) amphibian.

Ampulle [am'pulə] *f* (-/-n) ampoule.

Amput|ation [amputa'tsjo:n] *f* (-/-en) amputation; **2ieren** ♂ [~'ti:rən] *v/t.* (*no* -ge-, *h*) amputate; **~ierte** *m* (-n/-n) amputee.

Amsel *orn.* ['amzəl] *f* (-/-n) blackbird.

Amt [amt] *n* (-[e]s/=er) office; post; charge; office, board; official duty, function; (telephone) exchange; **2ieren** [~'ti:rən] *v/i.* (*no* -ge-, *h*) hold office; officiate; **'2lich** *adj.* official; **'~mann** *m* district administrator; *hist.* bailiff.

'Amts|arzt *m* medical officer of health; **'~befugnis** *f* competence, authority; **'~bereich** *m*, **'~bezirk** *m* jurisdiction; **'~blatt** *n* gazette; **'~eid** *m* oath of office; **'~einführung** *f* inauguration; **'~führung** *f* administration; **'~geheimnis** *n* official secret; **'~gericht** *n* *appr.* district court; **'~geschäfte** *n/pl.* official duties *pl.*; **'~gewalt** *f* (official) authority; **'~handlung** *f* official act; **'~niederlegung** *f* (-/%-en) resignation; **'~richter** *m* *appr.* district court judge; **'~siegel** *n* official seal; **'~vorsteher** *m* head official.

Amulett [amu'lɛt] *n* (-[e]s/-e) amulet, charm.

amüs|ant *adj.* [amy'zant] amusing, entertaining; **~ieren** [~'zi:rən] *v/t.* (*no* -ge-, *h*) amuse, entertain; *sich* ~ amuse *or* enjoy o.s., have a good time.

an [an] **1.** *prp.* (*dat.*) at; on, upon; in; against; to; by, near, close to; ~ der Themse on the Thames; ~ der Wand on *or* against the wall; es ist ~ dir zu *inf.* it is up to you to *inf.*; am Leben alive; am 1. März on March 1st; am Morgen in the morning; **2.** *prp.* (*acc.*) to; on; on to; at; against; about; bis ~ as far as, up to; **3.** *adv.* on; von heute ~ from this day forth, from today; von nun *or* jetzt ~ from now on.

analog *adj.* [ana'lo:k] analogous (*dat. or zu* to), with.

Analphabet [an⟨?⟩alfa'be:t] *m* (-en/-en) illiterate (person).

Analys|e [ana'ly:zə] *f* (-/-n) analysis; **2ieren** [~'zi:rən] *v/t.* (*no* -ge-, *h*) analy|se, *Am.* -ze.

Anämie ♂ [anɛ'mi:] *f* (-/-n) an(a)emia.

Ananas ['ananas] *f* (-/-, -se) pineapple.

Anarchie [anar'çi:] *f* (-/-n) anarchy.

Anatom|ie [anato'mi:] *f* (-/*no pl.*) anatomy; **2isch** *adj.* [~'to:miʃ] anatomical.

'anbahnen *v/t.* (*sep.*, -ge-, *h*) pave the way for, initiate; open up; *sich* ~ be opening up.

'Anbau *m* **1.** ♂ (-[e]s/*no pl.*) cultivation; **2.** △ (-[e]s/-ten) outbuilding, annex, extension, addition; **'2en** *v/t.* (*sep.*, -ge-, *h*) ♂ cultivate, grow; △ add (*an acc.* to); **'~fläche** *f* arable land.

'anbehalten *v/t.* (*irr.* halten, *sep.*, *no* -ge-, *h*) keep (*garment, etc.*) on.

an'bei ✝ *adv.* enclosed.

'an|beißen (*irr.* beißen, *sep.*, -ge-, *h*) **1.** *v/t.* bite into; **2.** *v/i.* *fish:* bite; **'~bellen** *v/t.* (*sep.*, -ge-, *h*) bark at; **'~beraumen** [~bəraumən] *v/t.* (*sep.*, *no* -ge-, *h*) appoint, fix; **'~beten** *v/t.* (*sep.*, -ge-, *h*) adore, worship.

'Anbetracht *m*: in ~ considering, in consideration of.

'**anbetteln** v/t. (sep., -ge-, h) beg from, solicit alms of.

'**Anbetung** f (-/%-en) worship, adoration; **2swürdig** adj. adorable.

'**an|bieten** v/t. (irr. bieten, sep., -ge-, h) offer; '**~binden** v/t. (irr. binden, sep., -ge-, h) bind, tie (up); **~** an (dat., acc.) tie to; s. angebunden; '**~blasen** v/t. (irr. blasen, sep., -ge-, h) blow at or (up)on.

'**Anblick** m look; view; sight, aspect; '**2en** v/t. (sep., -ge-, h) look at; glance at; view; eye.

'**an|blinzeln** v/t. (sep., -ge-, h) wink at; '**~brechen** (irr. brechen, sep., -ge-) 1. v/t. (h) break into (provisions, etc.); open (bottle, etc.); 2. v/i. (sein) begin; day: break, dawn; '**~brennen** (irr. brennen, sep., -ge-) 1. v/t. (h) set on fire; light (cigar, etc.); 2. v/i. (sein) catch fire; burn; '**~bringen** v/t. (irr. bringen, sep., -ge-, h) bring; fix (an dat. to), attach (to); place; ✝ dispose of (goods); lodge (complaint); s. angebracht.

'**Anbruch** m (-[e]s/no pl.) beginning; break (of day).

'**anbrüllen** v/t. (sep., -ge-, h) roar at.

Andacht ['andaxt] f (-/-en) devotion(s pl.); prayers pl.

andächtig adj. ['andɛçtiç] devout.

'**andauern** v/i. (sep., -ge-, h) last, continue, go on.

'**Andenken** n (-s/-) memory, remembrance; keepsake, souvenir; zum **~** an (acc.) in memory of.

ander adj. ['andər] other; different; next; opposite; am **~en** Tag (on) the next day; e-n Tag um den **~en** every other day; ein **~er** Freund another friend; nichts **~es** nothing else.

andererseits adv. ['andərər'zaɪts] on the other hand.

ändern ['ɛndərn] v/t. (ge-, h) alter; change; ich kann es nicht **~** I can't help it; sich **~** alter; change.

'**andern|falls** adv. otherwise, else.

'**anders** adv. ['andərs] otherwise; differently (als from); else; j. **~** somebody else; ich kann nicht **~**, ich muß weinen I cannot help crying; **~** werden change.

'**ander'seits** adv. s. andererseits.

'**anders'wo** adv. elsewhere.

anderthalb adj. ['andərt'halp] one and a half.

'**Änderung** f (-/-en) change, alteration.

ander|wärts adv. ['andər'verts] elsewhere; '**~weitig** 1. adj. other; 2. adv. otherwise.

'**andeut|en** v/t. (sep., -ge-, h) indicate; hint; intimate; imply; suggest; '**2ung** f intimation; hint; suggestion.

'**Andrang** m rush; 🠮 congestion.

andre adj. ['andrə] s. andere.

'**andrehen** v/t. (sep., -ge-, h) turn on (gas, etc.); ∮ switch on (light).

'**androh|en** v/t. (sep., -ge-, h) j-m et. **~** threaten s.o. with s.th.; '**2ung** f threat.

aneignen ['an⁹-] v/refl. (sep., -ge-, h) appropriate; acquire; adopt; seize; usurp.

aneinander adv. [an⁹aɪ'nandər] together; **~geraten** v/i. (irr. raten, sep., no -ge-, sein) clash (mit with).

anekeln ['an⁹-] v/t. (sep., -ge-, h) disgust, sicken.

Anerbieten ['an⁹-] n (-s/-) offer.

anerkannt adj. ['an⁹-] acknowledged, recognized.

anerkenn|en ['an⁹-] v/t. (irr. kennen, sep., no -ge-, h) acknowledge (als as), recognize; appreciate; own (child); hono(u)r (bill); '**2ung** f (-/-en) acknowledgement; recognition; appreciation.

'**anfahr|en** (irr. fahren, sep., -ge-) 1. v/i. (sein) start; 🠮 descend; angefahren kommen drive up; 2. v/t. (h) run into; carry, convey; j-n **~** let fly at s.o.; '**2t** f approach; drive.

'**Anfall** 🠮 m fit, attack; '**2en** (irr. fallen, sep., -ge-) 1. v/t. (h) attack; assail; 2. v/i. (sein) accumulate; money: accrue.

anfällig adj. ['anfɛliç] susceptible (für to); prone to (diseases, etc.).

'**Anfang** m beginning, start, commencement; **~** Mai at the beginning of May, early in May; '**2en** v/t. and v/i. (irr. fangen, sep., -ge-, h) begin, start, commence.

Anfäng|er ['anfɛŋər] m (-s/-) beginner; '**2lich 1.** adj. initial; 2. adv. in the beginning.

anfangs adv. ['anfaŋs] in the beginning; '**2buchstabe** m initial (letter); großer **~** capital letter; '**2grün|de** ['-grʏndə] m/pl. elements pl.

'**anfassen** (sep., -ge-, h) 1. v/t. seize; touch; handle; 2. v/i. lend a hand.

anfecht|bar adj. ['anfɛçtbaːr] contestable; '**~en** v/t. (irr. fechten, sep., -ge-, h) contest, dispute; ✝ avoid (contract); '**2ung** f (-/-en) contestation; ✝ avoidance; fig. temptation.

an|fertigen ['anfertigən] v/t. (sep., -ge-, h) make, manufacture; '**~feuchten** v/t. (sep., -ge-, h) moisten, wet, damp; '**~feuern** v/t. (sep., -ge-, h) fire, heat; sports: cheer; fig. encourage; '**~flehen** v/t. (sep., -ge-, h) implore; '**~fliegen** 🟊 v/t. (irr. fliegen, sep., -ge-, h) approach, head for (airport, etc.); '**2flug** m 🟊 approach (flight); fig. touch, tinge.

'**anforder|n** v/t. (sep., -ge-, h) demand; request; claim; '**2ung** f demand; request; claim.

'**Anfrage** f inquiry; '**2n** v/i. (sep., -ge-, h) ask (bei j-m s.o.); inquire (bei j-m nach et. of s.o. about s.th.).

an|freunden ['anfrɔyndən] v/refl. (sep., -ge-, h): sich ~ mit make friends with; '~frieren v/i. (irr. frieren, sep., -ge-, sein) freeze on (an dat. or acc. to); '~fügen v/t. (sep., -ge-, h) join, attach (an acc. to); '~fühlen v/t. (sep., -ge-, h) feel, touch; sich ~ feel.

Anfuhr ['anfu:r] f (-/-en) conveyance, carriage.

'anführ|en v/t. (sep., -ge-, h) lead; allege; ✗ command; quote, cite (authority, passage, etc.); dupe, fool, trick; '2er m (ring)leader; '2ungszeichen n/pl. quotation marks pl., inverted commas pl.

'Angabe f declaration; statement; instruction; F fig. bragging, showing off.

'angeb|en (irr. geben, sep., -ge-, h) 1. v/t. declare; state; specify; allege; give (name, reason); † quote (prices); denounce, inform against; 2. v/i. cards: deal first; F fig. brag, show off, Am. blow; '2er m (-s/-) informer; F braggart, Am. blowhard; '~lich adj. ['~pliç] supposed; pretended, alleged.

'angeboren adj. innate, inborn; ✗ congenital.

'Angebot n offer (a. †); at auction sale: bid; ✦ supply.

'ange|bracht adj. appropriate, suitable; well-timed; '~bunden adj.: kurz ~ sein be short (gegen with).

'angehen (irr. gehen, sep., -ge-) 1. v/i. (sein) begin; meat, etc.: go bad, go off; es geht an it will do; 2. v/t. (h): j-n ~ concern s.o.; das geht dich nichts an that is no business of yours.

'angehör|en v/i. (sep., no -ge-, h) belong to; '2ige ['~iga] m, f (-n/-n): seine ~n pl. his relations pl.; die nächsten ~n pl. the next of kin.

Angeklagte rt ['angəkla:ktə] m, f (-n/-n) the accused; prisoner (at the bar); defendant.

Angel ['anəl] f (-/-n) hinge; fishing-tackle, fishing-rod.

'angelegen adj.: sich et. ~ sein lassen make s.th. one's business; '2-heit f business, concern, affair, matter.

'Angel|gerät n fishing-tackle; '2n (ge-, h) 1. v/i. fish (nach for), angle (for) (both a. fig.); ~ in fish (river, etc.); 2. v/t. fish (trout); '~punkt fig. m pivot.

'Angel|sachse m Anglo-Saxon; '2-sächsisch adj. Anglo-Saxon.

'Angelschnur f fishing-line.

'ange|messen adj. suitable, appropriate; reasonable; adequate; '~-nehm adj. pleasant, agreeable, pleasing; sehr ~! glad or pleased to meet you; '~regt adj. ['~re:kt] stimulated; discussion: animated, lively; '~sehen adj. respected, esteemed.

'Angesicht n (-[e]s/-er, -e) face, countenance; von ~ zu ~ face to face; '2s prp. (gen.) in view of.

angestammt adj. ['angəʃtamt] hereditary, innate.

Angestellte ['angəʃtɛltə] m, f (-n/-n) employee; die ~n pl. the staff.

'ange|trunken adj. tipsy; '~wandt adj. ['~vant] applied; '~wiesen adj.: ~ sein auf (acc.) be dependent or thrown (up)on.

'angewöhnen v/t. (sep., -ge-, h): j-m et. ~ accustom s.o. to s.th.; sich et. ~ get into the habit of s.th.; take to (smoking).

'Angewohnheit f custom, habit.

Angina ✗ [an'gi:na] f (-/Anginen) angina; tonsillitis.

'angleichen v/t. (irr. gleichen, sep., -ge-, h) assimilate (an acc. to, with), adjust (to); sich ~ an (acc.) assimilate to or with, adjust or adapt o.s. to.

Angler ['anlər] m (-s/-) angler.

'angliedern v/t. (sep., -ge-, h) join; annex; affiliate.

Anglist [an'glist] m (-en/-en) professor or student of English, Angli(ci)st.

'angreif|en v/t. (irr. greifen, sep., -ge-, h) touch; draw upon (capital, provisions); attack; affect (health, material); ⚗ corrode; exhaust; '2er m (-s/-) aggressor, assailant.

'angrenzend adj. adjacent; adjoining.

'Angriff m attack, assault; in ~ nehmen set about; '~skrieg m offensive war; '2slustig adj. aggressive.

Angst [anst] f (-/=e) fear; anxiety; anguish; ich habe ~ I am afraid (vor dat. of); '~hase m coward.

ängstigen ['enstigən] v/t. (ge-, h) frighten, alarm; sich ~ be afraid (vor dat. of); be alarmed (um about).

ängstlich adj. ['enstliç] uneasy, nervous; anxious; afraid; scrupulous; timid; '2keit f (-/no pl.) anxiety; scrupulousness; timidity.

'an|haben v/t. (irr. haben, sep., -ge-, h) have (garment) on; das kann mir nichts ~ that can't do me any harm; '~haften v/i. (sep., -ge-, h) stick, adhere (dat. to); '~haken v/t. (sep., -ge-, h) hook on; tick (off), Am. check (off) (name, item).

'anhalten (irr. halten, sep., -ge-, h) 1. v/t. stop; j-n ~ zu et. keep s.o. to s.th.; den Atem ~ hold one's breath; 2. v/i. continue, last; stop; um ein Mädchen ~ propose to a girl; '~d adj. continuous; persevering.

'Anhaltspunkt m clue.

'Anhang m appendix, supplement (to book, etc.); followers pl., adherents pl.

'anhäng|en (sep., -ge-, h) 1. v/t. hang on; affix, attach, join; add; couple (on) (coach, vehicle); 2. v/i.

(irr. hängen) adhere to; '**2er** *m* (-s/-) adherent, follower; pendant *(of necklace, etc.)*; label, tag; trailer *(behind car, etc.)*.

anhänglich *adj.* ['anhɛnlɪç] devoted, attached; '**2keit** *f* (-/no *pl.*) devotion, attachment.

Anhängsel ['anhɛŋzəl] *n* (-s/-) appendage.

'**anhauchen** *v/t.* (*sep., -ge-, h*) breathe on; blow *(fingers)*.

'**anhäuf|en** *v/t. and v/refl.* (*sep., -ge-, h*) pile up, accumulate; '**2ung** *f* accumulation.

'**an|heben** *v/t.* *(irr. heben, sep., -ge-, h)* lift, raise; '**_heften** *v/t.* (*sep., -ge-, h*) fasten *(an acc.* to); stitch (to).

an'heim|fallen *v/i. (irr. fallen, sep., -ge-, sein)*: *j-m* \~ fall to s.o.; _**stellen** *v/t.* (*sep., -ge-, h*): *j-m et.* \~ leave s.th. to s.o.

'**Anhieb** *m*: *auf* \~ at the first go.

'**Anhöhe** *f* rise, elevation, hill.

'**anhören** *v/t.* (*sep., -ge-, h*) listen to; *sich* \~ sound.

Anilin ['ani'li:n] *n* (-s/no *pl.*) anilin(e).

'**ankämpfen** *v/i.* (*sep., -ge-, h*): \~ *gegen* struggle against.

'**Ankauf** *m* purchase.

Anker ⚓ ['aŋkər] *m* (-s/-) anchor; *vor* \~ *gehen* cast anchor; '**_kette** ⚓ *f* cable; '**2n** ⚓ *v/t. and v/i.* (ge-, h) anchor; '**_uhr** *f* lever watch.

'**anketten** *v/t.* (*sep., -ge-, h*) chain *(an dat. or acc.* to).

'**Anklage** *f* accusation, charge; ⚖️ *a.* indictment; '**2n** *v/t.* (*sep., -ge-, h*) accuse *(gen. or wegen* of), charge (with); ⚖️ *a.* indict (for).

'**Ankläger** *m* accuser; *öffentlicher* \~ ⚖️ public prosecutor; *Am.* district attorney.

'**anklammern** *v/t.* (*sep., -ge-, h*) clip *s.th.* on; *sich* \~ cling *(an dat. or acc.* to).

'**Anklang** *m*: \~ *an (acc.)* suggestion of; \~ *finden* meet with approval.

'**an|kleben** *v/t.* (*sep., -ge-, h*) stick on *(an dat. or acc.* to); glue on (to); paste on (to); gum on (to); '**_kleiden** *v/t.* (*sep., -ge-, h*) dress; *sich* \~ dress (o.s.); '**_klopfen** *v/i.* (*sep., -ge-, h*) knock *(an acc.* at); '**_knipsen** ⚡ *v/t.* (*sep., -ge-, h*) turn or switch on; '**_knüpfen** (*sep., -ge-, h*) **1.** *v/t.* tie *(an dat. or acc.* to); *fig.* begin; *Verbindungen* \~ form connexions or *(Am. only)* connections; **2.** *v/i.* refer *(an acc.* to); '**_kommen** *v/i.* *(irr. kommen, sep., -ge-, sein)* arrive; \~ *auf (acc.)* depend (up)on; *es darauf* \~ *lassen* run the risk, risk it; *darauf kommt es an* that is the point; *es kommt nicht darauf an* it does not matter.

Ankömmling ['ankœmlɪŋ] *m* (-s/-e) new-comer, new arrival.

'**ankündig|en** *v/t.* (*sep., -ge-, h*) announce; advertise; '**2ung** *f* announcement; advertisement.

Ankunft ['ankunft] *f* (-/no *pl.*) arrival.

'**an|kurbeln** *v/t.* (*sep., -ge-, h*) *mot.* crank up; *die Wirtschaft* \~ F boost the economy; '**_lächeln** *v/t.* (*sep., -ge-, h*), '**_lachen** *v/t.* (*sep., -ge-, h*) smile at.

'**Anlage** *f* construction; installation; ⊕ plant; grounds *pl.*, park; plan, arrangement, layout; enclosure *(to letter)*; ✝ investment, talent; predisposition, tendency, *öffentliche* \~*n pl.* public gardens *pl.*, '**_kapital** ✝ *n* invested capital.

'**anlangen** (*sep., -ge-, h*) **1.** *v/i. (sein)* arrive at; **2.** *v/t.* (*h*) F touch; concern; *was mich anlangt* as far as I am concerned, (speaking) for myself.

Anlaß ['anlas] *m* (Anlasses/Anlässe) occasion; *ohne allen* \~ without any reason.

'**anlass|en** *v/t. (irr. lassen, sep., -ge-, h)* F leave or keep *(garment, etc.)* on; leave *(light, etc.)* on; ⊕ start, set going; *sich gut* \~ promise well; '**2er** *mot. m* (-s/-) starter.

anläßlich *prp. (gen.)* ['anlɛslɪç] on the occasion of.

'**Anlauf** *m* start, run; '**2en** *(irr. laufen, sep., -ge-)* **1.** *v/i. (sein)* run up; start; tarnish, (grow) dim; \~ *gegen* run against; **2.** ⚓ *v/t.* (*h*) call or touch at *(port)*.

'**an|legen** (*sep., -ge-, h*) **1.** *v/t.* put *(an acc.* to, against); lay out *(garden)*; invest *(money)*; level *(gun)*, put on *(garment)*; found *(town)*; ⚡ apply *(dressing)*; lay in *(provisions)*; *Feuer* \~ *an (acc.)* set fire to; **2.** *v/i.* ⚓: land; moor; \~ *auf (acc.)* aim at; '**_lehnen** *v/t.* (*sep., -ge-, h*) lean *(an acc.* against); leave or set *(door)* ajar; *sich* \~ *an (acc.)* lean against or on.

Anleihe ['anlaɪə] *f* (-/-n) loan.

'**anleit|en** *v/t.* (*sep., -ge-, h*) guide *(zu* to); instruct *(in dat.* in); '**2ung** *f* guidance, instruction; guide.

'**Anliegen** *n* (-s/-) desire, request.

'**an|locken** *v/t.* (*sep., -ge-, h*) allure, entice; decoy; '**_machen** *v/t.* (*sep., -ge-, h*) fasten *(an acc.* to), fix (to); make, light *(fire)*; ⚡ switch on *(light)*; dress *(salad)*; '**_malen** *v/t.* (*sep., -ge-, h*) paint.

'**Anmarsch** *m* approach.

anmaß|en ['anmaːsən] *v/refl.* (*sep., -ge-, h*) arrogate *s.th.* to o.s.; assume *(right)*; presume; '**_end** *adj.* arrogant; '**2ung** *f* (-/-en) arrogance, presumption.

'**anmeld|en** *v/t.* (*sep., -ge-, h*) announce, notify; *sich* \~ *bei* make an appointment with; '**2ung** *f* announcement, notification.

'anmerk|en v/t. (sep., -ge-, h) mark; note down; j-m et. ~ observe or perceive s.th. in s.o.; '2ung f (-/-en) remark; note; annotation; comment.

'anmessen v/t. (irr. messen, sep., -ge-, h): j-m e-n Anzug ~ measure s.o. for a suit; s. angemessen.

'Anmut f (-/no pl.) grace, charm, loveliness; '2ig adj. charming, graceful, lovely.

'an|nageln v/t. (sep., -ge-, h) nail on (an acc. to); '~nähen v/t. (sep., -ge-, h) sew on (an acc. to).

annäher|nd adj. ['annɛːərnt] approximate; '2ung f (-/-en) approach.

Annahme ['annɑːmə] f (-/-n) acceptance; receiving-office; fig. assumption, supposition.

'annehm|bar adj. acceptable; price: reasonable; '~en (irr. nehmen, sep., -ge-, h) 1. v/t. accept, take; fig.: suppose, take it, Am. guess; assume; contract (habit); adopt (child); parl. pass (bill); sich (gen.) ~ attend to s.th.; befriend s.o.; 2. v/t. accept; '2lichkeit f (-/-en) amenity, agreeableness.

Annexion [anɛk'sjoːn] f (-/-en) annexation.

Annonce [a'nõːsə] f (-/-n) advertisement. [mous.]

anonym adj. [ano'nyːm] anony-)

anordn|en ['an'-] v/t. (sep., -ge-, h) order; arrange; direct; '2ung f arrangement; direction; order.

'anpacken v/t. (sep., -ge-, h) seize, grasp; fig. tackle.

'anpass|en v/t. (sep., -ge-, h) fit, adapt, suit; adjust; try or fit (garment) on; sich ~ adapt o.s. (dat. to); '2ung f (-/-en) adaptation; '~ungsfähig adj. adaptable.

'anpflanz|en v/t. (sep., -ge-, h) cultivate, plant; '2ung f cultivation; plantation.

Anprall ['anpral] m (-[e]s/%-e) impact; '2en v/i. (sep., -ge-, sein) strike (an acc. against).

'anpreisen v/t. (irr. preisen, sep., -ge-, h) commend, praise; boost, push.

'Anprobe f try-on, fitting.

'an|probieren v/t. (sep., no -ge-, h) try or fit on; '~raten v/t. (irr. raten, sep., -ge-, h) advise; '~rechnen v/t. (sep., -ge-, h) charge; hoch ~ value highly.

'Anrecht n right, title, claim (auf acc. to).

'Anrede f address; '2n v/t. (sep., -ge-, h) address, speak to.

'anreg|en v/t. (sep., -ge-, h) stimulate; suggest; '~end adj. stimulative, stimulating; suggestive; '2ung f stimulation; suggestion.

'Anreiz m incentive; '2en v/t. (sep., -ge-, h) stimulate; incite.

'an|rennen v/i. (irr. rennen, sep., -ge-, sein): ~ gegen run against; angerannt kommen come running; '~richten v/t. (sep., -ge-, h) prepare, dress (food, salad); cause, do (damage).

anrüchig adj. ['anryçiç] disreputable.

'anrücken v/i. (sep., -ge-, sein) approach.

'Anruf m call (a. teleph.); '2en v/t. (irr. rufen, sep., -ge-, h) call (zum Zeugen to witness); teleph. ring up, F phone, Am. call up; hail (ship); invoke (God, etc.); appeal to (s.o.'s help).

'anrühren v/t. (sep., -ge-, h) touch; mix.

'Ansage f announcement; '2n v/t. (sep., -ge-, h) announce; '~r m (-s/-) announcer; compère, Am. master of ceremonies.

'ansammeln v/t. (sep., -ge-, h) collect, gather; accumulate, amass; sich ~ collect, gather; accumulate.

ansässig adj. ['anzɛsiç] resident.

'Ansatz m start.

'an|schaffen v/t. (sep., -ge-, h) procure, provide; purchase; sich et. ~ provide or supply o.s. with s.th.; '~schalten ⨎ v/t. (sep., -ge-, h) connect; switch on (light).

'anschau|en v/t. (sep., -ge-, h) look at, view; '~lich adj. clear, vivid; graphic.

'Anschauung f (-/-en) view; perception; conception; intuition; contemplation; '~smaterial n illustrative material; '~sunterricht ['anʃauuŋs⁹-] m visual instruction, object-lessons pl.; '~svermögen n intuitive faculty.

'Anschein m (-[e]s/no pl.) appearance; '2end adj. apparent, seeming.

'an|schicken v/refl. (sep., -ge-, h): sich ~ et. zu tun get ready for s.th.; prepare for s.th.; set about doing s.th., '~schirren ['~ʃirən] v/t. (sep., -ge-, h) harness.

'Anschlag m ⨁ stop, catch; ♪ touch; notice; placard, poster, bill; estimate; calculation; plot; e-n ~ auf j-n verüben make an attempt on s.o.'s life; '~brett ['~k-] n noticeboard, Am. bulletin board; '2en ['~gən] (irr. schlagen, sep., -ge-, h) 1. v/t. strike (an dat. or acc. against), knock (against); post up (bill); ♪ touch; level (gun); estimate, rate; 2. v/i. strike (an acc. against), knock (against); dog: bark; 𝕗 take (effect); food: agree (bei with); '~säule ['~k-] f advertising pillar; '~zettel ['~k-] m notice; placard, poster, bill.

'anschließen v/t. (irr. schließen, sep., -ge-, h) fix with a lock; join, attach, annex; ⊕, ⨎ connect; sich j-m ~ join s.o.; sich e-r Meinung ~

follow an opinion; '~d adj. adjacent (an acc. to); subsequent (to).

'Anschluß m joining; ⚓, ⚡, teleph., gas, etc.: connexion, (Am. only) connection; ~ haben an (acc.) ⚓, boat: connect with; ⚓ run in connexion with; ~ finden make friends (an acc. with), F pal up (with); teleph.: ~ bekommen get through; '~dose ⚡ f (wall) socket; '~zug ⚓ m connecting train, connexion.

'an|schmiegen v/refl. (sep., -ge-, h): sich ~ an (acc.) nestle to; '~schmieren v/t. (sep., -ge-, h) (be)smear, grease; F fig. cheat; '~schnallen v/t. (sep., -ge-, h) buckle on; bitte ~! 🚗 fasten seat-belts, please!; '~schnauzen F v/t. (sep., -ge-, h) snap at, blow s.o. up, Am. a. bawl s.o. out; '~schneiden v/t. (irr. schneiden, sep., -ge-, h) cut; broach (subject).

'Anschnitt m first cut or slice.

'an|schrauben v/t. (sep., -ge-, h) screw on (an dat. or acc. to); '~schreiben v/t. (irr. schreiben, sep., -ge-, h) write down; sports, games: score; et. ~ lassen have s.th. charged to one's account; buy s.th. on credit; '~schreien v/t. (irr. schreien, sep., -ge-, h) shout at.

'Anschrift f address.

'an|schuldigen ['anʃuldigən] v/t. (sep., -ge-, h) accuse, incriminate; '~schwärzen v/t. (sep., -ge-, h) blacken; fig. a. defame.

'anschwell|en (irr. schwellen, sep., -ge-) 1. v/i. (sein) swell; increase, rise; 2. v/t. (h) swell; '2ung f swelling.

'anschwemm|en ['anʃvemən] v/t. (sep., -ge-, h) wash ashore; geol. deposit (alluvium); '2ung f (-/-en) wash; geol. alluvial deposits pl., alluvium.

'ansehen 1. v/t. (irr. sehen, sep., -ge-, h) (take a) look at; view; regard, consider (als as); et. mit ~ witness s.th.; ~ für take for; man sieht ihm sein Alter nicht an he does not look his age; 2. 2 n (-s/no pl.) authority, prestige; respect; F appearance, aspect.

ansehnlich adj. ['anzeːnliç] considerable; good-looking.

'an|seilen mount. v/t. and v/refl. (sep., -ge-, h) rope; '~sengen v/t. (sep., -ge-, h) singe; '~setzen (sep., -ge-, h) 1. v/t. put (an acc. to); add (to); fix, appoint (date); rate; fix, quote (prices); charge; put forth (leaves, etc.); put on (flesh); put (food) on (to boil); Rost ~ rust; 2. v/i. try; start; get ready.

'Ansicht f (-/-en) sight, view; fig. view, opinion; meiner ~ nach in my opinion; zur ~ 🏪 on approval; '~s-(post)karte f picture postcard; '~ssache f matter of opinion.

'ansied|eln v/t. and v/refl. (sep., -ge-, h) settle; '2ler m settler; '2lung f settlement.

'Ansinnen n (-s/-) request, demand.

'anspann|en v/t. (sep., -ge-, h) stretch; put or harness (horses, etc.) to the carriage, etc.; fig. strain, exert; '2ung fig. f strain, exertion.

'anspeien v/t. (irr. speien, sep., -ge-, h) spit (up)on or at.

'anspiel|en v/i. (sep., -ge-, h) cards: lead; sports: lead off; football: kick off; ~ auf (acc.) allude to, hint at; '2ung f (-/-en) allusion, hint.

'anspitzen v/t. (sep., -ge-, h) point, sharpen.

'Ansporn m (-[e]s/⚡ -e) spur; '2en v/t. (sep., -ge-, h) spur s.o. on.

'Ansprache f address, speech; e-e ~ halten deliver an address.

'ansprechen v/t. (irr. sprechen, sep., -ge-, h) speak to, address; appeal to; '~d adj. appealing.

'an|springen (irr. springen, sep., -ge-) 1. v/i. (sein) engine: start; 2. v/t. (h) jump (up)on, leap at; '~spritzen v/t. (sep., -ge-, h) splash (j-n mit et. s.th. on s.o.); (be)sprinkle.

'Anspruch m claim (a. 🔩) (auf acc. to), pretension (to); 🔩 title (to); ~ haben auf (acc.) be entitled to; in ~ nehmen claim s.th.; Zeit in ~ nehmen take up time; '2slos adj. unpretentious; unassuming; '2svoll adj. pretentious.

'an|spülen v/t. (sep., -ge-, h) s. anschwemmen; '~stacheln v/t. (sep., -ge-, h) goad (on).

Anstalt ['anʃtalt] f (-/-en) establishment, institution; ~en treffen zu make arrangements for.

'Anstand m 1. (-[e]s/⚡e) hunt. stand; objection; 2. (-[e]s/⚡, ⚡e) good manners pl.; decency, propriety.

anständig adj. ['anʃtɛndiç] decent; respectable; price: fair, handsome; '2keit f (-/⚡, -en) decency.

'Anstands|gefühl n sense of propriety; tact; '2los adv. unhesitatingly.

'anstarren v/t. (sep., -ge-, h) stare or gaze at.

anstatt prp. (gen.) and cj. [an'ʃtat] instead of.

'anstaunen v/t. (sep., -ge-, h) gaze at s.o. or s.th. in wonder.

'ansteck|en v/t. (sep., -ge-, h) pin on; put on (ring); 🏥 infect; set on fire; kindle (fire); light (candle, etc.); '~end adj. infectious; contagious; fig. a. catching; '2ung 🏥 f (-/-en) infection; contagion.

'an|stehen v/i. (irr. stehen, sep., -ge-, h) queue up (nach for), Am. stand in line (for); '~steigen v/i. (irr. steigen, sep., -ge-, sein) ground: rise, ascend; fig. increase.

'anstell|en v/t. (sep., -ge-, h) engage, employ, hire; make (ex-

periments); draw (*comparison*); turn on (*light, etc.*); manage; *sich ~* queue up (*nach for*), *Am.* line up (*for*); *sich dumm ~* set about *s.th.* stupidly; '*~ig adj.* handy, skil(l)ful; '**2ung** *f* place, position, job; employment.

Anstieg ['anʃtiːk] *m* (-[e]s/-e) ascent.

'**anstift|en** *v/t.* (*sep., -ge-, h*) instigate; '**2er** *m* instigator; '**2ung** *f* instigation.

'**anstimmen** *v/t.* (*sep., -ge-, h*) strike up (*tune*).

'**Anstoß** *m* football: kick-off; *fig.* impulse; offen|ce, *Am. -se; ~ erregen* give offence (*bei* to); *~ nehmen an* (*dat.*) take offence at; *~ geben zu* et. start s.th., initiate s.th.; '**2en** (*irr. stoßen, sep., -ge-*) 1. *v/t.* (h) push, knock (*acc. or on* against); nudge; 2. *v/i.* (sein) knock (*an acc.* against); border (*on, upon*); adjoin; 3. *v/i.* (h): *mit der Zunge ~* lisp; *auf j-s Gesundheit ~* drink (to) s.o.'s health; '**2end** *adj.* adjoining.

anstößig *adj.* ['anʃtøːsiç] shocking.

'**an|strahlen** *v/t.* (*sep., -ge-, h*) illuminate; floodlight (*building, etc.*); *fig.* beam at *s.o.*; '**~streben** *v/t.* (*sep., -ge-, h*) aim at, aspire to, strive for.

'**anstreich|en** *v/t.* (*irr. streichen, sep., -ge-, h*) paint; whitewash; mark; underline (*mistake*); '**2er** *m* (-s/-) house-painter; decorator.

anstreng|en ['anʃtrɛŋən] *v/t.* (*sep., -ge-, h*) exert; try (*eyes*); fatigue; *Prozeß ~* bring an action (*gegen j-n* against s.o.); *sich ~* exert o.s.; '**~end** *adj.* strenuous; trying (*für* to); '**2ung** *f* (-/-en) exertion, strain, effort.

'**Anstrich** *m* paint, colo(u)r; coat (-ing); *fig.*: tinge; air.

'**Ansturm** *m* assault; onset; *~ auf* (*acc.*) rush for; ✝ run on (*bank*).

'**anstürmen** *v/i.* (*sep., -ge-, sein*) storm, rush.

'**Anteil** *m* share, portion; *~ nehmen an* (*dat.*) take an interest in; sympathize with; *~nahme* ['~naːmə] *f* (-/*no pl.*) sympathy; interest; '**~schein** ✝ *m* share-certificate.

Antenne [an'tɛnə] *f* (-/-n) aerial.

Antialkoholiker [anti°alko'hoːlikər, '~] *m* (-s/-) teetotaller.

antik *adj.* [an'tiːk] antique.

Antilope *zo.* [anti'loːpə] *f* (-/-n) antelope.

Antipathie [antipa'tiː] *f* (-/-n) antipathy.

'**antippen** F *v/t.* (*sep., -ge-, h*) tap.

Antiquar [anti'kvaːr] *m* (-s/-e) second-hand bookseller; *~iat* [~ar-'jaːt] *n* (-[e]s/-e) second-hand bookshop; **2isch** *adj. and adv.* [~'kvaːriʃ] second-hand.

Antiquitäten [antikvi'tɛːtən] *f/pl.* antiques *pl.*

'**Anti-Rakete** *f* anti-ballistic missile.

antiseptisch ⚕ *adj.* [anti'zɛptiʃ] antiseptic.

Antlitz ['antlits] *n* (-es/✝ -e) face, countenance.

Antrag ['antraːk] *m* (-[e]s/-̈e) offer, proposal; application, request; *parl.* motion; *~ stellen auf* (*acc.*) make an application for; *parl.* put a motion for; '**~steller** *m* (-s/-) applicant; *parl.* mover; ⚖ petitioner.

'**an|treffen** *v/t.* (*irr. treffen, sep., -ge-, h*) meet with, find; '**~treiben** (*irr. treiben, sep., -ge-*) 1. *v/i.* (sein) drift ashore; 2. *v/t.* (h) drive (on); *fig.* impel; '**~treten** (*irr. treten, sep., -ge-*) 1. *v/t.* (h) enter upon (*office*); take up (*position*); set out on (*journey*); enter upon take possession of (*inheritance*); 2. *v/i.* (sein) take one's place; ✕ fall in.

'**Antrieb** *m* motive, impulse; ⊕ drive, propulsion.

'**Antritt** *m* (-[e]s/✝ -e) entrance (*into office*); taking up (*of position*); setting out (*on journey*); entering into possession (*of inheritance*).

'**antun** *v/t.* (*irr. tun, sep., -ge-, h*): *j-m* et. *~* do s.th. to s.o.; *sich* et. *~* lay hands on o.s.

'**Antwort** *f* (-/-en) answer, reply (*auf acc.* to); '**2en** (ge-, h) 1. *v/i.* answer (*j-m* s.o.), reply (*j-m* to s.o.; *both*: *auf acc.* to); 2. *v/t.* answer (*auf acc.* to), reply (to); '**~schein** *m* (international) reply coupon.

'**an|vertrauen** *v/t.* (*sep., no -ge-, h*): *j-m* et. *~* (en)trust s.o. with s.th., entrust s.th. to s.o.; confide s.th. to s.o.; '**~wachsen** *v/i.* (*irr. wachsen, sep., -ge-, sein*) take root; *fig.* increase; *~ an* (*acc.*) grow on to.

Anwalt ['anvalt] *m* (-[e]s/-̈e) lawyer; solicitor, *Am.* attorney; counsel; barrister, *Am.* counsel(l)or; *fig.* advocate.

'**Anwandlung** *f* fit; impulse.

'**Anwärter** *m* candidate, aspirant; expectant.

Anwartschaft ['anvartʃaft] *f* (-/-en) expectancy; candidacy; prospect (*auf acc.* of).

'**anweis|en** *v/t.* (*irr. weisen, sep., -ge-, h*) assign; instruct; direct; *s. angewiesen*; '**2ung** *f* assignment; instruction; direction; ✝: cheque, *Am.* check; draft; *s. Postanweisung*.

'**anwend|en** *v/t.* ([*irr. wenden,*] *sep., -ge-, h*) employ, use; apply (*auf acc.* to); *s. angewandt*; '**2ung** *f* application.

'**anwerben** *v/t.* (*irr. werben, sep., -ge-, h*) ✕ enlist, enrol(l); engage.

'**Anwesen** *n* estate; property.

'**anwesen|d** *adj.* present; '**2heit** *f* (-/*no pl.*) presence.

'**Anzahl** *f* (-/*no pl.*) number; quantity.

'anzahl|en v/t. (sep., -ge-, h) pay on account; pay a deposit; '2ung f (first) instal(l)ment; deposit.

'anzapfen v/t. (sep., -ge-, h) tap.

'Anzeichen n symptom; sign.

Anzeige ['antsaigə] f (-/-n) notice, announcement; ✝ advice; advertisement; ⅌ information; '2n v/t. (sep., -ge-, h) announce, notify; ✝ advise; advertise; indicate; ⊕ instrument: indicate, show; thermometer: read (degrees); j-n ~ denounce s.o., inform against s.o.

'anziehen (irr. ziehen, sep., -ge-, h) 1. v/t. draw, pull; draw (rein); tighten (screw); put on (garment); dress; fig. attract; 2. v/i. draw; prices: rise; '~d adj. attractive, interesting.

'Anziehung f attraction; '~skraft f attractive power; attraction.

'Anzug m 1. (-[e]s/~e) dress; suit; 2. (-[e]s/no pl.): im ~ sein storm: be gathering; danger: be impending.

anzüglich adj. ['antsy:klıç] personal; '2keit f (-/-en) personality.

'anzünden v/t. (sep., -ge-, h) light, kindle; strike (match); set (building) on fire.

apathisch adj. [a'pɑ:tıʃ] apathetic.

Apfel ['apfəl] m (-s/¨) apple; '~mus n apple-sauce; ~sine [~'zi:nə] f (-/-n) orange; '~wein m cider.

Apostel [a'pɔstəl] m (-s/-) apostle.

Apostroph [apo'stro:f] m (-s/-e) apostrophe.

Apotheke [apo'te:kə] f (-/-n) chemist's shop, pharmacy, Am. drugstore; ~r m (-s/-) chemist, Am. druggist, pharmacist.

Apparat [apa'rɑ:t] m (-[e]s/-e) apparatus; device; teleph.: am ~! speaking!; teleph.: am ~ bleiben hold the line.

Appell [a'pɛl] m (-s/-e) ✕: roll-call; inspection; parade; fig. appeal (an acc. to); 2ieren [~'li:rən] v/i. (no -ge-, h) appeal (an acc. to).

Appetit [ape'ti:t] m (-[e]s/-e) appetite; 2lich adj. appetizing, savo(u)ry, dainty.

Applaus [a'plaus] m (-es/¨, -e) applause.

Aprikose [apri'ko:zə] f (-/-n) apricot.

April [a'prıl] m (-[s]/-e) April.

Aquarell [akva'rɛl] n (-s/-e) watercolo(u)r (painting), aquarelle.

Aquarium [a'kvɑ:rıum] n (-s/ Aquarien) aquarium.

Äquator [ɛ'kvɑ:tɔr] m (-s/¨, -en) equator.

Ära ['ɛ:ra] f (-/¨, Ären) era.

Arab|er ['ɑrabər] m (-s/-) Arab; 2isch adj. [a'rɑ:bıʃ] Arabian, Arab(ic).

Arbeit ['arbaıt] f (-/-en) work; labo(u)r, toil; employment; job;

---

task; paper; workmanship; bei der ~ at work; sich an die ~ machen, an die ~ gehen set to work; (keine) ~ haben be in (out of) work; die ~ niederlegen stop work, down tools; '2en (ge-, h) 1. v/i. work; labo(u)r, toil; 2. v/t. work; make.

'Arbeiter m (-s/-) worker; workman, labo(u)rer, hand; '~in f (-/-nen) female worker; working woman, workwoman; '~klasse f working class(es pl.); '~partei f Labo(u)r Party; '~schaft f (-/-en), '~stand m working class(es pl.), labo(u)r.

'Arbeit|geber m (-s/-), '~geberin f (-/-nen) employer; '~nehmer m (-s/-), '~nehmerin f (-/-nen) employee.

'arbeitsam adj. industrious.

'Arbeits|amt n labo(u)r exchange; '~anzug m overall; '~beschaffung f (-/-en) provision of work; '~bescheinigung f certificate of employment; '~einkommen n earned income; '2fähig adj. able to work; '~gericht n labo(u)r or industrial court; '~kleidung f working clothes pl.; '~kraft f working power; worker, hand; Arbeitskräfte pl. a. labo(u)r; '~leistung f efficiency; power (of engine); output (of factory); '~lohn m wages pl., pay; '2los adj. out of work, unemployed; '~lose m (-n/-n): die ~n pl. the unemployed pl.; '~losenunterstützung f unemployment benefit; ~ beziehen F be on the dole; '~losigkeit f (-/no pl.) unemployment; '~markt m labo(u)r market; '~minister m Minister of Labour, Am. Secretary of Labor; '~nachweis(stelle f) m employment registry office, Am. labor registry office; ~niederlegung f (-/-en) strike, Am. F a. walkout; '~pause f break, intermission; '~platz m place of work; job; '~raum m workroom; '2scheu adj. work-shy; '~scheu f aversion to work; '~schutzgesetz n protective labo(u)r law; '~tag m working day, workday; '2unfähig adj. incapable of working; disabled; '~weise f practice, method of working; '~willige m (-n/-n) non-striker; '~zeit f working time; working hours pl.; '~zeug n tools pl.; '~zimmer n workroom; study.

Archäo|loge [arçeo'lo:gə] m (-n/-n) arch(a)eologist; ~logie [~o'gi:] f (-/no pl.) arch(a)eology.

Arche ['arçə] f (-/-n) ark.

Architekt [arçi'tɛkt] m (-en/-en) architect; ~ur [~'tu:r] f (-/-en) architecture.

Archiv [ar'çi:f] n (-s/-e) archives pl.; record office.

Areal [are'ɑ:l] n (-s/-e) area.

Arena [a're:na] *f* (-/Arenen) arena; bullring; (circus-)ring.

arg *adj.* [ark] bad; wicked; gross.

Ärger ['ɛrgər] *m* (-s/*no pl.*) vexation, annoyance; anger; '2lich *adj.* vexed, F mad, angry (*auf, über acc.* at *s.th.*, with *s.o.*); annoying, vexatious; '2n *v/t.* (ge-, h) annoy, vex, irritate, fret; bother; *sich ~* feel angry *or* vexed (*über acc.* at, about *s.th.*; with *s.o.*); ~nis *n* (-ses/-se) scandal, offen|ce, *Am.* -se.

Arg|list *f* (-/*no pl.*) cunning, craft (-iness); 2listig *adj.* crafty, cunning; 2los *adj.* guileless; artless, unsuspecting; ~wohn ['~vo:n] *m* (-[e]s/*no pl.*) suspicion; 2wöhnen ['~vø:nən] *v/t.* (ge-, h) suspect; 2wöhnisch *adj.* suspicious.

Arie *♪* ['a:rjə] *f* (-/-n) aria.

Aristokrat [aristo'kra:t] *m* (-en/-en), ~in *f* (-/-nen) aristocrat; ~le [~kra-'ti:] *f* (-/-n) aristocracy.

Arkade [ar'ka:də] *f* (-/-n) arcade.

arm[1] *adj.* [arm] poor.

Arm[2] [~] *m* (-[e]s/-e) arm; branch (*of river, etc.*); F: *j-n auf den ~ nehmen* pull *s.o.*'s leg.

Armaturenbrett [arma'tu:rənbrɛt] *n* instrument board, dash-board.

Arm|band ≈ bracelet, ~banduhr ['armbant⁹-] *f* wrist watch; '~bruch *m* fracture of the arm.

Armee [ar'me:] *f* (-/-en) army.

Ärmel ['ɛrməl] *m* (-s/-) sleeve; '~kanal *m the* English) Channel.

Armen|haus ≈ alms-house, *Brt.* a. workhouse; ~pflege *f* poor relief; ~pfleger *m* guardian of the poor; welfare officer; '~unterstützung *f* poor relief.

ärmlich *adj.* ['ɛrmliç] *s.* armselig.

armselig *adj.* poor; wretched; miserable, shabby; paltry.

Armut ['armu:t] *f* (-/*no pl.*) poverty.

Aroma [a'ro:ma] *n* (-s/Aromen, Aromata, -s) aroma, flavo(u)r; fragrance.

Arrest [a'rɛst] *m* (-es/-e) arrest; confinement; seizure (*of goods*); detention (*of pupil, etc.*); *~ bekommen* be kept in.

Art [a:rt] *f* (-/-en) kind, sort; ♀, *zo.* species; manner, way; nature; manners *pl.*; breed, race (*of animals*); *auf die(se) ~* in this way; '2en *v/i.* (ge-, sein): *~ nach* take after.

Arterie *anat.* [ar'te:rjə] *f* (-/-n) [artery.]

artig *adj.* ['a:rtiç] good, well-behaved; civil, polite; '2keit *f* (-/-en) good behavio(u)r; politeness; civility, *a.* civilities *pl.*

Artikel [ar'ti:kəl] *m* (-s/-) article; commodity.

Artillerie [artilə'ri:] *f* (-/-n) artillery.

Artist [ar'tist] *m* (-en/-en), ~in *f* (-/-nen) circus performer.

Arznei [arts'nai] *f* (-/-en) medicine, F physic; ~kunde *f* (-/*no pl.*) pharmaceutics; ~mittel *n* medicine, drug.

Arzt [a:rtst] *m* (-es/*=e) doctor, medical man; physician.

Ärztin ['ɛ:rtstin] *f* (-/-nen) woman *or* lady doctor.

ärztlich *adj.* ['ɛ:rtstliç] medical.

As [as] *n* (-ses/-se) ace.

Asche ['aʃə] *f* (-/-n) ash(es *pl.*); '~nbahn *f* *sports:* cinder-track, *mot.* dirt-track; '~nbecher *m* ash-tray; ~nbrödel ['~nbrø:dəl] *n* (-s/*no pl.*), ~nputtel ['~nputəl] *n* 1. (-s/*no pl.*) Cinderella; 2. (-s/-) drudge.

Ascher'mittwoch *m* Ash Wednesday.

'asch'grau *adj.* ash-grey, ashy, *Am.* ash-gray.

äsen *hunt.* ['ɛ:zən] *v/i.* (ge-, h) graze, browse.

Asiat [az'ja:t] *m* (-en/-en), ~in *f* (-/-nen) Asiatic, Asian; 2isch *adj.* Asiatic, Asian.

Asket [as'ke:t] *m* (-en/-en) ascetic.

Asphalt [as'falt] *m* (-[e]s/-e) asphalt; 2ieren [~'ti:rən] *v/t.* (*no* -ge-, h) asphalt.

aß [a:s] *pret. of* essen.

Assistent [asis'tɛnt] *m* (-en/-en), ~in *f* (-/-nen) assistant.

Ast [ast] *m* (-es/*=e) branch, bough; knot (*in timber*); '~loch *n* knot-hole.

Astro|naut [astro'naut] *m* (-en/-en) astronaut; ~nom [~'no:m] *m* (-en/-en) astronomer.

Asyl [a'zy:l] *n* (-s/-e) asylum; *fig.* sanctuary.

Atelier [atə'lje:] *n* (-s/-s) studio.

Atem ['a:təm] *m* (-s/*no pl.*) breath; *außer ~* out of breath, '2los *adj.* breathless; '~not *♀ f* difficulty in breathing; ~pause *f* breathing-space; ~zug *m* breath, respiration.

Äther ['ɛ:tər] *m* 1. (-s/*no pl.*) the ether; 2. *♠* (-s/-) ether; 2isch *adj.* [ɛ:'te:riʃ] ethereal, etheric.

Athlet [at'le:t] *m* (-en/-en), ~in *f* (-/-nen) athlete; ~ik *f* (-/*no pl.*) athletics *mst sg.*; 2isch *adj.* athletic.

atlantisch *adj* [at'lantiʃ] Atlantic.

Atlas ['atlas] *m* 1. *geogr.* (-/*no pl.*) Atlas; 2. (-, -ses/-se, Atlanten) *maps:* atlas; 3. (-, -ses/-se) *textiles:* satin.

atmen ['a:tmən] *v/i. and v/t.* (ge-, h) breathe.

Atmosphär|e [atmo'sfɛ:rə] *f* (-/-n) atmosphere; 2isch *adj.* atmospheric.

Atmung *f* (-/-en) breathing, respiration.

Atom [a'to:m] *n* (-s/-e) atom; 2ar *adj.* [ato'ma:r] atomic; ~bombe *f* atomic bomb, atom-bomb, A-bomb; ~energie *f* atomic *or* nuclear energy; ~forschung *f* atomic *or* nuclear research; ~kern *m* atomic nucleus; ~kraftwerk *n* nuclear power station; **∼meiler** *m* atomic pile, nuclear reactor; **∼physiker** *m* atomic physicist; **∼reaktor** *m* nuclear reactor, atomic pile; **∼versuch** *m* atomic test; **∼waffe** *f* atomic *or* nuclear weapon; **∼wissenschaftler** *m* atomic scientist; **∼zeitalter** *n* atomic age.

Attent|at [atɛn'taːt] *n* (-[e]s/-e) (attempted) assassination; *fig.* outrage; **∼äter** [‿ɛːtər] *m* (-s/-) assailant, assassin.

Attest [a'tɛst] *n* (-es/-e) certificate; **2ieren** [‿'tiːrən] *v/t.* (*no* -ge-, *h*) attest, certify.

Attraktion [atrak'tsjoːn] *f* (-/-en) attraction.

Attrappe [a'trapə] *f* (-/-n) dummy.

Attribut [atri'buːt] *n* (-[e]s/-e) attribute; *gr.* attributive.

ätz|en ['ɛtsən] *v/t.* (ge-, *h*) corrode; *⚘* cauterize; etch (*metal plate*); **'∼end** *adj.* corrosive; caustic (*a. fig.*); **'2ung** *f* (-/-en) corrosion; *⚘* cauterization; etching.

au *int.* [au] oh!; ouch!

auch *cj.* [aux] also, too, likewise; even; ∼ *nicht* neither, nor; *wo* ∼ (*immer*) wher(eso)ever; *ist es* ∼ *wahr?* is it really true?

Audienz [aodi'ɛnts] *f* (-/-en) audience, hearing.

auf [auf] **1.** *prp.* (*dat.*) (up)on; in; at; of; by; ∼ *dem Tisch* (up)on the table; ∼ *dem Markt* in the market; ∼ *der Universität* at the university; ∼ *e-m Ball* at a ball; **2.** *prp.* (*acc.*) on; in; at; to; towards (*a.* ∼ *... zu*); up; ∼ *deutsch* in German; ∼ *e-e Entfernung von* at a range of; ∼ *die Post etc.* gehen go to the post-office, etc.; ∼ *ein Pfund gehen 20 Schilling* 20 shillings go to a pound; *es geht* ∼ *neun* it is getting on to nine; ∼ *... hin* on the strength of; **3.** *adv.* up(wards); ∼ *und ab gehen* walk up and down *or* to and fro; **4.** *cj.:* ∼ *daß* (in order) that; ∼ *daß nicht* that not, lest; **5.** *int.:* ∼*!* up!

auf|arbeiten ['auf?-] *v/t.* (*sep.*, -ge-, *h*) work off (*arrears of work*); furbish up; F do up (*garments*); **∼atmen** *fig.* ['auf?-] *v/i.* (*sep.*, -ge-, *h*) breathe again.

'Aufbau *m* (-[e]s/*no pl.*) building up; construction (*of play*, *etc.*); F *esp. Am.* setup (*of organization*); *mot.* body (of car, *etc.*); **'2en** *v/t.* (*sep.*, -ge-, *h*) erect, build up; construct.

'auf|bauschen *v/t.* (*sep.*, -ge-, *h*) puff out; *fig.* exaggerate; **∼beißen** *v/t.* (*irr.* beißen, *sep.*, -ge-, *h*) crack; **'∼bekommen** *v/t.* (*irr.* kommen, *sep.*, *no* -ge-, *h*) get open (*door*); be given (*a task*); **'∼bessern** *v/t.* (*sep.*, -ge-, *h*) raise (*salary*); **'∼bewahren** *v/t.* (*sep.*, *no* -ge-, *h*) keep; preserve;

'∼bieten *v/t.* (*irr.* bieten, *sep.*, -ge-, *h*) summon; exert; ✗ raise; **'∼binden** *v/t.* (*irr.* binden, *sep.*, -ge-, *h*) untie; **'∼bleiben** *v/i.* (*irr.* bleiben, *sep.*, -ge-, *sein*) sit up; door, *etc.:* remain open; **'∼blenden** (*sep.*, -ge-, *h*) **1.** *mot. v/i.* turn up the headlights; **2.** *v/t.* fade in (*scene*); **'∼blicken** *v/i.* (*sep.*, -ge-, *h*) look up; raise one's eyes; **'∼blitzen** *v/i.* (*sep.*, -ge-, *h*, *sein*) flash (up); **'∼blühen** *v/i.* (*sep.*, -ge-, *sein*) bloom; flourish.

'aufbrausen *fig. v/i.* (*sep.*, -ge-, *sein*) fly into a passion; **'∼d** *adj.* hot-tempered.

'auf|brechen (*irr.* brechen, *sep.*, -ge-) **1.** *v/t.* (*h*) break open; force open; **2.** *v/i.* (*sein*) burst open; set out (*nach* for); leave (*party*); **'∼bringen** *v/t.* (*irr.* bringen, *sep.*, -ge-, *h*) raise (*money*, *troops*); capture (*ship*); rouse *or* irritate *s.o.*

'Aufbruch *m* departure, start.

'auf|bügeln *v/t.* (*sep.*, -ge-, *h*) iron; **'∼bürden** *v/t.* (*sep.*, -ge-, *h*): *j-m et.* ∼ impose s.th. on *s.o.*; **'∼decken** *v/t.* (*sep.*, -ge-, *h*) uncover; spread (*cloth*); *fig.* disclose; **'∼drängen** *v/t.* (*sep.*, -ge-, *h*) force, obtrude (*j-m* [*up*]*on s.o.*); **'∼drehen** *v/t.* (*sep.*, -ge-, *h*) turn on (*gas*, *etc.*).

'aufdringlich *adj.* obtrusive.

'Aufdruck *m* (-[e]s/-e) imprint; surcharge.

'aufdrücken *v/t.* (*sep.*, -ge-, *h*) impress.

aufeinander *adv.* [aof?aı'nandər] one after *or* upon another; **2folge** *f* succession; **∼folgend** *adj.* successive.

Aufenthalt ['aofɛnthalt] *m* (-[e]s/-e) stay; residence; delay; 🚊 stop; **'∼genehmigung** *f* residence permit.

auferlegen ['auf?ɛrle:gən] *v/t.* (*sep.*, *no* -ge-, *h*) impose (*j-m* on *s.o.*).

auferstehen ['auf?ɛrʃteːən] *v/i.* (*irr.* stehen, *sep.*, *no* -ge-, *sein*) rise (from the dead); **'2ung** *f* (-/-en) resurrection.

auf|essen ['auf?-] *v/t.* (*irr.* essen, *sep.*, -ge-, *h*) eat up; **'∼fahren** *v/i.* (*irr.* fahren, *sep.*, -ge-, *sein*) ascend; start up; *fig.* fly out; ⚓ run aground; *mot.* drive *or* run (*auf acc.* against, into).

'Auffahrt *f* ascent; driving up; approach; drive, *Am.* driveway; **'∼srampe** *f* ramp.

'auf|fallen *v/i.* (*irr.* fallen, *sep.*, -ge-, *sein*) be conspicuous; *j-m* ∼ strike *s.o.*; **'∼fallend** *adj.*, **'∼fällig** *adj.* striking; conspicuous; flashy.

'auffangen *v/t.* (*irr.* fangen, *sep.*, -ge-, *h*) catch (up); parry (*thrust*).

'auffass|en *v/t.* (*sep.*, -ge-, *h*) conceive; comprehend; interpret; **'2ung** *f* conception; interpretation; grasp.

'**auffinden** v/t. (irr. finden, sep., -ge-, h) find, trace, discover, locate.

'**auffforder|n** v/t. (sep., -ge-, h) ask, invite; call (up)on; esp. 🏛 summon; '**2ung** f invitation; esp. 🏛 summons.

'**auffrischen** (sep., -ge-) 1. v/t. (h) freshen up, touch up; brush up (knowledge); revive; 2. v/i. (sein) wind: freshen.

'**aufführ|en** v/t. (sep., -ge-, h) thea. represent, perform, act; enumerate; enter (in list); einzeln ~ specify; Am. itemize; sich ~ behave; '**2ung** f thea. performance; enumeration; entry; specification; conduct.

'**Aufgabe** f task; problem; school: homework; posting, Am. mailing (of letter); booking (of luggage), Am. checking (of baggage); resignation (from office); abandonment; giving up (business); es sich zur ~ machen make it one's business.

'**Aufgang** m ascent; ast. rising; staircase.

'**aufgeben** (irr. geben, sep., -ge-, h) 1. v/t. give up, abandon; resign from (office); insert (advertisement); post, Am. mail (letter); book (luggage), Am. check (baggage); hand in, send (telegram); ✦ give (order); set, Am. assign (homework); set (riddle); 2. v/i. give up or in.

'**Aufgebot** n public notice; 🗡 levy; fig. array; banns pl. (of marriage).

'**aufgehen** v/i. (irr. gehen, sep., -ge-, sein) open; 🜨 leave no remainder; sewing: come apart; paste, star, curtain: rise; seed: come up; ~ in (dat.) be merged in; fig. be devoted to (work); in Flammen ~ go up in flames.

'**aufgeklärt** adj. ['aufgɛklɛːrt] enlightened; '**2heit** f (-/no pl.) enlightenment.

'**Aufgeld** ✦ n agio, premium.

'**aufge|legt** adj. ['aufgɛleːkt] disposed (zu for); in the mood (zu inf. for ger., to inf.); gut (schlecht) ~ in a good (bad) humo(u)r; '**schlossen** fig. adj. open-minded; '**weckt** fig. adj. ['vɛkt] bright.

'**auf|gießen** v/t. (irr. gießen, sep., -ge-, h) pour (on); make (tea); '**greifen** v/t. (irr. greifen, sep., -ge-, h) snatch up, fig. take up; '**Aufguß** m infusion. [seize.]

'**auf|haben** (irr. haben, sep., -ge-, h) 1. v/t. have on (hat); have open (door); have to do (task); 2. F v/i.: das Geschäft hat auf the shop is open; '**haken** v/t. (sep., -ge-, h) unhook; '**halten** v/t. (irr. halten, sep., -ge-, h) keep open; stop, detain, delay; hold up (traffic); sich ~ stay; sich ~ bei dwell on; sich ~ mit spend one's time on; '**hängen** v/t. (irr. hängen, sep., -ge-, h) hang (up); ⊕ suspend.

'**aufheb|en** v/t. (irr. heben, sep., -ge-, h) lift (up), raise; pick up; raise (siege); keep, preserve; cancel, annul, abolish; break off (engagement); break up (meeting); sich ~ neutralize; die Tafel ~ rise from the table; gut aufgehoben sein be well looked after; viel Aufhebens machen make a fuss (von about); '**2ung** f (-/-en) raising; abolition; annulment; breaking up.

'**auf|heitern** v/t. (sep., -ge-, h) cheer up; sich ~ weather: clear up; face: brighten; '**hellen** v/t. and v/refl. (sep., -ge-, h) brighten.

'**aufhetz|en** v/t. (sep., -ge-, h) incite, instigate s.o.; '**2ung** f (-/-en) instigation, incitement.

'**auf|holen** (sep., -ge-, h) 1. v/t. make up (for); ⬧ haul up; 2. v/i. gain (gegen on); pull up (to); '**hören** v/i. (sep., -ge-, h) cease, stop; Am. quit (all: zu tun doing); F: da hört (sich) doch alles auf! that's the limit!, Am. that beats everything!; '**kaufen** v/t. (sep., -ge-, h) buy up.

'**aufklär|en** v/t. (sep., -ge-, h) clear up; enlighten (über acc. on); 🗡 reconnoit|re, Am. -er; sich ~ clear up; 2ung f enlightenment; 🗡 reconnaissance.

'**auf|kleben** v/t. (sep., -ge-, h) paste on, stick on, affix on; '**klinken** v/t. (sep., -ge-, h) unlatch; '**knöpfen** v/t. (sep., -ge-, h) unbutton.

'**aufkommen** 1. v/i. (irr. kommen, sep., -ge-, sein) rise; recover (from illness); come up; come into fashion or use; thought: arise; ~ für et. answer for s.th.; ~ gegen prevail against s.o.; 2. 2 n (-s/no pl.) recovery.

'**auf|krempeln** ['aufkrɛmpɛln] v/t. (sep., -ge-, h) turn up, roll up; tuck up; '**lachen** v/i. (sep., -ge-, h) burst out laughing; '**laden** v/t. (irr. laden, sep., -ge-, h) load; ⚡ charge.

'**Auflage** f edition (of book); circulation (of newspaper); ⊕ support.

'**auf|lassen** v/t. (irr. lassen, sep., -ge-, h) F leave open (door, etc.); F keep on (hat); 🏛 cede; '**lauern** v/i. (sep., -ge-, h): j-m ~ lie in wait for s.o.

'**Auflauf** m concourse; riot; dish: soufflé; '**2en** v/i. (irr. laufen, sep., -ge-, sein) interest: accrue; ⬧ run aground.

'**auflegen** (sep., -ge-, h) 1. v/t. put on, lay on; apply (auf acc. to); print, publish (book); teleph. hang up; 2. teleph. v/i. ring off.

'**auflehn|en** v/t. (sep., -ge-, h) lean (on); sich ~ lean (on); fig. rebel, revolt (gegen against); '**2ung** f (-/-en) rebellion.

'**auf|lesen** v/t. (irr. lesen, sep., -ge-, h) gather, pick up; '**~leuchten** v/i. (sep., -ge-, h) flash (up); '**~liegen** v/i. (irr. liegen, sep., -ge-, h) lie (auf dat. on).

'**auflös|bar** adj. (dis)soluble; '**~en** v/t. (sep., -ge-, h) undo (knot); break up (meeting); dissolve (salt, etc.; marriage, business, Parliament, etc.); solve (A, riddle); disintegrate; fig. aufgelöst upset; '**2ung** f (dis-)solution; disintegration.

aufmach|en v/t. (sep., -ge-, h) open; undo (dress, parcel); put up (umbrella); make up, get up; sich ~ wind: rise; set out (nach acc. for); make for; die Tür ~ answer the door; '**2ung** f (-/-en) make-up, get-up.

aufmarschieren v/i. (sep., no -ge-, sein) form into line; ~ lassen ✕ deploy.

aufmerksam adj. attentive (gegen to); j-n ~ machen auf (acc.) call s.o.'s attention to; '**2keit** f (-/-en) attention; token.

aufmuntern v/t. (sep., -ge-, h) rouse; encourage; cheer up.

Aufnahme ['aufnɑ:mə] f (-/-n) taking up (of work); reception; admission; phot.: taking; photograph, shot; shooting (of a film); '**2fähig** adj. capable of absorbing; mind: receptive (für of); '**~gebühr** f admission fee; '**~gerät** n phot. camera; recorder; '**~prüfung** f entrance examination.

'**aufnehmen** v/t. (irr. nehmen, sep., -ge-, h) take up; pick up; take s.o. in; take down (dictation, etc.); take s.th. in (mentally); receive (guests); admit; raise, borrow (money); draw up, record; shoot (film); phot. take (picture); gut (übel) ~ take well (ill); es ~ mit be a match for.

aufopfer|n ['auf⁹-] v/t. (sep., -ge-, h) sacrifice; '**2ung** f sacrifice.

'**auf|passen** v/i. (sep., -ge-, h) attend (auf acc. to); watch; at school: be attentive; look out; ~ auf (acc.) take care of; '**~platzen** v/i. (sep., -ge-, sein) burst (open); '**~polieren** v/t. (sep., no -ge-, h) polish up; '**~prallen** v/i. (sep., -ge-, sein): auf den Boden ~ strike the ground; '**~pumpen** v/t. (sep., -ge-, h) blow up (tyre, etc.); '**~raffen** v/t. (sep., -ge-, h) snatch up; sich ~ rouse o.s. (zu for); muster up one's energy; '**~räumen** (sep., -ge-, h) 1. v/t. put in order; tidy (up), Am. straighten up; clear away; 2. v/i. tidy up; ~ mit do away with.

'**aufrecht** adj. and adv. upright (a. fig.), erect; '**~erhalten** v/t. (irr. halten, sep., no -ge-, h) maintain, uphold; '**2erhaltung** f (-/no pl.) maintenance.

'**aufreg|en** v/t. (sep., -ge-, h) stir up, excite; sich ~ get excited or upset (über acc. about); aufgeregt excited; upset; '**2ung** f excitement, agitation.

'**auf|reiben** v/t. (irr. reiben, sep., -ge-, h) chafe (skin, etc.); fig.: destroy; exhaust, wear s.o. out; '**~reißen** (irr. reißen, sep., -ge-) 1. v/t. (h) rip or tear up or open; fling open (door); open (eyes) wide; 2. v/i. (sein) split open, burst.

'**aufreiz|en** v/t. (sep., -ge-, h) incite, stir up; '**~end** adj. provocative; '**2ung** f instigation.

'**aufrichten** v/t. (sep., -ge-, h) set up, erect; sich ~ stand up; straighten; sit up (in bed).

'**aufrichtig** adj. sincere, candid; '**2keit** f sincerity, cando(u)r.

'**aufriegeln** v/t. (sep., -ge-, h) unbolt.

'**Aufriß** △ m elevation.

'**aufrollen** v/t. and v/refl. (sep., -ge-, h) roll up; unroll.

'**Aufruf** m call, summons; '**2en** v/t. (irr. rufen, sep., -ge-, h) call up; call on s.o.

Aufruhr ['aufru:r] m (-[e]s/-e) uproar, tumult; riot, rebellion.

'**aufrühr|en** v/t. (sep., -ge-, h) stir up; revive; fig. rake up; '**2er** m (-s/-) rebel; '**~erisch** adj. rebellious.

'**Aufrüstung** ✕ f (re)armament.

'**auf|rütteln** v/t. (sep., -ge-, h) shake up; rouse; '**~sagen** v/t. (sep., -ge-, h) say, repeat; recite.

aufsässig adj. ['aufzɛsiç] rebellious.

'**Aufsatz** m essay; composition; ⊕ top.

'**auf|saugen** v/t. (sep., -ge-, h) suck up; 🜄 absorb; '**~scheuchen** v/t. (sep., -ge-, h) scare (away); disturb; rouse; '**~scheuern** v/t. (sep., -ge-, h) scour; 🜂 chafe; '**~schichten** v/t. (sep., -ge-, h) pile up; '**~schieben** v/t. (irr. schieben, sep., -ge-, h) slide open; fig.: put off; defer, postpone; adjourn.

'**Aufschlag** m striking; impact; additional or extra charge; facing (on coat), lapel (of coat); cuff (on sleeve); turn-up (on trousers); tennis: service; '**2en** ['-gən] (irr. schlagen, sep., -ge-) 1. v/t. (h) open; turn up (sleeve, etc.); take up (abode); pitch (tent); raise (prices); cut (one's knee) open; 2. v/i. (sein) strike, hit; ✝ rise, go up (in price); tennis: serve.

'**auf|schließen** v/t. (irr. schließen, sep., -ge-, h) unlock, open; '**~schlitzen** v/t. (sep., -ge-, h) slit or rip open.

'**Aufschluß** fig. m information.

'**auf|schnallen** v/t. (sep., -ge-, h) unbuckle; '**~schnappen** (sep., -ge-) 1. v/t. (h) snatch; fig. pick up; 2. v/i. (sein) snap open; '**~schnei-**

den (*irr. schneiden, sep.*, -ge-, h)
1. *v/t.* cut open; cut up (*meat*);
2. *fig. v/i.* brag, boast.

'**Aufschnitt** *m* (slices *pl.* of) cold
meat, *Am.* cold cuts *pl.*

'**auf|schnüren** *v/t.* (*sep.*, -ge-, h)
untie; unlace; '**~schrauben** *v/t.*
(*sep.*, -ge-, h) screw (*auf acc.* on);
unscrew; '**~schrecken** (*sep.*, -ge-)
1. *v/t.* (h) startle; 2. *v/i.* (*irr.
schrecken, sein*) start (up).

'**Aufschrei** *m* shriek, scream; *fig.*
outcry.

'**auf|schreiben** *v/t.* (*irr. schreiben,
sep.*, -ge-, h) write down; '**~
schreien** *v/i.* (*irr. schreien, sep.*,
-ge-, h) cry out, scream.

'**Aufschrift** *f* inscription; address,
direction (*on letter*); label.

'**Aufschub** *m* deferment; delay;
adjournment; respite.

'**auf|schürfen** *v/t.* (*sep.*, -ge-, h)
graze (*skin*); '**~schwingen** *v/refl.*
(*irr. schwingen, sep.*, -ge-, h) soar,
rise; *sich zu et.* **~** bring o.s. to do
s.th.

'**Aufschwung** *m fig.* rise, *Am.* up-
swing; ✝ boom.

'**aufsehen** 1. *v/i.* (*irr. sehen, sep.*,
-ge-, h) look up; 2. ♀ *n* (-s/no *pl.*)
sensation; **~** *erregen* cause a sensation; '**~erregend** *adj.* sensational.

'**Aufseher** *m* overseer; inspector.

'**aufsetzen** (*sep.*, -ge-, h) 1. *v/t.* set
up; put on (*hat, countenance*); draw
up (*document*); *sich* **~** sit up; 2. ✈
v/i. touch down.

'**Aufsicht** *f* (-/-en) inspection, supervision; *store*: shopwalker, *Am.* floor-
walker; '**~sbehörde** *f* board of control; '**~srat** *m* board of directors.

'**auf|sitzen** *v/i.* (*irr. sitzen, sep.*,
-ge-, h) *rider*: mount; '**~spannen**
v/t. (*sep.*, -ge-, h) stretch; put up
(*umbrella*); spread (*sails*); '**~sparen**
v/t. (*sep.*, -ge-, h) save; *fig.* reserve;
'**~speichern** *v/t.* (*sep.*, -ge-, h)
store up; '**~sperren** *v/t.* (*sep.*, -ge-,
h) open wide; '**~spielen** (*sep.*, -ge-,
h) 1. *v/t. and v/i.* strike up; 2. *v/refl.*
show off; *sich* **~** *als* set up for; '**~
spießen** *v/t.* (*sep.*, -ge-, h) pierce;
with horns: gore; run through,
spear; '**~springen** *v/i.* (*irr. springen, sep.*, -ge-, sein) jump up; *door*:
fly open; crack; *skin*: chap; '**~spü-
ren** *v/t.* (*sep.*, -ge-, h) hunt up;
track down; '**~stacheln** *fig. v/t.*
(*sep.*, -ge-, h) goad; incite, instigate;
'**~stampfen** *v/i.* (*sep.*, -ge-, h)
stamp (one's foot).

'**Aufstand** *m* insurrection; rebellion;
uprising, revolt.

aufständisch *adj.* ['aufʃtendiʃ] rebellious; '**2e** *m* (-n/-n) insurgent,
rebel.

'**auf|stapeln** *v/t.* (*sep.*, -ge-, h) pile
up; ✝ store (up); '**~stechen** *v/t.*
(*irr. stechen, sep.*, -ge-, h) puncture,

prick open; ✗ lance; '**~stecken** *v/t.*
(*sep.*, -ge-, h) pin up; put up (*hair*);
'**~stehen** *v/i.* (*irr. stehen, sep.*, -ge-)
1. (*sein*) stand up; rise, get up; revolt; 2. F (h) stand open; '**~steigen**
v/i. (*irr. steigen, sep.*, -ge-, sein) rise,
ascend; ✗ take off; *rider*: mount.

'**aufstell|en** *v/t.* (*sep.*, -ge-, h) set
up, put up; ✗ draw up; post (*sen-
tries*); make (*assertion*); set (*example*); erect (*column*); set (*trap*);
nominate (*candidate*); draw up
(*bill*); lay down (*rule*); make out
(*list*); set up, establish (*record*);
'**2ung** *f* putting up; drawing up;
erection; nomination; ✝ statement;
list.

Aufstieg ['aufʃti:k] *m* (-[e]s/-e)
ascent, *Am. a.* ascension; *fig.* rise.

'**auf|stöbern** *fig. v/t.* (*sep.*, -ge-, h)
hunt up; '**~stoßen** (*irr. stoßen, sep.*,
-ge-) 1. *v/t.* (h) push open; **~** *auf*
(*acc.*) knock against; 2. *v/i.* (h, sein)
of food: rise, repeat; belch; '**~strei-
chen** *v/t.* (*irr. streichen, sep.*, -ge-,
h) spread (*butter*).

'**Aufstrich** *m* spread (*for bread*).

'**auf|stützen** *v/t.* (*sep.*, -ge-, h) prop
up, support *s.th.*; *sich* **~** *auf* (*acc.*)
lean on; '**~suchen** *v/t.* (*sep.*, -ge-, h)
visit (*places*); go to see *s.o.*, look
s.o. up.

'**Auftakt** *m* ♪ upbeat; *fig.* prelude,
preliminaries *pl.*

'**auf|tauchen** *v/i.* (*sep.*, -ge-, sein)
emerge, appear, turn up; '**~tauen**
(*sep.*, -ge-) 1. *v/t.* (h) thaw; 2. *v/i.*
(sein) thaw (*a. fig.*); '**~teilen** *v/t.*
(*sep.*, -ge-, h) divide (up), share.

Auftrag ['auftra:k] *m* (-[e]s/=e)
commission; instruction; mission;
⅟₂ mandate; ✝ order; '**2en** ['~gən]
v/t. (*irr. tragen, sep.*, -ge-, h) serve
(up) (*meal*); lay on (*paint*); wear
out (*dress*); *j-m et.* **~** charge s.o.
with *s.th.*; '**~geber** ['~k-] *m* (-s/-)
employer; customer; principal; '**~
erteilung** ['~ks²ertailuŋ] *f* (-/-en)
placing of an order.

'**auf|treffen** *v/i.* (*irr. treffen, sep.*,
-ge-, sein) strike, hit; '**~treiben** *v/t.*
(*irr. treiben, sep.*, -ge-, h) hunt up;
raise (*money*); '**~trennen** *v/t.* (*sep.*,
-ge-, h) rip; unstitch (*seam*).

'**auftreten** 1. *v/i.* (*irr. treten, sep.*,
-ge-, sein) tread; *thea., witness, etc.*:
appear (*als* as); behave, act; *difficulties*: arise; 2. ♀ *n* (-s/no *pl.*) appearance; occurrence (*of events*);
behavio(u)r.

'**Auftrieb** *m phys. and fig.* buoyancy; ✗ lift; *fig.* impetus.

'**Auftritt** *m thea.* scene (*a. fig.*);
appearance (*of actor*).

'**auf|trumpfen** *fig. v/i.* (*sep.*, -ge-, h)
put one's foot down; '**~tun** *v/t.* (*irr.
tun, sep.*, -ge-, h) open; *sich* **~** open;
chasm: yawn; *society*: form; '**~tür-
men** *v/t.* (*sep.*, -ge-, h) pile *or* heap

up; *sich* ~ tower up; pile up; *difficulties*: accumulate; '~wachen *v/i.* (*sep.*, -ge-, sein) awake, wake up; '~wachsen *v/i.* (*irr. wachsen, sep.*, -ge-, sein) grow up.

'Aufwallung *f* ebullition, surge.

Aufwand ['aufvant] *m* (-[e]s/*no pl.*) expense, expenditure (*an dat.* of); pomp; splendid *or* great display (*of words, etc.*).

'aufwärmen *v/t.* (*sep.*, -ge-, h) warm up.

'Aufwarte|frau *f* charwoman, *Am. a.* cleaning woman; '2n *v/i.* (*sep.*, -ge-, h) wait (up)on *s.o.*, attend on *s.o.*; wait (at table).

aufwärts *adv.* ['aufverts] upward(s).

'Aufwartung *f* attendance; visit; *j-m* s-e ~ *machen* pay one's respects to *s.o.*, call on *s.o.*

'aufwasch|en *v/t.* (*irr. waschen, sep.*, -ge-, h) wash up; '2wasser *n* dish-water.

'auf|wecken *v/t.* (*sep.*, -ge-, h) awake(n), wake (up); '~weichen (*sep.*, -ge-) 1. *v/t.* (h) soften; soak; 2. *v/i.* (sein) soften, become soft; '~weisen *v/t.* (*irr. weisen, sep.*, -ge-, h) show, exhibit; produce; '~wenden *v/t.* ([*irr. wenden,*] *sep.*, -ge-, h) spend; *Mühe* ~ take pains; '~werfen *v/t.* (*irr. werfen, sep.*, -ge-, h) raise (*a. question*).

'aufwert|en *v/t.* (*sep.*, -ge-, h) revalorize; revalue; '2ung *f* revalorization; revaluation.

'aufwickeln *v/t. and v/refl.* (*sep.*, -ge-, h) wind up, roll up.

'aufwiegel|n ['aufvi:gəln] *v/t.* (*sep.*, -ge-, h) stir up, incite, instigate; '2ung *f* (-/-en) instigation.

'aufwiegen *fig. v/t.* (*irr. wiegen, sep.*, -ge-, h) make up for.

Aufwiegler ['aufvi:glər] *m* (-s/-) agitator; instigator.

'aufwirbeln ['aufvi-, *sep.*, -ge-) 1. *v/t.* (h) whirl up; raise (*dust*); *fig. viel Staub* ~ create a sensation; 2. *v/i.* (sein) whirl up.

'aufwisch|en *v/t.* (*sep.*, -ge-, h) wipe up; '2lappen *m* floor-cloth.

'aufwühlen *v/t.* (*sep.*, -ge-, h) turn up; *fig.* stir.

'aufzähl|en *v/t.* (*sep.*, -ge-, h) count up; *fig.* enumerate, *Am. a.* call off; specify, *Am.* itemize; '2ung *f* (-/-en) enumeration; specification.

'auf|zäumen *v/t.* (*sep.*, -ge-, h) bridle; '~zehren *v/t.* (*sep.*, -ge-, h) consume.

'aufzeichn|en *v/t.* (*sep.*, -ge-, h) draw; note down; record; '2ung *f* note; record.

'auf|zeigen *v/t.* (*sep.*, -ge-, h) show; demonstrate; point out (*mistakes, etc.*); disclose; '~ziehen (*irr. ziehen, sep.*, -ge-) 1. *v/t.* (h) draw *or* pull up; (pull) open; hoist (*flag*); bring up (*child*); mount (*picture*);

wind (up) (*clock, etc.*); *j-n* ~ tease *s.o.*, pull *s.o.'s* leg; *Saiten auf* e-e *Violine* ~ string a violin; 2. *v/i.* (sein) ✕ draw up; *storm*: approach.

'Aufzucht *f* rearing, breeding.

'Aufzug *m* ⊕ hoist; lift, *Am.* elevator; *thea.* act; attire; show.

'aufzwingen *v/t.* (*irr. zwingen, sep.*, -ge-, h): *j-m et.* ~ force s.th. upon *s.o.*

Augapfel ['auk?-] *m* eyeball.

Auge ['augə] *n* (-s/-n) eye; sight; ♀ bud; *in meinen* ~n in my view; *im* ~ *behalten* keep an eye on; keep in mind; *aus den* ~n *verlieren* lose sight of; *ein* ~ *zudrücken* turn a blind eye (*bei* to); *ins* ~ *fallen* strike the eye; *große* ~n *machen* open one's eyes wide; *unter vier* ~n face to face, privately; *kein* ~ *zutun* not to get a wink of sleep.

'Augen|arzt *m* oculist, eye-doctor; '~blick *m* moment, instant; '2blicklich 1. *adj.* instantaneous; momentary; present; 2. *adv.* instant(aneous)ly; at present; '~braue *f* eyebrow; '~entzündung ✗ *f* inflammation of the eye; '~heilkunde *f* ophthalmology; '~klinik *f* ophthalmic hospital; '~leiden ✗ *n* eye-complaint; '~licht *n* eyesight; '~lid *n* eyelid; '~maß *n*: *ein gutes* ~ a sure eye; *nach dem* ~ by eye; *~merk* ['~mɛrk] *n* (-[e]s/*no pl.*): *sein* ~ *richten auf* (*acc.*) turn one's attention to; *have* s.th. *in view*; '~schein *m* appearance; *in* ~ *nehmen* examine, view, inspect; '2scheinlich *adj.* evident; '~wasser *n* eyewash, eye-lotion; '~wimper *f* eyelash; '~zeuge *m* eyewitness.

August [au'gust] *m* (-[e]s, - /-e) August.

Auktion [auk'tsjo:n] *f* (-/-en) auction; ~ator [~o'na:tɔr] *m* (-s/-en) auctioneer.

Aula ['aula] *f* (-/*Aulen*, -s) (assembly) hall, *Am.* auditorium.

aus [aus] 1. *prp.* (*dat.*) out of; from; of; by; for; in; ~ *Achtung* out of respect; ~ *London kommen* come from London; ~ *diesem Grunde* for this reason; ~ *Ihrem Brief ersehe ich* I see from your letter; 2. *adv.* out; over; *die Schule ist* ~ school is over; F: *von mir* ~ for all I care; *auf et.* ~ *sein* be keen on s.th.; *es ist* ~ *mit ihm* it is all over with him; *das Spiel ist* ~! the game is up!; *er weiß weder ein noch* ~ he is at his wit's end; *on instruments, etc.*: *an* — ~ on — off.

ausarbeit|en ['aus?-] *v/t.* (*sep.*, -ge-, h) work out; elaborate; '2ung *f* (-/-en) working-out; elaboration; composition.

aus|arten ['aus?-] *v/i.* (*sep.*, -ge-, sein) degenerate; get out of hand; ~atmen ['aus?-] (*sep.*, -ge-, h)

1. *v/i.* breathe out; **2.** *v/t.* breathe out; exhale (*vapour, etc.*); '**~baggern** *v/t.* (*sep.*, -ge-, *h*) dredge (*river, etc.*); excavate (*ground*).

'**Ausbau** *m* (-[e]s/-ten) extension; completion; development; '**~en** *v/t.* (*sep.*, -ge-, *h*) develop; extend; finish, complete; ⊕ dismantle (*engine*).

'**ausbedingen** *v/t.* (*irr. bedingen, sep.*, *no* -ge-, *h*) stipulate.

'**ausbesser|n** *v/t.* (*sep.*, -ge-, *h*) mend, repair, *Am.* F a. fix; '**~ung** *f* repair, mending.

'**Ausbeut|e** *f* (-/~-n) gain, profit; yield; ⚒ output; '**~en** *v/t.* (*sep.*, -ge-, *h*) exploit; sweat (*workers*); '**~ung** *f* (-/~-en) exploitation.

'**ausbild|en** *v/t.* (*sep.*, -ge-, *h*) form, develop; train; instruct, educate; ⚔ drill; '**~ung** *f* development; training; instruction; education; ⚔ drill.

'**ausbitten** *v/t.* (*irr. bitten, sep.*, -ge-, *h*): *sich et.* **~** request s.th.; insist on s.th.

'**ausbleiben 1.** *v/i.* (*irr. bleiben, sep.*, -ge-, *sein*) stay away, fail to appear; **2.** ⚖ *n* (-s/*no pl.*) non-arrival, non-appearance; absence.

'**Ausblick** *m* outlook (*auf acc.* over, on), view (of), prospect (of); *fig.* outlook (on).

'**aus|bohren** *v/t.* (*sep.*, -ge-, *h*) bore, drill; '**~brechen** (*irr. brechen, sep.*, -ge-) **1.** *v/t.* (*h*) break out; vomit; **2.** *v/i.* (*sein*) break out; *fig.* burst out (*laughing, etc.*).

'**ausbreit|en** *v/t.* (*sep.*, -ge-, *h*) spread (out); stretch (out) (*arms, wings*); display; *sich* **~** spread; '**~ung** *f* (-/~-en) spreading.

'**ausbrennen** (*irr. brennen, sep.*, -ge-) **1.** *v/t.* (*h*) burn out; ⚕ cauterize; **2.** *v/i.* (*sein*) burn out.

'**Ausbruch** *m* outbreak; eruption (*of volcano*); escape (*from prison*); outburst (*of emotion*).

'**aus|brüten** *v/t.* (*sep.*, -ge-, *h*) hatch (*a. fig.*); '**~bürgern** *v/t.* (*sep.*, -ge-, *h*) denationalize, expatriate.

'**Ausdauer** *f* perseverance; '**~nd** *adj.* persevering; ⚘ perennial.

'**ausdehn|en** *v/t. and v/refl.* (*sep.*, -ge-, *h*) extend (*auf acc.* to); expand; stretch; '**~ung** *f* expansion; extension; extent.

'**aus|denken** *v/t.* (*irr. denken, sep.*, -ge-, *h*) think *s.th.* out, *Am. a.* think *s.th.* up, contrive, devise, invent; imagine; '**~dörren** *v/t.* (*sep.*, -ge-, *h*) dry up; parch; '**~drehen** *v/t.* (*sep.*, -ge-, *h*) turn off (*radio, gas*); ⚡ turn out, switch off (*light*).

'**Ausdruck** *m* **1.** (-[e]s/*no pl.*) expression; **2.** (-[e]s/=e) expression; term.

'**ausdrück|en** *v/t.* (*sep.*, -ge-, *h*) press, squeeze (out); stub out (*cig-*

arette); *fig.* express; '**~lich** *adj.* express, explicit.

'**ausdrucks|los** *adj.* inexpressive, expressionless; blank; '**~voll** *adj.* expressive; '**~weise** *f* mode of expression; style.

'**Ausdünstung** *f* (-/-en) exhalation; perspiration; odo(u)r, smell.

auseinander *adv.* [ausʔaɪˈnandər] asunder, apart; separate(d); **~bringen** *v/t.* (*irr. bringen, sep.*, -ge-, *h*) separate, sever; **~gehen** *v/i.* (*irr. gehen, sep.*, -ge-, *sein*) meeting, crowd: break up; *opinions*: differ; *friends*: part; *crowd*: disperse; *roads*: diverge; **~nehmen** *v/t.* (*irr. nehmen, sep.*, -ge-, *h*) take apart *or* to pieces; ⊕ disassemble, dismantle; **~setzen** *fig. v/t.* (*sep.*, -ge-, *h*) explain; *sich mit j-m* **~** ⚔ compound with s.o.; argue with s.o.; have it out with s.o.; *sich mit e-m Problem* **~** get down to a problem; come to grips with a problem; ⚖setzung *f* (-/-en) explanation; discussion; settlement (*with creditors, etc.*); *krigerische* **~** armed conflict.

auserlesen *adj.* [ˈausʔ-] exquisite, choice; select(ed).

auserwählen [ˈausʔ-] *v/t.* (*sep.*, *no* -ge-, *h*) select, choose.

'**ausfahr|en** (*irr. fahren, sep.*, -ge-) **1.** *v/i.* (*sein*) drive out, go for a drive; ⚓ leave (*port*); **2.** *v/t.* (*h*) take (*baby*) out (*in pram*); take *s.o.* for a drive; rut (*road*); ✈ lower (*undercarriage*); ⚖*t f* drive; excursion; way out, exit (*of garage, etc.*); gateway; departure.

'**Ausfall** *m* falling out; ⚕: loss; deficit; '**~en** *v/i.* (*irr. fallen, sep.*, -ge-, *sein*) fall out; not to take place; turn out, prove; **~ lassen** drop; cancel; *die Schule fällt aus* there is no school; '**~end** *adj.* offensive, insulting.

'**aus|fasern** *v/i.* (*sep.*, -ge-, *sein*) ravel out, fray; '**~fegen** *v/t.* (*sep.*, -ge-, *h*) sweep (out).

ausfertig|en [ˈausfɛrtɪgən] *v/t.* (*sep.*, -ge-, *h*) draw up (*document*); make out (*bill, etc.*); issue (*passport*); '**~ung** *f* (-/-en) drawing up; issue; draft; copy; *in doppelter* **~** in duplicate. [chen find out; discover.]

ausfindig *adj.* [ˈausfɪndɪç]: **~ ma-**]

'**Ausflucht** *f* (-/-e) excuse, evasion, shift, subterfuge.

'**Ausflug** *m* trip, excursion, outing.

Ausflügler [ˈausflyːklər] *m* (-s/-) excursionist, tripper, tourist.

'**Ausfluß** *m* flowing out; discharge (*a.* ⚕); outlet, outfall.

'**aus|fragen** *v/t.* (*sep.*, -ge-, *h*) interrogate, *Am. a.* quiz; sound; '**~fransen** *v/i.* (*sep.*, -ge-, *sein*) fray.

Ausfuhr ✝ [ˈausfuːr] *f* (-/-en) export(ation); '**~artikel** ✝ *m* export (article).

'ausführ|bar adj. practicable; ✝ exportable; '~en v/t. (sep., -ge-, h) execute, carry out, perform, Am. a. fill; ✝ export; explain; j-n ~ take s.o. out.

'Ausfuhr|genehmigung f export permit; '~handel m export trade.

'ausführlich 1. adj. detailed; comprehensive; circumstantial; 2. adv. in detail, at (some) length; '2keit f (-/no pl.) minuteness of detail; particularity; comprehensiveness; copiousness.

'Ausführung f execution, performance; workmanship; type, make; explanation; '~sbestimmungen ✝ f/pl. export regulations pl.

'Ausfuhr|verbot n embargo on exports; '~waren f/pl. exports pl.; '~zoll m export duty.

'ausfüllen v/t. (sep., -ge-, h) fill out or up; fill in, complete (form); Am. fill out (blank).

'Ausgabe f distribution; edition (of book); expense, expenditure; issue (of shares, etc.); issuing office.

'Ausgang m going out; exit; way out; outlet; end; result; '~skapital ✝ n original capital; '~spunkt m starting-point; '~sstellung f starting-position.

'ausgeben v/t. (irr. geben, sep., -ge-, h) give out; spend (money); issue (shares, etc.); sich ~ für pass o.s. off for, pretend to be.

ausge|beult adj. ['ausgəbɔylt] baggy; ~bombt adj. ['~bɔmpt] bombed out; ~dehnt adj. ['~de:nt] expansive, vast, extensive; ~dient adj. ['~di:nt] worn out; superannuated; retired, pensioned off; ~er Soldat ex-serviceman, veteran; '~fallen fig. adj. odd, queer, unusual.

'ausgehen v/i. (irr. gehen, sep., -ge-, sein) go out; take a walk; end; colour: fade; hair: fall out; money, provisions: run out; uns gehen die Vorräte aus we run out of provisions; darauf ~ aim at; gut etc. ~ turn out well, etc.; leer ~ come away empty-handed; von et. ~ start from s.th.

'ausge|lassen fig. adj. frolicsome, boisterous; '~nommen prp. 1. (acc.) except (for); 2. (nom.): Anwesende ~ present company excepted; '~prägt adj. ['~prɛːkt] marked, pronounced; ~rechnet fig. adv. ['~rɛçnət] just; ~ er he of all people; ~ heute today of all days; '~schlossen fig. adj. impossible.

'ausgestalten v/t. (sep., no -ge-, h) arrange (celebration); et. zu et. ~ develop or turn s.th. into s.th.

ausge|sucht fig. adj. ['ausgəzuːxt] exquisite, choice; '~wachsen adj. full-grown; ~zeichnet fig. adj. ['~tsaiçnət] excellent.

ausgiebig adj. ['ausgiːbiç] abundant, plentiful; meal: substantial.

'ausgießen v/t. (irr. gießen, sep., -ge-, h) pour out.

Ausgleich ['ausglaiç] m (-[e]s/-e) compromise; compensation; ✝ settlement; sports: equalization (of score); tennis: deuce (score of 40 all); '2en v/t. (irr. gleichen, sep., -ge-, h) equalize; compensate (loss); ✝ balance.

'aus|gleiten v/i. (irr. gleiten, sep., -ge-, sein) slip, slide; '~graben v/t. (irr. graben, sep., -ge-, h) dig out or up (a. fig.); excavate; exhume (body).

Ausguck ⚓ ['ausguk] m (-[e]s/-e) look-out.

'Ausguß m sink; '~eimer m slop-pail.

'aus|haken v/t. (sep., -ge-, h) unhook; '~halten (irr. halten, sep., -ge-, h) 1. v/t. endure, bear, stand; ♪ sustain (note); 2. v/i. hold out; last; '~händigen ['~hɛndigən] v/t. (sep., -ge-, h) deliver up, hand over, surrender.

'Aushang m notice, placard, poster.

'aushänge|n 1. v/t. (sep., -ge-, h) hang or put out; unhinge (door); 2. v/i. (irr. hängen, sep., -ge-, h) have been hung or put out; '2-schild n signboard.

aus|harren ['ausharən] v/i. (sep., -ge-, h) persevere; hold out; '~hauchen v/t. (sep., -ge-, h) breathe out, exhale; '~heben v/t. (irr. heben, sep., -ge-, h) dig (trench); unhinge (door); recruit, levy (soldiers); excavate (earth); rob (nest); clean out, raid (nest of criminals); '~helfen v/i. (irr. helfen, sep., -ge-, h) help out.

'Aushilf|e f (temporary) help or assistance; sie hat e-c ~ she has s.o. to help out; '2sweise adv. as a makeshift; temporarily.

'aushöhl|en v/t. (sep., -ge-, h) hollow out; '2ung f hollow.

'aus|holen (sep., -ge-, h) 1. v/i. raise one's hand (as if to strike); weit ~ go far back (in narrating s.th.); 2. v/t. sound, pump s.o.; '~horchen v/t. (sep., -ge-, h) sound, pump s.o.; '~hungern v/t. (sep., -ge-, h) starve (out); '~husten v/t. (sep., -ge-, h) cough up; '~kennen v/refl. (irr. kennen, sep., -ge-, h) know one's way (about place); be well versed, be at home (in subject); er kennt sich aus he knows what's what; '~kleiden v/t. (sep., -ge-, h) undress; ⊕ line, coat; sich ~ undress; '~klopfen v/t. (sep., -ge-, h) beat (out); dust (garment); knock out (pipe); '~klügeln ['~klyːgəln] v/t. (sep., -ge-, h) work s.th. out; contrive; puzzle s.th. out.

'auskommen 1. v/i. (irr. kommen, sep., -ge-, sein) get out; escape; ~

mit manage with *s.th.*; get on with *s.o.*; ~ *ohne* do without; *mit dem Geld* ~ make both ends meet; 2. ♀ *n* (-s/*no pl.*) competence, competency.

'**auskundschaften** *v/t.* (*sep.*, -ge-, *h*) explore; ✂ reconnoit|re, *Am.* -er, scout.

Auskunft ['auskunft] *f* (-/-e) information; inquiry office, inquiries *pl.*, *Am.* information desk; '~stelle *f* inquiry office, inquiries *pl.*, *Am.* information bureau.

'**aus|lachen** *v/t.* (*sep.*, -ge-, *h*) laugh at, deride; '~laden *v/t.* (*irr. laden*, *sep.*, -ge-, *h*) unload; discharge (*cargo from ship*); cancel *s.o.'s* invitation, put off (*guest*).

'**Auslage** *f* display, show (*of goods*); *in der* ~ in the (shop) window; ~*n pl.* expenses *pl.*

'**Ausland** *n* (-[e]s/*no pl.*): *das* ~ foreign countries *pl.*; *ins* ~, *im* ~ abroad.

Ausländ|er ['auslɛndər] *m* (-s/-), '~erin *f* (-/-nen) foreigner; alien; '2isch *adj.* foreign; ♀, *zo.* exotic.

'**Auslandskorrespondent** *m* foreign correspondent.

'**auslass|en** *v/t.* (*irr. lassen*, *sep.*, -ge-, *h*) let out (*water*); melt (down) (*butter*); render down (*fat*); let out (*garment*); let down (*hem*); leave out, omit (*word*); cut *s.th.* out; miss or cut out (*meal*); miss (*dance*); *s-n Zorn an j-m* ~ vent one's anger on *s.o.*; *sich* ~ *über* (*acc.*) say *s.th.* about; express one's opinion about; '2ung *f* (-/-en) omission; remark, utterance; '2ungszeichen *gr. n* apostrophe.

'**aus|laufen** *v/i.* (*irr. laufen*, *sep.*, -ge-, *sein*) run *or* leak out (*aus et.* of *s.th.*); leak; end (*in s.th.*); *machine*: run down; ⚓ (set) sail; '~leeren *v/t.* (*sep.*, -ge-, *h*) empty; ⚕ evacuate (*bowels*).

'**ausleg|en** *v/t.* (*sep.*, -ge-, *h*) lay out; display (*goods*); explain, interpret; advance (*money*); '2ung *f* (-/-en) explanation, interpretation.

'**aus|leihen** *v/t.* (*irr. leihen*, *sep.*, -ge-, *h*) lend (out), *esp. Am.* loan; '~lernen *v/i.* (*sep.*, -ge-, *h*) finish one's apprenticeship; *man lernt nie aus* we live and learn.

'**Auslese** *f* choice, selection; *fig.* pick; '2n *v/t.* (*irr. lesen*, *sep.*, -ge-, *h*) pick out, select; finish reading (*book*).

'**ausliefer|n** *v/t.* (*sep.*, -ge-, *h*) hand *or* turn over, deliver (up); extradite (*criminal*); *ausgeliefert sein* (*dat.*) be at the mercy of; '2ung *f* delivery; extradition.

'**aus|liegen** *v/i.* (*irr. liegen*, *sep.*, -ge-, *h*) be displayed, be on show; '~löschen *v/t.* (*sep.*, -ge-, *h*) put out, switch off (*light*); extinguish (*fire*) (*a. fig.*); efface (*word*); wipe out, erase; '~losen *v/t.* (*sep.*, -ge-, *h*) draw (lots) for.

'**auslös|en** *v/t.* (*sep.*, -ge-, *h*) ⊕ release; redeem, ransom (*prisoner*); redeem (*from pawn*); *fig.* cause, start; arouse (*applause*); '2er *m* (-s/-) ⊕ release, *esp. phot.* trigger.

'**aus|lüften** *v/t.* (*sep.*, -ge-, *h*) air, ventilate; '~machen *v/t.* (*sep.*, -ge-, *h*) make out, sight, spot; *sum:* amount to; constitute, make up; put out (*fire*); ⚡ turn out, switch off (*light*); agree on, arrange; settle; *es macht nichts aus* it does not matter; *würde es Ihnen et.* ~, *wenn* ...? would you mind (*ger.*) ...?; '~malen *v/t.* (*sep.*, -ge-, *h*) paint; *sich et.* ~ picture *s.th.* to o.s., imagine *s.th.*

'**Ausmaß** *n* dimension(s *pl.*), measurement(s *pl.*); *fig.* extent.

aus|mergeln ['ausmɛrgəln] *v/t.* (*sep.*, -ge-, *h*) emaciate; exhaust; ~**merzen** *f* ['~mɛrtsən] *v/t.* (*sep.*, -ge-, *h*) eliminate; eradicate; '~messen *v/t.* (*irr. messen*, *sep.*, -ge-, *h*) measure.

Ausnahm|e ['ausnɑːmə] *f* (-/-n) exception; '2sweise *adv.* by way of exception; exceptionally.

'**ausnehmen** *v/t.* (*irr. nehmen*, *sep.*, -ge-, *h*) take out; draw (*fowl*); F fleece *s.o.*; *fig.* except, exempt; '~d 1. *adj.* exceptional; 2. *adv.* exceedingly.

'**aus|nutzen** *v/t.* (*sep.*, -ge-, *h*) utilize; take advantage of; *esp.* ♘, ✕ exploit; '~packen (*sep.*, -ge-, *h*) 1. *v/t.* unpack; 2. F *fig.* speak one's mind; '~pfeifen *thea. v/t.* (*irr. pfeifen*, *sep.*, -ge-, *h*) hiss; '~plaudern *v/t.* (*sep.*, -ge-, *h*) blab or let out; '~polstern *v/t.* (*sep.*, -ge-, *h*) stuff, pad; wad; '~probieren *v/t.* (*sep.*, *no* -ge-, *h*) try, test.

Auspuff *mot.* ['auspuf] *m* -[e]s/-e) exhaust; '~gas *mot. n* exhaust gas; '~rohr *mot. n* exhaust-pipe; '~topf *mot. m* silencer, *Am.* muffler.

'**aus|putzen** *v/t.* (*sep.*, -ge-, *h*) clean; '~quartieren *v/t.* (*sep.*, *no* -ge-, *h*) dislodge; ✕ billet out; '~radieren *v/t.* (*sep.*, *no* -ge-, *h*) erase; '~rangieren *v/t.* (*sep.*, *no* -ge-, *h*) discard; '~rauben *v/t.* (*sep.*, -ge-, *h*) rob; ransack; '~räumen *v/t.* (*sep.*, -ge-, *h*) empty, clear (out); remove (*furniture*); '~rechnen *v/t.* (*sep.*, -ge-, *h*) calculate, compute; reckon (out), *Am.* figure out *or* up (*all a. fig.*).

'**Ausrede** *f* excuse, evasion, subterfuge; '2n (*sep.*, -ge-, *h*) 1. *v/i.* finish speaking; ~ *lassen* hear *s.o.* out; 2. *v/t.*: *j-m et.* ~ dissuade *s.o.* from *s.th.*

'**ausreichen** *v/i.* (*sep.*, -ge-, *h*) suffice; '~d *adj.* sufficient.

'**Ausreise** *f* departure; ⚓ voyage out.

'ausreiß|en (*irr. reißen, sep., -ge-*) 1. *v/t.* (*h*) pull *or* tear out; 2. *v/i.* (*sein*) run away; '~er *m* runaway.

aus|renken ['ausrɛŋkən] *v/t.* (*sep., -ge-, h*) dislocate; '~richten *v/t.* (*sep., -ge-, h*) straighten; ⚔ dress; adjust; deliver (*message*); do, effect; accomplish; obtain; arrange (*feast*); richte ihr e-n Gruß von mir aus! remember me to her!; ~rotten ['~rɔtən] *v/t.* (*sep., -ge-, h*) root out; *fig.* extirpate, exterminate.

'Ausruf *m* cry; exclamation; '2en (*irr. rufen, sep., -ge-,h*) 1. *v/i.* cry out, exclaim; 2. *v/t.* proclaim; '~e-zeichen *n* exclamation mark, *Am. a.* exclamation point; '~ung *f* (*-/-en*) proclamation; '~ungszeichen *n s.* Ausrufezeichen. [*-ge-, h*) rest.\

'ausruhen *v/i./v/t. and v/refl.* (*sep.,*\
'ausrüst|en *v/t.* (*sep., -ge-, h*) fit out; equip; '2ung *f* outfit, equipment, fittings *pl.* [disseminate.\

'aussäen *v/t.* (*sep., -ge-, h*) sow; *fig.*)

'Aussage *f* statement; declaration; ⅗ evidence; *gr.* predicate; '2n (*sep., -ge-, h*) 1. *v/t.* state, declare; ⅗ depose; 2. ~ *v/i.* give evidence.

'Aussatz *m* (*-es/no pl.*) leprosy.

'aus|saugen *v/t.* (*sep., -ge-, h*) suck (out); *fig.* exhaust (*land*); '~schalten *v/t.* (*sep., -ge-, h*) eliminate; ⚡ cut out, switch off, turn off *or* out (*light*).

Ausschank ['ausʃaŋk] *m* (*-[e]s/=e*) retail (*of alcoholic drinks*); public house, F pub.

'Ausschau *f* (*-/no pl.*): ~ halten nach be on the look-out for, watch for.

'ausscheid|en (*irr. scheiden, sep., -ge-*) 1. *v/t.* (*h*) separate; 🧪, ⚗, *physiol.* eliminate; ⚗ secrete; 2. *v/i.* (*sein*) retire; withdraw; *sports:* drop out; '2ung *f* separation; elimination (*a. sports*); ⚗ secretion.

'aus|schiffen *v/t. and v/refl.* (*sep., -ge-, h*) disembark; '~schimpfen *v/t.* (*sep., -ge-, h*) scold, tell *s.o.* off, berate; ~schirren ['~ʃirən] *v/t.* (*sep., -ge-, h*) unharness; '~schlach-ten *v/t.* (*sep., -ge-, h*) cut up; cannibalize (*car, etc.*); *fig.* exploit, make the most of; '~schlafen (*irr. schlafen, sep., -ge-, h*) 1. *v/i.* sleep one's fill; 2. *v/t.* sleep off (*effects of drink, etc.*).

'Ausschlag *m* 🏥 eruption, rash; deflexion (*of pointer*); den ~ geben settle it; 2en ['~gən] (*irr. schlagen, sep., -ge-*) 1. *v/t.* (*h*) knock *or* beat out; line; refuse, decline; 2. *v/i.* (*h*) *horse:* kick; *pointer:* deflect; 3. *v/i.* (*h, sein*) bud; 2gebend *adj.* ['~k-] decisive.

'ausschließ|en *v/t.* (*irr. schließen, sep., -ge-, h*) shut *or* lock out; *fig.:* exclude; expel; *sports:* disqualify; '~lich *adj.* exclusive.

'Ausschluß *m* exclusion; expulsion; *sports:* disqualification.

'ausschmücken *v/t.* (*sep., -ge-, h*) adorn, decorate; *fig.* embellish.

'Ausschnitt *m* cut; décolleté, (low) neck (*of dress*); cutting, *Am.* clipping (*from newspaper*); *fig.* part, section.

'ausschreib|en *v/t.* (*irr. schreiben, sep., -ge-, h*) write out; copy; write out (*word*) in full; make out (*invoice*); announce; advertise; '2ung *f* (*-/-en*) announcement; advertisement.

'ausschreit|en (*irr. schreiten, sep., -ge-*) 1. *v/i.* (*sein*) step out, take long strides; 2. *v/t.* (*h*) pace (*room*); measure by steps; '2ung *f* (*-/-en*) excess; ~en *pl.* riots *pl.*

'Ausschuß *m* refuse, waste, rubbish; committee, board.

'aus|schütteln *v/t.* (*sep., -ge-, h*) shake out; '~schütten *v/t.* (*sep., -ge-, h*) pour out; spill; 🕊 distribute (*dividend*); j-m sein Herz ~ pour out one's heart to s.o.; '~schwär-men *v/i.* (*sep., -ge-, sein*) swarm out; ~ (*lassen*) ⚔ extend, deploy.

'ausschweif|end *adj.* dissolute; '2ung *f* (*-/-en*) debauchery, excess.

'ausschwitzen *v/t.* (*sep., -ge-, h*) exude.

'aussehen 1. *v/i.* (*irr. sehen, sep., -ge-, h*) look; wie sieht er aus? what does he look like?; es sieht nach Regen aus it looks like rain; 2. 2 *n* (*-s/ no pl.*) look(s *pl.*), appearance.

außen *adv.* ['ausən] (on the) outside; von ~ her from (the) outside; nach ~ (*hin*) outward(s); '2auf-nahme *f film:* outdoor shot; '2bordmotor *m* outboard motor.

'aussenden *v/t.* (*irr. senden,*) sep., -ge-, h) send out.

'Außen|hafen *m* outport; '~handel *m* foreign trade; '~minister *m* foreign minister; Foreign Secretary, *Am.* Secretary of State; '~ministe-rium *n* foreign ministry; Foreign Office, *Am.* State Department; '~politik *f* foreign policy; 2poli-tisch *adj.* of *or* referring to foreign affairs; '~seite *f* outside, surface; '~seiter *m* (*-s/-*) outsider; '~stände ⚔ ['~ʃtɛndə] *pl.* outstanding debts *pl., Am.* accounts *pl.* receivable; '~welt *f* outer *or* outside world.

außer ['ausər] 1. *prp.* (*dat.*) out of; beside(s), *Am.* aside from; except; ~ sich sein be beside o.s. (*vor Freude* with joy); 2. *cj.*: ~ daß except that; ~ wenn unless; '~dem *cj.* besides, moreover.

äußere ['ɔysərə] 1. *adj.* exterior, outer, external, outward; 2. 2 *n* (*Äußer[e]n/no pl.*) exterior, outside, outward appearance.

'außer|gewöhnlich *adj.* extra-

ordinary; exceptional; **'~halb**
1. *prp.* (*gen.*) outside, out of; beyond; **2.** *adv.* on the outside.
äußerlich *adj.* ['ɔʏsərliç] external,
outward; **'2keit** *f* (*-/-en*) super-
ficiality; formality.
äußern ['ɔʏsərn] *v/t.* (*ge-*, h) utter,
express; advance; *sich ~ matter*:
manifest itself; *p.* express o.s.
'außer'ordentlich *adj.* extraordinary.
äußerst ['ɔʏsərst] **1.** *adj.* outermost;
fig. utmost, extreme; **2.** *adv.* extremely, highly.
außerstande *adj.* [ausər'ʃtandə]
unable, not in a position.
'Äußerung *f* (*-/-en*) utterance,
remark.
'aussetz|en (*sep.*, -ge-, h) **1.** *v/t.* set
or put out; lower (*boat*); promise
(*reward*); settle (*pension*); bequeath;
expose (*child*); expose (*dat.* to);
et. ~ an (*dat.*) find fault with;
2. *v/i.* intermit; fail; *activity*: stop;
suspend; *mot.* misfire; **'2ung** *f*
(*-/-en*) exposure (*of child, to weather, etc.*) (*a.* 🐦).
'Aussicht *f* (*-/-en*) view (*auf acc.*
of); *fig.* prospect (of), chance (of);
in ~ haben have in prospect; **'2slos**
adj. hopeless, desperate; **'2sreich**
adj. promising, full of promise.
aussöhn|en ['auszø:nən] *v/t.* (*sep.*,
-ge-, h) reconcile *s.o.* (*mit* to *s.th.*,
with *s.o.*); *sich ~* reconcile o.s. (to
s.th., with *s.o.*); **'2ung** *f* (*-/-en*)
reconciliation.
'aussondern *v/t.* (*sep.*, -ge-, h)
single out; separate.
'aus|spannen (*sep.*, -ge-, h) **1.** *v/t.*
stretch, extend; F *fig.* steal (*s.o.'s
girl friend*); unharness (*draught
animal*); **2.** *fig.* *v/i.* (take a) rest,
relax; **'~speien** *v/t.* and *v/i.* (*irr.
speien, sep.*, -ge-, h) spit out.
'aussperr|en *v/t.* (*sep.*, -ge-, h)
shut out; lock out (*workmen*); **'2ung**
f (*-/-en*) lock-out.
'aus|spielen (*sep.*, -ge-, h) **1.** *v/t.*
play (*card*); **2.** *v/i.* at cards: lead; *er
hat ausgespielt* he is done for;
'~spionieren *v/t.* (*sep.*, *no* -ge-, h)
spy out.   [cent; discussion.)
'Aussprache *f* pronunciation, ac-)
'aussprechen (*irr. sprechen, sep.*,
-ge-, h) **1.** *v/t.* pronounce, express;
sich ~ für (*gegen*) declare o.s. for
(against); **2.** *v/i.* finish speaking.
'Ausspruch *m* utterance; saying;
remark.
'aus|spucken *v/i.* and *v/t.* (*sep.*,
-ge-, h) spit out; **'~spülen** *v/t.* (*sep.*,
-ge-, h) rinse.
'Ausstand *m* strike, *Am.* F *a.* walkout; *in den ~ treten* go on strike,
Am. F *a.* walk out.
ausstatt|en ['aus ʃtatən] *v/t.* (*sep.*,
-ge-, h) fit out, equip; furnish;
supply (*mit* with); give a dowry to

(*daughter*); get up (*book*); **'2ung** *f*
(*-/-en*) outfit, equipment; furniture; supply; dowry; get-up (*of
book*).
'aus|stechen *v/t.* (*irr. stechen, sep.*,
-ge-, h) cut out (*a. fig.*); put out
(*eye*); **'~stehen** (*irr. stehen, sep.*,
-ge-, h) **1.** *v/i.* payments: be outstanding; **2.** *v/t.* endure, bear;
'~steigen *v/i.* (*irr. steigen, sep.*,
-ge-, sein) get out *or* off, alight.
'ausstell|en *v/t.* (*sep.*, -ge-, h) ex-
hibit; make out (*invoice*); issue
(*document*); draw (*bill*); **'2er** *m* (*-s/-*)
exhibitor; drawer; **'2ung** *f* exhibition, show; **'2ungsraum** *m*
show-room.
'aussterben *v/i.* (*irr. sterben, sep.*,
-ge-, sein) die out; become extinct.
'Aussteuer *f* trousseau, dowry.
'ausstopfen *v/t.* (*sep.*, -ge-, h) stuff;
wad, pad.
'ausstoß|en *v/t.* (*irr. stoßen, sep.*,
-ge-, h) thrust out, eject; expel;
utter (*cry*); heave (*sigh*); ✂ cashier;
'2ung *f* (*-/-en*) expulsion.
'aus|strahlen *v/t.* and *v/i.* (*sep.*,
-ge-, h) radiate; **'~strecken** *v/t.*
(*sep.*, -ge-, h) stretch (out); **'~strei-
chen** *v/t.* (*irr. streichen, sep.*, -ge-, h)
strike out; smooth (down); **'~
streuen** *v/t.* (*sep.*, -ge-, h) scatter;
spread (*rumours*); **'~strömen** (*sep.*,
-ge-, h) **1.** *v/i.* (sein) stream out; *gas,
light*: emanate; *gas, steam*: escape;
2. *v/t.* (h) pour (out); **'~suchen** *v/t.*
(*sep.*, -ge-, h) choose, select.
'Austausch *m* exchange; **'2bar** *adj.*
exchangeable; **'2en** *v/t.* (*sep.*, -ge-,
h) exchange.
'austeil|en *v/t.* (*sep.*, -ge-, h) dis-
tribute; deal out (*blows*); **'2ung** *f*
distribution.
Auster *zo.* ['austər] *f* (*-/-n*) oyster.
'austragen *v/t.* (*irr. tragen, sep.*,
-ge-, h) deliver (*letters, etc.*); hold
(*contest*).
Australi|er [au'stra:liər] *m* (*-s/-*)
Australian; **2sch** *adj.* Australian.
'austreib|en *v/t.* (*irr. treiben, sep.*,
-ge-, h) drive out; expel; **'2ung** *f*
(*-/-en*) expulsion.
'aus|treten (*irr. treten, sep.*, -ge-)
1. *v/t.* (h) tread *or* stamp out; wear
out (*shoes*); wear down (*steps*);
2. *v/i.* (sein) emerge, come out;
river: overflow its banks; retire
(*aus* from); F ease o.s.; *~ aus*
leave (*society, etc.*); **'~trinken** (*irr.
trinken, sep.*, -ge-, h) **1.** *v/t.* drink
up; empty, drain; **2.** *v/i.* finish
drinking; **'2tritt** *m* leaving; retirement; **'~trocknen** (*sep.*, -ge-) **1.** *v/t.*
(h) dry up; drain (*land*); parch
(*throat, earth*); **2.** *v/i.* (sein) dry up.
ausüb|en ['aus ʔ-] *v/t.* (*sep.*, -ge-, h)
exercise; practi|se, *Am.* -ce (*profes-
sion*); exert (*influence*); **'2ung** *f*
practice; exercise.

'**Ausverkauf** ✝ *m* selling off *or* out (*of stock*); sale; '**2t** ✝, *thea. adj.* sold out; *theatre notice*: 'full house'.

'**Auswahl** *f* choice; selection; ✝ assortment. [choose, select.⟩

'**auswählen** *v/t.* (*sep.*, -ge-, *h*)⟩

'**Auswander|er** *m* emigrant; '**2n** *v/i.* (*sep.*, -ge-, *sein*) emigrate; '**~ung** *f* emigration.

auswärt|ig *adj.* ['ausvertiç] out-of-town; non-resident; foreign; *das Auswärtige Amt s.* Außenministerium; **~s** *adv.* ['~s] outward(s); out of doors; out of town; abroad; **~** essen dine out.

'**auswechseln 1.** *v/t.* (*sep.*, -ge-, *h*) exchange; change; replace; **2.** 2 *n* (-*s/no pl.*) exchange; replacement.

'**Ausweg** *m* way out (*a. fig.*); outlet; *fig.* expedient.

'**ausweichen** *v/i.* (*irr.* weichen, *sep.*, -ge-, *sein*) make way (for); *fig.* evade, avoid; '**~d** *adj.* evasive.

Ausweis ['ausvais] *m* (-*es/-e*) (bank) return; identity card, *Am.* identification (card); **2en** ['~zən] *v/t.* (*irr.* weisen, *sep.*, -ge-, *h*) turn out, expel; evict; deport; show, prove; *sich* **~** prove one's identity; '**~papiere** *n/pl.* identity papers *pl.*; '**~ung** ['~zuŋ] *f* expulsion; '**~ungsbefehl** *m* expulsion order.

'**ausweiten** *v/t.* and *v/refl.* (*sep.*, -ge-, *h*) widen, stretch, expand.

'**auswendig 1.** *adj.* outward, outside; **2.** *adv.* outwardly, outside; *fig.* by heart.

'**aus|werfen** *v/t.* (*irr.* werfen, *sep.*, -ge-, *h*) throw out, cast; eject; 𝔰 expectorate; allow (*sum of money*); '**~werten** *v/t.* (*sep.*, -ge-, *h*) evaluate; analyze, interpret; utilize, exploit; '**~wickeln** *v/t.* (*sep.*, -ge-, *h*) unwrap; '**~wiegen** *v/t.* (*irr.* wiegen, *sep.*, -ge-, *h*) weigh out; '**~wirken** *v/refl.* (*sep.*, -ge-, *h*) take effect, operate; *sich* **~** *auf* (*acc.*) affect; '**2wirkung** *f* effect; '**~wischen** *v/t.* (*sep.*, -ge-, *h*) wipe out, efface; '**~wringen** *v/t.* (*irr.* wringen, *sep.*, -ge-, *h*) wring out.

'**Auswuchs** *m* excrescence, outgrowth (*a. fig.*), protuberance.

'**Auswurf** *m* 𝔰 expectoration; *fig.* refuse, dregs *pl.*

'**aus|zahlen** *v/t.* (*sep.*, -ge-, *h*) pay out; pay *s.o.* off; '**~zählen** *v/t.* (*sep.*, -ge-, *h*) count out.

'**Auszahlung** *f* payment.

'**Auszehrung** *f* (-*/-en*) consumption.

'**auszeichn|en** *v/t.* (*sep.*, -ge-, *h*) mark (out); *fig.* distinguish (*sich o.s.*); '**2ung** *f* marking; distinction; hono(u)r; decoration.

'**auszieh|en** (*irr.* ziehen, *sep.*, -ge-) **1.** *v/t.* (*h*) draw out, extract; take off (*garment*); *sich* **~** undress; **2.** *v/i.* (*sein*) set out; move (out), remove, move house; '**2platte** *f* leaf (*of table*).

'**Auszug** *m* departure; 𝔛 marching out; removal; extract, excerpt (*from book*); summary; ✝ statement (of account). [tic, genuine.⟩

authentisch *adj.* [au'tɛntiʃ] authen-⟩

Auto ['auto] *n* (-*s/-s*) (motor-)car, *Am. a.* automobile; **~** *fahren* drive, motor; '**~bahn** *f* motorway, autobahn; '**~biogra'phie** *f* autobiography; '**~bus** ['~bus] *m* (-*ses/-se*) (motor-)bus; (motor) coach; '**~bushaltestelle** *f* bus stop; '**~didakt** [~di'dakt] *m* (-*en/-en*) autodidact, self-taught person; '**~droschke** *f* taxi(-cab), *Am.* cab; '**~fahrer** *m* motorist; '**~gramm** *s* autograph; '**~grammjäger** *m* autograph hunter; '**~händler** *m* car dealer; '**~kino** *n* drive-in cinema; '**~krat** [~'kra:t] *m* (-*en/-en*) autocrat; '**~kratie** [~a-'ti:] *f* (-*/-n*) autocracy; '**~mat** [~'ma:t] *m* (-*en/-en*) automaton; slot-machine, vending machine; '**~matenrestaurant** *n* self-service restaurant, *Am.* automat; '**~mation** ⊕ [~ma'tsjo:n] *f* (-*/no pl.*) automation; **2'matisch** *adj.* automatic; '**~mechaniker** *m* car mechanic; '**~mobil** [~mo'bi:l] *n* (-*s/-e*) *s.* Auto; **2nom** *adj.* [~'no:m] autonomous; '**~nomie** [~o'mi:] *f* (-*/-n*) autonomy.

Autor ['auto:r] *m* (-*s/-en*) author.

'**Autoreparaturwerkstatt** *f* car repair shop, garage. [thor(ess).⟩

Autorin [au'to:rin] *f* (-*/-nen*) au-⟩ **autori|sieren** [autori'zi:rən] *v/t.* (*no* -ge-, *h*) authorize; '**~tär** *adj.* [~'tɛ:r] authoritarian; **2'tät** *f* (-*/-en*) authority.

'**Auto|straße** *f* motor-road; '**~vermietung** *f* (-*/-en*) car hire service.

avisieren ✝ [avi'zi:rən] *v/t.* (*no* -ge-, *h*) advise.

Axt [akst] *f* (-*/⁺e*) ax(e).

Azetylen 🜊 [atsety'le:n] *n* (-*s/no pl.*) acetylene. [2n *adj.* azure.⟩

Azur [a'tsu:r] *m* (-*s/no pl.*) azure;⟩

B

Bach [bax] *m* (-[*e*]*s/⁺e*) brook, *Am. a.* run. [port.⟩

Backbord ⊕ ['bak-] *n* (-[*e*]*s/-e*)⟩

Backe ['bakə] *f* (-*/-n*) cheek.

backen ['bakən] (*irr.*, ge-, *h*) **1.** *v/t.* bake; fry; dry (*fruit*); **2.** *v/i.* bake; fry.

'**Backen|bart** *m* (side-)whiskers *pl.*, *Am. a.* sideburns *pl.*; '**~zahn** *m* molar (tooth), grinder.

Bäcker ['bɛkər] *m* (-s/-) baker; **~ei** [~'raɪ] *f* (-/-en) baker's (shop), bakery.

'**Back|fisch** *m* fried fish; *fig.* girl in her teens, teenager, *Am. a.* bobby soxer; '**~obst** *n* dried fruit; '**~ofen** *m* oven; '**~pflaume** *f* prune; '**~pulver** *n* baking-powder; '**~stein** *m* brick; '**~ware** *f* baker's ware.

Bad [baːt] *n* (-[e]s/**~er**) bath; *in river, etc.*: a. bathe; *s. Badeort*; **ein ~ nehmen** take *or* have a bath.

Bade|anstalt ['baːdə-] *f* (public swimming) baths *pl.*; '**~anzug** *m* bathing-costume, bathing-suit; '**~hose** *f* bathing-drawers *pl.*, (bathing) trunks *pl.*; '**~kappe** *f* bathing-cap; '**~kur** *f* spa treatment; '**~mantel** *m* bathing-gown, *Am.* bathrobe; '**~meister** *m* bath attendant; swimming-instructor; '**2n** (ge-, h) **1.** *v/t.* bath (*baby, etc.*); bathe (*eyes, etc.*); **2.** *v/i.* bath, tub; have *or* take a bath; *in river, etc.*: bathe; **~ gehen** go swimming; '**~ofen** *m* geyser, boiler, *Am.* a. water heater; '**~ort** *m* watering-place; spa; seaside resort; '**~salz** *n* bath-salt; '**~strand** *m* bathing-beach; '**~tuch** *n* bathtowel; '**~wanne** *f* bath-tub; '**~zimmer** *n* bathroom.

Bagatell|e [baga'tɛlə] *f* (-/-n) trifle, trifling matter, bagatelle; **2i'sieren** *v/t.* (*no* -ge-, h) minimize (the importance of), *Am. a.* play down.

Bagger ['bagər] *m* (-s/-) excavator; dredge(r); '**2n** *v/i. and v/t.* (ge-, h) excavate; dredge.

Bahn [baːn] *f* (-/-en) course; path; **~~** railway, *Am.* railroad; *mot.* lane; trajectory (*of bullet, etc.*); *ast.* orbit; *sports*: track, course, lane; *skating*: rink; *bowling*: alley; '**2brechend** *adj.* pioneer(ing), epoch-making; *art*: avant-gardist; '**~damm** *m* railway embankment, *Am.* railroad embankment; '**2en** *v/t.* (ge-, h) clear, open (up) (*way*); **den Weg ~ prepare** *or* pave the way (*dat.* for); **sich e-n Weg ~** force *or* work *or* elbow one's way; '**~hof** *m* (railway-)station, *Am.* (railroad-)station; '**~linie** *f* railway-line, *Am.* railroad line; '**~steig** *m* platform; '**~steigkarte** *f* platform ticket; '**~übergang** *m* level crossing, *Am.* grade crossing.

Bahre ['baːrə] *f* (-/-n) stretcher, litter; bier.

Bai [baɪ] *f* (-/-en) bay; creek.

Baisse ✝ ['bɛːs(ə)] *f* (-/-n) depression (on the market); fall (in prices); **auf ~ spekulieren** ✝ bear, speculate for a fall, *Am.* sell short; '**~spekulant** *m* bear.

Bajonett ⚔ [bajo'nɛt] *n* (-[e]s/-e) bayonet; **das ~ aufpflanzen** fix the bayonet.

Bake ['baːkə] *f* (-/-n) ⚓ beacon; **~~** warning-sign.

Bakterie [bak'teːrjə] *f* (-/-n) bacterium, microbe, germ.

bald *adv.* [balt] soon; shortly; before long; F almost, nearly; early; **so ~ als möglich** as soon as possible; **~ hier, ~ dort** now here, now there; **~ig** *adj.* ['~dɪç] speedy; **~e Antwort** ✝ early reply.

Baldrian ['baldriaːn] *m* (-s/-e) valerian.

Balg [balk] **1.** *m* (-[e]s/**~e**) skin; body (*of doll*); bellows *pl.*; **2.** F *m, n* (-[e]s/**~er**) brat, urchin; **2en** ['balgən] *v/refl.* (ge-, h) scuffle (*um* for), wrestle (for).

Balken ['balkən] *m* (-s/-) beam; rafter.

Balkon [bal'kõː; ~'kɔːn] *m* (-s/-s; -s/-e) balcony; *thea.* dress circle, *Am.* balcony; **~tür** *f* French window.

Ball [bal] *m* (-[e]s/**~e**) ball; *geogr., ast.* a. globe; ball, dance; **auf dem ~** at the ball.

Ballade [ba'laːdə] *f* (-/-n) ballad.

Ballast ['balast] *m* (-es/**~~**-e) ballast; *fig.* burden, impediment; dead weight.

'**ballen¹** *v/t.* (ge-, h) (form into a) ball; clench (*fist*); **sich ~** (form into a) ball; cluster.

'**Ballen²** *m* (-s/-) bale; *anat.* ball; **~ Papier** ten reams *pl.*

Ballett [ba'lɛt] *n* (-[e]s/-e) ballet; **~änzer** [ba'lɛttɛntsər] *m* (-s/-) ballet-dancer.

ball|förmig ['balfœrmɪç] ball-shaped, globular; '**2kleid** *n* ball-dress.

Ballon [ba'lõː; ~'oːn] *m* (-s/-s; -s/-s, -e) balloon.

'**Ball|saal** *m* ball-room; '**~spiel** *n* ball-game, game of ball.

Balsam ['balzaːm] *m* (-s/-e) balsam, balm (*a. fig.*); **2ieren** [~a'miːrən] *v/t.* (*no* -ge-, h) embalm.

Balz [balts] *f* (-/-en) mating season; display (*by cock-bird*).

Bambus ['bambus] *m* (-ses/-se) bamboo; '**~rohr** *n* bamboo, cane.

banal *adj.* [ba'naːl] commonplace, banal, trite; trivial; **2ität** [~ali'tɛːt] *f* (-/-en) banality; commonplace; triviality.

Banane [ba'naːnə] *f* (-/-n) banana; **~nstecker** ⚡ *m* banana plug.

Band [bant] **1.** *m* (-[e]s/**~e**) volume; **2.** *n* (-[e]s/**~er**) band; ribbon; tape; *anat.* ligament; **3.** *fig. n* (-[e]s/-e) bond, tie; **4.** 2 *pret. of* binden.

Bandag|e [ban'daːʒə] *f* (-/-n) bandage; **2ieren** [~a'ʒiːrən] *v/t.* (*no* -ge-, h) (apply a) bandage.

Bande ['bandə] *f* (-/-n) billiards: cushion; *fig.* gang, band.

bändigen ['bɛndigən] *v/t.* (ge-, h)

tame; break in (*horse*); subdue (*a. fig.*); *fig.* restrain, master.

Bandit [ban'diːt] *m* (-en/-en) bandit.

'Band|maß *n* tape measure; **~säge** *f* band-saw; **~scheibe** *anat. f* intervertebral disc; **~wurm** *zo. m* tapeworm.

bang *adj.* [baŋ], **~e** *adj.* ['~ə] anxious (*um about*), uneasy (*about*), concerned (*for*); *mir ist* ~ I am afraid (*vor dat.* of); *j-m bange machen* frighten *or* scare s.o.; **~en** *v/i.* (ge-, h) be anxious *or* worried (*um about*).

Bank [baŋk] *f* 1. (-/~e) bench; *school*: desk; F *durch die* ~ without exception, all through; *auf die lange* ~ *schieben* put off, postpone; shelve; 2. ✝ (-/-en) bank; *Geld auf der* ~ money in the bank; **~anweisung** *f* cheque, *Am.* check; **~ausweis** *m* bank return *or* statement; **~beamte** *m* bank clerk *or* official; **~einlage** *f* deposit.

Bankett [baŋ'kɛt] *n* (-[e]s/-e) banquet.

'Bank|geheimnis *n* banker's duty of secrecy; **~geschäft** ✝ *n* bank (-ing) transaction, banking operation; **~haus** *n* bank(ing-house).

Bankier [baŋ'jeː] *m* (-s/-s) banker.

'Bank|konto *n* bank(ing) account; **~note** *f* (bank) note, *Am.* (bank) bill.

bankrott [baŋ'krɔt] 1. *adj.* bankrupt; 2. 2 *m* (-[e]s/-e) bankruptcy, insolvency, failure; ~ *machen* fail, go *or* become bankrupt.

'Bankwesen *n* banking.

Bann [ban] *m* (-[e]s/-e) ban; *fig.* spell; *eccl.* excommunication; **2en** *v/t.* (ge-, h) banish (*a. fig.*); exorcize (*devil*); avert (*danger*); *eccl.* excommunicate; spellbind.

Banner ['banər] *n* (-s/-) banner (*a. fig.*); standard; **~träger** *m* standard-bearer.

'Bann|fluch *m* anathema; **~meile** *f* precincts *pl.*; ⚖ *area around government buildings within which processions and meetings are prohibited.*

bar¹ [baːr] 1. *adj.*: e-r *Sache* ~ destitute *or* devoid of s.th.; **~es** *Geld* ready money, cash; **~er** *Unsinn* sheer nonsense; 2. *adv.*: ~ *bezahlen* pay in cash, pay money down.

Bar² [.] *f* (-/-s) bar; night-club.

Bär [bɛːr] *m* (-en/-en) bear; *j-m e-n* ~en *aufbinden* hoax s.o.

Baracke [ba'rakə] *f* (-/-n) barrack; **~nlager** *n* hutment.

Barbar [bar'baːr] *m* (-en/-en) barbarian; **~ei** [~a'raɪ] *f* (-/-en) barbarism; barbarity; **2isch** [~'baːrɪʃ] *adj.* barbarian; barbarous; *art, taste*: barbaric.

'Bar|bestand *m* cash in hand; **~betrag** *m* amount in cash.

'Bärenzwinger *m* bear-pit.

barfuß *adj. and adv.* ['baːr-], **~füßig** *adj. and adv.* ['~fyːsɪç] barefoot.

barg [bark] *pret.* of *bergen*.

'Bar|geld *n* cash, ready money; **2geldlos** *adj.* cashless; **~er** *Zahlungsverkehr* cashless money transfers *pl.*; **2häuptig** *adj. and adv.* ['~hɔʏptɪç] bare-headed, uncovered.

Bariton ♩ ['baːritɔn] *m* (-s/-e) baritone. [launch.]

Barkasse ⚓ [bar'kasə] *f* (-/-n))

barmherzig *adj.* [barm'hɛrtsɪç] merciful, charitable; *der* ~e *Samariter* the good Samaritan; 2e *Schwester* Sister of Mercy *or* Charity; 2keit *f* (-/-en) mercy, charity.

Barometer [baro'-] *n* barometer.

Baron [ba'roːn] *m* (-s/-e) baron; **~in** *f* (-/-nen) baroness.

Barre ['barə] *f* (-/-n) bar.

Barren ['barən] *m* (-s/-) *metall.* bar, ingot, bullion; *gymnastics*: parallel bars *pl.*

Barriere [bar'jɛːrə] *f* (-/-n) barrier.

Barrikade [bari'kuːdə] *f* (-/-n) barricade; **~n** *errichten* raise barricades.

barsch *adj.* [barʃ] rude, gruff, rough.

'Bar|schaft *f* (-/-en) ready money, cash; **~scheck** ✝ *m* open cheque, *Am.* open check.

barst [barst] *pret.* of *bersten*.

Bart [baːrt] *m* (-[e]s/~e) beard; bit (*of key*); *sich e-n* ~ *wachsen lassen* grow a beard.

bärtig *adj.* ['bɛːrtɪç] bearded.

'bartlos *adj.* beardless.

'Barzahlung *f* cash payment; *nur gegen* ~ ✝ terms strictly cash.

Basis ['baːzɪs] *f* (-/*Basen*) base; *fig.* basis.

Baß ♩ [bas] *m* (*Basses/Bässe*) bass; **~geige** *f* bass-viol.

Bassist [ba'sɪst] *m* (-en/-en) bass (singer).

Bast [bast] *m* (-es/-e) bast; velvet (*on antlers*).

Bastard ['bastart] *m* (-[e]s/-e) bastard; half-breed; *zo.,* ♀ hybrid.

bast|eln ['bastəln] (ge-, h) 1. *v/t.* build, F rig up; 2. *v/i.* build; **2ler** *m* (-s/-) amateur craftsman, do-it-yourself man.

bat [baːt] *pret.* of *bitten*.

Bataillon [batal'joːn] *n* (-s/-e) battalion.

Batist [ba'tɪst] *m* (-[e]s/-e) cambric.

Batterie ⚔ ⚡ [batə'riː] *f* (-/-n) battery.

Bau [baʊ] *m* 1. (-[e]s/*no pl.*) building, construction; build, frame; 2. (-[e]s/-ten) building, edifice; 3. (-[e]s/-e) burrow, den (*a. fig.*), earth.

'Bau|arbeiter *m* workman in the building trade; **~art** *f* architecture, style; method of construction; *mot.* type, model.

4*

Bauch [baux] *m* (-[e]s/=e) *anat.* abdomen, belly; paunch; *ship:* bottom; '2ig *adj.* big-bellied, bulgy; '~landung *f* belly landing; '~redner *m* ventriloquist; '~schmerzen *m/pl.*, '~weh *n* (-s/*no pl.*) belly-ache, stomach-ache.

bauen ['bauən] (ge-, *h*) **1.** *v/t.* build, construct; erect, raise; build, make (*nest*); make (*violin, etc.*); **2.** *v/i.* build; ~ *auf* (*acc.*) trust (in); rely or count *or* depend on.

Bauer ['bauər] **1.** *m* (-n, -s/-n) farmer; peasant, countryman; *chess:* pawn; **2.** *n, m* (-s/-) (bird-)cage.

Bäuerin ['bɔʏərin] *f* (-/-nen) farmer's wife; peasant woman.

Bauerlaubnis ['bauⁿ-] *f* building permit.

bäuerlich *adj.* ['bɔʏərliç] rural, rustic.

Bauern|fänger *contp.* ['bauərn-fɛŋər] *m* (-s/-) trickster, confidence man; '~haus *n* farm-house; '~hof *m* farm.

'**bau|fällig** *adj.* out of repair, dilapidated; '2gerüst *n* scaffold (-ing); '2handwerker *m* craftsman in the building trade; '2herr *m* owner; '2holz *n* timber, *Am.* lumber; '2jahr *n* year of construction; ~ *1969* 1969 model *or* make; '2kasten *m* box of bricks; '2kunst *f* architecture.

'**baulich** *adj.* architectural, structural; *in gutem* ~*en Zustand* in good repair.

Baum [baum] *m* (-[e]s/=e) tree.

'**Baumeister** *m* architect.

baumeln ['bauməln] *v/i.* (ge-, *h*) dangle, swing; *mit den Beinen* ~ dangle *or* swing one's legs.

'**Baum|schere** *f* (*eine a pair of*) pruning-shears *pl.*; '~schule *f* nursery (*of young trees*); '~stamm *m* trunk; '~wolle *f* cotton; '2wollen *adj.* (made of) cotton.

'**Bau|plan** *m* architect's *or* building plan; '~platz *m* building plot *or* site, *Am.* location; '~polizei *f* Board of Surveyors.

Bausch [bauʃ] *m* (-es/-e, =e) pad; bolster; wad; *in* ~ *und Bogen* altogether, wholesale, in the lump; '2en *v/t.* (ge-, *h*) swell; *sich* ~ bulge, swell out, billow (out).

'**Bau|stein** *m* brick, building stone; building block; *fig.* element; '~stelle *f* building site; '~stil *m* (architectural) style; '~stoff *m* building material; '~unternehmer *m* building contractor; '~zaun *m* hoarding.

Bay|er ['baiⁿr] *m* (-n/-n) Bavarian; '2(e)risch *adj.* Bavarian.

Bazill|enträger ² [ba'tsilən-] *m* (germ-)carrier; ~us [~us] *m* (-/Ba-zillen) bacillus, germ.

beabsichtigen [bə'apziçtiɡən] *v/t.*

(*no -ge-, h*) intend, mean, propose (*zu tun* to do, doing).

be'acht|en *v/t.* (*no -ge-, h*) pay attention to; notice; observe; ~ens-wert *adj.* noteworthy, remarkable; ~lich *adj.* remarkable; considerable; 2ung *f* attention; consideration; notice; observance.

Beamte [bə'amtə] *m* (-n/-n) official, officer, *Am. a.* officeholder; functionary; Civil Servant.

be'ängstigend *adj.* alarming, disquieting.

beanspruch|en [bə'anʃpruxən] *v/t.* (*no -ge-, h*) claim, demand; require (*efforts, time, space, etc.*); ⊕ stress; 2ung *f* (-/-en) claim; demand (*gen.* on); ⊕ stress, strain.

beanstand|en [bə'anʃtandən] *v/t.* (*no -ge-, h*) object to; 2ung *f* (-/-en) objection (*gen.* to).

beantragen [bə'antraːɡən] *v/t.* (*no -ge-, h*) apply for; ∯ *parl.* move, make a motion; propose.

be'antwort|en *v/t.* (*no -ge-, h*) answer (*a. fig.*), reply to; 2ung *f* (-/-en) answer, reply; *in* ~ (*gen.*) in answer *or* reply to.

be'arbeit|en *v/t.* (*no -ge-, h*) work; ∮ till; dress (*leather*); hew (*stone*); process; ∰ treat; ∯ be in charge of (*case*); edit, revise (*book*); adapt (*nach* from); *esp.* ∮ arrange; *j-n* ~ work on s.o.; batter s.o.; 2ung *f* (-/-en) working; revision (*of book*); *thea.* adaptation; *esp.* ∮ arrangement; processing; ∰ treatment.

be'argwöhnen *v/t.* (*no -ge-, h*) suspect, be suspicious of.

beaufsichtig|en [bə'aufziçtiɡən] *v/t.* (*no -ge-, h*) inspect, superintend, supervise, control; look after (*child*); 2ung *f* (-/-en) inspection, supervision, control.

be'auftrag|en *v/t.* (*no -ge-, h*) commission (*zu inf.* to *inf.*), charge (*mit* with); 2te [~ktə] *m* (-n/-n) commissioner; representative; deputy; proxy.

be'bauen *v/t.* (*no -ge-, h*) ⚠ build on; ∮ cultivate.

beben ['beːbən] *v/i.* (ge-, *h*) shake (*vor dat.* with), tremble (with); shiver (with); *earth:* quake.

Becher ['bɛçər] *m* (-s/-) cup (*a. fig.*).

Becken ['bɛkən] *n* (-s/-) basin, *Am. a.* bowl; ∮ cymbal(s *pl.*); *anat.* pelvis.

bedacht *adj.* [bə'daxt]: ~ *sein auf* (*acc.*) look after, be concerned about, be careful *or* mindful of; *darauf* ~ *sein zu inf.* be anxious to *inf.*

bedächtig *adj.* [bə'dɛçtiç] deliberate.

bedang [bə'daŋ] *pret. of* bedingen.

be'danken *v/refl.* (*no -ge-, h*): *sich bei j-m für et.* ~ thank s.o. for s.th.

Bedarf [bə'darf] m (-[e]s/no pl.) need (an dat. of), want (of); ✝ demand (for); ~sartikel [bə'darfs?-] m/pl. necessaries pl., requisites pl.

bedauerlich adj. [bə'dauərliç] regrettable, deplorable.

be'dauern 1. v/t. (no -ge-, h) feel or be sorry for s.o.; pity s.o.; regret, deplore s.th.; **2.** ⚖ n (-s/no pl.) regret; pity; ~swert adj. pitiable, deplorable.

be'deck|en v/t. (no -ge-, h) cover; ✕ escort; ⚓ convoy; ~t adj. sky: overcast; ⚖ung f cover(ing); ✕ escort; ⚓ convoy.

be'denken 1. v/t. (irr. denken, no -ge-, h) consider; think s.th. over; j-n in s-m Testament ~ remember s.o. in one's will; **2.** ⚖ n (-s/-) consideration; objection; hesitation; scruple; ~los adj. unscrupulous.

be'denklich adj. doubtful; character: a. dubious; situation, etc.: dangerous, critical; delicate; risky.

Be'denkzeit f time for reflection; ich gebe dir e-e Stunde ~ I give you one hour to think it over.

be'deut|en v/t. (no -ge-, h) mean, signify; stand for; ~end adj. important, prominent; sum, etc. considerable; ~sam adj. significant.

Be'deutung f meaning, significance; importance; ⚖slos adj. insignificant; meaningless; ⚖svoll adj. significant; ~swandel ling. m semantic change.

be'dien|en (no -ge-, h) **1.** v/t. serve; wait on; ⚙ operate, work (machine); ✕ serve (gun); answer (telephone); sich ~ at table: help o.s.; **2.** v/i. serve; wait (at table); cards: follow suit; ⚖ung f (-/-en) service, esp. ✝ attendance; in restaurant, etc.: service; waiter, waitress; shop assistant(s pl.).

beding|en [bə'diŋən] v/t. ([irr.,] no -ge-, h) condition; stipulate; require; cause; imply; ~t adj. conditional (durch on); restricted; ~ sein durch be conditioned by; ⚖ung f (-/-en) condition; stipulation; ~en pl. ✝ terms pl.; ~ungslos adj. unconditional.

be'dräng|en v/t. (no -ge-, h) press hard, beset; ⚖nis f (-/-se) distress.

be'droh|en v/t. (no -ge-, h) threaten; menace; ~lich adj. threatening; ⚖ung f threat, menace (gen. to).

be'drück|en v/t. (no -ge-, h) oppress; depress; deject; ⚖ung f (-/-en) oppression; depression; dejection.

bedungen [bə'duŋən] p.p. of bedingen.

be'dürf|en v/i. (irr. dürfen, no -ge-, h): e-r Sache ~ need or want or require s.th.; ⚖nis n (-ses/-se) need, want, requirement; sein ~ verrichten relieve o.s. or nature; ⚖nisan-

stalt [bə'dyrfnis?-] f public convenience, Am. comfort station; ~tig adj. needy, poor, indigent.

be'ehren v/t. (no -ge-, h) hono(u)r, favo(u)r; ich beehre mich zu inf. I have the hono(u)r to inf.

be'eilen v/refl. (no -ge-, h) hasten, hurry, make haste, Am. F a. hustle.

beeindrucken [bə'aindrukən] v/t. (no -ge-, h) impress, make an impression on.

beeinfluss|en [bə'ainflusən] v/t. (no -ge-, h) influence; affect; parl. lobby; ⚖ung f (-/-en) influence; parl. lobbying.

beeinträchtig|en [bə'aintrɛçtigən] v/t. (no -ge-, h) impair, injure, affect (adversely); ⚖ung f (-/-en) impairment (gen. of); injury (to).

be'end|en v/t. (no -ge-, h), ~igen [~igən] v/t. (no -ge-, h) (bring to an) end, finish, terminate; ⚖igung [~iguŋ] f (-/-en) ending, termination.

beengt adj. [bə'ɛŋkt] space: narrow, confined, cramped; sich ~ fühlen feel cramped (for room); feel oppressed or uneasy.

be'erben v/t. (no -ge-, h): j-n ~ be s.o.'s heir.

beerdig|en [bə'e:rdigən] v/t. (no -ge-, h) bury; ⚖ung f (-/-en) burial, funeral.

Beere ['be:rə] f (-/-n) berry.

Beet [be:t] n (-[e]s/-e) bed.

befähig|en [bə'fɛ:igən] v/t. (no -ge-, h) enable (zu inf. to inf.); qualify (für, zu for); ~t adj. [~çt] (cap)able; ⚖ung f (-/-en) qualification; capacity.

befahl [bə'fa:l] pret. of befehlen.

befahr|bar adj. [bə'fa:rba:r] passable, practicable, trafficable; ⚓ navigable; ~en v/t. (irr. fahren, no -ge-, h) drive or travel on; ⚓ navigate (river).

be'fallen v/t. (irr. fallen, no -ge-, h) attack; befall; disease: a. strike; fear: seize.

be'fangen adj. embarrassed; self-conscious; prejudiced (a. ⚖⚖); ⚖⚖ bias(s)ed; ⚖heit f (-/-en) embarrassment; self-consciousness; ⚖⚖ bias, prejudice.

be'fassen v/refl. (no -ge-, h): sich ~ mit occupy o.s. with; engage in; attend to; deal with.

Befehl [bə'fe:l] m (-[e]s/-e) command (über acc. of); order; ⚖en (irr., no -ge-, h) **1.** v/t. command; order; **2.** v/i. command; ⚖igen ✕ [~igən] v/t. (no -ge- h) command.

Be'fehlshaber m (-s/-) commander(-in-chief); ⚖isch adj. imperious.

be'festig|en v/t. (no -ge-, h) fasten (an dat. to), fix (to), attach (to); ✕ fortify; fig. strengthen; ⚖ung f (-/-en) fixing, fastening; ✕ fortification; fig. strengthening.

be'feuchten v/t. (no -ge-, h) moisten, damp; wet.

be'finden 1. v/refl. (irr. finden, no -ge-, h) be; **2.** 2 n (-s/no pl.) (state of) health.

be'flaggen v/t. (no -ge-, h) flag.

be'flecken v/t. (no -ge-, h) spot, stain (a. fig.); fig. sully.

beflissen adj. [bə'flisən] studious; **2heit** f (-/no pl.) studiousness, assiduity.

befohlen [bə'fo:lən] p.p. of befehlen.

be'folg|en v/t. (no -ge-, h) follow, take (advice); obey (rule); adhere to (principle); **2ung** f (-/♣-en) observance (of); adherence (to).

be'förder|n v/t. (no -ge-, h) convey, carry; haul (goods), transport; forward; ✝ ship (a. ♨); promote (to be) (a. ✗); **2ung** f conveyance, transport(ation), forwarding; promotion; **2ungsmittel** n (means of) transport, Am. (means of) transportation.

be'fragen v/t. (no -ge-, h) question, interview; interrogate.

be'frei|en v/t. (no -ge-, h) (set) free (von from); liberate (nation, mind, etc.) (from); rescue (captive) (from); exempt s.o. (from); deliver s.o. (aus, von from); **2er** m liberator; **2ung** f (-/-en) liberation, deliverance; exemption.

Befremden [bə'fremdən] n (-s/ no pl.) surprise.

befreund|en [bə'frɔyndən] v/refl. (no -ge-, h): sich mit j-m ~ make friends with s.o.; sich mit et. ~ get used to s.th.; reconcile o.s. to s.th.; **~et** adj. friendly; on friendly terms; ~ sein be friends.

befriedig|en [bə'fri:digən] v/t. (no -ge-, h) satisfy; appease (hunger); meet (expectations, demand); pay off (creditor); **~end** adj. satisfactory; **2ung** f (-/-en) satisfaction.

be'fristen v/t. (no -ge-, h) set a time-limit.

be'frucht|en v/t. (no -ge-, h) fertilize; fructify; fecundate; impregnate; **2ung** f (-/-en) fertilization; fructification; fecundation; impregnation.

Befug|nis [bə'fu:knis] f (-/-se) authority, warrant; esp. ⚖ competence; **2t** adj. authorized; competent.

be'fühlen v/t. (no -ge-, h) feel; touch, handle, finger.

Be'fund m (-[e]s/-e) result; finding(s pl.); ⚕ diagnosis.

be'fürcht|en v/t. (no -ge-, h) fear, apprehend; suspect; **2ung** f (-/-en) fear, apprehension, suspicion.

befürworten [bə'fy:rvɔrtən] v/t. (no -ge-, h) plead for, advocate.

begab|t adj. [bə'ga:pt] gifted, talented; **2ung** [bə'ga:buŋ] f (-/-en) gift, talent(s pl.).

begann [bə'gan] pret. of beginnen.

be'geben v/t. (irr. geben, no -ge-, h) ✝ negotiate (bill of exchange); sich ~ happen; sich ~ nach go to, make for; sich in Gefahr ~ expose o.s. to danger.

begegn|en [bə'ge:gnən] v/i. (no -ge-, sein) meet s.o. or s.th., meet with; incident: happen to; anticipate, prevent; **2ung** f (-/-en) meeting.

be'gehen v/t. (irr. gehen, no -ge-, h) walk (on); inspect; celebrate (birthday, etc.); commit (crime); make (mistake); ein Unrecht ~ do wrong.

begehr|en [bə'ge:rən] v/t. (no -ge-, h) demand, require; desire, crave (for); long for; **~lich** adj. desirous, covetous.

begeister|n [bə'gaistərn] v/t. (no -ge-, h) inspire, fill with enthusiasm; sich ~ für feel enthusiastic about; **2ung** f (-/no pl.) enthusiasm, inspiration.

Be'gier f, **~de** [~də] f (-/-n) desire (nach for), appetite (for); concupiscence; **2ig** adj. eager (nach for, auf acc. for; zu inf. to inf.), desirous (nach of; zu inf. to inf.), anxious (zu inf. to inf.).

be'gießen v/t. (irr. gießen, no -ge-, h) water; baste (roasting meat); F wet (bargain).

Beginn [bə'gin] m (-[e]s/no pl.) beginning, start, commencement; origin; **2en** v/t. and v/i. (irr. no -ge-, h) begin, start, commence.

beglaubig|en [bə'glaubigən] v/t. (no -ge-, h) attest, certify; legalize, authenticate; **2ung** f (-/-en) attestation, certification; legalization; **2ungsschreiben** n credentials pl.

be'gleichen ✝ v/t. (irr. gleichen, no -ge-, h) pay, settle (bill, debt).

be'gleit|en v/t. (no -ge-, h) accompany (a. ♪ auf dat. on), escort; attend (a. fig.); see (s.o. home, etc.); **2er** m (-s/-) companion, attendant; escort; ♪ accompanist; **2erscheinung** f attendant symptom; **2schreiben** n covering letter; **2ung** f (-/-en) company; attendants pl., retinue (of sovereign, etc.); esp. ✗ escort; ♨, ✗ convoy; ♪ accompaniment.

be'glückwünschen v/t. (no -ge-, h) congratulate (zu on).

begnadig|en [bə'gna:digən] v/t. (no -ge-, h) pardon; pol. amnesty; **2ung** f (-/-en) pardon; pol. amnesty.

begnügen [bə'gny:gən] v/refl. (no -ge-, h): sich ~ mit content o.s. with, be satisfied with.

begonnen [bə'gɔnən] p.p. of beginnen.

be'graben v/t. (irr. graben, no -ge-, h) bury (a. fig.); inter.

Begräbnis [bə'grɛ:pnis] n (-ses/-se) burial; funeral, obsequies pl.

begradigen [bə'grɑːdigən] v/t. (no -ge-, h) straighten (road, frontier, etc.).

be'greif|en v/t. (irr. greifen, no -ge-, h) comprehend, understand; **.lich** adj. comprehensible.

be'grenz|en v/t. (no -ge-, h) bound, border; fig. limit; **2theit** f (-/-en) limitation (of knowledge); narrowness (of mind); **2ung** f (-/-en) boundary; bound, limit; limitation.

Be'griff m idea, notion, conception; comprehension; im ~ sein zu inf. be about or going to inf.

be'gründ|en v/t. (no -ge-, h) establish, found; give reasons for, substantiate (claim charge); **2ung** f establishment, foundation; fig. substantiation (of claim or charge); reason.

be'grüß|en v/t. (no -ge-, h) greet, welcome; salute; **2ung** f (-/-en) greeting, welcome; salutation.

begünstig|en [bə'gynstigən] v/t. (no -ge-, h) favo(u)r; encourage; patronize; **2ung** (-/-en) f favo(u)r; encouragement; patronage.

begutachten [bə'guːtʔ-] v/t. (no -ge-, h) give an opinion on; examine; ~ lassen obtain expert opinion on, submit s.th. to an expert.

begütert adj. [bə'gyːtərt] wealthy, well-to-do.

be'haart adj. hairy.

behäbig adj. [bə'hɛːbiç] phlegmatic, comfort-loving; figure: portly.

be'haftet adj. afflicted (with disease, etc.).

behag|en [bə'hɑːgən] **1.** v/i. (no -ge-, h) please or suit s.o.; **2.** ⯑ n (-s/no pl.) comfort, ease; **.lich** adj. [..k-] comfortable; cosy, snug.

be'halten v/t. (irr. halten, no -ge-, h) retain; keep (für sich to o.s.); remember.

Behälter [bə'hɛltər] m (-s/-) container, receptacle; box; for liquid: reservoir; for oil, etc.: tank.

be'hand|eln v/t. (no -ge-, h) treat; deal with (a. subject); ⊕ process; ⚕ treat; dress (wound); **2ung** f treatment; handling; ⊕ processing.

be'hängen v/t. (no -ge-, h) hang, drape (mit with); sich ~ mit cover or load o.s. with (jewellery).

beharr|en [bə'harən] v/i. (no -ge-, h) persist (auf dat. in); **.lich** adj. persistent; **2lichkeit** f (-/no pl.) persistence.

be'hauen v/t. (no -ge-, h) hew; trim (wood).

behaupt|en [bə'hauptən] v/t. (no -ge-, h) assert; maintain; **2ung** f (-/-en) assertion; statement.

Behausung [bə'hauzuŋ] f (-/-en) habitation; lodging.

Be'helf m (-[e]s/-e) expedient, (make)shift; s. Notbehelf; **2en** v/refl. (irr. helfen, no -ge-, h): sich ~ mit make shift with; sich ~ ohne do without; **.sheim** n temporary home.

behend adj. [bə'hɛnt], **.e** adj. [..də] nimble, agile; smart; **2igkeit** [..d-] f (-/no pl.) nimbleness, agility; smartness. [lodge, shelter.)

be'herbergen v/t. (no -ge-, h))

be'herrsch|en v/t. (no -ge-, h) rule (over), govern; command (situation, etc.); have command of (language); sich ~ control o.s.; **2er** m ruler (gen. over, of); **2ung** f (-/-en) command, control.

beherzigen [bə'hɛrtsigən] v/t. (no -ge-, h) take to heart, (bear in) mind.

be'hexen v/t. (no -ge-, h) bewitch.

be'hilflich adj.: j-m ~ sein help s.o. (bei in).

be'hindern v/t. (no -ge-, h) hinder, hamper, impede; handicap; obstruct (a. traffic, etc.).

Behörde [bə'høːrdə] f (-/-n) authority, mst authorities pl.; board; council.

be'hüten v/t. (no -ge-, h) guard, preserve (vor dat. from).

behutsam adj. [bə'huːtzɑːm] cautious, careful; **2keit** f (-/no pl.) caution.

bei prp. (dat.) [baɪ] address: ~ Schmidt care of (abbr. c/o) Schmidt; **.m** Buchhändler at the bookseller's; ~ uns with us; ~ der Hand nehmen take by the hand; ich habe kein Geld ~ mir I have no money about or on me; ~ der Kirche near the church; ~ guter Gesundheit in good health; wie es ~ Schiller heißt as Schiller says; die Schlacht ~ Waterloo the Battle of Waterloo; ~ e-m Glase Wein over a glass of wine; ~ alledem for all that; Stunden nehmen ~ take lessons from or with; ~ günstigem Wetter weather permitting.

'beibehalten v/t. (irr. halten, sep., no -ge-, h) keep up, retain.

'Beiblatt n supplement (zu to).

'beibringen v/t. (irr. bringen, sep., -ge-, h) bring forward; produce (witness, etc.); j-m et. ~ impart (news, etc.) to s.o.; teach s.o. s.th.; inflict (defeat, wound, etc.) on s.o.

Beichte ['baɪçtə] f (-/-n) confession; **2n** v/t. and v/i. (ge-, h) confess.

beide adj. ['baɪdə] both; nur wir ~ just the two of us; in ~n Fällen in either case.

beider|lei adj. ['baɪdərlaɪ] of both kinds; ~ Geschlechts of either sex; **'.seitig** 1. adj. on both sides; mutual; **2.** adv. mutually; **'.seits 1.** prp. on both sides (gen. of); **2.** adv. mutually.

'Beifahrer m (-s/-) (front-seat) passenger; assistant driver; motor racing: co-driver.

'**Beifall** *m* (-[e]s/*no pl.*) approbation; applause; cheers *pl.*

'**beifällig** *adj.* approving; favo(u)rable.

'**Beifallsruf** *m* acclaim; ~*e pl.* cheers *pl.*

'**beifügen** *v/t.* (*sep.*, -ge-, h) add; enclose.

Beigeschmack *m* (-[e]s/*no pl.*) slight flavo(u)r; smack (of) (*a. fig.*).

Beihilfe *f* aid; allowance; *for study:* grant; *for project:* subsidy; ⚖ aiding and abetting; j-m ~ leisten ⚖ aid and abet s.o.

beikommen *v/i.* (*irr.* kommen, *sep.*, -ge-, sein) get at.

Beil [baɪl] *n* (-[e]s/-e) hatchet; chopper; cleaver; ax(e).

Beilage *f* supplement (*to newspaper*); F trimming* *pl.* (*of meal*); vegetables *pl.*

beiläufig *adj.* ['baɪlɔyfiç] casual; incidental.

beileg|en *v/t.* (*sep.*, -ge-, h) add (*dat.* to); enclose; settle (*dispute*); '**2ung** *f* (-/-en) settlement.

Beileid ['baɪlaɪt] *n* condolence; j-m sein ~ bezeigen condole with s.o. (zu on, upon).

beiliegen *v/i.* (*irr.* liegen, *sep.*, -ge-, h) be enclosed (*dat.* with).

beimessen *v/t.* (*irr.* messen, *sep.*, -ge-, h) attribute (*dat.* to), ascribe (to); attach (*importance*) (to).

beimisch|en *v/t.* (*sep.*, -ge-, h): e-r Sache et. ~ mix s.th. with s.th.; '**2ung** *f* admixture.

Bein [baɪn] *n* (-[e]s/-e) leg; bone.

beinah(e) *adv.* almost, nearly.

Beiname *m* appellation; nickname.

Beinbruch *m* fracture of the leg.

beiordnen ['baɪ'?-] *v/t.* (*sep.*, -ge-, h) adjoin; co-ordinate (*a. gr.*).

beipflichten *v/i.* (*sep.*, -ge-, h) agree with *s.o.*; assent to *s.th.*

Beirat *m* (-[e]s/⁼e) adviser, counsel(l)or; advisory board.

be'irren *v/t.* (*no* -ge-, h) confuse.

beisammen *adv.* [baɪ'zamən] together.

'**Beisein** *n* presence; im ~ (*gen.*) or von in the presence of *s.o.*, in *s.o.'s* presence.

bei'seite *adv.* aside ˌapart; Spaß ~! joking apart!

beisetz|en *v/t.* (*sep.*, -ge-, h) bury, inter; '**2ung** *f* (-/-en) burial, funeral.

'**Beisitzer** ⚖ *m* (-s/-) assessor; associate judge; member (*of committee*).

'**Beispiel** *n* example, instance; zum ~ for example or instance; '**2haft** *adj.* exemplary; '**2los** *adj.* unprecedented, unparalleled; unheard of.

beißen ['baɪsən] (*irr.*, ge-, h) **1.** *v/t.* bite; *fleas*, *etc.*: bite, sting; **2.** *v/i.* bite (*auf acc.* on; *in acc.* into); *fleas*, *etc.*: bite, sting; *smoke*: bite, burn (*in dat.* in); *pepper*, *etc.*: bite,

burn (*auf dat.* on); '~**d** *adj.* biting, pungent (*both a. fig.*); *pepper*, *etc.*: hot.

'**Beistand** *m* assistance.

'**beistehen** *v/i.* (*irr.* stehen, *sep.*, -ge-, h): j-m ~ stand by or assist or help s.o.

'**beisteuern** *v/t.* and *v/i.* (*sep.*, -ge-, h) contribute (zu to).

Beitrag ['baɪtraːk] *m* (-[e]s/⁼e) contribution; share; subscription, *Am.* dues *pl.*; article (*in newspaper*, *etc.*).

'**bei|treten** *v/i.* (*irr.* treten, *sep.*, -ge-, sein) join (*political party*, *etc.*); '**2tritt** *m* joining.

Beiwagen *m* side-car (*of motorcycle*); trailer (*of tram*).

Beiwerk *n* accessories *pl.*

'**beiwohnen** *v/i.* (*sep.*, -ge-, h) assist or be present at, attend.

bei'zeiten *adv.* early; in good time.

beizen ['baɪtsən] *v/t.* (*ge*-, h) corrode; *metall.* pickle; bate (*hides*); stain (*wood*); 🔬 cauterize; *hunt.* hawk.

bejahen [bə'jaːən] *v/t.* (*no* -ge-, h) answer in the affirmative, affirm; ~**d** *adj.* affirmative.

be'jahrt *adj.* aged.

Bejahung *f* (-/-en) affirmation, affirmative answer; *fig.* acceptance.

be'jammern s. beklagen.

be'kämpfen *v/t.* (*no* -ge-, h) fight (against), combat; *fig.* oppose.

bekannt *adj.* [bə'kant] known (*dat.* to); j-n mit j-m ~ machen introduce s.o. to s.o.; **2e** *m, f* (-n/-n) acquaintance, *mst* friend; ~**lich** *adv.* as you know; ~**machen** *v/t.* (*sep.*, -ge-, h) make known; **2machung** *f* (-/-en) publication; public notice; **2schaft** *f* (-/-en) acquaintance.

be'kehr|en *v/t.* (*no* -ge-, h) convert; **2te** *m, f* (-n/-n) convert; **2ung** *f* (-/-en) conversion (zu to).

be'kenn|en *v/t.* (*irr.* kennen, *no* -ge-, h) admit; confess; sich schuldig ~ ⚖ plead guilty; sich ~ zu declare o.s. for; profess *s.th.*; **2tnis** *n* (-ses/-se) confession; creed.

Beklagte [bə'klaːktə] *m, f* (-n/-n) civil case: defendant, *the* accused.

be'klatschen *v/t.* (*no* -ge-, h) applaud, clap.

be'kleben *v/t.* (*no* -ge-, h) glue or stick *s.th.* on *s.th.*; mit Etiketten ~ label *s.th.*; mit Papier ~ paste *s.th.* up with paper; e-e Mauer mit Plakaten ~ paste (up) posters on a wall.

bekleckern F [bə'klɛkərn] *v/t.* (*no* -ge-, h) stain (*garment*); sich ~ soil one's clothes.

be'klecksen *v/t.* (*no* -ge-, h) stain, daub; blot.

be'kleid|en v/t. (no -ge-, h) clothe, dress; hold, fill (office, etc.); ~ mit invest with; 2ung f clothing, clothes pl.

be'klemm|en v/t. (no -ge-, h) oppress; 2ung f (-/-en) oppression; anguish, anxiety.

be'kommen (irr. kommen, no -ge-) 1. v/t. (h) get, receive; obtain; get, catch (illness); have (baby); catch (train, etc.); Zähne ~ teethe, cut one's teeth; 2. v/i. (sein): j-m (gut) ~ agree with s.o.; j-m nicht or schlecht ~ disagree with s.o.

bekömmlich adj. [bə'kœmliç] wholesome (dat. to).

beköstig|en [bə'kœstigən] v/t. (no -ge-, h) board, feed; 2ung f (-/-en) board(ing).

be'kräftig|en v/t. (no -ge-, h) confirm; 2ung f (-/-en) confirmation.

be'kränzen v/t. (no -ge-, h) wreathe; festoon.

be'kritteln v/t. (no -ge-, h) carp at, criticize.

be'kümmern v/t. (no -ge-, h) afflict, grieve; trouble; s. kümmern.

be'laden v/t. (irr. laden, no -ge-, h) load; fig. burden.

Belag [bə'la:k] m (-[e]s/⁓e) covering; ⊕ coat(ing); surface (of road); foil (of mirror); ⊗ fur (on tongue); (slices of) ham, etc. (on bread); filling (of roll).

Belager|er [bə'la:gərər] m (-s/-) besieger; 2n v/t. (no -ge-, h) besiege, beleaguer; ~ung f siege.

Belang [bə'laŋ] m (-[e]s/-e) importance; ~e pl. interests pl.; 2en v/t. (no -ge-, h) concern; ⁂ sue; 2los adj. unimportant; ~losigkeit f (-/-en) insignificance.

be'lasten v/t. (no -ge-, h) load; fig. burden; ⁂ incriminate; mortgage (estate, etc.); j-s Konto (mit e-r Summe) ~ ⁑ charge or debit s.o.'s account (with a sum).

belästig|en [bə'lestigən] v/t. (no -ge-, h) molest; trouble, bother; 2ung f molestation; trouble.

Be'lastung f (-/-en) load (a. ⚡, ⊕); fig. burden; ⁑ debit; encumbrance; ⁂ incrimination; erbliche ~ hereditary taint; ~szeuge ⁑ m witness for the prosecution.

be'laufen v/refl. (irr. laufen, no -ge-, h): sich ~ auf (acc.) amount to.

be'lauschen v/t. (no -ge-, h) overhear, eavesdrop on s.o.

be'leb|en fig. v/t. (no -ge-, h) enliven, animate; stimulate; ~t adj. street: busy, crowded; stock exchange: brisk; conversation: lively, animated.

Beleg [bə'le:k] m (-[e]s/-e) proof; ⁑ (supporting) evidence; document; voucher; 2en [~gən] v/t. (no -ge-, h) cover; reserve (seat, etc.); prove, verify; univ. enrol(l) or register for,

Am. a. sign up for (course of lectures, term); ein Brötchen mit et. ~ put s.th. on a roll, fill a roll with s.th.; ~schaft f (-/-en) personnel, staff; labo(u)r force; ~stelle f reference; 2t adj. engaged, occupied; hotel, etc.: full; voice: thick, husky; tongue: coated, furred; ~es Brot (open) sandwich.

be'lehr|en v/t. (no -ge-, h) instruct, inform; sich ~ lassen take advice; ~end adj. instructive; 2ung f (-/-en) instruction; information; advice.

beleibt adj. [bə'laɪpt] corpulent, stout, bulky, portly.

beleidig|en [bə'laɪdigən] v/t. (no -ge-, h) offend (s.o.; ear, eye, etc.); insult; ~end adj. offensive; insulting; 2ung f (-/-en) offen|ce, Am. -se; insult.

be'lesen adj. well-read.

be'leucht|en v/t. (no -ge-, h) light (up), illuminate (a. fig.); fig. shed or throw light on; 2ung f (-/-en) light(ing); illumination; 2ungskörper m lighting appliance.

be'licht|en phot. v/t. (no -ge-, h) expose; 2ung phot. f exposure.

Be'lieb|en n (-s/no pl.) will, choice; nach ~ at will; es steht in Ihrem ~ I leave it you to; 2ig 1. adj. any; jeder ~e anyone; 2. adv. at pleasure; ~ viele as many as you like; 2t adj. [~pt] popular (bei with); ~theit f (-/no pl.) popularity.

be'liefer|n v/t. (no -ge-, h) supply, furnish (mit with); 2ung f (-/no pl.) supply.

bellen ['belən] v/i. (ge-, h) bark.

belobigen [bə'lo:bigən] v/t. (no -ge-, h) commend, praise.

be'lohn|en v/t. (no -ge-, h) reward; recompense; 2ung f (-/-en) reward; recompense.

be'lügen v/t. (irr. lügen, no -ge-, h): j-n ~ lie to s.o.

bclustig|en [bə'lustigən] v/t. (no -ge-, h) amuse, entertain; sich ~ amuse o.s.; 2ung f (-/-en) amusement, entertainment.

bemächtigen [bə'meçtigən] v/refl. (no -ge-, h): sich e-r Sache ~ take hold of s.th., seize s.th.; sich e-r Person ~ lay hands on s.o., seize s.o.

be'malen v/t. (no -ge-, h) cover with paint; paint; daub.

bemängeln [bə'meŋəln] v/t. (no -ge-, h) find fault with, cavil at.

be'mannen v/t. (no -ge-, h) man.

be'merk|bar adj. perceptible; ~en v/t. (no -ge-, h) notice, perceive; remark, mention; ~enswert adj. remarkable (wegen for); 2ung f (-/-en) remark.

bemitleiden [bə'mitlaɪdən] v/t. (no -ge-, h) pity, commiserate (with); ~swert adj. pitiable.

be'müh|en v/t. (no -ge-, h) trouble (j-n in or wegen et. s.o. about s.th.);

sich ~ trouble o.s.; endeavo(u)r; *sich um e-e Stelle* ~ apply for a position; 2ung *f* (-/-en) trouble; endeavo(u)r, effort.

be'nachbart *adj.* neighbo(u)ring; adjoining, adjacent (to).

benachrichtig|en [bə'naːxriçtigən] *v/t.* (*no -ge-, h*) inform, notify; † advise; 2ung *f* (-/-en) information; notification; † advice.

benachteilig|en [bə'naːxtailigən] *v/t.* (*no -ge-, h*) place *s.o.* at a disadvantage, discriminate against *s.o.*; handicap; *sich benachteiligt fühlen* feel handicapped *or* at a disadvantage; 2ung *f* (-/-en) disadvantage; discrimination; handicap.

be'nehmen 1. *v/refl.* (*irr. nehmen, no -ge-, h*) behave (o.s.); 2. 2 *n* (-s/no *pl.*) behavio(u)r, conduct.

be'neiden *v/t.* (*irr. nennen, no -ge-*) *um et. s.o. s.th.*); ~swert *adj.* enviable.

be'nennen *v/t.* (*irr. nennen, no -ge-, h*) name.   [rascal; urchin.\

Bengel ['bɛŋəl] *m* (-s/-) (little)\

benommen *adj.* [bə'nɔmən] bemused, dazed, stunned; ~ sein be in a daze.

be'nötigen *v/t.* (*no -ge-, h*) need, require, want.

be'nutz|en *v/t.* (*no -ge-, h*) use (*a. patent, etc.*); make use of; avail o.s. of (*opportunity*); take (*tram, etc.*); 2ung *f* use.

Benzin [bɛn'tsiːn] *n* (-s/-e) 🜍 benzine; *mot.* petrol, F juice, *Am.* gasoline, F gas; ~motor *m* petrol engine, *Am.* gasoline engine; *s.* Tank.

beobacht|en [bə'oːbaxtən] *v/t.* (*no -ge-, h*) observe; watch; *police:* shadow; 2er *m* (-s/-) observer; 2ung *f* (-/-en) observation.

beordern [bə'ɔrdərn] *v/t.* (*no -ge-, h*) order, command.

be'packen *v/t.* (*no -ge-, h*) load (*mit* with).   [(*mit* with).\

be'pflanzen *v/t.* (*no -ge-, h*) plant\

bequem *adj.* [bə'kveːm] convenient; comfortable; *p.:* easy-going; lazy; ~en *v/refl.* (*no -ge-, h*): *sich* ~ *zu* condescend to; consent to; 2lichkeit *f* (-/-en) convenience; comfort, ease; indolence.

be'rat|en (*irr. raten, no -ge-, h*) 1. *v/t.* advise *s.o.*; consider, debate, discuss *s.th.*; *sich* ~ confer (*mit j-m* with s.o.; *über et.* on *or* about s.th.); 2. *v/i.* confer; *über et.* ~ consider, debate, discuss s.th., confer on *or* about s.th.; 2er *m* (-s/-) adviser, counsel(l)or; consultant; ~schlagen (*no -ge-, h*) 1. *v/i. s.* beraten 2; 2. *v/refl.* confer (*mit j-m* with s.o.; *über et.* on *or* about s.th.); 2ung *f* (-/-en) advice; debate; consultation; conference; 2ungsstelle *f* advisory bureau.

be'raub|en *v/t.* (*no -ge-, h*) rob, deprive (*gen.* of); 2ung *f* (-/-en) robbery, deprivation.

be'rauschen *v/t.* (*no -ge-, h*) intoxicate (*a. fig.*).

be'rechn|en *v/t.* (*no -ge-, h*) calculate; † charge (*zu* at); ~end *adj.* calculating, selfish; 2ung *f* calculation.

berechtig|en [bə'rɛçtigən] *v/t.* (*no -ge-, h*) *j-n* ~ *zu* entitle s.o. to; authorize s.o. to; ~t *adj.* [~çt] entitled (*zu* to); qualified (to); *claim:* legitimate; 2ung *f* (-/-en) title (*zu* to); authorization.

be'red|en *v/t.* (*no -ge-, h*) talk *s.th.* over; persuade *s.o.*; gossip about *s.o.*; 2samkeit [~tzaːmkait] *f* (-/no *pl.*) eloquence; ~t *adj.* [~t] eloquent (*a. fig.*).

Be'reich *m, n* (-[e]s/-e) area; reach; *fig.* scope, sphere; *science, etc.:* field, province; 2ern *v/t.* (*no -ge-, h*) enrich; *sich* ~ enrich o.s.; ~erung *f* (-/-en) enrichment.

be'reif|en *v/t.* (*no -ge-, h*) hoop (*barrel*); tyre, (*Am. only*) tire (*wheel*); 2ung *f* (-/-en) (set of) tyres *pl.*, (*Am. only*) (set of) tires *pl.*

be'reisen *v/t.* (*no -ge-, h*) tour (in), travel (over); *commercial traveller:* cover (*district*).

bereit *adj.* [bə'rait] ready, prepared; ~en *v/t.* (*no -ge-, h*) prepare; give (*joy, trouble, etc.*); ~s *adv.* already; 2schaft *f* (-/-en) readiness; *police:* squad; ~stellen *v/t.* (*sep., -ge-, h*) place *s.th.* ready; provide; 2ung *f* (-/-en) preparation; ~willig *adj.* ready, willing; 2willigkeit *f* (-/no *pl.*) readiness, willingness.

be'reuen *v/t.* (*no -ge-, h*) repent (of); regret, rue.

Berg [bɛrk] *m* (-[e]s/-e) mountain; hill; ~e *pl. von* F heaps *pl.* of, piles *pl.* of; *über den* ~ *sein* be out of the wood, *Am.* be out of the woods; *über alle* ~e off and away; *die Haare standen ihm zu* ~e his hair stood on end; 2'ab *adv.* downhill (*a. fig.*); 2'an *adv. s.* bergauf; '~arbeiter *m* miner; 2'auf *adv.* uphill (*a. fig.*); '~bahn 🚠 *f* mountain railway; '~bau *m* (-[e]s/*pl.*) mining.

bergen ['bɛrgən] *v/t.* (*irr., ge-, h*) save; rescue *s.o.*; ⚓ salvage, salve.

bergig *adj.* ['bɛrgiç] mountainous, hilly.

'Berg|kette *f* mountain chain *or* range; '~mann ⚒ *m* (-[e]s/Bergleute) miner; '~predigt *f* (-/no *pl.*) *the* Sermon on the Mount; '~recht *n* mining laws *pl.*; '~rennen *mot. n* mountain race; '~rücken *m* ridge; '~rutsch *m* landslide, landslip; '~spitze *f* mountain peak; '~steiger *m* (-s/-) mountaineer; '~sturz *m s.* Bergrutsch.

'**Bergung** f (-/-en) ⚓ salvage; rescue; ~**sarbeiten** ['berguŋs'-] f/pl. salvage operations pl.; rescue work.

'**Bergwerk** n mine; ~**saktien** ['berkverks'-] f/pl. mining shares pl.

Bericht [bə'riçt] m (-[e]s/-e) report (über acc. on); account (of); ~**en** (no -ge-, h) 1. v/t. report; j-m et. ~ inform s.o. of s.th.; tell s.o. about s.th.; 2. v/i. report (über acc. on); journalist: a. cover (über et. s.th.); ~**erstatter** m (-s/-) reporter; correspondent; ~**erstattung** f reporting; report(s pl.).

berichtig|en [bə'riçtigən] v/t. (no -ge-, h) correct (s.o.; error, mistake, etc.); put right (mistake); emend (corrupt text); ✝ settle (claim, debt, etc.); 2**ung** f (-/-en) correction; emendation; settlement.

be'riechen v/t. (irr. riechen, no -ge-, h) smell or sniff at.

Berliner [ber'li:nər] 1. m (-s/-) Berliner; 2. adj. (of) Berlin.

Bernstein ['bernʃtam] m amber; schwarzer ~ jet.

bersten ['berstən] v/i. (irr., ge-, sein) burst (fig. vor dat. with).

berüchtigt adj. notorious (wegen for), ill-famed.

berücksichtig|en [bə'rykziçtigən] v/t. (no -ge-, h) take s.th. into consideration, pay regard to s.th.; consider s.o.; 2**ung** f (-/-en) consideration; regard.

Beruf [bə'ru:f] m (-[e]s/-e) calling; profession; vocation; trade; occupation; 2**en** 1. v/t. (irr. rufen, no -ge-, h): j-n zu e-m Amt ~ appoint s.o. to an office; sich auf j-n ~ refer to s.o.; 2. adj. competent; qualified; 2**lich** adj. professional; vocational.

Be'rufs|ausbildung f vocational or professional training; ~**beratung** f vocational guidance; ~**kleidung** f work clothes pl.; ~**krankheit** f occupational disease; ~**schule** f vocational school; ~**spieler** m sports: professional (player); 2**tätig** adj. working; ~**tätige** [~gə] pl. working people pl.

Be'rufung f (-/-en) appointment (zu to); 🏛 appeal (bei dat. to); reference (auf acc. to); ~**sgericht** n court of appeal.

be'ruhen v/i. (no -ge-, h): ~ auf (dat.) rest or be based on; et. auf sich ~ lassen let a matter rest.

beruhig|en [bə'ru:igən] v/t. (no -ge- h) quiet, calm; soothe; sich ~ calm down; 2**ung** f (-/-en) calming (down); soothing; comfort; 2**ungsmittel** ✱ n sedative.

berühmt adj. [bə'ry:mt] famous (wegen for); celebrated; 2**heit** f (-/-en) fame, renown; famous or celebrated person, celebrity; person of note.

be'rühr|en v/t. (no -ge-, h) touch (a. fig.); touch (up)on (subject); 2**ung** f (-/-en) contact; touch; in ~ kommen mit come into contact with.

be'sag|en v/t. (no -ge-, h) say; mean, signify; ~**t** adj. [~kt] (afore-) said; above(-mentioned).

besänftigen [bə'zɛnftigən] v/t. (no -ge-, h) appease, calm, soothe.

Be'satz m (-es/~e) trimming; braid.

Be'satzung f ✗ occupation troops pl.; ✗ garrison; ⚓, 🛬 crew; ~**smacht** ✗ f occupying power.

be'schädig|en v/t. (no -ge-, h) damage, injure; 2**ung** f damage, injury (gen. to).

be'schaffen 1. v/t. (no -ge-, h) procure; provide; raise (money); 2. adj.: gut (schlecht) ~ sein be in good (bad) condition or state; 2**heit** f (-/-en) state, condition; properties pl.

beschäftig|en [bə'ʃɛftigən] v/t. (no -ge-, h) employ, occupy; keep busy; sich ~ occupy or busy o.s.; 2**ung** f (-/-en) employment; occupation.

beschatten [bə'ʃatən] v/t. (no -ge-, h) shade; fig. shadow s.o., Am. sl. tail s.o.

be'schau|en v/t. (no -ge-, h) look at, view; examine, inspect (goods, etc.); ~**lich** adj. contemplative, meditative.

Bescheid [bə'ʃaIt] m (-[e]s/-e) answer; 🏛 decision; information (über acc. on, about); ~ geben let s.o. know; ~ bekommen be informed or notified; ~ hinterlassen leave word (bei with, at); ~ wissen be informed, know, F be in the know.

bescheiden adj. [bə'ʃaIdən] modest, unassuming; 2**heit** f (-/no pl.) modesty.

bescheinig|en [bə'ʃaInigən] v/t. (no -ge-, h) certify, attest; den Empfang ~ acknowledge receipt; es wird hiermit bescheinigt, daß this is to certify that; 2**ung** f (-/-en) certification, attestation; certificate; receipt; acknowledgement.

be'schenken v/t. (no -ge-, h): j-n ~ make s.o. a present; j-n mit et. ~ present s.o. with s.th.; j-n reichlich ~ shower s.o. with gifts.

be'scher|en v/t. (no -ge-, h): j-n ~ give s.o. presents (esp. for Christmas); 2**ung** f (-/-en) presentation of gifts; F fig. mess.

be'schieß|en v/t. (irr. schießen, no -ge-, h) fire or shoot at or on; bombard (a. phys.), shell; 2**ung** f (-/-en) bombardment.

be'schimpf|en v/t. (no -ge-, h) abuse, insult; call s.o. names; 2**ung** f (-/-en) abuse; insult, affront.

be'schirmen *v/t.* (*no -ge-, h*) shelter, shield, guard, protect (*vor dat.* from); defend (against).

be'schlafen *v/t.* (*irr. schlafen, no -ge-, h*): et. ~ sleep on a matter, take counsel of one's pillow.

Be'schlag *m* ⊕ metal fitting(s *pl.*); furnishing(s *pl.*) (*of door, etc.*); shoe (*of wheel, etc.*); (horse)shoe; ⚖ seizure, confiscation; *in* ~ *nehmen, mit* ~ *belegen* seize; ⚖ seize, attach (*real estate, salary, etc.*); confiscate (*goods, etc.*); monopolize *s.o.'s* attention.

be'schlagen 1. *v/t.* (*irr. schlagen, no -ge-, h*) cover (*mit* with); ⊕ fit, mount; shoe (*horse*); hobnail (*shoe*); **2.** *v/i.* (*irr. schlagen, no -ge-, h*) *window, wall, etc.*: steam up; *mirror, etc.*: cloud *or* film over; **3.** *adj.* *windows, etc.*: steamed-up; *fig.* well versed (*auf, in dat.* in).

Beschlagnahme [bə'ʃlɑːknɑːmə] *f* (*-/-n*) seizure; confiscation (*of contraband goods, etc.*); ⚖ sequestration, distraint (*of property*); ⚒ requisition (*of houses, etc.*); embargo, detention (*of ship*); **2n** *v/t.* (*no -ge-, h*) seize; attach (*real estate*); confiscate; ⚖ sequestrate, distrain upon (*property*); ⚒ requisition; ⚓ embargo.

beschleunig|en [bə'ʃlɔʏnɪgən] *v/t.* (*no -ge-, h*) *mot.* accelerate; hasten, speed up; *s-e Schritte* ~ quicken one's steps; **2ung** *f* (*-/-en*) acceleration.

be'schließen *v/t.* (*irr. schließen, no -ge-, h*) end, close, wind up; resolve, decide.

Be'schluß *m* decision, resolution, *Am. a.* resolve; ⚖ decree; **2fähig** *adj.*: ~ *sein* form *or* have a quorum; **~fassung** *f* (passing of a) resolution.

be'schmieren *v/t.* (*no -ge-, h*) (be)smear (*with grease, etc.*).

be'schmutzen *v/t.* (*no -ge-, h*) soil (*a. fig.*), dirty; bespatter.

be'schneiden *v/t.* (*irr. schneiden, no -ge-, h*) clip, cut; lop (*tree*); trim, clip (*hair, hedge, etc.*); dress (*vinestock, etc.*); *fig.* cut down, curtail, F slash.

beschönig|en [bə'ʃøːnɪgən] *v/t.* (*no -ge-, h*) gloss over, palliate; **2ung** *f* (*-/-en*) gloss, palliation.

beschränk|en [bə'ʃrɛŋkən] *v/t.* (*no -ge-, h*) confine, limit, restrict, *Am. a.* curb; *sich* ~ *auf* (*acc.*) confine o.s. to; **~t** *fig. adj.* of limited intelligence; **2ung** *f* (*-/-en*) limitation, restriction.

be'schreiben *v/t.* (*irr. schreiben, no -ge-, h*) write on (*piece of paper, etc.*), cover with writing; describe; give a description of; **2ung** *f* (*-/-en*) description; account.

be'schrift|en *v/t.* (*no -ge-, h*) in-

scribe; letter; **2ung** *f* (*-/-en*) inscription; lettering.

beschuldig|en [bə'ʃʊldɪgən] *v/t.* (*no -ge-, h*) accuse (*gen.* of [*doing*] *s.th.*), *esp.* ⚖ charge (with); **2te** [‚ktə] *m, f* (*-n/-n*) *the* accused; **2ung** *f* (*-/-en*) accusation, charge.

Be'schuß *m* (*Beschusses/no pl.*) bombardment.

be'schütz|en *v/t.* (*no -ge-, h*) protect, shelter, guard (*vor dat.* from); **2er** *m* (*-s/-*) protector; **2ung** *f* (*-/-en*) protection.

be'schwatzen *v/t.* (*no -ge-, h*) talk *s.o.* into (*doing*) *s.th.*, coax *s.o.* into (*doing s.th.*).

Beschwerde [bə'ʃveːrdə] *f* (*-/-n*) trouble; ⚖ complaint; complaint (*über acc.* about); ⚖ objection (*gegen* to); **~buch** *n* complaints book.

beschwer|en [bə'ʃveːrən] *v/t.* (*no -ge-, h*) burden (*a. fig.*); weight (*loose sheets, etc.*); lie heavy on (*stomach*); weigh on (*mind, etc.*); *sich* ~ complain (*über acc.* about, of; *bei* to); **~lich** *adj.* troublesome.

beschwichtigen [bə'ʃvɪçtɪgən] *v/t.* (*no -ge-, h*) appease, calm (down), soothe.

be'schwindeln *v/t.* (*no -ge-, h*) tell a fib *or* lie; cheat, F diddle (*um* out of).

be'schwipst F *adj.* tipsy.

be'schwör|en *v/t.* (*irr. schwören, no -ge-, h*) take an oath on *s.th.*; implore *or* entreat *s.o.*; conjure (up), invoke (*spirit*); **2ung** *f* (*-/-en*) conjuration.

be'seelen *v/t.* (*no -ge-, h*) animate, inspire.

be'sehen *v/t.* (*irr. sehen, no -ge-, h*) look at; inspect; *sich et.* ~ look at s.th.; inspect s.th.

beseitig|en [bə'zaɪtɪgən] *v/t.* (*no -ge-, h*) remove, do away with; **2ung** *f* (*-/-en*) removal.

Besen ['beːzən] *m* (*-s/-*) broom; **~stiel** *m* broomstick.

besessen *adj.* [bə'zɛsən] obsessed, possessed (*von* by, with); *wie* ~ like mad; **2e** *m, f* (*-n/-n*) demoniac.

be'setz|en *v/t.* (*no -ge-, h*) occupy (*seat, table, etc.*); fill (*post, etc.*); man (*orchestra*); *thea.* cast (*play*); ⚒ occupy; trim (*dress, etc.*); set (*crown with jewels, etc.*); **~t** *adj.* engaged, occupied; *seat*: taken; F *bus, etc.*: full up; *hotel*: full; *teleph.* engaged, *Am.* busy; **2ung** *f* (*-/-en*) *thea.* cast; ⚒ occupation.

besichtig|en [bə'zɪçtɪgən] *v/t.* (*no -ge-, h*) view, look over; inspect (*a.* ⚒); visit; **2ung** *f* (*-/-en*) sightseeing; visit (*gen.* to); inspection (*a.* ⚒).

be'sied|eln *v/t.* (*no -ge-, h*) colonize, settle; populate; **2lung** *f* (*-/-en*) colonization, settlement.

be'siegeln v/t. (no -ge-, h) seal (a. fig.).

be'siegen v/t. (no -ge-, h) conquer; defeat, beat (a. sports).

be'sinn|en v/refl. (irr. sinnen, no -ge-, h) reflect, consider; sich ~ auf (acc.) remember, think of; ~lich adj. reflective, contemplative.

Be'sinnung f (-/no pl.) reflection; consideration; consciousness; (wieder) zur ~ kommen recover consciousness; fig. come to one's senses; 2slos adj. unconscious.

Be'sitz m possession; in ~ nehmen, ~ ergreifen von take possession of; 2anzeigend gr. adj. possessive; 2en v/t. (irr. sitzen, no -ge-, h) possess; ~er m (-s/-) possessor, owner, proprietor; den ~ wechseln change hands; ~ergreifung f taking possession (von of), occupation; ~tum n (-s/~er), ~ung f (-/-en) possession; property; estate.

be'sohlen v/t. (no -ge-, h) sole.

besold|en [bə'zɔldən] v/t. (no -ge-, h) pay a salary to (civil servant, etc.); pay (soldier); 2ung f (-/-en) pay; salary.

besonder adj. [bə'zɔndər] particular, special; peculiar; separate; 2heit f (-/-en) particularity, peculiarity; ~s adv. especially, particularly; chiefly, mainly; separately.

besonnen adj. [bə'zɔnən] sensible, considerate, level-headed; prudent; discreet; 2heit f (-/no pl.) considerateness; prudence; discretion; presence of mind.

be'sorg|en v/t. (no -ge-, h) get (j-m et. s.o. s.th.), procure (s.th. for s.o.); do, manage; 2nis [~knis] f (-/-se) apprehension, fear, anxiety, concern (über acc. about, at); ~niserregend adj. alarming, ~t adj. [~kt] uneasy (um about); worried (about), concerned (about); anxious (um for, about); 2ung f (-/-en) procurement; management; errand; ~en machen go shopping.

be'sprech|en v/t. (irr. sprechen, no -ge-, h) discuss, talk s.th. over; arrange; review (book, etc.); sich ~ mit confer with (über acc. about); 2ung f (-/-en) discussion; review; conference.

be'spritzen v/t. (no -ge-, h) splash, (be)spatter.

besser ['besər] 1. adj. better; superior; 2. adv. better; '~n v/t. (ge-, h) (make) better, improve; reform; sich ~ get or become better, improve, change for the better; mend one's ways; '2ung f (-/-en) improvement; change for the better; reform (of character), etc.; ~ improvement, recovery; gute ~! I wish you a speedy recovery!

best [best] 1. adj. best; der erste ~e (just) anybody; ~en Dank thank

you very much; sich von s-r ~en Seite zeigen be on one's best behavio(u)r; 2. adv. best; am ~en best; aufs ~e, ~ens in the best way possible; zum ~en geben recite (poem), tell (story), oblige with (song); j-n zum ~en haben or halten make fun of s.o., F pull s.o.'s leg; ich danke ~ens! thank you very much!

Be'stand m (continued) existence; continuance; stock; ~ stock-intrade; ✝ cash in hand; ~ haben be lasting, last.

be'ständig adj. constant, steady; lasting; continual; weather: settled; 2keit f (-/-en) constancy, steadiness; continuance.

Bestand|saufnahme ✝ [bə-'ʃtants?-] f stock-taking, Am. inventory; ~teil m component, constituent; element, ingredient; part.

be'stärken v/t. (no -ge-, h) confirm, strengthen, encourage (in dat. in).

bestätig|en [bə'ʃtɛːtigən] v/t. confirm (a. ✝ verdict, ✝ order); attest; verify (statement, etc.); ratify (law, treaty); ✝ acknowledge (receipt); 2ung f (-/-en) confirmation; attestation; verification; ratification; acknowledgement.

bestatt|en [bə'ʃtatən] v/t. (no -ge-, h) bury, inter; 2ung f (-/-en) burial, interment; funeral; 2ungsinstitut [bə'ʃtatuŋs?-] n undertakers pl.

'Beste 1. n (-n/no pl.) the best (thing); zu deinem ~n in your interest; zum ~n der Armen for the benefit of the poor; das ~ daraus machen make the best of it; 2. m, f (-n/-n): er ist der ~ in s-r Klasse he is the best in his class.

Besteck [bə'ʃtek] n (-[e]s/-e) ✄ (case or set of) surgical instruments pl.; (single set of) knife, fork and spoon; (complete set of) cutlery, Am. a. flatware.

be'stehen 1. v/t. (irr. stehen, no -ge-, h) come off victorious in (combat, etc.); have (adventure); stand, undergo (well) (test, trial); pass (test, examination); 2. v/i. (irr. stehen, no -ge-, h) be, exist; continue, last; ~ auf (dat.) insist (up)on; ~ aus consist of; 3. 2 n (-s/no pl.) existence; continuance; passing.

be'stehlen v/t. (irr. stehlen, no -ge-, h) steal from, rob.

be'steig|en v/t. (irr. steigen, no -ge-, h) climb (up) (mountain, tree, etc.); mount (horse, bicycle, etc.); ascend (throne); get into or on, board (bus, train, plane); 2ung f ascent; accession (to throne).

be'stell|en v/t. (no -ge-, h) order; ✝ a. place an order for; subscribe to (newspaper, etc.); book, reserve (room, seat, etc.); make an appointment with s.o.; send for (taxi, etc.); cultivate, till (soil, etc.); give (message, greetings); j-n zu sich ~ send for s.o.; 2ung f order; subscription (to); booking, esp. Am. reservation; ✗ cultivation; message.

'besten'falls adv. at (the) best.

be'steuer|n v/t. (no -ge-, h) tax; 2ung f taxation.

besti|alisch adj. [best'ja:liʃ] bestial; brutal; inhuman; weather, etc.: F beastly; 2e ['.jə] f (-/-n) beast; fig. brute, beast, inhuman person.

be'stimmen (no -ge-, h) 1. v/t. determine, decide; fix (date, place, price, etc.); appoint (date, time, place, etc.); prescribe; define (species, word, etc.); j-n für or zu et. ~ designate or intend s.o. for s.th.; 2. v/i.: ~ über (acc.) dispose of.

be'stimmt 1. adj. voice, manner, etc.: decided, determined, firm; time, etc.: appointed, fixed; point, number, etc.: certain; answer, etc.: positive; tone, answer, intention, idea: definite (a. gr.); ~ nach ⊕ ✗ bound for; 2. adv. certainly, surely; 2heit f (-/-en) determination, firmness; certainty.

Be'stimmung f determination; destination (of s.o. for the church, etc.); designation, appointment (of s.o. as successor, etc.); definition; ⚙ provision (in document); (amtliche) ~en pl. (official) regulations pl.; ~sort [bə'ʃtimuŋs°-] m destination.

be'straf|en v/t. (no -ge-, h) punish (wegen, für for; mit with); 2ung f (-/-en) punishment.

be'strahl|en v/t. (no -ge-, h) irradiate (a. ✗); 2ung f irradiation; ✗ ray treatment, radiotherapy.

Be'streb|en n (-s/no pl.), ~ung f (-/-en) effort, endeavo(u)r.

be'streichen v/t. (irr. streichen, no -ge-, h) coat, cover; spread; mit Butter ~ butter.

be'streiten v/t. (irr. streiten, no -ge-, h) contest, dispute, challenge (point, right, etc.); deny (facts, guilt, etc.); defray (expenses, etc.); fill (programme).

be'streuen v/t. (no -ge-, h) strew, sprinkle (mit with); mit Mehl ~ flour; mit Zucker ~ sugar.

be'stürmen v/t. (no -ge-, h) storm, assail (a. fig.); pester, plague (s.o. with questions, etc.).

be'stürz|t adj. dismayed, struck with consternation (über acc. at); 2ung f (-/-en) consternation, dismay.

Besuch [bə'zu:x] m (-[e]s/-e) visit (gen., bei, in dat. to); call (bei on; in dat. at); attendance (gen. at) (lecture, church, etc.); visitor(s pl.); company; 2en v/t. (no -ge-, h) visit; call on, go to see; attend (school, etc.); frequent; ~er m visitor, caller; ~szeit f visiting hours pl.

be'tasten v/t. (no -ge-, h) touch, feel, finger; ✗ palpate.

be'tätigen [bə'tɛ:tigən] v/t. (no -ge-, h) ⊕ operate (machine, etc.); put on, apply (brake); sich ~ als act or work as; sich politisch ~ dabble in politics.

be'täub|en [bə'tɔybən] v/t. (no -ge-, h) stun (a. fig.), daze (by blow, noise, etc.); deafen (by noise, etc.); slaughtering: stun (animal); ✗ an(a)esthetize; 2ung f (-/-en) an(a)esthetization; ✗ an(a)esthesia; fig. stupefaction; 2ungsmittel ✗ n narcotic, an(a)esthetic.

beteilig|en [bə'tailigən] v/t. (no -ge-, h): j-n ~ give s.o. a share (an dat. in); sich ~ take part (an dat., bei in), participate (a. ⚙) (in); 2te [~çtə] m, f (-n/-n) person or party concerned; 2ung f (-/-en) participation (a. ⚙), partnership; share, interest (a. ✝).

beten ['be:tən] v/i. (ge-, h) pray (um for), say one's prayers; at table: say grace

be'teuer|n v/t. (no -ge-, h) protest (one's innocence); swear (to s.th.; that); 2ung f protestation; solemn declaration.

be'titeln v/t. (no -ge-, h) entitle (book, etc.); style (s.o. 'baron', etc.).

Beton ⊕ [be'tõ:; be'to:n] m (-s/-s; -s/-e) concrete.

be'tonen v/t. (no -ge-, h) stress; fig. a. emphasize.

betonieren [beto'ni:rən] v/t. (no -ge-, h) concrete.

Be'tonung f (-/-en) stress; emphasis.

betör|en [bə'tø:rən] v/t. (no -ge-, h) dazzle; infatuate, bewitch; 2ung f (-/-en) infatuation.

Betracht [bə'traxt] m (-[e]s/no pl.): in ~ ziehen take into consideration; (nicht) in ~ kommen (not to) come into question; 2en v/t. (no -ge-, h) view; contemplate; fig. a. consider.

beträchtlich adj. [bə'trɛçtliç] considerable.

Be'trachtung f (-/-en) view; contemplation; consideration.

Betrag [bə'tra:k] m (-[e]s/~e) amount, sum; 2en [~gən] 1. v/t. (irr. tragen, no -ge-, h) amount to; 2. v/refl. (irr. tragen, no -ge-, h) behave (o.s.); 3. 2 n (-s/no pl.) behavio(u)r, conduct.

be'trauen v/t. (no -ge-, h): j-n mit et. ~ entrust or charge s.o. with s.th.

be'trauern v/t. (no -ge-, h) mourn (for, over).

Betreff [bə'trɛf] m (-[e]s/-e) at head of letter: reference; 2en v/t. (irr. treffen, no -ge-, h) befall; refer to; concern; was ... betrifft as for, as to; 2end adj. concerning; das ~e Geschäft the business referred to or in question; 2s prp. (gen.) concerning; as to.

be'treiben 1. v/t. (irr. treiben, no -ge-, h) carry on (business, etc.); pursue (one's studies); operate (railway line, etc.); **2.** ⟨ n (-s/no pl.): auf ⁓ von at or by s.o.'s instigation.
be'treten 1. v/t. (irr. treten, no -ge-, h) step on; enter (room, etc.); **2.** adj. embarrassed, abashed.
betreu|en [bə'trɔʏən] v/t. (no -ge-, h) look after; attend to; care for; ⟨ung f (-/no pl.) care (gen. of, for).
Betrieb [bə'tri:p] m (-[e]s/-e) working, running, esp. Am. operation; business, firm, enterprise; plant, works sg., workshop, Am. a. shop; fig. bustle; in ⁓ working; ⟨sam adj. active; industrious.
Be'triebs|anleitung f operating instructions pl., ⁓ausflug m firm's outing; ⁓ferien pl. (firm's, works) holiday; ⁓führer m s. Betriebsleiter; ⁓kapital n working capital; ⁓kosten pl. working expenses pl., Am. operating costs pl. ⁓leiter m (works) manager, superintendent; ⁓leitung f management; ⁓material n working materials pl.; 🗃 rolling stock; ⁓rat m works council; ⟨sicher adj. safe to operate; foolproof; ⁓störung f breakdown; ⁓unfall m industrial accident, accident while at work.
be'trinken v/refl. (irr. trinken, no -ge-, h) get drunk.
betroffen adj. [bə'trɔfən] afflicted (von by), stricken (with); fig. disconcerted.
be'trüben v/t. (no -ge-, h) grieve, afflict.
Be'trug m cheat(ing); fraud (a. ⚖️); deceit.
be'trüg|en v/t. (irr. trügen, no -ge-, h) deceive; cheat (a. at games); defraud; F skin; ⟨er m (-s/-) cheat, deceiver, impostor, confidence man, swindler, trickster; ⁓erisch adj. deceitful, fraudulent.
be'trunken adj. drunken, pred. drunk; ⟨e m (-n/-n) drunk(en man).
Bett [bɛt] n (-[e]s/-en) bed; '⁓bezug m plumeau case; '⁓decke f blanket; bedspread, coverlet.
Bettel|brief [bɛtəl-] m begging letter; ⁓ei [⁓'laɪ] f (-/-en) begging, mendicancy; '⟨n v/i. (ge-, h) beg (um for); ⁓ gehen go begging; '⁓stab m: an den ⁓ bringen reduce to beggary.
'Bett|gestell n bedstead; ⟨lägerig adj. ['⁓lɛ:gəriç] bedridden, confined to bed, Am. a. bedfast; '⁓laken n sheet.
Bettler ['bɛtlər] m (-s/-) beggar, Am. sl. panhandler.
'Bett|überzug m plumeau case; ⁓uch ['bɛtu:x] n sheet; '⁓vorleger m bedside rug; '⁓wäsche f bedlinen; '⁓zeug n bedding.
be'tupfen v/t. (no -ge-, h) dab.

beug|en ['bɔʏgən] v/t. (ge-, h) bend, bow; fig. humble, break (pride); gr. inflect (word), decline (noun, adjective); sich ⁓ bend (vor dat. to), bow (to); ⟨ung f (-/-en) bending; gr. inflection, declension.
Beule ['bɔʏlə] f (-/-n) bump, swelling; boil; on metal, etc.: dent.
beunruhig|en [bə'unru:igən] v/t. (no -ge-, h) disturb, trouble, disquiet, alarm; sich ⁓ über (acc.) be uneasy about, worry about; ⟨ung f (-/no pl.) disturbance; alarm; uneasiness.
beurkund|en [bə'u:rkundən] v/t. (no -ge-, h) attest, certify, authenticate; ⟨ung f (-/-en) attestation, certification, authentication.
beurlaub|en [bə'u:rlaubən] v/t. (no -ge-, h) give or grant s.o. leave (of absence); give s.o. time off; suspend (civil servant, etc.); ⟨ung f (-/-en) leave (of absence); suspension.
beurteil|en [bə'urtailən] v/t. (no -ge-, h) judge (nach by); ⟨ung f (-/-en) judg(e)ment.
Beute ['bɔʏtə] f (-/no pl.) booty, spoil(s pl.); loot; prey; hunt. bag; fig. prey, victim (gen. to).
Beutel ['bɔʏtəl] m (-s/-) bag; purse; pouch.
'Beutezug m plundering expedition.
bevölker|n [bə'fœlkərn] v/t. (no -ge-, h) people, populate; ⟨ung f (-/-en) population.
bevollmächtig|en [bə'fɔlmɛçtigən] v/t. (no -ge-, h) authorize, empower; ⟨te [⁓çtə] m, f (-n/-n) authorized person or agent, deputy; pol. plenipotentiary; ⟨ung f (-/-en) authorization.
be'vor cj. before.
bevormund|en fig. [bə'fo:rmundən] v/t. (no -ge-, h) patronize, keep in tutelage; ⟨ung fig. f (-/-en) patronizing, tutelage.
be'vorstehen v/i. (irr. stehen, sep., -ge-, h) be approaching, be near; crisis, etc.: be imminent; j-m ⁓ be in store for s.o., await s.o.; ⁓d adj. approaching; imminent.
bevorzug|en [bə'fo:rtsu:gən] v/t. (no -ge-, h) prefer; favo(u)r; ⚖️ privilege; ⟨ung f (-/-en) preference.
be'wach|en v/t. (no -ge-, h) guard, watch; ⟨ung f (-/-en) guard; escort.
bewaffn|en [bə'vafnən] v/t. (no -ge-, h) arm; ⟨ung f (-/-en) armament; arms pl.
be'wahren v/t. (no -ge-, h) keep, preserve (mst fig.: secret, silence, etc.).
be'währen v/refl. (no -ge-, h) stand the test, prove a success; sich ⁓ als prove o.s. (as) (a good teacher, etc.); sich ⁓ in prove o.s. efficient in (one's profession, etc.); sich nicht ⁓ prove a failure.

be'wahrheiten v/refl. (no -ge-, h) prove (to be) true; prophecy, etc.: come true.

be'währt adj. friend, etc.: tried; solicitor, etc.: experienced; friendship, etc.: long-standing; remedy, etc.: proved, proven.

Be'währung f ⚔ probation; in Zeiten der ~ in times of trial; s. bewähren; ~sfrist ⚔ f probation.

bewaldet adj. [bə'valdət] wooded, woody, Am. a. timbered.

bewältigen [bə'vɛltigən] v/t. (no -ge-, h) overcome (obstacle); master (difficulty); accomplish (task).

be'wandert adj. (well) versed (in dat. in), proficient (in); in e-m Fach gut ~ sein have a thorough knowledge of a subject.

be'wässer|n v/t. (no -ge-, h) water (garden, lawn, etc.); irrigate (land, etc.); **2ung** f (-/-en) watering; irrigation.

bewegen¹ [bə've:gən] v/t. (irr., no -ge-, h): j-n ~ zu induce or get s.o. to.

beweg|en² [~] v/t. and v/refl. (no -ge-, h) move, stir; **2grund** [~k-] m motive (gen., für for); **~lich** adj. [~k-] movable; p., mind, etc.: agile, versatile; active; **2lichkeit** [~k-] f (-/no pl.) mobility; agility, versatility; **~t** adj. [~kt] sea: rough, heavy; fig. moved, touched; voice: choked, trembling; life: eventful; times, etc.: stirring, stormy; **2ung** f (-/-en) movement; motion (a. phys.); fig. emotion; in ~ setzen set going or in motion; **~ungslos** adj. motionless, immobile.

be'weinen v/t. (no -ge-, h) weep or cry over; lament (for, over).

Beweis [bə'vais] m (-es/-e) proof (für of); ~(e pl.) evidence (esp. ⚔); **2en** [~zən] v/t. (irr. weisen, no -ge-, h) prove; show (interest, etc.); ~führung f argumentation; ~grund m argument; ~material n evidence; ~stück n (piece of) evidence; ⚔ exhibit. [leave it at that.)

be'wenden vb.: es dabei ~ lassen

be'werb|en v/refl. (irr. werben, no -ge-, h): sich ~ um apply for, Am. run for; stand for; compete for (prize); court (woman); **2er** m (-s/-) applicant (um for); candidate; competitor; suitor; **2ung** f application; candidature; competition; courtship; **2ungsschreiben** n (letter of) application.

bewerkstelligen [bə'verkʃteligən] v/t. (no -ge-, h) manage, effect, bring about.

be'wert|en v/t. (no -ge-, h) value (auf acc. at; nach by); **2ung** f valuation.

bewillig|en v/t. (no -ge-, h) grant, allow; **2ung** f (-/-en) grant, allowance.

be'wirken v/t. (no -ge-, h) cause; bring about, effect.

be'wirt|en v/t. (no -ge-, h) entertain; ~schaften v/t. (no -ge-, h) farm (land); ⚭ cultivate (field); manage (farm, etc.); ration (food, etc.); control (foreign exchange, etc.); **2ung** f (-/-en) entertainment; hospitality.

bewog [bə'vo:k] pret. of bewegen¹; ~en [bə'vo:gən] p.p. of bewegen¹.

be'wohn|en v/t. (no -ge-, h) inhabit, live in; occupy; **2er** m (-s/-) inhabitant; occupant.

bewölk|en [bə'vœlkən] v/refl. (no -ge-, h) sky: cloud up or over; brow: cloud over, darken; ~t adj. sky: clouded, cloudy, overcast; brow: clouded, darkened; **2ung** f (-/no pl.) clouds pl.

be'wunder|n v/t. (no -ge-, h) admire (wegen for); ~nswert adj. admirable; **2ung** f (-/-en) admiration.

bewußt adj. [bə'vust] deliberate, intentional; sich e-r Sache ~ sein be conscious or aware of s.th.; die ~e Sache the matter in question; ~los adj. unconscious; **2sein** n (-s/no pl.) consciousness.

be'zahl|en (no -ge-, h) **1.** v/t. pay; pay for (s.th. purchased); pay off, settle (debt); **2.** v/i. pay (für for); **2ung** f payment; settlement.

be'zähmen v/t. (no -ge-, h) tame (animal); restrain (one's anger, etc.); sich ~ control or restrain o.s.

be'zauber|n v/t. (no -ge-, h) bewitch, enchant (a. fig.); fig. charm, fascinate; **2ung** f (-/-en) enchantment, spell; fascination.

be'zeichn|en v/t. (no -ge-, h) mark; describe (als as), call; ~end adj. characteristic, typical (für of); **2ung** f indication (of direction, etc.); mark, sign, symbol; name, designation, denomination.

be'zeugen v/t. (no -ge-, h) ⚔ testify to, bear witness to (both a. fig.); attest.

be'zieh|en v/t. (irr. ziehen, no -ge-, h) cover (upholstered furniture, etc.); put cover on (cushion, etc.); move into (flat, etc.); enter (university); draw (salary, pension, etc.); get, be supplied with (goods); take in (newspaper, etc.); sich ~ sky: cloud over; sich ~ auf (acc.) refer to; **2er** m (-s/-) subscriber (gen. to).

Be'ziehung f relation (zu et. to s.th.; zu j-m with s.o.); connexion, (Am. only) connection (zu with); in dieser ~ in this respect; **2sweise** adv. respectively; or rather.

Bezirk [bə'tsirk] m (-[e]s/-e) district, Am. a. precinct; s. Wahlbezirk.

Bezogene ✝ [bə'tso:gənə] m (-n/-n) drawee.

Bezug [bə'tsu:k] m cover(ing), case; purchase (of goods); subscription (to newspaper); in ~ auf (acc.) with regard or reference to, as to; ~ nehmen auf (acc.) refer to, make reference to.

bezüglich [bə'tsy:kliç] 1. adj. relative, relating (both auf acc. to); 2. prp. (gen.) regarding, concerning.

Be'zugsbedingungen † f/pl. terms pl. of delivery.

be'zwecken v/t. (no -ge-, h) aim at; ~ mit intend by.

be'zweifeln v/t. (no -ge-, h) doubt, question.

be'zwing|en v/t. (irr. zwingen, no -ge-, h) conquer (fortress, mountain, etc.); overcome, master (feeling, difficulty, etc.); sich ~ keep o.s. under control, restrain o.s.; 2ung f (-/-en) conquest, mastering.

Bibel ['bi:bəl] f (-/-n) Bible.

Biber zo. ['bi:bər] m (-s/-) beaver.

Bibliothek [biblio'te:k] f (-/-en) library; ~ar [~e'ka:r] m (-s/-e) librarian.

biblisch adj. ['bi:bliʃ] biblical, scriptural; ~e Geschichte Scripture.

bieder adj. ['bi:dər] honest, upright, worthy (a. iro.); simple-minded; '2-keit f (-/no pl.) honesty, uprightness; simple-mindedness

bieg|en ['bi:gən] (irr., ge-) 1. v/t. (h) bend; 2. v/refl. (h) bend; sich vor Lachen ~ double up with laughter; 3. v/i. (sein) um e-e Ecke turn (round) a corner; ~sam adj ['bi:kza:m] wire, etc.: flexible, body lithe, supple; pliant (a. fig.), '2samkeit f (-/no pl.) flexibility, suppleness; pliability, '2ung f (-/-en) bend, wind (of road, river); curve (of road, arch).

Biene zo. ['bi:nə] f (-/-n) bee; '~n-königin f queen bee; '~nkorb m (bee)hive; '~nschwarm m swarm of bees; '~nstock m (bee)hive; '~n-zucht f bee-keeping, ~nzüchter m bee-keeper.

Bier [bi:r] n (-[e]s/-e) beer; helles ~ pale beer, ale; dunkles dark beer; stout, porter; vom Faß beer on draught; '~brauer m brewer; '~brauerei f brewery, '~garten m beer-garden; '~krug m beer-mug, Am. stein.

Biest [bi:st] n (-es/-er) beast, brute.

bieten ['bi:tən] (irr., ge-, h) 1. v/t. offer; † at auction sale bid; sich ~ opportunity, etc. offer itself, arise, occur; 2. † v/i. at auction sale: bid.

Bigamie [biga'mi:] f (-/~-en) bigamy.

Bilanz [bi'lants] f (-/-en) balance; balance-sheet, Am a. statement; fig. result, outcome, die ~ ziehen strike a balance; fig. take stock (of one's life, etc.).

Bild [bilt] n (-[e]s/-er) picture; image; illustration; portrait; fig. idea, notion; '~bericht m press: picture story.

bilden ['bildən] v/t. (ge-, h) form; shape, fig.: educate, train (s.o., mind, etc.); develop (mind, etc.); form, be, constitute (obstacle, etc.); sich form; fig. educate o.s., improve one's mind; sich e-e Meinung form an opinion.

Bilder|buch ['bildər-] n picture-book, ~galerie f picture-gallery; '~rätsel n rebus.

'Bild|fläche f: F auf der ~ erscheinen appear on the scene; F von der ~ verschwinden disappear (from the scene), ~funk m radio picture transmission; television; ~hauer m (-s/-) sculptor, '~hauerei [~'rai] f (-/-en) sculpture, '2lich adj. pictorial; word, etc.: figurative, '~nis n (-ses/-se) portrait; ~röhre f picture or television tube; '~säule f statue; ~schirm m (television) screen, '2schön adj. most beautiful; '~seite f face, head (of coin); '~streifen m picture or film strip; '~telegraphie f (-/no pl.) phototelegraphy.

'Bildung f (-/-en) forming, formation (both a. gr.: of plural, etc.); constitution (of committee, etc.); education; culture; (good) breeding. [sg., billiard-table.)

Billard ['biljart] n (-s/-e) billiards}

billig adj. ['biliç] just, equitable; fair; price: reasonable, moderate; goods: cheap, inexpensive; recht und ~ right and proper, ~en [~gən] v/t. (ge-, h) approve of, Am. a. approbate; '2keit f (-/no pl.) justness, equity; fairness; reasonableness, moderateness; 2ung f [~gun] f (-/~-en) approval, sanction.

Binde ['bində] f (-/-n) band; tie; ⚕ bandage; (arm-)sling, s. Damenbinde; ~gewebe anat. n connective tissue; ~glied n connecting link; ~haut anat. f conjunctiva; '~hautentzündung ⚕ f conjunctivitis, '2n (irr., ge-, h) 1. v/t bind, tie (an acc. to); bind (book, etc.); make (broom, wreath, etc.), knot (tie); sich ~ bind or commit or engage o.s.; 2. v/i. bind, unite; ⊕ cement, etc.: set, harden; '~strich m hyphen; '~wort gr. n (-[e]s/~er) conjunction.

Bindfaden ['bint-] m string; packthread.

'Bindung f (-/-en) binding (a. of ski); ♩ slur, tie, ligature, fig. commitment (a. pol.); engagement; ~en pl. bonds pl., ties pl.

binnen prp. (dat., a. gen.) ['binən] within; ~ kurzem before long.

'Binnen|gewässer n inland water; '~hafen m close port, ~handel m domestic or home trade, Am. domestic commerce; ~land n inland, interior; ~verkehr m inland traffic or transport.

Binse ♀ ['binzə] f (-/-n) rush; F: *in die ~n gehen* go to pot; '~nwahrheit f, '~nweisheit f truism.
Biochemie [bioçe'mi:] f (-/*no pl.*) biochemistry.
Biograph|ie [biogra'fi:] f (-/-n) biography; 2isch *adj.* [~'gra:fiʃ] biographic(al).
Biolog|ie [biolo'gi:] f (-/*no pl.*) biology; 2isch *adj.* [~'lo:giʃ] biological.
Birke ♀ ['birkə] f (-/-n) birch(-tree).
Birne ['birnə] f (-/-n) ♀ pear; ≠ (electric) bulb; *fig. sl.* nob, *Am.* bean.
bis [bis] **1.** *prp. (acc.) space:* to, as far as; *time:* till, until, by; *zwei ~ drei* two or three, two to three; *~ auf weiteres* until further orders, for the meantime; *~ vier zählen* count up to four; *alle ~ auf drei* all but *or* except three; **2.** *cj.* till, until.
Bisamratte zo. ['bi:zam-] f muskrat.
Bischof ['biʃɔf] m (-s/-e) bishop.
bischöflich *adj.* ['biʃøfliç] episcopal.
bisher *adv.* [bis'he:r] hitherto, up to now, so far; '~ig *adj.* until now; hitherto existing; former.
Biß [bis] **1.** m (Bisses/Bisse) bite; **2.** 2 *pret. of* beißen.
bißchen ['bisçən] **1.** *adj.: ein ~* a little, a (little) bit of; **2.** *adv.: ein ~* a little (bit).
Bissen ['bisən] m (-s/-) mouthful; morsel; bite.
'**bissig** *adj.* biting (*a. fig.*); *remark:* cutting; *Achtung, ~er Hund!* beware of the dog!
Bistum ['bistu:m] n (-s/*er) bishopric, diocese.
bisweilen *adv.* [bis'vailən] sometimes, at times, now and then.
Bitte ['bitə] f (-/-n) request (*um* for); entreaty; *auf j-s ~ (hin)* at s.o.'s request.
'**bitten** (*irr.*, ge-, h) **1.** *v/t.: j-n um et. ~* ask *or* beg s.o. for s.th.; *j-n um Entschuldigung ~* beg s.o.'s pardon; *dürfte ich Sie um Feuer ~?* may I trouble you for a light?; *bitte* please; (*wie*) *bitte?* (I beg your) pardon?; *bitte! offering s.th.:* (please,) help yourself, (please,) do take some *or* one; *danke (schön) — bitte (sehr)!* thank you — not at all, you're welcome, don't mention it, F that's all right?; **2.** *v/i.: um et. ~* ask *or* beg for s.th.
bitter *adj.* ['bitər] bitter (*a. fig.*); *frost:* sharp; '2keit f (-/-en) bitterness; *fig. a.* acrimony; '~lich *adv.* bitterly.
'**Bitt|gang** *eccl.* m procession; '~schrift f petition; '~steller m (-s/-) petitioner.
bläh|en ['blɛ:ən] (ge-, h) **1.** *v/t.* inflate, distend, swell out; belly (out),

swell out (*sails*); *sich ~ sails:* belly (out), swell out; *skirt:* balloon out; **2.** ≠ *v/i.* cause flatulence; '~end *adj.* flatulent; '2ung ≠ f (-/-en) flatulence, F wind.
Blam|age [bla'ma:ʒə] f (-/-n) disgrace, shame; 2ieren [~'mi:rən] *v/t.* (no -ge-, h) make a fool of *s.o.*, disgrace; *sich ~* make a fool of o.s.
blank *adj.* [blaŋk] shining, shiny, bright; polished; F *fig.* broke.
blanko ✝ ['blaŋko] **1.** *adj.* form, *etc.*: blank, not filled in; in blank; **2.** *adv.*: *~ verkaufen stock exchange:* sell short; '2scheck m blank cheque, *Am.* blank check; '2unterschrift f blank signature; '2vollmacht f full power of attorney, carte blanche.
Bläschen ≠ ['blɛ:sçən] n (-s/-) vesicle, small blister.
Blase ['bla:zə] f (-/-n) bubble; blister (*a. ≠*); *anat.* bladder; bleb (*in glass*); ⊕ flaw; '~balg m (*ein a pair of*) bellows *pl.*; '2n (*irr.*, ge-, h) **1.** *v/t.* blow; blow, sound; play (*wind-instrument*); **2.** *v/i.* blow.
Blas|instrument ♩ ['bla:s-] n wind-instrument; '~kapelle f brass band.
blaß *adj.* [blas] pale (*vor dat.* with); *~ werden* turn pale; *keine blasse Ahnung* not the faintest idea.
Blässe ['blɛsə] f (-/*no pl.*) paleness.
Blatt [blat] n (-[e]s/*er) leaf (*of book, ♀*); petal (*of flower*); leaf, sheet (*of paper*); ♩ sheet; blade (*of oar, saw, airscrew, etc.*); sheet (*of metal*); *cards:* hand; (news)paper.
Blattern ≠ ['blatərn] *pl.* smallpox.
blättern ['blɛtərn] *v/i.* (ge-, h): *in e-m Buch ~* leaf through a book, thumb a book.
'**Blatternarb|e** f pock-mark; '2ig *adj.* pock-marked.
'**Blätterteig** m puff paste.
'**Blatt|gold** n gold-leaf, gold-foil; '~laus zo. f plant-louse; '~pflanze f foliage plant.
blau [blau] **1.** *adj.* blue; F *fig.* drunk, tight, boozy; *~er Fleck* bruise; *~es Auge* black eye; *mit e-m ~en Auge davonkommen* get off cheaply; **2.** 2 n (-s/*no pl.*) blue (colo[u]r); *Fahrt ins ~e* mystery tour. [blue.)
bläuen ['blɔyən] *v/t.* (ge-, h) (dye)
'**blau|grau** *adj.* bluish grey; '2jacke ♣ f bluejacket, sailor.
bläulich *adj.* bluish.
Blausäure ♠ f (-/*no pl.*) hydrocyanic *or* prussic acid.
Blech [blɛç] n (-[e]s/-e) sheet metal; metal sheet, plate; F *fig.* balderdash, rubbish, *Am. sl. a.* baloney; '~büchse f tin, *Am.* can; '2ern *adj.* (of tin; *sound:* brassy; *sound, voice:* tinny; '~musik f brass-band music; '~waren f/pl. tinware.
Blei [blai] (-[e]s/-e) **1.** n lead; **2.** F n, m (lead) pencil.

bleiben ['blaɪbən] v/i. (irr., ge-, sein) remain, stay; be left; ruhig ~ keep calm; ~ bei keep to s.th., stick to s.th.; bitte bleiben Sie am Apparat teleph. hold the line, please; '~d adj. lasting, permanent; '~lassen v/t. (irr. lassen, sep., no -ge-, h) leave s.th. alone; laß das bleiben! don't do it!; leave it alone!; stop that (noise, etc.)!

bleich adj. [blaɪç] pale (vor dat. with); ~en (ge-) 1. v/t. (h) make pale, bleach; blanch; 2. v/i. (irr., sein) bleach; lose colo(u)r, fade; '~süchtig ♂ adj. chlorotic. greensick.

'**bleiern** adj. (of) lead, leaden (a. fig.). '**Blei|rohr** n lead pipe; '~soldat m tin soldier; '~stift m (lead) pencil; '~stifthülse f pencil cap; '~stiftspitzer m (-s/-) pencil-sharpener; '~vergiftung ♂ f lead-poisoning.

Blend|e ['blɛndə] f (-/-n) phot. diaphragm, stop; ⚠ blind or sham window; '2en (ge-, h) 1. v/t. blind; dazzle (both a. fig.); 2. v/i. light: dazzle the eyes, ~laterne ['blɛnt-] f dark lantern.

blich [blɪç] pret. of bleichen 2.

Blick [blɪk] m (-[e]s/-e) glance, look; view (auf acc. of); auf den ersten ~ at first sight; ein böser ~ an evil or angry look; '2en v/i. (ge-, h) look, glance (auf acc., nach at); '~fang m eye-catcher.

blieb [bliːp] pret. of bleiben.

blies [bliːs] pret. of blasen.

blind adj. [blɪnt] blind (a. fig.: gegen, für to; vor dat. with); metal: dull, tarnished; window: opaque (with age, dirt); mirror: clouded, dull; cartridge: blank; ~er Alarm false alarm; ~er Passagier stowaway; auf e-m Auge ~ blind in one eye.

'**Blinddarm** anat. m blind gut; appendix; '~entzündung ♂ f appendicitis.

Blinde ['blɪndə] (-n/-n) 1. m blind man; 2. f blind woman; ~nanstalt ['blɪndən'-] f institute for the blind; ~nheim n home for the blind; ~nhund m guide dog, Am. a. seeing-eye dog; '~nschrift f braille.

'**blind|fliegen** ⚙ (irr. fliegen, sep., -ge-) v/t. (h) and v/i. (sein) fly blind or on instruments; '2flug ⚙ m blind flying or flight; '2gänger m ⚙ blind shell, dud; F fig. washout; '2heit f (-/no pl.) blindness; ~lings adv. ['~lɪŋs] blindly; at random; '2schleiche zo. f (-/-n) slow-worm, blind-worm; '~schreiben v/t. and v/i. (irr. schreiben, sep., -ge-, h) touch-type.

blink|en ['blɪŋkən] v/i. (ge-, h) star, light: twinkle; metal, leather, glass, etc.: shine; signal (with lamps),

flash; '2er mot. m (-s/-) flashing indicator; '2feuer n flashing light.

blinzeln ['blɪntsəln] v/i. (ge-, h) blink (at light, etc.); wink.

Blitz [blɪts] m (-es/-e) lightning; '~ableiter m (-s/-) lightning-conductor, '2en v/i. (ge-, h) flash; es blitzt it is lightening; '~gespräch teleph. n special priority call; '~licht phot. n flash-light; '2schnell adv. with lightning speed; '~strahl m flash of lightning.

Block [blɔk] m 1. (-[e]s/=e) block; slab (of cooking chocolate); block, log (of wood); ingot (of metal); parl., pol., ♟ bloc; 2. (-[e]s/=e, -s) block (of houses); pad, block (of paper), ~ade ⚓ ♆ [~'kaːdə] f (-/-n) blockade; ~adebrecher m (-s/-) blockade-runner; ~haus n log cabin; 2ieren [~'kiːrən] (no -ge-, h) 1. v/t. block (up); lock (wheel); 2. v/i. brakes, etc.: jam.

blöd adj. [bløːt], ~e adj. ['~də] imbecile, stupid, dull; silly; '2heit f (-/-en) imbecility; stupidity, dullness; silliness; 2sinn m imbecility; rubbish, nonsense; '~sinnig adj. imbecile, idiotic, stupid, foolish.

blöken ['bløːkən] v/i. (ge-, h) sheep, calf bleat.

blond adj. [blɔnt] blond, fair (-haired).

bloß [bloːs] 1. adj. bare, naked; mere; ~e Worte mere words; mit dem ~en Auge wahrnehmbar visible to the naked eye; 2. adv. only, merely, simply, just.

Blöße ['bløːsə] f (-/-n) bareness, nakedness; fig. weak point or spot; sich e-e ~ geben give o.s. away; lay o.s. open to attack; keine ~ bieten be invulnerable.

'**bloß|legen** v/t. (sep., -ge-, h) lay bare, expose; '~stellen v/t. (sep., -ge-, h) expose, compromise, unmask, sich ~ compromise o.s.

blühen ['blyːən] v/i. (ge-, h) blossom, flower, bloom; fig. flourish, thrive, prosper; ♟ boom.

Blume ['bluːmə] f (-/-n) flower; wine bouquet; beer: froth.

'**Blumen|beet** n flower-bed; '~blatt n petal; '~händler m florist; '~strauß m bouquet or bunch of flowers, ~topf m flowerpot; '~zucht f floriculture.

Bluse ['bluːzə] f (-/-n) blouse.

Blut [bluːt] n (-[e]s/no pl.) blood; ~ vergießen shed blood; böses ~ machen breed bad blood; '~andrang ♂ m congestion; '2arm adj. bloodless, ♂ an(a)emic; '~armut ♂ f an(a)emia; '~bad n carnage, massacre; '~bank f blood bank; '~blase f blood blister; '~druck m blood pressure; 2dürstig adj. ['~dyrstiç] bloodthirsty.

Blüte ['blyːtə] f (-/-n) blossom,

bloom, flower; *esp. fig.* flower; prime, heyday (*of life*).
Blutegel ['blu:tⁱe:gəl] *m* (-s/-) leech.
'bluten *v/i.* (ge-, *h*) bleed (*aus* from); *aus der Nase* ~ bleed at the nose.
Bluterguß ⚔ ['blu:tʔ-] *m* effusion of blood.
'Blütezeit *f* flowering period *or* time; *fig. a.* prime, heyday.
'Blut|gefäß *anat. n* blood-vessel; **~gerinnsel** ⚔ ['~gərinzəl] *n* (-s/-) clot of blood; **'~gruppe** *f* blood group; **'~hund** *zo. m* bloodhound.
'blutig *adj.* bloody, blood-stained; *es ist mein ~er Ernst* I am dead serious; *~er Anfänger* mere beginner, F greenhorn.
Blut|körperchen ['blu:tkœrpərçən] *n* (-s/-) blood corpuscle; **'~kreislauf** *m* (blood) circulation; **'~lache** *f* pool of blood; **'²leer** *adj.*, **'²los** *adj.* bloodless; **'~probe** *f* blood test; **'~rache** *f* blood feud *or* revenge *or* vengeance, vendetta; **'²-'rot** *adj.* blood-red; crimson; **²rünstig** *adj.* ['~rynstiç] bloodthirsty; bloody; **'~schande** *f* incest; **'~spender** *m* blood-donor; **'²stillend** *adj.* blood-sta(u)nching; **'~sturz** ⚔ *m* h(a)emorrhage; **'²verwandt** *adj.* related by blood (*mit* to); **'~sverwandtschaft** *f* blood-relationship, consanguinity; **'~übertragung** *f* blood-transfusion; **'~ung** *f* (-/-en) bleeding, h(a)emorrhage; **'²unterlaufen** *adj. eye:* blood-shot; **'~vergießen** *n* bloodshed; **'~vergiftung** *f* blood-poisoning.
Bö [bø] *f* (-/-en) gust, squall.
Bock [bok] *m* (-[e]s/*e) deer, hare, rabbit: buck; he-goat, F billy-goat; *sheep:* ram; *gymnastics:* buck; *e-n* ~ *schießen* commit a blunder, *sl.* commit a bloomer; *den* ~ *zum Gärtner machen* set the fox to keep the geese; **'²en** *v/i.* (ge-, *h*) *horse:* buck; *child:* sulk; *p.* be obstinate *or* refractory; *mot.* move jerkily, *Am.* F *a.* buck; **'²ig** *adj.* stubborn, obstinate, pigheaded; **'~sprung** *m* leap-frog; *gymnastics:* vault over the buck; *Bocksprünge machen* caper, cut capers.
Boden ['bo:dən] *m* (-s/*) ground; ⚔ soil; bottom; floor; loft; **'~kammer** *f* garret, attic; **'²los** *adj.* bottomless; *fig.* enormous; unheard-of; **'~personal** ✈ *n* ground personnel *or* staff, *Am.* ground crew; **'~reform** *f* land reform; **'~satz** *m* grounds *pl.*, sediment; **~schätze** ['~fɛtsə] *m/pl.* mineral resources *pl.*; **'²ständig** *adj.* native, indigenous.
bog [bo:k] *pret. of* biegen.
Bogen ['bo:gən] *m* (-s/-, ·) bow, bend, curve; ⩘ arc; ⩘ arch; *ski-ing:* turn; *skating:* curve; sheet (*of*

paper); **'²förmig** *adj.* arched; **'~gang** ⩘ *m* arcade; **'~lampe** ⚡ *f* arc-lamp; **'~schütze** *m* archer, bowman.
Bohle ['bo:lə] *f* (-/-n) thick plank, board.
Bohne ['bo:nə] *f* (-/-n) bean; *grüne* ~ *pl.* French beans *pl.*, *Am.* string beans *pl.*; *weiße* ~ *pl.* haricot beans *pl.*; F *blaue* ~ *pl.* bullets *pl.*; **'~nstange** *f* beanpole (*a.* F *fig.*).
bohnern ['bo:nərn] *v/t.* (ge-, *h*) polish (*floor, etc.*), (bees)wax (*floor*).
bohr|en ['bo:rən] (ge-, *h*) 1. *v/t.* bore, drill (*hole*); sink, bore (*well, shaft*); bore, cut, drive (*tunnel, etc.*); 2. *v/i.* drill (*a. dentistry*); bore; **'²er** ⊕ *m* (-s/-) borer, drill.
'böig *adj.* squally, gusty; ✈ bumpy.
Boje ['bo:jə] *f* (-/-n) buoy.
Bollwerk ✕ ['bolverk] *n* bastion, bulwark (*a. fig.*).
Bolzen ⊕ ['boltsən] *m* (-s/-) bolt.
Bombard|ement [bombardə'mã:] *n* (-s/-s) bombardment; bombing; shelling; **²ieren** [~'di:rən] *v/t.* (*no* -ge-, *h*) bomb; shell; bombard (*a. fig.*).
Bombe ['bombə] *f* (-/-n) bomb; *fig.* bomb-shell; **'²nsicher** *adj.* bomb-proof; F *fig.* dead sure; **'~nschaden** *m* bomb damage; **'~r** ✕: ✈ *m* (-s/-) bomber.
Bon ✚ [bõ:] *m* (-s/-s) coupon; voucher; credit note.
Bonbon [bõ'bõ:] *m, n* (-s/-s) sweet (-meat), bon-bon, F goody, *Am.* candy.
Bonze F ['bontsə] *m* (-n/-n) bigwig, *Am. a.* big shot.
Boot [bo:t] *n* (-[e]s/-e) boat; **'~shaus** *n* boat-house; **'~smann** *m* (-[e]s/*Bootsleute*) boatswain.
Bord [bort] (-[e]s/-e) 1. *n* shelf; 2. ⚓, ✕ *m:* *an* ~ *on board*, aboard (*ship, aircraft, etc.*); *über* ~ overboard; *von* ~ *gehen* go ashore; **'~funker** ⚓, ✕ *m* wireless *or* radio operator; **'~stein** *m* kerb, *Am.* curb.
borgen ['borgən] *v/t.* (ge-, *h*) borrow (*von, bei* from, of); lend, *Am. a.* loan (*j-m et.* s.th. to s.o.).
Borke ['borkə] *f* (-/-n) bark (*of tree*).
borniert *adj.* [bor'ni:rt] narrow-minded, *of* restricted intelligence.
Borsalbe ['bo:r-] *f* boracic ointment.
Börse ['bœrzə] *f* (-/-n) purse; ✚ stock exchange; stock-market; money-market; **'~nbericht** *m* market report; **'²nfähig** *adj.* stock: negotiable on the stock exchange; **'~nkurs** *m* quotation; **'~nmakler** *m* stock-broker; **'~nnotierung** *f* (official, stock exchange) quotation; **'~npapiere** *n/pl.* listed securities *pl.*; **'~nspekulant** *m* stock-jobber; **'~nzeitung** *f* financial newspaper.

Borst|e ['bɔrstə] f (-/-n) bristle (*of hog or brush, etc.*); '2ig *adj.* bristly.
Borte ['bɔrtə] f (-/-n) border (*of carpet, etc.*); braid, lace.
'**bösartig** *adj.* malicious, vicious; ⚕ malignant; '2keit f (-/-en) viciousness; ⚕ malignity.
Böschung ['bœʃuŋ] f (-/-en) slope; embankment (*of railway*); bank (*of river*).
böse ['bøːzə] 1. *adj.* bad, evil, wicked; malevolent, spiteful; angry (*über acc.* at, about; *auf j-n* with *s.o.*); *er meint es nicht* ~ he means no harm; 2. 2 n (-n/no pl.) evil; 2wicht ['~viçt] m (-[e]s/-er, -e) villain, rascal.
bos|haft *adj.* ['boːshaft] wicked; spiteful; malicious; '2heit f (-/-en) wickedness; malice; spite.
'**böswillig** *adj.* malevolent; ~e Absicht ⚖ malice prepense; ~es Verlassen ⚖ wilful desertion; '2keit f (-/-en) malevolence.
bot [boːt] *pret.* of bieten.
Botan|ik [bo'taːnik] f (-/no pl.) botany; ~iker m (-s/-) botanist; 2isch *adj.* botanical.
Bote ['boːtə] m (-n/-n) messenger; '~ngang m errand; Botengänge machen run errands.
'**Botschaft** f (-/-en) message; *pol.* embassy; '~er m (-s/-) ambassador; *in British Commonwealth countries:* High Commissioner.
Bottich ['bɔtiç] m (-[e]s/-e) tub; wash-tub; *brewing:* tun. vat.
Bouillon [bu'ljõː] f (-/-s) beef tea.
Bowle ['boːlə] f (-/-n) *vessel:* bowl; *cold drink consisting of fruit, hock and champagne or soda-water: appr.* punch.
box|en ['bɔksən] 1. *v/i.* (ge-, h) box; 2. *v/t.* (ge-, h) punch *s.o.*; 3. 2 n (-s/no pl.) boxing; pugilism; '2er m (-s/-) boxer; pugilist; '2handschuh m boxing-glove; '2kampf m boxing-match, bout, fight; '2sport m boxing.
Boykott [bɔy'kɔt] (-[e]s/-e) boycott; 2ieren [~'tiːrən] *v/t.* (no -ge-, h) boycott.
brach [braːx] 1. *pret.* of brechen; 2. ✒ *adv.* fallow; uncultivated (*both a. fig.*).
brachte ['braxtə] *pret.* of bringen.
Branche † ['brãːʃə] f (-/-n) line (of business), trade; branch.
Brand [brant] m (-[e]s/⸚e) burning; fire, blaze; ⚕ gangrene; ✒, ✿ blight, smut, mildew; '~blase f blister; '~bombe f incendiary bomb; 2en ['~dən] *v/i.* (ge-, h) surge (*a. fig.*), break (*an acc., gegen* against); '~fleck m burn; 2ig *adj.* ['~diç] ⚕, ✒ blighted, smutted; ⚕ gangrenous; '~mal n brand; *fig.* stigma, blemish; '2marken *v/t.* (ge-, h) brand (*animal*); *fig.* brand

or stigmatize *s.o.*; '~mauer f fire (-proof) wall; '~schaden m damage caused by *or* loss suffered by fire; '2schatzen *v/t.* (ge-, h) lay (*town*) under contribution; sack, pillage; '~stätte f, '~stelle f scene of fire; '~stifter m incendiary, *Am.* F a. firebug; ~stiftung f arson; ~ung ['~duŋ] f (-/-en) surf, surge, breakers *pl.*; '~wache f fire-watch; '~wunde f burn; scald; '~zeichen n brand
brannte ['brantə] *pret.* of brennen.
Branntwein ['brantvain] m brandy, spirits *pl.*, whisk(e)y; gin; '~brennerei f distillery.
braten ['braːtən] 1. *v/t.* (irr., ge-, h) *in oven:* roast; grill; *in frying-pan:* fry; bake (*apple*); *am Spieß* ~ roast on a spit, barbecue; 2. *v/i.* (irr., ge-, h) roast; grill; fry; *in der Sonne* ~ p. roast *or* grill in the sun; 3. 2 m (-s/-) roast (meat); joint; '2fett n dripping, '2soße f gravy.
'**Brat|fisch** m fried fish; '~hering m grilled herring; '~huhn n roast chicken, '~kartoffeln *pl.* fried potatoes *pl.*; '~ofen m (kitchen) oven; '~pfanne f frying-pan, *Am. a.* skillet; '~röhre f s. Bratofen.
Brauch [braux] m (-[e]s/⸚e) custom, usage, use, habit; practice; '2bar *adj.* f, thing: useful; p. capable, able; *thing:* serviceable; '2en (h) 1. *v/t.* (ge-) need, want; require; take (*time*); use; 2. *v/aux.* (*no -ge-*): *du brauchst es nur zu sagen* you only have to say so; *er hätte nicht zu kommen* ~ he need not have come; ~tum n (-[e]s/⸚er) custom; tradition, folklore.
Braue ['brauə] f (-/-n) eyebrow.
brau|en ['brauən] *v/t.* (ge-, h) brew; '2er m (-s/-) brewer; 2erei [~'rai] f (-/-en) brewery; '2haus n brewery.
braun *adj.* [braun] brown; *horse:* bay; *werden* get a tan (*on one's skin*)
Bräune ['brɔynə] f (-/no pl.) brown colo(u)r, (sun) tan; '2n (ge-, h) 1. *v/t.* make *or* dye brown; *sun:* tan; 2. *v/i.* tan
'**Braunkohle** f brown coal, lignite.
'**bräunlich** *adj.* brownish.
Brause ['brauzə] f (-/-n) rose, sprinkling-nozzle (*of watering can*); *s.* Brausebad; *s.* Brauselimonade; '~bad ✿ shower(-bath); '~limonade f fizzy lemonade; '2n *v/i.* (ge-, h) *wind, water, etc.:* roar; rush; have a shower(-bath); '~pulver n effervescent powder.
Braut [braut] f (-/⸚e) fiancée; *on wedding-day:* bride; '~führer m best man.
Bräutigam ['brɔytigam] m (-s/-e) fiancé, *on wedding-day:* bridegroom, *Am. a.* groom.
'**Braut|jungfer** f bridesmaid; '~

kleid n wedding-dress; '**~kranz** m bridal wreath; '**~leute** pl., '**~paar** n engaged couple; *on wedding-day*: bride and bridegroom; '**~schleier** m bridal veil.

brav adj. [braːf] honest, upright; good, well-behaved; brave.

bravo int. ['braːvo] bravo!, well done!

Bravour [bra'vuːr] f (-/no pl.) bravery, courage; brilliance.

Brecheisen ['brɛç⁹-] n crowbar; (burglar's) jemmy, Am. a. jimmy.

brechen (irr., ge-) **1.** v/t. (h) break; pluck (flower); refract (ray, etc.); fold (sheet of paper); quarry (stone); vomit; die Ehe ~ commit adultery; sich ~ break (one's leg, etc.); opt. be refracted; **2.** v/t. (h) break; vomit; mit j-m ~ break with s.o.; **3.** v/i. (sein) break, get broken; bones: break, fracture.

Brech|mittel ✶ n emetic; F fig. sickener; '**~reiz** m nausea; '**~stange** f crowbar, Am. a. pry; '**~ung** opt. f (-/-en) refraction.

Brei [brai] m (-[e]s/-e) paste; pulp; mash; pap (for babies); made of oatmeal: porridge; (rice, etc.) pudding; '**2ig** adj. pasty; pulpy; pappy.

breit adj. [brait] broad, wide; zehn Meter ~ ten metres wide; ~e Schichten der Bevölkerung large sections of or the bulk of the population; '**~beinig 1.** adj. with legs wide apart; **2.** adv.: ~ gehen straddle.

Breite ['braitə] f (-/-n) breadth, width; ast., geogr. latitude; '**2n** v/t. (ge-, h) spread; '**~ngrad** m degree of latitude; '**~nkreis** m parallel (of latitude).

breit|machen v/refl. (sep., -ge-, h) spread o.s.; take up room; '**~schlagen** v/t. (irr. schlagen, sep., -ge-, h): F j-n ~ persuade s.o.; F j-n zu et. ~ talk s.o. into (doing) s.th.; '**2seite** ✪ f broadside.

Bremse ['brɛmzə] f (-/-n) zo. gad-fly; horse-fly; ⊕ brake; '**2n** (ge-, h) v/i. brake, put on the brakes; slow down; **2.** v/t. brake, put on the brakes to; slow down; fig. curb.

Brems|klotz m brake-block; ⚡ wheel chock; '**~pedal** n brake pedal; '**~vorrichtung** f brake-mechanism; '**~weg** m braking distance.

brenn|bar adj. ['brɛnbaːr] combustible, burnable; '**2dauer** f burning time; '**~en** (irr., ge-, h) **1.** v/t. burn; distil(l) (brandy); roast (coffee); bake (brick, etc.); **2.** v/i. burn; be ablaze, be on fire; wound, eye: smart, burn; nettle: sting; vor Ungeduld ~ burn with impatience; F darauf ~ zu inf. be burning to inf.; es brennt! fire!

'**Brenn|er** m (-s/-) p. distiller; fixture: burner; '**~essel** ['brɛnnɛsəl] f

stinging nettle; '**~glas** n burning glass; '**~holz** n firewood; '**~material** n fuel; '**~öl** n lamp-oil; fuel-oil; '**~punkt** m focus, focal point; in den ~ rücken bring into focus a. fig.); im ~ des Interesses stehen be the focus of interest; **~schere** f curling-tongs pl.; '**~spiritus** 'n methylated spirit; '**~stoff** m combustible; mot. fuel.

brenzlig ['brɛntsliç] **1.** adj. burnt; matter: dangerous; situation: precarious; ~er Geruch burnt smell, smell of burning; **2.** adv.: es riecht ~ it smells of burning.

Bresche ['brɛʃə] f (-/-n) breach (a. fig.), gap; in die ~ springen help s.o. out of a dilemma.

Brett [brɛt] n (-[e]s/-er) board; plank, shelf; spring-board; '**~spiel** n game played on a board.

Brezel ['breːtsəl] f (-/-n) pretzel.

Brief [briːf] m (-[e]s/-e) letter; '**~aufschrift** f address (on a letter); '**~beschwerer** m (-s/-) paperweight; '**~bogen** m sheet of notepaper; '**~geheimnis** n secrecy of correspondence; '**~karte** f correspondence card (with envelope); '**~kasten** m letter-box; pillar-box; Am. mailbox; '**2lich** adj. and adv. by letter, in writing; '**~marke** f (postage) stamp; '**~markensammlung** f stamp-collection; '**~öffner** m letter-opener; '**~ordner** m letterfile; '**~papier** n notepaper; '**~porto** n postage; '**~post** f mail, post; '**~tasche** f wallet, Am. a. billfold; '**~taube** f carrier pigeon, homing pigeon, homer; '**~träger** m postman, Am. mailman; '**~umschlag** m envelope; '**~waage** f letter-balance; '**~wechsel** m correspondence; '**~zensur** f postal censorship.

briet [briːt] pret. of braten.

Brikett [bri'kɛt] n (-[e]s/-s) briquet (-te).

Brillant [bril'jant] **1.** m (-en/-en) brilliant, cut diamond; **2.** ⚙ adj. brilliant; '**~ring** m diamond ring.

Brille ['brilə] f (-/-n) (eine a pair of) glasses pl. or spectacles pl.; goggles pl.; lavatory seat; '**~nfutteral** n spectacle-case; '**~nträger** m person who wears glasses.

bringen ['briŋən] v/t. (irr., ge-, h) bring; take; see (s.o. home, etc.); put (in order); make (sacrifice); yield (interest); an den Mann ~ dispose of, get rid of; j-n dazu ~ et. zu tun make or get s.o. to do s.th.; et. mit sich ~ involve s.th.; j-n um et. ~ deprive s.o. of s.th.; j-n zum Lachen ~ make s.o. laugh.

Brise ['briːzə] f (-/-n) breeze.

Brit|e ['britə] m (-n/-n) Briton, Am. a. Britisher; die ~n pl. the British pl.; '**2isch** adj. British.

bröckeln ['brœkəln] v/i. (ge-, h) crumble; become brittle.

Brocken ['brɔkən] 1. m (-s/-) piece; lump (of earth or stone, etc.); morsel (of food); F ein harter ~ a hard nut; 2. ♀ v/t. (ge-, h): Brot in die Suppe ~ break bread into soup.

brodeln ['bro:dəln] v/i. (ge-, h) bubble, simmer.

Brombeer|e ['brɔm-] f blackberry; '~strauch m blackberry bush.

Bronch|ialkatarrh ♀ [brɔnçi'ɑːl-katar] m bronchial catarrh; '~ien anat. f/pl. bronchi(a) pl.; ~itis ♀ [~çi:tis] f (-/Bronchitiden) bronchitis.

Bronze ['brõːsə] f (-/-n) bronze; '~medaille f bronze medal.

Brosche ['brɔʃə] f (-/-n) brooch.

broschier|en [brɔ'ʃiːrən] v/i. (no -ge-, h) sew, stitch (book); ~t adj. book: paper-backed, paper-bound; fabric: figured.

Broschüre [brɔ'ʃyːrə] f (-/-n) booklet; brochure; pamphlet.

Brot [bro:t] n (-[e]s/-e) bread; loaf; sein ~ verdienen earn one's living; '~aufstrich m spread.

Brötchen ['brøːtçən] n (-s/-) roll.

'Brot|korb m: j-m den ~ höher hängen put s.o. on short allowance; 'Qlos fig. adj. unemployed; unprofitable; '~rinde f crust; '~schneidemaschine f bread-cutter; '~schnitte f slice of bread; '~studium n utilitarian study; '~teig m bread dough.

Bruch [brux] (-[e]s/-e) break(ing); breach; ♀ fracture (of bones); ♀ hernia; crack; fold (in paper); crease (in cloth); split (in silk); Å fraction; breach (of promise); violation (of oath, etc.); violation, infringement (of law, etc.); '~band ♀ n truss.

brüchig adj. ['bryçiç] fragile; brittle; voice: cracked.

'Bruch|landung ✈ f crash-landing; '~rechnung f fractional arithmetic, F fractions pl.; '~strich Å m fraction bar; '~stück n fragment (a. fig.); '~teil m fraction; im ~ e-r Sekunde in a split second; '~zahl f fraction(al) number.

Brücke ['brykə] f (-/-n) bridge; carpet: rug; sports: bridge; e-e ~ schlagen über (acc.) build or throw a bridge across, bridge (river); '~nkopf ✕ m bridge-head; '~npfeiler m pier (of bridge).

Bruder ['bruːdər] m (-s/-) brother; eccl. (lay) brother, friar; '~krieg m fratricidal or civil war; '~kuß m fraternal kiss.

brüderlich ['bryːdərliç] 1. adj. brotherly, fraternal; 2. adv.: ~ teilen share and share alike; '2keit f (-/no pl.) brotherliness, fraternity.

Brühe ['bryːə] f (-/-n) broth; stock;

beef tea; F dirty water; drink: F dishwater; '2heiß adj. scalding hot; '~würfel m beef cube.

brüllen ['brylən] v/i. (ge-, h) roar; bellow; cattle: low; bull: bellow; vor Lachen ~ roar with laughter; ~des Gelächter roar of laughter.

brumm|en ['brumən] v/i. (ge-, h) p. speak in a deep voice, mumble; growl (a. fig.); insect: buzz; engine: buzz, boom; fig. grumble, Am. F grouch; mir brummt der Schädel my head is buzzing; '2bär fig. m grumbler, growler, Am. F grouch; '2er m (-s/-) bluebottle; dung-beetle; '~ig adj. grumbling, Am. F grouchy.

brünett adj. [bry'nɛt] woman: brunette.

Brunft hunt. [brunft] f (-/-e) rut; '~zeit f rutting season.

Brunnen ['brunən] m (-s/-) well; spring, fountain (a. fig.); e-n ~ graben sink a well; '~wasser n pump-water, well-water.

Brunst [brunst] f (-/-e) zo. rut (of male animal), heat (of female animal); lust, sexual desire.

brünstig adj. ['brynstiç] zo. rutting, in heat, lustful.

Brust [brust] f (-/-e) chest, anat. thorax, breast; (woman's) breast(s pl.), bosom; aus voller ~ at the top of one's voice, lustily; '~bild n half-length portrait.

brüsten ['brystən] v/refl. (ge-, h) boast, brag.

'Brust|fell anat. n pleura; '~fellentzündung ♀ f pleurisy; '~kasten m, '~korb m chest, anat. thorax; ~schwimmen n (-s/no pl.) breast-stroke.

Brüstung ['brystuŋ] f (-/-en) balustrade, parapet.

'Brustwarze anat. f nipple.

Brut [bruːt] f (-/-en) brooding, sitting, brood; hatch; fry, spawn (of fish); fig. F brood, (bad) lot.

brutal adj. [bru'tɑːl] brutal; 2ität [~ali'tɛːt] f (-/-en) brutality.

Brutapparat zo. [bru:t'?-] m incubator.

brüten ['bryːtən] v/i. (ge-, h) brood, sit (on egg); incubate; ~ über (dat.) brood over.

'Brutkasten ♀ m incubator.

brutto ⊕ adv. ['bruto] gross; 2gewicht n gross weight; 2registertonne f gross register ton; 2verdienst m gross earnings pl.

Bube ['buːbə] m (-n/-n) boy, lad; knave, rogue; cards: knave, jack; '~nstreich m, '~nstück n boyish prank, knavish trick.

Buch [buːx] n (-[e]s/-er) book; volume; '~binder m (book-)binder; '~drucker m printer; ~druckerei [~'rai] f printing; printing-office, Am. print shop.

Buche ♀ ['buːxə] f (-/-n) beech.

buchen ['buːxən] v/t. (ge-, h) book, reserve (passage, flight, etc.); book-keeping: book (item, sum), enter (transaction) in the books; et. als Erfolg ~ count s.th. as a success.

Bücher|abschluß ✝ ['byːçər-] m closing of or balancing of books; '~brett n bookshelf; ~ei [~'raı] f (-/-en) library; '~freund m book-lover, bibliophil(e); '~revisor ✝ m (-s/-en) auditor; accountant; '~schrank m bookcase; '~wurm m bookworm.

'**Buch|fink** orn. m chaffinch; '~halter m (-s/-) book-keeper; '~haltung f book-keeping; '~handel m book-trade; '~händler m book-seller; '~handlung f bookshop, Am. bookstore.

Büchse ['byksə] f (-/-n) box, case; tin, Am. can; rifle; '~nfleisch n tinned meat, Am. canned meat; '~nöffner ['byksənʔ-] m tin-opener, Am. can opener.

Buchstab|e ['buːxʃtaːbə] m (-n/-n) letter, character; typ. type; 2ieren [~ə'biːrən] v/t. (no -ge-, h) spell.

buchstäblich ['buːxʃteːpliç] 1. adj. literal; 2. adv. literally; word for word.

Bucht [buxt] f (-/-en) bay; bight; creek, inlet.

'**Buchung** f (-/-en) booking, reservation; book-keeping: entry.

Buckel ['bukəl] 1. m (-s/-) hump, hunch; humpback, hunchback; boss, stud, knob; 2. f (-/-n) boss, stud, knob.

'**buckelig** adj. s. bucklig.

bücken ['bykən] v/refl. (ge-, h) bend (down), stoop.

bucklig adj. ['bukliç] humpbacked, hunchbacked.

Bückling ['byklin] m (-s/-e) bloater, red herring; fig. bow.

Bude ['buːdə] f (-/-en) stall, booth; hut, cabin, Am. shack; F: place; den; (student's, etc.) digs pl.

Budget [by'dʒeː] n (-s/-s) budget.

Büfett [by'feː; by'fɛt] n (-[e]s/-s; -[e]s/-e) sideboard, buffet; buffet, bar, Am. a. counter; kaltes ~ buffet supper or lunch.

Büffel ['byfəl] m (-s/-) zo. buffalo; F fig. lout, blockhead.

Bug [buːk] m (-[e]s/-e) ⚓ bow; ⚔ nose; fold; (sharp) crease.

Bügel ['byːgəl] m (-s/-) bow (of spectacles, etc.); handle (of handbag, etc.); coat-hanger; stirrup; '~brett n ironing-board; '~eisen n (flat-)iron; '~falte f crease; 2n v/t. (ge-, h) iron (shirt, etc.), press (suit, skirt, etc.).

Bühne ['byːnə] f (-/-n) platform (a. ⊕); scaffold; thea. stage; fig.: die ~ the stage; die politische ~ the political scene; ~nanweisungen ['byː-

nən]ʔ-] f/pl. stage directions pl.; '~nbild n scene(ry); décor; stage design; '~ndichter m playwright, dramatist; '~nlaufbahn f stage career; '~nstück n stage play.

buk [buːk] pret. of backen.

Bull|auge ⚓ ['bul-] n porthole, bull's eye; '~dogge zo. f bulldog.

Bulle ['bulə] 1. zo. m (-n/-n) bull; 2. eccl. f (-/-n) bull.

Bummel F ['buməl] m (-s/-) stroll; spree, pub-crawl, sl. binge; ~ei [~'laı] f (-/-en) dawdling; negligence; 2n v/i. (ge-) 1. (sein) stroll, saunter; pub-crawl; 2. (h) dawdle (on way, at work), waste time; '~streik m go-slow (strike), Am. slowdown; '~zug m slow train, Am. way train.

Bummler ['bumlər] m (-s/-) saunterer, stroller; loafer, Am. F a. bum; dawdler.

Bund [bunt] 1. m (-[e]s/-e) pol. union, federation, confederacy; (waist-, neck-, wrist)band; 2. n (-[e]s/-e) bundle (of faggots); bundle, truss (of hay or straw); bunch (of radishes, etc.).

Bündel ['byndəl] n (-s/-) bundle, bunch; 2n v/t. (ge-, h) make into a bundle, bundle up.

Bundes|bahn ['bundəs-] f Federal Railway(s pl.); '~bank f Federal Bank; '~genosse m ally; '~gerichtshof m Federal Supreme Court; '~kanzler m Federal Chancellor; '~ministerium n Federal Ministry; '~post f Federal Postal Administration; '~präsident m President of the Federal Republic; '~rat m Bundesrat, Upper House of German Parliament; '~republik f Federal Republic; '~staat m federal state; confederation; '~tag m Bundestag, Lower House of German Parliament.

bündig adj. ['byndiç] style, speech: concise, to the point, terse.

Bündnis ['byntnis] n (-ses/-se) alliance; agreement.

Bunker ['bunkər] m (-s/-) ⚒, coal, fuel, etc.: bunker; bin; air-raid shelter; ⚔ bunker, pill-box; ⚓ (submarine) pen.

bunt adj. [bunt] (multi-)colo(u)red, colo(u)rful; motley; bird, flower, etc.: variegated; bright, gay; fig. mixed, motley; full of variety; '2druck m colo(u)r-print(ing); '2stift m colo(u)red pencil, crayon.

Bürde ['byrdə] f (-/-en) burden (a. fig.: für j-n to s.o.), load.

Burg [burk] f (-/-en) castle; fortress, citadel (a. fig.).

Bürge ⚖ ['byrgə] m (-n/-n) guarantor, security, surety, bailsman; sponsor; 2n v/i. (ge-, h): für j-n ~ stand guarantee or surety or security for s.o., Am. a. bond s.o.; stand bail for s.o.; vouch or answer for s.o.; sponsor s.o.; für et. ~ stand security for s.th. guarantee s.th.; vouch or answer for s.th.

Bürger ['byrgǝr] m (-s/-) citizen; townsman; ~krieg m civil war.

bürgerlich adj. civic, civil; ~e Küche plain cooking; Verlust der ~en Ehrenrechte loss of civil rights; Bürgerliches Gesetzbuch German Civil Code; '2e m (-n/-n) commoner.

Bürger|meister m mayor; in Germany: a. burgomaster; in Scotland: provost; ~recht n civic rights pl.; citizenship; '~schaft f (-/-en) citizens pl.; '~steig m pavement, Am. sidewalk; '~wehr f militia.

Bürgschaft ['byrkʃaft] f (-/-en) security; bail; guarantee.

Büro [by'ro:] n (-s/-s) office; ~angestellte m, f (-n/-n) clerk; ~arbeit f office-work; ~klammer f paper-clip; ~krat [~o'kra:t] m (-en/-en) bureaucrat; ~kratie [~o-kra'ti:] f (-/-n) bureaucracy; red tape; 2kratisch adj. [~o'kra:tiʃ] bureaucratic; ~stunden f/pl. office hours pl.; ~vorsteher m head or senior clerk.

Bursch [burʃ] m (-en/-en), ~e ['~ǝ] m (-n/-n) boy, lad, youth; F chap, Am. a. guy; ein übler ~ a bad lot, F a bad egg.

burschikos adj. [burʃi'ko:s] free and easy; esp. girl: boyish, unaffected, hearty.

Bürste ['byrstǝ] f (-/-n) brush; '2n v/t. (ge-, h) brush.

Busch [buʃ] m (-es/=e) bush, shrub.

Büschel ['byʃǝl] n (-s/-) bunch;

tuft, handful (of hair); wisp (of straw or hair).

'Busch|holz n brushwood, underwood; '2ig adj. hair, eyebrows, etc.: bushy, shaggy; covered with bushes or scrub, bushy; '~messer n bushknife; machete; '~neger m maroon; '~werk n bushes pl., shrubbery, Am. a. brush.

Busen ['bu:zǝn] m (-s/-) bosom, breast esp. of woman); fig. bosom, heart, geog. bay, gulf; '~freund m bosom friend.

Bussard orn. ['busart] m (-[e]s/-e) buzzard.

Buße ['bu:sǝ] f (-/-n) atonement (for sin), penance; repentance; satisfaction; fine; ~ tun do penance.

büßen ['by:sǝn] (ge-, h) 1. v/t. expiate, atone for (sin, crime); er mußte es mit s-m Leben ~ he paid for it with his life; das sollst du mir ~! you'll pay for that!; 2. v/i. atone, pay für for).

Büßer m (-s/-) penitent.

buß|fertig adj. penitent, repentant, contrite; 2fertigkeit f (-/no pl.) repentance, contrition; 2tag m day of repentance; Buß- und Bettag day of prayer and repentance.

Büste ['bystǝ] f (-/-n) bust; '~halter m (-s/-) brassière, F bra.

Büttenpapier ['bytǝn-] n handmade paper.

Butter ['butǝr] f (-/no pl.) butter; ~blume ♀ f buttercup; '~brot n (slice or piece of) bread and butter; F: für ein ~ for a song; '~brotpapier i greaseproof paper; '~dose f butter-dish; '~faß n butter-churn; '~milch f buttermilk; '2n v/i. (ge-, h) churn.

C

Café [ka'fe:] n (-s/-s) café, coffee-house.

Cape [ke:p] n (-s/-s) cape.

Cell|ist ♪ [tʃe'list] m (-en/-en) violoncellist, ')cellist; ~o ♪ ['~o] n (-s/-s, Celli) violoncello, ')cello.

Celsius ['tselzius]: 5 Grad ~ (abbr. 5° C) five degrees centigrade.

Chaiselongue [ʃɛz(ǝ)'lõ:] f (-/-n, -s) chaise longue, lounge, couch.

Champagner [ʃam'panjǝr] m (-s/-) champagne.

Champignon ♀ ['ʃampinjõ] m (-s/-s) champignon, (common) mushroom.

Chance ['ʃã:s(ǝ)] f (-/-n) chance; keine ~ haben not to stand a chance; sich eine ~ entgehen lassen miss a chance or an opportunity; die ~n sind gleich the chances or odds are even.

Chaos ['ka:ɔs] n (-/no pl.) chaos.

Charakter [ka'raktǝr] m (-s/-e) character; nature; ~bild n character (sketch); ~darsteller thea. m character actor; ~fehler m fault in s.o.'s character; 2fest adj. of firm or strong character; 2i'sieren v/t. (no -ge-, h) characterize, describe (als acc. as); ~i'sierung f (-/-en), ~istik [~'ristik] f (-/-en) characterization; 2istisch adj. [~'ristiʃ] characteristic or typical (für of); 2lich adj. of or concerning (the) character; 2los adj. characterless, without (strength of) character, spineless; ~rolle thea. f character role; ~zug m characteristic, feature, trait.

charm|ant adj. [ʃar'mant] charming, winning; 2e [ʃarm] m (-s/no pl.) charm, grace.

Chassis [ʃa'si:] n (-/-) mot., radio: frame, chassis.

Chauffeur [ʃɔ'føːr] m (-s/-e) chauffeur, driver.

Chaussee [ʃo'se:] f (-/-n) highway, (high) road.

Chauvinismus [ʃovi'nismus] m (-/ no pl.) jingoism; chauvinism.

Chef [ʃɛf] m (-s/-s) head, chief; ✝ principal, F boss; senior partner.

Chem|ie [çe'mi:] f (-/no pl.) chemistry, **~efaser** f chemical fib|re, Am. -er; **~ikalien** [~i'ka:ljən] f/pl. chemicals pl.; **~iker** ['çe:mikər] m (-s/-) (analytical) chemist; **2isch** adj. ['çe:miʃ] chemical.

Chiffr|e ['ʃifər] f (-/-n) number; cipher; in advertisement: box number; **2ieren** [ʃi'fri:rən] v/t. (no -ge-, h) cipher, code (message, etc.); write in code or cipher.

Chines|e [çi'ne:zə] m (-n/-n) Chinese, contp. Chinaman; **2isch** adj. Chinese.

Chinin 🜊 [çi'ni:n] n (-s/no pl.) quinine.

Chirurg [çi'rurk] m (-en/-en) surgeon; **~ie** [~'gi:] f (-/-n) surgery; **2isch** adj. [~giʃ] surgical.

Chlor 🜊 [klo:r] n (-s/no pl.) chlorine; **2en** v/t. (ge-, h) chlorinate (water); **~kalk** 🜊 m chloride of lime

Chloroform 🜊 [kloro'fɔrm] n (-/no pl.) chloroform; **2ieren** 🜊 [~'mi:rən] v/t. (no -ge-, h) chloroform.

Cholera 🜊 ['ko:ləra] f (-/no pl.) cholera.

cholerisch adj. [ko'le:riʃ] choleric, irascible.

Chor [ko:r] m 1. 🜊 a. n (-[e]s/-e, ᴗe) chancel, choir; (organ-)loft; 2. (-[e]s/ᴗe) in drama: chorus; singers: choir. chorus; piece of music: chorus; **~al** [ko'ra:l] m (-s/ᴗe) cho-

ral(e); hymn; **~gesang** m choral singing, chorus; **~sänger** m member of a choir; chorister.

Christ [krist] m (-en/-en) Christian; **~baum** m Christmas-tree; **~enheit** f (-/no pl.): die ~ Christendom; **~entum** n (-s/no pl.) Christianity; **~kind** n (-[e]s/no pl.) Christ-child, Infant Jesus; **2lich** adj. Christian.

Chrom [kro:m] n (-s/no pl.) metal: chromium; pigment: chrome.

chromatisch ♪, opt. adj. [kro'ma:tiʃ] chromatic.

Chronik ['kro:nik] f (-/-en) chronicle

chronisch adj. ['kro:niʃ] disease: chronic (a fig.).

Chronist [kro'nist] m (-en/-en) chronicler

chronologisch adj. [krono'lo:giʃ] chronological.

circa adv. ['tsirka] about, approximately.

Clique ['klikə] f (-/-n) clique, set, group, coterie; **~nwirtschaft** f (-/no pl. cliquism.

Conférencier [kõferã'sje:] m (-s/-s) compère, Am. master of ceremonies.

Couch [kautʃ] f (-/-es) couch.

Coupé [ku'pe:] n (-s/-s) mot. coupé; 🜊 🚂 compartment.

Couplet [ku'ple:] n (-s/-s) comic or music-hall song.

Coupon [ku'põ:] m (-s/-s) coupon; dividend-warrant; counterfoil.

Courtage ✝ [kur'ta:ʒə] f (-/-n) brokerage

Cousin [ku'zɛ̃] m (-s/-s), **~e** [~i:nə] f (-/-n) cousin.

Creme [krɛːm, kre:m] f (-/-s) cream (a. fig. only sg.).

Cut [kœt, kat] m (-s/-s), **~away** ['kœtəve, 'katəve:] m (-s/-s) cutaway (coat), morning coat.

D

da [da:] 1. adv. space: there; ~ wo where; hier und ~ here and there; ~ bin ich here I am; ~ haben wir's! there we are!; von ~ an from there; time: ~ erst only then, not till then; von ~ an from that time (on), since then; hier und ~ now and then or again; 2. cj. time: as, when, while; nun, ~ du es einmal gesagt hast now (that) you have mentioned it; causal: as, since, because; ~ ich krank war, konnte ich nicht kommen as or since I was ill I couldn't come.

dabei adv. [da'baɪ. when emphatic: 'da:baɪ] near (at hand), by; about, going (zu inf. to inf.), on the point

(of ger.); besides; nevertheless, yet, for all that; was ist schon ~? what does it matter?; lassen wir es ~ let's leave it at that; ~ bleiben stick to one's point, persist in it.

da'bei|bleiben v/i. (irr. bleiben, sep., -ge-, sein) stay with it or them; **~sein** v/i. (irr. sein, sep., -ge-, sein) be present or there; **~stehen** v/i. (irr. stehen, sep., -ge-, h) stand by or near

'dableiben v/i. (irr. bleiben, sep., -ge-, sein) stay, remain.

da capo adv. [da'ka:po] at opera, etc., encore.

Dach [dax] n (-[e]s/ᴗer) roof; fig. shelter; **~antenne** f roof aerial;

'**~decker** m (-s/-) roofer; tiler; slater; '**~fenster** n skylight; dormer window; '**~garten** m roofgarden; '**~gesellschaft** † f holding company; '**~kammer** f attic, garret; '**~pappe** f roofing felt; '**~rinne** f gutter, eaves pl.

dachte ['daxtə] pret. of denken.

Dachs zo. [daks] m (-es/-e) badger; '**~bau** m (-[e]s/-e) badger's earth.

Dach|sparren m rafter; '**~stube** f attic, garret; '**~stuhl** m roof framework; '**~ziegel** m (roofing) tile.

dadurch [da'durç, when emphatic: 'da:durç] 1. adv. for this reason, in this manner or way, thus; by it or that; 2. cj.: ~, daß owing to (the fact that), because; by ger.

dafür [da'fy:r, when emphatic: 'da:fy:r] for it or that; instead (of it); in return (for it), in exchange; ~ sein be in favo(u)r of it; ~ sein zu inf. be for ger., be in favo(u)r of ger.; er kann nichts ~ it is not his fault; ~ sorgen, daß see to it that.

Da'fürhalten n (-s/no pl.): nach meinem ~ in my opinion.

dagegen [da'ge:gən, when emphatic: 'da:ge:gən] 1. adv. against it or that; in comparison with it, compared to it; ~ sein be against it, be opposed to it; ich habe nichts ~ I have no objection (to it); 2. cj. on the other hand, however.

daheim adv. [da'haim] at home.

daher [da'he:r, when emphatic: 'da:he:r] 1. adv. from there; prefixed to verbs of motion: along; fig. from this, hence; ~ kam es, daß thus it happened that; 2. cj. therefore; that is (the reason) why.

dahin adv. [da'hin, when emphatic: 'da:hin] there, to that place; gone, past; prefixed to verbs of motion: along; j-n ~ bringen, daß induce s.o. to inf.; m-e Meinung geht ~, daß my opinion is that.

da'hingestellt adj.: es ~ sein lassen (,ob) leave it undecided (whether).

dahinter adv. [da'hintər, when emphatic: 'da:hintər] behind it or that, at the back of it; es steckt nichts ~ there is nothing in it.

da'hinterkommen v/i. (irr. kommen, sep., -ge-, sein) find out about it.

damal|ig adj. ['da:ma:liç] then, of that time; der ~e Besitzer the then owner; '**~s** adv. then, at that time.

Damast [da'mast] m (-es/-e) damask.

Dame ['da:mə] f (-/-n) lady; dancing, etc.: partner; cards, chess: queen; s. Damespiel; '**~brett** n draught-board, Am. checkerboard.

'**Damen|binde** f (woman's) sanitary towel, Am. sanitary napkin; '**~doppel** n tennis: women's doubles pl.; '**~einzel** n tennis: women's

singles pl.; '**~haft** adj. ladylike; '**~konfektion** f ladies' ready-made clothes pl., **~mannschaft** f sports: women's team; **~schneider** m ladies' tailor, dressmaker.

'**Damespiel** n (game of) draughts pl., ⟨m. (game of) checkers pl.

damit 1. adv. [da'mit, when emphatic: da:mit] with it or that, therewith, herewith; by it or that; was will er ~ sagen? what does he mean by it?; wie steht es ~? how about it?; ~ einverstanden sein agree to it; 2. cj. (in order) that, in order to inf., so (that); ~ nicht lest, (so as) to avoid that; for fear that (all with subjunctive).

dämlich F adj. ['dɛ:mliç] silly, asinine.

Damm [dam] m (-[e]s/-e) dam; dike, dyke; ⚭ embankment; embankment, Am. levee (of river); roadway; fig. barrier; '**~bruch** m bursting of a dam or dike.

dämmer|ig adj. ['dɛməriç] dusky; '**Qlicht** n twilight; '**~n** v/i. (ge-, h) dawn (a. fig.: F j-m on s.o.); grow dark or dusky; '**Qung** f (-/-en) twilight, dusk; in the morning: dawn.

Dämon ['dɛ:mɔn] m (-s/-en) demon; **Qisch** adj. [dɛ'mo:niʃ] demoniac(al).

Dampf [dampf] m (-[e]s/-e) steam; vapo(u)r; '**~bad** n vapo(u)r-bath; '**~boot** n steamboat; '**Qen** v/i. (ge-, h) steam.

dämpfen ['dɛmpfən] v/t. (ge-, h) deaden (pain, noise, force of blow); muffle (bell, drum, oar); damp (sound, oscillation, fig. enthusiasm); ♪ mute (stringed instrument); soften (colour, light); attenuate (wave); steam (cloth, food); stew (meat, fruit); fig. suppress, curb (emotion).

'**Dampfer** m (-s/-) steamer, steamship.

'**Dämpfer** m (-s/-) damper (a. ♪ of piano); ♪ mute (for violin, etc.).

'**Dampf|heizung** f steam-heating; '**~kessel** m (steam-)boiler; '**~maschine** f steam-engine; '**~schiff** n steamer, steamship; '**~walze** f steam-roller.

danach adv. [da'na:x, when emphatic: 'da:na:x] after it or that; afterwards; subsequently; accordingly; ich fragte ihn ~ I asked him about it; iro. er sieht ganz ~ aus he looks very much like it.

Däne ['dɛ:nə] m (-n/-n) Dane.

daneben adv. [da'ne:bən, when emphatic: 'da:ne:bən] next to it or that, beside it or that; besides, moreover; beside the mark.

da'nebengehen F v/i. (irr. gehen, sep., -ge-, sein) bullet, etc.: miss the target or mark; remark, etc.: miss one's effect, F misfire.

daniederliegen [da'ni:dər-] v/i.

(*irr. liegen, sep., -ge-. h*) be laid up (*an dat* with); *trade:* be depressed.

dänisch *adj.* ['dε:niʃ] Danish.

Dank [daŋk] 1. *m* (-[e]s/*no pl.*) thanks *pl.*, gratitude; reward; *j-m ~ sagen* thank s.o.; *Gott sei ~!* thank God!; 2. ♀ *prp.* (*dat.*) owing *or* thanks to; **'2bar** *adj.* thankful, grateful (*j-m* to s.o.; *für* for); profitable; **'~barkeit** *f* (-/*no pl.*) gratitude; **'2en** *v/i.* (ge-, h) thank (*j-m für et.* s.o. for s.th.); *danke* (*schön*)*l* thank you (very much)!; *danke* thank you; |*nein, danke* no, thank you; *nichts zu ~* don't mention it; **'2enswert** *adj.* *thing* one can be grateful for; *efforts, etc.:* kind; *task, etc.:* rewarding, worth-while; **'~gebet** *n* thanksgiving (prayer); **'~schreiben** *n* letter of thanks.

dann *adv.* [dan] then; *~ und wann* (every) now and then.

daran *adv.* [da'ran, *when emphatic:* 'da:ran] at (*or* by, in, on, to) it *or* that; *sich ~ festhalten* hold on tight to it; *~ festhalten* stick to it; *nahe ~ sein zu inf.* be on the point *or* verge of *ger.*

da'rangehen *v/i.* (*irr. gehen, sep., -ge-, sein*) set to work; set about *ger.*

darauf *adv.* [da'rauf, *when emphatic:* 'da:rauf] *space:* on (top of) it *or* that; *time:* thereupon, after it *or* that; *am Tage ~* the day after, the next *or* following day, *zwei Jahre ~* two years later; *~ kommt es an* that's what matters; *~hin* *adv.* [darauf'hin, *when emphatic:* 'da:raufhin] thereupon.

daraus *adv.* [da'raus, *when emphatic* 'da:raus] out of it *or* that, from it *or* that; *~ folgt* hence it follows, *was ist ~ geworden?* what has become of it?; *ich mache mir nichts ~* I don't care *or* mind (about it).

darben ['darbən] *v/i.* (ge-, h) suffer want, starve.

darbiet|en ['da:r-] *v/t.* (*irr. bieten, sep., -ge-, h*) offer, present; perform, **'2ung** *f* (-/-en) *thea., etc.:* performance.

'darbringen *v/t.* (*irr. bringen, sep., -ge-, h*) offer; make (*sacrifice*).

darein *adv.* [da'rain, *when emphatic* 'da:rain] into it *or* that, therein.

da'rein|finden *v/refl.* (*irr. finden, sep., -ge-, h*) put up with it; **~mischen** *v/refl.* (*sep., -ge-, h*) interfere (with it); **~reden** *v/i.* (*sep., -ge-, h*) interrupt; *fig.* interfere.

darin *adv.* [da'rin, *when emphatic:* 'da:rin] in it *or* that; therein; *es war nichts ~* there was nothing in it *or* them.

darleg|en ['da:r-] *v/t.* (*sep., -ge-, h*) lay open, expose, disclose; show; explain; demonstrate; point out; **'2ung** *f* (-/-en) exposition; explanation, statement.

Darlehen ['da:rle:ən] *n* (-s/-) loan.

Darm [darm] *m* (-[e]s/*~e*) gut, *anat.* intestine; (*sausage-*)skin; *Därme pl.* intestines *pl.*, bowels *pl.*

'darstell|en *v/t.* (*sep., -ge-, h*) represent, show, depict; delineate; describe, *actor:* interpret (*character, part*), represent (*character*); *graphic arts:* graph, plot (*curve, etc.*); **'2er** *thea.* *m* (-s/-) interpreter (*of a part*); actor; **'2ung** *f* representation, *thea.* performance.

'dartun *v/t.* (*irr. tun, sep., -ge-, h*) prove, demonstrate; set forth.

darüber *adv.* [da'ry:bər, *when emphatic* da:ry:bər] over it *or* that; across it; in the meantime; *~ werden Jahre vergehen* it will take years, *wir sind ~ hinweg* we got over it, *ein Buch ~ schreiben* write a book about it.

darum *adv.* [da'rum, *when emphatic:* 'da:rum] 1. *adv.* around it *or* that; *er kümmert sich nicht ~* he does not care, *es handelt sich ~ zu inf.* the point is to *inf.*; 2. *cj.* therefore, for that reason; *~ ist er nicht gekommen* that's (the reason) why he hasn't come.

darunter *adv.* [da'runtər, *when emphatic* da:runtər] under it *or* that; beneath it; among them; less; *zwei Jahre und ~* two years and under, *was verstehst du ~?* what do you understand by it?

das [das] *s* der.

dasein [da:-] 1. *v/i.* (*irr. sein, sep., -ge-, sein*) be there *or* present; exist. 2. **2** *n* (-s/*no pl.*) existence, life; being.

daß *cj.* [das] that; *~ nicht* less; *es sei denn,* unless; *ohne ~* without *ger.*, *nicht ~ ich wüßte* not that I know of.

'dastehen *v/i.* (*irr. stehen, sep., -ge-, h*) stand (there).

Daten [da:tən] *pl.* data *pl.* (*a.* ⊕), facts *pl.*, particulars *pl.*; **'~verarbeitung** *f* (-/-en) data processing.

datieren [da'ti:rən] *v/t. and v/i.* (*no -ge-, h*) date. [(case).]

Dativ *gr.* ['da:ti:f] *m* (-s/-e) dative'

Dattel [datəl] *f* (-/-n) date.

Datum [da:tum] *n* (-s/*Daten*) date.

Dauer ['dauər] *f* (-/*no pl.*) length, duration, continuance; *auf die ~* in the long run; *für die ~ von* for a period *or* term of; *von ~ sein* last well; **'2haft** *adj.* *peace, etc.:* lasting; *material, etc.:* durable; *colour, dye:* fast; **~karte** *f* season ticket, *Am.* commutation ticket; **'~lauf** *m* jog-trot; endurance-run; **'2n** *v/i.* (ge-, h) continue, last; take (*time*); **'~welle** *f* permanent wave, F perm.

Daumen ['daumən] m (-s/-) thumb; j-m den ~ halten keep one's fingers crossed (for s.o.); '~abdruck m (-[e]s/~e) thumb-print.

Daune ['daunə] f (-/-n): ~(n pl.) down; '~ndecke f eiderdown (quilt).

davon adv. [da'fɔn, when emphatic: 'da:fɔn] of it or that; thereof; from it or that; off, away; was habe ich ~? what do I get from it?; das kommt ~! it serves you right!

da'von|kommen v/i. (irr. kommen, sep., -ge-, sein) escape, get off; ~laufen v/i. (irr. laufen, sep., -ge-, sein) run away.

davor adv. [da'fo:r, when emphatic: 'da:fo:r] space: before it or that, in front of it or that; er fürchtet sich ~ he is afraid of it.

dazu adv. [da'tsu:, when emphatic: 'da:tsu:] to it or that; for it or that; for that purpose; in addition to that; noch ~ at that; ~ gehört Zeit it requires time.

da'zu|gehörig adj. belonging to it; ~kommen v/i. (irr. kommen, sep., -ge-, sein) appear (on the scene); find time.

dazwischen adv. [da'tsviʃən] between (them), in between; ~kommen v/i. (irr. kommen, sep., -ge-, sein) thing: intervene, happen.

Debatt|e [de'batə] f (-/-n) debate; 2ieren [~'ti:rən] (no -ge-, h) 1. v/t. discuss; debate; 2. v/i. debate (über acc. on).

Debüt [de'by:] n (-s/-s) first appearance, début.

dechiffrieren [deʃi'fri:rən] v/t. (no -ge-, h) decipher, decode.

Deck ⚓ [dek] n (-[e]s/-s, ⚓-e) deck; '~adresse f cover (address); '~bett n feather bed.

Decke ['dekə] f (-/-n) cover(ing); blanket; (travel[l]ing) rug; ceiling; '~l m (-s/-) lid, cover (of box or pot, etc.); lid (of piano) (book-)cover; '2n (-ge-, h) 1. v/t. cover; den Tisch ~ lay the table; 2. v/i. paint: cover.

'Deck|mantel m cloak, mask, disguise; '~name m assumed name, pseudonym; '~ung f (-/-en) cover; security.

defekt [de'fekt] 1. adj. defective, faulty; 2. 2 m (-[e]s/-e) defect, fault.

defin|ieren [defi'ni:rən] v/t. (no -ge-, h) define; 2ition [~i'tsjo:n] f (-/-en) definition; ~itiv adj. [~i'ti:f] definite; definitive.

Defizit ✝ ['de:fitsit] n (-s/-e) deficit, deficiency.

Degen ['de:gən] m (-s/-) sword; fencing: épée.

degradieren [degra'di:rən] v/t. (no -ge-, h) degrade, Am. a. demote.

dehn|bar adj. ['de:nba:r] extensible; elastic; metal: ductile; notion,

etc.: vague; '~en v/t. (ge-, h) extend; stretch; '2ung f (-/-en) extension; stretch(ing).

Deich [daiç] m (-[e]s/-e) dike, dyke.

Deichsel ['daiksəl] f (-/-n) pole, shaft.

dein poss. pron. [dain] your; der (die, das) ~e yours; ich bin ~ I am yours; die Deinen pl. your family; ~erseits adv. ['~ər'zaits] for or on your part; ~esgleichen pron. your like, your (own) kind, F the like(s) of you.

Dekan eccl. and univ. [de'ka:n] m (-s/-e) dean.

Deklam|ation [deklama'tsjo:n] f (-/-en) declamation; reciting; 2ieren [~'mi:rən] v/t. and v/i. (no -ge-, h) recite; declaim.

Deklin|ation gr. [deklina'tsjo:n] f (-/-en) declension; 2ieren gr. [~'ni:rən] v/t. (no -ge-, h) decline.

Dekor|ateur [dekora'tø:r] m (-s/-e) decorator; window-dresser; thea. scene-painter; ~ation [~'tsjo:n] f (-/-en) decoration; (window-)dressing; thea. scenery; 2ieren [~'ri:rən] v/t. (no -ge-, h) decorate; dress (window).

Dekret [de'kre:t] n (-[e]s/-e) decree.

delikat adj. [deli'ka:t] delicate (a. fig.); delicious; fig. ticklish; 2esse [~a'tesə] f (-/-n) delicacy; dainty.

Delphin zo. [del'fi:n] m (-s/-e) dolphin.

Dement|i [de'menti] n (-s/-s) (formal) denial; 2ieren [~'ti:rən] v/t. (no -ge-, h) deny, give a (formal) denial of.

'dem|entsprechend adv., '~gemäß adv. correspondingly, accordingly; '~nach adv. therefore, hence; accordingly; '~nächst adv. soon, shortly, before long.

demobili'sier|en (no -ge-, h) 1. v/t. demobilize; disarm; 2. v/i. disarm; 2ung f (-/-en) demobilization.

Demokrat [demo'kra:t] m (-en/-en) democrat; ~ie [~a'ti:] f (-/-n) democracy; 2isch adj. [~'kra:tiʃ] democratic.

demolieren [demo'li:rən] v/t. (no -ge-, h) demolish.

Demonstr|ation [demɔnstra'tsjo:n] f (-/-en) demonstration; 2ieren [~'stri:rən] v/t. and v/i. (no -ge-, h) demonstrate.

Demont|age [demɔn'ta:ʒə] f (-/-n) disassembly; dismantling; 2ieren [~'ti:rən] v/t. (no -ge-, h) disassemble; dismantle.

Demut ['de:mu:t] f (-/no pl.) humility, humbleness.

demütig adj. ['de:my:tiç] humble; ~en ['~gən] v/t. (ge-, h) humble, humiliate.

denk|bar ['deŋkba:r] 1. adj. conceivable; thinkable, imaginable; 2. adv.: ~ einfach most simple;

'~en (*irr.*, ge-, *h*) 1. *v/i.* think; ~ *an* (*acc.*) think of; remember; ~ *über* (*acc.*) think about; *j-m zu* ~ *geben* set s.o thinking; 2. *v/t.* think, *sich et.* ~ imagine *or* fancy s.th; *das habe ich mir gedacht* I thought as much; '2mal *n* monument memorial; '2schrift *f* memorandum; memoir; '2stein *m* memorial stone; '~würdig *adj.* memorable; '2zettel *fig. m* lesson.

denn [dɛn] 1. *cj.* for; *mehr* ~ *je* more than ever; 2. *adv.* then; *es sei* ~, *daß* unless, except; *wieso* ~? how so.

dennoch *cj.* ['dɛnɔx] yet, still, nevertheless; though.

Denunz|iant [denun'tsjant] *m* (-en/ -en) informer; ~iation [—tsjoːn] *f* (-/-en) denunciation; 2ieren [—'tsiː- rən] *v/t.* (no -ge-, *h*) inform against, denounce.

Depesche [de'pɛʃə] *f* (-/-n) dispatch, telegram, F wire; wireless.

deponieren [depo'niːrən] *v/t.* (no -ge-, *h* deposit.

Depositen ✝ [depo'ziːtən] *pl.* deposits *pl.*; ~bank *f* deposit bank.

der [deːr], **die** [diː], **das** [das] 1. *art.* the; 2. *dem. pron* that, this, he, she, it; *die* *pl.* these, those, they, them; 3. *rel. pron.* who, which, that. 'der'**artig** *adj.* such, of such a kind of this *or* that kind.

derb *adj.* [dɛrp] *cloth:* coarse, rough; *shoes, etc.:* stout, strong; *ore, etc.:* massive; *p.:* sturdy; rough; *food:* coarse, *p., manners:* rough, coarse; *way of speaking:* blunt, unrefined; *joke* crude; *humour* broad.

der'gleichen *adj.* such, of that kind, *used as a noun:* the like, such a thing, *und* ~ and the like; *nichts* ~ nothing of the kind.

der- ['deːrjeːnigə], 'die-, 'dasjenige *dem. pron.* he who, she who, that *which*, diejenigen *pl.* those who, those *which*.

der- [deːr'zɛlbə], **die-**, **das'selbe** *dem. pron.* the same; he, she, it.

Desert|eur [dezɛr'təːr] *m* (-s/-e) deserter; 2ieren [—'tiːrən] *v/i.* (no -ge-, sein) desert.

desgleichen [dɛs'glaɪçən] 1. *dem. pron* such a thing; 2. *cj.* likewise.

deshalb ['dɛshalp] 1. *cj.* for this *or* that reason; therefore; 2. *adv.:* *ich tat es nur* ~, *weil* I did it only because.

desinfizieren [dɛs'ʔinfi'tsiːrən] *v/t.* (no -ge-, *h*) disinfect.

Despot [dɛs'poːt] *m* (-en/-en) despot; 2isch *adj.* despotic.

destillieren [dɛsti'liːrən] *v/t.* (no -ge-, *h*) distil.

desto *adv.* ['dɛsto] (all, so much) the; ~ *besser* all the better; ~ *erstaunter* (all) the more astonished.

deswegen *cj. and adv.* ['dɛs've:gən] *s.* deshalb.

Detail [de'taɪ] *n* (-s/-s) detail.

Detektiv [detɛk'tiːf] *m* (-s/-e) detective.

deuten ['dɔytən] (ge-, *h*) 1. *v/t.* interpret, read (*stars, dream, etc.*); 2. *v/i.* *auf* (*acc.*) point at.

'deutlich *adj.* clear, distinct, plain.

deutsch *adj.* [dɔytʃ] German; '2e *m, f* -*n/-n*) German.

'**Deutung** *f* (-/-en) interpretation, explanation.

Devise [de'viːzə] *f* (-/-n) motto; ~n *pl.* ✝ foreign exchange *or* currency.

Dezember [de'tsɛmbər] *m* (-[s]/-) December.

dezent *adj.* [de'tsɛnt] *attire, etc.:* decent, modest; *literature, etc.:* decent, *behaviour:* decent, proper; *music, colour:* soft, restrained; *lighting, etc.* subdued.

Dezernat [detsɛr'naːt] *n* (-[e]s/-e) (administrative) department.

dezimal *adj.* [detsi'maːl] decimal; 2bruch *m* decimal fraction; 2stelle *f* decimal place.

dezi'mieren *v/t.* (no -ge-, *h*) decimate *fig. a* reduce (drastically).

Diadem [dia'deːm] *n* (-s/-e) diadem.

Diagnose [dia'gnoːzə] *f* (-/-n) diagnosis

diagonal *adj.* [diago'naːl] diagonal; 2e *f* (—-n) diagonal.

Dialekt [dia'lɛkt] *m* (-[e]s/-e) dialect, 2isch *adj.* dialectal.

Dialog [dia'loːk] *m* (-[e]s/-e) dialogue *Am. a.* dialog.

Diamant [dia'mant] *m* (-en/-en) diamond

Diät [di'ɛːt] *f* (-/no *pl.*) diet; *diät leben* live on a diet. yourself.)

dich *pers. pron.* [diç] you; ~ (selbst)

dicht [diçt] 1. *adj.* fog, rain, etc.: dense fog, forest, hair: thick; eyebrows bushy, thick; crowd: thick, dense, shoes, etc.: (water)tight; 2. *adv* ~ *an* (*dat.*) *or* *bei* close to.

'dichten¹ *v/t.* (ge-, *h*) make tight.

'**dicht|en**² (ge-, *h*) 1. *v/t.* compose, write, 2 *v/i.* compose *or* write poetry; 2er *m* (-s/-) poet; author; ~erisch *adj.* poetic(al); '2kunst *f* poetry

'**Dichtung**¹ ⊕ *f* (-/-en) seal(ing).

'**Dichtung**² *f* (-/-en) poetry; fiction; poem, poetic work.

dick *adj.* [dik] *wall, material, etc.:* thick, *book:* thick, bulky; *p.* fat, stout. 2e *f* (-/-n) thickness; bulkiness; *p* fatness, stoutness; ~fellig *adj. p.* thick-skinned; ~flüssig *adj.* thick, viscid, viscous, syrupy; 2icht ['—içt] *n* -[e]s/-e) thicket; '2kopf *m* stubborn person, F pig-headed person; ~leibig *adj.* ['~laɪbiç] corpulent; *fig.* bulky.

die [diː] *s.* der.

Dieb [diːp] *m* (-[e]s/-e) thief, *Am.* F *a.* crook; ~erei [diːbə'raɪ] *f* (-/-en) thieving, thievery.

Diebes|bande ['di:bəs-] *f* band of thieves; **~gut** *n* stolen goods *pl.*

dieb|isch *adj.* ['di:biʃ] thievish; *fig.* malicious; **2stahl** ['di:p-] *m* (-[e]s/ ~e) theft, *tÿ mst* larceny.

Diele ['di:lə] *f* (-/-n) board, plank; hall, *Am. a.* hallway.

dienen ['di:nən] *v/i.* (ge-, h) serve (*j-m s.o.*; *als* as; *zu* for; *dazu, zu inf.* to *inf.*); *womit kann ich ~?* what can I do for you?

'Diener *m* (-s/-) (man-, domestic) servant; *fig.* bow (*vor dat.* to); **'~in** *f* (-/-nen) (woman-)servant, maid; **'~schaft** *f* (-/-en) servants *pl.*

'dienlich *adj.* useful, convenient; expedient, suitable.

Dienst [di:nst] *m* (-es/-e) service; duty; employment; *~ haben* be on duty; *im (außer) ~* on (off) duty.

'Dienstag ['di:nsta:k] *m* (-[e]s/-e) Tuesday.

'Dienst|alter *n* seniority, length of service; **'2bar** *adj.* subject (*j-m* to *s.o.*); subservient (to); **'~bote** *m* domestic (servant), *Am.* help; **'2eifrig** *adj.* (over-)eager (in one's duty); **'2frei** *adj.* off duty; *~er Tag* day off; **'~herr** *m* master; employer; **'~leistung** *f* service; **'2lich** *adj.* official; **'~mädchen** *n* maid, *Am.* help; **'~mann** *m* (street-)porter; **'~stunden** *f/pl.* office hours *pl.*; **'2tauglich** *adj.* fit for service *or* duty; **2tuend** *adj.* ['~tu:ənt] on duty; **2untauglich** *adj.* unfit for service *or* duty; **'~weg** *m* official channels *pl.*; **'~wohnung** *f* official residence.

dies [di:s], **~er** ['di:zər], **~e** ['di:zə], **~es** ['di:zəs] *adj. and dem. pron.* this; *diese pl.* these; *dieser Tage* one of these days; *used as a noun:* this one; he, she, it; *diese pl.* they.

Dieselmotor ['di:zəl-] *m* Diesel engine.

dies|jährig *adj.* ['di:sjɛ:riç] of this year, this year's; **'~mal** *adv.* this time; for (this) once; **~seits** ['~zaɪts] **1.** *adv.* on this side; **2.** *prp.* (*gen.*) on this side of.

Dietrich ['di:triç] *m* (-s/-e) skeleton key; picklock.

Differenz [difə'rɛnts] *f* (-/-en) difference; disagreement.

Diktat [dik'ta:t] *n* (-[e]s/-e) dictation; *nach ~* at *or* from dictation; **~or** [~ɔr] *m* (-s/-en) dictator; **2orisch** *adj.* [~a'to:riʃ] dictatorial; **~ur** [~a'tu:r] *f* (-/-en) dictatorship.

dik'tieren *v/t. and v/i.* (no -ge-, h) dictate.

Dilettant [dile'tant] *m* (-en/-en) dilettante, dabbler; amateur.

Ding [diŋ] *n* (-[e]s/-e) thing; *guter ~e* in good spirits; *vor allen ~en* first of all, above all.

Diphtherie *ℱ* [difte'ri:] *f* (-/-n) diphtheria.

Diplom [di'plo:m] *n* (-[e]s/-e) diploma, certificate.

Diplomat [diplo'ma:t] *m* (-en/-en) diplomat; diplomatist; **~ie** [~a'ti:] *f* (-/no *pl.*) diplomacy; **2isch** *adj.* [~'ma:tiʃ] diplomatic (*a. fig.*).

dir *pers. pron.* [di:r] (to) you.

direkt [di'rɛkt] **1.** *adj.* direct; **~er Wagen** ⚙ through carriage, *Am.* through car; **2.** *adv.* direct(ly); **2ion** [~'tsjo:n] *f* (-/-en) direction; management; board of directors; **2or** [di'rɛktɔr] *m* (-s/-en) director; manager; headmaster, *Am.* principal; **2orin** [~'to:rin] *f* (-/-nen) headmistress, *Am.* principal; **2rice** [~'tri:s(ə)] *f* (-/-n) directress; manageress.

Dirig|ent *♪* [diri'gɛnt] *m* (-en/-en) conductor; **2ieren** *♪* [~'gi:rən] *v/t. and v/i.* (no -ge-, h) conduct.

Dirne ['dirnə] *f* (-/-n) prostitute.

Disharmon|ie *♪* [disharmo'ni:] *f* (-/-n) disharmony, dissonance (*both a. fig.*); **2isch** *adj.* [~'mo:niʃ] discordant, dissonant.

Diskont *✝* [dis'kɔnt] *m* (-s/-e) discount, **2ieren** [~'ti:rən] *v/t.* (no -ge-, h) discount.

diskret *adj.* [dis'kre:t] discreet; **2ion** [~e'tsjo:n] *f* (-/no *pl.*) discretion.

Disku|ssion [disku'sjo:n] *f* (-/-en) discussion, debate; **2'tieren** (no -ge-, h) **1.** *v/t.* discuss, debate; **2.** *v/i.*: *~ über* (*acc.*) have a discussion about, debate (up)on.

dispo|nieren [dispo'ni:rən] *v/i.* (no -ge-, h) make arrangements; plan ahead; dispose (*über acc.* of); **2sition** [~zi'tsjo:n] *f* (-/-en) disposition, arrangement; disposal.

Distanz [di'stants] *f* (-/-en) distance (*a. fig.*); **2ieren** [~'ti:rən] *v/refl.* (no -ge-, h): *sich ~ von* dis(as)sociate o.s. from.

Distel *♣* ['distəl] *f* (-/-n) thistle.

Distrikt [di'strikt] *m* (-[e]s/-e) district, region; area.

Disziplin [distsi'pli:n] *f* (-/-en) discipline.

Divid|ende *✝* [divi'dɛndə] *f* (-/-n) dividend; **2ieren** [~'di:rən] *v/t.* (no -ge-, h) divide (*durch* by).

Diwan ['di:va:n] *m* (-s/-e) divan.

doch [dɔx] **1.** *cj.* but, though; however, yet; **2.** *adv.* *in answer to negative question:* yes; *bist du noch nicht fertig? — ~!* aren't you ready yet? — yes, I am; *also ~!* I knew it!, I was right after all!; *komm ~ herein!* do come in!; *nicht ~!* don't!

Docht [dɔxt] *m* (-[e]s/-e) wick.

Dock *⚓* [dɔk] *n* (-[e]s/-s) dock.

Dogge *zo.* ['dɔgə] *f* (-/-n) Great Dane.

Dohle *orn.* ['do:lə] *f* (-/-n) (jack)daw.

Doktor ['dɔktɔr] *m* (-s/-en) doctor.

Dokument [doku'mɛnt] *n* (-[e]s/-e)

document; $\frac{z}{z}$ instrument; ~arfilm [~'ta:r-] *m* documentary (film).

Dolch [dɔlç] *m* (-[e]s/-e) dagger; poniard; ~stoß *m* dagger-thrust.

Dollar ['dɔlar] *m* (-s/-s) dollar.

dolmetsch|en ['dɔlmɛtʃən] *v/i. and v/t.* (ge-, h) interpret; '2er *m* (-s/-) interpreter.

Dom [do:m] *m* (-[e]s/-e) cathedral.

Domäne [do'mɛ:nə] *f* (-/-n) domain (*a. fig.*), province.

Domino ['do:mino] (-s/-s) 1. *m* domino; 2. *n* (game of) dominoes *pl.*

Donner ['dɔnər] *m* (-s/-) thunder; '2n *v/i.* (ge-, h) thunder (*a. fig.*); '~schlag *m* thunderclap (*a. fig.*); '~stag *m* Thursday, ~wetter *n* thunderstorm; F *fig* telling off; F: ~*l* my word!, by Jove!, F zum ~*l* F confound it!, *sl.* damn it.

Doppel ['dɔpəl] *n* (-s/-) duplicate; *tennis, etc.* double. Am doubles *pl.*; '~bett *n* double bed, ~decker *m* (-s/-) ⚔ biplane, double-decker (bus); '~ehe *f* bigamy, ~gänger ['~gɛŋər] *m* (-s/-) double, ~punkt *m* colon; ~sinn *m* double meaning, ambiguity; '2sinnig *adj* ambiguous, equivocal; ~stecker ⚡ *m* two-way adapter, '2t 1. *adj.* double; 2. *adv.* doubly, twice; ~zentner *m* quintal; 2züngig *adj.* ['~tsyŋiç] two-faced.

Dorf [dɔrf] *n* (-[e]s/=er) village; '~bewohner *m* villager

Dorn [dɔrn] *m* 1. (-[e]s/-en) thorn (*a. fig.*), prickle, spine; *j-m ein ~ im Auge sein* be a thorn in s.o.'s flesh or side; 2. (-[e]s/-e) tongue (*of buckle*); spike (*of running-shoe, etc.*); ⊕ punch; '2ig *adj.* thorny (*a. fig.*).

dörr|en ['dœrən] *v/t.* (ge-, h) dry; '2fleisch *n* dried meat; '2gemüse *n* dried vegetables *pl.*; '2obst *n* dried fruit.

Dorsch *ichth.* [dɔrʃ] *m* (-es/-e) cod(fish).

dort *adv.* [dɔrt] there; over there; '~her *adv.* from there; '~hin *adv.* there, to that place; '~ig *adj.* there, in *or* of that place.

Dose ['do:zə] *f* (-/-n) box; tin, Am. can; ~nöffner ['do:zən⁹-] *m* (-s/-) tin-opener, Am. can opener.

Dosis ['do:zis] *f* (-/Dosen) dose (*a. fig.*).

dotieren [do'ti:rən] *v/t.* (no -ge-, h) endow.

Dotter ['dɔtər] *m, n* (-s/-) yolk.

Dozent [do'tsɛnt] *m* (-en/-en) (university) lecturer, Am. assistant professor.

Drache ['draxə] *m* (-n/-n) dragon; '~n *m* (-s/-) kite; *fig.* termagant, shrew, battle-axe.

Dragoner [dra'go:nər] *m* (-s/-) ⚔ dragoon (*a. fig.*).

Draht [dra:t] *m* (-[e]s/=e) wire; '2en

v/t. (ge-, h) telegraph, wire; '~geflecht *n* (-[e]s/-e) wire netting; '~hindernis ⚔ *n* wire entanglement; '2ig *adj. p.* wiry; '2los *adj.* wireless; '~seilbahn *f* funicular (railway); '~stift *m* wire tack; '~zieher F *fig. m* (-s/-) wire-puller.

drall *adj.* [dral] *girl, legs, etc.*: plump; *woman*: buxom.

Drama ['dra:ma] *n* (-s/Dramen) drama; ~tiker [dra'ma:tikər] *m* (-s/-) dramatist; 2tisch *adj.* [dra'ma:tiʃ] dramatic.

dran F *adv.* [dran] *s. daran; er ist gut (übel)* ~ he's well (badly) off; *ich bin* ~ it's my turn.

Drang [draŋ] 1. *m* (-[e]s/⍩=e) pressure, rush; *fig.* urge; 2. 2 *pret. of dringen.*

drängen ['drɛŋən] (ge-, h) 1. *v/t.* press (*a. fig.*), push; *fig.* urge; *creditor.* dun; *sich* ~ crowd, throng; 2. *v/i.* press, be pressing *or* urgent.

drangsalieren [draŋza'li:rən] *v/t.* (no -ge-, h) harass, vex, plague.

drastisch *adj.* ['drastiʃ] drastic.

drauf *adv.* [drauf] *s. darauf; ~ und dran sein zu inf.* be on the point of *ger.*; 2gänger ['~gɛŋər] *m* (-s/-) dare-devil, Am. *sl. a.* go-getter.

draus *adv.* [draus] *s. daraus.*

draußen *adv.* ['drausən] outside; out of doors, abroad; out at sea.

drechs|eln ['drɛksəln] *v/t.* (ge-, h) turn (*wood, etc.*); 2ler ['~slər] *m* (-s/-) turner.

Dreck F [drɛk] *m* (-[e]s/*no pl.*) dirt; mud; filth (*a. fig.*); *fig.* trash; F ~ am Stecken haben not to have a clean slate; F *das geht dich einen* ~ an that's none of your business; '2ig *adj.* dirty; filthy.

Dreh|bank ['dre:-] *f* (-/=e) (turning-)lathe; '2bar *adj.* revolving, rotating; '~bleistift *m* propelling pencil; '~buch *n* scenario; script; '~bühne *thea. f* revolving stage; '2en *v/t.* (ge-, h) turn; shoot (*film*); roll (*cigarette*); *es dreht sich darum zu inf.* it is a matter of *ger.*; *sich* ~ turn; '~kreuz *n* turnstile; '~orgel *f* barrel-organ; '~punkt *m* ⊕ centre of rotation, Am. center of rotation, pivot (*a. fig.*); '~strom ⚡ *m* three-phase current; '~stuhl *m* swivel-chair; ~tür *f* revolving door; '~ung *f* (-/-en) turn; rotation.

drei *adj.* [drai] three; '~beinig *adj.* three-legged; '2eck *n* triangle; '~eckig *adj.* triangular; '~erlei *adj.* ['~ər'lai] of three kinds *or* sorts; '~fach *adj.* ['~fax] threefold, treble, triple; '~farbig *adj.* three-colo(u)r(ed); '2fuß *m* tripod; '~jährig *adj.* ['~jɛ:riç] three-year-old; triennial; '~mal *adv.* three times; ~malig *adj.* done *or* repeated three times; three; 2'meilenzone ♏, ♐ *f* three-mile limit; '2rad *n* tricycle;

'**~seitig** adj. three-sided; trilateral; '**~silbig** adj. trisyllabic.

dreißig adj. ['draɪsɪç] thirty; '**~ste** adj. thirtieth.

dreist adj. [draɪst] bold, audacious; cheeky, saucy, '**2igkeit** f (-/-en) boldness, audacity; cheek, sauciness.

'**drei|stimmig** ♪ adj. for or in three voices; '**~tägig** adj. ['~tɛ:gɪç] three-day; '**~teilig** adj. in three parts, tripartite; '**~zehn(te)** adj. thirteen(th).

dresch|en ['drɛʃən] v/t. and v/i. (irr., ge-, h) thresh; thrash; '**2flegel** m flail; '**2maschine** f threshing-machine.

dressieren [drɛ'si:rən] v/t. (no -ge-, h) train; break in (horse).

drillen ⚔ ✗ ['drɪlən] v/t. (ge-, h) drill.

Drillinge ['drɪlɪŋə] m/pl. triplets pl.

drin F adv. [drɪn] s darin.

dringen ['drɪŋən] v/i. (irr., ge-) 1. (sein): ~ durch force one's way through s.th., penetrate or pierce s.th.; ~ aus break forth from s.th.; noise: come from, in (acc.) penetrate into; in j-n urge or press s.o.; an die Öffentlichkeit . get abroad; 2. (h): ~ auf (acc.) insist on, press for; '**~d** adj. urgent, pressing; suspicion: strong

'**dringlich** adj. urgent pressing; '**2keit** f (-/no pl.) urgency.

drinnen adv. ['drɪnən] inside; indoors.

dritt|e adj. ['drɪtə] third; '**2el** n (-s/-) third; '**~ens** adv. thirdly; '**2letzt** adj. last but two.

Droge ['dro:gə] f (-/-n) drug; **~erie** [drogə'ri:] f (-/-n) chemist's (shop), Am drugstore, **~ist** [dro'gɪst] m (-en/-en) (retail pharmaceutical) chemist.

drohen ['dro:ən] v/i. (ge-, h) threaten, menace

Drohne ['dro:nə] f (-/-n) zo. drone (a. fig.).

dröhnen ['drø:nən] v/i. (ge-, h) voice, etc. resound, cannon, drum, etc.: roar, voice, cannon boom.

Drohung ['dro:uŋ] f (-/-en) threat, menace

drollig adj. ['drɔlɪç] amusing, quaint, comical.

Dromedar zo. [drome'da:r] n (-s/-e) dromedary

drosch [drɔʃ] pret. of dreschen.

Droschke ['drɔʃkə] f (-/-n) taxi (-cab), Am a cab, hack, '**~nkutscher** m cabman, driver, Am. a. hackman

Drossel orn ['drɔsəl] f (-/-n) thrush; '**2n** ⊕ v/t (ge-, h) throttle.

drüben adv ['dry:bən] over there, yonder

drüber ⋅ adv. ['dry:bər] s. darüber.

Druck [druk] m 1. (-[e]s/~e) pres-

sure; squeeze (of hand, etc.); 2. typ. (-[e]s/-e) print(ing); '**~bogen** m printed sheet; '**~buchstabe** m block letter.

drucken ['drukən] v/t. (ge-, h) print; ~ lassen have s.th. printed, publish.

drücken ['drykən] (ge-, h) 1. v/t. press; squeeze (hand, etc.); force down (prices, wages, etc.); lower (record); press, push (button, etc.). F sich ~ vor (dat.) or von shirk (work, etc.); 2. v/i. shoe: pinch.

'**Drucker** m (-s/-) printer.

'**Drücker** m (-s/-) door-handle; trigger

Drucker|ei [drukə'raɪ] f (-/-en) printing office, Am. printery, print shop; **~schwärze** f printer's or printing-ink.

'**Druck|fehler** m misprint; '**~fehlerverzeichnis** n errata pl.; '**2fertig** adj. ready for press, **~kammer** f pressurized cabin, **~knopf** m patent fastener, snap-fastener; ⚡ push-button; '**~luft** f compressed air; **~pumpe** f pressure pump; '**~sache(n** pl.) ⚖ f printed matter, Am. a second-class or third-class matter, **~schrift** f block letters; publication; '**~taste** f press key.

drum ⊦ adv., cj. [drum] s. darum.

drunten F adv. ['druntər] s. darunter.

Drüse anat. ['dry:zə] f (-/-n) gland.

du pers. pron. [du:] you.

Dublette [du'blɛtə] f (-/-n) duplicate.

ducken ['dukən] v/refl. (ge-, h) duck, crouch; fig. cringe (vor dat. to, before).

Dudelsack ♪ ['du:dəl-] m bagpipes pl.

Duell [du'ɛl] n (-s/-e) duel; **2ieren** [duɛ'li:rən] v/refl. (no -ge-, h) (fight a) duel (mit with)

Duett ♪ [du'ɛt] n (-[e]s/-e) duet.

Duft [duft] m (-[e]s/~e) scent, fragrance, perfume, '**2en** v/i. (ge-, h) smell, have a scent, be fragrant, '**2end** adj. fragrant; '**2ig** adj. dainty, fragrant.

duld|en ['duldən] (ge-, h) 1. v/t. bear, stand, endure, suffer (pain, grief, etc.); tolerate, put up with; 2. v/i. suffer; '**~sam** adj. [.t-] tolerant; '**2samkeit** f (-/no pl.) tolerance; **2ung** [.duŋ] f (-/~-en) toleration; sufferance

dumm adj. [dum] stupid, dull, Am. F dumb; '**2heit** f (-/-en) stupidity, dullness; stupid or foolish action; '**2kopf** m fool, blockhead, Am. sl. a. dumbbell.

dumpf adj. [dumpf] smell, air, etc.: musty, fusty, atmosphere stuffy, heavy; sound, sensation, et. dull; '**~ig** adj. cellar, etc. damp, musty.

Düne ['dy:nə] f (-/-n) dune, sand-hill.

Dung [duŋ] *m* (-[e]s/*no pl.*) dung, manure.

düngen ['dyŋən] *v/t.* (ge-, h) dung, manure; fertilize; **'2r** *m* (-s/-) *s.* *Dung*; fertilizer.

dunkel ['duŋkəl] **1.** *adj.* dark; dim; *fig.* obscure; *idea, etc.*: dim, faint, vague; **2.** **2** *n* (-s/*no pl.*) *s.* *Dunkelheit.*

Dünkel ['dyŋkəl] *m* (-s/*no pl.*) conceit, arrogance; **'2haft** *adj.* conceited, arrogant.

'Dunkel|heit *f* (-/*no pl.*) darkness (*a. fig.*); *fig.* obscurity; **'_kammer** *phot. f* dark-room; **'2n** *v/i.* (ge-, h) grow dark, darken.

dünn *adj.* [dyn] *paper, material, voice, etc.*: thin; *hair, population, etc.*: thin, sparse; *liquid*: thin, watery; *air*: rare(fied).

Dunst [dunst] *m* (-es/=e) vapo(u)r; haze, mist; fume.

dünsten ['dynstən] (ge-, h) **1.** *v/t.* steam (*fish, etc.*); stew (*fruit, etc.*); **2.** *v/i.* steam.

'dunstig *adj.* vaporous; hazy.

Duplikat [dupli'ka:t] *n* (-[e]s/-e) duplicate.

Dur ♪ [du:r] *n* (-/-) major.

durch [durç] **1.** *prp.* (*acc.*) through; **2.** *adv.*: die ganze Nacht ~ all night long; ~ und ~ through and through; thoroughly.

durcharbeiten ['durç゚-] (sep., -ge-, h) **1.** *v/t.* study thoroughly; *sich* ~ *durch* work through (*book, etc.*); **2.** *v/i.* work without a break.

durch'aus *adv.* through and through; thoroughly; by all means; absolutely, quite; ~ *nicht* not at all, by no means.

'durch'|biegen *v/t.* (*irr. biegen, sep.,* -ge-, h) bend; deflect (*beam, etc.*); *sich* ~ *beam, etc.*: deflect, sag; **'_blättern** *v/t.* (sep., -ge-, h) glance or skim through (*book, etc.*), *Am.* thumb through, skim; **'2blick** *m*: ~ *auf* (*acc.*) view through to, vista over, view of; **'_blicken** *v/i.* (sep., -ge-, h) look through; ~ *lassen, daß* give to understand that.

durch|'bluten *v/t.* (*no* -ge-, h) supply with blood; **_'bohren** *v/t.* (*no* -ge-, h) pierce; perforate; *mit Blicken* ~ look daggers at *s.o.*

'durch|braten *v/t.* (*irr. braten, sep.,* -ge-, h) roast thoroughly; **_brechen** (*irr. brechen*) **1.** ['_brɛçən] *v/i.* (sep., -ge-, sein) break through or apart; **2.** ['_] *v/t.* (sep., -ge-, h) break apart or in two; **3.** [_'brɛçən] *v/t.* (*no* -ge-, h) break through, breach; run (*blockade*); crash (*sound barrier*); **_brennen** *v/i.* (*irr. brennen, sep.,* -ge-, sein) ≠ *fuse*: blow; F *fig.* run away; *woman*: elope; **_bringen** *v/t.* (*irr. bringen, sep.,* -ge-, h) bring or get through; dissipate, squander (*money*); **2bruch** *m* ✕ break-

through; rupture; breach; *fig.* ultimate success.

durch'denken *v/t.* (*irr. denken, no* -ge-, h) think *s.th.* over thoroughly.

'durch|drängen *v/refl.* (sep., -ge-, h) force or push one's way through; **_dringen** (*irr. dringen*) **1.** ['_drɪŋən] *v/i.* (sep., -ge-, sein) penetrate (through); win acceptance (*mit* for) (*proposal*); **2.** [_'drɪŋən] *v/t.* (*no* -ge-, h) penetrate, pierce; *water, smell, etc.*: permeate.

durcheinander [durç゚ar'nandər] **1.** *adv.* in confusion or disorder; pell-mell; **2.** **2** *n* (-s/-) muddle, mess, confusion; **_bringen** *v/t.* (*irr. bringen, sep., -ge-, h*) confuse *s.o.*; *fig.* mix (*things*) up; **_werfen** *v/t.* (*irr. werfen, sep., -ge-, h*) throw into disorder; *fig.* mix up.

durchfahr|en (*irr. fahren*) **1.** ['_fa:-rən] *v/i.* (sep., -ge-, sein) go or pass or drive through; **2.** [_'fa:rən] *v/t.* (*no* -ge-, h) go or pass or travel or drive through; traverse (*tract of country, etc.*); **'2t** *f* passage (through); gate(way); ~ *verboten!* no thoroughfare!

'Durchfall *m* ✿ diarrh(o)ea; F *fig.* failure, *Am. a.* flunk; **2en** (*irr. fallen*) **1.** ['_falən] *v/i.* (sep., -ge-, sein) fall through; fail, F get ploughed (*in examination*); *thea.* be a failure, *sl.* be a flop; ~ *lassen* reject, F plough; **2.** [_'falən] *v/t.* (*no* -ge-, h) fall or drop through (*space*).

'durch|fechten *v/t.* (*irr. fechten, sep., -ge-, h*) fight or see *s.th.* through; **_finden** *v/refl.* (*irr. finden, sep., -ge-, h*) find one's way (through).

durch|'flechten *v/t.* (*irr. flechten, no* -ge-, h) interweave, intertwine; **_'forschen** *v/t.* (*no* -ge-, h) search through, investigate; explore (*region, etc.*).

'Durchfuhr ✝ *f* (-/-en) transit.

durchführ|bar *adj.* ['durçfy:rba:r] practicable, feasible, workable; **_en** *v/t.* (sep., -ge-, h) lead or take through or across; *fig.* carry out or through; realize; **'2ungsbestimmung** *f* (implementing) regulation.

'Durchgang *m* passage; ✝ transit; *sports*: run; **'_sverkehr** *m* through traffic; ✝ transit traffic; **'_szoll** *m* transit duty.

'durchgebraten *adj.* well done.

'durchgehen (*irr. gehen, sep., -ge-*) **1.** *v/i.* (sein) go or walk through; *bill*: pass, be carried; run away or off; abscond; *woman*: elope; *horse*: bolt; **2.** *v/t.* (sein) go through (*street, etc.*); **3.** *v/t.* (h, sein) go or look or read through (*work, book, etc.*); **'_d** **1.** *adj.* continuous; *_er Zug* through train; **2.** *adv.* generally; throughout.

durch'geistigt *adj.* spiritual.

'durch|greifen *v/i.* (*irr. greifen,*

sep., -ge-, *h*) put one's hand through; *fig.* take drastic measures *or* steps; '**~greifend** *adj.* drastic; radical, sweeping; '**~halten** (*irr.* halten, *sep.,* -ge-, *h*) **1.** *v/t.* keep up (*pace, etc.*); **2.** *v/i.* hold out; '**~hauen** *v/t.* (*irr.* hauen, *sep.,* -ge-, *h*) cut *or* chop through; *fig.* give *s.o.* a good hiding; '**~helfen** *v/i.* (*irr.* helfen, *sep.,* -ge-, *h*) help through (*a. fig.*); '**~kämpfen** *v/t.* (*sep.,* -ge-, *h*) fight out; *sich ~* fight one's way through; '**~kneten** *v/t* (*sep.,* -ge-, *h*) knead *or* work thoroughly; '**~kommen** *v/i.* (*irr.* kommen, *sep.,* -ge-, *sein*) come *or* get *or* pass through; *sick person:* pull through; *in examination:* pass.

durch'kreuzen *v/t.* (*no -ge-, h*) cross, foil, thwart (*plan, etc.*).

Durch|laß ['durçlas] *m* (*Durchlasses/Durchlässe*) passage; **2lassen** *v/t.* (*irr.* lassen, *sep.,* -ge-, *h*) let pass, allow to pass, let through; *Wasser ~* leak; '**2lässig** *adj.* pervious (to), permeable (to); leaky.

durchlaufen (*irr.* laufen) **1.** ['**~lau**fən] *v/i.* (*sep.,* -ge-, *sein*) run *or* pass through; **2.** ['**~**] *v/t.* (*sep.,* -ge-, *h*) wear out (*shoes, etc.*); **3.** [**~**'laufən] *v/t.* (*no -ge-, h*) pass through (*stages, departments, etc.*); *sports:* cover (*distance*).

durch'leben *v/t.* (*no -ge-, h*) go or live through.

'**durchlesen** *v/t.* (*irr.* lesen, *sep.,* -ge-, *h*) read through.

durchleuchten (*h*) **1.** ['**~**lɔyçtən] *v/i.* (*sep.,* -ge-) shine through; **2.** [**~**'lɔyçtən] *v/t.* (*no -ge-*) ${\mathcal{J}}$ X-ray; *fig.* investigate.

durchlöchern [durç'lœçərn] *v/t.* (*no -ge-, h*) perforate, make holes into *s.th.*

'**durchmachen** *v/t.* (*sep.,* -ge-, *h*) go through (*difficult times, etc.*); undergo (*suffering*).

'**Durchmarsch** *m* march(ing) through.

'**Durchmesser** *m* (*-s/-*) diameter.

durch'nässen *v/t.* (*no -ge-, h*) wet through, soak, drench.

'**durch|nehmen** *v/t.* (*irr.* nehmen, *sep.,* -ge-, *h*) go through *or* over (*subject*); '**~pausen** *v/t.* (*sep.,* -ge-, *h*) trace, calk (*design, etc.*).

durchqueren [durç'kve:rən] *v/t.* (*no -ge-, h*) cross, traverse.

'**durch|rechnen** *v/t.* (*sep.,* -ge-, *h*) (re)calculate, check; '**2reise** *f* journey *or* way through; '**~reisen** **1.** ['**~**raizən] *v/i.* (*sep.,* -ge-, *sein*) travel *or* pass through; **2.** [**~**'raizən] *v/t.* (*no -ge-, h*) travel over *or* through *or* across; '**2reisende** *m, f* (*-n/-n*) person travel(l)ing through. *Am. a.* transient; $\overline{\mathfrak{m}}$ through passenger; '**~reißen** (*irr.* reißen, *sep.,* -ge-) **1.** *v/i.* (*sein*) tear, break; **2.** *v/t.* (*h*) tear

asunder, tear in two; **~schauen** (*h*) **1.** ['**~**Jauən] *v/i. and v/t.* (*sep.,* -ge-) look through; **2.** *fig.* [**~**'Jauən] *v/t.* (*no -ge-*) see through.

'**durchscheinen** *v/i.* (*irr.* scheinen, *sep.,* -ge-, *h*) shine through; '**~d** *adj.* translucent; transparent.

'**durchscheuern** *v/t.* (*sep.,* -ge-, *h*) rub through, **~schießen** (*irr.* schießen) **1.** ['**~**ʃi:sən] *v/t.* (*sep.,* -ge-, *h*) shoot through; **2.** ['**~**] *v/i.* (*sep.,* -ge-, *sein*) *water:* shoot *or* race through; **3.** [**~**'ʃi:sən] *v/t.* (*no -ge-, h*) shoot *s.th.* through; *typ.:* space out (*lines*); interleave (*book*).

'**Durchschlag** *m* colander, strainer; carbon copy; **2en** (*irr.* schlagen) **1.** ['**~**ʃlagən] *v/t.* (*sep.,* -ge-, *h*) break *or* pass through; strain (*peas, etc.*); *sich ~* get along, make one's way. **2.** ['**~**] *v/i.* (*sep.,* -ge-, *h*) *typ.* come through; take *or* have effect; **3.** [**~**'ʃlagən] *v/t.* (*no -ge-, h*) pierce; *bullet* penetrate; '**2end** adj. effective, telling; **~papier** ['**~**k-] *n* copying paper.

durchschneiden *v/t.* (*irr.* schneiden, *h*) **1.** [**~**'ʃnaɪdən] (*sep.,* -ge-) cut through, **2.** ['**~**ʃnaɪdən] (*no -ge*) cut through, cut in two.

'**Durchschnitt** *m* cutting through; ⊕ section, profile; ✗ intersection; *fig.* average; *im ~* on an average; '**2lich** **1.** *adj.* average; normal; **2.** *adv* on an average; normally; '**~swert** *m* average value.

'**durch|sehen** (*irr.* sehen, *sep.,* -ge-, *h*) **1.** *v/i.* see *or* look through; **2.** *v/t.* see *or* look through *s.th.*; look *s.th.* over, go over *s.th.*; '**~seihen** *v/t.* (*sep.,* -ge-, *h*) filter, strain; **~setzen** *v/t.* (*h*) **1.** [**~**'zetsən] (*sep.,* -ge-) put (*plan, etc.*) through; force through; *seinen Kopf ~* have one's way; *sich ~ opinion, etc.:* gain acceptance; **2.** [**~**'zetsən] (*no -ge-*) intersperse.

'**Durchsicht** *f* looking through *or* over, examination; correction; *typ.* reading, **2ig** adj. glass, water, *etc.*: transparent; *fig.* clear, lucid; '**~igkeit** *f -/no pl.*) transparency; *fig.* clarity, lucidity.

'**durch|sickern** *v/i.* (*sep.,* -ge-, *sein*) seep *or* ooze through; *news, etc.*: leak out, **~sieben** *v/t.* (*h*) **1.** ['**~**zi:bən] (*sep.,* -ge-) sieve, sift; bolt (*flour*), **2.** [**~**'zi:bən] (*no -ge-*) riddle (*with bullets*); '**~sprechen** *v/t.* (*irr.* sprechen, *sep.,* -ge-, *h*) discuss, talk over; **~stechen** *v/t.* (*irr.* stechen, *h*) **1.** ['**~**ʃteçən] (*sep.,* -ge-) stick (*needle, etc.*) through *s.th.*; stick through *s.th.*; **2.** [**~**'ʃteçən] (*no -ge-*) pierce, cut through (*dike, etc.*); **~stecken** *v/t.* (*sep.,* -ge-, *h*) pass *or* stick through.

'**Durchstich** *m* cut(ting).

durch'stöbern *v/t.* (*no -ge-, h*) ransack (*room, pockets, etc.*); rummage through (*drawers, papers, etc.*).

'durchstreichen v/t. (*irr. streichen, sep., -ge-. h*) strike or cross out, cancel.

durch'streifen v/t. (*no -ge-, h*) roam or wander through or over or across.

durch'such|en v/t. (*no -ge-, h*) search (*a. ⚷*); ℒung f (*-/-en*) search.

durchtrieben adj. [durç'tri:bən] cunning, artful; ℒheit f (*-/no pl.*) cunning, artfulness.

durch'wachen v/t. (*no -ge-, h*) pass (*the night*) waking.

durch'wachsen adj. bacon: streaky.

durchwandern 1. ['ˌvandərn] v/i. (*sep., -ge-, sein*) walk or pass through; **2.** [ˌ'vandərn] v/t. (*no -ge-, h*) walk or pass through (*place, area, etc.*).

durch'weben v/t. (*no -ge-, h*) interweave; *fig. a.* intersperse.

durchweg adv. ['durçvɛk] throughout, without exception.

durch|weichen 1. ['ˌvaiçən] v/i. (*sep., -ge-, sein*) soak; **2.** [ˌ'vaiçən] v/t. (*no -ge-, h*) soak, drench; '**ˌwinden** v/refl. (*irr. winden, sep., -ge-, h*) worm or thread one's way through; **ˌwühlen** (*h*) **1.** *fig.* ['ˌvy:lən] v/refl. (*sep., -ge-*) work one's way through; **2.** [ˌ'vy:lən] v/t. (*no -ge-*) rummage; '**ˌzählen** v/t. (*sep., -ge-, h*) count; **ˌziehen** (*irr. ziehen*) **1.** ['ˌtsi:ən] v/i. (*sep., -ge-, sein*) pass or go or come or march through; **2.** ['ˌ] v/t. (*sep., -ge-, h*) pull (*thread, etc.*) through; **3.** [ˌ'tsi:ən] v/t. (*no -ge-, h*) go or travel through; *scent, etc.*: fill, pervade (*room, etc.*).

durch'zucken v/t. (*no -ge-, h*) flash through.

'Durchzug m passage through; draught, *Am.* draft.

'durchzwängen v/refl. (*sep., -ge-, h*) squeeze o.s. through.

dürfen ['dyrfən] (*irr., h*) **1.** v/i. (*ge-*): *ich darf* (*nicht*) I am (not) allowed to; **2.** v/aux. (*no -ge-*): *ich darf inf.* I am permitted or allowed to *inf.*; I may *inf.*; *du darfst nicht inf.* you must not *inf.*; *iro.*: *wenn ich bitten darf* if you please.

durfte ['durftə] pret. of dürfen.

dürftig adj. ['dyrftiç] poor; scanty.

dürr adj. [dyr] wood, leaves, etc.: dry; land: barren, arid; p. gaunt, lean, skinny; '**ℒe** f (*-/-n*) dryness; barrenness; leanness.

Durst [durst] m (*-es/no pl.*) thirst (*nach for*); ˌ haben be thirsty.

dürsten ['dyrstən] v/i. (*ge-, h*): ˌ *nach* thirst for.

'durstig adj. thirsty (*nach for*).

Dusche ['duʃə] f (*-/-n*) shower (*-bath*); 'ℒn v/refl. and v/i. (*ge-, h*) have a shower(-bath).

Düse ['dy:zə] f (*-/-n*) ⊕ nozzle; ✈ jet; **ˌnantrieb** ['ˌnˀ-] m jet propulsion; *mit* ˌ jet-propelled; '**ˌnflugzeug** n (jet(-propelled) aircraft, F jet; '**ˌnjäger** ✈ m jet fighter.

düster adj. ['dy:stər] dark, gloomy (*both a. fig.*); light: dim; *fig.*: sad; depressing; 'ℒheit f (*-/no pl.*), 'ℒkeit f (*-/no pl.*) gloom(iness).

Dutzend ['dutsənt] n (*-s/-e*) dozen; *ein* ˌ *Eier* a dozen eggs; ˌe *von Leuten* dozens of people; 'ℒweise adv. by the dozen, in dozens.

Dynam|ik [dy'na:mik] f (*-/no pl.*) dynamics; ℒisch adj. dynamic(al).

Dynamit [dyna'mi:t] n (*-s/no pl.*) dynamite.

Dynamo [dy'na:mo] m (*-s/-s*), **ˌmaschine** f dynamo, generator.

D-Zug ['de:tsu:k] m express train.

E

Ebbe ['ɛbə] f (*-/-n*) ebb(-tide); low tide; 'ℒn v/i. (*ge-, sein*) ebb.

eben ['e:bən] **1.** adj. even; plain, level; ⚸ plane; *zu* ˌer *Erde* on the ground floor, *Am.* on the first floor; **2.** adv. exactly; just; ˌ *erst* just now; 'ℒbild n image, likeness; **ˌbürtig** adj. ['ˌbyrtiç] of equal birth; *j-m* ˌ *sein* be a match for s.o., be s.o.'s equal; 'ˌda adv., 'ˌdaselbst adv. at the very (same) place, just there; *quoting books*: ibidem (*abbr.* ib., ibid.); ˌ'der, 'ˌdie, 'ˌdas dem. pron. = 'ˌderselbe, 'ˌdieselbe, 'ˌdasselbe dem. pron. the very (same); 'ˌ

des'wegen adv. for that very reason.

Ebene ['e:bənə] f (*-/-n*) plain; ⚸ plane; *fig.* level.

'eben|erdig adj. and adv. at street level; on the ground floor, *Am.* on the first floor; '**ˌfalls** adv. likewise; 'ℒholz n ebony; '**ˌmaß** n symmetry; harmony; regularity (*of features*); '**ˌmäßig** adj. symmetrical; harmonious; regular; '**ˌso** adv. just so; just as ...; likewise; '**ˌsosehr** adv., '**ˌsoviel** adv. just as much; '**ˌsowenig** adv. just as little or few (*pl.*), no more.

Eber *zo.* ['e:bər] *m* (-s/-) boar; '~esche ♦ *f* mountain-ash.

ebnen ['e:bnən] *v/t.* (ge-, *h*) level; *fig.* smooth.

Echo ['ɛço] *n* (-s/-s) echo.

echt *adj.* [ɛçt] genuine; true; pure; real; *colour*: fast; *document*: authentic; '2heit *f* (-/*no pl.*) genuineness; purity; reality; fastness; authenticity.

Eck [ɛk] *n* (-[e]s/-e) *s.* Ecke; '~ball *m sports*: corner-kick; '~e *f* (-/-n) corner; edge; '2ig *adj.* angular; *fig.* awkward; '~platz *m* corner-seat; '~stein *m* corner-stone; '~zahn *m* canine tooth.

edel *adj.* ['e:dəl] noble; *min.* precious; *organs of the body*: vital; '~denkend *adj.* noble-minded; '2mann *m* nobleman; '2mut *m* generosity; '~mütig *adj.* ['~my:tiç] noble-minded, generous; '2stein *m* precious stone; gem.

Edikt [e'dikt] *n* (-[e]s/-e) edict.

Efeu ♦ ['e:fɔy] *m* (-s/*no pl.*) ivy.

Effekt [ɛ'fɛkt] *m* (-[e]s/-e) effect; '~en *pl.* effects *pl.*; ✝: securities *pl.*; stocks *pl.*; '~enhandel *m* dealing in stocks; '~hascherei [~haʃə'raɪ] *f* (-/-en) claptrap; 2iv *adj.* [~'ti:v] effective; 2uieren [~u'i:rən] *v/t.* (*no* -ge-, *h*) effect; execute, *Am. a.* fill; 2voll *adj.* effective, striking.

egal *adj.* [e'ga:l] equal; F all the same.

Egge ['ɛgə] *f* (-/-n) harrow; '2n *v/t.* (ge-, *h*) harrow.

Egois|mus [ego'ɪsmus] *m* (-/Egoismen) ego(t)ism; '~t *m* (-en/-en) ego(t)ist; 2tisch *adj.* selfish, ego(t)istic(al).

ehe[1] *cj.* ['e:ə] before.

Ehe[2] [~]*f*(-/-n) marriage; matrimony; '~anbahnung *f* (-/-en) matrimonial agency; '~brecher *m* (-s/-) adulterer; '~brecherin *f* (-/-nen) adulteress; '2brecherisch *adj.* adulterous; '~bruch *m* adultery; '~frau *f* wife; '~gatte *m*, '~gattin *f* spouse; '~leute *pl.* married people *pl.*; '2lich *adj.* conjugal; *child*: legitimate; '~losigkeit *f* (-/*no pl.*) celibacy; single life.

ehemal|ig *adj.* ['e:əma:liç] former, ex-...; old; '~s *adv.* formerly.

'Ehe|mann *m* husband; '~paar *n* married couple.

'eher *adv.* sooner; rather; more likely; *je* ~, *desto besser* the sooner the better.

'Ehering *m* wedding ring.

ehern *adj.* ['e:ərn] brazen, of brass.

'Ehe|scheidung *f* divorce; '~schließung *f* (-/-en) (contraction of) marriage; '~stand *m* (-[e]s/*no pl.*) married state, matrimony; '~stifter *m*, '~stifterin *f* (-/-nen) matchmaker; '~vermittlung *f s.* Eheanbahnung; '~versprechen *n* promise of marriage; '~vertrag *m* marriage contract.

Ehrabschneider ['e:r'apʃnaɪdər] *m* (-s/-) slanderer.

'ehrbar *adj.* hono(u)rable, respectable; modest; '2keit *f* (-/*no pl.*) respectability; modesty.

Ehre ['e:rə] *f* (-/-n) hono(u)r; *zu* ~n (*gen.*) in hono(u)r of; '2n *v/t.* (ge-, *h*) hono(u)r; esteem.

'ehren|amtlich *adj.* honorary; '2bürger *m* honorary citizen; '2doktor *m* honorary doctor; '2erklärung *f* (full) apology; '2gast *m* guest of hono(u)r; '2gericht *n* court of hono(u)r; '~haft *adj.* hono(u)rable; '2kodex *m* code of hono(u)r; '2legion ['~legio:n] *f* (-/*no pl.*) Legion of Hono(u)r; '2mann *m* man of hono(u)r; '2mitglied *n* honorary member; '2platz *m* place of hono(u)r; '2recht *n*: *bürgerliche* ~e *pl* civil rights *pl.*; '2rettung *f* rehabilitation; '~rührig *adj.* defamatory, '2sache *f* affair of hono(u)r; point of hono(u)r; '~voll *adj.* hono(u)rable; '~wert *adj.* hono(u)rable; '2wort *n* (-[e]s/-e) word of hono(u)r.

ehr|erbietig *adj.* ['e:r'ɛrbi:tiç] respectful; '2erbietung *f* (-/-en) reverence; '2furcht *f* (-/*no pl.*) respect; awe; '~furchtgebietend *adj.* awe-inspiring, awesome; '~fürchtig *adj.* ['~fyrçtiç] respectful; '2gefühl *n* (-[e]s/*no pl.*) sense of hono(u)r; '2geiz *m* ambition; '~geizig *adj.* ambitious.

'ehrlich *adj.* honest; *commerce, game*: fair; *opinion*: candid; ~ *währt am längsten* honesty is the best policy; '2keit *f* (-/*no pl.*) honesty; fairness.

'ehrlos *adj.* dishono(u)rable, infamous; '2igkeit *f* (-/-en) dishonesty, infamy

'ehr|sam *adj. s.* ehrbar; '2ung *f* (-/-en) hono(u)r (conferred on *s.o.*); '~vergessen *adj.* dishono(u)rable, infamous; '2verlust ⚖ *m* (-es/*no pl.*) loss of civil rights; '~würdig *adj.* venerable, reverend.

ei[1] *int.* [aɪ] ah!, indeed!

Ei[2] [~] *n* (-[e]s/-er) egg; *physiol.* ovum.

Eibe ♦ ['aɪbə] *f* (-/-n) yew(-tree).

Eiche ♦ ['aɪçə] *f* (-/-n) oak(-tree); '~l ['~l] *f* (-/-n) ♦ acorn; *cards*: club; '2lhäher *orn.* ['~hɛ:ər] *m* (-s/-) jay.

eichen[1] ['aɪçən] *v/t.* (ge-, *h*) ga(u)ge.

eichen[2] *adj.* [~] oaken, of oak.

Eich|hörnchen *zo.* ['aɪçhœrnçən] *n* (-s/-) squirrel; '~maß *n* standard.

Eid [aɪt] *m* (-es/-e) oath; '2brüchig *adj.* *werden* break one's oath.

Eidechse *zo.* ['aɪdɛksə] *f* (-/-n) lizard.

eidesstattlich ⚖ *adj.* ['aɪdəs-] in lieu of (an) oath; ~e *Erklärung* statutory declaration.

'eidlich 1. *adj.* sworn; **2.** *adv.* on oath.

'Eidotter *m, n* yolk.

'Eier|kuchen *m* omelet(te), pancake; **_schale** *f* egg-shell; **'_stock** *anat. m* ovary; **'_uhr** *f* egg-timer.

Eifer ['aıfər] *m* (-s/no pl.) zeal; eagerness; ardo(u)r; **'_er** *m* (-s/-) zealot; **'_sucht** *f* (-/no pl.) jealousy; **'2süchtig** *adj.* jealous (auf acc. of).

eifrig *adj.* ['aıfrıç] zealous, eager; ardent.

eigen *adj.* ['aıgən] own; particular; strange, odd; *in compounds:* ...-owned; peculiar (*dat.* to); **'2art** *f* peculiarity; **'_artig** *adj.* peculiar; singular; **2brötler** ['_brø:tlər] *m* (-s/-) odd *or* eccentric person, crank; **'2gewicht** *n* dead weight; **_händig** *adj. and adv.* [_hendıç] with one's own hands; **'2heim** *n* house of one's own; homestead; **'2heit** *f* (-/-en) peculiarity; oddity; *of language:* idiom; **'2liebe** *f* self-love; **'2lob** *n* self-praise; **'_mächtig** *adj.* arbitrary; **'2name** *m* proper name; **_nützig** *adj.* ['_nytsıç] self-interested, selfish; **'_s** *adv.* expressly, specially; on purpose.

Eigenschaft *f* (-/-en) quality (*of s.o.*); property (*of s.th.*); *in s-r _ als* in his capacity as; **'_swort** *gr. n* (-[e]s/_er) adjective.

Eigensinn *m* (-[e]s/no pl.) obstinacy; **'2ig** *adj.* wil(l)ful, obstinate.

eigentlich 1. *adj.* proper; actual; true, real; **2.** *adv.* properly (speaking).

Eigentum *n* (-s/_er) property.

Eigentüm|er ['aıgənty:mər] *m* (-s/-) owner, proprietor; **'2lich** *adj.* peculiar; odd; **'_lichkeit** *f* (-/-en) peculiarity.

'Eigentums|recht *n* ownership; copyright; **'_wohnung** *f* freehold flat.

eigenwillig *adj.* self-willed; *fig.* individual.

eign|en ['aıgnən] *v/refl.* (ge-, h): *sich _ für* be suited for; **'2ung** *f* (-/-en) aptitude, suitability.

'Eil|bote ['_] *m* express messenger; *durch _n* by special delivery; **'_brief** ['_] *m* express letter, *Am.* special delivery letter.

Eile ['aılə] *f* (-/no pl.) haste, speed; hurry; **'2n** *v/i.* (ge-, sein) hasten, make haste; hurry; *letter, affair:* be urgent; **2nds** *adv.* ['_ts] quickly, speedily.

'Eil|fracht *f,* **'_gut** *n* express goods *pl., Am.* fast freight; **'2ig** *adj.* hasty, speedy; urgent; *es _ haben* be in a hurry.

Eimer ['aımər] *m* (-s/-) bucket, pail.

ein [aın] **1.** *adj.* one; **2.** *indef. art.* a, an.

einander *adv.* [aı'nandər] one another; each other.

ein|arbeiten ['aın⁹-] *v/t.* (sep., -ge-, h): *j-n _ in* (acc.) make s.o. acquainted with; **_armig** *adj.* ['aın⁹-] one-armed; **_äschern** ['aın⁹εʃərn] *v/t.* (sep., -ge-, h) burn to ashes; cremate (*dead body*); **'2äscherung** *f* (-/-en) cremation; **_atmen** ['aın⁹-] *v/t.* (sep., -ge-, h) breathe, inhale; **_äugig** *adj.* ['aın⁹ɔygıç] one-eyed.

Einbahnstraße *f* one-way street.

einbalsamieren *v/t.* (sep., no -ge-, h) embalm.

Einband *m* (-[e]s/_e) binding; cover.

ein|bauen *v/t.* (sep., -ge-, h) build in; install (*engine, etc.*); **'_behalten** *v/t.* (irr. halten, sep., no -ge-, h) detain; **_berufen** *v/t.* (irr. rufen, sep., no -ge-, h) convene; ⚔ call up, *Am.* induct.

einbett|en *v/t.* (sep., -ge-, h) embed; **2zimmer** *n* single(-bedded) room.

einbild|en *v/refl.* (sep., -ge-, h) fancy, imagine; **'2ung** *f* imagination, fancy; conceit.

einbinden *v/t.* (irr. binden, sep., -ge-, h) bind (*books*).

Einblick *m* insight (*in acc.* into).

einbrechen (irr. brechen, sep., -ge-) **1.** *v/t.* (h) break open; **2.** *v/i.* (sein) break in; *of night, etc.*: set in; *_ in* (acc.) break into (*house*).

'Einbrecher *m* at night: burglar; *by day* housebreaker.

Einbruch *m* ⚔ invasion; housebreaking, burglary; *bei _ der Nacht* at nightfall; **'_(s)diebstahl** *m* house-breaking, burglary.

einbürger|n ['aınbyrgərn] *v/t.* (sep., -ge-, h) naturalize; **'2ung** *f* (-/-en) naturalization.

'Ein|buße *f* loss; **'2büßen** *v/t.* (sep., -ge-, h) lose, forfeit.

ein|dämmen ['aındemən] *v/t.* (sep., -ge-, h) dam (up); embank (*river*); *fig.* check; **_deutig** *adj.* unequivocal; clear, plain.

'eindring|en *v/i.* (irr. dringen, sep., -ge-, sein) enter; penetrate; intrude; *_ in* (acc.) penetrate (into); force one's way into; invade (*country*); **'_lich** *adj.* urgent; **2ling** ['_lıŋ] *m* (-s/-e) intruder; invader.

'Eindruck *m* (-[e]s/_e) impression.

'ein|drücken *v/t.* (sep., -ge-, h) press in; crush (in) (*hat*); break (*pane*); **'_drucksvoll** *adj.* impressive; **_engen** ['aın⁹-] *v/t.* (sep., -ge-, h) narrow; *fig.* limit.

einer¹ ['aınər], **'_e,** **'_(e)s** *indef. pron.* one.

Einer² ['_] *m* (-s/-) & unit, digit; *rowing:* single sculler, skiff.

einerlei ['aınər'laı] **1.** *adj.* of the same kind; immaterial; *es ist mir _* it is all the same to me; **2.** **2** *n* (-s/no pl.) sameness; monotony; humdrum (*of one's existence*).

einerseits *adv.* [ˈaɪnərˈzaɪts] on the one hand.

einfach *adj.* [ˈaɪnfax] simple; single; plain; *meal*: frugal; *ticket*: single, *Am.* one-way; '**²heit** *f* (-/*no pl.*) simplicity.

einfädeln [ˈaɪnfɛːdəln] *v/t.* (*sep.*, -ge-, *h*) thread; *fig.* start, set on foot; contrive.

'**Einfahrt** *f* entrance, entry.

'**Einfall** *m* ⚔ invasion; idea, inspiration; '**²en** *v/i.* (*irr. fallen*, *sep.*, -ge-, *sein*) fall in, collapse; break in (*on a conversation*), interrupt, cut short; chime in; ♩ join in; invade; *j-m* ~ occur to s.o.

Ein|falt [ˈaɪnfalt] *f* (-/*no pl.*) simplicity, silliness; **²fältig** *adj.* [ˈ~fɛltɪç] simple; silly; '**~faltspinsel** *m* simpleton, *Am.* F sucker.

'**ein|farbig** *adj.* one-colo(u)red, uni-colo(u)red; plain; '**~fassen** *v/t.* (*sep.*, -ge-, *h*) border; set (*precious stone*); '**²fassung** *f* border; setting; '**~fetten** *v/t.* (*sep.*, -ge-, *h*) grease; oil; '**~finden** *v/refl.* (*irr. finden*, *sep.*, -ge-, *h*) appear; arrive; '**~flechten** *fig. v/t.* (*irr. flechten*, *sep.*, -ge-, *h*) put in, insert; '**~fließen** *v/i.* (*irr. fließen*, *sep.*, -ge-, *h*) flow in; ~ in (*acc.*) flow into; ~ *lassen* mention in passing; '**~flößen** *v/t.* (*sep.*, -ge-, *h*) infuse.

'**Einfluß** *m* influx; *fig.* influence; '**²reich** *adj.* influential.

ein|förmig *adj.* [ˈaɪnfœrmɪç] uniform; monotonous; **~frieden** [ˈ~friːdən] *v/t.* (*sep.*, -ge-, *h*) fence, enclose; '**²friedung** *f* (-/-en) enclosure; '**~frieren** (*irr. frieren*, *sep.*, -ge-) 1. *v/i.* (*sein*) freeze (in); 2. *v/t.* (*h*) freeze (*food*); '**~fügen** *v/t.* (*sep.*, -ge-, *h*) put in; *fig.* insert; *sich* ~ fit in.

Einfuhr ✝ [ˈaɪnfuːr] *f* (-/-en) import(ation); '**~bestimmungen** *f/pl.* import regulations *pl.*

'**einführen** *v/t.* (*sep.*, -ge-, *h*) ✝ import; introduce (*s.o., custom*); insert; initiate; install (*s.o. in an office*).

'**Einfuhrwaren** ✝ *f/pl.* imports *pl.*

'**Eingabe** *f* petition; application.

'**Eingang** *m* entrance; entry; arrival (*of goods*); *mail* ~ on receipt; '**~sbuch** ✝ *n* book of entries.

'**eingeben** *v/t.* (*irr. geben*, *sep.*, -ge-, *h*) give, administer (*medicine*) (*dat.* to); prompt, suggest (to).

'**einge|bildet** *adj.* imaginary; conceited (*auf acc.* of); '**~boren** *adj.* native; '**²borene** *m*, *f* (-*n*/-*n*) native.

Eingebung [ˈaɪngəbuŋ] *f* (-/-en) suggestion; inspiration.

einge|denk *adj.* [ˈaɪngədɛŋk] mindful (*gen.* of); '**~fallen** *adj. eyes*, *cheeks*: sunken, hollow; emaciated; **~fleischt** *fig. adj.* [ˈ~gəflaɪʃt] inveterate; confirmed; **~er** *Junggeselle* confirmed bachelor.

'**eingehen** (*irr. gehen*, *sep.*, -ge-) 1. *v/i.* (*sein*) *mail*, *goods*: come in, arrive; ♣, *animal*: die; cease (to exist); *material*: shrink; ~ *auf* (*acc.*) agree to; enter into; 2. *v/t.* (*h*, *sein*) enter into (*relationship*); contract (*marriage*); *ein Risiko* ~ run a risk, *esp. Am.* take a chance; *ein Vergleich* ~ come to terms; *Verbindlichkeiten* ~ incur liabilities; *e-e Wette* ~ make a bet; *eingegangene Gelder* *n/pl.* receipts *pl.*; '**~d** *adj.* detailed; thorough; *examination*: close.

Eingemachte [ˈaɪngəmaxtə] *n* (-*n*/ *no pl.*) preserves *pl.*; pickles *pl.*

'**eingemeinden** *v/t.* (*sep.*, *no* -ge-, *h*) incorporate (*dat.* into).

'**einge|nommen** *adj.* partial (*für* to); prejudiced (*gegen* against); *von sich* ~ conceited; '**²sandt** *n* (-/-s) letter to the editor; **~schnappt** F *fig. adj.* [ˈ~gəʃnapt] offended, touchy; **~sessen** *adj.* long-established; '**²ständnis** *n* confession, avowal; '**~stehen** *v/t.* (*irr. stehen*, *sep.*, *no* -ge-, *h*) confess, avow.

Eingeweide *anat.* [ˈaɪngəvaɪdə] *pl.* viscera *pl.*; intestines *pl.*; bowels *pl.*; *esp of animals*: entrails *pl.*

'**einge|wöhnen** *v/refl.* (*sep.*, *no* -ge-, *h*) accustom o.s. (*in acc.* to); acclimatize o.s., *Am.* acclimate o.s. (to); get used (to).

eingewurzelt *adj.* [ˈ~gəvurtsəlt] deep-rooted, inveterate.

'**eingießen** *v/t.* (*irr. gießen*, *sep.*, -ge-, *h*) pour in *or* out.

eingleisig *adj.* [ˈaɪnglaɪzɪç] single-track.

'**ein|graben** *v/t.* (*irr. graben*, *sep.*, -ge-, *h*) dig in; bury; engrave; *sich* ~ ⚔ dig o.s. in, entrench o.s.; *fig.* engrave itself (*on one's memory*); '**~gravieren** *v/t.* (*sep.*, *no* -ge-, *h*) engrave.

'**eingreifen** 1. *v/i.* (*irr. greifen*, *sep.*, -ge-, *h*) intervene; ~ *in* (*acc.*) interfere with; encroach on (*s.o.'s rights*); *in die Debatte* ~ join in the debate; 2. ⚙ *n* (-*s*/*no pl.*) intervention.

'**Eingriff** *m fig.* encroachment; 💉 operation.

'**einhaken** *v/t.* (*sep.*, -ge-, *h*) fasten; *sich bei j-m* ~ take s.o.'s arm.

'**Einhalt** *m* (-[*e*]*s*/*no pl.*): ~ *gebieten* (*dat.*) put a stop to; '**²en** *fig.* (*irr. halten*, *sep.*, -ge-, *h*) 1. *v/t.* observe, keep; 2. *v/i.* stop, leave off (*zu tun* doing).

'**ein|hängen** [ˈaɪn·hɛŋən̩] *v/t.* (*sep.*, -ge-, *h*) 1. *v/t.* hang in; hang up, replace (*receiver*); *sich bei j-m* ~ take s.o.'s arm, link arms with s.o.; 2. *teleph. v/i.* hang up; '**~heften** *v/t.* (*sep.*, -ge-, *h*) sew *or* stitch in.

'**einheimisch** *adj.* native (*in dat.*

to), indigenous (to) (*a.* ♀); ♣ endemic; *product*: home-grown; '♀e *m, f* (-n/-n) native; resident.

'**Einheit** *f* (-/-en) unity; oneness; ♈, *phys.*, ✂ unit; '♀**lich** *adj.* uniform; '**⁀spreis** *m* standard price.

'**einheizen** (*sep.*, -ge-, *h*) 1. *v/i.* make a fire; 2. *v/t.* heat (*stove*).

einhellig *adj.* ['aɪnhelɪç] unanimous.

'**einholen** (*sep.*, -ge-, *h*) 1. *v/t.* catch up with, overtake; make up for (*lost time*); make (*inquiries*); take (*order*); seek (*advice*); ask for (*permission*); buy; 2. *v/i.*: ⁀ gehen go shopping.

'**Einhorn** *zo. n* unicorn.

einhüllen *v/t.* (*sep.*, -ge-, *h*) wrap (up *or* in); envelop.

einig *adj.* ['aɪnɪç] united; ⁀ sein agree; nicht ⁀ sein differ (*über acc.* about); ⁀e *indef. pron.* ['⁀ɡə] several; some; ⁀en ['⁀ɡən] *v/t.* (*ge-, h*) unite; sich ⁀ come to terms; ⁀ermaßen *adv.* ['⁀ɡər'maːsən] in some measure; somewhat; ⁀es *indef. pron.* ['⁀ɡəs] some(thing); '♀**keit** *f* (-/*no pl.*) unity; concord; ♀**ung** ['⁀ɡ-] *f* (-/-en) union; agreement.

ein|impfen ['aɪn⁀-] *v/t.* (*sep.*, -ge-, *h*) ♣ inoculate (*a. fig.*); '**⁀jagen** *v/t.* (*sep.*, -ge-, *h*): j-m Furcht ⁀ scare s.o.

einjährig *adj.* ['aɪnjɛːrɪç] one-year-old; *esp.* ♀ annual; *animal*: yearling.

ein|kalkulieren *v/t.* (*sep.*, no -ge-, *h*) take into account, allow for; '**⁀kassieren** *v/t.* (*sep.*, no -ge-, *h*) cash; collect.

'**Einkauf** *m* purchase; Einkäufe machen *s.* einkaufen 2; '♀**en** (*sep.*, -ge-, *h*) 1. *v/t.* buy; purchase; 2. *v/i.* make purchases, go shopping.

'**Einkäufer** *m* buyer.

'**Einkaufs|netz** *n* string bag; '**⁀preis** ✝ *m* purchase price; '**⁀tasche** *f* shopping-bag.

ein|kehren *v/i.* (*sep.*, -ge-, sein) put up *or* stop (*at an inn*); '**⁀kerben** *v/t.* (*sep.*, -ge-, *h*) notch; '**⁀kerkern** *v/t.* (*sep.*, -ge-, *h*) imprison; '**⁀klagen** *v/t.* (*sep.*, -ge-, *h*) sue for; '**⁀klammern** *v/t.* (*sep.*, -ge-, *h*) *typ.* bracket; put in brackets.

'**Einklang** *m* unison; harmony.

ein|kleiden *v/t.* (*sep.*, -ge-, *h*) clothe; fit out; '**⁀klemmen** *v/t.* (*sep.*, -ge-, *h*) squeeze (in); jam; '**⁀klinken** (*sep.*, -ge-) 1. *v/t.* (*h*) latch; 2. *v/i.* (sein) latch; engage; '**⁀knicken** (*sep.*, -ge-) *v/t.* (*h*) *and* *v/i.* (sein) bend in; break; '**⁀kochen** (*sep.*, -ge-) 1. *v/t.* (*h*) preserve; 2. *v/i.* (sein) boil down *or* away.

'**Einkommen** *n* (-s/-) income, revenue; '**⁀steuer** *f* income-tax.

'**einkreisen** *v/t.* (*sep.*, -ge-, *h*) encircle.

Einkünfte ['aɪnkynftə] *pl.* income, revenue.

'**einlad|en** *v/t.* (*irr. laden, sep.*, -ge-, *h*) load (in) (*goods*); *fig.* invite; '♀**ung** *f* invitation.

'**Einlage** *f* enclosure (*in letter*); ✝ investment; deposit (*of money*); *gambling*: stake; inserted piece; ♣ arch-support; temporary filling (*of tooth*); '♀**rn** ✝ *v/t.* (*sep.*, -ge-, *h*) store (up).

Einlaß ['aɪnlas] *m* (Einlasses/Einlässe) admission, admittance.

'**einlassen** *v/t.* (*irr. lassen, sep.*, -ge-, *h*) let in, admit; ⁀ in (*acc.*) ⊕ imbed in; sich ⁀ in *or* auf (*both acc.*) engage in, enter into.

ein|laufen *v/i.* (*irr. laufen, sep.*, -ge-, sein) come in, arrive; *ship*: enter; *material*: shrink; '**⁀leben** *v/refl.* (*sep.*, -ge-, *h*) accustom o.s. (*in acc.* to).

'**einlege|n** *v/t.* (*sep.*, -ge-, *h*) lay *or* put in; insert; ⊕ inlay; deposit (*money*); pickle; preserve (*fruit*); Berufung ⁀ lodge an appeal (*bei* to); Ehre ⁀ mit gain hono(u)r *or* credit by; ♀**sohle** *f* insole, sock.

einleit|en *v/t.* (*sep.*, -ge-, *h*) start; introduce; **⁀end** *adj.* introductory; '♀**ung** *f* introduction.

'**ein|lenken** *fig.* *v/i.* (*sep.*, -ge-, *h*) come round; '**⁀leuchten** *v/i.* (*sep.*, -ge-, *h*) be evident *or* obvious; '**⁀liefern** *v/t.* (*sep.*, -ge-, *h*) deliver (up); in ein Krankenhaus ⁀ take to a hospital, *Am.* hospitalize; '**⁀lösen** *v/t.* (*sep.*, -ge-, *h*) ransom (*prisoner*); redeem (*pledge*); ✝ hono(u)r (*bill*); cash (*cheque*); ✝ meet (*bill*); '**⁀machen** *v/t.* (*sep.*, -ge-, *h*) preserve (*fruit*); tin, *Am.* can.

'**einmal** *adv.* once; one day; auf ⁀ all at once; es war ⁀ once (upon a time) there was; nicht ⁀ not even; ♀'**eins** *n* (-/-) multiplication table; '**⁀ig** *adj.* single; unique.

'**Einmarsch** *m* marching in, entry; '♀**ieren** *v/i.* (*sep.*, no -ge-, sein) march in, enter.

ein|mengen *v/refl.* (*sep.*, -ge-, *h*), '**⁀mischen** *v/refl.* (*sep.*, -ge-, *h*) meddle, interfere (*in acc.* with), *esp. Am. sl.* butt in.

'**Einmündung** *f* junction (*of roads*); mouth (*of river*).

einmütig *adj.* ['aɪnmyːtɪç] unanimous; ♀**keit** *f* (-/*no pl.*) unanimity.

Einnahme ['aɪnnaːmə] *f* (-/-n) ✂ taking, capture; *mst* ⁀n *pl.* takings *pl.*, receipts *pl.*

'**einnehmen** *v/t.* (*irr. nehmen, sep.*, -ge-, *h*) take (*meal, position*, ✂); ✝ take (*money*); ✝ earn, make (*money*); take up, occupy (*room*); *fig.* captivate; '**⁀d** *adj.* taking, engaging, captivating.

'**einnicken** *v/i.* (*sep.*, -ge-, sein) doze *or* drop off.

Einöde ['aɪnˀ-] *f* desert, solitude.
ein|ordnen ['aɪnˀ-] *v/t.* (*sep.*, *-ge-*, *h*) arrange in proper order; classify; file (*letters*, *etc.*); **~packen** *v/t.* (*sep.*, *-ge-*, *h*) pack up; wrap up; **~pferchen** *v/t.* (*sep.*, *-ge-*, *h*) pen in; *fig.* crowd, cram; **~pflanzen** *v/t.* (*sep.*, *-ge-*, *h*) plant; *fig.* implant; **~pökeln** *v/t.* (*sep.*, *-ge-*, *h*) pickle, salt; **~prägen** *v/t.* (*sep.*, *-ge-*, *h*) imprint; impress; *sich* ~ imprint itself; commit *s.th.* to one's memory; **~quartieren** *v/t.* (*sep.*, *no -ge-*, *h*) quarter, billet; **~rahmen** *v/t.* (*sep.*, *-ge-*, *h*) frame; **~räumen** *fig. v/t.* (*sep.*, *-ge-*, *h*) grant, concede; **~rechnen** *v/t.* (*sep.*, *-ge-*, *h*) comprise, include; **~reden** (*sep.*, *-ge-*, *h*) **1.** *v/t.*: *j-m* ~ persuade *or* talk *s.o.* into (*doing*) *s.th.*; **2.** *v/i.*: *auf j-n* ~ talk insistently to *s.o.*; **~reichen** *v/t.* (*sep.*, *-ge-*, *h*) hand in, send in, present; **~reihen** *v/t.* (*sep.*, *-ge-*, *h*) insert (*unter acc.* in); class (with); place (among); *sich* ~ take one's place.

einreihig *adj.* ['aɪnraiç] *jacket*: single-breasted.

'Einreise *f* entry; **~erlaubnis** *f*, **~genehmigung** *f* entry permit.

'ein|reißen (*irr. reißen*, *sep.*, *-ge-*) **1.** *v/t.* (*h*) tear; pull down (*building*); **2.** *v/i.* (*sein*) tear; abuse, *etc.*: spread; **~renken** ['~rɛŋkən] *v/t.* (*sep.*, *-ge-*, *h*) ✗ set; *fig.* set right.

'einricht|en *v/t.* (*sep.*, *-ge-*, *h*) establish; equip; arrange; set up (*shop*); furnish (*flat*); *es* ~ manage; *sich* ~ establish o.s., settle down; economize; *sich* ~ *auf* (*acc.*) prepare for; **'2ung** *f* establishment; arrangement, *esp. Am.* setup; equipment; furniture; fittings *pl.* (*of shop*); institution.

'ein|rollen *v/t.* (*sep.*, *-ge-*, *h*) roll up *or* in; *sich* ~ roll up; curl up; **~rosten** *v/i.* (*sep.*, *-ge-*, *sein*) rust; *screw, etc.*: rust in; **~rücken** (*sep.*, *-ge-*) **1.** *v/i.* (*sein*) enter, march in; ✗ join the army; **2.** *v/t.* (*h*) insert (*advertisement in a paper*); *typ.* indent (*line, word, etc.*); **~rühren** *v/t.* (*sep.*, *-ge-*, *h*) stir (in).

eins *adj.* [aɪns] one.

'einsam *adj.* lonely, solitary; **'2keit** *f* (*-/~-en*) loneliness, solitude.

'einsammeln *v/t.* (*sep.*, *-ge-*, *h*) gather; collect.

'Einsatz *m* inset; insertion (*of piece of material*); gambling: stake, pool; ♪ striking, entry; employment; engagement (*a.* ✗); ✗ action, operation; *unter* ~ *s-s Lebens* at the risk of one's life.

'ein|saugen *v/t.* (*sep.*, *-ge-*, *h*) suck in; *fig.* imbibe; **~schalten** *v/t.* (*sep.*, *-ge-*, *h*) insert; ∮ switch *or* turn on; *den ersten Gang* ~ *mot.* go into first *or* bottom gear; *sich* ~

intervene; **'~schärfen** *v/t.* (*sep.*, *-ge-*, *h*) inculcate (*dat.* upon); **'~schätzen** *v/t.* (*sep.*, *-ge-*, *h*) assess, appraise, estimate (*auf acc.* at); value (*a. fig.*); **'~schenken** *v/t.* (*sep.*, *-ge-*, *h*) pour in *or* out; **'~schicken** *v/t.* (*sep.*, *-ge-*, *h*) send in; **'~schieben** *v/t.* (*irr. schieben*, *sep.*, *-ge-*, *h*) insert; **'~schiffen** *v/t. and v/refl.* (*sep.*, *-ge-*, *h*) embark; **'2schiffung** *f* (*-/-en*) embarkation; **'~schlafen** *v/i.* (*irr. schlafen*, *sep.*, *-ge-*, *sein*) fall asleep; **~schläfern** ['~ʃlɛːfərn] *v/t.* (*sep.*, *-ge-*, *h*) lull to sleep; ✍ narcotize.

'Einschlag *m* striking (*of lightning*); impact (*of missile*); *fig.* touch; **'2en** (*irr. schlagen*, *sep.*, *-ge-*, *h*) **1.** *v/t.* drive in (*nail*); break (*in*); smash (*in*); wrap up; take (*road*); tuck in (*hem, etc.*); enter upon (*career*); **2.** *v/i.* shake hands; lightning, missile: strike; *fig.* be a success; *nicht* ~ fail; (*wie e-e Bombe*) ~ cause a sensation; *auf j-n* ~ belabour *s.o.*

einschlägig *adj.* ['aɪnʃlɛːgiç] relevant, pertinent.

'Einschlagpapier *n* wrapping-paper.

'ein|schleichen *v/refl.* (*irr. schleichen*, *sep.*, *-ge-*, *h*) creep *or* sneak in; **'~schleppen** *v/t.* (*sep.*, *-ge-*, *h*) ⚓ tow in; import (*disease*); **'~schleusen** *fig. v/t.* (*sep.*, *-ge-*, *h*) channel *or* let in; **'~schließen** *v/t.* (*irr. schließen*, *sep.*, *-ge-*, *h*) lock in *or* up; enclose; ✗ surround, encircle; *fig.* include; **'~schließlich** *prp.* (*gen.*) inclusive of; including, comprising; **'~schmeicheln** *v/refl.* (*sep.*, *-ge-*, *h*) ingratiate o.s. (*bei* with); **'~schmeichelnd** *adj.* insinuating; **'~schmuggeln** *v/t.* (*sep.*, *-ge-*, *h*) smuggle in; **'~schnappen** *v/i.* (*sep.*, *-ge-*, *sein*) catch; *fig. s.* eingeschnappt; **'~schneidend** *fig. adj.* incisive, drastic.

'Einschnitt *m* cut, incision; notch.

'ein|schnüren *v/t.* (*sep.*, *-ge-*, *h*) lace (up); **~schränken** ['~ʃrɛŋkən] *v/t.* (*sep.*, *-ge-*, *h*) restrict, confine; reduce (*expenses*); *sich* ~ economize; **'2schränkung** *f* (*-/-en*) restriction; reduction.

'Einschreibe|brief *m* registered letter; **'2n** *v/t.* (*irr. schreiben*, *sep.*, *-ge-*, *h*) enter; book; enrol(l); ✗ enlist, enrol(l); ✉ register; *lassen* have registered; *sich* ~ enter one's name.

'einschreiten 1. *fig. v/i.* (*irr. schreiten*, *sep.*, *-ge-*, *sein*) step in, interpose, intervene; take action (*gegen* against); **2.** *2 n* (*-s/no pl.*) intervention.

'ein|schrumpfen *v/i.* (*sep.*, *-ge-*, *sein*) shrink; **'~schüchtern** *v/t.* (*sep.*, *-ge-*, *h*) intimidate; bully; **'2schüchterung** *f* (*-/-en*) intimidation; '~schulen v/t. (sep., -ge-, h) put to school.

'Einschuß m bullet-hole; † invested capital.

'ein|segnen v/t. (sep., -ge-, h) consecrate; confirm (children); '2segnung f consecration; confirmation.

'einsehen 1. v/t. (irr. sehen, sep., -ge-, h) look into; fig.: see, comprehend; realize; 2. 2 n (-s/no pl.): ein ~ haben show consideration.

'einseifen v/t. (sep., -ge-, h) soap; lather (beard); F fig. humbug (s.o.).

einseitig adj. ['aɪnzaɪtɪç] one-sided; ♂, pol., ♐ unilateral.

'einsend|en v/t. ([irr. senden], sep., -ge-, h) send in; '2er m (-s/-) sender; contributor (to a paper).

'einsetz|en (sep., -ge-, h) 1. v/t. set or put in; stake (money); insert; institute; instal(l), appoint (s.o.); fig. use, employ; risk (one's life); sich ~ für stand up for; 2. v/i. fever, flood, weather: set in; ♪ strike in; '2ung f (-/-en) insertion; appointment, installation.

'Einsicht f (-/-en) inspection; fig. insight, understanding; judiciousness; '2ig adj. judicious; sensible.

'einsickern v/i. (sep., -ge-, sein) soak in; infiltrate.

'Einsiedler m hermit.

einsilbig adj. ['aɪnzɪlbɪç] monosyllabic; fig. taciturn; '2keit f (-/no pl.) taciturnity.

'einsinken v/i. (irr. sinken, sep., -ge-, sein) sink (in).

Einspänn|er ['aɪnʃpɛnər] m (-s/-) one-horse carriage; '2ig adj. one-horse.

'ein|sparen v/t. (sep., -ge-, h) save, economize; '~sperren v/t. (sep., -ge-, h) imprison; lock up, confine; '~springen v/i. (irr. springen, sep., -ge-, sein) ⊕ catch; fig. step in, help out; für j-n ~ substitute for s.o.; '~spritzen v/t. (sep., -ge-, h) inject; '2spritzung f (-/-en) injection.

'Einspruch m objection, protest, veto; appeal; '~srecht n veto.

'einspurig adj. single-track.

einst adv. [aɪnst] once; one or some day.

'Einstand m entry; tennis: deuce.

'ein|stecken v/t. (sep., -ge-, h) put in; pocket; plug in; '~steigen v/i. (irr. steigen, sep., -ge-, sein) get in; ~! 🚃 take your seats!, Am. all aboard!

'einstell|en v/t. (sep., -ge-, h) put in; ✗ enrol(l), enlist, Am. muster in; engage, employ, Am. a. hire; give up; stop, cease, Am. a. quit (payment, etc.); adjust (mechanism) (auf acc. to); tune in (radio) (to); opt., focus (on) (a. fig.); die Arbeit ~ cease working; strike, Am. a. walk out; sich ~ appear; sich ~ auf (acc.) be

prepared for; adapt o.s. to; '2ung f ✗ enlistment; engagement; adjustment; focus; (mental) attitude, mentality.

'einstimm|en ♪ v/i. (sep., -ge-, h) join in; '~ig adj. unanimous; '2igkeit f (-/no pl.) unanimity.

einstöckig adj. ['aɪnʃtœkɪç] onestoried.

'ein|streuen fig. v/t. (sep., -ge-, h) intersperse; '~studieren v/t. (sep., no -ge-, h) study; thea. rehearse; '~stürmen v/i. (sep., -ge-, sein): auf j-n ~ rush at s.o.; '2sturz m falling in, collapse; '~stürzen v/i. (sep., -ge-, sein) fall in, collapse.

einst|weilen adv. ['aɪnst'vaɪlən] for the present; in the meantime; '~weilig adj. temporary.

'ein|tauschen v/t. (sep., -ge-, h) exchange (gegen for); '~teilen v/t. (sep., -ge-, h) divide (in acc. into); classify; '~teilig adj. one-piece; '2teilung f division; classification.

eintönig adj. ['aɪntø:nɪç] monotonous; '2keit f (-/♐ -en) monotony.

'Eintopf(gericht n) m hot-pot; stew.

'Eintracht f (-/no pl.) harmony, concord.

einträchtig adj. ['aɪntrɛçtɪç] harmonious.

'eintragen v/t. (irr. tragen, sep., -ge-, h) enter; register; bring in, yield (profit); sich ~ in (acc.) sign.

einträglich adj. ['aɪntrɛ:klɪç] profitable.

'Eintragung f (-/-en) entry; registration.

'ein|treffen v/i. (irr. treffen, sep., -ge-, sein) arrive; happen; come true; '~treiben v/t. (irr. treiben, sep., -ge-, h) drive in or home; collect (debts, taxes); '~treten (irr. treten, sep., -ge-) 1. v/i. (sein) enter; occur, happen; take place; ~ für stand up for; ~ in (acc.) enter into (rights); enter upon (possession); enter (room); join (the army, etc.); 2. v/t. (h) kick in (door); sich et. ~ run a. sth. into one's foot.

'Eintritt m entry, entrance; admittance; beginning, setting-in (of winter, etc.); ~ frei! admission free!; ~ verboten! no admittance!; '~sgeld n entrance or admission fee; sports: gate money; '~skarte f admission ticket.

'ein|trocknen v/i. (sep., -ge-, sein) dry (up); '~trüben v/refl. (sep., -ge-, h) become cloudy or overcast; '~üben ['aɪn?-] v/t. (sep., -ge-, h) practi|se, Am. -ce s.th.; train s.o.

einver|leiben ['aɪnfɛrlaɪbən] v/t. ([sep.,] no -ge-, h) incorporate (dat. in); annex (to); F sich et. ~ eat or drink s.th.; '2nehmen n (-s/no pl.) agreement, understanding; in gutem ~ on friendly terms; '~standen *adj.*: ~ *sein* agree; '2ständnis *n* agreement.

'Einwand *m* (-[e]s/-e) objection (*gegen* to).

Einwander|er *m* immigrant; '2n *v/i.* (*sep.*, -ge-, *sein*) immigrate; '~ung *f* immigration.

einwandfrei *adj.* unobjectionable; perfect; faultless; *alibi*: sound.

einwärts *adv.* ['aınvɛrts] inward(s).

Einwegflasche *f* one-way bottle, non-return bottle.

einweih|en *v/t.* (*sep.*, -ge-, *h*) *eccl.* consecrate; inaugurate; ~ *in* (*acc.*) initiate *s.o.* into; '~ung *f* (-/-en) consecration; inauguration; initiation.

einwend|en *v/t.* ([*irr.* wenden,] *sep.*, -ge-, *h*) object; '2ung *f* objection.

einwerfen (*irr.* werfen, *sep.*, -ge-, *h*) 1. *v/t.* throw in (*a. fig.*); smash, break (*window-pane*); post, *Am.* mail (*letter*); interject (*remark*); 2. *v/i.* football: throw in.

einwickel|n *v/t.* (*sep.*, -ge-, *h*) wrap (up), envelop; '2papier *n* wrapping-paper.

einwillig|en ['aınvılıgən] *v/i.* (*sep.*, -ge-, *h*) consent, agree (*in acc.* to); '2ung *f* (-/-en) consent, agreement.

einwirk|en *v/i.* (*sep.*, -ge-, *h*): ~ *auf* (*acc.*) act (up)on; influence; effect; '2ung *f* influence; effect.

Einwohner ['aınvoːnər] *m* (-s/-), '~in *f* (-/-nen) inhabitant, resident.

'Einwurf *m* throwing in; *football*: throw-in; *fig.* objection; slit (*for letters*, *etc.*); slot (*for coins*).

'Einzahl *gr. f* (-/~-en) singular (number); '2en *v/t.* (*sep.*, -ge-, *h*) pay in; '~ung *f* payment; deposit (*at bank*).

einzäunen ['aıntsɔynən] *v/t.* (*sep.*, -ge-, *h*) fence in.

Einzel ['aıntsəl] *n* (-s/-) *tennis*: single, *Am.* singles *pl.*; **~gänger** ['~gɛŋər] *m* (-s/-) outsider; F lone wolf; '~handel ✝ *m* retail trade; '~händler ✝ *m* retailer, retail dealer; '~heit *f* (-/-en) detail, item; *~en pl.* particulars *pl.*, details *pl.*; '2n 1. *adj.* single; particular; individual; separate; *of shoes, etc.*: odd; *im ~en* in detail; 2. *adv.*: ~ *angeben* or *aufführen* specify, *esp. Am.* itemize; '~ne *m* (-n/-n) *the* individual; '~verkauf *m* retail sale; '~wesen *n* individual.

einziehen (*irr.* ziehen, *sep.*, -ge-) 1. *v/t.* (*h*) draw in; *esp.* ⊕ retract; ✗ call up, *Am.* draft, induct; ⚖ seize, confiscate; make (*inquiries*) (*über acc.* on, about); 2. *v/i.* (*sein*) enter; move in; *liquid*: soak in; ~ *in* (*acc.*) move into (*flat, etc.*).

einzig *adj.* ['aıntsıç] only; single; sole; unique; '~artig *adj.* unique, singular.

'Einzug *m* entry, entrance; moving in.

'einzwängen *v/t.* (*sep.*, -ge-, *h*) squeeze, jam.

Eis [aıs] *n* (-es/*no pl.*) ice; ice-cream; '~bahn *f* skating-rink; '~bär *zo. m* polar bear; '~bein *n* pickled pork shank; ~berg *m* iceberg; '~decke *f* sheet of ice; '~diele *f* ice-cream parlo(u)r.

Eisen ['aızən] *n* (-s/-) iron.

Eisenbahn *f* railway, *Am.* railroad; *mit der ~* by rail, by train; '~er *m* (-s/-) railwayman; '~fahrt *f* railway journey; '~knotenpunkt *m* (railway) junction; '~unglück *n* railway accident; '~wagen *m* railway carriage, *Am.* railroad car; coach.

Eisen|blech *n* sheet-iron; '~erz *n* iron-ore; '~gießerei *f* iron-foundry; 2haltig *adj.* ferruginous; '~hütte *f* ironworks *sg.*, *pl.*; '~waren *f/pl.* ironmongery, *esp. Am.* hardware; '~warenhändler *m* ironmonger, *esp. Am.* hardware dealer.

eisern *adj.* ['aızərn] iron, of iron.

Eis|gang *m* breaking up of the ice; ice-drift; 2gekühlt *adj.* ['~gəkyːlt] iced; 2grau *adj.* hoary; '~hockey *n* ice-hockey; 2ig *adj.* ['aızıç] icy; '2kalt *adj.* icy (cold); '~kunstlauf *m* figure-skating; '~lauf *m*, '~laufen *n* -s/*no pl.*) skating; skate; '~läufer *m* skater; '~meer *n* polar sea; '~schnellauf *m* speed-skating; '~scholle *f* ice-floe; '~schrank *m s. Kühlschrank*; '~vogel *orn. m* kingfisher; '~zapfen *m* icicle; '2zeit *geol. f* ice-age.

eitel *adj.* ['aıtəl] vain (*auf acc.* of); conceited; mere; '2keit *f* (-/-en) vanity.

Eiter ✍ ['aıtər] *m* (-s/*no pl.*) matter, pus, ~beule ✍ *f* abscess; '2ig ✍ *adj.* purulent; '2n ✍ *v/i.* (ge-, *h*) fester, suppurate; '~ung ✍ *f* (-/-en) suppuration.

eitrig ✍ *adj.* ['aıtrıç] purulent.

Eiweiß *n* (-es/-e) white of egg; 🍳 albumen; '2haltig 🍳 *adj.* albuminous.

Eizelle *f* egg-cell, ovum.

Ekel ['eːkəl] 1. *m* (-s/*no pl.*) disgust (*vor dat.* at), loathing, aversion; ✍ nausea; 2. F *n* (-s/-) nasty person; '2erregend *adj.* nauseating, sickening; 2haft *adj.*, '2ig *adj.* revolting; *fig.* disgusting; '2n *v/refl.* (ge-, *h*): *sich ~* be nauseated (*vor dat.* at); *fig.* be or feel disgusted (at).

eklig *adj.* ['eːklıç] *s.* ekelhaft.

elasti|sch *adj.* [e'lastıʃ] elastic; 2zität [~tsi'tɛːt] *f* (-/*no pl.*) elasticity.

Elch *zo.* [ɛlç] *m* (-[e]s/-e) elk; moose.

Elefant *zo.* [ele'fant] *m* (-en/-en) elephant.

elegan|t *adj.* [ele'gant] elegant; smart; 2z [⁓ts] *f* (-/*no pl.*) elegance.

elektrifizier|en [elɛktrifi'tsi:rən] *v/t.* (*no* -ge-, *h*) electrify; 2ung *f* (-/-en) electrification.

Elektri|ker [e'lɛktrikər] *m* (-s/-) electrician; 2sch *adj.* electric(al); 2sieren [⁓'zi:rən] *v/t.* (*no* -ge-, *h*) electrify.

Elektrizität [elɛktritsi'tɛːt] *f* (-/*no pl.*) electricity; ⁓sgesellschaft *f* electricity supply company, ⁓swerk *n* (electric) power station, power-house, *Am.* power plant.

Elektrode [elɛk'tro:də] *f* (-/-n) electrode.

Elektro|gerät [e'lɛktro-] *n* electric appliance; ⁓lyse [⁓'ly:zə] *f* (-/-n) electrolysis.

Elektron ⚡ [e'lɛktrɔn] *n* (-s/-en) electron; ⁓engehirn [⁓'tro:nən-] *n* electronic brain; ⁓ik [⁓'tro:nik] *f* (-/*no pl.*) electronics *sg.*

Elektro'technik *f* electrical engineering; ⁓er *m* electrical engineer.

Element [ele'mɛnt] *n* (-[e]s/-e) element.

elementar *adj.* [elemɛn'taːr] elementary; 2schule elementary *or* primary school, *Am.* grade school.

Elend ['eːlɛnt] **1.** *n* (-[e]s/*no pl.*) misery; need, distress; **2.** ⚙ *adj.* miserable, wretched; needy, distressed; ⁓viertel *n* slums *pl.*

elf¹ [ɛlf] **1.** *adj.* eleven; **2.** ⚙ *f* (-/-en) eleven (*a. sports*).

Elf² [⁓] *m* (-en/-en), ⁓e ['ɛlfə] *f* (-/-n) elf, fairy.

'Elfenbein *n* (-[e]s/⚙-e) ivory; '2ern *adj.* ivory.

Elf'meter *m football*: penalty kick; ⁓marke *f* penalty spot.

'elfte *adj.* eleventh.

Elite [e'liːtə] *f* (-/-n) élite.

'Ellbogen *anat. m* (-s/-) elbow.

Elle ['ɛlə] *f* (-/-n) yard; *anat.* ulna.

Elster *orn.* ['ɛlstər] *f* (-/-n) magpie.

elter|lich *adj.* ['ɛltərlɪç] parental; '2n *pl.* parents *pl.*; ⁓nlos *adj.* parentless, orphaned; '2nteil *m* parent.   [(-/-n) enamel.]

Email [e'maːj] *n* (-s/-s), ⁓le [⁓] *f*)

Emanzipation [emantsipa'tsjoːn] *f* (-/-en) emancipation.

Embargo [ɛm'bargo] *n* (-s/-s) embargo.

Embolie ⚕ [ɛmbo'liː] *f* (-/-n) embolism.

Embryo *biol.* ['ɛmbryo] *m* (-s/-s, -nen) embryo.

Emigrant [emi'grant] *m* (-en/-en) emigrant.

empfahl [ɛm'pfaːl] *pret. of empfehlen.*

Empfang [ɛm'pfaŋ] *m* (-[e]s/⁓e) reception (*a. radio*); receipt (*of s.th.*); *nach or bei* ⁓ *on receipt*; '2en *v/t.* (*irr. fangen, no* -ge-, *h*) receive; welcome; conceive (*child*).

Empfänger [ɛm'pfɛŋər] *m* (-s/-) receiver, recipient; payee (*of money*); addressee (*of letter*); ✝ consignee (*of goods*).

em'pfänglich *adj.* susceptible (*für* to); 2keit *f* (-/*no pl.*) susceptibility.

Em'pfangs|dame *f* receptionist; ⁓gerät *n* receiver, receiving set; ⁓schein *m* receipt; ⁓zimmer *n* reception-room.

empfehl|en [ɛm'pfeːlən] *v/t.* (*irr., no* -ge-, *h*) recommend; commend; ⁓ *Sie mich* (*dat.*) please remember me to; ⁓enswert *adj.* (re)commendable, 2ung *f* (-/-en) recommendation; compliments *pl.*

empfinden [ɛm'pfindən] *v/t.* (*irr. finden, no* -ge-, *h*) feel; perceive.

empfindlich *adj.* [ɛm'pfintliç] sensitive (*a. phot.*, 🎵) (*für, gegen* to); *pred. a.* susceptible (*gegen* to); delicate; tender; *p.*: touchy, sensitive; *cold*: severe; *pain, loss, etc.*: grievous; *pain*: acute; 2keit *f* (-/-en) sensitivity; sensibility; touchiness; delicacy.

empfindsam *adj.* [ɛm'pfintzaːm] sensitive; sentimental; 2keit *f* (-/-en) sensitiveness; sentimentality.

Empfindung [ɛm'pfinduŋ] *f* (-/-en) perception, sensation; sentiment; 2slos *adj* insensible; *esp. fig.* unfeeling; ⁓svermögen *n* faculty of perception.

empfohlen [ɛm'pfoːlən] *p.p. of empfehlen.*

empor *adv.* [ɛm'poːr] up, upwards.

empören [ɛm'pøːrən] *v/t.* (*no* -ge-, *h*) incense; shock; *sich* ⁓ revolt (*a. fig.*), rebel; grow furious (*über acc.* at); *empört* indignant, shocked (*both über acc.* at).

em'por|kommen *v/i.* (*irr. kommen, sep.,* -ge-, *sein*) rise (in the world); 2kömmling [⁓kœmlɪŋ] *m* (-s/-e) upstart; ⁓ragen *v/i.* (*sep.,* -ge-, *h*) tower, rise; ⁓steigen *v/i.* (*irr. steigen, sep.,* -ge-, *sein*) rise, ascend

Em'pörung *f* (-/-en) rebellion, revolt, indignation.

emsig *adj.* ['ɛmzɪç] busy, industrious, diligent; '2keit *f* (-/*no pl.*) busyness, industry, diligence.

Ende ['ɛndə] *n* (-s/-n) end; *am* ⁓ *at or in the end; after all; eventually; zu* ⁓ *gehen end; expire; run short;* '2n *v/i.* (ge-, *h*) end; cease, finish.

end|gültig *adj.* ['ɛntgyltɪç] final, definitive; '⁓lich *adv.* finally, at last; ⁓los *adj.* ['⁓loːs] endless; '2punkt *m* final point; '2runde *f sports* final; '2station 🚉 *f* terminus, *Am.* terminal; '2summe *f* (*sum*) total.

Endung *ling.* ['ɛnduŋ] *f* (-/-en) ending, termination.

Endzweck ['ɛnt-] *m* ultimate object.

Energie [enɛr'giː] *f* (-/-*n*) energy; Ølos *adj.* lacking (in) energy.

e'nergisch *adj.* vigorous; energetic.

eng *adj.* [eŋ] narrow; *clothes*: tight; close; intimate; *im* ~*eren Sinne* strictly speaking.

engagieren [ăgā'ʒiːrən] *v/t.* (*no* -ge-, *h*) engage, *Am. a.* hire.

Enge ['eŋə] *f* (-/-*n*) narrowness; *fig.* straits *pl.*

Engel ['eŋəl] *m* (-*s*/-) angel.

'engherzig *adj.* ungenerous, petty.

Engländer ['eŋlɛndər] *m* (-*s*/-) Englishman; *die* ~ *pl.* the English *pl.*; ~**in** *f* (-/-*nen*) Englishwoman.

englisch *adj.* ['eŋliʃ] English; British.

'**Engpaß** *m* defile, narrow pass, *Am. a.* notch; *fig.* bottle-neck.

en gros † *adv.* [ă'groː] wholesale.

En'groshandel † *m* wholesale trade.

'engstirnig *adj.* narrow-minded.

Enkel ['eŋkəl] *m* (-*s*/-) grandchild; grandson; ~**in** *f* (-/-*nen*) grand-daughter.

enorm *adj.* [e'nɔrm] enormous; F *fig.* tremendous.

Ensemble *thea.*, ♪ [ă'sāːbəl] *n* (-*s*/-*s*) ensemble; company.

entart|en [ent'aːrtən] *v/i.* (*no* -ge-, *sein*) degenerate; Øung *f* (-/-*en*) degeneration.

entbehr|en [ent'beːrən] *v/t.* (*no* -ge-, *h*) lack; miss, want; do without; ~lich *adj.* dispensable; superfluous; Øung *f* (-/-*en*) want, privation.

ent'bind|en (*irr. binden, no* -ge-, *h*) 1. *v/t.* dispense, release (von from); deliver (*of a child*); 2. *v/i.* be confined; Øung *f* dispensation, release; delivery; Øungsheim *n* maternity hospital.

ent'blöß|en *v/t.* (*no* -ge-, *h*) bare, strip; uncover (*head*); ~t *adj.* bare.

ent'deck|en *v/t.* (*no* -ge-, *h*) discover; detect; disclose; ~er *m* (-*s*/-) discoverer; Øung *f* discovery.

Ente ['entə] *f* (-/-*n*) *orn.* duck; *false report*: F canard, hoax.

ent'ehr|en *v/t.* (*no* -ge-, *h*) dishono(u)r; Øung *f* degradation; rape.

ent'eign|en *v/t.* (*no* -ge-, *h*) expropriate; dispossess; Øung *f* expropriation; dispossession.

ent'erben *v/t.* (*no* -ge-, *h*) disinherit.

entern ['entərn] *v/t.* (ge-, *h*) board, grapple (*ship*).

ent'fachen *v/t.* (*no* -ge-, *h*) kindle; *fig. a.* rouse (*passions*); ~'fallen *v/i.* (*irr. fallen, no* -ge-, *sein*): *j-m* ~ escape s.o.; *fig.* slip s.o.'s memory; *auf j-n* ~ fall to s.o.'s share; *s. wegfallen*; ~'falten *v/t.* (*no* -ge-, *h*) unfold; *fig.*: develop; display; *sich* ~ unfold; *fig.* develop (zu into).

ent'fern|en *v/t.* (*no* -ge-, *h*) remove; *sich* ~ withdraw; ~t *adj.* distant;

remote (*both a. fig.*); Øung *f* (-/-*en*) removal; distance; range; Øungsmesser *phot. m* (-*s*/-) range-finder.

ent'flammen *v/t.* (*no* -ge-) *v/t.* (*h*) and *v/i.* (*sein*) inflame; ~'fliehen *v/i.* (*irr. fliehen, no* -ge-, *sein*) flee, escape (*aus or dat.* from); ~'fremden *v/t.* (*no* -ge-, *h*) estrange, alienate (*j-m* from s.o.).

ent'führ|en *v/t.* (*no* -ge-, *h*) abduct, kidnap; run away with; Øer *m* abductor, kidnap(p)er; Øung *f* abduction, kidnap(p)ing.

ent'gegen 1. *prp.* (*dat.*) in opposition to, contrary to; against; 2. *adv.* towards; ~gehen *v/i.* (*irr. gehen, sep.,* -ge-, *sein*) go to meet; ~gesetzt *adj.* opposite; *fig.* contrary; ~halten *v/t.* (*irr. halten, sep.,* -ge-, *h*) hold out; *fig.* object; ~kommen *v/i.* (*irr. kommen, sep.,* -ge-, *sein*) come to meet; *fig.* meet s.o.'(s wishes) halfway; Økommen *n* (-*s*/*no pl.*) obligingness; ~kommend *adj.* obliging; ~nehmen *v/t.* (*irr. nehmen, sep.,* -ge-, *h*) accept, receive; ~sehen *v/i.* (*dat.*) (*irr. sehen, sep.,* -ge-, *h*) await; look forward to; ~setzen *v/t.* (*sep.,* -ge-, *h*) oppose; ~stehen *v/i.* (*irr. stehen, sep.,* -ge-, *h*) be opposed (*dat.* to); ~strecken *v/t.* (*sep.,* -ge-, *h*) hold or stretch out (*dat.* to); ~treten *v/i.* (*dat.*) (*irr. treten, sep.,* -ge-, *sein*) step up to s.o.; oppose; face (*danger*).

entgegn|en [ent'geːgnən] *v/i.* (*no* -ge-, *h*) reply; return; retort; Øung *f* (-/-*en*) reply; retort.

ent'gehen *v/i.* (*irr. gehen, no* -ge-, *sein*) escape.

entgeistert *adj.* [ent'gaistərt] aghast, thunderstruck, flabbergasted.

Entgelt [ent'gelt] *n* (-[*e*]*s*/*no pl.*) recompense; Øen *v/t.* (*irr. gelten, no* -ge-, *h*) atone or suffer *or* pay for.

entgleis|en [ent'glaizən] *v/i.* (*no* -ge-, *sein*) run off the rails, be derailed; *fig.* (make a) slip; Øung *f* (-/-*en*) derailment; *fig.* slip.

ent'gleiten *v/i.* (*irr. gleiten, no* -ge-, *sein*) slip (*dat.* from).

ent'halt|en *v/t.* (*irr. halten, no* -ge-, *h*) contain, hold, include; *sich* ~ (*gen.*) abstain *or* refrain from; ~sam *adj.* abstinent; Øsamkeit *f* (-/*no pl.*) abstinence; Øung *f* abstention.

ent'haupten *v/t.* (*no* -ge-, *h*) behead, decapitate.

ent'hüll|en *v/t.* (*no* -ge-, *h*) uncover, unveil; *fig.* reveal, disclose; Øung *f* (-/-*en*) uncovering; unveiling; *fig.* revelation, disclosure.

Enthusias|mus [entuzi'asmus] *m* (-/*no pl.*) enthusiasm; ~t *m* (-*en*/-*en*) enthusiast; *film*, *sports*: F fan; Øtisch *adj.* enthusiastic.

ent'kleiden *v/t. and v/refl.* (*no* -ge-, *h*) undress.

ent'kommen 1. v/i. (irr. kommen, no -ge-, sein) escape (j-m s.o.; aus from), get away or off; 2. 2 n (-s/no pl.) escape.

entkräft|en [ɛnt'krɛftən] v/t. (no -ge-, h) weaken, debilitate; fig. refute; 2ung f (-/-en) weakening; debility; fig. refutation.

ent'lad|en v/t. (irr. laden, no -ge-, h) unload; esp. ⚓ discharge; explode; sich ⚓ esp. ⚓ discharge; gun: go off; anger: vent itself; 2ung f unloading; esp. ⚓ discharge; explosion.

ent'lang 1. prp. (dat.; acc.) along; 2. adv. along; er geht die Straße ⚓ he goes along the street.

ent'larven v/t. (no -ge-, h) unmask; fig. a. expose.

ent'lass|en v/t. (irr. lassen, no -ge-, h) dismiss, discharge; F give s.o. the sack, Am. a. fire; 2ung f (-/-en) dismissal, discharge; 2ungsgesuch n resignation.

ent'lasten v/t. (no -ge-, h) unburden; ⅌⅍ exonerate, clear (from suspicion).

Ent'lastung f (-/-en) relief; discharge; exoneration; ⚓straße f by-pass (road); ⚓szeuge m witness for the defen|ce, Am. -se.

ent'lauf|en v/i. (irr. laufen, no -ge-, sein) run away (dat. from); ⚓ledigen [⚓'le:digən] v/refl. (gen.) (no -ge-, h): rid o.s. of s.th., get rid of s.th.; acquit o.s. of (duty); execute (orders); ⚓'leeren v/t. (no -ge-, h) empty. [of-the-way.|

ent'legen adj. remote, distant, out-]

ent'|lehnen v/t. (no -ge-, h) borrow (dat. or aus from); ⚓'locken v/t. (no -ge-, h) draw, elicit (dat. from); ⚓'lohnen v/t. (no -ge-, h) pay (off); ⚓'lüften v/t. (no -ge-, h) ventilate; ⚓militarisieren [⚓militari'zi:rən] v/t. (no -ge-, h) demilitarize; ⚓mutigen [⚓'mu:tigən] v/t. (no -ge-, h) discourage; ⚓'nehmen v/t. (irr. nehmen, no -ge- h) take (dat. from); ⚓ aus (with)draw from; fig. gather or learn from; ⚓'rätseln v/t. (no -ge-, h) unriddle; ⚓'reißen v/t. (irr. reißen, no -ge-, h) snatch away (dat. from); ⚓'richten v/t. (no -ge-, h) pay; ⚓'rinnen v/i. (irr. rinnen, no -ge-, sein) escape (dat. from); ⚓'rollen v/t. (no -ge-, h) unroll; ⚓'rücken v/t. (no -ge-, h) remove (dat. from), carry off or away; ⚓'rückt adj. entranced; lost in thought.

ent'rüst|en v/t. (no -ge-, h) fill with indignation; sich ⚓ become angry or indignant (über acc. at s.th., with s.o.); ⚓et adj. indignant (über acc. at s.th., with s.o.); 2ung f indignation.

ent'sag|en v/i. (no -ge-, h) renounce, resign; 2ung f (-/-en) renunciation, resignation.

ent'schädig|en v/t. (no -ge-, h) indemnify, compensate; 2ung f indemnification, indemnity; compensation.

ent'scheid|en (irr. scheiden, no -ge-, h) 1. v/t. decide; sich ⚓ question, etc.: be decided; p.: decide (für for; gegen against; über acc. on); come to a decision; 2. v/i. decide; ⚓end adj. decisive; crucial; 2ung f decision.

entschieden adj. [ɛnt'ʃi:dən] decided; determined, resolute; 2heit f (-/no pl.) determination.

ent'schließen v/refl. (irr. schließen, no -ge-, h) resolve, decide, determine (zu on s.th.; zu inf. to inf.), make up one's mind (zu inf. to inf.).

ent'schlossen adj. resolute, determined; 2heit f (-/no pl.) resoluteness.

ent'schlüpfen v/i. (no -ge-, sein) escape, slip (dat. from).

Ent'schluß m resolution, resolve, decision, determination.

entschuldig|en [ɛnt'ʃuldigən] v/t. (no -ge-, h) excuse; sich ⚓ apologize (bei to; für for); sich ⚓ lassen beg to be excused; 2ung f (-/-en) excuse; apology; ich bitte (Sie) um ⚓ I beg your pardon.

ent'senden v/t. (irr. senden, no -ge-, h) send off, dispatch; delegate, depute.

ent'setz|en 1. v/t. (no -ge-, h) dismiss (from a position); ⚔ relieve; frighten, sich ⚓ be terrified or shocked (über acc. at); 2. 2 n (-/no pl.) horror, fright; ⚓lich adj. horrible, dreadful, terrible, shocking.

ent'sinnen v/refl. (gen.) (irr. sinnen, no -ge-, h) remember or recall s.o., s.th.

ent'spann|en v/t. (no -ge-, h) relax; unbend; sich ⚓ relax; political situation: ease; 2ung f relaxation; pol. détente.

ent'sprech|en v/i. (irr. sprechen, no -ge-, h) answer (description, etc.); correspond to; meet (demand); ⚓end adj. corresponding; appropriate, 2ung f (-/-en) equivalent.

ent'springen v/i. (irr. springen, no -ge-, sein) escape (dat. from); river: rise, Am. head; s. entstehen.

ent'stammen v/i. (no -ge-, sein) be descended from; come from or of, originate from.

ent'steh|en v/i. (irr. stehen. no -ge-, sein) arise, originate (both: aus from), 2ung f (-/-en) origin.

ent'stell|en v/t. (no -ge-, h) disfigure; deface, deform; distort; 2ung f disfigurement; distortion, misrepresentation.

ent'täusch|en v/t. (no -ge-, h) disappoint; 2ung f disappointment.

ent'thronen v/t. (no -ge-, h) dethrone.

entvölker|n [ɛnt'fœlkərn] v/t. (no

-ge-, h) depopulate; Qung f (-/-en) depopulation.

ent'wachsen v/i. (irr. wachsen, no -ge-, sein) outgrow.

entwaffn|en [ɛnt'vafnən] v/t. (no -ge-, h) disarm; Qung f (-/-en) disarmament.

ent'warnen v/i. (no -ge-, h) civil defence: sound the all-clear (signal).

ent'wässer|n v/t. (no -ge-, h) drain; Qung f (-/-en) drainage; ⚕ dehydration.

ent'weder cj.: ～ ... oder either ... or.

ent|'weichen v/i. (irr. weichen, no -ge-, sein) escape (aus from); ～'weihen v/t. (no -ge-, h) desecrate, profane; ～'wenden v/t. (no -ge-, h) pilfer, purloin (j-m et. s.th. from s.o.); ～'werfen v/t. (irr. werfen, no -ge-, h) draft, draw up (document); design; sketch, trace out, outline; plan.

ent'wert|en v/t. (no -ge-, h) depreciate, devaluate; cancel (stamp); Qung f depreciation, devaluation; cancellation.

ent'wickeln v/t. (no -ge-, h) develop (a. phot.); evolve; sich ～ develop.

Entwicklung [ɛnt'viklun] f (-/-en) development; evolution; ～shilfe f development aid.

ent|'wirren v/t. (no -ge-, h) disentangle, unravel; ～'wischen v/i. (no -ge-, sein) slip away, escape (j-m [from] s.o.; aus from); j-m ～ give s.o. the slip; ～'wöhnen [～'vø:nən] v/t. (no -ge-, h) wean.

Ent'wurf m sketch; design; plan; draft.

ent|'wurzeln v/t. (no -ge-, h) uproot; ～'ziehen v/t. (irr. ziehen, no -ge-, h) deprive (j-m et. s.o. of s.th.); withdraw (dat. from); sich ～ avoid, elude; evade (responsibility); ～'ziffern v/t. (no -ge-, h) decipher, make out; tel. decode.

ent'zücken 1. v/t. (no -ge-, h) charm, delight; 2. Q n (-s/no pl.) delight, rapture(s pl.), transport(s pl.).

ent'zückend adj. delightful; charming.

Ent'zug m (-[e]s/no pl.) withdrawal; cancellation (of licence); deprivation.

entzünd|bar adj. [ɛnt'tsyntbɑ:r] (in)flammable; ～en v/t. (no -ge-, h) inflame (a. ⚕), kindle; sich ～ catch fire; ⚕ become inflamed; Qung ⚕ f inflammation.

ent'zwei adv. asunder, in two, to pieces; ～en v/t. (no -ge-, h) disunite, set at variance; sich ～ quarrel, fall out (both: mit with); ～gehen v/i. (irr. gehen, sep., -ge-, sein) break, go to pieces; Qung f (-/-en) disunion.

Enzian ⚘ ['ɛntsjɑːn] m (-s/-e) gentian.

Enzyklopädie [ɛntsyklopɛ'di:] f (-/-n) (en)cyclop(a)edia.

Epidemie ⚕ [epide'mi:] f (-/-n) epidemic (disease).

Epilog [epi'lo:k] m (-s/-e) epilog(ue).

episch adj. ['e:piʃ] epic.

Episode [epi'zo:də] f (-/-n) episode.

Epoche [e'pɔxə] f (-/-n) epoch.

Epos ['e:pɔs] n (-/Epen) epic (poem).

er pers. pron. [e:r] he.

erachten [ɛr'-] 1. v/t. (no -ge-, h) consider, think, deem; 2. Q n (-s/no pl.) opinion; m-s ～s in my opinion.

erbarmen [ɛr'barmən] 1. v/refl. (gen.) (no -ge-, h) pity or commiserate s.o.; 2. Q n (-s/no pl.) pity, compassion, commiseration; mercy; ～swert adj. pitiable.

erbärmlich adj. [ɛr'bɛrmliç] pitiful, pitiable; miserable; behaviour: mean.

er'barmungslos adj. pitiless, merciless, relentless.

er'bau|en v/t. (no -ge-, h) build (up), construct, raise; fig. edify; Qer m (-s/-) builder; constructor; ～lich adj. edifying; Qung fig. f (-/-en) edification, Am. uplift.

Erbe ['ɛrbə] 1. m (-n/-n) heir; 2. n (-s/no pl.) inheritance, heritage.

er'beben v/i. (no -ge-, sein) tremble, shake, quake.

'erben v/t. (ge-, h) inherit.

er'beuten v/t. (no -ge-, h) capture.

er'bieten v/refl. (irr. bieten, no -ge-, h) offer, volunteer.

'Erbin f (-/-nen) heiress.

er'bitten v/t. (irr. bitten, no -ge-, h) beg or ask for, request, solicit.

er'bitter|n v/t. (no -ge-, h) embitter, exasperate; Qung f (-/～, -en) bitterness, exasperation.

Erbkrankheit ⚕ ['ɛrp-] f hereditary disease.

erblassen [ɛr'blasən] v/i. (no -ge-, sein) grow or turn pale, lose colo(u)r.

Erblasser ⚖ [ɛr'blasər] m (-s/-) testator; '～in f (-/-nen) testatrix.

er'bleichen v/i. (no -ge-, sein) s. erblassen.

erblich adj. ['ɛrpliç] hereditary; 'Qkeit physiol. f (-/no pl.) heredity.

er'blicken v/t. (no -ge-, h) perceive, see; catch sight of.

erblind|en [ɛr'blindən] v/i. (no -ge-, sein) grow blind; Qung f (-/-en) loss of sight.

er'brechen 1. v/t. (irr. brechen, no -ge-, h) break or force open; vomit; sich ～ vomit; 2. Q n (-s/no pl.) vomiting.

Erbschaft ['ɛrpʃaft] f (-/-en) inheritance, heritage.

Erbse ⚘ ['ɛrpsə] f (-/-n) pea; '～nbrei m pease-pudding, Am. pea purée; '～nsuppe f pea-soup.

Erb|stück ['ɛrp-] n heirloom; '～sünde f original sin; '～teil n (portion of an) inheritance.

Erd|arbeiter ['e:rt-] *m* digger, navvy; **~ball** *m* globe; **~beben** *n* (-s/-) earthquake; **~beere** & *f* strawberry; **~boden** *m* earth; ground, soil; **~e** ['e:rdə] *f* (-/~ -n) earth; ground; soil; world; **'~en** & *v/t.* (ge-, h) earth, ground.

er'denklich *adj* imaginable.

Erdgeschoß ['e:rt-] *n* ground-floor, *Am.* first floor.

er'dicht|en *v/t.* (no -ge-, h) invent, feign; **~et** *adj.* fictitious.

erdig *adj.* ['e:rdiç] earthy.

Erd|karte ['e:rt-] *f* map of the earth; **~kreis** *m* earth, world; **'~kugel** *f* globe; **~kunde** *f* geography; **~leitung** & *f* earth-connexion, earth-wire, *Am.* ground wire; **'~nuß** *f* peanut; **'~öl** *n* mineral oil, petroleum.

er'dolchen *v/t.* (no -ge-, h) stab (with a dagger).

Erdreich ['e:rt-] *n* ground, earth.

er'dreisten *v/refl.* (no -ge-, h) dare, presume.

er'drosseln *v/t.* (no-ge-, h) strangle, throttle.

er'drücken *v/t.* (no-ge-, h) squeeze *or* crush to death; **~d** *fig. adj.* overwhelming.

Erd|rutsch ['e:rt-] *m* landslip; landslide (*a. pol.*); **'~schicht** *f* layer of earth, stratum; **'~teil** *m* part of the world; *geogr.* continent.

er'dulden *v/t.* (no -ge-, h) suffer, endure.

er'eifern *v/refl.* (no -ge-, h) get excited, fly into a passion.

er'eignen *v/refl.* (no -ge-, h) happen, come to pass, occur.

Ereignis [ɛr'aiknis] *n* (-ses/-se) event, occurrence; **Sreich** *adj.* eventful.

Eremit [ere'mi:t] *m* (-en/-en) hermit, anchorite.

ererbt *adj.* [ɛr'ɛrpt] inherited.

er'fahr|en 1. *v/t.* (*irr. fahren, no* -ge-, h) learn, hear; experience; **2.** *adj.* experienced, expert, skil(l)ful; **Sung** *f* (-/-en) experience; practice; skill.

er'fassen *v/t.* (no -ge-, h) grasp (*a. fig.*), seize, catch; cover; register, record.

er'find|en *v/t.* (*irr. finden, no* -ge-, h) invent; **Ser** *m* inventor; **~erisch** *adj.* inventive; **Sung** *f* (-/-en) invention.

Erfolg [ɛr'fɔlk] *m* (-[e]s/-e) success; result; **Sen** [-gən] *v/i.* (no -ge-, sein) ensue follow, happen; **Slos** *adj.* [-k-] unsuccessful; vain; **Sreich** *adj.* [-k-] successful.

er'forder|lich *adj* necessary, required; **~n** *v/t* (no -ge-, h) require, demand; **Snis** *n* (-ses/-se) requirement, demand, exigence, exigency.

er'forsch|en *v/t.* (no -ge-, h) inquire into, investigate; explore

(*country*); **Ser** *m* investigator; explorer; **Sung** *f* investigation; exploration

er'freu|en *v/t.* (no -ge-, h) please; delight; gratify; rejoice; *sich* e-*r Sache ~* enjoy s.th.; **~lich** *adj.* delightful, pleasing, pleasant, gratifying.

er'frier|en *v/i.* (*irr. frieren, no* -ge-, sein) freeze to death; **Sung** *f* (-/-en) frost-bite.

er'frisch|en *v/t.* (no -ge-, h) refresh; **Sung** *f* (-/-en) refreshment.

er'froren *adj.* limb. frost-bitten.

er'füll|en *v/t.* (no -ge-, h) fill; *fig.* fulfil(l); perform (*mission*); comply with (*s.o.'s wishes*); meet (*requirements*); **Sung** *f* fulfil(l)ment; performance; compliance; **Sungsort** †, *pɔ* [ɛr'fylʊŋs³-] *m* place of performance (*of contract*).

ergänz|en [ɛr'gɛntsən] *v/t.* (no -ge-, h) complete, complement; supplement; replenish (*stores, etc.*); **~end** *adj.* complementary, supplementary; **Sung** *f* (-/-en) completion; supplement; replenishment; *gr.* complement; **Sungsband** *m* (-[e]s/~e) supplementary volume.

er'geben 1. *v/t.* (*irr. geben, no* -ge-, h) yield, give; prove; *sich ~* surrender; *difficulties* arise; devote o.s. *to s.th.*; *sich ~ aus* result from; *sich ~ in* (*acc.*) resign o.s. to; **2.** *adj.* devoted (*dat.* to); *adv.* respectfully; **Sheit** *f* (-/no *pl.*) devotion.

Ergeb|nis [ɛr'ge:pnis] *n* (-ses/-se) result, outcome; *sports:* score; **~ung** [-bʊŋ] *f* (-/-en) resignation; ⚔ surrender.

er'gehen *v/i.* (*irr. gehen, no* -ge-, sein) be issued; *~ lassen* issue, publish; *über sich ~ lassen* suffer, submit to; *wie ist es ihm ergangen?* how did he come off?; *sich ~ in* (*dat.*) indulge in.

ergiebig *adj.* [ɛr'gi:biç] productive, rich.

er'gießen *v/refl.* (*irr. gießen, no* -ge-, h) flow (*in acc.* into; *über acc.* over).

er'götz|en 1. *v/t.* (no -ge-, h) delight; *sich ~ an* (*dat.*) delight in; **2.** *S n* (-s/no *pl.*) delight; **~lich** *adj.* delightful.

er'greif|en *v/t.* (*irr. greifen, no* -ge-, h) seize; grasp; take (*possession, s.o.'s part, measures, etc.*); take to (*flight*); take up (*profession, pen, arms*); *fig.* move, affect, touch; **Sung** *f* (-/~ -en) seizure.

Er'griffenheit *f* (-/no *pl.*) emotion.

er'gründen *v/t.* (no -ge-, h) fathom; *fig.* penetrate, get to the bottom of.

Er'guß *m* outpouring, effusion.

er'haben *adj.* elevated; *fig.* exalted, sublime; *~ über* (*acc.*) be above; **Sheit** *f* (-/~ -en) elevation; *fig.* sublimity.

er'halt|en 1. v/t. (irr. halten, no -ge-, h) get; obtain; receive; preserve, keep; support, maintain; sich ~ von subsist on; 2. adj.: gut ~ in good repair or condition; 2ung f preservation; maintenance.

erhältlich adj. [ɛr'hɛltlíç] obtainable.

er|'hängen v/t. (no -ge-, h) hang; ~'härten v/t. (no -ge-, h) harden; fig. confirm; ~'haschen v/t. (no -ge-, h) snatch, catch.

er'heb|en v/t. (irr. heben, no -ge-, h) lift, raise; elevate; exalt; levy, raise, collect (taxes, etc.); Klage ~ bring an action; sich ~ rise; question, etc.: arise; ~end fig. adj. elevating; ~lich adj. [~p-] considerable; 2ung [~buŋ] f (-/-en) elevation; levy (of taxes); revolt; rising ground.

er|'heitern v/t. (no -ge-, h) cheer up, amuse; ~'hellen v/t. (no -ge-, h) light up; fig. clear up; ~'hitzen v/t. (no -ge-, h) heat; sich ~ get or grow hot; ~'hoffen v/t. (no -ge-, h) hope for.

er'höh|en v/t. (no -ge-, h) raise; increase; 2ung f (-/-en) elevation; rise (in prices, wages); advance (in prices); increase.

er'hol|en v/refl. (no -ge-, h) recover; (take a) rest, relax; 2ung f (-/-en) recovery; recreation; relaxation; 2ungsurlaub [er'ho:luŋs?-] m holiday, Am. vacation; recreation leave; ✠ convalescent leave, sickleave. [(request).\]

er'hören v/t. (no -ge-, h) hear; grant\]

erinner|n [er'inərn] v/t. (no -ge-, h): j-n ~ an (acc.) remind s.o. of; sich ~ (gen.), sich ~ an (acc.) remember s.o. or s.th., recollect s.th.; 2ung f (-/-en) remembrance; recollection; reminder; ~en pl. reminiscences pl.

er'kalten v/i. (no -ge-, sein) cool down (a. fig.), get cold.

erkält|en [er'kɛltən] v/refl. (no -ge-, h): sich (sehr) ~ catch a (bad) cold; 2ung f (-/-en) cold.

er'kennen v/t. (irr. kennen, no -ge-, h) recognize (an dat. by); perceive, discern; realize.

er'kenntlich adj. perceptible; sich ~ zeigen show one's appreciation; 2keit f (-/-en) gratitude; appreciation.

Er'kenntnis 1. f perception; realization; 2. ⚖ n (-ses/-se) decision, sentence, finding.

Erker ['ɛrkər] m (-s/-) bay; '~fenster n bay-window.

er'klär|en v/t. (no -ge-, h) explain; account for; declare, state; sich ~ declare (für for, gegen against); ~lich adj. explainable, explicable; ~t adj. professed, declared; 2ung f explanation; declaration.

er'klingen v/i. (irr. klingen, no -ge-, sein) (re)sound, ring (out).

erkoren adj. [ɛr'ko:rən] (s)elect, chosen.

er'krank|en v/i. (no -ge-, sein) fall ill, be taken ill (an dat. of, with); become affected; 2ung f (-/-en) illness, sickness, falling ill.

er|'kühnen v/refl. (no -ge-, h) venture, presume, make bold (zu inf. to inf.); ~'kunden v/t. (no -ge-, h) explore, ⚔ reconnoit|re, Am. -er.

erkundig|en [er'kundigən] v/refl. (no -ge-, h) inquire (über acc. after; nach after or for s.o.; about s.th.); 2ung f (-/-en) inquiry.

er|'lahmen fig. v/i. (no -ge-, sein) grow weary, tire; slacken; interest: wane, flag; ~'langen v/t. (no -ge-, h) obtain, get.

Er|laß [er'las] m (Erlasses/Erlasse) dispensation, exemption, remission (of debt, penalty, etc.); edict, decree; 2'lassen v/t. (irr. lassen, no -ge-, h) remit (debt, penalty, etc.); dispense (j-m et. s.o from s.th.); issue (decree); enact (law).

erlauben [er'laubən] v/t. (no -ge-, h) allow, permit; sich et. indulge in s.th., sich zu inf. ✠ beg to inf.

Erlaubnis [er'laupnis] f (-/no pl.) permission; authority; ~schein m permit.

er'läuter|n v/t. (no -ge-, h) explain, illustrate; comment (up)on; 2ung f explanation, illustration; comment.

Erle ['ɛrlə] f (-/-n) alder.

er'leb|en v/t. (no -ge-, h) (live to) see; experience; go through; 2nis [~pnis] n (-ses/-se) experience; adventure.

erledig|en [er'le:digən] v/t. (no -ge-, h) dispatch, execute; settle (matter); ~t adj. [~çt] finished, settled; fig. played out, done for; F: du bist für mich ~ I am through with you, 2ung [~guŋ] f (-/✠ -en) dispatch, settlement.

er'leichter|n v/t. (no -ge-, h) lighten (burden), fig. make easy, facilitate; relieve; 2ung f (-/-en) ease, relief; facilitation; ~en pl facilities pl.

er|'leiden v/t. (irr leiden, no -ge-, h) suffer, endure, sustain (damage, loss); ~'lernen v/t. (no -ge-, h) learn, acquire.

er'leucht|en v/t. (no -ge-, h) illuminate; fig enlighten; 2ung f (-/-en) illumination; fig. enlightenment.

er'liegen v/i. (irr liegen, no -ge-, sein) succumb (dat to).

erlogen adj. [ɛr'lo:gən] false, untrue.

Erlös [ɛr'lø:s] m (-es/-e) proceeds pl.

erlosch [ɛr'lɔʃ] pret of erlöschen; ~en 1. p.p. of erlöschen; 2. adj. extinct.

er'löschen v/i. (irr., no -ge-, sein) go out; fig. become extinct; contract: expire.

er'lös|en v/t. (no -ge-, h) redeem;

deliver; 2er m (-s/-) redeemer, deliverer; *eccl.* Redeemer, Saviour; 2ung f redemption; deliverance.

ermächtig|en [ɛr'mɛçtigən] v/t. (*no -ge-, h*) authorize; 2ung f (-/-en) authorization; authority; warrant.

er'mahn|en v/t. (*no -ge-, h*) admonish; 2ung f admonition.

er'mangel|n v/i. (*no -ge-, h*) be wanting (*gen.* in); 2ung f (-/*no pl.*): in ~ (*gen.*) in default of, for want of, failing.

er'mäßig|en v/t. (*no -ge-, h*) abate, reduce, cut (down); 2ung f (-/-en) abatement, reduction.

er'matt|en (*no -ge-*) 1. v/t. (h) fatigue, tire, exhaust; 2. v/i. (sein) tire, grow weary; *fig.* slacken; 2ung f (-/◌, -en) fatigue, exhaustion.

er'messen 1. v/t. (*irr.* messen, *no -ge-, h*) judge; 2. 2 n (-s/*no pl.*) judg(e)ment; discretion.

er'mitt|eln v/t. (*no -ge-, h*) ascertain, find out; ₫ investigate; 2(e)-lung [~(ə)luŋ] f (-/-en) ascertainment; inquiry; ₫ investigation.

er'möglichen v/t. (*no -ge-, h*) render or make possible.

er'mord|en v/t. (*no -ge-, h*) murder; assassinate; 2ung f (-/-en) murder; assassination.

er'müd|en (*no -ge-*) 1. v/t. (h) tire, fatigue; 2. v/i. (sein) tire, get tired or fatigued; 2ung f (-/◌-en) fatigue, tiredness.

er'munter|n v/t. (*no -ge-, h*) rouse, encourage; animate; 2ung f (-/-en) encouragement, animation.

ermutig|en [ɛr'muːtigən] v/t. (*no -ge-, h*) encourage; 2ung f (-/-en) encouragement.

er'nähr|en v/t. (*no -ge-, h*) nourish, feed; support; 2er m (-s/-) breadwinner, supporter; 2ung f(-/◌, -en) nourishment; support; *physiol.* nutrition.

er'nenn|en v/t. (*irr.* nennen, *no -ge-, h*) nominate, appoint; 2ung f nomination, appointment.

er'neu|ern v/t. (*no -ge-, h*) renew, renovate; revive; 2erung f renewal, renovation; revival; ~t *adv.* once more.

erniedrig|en [ɛr'niːdrigən] v/t. (*no -ge-, h*) degrade; humiliate; humble; 2ung f (-/-en) degradation; humiliation.

Ernst [ɛrnst] 1. m (-es/*no pl.*) seriousness; earnest(ness); gravity; im ~ in earnest; 2. 2 *adj.* - 2haft *adj.*, 2lich *adj.* serious, earnest; grave.

Ernte ['ɛrntə] f (-/-n) harvest; crop; ~'dankfest n harvest festival; 2n v/t. (*ge-, h*) harvest, gather (in), reap (*a. fig.*).

er'nüchter|n v/t. (*no -ge-, h*) (make) sober; *fig.* disillusion; 2ung f (-/-en) sobering; *fig.* disillusionment.

Er'ober|er m (-s/-) conqueror; 2n v/t. (*no -ge-, h*) conquer; ~ung f (-/-en) conquest.

er'öffn|en v/t. (*no -ge-, h*) open; inaugurate; disclose (*j-m et. s.th. to s.o.*); notify; 2ung f opening; inauguration; disclosure.

erörter|n [ɛr'œrtərn] v/t. (*no -ge-, h*) discuss; 2ung f (-/-en) discussion.

Erpel ~rn. ['ɛrpəl] m (-s/-) drake.

erpicht *adj.* [ɛr'piçt]: ~ auf (*acc.*) bent or intent or set or keen on.

er'press|en v/t. (*no -ge-, h*) extort (*von* from); blackmail; 2er m (-s/-), 2erin f (-/-nen) extort(ion)er; blackmailer; 2ung f (-/-en) extortion; blackmail.

er'proben v/t. (*no -ge-, h*) try, test.

erquick|en [ɛr'kvikən] v/t. (*no -ge-, h*) refresh; 2ung f (-/-en) refreshment.

er|'raten v/t. (*irr.* raten, *no -ge-, h*) guess, find out; ~'rechnen v/t. (*no -ge-, h*) calculate, compute, work out.

erreg|bar *adj.* [ɛr'reːkbaːr] excitable; ~en [~gən] v/t. (*no -ge-, h*) excite; cause; 2er m [~gər] m (-s/-) exciter *a. ∉*); ∉ germ, virus; 2ung [~guŋ] f excitation; excitement.

er'reich|bar *adj.* attainable; within reach or call; ~en v/t. (*no -ge-, h*) reach; *fig.* achieve, attain; catch (*train*); come up to (*certain standard*).

er'rett|en v/t. (*no -ge-, h*) rescue; 2ung f rescue.

er'richt|en v/t. (*no -ge-, h*) set up, erect, establish; 2ung f erection; establishment.

er|'ringen v/t. (*irr.* ringen, *no -ge-, h*) gain, obtain; achieve (*success*); ~'röten v/i. (*no -ge-, h, sein*) blush.

Errungenschaft [ɛr'ruŋənʃaft] f (-/-en) acquisition; achievement.

Er'satz m (-es/*no pl.*) replacement; substitute; compensation; amends *sg.*, damages *pl.*; indemnification; s. Ersatzmann, Ersatzmittel; ~ leisten make amends; ~mann m substitute; ~mine f refill (*for pencil*); ~mittel n substitute, surrogate; ~reifen *mot.* m spare tyre, (*Am. only*) spare tire; ~teil ⊕ n, m spare (part).

er'schaff|en v/t. (*irr.* schaffen, *no -ge-, h*) create; 2ung f (-/*no pl.*) creation.

er'schallen v/i. ([*irr.* schallen,] *no -ge-, sein*) (re)sound; ring.

er'schein|en 1. v/i. (*irr.* scheinen, *no -ge-, sein*) appear; 2. 2 n (-s/*no pl.*) appearance; 2ung f (-/-en) appearance; apparition; vision.

er|'schießen v/t. (*irr.* schießen, *no -ge-, h*) shoot (dead); ~'schlaffen v/i. (*no -ge-, sein*) tire; relax; *fig.* languish, slacken; ~'schlagen v/t. (*irr.* schlagen, *no -ge-, h*) kill, slay;

~'schließen v/t. (irr. schließen, no -ge-, h) open; open up (new market); develop (district).

er'schöpf|en v/t. (no -ge-, h) exhaust; 2ung f exhaustion.

erschrak [ɛr'ʃraːk] pret. of erschrecken 2.

er'schrecken 1. v/t. (no -ge-, h) frighten, scare; 2. v/i. (irr., no -ge-, sein) be frightened (über acc. at); ~d adj. alarming, startling.

erschrocken [ɛr'ʃrɔkən] 1. p.p. of erschrecken 2; 2. adj. frightened, terrified.

erschütter|n [ɛr'ʃytərn] v/t. (no -ge-, h) shake; fig. shock, move; 2ung f (-/-en) shock; fig. emotion; ✻ concussion; ⊕ percussion.

er'schweren v/t. (no -ge-, h) make more difficult; aggravate.

er'schwing|en v/t. (irr. schwingen, no -ge-, h) afford; ~lich adj. within s.o.'s means; prices: reasonable.

er|'sehen v/t. (irr. sehen, no -ge-, h) see, learn, gather (all: aus from); ~'sehnen v/t. (no -ge-, h) long for; ~'setzen v/t. (no -ge-, h) repair; make up for, compensate (for); replace; refund.

er'sichtlich adj. evident, obvious.

er'sinnen v/t. (irr. sinnen, no -ge-, h) contrive, devise.

er'spar|en v/t. (no -ge-, h) save; j-m et. ~ spare s.o. s.th.; 2nis f (-/-se) saving.

er'sprießlich adj. useful, beneficial.

erst [eːrst] 1. adj.: der (die, das) ~e the first; 2. adv. first; at first; only; not ~ till or until.

er'starr|en v/i. (no -ge-, sein) stiffen; solidify; congeal; set; grow numb; fig. blood: run cold; ~t adj. benumbed; 2ung f (-/-en) numbness; solidification; congealment; setting.

erstatt|en [ɛr'ʃtatən] v/t. (no -ge-, h) restore; s. ersetzen; Bericht ~ (make a) report; 2ung f (-/-en) restitution.

'Erstaufführung f thea. first night or performance, premiere; film: a. first run.

er'staun|en 1. v/i. (no -ge-, sein) be astonished (über acc. at); 2. v/t. (no -ge-, h) astonish; 3. 2 n astonishment; in ~ setzen astonish; ~lich adj. astonishing, amazing.

er'stechen v/t. (irr. stechen, no -ge-, h) stab.

er'steig|en v/t. (irr. steigen, no -ge-, h) ascend, climb; 2ung f ascent.

erstens adv. ['eːrstəns] first, firstly.

er'stick|en (no -ge-) v/t. (h) and v/i. (sein) choke, suffocate; stifle; 2ung f (-/-en) suffocation. [rate, ┌ A 1.)

'erstklassig adj. first-class, first-)

er'streben v/t. (no -ge-, h) strive after or for; ~swert adj. desirable.

er'strecken v/refl. (no -ge-, h) extend; sich ~ über (acc.) cover.

er'suchen 1. v/t. (no -ge-, h) request; 2. 2 n (-s/-) request.

er|'tappen v/t. (no -ge-, h) catch, surprise; s. frisch; ~'tönen v/i. (no -ge-, sein) (re)sound.

Ertrag [ɛr'traːk] m (-[e]s/-e) produce, yield; proceeds pl., returns pl.; ✗ output; 2en [~gən] v/t. (irr. tragen, no -ge-, h) bear, endure; suffer, stand.

erträglich adj. [ɛr'trɛːkliç] tolerable

er|'tränken v/t. (no -ge-, h) drown; ~'trinken v/i. (irr. trinken, no -ge-, sein) be drowned, drown; ~'übrigen [ɛr'yːbrigən] v/t. (no -ge-, h) save; spare (time); sich ~ be unnecessary; ~'wachen v/i. (no -ge-, sein) awake, wake up.

er'wachsen 1. v/i. (irr. wachsen, no -ge-, sein) arise (aus from); 2. adj. grown-up, adult; 2e m, f (-n/-n) grown-up, adult.

er'wäg|en v/t. (irr. wägen, no -ge-, h) consider, think s.th. over; 2ung f (-/-en) consideration.

er'wählen v/t. (no -ge-, h) choose, elect.

er'wähn|en v/t. (no -ge-, h) mention, 2ung f (-/-en) mention.

er'wärmen v/t. (no -ge-, h) warm, heat, sich ~ warm (up).

er'wart|en v/t. (no -ge-, h) await, wait for; fig. expect; 2ung f expectation.

er|'wecken v/t. (no -ge-, h) wake, rouse, fig. awake; cause (fear); arouse (suspicion); ~'wehren v/refl. (gen.) (no -ge-, h) keep or ward off; ~'weichen v/t. (no -ge-, h) soften; fig. move; ~'weisen v/t. (irr. weisen, no -ge-, h) prove; show (respect); render (service); do, pay (honour); do (favour).

er'weiter|n v/t. and v/refl. (no -ge-, h) expand, enlarge, extend, widen; 2ung f (-/-en) expansion, enlargement, extension.

Erwerb [ɛr'verp] m (-[e]s/-e) acquisition; living; earnings pl.; business; 2en [~bən] v/t. (irr. werben, no -ge-, h) acquire; gain; earn.

erwerbs|los adj. [ɛr'verpsloːs] unemployed; ~tätig adj. (gainfully) employed; ~unfähig adj. [ɛr-'verps?-] incapable of earning one's living, 2zweig m line of business.

Erwerbung [ɛr'verbuŋ] f acquisition.

erwider|n [ɛr'viːdərn] v/t. (no -ge-, h) return; answer, reply; retort; 2ung f (-/-en) return; answer, reply.

er'wischen v/t. (no -ge-, h) catch, trap, get hold of.

er'wünscht adj. desired; desirable; welcome.

er'würgen v/t. (no -ge-, h) strangle, throttle.

Erz ⚒ [eːrts] n (-es/-e) ore; *poet.* brass.

er'zähl|en v/t. (no -ge-, h) tell; relate; narrate; **2er** m, **2erin** f (-/-nen) narrator; writer; **2ung** f narration; (short) story, narrative.

'Erz|bischof *eccl.* m archbishop; **'_bistum** *eccl.* n archbishopric; **'_engel** *eccl.* m archangel.

er'zeug|en v/t. (no -ge-, h) beget; produce; make, manufacture; **2er** m (-s/-) father (of child); ♱ producer; **2nis** n produce; production; ⊕ product; **2ung** f production.

'Erz|feind m arch-enemy; **'_herzog** m archduke; **'_herzogin** f archduchess; **'_herzogtum** n archduchy.

er'zieh|en v/t. (irr. ziehen, no -ge-, h) bring up, rear, raise; educate; **2er** m (-s/-) educator; teacher, tutor; **2rin** f (-/-nen) teacher; governess; **_risch** adj. educational, pedagogic (-al).

Er'ziehung f (-/⚒ -en) upbringing; breeding; education; **_sanstalt** [er'tsiːuŋs⁹-] f reformatory, approved school; **_swesen** n (-s/no pl.) educational matters pl. or system.

er|'zielen v/t. (no -ge-, h) obtain; realize (price); achieve (success); *sports:* score (points, goal); **_'zürnen** v/t. (no -ge-, h) make angry, irritate, enrage; **_'zwingen** v/t. (irr. zwingen, no -ge-, h) (en)force; compel; extort (von from).

es *pers. pron.* [es] **1.** *pers.:* it, he, she; wo ist das Buch? — _ ist auf dem Tisch where is the book? — it is on the table; das Mädchen blieb stehen, als _ seine Mutter sah the girl stopped when she saw her mother; **2.** *impers.:* it; _ gibt there is, there are; _ ist kalt it is cold; _ klopft there is a knock at the door.

Esche ⚘ ['ɛʃə] f (-/-n) ash(-tree).

Esel *zo.* ['eːzəl] m (-s/-) donkey; *esp. fig.* ass; sl. **_ei** ['_'laɪ] f (-/-en) stupidity, stupid thing, folly; **'_sbrücke** f at school: crib, Am. pony; **_sohr** ['eːzəls⁹-] n dog's ear (of book).

Eskorte [ɛs'kɔrtə] f (-/-n) ⚔ escort; ⚓ convoy.

Espe ⚘ ['ɛspə] f (-/-n) asp(en).

'eßbar adj. eatable, edible.

Esse ⚒ ['ɛsə] f (-/-n) chimney.

essen ['ɛsən] **1.** v/i. (irr., ge-, h) eat; zu Mittag _ (have) lunch; dine, have dinner; zu Abend _ dine, have dinner; *esp. late at night:* sup, have supper; auswärts _ eat or dine out; **2.** v/t. (irr., ge-, h) eat; et. zu Mittag etc. _ have s.th. for lunch, etc.; **3.** **2** n (-s/-) eating; food; meal; dish; midday meal: lunch, dinner; evening meal: dinner; last meal of the day: supper; **'2szeit** f lunch-time; dinner-time; supper-time.

Essenz [ɛ'sɛnts] f (-/-en) essence.

Essig ['ɛsiç] m (-s/-e) vinegar; **'_gurke** f pickled cucumber, gherkin.

Eß|löffel m soup-spoon; **'_nische** f dining alcove, Am. dinette; **'_tisch** m dining-table; **'_waren** f/pl. eatables pl., victuals pl., food; **'_zimmer** n dining-room.

etablieren [eta'bliːrən] v/t. (no -ge-, h) establish, set up.

Etage [e'taːʒə] f (-/-n) floor, stor(e)y; **_nwohnung** f flat, Am. a. apartment.

Etappe [e'tapə] f (-/-n) ⚔ base; *fig.* stage, leg.

Etat [e'taː] m (-s/-s) budget, *parl. the* Estimates pl.; **_sjahr** n fiscal year. [or sg.)

Ethik ['eːtik] f (-/⚒ -en) ethics pl.)

Etikett [eti'kɛt] n (-[e]s/-e, -s) label, ticket; tag; gummed: Am. a. sticker; **_e** f (-/-n) etiquette; **2ieren** [_'tiːrən] v/t. (no -ge-, h) label.

etliche *indef. pron.* ['ɛtliçə] some, several.

Etui [e'tviː] n (-s/-s) case.

etwa adv. ['ɛtva] perhaps, by chance; about, Am. a. around; **_ig** adj. ['_⁹iç] possible, eventual.

etwas ['ɛtvas] **1.** *indef. pron.* something; anything; **2.** adj. some; any; **3.** adv. somewhat; **4.** **2** n (-/-): das gewisse _ that certain something.

euch *pers. pron.* [ɔʏç] you; _ (selbst) yourselves.

euer *poss. pron.* ['ɔʏər] your; der (die, das) eu(e)re yours.

Eule *orn.* ['ɔʏlə] f (-/-n) owl; **_n** nach Athen tragen carry coals to Newcastle.

euresgleichen *pron.* ['ɔʏrəs'glaɪçən] people like you, F the likes of you.

Europä|er [ɔʏro'pɛːər] m (-s/-) European; **2isch** adj. European.

Euter ['ɔʏtər] n (-s/-) udder.

evakuieren [evaku'iːrən] v/t. (no -ge-, h) evacuate.

evangeli|sch adj. [evaŋ'geːliʃ] evangelic(al); Protestant; Lutheran; **2um** [_jum] n (-s/Evangelien) gospel.

eventuell [eventu'ɛl] **1.** adj. possible; **2.** adv. possibly, perhaps.

ewig adj. ['eːviç] eternal; everlasting; perpetual; auf _ for ever; **'2keit** f (-/-en) eternity; F: seit e-r _ for ages.

exakt adj. [ɛ'ksakt] exact; **2heit** f (-/-en) exactitude, exactness; accuracy.

Exam|en [ɛ'ksaːmən] n (-s/-, Examina) examination, F exam; **2inieren** [_ami'niːrən] v/t. (no -ge-, h) examine.

Exekutive [ɛksəku'tiːvə] f (-/no pl.) executive power.

Exempel [ɛ'ksɛmpəl] n (-s/-) example, instance.

Exemplar [ɛksɛm'plɑ:r] *n* (-s/-e) specimen; copy (*of book*).

exerzier|en ✂ [ɛksɛr'tsi:rən] *v/i. and v/t.* (*no -ge-, h*) drill; **♀platz** ✂ *m* drill-ground, parade-ground.

Exil [ɛ'ksi:l] *n* (-s/-e) exile.

Existenz [ɛksis'tɛnts] *f* (-/-en) existence; living, livelihood; **∼minimum** *n* subsistence minimum.

exis'tieren *v/i.* (*no -ge-, h*) exist; subsist.

exotisch *adj.* [ɛ'kso:tiʃ] exotic.

exped|ieren [ɛkspe'di:rən] *v/t.* (*no -ge-, h*) dispatch; **♀ition** [∼i'tsjo:n] *f* (-/-en) dispatch, forwarding, expedition; **✝** dispatch *or* forwarding office.

Experiment [ɛksperi'mɛnt] *n* (-[e]s/-e) experiment; **♀ieren** [∼'ti:rən] *v/i.* (*no -ge-, h*) experiment.

explo|dieren [ɛksplo'di:rən] *v/i.* (*no -ge-, sein*) explode, burst; **♀sion** [∼'zjo:n] *f* (-/-en) explosion; **∼siv** *adj.* [∼'zi:f] explosive.

Export [ɛks'pɔrt] *m* (-[e]s/-e) export(ation), **♀ieren** [∼'ti:rən] *v/t.* (*no -ge-, h*) export.

extra *adj.* ['ɛkstra] extra; special; **♀blatt** *n* extra edition (*of newspaper*), *Am.* extra.

Extrakt [ɛks'trakt] *m* (-[e]s/-e) extract.

Extrem [ɛks'tre:m] **1.** *n* (-s/-e) extreme; **2.** ♀ *adj.* extreme.

Exzellenz [ɛkstsɛ'lɛnts] *f* (-/-en) Excellency.

exzentrisch *adj.* [ɛks'tsɛntriʃ] eccentric

Exzeß [ɛks'tsɛs] *m* (Exzesses/Exzesse) excess.

F

Fabel ['fɑ:bəl] *f* (-/-n) fable (*a. fig.*); plot (*of story, book, etc.*); **♀haft** *adj.* fabulous; marvellous; '**♀n** *v/i.* (*ge-, h*) tell (tall) stories.

Fabrik [fa'bri:k] *f* (-/-en) factory, works *sg., pl.*, mill; **∼ant** [∼i'kant] *m* (-en/-en) factory-owner, mill-owner; manufacturer; **∼arbeit** *f* factory work; *s.* Fabrikware; **∼arbeiter** *m* factory worker *or* hand; **∼at** [∼i'ka:t] *n* (-[e]s/-e) make; product; **∼ationsfehler** [∼a'tsjo:ns-] *m* flaw; **∼besitzer** *m* factory-owner; **∼marke** *f* trade mark; **∼stadt** *f* factory *or* industrial town; **∼ware** *f* manufactured article; **∼zeichen** *n s.* Fabrikmarke.

Fach [fax] *n* (-[e]s/∼er) section, compartment, shelf (*of bookcase, cupboard, etc.*); drawer; *fig.* subject; *s.* Fachgebiet; '**∼arbeiter** *m* skilled worker; '**∼arzt** *m* specialist (*für* in); '**∼ausbildung** *f* professional training; '**∼ausdruck** *m* technical term.

fächeln ['fɛçəln] *v/t.* (*ge-, h*) fan *s.o.*

Fächer ['fɛçər] *m* (-s/-) fan; **♀förmig** *adj.* ['∼fœrmiç] fan-shaped.

'**Fach|gebiet** *n* branch, field, province; '**∼kenntnisse** *f/pl.* specialized knowledge; '**∼kreis** *m*: in **∼en** among experts; '**♀kundig** *adj.* competent, expert; '**∼literatur** *f* specialized literature; '**∼mann** *m* expert; **♀männisch** *adj.* ['∼mɛniʃ] expert; '**∼schule** *f* technical school; '**∼werk** ⚠ *n* framework.

Fackel ['fakəl] *f* (-/-n) torch; '**♀n** F *v/i.* (*ge-, h*) hesitate, F shilly-shally; '**∼zug** *m* torchlight procession.

fad *adj.* [fɑ:t], **∼e** *adj.* ['fɑ:də] *food*: insipid, tasteless; stale; *p.* dull, boring.

Faden ['fɑ:dən] *m* (-s/∼) thread (*a. fig.*); *fig.* an e-m **∼** hängen hang by a thread; '**∼nudeln** *f/pl.* vermicelli *pl.*; **♀scheinig** *adj.* ['∼ʃainiç] threadbare; *excuse, etc.*: flimsy, thin.

fähig *adj.* ['fɛ:iç] capable (*zu inf.* of *ger.*; *gen* of); able (*to inf.*); **♀keit** *f* (-/-en) (cap)ability; talent, faculty.

fahl *adj.* [fɑ:l] pale, pallid; *colour:* faded; *complexion:* leaden, livid.

fahnd|en ['fɑ:ndən] *v/i.* (*ge-, h*): nach *j-m* **∼** search for s.o.; **♀ung** *f* (-/-en) search.

Fahne ['fɑ:nə] *f* (-/-n) flag; standard; banner; ⚓, ✂, *fig.* colo(u)rs *pl.*; *typ* galley-proof.

'**Fahnen|eid** *m* oath of allegiance; '**∼flucht** *f* desertion; '**♀flüchtig** *adj.* **∼** werden desert (the colo[u]rs); '**∼stange** *f* flagstaff, *Am. a.* flagpole

'**Fahr|bahn** *f*, '**∼damm** *m* roadway.

Fähre ['fɛ:rə] *f* (-/-n) ferry(-boat).

fahren ['fɑ:rən] (*irr., ge-*) **1.** *v/i.* (*sein*) *driver, vehicle, etc.*: drive, go, travel; *cyclist:* ride, cycle; ⚓ sail; *mot.* motor; *mit der Eisenbahn* **∼** go by train *or* rail; *spazieren* **∼** go for *or* take a drive; *mit der Hand* **∼** *über* (*acc.*) pass one's hand over; *∼ lassen* let go *or* slip; *gut* (*schlecht*) **∼** *bei* do *or* fare well (badly) at *or* with; *er ist gut dabei gefahren* he did very well out of it; **2.** *v/t.* (*h*) carry, convey; drive (*car, train, etc.*); ride (*bicycle, etc.*).

'**Fahrer** *m* (-s/-) driver; '**∼flucht** *f* (-/*no pl.*) hit-and-run offence, *Am.* hit-and-run offense.

'Fahr|gast *m* passenger; *in taxi*: fare; '~geld *n* fare; '~gelegenheit *f* transport facilities *pl.*; '~gestell *n* mot. chassis; 🜇 undercarriage, landing gear; '~karte *f* ticket; '~kartenschalter *m* booking-office, *Am.* ticket office; '2lässig *adj.* careless, negligent; '~lässigkeit *f* (-/🜆-en) carelessness, negligence; '~lehrer mot. *m* driving instructor; '~plan *m* timetable, *Am. a.* schedule; '2planmäßig 1. *adj.* regular, *Am.* scheduled; 2. *adv.* on time, *Am. a.* on schedule; '~preis *m* fare; '~rad *n* bicycle, F bike; '~schein *m* ticket; '~schule *mot. f* driving school, school of motoring; ~stuhl *m* lift, *Am.* elevator; '~stuhlführer *m* lift-boy, lift-man, *Am.* elevator operator; '~stunde *mot. f* driving lesson.

Fahrt [fa:rt] *f* (-/-en) ride, drive; journey; voyage, passage; trip; ~ ins Blaue mystery tour; *in voller ~* (at) full speed.

Fährte ['fɛ:rtə] *f* (-/-n) track (*a. fig.*); *auf der falschen ~ sein* be on the wrong track.

'Fahr|vorschrift *f* rule of the road; '~wasser *n* ⚓ navigable water; *fig.* track; '~weg *m* roadway; '~zeug *n* vehicle; ⚓ vessel.

Fakt|or ['faktor] *m* (-s/-en) factor; ~otum [~'to:tum] *n* (-s/-s, Faktoten) factotum; ~ur ✝ [~'tu:r] *f* (-/-en), ~ura ✝ [~'tu:ra] *f* (-/Fakturen) invoice.

Fakultät *univ.* [fakul'tɛ:t] *f* (-/-en) faculty.

Falke *orn.* ['falkə] *m* (-n/-n) hawk, falcon.

Fall [fal] *m* (-[e]s/ⁿe) fall (*of body, stronghold, city, etc.*); gr., 🜨ⁿ case; gesetzt den ~ suppose; *auf alle Fälle* at all events; *auf jeden ~* in any case, at any rate; *auf keinen ~* on no account, in no case.

Falle ['falə] *f* (-/-n) trap (*a. fig.*); pitfall (*a. fig.*); e-e ~ stellen set a trap (*j-m* for s.o.).

fallen ['falən] 1. *v/i.* (*irr.*, ge-, sein) fall, drop; ✕ be killed in action; *shot*: be heard; *flood water*: subside; *auf j-n ~ suspicion, etc.*: fall on s.o.; ~ *lassen* drop (*plate, etc.*); 2. 2 *n* (-s/*no pl.*) fall(ing).

fällen ['fɛlən] *v/t.* (ge-, h) fell, cut down (*tree*); ⚓ lower (*bayonet*); 🜨ⁿ pass (*judgement*), give (*decision*).

'fallenlassen *v/t.* (*irr. lassen, sep., no -ge-, h*) drop (*plan, claim, etc.*).

fällig ['fɛliç] *adj.* due; payable; '2keit *f* (-/🜆-en) maturity; '2keitstermin *m* date of maturity.

'Fall|obst *n* windfall; '~reep ⚓ ['~re:p] *n* (-[e]s/-e) gangway.

falls *cj.* [fals] if; in the event of *ger.*; in case.

'Fall|schirm *m* parachute; '~

schirmspringer *m* parachutist; '~strick *m* snare; '~tür *f* trap door.

falsch [falʃ] 1. *adj.* false; wrong; *bank-note, etc.*: counterfeit; *money*: base; *bill of exchange, etc.*: forged; *p.* deceitful; 2. *adv.*: ~ *gehen watch*: go wrong; ~ *verbunden! teleph.* sorry, wrong number.

fälsch|en ['fɛlʃən] *v/t.* (ge-, h) falsify; forge, fake (*document, etc.*); counterfeit (*bank-note, coin, etc.*); fake (*calculations, etc.*); tamper with (*financial account*); adulterate (*food, wine*); '2er *m* (-s/-) forger, faker; adulterator.

'Falsch|geld *n* counterfeit *or* bad *or* base money; '~heit *f* (-/-en) falseness, falsity; duplicity, deceitfulness; '~meldung *f* false report; '~münzer *m* (-s/-) coiner; '~münzerwerkstatt *f* coiner's den; '2spielen *v/i.* (*sep.*, -ge-, h) cheat (at cards); '~spieler *m* cardsharper.

'Fälschung *f* (-/-en) forgery; falsification; fake; adulteration.

Falt|boot ['falt-] *n* folding canoe, *Am.* foldboat, faltboat; ~e ['~ə] *f* (-/-n) fold; pleat (*in skirt, etc.*); crease (*in trousers*); wrinkle (*on face*); '2en *v/t.* (ge-, h) fold; clasp or join (*one's hands*); '2ig *adj.* folded; pleated; wrinkled.

Falz [fals] *m* (-es/-e) fold; rabbet (*for woodworking, etc.*); bookbinding: guard; '2en *v/t.* (ge-, h) fold; rabbet.

familiär *adj.* [famil'jɛ:r] familiar; informal.

Familie [fa'mi:ljə] *f* (-/-n) family (*a. zo.*, ♧).

Fa'milien|angelegenheit *f* family affair; ~anschluß *m*: ~ haben live as one of the family; ~nachrichten *f/pl. in newspaper*: birth, marriage and death announcements *pl.*; ~name *m* family name, surname, *Am. a.* last name; ~stand *m* marital status.

Fanati|ker [fa'na:tikər] *m* (-s/-) fanatic; 2sch *adj.* fanatic(al).

Fanatismus [fana'tismus] *m* (-/*no pl.*) fanaticism.

fand [fant] *pret. of* finden.

Fanfare [fan'fa:rə] *f* (-/-en) fanfare, flourish (*of trumpets*).

Fang [faŋ] *m* (-[e]s/ⁿe) capture, catch(ing); *hunt.* bag; '2en *v/t.* (*irr.* ge-, h) catch (*animal, ball, thief, etc.*); '~zahn *m* fang (*of dog, wolf, etc.*); tusk (*of boar*).

Farb|band ['farp-] *n* (typewriter) ribbon; ~e ['~bə] *f* (-/-n) colo(u)r; paint; dye; complexion; *cards*: suit; 2echt *adj.* ['farpᵈ-] colo(u)r-fast.

färben ['fɛrbən] *v/t.* (ge-, h) colo(u)r (*glass, food, etc.*); dye (*material, hair, Easter eggs, etc.*); tint (*hair, paper, glass*); stain (*wood, fabrics, glass, etc.*); *sich ~* take on *or* assume a colo(u)r; *sich rot ~* turn *or* go red.

'**farben|blind** *adj.* colo(u)r-blind; '~**druck** *m* (-[e]s/-e) colo(u)r print; '~**prächtig** *adj.* splendidly col-o(u)rful.

Färber ['fɛrbər] *m* (-s/-) dyer.

Farb|fernsehen ['farp-] *n* colo(u)r television; '~**film** *m* colo(u)r film; **⚇ig** *adj.* ['~bic] colo(u)red; *glass*: tinted, stained; *fig.* colo(u)red; **⚇los** *adj.* ['~p-] colo(u)rless; '~**photographie** *f* colo(u)r photography; '~**stift** *m* colo(u)red pencil; '~**stoff** *m* colo(u)ring matter; '~**ton** *m* tone; shade, tint.

Färbung ['fɛrbuŋ] *f* (-/-en) colo(u)r-ing (*a. fig.*); shade (*a. fig.*).

Farnkraut ⚇ ['farnkraut] *n* fern.

Fasan *orn.* [fa'zaːn] *m* (-[e]s/-e[n]) pheasant.

Fasching ['faʃiŋ] *m* (-s/-e, -s) carni-val.

Fasel|ei [fɑːzə'lai] *f* (-/-en) driv-elling, waffling; twaddle; '**⚇n** *v/i.* (ge-, h) blather; F waffle.

Faser ['faːzər] *f* (-/-n) anat., ⚇, *fig.* fib|re, *Am.* -er; *cotton, wool, etc.*: staple; '**⚇ig** *adj.* fibrous; '**⚇n** *v/i.* (ge-, h) *wool*: shed fine hairs.

Faß [fas] *n* (Fasses/Fässer) cask, barrel; tub; vat; '~**bier** *n* draught beer.

Fassade △ [fa'saːdə] *f* (-/-n) façade, front (*a. fig.*); ~**nkletterer** *m* (-s/-) cat burglar.

fassen ['fasən] (ge-, h) 1. *v/t.* seize, take hold of; catch, apprehend (*criminal*); hold; *s.* einfassen; *fig.* grasp, understand, believe; pluck up (*courage*); form (*plan*); make (*decision*); *sich ~* compose o.s.; *sich kurz ~* be brief; 2. *v/i.*: ~ *nach* reach for.   [ceivable.⎱

'**faßlich** *adj.* comprehensible, con-⎰

'**Fassung** *f* (-/-en) setting (*of jewels*); ⚡ socket; *fig.*: composure; draft (-ing); wording, version; *die ~ verlieren* lose one's self-control; *aus der ~ bringen* disconcert; '~**s-kraft** *f* (powers of) comprehension, mental capacity; '~**svermögen** *n* (holding) capacity; *fig. s. Fassungs-kraft.*

fast *adv.* [fast] almost, nearly; ~ *nichts* next to nothing; ~ *nie* hardly ever.

fasten ['fastən] *v/i.* (ge-, h) fast; abstain from food and drink; '**⚇zeit** *f* Lent.

'**Fast|nacht** *f* (-/no *pl.*) Shrovetide; carnival; '~**tag** *m* fast-day.

fatal *adj.* [fa'taːl] *situation, etc.*: awkward; *business, etc.*: unfortu-nate; *mistake, etc.*: fatal.

fauchen ['fauxən] *v/i.* (ge-, h) *cat, etc.*: spit; F *p.* spit (*with anger*); *locomotive, etc.*: hiss.

faul *adj.* [faul] *fruit, etc.*: rotten, bad; *fish, meat*: putrid, bad; *fig.* lazy, indolent, idle; fishy; ~*e Aus-rede* lame excuse; '~**en** *v/i.* (ge-, h) rot, go bad, putrefy.

faulenze|n ['faulɛntsən] *v/i.* (ge-, h) idle; laze, loaf; '**⚇r** *m* (-s/-) idler, sluggard, lazy-bones.

'**Faul|heit** *f* (-/no *pl.*) idleness, laziness; '**⚇ig** *adj.* putrid.

Fäulnis ['foylnis] *f* (-/no *pl.*) rotten-ness; putrefaction; decay.

'**Faul|pelz** *m s.* Faulenzer; '~**tier** *n* zo. sloth (*a. fig.*).

Faust [faust] *f* (-/~e) fist; *auf eigene ~ on one's own initiative*; '~**hand-schuh** *m* mitt(en); '~**schlag** *m* blow with the fist, punch, *Am.* F *a.* slug.

Favorit [favo'riːt] *m* (-en/-en) favo(u)rite.

Faxe ['faksə] *f* (-/-n): ~*n machen* (play the) fool; ~*n schneiden* pull *or* make faces.

Fazit ['faːtsit] *n* (-s/-e, -s) result, upshot; total; *das ~ ziehen* sum *or* total up

Februar ['feːbruaːr] *m* (-[s]/-e) February.

fecht|en ['fɛçtən] *v/i.* (*irr.*, ge-, h) fight, *fenc.* fence; '**⚇er** *m* (-s/-) fencer.

Feder ['feːdər] *f* (-/-n) feather; (*ornamental*) plume; pen; ⊕ spring; '~**bett** *n* feather bed; '~**busch** *m* tuft of feathers; plume; '~**gewicht** *n boxing, etc.* featherweight; '~**hal-ter** *m* (-s/-) penholder; '~**kiel** *m* quill; '~**kraft** *f* elasticity, resilience; '~**krieg** *m* paper war; literary con-troversy; '**⚇leicht** *adj.* (as) light as a feather; '**⚇lesen** *n* (-s/no *pl.*): *nicht viel s machen mit* make short work of; ~**messer** *n* penknife; '**⚇n** *v/i.* (ge-, h) be elastic; '**⚇nd** *adj.* springy, elastic; '~**strich** *m* stroke of the pen; '~**vieh** *n* poultry; '~**zeichnung** *f* pen-and-ink draw-ing.

Fee [feː] *f* (-/-n) fairy.

Fegefeuer ['feːgə-] *n* purgatory.

fegen ['feːgən] *v/t.* (ge-, h) sweep; clean

Fehde ['feːdə] *f* (-/-n) feud; private war; *in ~ liegen* be at feud; F be at daggers drawn.

Fehl [feːl] *m*: *ohne ~* without fault *or* blemish; '~**betrag** *m* deficit, deficiency.

fehlen ['feːlən] *v/i.* (ge-, h) be absent; be missing *or* lacking; do wrong; *es fehlt ihm an* (*dat.*) he lacks; *was fehlt Ihnen?* what is the matter with you?; *weit gefehlt!* far off the mark!

Fehler ['feːlər] *m* (-s/-) mistake, error, slip; fault; ⊕ defect, flaw; '**⚇frei** *adj.*, '**⚇los** *adj.* faultless, perfect, ⊕ flawless; '**⚇haft** *adj.* faulty, defective; incorrect.

'**Fehl|geburt** *f* miscarriage, abortion; '≈gehen v/i. (irr. gehen, sep., -ge-, sein) go wrong; '∼griff fig. m mistake, blunder; '∼schlag fig. m failure; '≈schlagen fig. v/i. (irr. schlagen, sep., -ge-, sein) fail, miscarry; '∼schuß m miss; '≈treten v/i. (irr. treten, sep., -ge- sein) make a false step; '∼tritt m false step; slip; fig. slip, fault; ∼urteil t'z n error of judg(e)ment; '∼zündung mot. f misfire, backfire.

Feier ['faɪər] f (-/-n) ceremony; celebration; festival; festivity; '∼abend m finishing or closing time; ∼ machen finish, F knock off; '≈lich adj. promise, oath, etc.: solemn; act: ceremonial; '∼lichkeit f (-/-en) solemnity; ceremony; '≈n (ge-, h) 1. v/t. hold (celebration); celebrate, observe (feast, etc.); 2. v/i. celebrate; rest (from work), make holiday; '∼tag m holiday; festive day.

feig adj. [faɪk] cowardly.
feige¹ adj. ['faɪɡə] cowardly.
Feige² f [∼] f (-/-n) fig; '∼nbaum ♀ m fig-tree; '∼nblatt n fig-leaf.
Feig|heit ['faɪkhaɪt] f (-/no pl.) cowardice, cowardliness; '∼ling ['∼klɪŋ] m (-s/-e) coward.
feil adj. [faɪl] for sale, to be sold; fig. venal; '∼bieten v/t. (irr. bieten, sep., -ge-, h) offer for sale.
Feile ['faɪlə] f (-/-n) file; '≈n (ge-, h) 1. v/t. file (a. fig.); fig. polish; 2. v/i.: ∼ an (dat.) file (at); fig. polish (up).
feilschen ['faɪlʃən] v/i. (ge-, h) bargain (um for), haggle (for, about), Am. a. dicker (about).
fein adj. [faɪn] fine; material, etc.: high-grade; wine, etc.: choice; fabric, etc.: delicate, dainty; manners: polished; p. polite; distinction: subtle.
Feind [faɪnt] m (-[e]s/-e) enemy (a. ✕); '≈lich adj. hostile, inimical; '∼schaft f (-/-en) enmity; animosity, hostility; '≈selig adj. hostile (gegen to); '∼seligkeit f (-/-en) hostility; malevolence.
'fein|fühlend adj., '∼fühlig adj. sensitive; '≈gefühl n sensitiveness; delicacy; '≈gehalt m (monetary) standard; '≈heit f (-/-en) fineness, delicacy, daintiness; politeness; elegance; '≈kost f high-class groceries pl., Am. delicatessen; '≈mechanik f precision mechanics; '≈schmecker m (-s/-) gourmet, epicure; '∼sinnig adj. subtle.
feist adj. [faɪst] fat, stout.
Feld [fɛlt] n (-[e]s/-er) field (a. ✕, ✕, sports); ground, soil; plain; chess: square; △, ⊕ panel, compartment; ins ∼ ziehen take the field; '∼arbeit f agricultural work; '∼bett n camp-bed; '∼blume f wild flower; '∼dienst ✕ m field service; '∼flasche f water-bottle;

'∼frucht f fruit of the field; '∼geschrei n war-cry, battle-cry; '∼herr m general; '∼kessel m camp-kettle; '∼lazarett ✕ n field-hospital; '∼lerche orn. f skylark; '∼marschall m Field Marshal; '≈marschmäßig ✕ adj. in full marching order; '∼maus zo. f field-mouse; '∼messer m (land) surveyor; '∼post ✕ f army postal service; '∼schlacht ✕ f battle; '∼stecher m (-s/-) (ein a pair of) field-glasses pl.; '∼stuhl m camp-stool; '∼webel ['∼ve:bəl] m (-s/-) sergeant; '∼weg m (field) path; '∼zeichen ✕ n standard; '∼zug m ✕ campaign (a. fig.), (military) expedition; Am. fig. a. drive.

Felge ['fɛlɡə] f (-/-n) felloe (of cart-wheel); rim (of car wheel, etc.).
Fell [fɛl] n (-[e]s/-e) skin, pelt, fur (of dead animal); coat (of cat, etc.); fleece (of sheep).
Fels [fɛls] m (-en/-en), ∼en ['∼zən] m (-s/-) rock; '∼block ['fɛls-] m rock; boulder; ≈ig adj. ['∼zɪç] rocky.
Fenchel ♀ ['fɛnçəl] m (-s/no pl.) fennel.
Fenster ['fɛnstər] n (-s/-) window; '∼brett n window-sill; '∼flügel m casement (of casement window); sash (of sash window); '∼kreuz n cross-bar(s) pl.; '∼laden m shutter; '∼rahmen m window-frame; '∼riegel m window-fastener; '∼scheibe f (window-)pane; '∼sims m, n window-sill.
Ferien ['fe:rjən] pl. holiday(s pl.), esp. Am. vacation; leave, Am. a. furlough; parl. recess; t'z vacation, recess; '∼kolonie f children's holiday camp.
Ferkel ['fɛrkəl] n (-s/-) young pig; contp. p. pig.
fern [fɛrn] 1. adj. far (off), distant; remote; 2. adv. far (away); von ∼ from a distance.
'Fernamt teleph. n trunk exchange, Am. long-distance exchange.
'fernbleiben 1. v/i. (irr. bleiben, sep., -ge-, sein) remain or stay away (dat. from); 2. ≈ n (-s/no pl.) absence (from school, etc.); absenteeism (from work).
Fern|e ['fɛrnə] f (-/-n) distance; remoteness; aus der ∼ from or at a distance; '≈er 1. adj. farther; fig.: further; future; 2. adv. further (-more), in addition, also; ∼ liefen ... also ran ...; '∼flug ✕ m long-distance flight; ≈gelenkt adj. ['∼ɡəlɛŋkt] missile: guided; aircraft, etc.: remote-control(l)ed; '∼gespräch teleph. n trunk call, Am. long-distance call; '≈gesteuert adj. s. ferngelenkt; '∼glas n binoculars pl.; '≈halten v/t. and v/refl. (irr. halten, sep., -ge-, h) keep away (von from); '∼heizung f district heating; '∼la-

ster F *mot. m* long-distance lorry, *Am.* long haul truck; '**.lenkung** *f* (-/-en) remote control; '**2liegen** *v/i.* (*irr.* liegen, *sep.*, -ge-, *h*): es liegt mir fern zu *inf.* I am far from *ger.*; '**.rohr** *n* telescope; '**.schreiber** *m* teleprinter, *Am.* teletypewriter; '**.sehen 1.** *n* (-s/no *pl.*) television; **2.** **2** *v/i.* (*irr.* sehen, *sep.*, -ge-, *h*) watch television; '**.seher** *m* television set; *p.* television viewer, televiewer; '**.sehsendung** *f* television broadcast, telecast; '**.sicht** *f* visual range.

'**Fernsprech|amt** *n* telephone exchange, *Am. a.* central; '**.anschluß** *m* telephone connection; '**.er** *m* telephone; '**.leitung** *f* telephone line; '**.zelle** *f* telephone box.

'**fern|stehen** *v/i.* (*irr.* stehen, *sep.*, -ge-, *h*) have no real (point of) contact (*dat.* with); '**2steuerung** *f* *s.* Fernlenkung; '**2unterricht** *m* correspondence course *or* tuition; '**2verkehr** *m* long-distance traffic.

Ferse ['fɛrzə] *f* (-/-n) heel.

fertig *adj.* ['fɛrtıç] ready; *article*, *etc.*: finished; *clothing*: ready-made; mit et. ~ werden get s.th. finished; mit et. ~ sein have finished s.th.; '**.bringen** *v/t.* (*irr.* bringen, *sep.*, -ge-, *h*) bring about; manage; '**2keit** *f* (-/-en) dexterity; skill; fluency (*in the spoken language*); '**.machen** *v/t.* (*sep.*, -ge-, *h*) finish, complete; get *s.th.* ready; *fig.* finish, settle *s.o.'s* hash; *sich* ~ get ready; '**2stellung** *f* completion; '**2waren** *f/pl.* finished goods *pl.* or products *pl.*

fesch F *adj.* [fɛʃ] *hat, dress. etc.*: smart, stylish, chic; dashing.

Fessel ['fɛsəl] *f* (-/-n) chain, fetter, shackle; *vet.* fetlock; *fig.* bond, fetter, tie; '**.ballon** *m* captive balloon; '**2n** *v/t.* (ge-, *h*) chain, fetter, shackle; *j-n* ~ hold *or* arrest *s.o.'s* attention; fascinate *s.o.*

fest [fɛst] **1.** *adj.* firm; solid; fixed; fast; *principle*: firm, strong; *sleep*: sound; *fabric*: close; **2.** **2** *n* (-es/-e) festival, celebration; holiday, *eccl.* feast; '**.binden** *v/t.* (*irr.* binden, *sep.*, -ge-, *h*) fasten, tie (an *dat.* to); '**2essen** *n* banquet, feast; '**.fahren** *v/refl.* (*irr.* fahren, *sep.*, -ge-, *h*) get stuck; *fig.* reach a deadlock; '**2halle** *f* (festival) hall; '**.halten** (*irr.* halten, *sep.*, -ge-, *h*) **1.** *v/i.* hold fast *or* tight; ~ an (*dat.*) adhere *or* keep to; **2.** *v/t.* hold on to; hold tight; *sich* ~ an (*dat.*) hold on to; '**.igen** ['.ıgən] *v/t.* (ge-, *h*) consolidate (*one's position, etc.*); strengthen (*friendship, etc.*); stabilize (*currency*); '**2igkeit** ['.ç-] *f* (-/no *pl.*) firmness; solidity; '**2land** *n* mainland, continent; '**.legen** *v/t.* (*sep.*, -ge-, *h*) fix, set; *sich auf* et. ~

commit o.s. to s.th.; '**.lich** *adj.* *meal, day, etc.*: festive; *reception etc.*: ceremonial; '**2lichkeit** *f* (-/-en) festivity; festive character; '**.machen** (*sep.*, -ge-, *h*) **1.** *v/t.* fix, fasten, attach (an *dat.* to); ♣ moor; **2.** ♣ *v/i.* moor; put ashore; '**2mahl** *n* banquet, feast; '**2nahme** ['.na:mə] *f* (-/-n) arrest; '**.nehmen** *v/t.* (*irr.* nehmen, *sep.*, -ge-, *h*) arrest, take into custody; '**2rede** *f* speech of the day; '**.setzen** *v/t.* (*sep.*, -ge-, *h*) fix, set; *sich* ~ dust, *etc.*: become ingrained; *p.* settle (down); '**2spiel** *n* festival; '**.stehen** *v/i.* (*irr.* stehen, *sep.*, -ge-, *h*) stand firm; *fact*: be certain; *stationary*; *fact*: established; '**.stehend** *adj.* fixed, stationary; *fact*: established; '**.stellen** *v/t.* (*sep.*, -ge-, *h*) establish (*fact, identity, etc.*); ascertain, find out (*fact, s.o.'s whereabouts, etc.*); state; see, perceive (*fact, etc.*); '**2stellung** *f* establishment; ascertainment; statement; '**2tag** *m* festive day; festival, holiday; *eccl.* feast; '**2ung** ✗ *f* (-/-en) fortress; '**2zug** *m* festive procession.

fett [fɛt] **1.** *adj.* fat; fleshy; *voice*: oily; *land, etc.*: rich; **2.** **2** *n* (-[e]s/-e) fat; grease (*a.* ⊕); '**2druck** *typ. m* bold type; '**2fleck** *m* grease-spot; '**.ig** *adj.* hair, skin, *etc.*: greasy, oily; *fingers, etc.*: greasy; *substance*: fatty.

Fetzen ['fɛtsən] *m* (-s/-) shred; rag, *Am. a.* frazzle; scrap (*of paper*); in ~ in rags.

feucht *adj.* [fɔʏçt] *climate, air, etc.*: damp, moist; *air, zone, etc.*: humid; '**2igkeit** *f* (-/no *pl.*) moisture (*of substance*); dampness (*of place, etc.*); humidity (*of atmosphere, etc.*).

Feuer ['fɔʏər] *n* (-s/-) fire; light; *fig.* ardo(u)r; ~ fangen catch fire; *fig.* fall for (*girl*); '**.alarm** *m* fire alarm; **2beständig** *adj.* fire-proof, fire-resistant; '**.bestattung** *f* cremation; '**.eifer** *m* ardo(u)r; '**2fest** *adj. s* feuerbeständig; '**2gefährlich** *adj.* inflammable; '**.haken** *m* poker; '**.löscher** *m* (-s/-) fire extinguisher; '**.melder** *m* (-s/-) fire-alarm; '**2n** (ge-, *h*) **1.** ✗ *v/i.* shoot, fire (auf *acc.* at, on); **2.** F *fig. v/t* hurl; '**.probe** *fig. f* crucial test; **2'rot** *adj.* fiery (red), (as) red as fire; '**.sbrunst** *f* conflagration; '**.schiff** ♣ *n* lightship; '**.schutz** *m* fire prevention; ✗ covering fire; '**.sgefahr** *f* danger *or* risk of fire; '**2speiend** *adj.*: ~er Berg volcano; '**.spritze** *f* fire engine; '**.stein** *m* flint; '**.versicherung** *f* fire insurance company); '**.wache** *f* fire station, *Am. a.* firehouse; '**.wehr** *f* fire-brigade, *Am. a.* fire department; '**.wehrmann** *m* fireman; '**.werk** *n* (display of) fireworks *pl.*; '**.werkskörper** *m* firework; '**.~**

zange f (e-e a pair of) firetongs pl.; '˷zeug n lighter.

feurig adj. ['fɔʏriç] fiery (a. fig.); fig. ardent.

Fiasko [fi'asko] n (-s/-s) (complete) failure, fiasco; sl. flop.

Fibel ['fi:bəl] f (-/-n) spelling-book, primer.

Fichte ♣ ['fiçtə] f (-/-n) spruce; '˷nadel f pine-needle.

fidel adj. [fi'de:l] cheerful, merry, jolly, Am. F a. chipper.

Fieber ['fi:bər] n (-s/-) temperature, fever; ˷ haben have or run a temperature; '˷anfall m attack or bout of fever; '2haft adj. feverish (a. fig.); febrile; '2krank adj. ill with fever; '˷mittel n febrifuge; '2n v/i. (ge-, h) have or run a temperature; ˷ nach crave or long for; '˷schauer m chill, shivers pl.; '˷tabelle f temperature-chart; '˷thermometer n clinical thermometer.

fiel [fi:l] pret. of fallen.

Figur [fi'gu:r] f (-/-en) figure; chess: chessman, piece.

figürlich adj. [fi'gy:rliç] meaning, etc. figurative.

Filet [fi'le:] n (-s/-s) fillet (of beef, pork, etc.).

Filiale [fili'ɑ:lə] f (-/-n) branch.

Filigran(arbeit f) [fili'grɑ:n(ʔ-)] n (-s/-e) filigree.

Film [film] m (-[e]s/-e) film, thin coating (of oil, wax, etc.); phot. film; film, (moving) picture, Am. a. motion picture, F movie; e-n ˷ einlegen phot. load a camera; '˷atelier n film studio; '˷aufnahme f filming, shooting (of a film); film (of sporting event, etc.); '2en (ge-, h) 1. v/t. film, shoot (scene, etc.); 2. v/i. film; make a film; '˷gesellschaft f film company, Am. motion-picture company, '˷kamera f film camera, Am. motion-picture camera; '˷regisseur m film director; '˷reklame f screen advertising; '˷schauspieler m film or screen actor, Am. F movie actor; '˷spule f (film) reel; '˷streifen m film strip; '˷theater n cinema, Am. motion-picture or F movie theater; '˷verleih m (-[e]s/-e) film distributors pl.; '˷vorführer m projectionist; '˷vorstellung f cinema performance, Am. F movie performance.

Filter ['filtər] (-s/-) 1. m (coffee-, etc.) filter; 2. ⊕ n filter; '2n v/t. (ge-, h) filter (water, air, etc.); filtrate (water, impurities, etc.); strain (liquid); '˷zigarette f filter-tipped cigarette.

Filz [filts] m (-es/-e) felt; fig. F skinflint; '2ig adj. felt-like; of felt; fig. F niggardly, stingy; '˷laus f crab louse.

Finanz|amt [fi'nants ʔamt] n (inland) revenue office, office of the Inspector of Taxes; '˷en f/pl. finances pl.; 2iell adj. [˷'tsjel] financial; 2ieren [˷'tsi:rən] v/t. (no -ge-, h) finance (scheme, etc.); sponsor (radio programme, etc.); '˷lage f financial position; '˷mann m financier; '˷minister m minister of finance; Chancellor of the Exchequer, Am. Secretary of the Treasury; '˷ministerium n ministry of finance; Exchequer, Am. Treasury Department; '˷wesen n (-s/no pl.) finances pl.; financial matters pl.

Findelkind ['fındəl-] n foundling.

finden ['fındən] (irr., ge-, h) 1. v/t. find; discover, come across; find, think, consider; wie ˷ Sie ...? how do you like ...?; sich ˷ thing: be found; of o.s.: ˷ zu find one's way to.

'**Finder** m (-s/-) finder; '˷lohn m finder's reward.

'**findig** adj. resourceful, ingenious.

Findling ['fıntlıŋ] m (-s/-e) foundling; geol erratic block, boulder.

fing [fıŋ] pret. of fangen.

Finger ['fıŋər] m (-s/-) finger; sich die ˷ verbrennen burn one's fingers; er rührte keinen ˷ he lifted no finger; '˷abdruck m fingerprint; '˷fertigkeit f manual skill; '˷hut m thimble; ♣ foxglove; '2n v/i. (ge-, h): ˷ nach fumble for; '˷spitze f finger-tip; '˷spitzengefühl fig. n sure instinct; '˷übung ♪ f finger exercise; '˷zeig [˷tsaık] m (-[e]s/-e) hint, F pointer.

Fink orn. [fıŋk] m (-en/-en) finch.

finster ['fınstər] adj. night, etc.: dark; shadows, wood, etc.: sombre; night, room, etc.. gloomy, murky; person, nature: sullen; thought, etc.: sinister, sombre, gloomy; '2nis f (-/no pl.) darkness, gloom.

Finte ['fıntə] f (-/-n) feint; fig. a. ruse, trick.

Firma ✝ ['fırma] f (-/Firmen) firm, business, company.

firmen eccl. ['fırmən] v/t. (ge-, h) confirm

'**Firmen|inhaber** m owner of a firm; '˷wert m goodwill.

Firn [fırn] m (-[e]s/-e) firn, névé.

First ⌂ [fırst] m (-es/-e) ridge; '˷ziegel m ridge tile.

Fisch [fıʃ] m (-es/-e) fish; '˷dampfer m trawler; '2en v/t. and v/i. (ge-, h) fish; '˷er m (-s/-) fisherman; '˷erboot n fishing-boat; '˷erdorf n fishing-village; '˷erei [˷'raı] f (-/-en) fishery; fishing; '˷fang m fishing, '˷geruch m fishy smell; '˷gräte f fish-bone; '˷grätenmuster n herring-bone pattern; '˷händler m fishmonger, Am. fish dealer, 2ig adj. fishy; '˷laich m spawn, '˷leim m fish-glue; '˷mehl n fish-meal; '˷schuppe f scale; '˷tran m train-oil; '˷vergiftung

♒ f fish-poisoning; '**~zucht** f pisci-culture, fish-hatching; '**~zug** m catch, haul, draught (of fish).

fiskalisch adj. [fis'ka:liʃ] fiscal, governmental.

Fiskus ['fiskus] m (-/♒ -se, Fisken) Exchequer, esp. Am. Treasury; government.

Fistel ♒ ['fistəl] f (-/-n) fistual; '**~stimme** ♪ f falsetto.

Fittich ['fitiç] m (-[e]s/-e) poet. wing; j-n unter s-e ~e nehmen take s.o. under one's wing.

fix adj. [fiks] salary, price, etc.: fixed; quick, clever, smart; e-e ~e Idee an obsession; ein ~er Junge a smart fellow; **2ierbad** phot. [fi-'ksi:rba:t] n fixing bath; **~ieren** [fi'ksi:rən] v/t. (no -ge-, h) fix (a. phot.); fix one's eyes (up)on, stare at s.o.; '**2stern** ast. m fixed star; '**2um** n (-s/Fixa) fixed or basic salary.

flach adj. [flax] roof, etc.: flat; ground, etc.: flat, level, even; water, plate, fig.: shallow; ⊕ plane.

Fläche ['fleçə] f (-/-n) surface, ⊕ a. plane; sheet (of water, snow, etc.); geom. area; tract, expanse (of land, etc.); '**~inhalt** ⊕ ['fleçən?-] m (surface) area; '**~nmaß** n square or surface measure.

'**Flach|land** n plain, flat country; '**~rennen** n turf: flat race.

Flachs ♀ [flaks] m (-es/no pl.) flax.

flackern ['flakərn] v/i. (ge-, h) light, flame, eyes, etc.: flicker, wave; voice: quaver, shake.

Flagge ['flagə] f (-/-n) flag, colo(u)rs pl.; '**2n** v/i. (ge-, h) fly or hoist a flag; signal (with flags).

Flak ⚒ [flak] f (-/-, -s) anti-aircraft gun; anti-aircraft artillery.

Flamme ['flamə] f (-/-n) flame; blaze; '**~nmeer** n sea of flames; '**~nwerfer ⚒** m (-s/-) flame-thrower.

Flanell [fla'nɛl] m (-s/-e) flannel; '**~anzug** m flannel suit; '**~hose** f flannel trousers pl., flannels pl.

Flank|e ['flankə] f (-/-n) flank (a. ⚔, ✕, mount.); side; **2ieren** [~'ki:rən] v/t. (no -ge-, h) flank.

Flasche ['flaʃə] f (-/-n) bottle; flask.

'**Flaschen|bier** n bottled beer; '**~hals** m neck of a bottle; '**~öffner** m (-s/-) bottle-opener; '**~zug** ⊕ m block and tackle.

flatter|haft adj. ['flatərhaft] girl, etc.: fickle, flighty; mind: fickle, volatile; '**~n** v/i. (ge-) 1. (h, sein) bird, butterfly, etc.: flutter (about); bird, bat, etc.: flit (about); 2. (h) hair, flag, garment, etc.: stream, fly; mot. wheel: shimmy, wobble; car steering: judder; 3. (sein): auf den Boden ~ flutter to the ground.

flau adj. [flau] weak, feeble, faint; sentiment, reaction, etc.: lukewarm;

drink: stale; colour: pale, dull; ✝ market, business, etc.: dull, slack; ~e Zeit slack period.

Flaum [flaum] m (-[e]s/no pl.) down, fluff; fuzz.

Flau|s [flaus] m (-es/-e), **~sch** [~ʃ] m (-es/-e) tuft (of wool, etc.); napped coating.

Flausen F ['flauzən] f/pl. whims pl., fancies pl., (funny) ideas pl.; F fibs pl.; j-m ~ in den Kopf setzen put funny ideas into s.o.'s head; j-m ~ vormachen tell s.o. fibs.

Flaute ['flautə] f (-/-n) ⚓ dead calm; esp. ✝ dullness, slack period.

Flecht|e ['fleçtə] f (-/-n) braid, plait (of hair); ♀ lichen; ♒ herpes; '**2en** v/t. (irr., ge-, h) braid, plait (hair, ribbon, etc.); weave (basket, wreath, etc.); wreath (flowers); twist (rope, etc.); '**~werk** n wickerwork.

Fleck [flek] m (-[e]s/-e, -en) 1. mark (of dirt, grease, etc.; zo.); spot (of grease, paint, etc.); smear (of oil, blood, etc.); stain (of wine, coffee, etc.); blot (of ink); place, spot; fig. blemish, spot, stain; 2. patch (of material); bootmaking: heel-piece; '**~en** m (-s/-) s. Fleck 1; small (market-)town, townlet; '**~enwasser** n spot or stain remover; '**~fieber ♒** n (epidemic) typhus; '**2ig** adj. spotted; stained.

Fledermaus zo. ['fle:dər-] f bat.

Flegel ['fle:gəl] m (-s/-) flail; fig. lout, boor; **~ei** [~'lai] f (-/-en) rude-ness; loutishness; '**2haft** adj. rude-ill-mannered; loutish; '**~jahre** pl. awkward age.

flehen ['fle:ən] 1. v/i. (ge-, h) en-treat, implore (zu j-m s.o.; um et. s.th.); 2. 2 n (-s/no pl.) supplication, imploration, entreaty.

Fleisch [flaiʃ] n (-es/no pl.) flesh; meat, ♀ pulp; '**~brühe** f meat-broth; beef tea; '**~er** m (-s/-) butcher; **~erei** [~'rai] f (-/-en) butcher's (shop), Am. butcher shop; '**~extrakt** m meat extract; '**2fressend** adj. carnivorous; '**~hackmaschine** f mincing machine, mincer, Am. meat grinder; '**2ig** adj. fleshy, ♀ pulpy; '**~konserven** f/pl. tinned or potted meat, Am. canned meat; '**~kost** f meat (food); '**2lich** adj. desires, etc.: carnal, fleshly; '**2los** adj. meatless; '**~pastete** f meat pie, Am. a. potpie; '**~speise** f meat dish; '**~vergiftung** f meat or ptomaine poisoning; '**~ware** f meat (product); '**~wolf** m s. Fleischhack-maschine.

Fleiß [flais] m (-es/no pl.) diligence, industry; '**2ig** adj. diligent, indus-trious, hard-working.

fletschen ['fletʃən] v/t. (ge-, h): die Zähne ~ animal: bare its teeth; p. bare one's teeth.

Flicken ['flikən] 1. m (-s/-) patch;

2. ⚓ *v/t.* (ge-, *h*) patch (*dress, tyre, etc.*); repair (*shoe, roof. etc.*); cobble (*shoe*).

'**Flick|schneider** *m* jobbing tailor; '**₋schuster** *m* cobbler; '**₋werk** *n* (-[e]s/*no pl.*) patchwork.

Flieder ⚘ ['fli:dər] *m* (-s/-) lilac.

Fliege ['fli:gə] *f* (-/-n) *zo.* fly; bow-tie.

'**fliegen 1.** *v/i.* (*irr.*, ge-, sein) fly; go by air; **2.** *v/t.* (*irr.*, ge-, *h*) fly, pilot (*aircraft, etc.*); convey (*goods, etc.*) by air; **3.** ⚓ *n* (-s/*no pl.*) flying; ✈ *a.* aviation.

Fliegen|fänger ['fli:gənfɛŋər] *m* (-s/-) fly-paper; '**₋fenster** *n* fly-screen; '**₋gewicht** *n* boxing, etc.: flyweight; '**₋klappe** *f* fly-flap, Am. fly swatter; '**₋pilz** ⚘ *m* fly agaric.

'**Flieger** *m* (-s/-) flyer; ✈ airman, aviator; pilot; F plane, bomber; *cycling:* sprinter; '**₋abwehr** ✕ *f* anti-aircraft defen|ce, Am. -se; '**₋alarm** ✕ *m* air-raid alarm *or* warning; '**₋bombe** *f* aircraft bomb; '**₋offizier** ✕ *m* air-force officer.

flieh|en ['fli:ən] (*irr.*, ge-) **1.** *v/i.* (sein) flee (*vor dat.* from), run away; **2.** *v/t.* (*h*) flee, avoid, keep away from; '**Ջkraft** *phys. f* centrifugal force.   [(floor-)tile.]

Fliese ['fli:zə] *f* (-/-n) (wall-)tile;)

Fließ|band ['fli:s-] *n* (-[e]s/*▪*e) conveyor-belt; assembly-line; '**Ջen** *v/i.* (*irr.*, ge-, sein) river, traffic, etc.: flow; *tap-water, etc.*: run; '**Ջend 1.** *adj. water:* running; *traffic:* moving; *speech, etc.*: fluent; **2.** *adv.*: ~ lesen (sprechen) read (speak) fluently; '**₋papier** *n* blotting-paper.

Flimmer ['flimər] *m* (-s/-) glimmer, glitter; '**Ջn** *v/i.* (ge-, *h*) glimmer, glitter; *television, film:* flicker; es flimmert mir vor den Augen everything is dancing in front of my eyes.

flink *adj.* [fliŋk] quick, nimble, brisk.

Flinte ['flintə] *f* (-/-n) shotgun; die ~ ins Korn werfen throw up the sponge.

Flirt [flœrt] *m* (-es/-s) flirtation; '**Ջen** *v/i.* (ge-, *h*) flirt (*mit* with).

Flitter ['flitər] *m* (-s/-) tinsel (*a. fig.*), spangle; '**₋kram** *m* cheap finery; '**₋wochen** *pl.* honeymoon.

flitzen F ['flitsən] *v/i.* (ge-, sein) whisk, scamper; dash (off, *etc.*).

flocht [flɔxt] *pret. of* flechten.

Flock|e ['flɔkə] *f* (-/-n) flake (*of snow, soap, etc.*); flock (*of wool*); '**Ջig** *adj.* fluffy, flaky.

flog [flo:k] *pret. of* fliegen.

floh[1] [flo:] *pret. of* fliehen.

Floh[2] *zo.* [~] *m* (-[e]s/*▪*e) flea.

Flor [flo:r] *m* (-s/-e) bloom, blossom; *fig.* bloom, prime; gauze; crêpe, crape.

Florett *fenc.* [flo'rɛt] *n* (-[e]s/-e) foil.

florieren [flo'ri:rən] *v/i.* (*no* -ge-, *h*) business, etc.: flourish, prosper, thrive.

Floskel ['flɔskəl] *f* (-/-n) flourish; empty phrase.

floß[1] [flɔs] *pret. of* fließen.

Floß[2] [flo:s] *n* (-es/*▪*e) raft, float.

Flosse ['flɔsə] *f* (-/-n) fin; flipper (*of penguin, etc.*).

flöß|en ['flø:sən] *v/t.* (ge-, *h*) raft, float (*timber, etc.*); '**Ջer** *m* (-s/-) rafter, raftsman.

Flöte ♩ ['flø:tə] *f* (-/-n) flute; '**Ջn** (ge-, *h*) **1.** *v/i.* (play the) flute; **2.** *v/t.* play on the flute.

flott *adj.* [flɔt] ⚓ floating, afloat; *pace, etc.*: quick, brisk; *music, etc.*: gay, lively; *dress, etc.*: smart, stylish; *car, etc.*: sporty, racy; *dancer, etc.*: excellent.

Flotte ['flɔtə] *f* (-/-n) ⚓ fleet; ✕ navy; '**₋nstützpunkt** ✕ *m* naval base.

Flotille ⚓ [flɔ'tiljə] *f* (-/-n) flotilla.

Flöz *geol.*, ✕ [flø:ts] *n* (-es/-e) seam; layer, stratum.

Fluch [flu:x] *m* (-[e]s/*▪*e) curse, malediction; *eccl.* anathema; curse, swear-word; '**Ջen** *v/i.* (ge-, *h*) swear, curse.

Flucht [fluxt] *f* (-/-en) flight (*vor dat.* from); escape (*aus dat.* from); line (*of windows, etc.*); suite (*of rooms*); flight (*of stairs*).

flücht|en ['flyçtən] (ge-) *v/i.* (sein) *and v/refl.* (*h*) flee (*nach, zu* to); run away; escape; '**₋ig** *adj.* fugitive (*a. fig.*); thought, etc.: fleeting; fame, etc.: transient; *p.* careless, superficial; *▪* volatile; '**Ջling** [' ̣liŋ] *m* (-s/-e) fugitive; *pol.* refugee; '**Ջ₋lingslager** *n* refugee camp.

Flug [flu:k] *m* (-[e]s/*▪*e) flight; im ~(e) rapidly; quickly; '**₋abwehr-rakete** *f* anti-aircraft missile; '**₋bahn** *f* trajectory (*of rocket, etc.*); ✕ flight path; '**₋ball** *m* tennis, etc.: volley; '**₋blatt** *n* handbill, leaflet, Am. a. flier; '**₋boot** ✕ *n* flying-boat; '**₋dienst** ✕ *m* air service.

Flügel ['fly:gəl] *m* (-s/-) wing (*a.* △, ✕, ✈); blade, vane (*of propeller, etc.*); s. Fensterflügel, Türflügel, Lungenflügel; sail (*of windmill, etc.*); ♩ grand piano; '**₋fenster** △ *n* casement-window; '**Ջlahm** *adj.* broken-winged; '**₋mann** ✕ *m* marker; flank man; '**₋tür** △ *f* folding door.

Fluggast ['flu:k-] *m* (*air*) passenger.

flügge *adj.* ['flygə] fledged; ~ werden fledge; *fig.* begin to stand on one's own feet.

'**Flug|hafen** *m* airport; '**₋linie** *f* air route; airline; '**₋platz** *m* airfield, aerodrome, Am. a. airdrome; airport; '**₋sand** *geol. m* wind-blown sand; '**₋schrift** *f* pamphlet; '**₋sicherung** *f* air traffic control; '**₋sport** *m* sporting aviation; '**₋wesen** *n* aviation, aeronautics.

'**Flugzeug** n aircraft, aeroplane, F plane, *Am. a.* airplane; '**~bau** m aircraft construction; '**~führer** m pilot; '**~halle** f hangar; '**~rumpf** m fuselage, body; '**~träger** m aircraft carrier, *Am. sl.* flattop; '**~unglück** n air crash *or* disaster.

Flunder *ichth.* ['flundər] f (-/-n) flounder.

Flunker|ei F [fluŋkə'raı] f (-/-en) petty lying, F fib(bing); '**2n** v/i. (ge-, h) F fib, tell fibs.

fluoreszieren [fluores'tsi:rən] v/i. (no -ge-, h) fluoresce.

Flur [flu:r] 1. f (-/-en) field, meadow; *poet.* lea; 2. m (-[e]s/-e) (entrance-)hall.

Fluß [flus] m (Flusses/Flüsse) river, stream; flow(ing); *fig.* fluency, flux; 2'**abwärts** adv. downriver, downstream; 2'**aufwärts** adv. upriver, upstream; '**~bett** n river bed.

flüssig adj. ['flysiç] fluid, liquid; *metal.*: molten, melted; ✝ *money, capital, etc.*: available, in hand; *style:* fluent, flowing; '**2keit** f (-/-en) fluid, liquid; fluidity, liquidity; availability; fluency.

'**Fluß|lauf** m course of a river; '**~mündung** f mouth of a river; '**~pferd** zo. n hippopotamus; '**~schiffahrt** f river navigation *or* traffic.

flüstern ['flystərn] v/i. and v/t. (ge-, h) whisper.

Flut [flu:t] f (-/-en) flood; high tide, (flood-)tide; *fig.* flood, torrent, deluge; '**2en** (ge-) 1. v/i. (sein) water, crowd, *etc.*: flood, surge (über acc. over); 2. v/t. (h) flood (dock, etc.); '**~welle** f tidal wave.

focht [foxt] pret. of fechten.

Fohlen ['fo:lən] 1. n (-s/-) foal; *male:* colt; *female:* filly; 2. 2 v/i. (ge-, h) foal.

Folge ['fɔlgə] f (-/-n) sequence, succession (of events); instalment, part (of radio series, etc.); consequence, result; series; set, suit; future; **~n** pl. aftermath.

'**folgen** v/i. (dat.) (ge-, sein) follow; succeed (j-m s.o.; auf acc. to); follow, ensue (aus from); obey (j-m s.o.); **~dermaßen** adv. ['.dərma:sən] as follows; '**~schwer** adj. of grave consequence, grave.

'**folgerichtig** adj. logical; consistent.

folger|n ['fɔlgərn] v/t. (ge-, h) infer, conclude, deduce (aus from); '**2ung** f (-/-en) inference, conclusion, deduction.

'**folgewidrig** adj. illogical; inconsistent.

folglich cj. ['fɔlkliç] therefore, consequently.

folgsam adj. ['fɔlkza:m] obedient; '**2keit** f (-/no pl.) obedience.

Folie ['fo:ljə] f (-/-n) foil.

Folter ['fɔltər] f (-/-n) torture; *auf die ~ spannen* put to the rack; *fig.* F a. keep on tenterhooks; '**2n** v/t. (ge-, h) torture, torment; '**~qual** f torture, fig. a. torment.

Fonds ✝ [fõ:] m (-/-) fund (a. fig.); funds pl.

Fontäne [fɔn'tɛ:nə] f (-/-n) fountain.

foppen ['fɔpən] v/t. (ge-, h) tease, F pull s.o.'s leg; hoax, fool.

forcieren [fɔr'si:rən] v/t. (no -ge-, h) force (up).

'**Förder|band** n (-[e]s/~er) conveyor-belt; '**2lich** adj. conducive (dat. to), promotive (of); '**~korb** ⚒ m cage.

fordern ['fɔrdərn] v/t. (ge-, h) demand; claim (compensation, etc.); ask (price, etc.); challenge (to duel).

fördern ['fœrdərn] v/t. (ge-, h) further, advance, promote; ⚒ haul, raise (coal, etc.); zutage ~ reveal, bring to light.

'**Forderung** f (-/-en) demand; claim, charge; challenge.

'**Förderung** f (-/-en) furtherance, advancement, promotion; ⚒ haulage; output. [trout.]

Forelle *ichth.* [fo'rɛlə] f (-/-n)\

Form [fɔrm] f (-/-en) form; figure, shape; model; ⊕ mo(u)ld; *sports:* form, condition; 2al adj. [.'ma:l] formal; **~alität** [.ali'tɛ:t] f (-/-en) formality; **~at** [.'ma:t] n (-[e]s/-e) size; *von ~* of distinction; **~el** ['.əl] f (-/-n) formula; 2ell adj. [.'mɛl] formal; '**2en** v/t. (ge-, h) form (object, character, etc.); shape, fashion (wood, metal, etc.); mo(u)ld (clay, character, etc.); '**~enlehre** gr. f accidence; '**~fehler** m informality; ⚖ flaw; 2ieren [.'mi:rən] v/t. (no -ge-, h) form; draw up, line up; sich ~ line up.

förmlich adj. ['fœrmliç] formal; ceremonious; '**2keit** f (-/-en) formality; ceremoniousness.

'**formlos** adj. formless, shapeless; *fig.* informal.

Formular [fɔrmu'la:r] n (-s/-e) form, *Am. a.* blank.

formu'lieren v/t. (no -ge-, h) formulate (question, etc.); word, phrase (question, contract, etc.).

forsch adj. [fɔrʃ] vigorous, energetic; smart, dashing.

forsch|en ['fɔrʃən] v/i. (ge-, h): ~ nach (dat.) search for *or* after; ~ in (dat.) search (through); '**2er** m (-s/-) researcher, research worker.

'**Forschung** f (-/-en) research (work); '**~sreise** f (exploring) expedition; '**~sreisende** m explorer.

Forst [fɔrst] m (-es/-e[n]) forest; '**~aufseher** m (forest-)keeper, gamekeeper.

Förster ['fœrstər] m (-s/-) forester; ranger.

'Forst|haus n forester's house; '~-
revier n forest district; '~wesen n,
'~wirtschaft f forestry.
Fort¹ ⚔ [fo:r] n (-s/-s) fort.
fort² adv. [fɔrt] away, gone; on;
gone, lost; in e-m ~ continuously;
und so ~ and so on or forth; s. a.
weg.
'fort|bestehen v/i. (irr. stehen, sep.,
no -ge-, h) continue, persist; '~be-
wegen v/t. (sep., no -ge-, h) move
(on, away); sich ~ move, walk; '2-
dauer f continuance; '~dauern v/i.
(sep., -ge-, h) continue, last; '~fah-
ren v/i. (irr. fahren, sep., -ge-) 1.
(sein) depart, leave; drive off; 2. (h)
continue, keep on (et. zu tun doing
s.th.); '~führen v/t. (sep., -ge-, h)
continue, carry on; '2gang m departure, leaving; continuance; '~-
gehen v/i. (irr. gehen, sep., -ge-,
sein) go (away), leave; '~geschrit-
ten adj. advanced; '2kommen n
(-s/no pl.) progress; '~laufend adj.
consecutive, continuous; '~pflan-
zen v/t. (sep., -ge-, h) propagate;
sich ~ biol. propagate, reproduce;
phys., disease, rumour: be propa-
gated; '2pflanzung f propagation;
reproduction; '~reißen v/t. (irr.
reißen, sep., -ge-, h) avalanche, etc.:
sweep or carry away; '~schaffen
v/t. (sep., -ge-, h) get or take away,
remove; '~schreiten v/i. (irr.
schreiten, sep., -ge-, sein) advance,
proceed, progress; '~schreitend
adj. progressive; '2schritt m progress; '~schrittlich adj. progressive;
'~setzen v/t. (sep., -ge-, h) continue, pursue; '2setzung f (-/-en)
continuation, pursuit; ~ folgt to be
continued; '~während 1. adj. continual, continuous; perpetual; 2.
adv. constantly, always.
Forum [fo:rum] n (-s/Foren, Fora
and -s) forum.
Foto... [fo:to-] s. Photo...
Foyer [foa'je:] n (-s/-s) thea. foyer,
Am. and parl. lobby; hotel: foyer,
lounge.
Fracht [fraxt] f (-/-en) goods pl.;
🚂 carriage, freight; ⚓, 🛥 freight
(-age); cargo; '~brief m ⚓ consignment note, Am., ⚓ bill of
lading; '~dampfer m cargo steamer, freighter; '~er m (-s/-) freighter;
'2frei adj. carriage or freight paid;
'~führer m carrier, Am. a. team-
ster; '~geld n carriage charges pl.,
🚂, ⚓, Am. freight; '~gut n goods
pl., freight; '~stück n package.
Frack [frak] m (-[e]s/-e, -s) dress
coat, tail-coat, F tails; '~anzug m
dress-suit.
Frag|e ['fra:gə] f (-/-n) question;
gr., reth. interrogation; problem,
point; e-e ~ stellen ask a question;
in ~ stellen question; '~ebogen m
questionnaire; form; '2en (ge-, h)

1. v/t. ask; question; es fragt sich,
ob it is doubtful whether; 2. v/i.
ask; '~er m (-s/-) questioner; '~e-
wort gr. n (-[e]s/~er) interrogative;
'~ezeichen n question-mark, point
of interrogation, Am. mst interrogation point; 2lich adj. ['fra:k-] doubtful, uncertain; in question; 2los
adv. ['fra:k-] undoubtedly, unques-
tionably.
Fragment [frag'mɛnt] n (-[e]s/-e)
fragment.
fragwürdig adj. ['fra:k-] doubtful,
dubious, questionable.
Fraktion parl. [frak'tsjo:n] f (-/-en)
(parliamentary) group.
frank|ieren [fraŋ'ki:rən] v/t. (no
-ge-, h) prepay, stamp; ~o adv.
['~o] free; post(age) paid; parcel:
carriage paid.
Franse ['franzə] f (-/-n) fringe.
Franz|ose [fran'tso:zə] m (-n/-n)
Frenchman; die ~n pl. the French
pl.; ~ösin [~ø:zin] f (-/-nen) French-
woman; 2ösisch adj. [~ø:zif]
French.
fräs|en ⊕ ['frɛ:zən] v/t. (ge-, h)
mill; 2maschine ['frɛ:s-] f milling-
machine
Fraß [fra:s] 1. F m (-es/-e) sl. grub;
2. 2 pret. of fressen.
Fratze ['fratsə] f (-/-n) grimace, F
face; ~n schneiden make grimaces.
Frau [frau] f (-/-en) woman; lady;
wife, ✗ Mrs ✗.
'Frauen|arzt m gyn(a)ecologist;
'~klinik f hospital for women; '~-
rechte n|pl. women's rights pl.;
'~stimmrecht pol. n women's suffrage; '~zimmer mst contp. n
female, woman.
Fräulein ['frɔylain] n (-s/-, F -s)
young lady; teacher; shop-assist-
ant; waitress; ~ ✗ Miss ✗.
'fraulich adj. womanly.
frech adj. [frɛç] impudent, insolent,
F saucy, cheeky, Am. F a. sassy, sl.
fresh; lie, etc.: brazen; thief, etc.:
bold, daring; '2heit f (-/-en) impudence, insolence; F sauciness,
cheek; boldness.
frei adj. [frai] free (von from, of);
position vacant; field: open; parcel:
carriage-paid; journalist, etc.: free-
lance; liberal; candid, frank; licentious; ~ Haus ✝ franco domicile;
~er Tag day off; im Freien in the
open air.
'Frei|bad n open-air bath; '~beuter
['~bɔytər] m (-s/-) freebooter;
'2bleibend ✝ adj. price, etc.: subject to alteration; offer: conditional;
'~brief m charter; fig. warrant;
'~denker m (-s/-) freethinker.
Freier ['fraiər] m (-s/-) suitor.
'Frei|exemplar n free or presenta-
tion copy; '~frau f baroness; '~ga-
be f release; '2geben (irr. geben,
sep., -ge-, h) 1. v/t. release; give

(*s.o. an hour, etc.*) off; 2. *v/i.*: j-m ~ give s.o. time off; '**2gebig** *adj.* generous, liberal; **~gebigkeit** *f* (-/-en) generosity, liberality; '**~gepäck** *n* free luggage; '**2haben** *v/i.* (*irr. haben, sep., -ge-, h*) have a holiday; have a day off; '**~hafen** *m* free port; '**2halten** *v/t.* (*irr. halten, sep., -ge-, h*) keep free *or* clear; in *restaurant, etc.*: treat; '**~handel** *m* free trade.

'**Freiheit** *f* (-/-en) liberty; freedom; *dichterische* ~ poetic licence, *Am.* poetic license.

'**Frei|herr** *m* baron; '**~karte** *f* free (*thea. a.* complimentary) ticket; '**2lassen** *v/t.* (*irr. lassen, sep., -ge-, h*) release, set free *or* at liberty; *gegen Kaution* ~ $\frac{r}{r}$ release on bail; '**~lassung** *f* (-/-en) release; '**~lauf** *m* free-wheel.

'**freilich** *adv.* indeed, certainly, of course; admittedly.

'**Frei|lichtbühne** *f* open-air stage *or* theat|re, *Am.* -er; '**2machen** *v/t.* (*sep., -ge-, h*) ✎ prepay, stamp (*letter, etc.*); *sich* ~ undress, take one's clothes off; '**~marke** *f* stamp; '**~maurer** *m* freemason; **~maurerei** [~'raɪ] *f* (-/no *pl.*) freemasonry; '**~mut** *m* frankness; **2mütig** *adj.* ['~my:tiç] frank; '**2schaffend** *adj.*: **~er** *Künstler* free-lance artist; **~schärler** ['~ʃɛrlər] *m* (-s/-) volunteer, irregular; '**~schein** *m* licen|ce, *Am.* -se; **2sinnig** *adj.* liberal; '**2sprechen** *v/t.* (*irr. sprechen, sep., -ge-, h*) *esp. eccl.* absolve (*von* from); $\frac{r}{r}$ acquit (*of*); release (*apprentice*) from his articles; '**~sprechung** *f* (-/-en) *esp. eccl.* absolution; release from articles; **~** '**~spruch** $\frac{r}{r}$ *m* acquittal; '**~staat** *pol. m* free state; '**2stehen** *v/i.* (*irr. stehen, sep., -ge-, h*) house, *etc.*: stand empty; *es steht Ihnen frei zu inf.* you are free *or* at liberty to *inf.*; '**2stellen** *v/t.* (*sep., -ge-, h*): j-n ~ exempt s.o. (*von* from) (*a.* ✗); j-m *et.* ~ leave s.th. open to s.o.; '**~stoß** *m football*: free kick; '**~tag** *m* Friday; '**~tod** *m* suicide; '**2tragend** ⚙ *adj.* cantilever; '**~treppe** *f* outdoor staircase; '**2willig** 1. *adj.* voluntary; 2. *adv. a.* of one's own free will; **~willige** ['~viligə] *m* (-n/-n) volunteer; '**~zeit** *f* free *or* spare *or* leisure time; **2zügig** *adj.* ['~tsy:giç] free to move; '**~zügigkeit** *f* (-/no *pl.*) freedom of movement.

fremd *adj.* [fremt] strange; foreign; alien; extraneous; '**~artig** *adj.* strange; exotic.

Fremde ['fremdə] 1. *f* (-/no *pl.*) distant *or* foreign parts; *in der* ~ far away from home, abroad; 2. *m, f* (-n/-n) stranger; foreigner; '**~buch** *n* visitors' book; '**~nführer** *m* guide, cicerone; '**~nheim** *n*

boarding house; **~nindustrie** ['fremdən⁹-] *f* tourist industry; '**~nlegion** ✗ *f* Foreign Legion; '**~nverkehr** *m* tourism, tourist traffic, **~nzimmer** *n* spare (bed-) room, *tourism*: room.

'**Fremd|herrschaft** *f* foreign rule; '**~körper** ✛ *m* foreign body; **2ländisch** *adj.* ['~lendiʃ] foreign, exotic; '**~sprache** *f* foreign language, **2sprachig** *adj.*, **2sprachlich** *adj.* foreign-language; '**~wort** *n* (-[e]s/~er) foreign word.

Frequenz *phys.* [fre'kvents] *f* (-/-en) frequency.

fressen ['fresən] 1. *v/t.* (*irr., ge-, h*) eat; *beast of prey*: devour; F *p.* devour, gorge; 2. *v/i.* (*irr., ge-, h*) eat; F *p.* gorge; 3. 2 *n* (-s/no *pl.*) feed, food.

'**Freß|gier** *f* voracity, gluttony; '**~napf** *m* feeding dish.

Freude ['frɔydə] *f* (-/-n) joy, gladness; delight; pleasure; ~ *haben an* (*dat.,* find *or* take pleasure in.

'**Freuden|botschaft** *f* glad tidings *pl.*; '**~fest** *n* happy occasion; '**~feuer** *n* bonfire; '**~geschrei** *n* shouts *pl.* of joy; '**~tag** *m* day of rejoicing, red-letter day; '**~taumel** *m* transports *pl.* of joy.

'**freud|estrahlend** *adj.* radiant with joy; '**~ig** *adj.* joyful; happy; **~es** *Ereignis* happy event; '**~los** *adj.* ['frɔytlo:s] joyless, cheerless.

freuen ['frɔyən] *v/t.* (*ge-, h*): *es freut mich, daß* I am glad *or* pleased (*that*); *sich* ~ *über* (*acc.*) be pleased about *or* with, be glad about; *sich* ~ *auf* (*acc.*) look forward to.

Freund [frɔynt] *m* (-es/-e) (boy-) friend; **~in** ['~din] *f* (-/-nen) (girl-) friend; **2lich** *adj.* friendly, kind, nice; cheerful, bright; *climate*: mild; **~lichkeit** *f* (-/-en) friendliness, kindness; '**~schaft** *f* (-/-en) friendship; ~ *schließen* make friends (*mit* with); **2schaftlich** *adj.* friendly.

Frevel ['fre:fəl] *m* (-s/-) outrage (*an dat., gegen* on), crime (*against*); '**2haft** *adj.* wicked, outrageous; impious; **2n** *v/i.* (*ge-, h*) commit a crime *or* outrage (*gegen* against).

Frevler ['fre:flər] *m* (-s/-) evil-doer, offender; blasphemer.

Friede(n) ['fri:də(n)] *m* (*Friedens/ Frieden*) peace; *im Frieden* in peacetime; *laß mich in Frieden* leave me alone!

'**Friedens|bruch** *m* violation of (the) peace; '**~stifter** *m* peacemaker; '**~störer** *m* (-s/-) disturber of the peace; '**~verhandlungen** *f/pl.* peace negotiations *pl.*; '**~vertrag** *m* peace treaty.

fried|fertig *adj.* ['fri:t-] peaceable, peace-loving; '**2hof** *m* cemetery, graveyard; churchyard; '**~lich** *adj.*

s. friedfertig; peaceful; **'~liebend** *adj.* peace-loving.

frieren ['fri:rən] *v/i.* (*irr.*, *ge-*) **1.** (*sein*) *liquid:* freeze, become frozen; *river, etc.:* freeze (over, up); *window-pane, etc.:* freeze over; **2.** (*h*) be *or* feel cold; *mich friert or ich friere an den Füßen* my feet are cold.

Fries △ [fri:s] *m* (*-es/-e*) frieze.

frisch [friʃ] **1.** *adj. food, flowers, etc.:* fresh; *egg:* new-laid; *linen, etc.:* clean; *auf ~er Tat ertappen* catch red-handed; **2.** *adv.:* ~ *gestrichen!* wet paint!, *Am.* fresh paint!; **2e** ['~ə] *f* (*-/no pl.*) freshness.

Friseu|r [fri'zø:r] *m* (*-s/-e*) hairdresser; (*men's*) barber; **~se** [~zə] *f* (*-/-n*) (woman) hairdresser.

fri'sier|en *v/t.* (*no -ge-, h*): *j-n* ~ do *or* dress s.o.'s hair; F: *einen Wagen* ~ *mot.* tune up *or* soup up *or* hot up a car; *sich* ~ do one's hair; **2kommode** *f* dressing-table; **2salon** *m* hairdressing saloon; **2tisch** *m s. Frisierkommode.*

Frist [frist] *f* (*-/-en*) (fixed *or* limited) period of time, time allowed; term; *t'z* prescribed time; *t'z,* ✝ respite, grace; **'2en** *v/t.* (*ge-, h*): *sein Dasein* ~ scrape along, scrape a living.

Frisur [fri'zu:r] *f* (*-/-en*) hair-style, hair-do, coiffure.

frivol *adj.* [fri'vo:l] frivolous, flippant; **2ität** [~oli'tɛ:t] *f* (*-/-en*) frivolity, flippancy.

froh *adj.* [fro:] joyful, glad; cheerful; happy, gay (*a. colour*).

fröhlich *adj* ['frø:liç] gay, merry, cheerful, happy, *Am.* F *a.* chipper; **'2keit** *f* (*-/~, -en*) gaiety, cheerfulness; merriment.

froh'locken *v/i.* (*no -ge-, h*) shout for joy, be jubilant; exult (*über acc.* at, in); gloat (over); **'2sinn** *m* (*-[e]s/no pl.*) gaiety, cheerfulness.

fromm *adj* [from] *p.* pious, religious; *life, etc.* godly; *prayer, etc.:* devout; *horse, etc.* docile; *~e Lüge* white lie; *~er Wunsch* wishful thinking, idle wish

Frömmelei [fræmə'laɪ] *f* (*-/-en*) affected piety, bigotry.

'Frömmigkeit *f* (*-/-en*) piety, religiousness; godliness; devoutness.

Fron [fro:n] *f* (*-/-en*), **'~arbeit** *f,* **'~dienst** *m* forced *or* compulsory labo(u)r *or* service; *fig.* drudgery.

frönen ['frø:nən] *v/i.* (*dat.*) (*ge-, h*) indulge in, be a slave to.

Front [front] *f* (*-/-en*) △ front, façade, face; ✕ front (line); line; *pol.,* ✱, *etc.* front.

fror [fro:r] *pret. of* frieren.

Frosch *zo.* [frɔʃ] *m* (*-es/~e*) frog; **'~perspektive** *f* worm's-eye view.

Frost [frɔst] *m* (*-es/~e*) frost; chill; **'~beule** *f* chilblain.

frösteln ['fræstəln] *v/i.* (*ge-, h*) feel chilly, shiver (with cold).

'frostig *adj.* frosty (*a. fig.*); *fig.* cold, frigid, icy.

'Frost|salbe ✻ *f* chilblain ointment; **'~schaden** *m* frost damage; **'~schutzmittel** *mot. n* anti-freezing mixture; **'~wetter** *n* frosty weather.

frottier|en [fro'ti:rən] *v/t.* (*no -ge-, h*) rub; **2(hand)tuch** *n* Turkish towel.

Frucht [fruxt] *f* (*-/~e*) ✻ fruit (*a. fig.*); corn; crop; *fig.* reward, result; **'2bar** *adj.* fruitful (*esp. fig.*); fertile (*a. biol.*); **~barkeit** *f* (*-/no pl.*) fruitfulness, fertility; **'2bringend** *adj.* fruit-bearing; *fig.* fruitful; **'2en** *fig. v/i.* (*ge-, h*) be of use; **'~knoten** *m* ovary; **'2los** *adj.* fruitless; *fig. a.* ineffective.

früh [fry:] **1.** *adj.* early; *am ~en Morgen* in the early morning; *~es Aufstehen* early rising; *~e Anzeichen* early symptoms, *~er* former; **2.** *adv.* in the morning, *aufstehen* rise early; *heute* ~ this morning; *morgen* ~ tomorrow morning, *~er* earlier; formerly, in former times; *~estens* at the earliest; **'2aufsteher** *m* (*-s/-*) early riser, F early bird; **'2e** *f* (*-/no pl.*): *in aller* ~ very early in the morning; **'2geburt** *f* premature birth; premature baby *or* animal; **'2gottesdienst** *m* early service; **'2jahr** *n,* **2ling** [liŋ] *m* (*-s/-e*) spring, **'~morgens** *adv* early in the morning, **~reif** *fig. adj.* precocious; **'2sport** *m* early morning exercises; **'2stück** *n* breakfast; **'~stücken** (*ge-, h*) **1.** *v/i.* (have) breakfast; **2.** *v/t.* have s.th. for breakfast; **'2zug** ✺ *m* early train.

Fuchs [fuks] *m* (*-es/~e*) *zo.* fox (*a. fig.*); *horse:* sorrel.

Füchsin *zo.* ['fyksin] *f* (*-/-nen*) she-fox, vixen.

'Fuchs|jagd *f* fox-hunt(ing); **'~pelz** *m* fox-fur; **'2rot** *adj.* foxy-red, sorrel; **'~schwanz** *m* foxtail; ⊕ pad-saw; ✻ amarant(h); **'2'teufels'wild** F *adj.* mad with rage, F hopping mad.

fuchteln ['fuxtəln] *v/i.* (*ge-, h*): ~ *mit* (*dat.*) wave (*one's hands*) about.

Fuder ['fu:dər] *n* (*-s/-*) cart-load; tun (*of wine*). [*♪* fugue.]

Fuge ['fu:gə] *f* (*-/-n*) ⊕ joint; seam;]

füg|en ['fy:gən] *v/refl.* (*ge-, h*) submit, give in, yield (*dat., in acc.* to); comply (with), **~sam** *adj.* ['fy:k-] (com)pliant; manageable

fühl|bar *adj* ['fy:lba:r] tangible, palpable, *fig.* sensible, noticeable; **'~en** (*ge-, h*) **1.** *v/t* feel; be aware of; *sich glücklich* ~ feel happy; **2.** *v/i.:* *mit j-m* ~ feel for *or* sympathize with s.o.; **'2er** *m* (*-s/-*) feeler

(a. fig.); '2ung f (-/-en) touch, contact (a. 🗙); ~ haben be in touch (mit with); ~ verlieren lose touch.

fuhr [fu:r] pret. of fahren.

Fuhre ['fu:rə] f (-/-n) cart-load.

führen ['fy:rən] (ge-, h) 1. v/t. lead, guide (blind person, etc.); show (zu dat. to); wield (paint-brush, etc.); 🗙 command (regiment, etc.); have, bear (title, etc.); carry on (conversation, etc.); conduct (campaign, etc.); ✝ run (shop, etc.); deal in (goods); lead (life); keep (diary, etc.); 𝄑𝄑 try (case); wage (war) (mit, gegen against); ~ durch show round; sich ~ conduct o.s., behave (o.s.); 2. v/i. path, etc. lead, run, go (nach, zu to); sports, etc.: (hold the) lead, be ahead; ~ zu lead to, result in; '~d adj. leading, prominent, Am. a. banner.

'Führer m (-s/-) leader (a. pol., sports); guide(-book); '~raum 🗙 m cockpit; '~schein mot. m driving licence, Am. driver's license; '~sitz m mot. driver's seat, 🗙 pilot's seat; '~stand 🚋 m (driver's) cab.

'Fuhr|geld n, '~lohn m cartage, carriage; '~mann m (-[e]s/~er, Fuhrleute) carter, carrier, wag(g)oner; driver; '~park m fleet (of lorries), Am. fleet (of trucks).

'Führung f (-/-en) leadership; conduct, management; guidance; conduct, behavio(u)r; sports, etc.: lead; '~szeugnis n certificate of good conduct.

'Fuhr|unternehmer m carrier, haulage contractor, Am. a. trucker, teamster; '~werk n (horse-drawn) vehicle; cart, wag(g)on.

Fülle ['fylə] f (-/no pl.) fullness (a. fig.); corpulence, plumpness, stoutness; fig. wealth, abundance, profusion.

füllen[1] ['fylən] v/t. (ge-, h) fill (a. tooth); stuff (cushion, poultry, etc.).

Füllen[2] zo. [~] n (-s/-) foal; male: colt; female: filly.

'Füll|er F m (-s/-), '~feder(halter m) f fountain-pen; '~horn n horn of plenty; '~ung f (-/-en) filling; panel (of door, etc.).

Fund [funt] m (-[e]s/-e) finding, discovery, find.

Fundament[funda'ment]n(-[e]s/-e) ⚒ foundation, fig basis.

'Fund|büro n lost-property office; '~gegenstand m object found; '~grube fig f rich source, mine.

fünf adj. [fynf] five; '2eck n pentagon; '~fach ['fax] fivefold, quintuple, '2kampf m sports: pentathlon; 2linge [~liŋə] m/pl. quintuplets pl.; ~te adj. fifth; '2tel '2tel n (-s/-) fifth; '~tens adv. fifthly, in the fifth place; '2zehn(te) adj. fifteen(th); '~zig adj. ['~tsiç] fifty; ~zigste adj. fiftieth.

fungieren [fuŋ'gi:rən] v/i. (no -ge-, h): ~ als officiate or act as.

Funk [fuŋk] m (-s/no pl.) radio, wireless; '~anlage f radio or wireless installation or equipment; '~bastler m do-it-yourself radio ham, '~bild n photo-radiogram.

Funke ['fuŋkə] m (-ns/-n) spark; fig. a. glimmer.

'funkeln v/i. (ge-, h) sparkle, glitter; star: twinkle, sparkle.

'Funken[1] esp. fig. m (-s/-) s. Funke.

'funken[2] v/t. (ge-, h) radio, wireless, broadcast.

'Funk|er m (-s/-) radio or wireless operator; '~gerät n radio (communication) set; '~spruch m radio or wireless message; '~station f radio or wireless station; '~stille f radio or wireless silence; '~streifenwagen m radio patrol car.

Funktion [fuŋk'tsjo:n] f (-/-en) function; '~är [~tsjo'ne:r] m (-s/-e) functionary, official; 2ieren [~o-'ni:rən] v/i. (no -ge-, h) function, work.

'Funk|turm m radio or wireless tower; '~verkehr m radio or wireless communication; '~wagen m radio car; '~wesen n (-s/no pl.) radio communication.

für prp. (acc.) [fy:r] for; in exchange or return for; in favo(u)r of; in s.o.'s place; Schritt ~ Schritt step by step; Tag ~ Tag day after day; ich ~ meine Person ... as for me, I ...; das Für und Wider the pros and cons pl.

'Fürbitte f intercession.

Furche ['furçə] f (-/-n) furrow (a. in face); rut; ⊕ groove; '2n v/t. (ge-, h) furrow (a. face); ⊕ groove.

Furcht[furçt] f (-/no pl.) fear, dread; aus ~ vor for fear of; '2bar adj. awful, terrible, dreadful.

fürchten ['fyrçtən] (ge-, h) 1. v/t. fear, dread; sich ~ vor (dat.) be afraid or scared of; 2. v/i.: ~ um fear for.

'fürchterlich adj. s. furchtbar.

'furcht|los adj. fearless; '2losigkeit f (-/no pl.) fearlessness; '~sam adj. timid, timorous; '2samkeit f (-/no pl.) timidity.

Furie fig. ['fu:rjə] f (-/-n) fury.

Furnier ⊕ [fur'ni:r] n (-s/-e) veneer; 2en v/t. (no -ge-, h) veneer.

'Für|sorge f care, öffentliche ~ public welfare work, '~sorgeamt n welfare department, '~sorgeerziehung f corrective training for juvenile delinquents; '~sorger m (-s/-) social or welfare worker; '2sorglich adj. considerate, thoughtful, solicitous; '~sprache f intercession (für for, bei with); '~sprecher m intercessor.

Fürst [fyrst] m (-en/-en) prince; sovereign; '~enhaus n dynasty;

'**～enstand** m prince's rank; '**～entum** n (-s/~er) principality; '**Ꝃlich** 1. adj. princely (a. fig.), royal; fig. magnificent, sumptuous; 2. adv.: ~ leben live like a lord or king; '**～lichkeiten** f/pl. royalties pl.

Furt [furt] f (-/-en) ford.

Furunkel ♂ [fu'ruŋkəl] m (-s/-) boil, furuncle.

'**Fürwort** gr. n (-[e]s/~er) pronoun.

Fusel F ['fu:zəl] m (-s/-) low-quality spirits, F rotgut.

Fusion ✝ [fu'zjo:n] f (-/-en) merger, amalgamation.

Fuß [fu:s] m (-es/~e) foot; ~ fassen find a foothold; fig. become established; auf gutem (schlechtem) ~ stehen mit be on good (bad) terms with; zu ~ on foot; zu ~ gehen walk; gut zu ~ sein be a good walker; '**～abstreifer** m (-s/-) door-scraper, door-mat; '**～angel** f mantrap; '**～ball** m (association) football, F and Am. soccer; '**～ballspieler** m football player, footballer; '**～bank** f footstool; '**～bekleidung** f footwear, footgear; '**～boden** m floor (-ing); '**～bodenbelag** m floor covering; '**～bremse** mot. f foot-brake;

'**Ꝃen** v/i. (ge-, h): ~ auf (dat.) be based or founded on; **～gänger** ['～gɛŋər] m (-s/-) pedestrian; '**～gelenk** anat. n ankle joint; '**～note** f footnote; '**～pfad** m footpath; '**～sack** m foot-muff; '**～sohle** anat. f sole of the foot; '**～soldat** ✗ m foot-soldier, infantryman; '**～spur** f footprint; track; **～stapfe** ['～ʃtapfə] f (-/-n) footprint, fig. a. footstep; '**～steig** m footpath; '**～tritt** m kick; '**～wanderung** f walking tour, hike; '**～weg** m footpath.

Futter ['futər] n 1. (-s/no pl.) food, sl. grub, Am. F a. chow; feed, fodder; 2. (-s/-) lining; ⚒ casing.

Futteral [futə'ra:l] n (-s/-e) case (for spectacles, etc.); cover (of umbrella); sheath (of knife).

'**Futtermittel** n feeding stuff.

füttern ['fytərn] v/t. (ge-, h) feed; line (dress, etc.); ⚒ case.

'**Futter|napf** m feeding bowl or dish; '**～neid** fig. m (professional) jealousy; '**～stoff** m lining (material).

'**Fütterung** f (-/-en) feeding; lining; ⚒ casing.

Futur gr. [fu'tu:r] n (-s/-e) future (tense).

G

gab [ga:p] pret. of geben.

Gabe ['ga:bə] f (-/-n) gift, present; alms; donation; ♣ dose; talent.

Gabel ['ga:bəl] f (-/-n) fork; '**Ꝃn** v/refl. (ge-, h) fork, bifurcate; '**～ung** f (-/-en) bifurcation.

gackern ['gakərn] v/i. (ge-, h) cackle.

gaffen ['gafən] v/i. (ge-, h) gape, stare.

Gage ['ga:ʒə] f (-/-n) salary, pay.

gähnen ['gɛ:nən] 1. v/i. (ge-, h) yawn; 2. ♀ n (-s/no pl.) yawning.

Gala ['gala] f (-/no pl.) gala; in ~ in full dress.

galant adj. [ga'lant] gallant; courteous; **Ꝃerie** [～ə'ri:] f (-/-n) gallantry; courtesy.

Galeere ⚓ [ga'le:rə] f (-/-n) galley.

Galerie [galə'ri:] f (-/-n) gallery.

Galgen ['galgən] m (-s/-) gallows, gibbet; '**～frist** f respite; '**～gesicht** n gallows-look, hangdog look; '**～humor** m grim humo(u)r; '**～strick** m, '**～vogel** m gallows-bird, hangdog.

Galle anat. ['galə] f (-/-n) bile (of person); gall (of animal) (a. fig.); '**～nblase** anat. f gall-bladder; '**～nleiden** ♣ n bilious complaint; '**～nstein** ♣ m gall-stone, bile-stone.

Gallert ['galərt] n (-[e]s/-e), **～e** [ga'lɛrtə] f (-/-n) gelatine, jelly.

'**gallig** fig. adj. bilious.

Galopp [ga'lɔp] m (-s/-s, -e) gallop; canter; **Ꝃieren** [～'pi:rən] v/i. (no -ge-, sein) gallop; canter.

galt [galt] pret. of gelten.

galvani|sch adj. [gal'va:niʃ] galvanic; **～sieren** [～ani'-] v/t. (no -ge-, h) galvanize.

Gang[1] [gaŋ] m (-[e]s/~e) walk; s. Gangart; fig. motion; running, working (of machine); errand; way, course (of events, of a meal, etc.); passage(-way); alley; corridor, gallery; in vehicle, between seats: gangway, esp. Am. aisle; 🚪 corridor, Am. aisle; fencing: pass; anat. duct; mot. gear; erster (zweiter, dritter, vierter) ~ low or bottom (second, third, top) gear; in ~ bringen or setzen set going or in motion, Am. operate; in ~ kommen get going, get started; im ~ sein be in motion; ⊕ be working or running; fig. be in progress; in vollem ~ in full swing.

gang[2] adj. [～]: ~ und gäbe customary, traditional.

'**Gang|art** f gait, walk (of person); pace (of horse); '**Ꝃbar** adj. road: practicable, passable; money: current; ✝ goods: marketable; s. gängig.

Gängelband ['gɛŋəl-] n leading-strings *pl.*; *am ~ führen* keep in leading-strings, lead by the nose.

gängig *adj.* ['gɛŋɪç] *money*: current; † *goods*: marketable; *~er Ausdruck* current word *or* phrase.

Gans *orn.* [gans] *f* (-/*e*) goose.

Gänse|blümchen ❦ ['gɛnzəbly:mçən] *n* (-*s*/-) daisy; '*~braten* *m* roast goose; '*~feder* *f* goose-quill; *~füßchen* ['~fy:sçən] *n/pl.* quotation marks *pl.*, inverted commas *pl.*; '*~haut* *f* goose-skin; *fig. a.* goose-flesh, *Am. a.* goose pimples *pl.*; '*~klein* *n* (-*s/no pl.*) (goose-)giblets *pl.*; '*~marsch* *m* single *or* Indian file; '*~rich* *orn.* ['~rɪç] *m* (-*s*/-*e*) gander; '*~schmalz* *n* goose-grease.

ganz [gants] **1.** *adj.* all; entire, whole; complete, total, full; *den ~en Tag* all day (long); **2.** *adv.* quite; entirely, etc. (*s.* **1.**); very; *~ Auge* (*Ohr*) all eyes (ears); *~ und gar* wholly, totally; *~ und gar nicht* not at all; *im ~en* on the whole, generally; in all; † in the lump; '*~e* *n* (-*n/no pl.*) whole; totality; *aufs ~ gehen* go all out, *esp. Am. sl.* go the whole hog.

gänzlich *adj.* ['gɛntslɪç] complete, total, entire.

'**Ganztagsbeschäftigung** *f* full-time job *or* employment.

gar [ga:r] **1.** *adj. food*: done; **2.** *adv.* quite, very; even; *~ nicht* not at all.

Garage [ga'ra:ʒə] *f* (-/-*n*) garage.

Garantie [garan'ti:] *f* (-/-*n*) guarantee, warranty, ‡‡ guaranty; *~ren* *v/t.* (*no -ge-, h*) guarantee, warrant.

Garbe ['garbə] *f* (-/-*n*) sheaf.

Garde ['gardə] *f* (-/-*n*) guard.

Garderobe [gardə'ro:bə] *f* (-/-*n*) wardrobe; cloakroom, *Am.* check-room; *thea.* dressing-room; *~nfrau* *f* cloak-room attendant, *Am.* hat-check girl; *~nmarke* *f* check; *~nschrank* *m* wardrobe; *~nständer* *m* coat-stand, hat-stand, hall-stand.

Garderobiere [gardəro'bje:rə] *f* (-/-*n*) *s. Garderobenfrau*; *thea.* wardrobe mistress.

Gardine [gar'di:nə] *f* (-/-*n*) curtain.

gär|en ['gɛ:rən] *v/i.* (*irr., ge-, h, sein*) ferment; '*2mittel* *n* ferment.

Garn [garn] *n* (-[*e*]*s*/-*e*) yarn; thread; cotton; net; *j-m ins ~ gehen* fall into s.o.'s snare.

Garnele *zo.* [gar'ne:lə] *f* (-/-*n*) shrimp.

garnieren [gar'ni:rən] *v/t.* (*no -ge-, h*) trim; garnish (*esp. a dish*).

Garnison ✕ [garni'zo:n] *f* (-/-*en*) garrison, post.

Garnitur [garni'tu:r] *f* (-/-*en*) trimming; ⊕ fittings *pl.*; set.

garstig *adj.* ['garstɪç] nasty, bad; ugly.

'**Gärstoff** *m* ferment.

Garten ['gartən] *m* (-*s/~*) garden; '*~anlage* *f* gardens *pl.*, park; '*~ar-*

beit *f* gardening; '*~bau* *m* horti-culture; '*~erde* *f* (garden-)mo(u)ld; '*~fest* *n* garden-party, *Am. a.* lawn party; '*~geräte* *n/pl.* gardening-tools *pl.*; '*~stadt* *f* garden city.

Gärtner ['gɛrtnər] *m* (-*s*/-) gardener; *~ei* [~'raɪ] *f* (-/-*en*) gardening, horticulture; nursery; *~in* *f* (-/-*nen*) gardener.

Gärung ['gɛ:ruŋ] *f* (-/-*en*) fermentation.

Gas [ga:s] *n* (-*es*/-*e*) gas; *~ geben* *mot.* open the throttle, *Am.* step on the gas; '*~anstalt* *f* gas-works, *Am. a.* gas plant; '*~behälter* *m* gasometer, *Am.* gas tank *or* container; *~beleuchtung* *f* gaslight; '*~brenner* *m* gas-burner; 2förmig *adj.* ['~fœrmɪç] gaseous; '*~hahn* *m* gas-tap; '*~herd* *m* gas-stove, *Am.* gas range; '*~leitung* *f* gas-mains *pl.*; '*~messer* *m* (-*s*/-) gas-meter; '*~ofen* *m* gas-oven; '*~pedal* *mot. n* accelerator (pedal), *Am.* gas pedal.

Gasse ['gasə] *f* (-/-*n*) lane, by-street, alley(-way); '*~nhauer* *m* (-*s*/-) street ballad, popular song; '*~njunge* *m* street arab.

Gast [gast] *m* (-*es*/-*e*) guest; visitor; customer (*of public house, etc.*); *thea.* guest (artist); guest star; '*~arbeiter* *m* foreign worker; '*~bett* *n* spare bed.

Gäste|buch ['gɛstə-] *n* visitors' book; *~zimmer* *n* guest-room; spare bed)room; *s. Gaststube.*

'**gast|freundlich** *adj.* hospitable; '2freundschaft *f* hospitality; '2geber *m* (-*s*/-) host; '2geberin *f* (-/-*nen*) hostess; '2haus *n*, '2hof *m* restaurant; inn, hotel; '2hörer *univ. m* guest student, *Am. a.* auditor.

gastieren *thea.* [gas'ti:rən] *v/i.* (*no -ge-, h*) appear as a guest.

'**gast|lich** *adj.* hospitable; '2mahl *n* feast, banquet; '2recht *n* right of *or* to hospitality; '2rolle *thea.* *f* guest part; starring part *or* role; '2spiel *thea.* *n* guest appearance *or* performance; starring (perform-ance); '2stätte *f* restaurant; '2stube *f* taproom; restaurant; '2wirt *m* innkeeper, landlord; '2wirtin *f* innkeeper, landlady; '2wirtschaft *f* inn, public house, restaurant; '2zimmer *n s. Gästezimmer.*

'**Gas|uhr** *f* gas-meter; '*~werk* *n s. Gasanstalt.*

Gatte ['gatə] *m* (-*n*/-*n*) husband; spouse, consort.

Gatter ['gatər] *n* (-*s*/-) lattice; railing, grating.

'**Gattin** *f* (-/-*nen*) wife; spouse, consort.

Gattung ['gatuŋ] *f* (-/-*en*) kind; sort; type; species; genus.

gaukeln ['gaʊkəln] *v/i.* (*ge-, h*) juggle; *birds, etc.*: flutter.

Gaul [gaʊl] *m* (-[e]s/ᵘe) (old) nag.
Gaumen *anat.* ['gaʊmən] *m* (-s/-)
palate.
Gauner ['gaʊnər] *m* (-s/-) scoundrel,
swindler, sharper, *sl.* crook; ~ei
[~'raɪ] *f* (-/-en) swindling, cheating,
trickery.
Gaze ['gɑːzə] *f* (-/-n) gauze.
Gazelle *zo.* [ga'tsɛlə] *f* (-/-n) gazelle.
Geächtete [gə'ɛçtətə] *m, f* (-n/-n)
outlaw.
Gebäck [gə'bɛk] *n* (-[e]s/-e) baker's
goods *pl.*; pastry; fancy cakes *pl.*
ge'backen *p.p. of* backen.
Gebälk [gə'bɛlk] *n* (-[e]s/*no pl.*)
framework, timber-work; beams *pl.*
gebar [gə'baːr] *pret. of* gebären.
Gebärde [gə'bɛːrdə] *f* (-/-n) gesture;
2n *v/refl.* (*no -ge-, h*) conduct o.s.,
behave; ~nspiel *n* (-[e]s/*no pl.*)
gesticulation; dumb show, panto-
mime; ~nsprache *f* language of
gestures.
Gebaren [gə'baːrən] *n* (-s/*no pl.*)
conduct, deportment, behavio(u)r.
gebären [gə'bɛːrən] *v/t.* (*irr., no
-ge-, h*) bear, bring forth (*a. fig.*);
give birth to.
Ge|bäude [gə'bɔʏdə] *n* (-s/-) build-
ing, edifice, structure; ~bell [~'bɛl]
n (-[e]s/*no pl.*) barking.
geben ['geːbən] *v/t.* (*irr., ge-, h*)
give (*j-m et. s.o. s.th.*); present
(*s.o. with s.th.*); put; yield *s.th.*;
deal (*cards*); pledge (*one's word*);
von sich ~ emit; utter (*words*); bring
up, vomit (*food*); et. (*nichts*) ~ *auf*
(*acc.*) set (no) great store by; *sich
geschlagen* ~ give in; *sich zufrieden*
~ content o.s. (*mit with*); *sich zu
erkennen* ~ make o.s. known; *es
gibt* there is, there are; *was gibt es?*
what is the matter?; *thea.*: gegeben
werden be on.
Gebet [gə'beːt] *n* (-[e]s/-e) prayer.
ge'beten *p.p. of* bitten.
Gebiet [gə'biːt] *n* (-[e]s/-e) territory;
district; region; area; *fig.*: field;
province; sphere.
ge'biet|en (*irr. bieten, no -ge-, h*)
1. *v/t.* order, command; 2. *v/i.* rule;
2er *m* (-s/-) master, lord, governor;
2erin *f* (-/-nen) mistress; ~erisch
adj. imperious; commanding.
Gebilde [gə'bɪldə] *n* (-s/-) form,
shape; structure; 2t *adj.* educated;
cultured, cultivated.
Gebirg|e [gə'bɪrɡə] *n* (-s/-) moun-
tains *pl.*; mountain chain *or* range;
2ig *adj.* mountainous; ~sbewoh-
ner *m* mountaineer; ~szug *m* mountain range.
Ge'biß *n* (*Gebisses/Gebisse*) (set of)
teeth; (set of) artificial *or* false
teeth, denture; *harness*: bit.
ge|'bissen *p.p. of* beißen; ~'blasen
p.p. of blasen; ~'blichen *p.p. of*
bleichen 2; ~'blieben *p.p. of*
bleiben; [~'bliːbən]
p.p. of bleiben; ~blümt *adj.*

[~'blyːmt] *pattern, design:* flowered;
material: sprigged; ~'bogen 1. *p.p.
of* biegen; 2. *adj.* bent, curved;
~boren [~'boːrən] 1. *p.p. of* gebären; 2. *adj.* born; *ein* ~er *Deutscher* German by birth; ~e *Schmidt*
née Smith.
ge'borgen 1. *p.p. of* bergen; 2. *adj.*
safe, sheltered; 2heit *f* (-/*no pl.*)
safety, security.
geborsten [gə'bɔrstən] *p.p. of* bersten.
Ge'bot *n* (-[e]s/-e) order; command;
bid(ding), offer; *eccl.*: *die Zehn* ~e
pl. the Ten Commandments *pl.*;
2en *p.p. of* bieten.
ge|bracht [gə'braxt] *p.p. of* bringen;
~brannt [~'brant] *p.p. of* brennen;
~'braten *p.p. of* braten.
Ge'brauch *m* 1. (-[e]s/*no pl.*) use;
ⁱ application; 2. (-[e]s/ᵘe) usage,
practice; custom; 2en *v/t.* (*no -ge-,
h*) use, employ; 2t *adj. clothes, etc.*:
second-hand.
gebräuchlich *adj.* [gə'brɔʏçlɪç] in
use; usual, customary.
Ge'brauchs|anweisung *f* direc-
tions *pl. or* instructions *pl.* for use;
~artikel *m* commodity, necessary,
requisite; personal article; 2fertig
adj. ready for use; *coffee, etc.*:
instant; ~muster † *n* sample;
registered design.
Ge'braucht|wagen *mot. m* used
car; ~waren *f/pl.* second-hand
articles *pl.*
Ge'brechen *n* (-s/-) defect, infirmity; affliction.
ge'brechlich *adj.* fragile; *p.*: frail,
weak; infirm; 2keit *f* (-/-en)
fragility; infirmity.
gebrochen [gə'brɔxən] *p.p. of* brechen.
Ge|brüder [gə'bryːdər] *pl.* brothers
pl.; ~brüll [~'brʏl] *n* (-[e]s/*no pl.*)
roaring; lowing (*of cattle*).
Gebühr [gə'byːr] *f* (-/-en) due; duty;
charge; rate; fee; ~en *pl.* fee(s *pl.*);
dues *pl.*; 2en *v/i.* (*no -ge-, h*) be
due (*dat.* to); *sich* ~ be proper *or*
fitting; 2end *adj.* due; becoming;
proper; 2enfrei *adj.* free of charge;
2enpflichtig *adj.* liable to charges,
chargeable.
gebunden [gə'bʊndən] 1. *p.p. of*
binden; 2. *adj.* bound.
Geburt [gə'buːrt] *f* (-/-en) birth;
~enkontrolle *f*, ~enregelung *f*
birth-control; ~enziffer *f* birth-
rate.
gebürtig *adj.* [gə'byrtɪç]: ~ *aus* a
native of.
Ge'burts|anzeige *f* announcement
of birth; ~fehler *m* congenital
defect; ~helfer *m* obstetrician;
~hilfe *f* obstetrics, midwifery;
~jahr *n* year of birth; ~land *n* native country; ~ort *m* birth-place;
~schein *m* birth certificate; ~tag *m*

birthday; **~urkunde** f birth certificate.

Gebüsch [gə'byʃ] n (-es/-e) bushes pl., undergrowth, thicket.

gedacht [gə'daxt] p.p. of denken.

Gedächtnis [gə'dɛçtnis] n (-ses/-se) memory; remembrance, recollection; im ~ behalten keep in mind; zum ~ (gen.) in memory of; **~feier** f commemoration.

Gedanke [gə'daŋkə] m (-ns/-n) thought; idea; in ~n (versunken or verloren) absorbed in thought; sich ~n machen über (acc.) worry about.

Ge'danken|gang m train of thought; **~leser** m, **~leserin** f (-/-nen) thought-reader; **2los** adj. thoughtless; **~strich** m dash; **2voll** adj. thoughtful, pensive.

Ge|därm [gə'dɛrm] n (-[e]s/-e) mst pl. entrails pl., bowels pl., intestines pl.; **~deck** [~'dɛk] n (-[e]s/-e) cover; menu; ein ~ auflegen lay a place.

gedeihen [gə'daɪən] 1. v/i. (irr., no -ge-, sein) thrive, prosper; 2. 2 n (-s/no pl.) thriving, prosperity.

ge'denken 1. v/i. (gen.) (irr. denken, no -ge-, h) think of; remember, recollect; commemorate; mention; ~ zu inf. intend to inf.; 2. 2 n (-s/no pl.) memory, remembrance (an acc. of).

Ge'denk|feier f commemoration; **~stein** m memorial stone; **~tafel** f commemorative or memorial tablet.

Ge'dicht n (-[e]s/-e) poem.

gediegen adj. [gə'di:gən] solid; pure; **2heit** f (-/no pl.) solidity; purity.

gedieh [gə'di:] pret. of gedeihen; **~en** p.p. of gedeihen.

Gedrängle [gə'drɛŋə] n (-s/no pl.) crowd, throng; **2t** adj. crowded, packed, crammed; style: concise.

ge|droschen [gə'drɔʃən] p.p. of dreschen; **~'drückt** fig. adj. depressed; **~drungen** [~'druŋən] 1. p.p. of dringen; 2. adj. compact; squat, stocky, thickset.

Geduld [gə'dult] f (-/no pl.) patience; **2en** [~dən] v/refl. (no -ge-, h) have patience; **2ig** adj. [~diç] patient.

ge|dunsen adj. [gə'dunzən] bloated; **~durft** [~'durft] p.p. of dürfen 1; **~ehrt** adj. [~'e:rt] hono(u)red; correspondence: Sehr ~er Herr N.! Dear Sir, Dear Mr N.; **~eignet** adj. [~'aɪgnət] fit (für, zu, als for s.th.); suitable (to, for); qualified (for).

Gefahr [gə'fa:r] f (-/-en) danger, peril; risk; auf eigene ~ at one's own risk; ~ laufen zu inf. run the risk of ger.

gefährden [gə'fɛːrdən] v/t. (no -ge-, h) endanger; risk.

ge'fahren p.p. of fahren.

gefährlich adj. [gə'fɛːrliç] dangerous.

ge'fahrlos adj. without risk, safe.

Gefährt|e [gə'fɛːrtə] m (-en/-en), **~in** f (-/-nen) companion, fellow.

Gefälle [gə'fɛlə] n (-s/-) fall, slope, incline, descent, gradient, esp. Am. a. grade; fall (of river, etc.).

Ge'fallen 1. m (-s/-) favo(u)r; 2. n (-s/no pl.): ~ finden an (dat.) take (a) pleasure in, take a fancy to or for; 3. 2 v/i. (irr. fallen, no -ge-, h) please (j-m s.o.); er gefällt mir I like him; sich et. ~ lassen put up with s.th.; 4. 2 p.p. of fallen.

gefällig adj. [gə'fɛliç] pleasing, agreeable; p.: complaisant, obliging; kind, **2keit** f (-/~-en) complaisance, kindness; favo(u)r; **~st** adv. (if you) please.

ge'fangen 1. p.p. of fangen; 2. adj. captive, imprisoned; **2e** m (-n/-n), f (-n/-n) prisoner, captive; **2en-lager** n prison(ers') camp; **2-nahme** f (-/no pl.) capture; seizure, arrest; **~nehmen** v/t. (irr. nehmen, sep., -ge-, h) take prisoner; fig. captivate; **2schaft** f (-/no pl.) captivity, imprisonment; **~setzen** v/t. (sep., -ge-, h) put in prison.

Gefängnis [gə'fɛŋnis] n (-ses/-se) prison, jail, gaol, Am. a. penitentiary; **~direktor** m governor, warden; **~strafe** f (sentence or term of) imprisonment; **~wärter** m warder, gaoler, jailer, (prison) guard.

Gefäß [gə'fɛːs] n (-es/-e) vessel.

gefaßt adj. [gə'fast] composed; ~ auf (acc.) prepared for.

Ge|fecht n (-[e]s/-e) engagement; combat, fight; action; **~fieder** [~'fi:dər] n (-s/-) plumage, feathers pl.

ge|'fleckt adj. spotted; **~flochten** [~'flɔxtən] p.p. of flechten; **~flogen** [~'flo:gən] p.p. of fliegen; **~flohen** [~'flo:ən] p.p. of fliehen; **~flossen** [~'flɔsən] p.p. of fließen.

Ge|'flügel n (-s/no pl.) fowl; poultry; **~flüster** [~'flystər] n (-s/no pl.) whisper(ing).

gefochten [gə'fɔxtən] p.p. of fechten.

Ge'folg|e n (-s/no pl.) retinue, train, followers pl.; attendants pl.; **~schaft** [~kʃaft] f (-/-en) followers pl.

gefräßig adj. [gə'frɛːsiç] greedy, voracious; **2keit** f (-/no pl.) greediness, gluttony, voracity.

ge'fressen p.p. of fressen.

ge'frier|en v/i. (irr. frieren, no -ge-, sein) congeal, freeze; **2fleisch** n frozen meat; **2punkt** m freezing-point; **2schutz(mittel** n) m antifreeze.

gefroren [gə'fro:rən] p.p. of frieren; **2e** [~ə] n (-n/no pl.) ice-cream.

Gefüge [gə'fy:gə] n (-s/-) structure; texture;

ge'fügig *adj.* pliant; &keit *f* (-/*no pl.*) pliancy.

Gefühl [gə'fy:l] *n* (-[e]s/-e) feeling; touch; sense (*für of*); sensation; &los *adj.* unfeeling, insensible (*gegen* to); &sbetont *adj.* emotional; &voll *adj.* (full of) feeling; tender; sentimental.

ge|funden [gə'fundən] *p.p. of finden*; ~gangen [\'gaŋən] *p.p. of gehen*.

ge'geben *p.p. of geben*; ~enfalls *adv.* in that case; if necessary.

gegen *prp.* (*acc.*) ['ge:gən] space, *time*: towards; against; r̃ʒ versus; about, *Am.* around; by; compared with; (in exchange) for; *remedy*: for; *freundlich sein* ~ be kind to (~wards); ~ *bar* for cash.

'Gegen|angriff *m* counter-attack; '~antrag *m* counter-motion; '~antwort *f* rejoinder; '~befehl *m* counter-order; '~beschuldigung *f* countercharge; '~besuch *m* return visit; '~bewegung *f* counter-movement; '~beweis *m* counter-evidence.

Gegend ['ge:gənt] *f* (-/-en) region; area.

'Gegen|dienst *m* return service, service in return; '~druck *m* counter-pressure; *fig.* reaction; &ei'nander *adv.* against one another *or* each other; '~erklärung *f* counterstatement; '~forderung *f* counterclaim; '~frage *f* counter-question; '~geschenk *n* return present; '~gewicht *n* counterbalance, counterpoise; '~gift ⚥ *n* antidote; '~kandidat *m* rival candidate; '~klage *f* countercharge; '~leistung *f* return (service), equivalent; ~lichtaufnahme *phot.* ['gə:gənlɪçˀ-] *f* back-lighted shot; '~liebe *f* requited love; *keine* ~ *finden* meet with no sympathy *or* enthusiasm; '~maßnahme *f* counter-measure; '~mittel *n* remedy (*gegen* for), antidote (against, for); '~partei *f* opposite party; '~probe *f* check-test; '~satz *m* contrast; opposition; *im* ~ *zu* in contrast to *or* with, in opposition to; &sätzlich *adj.* ['~zetslɪç] contrary, opposite; '~seite *f* opposite side; '~seitig *adj.* mutual, reciprocal; '~seitigkeit *f* (-/*no pl.*): *auf* ~ *assurance*: mutual; *auf* ~ *beruhen* be mutual; '~spieler *m* games, *sports*: opponent; antagonist; '~spionage *f* counter-espionage; '~stand *m* object; subject, topic; '~strömung *f* counter-current; '~stück *n* counterpart; match; '~teil *n* contrary, reverse; *im* ~ *on* the contrary; &teilig *adj.* contrary, opposite; &'über 1. *adv.* opposite; 2. *prp.* (*dat.*) opposite (to); to (~wards); as against; face to face with; ~'über *n* (-s/-) vis-à-vis;

&'überstehen *v/i.* (*irr. stehen, sep.*, -ge-, *h*) (*dat.*) be faced with, face; ~'überstellung *esp.* r̃ʒ *f* confrontation; ~vorschlag *m* counterproposal; ~wart ['~vart] *f* (-/*no pl.*) presence; present time; *gr.* present tense; &wärtig ['~vertiç] 1. *adj.* present; actual; 2. *adv.* at present; '~wehr *f* defen|ce, *Am.* -se; resistance; ~wert *m* equivalent; '~wind *m* contrary wind, head wind; '~wirkung *f* counter-effect, reaction; &'zeichnen *v/t.* (*sep.*, -ge-, *h*) countersign; '~zug *m* counter-move (*a. fig.*); 🚂 corresponding train.

ge|gessen [gə'gesən] *p.p. of essen*; ~glichen [\'glɪçən] *p.p. of gleichen*; ~gliedert *adj.* articulate, jointed; ~glitten [\'glɪtən] *p.p. of gleiten*; ~glommen [\'glɔmən] *p.p. of glimmen*.

Gegner ['ge:gnər] *m* (-s/-) adversary, opponent; '~schaft *f* (-/-en) opposition.

ge|golten [gə'gɔltən] *p.p. of gelten*; ~goren [\'go:rən] *p.p. of gären*; ~gossen [\'gɔsən] *p.p. of gießen*; ~graben *p.p. of graben*; ~griffen [\'grɪfən] *p.p. of greifen*; ~habt [\'ha:pt] *p.p. of haben*.

Gehalt [gə'halt] 1. *m* (-[e]s/-e) contents *pl.*; capacity; merit; 2. *n* (-[e]s/⸚er) salary; &en *p.p. of halten*; &los *adj.* empty; ~sempfänger [gə'haltsˀ-] *m* salaried employee *or* worker; ~serhöhung [gə'haltsˀ-] *f* rise (in salary), *Am.* raise; &voll *adj.* rich; substantial; *wine* racy.

gehangen [gə'haŋən] *p.p. of hängen* 1.

gehässig *adj.* [gə'hesɪç] malicious, spiteful; &keit *f* (-/-en) malice, spitefulness.

ge'hauen *p.p. of hauen*.

Ge|häuse [gə'hɔyzə] *n* (-s/-) case, box; cabinet; shell; core (*of apple*, etc.); ~hege [\'he:gə] *n* (-s/-) enclosure.

geheim *adj.* [gə'haɪm] secret; &dienst *m* secret service.

Ge'heimnis *n* (-ses/-se) secret; mystery; ~krämer *m* mysterymonger; &voll *adj.* mysterious.

Ge'heim|polizei *f* secret police; ~polizist *m* detective; plain-clothes man; ~schrift *f* cipher; *tel.* code.

ge'heißen *p.p. of heißen*.

gehen ['ge:ən] *v/i.* (*irr.*, ge-, *sein*) go; walk; leave; *machine*: go, work; *clock, watch*: go; *merchandise*: sell; *wind*: blow; *paste*: rise; *wie geht es Ihnen?* how are you (getting on)?; *das geht nicht* that won't do; *in sich* ~ repent; *wieviel Pfennige* ~ *auf e-e Mark?* how many pfennigs go to a mark?; *das Fenster geht nach Norden* the window faces *or* looks north; *es geht nichts über (acc.)* there is nothing like; *wenn es nach mir ginge* if I had my way.

Geheul [gə'hɔʏl] *n* (-[e]s/*no pl.*) howling.

Ge'hilf|e *m* (-n/-n), **~in** *f* (-/-nen) assistant; *fig.* helpmate.

Ge'hirn *n* (-[e]s/-e) brain(s *pl.*); **~erschütterung** 🩺 *f* concussion (of the brain); **~schlag** 🩺 *m* cerebral apoplexy.

gehoben [gə'ho:bən] **1.** *p.p.* of *heben*; **2.** *adj.* speech, *style:* elevated; **~e** *Stimmung* elated mood.

Gehöft [gə'hø:ft] *n* (-[e]s/-e) farm (-stead).

geholfen [gə'hɔlfən] *p.p.* of *helfen*.

Gehölz [gə'hœlts] *n* (-es/-e) wood, coppice, copse.

Gehör [gə'hø:r] *n* (-[e]s/*no pl.*) hearing; ear; *nach dem* ~ by ear; *j-m* ~ *schenken* lend an ear to s.o.; *sich* ~ *verschaffen* make o.s. heard.

ge'horchen *v/i.* (*no -ge-*, *h*) obey (*j-m* s.o.).

ge'hör|en *v/i.* (*no -ge-*, *h*) belong (*dat. or zu* to); *es gehört sich* it is proper *or* fit *or* right *or* suitable; *das gehört nicht hierher* that's not to the point; **~ig 1.** *adj.* belonging (*dat. or zu* to); fit, proper, right; due; F good; **2.** *adv.* duly; F thoroughly.

gehorsam [gə'ho:rzɑ:m] **1.** *adj.* obedient; **2.** ⚺ *m* (-s/*no pl.*) obedience.

'Geh|steig *m*, **'~weg** *m* pavement, *Am.* sidewalk; **'~werk** ⊕ *n* clockwork, works *pl.*

Geier *orn.* ['gaɪər] *m* (-s/-) vulture.

Geige 🎵 ['gaɪgə] *f* (-/-n) violin, F fiddle, (*auf der*) ~ *spielen* play (on) the violin; **'~nbogen** 🎵 *m* (violin-bow; **'~nkasten** 🎵 *m* violin-case; **'~r** *m* (-s/-), **'~rin** 🎵 *f* (-/-nen) violinist.

'Geigerzähler *phys. m* Geiger counter.

geil *adj.* [gaɪl] lascivious, wanton; luxuriant.

Geisel ['gaɪzəl] *f* (-/-n) hostage.

Geiß *zo.* [gaɪs] *f* (-/-en) (she-, nanny-)goat; **'~blatt** ♀ *n* (-[e]s/*no pl.*) honeysuckle, woodbine; **'~bock** *zo.* m he-goat, billy-goat.

Geißel ['gaɪsəl] *f* (-/-n) whip, lash; *fig.* scourge; **'⚺n** *v/t.* (*ge-*, *h*) whip, lash; *fig.* castigate.

Geist [gaɪst] *m* (-es/-er) spirit; mind, intellect; wit; ghost; sprite.

'Geister|erscheinung *f* apparition; **'⚺haft** *adj.* ghostly.

'geistes|abwesend *adj.* absent-minded; **'⚺arbeiter** *m* brain-worker, white-collar worker; **'⚺blitz** *m* brain-wave, flash of genius; **'⚺gabe** *f* talent; **'⚺gegenwart** *f* presence of mind; **'~gegenwärtig** *adj.* alert; quick-witted; **'~gestört** *adj.* mentally disturbed; **'~krank**

adj. insane, mentally ill; **'⚺krankheit** *f* insanity, mental illness; **'~schwach** *adj.* feeble-minded, imbecile; **'~verwandt** *adj.* congenial; **'⚺wissenschaften** *f/pl.* the Arts *pl.*, *the* Humanities *pl.*; **'⚺zustand** *m* state of mind.

'geistig *adj.* intellectual, mental; spiritual; **~e** *Getränke n/pl.* spirits *pl.*

'geistlich *adj.* spiritual; clerical; sacred; **'⚺e** *m* (-n/-n) clergyman; minister; **'⚺keit** *f* (-/*no pl.*) clergy.

'geist|los *adj.* spiritless; dull; stupid; **~reich** *adj.*, **'~voll** *adj.* ingenious, spirited.

Geiz [gaɪts] *m* (-es/*no pl.*) avarice; **'~hals** *m* miser, niggard; **'⚺ig** *adj.* avaricious, stingy, mean.

Gejammer [gə'jamər] *n* (-s/*no pl.*) lamentation(s *pl.*), wailing.

gekannt [gə'kant] *p.p.* of *kennen*.

Geklapper [gə'klapər] *n* (-s/*no pl.*) rattling.

Geklirr [gə'klir] *n* (-[e]s/*no pl.*), **~e** [~ə] *n* (-s/*no pl.*) clashing, clanking.

ge|klungen [~'kluŋən] *p.p.* of *klingen*; **~'kniffen** *p.p.* of *kneifen*; **~'kommen** *p.p.* of *kommen*; **~'konnt** [~'kɔnt] *p.p.* of *können* 1, 2.

Ge|kreisch [gə'kraɪʃ] *n* (-es/*no pl.*) screaming, screams *pl.*; shrieking; **~kritzel** [~'kritsəl] *n* (-s/*no pl.*) scrawl(ing), scribbling, scribble.

ge|krochen [gə'krɔxən] *p.p.* of *kriechen*; **~künstelt** *adj.* [~'kynstəlt] affected.

Gelächter [gə'lɛçtər] *n* (-s/-) laughter.

ge'laden *p.p.* of *laden*.

Ge'lage *n* (-s/-) feast; drinking-bout.

Gelände [gə'lɛndə] *n* (-s/-) ground; terrain; country; area; **⚺gängig** *mot. adj.* cross-country; **⚺lauf** *m* *sports:* cross-country race *or* run.

Geländer [gə'lɛndər] *n* (-s/-) railing, balustrade; banisters *pl.*

ge'lang *pret.* of *gelingen*.

ge'langen *v/i.* (*no -ge-*, *sein*): ~ *an* (*acc.*) *or in* (*acc.*) arrive at, get *or* come to; ~ *zu* attain (to), gain.

ge'lassen 1. *p.p.* of *lassen*; **2.** *adj.* calm, composed.

Gelatine [ʒela'ti:nə] *f* (-/*no pl.*) gelatin(e).

ge'laufen *p.p.* of *laufen*; **~läufig** *adj.* [~'lɔʏfiç] current; fluent, easy; *tongue:* voluble; familiar; **~launt** *adj.* [~'laʊnt] in a (*good, etc.*) humo(u)r *or Am.* mood.

Geläut [gə'lɔʏt] *n* (-[e]s/-e), **~e** [~ə] *n* (-s/-) ringing (*of bells*); chimes *pl.* (*of church bells*).

gelb *adj.* [gɛlp] yellow; **'~lich** *adj.* yellowish; **'⚺sucht** 🩺 *f* (-/*no pl.*) jaundice.

Geld [gɛlt] *n* (-[e]s/-er) money; im

~ schwimmen be rolling in money; zu ~ machen turn into cash; '~angelegenheit f money-matter; '~anlage f investment; '~ausgabe f expense; '~beutel m purse; '~entwertung f devaluation of the currency; '~erwerb m money-making; '~geber m (-s/-) financial backer, investor; '~geschäfte n/pl. money transactions pl.; '2gierig adj. greedy for money, avaricious; '~mittel n/pl. funds pl., resources pl.; '~schein m bank-note, Am. bill; '~schrank m strong-box, safe; '~sendung f remittance; '~strafe f fine; '~stück n coin; '~tasche f money-bag; notecase, Am. billfold; '~überhang m surplus money; '~umlauf m circulation of money; '~umsatz m turnover (of money); '~verlegenheit f pecuniary embarrassment; '~wechsel m exchange of money; '~wert m (-[e]s/no pl.) value of money, money value.

Gelee [ʒə'le:] n, m (-s/-s) jelly.

ge'legen 1. p.p. of liegen; 2. adj. situated, Am. a. located; convenient, opportune; 2heit f (-/-en) occasion; opportunity; chance; facility; bei ~ on occasion.

Ge'legenheits|arbeit f casual or odd job, Am. a. chore; ~arbeiter m casual labo(u)rer, odd-job man; ~kauf m bargain.

ge'legentlich 1. adj. occasional; 2. prp. (gen.) on the occasion of.

ge'lehr|ig adj. docile; 2igkeit f (-/no pl.) docility; 2samkeit f (-/no pl.) learning; ~t adj. [~t] learned; 2te [~ə] m (-n/-n) learned man, scholar.

Geleise [gə'laɪzə] n (-s/-) rut, track; 𝕲 rails pl., line, esp. Am. tracks pl.

Geleit [gə'laɪt] n (-[e]s/-e) escort; attendance; j-m das ~ geben accompany s.o.; 2en v/t. (no -ge-, h) accompany, conduct; escort; ~zug 𝕮 m convoy.

Gelenk anat., ⊕, 𝕾 [gə'lɛŋk] n (-[e]s/-e) joint; 2ig adj. pliable, supple.

ge'lernt adj. worker: skilled; trained; ~'lesen p.p. of lesen.

Geliebte [gə'li:ptə] (-n/-n) 1. m lover; 2 f mistress, sweetheart.

geliehen [gə'li:ən] p.p. of leihen.

ge'linde 1. adj. soft, smooth, gentle; 2. adv.: gelinde gesagt to put it mildly, to say the least.

gelingen [gə'liŋən] 1. v/i. (irr., no -ge-, sein) succeed; es gelingt mir zu inf. I succeed in ger.; 2. 2 n (-s/no pl.) success.

ge'litten p.p. of leiden.

gellen ['gɛlən] (ge- h) 1. v/i. shrill; yell; of ears: ring, tingle; 2. v/t. shrill; yell; '~d adj. shrill, piercing.

ge'loben v/t. (no -ge-, h) vow, promise.

Gelöbnis [gə'lø:pnis] n (-ses/-se) promise, pledge; vow.

ge'logen p.p. of lügen.

gelt|en ['gɛltən] (irr., ge-, h) 1. v/t. be worth; 2. v/i. be of value; be valid; go; count; money: be current; maxim, etc.: hold (good or true); et. ~ have credit or influence; j-m ~ concern s.o.; ~ für or als pass for, be reputed or thought or supposed to be; ~ für apply to; ~ lassen let pass, allow; ~d machen maintain, assert; s-n Einfluß bei j-m ~d machen bring one's influence to bear on s.o.; das gilt nicht that is not fair; that does not count; es galt unser Leben our life was at stake; 2ung f (-/~ -en) validity; value; currency; authority (of person); zur ~ kommen tell; take effect; show; 2ungsbedürfnis n desire to show off. [ise; vow.

Gelübde [gə'lypdə] n (-s/-) prom-

gelungen [gə'luŋən] 1. p.p. of gelingen; 2. adj. successful; amusing, funny; F: das ist ja ~l that beats everything!

gemächlich adj. [gə'mɛ:çlɪç] comfortable, easy; 2keit f (-/no pl.) ease, comfort.

Gemahl [gə'ma:l] m (-[e]s/-e) consort, husband.

ge'mahlen p.p. of mahlen.

Gemälde [gə'mɛ:ldə] n (-s/-) painting, picture; ~galerie f picture-gallery.

gemäß prp. (dat.) [gə'mɛ:s] according to; ~igt adj. moderate; temperate (a. geogr.).

gemein [gə'maɪn] common; general; low, vulgar, mean, coarse; et. ~ haben mit have s.th. in common with.

Gemeinde [gə'maɪndə] f (-/-n) community; parish; municipality; eccl. congregation; ~bezirk m district; municipality; ~rat m municipal council; ~steuer f rate, Am. local tax; ~vorstand m district council.

ge'mein|gefährlich adj. dangerous to the public; ~er Mensch public danger, 4m. public enemy; 2heit f (-/-en) vulgarity; meanness; mean trick; 2nützig adj. of public utility; 2platz m commonplace; ~sam adj. common; joint; mutual; 2schaft f (-/-en) community; intercourse; ~schaftlich adj. s. gemeinsam; 2-schaftsarbeit f [gə'maɪnʃafts?-] f team-work; 2sinn m (-[e]s/no pl.) public spirit; ~verständlich adj. popular, 2wesen n community; 2wohl n public welfare.

Ge'menge n (-s/-) mixture.

ge'messen 1. p.p. of messen; 2. adj. measured; formal; grave.

Gemetzel [gə'mɛtsəl] n (-s/-) slaughter, massacre.

gemieden [gə'mi:dən] p.p. of meiden.

Gemisch [gə'miʃ] n (-es/-e) mixture; ₰ compound, composition.

ge|mocht [gə'mɔxt] p.p. of mögen; ~molken [gə'mɔlkən] p.p. of melken.

Gemse zo. ['gɛmzə] f (-/-n) chamois.

Gemurmel [gə'murməl] n (-s/no pl.) murmur(ing).

Gemüse [gə'my:zə] n (-s/-) vegetable(s pl.); greens pl.; ~anbau m vegetable gardening, Am. truck farming; ~garten m kitchen garden; ~händler m greengrocer.

gemußt [gə'must] p.p. of müssen 1.

Gemüt [gə'my:t] n (-[e]s/-er) mind; feeling; soul; heart; disposition, temper; 2lich adj. good-natured; genial; comfortable, snug, cosy, cozy; ~lichkeit f (-/no pl.) snugness, cosiness; easy-going; genial temper.

Ge'müts|art f disposition, nature, temper, character; ~bewegung f emotion; 2krank adj. emotionally disturbed; melancholic; depressed; ~krankheit f mental disorder; melancholy; ~ruhe f composure; ~verfassung f, ~zustand m state of mind, humo(u)r.

ge'mütvoll adj. emotional; full of feeling.

genannt [gə'nant] p.p. of nennen.

genas [gə'nɑːs] pret. of genesen.

genau adj. [gə'nau] exact, accurate; precise; strict; es ~ nehmen (mit) be particular (about); 2eres full particulars pl.; 2igkeit f (-/-en) accuracy, exactness; precision; strictness.

genehm adj. [gə'neːm] agreeable, convenient; ~igen [~igən] v/t. (no -ge-, h) grant; approve (of); 2igung f (-/-en) grant; approval; licen|ce, Am. -se; permit; permission; consent.

geneigt adj. [gə'naikt] well disposed (j-m towards s.o.); inclined (zu to).

General ⚔ [genə'rɑːl] m (-s/-e, ⁓e) general; ~bevollmächtigte m chief representative or agent; ~direktor m general manager; managing director; ~'feldmarschall ⚔ m field-marshal; ~intendant thea. m (artistic) director; ~konsul m consul-general; ~konsulat n consulate-general; ~leutnant ⚔ m lieutenant-general; ~major ⚔ m major-general; ~probe thea. f dress rehearsal; ~stab ⚔ m general staff; ~stabskarte ⚔ f ordnance (survey) map, Am. strategic map; ~streik m general strike; ~versammlung f general meeting; ~vertreter m general agent; ~vollmacht f full power of attorney.

Generation [genərɑ'tsjoːn] f (-/-en) generation.

generell adj. [genə'rɛl] general.

genes|en [gə'neːzən] 1. v/i. (irr., no -ge-, sein) recover (von from); 2. p.p. of 1; 2ende m, f (-n/-n) convalescent; 2ung f (-/⁓, -en) recovery.

genial adj. [gen'jɑːl] highly gifted, ingenious; 2ität [~ali'tɛːt] f (-/no pl.) genius.

Genick [gə'nik] n (-[e]s/-e) nape (of the neck), (back of the) neck.

Genie [ʒe'niː] n (-s/-s) genius.

ge'nieren v/t. (no -ge-, h) trouble, bother; sich ~ feel or be embarrassed or shy; be self-conscious.

genießen [gə'niːsən] v/t. (irr., no -ge-, h) enjoy; eat; drink; et. ~ take some food or refreshments; j-s Vertrauen ~ be in s.o.'s confidence.

Genitiv gr. ['geːnitiːf] m (-s/-e) genitive (case); possessive (case).

ge|nommen [gə'nɔmən] p.p. of nehmen; ~normt adj. standardized; ~noß [~'nɔs] pret. of genießen.

Genoss|e [gə'nɔsə] m (-n/-n) companion, mate; comrade (a. pol.); 2en p.p. of genießen; ~enschaft f (-/-en) company, association; co(-)operative (society); ~in f (-/-nen) (female) companion; comrade (a. pol.).

genug adj. [gə'nuːk] enough, sufficient.

Genüg|e [gə'nyːgə] f (-/no pl.): zur ~ enough, sufficiently; 2en v/i. (no -ge-, h) be enough, suffice; das genügt that will do; j-m ~ satisfy s.o.; 2end adj. sufficient; 2sam adj. [~k-] easily satisfied; frugal; ~samkeit [~k-] f (-/no pl.) modesty; frugality.

Genugtuung [gə'nuːktuːuŋ] f (-/-en) satisfaction. [gender.]

Genus gr. ['geːnus] n (-/Genera)]

Genuß [gə'nus] m (Genusses/Genüsse) enjoyment; pleasure; use; consumption; taking (of food); fig. treat; ~mittel n semi-luxury; ~sucht f (-/no pl.) thirst for pleasure; 2süchtig adj. pleasure-seeking.

Geo|graph [geo'grɑːf] m (-en/-en) geographer; ~graphie [~a'fiː] f (-/no pl.) geography; 2graphisch adj. [~'grɑːfiʃ] geographic(al); ~loge [~'loːgə] m (-n/-n) geologist; ~logie [~lo'giː] f (-/no pl.) geology; 2logisch adj. [~'loːgiʃ] geologic(al); ~metrie [~me'triː] f (-/-n) geometry; 2metrisch adj. [~'meːtriʃ] geometric(al).

Gepäck [gə'pɛk] n (-[e]s/no pl.) luggage, ℬ or Am. baggage; ~annahme f luggage (registration) counter, Am. baggage (registration) counter; ~aufbewahrung f (-/-en) left-luggage office, Am. checkroom; ~ausgabe f luggage delivery office, Am. baggage room; ~netz n luggage-rack, *Am.* baggage rack; **schein** *m* luggage-ticket, *Am.* baggage check; **träger** *m* porter, *Am. a.* redcap; *on bicycle:* carrier; **wagen** *m* luggage van, *Am.* baggage car.

ge|pfiffen [gə'pfifən] *p.p. of* pfeifen; **pflegt** *adj.* [‿'pfle:kt] *appearance:* well-groomed; *hands, garden, etc.:* well cared-for; *garden, etc.:* well-kept.

Gepflogenheit [gə'pflo:gənhaɪt] *f* (-/-en) habit; custom; usage.

Ge|plapper [gə'plapər] *n* (-s/*no pl.*) babbling, chattering; **plauder** [‿-'plaudər] *n* (-s/*no pl.*) chatting, small talk; **polter** [‿'pɔltər] *n* (-s/*no pl.*) rumble; **präge** [‿'prɛ:-gə] *n* (-s/-) impression; stamp (*a. fig.*).

ge|priesen [gə'pri:zən] *p.p. of* preisen; **quollen** [‿'kvɔlən] *p.p. of* quellen.

gerade [gə'raːdə] 1. *adj.* straight (*a. fig.*); *number, etc.:* even; direct; *bearing:* upright, erect; 2. *adv.* just; er schrieb ~ he was (just) writing; nun ~ now more than ever; ~ an dem Tage on that very day; 3. 2 *f* (-n/-n) A straight line; straight(*ofrace-course*); linke(rechte) ~ *boxing:* straight left (right); ~aus *adv.* straight on *or* ahead; **he'raus** *adv.* frankly; **nwegs** *adv.* [‿no:ve:ks] directly; **stehen** *v/i.* (*irr.* stehen, *sep.*, -ge-, h) stand erect; ~ für answer for *s.th.*; **wegs** *adv.* [‿ve:ks] straight, directly; **zu** *adv.* straight; almost; downright.

ge'rannt *p.p. of* rennen.

Gerassel [gə'rasəl] *n* (-s/*no pl.*) clanking, rattling.

Gerät [gə'rɛ:t] *n* (-[e]s/-e) tool, implement, utensil; ⊕ gear; *teleph.*, *radio.* set; apparatus; equipment; elektrisches ~ electric(al) appliance.

ge'raten 1. *v/i.* (*irr.* raten, *no* -ge-, sein) come *or* fall *or* get (*an acc.* by, upon; *auf acc.* on, upon; *in acc.* in, into); (*gut*) ~ succeed, turn out well; *in* Brand ~ catch fire; *ins* Stocken ~ come to a standstill; *in* Vergessenheit ~ fall *or* sink into oblivion; *in* Zorn ~ fly into a passion; 2. *p.p. of* raten.

Gerate'wohl *n:* aufs ~ at random.

geräumig *adj.* [gə'rɔʏmiç] spacious.

Geräusch [gə'rɔʏʃ] *n* (-es/-e) noise; **2los** *adj.* noiseless; **2voll** *adj.* noisy.

gerb|en ['gɛrbən] *v/t.* (ge-, h) tan; **2er** *m* (-s/-) tanner; **2erei** [‿'raɪ] *f* (-/-en) tannery.

ge'recht *adj.* just; righteous; ~ werden (*dat.*) do justice to; be fair to; meet; please *s.o.*; fulfil (*requirements*); **2igkeit** *f* (-/*no pl.*) justice; righteousness; *j-m* ~ widerfahren lassen do *s.o.* justice.

Ge'rede *n* (-s/*no pl.*) talk; gossip; rumo(u)r.

ge'reizt *adj.* irritable, irritated; **2-heit** *f* (-/*no pl.*) irritation.

ge'reuen *v/t.* (*no* -ge-, h): es gereut mich I repent (of) it, I am sorry for it.

Gericht [gə'rɪçt] *n* (-[e]s/-e) dish, course; *s.* Gerichtshof; *mst rhet. and fig.* tribunal; **2lich** *adj.* judicial, legal.

Ge'richts|barkeit *f* (-/-en) jurisdiction; **bezirk** *m* jurisdiction; **diener** *m* (court) usher; **gebäude** *n* court-house; **hof** *m* lawcourt, court of justice; **kosten** *pl.* (law-)costs *pl.*; **saal** *m* courtroom; **schreiber** *m* clerk (of the court); **stand** *m* (legal) domicile; venue; **tag** *m* court-day; **verfahren** *n* legal proceedings *pl.*, lawsuit; **verhandlung** *f* (court) hearing, trial; **vollzieher** *m* (-s/-) (court-)bailiff.

gerieben [gə'ri:bən] *p.p. of* reiben.

gering *adj.* [gə'rɪŋ] little, small; trifling, slight; mean, low; poor; inferior; **achten** *v/t.* (*sep.*, -ge-, h) think little of; disregard; **er** *adj.* inferior less, minor; **fügig** *adj.* insignificant, trifling, slight; **schätzen** *v/t.* (*sep.*, -ge-, h) *s.* geringachten; **schätzig** *adj.* disdainful, contemptuous, slighting; **2schätzung** *f* (-/*no pl.*) disdain; disregard; **st** *adj.* least; *nicht im ~en* not in the least.

ge'rinnen *v/i.* (*irr.* rinnen, *no* -ge-, sein) curdle (*a. fig.*); congeal; coagulate clot.

Ge'rippe *n* (-s/-) skeleton (*a. fig.*); ⊕ framework.

ge|rissen [gə'rɪsən] 1. *p.p. of* reißen; 2. *fig* *adj* cunning, crafty, smart; **ritten** [‿rɪtən] *p.p. of* reiten.

germanis|ch *adj.* [gɛr'ma:nɪʃ] Germanic, Teutonic; **2t** [‿'nɪst] *m* (-en/-en) Germanist, German scholar, student of German.

gern(e) *adv.* ['gɛrn(ə)] willingly, gladly; haben *or* mögen be fond of, like, er singt ~ he is fond of singing, he likes to sing.

ge'rochen *p.p. of* riechen.

Geröll [gə'rœl] *n* (-[e]s/-e) boulders *pl.*

geronnen [gə'rɔnən] *p.p. of* rinnen.

Gerste ♀ ['gɛrstə] *f* (-/-n) barley; **nkorn** *n* barleycorn; ✿ sty(e).

Gerte ['gɛrtə] *f* (-/-n) switch, twig.

Geruch [gə'rux] *m* (-[e]s/-e) smell, odo(u)r; scent; *fig.* reputation; **2los** *adj.* odo(u)rless, scentless; **ssinn** *m* (-[e]s/*no pl.*) sense of smell.

Gerücht [gə'rʏçt] *n* (-[e]s/-e) rumo(u)r.

ge'ruchtilgend *adj.:* **es** Mittel deodorant.

ge'rufen *p.p. of* rufen.

ge'ruhen *v/i.* (*no* -ge-, h) deign, condescend, be pleased.

Gerümpel [gə'rympəl] *n* (-s/*no pl.*) lumber, junk.

Gerundium *gr.* [gə'rundjum] *n* (-s/*Gerundien*) gerund.

gerungen [gə'ruŋən] *p.p. of* ringen.

Gerüst [gə'ryst] *n* (-[e]s/-e) scaffold(ing); stage; trestle.

ge'salzen *p.p. of* salzen.

gesamt *adj.* [gə'zamt] whole, entire, total, all; **2ausgabe** *f* complete edition; **2betrag** *m* sum total; **~deutsch** *adj.* all-German.

gesandt [gə'zant] *p.p. of* senden; **2e** [~ə] *m* (-n/-n) envoy; **2schaft** *f* (-/-en) legation.

Ge'sang *m* (-[e]s/**~e**) singing; song; **~buch** *eccl. n* hymn-book; **~slehrer** *m* singing-teacher; **~verein** *m* choral society, *Am.* glee club.

Gesäß *anat.* [gə'zɛːs] *n* (-es/-e) seat, buttocks *pl.*, posterior, F bottom, behind.

ge'schaffen *p.p. of* schaffen 1.

Geschäft [gə'ʃɛft] *n* (-[e]s/-e) business; transaction; affair; occupation; shop, *Am.* store; **2ig** *adj.* busy, active; **~igkeit** *f* (-/*no pl.*) activity; **2lich 1.** *adj.* business ...; commercial; **2.** *adv.* on business.

Ge'schäfts|bericht *m* business report; **~brief** *m* business letter; **~frau** *f* business woman; **~freund** *m* business friend, correspondent; **~führer** *m* manager; **~haus** *n* business firm; office building; **~inhaber** *m* owner or holder of a business; shopkeeper; **~jahr** *n* financial or business year, *Am.* fiscal year; **~lage** *f* business situation; **~leute** *pl.* businessmen *pl.*; **~mann** *m* businessman; **2mäßig** *adj.* business-like; **~ordnung** *f* standing orders *pl.*; rules *pl.* (of procedure); **~papiere** *n/pl.* commercial papers *pl.*; **~partner** *m* (business) partner; **~räume** *m/pl.* business premises *pl.*; **~reise** *f* business trip; **~reisende** *m* commercial travel(l)er, *Am.* travel(l)ing salesman; **~schluß** *m* closing-time; *nach ~ a.* after business hours; **~stelle** *f* office; **~träger** *m pol.* chargé d'affaires; ✝ agent, representative; **2tüchtig** *adj.* efficient, smart; **~unternehmen** *n* business enterprise; **~verbindung** *f* business connexion *or* connection; **~viertel** *n* business cent|re, *Am.* -er; *Am.* downtown; shopping cent|re, *Am.* -er; **~zeit** *f* office hours *pl.*, business hours *pl.*; **~zimmer** *n* office, bureau; **~zweig** *m* branch (of business), line (of business).

geschah [gə'ʃaː] *pret. of* geschehen.

geschehen [gə'ʃeːən] **1.** *v/i.* (*irr., no* -ge-, *sein*) happen, occur, take place; be done; *es geschieht ihm recht* it serves him right; **2.** *p.p. of*

1; **3.** **2** *n* (-s/-) events *pl.*, happenings *pl.*

gescheit *adj.* [gə'ʃaɪt] clever, intelligent, bright.

Geschenk [gə'ʃɛŋk] *n* (-[e]s/-e) present, gift; **~packung** *f* gift-box.

Geschicht|e [gə'ʃɪçtə] *f* **1.** (-/-n) story; tale; *fig.* affair; **2.** (-/*no pl.*) history, **2lich** *adj.* historical; **~sforscher** *m*, **~sschreiber** *m* historian.

Ge'schick *n* **1.** (-[e]s/-e) fate; destiny; **2.** (-[e]s/*no pl.*) = **~lichkeit** *f* (-/-en) skill; dexterity; aptitude; **2t** *adj.* skil(l)ful; dexterous; apt; clever.

ge|schieden [gə'ʃiːdən] *p.p. of* scheiden; **~schienen** [~'ʃiːnən] *p.p. of* scheinen.

Geschirr [gə'ʃɪr] *n* (-[e]s/-e) vessel; dishes *pl.*; china; earthenware, crockery; service; *horse*: harness.

ge'schlafen *p.p. of* schlafen; **~'schlagen** *p.p. of* schlagen.

Ge'schlecht *n* (-[e]s/-er) sex; kind, species; race; family; generation; *gr.* gender; **2lich** *adj.* sexual.

Ge'schlechts|krankheit *♂ f* venereal disease; **~reife** *f* puberty; **~teile** *anat. n/pl.* genitals *pl.*; **~trieb** *m* sexual instinct *or* urge; **~verkehr** *m* (-[e]s/*no pl.*) sexual intercourse; **~wort** *gr. n* (-[e]s/**~er**) article.

ge|schlichen [gə'ʃlɪçən] *p.p. of* schleichen; **~schliffen** [~'ʃlɪfən] **1.** *p.p. of* schleifen; **2.** *adj. jewel:* cut; *fig.* polished; **~schlossen** [~'ʃlɔsən] **1.** *p.p. of* schließen; **2.** *adj. formation:* close; collective; **~e** *Gesellschaft* private party; **~schlungen** [~'ʃluŋən] *p.p. of* schlingen.

Geschmack [gə'ʃmak] *m* (-[e]s/**~e**, *co.* **~er**) taste (*a. fig.*); flavo(u)r; *~finden an* (*dat.*) take a fancy to; **2los** *adj.* tasteless; *pred. fig.* in bad taste; **~(s)sache** *f* matter of taste; **2voll** *adj.* tasteful; *pred. fig.* in good taste.

ge|schmeidig *adj.* [gə'ʃmaɪdɪç] supple, pliant; **~schmissen** [~'ʃmɪsən] *p.p. of* schmeißen; **~schmolzen** [~'ʃmɔltsən] *p.p. of* schmelzen.

Geschnatter [gə'ʃnatər] *n* (-s/*no pl.*) cackling (*of geese*); chatter(ing) (*of girls, etc.*).

ge|schnitten [gə'ʃnɪtən] *p.p. of* schneiden; **~schoben** [~'ʃoːbən] *p.p. of* schieben; **~scholten** [~'ʃɔltən] *p.p. of* schelten.

Geschöpf [gə'ʃœpf] *n* (-[e]s/-e) creature.

ge'schoren *p.p. of* scheren.

Geschoß [gə'ʃɔs] *n* (*Geschosses/Geschosse*) projectile; missile; stor(e)y, floor.

geschossen [gə'ʃɔsən] *p.p. of* schießen.

Ge'schrei n (-[e]s/no pl.) cries pl.; shouting; fig. noise, fuss.

ge|schrieben [gə'ʃriːbən] p.p. of schreiben; **~schrie(e)n** [~'ʃriː(ə)n] p.p. of schreien; **~schritten** [~'ʃrɪtən] p.p. of schreiten; **~schunden** [~'ʃundən] p.p. of schinden.

Geschütz ✗ [gə'ʃyts] n (-es/-e) gun, cannon; ordnance.

Geschwader ✗ [gə'ʃvaːdər] n (-s/-) ⚓ squadron; ✗ wing, Am. group.

Geschwätz [gə'ʃvɛts] n (-es/no pl.) idle talk; gossip; **⌘ig** adj. talkative.

geschweige cj. [gə'ʃvaɪɡə]: **~** (denn) not to mention; let alone, much less.

geschwiegen [gə'ʃviːɡən] p.p. of schweigen.

geschwind adj. [gə'ʃvɪnt] fast, quick, swift; **⌘igkeit** [~'dɪçkaɪt] f (-/-en) quickness; speed, pace; phys. velocity; rate; mit e-r **~** von ... at the rate of ...; **⌘igkeitsbegrenzung** f speed limit.

Geschwister [gə'ʃvɪstər] n (-s/-): **~** pl. brother(s pl.) and sister(s pl.).

ge|schwollen [gə'ʃvɔlən] **1.** p.p. of schwellen; **2.** adj. language bombastic, pompous; **~schwommen** [~'ʃvɔmən] p.p. of schwimmen.

geschworen [gə'ʃvoːrən] p.p. of schwören; **⌘e** [~ə] m, f (-n/-n) juror; die **~n** pl. the jury; **⌘engericht** n jury.

Geschwulst ✗ [gə'ʃvʊlst] f (-/-e) swelling; tumo(u)r.

ge|schwunden [gə'ʃvʊndən] p.p. of schwinden; **~schwungen** [~'ʃvʊŋən] p.p. of schwingen.

Geschwür ✗ [gə'ʃvyːr] n (-[e]s/-e) abscess, ulcer.

ge'sehen p.p. of sehen.

Gesell ✗ [gə'zɛl] m (-en/-en), **~e** [~ə] m (-n/-n) companion, fellow; ⊕ journeyman; **⌘en** v/refl. (no -ge-, h) associate, come together; sich zu j-m **~** join s.o.; **⌘ig** adj. social; sociable.

Ge'sellschaft f (-/-en) society; company (a. ✝); party; j-m **~** leisten keep s.o. company; **~er** m (-s/-) companion; ✝ partner; **~erin** f (-/-nen) (lady) companion; ✝ partner; **⌘lich** adj. social.

Ge'sellschafts|dame f (lady) companion; **~reise** f party tour; **~spiel** n party or round game; **~tanz** m ball-room dance.

gesessen [gə'zɛsən] p.p. of sitzen.

Gesetz [gə'zɛts] n (-es/-e) law; statute; **~buch** n code; statute-book; **~entwurf** m bill; **~eskraft** f legal force; **⌘gebend** adj. legislative; **~geber** m (-s/-) legislator; **~gebung** f (-/-en) legislation; **⌘lich 1.** adj. lawful, legal; **2.** adv.: **~** geschützt patented, registered; **⌘los** adj. lawless; **⌘mäßig** adj. legal; lawful.

ge'setzt 1. adj. sedate, staid; sober;

mature; **2.** cj.: **~** den Fall, (daß) ... suppose or supposing (that) ...

ge'setzwidrig adj. unlawful, illegal.

Ge'sicht n (-[e]s/-er) face; countenance; fig character; zu **~** bekommen catch sight or a glimpse of; set eyes on.

Ge'sichts|ausdruck m (facial) expression; **~farbe** f complexion; **~kreis** m horizon; **~punkt** m point of view, viewpoint, angle, esp. Am. angle; **~zug** m mst Gesichtszüge pl. feature(s pl.), lineament(s pl.).

Ge'sims n ledge.

Gesinde [gə'zɪndə] n (-s/-) (domestic) servants pl.; **~l** [~l] n (-s/no pl.) rabble, mob.

ge'sinn|t adj. in compounds: ...-minded; wohl **~** well disposed (j-m towards s.o.); **⌘ung** f (-/-en) mind; conviction; sentiment(s pl.); opinions pl.

gesinnungs|los adj. [gə'zɪnuŋsloːs] unprincipled; **~treu** adj. loyal; **⌘wechsel** m change of opinion; esp. pol. volte-face.

ge|sittet [gə'zɪtət] adj. civilized; well-bred, well-mannered; **~'soffen** p.p. of saufen; **~sogen** [~'zoːɡən] p.p. of saugen; **~sonnen** [~'zɔnən] **1.** p.p. of sinnen; **2.** adj. minded, disposed; **~sotten** [~'zɔtən] p.p. of sieden; **~spalten** p.p. of spalten.

Ge'spann n (-[e]s/-e) team, Am. a. span, oxen yoke; fig. pair, couple.

ge'spannt adj. tense (a. fig.); rope: tight, taut, fig. intent; attention: close; relations: strained; **~** sein auf (acc.) be anxious for; auf **~em** Fuß on bad terms; **⌘heit** f (-/no pl.) tenseness, tension.

Gespenst [gə'ʃpɛnst] n (-es/-er) ghost, spect|re, Am. -er; **⌘isch** adj. ghostly.

Ge'spiel|e m (-n/-n), **~in** f (-/-nen) playmate.

gespien [gə'ʃpiːn] p.p. of speien.

Gespinst [gə'ʃpɪnst] n (-es/-e) web, tissue (both a. fig.); spun yarn.

gesponnen [gə'ʃpɔnən] p.p. of spinnen.

Gespött [gə'ʃpœt] n (-[e]s/no pl.) mockery, derision, ridicule; zum **~** der Leute werden become a laughing-stock.

Gespräch [gə'ʃprɛːç] n (-[e]s/-e) talk, conversation; teleph. call; dialogue; **⌘ig** adj. talkative.

ge|sprochen [gə'ʃrɔxən] p.p. of sprechen; **~sprossen** p.p. of sprießen; **~sprungen** [~'ʃprʊŋən] p.p. of springen

Gestalt [gə'ʃtalt] f (-/-en) form, figure, shape; stature; **⌘en** v/t. and v/refl (no -ge-, h) form, shape; **~ung** f (-/-en) formation; arrangement, organization.

gestanden [gə'ʃtandən] p.p. of stehen.

ge'ständ|ig adj.: ~ sein confess; 2nis [~t-] n (-ses/-se) confession.
Ge'stank m (-[e]s/no pl.) stench.
gestatten [gə'ʃtatən] v/t. (no -ge-, h) allow, permit.
Geste ['gɛstə] f (-/-n) gesture.
ge'stehen (irr. stehen, no -ge-, h) 1. v/t. confess, avow; 2. v/i. confess.
Ge|'stein n (-[e]s/-e) rock, stone; ~stell [~'ʃtɛl] n (-[e]s/-e) stand, rack, shelf; frame; trestle, horse.
gestern adv. ['gɛstərn] yesterday; ~ abend last night.
gestiegen [gə'ʃti:gən] p.p. of steigen.
Ge'stirn n (-[e]s/-e) star; astr. constellation; 2t adj. starry.
ge|stoben [gə'ʃto:bən] p.p. of stieben; ~stochen [~'ʃtɔxən] p.p. of stechen; ~stohlen [~'ʃto:lən] p.p. of stehlen; ~storben [~'ʃtɔrbən] p.p. of sterben; ~'stoßen p.p. of stoßen; ~strichen [~'ʃtriçən] p.p. of streichen.
gestrig adj. ['gɛstriç] of yesterday, yesterday's ...
ge'stritten p.p. of streiten.
Gestrüpp [gə'ʃtryp] n (-[e]s/-e) brushwood; undergrowth.
gestunken [gə'ʃtuŋkən] p.p. of stinken.
Gestüt [gə'ʃty:t] n (-[e]s/-e) stud farm; horses kept for breeding, etc.: stud.
Gesuch [gə'zu:x] n (-[e]s/-e) application, request; petition; 2t adj. wanted; sought-after; politeness: studied.
gesund adj. [gə'zunt] sound, healthy; salubrious; wholesome (a. fig.); ~er Menschenverstand common sense; ~en [~dən] v/i. (no -ge-, sein) recover.
Ge'sundheit f (-/no pl.) health (-iness); wholesomeness (a. fig.); auf j-s ~ trinken drink (to) s.o.'s health; 2lich adj. sanitary; ~ geht es ihm gut he is in good health.
Ge'sundheits|amt n Public Health Department; ~pflege f hygiene; public health service; 2schädlich adj. injurious to health, unhealthy, unwholesome; ~wesen n Public Health; ~zustand m state of health, physical condition.
ge|sungen [gə'zuŋən] p.p. of singen; ~sunken [~'zuŋkən] p.p. of sinken; ~tan [~'ta:n] p.p. of tun.
Getöse [gə'tø:zə] n (-s/no pl.) din, noise.
ge'tragen 1. p.p. of tragen; 2. adj. solemn.
Getränk [gə'trɛŋk] n (-[e]s/-e) drink, beverage.
ge'trauen v/refl. (no -ge-, h) dare, venture.
Getreide [gə'traɪdə] n (-s/-) corn, esp. Am. grain; cereals pl.; ~(an)bau m corn-growing, esp. Am. grain growing; ~pflanze f cereal plant;

~speicher m granary, grain silo, Am. elevator.
ge'treten p.p. of treten.
ge'treu(lich) adj. faithful, loyal; true.
Getriebe [gə'tri:bə] n (-s/-) bustle; ⊕ gear(ing); ⊕ drive.
ge|trieben [gə'tri:bən] p.p. of treiben; ~troffen [~'trɔfən] p.p. of treffen; ~trogen [~'tro:gən] p.p. of trügen.
ge'trost adv. confidently.
ge'trunken p.p. of trinken.
Ge|tue [gə'tu:ə] n (-s/no pl.) fuss; ~tümmel [~'tyməl] n (-s/-) turmoil; ~viert [~'fi:rt] n (-[e]s/-e) square.
Gewächs [gə'vɛks] n (-es/-e) growth (a. ♀⁸); plant; vintage; ~haus n greenhouse, hothouse, conservatory.
ge|'wachsen 1. p.p. of wachsen; 2. adj.: j-m ~ sein be a match for s.o.; e-r Sache ~ sein be equal to s.th.; sich der Lage ~ zeigen rise to the occasion; ~wagt adj. [~'va:kt] risky, bold; ~wählt [~'vɛ:lt] style: refined; ~'wahr adj.: ~ werden (acc. or gen.) perceive s.th., become aware of s.th.; ~ werden, daß become aware that.
Gewähr [gə've:r] f (-/no pl.) guarantee, warrant, security; 2en v/t. (no -ge-, h) grant, allow; give, yield, afford; j-n ~ lassen let s.o. have his way; leave s.o. alone; 2leisten v/t. (no -ge-, h) guarantee.
Ge'wahrsam m (-s/-e) custody, safe keeping.
Ge'währsmann m informant, source.
Gewalt [gə'valt] f (-/-en) power; authority; control; force, violence; höhere ~ act of God; mit ~ by force; ~herrschaft f despotism, tyranny; 2ig adj. powerful, mighty; vehement; vast; ~maßnahme f violent measure; 2sam 1. adj. violent; 2. adv. a. forcibly; ~ öffnen force open; open by force; ~tat f act of violence; 2tätig adj. violent.
Gewand [gə'vant] n (-[e]s/-er) garment, robe; esp. eccl. vestment.
ge'wandt 1. p.p. of wenden 2; 2. adj. agile, nimble, dexterous, adroit; clever; 2heit f (-/no pl.) agility, nimbleness; adroitness, dexterity; cleverness.
ge'wann pret. of gewinnen.
Gewäsch F [gə'vɛʃ] n (-es/no pl.) twaddle, nonsense.
ge'waschen p.p. of waschen.
Gewässer [gə'vɛsər] n (-s/-) water(s pl.).
Gewebe [gə've:bə] n (-s/-) tissue (a. anat. and fig.); fabric, web; texture.
Ge'wehr n gun; rifle; ~kolben m (rifle-)butt; ~lauf m (rifle-, gun-) barrel.

Geweih [gə'vaɪ] n (-[e]s/-e) horns pl., head, antlers pl.

Gewerbe [gə'verbə] n (-s/-) trade, business; industry; **~freiheit** f freedom of trade; **~schein** m trade licen|ce, Am. -se; **~schule** f technical school; **~steuer** f trade tax; 2**treibend** adj. carrying on a business, engaged in trade; **~treibende** m (-n/-n) tradesman.

gewerb|lich adj. [gə'verplɪç] commercial, industrial; **~smäßig** adj. professional.

Ge'werkschaft f (-/-en) trade(s) union, Am. labor union; **~ler** m (-s/-) trade(s)-unionist; 2**lich** adj. trade-union; **~sbund** m Trade Union Congress, Am. Federation of Labor.

ge|wesen [gə've:zən] p.p. of sein; **~wichen** [~'vɪçən] p.p. of weichen.

Gewicht [gə'vɪçt] n (-[e]s/-e) weight, Am. F a. heft; e-r Sache **~** beimessen attach importance to s.th.; **~** haben carry weight (bei dat. with); **~** legen auf et. lay stress on s.th.; ins **~** fallen be of great weight, count, matter; 2**ig** adj. weighty (a fig.).

ge|wiesen [gə'vi:zən] p.p. of weisen; **~willt** adj. [~'vɪlt] willing.

Ge|wimmel [gə'vɪməl] n (-s/no pl.) swarm; throng; **~winde** ⊕ [~'vɪndə] n (-s/-) thread.

Gewinn [gə'vɪn] m (-[e]s/-e) gain; † gains pl.; profit; lottery ticket: prize; game: winnings pl., **~anteil** m dividend; **~beteiligung** f profit-sharing; 2**bringend** adj. profitable; 2**en** (irr., no -ge-, h) 1. v/t win; gain; get; 2. v/i. win; gain, fig. improve; 2**end** adj. manner, smile: winning, engaging; **~er** m (-s/-) winner.

gewiß [gə'vɪs] 1. adj. certain; ein gewisser Herr N. a certain Mr. N., one Mr. N.; 2. adv.: **~!** certainly!, to be sure!, Am. sure!

Ge'wissen n (-s/-) conscience; 2**haft** adj. conscientious; 2**los** adj. unscrupulous; **~sbisse** m/pl. remorse, pangs pl. of conscience; **~sfrage** f question of conscience.

gewissermaßen adv. [gəvɪsər-'ma:sən] to a certain extent.

Ge'wißheit f (-/-en) certainty; certitude.

Gewitter [gə'vɪtər] n (-s/-) (thunder)storm; 2**n** v/i. (no -ge-, h): es gewittert there is a thunderstorm; **~regen** m thunder-shower; **~wolke** f thundercloud.

ge|woben [gə'vo:bən] p.p. of weben; **~wogen** 1. p.p. of wägen and wiegen¹; 2. adj. (dat.) well or kindly disposed towards, favo(u)rably inclined towards.

gewöhnen [gə'vø:nən] v/t. (no -ge-, h) accustom, get used (an acc. to).

Gewohnheit [gə'vo:nhaɪt] f (-/-en) habit; custom; 2**smäßig** adj. habitual.

ge'wöhnlich adj. common; ordinary, usual, customary; habitual; common, vulgar.

ge'wohnt adj. customary, habitual; (es) **~** sein zu inf. be accustomed or used to inf.

Gewölbe [gə'vœlbə] n (-s/-) vault.

ge|wonnen [gə'vɔnən] p.p. of gewinnen; **~worben** [~'vɔrbən] p.p. of werben; **~worden** [~'vɔrdən] p.p. of werden; **~worfen** [~'vɔrfən] p.p. of werfen; **~wrungen** [~'vrʊŋən] p.p. of wringen.

Gewühl [gə'vy:l] n (-[e]s/no pl.) bustle; milling crowd.

gewunden [gə'vʊndən] 1. p.p. of winden; 2. adj. twisted; winding.

Gewürz [gə'vyrts] n (-es/-e) spice; condiment; **~nelke** ⚘ f clove.

ge'wußt p.p. of wissen.

Ge|'zeit f: mst **~en** pl. tide(s pl.); **~zeter** n (-s/no pl.) (shrill) clamo(u)r.

ge|'ziert adj. affected; **~zogen** [~'tso:gən] p.p. of ziehen.

Gezwitscher [gə'tsvɪtʃər] n (-s/no pl.) chirping, twitter(ing).

gezwungen [gə'tsvʊŋən] 1. p.p. of zwingen; 2. adj. forced, constrained.

Gicht ⚕ [gɪçt] f (-/no pl.) gout; 2**isch** ⚕ adj. gouty; **~knoten** ⚕ m gouty knot.

Giebel ['gi:bəl] m (-s/-) gable(-end).

Gier [gi:r] f (-/no pl.) greed(iness) (nach for); 2**ig** adj. greedy (nach for, of).

'Gießbach m torrent.

gieß|en ['gi:sən] (irr., ge-, h) 1. v/t. pour, ⊕ cast, found; water (flowers); 2. v/i.: es gießt it is pouring (with rain); 2**er** m (-s/-) founder; 2**erei** [~'raɪ] f (-/-en) foundry; '2**kanne** f watering-can or -pot.

Gift [gɪft] n (-[e]s/-e) poison; venom (esp. of snakes) (a. fig.); malice, spite; '2**ig** adj. poisonous; venomous; malicious, spiteful; '~**schlange** f venomous or poisonous snake; '~**zahn** m poison-fang.

Gigant [gi'gant] m (-en/-en) giant.

Gimpel orn. ['gɪmpəl] m (-s/-) bullfinch.

ging [gɪŋ] pret. of gehen.

Gipfel ['gɪpfəl] m (-s/-) summit, top, peak; '~**konferenz** pol. f summit meeting or conference; '2**n** v/i. (ge-, h) culminate.

Gips [gɪps] m (-es/-e) min. gypsum; ⊕ plaster (of Paris); '~**abdruck** m, '~**abguß** m plaster cast; '2**en** v/t. (ge-, h) plaster; '~**verband** ⚕ m plaster (of Paris) dressing.

Giraffe zo. [gi'rafə] f (-/-n) giraffe.

girieren ✝ [ʒi'ri:rən] v/t. (no -ge-, h) endorse, indorse (bill of exchange).

Girlande [gir'landə] f (-/-n) garland.

Giro ✝ ['ʒi:ro] n (-s/-s) endorsement, indorsement; '~bank f clearing-bank; '~konto n current account.

girren ['girən] v/i. (ge-, h) coo.

Gischt [giʃt] m (-es/~ -e) and f (-/~ -en) foam, froth; spray; spindrift.

Gitarre ♪ [gi'tarə] f (-/-n) guitar.

Gitter ['gitər] n (-s/-) grating; lattice; trellis; railing; '~bett n crib; '~fenster n lattice-window.

Glacéhandschuh [gla'se:-] m kid glove.

Glanz [glants] m (-es/no pl.) brightness; lust|re, Am. -er; brilliancy; splendo(u)r.

glänzen ['glentsən] v/i. (ge-, h) glitter, shine; '~d adj. bright, brilliant; fig. splendid.

'Glanz|leistung f brilliant achievement or performance; '~papier n glazed paper; '~punkt m highlight; '~zeit f golden age, heyday.

Glas [gla:s] n (-es/~er) glass; ~er ['~zər] m (-s/-) glazier.

gläsern adj. ['gle:zərn] of glass; fig. glassy.

'Glas|glocke f (glass) shade or cover; globe; bell-glass; '~hütte f glassworks sg., pl.

glasieren [gla'zi:rən] v/t. (no -ge-, h) glaze; ice, frost (cake).

glasig adj. ['gla:ziç] glassy, vitreous.

'Glasscheibe f pane of glass.

Glasur [gla'zu:r] f (-/-en) glaze, glazing; enamel; icing, frosting (on cakes).

glatt [glat] 1. adj. smooth (a. fig.); even; lie, etc.: flat, downright; road, etc.: slippery; 2. adv. smoothly, evenly; ~ anliegen fit closely or tightly; ~ rasiert clean-shaven; et. ~ ableugnen deny s.th. flatly.

Glätte ['gletə] f (-/-n) smoothness; road, etc.: slipperiness.

'Glatteis n glazed frost, icy glaze, Am. glaze; F: j-n aufs ~ führen lead s.o. up the garden path.

glätten v/t. (ge-, h) smooth.

Glatze ['glatsə] f (-/-n) bald head.

Glaube ['glaubə] m (-ns/~ -n) faith, belief (an acc. in); 2n (ge-, h) 1. v/t. believe; think, suppose, Am. a. guess; 2. v/i. believe (j-m s.o.; an acc. in).

'Glaubens|bekenntnis n creed, profession or confession of faith; '~lehre f, '~satz m dogma, doctrine.

glaubhaft adj. ['glaup-] credible; plausible; authentic.

gläubig adj. ['glɔybiç] believing, faithful; 2e ['~gə] m, f (-n/-n)

believer; 2er ✝ ['~gər] m (-s/-) creditor.

glaubwürdig adj. ['glaup-] credible.

gleich [glaiç] 1. adj. equal (an dat. in); the same; like; even, level; in ~er Weise likewise; zur ~en Zeit at the same time; es ist mir ~ it's all the same to me; das ~e the same; as much; er ist nicht (mehr) der ~e he is not the same man; 2. adv. alike, equally; immediately, presently, directly, at once; just; es ist ~ acht (Uhr) it is close on or nearly eight (o'clock); ~altrig adj. ['~altriç] (of) the same age; '~artig adj. homogeneous; similar; uniform; '~bedeutend adj. synonymous; equivalent (to); tantamount (mit to); '~berechtigt adj. having equal rights; ~bleibend adj. constant, steady; ~en v/i. (irr., ge-, h) equal; resemble.

'gleich|falls adv. also, likewise; ~förmig adj. ['~fœrmiç] uniform; ~gesinnt adj. like-minded; '2ge-wicht n balance (a. fig.); equilibrium, equipoise; pol.: ~ der Kräfte balance of power; '~gültig adj. indifferent (gegen to); es ist mir ~ I don't care; ~, was du tust no matter what you do; '2gültigkeit f indifference; '2heit f (-/-en) equality; likeness; '2klang m unison; consonance, harmony; '~kommen v/i. (irr. kommen, sep., -ge-, sein): e-r Sache ~ amount to s.th.; j-m ~ equal s.o.; '~laufend adj. parallel; '~lautend adj. consonant; identical; ~machen v/t. (sep., -ge-, h) make equal (dat. to), equalize (to or with); '2maß n regularity; evenness; fig. equilibrium; ~mäßig adj. equal; regular; constant; even; '2mut m equanimity; ~mütig adj. even-tempered; calm; ~namig adj. ['~na:miç] of the same name; '2nis n (-ses/-se) parable; rhet. simile; '~sam adv. as it were, so to speak; '~schalten v/t. (sep., -ge-, h) ⊕ synchronize; pol. co-ordinate, unify; '~seitig adj. equilateral; '~setzen v/t. (sep., -ge-, h) equate (dat. or mit with); '~stehen v/i. (irr. stehen, sep., -ge-, h) be equal; '~stellen v/t. (sep., -ge-, h) equalize, equate (dat. with); put s.o. on an equal footing (with); '2stellung f equalization, equation; '2strom ∮ m direct current; '2ung f (-/-en) equation; '~wertig adj. equivalent, of the same value, of equal value; '~zeitig adj. simultaneous; synchronous; contemporary.

Gleis [glais] n (-es/-e) s. Geleise.

gleiten ['glaitən] v/i. (irr., ge-, sein) glide, slide.

'Gleit|flug m gliding flight, glide, ✈ volplane; '~schutzreifen m non-skid tyre, (Am. only) non-skid tire; '~schutz(vorrichtung f) m anti-skid device.

Gletscher ['glɛtʃər] m (-s/-) glacier; '~spalte f crevasse.

glich [gliç] pret. of gleichen.

Glied [gli:t] n (-[e]s/-er) anat. limb; member (a. anat.); link; ⚔ rank, file; 2ern ['~dərn] v/t. (ge-, h) joint, articulate; arrange; divide (in acc. into); '~erung f (-/-en) articulation; arrangement; division; formation; ~maßen ['~tma:sən] pl. limbs pl., extremities pl.

glimmen ['glimən] v/i. ([irr.,] ge-, h) fire: smo(u)lder (a. fig.); glimmer; glow.

glimpflich ['glimpfliç] 1. adj. lenient, mild; 2. adv.: ~ davonkommen get off lightly.

glitschig adj. ['glitʃiç] slippery.

glitt [glit] pret. of gleiten.

glitzern ['glitsərn] v/i. (ge-, h) glitter, glisten.

Globus ['glo:bus] m (-, -ses/Globen, Globusse) globe.

Glocke ['glɔkə] f (-/-n) bell; shade; (glass) cover.

'Glocken|schlag m stroke of the clock; '~spiel n chime(s pl.); '~stuhl m bell-cage; '~turm m bell tower, belfry.

Glöckner ['glœknər] m (-s/-) bell-ringer.

glomm [glɔm] pret. of glimmen.

Glorie ['glo:rjə] f (-/-n) glory; '~schein fig m halo, aureola.

glorreich adj. ['glo:r-] glorious.

glotzen F ['glɔtsən] v/i. (ge-, h) stare.

Glück [glyk] n (-[e]s/no pl.) fortune; good luck; happiness, bliss, felicity; prosperity, auf gut on the off chance; ~ haben be lucky, succeed; das ~ haben zu inf. have the good fortune to inf.; j-m ~ wünschen congratulate s.o. (zu on); viel ~! good luck!, zum ~ fortunately; '2bringend adj. lucky.

Glucke orn. ['glukə] f (-/-n) sitting hen.   [gen.\]

'glücken v/i. (ge-, sein) s. gelin-

gluckern ['glukərn] v/i. (ge-, h) water, etc gurgle

'glücklich adj fortunate; happy; lucky, ~er'weise adv. fortunately.

'Glücksbringer m (-s/-) mascot.

glück'selig adj. blissful, blessed, happy.

glucksen ['gluksən] v/i. (ge-, h) gurgle.

'Glücks|fall m lucky chance, stroke of (good) luck; '~göttin f Fortune; '~kind n lucky person; '~pfennig m lucky penny, '~pilz m lucky person; '~spiel n game of chance; fig. gamble; '~stern m lucky star; '~tag m happy or lucky day, red-letter day.

'glück|strahlend adj. radiant(ly happy); '2wunsch m congratulation, good wishes pl.; compliments pl.; ~ zum Geburtstag many happy returns (of the day).

Glüh|birne ⚡ ['gly:-] f (electric-light) bulb; '2en v/i. (ge-, h) glow; '2end adj. glowing; iron: red-hot; coal: live; fig. ardent, fervid; '2(end)'heiß adj. burning hot; '~lampe f incandescent lamp; '~wein m mulled wine; ~würmchen zo. ['~vyrmçən] n (-s/-) glow-worm.

Glut [glu:t] f (-/-en) heat, glow (a. fig.); glowing fire, embers pl.; fig. ardo(u)r.

Gnade ['gna:də] f (-/-n) grace; favo(u)r; mercy; clemency; pardon; ⚔ quarter.

'Gnaden|akt m act of grace; '~brot n (-[e]s/no pl.) bread of charity; '~frist f reprieve; '~gesuch n petition for mercy.

gnädig adj. ['gnɛ:diç] gracious; merciful; address: 2e Frau Madam.

Gnom [gno:m] m (-en/-en) gnome, goblin.

Gobelin [gobə'lɛ̃:] m (-s/-s) Gobelin tapestry.

Gold [gɔlt] n (-[e]s/no pl.) gold; '~barren m gold bar, gold ingot, bullion; '~borte f gold lace; 2en adj. ['~dən] gold; fig. golden; '~feder f gold nib; '~fisch m goldfish; '2gelb adj. golden-(yellow); '~gräber ['~grɛ:bər] m (-s/-) gold-digger; '~grube f gold-mine; '2haltig adj. gold-bearing, containing gold; '2ig fig. adj. ['~diç] sweet, lovely, Am. F a. cute; '~mine f gold-mine; '~münze f gold coin; '~schmied m goldsmith; '~schnitt m gilt edge; mit ~ gilt-edged; '~stück n gold coin; '~waage f gold-balance; '~währung f gold standard.

Golf[1] geogr. [gɔlf] m (-[e]s/-e) gulf.

Golf[2] [~] n (-s/no pl.) golf; '~platz m golf-course, (golf-)links pl.; '~schläger m golf-club; '~spiel n golf; '~spieler m golfer.

Gondel ['gɔndəl] f (-/-n) gondola; ⚡ mst car.

gönnen ['gœnən] v/t. (ge-, h): j-m et. ~ allow or grant or not to grudge s.o. s.th.

'Gönner m (-s/-) patron; Am. a. sponsor; '2haft adj. patronizing.

gor [go:r] pret. of gären.

Gorilla zo. [go'rila] m (-s/-s) gorilla.

goß [gɔs] pret of gießen.

Gosse ['gɔsə] f (-/-n) gutter (a. fig.).

Gott [gɔt] m (-es, ⁀-es/⁀-er) God; god, deity; '2ergeben adj. resigned (to the will of God).

'Gottes|dienst eccl. m (divine) service; '2fürchtig adj. godfearing; '~haus n church, chapel; '~läste-

rer m (-s/-) blasphemer; '∼läste-
rung f blasphemy.
'Gottheit f (-/-en) deity, divinity.
Göttin ['gœtin] f (-/-nen) goddess.
göttlich adj. ['gœtliç] divine.
gott|'lob int. thank God or good-
ness!; '∼los adj. godless; impious;
F fig. deed· unholy, wicked; '2ver-
trauen n trust in God.
Götze ['gœtsə] m (-n/-n) idol;
'∼nbild n idol; '∼ndienst m idolatry.
Gouvern|ante [guvɛr'nantə] f (-/-n)
governess; '∼eur [∼'nøːr] m (-s/-e)
governor.
Grab [graːp] n (-[e]s/∼er) grave,
tomb, sepulch|re, Am. -er.
Graben ['graːbən] 1. m (-s/∼) ditch;
⚔ trench; 2. ⚙ v/t. (irr., ge-, h)
dig; animal burrow.
Grab|gewölbe ['graːp-] n vault,
tomb; '∼mal n monument; tomb,
sepulch|re, Am. -er; '∼rede f funeral
sermon; funeral oration or address;
'∼schrift f epitaph; '∼stätte f
burial-place; grave, tomb; '∼stein
m tombstone; gravestone.
Grad [graːt] m (-[e]s/-e) degree;
grade, rank; 15 ∼ Kälte 15 degrees
below zero; '∼einteilung f graduation; '∼messer m (-s/-) graduated
scale, graduator; fig. criterion;
'∼netz n map. grid.
Graf [graːf] m (-en/-en) in Britain:
earl; count.
Gräfin ['grɛːfin] f (-/-nen) countess.
'Grafschaft f (-/-en) county.
Gram [graːm] 1. m (-[e]s/no pl.)
grief, sorrow; 2. ⚙ adj.: j-m ∼
sein bear s.o. ill will or a grudge.
grämen ['grɛːmən] v/t. (ge-, h)
grieve; sich ∼ grieve (über acc. at,
for, over).
Gramm [gram] n (-s/-e) gramme,
Am. gram.
Grammati|k [gra'matik] f (-/-en)
grammar, 2sch adj. grammatical.
Granat min. [gra'naːt] m (-[e]s/-e)
garnet; ∼e ⚔ f(-/-n) shell; grenade;
∼splitter ⚔ m shell-splinter;
∼trichter ⚔ m shell-crater; ∼wer-
fer ⚔ m (-s/-) mortar.
Granit min. [gra'niːt] m (-s/-e)
granite.
Granne ⚘ ['granə] f (-/-n) awn,
beard.
Graphi|k ['graːfik] f (-/-en) graphic
arts pl., '2sch adj. graphic(al).
Graphit min. [gra'fiːt] m (-s/-e)
graphite.
Gras [graːs] n (-es/∼er) grass;
2bewachsen adj ['∼bəvaksən]
grass-grown, grass∼, 2en ['∼zən]
v/i. (ge-, h) graze; ∼halm m blade
of grass; ∼narbe f turf, sod;
'∼platz m grass-plot, lawn.
grassieren [gra'siːrən] v/i. (no -ge-,
h) rage, prevail.
gräßlich adj. ['grɛsliç] horrible;
hideous, atrocious.

Grassteppe ['graː-s] f prairie,
savanna(h).
Grat [graːt] m (-[e]s/-e) edge, ridge.
Gräte ['grɛːtə] f (-/-n) (fish-)bone.
Gratifikation [gratifika'tsjoːn] f
(-/-en) gratuity, bonus.
gratis adv. ['graːtis] gratis, free of
charge.
Gratul|ant [gratu'lant] m (-en/-en)
congratulator; ∼ation [∼'tsjoːn] f
(-/-en) congratulation; 2ieren [∼-
'liːrən] v/i. (no -ge-, h) congratulate
(j-m zu et. s.o. on s.th.); j-m zum
Geburtstag ∼ wish s.o. many happy
returns (of the day)
grau adj. [grau] grey, esp. Am. gray.
'grauen¹ v/i. (ge-, h) day: dawn.
'grauen² v/i. (ge-, h): mir graut
vor (dat.) I shudder at, I dread;
2. 2 n (-s/no pl.) horror (vor dat. of);
'∼erregend adj., ∼haft adj., '∼voll
adj. horrible, dreadful.
gräulich adj. ['grɔyliç] greyish, esp.
Am. grayish.
Graupe ['graupə] f (-/-n) (peeled)
barley, pot-barley; '∼ln 1. f/pl.
sleet; 2. 2 v/i. (ge-, h) sleet.
'grausam adj. cruel; 2keit f (-/-en)
cruelty.
grausen ['grauzən] 1. v/i. (ge-, h)
s. grauen² 1; 2. 2 n (-s/no pl.)
horror (vor dat. of).
'grausig adj. horrible.   [graver.]
Graveur [gra'vøːr] m (-s/-e en.)
gravieren [gra'viːrən] v/t. (no -ge-,
h) engrave; ∼d fig. adj. aggravating.
gravitätisch adj. [gravi'tɛːtiʃ] grave;
dignified, solemn; stately.
Grazie ['graːtsjə] f (-/-n) grace(fulness).
graziös adj. [gra'tsjøːs] graceful.
greifen ['graifən] (irr., ge-, h) 1. v/t.
seize, grasp, catch hold of; ♪ touch
(string); 2. v/i.: an den Hut ∼ touch
one's hat; ∼ nach grasp or snatch
at; um sich ∼ spread, j-m unter die
Arme ∼ give s.o. a helping hand;
zu strengen Mitteln ∼ resort to
severe measures; zu den Waffen ∼
take up arms
Greis [grais] m (-es/-e) old man;
2enhaft adj. [∼zən-] senile (a. ⚕);
∼in [∼in] f (-/-nen) old woman.
grell adj. [grɛl] light: glaring;
colour loud; sound shrill.
Grenze ['grɛntsə] f (-/-n) limit;
territory boundary; state frontier, borders pl., e-e ∼ ziehen draw
the line; '2n v/i. (ge-, h): ∼ an (acc.)
border on (a fig.); fig. verge on;
'2nlos adj boundless.
'Grenz|fall m border-line case;
'∼land n borderland; '∼linie f
boundary or border line; '∼schutz
m frontier or border protection;
frontier or border guard; ∼stein m
boundary stone; '∼übergang m
frontier or border crossing(-point).
Greuel ['grɔyəl] m (-s/-) horror;

abomination; atrocity; **∿tat** *f* atrocity.

Griech|e ['gri:çə] *m* (-n/-n) Greek; **'2isch** *adj.* Greek; **⚠**, *features*: Grecian.

griesgrämig *adj.* ['gri:sgrɛ:miç] morose, sullen.

Grieß [gri:s] *m* (-es/-e) gravel (*a.* **⚛**), grit; semolina; **'∿brei** *m* semolina pudding.

Griff [grif] **1.** *m* (-[e]s/-e) grip, grasp, hold; **♪** touch; handle (*of knife, etc.*); hilt (*of sword*); **2. 2** *pret. of greifen.*

Grille ['grilə] *f* (-/-n) *zo.* cricket; *fig.* whim, fancy; **'2nhaft** *adj.* whimsical.

Grimasse [gri'masə] *f* (-/-n) grimace; **∿n schneiden** pull faces.

Grimm [grim] *m* (-[e]s/*no pl.*) fury, rage; **'2ig** *adj.* furious, fierce, grim.

Grind [grint] *m* (-[e]s/-e) scab, scurf.

grinsen ['grinzən] **1.** *v/i.* (ge-, h) grin (*über acc.* at); sneer (at); **2. 2** *n* (-s/*no pl.*) grin; sneer.

Grippe ♪ ['gripə] *f* (-/-n) influenza, F flu(e), grippe.

grob *adj.* [grɔp] coarse; gross; rude; *work, skin*: rough; **'2heit** *f* (-/-en) coarseness; grossness; rudeness; **∿en** *pl.* rude things *pl.*

grölen F ['grø:lən] *v/t. and v/i.* (ge-, h) bawl.

Groll [grɔl] *m* (-[e]s/*no pl.*) grudge, ill will; **'2en** *v/i.* (ge-, h) *thunder*: rumble; *j-m* ∿ bear s.o. ill will *or* a grudge.

Gros[1] † [grɔs] *n* (-ses/-se) gross.

Gros[2] [gro:] *n* (-/-) main body.

Groschen ['grɔʃən] *m* (-s/-) penny.

groß *adj.* [gro:s] great; large; big; *figure*: tall; huge; *fig.* great, grand; *heat*: intense; *cold*: severe; *loss*: heavy; *die* **2en** *pl.* the grown-ups *pl.*; *im* ∿en wholesale, on a large scale; *im* ∿en (*und*) *ganzen* on the whole; ∿er Buchstabe capital (letter); *das* ∿e Los the first prize; *ich bin kein* ∿er Tänzer I am not much of a dancer; **'∿artig** *adj.* great, grand, sublime; first-rate; **'2aufnahme** *f film*: close-up.

Größe ['grø:sə] *f* (-/-n) size; largeness; height, tallness; quantity (*esp.* **Å**); *importance*: greatness; *p.* celebrity; *thea.* star.

'Großeltern *pl.* grandparents *pl.*

'großenteils *adv.* to a large *or* great extent, largely.

'Größenwahn *m* megalomania.

'Groß|grundbesitz *m* large landed property; **∿handel †** *m* wholesale trade; **∿handelspreis †** *m* wholesale price; **∿händler †** *m* wholesale dealer, wholesaler; **'∿handlung** *f* wholesale business; **'∿herzog** *m* grand duke; **'∿industrielle** *m* big industrialist.

Grossist [grɔ'sist] *m* (-en/-en) *s.* Großhändler.

groß|jährig *adj.* ['gro:sjɛ:riç] of age; ∿ *werden* come of age; **2jährigkeit** *f* (-/*no pl.*) majority, full (legal) age; **'2kaufmann** *m* wholesale merchant; **2kraftwerk ⚡** *n* super-power station; **2macht** *f* great power; **2maul** *n* braggart; **2mut** *f* (-/*no pl.*) generosity; **∿mütig** *adj.* ['∿my:tiç] magnanimous, generous; **2mutter** *f* grandmother; **2neffe** *m* great-nephew, grand-nephew; **2nichte** *f* great-niece, grand-niece; **2onkel** *m* great-uncle, grand-uncle; **2schreibung** *f* (-/-en) use of capital letters; capitalization; **∿sprecherisch** *adj.* boastful; **∿spurig** *adj.* arrogant; **'2stadt** *f* large town *or* city; **'∿städtisch** *adj.* of *or* in a large town *or* city; **2tante** *f* great-aunt, grand-aunt.

größtenteils *adv.* ['grø:stəntaɪls] mostly, chiefly, mainly.

'groß|tun *v/i.* (*irr.* tun, sep., -ge-, h) swagger, boast; *sich mit et.* ∿ boast *or* brag *of or* about s.th.; **'2vater** *m* grandfather; **2verdiener** *m* (-s/-) big earner; **2wild** *n* big game; **'∿ziehen** *v/i.* (*irr.* ziehen, sep., -ge-, h) bring up (*child*); rear, raise (*child, animal*); **∿zügig** *adj.* ['∿tsy:giç] liberal; generous; broad-minded; *planning: a.* on a large scale.

grotesk *adj.* [gro'tɛsk] grotesque.

Grotte ['grɔtə] *f* (-/-n) grotto.

grub [gru:p] *pret. of graben.*

Grübchen ['gry:pçən] *n* (-s/-) dimple.

Grube ['gru:bə] *f* (-/-n) pit; **⚒** mine, pit.

Grübel|ei [gry:bə'laɪ] *f* (-/-en) brooding, musing, meditation; **2n** ['∿ln] *v/i.* (ge-, h) muse, meditate, ponder (*all:* über *acc.* on, over); *Am.* F *a.* mull (over).

'Gruben|arbeiter ⚒ *m* miner; '∿**gas ⚒** *n* fire-damp; **'∿lampe ⚒** *f* miner's lamp.

Gruft [gruft] *f* (-/∿e) tomb, vault.

grün [gry:n] **1.** *adj.* green; ∿er *Hering* fresh herring; ∿er *Junge* greenhorn; ∿ *und blau schlagen* beat *s.o.* black and blue; *vom* ∿en Tisch aus armchair (*strategy, etc.*); **2. 2** *n* (-s/*no pl.*) green; verdure.

Grund [grunt] *m* (-[e]s/∿e) ground; soil; bottom (*a. fig.*); land, estate; foundation; *fig.*: motive; reason; argument; *von* ∿ *auf* thoroughly, fundamentally; **∿ausbildung** *f* basic instruction; **⚔** basic (military) training; **'∿bedeutung** *f* basic *or* original meaning; **∿bedingung** *f* basic *or* fundamental condition; **'∿begriff** *m* fundamental *or* basic idea; ∿e *pl.* principles *pl.*; rudiments *pl.*; **'∿besitz** *m* land(ed property);' '~besitzer *m* landowner; '~buch *n* land register.

gründ|en ['gryndən] *v/t.* (ge-, h) establish; ✝ promote; *sich ~ auf* (*acc.*) be based *or* founded on; '2er *m* (-s/-) founder; ✝ promoter.

'**grund'falsch** *adj.* fundamentally wrong; '2farbe *f* ground-colo(u)r; *opt.* primary colo(u)r; '2fläche *f* base; area (*of room, etc.*); '2gebühr *f* basic rate *or* fee; flat rate; '2gedanke *m* basic *or* fundamental idea; '2gesetz *n* fundamental law; ⅌ *appr.* constitution; '2kapital ✝ *n* capital (fund); '2lage *f* foundation, basis; '~legend *adj.* fundamental, basic.

gründlich *adj.* ['gryntliç] thorough; *knowledge*: profound.

'**Grund|linie** *f* base-line; '2los *adj.* bottomless; *fig.*: groundless; unfounded; '~mauer *f* foundation-wall. [Thursday.\

Grün'donnerstag *eccl. m* Maundy

'**Grund|regel** *f* fundamental rule; '~riß *m* ⚠ ground-plan; outline; compendium; '~satz *m* principle; 2sätzlich ['~zetsliç] **1.** *adj.* fundamental; **2.** *adv.* in principle; on principle; '~schule *f* elementary *or* primary school; '~stein *m* ⚠ foundation-stone; *fig.* corner-stone; '~steuer *f* land-tax; '~stock *m* basis, foundation; '~stoff *m* element; '~strich *m* down-stroke; '~stück *n* plot (of land); ⅌ (real) estate; premises *pl.*; '~stücksmakler *m* real estate agent, *Am.* realtor; '~ton *m* ♪ keynote; ground shade.

'**Gründung** *f* (-/-en) foundation, establishment.

'**grund|ver'schieden** *adj.* entirely different; '2wasser *geol. n* (under-)ground water; '2zahl *gr. f* cardinal number; '2zug *m* main feature, characteristic.

'**grünlich** *adj.* greenish.

'**Grün|schnabel** *fig. m* greenhorn; whipper-snapper; '~span *m* (-[e]s/*no pl.*) verdigris.

grunzen ['gruntsən] *v/i. and v/t.* (ge-, h) grunt.

Gruppe ['grupə] *f* (-/-n) group; '~ section, *Am.* squad; 2ieren [~'pi:rən] *v/t.* (*no* -ge-, h) group, arrange in groups; *sich ~* form groups.

Gruselgeschichte ['gru:zəl-] *f* tale of horror, spine-chilling story *or* tale, F creepy story *or* tale.

Gruß [gru:s] *m* (-es/*ue*e) salutation, greeting; *esp.* ⚔, ♇ salute; *mst* Grüße *pl.* regards *pl.*; respects *pl.*, compliments *pl.*

grüßen ['gry:sən] *v/t.* (ge-, h) greet, *esp.* ⚔ salute; hail; *~ Sie ihn von mir* remember me to him; *j-n ~ lassen* send one's compliments *or* regards to s.o.

9*

Grütze ['grytsə] *f* (-/-n) grits *pl.*, groats *pl.*

guck|en ['gukən] *v/i.* (ge-, h) look; peep, peer; '2loch *n* peep- *or* spy-hole.

Guerilla ⚔ [ge'ril(j)a] *f* (-/-s) guer(r)illa war.

gültig *adj.* ['gyltiç] valid; effective, in force; legal; *coin:* current; *ticket:* available; '2keit *f* (-/*no pl.*) validity; currency (*of money*); availability (*of ticket*).

Gummi ['gumi] *n, m* (-s/-s) gum; (india-)rubber; '~ball *m* rubber ball; '~band *n* elastic (band); rubber band; '~baum ♧ *m* gum-tree; (india-)rubber tree.

gum'mieren *v/t.* (*no* -ge-, h) gum.

'**Gummi|handschuh** *m* rubber glove; '~knüppel *m* truncheon, *Am.* club; '~schuhe *m/pl.* rubber shoes *pl.*, *Am.* rubbers *pl.*; '~sohle *f* rubber sole; '~stiefel *m* wellington (boot), *Am.* rubber boot; '~zug *m* elastic; elastic webbing.

Gunst [gunst] *f* (-/*no pl.*) favo(u)r, goodwill; *zu ~en* (*gen.*) in favo(u)r of.

günst|ig *adj.* ['gynstiç] favo(u)rable; *omen:* propitious; *im ~sten Fall* at best; *zu ~en Bedingungen* on easy terms; 2ling ['~liŋ] *m* (-s/-e) favo(u)rite.

Gurgel ['gurgəl] *f* (-/-n): *j-m an die ~ springen* leap *or* fly at s.o.'s throat; '2n *v/i.* (ge-, h) ⚕ gargle; gurgle.

Gurke ['gurkə] *f* (-/-n) cucumber; *pickled* gherkin.

gurren ['gurən] *v/i.* (ge-, h) coo.

Gurt [gurt] *m* (-[e]s/-e) girdle; *harness.* girth; strap; belt.

Gürtel ['gyrtəl] *m* (-s/-) belt; girdle; *geogr.* zone.

Guß [gus] *m* (Gusses/Güsse) ⊕ founding, casting; *typ.* fount, *Am.* font; *rain:* downpour, shower; '~eisen *n* cast iron; '2eisern *adj.* cast-iron; '~stahl *m* cast steel.

gut¹ [gu:t] **1.** *adj.* good; *~e Worte* fair words; *~es Wetter* fine weather; *~er Dinge or ~en Mutes sein* be of good cheer; *~e Miene zum bösen Spiel machen* grin and bear it; *~ so!* good!, well done!; *~ werden* get well, heal; *fig.* turn out well; *ganz ~* not bad; *schon ~!* never mind!, all right!; *sei so ~ und ... (will you) be so kind as to inf.*; *auf ~ deutsch* in plain German; *j-m ~ sein* love *or* like s.o.; **2.** *adv.* well; *ein ~ gehendes Geschäft* a flourishing business; *du hast ~ lachen* it's easy *or* very well for you to laugh; *es ~ haben* be lucky; be well off.

Gut² [~] *n* (-[e]s/*ue*er) possession, property; (landed) estate; ✝ goods *pl.*

'Gut|achten n (-s/-) (expert) opinion; '~achter m (-s/-) expert; consultant; '2artig adj. good-natured; **⚕** benign; ~dünken ['~dyŋkən] n (-s/no pl.): nach ~ at discretion or pleasure.

Gute 1. n (-n/no pl.) the good; ~s tun do good; 2. m, f (-n/-n): die ~n pl. the good pl.

Güte ['gy:tə] f (-/no pl.) goodness, kindness; ✝ class, quality; in ~ amicably; F: meine ~l good gracious!; haben Sie die ~ zu inf. be so kind as to inf.

'Güter|abfertigung f dispatch of goods; ~ annahme f goods office, Am. freight office; '~bahnhof m goods station, Am. freight depot or yard; '~gemeinschaft ₹₴ community of property; '~trennung ₹₴ f separation of property; '~verkehr m goods traffic, Am. freight traffic; '~wagen m (goods) wag(g)on, Am. freight car; offener ~ (goods) truck; geschlossener ~ (goods) van, Am. boxcar; '~zug m goods train, Am. freight train.

'gut|gelaunt adj. good-humo(u)red; '~gläubig adj. acting or done in good faith; s. leichtgläubig; '~haben v/t. (irr. haben, sep., -ge-, h) have credit for (sum of money); '2~haben ✝ n credit (balance); '~heißen v/t. (irr. heißen, sep., -ge-, h)

approve (of); '~herzig adj. good-natured, kind-hearted.

'gütig adj. good, kind(ly).

'gütlich adv.: sich ~ einigen settle s.th. amicably; sich ~ tun an (dat.) regale o.s. on.

'gut|machen v/t. (sep., -ge-, h) make up for, compensate, repair; ~mütig adj. ['~my:tiç] good-natured; '2mütigkeit f (-/**⚕** -en) good nature.

'Gutsbesitzer m landowner; owner of an estate.

'Gut|schein m credit note, coupon; voucher; '2schreiben v/t. (irr. schreiben, sep., -ge-, h): j-m e-n Betrag ~ put a sum to s.o.'s credit; '~schrift ✝ f credit(ing).

'Guts|haus n farm-house; manor house; '~herr m lord of the manor; landowner; '~hof m farmyard; estate, farm; '~verwalter m (landlord's) manager or steward.

'gutwillig adj. willing; obliging.

Gymnasi|albildung [gymna'zja:l-] f classical education; '~ast [~ast] m (-en/-en) appr. grammar-school boy; ~um [~'na:zjum] n (-s/Gymnasien) appr. grammar-school.

Gymnasti|k [gym'nastik] f (-/no pl.) gymnastics pl.; 2sch adj. gymnastic.

Gynäkologe **⚕** [gynɛ:ko'lo:gə] m (-n/-n) gyn(a)ecologist.

H

Haar [ha:r] n (-[e]s/-e) hair; sich die ~e kämmen comb one's hair; sich die ~e schneiden lassen have one's hair cut; aufs ~ to a hair; um ein ~ by a hair's breadth; '~ausfall m loss of hair; ~bürste f hairbrush; '2en v/i. and v/refl. (ge-, h) lose or shed one's hairs; '~esbreite f: um ~ by a hair's breadth; '2'fein adj. (as) fine as a hair; fig. subtle; ~gefäß anat. n capillary (vessel); 2ge'nau adj. exact to a hair; '2ig adj. hairy; in compounds: ...-haired; '2klein adv. to the last detail; '~klemme f hair grip, Am. bobby pin; '~nadel f hairpin; '~nadelkurve f hairpin bend; ~netz n hair-net; '~öl n hair-oil; '2'scharf 1. adj. very sharp; fig. very precise; 2. adv. by a hair's breadth; '~schneidemaschine f (e-e a pair of) (hair) clippers pl.; '~schneider m barber, (men's) hairdresser; '~schnitt m haircut; '~schwund m loss of hair; '~spalte'rei f (-/-en) hair-splitting; '2sträubend adj. hair-raising, horrifying; '~tracht f hair-style, coiffure; '~wäsche f hair-wash,

shampoo; '~wasser n hair-lotion; '~wuchs m growth of the hair; '~wuchsmittel n hair-restorer.

Habe ['ha:bə] f (-/no pl.) property; belongings pl.

haben ['ha:bən] 1. v/t. (irr., ge-, h) have; F fig.: sich ~ (make a) fuss; etwas (nichts) auf sich ~ be of (no) consequence; unter sich ~ be in control of, command; zu ~ be obtainable, to be had; da ~ wir's/ there we are!; 2. 2 ✝ n (-s/-) credit (side).

Habgier ['ha:p-] f avarice, covetousness; '2ig adj. avaricious, covetous.

habhaft adj. ['ha:phaft]: ~ werden (gen.) get hold of; catch, apprehend.

Habicht orn. ['ha:biçt] m (-[e]s/-e) (gos)hawk.

Hab|seligkeiten ['ha:p-] f/pl. property, belongings pl.; '~sucht f s. Habgier; '2süchtig adj. s. habgierig.

Hacke ['hakə] f (-/-n) **⚒** hoe, mattock; ⟨pick⟩axe; heel.

Hacken ['hakən] 1. m (-s/-) heel; die ~ zusammenschlagen **⚔** click one's heels; 2. 2 v/t. (ge-, h) **⚒**

hack (*soil*); mince (*meat*); chop (*wood*).
'Hackfleisch *n* minced meat, *Am.* ground meat.
Häcksel ['hɛksəl] *n, m* (-*s*/*no pl.*) chaff, chopped straw.
Hader ['hɑːdər] *m* (-*s*/*no pl.*) dispute, quarrel; discord; '**2n** *v/i.* (ge-, *h*) quarrel (*mit* with).
Hafen ['hɑːfən] *m* (-*s*/=) harbo(u)r; port; '**~anlagen** *f/pl.* docks *pl.*; '**~arbeiter** *m* docker, *Am. a.* longshoreman; '**~damm** *m* jetty; pier; '**~stadt** *f* seaport.
Hafer ['hɑːfər] *m* (-*s*/-) oats *pl.*; '**~brei** *m* (oatmeal) porridge; '**~flocken** *f/pl.* porridge oats *pl.*; '**~grütze** *f* groats *pl.*, grits *pl.*; '**~schleim** *m* gruel.
Haft ⚖ [haft] *f* (-/*no pl.*) custody; detention, confinement; '**2bar** *adj.* responsible, ⚖ liable (*für* for); '**~befehl** *m* warrant of arrest; '**2en** *v/i.* (ge-, *h*) stick, adhere (*an dat.* to); ~ *für* ⚖ answer for, be liable for.
Häftling ['hɛftliŋ] *m* (-*s*/-e) prisoner.
'Haftpflicht ⚖ *f* liability; '**2ig** *adj.* liable (*für* for); '**~versicherung** *f* third-party insurance.
'Haftung *f* (-/-en) responsibility, ⚖ liability; *mit beschränkter* ~ limited.
Hagel ['hɑːgəl] *m* (-*s*/-) hail; *fig. a.* shower, volley; '**~korn** *n* hailstone; '**2n** *v/i.* (ge-, *h*) hail (*a. fig.*); '**~schauer** *m* shower of hail, (brief) hailstorm.
hager *adj.* ['hɑːgər] lean, gaunt; scraggy, lank.
Hahn [hɑːn] *m* **1.** *orn.* (-[e]*s*/=e) cock; rooster; **2.** ⊕ (-[e]*s*/=e, -en) (stop)cock, tap, *Am. a.* faucet; '**~enkampf** *m* cock-fight; '**~enschrei** *m* cock-crow.
Hai *ichth.* [haɪ] *m* (-[e]*s*/-e), '**~fisch** *m* shark.
Hain *poet.* [haɪn] *m* (-[e]*s*/-e) grove; wood.
häkel|n ['hɛːkəln] *v/t. and v/i.* (ge-, *h*) crochet; '**2nadel** *f* crochet needle *or* hook.
Haken ['hɑːkən] **1.** *m* (-*s*/-) hook (*a. boxing*); peg; *fig.* snag, catch; **2.** 2 *v/i.* (ge-, *h*) get stuck, jam.
'hakig *adj.* hooked.
halb [halp] **1.** *adj.* half; *eine ~e Stunde* half an hour, a half-hour; *eine ~e Flasche Wein* a half-bottle of wine; *ein ~es Jahr* half a year; *~e Note* ♪ minim, *Am. a.* half note; *~er Ton* ♪ semitone, *Am. a.* half tone; **2.** *adv.* half; ~ *voll* half full; ~ *soviel* half as much; *es schlug* ~ it struck the half-hour.
'halb|amtlich *adj.* semi-official; '**2bruder** *m* half-brother; '**2dunkel** *n* semi-darkness; dusk, twilight; **~er** *prp.* (*gen.*) ['halbər] on account of; for the sake of; '**2fabrikat** ⊕ *n* semi-finished product; '**~gar** *adj.* underdone, *Am. a.* rare; '**2gott** *m* demigod; '**2heit** *f* (-/-en) half-measure.
halbieren [hal'biːrən] *v/t.* (*no* -ge-, *h*) halve, divide in half; & bisect.
'Halb|insel *f* peninsula; '**~jahr** *n* half-year, six months *pl.*; **2jährig** *adj.* ['~jɛːriç] half-year, six months; of six months; '**2jährlich 1.** *adj.* half-yearly; **2.** *adv. a.* twice a year; '**~kreis** *m* semicircle; '**~kugel** *f* hemisphere; '**2laut 1.** *adj.* low, subdued; **2.** *adv.* in an undertone; '**2mast** *adv.* (at) half-mast, *Am. a.* (at) half-staff; '**~messer** & *m* (-*s*/-) radius; '**~mond** *m* half-moon, crescent; '**2part** *adv.*: ~ *machen* go halves, F go fifty-fifty; '**~schuh** *m* (low) shoe; '**~schwester** *f* half-sister; **~tagsbeschäftigung** *f* part-time job *or* employment; '**2tot** *adj.* half-dead; **2wegs** *adv.* ['~'veːks] half-way, *fig.* to some extent, tolerably; '**~welt** *f* demi-monde; **2wüchsig** *adj.* ['~vyːksiç] adolescent, *Am. a.* teen-age; '**~zeit** *f* *sports* half(-time).
Halde ['haldə] *f* (-/-n) slope; ⚒ dump.
half [half] *pret. of helfen.*
Hälfte ['hɛlftə] *f* (-/-n) half, ⚖ moiety; *die ~ von* half of.
Halfter ['halftər] *m, n* (-*s*/-) halter.
Halle ['halə] *f* (-/-n) hall; *hotel*: lounge, *tennis*: covered court; ✈ hangar.
hallen ['halən] *v/i.* (ge-, *h*) (re)sound, ring, (re-)echo.
'Hallen|bad *n* indoor swimming-bath, *Am. a.* natatorium; '**~sport** *m* indoor sports *pl.*
hallo [ha'loː] **1.** *int.* hallo!, hello!, hullo!; **2.** 2 *fig. n* (-*s*/-*s*) hullabaloo.
Halm ♀ [halm] *m* (-[e]*s*/-e) blade; stem, stalk; straw.
Hals [hals] *m* (-es/=e) neck; throat; ~ *über Kopf* head over heels; *auf dem ~e haben* have on one's back, be saddled with; *sich den ~ verrenken* crane one's neck; '**~abschneider** *fig. m* extortioner, F shark; '**~band** *n* necklace; collar (*for dog, etc.*); '**~entzündung** ⚕ *f* sore throat; '**~kette** *f* necklace; string, chain; '**~kragen** *m* collar; '**~schmerzen** *m/pl.*: ~ *haben* have a sore throat; '**2starrig** *adj.* stubborn, obstinate; '**~tuch** *n* neckerchief, scarf; '**~weite** *f* neck size.
Halt [halt] *m* (-[e]*s*/-e) hold; foothold, handhold; support (*a. fig.*); *fig.*: stability; security, mainstay.
halt 1. *int.* stop!; ⚔ halt!; **2.** F *adv.* just; *das ist ~* so that's the way it is.
'haltbar *adj. material, etc.*: durable, lasting; *colour*: fast; *fig. theory, etc.*: tenable.
'halten (*irr.*, ge-, *h*) **1.** *v/t.* hold (*fort,*

position, water, etc.); maintain (*position, level, etc.*); keep (*promise, order, animal, etc.*); make, deliver (*speech*); give, deliver (*lecture*); take in (*newspaper*); ~ *für* regard as, take to be; take for; *es ~ mit* side with; be fond of; *kurz~* keep *s.o.* short; *viel* (*wenig*) ~ *von* think highly (little) of; *sich ~* hold out; last; *food:* keep; *sich gerade ~* hold o.s. straight; *sich gut ~ in examination, etc.:* do well; *p.* be well preserved; *sich ~ an* (*acc.*) adhere *or* keep to; 2. *v/i.* stop, halt; *ice:* bear; *rope, etc.:* stand the strain; ~ *zu* stick to *or* by; ~ *auf* (*acc.*) set store by, value; *auf sich ~* pay attention to one's appearance; have self-respect.

'Halte|punkt *m* 🚉, *etc.:* wayside stop, halt; *shooting:* point of aim; *phys.* critical point; '~r *m* (*-s/-*) keeper; *a.* owner; *devices:* ... holder; '~stelle *f* stop; 🚉 station, stop; '~signal 🚉 *n* stop signal.

halt|los *adj.* ['haltlo:s] *p.* unsteady, unstable; *theory, etc.:* baseless, without foundation; '~machen *v/i.* (*sep.*, *-ge-*, *h*) stop, halt; *vor nichts~* stick *or* stop; at nothing; 2ung *f* (*-/-en*) deportment, carriage; pose; *fig.* attitude (*gegenüber* towards); self-control; *stock exchange:* tone.

hämisch *adj.* ['hɛ:miʃ] spiteful, malicious.

Hammel ['haməl] *m* (*-s/-*, *¨*) wether; '~fleisch *n* mutton; '~keule *f* leg of mutton; '~rippchen *n* (*-s/-*) mutton chop.

Hammer ['hamər] *m* (*-s/¨*) hammer; (*auctioneer's*) gavel; *unter den ~ kommen* come under the hammer.

hämmern ['hɛmərn] (*ge-*, *h*) 1. *v/t.* hammer; 2. *v/i.* hammer (*a. an dat.* at *door, etc.*); hammer away (*auf dat.* at *piano*); *heart, etc.:* throb (*violently*), pound.

Hämorrhoiden 🖋 [hɛ:mɔrɔ'i:dən] *f/pl.* h(a)emorrhoids *pl.*, piles *pl.*

Hampelmann ['hampəlman] *m* jumping-jack; *fig.* (mere) puppet.

Hamster *zo.* ['hamstər] *m* (*-s/-*) hamster; '2n *v/t. and v/i.* (*ge-*, *h*) hoard.

Hand [hant] *f* (*-/¨e*) hand; *j-m die ~ geben* shake hands with *s.o.*; *an ~* (*gen.*) *or von* with the help *or* aid of; *aus erster ~* first-hand, at first hand; *bei der ~, zur ~* at hand; *~ und Fuß haben* be sound, hold water; *seine ~ im Spiele haben* have a finger in the pie; '~arbeit *f* manual labo(u)r *or* work; (handi)craft; needlework; '~arbeiter *m* manual labo(u)rer; '~bibliothek *f* reference library; '~breit 1. *f* (*-/-*) hand's breadth; 2. 2 *adj.* a hand's breadth across; '~bremse *mot.* *f* hand-brake; '~buch *n* manual, handbook.

Hände|druck ['hɛndə-] *m* (*-[e]s/¨e*) handshake; '~klatschen *n* (*-s/no pl.*) (hand-)clapping; applause.

Handel ['handəl] *m* 1. (*-s/no pl.*) commerce; trade; business; market; traffic; transaction, deal, bargain; 2. (*-s/¨*): *Händel pl.* quarrels *pl.*, contention; '2n *v/i.* (*ge-*, *h*) act, take action; ✝ trade (*mit* with *s.o.*, *in goods*), deal (*in goods*) bargain (*um* for), haggle (over); ~ *von* treat of, deal with; *es handelt sich um* it concerns, it is a matter of.

'Handels|abkommen *n* trade agreement; '~bank *f* commercial bank; '2einig *adj.:* ~ *werden* come to terms; '~genossenschaft *f* traders' co-operative association; '~gericht *n* commercial court; '~gesellschaft *f* (trading) company; '~haus *n* business house, firm; '~kammer *f* Chamber of Commerce; '~marine *f* mercantile marine; '~minister *m* minister of commerce; President of the Board of Trade, *Am.* Secretary of Commerce; '~ministerium *n* ministry of commerce; Board of Trade, *Am.* Department of Commerce; '~reisende *m* commercial traveller, *Am.* traveling salesman, *F* drummer; '~schiff *n* merchantman; '~schiffahrt *f* merchant shipping; '~schule *f* commercial school; '~stadt *f* commercial town; '2üblich *adj.* customary in trade; '~vertrag *m* commercial treaty, trade agreement.

'handeltreibend *adj.* trading.

'Hand|feger *m* (*-s/-*) hand-brush; '~fertigkeit *f* manual skill; '2fest *adj.* sturdy, strong; *fig.* well-founded, sound; '~feuerwaffen *f/pl.* small arms *pl.*; '~fläche *f* flat of the hand, palm; '2gearbeitet *adj.* hand-made; '~geld *n* earnest money; 🞄 bounty; '~gelenk *anat.* *n* wrist; '~gemenge *n* scuffle, mêlée; '~gepäck *n* hand luggage, *Am.* hand baggage; '~granate 🞄 *f* hand-grenade; '2greiflich *adj.* violent; *fig.* tangible, palpable; ~ *werden* turn violent, *Am. a.* get tough; '~griff *m* grasp; handle, grip; *fig.* manipulation; '~habe *fig. f* handle; '2haben *v/t.* (*ge-*, *h*) handle, manage; operate (*machine, etc.*); administer (*law*); '~karren *m* hand-cart; '~koffer *m* suitcase, *Am. a.* valise; '~kuß *m* kiss on the hand; '~langer *m* (*-s/-*) hodman, handy man; *fig.* dog's-body, henchman.

Händler ['hɛndlər] *m* (*-s/-*) dealer, trader.

'handlich *adj.* handy; manageable.

Handlung ['handluŋ] *f* (*-/-en*) act, action; deed; *thea.* action, plot; ✝ shop, *Am.* store.

'Handlungs|bevollmächtigte *m* proxy; '~gehilfe *m* clerk; shop-assistant, *Am.* salesclerk; '~reisende *m s. Handelsreisende*; '~weise *f* conduct; way of acting.

'Hand|rücken *m* back of the hand; '~schelle *f* handcuff, manacle; '~schlag *m* handshake; '~schreiben *n* autograph letter; '~schrift *f* handwriting; manuscript; '2-schriftlich 1. *adj.* hand-written; 2. *adv.* in one's own handwriting; '~schuh *m* glove; '~streich *m* surprise attack, coup de main; *im ~ nehmen* take by surprise; '~tasche *f* handbag, *Am. a.* purse; '~tuch *n* towel; '~voll *f* (-/-) handful; '~wagen *m* hand-cart; '~werk *n* (handi)craft, trade; '~werker *m* (-s/-) (handi)craftsman, artisan; workman; '~werkzeug *n* (kit of) tools *pl.*; '~wurzel *anat. f* wrist; '~zeichnung *f* drawing.

Hanf ♥ [hanf] *m* (-[e]s/*no pl.*) hemp.

Hang [haŋ] *m* (-[e]s/=e) slope, incline, declivity; hillside; *fig.* inclination, propensity (*zu* for; *zu inf.* to *inf.*); tendency (to).

Hänge|boden ['hɛŋə-] *m* hanging-loft; '~brücke △ *f* suspension bridge; '~lampe *f* hanging lamp; '~matte *f* hammock.

hängen ['hɛŋən] 1. *v/i.* (*irr.*, ge-, h) hang, be suspended; adhere, stick, cling (*an dat.* to); ~ *an* (*dat.*) be attached *or* devoted to; 2. *v/t.* (ge-, h) hang, suspend; '~bleiben *v/i.* (*irr.* bleiben, sep., -ge-, sein) get caught (up) (*an dat.* on, in); *fig.* stick (in the memory).

hänseln ['hɛnzəln] *v/t.* (ge-, h) tease (*wegen* about), F rag.

Hansestadt ['hanzə-] *f* Hanseatic town.

Hanswurst [hans'-] *m* (-es/-e, F =e) merry andrew; Punch; *fig. contp.* clown, buffoon.

Hantel ['hantəl] *f* (-/-n) dumb-bell.

hantieren [han'ti:rən] *v/i.* (*no* -ge-, h) be busy (*mit* with); work (*an dat.* on).

Happen ['hapən] *m* (-s/-) morsel, mouthful, bite; snack.

Harfe ♪ ['harfə] *f* (-/-n) harp.

Harke ✗ ['harkə] *f* (-/-n) rake; '2n *v/t. and v/i.* (ge-, h) rake.

harmlos *adj.* ['harmlo:s] harmless, innocuous; inoffensive.

Harmon|ie [harmo'ni:] *f* (-/-n) harmony (*a.* ♪); 2ieren *v/i.* (*no* -ge-, h) harmonize (*mit* with); *fig. a.* be in tune (with); ~ika ♪ [~'mo:nika] *f* (-/-s, *Harmoniken*) accordion; mouth-organ; 2isch *adj.* [~'mo:niʃ] harmonious.

Harn [harn] *m* (-[e]s/-e) urine; '~blase *anat. f* (urinary) bladder; '2en *v/i.* (ge-, h) pass water, urinate.

Harnisch ['harniʃ] *m* (-es/-e) armo(u)r; *in ~ geraten* be up in arms (*über acc.* about).

'**Harnröhre** *anat. f* urethra.

Harpun|e [har'pu:nə] *f* (-/-n) harpoon; 2ieren [~u'ni:rən] *v/t.* (*no* -ge-, h) harpoon.

hart [hart] 1. *adj.* hard; *fig. a.* harsh; heavy, severe; 2. *adv.* hard; ~ *arbeiten* work hard.

Härte ['hɛrtə] *f* (-/-n) hardness; *fig. a.* hardship; severity; '2n (ge-, h) 1. *v/t.* harden (*metal*); temper (*steel*); case-harden (*iron, steel*); 2. *v/i. and v/refl.* harden, become *or* grow hard; *steel*: temper.

'**Hart|geld** *n* coin(s *pl.*), specie; '~gummi *m* hard rubber; ✝ ebonite, vulcanite; '2herzig *adj.* hardhearted; 2köpfig *adj.* ['~kœpfiç] stubborn, headstrong; 2näckig *adj.* ['~nɛkiç] *p.* obstinate, obdurate; *effort:* dogged, tenacious; 𝔰 *ailment:* refractory.

Harz [ha:rts] *n* (-es/-e) resin; ♪ rosin; *mot* gum; '2ig *adj.* resinous.

Hasardspiel [ha'zart-] *n* game of chance, *fig.* gamble.

haschen ['haʃən] (ge-, h) 1. *v/t.* catch (hold of), snatch; *sich ~ children* play tag; 2. *v/i.*: ~ *nach* snatch at; *fig.* strain after (*effect*), fish for (*compliments*).

Hase ['ha:zə] *m* (-n/-n) zo. hare; *ein alter ~* an old hand, an old-timer.

Haselnuß ♥ ['ha:zəlnus] *f* hazelnut.

'**Hasen|braten** *m* roast hare; '~fuß F *fig. m* coward, F funk; '~panier F *n*: *das ~ ergreifen* take to one's heels; '~scharte 𝔰 *f* hare-lip.

Haß [has] *m* (*Hasses/no pl.*) hatred.

'**hassen** *v/t.* (ge-, h) hate.

häßlich *adj.* ['hɛsliç] ugly; *fig. a.* nasty, unpleasant.

Hast [hast] *f* (-/*no pl.*) hurry, haste; rush; *in wilder ~* in frantic haste; '2en *v/i.* (ge-, sein) hurry, hasten; rush; '2ig *adj.* hasty, hurried.

hätscheln ['hɛ:tʃəln] *v/t.* (ge-, h) caress, fondle, pet; pamper, coddle.

hatte ['hatə] *pret. of* haben.

Haube ['haubə] *f* (-/-n) bonnet (*a.* ⊕, *mot.*); cap; *orn.* crest, tuft; *mot. Am. a.* hood.

Haubitze ✗ [hau'bitsə] *f* (-/-n) howitzer.

Hauch [haux] *m* (-[e]s/✎, -e) breath; *fig.:* waft, whiff (*of perfume, etc.*); touch, tinge (*of irony, etc.*); '2en (ge-, h) 1. *v/i.* breathe; 2. *v/t.* breathe, whisper; *gr.* aspirate.

Haue ['hauə] *f* (-/-n) ✗ hoe, mattock; pick; F hiding, spanking; '2n ([*irr.*,] ge-, h) 1. *v/t.* hew (*coal, stone*); cut up (*meat*); chop (*wood*); cut (*hole, steps, etc.*); beat (*child*); *sich ~* (have a) fight; 2. *v/i.*: ~ *nach* cut at, strike out at.

Haufen ['haufən] *m* (-s/-) heap, pile (*both* F *a. fig.*); *fig.* crowd.

häufen ['hɔyfən] *v/t.* (ge-, h) heap

(up), pile (up); accumulate; *sich ~* pile up, accumulate; *fig.* become more frequent, increase.

'**häufig** *adj.* frequent; '**Ωkeit** *f* (-/no *pl.*) frequency.

'**Häufung** *fig. f* (-/-en) increase, *fig.* accumulation.

Haupt| [haupt] *n* (-[e]s/ᵘer) head; *fig.* chief, head, leader; '**~altar** *m* high altar; '**~anschluß** *teleph. m* subscriber's main station; '**~bahnhof** 🚂 *m* main *or* central station; '**~beruf** *m* full-time occupation; '**~buch** † *n* ledger; '**~darsteller** *thea. m* leading actor; '**~fach** *univ. n* main *or* principal subject, *Am. a.* major; '**~film** *m* feature · (film); '**~geschäft** *n* main transaction; main shop; '**~geschäftsstelle** *f* head *or* central office; '**~gewinn** *m* first prize; '**~grund** *m* main reason; **~handelsartikel** † ['haupthandəls⁹-] *m* staple.

Häuptling ['hɔyptliŋ] *m* (-s/-e) chief(tain).

'**Haupt|linie** 🚂 *f* main *or* trunk line; '**~mann** ✕ *m* (-[e]s/*Hauptleute*) captain; '**~merkmal** *n* characteristic feature; '**~postamt** *n* general post office, *Am.* main post office; '**~punkt** *m* main *or* cardinal point; '**~quartier** *n* headquarters *sg. or pl.*; '**~rolle** *thea. f* lead(ing part); '**~sache** *f* main thing *or* point; '**Ωsächlich** *adj.* main, chief, principal; '**~satz** *gr. m* main clause; '**~stadt** *f* capital; '**Ωstädtisch** *adj.* metropolitan; '**~straße** *f* main street; major road; '**~treffer** *m* first prize, jackpot; '**~verkehrsstraße** *f* main road; arterial road; '**~verkehrsstunden** *f/pl.*, '**~verkehrszeit** *f* rush hour(s *pl.*), peak hour(s *pl.*); '**~versammlung** *f* general meeting; '**~wort** *gr. n* (-[e]s/ᵘer) substantive, noun.

Haus [haus] *n* (-es/ᵘer) house; building; home, family, household; dynasty; † (business) house, firm; *parl.* House; *nach ~e* home; *zu ~e* at home, F in; **~angestellte** *f* (-n/-n) (house-)maid; **~apotheke** *f* (household) medicine-chest; '**~arbeit** *f* housework; '**~arrest** *m* house arrest; '**~arzt** *m* family doctor; '**~aufgaben** *f/pl.* homework, F prep; '**Ωbacken** *fig. adj.* homely; '**~bar** *f* cocktail cabinet; '**~bedarf** *m* household requirements *pl.*; '**~besitzer** *m* house-owner; '**~diener** *m* (man-)servant; *hotel:* porter, boots *sg.*

hausen ['hauzən] *v/i.* (ge-, h) live; play *or* work havoc (*in a place*).

'**Haus|flur** *m* (entrance-)hall, *esp. Am.* hallway; '**~frau** *f* housewife; '**~halt** *m* household; '**Ωhalten** *v/i.* (*irr. halten, sep.,* -ge-, h) be economical (*mit* with), economize (on);

~hälterin ['~hɛltərin] *f* (-/-nen) housekeeper; '**~halt(s)plan** *parl. m* budget; '**~haltung** *f* housekeeping; household, family; '**~haltwaren** *f/pl.* household articles *pl.*; '**~herr** *m* master of the family; landlord.

hausier|en [hau'zi:rən] *v/i.* (*no -ge-, h*) hawk, peddle (*mit et.* s.th.); *~ gehen* be a hawker *or* pedlar; **Ωer** *m* (-s/-) hawker, pedlar.

'**Haus|kleid** *n* house dress; '**~knecht** *m* boots; '**~lehrer** *m* private tutor.

häuslich *adj.* ['hɔysliç] domestic; domesticated; '**Ωkeit** *f* (-/no *pl.*) domesticity; family life; home.

'**Haus|mädchen** *n* (house-)maid; '**~mannskost** *f* plain fare; '**~meister** *m* caretaker; janitor; '**~mittel** *n* popular medicine; '**~ordnung** *f* rules *pl.* of the house; '**~rat** *m* household effects *pl.*; '**~recht** *n* domestic authority; '**~sammlung** *f* house-to-house collection; '**~schlüssel** *m* latchkey; front-door key; '**~schuh** *m* slipper.

Hauss|e † ['ho:s(ə)] *f* (-/-n) rise, boom; *~ier* [hos'je:] *m* (-s/-s) speculator for a rise, bull.

'**Haus|stand** *m* household; *e-n ~ gründen* set up house; '**~suchung** 🏛 *f* house search, domiciliary visit; *Am. a.* house check; '**~tier** *n* domestic animal; '**~tür** *f* front door; '**~verwalter** *m* steward; '**~wirt** *m* landlord; '**~wirtin** *f* (-/-nen) landlady.

Haut [haut] *f* (-/ᵘe) skin; hide; film; *bis auf die ~* to the skin; *aus der ~ fahren* jump out of one's skin; *F e-e ehrliche ~* an honest soul; '**~abschürfung** ᶿ *f* skin abrasion; '**~arzt** *m* dermatologist; '**~ausschlag** ᶿ *m* rash; '**Ωeng** *adj. garment:* skin-tight; '**~farbe** *f* complexion.

Hautgout [o'gu] *m* (-s/no *pl.*) high taste.

häutig *adj.* ['hɔytiç] membranous; covered with skin.

'**Haut|krankheit** *f* skin disease; '**~pflege** *f* care of the skin; '**~schere** *f* (e-e a pair of) cuticle scissors *pl.*

Havarie ⚓ [hava'ri:] *f* (-/-n) average.

H-Bombe ✕ ['ha:-] *f* H-bomb.

he *int.* [he:] hi!, hi there!; I say!

Hebamme ['he:p⁹amə] *f* midwife.

Hebe|baum ['he:bə-] *m* lever (*for raising heavy objects*); '**~bühne** *mot. f* lifting ramp; '**~eisen** *n* crowbar; '**~kran** *m* lifting crane.

Hebel ⊕ ['he:bəl] *m* (-s/-) lever; '**~arm** *m* lever arm.

heben ['he:bən] *v/t.* (*irr.,* ge-, h) lift (*a. sports*), raise (*a. fig.*); heave (*heavy load*); hoist; recover (*treas-*

ure); raise (sunken ship); fig. promote, improve, increase; sich ~ rise, go up.

Hecht ichth. [hɛçt] m (-[e]s/-e) pike.

Heck [hɛk] n (-[e]s/-e, -s) ⚓ stern; mot. rear; ✕ tail.

Hecke [ˈhɛkə] f (-/-n) ⚭ hedge; zo. brood, hatch; '2n v/t. and v/i. (ge-, h) breed, hatch; '~nrose ⚭ f dog-rose.   [(hallo!)

heda int. [ˈheːdaː] hi (there)!,]

Heer [heːr] n (-[e]s/-e) ✕ army; fig. a. host; '~esdienst m military service; '~esmacht f military force(s pl.); '~eszug m military expedition; '~führer m general; '~lager n (army) camp; '~schar f army, host; '~straße f military road; highway; '~zug m s. Heereszug.

Hefe [ˈheːfə] f (-/-n) yeast; barm.

Heft [hɛft] n (-[e]s/-e) dagger, etc.: haft; knife: handle; fig. reins pl.; exercise book; periodical, etc.: issue, number.

'**heft|en** v/t. (ge-, h) fasten, fix (an acc. on to); affix, attach (to); pin on (to); tack, baste (seam, etc.); stitch, sew (book); '2faden m basting thread.

'**heftig** adj. storm, anger, quarrel, etc.: violent, fierce; rain, etc.: heavy; pain, etc.: severe; speech, desire, etc.: vehement, passionate; p. irascible; '2keit f (-/-, -en) violence, fierceness; severity; vehemence; irascibility.

'**Heft|klammer** f paper-clip; '~pflaster n sticking plaster.

hegen [ˈheːgən] v/t. (ge-, h) preserve (game); nurse, tend (plants); have, entertain (feelings); harbo(u)r (fears, suspicions, etc.).

Hehler ⚖ [ˈheːlər] m (-s/-) receiver (of stolen goods); '~ei [~ˈraɪ] f (-/-en) receiving of stolen goods.

Heide [ˈhaɪdə] 1. m (-n/-n) heathen; 2. f (-/-n) heath(-land); — '~kraut ⚭ n heather; '~land n heath(-land).

'**Heiden|geld** F n pots pl. of money; '~lärm F m hullabaloo; '~spaß F m capital fun; '~tum n (-s/no pl.) heathenism.   [(-ish).]

heidnisch adj. [ˈhaɪdnɪʃ] heathen]

heikel adj. [ˈhaɪkəl] p. fastidious, particular; problem, etc.: delicate, awkward.

heil [haɪl] 1. adj. p. safe, unhurt; whole, sound; 2. 2 n (-[e]s/no pl.) welfare, benefit; eccl. salvation; 3. int. hail!

Heiland eccl. [ˈhaɪlant] m (-[e]s/-e) Saviour, Redeemer.

'**Heil|anstalt** f sanatorium, Am. a. sanitarium; '~bad n medicinal bath; spa; '2bar adj. curable; '2en (ge-) 1. v/t. (h) cure, heal; ~ von cure s.o. of; 2. v/i. (sein) heal (up); '~gehilfe m male nurse.

heilig adj. [ˈhaɪlɪç] holy; sacred; solemn; 2er Abend Christmas Eve; 2e [ˈ~gə] m, f (-n/-n) saint; '~en [ˈ~gən] v/t. (ge-, h) sanctify (a. fig.), hallow; '2keit f (-/no pl.) holiness; sacredness, sanctity; '~sprechen v/t. (irr. sprechen, sep., -ge-, h) canonize; '2sprechung f (-/-en) canonization; '2tum n (-[e]s/~er) sanctuary; sacred relic; 2ung f [ˈ~gʊŋ] f (-/-en) sanctification (a. fig.), hallowing.

'**Heil|kraft** f healing or curative power; '2kräftig adj. healing, curative; '~kunde f medical science; '2los fig. adj. confusion: utter, great; '~mittel n remedy, medicament; '~praktiker m non-medical practitioner; '~quelle f medicinal spring; '2sam adj. curative; fig. salutary.   [Army.]

Heilsarmee [ˈhaɪls?-] f Salvation]

'**Heil|ung** f (-/-en) cure, healing, successful treatment; '~verfahren n therapy.

heim [haɪm] 1. adv. home; 2. 2 n (-[e]s/-e) home; hostel; '2arbeit f homework, outwork.

Heimat [ˈhaɪmaːt] f (-/-, -en) home; own country; native land; '~land n own country; native land; '2lich adj. native; '2los adj. homeless; '~ort m home town or village; '~vertriebene m expellee.

Heimchen zo. [ˈhaɪmçən] n (-s/-) cricket.

'**heimisch** adj. trade, industry, etc.: home, local, domestic; ⚭, zo., etc.: native, indigenous; ~ werden settle down; become established; sich ~ fühlen feel at home.

Heim|kehr [ˈhaɪmkeːr] f (-/no pl.) return (home), homecoming; '2kehren v/i. (sep., -ge-, sein); '2kommen v/i. (irr. kommen, sep., -ge-, sein) return home.

'**heimlich** adj. plan, feeling, etc.: secret; meeting, organization, etc.: clandestine; glance, movement, etc.: stealthy, furtive.

'**Heim|reise** f homeward journey; '2suchen v/t. (sep., -ge-, h) disaster, etc.: afflict, strike; ghost: haunt; God: visit, punish; '~tücke f underhand malice, treachery; 2tückisch adj. malicious, treacherous, insidious; 2wärts adv. [ˈ~vɛrts] homeward(s); '~weg m way home; '~weh n homesickness, nostalgia; ~ haben be homesick.

Heirat [ˈhaɪraːt] f (-/-en) marriage; '2en (ge-, h) 1. v/t. marry; 2. v/i. marry, get married.

'**Heirats|antrag** m offer or proposal of marriage; '2fähig adj. marriageable; '~kandidat m possible marriage partner; '~schwindler m marriage impostor; '~vermittler m matrimonial agent.

heiser adj. ['haɪzər] hoarse; husky; '2keit f (-/no pl.) hoarseness; huskiness.

heiß adj. [haɪs] hot; fig. a. passionate, ardent; mir ist ~ I am or feel hot.

heißen ['haɪsən] (irr., ge-, h) 1. v/t.: e-n Lügner ~ call s.o. a liar; willkommen ~ welcome; 2. v/i. be called; mean; wie ~ Sie? what is your name?; was heißt das auf englisch? what's that in English?

heiter adj. ['haɪtər] day, weather: bright; sky: bright, clear; p., etc.: cheerful, gay, serene; '2keit f (-/no pl.) brightness; cheerfulness, gaiety; serenity.

heiz|en ['haɪtsən] (ge-, h) 1. v/t. heat (room, etc.); light (stove); fire (boiler); 2. v/i. stove, etc.: give out heat; turn on the heating; mit Kohlen ~ burn coal; '2er m (-s/-) stoker, fireman; '2kissen n electric heating pad; '2körper m central heating radiator; ⚙ heating element; '2material n fuel; '2ung f (-/-en) heating.

Held [hɛlt] m (-en/-en) hero.

'Helden|gedicht n epic (poem); '2haft adj. heroic, valiant; '_mut m heroism, valo(u)r; 2mütig adj. ['_my:tɪç] heroic; '_tat f heroic or valiant deed; '_tum n (-[e]s/no pl.) heroism.

helfen ['hɛlfən] v/i. (dat.) (irr., ge-, h) help, assist, aid; ~ gegen be good for; sich nicht zu ~ wissen be helpless.

'Helfer m (-s/-) helper, assistant; '_shelfer m accomplice.

hell adj. [hɛl] sound, voice, light, etc.: clear; light, flame, etc.: bright; hair: fair; colour: light; ale: pale; '_blau adj. light-blue; '_blond adj. very fair; '_hörig adj. p. quick of hearing; fig. perceptive; ⚠ poorly sound-proofed; '2seher m clairvoyant.

Helm [hɛlm] m ([-e]s/-e) ⚔ helmet; ⚠ dome, cupola; ⚓ helm; '_busch m plume.

Hemd [hɛmt] n (-[e]s/-en) shirt; vest; '_bluse f shirt-blouse, Am. shirtwaist. [hemisphere.\
Hemisphäre [he:mi'sfɛ:rə] f (-/-n)]

hemm|en ['hɛmən] v/t. (ge-, h) check, stop (movement, etc.); stem (stream, flow of liquid); hamper (free movement, activity); be a hindrance to; psych.: gehemmt sein be inhibited; '2nis n (-ses/-se) hindrance, impediment; '2schuh m slipper; fig. hindrance, F drag (für acc. on); '2ung f (-/-en) stoppage, check; psych.: inhibition.

Hengst zo. [hɛŋst] m (-es/-e) stallion.

Henkel ['hɛŋkəl] m (-s/-) handle, ear.

Henker ['hɛŋkər] m (-s/-) hangman, executioner; F: zum ~! hang it (all)!

Henne zo. ['hɛnə] f (-/-n) hen.

her adv. [he:r] here; hither; es ist schon ein Jahr ~, daß ... or seit ... it is a year since ...; wie lange ist es ~, seit ... how long is it since ...; hinter (dat.) ~ sein be after; ~ damit! out with it!

herab adv. [hɛ'rap] down, downward; _lassen v/t. (irr. lassen, sep., -ge-, h) let down, lower; fig. sich ~ condescend; _lassend adj. condescending; _setzen v/t. (sep., -ge-, h) take down; fig. belittle, disparage s.o.; ⚕ reduce, lower, cut (price, etc.); 2setzung fig. f (-/-en) reduction; disparagement; _steigen v/i. (irr. steigen, sep., -ge-, sein) climb down, descend; _würdigen v/t. (sep., -ge-, h) degrade, belittle, abase

heran adv. [hɛ'ran] close, near; up; nur ~! come on!; _bilden v/t. (sep., -ge-, h) train, educate (zu as s.th., to be s.th.); _kommen v/i. (irr. kommen, sep., -ge-, sein) come or draw near; approach; ~ an (acc.) come up to s.o.; measure up to; ~ wachsen v/i. (irr. wachsen, sep., -ge-, sein) grow (up) (zu into).

herauf adv. [hɛ'rauf] up(wards), up here; upstairs; _beschwören v/t. (irr. schwören, sep., no -ge-, h) evoke, call up, conjure up (spirit, etc.); fig. a. bring about, provoke, give rise to (war, etc.); _steigen v/i. (irr. steigen, sep., -ge-, sein) climb up (here), ascend; _ziehen v/t. (irr. ziehen, sep., -ge-, h) 1. v/t. (h) pull or hitch up (trousers, etc.); 2. v/i. (sein) cloud, etc.: come up.

heraus adv. [hɛ'raus] out, out here; zum Fenster ~ out of the window; ~ mit der Sprache! speak out!; _bekommen v/t. (irr. kommen, sep., no -ge-, h) get out; get (money) back; fig. find out; _bringen v/t. (irr. bringen, sep., -ge-, h) bring or get out; thea. stage; _finden v/t. (irr. finden, sep., -ge-, h) find out; fig. a. discover; 2forderer m (-s/-) challenger; _fordern v/t. (sep., -ge-, h) challenge (to a fight); provoke; 2forderung f (-/-en) challenge; provocation; _geben v/t. (irr. geben, sep., -ge-, h) 1. v/t. surrender; hand over; restore; edit (periodical, etc.); publish (book, etc.); issue (regulations, etc.); 2. v/i. give change (auf acc. for); 2geber m (-s/-) editor; publisher; _kommen v/i. (irr. kommen, sep., -ge-, sein) come out; fig. a. appear, be published; _nehmen v/t. (irr. nehmen, sep., -ge-, h) take out; sich viel ~ take liberties; _putzen v/t. (sep., -ge-, h) dress up; sich ~ dress (o.s.)

up; ~reden v/refl. (sep., -ge-, h) talk one's way out; ~stellen v/t. (sep., -ge-, h) put out; fig. emphasize, set forth; sich ~ emerge, turn out; ~strecken v/t. (sep., -ge-, h) stretch out; put out; ~streichen v/t. (irr. streichen, sep., -ge-, h) cross out, delete (word, etc.); fig. extol, praise; ~winden fig. v/refl. (irr. winden, sep., -ge-, h) extricate o.s. (aus from).

herb adj. [hɛrp] fruit, flavour, etc.: tart; wine, etc.: dry; features, etc.: austere; criticism, etc.: harsh; disappointment, etc.: bitter.

herbei adv. [hɛr'baɪ] here; ~! come here!; ~eilen [hɛr'baɪ⁹-] v/i. (sep., -ge-, sein) come hurrying; ~führen fig. v/t. (sep., -ge-, h) cause, bring about, give rise to; ~schaffen v/t. (sep., -ge-, h) bring along; procure.

Herberge ['hɛrbɛrgə] f (-/-n) shelter, lodging; inn.

'Herbheit f (-/no pl.) tartness; dryness; fig.: austerity; harshness, bitterness.

Herbst [hɛrpst] m (-[e]s/-e) autumn, Am. a. fall.

Herd [he:rt] m (-[e]s/-e) hearth, fireplace; stove; fig. seat, focus.

Herde ['he:rdə] f (-/-n) herd (of cattle, pigs, etc.) (contp. a. fig.); flock (of sheep, geese, etc.).

herein adv. [hɛ'raɪn] in (here); ~! come in!; ~brechen fig. v/i. (irr. brechen, sep., -ge-, sein) night: fall; ~ über (acc.) misfortune, etc.: befall; ~fallen fig. v/i. (irr. fallen, sep., -ge-, sein) be taken in.

'her|fallen v/i. (irr. fallen, sep., -ge-, sein): ~ über (acc.) attack (a. fig.), fall upon; F fig. pull to pieces; '2gang m course of events, details pl.; ~geben v/t. (irr. geben, sep., -ge-, h) give up, part with, return; yield; sich ~ zu lend o.s. to; ~gebracht fig. adj. traditional; customary; ~halten (irr. halten, sep., -ge-, h) 1. v/t. hold out; 2. v/i. ~ müssen be the one to pay or suffer (für for).

Hering ichth. ['he:rɪŋ] m (-s/-e) herring.

'her|kommen v/i. (irr. kommen, sep., -ge-, sein) come or get here; come or draw near; ~ von come from; fig. a. be due to, be caused by; ~kömmlich adj. ['~kœmlɪç] traditional; customary; '2kunft ['~kunft] f (-/no pl.) origin; birth, descent; ~leiten v/t. (sep., -ge-, h) lead here; fig. derive (von from); '2leitung fig. f derivation.

Herold ['he:rɔlt] m (-[e]s/-e) herald.

Herr [hɛr] m (-n, ⚓-en/-en) lord; master; eccl. the Lord; gentleman; ~ Maier Mr Maier; mein ~ Sir; m-e ~en gentlemen; ~ der Situation master of the situation.

'Herren|bekleidung f men's cloth-

ing; '~einzel n tennis: men's singles pl.; '~haus n manor-house; 2~los adj. ['~lo:s] ownerless; '~reiter m sports: gentleman-jockey; '~schneider m men's tailor; '~zimmer n study; smoking-room.

herrichten ['hɛ:r-] v/t. (sep., -ge-, h) arrange, prepare.

'herrisch adj. imperious, overbearing; voice, etc.: commanding, peremptory.

'herrlich adj. excellent, glorious, magnificent, splendid; '2keit f (-/-en) glory, splendo(u)r.

'Herrschaft f (-/-en) rule, dominion (über acc. of); fig. mastery; master and mistress; m-e ~en! ladies and gentlemen!; '2lich adj. belonging to a master or landlord; fig. high-class, elegant.

herrsch|en ['hɛrʃən] v/i. (ge-, h) rule (über acc. over); monarch: reign (over); govern; fig. prevail, be; '2er m (-s/-) ruler; sovereign, monarch; '2sucht f thirst for power; '~süchtig adj. thirsting for power; imperious.

'her|rühren v/i. (sep., -ge-, h): ~ von come from, originate with; '~sagen v/t. (sep., -ge-, h) recite; say (prayer); ~stammen v/i. (sep., -ge-, h): ~ von or aus be descended from; come from; be derived from; '~stellen v/t. (sep., -ge-, h) place here; ✝ make, manufacture, produce; '2stellung f (-/-en) manufacture, production.

herüber adv. [hɛ'ry:bər] over (here), across.

herum adv. [hɛ'rum] (a)round; about; ~führen v/t. (sep., -ge-, h) show a)round; ~ in (dat.) show over; ~lungern v/i. (sep., -ge-, h) loaf or loiter or hang about; ~reichen v/t. (sep., -ge-, h) pass or hand round; ~sprechen v/refl. (irr. sprechen, sep., -ge-, h) get about, spread; ~treiben v/refl. (irr. treiben, sep., -ge-, h) F gad or knock about.

herunter adv. [hɛ'runtər] down (here); downstairs; von oben ~ down from above; ~bringen v/t. (irr. bringen, sep., -ge-, h) bring down; fig. a. lower, reduce; ~kommen v/i. (irr. kommen, sep., -ge-, sein) come down(stairs); fig. come down in the world; deteriorate; ~machen v/t. (sep., -ge-, h) take down; turn (collar, etc.) down; fig. give s.o. a dressing-down; fig. pull to pieces; ~reißen v/t. (irr. reißen, sep., -ge-, h) pull or tear down; fig. pull to pieces; ~sein F fig. v/i. (irr. sein, sep., -ge-, sein) be low in health; ~wirtschaften v/t. (sep., -ge-, h) run down.

hervor adv. [hɛr'fo:r] forth, out; ~bringen v/t. (irr. bringen, sep.,

-ge-, h) bring out, produce (a. fig.); yield (fruit); fig. utter (word); ~ **gehen** v/i. (irr. gehen, sep., -ge-, sein) p. come (aus from); come off (victorious) (from); fact, etc.: emerge (from); be clear or apparent (from); ~**heben** fig. v/t. (irr. heben, sep., -ge-, h) stress, emphasize; give prominence to; ~**holen** v/t. (sep., -ge-, h) produce; ~**ragen** v/i. (sep., -ge-, h) project (über acc. over); fig. tower (above); ~**ragend** adj. projecting, prominent; fig. outstanding, excellent; ~**rufen** v/t. (irr. rufen, sep, -ge-, h) thea. call for; fig. arouse, evoke; ~**stechend** fig. adj. outstanding, striking; conspicuous.

Herz [herts] n (-ens/-en) anat. heart (a. fig.); cards: hearts pl.; fig. courage, spirit, sich ein ~ fasser take heart; mit ganzem ~en whole-heartedly, sich et. zu ~en nehmen take s.th. to heart; es nicht übers ~ bringen zu inf. not to have the heart to inf.; ~**anfall** m heart attack.

'**Herzens|brecher** m (-s/-) ladykiller; ~**lust** f: nach ~ to one's heart's content; '~**wunsch** m heart's desire.

'**herz|ergreifend** fig. adj. heartmoving, '~**fehler** ♂ m cardiac defect; '2**gegend** anat. f cardiac region; ~**haft** adj. hearty, good; ~**ig** adj. lovely, Am. a. cute; 2**Infarkt** ♂ ['~?infarkt] m (-[e]s/-e) cardiac infarction, '2**klopfen** ♂ n (-s/no pl.) palpitation; ~**krank** adj. having heart trouble; '~**lich** 1. adj. heartfelt; cordial, hearty; ~**es** Beileid sincere sympathy; 2. adv.: ~ gern with pleasure; '~**los** adj. heartless; unfeeling

Herzog ['hertso:k] m (-[e]s/~e, -e) duke, ~**in** f (-/-nen) duchess; '~**tum** n (-[e]s/~er) dukedom, duchy.

'**Herz|schlag** ♂ m heartbeat; ♂ heart failure; ~**schwäche** ♂ f cardiac insufficiency; ~**verpflanzung** ♂ f heart transplant; '2**zerreißend** adj. heart-rending.

Hetz|e ['hetsə] f (-/-n) hurry, rush; instigation (gegen acc. against); baiting (of); '2**en** (ge-) 1. v/t. (h) course (hare); bait (bear, etc.); hound hunt, chase (animal); fig. hurry, rush; sich ~ hurry, rush; e-n Hund auf j-n ~ set a dog at s.o.; 2. v/i. (h) fig.: cause discord; agitate (gegen against); 3. fig. v/i. (sein) hurry, rush; '~**er** fig. m (-s/-) instigator; agitator; '2**erisch** adj. virulent, inflammatory; '~**jagd** f hunt(ing); fig.: virulent campaign; rush, hurry; '~**presse** f yellow press.

Heu [hɔy] n (-[e]s/no pl.) hay; '~**boden** m hayloft.

Heuchel|ei [hɔyçə'laɪ] f (-/-en) hypocrisy; '2**n** (ge-, h) 1. v/t. sim-

ulate, feign, affect; 2. v/i. feign, dissemble; play the hypocrite. '**Heuchler** m (-s/-) hypocrite; '2**isch** adj. hypocritical.

heuer ['hɔyər] 1. adv. this year; 2. ♂ ♦ f (-/-n) pay, wages pl.; '~**n** v/t. (ge-, h) hire; ♦ engage, sign on (crew), charter (ship).

heulen ['hɔylən] v/i. (ge-, h) wind, etc. howl; storm, wind, etc.: roar; siren wail, p. howl, cry.

'**Heu|schnupfen** ♂ m hay-fever; ~**schrecke** zo. ['~frekə] f (-/-n) grasshopper, locust.

heut|e adv ['hɔytə] today; ~ abend this evening, tonight; ~ früh, ~ morgen this morning; ~ in acht Tagen today or this day week; ~ vor acht Tagen a week ago today; '~**ig** adj this day's, today's; present; ~**zutage** adv. ['hɔyttsutaːgə] nowadays, these days.

Hexe ['heksə] f (-/-n) witch, sorceress; fig hell-cat; hag; '2**n** v/i. (ge-, h) practice witchcraft; F fig. work miracles, ~**nkessel** fig. m inferno; '~**nmeister** m wizard, sorcerer; '~**nschuß** ♂ m lumbago; ~**rei** [~'raɪ] f (-/-en) witchcraft, sorcery, magic

Hieb [hi:p] 1. m (-[e]s/-e) blow, stroke, lash, cut (of whip, etc.); a. punch (with fist); fenc. cut; ~**e** pl. hiding, thrashing; 2. ♀ pret. of hauen

hielt [hi:lt] pret. of halten.

hier adv [hi:r] here; in this place; ~**!** present!; ~ entlang! this way!

hier|an adv. ['hi:'ran, when emphatic 'hi:ran] at or by or in or on or to it or this; ~**auf** adv. ['hi:'rauf, when emphatic 'hi:rauf] on it or this; after this or that, then; ~**aus** adv. ['hi:'raus, when emphatic 'hi:raus] from or out of it or this; ~**bei** adv. ['hi:r'baɪ, when emphatic 'hi:rbaɪ] here, in this case, in connection with this; ~**durch** adv. ['hi:r'durç, when emphatic 'hi:rdurç] through here, by this, hereby; ~**für** adv. ['hi:r'fy:r, when emphatic 'hi:rfy:r] for it or this; ~**her** adv. ['hi:r'he:r, when emphatic 'hi:rhe:r] here, hither, bis ~ as far as here; ~**in** adv. ['hi:'rin, when emphatic 'hi:rin] in it or this, in here, ~**mit** adv. ['hi:r'mit, when emphatic 'hi:rmit] with it or this, herewith; ~**nach** adv. ['hi:r'na:x, when emphatic 'hi:rna:x] after it or this; according to this; ~**über** adv. ['hi:'ry:bər, when emphatic 'hi:ry:bər] over it or this; over here; on this (subject); ~**unter** adv. ['hi:'runtər, when emphatic 'hi:runtər] under it or this; among these; by this or that; ~**von** adv. ['hi:r'fon, when emphatic 'hi:rfon] of or from it or this; ~**zu** adv. ['hi:r'tsu:, when emphatic 'hi:rtsu:]

with it *or* this; (in addition) to this.

hiesig *adj.* ['hi:ziç] of *or* in this place *or* town, local.

hieß [hi:s] *pret. of* heißen.

Hilfe ['hilfə] *f* (-/-n) help; aid, assistance; succour; relief (für to); **∼!** help!; *mit* **∼** *von* with the help *or* aid of; **'∼ruf** *m* shout *or* cry for help.

'hilf|los *adj.* helpless; **'∼reich** *adj.* helpful.

'Hilfs|aktion *f* relief measures *pl.*; **'∼arbeiter** *m* unskilled worker *or* labo(u)rer; **'2bedürftig** *adj.* needy, indigent; **'∼lehrer** *m* assistant teacher; **'∼mittel** *n* aid; device; remedy; expedient; **∼motor** *m*: *Fahrrad mit* **∼** motor-assisted bicycle; **'∼quelle** *f* resource; **'∼schule** *f* elementary school for backward children; **'∼werk** *n* relief organization. [berry.⟩

Himbeere ♀ ['himbe:rə] *f* rasp-⟩

Himmel ['himəl] *m* (-s/-) sky, heavens *pl.*; *eccl.*, *fig.* heaven; **∼bett** *n* tester-bed; **2blau** *adj.* sky-blue; **'∼fahrt** *eccl. f* ascension (of Christ); Ascension-day; **2schreiend** *adj.* crying.

'Himmels|gegend *f* region of the sky; cardinal point; **'∼körper** *m* celestial body; **'∼richtung** *f* point of the compass, cardinal point; direction; **'∼strich** *m* region, climate zone.

'himmlisch *adj.* celestial, heavenly.

hin *adv.* [hin] there; gone, lost; **∼** *und her* to and fro, *Am.* back and forth; **∼** *und wieder* now and again *or* then; **∼** *und zurück* there and back.

hinab *adv.* [hi'nap] down; **∼steigen** *v/i.* (*irr.* steigen, *sep.*, -ge-, sein) climb down, descend.

hinarbeiten ['hin°-] *v/i.* (*sep.*, -ge-, h): **∼** *auf* (*acc.*) work for *or* towards.

hinauf *adv.* [hi'nauf] up (there); upstairs; **∼gehen** *v/i.* (*irr.* gehen, *sep.*, -ge-, sein) go up(stairs) *or* prices, wages, *etc.*: go up, rise; **∼steigen** *v/i.* (*irr.* steigen, *sep.*, -ge-, sein) climb up, ascend.

hinaus *adv.* [hi'naus] out; **∼** *mit euch!* out with you!; *auf* (*viele*) *Jahre* **∼** for (many) years (to come); **∼gehen** *v/i.* (*irr.* gehen, *sep.*, -ge-, sein) go *or* walk out; **∼** *über* (*acc.*) go beyond, exceed; **∼** *auf* (*acc.*) *window, etc.*: look out on, overlook; *intention, etc.*: drive *or* aim at; **∼laufen** *v/i.* (*irr.* laufen, *sep.*, -ge-, sein) run *or* rush out; **∼** *auf* (*acc.*) come *or* amount to; **∼schieben** *fig.* *v/t.* (*irr.* schieben, *sep.*, -ge-, h) put off, postpone, defer; **∼werfen** *v/t.* (*irr.* werfen, *sep.*, -ge-, h) throw out (*aus* of); turn *or* throw *or* F chuck *s.o.* out.

'Hin|blick *m*: *im* **∼** *auf* (*acc.*) in view of, with regard to; **'2bringen** *v/t.* (*irr.* bringen, *sep.*, -ge-, h) take there; while away, pass (*time*).

hinder|lich *adj.* ['hindərliç] hindering, impeding; *j-m* **∼** *sein* be in s.o.'s way; **∼n** *v/t.* (ge-, h) hinder, hamper (*bei*, *in dat.* in); **∼** *an* (*dat.*) prevent from; **'2nis** *n* (-ses/-se) hindrance; *sports*: obstacle; turf, *etc.*: fence; **'2nisrennen** *n* obstacle-race.

hin'durch *adv.* through; all through, throughout; across.

hinein *adv.* [hi'nain] in; **∼** *mit dir!* in you go!; **∼gehen** *v/i.* (*irr.* gehen, *sep.*, -ge-, sein) go in; **∼** *in* (*acc.*) go into; *in den Topf gehen ... hinein* the pot holds *or* takes ...

'Hin|fahrt *f* journey *or* way there; **'2fallen** *v/i.* (*irr.* fallen, *sep.*, -ge-, sein) fall (down); **'2fällig** *adj. p.* frail; *regulation, etc.*: invalid; **∼** *machen* invalidate, render invalid.

hing [hiŋ] *pret. of* hängen 1.

'Hin|gabe *f* devotion (*an acc.* to); **'2geben** *v/t.* (*irr.* geben, *sep.*, -ge-, h) give up *or* away; *sich* **∼** (*dat.*) give o.s. to; devote o.s. to; **'∼gebung** *f* (-/-en) devotion; **'2gehen** *v/i.* (*irr.* gehen, *sep.*, -ge-, sein) go *or* walk there; go (*zu* to); *path, etc.*: lead there; lead (*zu to a place*); **'2halten** *v/t.* (*irr.* halten, *sep.*, -ge-, h) hold out (*object, etc.*); put *s.o.* off.

hinken ['hiŋkən] *v/i.* (ge-) **1.** (h) limp (*auf dem rechten Fuß* with one's right leg), have a limp; **2.** (sein) limp (along).

'hin|länglich *adj.* sufficient, adequate; **'∼legen** *v/t.* (*sep.*, -ge-, h) lay *or* put down; *sich* **∼** lie down; **∼nehmen** *v/t.* (*irr.* nehmen, *sep.*, -ge-, h) accept, take; put up with; **∼raffen** *v/t.* (*sep.*, -ge-, h) *death, etc.*: snatch *s.o.* away, carry *s.o.* off; **∼reichen** (*sep.*, -ge-, h) **1.** *v/t.* reach *or* stretch *or* hold out (*dat.* to); **2.** *v/i.* suffice; **∼reißen** *fig.* *v/t.* (*irr.* reißen, *sep.*, -ge-, h) carry away; enrapture, ravish; **∼reißend** *adj.* ravishing, captivating; **∼richten** *v/t.* (*sep.*, -ge-, h) execute, put to death; **2richtung** *f* execution; **'∼setzen** *v/t.* (*sep.*, -ge-, h) set *or* put down; *sich* **∼** sit down; **2sicht** *f* regard, respect; *in* **∼** *auf* (*acc.*) = **∼sichtlich** *prp.* (*gen.*) with regard to, as to, concerning; **'∼stellen** *v/t.* (*sep.*, -ge-, h) place; put; put down; *et.* **∼** *als* represent s.th. as; make s.th. appear (as).

hintan|setzen [hint'an-] *v/t.* (*sep.*, -ge-, h) set aside; **2setzung** *f* (-/-en) setting aside; **∼stellen** *v/t.* (*sep.*, -ge-, h) set aside; **2stellung** *f* (-/-en) setting aside.

hinten *adv.* ['hintən] behind, at the

back; in the background; in the rear.

hinter *prp.* ['hıntər] **1.** (*dat.*) behind, *Am. a.* back of; ~ *sich lassen* outdistance; **2.** (*acc.*) behind; '2**bein** *n* hind leg; 2**bliebenen** *pl.* [‿'bliːbənən] *the* bereaved *pl.*; surviving dependants *pl.*; ‿'**bringen** *v/t.* (*irr.* bringen, no -ge-, h): *j-m et.* ~ inform s.o. of s.th. (secretly); ‿ei'**nander** *adv.* one after the other; in succession; '2**gedanke** *m* ulterior motive; ‿'**gehen** *v/t.* (*irr.* gehen, no -ge-, h) deceive, F doublecross; 2'**gehung** *f* (-/-en) deception; '2**grund** *m* background (*a. fig.*); '2**halt** *m* ambush; ‿**hältig** *adj.* ['‿hɛltıç] insidious; underhand; '2**haus** *n* back *or* rear building; ‿'**her** *adv.* behind; afterwards; '2**hof** *m* backyard; '2**kopf** *m* back of the head; ‿'**lassen** *v/t.* (*irr.* lassen, no -ge-, h) leave (behind); 2'**lassenschaft** *f* (-/-en) property (left), estate; ‿'**legen** *v/t.* (no -ge-, h) deposit, lodge (*bei* with); 2'**legung** *f* (-/-en) deposit(ion); '2**list** *f* (-/-en) craftiness; insidiousness; '‿**listig** *adj.* deceitful; crafty; insidious; '2**mann** *m* ⚔ rear-rank man; *fig.*: ♱ subsequent endorser; *pol.* backer; wire-puller; instigator; '2**n** F *m* (-s/-) backside, behind, bottom; '2**rad** *n* rear wheel; ‿**rücks** *adv.* ['‿ryks] from behind; *fig.* behind his, *etc.* back; '2**seite** *f* back; '2**teil** *n* back (part); rear (part); F *s.* Hintern; ‿'**treiben** *v/t.* (*irr.* treiben, no -ge-, h) thwart, frustrate; '2**treppe** *f* backstairs *pl.*; '2**tür** *f* back door; ‿'**ziehen** ⅎ *v/t.* (*irr.* ziehen, no -ge-, h) evade (*tax, duty, etc.*); 2'**ziehung** *f* evasion.

hinüber *adv.* [hı'nyːbər] over (there); across.

Hin- und 'Rückfahrt *f* journey there and back, *Am.* round trip.

hinunter *adv.* [hı'nuntər] down (there); downstairs; ‿**schlucken** *v/t.* (*sep.*, -ge-, h) swallow (down); *fig.* swallow.

'**Hinweg**[1] *m* way there *or* out.

hinweg[2] *adv.* [hın'vɛk] away, off; ‿**gehen** *v/i.* (*irr.* gehen, *sep.*, -gesein): ~ *über* (*acc.*) go *or* walk over *or* across; *fig.* pass over, ignore; ‿**kommen** *v/i.* (*irr.* kommen, *sep.*, -ge-, sein): ~ *über* (*acc.*) get over (*a. fig.*); ‿**sehen** *v/i.* (*irr.* sehen, *sep.*, -ge-, h): ~ *über* (*acc.*) see *or* look over; *fig.* overlook, shut one's eyes to; ‿**setzen** *v/refl.* (*sep.*, -ge-, h): *sich* ~ *über* (*acc.*) ignore, disregard, make light of.

Hin|**weis** ['hınvaıs] *m* (-es/-e) reference (*auf acc.* to); hint (at); indication (of); '2**weisen** (*irr.* weisen, *sep.*, -ge-, h) **1.** *v/t.*: *j-n* ~ *auf* (*acc.*) draw *or* call s.o.'s attention to; **2.** *v/i.*: ~

auf (*acc.*) point at *or* to, indicate (*a. fig.*); *fig.*: point out; hint at; '2**werfen** *v/t.* (*irr.* werfen, *sep.*, -ge-, h) throw down; *fig.*: dash off (*sketch, etc.*); say *s.th.* casually; '2**wirken** *v/i.* (*sep.*, -ge-, h): ~ *auf* (*acc.*) work towards; use one's influence to; '2**ziehen** (*irr.* ziehen, *sep.*, -ge-) **1.** *fig. v/t.* (h) attract *or* draw there; *sich* ~ *space*: extend (*bis zu* to), stretch (to); *time*: drag on; **2.** *v/i.* (sein) go *or* move there; '2**zielen** *fig. v/i.* (*sep.*, -ge-, h): ~ *auf* (*acc.*) aim *or* drive at.

hin'zu *adv.* there; near; in addition; ‿**fügen** *v/t.* (*sep.*, -ge-, h) add (zu to) (*a. fig.*), 2'**fügung** *f* (-/-en) addition; ‿**kommen** *v/i.* (*irr.* kommen, *sep.*, -ge-, sein) come up (zu to); supervene; be added; *es kommt* (noch) *hinzu, daß* add to this that, (and) moreover; ‿**rechnen** *v/t.* (*sep.*, -ge-, h) add (zu to), include (in, among); ‿**setzen** *v/t.* (*sep.*, -ge-, h) *s.* hinzufügen; ‿**treten** *v/i.* (*irr.* treten, *sep.*, -ge-, sein) *s.* hinzukommen; join; ‿**ziehen** *v/t.* (*irr.* ziehen, *sep* , -ge-, h) call in (*doctor, etc.*).

Hirn [hırn] *n* (-[e]s/-e) *anat.* brain; *fig.* brains *pl.*, mind; '‿**gespinst** *n* figment of the mind, chimera; '2**los** *fig. adj.* brainless, senseless; '‿**schale** *anat.* f brain-pan, cranium; '‿**schlag** 🞗 *m* apoplexy; '2**verbrannt** *adj.* crazy, F crack-brained, cracky.

Hirsch *zo.* [hırʃ] *m* (-es/-e) *species*: deer; stag, hart; '‿**geweih** *n* (stag's) antlers *pl.*; '‿**kuh** *f* hind; '‿**leder** *n* buckskin, deerskin.

Hirse ♣ ['hırzə] *f* (-/-n) millet.

Hirt [hırt] *m* (-en/-en), ‿**e** ['‿ə] *m* (-n/-n) herdsman; shepherd.

hissen ['hısən] *v/t.* (*ge-*, h) hoist, raise (*flag*); ♣ *a.* trice up (*sail*).

Histori|**ker** [hı'stoːrıkər] *m* (-s/-) historian, **2sch** *adj.* historic(al).

Hitz|**e** ['hıtsə] *f* (-/*no pl.*) heat; '2**ebeständig** *adj.* heat-resistant, heat-proof; ‿**ewelle** *f* heat-wave, hot spell; '2**ig** *adj. p.* hot-tempered, hot-headed; *discussion*: heated; '‿**kopf** *m* hothead; '‿**schlag** 🞗 *m* heat-stroke.

hob [hoːp] *pret. of* heben.

Hobel ⊕ ['hoːbəl] *m* (-s/-) plane; '‿**bank** *f* carpenter's bench; '2**n** *v/t.* (ge-, h) plane.

hoch [hoːx] **1.** *adj.* high; *church spire, tree, etc.*: tall; *position, etc.*: high, important; *guest, etc.*: distinguished; *punishment, etc.*: heavy, severe; *age*: great, old; *hohe See* open sea, high seas *pl.*; **2.** *adv.*: ~ *lebe* ...! long live ...! **3.** 2 *n* (-s/-s) cheer; toast; *meteorology*: high (-pressure area).

'**hoch**|**achten** *v/t.* (*sep.*, -ge-, h) esteem highly; '2**achtung** *f* high esteem or respect; '‿achtungsvoll 1. adj. (most) respectful; 2. adv. correspondence: yours faithfully or sincerely, esp. Am. yours truly; '2adel m greater or higher nobility; '2amt eccl. n high mass; 2antenne f overhead aerial; '2bahn f elevated or overhead railway, Am. elevated railroad; 2betrieb m intense activity, rush; '2burg fig. f stronghold; '‿deutsch adj. High or standard German; 2druck m high pressure (a. fig.); mit ‿ arbeiten work at high pressure; 2ebene f plateau, tableland; '‿fahrend adj. highhanded, arrogant; ‿fein adj. superfine; '2form f in ‿ in top form; 2frequenz ≠ f high frequency; 2gebirge ⊣ high mountains pl.; 2genuß m great enjoyment; 2glanz m high polish; '2haus n multi-stor(e)y building, skyscraper; ‿herzig adj. nobleminded; generous; 2herzigkeit f (-/-en) noble-mindedness; generosity; '2konjunktur ✦ f boom, business prosperity; 2land n upland(s pl.), highlands pl.; '2mut m arrogance, haughtiness; ‿mütig adj. ['‿my:tiç] arrogant, haughty; ‿näsig ⌐ adj. ['‿nε:ziç] stuck up; '2ofen ⊕ m blast-furnace; '‿rot adj. bright red; 2saison f peak season, height of the season; '‿schätzen v/t. (sep.,-ge-, h) esteem highly; '2schule f university; academy; 2seefischerei f deep-sea fishing; '2sommer m midsummer; '2spannung ≠ f high tension or voltage; '2sprung m sports: high jump.

höchst [hø:çst] 1. adj. highest; fig. a.: supreme; extreme; 2. adv. highly, most, extremely.

Hochstap|elei [ho:x‖ta:pə'laɪ] f (-/-en) swindling; ‿ler m (-s/-) confidence man, swindler.

höchstens adv. ['hø:çstəns] at (the) most, at best.

'Höchst|form f sports: top form; '‿geschwindigkeit f maximum speed; speed limit; ‿leistung f sports: record (performance); ⊕ maximum output (of machine, etc.); '‿lohn m maximum wages pl.; '‿maß n maximum; '‿preis m maximum price.

'hoch|trabend fig. adj. high-flown, pompous; 2verrat m high treason; '2wald m high forest; 2wasser n high tide or water; flood; ‿wertig adj. high-grade, high-class; 2wild n big game; 2wohlgeboren m (-s/-) Right Hono(u)rable.

Hochzeit ['hɔxtsaɪt] f (-/-en) wedding; marriage; 2lich adj. bridal, nuptial; ‿sgeschenk n wedding present; '‿sreise f honeymoon (trip).

Hocke ['hɔkə] f (-/-n) gymnastics: squat-vault; skiing: crouch; '2n v/i. (ge-, h) squat, crouch; '‿r m (-s/-) stool.

Höcker ['hœkər] m (-s/-) surface, etc.: bump; camel, etc.: hump; p. hump, hunch; '2ig adj. animal: humped; p. humpbacked, hunchbacked; surface, etc.: bumpy, rough, uneven.

Hode anat. ['ho:də] m (-n/-n), f (-/-n), '‿n anat. m (-s/-) testicle.

Hof [ho:f] m (-[e]s/‿e) court(yard); farm; king, etc.: court; ast. halo; j-m den ‿ machen court s.o.; '‿dame f lady-in-waiting; '2fähig adj. presentable at court.

Hoffart ['hɔfart] f (-/no pl.) arrogance, haughtiness; pride.

hoffen ['hɔfən] (ge-, h) 1. v/i. hope (auf acc. for); trust (in); 2. v/t.: das Beste ‿ hope for the best; '‿tlich adv. it is to be hoped that, I hope, let's hope.

Hoffnung ['hɔfnuŋ] f (-/-en) hope (auf acc. for, of); in der ‿ zu inf. in the hope of ger., hoping to inf.; s-e ‿ setzen auf (acc.) pin one's hopes on; 2slos adj. hopeless; '2svoll adj. hopeful; promising.

'Hofhund m watch-dog.

höfisch adj. ['hø:fiʃ] courtly.

höflich adj. ['hø:fliç] polite, civil, courteous (gegen to); 2keit f (-/-en) politeness, civility, courtesy.

'Hofstaat m royal or princely household; suite, retinue.

Höhe ['hø:ə] f (-/-n) height; ✮, ⋏, ast., geogr. altitude; hill; peak; amount (of bill, etc.); size (of sum, fine, etc.); level (of price, etc.); severity (of punishment, etc.); ♪ pitch; in gleicher ‿ mit on a level with; auf der ‿ sein be up to the mark; in die ‿ up(wards).

Hoheit ['ho:haɪt] f (-/-en) pol. sovereignty; title: Highness; '‿sgebiet n (sovereign) territory; '‿sgewässer n/pl. territorial waters pl.; ‿szeichen n national emblem.

'Höhen|kurort m high-altidude health resort; ‿luft f mountain air; ‿sonne f mountain sun; ✗ ultra-violet lamp; ‿steuer ✘ n elevator; ‿zug m mountain range.

'Höhepunkt m highest point; ast., fig. culmination, zenith; fig. a.: climax; summit, peak.

hohl adj. [ho:l] hollow (a. fig.); cheeks, etc. sunken; hand: cupped; sound: hollow, dull.

Höhle ['hø:lə] f (-/-n) cave, cavern; den, lair (of bear, lion, etc.) (both a. fig.); hole, burrow (of fox, rabbit, etc.); hollow; cavity.

'Hohl|maß n dry measure; '‿raum m hollow, cavity; '‿spiegel m concave mirror.

Höhlung ['hø:luŋ] f (-/-en) excavation, hollow, cavity.

'**Hohlweg** m defile.

Hohn [ho:n] m (-[e]s/no pl.) scorn, disdain, derision.

höhnen ['hø:nən] v/i. (ge-, h) sneer, jeer, mock, scoff (über acc. at).

'**Hohngelächter** n scornful or derisive laughter.

'**höhnisch** adj. scornful; sneering, derisive.

Höker ['hø:kər] m (-s/-) hawker, huckster; '2n v/i. (ge-, h) huckster, hawk about.

holen ['ho:lən] v/t. (ge-, h) fetch; go for; a. ~ lassen send for; draw (breath); sich e-e Krankheit ~ catch a disease; sich bei j-m Rat ~ seek s.o.'s advice.

Holländer ['hɔlɛndər] m (-s/-) Dutchman.

Hölle ['hœlə] f (-/⁎-n) hell.

'**Höllen|angst** fig. f: e-e ~ haben be in a mortal fright or F blue funk; '**_lärm** F fig. m infernal noise; '**_maschine** f infernal machine, time bomb; '**_pein** F fig. f torment of hell.

'**höllisch** adj. hellish, infernal (both a. fig.).

holper|ig adj. ['hɔlpəriç] surface, road, etc. bumpy, rough, uneven; vehicle, etc.: jolty, jerky; verse, style, etc.: rough, jerky; **_n** (ge-) 1. v/i. (sein) vehicle: jolt, bump; 2. v/i. vehicle: jolt, bump; be jolty or bumpy.

Holunder ⚕ [ho'lundər] m (-s/-) elder.

Holz [hɔlts] n (-es/⁎er) wood; timber, Am. lumber; '**_bau** △ m wooden structure; **_bildhauer** m woodcarver; '**_blasinstrument** ♪ n woodwind instrument, **_boden** m wood(en) floor, wood-loft.

hölzern adj ['hœltsərn] wooden; fig. a. clumsy, awkward.

'**Holz|fäller** m (-s/-) woodcutter, woodman, Am. a. lumberjack, logger, **_hacker** m (-s/-) woodchopper, woodcutter, Am lumberjack; **_händler** m wood or timber merchant, Am lumberman, **_haus** n wooden house, Am frame house; '2ig adj woody, **_kohle** f charcoal; '**_platz** m wood or timber yard, Am. lumberyard, **_schnitt** m woodcut, wood-engraving, **_schnitzer** m wood-carver, **_schuh** m wooden shoe, clog, **_stoß** m pil⹁ or stack of wood, stake, **_weg** fig. m auf dem ~ sein be on the wrong track, **_wolle** f wood-wool, fine wood shavings pl., Am a excelsior

Homöopath ♂ [homœo'pa:t] m (-en/-en) hom(o)eopath(ist), **_ie** [_a'ti:] f (-/no pl.) hom(o)eopathy; 2isch adj. [_'pa:tif] hom(o)eopathic.

Honig ['ho:niç] m (-s/-e) honey; '**_kuchen** m honey-cake; gingerbread; '2süß adj. honey-sweet, honeyed (a. fig.); '**_wabe** f honeycomb.

Honor|ar [hono'ra:r] n (-s/-e) fee; royalties pl.; salary, **_atioren** [_a-'tsjo:rən] pl. notabilities pl.; 2ieren [_'ri:rən] v/t. (no -ge-, h) fee, pay a fee to; ✝ hono(u)r, meet (bill of exchange).

Hopfen ['hɔpfən] m (-s/-) ♀ hop; brewing hops pl.

hops|a int. ['hɔpsa] (wh)oops!; upsadaisy!; '**_en** F v/i. (ge-, sein) hop, jump.

hörbar adj. ['hø:rba:r] audible.

horch|en ['hɔrçən] v/i. (ge-, h) listen (auf acc. to); eavesdrop; '2er m (-s/-) eavesdropper.

Horde ['hɔrdə] f (-/-n) horde, gang.

hör|en ['hø:rən] (ge-, h) 1. v/t. hear; listen (in) to (radio); attend (lecture, etc.); hear, learn; 2. v/i. hear (von dat. from); listen; ~ auf (acc.) listen to; schwer ~ be hard of hearing; ~ Sie mal! look here!; I say!; '2er m (-s/-) hearer; radio listener(-in); univ. student; teleph. receiver; '2erschaft f (-/-en) audience; '2gerät n hearing aid; '_ig adj.: j-m ~ sein be enslaved to s.o.; '2igkeit f (-/no pl.) subjection.

Horizont [hori'tsɔnt] m (-[e]s/-e) horizon; skyline; s-n ~ erweitern broaden one's mind; das geht über meinen ~ that's beyond me; 2al adj. [_'ta:l] horizontal.

Hormon [hɔr'mo:n] n (-s/-e) hormone.

Horn [hɔrn] n 1. (-[e]s/⁎er) horn (of bull); ♪, mot., etc.: horn; ⚔ bugle, peak; 2. (-[e]s/-e) horn, horny matter; ♀ matt f horny skin; anat. cornea (on eye).

Hornisse zo. [hɔr'nisə] f (-/-n) hornet.

Hornist ♪ [hɔr'nist] m (-en/-en) horn-player; ⚔ bugler.

Horoskop [horo'sko:p] n (-s/-e) horoscope, j-m das ~ stellen cast s.o.'s horoscope.

'**Hör|rohr** n ear-trumpet; ♫ stethoscope; **_saal** m lecture-hall; '**_spiel** n radio play; '**_weite** f: in ~ within earshot.

Hose ['ho:zə] f (-/-n) (e-e a pair of) trousers pl. or Am. pants pl.; slacks pl.

'**Hosen|klappe** f flap; **_latz** ['_lats] m (-es/⁎e) flap, fly; '**_tasche** f trouser-pocket; **_träger** m: (ein Paar) ~ pl. (a pair of) braces pl. or Am. suspenders pl.

Hospital [hɔspi'ta:l] n (-s/-e, ⁎er) hospital.

Hostie eccl. ['hɔstjə] f (-/-n) host, consecrated or holy wafer.

Hotel [ho'tɛl] n (-s/-s) hotel; **_besitzer** m hotel owner or proprietor;

~gewerbe n hotel industry; ~ier [~'je:] m (-s/-s) hotel-keeper.

Hub ⊕ [hu:p] m (-[e]s/~e) mot. stroke (of piston); lift (of valve, etc.); ~raum mot m capacity.

hübsch adj. [hypʃ] pretty, nice; good-looking, handsome; attractive.

'Hubschrauber ✶ m (-s/-) helicopter.

Huf [hu:f] m (-[e]s/-e) hoof; ~eisen n horseshoe; '~schlag m hoof-beat; (horse's) kick; ~schmied m farrier.

Hüft|e anat. ['hyftə] f (-/-n) hip; esp. zo. haunch; ~gelenk n hip-joint; ~gürtel m girdle; suspender belt, Am. garter belt.

Hügel ['hy:gəl] m (-s/-) hill(ock); '2ig adj. hilly.

Huhn orn. [hu:n] n (-[e]s/~er) fowl, chicken; hen; junges ~ chicken.

Hühnchen ['hy:nçən] n (-s/-) chicken, ein ~ zu rupfen haben have a bone to pick (mit with).

Hühner|auge ✍ ['hy:nər-] n corn; '~ei n hen's egg; '~hof m poultry-yard, Am. chicken yard; '~hund zo. m pointer, setter; '~leiter f chicken-ladder.

Huld [hult] f (-/no pl.) grace, fa-vo(u)r, 2igen ['~digən] v/i. (dat.) (ge-, h) pay homage to (sovereign, lady, etc.); indulge in (vice, etc.); '~igung f (-/-en) homage; '2reich adj., '2voll adj. gracious.

Hülle ['hylə] f (-/-n) cover(ing), wrapper; letter, balloon, etc.: envelope; book, etc.: jacket; umbrella, etc.: sheath; '2n v/t. (ge-, h) wrap, cover, envelope (a. fig.); sich in Schweigen ~ wrap o.s. in silence.

Hülse ['hylzə] f (-/-n) legume, pod (of leguminous plant); husk, hull (of rice, etc.); skin (of pea, etc.); ✖ case; '~nfrucht f legume(n); leguminous plant; '~nfrüchte f/pl. pulse.

human adj. [hu'ma:n] humane; 2i-tät [~ani'tɛ:t] f (-/no pl.) humanity.

Hummel zo. ['huməl] f (-/-n) bumble-bee.

Hummer zo. ['humər] m (-s/-) lobster.

Humor [hu'mo:r] m (-s/✖ -e) humo(u)r; ~ist [~o'rist] m (-en/-en) humorist; 2istisch adj. [~o'risti ʃ] humorous.

humpeln ['humpəln] v/i. (ge-) 1. (sein) hobble (along), limp (along); 2. (h) (have a) limp, walk with a limp.

Hund [hunt] m (-[e]s/-e) zo. dog; ✖ tub; ast. dog, canis; auf den ~ kommen go to the dogs.

'Hunde|hütte f dog-kennel, Am. a. doghouse; '~kuchen m dog-biscuit; '~leine f (dog-)lead or leash; '~peitsche f dog-whip.

hundert ['hundərt] 1. adj. a or one

hundred; 2. 2 n (-s/-e) hundred; fünf vom ~ five per cent; zu ~en by hundreds; '~fach adj., '~fältig adj. hundredfold, 2'jahrfeier f centenary, Am a. centennial; ~jährig adj. ['~jɛ:riç] centenary, a hundred years old; '~st adj. hundredth.

'Hunde|sperre f muzzling-order; '~steuer f dog tax.

Hündi|n zo. ['hyndin] f (-/-nen) bitch, she-dog; '2sch adj. doggish; fig. servile; cringing.

'hunds|ge'mein adj. dirty, mean, scurvy; ~mise'rabel F adj. rotten, wretched, lousy; '2tage m/pl. dog-days pl.

Hüne ['hy:nə] m (-n/-n) giant.

Hunger ['huŋər] m (-s/no pl.) hunger (fig. nach for); ~ bekommen get hungry; haben be or feel hungry; '~kur f starvation cure; '~leider F m (-s/-) starveling, poor devil; '2lohn m starvation wages pl.; '2n v/i. (ge-, h) hunger (fig. nach after, for); go without food; ~ lassen starve s.o.; '~snot f famine; '~streik m hunger-strike; '~tod m death from starvation; '~tuch fig. n: am ~ nagen have nothing to bite.

'hungrig adj. hungry (fig. nach for).

Hupe mot. ['hu:pə] f (-/-n) horn, hooter, klaxon; '2n v/i. (ge-, h) sound one's horn, hoot.

hüpfen ['hypfən] v/i. (ge-, sein) hip, skip, gambol, frisk (about).

Hürde ! hyrdə] f (-/-n) hurdle; fold, pen; ~nrennen n hurdle-race.

Hure ['hu:rə] f (-/-n) whore, prostitute

hurtig adj. ['hurtiç] quick, swift; agile, nimble.

Husar ✖ [hu'za:r] m (-en/-en) hussar

husch int. [huʃ] in or like a flash; shoo!, ~en v/i. (ge-, sein) slip, dart; small animal: scurry, scamper; bat, etc.: flit.

hüsteln ['hy:stəln] 1. v/i. (ge-, h) cough slightly; 2. 2 n (-s/no pl.) slight cough.

husten ['hu:stən] 1. v/i. (ge-, h) cough, 2. 2 m (-s/✖ -) cough.

Hut [hu:t] 1. m (-[e]s/~e) hat; den ~ abnehmen take off one's hat; ~ ab vor (dat.)! hats off to ...!; 2. f (-/no pl.) care, charge; guard; auf der ~ sein be on one's guard (vor dat. against).

hüte|n ['hy:tən] v/t. (ge-, h) guard, protect, keep watch over; keep (secret); tend (sheep, etc.); das Bett ~ be confined to (one's) bed; sich ~ vor (dat.) beware of; '2r m (-s/-) keeper, guardian; herdsman.

'Hut|futter n hat-lining; '~krempe f hat-brim; '~macher m (-s/-) hatter; '~nadel f hat-pin.

Hütte ['hytə] f (-/-n) hut; cottage, cabin; ⊕ metallurgical plant; mount refuge; '~nwesen ⊕ *n* metallurgy, metallurgical engineering.

Hyäne *zo.* [hy'ɛːnə] *f* (-/-n) hy(a)ena.

Hyazinthe 𝄞 [hya'tsintə] *f* (-/-n) hyacinth.   [hydrant.|

Hydrant [hy'drant] *m* (-en/-en)|

Hydrauli|k *phys.* [hy'draulik] *f* (-/no *pl.*) hydraulics *pl.*; ♀sch *adj.* hydraulic.

Hygien|e [hy'gjeːnə] *f* (-/no *pl.*) hygiene; ♀isch *adj.* hygienic(al).

Hymne ['hymnə] *f* (-/-n) hymn.

Hypno|se [hyp'noːzə] *f* (-/-n) hypnosis; ♀tisieren [~oti'ziːrən] *v/t.* and *v/i.* (no -ge-, h) hypnotize.

Hypochond|er [hypo'xɔndər] *m* (-s/-) hypochondriac; ♀risch *adj.* hypochondriac.

Hypotenuse ⚭ [hypote'nuːzə] *f* (-/-n) hypotenuse.

Hypothek [hypo'teːk] *f* (-/-en) mortgage; e-e ~ *aufnehmen* raise a mortgage; ♀arisch *adj.* [~e'kaːriʃ]: ~e *Belastung* mortgage.

Hypothe|se [hypo'teːzə] *f* (-/-n) hypothesis; ♀tisch *adj.* hypothetical.

Hyster|ie *psych.* [hyste'riː] *f* (-/-n) hysteria; ♀isch *psych. adj.* [~'teːriʃ] hysterical.

I

ich [iç] **1.** *pers. pron.* I; **2.** ♀ *n* (-[s]/-[s]) self; *psych.* the ego.

Ideal [ide'aːl] **1.** *n* (-s/-e) ideal; **2.** ♀ *adj.* ideal; ♀isieren [~ali'ziːrən] *v/t.* (no -ge-, h) idealize; ~ismus [~a'lismus] *m* (-/*Idealismen* ideal-ism; ~ist [~a'list] *m* (-en/-en) ideal-ist.

Idee [i'deː] *f* (-/-n) idea, notion.

identi|fizieren [identifi'tsiːrən] *v/t.* (no -ge-, h) identify; *sich* ~ identify o.s.; ~sch *adj.* [i'dentiʃ] identical; ♀tät [~'tɛːt] *f* (-/no *pl.*) identity.

Ideolog|ie [ideolo'giː] *f* (-/-n) ideology; ♀isch *adj.* [~'loːgiʃ] ideological.

Idiot [idi'oːt] *m* (-en/-en) idiot; ~ie [~o'tiː] *f* (-/-n) idiocy; ♀isch *adj.* [~'oːtiʃ] idiotic.

Idol [i'doːl] *n* (-s/-e) idol.

Igel *zo.* ['iːgəl] *m* (-s/-) hedgehog.

Ignor|ant [igno'rant] *m* (-en/-en) ignorant person, ignoramus; ~anz [~ts] *f* (-/no *pl.*) ignorance; ♀ieren *v/t.* (no -ge-, h) ignore, take no notice of.

ihm *pers. pron.* [iːm] *p.* (to) him; *thing:* (to) it.

ihn *pers. pron.* [iːn] *p.* him; *thing:* it.

'ihnen *pers. pron.* (to) them; *Ihnen sg. and pl.* (to) you.

ihr [iːr] **1.** *pers. pron.:* (*2nd pl. nom.*) you; (*3rd sg. dat.*) (to) her; **2.** *poss. pron.:* her; their; *Ihr sg. and pl.* your; *der* (*die, das*) ~e hers; theirs; *der* (*die, das*) *Ihre sg. and pl.* yours; ~erseits ['~ərˈzaıts] *adv.* on her part; on their part; *Ihrerseits sg. and pl.* on your part; '~es'gleichen *pron.* (of) her *or* their kind, her *or* their equal; *Ihresgleichen sg.* (of) your kind, your equal; *pl.* (of) your kind, your equals; '~et'wegen *adv.* for her *or* their sake, on her *or* their account; *Ihretwegen sg. or pl.* for your sake, on your account; '~et-willen *adv.:* um ~ *s. ihretwegen;*

~ige *poss. pron.* ['~igə]: *der* (*die, das*) ~ hers; theirs; *der* (*die, das*) *Ihrige* yours.

illegitim *adj.* [ilegi'tiːm] illegiti-mate.

illusorisch *adj.* [ilu'zoːriʃ] illusory, deceptive.

illustrieren [ilu'striːrən] *v/t.* (no -ge-, h) illustrate.

Iltis *zo.* ['iltis] *m* (-ses/-se) fitchew, polecat.

im *prp.* [im] = *in dem.*

imaginär *adj.* [imagi'nɛːr] imag-inary.

'Imbiß *m* light meal, snack; '~stube *f* snack bar.

Imker ['imkər] *m* (-s/-) bee-master, bee-keeper.

immatrikulieren [imatriku'liːrən] *v/t.* (no -ge-, h) matriculate, enrol(l); *sich* ~ *lassen* matriculate, enrol(l).

immer *adv.* ['imər] always; ~ *mehr* more and more; ~ *wieder* again *or* time and again; *für* ~ for ever, for good; ♀grün 𝄞 *n* (-s/-e) evergreen; '~'hin *adv.* still, yet; '~'zu *adv.* always, continually.

Immobilien [imo'biːljən] *pl.* im-movables *pl.*, real estate; ~händler *m s.* Grundstücksmakler.

immun *adj.* [i'muːn] immune (*gegen* against, from); ♀ität [~uni'tɛːt] *f* (-/no *pl.*) immunity.

Imperativ *gr.* ['imperatiːf] *m* (-s/-e) imperative (mood).

Imperfekt *gr.* ['imperfɛkt] *n* (-s/-e) imperfect (tense), past tense.

Imperialis|mus [imperia'lismus] *m* (-/no *pl.*) imperialism; ~t *m* (-en/-en) imperialist; ♀tisch *adj.* imperial-istic.

impertinent *adj.* [imperti'nɛnt] impertinent, insolent.

impf|en 𝄪 ['impfən] *v/t.* (ge-, h) vaccinate, inoculate; '♀schein *m* certificate of vaccination *or* in-oculation; '♀stoff 𝄪 *m* vaccine;

serum; '²ung f (-/-en) vaccination; inoculation.

imponieren [impo'ni:rən] v/i. (no -ge-, h): j-m ~ impress s.o.

Import ✛ [im'port] m (-[e]s/-e) import(ation); ~eur ✛ [‿'tø:r] m (-s/-e) importer; ²ieren [‿'ti:rən] v/t. (no -ge-, h) import.

imposant adj. [impo'zant] imposing, impressive.

imprägnieren [impre'gni:rən] v/t. (no -ge-, h) impregnate; (water-) proof (raincoat, etc.).

improvisieren [improvi'zi:rən] v/t. and v/i. (no -ge-, h) improvise.

Im'puls m (-es/-e) impuls; ²iv adj. [‿'zi:f] impulsive; ²iv able.)

imstande adj. [im'ʃtandə] ~ sein in prp. (dat.; acc.) [in] **1.** place: in, at; within; into, in; with names of important towns: in, ਸ਼੍ at, of; with names of villages and less important towns: at; im Hause in the house, indoors, in; im ersten Stock on the first floor; ~ der Schule (im Theater) at school (the theat|re, Am. -er); ~ die Schule (~s Theater) to school (the theat|re, Am. -er); ~ England in England; waren Sie schon einmal in England? have you ever been to England? **2.** time: in, at, during; within; ~ drei Tagen (with)in three days; heute vierzehn Tagen today fortnight, im Jahre 1960 in 1960; im Februar in February; im Frühling in (the) spring; ~ der Nacht at night; ~ letzter Zeit lately, of late, recently; **3.** mode: großer Eile in great haste; ~ Frieden leben live at peace; ~ Reichweite within reach; **4.** condition, state: im Alter von fünfzehn Jahren at (the age of) fifteen; ~ Behandlung under treatment.

'**Inbegriff** m (quint)essence; embodiment, incarnation; paragon; '²en adj. included, inclusive (of).

Inbrunst f (-/no pl.) ardo(u)r, fervo(u)r.

'**inbrünstig** adj. ardent, fervent.

in'dem cj. whilst, while; by (ger.); ~ er mich ansah, sagte er looking at me he said.

Inder ['indər] m (-s/-) Indian.

in'des(sen) **1.** adv. meanwhile; **2.** cj. while; however.

Indianer [in'dja:nər] m (-s/-) (American or Red) Indian.

Indikativ gr. ['indikati:f] m (-s/-e) indicative (mood).

'**indirekt** adj. indirect.

'**indisch** adj. ['indiʃ] Indian.

'**indiskret** adj. indiscreet; ²ion [~e'tsjo:n] f (-/-en) indiscretion.

indiskutabel adj. ['indiskuta:bəl] out of the question.

individu|ell [E. [individu'ɛl] individual; ²um [‿'vi:duum] n (-s/Individuen) individual.

Indizienbeweis ਸ਼੍ [in'di:tsjən-] m circumstantial evidence.

Indoss|ament ✛ [indɔsa'mɛnt] n (-s/-e) endorsement, indorsement; ²ieren ✛ [‿'si:rən] v/t. (no -ge-, h) indorse, endorse.

Industrialisierung [industriali'zi:ruŋ] f (~ -en) industrialization.

Industrie [indus'tri:] f (-/-n) industry; ~anlage f industrial plant; ~arbeiter m industrial worker; ~ausstellung f industrial exhibition; ~erzeugnis n industrial product; ~gebiet n industrial district or area; ²II adj. [‿i'ɛl] industrial; ~lle [‿i'ɛlə] m (-n/-n) industrialist; ~staat m industrial country.

ineinander adv. [in'ʼaiˈnandər] into one another, ~greifen ⊕ v/i. (irr. greifen, sep., -ge-, h) gear into one another, interlock.

infam adj. [in'fɑ:m] infamous.

Infanter|ie ⚔ [infantə'ri:] f (-/-n) infantry, ~ist ⚔ m (-en/-en) infantryman.

Infektion ☤ [infɛk'tsjo:n] f (-/-en) infection; ~skrankheit ☤ f infectious disease.

Infinitiv gr. ['infiniti:f] m (-s/-e) infinitive (mood).

infizieren [infi'tsi:rən] v/t. (no -ge-, h) infect   (flation.)

Inflation [infla'tsjo:n] f (-/-en) in-}

in'folge prp. (gen.) in consequence of, owing or due to; ~'dessen adv. consequently.

Inform|ation [informa'tsjo:n] f (-/-en) information; ²ieren [‿'mi:rən] v/t (no -ge-, h) inform; falsch ~ misinform

Ingenieur [inʒe'njø:r] m (-s/-e) engineer

Ingwer ['invər] m (-s/no pl.) ginger.

Inhaber ['inha:bər] m (-s/-) owner, proprietor (of business or shop); occupant (of flat); keeper (of shop); holder (of office, share, etc.); bearer (of cheque, etc.).

'**Inhalt** m (-[e]s/-e) contents pl. (of bottle, book, etc.); tenor (of speech); geom volume, capacity (of vessel); '**Inhalts|angabe** f summary; '²los adj. empty, devoid of substance; '²reich adj. full of meaning; life: rich, full; ~verzeichnis n on parcel: list of contents; in book: table of contents

Initiative [initsja'ti:və] f (-/no pl.) initiative; die ~ ergreifen take the initiative.

Ink:sso ✛ [in'kaso] n (-s/-s, Inkassi) collection.

'**inkonsequen|t** adj. inconsistent; ²z [‿ts] f (-/-en) inconsistency.

In'krafttreten n (-s/no pl.) coming into force, taking effect (of new law, etc.).

'**Inland** n (-[e]s/no pl.) home (country); inland.

inländisch *adj.* ['inlendiʃ] native; inland; home; domestic; *product*: home-made.

Inlett ['inlet] *n* (-[e]s/-e) bedtick.

in'mitten *prp.* (*gen.*) in the midst of, amid(st).

'inne|haben *v/t.* (*irr. haben, sep.*, -ge-, h) possess, hold (*office, record, etc.*); occupy (*flat*); **'~halten** *v/i.* (*irr. halten, sep.*, -ge-, h) stop, pause.

innen *adv.* ['inən] inside, within; indoors; *nach* ~ inwards.

'Innen|architekt *m* interior decorator; **'~ausstattung** *f* interior decoration, fittings *pl.*, furnishing; **'~minister** *m* minister of the interior; Home Secretary, *Am.* Secretary of the Interior; **'~ministerium** *n* ministry of the interior; Home Office, *Am.* Department of the Interior; **'~politik** *f* domestic policy; **'~seite** *f* inner side, inside; **'~stadt** *f* city, *Am.* downtown.

inner *adj.* ['inər] interior; inner; 𝔾, *pol.* internal; 𝔾 *n* (-n/no *pl.*) interior; *Minister(ium) des Innern s.* Innenminister(ium); **2eien** [~'raıən] *f/pl.* offal(s *pl.*); **'~halb** 1. *prp.* (*gen.*) within; 2. *adv.* within, inside; **'~lich** *adv.* inwardly; *esp.* 𝔾 internally.

innig *adj.* ['iniç] intimate, close; affectionate.

Innung ['inuŋ] *f* (-/-en) guild, corporation.

inoffiziell *adj.* ['in?-] unofficial.

ins *prp.* [ins] = in das.

Insasse ['inzasə] *m* (-n/-n) inmate; occupant, passenger (*of car*).

'Inschrift *f* inscription; legend (*on coin, etc.*).

Insekt *zo.* [in'zɛkt] *n* (-[e]s/-en) insect.

Insel ['inzəl] *f* (-/-n) island; **'~bewohner** *m* islander.

Inser|at [inzə'ra:t] *n* (-[e]s/-e) advertisement, F ad; **2ieren** [~'ri:rən] *v/t. and v/i.* (*no* -ge-, h) advertise.

insge'heim *adv.* secretly; **~'samt** *adv.* altogether.

in'sofern *cj.* so far; ~ *als* in so far as.

insolvent † *adj.* ['inzolvent] insolvent.

Inspekt|ion [inspek'tsjo:n] *f* (-/-en) inspection; **~or** [in'spektər] *m* (-s/-en) inspector; surveyor; overseer.

inspirieren [inspi'ri:rən] *v/t.* (*no* -ge-, h) inspire.

inspizieren [inspi'tsi:rən] *v/t.* (*no* -ge-, h) inspect (*troops, etc.*); examine (*goods*); survey (*buildings*).

Install|ateur [instala'tø:r] *m* (-s/-e) plumber; (gas- *or* electrical) fitter; **2ieren** [~'li:rən] *v/t.* (*no* -ge-, h) install.

instand *adv.* [in'ʃtant]: ~ *halten* keep in good order; keep up; ⊕

maintain; ~ *setzen* repair; **2haltung** *f* maintenance; upkeep.

'inständig *adv.*: *j-n* ~ *bitten* implore *or* beseech s.o.

Instanz [in'stants] *f* (-/-en) authority; 𝔾 instance; **~enweg** 𝔾 *m* stages of appeal; *auf dem* ~ through the prescribed channels.

Instinkt [in'stiŋkt] *m* (-[e]s/-e) instinct; **2iv** *adv.* [~'ti:f] instinctively.

Institut [insti'tu:t] *n* (-[e]s/-e) institute.

Instrument [instru'mɛnt] *n* (-[e]s/-e) instrument.

inszenier|en *esp. thea.* [instse'ni:-rən] *v/t.* (*no* -ge-, h) (put on the) stage; **2ung** *thea.* *f* (-/-en) staging, production.

Integr|ation [integra'tsjo:n] *f* (-/-en) integration; **2ieren** [~'gri:rən] *v/t.* (*no* -ge-, h) integrate.

intellektuell *adj.* [intelɛktu'ɛl] intellectual, highbrow; **2e** *m* (-n/-n) intellectual, highbrow.

intelligen|t *adj.* [inteli'gɛnt] intelligent; **2z** [~ts] *f* (-/-en) intelligence.

Intendant *thea.* [inten'dant] *m* (-en/-en) director.

intensiv *adj.* [inten'zi:f] intensive; intense.

interess|ant *adj.* [interɛ'sant] interesting; **2e** [~'rɛsə] *n* (-s/-n) interest (*an dat., für* in); **2engebiet** [~'rɛsən-] *n* field of interest; **2engemeinschaft** [~'rɛsən-] *f* community of interests; combine, pool, trust; **~ent** [~'sɛnt] *m* (-en/-en) interested person *or* party; † prospective buyer, *esp. Am.* prospect; **~ieren** [~'si:rən] *v/t.* (*no* -ge-, h) interest (*für* in); *sich* ~ *für* take an interest in.

intern *adj.* [in'tern] internal; **2at** [~'na:t] *n* (-[e]s/-e) boarding-school.

international *adj.* [internatsjo'na:l] international.

inter|'nieren *v/t.* (*no* -ge-, h) intern; **2'nierung** *f* (-/-en) internment; **2'nist** 𝔾 *m* (-en/-en) internal specialist, *Am.* internist.

inter|pretieren [intərpre'ti:rən] *v/t.* (*no* -ge-, h) interpret; **2punktion** [~puŋk'tsjo:n] *f* (-/-en) punctuation; **2vall** [~'val] *n* (-s/-e) interval; **~venieren** [~ve'ni:rən] *v/i.* (*no* -ge-, h) intervene; **2'zonenhandel** *m* interzonal trade; **2'zonenverkehr** *m* interzonal traffic.

intim *adj.* [in'ti:m] intimate (*mit* with); **2ität** [~imi'tɛ:t] *f* (-/-en) intimacy.

'intoleran|t *adj.* intolerant; **2z** ['~ts] *f* (-/-en) intolerance.

intransitiv *gr.* *adj.* ['intranziti:f] intransitive.

I..trig|e [in'tri:gə] *f* (-/-n) intrigue, scheme, plot; **2ieren** [~i'gi:rən] *v/i* (*no* -ge-, h) intrigue, scheme, plot.

Invalid|e [inva'li:də] m (-n/-n) invalid; disabled person; **~enrente** f disability pension; **~ität** [~idi'tɛ:t] f (-/no pl.) disablement, disability.

Inventar [invɛn'ta:r] n (-s/-e) inventory, stock.

Inventur ✝ [invɛn'tu:r] f (-/-en) stock-taking; **~ machen** take stock.

invest|ieren ✝ [invɛs'ti:rən] v/t. (no -ge-, h) invest; **2ition** ✝ [~i'tsjo:n] f (-/-en) investment.

inwie'fern cj. to what extent; in what way or respect; **~'weit** cj. how far, to what extent.

in'zwischen adv. in the meantime, meanwhile.

Ion phys. [i'o:n] n (-s/-en) ion.

ird|en adj. ['irdən] earthen; **~isch** adj. earthly; worldly; mortal.

Ire ['i:rə] m (-n/-n) Irishman; die **~n** pl. the Irish pl.

irgend adv. ['irgənt] in compounds: some; any (a. negative and in questions); wenn ich **~** kann if I possibly can; **~'ein(e)** indef. pron. and adj. some(one); any(one); **'~'einer** indef. pron. s. irgend jemand; **'~'ein(e)s** indef. pron. some; any; **~etwas** indef. pron. something; anything; **~ jemand** indef. pron. someone; anyone; **'~'wann** adv. some time (or other); **'~'wie** adv. somehow; anyhow; **'~'wo** adv. somewhere; anywhere; **'~'wo'her** adv. from somewhere; from anywhere; **'~wo'hin** adv. somewhere; anywhere.

'irisch adj. Irish.

Iron|ie [iro'ni:] f (-/-n) irony; **2isch** adj. [i'ro:niʃ] ironic(al).

irre ['irə] 1. adj. confused; ☞ insane; mad; 2. 2 f (-/no pl.): in die **~** gehen go astray; 3. 2 m, f (-n/-n) lunatic; mental patient; wie ein **~r** like a madman; **'~führen** v/t. (sep., -ge-, h) lead astray; fig. mislead; **'~gehen** v/i. (irr. gehen, sep., -ge-, sein) go astray, stray; lose one's way; **'~machen** v/t. (sep., -ge-, h) puzzle, bewilder; perplex; confuse;

~n 1. v/i. (ge-, h) err; wander; 2. v/refl. (ge-, h) be mistaken (in dat. in s.o., about s.th.); be wrong.

'Irren|anstalt ☞ f lunatic asylum, mental home or hospital; **'~arzt** ☞ m alienist, mental specialist; **'~haus** ☞ n s. Irrenanstalt.

'irre|reden v/i. (sep., -ge-, h) rave.

'Irr|fahrt f wandering; Odyssey; **~garten** m labyrinth, maze; **'~glaube** m erroneous belief; false doctrin~, heterodoxy; heresy; **'2gläubig** adj. heterodox; heretical; **'2ig** adj. erroneous, mistaken, false, wrong.

irritieren [iri'ti:rən] v/t. (no -ge-, h) irritat~, annoy; confuse.

'Irr|lehre f false doctrine, heterodoxy; heresy; **'~licht** n will-o'-the-wisp, jack-o'-lantern; **~sinn** m insanity, madness; **'2sinnig** adj. insane; mad; fig.: fantastic; terrible; **'~sinnige** m, f (-n/-n) s. irre 3; **'~tum** m (-s/=er) error, mistake; im **~** sein be mistaken; **2tümlich** ['~ty:mliç] 1. adj. erroneous; 2. adv. = **2tümlicherweise** adv. by mistake; mistakenly, erroneously; **~wisch** m s. Irrlicht; p. flibbertigibbet.

Ischias ☞ ['iʃias] f, F a.: n, m (-/no pl.) sciatica.

Islam [islam, is'la:m] m (-s/no pl.) Islam.

Island|er ['i:slɛndər] m (-s/-) Icelander, **2isch** adj. Icelandic.

Isolator ⚡ [izo'la:tər] m (-s/-en) insulator.

Isolier|band ⚡ [izo'li:r~] n insulating tape, **2en** v/t. (no -ge-, h) isolate; **~masse** ⚡ f insulating compound, **~schicht** ⚡ f insulating layer, **~ung** f (-/-en) isolation (a. ☞); ⚡ quarantine; ⚡ insulation.

Isotop ⚛ phys. [izo'to:p] n (-s/-e) isotope.

Israeli [isra'e:li] m (-s/-s) Israeli.

Italien|er [ital'je:nər] m (-s/-) Italian; **2isch** adj. Italian.

I-Tüpfelchen fig. ['i:typfəlçən] n (-s/-): bis aufs **~** to a T.

J

ja [ja:] 1. adv. yes; ⚓, parl. aye, Am. parl. a. yea; **~** doch, **~** freilich yes, indeed; to be sure; da ist er **~** I well, there he is!; ich sagte es Ihnen **~** I told you so; tut es **~** nicht! don't you dare do it!; vergessen Sie es **~** nicht! be sure not to forget it!; 2. cj.: **~** sogar, **~** selbst nay (even); wenn **~** if so; er ist **~** mein Freund why, he is my friend; 3. int.: **~** weißt du

denn nicht, daß why, don't you know that.

Jacht ⚓ [jaxt] f (-/-en) yacht; **'~klub** m yacht-club.

Jacke [jakə] f (-/-n) jacket.

Jackett [ʒa'kɛt] n (-s/-e, -s) jacket.

Jagd [ja:kt] f (-/-en) hunt(ing); with a gun shoot(ing); chase; s. Jagdrevier, auf (die) **~** gehen go hunting or shooting, Am. a. be gunning; **~** machen auf (acc.) hunt after or for;

'~aufseher *m* gamekeeper, *Am.* game warden; **'~bomber** ✕ *m* (*-s*/-) fighter-bomber; **'~büchse** *f* sporting rifle; **'~flinte** *f* sporting gun; fowling-piece; **'~flugzeug** ✕ *n* fighter (aircraft); **'~geschwader** ✕ *n* fighter wing, *Am.* fighter group; **'~gesellschaft** *f* hunting *or* shooting party; **'~haus** *n* shooting-box *or* -lodge, hunting-box *or* -lodge; **'~hund** *m* hound; **'~hütte** *f* shooting-box, hunting-box; **~pächter** *m* game-tenant; **'~rennen** *n* steeplechase; **'~revier** *n* hunting-ground, shoot; **'~schein** *m* shooting licen|ce, *Am.* -se; **'~schloß** *n* hunting seat; **'~tasche** *f* game-bag.

jagen ['jɑːgən] (ge-, *h*) 1. *v/i.* go hunting *or* shooting, hunt; shoot; rush, dash; 2. *v/t.* hunt; chase; *aus dem Hause ~* turn *s.o.* out (of doors).

Jäger ['jeːgər] *m* (*-s*/-) hunter huntsman, sportsman; ✕ rifleman; **'~latein** F *fig. n* huntsmen's yarn, tall stories *pl.* [jaguar.)

Jaguar *zo.* ['jɑːguaːr] *m* (*-s*/-e)\

jäh *adj.* [jeː] sudden, abrupt; precipitous, steep.

Jahr [jɑːr] *n* (*-[e]s*/-e) year; *ein halbes ~* half a year, six months *pl.*; *einmal im ~* once a year; *im ~e* 1900 in 1900; *mit 18 ~en, im Alter von 18 ~en* at (the age of) eighteen; *letztes ~* last year; *das ganze ~ hindurch or über* all the year round; **2'aus** *adv.*: *~, jahrein* year in, year out; year after year; **'~buch** *n* yearbook, annual; **~'ein** *adv. s. jahraus*.

'jahrelang 1. *adv.* for years; 2. *adj.*: *~e Erfahrung* (many) years of experience.

jähren ['jeːrən] *v/refl.* (ge-, *h*): *es jährt sich heute, daß ... it is a year ago today that ..., it is a year today since ...*

'Jahres|abonnement *n* annual subscription (*to magazine, etc.*); *thea.* yearly season ticket; **'~abschluß** *m* annual statement of accounts; **'~anfang** *m* beginning of the year; *zum ~ die besten Wünsche!* best wishes for the New Year; **~bericht** *m* annual report; **~einkommen** *n* annual *or* yearly income; **~ende** *n* end of the year; **~gehalt** *n* annual salary; **'~tag** *m* anniversary; **'~wechsel** *m* turn of the year; **'~zahl** *f* date, year; **'~zeit** *f* season, time of the year.

'Jahrgang *m* volume, year (*of periodical, etc.*); *p.* age-group; *univ., school:* year, class; *wine:* vintage.

Jahr'hundert *n* (*-s*/-e) century; *~feier* *f* centenary, *Am.* centennial; *~wende* *f* turn of the century.

jährig *adj.* ['jeːrɪç] one-year-old.

jährlich ['jeːrlɪç] 1. *adj.* annual, yearly; 2. *adv.* every year; yearly, once a year.

'Jahr|markt *m* fair; **~tausend** *n* (*-s*/-e) millennium; **~'tausendfeier** *f* millenary; **~'zehnt** *n* (*-[e]s*/-e) decade.

'Jähzorn *m* violent (fit of) temper; irascibility; **'2ig** *adj.* hot-tempered; irascible.

Jalousie [ʒaluˈziː] *f* (*-/-n*) (Venetian) blind, *Am. a.* window shade.

Jammer ['jamər] *m* (*-s*/*no pl.*) lamentation; misery; *es ist ein ~ it is a pity.*

jämmerlich *adj.* ['jemərlɪç] miserable, wretched; piteous; pitiable (*esp. contp.*).

jammer|n ['jamərn] *v/i.* (ge-, *h*) lament (*nach, um* for; *über acc.* over); moan; wail, whine; **'~schade** *adj.*: *es ist ~ it is a thousand pities, it is a great shame.*

Januar ['januaːr] *m* (*-[s]*/-e) January.

Japan|er [jaˈpaːnər] *m* (*-s*/-) Japanese; *die ~ pl.* the Japanese *pl.*; **2isch** *adj.* Japanese.

Jargon [ʒarˈgõ] *m* (*-s*/-s) jargon, cant, slang.

Jasmin ♀ [jasˈmiːn] *m* (*-s*/-e) jasmin(e), jessamin(e).

'Jastimme *parl. f* aye, *Am. a.* yea.

jäten ['jeːtən] *v/t.* (ge-, *h*) weed.

Jauche ['jauxə] *f* (*-/-n*) ♀ liquid manure; sewage.

jauchzen ['jauxtsən] *v/i.* (ge-, *h*) exult, rejoice, cheer; *vor Freude ~* shout for joy.

jawohl *adv.* [jaˈvoːl] yes; yes, indeed; yes, certainly; that's right; ✕, *etc.*: yes, Sir!

'Jawort *n* consent; *j-m das ~ geben* accept *s.o.*'s proposal (of marriage).

je [jeː] 1. *adv.* ever, at any time; always; *ohne ihn ~ gesehen zu haben* without ever having seen him; *seit eh und ~* since time immemorial, always; *distributive with numerals:* *~ zwei* two at a time, two each, two by two, by *or* in twos; *sie bekamen ~ zwei Äpfel* they received two apples each; *für ~ zehn Wörter* for every ten words; *in Schachteln mit or zu ~ zehn Stück verpackt* packed in boxes of ten; 2. *cj.*: *~ nach Größe* according to *or* depending on size; *~ nachdem* it depends; *~ nachdem, was er für richtig hält* according as he thinks fit; *~ nachdem, wie er sich fühlt* depending on how he feels; *~ mehr, desto besser* the more the better; *~ länger, ~ lieber* the longer the better; 3. *prp.*: *die Birnen kosten e-e Mark ~ Pfund* the pears cost one mark a pound; *s. pro.*

jede|(r, -s) *indef. pron.* ['jeːdə(r, -s)] every; any; *of a group:* each; *of two persons:* either; jeder, der whoever; jeden zweiten Tag every other day; **'~n'falls** *adv.* at all events, in any case; '⌐rmann *indef. pron.* everyone, everybody; '⌐r'zeit *adv.* always, at any time; '⌐s'mal *adv.* each *or* every time; ⌐ *wenn* whenever.

jedoch *cj.* [je'dɔx] however, yet, nevertheless.

'jeher *adv.: von or seit* ⌐ at all times, always, from time immemorial.

jemals *adv.* ['je:ma:ls] ever, at any time.

jemand *indef. pron.* ['je:mant] someone, somebody; *with questions and negations:* anyone, anybody.

jene(r, -s) *dem. pron.* ['je:nə(r, -s)] that (one), jene *pl.* those *pl.*

jenseitig *adj* ['jɛnzaitiç] opposite.

'jenseits 1. *prp.* (*gen.*) on the other side of, beyond, across; 2. *adv.* on the other side, beyond; 3. ⌐ *n* (-/no *pl.*) *the* other *or* next world, *the* world to come, *the* beyond.

jetzig *adj* ['jetsiç] present, existing; *prices, etc.* current.

jetzt *adv* [jetst] now, at present; *bis* ⌐ until now; so far; *eben* ⌐ just now; *erst* ⌐ only now; *für* ⌐ for the present; *gleich* ⌐ at once, right away; *noch* ⌐ even now; *von* ⌐ *an* from now on.

jeweil|ig *adj.* ['je:'vailiç] respective; ⌐s *adv.* ['⌐s] respectively, at a time; from time to time (*esp. ₰₰*).

Joch [jɔx] *n* (-[e]s/-e) yoke; *in mountains* col, pass, saddle; △ bay; ⌐bein *anat. n* cheek-bone.

Jockel ['dʒɔki] *m* (-s/-s) jockey.

Jod ⚗ [jo:t] *n* (-[e]s/no *pl.*) iodine.

jodeln ['jo:dəln] *v/i.* (ge-, h) yodel.

Johanni [jo'hani] *n* (-/no *pl.*), ⌐s [⌐s] *n* (-/no *pl.*) Midsummer day; ⌐s-beere *f* currant; *rote* ⌐ red currant; ⌐stag *m eccl.* St John's day; Midsummer day.

johlen ['jo:lən] *v/i.* (ge-, h) bawl, yell, howl.

Jolle ⚓ ['jɔlə] *f* (-/-n) jolly-boat, yawl, dinghy.

Jongl|eur [ʒõ'glø:r] *m* (-s/-e) juggler; ⌐ieren *v/t. and v/i.* (no -ge-, h) juggle.

Journal [ʒur'na:l] *n* (-s/-e) journal; newspaper; magazine; diary; ⚓ log-book; ⌐ist [⌐a'list] *m* (-en/-en) journalist, *Am. a.* newspaperman.

Jubel ['ju:bəl] *m* (-s/no *pl.*) jubilation, exultation, rejoicing; cheering; ⌐n *v/i.* (ge-, h) jubilate; exult, rejoice (*über acc.* at).

Jubil|ar [jubi'la:r] *m* (-s/-e) person celebrating his jubilee, *etc.*; ⌐äum [⌐.ɛ:um] *n* (-s/ Jubiläen) jubilee.

Juchten ['juxtən] *m, n* (-s/no *pl.*), '⌐leder *n* Russia (leather).

jucken ['jukən] (ge-, h) 1. *v/i.* itch; 2. *v/t.* irritate, (make) itch; *F sich* ⌐ scratch (o.s.).

Jude ['ju:də] *m* (-n/-n) Jew; '⌐n-feindlich *adj.* anti-Semitic; '⌐n-

tum *n* (-s/no *pl.*) Judaism; '⌐nver-folgung *f* persecution of Jews, Jew-baiting; pogrom.

Jüd|in ['jy:din] *f* (-/-nen) Jewess; '⌐isch *adj.* Jewish.

Jugend ['ju:gənt] *f* (-/no *pl.*) youth; '⌐amt *n* youth welfare department; '⌐buch *n* book for the young; '⌐freund *m* friend of one's youth; school-friend; '⌐fürsorge *f* youth welfare; ⌐gericht *n* juvenile court; '⌐herberge *f* youth hostel; ⌐jahre *n/pl.* early years, youth; ⌐krimi-nalität *f* juvenile delinquency; '⌐lich *adj.* youthful, juvenile, young; '⌐liche *m, f* (-n/-n) young person; juvenile, young man, youth; young girl; teen-ager; ⌐liebe *f* early *or* first love, calf-love, *Am a.* puppy love; *old* sweetheart *or* flame; '⌐schriften *f/pl* books for the young; '⌐schutz *m* protection of children and young people; ⌐streich *m* youthful prank; ⌐werk *n* early work (*of author*); ⌐e *pl. a.* juvenilia *pl.*; '⌐zeit *f* (time *or* days of) youth.

Jugoslav|e [ju:go'sla:və] *m* (-en/-en) Jugoslav, Yugoslav, ⌐isch *adj.* Jugoslav, Yugoslav.

Juli ['ju:li] *m* (-[s]/-s) July.

jung *adj* [juŋ] young; youthful; *peas.* green; *beer, wine* new; ⌐es *Gemüse* young *or* early vegetables *pl.*; *F fig.* young people, small fry.

'Junge 1. *m* (-n/-n) boy, youngster; lad; fellow, chap, *Am.* guy; *cards:* knave, jack, *Am.* 2. *n* (-n/-n) young; puppy (*of dog*); kitten (*of cat*); calf (*of cow, elephant, etc.*); cub (*of beast of prey*); ⌐ *werfen* bring forth young; *ein* ⌐s *a* young one; '⌐nhaft *adj.* boyish; '⌐nstreich *m* boyish prank *or* trick.

jünger ['jyŋər] 1. *adj.* younger, junior; *er ist drei Jahre* ⌐ *als ich* he is my junior by three years, he is three years younger than I; 2. ⌐ *m* (-s/-) disciple.

Jungfer ['juŋfər] *f* (-/-n): *alte* ⌐ old maid *or* spinster.

'Jungfern|fahrt ⚓ *f* maiden voyage *or* trip, ⌐flug ✈ *m* maiden flight; '⌐rede *f* maiden speech.

'Jung|frau *f* maid(en), virgin; ⚸ fräulich *adj.* ['⌐frɔyliç] virginal; *fig.* virgin, ⌐fräulichkeit *f* (-/no *pl.*) virginity, maidenhood; '⌐ge-selle *m* bachelor; ⌐gesellenstand *m* bachelorhood; '⌐gesellin *f* (-/-nen) bachelor girl.

Jüngling ['jyŋliŋ] *m* (-s/-e) youth, young man.

jüngst [jyŋst] 1. *adj.* youngest; *time:* (most) recent, latest; *das* ⌐e *Ge-richt, der* ⌐e *Tag* Last Judg(e)ment, Day of Judg(e)ment; 2. *adv.* recently, lately.

'jungverheiratet *adj.* newly married; '⌐en *pl. the* newlyweds *pl.*

Juni [' juːni] *m* (-[s]/-s) June; '**käfer** *zo.* *m* cockchafer, June-bug.

Junior [' juːnjɔr] **1.** *adj.* junior; **2.** ♀ *m* (-s/-en) junior (*a. sports*).

Jura [' juːra] *n/pl.:* ∼ studieren read or study law.

Jurist [juˈrist] *m* (-en/-en) lawyer; law-student; ♀isch *adj.* legal.

Jury [ʒyˈriː] *f* (-/-s) jury.

justier|en ⊕ [jusˈtiːrən] *v/t.* (*no -ge-, h*) adjust; ♀ung ⊕ *f* (-/-en) adjustment.

Justiz [jusˈtiːts] *f* (-/*no pl.*) (administration of) justice; ∼beamte *m* judicial officer; ∼gebäude *n* courthouse; ∼inspektor *m* judicial officer; ∼irrtum *m* judicial error; ∼minister *m* minister of justice; Lord Chancellor, *Am.* Attorney General; ∼ministerium *n* ministry of justice; *Am.* Department of Justice; ∼mord *m* judicial murder.

Juwel [juˈveːl] *m, n* (-s/-en) jewel, gem; ∼en *pl.* jewel(le)ry; ∼ier [∼eˈliːr] *m* (-s/-e) jewel(l)er.

Jux F [juks] *m* (-es/-e) (practical) joke, fun, spree, lark; prank.

K

(Compare also C and Z)

Kabel [' kaːbəl] *n* (-s/-) cable.

Kabeljau *ichth.* [' kaːbəljau] *m* (-s/-e, -s) cod(fish).

'**kabeln** *v/t. and v/i.* (*ge-, h*) cable.

Kabine [kaˈbiːnə] *f* (-/-n) cabin; *at hairdresser's, etc.*: cubicle; cage (*of lift*).

Kabinett *pol.* [kabiˈnɛt] *n* (-s/-e) cabinet, government.

Kabriolett [kabrioˈlɛt] *n* (-s/-e) cabriolet, convertible.

Kachel [' kaxəl] *f* (-/-n) (Dutch *or* glazed) tile; '∼ofen *m* tiled stove.

Kadaver [kaˈdaːvər] *m* (-s/-) carcass.

Kadett [kaˈdɛt] *m* (-en/-en) cadet.

Käfer *zo.* [' kɛːfər] *m* (-s/-) beetle, chafer.

Kaffee [' kafe, kaˈfeː] *m* (-s/-s) coffee; (')∼bohne ♀ *f* coffee-bean; (')∼kanne *f* coffee-pot; (')∼mühle *f* coffee-mill *or* -grinder; (')∼satz *m* coffee-grounds *pl.*; (')∼tasse *f* coffee-cup.

Käfig [' kɛːfiç] *m* (-s/-e) cage (*a. fig.*).

kahl *adj.* [kaːl] *p.* bald; *tree, etc.*: bare; *landscape, etc.*: barren, bleak; *rock, etc.*: naked; ♀kopf *m* baldhead, baldpate; ∼köpfig *adj.* [' ∼kœpfiç] bald(-headed).

Kahn [kaːn] *m* (-[e]s/∼e) boat; riverbarge; ∼ fahren go boating; '∼fahren *n* (-s/*no pl.*) boating.

Kai [kai] *m* (-s/-e, -s) quay, wharf.

Kaiser [' kaizər] *m* (-s/-) emperor; '∼krone *f* imperial crown; ♀lich *adj.* imperial; '∼reich *n*, '∼tum *n* (-[e]s/∼er) empire; '∼würde *f* imperial status.

Kajüte ♨ [kaˈjyːtə] *f* (-/-n) cabin.

Kakao [kaˈkaːo] *m* (-s/-s) cocoa; ♀ *a.* cacao.

Kakt|ee ♀ [kakˈteː(ə)] *f* (-/-n), ∼us ♀ [' ∼us] *m* (-/Kakteen, F *Kaktusse*) cactus.

Kalauer [' kaːlauər] *m* (-s/-) stale joke; pun.

Kalb *zo.* [kalp] *n* (-[e]s/∼er) calf; ♀en [' ∼bən] *v/i.* (*ge-, h*) calve; '∼fell *n* calfskin; '∼fleisch *n* veal; '∼leder *n* calf(-leather).

'**Kalbs|braten** *m* roast veal; '∼keule *f* leg of veal; '∼leder *n s. Kalbleder*; '∼nierenbraten *m* loin of veal.

Kalender [kaˈlɛndər] *m* (-s/-) calendar; almanac; ∼block *m* dateblock; ∼jahr *n* calendar year; ∼uhr *f* calendar watch *or* clock.

Kali ♀ [' kaːli] *n* (-s/-s) potash.

Kaliber [kaˈliːbər] *n* (-s/-) calib|re, *Am.* -er (*a. fig.*), bore (*of firearm*).

Kalk [kalk] *m* (-[e]s/-e) lime; *geol.* limestone; '∼brenner *m* limeburner; '♀en *v/t.* (*ge-, h*) whitewash (*wall, etc.*); ♂ lime (*field*); ♀ig *adj.* limy; '∼ofen *m* limekiln; '∼stein *m* limestone; '∼steinbruch *m* limestone quarry.

Kalorie [kaloˈriː] *f* (-/-n) calorie.

kalt *adj.* [kalt] *climate, meal, sweat, etc.*: cold; *p.*, *manner, etc.*: cold, chilly, frigid; *mir ist* ∼ I am cold; ∼e *Küche* cold dishes *pl. or* meat, *etc.*; *j-m die* ∼e *Schulter zeigen* give s.o. the cold shoulder; ∼blütig *adj.* [' ∼blyːtiç] cold-blooded (*a. fig.*).

Kälte [' kɛltə] *f* (-/*no pl.*) cold; chill; coldness, chilliness (*both a. fig.*); *vor* ∼ *zittern* shiver with cold; *fünf Grad* ∼ five degrees below zero; '∼grad *m* degree below zero; '∼welle *f* cold spell.

'**kalt|stellen** *fig. v/t.* (*sep., -ge-, h*) shelve, reduce to impotence; '♀welle *f* cold wave.

kam [kaːm] *pret. of kommen.*

Kamel *zo.* [kaˈmeːl] *n* (-[e]s/-e) camel; ∼haar *n textiles:* camel hair.

Kamera *phot.* [' kamərə] *f* (-/-s) camera.

Kamerad [kamə'rɑːt] *m* (-en/-en) comrade; companion; mate, F pal, chum; **.schaft** *f* (-/-en) comradeship, companionship; **2schaftlich** *adj.* comradely, companionable.

Kamille ♣ [ka'milə] *f* (-/-n) camomile; **.ntee** *m* camomile tea.

Kamin [ka'miːn] *m* (-s/-e) chimney (*a. mount.*); fireplace, fireside; **.sims** *m, n* mantelpiece; **.vorleger** *m* hearth-rug; **.vorsetzer** *m* (-s/-) fender.

Kamm [kam] *m* (-[e]s/⁼e) comb; crest (*of bird or wave*); crest, ridge (*of mountain*).

kämmen ['kemən] *v/t.* (ge-, h) comb; **sich** (*die Haare*) **.** comb one's hair.

Kammer ['kamər] *f* (-/-n) (small) room; closet; *pol.* chamber; board; ⅞ division (*of court*); **.diener** *m* valet; **'.frau** *f* lady's maid; **.gericht** ⅞ *n* supreme court; **.herr** *m* chamberlain; **'.jäger** *m* vermin exterminator; **.musik** *f* chamber music; **'.zofe** *f* chambermaid.

'Kamm|garn *n* worsted (yarn); **'.rad ⊕** *n* cogwheel.

Kampagne [kam'panjə] *f* (-/-n) campaign.

Kampf [kampf] *m* (-[e]s/⁼e) combat, fight (*a. fig.*); struggle (*a. fig.*); battle (*a. fig.*); *fig.* conflict; *sports:* contest, match; *boxing:* fight, bout; **'.bahn** *f* *sports:* stadium, arena; **'2bereit** *adj.* ready for battle.

kämpfen ['kempfən] *v/i.* (ge-, h) fight (*gegen* against; *mit* with; *um* for) (*a. fig.*); struggle (*a. fig.*); *fig.* contend, wrestle (*mit* with).

Kampfer ['kampfər] *m* (-s/*no pl.*) camphor.

Kämpfer ['kempfər] *m* (-s/-) fighter (*a. fig.*); ✗ combatant, warrior.

'Kampf|flugzeug *n* tactical aircraft; **'.geist** *m* fighting spirit; **'.platz** *m* battlefield; *fig.*, *sports:* arena; **'.preis** *m* *sports:* prize; ✝ cut-throat price; **'.richter** *m* referee, judge, umpire; **'2unfähig** *adj.* disabled.

kampieren [kam'piːrən] *v/i.* (no -ge-, h) camp.

Kanal [ka'nɑːl] *m* (-s/⁼e) canal; channel (*a.* ⊕, *fig.*); *geogr.* **the** Channel; sewer, drain; **.isation** [.aliza'tsjoːn] *f* (-/-en) *river* canalization; *town, etc.:* sewerage; drainage; **2isieren** [.ali'ziːrən] *v/t.* (no -ge-, h) canalize; sewer (*town*).

Kanarienvogel *orn.* [ka'nɑːrjən-] *m* canary(-bird).

Kandare [kan'dɑːrə] *f* (-/-n) curb (-bit).

Kandid|at [kandi'dɑːt] *m* (-en/-en) candidate; applicant; **.atur** [.a'tuːr] *f* (-/-en) candidature, candidacy; **2ieren** [.'diːrən] *v/i.* (no -ge-, h) be a candidate (*für* for);

. *für* apply for, stand for, *Am.* run for (*office, etc.*).

Känguruh *zo.* ['keŋguruː] *n* (-s/-s) kangaroo.

Kaninchen *zo.* [ka'niːnçən] *n* (-s/-) rabbit; **.bau** *m* rabbit-burrow.

Kanister [ka'nistər] *m* (-s/-) can.

Kanne ['kanə] *f* (-/-n) milk, *etc.*: jug; coffee, tea: pot; oil, milk: can; **'.gießer** F *fig. m* political wiseacre.

Kannibal|e [kani'bɑːlə] *m* (-n/-n) cannibal; 2isch *adj.* cannibal.

kannte ['kantə] *pret. of* kennen.

Kanon ♪ ['kaːnɔn] *m* (-s/-s) canon.

Kanon|ade ✗ [kano'nɑːdə] *f* (-/-n) cannonade; **.e** [.'noːnə] *f* (-/-n) ✗ cannon, gun; F *fig.*: big shot; *esp. sports:* ace, crack.

Ka'nonen|boot ✗ *n* gunboat; **.donner** *m* boom of cannon; **.futter** *fig. n* cannon-fodder; **.kugel** *f* cannon-ball; **.rohr** *n* gun barrel.

Kanonier ✗ [kano'niːr] *m* (-s/-e) gunner.

Kant|e ['kantə] *f* (-/-n) edge; brim; **'.en** *m* (-s/-) end of loaf; **'2en** *v/t.* (ge-, h) square (*stone, etc.*); set on edge; tilt; edge (*skis*); **'2ig** *adj.* angular, edged; square(d).

Kantine [kan'tiːnə] *f* (-/-n) canteen.

Kanu ['kaːnu] *n* (-s/-s) canoe.

Kanüle ♣ [ka'nyːlə] *f* (-/-n) tubule, cannula.

Kanzel ['kantsəl] *f* (-/-n) eccl. pulpit; ✗ cockpit; ✗ (gun-)turret.; **'.redner** *m* preacher.

Kanzlei [kants'lai] *f* (-/-en) office.

'Kanzler *m* (-s/-) chancellor.

Kap *geogr.* [kap] *n* (-s/-s) headland.

Kapazität [kapatsi'tɛːt] *f* (-/-en) capacity; *fig.* authority.

Kapell|e [ka'pelə] *f* (-/-n) eccl. chapel; ♪ band; **.meister** *m* bandleader, conductor.

kaper|n ⚓ ['kaːpərn] *v/t.* (ge-, h) capture, seize; '2schiff *n* privateer.

kapieren F [ka'piːrən] *v/t.* (no -ge-, h) grasp, get.

Kapital [kapi'tɑːl] **1.** *n* (-s/-e, -ien) capital, stock, funds *pl.*; **.** *und* Zinsen principal and interest; **2.** 2 *adj.* capital; **.anlage** *f* investment; **.flucht** *f* flight of capital; **.gesellschaft** *f* joint-stock company; 2isieren [.ali'ziːrən] *v/t.* (no -ge-, h) capitalize; **.ismus** [.a'lismus] *m* (-/no pl.) capitalism; **.ist** [.a'list] *m* (-en/-en) capitalist; **.markt** [.'tɑːl-] *m* capital market; **.verbrechen** *n* capital crime.

Kapitän [kapi'tɛːn] *m* (-s/-e) captain; **.** *zur* See naval captain; **.leutnant** *m* (senior) lieutenant.

Kapitel [ka'pitəl] *n* (-s/-) chapter (*a. fig.*).

Kapitul|ation ✗ [kapitula'tsjoːn] *f* (-/-en) capitulation, surrender; 2ieren [.'liːrən] *v/i.* (no -ge-, h) capitulate, surrender.

Kaplan *eccl.* [ka'plɑ:n] *m* (-s/⁼e) chaplain.

Kappe ['kapə] *f* (-/-n) cap; hood (*a.* ⊕); bonnet; '⁓n *v/t.* (*ge-, h*) cut (*cable*); lop, top (*tree*).

Kapriole [kapri'o:lə] *f* (-/-n) equitation: capriole; *fig.*: caper; prank.

Kapsel ['kapsəl] *f* (-/-n) case, box; ♀, ♂, *anat., etc.*: capsule.

kaputt *adj.* [ka'put] broken; *elevator, etc.*: out of order; *fruit, etc.*: spoilt; *p.*: ruined; tired out, F fagged out; ⁓gehen *v/i.* (*irr. gehen, sep.*, -ge-, *sein*) break, go to pieces; spoil.

Kapuze [ka'pu:tsə] *f* (-/-n) hood; *eccl.* cowl.

Karabiner [kara'bi:nər] *m* (-s/-) carbine.

Karaffe [ka'rafə] *f* (-/-n) carafe (*for wine or water*); decanter (*for liqueur, etc.*).

Karambol|age [karambo'lɑ:ʒə] *f* (-/-n) collision, crash; *billiards*: cannon, *Am. a.* carom; ⁓ieren *v/i.* (*no -ge-, sein*) cannon, *Am. a.* carom; F *fig.* collide.

Karat [ka'rɑ:t] *n* (-[e]s/-e) carat.

Karawane [kara'vɑ:nə] *f* (-/-n) caravan.

Karbid [kar'bi:t] *n* (-[e]s/-e) carbide.

Kardinal *eccl.* [kardi'nɑ:l] *m* (-s/⁼e) cardinal.

Karfreitag *eccl.* [kɑ:r'-] *m* Good Friday.

karg *adj.* [kark] *soil*: meagre; *vegetation*: scant, sparse; *meal*: scanty, meagre, frugal; ⁓en ['-gən] *v/i.* (*ge-, h*): ⁓ *mit* be sparing of.

kärglich *adj.* ['kerkliç] scanty, meagre; poor.

kariert *adj.* [ka'ri:rt] check(ed), chequered, *Am.* checkered.

Karik|atur [karika'tu:r] *f* (-/-en) caricature, cartoon; ⁓ieren [⁓'ki:rən] *v/t.* (*no -ge-, h*) caricature, cartoon.

karmesin *adj.* [karme'zi:n] crimson.

Karneval ['karnəval] *m* (-s/-e, -s) Shrovetide, carnival.

Karo ['kɑ:ro] *n* (-s/-s) square, check; *cards*: diamonds *pl.*

Karosserie *mot.* [karɔsə'ri:] *f* (-/-n) body.

Karotte ♀ [ka'rɔtə] *f* (-/-n) carrot.

Karpfen *ichth.* ['karpfən] *m* (-s/-) carp.

Karre ['karə] *f* (-/-n) cart; wheelbarrow.

Karriere [kar'je:rə] *f* (-/-n) (successful) career.

Karte ['kartə] *f* (-/-n) card; postcard; map; chart; ticket; menu, bill of fare; list.

Kartei [kar'taɪ] *f* (-/-en) card-index; ⁓karte *f* index-card, filing-card; ⁓schrank *m* filing cabinet.

Kartell ♥ [kar'tel] *n* (-s/-e) cartel.

'Karten|brief *m* letter-card; '⁓haus *n* ⊕ chart-house; *fig.* house of cards; '⁓legerin *f* (-/-nen) fortune-teller from the cards; '⁓spiel *n* card-playing; card-game.

Kartoffel [kar'tɔfəl] *f* (-/-n) potato, F spud; ⁓brei *m* mashed potatoes *pl.*; ⁓käfer *m* Colorado *or* potato beetle, *Am. a.* potato bug; ⁓schalen *f/pl.* potato peelings *pl.*

Karton [kar'tõ, kar'to:n] *m* (-s/-s, -e) cardboard, pasteboard; cardboard box, carton.   [*Kartei.*\

Kartothek [karto'te:k] *f* (-/-en) *s.*\

Karussell [karu'sel] *n* (-s/-s, -e) roundabout, merry-go-round, *Am. a.* car(r)ousel.

Karwoche *eccl.* ['kɑ:r-] *f* Holy *or* Passion Week.

Käse ['kɛ:zə] *m* (-s/-) cheese.

Kasern|e ✕ [ka'zɛrnə] *f* (-/-n) barracks *pl.*; ⁓enhof *m* barrack-yard *or* -square; ⁓ieren [⁓'ni:rən] *v/t.* (*no -ge-, h*) quarter in barracks, barrack.

'käsig *adj.* cheesy; *complexion*: pale, pasty.

Kasino [ka'zi:no] *n* (-s/-s) casino, club(-house); (officers') mess.

Kasperle ['kasperlə] *n, m* (-s/-) Punch; '⁓theater *n* Punch and Judy show.

Kasse ['kasə] *f* (-/-n) cash-box; till (*in shop, etc.*); cash-desk, pay-desk (*in bank, etc.*); pay-office (*in firm*); *thea., etc.*: box-office, booking-office; cash; *bei* ⁓ in cash.

'Kassen|abschluß ♥ *m* balancing of the cash (accounts); '⁓anweisung *f* disbursement voucher; '⁓bestand *m* cash in hand; '⁓bote *m* bank messenger; '⁓buch *n* cash book; '⁓erfolg *m thea., etc.*: box-office success; '⁓patient ♂ *m* panel patient; '⁓schalter *m bank, etc.*: teller's counter.

Kasserolle [kasə'rɔlə] *f* (-/-n) stewpan, casserole.

Kassette [ka'sɛtə] *f* (-/-n) box (*for money, etc.*); casket (*for jewels, etc.*); slip-case (*for books*); *phot.* plateholder.

kassiere|n [ka'si:rən] (*no -ge-, h*) **1.** *v/i.* *waiter, etc.*: take the money (*für for*); **2.** *v/t.* take (*sum of money*); collect (*contributions, etc.*); annul; ⅛ quash (*verdict*); ⁓r *m* (-s/-) cashier; *bank*: *a.* teller; collector.

Kastanie ♀ [ka'stɑ:njə] *f* (-/-n) chestnut.

Kasten ['kastən] *m* (-s/⁼, ⁓) box; chest (*for tools, etc.*); case (*for violin, etc.*); bin (*for bread, etc.*).

Kasus *gr.* ['kɑ:sus] *m* (-/-) case.

Katalog [kata'lo:k] *m* (-[e]s/-e) catalogue, *Am. a.* catalog; ⁓isieren [⁓ogi'zi:rən] *v/t.* (*no -ge-, h*) catalogue, *Am. a.* catalog.

Katarrh ♂ [ka'tar] *m* (-s/-e) (common) cold, catarrh.

katastroph|al adj. [katastro'fɑːl] catastrophic, disastrous; 2e [↙'stroː- fə] f (-/-n) catastrophe, disaster.

Katechismus eccl. [kate'çismus] m (-/Katechismen) catechism.

Katego|rie [katego'riː] f (-/-n) category; 2**risch** adj. [↙'goːriʃ] categorical.

Kater ['kɑːtər] m (-s/-) zo. male cat, tom-cat; fig. s. Katzenjammer.

Katheder [ka'teːdər] n, m (-s/-) lecturing-desk. [cathedral.\

Kathedrale [kate'drɑːlə] f (-/-n)\

Katholi|k [kato'liːk] m (-en/-en) (Roman) Catholic; 2**sch** adj. [↙'toːliʃ] (Roman) Catholic.

Kattun [ka'tuːn] m (-s/-e) calico; cotton cloth or fabric; chintz.

Katze zo. ['katsə] f (-/-n) cat; '↙**n- jammer** F fig. m hangover, morn- ing-after feeling.

Kauderwelsch ['kaudərvelʃ] n (-[s]/ no pl.) gibberish, F double Dutch; 2**en** v/i. (ge-, h) gibber, F talk double Dutch.

kauen ['kauən] v/t. and v/i. (ge-, h) chew.

kauern ['kauərn] (ge-, h) 1. v/i. crouch; squat; 2. v/refl. crouch (down); squat (down); duck (down).

Kauf [kauf] m (-[e]s/٨e) purchase; bargain, F good buy; acquisition; purchasing, buying; '↙**brief** m deed of purchase; 2**en** v/t. (ge-, h) buy, purchase; acquire (by purchase); sich et. ∼ buy o.s. s.th., buy s.th. for o.s.

Käufer ['kɔyfər] m (-s/-) buyer, purchaser; customer.

'**Kauf|haus** n department store; '↙**laden** m shop, Am. a. store.

käuflich ['kɔyfliç] 1. adj. for sale; purchasable; fig. open to bribery, bribable; venal; 2. adv.: ∼ erwerben (acquire by) purchase; ∼ überlassen transfer by way of sale.

'**Kauf|mann** m (-[e]s/Kaufleute) businessman; merchant; trader, deal- er, shopkeeper; Am. a. storekeeper; 2**männisch** adj. ['↙meniʃ] com- mercial, mercantile; '↙**vertrag** m contract of sale.

'**Kaugummi** m chewing-gum.

kaum adv. [kaum] hardly, scarcely, barely; ∼ glaublich hard to believe.

'**Kautabak** m chewing-tobacco.

Kaution [kau'tsjoːn] f (-/-en) security, surety; mst bail.

Kautschuk ['kautʃuk] m (-s/-e) caoutchouc, pure rubber.

Kavalier [kava'liːr] m (-s/-e) gentle- man; beau, admirer.

Kavallerie ✕ [kavalə'riː] f (-/-n) cavalry, horse.

Kaviar ['kɑːviar] m (-s/-e) caviar(e).

keck adj. [kek] bold; impudent, saucy, cheeky; 2**heit** f (-/-en) bold- ness; impudence, sauciness, cheek- iness.

Kegel ['keːgəl] m (-s/-) games: skittle, pin; esp. ٨, ⊕ cone; ∼ schieben s. kegeln; '↙**bahn** f skittle, alley, Am. bowling alley; 2**förmig** adj. ['↙fœrmiç] conic(al), coniform; tapering; 2**n** v/i. (ge-, h) play (at) skittles or ninepins, Am. bowl.

Kegler ['keːglər] m (-s/-) skittle- player, Am. bowler.

Kehl|e ['keːlə] f (-/-n) throat; '↙**kopf** anat. m larynx.

Kehre ['keːrə] f (-/-n) (sharp) bend, turn; 2**n** v/t. (ge-, h) sweep, brush; turn (nach oben upwards); j-m den Rücken ∼ turn one's back on s.o.

Kehricht ['keːriçt] m, n (-[e]s/no pl.) sweepings pl., rubbish.

'**Kehrseite** f wrong side, reverse; esp. fig. seamy side.

'**kehrtmachen** v/i. (sep., -ge-, h) turn on one's heel; ✕ turn or face about.

keifen ['kaifən] v/i. (ge-, h) scold, chide.

Keil [kail] m (-[e]s/-e) wedge; gore, gusset; '↙**e** F f (-/no pl.) thrashing, hiding; ↙**er** zo. m (-s/-) wild-boar; ↙**erei** F [↙'rai] f (-/-en) row, scrap; 2**förmig** adj. ['↙fœrmiç] wedge- shaped, cuneiform; '↙**kissen** n wedge-shaped bolster; '↙**schrift** f cuneiform characters pl.

Keim [kaim] m (-[e]s/-e) ٩, biol. germ; ٩: seed-plant; shoot; sprout; fig. seeds pl., germ, bud; 2**en** v/i. (ge-, h) seeds, etc.: germinate; seeds, plants, potatoes, etc.: sprout; fig. b(o)urgeon; 2**frei** adj. sterilized, sterile; ↙**träger** m (germ-)car- rier; 2**zelle** f germ-cell.

kein indef. pron. [kain] as adj.: ∼(e) no, not any; ∼ anderer als none other but; as noun: ∼er, ∼e, ∼(e)s none, no one, nobody; ∼er von beiden neither (of the two); ∼er von uns none of us; '↙**es'falls** adv., ∼**es- wegs** adv. ['↙'veːks] by no means, not at all; '↙**mal** adv. not once, not a single time.

Keks [keːks] m, n (-, -es/-, -e) bis- cuit, Am. cookie; cracker.

Kelch [kelç] m (-[e]s/-e) cup, goblet; eccl. chalice, communion-cup; ٩ calyx.

Kelle ['kelə] f (-/-n) scoop; ladle; tool trowel.

Keller ['kelər] m (-s/-) cellar; base- ment, ↙**ei** [↙'rai] f (-/-en) wine-vault; '↙**geschoß** n basement; '↙**meister** m cellarman.

Kellner ['kelnər] m (-s/-) waiter; '↙**in** f (·/-nen) waitress.

Kelter ['keltər] f (-/-n) winepress; 2**n** v/t. (ge-, h) press.

kenn|en ['kenən] v/t. (irr., ge-, h) know, be acquainted with; have knowledge of s.th.; '↙**enlernen** v/t. (sep., -ge-, h) get or come to know;

make s.o.'s acquaintance, meet s.o.; '2er m (-s/-) expert; connoisseur; '~tlich adj. recognizable (an dat. by); ~ machen mark; label; '2tnis f (-/-se) knowledge; ~ nehmen von take not(ic)e of; '2zeichen n mark, sign; mot. registration (number), Am. license number; fig. hallmark, criterion; '~zeichnen v/t. (ge-, h) mark, characterize.

kentern ⚓ ['kɛntərn] v/i. (ge-, sein) capsize, keel over, turn turtle.

Kerbe ['kɛrbə] f (-/-n) notch, nick; slot; '2n v/t. (ge-, h) notch, nick, indent.

Kerker ['kɛrkər] m (-s/-) gaol, jail, prison; '~meister m gaoler, jailer.

Kerl F [kɛrl] m (-s, ⚓ -es/-e, F -s) man; fellow, F chap, bloke, esp. Am. guy.

Kern [kɛrn] m (-[e]s/-e) kernel (of nut, etc.); stone, Am. pit (of cherry, etc.); pip (of orange, apple, etc.); core (of the earth); phys. nucleus; fig. core, heart, crux; Kern... s. a. Atom...; '~energie f nuclear energy; '~forschung f nuclear research; '~gehäuse n core; '2ge'sund adj. thoroughly healthy, F as sound as a bell; '2ig adj. full of pips; fig.: pithy; solid; '~punkt m central or crucial point; '~spaltung f nuclear fission.

Kerze ['kɛrtsə] f (-/-n) candle; '~n-licht n candle-light; '~nstärke f candle-power.

keß F adj. [kɛs] pert, jaunty; smart.

Kessel ['kɛsəl] m (-s/-) kettle; cauldron; boiler; hollow.

Kette ['kɛtə] f (-/-n) chain; range (of mountains, etc.); necklace; '2n v/t. (ge-, h) chain (an acc. to).

'Ketten|hund m watch-dog; '~rau-cher m chain-smoker; '~reaktion f chain reaction.

Ketzer ['kɛtsər] m (-s/-) heretic; ~ei [~'raɪ] f (-/-en) heresy; '2isch adj. heretical.

keuch|en ['kɔʏçən] v/i. (ge-, h) pant, gasp; '2husten ♣ m (w)hooping cough.

Keule ['kɔʏlə] f (-/-n) club; leg (of mutton, pork, etc.).

keusch adj. [kɔʏʃ] chaste, pure; '2heit f (-/no pl.) chastity, purity.

kichern ['kiçərn] v/i. (ge-, h) giggle, titter.

Kiebitz ['ki:bits] m (-es/-e) orn. pe(e)wit; F fig. kibitzer; '2en f F fig. v/i. (ge-, h) kibitz.

Kiefer ['ki:fər] 1. anat. m (-s/-) jaw(-bone); 2. ♣ f (-/-n) pine.

Kiel [ki:l] m (-[e]s/-e) ⚓ keel; quill; '~raum m bilge, hold; '~wasser n wake (a. fig.).

Kieme zo. ['ki:mə] f (-/-n) gill.

Kies [ki:s] m (-es/-e) gravel; sl. fig. dough; '~el [~zəl] m (-s/-) pebble, flint; '~weg m gravel-walk.

Kilo ['ki:lo] n (-s/-[s]), ~gramm [kilo'gram] n kilogram(me); ~hertz [~'hɛrts] n (-/no pl.) kilocycle per second; ~meter m kilomet|re, Am. -er; ~watt n kilowatt.

Kimme ['kimə] f (-/-n) notch.

Kind [kint] n (-[e]s/-er) child; baby.

'Kinder|arzt m p(a)ediatrician; ~ei [~'raɪ] f (-/-en) childishness; child-ish trick; trifle; '~frau f nurse; '~fräulein n governess; '~funk m children's program(me); '~garten m kindergarten, nursery school; '~lähmung ♣ f infantile paralysis, polio(myelitis); '2leicht adj. very easy or simple, F as easy as winking or as ABC; '~lied n children's song; '2los adj. childless; '~mäd-chen n nurse(maid); '~spiel n children's game; ein ~ s. kinder-leicht; '~stube f nursery; fig. manners pl., upbringing; '~wagen m perambulator, F pram, Am. baby carriage; '~zeit f childhood; '~zim-mer n children's room.

'Kindes|alter n childhood, infancy; '~beine n/pl.: von ~n an from child-hood, from a very early age; '~kind n grandchild.

'Kind|heit f (-/no pl.) childhood; 2isch adj. ['~dɪʃ] childish; 2lich adj. childlike.

Kinn anat. [kin] n (-[e]s/-e) chin; '~backe f, '~backen m (-s/-) jaw (-bone); '~haken m boxing: hook to the chin; uppercut; '~lade f jaw(-bone).

Kino ['ki:no] n (-s/-s) cinema, F the pictures pl., Am. motion-picture theater, F the movies pl.; ins ~ gehen go to the cinema or F pictures, Am. F go to the movies; '~besu-cher m cinema-goer, Am. F moviegoer; '~vorstellung f cine-ma-show, Am. motion-picture show.

Kippe F ['kipə] f (-/-n) stub, fag-end, Am. a. butt; auf der ~ stehen or sein hang in the balance; '2n (ge-) 1. v/i. (sein) tip (over), topple (over), tilt (over); 2. v/t. (h) tilt, tip over or up.

Kirche ['kirçə] f (-/-n) church.

'Kirchen|älteste m (-n/-n) church-warden, elder; 2buch n parochial register, '~diener m sacristan, sexton; '~gemeinde f parish; '~jahr n ecclesiastical year; '~lied n hymn; '~musik f sacred music; '~schiff ⚓ n nave; '~steuer f church-rate; '~stuhl m pew; '~vor-steher m churchwarden.

'Kirch|gang m church-going; ~gän-ger [~gɛŋər] m (-s/-) church-goer; 2hof m churchyard; '2lich adj. ecclesiastical; '~spiel n parish; '~turm m steeple; ~weih f ['~vaɪ] f (-/-en) parish fair.

Kirsche ['kirʃə] f (-/-n) cherry.

Kissen ['kisən] *n* (-s/-) cushion; pillow; bolster, pad.

Kiste ['kistə] *f* (-/-n) box, chest; crate.

Kitsch [kitʃ] *m* (-es/*no pl.*) trash, rubbish; '2**ig** *adj.* shoddy, trashy.

Kitt [kit] *m* (-[e]s/-e) cement; putty.

Kittel ['kitəl] *m* (-s/-) overall; smock, frock.

'**kitten** *v/t.* (ge-, h) cement; putt.

kitz|eln ['kitsəln] (ge-, h) **1.** *v/t.* tickle; **2.** *v/i.:* meine Nase kitzelt my nose is tickling; '**~lig** *adj.* ticklish (*a. fig.*).

Kladde ['kladə] *f* (-/-n) rough notebook, waste-book.

klaffen ['klafən] *v/i.* (ge-, h) gape, yawn.

kläffen ['klɛfən] *v/i.* (ge-, h) yap, yelp.

klagbar ɪᵗᶻ *adj.* ['klɑːkbɑːr] *matter, etc.*: actionable; *debt, etc.*: suable.

Klage ['klɑːgə] *f* (-/-n) complaint; lament; *fig.* action, suit; '2**n** (ge-, h) **1.** *v/i.* complain (*über acc.* of, about; *bei* to); lament; ɪᵗᶻ take legal action (*gegen* against); **2.** *v/t.: j-m et.* ~ complain to s.o. of *or* about s.th.

Kläger ɪᵗᶻ ['klɛːgər] *m* (-s/-) plaintiff; complainant.

kläglich *adj.* ['klɛːkliç] pitiful, piteous, pitiable; *cries, etc.*: plaintive; *condition*: wretched, lamentable; *performance, result, etc.*: miserable, poor; *failure, etc.*: lamentable, miserable.

klamm [klam] **1.** *adj.* hands, *etc.*: numb *or* stiff with cold, clammy; **2.** 2 *f* (-/-en) ravine, gorge, canyon.

Klammer ['klamər] *f* (-/-n) ⊕ clamp, cramp; (paper-)clip; *gr., typ.,* A bracket, parenthesis; '2**n** (ge-, h) **1.** *v/t.* clip together; ⊕ close (*wound*) with clips; *sich* ~ *an* (*acc.*) cling to (*a. fig.*); **2.** *v/i. boxing:* clinch.

Klang [klaŋ] **1.** *m* (-[e]s/∸e) sound, tone (*of voice, instrument, etc.*); tone (*of radio, etc.*); clink (*of glasses, etc.*); ringing (*of bells, etc.*); timbre; **2.** 2 *pret. of klingen*; '**~fülle** ♪ *f* sonority; '2**los** *adj.* toneless; '2**voll** *adj.* sonorous.

Klappe ['klapə] *f* (-/-n) flap; flap, drop leaf (*of table, etc.*); shoulder strap (*of uniform, etc.*); tailboard (*of lorry, etc.*); ⊕, ♫, *anat.* valve; ♪ key; F *fig.*: bed; trap; '2**n** (ge-, h) **1.** *v/t.: nach oben* ~ tip up; *nach unten* ~ lower, put down; **2.** *v/i.* clap, flap; *fig.* come off well, work out fine, *Am. sl. a.* click.

Klapper ['klapər] *f* (-/-n) rattle; '2**ig** *adj. vehicle, etc.*: rattly, ramshackle; *furniture*: rickety; *person, horse, etc.*: decrepit; '**~kasten** F *m* wretched piano; rattletrap; '2**n** *v/i.* (ge-, h) clatter, rattle (*mit et. s.th.*); *er klapperte vor Kälte mit den Zäh-*

nen his teeth were chattering with cold; '**~schlange** *zo. f* rattlesnake, *Am. a.* rattler.

'**Klapp|kamera** *phot. f* folding camera; '**~messer** *n* clasp-knife, jack-knife; '**~sitz** *m* tip-up *or* flap seat; '**~stuhl** *m* folding chair; '**~tisch** *m* folding table, *Am. a.* gate-leg(ged) table; **~ult** ['klappult] *n* folding desk.

Klaps [klaps] *m* (-es/-e) smack, slap; '2**en** *v/t.* (ge-, h) smack, slap.

klar *adj.* [klɑːr] clear; bright; transparent, limpid; pure; *fig.*: clear, distinct; plain; evident, obvious; *sich* ~ *sein über* (*acc.*) be clear about; **~en Kopf bewahren** keep a clear head.

klären ['klɛːrən] *v/t.* (ge-, h) clarify; *fig.* clarify, clear up, elucidate.

'**klar|legen** *v/t.* (sep., -ge-, h), '**~stellen** *v/t.* (sep., -ge-, h) clear up.

'**Klärung** *f* (-/-en) clarification; *fig. a.* elucidation.

Klasse ['klasə] *f* (-/-n) class, category; *school*: class, form, *Am. a.* grade; (social) class.

'**Klassen|arbeit** *f* (test) paper; '2**bewußt** *adj.* class-conscious; '**~bewußtsein** *n* class-consciousness; '**~buch** *n* class-book; '**~haß** *m* class-hatred; '**~kamerad** *m* classmate; '**~kampf** *m* class-war(fare); '**~zimmer** *n* classroom, schoolroom.

klassifizier|en [klasifiˈtsiːrən] *v/t.* (no -ge-, h) classify; 2**ung** *f* (-/-en) classification.

Klass|iker ['klasikər] *m* (-s/-) classic; 2**isch** *adj.* classic(al).

klatsch [klatʃ] **1.** *int.* smack!, slap!; **2.** 2 *m* (-es/-e) smack, slap; F *fig.*: gossip; scandal; 2**base** ['~bɑːzə] *f* (-/-n) gossip; '2**e** *f* (-/-n) fly-flap; '**~en** (ge-, h) **1.** *v/t.* fling, hurl; *Beifall* ~ clap, applaud (*j-m* s.o.) **2.** *v/i.* splash; applaud, clap; F *fig.* gossip; '**~haft** *adj.* gossiping, gossipy; '2**maul** F *n s. Klatschbase*; '**~naß** F *adj.* soaking wet.

Klaue ['klauə] *f* (-/-n) claw; paw; *fig.* clutch.

Klause ['klauzə] *f* (-/-n) hermitage; cell.

Klausel ɪᵗᶻ ['klauzəl] *f* (-/-n) clause; proviso; stipulation.

Klaviatur ♪ [klavjaˈtuːr] *f* (-/-en) keyboard, keys *pl.*

Klavier ♪ [klaˈviːr] *n* (-s/-e) piano (-forte); **~konzert** *n* piano concert *or* recital; **~lehrer** *m* piano teacher; **~sessel** *m* music-stool; **~stimmer** *m* (-s/-) piano-tuner; **~stunde** *f* piano-lesson.

kleb|en ['kleːbən] (ge-, h) **1.** *v/t.* glue, paste, stick; **2.** *v/i.* stick, adhere (*an dat.* to); '**~end** *adj.* adhesive; '2**epflaster** *n* adhesive *or* sticking plaster; '**~rig** *adj.* adhesive, sticky; '2**stoff** *m* adhesive; glue.

Klecks [klɛks] m (-es/-e) blot (of ink); mark (of dirt, grease, paint, etc.); spot (of grease, paint, etc.); stain (of wine, coffee, etc.); '2en (ge-) 1. v/i. (h) make a mark or spot or stain; 2. v/i. (sein) ink, etc.: drip (down); 3. v/t. (h): et. auf et. ~ splash or spill s.th. on s.th.

Klee ⚘ [kle:] m (-s/no pl.) clover, trefoil.

Kleid [klaɪt] n (-[e]s/-er) garment; dress, frock; gown; ~er pl. clothes pl.; 2en ['~dən] v/t. (ge-, h) dress, clothe; sich ~ dress (o.s.); j-n gut ~ suit or become s.o.

Kleider|ablage ['klaɪdər-] f cloak-room, Am. a. checkroom; '~bügel m coat-hanger; '~bürste f clothes-brush; '~haken m clothes-peg; '~schrank m wardrobe; '~ständer m hat and coat stand; '~stoff m dress material.

'kleidsam adj. becoming.

Kleidung ['klaɪduŋ] f (-/-en) clothes pl., clothing; dress; '~sstück n piece or article of clothing; garment.

Kleie ['klaɪə] f (-/-n) bran.

klein [klaɪn] 1. adj. little (only attr.), small; fig. a. trifling, petty; 2. adv.: ~ schreiben write with a small (initial) letter; ~ anfangen start in a small or modest way; 3. noun: von ~ auf from an early age; '2auto n baby or small car; '2bahn f narrow-ga(u)ge railway; '2bildkamera f miniature camera; '2geld n (small) change; '~gläubig adj. of little faith; '2handel ✝ m retail trade; '2händler m retailer; '2heit f (-/no pl.) smallness, small size; '2holz n firewood, matchwood, kindling.

'Kleinigkeit f (-/-en) trifle, triviality; '~skrämer m pettifogger.

'Klein|kind n infant; '2laut adj. subdued; '2lich adj. paltry; pedantic, fussy; '~mut m pusillanimity; despondency; '2mütig adj. ['~my:tiç] pusillanimous; despondent; '2schneiden v/t. (irr. schneiden, sep., -ge-, h) cut into small pieces; '~staat m small or minor state; '~stadt f small town; '2städter m small-town dweller, Am. a. small-towner; '2städtisch adj. small-town, provincial; '~vieh n small livestock.

Kleister ['klaɪstər] m (-s/-) paste; '2n v/t. (ge-, h) paste.

Klemm|e ['klɛmə] f (-/-n) ⊕ clamp; ⚡ terminal; F in der ~ sitzen be in a cleft stick, F be in a jam; '2en v/t. (ge-, h) jam, squeeze, pinch; '~er m (-s/-) pince-nez; '~schraube ⊕ f set screw.

Klempner ['klɛmpnər] m (-s/-) tin-man, tin-smith, Am. a. tinner; plumber.

Klerus ['kle:rus] m (-/no pl.) clergy.

Klette ['klɛtə] f (-/-n) ⚘ bur(r); fig. a. leech.

Kletter|er ['klɛtərər] m (-s/-) climber; '2n v/i. (ge-, sein) climb, clamber (auf e-n Baum [up] a tree); '~pflanze f climber, creeper.

Klient [kli'ɛnt] m (-en/-en) client.

Klima ['kli:ma] n (-s/-s, -te) climate; fig. a. atmosphere; ~anlage f air-conditioning plant; 2tisch adj. ['~ma:tiʃ] climatic.

klimpern ['klɪmpərn] v/i. (ge-, h) jingle, chink (mit et. s.th.); F strum or tinkle away (auf acc. on, at piano, guitar).

Klinge ['klɪŋə] f (-/-n) blade.

Klingel ['klɪŋəl] f (-/-n) bell, hand-bell; ~knopf m bell-push; '2n v/i. (ge-, h) ring (the bell); doorbell, etc.: ring; es klingelt the doorbell is ringing; '~zug m bell-pull.

klingen ['klɪŋən] v/i. (irr., ge-, h) sound; bell, metal, etc.: ring; glasses, etc.: clink; musical instrument: speak.

Klini|k ['kli:nik] f (-/-en) nursing home, private hospital; clinic(al hospital); '2sch adj. clinical.

Klinke ['klɪŋkə] f (-/-n) latch; (door-) handle.

Klippe ['klɪpə] f (-/-n) cliff; reef; crag; rock; fig. rock, hurdle.

klirren ['klɪrən] v/i. (ge-, h) window-pane, chain, etc.: rattle; chain, swords, etc.: clank, jangle; keys, spurs, etc.: jingle; glasses, etc.: clink, chink; pots, etc.: clatter; ~ mit rattle, jingle.

Klistier ⚕ [kli'sti:r] n (-s/-e) enema.

Kloake [klo'a:kə] f (-/-n) sewer, cesspool (a. fig.).

Klob|en ['klo:bən] m (-s/-) ⊕ pulley, block; log; '2ig adj. clumsy (a. fig.).

klopfen ['klɔpfən] v/i. (ge-, h) 1. v/i. heart, pulse: beat, throb; knock (at door, etc.); tap (on shoulder); pat (on cheek); es klopft there's a knock at the door; 2. v/t. knock, drive (nail, etc.).

Klöppel ['klœpəl] m (-s/-) clapper (of bell); lacemaking: bobbin; beetle; '~spitze f pillow-lace, bone-lace.

Klops [klɔps] m (-es/-e) meat ball.

Klosett [klo'zɛt] n (-s/-e, -s) lavatory, (water-)closet, W.C., toilet; ~papier n toilet-paper.

Kloß [klo:s] m (-es/ᵘe) earth, clay, etc.: clod, lump; cookery: dumpling.

Kloster ['klo:stər] n (-s/ᵘ) cloister; monastery; convent, nunnery; '~bruder m friar; '~frau f nun; '~gelübde n monastic vow.

Klotz [klɔts] m (-es/ᵘe) block, log (a. fig.).

Klub [klup] m (-s/-s) club; '~kamerad m clubmate; '~sessel m lounge-chair.

Kluft [kluft] f 1. (-/ᵘe) gap (a. fig.),

crack; cleft; gulf, chasm (*both a. fig.*); **2.** F (-/-en) outfit, F togs *pl.*; uniform.

klug *adj.* [klu:k] clever; wise, intelligent, sensible; prudent; shrewd; cunning; **'2heit** *f* (-/*no pl.*) cleverness; intelligence; prudence; shrewdness; good sense.

Klump|en ['klumpən] *m* (-s/-) lump (*of earth, dough, etc.*); clod (*of earth, etc.*); nugget (*of gold, etc.*); heap; **'.fuß** *m* club-foot; **'2ig** *adj.* lumpy; cloddish.

knabbern ['knabərn] (ge-, h) **1.** *v/t.* nibble, gnaw; **2.** *v/i.* nibble, gnaw (*an dat.* at).

Knabe ['kna:bə] *m* (-n/-n) boy; lad; F *alter* ~ F old chap.

'Knaben|alter *n* boyhood; **'.chor** *m* boys' choir; **'2haft** *adj.* boyish.

Knack [knak] *m* (-[e]s/-e) crack, snap, click; **'2en** (ge-, h) **1.** *v/i. wood:* crack; *fire:* crackle; click; **2.** *v/t.* crack (*nut, etc.*); F crack open (*safe*); e-e harte Nuß zu ~ haben have a hard nut to crack; **~s** [~s] *m* (-es/-e) *s.* Knack; F *fig.* defect; **'2sen** *v/i.* (ge-, h) *s.* knacken 1.

Knall [knal] *m* (-[e]s/-e) crack, bang (*of shot*); bang (*of explosion*); crack (*of rifle or whip*); report (*of gun*); detonation, explosion, report; **'.bonbon** *m,n* cracker; **'.effekt** *m* sensation; **'2en** *v/i.* (ge-, h) *rifle, whip:* crack; *fireworks, door, etc.:* bang; *gun:* fire; *cork, etc.:* pop; *explosive, etc.:* detonate.

knapp *adj.* [knap] *clothes:* tight, close-fitting; *rations, etc.:* scanty, scarce; *style, etc.:* concise; *lead, victory, etc.:* narrow; *majority, etc.:* bare; mit ~er Not entrinnen have a narrow escape; ~ werden run short; **'2e** ⚒ *m* (-n/-n) miner; **'.halten** *v/t.* (*irr.* halten, *sep.*, -ge-, h) keep s.o. short; **'2heit** *f* (-/*no pl.*) scarcity, shortage; conciseness; **'.schaft** ⚒ *f* (-/-en) miners' society.

Knarre ['knarə] *f* (-/-n) rattle; F rifle, gun; **'2n** *v/i.* (ge-, h) creak; *voice:* grate.

knattern ['knatərn] *v/i.* (ge-, h) crackle; *machine-gun, etc.:* rattle; *mot.* roar.

Knäuel ['knɔʏəl] *m, n* (-s/-) clew, ball; *fig.* bunch, cluster.

Knauf [knauf] *m* (-[e]s/ᵘe) knob; pommel (*of sword*).

Knauser ['knauzər] *m* (-s/-) niggard, miser, skinflint; **~ei** [~'raɪ] *f* (-/-en) niggardliness, miserliness; **'2ig** *adj.* niggardly, stingy; **'2n** *v/i.* (ge-, h) be stingy.

Knebel ['kne:bəl] *m* (-s/-) gag; **'2n** *v/t.* (ge-, h) gag; *fig.* muzzle (*press*).

Knecht [knɛçt] *m* (-[e]s/-e) servant; farm-labo(u)rer, farm-hand; slave; **'2en** *v/t.* (ge-, h) enslave; tyrannize;

subjugate; **'.schaft** *f* (-/*no pl.*) servitude, slavery.

kneif|en ['knaɪfən] (*irr.*, ge-, h) **1.** *v/t.* pinch, nip; **2.** *v/i.* pinch; F *fig.* back out, *Am.* F *a.* crawfish; **'2er** *m* (-s/-) pince-nez; **'2zange** *f* (e-e a pair of) pincers *pl. or* nippers *pl.*

Kneipe ['knaɪpə] *f* (-/-n) public house, tavern, F pub, *Am. a.* saloon; **'2n** *v/i.* (ge-, h) carouse, tipple, F booze; **'.rei** *f* (-/-en) drinking-bout, carousal.

kneten ['kne:tən] *v/t.* (ge-, h) knead (*dough, etc.*); 🩺 *a.* massage (*limb, etc.*).

Knick [knik] *m* (-[e]s/-e) *wall, etc.:* crack; *paper, etc.:* fold, crease; *path, etc.:* bend; **'2en** *v/t.* (ge-, h) fold, crease; bend; break.

Knicker F ['knikər] *m* (-s/-) *s.* Knauser.

Knicks [kniks] *m* (-es/-e) curts(e)y; e-n ~ machen = **'2en** *v/i.* (ge-, h) (drop a) curts(e)y (*vor dat.* to).

Knie [kni:] *n* (-s/-) knee; **'2fällig** *adv.* on one's knees; **'.kehle** *anat.* *f* hollow of the knee; **'2n** *v/i.* (ge-, h) kneel, be on one's knees; **'.scheibe** *anat.* *f* knee-cap, knee-pan; **'.strumpf** *m* knee-length sock.

Kniff [knif] **1.** *m* (-[e]s/-e) crease, fold; *fig.* trick, knack; **2.** *2 pret. of* kneifen; **2(e)lig** *adj.* ['knif(-)liç] tricky; intricate.

knipsen ['knipsən] (ge-, h) **1.** *v/t.* clip, punch (*ticket, etc.*); F *phot.* take a snapshot of, snap; **2.** F *phot.* *v/i.* take snapshots.

Knirps [knirps] *m* (-es/-e) little man; little chap, F nipper; **'2ig** *adj.* very small.

knirschen ['knirʃən] *v/i.* (ge-, h) *gravel, snow, etc.:* crunch; grind; *teeth, etc.:* grate; mit den Zähnen ~ grind *or* gnash one's teeth.

knistern ['knistərn] *v/i.* (ge-, h) *woodfire, etc.:* crackle; *dry leaves, silk, etc.:* rustle.

knitter|frei *adj.* ['knitər-] crease-resistant; **'2n** *v/t. and v/i.* (ge-, h) crease, wrinkle.

Knoblauch 🌿 ['kno:plaux] *m* (-[e]s/*no pl.*) garlic.

Knöchel *anat.* ['knœçəl] *m* (-s/-) knuckle; ankle.

Knoch|en *anat.* ['knɔxən] *m* (-s/-) bone; **.enbruch** *m* fracture (*of a bone*); **2ig** *adj.* bony.

Knödel ['knø:dəl] *m* (-s/-) dumpling.

Knolle 🌿 ['knɔlə] *f* (-/-n) tuber; bulb.

Knopf [knɔpf] *m* (-[e]s/ᵉe) button.

knöpfen ['knœpfən] *v/t.* (ge-, h) button.

'Knopfloch *n* buttonhole.

Knorpel ['knɔrpəl] *m* (-s/-) cartilage, gristle.

Knorr|en ['knɔrən] *m* (-s/-) knot,

knag, gnarl; '2ig adj. gnarled, knotty.

Knospe ♀ ['knɔspə] f (-/-n) bud; '2n v/i. (ge-, h) (be in) bud.

Knot|en ['kno:tən] 1. m (-s/-) knot (a. fig., ♣); 2. ♀ v/t. (ge-, h) knot; '~enpunkt m 🚂 junction; intersection; '2ig adj. knotty.

Knuff F [knuf] m (-[e]s/⁻e) poke, cuff, nudge; '2en F v/t. (ge-, h) poke, cuff, nudge.

knülle|n ['knylən] v/t. and v/i. (ge-, h) crease, crumple; '2r F m (-s/-) hit.

knüpfen ['knypfən] v/t. (ge-, h) make, tie (knot, etc.); make (net); knot (carpet, etc.); tie (shoe-lace, etc.); strike up (friendship, etc.); attach (condition, etc.) (an acc. to).

Knüppel ['knypəl] m (-s/-) cudgel.

knurren ['knurən] v/i. (ge-, h) growl, snarl; fig. grumble (über acc. at, over about); stomach: rumble.

knusp(e)rig adj. ['knusp(ə)riç] crisp, crunchy

Knute ['knu:tə] f (-/-n) knout.

Knüttel ['knytəl] m (-s/-) cudgel.

Kobold ['ko:bɔlt] m (-[e]s/-e) (hob)goblin, imp.

Koch [kɔx] m (-[e]s/⁻e) cook; '~buch n cookery-book, Am. cookbook; '2en (ge-, h) 1. v/t. boil (water, egg, fish, etc.); cook (meat, vegetables, etc.) (by boiling); make (coffee, tea, etc.); 2. v/i. water, etc.: boil (a. fig.); do the cooking; be a (good, etc.) cook; '~er m (-s/-) cooker.

Köcher ['kœçər] m (-s/-) quiver.

'Koch|kiste f haybox; '~löffel m wooden spoon; '~nische f kitchenette; '~salz n common salt; '~topf m pot, saucepan.

Köder ['kø:dər] m (-s/-) bait (a. fig.); lure (a. fig.); '2n v/t. (ge-, h) bait; lure; fig. a. decoy.

Kodex ['ko:dɛks] m (-es, -/-e, Kodizes) code.

Koffer ['kɔfər] m (-s/-) (suit)case; trunk; '~radio n portable radio (set).

Kognak ['kɔnjak] m (-s/-s, ⚓-e) French brandy, cognac.

Kohl ♀ [ko:l] m (-[e]s/-e) cabbage.

Kohle ['ko:lə] f (-/-n) coal; charcoal; ⚡ carbon, wie auf (glühenden) ~n sitzer be on tenterhooks.

'Kohlen|bergwerk n coal-mine, coal-pit, colliery, ~eimer m coal-scuttle, ~händler m coal-merchant; ~kasten m coal-box; '~revier 🔨 n coal-district; '~säure f carbonic acid; '~stoff 🔥 m carbon

'Kohle|papier n carbon paper; '~zeichnung f charcoal-drawing.

'Kohl|kopf ♀ m (head of) cabbage; '~rübe ♀ f Swedish turnip.

Koje ⚓ ['ko:jə] f (-/-n) berth, bunk.

Kokain [koka'i:n] n (-s/no pl.) cocaine, sl. coke, snow.

kokett adj. [ko'kɛt] coquettish; 2erie [~ə'ri:] f (-/-n) coquetry, coquettishness; ~ieren [~'ti:rən] v/i. (no -ge-, h) coquet, flirt (mit with; a. fig.).

Kokosnuß ♀ ['ko:kɔs-] f coconut.

Koks [ko:ks] m (-es/-e) coke.

Kolben ['kɔlbən] m (-s/-) butt (of rifle); ⊕ piston; '~stange f piston-rod.

Kolchose [kɔl'ço:zə] f (-/-n) collective farm, kolkhoz.

Kolleg univ. [kɔ'le:k] n (-s/-s, -ien) course of lectures; ~e [~gə] m (-n/-n) colleague; 2ium [~gjum] n (-s/Kollegien) council, board; teaching staff.

Kollekt|e eccl. [kɔ'lɛktə] f (-/-n) collection; ~ion ♀ [~'tsjo:n] f (-/-en) collection, range.

Koller ['kɔlər] m (-s/-) vet. staggers pl.; F fig. rage, tantrum; '2n v/i. 1. (h) turkey-cock gobble; pigeon: coo; bowels: rumble; vet. have the staggers; 2. (sein) ball, tears, etc.: roll.

kolli|dieren [kɔli'di:rən] v/i. (no -ge-, sein) collide; fig. clash; 2sion [~'zjo:n] f (-/-en) collision; fig. clash, conflict.

Kölnischwasser ['kœlniʃ-] n eau-de-Cologne.

Kolonialwaren [kolo'nja:l-] f/pl. groceries pl.; ~händler m grocer; ~handlung f grocer's (shop), Am. grocery.

Kolon|ie [kolo'ni:] f (-/-n) colony; 2isieren [~i'zi:rən] v/t. (no -ge-, h) colonize

Kolonne [ko'lɔnə] f (-/-n) column; convoy; gang (of workers, etc.).

kolorieren [kolo'ri:rən] v/t. (no -ge-, h) colo(u)r.

Kolo|ß [ko'lɔs] m (Kolosses/Kolosse) colossus; 2ssal adj. [~'sa:l] colossal, huge (both a. fig.).

Kombin|ation [kɔmbina'tsjo:n] f (-/-en) combination; overall; ✈ flying-suit; football, etc.: combined attack; 2ieren [~'ni:rən] (no -ge-, h) 1. v/t. combine; 2. v/i. reason, deduce; football, etc.: combine, move.

Kombüse ⚓ [kɔm'by:zə] f (-/-n) galley, caboose.

Komet ast. [ko'me:t] m (-en/-en) comet.

Komfort [kɔm'fo:r] m (-s/no pl.) comfort; 2abel adj. [~r'ta:bəl] comfortable.

Komik ['ko:mik] f (-/no pl.) humo(u)r, fun(niness); '~er m (-s/-) comic actor, comedian.

komisch adj. ['ko:miʃ] comic(al), funny; fig. funny, odd, queer.

Komitee [komi'te:] n (-s/-s) committee.

Kommand|ant ✗ [kɔman'dant] *m*
(-en/-en), **~eur** ✗ [~'dø:r] *m* (-s/-e)
commander, commanding officer;
~ieren [~'di:rən] (*no* -ge-, *h*) 1. *v/i.*
order, command, be in command;
2. *v/t.* ✗ command, be in command
of; order; **~itgesellschaft** ✝ [~
'di:t-] *f* limited partnership; **~o**
[~'mando] *n* (-s/-s) ✗ command,
order; order(s *pl.*), directive(s *pl.*);
✗ detachment; **~obrücke** ⚓ *f*
navigating bridge.

kommen ['kɔmən] *v/i.* (*irr.*, ge-,
sein) come; arrive; **~** *lassen* send
for *s.o.*, order *s.th.*; *et.* **~** *sehen* foresee; *an die Reihe* **~** it is one's turn;
~ *auf* (*acc.*) think of, hit upon; remember; *zu dem Schluß* **~**, *daß* decide that; *hinter et.* **~** find s.th. out;
um et. **~** lose s.th.; *zu et.* **~** come by
s.th.; *wieder zu sich* **~** come round
or to; *wie* **~** *Sie dazu!* how dare you!

Komment|ar [kɔmen'ta:r] *m* (-s/-e)
commentary, comment; **~ator** [~
tɔr] *m* (-s/-en) commentator; **~ie-
ren** [~'ti:rən] *v/t.* (*no* -ge-, *h*) comment on.

Kommissar [kɔmi'sa:r] *m* (-s/-e)
commissioner; superintendent; *pol.*
commissar.

Kommißbrot F [kɔ'mis-] *n* army *or*
ration bread, *Am. a.* G.I. bread.

Kommission [kɔmi'sjo:n] *f* (-/-en)
commission (*a.* ✝); committee; **~är**
✝ [~'ɔ'ne:r] *m* (-s/-e) commission
agent.

Kommode [kɔ'mo:də] *f* (-/-n) chest
of drawers, *Am.* bureau.

Kommunis|mus *pol.* [kɔmu'nis-
mus] *m* (-/*no pl.*) communism; **~t** *m*
(-en/-en) communist; **~tisch** *adj.*
communist(ic).

Komöd|iant [kɔmø'djant] *m* (-en/
-en) comedian; *fig.* play-actor; **~ie**
[~'mø:djə] *f* (-/-n) comedy; **~** *spielen* play-act.

Kompagnon ✝ [kɔmpan'jõ:] *m*
(-s/-s) (business-)partner, associate.

Kompanie ✗ [kɔmpa'ni:] *f* (-/-n)
company.

Kompaß ['kɔmpas] *m* (*Kompasses/
Kompasse*) compass.

kompetent *adj.* [kɔmpe'tent] competent.

komplett *adj.* [kɔm'plet] complete.

Komplex [kɔm'pleks] *m* (-es/-e)
complex (*a.* *psych.*); block (*of
houses*).

Kompliment [kɔmpli'ment] *n*
(-[e]s/-e) compliment.

Komplize [kɔm'pli:tsə] *m* (-n/-n)
accomplice.

komplizier|en [kɔmpli'tsi:rən] *v/t.*
(*no* -ge-, *h*) complicate; **~t** *adj. machine, etc.*: complicated; *argument,
situation, etc.*: complex; **~er** *Bruch*
🦴 compound fracture.

Komplott [kɔm'plɔt] *n* (-[e]s/-e)
plot, conspiracy.

kompo|nieren ♪ [kɔmpo'ni:rən]
v/t. and v/i. (*no* -ge-, *h*) compose;
2'**nist** *m* (-en/-en) composer; 2si-
tion [~zi'tsjo:n] *f* (-/-en) composition.

Kompott [kɔm'pɔt] *n* (-[e]s/-e) com-
pote, stewed fruit, *Am. a.* sauce.

komprimieren [kɔmpri'mi:rən] *v/t.*
(*no* -ge-, *h*) compress.

Kompromi|ß [kɔmpro'mis] *m*
(*Kompromisses/Kompromisse*) compromise, 2Blos *adj.* uncompromising; 2ttieren [~'ti:rən] *v/t.* (*no* -ge-,
h) compromise.

Kondens|ator [kɔndɛn'za:tɔr] *m*
(-s/-en) 🔌 capacitor, condenser (*a.*
🔋); 2ieren [~'zi:rən] *v/t.* (*no* -ge-,
h) condense.

Kondens|milch [kɔn'dɛns-] *f* evap-
orated milk, **~streifen** ✈ *m* condensation *or* vapo(u)r trail; **~was-
ser** *n* water of condensation.

Konditor [kɔn'di:tɔr] *m* (-s/-en)
confectioner, pastry-cook; **~ei** [~i-
to'rai] *f* (-/-en) confectionery, confectioner's (shop); **~eiwaren** *f/pl.*
confectionery.

Konfekt [kɔn'fɛkt] *n* (-[e]s/-e) sweets
pl., sweetmeat, *Am. a.* soft candy;
chocolates *pl.*

Konfektion [kɔnfɛk'tsjo:n] *f* (-/-en)
(manufacture of) ready-made clothing; **~sanzug** [kɔnfɛk'tsjo:ns?-] *m*
ready-made suit; **~sgeschäft** *n*
ready-made clothes shop.

Konfer|enz [kɔnfe'rɛnts] *f* (-/-en)
conference, 2ieren [~'ri:rən] *v/i.*
(*no* -ge-, *h*) confer (*über acc. on*).

Konfession [kɔnfe'sjo:n] *f* (-/-en)
confession, creed, denomination,
2ell *adj.* [~o'nel] confessional, denominational, **~sschule** [~'sjo:ns-]
f denominational school.

Konfirm|and *eccl.* [kɔnfir'mant] *m*
(-en/-en) candidate for confirmation, confirmee, **~ation** [~'tsjo:n] *f*
(-/-en) confirmation; 2ieren [~
'mi:rən] *v/t* (*no* -ge-, *h*) confirm.

konfiszieren 🏛 [kɔnfis'tsi:rən] *v/t.*
(*no* -ge-, *h*) confiscate, seize.

Konfitüre [kɔnfi'ty:rə] *f* (-/-n) pre-
serve(s *pl.*), (whole-fruit) jam.

Konflikt [kɔn'flikt] *m* (-[e]s/-e) conflict.

konform *adv.* [kɔn'fɔrm]: **~** *gehen*
mit agree *or* concur with.

konfrontieren [kɔnfrɔn'ti:rən] *v/t.*
(*no* -ge-, *h*) confront (*mit* with).

konfus *adj.* [kɔn'fu:s] *p.*, *a. ideas*:
muddled; *p* muddle-headed.

Kongreß [kɔn'grɛs] *m* (*Kongresses/
Kongresse*) congress, *Am. parl.*
Congress, **~halle** *f* congress hall.

König ['kø:niç] *m* (-s/-e) king; 2lich
adj. [~k-] royal, regal, **~reich**
['~k-] *n* kingdom; **~swürde** ['~ks-] *f*
royal dignity, kingship; **~tum**
n (-s/~er) monarchy; kingship.

Konjug|ation *gr.* [kɔnjuga'tsjo:n] *f*

(-/-en); 2ieren [ˌ'giːrən] v/t. (no -ge-, h) conjugate.

Konjunkt|iv gr. ['kɔnjuŋktiːf] m (-s/-e) subjunctive (mood); ~ur ✝ [ˌ'tuːr] f (-/-en) trade or business cycle; economic or business situation.

konkret adj. [kɔn'kreːt] concrete.

Konkurrent [kɔnku'rɛnt] m (-en/-en) competitor, rival.

Konkurrenz [kɔnku'rɛnts] f (-/-en) competition; competitors pl., rivals pl.; sports: event; 2fähig adj. able to compete; competitive; ~geschäft n rival business or firm; ~kampf m competition.

konkur'rieren v/i. (no -ge-, h) compete (mit with; um for).

Konkurs ✝, ⚖ [kɔn'kurs] m (-es/-e) bankruptcy, insolvency, failure; ~ anmelden file a petition in bankruptcy; in ~ gehen or geraten become insolvent, go bankrupt; ~erklärung ⚖ f declaration of insolvency; ~masse ⚖ f bankrupt's estate; ~verfahren ⚖ n bankruptcy proceedings pl.; ~verwalter ⚖ m trustee in bankruptcy; liquidator.

können ['kœnən] 1. v/i. (irr., ge-, h): ich kann nicht I can't, I am not able to; 2. v/t. (irr., ge-, h) know, understand; e-e Sprache ~ know a language, have command of a language; 3. v/aux. (irr., no -ge-, h) be able to inf.; be capable of ger.; be allowed or permitted to inf.; es kann sein it may be; du kannst hingehen you may go there; er kann schwimmen he can swim, he knows how to swim, 4. 2 n (-s/no pl.) ability; skill; proficiency.

Konnossement ✝ [kɔnɔsə'mɛnt] n (-[e]s;-e) bill of lading.

konnte ['kɔntə] pret. of können.

konsequen|t adj. [kɔnze'kvɛnt] consistent; 2z [ˌts] f (-/-en) consistency; consequence; die ~en ziehen do the only thing one can.

konservativ adj. [kɔnzerva'tiːf] conservative.

Konserven [kɔn'zervən] f/pl. tinned or Am. canned foods pl.; ~büchse f, ~dose f tin, Am. can; ~fabrik f tinning factory, esp. Am. cannery.

konservieren [kɔnzer'viːrən] v/t. (no -ge-, h) preserve.

Konsonant gr. [kɔnzo'nant] m (-en/-en) consonant.

Konsortium ✝ [kɔn'zɔrtsjum] n (-s/Konsortien) syndicate.

konstruieren [kɔnstru'iːrən] v/t. (no -ge-, h) gr. construe; ⊕: construct; design.

Konstruk|teur ⊕ [kɔnstruk'tøːr] m (-s/-e) designer; ~tion ⊕ [ˌ'tsjoːn] f (-/-en) construction; ~'tionsfehler ⊕ m constructional defect.

Konsul pol. ['kɔnzul] m (-s/-n) con-

sul; ~at pol. [ˌ'laːt] n (-[e]s/-e) consulate; 2'tieren v/t. (no -ge-, h) consult, seek s.o.'s advice.

Konsum [kɔn'zuːm] m 1. (-s/no pl.) consumption; 2. (-s/-s) co-operative shop, Am. co-operative store, F co-op; 3. (-s/no pl.) consumers' co-operative society, F co-op; ~ent [ˌu'mɛnt] m (-en/-en) consumer; 2ieren [ˌu'miːrən] v/t. (no -ge-, h) consume; ~verein m s. Konsum 3.

Kontakt [kɔn'takt] m (-[e]s/-e) contact (a. ⚡); in ~ stehen mit be in contact or touch with.

Kontinent ['kɔntinɛnt] m (-[e]s/-e) continent.

Kontingent [kɔntiŋ'gɛnt] n (-[e]s/-e) ⚔ contingent, quota (a. ✝).

Konto ✝ ['kɔntoː] n (-s/Konten, Kontos, Konti) account; ~auszug ✝ m statement of account; ~korrentkonto ✝ [ˌkɔ'rɛnt-] n current account.

Kontor [kɔn'toːr] n (-s/-e) office; ~ist [ˌoˈrist] m (-en/-en) clerk.

Kontrast [kɔn'trast] m (-es/-e) contrast.

Kontroll|e [kɔn'trɔlə] f (-/-n) control; supervision; check; 2ieren [ˌ'liːrən] v/t. (no -ge-, h) control; supervise; check.

Kontroverse [kɔntro'vɛrzə] f (-/-n) controversy.

konventionell adj. [kɔnventsjo'nɛl] conventional.

Konversation [kɔnverza'tsjoːn] f (-/-en) conversation; ~slexikon n encyclop(a)edia.

Konzentr|ation [kɔntsentra'tsjoːn] f (-/-en) concentration; 2ieren [ˌˈtriːrən] v/t. (no -ge-, h) concentrate, focus (attention, etc.) (auf acc. on); sich ~ concentrate (auf acc. on).

Konzern ✝ [kɔn'tsern] m (-s/-e) combine, group.

Konzert ♪ [kɔn'tsert] n (-[e]s/-e) concert; recital; concerto; ~saal ♪ m concert-hall.

Konzession [kɔntsɛ'sjoːn] f (-/-en) concession; licen|ce, Am. -se; 2ieren [ˌo'niːrən] v/t. (no -ge-, h) license.

Kopf [kɔpf] m (-[e]s/-e) head; top; brains pl.; pipe: bowl; ein fähiger ~ a clever fellow; ~ hoch! chin up!; j-m über den ~ wachsen outgrow s.o.; fig. get beyond s.o.; ~arbeit f brain-work; ~bahnhof 🚉 m terminus, Am. terminal; ~bedeckung f headgear, headwear.

köpfen ['kœpfən] v/t. (ge-, h) behead, decapitate; football: head (ball).

'Kopf|ende n head; ~hörer m headphone, headset; ~kissen n pillow; 2los adj. headless; fig. confused; ~nicken n (-s/no pl.) nod; ~rechnen n (-s/no pl.) mental arithmetic; ~salat m cabbage-lettuce;

'**.schmerzen** m/pl. headache; '**.-sprung** m header; '**.tuch** n scarf; ²**über** adv. head first, headlong; **.weh** n (-[e]s/-e) s. Kopfschmerzen; **.zerbrechen** n (-s/no pl.): j-m ~ machen puzzle s.o.

Kopie [ko'pi:] f(-/-n) copy; duplicate; phot., film: print; **.rstift** m indelible pencil.

Koppel ['kɔpəl] **1.** f (-/-n) hounds: couple; horses: string; paddock; **2.** ⚥ n (-s/-) belt; ²n v/t. (ge-, h) couple (a. ⊕, ♂).

Koralle [ko'ralə] f (-/-n) coral; **.n-fischer** m coral-fisher.

Korb [kɔrp] m (-[e]s/⸚e) basket; fig. refusal; Hahn im ~ cock of the walk; **.möbel** n/pl. wicker furniture.

Kordel ['kɔrdəl] f (-/-n) string, twine, cord.

Korinthe [ko'rintə] f (-/-n) currant.

Kork [kɔrk] m (-[e]s/-e), '**.en** m (-s/-) cork; '**.(en)zieher** m (-s/-) corkscrew.

Korn [kɔrn] **1.** n (-[e]s/⸚er) seed; grain; **2.** n (-[e]s/-e) corn, cereals pl.; **3.** n (-[e]s/⚥-e) front sight; **4.** F m (-[e]s/-) (German) corn whisky.

körnig adj. ['kœrniç] granular; in compounds: ...-grained.

Körper ['kœrpər] m (-s/-) body (a. phys., ⚥); ♂ solid; '**.bau** m build, physique; ²**behindert** adj. ['.-bə-hindərt] (physically) disabled, handicapped; **.beschaffenheit** f constitution, physique; **.fülle** f corpulence; **.geruch** m body-odo(u)r; '**.größe** f stature; '**.kraft** f physical strength; '²**lich** adj. physical; corporal; bodily; '**.pflege** f care of the body, hygiene; '**.schaft** f (-/-en) body; ⚥ body (corporate), corporation; '**.verletzung** ⚥ f bodily harm, physical injury.

korrekt adj. [kɔ'rekt] correct; ²**or** [.ɔr] m (-s/-en) (proof-)reader; ²**ur** [.'tu:r] f (-/-en) correction; ²**ur-bogen** m proof-sheet.

Korrespond|ent [kɔrespɔn'dɛnt] m (-en/-en) correspondent; **.enz** [.ts] f (-/-en) correspondence; ²**ieren** [.'di:rən] v/i. (no -ge-, h) correspond (mit with).

korrigieren [kɔri'gi:rən] v/t. (no -ge-, h) correct.

Korsett [kɔr'zet] n (-[e]s/-e, -s) corset, stays pl.

Kosename ['ko:zə-] m pet name.

Kosmetik [kɔs'me:tik] f (-/no pl.) beauty culture; **.erin** f (-/-nen) beautician, cosmetician.

Kost [kɔst] f (-/no pl.) food, fare; board; diet; ²**bar** adj. present, dear.: costly, expensive; health, time, etc.: valuable; mineral, etc.: precious.

'**kosten**¹ v/t. (ge-, h) taste, try, sample.

'**Kosten**² **1.** pl. cost(s pl.); expense(s pl.), charges pl.; auf ~ (gen.) at the expense of; **2.** ² v/t. (ge-, h) cost; take, require (time, etc.); '**.an-schlag** m estimate, tender; '²**frei 1.** adj. free; **2.** adv. free of charge; '²**los** s. kostenfrei.

Kost|gänger ['kɔstgeŋər] m (-s/-) boarder; '**.geld** n board-wages pl.

köstlich adj. ['kœstliç] delicious.

'**Kost|probe** f taste, sample (a. fig.); ²**spielig** adj. ['.ʃpi:liç] expensive, costly.

Kostüm [kɔs'ty:m] n (-s/-e) costume, dress; suit; **.fest** n fancy-dress ball.

Kot [ko:t] m (-[e]s/no pl.) mud, mire, excrement.

Kotelett [kot(ə)'let] n (-[e]s/-s, ⚥ -e) pork, veal, lamb: cutlet; pork, veal, mutton chop; **.en** pl. sidewhiskers pl., Am. a. sideburns pl.

'**Kot|flügel** mot. m mudguard, Am. a. fender; '²**ig** adj. muddy, miry.

Krabbe zo. ['krabə] f (-/-n) shrimp; crab.

krabbeln ['krabəln] v/i. (ge-, sein) crawl.

Krach [krax] m (-[e]s/-e, -s) crack, crash (a. ♥); quarrel, sl. bust-up; F row; **.machen** kick up a row; '²**en** v/i. (ge-) **1.** (h) thunder; crash; cannon: roar, thunder; **2.** (sein) crash (a. ♥), smash.

krächzen ['krɛçtsən] v/t. and v/i. (ge-, h) croak.

Kraft [kraft] **1.** f (-/⸚e) strength; force (a. ♂); power (a. ⚥, ⊕); energy, vigo(u)r; efficacy; in ~ sein (setzen, treten) be in (put into, come into) operation or force; außer ~ setzen repeal, abolish (law); **2.** ² prp. (gen.) by virtue of; '**.an-lage** ⚥ f power plant; '**.brühe** f beef tea, **.fahrer** m driver, motorist; '**.fahrzeug** n motor vehicle.

kräftig adj. ['kreftiç] strong (a. fig.), powerful; fig. nutritious, rich; **.en** ['.gən] (ge-, h) **1.** v/t. strengthen; **2.** v/i. give strength.

'**kraft|los** adj. powerless, feeble; weak; '²**probe** f trial of strength; '²**rad** n motor cycle; '²**stoff** mot. m fuel; **.voll** adj. powerful (a. fig.); '²**wagen** m motor vehicle; '²**werk** ⚥ n power station.

Kragen ['kra:gən] m (-s/-) collar; '**.knopf** m collar-stud, Am. collar button.

Krähe orn. ['krɛ:ə] f (-/-n) crow; '²**n** v/i. (ge-, h) crow.

Kralle ['kralə] f (-/-n) claw (a. fig.); talon, clutch.

Kram [kra:m] m (-[e]s/no pl.) stuff, odds and ends pl.; fig. affairs pl., business.

Krämer ['krɛ:mər] m (-s/-) shopkeeper.

Krampf ⚕ [krampf] *m* (-[e]s/ᵘe) cramp; spasm, convulsion; '⸤ader ⚕ *f* varicose vein; '⸌haft *adj.* ⚕ spasmodic, convulsive; *laugh*: forced.

Kran ⊕ [kraːn] *m* (-[e]s/ᵘe, -e) crane.

krank *adj.* [kraŋk] sick; *organ, etc.*: diseased; ~ *sein p.* be ill, *esp. Am.* be sick; *animal*: be sick or ill; ~ *werden p.* fall ill *or esp. Am.* sick; *animal*: fall sick; '⸘e *m, f* (-n/-n) sick person, patient, invalid.

kränkeln ['krɛŋkəln] *v/i.* (ge-, h) be sickly, be in poor health.

'kranken *fig. v/i.* (ge-, h) suffer (*an dat.* from).

kränken ['krɛŋkən] *v/t.* (ge-, h) offend, injure; wound *or* hurt *s.o.'s* feelings; *sich* ~ feel hurt (*über acc.* at, about).

'Kranken|bett *n* sick-bed; '⸤geld *n* sick-benefit; '⸤haus *n* hospital; '⸤kasse *f* health insurance (fund); '⸤kost *f* invalid diet; '⸌lager *n s.* Krankenbett; '⸤pflege *f* nursing; '⸤pfleger *m* male nurse; '⸌schein *m* medical certificate; ⸌schwester *f* (sick-)nurse; ⸌versicherung *f* health *or* sickness insurance; '⸌wagen *m* ambulance; '⸌zimmer *n* sick-room.

'krank|haft *adj.* morbid, pathological; '⸘heit *f* (-/-en) illness, sickness; disease.

'Krankheits|erreger ⚕ *m* pathogenic agent; '⸌erscheinung *f* symptom (*a. fig.*).

'kränklich *adj.* sickly, ailing.

'Kränkung *f* (-/-en) insult, offen|ce, *Am.* -se.

Kranz [krants] *m* (-es/ᵘe) wreath; garland.

Kränzchen *fig.* ['krɛntsçən] *n* (-s/-) tea-party, *F* hen-party.

kraß *adj.* [kras] crass, gross.

kratzen ['kratsən] (ge-, h) 1. *v/i.* scratch; 2. *v/t.* scratch; *sich* ~ scratch (o.s.).

kraulen ['kraulən] (ge-) 1. *v/t.* (h) scratch gently; 2. *v/i.* (sein) *sports*: crawl.

kraus *adj.* [kraus] curly, curled; crisp; frizzy; *die Stirn* ~ *ziehen* knit one's brow; '⸘e *f* (-/-n) ruff(le), frill.

kräuseln ['krɔyzəln] *v/t.* (ge-, h) curl, crimp (*hair, etc.*); pucker (*lips*); *sich* ~ *hair*: curl; *waves, etc.*: ruffle; *smoke*: curl *or* wreath up.

Kraut ⚘ [kraut] *n* 1. (-[e]s/ᵘer) plant; herb; 2. (-[e]s/*no pl.*) tops *pl.*; cabbage; weed.

Krawall [kra'val] *m* (-[e]s/-e) riot; shindy, F row, *sl.* rumpus.

Krawatte [kra'vatə] *f* (-/-n) (neck-) tie.

Kreatur [krea'tuːr] *f* (-/-en) creature.

Krebs [kreːps] *m* (-es/-e) *zo.* crayfish, *Am. a.* crawfish; *ast.* Cancer, Crab; ⚕ cancer; ⸌e *pl.* † returns *pl.*

Kredit † [kre'diːt] *m* (-[e]s/-e) credit; *auf* ~ on credit; ⸘fähig † *adj.* credit-worthy.

Kreide ['kraɪdə] *f* (-/-n) chalk; *paint.* crayon.

Kreis [kraɪs] *m* (-es/-e) circle (*a. fig.*); *ast.* orbit; ⚡ circuit; district, *Am.* county; *fig.*: sphere; field; range.

kreischen ['kraɪʃən] (ge-, h) 1. *v/i.* screech, scream; squeal, shriek; *circular saw, etc.*: grate (on the ear); 2. *v/t.* shriek, screech (insult, etc.).

Kreisel ['kraɪzəl] *m* (-s/-) (whipping-)top; '⸌kompaß *m* gyro-compass.

kreisen ['kraɪzən] *v/i.* (ge-, h) (move in a) circle; revolve, rotate; ☾, *bird*: circle; *bird*: wheel; *blood, money*: circulate.

kreis|förmig *adj.* ['kraɪsfœrmiç] circular; '⸘lauf *m physiol., money, etc.*: circulation; *business, trade*: cycle; ⸘laufstörungen ⚕ *f/pl.* circulatory trouble; '⸌rund *adj.* circular; '⸘säge ⊕ *f* circular saw, *Am. a.* buzz saw; '⸘verkehr *m* roundabout (traffic).

Krempe ['krɛmpə] *f* (-/-n) brim (*of hat*).

Krempel F ['krɛmpəl] *m* (-s/*no pl.*) rubbish, stuff, lumber.

krepieren [kre'piːrən] *v/i.* (*no* -ge-, sein) *shell*: burst, explode; *sl.* kick the bucket, peg *or* snuff out; *animal*: die, perish.

Krepp [krɛp] *m* (-s/-s, -e) crêpe; crape; ⸌apier ['krɛppapiːr] *n* crêpe paper; '⸌sohle *f* crêpe(-rubber) sole.

Kreuz [krɔyts] 1. *n* (-es/-e) cross (*a. fig.*); crucifix; *anat.* small of the back; ⚑ sacral region; *cards*: club(s *pl.*); ♪ sharp; *zu* ~(e) *kriechen* eat humble pie; 2. ♀ *adv.*: ~ *und quer* in all directions; criss-cross.

'kreuzen (ge-, h) 1. *v/t.* cross, fold (*arms, etc.*); ♀, *zo.* cross(-breed), hybridize; *sich* ~ *roads*: cross, intersect; *plans, etc.*: clash; 2. ⚓ *v/i.* cruise.

'Kreuzer ⚓ *m* (-s/-) cruiser.

'Kreuz|fahrer *hist. m* crusader; '⸌fahrt *f hist.* crusade; ⚓ cruise; '⸌feuer *n* ⚔ cross-fire (*a. fig.*); ⸘igen [⸍igən] *v/t.* (ge-, h) crucify; ⸌igung *f* (-/-en) crucifixion; ⸌otter *zo. f* common viper; '⸌ritter *hist. m* knight of the Cross; '⸌schmerzen *m/pl.* back ache; '⸌spinne *zo. f* garden- *or* cross-spider; '⸌ung *f* (-/-en) ⚑, *roads, etc.*: crossing, intersection; *roads*: crossroads; ♀, *zo.* cross-breeding, hybridization; '⸌verhör ⚖ *n* cross-examination; *ins* ~ *nehmen* cross-examine; **'2weise** adv. crosswise, crossways; **'⁓worträtsel** n crossword (puzzle); **'⁓zug** hist. m crusade.

kriech|en ['kri:çən] v/i. (irr., ge-, sein) creep, crawl; fig. cringe (vor dat. to, before); **2er** contp. m (-s/-) toady; **2erei** contp. [⁓'raɪ] f (-/-en) toadyism.

Krieg [kri:k] m (-[e]s/-e) war; im ⁓ at war; s. führen.

kriegen F ['kri:gən] v/t. (ge-, h) catch, seize; get.

Krieg|er ['kri:gər] m (-s/-) warrior; **'⁓erdenkmal** n war memorial; **'2erisch** adj. warlike; militant; **'2führend** adj. belligerent; **⁓führung** f warfare.

'Kriegs|beil fig. n: das ⁓ begraben bury the hatchet; **2beschädigt** adj. ['⁓bəʃɛːdiçt] war-disabled; **'⁓beschädigte** m (-n/-n) disabled ex-serviceman; **'⁓dienst** ⚔ m war service; **'⁓dienstverweigerer** ⚔ m (-s/-) conscientious objector; **'⁓erklärung** f declaration of war; **'⁓flotte** f naval force; **'⁓gefangene** m prisoner of war; **'⁓gefangenschaft** ⚔ f captivity; **'⁓gericht** ⚔ n court martial; **⁓gewinner** ['⁓gəvinlər] m (-s/-) war profiteer; **'⁓hafen** m naval port; **'⁓kamerad** m wartime comrade; **'⁓list** f stratagem; **'⁓macht** f military forces pl.; **'⁓minister** hist. m minister of war; Am. Secretary of State for War, Am. Secretary of War; **'⁓ministerium** hist. n ministry of war; War Office, Am. War Department; **'⁓rat** m council of war; **'⁓schauplatz** ⚔ m theat|re or Am. -er of war; **'⁓schiff** n warship; **'⁓schule** f military academy; **'⁓teilnehmer** m combatant; ex-serviceman, Am. veteran; **'⁓treiber** m (-s/-) warmonger; **'⁓verbrecher** m war criminal; **'⁓zug** m (military) expedition, campaign.

Kriminal|beamte [krimi'nɑːl-] m criminal investigator, Am. plain-clothes man; **'⁓film** m crime film; thriller; **⁓polizei** f criminal investigation department; **⁓roman** m detective or crime novel, thriller, sl. whodun(n)it.

kriminell adj. [krimi'nɛl] criminal; **2e** m (-n/-n) criminal.

Krippe ['krɪpə] f (-/-n) crib, manger; crèche.

Krise ['kriːzə] f (-/-n) crisis.

Kristall [krɪs'tal] **1.** m (-s/-e) crystal; **2.** n (-s/no pl.) crystal(-glass); **2isieren** [⁓i'ziːrən] v/i. and v/refl. (no -ge-, h) crystallize.

Kriti|k [kri'tiːk] f (-/-en) criticism; ♪, thea., etc.: review, criticism; F unter aller ⁓ beneath contempt; ⁓ üben an (dat.) s. kritisieren; **⁓ker** ['kriːtikər] m (-s/-) critic; books: re-

viewer; **2sch** adj. ['kriːtiʃ] critical (gegenüber of); **2sieren** [kriti'ziːrən] v/t. (no -ge-, h) criticize; review (book).

kritt|eln ['kritəln] v/t. (ge-, h) find fault (an dat. with), cavil (at); **2ler** ['⁓lər] m (-s/-) fault-finder, caviller.

Kritzel|ei [kritsə'laɪ] f (-/-en) scrawl(ing), scribble, scribbling; **'2n** v/t and v/i. (ge-, h) scrawl, scribble.

kroch [krɔx] pret. of kriechen.

Krokodil zo. [kroko'diːl] n (-s/-e) crocodile.

Krone ['kroːnə] f (-/-n) crown; coronet (of duke, earl, etc.).

krönen ['krøːnən] v/t. (ge-, h) crown (zum König king) (a.fig.).

'Kron|leuchter m chandelier; lust|re, Am. -er; electrolier; **'⁓prinz** m crown prince; **'⁓prinzessin** f crown princess.

'Krönung f (-/-en) coronation; crowning, fig. climax, culmination.

'Kronzeuge ⚖ m chief witness; King's evidence, Am. State's evidence.

Kropf ✻ [krɔpf] goit|re, Am. -er.

Kröte zo. ['krøːtə] f (-/-n) toad.

Krücke ['krykə] f (-/-n) crutch.

Krug [kruːk] m (-[e]s/⁓e) jug, pitcher; jar, mug; tankard.

Krume ['kruːmə] f (-/-n) crumb; ♪ topsoil.

Krümel ['kryːməl] m (-s/-) small crumb; **'2n** v/t. and v/i. (ge-, h) crumble

krumm adj. [krum] p. bent, stooping; limb, nose, etc.: crooked; spine: curved; deal, business, etc.: crooked; **'⁓beinig** adj. bandy- or bow-legged.

krümmen ['krymən] v/t. (ge-, h) bend (arm, back, etc.); crook (finger, etc.); curve (metal sheet, etc.); sich ⁓ person, snake, etc.: writhe, worm, etc.: wriggle; sich vor Schmerzen ⁓ writhe with pain; sich vor Lachen ⁓ be convulsed with laughter.

'Krümmung f (-/-en) road, etc.: bend, arch, road, etc.: curve; river, path, etc.: turn, wind, meander; earth's surface, spine, etc.: curvature.

Krüppel ['krypəl] m (-s/-) cripple.

Kruste ['krustə] f (-/-n) crust.

Kübel ['kyːbəl] m (-s/-) tub; pail, bucket

Kubik|meter [ku'biːk-] n, m cubic met|re, Am. -er; **⁓wurzel** A f cube root.

Küche ['kyçə] f (-/-n) kitchen; cuisine, cookery; s. kalt.

Kuchen ['kuːxən] m (-s/-) cake, flan; pastry.

'Küchen|gerät n, **'⁓geschirr** n kitchen utensils pl.; **'⁓herd** m (kitchen-)range; cooker, stove; **'⁓schrank** m kitchen cupboard or cabinet; **~zettel** *m* bill of fare, menu.

Kuckuck *orn.* ['kukuk] *m* (-s/-e) cuckoo.

Kufe ['ku:fə] *f* (-/-n) ⚔ skid; *sleigh*, *etc.*: runner.

Küfer ['ky:fər] *m* (-s/-) cooper; cellarman.

Kugel ['ku:gəl] *f* (-/-n) ball; ⚒ bullet; ⚔, *geogr.* sphere; *sports*: shot, weight; **2förmig** *adj.* ['~fœr-miç] spherical, ball-shaped, globular; **~gelenk** ⊕, *anat.* *n* ball-and-socket joint; **~lager** ⊕ *n* ball-bearing; **2n** (ge-) 1. *v/i.* (sein) *ball*, *etc.*: roll; 2. *v/t.* (h) roll (*ball*, *etc.*); *sich ~ children*, *etc.*: roll about; F double up (*vor* with *laughter*); **'~schreiber** *m* ball-(point)-pen; **'~stoßen** *n* (-s/*no pl.*) *sports*: putting the shot *or* weight.

Kuh *zo.* [ku:] *f* (-/-e) cow.

kühl *adj.* [ky:l] cool (*a. fig.*); **2an-lage** *f* cold-storage plant; **'2e** *f* (-/*no pl.*) cool(ness); **~en** *v/t.* (ge-, h) cool (*wine*, *wound*, *etc.*); chill (*wine*, *etc.*); **2er** *mot.* *m* (-s/-) radiator; **'2raum** *m* cold-storage chamber; **2schrank** *m* refrigerator, F fridge.

kühn *adj.* [ky:n] bold (*a. fig.*), daring; audacious.

'Kuhstall *m* cow-house, byre, *Am.* *a.* cow barn.

Küken *orn.* ['ky:kən] *n* (-s/-) chick.

kulant ✝ *adj.* [ku'lant] firm, *etc.*: accommodating, obliging; *price*, *terms*, *etc.*: fair, easy.

Kulisse [ku'lisə] *f* (-/-n) *thea.* wing, side-scene; *fig.* front; **~n** *pl.* *a.* scenery; *hinter den ~n* behind the scenes.

Kult [kult] *m* (-[e]s/-e) cult, worship.

kultivieren [kulti'vi:rən] *v/t.* (*no -ge-*, h) cultivate (*a. fig.*).

Kultur [kul'tu:r] *f* (-/-en) 🌿 cultivation; *fig.* culture; civilization; **2ell** *adj.* [~u'rɛl] cultural; **~film** [~'tu:r-] *m* educational film; **~geschichte** *f* history of civilization; **~volk** *n* civilized people.

Kultus ['kultus] *m* (-/*Kulte*) s. *Kult*; **'~minister** *m* minister of education and cultural affairs; **'~ministe-rium** *n* ministry of education and cultural affairs.

Kummer ['kumər] *m* (-s/*no pl.*) grief, sorrow; trouble, worry.

kümmer|lich *adj.* ['kymərliç] *life*, *etc.*: miserable, wretched; *conditions*, *etc.*: pitiful, pitiable; *result*, *etc.*: poor; *resources*: scanty; **'~n** *v/t.* (ge-, h): *es kümmert mich* I bother, I worry; *sich ~ um* look after, take care of; *see to*; meddle with.

'kummervoll *adj.* sorrowful.

Kump|an F [kum'pɑ:n] *m* (-s/-e) companion; F mate, chum, *Am.* F *a.*

buddy; **~el** ['~pəl] *m* (-s/-, F -s) ⚒ pitman, collier; F work-mate; F *s.* *Kumpan*.

Kunde ['kundə] 1. *m* (-n/-n) customer, client; 2. *f* (-/-n) knowledge.

Kundgebung ['kunt-] *f* (-/-en) manifestation; *pol.* rally.

kündig|en ['kyndigən] (ge-, h) 1. *v/i.*: *j-m ~* give s.o. notice; 2. *v/t.* ✝ call in (*capital*); 🏦 cancel (*contract*); *pol.* denounce (*treaty*); **'2ung** *f* (-/-en) notice; ✝ calling in; 🏦 cancellation; *pol.* denunciation.

'Kundschaft *f* (-/-en) customers *pl.*, clients *pl.*; custom, clientele; **'~er** ⚒ *m* (-s/-) scout; spy.

künftig ['kynftiç] 1. *adj.* event, years, *etc.*: future; *event*, *programme*, *etc.*: coming; *life*, *world*, *etc.*: next; 2. *adv.* in future, from now on.

Kunst [kunst] *f* (-/-e) art; skill; **'~akademie** *f* academy of arts; **'~ausstellung** *f* art exhibition; **'~druck** *m* art print(ing); **'~dünger** *m* artificial manure, fertilizer; **'2fer-tig** *adj.* skilful, skilled; **'~fertig-keit** *f* artistic skill; **'~gegenstand** *m* objet d'art; **'2gerecht** *adj.* skilful; professional, expert; **'~ge-schichte** *f* history of art; **'~ge-werbe** *n* arts and crafts *pl.*; applied arts *pl.*; **'~glied** *n* artificial limb; **'~griff** *m* trick, dodge; artifice, knack; **'~händler** *m* art-dealer; **'~kenner** *m* connoisseur of *or* in art; **'~leder** *n* imitation *or* artificial leather.

Künstler ['kynstlər] *m* (-s/-) artist; ♪, *thea.* performer; **'2isch** *adj.* artistic.

künstlich *adj.* ['kynstliç] *eye*, *flower*, *light*, *etc.*: artificial; *teeth*, *hair*, *etc.*: false; *fibres*, *dyes*, *etc.*: synthetic.

Kunst|liebhaber *m* art-lover; **'~maler** *m* artist, painter; **'~reiter** *m* equestrian; circus-rider; **'~schätze** ['~ʃɛtsə] *m/pl.* art treasures *pl.*; **'~seide** *f* artificial silk, rayon; **'~stück** *n* feat, trick, F stunt; **'~tischler** *m* cabinet-maker; **'~verlag** *m* art publishers *pl.*; **'2voll** *adj.* artistic, elaborate; **'~werk** *n* work of art.

kunterbunt F *fig.* *adj.* ['kuntər-] higgledy-piggledy.

Kupfer ['kupfər] *n* (-s/*no pl.*) copper; **~geld** *n* copper coins *pl.*, F coppers *pl.*; **'2n** *adj.* (of) copper; **'2rot** *adj.* copper-colo(u)red; **'~stich** *m* copper-plate engraving.

Kupon [ku'põ:] *m* (-s/-s) *s.* Coupon.

Kuppe ['kupə] *f* (-/-n) rounded hilltop; *nail*: head.

Kuppel ⌂ ['kupəl] *f* (-/-n) dome, cupola; **~ei** 🏦 ['~'laı] *f* (-/-en) procuring; **2n** (ge-, h) 1. *v/t.* s. koppeln; 2. *mot.* *v/i.* declutch.

Kuppl|er ['kuplər] *m* (-s/-) pimp, procurer; **'~ung** *f* (-/-en) ⊕ coupling (*a.* 🚗); *mot.* clutch.

Kur [ku:r] *f* (-/-en) course of treatment, cure.

Kür [ky:r] *f* (-/-en) *sports*: s. *Kürlauf*; voluntary exercise.

Kuratorium [kura'to:rium] *n* (-s/ *Kuratorien*) board of trustees.

Kurbel ⊕ ['kurbəl] *f* (-/-n) crank, winch, handle; '2n (ge-, h) 1. *v/t.* shoot (*film*); *in die Höhe ~* winch up (*load*, *etc.*); wind up (*car window*, *etc.*); 2. *v/i.* crank.

Kürbis ♀ ['kyrbis] *m* (-ses/-se) pumpkin.

'**Kur|gast** *m* visitor to *or* patient at a health resort *or* spa; '**~haus** *n* spa hotel.

Kurier [ku'ri:r] *m* (-s/-e) courier, express (messenger).

kurieren [ku'ri:rən] *v/t.* (*no* -ge-, h) cure.

kurios *adj.* [ku'rjo:s] curious, odd, strange, queer.   [skating.\

'**Kürlauf** *m sports*: free (roller)

'**Kur|ort** *m* health resort; spa; '**~pfuscher** *m* quack (doctor); **~pfusche'rei** *f* (-/-en) quackery.

Kurs [kurs] *m* (-es/-e) ♣ currency; ♣ rate, price; ♣ *and fig.* course, course, class; '**~bericht** ♣ *m* market-report; '**~buch** 🕮 *n* railway guide, *Am.* railroad guide.

Kürschner ['kyrʃnər] *m* (-s/-) furrier.

kursieren [kur'zi:rən] *v/i.* (*no* -ge-, h) *money*, *etc.*: circulate, be in circulation; *rumour*, *etc.*: circulate, be afloat, go about.

Kursivschrift *typ.* [kur'zi:f-] *f* italics *pl.*

Kursus ['kurzus] *m* (-/*Kurse*) course, class.

'**Kurs|verlust** ♣ *m* loss on the stock exchange; '**~wert** ♣ *m* market value; '**~zettel** ♣ *m* stock exchange list.

Kurve ['kurvə] *f* (-/-n) curve; *road*, *etc.*: *a.* bend, turn.

kurz [kurts] 1. *adj. space*: short; *time*, *etc.*: short, brief; *~ und bündig* brief, concise; *~e Hose* shorts *pl.*; *mit ~en Worten* with a few words; *den kürzeren ziehen* get the worst of it; 2. *adv.* in short; *~ angebunden sein* be curt *or* sharp; *~ und gut* in short, in a word; *~ vor London* short of London; *sich ~ fassen* be brief *or* concise; *in ~em* before long, shortly; *vor ~em* a short time ago; *zu ~ kommen* come off badly, get a raw deal; *um es ~ zu sagen* to cut a long story short; '2arbeit ♣ *f* short-

time work; '2arbeiter ♣ *m* short-time worker; **~atmig** *adj.* ['~9a:t-miç] short-winded.

Kürze ['kyrtsə] *f* (-/*no pl.*) shortness; brevity; *in ~* shortly, before long; '2n *v/t.* (ge-, h) shorten (*dress*, *etc.*) (*um* by); abridge, condense (*book*, *etc.*); cut, reduce (*expenses*, *etc.*).

'**kurz|er'hand** *adv.* without hesitation; on the spot; '2film *m* short (film); '2form *f* shortened form; '**~fristig** *adj.* short-term; ♣ *bill*, *etc.*: short-dated; '2geschichte *f* (short) short story; **~lebig** *adj.* ['~le:biç] short-lived; '2nachrichten *f/pl.* news summary.

kürzlich *adv.* ['kyrtsliç] lately, recently, not long ago.

'**Kurz|schluß** ⚡ *m* short circuit, F short; '**~schrift** *f* shorthand, stenography; '2sichtig *adj.* short-sighted, near-sighted; '2um *adv.* in short, in a word.

'**Kürzung** *f* (-/-en) shortening (*of dress*, *etc.*); abridg(e)ment, condensation (*of book*, *etc.*); cut, reduction (*of expenses*, *etc.*).

'**Kurz|waren** *f/pl.* haberdashery, *Am.* dry goods *pl.*, notions *pl.*; '**~weil** *f* (-/*no pl.*) amusement, entertainment; '2weilig *adj.* amusing, entertaining; '**~welle** ♣ *f* short wave, *radio* short-wave band.

Kusine [ku'zi:nə] *f* (-/-n) s. *Cousine*.

Kuß [kus] *m* (*Kusses/Küsse*) kiss; '2echt *adj.* kiss-proof.

küssen ['kysən] *v/t. and v/i.* (ge-, h) kiss.

'**kußfest** *adj. s. kußecht.*

Küste ['kystə] *f* (-/-n) coast; shore.

'**Küsten|bewohner** *m* inhabitant of a coastal region; '**~fischerei** *f* inshore fishery *or* fishing; '**~gebiet** *n* coastal area *or* region; '**~schiffahrt** *f* coastal shipping.

Küster *eccl.* ['kystər] *m* (-s/-) verger, sexton, sacristan.

Kutsch|bock ['kutʃ-] *m* coach-box; '**~e** *f* (-/-n) carriage, coach; '**~en-schlag** *m* carriage-door, coach-door; '**~er** *m* (-s/-) coachman; 2ie-ren [~'tʃi:rən] (*no* -ge-) 1. *v/t.* (h) drive *s.o.* in a coach; 2. *v/i.* (h) (drive a) coach; 3. *v/i.* (sein) (drive *or* ride in a) coach.

Kutte ['kutə] *f* (-/-n) cowl.

Kutter ♣ ['kutər] *m* (-s/-) cutter.

Kuvert [ku'vert; ku've:r] *n* (-[e]s/-e; -s/-s) envelope; *at table*: cover.

Kux ⚒ [kuks] *m* (-es/-e) mining share.

L

Lab zo. [lɑːp] n (-[e]s/-e) rennet.
labil adj. [la'biːl] unstable (a. ⊕, ♂); phys., ♫ labile.
Labor [la'boːr] n (-s/-s, -e) s. Laboratorium; **~ant** [labo'rant] m (-en/-en) laboratory assistant; **~atorium** [labora'toːrjum] n (-s/ Laboratorien) laboratory; **2ieren** [ˌoˈriːrən] v/i. (no -ge-, h): ~ an (dat.) labo(u)r under, suffer from.
Labyrinth [laby'rint] n (-[e]s/-e) labyrinth, maze.
Lache ['laxə] f (-/-n) pool, puddle.
lächeln ['lɛçəln] 1. v/i. (ge-, h) smile (über acc. at); höhnisch ~ sneer (über acc. at); 2. 2 n (-s/no pl.) smile; höhnisches ~ sneer.
lachen ['laxən] 1. v/i. (ge-, h) laugh (über acc. at); 2. 2 n (-s/no pl.) laugh(ter).
lächerlich adj. ['lɛçərliç] ridiculous, laughable, ludicrous; absurd; derisory, scoffing; ~ machen ridicule; sich ~ machen make a fool of o.s.
Lachs ichth. [laks] m (-es/-e) salmon.
Lack [lak] m (-[e]s/-e) (gum-)lac; varnish; lacquer, enamel; **2ieren** [la'kiːrən] v/t. (no -ge-, h) lacquer, varnish, enamel; **~leder** n patent leather; **~schuhe** m/pl. patent leather shoes pl., F patents pl.
Lade|fähigkeit ['laːdə-] f loading capacity; **~fläche** f loading area; **~hemmung** ⚔ f jam, stoppage; **~linie** ⚓ f load-line.
laden[1] ['laːdən] v/t. (irr., ge-, h) load; load (gun), charge (a. ⚡); freight, ship; ⚖ cite, summon; invite, ask (guest).
Laden[2] [..] m (-s/⸗) shop, Am. store; shutter; **~besitzer** m s. Ladeninhaber; **~dieb** m shop-lifter; **~diebstahl** m shop-lifting; **~hüter** m drug on the market; **~inhaber** m shopkeeper, Am. storekeeper; **~kasse** f till; **~preis** m selling-price, retail price; **~schild** n shopsign; **~schluß** m closing time; nach ~ after hours; **~tisch** m counter.
'Lade|platz m loading-place; **'~rampe** f loading platform or ramp; **'~raum** m loading space; ⚓ hold; **'~schein** ⚓ m bill of lading.
'Ladung f (-/-en) loading; load, freight; ⚓ cargo; ⚡ charge (a. of gun); ⚖ summons.
lag [laːk] pret. of liegen.
Lage ['laːgə] f (-/-n) situation, position; site, location (of building); state, condition; attitude; geol. layer, stratum; round (of beer, etc.); in der ~ sein zu inf. be able to inf., be in a position to inf.; versetzen

Sie sich in meine ~ put yourself in my place.
Lager ['laːgər] n (-s/-) couch, bed; den, lair (of wild animals); geol. deposit; ⊕ bearing; warehouse, storehouse, depot; store, stock (🌲 pl. a. Läger); ⚔, etc.: camp, encampment; auf ~ 🌲 on hand, in stock; **~buch** n stock-book; **~feuer** n camp-fire; **~geld** n storage; **~haus** n warehouse; **2n** (ge-, h) 1. v/i. lie down, rest; ⚔ (en)camp; 🌲 be stored; 2. v/t. lay down; ⚔ (en)camp; 🌲 store, warehouse; sich ~ lie down, rest; **~platz** m 🌲 depot; resting-place; ⚔, etc.: camp-site; **~raum** m store-room; **~ung** f (-/-en) storage (of goods).
Lagune [la'guːnə] f (-/-n) lagoon.
lahm adj. [lɑːm] lame; **~en** v/i. (ge-, h) be lame.
lähmen ['lɛːmən] v/t. (ge-, h) (make) lame; paraly|se, Am. -ze (a. fig.).
'lahmlegen v/t. (sep., -ge-, h) paraly|se, Am. -ze; obstruct.
'Lähmung ♫ f (-/-en) paralysis.
Laib [laɪp] m (-[e]s/-e) loaf.
Laich [laɪç] m (-[e]s/-e) spawn; **2en** v/i. (ge-, h) spawn.
Laie ['laɪə] m (-n/-n) layman; amateur; **~nbühne** f amateur theat|re, Am. -er.
Lakai [la'kaɪ] m (-en/-en) lackey (a. fig.), footman.
Lake ['laːkə] f (-/-n) brine, pickle.
Laken ['laːkən] n (-s/-) sheet.
lallen ['lalən] v/i. and v/t. (ge-, h) stammer; babble.
Lamelle [la'melə] f (-/-n) lamella, lamina; ♣ gill (of mushrooms).
lamentieren [lamen'tiːrən] v/i. (no -ge-, h) lament (um for; über acc. over).
Lamm zo. [lam] n (-[e]s/⸗er) lamb; **~fell** n lambskin; **2fromm** adj. (as) gentle or (as) meek as a lamb.
Lampe ['lampə] f (-/-n) lamp.
'Lampen|fieber n stage fright; **'~licht** n lamplight; **'~schirm** m lamp-shade.
Lampion [lã'pjõː] m, n (-s/-s) Chinese lantern.
Land [lant] n (-[e]s/⸗er, poet. -e) land; country; territory; ground, soil; an ~ gehen go ashore; auf dem ~e in the country; aufs ~ gehen go into the country; außer ~es gehen go abroad; zu ~e by land; **~arbeiter** m farm-hand; **~besitz** m landed property; ⚖ real estate; **~besitzer** m landowner, landed proprietor; **~bevölkerung** f rural population.
Lande|bahn ✈ f ['landə-] f runway; **~deck** ✈ n flight-deck.

land'einwärts adv. upcountry, inland.

landen ['landən] (ge-) **1.** v/i. (sein) land; **2.** v/t. (h) ⚓ disembark (troups); ⚓ land, set down (troups).

'Landenge f neck of land, isthmus.

Landeplatz ⚓ ['landə-] m landingfield.

Ländereien [lɛndə'raiən] pl. landed property, lands pl., estates pl.

Länderspiel ['lɛndər-] n sports: international match.

Landes|grenze ['landəs-] f frontier, boundary; '~innere n interior, inland, upcountry; '~kirche f national church; Brt. Established Church; '~regierung f government; in Germany: Land government; '~sprache f native language, vernacular; '2üblich adj. customary; '~verrat m treason; '~verräter m traitor to his country; '~verteidigung f national defen|ce, Am. -se.

'Land|flucht f rural exodus; '~friedensbruch ⚖ m breach of the public peace; '~gericht n appr. district court; '~gewinnung f (-/-en) reclamation of land; '~gut n country-seat, estate; '~haus n country-house, cottage; '~karte f map; '~kreis m rural district; 2läufig adj. ['~lɔyfiç] customary, current, common.

ländlich adj. ['lɛntliç] rural, rustic.

'Land|maschinen f/pl. agricultural or farm equipment; '~partie f picnic, outing, excursion into the country; '~plage iro. f nuisance; '~rat m (-[e]s/ᵘe) appr. district president; '~ratte ⚓ f landlubber; '~recht n common law; '~regen m persistent rain.

'Landschaft f (-/-en) province, district, region; countryside, scenery; esp. paint. landscape; '2lich adj. provincial; scenic (beauty, etc.).

'Landsmann m (-[e]s/Landsleute) (fellow-)countryman, compatriot; was sind Sie für ein ~? what's your native country?

'Land|straße f highway, high road; '~streicher m (-s/-) vagabond, tramp, Am. sl. hobo; '~streitkräfte f/pl. land forces pl.; the Army; ground forces pl.; '~strich m tract of land, region; '~tag m Landtag, Land parliament.

Landung ['landuŋ] f (-/-en) ⚓, ⚓ landing; disembarkation; arrival; '~sbrücke ⚓ f floating: landingstage; pier; '~ssteg ⚓ m gangway, gang-plank.

'Land|vermesser m (-s/-) surveyor; '~vermessung f land-surveying; 2wärts adv. ['~vɛrts] landward(s); '~weg m: auf dem ~ by land; '~wirt m farmer, agriculturist; '~wirtschaft f agriculture, farming; '2wirtschaftlich adj. agri-

cultural; '~e Maschinen f/pl. s. Landmaschinen; '~zunge f spit.

lang [laŋ] **1.** adj. long; p. tall; er machte ein ~es Gesicht his face fell; **2.** adv. long; e-e Woche ~ for a week; über kurz oder ~ sooner or later; '~(e) anhaltend continuous; '~(e) entbehrt long-missed; '~(e) ersehnt long-wished-for; das ist schon ~(e) her that was a long time ago; ~ und breit at (full or great) length; noch ~(e) nicht not for a long time yet; far from ger.; wie ~e lernen Sie schon Englisch? how long have you been learning English?; '~atmig adj. ['~a:tmiç] long-winded; '~e adv. s. lang 2.

Länge ['lɛŋə] f (-/-n) length; tallness; geogr., ast. longitude; der ~ nach (at) full length, lengthwise.

langen ['laŋən] v/i. (ge-, h) suffice, be enough; ~ nach reach for.

'Längen|grad m degree of longitude; '~maß n linear measure.

'länger 1. adj. longer; '~e Zeit (for) some time; **2.** adv. longer; ich kann es nicht ~ ertragen I cannot bear it any longer; je ~, je lieber the longer the better.

'Langeweile f (-, Langenweile/no pl.) boredom, tediousness, ennui.

'lang|fristig adj. long-term; '~jährig adj. of long standing; '~e Erfahrung (many) years of experience; '2lauf m skiing: cross-country run or race.

'länglich adj. longish, oblong.

'Langmut f (-/no pl.) patience, forbearance.

längs [lɛŋs] **1.** prp. (gen., dat.) along(side of); ~ der Küste fahren ⚓ (soil along the) coast; **2.** adv. lengthwise; '2achse f longitudinal axis.

'lang|sam adj. slow; '2schläfer ['~ʃlɛːfər] m (-s/-) late riser, lie-abed; '2spielplatte f long-playing record.

längst adv. [lɛŋst] long ago or since; ich weiß es ~ I have known it for a long time; '~ens adv. at the longest; at the latest; at the most.

'lang|stielig adj. long-handled; ⚘ long-stemmed, long-stalked; '2streckenlauf m long-distance run or race; '2weile f (-, Langenweile/no pl.) s. Langeweile; '~weilen v/t. (ge-, h) bore; sich ~ be bored; '~weilig adj. tedious, boring, dull; '~e Person bore; '2welle f ⚡ long wave; radio: long wave band; '~wierig adj. ['~vi:riç] protracted, lengthy; ⚗ lingering.

Lanze ['lantsə] f (-/-n) spear, lance.

Lappalie [la'pa:ljə] f (-/-n) trifle.

Lapp|en ['lapən] m (-s/-) patch; rag; duster; (dish- or floor-)cloth; anat., ⚘ lobe; '2ig adj. flabby.

läppisch adj. ['lɛpiʃ] foolish, silly.

Lärche ♀ ['lɛrçə] f (-/-n) larch.

Lärm [lɛrm] m (-[e]s/no pl.) noise; din; ~ schlagen give the alarm; **'2en** v/i. (ge-, h) make a noise; **'2end** adj. noisy.

Larve ['larfə] f (-/-n) mask; face (often iro.); zo. larva, grub.

las [lɑːs] pret. of lesen.

lasch F adj. [laʃ] limp, lax.

Lasche ['laʃə] f (-/-n) strap; tongue (of shoe).

lassen ['lasən] (irr., h) 1. v/t. (ge-) let; leave; laß das! don't!; laß das Weinen! stop crying!; ich kann es nicht ~ I cannot help (doing) it; sein Leben ~ für sacrifice one's life for; 2. v/i. (ge-): von et. ~ desist from s.th., renounce s.th.; do without s.th.; 3. v/aux. (no -ge-) allow, permit, let; make, cause; drucken ~ have s. th. printed; gehen ~ let s.o. go; ich habe ihn dieses Buch lesen ~ I have made him read this book; von sich hören ~ send word; er läßt sich nichts sagen he won't take advice; es läßt sich nicht leugnen there is no denying (the fact).

lässig adj. ['lɛsiç] indolent, idle; sluggish; careless.

Last [last] f (-/-en) load; burden; weight; cargo, freight; fig. weight, charge, trouble; zu ~en von ✝ to the debit of; j-m zur ~ fallen be a burden to s.o.; j-m et. zur ~ legen lay s.th. at s.o.'s door or to s.o.'s charge; **'~auto** n s. Lastkraftwagen.

'lasten v/i. (ge-, h): ~ auf (dat.) weigh or press (up)on; **'2aufzug** m goods lift, Am. freight elevator.

Laster ['lastər] n (-s/-) vice.

Lästerer ['lɛstərər] m (-s/-) slanderer, backbiter.

'lasterhaft adj. vicious; corrupt.

Läster|maul ['lɛstər-] n s. Lästerer; **'2n** v/i. (ge-, h) slander, calumniate; defame; abuse; **'~ung** f (-/-en) slander, calumny.

lästig adj. ['lɛstiç] troublesome; annoying; uncomfortable, inconvenient.

'Last|kahn m barge, lighter; **'~kraftwagen** m lorry, Am. truck; **'~schrift** ✝ f debit; **'~tier** n pack animal; **'~wagen** m s. Lastkraftwagen.

Latein [la'taɪn] n (-s/no pl.) Latin; **2isch** adj. Latin.

Laterne [la'tɛrnə] f (-/-n) lantern; street-lamp; **'~npfahl** m lamp-post.

latschen F ['lɑːtʃən] v/i. (ge-, sein) shuffle (along).

Latte ['latə] f (-/-n) pale; lath; sports: bar; **'~nkiste** f crate; **'~nverschlag** m latticed partition; **'~nzaun** m paling, Am. picket fence.

Lätzchen ['lɛtsçən] n (-s/-) bib, feeder.

lau adj. [lau] tepid, lukewarm (a. fig.).

Laub [laup] n (-[e]s/no pl.) foliage, leaves pl.; **'~baum** m deciduous tree.

Laube ['laubə] f (-/-n) arbo(u)r, bower; **'~ngang** m arcade.

'Laub|frosch zo. m tree-frog; **'~säge** f fret-saw.

Lauch ♀ [laux] m (-[e]s/-e) leek.

Lauer ['lauər] f (-/no pl.): auf der ~ liegen or sein lie in wait or ambush, be on the look-out; **'2n** v/i. (ge-, h) lurk (auf acc. for); watch for; **'2nd** adj. louring, lowering.

Lauf [lauf] m (-[e]s/⸚e) run(ning); sports: a. run, heat; race; current (of water); course; barrel (of gun); ♪ run; im ~e der Zeit in (the) course of time; **'~bahn** f career; **'~bursche** m errand-boy, office-boy; **'~disziplin** f sports: running event.

'laufen (irr., ge-) 1. v/i. (sein) run; walk; flow; time: pass, go by, elapse, leak; die Dinge ~ lassen let things slide; j-n ~ lassen let s.o. go; 2. v/t. (sein, h) run; walk; **'~d** adj. running; current; regular; ~en Monats ✝ instant; auf dem ~en sein be up to date, be fully informed.

Läufer ['lɔyfər] m (-s/-) runner (a. carpet), chess: bishop; football: half-back.

'Lauf|masche f ladder, Am. a. run; **'~paß** F m sack, sl. walking papers pl.; **'~planke** ⚓ f gang-board, gang-plank; **'~schritt** m im ~ running; **'~steg** m footbridge; ⚓ gangway.

Lauge ['laugə] f (-/-n) lye.

Laun|e ['launə] f (-/-n) humo(u)r; mood; temper; caprice, fancy, whim; guter ~ in (high) spirits; **'2enhaft** adj. capricious; **'2isch** adj. moody; wayward.

Laus zo. [laus] f (-/⸚e) louse; **~bub** ['~buːp] m (-en/-en) young scamp, F young devil, rascal.

lausch|en ['lauʃən] v/i. (ge-, h) listen; eavesdrop; **'~ig** adj. snug, cosy; peaceful.

laut [laut] 1. adj. loud (a. fig.); noisy; 2. adv. aloud, loud(ly); (sprechen Sie) ~er! speak up!, Am. louder!; 3. prp. (gen., dat.) according to; ✝ as per; 4. ⌂ m (-[e]s/-e) sound; **'2e** ♪ f (-/-n) lute; **'~en** v/i. (ge-, h) sound; words, etc.: run; read; ~ auf (acc.) passport, etc.: be issued to.

läuten ['lɔytən] (ge-, h) 1. v/i. ring; toll; es läutet the bell is ringing; 2. v/t. ring; toll.

'lauter adj. pure; clear; genuine; sincere; mere, nothing but, only.

läuter|n ['lɔytərn] v/t. (ge-, h) purify; ⊕ cleanse; refine; **'2ung** f (-/-en) purification; refining.

'**laut|los** adj. noiseless; mute; silent; silence: hushed; '2**schrift** f phonetic transcription; '2**sprecher** m loud-speaker; '2**stärke** f sound intensity; radio: (sound-)volume; 2**stärkeregler** ['⸴re:glər] m (-s/-) volume control.

'**lauwarm** adj. tepid, lukewarm.

Lava geol. ['la:va] f (-/Laven) lava.

Lavendel ⚕ [la'vendəl] m (-s/-) lavender.

lavieren [la'vi:rən] v/i. (no -ge-, h, sein) ⚓ tack (a. fig.).

Lawine [la'vi:nə] f (-/-n) avalanche.

lax adj. [laks] lax, loose; morals: a. easy.

Lazarett [latsa'ret] n (-[e]s/-e) (military) hospital.

leben[1] ['le:bən] (ge-, h) 1. v/i. live; be alive; ~ Sie wohl! good-bye!, farewell!; j-n hochleben lassen cheer s.o.; at table: drink s.o.'s health; von et. ~ live on s.th.; hier lebt es sich gut it is pleasant living here; 2. v/t. live (one's life).

Leben[2] [⸴] n (-s/-) life; stir, animation, bustle; am ~ bleiben remain alive, survive; am ~ erhalten keep alive; ein neues ~ beginnen turn over a new leaf; ins ~ rufen call into being; sein ~ aufs Spiel setzen risk one's life; sein ~ lang all one's life; ums ~ kommen lose one's life; perish.

lebendig adj. [le'bendiç] living; pred. alive; quick; lively.

'**Lebens|alter** n age; '~**anschauung** f outlook on life; ~**art** f manners pl., behavio(u)r; ~**auffassung** f philosophy of life; ~**bedingungen** f/pl. living conditions pl.; '~**beschreibung** f life, biography; '~**dauer** f span of life; ⊕ durability; '2**echt** adj. true to life; '~**erfahrung** f experience of life; '2**fähig** adj. ⚕ and fig. viable; ~**gefahr** f danger of life; ~! danger of death)!; unter ~ at the risk of one's life; 2**gefährlich** adj. dangerous (to life), perilous; ~**gefährte** m life's companion; ~**größe** f life-size; in ~ at full length; ~**kraft** f vital power, vigo(u)r, vitality; '2**länglich** adj. for life, lifelong; '~**lauf** m course of life, personal record, curriculum vitae; 2**lustig** adj. gay, merry; ~**mittel** pl. food (-stuffs pl.), provisions pl., groceries pl., 2**müde** adj. weary or tired of life; 2**notwendig** adj. vital, essential; ~**retter** m life-saver, rescuer; ~**standard** m standard of living; ~**unterhalt** m livelihood; s-n ~ verdienen earn one's living; '~**versicherung** f life-insurance; '~**wandel** m life, (moral) conduct; '~**weise** f mode of living, habits pl.; gesunde ~ regimen; ~**weisheit** f worldly wisdom; '2**wichtig** adj. vital, essential; ~e Organe pl. vitals

pl.; '~**zeichen** n sign of life; '~**zeit** f lifetime; auf ~ for life.

Leber anat. ['le:bər] f (-/-n) liver; '~**fleck** m mole; '2**krank** adj., '2**leidend** adj. suffering from a liver-complaint; '~**tran** m cod-liver oil; '~**wurst** f liver-sausage, Am. liverwurst.

'**Lebewesen** n living being, creature.

Lebe'wohl n (-[e]s/-e, -s) farewell.

leb|haft adj. ['le:phaft] lively; vivid; spirited; interest: keen; traffic: busy; '2**kuchen** m gingerbread; '~**los** adj. lifeless; '2**zeiten** pl.: zu s-n ~ in his lifetime.

lechzen ['leçtsən] v/i. (ge-, h): ~ nach languish or yearn or pant for.

Leck [lek] 1. n (-[e]s/-s) leak; 2. 2 adj. leaky; ~ werden ⚓ spring a leak.

lecken ['lekən] (ge-, h) 1. v/t. lick; 2. v/i. lick; leak.

lecker adj. ['lekər] dainty; delicious; '2**bissen** m dainty, delicacy.

Leder ['le:dər] n (-s/-) leather; in ~ gebunden leather-bound; '2**n** adj. leathern, of leather.

ledig adj. ['le:diç] single, unmarried; child: illegitimate; '~**lich** adv. ['~k-] solely, merely.

Lee ⚓ [le:] f (-/no pl.) lee (side).

leer [le:r] 1. adj. empty; vacant; void; vain; blank; 2. adv.: ~ laufen ⊕ idle; '2**e** f (-/no pl.) emptiness, void (a. fig.); phys. vacuum; '~**en** v/t. (ge-, h) empty; clear (out); pour out; 2**gut** † n empties pl.; '2**lauf** m ⊕ idling; mot. neutral gear; fig. waste of energy; '~**stehend** adj. flat empty, unoccupied, vacant.

legal adj. [le'ga:l] legal, lawful.

Legat [le'ga:t] 1. m (-en/-en) legate; 2. 🕮 n (-[e]s/-e) legacy.

legen ['le:gən] (ge-, h) 1. v/t. lay; place, put; sich ~ wind, etc.: calm down, abate; cease; Wert ~ auf (acc.) attach importance to; 2. v/i. hen: lay.

Legende [le'gendə] f (-/-n) legend.

legieren [le'gi:rən] v/t. (no -ge-, h) ⊕ alloy; cookery: thicken (mit with).

Legislative [le:gisla'ti:və] f (-/-n) legislative body or power.

legitim adj. [legi'ti:m] legitimate; ~**ieren** [⸴i'mi:rən] v/t. (no -ge-, h) legitimate; authorize; sich ~ prove one's identity.

Lehm [le:m] m (-[e]s/-e) loam; mud; 2**ig** adj. loamy.

Lehn|e ['le:nə] f (-/-n) support; arm, back (of chair); '2**en** (ge-, h) 1. v/i. lean (an dat. against); 2. v/t. lean, rest (an acc., gegen against); sich ~ an (acc.) lean against; sich ~ auf (acc.) rest or support o.s. (up-)on; sich aus dem Fenster ~ lean out of the window; ~**sessel** m, '~**stuhl** m armchair, easy chair.

Lehrbuch ['le:r-] n textbook.
Lehre ['le:rə] f (-/-n) rule, precept; doctrine; system; science; theory; lesson, warning; moral (of fable); instruction, tuition; ⊕ ga(u)ge; ⊕ pattern; in der ~ sein be apprenticed (bei to); in die ~ geben apprentice, article (both: bei, zu to); ²n v/t. (ge-. h) teach, instruct; show.
'**Lehrer** m (-s/-) teacher; master, instructor; '~in f (-/-nen) (lady) teacher; (school)mistress; '~kollegium n staff (of teachers).
'**Lehr|fach** n subject; '~film m instructional film; '~gang m course (of instruction); '~geld n premium; '~herr m master, sl. boss; '~jahre n/pl. (years pl. of) apprenticeship; '~junge m s. Lehrling; '~körper m teaching staff; univ. professoriate, faculty; '~kraft f teacher; professor; '~ling m (-s/-e) apprentice; '~mädchen n girl apprentice; '~meister m master; '~methode f method of teaching; '~plan m curriculum, syllabus; ²reich adj. instructive; '~satz m ⅋ theorem; doctrine; eccl. dogma; '~stoff m subject-matter, subject(s pl.); '~stuhl m professorship; '~vertrag m articles pl. of apprenticeship, indenture(s pl.); '~zeit f apprenticeship.
Leib [laıp] m (-[e]s/-er) body; belly, anat. abdomen; womb; bei lebendigem ~e alive; mit ~ und Seele body and soul; sich j-n vom ~e halten keep s.o. at arm's length; '~arzt m physician in ordinary, personal physician; '~chen n (-s/-) bodice.
Leibeigen|e ['laıp?aıgənə] m (-n/-n) bond(s)man, serf; '~schaft f (-/no pl.) bondage, serfdom.
Leibes|erziehung ['laıbəs-] f physical training; '~frucht f f(o)etus; '~kraft f: aus Leibeskräften pl. with all one's might; '~übung f bodily or physical exercise.
'**Leib|garde** f body-guard; '~gericht n favo(u)rite dish; ²haftig adj. [~'haftıç]: der ~e Teufel the devil incarnate; ²lich adj. bodily, corpor(e)al; '~rente f life-annuity; '~schmerzen m/pl. stomach-ache, belly-ache, ♣ colic; '~wache f body-guard; '~wäsche f underwear.
Leiche ['laıçə] f (-/-n) (dead) body, corpse
Leichen|beschauer ⚕ ['laıçənbə-ʃaʊər] m (-s/-) appr. coroner; '~bestatter m (-s/-) undertaker, Am. a. mortician; '~bittermiene F f woebegone look or countenance; '²blaß adj. deadly pale; '~halle f mortuary; '~schau f appr. (coroner's) inquest; '~schauhaus n morgue; '~tuch n (-[e]s/⁼er) shroud; '~verbrennung f cremation; '~wagen m hearse.

Leichnam ['laıçna:m] m (-[e]s/-e) s. Leiche.
leicht [laıçt] 1. adj. light; easy; slight; tobacco: mild; 2. adv.: es ~ nehmen take it easy; '²athlet m athlete; '²athletik f athletics pl., Am. track and field events pl.;'~fertig adj. light(-minded); careless; frivolous, flippant; '²fertigkeit f levity; carelessness; frivolity, flippancy; '²gewicht n boxing: lightweight; '~gläubig adj. credulous; '~hin adv. lightly, casually; ²igkeit ['~ıç-] f (-/-en) lightness; ease, facility, '~lebig adj. easy-going; '²metall n light metal; '²sinn m (-[e]s/no pl.) frivolity, levity; carelessness; ~sinnig adj. light-minded, frivolous; careless; '~verdaulich adj. easy to digest; '~verständlich adj. easy to understand.
leid [laıt] 1. adv.: es tut mir ~ I am sorry (um for), I regret; 2. ♀ n (-[e]s/no pl.) injury, harm; wrong; grief, sorrow; ~en ['~dən] (irr., ge-, h) 1. v/i. suffer (an dat. from); 2. v/t.: (nicht) ~ können (dis)like; ²en ['~dən] n (-s/-) suffering; ♣ complaint; ~end adj. ['~dənt] ailing.
'**Leidenschaft** f (-/-en) passion; '²lich adj. passionate; ardent; vehement; '²slos adj. dispassionate.
'**Leidens|gefährte** m, '~gefährtin f fellow-sufferer.
leid|er adv. ['laıdər] unfortunately; int. alas!; ~ muß ich inf. I'm (so) sorry to inf.; ich muß ~ gehen I am afraid I have to go; '~ig adj. disagreeable; '~lich adj. ['laıt-] tolerable; fairly well; ²tragende ['laıt-] m, f (-n/-n) mourner; er ist der ~ dabei he is the one who suffers for it; ²wesen ['laıt-] n (-s/no pl.): zu meinem ~ to my regret.
Leier ♪ ['laıər] f (-/-n) lyre; '~kasten m barrel-organ; '~kastenmann m organ-grinder.
Leih|bibliothek ['laı-] f, '~bücherei f lending or circulating library, Am. a. rental library; '²en v/t. (irr. ge-, h) lend; borrow (von from); '~gebühr f lending fee(s pl.); '~haus n pawnshop, Am. a. loan office; '²weise adv. as a loan.
Leim [laım] m (-[e]s/-e) glue; F aus dem ~ gehen get out of joint; F: auf den ~ gehen fall for it, fall into the trap; '²en v/t. (ge-, h) glue; size.
Lein ♀ [laın] m (-[e]s/-e) flax.
Leine ['laınə] f (-/-n) line, cord; (dog-)lead, leash.
leinen ['laınən] 1. adj. (of) linen; 2. ♀ n (-s/-) linen; in ~ gebunden cloth-bound; '²schuh m canvas shoe.
'**Lein|öl** n linseed-oil; '~samen m linseed; '~wand f (-/no pl.) linen (cloth); paint. canvas; film: screen.

leise adj. ['laɪzə] low, soft; gentle; slight, faint; ~r stellen turn down (radio).

Leiste ['laɪstə] f (-/-n) border, ledge; ⚒ fillet; anat. groin.

leisten ['laɪstən] 1. v/t. (ge-, h) do; perform; fulfil(l); take (oath); render (service); ich kann mir das ~ I can afford it; 2. ♀ ⊕ m (-s/-) last; boot-tree, Am. a. shoetree; '2-bruch ♂ m inguinal hernia.

Leistung f (-/-en) performance; achievement; work(manship); result(s pl.); ⊕ capacity; output (of factory); benefit (of insurance company); '2fähig adj. productive; efficient, ⊕ a. powerful; '~fähigkeit f efficiency; ⊕ productivity; ⊕ capacity, producing-power.

Leit|artikel ['laɪt-] m leading article, leader, editorial; '~bild n image; example.

leiten ['laɪtən] v/t. (ge-, h) lead, guide; conduct (a. phys., ♪); fig. direct, run, manage, operate; preside over (meeting); '~d adj. leading; phys. conductive; ~e Stellung key position.

Leiter 1. m (-s/-) leader; conductor (a. phys., ♪); guide; manager; 2. f (-/-n) ladder; '~in f (-/-nen) leader; conductress, guide; manageress; '~wagen m rack-wag(g)on.

Leit|faden m manual, textbook, guide; '~motiv ♪ n leit-motiv; '~spruch m motto; '~tier n leader; '~ung f (-/-en) lead(ing), conducting, guidance; management, direction, administration, Am. a. operation; phys. conduction; ⚡ lead; circuit; tel. line; mains pl. (for gas, water, etc.); pipeline; die ~ ist besetzt teleph. the line is engaged or Am. busy.

'Leitungs|draht m conducting wire, conductor; '~rohr n conduit(-pipe); main (for gas, water, etc.); '~wasser n (-s/-) tap water.

'Leitwerk ✈ n tail unit or group, empennage.

Lekt|ion [lɛk'tsjoːn] f (-/-en) lesson; ~or ['lɛktɔr] m (-s/-en) lecturer; reader; ~üre [~'tyːrə] f 1. (-/no pl.) reading; 2. (-/-n) books pl.

Lende anat. ['lɛndə] f (-/-n) loin(s pl.).

lenk|bar adj. ['lɛŋkbaːr] guidable, manageable, tractable; docile; ⊕ steerable, dirigible; '~en v/t. (ge-, h) direct, guide; turn; rule; govern; drive (car); ⚓ steer; Aufmerksamkeit ~ auf (acc.) draw attention to; '2rad mot. n steering wheel; '2-säule mot. f steering column; '2-stange f handle-bar (of bicycle); '2ung mot. f (-/-en) steering-gear.

Lenz [lɛnts] m (-es/-e) spring.

Leopard zo. [leo'part] m (-en/-en) leopard.

Lepra ♨ ['leːpra] f (-/no pl.) leprosy.

Lerche orn. ['lɛrçə] f (-/-n) lark.

lern|begierig adj. ['lɛrn-] eager to learn, studious; '~en v/t. and v/i. (ge-, h) learn; study.

Lese ['leːzə] f (-/-n) gathering; s. Weinlese; '~buch n reader; '~lampe f reading-lamp.

lesen ['leːzən] (irr., ge-, h) 1. v/t. read; ~ gather; Messe ~ eccl. say mass; 2. v/i. read; univ. (give a) lecture (über acc. on); '~swert adj. worth reading.

'Leser m (-s/-), '~in f (-/-nen) reader; ♂ gatherer; vintager; '2lich adj. legible; '~zuschrift f letter to the editor.

'Lesezeichen n book-mark.

'Lesung parl. f (-/-en) reading.

letzt adj. [lɛtst] last; final; ultimate; ~e Nachrichten pl. latest news pl.; ~e Hand anlegen put the finishing touches (an acc. to); das ~e the last thing; der ~ere the latter; der (die, das) Letzte the last (one); zu guter Letzt last but not least; finally; '~ens adv., '~hin adv. lately, of late; '~lich adv. s. letztens; finally; ultimately.

Leucht|e ['lɔʏçtə] f (-/-n) (fig. shining) light, lamp (a. fig.); luminary (a. fig., esp. p.); '2en v/i. (ge-, h) (give) light, shine (forth); beam, gleam; '~en n (-s/no pl.) shining, light, luminosity; '2end adj. shining, bright; luminous; brilliant (a. fig.); '~er m (-s/-) candlestick; s. Kronleuchter; '~feuer n ⚓, ✈, etc.: beacon(-light), flare (light); '~käfer zo. m glow-worm; '~kugel ✕ f Very light; flare; '~turm m lighthouse; '~ziffer f luminous figure.

leugnen ['lɔʏɡnən] v/t. (ge-, h) deny; disavow; contest.

Leukämie ♨ [lɔʏkɛ'miː] f (-/-n) leuk(a)emia.

Leumund ['lɔʏmunt] m (-[e]s/no pl.) reputation, repute; character; '~szeugnis ⚖ n character reference.

Leute ['lɔʏtə] pl. people pl.; persons pl.; ✕, pol. men pl.; workers: hands pl.; F folks pl.; domestics pl., servants pl.

Leutnant ✕ ['lɔʏtnant] m (-s/-s, ✎ -e) second lieutenant.

leutselig adj. ['lɔʏtzeːliç] affable.

Lexikon ['lɛksikɔn] n (-s/Lexika, Lexiken) dictionary; encyclop(a)edia.

Libelle zo. [li'bɛlə] f (-/-n) dragonfly.

liberal adj. [libe'raːl] liberal.

Licht [liçt] 1. n (-[e]s/-er) light; brightness; lamp; candle; hunt. eye; ~ machen ⚡ switch or turn on the light(s pl.); das ~ der Welt erblicken see the light, be born; 2. ♀ adj. light, bright; clear; ~er Augenblick lucid interval; '~anlage f lighting plant; '~**bild** n photo (-graph); '~**bildervortrag** m slide lecture; ~**blick** fig. m bright spot; '~**bogen** ⚡ m arc; 'Q**durchlässig** adj. translucent; 'Q**echt** adj. fast (to light), unfading; 'Q**empfindlich** adj. sensitive to light, phot. sensitive; ~ **machen** sensitize.

'**lichten** v/t. (ge-, h) clear (forest); **den Anker** ~ ⚓ weigh anchor; sich ~ hair, crowd: thin.

lichterloh adv. ['liçtər'lo:] blazing, in full blaze.

'**Licht|geschwindigkeit** f speed of light; ~**hof** m glass-roofed court; patio, halo (a. phot.); '~**leitung** f lighting mains pl.; '~**maschine** mot. f dynamo, generator; '~**pause** f blueprint; '~**quelle** f light source, source of light; '~**reklame** f neon sign; ~**schacht** m well; '~**schalter** m (light) switch; '~**schein** m gleam of light; 'Q**scheu** adj. shunning the light; '~**signal** n light or luminous signal; ~**spieltheater** n s. **Film-theater**, **Kino**; '~**strahl** m ray or beam of light (a. fig.); 'Q**undurch-lässig** adj. opaque.

'**Lichtung** f (-/-en) clearing, opening, glade.

'**Lichtzelle** f s. Photozelle.

Lid [li:t] n (-[e]s/-er) eyelid.

lieb adj. [li:p] dear; nice, kind; child: good; in letters: ~**er Herr N.** dear Mr N.; ~**er Himmel!** good Heavens!, dear me!; es ist mir ~, daß I am glad that; 'Q**chen** n (-s/-) sweetheart.

Liebe ['li:bə] f (-/no pl.) love (zu of, for); aus ~ for love; aus ~ **zu** for the love of; 'Q**n** (ge-, h) 1. v/t. love; be in love with; be fond of, like; 2. v/i. (be in) love; '~**nde** m, f (-n/-n): die ~**n** pl. the lovers pl.

'**liebens|wert** adj. lovable; charming; ~**würdig** adj. lovable, amiable; das ist sehr ~ von Ihnen that is very kind of you; 'Q**würdigkeit** f (-/-en) amiability, kindness.

'**lieber** 1. adj. dearer; 2. adv. rather, sooner, ~ **haben** prefer, like better.

'**Liebes|brief** m love-letter; '~**dienst** m favo(u)r, kindness; good turn; ~**erklärung** f: e-e ~ **machen** declare one's love; '~**heirat** f love-match; ~**kummer** m lover's grief; '~**paar** n (courting) couple, lovers pl.; '~**verhältnis** n love-affair.

'**liebevoll** adj. loving, affectionate.

lieb|gewinnen ['li:p-] v/t. (irr. gewinnen, sep., no -ge-, h) get or grow fond of; '~**haben** v/t. (irr. haben, sep., -ge-, h) love, be fond of; 'Q**haber** m (-s/-) lover; beau; fig. amateur; Q**haberei** fig. [~'raɪ] f (-/-en) hobby; 'Q**haberpreis** m fancy price; 'Q**haberwert** m sentimental value; '~**kosen** v/t. (no -ge-, h) caress, fondle; 'Q**kosung** f (-/-en) caress;

~**lich** adj. lovely, charming, delightful.

Liebling ['li:plɪŋ] m (-s/-e) darling; favo(u)rite, esp. animals: pet; esp. form of address darling, esp. Am. honey; ~**sbeschäftigung** f favo(u)rite occupation, hobby.

lieb|los adj. ['li:p-] unkind; careless; 'Q**schaft** f (-/-en) (love-)affair; 'Q**ste** m, f (-n/-n) sweetheart; darling.

Lied [li:t] n (-[e]s/-er) song; tune.

liederlich adj. ['li:dərlɪç] slovenly, disorderly; careless; loose, dissolute.

lief [li:f] pret. of laufen.

Lieferant [li:fə'rant] m (-en/-en) supplier, purveyor; caterer.

Liefer|auto ['li:fər-] n s. Liefer-wagen, 'Q**bar** adj. to be delivered; available; ~**bedingungen** f/pl. terms pl. of delivery; '~**frist** f term of delivery; 'Q**n** v/t. (ge-, h) deliver; j-m et.~ furnish or supply s.o. with s.th.; ~**schein** m delivery note; '~**ung** f (-/-en) delivery; supply; consignment; instal(l)ment (of book); '~**ungsbedingungen** f/pl. s. Liefer-bedingungen; ~**wagen** m delivery-van, Am. delivery wagon.

Liege ['li:gə] f (-/-n) couch; bed-chair.

liegen ['li:gən] v/i. (irr., ge-, h) lie; house, etc.: be (situated); room: face; an wem liegt es? whose fault is it? es liegt an or bei ihm zu inf. it is for him to inf.; es liegt daran, daß the reason for it is that; es liegt mir daran zu inf. I am anxious to inf.; es liegt mir nichts daran it does not matter or it is of no consequence to me; ~**bleiben** v/i. (irr. bleiben, sep., -ge-, sein) stay in bed; break down (on the road, a. mot., etc.); work, etc.: stand over; fall behind; ✝ goods: remain on hand; '~**lassen** v/t. (irr. lassen, sep., [-ge-,] h) leave; leave behind; leave alone; leave off (work); j-n links ~ ignore s.o., give s.o. the cold shoulder; 'Q**schaften** f/pl. real estate.

'**Liege|stuhl** m deck-chair; '~**wagen** 🚂 m couchette coach.

lieh [li:] pret. of leihen.

ließ [li:s] pret. of lassen.

Lift [lɪft] m (-[e]s/-e, -s) lift, Am. elevator.

Liga ['li:ga] f (-/Ligen) league.

Likör [li'kø:r] m (-s/-e) liqueur, cordial.

lila adj. ['li:la] lilac.

Lilie ⚘ ['li:lɪə] f (-/-n) lily.

Limonade [limo'na:də] f (-/-n) soft drink, fruit-juice; lemonade.

Limousine mot. [limu'zi:nə] f (-/-n) limousine, saloon car, Am. sedan.

lind adj. [lɪnt] soft, gentle; mild.

Linde ⚘ ['lɪndə] f (-/-n) lime(-tree), linden(-tree).

linder|n ['lindərn] *v/t.* (ge-, h) soften; mitigate; alleviate, soothe; allay, ease (*pain*); '2ung *f* (-/⸱-en) softening; mitigation; alleviation; easing.

Lineal [line'ɑːl] *n* (-s/-e) ruler.

Linie ['liːnjə] *f* (-/-n) line; '⸱⸱npa-pier *n* ruled paper; '⸱nrichter *m* *sports*: linesman; '2ntreu *pol. adj.*: ~ sein follow the party line.

lin(i)ieren [li'niːrən; liniˈiːrən] *v/t.* (*no* -ge-, h) rule, line.

link *adj.* [liŋk] left; ~e Seite left (-hand) side, left; *of cloth*: wrong side; '2e *f* (-n/-n) the left (hand); *pol. the* Left (Wing); *boxing: the* left; '⸱isch *adj.* awkward, clumsy.

links *adv.* on *or* to the left; 2händer ['⸱hendər] *m* (-s/-) left-hander, *Am. a.* southpaw.

Linse ['linzə] *f* (-/-n) ⚜ lentil; *opt.* lens.

Lippe ['lipə] *f* (-/-n) lip; '⸱nstift *m* lipstick.

liquidieren [likvi'diːrən] *v/t.* (*no* -ge-, h) liquidate (*a. pol.*); wind up (*business company*); charge (*fee*).

lispeln ['lispəln] *v/i. and v/t.* (ge-, h) lisp; whisper.

List [list] *f* (-/-en) cunning, craft; artifice, ruse, trick; stratagem.

Liste ['listə] *f* (-/-n) list, roll.

listig *adj.* cunning, crafty, sly.

Liter ['liːtər] *n, m* (-s/-) lit|re, *Am.* -er.

literarisch *adj.* [lite'rɑːriʃ] literary.

Literatur [litera'tuːr] *f* (-/-en) literature; ⸱beilage *f* literary supplement (*in newspaper*); ⸱ge-schichte *f* history of literature; ⸱verzeichnis *n* bibliography.

litt [lit] *pret. of* leiden.

Litze ['litsə] *f* (-/-n) lace, cord, braid; ≩ strand(ed wire).

Livree [li'vre:] *f* (-/-n) livery.

Lizenz [li'tsɛnts] *f* (-/-en) licen|ce, *Am.* -se; ⸱inhaber *m* licensee.

Lob [loːp] *n* (-[e]s/*no pl.*) praise; commendation; 2en ['loːbən] *v/t.* (ge-, h) praise; 2enswert *adj.* ['loːbəns-] praise-worthy, laudable; ⸱gesang ['loːp-] *m* hymn, song of praise; ⸱hudelei [loːphuːdə'laɪ] *f* (-/-en) adulation, base flattery.

löblich *adj.* ['løːpliç] *s.* lobenswert.

Lobrede ['loːp-] *f* eulogy, panegyric.

Loch [lɔx] *n* (-[e]s/⸱er) hole; '2en *v/t.* (ge-, h) perforate, pierce; punch (*ticket, etc.*); '⸱er *m* (-s/-) punch, perforator; '⸱karte *f* punch(ed) card.

Locke ['lɔkə] *f* (-/-n) curl, ringlet.

'locken[1] *v/t. and v/refl.* (ge-, h) curl.

'locken[2] *v/t.* (ge-, h) *hunt.*: bait; decoy (*a. fig.*); *fig.* allure, entice.

'Locken|kopf *m* curly head; ⸱wick-ler ['⸱viklər] *m* (-s/-) curler, roller.

locker *adj.* ['lɔkər] loose, slack; '⸱n

v/t. (ge-, h) loosen; slacken; relax (*grip*); break up (*soil*); *sich* ~ loosen, (be)come loose; give way; *fig.* relax.

'lockig *adj.* curly.

'Lock|mittel *n s.* Köder; '⸱vogel *m* decoy (*a. fig.*); *Am. a.* stool pigeon (*a. fig.*).

lodern ['loːdərn] *v/i.* (ge-, h) flare, blaze.

Löffel ['lœfəl] *m* (-s/-) spoon; ladle; '2n *v/t.* (ge-, h) spoon up; ladle out; '⸱voll *m* (-/-) spoonful.

log [loːk] *pret. of* lügen.

Loge ['loːʒə] *f* (-/-n) *thea.* box; *free-masonry*: lodge; '⸱nschließer *thea. m* (-s/-) box-keeper.

logieren [loˈʒiːrən] *v/i.* (*no* -ge-, h) lodge, stay, *Am. a.* room (*all:* bei with; *in dat.* at).

logisch *adj.* ['loːgiʃ] logical; '⸱er-weise *adv.* logically.

Lohn [loːn] *m* (-[e]s/⸱e) wages *pl.*, pay(ment); hire; *fig.* reward; ⸱bü-ro *n* pay-office; ⸱empfänger *m* wage-earner; '2en *v/t.* (ge-, h) compensate, reward; *sich* ~ pay; es lohnt sich zu *inf.* it is worth while *ger.*, it pays to *inf.*; 2end *adj.* pay-ing; advantageous, *fig.* rewarding; '⸱erhöhung *f* increase in wages, rise, *Am.* raise; '⸱forderung *f* demand for higher wages; ⸱steuer *f* tax on wages *or* salary; ⸱stopp *m* (-s/*no pl.*) wage freeze; ⸱tarif *m* wage rate; '⸱tüte *f* pay envelope.

lokal [lo'kɑːl] **1.** *adj.* local; **2.** 2 *n* (-[e]s/-e) locality, place; restaurant; public house, F pub, F local, *Am.* saloon.

Lokomotiv|e [lokomo'tiːvə] *f* (-/-n) (railway) engine, locomotive; ⸱füh-rer [⸱ˈtiːf-] *m* engine-driver, *Am.* engineer.

Lorbeer ≩ ['lɔrbeːr] *m* (-s/-en) laurel, bay.

Lore ['loːrə] *f* (-/-n) lorry, truck.

Los[1] [loːs] *n* (-es/-e) lot; lottery ticket; *fig.* fate, destiny, lot; das Große ~ ziehen win the first prize, *Am. sl.* hit the jackpot; durchs ~ entscheiden decide by lot.

los[2] [~] **1.** *pred. adj.* loose; free; was ist ~? what is the matter?, F what's up?, *Am.* F what's cooking?; ~ sein be rid of; **2.** *int.*: ~! go (on *or* ahead)!

losarbeiten ['loːsʔ-] *v/i.* (*sep.*, -ge-, h) start work(ing).

lösbar *adj.* ['løːsbɑːr] soluble, ₳ *a.* solvable.

'los|binden *v/t.* (*irr.* binden, *sep.*, -ge-, h) untie, loosen; '⸱brechen (*irr.* brechen, *sep.*, -ge-) **1.** *v/t.* (h) break off; **2.** *v/i.* (sein) break *or* burst out.

Lösch|blatt ['lœʃ-] *n* blotting-paper; '2en *v/t.* (ge-, h) extinguish, put out (*fire, light*); blot out (*writing*);

erase (*tape recording*); cancel (*debt*); quench (*thirst*); slake (*lime*); ⚓ unload; **~er** *m* (-s/-) blotter; '**~papier** *n* blotting-paper.

lose *adj.* ['loːzə] loose.

'**Lösegeld** *n* ransom.

losen ['loːzən] *v/i.* (ge-, h) cast *or* draw lots (*um* for).

lösen ['løːzən] *v/t.* (ge-, h) loosen, untie; buy, book (*ticket*); solve (*task, doubt, etc.*); break off (*engagement*); annul (*agreement, etc.*); 🜩 dissolve; *ein Schuß löste sich* the gun went off.

'**los|fahren** *v/i.* (*irr.* fahren, sep., -ge-, sein) depart, drive off; '**~gehen** *v/i.* (*irr.* gehen, sep., -ge-, sein) go *or* be off; come off, get loose; *gun:* go off; begin, start; F *auf j-n ~* fly at s.o.; **~haken** *v/t.* (sep., -ge-, h) unhook; **~kaufen** *v/t.* (sep., -ge-, h) ransom, redeem; **~ketten** *v/t.* (sep., -ge-, h) unchain; **~kommen** *v/i.* (*irr.* kommen, sep., -ge-, sein) get loose *or* free; '**~lachen** *v/i.* (sep., -ge-, h) laugh out; '**~lassen** *v/t.* (*irr.* lassen, sep., -ge-, h) let go; release.

löslich 🜩 *adj.* ['løːsliç] soluble.

'**los|lösen** *v/t.* (sep., -ge-, h) loosen, detach; sever; '**~machen** *v/t.* (sep., -ge-, h) unfasten, loosen; *sich ~* disengange (o.s.) (*von* from); '**~reißen** *v/t.* (*irr.* reißen, sep., -ge-, h) tear off; *sich ~* break away, *esp. fig.* tear o.s. away (*both: von* from); '**~sagen** *v/refl.* (sep., -ge-, h): *sich ~ von* renounce; '**~schlagen** (*irr.* schlagen, sep., -ge-, h) **1.** *v/t.* knock off; **2.** *v/i.* open the attack; *auf j-n ~* attack s.o.; '**~schnallen** *v/t.* (sep., -ge-, h) unbuckle; '**~schrauben** *v/t.* (sep., -ge-, h) unscrew, screw off; '**~sprechen** *v/t.* (*irr.* sprechen, sep., -ge-, h) absolve (*von* of, from); acquit (of); free (from, of); '**~stürzen** *v/i.* (sep., -ge-, sein): *~ auf* (*acc.*) rush at.

Losung ['loːzuŋ] *f* **1.** (-/-en) ✕ password, watchword; *fig.* slogan; **2.** *hunt.* (-/*no pl.*) droppings *pl.*, dung.

Lösung ['løːzuŋ] *f* (-/-en) solution; '**~smittel** *n* solvent.

'**los|werden** *v/t.* (*irr.* werden, sep., -ge-, sein) get rid of, dispose of; '**~ziehen** *v/i.* (*irr.* ziehen, sep., -ge-, sein) set out, take off, march away.

Lot [loːt] *n* (-[e]s/-e) plumb(-line), plummet.

löten ['løːtən] *v/t.* (ge-, h) solder.

Lotse ⚓ ['loːtsə] *m* (-n/-n) pilot; '**2n** *v/t.* (ge-, h) ⚓ pilot (*a. fig.*).

Lotterie [lɔtə'riː] *f* (-/-en) lottery; **~gewinn** *m* prize; **~los** *n* lottery ticket.

Lotto ['lɔto] *n* (-s/-s) numbers pool, lotto.

Löwe *zo.* ['løːvə] *m* (-n/-n) lion.

'**Löwen|anteil** F *m* lion's share; '**~maul** ♦ *n* (-[e]s/*no pl.*) snapdragon; '**~zahn** ♦ *m* (-[e]s/*no pl.*) dandelion.

'**Löwin** *zo.* *f* (-/-nen) lioness.

loyal *adj.* [loa'jaːl] loyal.

Luchs *zo.* [luks] *m* (-es/-e) lynx.

Lücke ['lykə] *f* (-/-n) gap; blank, void (*a. fig.*); **~nbüßer** *m* stopgap; '**2nhaft** *adj.* full of gaps; *fig.* defective, incomplete; '**2nlos** *adj.* without a gap; *fig.* unbroken; complete, **~er Beweis** close argument.

lud [luːt] *pret. of* laden.

Luft [luft] *f* (-/**~e**) air; breeze; breath; *frische ~ schöpfen* take the air; *an die ~ gehen* go for an airing; *aus der ~ gegriffen* (totally) unfounded, fantastic; *es liegt et. in der ~* there is s.th. in the wind; *in die ~ fliegen* be blown up, explode; *in die ~ gehen* explode, *sl.* blow one's top; *in die ~ sprengen* blow up; F *j-n an die ~ setzen* turn s.o. out, *Am. sl.* give s.o. the air; *sich or s-n Gefühlen ~ machen* give vent to one's feelings.

'**Luft|alarm** *m* air-raid alarm; '**~angriff** *m* air raid; **~aufnahme** *f* aerial photograph; **~ballon** *m* (air-)balloon; **~bild** *n* aerial photograph, airview; **~blase** *f* air-bubble; **~brücke** *f* air-bridge; *for supplies, etc.* air-lift.

Lüftchen ['lyftçən] *n* (-s/-) gentle breeze.

'**luft|dicht** *adj.* air-tight; '**2druck** *phys. m* (-[e]s/*no pl.*) atmospheric *or* air pressure; '**2druckbremse** *f* air-brake; **~durchlässig** *adj.* permeable to air.

lüften ['lyftən] (ge-, h) **1.** *v/i.* air; **2.** *v/t.* air; raise (*hat*); lift (*veil*); disclose (*secret*).

'**Luft|fahrt** *f* aviation, aeronautics; '**~feuchtigkeit** *f* atmospheric humidity, '**2gekühlt** ⊕ *adj.* air-cooled; **~hoheit** *f* air sovereignty; '**2ig** *adj.* airy, breezy; flimsy; '**~kissen** *n* air-cushion; '**~klappe** *f* air-valve; '**~korridor** *m* air corridor; **~krankheit** *f* airsickness; '**~krieg** *m* aerial warfare; '**~kurort** *m* climatic health resort; '**~landetruppen** *f/pl.* airborne troops *pl.*; '**2leer** *adj.* void of air, evacuated; **~er Raum** vacuum; '**~linie** *f* air line, bee-line; **~loch** *n* ✈ air-pocket; vent(-hole); '**~post** *f* air mail; '**~pumpe** *f* air-pump; '**~raum** *m* airspace; **~röhre** *anat. f* windpipe, trachea; **~schacht** *m* air-shaft; **~schaukel** *f* swing-boat; '**~schiff** *n* airship; '**~schloß** *n* castle in the air *or* in Spain; '**~schutz** *m* air-raid protection; '**~schutzkeller** *m* air-raid shelter; **~sprünge** [~ʃpryŋə] *m/pl.*: *~ machen* cut capers *pl.*; gambol; '**~stützpunkt** *m* air base.

'**Lüftung** f (-/-en) airing; ventilation.
'**Luft|veränderung** f change of air;
'**~verkehr** m air-traffic; '**~verkehrsgesellschaft** f air transport
company, airway, *Am.* airline;
'**~verteidigung** ⚓ f air defen|ce,
Am. -se; '**~waffe** ⚓ f air force;
'**~weg** m airway; *auf dem* **~** by air;
'**~zug** m draught, *Am.* draft.
Lüge ['ly:gə] f (-/-n) lie, falsehood;
j-n **~** *n strafen* give the lie to s.o.
'**lügen** v/i. (*irr.*, ge-, h) (tell a) lie;
'**~haft** adj. lying, mendacious; untrue, false.
Lügner ['ly:gnər] m (-s/-), '**~in** f
(-/-nen) liar; '**2isch** adj. s. lügen-
haft.
Luke ['lu:kə] f (-/-n) dormer- *or*
garret-window; hatch.
Lümmel ['lyməl] m (-s/-) lout,
boor; saucy fellow; '**2n** v/refl. (ge-,
h) loll, lounge, sprawl.
Lump [lump] m (-en/-en) ragamuffin, beggar; cad, *Am. sl.* rat, heel;
scoundrel.
'**Lumpen** 1. m (-s/-) rag; 2. ⚓ vb.:
sich nicht **~** *lassen* come down
handsomely; '**~pack** n rabble, riff-
raff; '**~sammler** m rag-picker.
'**lumpig** adj. ragged; *fig.*: shabby,
paltry, mean.
Lunge ['luŋə] f (-/-n) anat. lungs
pl.; *of animals*: a. lights *pl.*
'**Lungen|entzündung** ⚕ f pneu-
monia; '**~flügel** anat. m lung;
'**2krank** ⚕ adj. suffering from consumption, consumptive; '**~kranke**
⚕ m, f consumptive (patient); '**~krankheit** ⚕ f lung-disease; '**~schwindsucht** ⚕ f (pulmonary)
consumption.

lungern ['luŋərn] v/i. (ge-, h) s.
herumlungern.
Lupe ['lu:pə] f (-/-n) magnifying-
glass, *unter die* **~** *nehmen* scrutinize,
take a good look at.
Lust [lust] f (-/‌-̈e) pleasure, delight;
desire, lust; **~** *haben zu inf.* have a
mind to *inf.*, feel like *ger.*; *haben Sie*
~ *auszugehen?* would you like to go
out?
lüstern adj. ['lystərn] desirous (*nach*
of), greedy (of, for); lewd, lascivious, lecherous.
'**lustig** adj. merry, gay; jolly, cheerful; amusing, funny; *sich* **~** *machen*
über (acc.) make fun of; '**2keit** f
(-/no *pl.*) gaiety, mirth; jollity,
cheerfulness; fun.
Lüstling ['lystliŋ] m (-s/-e) volup-
tuary, libertine.
'**lust|los** adj. dull, spiritless; ✝ flat;
'**2mord** m rape and murder; '**2spie**
n comedy.
lutschen ['lutʃən] v/i. *and* v/t. (ge-,
h) suck.
Luv ⚓ [lu:f] f (-/no *pl.*) luff, wind-
ward.
luxuriös adj. [luksu'rjø:s] luxurious.
Luxus ['luksus] m (-/no *pl.*) luxury
(*a. fig.*), **~artikel** m luxury; '**~ausgabe** f de luxe edition (*of books*);
'**~ware** f luxury (article); fancy
goods *pl.*
Lymph|drüse anat. ['lymf-] f
lymphatic gland; '**~e** f (-/-n) lymph;
⚕ vaccine; '**~gefäß** anat. n lymphatic vessel.
lynchen ['lynçən] v/t. (ge-, h) lynch.
Lyrik ['ly:rik] f (-/no *pl.*) lyric
verses *pl.*, lyrics *pl.*; '**~er** m (-s/-)
lyric poet.
'**lyrisch** adj. lyric; lyrical (*a. fig.*).

M

Maat ⚓ [ma:t] m (-[e]s/-e[n])
(ship's) mate.
Mache F ['maxə] f (-/no *pl.*) make-
believe, window-dressing, *sl.* eyewash; *et. in der* **~** *haben* have s.th.
in hand.
machen ['maxən] (ge-, h) 1. v/t.
make; do; produce, manufacture;
give (*appetite, etc.*); sit for, undergo
(*examination*); come *or* amount to;
make (*happy, etc.*); *was macht das*
(*aus*)? what does that matter?; *das*
macht nichts! never mind!, that's
(quite) all right!; *da(gegen) kann*
man nichts **~** that cannot be helped;
ich mache mir nichts daraus I don't
care about it; *mach, daß du fort-*
kommst! off with you!; *j-n* **~** *las-*
sen, was er will let s.o. do as he
pleases; *sich* **~** *an* (acc.) go *or* set

about; *sich et.* **~** *lassen* have s.th.
made; 2. F v/i.: *na, mach schon!*
hurry up!; '**2schaften** f/pl. machi-
nations *pl.*
Macht [maxt] f (-/‌-̈e) power; might;
authority; control (*über acc.* of); *an*
der **~** *pol.* in power; '**~befugnis** f
authority, power; '**~haber** *pol.* m
(-s/-) ruler.
mächtig adj. ['mɛçtiç] powerful (*a.*
fig.); mighty, immense, huge; **~**
sein (*gen.*) be master of *s.th.*; have
command of (*language*).
'**Macht|kampf** m struggle for pow-
er; '**2los** adj. powerless; '**~politik**
f power politics *sg.*, *pl.*; policy of
the strong hand; '**~spruch** m
authoritative decision; '**2voll** adj.
powerful (*a. fig.*); '**~vollkommen-**
heit f authority; '**~wort** n (-[e]s/-e)

word of command; *ein* ~ *sprechen* put one's foot down.

'**Machwerk** *n* concoction, F put-up job; *elendes* ~ bungling work.

Mädchen ['mɛːtçən] *n* (-s/-) girl; maid(-servant); ~ *für alles* maid of all work; *fig. a.* jack of all trades; '2haft *adj.* girlish; '~name *m* girl's name; maiden name; '~schule *f* girls' school.

Made *zo.* ['maːdə] *f* (-/-n) maggot, mite; *fruit:* worm.

Mädel ['meːdəl] *n* (-s/-, F -s) girl, lass(ie).

madig *adj.* ['maːdiç] maggoty, full of mites; *fruit:* wormeaten.

Magazin [maga'tsiːn] *n* (-s/-e) store, warehouse; ✕, *in rifle, periodical:* magazine.

Magd [maːkt] *f* (-/⸚e) maid(-servant).

Magen ['maːgən] *m* (-s/⸚, *a.* -) stomach, F tummy; *animals:* maw; '~beschwerden *f/pl.* stomach or gastric trouble, indigestion; '~bitter *m* (-s/-) bitters *pl.*; '~geschwür *s* *n* gastric ulcer; '~krampf *m* stomach cramp; '~krebs *s* *m* stomach cancer; '~leiden *n* gastric complaint; '~säure *f* gastric acid.

mager *adj.* ['maːgər] meag[re, *Am.* -er (*a. fig.*); *p., animal, meat:* lean, *Am. a.* scrawny; '2milch *f* skim milk.

Magie [ma'giː] *f* (-/no *pl.*) magic; ~r ['maːgjər] *m* (-s/-) magician.

magisch *adj.* ['maːgiʃ] magic(al).

Magistrat [magis'traːt] *m* (-[e]s/-e) municipal *or* town council.

Magnet [ma'gneːt] *m* (-[e]s, -en/ -e[n]) magnet (*a. fig.*); lodestone; 2isch *adj.* magnetic. 2isieren [~eti'ziːrən] *v/t.* (no -ge-, *h*) magnetize; '~nadel [~'gneːt-] *f* magnetic needle.

Mahagoni [maha'goːni] *n* (-s/no *pl.*) mahogany (wood).

mähen ['meːən] *v/t.* (ge-, *h*) cut, mow, reap.

Mahl [maːl] *n* (-[e]s/⸚er, -e) meal, repast.

'**mahlen** (*irr.*, ge-, *h*) **1.** *v/t.* grind, mill; **2.** *v/i. tyres:* spin.

'**Mahlzeit** *f s.* Mahl; F feed.

Mähne ['meːnə] *f* (-/-n) mane.

mahn|en ['maːnən] *v/t.* (ge-, *h*) remind, admonish (*both: an acc.* of); *j-n wegen e-r Schuld* ~ press s.o. for payment, dun s.o.; '2mal *n*(-[e]s/-e) memorial; '2ung *f* (-/-en) admonition; ✝ reminder, dunning; '2zettel *m* reminder.

Mai [maɪ] *m* (-[e]s, -/-e) May; '~baum *m* maypole; ~glöckchen ♀ [~'glœkçən] *n* (-s/-) lily of the valley; '~käfer *zo. m* cockchafer, may-beetle, may-bug.

Mais ♀ [maɪs] *m* (-es/-e) maize, Indian corn, *Am.* corn.

Majestät [maje'stɛːt] *f* (-/-en) majesty; *Your ~* Majesty; 2isch *adj.* majestic; ~s-beleidigung *f* lese-majesty.

Major ✕ [ma'joːr] *m* (-s/-e) major.

Makel ['maːkəl] *m* (-s/-) stain, spot; *fig. a.* blemish, fault; '2los *adj.* stainless, spotless; *fig. a.* unblemished, faultless, immaculate.

mäkeln F ['meːkəln] *v/i.* (ge-, *h*) find fault (*an dat.* with), carp (at), F pick (at).

Makler ✝ ['maːklər] *m* (-s/-) broker; ~gebühr ✝ *f* brokerage.

Makulatur ⊕ [makula'tuːr] *f* (-/-en) waste paper.

Mal[1] [maːl] *n* (-[e]s/-e, ⸚er) mark, sign; *sports:* start(ing-point), goal; spot, stain; mole.

Mal[2] [~] *n* (-[e]s/-e) time; *für dieses* ~ this time; *zum ersten* ~e for the first time; *mit e-m* ~e all at once, all of a sudden; **2.** 2 *adv.* times, multiplied by; *drei* ~ *fünf ist fünfzehn* three times five is *or* are fifteen; F *s.* einmal.

'**malen** *v/t.* (ge-, *h*) paint; portray.

'**Maler** *m* (-s/-) painter; artist; ~ei [~'raɪ] *f* (-/-en) painting; '2isch *adj.* pictorial, painting; *fig.* picturesque.

'**Malkasten** *m* paint-box.

'**malnehmen** *v/t.* (*irr.* nehmen, sep., -ge-, *h*) multiply (*mit* by).

Malz [malts] *n* (-es/no *pl.*) malt; '~bier *n* malt beer.

Mama [ma'maː, F 'mama] *f* (-/-s) mamma, mammy, F ma, *Am.* F *a.* mummy, mom.

man *indef. pron.* [man] one, you, we; they, people; ~ *sagte mir* I was told. [manager.\]

Manager ['mɛnidʒər] *m* (-s/-)\]

manch [manç], '~er, '~e, '~es *adj. and indef. pron.* many a; ~e *pl.* some, several; '~erlei *adj.* ['~ərlaɪ] diverse, different; *all sorts of, ... of* several sorts; *auf ~ Art* in various ways; *used as a noun:* many *or* various things; '~mal *adv.* sometimes, at times.

Mandant 🕀 [man'dant] *m* (-en/-en) client.

Mandarine ♀ [manda'riːnə] *f* (-/-n) tangerine.

Mandat [man'daːt] *n* (-[e]s/-e) authorization; 🕀 brief; *pol.* mandate; *parl.* seat.

Mandel ['mandəl] *f* (-/-n) ♀ almond; *anat.* tonsil; '~baum ♀ *m* almond-tree; '~entzündung ⚕ *f* tonsillitis.

Manege [ma'nɛːʒə] *f* (-/-n) (circus-) ring, manège.

Mangel[1] ['maŋəl] *m* **1.** (-s/no *pl.*) want, lack, deficiency; shortage; penury; *aus* ~ *an* for want of; ~ *leiden an* (*dat.*) be in want of; **2.** (-s/⸚) defect, shortcoming.

Mangel[2] [~] *f* (-/-n) mangle; calender.

'**mangelhaft** adj. defective; deficient; unsatisfactory; '**2igkeit** f (-/no pl.) defectiveness; deficiency.

'**mangeln**[1] v/i. (ge-, h): es mangelt an Brot there is a lack or shortage of bread, bread is lacking or wanting; es mangelt ihm an (dat.) he is in need of or short of or wanting in, he wants or lacks.

'**mangeln**[2] v/t. (ge-, h) mangle (clothes, etc.); ⊕ calender (cloth, paper).

'**mangels** prp. (gen.) for lack or want of; esp. ₰₣ in default of.

'**Mangelware** ✝ f scarce commodity; goods pl. in short supply.

Manie [ma'ni:] f (-/-n) mania.

Manier [ma'ni:r] f (-/-en) manner; 2lich adj. well-behaved; polite, mannerly. [manifesto.)

Manifest [mani'fɛst] n (-es/-e)

Mann [man] m (-[e]s/=er) man; husband.

'**mannbar** adj. marriageable; '**2-keit** f (-/no pl.) puberty, manhood.

Männchen ['mɛnçən] n (-s/-) little man; zo. male; birds: cock.

'**Mannes|alter** n virile age, manhood; ～**kraft** f virility.

mannig|fach adj. ['maniç-], '～**faltig** adj manifold, various, diverse; '**2faltigkeit** f (-/no pl.) manifoldness, variety, diversity.

männlich adj. ['mɛnliç] male; gr. masculine; fig. manly; '**2keit** f (-/no pl.) manhood, virility.

'**Mannschaft** f (-/-en) (body of) men; ⚓ crew; sports: team, side; '～**sführer** m sports: captain; '～**geist** m (-es/no pl.) sports: team spirit.

Manöv|er [ma'nø:vər] n (-s/-) manœuvre, Am. maneuver; 2rieren [～'vri:rən] v/i. (no -ge-, h) manœuvre, Am. maneuver.

Mansarde [man'zardə] f (-/-n) attic, garret; ～**nfenster** n dormer-window.

mansche|n F ['manʃən] (ge-, h) 1. v/t. mix, work; 2. v/i. dabble (in dat. in); '2**rei** F f (-/-en) mixing, F mess; dabbling.

Manschette [man'ʃɛtə] f (-/-n) cuff; ～**knopf** m cuff-link.

Mantel ['mantəl] m (-s/=) coat; overcoat, greatcoat; cloak, mantle (both a. fig.); ⊕ case, jacket; (outer) cover (of tyre).

Manuskript [manu'skript] n (-[e]s/-e) manuscript; typ. copy.

Mappe ['mapə] f (-/-n) portfolio, brief-case; folder; s. a. Schreibmappe, Schulmappe.

Märchen ['mɛːrçən] n (-s/-) fairy-tale; fig. (cock-and-bull) story, fib; '～**buch** n book of fairy-tales; '2**haft** adj. fabulous (a. fig.).

Marder zo. ['mardər] m (-s/-) marten.

Marine [ma'ri:nə] f (-/-n) marine; ⚔ navy, naval forces pl.; ～**minister** m minister of naval affairs; First Lord of the Admiralty, Am. Secretary of the Navy; ～**ministerium** n ministry of naval affairs; the Admiralty, Am. Department of the Navy.

marinieren [mari'ni:rən] v/t. (no -ge-, h) pickle, marinade.

Marionette [mario'nɛtə] f (-/-n) puppet, marionette; ～**ntheater** n puppet-show.

Mark [mark] 1. f (-/-) coin: mark; 2. n (-[e]s/no pl.) anat. marrow; ♀ pith; fig core.

markant adj [mar'kant] characteristic, striking; (well-)marked.

Marke ['markə] f (-/-n) mark, sign, token, ⚙, etc.: stamp; ✝ brand, trade-mark; coupon; '～**nartikel** ✝ m branded or proprietary article.

mar'kier|en (no -ge-, h) 1. v/t. mark (a. sports); brand (cattle, goods, etc.); 2. F fig. v/t. put it on; 2**ung** f (-/-en) mark(ing).

'**markig** adj marrowy; fig. pithy.

Markise [mar'ki:zə] f (-/-n) blind, (window-)awning.

'**Markstein** m boundary-stone, landmark ͺ fig.)

Markt [markt] m (-[e]s/=e) ✝ market; s. Marktplatz; fair; auf den ～ bringen ✝ put on the market; '～**flecken** m small market-town; '～**platz** m. market-place; '～**schreier** m (-s - quack; puffer.

Marmelade [marmə'la:də] f (-/-n) jam; marmalade (made of oranges).

Marmor [marmɔr] m (-s/-e) marble; 2**ieren** [ɔ'ri:rən] v/t. (no -ge-, h) marble, vein, grain; 2n adj. [ˈɔrn] (of) marble. [whim, caprice.)

Marotte [ma'rɔtə] f (-/-n) fancy,)

Marsch [marʃ] 1. m (-es/=e) march (a. ♪); 2. f (-/-en) marsh, fen.

Marschall ['marʃal] m (-s/=e) marshal.

'**Marsch|befehl** ⚔ m marching orders pl., 2**ieren** [ˌ'ʃi:rən] v/i. (no -ge-, sein) march; '～**land** n marshy land.

Marter ['martər] f (-/-n) torment, torture, 2**n** v/t. (ge-, h) torment, torture, ～**pfahl** m stake.

Märtyrer ['mɛrtyrər] m (-s/-) martyr; '～**tod** m martyr's death; '～**tum** n (-s/no pl.) martyrdom.

Marxis|mus pol. [mar'ksismus] m (-/no pl.) Marxism; 2**t** pol. m (-en/-en) Marxian, Marxist; 2**tisch** pol. adj. Marxian, Marxist.

März [mɛrts] m (-[e]s/-e) March.

Marzipan [martsi'pa:n] n, ⚙ m (-s/-e) marzipan, marchpane.

Masche [maʃə] f (-/-n) mesh; knitting: stitch; F fig. trick, line; 2**nfest** adj. ladder-proof, Am. runproof.

Maschine [ma'ʃiːnə] f (-/-n) machine; engine.

maschinell adj. [maʃi'nɛl] mechanical; ~e Bearbeitung machining.

Ma'schinen|bau ⊕ m (-[e]s/no pl.) mechanical engineering; ~gewehr ✗ n machine-gun; 2mäßig adj. mechanical; automatic; ~pistole ✗ f sub-machine-gun; ~schaden m engine trouble; ~schlosser m (engine) fitter; ~schreiberin f (-/-nen) typist; ~schrift f typescript.

Maschin|erie [maʃinə'riː] f (-/-n) machinery; ~ist [~'nist] m (-en/-en) machinist.

Masern ✗ ['maːzərn] pl. measles pl.

Mask|e ['maskə] f (-/-n) mask (a. fig.); ~enball m fancy-dress or masked ball; ~erade [~'raːdə] f (-/-n) masquerade; 2ieren [~'kiːrən] v/t. (no -ge-, h) mask; sich ~ put on a mask; dress o.s. up (als as).

Maß [maːs] 1. n (-es/-e) measure; proportion; fig. moderation; ~e pl. und Gewichte pl. weights and measures pl.; ~e pl. room, etc.: measurements pl.; 2. f (-/-[e]) appr. quart (of beer); 3. 2 pret. of messen.

Massage [ma'saːʒə] f (-/-n) massage.

'Maßanzug m tailor-made or bespoke suit, Am. a. custom(-made) suit.

Masse ['masə] f (-/-n) mass; bulk; substance; multitude; crowd; t͡t͡ assets pl., estate; die breite ~ the rank and file; F e-e ~ a lot of, F lots pl. or heaps pl. of.

'Maßeinheit f measuring unit.

'Massen|flucht f stampede; '~grab n common grave; ~güter ✝ ['~gyːtər] n/pl. bulk goods pl.; '2haft adj. abundant; '~produktion ✝ f mass production; '~versammlung f mass meeting, Am. a. rally; '2weise adv. in masses, in large numbers.

Masseu|r [ma'søːr] m (-s/-e) masseur; ~se [~zə] f (-/-n) masseuse.

'maß|gebend adj. standard; authoritative, decisive; board: competent; circles: influential, leading; '~halten v/i. (irr. halten, sep., -ge-, h) keep within limits, be moderate.

mas'sieren v/t. (no -ge-, h) massage, knead.

'massig adj. massy, bulky; solid.

mäßig adj. ['mɛːsiç] moderate; food, etc.: frugal; ✝ prices: moderate, reasonable; result, etc.: poor; ~en ['~gən] v/t. (ge-, h) moderate; sich ~ moderate or restrain o.s.; 2ung f (-/-en) moderation; restraint.

massiv [ma'siːf] 1. adj. massive, solid; 2. 2 geol. n (-s/-e) massif.

'Maß|krug m beer-mug, Am. a. stein; '2los adj. immoderate; boundless; exorbitant, excessive;

extravagant; ~nahme ['~naːmə] f (-/-n) measure, step, action; 2regeln v/t. (ge-, h) reprimand; inflict disciplinary punishment on; '~schneider m bespoke or Am. custom tailor; '~stab m measure, rule(r); maps, etc.: scale; fig. yardstick, standard; 2voll adj. moderate.

Mast¹ ⚓ [mast] m (-es/-e[n]) mast.

Mast² ✗ [~] f (-/-en) fattening; mast, food; '~darm anat. m rectum.

mästen ['mɛstən] v/t. (ge-, h) fatten, feed; stuff (geese, etc.).

'Mastkorb ⚓ m mast-head, crows-nest.

Material [mater'jaːl] n (-s/-ien) material; substance; stock, stores pl.; fig.: material, information; evidence; ~ismus phls. [~a'lismus] m (-/no pl.) materialism; ~ist [~a'list] m (-en/-en) materialist; 2istisch adj. [~a'listiʃ] materialistic.

Materie [ma'teːrjə] f (-/-n) matter (a. fig.), stuff; fig. subject; 2ll adj. [~er'jɛl] material.

Mathemati|k [matema'tiːk] f (-/no pl.) mathematics sg.; ~ker [~'maːtikər] m (-s/-) mathematician; 2sch adj. [~'maːtiʃ] mathematical.

Matinee thea. [mati'neː] f (-/-n) morning performance.

Matratze [ma'tratsə] f (-/-n) mattress.

Matrone [ma'troːnə] f (-/-n) matron; 2nhaft adj. matronly.

Matrose ⚓ [ma'troːzə] m (-n/-n) sailor, seaman.

Matsch [matʃ] m (-es/no pl.), ~e F ['~ə] f (-/no pl.) pulp, squash; mud, slush; '2ig adj. pulpy, squashy; muddy, slushy.

matt adj. [mat] faint, feeble; voice, etc.: faint; eye, colour, etc.: dim; colour, light, ✝ stock exchange, style, etc.: dull; metal: tarnished; gold, etc.: dead, dull; chess: mated; ⚡ bulb: non-glare; ~ geschliffen glass: ground, frosted, matted; ~ setzen at chess: (check)mate s.o.

Matte ['matə] f (-/-n) mat.

'Mattigkeit f (-/no pl.) exhaustion, feebleness; faintness.

'Mattscheibe f phot. focus(s)ing screen; television: screen.

Mauer ['mauər] f (-/-n) wall; ~blümchen fig. ['~blyːmçən] n (-s/-) wall-flower; '2n (ge-, h) 1. v/i. make a wall, lay bricks; 2. v/t. build (in stone or brick); '~stein m brick; '~werk n masonry, brickwork.

Maul [maul] n (-[e]s/=er) mouth; sl.: halt's ~! shut up!; '2n F v/i. (ge-, h) sulk, pout; '~esel zo. m mule, hinny; '~held F m braggart; '~korb m muzzle; '~schelle F f box on the ear; '~tier zo. n mule;

'~wurf zo. m mole; '~wurfshügel m molehill.

Maurer ['maurər] m (-s/-) bricklayer, mason; '~meister m master mason; '~polier m bricklayers' foreman.

Maus zo. [maus] f (-/¨e) mouse; ~efalle ['~zə-] f mousetrap; 2en ['~zən] (ge-, h) 1. v/i. catch mice; 2. F v/t. pinch, pilfer, F swipe.

Mauser ['mauzər] f (-/no pl.) mo(u)lt(ing); in der ~ sein be mo(u)lting; '2n v/refl. (ge-, h) mo(u)lt.

Maximum ['maksimum] n (-s/Maxima) maximum.

Mayonnaise [majo'nɛːzə] f (-/-n) mayonnaise.

Mechani|k [me'çaːnik] f 1. (-/no pl.) mechanics mst sg.; 2. ⊕ (-/-en) mechanism; ~ker m (-s/-) mechanic; 2sch adj. mechanical; 2sieren [~ani'ziːrən] v/t. (no -ge-, h) mechanize; '~smus ⊕ [~a'nismus] m (-/Mechanismen) mechanism; clock, watch, etc.: works pl.

meckern ['mɛkərn] v/i. (ge-, h) bleat; fig. grumble (über acc. over, at, about), carp (at); nag (at); sl. grouse, Am. sl. gripe.

Medaill|e [me'daljə] f (-/-n) medal; ~on [~'jõː] n (-s/-s) medallion, locket.

Medikament [medika'mɛnt] n (-[e]s/-e) medicament, medicine.

Medizin [medi'tsiːn] f 1. (-/no pl.) (science of) medicine; 2. (-/-en) medicine, F physic; ~er m (-s/-) medical man; medical student; 2isch adj. medical; medicinal.

Meer [meːr] n (-[e]s/-e) sea (a. fig.), ocean; '~busen m gulf, bay; '~enge f strait(s pl.); '~esspiegel m sea level; '~rettich m horse-radish; '~schweinchen zo. n guinea-pig.

Mehl [meːl] n (-[e]s/-e) flour; meal; '~brei m pap; '2ig adj. floury, mealy, farinaceous; '~speise f sweet dish, pudding; '~suppe f gruel.

mehr [meːr] 1. adj. more; er hat ~ Geld als ich he has (got) more money than I; 2. adv. more; nicht ~ no more, no longer, not any longer; ich habe nichts ~ I have nothing left; '2arbeit f additional work; overtime; '2ausgaben f/pl. additional expenditure; '2betrag m surplus; '~deutig adj. ambiguous; '2einnahme(n [n pl.) f additional receipts pl.; '~en v/t. (ge-, h) augment, increase; sich ~ multiply, grow; '~ere adj. and indef. pron. several, some; '~fach 1. adj. manifold, repeated; 2. adv. repeatedly, several times; '2gebot n higher bid; '2heit f (-/-en) majority, plurality; '2kosten pl. additional expense; '~malig adj. repeated, reiterated;

~mals adv. ['~maːls] several times, repeatedly; '~sprachig adj. polyglot; '~stimmig ♪ adj.: ~er Gesang part-song; '2verbrauch m excess consumption; '2wertsteuer † f (-/no pl.) value-added tax; '2-zahl f majority; gr. plural (form); die ~ (gen.) most of.

meiden ['maidən] v/t. (irr., ge-, h) avoid, shun, keep away from.

Meile ['mailə] f (-/-n) mile; '~n-stein m milestone.

mein poss. pron. [main] my; der (die, das) ~e my; die 2en pl. my family, F my people or folks pl.; ich habe das ~e getan I have done all I can; '~e Damen und Herren! Ladies and Gentlemen!

Meineid ṟi ['main?-] m perjury; '2ig adj. perjured.

meinen ['mainən] v/t. (ge-, h) think, believe, be of (the) opinion, Am. a. reckon, guess; say; mean; wie ~ Sie das? what do you mean by that?; ~ Sie das ernst? do you (really) mean it?; es gut ~ mean well.

meinetwegen adv. ['mainət'-] for my sake, on my behalf; because of me, on my account; for all I care; I don't mind or care.

'Meinung f (-/-en) opinion (über acc., von about, of); die öffentliche ~ (the) public opinion; meiner ~ nach in my opinion, to my mind; j-m (gehörig) die ~ sagen give s.o. a piece of one's mind; '~saustausch ['mainuns?-] m exchange of views (über acc. on); '~sverschiedenheit f difference of opinion (über acc. on); disagreement.

Meise orn. ['maizə] f (-/-n) titmouse.

Meißel ['maisəl] m (-s/-) chisel; '2n v/t. and v/i. (ge-, h) chisel; carve.

meist [maist] 1. adj. most; die ~en Leute most people; die ~e Zeit most of one's time; 2. adv.: s. meistens; am ~en most (of all); 2bietende ['~biːtəndə] m (-n/-n) highest bidder; ~ens adv. ['~əns], '~en'teils adv. mostly, in most cases; usually.

Meister ['maistər] m (-s/-) master, sl. boss, sports: champion; '2haft 1. adj. masterly; 2. adv. in a masterly manner or way; '2n v/t. (ge-, h) master; '~schaft f 1. (-/no pl.) mastery; 2. (-/-en) sports: championship, title; '~stück n, '~werk n masterpiece.

'Meistgebot n highest bid, best offer.

Melancholi|e [melaŋko'liː] f (-/-n) melancholy; 2sch adj. [~'koːliʃ] melancholy; ~ sein F have the blues.

Melde|amt ['mɛldə-] n registration office, ~liste f sports: list of entries; '2n v/t. (ge-, h) announce; j-m et. ~ inform s.o. of s.th.; officially: notify s.th. to s.o.; j-n ~

enter s.o.'s name (*für, zu* for); *sich* ~ report o.s. (*bei* to); *school, etc.*: put up one's hand; answer the telephone; enter (one's name) (*für, zu* for *examination, etc.*); *sich* ~ *zu* apply for; *sich auf ein Inserat* ~ answer an advertisement.

'**Meldung** *f* (-/-en) information, advice; announcement; report; registration; application; *sports*: entry.

melke|n ['mɛlkən] *v/t.* (*irr.*, ge-, *h*) milk; '**2r** *m* (-s/-) milker.

Melod|ie [melo'di:] *f* (-/-n) melody; tune, air; **2isch** *adj.* [~'lo:diʃ] melodious, tuneful.

Melone [me'lo:nə] *f* (-/-n) ♀ melon; F bowler(-hat), *Am.* derby.

Membran [mɛm'bra:n] *f* (-/-en), ~**e** *f* (-/-n) membrane; *teleph. a.* diaphragm.

Memme F ['mɛmə] *f* (-/-n) coward; poltroon.

Memoiren [memo'a:rən] *pl.* memoirs *pl.*

Menagerie [menaʒə'ri:] *f* (-/-n) menagerie.

Menge ['mɛŋə] *f* (-/-n) quantity; amount; multitude; crowd; *in großer* ~ in abundance; *persons, animals*: in crowds; e-e ~ *Geld* plenty of money, F lots *pl.* of money; e-e ~ *Bücher* a great many books; '**2n** *v/t.* (ge-, *h*) mix, blend; *sich* ~ mix (*unter acc.* with), mingle (with); *sich* ~ *in* (*acc.*) meddle *or* interfere with.

Mensch [mɛnʃ] *m* (-en/-en) human being; man; person, individual; *die* ~**en** *pl.* people *pl.*, the world, mankind; *kein* ~ nobody.

'**Menschen|affe** *zo. m* anthropoid ape; ~**alter** *n* generation, age; '~**feind** *m* misanthropist; '**2feindlich** *adj.* misanthropic; '~**fresser** *m* (-s/-) cannibal, man-eater; '~**freund** *m* philanthropist; '**2-freundlich** *adj.* philanthropic; '~**gedenken** *n* (-s/*no pl.*): *seit* ~ from time immemorial, within the memory of man; ~**geschlecht** *n* human race, mankind; ~**haß** *m* misanthropy; '~**kenner** *m* judge of men *or* human nature; ~**kenntnis** *f* knowledge of human nature; '~**leben** *n* human life; '**2leer** *adj.* deserted; '~**liebe** *f* philanthropy; '~**menge** *f* crowd (of people), throng; '**2möglich** *adj.* humanly possible; '~**raub** *m* kidnap(p)ing; '~**rechte** *n/pl.* human rights *pl.*; '**2scheu** *adj.* unsociable, shy; '~**seele** *f*: *keine* ~ not a living soul; '~**verstand** *m* human understanding; *gesunder* ~ common sense, F horse sense; '~**würde** *f* dignity of man.

'**Menschheit** *f* (-/*no pl.*) human race, mankind.

'**menschlich** *adj.* human; *fig.* humane; '**2keit** *f* (-/*no pl.*) human nature; humanity, humaneness.

Mentalität [mɛntali'tɛ:t] *f* (-/-en) mentality.

merk|bar *adj.* ['mɛrkba:r] *s.* **merklich**; '**2blatt** *n* leaflet, instructional pamphlet; '**2buch** *n* notebook; '~**en** (ge-, *h*) 1. *v/i.*: ~ *auf* (*acc.*) pay attention to, listen to; 2. *v/t.* notice, perceive; find out, discover; *sich et.* ~ remember s.th.; bear s.th. in mind; '~**lich** *adj.* noticeable, perceptible; '**2mal** *n* (-[e]s/-e) mark, sign; characteristic, feature.

'**merkwürdig** *adj.* noteworthy, remarkable; strange, odd, curious; ~**erweise** *adv.* ['~gər'] strange to say, strangely enough; '**2keit** *f* (-/-en) remarkableness; curiosity; peculiarity.

meßbar *adj.* ['mɛsba:r] measurable.

Messe ['mɛsə] *f* (-/-n) ✝ fair; *eccl.* mass; ⚓, ♣ mess.

messen ['mɛsən] *v/t.* (*irr.*, ge-, *h*) measure; ⚓ sound; *sich mit j-m* ~ compete with s.o.; *sich nicht mit j-m* ~ *können* be no match for s.o.; *gemessen an* (*dat.*) measured against, compared with.

Messer ['mɛsər] *n* (-s/-) knife; ✄ scalpel; *bis aufs* ~ to the knife; *auf des* ~*s Schneide* on a razor-edge *or* razor's edge; ~**griff** *m* knifehandle; ~**held** *m* stabber; '~**klinge** *f* knife-blade; ~**schmied** *m* cutler; '~**schneide** *f* knife-edge; ~**stecher** *m* (-s/-) stabber; ~**stecherei** [~ʃtɛçə'raɪ] *f* (-/-en) knifing, knife-battle; ~**stich** *m* stab with a knife.

Messing ['mɛsɪŋ] *n* (-s/*no pl.*) brass; '~**blech** *n* sheet-brass.

'**Meß|instrument** *n* measuring instrument; '~**latte** *f* surveyor's rod; '~**tisch** *m* surveyor's *or* plane table.

Metall [me'tal] *n* (-s/-e) metal; ~**arbeiter** *m* metal worker; **2en** *adj.* (of) metal, metallic; ~**geld** *n* coin(s *pl.*), specie; ~**glanz** *m* metallic lust|re, *Am.* -er; **2haltig** *adj.* metalliferous; ~**industrie** *f* metallurgical industry; ~**waren** *f/pl.* hardware.

Meteor *ast.* [mete'o:r] *m* (-s/-e) meteor; ~**ologe** [~oro'lo:gə] *m* (-n/-n) meteorologist; ~**ologie** [~orolo'gi:] *f* (-/*no pl.*) meteorology.

Meter ['me:tər] *n, m* (-s/-) met|re, *Am.* -er; '~**maß** *n* tape-measure.

Method|e [me'to:də] *f* (-/-n) method; ⊕ *a.* technique; **2isch** *adj.* methodical. [metropolis.\]

Metropole [metro'po:lə] *f* (-/-n)

Metzel|ei [mɛtsə'laɪ] *f* (-/-en) slaughter, massacre; '**2n** *v/t.* (ge-, *h*) butcher, slaughter, massacre.

Metzger ['mɛtsgər] *m* (-s/-) butcher; ~**ei** [~'raɪ] *f* (-/-en) butcher's (shop).

Meuchel|mord ['mɔʏçəl-] *m* assassination; '~**mörder** *m* assassin.

Meute ['mɔʏtə] f (-/-n) pack of hounds; fig. gang; **~rei** [~'raɪ] f (-/-en) mutiny; '**~rer** m (-s/-) mutineer; '**Qrisch** adj. mutinous; '**Qrn** v/i. (ge-, h) mutiny (gegen against).

mich pers. pron. [mɪç] me; ~ (selbst) myself.

mied [mi:t] pret. of meiden.

Mieder ['mi:dər] n (-s/-) bodice; corset; '**~waren** f/pl. corsetry.

Miene ['mi:nə] f (-/-n) countenance, air; feature; gute ~ zum bösen Spiel machen grin and bear it; ~ machen zu inf. offer or threaten to inf.

mies F adj. [mi:s] miserable, poor; out of sorts, seedy.

Miet|e ['mi:tə] f (-/-n) rent; hire; zur ~ wohnen live in lodgings, be a tenant; '**Qen** v/t. (ge-, h) rent (land, building, etc.); hire (horse, etc.); (take on) lease (land, etc.); ⚓, ✈ charter; '**~er** m (-s/-) tenant; lodger, Am. a. roomer; ⚖ lessee; '**Qfrei** adj. rent-free; '**~shaus** n block of flats, Am. apartment house; '**~vertrag** m tenancy agreement; lease; '**~wohnung** f lodgings pl., flat, Am. apartment.

Migräne ✿ [mi'grɛ:nə] f (-/-n) migraine, megrim; sick headache.

Mikrophon [mikro'fo:n] n (-s/-e) microphone, F mike.

Mikroskop [mikro'sko:p] n (-s/-e) microscope, **Qisch** adj. microscopic(al).

Milbe zo. ['milbə] f (-/-n) mite.

Milch [milç] f (-/no pl.) milk; milt, soft roe (of fish); '**~bar** f milk-bar; '**~bart** fig. m stripling; '**~brötchen** n (French) roll; '**~gesicht** n baby face; '**~glas** n frosted glass; '**Qig** adj. milky; '**~kanne** f milk-can; '**~kuh** f milk cow (a. fig.); '**~mädchen** F n milkmaid, dairymaid; '**~mann** F m milkman, dairyman; '**~pulver** n milk-powder; '**~reis** m rice-milk; '**~straße** ast. f Milky Way, Galaxy; '**~wirtschaft** f dairy-farm(ing); '**~zahn** m milktooth.

mild [milt] 1. adj. weather, punishment, etc.: mild; air, weather, light, etc.: soft; wine, etc.: mellow, smooth; reprimand, etc.: gentle; 2. adv.: et. ~ beurteilen take a lenient view of s. th.

milde ['mildə] 1. adj. s. mild 1; 2. adv.: ~ gesagt to put it mildly; 3. ⚖ f (-/no pl.) mildness; softness; smoothness; gentleness.

milder|n ['mildərn] v/t. (ge-, h) soften, mitigate; soothe, alleviate (pain, etc.); ~de Umstände ⚖ extenuating circumstances; '**Qung** f (-/-en) softening, mitigation; alleviation.

'**mild|herzig** adj. charitable; '**Qherzigkeit** f (-/no pl.) charitableness;

'**~tätig** adj. charitable; '**Qtätigkeit** f charity.

Milieu [mil'jø:] n (-s/-s) surroundings pl., environment; class, circles pl.; local colo(u)r.

Militär [mili'tɛ:r] 1. n (-s/no pl.) military, armed forces pl.; army; 2. m (-s/-s) military man, soldier; **~attaché** [~ataʃe:] m (-s/-s) military attaché; **~dienst** m military service; **Qisch** adj. military; **~musik** f military music; **~regierung** f military government; **~zeit** f (-/no pl.) term of military service.

Miliz ⚔ [mi'li:ts] f (-/-en) militia; **~soldat** ⚔ m militiaman.

Milliarde [mil'jardə] f (-/-n) thousand millions, milliard, Am. billion.

Millimeter [mili'-] n, m millimet|re, Am. -er.

Million [mil'jo:n] f (-/-en) million; **~är** [~o'nɛ:r] m (-s/-e) millionaire.

Milz anat. [milts] f (-/-en) spleen, milt.

minder ['mindər] 1. adv. less; nicht ~ no less, likewise; 2. adj. less(er); smaller; minor; inferior; **~begabt** adj. less gifted; **~bemittelt** adj. ['~bəmɪtəlt] of moderate means; '**Qbetrag** m deficit, shortage; '**Qeinnahme** f shortfall in receipts; '**Qgewicht** n short weight; '**Qheit** f (-/-en) minority; **~jährig** adj. ['~jɛ:rɪç] under age, minor; '**Qjährigkeit** f (-/no pl.) minority; '**~n** v/t. and v/refl. (ge-, h) diminish, lessen, decrease; '**Qung** f (-/-en) decrease, diminution; '**~wertig** adj. inferior, of inferior quality; '**Qwertigkeit** f (-/no pl.) inferiority; † inferior quality; '**Qwertigkeitskomplex** m inferiority complex.

mindest adj. ['mindəst] least; slightest; minimum; nicht die ~e Aussicht not the slightest chance; nicht im ~en not in the least, by no means; zum ~en at least; '**Qalter** n minimum age; '**Qanforderungen** f/pl. minimum requirements pl.; '**Qbetrag** m lowest amount; '**Qeinkommen** n minimum income; '**~ens** adv. at least; '**Qgebot** n lowest bid; '**Qlohn** m minimum wage; '**Qmaß** n minimum; auf ein ~ herabsetzen minimize; '**Qpreis** m minimum price.

Mine ['mi:nə] f (-/-n) ⚔, ⚒, ⚓ mine; pencil: lead; ball-point-pen: refill.

Mineral [minə'ra:l] n (-s/-e, -ien) mineral; **Qisch** adj. mineral; **~ogie** [~alo'gi:] f (-/no pl.) mineralogy; **~wasser** n (-s/~) mineral water.

Miniatur [minia'tu:r] f (-/-en) miniature; **~gemälde** n miniature.

Minirock ['mini-] m miniskirt.

Minister [mi'nistər] m (-s/-) minister; Secretary (of State), Am. Secretary; ~ium [~'te:rjum] n (-s/Ministerien) ministry; Office, Am. Department; ~präsident m prime minister, premier; in Germany, etc.: minister president; ~rat m (-[e]s/~e) cabinet council.

minus adv. ['mi:nus] minus, less, deducting.

Minute [mi'nu:tə] f (-/-n) minute; ~nzeiger m minute-hand.

mir pers. pron. [mi:r] (to) me.

Misch|ehe ['miʃ⁹-] f mixed marriage; intermarriage; ²en v/t. (ge-, h) mix, mingle; blend (coffee, tobacco, etc.); alloy (metal); shuffle (cards); sich ~ in (acc.) interfere in; join in (conversation); sich ~ unter (acc.) mix or mingle with (the crowd); ~ling ['~liŋ] m (-s/-e) half-breed, half-caste; ⚥, zo. hybrid; ~masch F ['~maʃ] m (-es/-e) hotchpotch, jumble; ~ung f (-/-en) mixture; blend; alloy.

miß|achten [mis'-] v/t. (no -ge-, h) disregard, ignore, neglect; slight, despise; ²achtung f disregard, neglect; ~behagen 1. v/i. (no -ge-, h) displease; 2. ² n discomfort, uneasiness; ²bildung f malformation, deformity; ~billigen v/t. (no -ge-, h) disapprove (of); ²billigung f disapproval; ²brauch m abuse; misuse; ~'brauchen v/t. (no -ge-, h) abuse; misuse; ~bräuchlich adj. ['~brɔyçliç] abusive; improper; ~deuten v/t. (no -ge-, h) misinterpret; ²deutung f misinterpretation.

missen ['misən] v/t. (ge-, h) miss; do without, dispense with.

'Miß|erfolg m failure; fiasco; '~ernte f bad harvest, crop failure.

Misse|tat ['misə-] f misdeed; crime; '~täter m evil-doer, offender; criminal.

miß|'fallen v/i. (irr. fallen, no -ge-, h): j-m ~ displease s.o.; '²fallen n (-s/no pl.) displeasure, dislike; '~fällig 1. adj. displeasing; shocking; disparaging; 2. adv.: sich ~ äußern über (acc.) speak ill of; '²geburt f monster, freak (of nature), deformity; ²geschick n bad luck, misfortune; mishap; ~gestimmt fig. adj. ['~gəʃtimt] s. mißmutig; ~'glücken v/i. (no -ge-, sein) fail; ~'gönnen v/t. (no -ge-, h): j-m et. ~ envy or grudge s.o. s.th.; ²griff m mistake, blunder; ²gunst f envy, jealousy; ~günstig adj. envious, jealous; ~ handeln v/t. (no -ge-, h) ill-treat; maul, sl. manhandle; ²handlung f ill-treatment; mauling, sl. manhandling; ⚔ assault and battery; ²heirat f misalliance; '~hellig adj. dissonant, dissentient; ²helligkeit f (-/-en) dissonance, discord.

Mission [mis'jo:n] f (-/-en) mission

(a. pol. and fig.); ~ar [~o'na:r] m (-s/-e) missionary.

'Miß|klang m dissonance, discord (both a. fig.); '~kredit fig. m (-[e]s/no pl.) discredit; in ~ bringen bring discredit upon s.o.

miß|'lang pret. of mißlingen; '~lich adj. awkward; unpleasant; ~liebig adj. ['~li:biç] unpopular; ~lingen [~'liŋən] v/i. (irr., no -ge-, sein) fail; ²lingen n (-s/no pl.) failure; '²mut m ill humo(u)r; discontent; '~mutig adj. ill-humo(u)red; discontented; ~'raten 1. v/i. (irr. raten, no -ge-, sein) fail; turn out badly; 2. adj. wayward; ill-bred; ²stand m nuisance; grievance; ²stimmung f ill humo(u)r; ²ton m (-[e]s/~e) dissonance, discord (both a. fig.); ~'trauen v/i. (no -ge-, h): j-m ~ distrust or mistrust s.o.; '²trauen n (-s/no pl.) distrust, mistrust; '~trauisch adj. distrustful; suspicious; ²vergnügen n (-s/no pl.) displeasure; '~vergnügt adj. discontented; '²verhältnis n disproportion; incongruity; '²verständnis n misunderstanding; dissension; '~verstehen v/t. (irr. stehen, no -ge-, h) misunderstand, mistake (intention, etc.); '²wirtschaft f maladministration, mismanagement.

Mist [mist] m (-es/-e) dung, manure; dirt; F fig. trash, rubbish; '~beet n hotbed.

Mistel ⚘ ['mistəl] f (-/-n) mistletoe.

'Mist|gabel f dung-fork; '~haufen m dung-hill.

mit [mit] 1. prp. (dat.) with; ~ 20 Jahren at the age of twenty; ~ e-m Schlage at a blow; ~ Gewalt by force; ~ der Bahn by train; 2. adv. also, too; ~ dabeisein be there too, be (one) of the party.

Mit|arbeiter ['mit⁹-] m co-worker; writing, art, etc.: collaborator; colleague; newspaper, etc.: contributor (an dat. to); ²benutzen v/t. (sep., no -ge-, h) use jointly or in common; '~besitzer m joint owner; '~bestimmungsrecht n right of co-determination; ~bewerber m competitor; ~bewohner m co-inhabitant, fellow-lodger; ²bringen v/t. (irr. bringen, sep., -ge-, h) bring along (with one); ~bringsel ['~briŋzəl] n (-s/-) little present; ~bürger m fellow-citizen; ²einander adv. [mit⁹ai'nandər] together, jointly; with each other, with one another; ~empfinden ['mit⁹-] n (-s/no pl.) sympathy; ~erbe ['mit⁹-] m co-heir; ~esser m ['mit⁹-] m (-s/-) blackhead; ²fahren v/i. (irr. fahren, sep., -ge-, sein): mit j-m ~ drive or go with s.o.; j-n ~ lassen give s.o. a lift; '²fühlen *v/i.* (*sep.*, -ge-, *h*) sympathize (*mit with*); '2geben *v/t.* (*irr. geben*, *sep.*, -ge-, *h*) give along (*dat. with*); '~gefühl *n* sympathy; '2gehen *v/i.* (*irr. gehen*, *sep.*, -ge-, *sein*): mit j-m ~ go with s.o.; '~gift *f* (-/-en) dowry, marriage portion.

'Mitglied *n* member; '~erversammlung *f* general meeting; '~erzahl *f* membership; '~sbeitrag *m* subscription; '~schaft *f* (-/no *pl.*) membership.

mit|'hin *adv.* consequently, therefore; 2inhaber ['mit?-] *m* copartner; '2kämpfer *m* fellowcombatant; '~kommen *v/i.* (*irr. kommen*, *sep.*, -ge-, *sein*) come along (*mit with*); *fig.* be able to follow; '2läufer *pol. m* nominal member; *contp.* trimmer.

'Mitleid *n* (-[e]s/no *pl.*) compassion, pity; sympathy; *aus ~* out of pity; ~ *haben* mit have or take pity on; '~enschaft *f* (-/no *pl.*): *in ~ ziehen* affect; implicate, involve; damage; '2ig *adj.* compassionate, pitiful; 2(s)los *adj.* ['~t-] pitiless, merciless; 2(s)voll *adj.* ['~t-] pitiful, compassionate.

'mit|machen (*sep.*, -ge-, *h*) 1. *v/i.* make one of the party; 2. *v/t.* take part in, participate in; follow, go with (*fashion*); go through (*hardships*); '2mensch *m* fellow creature; '~nehmen *v/t.* (*irr. nehmen*, *sep.*, -ge-, *h*) take along (with one); *fig.* exhaust, wear out; j-n (*im Auto*) ~ give s.o. a lift; '~nichten *adv.* [~'niçtən] by no means, not at all; '~rechnen *v/t.* (*sep.*, -ge-, *h*) include (in the account); *nicht* ~ leave out of account; *nicht mitgerechnet* not counting; ~reden (*sep.*, -ge-, *h*) 1. *v/i.* join in the conversation; 2. *v/t.* ein Wort or Wörtchen mitzureden haben have a say (*bei in*); '~reißen *v/t.* (*irr. reißen*, *sep.*, -ge-, *h*) tear or drag along; *fig.* sweep along.

'Mitschuld *f* complicity (*an dat.* in); '2ig *adj.* accessary (*an dat.* to *crime*); '~ige *m* accessary, accomplice.

'Mitschüler *m* schoolfellow.

'mitspiel|en (*sep.*, -ge-, *h*) 1. *v/i.* play (*bei with*); *sports:* be on the team; *thea.* appear, star (*in a play*); join in a game; *matter* be involved; j-m arg or übel ~ play s.o. a nasty trick; 2. *fig. v/t.* join in (*game*); '2er *m* partner.

'Mittag *m* midday, noon; *heute* 2 *at* noon today; *zu ~ essen* lunch, dine; '~essen *n* lunch(eon), dinner; '2s *adv.* at noon.

'Mittags|pause *f* lunch hour; '~ruhe *f* midday rest; '~schlaf *m*, '~schläfchen *n* after-dinner nap, siesta; '~stunde *f* noon; '~tisch

fig. m lunch, dinner; '~zeit *f* noontide; lunch-time, dinner-time.

Mitte ['mitə] *f* (-/-n) middle; cent|re, *Am.* -er; *die goldene ~* the golden or happy mean; *aus unserer ~* from among us; ~ *Juli* in the middle of July; ~ *Dreißig* in the middle of one's thirties.

'mittell|en *v/t.* (*sep.*, -ge-, *h*): j-m et. ~ communicate s.th. to s.o.; impart s.th. to s.o.; inform s.o. of s.th.; make s.th. known to s.o.; '~sam *adj.* communicative; '2ung *f* (-/-en) communication; information; communiqué.

Mittel ['mitəl] *n* (-s/-) means *sg.*, way; remedy (*gegen* for); average; *A* mean; *phys.* medium; ~ *pl. a.* means *pl.*, funds *pl.*, money; ~ *pl. und Wege* ways and means *pl.*; '~alter *n* Middle Ages *pl.*; '2alterlich *adj.* medi(a)eval; '2bar *adj.* mediate, indirect; '~ding *n*: *ein ~ zwischen ... und ...* something between ... and ...; '~finger *m* middle finger; '~gebirge *n* highlands *pl.*; '2groß *adj.* of medium height; medium-sized; '~läufer *m sports* centre half back, *Am.* center half back; '2los *adj.* without means, destitute; '2mäßig *adj.* middling; mediocre; '~mäßigkeit *f* (-/no *pl.*) mediocrity; '~punkt *m* cent|re, *Am.* -er; *fig. a.* focus; '2s *prp.* (*gen.*) by (means of), through; '~schule *f* intermediate school, *Am.* high school; '~smann *m* (-[e]s/~er, *Mittelsleute*) mediator, go-between; '~stand *m* middle classes *pl.*; '~stürmer *m sports:* centre forward, *Am.* center forward; '~weg *fig. m* middle course; '~wort *gr. n* (-[e]s/~er) participle.

mitten *adv.* ['mitən]: ~ *in* or *an* or *auf* or *unter* (*acc.*; *dat.*) in the midst or middle of; ~ *entzwei* right in two; ~ *im Winter* in the depth of winter; ~ *in der Nacht* in the middle or dead of night; ~ *ins Herz* right into the heart; ~'drin *F adv.* right in the middle; ~'durch *F adv.* right through or across.

Mitter|nacht ['mitər-] *f* midnight; *um ~* at midnight; 2nächtig *adj.* ['~neçtiç], 2nächtlich *adj.* midnight.

Mittler ['mitlər] 1. *m* (-s/-) mediator, intercessor; 2. 2 *adj.* middle, central; average, medium; '2'weile *adv.* meanwhile, (in the) meantime.

Mittwoch ['mitvɔx] *m* (-[e]s/-e) Wednesday; '2s *adv.* on Wednesday(s), every Wednesday.

mit|'unter *adv.* now and then, sometimes; '~verantwortlich *adj.* jointly responsible; '2welt *f* (-/no *pl.*): *die ~* our, *etc.* contemporaries *pl.*

'mitwirk|en v/i. (sep., -ge-, h) co-operate (bei in), contribute (to), take part (in); '2ende m (-n/-n) thea. performer, actor, player (a. ♪); die ~n pl. the cast; '2ung f (-/no pl.) co(-)operation, contribution.
'Mitwisser m (-s/-) confidant; z̄t accessary.   [rechnen.\
'mitzählen v/t. (sep., -ge-, h) s. mit-)
Mix|becher ['miks-] m (cocktail-) shaker; '2en v/t. (ge-, h) mix; ~tur [~'tu:r] f (-/-en) mixture.
Möbel ['mø:bəl] n (-s/-) piece of furniture; ~ pl. furniture; '~händ-ler m furniture-dealer; '~spedi-teur m furniture-remover; ~stück n piece of furniture; '~tischler m cabinet-maker; '~wagen m pan-technicon, Am. furniture truck.
mobil adj. [mo'bi:l] ⚔ mobile; F active, nimble; ~ machen ⚔ mobi-lize; 2iar [~il'ja:r] n (-s/-e) furni-ture; movables pl.; ~isieren [~ili-'zi:rən] v/t. (no -ge-, h) ⚔ mobilize; † realize (property, etc.); 2ma-chung [mo'bi:lmaxuŋ] f (-/-en) mobilization.
möblieren [mø'bli:rən] v/t. (no -ge-, h) furnish; möbliertes Zimmer furnished room, F bed-sitter.
mochte ['mɔxtə] pret. of mögen.
Mode ['mo:də] f (-/-n) fashion, vogue; use, custom; die neueste ~ the latest fashion; in ~ in fashion or vogue; aus der ~ kommen grow or go out of fashion; die ~ bestimmen set the fashion; in ~ bringen bring into fashion; out of fashion; die ~ bestimmen set the fashion; ~artikel m/pl. fancy goods pl., novelties pl.; '~far-be f fashionable colo(u)r.
Modell [mo'dɛl] n (-s/-e) ⊕, fashion, paint.: model; pattern, design; ⊕ mo(u)ld; j-m ~ stehen paint. pose for s.o.; ~eisenbahn f model rail-way; 2ieren [~'li:rən] v/t. (no -ge-, h) model, mo(u)ld, fashion.
'Moden|schau f dress parade, fashion-show; '~zeitung f fashion magazine.
Moder ['mo:dər] m (-s/no pl.) must, putrefaction; '~geruch m musty smell; '2ig adj. musty, putrid.
modern¹ ['mo:dərn] v/i. (ge-, h) putrefy, rot, decay.
modern² adj. [mo'dɛrn] modern; progressive; up-to-date; fashion-able; ~isieren [~i'zi:rən] v/t. (no -ge-, h) modernize, bring up to date.
'Mode|salon m fashion house; '~schmuck m costume jewel(le)ry; '~waren f/pl. fancy goods pl.; '~zeichner m fashion-designer.
modifizieren [modifi'tsi:rən] v/t. (no -ge-, h) modify.
modisch adj. ['mo:diʃ] fashionable, stylish.   [liner.\
Modistin [mo'distin] f (-/-nen) mil-)
Mogel|ei F [mo:gə'lai] f (-/-en) cheat; '2n F v/i. (ge-, h) cheat.

mögen ['mø:gən] (irr., h) 1. v/i. (ge-) be willing; ich mag nicht I don't like to; 2. v/t. (ge-) want, wish; like, be fond of; nicht ~ dislike; not to be keen on (food, etc.); lieber ~ like better, prefer; 3. v/aux. (no -ge-) may, might; ich möchte wissen I should like to know; ich möchte lieber gehen I would rather go; das mag (wohl) sein that's (well) pos-sible; wo er auch sein mag wherever he may be; mag er sagen, was er will let him say what he likes.
möglich ['mø:kliç] 1. adj. possible; practicable, feasible; market, crim-inal, etc.: potential; alle ~en all sorts of; alles ~e all sorts of things; sein ~stes tun do one's utmost or level best; nicht ~! you don't say (so)!; so bald etc. wie ~ ~ 2. adv.:~st bald etc as soon, etc., as possible; '~er'weise adv. possibly, if pos-sible; perhaps; '2keit f (-/-en) pos-sibility, chance; nach ~ if possible.
Mohammedan|er [mohame'da:-nər] m (-s/-) Muslim, Moslem, Mohammedan; 2isch adj. Muslim, Moslem, Mohammedan.
Mohn ♣ [mo:n] m (-[e]s/-e) poppy.
Möhre ♣ ['mø:rə] f (-/-n) carrot.
Mohrrübe ♣ ['mo:r-] f carrot.
Molch zo. [mɔlç] m (-[e]s/-e) sala-mander, newt.
Mole ♣ ['mo:lə] f (-/-n) mole, jetty.
molk [mɔlk] pret. of melken.
Molkerei [mɔlkə'rai] f (-/-en) dairy; ~produkte n/pl. dairy products pl.
Moll ♪ [mɔl] n (-/-) minor (key).
mollig F adj. ['mɔliç] snug, cosy; plump, rounded.
Moment [mo'mɛnt] (-[e]s/-e) 1. m moment, instant; im ~ at the moment, 2. n motive; fact(or); ⊕ momentum; ⊕ impulse (a. fig.); 2an [~'ta:n] 1. adj. momentary; 2. adv at the moment, for the time being, ~aufnahme phot. f snapshot, instantaneous photograph.
Monarch [mo'narç] m (-en/-en) monarch; ~ie [~çi:] f (-/-n) mon-archy
Monat ['mo:nat] m (-[e]s/-e) month; '2elang 1. adj. lasting for months; 2. adv for months; '2lich 1. adj. monthly, 2. adv. monthly, a month.
Mönch [mœnç] m (-[e]s/-e) monk, friar
'Mönchs|kloster n monastery; '~-kutte f (monk's) frock; '~leben n monastic life; '~orden m monastic order, ~zelle f monk's cell.
Mond [mo:nt] m (-[e]s/-e) moon; hinter dem ~ leben be behind the times, '~fähre f lunar module; '~finsternis f lunar eclipse; '2hell adj. moonlit; '~schein m (-[e]s/no pl.) moonlight; '~sichel f crescent; '2süchtig adj. moonstruck.
Mono|log [mono'lo:k] m (-s/-e)

monologue, *Am. a.* monolog;
soliloquy; ~'pol ✝ *n* (-s/-e) monopoly; 2polisieren [~oli'zi:rən] *v/t.*
(*no* -ge-, *h*) monopolize; 2'ton *adj.*
monotonous; ~tonie [~to'ni:] *f*
(-/-n) monotony.

Monstrum ['mɔnstrum] *n* (-s/Monstren, Monstra) monster.

Montag ['mo:n-] *m* Monday; 2s
adv. on Monday(s), every Monday.

Montage ⊕ [mɔn'ta:ʒə] *f* (-/-n)
mounting, fitting; setting up; assemblage, assembly.

Montan|industrie [mɔn'ta:n-] *f*
coal and steel industries *pl.*; ~union
f European Coal and Steel Community.

Mont|eur [mɔn'tø:r] *m* (-s/-e) ⊕
fitter, assembler; *esp. mot.,* 🗲
mechanic; ~eurazug *m* overall;
2ieren [~'ti:rən] *v/t.* (*no* -ge-, *h*)
mount, fit; set up; assemble; ~ur
🗲 [~'tu:r] *f* (-/-en) regimentals *pl.*

Moor [mo:r] *n* (-[e]s/-e) bog; swamp;
'~bad *n* mud-bath; '2ig *adj.* boggy,
marshy.

Moos 🗲 [mo:s] *n* (-es/-e) moss; '2ig
adj. mossy.

Moped *mot.* ['mo:pɛt] *n* (-s/-s)
moped.

Mops *zo.* [mɔps] *m* (-əs/¤e) pug;
'2en *v/t.* (ge-, *h*) 🗲 pilfer, pinch; *sl.:*
sich ~ be bored stiff.

Moral [mo'ra:l] *f* (-/🗲-en) morality; morals *pl.*; moral; 🗲, *etc.:*
morale; 2isch *adj.* moral; 2isieren
[~ali'zi:rən] *v/i.* (*no* -ge-, *h*) moralize.

Morast [mo'rast] *m* (-es/-e, ¤e)
slough, morass; *s.* Moor; mire, mud;
2ig *adj.* marshy; muddy, miry.

Mord [mɔrt] *m* (-[e]s/-e) murder
(*an dat.* of); e-n ~ begehen commit
murder; '~anschlag *m* murderous
assault; 2en ['~dən] *v/i.* (ge-, *h*)
commit murder(s).

Mörder ['mœrdər] *m* (-s/-) murderer; '2isch *adj.* murderous;
climate, etc.: deadly; ✝ *competition:*
cut-throat.

Mord|gier *f* lust of murder, bloodthirstiness; '2gierig *adj.* bloodthirsty; '~kommission *f* homicide
squad; '~prozeß 🗲 *m* murder trial.

Mords|angst F *f* blue funk, *sl.*
mortal fear; '~glück F *n* stupendous
luck; '~kerl F *m* devil of a fellow;
'~spek'takel F *m* hullabaloo.

Morgen ['mɔrgən] 1. *m* (-s/-) morning; *measure:* acre; *am* ~ *s.* morgens;
2. 2 *adv.* tomorrow; ~ früh (abend)
tomorrow morning (evening *or*
night); ~ *in acht Tagen* tomorrow
week; '~ausgabe *f* morning edition; ~blatt *n* morning paper;
'~dämmerung *f* dawn, daybreak;
'~gebet *n* morning prayer; '~gymnastik *f* morning exercises *pl.*;
'~land *n* (-[e]s/*no pl.*) Orient, East;

'~rock *m* peignoir, dressing-gown,
wrapper (*for woman*); '~röte *f*
dawn; '2s *adv.* in the morning; '~zeitung *f* morning paper.

'morgig *adj.* of tomorrow.

Morphium *pharm.* ['mɔrfium] *n*
(-s/*no pl.*) morphia, morphine.

morsch *adj.* [mɔrʃ] rotten, decayed;
brittle.

Mörser ['mœrzər] *m* (-s/-) mortar
(*a.* 🗲).

Mörtel ['mœrtəl] *m* (-s/-) mortar.

Mosaik [moza'i:k] *n* (-s/-en) mosaic;
~fußboden *m* mosaic *or* tessellated
pavement.

Moschee [mɔ'ʃe:] *f* (-/-n) mosque.

Moschus ['mɔʃus] *m* (-/*no pl.*) musk.

Moskito *zo.* [mɔs'ki:to] *m* (-s/-s)
mosquito; ~netz *n* mosquito-net.

Moslem ['mɔslem] *m* (-s/-s) Muslim, Moslem.

Most [mɔst] *m* (-es/-e) must, grapejuice; *of apples:* cider; *of pears:*
perry.

Mostrich ['mɔstriç] *m* (-[e]s/*no pl.*)
mustard.

Motiv [mo'ti:f] *n* (-s/-e) motive,
reason; *paint., ♪* motif; 2ieren
[~i'vi:rən] *v/t.* (*no* -ge-, *h*) motivate.

Motor ['mo:tɔr] *m* (-s/-en) engine,
esp. 🗲 motor; '~boot *n* motor boat;
'~defekt *m* engine *or* 🗲 motor
trouble; '~haube *f* bonnet, *Am.*
hood; 2isieren [motori'zi:rən] *v/t.*
(*no* -ge-, *h*) motorize; ~isierung
[motori'zi:ruŋ] *f* (-/*no pl.*) motorization; '~rad *n* motor (bi)cycle;
'~radfahrer *m* motor cyclist; '~roller *m* (motor) scooter; '~sport *m*
motoring.

Motte *zo.* ['mɔtə] *f* (-/-n) moth.

'Motten|kugel *f* moth-ball; '2sicher *adj.* mothproof; '2zerfressen
adj. moth-eaten.

Motto ['mɔto] *n* (-s/-s) motto.

Möwe *orn.* ['mø:və] *f* (-/-n) sea-gull,
(sea-)mew.

Mücke *zo.* ['mykə] *f* (-/-n) midge,
gnat, mosquito; *aus e-r* ~ *e-n Elefanten machen* make a mountain
out of a molehill; '~nstich *m* gnatbite.

Mucker ['mukər] *m* (-s/-) bigot,
hypocrite.

müd|e *adj.* ['my:də] tired, weary;
e-r Sache ~ weary *or* tired
of s.th.; '2igkeit *f* (-/*no pl.*) tiredness, weariness.

Muff [muf] *m* 1. (-[e]s/-e) muff;
2. (-[e]s/*no pl.*) mo(u)ldy *or* musty
smell; '~e ⊕ *f* (-/-n) sleeve, socket;
'2eln F *v/i.* (ge-, *h*) munch; mumble; 2ig *adj.* smell, *etc.:* musty,
fusty; *air:* close; *fig.* sulky, sullen.

Mühe ['my:ə] *f* (-/-n) trouble, pains
pl.; (*nicht*) *der* ~ *wert* (not) worth
while; *j-m* ~ *machen* give s.o.
trouble; *sich* ~ *geben* take pains
(*mit over, with s.th.*); '2los *adj.*

effortless, easy; '²n v/refl. (ge-, h) take pains, work hard; '²voll adj. troublesome, hard; laborious.

Mühle ['my:lə] f (-/-n) mill.

'Müh|sal f (-/-e) toil, trouble; hardship; '²sam, '²selig 1. adj. toilsome, troublesome; difficult; 2. adv. laboriously; with difficulty.

Mulatte [mu'latə] m (-n/-n) mulatto.

Mulde ['muldə] f (-/-n) trough; depression, hollow.

Mull [mul] m (-[e]s/-e) mull.

Müll [myl] m (-[e]s/no pl.) dust, rubbish, refuse, Am. a. garbage; '~abfuhr f removal of refuse; '~eimer m dust-bin, Am. garbage can.

Müller ['mylər] m (-s/-) miller.

'Müll|fahrer m dust-man, Am. garbage collector; '~haufen m dust-heap; '~kasten m s. Mülleimer; '~kutscher m s. Müllfahrer; '~wagen m dust-cart, Am. garbage cart.

Multipli|kation ₳ [multiplika-'tsjo:n] f (-/-en) multiplication; ²zieren ₳ [~'tsi:rən] v/t. (no -ge-, h) multiply (mit by).

Mumie ['mu:mjə] f (-/-n) mummy.

Mumps ⚕ [mumps] m, f f (-/no pl.) mumps.

Mund [munt] m (-[e]s/~er) mouth; den ~ halten hold one's tongue; den ~ voll nehmen talk big; sich den ~ verbrennen put one's foot in it; nicht auf den ~ gefallen sein have a ready or glib tongue; j-m über den ~ fahren cut s.o. short; '~art f dialect; '²artlich adj. dialectal.

Mündel ['myndəl] m, n (-s/-), girl: a. f (-/-n) ward, pupil; '²sicher adj.: ~e Papiere n/pl. ✝ gilt-edged securities pl.

münden ['myndən] v/i. (ge-, h): ~ in (acc.) river, etc.: fall or flow into; street, etc.: run into.

'mund|faul adj. too lazy to speak; '~gerecht adj. palatable (a. fig.); '²harmonika ♪ f mouth-organ; '²höhle anat. f oral cavity.

mündig ⚖ adj. ['myndiç] of age; ~ werden come of age; '²keit f (-/no pl.) majority.

mündlich ['myntliç] 1. adj. oral, verbal; 2. adv. a. by word of mouth.

'Mund|pflege f oral hygiene; '~raub ⚖ m theft of comestibles; '~stück n mouthpiece (of musical instrument, etc.); tip (of cigarette); '²tot adj.: ~ machen silence or gag s.o.

'Mündung f (-/-en) mouth; a. estuary (of river); muzzle (of fire-arms).

'Mund|vorrat m provisions pl.; victuals pl.; '~wasser n (-s/~) mouth-wash, gargle; '~werk F fig. n: ein gutes ~ haben have the gift of the gab.

Munition [muni'tsjo:n] f (-/-en) ammunition.

munkeln F ['muŋkəln] (ge-, h) 1. v/i. whisper; 2. v/t. whisper, rumo(u)r; man munkelt there is a rumo(u)r afloat. [lively; merry.]

munter adj. ['muntər] awake; fig.:]

Münz|e ['myntsə] f (-/-n) coin; (small) change; medal; mint; für bare ~ nehmen take at face value; j-m et. mit gleicher ~ heimzahlen pay s.o. back in his own coin; '~einheit f (monetary) unit, standard of currency; '²en v/t. (ge-, h) coin, mint; gemünzt sein auf (acc.) be meant for, be aimed at; '~fernsprecher teleph. m coin-box telephone; '~fuß m standard (of coinage); '~wesen n monetary system.

mürbe adj. ['myrbə] tender; pastry, etc.: crisp, short; meat: well-cooked; material: brittle; F fig. worn-out, demoralized; F j-n ~ machen break s.o.'s resistance; F ~ werden give in.

Murmel ['murməl] f (-/-n) marble; '²n v/t and v/i. (ge-, h) mumble, murmur; '~tier zo. n marmot.

murren ['murən] v/i. (ge-, h) grumble, F grouch (both: über acc. at, over, about).

mürrisch adj. ['myriʃ] surly, sullen.

Mus [mu:s] n (-es/-e) pap; stewed fruit

Muschel ['muʃəl] f (-/-n) zo.: mussel; shell, conch; teleph. ear-piece.

Museum [mu'ze:um] n (-s/Museen) museum.

Musik [mu'zi:k] f (-/no pl.) music; ~alienhandlung [~i'ka:ljən-] f music-shop; ²alisch adj. [~i'ka:liʃ] musical; ~ant [~i'kant] m (-en/-en) musician; ~automat m juke-box; ~er ['mu:zikər] m (-s/-) musician; bandsman; ~instrument n musical instrument; ~lehrer m music-master; ~stunde f music-lesson; ~truhe f radiogram(ophone), Am. radio-phonograph

musizieren [muzi'tsi:rən] v/i. (no -ge-, h) make or have music.

Muskat ♣ [mus'ka:t] m (-[e]s/-e) nutmeg; ~nuß ♣ f nutmeg.

Muskel [muskəl] m (-s/-n) muscle; '~kater m stiffness and soreness, Am. a. charley horse; '~kraft f muscular strength; '~zerrung ⚕ f pulled muscle.

Muskul|atur [muskula'tu:r] f (-/-en) muscular system, muscles pl.; ²ös adj. [~'lø:s] muscular, brawny.

Muß [mus] n (-/no pl.) necessity; es ist ein ~ it is a must.

Muße ['mu:sə] f (-/no pl.) leisure; spare time; mit ~ at one's leisure.

Musselin [musə'li:n] m (-s/-e) muslin.

müssen ['mysən] (irr., h) 1. v/i. (ge-): ich muß I must; 2. v/aux. (no -ge-): ich muß I must, I have to;

I am obliged *or* compelled *or* forced to; I am bound to; *ich habe gehen* ~ I had to go; *ich müßte (eigentlich) wissen* I ought to know.

müßig *adj.* ['my:siç] idle; superfluous; useless; '2gang *m* idleness, laziness; 2gänger ['~gεŋər] *m* (-s/-) idler, loafer; lazy-bones.

mußte ['mustə] *pret. of* müssen.

Muster ['mustər] *n* (-s/-) model; example, paragon; design, pattern; specimen; sample; '~betrieb *m* model factory *or* ✶ farm; ~gatte *m* model husband; '2gültig, '2haft 1. *adj.* model, exemplary, perfect; 2. *adv. sich* ~ *benehmen* be on one's best behavio(u)r; '~kollektion ✝ *f* range of samples; '2n *v/t.* (ge-, h) examine; eye; ⚓ inspect, review; figure, pattern (*fabric, etc.*); '~schutz *m* protection of patterns and designs; ~ung *f* (-/-en) examination; ⚓ review; pattern (*of fabric, etc.*); '~werk *n* standard work.

Mut [mu:t] *m* (-[e]s/*no pl.*) courage; spirit; pluck; ~ *fassen* pluck up courage, summon one's courage; *den* ~ *sinken lassen* lose courage *or* heart; *guten* ~(e)s of good cheer; '2ig *adj.* courageous; plucky; '2los *adj.* discouraged; despondent; '~losigkeit *f* (-/*no pl.*) discouragement; despondency; 2maßen ['~ma:sən] *v/t.* (ge-, h) suppose, guess, surmise; '2maßlich *adj.* presumable; supposed; *heir:* presumptive; '~maßung *f* (-/-en) supposition, surmise; *bloße* ~en *pl.* guesswork.

Mutter ['mutər] *f* 1. (-/ⁿ) mother; 2. ⊕ (-/-n) nut; '~brust *f* mother's breast; ~leib *m* womb.

mütterlich *adj.* ['mytərliç] motherly; maternal; ~erseits *adv.* ['~ər-'zaits] on *or* from one's mother's side; *uncle, etc.*: maternal.

'Mutter|liebe *f* motherly love; '2los *adj.* motherless; '~mal *n* birth-mark; mole; '~milch *f* mother's milk; '~schaft *f* (-/*no pl.*) maternity, motherhood; '2'seelenal'lein *adj.* all *or* utterly alone; ~söhnchen ['~zø:nçən] *n* (-s/-) milksop, *sl.* sissy; '~sprache *f* mother tongue; '~witz *m* (-es/*no pl.*) mother wit.

'Mutwill|e *m* wantonness; mischievousness; 2ig *adj.* wanton; mischievous; wilful.

Mütze ['mytsə] *f* (-/-n) cap.

Myrrhe ['myrə] *f* (-/-n) myrrh.

Myrte ⚘ ['myrtə] *f* (-/-n) myrtle.

mysteri|ös *adj.* [myster'jø:s] mysterious; 2um ['~'te:rjum] *n* (-s/ *Mysterien*) mystery.

Mystifi|kation [mystifika'tsjo:n] *f* (-/-en) mystification; 2zieren [~'tsi:rən] *v/t.* (*no* -ge-, h) mystify.

Mysti|k ['mystik] *f* (-/*no pl.*) mysticism; '2sch *adj.* mystic(al).

Myth|e ['my:tə] *f* (-/-n) myth; '2isch *adj.* mythic; *esp. fig.* mythical; ~ologie [mytolo'gi:] *f* (-/-en) mythology; 2ologisch *adj.* [myto-'lo:giʃ] mythological; ~os ['~ɔs] *m* (-/*Mythen*), ~us ['~us] *m* (-/*Mythen*) myth.

N

na *int.* [na] now!, then!, well!, *Am. a.* hey!

Nabe ['na:bə] *f* (-/-n) hub.

Nabel *anat.* ['na:bəl] *m* (-s/-) navel.

nach [na:x] 1. *prp. (dat.) direction, striving:* after; to(wards), for (*a.* ~ ... *hin or zu*); *succession:* after; *time:* after, past; *manner, measure, example:* according to; ~ *Gewicht* by weight; ~ *deutschem Geld in* German money; *e-r* ~ *dem andern* one by one; *fünf Minuten* ~ *eins* five minutes past one; 2. *adv.* after; ~ *und* ~ little by little, gradually; ~ *wie vor* little as before, still.

nachahm|en ['na:x⁹a:mən] *v/t.* (*sep.*, -ge-, h) imitate, copy; counterfeit; '~ens'wert *adj.* worthy of imitation, exemplary; '2er *m* (-s/-) imitator; '2ung *f* (-/-en) imitation; copy; counterfeit, fake.

Nachbar ['naxba:r] *m* (-n, -s/-n), '~in *f* (-/-nen) neighbo(u)r; '~-schaft *f* (-/-en) neighbo(u)rhood, vicinity.

'Nachbehandlung ✶ *f* after-treatment.

'nachbestell|en *v/t.* (*sep., no* -ge-, h) repeat one's order for *s.th.*; '2ung *f* repeat order).

'nachbeten *v/t.* (*sep.*, -ge-, h) echo.

'Nachbildung *f* copy, imitation; replica; dummy.

'nachblicken *v/i.* (*sep.*, -ge-, h) look after.

nachdem *cj.* [na:x'de:m] after, when; *je* ~ according as.

'nachdenk|en *v/i.* (*irr. denken, sep.,* -ge-, h) think (*über acc.* over, about); reflect, meditate (*über acc.* on); '2en *n* (-s/*no pl.*) reflection, meditation; musing; '~lich *adj.* meditative, reflecting; pensive.

'Nachdichtung *f* free version.

'Nachdruck *m* 1. (-[e]s/*no pl.*) stress, emphasis; 2. *typ.* (-[e]s/-e)

reprint; *unlawfully*: piracy, pirated edition; '2en *v/t.* (*sep.*, -ge-, h) reprint; *unlawfully*: pirate.
nachdrücklich ['naːxdryklɪç] 1. *adj.* emphatic, energetic; forcible; positive; 2. *adv.*: ~ betonen emphasize.
nacheifern ['naːxʔ-] *v/i.* (*sep.*, -ge-, h) emulate *s.o.*
nacheinander *adv.* [naːxʔaɪˈnandər] one after another, successively; by *or* in turns.
nachempfinden ['naːxʔ-] *v/t.* (*irr.* empfinden, *sep.*, no -ge-, h) s. nachfühlen.
nacherzähl|en ['naːxʔ-] *v/t.* (*sep.*, no -ge-, h) repeat; retell; *dem Englischen nacherzählt* adapted from the English; 2ung ['naːxʔ-] *f* repetition; story retold, reproduction.
'**Nachfolge** *f* succession; '2n *v/i.* (*sep.*, -ge-, sein) follow *s.o.*; *j-m im Amt* ~ succeed *s.o.* in his office; '~r *m* (-s/-) follower; successor.
'**nachforsch|en** *v/i.* (*sep.*, -ge-, h) investigate; search for; '2ung *f* investigation, inquiry, search.
'**Nachfrage** *f* inquiry; ✝ demand; '2n *v/i.* (*sep.*, -ge-, h) inquire (*nach* after).
'**nach|fühlen** *v/t.* (*sep.*, -ge-, h): es *j-m* ~ feel *or* sympathize with *s.o.*; '~füllen *v/t.* (*sep.*, -ge-, h) fill up, refill; ~geben *v/i.* (*irr.* geben, *sep.*, -ge-, h) give way (*dat.* to); *fig.* give in, yield (to); '2gebühr *f* surcharge; '~gehen *v/i.* (*irr.* gehen, *sep.*, -ge-, sein) follow (*s.o.*, business, trade, *etc.*); pursue (*pleasure*); attend to (*business*); investigate *s.th.*; *watch*: be slow; '2geschmack *m* (-[e]s/no *pl.*) after-taste.
nachgiebig *adj.* ['naːxɡiːbɪç] elastic, flexible; *fig.* a. yielding, compliant; '2keit *f* (-/-en) flexibility; compliance.
'**nachgrübeln** *v/i.* (*sep.*, -ge-, h) ponder, brood (*both*: über *acc.* over), muse (on).
nachhaltig *adj.* ['naːxhaltɪç] lasting, enduring.
nach'her *adv.* afterwards; then; *bis* ~! see you later!, so long!
'**Nachhilfe** *f* help, assistance; '~lehrer *m* coach, private tutor; '~unterricht *m* private lesson(s *pl.*), coaching.
'**nach|holen** *v/t.* (*sep.*, -ge-, h) make up for, make good; '2hut ✗ *f* (-/-en) rear-(guard); *die* ~ *bilden* bring up the rear (*a. fig.*); '~jagen *v/i.* (*sep.*, -ge-, sein) chase *or* pursue *s.o.*; '~klingen *v/i.* (*irr.* klingen, *sep.*, -ge-, h) resound, echo.
'**Nachkomme** *m* (-n/-n) descendant; ~n *pl. esp.* ✗ issue; '2n *v/i.* (*irr.* kommen, *sep.*, -ge-, sein) follow; come later; obey (*order*); meet (*liabilities*); '~nschaft *f* (-/-en) descendants *pl.*, *esp.* ✗ issue.

'**Nachkriegs...** post-war.
Nachlaß ['naːxlas] *m* (Nachlasses/ Nachlasse, Nachlässe) ✝ reduction, discount, assets *pl.*, estate, inheritance (*of deceased*).
'**nachlassen** (*irr.* lassen, *sep.*, -ge-, h) 1. *v/t* reduce (*price*); 2. *v/i.* deteriorate, slacken, relax; diminish; *pain, rain, etc.* abate; *storm*: calm down, *strength*: wane; *interest*: flag.
'**nachlässig** *adj.* careless, negligent.
'**nach|laufen** *v/i.* (*irr.* laufen, *sep.*, -ge-, sein) run (*dat.* after); '~lesen *v/t.* (*irr.* lesen, *sep.*, -ge-, h) in *book*: look up; ✗ glean; '~liefern ✝ *v/t.* (*sep.*, -ge-, h) deliver subsequently; repeat delivery of; '~lösen *v/t.* (*sep.*, -ge-, h): *e-e Fahrkarte* ~ take a supplementary ticket; buy a ticket en route; '~machen *v/t.* (*sep.*, -ge-, h) imitate (*art.* s.o. in s.th.); copy; counterfeit, forge; '~messen *v/t.* (*irr.* messen, *sep.*, -ge-, h) measure again.
'**Nachmittag** *m* afternoon; '2s *adv.* in the afternoon; '~svorstellung *thea. f* matinée.
Nach|nahme ['naːxnaːmə] *f* (-/-n) cash on delivery, *Am.* collect on delivery, *per* ~ *schicken* send C.O.D.; '~name *m* surname, last name; '~porto ✗ *n* surcharge.
'**nach|prüfen** *v/t.* (*sep.*, -ge-, h) verify, check; '~rechnen *v/t.* (*sep.*, -ge-, h) reckon over again; check (*bill*).
'**Nachrede** *f*: üble ~ ⚖ defamation (of character); *oral*: slander, *written* libel; '2n *v/t.* (*sep.*, -ge-, h): *j-m Übles* ~ slander *s.o.*
Nachricht [-naːxrɪçt] *f* (-/-en) news; message; report; information, notice; *geben* s. benachrichtigen; '~enagentur *f* news agency; '~endienst *m* news service; ✗ intelligence service; '~ensprecher *m* newscaster; '~enwesen *n* (-s/no *pl.*) communications *pl.*
'**nachrücken** *v/i.* (*sep.*, -ge-, sein) move along.
'**Nach|ruf** *m* obituary (notice); '~ruhm *m* posthumous fame.
'**nachsagen** *v/t.* (*sep.*, -ge-, h) repeat; *man sagt ihm nach, daß* he is said to *inf.*
'**Nachsaison** *f* dead *or* off season.
'**nachschicken** *v/t.* (*sep.*, -ge-, h) s. nachsenden.
'**nachschlage|n** *v/t.* (*irr.* schlagen, *sep.*, -ge-, h) consult (*book*); look up (*word*); '2werk *n* reference-book.
'**Nach|schlüssel** *m* skeleton key; '~schrift *f* in *letter*: postscript; '~schub ✗ *m* supplies *pl.*; '~schubweg ✗ *m* supply line.
'**nach|sehen** (*irr.* sehen, *sep.*, -ge-, h) 1. *v/i.* look after; ~, ob (go and) see whether; 2. *v/t.* look after; examine,

inspect; check; overhaul (machine); s. nachschlagen; j-m et. ~ indulge s.o. in s.th.; **'~senden** v/t. ([irr. senden,] sep., -ge-, h) send after; send on, forward (letter) (j-m to s.o.).

'Nachsicht f indulgence; **'2ig** adj., **'2svoll** adj. indulgent, forbearing.

'Nachsilbe gr. f suffix.

'nach|sinnen v/i. (irr. sinnen, sep., -ge-, h) muse, meditate (über acc. [up]on); **'~sitzen** v/i. (irr. sitzen, sep., -ge-, h) pupil: be kept in.

'Nach|sommer m St. Martin's summer, esp. Am. Indian summer; **'~speise** f dessert; **'~spiel** fig. n sequel.

'nach|spionieren v/i. (sep., no -ge-, h) spy (dat. on); **'~sprechen** v/i. and v/t. (irr. sprechen, sep., -ge-, h) repeat; **'~spülen** v/t. (sep., -ge-, h) rinse; **'~spüren** v/i. (sep., -ge-, h) (dat.) track, trace.

nächst [nɛːçst] 1. adj. succession, time: next; distance, relation: nearest; 2. prp. (dat.) next to, next after; **'2°beste** m, f, n (-n/-n): der (die) ~ anyone; das ~ anything; er fragte den ~n he asked the next person he met.

'nachstehen v/i. (irr. stehen, sep., -ge-, h): j-m in nichts ~ be in no way inferior to s.o.

'nachstell|en (sep., -ge-, h) 1. v/t. place behind; put back (watch); ⊕ adjust (screw, etc.); 2. v/i.: j-m ~ be after s.o.; **'2ung** fig. f persecution.

'Nächstenliebe f charity.

'nächstens adv. shortly, (very) soon, before long.

'nach|streben v/i. (sep., -ge-, h) s. nacheifern; **'~suchen** v/i. (sep., -ge-, h): ~ um apply for, seek.

Nacht [naxt] f (-/⸚e) night; bei ~, des ~s ~ nachts; **'~arbeit** f night-work; **'~asyl** n night-shelter; **'~ausgabe** f night edition (of newspaper); **'~dienst** m night-duty.

'Nachteil m disadvantage, drawback; im ~ sein be at a disadvantage; **'2ig** adj. disadvantageous.

'Nacht|essen n supper; **'~falter** zo. m (-s/-) moth; **'~gebet** n evening prayer; **'~geschirr** n chamberpot; **'~hemd** n night-gown, Am. a. night robe; for men: night-shirt.

Nachtigall orn. ['naxtigal] f (-/-en) nightingale.

'Nachtisch m (-es/no pl.) sweet, dessert.

'Nachtlager n (a) lodging for the night; bed.

nächtlich adj. ['nɛçtlíç] nightly, nocturnal.

'Nacht|lokal n night-club; **'~mahl** n supper; **'~portier** m night-porter; **'~quartier** n night-quarters pl.

Nachtrag ['naːxtraːk] m (-[e]s/⸚e) supplement; fig. (j-m et. s.th. after s.o.); add; ✝ post up (ledger); j-m et. ~ bear s.o. a grudge; **'2end** adj. unforgiving, resentful.

nachträglich adj. ['naːxtrɛːklíç] additional; subsequent.

nachts adv. [naxts] at or by night.

'Nacht|schicht f night-shift; **'2°schlafend** adj.: zu ~er Zeit in the middle of the night; **'~schwärmer** fig. m night-reveller; **'~tisch** m bedside table; **'~topf** m chamberpot; **'~vorstellung** thea. f night performance; **'~wache** f night-watch; **'~wächter** m (night-)watchman; **'~wandler** ['~vandlər] m (-s/-) sleep-walker; **'~zeug** n night-things pl.

'nachwachsen v/i. (irr. wachsen, sep., -ge-, h) grow again.

'Nachwahl parl. f by-election.

Nachweis ['naːxvais] m (-es/-e) proof, evidence; **'2bar** adj. demonstrable; traceable; **2en** ['~zən] v/t. (irr. weisen, sep., -ge-, h) point out, show; trace; prove; **'2lich** adj. s. nachweisbar.

'Nach|welt f posterity; **'~wirkung** f after-effect; consequences pl.; aftermath; **'~wort** n (-[e]s/-e) epilog(ue); **'~wuchs** m (-[e]s/no pl.) rising generation.

'nach|zahlen v/t. (sep., -ge-, h) pay in addition; **'~zählen** v/t. (sep., -ge-, h) count over (again), check; **'2zahlung** f additional payment.

Nachzügler ['naːxtsyːklər] m (-s/-) straggler, late-comer.

Nacken ['nakən] m (-s/-) nape (of the neck); neck.

nackt adj. [nakt] naked, nude; bare (a. fig.); young birds: unfledged; truth: plain.

Nadel ['naːdəl] f (-/-n) needle; pin; brooch; **'~arbeit** f needlework; **'~baum** ♣ m conifer(ous tree); **'~stich** m prick; stitch; fig. pin-prick.

Nagel ['naːgəl] m (-s/⸚) anat., ⊕ nail; of wood: peg; spike; stud; die Arbeit brennt mir auf den Nägeln it's a rush job; **'~haut** f cuticle; **'~lack** m nail varnish; **2n** v/t. (ge-, h) nail (an or auf acc. to); **~necessaire** ['~nesesɛːr] n (-s/-s) manicure-case; **'2neu** F adj. bran(d)-new; **'~pflege** f manicure.

nage|n ['naːgən] (ge-, h) 1. v/i. gnaw; ~ an (dat.) gnaw at; pick (bone); 2. v/t. gnaw; gnawer; **2tier** zo. n rodent, gnawer.

nah adj. [naː] near, close (bei to); nearby; danger: imminent.

Näharbeit ['nɛːʔ-] f needlework, sewing.

Nahaufnahme f film: close-up.

nahe adj. ['naːə] s. nah.

Nähe ['nɛːə] f (-/no pl.) nearness, proximity; vicinity; *in der ~* close by.

'**nahe|gehen** v/i. (irr. gehen, sep., -ge-, sein) (dat.) affect, grieve; '**~kommen** v/i. (irr. kommen, sep., -ge-, sein) (dat.) approach; get at (truth); '**~legen** v/t. (sep., -ge-, h) suggest; '**~liegen** v/i. (irr. liegen, sep., -ge-, h) suggest itself, be obvious.

nahen ['naːən] 1. v/i. (ge-, sein) approach; 2. v/refl. (ge-, h) approach (j-m s.o.).

nähen ['nɛːən] v/t. and v/i. (ge-, h) sew, stitch.

näher adj. ['nɛːər] nearer, closer; road shorter; *das Nähere* (further) particulars pl. or details pl.

'**Näherin** f (-/-nen) seamstress.

'**nähern** v/t. (ge-, h) approach (dat. to); sich ~ approach (j-m s.o.).

'**nahe'zu** adv. nearly, almost.

'**Nähgarn** n (sewing-)cotton.

'**Nahkampf** ✕ m close combat.

nahm [naːm] pret. of nehmen.

'**Näh|maschine** f sewing-machine; '**~nadel** f (sewing-)needle.

nähren ['nɛːrən] v/t. (ge-, h) nourish (a. fig.), feed; nurse (child); sich ~ von live or feed on.

nahrhaft adj. ['naːrhaft] nutritious, nourishing.

'**Nahrung** f (-/no pl.) food, nourishment, nutriment.

'**Nahrungs|aufnahme** f intake of food; '**~mittel** n/pl. food(-stuff), victuals pl.

'**Nährwert** m nutritive value.

Naht [naːt] f (-/=e) seam; ✍ suture.

'**Nahverkehr** m local traffic.

'**Nähzeug** n sewing-kit.

naiv adj. [na'iːf] naïve, naive, simple; 2**ität** [naivi'tɛːt] f (-/no pl.) naïveté, naivety, simplicity.

Name ['naːmə] m (-ns/-n) name; *im ~* (gen.) on behalf of; *dem ~n nach* nominal(ly), in name only; *dem ~n nach kennen* know by name; *die Dinge beim rechten ~n nennen* call a spade a spade; *darf ich um Ihren ~n bitten?* may I ask your name?

'**namen|los** adj. nameless, anonymous; fig. unutterable; '**~s** 1. adv. named, by the name of, called; 2. prp. (gen.) in the name of.

'**Namens|tag** m name-day; '**~vetter** m namesake, '**~zug** m signature.

namentlich ['naːməntlɪç] 1. adj. nominal; 2. adv. by name; especially, in particular.

'**namhaft** adj. notable; considerable; ~ machen name.

nämlich ['nɛːmlɪç] 1. adj. the same; 2. adv namely, that is (to say).

nannte ['nantə] pret. of nennen.

Napf [napf] m (-[e]s/=e) bowl, basin.

Narb|e ['narbə] f (-/-n) scar; '2**ig** adj. scarred; leather: grained.

Narko|se ✍ [nar'koːzə] f (-/-n) narcosis; 2**tisieren** [~oti'ziːrən] v/t. (no -ge-, h) narcotize.

Narr [nar] m (-en/-en) fool; jester; *zum ~en halten* = '2**en** v/t. (ge-) make a fool of, fool; '**Narren|haus** F n madhouse; '**~kappe** f fool's-cap; '2**sicher** adj. foolproof.

'**Narrheit** f (-/-en) folly.

Närrin ['nɛrɪn] f (-/-nen) fool, foolish woman.

'**närrisch** adj. foolish, silly; odd.

Narzisse ♣ [nar'tsɪsə] f (-/-n) narcissus; gelbe ~ daffodil.

nasal adj. [na'zaːl] nasal; ~e Sprechweise twang.

nasch|en ['naʃən] (ge-, h) 1. v/i. nibble (an dat. at); gern ~ have a sweet tooth; 2. v/t. nibble; eat s.th. on the sly; 2**ereien** [~'raɪən] f/pl. dainties pl., sweets pl.; '**~haft** adj. fond of dainties or sweets.

Nase ['naːzə] f (-/-n) nose; die ~ rümpfen turn up one's nose (über acc. at).

näseln ['nɛːzəln] v/i. (ge-, h) speak through the nose, nasalize; snuffle.

'**Nasen|bluten** n (-s/no pl.) nosebleeding, '**~loch** n nostril; '**~spitze** f tip of the nose.

naseweis adj. ['naːzəvaɪs] pert, saucy.

nasführen ['naːs-] v/t. (ge-, h) fool, dupe.

Nashorn zo. ['naːs-] n rhinoceros.

naß adj. [nas] wet; damp, moist.

Nässe [nɛsə] f (-/no pl.) wet(ness); moisture; ⚗ humidity; '2**n** (ge-, h) 1. v/t. wet; moisten; 2. ✍ v/i. discharge.

'**naßkalt** adj. damp and cold, raw.

Nation [na'tsjoːn] f (-/-en) nation.

national adj. [natsjo'naːl] national; 2**hymne** f national anthem; 2**ismus** [~a'lɪsmus] m (-/Nationalismen) nationalism; 2**ität** [~ali'tɛːt] f (-/-en) nationality; 2**mannschaft** f national team.

Natter ['natər] f (-/-n) zo. adder, viper; fig. serpent.

Natur [na'tuːr] f 1. (-/no pl.) nature; 2. (-/-en) constitution; temper(ament), disposition, nature; von ~ by nature.

Naturalien [natu'raːljən] pl. natural produce sg.; in ~ in kind.

naturalisieren [naturali'ziːrən] v/t. (no -ge-, h) naturalize.

Naturalismus [natura'lɪsmus] m (-/no pl.) naturalism.

Naturanlage [na'tuːr⁹-] f (natural) disposition

Naturell [natu'rɛl] n (-s/-e) natural disposition, nature, temper.

Na'tur|ereignis n, **~erscheinung** f phenomenon; **~forscher** m naturalist, scientist; 2gemäß *adj.* natural; .geschichte *f* natural history; .gesetz *n* law of nature, natural law; 2getreu *adj.* true to nature; life-like; .kunde *f* (natural) science.

natürlich [na'ty:rliç] 1. *adj.* natural; genuine; innate; unaffected; 2. *adv.* naturally, of course.

Na'tur|produkte *n/pl.* natural products *pl. or* produce *sg.*; .schutz *m* wild-life conservation; .schutzgebiet *n*, .schutzpark *m* national park, wild-life (p)reserve; .trieb *m* instinct; .wissenschaft *f* (natural) science; .wissenschaftler *m* (natural) scientist.

Nebel ['ne:bəl] *m* (-s/-) fog; mist; haze; smoke; 2haft *fig. adj.* nebulous, hazy, dim; '.horn *n* fog-horn.

neben *prp.* (*dat. or acc.*) ['ne:bən] beside, by (the side of); near to; against, compared with; apart *or Am. a.* aside from, besides.

neben|'an *adv.* next door; close by; 2anschluß *teleph.* ['ne:bən⁹-] *m* extension (line); 2arbeit ['ne:bən⁹-] *f* extra work; 2ausgaben ['ne:bən⁹-] *f/pl.* incidental expenses *pl.*, extras *pl.*; 2ausgang ['ne:bən⁹-] *m* side-exit, side-door; 2bedeutung *f* secondary meaning, connotation; .bei *adv.* by the way; besides; 2beruf *m* side-line; '.beruflich *adv.* as a side-line; in one's spare time; 2beschäftigung *f* s. Nebenberuf; 2buhler ['.bu:lər] *m* (-s/-) rival; .ei'nander *adv.* side by side; . bestehen co-exist; 2eingang ['ne:bən⁹-] *m* side-entrance; 2einkünfte ['ne:bən⁹-] *pl.*, 2einnahmen ['ne:bən⁹-] *f/pl.* casual emoluments *pl.*, extra income; 2erscheinung ['ne:bən⁹-] *f* accompaniment; 2fach *n* subsidiary subject, *Am.* minor (subject); 2fluß *m* tributary (river); 2gebäude *n* annex(e); outhouse; 2geräusch *n* radio: atmospherics *pl.*, interference, jamming; 2gleis *n* siding, side-track; 2handlung *thea. f* underplot; 2haus *n* adjoining house; .her *adv.*, .hin *adv.* by his *or* her side; *s. nebenbei*; 2kläger *m* co-plaintiff; 2kosten *pl.* extras *pl.*; 2mann *m* person next to one; 2produkt *n* by-product; 2rolle *f* minor part (*a. thea.*); 2sache *f* minor matter, side issue; 2sächlich *adj.* subordinate, incidental; unimportant; 2satz *gr. m* subordinate clause; '.stehend *adj.* in the margin; 2stelle *f* branch; agency; *teleph.* extension; 2straße *f* bystreet, by-road; 2strecke *f* branch line; 2tisch *m* next table; 2tür *f* side-door; 2verdienst *m* incidental *or* extra earnings *pl.*; 2zimmer *n* adjoining room.

'neblig *adj.* foggy, misty, hazy.

nebst *prp.* (*dat.*) [ne:pst] together with, besides; including.

neck|en ['nekən] *v/t.* (ge-, h) tease, banter, *sl.* kid; 2erei ['.rai] *f* (-/-en) teasing, banter; '.isch *adj.* playful; droll, funny.

Neffe ['nefə] *m* (-n/-n) nephew.

negativ [nega'ti:f] 1. *adj.* negative; 2. 2 *n* (-s/-e) negative.

Neger ['ne:gər] *m* (-s/-) negro; '.in *f* (-/-nen) negress.

nehmen ['ne:mən] *v/t.* (*irr.*, ge-, h) take; receive; charge (*money*); zu sich take, have (*meal*); j-m et. take s.th. from s.o.; *ein Ende* come to an end; *es sich nicht* *lassen zu inf.* insist upon *ger.*; *streng genommen* strictly speaking.

Neid [nait] *m* (-[e]s/*no pl.*) envy; 2en ['naidən] *v/t.* (ge-, h): j-m et. envy s.o. s.th.; '.er ['.dər] *m* (-s/-) envious person; .hammel F ['nait-] *m* dog in the manger; '.isch *adj.* ['.diʃ] envious (*auf acc.* of); 2los *adj.* ['nait-] ungrudging.

Neige ['naigə] *f* (-/-en) decline; *barrel:* dregs *pl.*; *glass:* heeltap; *zur* *gehen* (be on the) decline; *esp.* run short; 2n (ge-, h) 1. *v/t. and v/refl.* bend, incline; 2. *v/i.*: *er neigt zu Übertreibungen* he is given to exaggeration.

'Neigung *f* (-/-en) inclination (*a. fig.*); slope, incline.

nein *adv.* [nain] no.

Nektar ['nekta:r] *m* (-s/*no pl.*) nectar.

Nelke ['nelkə] *f* (-/-n) carnation, pink; *spice:* clove.

nennen ['nenən] *v/t.* (*irr.*, ge-, h) name; call; term; mention; nominate (*candidate*); *sports:* enter (*für* for); *sich* ... be called ...; '.swert *adj.* worth mentioning.

'Nenn|er *m* (-s/-) denominator; '.ung *f* (-/-en) naming; mentioning; nomination (*of candidates*); *sports:* entry; '.wert *m* nominal *or* face value; *zum* ↑ at par.

Neon ['ne:ɔn] *n* (-s/*no pl.*) neon; '.röhre *f* neon tube.

Nerv [nerf] *m* (-s/-en) nerve; *j-m auf die* .en *fallen or gehen* get on s.o.'s nerves.

'Nerven|arzt *m* neurologist; 2aufreibend *adj.* trying; '.heilanstalt *f* mental hospital; '.kitzel *m* (-s/*no pl.*) thrill, sensation; 2krank *adj.* neurotic; 2leidend *adj.* neuropathic, neurotic; '.schwäche *f* nervous debility; 2stärkend *adj.* tonic; '.system *n* nervous system; '.zusammenbruch *m* nervous breakdown.

nerv|ig *adj.* ['nerviç] sinewy, .ös *adj.* ['.vø:s] nervous; 2osität ['.ozi-'te:t] *f* (-/*no pl.*) nervousness.

Nerz *zo.* [nerts] *m* (-es/-e) mink.

Nessel ⚘ ['nɛsəl] f (-/-n) nettle.
Nest [nɛst] n (-es/-er) nest; F *fig.*
bed; F *fig.* hick *or* one-horse town.
nett *adj.* [nɛt] nice; neat, pretty,
Am. a. cute; pleasant, kind.
netto ✦ *adv.* ['nɛto] net, clear.
Netz [nɛts] n (-es -e) net; *fig.* network; **~anschluß** ⚡ m mains connection, power supply; **~haut**
anat. f retina; **~spannung** ⚡ f
mains voltage.

neu *adj.* [nɔy] new; fresh; recent;
modern; **~ere Sprachen** modern
languages; **~este Nachrichten** latest
news; **von ~em** anew, afresh; *ein*
~es Leben beginnen turn over a new
leaf; *was gibt es Neues?* what is
the news?, *Am.* what is new?
'**Neu|anschaffung** f -/-en) recent
acquisition, **2artig** *adj.* novel; '**~
auflage** *typ.* f, **~ausgabe** *typ.* f
new edition; reprint; **~bau** m
(-[e]s/-ten) new building, **2bear-**
beitet *adj.* revised; **~e ~n** (-n/-n)
new man; new-comer; novice;
'**2entdeckt** *adj.* recently discov-
ered.
neuer|dings *adv.* ['nɔyər'diŋs] of
late, recently; '**2er** m (-s/-) inno-
vator.
Neuerscheinung ['nɔyʔ-] f new
book *or* publication.
'**Neuerung** f (-/-en) innovation.
neu|geboren *adj.* new-born; '**~ge-**
stalten *v/t.* (*sep*, ge-, h) reorgan-
ize; '**2gestaltung** f reorganization;
'**2gier** f, **2gierde** ~də] f *no pl.*)
curiosity, inquisitiveness; **~gierig**
adj. curious (*auf acc* about, of), in-
quisitive, *sl.* nos(e)y; *ich bin* ~, *ob*
I wonder whether *or* if; **2heit** f
(-/-en) newness, freshness; novelty.
'**Neuigkeit** f (-/-en) (e-e a piece of)
news.
'**Neu|jahr** n New Year('s Day); '**~**
land n (-[e]s/*no pl.*): erschließen
break fresh ground (*a. fig.*); **~lich**
adv. the other day, recently, '**~ling**
m (-s/-e) novice; contp greenhorn;
'**2modisch** *adj.* fashionable; '**~**
mond m (-[e]s/*no pl.*) new moon.
neun *adj.* [nɔyn] nine; **~te** *adj.*
ninth; '**2tel** n -s/-) ninth part;
'**~tens** *adv.* ninthly; **~zehn** *adj.*
nineteen; '**~zehnte** *adj.* nineteenth;
~zig *adj.* ['~tsiç] ninety; **~zigste**
adj. ninetieth.
'**Neu|philologe** m student *or* teacher
of modern languages; **~regelung** f
reorganization, rearrangement.
neutr|al *adj.* [nɔy'trɑːl] neutral;
2alität [~ali'tɛːt] f -/*no pl.*) neu-
trality; **2um** gr. ['nɔytrum] n
(-s/Neutra, Neutren) neuter.
'**neu|vermählt** *adj.* newly married;
die **2en** *pl.* the newly-weds *pl.*; '**2-**
wahl *parl.* f new election; **~wer-**
tig *adj.* as good as new; '**2zeit** f
(-/*no pl.*) modern times *pl.*

nicht *adv.* [niçt] not; *auch* ~ nor;
~ **anziehend** unattractive; ~ **besser**
no better; ~ **bevollmächtigt** non-
commissioned; ~ **einlösbar** ✦ in-
convertible; ~ **erscheinen** fail to attend.
Nicht|achtung f disregard; '**2amt-**
lich *adj.* unofficial; '**~angriffspakt**
pol. m non-aggression pact; **~an-**
nahme f non-acceptance; '**~befol-**
gung f non-observance.
Nichte [niçtə] f (-/-n) niece.
nichtig *adj.* null, void; invalid;
vain, futile; *für* ~ **erklären** declare
null and void, annul; '**2keit** f (-/-en)
ggf nullity; vanity, futility.
Nichtraucher m non-smoker.
nichts [niçts] 1. *indef. pron.* nothing,
naught, not anything; 2. **2** n (-/*no
pl.*) nothing(ness); *fig.* nonentity;
void; **~ahnend** *adj.* unsuspecting;
~desto weniger *adv.* nevertheless;
~nutzig *adj.* ['~nutsiç] good-for-
nothing, worthless; **~sagend** *adj.*
insignificant; **2tuer** ['~tuːər] m
(-s/-) idler; **~würdig** *adj.* vile,
base, infamous.
Nicht|vorhandensein n absence;
lack; **~wissen** n ignorance.
nick|en ['nikən] *v/i.* (ge-, h) nod;
bow; **2erchen** F n (-s/-): *ein* ~
machen take a nap, have one's forty
winks.
nie *adv.* [niː] never, at no time.
nieder ['niːdər] 1. *adj.* low; base,
mean, vulgar; *value, rank:* inferior;
2. *adv.* down.
Nieder|gang m decline; '**2ge-**
drückt *adj.* dejected, downcast;
2gehen *v/i.* (*irr. gehen, sep.,* -ge-,
sein) go down; ✈ descend; *storm:*
break; **2geschlagen** *adj.* dejected,
downcast; '**2hauen** *v/t.* (*irr. hauen,
sep.,* -ge-, h) cut down; '**2kommen**
v/i. (*irr. kommen, sep.,* -ge-, sein)
be confined; be delivered (*mit of*);
~kunft ['~kunft] f (-/-e) confinement, delivery; '**2lage** f defeat; ✕
warehouse; branch; **2lassen** *v/t.*
(*irr. lassen, sep.,* -ge-, h) let down;
sich ~ settle (down); *bird:* alight;
sit down; establish o.s.; settle (*in
dat.* at); **~lassung** f (-/-en) establishment; settlement; branch, agency; **2legen** *v/t.* (*sep.,* -ge-, h) lay
or put down; resign (*position*); retire from (*business*); abdicate; *die
Arbeit* ~ (*a.* go on) strike, down tools,
Am. F *a.* walk out; *sich* ~ lie down,
go to bed; **2machen** *v/t.* (*sep.,*
-ge-, h) cut down; massacre; '**~**
schlag m 🜄 precipitate; sediment;
precipitation (*of rain, etc.*); *radio-*
active: fall-out; *boxing:* knock-
down, knock-out; '**2schlagen** *v/t.*
(*irr. schlagen, sep.,* -ge-, h) knock
down; *boxing: a.* floor; cast down
(*eyes*); suppress; put down, crush
(*rebellion*); 🜄🜄 quash; *sich* ~

⚇ precipitate; '⚇**schmettern** *fig.* *v/t.* (*sep.*, -ge-, *h*) crush; '⚇**setzen** *v/t.* (*sep.*, -ge-, *h*) set *or* put down; *sich ~* sit down; *birds:* perch, alight; '⚇**strecken** *v/t.* (*sep.*, -ge-, *h*) lay low, strike to the ground, floor; '⚇**trächtig** *adj.* base, mean; F beastly; '~**ung** *f* (-/-*en*) lowlands *pl.*

niedlich *adj.* ['niːtliç] neat, nice, pretty, *Am. a.* cute.

Niednagel ['niːt-] *m* agnail, hangnail.

niedrig *adj.* ['niːdriç] low (*a. fig.*); moderate; *fig.* mean, base.

niemals *adv.* ['niːmaːls] never, at no time.

niemand *indef. pron.* ['niːmant] nobody, no one, none; '⚇**sland** *n* (-[*e*]*s/no pl.*) no man's land.

Niere ['niːrə] *f* (-/-*n*) kidney; '~**braten** *m* loin of veal.

nieseln F ['niːzəln] *v/i.* (ge-, *h*) drizzle; '⚇**regen** F *m* drizzle.

niesen ['niːzən] *v/i.* (ge-, *h*) sneeze.

Niet ⊕ [niːt] *m* (-[*e*]*s/-e*) rivet; '~**e** *f* (-/-*n*) *lottery:* blank; F *fig.* washout; '⚇**en** ⊕ *v/t.* (ge-, *h*) rivet.

Nilpferd *zo.* ['niːl-] *n* hippopotamus.

Nimbus ['nimbus] *m* (-/-*se*) halo (*a. fig.*), nimbus.

nimmer *adv.* ['nimər] never; '~**mehr** *adv.* nevermore; '⚇**satt** *m* (-, -[*e*]*s/-e*) glutton; ⚇'**wiedersehen** F *n:* *auf ~* never to meet again; *er verschwand auf ~* he left for good. [*dat.* at).\

nippen ['nipən] *v/i.* (ge-, *h*) sip (*an*

Nipp|es ['nipəs] *pl.*, '~**sachen** *pl.* (k)nick-(k)nacks *pl.*

nirgend|s *adv.* ['nirgənts], '~(*s*)'*wo adv.* nowhere.

Nische ['niːʃə] *f* (-/-*n*) niche, recess.

nisten ['nistən] *v/i.* (ge-, *h*) nest.

Niveau [ni'voː] *n* (-*s*/-*s*) level; *fig. a.* standard.

nivellieren [nive'liːrən] *v/t.* (*no* -ge-, *h*) level, grade.

Nixe ['niksə] *f* (-/-*n*) water-nymph, mermaid.

noch [nɔx] **1.** *adv.* still; yet; *~ ein* another, one more; *~ einmal* once more *or* again; *~ etwas* something more; *~ etwas?* anything else?; *~ heute* this very day; *~ immer* still; *~ nicht* not yet; *~ nie* never before; *~ so* ever so; *~ im 19. Jahrhundert* as late as the 19th century; *es wird ~ 2 Jahre dauern* it will take two more *or* another two years; **2.** *cj.:* *s. weder;* ~**malig** *adj.* ['~maːliç] repeated; ~**mals** *adv.* ['~maːls] once more *or* again.

Nomad|e [no'maːdə] *m* (-*n*/-*n*) nomad; ⚇**isch** *adj.* nomadic.

Nominativ *gr.* ['noːminatiːf] *m* (-*s*/-*e*) nominative (case).

nominieren [nomi'niːrən] *v/t.* (*no* -ge-, *h*) nominate.

Nonne ['nɔnə] *f* (-/-*n*) nun; '~**nkloster** *n* nunnery, convent.

Nord *geogr.* [nɔrt], ~**en** ['~dən] *m* (-*s/no pl.*) north; ⚇**isch** *adj.* ['~diʃ] northern.

nördlich *adj.* ['nœrtliç] northern, northerly.

'**Nord|licht** *n* northern lights *pl.*; ~'**ost(en** *m*) north-east; '~**pol** *m* North Pole; ⚇**wärts** *adv.* ['~verts] northward(s), north; ~'**west(en** *m*) north-west.

nörg|eln ['nœrgəln] *v/i.* (ge-, *h*) nag, carp (*an dat.* at); grumble; ⚇**ler** ['~lər] *m* (-*s*/-) faultfinder, grumbler.

Norm [nɔrm] *f* (-/-*en*) standard; rule; norm.

normal *adj.* [nɔr'maːl] normal; regular; *measure, weight, time:* standard; ~**isieren** [~ali'ziːrən] *v/refl.* (*no* -ge-, *h*) return to normal.

'**norm|en** *v/t.* (ge-, *h*), ~**ieren** [~'miːrən] *v/t.* (*no* -ge-, *h*) standardize.

Not [noːt] *f* (-/⁼*e*) need, want; necessity; difficulty; trouble; misery; danger, emergency, distress (*a. ⚓*); *~ leiden* suffer privations; *in ~ geraten* become destitute, get into trouble; *in ~ sein* be in trouble; *zur ~* at a pinch; *es tut not, daß* it is necessary that.

Notar [no'taːr] *m* (-*s*/-*e*) (public) notary.

'**Not|ausgang** *m* emergency exit; '~**behelf** *m* makeshift, expedient, stopgap; '~**bremse** *f* emergency brake; '~**brücke** *f* temporary bridge; ~**durft** ['~durft] *f* (-/*no pl.*): *s-e ~ verrichten* relieve o.s.; ⚇**dürftig** *adj.* scanty, poor; temporary.

Note ['noːtə] *f* (-/-*n*) note (*a. ♪*); *pol.* note, memorandum; *school:* mark.

'**Noten|bank** ✝ *f* bank of issue; '~**schlüssel** ♪ *m* clef; '~**system** ♪ *n* staff.

'**Not|fall** *m* case of need, emergency; '⚇**falls** *adv.* if necessary; '⚇**gedrungen** *adv.* of necessity, needs.

notier|en [no'tiːrən] *v/t.* (*no* -ge-, *h*) make a note of, note (down); ✝ quote; ⚇**ung** *f* (-/-*en*) quotation.

nötig *adj.* ['nøːtiç] necessary; *~ haben* need; ~**en** ['~gən] *v/t.* (ge-, *h*) force, oblige, compel; press, urge (*guest*); '~**en'falls** *adv.* if necessary; '⚇**ung** *f* (-/-*en*) compulsion; pressing; *⚇⚇* intimidation.

Notiz [no'tiːts] *f* (-/-*en*) notice; note, memorandum; *~ nehmen von* take notice of; pay attention to; *keine ~ nehmen von* ignore; *sich ~ machen* take notes; ~**block** *m* pad, *Am. a.* scratch pad; ~**buch** *n* notebook.

'**Not|lage** *f* distress; emergency; '⚇**landen** ✈ *v/i.* (-ge-, *sein*) make a forced *or* emergency landing; '**~landung** ⚡ *f* forced *or* emergency landing; '**2leidend** *adj.* needy, destitute; distressed; **~lösung** *f* expedient; **~lüge** *f* white lie.

notorisch *adj.* [no to·riʃ] notorious.

'**Not|ruf** *teleph. m* emergency call; '**~signal** *n* emergency *or* distress signal; **~sitz** *mot m* dick·· v(~seat), *Am. a.* rumble seat, **~stand** *m* emergency; '**~standsarbeiten** *f/pl.* relief works *pl.*, **~standsgebiet** *n* distressed area, **~standsgesetze** *n/pl.* emergency laws *pl.*, **~verband** *m* first-aid dressing, **~verordnung** *f* emergency decree; '**~wehr** *f* self-defen|ce, **~**m. -se; '**2wendig** *adj.* necessary; **~wendigkeit** *f* -|-en) necessity; **~zucht** *f* (-/*no pl.*) rape.

Novelle [no'vɛlə] *f* (-/-n) short story, novella; *parl.* amendment.

November [no'vɛmbər] *m* (-[s]/-) November.

Nu [nu:] *m* (-/*no pl.*): im ~ in no time.

Nuance [ny'ã:sə] *f* (-/-n) shade.

nüchtern *adj.* ['nyçtərn] empty, fasting; sober (*a. fig.*); matter-of-fact; *writings:* jejune; prosaic; cool; plain; **2heit** *f* (-/*no pl.*) sobriety; *fig.* soberness.

Nudel ['nu:dəl] *f* (-/-n) noodle.

null [nul] **1.** *adj.* null; nil; *tennis:* love; **~ und nichtig** null and void; **2.** *f* (-/-en) nought, cipher (*a. fig.*); zero; **2punkt** *m* zero.

numerieren [numə'ri:rən] *v/t.* (*no* -ge-, *h*) number; **numerierter Platz** reserved seat.

Nummer ['numər] *f* (-/-n) number

(*a. newspaper, thea.*); size (*of shoes, etc.*); *thea.* turn; *sports:* event; '**~nschild** *mot. n* number-plate.

nun [nu:n] **1.** *adv.* now, at present; then; **~?** well?; ~ *also* well then; **2.** *int.* now then!; '**~'mehr** *adv.* now.

nur *adv.* [nu:r] only; (nothing) but; merely; ~ noch only.

Nuß [nus] *f* (-/Nüsse) nut; '**~kern** *m* kernel; **~knacker** *m* (-s/-) nutcracker; **~schale** *f* nutshell.

Nüstern ['ny:stərn] *f/pl.* nostrils *pl.*

nutz *adj.* [nuts] *n. sülze;* '**2anwendung** *f* practical application; '**~bar** *adj.* useful; **~bringend** *adj.* profitable.

nütze *adj.* ['nytsə] useful; **zu nichts ~ sein** be of no use, be good for nothing.

Nutzen ['nutsən] **1.** *m* (-s/-) use; profit, gain; advantage; utility; **2.** 2 *v/i. and v/t.* (ge-, *h*) s. nützen.

nützen ['nytsən] (ge-, *h*) **1.** *v/i.:* zu et. ~ be of use *or* useful for s.th.; *j-m* ~ serve s.o.; **es nützt nichts** *zu inf.* it is no use ger.; **2.** *v/t.* use, make use of; put to account; avail o.s. of, seize (*opportunity*).

'**Nutz|holz** *n* timber; '**~leistung** *f* capacity.

nützlich *adj.* ['nytsliç] useful, of use, advantageous.

nutz|los *adj.* useless; **2nießer** ['~ni:sər] *m* (-s/-) usufructuary; '**2nießung** *f* (-/-en) usufruct.

Nutzung *f* (-/-en) using; utilization.

Nylon [naɪlɔn] *n* (-s/*no pl.*) nylon; **~strümpfe** ['~ʃtrympfə] *m/pl.* nylons *pl.*, nylon stockings *pl.*

Nymphe ['nymfə] *f* (-/-n) nymph.

O

o *int.* [o:] oh!, ah!; ~ weh! alas!, oh dear (me)!

Oase [o'a:zə] *f* (-/-n) oasis.

ob *cj.* [ɔp] whether, if; *als* ~ as if, as though.

Obacht ['o:baxt] *f* (-/*no pl.*): ~ geben auf (*acc.*) pay attention to, take care of, heed.

Obdach ['ɔpdax] *n* (-[e]s/*no pl.*) shelter, lodging; **2los** *adj.* unsheltered, homeless; **~lose** *m, f* (-n/-n) homeless person; '**~losenasyl** *n* casual ward.

Obdu|ktion ʃ [ɔpdukˈtsjoːn] *f* (-/-en) post-mortem examination, autopsy; **2zieren** ꬲ [tsɪ·rən] *v/t.* (*no* -ge-, *h*) perform an autopsy on.

oben *adv.* ['o:bən] above, *mountain:* at the top; *house:* upstairs; on the surface; von ~ from above; von ~ bis unten from top to bottom;

von ~ herab behandeln treat haughtily; '**~'an** *adv.* at the top; '**~'auf** *adv.* on the top; on the surface; **~drein** *adv.* ['~'draɪn] into the bargain, at that; **~erwähnt** *adj.* ['o:bən'ɛrvɛ:nt], **~genannt** *adj.* above-mentioned, aforesaid; **~'hin** *adv.* superficially, perfunctorily.

ober [o:bər] **1.** *adj.* upper, higher; *fig. a* superior; **2.** 2 *m* (-s/-) (head) waiter, *German cards:* queen.

Ober|arm ['o:bər?-] *m* upper arm; **~arzt** [o:bər?-] *m* head physician; **~aufseher** ['o:bər?-] *m* superintendent; **~aufsicht** ['o:bər?-] *f* superintendence; **~befehl** ⚔ *m* supreme command; **~befehlshaber** ⚔ *m* commander-in-chief; **~bekleidung** *f* outer garments *pl.*, outer wear; **~bürgermeister** *m* chief burgomaster; Lord Mayor;

'**.deck** ⚓ *n* upper deck; '**.fläche** *f* surface; 2**flächlich** *adj.* ['.flɛçliç] superficial; *fig. a.* shallow; '2**halb** *prp.* (*gen.*) above; '**.hand** *fig. f:* die ~ *gewinnen über* (*acc.*) get the upper hand of; '**.haupt** *n* head, chief; '**.haus** *Brt. parl. n* House of Lords; '**.hemd** *n* shirt; '**.herrschaft** *f* supremacy.

'**Oberin** *f* (-/-nen) *eccl.* Mother Superior; *at hospital*: matron.

ober|irdisch *adj.* ['.o:bər?-] overground, above ground; ⚡ overhead; '2**kellner** *m* head waiter; '2**kiefer** *anat. m* upper jaw; '2**körper** *m* upper part of the body; '2**land** *n* upland; '2**lauf** *m* upper course (*of river*); '2**leder** *n* upper; '2**leitung** *f* chief management; ⚡ overhead wires *pl.*; '2**leutnant** ✕ *m* (*Am.* first) lieutenant; '2**licht** *n* skylight; '2**lippe** *f* upper lip; '2**schenkel** *m* thigh; '2**schule** *f* secondary school, *Am. a.* high school.

'**oberst** 1. *adj.* uppermost, topmost, top; highest (*a. fig.*); *fig.* chief, principal; *rank, etc.*: supreme; 2. 2 ✕ *m* (-en, -s/-en, -e) colonel.

'**Ober|staatsanwalt** ⚖ *m* chief public prosecutor; '**.stimme** ♪ *f* treble, soprano.

'**Oberst|leutnant** ✕ *m* lieutenant-colonel.

'**Ober|tasse** *f* cup; '**.wasser** *fig. n:* ~ *bekommen* get the upper hand.

obgleich *cj.* [ɔp'glaiç] (al)though.

'**Obhut** *f* (-/no *pl.*) care, guard; protection; custody; *in* (*scinc*) ~ *nehmen* take care or charge of.

obig *adj.* ['o:biç] above(-mentioned), aforesaid.

Objekt [ɔp'jɛkt] *n* (-[e]s/-e) object (*a. gr.*); project; ✝ *a.* transaction.

objektiv [ɔpjɛk'ti:f] 1. *adj.* objective; impartial, detached; actual, practical; 2. 2 *n* (-s/-e) object-glass, objective; *phot.* lens; 2**ität** [.ivi-'tɛ:t] *f* (-/no *pl.*) objectivity; impartiality.

obligat *adj.* [obli'ga:t] obligatory; indispensable; inevitable; 2**ion** ✝ [.a'tsjo:n] *f* (-/-en) bond, debenture; **.orisch** *adj.* [.a'to:riʃ] obligatory (*für* on), compulsory, mandatory.

'**Obmann** *m* chairman; ✕ foreman (*of jury*); umpire; ✝ shop-steward, spokesman.

Oboe ♪ [o'bo:ə] *f* (-/-n) oboe, hautboy.

Obrigkeit ['o:briçkait] *f* (-/-en) *the* authorities *pl.*; government; 2**lich** *adj.* magisterial, official; '**.sstaat** *m* authoritarian state.

ob'schon *cj.* (al)though.

Observatorium *ast.* [ɔpzɛrva'to:rjum] *n* (-s/*Observatorien*) observatory.

Obst [o:pst] *n* (-es/no *pl.*) fruit;

'**.bau** *m* fruit-culture, fruit-growing; '**.baum** *m* fruit-tree; '**.ernte** *f* fruit-gathering; fruit-crop; '**.garten** *m* orchard; '**.händler** *m* fruiterer, *Am.* fruitseller; '**.züchter** *m* fruiter, fruit-grower.

obszön *adj.* [ɔps'tsø:n] obscene, filthy.

ob'wohl *cj.* (al)though.

Ochse *zo.* ['ɔksə] *m* (-n/-n) ox; bullock; '**.nfleisch** *n* beef.

öde 1. *adj.* deserted, desolate; waste; *fig.* dull, tedious; 2. 2 *f* (-/-n) desert, solitude; *fig.* dullness, tedium.

oder *cj.* ['o:dər] or.

Ofen ['o:fən] *m* (-s/=) stove; oven; kiln; furnace; '**.heizung** *f* heating by stove; '**.rohr** *n* stove-pipe.

offen *adj.* ['ɔfən] open (*a. fig.*); *position*: vacant; *hostility*: overt; *fig.* frank, outspoken.

'**offen|bar** 1. *adj.* obvious, evident, apparent; 2. *adv. a.* it seems that; **.en** [ɔfən'-] *v/t.* (*no -ge-, h*) reveal, disclose; manifest; *sich j-m* ~ open one's heart to s.o.; 2**ung** [ɔfən'-] *f* (-/-en) manifestation; revelation; 2**ungseid** [ɔfən'ba:ruŋs?-] *m* oath of manifestation.

'**Offenheit** *fig. f* (-/no *pl.*) openness, frankness.

'**offen|herzig** *adj.* open-hearted, sincere; frank; '**.kundig** *adj.* public; notorious; '**.sichtlich** *adj.* manifest, evident, obvious.

offensiv *adj.* [ɔfɛn'zi:f] offensive; 2**e** [.və] *f* (-/-n) offensive.

'**offenstehen** *v/i.* (*irr. stehen, sep.,* *-ge-, h*) stand open; ✝ *bill:* be outstanding; *fig.* be open (*j-m* to s.o.); *es steht ihm offen zu inf.* he is free *or at liberty to inf.*

öffentlich ['œfəntliç] 1. *adj.* public; **.es Ärgernis** public nuisance; **.er** *Dienst* Civil Service; 2. *adv.* publicly, in public; ~ *auftreten* make a public appearance; 2**keit** *f* (-/no *pl.*) publicity; *the* public; *in aller* ~ in public.

offerieren [ɔfə'ri:rən] *v/t.* (*no -ge-,* *h*) offer.

Offerte [ɔ'fɛrtə] *f* (-/-n) offer; tender.

offiziell *adj.* [ɔfi'tsjɛl] official.

Offizier ✕ [ɔfi'tsi:r] *m* (-s/-e) (commissioned) officer; '**.skorps** ✕ [.sko:r] *n* (-/-) body of officers, *the* officers *pl.*; '**.smesse** *f* ✕ officers' mess; ⚓ *a.* wardroom.

offiziös *adj.* [ɔfi'tsjø:s] officious, semi-official.

öffn|en ['œfnən] *v/t.* (*ge-, h*) open; *a.* uncork (*bottle*); ⚕ dissect (*body*); *sich* ~ open; '2**er** *m* (-s/-) opener; '2**ung** *f* (-/-en) opening, aperture; '2**ungszeiten** *f/pl.* hours *pl.* of opening, business hours *pl.*

oft *adv.* [ɔft] often, frequently.

öfters *adv.* ['œftərs] *s.* oft.

'oftmal|lig *adj.* frequent, repeated; '.s *adv. s.* oft.

oh *int.* [o:] o(h)!

ohne ['o:nə] **1.** *prp.* (*acc.*) without; **2.** *cj.*: ~ daß, ~ zu *inf.* without *ger.*; ~'dies *adv.* anyhow, anyway; ~ gleichen *adv.* unequal(l)ed, matchless; ~'hin *adv. s.* ohnedies.

'Ohn|macht *f* (-/-en) powerlessness; impotence; *&* faint, unconsciousness; *in ~ fallen* faint, swoon; ~machtsanfall *&* [o:nmaxts'-] *m* fainting fit, swoon; 2mächtig *adj.* powerless; impotent; *&* unconscious; ~ werden faint, swoon.

Ohr [o:r] *n* (-[e]s/-en) ear; *fig. a.* hearing; *ein ~ haben für* have an ear for; *ganz ~ sein* be all ears; F *j-n übers ~ hauen* cheat s.o., *sl.* do s.o. (in the eye); *bis über die ~en* up to the ears *or* eyes.

Öhr [ø:r] *n* (-[e]s/-e) eye (*of needle*).

'Ohren|arzt *m* aurist, ear specialist; '2betäubend *adj.* deafening; ~leiden *n* ear-complaint; ~schmalz *n* ear-wax; ~schmaus *m* treat for the ears; ~schmerzen *m/pl.* earache; '~zeuge *m* ear-witness.

'Ohr|feige *f* box on the ear(s), slap in the face (*a. fig.*); 2feigen *v/t.* (*ge-, h*): *j-n ~* box s.o.'s ear(s), slap s.o.'s face; ~läppchen [~lɛpçən] *n* (-s/-) lobe of ear; '~ring *m* earring.

Ökonom|ie [økono'mi:] *f* (-/-n) economy; 2isch *adj.* [~'no:miʃ] economical.

Oktav [ɔk'ta:f] *n* (-s/-e) octavo; ~e *♪* [~və] *f* (-/-n) octave.

Oktober [ɔk'to:bər] *m* (-[s]/-) October.

Okul|ar *opt.* [oku'la:r] *n* (-s/-e) eyepiece, ocular; 2ieren *✗ v/t.* (*no -ge-, h*) inoculate, graft.

Öl [ø:l] *n* (-[e]s/-e) oil; ~ *ins Feuer gießen* add fuel to the flames; ~ *auf die Wogen gießen* pour oil on the (troubled) waters; ~baum *♀ m* olive-tree; ~berg *eccl. m* -[e]s/no *pl.*) Mount of Olives; 2en *v/t.* (*ge-, h*) oil; ⊕ *a.* lubricate; ~farbe *f* oil-colo(u)r, oil-paint; ~gemälde *n* oil-painting; ~heizung *f* oil heating; '2ig *adj.* oily (*a. fig.*).

Oliv|e [o'li:və] *f* (-/-n) olive; ~enbaum *♀ m* olive-tree; 2grün *adj.* olive(-green).

Öl|male'rei *f* oil-painting; '~quelle *f* oil-spring, gusher; oil-well; ~ung *f* (-/-en) oiling; ⊕ *a.* lubrication; *Letzte ~ eccl.* extreme unction.

Olympi|ade [olymp ja:də] *f* (-/-n) Olympiad; *a.* Olympic Games *pl.*; 2sch *adj.* [o'lympiʃ] Olympic; *Olympische Spiele pl.* Olympic Games *pl.*

Ölzweig *m* olive-branch.

Omelett [ɔm(ə)'lɛt] *n* (-[e]s/-e, -s), ~e [~'lɛt] *f* (-/-n) omelet(te).

Om|en ['o:mən] *n* (-s/-, *Omina*) omen, augury; 2inös *adj.* [omi'nø:s] ominous.

Omnibus ['ɔmnibus] *m* (-ses/-se) (omni)bus; (motor-)coach; '~haltestelle *f* bus-stop.

Onkel ['ɔŋkəl] *m* (-s/-, F -s) uncle.

Oper ['o:pər] *f* (-/-n) *♪* opera; opera-house.

Operat|eur [opəra'tø:r] *m* (-s/-e) operator; *&* surgeon; ~ion *&*, ✗ [~'tsjo:n] *f* (-/-en) operation; ~ionssaal *& m* operating room, *Am.* surgery; 2iv *& adj.* [~'ti:f] operative.

Operette *♪* [opə'retə] *f* (-/-n) operetta.

operieren [opə'ri:rən] (*no -ge-, h*) **1.** *v/t.*: *j-n ~* operate (up)on s.o. (*wegen* for); **2.** *&*, ✗ *v/i.* operate; *sich ~ lassen* undergo an operation.

'Opern|glas *n*, ~gucker F ['~gukər] *m* (-s/-) opera-glass(es *pl.*); '~haus *n* opera-house; '~sänger *m* opera-singer, operatic singer; '~text *m* libretto, book (of an opera).

Opfer [ɔpfər] *n* (-s/-) sacrifice; offering; victim (*a. fig.*); *ein ~ bringen* make a sacrifice; *j-m zum ~ fallen* be victimized by s.o.; ~gabe *f* offering; '2n (*ge-, h*) **1.** *v/t.* sacrifice; immolate; *sich für et.* ~ sacrifice o.s. for s.th.; **2.** *v/i.* (make a) sacrifice (*dat.* to); '~stätte *f* place of sacrifice; '~tod *m* sacrifice of one's life; '~ung *f* (-/-en) sacrificing, sacrifice; immolation.

Opium ['o:pjum] *n* (-s/no *pl.*) opium.

opponieren [ɔpo'ni:rən] *v/i.* (*no -ge-, h*) be opposed (*gegen* to), resist.

Opposition [ɔpozi'tsjo:n] *f* (-/-en) opposition (*a. parl.*); ~sführer *parl. m* opposition leader; ~spartei *parl. f* opposition party.

Optik ['ɔptik] *f* (-/,~-en) optics; *phot.* lens system; *fig.* aspect; '~er *m* (-s -) optician.

Optim|ismus [ɔpti'mismus] *m* (-/no *pl.*) optimism; ~ist *m* (-en/-en) optimist; 2istisch *adj.* optimistic.

'optisch *adj.* optic(al); ~e *Täuschung* optical illusion.

Orakel [o'ra:kəl] *n* (-s/-) oracle; 2haft *adj.* oracular; 2n *v/i.* (*no -ge-, h*) speak oracularly; '~spruch *m* oracle.

Orange [o'rã:ʒə] *f* (-/-n) orange; 2farben *adj.* orange(-colo[u]red); ~nbaum *♀ m* orange-tree.

Oratorium *♪* [ora'to:rjum] *n* (-s/ *Oratorien*) oratorio.

Orchester *♪* [ɔr'kɛstər] *n* (-s/-) orchestra.

Orchidee *♀* [ɔrçi'de:ə] *f* (-/-n) orchid.

Orden ['ɔrdən] *m* (-s/-) order (*a. eccl.*); order, medal, decoration.

'Ordens|band *n* ribbon (of an order); **'~bruder** *eccl. m* brother, friar; **'~gelübde** *eccl. n* monastic vow; **'~schwester** *eccl. f* sister, nun; **'~verleihung** *f* conferring (of) an order.

ordentlich *adj.* ['ɔrdəntliç] tidy; orderly; proper; regular; respectable; good, sound; **~er** *Professor univ.* professor in ordinary.

ordinär *adj.* [ɔrdi'nɛːr] common, vulgar, low.

ordn|en ['ɔrdnən] *v/t.* (ge-, h) put in order; arrange, fix (up); settle (*a.* † *liabilities*); **'2er** *m* (-s/-) *at festival, etc.*: steward; *for papers, etc.*: file.

'Ordnung *f* (-/-en) order; arrangement; system; rules *pl.*, regulations *pl.*; class; *in ~ bringen* put in order.

'ordnungs|gemäß, **'~mäßig 1.** *adj.* orderly, regular; **2.** *adv.* duly; **'2ruf** *parl. m* call to order; **'2strafe** *f* disciplinary penalty; fine; **'~widrig** *adj.* contrary to order, irregular; **'2zahl** *f* ordinal number.

Ordonnanz ✕ [ɔrdɔ'nants] *f* (-/-en) orderly.

Organ [ɔr'gaːn] *n* (-s/-e) organ.

Organisat|ion [ɔrganiza'tsjoːn] *f* (-/-en) organization; **~ionstalent** *n* organizing ability; **~or** [~'zaːtɔr] *m* (-s/-en) organizer; **2orisch** *adj.* [~ə'toːriʃ] organizational, organizing.

or'ganisch *adj.* organic.

organi'sieren *v/t.* (*no -ge-*, h) organize; *sl.* scrounge; (*nicht*) *organisiert(er Arbeiter*) (non-)unionist.

Organismus [ɔrga'nismus] *m* (-/Organismen) organism; *✻ a.* system.

Organist ♪ [ɔrga'nist] *m* (-en/-en) organist.

Orgel ♪ ['ɔrgəl] *f* (-/-n) organ, *Am. a.* pipe organ; **'~bauer** *m* organbuilder; **'~pfeife** *f* organ-pipe; **'~spieler** ♪ *m* organist.

Orgie ['ɔrgjə] *f* (-/-n) orgy.

Oriental|e [orien'taːlə] *m* (-n/-n) oriental; **2isch** *adj.* oriental.

orientier|en [orien'tiːrən] *v/t.* (*no -ge-*, h) inform, instruct; *sich ~* orient(ate) o.s. (*a. fig.*); inform o.s. (*über acc.* of); *gut orientiert sein über (acc.*) be well informed about, be familiar with; **2ung** *f* (-/-en) orientation; *fig. a.* information; *die ~ verlieren* lose one's bearings.

Origin|al [origi'naːl] **1.** *n* (-s/-e) original; **2.** 2 *adj.* original; **~alität** [~ali'tɛːt] *f* (-/-en) originality; **2ell** *adj.* [~'nɛl] original; *design, etc.*: ingenious.

Orkan [ɔr'kaːn] *m* (-[e]s/-e) hurricane; typhoon; **2artig** *adj.* storm: violent; *applause*: thunderous, frenzied.

Ornat [ɔr'naːt] *m* (-[e]s/-e) robe(s *pl.*), vestment.

Ort [ɔrt] *m* (-[e]s/-e) place; site; spot, point; locality; place, village, town; *~ der Handlung thea.* scene (of action); *an ~ und Stelle* on the spot; *höher(e)n ~(e)s* at higher quarters; **'2en** *v/t.* (ge-, h) locate.

ortho|dox *adj.* [ɔrto'dɔks] orthodox; **2graphie** [~gra'fiː] *f* (-/-n) orthography; **~graphisch** *adj.* [~'graː-fiʃ] orthographic(al); **2päde** ✻ [~'pɛːdə] *m* (-n/-n) orthop(a)edist; **2pädie** ✻ [~pɛ'diː] *f* (-/*no pl.*) orthop(a)edics, orthop(a)edy; **~pädisch** *adj.* [~'pɛːdiʃ] orthop(a)edic.

örtlich *adj* ['œrtliç] local; *✻ a.* topical; **'2keit** *f* (-/-en) locality.

'Orts|angabe *f* statement of place; **'2ansässig** *adj.* resident, local; **~ansässige** ['~gə] *m* (-n/-n) resident; **'~beschreibung** *f* topography; **'~besichtigung** *f* local inspection.

'Ortschaft *f* (-/-en) place, village.

'Orts|gespräch *teleph. n* local call; **'~kenntnis** *f* knowledge of a place; **'2kundig** *adj.* familiar with the locality; **'~name** *m* place-name; **'~verkehr** *m* local traffic; **'~zeit** *f* local time.

Öse ['øːzə] *f* (-/-n) eye, loop; eyelet (*of shoe*).

Ost *geogr.* [ɔst] east; **'~en** *m* (-s/*no pl.*) east; *the* East; *der Ferne (Nahe) ~* the Far (Near) East.

ostentativ *adj.* [ɔstɛnta'tiːf] ostentatious.

Oster|ei ['oːstar?-] *n* Easter egg; **'~fest** *n* Easter; **'~hase** *m* Easter bunny *or* rabbit; **'~lamm** *n* paschal lamb; **'~n** *n* (-/-) Easter.

Österreich|er ['øːstəraiçər] *m* (-s/-) Austrian; **2isch** *adj.* Austrian.

östlich ['œstliç] **1.** *adj.* eastern; *wind, etc.*: easterly; **2.** *adv.*: *~ von* east of.

ost|wärts *adv.* ['ɔstvɛrts] eastward(s); **'2wind** *m* east(erly) wind.

Otter zo. ['ɔtər] **1.** *m* (-s/-) otter; **2.** *f* (-/-n) adder, viper.

Ouvertüre ♪ [uver'tyːrə] *f* (-/-n) overture.

oval [o'vaːl] **1.** *adj.* oval; **2.** 2 *n* (-s/-e) oval.

Ovation [ova'tsjoːn] *f* (-/-en) ovation; *j-m ~en bereiten* give s.o. ovations.

Oxyd ♠ [ɔ'ksyːt] *n* (-[e]s/-e) oxide; **2ieren** [~y'diːrən] (*no -ge-*) **1.** *v/t.* (h) oxidize; **2.** *v/i.* (sein) oxidize.

Ozean ['oːtseaːn] *m* (-s/-e) ocean.

P

Paar [pɑːr] 1. *n* (-[e]s/-e) pair; couple; 2. 2 *adj.*: ein ~ a few, some; j-m ein ~ Zeilen schreiben drop s.o. a few lines; '2en *v/t.* (ge-, h) pair, couple; mate (*animals*); sich ~ (form a) pair; *animals*: mate; *fig.* join, unite; '~lauf *m sports*: pair-skating; '~läufer *m sports*: pair-skater; '2mal *adv.*: ein ~ several *or* a few times; '~ung *f* (-/-en) coupling; mating, copulation; *fig.* union; 2weise *adv.* in pairs *or* couples, by twos.

Pacht [paxt] *f* (-/-en) lease, tenure, tenancy; *money payment*: rent; '2en *v/t.* (ge-, h) (take on) lease; rent.

Pächter ['pɛçtər] *m* (-s/-), '~in *f* (-/-nen) lessee, lease-holder; tenant.

'**Pacht|ertrag** *m* rental; '~geld *n* rent; '~gut *n* farm; '~vertrag *m* lease; 2weise *adv.* on lease.

Pack [pak] 1. *m* -[e]s/-e, ~e) *s.* Packen²; 2. *n* (-[e]s/*no pl.*) rabble.

Päckchen ['pɛkçən] *n* (-s/-) small parcel, *Am. a.* package; ein ~ Zigaretten a pack(et) of cigarettes.

packen¹ ['pakən] (ge-, h) 1. *v/t.* pack (up); seize, grip, grasp, clutch; collar; *fig.* grip, thrill; F *pack dich!* F clear out!, *sl.* beat it!; 2. *v/i.* pack (up); 3. 2 *n* (-s/*no pl.*) packing.

Packen² [~] *m* (-s/-) pack(et), parcel; bale.

'**Packer** *m* (-s/-) packer; ~ei [~'raɪ] *f* 1. (-/-en) packing-room; 2. (-/*no pl.*) packing.

'**Pack|esel** *fig. m* drudge; '~material *n* packing materials *pl.*; '~papier *n* packing-paper, brown paper; '~pferd *n* pack-horse; ~ung *f* (-/-en) pack(age), packet; ~ pack; e-e ~ Zigaretten a pack(et) of cigarettes; '~wagen *m s.* Gepäckwagen.

Pädagog|e [pɛda'ɡoːɡə] *m* (-n/-n) pedagog(ue), education(al)ist; ~ik *f* (-/*no pl.*) pedagogics, pedagogy; 2isch *adj.* pedagogic(al).

Paddel ['padəl] *n* (-s/-) paddle; '~boot *n* canoe; '2n *v/i.* (ge-, h, sein) paddle, canoe.

Page ['pɑːʒə] *m* (-n/-n) page.

pah *int.* [pɑː] pah!, pooh!, pshaw!

Paket [pa'keːt] *n* (-[e]s/-e) parcel, packet, package; ~annahme ⍩ *f* parcel counter; ~karte ⍩ *f* dispatch-note; ~post ⍩ *f* parcel post; ~zustellung ⍩ *f* parcel delivery.

Pakt [pakt] *m* (-[e]s/-e) pact; agreement; treaty.

Palast [pa'last] *m* (-es/~e) palace.

Palm|e ⍩ ['palmə] *f* (-/-n) palm (-tree); '~öl *n* palm-oil; ~'sonntag *eccl. m* Palm Sunday.

panieren [pa'niːrən] *v/t.* (*no* -ge-, h) crumb.

Pani|k ['paːnik] *f* (-/-en) panic; stampede; '2sch *adj.* panic; von ~em Schrecken erfaßt panic-stricken.

Panne ['panə] *f* (-/-n) breakdown, *mot. a.* engine trouble; *tyres*: puncture; *fig.* blunder.

panschen ['panʃən] (ge-, h) 1. *v/i.* splash (about); 2. *v/t.* adulterate (*wine, etc.*).

Panther *zo.* ['pantər] *m* (-s/-) panther.

Pantine [pan'tiːnə] *f* (-/-n) clog.

Pantoffel [pan'tɔfəl] *m* (-s/-n, F -) slipper; *unter dem* ~ *stehen* be henpecked; ~held F *m* henpecked husband.

pantschen ['pantʃən] *v/i. and v/t.* (ge-, h) *s.* panschen.

Panzer ['pantsər] *m* (-s/-) armo(u)r; ✗ tank; *zo.* shell; '~abwehr ✗ *f* anti-tank defen|ce, *Am.* -se; '~glas *n* bullet-proof glass; '~hemd *n* coat of mail; ~kreuzer ⍩ *m* armo(u)red cruiser; 2n *v/t.* (ge-, h) armo(u)r; '~platte *f* armo(u)r-plate; ~schiff ✗ *n* ironclad; '~schrank *m* safe; '~ung *f* (-/-en) armo(u)r-plating; '~wagen *m* armo(u)red car; ✗ tank.

Papa [pa'pɑː, F 'papa] *m* (-s/-s) papa, F pa, dad(dy), *Am. a.* pop.

Papagei *orn.* [papa'ɡaɪ] *m* (-[e]s, -en/-e[n]) parrot.

Papier [pa'piːr] *n* (-s/-e) paper; ~e *pl.* papers *pl.*, documents *pl.*; papers *pl.*, identity card; ein Bogen ~ a sheet of paper; 2en *adj.* (of) paper; *fig.* dull; ~fabrik *f* paper-mill; ~geld *n* (-[e]s/*no pl.*) paper-money; banknotes *pl.*, *Am.* bills *pl.*; ~korb *m* waste-paper-basket; ~schnitzel F *n or m/pl.* scraps *pl.* of paper; ~tüte *f* paper-bag; ~waren *f/pl.* stationery.

Papp|band *m* (-[e]s/~e) paperback; ~deckel *m* pasteboard, cardboard.

Pappe ['papə] *f* (-/-n) pasteboard, cardboard.

Pappel ⍙ ['papəl] *f* (-/-n) poplar.

päppeln F ['pɛpəln] *v/t.* (ge-, h) feed (with pap).

papp|en F ['papən] (ge-, h) 1. *v/t.* paste; 2. *v/i.* stick; '~ig *adj.* sticky; '2karton *m*, '2schachtel *f* cardboard box, carton.

Papst [pɑːpst] *m* (-es/~e) pope.

päpstlich *adj.* ['pɛːpstliç] papal.

Papsttum *n* (-s/*no pl.*) papacy.

Parade [pa'rɑːdə] *f* (-/-n) parade; ✗ review; *fencing*: parry.

Paradies [para'diːs] *n* (-es/-e) paradise; ~isch *fig. adj.* [~'diːzɪʃ] heavenly, delightful.

paradox *adj.* [para'dɔks] paradoxical.

Paragraph [para'grɑːf] *m* (-en, -s/-en) article, section; paragraph; section-mark.

parallel *adj.* [para'leːl] parallel; 2e *f* (-/-n) parallel.

Paralys|e [para'lyːzə] *f* (-/-n) paralysis; 2ieren ⚡ [‿y'ziːrən] *v/t.* (*no* -ge-, *h*) paralyse.

Parasit [para'ziːt] *m* (-en/-en) parasite.

Parenthese [paren'teːzə] *f* (-/-n) parenthesis.

Parforcejagd [par'fɔrs-] *f* hunt (-ing) on horseback (with hounds), *after hares:* coursing.

Parfüm [par'fyːm] *n* (-s/-e, -s) perfume, scent; ‿erie [‿ymə'riː] *f* (-/-n) perfumery; 2ieren [‿y'miːrən] *v/t.* (*no* -ge-, *h*) perfume, scent.

pari ⁺ *adv.* ['paːri] par; *al* ‿ at par.

parieren [pa'riːrən] (*no* -ge-, *h*) **1.** *v/t.* fencing: parry (*a. fig.*); pull up (*horse*); **2.** *v/i.* obey (*j-m s.o.*).

Park [park] *m* (-s/-s, -e) park; ‿anlage *f* park; ‿aufseher *m* parkkeeper; 2en (ge-, *h*) **1.** *v/i.* park; ~ verboten! no parking!; **2.** *v/t.* park.

Parkett [par'kɛt] *n* (-[e]s/-e) parquet; *thea.* (orchestra) stalls *pl.*, *esp. Am.* orchestra *or* parquet.

Park|gebühr *f* parking-fee; ‿licht *n* parking light; ‿platz *m* (car-) park, parking lot; ‿uhr *mot. f* parking meter.

Parlament [parla'ment] *n* (-[e]s/-e) parliament; 2arisch *adj.* [‿'taːriʃ] parliamentary.

Parodie [paro'diː] *f* (-/-n) parody; 2ren *v/t.* (*no* -ge-, *h*) parody.

Parole [pa'roːlə] *f* (-/-n) ⚔ password, watchword; *fig.* slogan.

Partei [par'tai] *f* (-/-en) party (*a. pol.*); *j-s* ~ *ergreifen* take s.o.'s part, side with s.o.; ‿apparat *pol. m* party machinery; ‿gänger [‿genər] *m* (-s/-) partisan; 2isch *aay*, ‿lich *adj.* partial (*für* to); prejudiced (*gegen* against); 2los *pol. adj.* independent; ‿mitglied *pol. n* party member; ‿programm *pol. n* platform; ‿tag *pol. m* convention; ‿zugehörigkeit *pol. f* party membership.

Parterre [par'tɛr] *n* (-s/-s) ground floor, *Am.* first floor; *thea.:* pit, *Am.* parterre, *Am.* parquet circle.

Partie [par'tiː] *f* (-/-n) ⁺ parcel, lot; outing, excursion; *cards, etc.:* game; ♪ part; *marriage* match.

Partitur ♪ [parti'tuːr] *f* (-/-en) score.

Partizip *gr.* [parti'tsiːp] *n* (-s/-ien) participle.

Partner ['partnər] *m* (-s/-), ‿in *f* (-/-nen) partner; *film: a.* co-star; ‿schaft *f* (-/-en) partnership.

Parzelle [par'tsɛlə] *f* (-/-n) plot, lot, allotment.

Paß [pas] *m* (Passes/Pässe) pass;

passage; *football, etc.:* pass; passport.

Passage [pa'saːʒə] *f* (-/-n) passage; arcade.

Passagier [pasa'ʒiːr] *m* (-s/-e) passenger, *in taxis: a.* fare; ‿flugzeug *n* air liner.

Passah ['pasa] *n* (-s/*no pl.*), '‿fest *n* Passover.

Passant [pa'sant] *m* (-en/-en), ‿in *f* (-/-nen) passer-by.

'**Paßbild** *n* passport photo(graph).

passen ['pasən] (ge-, *h*) **1.** *v/i.* fit (*j-m s.o.*; *auf acc. or für or zu et. s.th.*); suit (*j-m s.o.*), be convenient; *cards, football:* pass; ~ *zu* go with, match (with); **2.** *v/refl.* be fit *or* proper; '‿d *adj.* fit, suitable; convenient (*für* for).

passier|bar *adj.* [pa'siːrbaːr] passable, practicable; ‿en (*no* -ge-) **1.** *v/i.* (*sein*) happen; **2.** *v/t.* (*h*) pass (over *or* through); 2schein *m* pass, permit.

Passion [pa'sjoːn] *f* (-/-en) passion; hobby; *eccl.* Passion.

passiv ['pasiːf] **1.** *adj.* passive; **2.** 2 *gr. n* (-s/-e) passive (voice); 2a ⁺ [pa'siːva] *pl.* liabilities *pl.*

Paste ['pastə] *f* (-/-n) paste.

Pastell [pa'stɛl] *n* (-[e]s/-e) pastel.

Pastete [pa'steːtə] *f* (-/-n) pie; ‿bäcker *m* pastry-cook.

Pate ['paːtə] **1.** *m* (-n/-n) godfather; godchild; **2.** *f* (-/-n) godmother; ‿nkind *n* godchild; '‿nschaft *f* (-/-en) sponsorship.

Patent [pa'tent] *n* (-[e]s/-e) ✕ commission; *ein* ~ *anmelden* apply for a patent; ‿amt *n* Patent Office; ‿anwalt *m* patent agent; 2ieren [‿'tiːrən] *v/t.* (*no* -ge-, *h*) patent; *et.* ‿ *lassen* take out a patent for s.th.; ‿inhaber *m* patentee; ‿urkunde *f* letters patent.

Patient [pa'tsjent] *m* (-en/-en), ‿in *f* (-/-nen) patient.

Patin [paːtin] *f* (-/-nen) godmother.

Patriot [patri'oːt] *m* (-en/-en), ‿in *f* (-/-nen) patriot.

Patron [pa'troːn] *m* (-s/-e) patron, protector; *contp.* fellow, bloke, customer; ‿at [‿o'naːt] *n* (-[e]s/-e) patronage; ‿e [pa'troːnə] *f* (-/-n) cartridge, *Am. a.* shell.

Patrouille ✕ [pa'truljə] *f* (-/-n) patrol; 2ieren [‿'jiːrən] *v/i.* (*no* -ge-, *h*) patrol.

Patsch|e F *fig.* ['patʃə] *f* (-/*no pl.*): *in der* ~ *sitzen* be in a fix *or* scrape; '2en F (ge-) **1.** *v/i.* (*h, sein*) splash; **2.** *v/t.* (*h*) slap; '2'naß *adj.* dripping wet, drenched.

patzig F *adj.* ['patsiç] snappish.

Pauke ♪ ['paukə] *f* (-/-n) kettledrum; '2n F *v/i. and v/t.* (ge-, *h*) *school:* cram.

Pauschal|e [pau'ʃaːlə] *f* (-/-n), ‿summe *f* lump sum.

Pause ['pauzə] *f* (-/-n) pause, stop, interval; *school*: break, *Am.* recess; *thea.* interval, *Am.* intermission; *♪* rest; *drawing*: tracing; '♀n *v/t.* (ge-, h) trace; '♀nlos *adj.* uninterrupted, incessant; '♀nzeichen *n wireless*: interval signal.

pau'sieren *v/i.* (no -ge-, h) pause.

Pavian *zo.* ['pɑːviaːn] *m* (-s/-e) baboon.

Pavillon ['paviljõ] *m* (-s/-s) pavilion.

Pazifist [patsi'fist] *m* (-en/-en) pacif(ic)ist.

Pech [pεç] *n* **1.** (-[e]s /-e) pitch; **2.** F *fig.* (-[e]s/no *pl.*) bad luck; '♀strähne F *f* run of bad luck; '♀vogel F *m* unlucky fellow.

pedantisch *adj.* [pe'dantiʃ] pedantic; punctilious, meticulous.

Pegel ['peːgəl] *m* (-s/-) water-ga(u)ge.

peilen ['pailən] *v/t.* (ge-, h) sound (*depth*); take the bearings of (*coast*).

Pein [pain] *f* (-/no *pl.*) torment, torture, anguish; ♀igen ['♀igən] *v/t.* (ge-, h) torment; ♀iger ['♀igər] *m* (-s/-) tormentor.

'peinlich *adj.* painful, embarrassing; particular, scrupulous, meticulous.

Peitsche ['paitʃə] *f* (-/-n) whip; '♀n *v/t.* (ge-, h) whip; '♀nhieb *m* lash.

Pelikan *orn.* ['peːlikaːn] *m* (-s/-e) pelican.

Pell|e ['pεlə] *f* (-/-n) skin, peel; '♀en *v/t.* (ge-, h) skin, peel; '♀kartoffeln *f/pl.* potatoes *pl.* (boiled) in their jackets *or* skins.

Pelz [pεlts] *m* (-es/-e) fur; *garment*: mst furs *pl.*; '♀gefüttert *adj.* furlined; '♀händler *m* furrier; '♀handschuh *m* furred glove; '♀ig *adj.* furry; *♀ tongue*: furred; '♀mantel *m* fur coat; '♀stiefel *m* fur-lined boot; '♀tiere *n/pl.* fur-covered animals *pl.*

Pendel ['pεndəl] *n* (-s/-) pendulum; '♀n *v/i.* (ge-, h) oscillate, swing; ♀ shuttle, *Am.* commute; '♀tür *f* swing-door; '♀verkehr *m* shuttle service.

Pension [pã'sjõː, pɛn'zjoːn] *f* (-/-en) (old-age) pension, retired pay; board; boarding-house; ♀är [♀o-'nɛːr] *m* (-s/-e) (old-age) pensioner; boarder; ♀at [♀o'naːt] *n* (-[e]s/-e) boarding-school; ♀ieren [♀o'niːrən] *v/t.* (no -ge-, h) pension (off); *sich ~ lassen* retire; ♀sgast *m* boarder.

Pensum ['pεnzum] *n* (-s/Pensen, Pensa) task, lesson.

perfekt 1. *adj.* [pεr'fεkt] perfect; *agreement*: settled; **2.** ♀ *gr.* ['~] *n* (-[e]s/-e) perfect (tense).

Pergament [pεrga'mεnt] *n* (-[e]s/-e) parchment.

Period|e [pe'rjoːdə] *f* (-/-n) period; *♀* periods *pl.*; ♀isch *adj.* periodic (-al).

Peripherie [perife'riː] *f* (-/-n) circumference; outskirts *pl.* (*of town*).

Perle ['pεrlə] *f* (-/-n) pearl; *of glass*: bead; '♀n *v/i.* (ge-, h) sparkle; '♀nkette *f* pearl necklace; '♀nschnur *f* string of pearls *or* beads.

'Perl|muschel *zo. f* pearl-oyster; ♀mutt ['♀mut] *n* (-s/no *pl.*), ♀'mutter *f* (-/no *pl.*) mother-of-pearl.

Person [pεr'zoːn] *f* (-/-en) person; *thea.* character.

Personal [pεrzo'naːl] *n* (-s/no *pl.*) staff, personnel; ♀abteilung *f* personnel office; ♀angaben *f/pl.* personal data *pl.*; ♀ausweis *m* identity card; ♀chef *m* personnel officer *or* manager *or* director; ♀ien [♀ɔən] *pl.* particulars *pl.*, personal data *pl.*; ♀pronomen *gr. n* personal pronoun.

Per'sonen|verzeichnis *n* list of persons; *thea.* dramatis personae *pl.*; ♀wagen *m* ♀ (passenger-)carriage *or Am.* car, coach; *mot.* (motor-)car; ♀zug ♀ *m* passenger train.

personifizieren [pεrzonifi'tsiːrən] *v/t.* (no -ge-, h) personify.

persönlich *adj.* [pεr'zøːnliç] personal; *opinion, letter*: *a.* private; ♀keit *f* (-/-en) personality; personage.

Perücke [pe'rykə] *f* (-/-n) wig.

Pest *♀* [pεst] *f* (-/no *pl.*) plague.

Petersilie *♀* [petər'ziːljə] *f* (-/-n) parsley.

Petroleum [pe'troːleum] *n* (-s/no *pl.*) petroleum; *for lighting, etc.*: paraffin, *esp. Am.* kerosene.

Pfad [pfaːt] *m* (-[e]s/-e) path, track; '♀finder *m* boy scout; '♀finderin *f* (-/-nen) girl guide, *Am.* girl scout.

Pfahl [pfaːl] *m* (-[e]s/¨e) stake, pale, pile.

Pfand [pfant] *n* (-[e]s/¨er) pledge; *♀* deposit, security; *real estate*: mortgage; *game*: forfeit; '♀brief *♀ m* debenture (bond).

pfänden *♀♀* ['pfεndən] *v/t.* (ge-, h) seize *s.th.*; distrain upon *s.o. or s.th.*

'Pfand|haus *n s.* Leihhaus; '♀leiher *m* (-s/-) pawnbroker; '♀schein *m* pawn-ticket.

'Pfändung *♀♀ f* (-/-en) seizure; distraint.

Pfann|e ['pfanə] *f* (-/-n) pan; '♀kuchen *m* pancake.

Pfarr|bezirk ['pfar-] *m* parish; '♀er *m* (-s/-) parson; *Church of England*: rector, vicar; *dissenters*: minister; '♀gemeinde *f* parish; '♀haus *n* parsonage; *Church of England*: rectory, vicarage; '♀kirche *f* parish church; '♀stelle *f* (-/-n) (church) living.

Pfau *orn.* [pfau] *m* (-[e]s/-en) peacock.

Pfeffer ['pfεfər] *m* (-s/-) pepper; '♀gurke *f* gherkin; '♀ig *adj.* peppery; '♀kuchen *m* gingerbread;

⁓minze ⚹ ['⁓mintsə] *f* (-/*no pl.*) peppermint; '⁓**minzplätzchen** *n* peppermint; '**⁊n** *v/t* (ge-, h) pepper; '⁓**streuer** *m* (-s/-) pepperbox, pepper-castor, pepper-caster.

Pfeife ['pfaifə] *f* (-/-*n*) whistle; ⚸ fife; pipe (*of organ, etc.*); ⚓ tobacco-) pipe; '**⊋n** (*irr.*, ge-, h) **1.** *v/i.* whistle (*dat.* to, for); radio. howl; pipe; **2.** *v/t.* whistle; pipe; ⁓**kopf** *m* pipe-bowl.

Pfeil [pfail] *m* (-[e]s/-e) arrow.

Pfeiler ['pfailər] *m* (-s/-) pillar (*a. fig.*); pier (*of bridge, etc.*).
'**pfeil**'**schnell** *adj.* (as) swift as an arrow; '⊋**spitze** *f* arrow-head.

Pfennig ['pfeniç] *m* -[e]s/-e) coin: pfennig; *fig.* penny, farthing.

Pferch [pferç] *m* (-[e]s/-e) fold, pen; '**⊋n** *v/t.* (ge-, h) fold, pen; *fig.* cram.

Pferd zo. [pfe:rt] *n* (-[e]s/-e) horse; zu ⁓e on horseback.

Pferde|geschirr ['pfe:rdə-] *n* harness; ⁓**koppel** *f* (-/-*n*) paddock, *Am. a.* corral; ⁓**rennen** *n* horse-race; ⁓**schwanz** *m* horse's tail; hair-style: pony-tail; ⁓**stall** *m* stable; '⁓**stärke** ⊕ *f* horsepower.

pfiff[1] [pfif] *pret. of* pfeifen.

Pfiff[2] *m* (-[e]s/-e) whistle; *fig.* trick; '⊋**ig** *adj.* cunning, artful.

Pfingst|en *eccl.* ['pfiŋstən] *n* (-/-), '⁓**fest** *eccl.* *n* Whitsun(tide); '⁓**'montag** *eccl.* *m* Whit Monday; '⁓**rose** ⚹ *f* peony; '⁓**sonntag** *eccl.* *m* Whit Sunday.

Pfirsich ['pfirziç] *m* (-[e]s/-e) peach.

Pflanz|e ['pflantsə] *f* (-/-*n*) plant; '⊋**en** *v/t.* (ge-, h) plant, set; pot; ⁓**enfaser** *f* vegetable fib|re, *Am.* -er; ⁓**enfett** *n* vegetable fat; ⊋**en**-**fressend** *adj.* herbivorous; ⁓**er** *m* (-s/-) planter; '⁓**ung** *f* (-/-*en*) plantation.

Pflaster ['pflastər] *n* (-s/-) ✚ plaster; road: pavement; '⁓**er** *m* (-s/-) paver, pavio(u)r; '⊋**n** *v/t.* (ge-, h) ✚ plaster; pave (road); ⁓**stein** *m* paving-stone; cobble.

Pflaume ['pflaumə] *f* (-/-*n*) plum; dried: prune.

Pflege ['pfle:gə] *f* (-/-*n*) care; ✚ nursing; cultivation (*of art, garden, etc.*); ⊕ maintenance; *in* geben put out (*child*) to nurse; *in* nehmen take charge of; ⊋**bedürftig** *adj.* needing care; ⁓**befohlne** ['⁓bəfo:lənə] *m*, *f* (-*n*/-*n*) charge; ⁓**eltern** *pl.* foster-parents *pl.*; '⁓**heim** ✚ *n* nursing home; ⁓**kind** *n* foster-child; '⊋**n** (ge-, h) **1.** *v/t.* take care of; attend (to); foster (*child*); ✚ nurse; maintain; cultivate (*art, garden*); **2.** *v/i. zu inf.* be accustomed *or* used *or* wont to *inf.*, be in the habit of *ger.*; *sie pflegte zu sagen* she used to say; '⁓**r** *m* (-s/-) fosterer; ✚ male nurse;

trustee; ✚ guardian, curator; '⁓**rin** *f* (-/-*nen*) nurse.

Pflicht [pfliçt] *f* (-/-en) duty (*gegen* to); obligation; '⊋**bewußt** *adj.* conscious of one's duty; ⊋**eifrig** *adj.*zealous; '⁓**erfüllung** *f* performance of one's duty; ⁓**fach** *n* school, univ.: compulsory subject; '⁓**gefühl** *n* sense of duty; ⊋**gemäß** *adj.* dutiful; ⊋**getreu** *adj.* dutiful, loyal; ⊋**schuldig** *adj.* in duty bound; ⊋**vergessen** *adj.* undutiful, disloyal; ⁓**verteidiger** ✚ *m* assigned counsel.

Pflock [pflɔk] *m* (-[e]s/⁓e) plug, peg.

pflücken ['pflykən] *v/t.* (ge-, h) pick, gather, pluck.

Pflug [pflu:k] *m* (-[e]s/⁓e) plough, *Am.* plow.

pflügen ['pfly:gən] *v/t. and v/i.* (ge-, h) plough, *Am.* plow.

Pforte ['pfɔrtə] *f* (-/-*n*) gate, door.

Pförtner ['pfœrtnər] *m* (-s/-) gate-keeper, door-keeper, porter, janitor.

Pfosten ['pfɔstən] *m* (-s/-) post.

Pfote [pfo:tə] *f* (-/-*n*) paw.

Pfropf [pfrɔpf] *m* (-[e]s/-e) *s.* Pfropfen.

Pfropfen 1. *m* (-s/-) stopper; cork; plug; ✚ clot (of blood); **2.** ⚹ *v/t.* (ge-, h) stopper; cork; *fig.* cram; ⚹ graft.

Pfründe *eccl.* ['pfryndə] *f* (-/-*n*) prebend; benefice, (church) living.

Pfuhl [pfu:l] *m* (-[e]s/-e) pool, puddle; *fig.* sink, slough.

pfui *int.* [pfui] fie!, for shame!

Pfund [pfunt] *n* (-[e]s/-e) pound; ⊋**ig** ⸿ *adj.* ['⁓diç] great, *Am.* swell; ⊋**weise** *adv.* by the pound.

pfusch|en F ['pfuʃən] (ge-, h) **1.** *v/i.* bungle; **2.** *v/t.* bungle, botch; ⊋**erei** F [⁓rai] *f* (-/-*en*) bungle, botch.

P'tutze ['pfytsə] *f* (-/-*n*) puddle, pool.

Phänomen [fɛno'me:n] *n* (-s/-e) phenomenon; ⊋**al** *adj.* [⁓e'na:l] phenomenal.

Phantasie [fanta'zi:] *f* (-/-*n*) imagination, fancy; vision; ♪ fantasia; ⊋**ren** (*no* -ge-, h) **1.** *v/i.* dream; ramble; ✚ be delirious *or* raving; ♪ improvise; **2.** *v/t.* dream; ♪ improvise.

Phantast [fan'tast] *m* (-en/-en) visionary, dreamer; ⊋**isch** *adj.* fantastic; F great, terrific.

Phase ['fa:zə] *f* (-/-*n*) phase (*a.* ⚡), stage.

Philanthrop [filan'tro:p] *m* (-en/-en) philanthropist.

Philolog|e [filo'lo:gə] *m* (-n/-n), ⁓**in** *f* (-/-*nen*) philologist; ⁓**ie** [⁓o-'gi:] *f* (-/-*n*) philology.

Philosoph [filo'zo:f] *m* (-en/-en) philosopher; ⁓**ie** [⁓o'fi:] *f* (-/-*n*) philosophy; ⊋**ieren** [⁓o'fi:rən] *v/i.* (*no* -ge-, h) philosophize (*über acc.* on); ⊋**isch** *adj.* [⁓'zo:fiʃ] philosophical.

Phlegma ['flɛgma] n (-s/no pl.) phlegm; ♀**tisch** adj. [~'maːtiʃ] phlegmatic.

phonetisch adj. [fo'neːtiʃ] phonetic.

Phosphor ♀ ['fɔsfɔr] m (-s/no pl.) phosphorus.

Photo F ['foːto] **1.** n (-s/-s) photo; **2.** m (-s/-s) = '~**apparat** m camera.

Photograph [foto'graːf] m (-en/-en) photographer; ~**ie** [~a'fiː] f **1.** (-/-n) photograph, F: photo, picture; **2.** (-/no pl.) as an art: photography; ♀**ieren** [~a'fiːrən] (no -ge-, h) **1.** v/t. photograph; take a picture of; sich ~ lassen have one's photo(graph) taken; **2.** v/i. photograph; ♀**isch** adj. [~'graːfiʃ] photographic.

Photo|ko'pie f photostat; ~**ko'pier-gerät** n photostat; '~**zelle** f photo-electric cell.

Phrase ['fraːzə] f (-/-n) phrase.

Physik [fy'ziːk] f (-/no pl.) physics sg.; ♀**alisch** adj. [~i'kaːliʃ] physical; ~**er** ['fyːzikər] m (-s/-) physicist.

physisch adj. ['fyːziʃ] physical.

Pian|ist [pia'nist] m (-en/-en) pianist; ~**o** [pi'aːno] n (-s/-s) piano.

Picke ⊕ ['pikə] f (-/-n) pick(axe).

Pickel ['pikəl] m (-s/-) ♀ pimple; ⊕ pick(axe); ice-pick; ♀**ig** adj. pimpled, pimply.

picken ['pikən] v/i. and v/t. (ge-, h) pick, peck.

picklig adj. ['pikliç] s. pickelig.

Picknick ['piknik] n (-s/-e, -s) pic-nic.

piekfein F adj. ['piːk'-] smart, tip-top, slap-up.

piep(s)en ['piːp(s)ən] v/i. (ge-, h) cheep, chirp, peep; squeak.

Pietät [pie'tɛːt] f (-/no pl.) reverence; piety; ♀**los** adj. irreverent; ♀**voll** adj. reverent.

Pik [piːk] **1.** m (-s/-e, -s) peak; ♀ F m (-s/-e): e-n ~ auf j-n haben bear s.o. a grudge; **3.** n (-s/-s) cards: spade(s pl.).

pikant adj. [pi'kant] piquant, spicy (both a. fig.); das Pikante the piquancy.

Pike ['piːkə] f (-/-n) pike; von der ~ auf dienen rise from the ranks.

Pilger ['pilgər] m (-s/-) pilgrim; '~**fahrt** f pilgrimage; ♀**n** v/i. (ge-, sein) go on or make a pilgrimage; wander.

Pille ['pilə] f (-/-n) pill.

Pilot [pi'loːt] m (-en/-en) pilot.

Pilz ♀ [pilts] m (-es/-e) fungus, edible: mushroom, inedible: toad-stool.

pimp(e)lig F adj. ['pimp(ə)liç] sickly; effeminate.

Pinguin orn. ['piŋguiːn] m (-s/-e) penguin.

Pinsel ['pinzəl] m (-s/-) brush; F fig. simpleton; ♀**n** v/t. and v/i. (ge-, h) paint; daub; '~**strich** m stroke of the brush.

Pinzette [pin'tsɛtə] f (-/-n) (e-e a pair of) tweezers pl.

Pionier [pio'niːr] m (-s/-e) pioneer, Am. a. trail blazer; ✗ engineer.

Pirat [pi'raːt] m (-en/-en) pirate.

Pirsch hunt. [pirʃ] f (-/no pl.) deer-stalking, Am. a. still hunt.

Piste ['pistə] f (-/-n) skiing, etc.: course; ✈ runway.

Pistole [pis'toːlə] f (-/-n) pistol, Am. F a. gun, rod; ~**ntasche** f holster.

placieren [pla'siːrən] v/t. (no -ge-, h) place; sich ~ sports: be placed (second, etc.).

Plackerei F [plakə'raɪ] f (-/-en) drudgery.

plädieren [plɛ'diːrən] v/i. (no -ge-, h) plead (für for).

Plädoyer ♫ [plɛdoa'jeː] n (-s/-s) pleading.

Plage ['plaːgə] f (-/-n) trouble, nuisance, F plague; torment; ♀**n** v/t. (ge-, h) torment; trouble, bother; F plague; sich ~ toil, drudge.

Plagiat [plag'jaːt] n (-[e]s/-e) plagiarism; ein ~ begehen plagiarize.

Plakat [pla'kaːt] n (-[e]s/-e) poster, placard, bill; ~**säule** f advertisement pillar.

Plakette [pla'kɛtə] f (-/-n) plaque.

Plan [plaːn] m (-[e]s/~e) plan; design, intention; scheme.

Plane ['plaːnə] f (-/-n) awning, tilt.

'**planen** v/t. (ge-, h) plan; scheme.

Planet [pla'neːt] m (-en/-en) planet.

planieren ⊕ [pla'niːrən] v/t. (no -ge-, h) level.

Planke ['plaŋkə] f (-/-n) plank, board.

plänkeln ['plɛŋkəln] v/i. (ge-, h) skirmish (a. fig.).

'**plan|los** **1.** adj. planless, aimless, desultory; **2.** adv. at random; '~**mäßig** **1.** adj. systematic, planned; **2.** adv. as planned.

planschen ['planʃən] v/i. (ge-, h) splash, paddle.

Plantage [plan'taːʒə] f (-/-n) plantation.

Plapper|maul F ['plapər-] n chatterbox; '♀**n** F v/i. (ge-, h) chatter, prattle, babble.

plärren F ['plɛrən] v/i. and v/t. (ge-, h) blubber; bawl.

Plasti|k [plastik] **1.** f (-/no pl.) plastic art; **2.** f (-/-en) sculpture; ♫ plastic; **3.** ⊕ n (-s/-s) plastic; '♀**sch** adj. plastic; three-dimensional.

Platin [pla'tiːn] n (-s/no pl.) platinum.

plätschern ['plɛtʃərn] v/i. (ge-, h) dabble, splash; water: ripple, murmur.

platt adj. [plat] flat, level, even; fig. trivial, commonplace, trite; F fig. flabbergasted.

Plättbrett ['plɛt-] n ironing-board.

Platte ['platə] f (-/-n) plate; dish; sheet (of metal, etc.); flag, slab (of stone); mountain: ledge; top (of table); tray, salver; disc, record; F fig. bald pate; kalte ~ cold meat.

plätten ['plɛtən] v/t. (ge-, h) iron.

'Platten|spieler m record-player; '~teller m turn-table.

'Platt|form f platform; '~fuß m ❦ flat-foot; F mot. flat; ~heit fig. f (-/-en) triviality; commonplace, platitude, Am. sl. a. bromide.

Platz [plats] m (-es/~e) place; spot, Am. a. point; room, space; site; seat; square; round: circus; sports: ground; tennis: court; ~ behalten remain seated; ~ machen make way or room (dat. for); ~ nehmen take a seat, sit down, Am. a. have a seat; ist hier noch ~? is this seat taken or engaged or occupied?; den dritten ~ belegen sports: be placed third, come in third; ~anweiserin f (-/-nen) usherette.

Plätzchen ['plɛtsçən] n (-s/-) snug place; spot; biscuit, Am. cookie.

'platzen v/i. (ge-, sein) burst; explode; crack, split.

'Platz|patrone f blank cartridge; '~regen m downpour.

Plauder|ei [plaudə'rai] f (-/-en) chat; talk; small talk; '2n v/i. (ge-, h) (have a) chat (mit with), talk (to); chatter.

plauz int. [plauts] bang!

Pleite F ['plaitə] 1. f (-/-n) smash; fig. failure; 2. 2 F adj. (dead) broke, Am. sl. bust.

Plissee [pli'se:] n (-s/-s) pleating; ~rock m pleated skirt.

Plomb|e ['plɔmbə] f (-/-n) (lead) seal; stopping, filling (of tooth); 2ieren [~'bi:rən] v/t. (no -ge-, h) seal; stop, fill (tooth).

plötzlich adj. ['plœtsliç] sudden.

plump adj. [plump] clumsy, ~s int. plump, plop; ~sen v/i. (ge-, sein) plump, plop, flop.

Plunder F ['plundər] m (-s/no pl.) lumber, rubbish, junk.

plündern ['plyndərn] (ge-, h) 1. v/t. plunder, pillage, loot, sack; 2. v/i. plunder, loot.

Plural gr. ['plu:ra:l] m (-s/-e) plural (number).

plus adv. [plus] plus.

Plusquamperfekt gr. ['pluskvamperfɛkt] n (-s/-e) pluperfect (tense), past perfect.

Pöbel ['pø:bəl] m (-s/no pl.) mob, rabble; 2haft adj. low, vulgar.

pochen ['pɔxən] v/i. (ge-, h) knock, rap, tap; heart: beat, throb, thump; auf sein Recht ~ stand on one's rights.

Pocke ❦ ['pɔkə] f (-/-n) pock; '~n ❦ pl. smallpox; '2nnarbig adj. pock-marked.

Podest [po'dɛst] n, m (-es/-e) pedestal (a. fig.).

Podium ['po:dium] n (-s/Podien) podium, platform, stage.

Poesie [poe'zi:] f (-/-n) poetry.

Poet [po'e:t] m (-en/-en) poet; 2isch adj. poetic(al).

Pointe [po'ɛ̃:tə] f (-/-n) point.

Pokal [po'ka:l] m (-s/-e) goblet; sports: cup; ~endspiel n sports: cup final; ~spiel n football: cup-tie.

Pökel|fleisch ['pø:kəl-] n salted meat; 2n v/t. (ge-, h) pickle, salt.

Pol [po:l] m (-s/-e) pole; ❦ a. terminal; 2ar adj. [po'la:r] polar (a. ❦).

Pole ['po:lə] m (-n/-n) Pole.

Polemi|k [po'le:mik] f (-/-en) polemic(s pl.); 2sch adj. polemic (-al); 2sieren [~emi'zi:rən] v/i. (no -ge-, h) polemize.

Police [po'li:s(ə)] f (-/-n) policy.

Polier ⊕ [po'li:r] m (-s/-e) foreman; 2en v/t. (no -ge-, h) polish, burnish; furbish.

Politi|k [poli'ti:k] f (-/~-en) policy; politics sg., pl.; ~ker [po'li:tikər] m (-s/-) politician; statesman; 2sch adj. [po'li:tiʃ] political; 2sieren [~iti'zi:rən] v/i. (no -ge-, h) talk politics.

Politur [poli'tu:r] f (-/-en) polish; lust|re, Am. -er, finish.

Polizei [poli'tsai] f (-/~-en) police; ~beamte m police officer; ~knüppel m truncheon, Am. club; ~kommissar m inspector; 2lich adj. (of or by the) police; ~präsident m president of police; Brt. Chief Constable, Am. Chief of Police; ~präsidium n police headquarters pl.; ~revier n police-station; police precinct; ~schutz m: unter ~ under police guard; ~streife f police patrol; police squad; ~stunde f (-/no pl.) closing-time; ~verordnung f police regulation(s pl.); ~wache f police-station.

Polizist [poli'tsist] m (-en/-en) policeman, constable, sl. bobby, cop; ~in f (-/-nen) policewoman.

polnisch adj. ['pɔlniʃ] Polish.

Polster ['pɔlstər] n (-s/-) pad; cushion; bolster; s. Polsterung; '~möbel n/pl. upholstered furniture; upholstery; '2n v/t. (ge-, h) upholster, stuff; pad, wad; '~sessel m, '~stuhl m upholstered chair; '~ung f (-/-en) padding, stuffing; upholstery.

poltern ['pɔltərn] v/i. (ge-, h) make a row; rumble; p. bluster.

Polytechnikum [poly'tɛçnikum] n (-s/Polytechnika, Polytechniken) polytechnic (school).

Pommes frites [pɔm'frit] pl. chips pl., Am. French fried potatoes pl.

Pomp [pɔmp] m (-[e]s/no pl.) pomp, splendo(u)r; 2haft adj., 2ös adj. [~'pø:s] pompous, splendid.

Pony ['pɔni] 1. *zo. n* (-s/-s) pony; 2. *m* (-s/-s) *hairstyle:* bang, fringe.

popul|är *adj.* [popu'lɛːr] popular; **2arität** [ˌari'tɛːt] *f* (-/no *pl.*) popularity.

Por|e ['poːrə] *f* (-/-n) pore; **2ös** *adj.* [po'røːs] porous; permeable.

Portemonnaie [pɔrtmɔ'neː] *n* (-s/-s) purse.

Portier [pɔr'tjeː] *m* (-s/-s) *s.* Pförtner.

Portion [pɔr'tsjoːn] *f* (-/-en) portion, share; ✕ ration; helping, serving; *zwei ~en Kaffee* coffee for two.

Porto ['pɔrto] *n* (-s/-s, Porti) postage; **2frei** *adj.* post-free; prepaid, *esp. Am.* postpaid; **2pflichtig** *adj.* subject to postage.

Porträt [pɔr'trɛː] ~t] *n* (-s/-s; -[e]s/-e) portrait, likeness; **2ieren** [ˌɛ'tiːrən] *v/t.* (no -ge-, h) portray.

Portugies|e [pɔrtu'giːzə] *m* (-n/-n) Portuguese; *die ~n pl.* the Portuguese *pl.*; **2isch** *adj.* Portuguese.

Porzellan [pɔrtse'laːn] *n* (-s/-e) porcelain, china.

Posaune [po'zaunə] *f* (-/-n) ♪ trombone; *fig.* trumpet.

Pose ['poːzə] *f* (-/-n) pose, attitude; *fig. s.* air.

Position [pozi'tsjoːn] *f* (-/-en) position; social standing; ⚓ station.

positiv *adj.* ['poːzitiːf] positive.

Positur [pozi'tuːr] *f* (-/-en) posture; *sich in ~ setzen* strike an attitude.

Posse *thea.* ['pɔsə] *f* (-/-n) farce.

'Possen *m* (-s/-) trick, prank; **2haft** *adj.* farcical, comical; **'~reißer** *m* (-s/-) buffoon, clown.

possessiv *gr. adj.* ['pɔsesiːf] possessive.

pos'sierlich *adj.* droll, funny.

Post [pɔst] *f* (-/-en) post, *Am.* mail; mail, letters *pl.*; post office; *mit der ersten ~ by* the first delivery; **'~amt** *n* post office; **'~anschrift** *f* mailing address; **'~anweisung** *f* postal order; **'~beamte** *m* post-office clerk; **'~bote** *m* postman, *Am.* mailman; **'~dampfer** *m* packet-boat.

Posten ['pɔstən] *m* (-s/-) post, place, station; job; ✕ sentry, sentinel; item; entry; *goods:* lot, parcel.

'Postfach *n* post-office box.

pos'tieren *v/t.* (no -ge-, h) post, station, place; *sich ~ station o.s.*

'Post|karte *f* postcard, *with printed postage stamp:* *Am. a.* postal card; **'~kutsche** *f* stage-coach; **'2lagernd** *adj.* to be (kept until) called for, poste restante, *Am.* (in care of) general delivery; **'~leitzahl** *f* postcode; **'~minister** *m* minister of post; *Brt. and Am.* Postmaster General; **'~paket** *n* postal parcel; **'~schalter** *m* (post-office) window; **'~scheck** *m* postal cheque, *Am.* postal check; **'~schließfach** *n*

post-office box; **'~sparbuch** *n* post-office savings-book; **'~stempel** *m* postmark; **2wendend** *adv.* by return of post; **'~wertzeichen** *n* (postage) stamp; **'~zug** 🚂 *m* mail-train.

Pracht [praxt] *f* (-/✕ -en, ⁿe) splendo(u)r, magnificence; luxury.

prächtig *adj.* ['prɛçtiç] splendid, magnificent; gorgeous; grand.

'prachtvoll *adj. s.* prächtig.

Prädikat [predi'kaːt] *n* (-[e]s/-e) predicate; *school, etc.:* mark.

prägen ['prɛːgən] *v/t.* (ge-, h) stamp; coin (*word, coin*).

prahlen ['praːlən] *v/i.* (ge-, h) brag, boast (*mit of*); *~ mit* show off *s.th.*

'Prahler *m* (-s/-) boaster, braggart; **~ei** [ˌɛ'raɪ] *f* (-/-en) boasting, bragging; **'2isch** *adj.* boastful; ostentatious.

Prakti|kant [prakti'kant] *m* (-en/-en) probationer, trainee; expert; **'~ker** *m* (-s/-) practical man; expert; **'~kum** *n* (-s/Praktika, Praktiken) practical course; **'2sch** *adj.* practical; useful, handy; *~er Arzt* general practitioner; **2zieren** 🎖, ⚖ [ˌ'tsiːrən] *v/i.* (no -ge-, h) practi|se, *Am.* -ce medicine *or* the law. [prelate.␣]

Prälat *eccl.* [prɛ'laːt] *m* (-en/-en)

Praline [pra'liːnə] *f* (-/-n): *~n pl.* chocolates *pl.*

prall *adj.* [pral] tight; plump; *sun:* blazing; **'~en** *v/i.* (ge-, sein) bounce *or* bound (*auf acc., gegen* against).

Prämi|e ['prɛːmjə] *f* (-/-n) ➕ premium; prize; bonus; **2(i)eren** [prɛ'miːrən, prɛmi'iːrən] *v/t.* (no -ge-, h) award a prize to.

prang|en ['praŋən] *v/i.* (ge-, h) shine, make a show; **'2er** *m* (-s/-) pillory.

Pranke ['praŋkə] *f* (-/-n) paw.

pränumerando *adv.* [prɛːnumə'rando] beforehand, in advance.

Präpa|rat [prepa'raːt] *n* (-[e]s/-e) preparation; *microscopy:* slide; **2'rieren** *v/t.* (no -ge-, h) prepare.

Präposition *gr.* [prɛpozi'tsjoːn] *f* (-/-en) preposition.

Prärie [prɛ'riː] *f* (-/-n) prairie.

Präsens *gr.* ['prɛːzɛns] *n* (-/Präsentia, Präsenzien) present (tense).

Präsi|dent [prezi'dɛnt] *m* (-en/-en) president; chairman; **2'dieren** *v/i.* (no -ge-, h) preside (*über acc.* over); be in the chair; **~dium** [ˌ'ziːdjum] *n* (-s/Präsidien) presidency, chair.

prasseln ['prasəln] *v/i.* (ge-, h) *fire:* crackle; *rain:* patter.

prassen ['prasən] *v/i.* (ge-, h) feast, carouse.

Präteritum *gr.* [prɛ'teːritum] *n* (-s/Präterita) preterite (tense); past tense.

Praxis ['praksis] *f* 1. (-/no *pl.*) practice; 2. (-/Praxen) practice (*of doctor or lawyer*).

Präzedenzfall [prɛtseˈdɛnts-] *m* precedent; ₰₷ *a.* case-law.

präzis *adj.* [prɛˈtsiːs], ~e *adj.* [~zə] precise.

predig|en [ˈpreːdigən] *v/i. and v/t.* (ge-, *h*) preach; '2er *m* (-s/-) preacher; clergyman; 2t [ˈ~diçt] *f* (-/-en) sermon (*a. fig.*); *fig.* lecture.

Preis [praɪs] *m* (-es/-e) price; cost; *competition*: prize; award; reward; praise; *um jeden* ~ at any price *or* cost; '~ausschreiben *n* (-s/-) competition.

preisen [ˈpraɪzən] *v/t.* (*irr.*, ge-, *h*) praise.

'Preis|erhöhung *f* rise *or* increase in price(s); '~gabe *f* abandonment; revelation (*of secret*); 2geben *v/t.* (*irr.* geben, *sep.*, -ge-, *h*) abandon; reveal, give away (*secret*); disclose, expose; '2gekrönt *adj.* prize-winning, prize (*novel, etc.*); '~gericht *n* jury; ~lage *f* range of prices; ~liste *f* price-list; ~nachlaß *m* price cut; discount, ~richter *m* judge, umpire; ~schießen *n* (-s/-) shooting competition; ~stopp *m* (-s/*no pl.*) price freeze; ~träger *m* prize-winner; '2wert *adj.*: ~ *sein* be a bargain.

prell|en [ˈprɛlən] *v/t.* (ge-, *h*) *fig.* cheat, defraud (*um of*); *sich et.* ~ ₰₷ contuse *or* bruise s.th.; '2ung ₰₷ *f* (-/-en) contusion.

Premier|e *thea.* [prəmˈjeːrə] *f* (-/-n) première, first night; ~minister [~ˈjeː-] *m* prime minister.

Presse [ˈprɛsə] *f* 1. (-/-n) ⊕, *typ.* press; squeezer; 2. (-/*no pl.*) *newspapers generally*: the press; ~amt *n* public relations office; ~freiheit *f* freedom of the press; ~meldung *f* news item; '2n *v/t.* (ge-, *h*) press; squeeze; ~photograph *m* press-photographer; ~vertreter *m* reporter; public relations man.

Preßluft [ˈprɛs-] *f* (-/*no pl.*) compressed air.

Prestige [prɛsˈtiːʒə] *n* (-s/*no pl.*) prestige; ~ *verlieren a.* lose face.

Preuße [ˈprɔʏsə] *m* (-n/-n) Prussian; '2isch *adj.* Prussian.

prickeln [ˈprɪkəln] *v/i.* (ge-, *h*) prick(le), tickle; itch; *fingers*: tingle.

Priem [priːm] *m* (-[e]s/-e) quid.

pries [priːs] *pret. of* preisen.

Priester [ˈpriːstər] *m* (-s/-) priest; '~in *f* (-/-nen) priestess; '2lich *adj.* priestly, sacerdotal; '~rock *m* cassock.

prim|a F *adj.* [ˈpriːma] first-rate, F A 1; ✝ *a.* prime; F swell; ~är *adj.* [priˈmɛːr] primary.

Primel ♣ [ˈpriːməl] *f* (-/-n) primrose.

Prinz [prɪnts] *m* (-en/-en) prince; ~essin [~ˈtsɛsɪn] *f* (-/-nen) princess; '~gemahl *m* prince consort.

Prinzip [prɪnˈtsiːp] *n* (-s/-ien)

principle; *aus* ~ on principle; *im* ~ in principle, basically.

Priorität [prioriˈtɛːt] *f* 1. (-/-en) priority; 2. (-/*no pl.*) *time*: priority.

Prise [ˈpriːzə] *f* (-/-n) ⚓ prize; e-e ~ a pinch of (*salt, snuff*).

Prisma [ˈprɪsma] *n* (-s/Prismen) prism.

privat *adj.* [priˈvaːt] private; 2adresse *f* home address; 2mann *m* (-[e]s/Privatmänner, Privatleute) private person *or* gentleman; 2patient ₰₷ *m* paying patient; 2person *f* private person; 2schule *f* private school.

Privileg [priviˈleːk] *n* (-[e]s/-ien, -e) privilege.

pro *prp.* [proː] per; ~ *Jahr* per annum; ~ *Kopf* per head; ~ *Stück* a piece.

Probe [ˈproːbə] *f* (-/-n) experiment; trial, test; *metall.* assay; sample; specimen; proof; probation; check; *thea.* rehearsal; audition; *auf* ~ on probation, on trial; *auf die* ~ *stellen* (put to the) test; ~abzug *typ.*, *phot. m* proof; ~exemplar *n* specimen copy; '~fahrt *f* ⊕ trial trip; *mot.* trial run; ~flug *m* test *or* trial flight; '2n *v/t.* (ge-, *h*) exercise; *thea.* rehearse; ~nummer *f* specimen copy *or* number; ~seite *typ. f* specimen page; ~sendung *f* goods on approval; 2weise *adv.* on trial; *p. a.* on probation; '~zeit *f* time of probation.

probieren [proˈbiːrən] *v/t.* (*no* -ge-, *h*) try, test; taste (*food*.)

Problem [proˈbleːm] *n* (-s/-e) problem; 2atisch *adj.* [~eˈmaːtɪʃ] problematic(al).

Produkt [proˈdʊkt] *n* (-[e]s/-e) product (*a.* A; *); ₰ produce; result; ~ion [~tsioːn] *f* (-/-en) production; output; 2iv *adj.* [~ˈtiːf] productive.

Produz|ent [produˈtsɛnt] *m* (-en/-en) producer; 2ieren [~ˈtsiːrən] *v/t.* (*no* -ge-, *h*) produce; *sich* ~ perform; *contp.* show off.

professionell *adj.* [profesioˈnɛl] professional, by trade.

Profess|or [proˈfɛsɔr] *m* (-s/-en) professor; ~ur [~ˈsuːr] *f* (-/-en) professorship, chair.

Profi [ˈproːfi] *m* (-s/-s) *sports*: professional, F pro. [*on tyre*: tread.]

Profil [proˈfiːl] *n* (-s/-e) profile;]

Profit [proˈfiːt] *m* (-[e]s/-e) profit; 2ieren [~ˈtiːrən] *v/i.* (*no* -ge-, *h*) profit (*von by*).

Prognose [proˈgnoːzə] *f* (-/-n) ₰₷ prognosis; *meteor.* forecast.

Programm [proˈgram] *n* (-s/-e) program(me); *politisches* ~ political program(me), *Am.* platform.

Projektion [projɛkˈtsioːn] *f* (-/-en) projection; ~sapparat [projɛkˈtsioːns?-] *m* projector.

proklamieren [prokla'mi:rən] *v/t.* (*no* -ge-, *h*) proclaim.

Prokur|a † [pro'ku:ra] *f* (-/*Prokuren*) procuration; ~ist [~ku'rist] *m* (-en/-en) confidential clerk.

Proletari|er [prole'ta:rjər] *m* (-s/-) proletarian; 2sch *adj.* proletarian.

Prolog [pro'lo:k] *m* (-[e]s/-e) prolog(ue).

prominen|t *adj.* [promi'nent] prominent; 2z [~ts] *f* (-/*no pl.*) notables *pl.*, celebrities *pl.*; high society.

Promo|tion *univ.* [promo'tsjo:n] *f* (-/-en) graduation; 2vieren [~'vi:rən] *v/i.* (*no* -ge-, *h*) graduate (*an dat.* from), take one's degree.

Pronomen *gr.* [pro'no:men] *n* (-s/-, *Pronomina*) pronoun.

Propeller [pro'pɛlər] *m* (-s/-) ⚓, ✈ (screw-)propeller, screw; ✈ airscrew.

Prophe|t [pro'fe:t] *m* (-en/-en) prophet; 2tisch *adj.* prophetic; 2zeien [~e'tsaiən] *v/t.* (*no* -ge-, *h*) prophesy; predict, foretell; ~'zeiung *f* (-/-en) prophecy; prediction.

Proportion [propor'tsjo:n] *f* (-/-en) proportion.

Prosa ['pro:za] *f* (-/*no pl.*) prose.

prosit *int.* ['pro:zit] your health!, here's to you!, cheers!

Prospekt [pro'spɛkt] *m* (-[e]s/-e) prospectus; brochure, leaflet, folder.

prost *int.* [pro:st] *s. prosit.*

Prostituierte [prostitu'i:rtə] *f* (-n/-n) prostitute.

Protest [pro'tɛst] *m* (-es/-e) protest; ~ einlegen *or* erheben gegen (enter a) protest against.

Protestant *eccl.* [protes'tant] *m* (-en/-en) Protestant; 2isch *adj.* Protestant.

protes'tieren *v/i.* (*no* -ge-, *h*): gegen et. ~ protest against s.th., object to s.th.

Prothese 🦷 [pro'te:zə] *f* (-/-n) pro(s)thesis; *dentistry: a.* denture; artificial limb.

Protokoll [proto'kɔl] *n* (-s/-e) record, minutes *pl.* (*of meeting*); *diplomacy:* protocol; *das* ~ *aufnehmen* take down the minutes; *das* ~ *führen* keep the minutes; *zu* ~ *geben* 🖪 depose, state in evidence; *zu* ~ *nehmen* take down, record; 2ieren [~'li:rən] (*no* -ge-, *h*) 1. *v/t.* record, take down (on record); 2. *v/i.* keep the minutes.

Protz *contp.* [prɔts] *m* (-en, -es/-e[n]) braggart, F show-off; 2en *v/i.* (ge-, *h*) show off (*mit dat.* with); 2ig *adj.* ostentatious, showy.

Proviant [pro'vjant] *m* (-s/✎ -e) provisions *pl.*, victuals *pl.*

Provinz [pro'vints] *f* (-/-en) province; *fig.* the provinces *pl.*; 2ial *adj.* [~'tsja:l], 2iell *adj.* [~'tsjɛl] provincial.

Provis|ion † [provi'zjo:n] *f* (-/-en) commission; 2orisch *adj.* [~'zo:riʃ] provisional, temporary.

provozieren [provo'tsi:rən] *v/t.* (*no* -ge-, *h*) provoke.

Prozent [pro'tsent] *n* (-[e]s/-e) per cent; ~satz *m* percentage; proportion; 2ual *adj.* [~u'a:l] percental; ~er Anteil percentage.

Prozeß [pro'tses] *m* (*Prozesses/Prozesse*) process; 🖪: action, lawsuit; trial; (legal) proceedings *pl.*; e-n ~ gewinnen win one's case; e-n ~ gegen j-n anstrengen bring an action against s.o., sue s.o.; j-m den ~ machen try s.o., put s.o. on trial; kurzen ~ machen mit make short work of.

prozessieren [protse'si:rən] *v/i.* (*no* -ge-, *h*): mit j-m ~ go to law against s.o., have the law of s.o.

Prozession [protse'sjo:n] *f* (-/-en) procession.

prüde *adj.* ['pry:də] prudish.

prüf|en ['pry:fən] *v/t.* (ge-, *h*) examine; try, test; quiz; check, verify; '~end *adj.* look: searching, scrutinizing; '2er *m* (-s/-) examiner; '2ling *m* (-s/-e) examinee; '2stein *fig. m* touchstone; '2ung *f* (-/-en) examination; *school, etc.: a.* F exam; test; quiz; verification, checking, check-up; e-e ~ machen go in for *or* sit for *or* take an examination.

'Prüfungs|arbeit *f*, '~aufgabe *f* examination-paper; '~ausschuß *m*, '~kommission *f* board of examiners.

Prügel ['pry:gəl] **1.** *m* (-s/-) cudgel, club, stick; **2.** F *fig. pl.* beating, thrashing; ~ei F [~'lai] *f* (-/-en) fight, row; '~knabe *m* scapegoat; '2n *v/t.* (ge-, *h*) cudgel, flog; beat (up); thrash; sich ~ (have) a fight.

Prunk [pruŋk] *m* (-[e]s/*no pl.*) splendo(u)r; pomp, show; '2en *v/i.* (ge-, *h*) make a show (*mit* of), show off (*mit* et. s.th.); '2voll *adj.* splendid, gorgeous.

Psalm *eccl.* [psalm] *m* (-s/-en) psalm.

Pseudonym [psɔʏdo'ny:m] *n* (-s/-e) pseudonym.

pst *int.* [pst] hush!

Psychi|ater [psyçi'a:tər] *m* (-s/-) psychiatrist, alienist; 2sch *adj.* ['psy:çiʃ] psychic(al).

Psycho|analyse [psyço?ana'ly:zə] *f* (-/*no pl.*) psychoanalysis; ~analytiker [~tikər] *m* (-s/-) psychoanalist; ~loge [~'lo:gə] *m* (-n/-n) psychologist; ~se [~'ço:zə] *f* (-/-n) psychosis; panic.

Pubertät [puber'tɛ:t] *f* (-/*no pl.*) puberty.

Publikum ['pu:blikum] *n* (-s/*no pl.*) *the* public; audience; spectators *pl.*, crowd; readers *pl.*

publiz|ieren [publi'tsi:rən] *v/t.* (*no*

-ge-, *h*) publish; 2ist *m* (-en/-en) publicist; journalist.

Pudding ['pudiŋ] *m* (-s/-e, -s) cream.

Pudel *zo.* ['pu:dəl] *m* (-s/-) poodle; '2'naß F *adj.* dripping wet, drenched.

Puder ['pu:dər] *m* (-s/-) powder; '~dose *f* powder-box; compact; '2n *v/t.* (ge-, *h*) powder; *sich* ~ powder o.s. *or* one's face; '~quaste *f* powder-puff; '~zucker *m* powdered sugar.

Puff F [puf] *m* (-[e]s/=e, -e) poke, nudge; '2en (ge-, *h*) 1. F *v/t.* nudge; 2. *v/i.* pop; '~er *m* (-s/-) buffer.

Pullover [pu'lo:vər] *m* (-s/-) pull-over, sweater.

Puls *#* [puls] *m* (-es/-e) pulse; '~ader *anat. f* artery; 2ieren [~'zi:-rən] *v/i.* (no -ge-, *h*) pulsate, throb; '~schlag *#* *m* pulsation.

Pult [pult] *n* (-[e]s/-e) desk.

Pulv|er ['pulfər] *n* (-s/-) powder; gunpowder; F *fig.* cash, *sl.* brass, dough; '2erig *adj.* powdery; 2eri-sieren [~vəri'zi:rən] *v/t.* (no -ge-, *h*) pulverize; 2rig *adj.* ['~friç] pow-dery.

Pump F [pump] *m* (-[e]s/-e): *auf* ~ on tick; '~e *f* (-/-n) pump; '2en (ge-, *h*) 1. *v/i.* pump; 2. *v/t.* pump; F *fig.*: give *s.th.* on tick; borrow (et. *von j-m* s.th. from s.o.).

Punkt [puŋkt] *m* (-[e]s/-e) point (*a. fig.*); dot; *typ.*, *gr.* full stop, period; spot, place; *fig.* item; article, clause (*of agreement*); *der springende* ~ the point; *toter* ~ deadlock, dead end; *wunder* ~ tender subject, sore point; ~ *zehn Uhr* on the stroke of ten, at 10 (o'clock) sharp; *in vielen* ~*en* on many points, in many respects; *nach* ~*en siegen sports*: win on points; 2ieren [~'ti:rən] *v/t.* (no -ge-, *h*) dot, point; *#* puncture, tap; *drawing*, *painting*: stipple.

pünktlich *adj.* ['pyŋktliç] punctual; ~ *sein* be on time; '2keit *f* (-/no *pl.*) punctuality.

Punsch [punʃ] *m* (-es/-e) punch.

Pupille *anat.* [pu'pilə] *f* (-/-n) pupil.

Puppe ['pupə] *f* (-/-n) doll (*a. fig.*); puppet (*a. fig.*); *tailoring*: dummy; *zo.* chrysalis, pupa; '~nspiel *n* puppet-show; '~nstube *f* doll's room; '~nwagen *m* doll's pram, *Am.* doll carriage *or* buggy.

pur *adj.* [pu:r] pure, sheer.

Püree [py're:] *n* (-s/-s) purée, mash.

Purpur ['purpur] *m* (-s/no *pl.*) purple; 2farben *adj.*, '2n *adj.*, '2rot *adj.* purple.

Purzel|baum ['purtsəl-] *m* somer-sault; *e-n* ~ *schlagen* turn a somer-sault; '2n *v/i.* (ge-, *sein*) tumble.

Puste F ['pu:stə] *f* (-/no *pl.*) breath; *ihm ging die* ~ *aus* he got out of breath.

Pustel *#* ['pustəl] *f* (-/-n) pustule, pimple.

pusten ['pu:stən] *v/i.* (ge-, *h*) puff, pant; blow.

Pute *orn.* ['pu:tə] *f* (-/-n) turkey (-hen); '~r *orn.* *m* (-s/-) turkey (-cock); '2r'rot *adj.* (as) red as a turkey-cock.

Putsch [putʃ] *m* (-es/-e) putsch, insurrection; riot; '2en *v/i.* (ge-, *h*) revolt, riot.

Putz [puts] *m* (-es/-e) *on garments*: finery; ornaments *pl.*; trimming; *Δ* roughcast, plaster; '2en *v/t.* (ge-, *h*) clean, cleanse; polish, wipe; adorn; snuff (*candle*); polish, *Am.* shine (*shoes*); *sich* ~ smarten *or* dress o.s. up; *sich die Nase* ~ blow *or* wipe one's nose; *sich die Zähne* ~ brush one's teeth; '~frau *f* char-woman, *Am. a.* scrubwoman; '2ig *adj.* droll, funny; '~lappen *m* cleaning rag; '~zeug *n* cleaning utensils *pl.*

Pyjama [pi'dʒɑ:ma] *m* (-s/-s) (*ein* a suit of) pyjamas *pl.* or *Am. a.* pajamas *pl.*

Pyramide [pyra'mi:də] *f* (-/-n) pyramid (*a. Å*); *✕* stack (*of rifles*); 2nförmig *adj.* [~nfœrmiç] pyram-idal.

Q

Quacksalber ['kvakzalbər] *m* (-s/-) quack (doctor); ~ei F [~'raɪ] *f* (-/-en) quackery; '2n *v/i.* (ge-, *h*) (play the) quack.

Quadrat [kva'drɑ:t] *n* (-[e]s/-e) square; 2 *Fuß im* ~ 2 feet square; *ins* ~ *erheben* square; 2isch *adj.* square; *Å equation*: quadratic; ~meile *f* square mile; ~meter *n*, *m* square met|re, *Am.* -er; ~wurzel *Å f* square root; ~zahl *Å f* square number.

quaken ['kvɑ:kən] *v/i.* (ge-, *h*) *duck*: quack; *frog*: croak.

quäken ['kve:kən] *v/i.* (ge-, *h*) squeak.

Quäker ['kve:kər] *m* (-s/-) Quaker, member of the Society of Friends.

Qual [kvɑ:l] *f* (-/-en) pain; torment; agony.

quälen ['kve:lən] *v/t.* (ge-, *h*) tor-ment (*a. fig.*); torture; ago-nize; *fig.* bother, pester; *sich* ~ toil, drudge.

Qualifikation [kvalifika'tsjo:n] f (-/-en) qualification.

qualifizieren [kvalifi'tsi:rən] v/t. and v/refl. (no -ge-, h) qualify (zu for).

Qualit|ät [kvali'tɛ:t] f (-/-en) quality; **2ativ** [..a'ti:f] 1. adj. qualitative; 2. adv. as to quality.

Quali'täts|arbeit f work of high quality; ~stahl m high-grade steel; ~ware f high-grade or quality goods pl.

Qualm [kvalm] m (-[e]s/no pl.) dense smoke; fumes pl.; vapo(u)r, steam; **2en** (ge-, h) 1. v/i. smoke, give out vapo(u)r or fumes; F p. smoke heavily; 2. F v/t. puff (away) at (cigar, pipe, etc.); **2ig** adj. smoky.

'qualvoll adj. very painful; pain: excruciating; fig. agonizing, harrowing.

Quantit|ät [kvanti'tɛ:t] f (-/-en) quantity; **2ativ** [..a'ti:f] 1. adj. quantitative; 2. adv. as to quantity.

Quantum ['kvantum] n -s/Quanten) quantity, amount; quantum (a. phys.).

Quarantäne [karan'tɛ:nə] f (-/-n) quarantine; in ~ legen (put in) quarantine; [curd(s pl.).)

Quark [kvark] m (-[e]s/no pl.)]

Quartal [kvar'ta:l] n (-s/-e) quarter (of a year); univ. term.

Quartett [kvar'tɛt] n (-[e]s/-e) ♪ quartet(te); cards: four.

Quartier [kvar'ti:r] n (-s/-e) accommodation; ✕ quarters pl., billet.

Quaste ['kvastə] f (-/-n) tassel; (powder-)puff.

Quatsch F [kvatʃ] m (-es/no pl.) nonsense, fudge, sl. bosh, rot, Am. sl. a. baloney; **2en** F v/i. (ge-, h) twaddle, blether, sl. talk rot; (have a) chat; ~kopf F m twaddler.

Quecksilber ['kvɛk-] n mercury, quicksilver.

Quelle ['kvɛlə] f (-/-n) spring, source (a. fig.); oil: well; fig. fountain, origin; **2n** v/i. (irr., ge-, sein) gush, well; ~nangabe ['kvɛlən?-] f mention of sources used; ~nforschung f original research.

Quengel|ei F [kvɛŋə'laɪ] f (-/-en) grumbling, whining, nagging; **2n** F v/i. (ge-, h) grumble, whine; nag.

quer adv. [kve:r] crossways, crosswise; F fig. wrong; F ~ gehen go wrong; ~ über (acc.) across.

Quer|e f (-/no pl.): der ~ nach crossways, crosswise; F j-m in die ~ kommen cross s.o.'s path; fig. thwart s.o.'s plans; ~frage f crossquestion; ~kopf fig. m wrongheaded fellow; **2schießen** F v/i. (irr. schießen, sep., -ge-, h) try to foil s.o.'s plans; ~schiff △ n transept; ~schläger ✕ m ricochet; ~schnitt m cross-section a. fig.); ~straße f cross-road; zweite ~ rechts second turning to the right; ~treiber m (-s/-) schemer; ~treibe'rei f (-/-en) intriguing, machination.

Querulant [kveru'lant] m (-en/-en) querulous person, grumbler, Am. sl. a. griper.

quetsch|en ['kvɛtʃən] v/t. (ge-, h) squeeze; ✗ bruise, contuse; sich den Finger ~ jam one's finger; **2ung** ✗ (-/-en), **2wunde** ✗ f bruise, contusion.

quick adj. [kvik] lively, brisk.

quieken ['kvi:kən] v/i. (ge-, h) squeak, squeal.

quietsch|en ['kvi:tʃən] v/i. (ge-, h) squeak, squeal; door-hinge, etc.: creak, squeak; brakes, etc.: screech; ~vergnügt F adj. (as) jolly as a sandboy.

Quirl [kvirl] m (-[e]s/-e) twirlingstick; **2en** v/t. (ge-, h) twirl.

quitt adj. [kvit]: ~ sein mit j-m be quits or even with s.o.; jetzt sind wir ~ that leaves us even; ~ieren [..'ti:rən] v/t. (no -ge-, h) receipt (bill, etc.); quit, abandon (post, etc.); **2ung** f (-/-en) receipt; fig. answer; gegen ~ against receipt.

Quot|e ['kvo:tə] f (-/-n) quota; share, portion; ~ient Å [kvo'tsjɛnt] m (-en/-en) quotient.

R

Rabatt ✝ [ra'bat] m (-[e]s/-e) discount, rebate.

Rabe orn. ['ra:bə] m (-n/-n) raven; **2nschwarz** F adj. raven, jet-black.

rabiat adj. [ra'bja:t] rabid, violent.

Rache ['raxə] f (-/no pl.) revenge, vengeance; retaliation.

Rachen anat. ['raxən] m (-s/-) throat, pharynx; jaws pl.

rächen ['rɛçən] v/t. (ge-, h) avenge, revenge; sich ~ an (dat.) revenge o.s. or be revenged on.

'Rachen|höhle anat. f pharynx; ~katarrh ✗ m cold in the throat.

'rach|gierig adj., ~süchtig adj. revengeful, vindictive.

Rad [ra:t] n (-[e]s/~er) wheel; (bi)cycle, F bike; (ein) ~ schlagen peacock: spread its tail; sports: turn cart-wheels; unter die Räder *kommen* go to the dogs; '**~achse** *f* axle(-tree).

Radar ['rɑːdɑːr, ra'dɑːr] *m, n* (-/s/-s) radar.

Radau F [ra'dau] *m* (-s/*no pl.*) row, racket, hubbub.

radebrechen ['rɑːdə-] *v/t.* (ge-, h) speak (*language*) badly, murder (*language*).

radeln ['rɑːdəln] *v/i.* (ge-, sein) cycle, pedal, F bike.

Rädelsführer ['rɛːdəls-] *m* ringleader.

Räderwerk ⊕ ['rɛːdər-] *n* gearing.

rad|fahren *v/i.* (*irr. fahren, sep.,* -ge-, sein) cycle, (ride a) bicycle, pedal, F bike; '**²fahrer** *m* cyclist, *Am. a.* cycler *or* wheelman.

radier|en [ra'diːrən] *v/t.* (no -ge-, h) rub out, erase; *art:* etch; **²gummi** *m* (india-)rubber, *esp. Am.* eraser; **²messer** *n* eraser; **²ung** *f* (-/-en) etching.

Radieschen ♀ [ra'diːsçən] *n* (-s/-) (red) radish.

radikal *adj.* [radi'kɑːl] radical.

Radio ['rɑːdjo] *n* (-s/-s) radio, wireless; *im ~* on the radio, on the air; **²aktiv** *phys. adj.* [radjoak'tiːf] radio(-)active; **~er** *Niederschlag* fall-out; '**~apparat** *m* radio *or* wireless (set).

Radium ⚗ ['rɑːdjum] *n* (-s/*no pl.*) radium.

Radius ⚗ ['rɑːdjus] *m* (-/Radien) radius.

'**Rad|kappe** *f* hub cap; '**~kranz** *m* rim; '**~rennbahn** *f* cycling track; '**~rennen** *n* cycle race; '**~sport** *m* cycling; '**~spur** *f* rut, track.

raffen ['rafən] *v/t.* (ge-, h) snatch up; gather (*dress*).

raffiniert *adj.* [rafi'niːrt] refined; *fig.* clever, cunning.

ragen ['rɑːgən] *v/i.* (ge-, h) tower, loom.

Ragout [ra'guː] *n* (-s/-s) ragout, stew, hash.

Rahe ⚓ ['rɑːə] *f* (-/-n) yard.

Rahm [rɑːm] *m* (-[e]s/*no pl.*) cream.

Rahmen ['rɑːmən] **1.** *m* (-s/-) frame; *fig.:* frame, background, setting; scope; *aus dem ~ fallen* be out of place; **2.** ♀ *v/t.* (ge-, h) frame.

Rakete [ra'keːtə] *f* (-/-n) rocket; *e-e ~ abfeuern or starten* launch a rocket; *dreistufige ~* three-stage rocket; '**~nantrieb** [ra'keːtən-] *m* rocket propulsion; *mit ~* rocket-propelled; '**~nflugzeug** *n* rocket (-propelled) plane; '**~ntriebwerk** *n* propulsion unit.

Ramm|bär ⊕ ['ram-] *m*, '**~bock** *m*, '**~e** *f* (-/-n) ram(mer); '**²en** *v/t.* (ge-, h) ram.

Rampe ['rampə] *f* (-/-n) ramp, ascent; '**~nlicht** *n* footlights *pl.*; *fig.* limelight.

Ramsch [ramʃ] *m* (-es/⚹ -e) junk,

---

trash; *im ~ kaufen* buy in the lump; '**~verkauf** *m* jumble-sale; '**~ware** *f* job lot.

Rand [rant] *m* (-[e]s/ᵘer) edge, brink (a. *fig.*); *fig.* verge; border; brim (of *hat, cup, etc.*); rim (of *plate, etc.*); margin (of *book, etc.*); lip (of *wound*); *Ränder pl. under the eyes:* rings *pl.*, circles *pl.*; *vor Freude außer ~ und Band geraten* be beside o.s. with joy; *er kommt damit nicht zu ~e* he can't manage it; '**~bemerkung** *f* marginal note; *fig.* comment.

rang[1] [raŋ] *pret. of* ringen.

Rang[2] [⌐] *m* (-[e]s/ᵘe) rank, order; ✕ rank; position; *thea.* tier; *erster ~ thea.* dress-circle, *Am.* first balcony; *zweiter ~ thea.* upper circle, *Am.* second balcony; *erster ~ es* first-class, first-rate; *j-m den ~ ablaufen* get the start *or* better of s.o.

Range ['raŋə] *m* (-n/-n), *f* (-/-n) rascal; romp.

rangieren [rã'ʒiːrən] (*no -ge-, h*) **1.** 🚂 *v/t.* shunt, *Am. a.* switch; **2.** *fig. v/i.* rank.

'**Rang|liste** *f sports, etc.:* ranking list; ✕ army-list, navy *or* air-force list; '**~ordnung** *f* order of precedence.

Ranke ♀ ['raŋkə] *f* (-/-n) tendril; runner.

Ränke ['rɛŋkə] *m/pl.* intrigues *pl.*

'**ranken** *v/refl.* (ge-, h) creep, climb.

rann [ran] *pret. of* rinnen.

rannte ['rantə] *pret. of* rennen.

Ranzen ['rantsən] *m* (-s/-) knapsack; satchel.

ranzig *adj.* ['rantsiç] rancid, rank.

Rappe *zo.* ['rapə] *m* (-n/-n) black horse.

rar *adj.* [rɑːr] rare, scarce.

Rarität [rari'tɛːt] *f* (-/-en) rarity; curiosity, curio.

rasch *adj.* [raʃ] quick, swift, brisk; hasty; prompt.

rascheln ['raʃəln] *v/i.* (ge-, h) rustle.

rasen[1] ['rɑːzən] *v/i.* (ge-) **1.** (h) rage, storm; rave; **2.** (sein) race, speed; '**~d** *adj.* raving; frenzied; *speed:* tearing; *pains:* agonizing; *headache:* splitting; *j-n ~ machen* drive s.o. mad.

Rasen[2] [⌐] *m* (-s/-) grass; lawn; turf; '**~platz** *m* lawn, grass-plot.

Raserei [rɑːzə'rai] *f* (-/-en) rage, fury; frenzy, madness; F *mot.* scorching; *j-n zur ~ bringen* drive s.o. mad.

Rasier|apparat [ra'ziːr-] *m* (safety) razor; **²en** *v/t.* (no -ge-, h) shave; *sich ~ (lassen* get a) shave; **~klinge** *f* razor-blade; **~messer** *n* razor; **~pinsel** *m* shaving-brush; **~seife** *f* shaving-soap; **~wasser** *n* after-shave lotion; **~zeug** *n* shaving kit.

Rasse ['rasə] *f* (-/-n) race; *zo.* breed.

rasseln ['rasəln] *v/i.* (ge-, h) rattle.

'Rassen|frage f (-/no pl.) racial issue; '~kampf m race conflict; '~problem n racial issue; '~schranke f colo(u)r bar; '~trennung f (-/no pl.) racial segregation; '~unruhen f/pl. race riots pl.

'rasserein adj. thoroughbred, pure-bred.

'rassig adj. thoroughbred; fig. racy.

Rast [rast] f (-/-en) rest, repose; break, pause; 2en v/i. (ge-, h) rest, repose; '2los adj. restless; ~platz m resting-place; mot. picnic area.

Rat [ra:t] m 1. (-[e]s/no pl.) advice, counsel; suggestion; fig. way out; zu ~e ziehen consult; j-n um ~ fragen ask s.o.'s advice; 2. (-[e]s/~e) council, board; council(l)or, alderman.

Rate ['ra:tə] f (-/-n) instal(l)ment (a. ✝); auf ~n ✝ on hire-purchase.

'raten (irr., ge-) 1. v/i. advise, counsel (j-m zu inf. s.o. to inf.); 2. v/t. guess, divine.

'raten|weise adv. by instal(l)ments; '2zahlung ✝ f payment by instal(l)ments.

'Rat|geber m (-s/-) adviser, counsel(l)or; '~haus n town hall, Am. a. city hall.

ratifizieren [ratifi'tsi:rən] v/t. (no -ge-, h) ratify.

Ration [ra'tsjo:n] f (-/-en) ration, allowance; 2ell adj. [~o'nɛl] rational; efficient; economical; 2ieren [~o'ni:rən] v/t. (no -ge-, h) ration.

'rat|los adj. puzzled, perplexed, at a loss; '~sam adj. advisable; expedient; '2schlag m (piece of) advice, counsel.

Rätsel ['rɛ:tsəl] n (-s/-) riddle, puzzle; enigma, mystery; '2haft adj. puzzling; enigmatic(al), mysterious.

Ratte zo. ['ratə] f (-/-n) rat.

rattern ['ratərn] v/i. (ge-, h, sein) rattle, clatter.

Raub [raup] m (-[e]s/no pl.) robbery; kidnap(p)ing; piracy (of intellectual property); booty, spoils pl.; '~bau m (-[e]s/no pl.): ~ treiben ✗ exhaust the land; ✗ rob a mine; ~ treiben mit undermine (one's health); 2en ['~bən] v/t. (ge-, h) rob, take by force, steal; kidnap; j-m et. ~ rob or deprive s.o. of s.th.

Räuber ['rɔybər] m (-s/-) robber; '~bande f gang of robbers; '2isch adj. rapacious, predatory.

'Raub|fisch ichth. m fish of prey; '~gier f rapacity; '2gierig adj. rapacious; '~mord m murder with robbery; '~mörder m murderer and robber; '~tier zo. n beast of prey; '~überfall m hold-up, armed robbery; '~vogel orn. m bird of prey; '~zug m raid.

Rauch [raux] m (-[e]s/no pl.) smoke; fume; 2en (ge-, h) 1. v/i. smoke;

fume; p. (have a) smoke; 2. v/t. smoke (cigarette); ~er m (-s/-) smoker; s. Raucherabteil.

Räucheraal ['rɔyçər⁹-] m smoked eel.

Raucherabteil 🚬 ['rauxər⁹-] n smoking-car(riage), smoking-compartment, smoker.

'Räucher|hering m red or smoked herring, kipper; '2n (ge-, h) 1. v/t. smoke, cure (meat, fish); 2. v/i. burn incense.

'Rauch|fahne f trail of smoke; '~fang m chimney, flue; '~fleisch n smoked meat; '2ig adj. smoky; '~tabak m tobacco; '~waren f/pl. tobacco products pl.; furs pl.; '~zimmer n smoking-room.

Räud|e ['rɔydə] f (-/-n) mange, scab; 2ig adj. mangy, scabby.

Rauf|bold contp. ['raufbɔlt] m (-[e]s/-e) brawler, rowdy, Am. sl. tough; 2en (ge-, h) 1. v/t. pluck, pull; sich die Haare ~ tear one's hair; 2. v/i. fight, scuffle; ~erei [~⁹'rai] f (-/-en) fight, scuffle.

rauh adj. [rau] rough; rugged; weather: inclement, raw; voice: hoarse; fig.: harsh; coarse, rude; F: in ~en Mengen galore; '2reif m (-[e]s/no pl.) hoar-frost, poet. rime.

Raum [raum] m (-[e]s/⁹e) room, space; expanse; area; room; premises pl.; '~anzug m space suit.

räumen ['rɔymən] v/t. (ge-, h) remove, clear (away); leave, give up, esp. ✗ evacuate; vacate (flat).

'Raum|fahrt f astronautics; '~flug m space flight; '~inhalt m volume, capacity; '~kapsel f capsule.

räumlich adj. ['rɔymlic] relating to space, of space, spatial.

'Raum|meter n, m cubic met|re, Am. -er; '~schiff n space craft or ship; '~sonde f space probe; '~station f space station.

'Räumung f (-/-en) clearing, removal; esp. ✝ clearance; vacating (of flat), by force: eviction; ✗ evacuation (of town); '~sverkauf ✝ m clearance sale.

raunen ['raunən] (ge-, h) 1. v/i. whisper, murmur; 2. v/t. whisper, murmur; man raunt rumo(u)r has it.

Raupe zo. ['raupə] f (-/-n) caterpillar; '~nschlepper ⊕ m caterpillar tractor.

raus int. [raus] get out!, sl. beat it!, scram!

Rausch [rauʃ] m (-es/⁹e) intoxication, drunkenness; fig. frenzy, transport(s pl.); e-n ~ haben be drunk; 2en v/i. (ge-) 1. (h) leaves, rain, silk: rustle; water, wind: rush; surf: roar; applause: thunder; 2. (sein) movement: sweep; '~gift n narcotic (drug), F dope.

räuspern ['rɔʏspərn] v/refl. (ge-, h) clear one's throat.

Razzia ['ratsja] f (-/Razzien) raid, round-up.

reagieren [rea'giːrən] v/i. (no -ge-, h) react (auf acc. [up]on; to); fig. and ⊕ a. respond (to).

Reaktion [reak'tsjoːn] f (-/-en) reaction (a. pol.); fig. a. response (auf acc. to); **~är** [~o'nɛːr] 1. m (-s/-e) reactionary; 2. ♀ adj. reactionary.

Reaktor phys. [re'aktɔr] m (-s/-en) (nuclear) reactor, atomic pile.

real adj. [re'aːl] real; concrete; **~isieren** [reali'ziːrən] v/t. (no -ge-, h) realize; **♀ismus** [rea'lismus] m (-/no pl.) realism; **~istisch** adj. [rea'listiʃ] realistic; **♀ität** [reali'tɛːt] f (-/-en) reality; **♀schule** f non-classical secondary school.

Rebe ♀ ['reːbə] f (-/-n) vine.

Rebell [re'bɛl] m (-en/-en) rebel; **♀ieren** [~'liːrən] v/i. (no -ge-, h) rebel, revolt, rise; **♀isch** adj. rebellious.

Reb|huhn orn. ['reːp-] n partridge; **~laus** zo. ['reːp-] f vine-fretter, phylloxera; **~stock** ♀ ['reːp-] m vine.

Rechen ['reçən] m (-s/-) rake; grid.

Rechen|aufgabe ['reçən-] f sum, (arithmetical) problem; **~fehler** m arithmetical error, miscalculation; **~maschine** f calculating-machine; **~schaft** f (-/no pl.): ~ ablegen give or render an account (über acc. of), account or answer (for); zur ~ ziehen call to account (wegen for); **~schieber** ⚔ m slide-rule.

rechne|n ['reçnən] (ge-, h) 1. v/t. reckon, calculate; estimate, value; charge; ~ zu rank with or among(st); 2. v/i. count; ~ auf (acc.) or mit count or reckon or rely (up)on; **~risch** adj. arithmetical.

'Rechnung f (-/-en) calculation, sum, reckoning; account, bill; invoice (of goods); in restaurant: bill, Am. check; score; auf ~ on account; ~ legen render an account (über acc. of); e-r Sache ~ tragen make allowance for s.th.; es geht auf meine ~ in restaurants: it is my treat, Am. F this is on me; **~sprüfer** m auditor.

recht¹ [reçt] 1. adj. right; real; legitimate; right, correct; zur ~en Zeit in due time, at the right moment; ein ~er Narr a regular fool; mir ist es ~ I don't mind; ~ haben be right; j-m ~ geben agree with s.o.; 2. adv. right(ly), well; very; rather; really; correctly; ganz ~! quite (so)!; es geschieht ihm ~ it serves him right; ~ gern gladly, with pleasure; ~ gut quite good or well; ich weiß nicht ~ I wonder.

Recht² [~] n (-[e]s/-e) right (auf

acc. to), title (to), claim (on), interest (in); privilege; power, authority; ⚖ law; justice; ~ sprechen administer justice; mit ~ justly.

'Rechte f (-n/-n) right hand; boxing: right; pol. the Right.

Rechteck ['reçt?-] n (-[e]s/-e) rectangle; **♀ig** adj. rectangular.

recht|fertigen ['reçtfɛrtigən] v/t. (ge-, h) justify; defend, vindicate; **♀fertigung** f (-/-en) justification; vindication, defen|ce, Am. -se; **~gläubig** adj. orthodox; **~haberisch** adj. ['~haːbəriʃ] dogmatic; **~lich** adj. legal, lawful, legitimate; honest, righteous; **~los** adj. without rights; outlawed; **♀losigkeit** f (-/no pl.) outlawry; **~mäßig** adj. legal, lawful, legitimate; **♀mäßigkeit** f (-/no pl.) legality, legitimacy.

rechts adv. [reçts] on or to the right (hand).

'Rechts|anspruch m legal right or claim (auf acc. on, to), title (to); **~anwalt** m lawyer, solicitor; barrister, Am. attorney (at law); **~außen** m (-/-) football: outside right; **~beistand** m legal adviser, counsel.

'recht|schaffen 1. adj. honest, righteous; 2. adv. thoroughly, downright, F awfully; **♀schreibung** f (-/-en) orthography, spelling.

'Rechts|fall m case, cause; **~frage** f question of law; issue of law; **~gelehrte** m jurist, lawyer; **♀gültig** adj. s. rechtskräftig; **~kraft** f (-/no pl.) legal force or validity; **♀kräftig** adj. valid, legal; judgement: final; **~kurve** f right-hand bend; **~lage** f legal position or status; **~mittel** n legal remedy; **~nachfolger** m assign, assignee; **~person** f legal personality; **~pflege** f administration of justice, judicature.

'Rechtsprechung f (-/-en) jurisdiction.

'Rechts|schutz m legal protection; **~spruch** m legal decision; judg(e)ment; sentence; verdict (of jury); **~steuerung** mot. f (-/-en) right-hand drive; **~streit** m action, lawsuit; **~verfahren** n (legal) proceedings pl.; **~verkehr** mot. m right-hand traffic; **~verletzung** f infringement; **~vertreter** m s. Rechtsbeistand; **~weg** m: den ~ beschreiten take legal action, go to law; unter Ausschluß des ~es eliminating legal proceedings; **♀widrig** adj. illegal, unlawful; **~wissenschaft** f jurisprudence.

'recht|wink(e)lig adj. right-angled; **~zeitig** 1. adj. punctual; opportune; 2. adv. in (due) time, punctually, Am. on time.

Reck [rɛk] *n* (-[e]s/-e) *sports*: horizontal bar.

recken ['rɛkən] *v/t.* (ge-, h) stretch; sich ~ stretch o.s.

Redakt|eur [redak'tø:r] *m* (-s/-e) editor; **~ion** [~'tsjo:n] *f* (-/-en) editorship; editing, wording; editorial staff, editors *pl.*; editor's or editorial office; **2ionell** *adj.* [~tsjo'nɛl] editorial.

Rede ['re:də] *f* (-/-n) speech; oration; language; talk, conversation; discourse; **direkte ~** *gr.* direct speech; **indirekte ~** *gr.* reported or indirect speech; **e-e ~ halten** make or deliver a speech; **~ zur stellen** call to account (**wegen** for); **davon ist nicht die ~** that is not the point; **davon kann keine ~ sein** that's out of the question; **es ist nicht der ~ wert** it is not worth speaking of; **'2gewandt** *adj.* eloquent, **kunst** *f* rhetoric; **'2n** (ge-, h) **1.** *t* speak; talk; **2.** *v/i.* speak mit to), talk (to), chat (with); discuss (**über et.** s.th.); **sie läßt nicht mit sich ~** she won't listen to reason.

Redensart ['re:dəns⁹-] *f* phrase, expression; idiom; proverb, saying.

redigieren [redi'gi:rən] *v/t.* (no -ge-, h) edit; revise.

redlich ['re:tliç] **1.** *adj.* honest, upright; sincere; **2.** *adv.*: **sich ~ bemühen** take great pains.

Redner ['re:dnər] *m* (-s/-) speaker; orator; **~bühne** *f* platform; **2isch** *adj.* oratorical, rhetorical; **~pult** *n* speaker's desk.

redselig *adj.* ['re:tze:liç] talkative.

reduzieren [redu'tsi:rən] *v/t.* (no -ge-, h) reduce (**auf** acc. to).

Reede ⚓ ['re:də] *f* (-/-n) roads *pl.*, roadstead; **~r** *m* (-s/-) shipowner; **~'rei** *f* (-/-en) shipping company or firm.

reell [re'ɛl] **1.** *adj.* respectable, honest; *business firm*: solid; *goods*: good; *offer*: real; **2.** *adv.*: **bedient werden** get good value for one's money.

Refer|at [refe'ra:t] *n* (-[e]s/-e) report; lecture; paper; **ein ~ halten** *esp. univ.* read a paper; **~endar** [~ɛn'da:r] *m* (-s/-e) ♣ junior lawyer; *at school*: junior teacher; **~ent** [~'rɛnt] *m* (-en/-en) reporter; speaker; **~enz** [~'rɛnts] *f* (-/-en) reference; **2ieren** [~ri:rən] *v/i.* (no -ge-, h) report (**über** acc. [up]on); (give a) lecture (on); *esp. univ.* read a paper (on).

reflektieren [reflɛk'ti:rən] (no -ge-, h) **1.** *phys. v/t.* reflect; **2.** *v/i.* reflect (**über** acc. [up]on); **~ auf** acc.) ✝ think of buying; be interested in.

Reflex [re'flɛks] *m* (-es -e) *phys.* reflection or reflexion; ✠ reflex (action); **2iv** *gr.* adj. [~'ksi:f] reflexive.

Reform [re'fɔrm] *f* (-/-en) reform; **~er** *m* (-s/-) reformer; **2ieren** [~'mi:rən] *v/t.* (no -ge-, h) reform.

Refrain [rə'frɛ:] *m* (-s/-s) refrain, chorus, burden.

Regal [re'ga:l] *n* (-s/-e) shelf.

rege *adj.* ['re:gə] active, brisk, lively; busy.

Regel ['re:gəl] *f* (-/-n) rule; regulation; standard; *physiol.* menstruation, menses *pl.*; **in der ~ as a rule**; **'2los** *adj.* irregular; disorderly; **'2mäßig** *adj.* regular; **'2n** *v/t.* (ge-, h) regulate, control; arrange, settle; put in order; **'2recht** *adj.* regular; **'~ung** *f* (-/-en) regulation, control; arrangement, settlement; **2widrig** *adj.* contrary to the rules, irregular; abnormal; *sports*: foul.

regen¹ ['re:gən] *v/t. and v/refl.* ~ (ge-, h) move, stir.

Regen² [~] *m* (-s/-) rain; **vom ~ in die Traufe kommen** jump out of the frying-pan into the fire, get from bad to worse; **'2arm** *adj.* dry; **'~bogen** *m* rainbow; **~bogenhaut** *anat. f* iris; **2dicht** *adj.* rain-proof; **~guß** *m* downpour; **~mantel** *m* waterproof, raincoat, mac(k)intosh, F mac; **2reich** *adj.* rainy; **~schauer** *m* shower (of rain); **~schirm** *m* umbrella; **~tag** *m* rainy day; **~tropfen** *m* raindrop; **~wasser** *n* rain-water; **'~wetter** *n* rainy weather; **~wolke** *f* rain-cloud; **~wurm** *zo. m* earthworm, Am. a. angleworm; **'~zeit** *f* rainy season.

Regie [re'ʒi:] *f* (-/-n) management; *thea., film*: direction; **unter der ~ von** directed by.

regier|en [re'gi:rən] (no -ge-, h) **1.** *v/i* reign; **2.** *v/t.* govern (*a. gr.*), rule; **~ung** *f* (-/-en) government, *Am.* administration; reign.

Re'gierungs|antritt *m* accession (to the throne); **~beamte** *m* government official; *Brt.* Civil Servant; **~bezirk** *m* administrative district; **~gebäude** *n* government offices *pl.*

Regiment [regi'mɛnt] *n* **1.** (-[e]s/-e) government, rule; **2.** ✠ (-[e]s/-er) regiment.

Regisseur [reʒi'sø:r] *m* (-s/-e) *thea.* stage manager, director; *film*: director.

Regist|er [re'gistər] *n* (-s/-) register (*a. ♪*); record; index; **~ratur** [~ra'tu:r] *f* (-/-en) registry; registration.

registrier|en [regis'tri:rən] *v/t.* (no -ge-, h) register, record; **2kasse** *f* cash register.

reglos *adj.* ['re:klo:s] motionless.

regne|n ['re:gnən] *v/i.* (ge-, h) rain; **es regnet in Strömen** it is pouring with rain; **'~risch** *adj.* rainy.

Regreß ✠, ✝ [re'grɛs] *m* (Regresses/Regresse) recourse; **2pflichtig** ✠, ✝ *adj.* liable to recourse.

regulär *adj.* [regu'lɛ:r] regular.

regulier|bar adj. [regu'li:rbɑ:r] adjustable, controllable; **~en** v/t. (no -ge-, h) regulate, adjust; control.
Regung ['re:guŋ] f (-/-en) movement, motion; emotion; impulse; **'2slos** adj. motionless.
Reh zo. [re:] n (-[e]s/-e) deer, roe; female: doe.
rehabilitieren [rehabili'ti:rən] v/t. (no -ge-, h) rehabilitate.
'Reh|bock zo. m roebuck; **'2braun** adj., **'2farben** adj. fawn-colo(u)red; **'~geiß** zo. f doe; **'~kalb** zo. n, **~kitz** zo. ['~kits] n (-es/-e) fawn.
Reib|e ['raibə] f (-/-n), **~eisen** ['raip°-] n grater.
reib|en ['raibən] (irr., ge-, h) 1. v/i. rub (an dat. [up]on), 2. v/t. rub, grate; pulverize; wund ~ chafe, gall; **2erei** F fig. [~'rai] f (-/-en) (constant) friction; **'2ung** f (-/-en) friction; **'~ungslos** adj. frictionless; fig. smooth.
reich¹ adj. [raiç] rich (an dat. in); wealthy; ample, abundant, copious.
Reich² [~] n (-es/-e) empire; kingdom (of animals, vegetables, minerals); poet., rhet., fig. realm.
reichen ['raiçən] (ge-, h) 1. v/t. offer; serve (food); j-m et. ~ hand or pass s.th. to s.o.; sich die Hände ~ join hands; 2. v/i. reach; extend; suffice; das reicht! that will do!
reich|haltig adj. ['raiçhaltiç] rich; abundant, copious; **'~lich** 1. adj. ample, abundant, copious, plentiful; ~ Zeit plenty of time; 2. F adv. rather, fairly, F pretty, plenty; **'2tum** m (-s/ᵘer) riches pl.; wealth (an dat. of).
'Reichweite f reach; ✗ range; in ~ within reach, near at hand.
reif¹ adj. [raif] ripe, mature.
Reif² [~] m (-[e]s/no pl.) white or hoar-frost, poet. rime.
'Reife f (-/no pl.) ripeness, maturity.
'reifen¹ v/i. (ge-) 1. (sein) ripen, mature; 2. (h): es hat gereift there is a white or hoar-frost.
'Reifen² m (-s/-) hoop; ring; tyre, (Am. only) tire; as ornament: circlet; ~ wechseln mot. change tyres; **'~panne** mot. f puncture, Am. a. blowout.
'Reife|prüfung f s. Abitur; **'~zeugnis** n s. Abschlußzeugnis.
'reiflich adj. mature, careful.
Reihe ['raiə] f (-/-n) row; line; rank; series; number; thea. row, tier; der ~ nach by turns; ich bin an der ~ it is my turn.
'Reihen|folge f succession, sequence; alphabetische ~ alphabetical order; **'~haus** n terrace-house, Am. row house; **'2weise** adv. in rows.
Reiher orn. ['raiər] m (-s/-) heron.
Reim [raim] m (-[e]s/-e) rhyme; **'2en** (ge-, h) 1. v/i. rhyme; 2. v/t. and v/refl. rhyme (auf acc. with).

rein adj. [rain] pure; clean; clear; ~e Wahrheit plain truth; **'2fall** F m letdown; **'2gewicht** n net weight; **'2gewinn** m net profit; **'2heit** f (-/no pl.) purity; cleanness.
'reinig|en v/t. (ge-, h) clean(se); fig. purify; **'2ung** f (-/-en) clean(s)ing; fig. purification; cleaners pl.; chemische ~ dry cleaning; **'2ungs-mittel** n detergent, cleanser.
'rein|lich adj. clean; cleanly; neat, tidy; **'2machefrau** f charwoman; **'~rassig** adj. pedigree, thoroughbred, esp. Am. purebred; **'2schrift** f fair copy.
Reis¹ ♀ [rais] m (-es/-e) rice.
Reis² ♀ [~] n (-es/-er) twig, sprig.
Reise ['raizə] f (-/-n) journey; ♐, ✗ voyage; travel; tour; trip; passage; **~büro** n travel agency or bureau; **'2decke** f travel(l)ing-rug; **'2fertig** adj. ready to start; **'~führer** m guide(-book); **'~gepäck** n luggage, Am. baggage; **'~gesellschaft** f tourist party; **'~kosten** pl. travel(l)ing-expenses pl.; **'~leiter** m courier; **'2n** v/i. (ge-, sein) travel, journey; ~ nach go to; ins Ausland ~ go abroad; **'~nde** m, f (-n/-n) (♠ commercial) travel(l)er; in trains: passenger; for pleasure: tourist; **~necessaire** [~nesesɛ:r] n (-s/-s) dressing-case; **'~paß** m passport; **'~scheck** m traveller's cheque, Am. traveler's check; **'~schreibmaschine** f portable typewriter; **'~tasche** f travel(l)ing-bag, Am. grip(sack).
Reisig ['raiziç] n (-s/no pl.) brushwood.
Reißbrett ['rais-] n drawing-board.
reißen ['raisən] 1. v/t. (irr., ge-, h) tear; pull; an dat. ~ seize; sich ~ scratch o.s. (an dat. with); sich ~ um scramble for; 2. v/i. (irr., ge-, sein) break; burst; split; tear; mir riß die Geduld I lost (all) patience; 3. ♀ F ⚕ n (-s/no pl.) rheumatism; **'~d** adj. rapid; animal: rapacious; pain: acute; ~en Absatz finden sell like hot cakes.
'Reiß|er F m (-s/-) draw, box-office success; thriller; **'~feder** f drawing-pen; **'~leine** ✈ f rip-cord; **'~nagel** m s. Reißzwecke; **'~schiene** f (T-)square; **'~verschluß** m zip-fastener, zipper, Am. a. slide fastener; **'~zeug** n drawing instruments pl.; **'~zwecke** f drawing-pin, Am. thumbtack.
Reit|anzug ['rait-] m riding-dress; **'~bahn** f riding-school, manège; riding-track; **'2en** (irr., ge-) 1. v/i. (sein) ride, go on horseback; 2. v/t. (h) ride; **'~er** m (-s/-) rider, horseman; ✗, police: trooper; filing: tab; **~e'rei** f (-/-en) cavalry; **'~erin** f (-/-nen) horsewoman; **'~gerte** f

riding-whip; '~hose f (riding-) breeches pl.; '~knecht m groom; '~kunst f horsemanship; ~lehrer m riding master; ~peitsche f riding-whip; '~pferd zo. n riding-horse, saddle-horse; ~schule f riding-school; '~stiefel m/pl. riding-boots pl.; '~weg m bridle-path.

Reiz [raɪts] m (-es/-e) irritation; charm, attraction; allurement; '2-bar adj. sensitive; irritable, excitable, Am. sore; 2en (ge-, h) 1. v/t. irritate (a. s'); excite; provoke; nettle; stimulate, rouse; entice, (al)lure, tempt, charm, attract; 2. v/i. cards: bid; 2end adj. charming, attractive; Am. cute; lovely; '2los adj. unattractive; ~mittel n stimulus; s' stimulant; ~ung f (-/-en) irritation; provocation; '2-voll adj. charming, attractive.

rekeln F ['re:kəln] v/refl. (ge-, h) loll, lounge, sprawl.

Reklamation [reklama'tsjo:n] f (-/-en) claim; complaint, protest.

Reklame [re'kla:mə] f (-/-n) advertising; advertisement, F ad; publicity; ~ machen advertise; ~ machen für et. advertise s.th.

rekla'mieren (no -ge-, h) 1. v/t. (re)claim; 2. v/i. complain (wegen about).

Rekonvaleszen|t [rekɔnvales'tsɛnt] m (-en/-en), ~tin f (-/-nen) convalescent; ~z [~ts] f (-/no pl.) convalescence.

Rekord [re'kɔrt] m (-[e]s/-e) sports, etc.: record.

Rekrut ✗ [re'kru:t] m (-en/-en) recruit; 2ieren ✗ [~u'ti:rən] v/t. (no -ge-, h) recruit.

Rektor ['rɛktɔr] m (-s/-en) headmaster, rector, Am. principal; univ. chancellor, rector, Am. president.

relativ adj. [rela'ti:f] relative.

Relief [rel'jɛf] n (-s/-s, -e) relief.

Religi|on [reli'gjo:n] f (-/-en) religion; 2ös adj. [~ø:s] religious; pious, devout; ~osität [~ozi'tɛ:t] f (-/no pl.) religiousness; piety.

Reling ⚓ ['re:lɪŋ] f (-/-s, -e) rail.

Reliquie [re'li:kviə] f (-/-n) relic.

Ren zo. [rɛn; re:n] n (-s/-s; -s/-e) reindeer.

Renn|bahn ['rɛn-] f racecourse, Am. race track, horse-racing: a. the turf; mot. speedway; '~boot n racing boat, racer.

rennen ['rɛnən] 1. v/i. (irr., ge-, sein) run; race; 2. v/t. (irr., ge-, h): j-n zu Boden ~ run s.o. down; 3. 2 n (-s/-) run(ning); race; heat.

'Renn|fahrer m mot. racing driver, racer; racing cyclist; ~läufer m ski racer; '~mannschaft f race-crew; '~pferd zo. n racehorse, racer; '~rad n racing bicycle, racer; '~sport m racing; horse-racing: a. the turf; '~stall m racing stable;

'~strecke f racecourse, Am. race track; mot. speedway; distance (to be run); '~wagen m racing car, racer.

renommiert adj. [reno'mi:rt] famous, noted (wegen for).

renovieren [reno'vi:rən] v/t. (no -ge-, h) renovate, repair; redecorate (interior of house).

rent|abel adj. [rɛn'ta:bəl] profitable, paying; '2e f (-/-n) income, revenue; annuity; (old-age) pension; rent; 2enempfänger ['rɛntən?-] m s. Rentner; rentier.

Rentier zo. ['rɛn-] n s. Ren.

rentieren [rɛn'ti:rən] v/refl. (no -ge-, h) pay.

Rentner ['rɛntnər] m (-s/-) (old-age) pensioner.

Reparatur [repara'tu:r] f (-/-en) repair; ~werkstatt f repair-shop; mot. a. garage, service station.

repa'rieren v/t. (no -ge-, h) repair, Am. F fix.

Report|age [repɔr'ta:ʒə] f (-/-n) reporting, commentary, coverage; ~er [re'pɔrtər] m (-s/-) reporter.

Repräsent|ant [reprezɛn'tant] m (-en/-en) representative; ~antenhaus Am. parl. n House of Representatives; 2ieren (no -ge-, h) 1. v/t. represent; 2. v/i. cut a fine figure.

Repressalie [reprɛ'sa:ljə] f (-/-n) reprisal.

reproduzieren [reprodu'tsi:rən] v/t. (no -ge-, h) reproduce.

Reptil zo. [rɛp'ti:l] n (-s/-ien, ✍-e) reptile.

Republik [repu'bli:k] f (-/-en) republic; ~aner pol. [~i'ka:nər] m (-s/-) republican; 2anisch adj. [~i'ka:nɪʃ] republican.

Reserve [re'zɛrvə] f (-/-n) reserve; ~rad mot. n spare wheel.

reser'vier|en v/t. (no -ge-, h) reserve; ~ lassen book (seat, etc.); ~t adj. reserved (a. fig.).

Resid|enz [rezi'dɛnts] f (-/-en) residence; 2ieren v/i. (no -ge-, h) reside.

resignieren [rezi'gni:rən] v/i. (no -ge-, h) resign.

Respekt [re'spɛkt] m (-[e]s/no pl.) respect; 2ieren [~'ti:rən] v/t. (no -ge-, h) respect; 2los adj. irreverent, disrespectful; 2voll adj. respectful.

Ressort [rɛ'so:r] n (-s/-s) department; province.

Rest [rɛst] m (-es/-e, ✝ -er) rest, remainder; residue (a. 🜊); esp. ✝ remnant (of cloth); leftover (of food); das gab ihm den ~ that finished him (off).

Restaurant [rɛsto'rã:] n (-s/-s) restaurant.

'Rest|bestand m remnant; '~betrag m remainder, balance; '2lich adj. remaining; '2los adv. completely; entirely; **'~zahlung** f payment of balance; final payment.

Resultat [rezul'taːt] n (-[e]s/-e) result, outcome; *sports:* score.

retten ['rɛtən] v/t. (ge-, h) save; deliver, rescue.

Rettich ♣ ['rɛtiç] m (-s/-e) radish.

Rettung f (-/-en) rescue; deliverance; escape.

Rettungs|boot n lifeboat; **'~gürtel** m lifebelt; **'2los** adj. irretrievable, past help or hope, beyond recovery; **'~mannschaft** f rescue party; **'~ring** m life-buoy.

Reue ['rɔyə] f (-/no pl.) repentance (über acc. of), remorse (at); **'2en** v/t. (ge-, h): et. reut mich I repent (of) s.th.; **'2evoll** adj. repentant; **2(müt)ig** adj. ['~(myːt)iç] repentant.

Revanche [re'vãːʃ(ə)] f (-/-n) revenge; **~spiel** n return match.

revan'chieren v/refl. (no -ge-, h) take or have one's revenge (an dat. on); return (für et. s.th.).

Revers 1. [re'veːr] n, m (-/-) lapel (of coat); 2. [re'vɛrs] m (-es/-e) declaration; ⚖ bond.

revidieren [revi'diːrən] v/t. (no -ge-, h) revise; check; ♦ audit.

Revier [re'viːr] n (-s/-e) district, quarter; s. Jagdrevier.

Revision [revi'zjoːn] f (-/-en) revision (a. typ.); ♦ audit; ⚖ appeal; ~ einlegen ⚖ lodge an appeal.

Revolt|e [re'vɔltə] f (-/-n) revolt, uprising; **2ieren** [~'tiːrən] v/i. (no -ge-, h) revolt, rise (in revolt).

Revolution [revolu'tsjoːn] f (-/-en) revolution; **~är** [~o'nɛːr] 1. m (-s/-e) revolutionary; 2. ♀ adj. revolutionary.

Revolver [re'vɔlvər] m (-s/-) revolver, Am. ⌐ u. gun.

Revue [rə'vyː] f (-/-n) review; *thea.* revue, (musical) show; ~ passieren lassen pass in review.

Rezens|ent [retsɛn'zɛnt] m (-en/-en) critic, reviewer; **2ieren** v/t. (no -ge-, h) review, criticize; **~ion** [~'zjoːn] f (-/-en) review, critique.

Rezept [re'tsɛpt] n (-[e]s/-e) ⚕ prescription; *cooking:* recipe (a. fig.).

Rhabarber ♣ [ra'barbər] m (-s/no pl.) rhubarb.

rhetorisch adj. [re'toːriʃ] rhetorical.

rheumati|sch ⚕ adj. [rɔy'maːtiʃ] rheumatic; **2smus** ⚕ [~a'tismus] m (-/Rheumatismen) rheumatism.

rhythm|isch adj. ['rytmiʃ] rhythmic(al); **2us** ['~us] m (-/Rhythmen) rhythm.

richten ['riçtən] v/t. (ge-, h) set right, arrange, adjust; level; point (gun) (auf acc. at); direct (gegen at); ⚖ judge; execute; zugrunde ~ ruin, destroy; in die Höhe ~ raise, lift up; sich ~ nach conform to, act according to; take one's bearings from;

gr. agree with; depend on; *price:* be determined by; ich richte mich nach Ihnen I leave it to you.

'Richter m (-s/-) judge; **2lich** adj. judicial; **'~spruch** m judg(e)ment, sentence.

'richtig 1. adj. right, correct, accurate; proper; true; just; ein ~er Londoner a regular cockney; 2. adv.: ~ gehen *clock:* go right; **'2keit** f (-/no pl.) correctness; accuracy; justness; **'stellen** v/t. (sep., -ge-, h) put or set right, rectify.

'Richt|linien f/pl. (general) directions pl., rules pl.; **'~preis** ♦ m standard price; **'~schnur** f ⊕ plumb-line; *fig.* rule of (conduct), guiding principle.

Richtung f (-s/-en) direction; course, way; *fig.* line; **~sanzeiger** *mot.* ['riçtuŋs~] m (-s/-) flashing indicator, trafficator; **'2weisend** adj. directive, leading, guiding.

Richtwaage ⊕ f level.

rieb [riːp] pret. of reiben.

riechen ['riːçən] (irr., ge-, h) 1. v/i. smell (nach of an acc. at); sniff (an dat. at); 2. v/t. smell; sniff.

rief [riːf] pret. of rufen.

riefeln ⊕ ['riːfəln] v/t. (ge-, h) flute, groove.

Riegel ['riːgəl] m (-s/-) bar, bolt; bar, cake (of soap); bar (of chocolate).

Riemen ['riːmən] m (-s/-) strap, thong; belt; ⊕ oar.

Ries [riːs] n (-es/-e) ream.

Riese ['riːzə] m (-n/-n) giant.

rieseln ⊕ ['riːzəln] v/i. (ge-) 1. (sein) *small stream:* purl, ripple; trickle; 2. (h) es rieselt it drizzles.

ries|engroß adj. ['riːzən'-], **'~en-haft** adj., **'~ig** adj. gigantic, huge; **'2in** f (-/-nen) giantess.

riet [riːt] pret. of raten.

Riff [rif] n (-[e]s/-e) reef.

Rille ['rilə] f (-/-n) groove; ⊕ a. flute.

Rimesse ♦ [ri'mɛsə] f (-/-n) remittance.

Rind *zo.* [rint] n (-[e]s/-er) ox; cow; neat; ~er pl. (horned) cattle pl.; zwanzig ~er twenty head of cattle.

Rinde ['rində] f (-/-n) ⊕ bark; rind (of fruit, bacon, cheese); crust (of bread).

Rinder|braten m roast beef; **'~herde** f herd of cattle; **'~hirt** m cowherd, Am. cowboy.

'Rind|fleisch n beef; **'~(s)leder** n neat's-leather, cow-hide; **'~vieh** n (horned) cattle pl., neat pl.

Ring [riŋ] m (-[e]s/-e) ring; circle; link (of chain); ♦ ring, pool, trust, Am. ⌐ combine; **'~bahn** f circular railway.

ringel|n ['riŋəln] v/refl. (ge-, h) curl, coil; **'2natter** *zo.* f ringsnake.

ring|en ['riŋən] (*irr.*, ge-, *h*) **1.** *v/i.* wrestle; struggle (*um* for); *nach Atem* ~ gasp (for breath); **2.** *v/t.* wring (*hands, washing*); '**~er** *m* (-s/-) wrestler.

ring|förmig *adj.* ['riŋfœrmiç] annular, ring-like; '**2kampf** *m sports:* wrestling(-match); '**2richter** *m boxing:* referee.

rings *adv.* [riŋs] around; '**~he'rum** *adv.,* '**~um** *adv.,* '**~um'her** *adv.* round about, all (a)round.

Rinn|e ['rinə] *f* (-/-n) groove, channel; gutter (*of roof or street*); gully; '**2en** *v/i.* (*irr.,* ge-, *sein*) run, flow; drip; leak; **~sal** [´~za:l] *n* (-[e]s/-e) watercourse, streamlet; '**~stein** *m* gutter; sink (*of kitchen unit*).

Rippe ['ripə] *f* (-/-n) rib, △ groin; bar (*of chocolate*); '**2n** *v/t.* (ge-, *h*) rib; '**~nfell** *anat.:* pleura; '**~nfell-entzündung** *f* pleurisy; '**~n-stoß** *m* dig in the ribs; nudge.

Risiko ['ri:ziko] *n* (-s/-s, *Risiken*) risk; *ein* ~ *eingehen* take a risk.

risk|ant *adj.* [ris'kant] risky; **~ieren** *v/t.* (*no* -ge-, *h*) risk.

Riß [ris] **1.** *m* (*Risses/Risse*) rent, tear; split (*a. fig.*); crack; *in skin:* chap; scratch; ⊕ draft, plan; *fig.* rupture; **2.** 2 *pret. of reißen.*

rissig *adj.* ['risiç] full of rents; *skin, etc.:* chappy; ~ *werden* crack.

Rist [rist] *m* (-es/-e) instep; back of the hand; wrist.

Ritt [rit] **1.** *m* (-[e]s/-e) ride; **2.** 2 *pret. of reiten.*

'**Ritter** *m* (-s/-) knight; *zum* ~ *schlagen* knight; '**~gut** *n* manor; '**2lich** *adj.* knightly, chivalrous; '**~lich-keit** *f* (-/-en) gallantry, chivalry.

rittlings *adv.* ['ritliŋs] astride (*auf e-m Pferd* a horse).

Ritz [rits] *m* (-es/-e) crack, chink; scratch; '**~e** *f* (-/-n) crack, chink; fissure; '**2en** *v/t.* (ge-, *h*) scratch; cut.

Rival|e [ri'vɑ:lə] *m* (-n/-n), **~in** *f* (-/-nen) rival; **2isieren** [~ali'zi:rən] *v/i.* (*no* -ge-, *h*) rival (*mit j-m* s.o.); **~ität** [~ali'tɛ:t] *f* (-/-en) rivalry.

Rizinusöl ['ri:tsinus ´~] *n* (-[e]s/*no pl.*) castor oil.

Robbe *zo.* ['rɔbə] *f* (-/-n) seal.

Robe ['ro:bə] *f* (-/-n) gown; robe.

Roboter ['rɔbɔtər] *m* (-s/-) robot.

robust *adj.* [ro'bust] robust, sturdy, vigorous.

roch [rɔx] *pret. of riechen.*

röcheln ['rœçəln] (ge-, *h*) **1.** *v/i.* rattle; **2.** *v/t.* gasp out (*words*).

Rock [rɔk] *m* (-[e]s/-e) skirt; coat, jacket; '**~schoß** *m* coat-tail.

Rodel|bahn ['ro:dəl-] *f* toboggan-run; '**2n** *v/i.* (ge-, *h*, *sein*) toboggan, *Am. a.* coast; '**~schlitten** *m* sled(ge), toboggan.

roden ['ro:dən] *v/t.* (ge-, *h*) clear (*land*); root up, stub (*roots*).

Rogen *ichth.* ['ro:gən] *m* (-s/-) roe, spawn.

Roggen ♀ ['rɔgən] *m* (-s/-) rye.

roh *adj.* [ro:] raw; *fig.:* rough, rude; cruel, brutal; *oil, metal:* crude; '**2bau** *m* (-[e]s/-ten) rough brick-work; '**2eisen** *n* pig-iron.

Roheit ['ro:hait] *f* (-/-en) rawness; roughness (*a. fig.*); *fig.:* rudeness; brutality.

'**Roh|ling** *m* (-s/-e) brute, ruffian; '**~material** *n* raw material; '**~pro-dukt** *n* raw product.

Rohr [ro:r] *n* (-[e]s/-e) tube, pipe; duct; ♀: reed; cane.

Röhre ['rø:rə] *f* (-/-n) tube, pipe; duct; *radio:* valve, *Am.* (electron) tube.

'**Rohr|leger** *m* (-s/-) pipe fitter, plumber; '**~leitung** *f* plumbing; pipeline; '**~post** *f* pneumatic dispatch *or* tube; '**~stock** *m* cane; '**~zucker** *m* cane-sugar.

'**Rohstoff** *m* raw material.

Rolladen ['rɔlla:dən] *m* (-s/=, -) rolling shutter.

'**Rollbahn** ♀ *f* taxiway, taxi-strip.

Rolle ['rɔlə] *f* (-/-n) roll; roller; coil (*of rope, etc.*); pulley; *beneath furniture:* cast|or, -er; mangle; *thea.* part, role; *fig.* figure; ~ *Garn* reel of cotton, *Am.* spool of thread; *das spielt keine* ~ that doesn't matter, it makes no difference; *Geld spielt keine* ~ money (is) no object; *aus der* ~ *fallen* forget o.s.

'**rollen** (ge-) **1.** *v/i.* (*sein*) roll; ♀ taxi; **2.** *v/t.* (*h*) roll; wheel; mangle (*laundry*).

'**Rollenbesetzung** *thea. f* cast.

'**Roller** *m* (-s/-) *children's toy:* scooter; *mot.* (motor) scooter.

'**Roll|feld** ♀ *n* manœuvring area, *Am.* maneuvering area; '**~film** *phot. m* roll film; '**~kragen** *m* turtle neck; '**~schrank** *m* roll-fronted cabinet; '**~schuh** *m* roller-skate; '**~schuhbahn** *f* roller-skating rink; '**~stuhl** *m* wheel chair; '**~treppe** *f* escalator; '**~wagen** *m* lorry, truck.

Roman [ro'ma:n] *m* (-s/-e) novel, (work of) fiction; *novel of adventure and fig.*: romance; '**~ist** [~a'nist] *m* (-en/-en) Romance scholar *or* student; **~schriftsteller** *m* novelist.

Romanti|k [ro'mantik] *f* (-/*no pl.*) romanticism; **2sch** *adj.* romantic.

Röm|er ['rø:mər] *m* (-s/-) Roman; '**2isch** *adj.* Roman.

röntgen ['rœntgən] *v/t.* (ge-, *h*) X-ray; '**2aufnahme** *f,* '**2bild** *n* X-ray; '**2strahlen** *m/pl.* X-rays *pl.*

rosa *adj.* ['ro:za] pink.

Rose ['ro:zə] *f* (-/-n) ♀ rose; *f* erysipelas.

'**Rosen|kohl** ♀ *m* Brussels sprouts *pl.*; '**~kranz** *eccl. m* rosary; '**2rot** *adj.* rose-colo(u)red, rosy; '**stock** ♀ *m* (-[e]s/=e) rose-bush.

'**rosig** *adj.* rosy (*a. fig.*), rose-colo(u)red, roseate.

Rosine [ro'zi:nə] *f* (-/-*n*) raisin.

Roß *zo.* [rɔs] *n* (Rosses/Rosse, F Rösser) horse, *poet.* steed; '**haar** *n* horsehair.

Rost [rɔst] *m* 1. (-es/*no pl.*) rust; 2. (-es/-e) grate; gridiron; grill; '**braten** *m* roast joint.

'**rosten** *v/i.* (ge-, *h*, sein) rust.

rösten ['rø:stən] *v/t.* (ge-, *h*) roast, grill; toast (*bread*); fry (*potatoes*).

'**Rost|fleck** *m* rust-stain; *in cloth*: iron-mo(u)ld; '**2frei** *adj.* rustless, rustproof; *esp. steel*: stainless; '**2ig** *adj.* rusty, corroded.

rot [ro:t] 1. *adj.* red; 2. ♀ *n* (-s/-, F -s) red.

Rotationsmaschine *typ.* [rota-'tsjo:ns-] *f* rotary printing machine.

'**rot|backig** *adj.* ruddy; '**blond** *adj.* sandy.

Röte ['rø:tə] *f* (-/*no pl.*) redness, red (colo[u]r); blush; '**2n** *v/t.* (ge-, *h*) redden; paint *or* dye red; *sich* ~ redden; flush, blush.

'**rot|gelb** *adj.* reddish yellow; '**glühend** *adj.* red-hot; '**2haut** *f* red-skin.

rotieren [ro'ti:rən] *v/i.* (*no* -ge-, *h*) rotate, revolve.

Rot|käppchen ['ro:tkɛpçən] *n* (-s/-) Little Red Riding Hood; **kehlchen** *orn.* *n* (-s/-) robin (redbreast).

rötlich ['rø:tliç] *adj.* reddish.

'**Rot|stift** *m* red crayon *or* pencil; '**tanne** ♀ *f* spruce (fir).

Rotte ['rɔtə] *f* (-/-*n*) band, gang.

'**Rot|wein** *m* red wine; claret; '**wild** *zo.* *n* red deer.

Rouleau [ru'lo:] *n* (-s/-s) *s.* Rollladen; blind, *Am.* (window) shade.

Route ['ru:tə] *f* (-/-*n*) route.

Routine [ru'ti:nə] *f* (-/*no pl.*) routine, practice.

Rübe ♀ ['ry:bə] *f* (-/-*n*) beet; weiße ~ (Swedish) turnip, *Am. a.* rutabaga; rote ~ red beet, beet(root); gelbe ~ carrot.

Rubin [ru'bi:n] *m* (-s/-e) ruby.

ruch|bar *adj.* ['ru:xba:r]: ~ werden become known, get about *or* abroad; '**los** *adj.* wicked, profligate.

Ruck [ruk] *m* (-[e]s/-e) jerk, *Am.* F yank; jolt (*of vehicle*).

Rück|antwort ['ryk?-] *f* reply; Postkarte mit ~ reply postcard; mit bezahlter ~ telegram: reply paid; '**2bezüglich** *gr. adj.* reflexive; '**blick** *m* retrospect(ive view) (*auf acc.* at); reminiscences *pl.*

rücken[1] ['rykən] (ge-) 1. *v/t.* (*h*) move, shift; 2. *v/i.* (sein) move; näher ~ near, approach.

Rücken[2] [~] *m* (-s/-) back; ridge (*of mountain*); '**deckung** *fig. f* backing, support; '**lehne** *f* back

(*of chair, etc.*); '**mark** *anat.* *n* spinal cord; '**schmerzen** *m/pl.* pain in the back, back ache; '**schwimmen** *n* (-s/*no pl.*) back-stroke swimming; '**wind** *m* following *or* tail wind; '**wirbel** *anat.* *n* dorsal vertebra.

Rück|erstattung ['ryk?-] *f* restitution; refund (*of money*), reimbursement (*of expenses*); '**fahrkarte** *f* return (ticket), *Am. a.* round-trip ticket; '**fahrt** *f* return journey *or* voyage; *auf der* ~ on the way back; '**fall** *m* relapse; '**2fällig** *adj.*: werden relapse; '**flug** *m* return flight; '**frage** *f* further inquiry; '**gabe** *f* return, restitution; '**gang** *fig. m* retrogression; ✝ recession, decline; '**2gängig** *adj.* retrograde; ~ machen cancel; '**grat** *anat.* ~ *n* (-[e]s/-e) spine, backbone (*both a. fig.*); '**halt** *m* support; '**2haltlos** *adj.* unreserved, frank; '**hand** *f* -/*no pl.*) *tennis*: backhand (stroke); '**kauf** *m* repurchase; '**kehr** f -/-/*no pl.*) return; '**kopp**e)**lung** *ƒ f* (-/-en) feedback; '**lage** *f* reserve(s *pl.*); savings *pl.*, '**2läufig** *fig. adj.* ['lɔyfiç] retrograde; '**licht** *mot.* *n* tail-light, tail-lamp, rear-light; '**2lings** *adv.* backwards, from behind; '**marsch** *m* march back *or* home; retreat; '**porto** ✉ *n* return postage; '**reise** *f* return journey, journey back *or* home.

Rucksack *m* knapsack, rucksack.

Rück|schlag *m* backstroke; *fig.* setback; '**schluß** *m* conclusion, inference; '**schritt** *fig. m* retrogression, set-back; *pol.* reaction; '**seite** *f* back, reverse; *a.* tail (*of coin*); '**sendung** *f* return; '**sicht** *f* respect, regard, consideration (*auf j-n* for s.o.); '**2sichtslos** *adj.* inconsiderate (*gegen* of), regardless (*of*); ruthless; reckless; *es Fahren mot.* reckless driving; '**2sichtsvoll** *adj.* regardful (*gegen* of); considerate, thoughtful; '**sitz** *mot.* *m* back-seat; '**spiegel** *mot.* *m* rearview mirror; '**spiel** *n sports*: return match; '**sprache** *f* consultation; ~ nehmen mit consult (*lawyer*), consult with (*fellow workers*); nach ~ mit on consultation with; '**stand** *m* arrears *pl.*; backlog; ✝ residue; im ~ sein mit be in arrears *or* behind with; '**ständig** *fig. adj.* old-fashioned, backward; *~e Miete* arrears of rent; '**stoß** *m* recoil; kick (*of gun*); '**strahler** *m* (-s/-) rear reflector, cat's eye; '**tritt** *m* withdrawal, retreat; resignation; '**trittbremse** *f* back-pedal brake, *Am.* coaster brake; '**versicherung** *f* reinsurance; '**2wärts** *adv.* ['verts] back, backward(s); '**wärtsgang**

mot. *m* reverse (gear); '**~weg** *m* way back, return.

'**ruckweise** *adv.* by jerks.

'**rück|wirkend** *adj.* reacting; $\frac{t}{t} \frac{t}{t}$, *etc.*: retroactive, retrospective; '**2wirkung** *f* reaction; '**2zahlung** *f* repayment; '**2zug** *m* retreat.

Rüde ['ry:də] 1. *zo.* *m* (-n/-n) male dog *or* fox *or* wolf; large hound; 2. 2 *adj.* rude, coarse, brutal.

Rudel ['ru:dəl] *n* (-s/-) troop; pack (*of wolves*); herd (*of deer*).

Ruder ['ru:dər] *n* (-s/-) oar; rudder (*a.* ⚓); helm; '**~boot** *n* row(ing)-boat; '**~er** *m* (-s/-) rower, oarsman; '**~fahrt** *f* row; '**2n** (ge-) 1. *v/i.* (h, sein) row; 2. *v/t.* (h) row; **~regatta** ['~regata] *f* (-/Ruderregatten) boat race, regatta; '**~sport** *m* rowing.

Ruf [ru:f] *m* (-[e]s/-e) call; cry, shout; summons, *univ.* call; reputation, repute; fame; standing, credit; '**2en** (*irr.*, ge-, h) 1. *v/i.* call; cry, shout; 2. *v/t.* call: ~ lassen send for.

'**Ruf|name** *m* Christian *or* first name; '**~nummer** *f* telephone number; '**~weite** *f* (-/no pl.): in ~ within call *or* earshot.

Rüge ['ry:gə] *f* (-/-n) rebuke, censure, reprimand; '**2n** *v/t.* (ge-, h) rebuke, censure, blame.

Ruhe ['ru:ə] *f* (-/no pl.) rest, repose; sleep; quiet, calm; tranquillity, silence; peace; composure; *sich zur* ~ *setzen* retire; ~! quiet!, silence!; *immer mit der* ~! take it easy!; *lassen Sie mich in* ~! let me alone!; '**2bedürftig** *adj.*: ~ *sein* want *or* need rest; '**~gehalt** *n* pension; '**2los** *adj.* restless; '**2n** *v/i.* (ge-, h) rest, repose; sleep; *laß die Vergangenheit* ~! let bygones be bygones!; '**~pause** *f* pause; lull; '**~platz** *m* resting-place; '**~stand** *m* (-[e]s/no pl.) retirement; *im* ~ retired; *in den* ~ *treten* retire; *in den* ~ *versetzen* superannuate, pension off, retire; '**~stätte** *f*: *letzte* ~ last resting-place; '**~störer** *m* (-s/-) disturber of the peace, peacebreaker; '**~störung** *f* disturbance (of the peace), disorderly behavio(u)r, riot.

'**ruhig** *adj.* quiet; *mind.*, *water*: tranquil, calm; silent; ⊕ smooth.

Ruhm [ru:m] *m* (-[e]s/no pl.) glory; fame, renown.

rühm|en ['ry:mən] *v/t.* (ge-, h) praise, glorify; *sich e-r Sache* ~ boast of s.th.; '**~lich** *adj.* glorious, laudable.

'**ruhm|los** *adj.* inglorious; '**~reich** *adj.* glorious.

Ruhr ⚕ [ru:r] *f* (-/no pl.) dysentery.

Rühr|ei ['ry:r⁹-] *n* scrambled egg; '**2en** (ge-, h) 1. *v/t.* stir, move; *fig.* touch, move, affect; *sich* ~ stir, move, bustle; 2. *v/i.*: *an et.* ~ touch s.th.; *wir wollen nicht daran* ~ *let* sleeping dogs lie; '**2end**

adj. touching, moving; '**2ig** *adj.* active, busy; enterprising; nimble; '**2selig** *adj.* sentimental; '**~ung** *f* (-/no pl.) emotion, feeling.

Ruin [ru'i:n] *m* (-s/no pl.) ruin; decay; **~e** *f* (-/-n) ruin(s *pl.*); *fig.* ruin, wreck; **2ieren** [rui'ni:rən] *v/t.* (*no* -ge-, h) ruin; destroy, wreck; spoil; *sich* ~ ruin o.s.

rülpsen ['rylpsən] *v/i.* (ge-, h) belch.

Rumän|e [ru'mɛ:nə] *m* (-n/-n) Ro(u)manian; **2isch** *adj.* Ro(u)manian.

Rummel *F* ['ruməl] *m* (-s/no pl.) hurly-burly, row; bustle; revel; *in publicity* F ballyhoo; '**~platz** *m* fun fair, amusement park.

rumoren [ru'mo:rən] *v/i.* (*no* -ge-, h) make a noise *or* row; *bowels*: rumble.

Rumpel|kammer *F* ['rumpəl-] *f* lumber-room; '**2n** *F* *v/i.* (ge-, h, sein) rumble.

Rumpf [rumpf] *m* (-[e]s/⁔e) *anat.* trunk, body; torso (*of statue*); ⚓ hull, frame, body; ✈ fuselage, body.

rümpfen ['rympfən] *v/t.* (ge-, h): *die Nase* ~ turn up one's nose, sniff (*über acc.* at).

rund [runt] 1. *adj.* round (*a. fig.*); circular; 2. *adv.* about; '**2blick** *m* panorama, view all (a)round; 2e ['rundə] *f* (-/-n) round; *sports*: lap; *boxing*: round; round, patrol; beat (*of policeman*); *in der or die* ~ (a)round; **~en** ['~dən] *v/refl.* (ge-, h) (grow) round; '**2fahrt** *f* drive round (*town, etc.*); *s. Rundreise*; '**2flug** *m* circuit (*über of*); '**2frage** *f* inquiry, poll.

'**Rundfunk** *m* broadcast(ing); broadcasting service; broadcasting company; radio, wireless; *im* ~ *over the* wireless, on the radio *or* air; '**~anstalt** *f* broadcasting company; '**~ansager** *m* (radio) announcer; '**~gerät** *n* radio *or* wireless set; '**~gesellschaft** *f* broadcasting company; '**~hörer** *m* listener(-in); ~ *pl.* *a.* (radio) audience; '**~programm** *n* broadcast *or* radio program(me); '**~sender** *m* broadcast transmitter; broadcasting *or* radio station; '**~sendung** *f* broadcast; '**~sprecher** *m* broadcaster, broadcast speaker, (radio) announcer; '**~station** *f* broadcasting *or* radio station; '**~übertragung** *f* radio transmission, broadcast(ing); broadcast (*of programme*).

'**Rund|gang** *m* tour, round, circuit; '**~gesang** *m* glee, catch; '**2he'raus** *adv.* in plain words, frankly, plainly; '**2he'rum** *adv.* round about, all (a)round; '**2lich** *adj.* round(ish); rotund, plump; **~reise** *f* circular tour *or* trip, sight-seeing trip, *Am.* *a.* round trip; '**~schau** *f* panorama;

newspaper: review; '~schreiben *n* circular (letter); '2'weg *adv.* flatly, plainly.

Runz|el ['runtsəl] *f* (-/-n) wrinkle; '2elig *adj.* wrinkled; 2eln *v/t.* (ge-, *h*) wrinkle; *die Stirn* ~ knit one's brows, frown; '2ig *adj.* wrinkled.

Rüpel ['ry:pəl] *m* (-s/-) boor, lout; '2haft *adj.* coarse, boorish, rude.

rupfen ['rupfən] *v/t.* (ge-, *h*) pull up *or* out, pick; pluck (*fowl*) (*a. fig.*).

ruppig *adj.* ['rupiç] ragged, shabby; *fig.* rude.

Rüsche ['ry:ʃə] *f* (-/-n) ruffle, frill.

Ruß [ru:s] *m* (-es/*no pl.*) soot.

Russe ['rusə] *m* (-n/-n) Russian.

Rüssel ['rysəl] *m* (-s/-) trunk (*of elefant*); snout (*of pig*).

'ruß|en *v/i.* (ge-, *h*) smoke; '~ig *adj.* sooty.

'russisch *adj.* Russian.

rüsten ['rystən] (ge-, *h*) **1.** *v/t. and v/refl.* prepare, get ready (*zu* for); **2.** *esp.* ⚔ *v/i.* arm.

rüstig *adj.* ['rystiç] vigorous, strong; 2keit *f* (-/*no pl.*) vigo(u)r.

Rüstung *f* (-/-en) preparations *pl.*; ⚔ arming, armament; armo(u)r; ~sindustrie ['rystuŋs²-/] *f* armament industry.

Rüstzeug *n* (set of) tools *pl.*, implements *pl.*; *fig.* equipment.

Rute [ru:tə] *f* (-/-n) rod; switch; *fox's tail* brush.

Rutsch [rutʃ] *m* (-es/-e) (land)slide; F short trip; ~bahn *f*, '~e *f* (-/-n) slide, chute; 2en *v/i.* (ge-, *sein*) glide, slide; slip; *vehicle*: skid; '2ig *adj.* slippery.

rütteln ['rytəln] (ge-, *h*) **1.** *v/t.* shake, jog; jolt; **2.** *v/i.* shake, jog; *car*: jolt; *an der Tür* ~ rattle at the door; *daran ist nicht zu* ~ that's a fact.

S

Saal [za:l] *m* (-[e]s/*Säle*) hall.

Saat 🌱 [za:t] *f* (-/-en) sowing; standing *or* growing crops *pl.*; seed (*a. fig.*); ~feld 🌱 *n* corn-field; '~gut 🌱 *n* (-[e]s/*no pl.*) seeds *pl.*; '~kartoffel 🌱 *f* seed-potato.

Sabbat ['zabat] *m* (-s/-e) Sabbath.

sabbern F ['zabərn] *v/i.* (ge-, *h*) slaver, slobber, *Am. a.* drool; twaddle, *Am. sl. a.* drool.

Säbel ['zɛ:bəl] *m* (-s/-) sab|re, *Am.* -er; *mit dem* ~ *rasseln pol.* rattle the sabre; '~beine *n/pl.* bandy legs *pl.*; 2beinig *adj.* bandy-legged; '~hieb *m* sabre-cut; '2n F *fig. v/t.* (ge-, *h*) hack.

Sabot|age [zabo'ta:ʒə] *f* (-/-n) sabotage; ~eur [~ø:r] *m* (-s/-e) saboteur; 2ieren *v/t.* (*no* -ge-, *h*) sabotage.

Sach|bearbeiter ['zax-] *m* (-s/-) official in charge; *social work*: case worker; ~beschädigung *f* damage to property; 2dienlich *adj.* relevant, pertinent, useful, helpful.

'Sache *f* (-/-n) thing, affair, matter, concern; ⚖ case; point, issue; ~n *pl.* things *pl.*; *beschlossene* foregone conclusion; e-e *für sich* a matter apart, (*nicht*) *zur gehörig* (ir)relevant, *pred. a.* to off) the point; *bei der* ~ *bleiben* stick to the point; *gemeinsame* ~ *machen mit* make common cause with.

'sach|gemäß *adj.* appropriate, proper; 2kenntnis *f* expert knowledge; '~kundig *adj. s.* sachverständig; '2lage *f* state of affairs, situation; '~lich **1.** *adj.* relevant,

pertinent, *pred. a.* to the point; matter-of-fact, business-like; unbias(s)ed; objective; **2.** *adv.*: ~ *einwandfrei od. richtig* factually correct.

sächlich *gr. adj.* ['zeçliç] neuter.

Sachlichkeit *f* (-/*no pl.*) objectivity; impartiality; matter-of-factness.

Sach register *n* (subject) index; ~schaden *m* damage to property.

Sachse [zaksə] *m* (-n/-n) Saxon.

sächsisch *adj.* ['zeksiʃ] Saxon.

sacht ~adj [zaxt] soft, gentle; slow.

Sach|verhalt ['zaxfərhalt] *m* (-[e]s/-e) facts *pl.* (of the case); 2verständig *adj.* expert; ~verständige *m* (-n/-n) expert, authority; ⚖ expert witness; ~wert *m* real value.

Sack [zak] *m* (-[e]s/*⁓e*) sack; bag; *mit und Pack* with bag and baggage, ~gasse *f* blind alley, cul-de-sac, impasse (*a. fig.*), *Am. a.* dead end *a fig.*); *fig.* deadlock; '~leinwand *f* sackcloth.

Sadis|mus [za'dismus] *m* (-/*no pl.*) sadism; ~t *m* (-en/-en) sadist; 2tisch *adj.* sadistic.

säen [zɛ:ən] *v/t. and v/i.* (ge-, *h*) sow *a. fig.*).

Saffian ['zafja:n] *m* (-s/*no pl.*) morocco.

Saft [zaft] *m* (-[e]s/*⁓e*) juice (*of vegetables or fruits*); sap (*of plants*) (*a. fig.*); 2ig *adj. fruits, etc.*: juicy; *meadow, etc.*: lush; *plants* sappy (*a. fig.*); joke, *etc.*: spicy, coarse; '2los *adj.* juiceless; sapless (*a. fig.*).

Sage [za:gə] *f* (-/-n) legend, myth; *die* ~ *geht* the story goes.

Säge ['zɛ:gə] *f* (-/-*n*) saw; **'~blatt** *n* saw-blade; **'~bock** *m* saw-horse, *Am. a.* sawbuck; **'~fisch** *ichth. m* sawfish; **'~mehl** *n* sawdust.

sagen ['za:gən] (*ge-*, *h*) **1.** *v/t.* say; *j-m et.* ~ tell s.o. s.th., say s.th. to s.o.; *j-m* ~ *lassen,* daß send s.o. word that; *er läßt sich nichts* ~ he will not listen to reason; *das hat nichts zu* ~ that doesn't matter; *j-m gute Nacht* ~ bid s.o. good night; **2.** *v/i.* say; *es ist nicht zu* ~ it is incredible *or* fantastic; *wenn ich so* ~ *darf* if I may express myself in these terms; *sage und schreibe* believe it or not; no less than, as much as.

'sägen *v/t. and v/i.* (*ge-*, *h*) saw.

'sagenhaft *adj.* legendary, mythical; *F fig.* fabulous, incredible.

Säge|späne ['zɛ:gəʃpɛ:nə] *m/pl.* sawdust; **'~werk** *n* sawmill.

sah [za:] *pret. of* sehen.

Sahne ['za:nə] *f* (-/no *pl.*) cream.

Saison [zɛ'zõ:] *f* (-/-*s*) season; **2bedingt** *adj.* seasonal.

Saite ['zaɪtə] *f* (-/-*n*) string, chord (*a. fig.*); **~ninstrument** ['zaɪtən?-] *n* stringed instrument.

Sakko ['zako] *m*, *n* (-*s*/-*s*) lounge coat; **'~anzug** *m* lounge suit.

Sakristei [zakris'taɪ] *f* (-/-*en*) sacristy, vestry.

Salat [za'la:t] *m* (-[*e*]*s*/-*e*) salad; **♀** lettuce.

Salb|e ['zalbə] *f* (-/-*n*) ointment; **2en** *v/t.* (*ge-*, *h*) rub with ointment; anoint; **'~ung** *f* (-/-*en*) anointing, unction (*a. fig.*); **'2ungsvoll** *fig. adj.* unctuous.

saldieren † [zal'di:rən] *v/t.* (*no -ge-*, *h*) balance, settle.

Saldo † ['zaldo] *m* (-*s*/*Salden, Saldos, Saldi*) balance; *den* ~ *ziehen* strike the balance; **'~vortrag †** *m* balance carried down.

Saline [za'li:nə] *f* (-/-*n*) salt-pit, salt-works.

Salmiak [zal'mjak] *m*, *n* (-*s*/no *pl.*) sal-ammoniac, ammonium chloride; **~geist** *m* (-*es*/no *pl.*) liquid ammonia.

Salon [za'lõ:] *m* (-*s*/-*s*) drawing-room, *Am. a.* parlor; **♣** saloon; **2fähig** *adj.* presentable; **~löwe** *fig. m* lady's man, carpet-knight; **~wagen 🚗** *m* saloon-carriage, *Am.* parlor car.

Salpeter 🧪 [zal'pe:tər] *m* (-*s*/no *pl.*) saltpet|re *Am.* -er; nit|re, *Am.* -er.

Salto ['zalto] *m* (-*s*/-*s*, *Salti*) somersault; ~ *mortale* break-neck leap; *e-n* ~ *schlagen* turn a somersault.

Salut [za'lu:t] *m* (-[*e*]*s*/-*e*) salute; ~ *schießen* fire a salute; **2ieren** [~u'ti:rən] *v/i.* (*no -ge-*, *h*) (stand at the) salute.

Salve ['zalvə] *f* (-/-*n*) volley; **♣** broadside; salute.

Salz [zalts] *n* (-*es*/-*e*) salt; **~berg-werk** *n* salt-mine; **'2en** *v/t.* ([*irr.,*] *ge-*, *h*) salt; **'~faß** *n*, **~fäßchen** ['~fɛsçən] *n* (-*s*/-) salt-cellar; **~gurke** *f* pickled cucumber; **'2haltig** *adj.* saline, saliferous; **'~hering** *m* pickled herring; **'2ig** *adj.* salt(y); *s. salzhaltig;* **'~säure 🧪** *f* hydrochloric *or* muriatic acid; **'~wasser** *n* (-*s*/⁼) salt water, brine; **'~werk** *n* salt-works, saltern.

Same ['za:mə] *m* (-*ns*/-*n*), **'~n** *m* (-*s*/-) **♀** seed (*a. fig.*); *biol.* sperm, semen; **~nkorn ♀** *n* grain of seed.

Sammel|büchse ['zaml-] *f* collecting-box; **'~lager** *n* collecting point; *refugees, etc.:* assembly camp; **'2n** (*ge-*, *h*) **1.** *v/t.* gather; collect (*stamps, etc.*); *sich* ~ gather; *fig.:* concentrate; compose o.s.; **2.** *v/i.* collect money (*für for*) **'~platz** *m* meeting-place, place of appointment; ✕, **♣** rendezvous.

Samml|er ['zamlər] *m* (-*s*/-) collector; **'~ung** *f* **1.** (-/-*en*) collection; **2.** *fig.* (-/no *pl.*) composure; concentration.

Samstag ['zams-] *m* Saturday.

samt¹ [zamt] **1.** *adv.:* ~ *und sonders* one and all; **2.** *prp.* (*dat.*) together *or* along with.

Samt² [~] *m* (-[*e*]*s*/-*e*) velvet.

sämtlich ['zɛmtlɪç] **1.** *adj.* all (together); complete; **2.** *adv.* all (together *or* of them).

Sanatorium [zana'to:rjum] *n* (-*s*/ *Sanatorien*) sanatorium, *Am. a.* sanitarium.

Sand [zant] *m* (-[*e*]*s*/-*e*) sand; *j-m* ~ *in die Augen streuen* throw dust into s.o.'s eyes; *im* ~ *e verlaufen* end in smoke, come to nothing.

Sandale [zan'da:lə] *f* (-/-*n*) sandal.

'Sand|bahn *f sports:* dirt-track; **'~bank** *f* sandbank; **'~boden** *m* sandy soil; **'~grube** *f* sand-pit; **'2ig** *adj.* ['~dɪç] sandy; **'~korn** *n* grain of sand; **'~mann** *fig. m* (-[*e*]*s*/no *pl.*) sandman, dustman; **'~papier** *n* sandpaper; **'~sack** *m* sand-bag; **'~stein** *m* sandstone.

sandte ['zantə] *pret. of* senden.

'Sand|torte *f* Madeira cake; **'~uhr** *f* sand-glass; **'~wüste** *f* sandy desert.

sanft *adj.* [zanft] soft; gentle; mild; smooth; *slope, death, etc.:* easy; **~er** *Zwang* non-violent coercion; *mit* **~er** *Stimme* softly, gently; **~mütig** *adj.* ['~my:tɪç] gentle, mild; meek.

sang [zaŋ] *pret. of* singen.

Sänger ['zɛŋər] *m* (-*s*/-) singer.

Sanguini|ker [zaŋgu'i:nɪkər] *m* (-*s*/-) sanguine person; **2sch** *adj.* sanguine.

sanier|en [za'ni:rən] *v/t.* (*no -ge-*, *h*) improve the sanitary conditions of; *esp.* ✝: reorganize; readjust; **2ung** *f* (-/-*en*) sanitation; *esp.* ✝: reorganization; readjustment.

sanitär adj. [zani'tɛːr] sanitary.
Sanität|er [zani'tɛːtər] m (-s/-) ambulance man; ✠ medical orderly.
sank [zaŋk] pret. of sinken.
Sankt [zaŋkt] Saint, St.
sann [zan] pret. of sinnen.
Sard|elle ichth. [zar'dɛlə] f (-/-n) anchovy; ~ine ichth. [~iːnə] f (-/-n) sardine.
Sarg [zark] m (-[e]s/⁀e) coffin, Am. a. casket; ~deckel m coffin-lid.
Sarkas|mus [zar'kasmus] m (-/⁀ Sarkasmen) sarcasm; ⁀tisch adj. [~tiʃ] sarcastic.
saß [zaːs] pret. of sitzen.
Satan ['zaːtan] m (-s/-e) Satan; fig. devil; ⁀isch fig. adj. [za'taːniʃ] satanic.
Satellit ast.,pol. [zate'liːt] m (-en/-en) satellite; ~enstaat pol. m satellite state.
Satin [sa'tɛ̃ː] m (-s/-s) satin; sateen.
Satir|e [za'tiːrə] f (-/-n) satire; ~iker [~ikər] m (-s/-) satirist; ⁀isch adj. satiric(al).
satt adj. [zat] satisfied, satiated, full; colour: deep, rich; sich ~ essen eat one's fill; ich bin ~ I have had enough; F et. ~ haben be tired or sick of s.th., sl. be fed up with s.th.
Sattel ['zatəl] m (-s/⁀) saddle; ~gurt m girth; ⁀n v/t. (ge-, h) saddle.
'Sattheit f (-/no pl.) satiety, fullness; richness, intensity of colours).
sättig|en ['zɛtigən] (ge-, h) 1. v/t. satisfy, satiate; ⁀, phys. saturate; 2. v/i. food: be substantial; ⁀ung f (-/-en) satiation; ⁀, fig. saturation.
Sattler ['zatlər] m (-s/-) saddler; ~ei [~'rai] f (-/-en) saddlery.
'sattsam adv. sufficiently.
Satz [zats] m (-es/⁀e) gr. sentence, clause; phls. maxim; ♪ proposition, theorem; ♪ movement, tennis, etc.: set; typ. setting, composition; sediment, dregs pl., grounds pl.; rate (of prices, etc.); set (of stamps, tools, etc.); leap, bound.
'Satzung f (-/-en) statute, by-law; ⁀sgemäß adj. statutory.
'Satzzeichen gr. n punctuation mark.
Sau [zau] f 1. (-/⁀e) zo. sow; fig. contp. filthy swine; 2. hunt. (-/-en) wild sow.
sauber adj. ['zaubər] clean; neat (a. fig.), tidy; attitude: decent; iro. fine, nice; ⁀keit f (-/no pl.) clean(li)ness; tidiness, neatness; decency (of attitude).
säuber|n ['zɔybərn] v/t. (ge-, h) clean(se); tidy, clean up (room, etc.); clear (von of); purge (of, from) (a. fig., pol.); '⁀ungsaktion pol. f purge.
sauer ['zauər] 1. adj. sour (a. fig.), acid (a. ⁀); cucumber: pickled; task, etc.: hard, painful; fig. morose,

surly; 2. adv.: ~ reagieren auf et. take s.th. in bad part.
säuer|lich adj. ['zɔyərliç] sourish, acidulous; '~n v/t. (ge-, h) (make) sour, acidify (a. ⁀); leaven (dough).
'Sauer|stoff ⁀ m (-[e]s/no pl.) oxygen; ~teig m leaven.
saufen ['zaufən] v/t. and v/i. (irr., ge-, h) animals: drink; F p. sl. soak, lush.
Säufer F ['zɔyfər] m (-s/-) sot, sl. soak.
saugen ['zaugən] ([irr.,] ge-, h) 1. v/i. suck (an et. s.th.); 2. v/t. suck.
säuge|n ['zɔygən] v/t. (ge-, h) suckle, nurse; ⁀tier n mammal.
Säugling ['zɔyklɪŋ] m (-s/-e) baby, suckling; ~sheim n baby-farm, baby-nursery.
Saug|papier n absorbent paper; ~pumpe f suction-pump; '~wirkung f suction-effect.
Säule [zɔylə] f (-/-n) ⚠, anat. column a. of smoke, mercury, etc.); pillar, support (both a. fig.); '~ngang m colonnade; ~nhalle f pillared hall; portico.
Saum [zaum] m (-[e]s/⁀e) seam, hem, border, edge.
säum|en ['zɔymən] v/t. (ge-, h) hem, border, edge; die Straßen ~ line the streets; '~ig adj. payer: dilatory.
Saum|pfad m mule-track; '~tier n sumpter-mule.
Säure [zɔyrə] f (-/-n) sourness; acidity (a. ⚙ of stomach); ⁀ acid.
Saure gurkenzeit f silly or slack season.
säuseln ['zɔyzəln] (ge-, h) 1. v/i. leaves, wind: rustle, whisper; 2. v/t. p. say airily, purr.
sausen [zauzən] v/i. (ge-) 1. (sein) F rush, dash; bullet, etc.: whiz(z), whistle; 2. (h) wind: whistle, sough.
'Saustall m pigsty; F fig. a. horrid mess.
Saxophon ♪ [zakso'foːn] n (-s/-e) saxophone.
Schab|e ['ʃaːbə] f (-/-n) zo. cockroach; ⊕ s. Schabeisen; '~efleisch n scraped meat; '~eisen ⊕ n scraper, shaving-tool; '~emesser ⊕ n scraping-knife; '⁀en v/t. (ge-, h) scrape a. ⊕); grate, rasp; scratch; '~er ⊕ m (-s/-) scraper.
Schabernack ['ʃaːbərnak] m (-[e]s/-e) practical joke, hoax, prank.
schäbig adj. ['ʃɛːbiç] shabby (a. fig.), F seedy, Am. F a. dowdy, tacky; fig. mean.
Schablone [ʃa'bloːnə] f (-/-n) model, pattern, stencil; fig.: routine; cliché; ⁀nhaft adj., ⁀nmäßig adj. according to pattern; fig.: mechanical; attr. a. routine.
Schach [ʃax] n (-s/-s) chess; ~! check!; ~ und matt! checkmate!;

in or im ~ *halten* keep *s.o.* in check;
'~brett *n* chessboard.

schachern ['ʃaxərn] *v/i.* (ge-, h)
haggle (*um* about, over), chaffer
(about, over), *Am. a.* dicker; ~ *mit*
barter (away).

'**Schach|feld** *n* square; '~figur *f*
chess-man, piece; *fig.* pawn; '2-
matt *adj.* (check)mated; *fig.* tired
out, worn out; '~spiel *n* game of
chess. [*a.* pit.]

Schacht [ʃaxt] *m* (-[e]s/=e) shaft; ⚒

Schachtel ['ʃaxtəl] *f* (-/-n) box; F
alte ~ old frump.

'**Schachzug** *m* move (at chess); *ge-
schickter* ~ clever move (*a. fig.*).

schade *pred. adj.* ['ʃa:də]: *es ist* ~
it is a pity; *wie* ~*!* what a pity!; *zu*
~ *für* too good for.

Schädel ['ʃɛ:dəl] *m* (-s/-) skull,
cranium; '~bruch ⚕ *m* fracture of
the skull.

schaden ['ʃa:dən] 1. *v/i.* (ge-, h)
damage, injure, harm, hurt (*j-m*
s.o.); be detrimental (to *s.o.*); *das
schadet nichts* it does not matter,
never mind; 2. ♀ *m* (-s/=) damage
(*an dat.* to); injury, harm; infirmity; hurt; loss; '2ersatz *m* indemnification, compensation; damages
pl.; ~ *verlangen* claim damages; ~
leisten pay damages; *auf* ~ *(ver)kla-
gen* ⚖ sue for damages; '2freude *f*
malicious enjoyment of others'
misfortunes, schadenfreude; '~froh
adj. rejoicing over others' misfortunes.

schadhaft *adj.* ['ʃa:thaft] damaged;
defective, faulty; *building, etc.*:
dilapidated; *pipe, etc.*: leaking;
tooth, etc.: decayed.

schädig|en ['ʃɛ:digən] *v/t.* (ge-, h)
damage, impair; wrong, harm;
'2ung *f* (-/-en) damage (*gen.* to),
impairment (of); prejudice (to).

schädli|ch *adj.* ['ʃɛ:tliç] harmful,
injurious; noxious; detrimental,
prejudicial; '2ng *f* [~ŋ] *m* (-s/-e) zo.
pest; ✿ destructive weed; noxious
person; ~*e pl.* ✿ *a.* vermin.

schadlos *adj.* ['ʃa:tlo:s]: *sich* ~ *halten* recoup *or* idemnify o.s. (*für* for).

Schaf [ʃa:f] *n* (-[e]s/-e) zo. sheep;
fig. simpleton; '~bock zo. *m* ram.

Schäfer ['ʃɛ:fər] *m* (-s/-) shepherd;
'~hund *m* sheep-dog; Alsatian
(wolf-hound).

Schaffell ['ʃa:fᵊ·] *n* sheepskin.

schaffen ['ʃafən] 1. *v/t.* (*irr.*, ge-, h)
create, produce; 2. *v/t.* (ge-, h)
convey, carry, move; take, bring;
cope with, manage; 3. *v/i.* (ge-, h)
be busy, work.

Schaffner ['ʃafnər] *m* (-s/-) ☷
guard, *Am.* conductor; *tram, bus:*
conductor.

'**Schafhirt** *m* shepherd.

Schafott [ʃa'fɔt] *n* (-[e]s/-e) scaffold.

'**Schaf|pelz** *m* sheepskin coat;
'~stall *m* fold.

Schaft [ʃaft] *m* (-[e]s/=e) shaft (*of
lance, column, etc.*); stick (*of flag*);
stock (*of rifle*); shank (*of tool, key,
etc.*); leg (*of boot*); '~stiefel *m*
high boot; ~ *pl. a.* Wellingtons *pl.*

'**Schaf|wolle** *f* sheep's wool;
'~zucht *f* sheep-breeding, sheep-
farming.

schäkern ['ʃɛ:kərn] *v/i.* (ge-, h) jest,
joke; flirt.

schal[1] *adj.* [ʃa:l] insipid; stale; *fig.
a.* flat.

Schal[2] [~] *m* (-s/-e, -s) scarf, muffler; comforter.

Schale ['ʃa:lə] *f* (-/-n) bowl; ⊕
scale (*of scales*); shell (*of eggs, nuts,
etc.*); peel, skin (*of fruit*); shell, crust
(*of tortoise*); paring, peeling; F:
sich in ~ *werfen* doll o.s. up.

schälen ['ʃɛ:lən] *v/t.* (ge-, h) remove
the peel *or* skin from; pare, peel
(*fruit, potatoes, etc.*); *sich* ~ *skin:*
peel *or* come off.

Schalk [ʃalk] *m* (-[e]s/-e, =e) rogue,
wag; '2haft *adj.* roguish, waggish.

Schall [ʃal] *m* (-[e]s/-e, =e) sound;
'~dämpfer *m* sound absorber;
mot. silencer, *Am.* muffler; silencer
(*on fire-arms*); '2dicht *adj.* sound-
proof; '2en *v/i.* (*irr.*⁏] ge-, h)
sound; ring, peal; '2end *adj.*: ~*es
Gelächter* roars *pl. or* a peal of
laughter; '~mauer *f* sound barrier;
'~platte *f* record, disc, disk;
'~welle *f* sound-wave.

schalt [ʃalt] *pret. of* schelten.

'**Schaltbrett** ⚡ *n* switchboard.

schalten ['ʃaltən] (ge-, h) 1. *v/i.* ⚡
switch; *mot.* change *or* shift gears;
direct, rule; 2. *v/t.* ⚡ actuate;
operate, control.

'**Schalter** *m* (-s/-) ☷, *theatre, etc.*:
booking-office; ✿, *bank, etc.*:
counter; ⚡ switch; ⊕, *mot.* con-
troller.

'**Schalt|hebel** *m mot.* gear lever;
⊕, ⚙ control lever; ⚡ switch
lever; '~jahr *n* leap-year; '~tafel
⚡ *f* switchboard, control panel;
'~tag *m* intercalary day.

Scham [ʃa:m] *f* (-/*no pl.*) shame;
bashfulness, modesty; *anat.* privy
parts *pl.*, genitals *pl.*

schämen ['ʃɛ:mən] *v/refl.* (ge-, h)
be *or* feel ashamed (*gen. or wegen* of).

'**Scham|gefühl** *n* sense of shame;
'2haft *adj.* bashful, modest; '~haf-
tigkeit *f* (-/*no pl.*) bashfulness,
modesty; '2los *adj.* shameless; impudent; '~losigkeit *f* (-/-en) shame-
lessness; impudence; '2rot *adj.*
blushing; ~ *werden* blush; '~röte *f*
blush; '~teile *anat. m/pl.* privy
parts *pl.*, genitals *pl.*

Schande ['ʃandə] *f* (-/✕, -n) shame,
disgrace.

schänden ['ʃɛndən] *v/t.* (ge-, h)

dishono(u)r, disgrace; desecrate, profane; rape, violate; disfigure.

Schandfleck fig. ['ʃant-] m blot, stain; eyesore.

schändlich adj. ['ʃentliç] shameful, disgraceful, infamous; '2keit f (-/-en) infamy.

'**Schandtat** f infamous act(ion).

'**Schändung** f (-/-en) dishono(u)ring; profanation, desecration; rape, violation; disfigurement.

Schanze ['ʃantsə] f (-/-n) 🛠 entrenchment; ⚓ quarter-deck; sports: ski-jump; '2n v/i. (ge-, h) throw up entrenchments, entrench.

Schar [ʃaːr] f (-/-en) troop, band; geese, etc.: flock; 🛠 ploughshare, Am. plowshare; '2en v/t. (ge-, h) assemble, collect; sich ~ a. flock (um round).

scharf [ʃarf] 1. adj. sharp; edge: keen; voice, sound: piercing, shrill; smell, taste: pungent; pepper, etc.: hot; sight, hearing, intelligence, etc.: keen; answer, etc.: cutting; 🛠 ammunition: live; ~ sein auf (acc.) be very keen on; 2. adv.: ~ ansehen look sharply at; ~ reiten ride hard; '2blick fig. m (-[e]s/no pl.) clear-sightedness.

Schärfe ['ʃerfə] f (-/-n) sharpness; keenness; pungency; '2n v/t. (ge-, h) put an edge on, sharpen; strengthen (memory); sharpen (sight, hearing, etc.).

'**Scharf|macher** fig. m (-s/-) firebrand, agitator; '~richter m executioner; '~schütze 🛠 m sharpshooter, sniper; '2sichtig adj. sharp-sighted; fig. clear-sighted; '~sinn m (-[e]s/no pl.) sagacity; '2sinnig adj. sharp-witted, shrewd; sagacious.

Scharlach ['ʃarlax] m 1. (-s/-e) scarlet; 2. ✿ (-s/no pl.) scarlet fever; '2rot adj. scarlet.

Scharlatan ['ʃarlatan] m (-s/-e) charlatan, quack (doctor); mountebank.

Scharmützel [ʃar'mytsəl] n (-s/-) skirmish.

Scharnier ⊕ [ʃar'niːr] n (-s/-e) hinge, joint.

Schärpe ['ʃerpə] f (-/-n) sash.

scharren ['ʃarən] (ge-, h) 1. v/i. scrape (mit den Füßen one's feet); hen, etc.: scratch; horse: paw; 2. v/t. horse: paw (ground).

Schart|e ['ʃartə] f (-/-n) notch, nick; mountains: gap, Am. notch; e-e ~ auswetzen repair a fault; wipe out a disgrace; '2ig adj. jagged, notchy.

Schatten ['ʃatən] m (-s/-) shadow (a. fig.); shade (a. paint.); '~bild n silhouette; '2haft adj. shadowy; '~kabinett pol. n shadow cabinet; '~riß m silhouette; '~seite f shady side; fig. seamy side.

schattier|en [ʃa'tiːrən] v/t. (no -ge-, h) shade, tint; 2ung f (-/-en) shading; shade (a. fig.), tint.

'**schattig** adj. shady.

Schatz [ʃats] m (-es/ᵘe) treasure; fig. sweetheart, darling; '~amt ✝ n Exchequer, Am. Treasury (Department); '~anweisung ✝ f Treasury Bond, Am. a. Treasury Note.

schätzen ['ʃetsən] v/t. (ge-, h) estimate; value (auf acc. at); price (at); rate; appreciate; esteem; sich glücklich ~ zu inf. be delighted to inf.; '~swert adj. estimable.

'**Schatz|kammer** f treasury; '~meister m treasurer.

'**Schätzung** f 1. (-/-en) estimate, valuation; rating; 2. (-/no pl.) appreciation, estimation; esteem.

'**Schatzwechsel** ✝ m Treasury Bill.

Schau [ʃau] f (-/-en) inspection; show, exhibition; zur ~ stellen exhibit, display.

Schauder ['ʃaudər] m (-s/-) shudder(ing), shiver, tremor; fig. horror, terror; '2haft adj. horrible, dreadful; F fig. a. awful; '2n v/i. (ge-, h) shudder, shiver (both: vor dat. at).

schauen ['ʃauən] v/i. (ge-, h) look (auf acc. at).

Schauer ['ʃauər] m (-s/-) rain, etc.: shower (a. fig.); shudder(ing), shiver; attack, fit; thrill; '2lich adj. dreadful, horrible; '2n v/i. (ge-, h) s. schaudern; '~roman m penny dreadful, thriller.

Schaufel ['ʃaufəl] f (-/-n) shovel; dust-pan; '2n v/t. and v/i. (ge-, h) shovel.

'**Schaufenster** n shop window, Am. a. show-window; '~bummel m: e-n ~ machen go window-shopping; '~dekoration f window-dressing; '~einbruch m smash-and-grab raid.

Schaukel ['ʃaukəl] f (-/-n) swing; '2n (ge-, h) 1. v/i. swing; ship, etc.: rock; 2. v/t. rock (baby, etc.); '~pferd n rocking-horse; '~stuhl m rocking-chair, Am. a. rocker.

Schaum [ʃaum] m (-[e]s/ᵘe) foam; beer, etc.: froth, head; soap: lather; '~bad n bubble bath.

schäumen ['ʃɔymən] v/i. (ge-, h) foam, froth; lather; wine, etc.: sparkle.

'**Schaum|gummi** n, m foam rubber; '2ig adj. foamy, frothy; '~wein m sparkling wine.

'**Schau|platz** m scene (of action), theat|re, Am. -er; '~prozeß 🏛 m show trial.

schaurig adj. ['ʃauriç] horrible, horrid.

'**Schau|spiel** n spectacle; thea. play; '~spieler m actor, player; '~spielhaus n playhouse, theat|re, Am. -er; '~spielkunst f (-/no pl.) dramatic art, *the* drama; '~steller *m* (-s/-) showman.

Scheck † [ʃɛk] *m* (-s/-s) cheque, *Am.* check; '~buch *n*, '~heft *n* cheque-book, *Am.* checkbook.

'**scheckig** *adj.* spotted; *horse:* piebald.

scheel [ʃeːl] **1.** *adj.* squint-eyed, cross-eyed; *fig.* jealous, envious; **2.** *adv.:* j-n ~ ansehen look askance at s.o.

Scheffel ['ʃɛfəl] *m* (-s/-) bushel; '~n *v/t.* (ge-, h) amass (*money, etc.*).

Scheibe ['ʃaɪbə] *f* (-/-n) disk, disc (*a. of sun, moon*); *esp. ast.* orb; slice (*of bread, etc.*); pane (*of window*); *shooting:* target; ~nhonig *m* honey in combs; '~nwischer *mot. m* (-s/-) wind-screen wiper, *Am.* windshield wiper.

Scheide ['ʃaɪdə] *f* (-/-n) sword, *etc.*: sheath, scabbard; border, boundary; '~münze *f* small coin; '2n (*irr.*, ge-) **1.** *v/t.* (h) separate; ⚗ analyse; ⚖ divorce; *sich ~ lassen von* ⚖ divorce (*one's husband or wife*); **2.** *v/i.* (sein) depart; part (*von* with); *aus dem Dienst ~* retire from service; *aus dem Leben ~* depart from this life; ~wand *f* partition; '~weg *fig. m* cross-roads *sg.*

'**Scheidung** *f* (-/-en) separation; ⚖ divorce; '~sgrund ⚖ *m* ground for divorce; '~sklage ⚖ *f* divorce-suit; *die ~ einreichen* file a petition for divorce.

Schein [ʃaɪn] *m* **1.** (-[e]s/*no pl.*) shine; *sun, lamp, etc.:* light; *fire:* blaze; *fig.* appearance; **2.** (-[e]s/-e) certificate; receipt; bill; (bank-)note; '2bar *adj.* seeming, apparent; '2en *v/i.* (*irr.*, ge-, h) shine; *fig.* seem, appear, look; ~grund *m* pretext, preten|ce, *Am.* -se; '2heilig *adj.* sanctimonious, hypocritical; ~tod ⚕ *m* suspended animation; '2tot *adj.* in a state of suspended animation; '~werfer *m* (-s/-) reflector, projector; 🚗, ⚓, ✈ searchlight; *mot.* headlight; *thea.* spotlight.

Scheit [ʃaɪt] *n* (-[e]s/-e) log, billet.

Scheitel ['ʃaɪtəl] *m* (-s/-) crown or top of the head; *hair:* parting; summit, peak; *esp.* Å vertex; '2n *v/t.* (ge-, h) part (*hair*).

Scheiterhaufen ['ʃaɪtər-] *m* (funeral) pile; stake.

'**scheitern** *v/i.* (ge-, sein) ⚓ run aground, be wrecked; *fig.* fail, miscarry. [box on the ear.]

Schelle ['ʃɛlə] *f* (-/-n) (little) bell;)

'**Schellfisch** *ichth. m* haddock.

Schelm [ʃɛlm] *m* (-[e]s/-e) rogue; '~enstreich *m* roguish trick; '2isch *adj.* roguish, arch.

Schelte ['ʃɛltə] *f* (-/-n) scolding; '2n (*irr.*, ge-, h) **1.** *v/t.* scold, rebuke; **2.** *v/i.* scold.

Schema ['ʃeːma] *n* (-s/-s, -ta, *Schemen*) scheme; model, pattern; arrangement; 2tisch *adj.* [ʃeˈmaːtiʃ] schematic.

Schemel ['ʃeːməl] *m* (-s/-) stool.

Schemen ['ʃeːmən] *m* (-s/-) phantom, shadow; '2haft *adj.* shadowy.

Schenke ['ʃɛnkə] *f* (-/-n) public house, F pub; tavern, inn.

Schenkel ['ʃɛnkəl] *m* (-s/-) *anat.* thigh; *anat.* shank; *triangle, etc.*: leg; Å *angle:* side.

schenken ['ʃɛnkən] *v/t.* (ge-, h) give; remit (*penalty, etc.*); j-m et. ~ give s.o. s.th., present s.o. with s.th., make s.o. a present of s.th.

'**Schenkung** ⚖ *f* (-/-en) donation; ~surkunde ⚖ ['ʃɛnkuns⁹-] *f* deed of gift.

Scherbe ['ʃɛrbə] *f* (-/-n), '~n *m* (-s/-) (broken) piece, fragment.

Schere ['ʃeːrə] *f* (-/-n) (e-e a pair of) scissors *pl.*; *zo.* crab, *etc.*: claw; '2n *v/t.* **1.** (*irr.*, ge-, h) shear (*a. sheep*), clip; shave (*beard*); cut (*hair*); clip, prune (*hedge*); **2.** (ge-, h): *sich um et. ~* trouble about s.th.; '~nschleifer *m* (-s/-) knife-grinder; ~rei [~ˈraɪ] *f* (-/-en) trouble, bother.

Scherz [ʃɛrts] *m* (-es/-e) jest, joke; ~ *beiseite* joking apart; *im* ~, *zum* ~ in jest *or* joke; '2en *v/i.* (ge-, h) jest, joke; '2haft *adj.* joking, sportive.

scheu [ʃɔy] **1.** *adj.* shy, bashful, timid; *horse:* skittish; ~ *machen* frighten; **2.** 2 *f* (-/*no pl.*) shyness; timidity; aversion (*vor dat.* to).

scheuchen ['ʃɔyçən] *v/t.* (ge-, h) scare, frighten (away).

'**scheuen** (ge-, h) **1.** *v/i.* shy (*vor dat.* at), take fright (at); **2.** *v/t.* shun, avoid; fear; *sich ~ vor* (*dat.*) shy at, be afraid of.

Scheuer|lappen ['ʃɔyər-] *m* scouring-cloth, floor-cloth; '~leiste *f* skirting-board; '2n (ge-, h) **1.** *v/t.* scour, scrub; chafe; **2.** *v/i.* chafe.

'**Scheuklappe** *f* blinker, *Am.* a. blinder.

Scheune ['ʃɔynə] *f* (-/-n) barn.

Scheusal ['ʃɔyzaːl] *n* (-[e]s/-e) monster.

scheußlich *adj.* ['ʃɔyslɪç] hideous, atrocious (F *a. fig.*), abominable (F *a. fig.*); '2keit *f* **1.** (-/*no pl.*) hideousness; **2.** (-/-en) abomination; atrocity.

Schi [ʃiː] *m* (-s/-er) *etc. s.* Ski, *etc.*

Schicht [ʃɪçt] *f* (-/-en) layer; *geol.* stratum (*a. fig.*); *at work:* shift; (social) class, rank, walk of life; '2en *v/t.* (ge-, h) arrange *or* put in layers, pile up; classify; '2weise *adv.* in layers; *work:* in shifts.

Schick [ʃɪk] **1.** *m* (-[e]s/*no pl.*) chic, elegance, style; **2.** 2 *adj.* chic, stylish, fashionable.

schicken ['ʃɪkən] *v/t.* (ge-, h) send

(*nach, zu* to); remit (*money*); *nach j-m* ~ send for s.o.; *sich* ~ *für* become, suit, befit *s.o.*; *sich* ~ *in* put up with, resign o.s. to *s.th.*

'schicklich *adj.* becoming, proper, seemly; '2keit *f* (-/*no pl.*) propriety, seemliness.

'Schicksal *n* (-[e]s/-e) fate, destiny.

Schiebe|dach *mot.* ['ʃiːbə-] *n* sliding roof; '~fenster *n* sash-window; '2n (*irr.*, ge-, h) 1. *v/t.* push, shove; shift (*blame*) (*auf acc.* on to); F *fig.* sell on the black market; 2. F *fig. v/i.* profiteer; '~r *m* (-s/-) bolt (*of door*); ⊕ slide; *fig.* profiteer, black marketeer, *sl.* spiv; '~tür *f* sliding door.

'Schiebung *fig. f* (-/-en) black marketeering, profiteering; put-up job.

schied [ʃiːt] *pret.* of scheiden.

Schieds|gericht ['ʃiːts-] *n* court of arbitration, arbitration committee; '~richter *m* arbitrator; *tennis, etc.*: umpire; *football, etc.*: referee; '2richterlich *adj.* arbitral; '~spruch *m* award, arbitration.

schief [ʃiːf] 1. *adj.* sloping, slanting; oblique; *face, mouth*: wry; *fig.* false, wrong; ~e *Ebene* A inclined plane; 2. *adv.*: *j-n* ~ ansehen look askance at s.o.

Schiefer ['ʃiːfər] *m* (-s/-) slate; splinter; '~stift *m* slate-pencil; '~tafel *f* slate.

'schiefgehen *v/i.* (*irr. gehen, sep.*, -ge-, sein) go wrong or awry.

schielen ['ʃiːlən] *v/i.* (ge-, h) squint, be cross-eyed; ~ *auf* (*acc.*) squint at; leer at.

schien [ʃiːn] *pret.* of scheinen.

Schienbein ['ʃiːn-] *n* shin(-bone), tibia.

Schiene ['ʃiːnə] *f* (-/-n) 🚃, *etc.*: rail; ⚕ splint; '2n ⚕ *v/t.* (ge-, h) splint.

schießen ['ʃiːsən] (*irr.*, ge-) 1. *v/t.* (h) shoot; tot ~ shoot dead; *ein Tor* ~ score (a goal); *Salut* ~ fire a salute; 2. *v/i.* (h): *auf j-n* ~ shoot or fire at; *gut* ~ be a good shot; 3. *v/i.* (sein) shoot, dart, rush.

'Schieß|pulver *n* gunpowder; '~scharte *f* loop-hole, embrasure; '~scheibe *f* target; '~stand *m* shooting-gallery or -range.

Schiff [ʃif] *n* (-[e]s/-e) ⚓ ship, vessel; ∆ *church:* nave.

Schiffahrt ['ʃifaːrt] *f* (-/-en) navigation.

'schiff|bar *adj.* navigable; '2bau *m* shipbuilding; '2bauer *m* (-s/-) shipbuilder; '2bruch *m* shipwreck (*a. fig.*); ~ *erleiden* be shipwrecked; *fig.* make or suffer shipwreck; '~brüchig *adj.* shipwrecked; '2-brücke *f* pontoon-bridge; '~en *v/i.* (ge-, sein) navigate, sail; '2er

m (-s/-) sailor; boatman; navigator; skipper.

'Schiffs|junge *m* cabin-boy; '~kapitän *m* (sea-)captain; '~ladung *f* shipload; cargo; '~makler *m* shipbroker; '~mannschaft *f* crew; '~raum *m* hold; tonnage; '~werft *f* shipyard, *esp.* ⚓ dockyard, *Am. a.* navy yard.

Schikan|e [ʃiˈkaːnə] *f* (-/-n) vexation, nasty trick; 2ieren [~kaˈniːrən] *v/t.* (*no* -ge-, h) vex, ride.

Schild [ʃilt] 1. ⚔ *m* (-[e]s/-e) shield, buckler; 2. *n* (-[e]s/-er) *shop, etc.*: sign(board), facia; name-plate; *traffic:* signpost; label; *cap:* peak; '~drüse *anat. f* thyroid gland.

'Schilder|haus ⚔ *n* sentry-box; '~maler *m* sign-painter; '2n *v/t.* (ge-, h) describe, delineate; '~ung *f* (-/-en) description, delineation.

'Schild|kröte *zo. f* tortoise; turtle; '~wache ⚔ *f* sentinel, sentry.

Schilf ⚕ [ʃilf] *n* (-[e]s/-e) reed; '2ig *adj.* reedy; '~rohr *n* reed.

schillern ['ʃilərn] *v/i.* (ge-, h) show changing colo(u)rs; be iridescent.

Schimmel ['ʃiməl] *m* 1. *zo.* (-s/-) white horse; 2. ⚕ (-s/*no pl.*) mo(u)ld, mildew; '2ig *adj.* mo(u)ldy, musty; '2n *v/i.* (ge-, h) become mo(u)ldy, *Am. a.* mo(u)ld.

Schimmer ['ʃimər] *m* (-s/*no pl.*) glimmer, gleam (*a. fig.*); '2n *v/i.* (ge-, h) glimmer, gleam.

Schimpanse *zo.* [ʃimˈpanzə] *m* (-n/-n) chimpanzee.

Schimpf [ʃimpf] *m* (-[e]s/-e) insult; disgrace; *mit* ~ *und Schande* ignominiously; '2en (ge-, h) 1. *v/i.* rail (*über acc., auf acc.* at, against); 2. *v/t.* scold; *j-n e-n Lügner* ~ call s.o. a liar; '2lich *adj.* disgraceful (*für* to), ignominious (to); '~name *m* abusive name; '~wort *n* term of abuse; ~e *pl. a.* invectives *pl.*

Schindel ['ʃindəl] *f* (-/-n) shingle.

schinden ['ʃindən] *v/t.* (*irr.*, ge-, h) flay, skin (*rabbit, etc.*); sweat (*worker*); *sich* ~ drudge, slave, sweat.

'Schinder *m* (-s/-) knacker; *fig.* sweater, slave-driver; ~ei [~'rai] *f* (-/-en) sweating; drudgery, grind.

Schinken ['ʃiŋkən] *m* (-s/-) ham.

Schippe ['ʃipə] *f* (-/-n) shovel; '2n *v/t.* (ge-, h) shovel.

Schirm [ʃirm] *m* (-[e]s/-e) umbrella; parasol, sunshade; *wind, television, etc.*: screen; *lamp:* shade; *cap:* peak, visor; '~futteral *n* umbrella-case; '~herr *m* protector; patron; '~herrschaft *f* protectorate; patronage; *unter der* ~ *von event:* under the auspices of; '~mütze *f* peaked cap; '~ständer *m* umbrella-stand.

Schlacht ⚔ [ʃlaxt] *f* (-/-en) battle (*bei* of); '~bank *f* shambles; '2en *v/t.* (ge-, h) slaughter, butcher.

Schlächter ['ʃlɛçtər] *m* (-s/-) butcher.

'Schlacht|feld ⚔ *n* battle-field; **'~haus** *n*, **'~hof** *m* slaughter-house, abattoir; **'~kreuzer** ⚓ *m* battlecruiser; **'~plan** *m* ⚔ plan of action (*a. fig.*); **'~schiff** ⚓ *n* battleship; **'~vieh** *n* slaughter cattle.

Schlack|e ['ʃlakə] *f* (-/-n) wood, coal: cinder; *metall.* dross (*a. fig.*), slag; *geol.* scoria; **2ig** *adj.* drossy, slaggy; F *weather* slushy.

Schlaf [ʃlɑːf] *m* (-[e]s/no *pl.*) sleep; *im* ~(e) in one's sleep; *e-n leichten (festen)* ~ *haben* be a light (sound) sleeper; *in tiefem* ~*e liegen* be fast asleep; **'~abteil** *n* sleepingcompartment; **'~anzug** *m* ein a pair of) pyjamas *pl. or Am.* pajamas *pl.*

Schläfchen ['ʃlɛːfçən] *n* (-s/-) doze, nap, F forty winks *pl.*; *ein* ~ *machen* take a nap, F have one's forty winks.

'Schlafdecke *f* blanket.

Schläfe ['ʃlɛːfə] *f* (-/-n) temple.

'schlafen *v/i.* (*irr.,* ge-, h) sleep; ~ *gehen, sich* ~ *legen* go to bed.

schlaff *adj.* [ʃlaf] slack, loose; *muscles, etc.*: flabby, flaccid; *plant, etc.*: limp; *discipline, morals, etc.*: lax; **'2heit** *f* (-/no *pl.*) slackness, flabbiness; limpness; *fig.* laxity.

'Schlaf|gelegenheit *f* sleeping accommodation; **'~kammer** *f* bedroom; **'~krankheit** ♂ *f* sleepingsickness; **'~lied** *n* lullaby; **2los** *adj.* sleepless; **~losigkeit** *f* (-/no *pl.*) sleeplessness, insomnia; **'~mittel** ♂ *n* soporific; **~mütze** *f* nightcap; *fig.* sleepyhead.

schläfrig *adj.* ['ʃlɛːfriç] sleepy, drowsy; **'2keit** *f* (-/no *pl.*) sleepiness, drowsiness.

'Schlaf|rock *m* dressing-gown, *Am. a.* robe; **'~saal** *m* dormitory; **'~sack** *m* sleeping-bag; **'~stelle** *f* sleepingplace; night's lodging; **~tablette** ♂ *f* sleeping-tablet; **2trunken** *adj.* very drowsy; **~wagen** ⚓ *m* sleeping-car(riage), *Am. a.* sleeper; **~wandler** ['~vandlər] *m* (-s/-) sleep-walker, somnambulist; **'~zimmer** *n* bedroom.

Schlag [ʃlɑːk] *m* (-[e]s/⸚e) blow (*a. fig.*); stroke (*of clock, piston*) (*a. tennis, etc.*); slap (*with palm of hand*); punch (*with fist*); kick (*of horse's hoof*); ⚡ shock; beat (*of heart or pulse*); clap (*of thunder*); warbling (*of bird*); door (*of carriage*); ♂ apoplexy; *fig.* race, kind, sort; breed (*esp. of animals*); *Schläge bekommen* get a beating; *sechs Uhr* on the stroke of six; **~ader** *anat. f* artery; **'~anfall** ♂ *m* (stroke of) apoplexy, stroke; **2artig 1.** *adj.* sudden, abrupt; **2.** *adv.* all of a sudden; **'~baum** *m* turnpike.

schlagen ['ʃlɑːgən] (*irr.,* ge-, h) **1.** *v/t.* strike, beat, hit; punch; slap;

beat, defeat; fell (*trees*); fight (*battle*); *Alarm* ~ sound the alarm; *zu Boden* ~ knock down; *in den Wind* ~ cast *or* fling to the winds; *sich* ~ (have a) fight; *sich et. aus dem Kopf or Sinn* ~ put s.th. out of one's mind, dismiss s.th. from one's mind; **2.** *v/i.* strike, beat; *heart, pulse*: beat, throb; *clock*: strike; *bird*: warble; *das schlägt nicht in mein Fach* that is not in my line; *um sich* ~ lay about one; **'~d** *fig. adj.* striking.

Schlager ['ʃlɑːgər] *m* (-s/-) ♪ song hit; *thea.* hit, draw, box-office success; *book*: best seller.

Schläger ['ʃlɛːgər] *m* (-s/-) rowdy, hooligan; *cricket, etc.*: batsman; *horse*: kicker; *cricket, etc.*: bat; *golf*: club; *tennis, etc.*: racket; *hockey, etc.*: stick; **~ei** [~'raɪ] *f* (-/-en) tussle, fight.

'schlag|fertig *fig. adj.* quick at repartee; **~e** Antwort repartee; **'2fertigkeit** *fig. f* (-/no *pl.*) quickness at repartee; **'2instrument** ♪ *n* percussion instrument; **'2kraft** *f* (-/no *pl.*) striking power (*a.* ⚔); **'2loch** *n* pot-hole; **'2mann** *m* rowing: stroke; **'2ring** *m* knuckleduster, *Am. a.* brass knuckles *pl.*; **'2sahne** *f* whipped cream; **'2schatten** *m* cast shadow; **'2seite** ⚓ *f* list; ~ *haben* ⚓ list; F *fig.* be halfseas-over; **'2uhr** *f* striking clock; **'2werk** *n* clock: striking mechanism; **'2wort** *n* catchword, slogan; **'2zeile** *f* headline; banner headline, *Am.* banner; **'2zeug** ♪ *n in orchestra*: percussion instruments *pl.*; *in band*: drums *pl.*, percussion; **'2zeuger** ♪ *m* (-s/-) *in orchestra*: percussionist; *in band*: drummer.

schlaksig *adj.* ['ʃlaːksɪç] gangling.

Schlamm [ʃlam] *m* (-[e]s/⸚e, ⸚e) mud, mire; **'~bad** *n* mud-bath; **2ig** *adj.* muddy, miry.

Schlämmkreide ['ʃlɛm-] *f* (-/no *pl.*) whit(en)ing.

Schlamp|e ['ʃlampə] *f* (-/-n) slut, slattern; **'2ig** *adj.* slovenly, slipshod.

schlang [ʃlaŋ] *pret. of* schlingen.

Schlange ['ʃlaŋə] *f* (-/-n) *zo.* snake, *rhet.* serpent (*a. fig.*); *fig.*: snake in the grass; queue, *Am. a.* line; ~ *stehen* queue up (um for), *Am.* line up (for).

schlängeln ['ʃlɛŋəln] *v/refl.* (ge-, h): *sich* ~ *durch person*: worm one's way or o.s. (through); *path, river, etc.*: wind (one's way) through, meander through.

'Schlangenlinie *f* serpentine line.

schlank *adj.* [ʃlaŋk] slender, slim; **'2heit** *f* (-/no *pl.*) slenderness, slimness; **'2heitskur** *f*: *e-e* ~ *machen* slim.

schlapp F *adj.* [ʃlap] tired, exhausted,

worn out; '2e F ƒ (-/-n) reverse, set-back; defeat; '.machen F v/i. (sep., -ge-, h) break down, faint.

schlau adj. [ʃlaʊ] sly, cunning; crafty, clever, F cute.

Schlauch [ʃlaux] m (-[e]s/-e) tube; hose; car, etc.: inner tube; '.boot n rubber dinghy, pneumatic boat.

Schlaufe [ˈʃlaʊfə] ƒ (-/-n) loop.

schlecht [ʃleçt] 1. adj. bad; wicked; poor; temper: ill; quality: inferior; .e Laune haben be in a bad temper; .e Aussichten poor prospects; .e Zeiten hard times; mir ist ~ I feel sick; 2. adv. badly, ill; .erdings adv. ['.ər'dɪŋs] absolutely, down-right, utterly; .gelaunt adj. ['.gə-laʊnt] ill-humo(u)red, in a bad temper; '.hin adv. plainly, simply; '2igkeit ƒ (-/-en) badness; wicked-ness; .en pl. base acts pl., mean tricks pl.; '.machen v/t. (sep., -ge-, h) run down, backbite; .weg adv. ['.vek] plainly, simply.

schleich|en [ˈʃlaɪçən] v/i. (irr., ge-, sein) creep (a. fig.); sneak, steal; '2er m (-s/-) creeper; fig. sneak; '2handel m illicit trade; smuggling, contraband; '2händler m smuggler, contrabandist; black marketeer; '2weg m secret path.

Schleier [ˈʃlaɪər] m (-s/-) veil (a. fig.); mist: a. haze; den ~ nehmen take the veil; '2haft fig. adj. mys-terious, inexplicable.

Schleife [ˈʃlaɪfə] ƒ (-/-n) loop (a. ✗); slip-knot; bow; wreath: streamer; loop, horse-shoe bend.

'schleif|en 1. v/t. (irr., ge-, h) whet (knife, etc.); cut (glass, precious stones); polish (a. fig.); 2. v/t. (ge-, h) ɟ slur; drag, trail; ✗ raze (for-tress, etc.); 3. v/i. (ge-, h) drag, trail; '2stein m grindstone, whet-stone.

Schleim [ʃlaɪm] m (-[e]s/-e) slime; ✗ mucus, phlegm; '.haut anat. ƒ mucous membrane; '2ig adj. slimy (a. fig.); mucous.

schlemm|en [ˈʃlemən] v/i. (ge-, h) feast, gormandize; '2er m (-s/-) glutton, gormandizer; 2erei [.ˈraɪ] ƒ (-/-en) feasting, gluttony.

schlen|dern [ˈʃlendərn] v/i. (ge-, sein) stroll, saunter; 2drian [ˈ.driːan] m (-[e]s/no pl.) jogtrot; beaten track.

schlenkern [ˈʃleŋkərn] (ge-, h) 1. v/t. dangle, swing; 2. v/i.: mit den Armen ~ swing one's arms.

Schlepp|dampfer [ˈʃlep-] m steam tug, tug(boat); '.e ƒ (-/-n) train (of woman's dress); '2en (ge-, h) 1. v/t. carry with difficulty, haul, Am. F a. tote; ✗, ✗, mot. tow, haul; ✗ tug; ✝ tout (customers); sich ~ drag o.s.; 2. v/i. dress: drag, trail; '2end adj. speech: drawling; gait: shuffling; style: heavy; con-

versation, etc.: tedious; '.er ✗ m (-s/-) steam tug, tug(boat); '.tau n tow(ing)-rope; ins ~ nehmen take in or on tow (a. fig.).

Schleuder [ˈʃlɔydər] ƒ (-/-n) sling, catapult (a. ✗), Am. a. slingshot; spin drier; '2n (ge-, h) 1. v/t. fling, hurl (a. fig.); sling, catapult (a. ✗); spin-dry (washing); 2. mot. v/i. skid; '.preis ✝ m ruinous or give-away price; zu .en dirt-cheap.

schleunig adj. [ˈʃlɔynɪç] prompt, speedy, quick.

Schleuse [ˈʃlɔyzə] ƒ (-/-n) lock, sluice; '2n v/t. (ge-, h) lock (boat) (up or down); fig. manœuvre, Am. maneuver.

schlich [ʃlɪç] pret. of schleichen.

schlicht adj. [ʃlɪçt] plain, simple; modest, unpretentious; hair: smooth, sleek; '.en fig. v/t. (ge-, h) settle, adjust; settle by arbitration; '2er fig. m (-s/-) mediator; arbitra-tor.

schlief [ʃliːf] pret. of schlafen.

schließ|en [ˈʃliːsən] (irr., ge-, h) 1. v/t. shut, close; shut down (factory, etc.); shut up (shop); con-tract (marriage); conclude (treaty, speech, etc.); parl. close (debate); in die Arme ~ clasp in one's arms; in sich ~ comprise, include; Freund-schaft ~ make friends (mit with); 2. v/i. shut, close; school: break up; aus et. ~ auf (acc.) infer or conclude s.th. from s.th.; '2fach ✆ n post-office box; '.lich adv. finally, eventually; at last; after all.

Schliff [ʃlɪf] 1. m (-[e]s/-e) polish (a. fig.); precious stones, glass: cut; 2. 2 pret. of schleifen 1.

schlimm [ʃlɪm] 1. adj. bad; evil, wicked, nasty; serious; Γ ✗ bad, sore; .er worse; am .sten, das 2ste the worst; es wird immer .er things are going from bad to worse; 2. adv.: daran sein be badly off; '.sten'falls adv. at (the) worst.

Schling|e [ˈʃlɪŋə] ƒ (-/-n) loop, sling (a. ✗); noose; coil (of wire or rope); hunt. snare (a. fig.); den Kopf in die ~ stecken put one's head in the noose; '.el m (-s/-) rascal, naughty boy; '2en v/t. (irr., ge-, h) wind, twist; plait; die Arme ~ um (acc.) fling one's arms round; sich um et. ~ wind round; '.pflanze ✿ ƒ creeper, climber.

Schlips [ʃlɪps] m (-es/-e) (neck)tie.

Schlitten [ˈʃlɪtən] m (-s/-) sled(ge); sleigh; sports: toboggan.

'Schlittschuh m skate; ~ laufen skate, .läufer m skater.

Schlitz [ʃlɪts] m (-es/-e) slit, slash; slot; '2en v/t. (ge-, h) slit, slash.

Schloß [ʃlɔs] 1. n (Schlosses/Schlös-ser) lock (of door, gun, etc.); castle, palace; ins ~ fallen door: snap to;

hinter ~ und Riegel behind prison bars; 2. 2 *pret. of* schließen.

Schlosser ['ʃlɔsər] *m* (-s/-) locksmith; mechanic, fitter.

Schlot [ʃloːt] *m* (-[e]s/-e, ⁓e) chimney; flue; ♿, 🚂 funnel; '⁓feger *m* (-s/-) chimney-sweep(er).

schlotter|ig *adj.* ['ʃlɔtəriç] shaky, tottery; loose; ⁓n *v/i.* ('ge-, h) *garment*: hang loosely; *p.* shake, tremble (*both: vor dat.* with).

Schlucht [ʃluxt] *f* (-/-en) gorge, mountain cleft; ravine, *Am. a.* gulch.

schluchzen ['ʃluxtsən] *v/i.* (ge-, h) sob.

Schluck [ʃluk] *m* (-[e]s/-e, ⁓e) draught, swallow; mouthful, sip; '⁓auf *m* (-s/no *pl.*) hiccup(s *pl.*).

schlucken 1. *v/t. and v/i.* (ge-, h) swallow (*a. fig.*); 2. 2 *m* (-s/no *pl.*) hiccup(s *pl.*).

schlug [ʃluːk] *pret. of* schlagen.

Schlummer ['ʃlumər] *m* (-s/no *pl.*) slumber; '2n *v/i.* (ge-, h) slumber.

Schlund [ʃlunt] *m* '-[e]s/⁓e *anat.* pharynx; *fig.* abyss, chasm, gulf.

schlüpf|en ['ʃlypfən] *v/i.* ge-, sein) slip, slide; *in die Kleider* slip on one's clothes; *aus den Kleidern* ~ slip out of *or* slip off one's clothes; '2er *m* (-s/-) (*ein paar*) (*ein pair of*) knickers *pl. or* drawers *pl. or* F panties *pl.*; briefs *pl.*

Schlupfloch ['ʃlupf-] *n* loop-hole.

schlüpfrig *adj.* slippery; *fig.* lascivious.

Schlupfwinkel *m* hiding-place.

schlurfen ['ʃlurfən] *v/i.* (ge-, sein) shuffle, drag one's feet.

schlürfen ['ʃlyrfən] *v/t. and v/i.* (ge-, h) drink *or* eat noisily; sip.

Schluß [ʃlus] *m* (Schlusses/Schlüsse) close, end; conclusion; *parl.* closing (*of debate*).

Schlüssel ['ʃlysəl] *m* (-s/-) key (zu of; *fig.* to); ♪ clef; *fig.* code; quota; '⁓bart *m* key-bit; '⁓bein *anat. n* collar-bone, clavicle; '⁓bund *m, n* (-[e]s/-e) bunch of keys; ⁓industrie *fig. f* key industry; '⁓loch *n* keyhole; '⁓ring *m* key-ring.

'**Schluß|folgerung** *f* conclusion, inference; '⁓formel *f in letter*: complimentary close.

schlüssig *adj.* ['ʃlysiç] *evidence*: conclusive; *sich* ~ *werden* make up one's mind (*über acc.* about).

'**Schluß|licht** *n* ⚙, *mot., etc.*: tail-light; *sports*: last runner; bottom club; '⁓runde *f sports*: final; '⁓schein ✝ *m* contract-note.

Schmach [ʃmaːx] *f* (-/no *pl.*) disgrace; insult; humiliation.

schmachten ['ʃmaxtən] *v/i.* (ge-, h) languish (*nach* for), pine (for).

schmächtig *adj.* ['ʃmɛçtiç] slender, slim; *ein ⁓er Junge* a (mere) slip of a boy.

'**schmachvoll** *adj.* disgraceful; humiliating.

schmackhaft *adj.* ['ʃmakhaft] palatable, savo(u)ry.

schmäh|en ['ʃmɛːən] *v/t.* (ge-, h) abuse, revile; decry, disparage; slander, defame; '⁓lich *adj.* ignominious, disgraceful; '2schrift *f* libel, lampoon; '2ung *f* (-/-en) abuse; slander, defamation.

schmal *adj.* [ʃmaːl] narrow; *figure*: slender, slim; *face*: thin; *fig.* poor, scanty.

schmäler|n ['ʃmɛːlərn] *v/t.* (ge-, h) curtail; impair; belittle; '2ung *f* (-/-en) curtailment; impairment; detraction.

Schmal|film *phot. m* substandard film; '⁓spur ♿ *f* narrow ga(u)ge; '⁓spurbahn ♿ *f* narrow-ga(u)ge railway; '2spurig ♿ *adj.* narrow-ga(u)ge.

Schmalz [ʃmalts] *n* (-es/-e) grease; lard; 2ig *adj.* greasy; lardy; F *fig.* soppy, sentimental.

schmarotz|en [ʃmaˈrɔtsən] *v/i.* (no -ge-, h) sponge (*bei* on); 2er *m* (-s/-) ♿, *zo.* parasite; *fig. a.* sponge.

Schmarre F ['ʃmarə] *f* (-/-n) slash, cut; scar.

Schmatz [ʃmats] *m* (-es/-e) smack, loud kiss; '2en *v/i.* (ge-, h) smack (*mit den Lippen* one's lips); eat noisily.

Schmaus [ʃmaus] *m* (-es/⁓e) feast, banquet; *fig.* treat; 2en *v/i.* ['⁓zən] (ge-, h) feast, banquet.

schmecken ['ʃmekən] (ge-, h) 1. *v/t.* taste, sample; 2. *v/i.*: ~ *nach* taste *or* smack of (*both a. fig.*); *dieser Wein schmeckt mir* I like *or* enjoy this wine.

Schmeichel|ei [ʃmaiçəˈlai] *f* (-/-en) flattery; cajolery; '2haft *adj.* flattering; '2n *v/i.* (ge-, h): *j-m* ~ flatter s.o.; cajole s.o.

Schmeichler ['ʃmaiçlər] *m* (-s/-) flatterer; '2isch *adj.* flattering; cajoling.

schmeiß|en F ['ʃmaisən] (*irr.*, ge-, h) 1. *v/t.* throw, fling, hurl; slam, bang (*door*); 2. *v/i.*: *mit Geld um sich* ~ squander one's money; '2fliege *zo. f* blowfly, bluebottle.

Schmelz [ʃmelts] *m* 1. (-es/-e) enamel; 2. *fig.* (-es/no *pl.*) bloom; ♪ sweetness, mellowness; '2en (*irr.*, ge-) 1. *v/i.* (sein) melt (*a. fig.*); liquefy; *fig.* melt away, dwindle; 2. *v/t.* (h) melt; smelt, fuse (*ore, etc.*); liquefy; '⁓erei [⁓'rai] *f* (-/-en), '⁓hütte *f* foundry; '⁓ofen *m* smelting furnace; '⁓tiegel *m* melting-pot, crucible.

Schmerbauch ['ʃmeːr-] *m* paunch, pot-belly, F corporation, *Am. sl. a.* bay window.

Schmerz [ʃmerts] *m* (-es/-en) pain (*a. fig.*); ache; *fig.* grief, sorrow;

'**Øen** (ge-, h) 1. v/i. pain (a. fig.), hurt; ache; 2. v/t. pain (a. fig.); hurt; fig. grieve, afflict; '**Øhaft** adj. painful; '**Ølich** adj. painful, grievous; '**Ølindernd** adj. soothing; '**Ølos** adj. painless.

Schmetter|ling zo. ['ʃmetərliŋ] m (-s/-e) butterfly; '**Øn** (ge-, h) 1. v/i. dash (zu Boden to the ground); in Stücke to pieces); 2. v/i. crash; trumpet, etc.: bray, blare; bird: warble.

Schmied [ʃmi:t] m (-[e]s/-e) (black)smith; **~e** ['ˌdə] f (-/-n) forge, smithy; **~eeisen** ['ˌdəʔ-] n wrought iron; '**~ehammer** m sledge(-hammer); **Øen** ['ˌdən] v/t. (ge-, h) forge; make, devise, hatch (plans).

schmiegen ['ʃmi:gən] v/refl. (ge-, h) nestle (an acc. to).

schmiegsam adj. ['ʃmi:kza:m] pliant, flexible; supple (a. fig.); **Økeit** f (-/no pl.) pliancy, flexibility; suppleness (a. fig.).

Schmier|e ['ʃmi:rə] f (-/-n) grease; thea. contp. troop of strolling players, sl. penny gaff; '**Øen** v/t. (ge-, h) smear; ⊕ grease, oil, lubricate; butter (bread); spread (butter, etc.); scrawl, scribble; painter: daub; **~enkomödiant** ['ˌkɔmødjant] m (-en/-en) strolling actor, barnstormer, sl. ham (actor); **~erei** [ˌˈraɪ] f (-/-en) scrawl; paint. daub; '**Øig** adj. greasy; dirty; fig.: filthy; F smarmy; '**~mittel** ⊕ n lubricant.

Schminke ['ʃmiŋkə] f (-/-n) make-up (a. thea.); paint; rouge; thea. grease-paint; '**Øn** v/t. and v/refl. (ge-, h) paint, make up; rouge (o.s.); put on lipstick.

Schmirgel ['ʃmirgəl] m (-s/no pl.) emery; '**Øn** v/t. (ge-, h) (rub with) emery; '**~papier** n emery-paper.

Schmiß [ʃmis] 1. m (Schmisses/Schmisse) gash, cut; (duelling-)scar; 2. F m (Schmisses/no pl.) verve, go, Am. sl. a. pep; 3. ♀ pret. of schmeißen.

schmoll|en ['ʃmɔlən] v/i. (ge-, h) sulk, pout; '**Øwinkel** m sulking-corner.

schmolz [ʃmɔlts] pret. of schmelzen.

Schmor|braten ['ʃmo:r-] m stewed meat; '**Øen** v/t. and v/i. (ge-, h) stew (a. fig.).

Schmuck [ʃmuk] 1. m (-[e]s/ˋ-e) ornament; decoration; jewel(le)ry, jewels pl.; 2. ♀ adj. neat, smart, spruce, trim.

schmücken ['ʃmykən] v/t. (ge-, h) adorn, trim; decorate.

'**schmuck|los** adj. unadorned; plain; '**Øsachen** f/pl. jewel(le)ry, jewels pl.

Schmuggel ['ʃmugəl] m (-s/no pl.), **~ei** [ˌˈlaɪ] f (-/-en) smuggling; '**Øn** v/t. and v/i. (ge-, h) smuggle; '**~ware** f contraband, smuggled goods pl.

Schmuggler ['ʃmuglər] m (-s/-) smuggler.

schmunzeln ['ʃmuntsəln] v/i. (ge-, h) smile amusedly.

Schmutz [ʃmuts] m (-es/no pl.) dirt; filth; fig. a. smut; '**Øen** v/i. (ge-, h) soil, get dirty; '**~fink** fig. m mudlark; '**~fleck** m smudge, stain; fig. blemish; '**Øig** adj. dirty; filthy; fig. a. mean, shabby.

Schnabel ['ʃna:bəl] m (-s/ˋ-) bill, esp. bird of prey: beak.

Schnalle ['ʃnalə] f (-/-n) buckle; '**Øn** v/t. (ge-, h) buckle; strap.

schnalzen ['ʃnaltsən] v/i. (ge-, h): mit den Fingern ~ snap one's fingers; mit der Zunge ~ click one's tongue.

schnappen ['ʃnapən] (ge-, h) 1. v/i. lid, spring, etc.: snap; lock: catch; nach et. ~ snap or snatch at; nach Luft ~ gasp for breath; 2. F v/t. catch, sl. nab (criminal).

'**Schnapp|messer** n flick-knife; '**~schloß** n spring-lock; '**~schuß** phot. m snapshot.

Schnaps [ʃnaps] m (-es/ˋ-e) strong liquor, Am. hard liquor; brandy; ein (Glas) ~ a dram.

schnarch|en ['ʃnarçən] v/i. (ge-, h) snore; '**Øer** m (-s/-) snorer.

schnarren ['ʃnarən] v/i. (ge-, h) rattle; jar.

schnattern ['ʃnatərn] v/i. (ge-, h) cackle; fig. a. chatter, gabble.

schnauben ['ʃnaubən] (ge-, h) 1. v/i. snort; vor Wut ~ foam with rage; 2. v/t.: sich die Nase ~ blow one's nose.

schnaufen ['ʃnaufən] v/i. (ge-, h) pant, puff, blow; wheeze.

Schnauz|bart ['ʃnauts-] m m(o)ustache; **~e** f (-/-n) snout, muzzle; ⊕ nozzle; teapot, etc.: spout; sl. fig. potato-trap; '**Øen** F v/i. (ge-, h) jaw.

Schnecke zo. ['ʃnɛkə] f (-/-n) snail; slug; '**~nhaus** n snail's shell; '**~ntempo** n: im ~ at a snail's pace.

Schnee [ʃne:] m (-s/no pl.) snow; '**~ball** m snowball; '**~ballschlacht** f pelting-match with snowballs; **Øbedeckt** adj. ['ˌbədɛkt] snow-covered, mountain-top: snow-capped; '**Øblind** adj. snow-blind; '**~blindheit** f snow-blindness; '**~brille** f (e-e a pair of) snow-goggles pl.; '**~fall** m snow-fall; '**~flocke** f snow-flake; '**~gestöber** n (-s/-) snow-storm; '**~glöckchen** ['ˌglœkçən] n (-s/-) snowdrop; '**~grenze** f snow-line; '**~mann** m snow man; '**~pflug** m snow-plough, Am. snowplow; '**~schuh** m snow-shoe; '**~sturm** m snow-storm, blizzard; '**~wehe** f (-/-n) snow-drift; '**Øweiß** adj. snow-white.

Schneid F [ʃnaɪt] m (-[e]s/no pl.) pluck, dash, sl. guts pl.

Schneide ['ʃnaɪdə] f (-/-n) edge; '**~mühle** f sawmill; '**Øn** (irr., ge-, h)

1. v/t. cut; carve (*meat*); pare, clip (*finger-nails, etc.*); **2.** v/i. cut.

'**Schneider** m (-s/-) tailor; **~ei** [~'raɪ] f **1.** (-/*no pl.*) tailoring; dressmaking; **2.** (-/-en) tailor's shop; dressmaker's shop; **~in** f (-/-nen) dressmaker; '**~meister** m master tailor; '**2n** (ge-, h) **1.** v/i. tailor; do tailoring; do dressmaking; **2.** v/t. make, tailor.

'**Schneidezahn** m incisor.

'**schneidig** *fig. adj.* plucky; dashing, keen; smart, *Am. sl. a.* nifty.

schneien ['ʃnaɪən] v/i. (ge-, h) snow.

schnell [ʃnɛl] **1.** *adj.* quick, fast; rapid; swift, speedy; *reply, etc.*: prompt; sudden; **2.** *adv.*: **~** fahren drive fast; **~** handeln act promptly or without delay; (*mach*) **~!** be quick!, hurry up!

Schnelläufer ['ʃnɛlˌɔyfər] m sprinter; speed skater.

'**schnell|en** (ge-) v/t. (h) and v/i. (sein) jerk; '**2feuer** ⚔ n rapid fire; '**2hefter** m (-s/-) folder.

'**Schnelligkeit** f (-/*no pl.*) quickness, fastness; rapidity; swiftness; promptness; speed, velocity.

'**Schnell|imbiß** m snack (bar); '**~imbißstube** f snack bar; '**~kraft** f (-/*no pl.*) elasticity; '**~verfahren** n ⚖ summary proceeding; ⊕ highspeed process; '**~zug** 🚂 m fast train, express (train).

schneuzen ['ʃnɔytsən] v/refl. (ge-, h) blow one's nose.

schniegeln ['ʃniːgəln] v/refl. (ge-, h) dress or smarten or spruce (o.s.) up.

Schnipp|chen ['ʃnɪpçən] n: F j-m ein **~** schlagen outwit or overreach s.o.; '**2isch** *adj.* pert, snappish, *Am.* F a. snippy.

Schnitt [ʃnɪt] **1.** m (-[e]s/-e) cut; *dress, etc.*: cut, make, style; pattern; *book*: edge; Å (inter)section; *fig.*: average; F profit; **2.** 2 *pret. of* schneiden; '**~blumen** f/pl. cut flowers pl.; '**~e** f (-/-n) slice; '**~er** m (-s/-) reaper, mower; '**~fläche** Å f section(al plane); '**2ig** *adj.* streamline(d); '**~muster** n pattern; '**~punkt** m (point of) intersection; '**~wunde** f cut, gash.

Schnitzel ['ʃnɪtsəl] **1.** n (-s/-) schnitzel; 2 f (-s/-) chip; *paper*: scrap; **~** pl. ⊕ parings pl., shavings pl.; *paper*: a. clippings pl.; '**2n** v/t. (ge-, h) chip, shred, whittle.

schnitzen ['ʃnɪtsən] v/t. (ge-, h) carve, cut (in wood).

'**Schnitzer** m (-s/-) carver; F *fig.* blunder, *Am. sl. a.* boner; **~ei** [~'raɪ] f **1.** (-/-en) carving, carved work; **2.** (-/*no pl.*) carving.

schnöde *adj.* ['ʃnøːdə] contemptuous; disgraceful; base, vile; **~r** Mammon filthy lucre.

Schnörkel ['ʃnœrkəl] m (-s/-) flourish (*a. fig.*), scroll (*a.* △).

schnorr|en F ['ʃnɔrən] v/t. and v/i. (ge-, h) cadge; '**2er** m (-s/-) cadger.

schnüff|eln ['ʃnYfəln] v/i. (ge-, h) sniff, nose (*both: an dat.* at); *fig.* nose about, *Am.* F a. snoop around; '**2ler** *fig.* m (-s/-) spy, *Am.* F a. snoop; F sleuth(-hound).

Schnuller ['ʃnʊlər] m (-s/-) dummy, comforter.

Schnulze F ['ʃnʊltsə] f (-/-n) sentimental song or film or play, F tearjerker.

Schnupf|en ['ʃnʊpfən] **1.** m (-s/-) cold, catarrh; 2 v/i. (ge-, h) take snuff; '**~er** m (-s/-) snuff-taker; '**~tabak** m snuff.

schnuppe F *adj.* ['ʃnʊpə]: *das ist mir* **~** I don't care (F a damn); '**~rn** v/i. (ge-, h) sniff, nose (*both: an dat.* at).

Schnur [ʃnuːr] f (-/⸚e, ⚓-en) cord; string, twine; line; ⚡ flex.

Schnür|band ['ʃnyːr-] n lace; **~chen** ['~çən] n (-s/-): *wie am* **~** *like clockwork*; '2en v/t. (ge-, h) lace (up); (bind with) cord, tie up.

'**schnurgerade** *adj.* dead straight.

Schnurr|bart ['ʃnʊr-] m m(o)ustache; '2en (ge-, h) **1.** v/i. *wheel, etc.*: whir(r); *cat*: purr (*a. fig.*); F *fig.* cadge; **2.** F *fig.* v/t. cadge.

Schnür|senkel ['ʃnyːrzɛŋkəl] m (-s/-) shoe-lace, shoe-string; '**~stiefel** m lace-boot.

schnurstracks *adv.* ['ʃnuːr'ʃtraks] direct, straight; on the spot, at once, *sl.* straight away.

schob [ʃoːp] *pret. of* schieben.

Schober ['ʃoːbər] m (-s/-) rick, stack.

Schock [ʃɔk] **1.** n (-[e]s/-e) threescore; **2.** ⚕ m (-[e]s/-s, ⚓-e) shock; 2ieren [~'kiːrən] v/t. (no -ge-, h) shock, scandalize.

Schokolade [ʃokoˈlaːdə] f (-/-n) chocolate.

scholl [ʃɔl] *pret. of* schallen.

Scholle ['ʃɔlə] f (-/-n) clod (*of earth*), *poet.* glebe; floe (*of ice*); *ichth.* plaice.

schon *adv.* [ʃoːn] already; **~** *lange* for a long time; **~** *gut!* all right!; **~** *der Gedanke* the very idea; **~** *der Name* the bare name; *hast du* **~** *einmal ...?* have you ever ...?; *mußt du* **~** *gehen?* need you go yet?; **~** *um 8 Uhr* as early as 8 o'clock.

schön [ʃøːn] **1.** *adj.* beautiful; *man*: handsome (*a. fig.*); *weather*: fair, fine (*a. iro.*); *das* **~e** *Geschlecht* the fair sex; *die* **~en** *Künste* the fine arts; **~e** *Literatur* belles-lettres pl.; **2.** *adv.*: **~** *warm* nice and warm; *du hast mich ...* **~** *erschreckt* you gave me quite a start.

schonen ['ʃoːnən] v/t. (ge-, h) spare (*j-n s.o.*; *j-s Leben s.o.'s life*); take

care of; husband (*strength*, etc.);
sich ~ take care of o.s., look after
o.s.

'**Schönheit** *f* 1. (-/no *pl.*) beauty;
of woman: a. pulchritude; 2. (-/-en)
beauty; beautiful woman, belle; '~spflege *f* beauty treatment.

'**schöntun** *v/i.* (*irr.* tun, *sep.*, -ge-, h)
flatter (*j-m* s.o.); flirt (*dat.* with).

'**Schonung** *f* 1. (-/no *pl.*) mercy;
sparing, forbearance; careful treatment; 2. (-/-en) tree-nursery;
'**2slos** *adj.* unsparing, merciless,
relentless.

Schopf [ʃɔpf] *m* (-[e]s/ᵃe) tuft; *orn.*
a. crest.

schöpfen ['ʃœpfən] *v/t.* (ge-, h)
scoop, ladle; draw (*water at well*);
draw, take (*breath*); take (*courage*);
neue Hoffnung ~ gather fresh hope;
Verdacht ~ become suspicious.

'**Schöpf|er** *m* (-s/-) creator; '**2e-
risch** *adj.* creative; '~ung *f* (-/-en)
creation.

schor [ʃoːr] *pret.* of scheren.

Schorf ♣ [ʃɔrf] *m* (-[e]s/-e) scurf;
scab, crust; '**2ig** *adj.* scurfy; scabby.

Schornstein ['ʃɔrn-] *m* chimney;
♣, ⚓ funnel; '~feger *m* (-s/-)
chimney-sweep(er).

Schoß [ʃoːs] *m* (-es/ᵉe) lap; womb;
coat: tail; 2. ⚓ [ʃɔs] *pret.* of schießen.

Schote ♣ ['ʃoːtə] *f* (-/-n) pod, husk.

Schott|e ['ʃɔtə] *m* (-n/-n) Scot,
Scotchman, Scotsman; *die* ~*n pl.*
the Scotch *pl.*; '~er *m* (-s/-) gravel;
(road-)metal; '**2isch** *adj.* Scotch,
Scottish.

schräg [ʃrɛːk] 1. *adj.* oblique, slanting; sloping; 2. *adv.*: ~ *gegenüber*
diagonally across (*von* from).

schrak [ʃraːk] *pret.* of schrecken 2.

Schramme ['ʃramə] *f* (-/-n) scratch;
skin: a. abrasion; '**2n** *v/t.* (ge-, h)
scratch; graze, abrade (*skin*).

Schrank [ʃraŋk] *m* (-[e]s/ᵃe) cupboard, *esp. Am.* closet; wardrobe.

'**Schranke** *f* (-/-n) barrier (*a. fig.*);
⚙ a. (railway-)gate; ⚓ bar; ~*n pl.
fig.* bounds *pl.*, limits *pl.*; '**2nlos**
fig. adj. boundless; unbridled; '~n-
wärter *m* gate-keeper.

'**Schrankkoffer** *m* wardrobe trunk.

Schraube ['ʃraubə] *f* (-/-n) ⚙ screw;
⚓ screw(-propeller); '**2n** *v/t.* (ge-,
h) screw.

'**Schrauben|dampfer** ⚓ *m* screw
(steamer); '~mutter ⊕ *f* nut;
'~schlüssel ⊕ *m* spanner, wrench;
'~zieher ⊕ *m* screwdriver.

Schraubstock ⊕ ['ʃraup-] *m* vice,
Am. vise.

Schrebergarten ['ʃreːbər-] *m* allotment garden.

Schreck [ʃrɛk] *m* (-[e]s/-e) fright,
terror; consternation; '~bild *n*
bugbear; '~en *m* (-s/-) fright, terror;
consternation; '**2en** (ge-) 1. *v/t.* (h)
frighten, scare; 2. *v/i.* (*irr.*, sein):

only in compounds; '~ensbotschaft
f alarming or terrible news; '~ens-
herrschaft *f* reign of terror; '**2haft**
adj. fearful, timid; '**2lich** *adj.* terrible, dreadful (*both a.* F *fig.*);
'~schuß *m* scare shot; *fig.* warning
shot.

Schrei [ʃraɪ] *m* (-[e]s/-e) cry; shout;
scream.

schreiben ['ʃraɪbən] 1. *v/t. and v/i.*
(*irr.*, ge-, h) write (*j-m* to s.o.; *über
acc.* on); *mit der Maschine* ~
type(write); 2. *v/t.* (*irr.*, ge-, h)
spell; 3. ♀ *n* (-s/-) letter.

'**Schreiber** *m* (-s/-) writer; secretary, clerk.

schreib|faul *adj.* ['ʃraɪp-] lazy in
writing; '**2feder** *f* pen; '**2fehler** *m*
mistake in writing or spelling, slip
of the pen; '**2heft** *n* exercise-book;
'**2mappe** *f* writing-case; '**2ma-
schine** *f* typewriter; (*mit der*) ~
schreiben type(write); '**2material**
n writing-materials *pl.*, stationery;
'**2papier** *n* writing-paper; '**2-
schrift** *typ. f* script; '**2tisch** *m*
(writing-)desk; '**2ung** ['.bʊŋ] *f*
(-/-en) spelling; '**2unterlage** *f*
desk pad; '**2waren** *f/pl.* writing-
materials *pl.*, stationery; '**2waren-
händler** *m* stationer; '**2zeug** *n*
writing-material *n*.

'**schreien** (*irr.*, ge-, h) 1. *v/t.* shout;
scream; 2. *v/i.* cry (out) (*vor dat.*
with *pain*, etc.); *nach for bread*,
etc.); shout (*vor* with); scream
(with); '~d *adj. colour*: loud; *injustice*: flagrant.

schreiten ['ʃraɪtən] *v/i.* (*irr.*, ge-,
sein) step, stride (*über acc.* across);
fig. proceed (*zu* to).

schrie [ʃriː] *pret.* of schreien.

schrieb [ʃriːp] *pret.* of schreiben.

Schrift [ʃrɪft] *f* (-/-en) (hand-)
writing, hand; *typ.* type; character,
letter; writing; publication; *die
Heilige* ~ the (Holy) Scriptures *pl.*;
'~art *f* type; '**2deutsch** *adj.*
literary German; '~führer *m*
secretary; '~leiter *m* editor; '**2lich**
1. *adj.* written, in writing; 2. *adv.*
in writing; '~satz *m* ⚖ pleadings
pl.; *typ.* composition, type-setting;
'~setzer *m* compositor, type-setter;
'~sprache *f* literary language;
'~steller *m* (-s/-) author, writer;
'~stück *n* piece of writing, paper,
document; '~tum *n* (-s/no *pl.*)
literature; '~wechsel *m* exchange
of letters, correspondence; '~zei-
chen *n* character, letter.

schrill *adj.* [ʃrɪl] shrill, piercing.

Schritt [ʃrɪt] *m* (-[e]s/-e) step
(*a. fig.*); pace (*a. fig.*); ~*e unternehmen* take steps; 2. ♀ *pret.* of
schreiten; '~macher *m* (-s/-) *sports*:
pace-maker; '~weise 1. *adj.* gradual;
2. *adv. a.* step by step.

schroff *adj.* [ʃrɔf] rugged, jagged;

steep, precipitous; *fig.* harsh, gruff; **~**er *Widerspruch* glaring contradiction.

schröpfen ['ʃrœpfən] *v/t.* (ge-, h) **⚕** cup; *fig.* milk, fleece.

Schrot [ʃro:t] *m, n* (-[e]s/-e) crushed grain; small shot; '**~brot** *n* wholemeal bread; '**~flinte** *f* shotgun.

Schrott [ʃrɔt] *m* (-[e]s/-e) scrap (-iron *or* -metal).

schrubben ['ʃrubən] *v/t.* (ge-, h) scrub.

Schrulle ['ʃrulə] *f* (-/-n) whim, fad.

schrumpf|en ['ʃrumpfən] *v/i.* (ge-, sein) shrink (*a.* ⊕, **⚕**, *fig.*); '**2ung** *f* (-/-en) shrinking; shrinkage.

Schub [ʃu:p] *m* (-[e]s/**~**e) push, shove; *phys.*, ⊕ thrust; *bread, people, etc.*: batch; '**~fach** *n* drawer; '**~karren** *m* wheelbarrow; '**~kasten** *m* drawer; '**~kraft** *phys.*, ⊕ *f* thrust; '**~lade** *f* (-/-n) drawer.

Schubs F [ʃups] *m* (-es/-e) push; '**2en** F *v/t.* (ge-, h) push.

schüchtern *adj.* ['ʃyçtərn] shy, bashful, timid; *girl:* coy; '**2heit** *f* (-/no *pl.*) shyness, bashfulness, timidity; coyness (*of girl*).

schuf [ʃu:f] *pret. of* **schaffen 1.**

Schuft [ʃuft] *m* (-[e]s/-e) scoundrel, rascal; cad; '**2en** F *v/i.* (ge-, h) drudge, slave, plod; '**2ig** *adj.* scoundrelly, rascally; caddish.

Schuh [ʃu:] *m* (-[e]s/-e) shoe; *j-m et. in die* **~**e *schieben* put the blame for s.th. on s.o.; *wissen, wo der* **~** *drückt* know where the shoe pinches; '**~anzieher** *m* (-s/-) shoehorn; '**~band** *n* shoe-lace *or* -string; '**~creme** *f* shoe-cream, shoe-polish; '**~geschäft** *n* shoe-shop; '**~löffel** *m* shoehorn; '**~macher** *m* (-s/-) shoemaker; '**~putzer** *m* (-s/-) shoeblack, *Am. a.* shoeshine; '**~sohle** *f* sole; '**~spanner** *m* (-s/-) shoetree; '**~werk** *n*, '**~zeug** F *n* foot-wear, boots and shoes *pl.*

'**Schul|amt** *n* school-board; '**~arbeit** *f* homework; '**~bank** *f* (school-) desk; '**~beispiel** *n* test-case, typical example; '**~besuch** *m* (-[e]s/no *pl.*) attendance at school; '**~bildung** *f* education; *höhere* **~** secondary education; '**~buch** *n* school-book.

Schuld [ʃult] *f* **1.** (-/no *pl.*) guilt; fault, blame; *es ist s-e* **~** it is his fault, he is to blame for it; **2.** (-/-en) debt; **~**en *machen* contract *or* incur debts; '**2bewußt** *adj.* conscious of one's guilt; **2en** ['∫ɔldən] *v/t.* (ge-, h): *j-m et.* **~** owe s.o. s.th.; *j-m Dank* **~** be indebted to s.o. (*für* for); **2haft** *adj.* ['∫thaft] culpable.

'**Schuldiener** *m* school attendant *or* porter.

schuldig *adj.* ['ʃuldiç] guilty (*e-r Sache* of s.th.); *respect, etc.:* due; *j-m et.* **~** *sein* owe s.o. s.th.; *Dank* **~** *sein* be indebted *to* s.o. (*für* for);

für **~** *befinden* **⚖** find guilty; **2e** ['**~**gə] *m, f* (-n/-n) guilty person; culprit; '**2keit** *f* (-/no *pl.*) duty, obligation.

'**Schuldirektor** *m* headmaster, *Am. a.* principal.

'**schuld|los** *adj.* guiltless, innocent; '**2losigkeit** *f* (-/no *pl.*) guiltlessness, innocence; **2ner** ['∫ʊldnər] *m* (-s/-) debtor; '**2schein** *m* evidence of debt, certificate of indebtedness, IOU (= I owe you); '**2verschreibung** *f* bond, debt certificate.

Schule ['ʃu:lə] *f* (-/-n) school; *höhere* **~** secondary school, *Am. a.* high school; *auf or in der* **~** at school; *in die* **~** *gehen* go to school; '**2n** *v/t.* (ge-, h) train, school; *pol.* indoctrinate.

Schüler ['ʃy:lər] *m* (-s/-) schoolboy, pupil; *phls., etc.:* disciple; '**~austausch** *m* exchange of pupils; '**~in** *f* (-/-nen) schoolgirl.

'**Schul|ferien** *pl.* holidays *pl.*, vacation; '**~fernsehen** *n* educational TV; '**~funk** *m* educational broadcast; '**~gebäude** *n* school(house); '**~geld** *n* school fee(s *pl.*), tuition; '**~hof** *m* playground, *Am. a.* schoolyard; '**~kamerad** *m* schoolfellow; '**~lehrer** *m* schoolmaster, teacher; '**~mappe** *f* satchel; '**2meistern** *v/t.* (ge-, h) censure pedantically; '**~ordnung** *f* school regulations *pl.*; '**2pflichtig** *adj.* schoolable; '**~rat** *m* supervisor of schools, school inspector; '**~schiff** *n* training-ship; '**~schluß** *m* end of school; end of term; '**~schwänzer** *m* (-s/-) truant; '**~stunde** *f* lesson.

Schulter ['ʃultər] *f* (-/-n) shoulder; '**~blatt** *anat. n* shoulder-blade; '**2n** *v/t.* (ge-, h) shoulder.

'**Schul|unterricht** *m* school, lessons *pl.*; school instruction; '**~versäumnis** *f* (-/no *pl.*) absence from school; '**~wesen** *n* educational system; '**~zeugnis** *n* report.

schummeln F ['ʃuməln] *v/i.* (ge-, h) cheat, *Am.* F *a.* chisel.

Schund [ʃunt] **1.** *m* (-[e]s/no *pl.*) trash, rubbish (*both a. fig.*); **2.** **2** *pret. of* **schinden**; '**~literatur** *f* trashy literature; '**~roman** *m* trashy novel, *Am. a.* dime novel.

Schupp|e ['ʃupə] *f* (-/-n) scale; **~**n *pl. on head:* dandruff; '**~en 1.** *m* (-s/-) shed; *mot.* garage; **✈** hangar; **2. 2** *v/t.* (ge-, h) scale (*fish*); *sich* **~** *skin:* scale off; '**2ig** *adj.* scaly.

Schür|eisen ['ʃy:r?-] *n* poker; '**2en** *v/t.* (ge-, h) poke; stoke; *fig.* fan, foment.

schürfen ['ʃyrfən] (ge-, h) **1. ⚒** *v/i.* prospect (*nach* for); **2.** *v/t.* **⚒** prospect for; *sich den Arm* **~** graze one's arm.

Schurk|e ['ʃurkə] *m* (-n/-n) scoundrel, knave; **~**erei [**~**'raɪ] *f* (-/-en) rascality, knavish trick; '⌀isch adj. scoundrelly, knavish.

Schürze ['ʃyrtsə] f (-/-n) apron; children: pinafore; '⌀n v/t. (ge-, h) tuck up (skirt); tie (knot); purse (lips); '⌀njäger m skirt-chaser, Am. sl. wolf.

Schuß [ʃus] m (Schusses/Schüsse) shot (a. sports); ammunition: round; sound: report; charge; wine, etc.: dash (a. fig.); in ~ sein be in full swing, be in full working order.

Schüssel ['ʃysəl] f (-/-n) basin (for water, etc.); bowl, dish, tureen (for soup, vegetables, etc.).

'**Schuß|waffe** f fire-arm; '⌀weite f range; '⌀wunde f gunshot wound.

Schuster ['ʃuːstər] m (-s/-) shoemaker; '⌀n fig. v/i. (ge-, h) s. pfuschen.

Schutt [ʃut] m (-[e]s/no pl.) rubbish, refuse; rubble, debris.

Schüttel|frost ['ʃytəl-] m shivering-fit; '⌀n v/t. (ge-, h) shake; den Kopf ~ shake one's head; j-m die Hand ~ shake hands with s.o.

schütten ['ʃytən] (ge-, h) 1. v/t. pour; spill (auf acc. on); 2. v/i.: es schüttet it is pouring with rain.

Schutz [ʃuts] m (-es/no pl.) protection (gegen, vor dat. against), defen|ce, Am. -se (against, from); shelter (from); safeguard; cover; '⌀brille f (e-e a pair of) goggles pl.

Schütze ['ʃytsə] m (-n/-n) marksman, shot; ♐ rifleman; '⌀n v/t. (ge-, h) protect (gegen, vor dat. against, from), defend (against, from), guard (against, from); shelter (from); safeguard (rights, etc.).

Schutzengel ['ʃuts⁹-] m guardian angel.

'**Schützen|graben** ♐ m trench; '⌀könig m champion shot.

'**Schutz|haft** ♐♐ f protective custody; '⌀heilige m patron saint; '⌀herr m patron, protector; '⌀impfung ♐ f protective inoculation; smallpox: vaccination.

Schützling ['ʃytslɪŋ] m (-s/-e) protégé, female: protégée.

'**schutz|los** adj. unprotected; defen|celess, Am. -seless; '⌀mann m (-[e]s/⌀er, Schutzleute) policeman, (police) constable, sl. bobby, sl. cop; '⌀marke f trade mark, brand; '⌀mittel n preservative; ♐ prophylactic; '⌀patron m patron saint; '⌀umschlag m (dust-)jacket, wrapper; '⌀zoll m protective duty.

Schwabe ['ʃvaːbə] m (-n/-n) Swabian.

schwäbisch adj. ['ʃvɛːbɪʃ] Swabian.

schwach adj. [ʃvax] resistance, team, knees (a. fig.), eyes, heart, voice, character, tea, gr. verb, ♐ demand, etc.: weak; person, etc.: infirm; person, recollection, etc.: feeble; sound, light, hope, idea, etc.: faint;

consolation, attendance, etc.: poor; light, recollection, etc.: dim; resemblance: remote; das ⌀e Geschlecht the weaker sex; ⌀e Seite weak point or side.

Schwäche ['ʃvɛçə] f (-/-n) weakness (a. fig.); infirmity; fig. foible; e-e ~ haben für have a weakness for; '⌀n v/t. (ge-, h) weaken (a. fig.); impair (health).

'**Schwach|heit** f (-/-en) weakness; fig. a. frailty; '⌀kopf m simpleton, soft(y), Am. F a. sap(head); '⌀köpfig adj. ['⌀køpfɪç] weak-headed, soft, Am. sl. a. sappy.

schwäch|lich adj. ['ʃvɛçlɪç] weakly, feeble; delicate, frail; '⌀ling m (-s/-e) weakling (a. fig.).

'**schwach|sinnig** adj. weak- or feeble-minded; '⌀strom ∉ m (-[e]s/no pl.) weak current.

Schwadron [ʃvaˈdroːn] f (-/-en) squadron; ⌀ieren [⌀oˈniːrən] v/t. (no -ge-, h) swagger, vapo(u)r.

Schwager ['ʃvaːgər] m (-s/⌀) brother-in-law.

Schwägerin ['ʃvɛːgərin] f (-/-nen) sister-in-law.

Schwalbe orn. ['ʃvalbə] f (-/-n) [swallow.]

Schwall [ʃval] m (-[e]s/-e) swell, flood; words: torrent.

Schwamm [ʃvam] 1. m (-[e]s/⌀e) sponge; ♣ fungus; ♣ dry-rot; 2. ⌀ pret. of schwimmen; '⌀ig adj. spongy; face, etc.: bloated.

Schwan orn. [ʃvaːn] m (-[e]s/⌀e) swan.

schwand [ʃvant] pret. of schwinden.

schwang [ʃvaŋ] pret. of schwingen.

schwanger adj. ['ʃvaŋər] pregnant, with child, in the family way.

schwängern ['ʃvɛŋərn] v/t. (ge-, h) get with child, impregnate (a. fig.).

'**Schwangerschaft** f (-/-en) pregnancy.

schwanken ['ʃvaŋkən] v/i. (ge-) 1. (h) earth, etc.: shake, rock; ♦ prices: fluctuate; branches, etc.: sway; fig. waver, oscillate, vacillate; 2. (sein) stagger, totter.

Schwanz [ʃvants] m (-es/⌀e) tail (a. ♐, ast.); fig. train.

schwänz|eln ['ʃvɛntsəln] v/i. (ge-, h) wag one's tail; fig. fawn (um [up]on); '⌀en v/t. (ge-, h) cut (lecture, etc.); die Schule ~ play truant, Am. a. play hooky.

Schwarm [ʃvarm] m (-[e]s/⌀e) bees, etc.: swarm; birds: a. flight, flock; fish: school, shoal; birds, girls, etc.: bevy; F fig. fancy, craze; p.: idol, hero; flame.

schwärmen ['ʃvɛrmən] v/i. (ge-) bees, etc.: swarm; fig.: revel; rave (von about, of), gush (over); ~ für be wild about, adore s.o.

'**Schwärmer** m (-s/-) enthusiast; esp. eccl. fanatic; visionary; fireworks: cracker, squib; zo. hawkmoth; **~ei** [~'raɪ] f (-/-en) enthusiasm (für for); idolization; ecstasy; esp. eccl. fanaticism; **'2isch** adj. enthusiastic; gushing, raving; adoring; esp. eccl. fanatic(al).

Schwarte ['ʃvartə] f (-/-n) bacon: rind; F fig. old book.

schwarz adj. [ʃvarts] black (a. fig.); dark; dirty; **~es Brett** notice-board, Am. bulletin board; **~es Brot** brown bread; **~er Mann** bog(e)y; **~er Markt** black market; **~ auf weiß** in black and white; **auf die ~e Liste setzen** blacklist; **'2arbeit** f illicit work; **'2brot** n brown bread; **'2e m**, f (-n/-n) black.

Schwärze ['ʃvɛrtsə] f (-/no pl.) blackness (a. fig.); darkness; **'2n** v/t. (ge-, h) blacken.

'**schwarz|fahren** F v/i. (irr. fahren, sep., -ge-, sein) travel without a ticket; mot. drive without a licence; '**2fahrer** m fare-dodger; mot. person driving without a licence; '**2fahrt** f ride without a ticket; mot. drive without a licence; '**2handel** m illicit trade, black marketeering; '**2händler** m black marketeer; '**2hörer** m listener without a licence.

'**schwärzlich** adj. blackish.

'**Schwarz|markt** m black market; **~seher** m pessimist; TV: viewer without a licence; **~sender** m pirate broadcasting station; **~weiß-film** m black-and-white film.

schwatzen ['ʃvatsən] v/i. (ge-, h) chat; chatter, tattle.

schwätz|en ['ʃvɛtsən] v/i. (ge-, h) s. schwatzen; '**2er** m (-s/-) chatterbox; tattler, prattler; gossip.

'**schwatzhaft** adj. talkative, garrulous.

Schwebe fig. ['ʃve:bə] f (-/no pl.): in der **~ sein** be in suspense; law, rule, etc.: be in abeyance; '**~bahn** f aerial railway or ropeway; '**2n** v/i. (ge-, h) be suspended; bird: hover (a. fig.); glide; fig. be pending (a. ½½); in Gefahr **~** be in danger.

Schwed|e ['ʃve:də] m (-n/-n) Swede; '**2isch** adj. Swedish.

Schwefel ['ʃve:fəl] m (-s/no pl.) sulphur, Am. a. sulfur; '**~säure** f (-/no pl.) sulphuric acid, Am. a. sulfuric acid.

Schweif [ʃvaɪf] m (-[e]s/-e) tail (a. ast.); fig. train; '**2en** (ge-) 1. v/i. (sein) rove, ramble; 2. ⊕ v/t. (h) curve; scallop.

schweigen ['ʃvaɪgən] 1. v/i. (irr., ge-, h) be silent; 2. 2 n (-s/no pl.) silence; '**~d** adj. silent.

schweigsam adj. ['ʃvaɪkza:m] taciturn; '**2keit** f (-/no pl.) taciturnity.

Schwein [ʃvaɪn] n 1. (-[e]s/-e) zo. pig, hog, swine (all a. contp. fig.); 2. F (-[e]s/no pl.): **~ haben** be lucky.

'**Schweine|braten** m roast pork;

~fleisch n pork; '**~hund** F contp. m swine; **~rei** [~'raɪ] f (-/-en) mess; dirty trick; smut(ty story); '**~stall** m pigsty (a. fig.).

'**schweinisch** fig. adj. swinish; smutty.

'**Schweinsleder** n pigskin.

Schweiß [ʃvaɪs] m (-es/-e) sweat, perspiration; '**2en** ⊕ v/t. (ge-, h) weld; '**~er** ⊕ m (-s/-) welder; '**~fuß** m perspiring foot; '**2ig** adj. sweaty, damp with sweat.

Schweizer ['ʃvaɪtsər] m (-s/-) Swiss; on farm: dairyman.

schwelen ['ʃve:lən] v/i. (ge-, h) smo(u)lder (a. fig.).

schwelg|en ['ʃvɛlgən] v/i. (ge-, h) lead a luxurious life; revel; fig. revel (in dat. in); '**2er** m (-s/-) revel(l)er; epicure; **2erei** [~'raɪ] f (-/-en) revel(ry), feasting; '**~erisch** adj. luxurious; revel(l)ing.

Schwell|e ['ʃvɛlə] f (-/-n) sill, threshold (a. fig.); ⚊ sleeper, Am. tie; '**2en 1.** v/i. (irr., ge-, sein) swell (out); 2. v/t. (ge-, h) swell; '**~ung** f (-/-en) swelling.

Schwemme ['ʃvɛmə] f (-/-n) watering-place; horse-pond; at tavern, etc.: taproom; † glut (of fruit, etc.).

Schwengel ['ʃvɛŋəl] m (-s/-) clapper (of bell); handle (of pump).

schwenk|en ['ʃvɛŋkən] (ge-) 1. v/t. (h) swing; wave (hat, etc.); brandish (stick, etc.); rinse (washing); 2. v/i. (sein) turn, wheel; '**2ung** f (-/-en) turn; fig. change of mind.

schwer [ʃve:r] 1. adj. heavy; problem, etc.: hard, difficult; illness, mistake, etc.: serious; punishment, etc.: severe; fault, etc.: grave; wine, cigar, etc.: strong; **~e Zeiten** hard times; **2 Pfund ~ sein** weigh two pounds; 2. adv.: **~ arbeiten** work hard; **~ hören** be hard of hearing; '**2e** f (-/no pl.) heaviness; phys. gravity (a. fig.); severity; '**~fällig** adj. heavy, slow; clumsy; '**2gewicht** n sports: heavy-weight; fig. main emphasis; '**2gewichtler** m (-s/-) sports: heavy-weight; '**~hörig** adj. hard of hearing; '**2industrie** f heavy industry; '**2kraft** phys. f (-/no pl.) gravity; '**~lich** adv. hardly, scarcely; '**2mut** f (-/no pl.) melancholy; '**~mütig** adj. ['~my:tiç] melancholy; '**2punkt** m centre of gravity, Am. center of gravity; fig.: crucial point; emphasis.

Schwert [ʃve:rt] n (-[e]s/-er) sword.

'**Schwer|verbrecher** m felon; '**2verdaulich** adj. indigestible, heavy; '**2verständlich** adj. difficult or hard to understand; '**2verwundet** adj. seriously wounded; '**2wiegend** fig. adj. weighty, momentous.

Schwester ['ʃvɛstər] f (-/-n) sister; nurse.

schwieg [ʃviːk] pret. of schweigen.

Schwieger|eltern ['ʃviːgər-] pl. parents-in-law pl.; '~mutter f mother-in-law; '~sohn m son-in-law; '~tochter f daughter-in-law; '~vater m father-in-law.

Schwiel|e ['ʃviːlə] f (-/-n) callosity; 'ℒig adj. callous.

schwierig adj. ['ʃviːriç] difficult, hard; 'ℒkeit f (-/-en) difficulty, trouble.

Schwimm|bad ['ʃvim-] n swimming-bath, Am. swimming pool; 'ℒen v/i. (irr., ge-) 1. (sein) swim; thing: float; ich bin über den Fluß geschwommen I swam across the river; in Geld ~ be rolling in money; 2. (h) swim; ich habe lange unter Wasser geschwommen I swam under water for a long time; '~gürtel m swimming-belt; lifebelt; '~haut f web; '~lehrer m swimming-instructor; '~weste f life-jacket.

Schwindel ['ʃvindəl] m (-s/no pl.) ꝰ vertigo, giddiness, dizziness; F fig.: swindle, humbug, sl. eyewash; cheat, fraud; '~anfall ꝰ m fit of dizziness; 'ℒerregend adj. dizzy (a. fig.); '~firma ✝ f long firm, Am. wildcat firm; 'ℒn v/i. (ge-, h) cheat, humbug, swindle.

schwinden ['ʃvindən] v/i. (irr., ge-, sein) dwindle, grow less; strength, colour, etc.: fade.

'Schwindl|er m (-s/-) swindler, cheat, humbug; liar; 'ℒig ꝰ adj. giddy, dizzy.

Schwind|sucht ꝰ ['ʃvint-] f (-/no pl.) consumption; 'ℒsüchtig ꝰ adj. consumptive.

Schwing|e ['ʃviŋə] f (-/-n) wing, poet. pinion; swingle; 'ℒen (irr., ge-, h) 1. v/t. swing; brandish (weapon); swingle (flax); 2. v/i. swing; ⊕ oscillate; sound, etc.: vibrate; '~ung f (-/-en) oscillation; vibration.

Schwips F [ʃvips] m (-es/-e): e-n ~ haben be tipsy, have had a drop too much.

schwirren ['ʃvirən] v/i. (ge-) 1. (sein) whir(r); arrow, etc.: whiz(z); insects: buzz; rumours, etc.: buzz, circulate; 2. (h): mir schwirrt der Kopf my head is buzzing.

'Schwitz|bad n sweating-bath, hot-air bath, vapo(u)r bath; 'ℒen (ge-, h) 1. v/i. sweat, perspire; fig. v/t.: Blut und Wasser ~ be in great anxiety.

schwoll [ʃvɔl] pret. of schwellen.

schwor [ʃvoːr] pret. of schwören.

schwören ['ʃvøːrən] (irr., ge-, h) 1. v/t. swear; e-n Meineid ~ commit perjury; j-m Rache ~ vow vengeance against s.o.; 2. v/i. swear (bei by);

~ auf (acc.) have great belief in, F swear by.

schwül adj. [ʃvyːl] sultry, oppressively hot; 'ℒe f (-/no pl.) sultriness.

Schwulst [ʃvulst] m (-es/ꝰe) bombast.

schwülstig adj. ['ʃvylstiç] bombastic, turgid.

Schwund [ʃvunt] m (-[e]s/no pl.) dwindling; wireless, etc.: fading; ꝰ atrophy.

Schwung [ʃvuŋ] m (-[e]s/ꝰe) swing; fig. verve, go; flight (of imagination); buoyancy; 'ℒhaft ✝ adj. flourishing, brisk; '~rad ⊕ n flywheel; watch, clock: balance-wheel; 'ℒvoll adj. full of energy or verve; attack, translation, etc.: spirited; style, etc.: racy.

Schwur [ʃvuːr] m (-[e]s/ꝰe) oath; '~gericht ᴢᴛᴢ in England, Wales: appr. court of assize.

sechs [zɛks] 1. adj. six; 2. ℒ f (-/-en) six; 'ℒeck n (-[e]s/-e) hexagon; '~eckig adj. hexagonal; '~fach adj. sixfold, sextuple; '~mal adv. six times; '~monatig adj. lasting or of six months, six-months ...; '~monatlich 1. adj. six-monthly; 2. adv. every six months; '~stündig adj. ['~ʃtyndiç] lasting or of six hours, six-hour ...; ℒ'tagerennen n cycling: six-day race; '~tägig adj. ['~tɛːgiç] lasting or of six days.

sechs|te adj. ['zɛkstə] sixth; 'ℒtel n (-s/-) sixth (part); '~tens adv. sixthly, in the sixth place.

sech|zehn(te) adj.['zɛç-] sixteen(th); '~zig adj. ['~tsiç] sixty; '~zigste adj. sixtieth.

See [zeː] 1. m (-s/-n) lake; 2. f (-/no pl.) sea; an die ~ gehen go to the seaside; in ~ gehen or stechen put to sea; auf ~ at sea; auf hoher ~ on the high seas; zur ~ gehen go to sea; 3. f (-/-n) sea, billow; '~bad n seaside resort; '~fahrer m sailor, navigator; '~fahrt f navigation; voyage; 'ℒfest adj. seaworthy; ~ sein be a good sailor; '~gang m (motion of the sea); '~hafen m seaport; '~handel ✝ m maritime trade; '~herrschaft f naval supremacy; '~hund zo. m seal; 'ℒkrank adj. seasick; '~krankheit f (-/no pl.) seasickness; '~krieg m naval war(fare).

Seele ['zeːlə] f (-/-n) soul (a. fig.); mit or von ganzer ~ with all one's heart.

'Seelen|größe f (-/no pl.) greatness of soul or mind; '~heil n salvation, spiritual welfare; 'ℒlos adj. soulless; '~qual f anguish of mind, (mental) agony; '~ruhe f peace of mind; coolness.

'seelisch adj. psychic(al), mental.

'Seelsorge f (-/no pl.) cure of souls;

ministerial work; '**∿r** m (-s/-) pastor, minister.

'**See|macht** f naval power; '**∿mann** m (-[e]s/*Seeleute*) seaman, sailor; '**∿meile** f nautical mile; '**∿not** f (-/no pl.) distress (at sea); '**∿räuber** m pirate; '**∿räuberei** [∿'raɪ] f (-/-en) piracy; '**∿recht** n maritime law; '**∿reise** f voyage; '**∿schiff** n seagoing ship; '**∿schlacht** f naval battle; '**∿schlange** f sea serpent; '**∿sieg** m naval victory; '**∿stadt** f seaside town; '**∿streitkräfte** f/pl. naval forces pl.; '**♀tüchtig** adj. seaworthy; '**∿warte** f naval observatory; '**∿weg** m sea-route; auf dem ∿ by sea; '**∿wesen** n (-s/no pl.) maritime or naval affairs pl.

Segel ['ze:gəl] n (-s/-) sail; unter ∿ gehen set sail; '**∿boot** n sailing-boat, Am. sailboat; sports: yacht; '**∿fliegen** n (-s/no pl.) gliding, soaring; '**∿flug** m gliding flight, glide; '**∿flugzeug** n glider; '**♀n** (ge-) 1. v/i. (h, sein) sail; sports: yacht; 2. v/t. (h) sail; '**∿schiff** n sailing-ship, sailing-vessel; '**∿sport** m yachting; '**∿tuch** n (-[e]s/-e) sailcloth, canvas.

Segen ['ze:gən] m (-s/-) blessing (a. fig.), esp. eccl. benediction; '**♀s-reich** adj. blessed.

Segler ['ze:glər] m (-s/-) sailing-vessel, sailing-ship; fast, good, etc. sailer; yachtsman.

segn|en ['ze:gnən] v/t. (ge-, h) bless; '**♀ung** f (-/-en) s. Segen.

sehen ['ze:ən] (irr., ge-, h) 1. v/i. see; gut ∿ have good eyes; ∿ auf (acc.) look at; be particular about; ∿ nach look for; look after; 2. v/t. see; notice; watch, observe; '**∿swert** adj. worth seeing; '**♀swürdigkeit** f (-/-en) object of interest, curiosity; ∿en pl. sights pl. (of a place).

Seher ['ze:ər] m (-s/-) seer, prophet; '**∿blick** m (-[e]s/no pl.) prophetic vision; '**∿gabe** f (-/no pl.) gift of prophecy.

'**Seh|fehler** m visual defect; '**∿kraft** f vision, eyesight.

Sehne ['ze:nə] f (-/-n) anat. sinew, tendon; string (of bow); ♪ chord.

'**sehnen** v/refl. (ge-, h) long (nach for), yearn (for, after); sich danach ∿ zu inf. be longing to inf.

'**Sehnerv** anat. m visual or optic nerve.

'**sehnig** adj. sinewy (a. fig.), stringy.

'**sehn|lich** adj. longing; ardent; passionate; '**♀sucht** f longing, yearning; '**∿süchtig** adj., '**∿suchtsvoll** adj. longing, yearning; eyes, etc.: a. wistful.

sehr adv. [ze:r] before adj. and adv.: very, most; with vb.: (very) much, greatly.

'**Seh|rohr** ⚓ n periscope; '**∿weite** f range of sight, visual range; in ∿ within eyeshot or sight.

seicht adj. [zaɪçt] shallow; fig. a. superficial.

Seide ['zaɪdə] f (-/-n) silk.

'**seiden** adj. silk, silken (a. fig.); '**♀flor** m silk gauze; '**♀glanz** m silky lust|re, Am. -er; '**♀händler** m mercer; '**♀papier** n tissue(-paper); '**♀raupe** zo. f silkworm; '**♀spinnerei** f silk-spinning mill; '**♀stoff** m silk cloth or fabric.

'**seidig** adj. silky.

Seife ['zaɪfə] f (-/-n) soap.

'**Seifen|blase** f soap-bubble; '**∿kistenrennen** n soap-box derby; '**∿lauge** f (soap-)suds pl.; '**∿pulver** n soap-powder; '**∿schale** f soap-dish; '**∿schaum** m lather.

'**seifig** adj. soapy.

seih|en ['zaɪən] v/t. (ge-, h) strain, filter; '**♀er** m (-s/-) strainer, colander.

Seil [zaɪl] n (-[e]s/-e) rope; '**∿bahn** f funicular or cable railway; '**∿er** m (-s/-) rope-maker; '**∿tänzer** m ropedancer.

sein¹ [zaɪn] 1. v/i. (irr., ge-, sein) be; exist; 2. ♀ n (-s/no pl.) being; existence.

sein² poss. pron. [∿] his, her, its (in accordance with gender of possessor); der (die, das) ∿e his, hers, its; ∿ Glück machen make one's fortune; die Seinen pl. his family or people.

'**seiner**'**seits** adv. for his part; '**∿zeit** adv. then, at that time; in those days.

'**seines**'**gleichen** pron. his equal(s pl.); j-n wie ∿ behandeln treat s.o. as one's equal; er hat nicht ∿ he has no equal; there is no one like him.

seit [zaɪt] 1. prp. (dat.): ∿ 1945 since 1945; ∿ drei Wochen for three weeks; 2. cj. since; es ist ein Jahr her, ∿ ... it is a year now since ...; ∿**dem** [∿'de:m] 1. adv. since or from that time, ever since; 2. cj. since.

Seite ['zaɪtə] f (-/-n) side (a. fig.); flank (a. ✕, ♙); page (of book).

'**Seiten|ansicht** f profile, side-view; '**∿blick** m side-glance; '**∿flügel** ⚖ m wing; '**∿hieb** fig. m innuendo, sarcastic remark; '**♀s** prp. (gen.) on the part of; by; '**∿schiff** ⚖ n church: aisle; '**∿sprung** fig. m extra-marital adventure; '**∿straße** f bystreet; '**∿stück** fig. n counterpart (zu of); '**∿weg** m by-way.

seit'**her** adv. since (then, that time).

'**seit**'**lich** adj. lateral; '**∿wärts** adv. ['∿verts] sideways; aside.

Sekret|är [zekre'te:r] m (-s/-e) secretary; bureau; '**∿ariat** [∿'ari'a:t] n (-[e]s/-e) secretary's office; secretariat(e); '**∿ärin** f (-/-nen) secretary.

Sekt [zekt] *m* (-[e]s/-e) champagne.

Sekt|e ['zɛktə] *f* (-/-n) sect; **~ierer** [~'tiːrər] *m* (-s/-) sectarian.

Sektor ['zɛktɔr] *m* (-s/-en) ⚔, ✂, *pol.* sector; *fig.* field, branch.

Sekunde [ze'kundə] *f* (-/-n) second; **~nbruchteil** *m* split second; **~nzeiger** *m* second-hand.

selb *adj.* [zɛlp] same; **~er** F *pron.* ['~bər] *s. selbst 1.*

selbst [zɛlpst] 1. *pron.* self; personally; *ich ~ I* myself; *von ~ p.* of one's own accord; *thing:* by itself, automatically; 2. *adv.* even; 3. ♀ *n* (-/no *pl.*) (one's own) self; ego.

selbständig *adj.* ['zɛlpʃtɛndiç] independent; *sich ~ machen* set up for o.s.; **♀keit** *f* (-/no *pl.*) independence.

'Selbst|anlasser *mot. m* self-starter; **~anschluß** *teleph. m* automatic connection; **~bedienungsladen** *m* self-service shop; **~beherrschung** *f* self-command, self-control; **~bestimmung** *f* self-determination; **~betrug** *m* self-deception; **♀bewußt** *adj.* self-confident, self-reliant; **~bewußtsein** *n* self-confidence, self-reliance; **~binder** *m* (-s/-) tie, **~erhaltung** *f* self-preservation; **~erkenntnis** *f* self-knowledge; **~erniedrigung** *f* self-abasement, **♀gefällig** *adj.* (self-)complacent; **~gefälligkeit** *f* (-/no *pl.*) (self-)complacency; **~gefühl** *n* (-[e]s/no *pl.*) self-reliance; **♀gemacht** *adj.* [..~gəmaxt] homemade; **♀gerecht** *adj.* self-righteous; **~gespräch** *n* soliloquy, monolog(ue); **♀herrlich** 1. *adj.* high-handed, autocratic(al); 2. *adv.* with a high hand; **~hilfe** *f* self-help; **~kostenpreis** ✦ *m* cost price; **~laut** *gr. m* vowel; **♀los** *adj.* unselfish, disinterested; **~mord** *m* suicide; **~mörder** *m* suicide; **♀mörderisch** *adj.* suicidal; **♀sicher** *adj.* self-confident, self-assured; **~sucht** *f* (-/no *pl.*) selfishness, ego(t)ism; **♀süchtig** *adj.* selfish, ego(t)istic(al); **♀tätig** ⊕ *adj.* self-acting, automatic; **~täuschung** *f* self-deception; **~überwindung** *f* (-/no *pl.*) self-conquest; **~unterricht** *m* self-instruction; **~verleugnung** *f* self-denial; **'~versorger** *m* (-s/-) self-supporter; **♀verständlich** 1. *adj.* self-evident, obvious; 2. *adv.* of course, naturally; **~l a.** by all means!; **~verständlichkeit** *f* 1. (-/-en) matter of course; 2. (-/no *pl.*) matter-of-factness; **~verteidigung** *f* self-defen|ce, *Am.* -se; **'~vertrauen** *n* self-confidence, self-reliance; **~verwaltung** *f* self-government, autonomy; **♀zufrieden** *adj.* self-satisfied; **~zufriedenheit** *f* self-satisfaction; **'~zweck** *m* (-[e]s/no *pl.*) end in itself.

selig *adj.* ['zeːliç] *eccl.* blessed; late, deceased; *fig.* blissful, overjoyed; **♀keit** *fig. f* (-/-en) bliss, very great joy.

Sellerie ♀ ['zɛləri:] *m* (-s/-[s]), *f* (-/-) celery.

selten ['zɛltən] 1. *adj.* rare; scarce; 2. *adv.* rarely, seldom; **'♀heit** *f* (-/-en) rarity, scarcity; rarity, curio(sity); **♀heitswert** *m* (-[e]s/no *pl.*) scarcity value.

Selterswasser ['zɛltərs-] *n* (-s/⁻) seltzer (water), soda-water.

seltsam *adj.* ['zɛltzaːm] strange, odd.

Semester *univ.* [ze'mɛstər] *n* (-s/-) term.

Semikolon *gr.* [zemi'koːlɔn] *n* (-s/-s, *Semikola*) semicolon.

Seminar [zemi'naːr] *n* (-s/-e) *univ.* seminar; seminary (*for priests*).

Senat [ze'naːt] *m* (-[e]s/-e) senate; *parl.* Senate.

send|en ['zɛndən] *v/t.* 1. [*irr.*,] ge-, *h*) send; forward; 2. (ge-, *h*) transmit; broadcast, *Am. a.* radio(broadcast); telecast; **'♀er** *m* (-s/-) transmitter, broadcasting station.

'Sende|raum *m* (broadcasting) studio, **~zeichen** *n* interval signal.

Sendung *f* (-/-en) ✝ consignment; shipment; broadcast; telecast; *fig.* mission. [♀.]

Senf [zɛnf] *m* (-[e]s/-e) mustard (*a.*)

sengen ['zɛŋən] *v/t.* (ge-, *h*) singe, scorch; **~d** *adj. heat:* parching.

senil *adj.* [ze'niːl] senile; **♀ität** [~ili'tɛːt] *f* (-/no *pl.*) senility.

senior *adj.* ['zeːniɔr] senior.

Senk|blei ['zɛŋk-] *n* ⚓ plumb, plummet; ⚓ *a.* sounding-lead; **'♀e** *geogr. f* (-/-n) depression, hollow; **'♀en** *v/t.* (ge-, *h*) lower; sink (*a. voice*); let down; bow (*head*); cut (*prices, etc.*); *sich ~ land, buildings, etc.:* sink, subside; *ceiling, etc.:* sag; **'~fuß** ⚕ *m* flat-foot; **'~fußeinlage** *f* arch support; **~grube** *f* cesspool; **'♀recht** *adj.* vertical, *esp.* ⚔ perpendicular; **'~ung** *f* (-/-en) *geogr.* depression, hollow; lowering, reduction (*of prices*); ⚒ sedimentation.

Sensation [zɛnza'tsjoːn] *f* (-/-en) sensation; **♀ell** *adj.* [~o'nɛl] sensational; **~slust** *f* (-/no *pl.*) sensationalism; **~spresse** *f* yellow press.

Sense ['zɛnzə] *f* (-/-n) scythe.

sensi|bel *adj.* [zɛn'ziːbəl] sensitive; **♀bilität** [~ibili'tɛːt] *f* (-/no *pl.*) sensitiveness.

sentimental *adj.* [zɛntimen'taːl] sentimental; **♀ität** [~ali'tɛːt] *f* (-/-en) sentimentality.

September [zɛp'tɛmbər] *m* (-[s]/-) September.

Serenade ♪ [zere'nɑːdə] *f* (-/-n) serenade.

Serie ['zeːrjə] *f* (-/-n) series; set; *billiards*: break; '**²nmäßig 1.** *adj.* standard; **2.** *adv.*: ~ *herstellen* produce in mass; '**~nproduktion** *f* mass production.

seriös *adj.* [zeˈrjøːs] serious; trustworthy, reliable.

Serum ['zeːrum] *n* (-s/Seren, Sera) serum.

Service[1] [zɛrˈviːs] *n* (-s/-) service, set.

Service[2] ['zøːrvis] *m*, *n* (-/-s) service.

servier|en [zɛrˈviːrən] *v/t.* (*no* -ge-, h) serve; **²wagen** *m* trolley(-table).

Serviette [zɛrˈvjɛta] *f* (-/-n) (table-) napkin.

Sessel ['zɛsəl] *m* (-s/-) armchair, easy chair; '**~lift** *m* chair-lift.

seßhaft *adj.* ['zɛshaft] settled, established; resident.

Setzei ['zɛts⁹-] *n* fried egg.

'**setzen** (ge-) **1.** *v/t.* (h) set, place, put; *typ.* compose; ♣ plant; erect, raise (*monument*); stake (*money*) (*auf acc.* on); *sich* ~ sit down, take a seat; *bird*: perch; *foundations of house, sediment, etc.*: settle; **2.** *v/i.* (h): ~ *auf* (*acc.*) back (*horse, etc.*); **3.** *v/i.* (sein): ~ *über* (*acc.*) leap (*wall, etc.*); clear (*hurdle, etc.*); take (*ditch, etc.*).

'**Setzer** *typ.* *m* (-s/-) compositor, type-setter; **~ei** *typ.* [~'raɪ] *f* (-/-en) composing-room.

Seuche ['zɔʏçə] *f* (-/-n) epidemic (disease).

seufz|en ['zɔʏftsən] *v/i.* (ge-, h) sigh; '**²er** *m* (-s/-) sigh.

sexuell *adj.* [zɛksuˈɛl] sexual.

sezieren [zeˈtsiːrən] *v/t.* (*no* -ge-, h) dissect (*a. fig.*).

sich *refl. pron.* [zɪç] oneself; *sg.* himself, herself, itself; *pl.* themselves; *sg.* yourself, *pl.* yourselves; each other, one another; *sie blickte* ~ *um* she looked about her.

Sichel ['zɪçəl] *f* (-/-n) sickle; *s.* Mondsichel.

sicher ['zɪçər] **1.** *adj.* secure (*vor dat.* from), safe (from); proof (against); *hand*: steady; certain, sure; positive; *aus* ~*er Quelle* from a reliable source; *e-r Sache* ~ *sein* be sure of s.th.; **2.** *adv. s. sicherlich*; *um* ~ *zu gehen* to be on the safe side, to make sure.

'**Sicherheit** *f* (-/-en) security; safety; surety, certainty; positiveness; assurance (*of manner*); *in* ~ *bringen* place in safety; '**~snadel** *f* safety-pin; '**~schloß** *n* safety-lock.

'**sicher|lich** *adv.* surely, certainly; undoubtedly; *er wird* ~ *kommen* he is sure to come; '**~n** *v/t.* (ge-, h) secure (*a.* ⚔, ⊕); guarantee (*a.* ✝); protect, safeguard; *sich et.* ~ secure (*prize, seat, etc.*); '**~stellen** *v/t.* (*sep.*, -ge-, h) secure; '**²ung** *f* (-/-en) securing; safeguard(ing); ✝ security, guaranty; ⊕ safety device; ⚡ fuse.

Sicht [zɪçt] *f* (-/*no pl.*) visibility; view; *in* ~ *kommen* come in(to) view *or* sight; *auf lange* ~ in the long run; *auf or bei* ~ ✝ at sight; '**²bar** *adj.* visible; '**²en** *v/t.* (ge-, h) ⚓ sight; *fig.* sift; '**²lich** *adv.* visibly; '**~vermerk** *m* visé, visa (*on passport*).

sickern ['zɪkərn] *v/i.* (ge-, sein) trickle, ooze, seep.

sie *pers. pron.* [ziː] *nom.*: *sg.* she, *pl.* they; *acc.*: *sg.* her, *pl.* them; *Sie nom. and acc.*: *sg. and pl.* you.

Sieb [ziːp] *n* (-[e]s/-e) sieve; riddle (*for soil, gravel, etc.*).

sieben[1] ['ziːbən] *v/t.* (ge-, h) sieve, sift; riddle.

sieben[2] [~] **1.** *adj.* seven; **2.** *f* (-/-) (number) seven; *böse* ~ shrew, vixen; '**~fach** *adj.* sevenfold; '**~mal** *adv.* seven times; '**²sachen** F *f/pl.* belongings *pl.*, F traps *pl.*; '**~te** *adj.* seventh; '**²tel** *n* (-s/-) seventh (part); '**~tens** *adv.* seventhly, in the seventh place.

sieb|zehn(te) *adj.* ['ziːp-] seventeen(th); '**~zig** *adj.* ['~tsɪç] seventy; '**~zigste** *adj.* seventieth.

siech *adj.* [ziːç] sickly; '**²tum** *n* (-s/*no pl.*) sickliness, lingering illness.

Siedehitze ['ziːdə-] *f* boiling-heat.

siedeln ['ziːdəln] *v/i.* (ge-, h) settle; *Am. a.* homestead.

siede|n ['ziːdən] *v/t. and v/i.* ([*irr.*,] ge-, h) boil, simmer; '**²punkt** *m* boiling-point (*a. fig.*).

Siedler ['ziːdlər] *m* (-s/-) settler; *Am. a.* homesteader; '**~stelle** *f* settler's holding; *Am. a.* homestead.

'**Siedlung** *f* (-/-en) settlement; housing estate.

Sieg [ziːk] *m* (-[e]s/-e) victory (*über acc.* over); *sports*: *a.* win; *den* ~ *davontragen* win the day, be victorious.

Siegel ['ziːgəl] *n* (-s/-) seal (*a. fig.*); signet; '**~lack** *m* sealing-wax; '**²n** *v/t.* (ge-, h) seal; '**~ring** *m* signet-ring.

sieg|en ['ziːgən] *v/i.* (ge-, h) be victorious (*über acc.* over), conquer *s.o.*; *sports*: win; '**²er** *m* (-s/-) conqueror, *rhet.* victor; *sports*: winner.

Siegeszeichen ['ziːgəs-] *n* trophy. '**siegreich** *adj.* victorious, triumphant.

Signal [zɪˈgnaːl] *n* (-s/-e) signal; **²isieren** [~ali'ziːrən] *v/t.* (*no* -ge-, h) signal.

Silbe ['zɪlbə] *f* (-/-n) syllable; '**~ntrennung** *f* syllabi(fi)cation.

Silber ['zɪlbər] *n* (-s/*no pl.*) silver; *s.* Tafelsilber; '**²n** *adj.* (of) silver;

'**zeug** F n silver plate, Am. a. silverware.

Silhouette [zilu'ɛtə] f (-/-n) silhouette; skyline.

Silvester [zil'vɛstər] n (-s/-), ~abend m new-year's eve.

simpel ['zimpəl] 1. adj. plain, simple; stupid, silly; 2. ♀ m (-s/-) simpleton.

Sims [zims] m, n (-es/-e) ledge; sill (of window); mantelshelf (of fireplace); shelf; △ cornice.

Simul|ant [zimu'lant] m (-en/-en) esp. ✗, ♣ malingerer; **2ieren** (no -ge-, h) 1. v/t. sham, feign, simulate (illness, etc.); 2. v/i. sham, feign; esp. ✗, ♣ malinger.

Sinfonie ♪ [zinfo'ni:] f (-/-n) symphony.

sing|en ['ziŋən] v/t. and v/i. (irr., ge-, h) sing; vom Blatt ~ sing at sight; nach Noten ~ sing from music; **2sang** F m (-[e]s/no pl.) singsong; **2spiel** n musical comedy; **2stimme** ♪ f vocal part.

Singular gr. ['ziŋgula:r] m (-s/-e) singular (number).

'**Singvogel** m song-bird, songster.

sinken ['ziŋkən] v/i. (irr., ge-, sein) sink; ship: a. founder, go down; ✝ prices: fall, drop, go down; den Mut ~ lassen lose courage.

Sinn [zin] m (-[e]s/-e) sense; taste (für for); tendency; sense, meaning; von ~en sein be out of one's senses; im ~ haben have in mind; in gewissem ~e in a sense; '~bild n symbol, emblem; **2bildlich** adj. symbolic(al), emblematic; **2en** v/i. (irr., ge-, h): auf Rache ~ meditate revenge.

'**Sinnen|lust** f sensuality; '~mensch m sensualist; '~rausch m intoxication of the senses.

sinnentstellend adj. ['zin⁹-] garbling, distorting.   [world.)

'**Sinnenwelt** f (-/no pl.) material)

'**Sinnes|änderung** f change of mind; '~art f disposition, mentality; '~organ n sense-organ; '~täuschung f illusion, hallucination.

'**sinn|lich** adj. sensual; material; **2lichkeit** f (-/no pl.) sensuality; '~los adj. senseless; futile, useless; **2losigkeit** f (-/-en) senselessness; futility, uselessness; '~reich adj. ingenious; '~verwandt adj. synonymous.

Sipp|e ['zipə] f (-/-n) tribe; (blood-) relations pl.; family; '~schaft contp. f (-/-en) relations pl.; fig. clan, clique; die ganze ~ the whole lot.

Sirene [zi're:nə] f (-/-n) siren.

Sirup ['zi:rup] m (-s/-e) syrup, Am. sirup; treacle, molasses sg.

Sitte ['zitə] f (-/-n) custom; habit; usage; ~n pl. morals pl.; manners pl.

'**Sitten|bild** n, '~gemälde n genre (-painting); fig. picture of manners and morals; '~gesetz n moral law; '~lehre f ethics pl.; **2los** adj. immoral; '~losigkeit f (-/-en) immorality; '~polizei f appr. vice squad; '~prediger m moralizer; '~richter fig. m censor, moralizer; **2streng** adj. puritanic(al).

'**sittlich** adj. moral; **2keit** f (-/no pl.) morality; **2keitsverbrechen** n sexual crime.

'**sittsam** adj. modest; **2keit** f (-/no pl.) modesty.

Situation [zitua'tsjo:n] f (-/-en) situation.

Sitz [zits] m (-es/-e) seat (a. fig.); fit (of dress, etc.).

'**sitzen** v/i. (irr., ge-, h) sit, be seated; dress, etc.: fit; blow, etc.: tell; F fig. do time; ~ bleiben remain seated, keep one's seat; '~bleiben v/i. (irr. bleiben, sep., -ge-, sein) girl at dance: F be a wallflower; girl: be left on the shelf; at school: not to get one's remove; ~ auf (dat.) be left with (goods) on one's hands; '~d adj.: ~e Tätigkeit sedentary work; '~lassen v/t. (irr. lassen, sep., [no] -ge-, h) leave s.o. in the lurch, let s.o. down; girl: jilt (lover); leave (girl) high and dry; auf sich ~ pocket (insult, etc.).

'**Sitz|gelegenheit** f seating accommodation, seat(s pl.); ~ bieten für seat; '~platz m seat; '~streik m sit-down or stay-in strike.

'**Sitzung** f (-/-en) sitting (a. parl., paint.); meeting, conference; '~periode f session.

Skala ['ska:la] f (-/Skalen, Skalas) scale (a. ♪); dial (of radio set); fig. gamut; gleitende ~ sliding scale.

Skandal [skan'da:l] m (-s/-e) scandal; row, riot; **2ös** adj. [~a'lø:s] scandalous.

Skelett [ske'lɛt] n (-[e]s/-e) skeleton.

Skep|sis ['skɛpsis] f (-/no pl.) scepticism, Am. a. skepticism; ~**tiker** ['~tikər] m (-s/-) sceptic, Am. a. skeptic; **2tisch** adj. sceptical, Am. a. skeptical.

Ski [ʃi:] m (-s/-er, ✎-) ski; ~ laufen or fahren ski; '~fahrer m, '~läufer m skier; '~lift m ski-lift; '~sport m (-[e]s/no pl.) skiing.

Skizz|e ['skitsə] f (-/-n) sketch (a. fig.); **2ieren** [~'tsi:rən] v/t. (no -ge-, h) sketch, outline (both a. fig.).

Sklav|e ['skla:və] m (-n/-n) slave (a. fig.); '~enhandel m slave-trade; '~enhändler m slave-trader; ~e'rei f (-/-en) slavery; **2isch** adj. slavish.

Skonto ✝ ['skɔnto] m, n (-s/-s, ✎ Skonti) discount.

Skrupel ['skru:pəl] m (-s/-) scruple; **2los** adj. unscrupulous.

Skulptur [skulp'tu:r] f (-/-en) sculpture.

Slalom ['sla:lɔm] *m* (-s/-s) *skiing, etc.*: slalom.

Slaw|e ['sla:və] *m* (-n/-n) Slav; **'2isch** *adj.* Slav(onic).

Smaragd [sma'rakt] *m* (-[e]s/-e) emerald; **2grün** *adj.* emerald.

Smoking ['smo:kiŋ] *m* (-s/-s) dinner-jacket, *Am.* a. tuxedo, F tux.

so [zo:] 1. *adv.* so, thus; like this *or* that; as; ~ *ein* such a; ~ ... *wie* as ... as; *nicht* ~ ... *wie* not so ... as; ~ *oder* ~ by hook or by crook; 2. *cj.* so, therefore, consequently; ~ *daß* so that; **'~bald** *cj.* [zo'-]: ~ (*als*) as soon as.

Socke ['zɔkə] *f* (-/-n) sock; **'~l** *m* (-s/-) △ pedestal, socle; socket (*of lamp*); **'~n** *m* (-s/-) sock; **'~nhalter** *m/pl.* suspenders *pl.*, *Am.* garters *pl.*

Sodawasser ['zo:da-] *n* (-s/ᵘ) soda(-water).

Sodbrennen ⚕ ['zo:t-] *n* (-s/*no pl.*) heartburn.

soeben *adv.* [zo'-] just (now).

Sofa ['zo:fa] *n* (-s/-s) sofa.

sofern *cj.* [zo'-] if, provided that; ~ *nicht* unless.

soff [zɔf] *pret. of saufen.*

sofort *adv.* [zo'-] at once, immediately, directly, right *or* straight away; **'~ig** *adj.* immediate, prompt.

Sog [zo:k] 1. *m* (-[e]s/-e) suction; ♣ wake (*a. fig.*), undertow; 2. 2 *pret. of saugen.*

so|gar *adv.* [zo'-] even; **~genannt** *adj.* ['zo:-] so-called; **~gleich** *adv.* [zo'-] *s. sofort.*

Sohle ['zo:lə] *f* (-/-n) sole; bottom (*of valley, etc.*); ☆ floor.

Sohn [zo:n] *m* (-[e]s/ᵘe) son.

solange *cj.* [zo'-]: ~ (*als*) so *or* as long as.   [such.]

solch *pron.* [zɔlç] such; *als* ~e(*r*) a.]

Sold ✕ [zɔlt] *m* (-[e]s/-e) pay.

Soldat [zɔl'da:t] *m* (-en/-en) soldier; *der unbekannte* ~ the Unknown Warrior *or* Soldier.

Söldner ['zœldnər] *m* (-s/-) mercenary.

Sole ['zo:lə] *f* (-/-n) brine, salt water.

solid [zo'li:t] solid (*a. fig.*); *basis, etc.*: sound; ✝ *firm, etc.*: sound, solvent; *prices*: reasonable, fair; *p.* steady, staid, respectable.

solidarisch *adj.* [zoli'da:riʃ] *sich* ~ *erklären mit* declare one's solidarity with.

solide *adj.* [zo'li:də] *s. solid.*

Solist [zo'list] *m* (-en/-en) soloist.

Soll ✝ [zɔl] *n* (-[s]/-[s]) debit; (output) target.

'sollen (*h*) 1. *v/i.* (ge-): *ich sollte* (*eigentlich*) I ought to; 2. *v/aux.* (*irr., no* -ge-): *er soll* he shall; he is to; he is said to; *ich sollte* I should; *er sollte* (*eigentlich*) *zu Hause sein* he ought to be at home; *er sollte seinen Vater niemals wiedersehen* he was never to see his father again.

Solo ['zo:lo] *n* (-s/-s, *Soli*) solo.

somit *cj.* [zo'-] thus; consequently.

Sommer ['zɔmər] *m* (-s/-) summer; **'~frische** *f* (-/-n) summer-holidays *pl.*; summer-resort; **'2lich** *adj.* summer-like, summer(ly); **'~sprosse** *f* freckle; **'2sprosslig** *adj.* freckled; **~wohnung** *f* summer residence, *Am.* cottage, summer house; **'~zeit** *f* 1. (-/-en) *season*: summertime; 2. (-/*no pl.*) summer time, *Am.* daylight-saving time.

Sonate ♪ [zo'na:tə] *f* (-/-n) sonata.

Sonde ['zɔndə] *f* (-/-n) probe.

Sonder|angebot ['zɔndər-] *n* special offer; **'~ausgabe** *f* special (edition); **'2bar** *adj.* strange, odd; **'~beilage** *f* inset, supplement (*of newspaper*); **'~berichterstatter** *m* special correspondent; **'2lich** 1. *adj.* special, peculiar; 2. *adv.* · *nicht* ~ not particularly; **'~ling** *m* (-s/-e) crank, odd person; **'2n** 1. *cj.* but; *nicht nur,* ~ *auch* not only, but (also); 2. *v/t.* (ge-, h): *die Spreu vom Weizen* ~ sift the chaff from the wheat; **'~recht** *n* privilege; **'~zug** 🚂 *m* special (train).

sondieren [zɔn'di:rən] (*no* -ge-, h) 1. *v/t.* 🕮 probe (*a. fig.*); 2. *fig. v/i.* make tentative inquiries.

Sonn|abend ['zɔn²-] *m* (-s/-e) Saturday; **'~e** *f* (-/-n) sun; **'2en** *v/t.* (ge-, h) (expose to the) sun; *sich* ~ sun o.s. (*a. fig. in dat.* in), bask in the sun.

'Sonnen|aufgang *m* sunrise; **'~bad** *n* sun-bath; **'~brand** *m* sunburn; **'~bräune** *f* sunburn, tan, *Am.* (sun) tan; **'~brille** *f* (-e-e a pair of) sunglasses *pl.*; **'~finsternis** *f* solar eclipse; **'~fleck** *m* sun-spot; **'2klar** *fig. adj.* (as) clear as daylight; **'~licht** *n* (-[e]s/*no pl.*) sunlight; **'~schein** *m* (-[e]s/*no pl.*) sunshine; **'~schirm** *m* sunshade, parasol; **'~segel** *n* awning; **'~seite** *f* sunny side (*a. fig.*); **'~stich** ⚕ *m* sunstroke; **'~strahl** *m* sunbeam; **'~uhr** *f* sun-dial; **'~untergang** *m* sunset, sundown; **'2verbrannt** *adj.* sunburnt, tanned; **'~wende** *f* solstice.

'sonnig *adj.* sunny (*a. fig.*).

'Sonntag *m* Sunday.

'Sonntags|anzug *m* Sunday suit *or* best; **~fahrer** *mot. contp. m* Sunday driver; **~kind** *n* person born on a Sunday; *fig.* person born under a lucky star; **'~rückfahrkarte** 🚂 *f* week-end ticket; **'~ruhe** *f* Sunday rest; **'~staat** F *co. m* (-[e]s/*no pl.*) Sunday go-to-meeting clothes *pl.*

sonor *adj.* [zo'no:r] sonorous.

sonst [zɔnst] 1. *adv.* otherwise, *with pron.* else; usually; normally; *wer* ~? who else?; *wie* ~ as usual; ~ *nichts* nothing else; 2. *cj.* otherwise, or else; **'~ig** *adj.* other; **'~wie** *adv.*

in some other way; '**~wo** *adv.* elsewhere, somewhere else.

Sopran ♩ [zo'praːn] *m* (-s/-e) soprano; **~ist** ~ [~a'nistn] *f* (-/-nen) soprano, sopranist.

Sorge ['zɔrgə] *f* (-/-n) care; sorrow; uneasiness, anxiety; ~ *tragen für* take care of; *sich* **~n** *machen um* be anxious or worried about; *mach dir keine* **~n** don't worry.

'**sorgen** (ge-, h) **1.** *v/i.*: ~ *für* care for, provide for; take care of, attend to; *dafür* **~,** *daß* take care that; **2.** *v/refl.*: *sich* ~ *um* be anxious or worried about; '**~frei** *adj.*, '**~los** *adj.* carefree, free from care; '**~voll** *adj.* full of cares; *face:* worried, troubled.

Sorg|falt ['zɔrkfalt] *f* (-/no *pl.*) care(fulness); **2fältig** *adj.* ['~fɛltiç] careful; '**2lich** *adj.* careful, anxious; '**2los** *adj.* carefree; thoughtless; negligent; careless; '**2sam** *adj.* careful.

Sort|e ['zɔrtə] *f* (-/-n) sort, kind, species, *Am.* ~ stripe; **2ieren** [~'tiːrən] *v/t.* (no -ge-, h) (as)sort; arrange; **~iment** [~i'mɛnt] *n* (-[e]s/-e) assortment.

Soße ['zoːsə] *f* (-/-n) sauce; gravy.

soll [zɔl] *pret. of* sieden.

Souffl|eurkasten *thea.* [su'fløːr-] *m* prompt-box, prompter's box; **~euse** *thea.* [~zə] *f* (-/-n) prompter; **2ieren** *thea.* (no -ge-, h) **1.** *v/i.* prompt (*j-m* s.o.); **2.** *v/t.* prompt.

Souverän [suvə'rɛːn] **1.** *m* (-s/-e) sovereign; **2.** *adj.* sovereign; *fig.* superior; **~ität** [~ɛni'tɛːt] *f* (-/no *pl.*) sovereignty.

so|viel [zo'-] **1.** *cj.* so *or* as far as; ~ *ich weiß* so far as I know; **2.** *adv.*: *doppelt* ~ *viel* twice as much; **~'weit 1.** *cj.*: ~ *es mich betrifft* in so far as it concerns me, so far as I am concerned; **2.** *adv.*: ~ *ganz gut* not bad (for a start); **~wieso** *adv.* [zovi'zoː] in any case, anyhow, anyway.

Sowjet [zɔ'vjɛt] *m* (-s/-s) Soviet; **2isch** *adj.* Soviet.

sowohl *cj.* [zo'-]: ~ ... *als* (*auch*) ... both ... and ..., ~ ... as well as ...

sozial *adj.* [zo'tsjaːl] social; **2demokrat** *m* social democrat; **~isieren** [~ali'ziːrən] *v/t.* (no -ge-, h) socialize; **2isierung** [~ali'ziːruŋ] *f* (-/-en) socialization; **2ist** [~a'list] *m* (-en/-en) socialist; **~istisch** *adj.* [~a'listiʃ] socialist.

Sozius ['zoːtsjus] *m* (-/-se) ✝ partner; *mot.* pillion-rider; '**~sitz** *mot. m* pillion.

sozusagen *adv.* [zotsu'zaːgən] so to speak, as it were.

Spachtel ['ʃpaxtəl] *m* (-s/-), *f* (-/-n) spatula.

spähe|n ['ʃpɛːən] *v/i.* (ge-, h) look out (*nach* for); peer; '**2r** *m* (-s/-) look-out; ✕ scout.

Spalier [ʃpa'liːr] *n* (-s/-e) trellis, espalier; *fig.* lane; ~ *bilden* form a lane.

Spalt [ʃpalt] *m* (-[e]s/-e) crack, split, rift, crevice, fissure; '**~e** *f* (-/-n) *s. Spalt; typ.* column; '**2en** *v/t.* ([*irr.*,] ge-, h) split (*a. fig.* hairs), cleave (*block of wood, etc.*); *sich* ~ split (up); '**~ung** *f* (-/-en) splitting, cleavage; *fig.* split; *eccl.* schism.

Span [ʃpaːn] *m* (-[e]s/**~e**) chip, shaving, splinter.

Spange ['ʃpaŋə] *f* (-/-n) clasp; buckle; clip; slide (*in hair*); strap (*of shoes*); bracelet.

Span|ier ['ʃpaːnjər] *m* (-s/-) Spaniard; **2isch** *adj.* Spanish.

Spann [ʃpan] **1.** *m* (-[e]s/-e) instep; **2.** ♀ *pret. of* spinnen; '**~e** *f* (-/-n) span; ✕, *orn.* spread (*of wings*); ✝ margin; '**2en** (ge-, h) **1.** *v/t.* stretch (*rope, muscles, etc.*); cock (*rifle*); bend (*bow, etc.*); tighten (*spring, etc.*); *vor den Wagen* ~ harness to the carriage; *s. gespannt;* **2.** *v/i.* be (too) tight; '**2end** *adj.* exciting, thrilling, gripping; '**~kraft** *f* (-/no *pl.*) elasticity; *fig.* energy; '**~ung** *f* (-/-en) tension (*a. fig.*); ✝ voltage; ⊕ strain, stress; ⚠ span; *fig.* close attention.

Spar|büchse ['ʃpaːr-] *f* money-box; '**2en** (ge-, h) **1.** *v/t.* save (*money, strength, etc.*); put by; **2.** *v/i.* save; economize, cut down expenses; ~ *mit* be chary of (*praise, etc.*); '**~er** *m* (-s/-) saver.

Spargel ♀ ['ʃpargəl] *m* (-s/-) asparagus.

'**Spar|kasse** *f* savings-bank; '**~konto** *n* savings-account.

spärlich *adj.* ['ʃpɛːrliç] *crop, dress, etc.*: scanty; *population, etc.*: sparse; *hair:* thin.

Sparren ['ʃparən] *m* (-s/-) rafter, spar.

'**sparsam 1.** *adj.* saving, economical (*mit* of); **2.** *adv.*: ~ *leben* lead a frugal life, economize; ~ *umgehen mit* use sparingly, be frugal of; '**2keit** *f* (-/no *pl.*) economy, frugality.

Spaß [ʃpaːs] *m* (-es/**~e**) joke, jest; fun, lark; amusement; *aus or im or zum* ~ *in fun;* ~ *beiseite* joking apart; *er hat nur* ~ *gemacht* he was only joking; '**2en** *v/i.* (ge-, h) joke, jest, make fun; *damit ist nicht zu* ~ that is no joking matter; '**2haft** *adj.*, '**2ig** *adj.* facetious, waggish; funny; '**~macher** *m* (-s/-), '**~vogel** *m* wag, joker.

spät [ʃpɛːt] **1.** *adj.* late; advanced; *zu* ~ too late; *am* ~*en Nachmittag* late in the afternoon; *wie* ~ *ist es?* what time is it?; **2.** *adv.* late; *er kommt 5 Minuten zu* ~ he is five minutes late (zu for); ~ *in der Nacht* late at night.

Spaten ['ʃpaːtən] *m* (-s/-) spade.

'späte|r 1. *adj.* later; **2.** *adv.* later on; afterward(s); *früher oder* ~ sooner or later; ~**stens** *adv.* ['~stəns] at the latest.

Spatz *orn.* [ʃpats] *m* (-en, -es/-en) sparrow.

spazieren [ʃpa'tsiːrən] *v/i.* (*no* -ge-, *sein*) walk, stroll; ~**fahren** (*irr. fahren, sep.,* -ge-) **1.** *v/i.* (*sein*) go for a drive; **2.** *v/t.* (*h*) take for a drive; take (*baby*) out (in pram); ~**gehen** *v/i.* (*irr. gehen, sep.,* -ge-, *sein*) go for a walk.

Spa'zier|fahrt *f* drive, ride; ~**gang** *m* walk, stroll; *e-n* ~ *machen* go for a walk; ~**gänger** [~gɛŋər] *m* (-s/-) walker, stroller; ~**weg** *m* walk.

Speck [ʃpɛk] *m* (-[e]s/-e) bacon.

Spedi|teur [ʃpedi'tøːr] *m* (-s/-e) forwarding agent; (*furniture*) remover; ~**tion** [~'tsjoːn] *f* (-/-en) forwarding agent *or* agency.

Speer [ʃpeːr] *m* (-[e]s/-e) spear; *sports:* javelin; ~**werfen** *n* (-s/*no pl.*) javelin-throw(ing); '~**werfer** *m* (-s/-) javelin-thrower.

Speiche ['ʃpaɪçə] *f* (-/-n) spoke.

Speichel ['ʃpaɪçəl] *m* (-s/*no pl.*) spit(tle), saliva; '~**lecker** *fig. m* (-s/-) lickspittle, toady.

Speicher ['ʃpaɪçər] *m* (-s/-) granary; warehouse; garret, attic.

speien ['ʃpaɪən] (*irr.,* ge-, *h*) **1.** *v/t.* spit out (*blood, etc.*); *volcano, etc.:* belch (*fire, etc.*); **2.** *v/i.* spit; vomit, be sick.

Speise ['ʃpaɪzə] *f* (-/-n) food, nourishment; meal; dish; '~**eis** *n* ice-cream; '~**kammer** *f* larder, pantry; '~**karte** *f* bill of fare, menu; '♀**n** (ge-, *h*) **1.** *v/i. ⓢ essen 1; at restaurants:* take one's meals; **2.** *v/t.* feed; ⊕, ⚡ *a.* supply (*mit* with); '~**nfolge** *f* menu; ~**röhre** *anat. f* gullet, ⊕esophagus; ~**saal** *m* dining-hall; '~**schrank** *m* (meat-)safe; ~**wagen** ⛉ *m* dining-car, diner; '~**zimmer** *n* dining-room.

Spektakel F [ʃpɛk'taːkəl] *m* (-s/-) noise, din.

Spekul|ant [ʃpeku'lant] *m* (-en/-en) speculator; ~**ation** [~a'tsjoːn] *f* (-/-en) speculation; ⊕ *a.* venture; ♀**ieren** [~'liːrən] *v/i.* (*no* -ge-, *h*) speculate (*auf acc. on*).

Spelunke [ʃpe'luŋkə] *f* (-/-n) den; drinking-den, *Am.* F *a.* dive.

Spende ['ʃpɛndə] *f* (-/-n) gift; alms *pl.*; contribution; '♀**n** *v/t.* (ge-, *h*) give; donate (*money* to charity, *blood, etc.*); *eccl.* administer (*sacraments*); bestow (*praise*) (*dat.* on); '~**r** *m* (-s/-) giver; donor.

spen'dieren *v/t.* (*no* -ge-, *h*): *j-m et.* ~ treat s.o. to s.th., stand s.o. s.th.

Sperling *orn.* ['ʃpɛrliŋ] *m* (-s/-e) sparrow.

Sperr|e ['ʃpɛrə] *f* (-/-n) barrier; ⛉ barrier, *Am.* gate; toll-bar; ⊕ lock(ing device), detent; barricade; ✝, ⚓ embargo; ✖ blockade; *sports:* suspension; '♀**en** '(ge-, *h*) **1.** *v/t.* close; ✝, ⚓ embargo; cut off (*gas supply, electricity, etc.*); stop (*cheque, etc.*); *sports:* suspend; **2.** *v/i.* jam, be stuck; '~**holz** *n* plywood; '~**konto** ✝ *n* blocked account; '~**kreis** ⚡ *m* wave-trap; '~**sitz** *thea. m* stalls *pl., Am.* orchestra; '~**ung** *f* (-/-en) closing; stoppage (*of cheque, etc.*); ✝, ⚓ embargo; ✖ blockade; '~**zone** *f* prohibited area.

Spesen ['ʃpeːzən] *pl.* expenses *pl.,* charges *pl.*

Spezial|ausbildung [ʃpe'tsjaːl-?] *f* special training; ~**fach** *n* special(i)ty; ~**geschäft** ✝ *n* one-line shop, *Am.* specialty store; ♀**isieren** [~ali'ziːrən] *v/refl.* (*no* -ge-, *h*) specialize (*auf acc. in*); ~**ist** [~a'list] *m* (-en/-en) specialist; ~**ität** [~ali-'tɛːt] *f* (-/-en) special(i)ty.

speziell *adj.* [ʃpe'tsjɛl] specific, special, particular.

spezifisch *adj.* [ʃpe'tsiːfiʃ]: ~*es Gewicht* specific gravity.

Sphäre ['sfɛːrə] *f* (-/-n) sphere (*a. fig.*).

Spick|aal ['ʃpik-] *m* smoked eel; '♀**en** (ge-, *h*) **1.** *v/t.* lard; *fig.* (inter-)lard (*mit* with); F: *j-n* ~ grease s.o.'s palm; **2.** F *fig. v/i.* crib.

spie [ʃpiː] *pret. of* **speien**.

Spiegel ['ʃpiːgəl] *m* (-s/-) mirror (*a. fig.*), looking-glass; '~**bild** *n* reflected image; '♀**blank** *adj.* mirror-like; ~**ei** ['ʃpiːgəl?-] *n* fried egg; '♀**glatt** *adj. water:* glassy, unrippled; *road, etc.:* very slippery; '♀**n** (ge-, *h*) **1.** *v/i.* shine; **2.** *v/refl.* be reflected; '~**schrift** *f* mirror-writing.

Spieg(e)lung ['ʃpiːg(ə)luŋ] *f* (-/-en) reflection, reflexion; mirage.

Spiel [ʃpiːl] *n* (-[e]s/-e) play (*a. fig.*); game (*a. fig.*); match; ♪ playing; *ein* ~ *Karten* a pack of playing-cards, *Am. a.* a deck; *auf dem* ~ *stehen* be at stake; *aufs* ~ *setzen* jeopardize, stake; '~**art** ♀, *zo. f* variety; '~**ball** *m tennis:* game ball; *billiards:* red ball; *fig.* plaything, sport; '~**bank** *f* (-/-en) gaming-house; '♀**en** (ge-, *h*) **1.** *v/i.* play; gamble; ~ *mit* play with; *fig. a.* toy with; **2.** *v/t.* play (*tennis, violin, etc.*); *thea.* act, play (*part*); *mit j-m Schach* ~ play s.o. at chess; *den Höflichen* ~ do the polite; '♀**end** *fig. adv.* easily; '~**er** *m* (-s/-) player; gambler; ~**e'rei** *f* (-/-en) pastime; child's amusement; '~**ergebnis** *n sports:* result, score; '~**feld** *n sports:* (playing-)field; pitch; '~**film** *m* feature film *or* picture; '~gefährte *m* playfellow, playmate; '~karte *f* playing-card; '~leiter *m thea.* stage manager; *cinematography*: director; *sports*: referee; '~marke *f* counter, *sl.* chip; '~plan *m thea.*, *etc.*: pro-gram(me); repertory; '~platz *m* playground; '~raum *fig. m* play, scope; '~regel *f* rule (of the game); '~sachen *f/pl.* playthings *pl.*, toys *pl.*; '~schuld *f* gambling-debt; '~schule *f* infant-school, kinder-garten; '~tisch *m* card-table; gambling-table; '~uhr *f* musical box, *Am.* music box; '~verderber *m* (-s/-) spoil-sport, killjoy, wet blanket; '~waren *f/pl.* playthings *pl.*, toys *pl.*; '~zeit *f thea.* season; *sports*: time of play; '~zeug *n* toy(s *pl.*), plaything(s *pl.*).

Spieß [ʃpiːs] *m* (-es/-e) spear, pike; spit; den ~ umdrehen turn the tables; '~bürger *m* bourgeois, Philistine, *Am. a.* Babbit; '2bür-gerlich *adj.* bourgeois, Philistine; '~er *m* (-s/-) *s.* Spießbürger; '~ge-selle *m* accomplice; '~ruten *f/pl.*: ~ laufen run the gauntlet (*a. fig.*).

spinal *adj.* [ʃpiˈnaːl]: ~e *Kinder-lähmung* 𝕏 infantile paralysis, poliomyelitis, F polio.

Spinat 𝕏 [ʃpiˈnaːt] *m* (-[e]s/-e) spinach.

Spind [ʃpint] *n, m* (-[e]s/-e) ward-robe, cupboard; 𝕏, *sports*, *etc.*: locker.

Spindel ['ʃpindəl] *f* (-/-n) spindle; '2dürr *adj.* (as) thin as a lath.

Spinn|e *zo.* ['ʃpinə] *f* (-/-n) spider; '2en (*irr.*, ge-, h) 1. *v/t.* spin (*a. fig.*); hatch (*plot*, *etc.*); 2. *v/i. cat*: purr; F *fig.* be crazy, *sl.* be nuts; '~engewebe *n* cobweb; '~er *m* (-s/-) spinner; F *fig.* silly; ~e'rei *f* (-/-en) spinning; spinning-mill; '~maschine *f* spinning-machine; '~webe *f* (-/-n) cobweb.

Spion [ʃpiˈoːn] *m* (-s/-e) spy, intel-ligencer; *fig.* judas; ~age [~oˈnaːʒə] *f* (-/no *pl.*) espionage; 2ieren [~oˈniːrən] *v/i.* (no -ge-, h) (play the) spy.

Spiral|e [ʃpiˈraːl] *f* (-/-n) spiral (*a.* ✝), helix; 2förmig *adj.* [~fœr-miç] spiral, helical.

Spirituosen [ʃpirituˈoːzən] *pl.* spir-its *pl.*

Spiritus ['ʃpiːritus] *m* (-/-se) spirit, alcohol; '~kocher *m* (-s/-) spirit stove.

Spital [ʃpiˈtaːl] *n* (-s/=er) hospital; alms-house; home for the aged.

spitz [ʃpits] 1. *adj.* pointed (*a. fig.*); 𝔸 *angle*: acute; *fig.* poignant; ~e Zunge sharp tongue; 2. *adv.*: ~ zu-laufen taper (off); '2bube *m* thief; rogue, rascal (*both a. co.*); 2büberei [~byˈbəˈraɪ] *f* (-/-en) roguery, ras-

cality (*both a. co.*); ~bübisch *adj.* [~byːbɪʃ] *eyes*, *smile*, *etc.*: roguish.

'Spitz|e *f* (-/-n) point (*of pencil*, *weapon*, *jaw*, *etc.*); tip (*of nose*, *finger*, *etc.*); nib (*of tool*, *etc.*); spire; head (*of enterprise*, *etc.*); lace; an der ~ liegen *sports*: be in the lead; j-m die ~ bieten make head against s.o.; auf die ~ treiben carry to an extreme; '~el *m* (-s/-) (common) informer; 2en *v/t.* (ge-, h) point, sharpen; den Mund ~ purse (up) one's lips; die Ohren ~ prick up one's ears (*a. fig.*).

'Spitzen|leistung *f* top perform-ance; ⊕ maximum capacity; '~lohn *m* top wages *pl.*

'spitz|findig *adj.* subtle, captious; '2findigkeit *f* (-/-en) subtlety, captiousness; '2hacke *f* pickax(e), pick; '~ig *adj.* pointed; *fig. a.* poignant; '2marke *typ. f* head(ing); '2name *m* nickname.

Splitter ['ʃplitər] *m* (-s/-) splinter, shiver; chip; '2frei *adj. glass*: shatterproof; '2ig *adj.* splintery; '2n *v/i.* (ge-, h, sein) splinter, shiver; '2'nackt F *adj.* stark naked, *Am. a.* mother-naked; '~partei *pol. f* splinter party.

spontan *adj.* [ʃponˈtaɪn] spontane-ous.

sporadisch *adj.* [ʃpoˈraːdɪʃ] sporad-ic.

Sporn [ʃpɔrn] *m* (-[e]s/Sporen) spur; die Sporen geben put *or* set spurs to (*horse*); sich die Sporen verdienen win one's spurs; '2en *v/t.* (ge-, h) spur.

Sport [ʃpɔrt] *m* (-[e]s/🔍-e) sport; *fig.* hobby; ~ treiben go in for sports; '~ausrüstung *f* sports equipment; '~geschäft *n* sporting-goods shop; '~kleidung *f* sport clothes *pl.*, sportswear; '~lehrer *m* games-master; '2lich *adj.* sporting, sportsmanlike; *figure*: athletic; '~nachrichten *f/pl.* sports news *sg.*, *pl.*; '~platz *m* sports field; stadium.

Spott [ʃpɔt] *m* (-[e]s/no *pl.*) mockery; derision; scorn; (s-n) ~ treiben mit make sport of; '2billig F *adj.* dirt-cheap.

Spötte|lei [ʃpœtəˈlaɪ] *f* (-/-en) raillery, sneer, jeer; '2ln *v/i.* (ge-, h) sneer (*über acc.* at), jeer (at).

'spotten *v/i.* (ge-, h) mock (*über acc.* at); jeer (at); jeder Beschreibung ~ beggar description.

Spötter ['ʃpœtər] *m* (-s/-) mocker, scoffer; ~ei [~ˈraɪ] *f* (-/-en) mockery.

'spöttisch *adj.* mocking; sneering; ironical.

'Spott|name *m* nickname; '~preis *m* ridiculous price; für e-n ~ for a mere song; '~schrift *f* lampoon, satire.

sprach [ʃpraːx] *pret. of* sprechen.

'Sprache *f* (-/-n) speech; language

(a. *fig.*); diction; zur ~ bringen bring up, broach; zur ~ kommen come up (for discussion).

'Sprach|eigentümlichkeit *f* idiom; '~fehler ⚡ *m* impediment (in one's speech); '~führer *m* language guide; '~gebrauch *m* usage; '~gefühl *n* (-[e]s/*no pl.*) linguistic instinct; 2kundig *adj.* [_kundic] versed in languages; ~lehre *f* grammar; '~lehrer *m* teacher of languages; '2lich *adj.* linguistic; grammatical; '2los *adj.* speechless; '~rohr *n* speaking-trumpet, megaphone; *fig.*: mouthpiece; organ; '~schatz *m* vocabulary; ~störung ⚡ *f* impediment (in one's speech); '~wissenschaft *f* philology, science of language; linguistics *pl.*; ~wissenschaftler *m* philologist; linguist; '2wissenschaftlich *adj.* philological; linguistic.

sprang [ʃpraŋ] *pret. of* springen.

Sprech|chor ['ʃprɛç-] *m* speaking chorus; '2en (*irr.*, ge-, h) 1. *v/t.* speak (*language, truth, etc.*); ⚡ pronounce (*judgement*); say (*prayer*); j-n zu ~ wünschen wish to see s.o.; j-n schuldig ⚡ pronounce s.o. guilty; F Bände ~ speak volumes (für for); 2. *v/i.* speak; talk (*both:* mit to, with; über *acc.*, von of, about); er ist nicht zu ~ you cannot see him; '~er *m* (-s/-) speaker; *radio*: announcer; spokesman; '~fehler *m* slip of the tongue; '~stunde *f* consulting-hours *pl.*; '~übung *f* exercise in speaking; '~zimmer *n* consulting-room, surgery.

spreizen ['ʃpraɪtsən] *v/t.* (ge-, h) spread (out); *a.* straddle (*legs*); sich ~ pretend to be unwilling.

Spreng|bombe ⚔ ['ʃprɛŋ-] *f* high-explosive bomb, demolition bomb; '~el *eccl. m* (-s/-) diocese, see; parish; '2en (ge-) 1. *v/t.* (h) sprinkle, water (*road, lawn, etc.*); blow up, blast (*bridge, rocks, etc.*); burst open (*door, etc.*); spring (*mine, etc.*); *gambling*: break (*bank*); break up (*meeting, etc.*); 2. *v/i.* (sein) gallop; '~stoff *m* explosive; '~ung *f* (-/-en) blowing-up, blasting; explosion; '~wagen *m* water(ing)-cart.

Sprenkel ['ʃprɛŋkəl] *m* (-s/-) speckle, spot; '2n *v/t.* (ge-, h) speckle, spot.

Spreu [ʃprɔy] *f* (-/*no pl.*) chaff; *s. sondern* 2.

Sprich|wort ['ʃpriç-] *n* (-[e]s/=er) proverb, adage; '2wörtlich *adj.* proverbial (*a. fig.*).

sprießen ['ʃpriːsən] *v/i.* (*irr.*, ge-, sein) sprout; germinate.

Spring|brunnen ['ʃpriŋ-] *m* fountain; '2en *v/i.* (*irr.*, ge-, sein) jump, leap; *ball, etc.*: bounce; *swimming*: dive; burst, crack, break; *in die Augen ~* strike the eye; ~ über (*acc.*)

jump (over), leap, clear; '~er *m* (-s/-) jumper; *swimming*: diver; *chess*: knight; '~flut *f* spring tide.

Sprit [ʃprit] *m* (-[e]s/-e) spirit, alcohol; F *mot.* fuel, petrol, *sl.* juice, *Am.* gasoline, F gas.

Spritz|e ['ʃpritsə] *f* (-/-n) syringe (*a.* ⚡), squirt; ⊕ fire-engine; *j-m e-e ~ geben* ⚡ give s.o. an injection; '2en (ge-) 1. *v/t.* (h) sprinkle, water (*road, lawn, etc.*); splash (*water, etc.*) (*über acc.* on, over); 2. *v/i.* (h) splash; *pen*: splutter; 3. *v/i.* (sein) F *fig.* dash, flit; ~ aus blood, *etc.*: spurt or spout from (*wound, etc.*); '~er *m* (-s/-) splash; '~tour F *f*: e-e ~ machen go for a spin.

spröde *adj.* ['ʃprøːdə] glass, *etc.*: brittle; *skin*: chapped, chappy; *esp. girl*: prudish, prim, coy.

Sproß [ʃprɔs] 1. *m* (Sprosses/Sprosse) ♀ shoot, sprout, scion (*a. fig.*); *fig.* offspring; 2. 2 *pret. of* sprießen.

Sprosse ['ʃprɔsə] *f* (-/-n) rung, round, step.

Sprößling ['ʃprœsliŋ] *m* (-s/-e) ♀ *s. Sproß* 1.; *co.* son.

Spruch [ʃprux] *m* (-[e]s/=e) saying; dictum; ⚡ sentence; ⚡ verdict; '~band *n* banner; '2reif *adj.* ripe for decision.

Sprudel ['ʃpruːdəl] *m* (-s/-) mineral water; '2n *v/i.* (ge-) 1. (h) bubble, effervesce; 2. (sein): ~ aus or von gush from.

sprüh|en ['ʃpryːən] (ge-) 1. *v/t.* (h) spray, sprinkle (*liquid*); throw off (*sparks*); Feuer ~ *eyes*: flash fire; 2. *v/i.* (h): ~ vor sparkle with (*wit, etc.*); es sprüht it is drizzling; 3. *v/i.* (sein) *sparks*: fly; '2regen *m* drizzle.

Sprung [ʃpruŋ] *m* (-[e]s/=e) jump, leap, bound; *swimming*: dive; crack, fissure; '~brett *n* *sports*: spring-board; *fig.* stepping-stone; '~feder *f* spiral spring.

Spuck|e F ['ʃpukə] *f* (-/*no pl.*) spit(tle); '2en (ge-, h) 1. *v/t.* spit (out) (*blood, etc.*); 2. *v/i.* spit; *engine* splutter; '~napf *m* spittoon, *Am. a.* cuspidor.

Spuk [ʃpuːk] *m* (-[e]s/-e) apparition, ghost, *co.* spook; F *fig.* noise; '2en *v/i.* (ge-, h): ~ in (*dat.*) haunt (*a place*); *hier spukt es* this place is haunted.

Spule ['ʃpuːlə] *f* (-/-n) spool, reel; bobbin; ⚡ coil; '2n *v/t.* (ge-, h) spool, reel.

spülen ['ʃpyːlən] (ge-, h) 1. *v/t.* rinse (*clothes, mouth, cup, etc.*); wash up (*dishes, etc.*); *an Land ~* wash ashore; 2. *v/i.* flush the toilet.

Spund [ʃpunt] *m* (-[e]s/=e) bung; plug; '~loch *n* bunghole.

Spur [ʃpuːr] *f* (-/-en) trace (*a. fig.*); track (*a. fig.*); print (*a. fig.*); rut (*of wheels*); *j-m auf der ~ sein* be on s.o.'s track.

spür|en ['ʃpy:rən] v/t. (ge-, h) feel; sense; perceive; '2sinn m (-[e]s/no pl.) scent; fig. a. flair (für for).

Spurweite ⚙ f ga(u)ge.

sputen ['ʃpu:tən] v/refl. (ge-, h) make haste, hurry up.

Staat [ʃta:t] m 1. F (-[e]s/no pl.) pomp, state; finery; ~ machen mit make a parade of; 2. (-[e]s/-en) state; government; '~enbund m (-[e]s/¨e) confederacy, confederation; '2enlos adj. stateless; '2lich adj. state; national; political; public.

'Staats|angehörige m, f (-n/-n) national, citizen, esp. Brt. subject; '~angehörigkeit f (-/no pl.) nationality, citizenship; '~anwalt ⚖ m public prosecutor, Am. prosecuting attorney; '~beamte m Civil Servant, Am. a. public servant; '~begräbnis n state or national funeral; '~besuch m official or state visit; '~bürger m citizen; '~bürgerkunde f (-/no pl.) civics sg.; '~bürgerschaft f (-/-en) citizenship; '~dienst m Civil Service; '2eigen adj. state-owned; '~feind m public enemy; '2feindlich adj. subversive; '~gewalt f (-/no pl.) supreme power; '~haushalt m budget; '~hoheit f (-/no pl.) sovereignty; '~kasse f treasury, Brt. exchequer; '~klugheit f political wisdom; '~kunst f (-/no pl.) statesmanship; '~mann m statesman, 2männisch adj. ['~mɛnɪʃ] statesmanlike; '~oberhaupt n head of (the) state; '~papiere n/pl. Government securities pl.; '~rat m Privy Council; '~recht n public law; '~schatz m s. Staatskasse; '~schulden f/pl. national debt; '~sekretär m under-secretary of state; '~streich m coup d'état; '~trauer f national mourning; '~vertrag m treaty; '~wesen n polity; '~wirtschaft f public sector of the economy; '~wissenschaft f political science; '~wohl n public weal.

Stab [ʃta:p] m (-[e]s/¨e) staff (a. fig.); bar (of metal, wood); crosier, staff (of bishop); wand (of magician); relay-race, ♪ conducting: baton; pole-vaulting: pole.

stabil adj. [ʃta'bi:l] stable (a. ✝); health: robust.

stabilisier|en [ʃtabili'zi:rən] v/t. (no -ge-, h) stabilize (a. ✝); 2ung f (-/-en) stabilization (a. ✝).

stach [ʃta:x] pret. of stechen.

Stachel ['ʃtaxəl] m (-s/-n) prickle (of plant, hedgehog, etc.); sting (of bee, etc.); tongue (of buckle); spike (of sports shoe); fig.: sting; goad; '~beere ⚘ f gooseberry; '~draht m barbed wire; '2ig adj. prickly, thorny.

'stachlig adj. s. stachelig.

Stadi|on ['ʃta:djɔn] n (-s/Stadien) stadium; ~um ['~um] n (-s/Stadien) stage, phase.

Stadt [ʃtat] f (-/¨e) town; city.

Städt|chen ['ʃtɛːtçən] n (-s/-) small town; '~ebau m (-[e]s/no pl.) town-planning; '~er m (-s/-) townsman; ~ pl. townspeople pl.

'Stadt|gebiet n urban area; '~gespräch n teleph. local call; fig. town talk, talk of the town; '~haus n town house.

städtisch adj. ['ʃtɛːtiʃ] municipal.

'Stadt|plan m city map; plan (of a town); '~planung f town-planning; '~rand m outskirts pl. (of a town); '~rat m (-[e]s/¨e) town council; town council(l)or; '~teil m, '~viertel n quarter.

Staffel ['ʃtafəl] f (-/-n) relay; relay-race; '~ei paint. [~'lai] f (-/-en) easel; '~lauf m relay-race; '2n v/t. (ge-, h) graduate (taxes, etc.); stagger (hours of work, etc.).

Stahl¹ [ʃta:l] m (-[e]s/¨e, -e) steel.

stahl² [~] pret. of stehlen.

stählen ['ʃtɛːlən] v/t. (ge-, h) ⊕ harden (a. fig.), temper.

'Stahl|feder f steel pen; steel spring; '~kammer f strong-room; '~stich m steel engraving.

stak [ʃta:k] pret. of stecken 2.

Stall [ʃtal] m (-[e]s/¨e) stable (a. fig.); cow-house, cowshed; pigsty, Am. a. pigpen; shed; '~knecht m stableman; '~ung f (-/-en) stabling; ~en pl. stables pl.

Stamm [ʃtam] m (-[e]s/¨e) ⚘ stem (a. gr.), trunk; fig.: race; stock; family; tribe; '~aktie ✝ f ordinary share, Am. common stock; '~baum m family or genealogical tree, pedigree (a. zo.); '~buch n album; book that contains the births, deaths, and marriages in a family; zo. stud-book; '2eln (ge-, h) 1. v/t. stammer (out); 2. v/i. stammer; '~eltern pl. ancestors pl., first parents pl.; '2en v/i. (ge-, sein): ~ von or aus come from (town, etc.), Am. a. hail from; date from (certain time); gr. be derived from; aus gutem Haus ~ be of good family; '~gast m regular customer or guest, F regular.

stämmig adj. ['ʃtɛmiç] stocky; thickset, squat(ty).

'Stamm|kapital ✝ n share capital, Am. capital stock; '~kneipe F f one's favo(u)rite pub, local; '~kunde m regular customer, patron; '~tisch m table reserved for regular guests; '~utter f (-/¨) ancestress; '~vater m ancestor; '2verwandt adj. cognate, kindred; pred. of the same race.

stampfen ['ʃtampfən] (ge-) 1. v/t. (h) mash (potatoes, etc.); aus dem Boden ~ conjure up; 2. v/i. (h) stamp (one's foot); horse: paw;

3. v/i. (sein): ~ durch plod through; ⚓ pitch through.

Stand [ʃtant] **1.** m (-[e]s/ᵘe) stand (-ing), standing or upright position; footing, foothold; s. Standplatz; stall; fig.: level; state; station, rank, status; class; profession; reading (of thermometer, etc.); ast. position; sports: score; auf den neuesten ~ bringen bring up to date; e-n schweren ~ haben have a hard time (of it); **2.** ⚲ pret. of stehen.

Standarte [ʃtan'dartə] f (-/-n) standard, banner.

¹**Standbild** n statue.

Ständchen ['ʃtɛntçən] n (-s/-) serenade; j-m ein ~ bringen serenade s.o.

Ständer ['ʃtɛndər] m (-s/-) stand; post, pillar, standard.

Standes|amt n registry (office), register office; '⊵amtlich adj.: ~e Trauung civil marriage; ⵥbeamte m registrar; ⵥdünkel m pride of place; '⊵gemäß adj., ⵥmäßig adj. in accordance with one's rank; 'ⵥperson f person of rank or position; 'ⵥunterschied m social difference.

¹**standhaft** adj. steadfast; firm; constant; ~ bleiben stand pat; resist temptation; '⊵igkeit f (-/no pl.) steadfastness; firmness.

¹**standhalten** v/i. (irr. halten, sep., -ge-, h) hold one's ground; j-m or e-r Sache ~ resist s.o. or s.th.

ständig adj. ['ʃtɛndiç] permanent; constant; income, etc. fixed.

¹**Stand|ort** m position (of ship, etc.); ✗ garrison, post; ⵥplatz m stand; ⵥpunkt m point of view, standpoint, angle, Am. a. slant; ⵥquartier ✗ n fixed quarters pl.; ⵥrecht ✗ n martial law; 'ⵥuhr f grandfather's clock.

Stange ['ʃtaŋə] f (-/-n) pole; rod, bar (of iron, etc.); staff (of flag); Anzug or Kleid von der ~ sl. reach-me-down, Am. F hand-me-down.

stank [ʃtaŋk] pret. of stinken.

Stänker|(er) contp. ['ʃtɛŋkər(ər)] m (-s/-) mischief-maker, quarrel(l)er; '⊵n F v/i. (ge-, h) make mischief.

Stanniol [ʃta'njoːl] n (-s/-e) tin foil.

Stanze ['ʃtantsə] f (-/-n) stanza; ⊕ punch, stamp, die; '⊵n ⊕ v/t. (ge-, h) punch, stamp.

Stapel ['ʃtaːpəl] m (-s/-) pile, stack; ⚓ stocks pl.; vom or von ~ lassen ⚓ launch; vom or von ~ laufen ⚓ be launched; 'ⵥlauf ⚓ m launch; '⊵n v/t. (ge-, h) pile (up), stack; 'ⵥplatz m dump; emporium.

stapfen ['ʃtapfən] v/i. (ge-, sein) plod (durch through).

Star 1. [ʃtaːr] m (-[e]s/-e) orn. starling; ⚕ cataract; j-m den ~ stechen open s.o.'s eyes; **2.** [staːr] m (-s/-s) thea., etc.: star.

starb [ʃtarp] pret. of sterben.

stark [ʃtark] **1.** adj. strong (a. fig.); stout, corpulent; fig.: intense; large; ~e Erkältung bad cold; ~er Raucher heavy smoker; ~e Seite strong point, forte; **2.** adv. very much; ~ erkältet sein have a bad cold; ~ übertrieben grossly exaggerated.

Stärke ['ʃtɛrkə] f (-/-n) strength (a. fig.); stoutness, corpulence; fig.: intensity; largeness; strong point, forte; ⚗ starch; '⊵n v/t. (ge-, h) strengthen (a. fig.); starch (linen, etc.); sich ~ take some refreshment(s).

¹**Starkstrom** ⚡ m heavy current.

¹**Stärkung** f (-/-en) strengthening; fig. a. refreshment; 'ⵥsmittel n restorative; ⚕ a. tonic.

starr [ʃtar] **1.** adj. rigid (a. fig.), stiff; gaze: fixed; ~ vor (dat.) numb with (cold, etc.); transfixed with (horror, etc.); dumbfounded with (amazement, etc.); **2.** adv.: j-n ~ ansehen stare at s.o.; 'ⵥen v/i. (ge-, h) stare (auf acc. at s.o.; vor Schmutz ~ be covered with dirt; '⊵heit f (-/no pl.) rigidity (a. fig.), stiffness; '⊵kopf m stubborn or obstinate fellow; '~köpfig adj. ['~kœpfiç] stubborn, obstinate; ⵥkrampf ⚕ m (-[e]s/no pl.) tetanus; '⊵sinn m (-[e]s/no pl.) stubbornness, obstinacy; '~sinnig adj. stubborn, obstinate.

Start [ʃtart] m (-[e]s/-s, ~-e) start (a. fig.); ✈ take-off; '~bahn ✈ f runway; '⊵bereit adj. ready to start; ✈ ready to take off; '⊵en (ge-) **1.** v/i. (sein) start; ✈ take off; **2.** v/t. (h) start; fig. a. launch; '~er m (-s/-) sports: starter; '~platz m starting-place.

Station [ʃta'tsjoːn] f (-/-en) station; ward (of hospital); (gegen) freie ~ board and lodging (found); ~ machen break one's journey; 'ⵥvorsteher 🚂 m station-master, Am. a. station agent.

Statist [ʃta'tist] m (-en/-en) thea. supernumerary (actor), F super; film: extra; 'ⵥik f (-/-en) statistics pl., sg.; 'ⵥiker m (-s/-) statistician; '⊵isch adj. statistic(al).

Stativ [ʃta'tiːf] n (-s/-e) tripod.

Statt [ʃtat] **1.** f (-/no pl.): an Eides ~ in lieu of an oath; an Kindes ~ annehmen adopt; **2.** ⚲ prp. (gen.) instead of; ~ zu inf. instead of ger.; ~ meiner in my place.

Stätte ['ʃtɛtə] f (-/-n) place, spot; scene (of events).

¹**statt|finden** v/i. (irr. finden, sep., -ge-, h) take place, happen; '~haft adj. admissible, allowable; legal.

¹**Statthalter** m (-s/-) governor.

stattlich adj. stately; impressive; sum of money, etc.: considerable.

Statue ['ʃtaːtuə] f (-/-n) statue.

statuieren [ʃtatu'iːrən] v/t. (no -ge-,

h): *ein Exempel ~* make an example (*an dat.* of).

Statur [ʃtaˈtuːr] *f* (-/-en) stature, size.

Statut [ʃtaˈtuːt] *n* (-[e]s/-en) statute; *~en pl.* regulations *pl.*; ✝ articles *pl.* of association.

Staub [ʃtaup] *m* (-[e]s/⊕ -e, ~e) dust; powder.

Staubecken [ˈʃtauʔ-] *n* reservoir.

stauben [ˈʃtaubən] *v/i.* (ge-, h) give off dust, make *or* raise a dust.

stäuben [ˈʃtɔybən] (ge-, h) 1. *v/t.* dust; 2. *v/i.* spray.

'**Staub|faden** ♀ *m* filament; ♀ig *adj.* [ˈ~bɪç] dusty; **~sauger** [ˈ~p-] *m* (-s/-) vacuum cleaner; **~tuch** [ˈ~p-] *n* (-[e]s/~er) duster.

stauchen ⊕ [ˈʃtauxən] *v/t.* (ge-, h) upset, jolt.

'**Staudamm** *m* dam.

Staude ♀ [ˈʃtaudə] *f* (-/-n) perennial (plant); head (of lettuce).

stau|en [ˈʃtauən] *v/t.* (ge-, h) dam (up) (*river, etc.*); ⚓ stow; *sich ~ waters, etc.:* be dammed (up); *vehicles:* be jammed; '**2er** ⚓ *m* (-s/-) stevedore.

staunen [ˈʃtaunən] 1. *v/i.* (ge-, h) be astonished (*über acc.* at); 2. ♀ *n* (-s/*no pl.*) astonishment; '**~swert** *adj.* astonishing. [temper.]

Staupe *vet.* [ˈʃtaupə] *f* (-/-n) dis-

'**Stau|see** *m* reservoir; '**~ung** *f* (-/-en) damming (up) (*of water*); stoppage; ☟ congestion (*a.* of traffic); jam; ⚓ stowage.

stechen [ˈʃtɛçən] (irr., ge-, h) 1. *v/t.* prick; *insect, etc.:* sting; *flea, mosquito, etc.:* bite; *card:* take, trump (*other card*); ⊕ engrave (*in or auf acc.* on); cut (*lawn, etc.*); *sich in den Finger ~* prick one's finger; 2. *v/i.* prick; stab (*nach* at); *insect, etc.:* sting; *flea, mosquito, etc.:* bite; *sun:* burn; *j-m in die Augen ~* strike s.o.'s eye; '**~d** *adj. pain, look, etc.:* piercing; *pain:* stabbing.

Steck|brief ⚖ [ˈʃtɛk-] *m* warrant of apprehension; '**2brieflich** ⚖ *adv.:* *er wird ~ gesucht* a warrant is out against him; '**~dose** ⚡ *f* (wall) socket; '**2en** 1. *v/t.* (ge-, h) put; *esp.* ⊕ insert (*in acc.* into); F stick; pin (*an acc.* to, on); ☟ set, plant; 2. *v/i.* (*irr.,*) ge-, h) be; stick, be stuck; *tief in Schulden ~* be deeply in debt; '**~en** *m* (-s/-) stick; '**2enbleiben** *v/i.* (irr. bleiben, sep., -ge-, sein) get stuck; *speaker, etc.:* break down; '**~enpferd** *n* hobby-horse; *fig.* hobby; '**~er** ⚡ *m* (-s/-) plug; '**~kontakt** ⚡ *m s.* Steckdose; '**~nadel** *f* pin.

Steg [ʃteːk] *m* (-[e]s/-e) foot-bridge; ⚓ landing-stage; '**~reif** *m* (-[e]s/-e): *aus dem ~* extempore, offhand (*both a. attr.*); *aus dem ~ sprechen* extemporize, F ad-lib.

stehen [ˈʃteːən] *v/i.* (irr., ge-, h) stand; be; be written; *dress:* suit, become (*j-m s.o.*); *~ vor* be faced with; *gut ~ mit* be on good terms with; *es kam ihn or ihn teuer zu ~* it cost him dearly; *wie steht's mit ...?* what about ...?; *wie steht das Spiel?* what's the score?; *~ bleiben* remain standing; '**~bleiben** *v/i.* (irr. bleiben, sep., -ge-, sein) stand (still), stop; leave off reading, *etc.*; '**~lassen** *v/t.* (irr. lassen, sep., [no] -ge-, h) turn one's back (up)on; leave (*meal*) untouched; leave (behind), forget; leave alone.

'**Steher** *m* (-s/-) *sports:* stayer.

'**Steh|kragen** *m* stand-up collar; '**~lampe** *f* standard lamp; '**~leiter** *f* (e-e a pair of) steps *pl.*, step-ladder.

stehlen [ˈʃteːlən] (irr., ge-, h) 1. *v/t.* steal; *j-m Geld ~* steal s.o.'s money; 2. *v/i.* steal.

'**Stehplatz** *m* standing-room; '**~inhaber** *m Am.* F standee; *in bus, etc.:* straphanger.

steif *adj.* [ʃtaɪf] stiff (*a. fig.*); numb (*vor Kälte* with cold); '**~halten** *v/t.* (irr. halten, sep. -ge-, h): F *die Ohren ~* keep a stiff upper lip.

Steig [ʃtaɪk] *m* (-[e]s/-e) steep path; '**~bügel** *m* stirrup.

steigen [ˈʃtaɪgən] 1. *v/i.* (irr., ge-, sein) flood, barometer, spirits, prices, etc.: rise; mists, etc.: ascend; blood, tension, etc.: mount; prices, etc.: increase; *auf e-n Baum ~* climb a tree; 2. ♀ *n* (-s/*no pl.*) rise; *fig. a.* increase.

steigern [ˈʃtaɪgərn] *v/t.* (ge-, h) raise; increase; enhance; *gr.* compare.

'**Steigerung** *f* (-/-en) raising; increase; enhancement; *gr.* comparison; '**~sstufe** *gr. f* degree of comparison.

Steigung [ˈʃtaɪguŋ] *f* (-/-en) rise, gradient, ascent, grade.

steil *adj.* [ʃtaɪl] steep; precipitous.

Stein [ʃtaɪn] *m* (-[e]s/-e) stone (*a.* ♀, ⚫), *Am.* F *a.* rock; *s.* Edel2; '2'alt *f adj.* (as) old as the hills; '**~bruch** *m* quarry; '**~druck** *m* 1. (-[e]s/*no pl.*) lithography; 2. (-[e]s/-e) lithograph; '**~drucker** *m* lithographer; '2ern *adj.* stone-..., of stone; *fig.* stony; '**~gut** *n* (-[e]s/-e) crockery, stoneware, earthenware; '2ig *adj.* stony; '2igen [ˈ~gən] *v/t.* (ge-, h) stone; **~igung** [ˈ~guŋ] *f* (-/-en) stoning; '**~kohle** *f* mineral coal; pit-coal; '**~metz** [ˈ~mɛts] *m* (-en/-en) stonemason; '**~obst** *n* stone-fruit; '2reich F *adj.* immensely rich; '**~salz** *n* (-es/*no pl.*) rock-salt; '**~setzer** *m* (-s/-) pavio(u)r; '**~wurf** *m* throwing of a stone; *fig.* stone's throw; '**~zeit** *f* (-/*no pl.*) stone age.

Steiß [ʃtaɪs] *m* (-es/-e) buttocks *pl.*, rump; '**~bein** *anat. n* coccyx.

Stelldichein *co.* ['ʃtɛldiçˀaɪn] *n* (-[s]/-[s]) meeting, appointment, rendezvous, *Am.* F *a.* date.

Stelle ['ʃtɛlə] *f* (-/-n) place; spot; point; employment, situation, post, place, F job; agency, authority; passage *(of book, etc.)*; freie ~ vacancy; *an deiner* ~ in your place, if I were you; *auf der* ~ on the spot; *zur* ~ *sein* be present.

'**stellen** *v/t.* (ge-, h) put, place, set, stand; regulate *(watch, etc.)*; set *(watch, trap, task, etc.)*; stop *(thief, etc.)*; hunt down *(criminal)*; furnish, supply, provide; *Bedingungen* ~ make conditions; *e-e Falle* ~ *a.* lay a snare; *sich* ~ give o.s. up (to the police); stand, place o.s. *(somewhere)*; *sich krank* ~ feign or pretend to be ill.

'**Stellen|angebot** *n* position offered, vacancy; '~**gesuch** *n* application for a post; '~**2weise** *adv.* here and there, sporadically.

'**Stellung** *f* (-/-en) position, posture; position, situation, (place of) employment; position, rank, status; arrangement *(a. gr.)*; ✕ position; ~ *nehmen* give one's opinion *(zu on)*, comment (upon); ~**nahme** ['~nɑː-mə] *f* (-/-n) attitude *(zu* to[wards]); opinion (on); comment (on); **2slos** *adj.* unemployed.

'**stellvertret|end** *adj.* vicarious, representative; acting, deputy; ~**er** *Vorsitzender* vice-chairman, deputy chairman; '**2er** *m* representative; deputy; proxy; '**2ung** *f* representation; substitution; proxy.

Stelz|bein *contp.* ['ʃtɛlts-] *n* wooden leg; '~**e** *f* (-/-n) stilt; '**2en** *mst iro.* *v/i.* (ge-, sein) stalk.

stemmen ['ʃtɛmən] *v/t.* (ge-, h) lift *(weight)*; *sich* ~ press (gegen against); *fig.* resist or oppose *s.th.*

Stempel ['ʃtɛmpəl] *m* (-s/-) stamp; ⊕ piston; ♀ pistil; '~**geld** F *n the* dole; '~**kissen** *n* ink-pad; '**2n** (ge-, h) 1. *v/t.* stamp; hallmark *(gold, silver)*; 2. *v/i.* F: ~ *gehen* be on the dole.

Stengel ♀ ['ʃtɛŋəl] *m* (-s/-) stalk, stem.

Steno F ['ʃteno] *f* (-/no *pl.*) *s.* Stenographie; ~'**gramm** *n* (-s/-e) stenograph; ~**graph** [~'grɑːf] *m* (-en/-en) stenographer; ~**graphie** [~ɑ'fiː] *f* (-/-n) stenography, shorthand; **2graphieren** [~ɑ'fiːrən] *(no -ge-, h)* 1. *v/t.* take down in shorthand; 2. *v/i.* know shorthand; **2graphisch** [~'grɑːfiʃ] 1. *adj.* shorthand, stenographic; 2. *adv.* in shorthand; ~**typistin** [~ty'pistin] *f* (-/-nen) shorthand-typist.

Stepp|decke ['ʃtɛp-] *f* quilt, *Am. a.* comforter; '**2en** (ge-, h) 1. *v/t.* quilt; stitch; 2. *v/i.* tap-dance.

Sterbe|bett ['ʃtɛrbə-] *n* deathbed; '~**fall** *m* (case of) death; '~**kasse** *f* burial-fund.

'**sterben** 1. *v/i.* (irr., ge-, sein) die *(a. fig.)* *(an dat.* of); *esp.* ⚕ decease; 2. ⚕ *n* (-s/no *pl.*): *im* ~ *liegen* be dying.

sterblich ['ʃtɛrpliç] 1. *adj.* mortal; 2. *adv.*: ~ *verliebt sein* be desperately in love *(in acc.* with); '**2keit** *f* (-/no *pl.*) mortality; '**2keitsziffer** *f* death-rate, mortality.

stereotyp *adj.* [ʃtereo'tyːp] *typ.* stereotyped *(a. fig.)*; ~**ieren** *typ.* [~y'piːrən] *v/t.* (no -ge-, h) stereotype.

steril *adj.* [ʃte'riːl] sterile; ~**isieren** [~ili'ziːrən] *v/t.* (no -ge-, h) sterilize.

Stern [ʃtɛrn] *m* (-[e]s/-e) star *(a. fig.)*; '~**bild** *ast. n* constellation; '~**deuter** *m* (-s/-) astrologer; '~**deutung** *f* astrology; '~**enbanner** *n* Star-Spangled Banner, Stars and Stripes *pl.*, Old Glory; '~**fahrt** *mot. f* motor rally; '~**gucker** F *m* (-s/-) star-gazer; **2hell** *adj.* starry, starlit; '~**himmel** *m* (-s/no *pl.*) starry sky; '~**kunde** *f* (-/no *pl.*) astronomy; '~**schnuppe** *f* (-/-n) shooting star; '~**warte** *f* observatory.

stet *adj.* [ʃteːt], '~**ig** *adj.* continual, constant; steady; '**2igkeit** *f* (-/no *pl.*) constancy, continuity; steadiness; ~**s** *adv.* always; constantly.

Steuer ['ʃtɔʏər] 1. *n* (-s/-) ⚓ helm, rudder; steering-wheel; 2. *f* (-/-n) tax; duty; rate, local tax; '~**amt** *n s. Finanzamt*; '~**beamte** *m* revenue officer; '~**berater** *m* (-s/-) tax adviser; '~**bord** ⚓ *n* (-[e]s/-e) starboard; '~**erhebung** *f* levy of taxes; '~**erklärung** *f* tax-return; '~**ermäßigung** *f* tax allowance; '**2frei** *adj.* tax-free; *goods:* duty-free; '~**freiheit** *f* (-/no *pl.*) exemption from taxes; '~**hinterziehung** *f* tax-evasion; '~**jahr** *n* fiscal year; '~**klasse** *f* tax-bracket; '~**knüppel** ✈ *m* control lever or stick; '~**mann** *m* (-[e]s/-er, Steuerleute) ⚓ helmsman, steersman, *Am. a.* wheelsman; coxwain *(a. rowing)*; '**2n** (ge-) 1. *v/t.* (h) ⚓, ✈ steer, navigate, pilot; ⊕ control; *fig.* direct, control; 2. *v/i.* (h) check *s.th.*; 3. *v/i.* (sein): ~ *in (acc.)* ⚓ enter *(harbour, etc.)*; ~ *nach* ⚓ be bound for; '**2pflichtig** *adj.* taxable; *goods:* dutiable; '~**rad** *n* steering-wheel; '~**ruder** ⚓ *n* helm, rudder; '~**satz** *m* rate of assessment; '~**ung** *f* (-/-en) ⚓, ✈ steering; ⊕, ✈ control *(a. fig.)*; ✈ controls *pl.*; '~**veranlagung** *f* tax assessment; '~**zahler** *m* (-s/-) taxpayer; ratepayer.

Steven ⚓ ['ʃteːvən] *m* (-s/-) stem; stern-post.

Stich [ʃtiç] *m* (-[e]s/-e) prick *(of needle, etc.)*; sting *(of insect, etc.)*;

stab (of knife, etc.); sewing: stitch; cards: trick; ⊕ engraving; ⚓ stab; ~ halten hold water; im ~ lassen abandon, desert, forsake.

Stichel|ei fig. [ʃtiçə'laɪ] f (-/-en) gibe, jeer; '2n fig. v/i. (ge-, h) gibe (gegen at), jeer (at).

'**Stich|flamme** f flash; '2haltig adj. valid, sound; ~ sein hold water; '~probe f random test or sample, Am. a. spot check; '~tag m fixed day; '~wahl f second ballot; '~wort n 1. typ. (-[e]s/~er) head-word; 2. thea. (-[e]s/-e) cue; '~wunde f stab.

sticken ['ʃtɪkən] v/t. and v/i. (ge-, h) embroider.

'**Stick|garn** n embroidery floss; '~husten ⚕ m (w)hooping cough; '2ig adj. stuffy, close; '~stoff ⚕ m (-[e]s/no pl.) nitrogen.

stieben ['ʃtiːbən] v/i. ([irr.,] ge-, h, sein) sparks, etc.: fly about.

Stief... ['ʃtiːf-] step...

Stiefel ['ʃtiːfəl] m (-s/-) boot; '~knecht m bootjack; '~schaft m leg of a boot.

'**Stief|mutter** f (-/=) stepmother; '~mütterchen ⚘ ['~mytərçən] n (-s/-) pansy; '~vater m stepfather.

stieg [ʃtiːk] pret. of steigen.

Stiel [ʃtiːl] m (-[e]s/-e) handle; helve (of weapon, tool); haft (of axe); stick (of broom); ⚘ stalk.

Stier [ʃtiːr] 1. zo. m (-[e]s/-e) bull; 2. 2 adj. staring; '2en v/i. (ge-, h) stare (auf acc. at); '~kampf m bull-fight.

stieß [ʃtiːs] pret. of stoßen.

Stift [ʃtɪft] 1. m (-[e]s/~e) pin; peg; tack; pencil, crayon; F fig.: young-ster; apprentice; 2. n (-[e]s/-e, -er) charitable institution; '2en v/t. (ge-, h) endow, give, Am. a. donate; found; fig. cause; make (mischief, peace); '~er m (-s/-) donor; found-er; fig. author; '~ung f (-/-en) (charitable) endowment, donation; foundation.

Stil [ʃtiːl] m (-[e]s/-e) style (a. fig.); '2gerecht adj. stylish; 2isieren [ʃtili'ziːrən] v/t. (no -ge-, h) stylize; 2istisch adj. [ʃti'listiʃ] stylistic.

still adj. [ʃtɪl] still, quiet; silent; ⊹ dull, slack; secret; ~! silence!; im ~en secretly; der Gesellschafter ~ sleeping or silent partner; der 2e Ozean the Pacific (Ocean); '2e f (-/no pl.) stillness, quiet(ness); silence; in aller ~ quietly, silently; privately; 2eben paint. ['ʃtile:bən] n (-s/-) still life; 2egen [ʃtille:gən] v/t. (sep., -ge-, h) shut down (fac-tory, etc.); stop (traffic); '~en v/t. (ge-, h) soothe (pain); appease (ap-petite); quench (thirst); sta(u)nch (blood); nurse (baby); '~halten v/i. (irr. halten, sep., -ge-, h) keep still; '~liegen [ʃtilli:gən] v/i.

(irr. liegen, sep., -ge-, h) factory, etc.: be shut down; traffic: be suspended; machines, etc.: be idle.

stillos adj. ['ʃtiːlloːs] without style.

'**stillschweigen 1.** v/i. (irr. schwei-gen, sep., -ge-, h) be silent; ~ zu et. ignore s.th.; 2. 2 n (-s/no pl.) silence; secrecy; ~ bewahren ob-serve secrecy; et. mit ~ übergehen pass s.th. over in silence; '~d adj. silent; agreement, etc.: tacit.

'**Still|stand** m (-[e]s/no pl.) standstill; fig.: stagnation (a. ⊹); deadlock; '2stehen v/i. (irr. stehen, sep., -ge-, h) stop; be at a standstill; still-gestanden! ⚔ attention!

'**Stil|möbel** n/pl. period furniture; '2voll adj. stylish.

Stimm|band anat. ['ʃtɪm-] n (-[e]s/~er) vocal c(h)ord; '2berech-tigt adj. entitled to vote; '2e f (-/-n) voice (a. ♪, fig.); vote; comment; ♪ part; '2en (ge-, h) 1. v/t. tune (piano, etc.); j-n fröhlich ~ put s.o. in a merry mood; 2. v/i. be true or right; sum, etc.: be correct; ~ für vote for; '~enmehrheit f majority or plurality of votes; '~enthaltung f abstention; '~enzählung f count-ing of votes; '~gabel ♪ f tuning-fork; '~recht n right to vote; pol. franchise; '~ung f (-/-en) ♪ tune; fig. mood, humo(u)r; 2ungsvoll adj. impressive; '~zettel m ballot, voting-paper.

stinken ['ʃtɪŋkən] v/i. (irr., ge-, h) stink (nach of); F fig. be fishy.

Stipendium univ. [ʃti'pendjʊm] n (-s/Stipendien) scholarship; ex-hibition.

stipp|en ['ʃtɪpən] v/t. (ge-, h) dip, steep; 2visite f F flying visit.

Stirn [ʃtɪrn] f (-/-en) forehead, brow; fig. face, cheek; j-m die ~ bieten make head against s.o.; s. runzeln; '~runzeln n (-s/no pl.) frown(ing).

stob [ʃtoːp] pret. of stieben.

stöbern F ['ʃtøːbərn] v/i. (ge-, h) rummage (about) (in dat. in).

stochern ['ʃtɔxərn] v/i. (ge-, h): ~ in (dat.) poke (fire); pick (teeth).

Stock [ʃtɔk] m 1. (-[e]s/~e) stick; cane; ♪ baton; beehive; ⚘ stalk; 2. (-[e]s/-) stor(e)y, floor; im ersten ~ on the first floor, Am. on the sec-ond floor; '2be'trunken F adj. dead drunk; '2blind F adj. stone-blind; '2dunkel F adj. pitch-dark.

Stöckelschuh ['ʃtœkəl-] m high-heeled shoe.

stocken v/i. (ge-, h) stop; liquid: stagnate (a. fig.); speaker: break down; voice: falter; traffic: be blocked; ihm stockte das Blut his blood curdled.

'**Stock|** engländer F m thorough or true-born Englishman; '2finster F adj. pitch-dark; '~fleck m spot of mildew; '♀(fleck)ig adj. foxy, mildewy; '♀'nüchtern F adj. (as) sober as a judge; '⁓schnupfen ⚕ m chronic rhinitis; '♀'taub F adj. stone-deaf; '⁓ung f (-/-en) stop (-page); stagnation (of liquid) (a. fig.); block (of traffic); '⁓werk n stor(e)y, floor.

Stoff [ʃtɔf] m (-[e]s/-e) matter, substance; material, fabric, textile; material, stuff, fig.: subject(-matter); food; '♀lich adj. material.

stöhnen ['ʃtøːnən] v/i. (ge-, h) groan, moan.

Stolle ['ʃtɔlə] f (-/-n) loaf-shaped Christmas cake; '⁓n m (-s/-) s. Stolle; ⚒ tunnel, gallery (a. ⚒).

stolpern ['ʃtɔlpərn] v/i. (ge-, sein) stumble (über acc. over), trip (over) (both a. fig.).

stolz [ʃtɔlts] 1. adj. proud (auf acc. of) (a. fig.); haughty; 2. ♀ m (-es/no pl.) pride (auf acc. in); haughtiness, ⁓ieren [⁓'tsiːrən] v/i. (no -ge-, sein) strut, flaunt.

stopfen ['ʃtɔpfən] (ge-, h) 1. v/t. stuff; fill (pipe); cram (poultry, etc.); darn (sock, etc.); j-m den Mund ⁓ stop s.o.'s mouth; 2. ⚕ v/i. cause constipation.

'Stopf|garn n darning-yarn; '⁓nadel f darning-needle.

Stoppel ['ʃtɔpəl] f (-/-n) stubble; '⁓bart F m stubbly beard; '♀ig adj. stubbly.

stopp|en ['ʃtɔpən] (ge-, h) 1. v/t. stop; time, F clock; 2. v/i. stop; '♀licht mot. n stop-light; '♀uhr f stop-watch.

Stöpsel ['ʃtøpsəl] m (-s/-) stopper, cork; plug (a. ⚡); F fig. whippersnapper; '♀n v/t. (ge-, h) stopper, cork; plug (up).

Storch orn. [ʃtɔrç] m (-[e]s/⁓e) stork.

stören ['ʃtøːrən] (ge-, h) 1. v/t. disturb; trouble; radio: jam (reception); lassen Sie sich nicht ⁓! don't let me disturb you!; darf ich Sie kurz ⁓? may I trouble you for a minute?; 2. v/i. be intruding; be in the way; ♀fried ['⁓friːt] m (-[e]s/-e) troublemaker; intruder.

störr|ig adj. ['ʃtœːrɪç], '⁓isch adj. stubborn, obstinate; a. horse: restive.

'Störung f (-/-en) disturbance; trouble (a. ⊕); breakdown; radio: jamming, interference.

Stoß [ʃtoːs] m (-es/⁓e) push, shove; thrust (a. fencing); kick; butt; shock; knock, strike; blow; swimming, billiards: stroke; jolt (of car, etc.); pile, stock, heap; '⁓dämpfer mot. m shock-absorber; ♀en (irr., ge-) 1. v/t. (h) push, shove; thrust (weapon, etc.); kick; butt; knock, strike; pound (pepper, etc.); sich ⁓ an (dat.) strike or knock against; fig. take offence at; 2. v/i. (h) thrust

(nach at); kick (at); butt (at); goat, etc.: butt; car: jolt; ⁓ an (acc.) adjoin, border on; 3. v/i. (sein): F ⁓ auf (acc.) come across; meet with (opposition, etc.); ⁓ gegen or an (acc.) knock or strike against.

'Stoß|seufzer m ejaculation; '⁓stange mot. f bumper; '♀weise adv. by jerks; by fits and starts; '⁓zahn m tusk.

stottern ['ʃtɔtərn] (ge-, h) 1. v/t. stutter (out); stammer; 2. v/i. stutter; stammer; F mot. conk (out).

Straf|anstalt ['ʃtraːf⁹-] f penal institution; prison; Am. penitentiary; '⁓arbeit f imposition, F impo(t); '♀bar adj. punishable, penal; '⁓e f (-/-n) punishment; ⚖, ♱, sports, fig. penalty; fine; bei ⁓ von on or under pain of; zur ⁓ as a punishment; '♀en v/t. (ge-, h) punish.

straff adj. [ʃtraf] tight; rope: a. taut; fig. strict, rigid.

'straf|fällig adj. liable to prosecution; '♀gesetz n penal law; '♀gesetzbuch n penal code.

sträf|lich adj. ['ʃtrɛːflɪç] culpable; reprehensible; inexcusable; ♀ling ['⁓lɪŋ] m (-s/-e) convict, Am. sl. a. lag.

'straf|los adj. unpunished; '♀losigkeit f (-/no pl.) impunity; '♀porto n surcharge; '♀predigt f severe lecture; j-m e-e ⁓ halten lecture s.o. severely; '♀prozeß m criminal action; '♀raum m football: penalty area; '♀stoß m football: penalty kick; '♀verfahren n criminal proceedings pl.

Strahl [ʃtraːl] m (-[e]s/-en) ray (a. fig.); beam; flash (of lightning, etc.); jet (of water, etc.); '♀en v/i. (ge-, h) radiate; shine (vor dat. with); fig. beam (vor dat. with), shine (with); '⁓ung f (-/-en) radiation, rays pl.

Strähne ['ʃtrɛːnə] f (-/-n) lock, strand (of hair); skein, hank (of yarn); fig. stretch.

stramm adj. [ʃtram] tight; rope: a. taut; stalwart; soldier: smart.

strampeln ['ʃtrampəln] v/i. (ge-, h) kick.

Strand [ʃtrant] m (-[e]s/⚓-e, ⁓e) beach; '⁓anzug m beach-suit; ♀en ['⁓dən] v/i. (ge-, sein) ⚓ strand, run ashore; fig. fail, founder; '⁓gut n stranded goods pl.; fig. wreckage; '⁓korb m roofed wicker chair for use on the beach; ⁓promenade ['⁓promənaːdə] f (-/-n) promenade, Am. boardwalk.

Strang [ʃtraŋ] m (-[e]s/⁓e) cord (a. anat.); rope; halter (for hanging s.o.); trace (of harness); ⚒ track; über die Stränge schlagen kick over the traces.

Strapaz|e [ʃtra'paːtsə] f (-/-n) fatigue; toil; ♀ieren [⁓a'tsiːrən] v/t.

(no -ge-, h) fatigue, strain (a. fig.); wear out (fabric, etc.); **2ierfähig** adj. [~a'tsi:r-] long-lasting; **2iös** adj. [~a'tsjø:s] fatiguing.

Straße ['ʃtra:sə] f (-/-n) road, highway; street (of town, etc.); strait; auf der ~ on the road; in the street.

'Straßen|anzug m lounge-suit, Am. business suit; **'~bahn** f tram(way), tram-line, Am. street railway, streetcar line; s. Straßenbahnwagen; **'~bahnhaltestelle** f tram stop, Am. streetcar stop; **~bahnwagen** m tram(-car), Am. streetcar; **~beleuchtung** f street lighting; **'~damm** m roadway; **'~händler** m hawker; **'~junge** m street arab, Am. street Arab; **'~kehrer** m (-s/-) scavenger, street orderly; **~kreuzung** f crossing, cross roads; **'~reinigung** f street-cleaning, scavenging; **'~rennen** n road-race.

strategisch adj. [ʃtra'te:giʃ] strategic(al).

sträuben ['ʃtrɔybən] v/t. (ge-, h) ruffle up (its feathers, etc.); sich ~ hair: stand on end; sich ~ gegen kick against or at.

Strauch [ʃtraux] m (-[e]s/~er) shrub; bush.

straucheln ['ʃtrauxəln] v/i. (ge-, sein) stumble (über acc. over, at), trip (over) (both a. fig.).

Strauß [ʃtraus] m 1. orn. (-es/-e) ostrich; 2. (-es/~e) bunch (of flowers), bouquet; strife, combat.

Strebe ['ʃtre:bə] f (-/-n) strut, support, brace.

'streben 1. v/i. (ge-, h): ~ nach strive for or after, aspire to or after; 2. 2 n (-s/no pl.) striving (nach for, after), aspiration (for, after); effort, endeavo(u)r.

'Streber m (-s/-) pusher, careerist; at school: sl. swot.

strebsam adj. ['ʃtre:pza:m] assiduous; ambitious; **2keit** f (-/no pl.) assiduity; ambition.

Strecke ['ʃtrekə] f (-/-n) stretch; route; tract, extent; distance (a. sports); course; 🚂 etc.: section, line; hunt. bag; zur ~ bringen hunt. bag, hunt down (a. fig.); 2n v/t. (ge-, h) stretch, extend; dilute (fluid); sich ~ stretch (o.s.); die Waffen ~ lay down one's arms; fig. a. give in.

Streich [ʃtraiç] m (-[e]s/-e) stroke; blow; fig. trick, prank; j-m e-n ~ spielen play a trick on s.o.; 2eln ['~əln] v/t. (ge-, h) stroke; caress; pat; '2en (irr., ge-) 1. v/t. (h) rub; spread (butter, etc.); paint; strike out, delete, cancel (a. fig.); strike, lower (flag, sail); 2. v/i. (sein) prowl (um round); 3. v/i.(h): mit der Hand über et. ~ pass one's hand over s.th.; '~holz n match; '~instrument ♪ n stringed instrument;

'~orchester n string band; **'~riemen** m strop.

Streif [ʃtraif] m (-[e]s/-e) s. Streifen; **'~band** n (-[e]s/~er) wrapper; **'~e** f (-/-n) patrol; patrolman; raid.

'streifen (ge-) 1. v/t. (h) stripe, streak; graze, touch lightly in passing, brush; touch (up)on (subject); 2. v/i. (sein): ~ durch rove, wander through; 3. v/i. (h): ~ an (acc.) graze, brush; fig. border or verge on; 4. 2 m (-s/-) strip; stripe; streak.

'streif|ig adj. striped; **'2licht** n sidelight; **'2schuß** ✕ m grazing shot; **'2zug** m ramble; ✕ raid.

Streik [ʃtraik] m (-[e]s/-s) strike, Am. F a. walkout; in den ~ treten go on strike, Am. F a. walk out; **'~brecher** m (-s/-) strike-breaker, blackleg, scab; **'2en** v/i. (ge-, h) (be on) strike; go on strike, Am. F a. walk out; **~ende** ['~əndə] m, f (-n/-n) striker; **'~posten** m picket.

Streit [ʃtrait] m (-[e]s/-e) quarrel; dispute; conflict; 🏛 litigation; **'2bar** adj. pugnacious; **'2en** v/i. and v/refl. (irr., ge-, h) quarrel (mit with; wegen for; über acc. about); **'~frage** f controversy, (point of) issue; **'2ig** adj. debatable, controversial; j-m et. ~ machen dispute s.o.'s right to s.th.; **'~igkeiten** f/pl. quarrels pl.; disputes pl.; **'~kräfte** ✕ ['~kreftə] f/pl. (military or armed) forces pl.; **'2lustig** adj. pugnacious, aggressive; **'2süchtig** adj. quarrelsome; pugnacious.

streng [ʃtreŋ] 1. adj. severe; stern; strict; austere; discipline, etc.: rigorous; weather, climate: inclement; examination: stiff; 2. adv.: ~ vertraulich in strict confidence; **'2e** f (-/no pl.) s. streng 1: severity; sternness; strictness; austerity; rigo(u)r; inclemency; stiffness; **'~genommen** adv. strictly speaking; **'~gläubig** adj. orthodox.

Streu [ʃtrɔy] f (-/-en) litter; **'2en** v/t. (ge-, h) strew, scatter; **'~zucker** m castor sugar.

Strich [ʃtriç] 1. m (-[e]s/-e) stroke; line; dash; tract (of land); j-m e-n ~ durch die Rechnung machen queer s.o.'s pitch; 2. 2 pret. of streichen; **'~regen** m local shower; **'2weise** adv. here and there.

Strick [ʃtrik] m (-[e]s/-e) cord; rope; halter, rope (for hanging s.o.); F fig. (young) rascal; **'2en** v/t. and v/i. (ge-, h) knit; **'~garn** n knitting-yarn; **'~jacke** f cardigan, jersey; **'~leiter** f rope-ladder; **'~nadel** f knitting-needle; **'~waren** f/pl. knit-wear; **'~zeug** n knitting(-things pl.).

Striemen ['ʃtri:mən] m (-s/-) weal, wale.

Strippe F ['ʃtripə] f (-/-n) band; string; shoe-lace; an der ~ hängen be on the phone.

stritt [ʃtrit] *pret. of* streiten; '⏼ig *adj.* debatable, controversial; ⏼er Punkt (point of) issue.

Stroh [ʃtro:] *n* (-[e]s/*no pl.*) straw; thatch; '⏼dach *n* thatch(ed roof); '⏼halm *m* straw; *nach* e-m ⏼ greifen catch at a straw; '⏼hut *m* straw hat; '⏼mann *m* man of straw; scarecrow; *fig.* dummy; '⏼sack *m* straw mattress; '⏼witwe F *f* grass widow.

Strolch [ʃtrɔlç] *m* (-[e]s/-e) scamp, F vagabond; '2en *v/i.* (ge-, sein): ⏼ durch rove.

Strom [ʃtro:m] *m* (-[e]s/=e) stream (*a. fig.*); (large) river; ≸ current (*a. fig.*); es regnet in Strömen it is pouring with rain; 2'ab(wärts) *adv.* down-stream; 2'auf(wärts) *adv.* up-stream.

strömen ['ʃtrø:mən] *v/i.* (ge-, sein) stream; flow, run; *rain:* pour; *people:* stream, pour (*aus* out of; *in* acc. into).

'**Strom|kreis** ≸ *m* circuit; '⏼linienform *f* (-/*no pl.*) streamline shape; '2linienförmig *adj.* streamline(d); '⏼schnelle *f* (-/-n) rapid, *Am.* ⏼ riffle; '⏼sperre ≸ *f* stoppage of current.

'**Strömung** *f* (-/-en) current; *fig. a.* trend, tendency.

'**Stromzähler** ≸ *m* electric meter.

Strophe [ʃtro:fə] *f* (-/-n) stanza, verse.

strotzen ['ʃtrɔtsən] *v/i.* (ge-, h): ⏼ von abound in; teem with (*blunders, etc.*); burst with (*health, etc.*).

Strudel ['ʃtru:dəl] *m* (-s/-) eddy, whirlpool; *fig.* whirl; '2n *v/i.* (ge-, h) swirl, whirl. [ture.]

Struktur [ʃtruk'tu:r] *f* (-/-en) struc-)

Strumpf [ʃtrumpf] *m* (-[e]s/=e) stocking; '⏼band *n* (-[e]s/=er) garter; '⏼halter *m* (-s/-) suspender, *Am.* garter; '⏼waren *f/pl.* hosiery.

struppig *adj.* ['ʃtrupiç] *hair:* rough, shaggy; *dog, etc.:* shaggy.

Stube ['ʃtu:bə] *f* (-/-n) room.

'**Stuben|hocker** *fig. m* (-s/-) stay-at-home; '⏼mädchen *n* chambermaid; '2rein *adj.* house-trained.

Stück [ʃtyk] *n* (-[e]s/-e) piece (*a. ♪*); fragment; head (*of cattle*); lump (*of sugar*); *thea.* play; *aus freien ⏼n* of one's own accord; *in ⏼e gehen or schlagen* break to pieces; '⏼arbeit *f* piece-work; '2weise *adv.* piece by piece; (by) piecemeal; ✝ by the piece; '⏼werk *fig. n* patchwork.

Student [ʃtu'dɛnt] *m* (-en/-en), ⏼in *f* (-/-nen) student, undergraduate.

Studie ['ʃtu:djə] *f* (-/-n) study (*über acc.*, zu of, in) (*a. art, literature*); *paint., etc.:* sketch; '⏼nrat *m* (-[e]s/=e) *appr.* secondary-school teacher; '⏼nreise *f* study trip.

studier|en [ʃtu'di:rən] (*no* -ge-, h) 1. *v/t.* study, read (*law, etc.*); 2. *v/i.*

study; be a student; 2zimmer *n* study.

Studium ['ʃtu:djum] *n* (-s/Studien) study (*a. fig.*); studies *pl.*

Stufe ['ʃtu:fə] *f* (-/-n) step; *fig.:* degree; grade; stage.

'**Stufen|folge** *fig. f* gradation; '⏼leiter *f* step-ladder; *fig.* scale; '2weise 1. *adj.* gradual; 2. *adv.* gradually, by degrees.

Stuhl [ʃtu:l] *m* (-[e]s/=e) chair, seat; *in a church:* pew; *weaving:* loom; ≸ *s.* Stuhlgang; '⏼bein *n* leg of a chair; '⏼gang ≸ *m* (-[e]s/*no pl.*) stool; motion; '⏼lehne *f* back of a chair.

stülpen ['ʃtylpən] *v/t.* (ge-, h) put (*über acc.* over); clap (*hat*) (*auf acc.* on).

stumm *adj.* [ʃtum] dumb, mute; *fig. a.* silent; *gr.* silent, mute.

Stummel ['ʃtuməl] *m* (-s/-) stump; stub.

'**Stummfilm** *m* silent film.

Stümper F ['ʃtympər] *m* (-s/-) bungler; ⏼ei F [⏼'rai] *f* (-/-en) bungling; bungle; '2haft *adj.* bungling; '2n F *v/i.* (ge-, h) bungle, botch.

stumpf [ʃtumpf] 1. *adj.* blunt; ⅍ *angle:* obtuse; *senses:* dull, obtuse; apathetic; 2. 2 *m* (-[e]s/=e) stump, stub; *mit ⏼ und Stiel* root and branch; '2sinn *m* (-[e]s/*no pl.*) stupidity, dul(l)ness; '⏼sinnig *adj.* stupid, dull.

Stunde ['ʃtundə] *f* (-/-n) hour; lesson, *Am. a.* period; '2n *v/t.* (ge-, h) grant respite for.

'**Stunden|kilometer** *m* kilometre per hour, *Am.* kilometer per hour; '2lang 1. *adj.:* *nach ⏼em Warten* after hours of waiting; 2. *adv.* for hours (and hours); '⏼lohn *m* hourly wage; '⏼plan *m* time-table, *Am.* schedule; '2weise 1. *adj.:* ⏼ Beschäftigung part-time employment; 2. *adv.* by the hour; '⏼zeiger *m* hour-hand.

stündlich ['ʃtyntliç] 1. *adj.* hourly; 2. *adv.* hourly, every hour; at any hour.

'**Stundung** *f* (-/-en) respite.

stur F *adj.* [ʃtu:r] *gaze:* fixed, staring; *p.* pigheaded, mulish.

Sturm [ʃturm] *m* (-[e]s/=e) storm (*a. fig.*); ⏻ gale.

stürm|en ['ʃtyrmən] (ge-) 1. *v/t.* (h) ⅍ storm (*a. fig.*); 2. *v/i.* (h) *wind:* storm, rage; es stürmt it is stormy weather; 3. *v/i.* (sein) rush; '2er *m* (-s/-) football, *etc.:* forward; '⏼isch *adj.* stormy; *fig.:* impetuous; tumultuous.

'**Sturm|schritt** ⅍ *m* double-quick step; '⏼trupp ⅍ *m* storming-party; '⏼wind *m* storm-wind.

Sturz [ʃturts] *m* (-es/=e) fall, tumble; overthrow (*of government, etc.*);

fig. ruin; † slump; '**~bach** *m* torrent.

stürzen ['ʃtyrtsən] (ge-) 1. *v/i.* (sein) (have a) fall, tumble; *fig.* rush, plunge (*in acc.* into); 2. *v/t.* (h) throw; overthrow (*government, etc.*); *fig.* plunge (*in acc.* into), precipitate (into); *j-n ins Unglück* ~ ruin s.o.; *sich in Schulden* ~ plunge into debt.

'**Sturz|flug** ✈ *m* (nose)dive; '**~helm** *m* crash-helmet.

Stute *zo.* ['ʃtuːtə] *f* (-/-n) mare.

Stütze ['ʃtytsə] *f* (-/-n) support, prop, stay (*all a. fig.*).

stutzen ['ʃtutsən] (ge-, h) 1. *v/t.* cut (*hedge*); crop (*ears, tail, hair*); clip (*hedge, wing*); trim (*hair, beard, hedge*); dock (*tail*); lop (*tree*); 2. *v/i.* start (*bei* at); stop dead or short.

'**stützen** *v/t.* (ge-, h) support, prop, stay (*all a. fig.*); ~ *auf* (*acc.*) base or found on; *sich* ~ *auf* (*acc.*) lean on; *fig.* rely (up)on; *argument, etc.*: be based on.

'**Stutz|er** *m* (-s/-) dandy, fop, *Am. a.* dude; '**~ig** *adj.* suspicious; ~ *machen* make suspicious.

'**Stütz|pfeiler** ⚒ *m* abutment; '**~punkt** *m* phys. fulcrum; ✕ base.

Subjekt [zup'jɛkt] *n* (-[e]s/-e) gr. subject; *contp.* individual; **2iv** *adj.* [~'tiːf] subjective; **~ivität** [~ivi'tɛːt] *f* (-/no pl.) subjectivity.

Substantiv gr. ['zupstantiːf] *n* (-s/-e) noun, substantive; **2isch** gr. *adj.* ['~viʃ] substantival.

Substanz [zup'stants] *f* (-/-en) substance (*a. fig.*).

subtra|hieren [zuptra'hiːrən] *v/t.* (no -ge-, h) subtract; **2ktion** [~k'tsjoːn] *f* (-/-en) subtraction.

Such|dienst ['zuːx-] *m* tracing service; '**~e** *f* (-/no pl.) search (*nach* for); *auf der* ~ *nach* in search of; **2en** (ge-, h) 1. *v/t.* seek (*advice, etc.*); search for; look for; *Sie haben hier nichts zu* ~ you have no business to be here; 2. *v/i.*: ~ *nach* seek for or after; search for; look for; '**~er** *phot. m* (-s/-) view-finder.

Sucht [zuxt] *f* (-/-e) mania (*nach* for), rage (for), addiction (to).

süchtig *adj.* ['zyçtiç] having a mania (*nach* for); ~ *sein* be a drug addict; **2e** ['~gə] *m, f* (-n/-n) drug addict or fiend.

Süd geogr. [zyːt], **~en** ['~dən] *m* (-s/no pl.) south; **~früchte** ['zyːt-fryçtə] *f/pl.* fruits from the south; '**2lich** 1. *adj.* south(ern); southerly; 2. *adv.*: ~ *von* (to the) south of; ~'*ost* geogr., ~'*osten* *m* (-s/no pl.) south-east; **2'östlich** *adj.* south-east(ern); '**~pol** geogr. *m* (-s/no pl.) South Pole; **2wärts** adv. ['~verts] southward(s); ~'*west* geogr., ~'*westen* *m* (-s/no pl.) south-west;

2'westlich *adj.* south-west(ern); '**~wind** *m* south wind.

süffig F *adj.* ['zyfiç] palatable, tasty.

suggerieren [zugeˈriːrən] *v/t.* (no -ge-, h) suggest.

suggestiv *adj.* [zugesˈtiːf] suggestive.

Sühne ['zyːnə] *f* (-/-n) expiation, atonement; '**2en** *v/t.* (ge-, h) expiate, atone for.

Sülze ['zyltsə] *f* (-/-n) jellied meat.

summ|arisch *adj.* [zuˈmaːriʃ] summary (*a. ᵗⁱᵇ*); '**2e** *f* (-/-n) sum (*a. fig.*); (sum) total; amount.

'**summen** (ge-, h) 1. *v/i.* bees, etc.: buzz, hum; 2. *v/t.* hum (*song, etc.*).

sum'mieren *v/t.* (no -ge-, h) sum or add up; *sich* ~ run up.

Sumpf [zumpf] *m* (-[e]s/-e) swamp, bog, marsh; '**2ig** *adj.* swampy, boggy, marshy.

Sünd|e ['zyndə] *f* (-/-n) sin (*a. fig.*); '**~enbock** F *m* scapegoat; '**~er** *m* (-s/-) sinner; '**2haft** ['~t-] 1. *adj.* sinful; 2. *adv.*: F ~ *teuer* awfully expensive; '**2ig** ['~diç] *adj.* sinful; '**2igen** ['~digən] *v/i.* (ge-, h) (commit a) sin.

Superlativ ['zuːperlatiːf] *m* (-s/-e) gr. superlative degree; *in* ~*en sprechen* speak in superlatives.

Suppe ['zupə] *f* (-/-n) soup; broth.

'**Suppen|löffel** *m* soup-spoon; '**~schöpfer** *m* soup ladle; '**~schüssel** *f* tureen; '**~teller** *m* soup-plate.

surren ['zurən] *v/i.* (ge-, h) whir(r); *insects* buzz.

Surrogat [zuroˈgaːt] *n* (-[e]s/-e) substitute.

suspendieren [zuspɛnˈdiːrən] *v/t.* (no -ge-, h) suspend.

süß *adj.* [zyːs] sweet (*a. fig.*); '**2e** *f* (-/no pl.) sweetness; '**~en** *v/t.* (ge-, h) sweeten; '**2igkeiten** *pl.* sweets *pl.*, sweetmeats *pl.*, *Am. a.* candy; '**~lich** *adj.* sweetish; mawkish (*a. fig.*); '**2stoff** *m* saccharin(e); '**2-wasser** *n* (-s/-) fresh water.

Symbol [zymˈboːl] *n* (-s/-e) symbol; '**~ik** *f* (-/no pl.) symbolism; **2isch** *adj.* symbolic(al).

Symmetr|ie [zymeˈtriː] *f* (-/-n) symmetry; **2isch** *adj.* [~ˈmeːtriʃ] symmetric(al).

Sympath|ie [zympaˈtiː] *f* (-/-n) liking; **2isch** *adj.* [~ˈpaːtiʃ] likable; *er ist mir* ~ I like him; **2isieren** [~iˈziːrən] *v/i.* (no -ge-, h) sympathize (*mit* with).

Symphonie ♪ [zymfoˈniː] *f* (-/-n) symphony; **~orchester** *n* symphony orchestra.

Symptom [zympˈtoːm] *n* (-s/-e) symptom; **2atisch** *adj.* [~oˈmaːtiʃ] symptomatic (*für* of).

Synagoge [zynaˈgoːgə] *f* (-/-n) synagogue.

synchronisieren [zynkroniˈziːrən] *v/t.* (no -ge-, h) synchronize; dub.

Syndik|at [zyndi'ka:t] *n* (-[e]s/-e) syndicate; **~us** ['zyndikus] *m* (-/-se, *Syndizi*) syndic.

Synkope ♪ [zyn'ko:pə] *f* (-/-n) syncope.

synonym [zyno'ny:m] **1.** *adj.* synonymous; **2.** ♀ *n* (-s/-e) synonym.

Syntax *gr.* ['zyntaks] *f* (-/-en) syntax.

synthetisch *adj.* [zyn'te:tiʃ] synthetic.

System [zys'te:m] *n* (-s/-e) system; scheme; **♀atisch** *adj.* [~e'ma:tiʃ] systematic(al), methodic(al).

Szene ['stse:nə] *f* (-/-n) scene (*a. fig.*); *in ~ setzen* stage; **~rie** [stsenə-'ri:] *f* (-/-n) scenery.

T

Tabak ['ta:bak, 'tabak, ta'bak] *m* (-s/-e) tobacco; (')**~händler** *m* tobacconist; (')**~sbeutel** *m* tobacco-pouch; (')**~sdose** *f* snuff-box; (')**~waren** *pl.* tobacco products *pl.*, F smokes *pl.*

tabellarisch [tabɛ'la:riʃ] **1.** *adj.* tabular; **2.** *adv.* in tabular form.

Tabelle [ta'bɛlə] *f* (-/-n) table; schedule.

Tablett [ta'blɛt] *n* (-[e]s/-e, -s) tray; *of metal*: salver; **~e** *pharm. f* (-/-n) tablet; lozenge.

Tachometer [taxo'-] *n*, *m* (-s/-) ⊕ tachometer; *mot. a.* speedometer.

Tadel ['ta:dəl] *m* (-s/-) blame; censure; reprimand, rebuke, reproof; reproach; *at school*: bad mark; **♀los** *adj.* faultless, blameless; excellent, splendid; **♀n** *v/t.* (ge-, h) blame (*wegen for*); censure; reprimand, rebuke, reprove; scold; find fault with.

Tafel ['ta:fəl] *f* (-/-n) table; plate (*a. book illustration*); slab; *on houses, etc.*: tablet, plaque; slate; blackboard; signboard, notice-board, *Am.* billboard; cake, bar (*of chocolate, etc.*); dinner-table; dinner; **♀förmig** *adj.* ['~fœrmiç] tabular; **~geschirr** *n* dinnerservice, dinner-set; **~land** *n* tableland, plateau; **♀n** *v/i.* (ge-, h) dine; feast, banquet; **~service** *n s. Tafelgeschirr*; **~silber** *n* silver plate, *Am.* silverware.

Täf(e)lung ['tɛ:f(ə)luŋ] *f* (-/-en) wainscot, panelling.

Taft [taft] *m* (-[e]s/-e) taffeta.

Tag [ta:k] *m* (-[e]s/-e) day; *officially*: *a.* date; *am or bei ~e* by day; *e-s ~es* one day; *den ganzen ~* all day long; *~ für ~* day by day; *über ~e* aboveground; *unter ~e* ☓ underground; *heute vor acht ~en* a week ago; *heute in acht (vierzehn) ~en* today *or* this day week (fortnight), a week (fortnight) today; *denkwürdiger or freudiger ~* red-letter day; *freier ~* day off; *guten ~!* how do you do?; good morning!; good afternoon!; F hallo!, hullo!, *Am.* hello!; *am hellichten ~e* in broad daylight; *es wird ~* it dawns; *an den*

~ bringen (kommen) bring (come) to light; *bis auf den heutigen ~* to this day; **♀'aus** *adv.*: *~, tagein* day in, day out.

Tage|blatt ['ta:gə-] *n* daily (paper); **~buch** *n* journal, diary.

tagein *adv.* [ta:k'aın] *s. tagaus*.

tage|lang *adv.* ['ta:gə-] day after day, for days together; **♀lohn** *m* day's *or* daily wages *pl.*; **♀löhner** ['~lø:nər] *m* (-s/-) day-labo(u)rer; **~n** *v/i.* (ge-, h) dawn; hold a meeting, meet, sit; ½½ be in session; **♀reise** *f* day's journey.

Tages|anbruch ['ta:gəs ʔ-] *m* daybreak, dawn; *bei ~* at daybreak *or* dawn; **~befehl** ☓ *m* order of the day; **~bericht** *m* daily report, bulletin; **~einnahme** ♰ *f* receipts *pl. or* takings *pl.* of the day; **~gespräch** *n* topic of the day; **~kasse** *f thea.* box-office, booking-office; *s. Tageseinnahme*; **~kurs** ♰ *m* current rate; *stock exchange*: quotation of the day; **~licht** *n* daylight; **~ordnung** *f* order of the day, agenda; *das ist an der ~* that is the order of the day, that is quite common; **~presse** *f* daily press; **~zeit** *f* time of day; daytime; *zu jeder ~* at any hour, at any time of the day; **~zeitung** *f* daily (paper).

tage|weise *adv.* ['ta:gə-] by the day; **♀werk** *n* day's work; man-day.

täglich *adj.* ['tɛ:kliç] daily.

tags *adv.* ['ta:ks]: *~ darauf* the following day, the day after; *~ zuvor* (on) the previous day, the day before.

'Tagschicht *f* day shift.

tagsüber *adv.* ['ta:ks ʔ-] during the day, in the day-time.

Tagung ['ta:guŋ] *f* (-/-en) meeting.

Taille ['taljə] *f* (-/-n) waist; bodice (*of dress*).

Takel ⊕ ['ta:kəl] *n* (-s/-) tackle; **~age** ⊕ [takə'la:ʒə] *f* (-/-n) rigging, tackle; **♀n** *v/t.* (ge-, h) rig (*ship*); **~werk** ⊕ *n s. Takelage*.

Takt [takt] *m* **1.** (-[e]s/-e) ♪ time, measure; bar; *mot.* stroke; *den ~ halten* ♪ keep time; *den ~ schlagen* ♪ beat time; **2.** (-[e]s/*no pl.*) tact; **♀fest** *adj.* steady in keeping time;

fig. firm; '~ik ✕ *f* (-/-en) tactics *pl. and sg.* (*a. fig.*); '~iker *m* (-s/-) tactician; '2isch *adj.* tactical; '2los *adj.* tactless; '~stock *m* baton; '~strich ♪ *m* bar; '2voll *adj.* tactful.

Tal [ta:l] *n* (-[e]s/~er) valley, *poet. a.* dale; *enges ~* glen.

Talar [ta'la:r] *m* (-s/-e) 鲜, *eccl.*, *univ.* gown; 鲜 robe.

Talent [ta'lɛnt] *n* (-[e]s/-e) talent, gift, aptitude, ability; 2iert *adj.* [~'ti:rt] talented, gifted.

'**Talfahrt** *f* downhill journey; ⚓ passage downstream.

Talg [talk] *m* (-[e]s/-e) suet; *melted*: tallow; '~drüse *anat.* *f* sebaceous gland; 2ig *adj.* ['~gɪç] suety; tallowish, tallowy; '~licht *n* tallow candle.

Talisman ['ta:lisman] *m* (-s/-e) talisman, (good-luck) charm.

'**Talsperre** *f* barrage, dam.

Tampon [*tã'pɔ̃*, 'tampɔn] *m* (-s/-s) tampon, plug.

Tang ♣ [taŋ] *m* (-[e]s/-e) seaweed.

Tank [taŋk] *m* (-[e]s/-s, -e) tank; '2en *v/i.* (ge-, *h*) get (some) petrol, *Am.* get (some) gasoline; '~er ⚓ *m* (-s/-) tanker; '~stelle *f* petrol station, *Am.* gas *or* filling station; '~wagen *m* *mot.* tank truck, *Am. a.* gasoline truck, tank trailer; 鲜 tank-car; '~wart ['~vart] *m* (-[e]s/-e) pump attendant.

Tanne ♣ ['tanə] *f* (-/-n) fir(-tree).

'**Tannen|baum** *m* fir-tree; '~nadel *f* fir-needle; '~zapfen *m* fir-cone.

Tante ['tantə] *f* (-/-n) aunt.

Tantieme [tã'tjɛ:mə] *f* (-/-n) royalty, percentage, share in profits.

Tanz [tants] *m* (-es/~e) dance.

tänzeln ['tɛntsəln] *v/i.* (ge-, *h*, *sein*) dance, trip, frisk.

'**tanzen** (ge-) *v/i.* (*h*, *sein*) *and v/t.* (*h*) dance.

Tänzer ['tɛntsər] *m* (-s/-), '~in *f* (-/-nen) dancer; *thea.* ballet-dancer; partner.

'**Tanz|lehrer** *m* dancing-master; '~musik *f* dance-music; '~saal *m* dancing-room, ball-room, dance-hall; '~schule *f* dancing-school; '~stunde *f* dancing-lesson.

Tapete [ta'pe:tə] *f* (-/-n) wallpaper, paper-hangings *pl.*

tapezier|en [tape'tsi:rən] *v/t.* (*no* -ge-, *h*) paper; 2er *m* (-s/-) paperhanger; upholsterer.

tapfer *adj.* ['tapfər] brave, valiant, heroic; courageous; '2keit *f* (-/*no pl.*) bravery, valo(u)r; heroism; courage.

tappen ['tapən] *v/i.* (ge-, *sein*) grope (about), fumble. [awkward.)

täppisch *adj.* ['tɛpiʃ] clumsy,)

tapsen F ['tapsən] *v/i.* (ge-, *sein*) walk clumsily.

Tara ✝ ['ta:ra] *f* (-/Taren) tare.

Tarif [ta'ri:f] *m* (-s/-e) tariff, (table of) rates *pl.*, price-list; 2lich *adv.* according to tariff; 2lohn *m* standard wage(s *pl.*); ~vertrag *m* collective *or* wage agreement.

tarn|en ['tarnən] *v/t.* (ge-, *h*) camouflage; *esp. fig.* disguise; '2ung *f* (-/-en) camouflage.

Tasche ['taʃə] *f* (-/-n) pocket (*of garment*); (hand)bag; pouch; *s.* Aktentasche, Schultasche.

'**Taschen|buch** *n* pocket-book; '~dieb *m* pickpocket, *Am. sl.* dip; '~geld *n* pocket-money; *monthly:* allowance; '~lampe *f* (electric) torch, *esp. Am.* flashlight; '~messer *n* pocket-knife; '~spielerei *f* juggle(ry); '~tuch *n* (pocket) handkerchief; '~uhr *f* (pocket-)watch; '~wörterbuch *n* pocket dictionary.

Tasse ['tasə] *f* (-/-n) cup.

Tastatur [tasta'tu:r] *f* (-/-en) keyboard, keys *pl.*

Tast|e ['tastə] *f* (-/-n) key; '2en (ge-, *h*) 1. *v/i.* touch, grope (*nach* for, after), fumble (for); 2. *v/t.* touch, feel; *sich ~* feel *or* grope one's way; '~sinn *m* (-[e]s/*no pl.*) sense of touch.

Tat [ta:t] 1. *f* (-/-en) action, act, deed; offen|ce, *Am.* -se, crime; *in der ~* indeed, in fact, as a matter of fact, really; *auf frischer ~ ertappen* catch *s.o.* red-handed; *zur ~ schreiten* proceed to action; *in die ~ umsetzen* implement, carry into effect; 2. 2 *pret.* of tun; '~bestand 鲜 *m* facts *pl.* of the case; '2enlos *adj.* inactive, idle.

Täter ['tɛ:tər] *m* (-s/-) perpetrator; offender, culprit.

tätig *adj.* ['tɛ:tiç] active; busy; *~ sein bei* work at; be employed with; '~en ['~gən] *v/t.* (ge-, *h*) effect, transact; conclude; '2keit *f* (-/-en) activity; occupation, business, job; profession.

'**Tat|kraft** *f* (-/*no pl.*) energy; enterprise; '2kräftig *adj.* energetic, active.

tätlich *adj.* ['tɛ:tliç] violent; *~ werden gegen* assault; '2keiten *f/pl.* (acts *pl.* of) violence; 鲜 assault (and battery).

Tatort 鲜 ['ta:t?~] *m* (-[e]s/-e) place *or* scene of a crime.

tätowieren [teto'vi:rən] *v/t.* (*no* -ge-, *h*) tattoo.

'**Tat|sache** *f* (matter of) fact; '~sachenbericht *m* factual *or* documentary report, matter-of-fact account; '2sächlich *adj.* actual, real. [pat.)

tätscheln ['tɛtʃəln] *v/t.* (ge-, *h*) pet,)

Tatze ['tatsə] *f* (-/-n) paw, claw.

Tau[1] [tau] *n* (-[e]s/-e) rope, cable.

Tau[2] [~] *m* (-[e]s/*no pl.*) dew.

taub *adj.* [taup] deaf (*fig.*: *gegen* to); *fingers, etc.*: benumbed, numb; *nut:*

deaf, empty; *rock*: dead; ~es Ei
addle egg; *auf e-m Ohr* ~ *sein* be
deaf of *or* in one ear.

Taube *orn.* ['taubə] f (-/-n) pigeon;
'~nschlag m pigeon-house.

'**Taub|heit** f (-/*no pl.*) deafness;
numbness; '2**stumm** *adj.* deaf and
dumb; '~**stumme** m, f (-n/-n) deaf
mute.

tauch|en ['tauxən] (*ge-*) 1. *v/t.*
(h) dip, plunge; 2. *v/i.* (h, sein) dive,
plunge; dip; *submarine*: submerge;
'2**er** m (-s/-) diver; '2**sieder** m (-s/-)
immersion heater.

tauen ['tauən] *v/i.* (*ge-*) 1. (h, sein):
der Schnee or es taut the snow *or*
it is thawing; *der Schnee ist von
den Dächern getaut* the snow has
melted off the roofs; 2. (h): *es taut*
dew is falling.

Taufe ['taufə] f (-/-n) baptism,
christening; '2**n** *v/t.* (*ge-*, h) baptize,
christen.

Täufling ['tɔyfliŋ] m (-s/-e) child *or*
person to be baptized.

'**Tauf|name** m Christian name, *Am.*
a. given name; '~**pate** 1. m godfather; 2. f godmother; '~**patin** f
godmother; '~**schein** m certificate
of baptism.

taug|en ['taugən] *v/i.* (*ge-*, h) be
good, be fit, be of use (*all: zu* for);
(*zu*) *nichts* ~ be good for nothing,
be no good, be of no use; '2**enichts**
m (-, -es/-e) good-for-nothing, *Am.
sl.* dead beat; '~**lich** *adj.* ['tauk-]
good, fit, useful (*all: für, zu* for, to
inf.); able; ✕, ⚓ able-bodied.

Taumel ['tauməl] m (-s/*no pl.*)
giddiness; rapture, ecstasy; '2**ig**
adj. reeling; giddy; '2**n** *v/i.* (*ge-*,
sein) reel, stagger; be giddy.

Tausch [tauʃ] m (-es/-e) exchange;
barter; '2**en** *v/t.* (*ge-*, h) exchange;
barter (*gegen* for).

täuschen ['tɔyʃən] *v/t.* (*ge-*, h)
deceive, delude, mislead (on purpose); cheat; *sich* ~ deceive o.s.; be
mistaken; *sich* ~ *lassen* let o.s. be
deceived; '~**d** *adj.* deceptive, delu-
sive; *resemblance*: striking.

'**Tauschhandel** m barter.

'**Täuschung** f (-/-en) deception,
delusion.

tausend *adj.* ['tauzənt] a thousand;
'~**fach** *adj.* thousandfold; '2**fuß** *zo.*
m, 2**füß(l)er** *zo.* ['~fy:s(l)ər] m
(-s/-) millepede, milliped(e), *Am. a.*
wireworm; '~**st** *adj.* thousandth;
'2**stel** n (-s/-) thousandth (part).

'**Tau|tropfen** m dew-drop; '~**wetter**
n thaw.

Taxameter [taksa'-] m taximeter.

Taxe ['taksə] f (-/-n) rate; fee;
estimate; s. *Taxi*.

Taxi ['taksi] n (-[s]/-[s]) taxi(-cab),
cab, *Am. a.* hack.

ta'xieren *v/t.* (*no -ge-*, h) rate,
estimate; *officially*: value, appraise.

'**Taxistand** m cabstand.

Technik ['tɛçnik] f 1. (-/*no pl.*)
technology; engineering; 2. (-/-en)
skill, workmanship; technique,
practice; ♪ execution; '~**er** m (-s/-)
(technical) engineer; technician;
'~**um** ['~um] n (-s/*Technika*, *Tech-
niken*) technical school.

'**technisch** *adj.* technical; ~**e** *Hochschule* school of technology.

Tee [te:] m (-s/-s) tea; '~**büchse** f
tea-caddy; '~**gebäck** n scones *or*
biscuits *pl.*, *Am. a.* cookies *pl.*;
'~**kanne** f teapot; '~**kessel** m tea-
kettle; '~**löffel** m tea-spoon.

Teer [te:r] m (-[e]s/-e) tar; '2**en** *v/t.*
(*ge-*, h) tar.

'**Tee|rose** ♀ f tea-rose; '~**sieb** n
tea-strainer; '~**tasse** f teacup;
'~**wärmer** m (-s/-) tea-cosy.

Teich [taiç] m (-[e]s/-e) pool,
pond.

Teig [taik] m (-[e]s/-e) dough, paste;
2**ig** *adj.* ['~giç] doughy, pasty;
'~**waren** f/pl. farinaceous food;
noodles *pl.*

Teil [tail] m, n (-[e]s/-e) part; portion, share; component; ⚖ party;
zum ~ partly, in part; *ich für mein*
~ ... for my part I ...; '2**bar** *adj.*
divisible; '~**chen** n (-s/-) particle;
'2**en** *v/t.* (*ge-*, h) divide; *fig.* share;
'2**haben** *v/i.* (*irr. haben, sep.*, *-ge-*,
h) participate, (have a) share (*both:
an dat.* in); '~**haber** ✝ m (-s/-)
partner; '~**nahme** f (-/*no pl.*)
participation (*an dat.* in); *fig.*:
interest (in); sympathy (with);
2**nahmslos** *adj.* ['~na:mslo:s] in-
different, unconcerned, passive;
apathetic; '~**nahmslosigkeit** f
(-/*no pl.*) indifference; passiveness;
apathy; '2**nehmen** *v/i.* (*irr. nehmen,
sep.*, *-ge-*, h): ~ *an* (*dat.*) take part *or*
participate in; join in; be present
at, attend at; *fig.* sympathize with;
'~**nehmer** m (-s/-) participant;
member; *univ.*, *etc.*: student; contestant; *sports*: competitor; *teleph.*
subscriber; 2**s** *adv.* [~s] partly;
'~**strecke** f section; stage, leg; ⬡
fare stage; '~**ung** f (-/-en) division;
2**weise** *adv.* partly, partially, in
part; '~**zahlung** f (payment by)
instal(l)ments.

Teint [tɛ̃:] m (-s/-s) complexion.

Tele|fon [tele'fo:n] n (-s/-e) *etc.* s.
Telephon, etc.; 2**graf** [~'gra:f] m
(-en/-en) *etc.* s. *Telegraph, etc.*;
~**gramm** [~'gram] n (-s/-e) telegram, wire; *overseas*: cable(gram).

Telegraph [tele'gra:f] m (-en/-en)
telegraph; 2**enamt** [~ən-] n telegraph office; 2**ieren** [~'fi:rən] *v/t.
and v/i.* (*no -ge-*, h) telegraph, wire;
overseas: cable; 2**isch** [~'gra:fiʃ]
1. *adj.* telegraphic; 2. *adv.* by telegram, by wire; by cable; '~**ist**
[~a'fist] m (-en/-en), ~**istin** f (-/-nen)

telegraph operator, telegrapher, telegraphist.

Teleobjektiv *phot.* ['te:le-] *n* telephoto lens.

Telephon [tele'fo:n] *n* (-s/-e) telephone, F phone; *am ~* on the (tele)phone; *ans ~ gehen* answer the (tele)phone; *~ haben* be on the (tele)phone; *~anschluß m* telephone connexion *or* connection; *~buch n* telephone directory; *~gespräch n* (tele)phone call; conversation *or* chat over the (tele)phone; *~hörer m* (telephone) receiver, handset; **2ieren** [~o'ni:rən] *v/i.* (*no -ge-, h*) telephone, F phone; *mit j-m ~ ring s.o. up, Am.* call s.o. up; **2isch** *adv.* [~'fo:niʃ] by (tele)phone, over the (tele)phone; *~ist* [~o'nist] *m* (-en/-en), *~istin f* (-/-nen) (telephone) operator, telephonist; *~vermittlung f* s. *Telephonzentrale; ~zelle f* telephone kiosk *or* box, call-box, *Am.* telephone booth; *~zentrale f* (telephone) exchange.

Teleskop *opt.* [tele'sko:p] *n* (-s/-e) telescope.

Teller ['tɛlər] *m* (-s/-) plate.

Tempel ['tɛmpəl] *m* (-s/-) temple.

Temperament [tɛmpəra'mɛnt] *n* (-[e]s/-e) temper(ament); *fig.* spirit(s *pl.*); **2los** *adj.* spiritless; **2voll** *adj.* (high-)spirited.

Temperatur [tɛmpəra'tu:r] *f* (-/-en) temperature; *j-s ~ messen* take s.o.'s temperature.

Tempo ['tɛmpo] *n* (-s/-s, *Tempi*) time; pace; speed; rate.

Tendenz [tɛn'dɛnts] *f* (-/-en) tendency; trend; **2iös** *adj.* [~'tsjø:s] tendentious.

Tennis ['tɛnis] *n* (-/*no pl.*) (lawn) tennis; *'~ball m* tennis-ball; *'~platz m* tennis-court; *'~schläger m* (tennis-)racket; *'~spieler m* tennis player; *'~turnier n* tennis tournament.

Tenor ♪ [te'no:r] *m* (-s/-e) tenor.

Teppich ['tɛpiç] *m* (-s/-e) carpet; *'~kehrmaschine f* carpet-sweeper.

Termin [tɛr'mi:n] *m* (-s/-e) appointed time *or* day; ¾, † date, term; *sports:* fixture; *äußerster ~* final date, dead(-)line; *~geschäfte* † *n/pl.* futures *pl.*; *~kalender m* appointment book *or* pad; ¾ causelist, *Am.* calendar; *~liste* ¾ *f* causelist, *Am.* calendar.

Terpentin [tɛrpən'ti:n] *n* (-s/-e) turpentine.

Terrain [tɛ'rɛ̃:] *n* (-s/-s) ground; plot; building site.

Terrasse [tɛ'rasə] *f* (-/-n) terrace; **2nförmig** *adj.* [~nfœrmiç] terraced, in terraces.

Terrine [tɛ'ri:nə] *f* (-/-n) tureen.

Territorium [tɛri'to:rjum] *n* (-s/*Territorien*) territory.

Terror ['tɛror] *m* (-s/*no pl.*) terror; **2isieren** [~ori'zi:rən] *v/t.* (*no -ge-, h*) terrorize.

Terz ♪ [tɛrts] *f* (-/-en) third; *~ett ♪* [~'tsɛt] *n* (-[e]s/-e) trio.

Testament [tɛsta'mɛnt] *n* (-[e]s/-e) (last) will, (*often:* last will and) testament; *eccl.* Testament; **2arisch** [~'ta:riʃ] **1.** *adj.* testamentary; **2.** *adv.* by will; *~svollstrecker m* (-s/-) executor; *officially:* administrator.

testen ['tɛstən] *v/t.* (ge-, *h*) test.

teuer *adj.* ['tɔyər] dear (*a. fig.*), expensive; *wie ~ ist es?* how much is it?

Teufel ['tɔyfəl] *m* (-s/-) devil; *der ~* the Devil, Satan; *zum ~!* F dickens!, hang it!; *wer zum ~?* F who the devil *or* deuce?; *der ~ ist los* the fat's in the fire; *scher dich zum ~!* F go to hell!, go to blazes!; *~ei* [~'lai] *f* (-/-en) devilment, mischief, devilry, *Am.* deviltry; *'~skerl* F *m* devil of a fellow.

'teuflisch *adj.* devilish, diabolic(al).

Text [tɛkst] *m* (-es/-e) text; words *pl.* (*of song*); book, libretto (*of opera*); *'~buch n* book; libretto.

Textil|ien [tɛks'ti:ljən] *pl.*, *~waren pl.* textile fabrics *pl.*, textiles *pl.*

'textlich *adv.* concerning the text.

Theater [te'a:tər] *n* **1.** (-s/-) theat|re, *Am.* -er; stage; **2.** F (-s/*no pl.*) playacting; *~besucher m* playgoer; *~karte f* theatre ticket; *~kasse f* box-office; *~stück n* play; *~vorstellung f* theatrical performance; *~zettel m* playbill.

theatralisch *adj.* [tea'tra:liʃ] theatrical, stagy.

Theke ['te:kə] *f* (-/-n) *at inn:* bar, *Am. a.* counter; *at shop:* counter.

Thema ['te:ma] *n* (-s/*Themen, Themata*) theme, subject; topic (*of discussion*).

Theolog|e [teo'lo:gə] *m* (-n/-n) theologian, divine; *~ie* [~o'gi:] *f* (-/-n) theology.

Theoret|iker [teo're:tikər] *m* (-s/-) theorist; **2isch** *adj.* theoretic(al).

Theorie [teo'ri:] *f* (-/-n) theory.

Therapie [tera'pi:] *f* (-/-n) therapy. [spa.]

Thermalbad [tɛr'ma:l-] *n* thermal]

Thermometer [tɛrmo'-] *n* (-s/-) thermometer; *~stand m* (thermometer) reading.

Thermosflasche ['tɛrmɔs-] *f* vacuum bottle *or* flask, thermos (flask).

These ['te:zə] *f* (-/-n) thesis.

Thrombose ♂ [trɔm'bo:zə] *f* (-/-n) thrombosis.

Thron [tro:n] *m* (-[e]s/-e) throne; *'~besteigung f* accession to the throne; *~erbe m* heir to the throne, heir apparent; *'~folge f* succession to the throne; *'~folger m* (-s/-) successor to the throne; *~rede parl. f* Queen's *or* King's Speech.

Thunfisch *ichth.* ['tu:n-] *m* tunny, tuna.

Tick F [tik] *m* (-[e]s/-s, -e) crotchet, fancy, kink; e-n ~ haben have a bee in one's bonnet.

ticken ['tikən] *v/i.* (ge-, h) tick.

tief [ti:f] **1.** *adj.* deep (*a. fig.*); *fig.*: profound; low; *im ~sten Winter* in the dead *or* depth of winter; **2.** *adv.*: *bis ~ in die Nacht* far into the night; *das läßt ~ blicken* that speaks volumes; *zu ~ singen* sing flat; **3.** ♀ *meteor. n* (-[e]s/-s) depression, low(-pressure area); '♀**bau** *m* civil *or* underground engineering; '♀**druckgebiet** *meteor. n s. Tief;* '♀**e** *f* (-/-n) depth (*a. fig.*); *fig.* profundity; '♀**ebene** *f* low plain, lowland; '♀**enschärfe** *phot. f* depth of focus; '♀**flug** *m* low-level flight; '♀**gang** ♃ *m* draught, *Am.* draft; ~**gebeugt** *fig. adj.* ['~gəbɔʏkt] deeply afflicted, bowed down; ~**gekühlt** *adj.* deep-frozen; ~**greifend** *adj.* fundamental, radical; ♀**land** *n* lowland(s *pl.*); '~**liegend** *adj. eyes:* sunken; *fig.* deep-seated; '♀**schlag** *m boxing:* low hit; '~**schürfend** *fig. adj.* profound; thorough; '♀**see** *f* deep sea; '~**sinnig** *adj.* thoughtful, pensive; F melancholy; '♀**stand** *m* (-[e]s/*no pl.*) low level.

Tiegel ['ti:gəl] *m* (-s/-) saucepan, stew-pan; ⊕ crucible.

Tier [ti:r] *n* (-[e]s/-e) animal; beast; brute; *großes ~ fig. sl.* bigwig, big bug, *Am.* big shot; '~**arzt** *m* veterinary (surgeon), F vet, *Am. a.* veterinarian; '~**garten** *m* zoological gardens *pl.*, zoo; '~**heilkunde** *f* veterinary medicine; '♀**isch** *adj.* animal; *fig.* bestial, brutish, savage; '~**kreis** *ast. m* zodiac; ~**quälerei** [~kvɛːləˈraɪ] *f* (-/-en) cruelty to animals; '~**reich** *n* (-[e]s/*no pl.*) animal kingdom; '~**schutzverein** *m* Society for the Prevention of Cruelty to Animals.

Tiger *zo.* ['ti:gər] *m* (-s/-) tiger; '~**in** *zo. f* (-/-nen) tigress.

tilgen ['tilgən] *v/t.* (ge-, h) extinguish; efface; wipe *or* blot out, erase; *fig.* obliterate; annul, cancel; discharge, pay (*debt*); redeem (*mortgage, etc.*); '♀**ung** *f* (-/-en) extinction; extermination; cancel(l)ing; discharge, payment; redemption.

Tinktur [tiŋkˈtu:r] *f* (-/-en) tincture. *[sitzen* F be in a scrape.*]*

Tinte ['tintə] *f* (-/-n) ink; *in der ~]*

'**Tinten|faß** *n* ink-pot, desk: inkwell; '~**fisch** *ichth. m* cuttle-fish; '~**fleck** *m,* '~**klecks** *m* (ink-)blot; '~**stift** *m* indelible pencil.

Tip [tip] *m* (-s/-s) hint, tip; '♀**pen** (ge-, h) **1.** *v/i.* F type; *fig.* guess; *j-m auf die Schulter ~* tap s.o. on his shoulder; **2.** *v/t.* tip; foretell, predict; F type.

Tiroler [tiˈrö:lər] **1.** *m* (-s/-) Tyrolese; **2.** *adj.* Tyrolese.

Tisch [tiʃ] *m* (-es/-e) table; *bei ~* at table; *den ~ decken* lay the table *or* cloth, set the table; *reinen ~ machen* make a clean sweep (*damit of it*); *zu ~ bitten* invite *or* ask to dinner *or* supper; *bitte zu ~!* dinner is ready!; '~**decke** *f* tablecloth; '♀**fertig** *adj.* food: ready-prepared; '~**gast** *m* guest; '~**gebet** *n*: *das ~ sprechen* say grace; '~**gesellschaft** *f* dinner-party; '~**gespräch** *n* table-talk; '~**lampe** *f* table-lamp; desk lamp.

Tischler ['tiʃlər] *m* (-s/-) joiner; carpenter; cabinet-maker; ~**ei** [~'rai] *f* (-/-en) joinery; joiner's workshop.

'**Tisch|platte** *f* top (of a table), table top; leaf (*of extending table*); '~**rede** *f* toast, after-dinner speech; '~**tennis** *n* table tennis, ping-pong; '~**tuch** *n* table-cloth; '~**zeit** *f* dinner-time.

Titan [tiˈta:n] *m* (-en/-en) Titan; ♀**isch** *adj.* titanic.

Titel ['ti:təl] *m* (-s/-) title; e-n ~ (*inne*)*haben sports:* hold a title; '~**bild** *n* frontispiece; cover picture (*of magazine, etc.*); '~**blatt** *n* title-page; cover (*of magazine*); '~**halter** *m* (-s/-) *sports:* title-holder; '~**kampf** *m boxing:* title fight; '~**rolle** *thea. f* title-role.

titulieren [titu'li:rən] *v/t.* (*no -ge-, h*) style, call, address as.

Toast [to:st] *m* (-es/-e, -s) toast (*a. fig.*).

tob|en ['to:bən] *v/i.* (ge-, h) rage, rave, storm, bluster; *children:* romp; ♀**sucht** ♂ (-/*no pl.*) raving madness, frenzy; ~**süchtig** *adj.* ['to:p-] raving mad, frantic.

Tochter ['tɔxtər] *f* (-/⸚) daughter; '~**gesellschaft** ♀ *f* subsidiary company.

Tod [to:t] *m* (-[e]s/⸚ -e) death; ⁂ decease.

Todes|angst ['to:dəsˀ-] *f* mortal agony; *fig.* mortal fear; *Todesängste ausstehen* be scared to death, be frightened out of one's wits; '~**anzeige** *f* obituary (notice); '~**fall** *m* (case of) death; *Todesfälle pl.* deaths *pl.,* ⚔ casualties *pl.*; '~**kampf** *m* death throes *pl.*, mortal agony; '~**strafe** *f* capital punishment, death penalty; *bei ~ verboten* forbidden on *or* under pain *or* penalty of death; '~**ursache** *f* cause of death; '~**urteil** *n* death *or* capital sentence, death-warrant.

'**Tod|feind** *m* deadly *or* mortal enemy; '♀**krank** *adj.* dangerously ill.

tödlich *adj.* ['tø:tliç] deadly; fatal; *wound: a.* mortal.

'**tod|'müde** *adj.* dead tired; '~

'schick F adj. dashing, gorgeous; '~sicher F adj. cock-sure; '2sünde f deadly or mortal sin.

Toilette [toa'letə] f (-/-n) dress(ing): toilet; lavatory, gentlemen's or ladies' room, esp. Am. toilet.

Toi'letten|artikel m/pl. toilet articles pl., Am. a. toiletry; ~papier n toilet-paper; ~tisch m toilet (-table), dressing-table, Am. a. dresser.

toleran|t adj. [tole'rant] tolerant (gegen of); 2z [~ts] f 1. (-/no pl.) tolerance, toleration (esp. eccl.); 2. ⊕ (-/-en) tolerance, allowance.

toll [tɔl] 1. adj. (raving) mad, frantic; mad, crazy, wild (all a. fig.); fantastic; noise, etc.: frightful, F awful; das ist ja ~ F that's (just) great; 2. adv.: es ~ treiben carry on like mad; es zu ~ treiben go too far; '~en v/i. (ge-, h, sein) children: romp; '2haus fig. n bedlam; '2heit f (-/-en) madness; mad trick; '~kühn adj. foolhardy, rash; '2wut vet. f rabies.

Tolpatsch F ['tɔlpatʃ] m (-es/-e) awkward or clumsy fellow; '2ig F adj. awkward, clumsy.

Tölpel F ['tœlpəl] m (-s/-) awkward or clumsy fellow; boob(y).

Tomate F [to'ma:tə] f (-/-n) tomato.

Ton¹ [to:n] m (-[e]s/-e) clay.

Ton² [~] m (-[e]s/-e) sound; ♪ tone (a. of language); ♪ single: note; accent, stress; fig. tone; paint. tone, tint, shade; guter ~ good form; den ~ angeben set the fashion; zum guten ~ gehören be the fashion; große Töne reden or F spucken F talk big, boast; '~abnehmer m pick-up; '2angebend adj. setting the fashion, leading; '~arm m pick-up arm (of record-player); '~art ♪ f key; '~band n recording tape; '~bandgerät n tape recorder.

tönen ['tø:nən] (ge-, h) 1. v/i. sound, ring; 2. v/t. tint, tone, shade.

tönern adj. ['tø:nərn] (of) clay, earthen.

'Ton|fall m in speaking: intonation, accent; '~film m sound film; '~lage f pitch; '~leiter ♪ f scale, gamut; '2los adj. soundless; fig. toneless; '~meister m sound engineer.

Tonne ['tɔnə] f (-/-n) large: tun; smaller: barrel, cask; ⚓ measure of weight: ton.

'Tonsilbe gr. f accented syllable.

Tonsur [tɔn'zu:r] f (-/-en) tonsure.

'Tönung paint. f (-/-en) tint, tinge, shade.

'Tonwaren f/pl. s. Töpferware.

Topf [tɔpf] m (-[e]s/~e) pot.

Töpfer ['tœpfər] m (-s/-) potter; stove-fitter; '~ei [~'raɪ] f (-/-en) pottery; '~ware f pottery, earthenware, crockery.

topp¹ int. [tɔp] done!, agreed!

Topp² ⚓ [~] m (-s/-e, -s) top, mast-head.

Tor¹ [to:r] n (-[e]s/-e) gate; gateway (a. fig.); football: goal; skiing: gate.

Tor² [~] m (-en/-en) fool.

Torf [tɔrf] m (-[e]s/no pl.) peat.

Torheit ['to:rhaɪt] f (-/-en) folly.

'Torhüter m gate-keeper; sports: goalkeeper.

töricht adj. ['tø:rɪçt] foolish, silly.

Törin ['tø:rɪn] f (-/-nen) fool(ish woman).

torkeln ['tɔrkəln] v/i. (ge-, h, sein) reel, stagger, totter.

'Tor|latte f sports: cross-bar; '~lauf m skiing: slalom; '~linie f sports: goal-line.

Tornister [tɔr'nɪstər] m (-s/-) knapsack; satchel.

torpedieren [tɔrpe'di:rən] v/t. (no -ge-, h) torpedo (a. fig.).

Torpedo [tɔr'pe:do] m (-s/-s) torpedo; ~boot n torpedo-boat.

'Tor|pfosten m gate-post; sports: goal-post; '~schuß m shot at the goal; '~schütze m sports: scorer.

Torte ['tɔrtə] f (-/-n) fancy cake, Am. layer cake; tart, Am. pie.

Tortur [tɔr'tu:r] f (-/-en) torture; fig. ordeal.

Tor|wart ['to:rvart] m (-[e]s/-e) sports: goalkeeper; '~weg m gateway.

tosen ['to:zən] v/i. (ge-, h, sein) roar, rage; '~d adj. applause: thunderous.

tot adj. [to:t] dead (a. fig.); deceased; ~er Punkt ⊕ dead centre, Am. -er; fig.: deadlock; fatigue; ~es Rennen sports: dead heat.

total adj. [to'ta:l] total, complete.

'tot|arbeiten v/refl. (sep., -ge-, h) work o.s. to death; '2e (-n/-n) 1. m dead man; (dead) body, corpse; die ~n pl. the dead pl., the deceased pl. or departed pl.; ⚔ casualties pl.; 2. f dead woman.

töten ['tø:tən] v/t. (ge-, h) kill; destroy; murder; deaden (nerve, etc.).

'Toten|bett n deathbed; '2blaß adj. deadly or deathly pale; '~blässe f deadly paleness or pallor; '2bleich adj. s. totenblaß; ~gräber ['~grɛ:bər] m (-s/-) grave-digger (a. zo.); '~hemd n shroud; '~kopf m death's-head (a. zo.); emblem of death: a. skull and cross-bones; '~liste f death-roll (a. ⚔), esp. ⚔ casualty list; '~maske f death-mask; '~messe eccl. f mass for the dead, requiem; '~schädel m death's-head, skull; '~schein m death certificate; '2still adj. (as) still as the grave; '~stille f dead(ly) silence, deathly stillness.

'tot|geboren adj. still-born; '2geburt f still birth; '~lachen v/refl. (sep., -ge-, h) die of laughing.

Toto ['to:to] *m*, F *a. n* (-*s*/-*s*) football pools *pl.*

'**tot|schießen** *v/t.* (*irr. schießen, sep., -ge-, h*) shoot dead, kill; '**Qschlag** *gtg m* manslaughter, homicide; '**Qschlagen** *v/t.* (*irr. schlagen, sep., -ge-, h*) kill (*a. time*), slay; '**Qschweigen** *v/t.* (*irr. schweigen, sep., -ge-, h*) hush up; '**Qstechen** *v/t.* (*irr. stechen, sep., -ge-, h*) stab to death; '**Qstellen** *v/refl.* (*sep., -ge-, h*) feign death.

'**Tötung** *f* (-/-en) killing, slaying; *gtg* homicide; *fahrlässige* ~ *gtg* manslaughter.

Tour [tu:r] *f* (-/-en) tour; excursion, trip; ⊕ turn, revolution; *auf* ~*en kommen mot.* pick up speed; '~**en-wagen** *mot. m* touring car.

Tourist [tu'rist] *m* (-en/-en), ~**in** *f* (-/-nen) tourist.

Tournee [tur'ne:] *f* (-/-s, -n) tour.

Trab [tra:p] *m* (-[e]s/*no pl.*) trot.

Trabant [tra'bant] *m* (-en/-en) satellite.

trab|en ['tra:bən] *v/i.* (*ge-, h, sein*) trot; **Qrennen** ['tra:p-] *n* trotting race.

Tracht [traxt] *f* (-/-en) dress, costume; uniform; fashion; load; e-e (*gehörige*) ~ *Prügel* a (sound) thrashing; '**Qen** *v/i.* (*ge-, h*): ~ *nach et.* strive for; *j-m nach dem Leben* ~ seek s.o.'s life.

trächtig *adj.* ['treçtiç] (big) with young, pregnant. [tradition.)

Tradition [tradi'tsjo:n] *f* (-/-en))

traf [tra:f] *pret. of* treffen.

Trag|bahre ['tra:k-] *f* stretcher, litter; '**Qbar** *adj.* portable; *dress:* wearable; *fig.:* bearable; reasonable; ~*e* ['~gə] *f* (-/-n) hand-barrow; *s.* Tragbahre.

träge *adj.* ['tre:gə] lazy, indolent; *phys.* inert (*a. fig.*).

tragen ['tra:gən] (*irr., ge-, h*) **1.** *v/t.* carry; bear (*costs, name, responsibility, etc.*); bear, endure; support; bear, yield (*fruit,* ✝ *interest, etc.*); wear (*dress, etc.*); *bei sich* ~ have about one; *sich gut* ~ *material:* wear well; *zur Schau* ~ show off; **2.** *v/i. tree:* bear, yield; *gun, voice:* carry; *ice:* bear.

Träger ['tre:gər] *m* (-s/-) carrier; porter (*of luggage*); holder, bearer (*of name, licence, etc.*); wearer (*of dress*); (shoulder-)strap (*of slip, etc.*); ⊕ support; ⚠ girder.

Trag|fähigkeit ['tra:k-] *f* carrying or load capacity; ⚓ tonnage; '~**fläche** ✈ *f*, '~**flügel** ✈ *m* wing, plane.

Trägheit ['tre:khart] *f* (-/*no pl.*) laziness, indolence; *phys.* inertia (*a. fig.*).

tragisch *adj.* ['tra:giʃ] tragic (*a. fig.*); *fig.* tragical.

Tragödie [tra'gø:djə] *f* (-/-n) tragedy.

Trag|riemen ['tra:k-] *m* (carrying) strap; sling (*of gun*); '~**tier** *n* pack animal; '~**tüte** *f* carrier-bag; '~**weite** *f* range; *fig.* import(ance), consequences *pl.*; *von großer* ~ of great moment.

Train|er ['tre:nər] *m* (-s/-) trainer; coach; **Qieren** [~'ni:rən] (*no -ge-, h*) **1.** *v/t.* train; coach; **2.** *v/i.* train; ~**ing** ['~iŋ] *n* (-s/-s) training; '~**ings-anzug** *m sports:* track suit.

traktieren [trak'ti:rən] *v/t.* (*no -ge-, h*) treat (badly).

Traktor ⊕ ['traktɔr] *m* (-s/-en) tractor.

trällern ['trelərn] *v/t. and v/i.* (*ge-, h*) troll.

trampel|n ['trampəln] *v/i.* (*ge-, h*) trample, stamp; **Qpfad** *m* beaten track.

Tran [tra:n] *m* (-[e]s/-e) train-oil, whale-oil.

Träne ['tre:nə] *f* (-/-n) tear; *in* ~*n ausbrechen* burst into tears; **Qn** *v/i.* (*ge-, h*) water; '~**ngas** *n* tear-gas.

Trank [traŋk] **1.** *m* (-[e]s/-e) drink, beverage; *g* potion; **2.** ♀ *pret. of* trinken.

Tränke ['treŋkə] *f* (-/-n) watering-place; **Qn** *v/t.* (*ge-, h*) water (*animals*); soak, impregnate (*material*).

Trans|formator ⚡ [transfɔr'ma:-tɔr] *m* (-s/-en) transformer; ~**fusion** *g* [~u'zjo:n] *f* (-/-en) transfusion.

Transistorradio [tran'zistɔr-] *n* transistor radio *or* set.

transitiv *gr. adj.* ['tranziti:f] transitive.

transparent [transpa'rent] **1.** *adj.* transparent; **2.** ♀ *n* (-[e]s/-e) transparency; *in political processions, etc.:* banner.

transpirieren [transpi'ri:rən] *v/i.* (*no -ge-, h*) perspire.

Transplantation *g* [transplanta-'tsjo:n] *f* transplant (operation).

Transport [trans'pɔrt] *m* (-[e]s/-e) transport(ation), conveyance, carriage; **Qabel** *adj.* [~'ta:bəl] (trans-)portable; ~**er** *m* (-s/-) ⚓, ✈ (troop-)transport; ✈ transport (aircraft *or* plane); **Qfähig** *adj.* transportable, *sick person:* a. transferable; **Qieren** [~'ti:rən] *v/t.* (*no -ge-, h*) transport, convey, carry; ~**unternehmen** *n* carrier.

Trapez [tra'pe:ts] *n* (-es/-e) ⚠ trapezium, *Am.* trapezoid; *gymnastics:* trapeze.

trappeln ['trapəln] *v/i.* (*ge-, h, sein*) *horse:* clatter; *children, etc.:* patter.

Trass|ant [tra'sant] *m* (-en/-en) drawer; ~**at** ✝ [~'sa:t] *m* (-en/-en) drawee; ~**e** ⊕ *f* (-/-n) line; **Qieren** [~'si:rən] *v/t.* (*no -ge-, h*) ⊕ lay *or* trace out; ~ *auf* (*acc.*) ✝ draw on.

trat [tra:t] *pret. of* treten.

Tratte ✝ ['tratə] *f (-/-n)* draft.

Traube ['traubə] *f (-/-n)* bunch of grapes; grape; cluster; '**∼nsaft** *m* grape-juice; '**∼nzucker** *m* grape-sugar, glucose.

trauen ['trauən] *(ge-, h)* **1.** *v/t.* marry; *sich ∼ lassen* get married; **2.** *v/i.* trust *(j-m s.o.)*, confide *(dat. in)*; *ich traute meinen Ohren nicht* I could not believe my ears.

Trauer ['trauər] *f (-/no pl.)* sorrow, affliction; *for dead person:* mourning; '**∼botschaft** *f* sad news; '**∼fall** *m* death; '**∼feier** *f* funeral ceremonies *pl.,* obsequies *pl.;* '**∼flor** *m* mourning-crape; '**∼geleit** *n* funeral procession; '**∼gottesdienst** *m* funeral service; '**∼kleid** *n* mourning (-dress); '**∼marsch** *m* funeral march; '**2n** *v/i. (ge-, h)* mourn *(um* for); be in mourning; '**∼spiel** *n* tragedy; '**∼weide** ♀ *f* weeping willow; '**∼zug** *m* funeral procession.

Traufe ['traufə] *f (-/-n)* eaves *pl.;* gutter; *s. Regen².*

träufeln ['trɔyfəln] *v/t. (ge-, h)* drop, drip, trickle.   [cosy, snug.|

traulich *adj.* ['trauliç] intimate;|

Traum [traum] *m (-[e]s/ⁿe)* dream *(a. fig.)*; reverie; *das fällt mir nicht im ∼ ein!* I would not dream of (doing) it!; '**∼bild** *n* vision; '**∼deuter** *m (-s/-)* dream-reader.

träum|en ['trɔymən] *v/i. and v/t. (ge-, h)* dream; '**2er** *m (-s/-)* dreamer *(a. fig.)*; '**2erei** [∼'raɪ] *f (-/-en)* dreaming; *fig. a.* reverie *(a. ♪)*, day-dream, musing; '**∼erisch** *adj.* dreamy; musing.

traurig *adj.* ['trauriç] sad *(über acc. at)*, *Am.* F blue; wretched.

'**Trau|ring** *m* wedding-ring; '**∼schein** *m* marriage certificate *or* lines *pl.;* '**∼ung** *f (-/-en)* marriage, wedding; '**∼zeuge** *m* witness to a marriage.

Trecker ⊕ ['trekər] *m (-s/-)* tractor.

Treff [tref] *n (-s/-s) cards:* club(s *pl.*).

treffen¹ ['trefən] *(irr., ge-)* **1.** *v/t. (h)* hit *(a. fig.)*, strike; concern, *disadvantageously:* affect; meet; *nicht ∼* miss; *e-e Entscheidung ∼* come to a decision; *Maßnahmen ∼* take measures *or* steps; *Vorkehrungen ∼* take precautions *or* measures; *sich ∼* happen; meet; gather, assemble; *a.* have an appointment *(mit* with), F have a date (with); *das trifft sich gut!* that's lucky!, how fortunate!; *sich getroffen fühlen* feel hurt; *wen trifft die Schuld?* who is to blame?; *das Los traf ihn* the lot fell on him; *du bist gut getroffen paint., phot.* this is a good likeness of you; *vom Blitz getroffen* struck by lightning; **2.** *v/i. (h)* hit; **3.** *v/i. (sein): ∼ auf (acc.)* meet with; encounter *(a. ✗)*.

Treffen² [∼] *n (-s/-)* meeting; rally; gathering; ✗ encounter; '**2d** *adj. remark:* appropriate, to the point.

'**Treff|er** *m (-s/-)* hit *(a. fig.)*; prize; '**∼punkt** *m* meeting-place.

Treibeis ['traɪp⁹-] *n* drift-ice.

treiben¹ ['traɪbən] *(irr., ge-)* **1.** *v/t. (h)* drive; ⊕ put in motion, propel; drift *(smoke, snow)*; put forth *(leaves)*; force *(plants)*; *fig.* impel, urge, press *(j-n zu inf. s.o.* to *inf.*); carry on *(business, trade)*; Musik *(Sport) ∼* go in for music (sports); *Sprachen ∼* study languages; *es zu weit ∼* go too far; *wenn er es weiterhin so treibt* if he carries *or* goes on like that; *was treibst du da?* what are you doing there?; **2.** *v/i. (sein)* drive; float, drift; **3.** *v/i. (h)* ♀ shoot; *dough:* ferment, work.

Treiben² [∼] *n (-s/no pl.)* driving; doings *pl.,* goings-on *pl.;* geschäftiges *∼* bustle; '**2d** *adj.: ∼e Kraft* driving force.

Treib|haus ['traɪp-] *n* hothouse; '**∼holz** *n* drift-wood; '**∼jagd** *f* battue; '**∼riemen** *m* driving-belt; '**∼stoff** *m* fuel; propell|ant, -ent *(of rocket)*.

trenn|en ['trenən] *v/t. (ge-, h)* separate, sever; rip *(seam)*; *teleph., ⚡* cut off, disconnect; isolate, segregate; *sich ∼* separate *(von* from), part *(from or with s.o.;* with *s.th.)*; '**2schärfe** *f radio:* selectivity; '**2ung** *f (-/-en)* separation; disconne|xion, -ction; segregation *(of races, etc.)*; '**2(ungs)wand** *f* partition (wall).   [(-bit.|

Trense ['trenzə] *f (-/-n)* snaffle|

Treppe ['trepə] *f (-/-n)* staircase, stairway, (e-e a flight *or* pair of) stairs *pl.;* zwei *∼n* hoch on the second floor, *Am.* on the third floor.

'**Treppen|absatz** *m* landing; '**∼geländer** *n* banisters *pl.;* '**∼haus** *n* staircase; '**∼stufe** *f* stair, step.

Tresor [tre'zo:r] *m (-s/-e)* safe; *bank:* strong-room, vault.

treten ['tre:tən] *(irr., ge-)* **1.** *v/i. (h)* tread, step *(j-n or j-m auf die Zehen* on s.o.'s toes); **2.** *v/i. (sein)* tread, step *(j-m auf die Zehen* on s.o.'s toes); walk; *ins Haus ∼* enter the house; *j-m unter die Augen ∼* appear before s.o., face s.o.; *j-m zu nahe ∼* offend s.o.; *zu j-m ∼* step *or* walk up to s.o.; *über die Ufer ∼* overflow its banks; **3.** *v/t. (h)* tread; kick; *mit Füßen ∼* trample upon.

treu *adj.* [trɔy] faithful, loyal; '**2bruch** *m* breach of faith, perfidy; '**2e** *f (-/no pl.)* fidelity, faith(fulness), loyalty; '**2händer** ['∼hendər] *m (-s/-)* trustee; '**∼herzig** *adj.* guileless; ingenuous, simpleminded; '**∼los** *adj.* faithless *(gegen* to), disloyal (to); perfidious.

Tribüne [tri'by:nə] *f* (-/-n) platform; *sports, etc.*: (grand) stand.

Tribut [tri'bu:t] *m* (-[e]s/-e) tribute.

Trichter ['trictər] *m* (-s/-) funnel; *made by bomb, shell, etc.*: crater; horn (*of wind instruments, etc.*).

Trick [trik] *m* (-s/-e, -s) trick; '~film *m* animation, animated cartoon.

Trieb [tri:p] 1. *m* (-[e]s/-e) 💠 sprout, (new) shoot; driving force; impulse; instinct; (sexual) urge; desire; 2. ♀ *pret.* of **treiben**; '~feder *f* main-spring; *fig.* driving force, motive; '~kraft *f* motive power; *fig.* driving force, motive; '~wagen 🚋 *m* rail-car, rail-motor; '~werk ⊕ *n* gear (drive), (driving) mechanism, transmission; engine.

triefen ['tri:fən] *v/i.* (*irr.*, ge-, *h* and *sein*) drip (von with); *eye*: run.

triftig *adj.* ['triftiç] valid.

Trigonometrie ⚠ [trigonome'tri:] *f* (-/no pl.) trigonometry.

Trikot [tri'ko:] (-s/-s) 1. *m* stockinet; 2. *n* tights *pl.*; vest; ~agen [~o'ta:ʒən] *f/pl.* hosiery.

Triller ♪ ['trilər] *m* (-s/-) trill, shake, quaver; '~n ♪ *v/i.* and *v/t.* (ge-, *h*) trill, shake, quaver; *bird*: *a.* warble.

trink|bar *adj.* ['triŋkba:r] drinkable; '~becher *m* drinking-cup; '~en (*irr.*, ge-, *h*) 1. *v/t.* drink; take, have (*tea, etc.*); 2. *v/i.* drink; ~ auf (*acc.*) drink to, toast; '~er *m* (-s/-) drinker; drunkard; '~gelage *n* drinking-bout; '~geld *n* tip, gratuity; *j-m e-e Mark ~ geben* tip s.o. one mark; '~glas *n* drinking-glass; '~halle *f at spa*: pump-room; '~kur *f*: e-e ~ machen drink the waters; '~spruch *m* toast; '~wasser *n* (-s/no pl.) drinking-water.

Trio ['tri:o] *n* (-s/-s) trio (*a.* ♪).

trippeln ['tripəln] *v/i.* (ge-, *sein*) trip.

Tritt [trit] *m* (-[e]s/-e) tread, step; footprint; *noise*: footfall, (foot)step; kick; ⊕ treadle; *s. Trittbrett, Trittleiter*; *im (falschen)* ~ in (out of) step; ~ halten keep step; '~brett *n* step, footboard; *mot.* running-board; '~leiter *f* stepladder, (e-e *a* pair *or* set of) steps *pl.*

Triumph [tri'umf] *m* (-[e]s/-e) triumph; ~al *adj.* [~'fɑ:l] triumphant; ~bogen *m* triumphal arch; ~ieren [~'fi:rən] *v/i.* (no -ge-, *h*) triumph (*über acc.* over).

trocken *adj.* ['trɔkən] dry (*a. fig.*); *soil, land*: arid; '~dock ⚓ *n* dry dock; '~haube *f* (hood of) hairdrier; '~heit *f* (-/no pl.) dryness; drought, aridity; '~legen *v/t.* (sep., -ge-, *h*) dry up; drain (*land*); *change the napkins of, Am.* change the diapers of (*baby*); '~obst *n* dried fruit.

trocknen ['trɔknən] (ge-) 1. *v/i.* (sein) dry; 2. *v/t.* (*h*) dry.

Troddel ['trɔdəl] *f* (-/-n) tassel.

Trödel F ['trø:dəl] *m* (-s/no pl.) second-hand articles *pl.*; lumber, *Am.* junk; rubbish; '~n F *fig. v/i.* (ge-, *h*) dawdle, loiter.

Trödler ['trø:dlər] *m* (-s/-) second-hand dealer, *Am.* junk dealer, junkman; *fig.* dawdler, loiterer.

troff [trɔf] *pret.* of **triefen**.

Trog[1] [tro:k] *m* (-[e]s/-e) trough.

trog[2] [~] *pret.* of **trügen**.

Trommel ['trɔməl] *f* (-/-n) drum; ⊕ *a.* cylinder, barrel; '~fell *n* drumskin; *anat.* ear-drum; '~n *v/i.* and *v/t.* (ge-, *h*) drum.

Trommler ['trɔmlər] *m* (-s/-) drummer.

Trompete [trɔm'pe:tə] *f* (-/-n) trumpet; ~n *v/i.* and *v/t.* (no -ge-, *h*) trumpet; ~r *m* (-s/-) trumpeter.

Tropen ['tro:pən]: *die* ~ *pl.* the tropics *pl.*

Tropf F [trɔpf] *m* (-[e]s/-e) simpleton; *armer* ~ poor wretch.

tröpfeln ['trœpfəln] (ge-) 1. *v/i.* (h) drop, drip, trickle; *tap*: *a.* leak; *es tröpfelt rain*: a few drops are falling; 2. *v/i.* (sein): ~ aus *or* von trickle *or* drip from; 3. *v/t.* (h) drop, drip.

tropfen[1] ['trɔpfən] (ge-) 1. *v/i.* (h) drop, drip, trickle; *tap*: *a.* leak; *candle*: gutter; 2. *v/i.* (sein): ~ aus *or* von trickle *or* drip from; 3. *v/t.* (h) drop, drip.

Tropfen[2] [~] *m* (-s/-) drop; *ein* ~ *auf den heißen Stein* a drop in the ocean *or* bucket; ~förmig *adj.* ['~fœrmiç] drop-shaped; '~weise *adv.* drop by drop, by drops.

Trophäe [tro'fɛ:ə] *f* (-/-n) trophy.

tropisch *adj.* ['tro:piʃ] tropical.

Trosse ['trɔsə] *f* (-/-n) cable; ⚓ *a.* hawser.

Trost [tro:st] *m* (-es/no pl.) comfort, consolation; *das ist ein schlechter* ~ that is cold comfort; *du bist wohl nicht (recht) bei* ~! F you must be out of your mind!

tröst|en ['trø:stən] *v/t.* (ge-, *h*) console, comfort; *sich* ~ console o.s. (mit with); ~ Sie sich! be of good comfort!, cheer up!; '~lich *adj.* comforting.

'trost|los *adj.* disconsolate, inconsolable; *land, etc.*: desolate; *fig.* wretched; '~losigkeit *f* (-/no pl.) desolation; *fig.* wretchedness; '~preis *m* consolation prize, booby prize; '~reich *adj.* consolatory, comforting.

Trott [trɔt] *m* (-[e]s/-e) trot; F *fig.* jogtrot, routine; '~el F *m* (-s/-) idiot, fool, ninny; '~en *v/i.* (ge-, *sein*) trot.

trotz [trɔts] 1. *prp.* (*gen.*) in spite of, despite; ~ alledem for all that; 2. ♀ *m* (-es/no pl.) defiance; obstinacy; **~dem** *cj.* ['~de:m] never-theless; (al)though; '**~en** *v/i.* (ge-, h) (*dat.*) defy, dare; brave (*danger*); be obstinate; sulk; '**~ig** *adj.* defiant; obstinate; sulky.

trüb *adj.* [try:p], **~e** *adj.* ['~bə] *liquid*: muddy, turbid, thick; *mind, thinking*: confused, muddy, turbid; *eyes, etc.*: dim, dull; *weather*: dull, cloudy, dreary (*all a. fig.*); *experiences*: sad.

Trubel ['tru:bəl] *m* (-s/*no pl.*) bustle.

trüben ['try:bən] *v/t.* (ge-, h) make thick *or* turbid *or* muddy; dim; darken; spoil (*pleasures, etc.*); blur (*view*); dull (*mind*); *sich ~ liquid*: become thick *or* turbid *or* muddy; dim, darken; *relations*: become strained.

Trüb|sal ['try:pza:l] *f* (-/~-e): ~ *blasen* mope, F be in the dumps, have the blues; '**2selig** *adj.* sad, gloomy, melancholy; wretched, miserable; dreary; '**~sinn** *m* (-[e]s/ *no pl.*) melancholy, sadness, gloom; '**2sinnig** *adj.* melancholy, gloomy, sad; **~ung** ['~buŋ] *f* (-/-en) *liquid*: muddiness, turbidity (*both a. fig.*); dimming, darkening.

Trüffel ['tryfəl] *f* (-/-n), F *m* (-s/-) truffle.

Trug[1] [tru:k] *m* (-[e]s/*no pl.*) deceit, fraud; delusion (*of senses*).

trug[2] [~] *pret. of* tragen.

'**Trugbild** *n* phantom; illusion.

trüg|en ['try:gən] (*irr.*, ge-, h) **1.** *v/t.* deceive; **2.** *v/i.* be deceptive; '**~e-risch** *adj.* deceptive, delusive; treacherous.

'**Trugschluß** *m* fallacy, false conclusion.

Truhe ['tru:ə] *f* (-/-n) chest, trunk; *radio, etc.*: cabinet, console.

Trümmer ['trymər] *pl.* ruins *pl.*; rubble, debris; **&**, **&** wreckage; '**~haufen** *m* heap of ruins *or* rubble.

Trumpf [trumpf] *m* (-[e]s/~e) *cards*: trump (card) (*a. fig.*); *s-n ~ ausspielen* play one's trump card.

Trunk [truŋk] *m* (-[e]s/~e) drink; draught; drinking; '**2en** *adj.* drunken; *pred.* drunk (*a. fig. von, vor* with); intoxicated; **~enbold** *contp.* ['~bolt] *m* (-[e]s/-e) drunkard, sot; '**~enheit** *f* (-/*no pl.*) drunkenness, intoxication; *~ am Steuer* **🚗** drunken driving, drunkenness at the wheel; '**~sucht** *f* alcoholism, dipsomania; '**2süchtig** *adj.* addicted to drink, given to drinking.

Trupp [trup] *m* (-s/-s) troop, band, gang; **✕** detachment.

'**Truppe** *f* (-/-n) **✕** troop, body; **✕** unit; *thea.* company, troupe; **~n** *pl.* **✕** troops *pl.*, forces *pl.*; *die ~n pl.* **✕** the (fighting) services *pl.*, the armed forces *pl.*

'**Truppen|gattung** *f* arm, branch, division; '**~schau** *f* military review;

'**~transporter** **&**, **✈** *m* (troop-) transport; '**~übungsplatz** *m* training area.

Truthahn *orn.* ['tru:t-] *m* turkey (-cock).

Tschech|e ['tʃɛçə] *m* (-n/-n), '**~in** *f* (-/-nen) Czech; '**2isch** *adj.* Czech.

Tube ['tu:bə] *f* (-/-n) tube.

tuberkul|ös **&** *adj.* [tuberku'lø:s] tuberculous, tubercular; **2ose** **&** [~o:zə] *f* (-/-n) tuberculosis.

Tuch [tu:x] *n* **1.** (-[e]s/-e) cloth; fabric; **2.** (-[e]s/~er) *head covering*: kerchief; shawl, scarf; *round neck*: neckerchief; duster; rag; '**~fühlung** *f* (-/*no pl.*) close touch.

tüchtig ['tyçtiç] **1.** *adj.* able, fit; clever; proficient; efficient; excellent; good; thorough; **2.** *adv.* vigorously; thoroughly; F awfully; '**2keit** *f* (-/*no pl.*) ability, fitness; cleverness; proficiency; efficiency; excellency.

'**Tuchwaren** *f/pl.* drapery, cloths *pl.*

Tück|e ['tykə] *f* (-/-n) malice, spite; '**2isch** *adj.* malicious, spiteful; treacherous.

tüfteln F ['tyftəln] *v/i.* (ge-, h) puzzle (*an dat.* over).

Tugend ['tu:gənt] *f* (-/-en) virtue; **~bold** ['~bolt] *m* (-[e]s/-e) paragon of virtue; '**2haft** *adj.* virtuous.

Tüll [tyl] *m* (-s/-e) tulle.

Tulpe ['tulpə] *f* (-/-n) tulip.

tummel|n ['tuməln] *v/refl.* (ge-, h) *children*: romp; hurry; bestir o.s.; '**2platz** *m* playground; *fig.* arena.

Tümmler ['tymlər] *m* (-s/-) *orn.* tumbler; *zo.* porpoise.

Tumor **&** ['tu:mɔr] *m* (-s/-en) tumo(u)r.

Tümpel ['tympəl] *m* (-s/-) pool.

Tumult [tu'mult] *m* (-[e]s/-e) tumult; riot, turmoil, uproar; row.

tun [tu:n] **1.** *v/t.* (*irr.*, ge-, h) do; make; put (*to school, into the bag, etc.*); *dazu ~* add to it; contribute; *ich kann nichts dazu ~* I cannot help it; *es ist mir darum zu ~* I am anxious about (it); *zu ~ haben* have to do; be busy; *es tut nichts* it doesn't matter; **2.** *v/i.* (*irr.*, ge-, h) do; make; *so ~ als ob* make as if; pretend to *inf.*; *das tut gut!* that is a comfort!; that's good!; **3.** **2** *n* (-s/*no pl.*) doings *pl.*; proceedings *pl.*; action; *~ und Treiben* ways and doings *pl.*

Tünche ['tynçə] *f* (-/-n) whitewash (*a. fig.*); '**2n** *v/t.* (ge-, h) whitewash.

Tunichtgut ['tu:niçtgu:t] *m* (-, -[e]s/-e) ne'er-do-well, good-for-nothing.

Tunke ['tuŋkə] *f* (-/-n) sauce; '**2n** *v/t.* (ge-, h) dip, steep.

tunlichst *adv.* ['tu:nliçst] if possible.

Tunnel ['tunəl] *m* (-s/-, -s) tunnel; subway.

Tüpfel ['typfəl] *m, n* (-s/-) dot, spot; '**₂n** *v/t.* (ge-, h) dot, spot.

tupfen ['tupfən] **1.** *v/t.* (ge-, h) dab; dot, spot; **2.** **♀** *m* (-s/-) dot, spot.

Tür [ty:r] *f* (-/-en) door; *mit der ~ ins Haus fallen* blurt (things) out; *j-n vor die ~ setzen* turn s.o. out; *vor der ~ stehen* be near *or* close at hand; *zwischen ~ und Angel* in passing; '**~angel** *f* (door-)hinge.

Turbine ⊕ [tur'bi:nə] *f* (-/-n) turbine; **~nflugzeug** *n* turbo-jet.

Turbo-Prop-Flugzeug ['turbo-'prɔp-] *n* turbo-prop.

'**Tür|flügel** *m* leaf (of a door); '**~füllung** *f* (door-)panel; '**~griff** *m* door-handle.

Türk|e ['tyrkə] *m* (-n/-n) Turk; '**~in** *f* (-/-nen) Turk(ish woman); **~is** *min.* [~'ki:s] *m* (-es/-e) turquoise; **2isch** *adj.* Turkish.

'**Türklinke** *f* door-handle; latch.

Turm [turm] *m* (-[e]s/ⁱ-e) tower; *a.* steeple (*of church*); *chess*: castle, rook.

Türm|chen ['tyrmçən] *n* (-s/-) turret; '**2en** (ge-) **1.** *v/t.* (h) pile up; *sich ~* tower; **2.** F *v/i.* (sein) bolt, F skedaddle, *Am. sl. a.* skiddoo.

'**turm|hoch** *adv.*: *j-m ~ überlegen sein* stand head and shoulders above s.o.; '**2spitze** *f* spire; '**2-springen** *n* (-s/*no pl.*) swimming: high diving; '**2uhr** *f* tower-clock; church-clock.

turnen ['turnən] **1.** *v/i.* (ge-, h) do gymnastics; **2.** **♀** *n* (-s/*no pl.*) gymnastics *pl.*

'**Turn|er** *m* (-s/-), '**~erin** *f* (-/-nen) gymnast; '**~gerät** *n* gymnastic apparatus; '**~halle** *f* gym(nasium); '**~hemd** *n* (gym-)shirt; '**~hose** *f* shorts *pl.*

Turnier [tur'ni:r] *n* (-s/-e) tournament.

'**Turn|lehrer** *m* gym master; '**~lehrerin** *f* gym mistress; '**~schuh** *m* gym-shoe; '**~stunde** *f* gym lesson; '**~unterricht** *m* instruction in gymnastics; '**~verein** *m* gymnastic *or* athletic club.

'**Tür|pfosten** *m* door-post; '**~rahmen** *m* door-case, door-frame; '**~schild** *n* door-plate.

Tusche ['tuʃə] *f* (-/-n) India(n) *or* Chinese ink; '**2n** *v/t.* (ge-, h) whisper; '**2n** *v/t.* (ge-, h) draw in India(n) ink.

Tüte ['ty:tə] *f* (-/-n) paper-bag.

tuten ['tu:tən] *v/i.* (ge-, h) toot(le); *mot.* honk, blow one's horn.

Typ [ty:p] *m* (-s/-en) type; ⊕ *a.* model; **~e** *f* (-/-n) *typ.* type; F *fig.* (queer) character.

Typhus 𝒔 ['ty:fus] *m* (-/*no pl.*) typhoid (fever).

'**typisch** *adj.* typical (*für* of).

Tyrann [ty'ran] *m* (-en/-en) tyrant; **~ei** [~'naɪ] *f* (-/*no pl.*) tyranny; **2isch** *adj.* [ty'raniʃ] tyrannical; **2isieren** [~i'zi:rən] *v/t.* (*no* -ge-, h) tyrannize (over) *s.o.*, oppress, bully.

U

U-Bahn ['u:-] *f s. Untergrundbahn.*

übel ['y:bəl] **1.** *adj.* evil, bad; *nicht ~* not bad, pretty good; *mir ist ~* I am *or* feel sick; **2.** *adv.* ill; *~ gelaunt sein* be in a bad mood; *es gefällt mir nicht ~* I rather like it; **3.** **♀** *n* (-s/-) evil; *s.* Übelstand; *das kleinere ~ wählen* choose the lesser evil; '**~gelaunt** *adj.* ill-humo(u)red; '**2keit** *f* (-/-en) sickness, nausea; '**~nehmen** *v/t.* (*irr. nehmen, sep.*, -ge-, h) take *s.th.* ill *or* amiss; '**2stand** *m* grievance; '**2täter** *m* evil-doer, wrongdoer.

'**übelwollen** **1.** *v/i.* (*sep.*, -ge-, h): *j-m ~* wish s.o. ill; be ill-disposed towards s.o.; **2.** **♀** *n* (-s/*no pl.*) ill will, malevolence; '**~d** *adj.* malevolent.

üben ['y:bən] (ge-, h) **1.** *v/t.* exercise; practi|se, *Am. a.* -ce; *Geduld ~* exercise patience; *Klavier ~* practise the piano; **2.** *v/i.* exercise; practi|se, *Am. a.* -ce.

über ['y:bər] **1.** *prp.* (*dat.; acc.*) over, above; across (*river, etc.*); via,

by way of (*Munich, etc.*); *sprechen ~* (*acc.*) talk about *or* of; *~ Politik sprechen* talk politics; *nachdenken ~* (*acc.*) think about *or* of; *ein Buch schreiben ~* (*acc.*) write a book on; *~ Nacht bleiben bei* stay overnight at; *~ s-e Verhältnisse leben* live beyond one's income; *~ kurz oder lang* sooner *or* later; **2.** *adv.*: *die ganze Zeit ~* all along; *j-m in et. ~ sein* excel s.o. in s.th.

über'all *adv.* everywhere, anywhere, *Am. a.* all over.

über|'anstrengen *v/t.* (*no* -ge-, h) overstrain; *sich ~* overstrain o.s.; **~'arbeiten** *v/t.* (*no* -ge-, h) retouch (*painting, etc.*), revise (*book, etc.*); *sich ~* overwork o.s.

überaus *adv.* ['y:bər⁹-] exceedingly, extremely.

'**überbelichten** *phot. v/t.* (*no* -ge-, h) over-expose.

über'bieten *v/t.* (*irr. bieten, no* -ge-, h) *at auction*: outbid; *fig.*: beat; surpass.

Überbleibsel ['y:bərblaɪpsəl] *n*

(-s/-) remnant, *Am.* F *a.* holdover; ~ *pl. a.* remains *pl.*

'**Überblick** *fig. m* survey, general view (*both:* über *acc.* of).

über|'blicken *v/t.* (*no -ge-, h*) overlook; *fig.* survey, have a general view of; ~'**bringen** *v/t.* (*irr. bringen, no -ge-, h*) deliver; 2'**bringer** *m* (-s/-) bearer; ~'**brücken** *v/t.* (*no -ge-, h*) bridge; *fig.* bridge over *s.th.*; ~'**dachen** *v/t.* (*no -ge-, h*) roof over; ~'**dauern** *v/t.* (*no -ge-, h*) outlast, outlive; ~'**denken** *v/t.* (*irr. denken, no -ge-, h*) think *s.th.* over.

über|dies *adv.* besides, moreover.

über|drehen *v/t.* (*no -ge-, h*) overwind (*watch, etc.*); strip (*screw*).

'**Überdruck** *m* 1. (-[e]s/-e) overprint; ✝ *a.* surcharge; 2. ⊕ (-[e]s/~e) overpressure.

Über|druß ['y:bərdrus] *m* (Überdrusses/*no pl.*) satiety; *bis zum* ~ *to* satiety; 2**drüssig** *adj.* (*gen.*) ['~ysiç] disgusted with, weary *or* sick of.

Über|eifer ['y:bər²-] *m* over-zeal; 2**rig** *adj.* ['y:bər²-] over-zealous.

über|eil|en *v/t.* (*no -ge-, h*) precipitate, rush; *sich* ~ hurry too much; ~**t** *adj.* precipitate, rash.

übereinander *adv.* [y:bər²ai'nandər] one upon the other; ~**schlagen** *v/t.* (*irr. schlagen, sep., -ge-, h*) cross (*one's legs*).

über|ein|kommen *v/i.* (*irr. kommen, sep., -ge-, sein*) agree; 2**kommen** *n* (-s/-), 2**kunft** [~kunft] *f* (-/~e) agreement; ~**stimmen** *v/i.* (*sep., -ge-, h*) *p.* agree (*mit* with); *thing:* correspond (with; to); 2**stimmung** *f* agreement; correspondence; *in* ~ *mit* in agreement *or* accordance with.

über|fahren 1. ['~faːrən] *v/i.* (*irr. fahren, sep., -ge-, sein*) cross; 2. [~'faːrən] *v/t.* (*irr. fahren, no -ge-, h*) run over; disregard (*traffic sign, etc.*); 2**fahrt** *f* passage; crossing.

'**Überfall** *m* ✕ surprise; ✕ invasion (*auf acc.* of); ✕ raid; hold-up; assault ([up]on).

über|fallen *v/t.* (*irr. fallen, no -ge-, h*) ✕ surprise; ✕ invade; ✕ raid; hold up; assault.

über|fällig *adj.* overdue; 2**fallkommando** *n* flying squad, *Am.* riot squad.

über|fliegen *v/t.* (*irr. fliegen, no -ge-, h*) fly over *or* across; *fig.* glance over, skim (through); *den Atlantik* ~ fly (across) the Atlantic.

'**überfließen** *v/i.* (*irr. fließen, sep., -ge-, sein*) overflow.

über|flügeln *v/t.* (*no -ge-, h*) ✕ outflank; *fig.* outstrip, surpass.

'**Überfluß** *m* (Überflusses/*no pl.*) abundance (*an dat.* of); superfluity (of); ~ *haben an* (*dat.*) abound in;

2**flüssig** *adj.* superfluous; redundant.

über|'fluten *v/t.* (*no -ge-, h*) overflow, flood (*a. fig.*).

'**Überfracht** *f* excess freight.

über|führen *v/t.* 1. ['~fyːrən] (*sep., -ge-, h*) convey (*dead body*); 2. [~'fyːrən] (*no -ge-, h*) *s.* 1; ⅀ convict (*gen.* of); 2**führung** *f* (-/-en) conveyance (*of dead body*); bridge, *Am.* overpass; ⅀ conviction (*gen.* of).

'**Überfülle** *f* superabundance (*an*)

über|füllen *v/t.* (*no -ge-, h*) overfill; cram; overcrowd; *sich den Magen* ~ glut o.s.; ~'**füttern** *v/t.* (*no -ge-, h*) overfeed.

'**Übergabe** *f* delivery; handing over; surrender (*a.* ✕).

'**Übergang** *m* bridge; ⚇ crossing; *fig.* transition (*a.* ♪); *esp.* ⅀ devolution; ~**sstadium** *n* transition stage.

über|geben *v/t.* (*irr. geben, no -ge-, h*) deliver up; hand over; surrender (*a.* ✕); *sich* ~ vomit, be sick; ~**gehen** 1. ['~geːən] *v/i.* (*irr. gehen, sep., -ge-, sein*) pass over; *work, duties:* devolve (*auf acc.* [up]on); ~ *in* (*acc.*) pass into; ~ *zu et.* proceed to *s.th.*; 2. [~'geːən] *v/t.* (*irr. gehen, no -ge-, h*) pass over, ignore.

'**Übergewicht** *n* (-[e]s/*no pl.*) overweight; *fig. a.* preponderance (*über acc.* over).

über|gießen *v/t.* (*irr. gießen, no -ge-, h*): *mit Wasser* ~ pour water over *s.th.*; *mit Fett* ~ baste (*roasting meat*).

'**über|greifen** *v/i.* (*irr. greifen, sep., -ge-, h*): ~ *auf* (*acc.*) encroach (up)on (*s.o.'s rights*); *fire, epidemic, etc.:* spread to; 2**griff** *m* encroachment (*auf acc.* [up]on), inroad (on); ~**haben** F *v/t.* (*irr. haben, sep., -ge-, h*) have (*coat, etc.*) on; *fig.* have enough of, *sl.* be fed up with.

über|handnehmen *v/i.* (*irr. nehmen, sep., -ge-, h*) be rampant, grow *or* wax rife.

'**überhängen** 1. *v/i.* (*irr. hängen, sep., -ge-, h*) overhang; 2. *v/t.* (*sep., -ge-, h*) put (*coat, etc.*) round one's shoulders; sling (*rifle*) over one's shoulder.

über|häufen *v/t.* (*no -ge-, h*): ~ *mit* swamp with (*letters, work, etc.*); overwhelm with (*inquiries, etc.*).

über|haupt *adv.:* wer will denn ~ daß er kommt? who wants him to come anyhow?; *wenn* ~ if at all; ~ *nicht* not at all; ~ *kein* no ... whatever.

überheblich *adj.* [y:bər'heːpliç] presumptuous, arrogant; 2**keit** *f* (-/~-en) presumption; arrogance.

über|'hitzen *v/t.* (*no -ge-, h*) overheat (*a.* ✝); ⊕ superheat; ~'**holen** *v/t.* (*no -ge-, h*) overtake (*a. mot.*);

esp. sports: outstrip (*a. fig.*); over-haul, *esp. Am. a.* service; ~'holt *adj.* outmoded; *pred. a.* out of date; ~'hören *v/t.* (*no -ge-, h*) fail to hear, miss; ignore.

'**überirdisch** *adj.* supernatural; un-earthly.

'**überkippen** *v/i.* (*sep., -ge-, sein*) *p.* overbalance, lose one's balance.

über'kleben *v/t.* (*no -ge-, h*) paste over.

'**Überkleidung** *f* outer garments *pl.*

'**überklug** *adj.* would-be wise, sapient.

'**überkochen** *v/i.* (*sep., -ge-, sein*) boil over; F *leicht* ~ be very irritable.

über'kommen *v/t.* (*irr. kommen, no -ge-, h*): *Furcht überkam ihn he* was seized with fear; ~'laden *v/t.* (*irr. laden, no -ge-, h*) overload; overcharge (*battery, picture, etc.*).

'**Überland|flug** *m* cross-country flight; '~zentrale *⚡ f* long-distance power-station.

über'lassen *v/t.* (*irr. lassen, no -ge-, h*): *j-m et.* ~ let s.o. have s.th.; *fig.* leave s.th. to s.o.; *j-n sich selbst* ~ leave s.o. to himself; *j-n s-m Schicksal* ~ leave or abandon s.o. to his fate; ~'lasten *v/t.* (*no -ge-, h*) overload; *fig.* overburden.

über|laufen 1. ['~laufən] *v/i.* (*irr. laufen, sep., -ge-, sein*) run over; boil over; ✗ desert (*zu* to); **2.** [~'laufən] *v/t.* (*irr. laufen, no -ge-, h*): *es überlief mich kalt* a shudder passed over me; *überlaufen werden von doctor, etc.*: be besieged by (*patients, etc.*); **3.** *adj.* [~'laufən] *place, profession, etc.*: overcrowded; '2läufer *m* ✗ deserter; *pol.* renegade, turncoat.

'**überlaut** *adj.* too loud.

über'leben (*no -ge-, h*) **1.** *v/t.* survive, outlive; **2.** *v/i.* survive; 2de *m, f* (*-n/-n*) survivor.

'**überlebensgroß** *adj.* bigger than life-size(d).

überlebt *adj.* [y:bər'le:pt] outmoded, disused, out of date.

'**überlegen¹** F *v/t.* (*sep., -ge-, h*) give (*child*) a spanking.

über'leg|en² *v/t. and v/refl.* (*no -ge-, h*) consider, reflect upon, think about; *ich will es mir* ~ I will think it over; *es sich anders* ~ change one's mind; **2.** *v/i.* (*no -ge-, h*) *er überlegt noch* he hasn't made up his mind yet; **3.** *adj.* superior (*dat.* to; *an dat.* in); 2enheit *f* (*-/no pl.*) superiority; preponderance; ~t *adj.* [~kt] deliberate; prudent; 2ung [~guŋ] *f* (*-/-en*) consideration, reflection; *nach reiflicher* ~ after mature deliberation.

über'lesen *v/t.* (*irr. lesen, no -ge-, h*) read s.th. through quickly, run over s.th.; overlook.

über'liefer|n *v/t.* (*no -ge-, h*) hand down or on (*dat.* to); 2ung *f* tradition.

über'listen *v/t.* (*no -ge-, h*) outwit, F outsmart.

'**Über|macht** *f* (*-/no pl.*) superiority; *esp.* ✗ superior forces *pl.*; *in der* ~ *sein* be superior in numbers; '2mächtig *adj.* superior.

über'malen *v/t.* (*no -ge-, h*) paint out; ~'mannen *v/t.* (*no -ge-, h*) overpower, overcome, overwhelm (*all. a. fig.*).

'**Über|maß** *n* (*-es/no pl.*) excess (*an dat.* of); '2mäßig **1.** *adj.* excessive; immoderate; **2.** *adv.* excessively, *Am. a.* overly; ~ *trinken* drink to excess.

'**Übermensch** *m* superman; '2lich *adj.* superhuman.

über'mitt|eln *v/t.* (*no -ge-, h*) transmit; convey; 2lung *f* (*-/-en*) transmission; conveyance.

'**übermorgen** *adv.* the day after tomorrow.

über'müd|et *adj.* overtired; 2ung *f* (*-/⌐-en*) overfatigue.

'**Über|mut** *m* wantonness; frolicsomeness; 2mütig *adj.* ['~my:tiç] wanton; frolicsome.

'**übernächst** *adj.* the next but one; ~e *Woche* the week after next.

über'nacht|en *v/i.* (*no -ge-, h*) stay overnight (*bei at a friend's* [*house*], with *friends*), spend the night (at, with); 2ung *f* (*-/-en*) spending the night; ~ *und Frühstück* bed and breakfast.

Übernahme ['y:bərna:mə] *f* (*-/-n*) field of application *s.* übernehmen **1**: taking over; undertaking; assumption; adoption.

'**übernatürlich** *adj.* supernatural.

übernehmen *v/t.* **1.** [~'ne:mən] (*irr. nehmen, no -ge-, h*) take over (*business, etc.*); undertake (*responsibility, etc.*); take (*lead, risk, etc.*); assume (*direction of business, office, etc.*); adopt (*idea, custom, etc.*); *sich* ~ overreach o.s.; **2.** ✗ ['~ne:mən] (*irr. nehmen, sep., -ge-, h*) slope, shoulder (*arms*).

'**über|ordnen** *v/t.* (*sep., -ge-, h*): *j-n j-m* ~ set s.o. over s.o.; '~parteilich *adj.* non-partisan; '2produktion *f* over-production.

über'prüf|en *v/t.* (*no -ge-, h*) reconsider; verify; check; review; screen *s.o.*; 2ung *f* reconsideration; checking; review.

über'queren *v/t.* (*no -ge-, h*) cross; ~'ragen (*no -ge-, h*) tower above (*a. fig.*), overtop; *fig.* surpass.

überrasch|en [y:bər'raʃən] *v/t.* (*no -ge-, h*) surprise; catch (*bei at, in*); 2ung *f* (*-/-en*) surprise.

über'red|en *v/t.* (*no -ge-, h*) persuade (*zu inf.* to *inf.*, into *ger.*);

talk (into *ger.*); 2ung *f* (-/ℛ-en)
persuasion.

über'reich|en *v/t.* (*no* -ge-, *h*)
present; 2ung *f* (-/ℛ-en) presentation.

über|'reizen *v/t.* (*no* -ge-, *h*) over-
excite; ~'reizt *adj.* overstrung;
~'rennen *v/t.* (*irr.* rennen, *no* -ge-,
h) overrun.

'Überrest *m* remainder; ~e *pl.*
remains *pl.*; sterbliche ~e *pl.* mortal
remains *pl.*

über'rump|eln *v/t.* (*no* -ge-, *h*)
(take by) surprise; 2(e)lung *f*
(-/ℛ-en) surprise.

über'rund|en *v/t.* (*no* -ge-, *h*)
sports: lap; *fig.* surpass; 2ung *f*
(-/-en) lapping.

übersät *adj.* [y:bər'zɛ:t] studded,
dotted.

über'sättig|en *v/t.* (*no* -ge-, *h*)
surfeit (*a. fig.*); ⚗ supersaturate;
2ung *f* (-/-en) surfeit (*a. fig.*); ⚗
supersaturation.

'Überschallgeschwindigkeit *f* su-
personic speed.

über|'schatten *v/t.* (*no* -ge-, *h*)
overshadow (*a. fig.*); ~'schätzen
v/t. (*no* -ge-, *h*) overrate, overesti-
mate.

'Überschlag *m gymnastics:* somersault; ⚡ loop; ⚔ flashover; *fig.*
estimate, approximate calculation;
2en (*irr.* schlagen) 1. ['~ʃla:gən] *v/t.*
(*sep.*, -ge-, *h*) cross (*one's legs*);
2. ['~ʃla:gən] *v/i.* (*sep.*, -ge-, *sein*)
voice: become high-pitched; 3.
[~'ʃla:gən] *v/t.* (*no* -ge-, *h*) skip
(*page, etc.*); make a rough estimate
of (*cost, etc.*); sich ~ fall head over
heels; *car, etc.:* (be) turn(ed) over;
⚡ loop the loop; *voice:* become
high-pitched; sich ~ vor (*dat.*) outdo
(*one's friendliness, etc.*); 4. *adj.*
[~'ʃla:gən] lukewarm, tepid.

'überschnappen *v/i.* (*sep.*, -ge-,
sein) *voice:* become high-pitched;
F *p.* go mad, turn crazy.

über|'schneiden *v/refl.* (*irr.* schnei-
den, *no* -ge-, *h*) overlap; intersect;
~'schreiben *v/t.* (*irr.* schreiben, *no*
-ge-, *h*) superscribe; entitle; make
s.th. over (*dat.* to); ~'schreiten
v/t. (*irr.* schreiten, *no* -ge-, *h*) cross;
transgress (*limit, bound*); infringe
(*rule, etc.*); exceed (*speed limit, one's
instructions, etc.*); sie hat die 40 bereits überschritten she is on the
wrong side of 40.

'Über|schrift *f* heading, title;
headline; '~schuh *m* overshoe.

'Über|schuß *m* surplus, excess;
profit; 2schüssig *adj.* ['~ʃysiç]
surplus, excess.

über'schütten *v/t.* (*no* -ge-, *h*): ~
mit pour (*water, etc.*) on; *fig.:* overwhelm with (*inquiries, etc.*); shower
(*gifts, etc.*) upon.

überschwemm|en [y:bər'ʃvemən]

v/t. (*no* -ge-, *h*) inundate, flood
(*both a. fig.*); 2ung *f* (-/-en) inunda-
tion, flood(ing).

überschwenglich *adj.* ['y:bər-
ʃveŋliç] effusive, gushy.

'Übersee: nach ~ gehen go overseas; '~dampfer ⚓ *m* transoceanic
steamer; '~handel *m* (-s/*no pl.*)
oversea(s) trade.

über|'sehen *v/t.* (*irr.* sehen, *no* -ge-,
h) survey; overlook (*printer's error,
etc.*); *fig.* ignore, disregard.

über|'send|en *v/t.* (*irr.* senden,] *no*
-ge-, *h*) send, transmit; consign;
2ung *f* sending, transmission; ✝
consignment.

'übersetzen[1] (*sep.*, -ge-) 1. *v/i.* (*sein*)
cross; 2. *v/t.* (*h*) ferry.

über'setz|en[2] *v/t.* (*no* -ge-, *h*)
translate (*in acc.* into), render (into);
⊕ gear; 2er *m* (-s/-) translator;
2ung *f* (-/-en) translation (*aus
from; in acc.* into); rendering; ⊕
gear(ing), transmission.

'Übersicht *f* (-/-en) survey (*über
acc.* of); summary; 2lich *adj.*
clear(ly arranged).

über|siedeln ['y:bərzi:dəln] *v/i.*
(*sep.*, -ge-, *sein*) and [~'zi:dəln] *v/i.*
(*no* -ge-, *sein*) remove (nach to);
2siedelung [~'zi:dəluŋ] *f* (-/-en),
2siedlung ['~zi:dluŋ, ~'zi:dluŋ] *f*
(-/-en) removal (nach to).

'übersinnlich *adj.* transcendental;
forces: psychic.

über|'spann|en *v/t.* (*no* -ge-, *h*)
cover (*mit* with); den Bogen ~ go
too far; ~t *adj.* extravagant; *p.*
eccentric; *claims, etc.:* exaggerated;
2theit *f* (-/ℛ-en) extravagance;
eccentricity.

über|'spitzt *adj.* oversubtle; ex-
aggerated.

überspringen 1. ['~ʃpriŋən] *v/i.*
(*irr.* springen, *sep.*, -ge-, *sein*) ⚡
spark: jump; *in a speech, etc.:* ~ von
... zu ... jump or skip from (*one
subject*) to (*another*); 2. [~'ʃpriŋən]
v/t. (*irr.* springen, *no* -ge-, *h*) jump,
clear; skip (*page, etc.*); jump (*class*).

überstehen (*irr.* stehen) 1. ['~ʃte:ən]
v/i. (*sep.*, -ge-, *h*) jut (out or forth),
project; 2. [~'ʃte:ən] *v/t.* (*no* -ge-, *h*)
survive (*misfortune, etc.*); weather
(*crisis*); get over (*illness*).

über|'steigen *v/t.* (*irr.* steigen, *no*
-ge-, *h*) climb over; *fig.* exceed;
~'stimmen *v/t.* (*no* -ge-, *h*) out-
vote, vote down.

'überstreifen *v/t.* (*sep.*, -ge-, *h*)
slip *s.th.* over.

überströmen 1. ['~ʃtrø:mən] *v/i.*
(*sep.*, -ge-, *sein*) overflow (vor *dat.*
with); 2. [~'ʃtrø:mən] *v/t.* (*no* -ge-,
h) flood, inundate.

'Überstunden *f/pl.* overtime; ~
machen work overtime.

über'stürz|en *v/t.* (*no* -ge-, *h*)
rush, hurry (up or on); sich ~ act

rashly; *events*: follow in rapid succession; **.t** *adj.* precipitate, rash; **2ung** *f* (-/-⁓-en) precipitancy.

über'|teuern *v/t.* (*no* -ge-, *h*) overcharge; **.'tölpeln** *v/t.* (*no* -ge-, *h*) dupe, take in; **.'tönen** *v/t.* (*no* -ge-, *h*) drown.

Übertrag † ['y:bɔrtra:k] *m* (-[e]s/ ⁓e) carrying forward; *sum carried forward.*

über'trag|bar *adj.* transferable; **†** negotiable; **⁓** communicable; **⁓en** [⁓gɔn] 1. *v/t.* (*irr.* tragen, *no* -ge-, *h*) **†** carry forward; make over (*property*) (*auf acc.* to); **⁓** transfuse (*blood*); delegate (*rights, etc.*) (*dat.* to); render (*book, etc.*) (*in acc.* into); transcribe (*s.th. written in shorthand*); **⁓**, ⊕, *phys.*, *radio*: transmit; *radio*: *a.* broadcast; *im Fernsehen* ⁓ televise; *ihm wurde eine wichtige Mission* ⁓ he was charged with an important mission; 2. *adj.* figurative; **2ung** [⁓guŋ] *f* (-/-en) *field of application s.* Übertragen 1: carrying forward; making over; transfusion; delegation; rendering; free translation; transcription; transmission; broadcast; ⁓ *im Fernsehen* telecast.

über'treffen *v/t.* (*irr.* treffen, *no* -ge-, *h*) excel *s.o.* (*an dat.* in; *in dat.* in, at); surpass (in), exceed (in).

über'treib|en (*irr.* treiben, *no* -ge-, *h*) 1. *v/t.* overdo; exaggerate, overstate; 2. *v/i.* exaggerate, draw the long bow; **2ung** *f* (-/-en) exaggeration, overstatement.

'übertreten¹ *v/i.* (*irr.* treten, *sep.*, -ge-, *sein*) *sports*: cross the take-off line; *fig.* go over (*zu* to); *zum Katholizismus* ⁓ turn Roman Catholic.

über'tret|en² *v/t.* (*irr.* treten, *no* -ge-, *h*) transgress, violate, infringe (*law, etc.*); *sich den Fuß* ⁓ sprain one's ankle; **2ung** *f* (-/-en) transgression, violation, infringement.

'Übertritt *m* going over (*zu* to); *eccl.* conversion (to).

übervölker|n [y:bɔr'fœlkɔrn] *v/t.* (*no* -ge-, *h*) over-populate; **2ung** *f* (-/-⁓-en) over-population.

über'vorteilen *v/t.* (*no* -ge-, *h*) overreach, F do.

über'wach|en *v/t.* (*no* -ge-, *h*) supervise, superintend; control; *police*: keep under surveillance, shadow; **2ung** *f* (-/-⁓-en) supervision, superintendence; control; surveillance.

überwältigen [y:bɔr'vɛltigɔn] *v/t.* (*no* -ge-, *h*) overcome, overpower, overwhelm (*all a. fig.*); **⁓d** *fig. adj.* overwhelming.

über'weis|en *v/t.* (*irr.* weisen, *no* -ge-, *h*) remit (*money*) (*dat. or an acc.* to); (*zur Entscheidung etc.*) ⁓ refer (to); **2ung** *f* (-/-en) remittance;

reference (*an acc.* to); *parl.* devolution.

überwerfen (*irr.* werfen) 1. ['⁓verfɔn] *v/t.* (*sep.*, -ge-, *h*) slip (*coat*) on; 2. [⁓'verfɔn] *v/refl.* (*no* -ge-, *h*) fall out (*mit* with).

über'wieg|en (*irr.* wiegen, *no* -ge-, *h*) 1. *v/t.* outweigh; 2. *v/i.* preponderate; predominate; **⁓end** *adj.* preponderant; predominant; ⁓ **'winden** *v/t.* (*irr.* winden, *no* -ge-, *h*) overcome (*a. fig.*), subdue; *sich* ⁓ *zu inf.* bring o.s. to *inf.*; **.'wintern** *v/i.* (*no* -ge-, *h*) (pass the) winter.

'Über|wurf *m* wrap; **'.zahl** *f* (-/-⁓-en) numerical superiority; *in der* ⁓ superior in numbers; **2zählig** *adj.* ['.tse:liç] supernumerary; surplus.

über'zeug|en *v/t.* (*no* -ge-, *h*) convince (*von* of); satisfy (of); **2ung** *f* (-/-en) conviction.

überziehe|n *v/t.* (*irr.* ziehen) 1. ['.tsi:ɔn] (*sep.*, -ge-, *h*) put on; 2. [⁓'tsi:ɔn] (*no* -ge-, *h*) cover; put clean sheets on (*bed*); **†** overdraw (*account*); *sich* ⁓ *sky*: become overcast; **'2r** *m* (-s/-) overcoat, topcoat.

'Überzug *m* cover; case, tick; ⊕ coat(ing).

üblich *adj.* ['y:pliç] usual, custom-)

U-Boot ⊕, ✕ ['u:-] *n* submarine, *in Germany*: *a.* U-boat.

übrig *adj.* ['y:briç] left, remaining; *die* ⁓*e Welt* the rest of the world; *die* ⁓*en pl.* the others *pl.*, the rest; *im* ⁓*en* for the rest; by the way; ⁓ *haben have s.th.* left; *keine Zeit* ⁓ *haben* have no time to spare; *etwas* ⁓ *haben für* care for, have a soft spot for; *eins tun* go out of one's way; **'.bleiben** *v/i.* (*irr.* bleiben, *sep.*, -ge-, *sein*) be left; remain; *es blieb ihm nichts anderes übrig* he had no (other) alternative (*als* but); **⁓ens** *adv.* ['⁓gɔns] by the way; **.lassen** ['.⁓-] *v/t.* (*irr.* lassen, *sep.*, -ge-, *h*) leave; *viel zu wünschen* ⁓ leave much to be desired.

'Übung *f* (-/-en) exercise; practice; drill; **'.shang** *m skiing*: nursery slope.

Ufer ['u:fɔr] *n* (-s/-) shore (*of sea, lake*); bank (*of river, etc.*).

Uhr [u:r] *f* (-/-en) clock; watch; *um vier* ⁓ at four o'clock; **'.armband** *n* (-[e]s/⁓er) watch-strap; **'.feder** *f* watch-spring; **'.macher** *m* (-s/-) watch-maker; **'.werk** *n* clockwork; watch-work; **'.zeiger** *m* hand (*of clock or watch*); **'.zeigersinn** *m* (-[e]s/*no pl.*): *im* ⁓ clockwise; *entgegen dem* ⁓ counter-clockwise.

Uhu *orn.* ['u:hu:] *m* (-s/-s) eagle-owl.

Ulk [ulk] *m* (-[e]s/-e) fun, lark; **'2en** *v/i.* (ge-, *h*) (sky)lark, joke; **'2ig** *adj.* funny.

Ulme ♀ ['ulmɔ] *f* (-/-n) elm.

Ultimatum [ulti'ma:tum] *n* (-s/Ul-)

timaten, -s) ultimatum; *j-m ein ~ stellen* deliver an ultimatum to s.o.

Ultimo ✝ ['ultimo] *m (-s/-s)* last day of the month.

Ultrakurzwelle *phys.* [ultra'-] *f* ultra-short wave, very-high-frequency wave.

um [um] **1.** *prp. (acc.)* round, about; *~ vier Uhr* at four o'clock; *~ sein Leben laufen* run for one's life; *et. ~ einen Meter verfehlen* miss s.th. by a metre; *et. ~ zwei Mark verkaufen* sell s.th. at two marks; **2.** *prp. (gen.): ~ seinetwillen* for his sake; **3.** *cj.: ~ so besser* all the better, so much the better; *~ so mehr (weniger)* all the more (less); *~ zu* (in order) to; **4.** *adv.:* er drehte sich *~* he turned round.

um|ändern ['um?-] *v/t. (sep., -ge-, h)* change, alter; **~arbeiten** ['um?-] *v/t. (sep., -ge-, h)* make over *(coat, etc.);* revise *(book, etc.); ~ zu* make into.

um'arm|en *v/t. (no -ge-, h)* hug, embrace; *sich ~* embrace; **2ung** *f (-/-en)* embrace, hug.

'Umbau *m (-[e]s/-e, -ten)* rebuilding; reconstruction; **'2en** *v/t. (sep., -ge-, h)* rebuild; reconstruct.

'umbiegen *v/t. (irr. biegen, sep., -ge-, h)* bend; turn up *or* down.

'umbild|en *v/t. (sep., -ge-, h)* remodel, reconstruct; reorganize, reform; reshuffle *(cabinet);* **'2ung** *f (-/-en)* remodel(l)ing, reconstruction; reorganization, *pol.* reshuffle.

'um|binden *v/t. (irr. binden, sep., -ge-, h)* put on *(apron, etc.);* **'~blättern** *v/t. (sep., -ge-, h)* **1.** *v/t.* turn over; **2.** *v/i.* turn over the page; **~brechen** *v/t. (irr. brechen)* **1.** ↗ ['~brɛçən] *(sep., -ge-, h)* dig, break up *(ground);* **2.** *typ.* [~'brɛçən] *(no -ge-, h)* make up; **'~bringen** *v/t. (irr. bringen, sep., -ge-, h)* kill; *sich ~* kill o.s.; **'2bruch** *m typ.* make-up; *fig.:* upheaval; radical change; **'~buchen** *v/t. (sep., -ge-, h)* ✝ transfer *or* switch to another account; book for another date; **'~disponieren** *v/i. (sep., no -ge-, h)* change one's plans.

'umdreh|en *v/t. (sep., -ge-, h)* turn; *s. Spieß; sich ~* turn round; **2ung** [um'-] *f (-/-en)* turn; *phys.,* ⊕ rotation, revolution.

um|fahren *(irr. fahren)* **1.** ['~faːrən] *v/t. (sep., -ge-, h)* run down; **2.** ['~faːrən] *v/i. (sep., -ge-, sein)* go a roundabout way; **3.** [~'faːrən] *v/t. (no -ge-, h)* drive round; ⚓ sail round; ⚓ double *(cape);* **'~fallen** *v/i. (irr. fallen, sep., -ge-, sein)* fall; collapse; *tot ~* drop dead.

'Umfang *m (-[e]s/no pl.)* circumference, circuit; perimeter; girth *(of body, tree, etc.); fig.:* extent; volume; *in großem ~* on a large

scale; **'2reich** *adj.* extensive; voluminous; spacious.

um'fassen *v/t. (no -ge-, h)* clasp; embrace *(a. fig.);* ⚔ envelop; *fig.* comprise, cover, comprehend; **'~d** *adj.* comprehensive, extensive; sweeping, drastic.

'umform|en *v/t. (sep., -ge-, h)* remodel, recast, transform *(a. ⚡);* ⚡ convert; **'2er** ⚡ *m (-s/-)* transformer; converter.

'Umfrage *f* poll; *öffentliche ~* public opinion poll.

'Umgang *m* **1.** *(-[e]s/=e)* △ gallery, ambulatory; *eccl.* procession *(round the fields, etc.);* **2.** *(-[e]s/no pl.)* intercourse *(mit* with); company; *~ haben mit* associate with.

umgänglich *adj.* ['umgɛŋliç] sociable, companionable, affable.

'Umgangs|formen *f/pl.* manners *pl.;* **'~sprache** *f* colloquial usage; *in der deutschen ~* in colloquial German.

um'garnen *v/t. (no -ge-, h)* ensnare.

um'geb|en **1.** *v/t. (irr. geben, no -ge-, h)* surround; *mit e-r Mauer ~* wall in; **2.** *adj.* surrounded *(von* with, by) *(a. fig.);* **2ung** *f (-/-en)* environs *pl. (of town, etc.);* surroundings *pl.,* environment *(of place, person, etc.).*

umgeh|en *(irr. gehen)* **1.** ['~geːən] *v/i. (sep., -ge-, sein)* make a detour; *rumour, etc.:* go about, be afloat; *ghost:* walk; *~ mit* use *s.th.;* deal with *s.o.;* keep company with; *ein Gespenst soll im Schlosse ~* the castle is said to be haunted; **2.** [~'geːən] *v/t. (no -ge-, h)* go round; ⚔ flank; bypass *(town, etc.); fig.* avoid, evade; circumvent, elude *(law, etc.);* **'~end** *adj.* immediate; **2ungsstraße** [um'geːuŋs-] *f* bypass.

umgekehrt ['umgəkeːrt] **1.** *adj.* reverse; inverse, inverted; *in ~er Reihenfolge* in reverse order; *im ~en Verhältnis zu* in inverse proportion to; **2.** *adv.* vice versa.

'umgraben *v/t. (irr. graben, sep., -ge-, h)* dig (up).

um'grenzen *v/t. (no -ge-, h)* encircle; enclose; *fig.* circumscribe, limit.

'umgruppier|en *v/t. (sep., no -ge-, h)* regroup; **'2ung** *f (-/-en)* regrouping.

'um|haben *F v/t. (irr. haben, sep., -ge-, h)* have *(coat, etc.)* on; **'2hang** *m* wrap; cape; **'~hängen** *v/t. (sep., -ge-, h)* rehang *(pictures);* sling *(rifle)* over one's shoulder; *sich den Mantel ~* put one's coat round one's shoulders; **'~hauen** *v/t. (irr. hauen, sep., -ge-, h)* fell, cut down; *F: die Nachricht hat mich umgehauen* I was bowled over by the news.

um'her|blicken v/i. (sep., -ge-, h) look about (one); **~streifen** v/i. (sep., -ge-, sein) rove.

um'hinkönnen v/i. (irr. können, sep., -ge-, h): ich kann nicht umhin, zu sagen I cannot help saying.

um'hüll|en v/t. (no -ge-, h) wrap up (mit in), envelop (in); **Qung** f (-/-en) wrapping, wrapper, envelopment.

Umkehr ['umke:r] f (-/no pl.) return; **2en** (sep., -ge-) 1. v/i. (sein) return, turn back; 2. v/t. (h) turn out (one's pocket, etc.); invert (a. ♪); reverse (a. ♪, ♪); **'~ung** f (-/-en) reversal; inversion.

'umkippen (sep., -ge-) 1. v/t. (h) upset, tilt; 2. v/i. (sein) upset, tilt (over); F faint.

um'klammer|n v/t. (no -ge-, h) clasp; boxing: clinch; **Qung** f (-/-en) clasp; boxing: clinch.

'umkleid|en v/refl. (sep., -ge-, h) change (one's clothes); **'2eraum** m dressing-room.

'umkommen v/i. (irr. kommen, sep., -ge-, sein) be killed (bei in), die (in), perish (in); vor Langeweile ~ die of boredom.

'Umkreis m (-es/no pl.) ♔ circumscribed circle; im ~ von within a radius of. [round.]

um'kreisen v/t. (no -ge-, h) circle)

'um|krempeln v/t. (sep., -ge-, h) tuck up (shirt-sleeves, etc.); change (plan, etc.); (völlig) ~ turn s.th. inside out; **'~laden** v/t. (irr. laden, sep., -ge-, h) reload; ⚓, ⚓ transship.

'Umlauf m circulation; phys., ⊕ rotation; circular (letter); in ~ setzen or bringen circulate, put into circulation; im ~ sein circulate, be in circulation; rumours: a. be afloat; außer ~ setzen withdraw from circulation; **'~bahn** f orbit; **2en** (irr. laufen) 1. ['~laufen] v/t. (sep., -ge-, h) knock over; 2. ['~laufen] v/i. (sep., -ge-, sein) circulate; make a detour; 3. [~'laufen] v/t. (no -ge-, h) run round.

'Umlege|kragen m turn-down collar; **'2n** v/t. (sep., -ge-, h) lay down; ⊕ throw (lever); storm, etc.: beat down (wheat, etc.); re-lay (cable, etc.); put (coat, etc.) round one's shoulders; apportion (costs, etc.); fig. sl. do s.o. in.

'umleit|en v/t. (sep., -ge-, h) divert; **'2ung** f diversion, detour.

'umliegend adj. surrounding, circumjacent.

um'nacht|et adj.: geistig ~ mentally deranged; **Qung** f (-/~-en): geistige ~ mental derangement.

'um|packen v/t. (sep., -ge-, h) repack; **~pflanzen** v/t. 1. ['~pflantsən] (sep., -ge-, h) transplant; 2. [~'pflantsən] (no -ge-, h): ~ mit

plant s.th. round with; **'~pflügen** v/t. (sep., -ge-, h) plough, Am. plow.

um'rahmen v/t. (no -ge-, h) frame; musikalisch ~ put into a musical setting.

umrand|en [um'randən] v/t. (no -ge-, h) edge, border; **Qung** f (-/-en) edge, border.

um'ranken v/t. (no -ge-, h) twine (mit with).

'umrechn|en v/t. (sep., -ge-, h) convert (in acc. into); **'Qung** f (-/no pl.) conversion; **'Qungskurs** m rate of exchange.

umreißen v/t. (irr. reißen) 1. ['~raisən] (sep., -ge-, h) pull down; knock s.o. over; 2. [~'raisən] (no -ge-, h) outline. [round (a. fig.).\]

um'ringen v/t. (no -ge-, h) sur-)

'Um|riß m outline (a. fig.), contour; **'2rühren** v/t. (sep., -ge-, h) stir; **'2satteln** (sep., -ge-, h) 1. v/t. resaddle; 2. v/i. fig. change one's studies or occupation; **~ von ... auf** (acc.) change from ... to ...; **'~satz** ♔ m turnover; sales pl.; return(s pl.); stock exchange: business done.

umschalt|en (sep., -ge-, h) 1. v/t. ⊕ change over; ⚡ commutate; ⚡, ⊕ switch; 2. ⚡, ⊕ v/i. switch over; **'2er** m ⊕ change-over switch; ⚡ commutator; **'Qung** f (-/-en) ⊕ change-over; ⚡ commutation.

'Umschau f (-/no pl.): ~ halten nach look out for, be on the look-out for; **2en** v/refl. (sep., -ge-, h) look round (nach for); look about (for) (a. fig.), look about one.

'umschicht|en v/t. (sep., -ge-, h) pile afresh; fig. regroup (a. ♠); **'~ig** adv. by or in turns; **'Qung** fig. f (-/-en) regrouping; soziale **~en** pl. social upheavals pl.

um'schiff|en v/t. (no -ge-, h) circumnavigate; double (cape); **Qung** f (-/♖-en) circumnavigation; doubling.

'Umschlag m envelope; cover, wrapper; jacket; turn-up, Am. a. cuff (of trousers); ♣ compress; poultice; trans-shipment (of goods); fig. change, turn; **'2en** (irr. schlagen, sep., -ge-) 1. v/t. (h) knock s.o. down; cut down, fell (tree); turn (leaf); turn up (sleeves, etc.); turn down (collar); trans-ship (goods); 2. v/i. (sein) turn over, upset; ⚓ capsize, upset; wine, etc.: turn sour; fig. turn (in acc. into); **'~hafen** m port of trans-shipment.

um'schließen v/t. (irr. schließen, no -ge-, h) embrace, surround (a. ✕), enclose; ✕ invest; **~'schlingen** v/t. (irr. schlingen, no -ge-, h) embrace.

'um|schmeißen F v/t. (irr. schmeißen, sep., -ge-, h) s. umstoßen; **'~**

schnallen v/t. (sep., -ge-, h) buckle on.

umschreib|en v/t. (irr. schreiben) 1. ['~ʃraibən] (sep., -ge-, h) rewrite; transfer (property, etc.) (auf acc. to); 2. [~'ʃraibən] (no -ge-, h) ⅋ circumscribe; paraphrase; ⒉ung f (-/-en) 1. ['~'ʃraibuŋ] rewriting; transfer (auf acc. to); 2. [~'ʃraibuŋ] ⅋ circumscription; paraphrase.

'Umschrift f circumscription; phonetics: transcription.

'umschütten v/t. (sep., -ge-, h) pour into another vessel; spill.

'Um|schweife pl.: ~ machen beat about the bush; ohne ~ pointblank; ⒉schwenken fig. v/i. (sep., -ge-, sein) veer or turn round; '~schwung fig. m revolution; revulsion (of public feeling, etc.); change (in the weather, etc.); reversal (of opinion, etc.).

um'seg|eln v/t. (no -ge-, h) sail round; double (cape); circumnavigate (globe, world); ⒉(e)lung f (-/-en) sailing round (world, etc.); doubling; circumnavigation.

'um|sehen v/refl. (irr. sehen, sep., -ge-, h) look round (nach for); look about (for) (a. fig.), look about one; '~sein F v/i. (irr. sein, sep., -ge-, sein) time: be up; holidays, etc.: be over; '~setzen v/t. (sep., -ge-, h) transpose (a. ♪); ⤢ transplant; ✝ turn over; spend (money) (in acc. on books, etc.); in die Tat ~ realize, convert into fact.

'Umsicht f (-/no pl.) circumspection; **⒉ig** adj. circumspect.

'umsied|eln (sep., -ge-) 1. v/t. (h) resettle; 2. v/i. (sein) (re)move (nach, in acc. to); ⒉lung f(-/⅋ -en) resettlement; evacuation; removal.

um'sonst adv. gratis, free of charge; in vain; to no purpose; nicht ~ not without good reason.

umspann|en v/t. 1. ['~ʃpanən] (sep., -ge-, h) change (horses); ⅋ transform; 2. [~'ʃpanən] (no -ge-, h) span; fig. a. embrace; ⒉er ⅋ m (-s/-) transformer.

'umspringen v/i. (irr. springen, sep., -ge-, sein) shift, veer (round); ~ mit treat badly, etc.

'Umstand m circumstance; fact, detail; unter diesen Umständen in or under the circumstances; unter keinen Umständen in or under no circumstances, on no account; unter Umständen possibly; ohne Umstände without ceremony; in anderen Umständen sein be in the family way.

umständlich adj. ['umʃtɛntliç] story, etc.: long-winded; method, etc.: roundabout; p. fussy; das ist (mir) viel zu ~ that is far too much trouble (for me); ⒉keit f (-/⅋ -en) long-windedness; fussiness.

'Umstands|kleid n maternity robe; '~wort gr. n (-[e]s/⁻er) adverb.

'umstehend 1. adj.: auf der ~en Seite overleaf; 2. adv. overleaf; ⒉en ['~dən] pl. the bystanders pl.

'Umsteige|karte f transfer; ⒉n v/i. (irr. steigen, sep., -ge-, sein) change (nach for); ⤢ a. change⁓trains (for). **Umsteigkarte** ['umʃtaik-] f s. Umsteigekarte.

umstell|en v/t. 1. ['~ʃtɛlən] (sep., -ge-, h) transpose (a. gr.); shift (furniture) about or round; convert (currency, production) (auf acc. to); sich ~ change one's attitude; accommodate o.s. to new conditions; adapt o.s. (auf acc. to); 2. [~'ʃtɛlən] (no -ge-, h) surround; ⒉ung ['~ʃtɛluŋ] f transposition; fig.: conversion; adaptation; change.

'um|stimmen v/t. (sep., -ge-, h) ♪ tune to another pitch; j-n ~ change s.o.'s mind, bring s.o. round; '~stoßen v/t. (irr. stoßen, sep., -ge-, h) knock over; upset; fig. annul; ⅋⅋ overrule, reverse; upset (plan).

um|'stricken fig. v/t. (no -ge-, h) ensnare; ~stritten adj. [~'ʃtritən] disputed, contested; controversial; **'Um|sturz** m subversion, overturn; ⒉stürzen (sep., -ge-) 1. v/t. (h) upset, overturn (a. fig.); fig. subvert; 2. v/i. (sein) upset, overturn; fall down; ⒉stürzlerisch adj. ['~ləriʃ] subversive.

'Umtausch m (-es/⅋ -e) exchange; ⅋ conversion (of currency, etc.); ⒉en v/t. (sep., -ge-, h) exchange (gegen for); ✝ convert.

'umtun F v/t. (irr. tun, sep., -ge-, h) put (coat, etc.) round one's shoulders; sich ~ nach look about for.

'umwälz|en v/t. (sep., -ge-, h) roll round; fig. revolutionize; '~end adj. revolutionary; ⒉ung fig. f (-/-en) revolution, upheaval.

'umwand|eln v/t. (sep., -ge-, h) transform (in acc. into); ⅋, ✝ convert (into); ⅋⅋ commute (into); ⒉lung f transformation; ⅋, ✝ conversion; ⅋⅋ commutation.

'um|wechseln v/t. (sep., -ge-, h) change; ⒉weg m roundabout way or route; detour; auf ~en in a roundabout way; '~wehen v/t. (sep., -ge-, h) blow down or over; ⒉welt f (-/⅋ -en) environment; '~wenden 1. v/t. (sep., -ge-, h) turn over; 2. v/refl. (irr. wenden, sep., -ge-, h) look round (nach for).

um'werben v/t. (irr. werben, no -ge-, h) court, woo.

'umwerfen v/t. (irr. werfen, sep., -ge-, h) upset (a. fig.), overturn; sich e-n Mantel ~ throw a coat round one's shoulders.

um|'wickeln v/t. (no -ge-, h): et. mit Draht ~ wind wire round s.th.;

~wölken [~'vœlkən] *v/refl.* *(no -ge-, h)* cloud over *(a. fig.)*; **~zäunen** [~'tsɔynən] *v/t.* *(no -ge-, h)* fence (in).

umziehen *(irr. ziehen)* **1.** ['~tsi:ən] *v/i.* *(sep., -ge-, sein)* (re)move *(nach* to); move house; **2.** ['~tsi:ən] *v/refl.* *(sep., -ge-, h)* change (one's clothes); **3.** [~'tsi:ən] *v/refl.* *(no -ge-, h)* cloud over.

umzingeln [um'tsiŋəln] *v/t.* *(no -ge-, h)* surround, encircle.

'Umzug *m* procession; move *(nach* to), removal (to); change of residence.

unab|änderlich *adj.* [un⁹ap'ɛndərliç] unalterable; **~hängig** ['~hɛŋiç] **1.** *adj.* independent *(von* of); **2.** *adv.:* ~ von irrespective of; **'2hängigkeit** *f* *(-/no pl.)* independence *(von* of); **~kömmlich** *adj.* ['~kœmliç]: er ist im Moment ~ we cannot spare him at the moment, we cannot do without him at the moment; **~lässig** *adj.* incessant, unremitting; **~sehbar** *adj.* [~'ze:ba:r] incalculable; *in ~er Ferne* in a distant future; **~sichtlich** *adj.* unintentional; inadvertent; **~wendbar** *adj.* [~'vɛntba:r] inevitable, inescapable.

unachtsam *adj.* ['un⁹-] careless, heedless; **'2keit** *f* *(-/% -en)* carelessness, heedlessness.

unähnlich *adj.* ['un⁹-] unlike, dissimilar *(dat.* to).

unan|fechtbar *adj.* [un⁹an'-] unimpeachable, unchallengeable, incontestable; **~gebracht** *adj.* inappropriate; *pred. a.* out of place; **~gefochten** **1.** *adj.* undisputed; unchallenged; **2.** *adv.* without any hindrance; **~gemessen** *adj.* unsuitable; improper; inadequate; **'~genehm** *adj.* disagreeable, unpleasant; awkward; troublesome; **~nehmbar** *adj.* unacceptable *(für* to); **'2nehmlichkeit** *f* *(-/-en)* unpleasantness; awkwardness; troublesomeness; **~en** *pl.* trouble, inconvenience; **~sehnlich** *adj.* unsightly; plain; **~ständig** *adj.* indecent; obscene; **2ständigkeit** *f* *(-/-en)* indecency; obscenity; **'tastbar** *adj.* unimpeachable; inviolable.

unappetitlich *adj.* ['un⁹-] *food, etc.:* unappetizing; *sight, etc.:* distasteful, ugly.

Unart ['un⁹-] **1.** *f* bad habit; **2.** *m* *(-[e]s/-e)* naughty child; **'2ig** *adj.* naughty; **'~igkeit** *f* *(-/-en)* naughty behavio(u)r, naughtiness.

unauf|dringlich *adj.* ['un⁹auf-] unobtrusive; unostentatious; **'~fällig** *adj.* inconspicuous; unobtrusive; **~findbar** *adj.* [~'fintba:r] undiscoverable, untraceable; **~gefordert** ['~gəfordərt] **1.** *adj.* un-

---

asked; **2.** *adv.* without being asked, of one's own accord; **~'hörlich** *adj.* incessant, continuous, uninterrupted; **'~merksam** *adj.* inattentive; **'2merksamkeit** *f* *(-/-en)* inattention, inattentiveness; **'~richtig** *adj.* insincere; **2richtigkeit** *f* *(-/-en)* insincerity; **~schiebbar** *adj.* [~'ʃi:pba:r] urgent; ~ sein brook no delay.

unaus|bleiblich *adj.* [un⁹aus'blaipliç] inevitable; *das war ~* that was bound to happen; **~führbar** *adj.* impracticable; **~geglichen** *adj.* ['~gəgliçən] unbalanced *(a.* ✝); **~löschlich** *adj.* indelible; *fig. a.* inextinguishable; **~sprechlich** *adj.* unutterable; unspeakable; inexpressible; **~stehlich** *adj.* unbearable, insupportable.

'unbarmherzig *adj.* merciless, unmerciful; **'2keit** *f* *(-/no pl.)* mercilessness, unmercifulness.

unbe|absichtigt *adj.* ['unbə⁹apziçtiçt] unintentional, undesigned; **'~achtet** *adj.* unnoticed; **~anstandet** *adj.* ['unbə⁹-] unopposed, not objected to; **'~baut** *adj.* ♀ untilled; *land:* undeveloped; **'~dacht** *adj.* inconsiderate; imprudent; **'~denklich** **1.** *adj.* unobjectionable; **2.** *adv.* without hesitation; **'~deutend** *adj.* insignificant; slight; **'~dingt** **1.** *adj.* unconditional; *obedience, etc.:* implicit; **2.** *adv.* by all means; under any circumstances; **~fahrbar** *adj.* impracticable, impassable; **~fangen** *adj.* unprejudiced, unbias(s)ed; ingenuous; unembarrassed; **~friedigend** *adj.* unsatisfactory; **~friedigt** *adj.* ['~çt] dissatisfied; disappointed; **~fugt** *adj.* unauthorized; incompetent; **'2fugte** *m* *(-n/-n)* unauthorized person; *~n ist der Zutritt verboten!* no trespassing!; **~gabt** *adj.* untalented; **~greiflich** *adj.* inconceivable, incomprehensible; **~grenzt** *adj.* unlimited; boundless; **~gründet** *adj.* unfounded; **2hagen** *n* uneasiness; discomfort; **~haglich** *adj.* uneasy; uncomfortable; **~heiligt** *adj.* [~'heliçt] unmolested; **~herrscht** *adj.* lacking self-control; **'2herrschtheit** *f* *(-/no pl.)* lack of self-control; **~hindert** *adj.* unhindered, free; **~holfen** *adj.* ['~bəholfən] clumsy, awkward; **'2holfenheit** *f* *(-/no pl.)* clumsiness, awkwardness; **~irrt** *adj.* unswerving; **~kannt** *adj.* unknown; **~e** *Größe* ♬ unknown quantity *(a. fig.)*; **~kümmert** *adj.* unconcerned *(um, wegen* about), careless (of, about); **'~lebt** *adj.* inanimate; *street, etc.:* unfrequented; **~'lehrbar** *adj.:* ~ *sein* take no advice; **'~liebt** *adj.* unpopular; *sich ~ machen* get o.s. disliked; **'~mannt** *adj.* unmanned;

'**~merkt** adj. unnoticed; '**~mittelt** adj. impecunious, without means; **~nommen** adj. [~ˈnɔmən]: es bleibt ihm ~ zu inf. he is at liberty to inf.; '**~nutzt** adj. unused; '**~quem** adj. uncomfortable; inconvenient; '**2quemlichkeit** f lack of comfort; inconvenience; '**~rechtigt** adj. unauthorized; unjustified; **~schadet** prp. (gen.) [~ˈʃaːdət] without prejudice to; **~schädigt** adj. ['~çt] uninjured, undamaged; '**~scheiden** adj. immodest; **~scholten** adj. ['~ʃɔltən] blameless, irreproachable; **~schränkt** adj. unrestricted; absolute; **~schreiblich** adj. ['~ʃraiplıç] indescribable; '**~sehen** adv. unseen; without inspection; '**~setzt** adj. unoccupied; vacant; **~siegbar** adj. [~ˈziːkbaːr] invincible; '**~sonnen** adj. thoughtless, imprudent; rash; '**2sonnenheit** f (-/-en) thoughtlessness, rashness; '**~ständig** adj. inconstant; unsteady; weather: changeable, unsettled (a. ✝); p. erratic; '**2ständigkeit** f (-/no pl.) inconstancy; changeability; **~stätigt** adj. ['~çt] unconfirmed; letter, etc.: unacknowledged; **~stechlich** adj. incorruptible, unbribable; '**2stechlichkeit** f (-/no pl.) incorruptibility; '**~stimmt** adj. indeterminate (a. Å); indefinite (a. gr.); uncertain; feeling, etc.: vague; '**2stimmtheit** f (-/no pl.) indeterminateness, indetermination; indefiniteness; uncertainty; vagueness; **~streitbar** adj. incontestable, indisputable; **~stritten** adj. uncontested, undisputed; **~teiligt** adj. unconcerned (an dat. in); indifferent; **~trächtlich** adj. inconsiderable, insignificant; [flexible.] **unbeugsam** adj. [unˈbɔʏkzaːm] in-] '**unbe|wacht** adj. unwatched, unguarded (a. fig.); '**~waffnet** adj. unarmed; eye: naked; '**~weglich** adj. immovable; motionless; '**~wiesen** adj. unproven; '**~wohnt** adj. uninhabited; unoccupied, vacant; '**~wußt** adj. unconscious; **~zähmbar** adj. indomitable.

'**Un|bilden** pl.: ~ der Witterung inclemency of the weather; '**~bildung** f lack of education.

'**un|billig** adj. unfair; '**~blutig** 1. adj. bloodless; 2. adv. without bloodshed.

unbotmäßig adj. ['unboːt-] insubordinate; '**2keit** f (-/-en) insubordination.

'**un|brauchbar** adj. useless; '**~christlich** adj. unchristian.

und cj. [unt] and; F: na ~? so what?

'**Undank** m ingratitude; '**2bar** adj. ungrateful (gegen to); task, etc.: thankless; '**~barkeit** f ingratitude, ungratefulness; fig. thanklessness.

un|'denkbar adj. unthinkable; inconceivable; **~'denklich** adj.: seit ~en Zeiten from time immemorial; '**~deutlich** adj. indistinct; speech: a. inarticulate; fig. vague, indistinct; '**~deutsch** adj. un-German; '**~dicht** adj. leaky; '**2ding** n: es wäre ein ~, zu behaupten, daß ... it would be absurd to claim that ...

unduldsam adj. intolerant; '**2keit** f intolerance.

undurch|'dringlich adj. impenetrable; countenance: impassive; **~'führbar** adj. impracticable; **~'lässig** adj. impervious, impermeable; **~'sichtig** adj. opaque; fig. mysterious.

uneben adj. ['unˀ-] ground: uneven, broken; way, etc.: bumpy; '**2heit** f 1. (-/no pl.) unevenness; 2. (-/-en) bump.

un|echt adj. ['unˀ-] jewellery, etc.: imitation; hair, teeth, etc.: false; money, jewellery, etc.: counterfeit; picture, etc.: fake; & fraction: improper; '**~ehelich** adj. illegitimate.

Unehr|e f ['unˀ-] dishono(u)r; j-m ~ machen discredit s.o.; '**2enhaft** adj. dishono(u)rable; '**2lich** adj. dishonest; '**~lichkeit** f dishonesty.

uneigennützig adj. ['unˀ-] disinterested, unselfish.

uneinig adj. ['unˀ-]: ~ sein be at variance (mit with); disagree (über acc. on); '**2keit** f variance, disagreement.

un|ein'nehmbar adj. impregnable; '**~empfänglich** adj. insusceptible (für of, to).

unempfindlich adj. ['unˀ-] insensitive (gegen to); '**2keit** f insensitiveness (gegen to).

un'endlich 1. adj. endless, infinite (both a. fig.); 2. adv. infinitely (a. fig.); ~ lang endless; ~ viel no end of (money, etc.); **2keit** f (-/no pl.) endlessness, infinitude, infinity (all a. fig.).

unent|behrlich adj. [unˀɛntˈbeːrlıç] indispensable; **~geltlich** 1. adj gratuitous, gratis; 2. adv. gratis, free of charge; **~rinnbar** adj. ineluctable; **~schieden** 1. adj. undecided; ~ enden game: end in a draw or tie; 2. 2 n (-s/-) draw, tie; '**~schlossen** adj. irresolute; '**2schlossenheit** f irresoluteness, irresolution; **~schuldbar** adj. [~ˈʃultbaːr] inexcusable; **~wegt** adv. [~ˈveːkt] untiringly; continuously; '**~wirrbar** adj. inextricable.

uner|bittlich adj. [unˀɛrˈbıtlıç] inexorable; fact: stubborn; **~fahren** adj. inexperienced; **~findlich** adj. [~ˈfıntlıç] incomprehensible; **~'forschlich** adj. inscrutable; **~'freulich** adj. unpleasant; **~'füllbar** adj. unrealizable; **~'giebig** adj. unproductive (an dat. of); '**~heb-**

lich *adj.* irrelevant (*für* to); inconsiderable; **hört** *adj.* 1. [*'ho:rt*] unheard; 2. [*'ho:rt*] unheard-of; outrageous; **kannt** *adj.* unrecognized; **klärlich** *adj.* inexplicable; **läßlich** *adj.* [*'lesliç*] indispensable (*für* to, for); **laubt** *adj.* [*'laupt*] unauthorized; illegal, illicit; *e Handlung* ½½ tort; **ledigt** *adj.* [*'le:diçt*] unsettled (*a.* ♦); **meßlich** *adj.* [*'mesliç*] immeasurable, immense; **müdlich** *adj.* [*'my:tliç*] *p.* indefatigable, untiring; *efforts,* etc.: untiring, unremitting; **quicklich** *adj.* unpleasant, unedifying; **reichbar** *adj.* inattainable; inaccessible; *pred. a.* above *or* beyond *or* out of reach; **reicht** *adj.* unrival(l)ed, unequal(l)ed; **sättlich** *adj.* [*'zetliç*] insatiable, insatiate; **schöpflich** *adj.* inexhaustible.

unerschrocken *adj.* [*'un²-*] intrepid, fearless; **heit** *f* (*-/no pl.*) intrepidity, fearlessness.

uner|schütterlich *adj.* [*un²er'-ʃytərliç*] unshakable; **schwinglich** *adj.* price: prohibitive; *pred. a.* above *or* beyond *or* out of reach (*für of*); **setzlich** *adj.* irreplaceable; *loss,* etc.: irreparable; **träglich** *adj.* intolerable, unbearable; **wartet** *adj.* unexpected; **wünscht** *adj.* undesirable, undesired.

'unfähig *adj.* incapable (*zu inf.* of *ger.*); unable (*to inf.*); inefficient; **heit** *f* incapability (*zu inf.* of *ger.*); inability (*to inf.*); inefficiency.

'Unfall *m* accident; *e-n ~ haben* meet with *or* have an accident; **station** *f* emergency ward; **versicherung** *f* accident insurance.

un'faßlich *adj.* incomprehensible, inconceivable; *das ist mir ~* that is beyond me.

un'fehlbar 1. *adj.* infallible (*a. eccl.*); *decision,* etc.: unimpeachable; *instinct,* etc.: unfailing; 2. *adv.* without fail; inevitably; **heit** *f* (*-/no pl.*) infallibility.

'un|fein *adj.* indelicate; *pred. a.* lacking in refinement; **fern** *prp.* (*gen. or von*) not far from; **fertig** *adj.* unfinished; *fig. a.* half-baked; **flätig** *adj.* [*'fle:tiç*] dirty, filthy.

'unfolgsam *adj.* disobedient; **keit** *f* disobedience.

un|förmig *adj.* [*'unfœrmiç*] misshapen; shapeless; **frankiert** *adj.* unstamped; **frei** *adj.* not free; ♣ unstamped; **freiwillig** *adj.* involuntary; *humour:* unconscious; **freundlich** *adj.* unfriendly (*zu* with), unkind (*to*); *climate, weather:* inclement; *room, day:* cheerless; **friede(n)** *m* discord.

'unfruchtbar *adj.* unfruitful; ster-

ile; **keit** *f* (*-/no pl.*) unfruitfulness; sterility.

Unfug [*'unfu:k*] *m* (*-[e]s/no pl.*) mischief.

Ungar [*'ungar*] *m* (*-n/-n*) Hungarian; **isch** *adj.* Hungarian.

'ungastlich *adj.* inhospitable.

unge|achtet *prp.* (*gen.*) [*'unga²axtət*] regardless of; despite; **ahnt** *adj.* [*'unga²-*] undreamt-of; unexpected; **bärdig** *adj.* [*'be:rdiç*] unruly; **beten** *adj.* uninvited, unasked; *er Gast* intruder, *sl.* gatecrasher; **bildet** *adj.* uneducated; **bräuchlich** *adj.* unusual; **braucht** *adj.* unused; **bührlich** *adj.* improper, undue, unseemly; **bunden** *adj.* book: unbound; *fig.:* free; single; **deckt** *adj.* table: unlaid; *sports,* ✕, ♦: uncovered; *paper currency:* fiduciary.

'Ungeduld *f* impatience; **ig** *adj.* impatient.

'ungeeignet *adj.* unfit (*für* for *s.th.,* *to* do *s.th.*); *p. a.* unqualified; *moment:* inopportune.

ungefähr [*'ungəfe:r*] 1. *adj.* approximate, rough; 2. *adv.* approximately, roughly, about, *Am.* F *a.* around; *von ~* by chance; **det** *adj.* unendangered, safe; **lich** *adj.* harmless; *pred. a.* not dangerous.

unge|fällig *adj.* disobliging; **halten** *adj.* displeased (*über acc.* at); **hemmt** 1. *adj.* unchecked; 2. *adv.* without restraint; **heuchelt** *adj.* unfeigned.

ungeheuer [*'ungəhɔʏər*] 1. *adj.* vast, huge, enormous; 2. Ձ *n* (*-s/-*) monster; **lich** [*'hɔʏərliç*] monstrous.

'ungehobelt *adj.* not planed; *fig.* uncouth, rough.

'ungehörig *adj.* undue, improper; **keit** *f* (*-/½-en*) impropriety.

'ungehorsam 1. *adj.* disobedient; 2. Ձ *m* disobedience.

'unge|künstelt *adj.* unaffected; **kürzt** *adj.* unabridged.

'ungelegen *adj.* inconvenient, inopportune; **heiten** *f/pl.* inconvenience; trouble; *j-m ~ machen* put *s.o.* to inconvenience.

'unge|lehrig *adj.* indocile; **lenk** *adj.* awkward, clumsy; **lernt** *adj.* unskilled; **mütlich** *adj.* uncomfortable; *room: a.* cheerless; *p.* nasty; **nannt** *adj.* unnamed; *p.* anonymous.

'ungenau *adj.* inaccurate, inexact; **igkeit** *f* inaccuracy, inexactness.

'ungeniert *adj.* free and easy, unceremonious; undisturbed.

unge|nießbar *adj.* [*'ungəni:sba:r*] uneatable; undrinkable; F *p.* unbearable; *pred. a.* in a bad humo(u)r; **nügend** *adj.* insufficient; **pflegt** *adj.* unkempt; **rade** *adj.* odd; **raten** *adj.* spoilt, undutiful.

'ungerecht adj. unjust (gegen to); 'Qigkeit f (-/-en) injustice.

'un|gern adv. unwillingly, grudgingly; reluctantly; ~geschehen adj.: ~ machen undo s.th.

'Ungeschick n (-[e]s/no pl.), '~lichkeit f awkwardness, clumsiness, maladroitness; 'Qt adj. awkward, clumsy, maladroit.

unge|schlacht adj. ['ungəʃlaxt] hulking; uncouth; '~schliffen adj. unpolished, rough (both a. fig.); '~schminkt adj. not made up; fig. unvarnished.

'ungesetzlich adj. illegal, unlawful, illicit; 'Qkeit f (-/-en) illegality, unlawfulness.

'unge|sittet adj. uncivilized; unmannerly; '~stört adj. undisturbed, uninterrupted; '~straft 1. adj. unpunished; 2. adv. with impunity; ~ davonkommen get off or escape scot-free.

ungestüm ['ungəʃty:m] 1. adj. impetuous; violent; 2. Ω n (-[e]s/no pl.) impetuosity; violence.

'unge|sund adj. climate: unhealthy; appearance: a. unwholesome; food: unwholesome; '~teilt adj. undivided (a. fig.); ~trübt adj. ['~try:pt] untroubled; unmixed; Ωtüm ['~ty:m] n (-[e]s/-e) monster; ~übt adj. ['~'y:pt] untrained; inexperienced; '~waschen adj. unwashed.

'ungewiß adj. uncertain; j-n im ungewissen lassen keep s.o. in suspense; 'Qheit f (-/'~-en) uncertainty; suspense.

'unge|wöhnlich adj. unusual, uncommon; '~wohnt adj. unaccustomed; unusual; '~zählt adj. numberless, countless; Qziefer ['~tsi:fər] n (-s/-) vermin; '~ziemend adj. improper, unseemly; '~zogen adj. ill-bred, rude, uncivil; child: naughty; '~zügelt adj. unbridled.

'ungezwungen adj. unaffected, easy; 'Qheit f (-/'~-en) unaffectedness, ease, easiness.

'Unglaube(n) m unbelief, disbelief.

'ungläubig adj. incredulous, unbelieving (a. eccl.); infidel; 'Qe m, f unbeliever; infidel.

unglaub|lich adj. ['un'glauplıç] incredible; '~würdig adj. p. untrustworthy; thing: incredible; ~e Geschichte cock-and-bull story.

'ungleich 1. adj. unequal, different; uneven; unlike; 2. adv. (by) far, much; '~artig adj. heterogeneous; 'Qheit f difference, inequality; unevenness, unlikeness; '~mäßig adj. uneven; irregular.

'Unglück n (-[e]s/'~-e) misfortune; bad or ill luck; accident; calamity, disaster; misery; 'Qlich adj. unfortunate, unlucky; unhappy; Qlicher'weise adv. unfortunately,

unluckily; 'Qselig adj. unfortunate; disastrous.

'Unglücks|fall m misadventure; accident; '~rabe F m unlucky fellow.

'Un|gnade f (-/no pl.) disgrace, disfavo(u)r; in ~ fallen bei fall into disgrace with, incur s.o.'s disfavo(u)r; 'Qgnädig adj. ungracious, unkind.

'ungültig adj. invalid; ticket: not available; money: not current; ťť (null and void); 'Qkeit f invalidity; ťť a. voidness.

'Un|gunst f disfavo(u)r; inclemency (of weather); zu meinen ~en to my disadvantage; 'Qgünstig adj. unfavo(u)rable; disadvantageous.

'un|gut adj.: ~es Gefühl misgiving; nichts für ~! no offen|ce, Am. ~se!; '~haltbar adj. shot: unstoppable; theory, etc.: untenable; '~handlich adj. unwieldy, bulky.

'Unheil n mischief; disaster, calamity; 'Qbar adj. incurable; 'Qvoll adj. sinister, ominous.

'unheimlich 1. adj. uncanny (a. fig.), weird; sinister; F fig. tremendous, terrific; 2. F fig. adv.: ~ viel heaps of, an awful lot of.

'unhöflich adj. impolite, uncivil; 'Qkeit f impoliteness, incivility.

Unhold ['unhɔlt] m (-[e]s/-e) fiend.

'un|hörbar adj. inaudible; '~hygienisch adj. unsanitary, insanitary.

Uni ['uni] f (-/-s) F varsity.

Uu|form [uni'form] f (-/-en) uniform.

Unikum ['u:nikum] n (-s/Unika, -s) unique (thing); queer fellow.

uninteress|ant adj. ['un?-] uninteresting, boring; '~iert adj. uninterested (an dat. in).

Universität [univerzi'tɛ:t] f (-/-en) university.

Universum [uni'verzum] n (-s/no pl.) universe.

Unke ['unkə] f (-/-n) zo. fire-bellied toad; F fig. croaker; 'Qn F v/i. (ge-, h) croak.

'unkennt|lich adj. unrecognizable; 'Qlichkeit f (-/no pl.): bis zur ~ past all recognition; 'Qnis f (-/no pl.) ignorance.

'unklar adj. not clear; meaning, etc.: obscure; answer, etc.: vague; im ~en sein to be in the dark (über acc. about); 'Qheit f want of clearness; vagueness; obscurity.

'unklug adj. imprudent, unwise.

'Unkosten pl. cost(s pl.), expenses pl.; sich in (große) ~ stürzen go to great expense.

'Unkraut n weed.

un|kündbar adj. ['unkyntba:r] loan, etc.: irredeemable; employment: permanent; ~kundig adj. ['~kundiç] ignorant (gen. of); '~längst

adv. lately, recently, the other day;
'**~lauter** *adj.* competition: unfair;
'**~leidlich** *adj.* intolerable, insufferable; '**~leserlich** *adj.* illegible;
~leugbar *adj.* ['**~**ɔykbɑːr] undeniable; '**~logisch** *adj.* illogical; '**~**lösbar *adj.* unsolvable, insoluble.
'**Unlust** *f* (-/*no pl.*) reluctance (*zu inf.* to *inf.*); '**2ig** *adj.* reluctant.
'**un|manierlich** *adj.* unmannerly;
'**~männlich** *adj.* unmanly; **~maßgeblich** *adj.* ['**~**ge:plɪç]: *nach m-r ~en Meinung* in my humble opinion; '**~mäßig** *adj.* immoderate; intemperate; '**2menge** *f* enormous *or* vast quantity *or* number.
'**Unmensch** *m* monster, brute; '**2lich** *adj.* inhuman, brutal; '**~lichkeit** *f* inhumanity, brutality.
'**un|mißverständlich** *adj.* unmistakable; '**~mittelbar** *adj.* immediate, direct; '**~möbliert** *adj.* unfurnished; '**~modern** *adj.* unfashionable, outmoded.
'**unmöglich** *adj.* impossible; '**2keit** *f* impossibility.
'**Unmoral** *f* immorality; '**2isch** *adj.* immoral.
'**unmündig** *adj.* under age.
'**un|musikalisch** *adj.* unmusical;
'**2mut** *m* (-[e]s/*no pl.*) displeasure (*über acc.* at, over); '**~nachahmlich** *adj.* inimitable; '**~nachgiebig** *adj.* unyielding; '**~nachsichtig** *adj.* strict, severe; inexorable; **~nahbar** *adj.* inaccessible, unapproachable; '**~natürlich** *adj.* unnatural; affected; '**~nötig** *adj.* unnecessary, needless; '**~nütz** *adj.* useless; **~ordentlich** *adj.* ['un²-] untidy; *room, etc.*: *a.* disorderly; '**2ordnung** ['un²-] *f* disorder, mess.
'**unpartei|isch** *adj.* impartial, unbias(s)ed; '**2ische** *m* (-n/-n) referee; umpire; '**2lichkeit** *f* impartiality.
'**un|passend** *adj.* unsuitable; improper; inappropriate; '**~passierbar** *adj.* impassable.
unpäßlich *adj.* ['unpeslɪç] indisposed, unwell; '**2keit** *f* (-/-en) indisposition.
'**un|persönlich** *adj.* impersonal (*a. gr.*); '**~politisch** *adj.* unpolitical; '**~praktisch** *adj.* unpractical, *Am. a.* impractical; '**2rat** *m* (-[e]s/*no pl.*) filth; rubbish; **~wittern** smell a rat.
'**unrecht 1.** *adj.* wrong; ~ *haben* be wrong; *j-m* ~ *tun* wrong s.o.; **2.** **2** *n* (-[e]s/*no pl.*): *mit or zu* ~ wrongly; *ihm ist* ~ *geschehen* he has been wronged; '**~mäßig** *adj.* unlawful; '**2mäßigkeit** *f* unlawfulness.
'**unreell** *adj.* dishonest; unfair.
'**unregelmäßig** *adj.* irregular (*a. gr.*); '**2keit** *f* (-/-en) irregularity.
'**unreif** *adj.* unripe, immature (*both a. fig.*); '**2e** *f* unripeness, immaturity (*both a. fig.*).

'**un|rein** *adj.* impure (*a. eccl.*); unclean (*a. fig.*); '**~reinlich** *adj.* uncleanly; **~rettbar** *adv.*: ~ *verloren* irretrievably lost; '**~richtig** *adj.* incorrect, wrong.
Unruh ['unruː] *f* (-/-en) balance (-wheel); '**~e** *f* (-/-n) restlessness, unrest (*a. pol.*); uneasiness; disquiet(ude); flurry; alarm; ~*n pl.* disturbances *pl.*, riots *pl.*; '**2ig** *adj.* restless; uneasy; *sea:* rough, choppy.
'**unrühmlich** *adj.* inglorious.
uns *pers. pron.* [uns] us; *dat.:* a. to us; ~ (*selbst*) ourselves, *after prp.:* us; *ein Freund von* ~ a friend of ours.
'**un|sachgemäß** *adj.* inexpert; '**~sachlich** *adj.* not objective; personal; **~säglich** *adj.* [**~**'zeːklɪç] unspeakable; untold; '**~sanft** *adj.* ungentle; '**~sauber** *adj.* dirty; *fig. a.* unfair (*a. sports*); '**~schädlich** *adj.* innocuous, harmless; '**~scharf** *adj.* blurred; *pred. a.* out of focus; **~schätzbar** *adj.* inestimable, invaluable; '**~scheinbar** *adj.* plain, *Am. a.* homely.
'**unschicklich** *adj.* improper, indecent; '**2keit** *f* (-/-en) impropriety, indecency.
unschlüssig *adj.* ['unʃlʏsɪç] irresolute; '**2keit** *f* (-/*no pl.*) irresoluteness, irresolution.
'**un|schmackhaft** *adj.* insipid; unpalatable, unsavo(u)ry; '**~schön** *adj.* unlovely, unsightly; *fig.* unpleasant.
'**Unschuld** *f* (-/*no pl.*) innocence; '**2ig** *adj.* innocent (*an dat.* of).
'**unselbständig** *adj.* dependent (on others); '**2keit** *f* (lack of in)dependence.
unser ['unzər] **1.** *poss. pron.* our; *der* (*die, das*) ~*e* our; *die* ~*en pl.* our relations *pl.*; **2.** *pers. pron.* of us; *wir waren* ~ *drei* there were three of us.
'**unsicher** *adj.* unsteady; unsafe, insecure; uncertain; '**2heit** *f* unsteadiness; insecurity, unsafeness; uncertainty.
'**unsichtbar** *adj.* invisible.
'**Unsinn** *m* (-[e]s/*no pl.*) nonsense; '**2ig** *adj.* nonsensical.
'**Unsitt|e** *f* bad habit; abuse; '**2lich** *adj.* immoral; indecent (*a.* ¾); '**~lichkeit** *f* (-/-en) immorality.
'**un|solid(e)** *adj. p.* easy-going; *life:* dissipated; † unreliable; '**~sozial** *adj.* unsocial, antisocial; '**~sportlich** *adj.* unsportsmanlike; unfair (*gegenüber* to).
'**unstatthaft** *adj.* inadmissible.
'**unsterblich** *adj.* immortal.
Un'sterblichkeit *f* immortality.
'**un|stet** *adj.* unsteady; *character, life:* unsettled; '**2timmigkeit** ['**~**ʃtimɪçkaɪt] *f* (-/-en) discrepancy; dissension; '**~sträflich** *adj.* blame-

less; '~streitig adj. incontestable; '~sympathisch adj. disagreeable; er ist mir ~ I don't like him; '~tätig adj. inactive; idle.

'untauglich adj. unfit (a. ✗); unsuitable; '2keit f (-/no pl.) unfitness (a. ✗).

un'teilbar adj. indivisible.

unten adv. ['untən] below; downstairs; von oben bis ~ from top to bottom.

unter ['untər] 1. prp. (dat.; acc.) below, under; among; ~ anderem among other things; ~ zehn Mark (for) less than ten marks; ~ Null below zero; ~ aller Kritik beneath contempt; ~ diesem Gesichtspunkt from this point of view; 2. adj. lower; inferior; die ~en Räume the downstair(s) rooms.

Unter|abteilung ['untər?-] f subdivision; ~arm ['untər?-] m forearm; '~bau m (-[e]s/-ten) ⚒ substructure (a. 🛢), foundation.

unter|'bieten v/t. (irr. bieten, no -ge-, h) underbid; ✝ undercut, undersell (competitor); lower (record); ~'binden v/t. (irr. binden, no -ge-, h) ✄ ligature; fig. stop; ~'bleiben v/i. (irr. bleiben, no -ge-, sein) remain undone; not to take place.

unter'brech|en v/t. (irr. brechen, no -ge-, h) interrupt (a. 🎜); break, Am. a. stop over; ⚡ break (circuit); 2ung f (-/-en) interruption; break, Am. a. stopover.   [mit.\

unter'breiten v/t. (no -ge-, h) sub-\

unter'bring|en v/t. (irr. bringen, sep., -ge-, h) place (a. ✝); accommodate, lodge; '2ung f (-/-en) accommodation; ✝ placement.

unterdessen adv. [untər'dɛsən] (in the) meantime, meanwhile.

unter'drück|en v/t. (no -ge-, h) oppress (subjects, etc.); repress (revolt, sneeze, etc.); suppress (rising, truth, yawn, etc.); put down (rebellion, etc.); 2ung f (-/-en) oppression; repression; suppression; putting down.

unterernähr|t adj. ['untər?-] underfed, undernourished; '2ung f (-/no pl.) underfeeding, malnutrition.

Unter'führung f subway, Am. underpass.

'Untergang m (-[e]s/✗ ⁼e) ast. setting; ⚓ sinking; fig. ruin.

Unter'gebene m (-n/-n) inferior, subordinate; ✝ underling.

'untergehen v/i. (irr. gehen, sep., -ge-, sein) ast. set; ⚓ sink, founder; fig. be ruined.

untergeordnet adj. ['untərgə?ɔrdnət] subordinate; importance: secondary.

'Untergewicht n (-[e]s/no pl.) underweight.

unter'graben fig. v/t. (irr. graben, no -ge-, h) undermine.

'Untergrund m (-[e]s/no pl.) subsoil; '~bahn f underground (railway), in London: tube; Am. subway; '~bewegung f underground movement.

'unterhalb prp. (gen.) below, underneath.

'Unterhalt m (-[e]s/no pl.) support, subsistence, livelihood; maintenance.

unter'halt|en v/t. (irr. halten, no -ge-, h) maintain; support; entertain, amuse; sich ~ converse (mit with; über acc. on, about), talk (with; on, about); sich gut ~ enjoy o.s.; 2ung f maintenance, upkeep; conversation, talk; entertainment.

'Unterhändler m negotiator; ✗ Parlementaire.

'Unter|haus parl. n (-es/no pl.) House of Commons; '~hemd n vest, undershirt; '~holz n (-es/no pl.) underwood, brushwood; '~hose f (e-e a pair of) drawers pl., pants pl.; '2irdisch adj. subterranean, underground (both a. fig.).

unter'joch|en v/t. (no -ge-, h) subjugate, subdue; 2ung f (-/-en) subjugation.

'Unter|kiefer m lower jaw; '~kleid n slip; '~kleidung f underclothes pl., underclothing, underwear.

'unterkommen 1. v/i. (irr. kommen, sep., -ge-, sein) find accommodation; find employment; 2. n (-s/✗ -) accommodation; employment, situation.

'unter|kriegen F v/t. (sep., -ge-, h) bring to heel; sich nicht ~ lassen not to knuckle down or under; 2kunft ['~kunft] f (-/⁼e) accommodation, lodging; ✗ quarters pl.; '2lage f base; pad; fig.: voucher; ~n pl. documents pl.; data pl.

unter'lass|en v/t. (irr. lassen, no -ge-, h) omit (zu tun doing, to do); neglect (to do, doing); fail (to do); 2ung f (-/-en) omission; neglect; failure; 2ungssünde f sin of omission.

'unterlegen[1] v/t. (sep., -ge-, h) lay or put under; give (another meaning).

unter'legen[2] adj. inferior (dat. to); 2e m (-n/-n) loser; underdog; 2heit f (-/no pl.) inferiority.

'Unterleib m abdomen, belly.

unter'liegen v/i. (irr. liegen, no -ge-, sein) be overcome (dat. by); be defeated (by), sports: a. lose (to); fig.: be subject to; be liable to; es unterliegt keinem Zweifel, daß ... there is no doubt that ...

'Unter|lippe f lower lip; '~mieter m subtenant, lodger, Am. a. roomer.

unter'nehmen 1. v/t. (irr. nehmen, no -ge-, h) undertake; take (steps);

2. 2 n (-s/-) enterprise; **⊕** a. business; ⚓ operation.

unter'nehm|end adj. enterprising; **2er ⊕** m (-s/-) entrepreneur; contractor; employer; **2ung** f (-/-en) enterprise, undertaking; ⚓ operation; **~ungslustig** adj. enterprising.

'Unter|offizier ⚔ m non-commissioned officer; '**2ordnen** v/t. (sep., -ge-, h) subordinate (dat. to); sich ~ submit (to).

Unter'redung f (-/-en) conversation, conference.

Unterricht ['untərriçt] m (-[e]s/⚓ -e) instruction, lessons pl.

unter'richt|en v/t. (no -ge-, h): ~ in (dat.) instruct in, teach (English, etc.); ~ von inform s.o. of.

'Unterrichts|ministerium n ministry of education; '~stunde f lesson, (teaching period) ; '~wesen n (-s/no pl.) education; teaching.

'Unterrock m slip.

unter'sagen v/t. (no -ge-, h) forbid (j-m et. s.o. to do s.th.).

'Untersatz m stand; saucer.

unter'schätz|en v/t. (no -ge-, h) undervalue; underestimate, underrate.

unter'scheid|en v/t. and v/i. (irr. scheiden, no -ge-, h) distinguish (zwischen between; von from); sich ~ differ (von from); **2ung** f distinction.

'Unterschenkel m shank.

'unterschieb|en v/t. (irr. schieben, sep., -ge-, h) push under; fig.: attribute (dat. to); substitute (statt for); **2ung** f substitution.

Unterschied ['untərʃiːt] m (-[e]s/-e) difference; distinction; zum ~ von in distinction from or to; '**2lich** adj. different; differential; variable, varying; '**2slos** adj. indiscriminate; undiscriminating.

unter'schlag|en v/t. (irr. schlagen, no -ge-, h) embezzle; suppress (truth, etc.); **2ung** f (-/-en) embezzlement; suppression.

'Unterschlupf m (-[e]s/⚓e, -e) shelter, refuge.

unter'schreiben v/t. and v/i. (irr. schreiben, no -ge-, h) sign.

'Unterschrift f signature.

'Untersee|boot ⚓, ⚔ n s. U-Boot; '~kabel n submarine cable.

unter'setzt adj. thick-set, squat.

unterst adj. ['untərst] lowest, undermost.

'Unterstand ⚔ m shelter, dug-out.

unter'stehen v/i. (irr. stehen, no -ge-, h) 1. v/i. (dat.) be subordinate to; be subject to (law, etc.); 2. v/refl. dare; untersteh dich! don't you dare!; '~stellen v/t. (dat. to) ['~ʃtɛlən] (sep., -ge-, h) put or place under; garage (car); sich ~ take shelter (vor dat. from); 2. [~'ʃtɛlən] (no -ge-, h) (pre)suppose, assume; impute (dat.

to); j-m ~ ⚔ put (troops, etc.) under s.o.'s command; **2'stellung** f (-/-en) assumption, supposition; imputation; **~'streichen** v/t. (irr. streichen, no -ge-, h) underline, underscore (both a. fig.).

unter'stütz|en v/t. (no -ge-, h) support; back up; **2ung** f (-/-en) support (a. ⚓); assistance, aid; relief.

unter'such|en v/t. (no -ge-, h) examine (a. ⚕); inquire into, investigate (a. ⚖); explore; ⚖ try; analy|se, Am. -ze (a. ⚕); **2ung** f (-/-en) examination (a. ⚕); inquiry (gen. into), investigation (a. ⚖); exploration; analysis (a. ⚕).

Unter'suchungs|gefangene m prisoner on remand; **~gefängnis** n remand prison; **~haft** f detention on remand; **~richter** m investigating judge.

Untertan ['untərtaːn] m (-s, -en/ -en) subject.

untertänig adj. ['untərtɛːniç] submissive.

'Unter|tasse f saucer; '**2tauchen** (sep., -ge-, h) 1. v/i. (sein) dive, dip; duck; fig. disappear; 2. v/t. (h) duck.

'Unterteil n, m lower part.

unter'teil|en v/t. (no -ge-, h) subdivide; **2ung** f subdivision.

'Unter|titel m subheading; subtitle; a. caption (of film); '~ton m undertone; '**2vermieten** v/t. (no -ge-, h) sublet.

unter'wander|n pol. v/t. (no -ge-, h) infiltrate; **2ung** pol. f infiltration.

'Unterwäsche f s. Unterkleidung.

unterwegs adv. [untər'veːks] on the or one's way.

unter'weis|en v/t. (irr. weisen, no -ge-, h) instruct (in dat. in); **2ung** f instruction.

'Unterwelt f underworld (a. fig.).

unter'werf|en v/t. (irr. werfen, no -ge-, h) subdue (dat. to), subjugate (to); subject (to); submit (to); sich ~ submit (to); **2ung** f (-/-en) subjugation, subjection; submission (unter acc. to).

unterworfen adj. [untər'vorfən] subject (dat. to).

unterwürfig adj. [untər'vyrfiç] submissive; subservient; **2keit** f (-/no pl.) submissiveness; subservience.

unter'zeichn|en v/t. (no -ge-, h) sign; **2er** m signer, the undersigned; subscriber (gen. to); signatory (gen. to treaty); **2erstaat** m signatory state; **2ete** m, f (-n/-n) the undersigned; **2ung** f signature, signing.

unterziehen v/t. (irr. ziehen) 1. ['~tsiːən] (sep., -ge-, h) put on underneath; 2. [~'tsiːən] (no -ge-, h) subject (dat. to); sich e-r Operation ~ undergo an operation; sich e-r Prüfung ~ go in or sit for an examination; sich der Mühe ~ zu inf. take the trouble to inf.

'**Untiefe** f shallow, shoal.
'**Untier** n monster (a. fig.).
un|tilgbar adj. [un'tilkbɑ:r] indelible; † government annuities: irredeemable; ~'**tragbar** adj. unbearable, intolerable; costs: prohibitive; ~'**trennbar** adj. inseparable.
'**untreu** adj. untrue (dat. to), disloyal (to); husband, wife: unfaithful (to); '~**e** f disloyalty; unfaithfulness, infidelity.
un|'tröstlich adj. inconsolable, disconsolate; ~**trüglich** adj. [~'try:kliç] infallible, unerring.
'**Untugend** f vice, bad habit.
unüber|legt adj. ['un'y:bər-] inconsiderate, thoughtless; ~**sichtlich** adj. badly arranged; difficult to survey; involved; mot. corner: blind; ~'**trefflich** adj. unsurpassable; ~**windlich** adj. [~'vintliç] invincible; fortress: impregnable; obstacle, etc.: insurmountable; difficulties, etc.: insuperable.
unum|gänglich adj. [un'um'gɛnliç] absolutely necessary; ~**schränkt** adj. [~'frɛŋkt] absolute; ~**stößlich** adj. [~'ʃtø:sliç] irrefutable; incontestable; irrevocable; ~**wunden** adj. ['~vundən] frank, plain.
ununterbrochen adj. ['un'unterbrɔxən] uninterrupted; incessant.
unver|'änderlich adj. unchangeable; invariable; ~'**antwortlich** adj. irresponsible; inexcusable; ~'**besserlich** adj. incorrigible; '~**bindlich** adj. not binding or obligatory; answer, etc.: non-committal; ~**blümt** adj. [~'bly:mt] plain, blunt; ~**bürgt** adj. [~'byrkt] unwarranted; news: unconfirmed; '~**dächtig** adj. unsuspected; '~**daulich** adj. indigestible (a. fig.); '~**dient** adj. undeserved; '~**dorben** adj. unspoiled, unspoilt; fig.: uncorrupted; pure, innocent; '~**drossen** adj. indefatigable, unflagging; '~**dünnt** adj. undiluted; Am. a. straight; ~'**einbar** adj. incompatible; '~**fälscht** adj. unadulterated; fig. genuine; ~**fänglich** adj. ['~fɛnliç] not captious; ~**froren** adj. ['~fro:rən] unabashed, impudent; '~**frorenheit** f (-/-en) impudence, f cheek; '~**gänglich** adj. imperishable; ~**geßlich** adj. unforgettable; ~**gleichlich** adj. incomparable; '~**hältnismäßig** adj. disproportionate; '~**heiratet** adj. unmarried, single; '~**hofft** adj. unhoped-for, unexpected; '~**hohlen** adj. unconcealed; '~**käuflich** adj. unsal(e)able; not for sale; '~'**kennbar** adj. unmistakable; '~**letzbar** adj. invulnerable; fig. a. inviolable; ~**meidlich** adj. [~'maitliç] inevitable; '~**mindert** adj. undiminished; '~**mittelt** adj. abrupt.

'**Unvermögen** n (-s/no pl.) inability; impotence; '~**d** adj. impecunious, without means.
'**unvermutet** adj. unexpected.
'**Unver|nunft** f unreasonableness, absurdity; ~**nünftig** adj. unreasonable, absurd; '~**richteterdinge** adv. without having achieved one's object.
'**unverschämt** adj. impudent, impertinent; '~**heit** f (-/-en) impudence, impertinence.
'**unver|schuldet** adj. not in debt; through no fault of mine, etc.; '~**sehens** adv. unawares, suddenly, all of a sudden; ~**sehrt** adj. ['~ze:rt] uninjured; '~**söhnlich** adj. implacable, irreconcilable; '~**sorgt** adj. unprovided for; '~**stand** m injudiciousness; folly, stupidity; '~**ständig** adj. injudicious; foolish; '~**ständlich** adj. unintelligible; incomprehensible; das ist mir ~ that is beyond me; '~**sucht** adj.: nichts ~ lassen leave nothing undone; '~**träglich** adj. unsociable; quarrelsome; '~**wandt** adj. steadfast; ~**wundbar** adj. [~'vuntba:r] invulnerable; ~**wüstlich** adj. [~'vy:stliç] indestructible; fig. irrepressible; ~**zagt** adj. ['~tsa:kt] intrepid, undaunted; '~**zeihlich** adj. unpardonable; ~**zinslich** adj. bearing no interest; non-interest-bearing; ~**züglich** adj. [~'tsy:kliç] immediate, instant.
'**unvollendet** adj. unfinished.
'**unvollkommen** adj. imperfect; '~**heit** f imperfection.
'**unvollständig** adj. incomplete; '~**keit** f (-/no pl.) incompleteness.
'**unvorbereitet** adj. unprepared; extempore.
'**unvoreingenommen** adj. unbias(s)ed, unprejudiced; '~**heit** f freedom from prejudice.
'**unvor|hergesehen** adj. unforoseseen; ~**schriftsmäßig** adj. irregular.
'**unvorsichtig** adj. incautious; imprudent; '~**keit** f incautiousness; imprudence.
unvor|'stellbar adj. unimaginable; '~**teilhaft** adj. unprofitable; dress, etc.: unbecoming.
'**unwahr** adj. untrue; '~**heit** f untruth.
'**unwahrscheinlich** adj. improbable, unlikely; '~**keit** f (-/-en) improbability, unlikelihood.
'**un|wegsam** adj. pathless, impassable; '~**weit** prp. (gen. or von) not far from; '~**wesen** n (-s/no pl.) nuisance; sein ~ treiben be up to one's tricks; '~**wesentlich** adj. unessential, immaterial (für to); '~**wetter** n thunderstorm; '~**wichtig** adj. unimportant, insignificant.
unwider|legbar adj. [unvi:dər'le:k

baːr] irrefutable; **~'ruflich** *adj.* irrevocable (*a.* ✝).

unwider'stehlich *adj.* irresistible; **2keit** *f* (*-/no pl.*) irresistibility.

unwieder'bringlich *adj.* irretrievable.

'Unwill|e *m* (*-ns/no pl.*), **'~en** *m* (*-s/no pl.*) indignation (*über acc.* at), displeasure (at, over); **2ig** *adj.* indignant (*über acc.* at), displeased (at, with); unwilling; **'2kürlich** *adj.* involuntary.

unwirklich *adj.* unreal.

'unwirksam *adj.* ineffective, inefficient; *laws, rules, etc.*: inoperative; ⚙ inactive; **'2keit** *f* (*-/no pl.*) ineffectiveness, inefficiency; ⚙ inactivity.

unwirsch *adj.* ['unvirʃ] testy.

'unwirt|lich *adj.* inhospitable, desolate; **'~schaftlich** *adj.* uneconomic(al).

'unwissen|d *adj.* ignorant; **'2heit** *f* (*-/no pl.*) ignorance; **'~tlich** *adj.* unwitting, unknowing.

unwohl *adj.* unwell, indisposed; **'2sein** *n* (*-s/no pl.*) indisposition.

'unwürdig *adj.* unworthy (*gen.* of).

un|zählig *adj.* [un'tsɛːliç] innumerable; **'2zart** *adj.* indelicate.

Unze ['untsə] *f* (*-/-n*) ounce.

'Unzeit *f:* zur ~ inopportunely; **'2-gemäß** *adj.* old-fashioned; inopportune; **'2ig** *adj.* untimely; unseasonable; *fruit:* unripe.

unzer|'brechlich *adj.* unbreakable, **~'reißbar** *adj.* untearable; **~'stör-bar** *adj.* indestructible; **~'trenn-lich** *adj.* inseparable.

'un|ziemlich *adj.* unseemly; **'2-zucht** *f* (*-/no pl.*) lewdness; ⚕ sexual offen|ce, *Am.* -se; **'~züchtig** *adj.* lewd; obscene.

unzufrieden *adj.* discontented (*mit* with), dissatisfied (with, at); **'2heit** *f* discontent, dissatisfaction.

'unzugänglich *adj.* inaccessible.

unzulänglich *adj.* ['untsuleŋliç] insufficient; **'2keit** *f* (*-/-en*) insufficiency; shortcoming.

'unzulässig *adj.* inadmissible; *esp.* ⚕ *influence:* undue.

'unzurechnungsfähig *adj.* irresponsible; **'2keit** *f* irresponsibility.

'unzu|reichend *adj.* insufficient; **'~sammenhängend** *adj.* incoherent; **'~träglich** *adj.* unwholesome; **'~treffend** *adj.* incorrect; inapplicable (*auf acc.* to).

'unzuverlässig *adj.* unreliable, untrustworthy; *friend: a.* uncertain; **'2keit** *f* unreliability, untrustworthiness.

'unzweckmäßig *adj.* inexpedient; **'2keit** *f* inexpediency.

'un|zweideutig *adj.* unequivocal; unambiguous; **'~zweifelhaft 1.** *adj.* undoubted, undubitable; **2.** *adv.* doubtless.

üppig *adj.* ['ypiç] ❀ luxuriant, exuberant, opulent; *food:* luxurious, opulent; *figure:* voluptuous; **'2keit** *f* (*-/~-en*) luxuriance, luxuriancy, exuberance; voluptuousness.

ur|alt *adj.* ['uːr'ʔalt] very old; (as) old as the hills; **2aufführung** ['uːrʔ-] *f* world première.

Uran [u'raːn] *n* (*-s/no pl.*) uranium.

urbar *adj.* ['uːrbaːr] arable, cultivable; ~ *machen* reclaim; **'2ma-chung** *f* (*-/-en*) reclamation.

'Ur|bevölkerung *f* aborigines *pl.*; **'~bild** *n* original, prototype; **'2-eigen** *adj.* one's very own; **'~enkel** *m* great-grandson; **'~großeltern** *pl.* great-grandparents *pl.*; **'~groß-mutter** *f* great-grandmother; **'~ großvater** *m* great-grandfather.

'Urheber *m* (*-s/-*) author; **'~recht** *n* copyright (*an dat.* in); **'~schaft** *f* (*-/no pl.*) authorship.

Urin [u'riːn] *m* (*-s/-e*) urine; **2ieren** [~i'niːrən] *v/i.* (*no -ge-, h*) urinate.

'Urkund|e *f* document; deed; **'~en-fälschung** *f* forgery of documents; **2lich** *adj.* ['~tliç] documentary.

Urlaub ['uːrlaup] *m* (*-[e]s/-e*) leave (of absence) (*a.* ⚔); holiday(s *pl.*), *esp. Am.* vacation; **'~er** ['~bər] *m* (*-s/-*) holiday-maker, *esp. Am.* vacationist, vacationer.

Urne ['urnə] *f* (*-/-n*) urn; ballotbox.

'ur|plötzlich 1. *adj.* very sudden, abrupt; **2.** *adv.* all of a sudden; **'2sache** *f* cause; reason; *keine ~l* don't mention it, *Am. a.* you are welcome; **'~sächlich** *adj.* causal; **'2schrift** *f* original (text); **'2-sprung** *m* origin, source; **'~sprünglich** *adj.* ['~ʃpryŋliç] original; **'2stoff** *m* primary matter.

Urteil ['urtaɪl] *n* (*-s/-e*) judg(e)-ment; ⚖ *a.* sentence; *meinem ~ nach* in my judg(e)ment; *sich ein ~ bilden* form a judg(e)ment (*über acc.* of, on); **'2en** *v/i.* (*ge-, h*) judge (*über acc.* of; *nach* by, from); **'~s-kraft** *f* (*-/~-e*) discernment.

'Ur|text *m* original (text); **'~wald** *m* primeval *or* virgin forest; **2-wüchsig** *adj.* ['~vyːksiç] original; *fig.:* natural; rough; **'~zeit** *f* primitive times *pl.*

Utensilien [uten'ziːljən] *pl.* utensils *pl.*

Utop|ie [uto'piː] *f* (*-/-n*) Utopia; **2isch** *adj.* [u'toːpiʃ] Utopian, utopian.

V

Vagabund [vaga'bunt] *m* (-en/-en) vagabond, vagrant, tramp, *Am.* hobo, F bum.

Vakuum ['vaːkuʔum] *n* (-s/*Vakua, Vakuen*) vacuum.

Valuta ✝ [va'luːta] *f* (-/*Valuten*) value; currency.

Vanille [va'niljə] *f* (-/*no pl.*) vanilla.

variabel *adj.* [vari'aːbəl] variable.

Varia|nte [vari'antə] *f* (-/-n) variant; **~tion** [~'tsjoːn] *f* (-/-en) variation.

Varieté [varie'teː] *n* (-s/-s), **~thea-ter** *n* variety theatre, music-hall, *Am.* vaudeville theater.

variieren [vari'iːrən] *v/i. and v/t.* (*no -ge-, h*) vary.

Vase ['vaːzə] *f* (-/-n) vase.

Vater ['faːtər] *m* (-s/~) father; '**~land** *n* native country *or* land, mother country; '**~landsliebe** *f* patriotism.

väterlich *adj.* ['fɛːtərliç] fatherly, paternal.

'**Vater|schaft** *f* (-/*no pl.*) paternity, fatherhood; '**~unser** *eccl. n* (-s/-) Lord's Prayer.

Vati ['faːti] *m* (-s/-s) dad(dy).

Veget|arier [vege'taːrjər] *m* (-s/-) vegetarian; **&arisch** *adj.* vegetarian; **~ation** [~a'tsjoːn] *f* (-/-en) vegetation; **&ieren** [~'tiːrən] *v/i.* (*no -ge-, h*) vegetate.

Veilchen ❧ ['faɪlçən] *n* (-s/-) violet.

Vene *anat.* ['veːnə] *f* (-/-n) vein.

Ventil [vɛn'tiːl] *n* (-s/-e) valve (*a. ♪*); ♪ stop (*of organ*); *fig.* vent, outlet; **~ation** [~ila'tsjoːn] *f* (-/-en) ventilation; **~ator** [~i'laːtər] *m* (-s/-en) ventilator, fan.

verab|folgen [fɛr'apˈ] *v/t.* (*no ge-, h*) deliver; give; *✽* administer (*medicine*); **~reden** *v/t.* (*no -ge-, h*) agree upon, arrange; appoint, fix (*time, place*); *sich* ~ make an appointment, *Am.* F (have a) date; **&redung** *f* (-/-en) agreement; arrangement; appointment, *Am.* F date; **~reichen** *v/t.* (*no -ge-, h*) s. *verabfolgen*; **~scheuen** *v/t.* (*no -ge-, h*) abhor, detest, loathe; **~schieden** [~ʃiːdən] *v/t.* (*no -ge-, h*) dismiss; retire (*officer*); ✗ discharge (*troops*); *parl.* pass (*bill*); *sich* ~ take leave (*von of*), say goodbye (*to*); **&schiedung** *f* (-/-en) dismissal; discharge; passing.

ver|'achten *v/t.* (*no -ge-, h*) despise; **~ächtlich** *adj.* [~'ɛçtliç] contemptuous; contemptible; **&'achtung** *f* contempt; **~allgemeinern** [~ʔalgə'maɪnərn] *v/t.* (*no -ge-, h*) generalize; **~'altet** *adj.* antiquated, obsolete, out of date.

Veranda [ve'randa] *f* (-/*Veranden*) veranda(h), *Am. a.* porch.

veränder|lich *adj.* [fɛr'endərliç] changeable; variable (*a. ♀, gr.*); **~n** *v/t. and v/refl.* (*no -ge-, h*) alter, change; vary; **&ung** *f* change, alteration (*in dat.* in; *an dat.* to); variation.

verängstigt *adj.* [fɛr'ɛŋstiçt] intimidated, scared.

ver'anlag|en *v/t.* (*no -ge-, h*) of *taxation*: assess; **~t** *adj.* [~kt] talented; **&ung** *f* change, assessment; *fig.* talent(s *pl.*); *✽* predisposition.

ver'anlass|en *v/t.* (*no -ge-, h*) cause, occasion; arrange; **&ung** *f* (-/-en) occasion, cause; *auf m-e* ~ at my request *or* suggestion.

ver|'anschaulichen *v/t.* (*no -ge-, h*) illustrate; **~'anschlagen** *v/t.* (*no -ge-, h*) rate, value, estimate (*all: auf acc.* at).

ver'anstalt|en *v/t.* (*no -ge-, h*) arrange, organize; give (*concert, ball, etc.*); **&ung** *f* (-/-en) arrangement; event; *sports*: event, meeting, *Am.* meet.

ver'antwort|en *v/t.* (*no -ge-, h*) take the responsibility for; account for; **~lich** *adj.* responsible; *j-n* ~ *machen für* hold s.o. responsible for.

Ver'antwortung *f* (-/-en) responsibility; *die* ~ *tragen* be responsible; *zur* ~ *ziehen* call to account; **&slos** *adj.* irresponsible.

ver|'arbeiten *v/t.* (*no -ge-, h*) work up; ⊕ process, manufacture (*both: zu* into); digest (*food*) (*a. fig.*); **~'ärgern** *v/t.* (*no -ge-, h*) vex, annoy.

ver|'arm|en *v/i.* (*no -ge-, sein*) become poor; **~t** *adj.* impoverished.

ver|'ausgaben *v/t.* (*no -ge-, h*) spend (*money*); *sich* ~ run short of money; *fig.* spend o.s.; **~'äußern** *v/t.* (*no -ge-, h*) sell; alienate.

Verb *gr.* [vɛrp] *n* (-s/-en) verb.

Ver'band *m* (-[e]s/~e) *✽* dressing, bandage; association, union; ✗ formation, unit; **~(s)kasten** *m* first-aid box; **~(s)zeug** *n* dressing (material).

ver'bann|en *v/t.* (*no -ge-, h*) banish (*a. fig.*), exile; **&ung** *f* (-/-en) banishment, exile.

ver|barrikadieren [fɛrbarika'diːrən] *v/t.* (*no -ge-, h*) barricade; block (*street, etc.*); **~'bergen** *v/t.* (*irr. bergen, no -ge-, h*) conceal, hide.

ver'besser|n *v/t.* (*no -ge-, h*) improve; correct; **&ung** *f* improvement; correction.

ver'beug|en *v/refl.* (*no -ge-, h*) bow (*vor dat.* to); **&ung** *f* bow.

ver|'biegen *v/t.* (*irr. biegen, no*

-ge-, h) bend, twist, distort; ~'**bieten** v/t. (irr. bieten, no -ge-, h) forbid, prohibit; ~'**billigen** v/t. (no -ge-, h) reduce in price, cheapen.

ver|bind|en v/t. (irr. binden, no -ge-, h) ✗ dress; tie (together); bind (up); link (mit to); join, unite, combine; connect (a. teleph.); teleph. put s.o. through (mit to); j-m die Augen ~ blindfold s.o.; sich ~ join, unite, combine (a. 🜍); ich bin Ihnen sehr verbunden I am greatly obliged to you; falsch verbunden! teleph. wrong number!; ~**lich** adj. [~tliç] obligatory; obliging; 2**lichkeit** f (-/-en) obligation, liability; obligingness, civility.

Ver'bindung f union; alliance; combination; association (of ideas); connexion, (Am. only) connection (a. teleph., ⚙, ♠, ⊕); relation; communication (a. teleph.); 🜍 compound; geschäftliche ~ business relations pl.; teleph.: ~ bekommen (haben) get (be) through; die ~ verlieren mit lose touch with; in ~ bleiben (treten) keep (get) in touch (mit with); sich in ~ setzen mit communicate with, esp. Am. contact s.o.; ~**sstraße** f communication road, feeder road; ~**stür** f communication door.

ver|bissen adj. [fer'bisən] dogged; crabbed; ~'**bitten** v/refl. (irr. bitten, no -ge-, h): das verbitte ich mir! I won't suffer or stand that!

ver'bitter|n v/t. (no -ge-, h) embitter; 2**ung** f (-/⚡-en) bitterness (of heart).

verblassen [fer'blasən] v/i. (no -ge-, sein) fade (a. fig.).

Verbleib [fer'blaıp] m (-[e]s/no pl.) whereabouts sg., pl.; 2**en** [~bən] v/i. (irr. bleiben, no -ge-, sein) be left, remain.

ver'blend|en v/t. (no -ge-, h) 🜙 face (wall, etc.); fig. blind, delude; 2**ung** f (-/⚡-en) 🜙 facing; fig. blindness, delusion. [faded.\

verblichen adj. [fer'bliçən] colour:]

verblüff|en [fer'blyfən] v/t. (no -ge-, h) amaze; perplex, puzzle; dumbfound; 2**ung** f (-/⚡-en) amazement, perplexity.

ver|'blühen v/i. (no -ge-, sein) fade, wither; ~'**bluten** v/i. (no -ge-, sein) bleed to death.

ver'borgen adj. hidden; secret; 2**heit** f (-/no pl.) concealment; secrecy.

Verbot [fer'bo:t] n (-[e]s/-e) prohibition; 2**en** adj. forbidden, prohibited; Rauchen ~ no smoking.

Ver'brauch m (-[e]s/⚡-e) consumption (an dat. of); 2**en** v/t. (no -ge-, h) consume, use up; wear out; ~**er** m (-s/-) consumer; 2**t** adj. air: stale; p. worn out.

ver'brechen 1. v/t. (irr. brechen, no -ge-, h) commit; was hat er verbrochen? what is his offen|ce, Am. -se?, what has he done?; 2. 2 n (-s/-) crime, offen|ce, Am. -se.

Ver'brecher m (-s/-) criminal; 2**isch** adj. criminal; ~**tum** n (-s/no pl.) criminality.

ver'breit|en v/t. (no -ge-, h) spread, diffuse; shed (light, warmth, happiness); sich ~ spread; sich ~ über (acc.) enlarge (up)on (theme); ~**ern** v/t. and v/refl. (no -ge-, h) widen, broaden; 2**ung** f (-/⚡-en) spread (-ing), diffusion.

ver'brenn|en (irr. brennen, no -ge-) 1. v/i. (sein) burn; 2. v/t. (h) burn (up); cremate (corpse); 2**ung** f (-/-en) burning, combustion; cremation (of corpse); wound: burn.

ver'bringen v/t. (irr. bringen, no -ge-, h) spend, pass.

verbrüder|n [fer'bry:dərn] v/refl. (no -ge-, h) fraternize; 2**ung** f (-/-en) fraternization.

ver|'brühen v/t. (no -ge-, h) scald; sich ~ scald o.s.; ~'**buchen** v/t. (no -ge-, h) book.

Verbum gr. ['verbum] n (-s/Verba) verb.

verbünden [fer'byndən] v/refl. (no -ge-, h) ally o.s. (mit to, with).

Verbundenheit [fer'bundənhaıt] f (-/no pl.) bonds pl., ties pl.; solidarity; affection.

Ver'bündete m, f (-n/-n) ally, confederate; die ~n pl. the allies pl.

ver|'bürgen v/t. (no -ge-, h) guarantee, warrant; sich ~ für answer or vouch for; ~'**büßen** v/t. (no -ge-, h): e-e Strafe ~ serve a sentence, serve (one's) time.

Verdacht [fer'daxt] m (-[e]s/no pl.) suspicion; in ~ haben suspect.

verdächtig adj. [fer'deçtiç] suspected (gen. of); pred. suspect; suspicious; ~**en** [~gən] v/t. (no -ge-, h) suspect s.o. (gen. of); cast suspicion on; 2**ung** f (-/-en) suspicion; insinuation.

verdamm|en [fer'damən] v/t. (no -ge-, h) condemn, damn (a. eccl.); 2**nis** f (-/no pl.) damnation; ~**t** 1. adj. damned; F: ~! damn (it)!, confound it!; 2. F adv.: ~ kalt beastly cold; 2**ung** f (-/⚡-en) condemnation, damnation.

ver|'dampfen (no -ge-) v/t. (h) and v/i. (sein) evaporate; ~'**danken** v/t. (no -ge-, h): j-m et. ~ owe s.th. to s.o.

verdarb [fer'darp] pret. of verderben.

verdau|en [fer'dauən] v/t. (no -ge-, h) digest; ~**lich** adj. digestible; leicht ~ easy to digest, light; 2**ung** f (-/no pl.) digestion; 2**ungsstörung** f indigestion.

Ver'deck n (-[e]s/-e) ⚓ deck;

hood (*of carriage, car, etc.*); top (*of vehicle*); 2en *v/t.* (*no* -ge-, h) cover; conceal, hide.

ver'denken *v/t.* (*irr.* denken, *no* -ge-, h): ich kann es ihm nicht ~, daß I cannot blame him for *ger*.

Verderb [fɛr'dɛrp] *m* (-[e]s/*no pl.*) ruin; 2en [~bən] 1. *v/i.* (*irr.*, *no* -ge-, sein) spoil (*a. fig.*); rot; meat, *etc.*: go bad; *fig.* perish; 2. *v/t.* (*irr.*, *no* -ge-, h) spoil; *fig. a.*: corrupt; ruin; er will es mit niemandem ~ he tries to please everybody; sich den Magen ~ upset one's stomach; ~en [~bən] *n* (-s/*no pl.*) ruin; 2lich *adj.* [~plɪç] pernicious; *food*: perishable; ~nis [~pnɪs] *f* (-/~-se) corruption; depravity; 2t *adj.* [~pt] corrupted, depraved.

ver|'deutlichen *v/t.* (*no* -ge-, h) make plain *or* clear; ~'dichten *v/t.* (*no* -ge-, h) condense; sich ~ condense; *suspicion*: grow stronger; ~'dicken *v/t. and v/refl.* (*no* -ge-, h) thicken; ~'dienen *v/t.* (*no* -ge-, h) merit, deserve; earn (*money*).

Ver'dienst (-es/-e) 1. *m* gain, profit; earnings *pl.*; 2. *n* merit; es ist sein ~, daß it is owing to him that; 2voll *adj.* meritorious, deserving; ~spanne † *f* profit margin.

ver|'dient *adj. p.* of merit; (well-) deserved; sich ~ gemacht haben um deserve well of; ~'dolmetschen *v/t.* (*no* -ge-, h) interpret (*a. fig.*); ~'doppeln *v/t. and v/refl.* (*no* -ge-, h) double.

verdorben [fɛr'dɔrbən] 1. *p.p.* of verderben; 2. *adj. meat*: tainted; *stomach*: disordered, upset; *fig.* corrupt, depraved.

ver|'dorren [fɛr'dɔrən] *v/i.* (*no* -ge-, sein) wither (up); ~'drängen *v/t.* (*no* -ge-, h) push away, thrust aside; *fig.* displace; *psych.* repress; ~'drehen *v/t.* (*no* -ge-, h) distort, twist (*both a. fig.*); roll (*eyes*); *fig.* pervert; j-m den Kopf ~ turn s.o.'s head; ~'dreht F *fig. adj.* crazy; ~'dreifachen *v/t. and v/refl.* (*no* -ge-, h) triple.

verdrieß|en [fɛr'driːsən] *v/t.* (*irr.*, *no* -ge-, h) vex, annoy; ~lich *adj.* vexed, annoyed; sulky; *thing*: annoying.

ver'droß [fɛr'drɔs] *pret.* of verdrießen; ~drossen [~'drɔsən] 1.*p.p.* of verdrießen; 2. *adj.* sulky; listless.

ver'drucken *typ. v/t.* (*no* -ge-, h) misprint.

Verdruß [fɛr'drus] *m* (Verdrusses/~ Verdrusse) vexation, annoyance.

ver'dummen (*no* -ge-) 1. *v/t.* (h) make stupid; 2. *v/i.* (sein) become stupid.

ver'dunk|eln *v/t.* (*no* -ge-, h) darken, obscure (*both a. fig.*); black out (*window*); sich ~ darken;

2(e)lung *f* (-/~-en) darkening; obscuration; black-out; †† collusion.

ver|'dünnen *v/t.* (*no* -ge-, h) thin; dilute (*liquid*); ~'dunsten *v/i.* (*no* -ge-, sein) volatilize, evaporate; ~'dursten *v/i.* (*no* -ge-, sein) die of thirst; ~dutzt *adj.* [~'dutst] nonplussed.

ver'ed|eln *v/t.* (*no* -ge-, h) ennoble; refine; improve; ♦ graft; process (*raw materials*); 2(e)lung *f* (-/~-en) refinement; improvement; processing.

ver'ehr|en *v/t.* (*no* -ge-, h) revere, venerate; worship; admire, adore; 2er *m* (-s/-) worship(p)er; admirer, adorer; 2ung *f* (-/~-en) reverence, veneration; worship; adoration.

vereidigen [fɛr'aɪdɪɡən] *v/t.* (*no* -ge-, h) swear (*witness*); at entrance into office: swear *s.o.* in.

Verein [fɛr'aɪn] *m* (-[e]s/-e) union; society, association; club.

ver'einbar *adj.* compatible (*mit* with), consistent (with); ~en *v/t.* (*no* -ge-, h) agree upon, arrange; 2ung *f* (-/-en) agreement, arrangement.

ver'einen *v/t.* (*no* -ge-, h) *s.* vereinigen.

ver'einfach|en *v/t.* (*no* -ge-, h) simplify; 2ung *f* (-/-en) simplification.

ver'einheitlichen *v/t.* (*no* -ge-, h) unify, standardize.

ver'einig|en *v/t.* (*no* -ge-, h) unite, join; associate; sich ~ unite, join; associate o.s.; 2ung *f* (-/~-en) union; 2. (-/-en) union; society, association.

ver'ein|samen *v/i.* (*no* -ge-, sein) grow lonely *or* solitary; ~zelt *adj.* isolated; sporadic.

ver|'eiteln *v/t.* (*no* -ge-, h) frustrate; ~'ekeln *v/t.* (*no* -ge-, h): er hat mir das Essen verekelt he spoilt my appetite; ~'enden *v/i.* (*no* -ge-, sein) *animals*: die, perish; ~enge(r)n [~'ɛŋə(r)n] *v/t. and v/refl.* (*no* -ge-, h) narrow.

ver'erb|en *v/t.* (*no* -ge-, h) leave, bequeath; *biol.* transmit; sich ~ be hereditary; sich ~ auf (*acc.*) descend (up)on; 2ung *f* (-/~-en) *biol.* transmission; *physiol.* heredity; 2ungslehre *f* genetics.

verewig|en [fɛr'eːviɡən] *v/t.* (*no* -ge-, h) perpetuate; ~t *adj.* [~çt] deceased, late.

ver'fahren 1. *v/i.* (*irr.* fahren, *no* -ge-, sein) proceed; ~ mit deal with; 2. *v/t.* (*irr.* fahren, *no* -ge-, h) mismanage, muddle, bungle; sich ~ miss one's way; 3. 2 *n* (-s/-) procedure; proceeding(s *pl.* ††); ⊕ process.

Ver'fall *m* (-[e]s/*no pl.*) decay, decline; dilapidation (*of house, etc.*);

ǎ̃ forfeiture; expiration; maturity (*of bill of exchange*); ℒen 1. *v/i.* (irr. fallen, *no -ge-*, sein) decay; *house*: dilapidate; *document, etc.*: expire; *pawn*: become forfeited; *right*: lapse; *bill of exchange*: fall due; *sick person*: waste away; ~ auf (*acc.*) hit upon (*idea, etc.*); ~ in (*acc.*) fall into; j-m ~ become s.o.'s slave; 2. *adj.* ruinous; addicted (*dat.* to *drugs, etc.*); ~serscheinung [fer'fals°-] *f* symptom of decline; ~tag *m* day of payment.

ver|'fälschen *v/t.* (*no -ge-*, h) falsify; adulterate (*wine, etc.*); ~fänglich *adj.* [~'feŋliç] *question*: captious, insidious; risky; embarrassing; ~'färben *v/refl.* (*no -ge-*, h) change colo(u)r.

ver|'fass|en *v/t.* (*no -ge-*, h) compose, write; ℒer *m* (*-s/-*) author.

Ver'fassung *f* state, condition; *pol.* constitution; disposition (*of mind*); ℒsmäßig *adj.* constitutional; ℒs-widrig *adj.* unconstitutional.

ver|'faulen *v/i.* (*no -ge-*, sein) rot, decay; ~'fechten *v/t.* (*irr. fechten, no -ge-*, h) defend, advocate.

ver|'fehl|en *v/t.* (*no -ge-*, h) miss; ℒung *f* (*-/-en*) offen|ce, *Am.* -se.

ver|'feinden [fer'fainden] *v/t.* (*no -ge-*, h) make enemies of; sich ~ mit make an enemy of; ~feinern [~'fainern] *v/t. and v/refl.* (*no -ge-*, h) refine; ~fertigen [~'fertigen] *v/t.* (*no -ge-*, h) make, manufacture; compose.

ver|'film|en *v/t.* (*no -ge-*, h) film, screen; ℒung *f* (*-/-en*) film-version.

ver|'finstern *v/t.* (*no -ge-*, h) darken, obscure; sich ~ darken; ~'flachen (*no -ge-*) *v/i.* (sein) and *v/refl.* (h) (become) shallow (*a. fig.*); ~'flechten *v/t.* (*irr. flechten, no -ge-*, h) interlace; *fig.* involve; ~'fliegen *v/i.* (*irr. fliegen, no -ge-*) 1. *v/i.* (sein) evaporate; *time*: fly; *fig.* vanish; 2. *v/refl.* (h) *bird*: stray; ⚔ lose one's bearings, get lost; ~'fließen *v/i.* (*irr. fließen, no -ge-*, sein) *colours*: blend; *time*: elapse; ~'flossen *adj.* [~'flɔsən] *time*: past; F ein ~er Freund a late friend, an ex-friend.

ver|'fluch|en *v/t.* (*no -ge-*, h) curse, *Am.* F cuss; ~t *adj.* damned; ~! damn (it)!, confound it!

ver|'flüchtigen [fer'flyçtigən] *v/t.* (*no -ge-*, h) volatilize; sich ~ evaporate (*a. fig.*); F *fig.* vanish; ~'flüssigen [~'flysigən] *v/t. and v/refl.* (*no -ge-*, h) liquefy.

ver|'folg|en *v/t.* (*no -ge-*, h) pursue; persecute; follow (*tracks*); trace; *thoughts, dream*: haunt; *gerichtlich* ~ prosecute; ℒer *m* (*-s/-*) pursuer; persecutor; ℒung *f* (*-/-en*) pursuit; persecution; pursuance; *gericht-*

liche ~ prosecution; ℒungswahn ⚗ *m* persecution mania.

ver|'frachten [fer'fraxtən] *v/t.* (*no -ge-*, h) freight, *Am. a.* ship (*goods*); ⚓ ship; F j-n ~ in (*acc.*) bundle s.o. in(to) (*train, etc.*); ~'froren *adj.* chilled through; ~'früht *adj.* premature.

verfüg|bar *adj.* [fer'fy:kba:r] available; ~en [~gən] (*no -ge-*, h) 1. *v/t.* decree, order; 2. *v/i.*: ~ über (*acc.*) have at one's disposal; dispose of; ℒung [~guŋ] *f* (*-/-en*) decree, order; disposal; j-m zur ~ stehen (*stellen*) be (place) at s.o.'s disposal.

ver|'führ|en *v/t.* (*no -ge-*, h) seduce; ℒer *m* (*-s/-*) seducer; ~erisch *adj.* seductive; enticing; tempting; ℒung *f* seduction.

vergangen *adj.* [fer'gaŋən] gone, past; im ~en Jahr last year; ℒheit *f* (*-/-en*) past; *gr.* past tense.

vergänglich *adj.* [fer'geŋliç] transient, transitory.

vergas|en [fer'ga:zən] *v/t.* (*no -ge-*, h) gasify; gas *s.o.*; ℒer *mot. m* (*-s/-*) carburet(t)or.

vergaß [fer'ga:s] *pret.* of vergessen.

ver|geb|en [fer'ge:bən] *v/t.* (*irr. geben, no -ge-*, h) give away (*an j-n* to s.o.); confer (on), bestow (on); place (*order*); forgive; sich et. ~ compromise one's dignity; ~ens *adv.* [~s] in vain; ~lich [~pliç] 1. *adj.* vain; 2. *adv.* in vain; ℒung [~buŋ] *f* (*-/⚒-en*) bestowal, conferment (*both: an acc.* on); forgiveness, pardon.

ver|'gegenwärtigen [fergeː'gən'vertigən] *v/t.* (*no -ge-*, h) represent; sich et. ~ visualize s.th.

ver|'gehen 1. *v/i.* (*irr. gehen, no -ge-*, sein) pass (away); fade (away); ~ vor (*dat.*) die of; 2. *v/refl.* (*irr. gehen, no -ge-*, h): sich an j-m ~ assault s.o.; violate s.o.; sich gegen das Gesetz ~ offend against or violate the law; 3. ℒ *n* (*-s/-*) offen|ce, *Am.* -se.

ver|'gelt|en *v/t.* (*irr. gelten, no -ge-*, h) repay, requite; reward; retaliate; ℒung *f* (*-/-en*) requital; retaliation; retribution.

vergessen [fer'gesən] 1. *v/t.* (*irr., no -ge-*, h) forget; leave; 2. *p.p.* of 1; ℒheit *f* (*-/no pl.*): in ~ geraten sink *or* fall into oblivion.

vergeßlich *adj.* [fer'gesliç] forgetful.

vergeud|en [fer'gɔrdən] *v/t.* (*no -ge-*, h) dissipate, squander, waste (*time, money*); ℒung *f* (*-/⚒-en*) waste.

vergewaltig|en [fergə'valtigən] *v/t.* (*no -ge-*, h) violate; rape; ℒung *f* (*-/-en*) violation; rape.

ver|gewissern [fergə'wisərn] *v/refl.* (*no -ge-*, h) make sure (e-r Sache of s.th.); ~'gießen v/t. (irr. gießen, no -ge-, h) shed (tears, blood); spill (liquid).

ver'gift|en v/t. (no -ge-, h) poison (a. fig.); sich ~ take poison; 2ung f (-/-en) poisoning.

Vergißmeinnicht ♀ [fɛr'gismaɪn-nɪçt] n (-[e]s/-[e]) forget-me-not.

vergittern [fɛr'gitərn] v/t. (no -ge-, h) grate.

Vergleich [fɛr'glaɪç] m (-[e]s/-e) comparison; ⅔: agreement; compromise, composition; 2bar adj. comparable (mit to); 2en v/t. (irr. gleichen, no -ge-, h) compare (mit with, to); sich ~ mit ⅔ come to terms with; verglichen mit as against, compared to; 2sweise adv. comparatively.

vergnügen [fɛr'gny:gən] 1. v/t. (no -ge-, h) amuse; sich ~ enjoy o.s.; 2. 2 n (-s/-) pleasure, enjoyment; entertainment; ~ finden an (dat.) take pleasure in; viel ~! have a good time! [gay.]
vergnügt adj. [fɛr'gny:kt] merry,)

Ver'gnügung f (-/-en) pleasure, amusement, entertainment; ~s-reise f pleasure-trip, tour; 2s-süchtig adj. pleasure-seeking.

ver'golden [fɛr'gɔldən] v/t. (no -ge-, h) gild; ~göttern fig. [~'gœt-tərn] v/t. (no -ge-, h) idolize, adore; ~'graben v/t. (irr. graben, no -ge-, h) bury (a. fig.); sich ~ bury o.s.; ~'greifen v/refl. (irr. greifen, no -ge-, h) sprain (one's hand, etc.); sich ~ an (dat.) lay (violent) hands on, attack, assault; embezzle (money); encroach upon (s.o.'s property); ~griffen adj. [~'grifən] goods: sold out; book: out of print.

vergrößer|n [fɛr'grø:sərn] v/t. (no -ge-, h) enlarge (a. phot.); opt. magnify; sich ~ enlarge; 2ung f 1. (-/-en) phot. enlargement; opt. magnification; 2. (-/-en) enlargement; increase; extension; 2ungs-glas n magnifying glass.

Vergünstigung [fɛr'gynstiguŋ] f (-/-en) privilege.

vergüt|en [fɛr'gy:tən] v/t. (no -ge-, h) compensate (j-m et. s.o. for s.th.); reimburse (money spent); 2ung f (-/-en) compensation; reimbursement.

ver'haft|en v/t. (no -ge-, h) arrest; 2ung f (-/-en) arrest.

ver'halten 1. v/t. (irr. halten, no -ge-, h) keep back; catch or hold (one's breath); suppress, check; sich ~ thing: be; p. behave; sich ruhig ~ keep quiet; 2. 2 n (-s/no pl.) behavio(u)r, conduct.

Verhältnis [fɛr'hɛltnis] n (-ses/-se) proportion, rate; relation(s pl.) (zu with); F liaison, love-affair; F mistress; ~se pl. conditions pl., circumstances pl.; means pl.; 2mäßig

adv. in proportion; comparatively; ~wort gr. n (-[e]s/~er) preposition.

Ver'haltungsmaßregeln f/pl. instructions pl.

ver'hand|eln (no -ge-, h) 1. v/i. negotiate, treat (über acc., wegen for); ⅔ try (über et. s.th.); 2. v/t. discuss; 2lung f negotiation; discussion; ⅔ trial, proceedings pl.

ver'häng|en v/t. (no -ge-, h) cover (over), hang; inflict (punishment) (über acc. upon); 2nis n (-ses/-se) fate; ~nisvoll adj. fatal; disastrous.

ver'härmt adj. [fɛr'hɛrmt] careworn; ~harren [~'harən] v/i. (no -ge-, h, sein) persist (auf dat., bei, in dat. in), stick (to); ~'härten v/t. and v/refl. (no -ge-, h) harden; ~haßt adj. [~'hast] hated; hateful, odious; ~'hätscheln v/t. (no -ge-, h) coddle, pamper, spoil; ~'hauen v/t. (irr. hauen, no -ge-, h) thrash.

verheer|en [fɛr'he:rən] v/t. (no -ge-, h) devastate, ravage, lay waste; ~end fig. adj. disastrous; 2ung f (-/-en) devastation.

ver'hehlen [fɛr'he:lən] v/t. (no -ge-, h) s. verheimlichen; ~'heilen v/i. (no -ge-, sein) heal (up).

ver'heimlich|en [fɛr'haɪmlɪçən] v/t. (no -ge-, h) hide, conceal; 2ung f (-/~-en) concealment.

ver'heirat|en v/t. (no -ge-, h) marry (mit to); sich ~ marry; 2ung f (-/~-en) marriage.

ver'heiß|en v/t. (irr. heißen, no -ge-, h) promise; 2ung f (-/-en) promise; ~ungsvoll adj. promising.

ver'helfen v/i. (irr. helfen, no -ge-, h): j-m zu et. ~ help s.o. to s.th.

ver'herrlich|en v/t. (no -ge-, h) glorify; 2ung f (-/~-en) glorification.

ver|'hetzen v/t. (no -ge-, h) instigate; ~'hexen v/t. (no -ge-, h) bewitch.

ver'hinder|n v/t. (no -ge-, h) prevent; 2ung f (-/~-en) prevention.

ver'höhn|en v/t. (no -ge-, h) deride, mock (at), taunt; 2ung f (-/-en) derision, mockery.

Verhör ⅔ [fɛr'hø:r] n (-[e]s/-e) interrogation, questioning (of prisoners, etc.); examination; 2en v/t. (no -ge-, h) examine, hear; interrogate; sich ~ hear it wrong.

ver|'hüllen v/t. (no -ge-, h) cover, veil; ~'hungern v/i. (no -ge-, sein) starve; ~'hüten v/t. (no -ge-, h) prevent.

ver'irr|en v/refl. (no -ge-, h) go astray, lose one's way; ~t adj.: ~es Schaf stray sheep; 2ung fig. f (-/-en) aberration; error.

ver'jagen v/t. (no -ge-, h) drive away.

verjähr|en ⅔ [fɛr'jɛ:rən] v/i. (no -ge-, sein) become prescriptive;

Qung f (-/-en) limitation, (negative) prescription.

verjüngen [fɛr'jyŋən] v/t. (no -ge-, h) make young again, rejuvenate; reduce (scale); sich ~ grow young again, rejuvenate; taper off.

Ver'kauf m sale; Qen v/t. (no -ge-, h) sell; zu ~ for sale; sich gut ~ sell well.

Ver'käuf|er m seller; vendor; shop-assistant, salesman, Am. a. (sales-) clerk; ~erin f (-/-nen) seller; vendor; shop-assistant, saleswoman, shop girl, Am. a. (sales)clerk; Qlich adj. sal(e)able; for sale.

Ver'kaufs|automat m slot-machine, vending machine; ~schlager m best seller.

Verkehr [fɛr'keːr] m (-[e]s/~ -e) traffic; transport(ation); communication; correspondence; ⚓, ✈, ✎, etc.: service; commerce, trade; intercourse (a. sexually); aus dem ~ ziehen withdraw from service; withdraw (money) from circulation; Qen (no -ge-, h) 1. v/t. convert (in acc. into), turn (into); 2. v/i. ship, bus, etc.: run, ply (zwischen dat. between); bei j-m ~ go to or visit s.o.'s house; ~ in (dat.) frequent (public house, etc.); ~ mit associate or mix with; have (sexual) intercourse with.

Ver'kehrs|ader f arterial road; ~ampel f traffic lights pl., traffic signal; ~büro n tourist bureau; ~flugzeug n air liner; ~insel f refuge, island; ~minister m minister of transport; ~mittel n (means of) conveyance or transport, Am. transportation; ~polizist m traffic policeman or constable, sl. traffic cop; Qreich adj. congested with traffic, busy; ~schild n traffic sign; ~schutzmann m s. Verkehrspolizist; ~stauung f, ~stockung f traffic block, traffic jam; ~störung f interruption of traffic; ⚓, etc.: breakdown; ~straße f thoroughfare; ~teilnehmer m road user; ~unfall m traffic accident; ~verein m tourist agency; ~verhältnisse pl. traffic conditions pl.; ~vorschrift f traffic regulation; ~wesen n (-s/no pl.) traffic; ~zeichen n traffic sign.

ver'|kehrt adj. inverted, upside down; fig. wrong; ~'kennen v/t. (irr. kennen, no -ge-, h) mistake; misunderstand, misjudge.

Ver'kettung f (-/-en) concatenation (a. fig.).

ver'|klagen ⚖ v/t. (no -ge-, h) sue (auf acc., wegen for); bring an action against s.o.; ~'kleben v/t. (no -ge-, h) paste s.th. up.

ver'kleid|en v/t. (no -ge-, h) disguise; ⊕: line; face; wainscot; encase; sich ~ disguise o.s.; Qung f

(-/-en) disguise; ⊕: lining; facing; panel(l)ing, wainscot(t)ing.

verkleiner|n [fɛr'klaɪnərn] v/t. (no -ge-, h) make smaller, reduce, diminish; fig. belittle, derogate; Qung f (-/-en) reduction, diminution; fig. derogation.

ver'|klingen v/i. (irr. klingen, no -ge-, sein) die away; ~knöchern [~'knœçərn] (no -ge-) 1. v/t. (h) ossify; 2. v/i. (sein) ossify; fig. a. fossilize; ~'knoten v/t. (no -ge-, h) knot; ~'knüpfen v/t. (no -ge-, h) knot or tie (together); fig. connect, combine; ~'kohlen (no -ge-) 1. v/t. (h) carbonize; char; F: j-n ~ pull s.o.'s leg; 2. v/i. (sein) char; ~'kommen 1. v/i. (irr. kommen, no -ge-, sein) decay; p.: go downhill or to the dogs; become demoralized; 2. adj. decayed; depraved, corrupt; ~'korken v/t. (no -ge-, h) cork (up).

ver'körper|n v/t. (no -ge-, h) personify, embody; represent; esp. thea. impersonate; Qung f (-/-en) personification, embodiment; impersonation.

ver'|krachen F v/refl. (no -ge-, h) fall out (mit with); ~'krampft adj. cramped; fig. tense; ~'kriechen v/refl. (irr. kriechen, no -ge-, h) hide; ~'krümmt adj. crooked; ~krüppelt adj. [~'krypəlt] crippled; stunted; ~krustet adj. [~'krʊstət] (en)crusted; caked; ~'kühlen v/refl. (no -ge-, h) catch (a) cold.

ver'kümmer|n v/i. (no -ge-, sein) ♨, ⚘ become stunted; ⚘ atrophy; fig. waste away; ~t adj. stunted; atrophied; rudimentary (a. biol.).

verkünd|en [fɛr'kyndən] v/t. (no -ge-, h), ~igen v/t. (no -ge-, h) announce; publish, proclaim; pronounce (judgement); Qigung f, Qung f (-/-en) announcement; proclamation; pronouncement.

ver'|kuppeln v/t. (no -ge-, h) ⊕ couple; fig. pander; ~'kürzen v/t. (no -ge-, h) shorten; abridge; beguile (time, etc.); ~'lachen v/t. (no -ge-, h) laugh at; ~'laden v/t. (irr. laden, no -ge-, h) load, ship; ⚓ entrain (esp. troops).

Verlag [fɛr'laːk] m (-[e]s/-e) publishing house, the publishers pl.; im ~ von published by.

ver'lagern v/t. (no -ge-, h) displace, shift; sich ~ shift.

Ver'lags|buchhändler m publisher; ~buchhandlung f publishing house; ~recht n copyright.

ver'langen 1. v/t. (no -ge-, h) demand; require; desire; 2. v/i. (no -ge-, h) ~ nach ask for; long for; 3. Q n (-s/~ -) desire; longing (nach for); demand, request; auf ~ by request, ✝ on demand; auf ~ von at the request of, at s.o.'s request.

verlänger|n [fɛr'lɛŋərn] v/t. (no

-ge-, h) lengthen; prolong, extend; 2ung f (-/-en) lengthening; prolongation, extension.
ver'langsamen v/t. (no -ge-, h) slacken, slow down.
ver'lassen v/t. (irr. lassen, no -ge-, h) leave; forsake, abandon, desert; sich ~ auf (acc.) rely on; 2heit f (-/no pl.) abandonment; loneliness.
verläßlich adj. [fɛr'lɛsliç] reliable.
Ver'lauf m lapse, course (of time); progress. development (of matter); course (of disease, etc.); im ~ (gen.) or von in the course of; e-n schlimmen ~ nehmen take a bad turn; 2en (irr. laufen, no -ge-) 1. v/i. (sein) time: pass, elapse; matter: take its course; turn out, develop; road, etc.: run, extend; 2. v/refl. (h) lose one's way, go astray; crowd: disperse; water: subside.
ver'lauten v/i. (no -ge-, sein): ~ lassen give to understand, hint; wie verlautet as reported.
ver'leb|en v/t. (no -ge-, h) spend, pass; ~t adj. [~pt] worn out.
ver'leg|en 1. v/t. (no -ge-, h) mislay; transfer, shift, remove; ⊕ lay (cable, etc.); bar (road); put off, postpone; publish (book); sich ~ auf (acc.) apply o.s. to; 2. adj. embarrassed; at a loss (um for answer, etc.); 2enheit f (-/~-en) embarrassment; difficulty; predicament; 2er m (-s/-) publisher; 2ung f (-/-en) transfer, removal; ⊕ laying; time: postponement.
ver'leiden v/t. (no -ge-, h) s. verekeln.
ver'leih|en v/t. (irr. leihen, no -ge-, h) lend, Am. a. loan; hire or let out; bestow (right, etc.) (j-m on s.o.); award (price); 2ung f (-/-en) lending, loan; bestowal.
ver'|leiten v/t. (no -ge-, h) mislead; induce; seduce; ⚖ suborn; ~'lernen v/t. (no -ge-, h) unlearn, forget; ~'lesen v/t. (irr. lesen, no -ge-, h) read out; call (names) over; pick (vegetables, etc.); sich ~ read wrong.
verletz|en [fɛr'lɛtsən] v/t. (no -ge-, h) hurt, injure; fig. a.: offend; violate; ~end adj. offensive; 2te [~tə] m, f (-n/-n) injured person; die ~n pl. the injured pl.; 2ung f (-/-en) hurt, injury, wound; fig. violation.
ver'leugn|en v/t. (no -ge-, h) deny; disown; renounce (belief, principle, etc.); sich ~ lassen have o.s. denied (vor j-m to s.o.); 2ung f (-/-en) denial; renunciation.
verleumd|en [fɛr'ɔymdən] v/t. (no -ge-, h) slander, defame; ~erisch adj. slanderous; 2ung f (-/-en) slander, defamation, in writing: libel.
ver'lieb|en v/refl. (no -ge-, h): sich ~ in (acc.) fall in love with; ~t adj.

[~pt] in love (in acc. with); amorous; 2theit f (-/~-en) amorousness.
verlieren [fɛr'li:rən] (irr., no -ge-, h) 1. v/t. lose; shed (leaves, etc.); sich ~ lose o.s.; disappear; 2. v/i. lose.
ver'lob|en v/t. (no -ge-, h) engage (mit to); sich ~ become engaged; 2te [~ptə] (-n/-n) 1. m fiancé; die ~n pl. the engaged couple sg.; 2. f fiancée; 2ung f (-/-en) engagement.
ver'lock|en v/t. (no -ge-, h) allure, entice; tempt; ~end adj. tempting; 2ung f (-/-en) allurement, enticement.
verlogen adj. [fɛr'lo:gən] mendacious; 2heit f (-/~-en) mendacity.
verlor [fɛr'lo:r] pret. of verlieren; ~en 1. p.p. of verlieren; 2. adj. lost; fig. forlorn; ~e Eier poached eggs; ~engehen v/i. (irr. gehen, sep., -ge-, sein) be lost.
ver'los|en v/t. (no -ge-, h) raffle; 2ung f (-/-en) lottery, raffle.
ver'löten v/t. (no -ge-, h) solder.
Verlust [fɛr'lust] m (-es/-e) loss; ~e pl. ⚔ casualties pl.
ver'machen v/t. (no -ge-, h) bequeath, leave s.th. (dat. to).
Vermächtnis [fɛr'mɛçtnis] n (-ses/-se) will; legacy, bequest.
vermähl|en [fɛr'mɛ:lən] v/t. (no -ge-, h) marry (mit to); sich ~ (mit) marry (s.o.); 2ung f (-/-en) wedding, marriage.
ver'mehr|en v/t. (no -ge-, h) increase (um by), augment; multiply; add to; durch Zucht ~ propagate; breed; sich ~ increase, augment; multiply (a. biol.); propagate (itself), zo. breed; 2ung f (-/~-en) increase; addition (gen. to); propagation.
ver'meid|en v/t. (irr. meiden, no -ge-, h) avoid; 2ung f (-/~-en) avoidance.
ver|meintlich adj. [fɛr'maintliç] supposed; ~'mengen v/t. (no -ge-, h) mix, mingle, blend.
Vermerk [fɛr'mɛrk] m (-[e]s/-e) note, entry; 2en v/t. (no -ge-, h) note down, record.
ver'mess|en 1. v/t. (irr. messen, no -ge-, h) measure; survey (land); 2. adj. presumptuous; 2enheit f (-/~-en) presumption; 2ung f (-/-en) measurement; survey (of land).
ver'miete|n v/t. (no -ge-, h) let, esp. Am. rent; hire (out); ⚖ lease; zu ~ on or for hire; Haus zu ~ house to (be) let; 2r m landlord, ⚖ lessor; letter, hirer.
ver'mindern v/t. (no -ge-, h) diminish, lessen; reduce, cut.
ver'misch|en v/t. (no -ge-, h) mix, mingle, blend; ~t adj. mixed; news,

etc.: miscellaneous; 2ung *f* (-/~-en) mixture.

ver'mi|ssen *v/t.* (no -ge-, h) miss; ~ßt *adj.* [~'mist] missing; 2ßte *m, f* (-n/-n) missing person; die ~n *pl.* the missing *pl.*

vermitt|eln [fɛr'mitəln] (no -ge-, h) **1.** *v/t.* mediate (*settlement, peace*); procure, get; give (*impression, etc.*); impart (*knowledge*) (*j-m* to s.o.); **2.** *v/i.* mediate (zwischen *dat.* between); intercede (bei with, für for), intervene; 2ler *m* mediator; go-between; † agent; 2lung *f* (-/-en) mediation; intercession, intervention; *teleph.* (telephone) exchange.

ver'modern *v/i.* (no -ge-, sein) mo(u)lder, decay, rot.

ver'mögen 1. *v/t.* (*irr. mögen, no -ge-, h*): ~ zu *inf.* be able to *inf.*; et. ~ bei *j-m* have influence with s.o.; **2.** 2 *n* (-s/-) ability, power; property; fortune; means *pl.*; ‡‡ assets *pl.*; ~d *adj.* wealthy; *pred.* well off; 2sverhältnisse *pl.* pecuniary circumstances *pl.*

vermut|en [fɛr'mu:tən] *v/t.* (no -ge-, h) suppose, presume, *Am. a.* guess; conjecture, surmise; ~lich **1.** *adj.* presumable; **2.** *adv.* presumably; I suppose; 2ung *f* (-/-en) supposition, presumption; conjecture, surmise.

vernachlässig|en [fɛr'nɑ:xlɛsigən] *v/t.* (no -ge-, h) neglect; 2ung *f* (-/~-en) neglect(ing).

ver'narben *v/i.* (no -ge-, sein) cicatrize, scar over. [with.\]

ver'narrt *adj.*: ~ in (*acc.*) infatuated/

ver'nehm|en *v/t.* (*irr. nehmen, no -ge-, h*) hear, learn; examine, interrogate; ~lich *adj.* audible, distinct; 2ung ‡‡ *f* (-/-en) interrogation, questioning; examination.

ver'neig|en *v/refl.* (no -ge-, h) bow (vor *dat.* to); 2ung *f* bow.

vernein|en [fɛr'naɪnən] (no -ge-, h) **1.** *v/t.* answer in the negative; deny; **2.** *v/i.* answer in the negative; ~end *adj.* negative; 2ung *f* (-/-en) negation; denial; *gr.* negative.

vernicht|en [fɛr'niçtən] *v/t.* (no -ge-, h) annihilate; destroy; dash (*hopes*); ~end *adj.* destructive (*a. fig.*); *look*: withering; *criticism*: scathing; *defeat, reply*: crushing; 2ung *f* (-/~-en) annihilation; destruction.

ver|nickeln [fɛr'nikəln] *v/t.* (no -ge-, h) nickel(-plate); ~'nieten *v/t.* (no -ge-, h) rivet.

Vernunft [fɛr'nunft] *f* (-/no *pl.*) reason; ~ annehmen listen to *or* hear reason; *j-n* zur ~ bringen bring s.o. to reason *or* to his senses.

vernünftig *adj.* [fɛr'nynftiç] rational; reasonable; sensible.

ver'öden (no -ge-) **1.** *v/t.* (h) make

desolate; **2.** *v/i.* (sein) become desolate.

ver'öffentlich|en *v/t.* (no -ge-, h) publish; 2ung *f* (-/-en) publication.

ver'ordn|en *v/t.* (no -ge-, h) decree; order (*a.* ♫); ♫ prescribe (*j-m* to *or* for s.o.); 2ung *f* decree, order; ♫ prescription.

ver'pachten *v/t.* (no -ge-, h) rent, ‡‡ lease (*building, land*).

Ver'pächter *m* landlord, ‡‡ lessor.

ver'pack|en *v/t.* (no -ge-, h) pack (up); wrap up; 2ung *f* packing (material); wrapping.

ver'|passen *v/t.* (no -ge-, h) miss (*train, opportunity, etc.*); ~patzen F [~'patsən] *v/t.* (no -ge-, h) *s.* verpfuschen; ~'pesten *v/t.* (no -ge-, h) *fumes*: contaminate (*the air*); ~'pfänden *v/t.* (no -ge-, h) pawn, pledge (*a. fig.*); mortgage.

ver'pflanz|en *v/t.* (no -ge-, h) transplant (*a.* ♫); 2ung *f* transplantation; ♫ *a.* transplant.

ver'pfleg|en *v/t.* (no -ge-, h) board; supply with food, victual; 2ung *f* (-/~-en) board; food-supply; provisions *pl.*

ver'pflicht|en *v/t.* (no -ge-, h) oblige; engage; 2ung *f* (-/-en) obligation, duty; †, ‡‡ liability; engagement, commitment.

ver'pfusch|en F *v/t.* (no -ge-, h) bungle, botch; make a mess of; ~t *adj. life*: ruined, wrecked.

ver|pönt *adj.* [fɛr'pø:nt] taboo; ~'prügeln F *v/t.* (no -ge-, h) thrash, flog, F wallop; ~'puffen *fig. v/i.* (no -ge-, sein) fizzle out.

Ver'putz ⚒ *m* (-es/~-e) plaster; 2en ⚒ *v/t.* (no -ge-, h) plaster.

ver|quicken [fɛr'kvikən] *v/t.* (no -ge-, h) mix up; ~'quollen *adj. wood*: warped; *face*: bloated; *eyes*: swollen; ~'rammeln [~'raməln] *v/t.* (no -ge-, h) bar(ricade).

Verrat [fɛr'ra:t] *m* (-[e]s/no *pl.*) betrayal (*an dat.* of); treachery (to); ‡‡ treason (to); 2en *v/t.* (*irr. raten, no -ge-, h*) betray, give s.o. away; give away (*secret*); sich ~ betray o.s., give o.s. away.

Verräter [fɛr'rɛ:tər] *m* (-s/-) traitor (*an dat.* to); 2isch *adj.* treacherous; *fig.* telltale.

ver'rechn|en *v/t.* (no -ge-, h) reckon up; charge; settle; set off (*mit* against); account for; ~ *mit* offset against; sich ~ miscalculate, make a mistake (*a. fig.*); *fig.* be mistaken; sich um e-e Mark ~ be one mark out; 2ung *f* settlement; clearing; booking *or* charging (to *account*); 2ungsscheck *m* collection-only cheque *or Am.* check.

ver'regnet *adj.* rainy, rain-spoilt.

ver'reis|en *v/i.* (no -ge-, sein) go on a journey; ~t *adj.* out of town; (geschäftlich) ~ away (on business).

verrenk|en [fɛr'rɛŋkən] v/t. (no -ge-, h) ⚜: wrench; dislocate, luxate; sich et. ~ ⚜ dislocate or luxate s.th.; sich den Hals ~ crane one's neck; ℒung ⚜ f (-/-en) dislocation, luxation.

ver|'richten v/t. (no -ge-, h) do, perform; execute; sein Gebet ~ say one's prayer(s); ~'riegeln v/t. (no -ge-, h) bolt, bar.

verringer|n [fɛr'riŋərn] v/t. (no -ge-, h) diminish, lessen; reduce, cut; sich ~ diminish, lessen; ℒung f (-/-en) diminution; reduction, cut.

ver|'rosten v/i. (no -ge-, sein) rust; ~rotten [~'rɔtən] v/i. (no -ge-, sein) rot.

ver|'rück|en v/t. (no -ge-, h) displace, (re)move, shift; ~t adj. mad, crazy (both a. fig.: nach about); wie ~ like mad; j-n ~ machen drive s.o. mad; ℒte (-n/-n) 1. m lunatic, madman; 2. f lunatic, madwoman; ℒtheit f (-/-en) madness; foolish action; craze.

Ver'ruf m (-[e]s/no pl.): in ~ bringen bring discredit (up)on; in ~ kommen get into discredit; ℒen adj. ill-reputed, ill-famed.

ver|'rutsch|en v/i. (no -ge-, sein) slip; ~t adj. not straight.

Vers [fɛrs] m (-es/-e) verse.

ver|'sagen 1. v/t. (no -ge-, h) refuse, deny (j-m et. s.o. s.th.); sich et. ~ deny o.s. s.th.; 2. v/i. (no -ge-, h) fail, break down; gun: misfire; 3. ℒn (-s/no pl.) failure. [ure.|

ver'sager m (-s/-) misfire; p. fail-|

ver'salzen v/t. ([irr. salzen,] no -ge-, h) oversalt; Γ fig. spoil.

ver'samm|eln v/t. (no -ge-, h) assemble; sich ~ assemble, meet; ℒung f assembly, meeting.

Versand [fɛr'zant] m (-[e]s/no pl.) dispatch, Am. a. shipment; mailing; ~ ins Ausland a. export(ation); ~abteilung f forwarding department; ~geschäft n, ~haus n mailorder business or firm or house.

ver'säum|en v/t. (no -ge-, h) neglect (one's duty, etc.); miss (opportunity, etc.); lose (time); ~ zu inf. fail or omit to inf.; ℒnis n (-ses/-se) neglect, omission, failure.

ver|'schachern F v/t. (no -ge-, h) barter (away); ~'schaffen v/t. (no -ge-, h) procure, get; sich ~ obtain, get; raise (money); sich Respekt ~ make o.s. respected; ~'schämt adj. bashful; ~'schanzen v/refl. (no -ge-, h) entrench o.s.; sich ~ hinter (dat.) (take) shelter behind; ~'schärfen v/t. (no -ge-, h) heighten, intensify; aggravate; sich ~ get worse; ~'scheiden v/i. (irr. scheiden, no -ge-, sein) pass away; ~'schenken v/t. (no -ge-, h) give s.th. away; make a present of; ~'scherzen v/t. and v/refl. (no

-ge-, h) forfeit; ~'scheuchen v/t. (no -ge-, h) frighten or scare away; fig. banish; ~'schicken v/t. (no -ge-, h) send (away), dispatch, forward.

ver'schieb|en v/t. (irr. schieben, no -ge-, h) displace, shift, (re)move; ⚙ shunt; put off, postpone; F fig. ✝ sell underhand; sich ~ shift; ℒung f shift(ing); postponement.

verschieden adj. [fɛr'ʃiːdən] different (von from); dissimilar, unlike; aus ~en Gründen for various or several reasons; Verschiedenes various things pl., esp. ✝ sundries pl.; ~artig adj. of a different kind, various; ℒheit f (-/-en) difference; diversity, variety; ~tlich adv. repeatedly; at times.

ver'schiff|en v/t. (no -ge-, h) ship; ℒung f (-/⚓ -en) shipment.

ver|'schimmeln v/i. (no -ge-, sein) get mo(u)ldy, Am. mo(u)ld; ~'schlafen 1. v/t. (irr. schlafen, no -ge-, h) miss by sleeping; sleep (afternoon, etc.) away; sleep off (headache, etc.); 2. v/i. (irr. schlafen, no -ge-, h) oversleep (o.s.); 3. adj. sleepy, drowsy.

Ver'schlag m shed; box; crate; ℒen [~gən] 1. v/t. (irr. schlagen, no -ge-, h) board up; nail up; es verschlug ihm die Sprache it dum(b)-founded him; 2. adj. cunning; eyes: a. shifty; ~enheit f (-/no pl.) cunning.

verschlechter|n [fɛr'ʃlɛçtərn] v/t. (no -ge-, h) deteriorate, make worse; sich ~ deteriorate, get worse; ℒung f (-/⚓ -en) deterioration; change for the worse.

ver'schleiern v/t. (no -ge-, h) veil (a. fig.).

Verschleiß [fɛr'ʃlaɪs] m (-es/⚓ -c) wear (and tear); ℒen v/t. ([irr.,] no -ge-, h) wear out.

ver|'schleppen v/t. (no -ge-, h) carry off; pol. displace (person); abduct, kidnap; delay, protract; neglect (disease); ~'schleudern v/t. (no -ge-, h) dissipate, waste; ✝ sell at a loss, sell dirt-cheap; ~'schließen v/t. (irr. schließen, no -ge-, h) shut, close; lock (door); lock up (house).

verschlimmern [fɛr'ʃlimərn] v/t. (no -ge-, h) make worse, aggravate; sich ~ get worse.

ver'schlingen v/t. (irr. schlingen, no -ge-, h) devour; wolf (down) (one's food); intertwine, entwine, interlace; sich ~ intertwine, entwine, interlace.

verschli|ß [fɛr'ʃlis] pret. of verschleißen; ~ssen [~sən] p.p. of verschleißen.

verschlossen adj. [fɛr'ʃlɔsən] closed, shut; fig. reserved; ℒheit f (-/no pl.) reserve.

19*

ver'schlucken v/t. (no -ge-, h) swallow (up); sich ~ swallow the wrong way.

Ver'schluß m lock; clasp; lid; plug; stopper (of bottle); seal; fastener, fastening; phot. shutter; unter ~ under lock and key.

ver|'schmachten v/i. (no -ge-, sein) languish, pine away; vor Durst ~ die or be dying of thirst, be parched with thirst; ~'schmähen v/t. (no -ge-, h) disdain, scorn.

ver'schmelz|en (irr. schmelzen, no -ge-) v/t. (h) and v/i. (sein) melt, fuse (a. fig.); blend; fig.: amalgamate; merge (mit in, into); 2ung f (-/~-en) fusion; ✝ merger; fig. amalgamation.

ver|'schmerzen v/t. (no -ge-, h) get over (the loss of); ~'schmieren v/t. (no -ge-, h) smear (over); blur; ~schmitzt adj. [~'ʃmitst] cunning; roguish; arch; ~'schmutzen (no -ge-) 1. v/t. (h) soil, dirty; pollute (water); 2. v/i. (sein) get dirty; ~'schnaufen F v/i. and v/refl. (no -ge-, h) stop for breath; ~'schneiden v/t. (irr. schneiden, no -ge-, h) cut badly; blend (wine, etc.); geld, castrate; ~'schneit adj. covered with snow; mountains: a. snow-capped; roofs: a. snow-covered.

Ver'schnitt m (-[e]s/no pl.) blend.

ver'schnupf|en F fig. v/t. (no -ge-, h) nettle, pique; ~t ♀ adj.: ~ sein have a cold.

ver|'schnüren v/t. (no -ge-, h) tie up, cord; ~schollen adj. [~'ʃɔlən] not heard of again; missing; ⚖ presumed dead; ~'schonen v/t. (no -ge-, h) spare; j-n mit et. ~ spare s.o. s.th.

verschöne(r)n [fer'ʃø:nə(r)n] v/t. (no -ge-, h) embellish, beautify; 2rung f (-/-en) embellishment.

ver|schossen adj. [fer'ʃɔsən] colour: faded; F ~ sein in (acc.) be madly in love with; ~schränken [~'ʃreŋkən] v/t. (no -ge-, h) cross, fold (one's arms).

ver'schreib|en v/t. (irr. schreiben, no -ge-, h) use up (in writing); ♀ prescribe (j-m for s.o.); ⚖ assign (j-m to s.o.); sich ~ make a slip of the pen; sich e-r Sache ~ devote o.s. to s.th.; 2ung f (-/-en) assignment; prescription.

ver|schroben adj. [fer'ʃro:bən] eccentric, queer, odd; ~'schrotten v/t. (no -ge-, h) scrap; ~schüchtert adj. [~'ʃyçtərt] intimidated.

ver'schulden 1. v/t. (no -ge-, h) be guilty of; be the cause of; 2. 2 n (-s/no pl.) fault.

ver|'schuldet adj. indebted, in debt; ~'schütten v/t. (no -ge-, h) spill (liquid); block (up) (road); bury s.o. alive; ~schwägert adj. [~'ʃvɛ:gərt] related by marriage;

~'schweigen v/t. (irr. schweigen, no -ge-, h) conceal (j-m et. s.th. from s.o.).

verschwend|en [fer'ʃvɛndən] v/t. (no -ge-, h) waste, squander (an acc. on); lavish (on); 2er m (-s/-) spendthrift, prodigal; ~erisch adj. prodigal, lavish (both: mit of); wasteful; 2ung f (-/~-en) waste; extravagance.

verschwiegen adj. [fer'ʃvi:gən] discreet; place: secret, secluded; 2heit f (-/no pl.) discretion; secrecy.

ver|'schwimmen v/i. (irr. schwimmen, no -ge-, sein) become indistinct or blurred; ~'schwinden v/i. (irr. schwinden, no -ge-, sein) disappear, vanish; F verschwinde! go away!, sl. beat it!; 2'schwinden n (-s/no pl.) disappearance; ~schwommen adj. [~'ʃvɔmən] vague (a. fig.); blurred; fig. woolly.

ver'schwör|en v/refl. (irr. schwören, no -ge-, h) conspire; 2er m (-s/-) conspirator; 2ung f (-/-en) conspiracy, plot.

ver'sehen 1. v/t. (irr. sehen, no -ge-, h) fill (an office); look after (house, etc.); mit et. ~ furnish or supply with; sich ~ make a mistake; ehe man sich's versieht all of a sudden; 2. 2 n (-s/-) oversight, mistake, slip; aus ~ = ~tlich adv. by mistake; inadvertently.

Versehrte [fer'ze:rtə] m (-n/-n) disabled person.

ver'send|en v/t. ([irr. senden,] no -ge-, h) send, dispatch, forward, Am. ship; by water: ship; ins Ausland ~ a. export; 2ung f (-/~-en) dispatch, shipment, forwarding.

ver|'sengen v/t. (no -ge-, h) singe, scorch; ~'senken v/t. (no -ge-, h) sink; sich ~ in (acc.) immerse o.s. in; ~sessen adj. [~'zesən]: ~ auf (acc.) bent on, mad after.

ver'setz|en v/t. (no -ge-, h) displace, remove; transfer (officer); at school: remove, move up, Am. promote; transplant (tree, etc.); pawn, pledge; F fig. stand (lover, etc.) up; ~ in (acc.) put or place into (situation, condition); j-m e-n Schlag ~ give or deal s.o. a blow; in Angst ~ frighten or terrify s.o.; in den Ruhestand ~ pension s.o. off, retire s.o.; versetzt werden be transferred; at school: go up; ~ Sie sich in m-e Lage put or place yourself in my position; Wein mit Wasser ~ mix wine with water, add water to wine; et. ~ reply s.th.; 2ung f (-/-en) removal; transfer; at school: remove, Am. promotion.

ver'seuch|en v/t. (no -ge-, h) infect; contaminate; 2ung f (-/~-en) infection; contamination.

ver'sicher|n v/t. (no -ge-, h) assure

(a. one's life); protest, affirm; insure (one's property or life); sich ~ insure or assure o.s.; sich ~ (, daß) make sure (that); 2te m, f (-n/-n) insurant, the insured or assured, policy-holder; 2ung f assurance, affirmation; insurance; (life-)assurance; insurance company.

Ver'sicherungs|gesellschaft f insurance company; ~police f, ~schein m policy of assurance, insurance policy.

ver'|sickern v/i. (no -ge-, sein) trickle away; ~'siegeln v/t. (no -ge-, h) seal (up); ~'siegen v/i. (no -ge-, sein) dry up, run dry; ~'silbern v/t. (no -ge-, h) silver; F fig. realize, convert into cash; ~ 'sinken v/i. (irr. sinken, no -ge-, sein) sink; s. versunken; ~'sinnbildlichen v/t. (no -ge-, h) symbolize.

Version [vɛr'zjoːn] f (-/-en) version. 'Versmaß n met|re, Am. -er.

versöhn|en [fɛr'zøːnən] v/t. (no -ge-, h) reconcile (mit to, with); sich (wieder) ~ become reconciled; ~lich adj. conciliatory; 2ung f (-/-en) reconciliation.

ver'sorg|en v/t. (no -ge-, h) provide (mit with), supply (with); take care of, look after; ~t adj. [~kt] provided for; 2ung f [~guŋ] f (-/-en) providing (mit with), supplying (with); supply, provision.

ver'spät|en v/refl. (no -ge-, h) be late; ~et adj. belated, late, Am. tardy; 2ung f (-/-en) lateness, Am. tardiness; ~ haben he late; mit 2 Stunden ~ two hours behind schedule.

ver'|speisen v/t. (no -ge-, h) eat (up); ~'sperren v/t. (no -ge-, h) lock (up); bar, block (up), obstruct (a. view); ~'spielen v/t. (no -ge-, h) at cards, etc.: lose (money); ~'spielt adj. playful; ~'spotten v/t. (no -ge-, h) scoff at, mock (at), deride, ridicule; ~'sprechen v/t. (irr. sprechen, no -ge-, h) promise; sich viel ~ von expect much of; 2'sprechen n (-s/~) promise; ~'sprühen v/t. (no -ge-, h) spray; ~'spüren v/t. (no -ge-, h) feel; perceive, be conscious of.

ver'staatlich|en v/t. (no -ge-, h) nationalize; 2ung f (-/-en) nationalization.

Verstand [fɛr'ʃtant] m (-[e]s/no pl.) understanding; intelligence, intellect, brains pl.; mind, wits pl.; reason; (common) sense.

Verstandes|kraft [fɛr'ʃtandəs-] f intellectual power or faculty; 2mäßig adj. rational; intellectual; ~mensch m matter-of-fact person.

verständ|ig adj. [fɛr'ʃtɛndiç] intelligent; reasonable, sensible; judi-

cious; ~igen [~gən] v/t. (no -ge-, h) inform (von of), notify (of); sich mit j-m ~ make o.s. understood to s.o.; come to an understanding with s.o.; 2igung [~guŋ] f (-/~-en) information; understanding, agreement; teleph. communication; ~lich adj. [~tliç] intelligible; understandable; j-m et. ~ machen make s.th. clear to s.o.; sich ~ machen make o.s. understood.

Verständnis [fɛr'ʃtɛntnis] n (-ses/~-se) comprehension, understanding; insight; appreciation (für of); ~ haben für appreciate; 2los adj. uncomprehending; look, etc.: blank; unappreciative; 2voll adj. understanding; appreciative; sympathetic; look: knowing.

ver'stärk|en v/t. (no -ge-, h) strengthen, reinforce (a. ✕); amplify (radio signals, etc.); intensify; 2er m (-s/-) in radio, etc.: amplifier; 2ung f (-/~-en) strengthening, reinforcement (a. ✕); amplification; intensification.

ver'staub|en v/i. (no -ge-, sein) get dusty; ~t adj. [~pt] dusty.

ver'stauch|en 𝒮 v/t. (no -ge-, h) sprain; sich den Fuß ~ sprain one's foot; 2ung 𝒮 f (-/-en) sprain.

ver'stauen v/t. (no gc-, h) stow away.

Versteck [fɛr'ʃtɛk] n (-[e]s/-e) hiding-place; for gangsters, etc.: Am. F a. hide-out; ~ spielen play at hide-and-seek; 2en v/t. (no -ge-, h) hide, conceal; sich ~ hide.

ver'stehen v/t. (irr. stehen, no -ge-, h) understand, see, F get; comprehend; realize; know (language); es ~ zu inf. know how to inf.; Spaß ~ take a joke; zu ~ geben intimate; ~ Sie? do you see?; ich ~! I see!; verstanden? (do you) understand?, F (do you) get me?; falsch ~ misunderstand; ~ Sie mich recht! don't misunderstand me!; was ~ Sie unter (dat.)? what do you mean or understand by ...?; er versteht et. davon he knows a thing or two about it; sich ~ understand one another; sich ~ auf (acc.) know well, be an expert at or in; sich mit j-m gut ~ get on well with s.o.; es versteht sich von selbst it goes without saying.

ver'steifen v/t. (no -ge-, h) ⊕ strut, brace; stiffen; sich ~ stiffen; sich ~ auf (acc.) make a point of, insist on.

ver'steiger|n v/t. (no -ge-, h) (sell by or Am. at) auction; 2ung f (sale by or Am. at) auction, auction-sale.

ver'steinern (no -ge-) v/t. (h) and v/i. (sein) turn into stone, petrify (both a. fig.).

ver'stell|bar adj. adjustable; ~en v/t. (no -ge-, h) shift; adjust; disarrange; bar, block (up), obstruct; disguise (voice, etc.); sich ~ play or act a part; dissemble, feign; 2ung f (-/~-en) disguise; dissimulation.

ver|'steuern v/t. (no -ge-, h) pay duty or tax on; ~stiegen fig. adj. [~'fti:gən] eccentric.

ver'stimm|en v/t. (no -ge-, h) put out of tune; fig. put out of humo(u)r; ~t adj. out of tune; fig. out of humo(u)r, F cross; 2ung f ill humo(u)r; disagreement; ill feeling.

ver'stockt adj. stubborn, obdurate; 2heit f (-/no pl.) obduracy.

verstohlen adj. [fɛr'fto:lən] furtive.

ver'stopf|en v/t. (no -ge-, h) stop (up); clog, block (up), obstruct; jam, block (passage, street); ☼ constipate; 2ung ☼ f (-/~-en) constipation.

verstorben adj. [fɛr'ftɔrbən] late, deceased; 2e m, f (-f/-n) the deceased, Am. ☼☼ a. decedent; die ~n pl. the deceased pl., the departed pl.

ver'stört adj. scared; distracted, bewildered; 2heit f (-/no pl.) distraction, bewilderment.

Ver'stoß m offen|ce, Am. -se; contravention (gegen of law); infringement (on trade name, etc.); blunder; 2en (irr. stoßen, no -ge-, h) 1. v/t. expel (aus from); repudiate, disown (wife, child, etc.); 2. v/i.: ~ gegen offend against; contravene (law); infringe (rule, etc.).

ver|'streichen (irr. streichen, no -ge-) 1. v/i. (sein) time: pass, elapse; expire; 2. v/t. (h) spread (butter, etc.); ~'streuen v/t. (no -ge-, h) scatter.

verstümmel|n [fɛr'ftyməln] v/t. (no -ge-, h) mutilate; garble (text, etc.); 2ung f (-/~-en) mutilation.

ver'stummen v/i. (no -ge-, sein) grow silent or dumb.

Verstümmlung [fɛr'ftymluŋ] f (-/~-en) mutilation.

Versuch [fɛr'zu:x] m (-[e]s/-e) attempt, trial; phys., etc.: experiment; e-n ~ machen mit give s.o. or s.th. a trial; try one's hand at s.th., have a go at s.th.; 2en v/t. (no -ge-, h) try, attempt; taste; ~ tempt s.o.; es ~ mit give s.o. or s.th. a trial.

Ver'suchs|anstalt f research institute; ~kaninchen fig. n guinea-pig; 2weise adv. by way of trial or (an) experiment; on trial; ~zweck m: zu ~en pl. for experimental purposes pl.

Ver'suchung f (-/-en) temptation; j-n in ~ bringen tempt s.o.; in ~ sein be tempted.

ver|'sündigen v/refl. (no -ge-, h) sin (an dat. against); ~sunken fig. adj. [~'zuŋkən]: ~ in (acc.) absorbed

or lost in; ~'süßen v/t. (no -ge-, h) sweeten.

ver'tag|en v/t. (no -ge-, h) adjourn; parl. prorogue; sich ~ adjourn, Am. a. recess; 2ung f adjournment; parl. prorogation.

ver'tauschen v/t. (no -ge-, h) exchange (mit for).

verteidig|en [fɛr'taidigən] v/t. (no -ge-, h) defend; sich ~ defend o.s.; 2er m (-s/-) defender; ☼☼, fig. advocate; ☼☼ counsel for the defen|ce, Am. -se, Am. attorney for the defendant or defense; football: fullback; 2ung f (-/~-en) defen|ce, Am. -se.

Ver'teidigungs|bündnis n defensive alliance; ~minister m minister of defence; Brt. Minister of Defence, Am. Secretary of Defense; ~ministerium n ministry of defence; Brt. Ministry of Defence, Am. Department of Defense.

ver'teil|en v/t. (no -ge-, h) distribute; spread (colour, etc.); 2er m (-s/-) distributor; 2ung f (-/~-en) distribution.

ver'teuern v/t. (no -ge-, h) raise or increase the price of.

ver'tief|en v/t. (no -ge-, h) deepen (a. fig.); sich ~ deepen; sich ~ in (acc.) plunge in(to); become absorbed in; 2ung f (-/-en) hollow, cavity; recess.

vertikal adj. [vɛrti'ka:l] vertical.

ver'tilg|en v/t. (no -ge-, h) exterminate; F consume, eat (up) (food); 2ung f (-/~-en) extermination.

ver'tonen ♪ v/t. (no -ge-, h) set to music.

Vertrag [fɛr'tra:k] m (-[e]s/~e) agreement, contract; pol. treaty; 2en [~gən] v/t. (irr. tragen, no -ge-, h) endure, bear, stand; diese Speise kann ich nicht ~ this food does not agree with me; sich ~ things: be compatible or consistent; colours: harmonize; p.: agree; get on with one another; sich wieder ~ be reconciled, make it up; 2lich [~kliç] 1. adj. contractual, stipulated; 2. adv. as stipulated; ~ verpflichtet sein to be bound by contract; sich ~ verpflichten contract (zu for s.th.; zu inf. to inf.).

verträglich adj. [fɛr'trɛ:kliç] sociable.

Ver'trags|bruch m breach of contract; 2brüchig adj.: ~ werden commit a breach of contract; ~entwurf m draft agreement; ~partner m party to a contract.

ver'trauen 1. v/i. (no -ge-, h) trust (j-m s.o.); ~ auf (acc.) trust or confide in; 2. 2 n (-s/no pl.) confidence, trust; im ~ confidentially, between you and me; ~erweckend adj. inspiring confidence; promising.

Ver'trauens|bruch m breach or

betrayal of trust; ~frage *parl. f*: *die ~ stellen* put the question of confidence; ~**mann** *m* (-[e]s/~er, *Vertrauensleute*) spokesman; shop-steward; confidential agent; ~**sache** *f*: *das ist ~* that is a matter of confidence; ~**stellung** *f* position of trust; 2**voll** *adj.* trustful, trusting; ~**votum** *parl. n* vote of confidence; 2**würdig** *adj.* trustworthy, reliable.

ver'**traulich** *adj.* confidential, in confidence; intimate, familiar; 2-**keit** *f* (-/-en) confidence; intimacy, familiarity.

ver'**traut** *adj.* intimate, familiar; 2e (-n/-n) **1.** *m* confidant, intimate friend; 2 *f* confidante, intimate friend; 2**heit** *f* (-/~-en) familiarity.

ver'**treib|en** *v/t.* (*irr.* treiben, *no -ge-, h*) drive away; expel (*aus* from); turn out; † sell, distribute (*goods*); *sich die Zeit ~* pass one's time, kill time; 2**ung** *f* (-/~-en) expulsion.

ver'**tret|en** *v/t.* (*irr.* treten, *no -ge-, h*) represent (*s.o., firm, etc.*); substitute for *s.o.*; attend to, look after (*s.o.'s interests*); hold (*view*); *parl.* sit for (*borough*); answer for *s.th.*; *j-s Sache ~* 🏛 plead s.o.'s case *or* cause; *sich den Fuß ~* sprain one's foot; F *sich die Beine ~* stretch one's legs; 2**er** *m* (-s/-) representative; † *a.* agent; proxy, agent; substitute, deputy; exponent; (*sales*) representative; door-to-door salesman; commercial travel(l)er, *esp. Am.* travel(l)ing salesman; 2**ung** *f* (-/-en) representation (*a. pol.*); † agency; *in office*: substitution; *in ~* by proxy; *gen.*: acting for.

Vertrieb † [fer'tri:p] *m* (-[e]s/-e) sale; distribution; ~**ene** [~bənə] *m, f* (-n/-n) expellee.

ver'**trocknen** *v/i.* (*no -ge-, sein*) dry up; ~'**trödeln** F *v/t.* (*no -ge-, h*) dawdle away, waste (*time*); ~'**trösten** *v/t.* (*no -ge-, h*) put off; ~'**tuschen** F *v/t.* (*no -ge-, h*) hush up; ~'**übeln** *v/t.* (*no -ge-, h*) take *s.th.* amiss; ~'**üben** *v/t.* (*no -ge-, h*) commit, perpetrate.

ver'**unglück|en** *v/i.* (*no -ge-, sein*) meet with *or* have an accident; F *fig.* fail, go wrong; *tödlich ~* be killed in an accident; 2**te** *m, f* (-n/-n) casualty.

ver**un|reinigen** [fer'unraınıgən] *v/t.* (*no -ge-, h*) soil, dirty; defile; contaminate (*air*); pollute (*water*); ~**stalten** [~ʃtaltən] *v/t.* (*no -ge-, h*) disfigure.

ver'**untreu|en** *v/t.* (*no -ge-, h*) embezzle; 2**ung** *f* (-/-en) embezzlement.

ver'**ursachen** *v/t.* (*no -ge-, h*) cause.

ver'**urteil|en** *v/t.* (*no -ge-, h*) condemn (*zu* to) (*a. fig.*), sentence (to);

convict (*wegen* of); 2**te** *m, f* (-n/-n) convict; 2**ung** *f* (-/-en) condemnation (*a. fig.*), conviction.

ver|**vielfältigen** [fer'fi:lfɛltıgən] *v/t.* (*no -ge-, h*) manifold; ~**vollkommnen** [~'fɔlkɔmnən] *v/t.* (*no -ge-, h*) perfect; *sich ~* perfect o.s.

vervollständig|en [fer'fɔlʃtɛndıgən] *v/t.* (*no -ge-, h*) complete; 2**ung** *f* (-/~-en) completion.

ver|**wachsen 1.** *v/i.* (*irr.* wachsen, *no -ge-, sein*): *miteinander ~* grow together; **2.** *adj.* deformed; 🎽 humpbacked, hunchbacked; ~**wackeln** *phot. v/t.* (*no -ge-, h*) blur.

ver'**wahr|en** *v/t.* (*no -ge-, h*) keep; *sich ~ gegen* protest against; ~**lost** *adj.* [~'lo:st] child, garden, *etc.*: uncared-for, neglected; degenerate; 2**ung** *f* keeping; charge; custody; *fig.* protest; *j-m et. in ~ geben* give s.th. into s.o.'s charge; *in ~ nehmen* take charge of.

ver**waist** *adj.* [fer'vaıst] orphan(ed); *fig.* deserted.

ver'**walt|en** *v/t.* (*no -ge-, h*) administer, manage; 2**er** *m* (-s/-) administrator, manager; steward (*of estate*); 2**ung** *f* (-/-en) administration; management.

ver'**wand|eln** *v/t.* (*no -ge-, h*) change, turn, transform; *sich ~* change (*all: in acc.* into); 2**lung** *f* (-/-en) change; transformation.

ver**wandt** *adj.* [fer'vant] related (*mit* to); languages, tribes, *etc.*: kindred; languages, sciences: cognate (*with*); *pred.* akin (to) (*a. fig.*); 2e *m, f* (-n/-n) relative, relation; 2**schaft** *f* (-/-en) relationship; relations *pl.*; *geistige ~* congeniality.

ver'**warn|en** *v/t.* (*no -ge-, h*) caution; 2**ung** *f* caution.

ver'**wässern** *v/t.* (*no -ge-, h*) water (down), dilute; *fig.* water down, dilute.

ver'**wechs|eln** *v/t.* (*no -ge-, h*) mistake (*mit* for); confound, mix up, confuse (*all: mit* with); 2(e)**lung** *f* (-/-en) mistake; confusion.

ver**wegen** *adj.* [fer've:gən] daring, bold, audacious; 2**heit** *f* (-/~-en) boldness, audacity, daring.

ver|'**wehren** *v/t.* (*no -ge-, h*): *j-m et. ~* (de)bar s.o. from (doing) s.th.; *den Zutritt ~* deny *or* refuse admittance (*zu* to); ~'**weichlicht** *adj.* effeminate, soft.

ver'**weiger|n** *v/t.* (*no -ge-, h*) deny, refuse; disobey (*order*); 2**ung** *f* denial, refusal.

ver'**weilen** *v/i.* (*no -ge-, h*) stay, linger; *bei et. ~* dwell (up)on s.th.

Verweis [fer'vaıs] *m* (-es/-e) reprimand; rebuke, reproof; reference (*auf acc.* to); 2en [~zən] *v/t.* (*irr.* weisen, *no -ge-, h*): *j-n des Landes ~* expel s.o. from Germany, *etc.*;

j-m et. ~ reprimand s.o. for s.th.;
j-n ~ auf (acc.) or an (acc.) refer s.o.
to.

ver'welken v/i. (no -ge-, sein) fade,
wither (up).

ver'wend|en v/t. ([irr. wenden,] no
-ge-, h) employ, use; apply (für
for); spend (time, etc.) (auf acc.
on); sich bei j-m ~ für intercede
with s.o. for; 2ung f (-/~-en) use,
employment; application; keine ~
haben für have no use for.

ver'werf|en v/t. (irr. werfen, no
-ge-, h) reject; ₤₤ quash (verdict);
~lich adj. abominable.

ver'werten v/t. (no -ge-, h) turn to
account, utilize.

verwes|en [fɛr'veːzən] v/i. (no -ge-,
sein) rot, decay; 2ung f (-/~-en)
decay.

ver'wick|eln v/t. (no -ge-, h) entan-
gle (in acc. in); sich ~ entangle o.s.
(in) (a. fig.); ~elt fig. adj. complicated; 2(e)lung f (-/-en) entanglement; fig. a. complication.

ver'wilder|n v/i. (no -ge-, sein) run
wild; ~t adj. garden, etc.: uncultivated, weed-grown; fig. wild, unruly.

ver'winden v/t. (irr. winden, no
-ge-, h) get over s.th.

ver'wirklich|en v/t. (no -ge-, h)
realize; sich ~ be realized, esp. Am.
materialize; come true; 2ung f
(-/~-en) realization.

ver'wirr|en v/t. (no -ge-, h) entan-
gle; j-n ~ confuse s.o.; embarrass
s.o.; ~t fig. adj. confused; embarrassed; 2ung fig. f (-/-en) confusion.

ver'wischen v/t. (no -ge-, h) wipe or
blot out; efface (a. fig.); blur,
obscure; cover up (one's tracks).

ver'witter|n geol. v/i. (no -ge-, sein)
weather; ~t adj. geol. weathered;
weather-beaten (a. fig.).

ver'witwet adj. widowed.

verwöhn|en [fɛr'vøːnən] v/t. (no
-ge-, h) spoil; ~t adj. fastidious,
particular.

verworren adj. [fɛr'vɔrən] ideas,
etc.: confused; situation, plot: intricate.

verwund|bar adj. [fɛr'vuntbaːr]
vulnerable (a. fig.); ~en [~dən] v/t.
(no -ge-, h) wound.

ver'wunder|lich adj. astonishing;
2ung f (-/~-en) astonishment.

Ver'wund|ete ✕ m (-n/-n) wounded
(soldier), casualty; ~ung f (-/-en)
wound, injury.

ver'wünsch|en v/t. (no -ge-, h)
curse; 2ung f (-/-en) curse.

ver'wüst|en v/t. (no -ge-, h) lay
waste, devastate, ravage (a. fig.);
2ung f (-/-en) devastation, ravage.

verzag|en [fɛr'tsaːgən] v/i. (no -ge-,
h) despond (an dat. of); ~t adj. [~kt]
despondent; 2theit [~kt-] f (-/no
pl.) despondenc|e, -cy.

---

ver|'zählen v/refl. (no -ge-, h)
miscount; ~zärteln [~'tsɛːrtəln]
v/t. (no -ge-, h) coddle, pamper;
~'zaubern v/t. (no -ge-, h) bewitch,
enchant, charm; ~'zehren v/t. (no
-ge-, h) consume (a. fig.).

ver'zeichn|en v/t. (no -ge-, h) note
down; record; list; fig. distort; ~
können, zu ~ haben score (success,
etc.); ~et paint. adj. out of drawing;
2is n (-ses/-se) list, catalog(ue);
register; inventory; index (of book)
table, schedule.

verzeih|en [fɛr'tsaɪən] (irr., no -ge-,
h) 1. v/i. pardon, forgive; ~ Sie!
I beg your pardon!; excuse me!;
sorry!; 2. v/t. pardon, forgive (j-m
et. s.o. s.th.); ~lich adj. pardonable;
2ung f (-/no pl.) pardon; ~! I beg
your pardon!, sorry!

ver'zerr|en v/t. (no -ge-, h) distort;
sich ~ become distorted; 2ung f
distortion.

ver'zetteln v/t. (no -ge-, h) enter on
cards; sich ~ fritter away one's
energies.

Verzicht [fɛr'tsɪçt] m (-[e]s/-e)
renunciation (auf acc. of); 2en v/i.
(no -ge-, h) renounce (auf acc. s.th.);
do without (s.th.).

verzieh [fɛr'tsiː] pret. of verzeihen.

ver'ziehen[1] (irr. ziehen, no -ge-)
1. v/i. (sein) (re)move (nach to);
2. v/t. (h) spoil (child); distort; das
Gesicht ~ make a wry face, screw
up one's face, grimace; ohne e-e
Miene zu ~ without betraying the
least emotion; sich ~ wood: warp;
crowd, clouds: disperse; storm,
clouds: blow over; F disappear.

ver'ziehen[2] p.p. of verzeihen.

ver'zier|en v/t. (no -ge-, h) adorn,
decorate; 2ung f (-/-en) decoration;
ornament.

verzins|en [fɛr'tsɪnzən] v/t. (no
-ge-, h) pay interest on; sich ~ yield
interest; 2ung f (-/~-en) interest.

ver'zöger|n v/t. (no -ge-, h) delay,
retard; sich ~ be delayed; 2ung f
(-/-en) delay, retardation.

ver'zollen v/t. (no -ge-, h) pay duty
on; haben Sie et. zu ~? have you
anything to declare?

verzück|t adj. [fɛr'tsʏkt] ecstatic,
enraptured; 2ung f (-/~-en)
ecstasy, rapture; in ~ geraten go
into ecstasies (wegen over).

Ver'zug m (-[e]s/no pl.) delay; ✝
default; in ~ geraten ✝ come in
default; im ~ sein (be in) default.

ver'zweif|eln v/i. (no -ge-, h, sein)
despair (an dat. of); es ist zum Verzweifeln it is enough to drive one
mad; ~elt adj. hopeless; desperate;
2lung [~luŋ] f (-/no pl.) despair;
j-n zur ~ bringen drive s.o. to despair.

verzweig|en [fɛr'tsvaɪgən] v/refl.
(no -ge-, h) ramify; trees: branch
(out); road: branch; business firm,

etc.: branch out; **~ung** *f* (-/-en) ramification; branching.
verzwickt *adj.* [fɛr'tsvikt] intricate, complicated.
Veteran [vete'raːn] *m* (-en/-en) ✕ veteran (*a. fig.*), ex-serviceman.
Veterinär [veteri'nɛːr] *m* (-s/-e) veterinary (surgeon), F vet.
Veto ['veːto] *n* (-s/-s) veto; *ein ~ einlegen gegen* put a veto on, veto *s.th.*
Vetter ['fɛtər] *m* (-s/-n) cousin; **~nwirtschaft** *f* (-/no *pl.*) nepotism.
vibrieren [vi'briːrən] *v/i.* (*no -ge-, h*) vibrate.
Vieh [fiː] *n* (-[e]s/no *pl.*) livestock, cattle; animal, brute, beast; F *fig.* brute, beast; **~bestand** *m* livestock; **~händler** *m* cattle-dealer; **~hof** *m* stockyard; **Qisch** *adj.* bestial, beastly, brutal; **~wagen** 🚂 *m* stock-car; **~weide** *f* pasture; **~zucht** *f* stock-farming, cattle-breeding; **~züchter** *m* stock-breeder, stock-farmer, cattle-breeder, *Am. a.* rancher.
viel [fiːl] **1.** *adj.* much; **~e** *pl.* many; a lot (of), lots of; plenty of (*cake, money, room, time, etc.*); *das ~e Geld* all that money; *seine ~en Geschäfte* his numerous affairs *pl.*; *sehr ~e pl.* a great many *pl.*; *ziemlich ~ a good deal of; ziemlich ~e pl.* a good many *pl.*; *~ zuviel* far too much; *sehr ~* a great *or* good deal; **2.** *adv.* much; **~** *besser* much *or* a good deal *or* a lot better; *et. ~ lieber tun* prefer to do *s.th.*
viel|beschäftigt *adj.* ['fiːlbəʃɛftiçt] very busy; **~deutig** *adj.* ambiguous; **~erlei** *adj.* ['~ər'laɪ] of many kinds, many kinds of; multifarious; **~fach** ['~faɪx] **1.** *adj.* multiple; **2.** *adv.* in many cases, frequently; **~fältig** *adj.* ['~fɛltiç] multiple, manifold, multifarious; **~leicht** *adv.* perhaps, maybe; **~mals** *adv.* ['~maːls]: *ich danke ihnen ~* many thanks, thank you very much; *sie läßt (dich) ~ grüßen* she sends you her kind regards; *ich bitte ~ um Entschuldigung* I am very sorry, I do beg your pardon; **~mehr** *cj.* rather; **~sagend** *adj.* significant, suggestive; **~seitig** *adj.* ['~zartiç] many-sided, versatile; **~versprechend** *adj.* (very) promising.
vier *adj.* [fiːr] four; *zu ~t* four of us *or* them; *auf allen ~en* on all fours; *unter ~ Augen* confidentially, privately; *um halb ~* at half past three; **~beinig** *adj.* four-legged; **~eck** *n* square, quadrangle; **~eckig** *adj.* square, quadrangular; **~erlei** *adj.* ['~ər'laɪ] of four different kinds, four kinds of; **~fach** *adj.* ['~faɪx] fourfold; *~ Ausfertigung* four copies; **Qfüßer** *zo.* ['~fyːsər] *m* (-s/-) quadruped; **~füßig** *adj.* ['~fyːsiç]

four-footed; *zo.* quadruped; **Qfüßler** *zo.* ['~fyːslər] *m* (-s/-) quadruped; **~händig** *♪ adv.* ['~hɛndiç]: *~ spielen* play a duet; **~jährig** *adj.* ['~jɛːriç] four-year-old, of four; **Qlinge** ['~liŋə] *m/pl.* quadruplets *pl.*, F quads *pl.*; **~mal** *adv.* four times; **~schrötig** *adj.* ['~ʃrøːtiç] square-built, thickset; **~seitig** *adj.* ['~zartiç] four-sided; *A* quadrilateral; **Qsitzer** *esp. mot. m* (-s/-) four-seater; **~stöckig** *adj.* ['~ʃtœkiç] four-storeyed, four-storied; **Qtaktmotor** *mot. m* four-stroke engine; **~te** *adj.* fourth; **~teilen** *v/t.* (*ge-, h*) quarter.
Viertel ['fɪrtəl] *n* (-s/-) fourth (part); quarter; *~ fünf, (ein) ~ nach vier* a quarter past four; *drei ~ vier* a quarter to four; **~jahr** *n* three months *pl.*, quarter (of a year); **Qjährlich, Qjährlich 1.** *adj.* quarterly; **2.** *adv.* every three months, quarterly; **~note** *♪ f* crotchet, *Am. a.* quarter note; **~pfund** *n*, **~pfund** *n* quarter of a pound; **~stunde** *f* quarter of an hour, *Am.* quarter hour.
vier|tens *adv.* ['fɪrtəns] fourthly; **Qvierteltakt** *♪ m* common time.
vierzehn *adj.* ['fɪrtseːn] fourteen; *~ Tage pl.* a fortnight, *Am.* two weeks *pl.*; **~te** *adj.* fourteenth.
vierzig *adj.* ['fɪrtsiç] forty; **~ste** *adj.* fortieth.
Vikar *eccl.* [vi'kaːr] *m* (-s/-e) curate; vicar.
Villa ['vila] *f* (-/Villen) villa.
violett *adj.* [vio'lɛt] violet.
Violine *♪* [vio'liːnə] *f* (-/-n) violin.
Viper *zo.* ['viːpər] *f* (-/-n) viper.
virtuos *adj.* [virtu'oːs] masterly; **Qe** [~zə] *m* (-n/-n), **Qin** [~'ziːn] *f* (-/-nen) virtuoso; **Qität** [~ozi'tɛːt] *f* (-/no *pl.*) virtuosity.
Virus 🧫 ['viːrus] *n*, *m* (-/Viren) virus.
Vision [vi'zjoːn] *f* (-/-en) vision.
Visitation [vizita'tsjoːn] *f* (-/-en) search; inspection.
Visite 🩺 [vi'ziːtə] *f* (-/-n) visit; **~nkarte** *f* visiting-card, *Am.* calling card.
Visum ['viːzum] *n* (-s/Visa, Visen) visa, visé.
Vitalität [vitali'tɛːt] *f* (-/no *pl.*) vitality.   [min.\
Vitamin [vita'miːn] *n* (-s/-e) vita-/
Vize|kanzler ['fiːtsə-] *m* vice-chancellor; **~könig** *m* viceroy; **~konsul** *m* vice-consul; **~präsident** *m* vice-president.
Vogel ['foːgəl] *m* (-s/-) bird; F *e-n ~ haben* have a bee in one's bonnet, *sl.* have bats in the belfry; *den ~ abschießen* carry off the prize, *Am. sl.* take the cake; **~bauer** *n*, *m* (-s/-) bird-cage; **~flinte** *f* fowling-piece; **Qfrei** *adj.* outlawed; **~futter** *n* food for birds, bird-seed; **~kunde**

f (-/no *pl.*) ornithology; **'~liebhaber** *m* bird-fancier; **'~nest** *n* bird's nest, bird-nest; **'~perspektive** *f* (-/no *pl.*), **'~schau** *f* (-/no *pl.*) bird's-eye view; **'~scheuche** *f* (-/-*n*) scarecrow (*a. fig.*); **~'Strauß-Politik** *f* ostrich policy; ~ *betreiben* hide one's head in the sand (like an ostrich); **'~warte** *f* ornithological station; **'~zug** *m* passage *or* migration of birds.

Vokab|el [vo'ka:bəl] *f* (-/-*n*) word; **~ular** [~abu'la:r] *n* (-s/-e) vocabulary.

Vokal *ling.* [vo'ka:l] *m* (-s/-e) vowel.

Volk [fɔlk] *n* **1.** (-[e]s/-er) people; nation; swarm (*of bees*); covey (*of partridges*); **2.** (-[e]s/no *pl.*) populace, *the* common people; *contp. the* common *or* vulgar herd; *der Mann aus dem ~e* the man in the street *or Am.* on the street.

Völker|bund ['fœlkər-] *m* (-[e]s/no *pl.*) League of Nations; **'~kunde** *f* (-/no *pl.*) ethnology; **'~recht** *n* (-[e]s/no *pl.*) international law, law of nations; **'~wanderung** *f* age of national migrations.

'Volks|abstimmung *pol. f* plebiscite; **'~ausgabe** *f* popular edition (*of book*); **'~bücherei** *f* free *or* public library; **'~charakter** *m* national character; **'~dichter** *m* popular *or* national poet; **'~entscheid** *pol.* ['~ɛntʃaɪt] *m* (-[e]s/-e) referendum; plebiscite; **'~fest** *n* fun fair, amusement park *or* grounds *pl.*; public merry-making; national festival; **'~gunst** *f* popularity; **'~herrschaft** *f* democracy; **'~hochschule** *f* adult education (courses *pl.*); **'~lied** *n* folk-song; **'~menge** *f* crowd (of people), multitude; **'~partei** *f* people's party; **'~republik** *f* people's republic; **'~schule** *f* elementary *or* primary school, *Am. a.* grade school; **'~schullehrer** *m* elementary *or* primary teacher, *Am.* grade teacher; **'~sprache** *f* vernacular; **'~stamm** *m* tribe, race; **'~stück** *thea. n* folk-play; **'~tanz** *m* folk-dance; **'~tracht** *f* national costume; **2tümlich** *adj.* ['~ty:mlɪç] national; popular; **'~versammlung** *f* public meeting; **'~vertreter** *parl. m* deputy, representative, member of parliament; *Brt.* Member of Parliament, *Am.* Representative; **'~vertretung** *parl. f* representation of the people; parliament; **'~wirt** *m* (political) economist; **'~wirtschaft** *f* economics, political economy; **~wirtschaftler** ['~tlər] *m* (-s/-) *s.* Volkswirt; **'~zählung** *f* census.

voll [fɔl] **1.** *adj.* full; filled; whole, complete, entire; *figure, face:* full, round; *figure:* buxom; *~er Knospen* full of buds; *aus ~em Halse* at the top of one's voice; *aus ~em Herzen* from the bottom of one's heart; *in ~er Blüte* in full blossom; *in ~er Fahrt* at full speed; *mit ~en Händen* lavishly, liberally; *mit ~em Recht* with perfect right; *um das Unglück ~zumachen* to make things worse; **2.** *adv.* fully, in full; ~ *und ganz* fully, entirely; *j-n nicht für ~ ansehen or nehmen* have a poor opinion of s.o., think little of s.o.

'voll|auf *adv.*, **~'auf** *adv.* abundantly, amply, F plenty; **'~automatisch** *adj.* fully automatic; **'2bad** *n* bath; **'2bart** *m* beard; **'2beschäftigung** *f* full employment; **'2besitz** *m* full possession; **'2blut(pferd)** *zo. n* thoroughbred (horse); **'~bringen** *v/t.* (*irr.* bringen, no -ge-, h) accomplish, achieve; perform; **'2dampf** *m* full steam; F: *mit ~ at* or in full blast; **'~enden** *v/t.* (no -ge-, h) finish, complete; **'~endet** *adj.* perfect; **~ends** *adv.* ['~ɛnts] entirely, wholly, altogether; **2'endung** *f* (-/~ -en) finishing, completion; *fig.* perfection.

Völlerei [fœlə'raɪ] *f* (-/~ -en) gluttony.

voll|'führen *v/t.* (no -ge-, h) execute, carry out; **'~füllen** *v/t.* (*sep.*, -ge-, h) fill (up); **'2gas** *mot. n:* ~ *geben* open the throttle; *mit ~ with* the throttle full open; at full speed; **~gepfropft** *adj.* ['~gəpfrɔpft] crammed, packed; **'~gießen** *v/t.* (*irr.* gießen, *sep.*, -ge-, h) fill (up); **'2gummi** *n, m* solid rubber.

völlig *adj.* ['fœliç] entire, complete; silence, calm, *etc.*: dead.

voll|jährig *adj.* ['fɔljɛːriç]: ~ *sein* be of age; ~ *werden* come of age; **'2jährigkeit** *f* (-/no *pl.*) majority; **'~kommen** *adj.* perfect; **2'kommenheit** *f* (-/~ -en) perfection; **'2kornbrot** *n* whole-meal bread; **'~machen** *v/t.* (*sep.*, -ge-, h) fill (up); F soil, dirty; *um das Unglück vollzumachen* to make things worse; **'2macht** *f* (-/-en) full power, authority; **s̄t̄s̄** power of attorney; ~ *haben* be authorized; **'2matrose** ⚓ *m* able-bodied seaman; **'2milch** *f* whole milk; **'2mond** *m* full moon; **'~packen** *v/t.* (*sep.*, -ge-, h) stuff, cram; **'2pension** *f* (-/-en) full board; **'~schenken** *v/t.* (*sep.*, -ge-, h) fill (up); **'~schlank** *adj.* stout, corpulent; **'~ständig** *adj.* complete; **'~stopfen** *v/t.* (*sep.*, -ge-, h) stuff, cram; *sich ~ stuff o.s.; sich die Taschen ~ stuff* one's pockets; **~'strecken** *v/t.* (no -ge-, h) execute; **2'streckung** *f* (-/-en) execution; **'~tönend** *adj.* sonorous, rich; **'2treffer** *m* direct hit; **'2versammlung** *f* plenary meeting *or* assembly; General Assembly (*of the United Nations*); **'~wertig** *adj.* equivalent, equal in value; full; **'‿zählig** adj. complete; **‿ziehen** v/t. (irr. ziehen, no -ge-, h) execute; consummate (marriage); sich ‿ take place; **Ջziehung** f (-/‿-en), **Ջzug** m (-[e]s/no pl.) execution.

Volontär [volɔn'tɛːr] m (-s/-e) unpaid assistant.

Volt ⚡ [vɔlt] n (-, -[e]s/-) volt.

Volumen [vo'luːmən] n (-s/-, Volumina) volume.

vom prp. [fɔm] = **von dem**

von prp. (dat.) [fɔn] space, time: from; instead of gen.: of; passive: by; ‿ Hamburg from Hamburg; ‿ nun an from now on; ‿ morgen an from tomorrow (on), beginning tomorrow; ein Freund ‿ mir a friend of mine; die Einrichtung ‿ Schulen the erection of schools; ‿ dem or vom Apfel essen eat (some) of the apple; der Herzog ‿ Edinburgh the Duke of Edinburgh; ein Gedicht ‿ Schiller a poem by Schiller; ‿ selbst by itself; ‿ selbst, ‿ sich aus by oneself; ‿ drei Meter Länge three metres long; ein Betrag ‿ 300 Mark a sum of 300 marks; e-e Stadt ‿ 10 000 Einwohnern a town of 10,000 inhabitants; reden ‿ talk of or about s.th.; speak on (scientific subject); ‿ mir aus as far as I am concerned; I don't mind, for all I care; das ist nett ‿ ihm that is nice of him; ich habe ‿ ihm gehört I have heard of him; **‿statten** adv. [‿'ʃtatən]: gut ‿ gehen go well.

vor prp. (dat.; acc.) [foːr] space: in front of, before; time: before; ‿ langer Zeit a long time ago; ‿ einigen Tagen a few days ago; (heute) ‿ acht Tagen a week ago (today); am Tage ‿ (on) the day before, on the eve of; 5 Minuten ‿ 12 five minutes to twelve, Am. five minutes of twelve; fig. at the eleventh hour; ‿ der Tür stehen be imminent, be close at hand; ‿ e-m Hintergrund against a background; ‿ Zeugen in the presence of witnesses; ‿ allen Dingen above all; (dicht) ‿ dem Untergang stehen be on the brink or verge of ruin; ‿ Hunger sterben die of hunger; ‿ Kälte zittern tremble with cold; schützen (verstecken) ‿ protect (hide) from or against; ‿ sich gehen take place, pass off; ‿ sich hin lächeln smile to o.s.; sich fürchten ‿ be afraid of, fear.

Vor|abend ['foːr⁹-] m eve; **‿ahnung** f presentiment, foreboding.

voran adv. [fo'ran] at the head (dat. of), in front (of), before; Kopf ‿ head first; **‿gehen** v/i. (irr. gehen, sep., -ge-, sein) lead the way; precede; **‿kommen** v/i. (irr. kommen, sep., -ge-, sein) make progress; fig. get on (in life).

Voran|schlag ['foːr⁹an-] m (rough) estimate; **‿zeige** f advance notice; film: trailer.

vorarbeite|n ['foːr⁹-] v/t. and v/i. (sep., -ge-, h) work in advance; **Ջr** m foreman.

voraus adv. [fo'raus] in front (dat. of), ahead (of); im ‿ in advance, beforehand; **‿bestellen** v/t. (sep., no -ge-, h) s. vorbestellen; **‿bezahlen** v/t. (sep., no -ge-, h) pay in advance, prepay; **‿gehen** v/i. (irr. gehen, sep., -ge-, sein) go on before; s. vorangehen; **Ջsage** f prediction; prophecy; forecast (of weather); **‿sagen** v/t. (sep., -ge-, h) foretell, predict; prophesy; forecast (weather, etc.); **‿schicken** v/t. (sep., -ge-, h) send on in advance; fig. mention beforehand, premise; **‿sehen** v/t. (irr. sehen, sep., -ge-, h) foresee; **‿setzen** v/t. (sep., -ge-, h) (pre)suppose, presume, assume; vorausgesetzt, daß provided that; **Ջsetzung** f (-/-en) (pre)supposition, assumption; prerequisite; **Ջsicht** f foresight; aller ‿ nach in all probability; **‿sichtlich** adj. presumable, probable, likely; **Ջzahlung** f advance payment or instal(l)ment.

'Vor|bedacht 1. m (-[e]s/no pl.): mit ‿ deliberately, on purpose; **2. Ջ** adj. premeditated; **'‿bedeutung** f foreboding, omen, portent; **'‿bedingung** f prerequisite.

Vorbehalt ['foːrbəhalt] m (-[e]s/-e) reservation, reserve; **Ջen 1.** v/t. (irr. halten, sep., no -ge-, h): sich ‿ reserve (right, etc.); **2.** adj.: Änderungen ‿ subject to change (without notice); **Ջlos** adj. unreserved, unconditional.

vorbei adv. [foːr'bai] space: along, by, past (all: an dat. s.o., s.th.); time: over, gone; 3 Uhr ‿ past three (o'clock); **‿fahren** v/i. (irr. fahren, sep., -ge-, sein) drive past; **‿gehen** v/i. (irr. gehen, sep., -ge-, sein) pass, go by; pain: pass (off); storm: blow over; ‿ an (dat.) pass; im Vorbeigehen in passing; **‿kommen** v/i. (irr. kommen, sep., -ge-, sein) pass by; F drop in; F ‿ an (dat.) get past (obstacle, etc.); **‿lassen** v/t. (irr. lassen, sep., -ge-, h) let pass.

'Vorbemerkung f preliminary remark or note.

'vorbereit|en v/t. (sep., no -ge-, h) prepare (für, auf acc. for); **Ջung** f preparation (für, auf acc. for).

'Vorbesprechung f preliminary discussion or talk.

'vor|bestellen v/t. (sep., no -ge-, h) order in advance; book (room, etc.); **'‿bestraft** adj. previously convicted.

'vorbeug|en (sep., -ge-, h) **1.** v/i. prevent (e-r Sache s.th.); **2.** v/t. and v/refl. bend forward; **'‿end**

adj. preventive; $\mathscr{F}$ *a.* prophylactic; **'Ωung** *f* prevention.

'Vorbild *n* model; pattern; example; prototype; **'Ωlich** *adj.* exemplary; **~ung** ['~duŋ] *f* preparatory training.

'vor|bringen *v/t.* (*irr.* bringen, *sep.*, -ge-, h) bring forward, produce; advance (*opinion*); ᵗᵗₓ prefer (*charge*); utter, say, state; **'~datieren** *v/t.* (*sep.*, *no* -ge-, h) post-date.

vorder *adj.* ['fɔrdər] front, fore.

'Vorder|achse *f* front axle; **'~ansicht** *f* front view; **'~bein** *n* foreleg; **'~fuß** *m* forefoot; **'~grund** *m* foreground (*a. fig.*); **'~haus** *n* front building; **'~mann** *m* man in front (*of s.o.*); **'~rad** *n* front wheel; **~radantrieb** *mot.* ['fɔrdərraːtʔ-] *m* front-wheel drive; **'~seite** *f* front (side); obverse (*of coin*); **'~sitz** *m* front seat; **'Ωst** *adj.* foremost; **'~teil** *n, m* front (part); **'~tür** *f* front door; **'~zahn** *m* front tooth; **'~zimmer** *n* front room.

'vordrängen *v/refl.* (*sep.*, -ge-, h) press *or* push forward.

'vordring|en *v/i.* (*irr.* dringen, *sep.*, -ge-, sein) advance; **'~lich** *adj.* urgent. [blank.)

'Vordruck *m* (-[e]s/-e) form, *Am. a.*)

voreilig *adj.* ['foːrʔ-] hasty, rash, precipitate; **~e** *Schlüsse ziehen* jump to conclusions.

voreingenommen *adj.* ['foːrʔ-] prejudiced, bias(s)ed; **'Ωheit** *f* (-/*no pl.*) prejudice, bias.

vor|enthalten ['foːrʔ-] *v/t.* (*irr.* halten, *sep.*, *no* -ge-, h) keep back, withhold (*j-m* et. s.th. from s.o.); **Ωentscheidung** ['foːrʔ-] *f* preliminary decision; **~erst** *adv.* ['foːrʔ-] for the present, for the time being.

Vorfahr ['foːrfaːr] *m* (-en/-en) ancestor.

'vorfahr|en *v/i.* (*irr.* fahren, *sep.*, -ge-, sein) drive up; pass; *den Wagen ~ lassen* order the car; **'Ωt(srecht** *n)* *f* right of way, priority.

'Vorfall *m* incident, occurrence, event; **'Ωen** *v/i.* (*irr.* fallen, *sep.*, -ge-, sein) happen, occur.

'vorfinden *v/t.* (*irr.* finden, *sep.*, -ge-, h) find.

'Vorfreude *f* anticipated joy.

'vorführ|en *v/t.* (*sep.*, -ge-, h) bring forward, produce; bring (*dat.* before); show, display, exhibit; demonstrate (*use of s.th.*); show, present (*film*); **'Ωer** *m* projectionist (*in cinema theatre*); **'Ωung** *f* presentation, showing; ⊕ demonstration; ᵗᵗₓ production (*of prisoner*); *thea.*, *film:* performance.

'Vor|gabe *f* *sports:* handicap; *athletics:* stagger; *golf, etc.:* odds *pl.*; **'~gang** *m* incident, occurrence, event; facts *pl.*; file, record(s *pl.*); *biol.*, ⊕ process; **~gänger** ['~geŋər]

m (-s/-), **'~gängerin** *f* (-/-nen) predecessor; **'~garten** *m* front garden.

'vorgeben *v/t.* (*irr.* geben, *sep.*, -ge-, h) *sports:* give (*j-m* s.o.); *fig.* pretend, allege.

'Vor|gebirge *n* promontory, cape, headland; foot-hills *pl.*; **'~gefühl** *n* presentiment, foreboding.

'vorgehen 1. *v/i.* (*irr.* gehen, *sep.*, -ge-, sein) ⚔ advance; F lead the way; go on before; *watch, clock:* be fast, gain (*fünf Minuten* five minutes); take precedence (*dat.* of, over), be more important (*than*); take action, act; proceed (*a.* ᵗᵗₓ *gegen against*); go on, happen, take place; **2.** Ω *n* (-s/*no pl.*) action, proceeding.

'Vor|geschmack *m* (-[e]s/*no pl.*) foretaste; **~gesetzte** ['~gəzetstə] *m* (-n/-n) superior; *esp. Am.* F boss; **'Ωgestern** *adv.* the day before yesterday; **'Ωgreifen** *v/i.* (*irr.* greifen, *sep.*, -ge-, h) anticipate (*j-m* *or* e-r *Sache* s.o. *or* s.th.).

'vorhaben 1. *v/t.* (*irr.* haben, *sep.*, -ge-, h) intend, mean; be going to do *s.th.*; *nichts* ~ be at a loose end; *haben Sie heute abend et. vor?* have you anything on tonight?; *was hat er jetzt wieder vor?* what is he up to now?; *was hast du mit ihm vor?* what are you going to do *with* him?; **2.** Ω *n* (-s/-) intention, purpose, ᵗᵗₓ intent; plan; project.

'Vorhalle *f* vestibule, (entrance-) hall; lobby; porch.

'vorhalt|en (*irr.* halten, *sep.*, -ge-, h) **1.** *v/t.*: *j-m* et. ~ hold s.th. before s.o.; *fig.* reproach s.o. with s.th.; **2.** *v/i.* last; **'Ωung** *f* remonstrance; *j-m* ~en *machen* remonstrate with s.o. (*wegen on*).

vorhanden *adj.* [for'handən] at hand, present; available (*a.* †); † on hand, in stock; ~ *sein* exist; **Ω-sein** *n* presence, existence.

'Vor|hang *m* curtain; **'~hänge-schloß** *n* padlock.

'vorher *adv.* before, previously; in advance, beforehand.

vor'her|bestellen *v/t.* (*sep.*, *no* -ge-, h) *s.* vorbestellen; **~bestimmen** *v/t.* (*sep.*, *no* -ge-, h) determine beforehand, predetermine; **~gehen** *v/i.* (*irr.* gehen, *sep.*, -ge-, sein) precede; **~ig** *adj.* preceding, previous.

'Vorherr|schaft *f* predominance; **'Ωschen** *v/i.* (*sep.*, -ge-, h) predominate, prevail; **'Ωschend** *adj.* predominant, prevailing.

Vor'her|sage *f s.* Voraussage; **Ωsagen** *v/t.* (*sep.*, -ge-, h) *s.* voraussagen; **Ωsehen** *v/t.* (*irr.* sehen, *sep.*, -ge-, h) foresee; **Ωwissen** *v/t.* (*irr.* wissen, *sep.*, -ge-, h) know beforehand, foreknow.

'vor|hin *adv.*, ͵'hin *adv.* a short
while ago, just now.
'Vor|hof *m* outer court, forecourt;
anat. auricle (*of heart*); '͵hut ⚔ *f*
vanguard.
'vor|ig *adj.* last; ͵jährig *adj.* ['͵-
je:riç] of last year, last year's.
'Vor|kämpfer *m* champion, pio-
neer; '͵kehrung *f* (-/-en) precaution; ͵en treffen take precautions;
'͵kenntnisse *f/pl.* preliminary or
basic knowledge (*in dat.* of); *mit
guten ͵n in* (*dat.*) well grounded in.
'vorkommen 1. *v/i.* (*irr. kommen,
sep.*, -ge-, *sein*) be found; occur,
happen; *es kommt mir vor* it seems
to me; 2. ♀ *n* (-*s/-*) occurrence.
'Vor|kommnis *n* (-*ses/-se*) occur-
rence; event; '͵kriegszeit *f* pre-
war times *pl.*
'vorlad|en ⚖ *v/t.* (*irr. laden, sep.*,
-ge-, *h*) summon; '♀ung ⚖ *f* summons.
'Vorlage *f* copy; pattern; *parl.* bill;
presentation; production (*of document*); *football:* pass.
'vorlassen *v/t.* (*irr. lassen, sep.*, -ge-,
h) let *s.o.* pass, allow *s.o.* to pass;
admit.
'Vorläuf|er *m*, '͵erin *f* (-/-nen)
forerunner; '♀ig 1. *adj.* provisional,
temporary; 2. *adv.* provisionally,
temporarily; for the present, for
the time being.
'vorlaut *adj.* forward, pert.
'Vorleben *n* past (life), antecedents *pl.*
'vorlege|n *v/t.* (*sep.*, -ge-, *h*) put
(*lock*) on; produce (*document*); submit (*plans, etc. for discussion, etc.*);
propose (*plan, etc.*); present (*bill,
etc.*); *j-m et. ͵* lay or place or put
s.th. before *s.o.*; show *s.o. s.th.*;
at table: help *s.o.* to *s.th.*; *j-m e-e
Frage ͵* put a question to *s.o.*; *sich
͵ lean forward;* '♀r *m* (-*s/-*) rug.
'vorles|en *v/t.* (*irr. lesen, sep.*, -ge-,
h) read aloud; *j-m et. ͵* read (*out*)
s.th. to *s.o.*; '♀ung *f* lecture (*über
acc.* on; *vor dat.* to); *e-e ͵ halten*
(give a) lecture.
'vorletzt *adj.* last but one; *͵e Nacht*
the night before last.
'Vorlieb|e *f* (-/*no pl.*) predilection,
preference; ♀nehmen [͵'li:p-] *v/i.*
(*irr. nehmen, sep.*, -ge-, *h*) be satisfied (*mit* with); *͵ mit dem, was da
ist at meals:* take pot luck.
'vorliegen *v/i.* (*irr. liegen, sep.*, -ge-,
h) lie before *s.o.*; be there, exist;
da muß ein Irrtum ͵ there must be
a mistake; *was liegt gegen ihn vor?*
what is the charge against him?;
'͵d *adj.* present, in question.
'vor|lügen *v/t.* (*irr. lügen, sep.*, -ge-,
h): *j-m et. ͵* tell *s.o.* lies; '͵machen
v/t. (*sep.*, -ge-, *h*): *j-m et. ͵* show
s.o. how to do *s.th.*; *fig.* impose
upon *s.o.*; *sich* (*selbst*) *et. ͵* fool
o.s.

'Vormacht *f* (-/'⚔ ͵e), '͵stellung *f*
predominance; supremacy; hegem-
ony.
'Vormarsch ⚔ *m* advance.
'vormerken *v/t.* (*sep.*, -ge-, *h*) note
down, make a note of; reserve;
sich ͵ lassen für put one's name
down for.
'Vormittag *m* morning, forenoon;
'♀s *adv.* in the morning.
'Vormund *m* (-[e]s/-e, *͵*er) guardian; '͵schaft *f* (-/-en) guardian-
ship.
vorn *adv.* [fɔrn] in front; *nach ͵*
forward; *von ͵* from the front; *ich
sah sie von ͵* I saw her face; *von ͵
anfangen* begin at the beginning;
noch einmal von ͵ anfangen begin
anew, make a new start.
'Vorname *m* Christian name, first
name, *Am. a.* given name.
vornehm ['fo:rne:m] 1. *adj.* of
(superior) rank, distinguished; aris-
tocratic; noble; fashioanble; *͵e Gesinnung* high character; *aus.:
tun* give *o.s.* airs; '͵en *v/t.* (*irr.
nehmen, sep.*, -ge-, *h*) take *s.th.* in
hand; deal with; make (*changes,
etc.*); take up (*book*); *F sich j-n ͵*
take *s.o.* to task (*wegen for, about*);
sich ͵ resolve (up)on *s.th.*; resolve
(*zu inf.* to *inf.*), make up one's
mind (*zu inf.* to *inf.*); *sich vorgenommen
haben a.* be determined (*zu inf.* to
inf.); '♀heit *f* (-/*no pl.*) refinement;
elegance; high-mindedness.
'vorn|herein *adv.*, ͵'her'rein *adv.*:
von ͵ from the first or start or beginning.
Vorort ['fo:rʔ-] *m* (-[e]s/-e) suburb;
'͵(s)verkehr *m* suburban traffic;
'͵(s)zug *m* local (train).
'Vor|posten *m* outpost (*a.* ⚔);
'͵rang *m* (-[e]s/*no pl.*) precedence
(*vor dat.* of, over); priority (over);
'͵rat *m* store, stock (*an dat.* of);
Vorräte pl. a. provisions *pl.*, supplies *pl.*; ♀rätig *adj.* ['͵re:tiç]
available; *٠ a.* on hand, in stock;
'♀rechnen *v/t.* (*sep.*, -ge-, *h*) reckon
up (*j-m* to *s.o.*); '͵recht *n* privilege;
'͵rede *f* preface, introduction; '͵-
redner *m* previous speaker; '͵-
richtung ⊕ *f* contrivance, device;
'♀rücken (*sep.*, -ge-) 1. *v/t.* (*h*)
move (*chair, etc.*) forward; 2. *v/i.*
(*sein*) advance; '͵runde *f* sports:
preliminary round; '♀sagen *v/i.*
(*sep.*, -ge-, *h*); *j-m et. ͵* prompt *s.o.*;
'͵saison *f* off or dead season; '͵-
satz *m* intention, purpose, design;
♀sätzlich *adj.* ['͵zetsliç] intentional, deliberate; *͵er Mord* ⚖
wil(l)ful murder; '͵schein *m*: *zum
͵ bringen* bring forward, produce;
zum ͵ kommen appear, turn up;
'♀schieben *v/t.* (*irr. schieben, sep.*,
-ge-, *h*) push *s.th.* forward; slip
(*bolt*); *s. vorschützen*; '♀schießen

v/t. (*irr. schießen, sep., -ge-, h*) advance (*money*).

'**Vorschlag** *m* proposition, proposal; suggestion; offer; $\mathfrak{L}$en ['$\sim$gən] *v/t.* (*irr. schlagen, sep., -ge-, h*) propose; suggest; offer.

'**Vor|schlußrunde** *f sports:* semifinal; '$\mathfrak{L}$schnell *adj.* hasty, rash; '$\mathfrak{L}$schreiben *v/t.* (*irr. schreiben, sep., -ge-, h*): j-m et. $\sim$ write s.th. out for s.o.; *fig.* prescribe.

'**Vorschrift** *f* direction, instruction; prescription (*esp.* $\mathscr{Z}$); order (*a.* $\mathscr{Z}$); regulation(s *pl.*); '$\mathfrak{L}$smäßig *adj.* according to regulations; $\sim$e *Kleidung* regulation dress; '$\mathfrak{L}$swidrig *adj.* and *adv.* contrary to regulations.

'**Vor|schub** *m:* $\sim$ leisten (*dat.*) countenance (*fraud, etc.*); further, encourage; $\Sigma\frac{1}{\Sigma}$ aid and abet; '$\sim$schule *f* preparatory school; '$\sim$schuß *m* advance; *for barrister:* retaining fee, retainer; '$\mathfrak{L}$schützen *v/t.* (*sep., -ge-, h*) pretend, plead (*sickness, etc. as excuse*); '$\mathfrak{L}$schweben *v/i.* (*sep., -ge-, h*): mir schwebt et. vor I have s.th. in mind.

'**vorseh|en** *v/t.* (*irr. sehen, sep., -ge-, h*) plan; design; $\Sigma\frac{1}{\Sigma}$ provide; *sich* $\sim$ take care, be careful; *sich* $\sim$ vor (*dat.*) guard against; '$\mathfrak{L}$ung *f* (-/$\sim$-en) providence.

'**vorsetzen** *v/t.* (*sep., -ge-, h*) put forward; place or put or set before, offer.

'**Vorsicht** *f* caution; care; $\sim$*!* caution!, danger!; look out!, be careful!; $\sim$, *Glas!* Glass, with care!; $\sim$, *Stufe!* mind the step!; '$\mathfrak{L}$ig *adj.* cautious; careful; $\sim$*!* F steady!

'**vorsichts|halber** *adv.* as a precaution; '$\mathfrak{L}$maßnahme *f*, '$\mathfrak{L}$maßregel *f* precaution(ary measure); $\sim$n treffen take precautions.

'**Vorsilbe** *gr. f* prefix.

'**vorsingen** *v/t.* (*irr. singen, sep., -ge-, h*): j-m et. $\sim$ sing s.th. to s.o.

'**Vorsitz** *m* (-es/*no pl.*) chair, presidency; den $\sim$ führen or haben be in the chair, preside (*bei over;* at); den $\sim$ übernehmen take the chair; $\sim$ende ['$\sim$əndə] (-n/-n) **1.** *m* chairman, president; **2.** *f* chairwoman.

'**Vorsorg|e** *f* (-/*no pl.*) provision, providence; precaution; $\sim$ treffen make provision; '$\mathfrak{L}$en *v/i.* (*sep., -ge-, h*) provide; $\mathfrak{L}$lich ['$\sim$kliç] **1.** *adj.* precautionary; **2.** *adv.* as a precaution.

'**Vorspeise** *f* appetizer, hors d'œuvre.

'**vorspieg|eln** *v/t.* (*sep., -ge-, h*) pretend; j-m et. $\sim$ delude s.o. (with false hopes, *etc.*); '$\mathfrak{L}$(e)lung *f* preten|ce, *Am.* -se.

'**Vorspiel** *n* prelude; '$\mathfrak{L}$en *v/t.* (*sep., -ge-, h*): j-m et. $\sim$ play s.th. to s.o.

'**vor|sprechen** (*irr. sprechen, sep., -ge-, h*) **1.** *v/t.* pronounce (j-m et.

s.th. to or for s.o.); **2.** *v/i.* call (*bei on s.o.;* at *an office*); *thea.* audition; '$\sim$**springen** *v/i.* (*irr. springen, sep., -ge-, sein*) jump forward; project; '$\mathfrak{L}$**sprung** *m* $\triangle$ projection; *sports:* lead; *fig.* start, advantage (*vor dat.* of); '$\mathfrak{L}$**stadt** *f* suburb; '$\sim$**städtisch** *adj.* suburban; '$\mathfrak{L}$**stand** *m* board of directors; managing directors *pl.*

'**vorsteh|en** *v/i.* (*irr. stehen, sep., -ge-, h*) project, protrude; *fig.:* direct; manage (*both:* e-r Sache s.th.); '$\mathfrak{L}$er *m* director, manager; head, chief.

'**vorstell|en** *v/t.* (*sep., -ge-, h*) put forward; put (*clock*) on; introduce (j-n j-m s.o. to s.o.); mean, stand for; represent; *sich* $\sim$ have an interview with; *sich et.* $\sim$ imagine or fancy s.th.; '$\mathfrak{L}$ung *f* introduction, presentation; interview (*of applicant for post*); *thea.* performance; *fig.:* remonstrance; idea, conception; imagination; '$\mathfrak{L}$ungsvermögen *n* imagination.

'**Vor|stoß** $\times$ *m* thrust, advance; '$\sim$**strafe** *f* previous conviction; '$\mathfrak{L}$**strecken** *v/t.* (*sep., -ge-, h*) thrust out, stretch forward; advance (*money*); '$\sim$**stufe** *f* first step or stage; '$\mathfrak{L}$**täuschen** *v/t.* (*sep., -ge-, h*) feign, pretend.

Vorteil ['fɔrtaɪl] *m* advantage (*a. sports*); profit; *tennis:* (ad)vantage; '$\mathfrak{L}$**haft** *adj.* advantageous (*für* to), profitable (to).

Vortrag ['fo:rtraːk] *m* (-[e]s/$\sim$e) performance; execution (*esp.* $\text♪$); recitation (*of poem*); $\text♪$ recital; lecture; report; $\dagger$ balance carried forward; e-n $\sim$ halten (give a) lecture (*über acc.* on); '$\mathfrak{L}$en ['$\sim$gən] *v/t.* (*irr. tragen. sep., -ge-, h*) $\dagger$ carry forward; report on; recite (*poem*); perform, *esp.* $\text♪$ execute; lecture on; state, express (*opinion*); $\sim$ende ['$\sim$gəndə] *m* (-n/-n) performer; lecturer; speaker.

vor|trefflich *adj.* [fo:r'trefliç] excellent; '$\sim$**treten** *v/i.* (*irr. treten, sep., -ge-, sein*) step forward; *fig.* project, protrude, stick out; '$\mathfrak{L}$**tritt** *m* (-[e]s/*no pl.*) precedence.

vorüber *adv.* [fo'ry:bər] *space:* by, past; *time:* gone by, over; $\sim$**gehen** *v/i.* (*irr. gehen, sep., -ge-, sein*) pass, go by; $\sim$**gehend** *adj.* passing; temporary; $\mathfrak{L}$**gehende** [$\sim$də] *m* (-n/-n) passer-by; $\sim$**ziehen** *v/i.* (*irr. ziehen, sep., -ge-, sein*) march past, pass by; *storm:* blow over.

Vor|übung ['fo:r$^\text{?}$-] *f* preliminary practice; $\sim$**untersuchung** $\Sigma\frac{1}{\Sigma}$ ['fo:r$^\text{?}$-] *f* preliminary inquiry.

Vorurteil ['fo:r$^\text{?}$-] *n* prejudice; '$\mathfrak{L}$s-los *adj.* unprejudiced, unbias(s)ed.

'**Vor|verkauf** *thea. m* booking in advance; *im* $\sim$ bookable (*bei* at);

'**Qverlegen** v/t. (sep., no -ge-, h) advance; **~wand** m (-[e]s/=e) pretext, preten|ce, Am. -se.

vorwärts adv. ['fo:rverts] forward, onward, on; **~l** go ahead!; **~kommen** v/i. (irr. kommen, sep., -ge-, sein) (make) progress; fig. make one's way, get on (in life).

vorweg adv. [for'vek] beforehand; **~nehmen** v/t. (irr. nehmen, sep., -ge-, h) anticipate.

vor|weisen v/t. (irr. weisen, sep., -ge-, h) produce, show; **~werfen** v/t. (irr. werfen, sep., -ge-, h) throw or cast before; j-m et. ~ reproach s.o. with s.th.; **~wiegend** 1. adj. predominant, preponderant; 2. adv. predominantly, chiefly, mainly, mostly; '**~witzig** adj. forward, pert; inquisitive.

'**Vorwort** n (-[e]s/-e) preface (by author); foreword.

'**Vorwurf** m reproach; subject (of drama, etc.); j-m e-n ~ or Vorwürfe machen reproach s.o. (wegen with); '**Qsvoll** adj. reproachful.

'**vor|zählen** v/t. (sep., -ge-, h) enumerate, count out (both: j-m to s.o.); '**Qzeichen** n omen; '**~zeichnen** v/t. (sep., -ge-, h): j-m et. ~ draw or sketch s.th. for s.o.; show s.o. how to draw s.th.; fig. mark out, destine; '**~zeigen** v/t. (sep., -ge-, h) produce, show.

'**Vorzeit** f antiquity; in literature often: times of old, days of yore; '**Qig** adj. premature.

'**vor|ziehen** v/t. (irr. ziehen, sep., -ge-, h) draw forth; draw (curtains); fig. prefer; '**Qzimmer** n antechamber, anteroom; waiting-room; '**Qzug** fig. m preference; advantage; merit; priority; **~züglich** adj. [~'tsy:kliç] excellent, superior, exquisite.

'**Vorzugs|aktie** f preference share or stock, Am. preferred stock; '**~preis** m special price; '**Qweise** adv. preferably; chiefly.

Votum ['vo:tum] n (-s/Voten, Vota) vote.

vulgär [vul'gɛ:r] vulgar.

Vulkan [vul'ka:n] m (-s/-e) volcano; **Qisch** adj. volcanic.

W

Waag|e ['va:gə] f (-/-n) balance, (e-e a pair of) scales pl.; die ~ halten (dat.) counterbalance; '**Qerecht** adj., **Qrecht** adj. ['va:k-] horizontal, level; **~schale** ['va:k-] f scale.

Wabe ['va:bə] f (-/-n) honeycomb.

wach adj. (vax) awake; hell~ wide awake; ~ werden awake, wake up; '**Qe** f (-/-n) watch; guard; guardhouse, guardroom; police-station; sentry, sentinel; ~ haben be on guard; ~ halten keep watch; '**~en** v/i. (ge-, h) (keep) watch (über acc. over); sit up (bei with); '**Qhund** m watch-dog.

Wacholder ♀ [va'xɔldər] m (-s/-) juniper.

'**wach|rufen** v/t. (irr. rufen, sep., -ge-, h) rouse, evoke; '**~rütteln** v/t. (sep., -ge-, h) rouse (up); fig. rouse, shake up.

Wachs [vaks] n (-es/-e) wax.

'**wachsam** adj. watchful, vigilant; '**Qkeit** f (-/no pl.) watchfulness, vigilance.

wachsen[1] ['vaksən] v/i. (irr., ge-, sein) grow; fig. increase.

wachsen[2] [~] v/t. (ge-, h) wax.

wächsern adj. ['vɛksərn] wax; fig. waxen, waxy.

'**Wachs|kerze** f, '**~licht** n wax candle; '**~tuch** n waxcloth, oilcloth.

Wachstum ['vakstu:m] n (-s/no pl.) growth; fig. increase.

Wächte mount. ['vɛçtə] f (-/-n) cornice.

Wachtel orn. ['vaxtəl] f (-/-n) quail.

Wächter ['vɛçtər] m (-s/-) watcher, guard(ian); watchman.

'**Wacht|meister** m sergeant; '**~turm** m watch-tower.

wackel|ig adj. ['vakəliç] shaky (a. fig.), tottery; furniture, etc.: rickety; tooth, etc.: loose; '**Qkontakt** ⚡ m loose connexion or (Am. only) connection; '**~n** v/i. (ge-, h) shake; table, etc.: wobble; tooth, etc.: be loose; tail, etc.: wag; ~ mit wag s.th.

wacker adj. ['vakər] honest, upright; brave, gallant.

wacklig adj. ['vakliç] s. wackelig.

Wade ['va:də] f (-/-n) calf; '**~nbein** anat. n fibula.

Waffe ['vafə] f (-/-n) weapon (a. fig.); **~n** pl. a. arms pl.

Waffel ['vafəl] f (-/-n) waffle; wafer.

'**Waffen|fabrik** f armaments factory, Am. a. armory; '**~gattung** f arm; '**~gewalt** f (-/no pl.): mit ~ by force of arms; '**Qlos** adj. weaponless, unarmed; '**~schein** m firearm certificate, Am. gun license; '**~stillstand** m armistice (a. fig.), truce.

Wage|hals ['va:gəhals] m daredevil; '**Qhalsig** adj. daring, foolhardy; attr. a. daredevil; '**~mut** m daring

wagen¹ ['vɑːgən] v/t. (ge-, h) venture; risk, dare; sich ~ venture (an acc. [up]on).

Wagen² [~] m (-s/-, ¨) carriage (a. ☺); Am. ☺ car; ☺ coach; wag(g)on; cart; car; lorry, truck; van.

wägen ['vɛːgən] v/t. ([irr.,] ge-, h) weigh (a. fig.).

Wagen|heber m (-s/-) (lifting) jack; '~park m (-[e]s/no pl.) fleet of vehicles; '~schmiere f grease; '~spur f rut.

Waggon ☺ [va'gõː] m (-s/-s) (railway) carriage, Am. (railroad) car.

wag|halsig adj. ['vɑːkhalsiç] s. wagehalsig; '~nis n (-ses/-se) venture, risk.

Wahl [vɑːl] f (-/-en) choice; alternative; selection; pol. election; e-e ~ treffen make a choice; s-e ~ treffen take one's choice; ich hatte keine (andere) ~ I had no choice.

wählbar adj. ['vɛːlbɑːr] eligible; '**2keit** f (-/no pl.) eligibility.

wahl|berechtigt adj. ['vɑːlbərɛçtiçt] entitled to vote; '**2beteiligung** f percentage of voting, F turn-out; '**2bezirk** m constituency.

wählen (ge-, h) 1. v/t. choose; pol. elect; teleph. dial; 2. v/i. choose, take one's choice; teleph. dial (the number).

'**Wahlergebnis** n election return.

Wähler m (-s/-) elector, voter; '**2isch** adj. particular (in dat. in, about, as to), nice (about), fastidious, F choosy; '~schaft f (-/-en) constituency, electorate.

'**Wahl|fach** n optional subject, Am. a. elective; '**2fähig** adj. having a vote; eligible; '~gang m ballot; '~kampf m election campaign; '~kreis m constituency; '~lokal n polling station; '**2los** adj. indiscriminate; '~recht n (-[e]s/no pl.) franchise; '~rede f electoral speech.

'**Wahlscheibe** teleph. f dial.

'**Wahl|spruch** m device, motto; '~stimme f vote; '~urne f ballot-box; '~versammlung f electoral rally; '~zelle f polling-booth; '~zettel m ballot, voting-paper.

Wahn [vɑːn] m (-[e]s/no pl.) delusion, illusion; mania; '~sinn m (-[e]s/no pl.) insanity, madness (both a. fig.); '**2sinnig** adj. insane, mad (vor dat. with) (both a. fig.); '~sinnige ['~ɡə] m (-n/-n) madman, lunatic; '~vorstellung f delusion, hallucination; '~witz m (-es/no pl.) madness, insanity; '**2witzig** adj. mad, insane.

wahr adj. [vɑːr] true; real; genuine; '~en v/t. (ge-, h) safeguard (interests, etc.); maintain (one's dignity); den Schein ~ keep up or save appearances.

währen ['vɛːrən] v/i. (ge-, h) last, continue.

'**während** 1. prp. (gen.) during; pending; 2. cj. while, whilst; while, whereas.

'**wahrhaft** adv. really, truly, indeed; '~ig [~'haftiç] 1. adj. truthful, veracious; 2. adv. really, truly, indeed.

'**Wahrheit** f (-/-en) truth; in ~ in truth; j-m die ~ sagen give s.o. a piece of one's mind; '**2getreu** adj. true, faithful; '~sliebe f (-/no pl.) truthfulness, veracity; '**2sliebend** adj. truthful, veracious.

'**wahr|lich** adv. truly, really; '~nehmbar adj. perceivable, perceptible; '~nehmen v/t. (irr. nehmen, sep., -ge-, h) perceive, notice; avail o.s. of (opportunity); safeguard (interests); '**2nehmung** f (-/-en) perception, observation; '~sagen v/i. (sep., -ge-, h) tell or read fortunes; sich ~ lassen have one's fortune told; '**2sagerin** f (-/-nen) fortuneteller; '~scheinlich 1. adj. probable; likely; 2. adv.: ich werde ~ gehen I am likely to go; **2'scheinlichkeit** f (-/-ꬱ-en) probability, likelihood; aller ~ nach in all probability or likelihood.

'**Wahrung** f (-/no pl.) maintenance; safeguarding.

Währung ['vɛːruŋ] f (-/-en) currency; standard; '~sreform f currency or monetary reform.

'**Wahrzeichen** n landmark.

Waise ['vaizə] f (-/-n) orphan; '~n-haus n orphanage.

Wal zo. [vɑːl] m (-[e]s/-e) whale.

Wald [valt] m (-[e]s/¨er) wood, forest; '~brand m forest fire; **2ig** adj. ['~diç] wooded, woody; **2reich** adj. ['~t-] rich in forests; ~ung ['~duŋ] f (-/-en) forest.

Walfänger ['vɑːlfɛŋər] m (-s/-) whaler.

walken ['valkən] v/t. (ge-, h) full (cloth); mill (cloth, leather).

Wall [val] m (-[e]s/¨e) ⚔ rampart (a. fig.); dam; mound.

Wallach ['valax] m (-[e]s/-e) gelding.

wallen ['valən] v/i. (ge-, h, sein) hair, articles of dress, etc.: flow; simmer; boil (a. fig.).

wall|fahren ['valfɑːrən] v/i. (ge-, sein) (go on a) pilgrimage; '**2fahrer** m pilgrim; '**2fahrt** f pilgrimage; '~fahrten v/i. (ge-, sein) (go on a) pilgrimage.

'**Wallung** f (-/-en) ebullition; ⚗ congestion; (Blut) in ~ bringen make s.o.'s blood boil, enrage.

Walnuß ['val-] f walnut; '~baum ⚘ m walnut(-tree).

Walroß zo. ['val-] n walrus.

walten ['valtən] v/i. (ge-, h): s-s Amtes ~ attend to one's duties; Gnade ~ lassen show mercy.

Walze ['valtsə] f (-/-n) roller, cylinder; ⊕ a. roll; ⊕, ♪ barrel; '2n v/t. (ge-, h) roll (a. ⊕).

wälzen ['veltsən] v/t. (ge-, h) roll; roll (problem) round in one's mind; shift (blame) (auf acc. [up]on); sich ~ roll; wallow (in mud, etc.); welter (in blood, etc.).

Walzer ♪ ['valtsər] m (-s/-) waltz.

Wand [vant] 1. f (-/⁻e) wall; partition; 2. 2 pret. of winden.

Wandel ['vandəl] m (-s/no pl.) change; '2bar adj. changeable; variable; '~gang m, '~halle f lobby; '2n (ge-) 1. v/i. (sein) walk; 2. v/refl. (h) change.

Wander|er ['vandərər] m (-s/-) wanderer; hiker; '~leben n (-s/no pl.) vagrant life; '2n v/i. (ge-, sein) wander; hike; '~niere ⚕ f floating kidney; '~prediger m itinerant preacher; '~preis m challenge trophy; '~schaft f (-/no pl.) wanderings pl.; auf (der) ~ on the tramp; '~ung f (-/-en) walking-tour; hike.

'Wand|gemälde n mural (painting); '~kalender m wall-calendar; '~karte f wall-map.

Wandlung ['vandluŋ] f (-/-en) change, transformation; eccl. transubstantiation; ⚖ redhibition.

'Wand|schirm m folding-screen; '~schrank m wall-cupboard; '~spiegel m wall-mirror; '~tafel f blackboard; '~teppich m tapestry; '~uhr f wall-clock.

wandte ['vantə] pret. of wenden 2.

Wange ['vaŋə] f (-/-n) cheek.

Wankel|mut ['vaŋkəlmu:t] m fickleness, inconstancy; 2mütig adj. ['~my:tiç] fickle, inconstant.

wanken ['vaŋkən] v/i. (ge-, h, sein) totter, stagger (a. fig.); house, etc.: rock; fig. waver.

wann adv. [van] when; s. dann; seit ~? how long?, since when?

Wanne ['vanə] f (-/-n) tub; bath (-tub), F tub; '~nbad n bath, F tub.

Wanze zo. ['vantsə] f (-/-n) bug, Am. a. bedbug.

Wappen ['vapən] n (-s/-) (coat of) arms pl.; '~kunde f (-/no pl.) heraldry; '~schild m, n escutcheon; '~tier n heraldic animal.

wappnen fig. ['vapnən] v/refl. (ge-, h): sich ~ gegen be prepared for; sich mit Geduld ~ have patience.

war [va:r] pret. of sein[1].

warb [varp] pret. of werben.

Ware ['va:rə] f (-/-n) commodity, article of trade; ~n pl. a. goods pl., merchandise, wares pl.

'Waren|aufzug m hoist; '~bestand m stock (on hand); '~haus n department store; '~lager n stock; warehouse, Am. a. stock room; '~probe f sample; '~zeichen n trade mark.

warf [varf] pret. of werfen.

warm adj. [varm] warm (a. fig.); meal: hot; schön ~ nice and warm.

Wärme ['vɛrmə] f (-/⚛-n) warmth; phys. heat; '~grad m degree of heat; '2n v/t. (ge-, h) warm; sich die Füße ~ warm one's feet.

'Wärmflasche f hot-water bottle.

'warmherzig adj. warm-hearted.

Warm'wasser|heizung f hot-water heating; '~versorgung f hot-water supply.

warn|en ['varnən] v/t. (ge-, h) warn (vor dat. of, against), caution (against); '2signal n danger-signal (a. fig.); '2streik m token strike; '2ung f (-/-en) warning, caution; 2ungstafel ['varnuŋs-] f notice-board.

Warte fig. ['vartə] f (-/-n) point of view.

warten ['vartən] v/i. (ge-, h) wait (auf acc. for); be in store (for s.o.); j-n ~ lassen keep s.o. waiting.

Wärter ['vɛrtər] m (-s/-) attendant; keeper; (male) nurse.

'Warte|saal m, '~zimmer n waiting-room.

Wartung ⊕ ['vartuŋ] f (-/⚛-en) maintenance.

warum adv. [va'rum] why.

Warze ['vartsə] f (-/-n) wart; nipple.

was [vas] 1. interr. pron. what; ~ kostet das Buch? how much is this book?; F ~ rennst du denn so (schnell)? why are you running like this?; ~ für (ein) ...! what a(n) ...!; ~ für ein ...? what ...?; 2. rel. pron. what; ~ (auch immer), alles ~ what(so)ever; ...; ~ ihn völlig kalt ließ ... which left him quite cold; 3. F indef. pron. something; ich will dir mal ~ sagen I'll tell you what.

wasch|bar adj. ['vaʃba:r] washable; '2becken n wash-basin, Am. washbowl.

Wäsche ['vɛʃə] f (-/-n) wash(ing); laundry; linen (a. fig.); underwear; in der ~ sein be at the wash; sie hat heute große ~ she has a large wash today.

waschecht adj. ['vaʃʔ-] washable; colour: a. fast; fig. dyed-in-the-wool.

'Wäsche|klammer f clothes-peg, clothes-pin; '~leine f clothes-line.

'waschen v/t. (irr., ge-, h) wash; sich ~ (have a) wash; sich das Haar or den Kopf ~ wash or shampoo one's hair or head; sich gut ~ (lassen) wash well.

Wäscher|ei [vɛʃə'raɪ] f (-/-en) laundry; '~in f (-/-nen) washerwoman, laundress.

'Wäscheschrank m linen closet.

'Wasch|frau f s. Wäscherin; '~haus n wash-house; '~kessel m copper; '~korb m clothes-basket;

'**küche** f wash-house; '**lappen** m face-cloth, Am. washrag, washcloth; '**maschine** f washing machine, washer; '**pulver** n washing powder; '**raum** m lavatory, Am. a. washroom; '**schüssel** f wash-basin; '**tag** m wash(ing)-day; '**ung** f (-/-en) ⚓ wash; ablution; '**weib** contp. n gossip; '**wanne** f wash-tub.

Wasser ['vasər] n (-s/-, ⚓) water; ~ lassen make water; zu ~ und zu Land(e) by sea and land; '**ball** m 1. beach-ball; water-polo ball; 2. (-[e]s/no pl.) water-polo; '**ballspiel** n 1. (-[e]s/no pl.) water-polo; 2. water-polo match; '**behälter** m reservoir, water-tank; '**blase** ⚓ f water-blister; '**dampf** m steam; '²**dicht** adj. waterproof; watertight; '**eimer** m water-pail, bucket; '**fall** m waterfall, cascade; cataract; '**farbe** f water-colo(u)r; '**flugzeug** n waterplane, seaplane; '**glas** n 1. tumbler; 2. ⚓ (-es/no pl.) water-glass; '**graben** m ditch; '**hahn** m tap, Am. a. faucet; '~**hose** f waterspout.

wässerig adj. ['vɛsəriç] watery, washy (a. fig.); j-m den Mund ~ machen make s.o.'s mouth water.

'**Wasser**|**kanne** f water-jug, ewer; '**kessel** m kettle; '**klosett** n water-closet, W.C.; '**kraft** f water-power; '**kraftwerk** n hydroelectric power station or plant, water-power station; '**krug** m water-jug, ewer; '**kur** f water-cure, hydropathy; '**lauf** m watercourse; '**leitung** f water-supply; '**leitungsrohr** n water-pipe; '²**n**|**mangel** m shortage of water; '²**n** v/i. (ge-, h) alight on water; splash down. [(salted herring, etc.).]

wässern ['vɛsərn] v/t. (ge-, h) soak

'**Wasser**|**pflanze** f aquatic plant; '**rinne** f gutter; '**rohr** n waterpipe; '**schaden** m damage caused by water; '**scheide** f watershed, Am. a. divide; '²**scheu** adj. afraid of water; '**schlauch** m water-hose; '**spiegel** m water-level; '**sport** m aquatic sports pl.; '**spülung** f (-/-en) flushing (system); '**stand** m water-level; '**standsanzeiger** ['vasərʃtants-] m water-gauge; '**stiefel** m/pl. waders pl.; '**stoff** ⚓ m (-[e]s/no pl.) hydrogen; '**stoffbombe** f hydrogen bomb, H-bomb; '**strahl** m jet of water; '**straße** f waterway; '**tier** n aquatic animal; '**verdrängung** f (-/-en) displacement; '**versorgung** f water-supply; '**waage** f spirit-level, water-level; '**weg** m waterway; auf dem ~ by water; '**welle** f water-wave; '**werk** n waterworks sg., pl.; '**zeichen** n watermark.

wäßrig adj. ['vɛsriç] s. wässerig.

waten ['va:tən] v/i. (ge-, sein) wade.

watscheln ['va:tʃəln] v/i. (ge-, sein, h) waddle.

Watt ⚓ f [vat] n (-s/-) watt.

Watt|**e** ['vatə] f (-/-n) cotton-wool; surgical cotton; wadding; '~**ebausch** m wad; **2ieren** [~'ti:rən] v/t. wad, pad.

weben ['ve:bən] v/t. and v/i. ([irr.,] ge-, h) weave.

Weber m (-s/-) weaver; '~**ei** [~'raɪ] f 1. (-/no pl.) weaving; 2. (-/-en) weaving-mill.

Webstuhl ['ve:pʃtu:l] m loom.

Wechsel ['vɛksəl] m (-s/-) change; allowance; ✝ bill (of exchange); hunt. runway; eigener ~ ✝ promissory note; '**beziehung** f correlation; '**fälle** ['~fɛlə] pl. vicissitudes pl.; '**fieber** ⚓ n (-s/no pl.) intermittent fever; malaria; '**frist** f usance; '**geld** n change; '**kurs** m rate of exchange; '**makler** ✝ m bill-broker; '²**n** (ge-, h) 1. v/t. change; vary; exchange (words, etc.); den Besitzer ~ change hands; die Kleider ~ change (one's clothes); 2. v/i. change; vary; alternate; '~**nehmer** ✝ m (-s/-) payee; ²**seitig** adj. ['~zaɪtiç] mutual, reciprocal; '**strom** ⚓ m alternating current; '**stube** f exchange office; '²**weise** adv. alternately, by or in turns; '~**wirkung** f interaction.

wecke|**n** ['vɛkən] v/t. (ge-, h) wake (up), waken; arouse (a. fig.); '²**r** m (-s/-) alarm-clock.

wedeln ['ve:dəln] v/i. (ge-, h): ~ mit wag (tail).

weder cj. ['ve:dər]: ~ ... noch neither ... nor.

Weg[1] [ve:k] m (-[e]s/-e) way (a. fig.); road (a. fig.); path; route; walk; auf halbem ~ half-way; am ~e by the roadside; aus dem ~e gehen steer clear of; aus dem ~e räumen remove (a. fig.); in die ~e leiten set on foot, initiate.

weg[2] adv. [vɛk] away, off; gone; geh ~! be off (with you)!; ~ mit ihm! off with him!; Hände ~! hands off!; F ich muß ~ I must be off; F ganz ~ sein be quite beside o.s.; '**bleiben** F v/i. (irr. bleiben, sep., -ge-, sein) stay away; be omitted; '**bringen** v/t. (irr. bringen, sep., -ge-, h) take away; a. remove (things).

wegen prp. (gen.) ['ve:gən] because of, on account of, owing to.

weg|**fahren** ['vɛk-] (irr. fahren, sep., -ge-) 1. v/t. (h) remove; cart away; 2. v/i. (sein) leave; '**fallen** v/i. (irr. fallen, sep., -ge-, sein) be omitted; be abolished; '²**gang** m (-[e]s/no pl.) going away; departure; '~**gehen** v/i. (irr. gehen, sep., -ge-, sein) go away or off; merchandise:

sell; '~haben F v/t. (irr. haben, sep., -ge-, h): e-n ~ be tight; have a screw loose; er hat noch nicht weg, wie man es machen muß he hasn't got the knack of it yet; '~jagen v/t. (sep., -ge-, h) drive away; '~kommen F v/i. (irr. kommen, sep., -ge-, sein) get away; be missing; gut (schlecht) ~ come off well (badly); mach, daß du wegkommst! be off (with you)!; '~lassen v/t. (irr. lassen, sep., -ge-, h) let s.o. go; leave out, omit; '~laufen v/i. (irr. laufen, sep., -ge-, sein) run away; '~legen v/t. (sep., -ge-, h) put away; '~machen F v/t. (sep., -ge-, h) remove; a. take out (stains); '~müssen F v/i. (irr. müssen 1, sep., -ge-, h): ich muß weg I must be off; 2nahme ['~nɑːmə] f (-/-n) taking (away); '~nehmen v/t. (irr. nehmen, sep., -ge-, h) take up, occupy (time, space); j-m et. ~ take s.th. away from s.o.; '~raffen fig. v/t. (sep., -ge-, h) carry off.

Wegrand ['veːk-] m wayside.

weg|räumen ['vɛk-] v/t. (sep., -ge-, h) clear away, remove; '~schaffen v/t. (sep., -ge-, h) remove; '~schicken v/t. (sep., -ge-, h) send away or off; '~sehen v/i. (irr. sehen, sep., -ge-, h) look away; ~ über (acc.) overlook, shut one's eyes to; '~setzen v/t. (sep., -ge-, h) put away; sich ~ über (acc.) disregard, ignore; '~streichen v/t. (irr. streichen, sep., -ge-, h) strike off or out; '~tun v/t. (irr. tun, sep., -ge-, h) put away or aside.

Wegweiser ['veːkvaɪzər] m (-s/-) signpost, finger-post; fig. guide.

weg|wenden ['vɛk-] v/t. ([irr. wenden], sep., -ge-, h) turn away, avert (one's eyes); sich ~ turn away; '~werfen v/t. (irr. werfen, sep., -ge-, h) throw away; '~werfend adj. disparaging; '~wischen v/t. (sep., -ge-, h) wipe off; '~ziehen (irr. ziehen, sep., -ge-) 1. v/t. (h) pull or draw away; 2. v/i. (sein) (re)move.

weh [veː] 1. adj. sore; 2. adv.: ~ tun ache, hurt; j-m ~ tun pain or hurt s.o.; fig. a. grieve s.o.; ~ tun hurt o.s.; mir tut der Finger ~ my finger hurts.

Wehen[1] ♀ ['veːən] f/pl. labo(u)r, travail.

wehen[2] f (ge-, h) 1. v/t. blow; 2. v/i. blow; es weht ein starker Wind it is blowing hard.

'weh|klagen v/i. (ge-, h) lament (um for, over); '~leidig adj. snivel(l)ing; voice: plaintive; '2mut f (-/no pl.) wistfulness; ~mütig adj. ['~myːtiç] wistful.

Wehr [veːr] 1. f (-/-en): sich zur ~ setzen offer resistance (gegen to), show fight; 2. n (-[e]s/-e) weir; '~dienst ⚔ m military service; '2en v/refl. (ge-, h) defend o.s.; offer resistance (gegen to); '2fähig ⚔ adj. able-bodied; '2los adj. defenceless, Am. defenseless; '~pflicht ⚔ f (-/no pl.) compulsory military service, conscription; '2pflichtig ⚔ adj. liable to military service.

Weib [vaɪp] n (-[e]s/-er) woman; wife; '~chen zo. n (-s/-) female.

Weiber|feind ['vaɪbər-] m womanhater; '~held contp. m ladies' man; '~volk F n (-[e]s/no pl.) womenfolk.

weib|isch adj. ['vaɪbɪʃ] womanish, effeminate; '~lich adj. ['~p-] female; gr. feminine; womanly, feminine.

weich adj. [vaɪç] soft (a. fig.); meat, etc.: tender; egg: soft-boiled; ~ werden soften; fig. relent.

Weiche[1] ⛬ ['vaɪçə] f (-/-n) switch; ~n pl. points pl.

Weiche[2] anat. [~] f (-/-n) flank, side.

weichen[1] ['vaɪçən] v/i. (irr., ge-, sein) give way, yield (dat. to); nicht von der Stelle ~ not to budge an inch; j-m nicht von der Seite ~ stick to s.o.

weichen[2] [~] v/i. (ge-, h, sein) soak.

'Weichensteller ⛬ m (-s/-) pointsman, switch-man.

'weich|herzig adj. soft-hearted, tender-hearted; '~lich adj. somewhat soft; fig. effeminate; '2ling ['~lɪŋ] m (-s/-e) weakling, milksop, molly(-coddle), sl. sissy; '2tier n mollusc.

Weide[1] ♀ ['vaɪdə] f (-/-n) willow.

Weide[2] ♪ [~] f (-/-n) pasture; auf der ~ out at grass; '~land n pasture(-land); '2n (ge-, h) 1. v/t. feed, pasture, graze; sich ~ an (dat.) gloat over; feast on; 2. v/i. pasture, graze.

'Weiden|korb m wicker basket, osier basket; '~rute f osier switch.

weidmännisch hunt. adj. ['vaɪtmɛnɪʃ] sportsmanlike.

weiger|n ['vaɪgərn] v/refl. (ge-, h) refuse, decline; '2ung f (-/-en) refusal.

Weihe eccl. ['vaɪə] f (-/-n) consecration; ordination; '2n eccl. v/t. (ge-, h) consecrate; j-n zum Priester ~ ordain s.o. priest.

Weiher ['vaɪər] m (-s/-) pond.

'weihevoll adj. solemn.

Weihnachten ['vaɪnaxtən] n (-s/no pl.) Christmas, Xmas.

'Weihnachts|abend m Christmas eve; '~baum m Christmas-tree; '~ferien pl. Christmas holidays pl.; '~fest n Christmas; '~geschenk n Christmas present; '~gratifikation f Christmas bonus; '~karte f Christmas card; '~lied n carol, Christmas hymn; '~mann m Father Christmas, Santa Claus; '~markt m Christmas fair; '~zeit f

(-/no pl.) Christmas(-tide) (in Germany beginning on the first Advent Sunday).

'**Weih|rauch** eccl. m incense; '**~wasser** eccl. n (-s/no pl.) holy water.

weil cj. [vaɪl] because, since, as.

Weil|chen ['vaɪlçən] n (-s/-): ein ~ a little while, a spell; '**~e** f (-/no pl.): e-e ~ a while.

Wein [vaɪn] m (-[e]s/-e) wine; ♀ vine; wilder ~ ♀ Virginia creeper; '**~bau** m (-[e]s/no pl.) vine-growing, viticulture; '**~beere** f grape; '**~berg** m vineyard; '**~blatt** n vine-leaf.

wein|en ['vaɪnən] v/i. (ge-, h) weep (um, vor dat. for), cry (vor dat. for joy, etc., with hunger, etc.); '**~erlich** adj. tearful, lachrymose; whining.

'**Wein|ernte** f vintage; '**~essig** m vinegar; '**~faß** n wine-cask; '**~flasche** f wine-bottle; '**~geist** m (-[e]s/-e) spirit(s pl.) of wine; '**~glas** n wineglass; '**~handlung** f wine-merchant's shop; '**~karte** f wine-list; '**~keller** m wine-vault; '**~kelter** f winepress; '**~kenner** m connoisseur of or in wines.

'**Weinkrampf** ♀ m paroxysm of weeping.

'**Wein|kühler** m wine-cooler; '**~lese** f vintage; '**~presse** f winepress; '**~ranke** f vine-tendril; '**~rebe** f vine; '**²rot** adj. claret-colo(u)red; '**~stock** m vine; '**~traube** f grape, bunch of grapes.

weise[1] ['vaɪzə] 1. adj. wise; sage; 2. ♀ m (-n/-n) wise man, sage.

Weise[2] [~] f (-/-n) ♪ melody, tune; fig. manner, way; auf diese ~ in this way.

weisen ['vaɪzən] (irr., ge-, h) 1. v/t.: j-m die Tür ~ show s.o. the door; von der Schule ~ expel from school; von sich ~ reject (idea, etc.); deny (charge, etc.); 2. v/i.: ~ auf (acc.) point at or to.

Weis|heit ['vaɪshaɪt] f (-/%-en) wisdom; am Ende s-r ~ sein be at one's wit's end; '**~heitszahn** m wisdom-tooth; '**²machen** v/t. (sep., -ge-, h): j-m et. ~ make s.o. believe s.th.

weiß adj. [vaɪs] white; '**²blech** n tin(-plate); '**²brot** n white bread; '**²e** m (-n/-n) white (man); '**~en** v/t. (ge-, h) whitewash; '**~glühend** adj. white-hot, incandescent; '**²kohl** m white cabbage; '**~lich** adj. whitish; '**²waren** pl. linen goods pl.; '**²wein** m white wine.

Weisung ['vaɪzuŋ] f (-/-en) direction, directive.

weit [vaɪt] 1. adj. distant (von from); world, garment: wide; area, etc.: vast; garment: loose; journey, way: long; conscience: elastic; 2. adv.: ~ entfernt far away; ~ entfernt von a. a long distance from; fig. far from;

~ und breit far and wide; ~ über sechzig (Jahre alt) well over sixty; bei ~em (by) far; von ~em from a distance.

weit|ab adv. ['vaɪt'-] far away (von from); '**~aus** adv. (by) far, much; '**²blick** m (-[e]s/no pl.) far-sightedness; '**~blickend** adj. far-sighted, far-seeing; '**~en** v/t. and v/refl. (ge-, h) widen.

'**weiter** 1. adj. particulars, etc.: further; charges, etc.: additional, extra; ~e fünf Wochen another five weeks; bis auf ~es until further notice; ohne ~es without any hesitation; off-hand; 2. adv. furthermore, moreover; ~! I go on!; nichts ~ nothing more; und so ~ and so on; bis hierher und nicht ~ so far and no farther; '**²e** n (-n/no pl.) the rest; further details pl.

'**weiter|befördern** v/t. (sep., no -ge-, h) forward; '**~bestehen** v/i. (irr. stehen, sep., no -ge-, h) continue to exist, survive; '**~bilden** v/t. (sep., -ge-, h) give s.o. further education; sich ~ improve one's knowledge; continue one's education; '**~geben** v/t. (irr. geben, sep., -ge-, h) pass (dat., an acc. to); '**~gehen** v/i. (irr. gehen, sep., -ge-, sein) pass or move on, walk along; fig. continue, go on; '**~hin** adv. in (the) future; furthermore; et. ~ tun continue doing or to do s.th.; '**~kommen** v/i. (irr. kommen, sep., -ge-, sein) get on; '**~können** v/i. (irr. können, sep., -ge-, h) be able to go on; '**~leben** v/i. (sep., -ge-, h) live on, survive (a. fig.); '**~machen** v/t. and v/i. (sep., -ge-, h) carry on.

'**weit|gehend** adj. powers: large; support: generous; '**~gereist** adj. travel(l)ed; '**~greifend** adj. far-reaching; '**~herzig** adj. broad-minded; '**~hin** adv. far off; '**~läufig** ['~lɔʏfiç] 1. adj. house, etc.: spacious; story, etc.: detailed; relative: distant; 2. adv.: ~ erzählen (tell in) detail; er ist ~ verwandt mit mir he is a distant relative of mine; '**~reichend** adj. far-reaching; '**~schweifig** adj. diffuse, prolix; '**~sichtig** adj. ♀ far-sighted; fig. a. far-seeing; '**²sichtigkeit** ♀ f (-/%-en) far-sightedness; '**²sprung** m (-[e]s/no pl.) long jump, Am. broad jump; '**~tragend** adj. ✕ long-range; fig. far-reaching; '**~verbreitet** adj. widespread.

Weizen ♀ m (-s/-) wheat; '**~brot** n wheaten bread; '**~mehl** n wheaten flour.

welch [vɛlç] 1. interr. pron. what; which; ~er? which one?; ~er von beiden? which of the two?; 2. rel. pron. who, that; which, that; 3. F indef. pron.: es gibt ~e, die sagen, daß ... there are some who say that ...; *es sollen viele Ausländer hier sein, hast du schon ~e gesehen?* many foreigners are said to be here, have you seen any yet?

welk *adj.* [vɛlk] faded, withered; *skin:* flabby, flaccid; **'~en** *v/i.* (ge-, sein) fade, wither.

Wellblech ['vɛlblɛç] *n* corrugated iron.

Welle ['vɛlə] *f* (-/-n) wave (*a. fig.*); ⊕ shaft.

'wellen *v/t. and v/refl.* (ge-, h) wave; **'2bereich** ⚡ *m* wave-range; **~förmig** *adj.* ['~fœrmiç] undulating, undulatory; **'2länge** ⚡ *f* wavelength; **'2linie** *f* wavy line; **'2reiten** *n* (-s/no *pl.*) surf-riding.

'wellig *adj.* wavy.

'Wellpappe *f* corrugated cardboard *or* paper.

Welt [vɛlt] *f* (-/-en) world; *die ganze ~* the whole world, all the world; *auf der ~* in the world, *auf der ganzen ~* all over the world; *zur ~ bringen* give birth to, bring into the world.

'Welt|all *n* universe, cosmos; **'~anschauung** *f* Weltanschauung; **'~ausstellung** *f* world fair; **'2bekannt** *adj.* known all over the world; **'2berühmt** *adj.* world-famous; **'~bürger** *m* cosmopolite; **'2erschütternd** *adj.* world-shaking; **'2fremd** *adj.* wordly innocent; **'~friede(n)** *m* universal peace; **'~geschichte** *f* (-/no *pl.*) universal history; **'2gewandt** *adj.* knowing the ways of the world; **'~handel** † *m* (-s/no *pl.*) world trade; **'~karte** *f* map of the world; **'2klug** *adj.* wordly-wise; **'~krieg** *m* world war; *der zweite ~* World War II; **'~lage** *f* international situation; **'~lauf** *m* course of the world; **'2lich** 1. *adj.* wordly; secular, temporal; 2. *adv.*: *~ gesinnt* wordly-minded; **'~literatur** *f* world literature; **'~macht** *f* world-power; **2männisch** *adj.* ['~mɛniʃ] man-of-the-world; **'~markt** *m* (-[e]s/no *pl.*) world market; **'~meer** *n* ocean; **'~meister** *m* world champion; **'~meisterschaft** *f* world championship; **'~raum** *m* (-[e]s/no *pl.*) (outer) space; **'~reich** *n* universal empire; *das Britische ~* the British Empire; **'~reise** *f* journey round the world; **'~rekord** *m* world record; **'~ruf** *m* (-[e]s/no *pl.*) world-wide reputation; **'~schmerz** *m* Weltschmerz; **'~sprache** *f* world *or* universal language; **'~stadt** *f* metropolis; **'2weit** *adj.* world-wide; **'~wunder** *n* wonder of the world.

Wende ['vɛndə] *f* (-/-n) turn (*a. swimming*); *fig. a.* turning-point; **'~kreis** *m geogr.* tropic; *mot.* turning-circle.

Wendeltreppe ['vɛndəl-] *f* winding staircase, (e-e a flight of) winding stairs *pl.*, spiral staircase.

'Wende|marke *f sports:* turning-point; **'2n 1.** *v/t.* (ge-, h) turn (*coat, etc.*); turn (*hay*) about; 2. *v/refl.* ([irr.,] ge-, h): *sich ~ an* (*acc.*) turn to; address o.s. to; apply to (*wegen* for); 3. *v/i.* (ge-, h) ⊕, *mot.* turn; *bitte ~!* please turn over!; **'~punkt** *m* turning-point.

'wend|ig *adj.* nimble, agile (*both a. fig.*); *mot.*, ⊕ easily steerable; *mot.* flexible; **'2ung** *f* (-/-en) turn (*a. fig.*); ⚔ facing; *fig.:* change; expression; idiom.

wenig ['ve:niç] 1. *adj.* little; *~e pl.* few *pl.*; *~er* less; *~er pl.* fewer; *ein klein ~* Geduld a little bit of patience; *das ~e* the little; 2. *adv.* little; *~er* less; ♫ *a.* minus; *am ~sten* least (of all); **'2keit** *f* (-/-en): *meine ~* my humble self; **'~stens** *adv.* ['~stəns] at least.

wenn *cj.* [vɛn] when; if; *~ ... nicht* if ... not, unless; *~ auch* (al)though, even though; *~ auch noch so however; und ~ nun ...?* what if ...?; *wie wäre es, ~ wir jetzt heimgingen?* what about going home now?

wer [ve:r] 1. *interr. pron.* who; which; *~ von euch?* which of you?; 2. *rel. pron.* who; *~ auch (immer)* who(so)ever; 3. F *indef. pron.* somebody; anybody; *ist schon ~ gekommen?* has anybody come yet?

Werbe|abteilung ['vɛrbə-] *f* advertising *or* publicity department; **'~film** *m* advertising film.

'werb|en (*irr.*, ge-, h) 1. *v/t.* canvass (*votes, subscribers, etc.*); ⚔ recruit, enlist; 2. *v/i.*: *~ für* advertise, *Am. a.* advertize; make propaganda for; canvass for; **'2ung** *f* (-/-en) advertising, publicity, *Am. a.* advertizing; propaganda; canvassing; ⚔ enlistment, recruiting.

Werdegang ['ve:rdə-] *m* career; ⊕ process of manufacture.

'werden 1. *v/i.* (*irr.*, ge-, sein) become, get; grow; turn (*pale, sour, etc.*); *was ist aus ihm geworden?* what has become of him?; *was will er (einmal) ~?* what is he going to be?; 2. ♫ *n* (-s/no *pl.*): *noch im ~ sein* be in embryo.

werfen ['vɛrfən] (*irr.*, ge-, h) 1. *v/t.* throw (*nach at*); *zo.* throw (*young*); cast (*shadow, glance, etc.*); *Falten ~* fall in folds; set badly; 2. *v/i.* throw; *zo.* litter; *~ mit* throw (*auf acc., nach at*).

Werft ⚓ [vɛrft] *f* (-/-en) shipyard, dockyard.

Werk [vɛrk] *n* (-[e]s/-e) work; act; ⊕ works *pl.*; works *sg., pl.*, factory; *das ~ e-s Augenblicks* the work of a moment; *zu ~e gehen* proceed; **'~bank** ⊕ *f* work-bench; **'~meister** *m* foreman; **~statt** ['~ʃtat] *f*

(-/~en) workshop; '~tag m work-
day; '2tätig adj. working; '~zeug
n tool; implement; instrument.

Wermut ['ve:rmu:t] m (-[e]s/no pl.)
♀ wormwood; verm(o)uth.

wert [ve:rt] 1. adj. worth; worthy
(gen. of); ~, getan zu werden worth
doing; 2. 2 m (-[e]s/-e) value (a. ♭,
♩, phys., fig.); worth (a. fig.); Briefmarken im ~ von 2 Schilling 2 shillings' worth of stamps; großen ~
legen auf (acc.) set a high value
(up)on.

'Wert|brief m money-letter; '2en
v/t. (ge-, h) value; appraise; '~ge-
genstand m article of value; '2los
adj. worthless, valueless; '~pa-
piere n/pl. securities pl.; '~sachen
pl. valuables pl.; '~ung f (-/-en)
valuation; appraisal; sports: score;
'2voll adj. valuable, precious.

Wesen ['ve:zən] n 1. (-s/no pl.)
entity, essence; nature, character;
viel ~s machen um make a fuss of;
2. (-s/-) being, creature; '2los adj.
unreal; '2tlich adj. essential, substantial.

weshalb [vɛs'halp] 1. interr. pron.
why; 2. cj. that's why.

Wespe zo. ['vɛspə] f (-/-n) wasp.

West geogr. [vɛst] west; '~en m
(-s/no pl.) west; the West.

Weste ['vɛstə] f (-/-n) waistcoat, ✝
and Am. vest; e-e reine ~ haben
have a clean slate.

'west|lich adj. west; westerly;
western; '2wind m west(erly) wind.

Wett|bewerb ['vɛtbəvɛrp] m (-[e]s/
-e) competition (a. ✝); '~büro n
betting office; '~e f (-/-n) wager,
bet; e-e ~ eingehen lay or make a
bet; '~eifer m emulation, rivalry;
'2eifern v/i. (ge-, h) vie (mit with;
in dat. in; um for); '2en (ge-, h)
1. v/t. wager, bet; 2. v/i.: mit j-m
um et. ~ wager or bet s.o. s.th.; ~
auf (acc.) wager or bet on, back.

Wetter[1] ['vɛtər] n (-s/-) weather.

Wetter[2] [~] m (-s/-) better.

'Wetter|bericht m weather-fore-
cast; '2fest adj. weather-proof;
'~karte f weather-chart; '~lage f
weather-conditions pl.; '~leuchten
n (-s/no pl.) sheet-lightning; '~vor-
hersage f (-/-n) weather-forecast;
'~warte f weather-station.

'Wett|kampf m contest, competi-
tion; '~kämpfer m contestant;
'~lauf m race; '~läufer m racer,
runner; '2machen v/t. (sep., -ge-,
h) make up for; '~rennen n race;
'~rüsten n (-s/no pl.) armament
race; '~spiel n match, game;
'~streit m contest.   [sharpen.]

wetzen ['vɛtsən] v/t. (ge-, h) whet,]

wich [viç] pret. of weichen[1].

Wichse ['viksə] f 1. (-/-n) blacking;
polish; 2. F fig. (-/no pl.) thrashing;
'2n v/t. (ge-, h) black; polish.

wichtig adj. ['viçtiç] important;
sich ~ machen show off; '2keit f
(-/~-en) importance; 2tuer ['~tu:-
ər] m (-s/-) pompous fellow; '~tue-
risch adj. pompous.

Wickel ['vikəl] m (-s/-) roll(er); ♀:
compress; packing; '2n v/t. (ge-, h)
wind; swaddle (baby); wrap.

Widder zo. ['vidər] m (-s/-) ram.

wider prp. (acc.) ['vi:dər] against,
contrary to; '~borstig adj. cross-
grained; '~fahren v/i. (irr. fahren,
no -ge-, sein) happen (dat. to);
'2haken m barb; 2hall ['~hal] m
(-[e]s/-e) echo, reverberation; fig.
response; '~hallen v/i. (sep., -ge-,
h) (re-)echo (von with), resound
(with); '~legen v/t. (no -ge-, h)
refute, disprove; '~lich adj. repugnant, repulsive; disgusting; '~na-
türlich adj. unnatural; '~recht-
lich adj. illegal, unlawful; '2rede f
contradiction; '2ruf m revocation; retraction; '~rufen v/t. (irr.
rufen, no -ge-, h) revoke; retract (a.
♱); '~ruflich adj. revocable; 2sa-
cher ['~zaxər] m (-s/-) adversary;
'2schein m reflection; '~setzen
v/refl. (no -ge-, h): sich e-r Sache ~
oppose or resist s.th.; '~setzlich
adj. refractory; insubordinate; '~-
sinnig adj. absurd; ~spenstig adj.
['~ʃpɛnstiç] refractory; '2spenstig-
keit f (-/~-en) refractoriness;
'~spiegeln v/t. (sep., -ge-, h)
reflect (a. fig.); sich ~ in (dat.) be
reflected in; '~sprechen v/i. (irr.
sprechen, no -ge-, h): j-m ~ contradict s.o.; '2spruch m contradiction; opposition; im ~ zu in contradiction to; '~sprüchlich adj.
['~ʃpry:çliç] contradictory; '~-
spruchslos 1. adj. uncontradicted;
2. adv. without contradiction;
'2stand m resistance (a. ♫); opposition; ~ leisten offer resistance
(dat. to); auf heftigen ~ stoßen meet
with stiff opposition; '~stands-
fähig adj. resistant (a. ⊕); ~'stehen v/i. (irr. stehen, no -ge-, h)
resist (e-r Sache s.th.); ~'streben
v/i. (no -ge-, h): es widerstrebt mir,
dies zu tun I hate doing or to do
that, I am reluctant to do that;
~'strebend adv. reluctantly; '2-
streit m (-[e]s/✫-e) antagonism;
fig. conflict; ~wärtig adj. ['~vɛrtiç]
unpleasant, disagreeable; disgusting; '2wille m aversion (gegen to,
for, from); dislike (to, of, for);
disgust (at, for); reluctance, un-
willingness; '~willig adj. reluctant,
unwilling.

widm|en ['vitmən] v/t. (ge-, h)
dedicate; '2ung f (-/-en) dedica-
tion.

widrig adj. ['vi:driç] adverse; ~en-
falls adv. ['~gən'-] failing which,
in default of which.

wie [vi:] **1.** *adv.* how; ~ *alt ist er?* what is his age?; ~ *spät ist es?* what is the time?; **2.** *cj.*: *ein Mann* ~ *er* a man such as he, a man like him; ~ *er dies hörte* hearing this; *ich hörte,* ~ *er es sagte* I heard him saying so.

wieder *adv.* ['vi:dər] again, anew; *immer* ~ again and again; 2'**aufbau** *m* (-[e]s/*no pl.*) reconstruction; rebuilding; ~'**aufbauen** *v/t.* (*sep.*, -ge-, *h*) reconstruct; ~'**aufleben** *v/i.* (*sep.*, -ge-, *sein*) revive; 2'**aufleben** *n* (-s/*no pl.*) revival; 2'**aufnahme** *f* resumption; ~'**aufnehmen** *v/t.* (*irr. nehmen, sep.*, -ge-, *h*) resume; '2**beginn** *m* recommencement; re-opening; ~'**bekommen** *v/t.* (*irr. kommen, sep., no -ge-, h*) get back; ~'**beleben** *v/t.* (*sep., no -ge-, h*) resurrect; 2'**belebung** *f* (-/-*en*) revival; *fig. a.* resurrection; 2'**belebungsversuch** *m* attempt at resuscitation; ~'**bringen** *v/t.* (*irr. bringen, sep.*, -ge-, *h*) bring back; restore, give back; ~'**einsetzen** *v/t.* (*sep.*, -ge-, *h*) restore; ~'**einstellen** *v/t.* (*sep.*, -ge-, *h*) re-engage; '2**ergreifung** *f* reseizure; ~'**erkennen** *v/t.* (*irr. kennen, sep., no -ge-, h*) recognize (*an dat.* by); '**erstatten** *v/t.* (*sep., no -ge-, h*) restore; reimburse, refund (*money*); ~'**geben** *v/t.* (*irr. geben, sep.*, -ge-, *h*) give back, return; render, reproduce; ~'**gutmachen** *v/t.* (*sep.*, -ge-, *h*) make up for; 2'**gutmachung** *f* (-/-*en*) reparation; ~'**herstellen** *v/t.* (*sep.*, -ge-, *h*) restore; ~**holen** *v/t.* (*h*) **1.** [~'ho:lən] (*no* -ge-) repeat; **2.** ['~ho:lən] (*sep.*, -ge-) fetch back; 2'**holung** *f* (-/-*en*) repetition; ~'**käuen** ['~kɔyən] (*sep.*, -ge-, *h*) **1.** *v/t.* ruminate, chew the cud; **2.** F *fig. v/t.* repeat over and over; 2**kehr** ['~ke:r] *f* (-/*no pl.*) return; recurrence; '**kehren** *v/i.* (*sep.*, -ge-, *sein*) return; recur; '**kommen** *v/i.* (*irr. kommen, sep.*, -ge-, *sein*) come back; return; '~**sehen** *v/t. and v/refl.* (*irr. sehen, sep.*, -ge-, *h*) see or meet again; '2**sehen** *n* (-s/*no pl.*) meeting again; *auf* ~*I* good-bye!; '~**tun** *v/t.* (*irr. tun, sep.*, -ge-, *h*) do again, repeat; '~**um** *adv.* again, anew; '~**vereinigen** *v/t.* (*sep., no -ge-, h*) reunite; '2**vereinigung** *f* reunion; *pol.* reunification; '2**verheiratung** *f* remarriage; '2**verkäufer** *m* reseller; retailer; '2**wahl** *f* re-election; '~**wählen** *v/t.* (*sep.*, -ge-, *h*) re-elect; 2'**zulassung** *f* readmission.

Wiege ['vi:gə] *f* (-/-*en*) cradle.

wiegen[1] ['vi:gən] *v/t. and v/i.* (*irr.*, ge-, *h*) weigh.

wiegen[2] [~] *v/t.* (ge-, *h*) rock; *in Sicherheit* ~ rock in security, lull into (a false sense of) security.

'**Wiegenlied** *n* lullaby.

wiehern ['vi:ərn] *v/i.* (ge-, *h*) neigh.

Wiener ['vi:nər] *m* (-s/-) Viennese; '2**isch** *adj.* Viennese.

wies [vi:s] *pret. of* weisen.

Wiese ['vi:zə] *f* (-/-*n*) meadow.

wie'so *interr. pron.* why; why so.

wie'viel *adv.* how much; ~ *pl.* how many *pl.*; ~**te** *adv.* [~tə]: *den* ~*ten haben wir heute?* what's the date today?

wild [vilt] **1.** *adj.* wild; savage; ~*es Fleisch* ⚕ proud flesh; ~*e Ehe* concubinage; ~*er Streik* ✝ wildcat strike; **2.** 2 *n* (-[e]s/*no pl.*) game. '**Wild**|**bach** *m* torrent; ~**bret** ['~brɛt] *n* (-s/*no pl.*) game; venison.

Wilde ['vildə] *m* (-n/-*n*) savage.

Wilder|**er** ['vildərər] *m* (-s/-) poacher; '2**n** *v/i.* (ge-, *h*) poach.

'**Wild**|**fleisch** *n s.* Wildbret; '2**fremd** *Z adj.* quite strange; ~**hüter** *m* gamekeeper; '**leder** *n* buckskin; 2**ledern** *adj.* buckskin; doeskin; '~**nis** *f* (-/-*se*) wilderness, wild (*a. fig.*); ~**schwein** *n* wildboar.

Wille ['vilə] *m* (-ns/-, -*n*) will; *s-n* ~*n durchsetzen* have one's way; *gegen s-n* ~*n* against one's will; *j-m s-n* ~*n lassen* let s.o. have his (own) way; '2**nlos** *adj.* lacking will-power.

'**Willens**|**freiheit** *f* (-/*no pl.*) freedom of (the) will; '**kraft** *f* (-/*no pl.*) will-power; ~**schwäche** *f* (-/*no pl.*) weak will; 2**stark** *adj.* strong-willed; '**stärke** *f* (-/*no pl.*) strong will, will-power.

'**will**|**ig** *adj.* willing, ready; ~'**kommen** *adj.* welcome; 2**kür** ['~ky:r] *f* (-/*no pl.*) arbitrariness; '~**kürlich** *adj.* arbitrary.

wimmeln ['viməln] *v/i.* (ge-, *h*) swarm (*von* with), teem (with).

wimmern ['vimərn] *v/i.* (ge-, *h*) whimper, whine.

Wimpel ['vimpəl] *m* (-s/-) pennant, pennon, streamer.

Wimper ['vimpər] *f* (-/-*n*) eyelash.

Wind [vint] *m* (-[e]s/-*e*) wind; '~**beutel** *m* cream-puff; F *fig.* windbag.

Winde ['vində] *f* (-/-*n*) windlass; reel.

Windel ['vindəl] *f* (-/-*n*) diaper, (baby's) napkin; ~*n pl. a.* swaddling-clothes *pl.*

'**winden** *v/t.* (*irr.*, ge-, *h*) wind; twist, twirl; make, bind (*wreath*); *sich* ~ *vor* (*dat.*) writhe with.

'**Wind**|**hose** *f* whirlwind, tornado; '~**hund** *m* greyhound; 2**ig** *adj.* ['~diç] windy; F *fig. excuse:* thin, lame; '~**mühle** *f* windmill; '~**pocken** ⚕ *pl.* chicken-pox; '~**richtung** *f* direction of the wind; '~**rose** ⚓ *f* compass card; '~**schutzscheibe** *f* wind-screen, *Am.* windshield; '~**stärke** *f* wind velocity; '♀still adj. calm; '✲stille f calm; '✲stoß m blast of wind, gust.

'**Windung** f (-/-en) winding, turn; bend (of way, etc.); coil (of snake, etc.).

Wink [viŋk] m (-[e]s/-e) sign; wave; wink; fig.: hint; tip.

Winkel ['viŋkəl] m (-s/-) Å angle; corner, nook; '♀ig adj. angular; street: crooked; '✲zug m subterfuge, trick, shift.

'**winken** v/i. (ge-, h) make a sign; beckon; mit dem Taschentuch ✲ wave one's handkerchief.

winklig adj. ['viŋkliç] s. winkelig.

winseln ['vinzəln] v/i. (ge-, h) whimper, whine.

Winter ['vintər] m (-s/-) winter; im ✲ in winter; '♀lich adj. wintry; '✲schlaf m hibernation; '✲sport m winter sports pl.

Winzer ['vintsər] m (-s/-) vine-dresser; vine-grower; vintager.

winzig adj. ['vintsiç] tiny, diminutive.

Wipfel ['vipfəl] m (-s/-) top.

Wippe ['vipə] f (-/-n) seesaw; '♀n v/i. (ge-, h) seesaw.

wir pers. pron. [viːr] we; ✲ drei the three of us.

Wirbel ['virbəl] m (-s/-) whirl, swirl; eddy; flurry (of blows, etc.); anat. vertebra; '♀ig adj. giddy, vertiginous; wild; '♀n v/i. (ge-, h) whirl; drums: roll; '✲säule anat. f spinal or vertebral column; '✲sturm m cyclone, tornado, Am. a. twister; '✲tier n vertebrate; '✲wind m whirlwind (a. fig.).

wirk|en ['virkən] (ge-, h) 1. v/t. knit, weave; work (wonders); 2. v/i.: ✲ als act or function as; ✲ auf (acc.) produce an impression on; beruhigend ✲ have a soothing effect; '✲lich adj. real, actual; true, genuine; '♀lichkeit f (-/-en) reality; in ✲ in reality; '✲sam adj. effective, efficacious; '♀samkeit f (-/✲-en) effectiveness, efficacy; '♀ung f (-/-en) effect.

'**Wirkungs|kreis** m sphere or field of activity; '♀los adj. ineffective, inefficacious; '✲losigkeit f (-/no pl.) ineffectiveness, inefficacy; '♀voll adj. s. wirksam.

wirr adj. [vir] confused; speech: incoherent; hair: dishevel(l)ed; '♀en pl. disorders pl.; troubles pl.; ♀warr ['✲var] m (-s/no pl.) confusion, muddle.

Wirsingkohl ['virziŋ-] m (-[e]s/no pl.) savoy.

Wirt [virt] m (-[e]s/-e) host; landlord; innkeeper.

'**Wirtschaft** f (-/-en) housekeeping; economy; trade and industry; economics pl.; s. Wirtshaus; F mess; '♀en v/i. (ge-, h) keep house; economize; F bustle (about); '✲erin

f (-/-nen) housekeeper; '♀lich adj. economic; economical.

'**Wirtschafts|geld** n housekeeping money; '✲jahr n financial year; '✲krise f economic crisis; '✲politik f economic policy; '✲prüfer m (-s/-) chartered accountant, Am. certified public accountant.

'**Wirtshaus** n public house, F pub.

Wisch [viʃ] m (-es/-e) wisp (of straw, etc.); contp. scrap of paper; '♀en v/t. (ge-, h) wipe.

wispern ['vispərn] v/t. and v/i. (ge-, h) whisper.

Wiß|begierde ['vis-] f (-/no pl.) thirst for knowledge; '♀begierig adj. eager for knowledge.

wissen ['visən] 1. v/t. (irr., ge-, h) know; man kann nie ✲ you never know, you never can tell; 2. ♀ n (-s/no pl.) knowledge; meines ✲s to my knowledge, as far as I know.

'**Wissenschaft** f (-/-en) science; knowledge; '✲ler m (-s/-) scholar; scientist; researcher; '♀lich adj. scientific.

'**Wissens|drang** m (-[e]s/no pl.) urge or thirst for knowledge; '♀-wert adj. worth knowing.

'**wissentlich** adj. knowing, conscious.

wittern ['vitərn] v/t. (ge-, h) scent, smell; fig. a. suspect.

'**Witterung** f (-/✲-en) weather; hunt. scent; '✲sverhältnisse ['✲sferheltnisə] pl. meteorological conditions pl.   [m (-s/-) widower.)

Witwe ['vitvə] f (-/-n) widow; '✲r)

Witz [vits] m 1. (-es/no pl.) wit; 2. (-es/-e) joke; ✲e reißen crack jokes; '✲blatt n comic paper; '♀ig adj. witty; funny.

wo [voː] 1. adv. where?; 2. cj.: F ach ✲! nonsense!

wob [voːp] pret. of weben.

wo'bei adv. at what?; at which; in doing so.

Woche ['vɔxə] f (-/-n) week; heute in e-r ✲ today week.

'**Wochen|bett** n childbed; '✲blatt n weekly (paper); '✲ende n weekend; '♀lang 1. adj.: nach ✲em Warten after many) weeks of waiting; 2. adv. for weeks; '✲lohn m weekly pay or wages pl.; '✲markt m weekly market; '✲schau f news-reel; '✲tag m week-day.

wöchentlich ['vœçəntliç] 1. adj. weekly; 2. adv. weekly, every week; einmal ✲ once a week.

Wöchnerin ['vœçnərin] f (-/-nen) woman in childbed.

wo'durch adv. by what?, how?; by which, whereby; '✲für adv. for what?, what ... for?; (in return) for which.   [gen¹.)

wog [voːk] pret. of wägen and wie-)

Woge ['voːgə] f (-/-n) wave (a. fig.), billow; die ✲n glätten pour oil on troubled waters; '²n v/i. (ge-, h) surge (a. fig.), billow; wheat: a. wave; heave.

wo|'her adv. from where?, where ... from?; ~ wissen Sie das? how do you (come to) know that?; ~'hin adv. where (... to)?

wohl [vo:l] 1. adv. well; sich nicht ~ fühlen be unwell; ~ oder übel willy-nilly; leben Sie ~! farewell!; er wird ~ reich sein he is rich, I suppose; 2. ~ n (-[e]s/no pl.): ~ und Wehe weal and woe; auf Ihr ~! your health!, here is to you!

'Wohl|befinden n well-being; good health; '~behagen n comfort, ease; '²behalten adj. safe; '²bekannt adj. well-known; '~ergehen n (-s/no pl.) welfare, prosperity; ²er-zogen adj. ['~²ertso:gən] well-bred, well-behaved; '~fahrt f (-/no pl.) welfare; public assistance; '~ge-fallen n (-s/no pl.) pleasure; sein ~ haben an (dat.) take delight in; '²gemeint adj. well-meant, well-intentioned; ²gemut adj. ['~gə-mu:t] cheerful; '²genährt adj. well-fed; '~geruch m scent, perfume; '²gesinnt adj. well-disposed (j-m towards s.o.); '²habend adj. well-to-do; '²ig adj. comfortable; cosy, snug; '~klang m (-[e]s/no pl.) melodious sound, harmony; '²-klingend adj. melodious, harmonious; '~laut m s. Wohlklang; '~leben n (-s/no pl.) luxury; ²'riechend adj. fragrant; '²schmeckend adj. savo(u)ry; '~sein n well-being; good health; '~stand m (-[e]s/no pl.) prosperity, wealth; '~tat f kindness, charity; fig. comfort, treat; '~täter m benefactor; '²tätig adj. charitable, beneficient; '~tä-tigkeit f charity; ²tuend adj. ['~tu:ənt] pleasant, comfortable; '²tun v/i. (irr. tun, sep., -ge-, h) do good; '²verdient adj. well-deserved; p. of great merit; '~wollen n (-s/no pl.) goodwill; benevolence; favo(u)r; '²wollen v/i. (sep., -ge-, h) be well-disposed (j-m towards s.o.).

wohn|en ['vo:nən] v/i. (ge-, h) live (in dat. in, at; bei j-m with s.o.); reside (in, at; with); '²haus n dwelling-house; block of flats, Am. apartment house; '~haft adj. resident, living; '~lich adj. comfortable; cosy, snug; '²ort m dwelling-place, residence; esp. ₺₺ domicile; '²sitz m residence; mit ~ in resident in or at; ohne festen ~ without fixed abode; '²ung f (-/-en) dwelling, habitation; flat, Am. apartment.

'Wohnungs|amt n housing office; '~not f housing shortage; '~pro-blem n housing problem.

'Wohn|wagen m caravan, trailer; '~zimmer n sitting-room, esp. Am. living room.

wölb|en ['vœlbən] v/t. (ge-, h) vault; arch; sich ~ arch; '²ung f (-/-en) vault, arch; curvature.

Wolf zo. [vɔlf] m (-[e]s/≈e) wolf.

Wolke ['vɔlkə] f (-/-n) cloud.

'Wolken|bruch m cloud-burst; '~kratzer m (-s/-) skyscraper; '²los adj. cloudless.

'wolkig adj. cloudy, clouded.

Woll|decke ['vɔl-] f blanket; '~e f (-/-n) wool.

wollen¹ ['vɔlən] (h) 1. v/t. (ge-) wish, desire; want; lieber ~ prefer; nicht ~ refuse; er weiß, was er will he knows his mind; 2. v/i. (ge-): ich will schon, aber ... I want to, but ...; 3. v/aux. (no -ge-) be willing; intend, be going to; be about to; lieber ~ prefer; nicht ~ refuse; er hat nicht gehen ~ he refused to go.

woll|en² adj. [~] wool(l)en; '~ig adj. wool(l)y; '²stoff m wool(l)en.

Woll|lust ['vɔlust] f (-/-e) voluptuousness; ²lüstig adj. ['~lystiç] voluptuous.

'Wollwaren pl. wool(l)en goods pl.

wo|'mit adv. with what?, what ... with?; with which; ~'möglich adv. perhaps, maybe.

Wonn|e ['vɔnə] f (-/-n) delight, bliss; '²ig adj. delightful, blissful.

wo|'ran adv. [vo:'ran]: ~ denkst du? what are you thinking of?; ich weiß nicht, ~ ich mit ihm bin I don't know what to make of him; ~ liegt es, daß ...? how is it that ...?; ~'rauf adv. on what?, what ... on?; whereupon, after which; ~ wartest du? what are you waiting for?; ~'raus adv. from what?; what ... of?; from which; ~rin adv. [~'rin] in what?; in which.

Wort [vɔrt] n 1. (-[e]s/≈er) word; er kann seine Wörter noch nicht he hasn't learnt his words yet; 2. (-[e]s/-e) word; term, expression; ums ~ bitten ask permission to speak; das ~ ergreifen begin to speak; parl. rise to speak, address the House, esp. Am. take the floor; das ~ führen be the spokesman; ~ halten keep one's word; '²brüchig adj.: er ist ~ geworden he has broken his word.

Wörter|buch ['vœrtər-] n dictionary; '~verzeichnis n vocabulary, list of words.

'Wort|führer m spokesman; '²ge-treu adj. literal; '²karg adj. taciturn; ~klauberei [~klaubə'raɪ] f (-/-en) word-splitting; '~laut m (-[e]s/no pl.) wording; text. [eral.]

wörtlich adj. ['vœrtliç] verbal, lit-

'Wort|schatz m (-es/no pl.) vocabulary; '~schwall m (-[e]s/no pl.) verbiage; '~spiel n pun (über acc., mit [up]on), play upon words; '~stellung gr. f word order, order of words; '~stamm ling. m stem; '~streit m, '~wechsel m dispute.

wo|rüber adv. [voː'ryːbər] over or upon what?, what ... over or about or on?; over or upon which, about which; **~rum** adv. [~'rum] about what?, what ... about?; about or for which; **~** handelt es sich? what is it about?; **~runter** adv. [~'runtər] under or among what?, what ... under?; under or among which; **~von** adv. of or from what?, what ... from or of?; about what?, what ... about?; of or from which; **~vor** adv. of what?, what ... of?; of which; **~zu** adv. for what?, what ... for?; for which.

Wrack [vrak] n (-[e]s/-e, -s) ⚓ wreck (a. fig.).

wrang [vraŋ] pret. of wringen.

wring|en ['vriŋən] v/t. (irr., ge-, h) wring; **~maschine** f wringing-machine.

Wucher ['vuːxər] m (-s/no pl.) usury; **~** treiben practise usury; **~er** m (-s/-) usurer; **~gewinn** m excess profit; **~isch** adj. usurious; **~n** v/i. (ge-, h) grow exuberantly; **~ung** f (-/-en) ⚕ exuberant growth; ⚘ growth; **~zinsen** m/pl. usurious interest.

Wuchs [vuːks] 1. m (-es/ⁿe) growth; figure, shape; stature; 2. ♀ pret. of wachsen.

Wucht [vuxt] f (-/⚓-en) weight; force; **~ig** adj. heavy.

Wühl|arbeit fig. ['vyːl-] f insidious agitation, subversive activity; **~en** v/i. (ge-, h) dig; pig: root; fig. agitate; **~** in (dat.) rummage (about) in; **~er** m (-s/-) agitator.

Wulst [vulst] m (-es/ⁿe), f (-/ⁿe) pad; bulge; ⊕ roll(-mo[u]lding); ⊕ bead; **~ig** adj. lips: thick.

wund adj. [vunt] sore; **~e** Stelle sore; **~er** Punkt tender spot; 2e ['~də] f (-/-n) wound; alte **~n** wieder aufreißen reopen old sores.

Wunder ['vundər] n (-s/-) miracle; fig. a. wonder, marvel; **~** wirken pills, etc.: work marvels; kein **~**, wenn man bedenkt ... no wonder, considering ...; **2bar** adj. miraculous; fig. a. wonderful, marvel-(l)ous; **~kind** n infant prodigy; **2lich** adj. queer, odd; **2n** v/t. (ge-, h) surprise, astonish; sich **~** be surprised or astonished (über acc. at); **2schön** adj. very beautiful; **~tat** f wonder, miracle; **~täter** m wonder-worker; **2tätig** adj. wonderworking; **2voll** adj. wonderful; **~werk** n marvel, wonder.

'Wund|fieber n wound-fever; **~starrkrampf** ⚕ m tetanus.

Wunsch [vunʃ] m (-es/ⁿe) wish, desire; request; auf **~** by or on request; if desired; nach **~** as desired; mit den besten Wünschen zum Fest with the compliments of the season.

Wünschelrute ['vynʃəl-] f divin-

ing-rod, dowsing-rod; **~gänger** ['~gɛŋər] m (-s/-) diviner, dowser.

wünschen ['vynʃən] v/t. (ge-, h) wish, desire; wie Sie **~** as you wish; was **~** Sie? what can I do for you?; **~swert** adj. desirable.

'wunsch|gemäß adv. as requested or desired, according to one's wishes; **2zettel** m list of wishes.

wurde ['vurdə] pret. of werden.

Würde ['vyrdə] f (-/-n) dignity; unter seiner **~** beneath one's dignity; **2los** adj. undignified; **~nträger** m dignitary; **2voll** adj. dignified; grave.

'würdig adj. worthy (gen. of); dignified; grave; **~en** ['~gən] v/t. (ge-, h) appreciate, value; mention hono(u)rably; laud, praise; j-n keines Blickes **~** ignore s.o. completely; 2ung f (-/-en) appreciation, valuation.

Wurf [vurf] m (-[e]s/ⁿe) throw, cast; zo. litter.

Würfel ['vyrfəl] m (-s/-) die; cube (a. Å); **~becher** m dice-box; **2n** v/i. (ge-, h) (play) dice; **~spiel** n game of dice; **'~zucker** m lump sugar. [tile.]

'Wurfgeschoß n missile, projec-)

würgen ['vyrgən] (ge-, h) 1. v/t. choke, strangle; 2 v/i. choke; retch.

Wurm zo. [vurm] m (-[e]s/ⁿer) worm; **2en** F v/t. (ge-, h) vex; rankle (j-n in s.o.'s mind); **2-stichig** adj. worm-eaten.

Wurst [vurst] f (-/ⁿe) sausage; F das ist mir ganz **~** I don't care a rap.

Würstchen ['vyrstçən] n (-s/-) sausage; heißes **~** hot sausage, Am. hot dog.

Würze ['vyrtsə] f (-/-n) seasoning, flavo(u)r; spice, condiment; fig. salt.

Wurzel ['vurtsəl] f (-/-n) root (a. gr., Å); **~** schlagen strike or take root (a. fig.); **2n** v/i. (ge-, h) (strike or take) root; **~** in (dat.) take one's root in, be rooted in.

'würz|en v/t. (ge-, h) spice, season, flavo(u)r; **~ig** adj. spicy, well-seasoned, aromatic.

wusch [vuːʃ] pret. of waschen.

wußte ['vustə] pret. of wissen.

Wust F [vuːst] m (-es/no pl.) tangled mass; rubbish; mess.

wüst adj. [vyːst] desert, waste; confused; wild, dissolute; rude; **2e** f (-/-n) desert, waste; **2ling** ['~liŋ] m (-s/-e) debauchee, libertine, rake.

Wut [vuːt] f (-/no pl.) rage, fury; in **~** in a rage; **~anfall** m fit of rage.

wüten ['vyːtən] v/i. (ge-, h) rage (a. fig.); **~d** adj. furious, enraged (über acc. at; auf acc. with), esp. Am. F a. mad (über acc., auf acc. at).

Wüterich ['vyːtəriç] m (-[e]s/-e) berserker; bloodthirsty man.

'wutschnaubend adj. foaming with rage.

X, Y

X-Beine ['iks-] *n/pl.* knock-knees *pl.*; **'X-beinig** *adj.* knock-kneed.

x-beliebig *adj.* [iksbə'li:biç] any (... you please); *jede(r, -s)* ~e ... any ...

x-mal *adv.* ['iks-] many times, *sl.* umpteen times.

X-Strahlen ['iks-] *m/pl.* X-rays *pl.*

x-te *adj.* ['ikstə]: *zum* ~*n Male* for the umpteenth time.

Xylophon ♪ [ksylo'fo:n] *n* (-s/-e) xylophone.

Yacht ⚓ [jaxt] *f* (-/-en) yacht.

Z

Zacke ['tsakə] *f* (-/-n) *s.* Zacken.

'Zacken 1. *m* (-s/-) (sharp) point; prong; tooth (*of comb, saw, rake*); jag (*of rock*); **2.** ⚙ *v/t.* (ge-, h) indent, notch; jag.

'zackig *adj.* indented, notched; *rock:* jagged; pointed; ✂ F *fig.* smart.

zaghaft *adj.* ['tsa:khaft] timid; **'2igkeit** *f* (-/*no pl.*) timidity.

zäh *adj.* [tsɛ:] tough, tenacious (*both a. fig.*); *liquid:* viscid, viscous; *fig.* dogged; **'~flüssig** *adj.* viscid, viscous, sticky; **'2igkeit** *f* (-/*no pl.*) toughness, tenacity (*both a. fig.*); viscosity; *fig.* doggedness.

Zahl [tsa:l] *f* (-/-en) number; figure, cipher; **'2bar** *adj.* payable.

'zählbar *adj.* countable.

zahlen ['tsa:lən] (ge-, h) **1.** *v/i.* pay; *at restaurant:* ~ (, bitte)! the bill, please!, *Am.* the check, please!; **2.** *v/t.* pay.

zählen ['tsɛ:lən] (ge-, h) **1.** *v/t.* count, number; ~ *zu* count or number among; **2.** *v/i.* count; ~ *auf* (*acc.*) count (up)on, rely (up)on.

'Zahlen|lotto *n s.* Lotto; **'2mäßig 1.** *adj.* numerical; **2.** *adv.*: *j-m* ~ *überlegen sein* outnumber s.o.

'Zähler *m* (-s/-) counter; ⚗ numerator; *for gas, etc.*: meter.

'Zahl|karte *f* money-order form (*for paying direct into the postal cheque account*); **'2los** *adj.* numberless, innumerable, countless; **'~meister** ✂ *m* paymaster; **'2reich 1.** *adj.* numerous; **2.** *adv.* in great number; **'~tag** *m* pay-day; **'~ung** *f* (-/-en) payment.

'Zählung *f* (-/-en) counting.

'Zahlungs|anweisung *f* order to pay; **'~aufforderung** *f* request for payment; **'~bedingungen** *f/pl.* terms *pl.* of payment; **'~befehl** *m* order to pay; **'~einstellung** *f* suspension of payment; **'2fähig** *adj.* solvent; **'~fähigkeit** *f* solvency; **'~frist** *f* term for payment; **'~mittel** *n* currency; *gesetzliches* ~ legal tender; **'~schwierigkeiten** *f/pl.* financial *or* pecuniary difficulties *pl.*; **'~termin** *m* date of payment; **'2unfähig** *adj.* insolvent; **'~unfähigkeit** *f* insolvency.

'Zahlwort *gr. n* (-[e]s/~er) numeral.

zahm *adj.* [tsa:m] tame (*a. fig.*), domestic(ated).

zähm|en ['tsɛ:mən] *v/t.* (ge-, h) tame (*a. fig.*), domesticate; **'2ung** *f* (-/~-en) taming (*a. fig.*), domestication.

Zahn [tsa:n] *m* (-[e]s/~e) tooth; ⊕ tooth, cog; *Zähne bekommen* cut one's teeth; **'~arzt** *m* dentist, dental surgeon; **'~bürste** *f* toothbrush; **'~creme** *f* tooth-paste; **'2en** *v/i.* (ge-, h) teethe, cut one's teeth; **'~ersatz** *m* denture; **'~fäule** ['~fɔylə] *f* (-/*no pl.*) dental caries; **'~fleisch** *n* gums *pl.*; **'~füllung** *f* filling, stopping; **'~geschwür** *n* gumboil; **'~heilkunde** *f* dentistry; **'2los** *adj.* toothless; **'~lücke** *f* gap between the teeth; **'~pasta** ['~pasta] *f* (-/Zahnpasten), **'~paste** *f* toothpaste; **'~rad** ⊕ *n* cog-wheel; **'~radbahn** /rack-railway/; **'~schmerzen** *m/pl.* toothache; **'~stocher** *m* (-s/-) toothpick.

Zange ['tsaŋə] *f* (-/-n) (e-e pair of) tongs *pl.* or pliers *pl.* or pincers *pl.*; ♂, *zo.* forceps *sg.*, *pl.*

Zank [tsaŋk] *m* (-[e]s/*no pl.*) quarrel, F row; **'~apfel** *m* bone of contention; **'2en** (ge-, h) **1.** *v/i.* scold (*mit j-m* s.o.); **2.** *v/refl.* quarrel, wrangle.

zänkisch *adj.* ['tsɛŋkiʃ] quarrelsome.

Zäpfchen ['tsɛpfçən] *n* (-s/-) small peg; *anat.* uvula.

Zapfen ['tsapfən] **1.** *m* (-s/-) plug; peg, pin; bung (*of barrel*); pivot; ♣ cone; **2.** *v/t.* (ge-, h) tap; **'~streich** ✂ *m* tattoo, retreat, *Am. a.* taps *pl.*

'Zapf|hahn *m* tap, *Am.* faucet; **'~säule** *mot. f* petrol pump.

zappel|ig *adj.* ['tsapəliç] fidgety; **'~n** *v/i.* (ge-, h) struggle; fidget.

zart *adj.* [tsa:rt] tender; soft; gentle; delicate; **'2fühlend** *adj.* delicate; **'2gefühl** *n* (-[e]s/*no pl.*) delicacy (of feeling).

zärtlich adj. ['tsɛːrtliç] tender; fond, loving; '2keit f 1. (-/no pl.) tenderness; fondness; 2. (-/-en) caress.

Zauber ['tsaubər] m (-s/-) spell, charm, magic (all a. fig.); fig.: enchantment; glamo(u)r; **~ei** [~'raɪ] f (-/-en) magic, sorcery; witchcraft; conjuring; '**~er** m (-s/-) sorcerer, magician; conjurer; '**~flöte** f magic flute; '**~formel** f spell; '2**haft** adj. magic(al); fig. enchanting; **~in** f (-/-nen) sorceress, witch; fig. enchantress; '**~kraft** f magic power; '**~kunststück** n conjuring trick; '2**n** (ge-, h) 1. v/i. practise magic or witchcraft; do conjuring tricks; 2. v/t. conjure; '**~spruch** m spell; '**~stab** m (magic) wand; '**~wort** n (-[e]s/-er) magic word, spell.

zaudern ['tsaudərn] v/i. (ge-, h) hesitate; linger, delay.

Zaum [tsaum] m (-[e]s/ᵘe) bridle; im ~ halten keep in check.

zäumen ['tsɔʏmən] v/t. (ge-, h) bridle.

'**Zaumzeug** n bridle.

Zaun [tsaun] m (-[e]s/ᵘe) fence; '**~gast** m deadhead; '**~könig** orn. m wren; '**~pfahl** m pale.

Zebra zo. ['tseːbra] n (-s/-s) zebra; '**~streifen** m zebra crossing.

Zech|e ['tseçə] f (-/-n) score, reckoning, bill; ⚒ mine; coal-pit, colliery; F die ~ bezahlen foot the bill, F stand treat; '2**en** v/i. (ge-, h) carouse, tipple; '**~gelage** n carousal, carouse; '**~preller** m (-s/-) bilk(er).

Zeh [tseː] m (-[e]s/-en), '**~e** f (-/-n) toe; '**~enspitze** f point or tip of the toe; auf ~n on tiptoe.

zehn adj. [tseːn] ten; '2**er** m (-s/-) ten; coin: F ten-pfennig piece; '**~fach** adj. ['~fax] tenfold; '**~jährig** adj. ['~jɛːriç] ten-year-old, of ten (years); '2**kampf** m sports: decathlon; '**~mal** adv. ten times; '**~te** ['~tə] 1. adj. tenth; 2. ⚹ † m (-n/-n) tithe; '2**tel** ['~təl] n (-s/-) tenth (part); **~tens** adv. ['~təns] tenthly.

zehren ['tseːrən] v/i. (ge-, h) make thin; ~ von live on s.th.; fig. live off (the capital); ~ an prey (up)on (one's mind); undermine (one's health).

Zeichen ['tsaɪçən] n (-s/-) sign; token; mark; indication, symptom; signal; zum ~ (gen.) in sign of, as a sign of; '**~block** m drawing-block; '**~brett** n drawing-board; '**~lehrer** m drawing-master; '**~papier** n drawing-paper; '**~setzung** gr. f (-/no pl.) punctuation; '**~sprache** f sign-language; '**~stift** m pencil, crayon; '**~trickfilm** m animation, animated cartoon; '**~unterricht** m drawing-lessons pl.

zeichn|en ['tsaɪçnən] (ge-, h) 1. v/t. draw (plan, etc.); design (pattern); mark; sign; subscribe (sum of money) (zu to); subscribe for (shares); 2. v/i. draw; sie zeichnet gut she draws well; '2**er** m (-s/-) draftsman, draughtsman; designer; subscriber (gen. for shares); '2**ung** f (-/-en) drawing; design; illustration; zo. marking (of skin, etc.); subscription.

Zeige|finger ['tsaɪgə-] m forefinger, index (finger); '2**n** (ge-, h) 1. v/t. show; point out; indicate; demonstrate; sich ~ appear; 2. v/i.: ~ auf (acc.) point at; ~ nach point to; '**~r** m (-s/-) hand (of clock, etc.); pointer (of dial, etc.); '**~stock** m pointer.

Zeile ['tsaɪlə] f (-/-n) line; row; j-m ein paar ~n schreiben drop s.o. a line or a few lines. [siskin.]

Zeisig orn. ['tsaɪziç] m (-[e]s/-e)}

Zeit [tsaɪt] f (-/-en) time; epoch, era, age; period, space (of time); term; freie ~ spare time; mit der ~ in the course of time; von ~ zu ~ from time to time; vor langer ~ long ago, a long time ago; zur ~ (gen.) in the time of; at (the) present; zu meiner ~ in my time; zu s-r ~ in due course (of time); das hat ~ there is plenty of time for that; es ist höchste ~ it is high time; j-m ~ lassen give s.o. time; laß dir ~! take your time!; sich die ~ vertreiben pass the time, kill time. '**Zeit|abschnitt** m epoch, period; '**~alter** n age; '**~angabe** f exact date and hour; date; '**~aufnahme** phot. f time-exposure; '**~dauer** f length of time, period (of time); '**~enfolge** gr. f sequence of tenses; '**~geist** m (-es/no pl.) spirit of the time(s), zeitgeist; '2**gemäß** adj. modern, up-to-date; '**~genosse** m contemporary; 2**genössisch** adj. ['~gənœsiʃ] contemporary; '**~geschichte** f contemporary history; '**~gewinn** m gain of time; '2**ig** 1. adj. early; 2. adv. on time; '**~karte** f season-ticket, Am. commutation ticket; '**~lang** f: e-e ~ for some time, for a while; 2**lebens** adv. for life, all one's life; '2**lich** 1. adj. temporal; 2. adv. as to time; ~ zusammenfallen coincide; '2**los** adj. timeless; '**~lupe** phot. f slow motion; '**~lupenaufnahme** phot. f slow-motion picture; '2**nah** adj. current, up-to-date; '**~ordnung** f chronological order; '**~punkt** m moment; time; date; '**~rafferaufnahme** phot. f time-lapse photography; '2**raubend** adj. time-consuming; pred. a. taking up much time; '**~raum** m space (of time), period; '**~rechnung** f chronology; era; '**~schrift** f journal, periodical, magazine; review; '**~tafel** f chronological table.

'Zeitung f (-/-en) (news)paper, journal.
'Zeitungs|abonnement n subscription to a paper; '~artikel m newspaper article; '~ausschnitt m (press or newspaper) cutting, (Am. only) (newspaper) clipping; ~kiosk ['~kiosk] m (-[e]s/-e) news-stand; '~notiz f press item; '~papier n newsprint; '~verkäufer m newsvendor; news-boy, news-man; '~wesen n journalism, the press.
'Zeit|verlust m loss of time; '~verschwendung f waste of time; ~vertreib ['~fɛrtraip] m (-[e]s/-e) pastime; zum ~ to pass the time; 2weilig adj. ['~vailiç] temporary; '2weise adv. for a time; at times, occasionally; '~wort pr. n (-[e]s/~er) verb; '~zeichen n time-signal.
Zell|e ['tsɛlə] f (-/-n) cell; '~stoff m, ~ulose ⊕ [~u'lo:zə] f (-/-n) cellulose.
Zelt [tsɛlt] n (-[e]s/-e) tent; '2en v/i. (ge-, h) camp; '~leinwand f canvas; '~platz m camping-ground.
Zement [tse'mɛnt] m (-[e]s/-e) cement; 2ieren [~'ti:rən] v/t. (no -ge-, h) cement.
Zenit [tse'ni:t] m (-[e]s/no pl.) zenith (a. fig.).
zens|ieren [tsɛn'zi:rən] v/t. (no -ge-, h) censor (book, etc.); at school: mark, Am. a. grade; 2or ['~ɔr] m (-s/-en) censor; 2ur [~'zu:r] f 1. (-/no pl.) censorship; 2. (-/-en) at school: mark, Am. a. grade; (school) report, Am. report card.
2entimeter [tsɛnti'-] n, m centimet|re, Am. -er.
Zentner ['tsɛntnər] m (-s/-) (Brt. appr.) hundredweight.
zentral adj. [tsɛn'tra:l] central; 2e f (-/-n) central office; teleph. (telephone) exchange, Am. a. central; 2heizung f central heating.
Zentrum ['tsɛntrum] n (-s/Zentren) cent|re, Am. -er. [Am. -er.
Zepter ['tsɛptər] n (-s/-) scept|re,]
zer'beißen [tsɛr'-] v/t. (irr. beißen, no -ge-, h) bite to pieces; ~'bersten v/i. (irr. bersten, no -ge-, sein) burst asunder.
zer'brech|en (irr. brechen, no -ge-) 1. v/t. (h) break (to pieces); sich den Kopf ~ rack one's brains; 2. v/i. (sein) break; ~lich adj. breakable, fragile.
zer|'bröckeln v/t. (h) and v/i. (sein) (no -ge-) crumble; ~'drücken v/t. (no -ge-, h) crush; crease (dress).
Zeremon|ie [tseremo'ni:, ~'mo:njə] f (-/-n) ceremony; 2iell adj. [~o'njɛl] ceremonial; ~iell [~o'njɛl] n (-s/-e) ceremonial.
zer'fahren adj. road: rutted; p.: flighty, giddy; scatter-brained; absent-minded.
Zer'fall m (-[e]s/no pl.) ruin, decay;

disintegration; 2en v/i. (irr. fallen, no -ge-, sein) fall to pieces, decay; disintegrate; in mehrere Teile ~ fall into several parts.
zer|'fetzen v/t. (no -ge-, h) tear in or to pieces; ~'fleischen v/t. (no -ge-, h) mangle; lacerate; ~'fließen v/i. (irr. fließen, no -ge-, sein) melt (away); ink, etc.: run; ~'fressen v/t. (irr. fressen, no -ge-, h) eat away; 🜄 corrode; ~'gehen v/i. (irr. gehen, no -ge-, sein) melt, dissolve; ~'gliedern v/t. (no -ge-, h) dismember; anat. dissect; fig. analy|se, Am. -ze; ~'hacken v/t. (no -ge-, h) cut (in)to pieces; mince; chop (up) (wood, meat); ~'kauen v/t. (no -ge-, h) chew; ~'kleinern v/t. (no -ge-, h) mince (meat); chop up (wood); grind.
zer'knirsch|t adj. contrite; 2ung f (-/🜄-en) contrition.
zer|'knittern v/t. (no -ge-, h) (c)rumple, wrinkle, crease; ~'knüllen v/t. (no -ge-, h) crumple up (sheet of paper); ~'kratzen v/t. (no -ge-, h) scratch; ~'krümeln v/t. (no -ge-, h) crumble; ~'lassen v/t. (irr. lassen, no -ge-, h) melt; ~'legen v/t. (no -ge-, h) take apart or to pieces; carve (joint); 🜄, gr., fig. analy|se, Am. -ze; ~'lumpt adj. ragged, tattered; ~'mahlen v/t. (irr. mahlen, no -ge-, h) grind; ~'malmen [~'malmən] v/t. (no -ge-, h) crush; crunch; ~'mürben v/t. (no -ge-, h) wear down or out; ~'platzen v/i. (no -ge-, sein) burst; explode; ~'quetschen v/t. (no -ge-, h) crush, squash; mash (esp. potatoes).
Zerrbild ['tsɛr-] n caricature.
zer|'reiben v/t. (irr. reiben, no -ge-, h) rub to powder, grind down, pulverize; ~'reißen (irr. reißen, no -ge-) 1. v/t. (h) tear, rip up; in Stücke ~ tear to pieces; 2. v/i. (sein) tear; rope, string: break.
zerren ['tsɛrən] (ge-, h) 1. v/t. tug, pull; drag; 🜄 strain; 2. v/i.: ~ an (dat.) pull at.
zer'rinnen v/i. (irr. rinnen, no -ge-, sein) melt away; fig. vanish.
'Zerrung 🜄 f (-/-en) strain.
zer|'rütten [tsɛr'rytən] v/t. (no -ge-, h) derange, unsettle; disorganize; ruin, shatter (one's health or nerves); wreck (marriage); ~'sägen v/t. (no -ge-, h) saw up; ~'schellen [~'ʃɛlən] v/i. (no -ge-, sein) be dashed or smashed; 🜄 be wrecked; 🜄 crash; ~'schlagen 1. v/t. (irr. schlagen, no -ge-, h) break or smash (to pieces); sich ~ come to nothing; 2. adj. battered; fig. knocked up; ~'schmettern v/t. (no -ge-, h) smash, dash, shatter; ~'schneiden v/t. (irr. schneiden, no -ge-, h) cut in two; cut up, cut to pieces.

zer'setz|en v/t. and v/refl. (no -ge-, h) decompose; **2ung** f (-/~-en) decomposition.

zer|'spalten v/t. ([irr. spalten,] no -ge-, h) cleave, split; **~'splittern** (no -ge-) 1. v/t. (h) split (up), splinter; fritter away (one's energy, etc.); 2. v/i. (sein) split (up), splinter; **~'sprengen** v/t. (no -ge-, h) burst (asunder); disperse (crowd); **~'springen** v/i. (irr. springen, no -ge-, sein) burst; glass: crack; mein Kopf zerspringt mir I've got a splitting headache; **~'stampfen** v/t. (no -ge-, h) crush; pound.

zer'stäub|en v/t. (no -ge-, h) spray; **2er** m (-s/-) sprayer, atomizer.

zer'stör|en v/t. (no -ge-, h) destroy; **2er** m (-s/-) destroyer (a. ⊕); **2ung** f destruction.

zer'streu|en v/t. (no -ge-, h) disperse, scatter; dissipate (doubt, etc.); fig. divert; sich ~ disperse, scatter; fig. amuse o.s.; **~t** fig. adj. absent(-minded); **2theit** f (-/~-en) absent-mindedness; **2ung** f 1. (-/-en) dispersion; diversion; amusement; 2. phys. (-/no pl.) dispersion (of light).

zerstückeln [tser'ʃtykəln] v/t. (no -ge-, h) cut up, cut (in)to pieces; dismember (body, etc.).

zer|'teilen v/t. and v/refl. (no -ge-, h) divide (in acc. into); **~'trennen** v/t. (no -ge-, h) rip (up) (dress); **~'treten** v/t. (irr. treten, no -ge-, h) tread down; crush; tread or stamp out (fire); **~'trümmern** v/t. (no -ge-, h) smash.

Zerwürfnis [tser'vyrfnis] n (-ses/-se) dissension, discord.

Zettel ['tsetəl] m (-s/-) slip (of paper), scrap of paper; note; ticket; label, sticker; tag; s. Anschlagzettel; s. Theaterzettel; **'~kartei** f, **'~kasten** m card index.

Zeug [tsɔʏk] n (-[e]s/-e) stuff (a. fig. contp.), material; cloth; tools pl.; things pl.

Zeuge ['tsɔʏgə] m (-n/-n) witness; **'2n** (ge-, h) 1. v/i. witness; ﬆ give evidence; für (gegen, von) et. ~ testify for (against, of) s.th.; ~ von be evidence of, bespeak (courage, etc.); 2. v/t. beget.

'Zeugen|aussage ﬆ f testimony, evidence; **'~bank** f (-/~e) witness-box, Am. witness stand.

Zeugin ['tsɔʏgin] f (-/-nen) (female) witness.

Zeugnis ['tsɔʏknis] n (-ses/-se) ﬆ testimony, evidence; certificate; (school) report, Am. report card.

Zeugung ['tsɔʏgun] f (-/-en) procreation; **2sfähig** adj. capable of begetting; **'~skraft** f generative power; **2sunfähig** adj. ['tsɔʏguns-?] impotent.

Zick|lein zo. ['tsiklaɪn] n (-s/-) kid;

~zack ['~tsak] m (-[e]s/-e) zigzag; im ~ fahren etc. zigzag.

Ziege zo. ['tsi:gə] f (-/-n) (she-)goat, nanny(-goat).

Ziegel ['tsi:gəl] m (-s/-) brick; tile (of roof); **'~dach** n tiled roof; **~ei** ['~'laɪ] f (-/-en) brickworks sg., pl., brickyard; **'~stein** m brick.

'Ziegen|bock zo. m he-goat; **'~fell** n goatskin; **'~hirt** m goatherd; **'~leder** n kid(-leather); **'~peter** 〆 m (-s/-) mumps.

Ziehbrunnen ['tsi:-] m draw-well.

ziehen ['tsi:ən] (irr., ge-) 1. v/t. (h) pull, draw; draw (line, weapon, lots, conclusion, etc.); drag; 〆 cultivate; zo. breed; take off (hat); dig (ditch); draw, extract (tooth); A extract (root of number); Blasen ~ raise blisters; e-n Vergleich ~ draw or make a comparison; j-n ins Vertrauen ~ take s.o. into one's confidence; in Erwägung ~ take into consideration; in die Länge ~ draw out; fig. protract; Nutzen ~ aus derive profit or benefit from; an sich ~ draw to one; Aufmerksamkeit etc. auf sich ~ attract attention, etc.; et. nach sich ~ entail or involve s.th.; 2. v/i. (h) pull (an dat. at); chimney, cigar, etc.: draw; puff (an e-r Zigarre at a cigar); tea: infuse, draw; play: draw (large audiences); F ✝ goods: draw (customers), take; es zieht there is a draught, Am. there is a draft; 3. v/i. (sein) move, go; march; (re)move (nach to); birds: migrate; 4. v/refl. (h) extend, stretch, run; wood: warp; sich in die Länge ~ drag on.

'Zieh|harmonika ♪ f accordion; **'~ung** f (-/-en) drawing (of lots).

Ziel [tsi:l] n (-[e]s/-e) aim (a. fig.); mark; sports: winning-post, goal (a. fig.); target; 〆 objective; destination (of voyage); fig. end, purpose, target, object(ive); term; sein ~ erreichen gain one's end(s pl.); über das ~ hinausschießen overshoot the mark; zum ~e führen succeed, be successful; sich zum ~ setzen zu inf. aim at ger., Am. aim to inf.; '~band m sports: tape; es zieht there is a draught, Am. **2bewußt** adj. purposeful; **'2en** v/i. (ge-, h) (take) aim (auf acc. at); **'~fernrohr** n telescopic sight; **'2los** adj. aimless, purposeless; **'~scheibe** f target, butt; ~ des Spottes butt or target (of derision); **'2strebig** adj. purposive.

ziemlich ['tsi:mlɪç] 1. adj. fair, tolerable; considerable; 2. adv. pretty, fairly, tolerably; rather; about.

Zier [tsi:r] f (-/no pl.), **~de** f (-/-n) ornament; fig. a. hono(u)r (für to); **'2en** v/t. (ge-, h) ornament, adorn; decorate; sich ~ be affected; esp. of woman: be prudish; refuse; '♀lich adj. delicate; neat; graceful, elegant; '⚲lichkeit f (-/♀-en) delicacy; neatness; gracefulness, elegance; '⚲pflanze f ornamental plant.

Ziffer ['tsifər] f (-/-n) figure, digit; '⚲blatt n dial(-plate), face.

Zigarette [tsiga'retə] f (-/-n) cigaret(te); ⚲**automat** [⚲n♀-] m cigarette slot-machine; ⚲**netui** [⚲n♀-] n cigarette-case, ⚲**nspitze** f cigaretteholder; ⚲**nstummel** m stub, Am. a. butt.

Zigarre [tsi'garə] f (-/-n) cigar.

Zigeuner [tsi'gɔynər] m (-s/-), ⚲**inf** (-/-nen) gipsy, gypsy.

Zimmer ['tsimər] n (-s/-) room; apartment, ⚲**antenne** f radio, etc.: indoor aerial, Am. a. indoor antenna; ⚲**einrichtung** f furniture; '⚲**flucht** f suite (of rooms); '⚲**mädchen** n chamber-maid; '⚲**mann** m (-[e]s/Zimmerleute) carpenter; '♀n (ge-, h) v/t. carpenter; fig. frame; 2.v/i. carpenter; ⚲**pflanze** f indoor plant; '⚲**vermieterin** f (-/-nen) landlady.

zimperlich adj. ['tsimpərliç] prim; prudish; affected.

Zimt [tsimt] m (-[e]s/-e) cinnamon.

Zink ⚲ [tsiŋk] n (-[e]s/no pl.) zinc; '⚲**blech** n sheet zinc.

Zinke ['tsiŋkə] f (-/-n) prong; tooth (of comb or fork); '⚲n m (-s/-) s. Zinke.

Zinn ⚲ [tsin] n (-[e]s/no pl.) tin.

Zinne ['tsinə] f (-/-n) ⚔ pinnacle; ✕ battlement.

Zinnober [tsi'no:bər] m (-s/-) cinnabar; ♀rot adj. vermilion.

Zins [tsins] m (-es/-en) rent; tribute; mst ⚲en pl. interest; ⚲en tragen yield or bear interest; '♀**bringend** adj. bearing interest; ⚲**eszins** ['⚲zəs-] m compound interest; '♀**frei** adj. rent-free; free of interest; '⚲**fuß** m, '⚲**satz** m rate of interest.

Zipf|el ['tsipfəl] m (-s/-) tip, point, end; corner (of handkerchief, etc.); lappet (of garment); '♀**elig** adj. having points or ends; '⚲**elmütze** f jelly-bag cap; nightcap.

Zirkel ['tsirkəl] m (-s/-) circle (a. fig.); ⚲ (ein a pair of) compasses pl. or dividers pl.

zirkulieren [tsirku'li:rən] v/i. (no -ge-, h) circulate.

Zirkus ['tsirkus] m (-/-se) circus.

zirpen ['tsirpən] v/i. (ge-, h) chirp, cheep.

zisch|en ['tsiʃən] v/t. and v/i. (ge-, h) whisper; '⚲**en** v/i. (ge-, h) hiss; whiz(z).

ziselieren [tsize'li:rən] v/t. (no -ge-, h) chase.

Zit|at [tsi'tɑːt] n (-[e]s/-e) quotation; ♀**ieren** [⚲'ti:rən] v/t. (no -ge-, h) summon; quote.

Zitrone [tsi'tro:nə] f (-/-n) lemon;

⚲**nlimonade** f lemonade; lemon squash; ⚲**npresse** f lemon-squeezer; ⚲**nsaft** m lemon juice.

zittern ['tsitərn] v/i. (ge-, h) tremble, shake (vor dat. with).

zivil [tsi'vi:l] 1. adj. civil; civilian; price: reasonable; 2. ♀ n (-s/no pl.) civilians pl., s Zivilkleidung; ♀**bevölkerung** f civilian population, civilians pl., ♀**isation** [⚲iliza'tsjo:n] f (-/♀-en) civilization; ⚲**isieren** [⚲ili'zi:rən] v/t. (no -ge-, h) civilize; ♀**ist** [⚲i'list] m (-en/-en) civilian; ♀**kleidung** f civilian or plain clothes pl.

Zofe ['tso:fə] f (-/-n) lady's maid.

zog [tso:k] pret of ziehen.

zögern ['tsø:gərn] 1. v/i. (ge-, h) hesitate, linger, delay; 2. ♀ n (-s/no pl.) hesitation, delay.

Zögling ['tsø:kliŋ] m (-s/-e) pupil.

Zoll [tsɔl] m 1. (-[e]s/-) inch; 2. (-[e]s/⚲e) customs pl., duty; the Customs pl., ⚲**abfertigung** f customs clearance, ⚲**amt** n customhouse; ⚲**beamte** m customs officer; ⚲**behörde** f the Customs pl.; '⚲**erklärung** f customs declaration; ♀**frei** adj. duty-free; '⚲**kontrolle** f customs examination; ♀**pflichtig** adj. liable to duty; '⚲**stock** m footrule; '⚲**tarif** m tariff.

Zone ['tso:nə] f (-/-n) zone.

Zoo [tso:] m (-[s]/-s) zoo.

Zoolog|e [tso⚲o'lo:gə] m (-n/-n) zoologist; ⚲**ie** [⚲o'gi:] f (-/no pl.) zoology, ♀**isch** adj. [⚲'lo:giʃ] zoological.

Zopf [tsɔpf] m (-[e]s/⚲e) plait, tress; pigtail; alter ⚲ antiquated ways pl. or custom.

Zorn [tsɔrn] m (-[e]s/no pl.) anger; '♀**ig** adj. angry (auf j-n with s.o.; auf et. at s.th.).

Zote ['tso:tə] f (-/-n) filthy or smutty joke, obscenity.

Zott|el ['tsɔtəl] f (-/-n) tuft (of hair); tassel; '♀**(e)lig** adj. shaggy.

zu [tsu:] 1. prp. (dat.) direction: to, towards, up to; at, in; on; in addition to, along with; purpose: for; ⚲ Beginn at the beginning or outset; ⚲ Weihnachten at Christmas; zum ersten Mal for the first time; ⚲ e-m ... Preise at a ... price; ⚲ meinem Erstaunen to my surprise; ⚲ Tausenden by thousands; ⚲ Wasser by water; ⚲ zweien by twos; zum Beispiel for example; 2. adv. too; direction: towards, to; F closed, shut; with inf. to; ich habe ⚲ arbeiten I have to work.

'**zubauen** v/t. (sep., -ge-, h) build up or in, block.

Zubehör ['tsu:bəhø:r] n, m (-[e]s/-e) appurtenances pl., fittings pl., Am. F fixings pl., esp. ⊕ accessories pl.

'**zubereit|en** v/t. (sep., no -ge-, h) prepare; ♀**ung** f preparation.

'**zu**|**billigen** v/t. (sep., -ge-, h) grant; '**binden** v/t. (irr. binden, sep., -ge-, h) tie up; '**blinzeln** v/i. (sep., -ge-, h) wink at s.o.; '**bringen** v/t. (irr. bringen, sep., -ge-, h) pass, spend (time).

Zucht [tsuxt] f 1. (-/no pl.) discipline; breeding, rearing; rearing of bees, etc.: culture; ♀ cultivation; 2. (-/-en) breed, race; '**bulle** zo. m bull (for breeding).

zücht|**en** ['tsʏçtən] v/t. (ge-, h) breed (animals); grow, cultivate (plants); '**2er** m (-s/-) breeder (of animals); grower (of plants).

'**Zucht**|**haus** n penitentiary; punishment: penal servitude; '**häusler** ['-hɔʏslər] m (-s/-) convict; '**hengst** zo. m stud-horse, stallion.

züchtig adj. ['tsʏçtiç] chaste, modest; '**en** ['-gən] v/t. (ge-, h) flog. '**zucht**|**los** adj. undisciplined; '**2losigkeit** f (-/*-en) want of discipline; '**2stute** zo. f brood-mare.

zucken ['tsukən] v/i. (ge-, h) jerk; move convulsively, twitch (all: mit et. s.th.); with pain: wince; lightning: flash.

zücken ['tsʏkən] v/t. (ge-, h) draw (sword); F pull out (purse, pencil).

Zucker ['tsukər] m (-s/no pl.) sugar; '**dose** f sugar-basin, Am. sugar bowl; '**erbse** ♀ f green pea; '**guß** m icing, frosting; '**hut** m sugarloaf; '**2ig** adj. sugary; '**2krank** adj. diabetic; '**2n** v/t. (ge-, h) sugar; '**rohr** ♀ n sugar-cane; '**rübe** ♀ f sugar-beet; '**2süß** adj. (as) sweet as sugar; '**wasser** n sugared water; '**zange** f (e-e a pair of) sugar-tongs pl.

zuckrig adj. ['tsukriç] sugary.
'**Zuckung** ✺ f (-/-en) convulsion. '**zudecken** v/t. (sep., -ge-, h) cover (up).

zudem adv. [tsu'de:m] besides, moreover.

'**zu**|**drehen** v/t. (sep., -ge-, h) turn off (tap); j-m den Rücken ~ turn one's back on s.o.; '**dringlich** adj. importunate, obtrusive; '**drücken** v/t. (sep., -ge-, h) close, shut; '**erkennen** v/t. (irr. kennen, sep., no -ge-, h) award (a. ♯♯); adjudge (dat. to) (a. ♯♯).

zuerst adv. [tsu'-] first (of all); at first; er kam ~ an he was the first to arrive.

'**zufahr**|**en** v/i. (irr. fahren, sep., -ge-, sein) drive on; ~ auf (acc.) drive to (-wards); fig. rush at s.o.; '**2t** f approach; drive, Am. driveway; '**2tsstraße** f approach (road).

'**Zufall** m chance, accident; durch ~ by chance, by accident; '**2en** v/i. (irr. fallen, sep., -ge-, sein) eyes: be closing (with sleep); door: shut (of itself); j-m ~ fall to s.o.('s share).

'**zufällig** 1. adj. accidental; attr.

chance; casual; 2. adv. accidentally, by chance.

'**zufassen** v/i. (sep., -ge-, h) seize (hold of) s.th.; (mit) ~ lend or give a hand.

'**Zuflucht** f (-/*ᵘe) refuge, shelter, resort; s-e ~ nehmen zu have recourse to s.th., take refuge in s.th. '**Zufluß** m afflux; influx (a. ♥); affluent, tributary (of river); ♥ supply.

'**zuflüstern** v/t. (sep., -ge-, h): j-m et. ~ whisper s.th. to s.o.

zufolge prp. (gen.; dat.) [tsu'fɔlgə] according to.

zufrieden adj. [tsu'-] content(ed), satisfied; **2heit** f (-/no pl.) contentment, satisfaction; '**lassen** v/t. (irr. lassen, sep., -ge-, h) let s.o. alone; '**stellen** v/t. (sep., -ge-, h) satisfy; '**stellend** adj. satisfactory.

'**zu**|**frieren** v/i. (irr. frieren, sep., -ge-, sein) freeze up or over; '**fügen** v/t. (sep., -ge-, h) add; do, cause; inflict (wound, etc.) (j-m [up]on s.o.); **2fuhr** ['-fu:r] f (-/-en) supply; supplies pl.; influx; '**führen** v/t. (sep., -ge-, h) carry, lead, bring; ⊕ feed; supply (a. ⊕).

Zug [tsu:k] m (-[e]s/*ᵘe) draw(ing), pull(ing); ⊕ traction; ✗ expedition, campaign; procession; migration (of birds); drift (of clouds); range (of mountains); ⊕ train; feature; trait (of character); bent, tendency, trend; draught, Am. draft (of air); at chess: move; drinking: draught, Am. draft; at cigarette, etc.: puff.

'**Zu**|**gabe** f addition; extra; thea. encore; '**gang** m entrance; access; approach; **2gänglich** adj. ['-gɛŋliç] accessible (für to); '**2geben** v/t. (irr. geben, sep., -ge-, h) add; fig.: allow; confess; admit.

zugegen adj. [tsu'-] present (bei at.). '**zugehen** v/i. (irr. gehen, sep., -ge-, sein) door, etc.: close, shut; p. move on, walk faster; happen; auf j-n ~ go up to s.o., move or walk towards s.o.

'**Zugehörigkeit** f (-/no pl.) membership (zu to) (society, etc.); belonging (to).

Zügel ['tsy:gəl] m (-s/-) rein; bridle (a. fig.); '**2los** adj. unbridled; fig.: unrestrained; licentious; '**2n** v/t. (ge-, h) rein (in); fig. bridle, check.

'**Zuge**|**ständnis** n concession; '**2stehen** v/t. (irr. stehen, sep., -ge-, h) concede.

'**zugetan** adj. attached (dat. to).
'**Zugführer** 🚂 m guard, Am. conductor.   [-ge-, h) add.\
'**zugießen** v/t. (irr. gießen, sep.,)

zug|**ig** adj. ['tsu:giç] draughty, Am. drafty; **2kraft** ['-k-] f ⊕ traction; fig. attraction, draw, appeal; '**kräftig** adj. ['-k-]: ~ sein be a draw.

zugleich adv. [tsu'-] at the same time; together.

'Zug|luft f (-/no pl.) draught, Am. draft; **~maschine** f traction-engine, tractor; **~pflaster** n blister.

'zu|greifen v/i. (irr. greifen, sep., -ge-, h) grasp or grab at s.th.; at table: help o.s.; lend a hand; **2griff** m grip, clutch.

zugrunde adv. [tsu'grundə]: ~ gehen perish; ~ richten ruin.

'Zugtier n draught animal, Am. draft animal.

zu|gunsten prp. (gen.) [tsu'gunstən] in favo(u)r of; **~gute** adv.: j-m et. ~ halten give s.o. credit for s.th.; ~ kommen be for the benefit (dat. of).

'Zugvogel m bird of passage.

'zuhalten v/t. (irr. halten, sep., -ge-, h) hold (door) to; sich die Ohren ~ stop one's ears. [home.)

Zuhause [tsu'hauzə] n (-/no pl.)

'zu|heilen v/i. (sep., -ge-, sein) heal up, skin over; **~hören** v/i. (sep., -ge-, h) listen (dat. to).

'Zuhörer m hearer, listener; ~ pl. audience; **~schaft** f (-/~-en) audience.

'zu|jubeln v/i. (sep., -ge-, h) cheer; **~kleben** v/t. (sep., -ge-, h) paste or glue up; gum (letter) down; **~knallen** v/t. (sep., -ge-, h) bang, slam (door, etc.); **~knöpfen** v/t. (sep., -ge-, h) button (up); **~kommen** v/i. (irr. kommen, sep., -ge-, sein): auf j-n ~ come up to s.o.; j-m ~ be due to s.o.; j-m et. ~ lassen let s.o. have s.th.; send s.o. s.th.; **~korken** v/t. (sep., -ge-, h) cork (up).

'Zu|kunft f (-/no pl.) future; gr. future (tense); **2künftig** 1. adj. future; mein Vater father-to-be; 2. adv. in future.

'zu|lächeln v/i. (sep., -ge-, h) smile at or (up)on; **2lage** f extra pay, increase; rise, Am. raise (in salary or wages); **~langen** v/i. (sep., -ge-, h) at table: help o.s.; **~lassen** v/t. (irr. lassen, sep., -ge-, h) leave (door) shut; keep closed; fig.: admit s.o.; license; allow, suffer; admit of (only one interpretation, etc.); **~lässig** adj. admissible, allowable; **2lassung** f (-/-en) admission; permission; licen|ce, Am. -se.

zulegen v/t. (sep., -ge-, h) add; F sich et. ~ get o.s. s.th.

zuleide adv. [tsu'laɪdə]: j-m et. ~ tun do s.o. harm, harm or hurt s.o.

'zuleiten v/t. (sep., -ge-, h) let in (water, etc.); conduct to; pass on to s.o.

zu|letzt adv. [tsu'-] finally, at last; er kam ~ an he was the last to arrive; **~liebe** adv.: j-m ~ for s.o.'s sake.

zum prp. [tsum] = zu dem.

'zumachen v/t. (sep., -ge-, h) close, shut; button (up) (coat); fasten.

zumal cj. [tsu'-] especially, particularly. [up.)

'zumauern v/t. (sep., -ge-, h) wall)

zumut|en ['tsu:mu:tən] v/t. (sep., -ge-, h): j-m et. ~ expect s.th. of s.o.; sich zuviel ~ overtask o.s., overtax one's strength, etc.; **2ung** f (-/-en) exacting demand, exaction; fig. impudence.

zunächst [tsu'-] 1. prp. (dat.) next to; 2. adv. first of all; for the present.

'zu|nageln v/t. (sep., -ge-, h) nail up; **~nähen** v/t. (sep., -ge-, h) sew up; **2nahme** ['-na:mə] f (-/-n) increase, growth; **2name** m surname.

zünden ['tsyndən] v/i. (ge-, h) kindle; esp. mot. ignite; fig. arouse enthusiasm.

'Zünd|holz ['tsynt-] n match; **~kerze** f spark(ing)-plug, Am. spark plug; **~schlüssel** mot. m ignition key; **~schnur** f fuse; **~stoff** fig. m fuel; **~ung** mot. ['-duŋ] f (-/-en) ignition.

'zunehmen v/i. (irr. nehmen, sep., -ge-, h) increase (an dat. in); grow; put on weight; moon: wax; days: grow longer.

'zuneig|en (sep., -ge-, h) 1. v/i. incline to(wards); 2. v/refl. incline to(wards); sich dem Ende ~ draw to a close; **2ung** f (-/~-en) affection.

Zunft [tsunft] f (-/-e) guild, corporation.

Zunge ['tsuŋə] f (-/-n) tongue.

züngeln ['tsyŋəln] v/i. (ge-, h) play with its tongue; flame: lick.

'zungen|fertig adj. voluble; **2fertigkeit** f (-/no pl.) volubility; **2spitze** f tip of the tongue.

zunichte adv. [tsu'niçtə]: ~ machen or werden bring or come to nothing.

'zunicken v/i. (sep., -ge-, h) nod to.

zu|nutze [tsu'nutsə]: sich et. ~ machen turn s.th. to account, utilize s.th.; **~'oberst** adv. at the top, uppermost.

zupfen ['tsupfən] (ge-, h) 1. v/t. pull, tug, twitch; 2. v/i. pull, tug, twitch (all: an dat. at).

zur prp. [tsu:r] = zu der.

'zurechnungsfähig adj. of sound mind; responsible; **2keit** f (-/no pl.) responsibility.

zurecht|finden [tsu'-] v/refl. (irr. finden, sep., -ge-, h) find one's way; **~kommen** v/i. (irr. kommen, sep., -ge-, sein) arrive in time; ~ (mit) get on (well) (with); manage s.th.; **~legen** v/t. (sep., -ge-, h) arrange; sich e-e Sache ~ think s.th. out; **~machen** F v/t. (sep., -ge-, h) get ready, prepare, Am. F fix; adapt (für to, for purpose); sich ~ of *woman*: make (o.s.) up; **~weisen** *v/t.* (*irr.* weisen, sep., -ge-, h) reprimand; **2weisung** *f* reprimand.

'zu|reden *v/i.* (sep., -ge-, h): j-m ~ try to persuade s.o.; encourage s.o.; **'~reiten** *v/t.* (*irr.* reiten, sep., -ge-, h) break in; **'~riegeln** *v/t.* (sep., -ge-, h) bolt (up).

zürnen ['tsyrnən] *v/i.* (ge-, h) be angry (*j-m* with s.o.).

zurück *adv.* [tsu'ryk] back; backward(s); behind; **~behalten** *v/t.* (*irr.* halten, sep., no -ge-, h) keep back, retain; **~bekommen** *v/t.* (*irr.* kommen, sep., no -ge-, h) get back; **~bleiben** *v/i.* (*irr.* bleiben, sep., -ge-, sein) remain or stay behind; fall behind, lag; **~blicken** *v/i.* (sep., -ge-, h) look back; **~bringen** *v/t.* (*irr.* bringen, sep., -ge-, h) bring back; **~datieren** *v/t.* (sep., no -ge-, h) date back, antedate; **~drängen** *v/t.* (sep., -ge-, h) push back; *fig.* repress; **~erobern** *v/t.* (sep., no -ge-, h) reconquer; **~erstatten** *v/t.* (sep., no -ge-, h) restore, return; refund (*expenses*); **~fahren** (*irr.* fahren, sep., -ge-) 1. *v/i.* (sein) drive back; *fig.* start; 2. *v/t.* (h) drive back; **~fordern** *v/t.* (sep., -ge-, h) reclaim; **~führen** *v/t.* (sep., -ge-, h) lead back; **~ auf** (*acc.*) reduce to (*rule*, etc.); refer to (*cause*, etc.); **~geben** *v/t.* (*irr.* geben, sep., -ge-, h) give back, return, restore; **~gehen** *v/i.* (*irr.* gehen, sep., -ge-, sein) go back; return; **~gezogen** *adj.* retired; **~greifen** *fig. v/i.* (*irr.* greifen, sep., -ge-, h): ~ auf (*acc.*) fall back (up)on; **~halten** (*irr.* halten, sep., -ge-, h) 1. *v/t.* hold back; 2. *v/i.*: ~ mit keep back; **~haltend** *adj.* reserved; **2haltung** *f* (-/~-en) reserve; **~kehren** *v/i.* (sep., -ge-, sein) return; **~kommen** *v/i.* (*irr.* kommen, sep., -ge-, sein) come back; return (*fig. auf acc.* to); **~lassen** *v/t.* (*irr.* lassen, sep., -ge-, h) leave (behind); **~legen** *v/t.* (sep., -ge-, h) lay aside; cover (*distance*, *way*); **~nehmen** *v/t.* (*irr.* nehmen, sep., -ge-, h) take back; withdraw, retract (*words*, etc.); **~prallen** *v/i.* (sep., -ge-, sein) rebound; start; **~rufen** *v/t.* (*irr.* rufen, sep., -ge-, h) call back; *sich ins Gedächtnis* ~ recall; **~schicken** *v/t.* (sep., -ge-, h) send back; **~schlagen** (*irr.* schlagen, sep., -ge-, h) 1. *v/t.* drive (*ball*) back; repel (*enemy*); turn down (*blanket*); 2. *v/i.* strike back; **~schrecken** *v/i.* (sep., -ge-, sein) 1. (*irr.* schrecken) shrink back (*vor dat.* from *spectacle*, etc.); 2. shrink (*vor dat.* from *work*, etc.); **~setzen** *v/t.* (sep., -ge-, h) put back; *fig.* slight, neglect; **~stellen** *v/t.* (sep., -ge-, h) put back (*a. clock*); *fig.* defer, postpone; **~strahlen** *v/t.* (sep., -ge-, h) reflect;

~streifen *v/t.* (sep., -ge-, h) turn or tuck up (*sleeve*); **~treten** *v/i.* (*irr.* treten, sep., -ge-, sein) step or stand back; *fig.*: recede; resign; withdraw; **~weichen** *v/i.* (*irr.* weichen, sep., -ge-, sein) fall back; recede (*a. fig.*); **~weisen** *v/t.* (*irr.* weisen, sep., -ge-, h) decline, reject; repel (*attack*); **~zahlen** *v/t.* (sep., -ge-, h) pay back (*a. fig.*); **~ziehen** (*irr.* ziehen, sep., -ge-) 1. *v/t.* (h) draw back; *fig.* withdraw; *sich* ~ retire, withdraw; ✕ retreat; 2. *v/i.* (sein) move or march back.

'Zuruf *m* call; **'2en** *v/t.* (*irr.* rufen, sep., -ge-, h) call (out), shout (*j-m et.* s.th. to s.o.).

'Zusage *f* promise; assent; **'2n** (sep., -ge-, h) 1. *v/t.* promise; 2. *v/i.* promise to come; *j-m* ~ *food*, etc.: agree with s.o.; accept s.o.'s invitation; suit s.o.

zusammen *adv.* [tsu'zamən] together; at the same time; *alles* ~ (all) in all; ~ *betragen* amount to, total (up to); **2arbeit** *f* (-/*no pl.*) co-operation; team-work; **~arbeiten** *v/i.* (sep., -ge-, h) work together; co-operate; **~beißen** *v/t.* (*irr.* beißen, sep., -ge-, h): die Zähne ~ set one's teeth; **~brechen** *v/i.* (*irr.* brechen, sep., -ge-, sein) break down; collapse; **2bruch** *m* breakdown; collapse; **~drücken** *v/t.* (sep., -ge-, h) compress, press together; **~fahren** *fig. v/i.* (*irr.* fahren, sep., -ge-, sein) start (*bei* or *vor dat.* with); **~fallen** *v/i.* (*irr.* fallen, sep., -ge-, sein) fall in, collapse; coincide; **~falten** *v/t.* (sep., -ge-, h) fold up; **~fassen** *v/t.* (sep., -ge-, h) summarize, sum up; **2fassung** *f* (-/-en) summary; **~fügen** *v/t.* (sep., -ge-, h) join (together); **~halten** (*irr.* halten, sep., -ge-, h) 1. *v/t.* hold together; 2. *v/i.* hold together; *friends*: F stick together; **2hang** *m* coherence, coherency; connection; context; **~hängen** (sep., -ge-, h) 1. *v/i.* (*irr.* hängen) cohere; *fig.* be connected; 2. *v/t.* hang together; **~klappen** *v/t.* (sep., -ge-, h) fold up; close (*clasp-knife*); **~kommen** *v/i.* (*irr.* kommen, sep., -ge-, sein) meet; **2kunft** [~kunft] *f* (-/~e) meeting; **~laufen** *v/i.* (*irr.* laufen, sep., -ge-, sein) run or crowd together; ⚛ converge; *milk*: curdle; **~legen** *v/t.* (sep., -ge-, h) lay together; fold up; club (*money*) (together); **~nehmen** *v/t.* (*irr.* nehmen, sep., -ge-, h) collect (*one's wits*); *sich* ~ be on one's good behavio(u)r; pull o.s. together; **~packen** *v/t.* (sep., -ge-, h) pack up; **~passen** *v/i.* (sep., -ge-, h) match, harmonize; **~rechnen** *v/t.* (sep., -ge-, h) add up; **~reißen** F *v/refl.* (*irr.* reißen, sep., -ge-, h) pull o.s. together; **~rollen**

v/t. and v/refl. (sep., -ge-, h) coil (up); **~rotten** *v/refl. (sep., -ge-, h)* band together; **~rücken** *(sep., -ge-)* **1.** *v/t. (h)* move together; **2.** *v/i. (sein)* close up; **~schlagen** *(irr. schlagen, sep., -ge-)* **1.** *v/t. (h)* clap *(hands)* (together); F smash to pieces; beat *s.o.* up; **2.** *v/i. (sein):* **~** *über (dat.)* close over; **~schließen** *v/refl. (irr. schließen, sep., -ge-, h)* join; unite; **2schluß** *m* union; **~schrumpfen** *v/i. (sep., -ge-, sein)* shrivel (up), shrink; **~setzen** *v/t. (sep., -ge-, h)* put together; compose; compound *(a.* ⚛, *word);* ⊕ assemble; *sich ~ aus* consist of; **2setzung** *f (-/-en)* composition; compound; ⊕ assembly; **~stellen** *v/t. (sep., -ge-, h)* put together; compile; combine; **2stoß** *m* collision *(a. fig.);* ✗ encounter; *fig.* clash; **~stoßen** *v/i. (irr. stoßen, sep., -ge-, sein)* collide *(a. fig.);* adjoin; *fig.* clash; **~** *mit* knock *(heads, etc.)* together; **~stürzen** *v/i. (sep., -ge-, sein)* collapse; *house, etc.:* fall in; **~tragen** *v/t. (irr. tragen, sep., -ge-, h)* collect; compile *(notes);* **~treffen** *v/i. (irr. treffen, sep., -ge-, sein)* meet; coincide; **2treffen** *n (-s/no pl.)* meeting; encounter *(of enemies);* coincidence; **~treten** *v/i. (irr. treten, sep., -ge-, sein)* meet; *parl. a.* convene; **~wirken** *v/i. (sep., -ge-, h)* co-operate; **2wirken** *n (-s/no pl.)* co-operation; **~zählen** *v/t. (sep., -ge-, h)* add up, count up; **~ziehen** *v/t. (irr. ziehen, sep., -ge-, h)* draw together; contract; concentrate *(troops); sich ~* contract.

'Zusatz *m* addition; admixture, *metall.* alloy; supplement.

zusätzlich *adj.* ['tsuːzɛtslɪç] additional.

'zuschau|en *v/i. (sep., -ge-, h)* look on *(e-r Sache at s.th.); j-m ~* watch *s.o. (bei et.* doing *s.th.);* **2er** *m (-s/-)* spectator, looker-on, onlooker; **2erraum** *thea. m* auditorium.

'zuschicken *v/t. (sep., -ge-, h)* send *(dat.* to); mail; consign *(goods).*

'Zuschlag *m* addition; extra charge; excess fare; ✆ surcharge; *at auction:* knocking down; **2en** ['~gən] *(irr. schlagen, sep., -ge-)* **1.** *v/t. (h)* strike; **2.** *v/i. (sein) door:* slam (to); **3.** *v/t. (h)* bang, slam *(door)* (to); *at auction:* knock down *(dat.* to).

'zu|schließen *v/t. (irr. schließen, sep., -ge-, h)* lock (up); **~schnallen** *v/t. (sep., -ge-, h)* buckle (up); **~schnappen** *(sep., -ge-)* **1.** *v/i. (h) dog:* snap; **2.** *v/i. (sein) door:* snap to; **~schneiden** *v/t. (irr. schneiden, sep., -ge-, h)* cut up; cut *(suit)* (to size); **2schnitt** *m (-[e]s/*✻*-e)* cut; style; **~schnüren** *v/t. (sep., -ge-, h)* lace up; cord up; **~schrauben** *v/t.*

(sep., -ge-, h) screw up *or* tight; **~schreiben** *v/t. (irr. schreiben, sep., -ge-, h): j-m et. ~* ascribe *or* attribute *s.th.* to *s.o.;* **2schrift** *f* letter.

zuschulden *adv.* [tsuː-]: *sich et. kommen lassen* make *o.s.* guilty of *s.th.*

'Zu|schuß *m* allowance; subsidy, grant *(of government);* **2schütten** *v/t. (sep., -ge-, h)* fill up *(ditch);* F add; **2sehen** *v/i. (irr. sehen, sep., -ge-, h) s.* zuschauen; **~,** *daß* see (to it) that; **2sehends** *adv.* ['~ts] visibly; **2senden** *v/t. ([irr. senden,] sep., -ge-, h) s.* zuschicken; **2setzen** *(sep., -ge-, h)* **1.** *v/t.* add; lose *(money);* **2.** *v/i.* lose money; *j-m ~* press *s.o.* hard.

'zusicher|n *v/t. (sep., -ge-, h): j-m et. ~* assure *s.o.* of *s.th.;* promise *s.o. s.th.;* **2ung** *f* promise, assurance.

'zu|spielen *v/t. (sep., -ge-, h) sports:* pass *(ball) (dat.* to); **~spitzen** *v/t. (sep., -ge-, h)* point; *sich ~* taper (off); *fig.* come to a crisis; **2spruch** *m (-[e]s/no pl.)* encouragement; consolation; ✝ custom; **2stand** *m* condition, state; *in gutem ~ house:* in good repair.

zustande *adv.* [tsuː'ʃtandə]: *~ bringen* bring about; *~ kommen* come about; *nicht ~ kommen* not to come off.

'zuständig *adj.* competent; **2keit** *f (-/-en)* competence.

zustatten *adv.* [tsuː'ʃtatən]: *j-m ~ kommen* be useful to *s.o.*

'zustehen *v/i. (irr. stehen, sep., -ge-, h)* be due *(dat.* to).

'zustell|en *v/t. (sep., -ge-, h)* deliver *(a.* ✉); ✈ serve *(j-m on s.o.);* **2ung** *f* delivery; ✈ service.

'zustimm|en *v/i. (sep., -ge-, h)* agree *(dat.:* to *s.th.;* with *s.o.);* consent (to *s.th.);* **2ung** *f* consent.

'zustoßen *fig. v/i. (irr. stoßen, sep., -ge-, sein): j-m ~* happen to *s.o.*

zutage *adv.* [tsuː'taːgə]: *~ treten* come to light.

Zutaten ['tsuːtaːtən] *f/pl.* ingredients *pl. (of food);* trimmings *pl. (of dress).* **~** (hold to *s.o.'s* share.)

zuteil *adv.* [tsuː'taɪl]: *j-m ~ werden*) **'zuteil|en** *v/t. (sep., -ge-, h)* allot, apportion; **2ung** *f* allotment, apportionment; ration.

'zutragen *v/refl. (irr. tragen, sep., -ge-, h)* happen.

'zutrauen **1.** *v/t. (sep., -ge-, h): j-m et. ~* credit *s.o.* with *s.th.; sich zuviel ~* overrate *o.s.;* **2.** **2** *n (-s/no pl.)* confidence *(zu* in).

'zutraulich *adj.* confiding, trustful, trusting; *animal:* friendly, tame.

'zutreffen *v/i. (irr. treffen, sep., -ge-, h)* be right, be true; *~ auf (acc.)* be true of; **'~d** *adj.* right, correct; applicable.

'zutrinken v/i. (irr. trinken, sep., -ge-, h): j-m ~ drink to s.o.

'Zutritt m (-[e]s/no pl.) access; admission; ~ verboten! no admittance! [bottom.]

zuunterst adv. [tsu'-] right at the

zuverlässig adj. ['tsu:ferlɛsiç] reliable; certain; **'2keit** f (-/no pl.) reliability; certainty.

Zuversicht ['tsu:ferziçt] f (-/no pl.) confidence; **'2lich** adj. confident.

zuviel adv. [tsu'-] too much; e-r ~ one too many.

zuvor adv. [tsu'-] before, previously; first; **~kommen** v/i. (irr. kommen, sep., -ge-, sein): j-m ~ anticipate s.o.; e-r Sache ~ anticipate or prevent s.th.; **~kommend** adj. obliging; courteous.

Zuwachs ['tsu:vaks] m (-es/no pl.) increase; **2en** v/i. (irr. wachsen, sep., -ge-, sein) become overgrown; wound: close.

zu|wege adv. [tsu've:gə]: ~ bringen bring about; **~'weilen** adv. sometimes.

'zu|weisen v/t. (irr. weisen, sep., -ge-, h) assign; **~wenden** v/t. (irr. wenden) sep., -ge-, h) (dat.) turn to(wards); fig.: give; bestow on; sich ~ (dat.) turn to(wards).

zuwenig adv. [tsu'-] too little.

'zuwerfen v/t. (irr. werfen, sep., -ge-, h) fill up (pit); slam (door) (to); j-m ~ throw (ball, etc.) to s.o.; cast (look) at s.o.

zuwider prp. (dat.) [tsu'-] contrary to, against; repugnant, distasteful; **~handeln** v/i. (sep., -ge-, h) (dat.) act contrary or in opposition to; esp. ⚖ contravene; **2handlung** ⚖ f contravention.

'zu|winken v/i. (sep., -ge-, h) (dat.) wave to; beckon to; **~zahlen** v/t. (sep., -ge-, h) pay extra; **~zählen** v/t. (sep., -ge-, h) add; **~ziehen** (irr. ziehen, sep., -ge-, h) **1.** v/t. (h) draw together; draw (curtains); consult (doctor, etc.); sich ~ incur (s.o.'s displeasure, etc.); ⚕ catch (disease); **2.** v/i. (sein) move in; **~züglich** prp. (gen.) ['~tsy:k-] plus.

Zwang [tsvaŋ] **1.** m (-[e]s/⸚e) compulsion, coercion; constraint; ⚖ duress(e); force; sich ~ antun check or restrain o.s.; **2.** 2 pret. of zwingen.

zwängen ['tsvɛŋən] v/t. (ge-, h) press, force.

'zwanglos fig. adj. free and easy, informal; **'2igkeit** f (-/-en) ease, informality.

'Zwangs|arbeit f hard labo(u)r; **~jacke** f strait waistcoat or jacket; **~lage** f embarrassing situation; **2läufig** fig. adj. ['~lɔyf-] necessary; **~maßnahme** f coercive measure; **~vollstreckung** ⚖ f distraint, execution; **~vorstellung** ✻ f

obsession, hallucination; **2weise** adv. by force; **'~wirtschaft** f (-/⚑ -en) controlled economy.

zwanzig adj. ['tsvantsiç] twenty; **~ste** adj. ['~stə] twentieth.

zwar cj. [tsva:r] indeed, it is true; und ~ and that, that is.

Zweck [tsvek] m (-[e]s/-e) aim, end, object, purpose; design; keinen ~ haben be of no use; s-n ~ erfüllen answer its purpose; zu dem ~ (gen.) for the purpose of; **2dienlich** adj. serviceable, useful, expedient.

Zwecke ['tsvekə] f (-/-n) tack; drawing-pin, Am. thumbtack.

'zweck|los adj. aimless, purposeless, useless; **~mäßig** adj. expedient, suitable; **2mäßigkeit** f (-/no pl.) expediency.

zwei adj. [tsvaɪ] two; **'~beinig** adj. two-legged; **'2bettzimmer** n double (bedroom); **~deutig** adj. ['~dɔr-tiç] ambiguous; suggestive; **~erlei** adj. ['~ər'laɪ] of two kinds, two kinds of; **~fach** adj. ['~fax] double, twofold.

Zweifel ['tsvaɪfəl] m (-s/-) doubt; **2haft** adj. doubtful, dubious; **2los** adj. doubtless; **2n** v/i. (ge-, h) doubt (an e-r Sache s.th.; an j-m s.o.).

Zweig [tsvaɪk] m (-[e]s/-e) branch (a. fig.); kleiner ~ twig; **~geschäft** n, **~niederlassung** f, **~stelle** f branch.

zwei|jährig adj. ['tsvaɪjɛ:riç] two-year-old, of two (years); **2kampf** m duel, single combat; **~mal** adv. twice; **~malig** adj. (twice) repeated; **~motorig** adj. ['~mo:to:riç] two- or twin-engined; **~reihig** adj. having two rows; suit: double-breasted; **~schneidig** adj. double- or two-edged (both a. fig.); **~seitig** adj. two-sided; contract, etc.: bilateral; fabric: reversible, **2sitzer** esp. mot. m (-s/-) two-seater; **~sprachig** adj. bilingual; **~stimmig** adj. for two voices; **~stöckig** adj. ['~ʃtœkiç] two-stor[e]yed, -ied; **~stufig** ⊕ adj. two-stage; **~stündig** adj. ['~ʃtyndiç] of or lasting two hours, two-hour.

zweit adj. [tsvaɪt] second; ein ~er another; aus ~er Hand second-hand; zu ~ by twos; wir sind zu ~ there are two of us. [engine.]

'Zweitaktmotor mot. m two-stroke)

'zweit'best adj. second-best.

'zweiteilig adj. garment: two-piece.

zweitens adv. ['tsvaɪtəns] secondly.

'zweitklassig adj. second-class, second-rate.

Zwerchfell anat. ['tsverç-] n diaphragm.

Zwerg [tsverk] m (-[e]s/-e) dwarf; **2enhaft** adj. ['~gən-] dwarfish.

Zwetsch(g)e ['tsvetʃ(g)ə] f (-/-n) plum.

Zwick|el ['tsvikəl] m (-s/-) sewing: gusset; **'2en** v/t. and v/i. (ge-, h) pinch, nip; **'~er** m (-s/-) (ein a pair of) eye-glasses pl., pince-nez; **'~mühle** fig. f dilemma, quandary, fix.

Zwieback ['tsviːbak] m (-[e]s/ʉe, -e) rusk, zwieback.

Zwiebel ['tsviːbəl] f (-/-n) onion; bulb (of flowers, etc.).

Zwie|gespräch ['tsviː-] n dialog(ue); **'~licht** n (-[e]s/no pl.) twilight; **'~spalt** m (-[e]s/-e, ʉe) disunion; conflict; **2spältig** adj. ['~ʃpeltiç] disunited; emotions: conflicting; **'~tracht** f (-/no pl.) discord.

Zwilling|e ['tsviliŋə] m/pl. twins pl.; **'~sbruder** m twin brother; **'~sschwester** f twin sister.

Zwinge ['tsviŋə] f (-/-n) ferrule (of stick, etc.); ⊕ clamp; **2n** v/t. (irr., ge-, h) compel, constrain; force; **'2nd** adj. forcible; arguments: cogent, compelling; imperative; **'~r** m (-s/-) outer court; kennel(s pl.); bear-pit.

zwinkern ['tsviŋkərn] v/i. (ge-, h) wink, blink.

Zwirn [tsvirn] m (-[e]s/-e) thread, cotton; **'~sfaden** m thread.

zwischen prp. (dat.; acc.) ['tsviʃən] between (two); among (several); **'2bilanz** ✝ f interim balance; **'2deck** ⚓ n steerage; **~'durch** F adv. in between; for a change; **'2ergebnis** n provisional result; **'2fall** m incident; **'2händler** ✝ m middleman; **'2landung** ✈ f intermediate landing, stop, Am. a. stopover; (Flug) ohne ~ non-stop (flight);

'2pause f interval, intermission; **'2prüfung** f intermediate examination; **'2raum** m space, interval; **'2ruf** m (loud) interruption; **'2spiel** n interlude; **'~staatlich** adj. international; Am. between States: interstate; **'2station** f intermediate station; **'2stecker** ⚡ m adapter; **'2stück** n intermediate piece, connexion, (Am. only) connection; **'2stufe** f intermediate stage; **'2-wand** f partition (wall); **'2zeit** f interval; in der ~ in the meantime.

Zwist [tsvist] m (-es/-e), **'~igkeit** f (-/-en) discord; disunion; quarrel.

zwitschern ['tsvitʃərn] v/i. (ge-, h) twitter, chirp.

Zwitter ['tsvitər] m (-s/-) hermaphrodite.

zwölf adj. [tsvœlf] twelve; um ~ (Uhr) at twelve (o'clock); (um) ~ Uhr mittags (at) noon; (um) ~ Uhr nachts (at) midnight; **2'finger-darm** anat. m duodenum; **~te** adj. ['~tə] twelfth.

Zyankali [tsyan'kaːli] n (-s/no pl.) potassium cyanide.

Zyklus ['tsyːklus, 'tsyk-] m (-/Zyklen) cycle; course, set (of lectures, etc.).

Zylind|er [tsi'lindər, tsy'-] m (-s/-) ⚙, ⊕ cylinder; chimney (of lamp); top hat; **2risch** adj. ['~driʃ] cylindrical.

Zyni|ker ['tsyːnikər] m (-s/-) cynic; **'2sch** adj. cynical; **~smus** [tsy-'nismus] m (-/Zynismen) cynicism.

Zypresse ♀ [tsy'prɛsə] f (-/-n) cypress.

Zyste ♣ ['tsystə] f (-/-n) cyst.

PART II

ENGLISH-GERMAN
DICTIONARY

A

a [ei, ə] *Artikel*: ein(e); per, pro, je; *all of a size* alle gleich groß; *twice a week* zweimal wöchentlich.

A 1 F [ei'wʌn] Ia, prima.

aback [ə'bæk] rückwärts; *taken ~ fig.* überrascht, verblüfft, bestürzt.

abandon [ə'bændən] auf-, preisgeben; verlassen; überlassen; ~ed verworfen; ~ment [~nmənt] Auf-, Preisgabe *f*; Unbeherrschtheit *f*.

abase [ə'beis] erniedrigen, demütigen; ~ment [~smənt] Erniedrigung *f*.

abash [ə'bæʃ] beschämen, verlegen machen; ~ment [~ʃmənt] Verlegenheit *f*.

abate [ə'beit] *v/t.* verringern; *Mißstand* abstellen; *v/i.* abnehmen, nachlassen; ~ment [~tmənt] Verminderung *f*; Abschaffung *f*.

abattoir [ˈæbətwɑ:] Schlachthaus *n*.

abb|ess [ˈæbis] Äbtissin *f*; ~ey [ˈæbi] Abtei *f*; ~ot [ˈæbət] Abt *m*.

abbreviat|e [ə'bri:vieit] (ab)kürzen; ~ion [əbri:vi'eiʃən] Abkürzung *f*.

ABC [ˈeibiːˈsiː] Abc *n*, Alphabet *n*.

ABC weapons *pl.* ABC-Waffen *f/pl.*

abdicat|e [ˈæbdikeit] entsagen (*dat.*); abdanken; ~ion [æbdi-ˈkeiʃən] Verzicht *m*; Abdankung *f*.

abdomen [ˈæbdəmen] Unterleib *m*, Bauch *m*.

abduct [æb'dʌkt] entführen.

aberration [æbə'reiʃən] Abweichung *f*; *fig.* Verirrung *f*.

abet [ə'bet] aufhetzen; anstiften; unterstützen; ~tor [~tə] Anstifter *m*; (Helfers)Helfer *m*.

abeyance [ə'beiəns] Unentschiedenheit *f*; *in ~* ⚖ in der Schwebe.

abhor [əb'hɔ:] verabscheuen; ~rence [əb'hɔrəns] Abscheu *m* (*of* vor *dat.*); ~rent □ [~nt] zuwider (*to dat.*); abstoßend.

abide [ə'baid] [*irr.*] *v/i.* bleiben (*by* bei); *v/t.* erwarten; (v)ertragen.

ability [ə'biliti] Fähigkeit *f*.

abject □ [ˈæbdʒekt] verächtlich, gemein.

abjure [əb'dʒuə] abschwören; entsagen (*dat.*).

able □ [ˈeibl] fähig, geschickt; *be ~* imstande sein, können; ~-bodied kräftig.

abnegat|e [ˈæbnigeit] ableugnen; verzichten auf (*acc.*); ~ion [æbni-ˈgeiʃən] Ableugnung *f*; Verzicht *m*.

abnormal □ [æb'nɔ:məl] abnorm.

aboard [ə'bɔːd] ⚓ an Bord (*gen.*); *all ~! Am.* 🚃 *etc.* einsteigen!

abode [ə'boud] **1.** *pret. u. p.p. von* abide; **2.** Aufenthalt *m*; Wohnung *f*.

aboli|sh [ə'bɔliʃ] abschaffen, aufheben; ~tion [æbə'liʃən] Abschaffung *f*, Aufhebung *f*; ~tionist [~nist] Gegner *m* der Sklaverei.

A-bomb [ˈeibɔm] = *atomic bomb*.

abomina|ble □ [ə'bɔminəbl] abscheulich; ~te [~neit] verabscheuen; ~tion [əbɔmi'neiʃən] Abscheu *m*.

aboriginal □ [æbə'ridʒənl] einheimisch; Ur...

abortion ⚕ [ə'bɔːʃən] Fehlgeburt *f*; Abtreibung *f*.

abortive □ [ə'bɔːtiv] vorzeitig; erfolglos, fehlgeschlagen; verkümmert.

abound [ə'baund] reichlich vorhanden sein; Überfluß haben (*in* an *dat.*).

about [ə'baut] **1.** *prp.* um (...herum); bei; im Begriff; über (*acc.*); *I had no money ~ me* ich hatte kein Geld bei mir; *what are you ~?* was macht ihr da?; **2.** *adv.* herum, umher; in der Nähe; etwa; ungefähr um, gegen; *bring ~* zustande bringen.

above [ə'bʌv] **1.** *prp.* über; *fig.* erhaben über; *~ all* vor allem; *~ ground fig.* am Leben; **2.** *adv.* oben; darüber; **3.** *adj.* obig.

abreact [æbri'ækt] abreagieren.

abreast [ə'brest] nebeneinander.

abridg|e [ə'bridʒ] (ver)kürzen; ~(e)ment [~dʒmənt] (Ver)Kürzung *f*; Auszug *m*.

abroad [ə'brɔːd] im (ins) Ausland; überall(hin); *there is a report ~* es geht das Gerücht; *all ~* ganz im Irrtum.

abrogate [ˈæbrougeit] aufheben.

abrupt □ [ə'brʌpt] jäh; zs.-hanglos; schroff.

abscess ⚕ [ˈæbsis] Geschwür *n*.

abscond [əb'skɔnd] sich davonmachen.

absence [ˈæbsəns] Abwesenheit *f*; Mangel *m*; *~ of mind* Zerstreutheit *f*.

absent **1.** □ [ˈæbsənt] abwesend; nicht vorhanden; **2.** [æb'sent]: *~ o.s.* fernbleiben; ~-minded □ [ˈæbsənt'maindid] zerstreut, geistesabwesend.

absolut|e □ [ˈæbsəluːt] absolut; unumschränkt; vollkommen; unvermischt; unbedingt; ~ion [æbsə-ˈluːʃən] Lossprechung *f*.

absolve [əb'zɔlv] frei-, lossprechen.

absorb [əb'sɔːb] aufsaugen; *fig.* ganz in Anspruch nehmen.

absorption [əb'sɔːpʃən] Aufsaugung *f*; *fig.* Vertieftsein *n*.

abstain [əb'stein] sich enthalten.

abstemious □ [æb'sti:mjəs] enthaltsam; mäßig.

abstention [æb'stenʃən] Enthaltung f.

abstinen|ce ['æbstinəns] Enthaltsamkeit f; ~t □ [~nt] enthaltsam.

abstract 1. □ ['æbstrækt] abstrakt; **2.** [~] Auszug m; gr. Abstraktum n; **3.** [æb'strækt] abstrahieren; ablenken; entwenden; *Inhalt* kurz zs.-fassen; ~ed □ zerstreut; ~ion [~kʃən] Abstraktion f; (abstrakter) Begriff.

abstruse □ [æb'stru:s] fig. dunkel, schwer verständlich; tiefgründig.

absurd [əb'sə:d] absurd, sinnwidrig; lächerlich.

abundan|ce [ə'bʌndəns] Überfluß m; Fülle f; Überschwang m; ~t □ [~nt] reich(lich).

abus|e 1. [ə'bju:s] Mißbrauch m; Beschimpfung f; **2.** [~u:z] mißbrauchen; beschimpfen; ~ive □ [~u:siv] schimpfend; Schimpf...

abut [ə'bʌt] (an)grenzen (*upon* an).

abyss [ə'bis] Abgrund m.

academic|(al □) [ækə'demik(əl)] akademisch; ~ian [əkædə'miʃən] Akademiemitglied n.

academy [ə'kædəmi] Akademie f.

accede [æk'si:d]: ~ to beitreten (*dat.*); *Amt* antreten; *Thron* besteigen.

accelerat|e [æk'seləreit] beschleunigen; fig. ankurbeln; ~or [æk'seləreitə] Gaspedal n.

accent 1. ['æksənt] Akzent m (*a. gr.*); **2.** [æk'sent] v/t. akzentuieren, betonen; ~uate [~tjueit] akzentuieren, betonen.

accept [æk'sept] annehmen; † akzeptieren; hinnehmen; ~able □ [~təbl] annehmbar; ~ance [~əns] Annahme f; † Akzept n.

access ['ækses] Zugang m; ❡ Anfall m; easy of ~ zugänglich; ~ road Zufahrtsstraße f; ~ary [æk'sesəri] Mitwisser(in), Mitschuldige(r m) f; = accessory 2; ~ible □ [~səbl] zugänglich; ~ion [~eʃən] Antritt m (to gen.); Eintritt m (to in acc.); ~ to the throne Thronbesteigung f.

accessory [æk'sesəri] **1.** □ zusätzlich; **2.** Zubehörteil n.

accident ['æksidənt] Zufall m; Unglücks(fall m; ~al □ [æksi'dentl] zufällig; nebensächlich.

acclaim [ə'kleim] j-m zujubeln.

acclamation [æklə'meiʃən] Zuruf m.

acclimatize [ə'klaimətaiz] akklimatisieren, eingewöhnen.

acclivity [ə'kliviti] Steigung f; Böschung f.

accommodat|e [ə'kɔmədeit] anpassen; unterbringen; *Streit* schlichten; versorgen; j-m aushelfen (*with* mit *Geld*); ~ion [əkɔmə'deiʃən] Anpassung f; Aushilfe f; Bequemlich-

keit f; Unterkunft f; Beilegung f; ~ seating ~ Sitzgelegenheit f; ~ train Am. Personenzug m.

accompan|iment [ə'kʌmpənimənt] Begleitung f; ~y [ə'kʌmpəni] begleiten; accompanied with verbunden mit.

accomplice [ə'kɔmplis] Komplice m.

accomplish [ə'kɔmpliʃ] vollenden; ausführen; ~ed vollendet, perfekt; ~ment [~mənt] Vollendung f; Ausführung f; Tat f, Leistung f; Talent n.

accord [ə'kɔ:d] **1.** Übereinstimmung f; with one ~ einstimmig; **2.** v/i. übereinstimmen; v/t. gewähren; ~ance [~dəns] Übereinstimmung f; ~ant □ [~nt] übereinstimmend; ~ing [~diŋ]: ~ to gemäß (dat.); ~ingly [~ŋli] demgemäß.

accost [ə'kɔst] j-n bsd. auf der Straße ansprechen.

account [ə'kaunt] **1.** Rechnung f; Berechnung f; † Konto n; Rechenschaft f; Bericht m; of no ~ ohne Bedeutung; on no ~ auf keinen Fall; on ~ of wegen; take into ~, take ~ of in Betracht ziehen, berücksichtigen; turn to ~ ausnutzen; keep ~s die Bücher führen; call to ~ zur Rechenschaft ziehen; give a good ~ of o.s. sich bewähren; make ~ of Wert auf et. (acc.) legen; **2.** v/i.: ~ for Rechenschaft über et. (acc.) ablegen; (sich) erklären; be much ~ed of hoch geachtet sein; v/t. ansehen als; ~able □ [~təbl] verantwortlich; erklärlich; ~ant [~ənt] Buchhalter m; chartered ~, Am. certified public ~ vereidigter Bücherrevisor; ~ing [~tiŋ] Buchführung f.

accredit [ə'kredit] beglaubigen.

accrue [ə'kru:] erwachsen (from aus).

accumulat|e [ə'kju:mjuleit] (sich) (an)häufen; ansammeln; ~ion [əkju:mju'leiʃən] Anhäufung f.

accura|cy ['ækjurəsi] Genauigkeit f; ~te □ [~rit] genau; richtig.

accurs|ed [ə'kə:sid], ~t [~st] verflucht, verwünscht.

accus|ation [ækju(:)'zeiʃən] Anklage f, Beschuldigung f; ~ative gr. [ə'kju:zətiv] a. ~ case Akkusativ m; ~e [ə'kju:z] anklagen, beschuldigen; ~er [~zə] Kläger(in).

accustom [ə'kʌstəm] gewöhnen (to an acc.); ~ed gewohnt, üblich; gewöhnt (to an acc., zu inf.).

ace [eis] As n (a. fig.); ~ in the hole Am. F fig. Trumpf m in Reserve; within an ~ um ein Haar.

acerbity [ə'sə:biti] Herbheit f.

acet|ic [ə'si:tik] essigsauer; ~ify [ə'setifai] säuern.

ache [eik] **1.** schmerzen; sich sehnen (for nach; to do zu tun); **2.** anhaltende Schmerzen m/pl.

achieve [ə'tʃiːv] ausführen; erreichen; **~ment** [~vmənt] Ausführung f; Leistung f.

acid ['æsid] 1. sauer; 2. Säure f; **~ity** [ə'siditi] Säure f.

acknowledg|e [ək'nɔlidʒ] anerkennen; zugeben; ✝ bestätigen; **~(e)ment** [~dʒmənt] Anerkennung f; Bestätigung f; Eingeständnis n.

acme ['ækmi] Gipfel m; 🞉 Krisis f.

acorn ['eikɔːn] Eichel f.

acoustics [ə'kuːstiks] pl. Akustik f.

acquaint [ə'kweint] bekannt machen; j-m mitteilen; be **~ed** with kennen; **~ance** [~təns] Bekanntschaft f; Bekannte(r m) f.

acquiesce [ækwi'es] (in) hinnehmen (acc.); einwilligen (in acc.).

acquire [ə'kwaiə] erwerben; **~ment** [~əmənt] Fertigkeit f.

acquisition [ækwi'ziʃən] Erwerbung f; Errungenschaft f.

acquit [ə'kwit] freisprechen; **~** o.s. of Pflicht erfüllen; **~** o.s. well s-e Sache gut machen; **~tal** [~tl] Freisprechung f, Freispruch m; **~tance** [~təns] Tilgung f.

acre ['eikə] Morgen m (4047 qm).

acrid ['ækrid] scharf, beißend.

across [ə'krɔs] 1. adv. hin-, herüber; (quer) durch; drüben; überkreuz; 2. prp. (quer) über (acc.); jenseits (gen.), über (dat.); come **~**, run **~** stoßen auf (acc.).

act [ækt] 1. v/i. handeln; sich benehmen; wirken; funktionieren; thea. spielen; v/t. thea. spielen; 2. Handlung f, Tat f; thea. Akt m; Gesetz n; Beschluß m; Urkunde f, Vertrag m; **~ing** [~tiŋ] 1. Handeln n; thea. Spiel(en) n; 2. tätig, amtierend.

action ['ækʃən] Handlung f (a. thea.); Tätigkeit f; Tat f; Wirkung f; Klage f, Prozeß m; Gang m (Pferd etc.); Gefecht n; Mechanismus m; take **~** Schritte unternehmen.

activ|e □ ['æktiv] aktiv; tätig; rührig, wirksam; ✝ lebhaft; **~ity** [æk'tiviti] Tätigkeit f; Betriebsamkeit f; bsd. ✝ Lebhaftigkeit f.

act|or ['æktə] Schauspieler m; **~ress** ['æktris] Schauspielerin f.

actual ['æktjuəl] wirklich, tatsächlich, eigentlich.

actuate ['æktjueit] in Gang bringen.

acute □ [ə'kjuːt] spitz; scharf(sinnig); brennend (Frage); 🞉 akut.

ad F [æd] = advertisement.

adamant fig. ['ædəmənt] unerbittlich.

adapt [ə'dæpt] anpassen (to, for dat.); Text bearbeiten (from nach); zurechtmachen; **~ation** [ædæp'teiʃən] Anpassung f, Bearbeitung f.

add [æd] v/t. hinzufügen; addieren; v/i.: **~** to vermehren; hinzukommen zu.

addict ['ædikt] Süchtige(r m) f; **~ed** [ə'diktid] ergeben (to dat.); **~** to e-m Laster verfallen.

addition [ə'diʃən] Hinzufügen n; Zusatz m; An-, Ausbau m; Addition f; in **~** außerdem; in **~** to außer, zu; **~al** [[~nl] zusätzlich.

address [ə'dres] 1. Worte richten (to an acc.); sprechen zu; 2. Adresse f; Ansprache f; Anstand m, Manieren f/pl.; pay one's **~es** to a lady e-r Dame den Hof machen; **~ee** [ædre'siː] Adressat m, Empfänger m.

adept ['ædept] 1. erfahren; geschickt; 2. Eingeweihte(r m) f; Kenner m.

adequa|cy ['ædikwəsi] Angemessenheit f; **~te** □ [~kwit] angemessen.

adhere [əd'hiə] (to) haften (an dat.); fig. festhalten (an dat.); **~nce** [~rəns] Anhaften n, Festhalten n; **~nt** [~nt] Anhänger(in).

adhesion [əd'hiːʒən] = adherence; fig. Einwilligung f.

adhesive [əd'hiːsiv] 1. □ klebend; **~** plaster, **~** tape Heftpflaster n; 2. Klebstoff m.

adjacent [[ə'dʒeisənt] (to) anliegend (dat.); anstoßend (an acc.); benachbart

adjective gr. ['ædʒiktiv] Adjektiv n, Eigenschaftswort n.

adjoin [ə'dʒɔin] angrenzen an (acc.).

adjourn [ə'dʒəːn] aufschieben; (v/i. sich) vertagen; **~ment** [~mənt] Aufschub m; Vertagung f.

adjudge [ə'dʒʌdʒ] zuerkennen; verurteilen.

adjust [ə'dʒʌst] in Ordnung bringen; anpassen; Streit schlichten; Mechanismus u. fig. einstellen (to auf acc.); **~ment** [~tmənt] Anordnung f; Einstellung f; Schlichtung f.

administ|er [əd'ministə] verwalten; spenden; ✝ verabfolgen; **~** justice Recht sprechen; **~ration** [ədminis'treiʃən] Verwaltung f; Regierung f; bsd. Am. Amtsperiode f e-s Präsidenten; **~rative** [əd'ministrətiv] Verwaltungs...; **~rator** [~reitə] Verwalter m.

admir|able [['ædmərəbl] bewundernswert; (vor)trefflich; **~ation** [ædmə'reiʃən] Bewunderung f; **~e** [əd'maiə] bewundern; verehren.

admiss|ible [əd'misəbl] zulässig; **~ion** [~iʃən] Zulassung f; F Eintritt(sgeld n) m; Eingeständnis n.

admit [əd'mit] v/t. (her)einlassen (to, into in acc.), eintreten lassen; zulassen (to zu); zugeben; **~tance** [~təns] Einlaß m, Zutritt m.

admixture [əd'mikstʃə] Beimischung f, Zusatz m.

admon|ish [əd'mɔniʃ] ermahnen; warnen (of, against vor dat.); **~ition** [ædmə'niʃən] Ermahnung f; Warnung f.

ado [ə'du:] Getue *n*; Lärm *m*; Mühe *f*.

adolescen|ce [ædou'lesns] Adoleszenz *f*, Reifezeit *f*; ~t [~nt] 1. jugendlich, heranwachsend; 2. Jugendliche(r *m*) *f*.

adopt [ə'dɔpt] adoptieren; sich aneignen; ~ion [~pʃən] Annahme *f*.

ador|able □ [ə'dɔ:rəbl] verehrungswürdig; ~ation [ædɔ:'reiʃən] Anbetung *f*; ~e [ə'dɔ:] anbeten.

adorn [ə'dɔ:n] schmücken, zieren; ~ment [~mənt] Schmuck *m*.

adroit □ [ə'drɔit] gewandt.

adult ['ædʌlt] 1. erwachsen; 2. Erwachsene(r *m*) *f*.

adulter|ate [ə'dʌltəreit] (ver)fälschen; ~er [~rə] Ehebrecher *m*; ~ess [~ris] Ehebrecherin *f*; ~ous □ [~rəs] ehebrecherisch; ~y [~ri] Ehebruch *m*.

advance [əd'vɑ:ns] 1. *v/i.* vorrücken, vorgehen; steigen; Fortschritte machen; *v/t.* vorrücken; vorbringen; vorausbezahlen; vorschießen; (be)fördern; *Preis* erhöhen; beschleunigen; 2. Vorrücken *n*; Fortschritt *m*; Angebot *n*; Vorschuß *m*; Erhöhung *f*; in ~ im voraus; ~d vor-, fortgeschritten; ~ in years im vorgerücktem Alter; ~ment [~smənt] Förderung *f*; Fortschritt *m*.

advantage [əd'vɑ:ntidʒ] Vorteil *m*; Überlegenheit *f*; Gewinn *m*; take ~ of ausnutzen; ~ous □ [ædvən'teidʒəs] vorteilhaft.

adventur|e [əd'ventʃə] Abenteuer *n*, Wagnis *n*; Spekulation *f*; ~er [~ərə] Abenteurer *m*; Spekulant *m*; ~ous □ [~rəs] abenteuerlich; wagemutig.

adverb *gr.* ['ædvə:b] Adverb *n*, Umstandswort *n*.

advers|ary ['ædvəsəri] Gegner *m*, Feind *m*; ~e □ ['ædvə:s] widrig; feindlich; ungünstig, nachteilig (to für); ~ity [əd'və:siti] Unglück *n*.

advertis|e ['ædvətaiz] ankündigen; inserieren; Reklame machen (für); ~ement [əd'və:tismənt] Ankündigung *f*, Inserat *n*; Reklame *f*; ~ing ['ædvətaiziŋ] Reklame *f*, Werbung *f*; ~ agency Annoncenbüro *n*; ~ designer Reklamezeichner *m*; ~ film Reklamefilm *m*; ~ screen ~ Filmreklame *f*.

advice [əd'vais] Rat(schlag) *m*; (*mst pl.*) Nachricht *f*, Meldung *f*; take medical ~ e-n Arzt zu Rate ziehen.

advis|able □ [əd'vaizəbl] ratsam; ~e [əd'vaiz] *v/t.* j-n beraten; j-m raten; † benachrichtigen, avisieren; *v/i.* (sich) beraten; ~er [~zə] Ratgeber(in).

advocate 1. ['ædvəkit] Anwalt *m*; Fürsprecher *m*; 2. [~keit] verteidigen, befürworten.

aerial ['ɛəriəl] 1. □ luftig; Luft...;

~ view Luftaufnahme *f*; 2. *Radio, Fernsehen*: Antenne *f*.

aero|... ['ɛərou] Luft...; ~cab *Am.* F ['ɛərəkæb] Lufttaxi *n* (*Hubschrauber als Zubringer*); ~drome [~ədroum] Flugplatz *m*; ~naut [~ənɔ:t] Luftschiffer *m*; ~nautics [ɛərə'nɔ:tiks] *pl.* Luftfahrt *f*; ~plane ['ɛərəplein] Flugzeug *n*; ~stat ['ɛəroustæt] Luftballon *m*.

aesthetic [i:s'θetik] ästhetisch; ~s *sg.* Ästhetik *f*.

afar [ə'fɑ:] fern, weit (weg).

affable □ ['æfəbl] leutselig.

affair [ə'fɛə] Geschäft *n*; Angelegenheit *f*; Sache *f*; F Ding *n*; Liebschaft *f*.

affect [ə'fekt] (ein- *od.* sich aus-) wirken auf (*acc.*); (be)rühren; *Gesundheit* angreifen; gern mögen; vortäuschen, nachahmen; ~ation [æfek'teiʃən] Vorliebe *f*; Ziererei *f*; Verstellung *f*; ~ed □ geziert; befallen (*von Krankheit*); angegriffen (*Augen etc.*); geziert, affektiert; ~ion [~kʃən] Gemütszustand *m*; (Zu)Neigung *f*; Erkrankung *f*; ~ionate □ [~ʃnit] liebevoll.

affidavit [æfi'deivit] *schriftliche* beeidigte Erklärung.

affiliate [ə'filieit] *als Mitglied* aufnehmen; angliedern; ~d company Tochtergesellschaft *f*.

affinity [ə'finiti] *fig.* (geistige) Verwandtschaft; 🕭 Affinität *f*.

affirm [ə'fə:m] bejahen; behaupten; bestätigen; ~ation [æfə:'meiʃən] Behauptung *f*; Bestätigung *f*; ~ative [ə'fə:mətiv] 1. □ bejahend; 2.: answer in the ~ bejahen.

affix [ə'fiks] (to) anheften (an *acc.*); befestigen (an *dat.*); *Siegel* aufdrücken (*dat.*); bei-, zufügen (*dat.*).

afflict [ə'flikt] betrüben; plagen; ~ion [~kʃən] Betrübnis *f*; Leiden *n*.

affluen|ce ['æfluəns] Überfluß *m*; Wohlstand *m*; ~t [~nt] 1. □ reich (-lich); ~ society Wohlstandsgesellschaft *f*; 2. Nebenfluß *m*.

afford [ə'fɔ:d] liefern; erschwingen; I can ~ it ich kann es mir leisten.

affront [ə'frʌnt] 1. beleidigen; trotzen (*dat.*); 2. Beleidigung *f*.

afield [ə'fi:ld] im Felde; (weit) weg.

afloat [ə'flout] 🕭 *u. fig.* flott; schwimmend; auf See; umlaufend; set ~ flottmachen; *fig.* in Umlauf setzen.

afraid [ə'freid] bange; be ~ of sich fürchten *od.* Angst haben vor (*dat.*).

afresh [ə'freʃ] von neuem.

African ['æfrikən] 1. afrikanisch; 2. Afrikaner(in); *Am. a.* Neger(in).

after ['ɑ:ftə] 1. *adv.* hinterher; nachher; 2. *prp.* nach; hinter (... her); ~ all schließlich (doch); 3. *cj.* nachdem; 4. *adj.* später; Nach...; ~crop Nachernte *f*; ~glow Abendrot *n*; ~math [~əmæθ]

Nachwirkung(en pl.) f, Folgen f/pl.; **~noon** [~ə'nu:n] Nachmittag m; **~season** Nachsaison f; **~taste** Nachgeschmack m; **~thought** nachträglicher Einfall; **~wards** [~əwədz] nachher; später.

again [ə'gen] wieder(um); ferner; dagegen; **~** and **~**, time and **~** immer wieder; as much **~** noch einmal soviel.

against [ə'genst] gegen; räumlich: gegen; an, vor (dat. od. acc.); fig. in Erwartung (gen.), für; as **~** verglichen mit.

age [eidʒ] 1. (Lebens)Alter n; Zeit (-alter n) f; Menschenalter n; (old) **~** Greisenalter n; of **~** mündig; over **~** zu alt; under **~** unmündig; wait for **~**s F e-e Ewigkeit warten; 2. alt werden od. machen; **~d** ['eidʒid] alt; [eidʒd]: **~** twenty 20 Jahre alt.

agency ['eidʒənsi] Tätigkeit f; Vermittlung f; Agentur f, Büro n.

agenda [ə'dʒendə] Tagesordnung f.

agent ['eidʒənt] Handelnde(r m) f; Agent m; wirkende Kraft, Agens n.

age-worn ['eidʒwɔːn] altersschwach.

agglomerate [ə'glɔməreit] (sich) zs.-ballen; (sich) (an)häufen.

agglutinate [ə'gluːtineit] zs.-, an-, verkleben.

aggrandize [ə'grændaiz] vergrößern; erhöhen.

aggravate ['ægrəveit] erschweren; verschlimmern; F ärgern.

aggregate 1. F ['ægrigeit] (sich) anhäufen; vereinigen (to mit); sich belaufen auf (acc.); 2. □ [~git] gehäuft; gesamt; 3. [~] Anhäufung f; Aggregat n.

aggress|ion [ə'greʃən] Angriff m; **~or** [~esə] Angreifer m.

aggrieve [ə'griːv] kränken; schädigen. [setzt.]

aghast [ə'gɑːst] entgeistert, ent-)

agil|e ['ædʒail] flink, behend; **~ity** [ə'dʒiliti] Behendigkeit f.

agitat|e ['ædʒiteit] v/t. bewegen, schütteln; fig. erregen; erörtern; v/i. agitieren; **~ion** [ædʒi'teiʃən] Bewegung f, Erschütterung f; Aufregung f; Agitation f; **~or** ['ædʒiteitə] Agitator m, Aufwiegler m.

ago [ə'gou]: a year **~** vor e-m Jahr.

agonize ['ægənaiz] (sich) quälen.

agony ['ægəni] Qual f, Pein f; Ringen n; Todeskampf m.

agree [ə'griː] v/i. übereinstimmen; sich vertragen; einig werden (on, upon über acc.); übereinkommen, **~** to zustimmen (dat.); einverstanden sein mit; **~able** [ə'griəbl] (to) angenehm (für); übereinstimmend (mit); **~ment** [ə'griːmənt] Übereinstimmung f; Vereinbarung f, Abkommen n; Vertrag m.

agricultur|al [ægri'kʌltʃərəl] land-

wirtschaftlich; **~e** ['ægrikʌltʃə] Landwirtschaft f; **~ist** [ægri'kʌltərist] Landwirt m.

aground ⚓ [ə'graund] gestrandet; run **~** stranden, auflaufen.

ague ♣ ['eigjuː] Wechselfieber n; Schüttelfrost m.

ahead [ə'hed] vorwärts; voraus; vorn; straight **~** geradeaus.

aid [eid] 1. helfen (dat.; in bei et.); fördern; 2. Hilfe f, Unterstützung f.

ail [eil] v/i. kränkeln; v/t. schmerzen, weh(e) tun (dat.); what **~**s him? was fehlt ihm?; **~ing** ['eilin] leidend; **~ment** ['eilmənt] Leiden n.

aim [eim] 1. v/i. zielen (at auf acc.); **~** at fig. streben nach; **~** to do bsd. Am. beabsichtigen od. versuchen zu tun, tun wollen; v/t. **~** at Waffe etc. richten auf gegen (acc.); 2. Ziel n; Absicht f; **~less** □ ['eimlis] ziellos.

air[1] [ɛə] 1. Luft f; Luftzug m; by **~** auf dem Luftwege; in the open **~** im Freien; be in the **~** fig. in der Luft liegen; ungewiß sein; on the **~** im Rundfunk (senden); be on (off) the **~** in (außer) Betrieb sein (Sender); put on the **~** im Rundfunk senden; 2. (aus)lüften; fig. an die Öffentlichkeit bringen; erörtern.

air[2] [~] Miene f; Aussehen n; give o.s. **~**s vornehm tun.

air[3] ♪ [~] Arie f, Weise f, Melodie f.

air|-base ⚔ ['ɛəbeis] Luftstützpunkt m; **~bed** Luftmatratze f; **~borne** ⚔ in der Luft (Flugzeug); ⚔ Luftlande...; **~brake** Druckluftbremse f; **~conditioned** mit Klimaanlage; **~craft** Flugzeug (-e pl.) n; **~field** ⚔ Flugplatz m; **~force** ⚔ Luftwaffe f; **~hostess** ⚔ Stewardess f; **~jacket** Schwimmweste f; **~lift** Luftbrücke f; **~liner** ⚔ Verkehrsflugzeug n; **~mail** Luftpost f; **~man** ['ɛəmən] Flieger m; **~plane** Am. Flugzeug n; **~pocket** ⚔ Luftloch n; **~port** ⚔ Flughafen m; **~raid** ⚔ Luftangriff m; **~raid precautions** pl. Luftschutz m; **~raid shelter** Luftschutzraum m; **~route** ⚔ Luftweg m; **~tight** luftdicht; **~** case sl. todsicherer Fall; **~tube** Luftschlauch m; **~umbrella** ⚔ Luftsicherung f; **~way** ⚔ Luftverkehrslinie f.

airy □ ['ɛəri] luftig; leicht(fertig).

aisle ⚛ [ail] Seitenschiff n; Gang m.

ajar [ə'dʒɑː] halb offen, angelehnt.

akin [ə'kin] verwandt (to mit).

alacrity [ə'lækriti] Munterkeit f; Bereitwilligkeit f, Eifer m.

alarm [ə'lɑːm] 1. Alarm(zeichen n) m; Angst f; 2. alarmieren; beunruhigen; **~clock** Wecker m.

albuminous [æl'bjuːminəs] eiweißartig, -haltig.

alcohol ['ælkəhɔl] Alkohol m; **~ic**

[ælkə'hɔlik] alkoholisch; ~ism ['æl-kəhɔlizəm] Alkoholvergiftung f.

alcove ['ælkouv] Nische f; Laube f.

alderman ['ɔːldəmən] Stadtrat m.

ale [eil] Ale n (Art engl. Bier).

alert [ə'ləːt] 1. □ wachsam; munter; 2. Alarm(bereitschaft f) m; on the ~ auf der Hut; in Alarmbereitschaft.

alibi ['ælibai] Alibi n; Am. F Entschuldigung f; Ausrede f.

alien ['eiljən] 1. fremd, ausländisch; 2. Ausländer(in); ~able [~nəbl] veräußerlich; ~ate [~neit] veräußern; fig. entfremden (from dat.); ~ist [~nist] Irrenarzt m, Psychiater m.

alight [ə'lait] 1. brennend; erhellt; 2. ab~, aussteigen; ✗ niedergehen, landen; sich niederlassen.

align [ə'lain] (sich) ausrichten (with nach); surv. abstecken; ~ o.s. with sich anschließen an (acc.).

alike [ə'laik] 1. adj. gleich, ähnlich; 2. adv. gleich; ebenso.

aliment ['elimənt] Nahrung f; ~ary [æli'mentəri] nahrhaft; ~ canal Verdauungskanal m.

alimony ♂♀ ['æliməni] Unterhalt m.

alive [ə'laiv] lebendig; in Kraft, gültig; empfänglich (to für); lebhaft; belebt (with von).

all [ɔːl] 1. adj. all; ganz; jede(r, -s); for ~ that dessenungeachtet, trotzdem; 2. pron. alles; alle pl.; at ~ gar, überhaupt; not at ~ durchaus nicht; for ~ (that) I care meinetwegen; for ~ I know soviel ich weiß; 3. adv. ganz, völlig; ~ at once auf einmal; ~ the better desto besser; ~ but beinahe, fast; ~ in Am. F fertig, ganz erledigt; ~ right (alles) in Ordnung.

all-American [ɔːlə'merikən] rein amerikanisch; die ganzen USA vertretend.

allay [ə'lei] beruhigen; lindern.

alleg|ation [æle'geiʃən] unerwiesene Behauptung f; ~e [ə'ledʒ] behaupten; ~ed angeblich.

allegiance [ə'liːdʒəns] Lehnspflicht f; (Untertanen)Treue f.

alleviate [ə'liːvieit] erleichtern, lindern.

alley ['æli] Allee f; Gäßchen n; Gang m; bsd. Am. schmale Zufahrtsstraße.

alliance [ə'laiəns] Bündnis n.

allocat|e ['æləkeit] zuteilen, anweisen; ~ion [ælə'keiʃən] Zuteilung f.

allot [ə'lɔt] zuweisen; ~ment [~t-mənt] Zuteilung f; Los n; Parzelle f.

allow [ə'lau] erlauben, bewilligen, gewähren, zugeben; ab~, anrechnen; vergüten; ~ for berücksichtigen; ~able [~'lauəbl] erlaubt, zulässig; ~ance [~əns] Erlaubnis f; Bewilligung f; Taschengeld n, Zuschuß m; Vergütung f; Nachsicht f;

make ~ for s.th. et. in Betracht ziehen.

alloy 1. ['ælɔi] Legierung f; 2. [ə'lɔi] legieren; fig. verunedeln.

all-red ['ɔːl'red] rein britisch.

all-round ['ɔːl'raund] zu allem brauchbar; vielseitig.

all-star Am. ['ɔːl'staː] Sport u. thea.: aus den besten (Schau)Spielern bestehend.

allude [ə'luːd] anspielen (to auf acc.).

allure [ə'ljuə] (an~, ver)locken; ~ment [~əmənt] Verlockung f.

allusion [ə'luːʒən] Anspielung f.

ally 1. [ə'lai] (sich) vereinigen, verbünden (to, with mit); 2. ['ælai] Verbündete(r m) f, Bundesgenosse m; the Allies pl. die Alliierten pl.

almanac ['ɔːlmənæk] Almanach m.

almighty [ɔːl'maiti] 1. □ allmächtig; 2 ♀ Allmächtige(r) m.

almond ♀ ['aːmənd] Mandel f.

almoner ['aːmənə] Krankenhausfürsorger(in).

almost ['ɔːlmoust] fast, beinahe.

alms [aːmz] sg. u. pl. Almosen n; ~house ['aːmzhaus] Armenhaus n.

aloft [ə'lɔft] (hoch) (dr)oben.

alone [ə'loun] allein; let od. leave ~ in Ruhe od. bleiben lassen; let ~ ... abgesehen von ...

along [ə'lɔŋ] 1. adv. weiter, vorwärts, her; mit, bei (sich); all ~ die ganze Zeit; ~ with zs. mit; get ~ with you! F scher dich weg! 2. prp. entlang, längs; ~side [~ŋ'said] Seite an Seite; neben.

aloof [ə'luːf] fern; weitab; stand ~ abseits stehen.

aloud [ə'laud] laut; hörbar.

alp [ælp] Alp(e) f; 2s pl. Alpen pl.

already [ɔːl'redi] bereits, schon.

also ['ɔːlsou] auch; ferner.

altar ['ɔːltə] Altar m.

alter ['ɔːltə] (sich) (ver)ändern; ab~ umändern; ~ation [~ɔːltə'reiʃən] Änderung f (to an dat.).

alternat|e 1. ['ɔːltəːneit] abwechseln (lassen); alternating current ∉ Wechselstrom m; 2. □ [ɔːl'təːnit] abwechselnd; 3. [~] Am. Stellvertreter m; ~ion [ɔːltəː'neiʃən] Abwechslung f; Wechsel m; ~ive [ɔːl'təːnə-tiv] 1. □ nur eine Wahl zwischen zwei Möglichkeiten lassend; 2. Alternative f; Wahl f; Möglichkeit f.

although [ɔːl'ðou] obgleich.

altitude ['æltitjuːd] Höhe f.

altogether [ɔːltə'geðə] im ganzen (genommen), alles in allem; gänzlich.

aluminium [ælju'minjəm] Aluminium n.

aluminum Am. [ə'luːminəm] = aluminium.

always ['ɔːlwəz] immer, stets.

am [æm; im Satz əm] 1. sg. pres. von be.

amalgamate [ə'mælgɔmeit] amalgamieren; (sich) verschmelzen.

amass [ə'mæs] (an-, auf)häufen.

amateur ['æmətə:] Amateur m; Liebhaber m; Dilettant m.

amaz|e [ə'meiz] in Staunen setzen, verblüffen; ~ement [ˌzmənt] Staunen n, Verblüffung f; ~ing □ [ˌziŋ] erstaunlich, verblüffend.

ambassador [æm'bæsədə] Botschafter m, Gesandte(r) m.

amber ['æmbə] Bernstein m.

ambigu|ity [æmbi'gju(:)iti] Zwei-, Vieldeutigkeit f; ~ous □ [ˌ.ʃəs] 'bigjuəs] zwei-, vieldeutig; doppelsinnig.

ambitio|n [æm'biʃən] Ehrgeiz m; Streben n (of nach); ~us □ [ˌʃəs] ehrgeizig; begierig (of, for nach).

amble ['æmbl] 1. Paßgang m; 2. im Paßgang gehen od. reiten; schlendern.

ambulance ['æmbjuləns] Feldlazarett n; Krankenwagen m; ~ station Sanitätswache f, Unfallstation f.

ambus|cade [æmbəs'keid], ~h ['æmbuʃ] 1. Hinterhalt m; be od. lie in ambush for s.o. j-m auflauern; 2. auflauern (dat.); überfallen.

ameliorate [ə'mi:ljəreit] v/t. verbessern; v/i. besser werden.

amend [ə'mend] (sich) (ver)bessern; berichtigen; Gesetz (ab)ändern; ~ment [ˌdmənt] Besserung f; ₤ Berichtigung f; parl. Änderungsantrag m; Am. Zusatzartikel m zur Verfassung der USA; ~s sg. (Schaden)Ersatz m.

amenity [ə'mi:niti] Annehmlichkeit f; Anmut f; amenities pl. angenehmes Wesen.

American [ə'merikən] 1. amerikanisch; ~ cloth Wachstuch n; ~ plan Hotelzimmervermietung mit voller Verpflegung; 2. Amerikaner(in); ~ism [ˌnizəm] Amerikanismus m; ~ize [ˌnaiz] (sich) amerikanisieren.

amiable □ ['eimjəbl] liebenswürdig, freundlich.

amicable □ ['æmikəbl] freundschaftlich; gütlich.

amid(st) [ə'mid(st)] inmitten (gen.); (mitten) unter; mitten in (dat.).

amiss [ə'mis] verkehrt; übel; ungelegen; take ~ übelnehmen.

amity ['æmiti] Freundschaft f.

ammonia [ə'mounjə] Ammoniak n.

ammunition [æmju'niʃən] Munition f.

amnesty ['æmnesti] 1. Amnestie f (Straferlaß); 2. begnadigen.

among(st) [ə'mʌŋ(st)] (mitten) unter, zwischen. [in acc.).]

amorous □ ['æmərəs] verliebt (of)

amount [ə'maunt] 1. (to) sich belaufen (auf acc.); hinauslaufen (auf acc.); 2. Betrag m, (Gesamt-)

Summe f; Menge f; Bedeutung f, Wert m.

amour [ə'muə] Liebschaft f; ~-propre Selbstachtung f; Eitelkeit f.

ample □ ['æmpl] weit, groß; geräumig; reichlich.

ampli|fication [æmplifi'keiʃən] Erweiterung f; rhet. weitere Ausführung f; phys. Verstärkung f; ~fier ['æmplifaiə] Radio: Verstärker m; ~fy [ˌfai] erweitern; verstärken; weiter ausführen; ~tude [ˌitju:d] Umfang m, Weite f, Fülle f.

amputate ['æmpjuteit] amputieren.

amuse [ə'mju:z] amüsieren; unterhalten; belustigen; ~ment [ˌzmənt] Unterhaltung f; Zeitvertreib m.

an [æn, ən] Artikel: ein(e).

an(a)emia [ə'ni:mjə] Blutarmut f.

an(a)esthetic [ænis'θetik] 1. betäubend, Narkose...; 2. Betäubungsmittel n.

analog|ous [ə'næləgəs] analog, ähnlich; ~y [ˌədʒi] Ähnlichkeit f, Analogie f.

analys|e ['ænəlaiz] analysieren; zerlegen; ~is [ə'næləsis] Analyse f.

anarchy ['ænəki] Anarchie f, Gesetzlosigkeit f; Zügellosigkeit f.

anatom|ize [ə'nætəmaiz] zergliedern; ~y [ˌmi] Anatomie f; Zergliederung f, Analyse f.

ancest|or ['ænsistə] Vorfahr m, Ahn m; ~ral [æn'sestrəl] angestammt; ~ress ['ænsistris] Ahne f; ~ry [ˌri] Abstammung f; Ahnen m/pl.

anchor ['æŋkə] 1. Anker m; at ~ vor Anker; 2. (ver)ankern; ~age [ˌəridʒ] Ankerplatz m.

anchovy ['æntʃəvi] Sardelle f.

ancient ['einʃənt] 1. alt, antik; uralt; 2. the ~s pl. hist. die Alten, die antiken Klassiker.

and [ænd, ənd] und.

anew [ə'nju:] von neuem.

angel ['eindʒəl] Engel m; ~ic(al □) [æn'dʒelik(əl)] engelgleich.

anger ['æŋgə] 1. Zorn m, Ärger m (at über acc.); 2. erzürnen, ärgern.

angina ⚕ [æn'dʒainə] Angina f, Halsentzündung f.

angle ['æŋgl] 1. Winkel m; fig. Standpunkt m; 2. angeln (for nach).

Anglican ['æŋglikən] 1. anglikanisch; Am. a. englisch; 2. Anglikaner(in).

Anglo-Saxon ['æŋglou'sæksən] 1. Angelsachse m; 2. angelsächsisch.

angry ['æŋgri] zornig, böse (a. ⚕) (with s.o., at s.th. über, auf acc.).

anguish ['æŋgwiʃ] Pein f, (Seelen-) Qual f, Schmerz m.

angular □ ['æŋgjulə] winkelig; Winkel...; fig. eckig.

animadver|sion [ænimæd'və:ʃən]

Verweis *m*, Tadel *m*; ~t [~ɔːt] tadeln, kritisieren.

animal ['æniməl] 1. Tier *n*; 2. tierisch.

animat|e ['ænimeit] beleben; beseelen; aufmuntern; ~ion [æni'meiʃən] Leben *n* (und Treiben *n*), Lebhaftigkeit *f*, Munterkeit *f*.

animosity [æni'mɔsiti] Feindseligkeit *f*.

ankle ['æŋkl] Fußknöchel *m*.

annals ['ænlz] *pl.* Jahrbücher *n/pl.*

annex 1. [ə'neks] anhängen; annektieren; 2. ['æneks] Anhang *m*; Anbau *m*; ~ation [ænek'seiʃən] Annexion *f*, Aneignung *f*; Einverleibung *f*.

annihilate [ə'naiəleit] vernichten; = *annul.*

anniversary [æni'vəːsəri] Jahrestag *m*; Jahresfeier *f.*

annotat|e ['ænouteit] mit Anmerkungen versehen; kommentieren; ~ion [ænou'teiʃən] Kommentieren *n*; Anmerkung *f.*

announce [ə'nauns] ankündigen; ansagen; ~ment [~smənt] Ankündigung *f*; Ansage *f*; *Radio:* Durchsage *f*; Anzeige *f*; ~r [~sə] *Radio:* Ansager *m.*

annoy [ə'nɔi] ärgern; belästigen; ~ance [ə'nɔiəns] Störung *f*; Plage *f*; Ärgernis *n.*

annual ['ænjuəl] 1. □ jährlich; Jahres...; 2. einjährige Pflanze; Jahrbuch *n.* [Rente *f.*]

annuity [ə'nju(ː)iti] (Jahres-)]

annul [ə'nʌl] für ungültig erklären, annullieren; ~ment [~lmənt] Aufhebung *f.*

anodyne ['ænoudain] 1. schmerzstillend; 2. schmerzstillendes Mittel.

anoint [ə'nɔint] salben.

anomalous □ [ə'nɔmələs] anomal, unregelmäßig, regelwidrig.

anonymous □ [ə'nɔniməs] anonym, ungenannt.

another [ə'nʌðə] ein anderer; ein zweiter; noch ein.

answer ['ɑːnsə] 1. *v/t. et.* beantworten; *j-m* antworten; entsprechen (*dat.*); *Zweck* erfüllen; *dem Steuer* gehorchen; *e-r Vorladung* Folge leisten; ~ *the bell od. door* (die Haustür) aufmachen; *v/i.* antworten (*to s.o.* j-m; *to a question* auf e-e Frage); entsprechen (*to dat.*); Erfolg haben; sich lohnen; ~ *for* einstehen für; bürgen für; 2. Antwort *f* (*to* auf *acc.*); ~able □ [~ərəbl] verantwortlich.

ant [ænt] Ameise *f.*

antagonis|m [æn'tægənizm] Widerstreit *m*; Widerstand *m*; Feindschaft *f*; ~t [~ist] Gegner(in).

antagonize [æn'tægənaiz] ankämpfen gegen; sich *j-n* zum Feind machen.

antecedent [ænti'siːdənt] 1. □ vor-

hergehend; früher (*to* als); 2. Vorhergehende(s) *n.*

anterior [æn'tiəriə] vorhergehend; früher (*to* als); vorder.

ante-room ['æntirum] Vorzimmer *n.*

anthem ['ænθəm] Hymne *f.*

anti|... ['ænti] Gegen...; gegen ... eingestellt *od.* wirkend; ~aircraft Fliegerabwehr...; ~biotic [~ibai-'ɔtik] Antibiotikum *n.*

antic ['æntik] Posse *f*; ~s *pl.* Mätzchen *n/pl.*; (tolle) Sprünge *m/pl.*

anticipat|e [æn'tisipeit] vorwegnehmen; zuvorkommen (*dat.*); voraussehen, ahnen; erwarten; ~ion [æntisi'peiʃən] Vorwegnahme *f*; Zuvorkommen *n*; Voraussicht *f*; Erwartung *f*; *in* ~ im voraus.

antidote ['æntidout] Gegengift *n.*

antipathy [æn'tipəθi] Abneigung *f.*

antiqua|ry ['æntikwəri] Altertumsforscher *m*; Antiquitätensammler *m*, -händler *m*; ~ted [~kweitid] veraltet, überlebt.

antiqu|e [æn'tiːk] 1. □ antik, alt (-modisch); 2. alter Kunstgegenstand; ~ity [æn'tikwiti] Altertum *n*; Vorzeit *f.*

antiseptic [ænti'septik] 1. antiseptisch; 2. antiseptisches Mittel.

antlers ['æntləz] *pl.* Geweih *n.*

anvil ['ænvil] Amboß *m.*

anxiety [æŋ'zaiəti] Angst *f*; *fig.* Sorge *f* (*for* um); Beklemmung *f.*

anxious □ ['æŋkʃəs] ängstlich, besorgt (*about* um, wegen); begierig, gespannt (*for* auf *acc.*); bemüht (*for* um).

any ['eni] 1. *pron.* (irgend)einer; einige *pl.*; (irgend)welcher; (irgend) etwas; jeder (beliebige); *not* ~ keiner; 2. *adv.* irgend(wie); ~body (irgend) jemand; jeder; ~how irgendwie; jedenfalls; ~one = *anybody*; ~thing (irgend) etwas, alles; ~ *but* alles andere als; ~way = *anyhow*; ohnehin; ~where irgendwo(hin); überall.

apart [ə'pɑːt] einzeln; getrennt; für sich; beiseite; ~ *from* abgesehen von.

apartheid *pol.* [ə'pɑːtheit] Apartheid *f*, Rassentrennung(spolitik) *f.*

apartment [ə'pɑːtmənt] Zimmer *n*, *Am. a.* Wohnung *f*; ~s *pl.* Wohnung *f*; ~ *house Am.* Mietshaus *n.*

apathetic [æpə'θetik] apathisch, gleichgültig.

ape [eip] 1. Affe *m*; 2. nachäffen.

aperient [ə'piəriənt] Abführmittel*n.*

aperture ['æpətjuə] Öffnung *f.*

apiary ['eipjəri] Bienenhaus *n.*

apiculture ['eipikʌltʃə] Bienenzucht *f.*

apiece [ə'piːs] (für) das Stück; je.

apish □ ['eipiʃ] affig; äffisch.

apolog|etic [əpɔlə'dʒetik] (~ally) verteidigend; rechtfertigend; entschuldigend; ~ize [ə'pɔlədʒaiz] sich entschuldigen (for wegen; to bei); ~y [~dʒi] Entschuldigung f; Rechtfertigung f; F Notbehelf m.

apoplexy ['æpəpleksi] Schlag(anfall) m.

apostate [ə'pɔstit] Abtrünnige(r m)f.

apostle [ə'pɔsl] Apostel m.

apostroph|e [ə'pɔstrəfi] Anrede f; Apostroph m; ~ize [~faiz] anreden, sich wenden an (acc.).

appal [ə'pɔ:l] erschrecken.

apparatus [æpə'reitəs] Apparat m, Vorrichtung f, Gerät n.

apparel [ə'pærəl] 1. Kleidung f; 2. (be)kleiden.

appar|ent □ [ə'pærənt] anscheinend; offenbar; ~ition [æpə'riʃən] Erscheinung f; Gespenst n.

appeal [ə'pi:l] 1. (to) ᵗᵗ appellieren (an acc.); sich berufen (auf e-n Zeugen); sich wenden (an acc.); wirken (auf acc.); Anklang finden (bei); ~ to the country parl. Neuwahlen ausschreiben; 2. ᵗᵗ Revision f, Berufung(sklage) f; ᵗᵗ Rechtsmittel n; fig. Appell m (to an acc.); Wirkung f, Reiz m; ~ for mercy ᵗᵗ Gnadengesuch n; ~ing □ [~liŋ] flehend; ansprechend.

appear [ə'piə] (er)scheinen; sich zeigen; öffentlich auftreten; ~ance [~ərəns] Erscheinen n, Auftreten n; Außere(s) n, Erscheinung f; Anschein m; ~s pl. äußerer Schein; to od. by all ~s allem Anschein nach.

appease [ə'pi:z] beruhigen; beschwichtigen; stillen; mildern; beilegen.

appellant [ə'pelənt] 1. appellierend; 2. Appelant(in), Berufungskläger (-in).

append [ə'pend] anhängen; hinzu-, beifügen; ~age [~didʒ] Anhang m; Anhängsel n; Zubehör n, m; ~icitis [əpendi'saitis] Blinddarmentzündung f; ~ix [ə'pendiks] Anhang m; a. vermiform ~ ⚕ Wurmfortsatz m, Blinddarm m.

appertain [æpə'tein] gehören (to zu).

appetite ['æpitait] (for) Appetit m (auf acc.); fig. Verlangen n (nach).

appetizing ['æpitaiziŋ] appetitanregend.

applaud [ə'plɔ:d] applaudieren, Beifall spenden; loben.

applause [ə'plɔ:z] Applaus m, Beifall m.

apple ['æpl] Apfel m; ~cart Apfelkarren m; upset s.o.'s ~ F j-s Pläne über den Haufen werfen; ~pie gedeckter Apfelkuchen; in ~ order F in schönster Ordnung; ~sauce Apfelmus n; Am. sl. Schmus m, Quatsch m.

appliance [ə'plaiəns] Vorrichtung f; Gerät n; Mittel n.

applica|ble ['æplikəbl] anwendbar

(to auf acc.); ~nt [~ənt] Bittsteller (-in); Bewerber(in) (for um); ~tion [æpli'keiʃən] (to) Auf-, Anlegung f (auf acc.); Anwendung f (of auf acc.); Bedeutung f (für); Gesuch n (for um); Bewerbung f.

apply [ə'plai] v/t. (to) (auf)legen (auf acc.); anwenden (auf acc.); verwenden (für); ~ o.s. to sich widmen (dat.); v/i. (to) passen, sich anwenden lassen (auf acc.); gelten (für); sich wenden (an acc.); (for) sich bewerben (um); nachsuchen (um).

appoint [ə'pɔint] bestimmen; festsetzen; verabreden; ernennen (s.o. governor j-n zum ...); berufen (to auf e-n Posten); well ~ed gut eingerichtet; ~ment [~tmənt] Bestimmung f; Stelldichein n; Verabredung f; Ernennung f, Berufung f; Stelle f; ~s pl. Ausstattung f, Einrichtung f.

apportion [ə'pɔ:ʃən] ver-, zuteilen; ~ment [~mənt] Verteilung f.

apprais|al [ə'preizl] Abschätzung f; ~e [ə'preiz] abschätzen, taxieren.

apprecia|ble [ə'pri:ʃəbl] (ab)schätzbar; merkbar; ~te [~ʃieit] v/t. schätzen; würdigen; dankbar sein für; v/i. im Werte steigen; ~tion [əpri:ʃi'eiʃən] Schätzung f, Würdigung f; Verständnis n (of für); Einsicht f; Dankbarkeit f; Aufwertung f.

apprehen|d [æpri'hend] ergreifen; fassen, begreifen; befürchten; ~sion [~nʃən] Ergreifung f, Festnahme f; Fassungskraft f, Auffassung f; Besorgnis f; ~sive [~nsiv] schnell begreifend (of acc.); ängstlich; besorgt (of, for um, wegen; that daß).

apprentice [ə'prentis] 1. Lehrling m; 2. in die Lehre geben (to dat.); ~ship [~ʃip] Lehrzeit f; Lehre f.

approach [ə'prəutʃ] 1. v/i. näherkommen, sich nähern; v/t. sich nähern (dat.), herangehen od. herantreten an (acc.); 2. Annäherung f; fig. Herangehen n; Methode f; Zutritt m; Auffahrt f.

approbation [æprə'beiʃən] Billigung f, Beifall m.

appropriat|e 1. [ə'prəuprieit] sich aneignen; verwenden; parl. bewilligen; 2. □ [~iit] (to) angemessen (dat.); passend (für); eigen (dat.); ~ion [əproupri'eiʃən] Aneignung f; Verwendung f.

approv|al [ə'pru:vəl] Billigung f, Beifall m; ~e [~u:v] billigen, anerkennen; (~ o.s. sich) erweisen als; ~ed □ bewährt.

approximate 1. [ə'prɔksimeit] sich nähern; 2. □ [~mit] annähernd; ungefähr; nahe.

apricot ['eiprikɔt] Aprikose f.

April ['eiprəl] April m.

apron ['eiprən] Schürze *f*; ~**string** Schürzenband *n*; *be tied to one's wife's (mother's)* ~**s** *fig.* unterm Pantoffel stehen (der Mutter am Rockzipfel hängen).

apt [[æpt] geeignet, passend; begabt; ~ **to** geneigt zu; ~**itude** ['æptitjuːd], ~**ness** ['æptnis] Neigung *f* (to zu); Befähigung *f*.

aquatic [ə'kwætik] Wasserpflanze *f*; ~*s pl* Wassersport *m*.

aque|duct ['ækwidʌkt] Aquädukt *m*, Wasserleitung *f*; ~**ous** □ ['eikwiəs] wässerig

aquiline ['ækwilain] Adler...; gebogen; ~ *nose* Adlernase *f*.

Arab ['ærəb] Araber(in); ~**ic** [~bik] 1. arabisch; 2. Arabisch *n*.

arable ['ærəbl] pflügbar; Acker...

arbit|er ['aːbitə] Schiedsrichter *m*; *fig.* Gebieter *m*; ~**rariness** [~trɛərinis] Willkür *f*; ~**rary** [~trəri] willkürlich; eigenmächtig; ~**rate** [~reit] entscheiden, schlichten; ~**ration** [aːbi'treiʃən] Schiedsspruch *m*; Entscheidung *f*; ~**rator** ['aːbitreitə] Schiedsrichter *m*.

arbo(u)r ['aːbə] Laube *f*.

arc *ast.*, **A** *etc* [aːk] (*𝇇* Licht-) Bogen *m*; ~**ade** [aː'keid] Arkade *f*; Bogen-, Laubengang *m*

arch¹ [aːtʃ] 1. Bogen *m*; Gewölbe *n*; 2. (sich) wölben; überwölben.

arch² [~] erst; schlimmst; Haupt...; Erz...

arch³ [[~] schelmisch.

archaic [aː'keiik] (~*ally*) veraltet.

archangel [aː'keindʒəl] Erzengel *m*.

archbishop ['aːtʃ'biʃəp] Erzbischof *m*.

archer ['aːtʃə] Bogenschütze *m*; ~**y** [~əri] Bogenschießen *n*.

architect ['aːkitekt] Architekt *m*; Urheber(in), Schöpfer(in); ~**onic** [aːkitek'tɔnik] (~*ally*) architektonisch; *fig* aufbauend; ~**ure** ['aːkitektʃə] Architektur *f*, Baukunst *f*.

archives ['aːkaivz] *pl.* Archiv *n*.

archway ['aːtʃwei] Bogengang *m*.

arc|-lamp ['aːklæmp], ~**light** *𝇇* Bogenlampe *f*.

arctic ['aːktik] 1. arktisch, nördlich; Nord. , Polar...; 2. *Am.* wasserdichter Überschuh.

arden|cy ['aːdənsi] Hitze *f*, Glut *f*; Innigkeit *f*; ~**t** □ [~nt] *mst fig.* heiß, glühend; *fig.* feurig; eifrig.

ardo(u)r ['aːdə] Fig. Glut *f*; Eifer *m*.

arduous □ ['aːdjuəs] mühsam; zäh.

are [aː; *im Satz* ə] *pres. pl. u. 2. sg. von* be.

area ['ɛəriə] Areal *n*; (Boden-) Fläche *f*; Flächenraum *m*; Gegend *f*; Gebiet *n*; Bereich *m*.

Argentine ['aːdʒəntain] 1. argentinisch; 2. Argentinier(in); *the* ~ Argentinien *n*.

argue ['aːgjuː] *v/t.* erörtern; beweisen; begründen; einwenden; ~

s.o. into j-n zu *et.* bereden; *v/i.* streiten; Einwendungen machen.

argument ['aːgjumənt] Beweis (-grund) *m*; Streit(frage *f*) *m*; Erörterung *f*, Thema *n*; ~**ation** [aːgjumen'teiʃən] Beweisführung *f*.

arid ['ærid] dürr, trocken (*a. fig.*).

arise [ə'raiz] [*irr.*] sich erheben (*a. fig.*); ent-, erstehen (from aus); ~**n** [ə'rizn] *p.p von* arise.

aristocra|cy [æris'tɔkrəsi] Aristokratie *f* (*a fig*), Adel *m*; ~**t** ['æristəkræt] Aristokrat(in); ~**tic(al** □) [æristə'krætik(əl)] aristokratisch.

arithmetic [ə'riθmətik] Rechnen *n*.

ark [aːk] Arche *f*.

arm¹ [aːm] Arm *m*; Armlehne *f*; *keep s.o. at* ~*'s length* sich j-n vom Leibe halten; *infant in* ~*s* Säugling *m*.

arm² [~] 1. Waffe *f* (*mst pl.*); Waffengattung *f*; *be (all) up in* ~*s* in vollem Aufruhr sein; in Harnisch geraten. 2. (sich) (be)waffnen; (aus)rüsten, ⊕ armieren.

armada [aː'maːdə] Kriegsflotte *f*.

arma|ment [aː'maːmənt] (Kriegsaus)Rüstung *f*, Kriegsmacht *f*; ~**race** Wettrüsten *n*; ~**ture** [aː'maːtjuə] Rüstung *f*; ⊿, *phys.* Armatur *f*.

armchair [aːm'tʃɛə] Lehnstuhl *m*, Sessel *m*

armistice [aː'mistis] Waffenstillstand *m* (*a fig.*).

armo(u)r [[aː'maːə] 1. ⚔ Rüstung *f*, Panzer *m* (*a fig.*, *zo.*); 2. panzern; ~**ed car** Panzerwagen *m*; ~**y** ['aːməri] Rüstkammer *f* (*a. fig.*); *Am.* Rüstungsbetrieb *m*, Waffenfabrik *f*

armpit [[ʌ mpit] Achselhöhle *f*.

army ['aːmi] Heer *n*, Armee *f*; *fig.* Menge *f*, ~ *chaplain* Militärgeistliche(r) *m*

arose [ə rouz] *pret. von* arise.

around [ə'raund] 1. *adv.* rund-(her)um, *Am* F hier herum; 2. *prp.* um . her(um), *bsd. Am.* F ungefähr, etwa (*bei Zahlenangaben*).

arouse [ə rauz] aufwecken; *fig.* aufrütteln, erregen.

arraign [ə rein] vor Gericht stellen, anklagen, *fig* rügen.

arrange [ə reindʒ] (an)ordnen, *bsd.* ♪ einrichten, festsetzen; *Streit* schlichten, vereinbaren; erledigen; ~**ment** [~dʒmənt] Anordnung *f*; Disposition *f*, Übereinkommen *n*; Vorkehrung *f*, ♪ Arrangement *n*.

array [ə rei] 1. (Schlacht)Ordnung *f*; *fig* Aufgebot *n*; 2. ordnen, aufstellen, aufbieten; kleiden, putzen.

arrear [ə'riə] *mst pl.* Rückstand *m*, *bsd.* Schulden *f*/*pl.*

arrest [ə'rest] 1. Verhaftung *f*; Haft *f*; Beschlagnahme *f*; 2. verhaften; beschlagnahmen; anhalten, hemmen.

arriv|al [ə'raivəl] Ankunft *f*; Auftreten *n*; Ankömmling *m*; ~*s pl.* angekommene Personen f/pl., Züge m/pl., Schiffe n/pl.; ~e [ə'raiv] (an-) kommen, eintreffen; erscheinen; eintreten (Ereignis); ~ at erreichen (acc.).

arroga|nce ['ærəgəns] Anmaßung f; Überheblichkeit f; ~nt □ [~nt] anmaßend; überheblich; ~te ['ærougeit] sich et. anmaßen.

arrow ['ærou] Pfeil m; ~-head Pfeilspitze f; ~y ['æroui] pfeilartig.

arsenal ['ɑːsinl] Zeughaus n.

arsenic ['ɑːsnik] Arsen(ik) n.

arson ꜧ ['ɑːsn] Brandstiftung f.

art [ɑːt] Kunst f; fig. List f; Kniff m; ~s pl. Geisteswissenschaften f/pl.; Faculty of ~s philosophische Fakultät f.

arter|ial [ɑː'tiəriəl] Pulsader...; ~ road Hauptstraße f; ~y ['ɑːtəri] Arterie f, Pulsader f; fig. Verkehrsader f.   [schmitt.]

artful □ ['ɑːtful] schlau, ver-

article ['ɑːtikl] Artikel m; fig. Punkt m; ~d to in der Lehre bei.

articulat|e 1. [ɑː'tikjuleit] deutlich (aus)sprechen; Knochen zs.-fügen; 2. □ [~lit] deutlich; gegliedert; ~ion [ɑːtikju'leiʃən] deutliche Aussprache; anat. Gelenkfügung f.

artific|e ['ɑːtifis] Kunstgriff m, List f; ~ial □ [ɑːti'fiʃəl] künstlich; Kunst...; ~ person ꜧ juristische Person.

artillery [ɑː'tiləri] Artillerie f; ~man Artillerist m.

artisan [ɑːti'zæn] Handwerker m.

artist ['ɑːtist] Künstler(in); ~e [ɑː'tiːst] Artist(in); ~ic(al) □ [ɑː'tistik(əl)] künstlerisch; Kunst...

artless □ ['ɑːtlis] ungekünstelt, schlicht; arglos.

as [æz, əz] 1. adv. so; (ebenso) wie; (in der Eigenschaft) als; ~ big ~ so groß wie; ~ well ebensogut; auch; ~ well ~ sowohl ... als auch; 2. cj. (so-) wie; ebenso; (zu der Zeit) als, während; da, weil, indem; sofern; ~ it were sozusagen; such ~ to derart, daß; ~ for, ~ to was (an)betrifft; ~ from von ... an.

ascend [ə'send] v/i. (auf-, empor-, hinauf)steigen; zeitlich: zurückgehen (to bis zu); v/t. be-, ersteigen; hinaufsteigen; Fluß etc. hinauffahren, ~ancy, ~ency [~dənsi] Überlegenheit f, Einfluß m; Herrschaft f.

ascension [ə'senʃən] Aufsteigen n (bsd. ast.); Am. a. Aufstieg m (e-s Ballons etc.); ♈ (Day) Himmelfahrt(stag m) f.

ascent [ə'sent] Aufstieg m; Besteigung f; Steigung f; Aufgang m.

ascertain [æsə'tein] ermitteln.

ascetic [ə'setik] (~ally) asketisch.

ascribe [əs'kraib] zuschreiben.

aseptic ꜧ [æ'septik] 1. aseptisch; 2. aseptisches Mittel.

ash[1] [æʃ] ♃ Esche f; Eschenholz n.

ash[2] (~), mst. pl. ~es ['æʃiz] Asche f; Ash Wednesday Aschermittwoch m.

ashamed [ə'ʃeimd] beschämt; be ~ of sich e-r Sache od. j-s schämen.

ash can Am. ['æʃkæn] = dust-bin.

ashen ['æʃn] Aschen...; aschfahl.

ashore [ə'ʃɔː] am od. ans Ufer od. Land; run ~, be driven ~ stranden.

ash|-pan ['æʃpæn] Asch(en)kasten m; ~-tray Asch(en)becher m.

ashy ['æʃi] aschig; aschgrau.

Asiatic [eiʃi'ætik] 1. asiatisch; 2. Asiat(in).

aside [ə'said] 1. beiseite (a. thea.); abseits; seitwärts; ~ from Am. abgesehen von; 2. thea. Aparte n.

ask [ɑːsk] v/t. fragen (s.th. nach et.); verlangen (of, from s.o. von j-m); bitten (s.o. [for] s.th. j. um et., that darum, daß); erbitten; ~ (s.o.) a question (j-m) e-e Frage stellen; v/i.: ~ for bitten um, fragen nach; he ~ed for it od. for trouble er wollte es ja so haben; to be had for the ~ing umsonst zu haben.

askance [əs'kæns], askew [əs'kjuː] von der Seite, seitwärts; schief.

asleep [ə'sliːp] schlafend; in den Schlaf; eingeschlafen, be ~ schlafen; fall ~ einschlafen.

asparagus ♃ [əs'pærəgəs] Spargel m.

aspect ['æspekt] Äußere n; Aussicht f, Lage f; Aspekt m, Seite f, Gesichtspunkt m.

asperity [æs'periti] Rauheit f; Unebenheit f; fig. Schroffheit f.

asphalt ['æsfælt] 1. Asphalt m; 2. asphaltieren.

aspic ['æspik] Aspik m, Sülze f.

aspir|ant [əs'paiərənt] Bewerber (-in); ~ate ling. ['æspəreit] aspirieren; ~ation [æspə'reiʃən] Aspiration f; Bestrebung f; be [əs'paiə] streben, trachten (to, after, at nach).

ass [æs] Esel m.

assail [ə'seil] angreifen, überfallen (a. fig.); befallen (Zweifel etc.); ~ant [~lənt] Angreifer(in).

assassin [ə'sæsin] (Meuchel)Mörder(in); ~ate [~neit] (meuchlings) ermorden; ~ation [əsæsi'neiʃən] Meuchelmord m.

assault [ə'sɔːlt] 1. Angriff m (a. fig.); 2. anfallen; ꜧ tätlich angreifen od. beleidigen; ✕ bestürmen (a. fig.).

assay [ə'sei] 1. (Erz-, Metall-) Probe f; 2. v/t. untersuchen; v/i. Am. Edelmetall enthalten.

assembl|age [ə'semblidʒ] (An-) Sammlung f; ⊕ Montage f; ~e [ə'sembl] (sich) versammeln; zs.-berufen; ⊕ montieren; ~y [~li] Versammlung f; Gesellschaft f; ⊕ Montage f; ~ line ⊕ Fließband n; ~ man pol. Abgeordnete(r) m.

assent [ə'sent] **1.** Zustimmung *f*; **2.** (*to*) zustimmen (*dat*.); billigen.

assert [ə'sə:t] (sich) behaupten; **~ion** [ə'sə:ʃən] Behauptung *f*; Erklärung *f*; Geltendmachung *f*.

assess [ə'ses] besteuern; zur Steuer veranlagen (*at* mit); **~able** [~'səbl] steuerpflichtig; **~ment** [~smənt] (Steuer)Veranlagung *f*; Steuer *f*.

asset ['æset] ♦ Aktivposten *m*; *fig.* Gut *n*, Gewinn *m*; **~s** *pl.* Vermögen *n*; ♦ Aktiva *pl.*; ♦ Konkursmasse *f*.

asseverate [ə'sevəreit] beteuern.

assiduous □ [ə'sidjuəs] emsig, fleißig; aufmerksam.

assign [ə'sain] an-, zuweisen; bestimmen; zuschreiben; **~ation** [æsig'neiʃən] Verabredung *f*, Stelldichein *n*; = **~ment** [ə'sainmənt] An-, Zuweisung *f*; *bsd. Am.* Auftrag *m*; ♦♦ Übertragung *f*.

assimilat|e [ə'simileit] (sich) angleichen (*to, with dat*.); **~ion** [əsimi'leiʃən] Assimilation *f*, Angleichung *f*.

assist [ə'sist] *j-m* beistehen, helfen; unterstützen; **~ance** [~təns] Beistand *m*; Hilfe *f*; **~ant** [~nt] **1.** behilflich; **2.** Assistent(in).

assize ♦♦ [ə'saiz] (Schwur)Gerichtssitzung *f*; **~s** *pl. periodisches* Geschworenengericht *n*.

associa|te 1. [ə'souʃieit] (sich) zugesellen (*with dat*.), (sich) vereinigen; Umgang haben (*with* mit); **2.** [~ʃiit] verbunden; **3.** [~] (Amts)Genosse *m*; Teilhaber *m*; **~tion** [əsousi'eiʃən] Vereinigung *f*, Verbindung *f*; *Handels- etc.* Gesellschaft *f*; Genossenschaft *f*; Verein *m*.

assort [ə'sɔ:t] *v/t.* sortieren, zs.-stellen; *v/i.* passen (*with* zu); **~ment** [~tmənt] Sortieren *n*; ♦ Sortiment *n*, Auswahl *f*.

assum|e [ə'sju:m] annehmen; vorgeben; übernehmen; **~ption** [ə'sʌmpʃən] Annahme *f*; Übernahme *f*; *eccl.* ♀ (*Day*) Mariä Himmelfahrt *f*.

assur|ance [ə'ʃuərəns] Zu-, Versicherung *f*; Zuversicht *f*; Sicherheit *f*, Gewißheit *f*; Selbstsicherheit *f*; Dreistigkeit *f*; **~e** [ə'ʃuə] (*Leben* ver)sichern; sicherstellen; **~ed 1.** (*adv.* **~edly** [~ridli]) sicher; dreist; **2.** Versicherte(r *m*) *f*.

asthma ['æsmə] Asthma *n*.

astir [ə'stə:] auf (den Beinen) in Bewegung, rege.

astonish [əs'tɔniʃ] in Erstaunen setzen; verwundern; befremden; *be* **~ed** erstaunt sein (*at* über *acc*.); **~ing** □ [~ʃiŋ] erstaunlich; **~ment** [~ʃmənt] (Er)Staunen *n*; Verwunderung *f*.

astound [əs'taund] verblüffen.

astray [əs'trei] vom (rechten) Wege

ab (*a. fig.*); irre; *go* **~** sich verlaufen, fehlgehen.

astride [əs'traid] mit gespreizten Beinen; rittlings (*of* auf *dat*.).

astringent ♫ [əs'trindʒənt] **1.** □ zs.-ziehend; **2.** zs.-ziehendes Mittel.

astro|logy [əs'trɔlədʒi] Astrologie *f*; **~naut** ['æstrənɔ:t] Astronaut *m*, Raumfahrer *m*; **~nomer** [əs'trɔnəmə] Astronom *m*; **~nomy** [~mi] Astronomie *f*.

astute □ [əs'tju:t] scharfsinnig; schlau; **~ness** [~tnis] Scharfsinn *m*.

asunder [ə'sʌndə] auseinander; entzwei.

asylum [ə'sailəm] Asyl *n*.

at [æt; *unbetont* ət] *prp.* an; auf; aus; bei; für; in; mit; nach; über; um; von; vor; zu; **~** *school* in der Schule; **~** *the age of* im Alter von.

ate [et] *pret von* eat 1.

atheism [ˈeiθiizm] Atheismus *m*.

athlet|e ['æθli:t] Sport. Leicht-) Athlet *m*; **~ic(al** □) [æθ'letik(əl)] athletisch; **~ics** *pl.* (*bsd.* Leicht-) Athletik *f*.

Atlantic [ət'læntik] **1.** atlantisch; **2.** *a.* **~** *Ocean* Atlantik *m*.

atmospher|e ['ætməsfiə] Atmosphäre *f* (*a. fig.*); **~ic(al** □) [ætməs-'ferik(əl)] atmosphärisch.

atom ⚛ ['ætəm] Atom *n* (*a. fig.*); **~ic** [ə'tɔmik] atomar(ig, atom-.); atomistisch; **~ age** Atomzeitalter *n*; **~** (*a. atom*) *bomb* Atombombe *f*; **~** *pile* Atomreaktor *m*; **~ic-powered** durch Atomkraft betrieben; **~ize** ['ætəmaiz] in Atome auflösen, atomisieren; **~izer** [~zə] Zerstäuber *m*.

atone [ə'toun]: **~** *for* büßen für *et.*; **~ment** [~nmənt] Buße *f*; Sühne *f*.

atroci|ous □ [ə'trouʃəs] scheußlich, gräßlich; grausam; **~ty** [ə'trositi] Scheußlichkeit *f*, Gräßlichkeit *f*; Grausamkeit *f*.

attach [ə'tætʃ] *v/t.* (*to*) anheften (an, *acc.*), befestigen (an); *Wert, Wichtigkeit etc.* beilegen (*dat.*); ♦♦ *j-n* verhaften; *et.* beschlagnahmen; **~** *o.s. to* sich anschließen an (*acc.*); **~ed**: **~** *to* gehörig zu; *j-m* zugetan, ergeben; **~ment** [~mənt] Befestigung *f*; Bindung *f* (*to, for an acc.*); Anhänglichkeit *f* (*an acc.*), Neigung *f* (zu); Anhängsel *n* (*to gen.*); ♦♦ Verhaftung *f*; Beschlagnahme *f*.

attack [ə'tæk] **1.** angreifen (*a. fig.*); befallen (*Krankheit*); *Arbeit* in Angriff nehmen; **2.** Angriff *m*; ♫ Anfall *m*; Inangriffnahme *f*.

attain [ə'tein] *v/t.* Ziel erreichen; *v/i.* **~** *to* gelangen zu; **~ment** [~nmənt] Erreichung *f*; *fig.* Aneignung *f*; *pl.* Kenntnisse *f/pl.*; Fertigkeiten *f/pl.*

attempt [ə'tempt] **1.** versuchen; **2.** Versuch *m*; Attentat *n*.

attend [ə'tend] *v/t.* begleiten; bedienen; pflegen; ✗ behandeln; *j-m* aufwarten; beiwohnen *(dat.)*; *Vorlesung etc.* besuchen; *v/i.* achten, hören (to auf *acc.*); anwesend sein (*at bei*); ~ to erledigen; **~ance** [~dəns] Begleitung *f*; Aufwartung *f*; Pflege *f*; ✗ Behandlung *f*; Gefolge *n*; Anwesenheit *f* (*at bei*); Besuch *m* (*der Schule etc.*); Besucher(zahl *f*) *m/pl.*; Publikum *n*; *be in* ~ zu Diensten stehen; **~ant** [~nt] **1.** begleitend (*on, upon acc.*); anwesend (*at bei*); **2.** Diener(in); Begleiter(in); Wärter(in); Besucher(in) (*at gen.*); ⊕ Bedienungsmann *m*; ~s *pl.* Dienerschaft *f*.

attent|ion [ə'tenʃən] Aufmerksamkeit *f* (*a. fig.*); ~! ✗ Achtung!; **~ive** [~ntiv] aufmerksam.

attest [ə'test] bezeugen; beglaubigen; *bsd.* ✗ vereidigen.

attic ['ætik] Dachstube *f*. [dung *f*.⟨

attire [ə'taiə] **1.** kleiden; **2.** Klei-⟩

attitude ['ætitju:d] (Ein)Stellung *f*; Haltung *f*; *fig.* Stellungnahme *f*.

attorney [ə'tə:ni] Bevollmächtigte(r) *m*; *Am.* Rechtsanwalt *m*; *power of* ~ Vollmacht *f*; ♀ *General* Generalstaats- *od.* Kronanwalt *m*, *Am.* Justizminister *m*.

attract [ə'trækt] anziehen, *Aufmerksamkeit* erregen; *fig.* reizen; **~ion** [~kʃən] Anziehung(skraft) *f*; *fig.* Reiz *m*; Zugartikel *m*; *thea.* Zugstück *n*; **~ive** [~ktiv] anziehend; reizvoll; zugkräftig; **~iveness** [~vnis] Reiz *m*.

attribute **1.** [ə'tribju(:)t] beimessen, zuschreiben; zurückführen (*to* auf *acc.*); **2.** ['ætribju:t] Attribut *n* (*a. gr.*), Eigenschaft *f*, Merkmal *n*.

attune [ə'tju:n] (ab)stimmen.

auburn ['ɔ:bən] kastanienbraun.

auction ['ɔ:kʃən] **1.** Auktion *f*; *sell by* ~, *put up for* ~ versteigern, versteigern lassen; **2.** *mst* ~ *off* versteigern; **~eer** [ɔ:kʃə'niə] Auktionator *m*.

audaci|ous □ [ɔ:'deiʃəs] kühn; unverschämt; **~ty** [ɔ:'dæsiti] Kühnheit *f*; Unverschämtheit *f*.

audible □ ['ɔ:dəbl] hörbar; Hör...

audience ['ɔ:djəns] Publikum *n*, Zuhörerschaft *f*; Leserkreis *m*; Audienz *f*; Gehör *n*; *give* ~ *to* Gehör schenken (*dat.*).

audit ['ɔ:dit] **1.** Rechnungsprüfung *f*; **2.** *Rechnungen* prüfen; **~or** [~tə] Hörer *m*; Rechnungs-, Buchprüfer *m*; **~orium** [ɔ:di'tɔ:riəm] Hörsaal *m*; *Am.* Vortrags-, Konzertsaal *m*.

auger ⊕ ['ɔ:gə] *großer* Bohrer.

aught [ɔ:t] (irgend) etwas; *for* ~ *I care* meinetwegen; *for* ~ *I know* soviel ich weiß.

augment [ɔ:g'ment] vergrößern; **~ation** [ɔ:gmen'teiʃən] Vermehrung *f*, Vergrößerung *f*; Zusatz *m*.

augur ['ɔ:gə] **1.** Augur *m*; **2.** weissagen, voraussagen (*well Gutes, ill*

Übles); **~y** ['ɔ:gjuri] Prophezeiung *f*; An-, Vorzeichen *n*; Vorahnung *f*.

August[1] ['ɔ:gəst] *Monat* August *m*.

august[2] □ [ɔ:'gʌst] erhaben.

aunt [ɑ:nt] Tante *f*.

auspic|e ['ɔ:spis] Vorzeichen *n*; **~s** *pl.* Auspizien *pl.*; Schirmherrschaft *f*; **~ious** □ [ɔ:s'piʃəs] günstig.

auster|e □ [ɔs'tiə] streng; herb; hart; einfach; **~ity** [ɔs'teriti] Strenge *f*; Härte *f*; Einfachheit *f*.

Australian [ɔs'treiljən] **1.** australisch; **2.** Australier(in).

Austrian ['ɔstriən] **1.** österreichisch; **2.** Österreicher(in).

authentic [ɔ:'θentik] (~ally) authentisch; zuverlässig; echt.

author ['ɔ:θə] Urheber(in); Autor (-in); Verfasser(in); **~itative** □ [ɔ:'θɔritətiv] maßgebend; gebieterisch; zuverlässig; **~ity** [ɔ:'θɔriti] Autorität *f*; (Amts)Gewalt *f*, Vollmacht *f*; Einfluß *m* (*over* auf *acc.*); Ansehen *n*; Glaubwürdigkeit *f*; Quelle *f*; Fachmann *m*; Behörde *f* (*mst pl.*); *on the* ~ *of* auf *j-s* Zeugnis hin; **~ize** ['ɔ:θəraiz] *j-n* autorisieren, bevollmächtigen; *et.* gutheißen, **~ship** ['ɔ:θəʃip] Urheberschaft *f*.

autocar ['ɔ:touka:] Kraftwagen *m*.

autocra|cy [ɔ:'tɔkrəsi] Autokratie *f*; **~tic(al** □) [ɔ:tə'krætik(əl)] autokratisch, despotisch.

autogiro ✈ ['ɔ:tou'dʒaiərou] Autogiro *n*, Tragschrauber *m*.

autograph ['ɔ:təgra:f] Autogramm *n*. [Restaurant *n.*⟨

automat ['ɔ:təmæt] Automaten-⟩

automat|ic [ɔ:tə'mætik] (~ally) **1.** automatisch; ~ *machine* (Verkaufs)Automat *m*; **2.** *Am.* Selbstladepistole *f*, -gewehr *n*; **~ion** [~'meiʃən] Automation *f*; **~on** *fig.* [ɔ:'tɔmətən] Roboter *m*.

automobile *bsd. Am.* ['ɔ:təməbi:l] Automobil *n*.

autonomy [ɔ:'tɔnəmi] Autonomie *f*.

autumn ['ɔ:təm] Herbst *m*; **~al** □ [ɔ:'tʌmnəl] herbstlich; Herbst...

auxiliary [ɔ:g'ziljəri] helfend; Hilfs...

avail [ə'veil] **1.** nützen, helfen; ~ *o.s. of* sich *e-r S.* bedienen; **2.** Nutzen *m*; *of no* ~ nutzlos; **~able** □ [~ləbl] benutzbar; verfügbar; *pred.* erhältlich, vorhanden; gültig.

avalanche ['ævəla:nʃ] Lawine *f*.

avaric|e ['ævəris] Geiz *m*; Habsucht *f*; **~ious** □ [ævə'riʃəs] geizig; habgierig.

avenge [ə'vendʒ] rächen, *et.* ahnden; **~r** [~dʒə] Rächer(in).

avenue ['ævinju:] Allee *f*; Prachtstraße *f*; *fig.* Weg *m*, Straße *f*.

aver [ə'və:] behaupten.

average ['ævəridʒ] **1.** Durchschnitt *m*; ♺ Havarie *f*; **2.** □ durchschnittlich; Durchschnitts...; **3.** durchschnittlich schätzen (*at* auf *acc.*); durchschnittlich betragen *od.* arbeiten *etc.*

avers|e □ [ə'vəːs] abgeneigt (*to, from dat.*); widerwillig; **~ion** [ə'vəːʃən] Widerwille *m.*

avert [ə'vəːt] abwenden (*a. fig.*).

aviat|ion ✈ [eivi'eiʃən] Fliegen *n;* Flugwesen *n;* Luftfahrt *f;* **~or** ['eivieitə] Flieger *m.*

avid □ ['ævid] gierig (*of* nach; *for* auf *acc.*).

avoid [ə'vɔid] (ver)meiden; *j-m* ausweichen; ⚖ anfechten; ungültig machen; **~ance** [~dəns] Vermeidung *f.*

avouch [ə'vautʃ] verbürgen, bestätigen; **~** *avow.*

avow [ə'vau] bekennen, (ein)gestehen; anerkennen; **~al** [ə'vauəl] Bekenntnis *n,* (Ein)Geständnis *n;* **~edly** [ə'vauidli] eingestandenermaßen.

await [ə'weit] erwarten (*a. fig.*).

awake [ə'weik] 1. wach, munter; *be* **~** *to* sich *e-r S.* bewußt sein; 2. [*irr.*] *v/t.* (*mst* **~n** [~kən]) (er)wecken; *v/i.* erwachen; gewahr werden (*to s.th.* et.).

award [ə'wɔːd] 1. Urteil *n,* Spruch

m; Belohnung *f;* Preis *m;* 2. zuerkennen, *Orden etc.* verleihen.

aware [ə'wɛə]: *be* **~** *wissen* (*of von od. acc.*), sich bewußt sein (*of gen.*); *become* **~** *of et.* gewahr werden, merken.

away [ə'wei] (hin)weg; fort; immer weiter, darauflos; **~** *back Am.* F (schon) damals, weit zurück.

awe [ɔː] 1. Ehrfurcht *f,* Scheu *f* (*of* vor *dat.*); 2. (Ehr)Furcht einflößen (*dat.*).

awful □ ['ɔːful] ehrfurchtgebietend; furchtbar; F *fig.* schrecklich.

awhile [ə'wail] e-e Weile.

awkward □ ['ɔːkwəd] ungeschickt, unbeholfen; linkisch; unangenehm; dumm, ungünstig, unpraktisch.

awl [ɔːl] Ahle *f,* Pfriem *m.*

awning [' ɔːniŋ] Plane *f;* Markise *f.*

awoke [ə'wouk] *pret. u. p.p. von* awake 2.

awry [ə'rai] schief; *fig.* verkehrt.

ax(e) [æks] Axt *f,* Beil *n.*

axis ['æksis], *pl.* axes ['æksiːz] Achse *f.*

axle ⊕ ['æksl] *a.* **~-tree** (Rad-) Achse *f,* Welle *f.*

ay(e) [ai] Ja *n; parl.* Jastimme *f; the* **~s** *have it* die Mehrheit ist dafür.

azure ['æʒə] azurn, azurblau.

B

babble ['bæbl] 1. stammeln; (nach-) plappern; schwatzen; plätschern (*Bach*); 2. Geplapper *n;* Geschwätz *n.*

baboon *zo.* [bə'buːn] Pavian *m.*

baby ['beibi] 1. Säugling *m,* kleines Kind, Baby *n; Am. sl.* Süße *f* (*Mädchen*); 2. Baby...; Kinder...; klein; **~hood** [~ihud] frühe Kindheit.

bachelor ['bætʃələ] Junggeselle *m; univ.* Bakkalaureus *m* (*Grad*).

back [bæk] 1. Rücken *m;* Rückseite *f;* Rücklehne *f;* Hinterende *n; Fußball:* Verteidiger *m;* 2. *adj.* Hinter..., Rück...; hinter; rückwärtig; entlegen; rückläufig; rückständig; 3. *adv.* zurück; 4. *v/t.* mit e-m Rücken versehen; unterstützen; hinten anstoßen an (*acc.*); zurückbewegen; wetten *od.* setzen auf (*acc.*); ✝ indossieren; *v/i.* sich rückwärts bewegen, zurückgehen *od.* zurückfahren; **~** *alley Am.* finstere Seitengasse; **~bite** ['bækbait] [*irr.* (*bite*)] verleumden; **~bone** Rückgrat *n;* **~er** ['bækə] Unterstützer (-in); ✝ Indossierer *m;* Wetter(in); **~-fire** *mot.* Frühzündung *f;* **~ground** Hintergrund *m;* **~ number** alte Nummer (*e-r Zeitung*); **~**

pedal rückwärtstreten (*Radfahren*); **~ling** brake Rücktrittbremse *f;* **~side** Hinter-, Rückseite *f;* **~slapper** *Am.* [~slæpə] plump vertraulicher Mensch; **~slide** [*irr.* (*slide*)] rückfällig werden; **~stairs** Hintertreppe *f;* **~stop** *Am. Baseball* Gitter *n* hinter dem Fänger; *Schießstand:* Kugelfang *m;* **~stroke** Rückenschwimmen *n;* **~talk** *Am.* F freche Antworten; **~track** *Am.* F *fig.* e-n Rückzieher machen; **~ward** ['bækwəd] 1. *adj.* Rück(wärts)...; langsam; zurückgeblieben, rückständig; zurückhaltend; 2. *adv.* (*a.* **~wards** [~dz]) rückwärts, zurück; **~water** Stauwasser *n;* **~woods** *pl.* weit abgelegene Waldgebiete; *fig.* Provinz *f;* **~woodsman** Hinterwäldler *m.*

bacon ['beikən] Speck *m.*

bacteri|ologist [bæktiəri'ɔlədʒist] Bakteriologe *m;* **~um** [bæk'tiəriəm], *pl.* **~a** [~iə] Bakterie *f.*

bad ∟ [bæd] schlecht, böse, schlimm; falsch (*Münze*); faul (*Schuld*); *he is* **~ly** *off* er ist übel dran; **~ly** *wounded* schwerverwundet; *want* **~ly** F dringend brauchen; *be in* **~** *with Am.* F in Ungnade bei.

bade [beid] *pret. von* bid 1.

badge [bædʒ] Ab-, Kennzeichen *n*.

badger ['bædʒə] 1. *zo*. Dachs *m*; 2. hetzen, plagen, quälen.

badlands *Am*. ['bædlændz] *pl*. Ödland *n*.

badness ['bædnis] schlechte Beschaffenheit; Schlechtigkeit *f*.

baffle ['bæfl] *j-n* verwirren; *Plan etc.* vereiteln, durchkreuzen.

bag [bæg] 1. Beutel *m*, Sack *m*; Tüte *f*; Tasche *f*; ~ and baggage mit Sack und Pack; 2. in e-n Beutel *etc.* tun, einsacken; *hunt.* zur Strecke bringen; (sich) bauschen.

baggage *Am*. ['bægidʒ] (Reise-) Gepäck *n*; ~ **car** *Am*. 🚂 Gepäckwagen *m*; ~ **check** *Am*. Gepäckschein *m*.

bagpipe ['bægpaip] Dudelsack *m*.

bail [beil] 1. Bürge *m*; Bürgschaft *f*; Kaution *f*; admit to ~ 🚓 gegen Bürgschaft freilassen; 2. bürgen für; ~ out *j-n* freibürgen; 🪂 mit dem Fallschirm abspringen.

bailiff ['beilif] Gerichtsdiener *m*; (Guts)Verwalter *m*; Amtmann *m*.

bait [beit] 1. Köder *m*; *fig.* Lockung *f*; 2. *v/t.* Falle *etc.* beködern; *hunt.* hetzen; *fig.* quälen; reizen; *v/i.* rasten; einkehren.

bak|e [beik] 1. backen; braten; Ziegel brennen; (aus)dörren; 2. *Am.* gesellige Zusammenkunft; **~er** ['beikə] Bäcker *m*; **~ery** [~əri] Bäckerei *f*; **~ing-powder** [~kiŋpaudə] Backpulver *n*.

balance ['bæləns] 1. Waage *f*; Gleichgewicht *n* (*a. fig.*); Harmonie *f*; ✝ Bilanz *f*, Saldo *m*, Überschuß *m*; Restbetrag *m*; ✝ Rest *m*; *a.* ~ wheel Unruh(e) *f der Uhr*; ~ of power *pol.* Kräftegleichgewicht *n*; ~ of trade (Außen-) Handelsbilanz *f*; 2. *v/t.* (ab-) er)wägen; im Gleichgewicht halten; ausgleichen; ✝ bilanzieren; saldieren; *v/i.* balancieren; sich ausgleichen.

balcony ['bælkəni] Balkon *m*.

bald [bɔːld] kahl; *fig.* nackt; dürftig.

bale ✝ [beil] Ballen *m*.

baleful □ ['beilful] verderblich; unheilvoll.

balk [bɔːk] 1. (Furchen)Rain *m*; Balken *m*; Hemmnis *n*; 2. *v/t.* (ver-) hindern; enttäuschen; vereiteln; *v/i.* stutzen, scheuen.

ball¹ [bɔːl] 1. Ball *m*; Kugel *f*; (Hand-, Fuß)Ballen *m*; Knäuel *m*, *n*; Kloß *m*; *Sport*: Wurf *m*; keep the ~ rolling das Gespräch in Gang halten; *play* ~ *Am.* F mitmachen; 2. (sich) (zs.-)ballen.

ball² [~] Ball *m*, Tanzgesellschaft *f*.

ballad ['bæləd] Ballade *f*; Lied *n*.

ballast ['bæləst] 1. Ballast *m*; 🚂 Schotter *m*, Bettung *f*; 2. mit Ballast beladen; 🚂 beschottern, betten.

ball-bearing(s *pl.*) ⊕ ['bɔːl-'bɛəriŋ(z)] Kugellager *n*.

ballet ['bælei] Ballett *n*.

balloon [bə'luːn] 1. Ballon *m*; 2. im Ballon aufsteigen; sich blähen; **~ist** [~nist] Ballonfahrer *m*.

ballot ['bælət] 1. Wahlzettel *m*; (geheime) Wahl; 2. (geheim) abstimmen; ~ for losen um; **~-box** Wahlurne *f*.

ball(-point) pen ['bɔːl(pɔint)pen] Kugelschreiber *m*.

ball-room ['bɔːlrum] Ballsaal *m*.

balm [bɑːm] Balsam *m*; *fig.* Trost *m*.

balmy □ ['bɑːmi] balsamisch (*a. fig.*).

baloney *Am. sl.* [bə'louni] Quatsch *m*.

balsam ['bɔːlsəm] Balsam *m*.

balustrade [bæləs'treid] Balustrade *f*, Brüstung *f*; Geländer *n*.

bamboo [bæm'buː] Bambus *m*.

bamboozle F [bæm'buːzl] beschwindeln.

ban [bæn] 1. Bann *m*; Acht *f*; (amtliches) Verbot; 2. verbieten.

banal [bə'nɑːl] banal, abgedroschen.

banana [bə'nɑːnə] Banane *f*.

band [bænd] 1. Band *n*; Streifen *m*; Schar *f*; ♪ Kapelle *f*; 2. zs.-binden; ~ o.s. sich zs.-tun *od.* zs.-rotten.

bandage ['bændidʒ] 1. Binde *f*; Verband *m*; 2. bandagieren; verbinden.

bandbox ['bændbɔks] Hutschachtel *f*.

bandit ['bændit] Bandit *m*.

band|-master ['bændmɑːstə] Kapellmeister *m*; **~stand** Musikpavillon *m*; **~ wagon** *Am.* Wagen *m* mit Musikkapelle; *jump on the* ~ sich der erfolgversprechenden Sache anschließen.

bandy ['bændi] *Worte etc.* wechseln; **~legged** säbelbeinig.

bane [bein] Ruin *m*; **~ful** □ ['beinful] verderblich.

bang [bæŋ] 1. Knall *m*; Ponyfrisur *f*; 2. dröhnend (zu)schlagen; **~up** *Am. sl.* ['bæŋ'ʌp] Klasse, prima.

banish ['bæniʃ] verbannen; **~ment** [~ʃmənt] Verbannung *f*.

banisters ['bænistəz] *pl.* Treppengeländer *n*.

bank [bæŋk] 1. Damm *m*; Ufer *n*; (Spiel-, Sand-, Wolken- *etc.*)Bank *f*; ~ of issue Notenbank *f*; 2. *v/t.* eindämmen; ✝ *Geld* auf die Bank legen; 🪂 in die Kurve bringen; *v/i.* Bankgeschäfte machen; ein Bankkonto haben; 🪂 in die Kurve gehen; ~ on sich verlassen auf (*acc.*); **~bill** [~bil] Bankwechsel *m*; *Am. s.* banknote; **~er** [~kə] Bankier *m*; **~ing** [~kiŋ] Bankgeschäft *n*; Bankwesen *n*; *attr.* Bank...; **~-note** Banknote *f*; Kassenschein *m*; ~

rate Diskontsatz m; **~rupt** [~krɔpt]
1. Bankrotteur m; 2. bankrott;
3. bankrott machen; **~ruptcy**
[~tsi] Bankrott m, Konkurs m.
banner ['bænə] Banner n; Fahne f.
banns [bænz] pl. Aufgebot n.
banquet ['bæŋkwit] 1. Festmahl n;
2. v/t. festlich bewirten; v/i. tafeln.
banter ['bæntə] necken, hänseln.
baptism ['bæptizəm] Taufe f.
baptist ['bæptist] Täufer m.
baptize [bæp'taiz] taufen.
bar [ba:] 1. Stange f; Stab m;
Barren m; Riegel m; Schranke f;
Sandbank f; fig. Hindernis n; ✗
Spange f; ♪ Takt(strich) m; (Gerichts)Schranke f; fig. Urteil n;
Anwaltschaft f; Bar f im Hotel etc.;
2. verriegeln; (ver-, ab)sperren;
verwehren; einsperren; (ver)hin-
dern; ausschließen.
barb [ba:b] Widerhaken m; **~ed**
wire Stacheldraht m.
barbar|ian [ba:'bɛəriən] 1. bar-
barisch; 2. Barbar(in); **~ous** □
['ba:bərəs] barbarisch; roh; grausam.
barbecue ['ba:bikju:] 1. großer
Bratrost; Am. Essen n (im Freien),
bei dem Tiere ganz gebraten
werden; 2. im ganzen braten.
barber ['ba:bə] (Herren)Friseur m.
bare [bɛə] 1. nackt, bloß; kahl; bar,
leer; arm, entblößt; 2. entblößen;
~faced ☐ ['bɛəfeist] frech; **~foot**,
~footed barfuß; **~headed** bar-
häuptig; **~ly** ['bɛəli] kaum.
bargain ['ba:gin] 1. Geschäft n;
Handel m, Kauf m; vorteilhafter
Kauf; a (dead) ~ spottbillig; it's a ~!
f abgemacht!; into the ~ obendrein;
2. handeln, übereinkommen.
barge [ba:dʒ] Flußboot n, Lastkahn
m; Hausboot n; **~man** ['ba:dʒmən]
Kahnführer m.
bark[1] [ba:k] 1. Borke f, Rinde f;
2. abrinden; Haut abschürfen.
bark[2] [~] 1. bellen; 2. Bellen n.
bar-keeper ['ba:ki:pə] Barbesitzer
m; Barkellner m.
barley ['ba:li] Gerste f; Graupe f.
barn [ba:n] Scheune f; bsd. Am.
(Vieh)Stall m; **~storm** Am. pol.
['ba:nstɔ:m] herumreisen u. (Wahl-)
Reden halten.
barometer [bə'rɔmitə] Barometer n.
baron ['bærən] Baron m, Freiherr
m; **~ess** [~nis] Baronin f.
barrack(s pl.) ['bærək(s)] (Miets-)
Kaserne f.
barrage ['bæra:ʒ] Staudamm m.
barrel ['bærəl] 1. Faß n, Tonne f;
Gewehr- etc. Lauf m; ⊕ Trommel
f; Walze f; 2. in Fässer füllen;
~organ ♪ Drehorgel f.
barren ☐ ['bærən] unfruchtbar;
dürr, trocken; tot (Kapital).
barricade [bæri'keid] 1. Barrikade
f; 2. verbarrikadieren; sperren.

barrier ['bæriə] Schranke f (a. fig.);
Barriere f, Sperre f; Hindernis
n.
barrister ['bæristə] (plädierender)
Rechtsanwalt, Barrister m.
barrow[1] ['bærou] Trage f; Karre f.
barrow[2] [~] Hügelgrab n, Tumulus
m.
barter ['ba:tə] 1. Tausch(handel)
m; 2. tauschen (for gegen); F
schachern.
base[1] ' [beis] gemein; unecht.
base[2] [~] 1. Basis f; Grundlage f;
Fundament n; Fuß m; ⚔ Base f;
Stützpunkt m; 2. gründen, stützen.
base|ball ['beisbɔ:l] Baseball m;
~born von niedriger Abkunft;
unehelich; **~less** ['beislis] grundlos;
~ment ['beismənt] Fundament n;
Kellergeschoß n.
baseness ['beisnis] Gemeinheit f.
bashful ☐ ['bæʃful] schüchtern.
basic ['beisik] (**~ally**) grundlegend;
Grund..; ⚔ basisch.
basin ['beisn] Becken n; Schüssel f;
Tal-, Wasser-, Hafenbecken n.
bas|is ['beisis], pl. **~es** ['beisi:z]
Basis f; Grundlage f; ✗, ⚓ Stützpunkt m.
bask [ba:sk] sich sonnen (a. fig.).
basket ['ba:skit] Korb m; **~ball**
Korbball(spiel n) m; **~ dinner**, **~
supper** Am. Picknick n.
bass ♪ [beis] Baß m.
basso ♪ ['bæsou] Baß(sänger) m.
bastard ['bæstəd] 1. ☐ unehelich;
unecht, Bastard...; 2. Bastard m.
baste[1] [beist] Braten begießen;
durchprügeln.
baste[2] [~] lose nähen, (an)heften.
bat[1] [bæt] Fledermaus f; as blind
as a ~ stockblind.
bat[2] [~] Sport: 1. Schlagholz n;
Schläger m; 2. den Ball schlagen.
batch [bætʃ] Schub m Brote (a. fig.);
Stoß m Briefe etc. (a. fig.).
bate [beit] verringern; verhalten.
bath [ba:θ] 1. Bad n; ⚲ chair Rollstuhl m; 2. baden.
bathe [beið] baden.
bathing ['beiðiŋ] Baden n, Bad n;
attr. Bade...; **~suit** Badeanzug m.
bath|robe Am. ['ba:θroub] Bade-
mantel m; **~room** Badezimmer n;
~sheet Badelaken n; **~towel**
Badetuch n; **~tub** Badewanne f.
batiste ✦ [bæ'ti:st] Batist m.
baton ['bætən] Stab m; Taktstock
m.
battalion ✗ [bə'tæljən] Bataillon n.
batten ['bætn] 1. Latte f; 2. sich
mästen.
batter ['bætə] 1. Sport: Schläger m;
Rührteig m; 2. heftig schlagen;
verbeulen; **~ down** od. in Tür einschlagen; **~y** [~əri] Schlägerei f;
Batterie f; ⚡ Akku m; fig. Satz m;
assault and **~** ⚖ tätlicher Angriff.
battle ['bætl] 1. Schlacht f (of bei);

2. streiten, kämpfen; ~ax(e) Streitaxt *f*; F Xanthippe *f*; ~field Schlachtfeld *n*; ~ments [~lmənts] *pl.* Zinnen *f/pl.*; ~plane ✕ Kriegsflugzeug *n*; ~ship ✕ Schlachtschiff *n*.

Bavarian [bə'vɛəriən] **1.** bay(e)-risch; **2.** Bayer(in).

bawdy ['bɔ:di] unzüchtig.

bawl [bɔ:l] brüllen; johlen, grölen; ~ out auf~, losbrüllen.

bay[1] [bei] **1.** rotbraun; **2.** Braune(r) *m* (*Pferd*).

bay[2] [~] Bai *f*, Bucht *f*; Erker *m*.

bay[3] [~] Lorbeer *m*.

bay[4] [~] **1.** bellen, anschlagen; **2.** *stand at ~* sich verzweifelt wehren; *bring to ~ Wild etc.* stellen.

bayonet ✕ ['beiənit] **1.** Bajonett *n*; **2.** mit dem Bajonett niederstoßen.

bayou *Am.* ['baiu:] sumpfiger Nebenarm.

bay window ['bei'windou] Erkerfenster *n*; *Am. sl.* Vorbau *m* (*Bauch*).

baza(a)r [bə'zɑ:] Basar *m*.

be [bi:, bi] [*irr.*] **1.** *v/i.* sein; *there is od. are es gibt*; *here you are again!* da haben wir's wieder!; ~ *about* beschäftigt sein mit; ~ *at* s.th. et. vorhaben; ~ *off* aus sein, sich fortmachen; **2.** *v/aux.*: ~ *reading* beim Lesen sein, gerade lesen; *I am to inform you* ich soll Ihnen mitteilen; **3.** *v/aux. mit p.p. zur Bildung des Passivs.* werden.

beach [bi:tʃ] **1.** Strand *m*; **2.** ⚓ auf den Strand setzen *od.* ziehen; ~comber ['bi:tʃkoumə] *fig.* Nichtstuer *m*.

beacon ['bi:kən] Blinklicht *n*; Leuchtfeuer *n*, Leuchtturm *m*.

bead [bi:d] Perle *f*; Tropfen *m*; Visier-Korn *n*; ~s *pl. a.* Rosenkranz *m*.

beak [bi:k] Schnabel *m*; Tülle *f*.

beaker ['bi:kə] Becher(glas *n*) *m*.

beam [bi:m] **1.** Balken *m*; Waagebalken *m*; Strahl *m*; Glanz *m*; *Radio* Richtstrahl *m*; **2.** (aus-)strahlen.

bean [bi:n] Bohne *f*; *Am. sl.* Birne *f* (*Kopf*); *full of ~s* F lebensprühend.

bear[1] [bɛə] Bär *m*; ✝ *sl.* Baissier *m*.

bear[2] [~] [*irr.*] *v/t.* tragen; hervorbringen, gebären; *Liebe etc.* hegen; ertragen; ~ *down* überwältigen; ~ *out* unterstützen, bestätigen; *v/i.* tragen; fruchtbar *od.* trächtig sein; leiden, dulden; ~ *up* standhalten, fest bleiben; ~ (*up*)*on* einwirken auf (*acc.*); *bring to* ~ zur Anwendung bringen, einwirken lassen, *Druck etc.* ausüben.

beard [biəd] **1.** Bart *m*; ♀ Granne *f*; **2.** *v/t. j-m* entgegentreten, trotzen.

bearer ['bɛərə] Träger(in); Überbringer(in), *Wechsel*-Inhaber(in).

bearing ['bɛəriŋ] (Er)Tragen *n*;

Betragen *n*; Beziehung *f*; Richtung *f*.

beast [bi:st] Vieh *n*, Tier *n*; Bestie *f*; ~ly ['bi:stli] viehisch; scheußlich.

beat [bi:t] **1.** [*irr.*] *v/t.* schlagen; prügeln; besiegen, *Am.* F *j-m* zuvorkommen; übertreffen; *Am.* F betrügen; ~ *it! Am. sl.* hau ab!; ~ *the band Am.* F wichtig *od.* großartig sein; ~ *a retreat* den Rückzug antreten; ~ *one's way Am.* F sich durchschlagen; ~ *up* auftreiben, *v/i.* schlagen; ~ *about the bush* wie die Katze um den heißen Brei herumgehen; **2.** Schlag *m*; ♪ Takt(schlag) *m*; Pulsschlag *m*; Runde *f*, Revier *n* *e-s Schutzmannes etc.*; *Am.* sensationelle Erstmeldung *e-r Zeitung*; **3.** F baff, verblüfft; ~en ['bi:tn] *p.p. von beat 1*; (aus)getreten (*Weg*).

beatitude [bi(:)'ætitju:d] (Glück-)Seligkeit *f*.

beatnik ['bi:tnik] Beatnik *m*, junger Antikonformist und Bohemien.

beau [bou] Stutzer *m*; Anbeter *m*.

beautiful ['bju:təful] schön.

beautify ['bju:tifai] verschönern.

beauty ['bju:ti] Schönheit *f*; *Sleeping ~* Dornrös-chen *n*; ~ *parlo(u)r*, ~ *shop* Schönheitssalon *m*.

beaver ['bi:və] Biber *m*; Biberpelz *m*.

becalm [bi'ka:m] beruhigen.

became [bi'keim] *pret. von become*

because [bi'kɔz] weil; ~ *of* wegen.

beckon ['bekən] (*j-m zu*)winken.

becom|**e** [bi'kʌm] [*irr.*] *v/i.* werden (*of aus*), *v/t.* anstehen, ziemen (*dat.*); sich schicken für; kleiden (*Hut etc.*); ~**ing** [~miŋ] passend; schicklich, kleidsam.

bed [bed] **1.** Bett *n*; Lager *n* *e-s Tieres*; ♂ Beet *n*; Unterlage *f*; **2.** betten.

bed-clothes ['bedkloudz] *pl.* Bettwäsche *f*

bedding [bediŋ] Bettzeug *n*; Streu *f*.

bedevil [bi'devl] behexen; quälen.

bedlam ['bedləm] Tollhaus *n*.

bed|**rid**|**den** ['bedrid(n)] bettlägerig. ~**room** Schlafzimmer *n*; ~**spread** Bett-, Tagesdecke *f*; ~**stead** Bettstelle *f*; ~**time** Schlafenszeit *f*

bee [bi:] *zo.* Biene *f*; *Am.* nachbarliches Treffen; Wettbewerb *m*; *have a ~ in one's bonnet* F *e-e* fixe Idee haben.

beech ♀ [bi:tʃ] Buche *f*; ~**nut** Bucheicker *f*.

beef [bi:f] **1.** Rindfleisch *n*; **2.** *Am.* F nörgeln; ~ *tea* Fleischbrühe *f*; ~**y** ['bi:fi] fleischig; kräftig.

bee|**hive** ['bi:haiv] Bienenkorb *m*, -stock *m*; ~**keeper** Bienenzüchter *m*; ~**line** kürzester Weg; *make a ~ for Am.* schnurstracks losgehen auf (*acc.*).

been [bi:n, bin] *p.p. von* be.
beer [biə] Bier *n*; *small* ~ Dünnbier
n. [Bete *f*.]
beet ♀ [bi:t] (Runkel)Rübe *f*,]
beetle¹ ['bi:tl] Käfer *m*.
beetle² [~] **1.** überhängend; buschig
(*Brauen*); **2.** *v/i.* überhängen.
beetroot ['bi:tru:t] rote Rübe.
befall [bi'fɔ:l] [*irr.* (*fall*)] *v/t.* zustoßen (*dat.*); *v/i.* sich ereignen.
befit [bi'fit] sich schicken für.
before [bi'fɔ:] **1.** *adv. Raum:* vorn;
voran; *Zeit:* vorher, früher; schon
(früher); **2.** *cj.* bevor, ehe, bis;
3. *prp.* vor; ~hand vorher, zuvor;
voraus (*with dat.*).
befriend [bi'frend] sich *j-m* freundlich erweisen.
beg [beg] *v/t. et.* erbetteln; erbitten
(*of von*); *j-n* bitten; ~ *the question*
um den Kern der Frage herum-
gehen; *v/i.* betteln; bitten; betteln
gehen; sich gestatten.
began [bi'gæn] *pret. von* begin.
beget [bi'get] [*irr.* (*get*)] (er)zeugen.
beggar ['begə] **1.** Bettler(in) *f*;
F Kerl *m*; **2.** zum Bettler machen;
fig. übertreffen; *it* ~*s all description*
es spottet jeder Beschreibung.
begin [bi'gin] [*irr.*] beginnen (*at*
bei, mit); ~ner [~nə] Anfänger(in);
~ning [~niŋ] Beginn *m*, Anfang *m*.
begone [bi'gɔn] fort!, F pack dich!
begot [bi'gɔt] *pret. von* beget; ~ten
[~tn] **1.** *p.p. von* beget; **2.** *adj.* er-
zeugt.
begrudge [bi'grʌdʒ] mißgönnen.
beguile [bi'gail] täuschen; betrügen
(*of, out of* um); *Zeit* vertreiben.
begun [bi'gʌn] *p.p. von* begin.
behalf [bi'hɑ:f]: *on* ~. *in* ~ *of* im
Namen von; *um* ... (*gen.*) willen.
behav|e [bi'heiv] sich benehmen;
~io(u)r [~vjə] Benehmen *n*, Betragen *n*.
behead [bi'hed] enthaupten.
behind [bi'haind] **1.** *adv.* hinten;
dahinter; zurück; **2.** *prp.* hinter;
~hand zurück, im Rückstand.
behold [bi'hould] [*irr.* (*hold*)] **1.** erblicken; **2.** siehe (da)!; ~en [~dən]
verpflichtet, verbunden.
behoof [bi'hu:f]: *to* (*for, on*) (*the*) ~
of in *j-s* Interesse, um *j-s* willen.
behoove *Am.* [bi'hu:v] = behove.
behove [bi'houv]: *it* ~*s s.o. to inf.*
es ist *j-s* Pflicht, zu *inf.*
being ['bi:iŋ] (Da)Sein *n*; Wesen
n; *in* ~ lebend; wirklich (vorhanden).
belabo(u)r F [bi'leibə] verbleuen.
belated [bi'leitid] verspätet.
belch [beltʃ] **1.** rülpsen; ausspeien;
2. Rülpsen *n*; Ausbruch *m*.
beleaguer [bi'li:gə] belagern.
belfry ['belfri] Glockenturm *m*,
-stuhl *m*. [2. Belgier(in).]
Belgian ['beldʒən] **1.** belgisch;]
belie [bi'lai] Lügen strafen.
belief [bi'li:f] Glaube *m* (*in an acc.*).

believable [bi'li:vəbl] glaubhaft.
believe [bi'li:v] glauben (*in an acc.*);
~r [~və] Gläubige(r *m*) *f*.
belittle *fig.* [bi'litl] verkleinern.
bell [bel] Glocke *f*; Klingel *f*; ~boy
Am. ['belbɔi] Hotelpage *m*.
belle [bel] Schöne *f*, Schönheit *f*.
belles-lettres ['bel'letr] *pl.* Belle-
tristik *f*, schöne Literatur.
bellhop *Am. sl.* ['belhɔp] Hotelpage *m*.
bellied ['belid] bauchig.
belligerent [bi'lidʒərənt] **1.** krieg-
führend; **2.** kriegführendes Land.
bellow ['belou] **1.** brüllen; **2.** Gebrüll *n*; ~*s pl.* Blasebalg *m*.
belly ['beli] **1.** Bauch *m*; **2.** (sich)
bauchen; (an)schwellen.
belong [bi'lɔŋ] (an)gehören; ~ *to*
gehören *dat. od.* zu; sich gehören
für; *j-m* gebühren; ~ings [~giŋz]
pl. Habseligkeiten *f/pl.*
beloved [bi'lʌvd] **1.** geliebt; **2.** Ge-
liebte(r *m*) *f*.
below [bi'lou] **1.** *adv.* unten; **2.** *prp.*
unter.
belt [belt] **1.** Gürtel *m*; ✂ Koppel *n*;
Zone *f*, Bezirk *m*; ⊕ Treibriemen
m; **2.** umgürten; ~ *out Am.* F
herausschmettern, loslegen (*singen*).
bemoan [bi'moun] betrauern, beklagen.
bench [bentʃ] Bank *f*; Richterbank
f; Gerichtshof *m*; Arbeitstisch *m*.
bend [bend] **1.** Biegung *f*, Kurve *f*;
♧ Seemannsknoten *m*; **2.** [*irr.*]
(sich) biegen; *Geist etc.* richten (*to,
on auf acc.*); (sich) beugen; sich
neigen (*to vor dat.*).
beneath [bi'ni:θ] = below.
benediction [beni'dikʃən] Segen *m*.
benefact|ion [beni'fækʃən] Wohltat
f; ~or ['benifæktə] Wohltäter *m*.
beneficen|ce [bi'nefisəns] Wohl-
tätigkeit *f*; ~t □ [~nt] wohltätig.
beneficial □ [beni'fiʃəl] wohltuend;
zuträglich; nützlich.
benefit ['benifit] **1.** Wohltat *f*;
Nutzen *m*, Vorteil *m*; Wohltätig-
keitsveranstaltung *f*; (Wohlfahrts-)
Unterstützung *f*; **2.** nützen; begünstigen; Nutzen ziehen.
benevolen|ce [bi'nevələns] Wohl-
wollen *n*; ~t □ [~nt] wohlwollend;
gütig, mildherzig.
benign □ [bi'nain] freundlich,
gütig; zuträglich; ✿ gutartig.
bent [bent] **1.** *pret. u. p.p. von*
bend 2; ~ *on versessen auf* (*acc.*);
2. Hang *m*; Neigung *f*.
benzene 🜂 ['benzi:n] Benzol *n*.
benzine 🜂 ['benzi:n] Benzin *n*.
bequeath [bi'kwi:ð] vermachen.
bequest [bi'kwest] Vermächtnis *n*.
bereave [bi'ri:v] [*irr.*] berauben.
bereft [bi'reft] *pret. u. p.p. von*
bereave.
beret ['berei] Baskenmütze *f*.

berry ['bɛri] Beere f.

berth [bəːθ] **1.** ⚓ Ankergrund m; Koje f; fig. (gute) Stelle; **2.** vor Anker gehen.

beseech [bi'siːtʃ] [irr.] ersuchen; bitten; um et. bitten; flehen.

beset [bi'set] [irr. (set)] umgeben; bedrängen; verfolgen.

beside prp. [bi'said] neben; weitab von; ~ o.s. außer sich (with vor); ~ the point, ~ the question nicht zur Sache gehörig; ~s [~dz] **1.** adv. außerdem; **2.** prp. abgesehen von, außer.

besiege [bi'siːdʒ] belagern.

besmear [bi'smiə] beschmieren.

besom [bi'zzəm] (Reisig)Besen m.

besought [bi'sɔːt] pret. u. p.p. von beseech.

bespatter [bi'spætə] (be)spritzen.

bespeak [bi'spiːk] [irr. (speak)] vorbestellen; verraten, (an)zeigen; bespoke tailor Maßschneider m.

best [best] **1.** adj. best; höchst; größt, meist; ~ man Brautführer m; **2.** adv. am besten, aufs beste; **3.** Beste(r m, -s n) f, Besten pl.; to the ~ of ... nach bestem ...; make the ~ of tun, was man kann, mit; at ~ im besten Falle.

bestial [['bestjəl] tierisch, viehisch.

bestow [bi'stou] geben, schenken, verleihen (on, upon dat.).

bet [bet] **1.** Wette f; **2.** [irr.] wetten; you ~ F sicherlich.

betake [bi'teik] [irr. (take)]: ~ o.s. to sich begeben nach; fig. s-e Zuflucht nehmen zu.

bethink [bi'θiŋk] [irr. (think)]: ~ o.s. sich besinnen (of auf acc.); ~ o.s. to inf. sich in den Kopf setzen zu inf.

betimes [bi'taimz] beizeiten.

betray [bi'trei] verraten (a. fig.); verleiten; ~er [~eiə] Verräter(in).

betrothal [bi'trouðəl] Verlobung f.

better ['betə] **1.** adj. besser, he is ~ es geht ihm besser; **2.** Bessere(s) n; ~s pl. Höherstehenden pl., Vorgesetzten pl.; get the ~ of die Oberhand gewinnen über (acc.); überwinden; **3.** adv. besser; mehr; so much the ~ desto besser; you had ~ go es wäre besser, wenn du gingest; **4.** v/t. (ver)bessern; v/i. sich bessern; ~ment [~əmənt] Verbesserung f.

between [bi'twiːn] (a. **betwixt** [bi'twikst]) **1.** adv. dazwischen; **2.** prp. zwischen, unter.

bevel ['bevəl] schräg, schief.

beverage ['bevəridʒ] Getränk n.

bevy ['bevi] Schwarm m; Schar f.

bewail [bi'weil] be-, wehklagen.

beware [bi'weə] sich hüten (of vor).

bewilder [bi'wildə] irremachen; verwirren; bestürzt machen; ~ment [~əmənt] Verwirrung f; Bestürzung f.

bewitch [bi'witʃ] bezaubern, behexen

beyond [bi'jɔnd] **1.** adv. darüber hinaus, **2.** prp. jenseits, über (... hinaus); mehr als; außer.

bi... [bai] zwei ...

bias ['baiəs] **1.** adj. u. adv. schief, schräg. **2.** Neigung f; Vorurteil n; **3.** beeinflussen, ~sed befangen.

bib [bib] (Sabber)Lätzchen n.

Bible ['baibl] Bibel f.

biblical [['biblikəl] biblisch; Bibel

bibliography [bibli'ɔgrəfi] Bibliographie f

bicarbonate 🜔 [bai'kɑːbənit] doppeltkohlensaures Natron.

biceps ['baiseps] Bizeps m.

bicker ['bikə] (sich) zanken; flackern, plätschern; prasseln.

bicycle ['baisikl] **1.** Fahrrad n; **2.** radfahren, radeln.

bid [bid] **1.** [irr.] gebieten, befehlen; (ent)bieten, Karten: reizen; ~ fair versprechen, ~ farewell Lebewohl sagen. **2.** Gebot n, Angebot n; ~den [bidn] p.p. von bid **1.**

bide [baid] [irr.]: ~ one's time den rechten Augenblick abwarten.

biennial [bai'eniəl] zweijährig.

bier [biə] (Toten)Bahre f.

big [big] groß, erwachsen; schwanger; ' wichtig(tuerisch); ~ business Großunternehmertum n; ~ shot F hohes Tier, ~ stick Am. Macht (-entfaltung) f; talk ~ den Mund vollnehmen

bigamy ['bigəmi] Doppelehe f.

bigot ['bigət] Frömmler(in); blinder Anhänger, ~ry [~tri] Frömmelei f.

bigwig ['bigwig] hohes Tier (P.).

bike [baik] (Fahr)Rad n.

bilateral [bai'lætərəl] zweiseitig.

bile [bail] Galle f (a. fig.).

bilious ['biljəs] gallig (a. fig.).

bill [bil] Schnabel m; Spitze f.

bill² [~] **1.** Gesetzentwurf m; Klage-, Rechtsschrift f; a. ~ of exchange Wechsel m, Zettel m; Am. Banknote f; ~ of fare Speisekarte f; ~ of lading Seefrachtbrief m, Konnossement n; ~ of sale Kaufvertrag m; 2 of Rights englische Freiheitsurkunde (1689); Am. die ersten 10 Zusatzartikel zur Verfassung der USA; **2.** (durch Anschlag) ankündigen

billboard Am. ['bilbɔːd] Anschlagbrett n

billfold Am. ['bilfould] Brieftasche f für Papiergeld.

billiards ['biljədz] pl. od. sg. Billiard(spiel) n.

billion ['biljən] Billion f; Am. Milliarde f.

billow ['bilou] **1.** Woge f (a. fig.); **2.** wogen; ~y [~oui] wogend.

billy Am. ['bili] (Gummi)Knüppel m.

bin [bin] Kasten *m*, Behälter *m*.

bind [baind] [*irr.*] *v/t.* (an-, ein-, um-, auf-, fest-, ver)binden; verpflichten; *Handel* abschließen; *Saum* einfassen; *v/i.* binden; **~er** ['baində] Binder *m*; Binde *f*; **~ing** [~diŋ] 1. bindend; 2. Binden *n*; Einband *m*; Einfassung *f*.

binocular [bi'nɔkjulə] *mst* **~s** *pl.* Feldstecher *m*, Fern-, Opernglas *n*.

biography [bai'ɔgrəfi] Biographie *f*.

biology [bai'ɔlədʒi] Biologie *f*.

biped *zo.* ['baiped] Zweifüßer *m*.

birch [bə:tʃ] 1. ♀ Birke *f*; (Birken-) Rute *f*; 2. mit der Rute züchtigen.

bird [bə:d] Vogel *m*; **~'s-eye** ['bə:dzai]: ~ view Vogelperspektive *f*.

birth [bə:θ] Geburt *f*; Ursprung *m*; Entstehung *f*; Herkunft *f*; **bring to** ~ entstehen lassen, veranlassen; **give** ~ **to** gebären, zur Welt bringen; ~ **control** Geburtenregelung *f*; **~day** ['bə:θdei] Geburtstag *m*; **~place** Geburtsort *m*.

biscuit ['biskit] Zwieback *m*; Keks *m*, *n*; Biskuit *n* (*Porzellan*).

bishop ['biʃəp] Bischof *m*; Läufer *m* im *Schach*; **~ric** [~prik] Bistum *n*.

bison *zo.* ['baisn] Wisent *m*.

bit [bit] 1. Bißchen *n*, Stückchen *n*; Gebiß *n am Zaum*; *Schlüssel*-Bart *m*; **a** (*little*) ~ ein (kleines) bißchen; 2. zäumen; zügeln; 3. *pret. von* bite 2.

bitch [bitʃ] Hündin *f*; V Hure *f*.

bite [bait] 1. Beißen *n*; Biß *m*; Bissen *m*; ⊕ Fassen *n*; 2. [*irr.*] (an)beißen; brennen (*Pfeffer*); schneiden (*Kälte*); ⊕ fassen; *fig.* verletzen.

bitten ['bitn] *p.p. von* bite 2.

bitter ['bitə] 1. □ bitter; streng; *fig.* verbittert; 2. **~s** *pl.* Magenbitter *m*.

biz F [biz] Geschäft *n*.

blab F [blæb] (aus)schwatzen.

black [blæk] 1. □ schwarz; dunkel; finster; ~ **eye** blaues Auge; 2. schwärzen; wichsen; ~ **out** verdunkeln; 3. Schwarz *n*; Schwärze *f*; Schwarze(r *m*) *f* (*Neger*); **~amoor** ['blækəmuə] Neger *m*; **~berry** Brombeere *f*; **~bird** Amsel *f*; **~board** Wandtafel *f*; **~en** [~kən] *v/t.* schwärzen; *fig.* anschwärzen; *v/i.* schwarz werden; **~guard** ['blægɑ:d] 1. Lump *m*, Schuft *m*; 2. □ schuftig; **~head** ♀ Mitesser *m*; **~ing** [~kiŋ] Schuhwichse *f*; **~ish** [~lʃ] □ schwärzlich; **~jack** 1. *bsd. Am.* Totschläger *m* (*Instrument*); 2. niederknüppeln; **~leg** Betrüger *m*; **~-letter** *typ.* Fraktur *f*; **~mail** 1. Erpressung *f*; 2. *j-n* erpressen; ~ **market** schwarzer Markt; **~ness** [~knis] Schwärze *f*; **~out** Verdunkelung *f*; ~ **pudding** Blutwurst *f*; **~smith** Grobschmied *m*.

bladder *anat.* ['blædə] Blase *f*.

blade [bleid] Blatt *n*, ♀ Halm *m*; *Säge-, Schulter- etc.* Blatt *n*; Propellerflügel *m*; Klinge *f*.

blame [bleim] 1. Tadel *m*; Schuld *f*; 2. tadeln; **be to** ~ **for** schuld sein an (*dat.*); **~ful** ['bleimful] tadelnswert; **~less** □ [~mlis] tadellos.

blanch [blɑ:ntʃ] bleichen; erbleichen (lassen); ~ **over** beschönigen.

bland □ [blænd] mild, sanft.

blank [blæŋk] 1. □ blank; leer; unausgefüllt; unbeschrieben; ✝ Blanko...; verdutzt; ~ **cartridge** ✗ Platzpatrone *f*; 2. Weiße *n*; Leere *f*; leerer Raum; Lücke *f*; unbeschriebenes Blatt, Formular *n*; Niete *f*.

blanket ['blæŋkit] 1. Wolldecke *f*; **wet** ~ *fig.* Dämpfer *m*; Spielverderber *m*; 2. (mit e-r Wolldecke) zudecken; 3. *Am.* umfassend, Gesamt...

blare [blεə] schmettern; grölen.

blasphem|e [blæs'fi:m] lästern (*against* über *acc.*); **~y** ['blæsfimi] Gotteslästerung *f*.

blast [blɑ:st] 1. Windstoß *m*; Ton *m* **e-s Blasinstruments**; ⊕ Gebläse (-luft *f*) *n*; Luftdruck *m* **e-r Explosion**; ♀ Meltau *m*; 2. (in die Luft) sprengen; zerstören (*a. fig.*); ~ (**it**)! verdammt; **~-furnace** ⊕ ['blɑ:st'fə:nis] Hochofen *m*.

blatant □ ['bleitənt] lärmend.

blather *Am.* ['blæðə] schwätzen.

blaze [bleiz] 1. Flamme(n *pl.*) *f*; Feuer *n*; **~s** *pl. sl.* Teufel *m*, Hölle *f*; heller Schein; *fig.* Ausbruch *m*; **go to** ~**s!** zum Teufel mit dir!; 2. *v/i.* brennen, flammen, lodern; leuchten; *v/t.* ~ **abroad** ausposaunen; **~r** ['bleizə] Blazer *m*.

blazon ['bleizn] Wappen(kunde *f*) *n*.

bleach [bli:tʃ] bleichen; **~er** ['bli:tʃə] Bleicher(in); *mst* **~s** *pl. Am.* nichtüberdachte Zuschauerplätze.

bleak □ [bli:k] öde, kahl; rauh; *fig.* trüb, freudlos, finster.

blear [bliə] 1. trüb; 2. trüben; **~-eyed** ['bliəraid] triefäugig.

bleat [bli:t] 1. Blöken *n*; 2. blöken.

bleb [bleb] Bläs-chen *n*, Pustel *f*.

bled [bled] *pret. u. p.p. von* bleed.

bleed [bli:d] [*irr.*] *v/i.* bluten; *v/t.* zur Ader lassen; *fig.* schröpfen; **~ing** ['bli:diŋ] 1. Bluten *n*; Aderlaß *m*; 2. *sl.* verflixt.

blemish ['blemiʃ] 1. Fehler *m*; Makel *m*, Schande *f*; 2. verunstalten; brandmarken.

blench [blentʃ] *v/i.* zurückschrecken; *v/t.* die Augen schließen vor.

blend [blend] 1. [*irr.*] (sich) (ver)mischen; *Wein etc.* verschneiden; 2. Mischung *f*; ✝ Verschnitt *m*.

blent [blent] *pret. u. p.p. von* blend 1.

bless [bles] segnen; preisen; be-

glücken; ~ me! herrje!; ~ed □
[pret. u. p.p. blest; adj. 'blesid]
glückselig; gesegnet; ~ing [~siŋ]
Segen m.

blew [blu:] pret. von blow² u. blow³1.

blight [blait] 1. ♀ Mehltau m; fig.
Gifthauch m; 2. vernichten.

blind [blaind] 1. blind (fig. to
gegen); geheim; nicht erkennbar;
~ alley Sackgasse f; ~ly fig. blindlings; 2. Blende f; Fenster-Vor-
hang m, Jalousie f; Am. Versteck
n; Vorwand m; 3. blenden; ver-
blenden (to gegen); abblenden;
~fold ['blaindfould] 1. blindlings;
2. j-m die Augen verbinden;
~worm Blindschleiche f.

blink [bliŋk] 1. Blinzeln n; Schimmer m; 2. v/i. blinzeln; blinken;
schimmern; v/t. absichtlich übersehen; ~er ['bliŋkə] Scheuklappe f.

bliss [blis] Seligkeit f, Wonne f.

blister ['blistə] 1. Blase f (auf der
Haut, im Lack); Zugpflaster n;
2. Blasen bekommen od. ziehen
(auf dat.).

blithe □ mst poet. [blaið] lustig.

blizzard ['blizəd] Schneesturm m.

bloat [blout] aufblasen; aufschwel-
len; ~er ['bloutə] Bückling m.

block [blɔk] 1. (Häuser-, Schreib-
etc.)Block m; Klotz m; Druckstock
m; Verstopfung f, Stockung f;
2. formen; verhindern; ~ in entwerfen, skizzieren; mst ~ up (ab-, ver-)
sperren; blockieren.

blockade [blɔ'keid] 1. Blockade f;
2. blockieren.

block|head ['blɔkhed] Dummkopf
m; ~ letters Druckschrift f.

blond(e f) [blɔnd] 1. blond;
2. Blondine f.

blood [blʌd] Blut n; fig. Blut n;
Abstammung f; in cold ~ kalten
Blutes, kaltblütig; ~-curdling
['blʌdkə:dliŋ] haarsträubend; ~-
horse Vollblutpferd n; ~shed Blut-
vergießen n; ~shot blutunterlaufen;
~thirsty blutdürstig; ~-vessel
Blutgefäß n; ~y □ ['blʌdi] blutig;
blutdürstig.

bloom [blu:m] 1. Blüte f; Reif m auf
Früchten; fig. Schmelz m; 2. (er-)
blühen (a. fig.).

blossom ['blɔsəm] 1. Blüte f;
2. blühen.

blot [blɔt] 1. Klecks m; fig. Makel m;
2. v/t. beklecksen, beflecken; (ab-)
löschen; ausstreichen; v/i. klecksen.

blotch [blɔtʃ] Pustel f; Fleck m.

blotter ['blɔtə] Löscher m; Am.
Protokollbuch n. [Löschpapier n.\

blotting-paper ['blɔtiŋpeipə]

blouse [blauz] Bluse f.

blow¹ [blou] Schlag m, Stoß m.

blow² [~] irr.] blühen.

blow³ [~] 1. [irr.] v/i. blasen; wehen;
schnaufen; ~ up in die Luft fliegen;
v/t. (weg- etc.)blasen; wehen; ♀

durchbrennen; ~ one's nose sich die
Nase putzen; ~ up sprengen;
2. Blasen n, Wehen n; ~er ['blouə]
Bläser m.

blown [bloun] p.p. von blow² und
blow³1.

blow|-out mot. ['blouaut] Reifen-
panne f, ~pipe Gebläsebrenner m.

bludgeon ['blʌdʒən] Knüppel m.

blue [blu:] 1. blau; F trüb,
schwermütig, 2. Blau n; 3. blau
färben, blauen; ~bird ['blu:bə:d]
amerikanische Singdrossel; ~ laws
Am. strenge (puritanische) Gesetze;
~s [blu:z] pl. Trübsinn m; ♪
Blues m.

bluff [blʌf] 1. □ schroff; steil; derb;
2. Steilufer n; Irreführung f;
3. bluffen, irreführen.

bluish ['blu(:)iʃ] bläulich.

blunder ['blʌndə] 1. Fehler m,
Schnitzer m; 2. e-n Fehler machen;
stolpern, stümpern; verpfuschen.

blunt [blʌnt] 1. □ stumpf (a. fig.);
plump, grob, derb; 2. abstumpfen.

blur [blə:] 1. Fleck(en) m; fig. Ver-
schwommenheit f; 2. v/t. beflecken;
verwischen, Sinn trüben.

blush [blʌʃ] 1. Schamröte f; Erröten n, flüchtiger Blick; 2. erröten, (vor Scham) röten.

bluster ['blʌstə] 1. Brausen n, Getöse n, Prahlerei f; 2. brausen;
prahlen

boar [bɔ:] Eber m; hunt. Keiler m.

board [bɔ:d] 1. (Anschlag)Brett n;
Konferenztisch m; Ausschuß m;
Gremium n, Behörde f; Verpflegung f, Pappe f; on ~ a train Am.
in e-m Zug, ~ of Trade Handels-
ministerium n, 2. v/t. dielen, verschalen, beköstigen; an Bord gehen; ♣ entern; bsd. Am. einsteigen
in (ein Fahr- od. Flugzeug); v/i. in
Kost sein; ~er ['bɔ:də] Kost-
gänger(in); Internatsschüler(in);
~ing-house ['bɔ:diŋhaus] Pension
f; ~ing-school ['bɔ:diŋsku:l] Internatsschule f; ~walk bsd. Am.
Strandpromenade f.

boast [boust] 1. Prahlerei f; 2. (of,
about) sich rühmen (gen.), prahlen
(mit); ~ful □ ['boustful] prahlerisch

boat [bout] Boot n; Schiff n; ~ing
['boutiŋ] Bootfahrt f.

bob [bɔb] 1. Quaste f; Ruck m;
Knicks m, Schopf m; sl. Schilling
m; 2. v/t. Haar stutzen; ~bed hair
Bubikopf m; v/i. springen, tanzen;
knicksen

bobbin ['bɔbin] Spule f (a. ♀).

bobble Am f ['bɔbl] Fehler m.

bobby sl. ['bɔbi] Schupo m, Polizist
m.

bobsleigh ['bɔbslei] Bob(sleigh) m
(Rennschlitten).

bode¹ [boud] prophezeien.

bode² [~] pret. von bide.

bodice ['bɔdis] Mieder n; Taille f.
bodily ['bɔdili] körperlich.
body ['bɔdi] Körper m, Leib m; Leichnam m; Körperschaft f; Hauptteil m; mot. Karosserie f; ✂ Truppenkörper m; **~guard** Leibwache f.
Boer ['bouə] Bure m; attr. Buren...
bog [bɔg] 1. Sumpf m, Moor n; 2. im Schlamm versenken.
boggle ['bɔgl] stutzen; pfuschen.
bogus ['bougəs] falsch; Schwindel...
boil [bɔil] 1. kochen, sieden; (sich) kondensieren; 2. Sieden n; Beule f, Geschwür n; **~er** ['bɔilə] (Dampf-) Kessel m.
boisterous □ ['bɔistərəs] ungestüm; heftig, laut; lärmend.
bold □ [bould] kühn; keck, dreist; steil; typ. fett; make ~ sich erkühnen; **~ness** ['bouldnis] Kühnheit f; Keckheit f, Dreistigkeit f.
bolster ['boulstə] 1. Kopfkeil m, Unterlage f; 2. polstern; (unter-) stützen.
bolt [boult] 1. Bolzen m; Riegel m; Blitz(strahl) m; Ausreißen n; 2. adv. ~ upright kerzengerade; 3. v/t. verriegeln; F hinunterschlingen; sieben; v/i. eilen; durchgehen (Pferd); Am. pol. abtrünnig werden; **~er** ['boultə] Ausreißer(in).
bomb [bɔm] 1. Bombe f; 2. mit Bomben belegen.
bombard [bɔm'bɑ:d] bombardieren.
bombastic [bɔm'bæstik] schwülstig.
bomb-proof ['bɔmpru:f] bombensicher.
bond [bɔnd] Band n; Fessel f; Bündnis n; Schuldschein m; ✝ Obligation f; in ~ unter Zollverschluß; **~age** ['bɔndidʒ] Hörigkeit f; Knechtschaft f; **~(s)man** [~d(z)mən] Leibeigene(r) m.
bone [boun] 1. Knochen m; Gräte f; ~s pl. a. Gebeine n/pl.; ~ of contention Zankapfel m; make no ~s about F nicht lange fackeln mit; 2. die Knochen auslösen (aus); aus-, entgräten.
bonfire ['bɔnfaiə] Freudenfeuer n.
bonnet ['bɔnit] Haube f, Schute(nhut m) f; ⊕ (Motor)Haube f.
bonus ✝ ['bounəs] Prämie f; Gratifikation f; Zulage f.
bony ['bouni] knöchern; knochig.
boob Am. [bu:b] Dummkopf m.
booby ['bu:bi] Tölpel m.
book [buk] 1. Buch n; Heft n; Liste f; Block m; 2. buchen; eintragen; Fahrkarte etc. lösen; e-n Platz etc. bestellen; Gepäck aufgeben; **~burner** Am. F ['bukbə:nə] intoleranter Mensch; **~case** Bücherschrank m; **~ing-clerk** ['bukiŋklɑ:k] Schalterbeamt|e(r) m, -in f; **~ing-office** ['bukiŋɔfis] Fahrkartenausgabe f, -schalter m; thea.

Kasse f; **~ish** □ [~iʃ] gelehrt; **~keeping** Buchführung f; **~let** ['buklit] Büchlein n; Broschüre f; **~seller** Buchhändler m.
boom¹ [bu:m] 1. ✝ Aufschwung m, Hochkonjunktur f, Hausse f; Reklamerummel m; 2. in die Höhe treiben od. gehen; für et. Reklame machen.
boom² [~] brummen; dröhnen.
boon¹ [bu:n] Segen m, Wohltat f.
boon² [~] freundlich, munter.
boor fig. [buə] Bauer m, Lümmel m; **~ish** □ ['buəriʃ] bäuerisch, lümmel-, flegelhaft.
boost [bu:st] heben; verstärken (a. ∮); Reklame machen.
boot¹ [bu:t]: to ~ obendrein.
boot² [~] Stiefel m; Kofferraum m; **~black** Am. ['bu:tblæk] = shoeblack; **~ee** ['bu:ti:] Damen-Halbstiefel m.
booth [bu:ð] (Markt- etc.)Bude f; Wahlzelle f; Am. Fernsprechzelle f.
boot|lace ['bu:tleis] Schnürsenkel m; **~legger** Am. [~legə] Alkoholschmuggler m.
booty ['bu:ti] Beute f, Raub m.
border ['bɔ:də] 1. Rand m, Saum m; Grenze f; Einfassung f; Rabatte f; 2. einfassen; grenzen (upon an acc.).
bore¹ [bɔ:] 1. Bohrloch n; Kaliber n; fig. langweiliger Mensch; Plage f; 2. bohren; langweilen; belästigen.
bore² [~] pret. von bear².
born [bɔ:n] p.p. von bear¹ gebären.
borne [bɔ:n] p.p. von bear² tragen.
borough ['bʌrə] Stadt(teil m) f; Am. a. Wahlbezirk m von New York City; municipal ~ Stadtgemeinde f.
borrow ['bɔrou] borgen, entleihen.
bosom ['buzəm] Busen m; fig. Schoß m.
boss F [bɔs] 1. Boss m, Chef m; bsd. Am. pol. (Partei)Bonze m; 2. leiten; **~y** Am. F ['bɔsi] tyrannisch, herrisch.
botany ['bɔtəni] Botanik f.
botch [bɔtʃ] 1. Flicken m; Flickwerk n; 2. flicken; verpfuschen.
both [bouθ] beide(s); ~ ... and sowohl ... als (auch).
bother F ['bɔðə] 1. Plage f; 2. (sich) plagen, (sich) quälen.
bottle ['bɔtl] 1. Flasche f; 2. auf Flaschen ziehen.
bottom ['bɔtəm] 1. Boden m, Grund m; Grundfläche f, Fuß m, Ende n; F Hintern m; fig. Wesen n, Kern m; at the ~ ganz unten; fig. im Grunde; 2. grundlegend, Grund...
bough [bau] Ast m, Zweig m.
bought [bɔ:t] pret. u. p.p von buy.
boulder ['bouldə] Geröllblock m.
bounce [bauns] 1. Sprung m, Rückprall m; F Aufschneiderei f; Auftrieb m; 2. (hoch)springen; F aufschneiden; **~r** F ['baunsə] F Mordskerl m; Am. sl. Rausschmeißer m.

bound¹ [baund] **1.** *pret. u. p.p von* **bind**; **2.** *adj.* verpflichtet; bestimmt, unterwegs (for nach).
bound² [..] **1.** Grenze *f*, Schranke *f*; **2.** begrenzen; beschränken.
bound³ [..] **1.** Sprung *m*; **2.** (hoch-)springen; an-, abprallen.
boundary ['baundəri] Grenze *f*.
boundless ['baundlis] grenzenlos.
bount|eous ['bauntiəs], **~iful** □ [..iful] freigebig; reichlich
bounty ['baunti] Freigebigkeit *f*; Spende *f*, ✦ Prämie *f*.
bouquet ['bukei] Bukett *n*, Strauß *m*; Blume *f des Weines*.
bout [baut] *Fecht-*Gang *m*; *Tanz-*Tour *f*; ♂ Anfall *m*; Kraftprobe *f*.
bow¹ [bau] **1.** Verbeugung *f*; **2.** *v/i.* sich (ver)beugen; *v/t.* biegen; beugen.
bow² ⚓ [..] Bug *m*.
bow³ [bou] **1.** Bogen *m*; Schleife *f*; **2.** geigen
bowdlerize ['baudləraiz] *Text* von anstößigen Stellen reinigen.
bowels ['bauəlz] *pl.* Eingeweide *n*; *das Innere*, *fig* Herz *n*.
bower ['bauə] Laube *f*.
bowl¹ [boul] Schale *f*, Schüssel *f*; *Pfeifen*-Kopf *m*.
bowl² [..] **1.** Kugel *f*; **~s** *pl.* Bowling *n*; **2.** *v/t* Ball etc. werfen; *v/i.* rollen; kegeln.
box¹ [bɔks] Buchsbaum *m*; Büchse *f*, Schachtel *f*, Kasten *m*; Koffer *m*; ⊕ Gehäuse *n*; *thea.* Loge *f*; Abteilung *f*; **2.** in Kästen etc. tun.
box² [..] **1.** boxen; **2.:** **~** on the ear Ohrfeige *f*
Boxing-Day ['bɔksiŋdei] zweiter Weihnachtsfeiertag.
box|-keeper ['bɔkski:pə] Logenschließer(in); **~-office** Theaterkasse *f*.
boy [bɔi] Junge *m*, junger Mann; Bursche *m* (*a. Diener*); **~-friend** Freund *m*; **~** scout Pfadfinder *m*; **~hood** ['bɔihud] Knabenalter *n*; **~ish** [['bɔiiʃ] knabenhaft; kindisch.
brace [breis] **1.** ⊕ Strebe *f*; Stützbalken *m*; Klammer *f*; Paar *n* (*Wild, Geflügel*); **~s** *pl.* Hosenträger *m/pl.*; **2.** absteifen; verankern; (an)spannen; *fig.* stärken.
bracelet ['breislit] Armband *n*.
bracket ['brækit] **1.** △ Konsole *f*; Winkelstütze *f*; *typ.* Klammer *f*; *Leuchter-*Arm *m*; lower income **~** niedrige Einkommensstufe; **2.** einklammern; *fig.* gleichstellen.
brackish ['brækiʃ] brackig, salzig.
brag [bræg] **1.** Prahlerei *f*; **2.** prahlen.
braggart ['brægət] **1.** Prahler *m*;
braid [breid] **1.** *Haar-*Flechte *f*; Borte *f*, Tresse *f*; **2.** flechten; mit Borte besetzen.
brain [brein] **1.** Gehirn *n*; Kopf *m*

(*fig. mst* **~s** = *Verstand*); **2.** *j-m* den Schädel einschlagen; **~-pan** ['breinpæn] Hirnschale *f*; **~(s)** trust *Am.* [..n(z)trʌst] Expertenrat *m* (*mst pol.*); **~-wave** ⌐ Geistesblitz *m*.
brake [breik] **1.** ⊕ Bremse *f*; **2.** bremsen; **~(s)man** ⛟ ['breik(s)mən] Bremser *m*; *Am.* Schaffner *m*.
bramble ['bræmbl] Brombeerstrauch *m*
bran [bræn] Kleie *f*.
branch [brɑːntʃ] **1.** Zweig *m*; Fach *n*; Linie *f des Stammbaumes*; Zweigstelle *f*; **2.** sich ver-, abzweigen
brand [brænd] **1.** (Feuer)Brand *m*; Brandmal *n*, Marke *f*; Sorte *f*; **2.** einbrennen; brandmarken.
brandish [['brændiʃ] schwingen.
bran(d)-new ['bræn(d)'nju:] nagelneu.
brandy ['brændi] Kognak *m*; Weinbrand *m*
brass [brɑːs] Messing *n*; F Unverschämtheit *f*; **~** band Blechblaskapelle *f*, **~-knuckles** *pl. Am.* Schlagring *m*
brassière ['bræsiə] Büstenhalter *m*.
brave [breiv] **1.** tapfer; prächtig; **2.** trotzen, mutig begegnen (*dat.*); **~ry** ['breivəri] Tapferkeit *f*; Pracht *f*
brawl [brɔːl] **1.** Krakeel *m*, Krawall *m*; **2.** krakeelen, Krawall machen.
brawny [broni] muskulös.
bray [brei] **1.** Eselsschrei *m*; **2.** schreien, schmettern; dröhnen.
bray² [(zer)stoßen, zerreiben.
brazen [breizn] bronzen; metallisch, **~-faced** unverschämt.
Brazilian [brə ziljən] **1.** brasilianisch, 2. brasilianer(in).
breach [briːtʃ] **1.** Bruch *m*; *fig.* Verletzung *f*, △ Bresche *f*; **2.** e-e Bresche schlagen in (*acc.*).
bread [bred] Brot *n*; know which side one's is buttered s-n Vorteil (er)kennen
breadth [bredθ] Breite *f*, Weite *f*, Größe *f des Geistes*; *Tuch-*Bahn *f*.
break [breik] **1.** Bruch *m*; Lücke *f*; Pause *f*, Absatz *m*; ✦ *Am.* (Preis-)Rückgang *m*; *Tages-*Anbruch *m*; a bad **~** e-e Dummheit; Pech *n*; a lucky **~** Glück *m*; **2.** [*irr.*] *v/t.* (zer)brechen, unterbrechen; übertreten; *Tier* abrichten; *Bank* sprengen; *Brief* erbrechen; *Tür* aufbrechen, abbrechen; *Vorrat* anbrechen, *Nachricht* schonend mitteilen; ruinieren; **~** up zerbrechen; auflösen; *v/i.* (zer)brechen; aus-, los-, an-, auf-; hervorbrechen; umschlagen (*Wetter*); **~** away sich losreißen, **~** down zs.-brechen; steckenbleiben; versagen; **~able** ['breikəbl] zerbrechlich; **~age** [..kidʒ] (*a.* ✦ *Waren*)Bruch *m*; **~down** Zs.-bruch *m*; Maschinen-

schaden *m*; *mot.* Panne *f*; ~fast
['brekfəst] **1.** Frühstück *n*; **2.** früh-
stücken; ~up ['breik'ʌp] Verfall
m; Auflösung *f*; Schulschluß *m*;
~water ['ˌkwɔ:tə] Wellenbrecher
m.

breast [brest] Brust *f*; Busen *m*;
Herz *n*; *make a clean ~ of s.th.* et.
offen gestehen; ~stroke ['brest-
strouk] Brustschwimmen *n*.

breath [breθ] Atem(zug) *m*; Hauch
m; *waste one's ~* s-e Worte verschwenden; ~e [bri:ð] *v/i.* atmen;
fig. leben; *v/t.* (aus-, ein)atmen;
hauchen; flüstern; ~less □ ['breθ-
lis] atemlos.

bred [bred] *pret. u. p.p. von*
breed 2.

breeches ['britʃiz] *pl.* Knie-, Reit-
hosen *f/pl.*

breed [bri:d] **1.** Zucht *f*; Rasse *f*;
Herkunft *f*; *Am.* Mischling *m bsd.*
weiß-indianisch; **2.** [*irr.*] *v/t.* erzeugen; auf-, erziehen; züchten; *v/i.*
sich fortpflanzen; ~er ['bri:də] Er-
zeuger(in); Züchter(in); ~ing [~diŋ]
Erziehung *f*; Bildung *f*; (Tier-)
Zucht *f*.

breez|e [bri:z] Brise *f*; ~y ['bri:zi]
windig, luftig; frisch, flott.

brethren ['breðrin] *pl.* Brüder *m/pl.*

brevity ['breviti] Kürze *f*.

brew [bru:] **1.** *v/t. u. v/i.* brauen;
zubereiten; *fig.* anzetteln; **2.** Gebräu *n*; ~ery ['bruəri] Brauerei *f*.

briar ['braiə] = brier.

brib|e [braib] **1.** Bestechung(sgeld
n, -geschenk *n*) *f*; **2.** bestechen;
~ery ['braibəri] Bestechung *f*.

brick [brik] **1.** Ziegel(stein) *m*; *drop
a ~ sl.* ins Fettnäpfchen treten;
2. mauern; ~layer ['brikleiə] Maurer *m*; ~works *sg.* Ziegelei *f*.

bridal □ ['braidl] bräutlich; Braut-
...; *~ procession* Brautzug *m*.

bride [braid] Braut *f*, Neuvermählte
f; ~groom ['braidgrum] Bräutigam
m, Neuvermählte(r) *m*; ~smaid
[~dzmeid] Brautjungfer *f*.

bridge [bridʒ] **1.** Brücke *f*; **2.** e-e
Brücke schlagen über (*acc.*); *fig.*
überbrücken.

bridle ['braidl] **1.** Zaum *m*; Zügel
m; **2.** *v/t.* (auf)zäumen; zügeln; *v/i.*
a. ~ up den Kopf zurückwerfen;
~path, ~road Reitweg *m*.

brief [bri:f] **1.** □ kurz, bündig; **2.** *st*
schriftliche Instruktion; *hold a ~
for* einstehen für; ~case ['bri:f-
keis] Aktenmappe *f*.

brier ♦ ['braiə] Dorn-, Hagebutten-
strauch *m*, wilde Rose.

brigade ✕ [bri'geid] Brigade *f*.

bright □ [brait] hell, glänzend, klar;
lebhaft; gescheit; ~en ['braitn] *v/t.*
auf-, erhellen; polieren; aufheitern;
v/i. sich aufhellen; ~ness [~nis]
Helligkeit *f*; Glanz *m*; Klarheit *f*;
Heiterkeit *f*; Aufgewecktheit *f*.

brillian|ce, ~cy ['briljəns, ~si]
Glanz *m*; ~t [~nt] **1.** □ glänzend;
prächtig; **2.** Brillant *m*.

brim [brim] **1.** Rand *m*; Krempe *f*;
2. bis zum Rande füllen *od.* voll
sein; ~full, ~ful ['brim'ful] ganz
voll; ~stone † ['brimstən] Schwefel
m.

brindle(d) ['brindl(d)] scheckig.

brine [brain] Salzwasser *n*, Sole *f*.

bring [briŋ] [*irr.*] bringen; *j.* veranlassen; *Klage* erheben; *Grund etc.*
vorbringen; *~ about, ~ to pass* zustande bringen; *~ down Preis* herabsetzen; *~ forth* hervorbringen; gebären; *~ home to j.* überzeugen; *~
round* wieder zu sich bringen; *~ up*
auf-, erziehen.

brink [briŋk] Rand *m*.

brisk □ [brisk] lebhaft, munter;
frisch; flink; belebend.

bristl|e ['brisl] **1.** Borste *f*; **2.** (sich)
sträuben; hochfahren, zornig wer-
den; *~ with fig.* starren von; ~ed,
~y [~li] gesträubt; struppig.

British ['britiʃ] britisch; *the ~ pl.* die
Briten *pl.*; ~er *bsd. Am.* [~ʃə] Ein-
wohner(in) Großbritanniens.

brittle ['britl] zerbrechlich, spröde.

broach [broutʃ] *Faß* anzapfen; vorbringen; *Thema* anschneiden.

broad □ [brɔ:d] breit; weit; hell
(*Tag*); deutlich (*Wink etc.*); derb
(*Witz*); allgemein; weitherzig, liberal; ~cast ['brɔ:dkɑ:st] **1.** weitverbreitet; **2.** [*irr.* (cast)] weit verbreiten; *Radio:* senden; **3.** Rundfunk
(-sendung *f*) *m*; ~cloth feiner
Wollstoff; ~minded großzügig.

brocade † [brə'keid] Brokat *m*.

broil [brɔil] **1.** Lärm *m*, Streit *m*;
2. auf dem Rost braten; *fig.*
schmoren.

broke [brouk] **1.** *pret. von* break 2;
2. *sl.* pleite, ohne e-n Pfennig; ~n
['broukən] **1.** *p.p. von* break 2; **2.**:
~ health zerrüttete Gesundheit.

broker ['broukə] Altwarenhändler
m; Zwangsversteigerer *m*; Makler
m.

bronc(h)o *Am.* ['brɔŋkou] (halb-)
wildes Pferd; ~buster [~oubʌstə]
Zureiter *m*.

bronze [brɔnz] **1.** Bronze *f*; **2.** bronzen, Bronze...; **3.** bronzieren.

brooch [broutʃ] Brosche *f*; Spange *f*.

brood [bru:d] **1.** Brut *f*; *attr.*
Zucht...; **2.** brüten (*a. fig.*); ~er
Am. ['bru:də] Brutkasten *m*.

brook [bruk] Bach *m*.

broom [brum] Besen *m*; ~stick
['brumstik] Besenstiel *m*.

broth [brɔθ] Fleischbrühe *f*.

brothel ['brɔθl] Bordell *n*.

brother ['brʌðə] Bruder *m*; ~(s) *and
sister(s)* Geschwister *pl.*; ~hood
[~ʃud] Bruderschaft *f*; ~in-law
[~ərinlɔ:] Schwager *m*; ~ly [~əli]
brüderlich.

brought [brɔːt] *pret. u. p.p. von*
bring.

brow [brau] (Augen)Braue *f*; Stirn
f; Rand *m e-s* Steilhanges; **~beat**
['braubiːt] [*irr.* (*beat*)] einschüchtern; tyrannisieren.

brown [braun] 1. braun; 2. Braun *n*;
3. (sich) bräunen.

browse [brauz] 1. Grasen *n*; *fig.*
Schmökern *n*; 2. grasen, weiden;
fig. schmökern.

bruise [bruːz] 1. Quetschung *f*;
2. (zer)quetschen.

brunt [brʌnt] Hauptstoß *m*, (volle)
Wucht; *das* Schwerste.

brush [brʌʃ] 1. Bürste *f*; Pinsel *m*;
Fuchs-Rute *f*; Scharmützel *n*; Unterholz *n*; 2. *v/t.* (ab-, aus)bürsten;
streifen; *j.* abbürsten; **~** *up* wieder
aufbürsten, *fig.* auffrischen; *v/i.*
bürsten; (davon)stürzen; **~** *against*
s.o. j. streifen; **~wood** ['brʌʃwud]
Gestrüpp *n*, Unterholz *n*.

brusque □ [brusk] brüsk, barsch.

Brussels sprouts ♀ ['brʌsl'sprauts]
pl. Rosenkohl *m*.

brut|al □ ['bruːtl] viehisch; roh,
gemein; **~ality** [bruːˈtæliti] Bruta-
lität *f*, Roheit *f*; **~e** [bruːt] 1. tierisch; unvernünftig; gefühllos;
2. Vich *n*; F Untier *n*, Scheusal *n*.

bubble ['bʌbl] 1. Blase *f*; Schwindel
m; 2. sieden; sprudeln.

buccaneer [bʌkəˈniə] Seeräuber *m*.

buck [bʌk] 1. *zo.* Bock *m*; Stutzer *m*;
Am. sl. Dollar *m*; 2. *v/i.* bocken;
~ *for Am.* sich bemühen um; **~** *up*
F sich zs.-**reißen**; *v/t. Am.* F sich
stemmen gegen; *Am.* F die Oberhand gewinnen wollen über *et.*

bucket ['bʌkit] Eimer *m*, Kübel *m*.

buckle ['bʌkl] 1. Schnalle *f*; 2. *v/t.*
(an-, auf-, um-, zu)schnallen; *v/i.*
⊕ sich (ver)biegen; **~** *to a task* sich
ernsthaft an eine Aufgabe machen.

buck|shot *hunt.* ['bʌkʃɔt] Rehposten
m; **~skin** Wildleder *n*.

bud [bʌd] 1. Knospe *f*; *fig.* Keim *m*;
2. *v/t.* ✍ veredeln; *v/i.* knospen.

buddy *Am.* F ['bʌdi] Kamerad *m*.

budge [bʌdʒ] (sich) bewegen.

budget ['bʌdʒit] Vorrat *m*; Staats-
haushalt *m*; *draft.* **~** Haushaltsplan *m*.

buff [bʌf] 1. Ochsenleder *n*; Leder-
farbe *f*; 2. lederfarben.

buffalo *zo.* ['bʌfəlou] Büffel *m*.

buffer ⚙ ['bʌfə] Puffer *m*; Prellbock
m.

buffet¹ ['bʌfit] 1. Puff *m*, Stoß *m*,
Schlag *m*; 2. puffen, schlagen;
kämpfen.

buffet² [~] Büfett *n*; Anrichte *f*.

buffet³ ['bufei] Büfett *n*, Theke *f*;
Tisch *m* mit Speisen u. Getränken;
Erfrischungsraum *m*.

buffoon [bʌˈfuːn] Possenreißer *m*.

bug [bʌg] Wanze *f*; *Am.* Insekt *n*,
Käfer *m*; *Am. sl.* Defekt *m*, Fehler
m; *big* **~** *sl.* hohes Tier.

bugle ['bjuːgl] Wald-, Signalhorn *n*.

build [bild] 1. [*irr.*] bauen; errichten; 2. Bauart *f*; Schnitt *m*; **~er**
['bildə] Erbauer *m*, Baumeister *m*;
~ing [~diŋ] Erbauen *n*; Bau *m*, Gebäude *n*; *attr.* Bau...

built [bilt] *pret. u. p.p. von* build 1.

bulb [bʌlb] ♀ Zwiebel *f*, Knolle *f*;
(Glüh)Birne *f*.

bulge [bʌldʒ] 1. (Aus)Bauchung *f*;
Anschwellung *f*; 2. sich (aus)bau-
chen; (an)schwellen; hervorquel-
len.

bulk [bʌlk] Umfang *m*; Masse *f*;
Hauptteil *m*; ♻ Ladung *f*; *in* **~** lose;
in großer Menge; **~y** ['bʌlki] umfangreich; unhandlich; ♻ sperrig.

bull¹ [bul] 1. Bulle *m*, Stier *m*; ✝ *sl.*
Haussier *m*; 2. ✝ *die Kurse* treiben.

bull² [~] *päpstliche* Bulle.

bulldog ['buldɔg] Bulldogge *f*.

bulldoze *Am.* F ['buldouz] terrorisieren; **~r** ⊕ [~zə] Bulldozer *m*,
Planierraupe *f*.

bullet ['bulit] Kugel *f*, Geschoß *n*.

bulletin ['bulitin] Tagesbericht *m*;
~ *board Am.* Schwarzes Brett.

bullion ['buljən] Gold-, Silberbar-
ren *m*; Gold-, Silberlitze *f*.

bully ['buli] 1. Maulheld *m*; Tyrann
m; 2. prahlerisch; *Am.* F prima;
3. einschüchtern; tyrannisieren.

bulwark *mst fig.* ['bulwək] Bollwerk
n.

bum *Am.* F [bʌm] 1. Nichtstuer
m, Vagabund *m*; 2. *v/i.* nassauern.

bumble-bee ['bʌmblbiː] Hummel *f*.

bump [bʌmp] 1. Schlag *m*; Beule *f*;
fig. Sinn *m* (*of* für); 2. (zs.-)stoßen;
holpern; *Rudern:* überholen.

bumper ['bʌmpə] volles Glas
(*Wein*); F *et.* Riesiges; *mot.* Stoß-
stange *f*; **~** *crop* Rekordernte *f*; **~**
house thea. volles Haus.

bun [bʌn] Rosinenbrötchen *n*;
Haar-Knoten *m*.

bunch [bʌntʃ] 1. Bund *n*; Büschel *n*;
Haufen *m*; **~** *of grapes* Weintraube
f; 2. (zs.-)bündeln; bauschen.

bundle ['bʌndl] 1. Bündel *n*, Bund
n; 2. *v/t. a.* **~** *up* (zs.-)bündeln.

bung [bʌŋ] Spund *m*.

bungalow ['bʌŋgəlou] Bungalow *m*
(*einstöckiges Haus*).

bungle ['bʌŋgl] 1. Pfuscherei *f*;
2. (ver)pfuschen.

bunion ⚕ ['bʌnjən] entzündeter
Fußballen.

bunk¹ *Am. sl.* [bʌŋk] Quatsch *m*.

bunk² [~] Schlafkoje *f*.

bunny ['bʌni] Kaninchen *n*.

buoy ⚓ [bɔi] 1. Boje *f*; 2. *Fahrwas-
ser* betonnen; *mst* **~** *up fig.* aufrechterhalten; **~ant** □ ['bɔiənt]
schwimmfähig; hebend; spannkräftig; *fig.* heiter.

burden ['bəːdn] 1. Last *f*; Bürde *f*;
♻ Ladung *f*; ♻ Tragfähigkeit *f*;

2. beladen; belasten; **~some** [~n-səm] lästig; drückend.

bureau [bjuə'rou] Büro *n*, Geschäftszimmer *n*; Schreibpult *n*; *Am.* Kommode *f*; **~cracy** [~'rɔkrəsi] Bürokratie *f*.

burg *Am* F [bəːg] Stadt *f*.

burgess [ˈbəːdʒis] Bürger *m*.

burglar [ˈbəːglə] Einbrecher *m*; **~y** [~əri] Einbruch(sdiebstahl) *m*.

burial [ˈberiəl] Begräbnis *n*.

burlesque [bəːˈlesk] **1.** possenhaft; **2.** Burleske *f*, Posse *f*; **3.** parodieren.

burly [ˈbəːli] stämmig, kräftig.

burn [bəːn] **1.** Brandwunde *f*; Brandmal *n*; **2.** [*irr.*] (ver-, an-) brennen, **~er** [ˈbəːnə] Brenner *m*.

burnish [ˈbəːniʃ] polieren, glätten.

burnt [bəːnt] *pret. u. p.p. von* burn **2.**

burrow [ˈbʌrou] **1.** Höhle *f*, Bau *m*; **2.** (sich ein-, ver)graben.

burst [bəːst] **1.** Bersten *n*; Krach *m*; Riß *m*, Ausbruch *m*; **2.** [*irr.*] *v/i.* bersten, platzen; zerspringen; explodieren; **~ from** sich losreißen von; **~ forth, ~ out** hervorbrechen; **~ into tears** in Tränen ausbrechen; *v/t.* (zer)sprengen.

bury [ˈberi] be-, vergraben; beerdigen; verbergen.

bus F [bʌs] (Omni)Bus *m*; **~ boy** *Am.* Kellnergehilfe *m*.

bush [buʃ] Busch *m*; Gebüsch *n*.

bushel [ˈbuʃl] Scheffel *m* (36,37 Liter).

bushy [ˈbuʃi] buschig.

business [ˈbiznis] Geschäft *n*; Beschäftigung *f*; Beruf *m*; Angelegenheit *f*, Aufgabe *f*; ✝ Handel *m*; **~ of the day** Tagesordnung *f*, on **~** geschäftlich; have no **~** to *inf* nicht befugt sein zu *inf*; mind one's own **~** sich um s-e eigenen Angelegenheiten kümmern; **~ hours** *pl* Geschäftszeit *f*; **~-like** geschäftsmäßig; sachlich; **~man** Geschäftsmann *m*; **~ tour, ~ trip** Geschäftsreise *f*.

bust¹ [bʌst] Büste *f*.

bust² *Am.* F [~] Bankrott *m*.

bustle [ˈbʌsl] **1.** Geschäftigkeit *f*; geschäftiges Treiben *n*; **2.** *v/i.* (umher)wirtschaften; hasten; *v/t.* hetzen, jagen.

busy [['bizi] **1.** beschäftigt; geschäftig; fleißig (*at* bei, an *dat.*); lebhaft; *Am. teleph.* besetzt; **2.** (*mst* **~ o.s.** sich) beschäftigen (*with, in, at, about, ger.* mit).

but [bʌt, bət] **1.** *cj.* aber, jedoch, sondern; *a.* **~** *that* wenn nicht; indessen; **2.** *prp.* außer; *the last* **~** *one* der vorletzte; *the next* **~** *one* der übernächste; **~** *for* wenn nicht ... gewesen wäre; ohne; **3.** *nach Negation:* der (die *od.* das) nicht; *there is*

no one **~** *knows* es gibt niemand, der nicht wüßte; **4.** *adv.* nur; **~** *just* soeben, eben erst; **~** *now* erst jetzt; *all* **~** fast, nahe daran; *nothing* **~** nur; *I cannot* **~** *inf.* ich kann nur *inf.*

butcher [ˈbutʃə] **1.** Schlächter *m*, Fleischer *m*, Metzger *m*; *fig.* Mörder *m*; **2.** (*fig* ab-, hin)schlachten; **~y** [~əri] Schlächterei *f*; Schlachthaus *n*

butler [ˈbʌtlə] Butler *m*; Kellermeister *m*

butt [bʌt] **1.** Stoß *m*; *a.* **~** *end* (dickes) Ende *e-s Baumes etc.*; Stummel *m*, Kippe *f*, *Gewehr*-Kolben *m*; Schießstand *m*, (End)Ziel *n*; *fig.* Zielscheibe *f*; **2.** (mit dem Kopf) stoßen

butter [ˈbʌtə] **1.** Butter *f*; F Schmeichelei *f*, **2.** mit Butter bestreichen; **~cup** Butterblume *f*; **~fingered** tolpatschig; **~fly** Schmetterling *m*; **~y** [~əri] butter(art)ig; Butter...; **2.** Speisekammer *f*

buttock [ˈbʌtək] *pl.* Gesäß *n*.

button [ˈbʌtn] **1.** Knopf *m*; Knospe *f*; **2.** an **~** zuknöpfen

buttress [ˈbʌtris] **1.** Strebepfeiler *m*; *fig* Stütze *f* **2.** (unter)stützen

buxom [ˈbʌksəm] drall, stramm.

buy [bai] [*irr*] *v/t* (an-, ein)kaufen (*from* bei), **~er** [ˈbaiə] (Ein)Käufer (-in).

buzz [bʌz] **1.** Gesumm *n*; Geflüster *n*; **~ saw** *Am* Kreissäge *f*; **2.** *v/i.* summen; surren; **~ about** herumschwirren; herumeilen.

buzzard [ˈbʌzəd] Bussard *m*.

by [bai] **1.** *prp* Raum bei; an, neben, *Richtung* durch, über; an (*dat.*) entlang *od* vorbei; *Zeit:* an, bei; spätestens *bis*, bis zu; *Urheber, Ursache* von, durch (*bsd.* beim *pass.*); *Mittel, Werkzeug* durch, mit; *Art u Weise:* bei; *Schwur:* bei; *Maß* um, bei; *Richtschnur:* gemäß, bei, **~** the *dozen* dutzendweise, **~** *s* allein; **~** *land* zu Lande, **~** *rail* per Bahn, *day* **~** *day* Tag für Tag; **~** *twos* zu zweien; **2.** *adv.* dabei; vorbei, beiseite; **~** *and* **~** nächstens, bald, nach und nach; **~** *the* **~** nebenbei bemerkt; **~** *and large Am.* im großen und ganzen; **3.** *adj.* Neben..., Seiten...; **~-election** [ˈbaiilekʃən] Nachwahl *f*; **~-gone** vergangen, **~-law** Ortsstatut *n*; **~.pl.** Satzung *f*, Statuten *n/pl.*; **~-line** *Am.* Verfasserangabe *f* *zu e-m* Artikel; **~-name** Bei-, Spitzname *m*; **~-pass** Umgehungsstraße *f*; **~-path** Seitenpfad *m*; **~-product** Nebenprodukt *n*; **~-road** Seitenweg *m*, **~-stander** Zuschauer *m*; **~-street** Neben-, Seitenstraße *f*; **~-way** Seitenweg *m*; **~-word** Sprichwort *n*, Inbegriff *m*; be *a* **~** *for* sprichwörtlich bekannt sein wegen.

C

cab [kæb] Droschke *f*, Mietwagen *m*, Taxi *n*; 🚂 Führerstand *m*.

cabbage 🌹 ['kæbidʒ] Kohl *m*.

cabin ['kæbin] **1.** Hütte *f*; ⚓ Kabine *f*, Kajüte *f*; Kammer *f*; **2.** einpferchen; **~boy** Schiffsjunge *m*; **~ cruiser** ⚓ Kabinenkreuzer *m*.

cabinet ['kæbinit] Kabinett *n*, Ministerrat *m*; Schrank *m*, Vitrine *f*; (Radio)Gehäuse *n*; **~ council** Kabinettssitzung *f*; **~-maker** Kunsttischler *m*.

cable ['keibl] **1.** Kabel *n*; ⚓ Ankertau *n*; **2.** *tel.* kabeln; **~-car** Kabine *f*, Gondel *f*; Drahtseilbahn *f*; **~-gram** [~lgræm] Kabeltelegramm *n*.

cabman ['kæbmən] Droschkenkutscher *m*, Taxifahrer *m*.

caboose [kə'buːs] ⚓ Kombüse *f*; *Am.* 🚂 Eisenbahnerwagen *m* am *Güterzug*.

cab-stand ['kæbstænd] Taxi-, Droschkenstand *m*.

cacao 🌹 [kə'kɑːou] Kakaobaum *m*, -bohne *f*.

cackle ['kækl] **1.** Gegacker *n*, Geschnatter *n*; **2.** gackern, schnattern.

cad F [kæd] Prolet *m*; Kerl *m*.

cadaverous ☐ [kə'dævərəs] leichenhaft; leichenblaß.

cadence ♪ ['keidəns] Kadenz *f*; Tonfall *m*; Rhythmus *m*.

cadet [kə'det] Kadett *m*.

café ['kæfei] Café *n*.

cafeteria *bsd. Am.* [kæfi'tiəriə] Restaurant *n* mit Selbstbedienung.

cage [keidʒ] **1.** Käfig *m*; Kriegsgefangenenlager *n*; ⚒ Förderkorb *m*; **2.** einsperren.

cagey ☐ *bsd. Am.* F ['keidʒi] gerissen, raffiniert.

cajole [kə'dʒoul] *j-m* schmeicheln; *j-n* beschwatzen.

cake [keik] **1.** Kuchen *m*; Tafel *f* *Schokolade*, Riegel *m* *Seife etc.*; **2.** zs.-backen.

calami|tous ☐ [kə'læmitəs] elend; katastrophal; **~ty** [~ti] Elend *n*, Unglück *n*; Katastrophe *f*.

calcify ['kælsifai] (sich) verkalken.

calculat|e ['kælkjuleit] *v/t.* kalkulieren; be-, aus-, errechnen; *v/i.* rechnen (*on, upon* auf *acc.*); *Am.* F vermuten; **~ion** [kælkju'leiʃən] Kalkulation *f*, Berechnung *f*; Voranschlag *m*; Überlegung *f*.

caldron ['kɔːldrən] Kessel *m*.

calendar ['kælində] **1.** Kalender *m*; Liste *f*; **2.** registrieren.

calf [kɑːf], *pl.* **calves** [kɑːvz] Kalb *n*; Wade *f*; *a.* **~-leather** ['kɑːfleðə] Kalbleder *n*; **~skin** Kalbfell *n*.

calibre ['kælibə] Kaliber *n*.

calico 🌹 ['kælikou] Kaliko *m*.

call [kɔːl] **1.** Ruf *m*; *teleph.* Anruf *m*,

Gespräch *n*; *fig.* Berufung *f* (*to* in *ein Amt*; auf *e-n Lehrstuhl*); Aufruf *m*; Aufforderung *f*; Signal *n*; Forderung *f*; Besuch *m*; Nachfrage *f* (*for* nach); Kündigung *f* *v. Geldern*; *on* ~ 🕇 auf Abruf; **2.** *v/t.* (herbei-) rufen; (an)rufen; (ein)berufen; *Am. Baseball:* Spiel abbrechen; *fig.* berufen (*to* in *ein Amt*); nennen; wecken; *Aufmerksamkeit lenken* (*to* auf *acc.*); be ~ed heißen; ~ *s.o. names* j. beschimpfen, beleidigen; ~ *down bsd. Am.* F anpfeifen; ~ in *Geld* kündigen; ~ *over Namen* verlesen; ~ *up* aufrufen; *teleph.* anrufen; *v/i.* rufen; *teleph.* anrufen; vorsprechen (*at* an *e-m Ort*; *on s.o.* bei j-m); ~ *at* a port e-n Hafen anlaufen; ~ *for* rufen nach; *et.* fordern; abholen; *to be (left till)* ~ed *for* postlagernd; ~ *on sich* an j. wenden (*for* wegen); *j.* berufen, auffordern (*to inf.* zu); **~-box** ['kɔːlbɔks] Fernsprechzelle *f*; **~er** ['kɔːlə] *teleph.* Anrufer(in); Besucher(in).

calling ['kɔːliŋ] Rufen *n*; Berufung *f*; Beruf *m*; **~ card** *Am.* Visitenkarte *f*.

call-office ['kɔːlɔfis] Fernsprechstelle *f*.

callous ☐ ['kæləs] schwielig; *fig.* dickfellig; herzlos.

callow ['kælou] nackt (*ungefiedert*); *fig.* unerfahren.

calm [kɑːm] **1.** ☐ still, ruhig; **2.** (Wind)Stille *f*, Ruhe *f*; **3.** (~ *down* sich) beruhigen; besänftigen.

calori|c [kə'lɔrik] Wärme *f*; **~e** *phys.* ['kælɔri] Wärmeeinheit *f*.

calumn|iate [kə'lʌmnieit] verleumden; **~iation** [kəlʌmni'eiʃən], **~y** ['kæləmni] Verleumdung *f*.

calve [kɑːv] kalben; **~s** [kɑːvz] *pl. von calf.*

cambric 🕇 ['keimbrik] Batist *m*.

came [keim] *pret. von come.*

camel *zo.*, ⚓ ['kæməl] Kamel *n*.

camera ['kæmərə] Kamera *f*; *in* ~ 🕇🕇 unter Ausschluß der Öffentlichkeit.

camomile 🌹 ['kæməmail] Kamille *f*.

camouflage ✗ ['kæmuflɑːʒ] **1.** Tarnung *f*; **2.** tarnen.

camp [kæmp] **1.** Lager *n*; ✗ Feldlager *n*; ~ *bed* Feldbett *n*; **2.** lagern; ~ *out* zelten.

campaign [kæm'pein] **1.** Feldzug *m*; **2.** e-n Feldzug mitmachen *od.* führen.

camphor ['kæmfə] Kampfer *m*.

campus *Am.* ['kæmpəs] Universitätsgelände *n*.

can¹ [kæn] [*irr.*] *v/aux.* können, fähig sein zu; dürfen.

can² [~] **1.** Kanne *f*; *Am.* Büchse *f*; **2.** *Am.* in Büchsen konservieren.

Canadian [kə'neidjən] **1.** kanadisch; **2.** Kanadier(in).

canal [kə'næl] Kanal m (a. ⚕).

canard [kæ'naːd] (Zeitungs)Ente f.

canary [kə'neəri] Kanarienvogel m.

cancel ['kænsəl] (durch)streichen; entwerten; absagen; a. ~ out fig. aufheben; be ~led ausfallen.

cancer ast., ⚕ [kænsə] Krebs m; ~ous [~rəs] krebsartig.

candid □ ['kændid] aufrichtig; offen.

candidate ['kændidit] Kandidat m (for für), Bewerber m (for um).

candied ['kændid] kandiert.

candle ['kændl] Licht n, Kerze f; burn the ~ at both ends mit s-n Kräften Raubbau treiben; ~stick Leuchter m.

cando(u)r ['kændə] Aufrichtigkeit f.

candy ['kændi] **1.** Kandis(zucker) m; Am. Süßigkeiten f/pl.; **2.** v/t. kandieren.

cane [kein] **1.** ⚕ Rohr n; (Rohr-) Stock m; **2.** prügeln.

canine ['keinain] Hunde...

canker ['kæŋkə] ⚕ Mundkrebs m; ⚕ Brand m.

canned Am. [kænd] Büchsen...

cannery Am. ['kænəri] Konservenfabrik f.

cannibal ['kænibəl] Kannibale m.

cannon ['kænən] Kanone f.

cannot ['kænət] nicht können etc.; s. can[1].

canoe [kə'nuː] Kanu n; Paddelboot n.

canon ['kænən] Kanon m; Regel f; Richtschnur f; ~ize [~naiz] heiligsprechen.

canopy ['kænəpi] Baldachin m; fig. Dach n; △ Überdachung f.

cant[1] [kænt] **1.** Schrägung f; Stoß m; **2.** kippen; kanten.

cant[2] [~] **1.** Zunftsprache f; Gewäsch n; scheinheiliges Gerede f; **2.** zunftmäßig od. scheinheilig reden.

can't F [kɑːnt] = cannot.

cantankerous F □ [kən'tæŋkərəs] zänkisch, mürrisch.

canteen [kæn'tiːn] ✕ Feldflasche f; Kantine f; ✕ Kochgeschirr n; Besteckkasten m.

canton 1. ['kæntən] Bezirk m; **2.** ✕ [kən'tuːn] (sich) einquartieren.

canvas ['kænvəs] Segeltuch n; Zelt (-e pl.) n; Zeltbahn f; Segel n/pl.; paint. Leinwand f; Gemälde n.

canvass [~] **1.** (Stimmen)Werbung f; Am. a. Wahlnachprüfung f; **2.** v/t. erörtern; v/i. (Stimmen, a. Kunden) werben.

caoutchouc ['kautʃuk] Kautschuk m.

cap [kæp] **1.** Kappe f; Mütze f; Haube f; ⊕ Aufsatz m; Zündhütchen n; set one's ~ at sich e-n Mann

angeln (Frau); **2.** mit e-r Kappe etc. bedecken; fig. krönen; F übertreffen; die Mütze abnehmen.

capab|ility [keipə'biliti] Fähigkeit f; ~le ['keipəbl] fähig (of zu).

capaci|ous [kə'peiʃəs] geräumig; ~ty [kə'pæsiti] Inhalt m; Aufnahmefähigkeit f; geistige (od. ⊕ Leistungs)Fähigkeit f (for ger. zu inf.); Stellung f; in my ~ as in meiner Eigenschaft als.

cape[1] [keip] Kap n, Vorgebirge n.

cape[2] [~] Cape n, Umhang m.

caper ['keipə] **1.** Kapriole f, Luftsprung m; cut ~s = **2.** Kapriolen od. Sprünge machen.

capital ['kæpitl] **1.** □ Kapital...; todeswürdig, Todes...; hauptsächlich, Haupt...; vortrefflich; ~ crime Kapitalverbrechen n; ~ punishment Todesstrafe f; **2.** Hauptstadt f; Kapital m; mst ~ letter Großbuchstabe m; ~ism [~təlizəm] Kapitalismus m; ~ize [kə'pitəlaiz] kapitalisieren.

capitulate [kə'pitjuleit] kapitulieren (to vor dat.).

capric|e [kə'priːs] Laune f; ~ious □ [~iʃəs] kapriziös, launisch.

Capricorn ast. ['kæprikɔːn] Steinbock m.

capsize [kæp'saiz] v/i. kentern; v/t. zum Kentern bringen.

capsule ['kæpsjuːl] Kapsel f.

captain ['kæptin] Führer m; Feldherr m; ⚓ Kapitän m; ✕ Hauptmann m.

caption ['kæpʃən] **1.** Überschrift f; Titel m; Film: Untertitel m; **2.** v/t. Am. mit Überschrift etc. versehen.

captious □ ['kæpʃəs] spitzfindig.

captiv|ate ['kæptiveit] fig. gefangennehmen, fesseln; ~e ['kæptiv] **1.** gefangen, gefesselt; **2.** Gefangene(r m) od. ~ity [kæp'tiviti] Gefangenschaft f.

capture ['kæptʃə] **1.** Eroberung f; Gefangennahme f; **2.** (ein)fangen; erobern; erbeuten; ⚓ kapern.

car [kɑː] Auto n; (Eisenbahn-, Straßenbahn)Wagen m; Ballonkorb m; Luftschiff-Gondel f; Kabine f e-s Aufzugs.

caramel ['kærəmel] Karamel m; Karamelle f.

caravan ['kærəvæn] Karawane f; Wohnwagen m.

caraway ⚕ ['kærəwei] Kümmel m.

carbine ['kɑːbain] Karabiner m.

carbohydrate ⚗ ['kɑːbou'haidreit] Kohle(n)hydrat n.

carbon ['kɑːbən] ⚗ Kohlenstoff m; ~ copy Brief-Durchschlag m; ~ paper Kohlepapier n.

carburet(t)or mot. ['kɑːbjuretə] Vergaser m.

car|case, mst ~cass ['kɑːkəs] (Tier-) Kadaver m; Fleischerei: Rumpf m.

card [kɑːd] Karte f; have a ~ up

one's *sleeve* et. in petto haben;
~board ['kɑ:dbɔ:d] Kartonpapier
n; Pappe *f*; ~ *box* Pappkarton *m*.
cardigan ['kɑ:digən] Wolljacke *f*.
cardinal □ ['kɑ:dinl] 1. Haupt...;
hochrot; ~ *number* Grundzahl *f*; 2.
Kardinal *m*.
card-index ['kɑ:dindeks] Kartei *f*.
card-sharper ['kɑ:dʃɑ:pə] Falsch-
spieler *m*.
care [keə] 1. Sorge *f*; Sorgfalt *f*,
Obhut *f*, Pflege *f*; *medical* ~ ärztliche Behandlung; ~ *of (abbr.* c/o) ...
per Adresse, bei ...; *take* ~ *of*
acht(geb)en auf *(acc.); with* ~*!* Vorsicht!; 2. Lust haben (*to inf.* zu);
~ *for* sorgen für; sich kümmern um;
sich etwas machen aus; *I don't* ~*!*
F meinetwegen!; *I couldn't* ~ *less* F
es ist mir völlig egal; *well* ~*d-for*
gefIegt. Pflege *f*; 2. rasen.|
career [kə'riə] 1. Karriere *f*; Lauf-
carefree ['keəfri:] sorgenfrei.
careful □ ['keəful] besorgt *(for* um),
achtsam *(of* auf *acc.);* vorsichtig;
sorgfältig; ~**ness** [~lnis] Sorgsam-
keit *f*; Vorsicht *f*; Sorgfalt *f*.
careless □ ['keəlis] sorglos; nachlässig; unachtsam; leichtsinnig;
~**ness** [~snis] Sorglosigkeit *f*; Nachlässigkeit *f*.
caress [kə'res] 1. Liebkosung *f*;
2. liebkosen; *fig.* schmeicheln.
caretaker ['keəteikə] Wärter(in);
(Haus)Verwalter(in).
care-worn ['keəwɔ:n] abgehärmt.
carfare *Am.* ['kɑ:feə] Fahrgeld *n*.
cargo ⊕ ['kɑ:gou] Ladung *f*.
caricature [kærikə'tjuə] 1. Karikatur *f*; 2. karikieren.
carmine ['kɑ:main] Karmin(rot) *n*.
carn|al □ ['kɑ:nl] fleischlich; sinn-
lich; ~**ation** [kɑ:'neiʃən] 1. Fleisch-
ton *m*; ♀ Nelke *f*; 2. blaßrot.
carnival ['kɑ:nivəl] Karneval *m*.
carnivorous [kɑ:'nivərəs] fleisch-
fressend.
carol ['kærəl] 1. Weihnachtslied *n*;
2. Weihnachtslieder singen.
carous|e [kə'rauz] 1. *a.* ~**al** [~əl]
(Trink)Gelage *n*; 2. zechen.
carp [kɑ:p] Karpfen *m*.
carpent|er ['kɑ:pintə] Zimmer-
mann *m*; ~**ry** [~tri] Zimmerhand-
werk *n*; Zimmermannsarbeit *f*.
carpet ['kɑ:pit] 1. Teppich *m*;
bring on the ~ aufs Tapet bringen;
2. mit e-m Teppich belegen; ~**bag**
Reisetasche *f*; ~**bagger** [~tbægə]
politischer Abenteurer.
carriage ['kærid3] Beförderung *f*,
Transport *m*; Fracht *f*; Wagen *m*;
Fuhr-, Frachtlohn *m*; Haltung *f*;
Benehmen *n*; ~**drive** Anfahrt *f*
(*vor e-m Hause*); ~**free**, ~**paid**
frachtfrei; ~**way** Fahrbahn *f*.
carrier ['kæriə] Fuhrmann *m*;
Spediteur *m*; Träger *m*; Gepäckträger *m*; ~**pigeon** Brieftaube *f*.

carrion ['kæriən] Aas *n*; *attr.* Aas...
carrot ['kærət] Mohrrübe *f*.
carry ['kæri] 1. *v/t. wohin* bringen,
führen, tragen *(a. v/i.),* fahren, befördern; (bei sich) haben; *Ansicht*
durchsetzen; *Gewinn, Preis* davontragen; *Zahlen* übertragen; *Ernte,*
Zinsen tragen; *Mauer etc.* weiter-
führen; *Benehmen* fortsetzen; *An-*
trag, Kandidaten durchbringen; ⚔
erobern; *be carried* angenommen
werden *(Antrag);* durchkommen
(Kandidat); ~ *the day* den Sieg
davontragen; ~ *forward od. over* ♱
übertragen; ~ *on* fortsetzen, weiter-
führen; *Geschäft etc.* betreiben; ~
out od. through durchführen; 2.
Trag-, Schußweite *f*.
cart [kɑ:t] 1. Karren *m*; Wagen *m*;
put the ~ *before the horse fig.* das
Pferd beim Schwanz aufzäumen;
2. karren, fahren; ~**age** ['kɑ:tid3]
Fahren *n*; Fuhrlohn *m*.
carter ['kɑ:tə] Fuhrmann *m*.
cartilage ['kɑ:tilid3] Knorpel *m*.
carton ['kɑ:tən] Karton *m*.
cartoon [kɑ:'tu:n] *paint.* Karton *m*;
⊕ Musterzeichnung *f*; Karikatur *f*;
Zeichentrickfilm *m*; ~**ist** [~nist]
Karikaturist *m*.
cartridge ['kɑ:trid3] Patrone *f*;
~**paper** Zeichenpapier *n*.
cart-wheel ['kɑ:twi:l] Wagenrad *n*;
Am. Silberdollar *m*; *turn* ~**s** rad-
schlagen.
carve [kɑ:v] *Fleisch* vorschneiden,
zerlegen; schnitzen; meißeln; ~**r**
['kɑ:və] (Bild)Schnitzer *m*; Vor-
schneider *m*; Vorlegemesser *m*.
carving ['kɑ:viŋ] Schnitzerei *f*.
cascade [kæs'keid] Wasserfall *m*.
case[1] [keis] *m* Behälter *m*; Kiste *f*;
Etui *n*; Gehäuse *n*; Schachtel *f*;
Fach *n*; *typ.* Setzkasten *m*; 2. (ein-)
stecken; ver-, umkleiden.
case[2] [~] Fall *m (a. gr., ♠, ✝);* gr.
Kasus *m*; ✝ *a.* Kranke(r *m*) *f*; *Am.*
F komischer Kauz; ✝ Schriftsatz
m; Hauptargument *n*; Sache *f*, Angelegenheit *f*.
case-harden ⊕ ['keishɑ:dn] hart-
gießen; ~**ed** *fig.* hartgesotten.
case-history ['keishistəri] Vor-
geschichte *f*; Krankengeschichte *f*.
casement ['keismənt] Fensterflügel
m; ~ *window* Flügelfenster *n*.
cash [kæʃ] 1. Bargeld *n*, Kasse *f*;
~ *down, for* ~ gegen bar; ~ *on deli-*
very Lieferung *f* gegen bar; (per)
Nachnahme *f*; ~ *register* Registrierkasse *f*; 2. einkassieren, einlösen; ~**book** ['kæʃbuk] Kassa-
buch *n*; ~**ier** [kæ'ʃiə] Kassierer(in).
casing ['keisiŋ] Überzug *m*, Gehäuse *n*, Futteral *n*; △ Verkleidung *f*.
cask [kɑ:sk] Faß *n*.
casket ['kɑ:skit] Kassette *f*; *Am.*
Sarg *m*.

casserole ['kæsəroul] Kasserolle *f.*
cassock *eccl.* ['kæsək] Soutane *f.*
cast [ka:st] **1.** Wurf *m;* ⊕ Guß
(-form *f*) *m;* Abguß *m,* Abdruck *m;*
Schattierung *f,* Anflug *m;* Form *f,*
Art *f;* ⚓ Auswerfen *n von Senkblei
etc.; thea.* (Rollen)Besetzung *f;*
2. [*irr.*] *v/t.* (ab-, aus-, hin-, um-,
weg)werfen; *zo. Haut etc.* abwerfen; *Zähne etc.* verlieren; verwerfen; gestalten; ⊕ gießen; *a.*
~ *up* aus-, zs.-rechnen; *thea. Rolle*
besetzen; *Rolle* übertragen (*to
dat.*); *be* ~ *in a lawsuit* ⚖ e-n
Prozeß verlieren; ~ *lots* losen (*for
um); ~ in one's lot with s.o.* j-s Los
teilen; *be* ~ *down* niedergeschlagen
sein; *v/i.* sich gießen lassen; ⊕
sich (ver)werfen; ~ *about for* sinnen
auf (*acc.*); sich *et.* überlegen.
castanet [kæstə'net] Kastagnette *f.*
castaway ['ka:stəwei] **1.** verworfen,
⚓ schiffbrüchig; **2.** Verworfene(r
m) f; Schiffbrüchige(r *m) f.*
caste [ka:st] Kaste *f* (*a. fig.*).
castigate ['kæstigeit] züchtigen;
fig. geißeln.
cast iron ['ka:st'aiən] Gußeisen *n;*
cast-iron gußeisern.
castle ['ka:sl] Burg *f,* Schloß *n;*
Schach: Turm *m.*
castor[1] ['ka:stə]: ~ *oil* Rizinusöl *n.*
castor[2] [~] Laufrolle *f unter Möbeln;*
(Salz-, Zucker- *etc.*) Streuer *m.*
castrate [kæs'treit] kastrieren.
cast steel ['ka:ststi:l] Gußstahl *m;*
cast-steel aus Gußstahl.
casual □ ['kæʒjuəl] zufällig; gelegentlich; F lässig; ~**ty** [~lti] Unfall *m;* ✗ Verlust *m.*
cat [kæt] Katze *f;* ~ *burglar* Fas-
sadenkletterer *m.*
catalo|gue, *Am.* ~**g** ['kætəlog] **1.** Ka-
talog *m; Am. univ.* Vorlesungs-
verzeichnis *n;* **2.** katalogisieren.
catapult ['kætəpʌlt] Schleuder *f;*
✗ Katapult *m, n.*
cataract ['kætərækt] Katarakt *m,*
Wasserfall *m;* ⚚ grauer Star.
catarrh [kə'ta:] Katarrh *m;* Schnupfen *m.*
catastrophe [kə'tæstrəfi] Kata-
strophe *f.*
catch [kætʃ] **1.** Fang *m;* Beute *f,*
fig. Vorteil *m;* ♪ Rundgesang *m;*
Kniff *m;* ⊕ Haken *m,* Griff *m,*
Klinke *f;* **2.** [*irr.*] *v/t.* fassen, F
kriegen; fangen, ergreifen; ertappen; *Blick etc.* auffangen; *Zug
etc.* erreichen; bekommen; sich
Krankheit zuziehen, holen; *fig.* erfassen; ~ (*a*) *cold* sich erkälten; ~
s.o.'s eye j-m ins Auge fallen; ~ *up*
auffangen; F j. unterbrechen; einholen; **3.** *v/i.* sich verfangen, hängenbleiben; fassen, einschnappen
(*Schloß etc.*); ~ *on* F Anklang
finden; *Am.* F kapieren; ~ *up with*
∴ einholen; ~**all** ['kætʃɔ:l] *Am.*

Platz *m od.* Behälter *m* für alles
mögliche (*a. fig. u. attr.*); ~**er** [~ʃə]
Fänger(in); ~**ing** [~ʃiŋ] packend; ✗
ansteckend; ~**line** Schlagzeile *f;*
~**word** Schlagwort *n;* Stichwort *n.*
catechism ['kætikizəm] Katechismus *m*
categor|ical □ [kæti'gɔrikəl] kate-
gorisch, ~**y** ['kætigəri] Kategorie *f.*
cater ['keitə]: ~ *for* Lebensmittel
liefern für; *fig.* sorgen für; ~**ing**
[~əriŋ] Verpflegung *f.*
caterpillar ['kætəpilə] *zo.* Raupe *f;*
⊕ Raupe(nschlepper *m) f.*
catgut ['kætgʌt] Darmsaite *f.*
cathedral [kə'θi:drəl] Dom *m,*
Kathedrale *f.*
Catholic ['kæθəlik] **1.** katholisch;
2. Katholik(in).
catkin ♀ ['kætkin] Kätzchen *n.*
cattish *fig.* ['kætiʃ] falsch.
cattle ['kætl] Vieh *n;* ~**breeding**
Viehzucht *f;* ~**plague** *vet.* Rinder-
pest *f.*   [*catch* 2.)
caught [kɔ:t] *pret. u. p.p. von)*
ca(u)ldron ['kɔ:ldrən] Kessel *m.*
cauliflower ♀ ['kɔliflauə] Blumen-
kohl *m*
caulk ⚓ [kɔ:k] kalfatern (*abdichten*).
caus|al ['kɔ:zəl] ursächlich; ~**e**
[kɔ:z] **1.** Ursache *f,* Grund *m;* ⚖
Klage(grund *m) f;* Prozeß *m;* Angelegenheit *f,* Sache *f;* **2.** verursachen, veranlassen; ~**eless** □
['kɔ:zlis] grundlos.
causeway ['kɔ:zwei] Damm *m.*
caustic ⚕ ['kɔ:stik] (~*ally*) ätzend;
fig. beißend, scharf.
caution ['kɔ:ʃən] **1.** Vorsicht *f;*
Warnung *f;* Verwarnung *f;* ~
money Kaution *f;* **2.** warnen; verwarnen
cautious ['kɔ:ʃəs] behutsam, vorsichtig, ~**ness** [~snis] Behutsam-
keit *f,* Vorsicht *f.*
cavalry ✗ ['kævəlri] Reiterei *f.*
cave [keiv] **1.** Höhle *f;* **2.** *v/i.* ~ *in*
einstürzen; klein beigeben.
cavern ['kævən] Höhle *f;* ~**ous** *fig.*
[~nəs] hohl.
cavil ['kævil] **1.** Krittelei *f;* **2.** kritteln (*at, about an dat.*).
cavity ['kæviti] Höhle *f;* Loch *n.*
cavort *Am.* F [kə'vɔ:t] sich auf-
bäumen, umherspringen.
caw [kɔ:] **1.** krächzen; **2.** Krächzen *n.*
cayuse *Am.* F ['kaiju:s] kleines
(Indianer)Pferd.
cease [si:s] *v/i.* (*from*) aufhören
(mit), ablassen (von); *v/t.* aufhören
mit; ~**less** □ ['si:slis] unaufhörlich.
cede [si:d] abtreten, überlassen.
ceiling ['si:liŋ] Zimmer-Decke *f; fig.*
Höchstgrenze *f;* ~ *price* Höchst-
preis *m.*
celebrat|e ['selibreit] feiern; ~**ed**
gefeiert, berühmt (*for wegen*);
~**ion** [seli'breiʃən] Feier *f.*

celebrity [si'lebriti] Berühmtheit *f.*

celerity [si'leriti] Geschwindigkeit *f.*

celery ♀ ['seləri] Sellerie *m, f.*

celestial ☐ [si'lestjəl] himmlisch.

celibacy ['selibəsi] Ehelosigkeit *f.*

cell [sel] *allg.* Zelle *f; ≴* Element *n.*

cellar ['selə] Keller *m.*

cement [si'ment] 1. Zement *m*; Kitt *m*; 2. zementieren; (ver)kitten.

cemetery ['semitri] Friedhof *m.*

censor ['sensə] 1. Zensor *m*; 2. zensieren; ⁓ious ☐ [sen'sɔ:riəs] kritisch; kritt(e)lig; ⁓ship ['sensəʃip] Zensur *f*; Zensoramt *n.*

censure ['senʃə] 1. Tadel *m*; Verweis *m*; 2. tadeln.

census ['sensəs] Volkszählung *f.*

cent [sent] Hundert *n; Am.* Cent *m* = ¹/₁₀₀ Dollar; *per* ⁓ Prozent *n.*

centenary [sen'ti:nəri] Hundertjahrfeier *f.*

centennial [sen'tenjəl] 1. hundertjährig; 2. hundertjähriges Jubiläum.

centi|grade ['sentigreid]: *10 degrees* ⁓ 10 Grad Celsius; ⁓metre, *Am.* ⁓meter Zentimeter *n, m*; ⁓pede *zo.* [.ipi:d] Hundertfüßer *m.*

central ☐ ['sentrəl] zentral; ⁓ *heating* Zentralheizung *f;* ⁓ *office, ≴* ⁓ *station* Zentrale *f;* ⁓ize [.aiz] zentralisieren.

cent|re, *Am.* ⁓er ['sentə] 1. Zentrum *n*, Mittelpunkt *m*; 2. zentral; 3. (sich) konzentrieren; zentralisieren; zentrieren.

century ['sentʃuri] Jahrhundert *n.*

cereal ['siəriəl] 1. Getreide...; 2. Getreide(pflanze *f*) *n*; Hafer-, Weizenflocken *f/pl.*; Corn-flakes *pl.*

cerebral *anat.* ['seribrəl] Gehirn...

ceremon|ial [seri'mounjəl] 1. ☐ *a.* ⁓ious ☐ [.jəs] zeremoniell; förmlich; 2. Zeremoniell *n*; ⁓y ['seriməni] Zeremonie *f*; Feierlichkeit *f*; Förmlichkeit(en *pl.*) *f.*

certain ☐ ['sə:tn] sicher, gewiß; zuverlässig; bestimmt; gewisse(r, -s); ⁓ty [.nti] Sicherheit *f*, Gewißheit *f*; Zuverlässigkeit *f.*

certi|ficate 1. [sə'tifikit] Zeugnis *n*, Schein *m*; ⁓ *of birth* Geburtsurkunde *f; medical* ⁓ ärztliches Attest; 2. [.keit] bescheinigen; ⁓fication [sə:tifi'keiʃən] Bescheinigung *f*; ⁓fy ['sə:tifai] *et.* bescheinigen; bezeugen; ⁓tude [.itju:d] Gewißheit *f.*

cessation [se'seiʃən] Aufhören *n.*

cession ['seʃən] Abtretung *f.*

cesspool ['sespu:l] Senkgrube *f.*

chafe [tʃeif] *v/t.* reiben; wundreiben; erzürnen; *v/i.* sich scheuern; sich wundreiben; toben.

chaff [tʃɑ:f] 1. Spreu *f*; Häcksel *n*; F Neckerei *f*; 2. zu Häcksel schneiden; F necken.

chaffer ['tʃæfə] feilschen.

chaffinch ['tʃæfintʃ] Buchfink *m.*

chagrin ['ʃægrin] 1. Ärger *m*; 2. ärgern.

chain [tʃein] 1. Kette *f; fig.* Fessel *f*; ⁓ *store bsd. Am.* Kettenladen *m*, Zweiggeschäft *n*; 2. (an)ketten; *fig.* fesseln.

chair [tʃeə] Stuhl *m*; Lehrstuhl *m*; Vorsitz *m*; *be in the* ⁓ den Vorsitz führen; ⁓man ['tʃeəmən] Vorsitzende(r) *m*; Präsident *m.*

chalice ['tʃælis] Kelch *m.*

chalk [tʃɔ:k] 1. Kreide *f*; 2. mit Kreide (be)zeichnen; *mst* ⁓ *up* ankreiden; ⁓ *out* entwerfen.

challenge ['tʃælindʒ] 1. Herausforderung *f;* ⚔ Anruf *m; bsd.* ⚖ Ablehnung *f*; 2. herausfordern; anrufen; ablehnen; anzweifeln.

chamber ['tʃeimbə] *parl., zo.,* ♀, ⊕, *Am.* Kammer *f*; ⁓s *pl.* Geschäftsräume *m/pl.*; ⁓maid Zimmermädchen *n.*

chamois ['ʃæmwɑ:] 1. Gemse *f; a.* ⁓-leather [*oft a.* 'ʃæmileðə] Wildleder *n*; 2. chamois (*gelbbraun*).

champagne [ʃæm'pein] Champagner *m.*

champion ['tʃæmpjən] 1. Vorkämpfer *m*, Verfechter *m*; Verteidiger *m; Sport:* Meister *m*; 2. verteidigen; kämpfen für; *fig.* stützen; 3. großartig; ⁓ship Meisterschaft *f.*

chance [tʃɑ:ns] 1. Zufall *m*; Schicksal *n*; Glück(sfall *m*) *n*; Chance *f*; Aussicht *f* (*of* auf *acc.*); (günstige) Gelegenheit; Möglichkeit *f; by* ⁓ zufällig; *take a* ⁓ *take one's* ⁓ es darauf ankommen lassen; 2. zufällig; gelegentlich; 3. *v/i.* geschehen; sich ereignen; ⁓ *upon* stoßen auf (*acc.*); *v/t.* F wagen.

chancellor ['tʃɑ:nsələ] Kanzler *m.*

chancery ['tʃɑ:nsəri] Kanzleigericht *n; fig. in* ⁓ in der Klemme.

chandelier [ʃændi'liə] Lüster *m.*

chandler ['tʃɑ:ndlə] Krämer *m.*

change [tʃeindʒ] 1. Veränderung *f*, Wechsel *m*, Abwechs(e)lung *f*; Tausch *m*; Wechselgeld *n*; Kleingeld *n*; 2. *v/t.* (ver)ändern; (aus-)wechseln, (aus-)wechseln (*for* gegen); ⁓ *trains* umsteigen; *v/i.* sich ändern, wechseln; sich umziehen; ⁓able ☐ ['tʃeindʒəbl] veränderlich; ⁓less ☐ [.dʒlis] unveränderlich; ⁓ling [.liŋ] Wechselbalg *m*; ⁓ *over* Umstellung *f.*

channel ['tʃænl] 1. Kanal *m*; Flußbett *n*; Rinne *f; fig.* Weg *m*; 2. furchen; aushöhlen.

chant [tʃɑ:nt] 1. (Kirchen)Gesang *m; fig.* Singsang *m*; 2. singen.

chaos ['keiɔs] Chaos *n.*

chap¹ [tʃæp] 1. Riß *m*, Sprung *m*; 2. rissig machen *od.* werden.

chap² F [.] Bursche *m*, Kerl *m*, Junge *m.*

chap³ [⌣] Kinnbacken m; ~s pl. Maul n; ⊕ Backen f/pl.

chapel ['tʃæpəl] Kapelle f; Gottesdienst m.

chaplain ['tʃæplin] Kaplan m.

chapter ['tʃæptə] Kapitel n; Am. Orts-, Untergruppe f e-r Vereinigung.

char [tʃɑː] verkohlen.

character ['kæriktə] Charakter m; Merkmal n; Schrift(zeichen n) f; Sinnesart f; Persönlichkeit f; Original n; thea., Roman: Person f; Rang m, Würde f; (bsd. guter) Ruf; Zeugnis n; ~istic [kærikt'ristik] 1. (~ally) charakteristisch (of für); 2. Kennzeichen n; ~ize ['kæriktəraiz] charakterisieren.

charcoal ['tʃɑːkoul] Holzkohle f.

charge [tʃɑːdʒ] 1. Ladung f; fig. Last f (on für); Verwahrung f, Obhut f; Schützling m; Mündel m, f, n; Amt n, Stelle f; Auftrag m, Befehl m; Angriff m; Ermahnung f; Beschuldigung f, Anklage f; Preis m, Forderung f; ~s pl. ✝ Kosten pl.; be in ~ of et. in Verwahrung haben; mit et. beauftragt sein; für et. sorgen; 2. v/t. laden; beladen, belasten; beauftragen; j-m et. einschärfen, befehlen; ermahnen; beschuldigen, anklagen (with gen.); zuschreiben (on, upon dat.); fordern, verlangen; an-, berechnen, in Rechnung stellen (to dat.); angreifen (a. v/i.); behaupten.

chariot poet. od. hist. ['tʃæriət] Streit-, Triumphwagen m.

charitable □ ['tʃæritəbl] mild(tätig), wohltätig.

charity ['tʃæriti] Nächstenliebe f; Wohltätigkeit f; Güte f; Nachsicht f; milde Gabe.

charlatan ['ʃɑːlətən] Marktschreier m.

charm [tʃɑːm] 1. Zauber m; fig. Reiz m; 2. bezaubern; fig. entzücken; ~ing □ ['tʃɑːmiŋ] bezaubernd.

chart [tʃɑːt] 1. ♎ Seekarte f; Tabelle f; 2. auf e-r Karte einzeichnen.

charter ['tʃɑːtə] 1. Urkunde f; Freibrief m; Patent n; Frachtvertrag m; 2. privilegieren; ♎, ⚓ chartern, mieten.

charwoman ['tʃɑːwumən] Putz-, Reinemachefrau f.

chary [['tʃɛəri] vorsichtig.

chase [tʃeis] 1. Jagd f; Verfolgung f; gejagtes Wild; 2. jagen, hetzen; Jagd machen auf (acc.).

chasm ['kæzəm] Kluft f (a. fig.); Lücke f.

chaste □ ['tʃeist] rein, keusch, unschuldig; schlicht (Stil).

chastise [tʃæs'taiz] züchtigen.

chastity ['tʃæstiti] Keuschheit f.

chat [tʃæt] 1. Geplauder n, Plauderei f; 2. plaudern.

chattels ['tʃætlz] pl. mst goods and ~ Hab n und Gut n; Vermögen n.

chatter ['tʃætə] 1. plappern; schnattern; klappern; 2. Geplapper n; ~box F Plaudertasche f; ~er [~ərə] Schwätzer(in).

chatty [tʃæti] gesprächig.

chauffeur ['ʃoufə] Chauffeur m.

chaw sl [tʃɔː] kauen; ~ up Am. mst fig. fix und fertig machen.

cheap □ [tʃiːp] billig; fig. gemein; ~en ['tʃiːpən] (sich) verbilligen; fig herabsetzen.

cheat [tʃiːt] 1. Betrug m, Schwindel m; Betrüger(in); 2. betrügen.

check [tʃek] 1. Schach(stellung f) n; Hemmnis n (on für); Zwang m, Aufsicht f; Kontrolle f (on gen.); Kontrollmarke f; Am. (Gepäck-) Schein m; Am. ✝ = cheque; Am. Rechnung f im Restaurant; karierter Stoff; 2. v/i. an-, innehalten; Am. e-n Scheck ausstellen; ~ in Am. (in e-m Hotel) absteigen; ~ out Am. das Hotel (nach Bezahlung der Rechnung) verlassen; v/t. hemmen; kontrollieren; nachprüfen; Kleider in der Garderobe abgeben; Am. Gepäck aufgeben; ~er ['tʃekə] Aufsichtsbeamte(r) m; ~s pl. Am. Damespiel n; ~ing-room [~kiŋrum] Am. Gepäckaufbewahrung f; ~mate 1. Schachmatt n; 2. matt setzen; ~-up Am. scharfe Kontrolle.

cheek [tʃiːk] Backe f, Wange f; F Unverschämtheit f; cheeky F ['tʃiːki] frech.

cheer [tʃiə] 1. Stimmung f, Fröhlichkeit f; Hoch(ruf m n); Beifall(sruf) m; Speisen f/pl., Mahl n; three ~s! dreimal hoch!; 2. v/t. a. ~ up aufheitern; mit Beifall begrüßen; a. ~ on ansporen; v/i. hoch rufen; jauchzen; a. ~ up Mut fassen; ~ful □ ['tʃiəful] heiter; ~io [~ri'ou] mach dir's gut!, tschüs!; prosit!; ~less [~lis] freudlos; ~y □ [~əri] heiter, froh.

cheese [tʃiːz] Käse m.

chef [ʃef] Küchenchef m.

chemical ['kemikəl] 1. □ chemisch; 2. ~s pl Chemikalien pl.

chemise [ʃi'miːz] (Frauen)Hemd n.

chemist ['kemist] Chemiker(in); Apotheker m; Drogist m; ~ry [~tri] Chemie f.

cheque ✝ [tʃek] Scheck m; crossed ~ Verrechnungsscheck m.

chequer ['tʃekə] 1. mst ~s pl. Karomuster n; 2. karieren; ~ed gewürfelt; fig. bunt.

cherish ['tʃeriʃ] hegen, pflegen.

cherry ['tʃeri] Kirsche f.

chess [tʃes] Schach(spiel) n; ~board ['tʃesbɔːd] Schachbrett n; ~man Schachfigur f.

chest [tʃest] Kiste f, Lade f; anat. Brustkasten m; ~ of drawers Kommode f.

chestnut ['tʃesnʌt] 1. ♀ Kastanie *f*; F alter Witz; 2. kastanienbraun.

chevy F ['tʃevi] 1. Hetzjagd *f*; Barlaufspiel *n*; 2. hetzen, jagen.

chew [tʃuː] kauen; sinnen; ~ the fact od. rag Am. sl. die Sache durchkauen; ~ing-gum ['tʃu(ː)iŋgʌm] Kaugummi *m*.

chicane [ʃi'kein] 1. Schikane *f*; 2. schikanieren.

chicken ['tʃikin] Hühnchen *n*, Küken *n*; ~-hearted furchtsam, feige; ~-pox ♣ [~npɔks] Windpocken *f/pl.*

chid [tʃid] *pret. u. p.p. von* chide; ~den ['tʃidn] *p.p. von* chide.

chide *lit.* [tʃaid] [*irr.*] schelten.

chief [tʃiːf] 1. ☐ oberst; Ober...; Haupt...; hauptsächlich; ~ clerk Bürovorsteher *m*; 2. Oberhaupt *n*, Chef *m*; Häuptling *m*; ...-in-~ Ober...; ~tain ['tʃiːftən] Häuptling *m*.

chilblain ['tʃilblein] Frostbeule *f*.

child [tʃaild] Kind *n*; from a ~ von Kindheit an; with ~ schwanger; ~birth ['tʃaildbəːθ] Niederkunft *f*; ~hood [~dhud] Kindheit *f*, ~ish ☐ [~diʃ] kindlich; kindisch; ~like kindlich; ~ren ['tʃildrən] *pl. v* child.

chill [tʃil] 1. eisig, frostig; 2. Frost *m*, Kälte *f*; ♣ Fieberfrost *m*; Erkältung *f*; 3. *v/t.* erkalten lassen; abkühlen; *v/i.* erkalten; erstarren; ~y ['tʃili] kalt, frostig.

chime [tʃaim] 1. Glockenspiel *n*; Geläut *n*; *fig.* Einklang *m*; 2. läuten; *fig.* harmonieren, übereinstimmen.

chimney ['tʃimni] Schornstein *m*; Rauchfang *m*; Lampen-Zylinder *m*; ~-sweep(er) Schornsteinfeger *m*.

chin [tʃin] 1. Kinn *n*; take it on the ~ Am. ⌐ se standhaft ertragen; 2.; ~ o.s. Am. e-n Klimmzug machen.

china ['tʃainə] Porzellan *n*.

Chinese [tʃai'niːz] 1. chinesisch; 2. Chinese(n *pl.*) *m*, Chinesin *f*.

chink [tʃiŋk] Ritz *m*, Spalt *m*.

chip [tʃip] 1. Schnitzel *n*, Stückchen *n*; Span *m*; Glas- etc. Splitter *m*; Spielmarke *f*; have a ~ on one's shoulder Am. F aggressiv sein; ~s *pl.* Pommes frites *pl.*; 2. *v/t.* schnitzeln; an-, abschlagen; *v/i.* abbröckeln; ~muck ['tʃipmʌk], ~munk [~ʌŋk] nordamerikanisches gestreiftes Eichhörnchen.

chirp [tʃəːp] 1. zirpen; zwitschern; 2. Gezirp *n*.

chisel ['tʃizl] 1. Meißel *m*; 2. meißeln; sl. (be)mogeln.

chit-chat ['tʃittʃæt] Geplauder *n*.

chivalr|ous ☐ ['ʃivəlrəs] ritterlich; ~y [~ri] Ritterschaft *f*, Rittertum *n*; Ritterlichkeit *f*.

chive ♀ [tʃaiv] Schnittlauch *m*.

chlor|ine ['klɔːriːn] Chlor *n*; ~oform ['klɔrəfɔːm] 1. Chloroform *n*; 2. chloroformieren.

chocolate ['tʃɔkəlit] Schokolade *f*.

choice [tʃɔis] 1. Wahl *f*; Auswahl *f*; 2. ☐ auserlesen, vorzüglich.

choir ['kwaiə] Chor *m*.

choke [tʃouk] 1. *v/t.* (er)würgen, (a. *v/i*) ersticken; ♂ (ab)drosseln; (ver)stopfen; *mst* ~ down hinunterwürgen. 2. Erstickungsanfall *m*; ⊕ Würgung *f*; *mot.* Choke *m*, Starterklappe *f*

choose [tʃuːz] [*irr.*] (aus)wählen; ~ to *inf* vorziehen zu *inf*.

chop [tʃɔp] 1. Hieb *m*; Kotelett *n*; ~s *pl* Maul *n*, Rachen *m*; ⊕ Backen *f/pl*.; 2. *v/t.* hauen, hacken, zerhacken, austauschen; *v/i.* wechseln; ~per ['tʃɔpə] Hackmesser *n*; ~py [~pi] unstet; unruhig (*See*); böig (*Wind*).

choral ☐ ['kɔːrəl] chormäßig; Chor..; ~(e) *f* [kɔ'rɑːl] Choral *m*.

chord [kɔːd] Saite *f*; Akkord *m*.

chore Am. [tʃɔː] Hausarbeit *f* (*mst pl.*).

chorus ['kɔːrəs] 1. Chor *m*; Kehrreim *m*; 2. im Chor singen od. sprechen

chose [tʃouz] *pret. von* choose; ~n ['tʃouzn] *p.p. von* choose.

chow Am. sl [tʃau] Essen *n*.

Christ [kraist] Christus *m*.

christen ['krisn] taufen; ~ing [~niŋ] ⏋aufe *f*; attr. Tauf...

Christian ['kristjən] 1. ☐ christlich; ~ name Vor-, Taufname *m*; 2. Christ(in); ~ity [kristi'æniti] Christentum *n*.

Christmas ['krisməs] Weihnachten *n*

chromium ['kroumjəm] Chrom *n* (Metall); ~-plated verchromt.

chronic [krɔnik] (~ally) chronisch (*mst* ♣ dauernd; sl. ekelhaft; ~le [~kl] 1. ~hronik *f*; 2. aufzeichnen.

chronolog|ical [krɔnə'bdʒikəl] chronologisch; ~y [krə'nɔlədʒi] Zeitrechnung *f*, Zeitfolge *f*.

chubby ['tʃʌbi] rundlich; pausbäckig plump (a. fig.).

chuck¹ [tʃʌk] 1. Glucken *n*; my ~! mein Täubchen!; 2. glucken.

chuck² [~] 1. schmeißen; 2. (Hinaus)Wurf *m*.

chuckle [tʃʌkl] kichern, glucksen.

chum [tʃʌm] 1. (Stuben)Kamerad *m*, 2. zs.-wohnen.

chump [tʃʌmp] Holzklotz *m*.

chunk [tʃʌnk] Klotz *m*.

church [tʃəːtʃ] Kirche *f*; attr. Kirch(en)...; ~ service Gottesdienst *m*; ~warden ['tʃəːtʃ'wɔːdn] Kirchenvorsteher *m*; ~yard Kirchhof *m*.

churl [tʃəːl] Grobian *m*; Flegel *m*; ~ish ['tʃəːliʃ] grob, flegelhaft.

churn [tʃəːn] 1. Butterfaß *n*; 2. buttern; aufwühlen.

chute [ʃuːt] Stromschnelle *f*; Gleit-, Rutschbahn *f*; Fallschirm *m*.

cider ['saidə] Apfelmost m.

cigar [si'gɑː] Zigarre f.

cigarette [sigə'ret] Zigarette f; ~-case Zigarettenetui n.

cigar-holder [si'gaːhouldə] Zigarrenspitze f.

cilia ['siliə] pl. (Augen)Wimpern f/pl.

cinch Am. sl. [sintʃ] sichere Sache.

cincture ['siŋktʃə] Gürtel m, Gurt m.

cinder ['sində] Schlacke f; ~s pl. Asche f; 2ella [sində'relə] Aschenbrödel n; ~-path Sport: Aschenbahn f.

cine-camera ['sini'kæmərə] Filmkamera f.

cinema ['sinəmə] Kino n; Film m.

cinnamon ['sinəmən] Zimt m.

cipher ['saifə] 1. Ziffer f; Null f (a. fig.); Geheimschrift f, Chiffre f; 2. chiffrieren; (aus)rechnen.

circle ['səːkl] 1. Kreis m; Bekanntenetc. Kreis m; Kreislauf m; thea. Rang m; Ring m; 2. (um)kreisen.

circuit ['səːkit] Kreislauf m; ⚡ Stromkreis m; Rundreise f; Gerichtsbezirk m; 🛫 Rundflug m; short ~ ⚡ Kurzschluß m; ~ous □ [sə(ː)'kjuː(ː)itəs] weitschweifig; Um...

circular ['səːkjulə] 1. □ kreisförmig; Kreis...; ~ letter Rundschreiben n; ~ note ✝ Kreditbrief m; 2. Rundschreiben n; Laufzettel m.

circulat|e ['səːkjuleit] v/i. umlaufen, zirkulieren; v/t. in Umlauf setzen; ~ing [~tiŋ]: ~ library Leihbücherei f; ~ion [səːkju'leiʃən] Zirkulation f, Kreislauf m; fig. Umlauf m; Verbreitung f; Zeitungs-Auflage f.

circum|... ['səːkəm] (her)um; ~ference [se'kʌmfərəns] (Kreis-)Umfang m, Peripherie f; ~jacent [səːkəm'dʒeisənt] umliegend; ~locution [~mlə'kjuːʃən] Umständlichkeit f; Weitschweifigkeit f; ~navigate [~m'nævigeit] umschiffen; ~scribe ['səːkəmskraib] ⅍ umschreiben; fig. begrenzen; ~spect □ [~spekt] um-, vorsichtig; ~stance [~stəns] Umstand m (~s pl. a. Verhältnisse n/pl.); Einzelheit f; Umständlichkeit f; ~stantial □ [səːkəm'stænʃəl] umständlich; ~ evidence ⅍ Indizienbeweis m; ~vent [~m'vent] überlisten; vereiteln.

circus ['səːkəs] Zirkus m; (runder) Platz.

cistern ['sistən] Wasserbehälter m.

cit|ation [sai'teiʃən] Vorladung f; Anführung f, Zitat n; Am. öffentliche Ehrung; ~e [sait] ⅍ vorladen; anführen; zitieren.

citizen ['sitizn] (Staats)Bürger(in); Städter(in); ~ship [~nʃip] Bürgerrecht n, Staatsangehörigkeit f.

citron ['sitrən] Zitrone f.

city ['siti] 1. Stadt f; the 2 die City, das Geschäftsviertel; 2. städtisch, Stadt...; 2 article Börsen-, Handelsbericht m; ~ editor Am. Lokalredakteur m; ~ hall Am. Rathaus n; ~ manager Am. Oberstadtdirektor m.

civic ['sivik] (staats)bürgerlich; städtisch; ~s sg. Staatsbürgerkunde f.

civil [ ] ['sivl] bürgerlich, Bürger...; zivil; ⅍ zivilrechtlich; höflich; 2 Servant Verwaltungsbeamt|e(r) m, -in f; 2 Service Staatsdienst m; ~ian ✗ [si'viljən] Zivilist m; ~ity [~liti] Höflichkeit f; ~ization [sivilai'zeiʃən] Zivilisation f, Kultur f; ~ize ['sivilaiz] zivilisieren.

clad [klæd] 1. pret. u. p.p. von clothe; 2. adj. gekleidet.

claim [kleim] 1. Anspruch m; Anrecht n (to auf acc.); Forderung f; Am. Parzelle f; 2. beanspruchen; fordern; sich berufen auf (acc.); ~ to be sich ausgeben für; ~ant ['kleimənt] Beanspruchende(r m) f; ⅍ Kläger m.

clairvoyant(e) [klɛə'vɔiənt] Hellseher(in).

clamber ['klæmbə] klettern.

clammy ['klæmi] feuchtkalt, klamm.

clamo(u)r ['klæmə] 1. Geschrei n, Lärm m; 2. schreien (for nach).

clamp ⊕ [klæmp] 1. Klammer f; 2. verklammern; befestigen.

clan [klæn] Clan m, Sippe f (a. fig.).

clandestine □ [klæn'destin] heimlich; Geheim...

clang [klæŋ] 1. Klang m, Geklirr n; 2. schallen; klirren (lassen).

clank [klæŋk] 1. Gerassel n, Geklirr n; 2. rasseln, klirren (mit).

clap [klæp] 1. Klatschen n; Schlag m, Klaps m; 2. schlagen (mit); klatschen; ~board Am. ['klæpbɔːd] Schaltbrett n; ~trap Effekthascherei f.

claret ['klærət] roter Bordeaux; allg. Rotwein m; Weinrot n; sl. Blut n.

clarify ['klærifai] v/t. (ab)klären; fig. klären; v/i. sich klären.

clarity ['klæriti] Klarheit f.

clash [klæʃ] 1. Geklirr n; Zs.-stoß m; Widerstreit m; 2. klirren (mit); zs.-stoßen.

clasp [klɑːsp] 1. Haken m, Klammer f; Schnalle f; Spange f; fig. Umklammerung f; Umarmung f; 2. v/t. an-, zuhaken; fig. umklammern; umfassen; v/i. festhalten; ~-knife ['klɑːspnaif] Taschenmesser n.

class [klɑːs] 1. Klasse f; Stand m; (Unterrichts)Stunde f; Kurs m; Am. univ. Jahrgang m; 2. (in Klassen) einteilen, einordnen.

classic ['klæsik] Klassiker m; ~s

pl. die alten Sprachen; ~(al □) [~k(əl)] klassisch.

classi|fication [klæsifi'keiʃən] Klassifizierung *f*; Einteilung *f*; ~**fy** ['klæsifai] klassifizieren, einstufen.

clatter ['klætə] 1. Geklapper *n*; 2. klappern (mit); *fig.* schwatzen.

clause [klɔːz] Klausel *f*, Bestimmung *f*; *gr.* (Neben)Satz *m*.

claw [klɔː] 1. Klaue *f*, Kralle *f*, Pfote *f*; *Krebs*-Schere *f*; 2. (zer-) kratzen; (um)krallen.

clay [klei] Ton *m*; *fig.* Erde *f*.

clean [kliːn] 1. *adj.* □ rein; sauber; 2. *adv.* rein, völlig; 3. reinigen (*of* von); ~ *up* aufräumen; ~**er** ['kliːnə] Reiniger *m*; *mst* ~*s pl.* (chemische) Reinigung; ~**ing** [~niŋ] Reinigung *f*; ~**liness** ['klenlinis] Reinlichkeit *f*; ~**ly** 1. *adv.* ['kliːnli] rein; sauber; 2. *adj.* ['klenli] reinlich; ~**se** [klenz] reinigen; säubern.

clear [kliə] 1. □ klar; hell, rein; *fig.* rein (*from* von); frei (*of* von); ganz, voll; ~ rein, netto; 2. *v/t.* er-, aufhellen; (auf)klären; reinigen (*of, from* von); *Wald* lichten, roden; wegräumen (*a.* ~ *away od. off*); *Hindernis* nehmen; *Rechnung* bezahlen; ✈ (aus)klarieren, verzollen; ✈ freisprechen; befreien; rechtfertigen (*from* von); *v/i.* ~ *up* sich aufhellen; sich verziehen; ~**ance** ['kliərəns] Aufklärung *f*; Freilegung *f*; Räumung *f*; ✈ Abrechnung *f*; ⚓, ✈ Verzollung *f*; ~**ing** [~riŋ] Aufklärung *f*; Lichtung *f*, Rodung *f*; ✈ Ab-, Verrechnung *f*; ⚓ *House* Ab-, Verrechnungsstelle *f*.

cleave[1] [kliːv] [*irr.*] (sich) spalten; *Wasser*, *Luft* (zer)teilen.

cleave[2] [~] *fig.* festhalten (*to an dat.*); treu bleiben (*dat.*).

cleaver ['kliːvə] Hackmesser *n*.

clef ♪ [klef] Schlüssel *m*.

cleft [kleft] 1. Spalte *f*; Sprung *m*, Riß *m*; 2. *pret. u. p.p. von cleave*[1].

clemen|cy ['klemənsi] Milde *f*; ~**t** □ [~nt] mild.

clench [klentʃ] *Lippen etc.* fest zs.-pressen; *Zähne* zs.-beißen; *Faust* ballen; festhalten.

clergy ['klɜːdʒi] Geistlichkeit *f*; ~**man** Geistliche(r) *m*.

clerical ['klerikəl] 1. □ geistlich; Schreib(er)...; 2. Geistliche(r) *m*.

clerk [klɑːk] Schreiber(in); Büroangestellte(r *m f*); Sekretär(in); ✚ kaufmännische(r) Angestellte(r); *Am.* Verkäufer(in); Küster *m*.

clever □ ['klevə] gescheit; geschickt.

clew [kluː] Knäuel *m, n*; = *clue.*

click [klik] 1. Knacken *n*; ⊕ Sperrhaken *m*, -klinke *f*; 2. knacken; zu-, einschnappen; klappen.

client ['klaiənt] Klient(in); Kund|e

m, -in *f*; ~**ele** [kliːɑːn'teil] Kundschaft *f*.

cliff [klif] Klippe *f*; Felsen *m*.

climate ['klaimit] Klima *m*.

climax ['klaimæks] 1. *rhet.* Steigerung *f*, Gipfel *m*, Höhepunkt *m*; 2. (sich steigern.

climb [klaim] (er)klettern, (er-) klimmen, (er)steigen; ~**er** ['klaimə] Kletterer *m*, Bergsteiger(in); *fig.* Streber(in); ♣ Kletterpflanze *f*; ~**ing** [~miŋ] Klettern *n*; *attr.* Kletter...

clinch [klintʃ] 1. ⊕ Vernietung *f*; Festhalten *n*; *Boxen*: Umklammerung *f*, 2. *v/t* vernieten; festmachen, ~ *s clench*; *v/i.* festhalten.

cling [kliŋ] [*irr.*] (*to*) festhalten (an *dat.*), sich klammern (an *acc.*); sich (an)schmiegen (an *acc.*); *j-m* anhängen

clinic ['klinik] Klinik *f*; klinisches Praktikum, ~**al** □ [~kəl] klinisch.

clink [kliŋk] 1. Geklirr *n*; 2. klingen, klirren (lassen); klimpern mit; ~**er** ['kliŋkə] Klinker(stein) *m*.

clip[1] [klip] 1. Schur *f*; *at one* ~ *Am.* F auf einmal; 2. ab-, aus-, beschneiden; *Schafe etc* scheren.

clip[2] [~] 1. Klammer *f*; Spange *f*.

clipp|er ['klipə] (*a. pair of*) ~*s pl.* Haarschneide-, Schermaschine *f*; Klipper *m*, ⚓ Schnellsegler *m*; ✈ Verkehrsflugzeug *n*; ~**ings** [~piŋz] *pl.* Abfäll *m/pl.*; *Zeitungs- etc.* Ausschnitt *m/pl.*

cloak [klouk] 1. Mantel *m*; 2. *fig.* bemänteln, verhüllen; ~**room** ['kloukruːm] Garderobe(nraum *m*) *f*; Toilette *f*, ⚓ Gepäckabgabe *f*.

clock [klɔk] *Schlag-, Wand-*Uhr *f*; ~**wise** ['klɔkwaiz] im Uhrzeigersinn, ~**work** Uhrwerk *n*; *like* ~ wie am Schnürchen.

clod [klɔd] Erdklumpen *m*; *a.* ~**hopper** (Bauern)Tölpel *m*.

clog [klɔg] 1. Klotz *m*; Holzschuh *m*, Pantine *f*, 2. belasten; hemmen; (sich) verstopfen.

cloister ['klɔistə] Kreuzgang *m*; Kloster *n*

close 1. [klous] geschlossen; verborgen, verschwiegen; knapp, eng; begrenzt, nah, eng; bündig; dicht; gedrängt, schwül; knickerig; genau; fest (*Griff*); ~ *by*, ~ *to* dicht bei; ~ *fight*, ~ *quarters pl.* Handgemenge *n*, Nahkampf *m*; ~(*ed*) *season*, ~ *time hunt.* Schonzeit *f*; *sail* ~ *to the wind fig.* sich hart an der Grenze des Erlaubten bewegen; 2. [klouz] Schluß *m*; Abschluß *m*; [klous] Einfriedung *f*; Hof *m*; 3. [klouz] *v/t* (ab-, ein-, ver-, zu-) schließen, beschließen; *v/i.* (sich) schließen, abschließen; handgemein werden; ~ *in* hereinbrechen (*Nacht*); kürzer werden (*Tage*); ~ *on* (*prp.*) sich schließen um, um-

fassen; **~ness** ['klousnis] Genauigkeit *f*, Geschlossenheit *f*.
closet ['klɔzit] **1.** Kabinett *n*; (Wand)Schrank *m*; = water-~; **2.**: be ~ed with mit *j-m* e-e geheime Beratung haben.   [nahme *f*.\
close-up ['klousʌp] *Film*: Großauf-\
closure ['klouʒə] Verschluß *m*; *parl.* (Antrag *m* auf) Schluß *m* e-r *Debatte*.
clot [klɔt] **1.** Klümpchen *n*; **2.** zu Klümpchen gerinnen (lassen).
cloth [klɔθ] Stoff *m*, Tuch *n*; Tischtuch *n*; Kleidung *f*, *Amts*-Tracht *f*; *the ~* F der geistliche Stand; *lay the* ~ den Tisch decken; **~-binding** Leineneinband *m*; **~-bound** in Leinen gebunden.
clothe [klouð] [*irr.*] (an-, be)kleiden; einkleiden.
clothes [klouðz] *pl.* Kleider *n/pl.*; Kleidung *f*; Anzug *m*; Wäsche *f*; **~-basket** ['klouðbɑːskit] Waschkorb *m*; **~-line** Wäscheleine *f*; **~-peg** Kleiderhaken *m*; Wäscheklammer *f*; **~pin** *bsd. Am.* Wäscheklammer *f*; **~press** Kleider-, Wäscheschrank *m*.
clothier ['klouðiə] Tuch-, Kleiderhändler *m*.
clothing ['klouðiŋ] Kleidung *f*.
cloud [klaud] **1.** Wolke *f* (*a. fig.*); Trübung *f*; Schatten *m*; **2.** (sich) be-, umwölken (*a. fig.*); **~-burst** ['klaudbəːst] Wolkenbruch *m*; **~less** □ [.dlis] wolkenlos; **~y** □ [.di] wolkig; Wolken...; trüb; unklar.
clout [klaut] Lappen *m*; F Kopfnuß *f*.
clove[1] [klouv] (Gewürz)Nelke *f*.
clove[2] [.] *pret. von cleave*[1]; **~n** ['klouvn] **1.** *p.p. von cleave*[1]; **2.** *adj.* gespalten.
clover ♧ ['klouvə] Klee *m*.
clown [klaun] Hanswurst *m*; Tölpel *m*; **~ish** □ ['klauniʃ] bäurisch; plump; clownhaft.
cloy [klɔi] übersättigen, überladen.
club [klʌb] **1.** Keule *f*; (Gummi-) Knüppel *m*; Klub *m*; ~s *pl. Karten*: Kreuz *n*; **2.** *v/t.* mit e-r Keule schlagen; *v/i.* sich zs.-tun; **~-foot** ['klʌbˈfut] Klumpfuß *m*.
clue [klu:] Anhaltspunkt *m*, Fingerzeig *m*.
clump [klʌmp] **1.** Klumpen *m*; *Baum*-Gruppe *f*; **2.** trampeln; zs.-drängen.
clumsy □ ['klʌmzi] unbeholfen, ungeschickt; plump.
clung [klʌŋ] *pret. u. p.p. von cling.*
cluster ['klʌstə] **1.** Traube *f*; Büschel *n*; Haufen *m*; **2.** büschelweise wachsen; (sich) zs.-drängen.
clutch [klʌtʃ] **1.** Griff *m*; ⊕ Kupplung *f*; Klaue *f*; **2.** (er)greifen.
clutter ['klʌtə] **1.** Wirrwarr *m*; **2.** durch-ea.-rennen; durch-ea.-bringen.

coach [koutʃ] **1.** Kutsche *f*; 🚌 Wagen *m*; Reisebus *m*; Einpauker *m*; Trainer *m*; **2.** in e-r Kutsche fahren; (ein)pauken; trainieren; **~man** ['koutʃmən] Kutscher *m*.
coagulate [kou'ægjuleit] gerinnen (lassen).
coal [koul] **1.** (Stein)Kohle *f*; *carry* ~s *to Newcastle* Eulen nach Athen tragen; **2.** ♣ (be)kohlen.
coalesce [kouə'les] zs.-wachsen; sich vereinigen.
coalition [kouə'liʃən] Verbindung *f*; Bund *m*, Koalition *f*.
coal-pit ['koulpit] Kohlengrube *f*.
coarse] [kɔːs] grob; ungeschliffen.
coast [koust] **1.** Küste *f*; *bsd. Am.* Rodelbahn *f*; **2.** die Küste entlangfahren; im Freilauf fahren; rodeln; **~er** ['koustə] *Am.* Rodelschlitten; ♣ Küstenfahrer *m*.
coat [kout] **1.** Jackett *n*, Jacke *f*, Rock *m*; Mantel *m*; Pelz *m*, Gefieder *n*; Überzug *m*; ~ *of arms* Wappen(schild *m*, *n*) *n*; **2.** überziehen; anstreichen; **~-hanger** ['kouthæŋə] Kleiderbügel *m*; **~ing** ['koutiŋ] Überzug *m*; Anstrich *m*; Mantelstoff *m*.
coax [kouks] schmeicheln (*dat.*); beschwatzen (*into* zu).
cob [kɔb] kleines starkes Pferd; Schwan *m*; *Am.* Maiskolben *m*.
cobbler ['kɔblə] Schuhmacher *m*; Stümper *m*.
cobweb ['kɔbweb] Spinn(en)gewebe *n*.
cock [kɔk] **1.** Hahn *m*; Anführer *m*; Heuhaufen *m*; **2.** *a.* ~ *up* aufrichten; *Gewehrhahn* spannen.
cockade [kɔ'keid] Kokarde *f*.
cockatoo [kɔkə'tuː] Kakadu *m*.
cockboat ♣ ['kɔkbout] Jolle *f*.
cockchafer ['kɔktʃeifə] Maikäfer *m*.
cock|-eyed *sl.* ['kɔkaid] schieläugig; *Am.* blau (*betrunken*); **~horse** Steckenpferd *n*.
cockney ['kɔkni] waschechter Londoner.
cockpit ['kɔkpit] Kampfplatz *m* für Hähne; ♣ Raumdeck *n*; ✈ Führerraum *m*, Kanzel *f*.
cockroach *zo.* ['kɔkroutʃ] Schabe *f*.
cock|sure F ['kɔk'ʃuə] absolut sicher; überheblich; **~tail** Cocktail *m*; **~y** □ F ['kɔki] selbstbewußt; frech.
coco ['koukou] Kokospalme *f*.
cocoa ['koukou] Kakao *m*.
coco-nut ['koukənʌt] Kokosnuß *f*.
cocoon [kə'kuːn] Seiden-Kokon *m*.
cod [kɔd] Kabeljau *m*.
coddle ['kɔdl] verhätscheln.
code [koud] **1.** Gesetzbuch *n*; Kodex *m*; *Telegramm*-, *Signal*-Schlüssel *m*; **2.** chiffrieren.
codger F ['kɔdʒə] komischer Kauz.
cod-liver ['kɔdlivə]: ~ *oil* Lebertran *m*.

co-ed *Am.* F ['kou'ed] Schülerin *f* e-r Koedukationsschule, *allg.* Studentin *f.*

coerc|e [kou'ə:s] (er)zwingen; **~ion** [kou'ə:ʃən] Zwang *m.*

coeval [kou'i:vəl] gleichzeitig; gleichalt(e)rig.

coexist ['kouig'zist] gleichzeitig bestehen.

coffee ['kɔfi] Kaffee *m;* **~-pot** Kaffeekanne *f;* **~-room** Speisesaal *m e-s Hotels;* **~-set** Kaffeeservice *n.*

coffer ['kɔfə] (Geld)Kasten *m.*

coffin ['kɔfin] Sarg *m.*

cogent ['koudʒənt] zwingend.

cogitate ['kɔdʒiteit] *v/i.* nachdenken; *v/t* (er)sinnen.

cognate ['kɔgneit] verwandt.

cognition [kɔg'niʃən] Erkenntnis *f.*

cognizable ['kɔgnizəbl] erkennbar.

coheir ['kou'eə] Miterbe *m.*

coheren|ce [kou'hiərəns] Zs.-hang *m;* **~t** [~nt] zs.-hängend.

cohesi|on [kou'hi:ʒən] Kohäsion *f;* **~ve** [~i:siv] (fest) zs.-hängend.

coiff|eur [kwa:'fə:] Friseur *m;* **~ure** [~'fjuə] Frisur *f.*

coil [kɔil] 1. *a.* **~ up** aufwickeln; (sich) zs.-rollen; 2. Rolle *f,* Spirale *f;* Wicklung *f;* ⚡ Spule *f;* Windung *f;* ⊕ (Rohr)Schlange *f.*

coin [kɔin] 1. Münze *f;* 2. prägen (*a. fig.*); münzen; **~age** ['kɔinidʒ] Prägung *f;* Geld *n,* Münze *f.*

coincide [kouin'said] zs.-treffen; übereinstimmen; **~nce** [kou'insidəns] Zs.-treffen *n; fig.* Übereinstimmung *f.*

coke [kouk] Koks *m* (*a. sl.* = *Kokain*); *Am.* F Coca-Cola *n, f.*

cold [kould] 1. ☐ kalt; 2. Kälte *f,* Frost *m;* Erkältung *f;* **~ness** ['kouldnis] Kälte *f.*

coleslaw *Am.* ['koulslɔ:] Krautsalat *m.*

colic 𝔰 ['kɔlik] Kolik *f.*

collaborat|e [kə'læbəreit] zs.-arbeiten; **~ion** [kəlæbə'reiʃən] Zs.-; Mitarbeit *f; in* ~ gemeinsam.

collaps|e [kə'læps] 1. zs.-, einfallen; zs.-brechen; 2. Zs.-bruch *m;* **~ible** [~səbl] zs.-klappbar.

collar ['kɔlə] 1. Kragen *m;* Halsband *n;* Kum(me)t *n;* ⊕ Lager *n;* 2. beim Kragen packen; *Fleisch* zs.-rollen; **~-bone** Schlüsselbein *n;* **~-stud** Kragenknopf *m.*

collate [kɔ'leit] *Texte* vergleichen.

collateral [kɔ'lætərəl] 1. ☐ parallel laufend, Seiten..., Neben...; indirekt; 2. Seitenverwandte(r *m f*) *f.*

colleague ['kɔli:g] Kollege *m,* -in *f.*

collect *s. eccl.* ['kɔlekt] Kollekte *f;* 2. *v/t.* [kə'lekt] (ein)sammeln; *Gedanken etc.* sammeln; einkassieren; abholen; *v/i.* sich (ver)sammeln; **~ed** ☐ *fig.* gefaßt; **~ion** [~kʃən] Sammlung *f;* Einziehung *f;* **~ive** [~ktiv] gesammelt; Sammel...; ~

bargaining Tarifverhandlungen *f/pl.;* **~ively** [~vli] insgesamt; zs.-fassend; **~or** [~tə] Sammler *m;* Steuereinnehmer *m;* 🔚 Fahrkartenabnehmer *m;* ⚡ Stromabnehmer *m.*

college ['kɔlidʒ] College *n* (*Teil e-r Universstät*). höhere Schule *od.* Lehranstal· *j·* Hochschule *f;* Akademi· *f.* Kollegium *n.*

collide [kə laid] zs.-stoßen.

collie |⃗ k lij] Collie *m,* schottischer Schä·erhund

collier ['kɔliə] Bergmann *m;* ⚓ Kohlenschiff *n;* **~y** ['kɔljəri] Kohlengrul·· *f*

collision [k· liʒən] Zs.-stoß *m.*

colloquial [ka'loukwiəl] umgangssprachlic··· ·amiliär

colloquy | · ·l·kwi] Gespräch *n.*

colon *typ* [·'koulən] Doppelpunkt *m.*

colonel ✗ [· kə:nl] Oberst *m.*

coloni|al [kə lounjəl] Kolonial...; **~alism** *pol.* [·.·lizəm] Kolonialismus *m;* **~ze** ['kɔlənaiz] kolonisieren; (sich) ansiedeln; besiedeln.

colony ['kɔləni] Kolonie *f;* Siedlung *f*

colossal [kə'lɔsl] kolossal.

colo(u)r ['kʌlə] 1. Farbe *f; fig.* Färbun· *f,* Anschein *m;* Vorwand *m;* **~s** *pl.* ✗ Fahne *f,* Flagge *f;* 2. *v/t.* färben, anstreichen; *fig.* beschönigen; *v/i.* sich (ver)färben; erröten; **~-bar** Rassenschranke *f;* **~ed** gefärbt, farbig... *man* Farbige(r) *m;* **~ful** [·əful] farbenreich, ~freudig; lebhaft; **~ing** [·əriŋ] Färbung *f;* Farbton *m, fig* Beschönigung *f;* **~less** [·əlis] farblos; **~ line** *bsd. Am.* Rassenschranke *f.*

colt [koult] Hengstfüllen *n; fig.* Neuling *m*

column ['kɔləm] Säule *f; typ.* Spalte *f;* ✗ kolonne *f;* **~ist** *Am.* [·əmnist] Kolumnist *m.*

comb [koum] 1. Kamm *m;* ⊕ Hechel *f;* 2. *v/t.* kämmen; striegeln; *Flachs* hecheln.

combat ['kɔmbət] 1. Kampf *m;* *single* Zweikampf *m;* 2. (be)kämpfe·· **~ant** [·tənt] Kämpfer *m.*

combin|ation [kɔmbi'neiʃən] Verbindung *f, mst ~s pl.* Hemdhose *f;* **~e** [kəm'bain] (sich) verbinden, vereinigen

combust|ible [kəm'bʌstəbl] 1. brennbar *f;* 2. *pl.* Brennmaterial *n;* *mot.* Betriebsstoff *m;* **~ion** [·tʃən] Verbrennung *f.*

come [kʌm] [*irr.*] kommen; *to ~* künftig, kommend; ~ *about* sich zutragen, ~ *across* auf *j.* od. *et.* stoßen; ~ *at* erreichen; ~ *by* vorbeikommen; zu *et.* kommen; ~ *down* herunterkommen (*a. fig.*); *Am.* F erkranken (*with an dat.*); ~ *for* abholen; ~ *off* davonkommen; losgehen (*Knopf*), ausfallen (*Haare etc.*); stattfinden,

~ round vorbeikommen (bsd. zu Besuch); wiederkehren; F zu sich kommen; fig. einlenken; ~ to adv. dazukommen; ⚓ beidrehen; prp. betragen; ~ up to entsprechen (dat.); es j-m gleichtun; Stand, Maß erreichen; ~back ['kʌmbæk] Wiederkehr f, Comeback n; Am. sl. schlagfertige Antwort.

comedian [kə'miːdjən] Schauspieler(in); Komiker(in); Lustspieldichter m.

comedy ['kɔmidi] Lustspiel n.

comeliness ['kʌmlinfs] Anmut f.

comfort ['kʌmfət] 1. Bequemlichkeit f; Behaglichkeit f; Trost m; fig. Beistand m; Erquickung f; 2. trösten; erquicken; beleben; ~able □ [~təbl] behaglich; bequem; tröstlich; ~er [~tə] Tröster m; fig. wollenes Halstuch; Schnuller m; Am. Steppdecke f; ~less □ [~tlis] unbehaglich; trostlos; ~ station Am. Bedürfnisanstalt f.

comic(al □) ['kɔmik(əl)] komisch; lustig, drollig.

coming ['kʌmiŋ] 1. kommend; künftig; 2. Kommen n.

comma ['kɔmə] Komma n.

command [kə'mɑːnd] 1. Herrschaft f, Beherrschung f (a. fig.); Befehl m; ✕ Kommando n; be (have) at ~ zur Verfügung stehen (haben); 2. befehlen; ✕ kommandieren; verfügen über (acc.); beherrschen; ~er [~də] Kommandeur m, Befehlshaber m; ⚓ Fregattenkapitän m; ~er-in-chief [~ərin-'tʃiːf] Oberbefehlshaber m; ~ment [~dmənt] Gebot n.

commemorat|e [kə'meməreit] gedenken (gen.), feiern; ~ion [kəme-mə'reiʃən] Gedächtnisfeier f.

commence [kə'mens] anfangen, beginnen; ~ment [~smənt] Anfang m. [loben; anvertrauen.)

commend [kə'mend] empfehlen;)

commensurable □ [kə'menʃərəbl] vergleichbar (with, to mit).

comment ['kɔment] 1. Kommentar m; Erläuterung f; An-, Bemerkung f; 2. (upon) erläutern (acc.); sich auslassen (über acc.); ~ary [~'kɔməntəri] Kommentar m; ~ator ['kɔmenteitə] Kommentator m; Radio: Berichterstatter m.

commerc|e ['kɔmə(:)s] Handel m; Verkehr m; ~ial □ [kə'məːʃəl] 1. kaufmännisch; Handels..., Geschäfts...; gewerbsmäßig; ~ traveller Handlungsreisende(r) m; 2. bsd. Am. Radio, Fernsehen: kommerzielle (Werbe)Sendung.

commiseration [kəmizə'reiʃən] Mitleid n (for mit).

commissary ['kɔmisəri] Kommissar m; ✕ Intendanturbeamte(r) m.

commission [kə'miʃən] 1. Auftrag m; Übertragung f von Macht etc.;

Begehung f e-s Verbrechens; Provision f; Kommission f; (Offiziers-) Patent n; 2. beauftragen; bevollmächtigen; ✕ bestallen; ⚓ in Dienst stellen; ~er [~ʃnə] Bevollmächtigte(r m) f; Kommissar m.

commit [kə'mit] anvertrauen; übergeben, überweisen; Tat begehen; bloßstellen; ~ (o.s. sich) verpflichten; ~ (to prison) in Untersuchungshaft nehmen; ~ment [~tmənt], ~tal [~tl] Überweisung f; Verpflichtung f; Verübung f; ~tee [~ti] Ausschuß m, Komitee n.

commodity [kə'mɔditi] Ware f (mst pl.), Gebrauchsartikel m.

common ['kɔmən] 1. □ (all)gemein; gewöhnlich; gemeinschaftlich; öffentlich; gemein (niedrig); 2 Council Gemeinderat m; 2. Gemeindewiese f; in ~ gemeinsam; in ~ with fig. genau wie; ~er [~nə] Bürger m, Gemeine(r) m; Mitglied n des Unterhauses; ~ law Gewohnheitsrecht n; 2 Market Gemeinsamer Markt; ~place 1. Gemeinplatz m; 2. gewöhnlich; F abgedroschen; ~s pl. das gemeine Volk; Gemeinschaftsverpflegung f; (mst House of) 2 Unterhaus n; ~ sense gesunder Menschenverstand; ~wealth [~nwelθ] Gemeinwesen n, Staat m; bsd. Republik f; the British 2 das Commonwealth.

commotion [kə'mouʃən] Erschütterung f; Aufruhr m; Aufregung f.

communal □ ['kɔmjunl] gemeinschaftlich; Gemeinde...

commune 1. [kə'mjuːn] sich vertraulich besprechen; 2. ['kɔmjuːn] Gemeinde f.

communicat|e [kə'mjuːnikeit] v/t. mitteilen; v/i. das Abendmahl nehmen, kommunizieren; in Verbindung stehen; ~ion [kəmjuːni'kei-ʃən] Mitteilung f; Verbindung f; ~ive [kə'mjuːnikətiv] gesprächig.

communion [kə'mjuːnjən] Gemeinschaft f; eccl. Kommunion f, Abendmahl n.

communis|m ['kɔmjunizəm] Kommunismus m; ~t [~ist] 1. Kommunist(in); 2. kommunistisch.

community [kə'mjuːniti] Gemeinschaft f; Gemeinde f; Staat m.

commut|ation [kɔmju(:)'teiʃən] Vertauschung f; Umwandlung f; Ablösung f; Strafmilderung f; ~ ticket Am. Zeitkarte f; ~e [kə'mjuːt] ablösen; Strafe (mildernd) umwandeln; Am. pendeln im Arbeitsverkehr.

compact 1. ['kɔmpækt] Vertrag m; 2. [kəm'pækt] adj. dicht, fest; knapp, bündig; v/t. fest verbinden.

companion [kəm'pænjən] Gefährt|e m, -in f; Gesellschafter(in); ~able □ [~nəbl] gesellig; ~ship [~nʃip] Gesellschaft f.

company ['kʌmpəni] Gesellschaft f; Kompanie f; Handelsgesellschaft f; Genossenschaft f; ⚓ Mannschaft f; thea. Truppe f; have ~ Gäste haben; keep ~ with verkehren mit.

compar|able □ ['kɔmpərəbl] vergleichbar; ~ative [kəm'pærətiv] 1. □ vergleichend; verhältnismäßig; 2. a. ~ degree gr Komparativ m; ~e [~'pɛə] 1.: beyond ~, without ~, past ~ unvergleichlich; 2. v/t. vergleichen; gleichstellen (to mit); v/i. sich vergleichen (lassen); ~ison [~'pærisn] Vergleich(ung f) m.

compartment [kəm'pɑ:tmənt] Abteilung f; ⚔ Fach n; 🚃 Abteil n.

compass ['kʌmpəs] 1. Bereich m; ♩ Umfang m; Kompaß m; oft pair of ~es pl. Zirkel m; 2. herumgehen um; einschließen; erreichen; planen.

compassion [kəm'pæʃən] Mitleid n; ~ate [[~nit] mitleidig.

compatible □ [kəm'pætəbl] vereinbar, verträglich; schicklich.

compatriot [kəm'pætriət] Landsmann m.

compel [kəm'pel] (er)zwingen.

compensat|e ['kɔmpenseit] j-n entschädigen; et. ersetzen; ausgleichen; ~ion [kɔmpen'seiʃən] Ersatz m; Ausgleich(ung f) m; Entschädigung f; Am. Vergütung f (Gehalt).

compère ['kɔmpɛə] 1. Conférencier m; 2. ansagen (bei).

compete [kəm'pi:t] sich mitbewerben (for um), konkurrieren.

competen|ce, ~cy ['kɔmpitəns, ~si] Befugnis f, Zuständigkeit f; Auskommen n; ~t [[~nt] hinreichend; (leistungs)fähig; fachkundig; berechtigt, zuständig.

competit|ion [kɔmpi'tiʃən] Mitbewerbung f; Wettbewerb m; ✝ Konkurrenz f; ~ive [kəm'petitiv] wetteifernd; ~or [~tə] Mitbewerber (-in); Konkurrent(in).

compile [kəm'pail] zs.-tragen, zs.-stellen (from aus); sammeln.

complacen|ce, ~cy [kəm'pleisns, ~si] Selbstzufriedenheit f.

complain [kəm'plein] (sich be-)klagen; ~ant [~nənt] Kläger(in); ~t [~nt] Klage f, Beschwerde f; ⚕ Leiden n.

complaisan|ce [kəm'pleizənz] Gefälligkeit f; Entgegenkommen n; ~t □ [~nt] gefällig; entgegenkommend.

complement 1. ['kɔmplimənt] Ergänzung f; volle Anzahl; 2. [~ment] ergänzen.

complet|e [kəm'pli:t] 1. □ vollständig, ganz; vollkommen; 2. vervollständigen; vervollkommnen; abschließen; ~ion [~'i:ʃən] Vervollständigung f; Abschluß m; Erfüllung f.

complex ['kɔmpleks] 1. □ zs.-gesetzt; fig kompliziert; 2. Gesamtheit f, Komplex m; ~ion [kəm'plekʃən] Aussehen n; Charakter m, Zug m, Gesichtsfarbe f, Teint m; ~ity [~ksiti] Kompliziertheit f.

complian|ce [kəm'plaiəns] Einwilligung f, Einverständnis n; in ~ with gemäß; ~t □ [~nt] gefällig.

complicate ['kɔmplikeit] komplizieren, erschweren.

complicity [kəm'plisiti] Mitschuld f (in an dat.)

compliment 1. ['kɔmplimənt] Kompliment n; Schmeichelei f; Gruß m, 2. [~ment] v/t. (on) beglückwünschen (zu); j-m Komplimente machen (über acc.); ~ary [kɔmpli'mentəri] höflich.

comply [kəm'plai] sich fügen; nachkommen, entsprechen (with dat.).

component [kəm'pounənt] 1. Bestandteil m, 2. zs.-setzend.

compos|e [kəm'pouz] zs.-setzen; komponieren, verfassen; ordnen; beruhigen, typ setzen; ~ed □ ruhig, gesetzt, ~er [~zə] Komponist(in), Verfasser(in); ~ition [kɔmpə'ziʃən] Zs.-setzung f; Abfassung f, Komposition f; (Schrift-) Satz m, Aufsatz m; ✝ Vergleich m; ~t ['kɔmpɔst] Kompost m; ~ure [kəm'pouʒə] Fassung f, Gemütsruhe f.

compound 1. ['kɔmpaund] zs.-gesetzt, ~ interest Zinseszinsen m/pl.; 2. Zs.-setzung f, Verbindung f; 3. [kəm'paund] v/t. zs.-setzen; Streit beilegen, v/i sich einigen.

comprehend [kɔmpri'hend] umfassen, begreifen, verstehen.

comprehen|sible □ [kɔmpri'hensəbl] verständlich; ~sion [~nʃən] Verständnis n; Fassungskraft f; Umfang m, ~sive □ [~nsiv] umfassend

compress [kəm'pres] zs.-drücken; ~ed air Druckluft f; ~ion [~eʃən] phys Verdichtung f; ⊕ Druck m.

comprise [kəm praiz] in sich fassen, einschließen, enthalten.

compromise ['kɔmprəmaiz] 1. Kompromiß m, n; 2. v/t. Streit beilegen, bloßstellen; v/i. e-n Kompromiß schließen.

compuls|ion [kəm'pʌlʃən] Zwang m; ~ory [~'lsəri] obligatorisch; Zwangs_, Pflicht...

compunction [kəm'pʌŋkʃən] Gewissensbisse m/pl.; Reue f; Bedenken n

comput|ation [kɔmpju(:)'teiʃən] (Be)Rechnung f; ~e [kəm'pju:t] (be-, er)rechnen; schätzen; ~er [~tə] Computer m.

comrade ['kɔmrid] Kamerad m.

con[1] abbr. [kɔn] = contra.

con² *Am. sl.* [‿] **1.**: ~ *man* = confidence *man*; **2.** 'reinlegen (*betrügen*).

conceal [kən'si:l] verbergen; *fig.* verhehlen, verheimlichen, verschweigen.

concede [kən'si:d] zugestehen; einräumen; gewähren, nachgeben.

conceit [kən'si:t] Einbildung *f*; spitzfindiger Gedanke; übertriebenes sprachliches Bild; **~ed** □ eingebildet (*of* auf *acc.*).

conceiv|able □ [kən'si:vəbl] denkbar; begreiflich; **~e** [kən'si:v] *v/i.* empfangen (*schwanger werden*); sich denken (*of acc.*); *v/t. Kind* empfangen; sich denken; aussinnen.

concentrate ['kɔnsentreit] (sich) zs.-ziehen, (sich) konzentrieren.

conception [kən'sepʃən] Begreifen *n*; Vorstellung *f*, Begriff *m*, Idee *f*; *biol.* Empfängnis *f*.

concern [kən'sɔːn] **1.** Angelegenheit *f*; Interesse *n*; Sorge *f*; Beziehung *f* (*with* zu); ✝ Geschäft *n*, (industrielles) Unternehmen; **2.** betreffen, angehen, interessieren; ~ *o.s. about od. for* sich kümmern um; *be* ~*ed* in Betracht kommen; ~*ed* □ interessiert, beteiligt (*in an dat.*); bekümmert; **~ing** *prp.* [~niŋ] betreffend, über, wegen, hinsichtlich.

concert 1. ['kɔnsət] Konzert *n*; **2.** [~sə(:)t] Einverständnis *n*; **3.** [kən'sɔːt] sich einigen, verabreden; **~ed** gemeinsam; ♪ mehrstimmig.

concession [kən'seʃən] Zugeständnis *n*; Erlaubnis *f*. [räumend.)

concessive □ [kən'sesiv] ein-)

concil|iate [kən'silieit] aus-, versöhnen; ausgleichen; **~or** [~tə] Vermittler *m*; **~ory** [~iətəri] versöhnlich, vermittelnd.

concise □ [kən'sais] kurz, bündig, knapp; **~ness** [~snis] Kürze *f*.

conclude [kən'klu:d] schließen, beschließen; abschließen; folgern; sich entscheiden; *to be* ~*d* Schluß folgt.

conclusi|on [kən'klu:ʒən] Schluß *m*, Ende *n*; Abschluß *m*; Folgerung *f*; Beschluß *m*; **~ve** □ [~u:siv] schlüssig; endgültig.

concoct [kən'kɔkt] zs.-brauen; *fig.* aussinnen; **~ion** [~kʃən] Gebräu *n*; *fig.* Erfindung *f*.

concord ['kɔŋkɔːd] Eintracht *f*; Übereinstimmung *f* (*a. gr.*); ♪ Harmonie *f*; **~ant** □ [kən'kɔːdənt] übereinstimmend; einstimmig; ♪ harmonisch.

concourse ['kɔŋkɔːs] Zusammen-, Auflauf *m*; Menge *f*; *Am.* Bahnhofs-, Schalterhalle *f*.

concrete 1. ['kɔŋkriːt] konkret; Beton...; **2.** [~] Beton *m*; **3.** [kən'kriːt] *zu e-r Masse* verbinden; ['kɔŋkriːt] betonieren.

concur [kən'kəː] zs.-treffen, zs.-wirken; übereinstimmen; **~rence** [~'kʌrəns] Zusammentreffen *n*; Übereinstimmung *f*; Mitwirkung *f*.

concussion [kən'kʌʃən] ~ *of the brain* Gehirnerschütterung *f*.

condemn [kən'dem] verdammen; verurteilen; verwerfen; *Kranke* aufgeben; beschlagnahmen; **~ation** [kɔndem'neiʃən] Verurteilung *f*; Verdammung *f*; Verwerfung *f*.

condens|ation [kɔnden'seiʃən] Verdichtung *f*; **~e** [kən'dens] (sich) verdichten; ⊕ kondensieren; zs.-drängen; **~er** [~sə] ⊕ Kondensator *m*.

condescen|d [kɔndi'send] sich herablassen; geruhen; **~sion** [~nʃən] Herablassung *f*.

condiment ['kɔndimənt] Würze *f*.

condition [kən'diʃən] **1.** Zustand *m*, Stand *m*; Stellung *f*, Bedingung *f*; ~*s pl.* Verhältnisse *n/pl.*; **2.** bedingen; in e-n bestimmten Zustand bringen; **~al** □ [~l] bedingt (*on*, *upon* durch); Bedingungs...; ~ *clause gr.* Bedingungssatz *m*; ~ *mood gr.* Konditional *m*.

condol|e [kən'doul] kondolieren (*with dat.*); **~ence** [~əns] Beileid *n*.

conduc|e [kən'djuːs] führen, dienen; **~ive** [~siv] dienlich, förderlich.

conduct 1. ['kɔndəkt] Führung *f*; Verhalten *n*, Betragen *n*; **2.** [kən'dʌkt] führen; ♪ dirigieren; **~ion** [~kʃən] Leitung *f*; **~or** [~ktə] Führer *m*; Leiter *m*; Schaffner *m*; ♪ Dirigent *m*; ⚡ Blitzableiter *m*.

conduit ['kɔndit] (Leitungs-) Röhre *f*.

cone [koun] Kegel *m*; ♣ Zapfen *m*.

confabulation [kɔnfæbju'leiʃən] Plauderei *f*.

confection [kən'fekʃən] Konfekt *n*; **~er** [~ʃnə] Konditor *m*; **~ery** [~əri] Konfekt *n*; Konditorei *f*; *bsd. Am.* Süßwarengeschäft *n*.

confedera|cy [kən'fedərəsi] Bündnis *n*; *the* ♀ *bsd. Am.* die 11 Südstaaten *bei der Sezession 1860—61*; **~te 1.** [~rit] verbündet; **2.** [~] Bundesgenosse *m*; **3.** [~reit] (sich) verbünden; **~tion** [kɔnfedə'reiʃən] Bund *m*, Bündnis *n*; *the* ♀ *bsd. Am.* die Staatenkonföderation *f* von 1781—1789.

confer [kən'fəː] *v/t.* übertragen, verleihen; *v/i.* sich besprechen; **~ence** ['kɔnfərəns] Konferenz *f*.

confess [kən'fes] bekennen, gestehen; beichten; **~ion** [~eʃən] Geständnis *n*; Bekenntnis *n*; Beichte *f*; **~ional** [~nl] Beichtstuhl *m*; **~or** [~esə] Bekenner *m*; Beichtvater *m*.

confide [kən'faid] *v/t.* anvertrauen; *v/i.* vertrauen (*in* auf *acc.*); **~nce** ['kɔnfidəns] Vertrauen *n*; Zuversicht *f*; **~nce man** Schwindler *m*;

Hochstapler *m*; ~nce trick Bauernfängerei *f*; ~nt □ [~nt] vertrauend; zuversichtlich; ~ntial □ [konfi-'denʃəl] vertraulich.

confine [kən'fain] begrenzen; beschränken; einsperren; *be ~d* niederkommen (*of* mit); *be ~d to bed* das Bett hüten müssen; ~ment [~nmənt] Haft *f*; Beschränkung *f*; Entbindung *f*.

confirm [kən'fəːm] (be)kräftigen; bestätigen; konfirmieren; firmen; ~ation [kɔnfə'meiʃən] Bestätigung *f*; *eccl.* Konfirmation *f*; *eccl.* Firmung *f*.

confiscat|e ['kɔnfiskeit] beschlagnahmen; ~ion [kɔnfis'keiʃən] Beschlagnahme *f*. [ßer Brand.\

conflagration [kɔnflə'greiʃən] gro-)

conflict 1. ['kɔnflikt] Konflikt *m*; **2.** [kən'flikt] im Konflikt stehen.

conflu|ence ['kɔnfluəns], ~x [~ʌks] Zs.-fluß *m*; Auflauf *m*; ~ent [~luənt] **1.** zs.-fließend, zs.-laufend; **2.** Zu-, Nebenfluß *m*.

conform [kən'fɔːm] (sich) anpassen; ~able □ [~məbl] (to) übereinstimmend (mit); entsprechend (*dat.*); nachgiebig (gegen); ~ity [~miti] Übereinstimmung *f*.

confound [kən'faund] vermengen; verwechseln; *j-n* verwirren; ~ *it!* F verdammt!; ~ed □ F verdammt.

confront [kən'frʌnt] gegenüberstellen; entgegentreten (*dat.*).

confus|e [kən'fjuːz] verwechseln; verwirren; ~ion [~uːʒən] Verwirrung *f*; Verwechs(e)lung *f*.

confut|ation [kɔnfjuː'teiʃən] Widerlegung *f*; ~e [kən'fjuːt] widerlegen.

congeal [kən'dʒiːl] erstarren (lassen); gerinnen (lassen).

congenial □ [kən'dʒiːnjəl] (geistes-) verwandt (*with dat.*); zusagend.

congenital [kən'dʒenitl] angeboren.

congestion [kən'dʒestʃən] (Blut-) Andrang *m*; Stauung *f*; *traffic* ~ Verkehrsstockung *f*.

conglomeration [kɔnglɔmə'reiʃən] Anhäufung *f*; Konglomerat *n*.

congratulat|e [kən'grætjuleit] beglückwünschen; *j-m* gratulieren; ~ion [kəngrætju'leiʃən] Glückwunsch *m*.

congregat|e ['kɔngrigeit] (sich) (ver)sammeln; ~ion [kɔngri'geiʃən] Versammlung *f*; *eccl.* Gemeinde *f*.

congress ['kɔngres] Kongreß *m*; ♀ Kongreß *m*, *gesetzgebende Körperschaft der USA*; ♀man, ♀woman *Am. pol.* Mitglied *n* des Repräsentantenhauses.

congruous □ ['kɔngruəs] angemessen (to für); übereinstimmend; folgerichtig.

conifer ['kounifə] Nadelholzbaum *m*.

conjecture [kən'dʒektʃə] **1.** Mutmaßung *f*; **2.** mutmaßen.

conjoin [kən'dʒɔin] (sich) verbinden; ~t ['kɔndʒɔint] verbunden.

conjugal □ ['kɔndʒugəl] ehelich.

conjugat|e *gr.* ['kɔndʒugeit] konjugieren, beugen; ~ion *gr.* [kɔndʒu'geiʃən] Konjugation *f*, Beugung *f*.

conjunction [kən'dʒʌŋkʃən] Verbindung *f*; Zs.-treffen *n*; *gr.* Konjunktion *f*.

conjunctivitis [kəndʒʌŋkti'vaitis] Bindehautentzündung *f*.

conjure¹ [kən'dʒuə] beschwören, inständig bitten.

conjur|e² ['kʌndʒə] *v/t.* beschwören; *et. wohin* zaubern; *v/i.* zaubern; ~er [~ərə] Zauber|er *m*, -in *f*; Taschenspieler(in); ~ing-trick [~riŋtrik] Zauberkunststück *n*; ~or [~rə] = conjurer.

connect [kə'nekt] (sich) verbinden; ∮ schalten; ~ed □ verbunden; zs.-hängend (*Rede etc.*); *be ~ with* in Verbindung stehen mit *j-m*; ~ion [~kʃən] = connexion.

connexion [kə'nekʃən] Verbindung *f*; ∮ Schaltung *f*; Anschluß *m* (*a.* ⚙, ∮); Zs.-hang *m*; Verwandtschaft *f*.

connive [kə'naiv]: ~ *at* ein Auge zudrücken bei.

connoisseur [kɔni'səː] Kenner(in).

connubial □ [kə'njuːbjəl] ehelich.

conquer ['kɔŋkə] erobern; (be)siegen; ~or [~ərə] Eroberer *m*; Sieger *m*.

conquest ['kɔŋkwest] Eroberung *f*; Errungenschaft *f*; Sieg *m*.

conscience ['kɔnʃəns] Gewissen *n*.

conscientious □ [kɔnʃi'enʃəs] gewissenhaft; Gewissens...; ~ *objector* Kriegsdienstverweigerer *m* aus Überzeugung; ~ness [~snis] Gewissenhaftigkeit *f*.

conscious □ ['kɔnʃəs] bewußt; *be ~ of* sich bewußt sein (*gen.*); ~ness [~snis] Bewußtsein *n*.

conscript ∦ ['kɔnskript] Wehrpflichtige(r) *m*; ~ion ∦ [kən'skripʃən] Einberufung *f*.

consecrat|e ['kɔnsikreit] weihen, einsegnen; heiligen; widmen; ~ion [kɔnsi'kreiʃən] Weihung *f*, Einsegnung *f*; Heiligung *f*.

consecutive □ [kən'sekjutiv] aufea.-folgend; fortlaufend.

consent [kən'sent] **1.** Zustimmung *f*; **2.** einwilligen, zustimmen (*dat.*).

consequen|ce ['kɔnsikwəns] (to) Folge *f*, Konsequenz *f* (für); Wirkung *f*, Einfluß *m* (auf *acc.*); Bedeutung *f* (für); ~t [~nt] **1.** folgend; **2.** Folge(rung) *f*; ~tial □ [kɔnsi'kwenʃəl] sich ergebend (*on* aus); folgerichtig; wichtigtuerisch; ~tly ['kɔnsikwəntli] folglich, daher.

conserv|ation [kɔnsə(ː)'veiʃən] Erhaltung *f*; ~ative □ [kən'səːvətiv] **1.** erhaltend (*of acc.*); konservativ; vorsichtig; **2.** Konservative(r) *m*;

~atory [kən'sɔːvətri] Treib-, Gewächshaus n; ♪ Konservatorium n; ~e [kən'sɔːv] erhalten.

consider [kən'sidə] v/t. betrachten; erwägen; überlegen; in Betracht ziehen; berücksichtigen; meinen, glauben; v/i. überlegen; *all things* ~ed wenn man alles in Betracht zieht; ~able [⌐ [⌐ərəbl] ansehnlich, beträchtlich; ~ably [⌐li] bedeutend, ziemlich, (sehr) viel; ~ate [⌐rit] rücksichtsvoll; ~ation [kənsidə'reiʃən] Betrachtung f, Erwägung f, Überlegung f; Rücksicht f; Wichtigkeit f; Entschädigung f; Entgelt n; *be under* ~ erwogen werden; in Betracht kommen; *on no* ~ unter keinen Umständen; ~ing [kən'sidəriŋ] **1.** *prp.* in Anbetracht (*gen.*); **2.** F *adv.* den Umständen entsprechend.

consign [kən'sain] übergeben, überliefern; anvertrauen; ✝ konsignieren; ~ment ✝ [⌐nmənt] Übersendung f; Konsignation f.

consist [kən'sist] bestehen (*of* aus); in Einklang stehen (*with* mit); ~ence, ~ency [⌐təns, ~si] Festigkeit(sgrad m) f; Übereinstimmung f; Konsequenz f; ~ent [⌐nt] fest; übereinstimmend, vereinbar (*with* mit); konsequent.

consol|ation [kɔnsə'leiʃən] Trost m; ~e [kən'soul] trösten.

consolidate [kən'sɔlideit] festigen; *fig.* vereinigen; zs.-legen.

consonan|ce ['kɔnsənəns] Konsonanz f; Übereinstimmung f; ~t [⌐nt] **1.** [übereinstimmend; **2.** *gr.* Konsonant m, Mitlaut m.

consort ['kɔnsɔːt] Gemahl(in); ♣ Geleitschiff n.

conspicuous [[kən'spikjuəs] sichtbar; auffallend; hervorragend; *make o.s.* ~ sich auffällig benehmen.

conspir|acy [kən'spirəsi] Verschwörung f; ~ator [⌐rətə] Verschwörer m; ~e [⌐'spaiə] sich verschwören.

constab|le ['kʌnstəbl] Polizist m; Schutzmann m; ~ulary [kən'stæbjuləri] Polizei(truppe) f.

constan|cy ['kɔnstənsi] Standhaftigkeit f; Beständigkeit f; ~t [[⌐nt] beständig, fest; unveränderlich; treu.

consternation [kɔnstə(ː)'neiʃən] Bestürzung f.

constipation ⚕ [kɔnsti'peiʃən] Verstopfung f.

constituen|cy [kən'stitjuənsi] Wählerschaft f; Wahlkreis m; ~t [[⌐nt] **1.** wesentlich; Grund..., Bestand...; konstituierend; **2.** wesentlicher Bestandteil m; Wähler m.

constitut|e ['kɔnstitjuːt] ein-, errichten; ernennen; bilden, ausmachen; ~ion [kɔnsti'tjuːʃən] Ein-, Errichtung f; Bildung f; Körper-

bau m; Verfassung f; ~ional □ [⌐nl] konstitutionell; natürlich; verfassungsmäßig.

constrain [kən'strein] zwingen; *et.* erzwingen, ⌐; ~t [⌐nt] Zwang m.

constrict [kən'strikt] zs.-ziehen; ~ion [⌐kʃən] Zs.-ziehung f.

constringent [kən'strindʒənt] zs.-ziehend

construct [kən'strʌkt] bauen, errichten, *fig* bilden; ~ion [⌐kʃən] Konstruktion f; Bau m; Auslegung f; ~ive [⌐ktiv] aufbauend, schöpferisch, konstruktiv, positiv; Bau...; ~or [⌐tə] Erbauer m, Konstrukteur m

construe [kən'struː] *gr.* konstruieren; auslegen, auslegen; übersetzen

consul ['kɔnsəl] Konsul m; ~-*general* Generalkonsul m; ~ate [⌐sjulit] Konsulat n (*a Gebäude*).

consult [kən sʌlt] v/t. konsultieren, um Rat fragen; in *e-m Buch* nachschlagen, v/i sich beraten; ~ation [kɔnsəl'teiʃən] Konsultation f, Beratung f, Rücksprache f; ~ hour Sprechstunde f; ~ative [kən'sʌltətiv] beratend

consume [kən'sjuːm] v/t. verzehren; verbrauchen; vergeuden; ~r [⌐mə] Verbraucher m; Abnehmer m.

consummate 1. □ [kən'sʌmit] vollendet, **2.** [kɔnsʌmeit] vollenden.

consumpti|on [kən'sʌmpʃən] Verbrauch m, ⚕ Schwindsucht f; ~ve □ [⌐ptiv] verzehrend; ⚕ schwindsüchtig

contact 1. ['kɔntækt] Berührung f; Kontakt m, ~ *lenses pl.* Haft-, Kontaktschalen f/pl; **2.** [kən'tækt] Fühlung nehmen mit.

contagi|on ⚕ [kən'teidʒən] Ansteckung f, Übertragung f; Seuche f; ~ous [⌐əs] ansteckend.

contain [kən'tein] (ent)halten, (um-) fassen; ~ *o.s* an sich halten; ~er [⌐nə] Behälter m; Großbehälter m (*im Frachtverkehr*).

contaminat|e [kən'tæmineit] verunreinigen, *fig* anstecken, vergiften; verseuchen; ~ion [kəntæmi-'neiʃən] Verunreinigung f; (radioaktive) Verseuchung f.

contemplat|e *fig.* ['kɔntempleit] betrachten, beabsichtigen; ~ion [kɔntəm pleiʃən] Betrachtung f; Nachsinnen n; ~ive □ ['kɔntempleitiv] nachdenklich; [kən'templətiv] beschaulich.

contempora|neous □ [kəntempə-'reinjəs] gleichzeitig; ~ry [kən-'tempərəri] **1.** zeitgenössisch; gleichzeitig, **2.** Zeitgenoss|e m, -in f.

contempt [kən'tempt] Verachtung f; ~ible □ [⌐təbl] verachtenswert; ~uous [[⌐tjuəs] geringschätzig (*of* gegen); verächtlich.

contend [kən'tend] *v/i.* streiten, ringen (*for* um); *v/t.* behaupten.

content [kən'tent] **1.** zufrieden; **2.** befriedigen; ~ *o.s.* sich begnügen; **3.** Zufriedenheit *f*; *to one's heart's* ~ nach Herzenslust; ['kɔntent] Umfang *m*; Gehalt *m*; ~s *pl.* stofflicher Inhalt; ~**ed** □ [kən'tentid] zufrieden; genügsam.

contention [kən'tenʃən] (Wort-)Streit *m*; Wetteifer *m*.

contentment [kən'tentmənt] Zufriedenheit *f*, Genügsamkeit *f*.

contest 1. ['kɔntest] Streit *m*; Wettkampf *m*; **2.** [kən'test] (be)streiten; anfechten; um *et.* streiten.   [*m.*]

context [kɔn'tekst] Zusammenhang

contiguous □ [kən'tigjuəs] anstoßend (*to* an *acc.*); benachbart.

continent ['kɔntinənt] **1.** □ enthaltsam; mäßig; **2.** Kontinent *m*, Erdteil *m*; Festland *n*; ~**al** [kɔnti'nentl] **1.** □ kontinental; Kontinental...; **2.** Kontinentaleuropäer(in).

contingen|cy [kən'tindʒənsi] Zufälligkeit *f*; Zufall *m*; Möglichkeit *f*; ~**t** [~nt] **1.** □ zufällig; möglich (*to* bei); **2.** ✕ Kontingent *n*.

continu|al □ [kən'tinjuəl] fortwährend, unaufhörlich; ~**ance** [~əns] (Fort)Dauer *f*; ~**ation** [kəntinju-'eiʃən] Fortsetzung *f*; Fortdauer *f*; ~ *school* Fortbildungsschule *f*; ~**e** [kən'tinju(:)] *v/t.* fortsetzen; beibehalten; *to be* ~**d** Fortsetzung folgt; *v/i.* andauern; fortfahren; ~**ity** [kɔnti'nju(:)iti] Kontinuität *f*; *Film:* Drehbuch *n*; *Radio:* verbindende Worte; ~ *girl* Skriptgirl *n*; ~**ous** □ [kən'tinjuəs] ununterbrochen.

contort [kən'tɔːt] verdrehen; verzerren; ~**ion** [~ɔːʃən] Verdrehung *f*; Verzerrung *f*.

contour ['kɔntuə] Umriß *m*.

contra ['kɔntrə] wider.

contraband ['kɔntrəbænd] Schmuggelware *f*; Schleichhandel *m*; *attr.* Schmuggel...

contraceptive [kɔntrə'septiv] **1.** empfängnisverhütend; **2.** empfängnisverhütendes Mittel.

contract 1. [kən'trækt] *v/t.* zs.-ziehen; sich *et.* zuziehen; *Schulden* machen; *Heirat etc.* (ab)schließen; *v/i.* einschrumpfen; e-n Vertrag schließen; sich verpflichten; **2.** ['kɔntrækt] Kontrakt *m*, Vertrag *m*; ~**ion** [kən'trækʃən] Zs.-ziehung *f*; *gr.* Kurzform *f*; ~**or** [~ktə] Unternehmer *m*; Lieferant *m*.

contradict [kɔntrə'dikt] widersprechen (*dat.*); ~**ion** [~kʃən] Widerspruch *m*; ~**ory** □ [~ktəri] (sich) widersprechend.

contrar|iety [kɔntrə'raiəti] Widerspruch *m*; Widrigkeit *f*; ~**y** ['kɔntrəri] **1.** entgegengesetzt; widrig; ~ *to* zuwider (*dat.*); gegen; **2.** Gegenteil *n*; *on the* ~ im Gegenteil.

contrast 1. ['kɔntrɑːst] Gegensatz *m*; **2.** [kən'trɑːst] *v/t.* gegenüberstellen; vergleichen; *v/i.* sich unterscheiden, abstechen (*with* von).

contribut|e [kən'tribju(:)t] beitragen, beisteuern; ~**ion** [kɔntri'bju:ʃən] Beitrag *m*; ~**or** [kən'tribjutə] Beitragende(r *m*) *f*; Mitarbeiter(in) *an e-r Zeitung*; ~**ory** [~əri] beitragend.

contrit|e □ ['kɔntrait] reuevoll; ~**ion** [kən'triʃən] Zerknirschung *f*.

contriv|ance [kən'traivəns] Erfindung *f*; Plan *m*; Vorrichtung *f*; Kunstgriff *m*; Scharfsinn *m*; ~**e** [kən'traiv] *v/t.* ersinnen; planen; zuwegebringen; *v/i.* es fertig bringen (*to inf.* zu *inf.*); ~**er** [~və] Erfinder(in).

control [kən'troul] **1.** Kontrolle *f*, Aufsicht *f*; Befehl *m*; Zwang *m*; Gewalt *f*; Zwangswirtschaft *f*; Kontrollvorrichtung *f*; Steuerung *f*; ~ *board* ⊕ Schaltbrett *n*; **2.** einschränken; kontrollieren; beaufsichtigen, überwachen; beherrschen; (nach)prüfen; bewirtschaften; regeln; ✕ steuern (*a. fig. dat.*); ~**ler** [~lə] Kontrolleur *m*, Aufseher *m*; Leiter *m*; Rechnungsprüfer *m*.

controver|sial □ [kɔntrə'vəːʃəl] umstritten; streitsüchtig; ~**sy** ['kɔntrəvəːsi] Streit(frage *f*) *m*; ~**t** [~ɔːt] bestreiten.

contumacious □ [kɔntju(:)'meiʃəs] widerspenstig; ✝✝ ungehorsam.

contumely ['kɔntjuːmli] Beschimpfung *f*; Schmach *f*.

contuse ✝ [kən'tjuːz] quetschen.

convalesce [kɔnvə'les] genesen; ~**nce** [~sns] Genesung *f*; ~**nt** [~nt] **1.** □ genesend; **2.** Genesende(r *m*) *f*.

convene [kən'viːn] (sich) versammeln; zs.-rufen; ✝✝ vorladen.

convenien|ce [kən'viːnjəns] Bequemlichkeit *f*; Angemessenheit *f*; Vorteil *m*; Klosett *n*; *at your earliest* ~ möglichst bald; ~**t** □ [~nt] bequem; passend; brauchbar.

convent [kən'vent] (Nonnen)Kloster *n*; ~**ion** [kən'venʃən] Versammlung *f*; Konvention *f*, Übereinkommen *n*, Vertrag *m*; Herkommen *n*; ~**ional** [~nl] vertraglich; herkömmlich, konventionell.

converge [kən'vəːdʒ] konvergieren, zs.-laufen (lassen).

convers|ant [kən'vəːsənt] vertraut; ~**ation** [kɔnvə'seiʃən] Gespräch *n*, Unterhaltung *f*; ~**ational** [~nl] Unterhaltungs...; umgangssprachlich; ~**e 1.** □ ['kɔnvəːs] umgekehrt; **2.** [kən'vəːs] sich unterhalten; ~**ion** [~əːʃən] Um-, Verwandlung *f*; ⊕, ✈ Umformung *f*; *eccl.* Bekehrung *f*; *pol.* Meinungswechsel *m*, Übertritt *m*; ✝ Konvertierung *f*; Umstellung *f* e-r Währung *etc.*

convert 1. ['kɔnvə:t] Bekehrte(r *m*)
f, Konvertit *m*; **2.** [kən'və:t] (sich)
um-, verwandeln; ⊕, ⚡ umformen;
eccl. bekehren; ✝ konvertieren;
Währung etc. umstellen; **~er** ⊕, ⚡
[~tə] Umformer *m*; **~ible 1.** □
[~təbl] um-, verwandelbar; ✝ kon-
vertierbar; **2.** *mot.* Kabrio(lett) *n*.
convey [kən'vei] befördern, bringen, schaffen; übermitteln, mitteilen; ausdrücken; übertragen;
~ance [~eiəns] Beförderung *f*; ✝
Spedition *f*; Übermittlung *f*; Ver-
kehrsmittel *n*; Fuhrwerk *n*; Übertragung *f*; **~er, ~or** ⊕ [~eiə] *a.* **~**
belt Förderband *n*.
convict 1. ['kɔnvikt] Sträfling *m*;
2. [kən'vikt] *j-n* überführen; **~ion**
[~kʃən] ⚡ Überführung *f*; Überzeugung *f* (*of* von).
convince [kən'vins] überzeugen.
convivial □ [kən'viviəl] festlich;
gesellig.
convocation [kɔnvə'keiʃən] Einberufung *f*; Versammlung *f*.
convoke [kən'vouk] einberufen.
convoy ['kɔnvɔi] **1.** Geleit *n*; Ge-
leitzug *m*; (Geleit)Schutz *m*;
2. geleiten.
convuls|ion [kən'vʌlʃən] Zuckung
f, Krampf *m*; **~ive** □ [~lsiv]
krampfhaft, -artig, konvulsiv.
coo [ku:] girren, gurren.
cook [kuk] **1.** Koch *m*; Köchin *f*;
2. kochen; *Bericht etc* frisieren;
~book *Am.* ['kukbuk] Kochbuch *n*;
~ery ['kukəri] Kochen *n*; Koch-
kunst *f*; **~ie** *Am.* ['kuki] Plätzchen
n; **~ing** [~iŋ] Küche *f* (*Kochweise*);
~y *Am.* ['kuki] = *cookie*.
cool [ku:l] **1.** □ kühl; *fig.* kaltblütig,
gelassen; unverfroren; **2.** Kühle *f*;
3. (sich) abkühlen.
coolness ['ku:lnis] Kühle *f* (*a. fig.*);
Kaltblütigkeit *f*.
coon *Am.* F [ku:n] *zo.* Waschbär *m*;
Neger *m*; (schlauer) Bursche.
coop [ku:p] **1.** Hühnerkorb *m*;
2. **~** *up od. in* einsperren.
co-op F [kou'ɔp] = *co-operative*
(*store*).
cooper ['ku:pə] Böttcher *m*, Küfer
m.
co(-)operat|e [kou'ɔpəreit] mitwir-
ken; zs.-arbeiten; **~ion** [kouɔpə-
'reiʃən] Mitwirkung *f*; Zs.-arbeit *f*;
~ive [kou'ɔpərəti] zs.-wirkend; **~**
society Konsumverein *m*; **~** *store*
Konsum(vereinsladen) *m*; **~or**
[~reitə] Mitarbeiter *m*.
co-ordinat|e 1. □ [kou'ɔ:dnit]
gleichgeordnet; **2.** [~dineit] koordi-
nieren, gleichordnen; auf-e-a einstellen; **~ion** [kouɔ:di'neiʃən]
Gleichordnung *f*, -schaltung *f*.
copartner ['kou'pɑ:tnə] Teilhaber
m.
cope [koup]: **~** *with* sich messen mit,
fertig werden mit.

copious □ ['koupjəs] reich(lich);
weitschweifig; **~ness** [~snis] Fülle
f.
copper[1] ['kɔpə] **1.** Kupfer *n*; Kup-
fermünze *f*; **2.** kupfern; Kupfer...
copper[2] *sl* [~] Polyp *m* (*Polizist*).
coppice, copse ['kɔpis, kɔps] Unterholz *n*, Dickicht *n*.
copy ['kɔpi] **1.** Kopie *f*; Nachbildung *f*, Abschrift *f*; Durchschlag
m; Muster *n*; Exemplar *n* e-s *Buches*; *Zeitungs*-Nummer *f*; druck-
fertiges Manuskript; *fair od. clean*
~ Reinschrift *f*; **2.** kopieren; abschreiben, nachbilden, nachahmen;
~book Schreibheft *n*; **~ing** [~iŋ]
Kopier ...; **~ist** [~ist] Abschreiber
m; Nachahmer *m*; **~right** Verlags-
recht *n*, Copyright *n*.
coral ['kɔrəl] Koralle *f*.
cord [kɔ:d] **1.** Schnur *f*, Strick *m*;
anat Strang *m*; **2.** (zu)schnüren,
binden... **~ed** ['kɔ:did] gerippt.
cordial □ ['kɔ:djəl] **1.** □ herzlich;
herzstärkend, *a.* (Magen)Likör *m*;
~ity [kɔ:di'æliti] Herzlichkeit *f*.
cordon ['kɔ:dən] **1.** Postenkette *f*;
2. **~** *off* abriegeln, absperren.
corduroy ['kɔ:dərɔi] Kord *m*; **~s**
pl. Kordhosen *f*/*pl.*; **~** *road* Knüp-
peldamm *m*.
core [kɔ:] **1.** Kerngehäuse *n*; *fig.*
Herz *n*; Kern *m*; **2.** entkernen.
cork [kɔ:k] **1.** Kork *m*; **2.** (ver)kor-
ken; **~ing** *Am* F ['kɔ:kiŋ] fabelhaft,
prima; **~jacket** Schwimmweste *f*;
~screw Kork(en)zieher *m*.
corn [kɔ:n] **1.** Korn *n*; Getreide *n*;
a. Indian **~** *Am.* Mais *m*; ⚕ Hühner-
auge *n*; **2.** einpökeln.
corner ['kɔ:nə] **1.** Ecke *f*, Winkel *m*;
Kurve *f*, *fig* Enge *f*; ✝ Aufkäufer-
Ring *m*, **2.** Eck...; **3.** in die Ecke
(*fig.* Enge) treiben; ✝ aufkaufen;
~ed eckig.
cornet ♪ ['kɔ:nit] (kleines) Horn.
cornice △ ['kɔ:nis] Gesims *n*.
corn|-juice *Am.* *sl.* ['kɔ:ndʒu:s]
Maisschnaps *m*; **~ pone** *Am.*
['kɔ:npoun] Maisbrot *n*; **~stalk**
Getreidehalm *m*; *Am.* Maisstengel
m; **~starch** *Am.* Maisstärke *f*.
coron|ation [kɔrə'neiʃən] Krönung
f; **~er** ['kɔrənə] Leichenbeschauer
m; **~et** [~nit] Adelskrone *f*.
corpor|al ['kɔ:pərəl] **1.** □ körper-
lich; **2.** ⚡ Korporal *m*; **~ation**
[kɔ:pə reiʃən] Körperschaft *f*, Innung *f*, Zunft *f*; Stadtverwaltung *f*;
Am. Aktiengesellschaft *f*.
corpse [kɔ:ps] Leichnam *m*.
corpulen|ce, ~cy ['kɔ:pjuləns, ~si]
Beleibtheit *f*, **~t** [~nt] beleibt.
corral *Am* [kɔ:'rɑ:l] **1.** Einzäunung
f; **2.** zs -pferchen, einsperren.
correct [kə'rekt] **1.** *adj.* □ korrekt,
richtig, **2.** *v/t.* korrigieren; zurecht-
weisen, strafen; **~ion** [~kʃən] Berichtigung *f*; Verweis *m*; Strafe *f*;

Korrektur *f*; *house of* ~ Besserungs-
anstalt *f*.
correlate ['kɔrileit] in Wechselbe-
ziehung stehen *od.* bringen.
correspond [kɔris'pɔnd] entsprechen (*with, to dat.*); korrespondie-
ren; **~ence** [~dəns] Übereinstimmung *f*; Briefwechsel *m*; **~ent** [~nt]
1. □ entsprechend; **2.** Briefschrei-
ber(in); Korrespondent(in).
corridor ['kɔridɔ:] Korridor *m*;
Gang *m*; ~ *train* D-Zug *m*.
corrigible □ ['kɔridʒəbl] verbesser-
lich; zu verbessern(d).
corroborate [kə'rɔbəreit] stärken;
bestätigen.
corro|de [kə'roud] zerfressen; weg-
ätzen; **~sion** [~ouʒən] Ätzen *n*,
Zerfressen *n*; ⊕ Korrosion *f*; Rost
m; **~sive** [~ousiv] **1.** □ zerfressend,
ätzend; **2.** Ätzmittel *n*.
corrugate ['kɔrugeit] runzeln; ⊕
riefen; **~d** *iron* Wellblech *n*.
corrupt [kə'rʌpt] **1.** ╽ verdorben;
verderbt; bestechlich; **2.** *v/t.* verderben; bestechen; anstecken; *v/i.*
(ver)faulen, verderben; **~ible** □
[~təbl] verderblich; bestechlich;
~ion [~pʃən] Verderbnis *f*, Verdor-
benheit *f*; Fäulnis *f*; Bestechung *f*.
corsage [kɔ:'sɑ:ʒ] Taille *f*, Mieder
n; *Am.* Ansteckblume(n *pl.*) *f*.
corset ['kɔ:sit] Korsett *n*.
coruscate ['kɔrəskeit] funkeln.
co-signatory ['kou'signətəri] **1.** mit-
unterzeichnend; **2.** Mitunterzeich-
ner *m*.
cosmetic [kɔz'metik] **1.** kosme-
tisch; **2.** Schönheitsmittel *n*; Kosmetik *f*; **~ian** [kɔzme'tiʃən] Kos-
metiker(in).
cosmonaut ['kɔzmənɔ:t] Kosmo-
naut *m*, Weltraumfahrer *m*.
cosmopolit|an [kɔzmə'pɔlitən], **~e**
[kɔz'mɔpəlait] **1.** kosmopolitisch;
2. Weltbürger(in).
cost [kɔst] **1.** Preis *m*; Kosten *pl.*;
Schaden *m*; *first od. prime* ~ An-
schaffungskosten *pl.*; **2.** [*irr.*] kosten.
costl|iness ['kɔstlinis] Kostbarkeit
f; **~y** ['kɔstli] kostbar; kostspielig.
costume ['kɔstju:m] Kostüm *n*;
Kleidung *f*; Tracht *f*.
cosy ['kouzi] **1.** □ behaglich, gemütlich; **2.** = *tea-cosy*.
cot [kɔt] Feldbett *n*; ♣ Hängematte
f mit Rahmen, Koje *f*; Kinderbett *n*.
cottage ['kɔtidʒ] Hütte *f*; kleines
Landhaus, Sommerhaus *n*; ~ *cheese*
Am. Quark(käse) *m*; ~ *piano* Piani-
no *n*; **~r** [~dʒə] Häusler *m*; Hütten-
bewohner *m*; *Am.* Sommergast *m*.
cotton ['kɔtn] **1.** Baumwolle *f*; †
Kattun *m*; *Näh*-Garn *n*; **2.** baum-
wollen; Baumwoll...; ~ *wool* Watte
f; **3.** F sich vertragen; sich anschließen; **~-wood** ♣ *e-e* amerikanische Pappel.

couch [kautʃ] **1.** Lager *n*; Couch *f*,
Sofa *n*, Liege *f*; Schicht *f*; **2.** *v/t.*
Meinung etc. ausdrücken; *Schriftsatz etc.* abfassen; ⚔ *Star* stechen;
v/i. sich (nieder)legen; versteckt
liegen; kauern.
cough [kɔf] **1.** Husten *m*; **2.** husten.
could [kud] *pret. von can*[1].
coulee *Am.* ['ku:li] (trockenes)
Bachbett.
council ['kaunsl] Rat(sversammlung
f) *m*; **~(l)or** [~silə] Ratsmitglied *n*,
Stadtrat *m*.
counsel ['kaunsl] **1.** Beratung *f*;
Rat(schlag) *m*; ♣ Anwalt *m*; ~ *for
the defense* Verteidiger *m*; ~ *for the
prosecution* Anklagevertreter *m*;
2. *j-n* beraten; *j-m* raten; **~(l)or**
[~silə] Ratgeber(in); Anwalt *m*;
Am. Rechtsbeistand *m*.
count[1] [kaunt] **1.** Rechnung *f*;
Zahl *f*; ♣ Anklagepunkt *m*; **2.** *v/t.*
zählen; rechnen; dazurechnen; *fig.*
halten für; *v/i.* zählen; rechnen;
gelten (*for little* wenig).
count[2] [~] *nichtbritischer* Graf.
count-down ['kauntdaun] Count-
down *m, n*, Startzählung *f* (*beim
Raketenstart*).
countenance ['kauntinəns] **1.** Gesicht *n*; Fassung *f*; Unterstützung
f; **2.** begünstigen, unterstützen.
counter[1] ['kauntə] Zähler *m*, Zähl-
apparat *m*; Spielmarke *f*; Zahl-
pfennig *m*; Ladentisch *m*; Schalter
m.
counter[2] [~] **1.** entgegen, zuwider
(*to dat.*); Gegen...; **2.** Gegenschlag
m; **3.** Gegenmaßnahmen treffen.
counteract [kauntə'rækt] zuwider-
handeln (*dat.*).
counterbalance 1. ['kauntəbæləns]
Gegengewicht *n*; **2.** [kauntə'bæləns]
aufwiegen; ╈ ausgleichen.
counter-espionage ['kauntər'espiə-
na:ʒ] Spionageabwehr *f*.
counterfeit ['kauntəfit] **1.** □ nachgemacht; falsch, unecht; **2.** Nachahmung *f*; Fälschung *f*; Falschgeld *n*; **3.** nachmachen; fälschen;
heucheln.
counterfoil ['kauntəfɔil] Kontrollabschnitt *m*.
countermand [kauntə'mɑ:nd]
1. Gegenbefehl *m*; Widerruf *m*;
2. widerrufen; abbestellen.
counter-move *fig.* ['kauntəmu:v]
Gegenzug *m*, -maßnahme *f*.
counterpane ['kauntəpein] Bett-
decke *f*.
counterpart ['kauntəpa:t] Gegenstück *n*.
counterpoise ['kauntəpɔiz] **1.** Gegengewicht *n*; **2.** das Gleichgewicht
halten (*dat.*) (*a. fig.*), ausbalancie-
ren.
countersign ['kauntəsain] **1.** Ge-
genzeichen *n*; ⚔ Losung(swort *n*)
f; **2.** gegenzeichnen.

countervail ['kauntəveil] aufwiegen.

countess ['kauntis] Gräfin f.

counting-house ['kauntiŋhaus] Kontor n.

countless ['kauntlis] zahllos.

countrified ['kʌntrifaid] ländlich; bäurisch.

country ['kʌntri] 1. Land n; Gegend f; Heimatland n; 2. Land(s)..., ländlich; **~man** Landmann m (Bauer); Landsmann m; **~side** Gegend f; Land(bevölkerung f) n.

county ['kaunti] Grafschaft f, Kreis m; **~ seat** Am. = **~ town** Kreisstadt f.

coup [ku:] Schlag m, Streich m.

couple ['kʌpl] 1. Paar n; Koppel f; 2. (ver)koppeln; ⊕ kuppeln, (sich) paaren; **~r** [.lə] Radio Koppler m.

coupling ['kʌpliŋ] Kupplung f; Radio: Kopplung f; attr. Kupplungs...

coupon ['ku:pɔn] Abschnitt m.

courage ['kʌridʒ] Mut m; **~ous** □ [kə'reidʒəs] mutig, beherzt.

courier ['kuriə] Kurier m, Eilbote m; Reiseführer m.

course [kɔ:s] 1. Lauf m, Gang m; Weg m; ⚓, fig. Kurs m; Rennbahn f; Gang m (Speisen); Kursus m; univ. Vorlesung f; Ordnung f, Folge f; of **~** selbstverständlich; 2. v/t. hetzen; jagen; v/i rennen.

court [kɔ:t] 1. Hof m, Hofgesellschaft f; Gericht(shof m) n, General ♀ Am. gesetzgebende Versammlung; pay (one's) **~** to j-m den Hof machen; 2. j-m den Hof machen; werben um; **~day** ['kɔ:tdei] Gerichtstag m; **~eous** [ˈkɔ:tjəs] höflich; **~esy** ['kɔ:tisi] Höflichke.t f; Gefälligkeit f; **~house** ['kɔ:t-'haus] Gerichtsgebäude n; Am. a. Amtshaus n e-s Kreises, **~ier** ['kɔ:tjə] Höfling m; **~ly** ['kɔ:tli] höfisch; höflich; **~ martial** ⚔ Kriegs-, Militärgericht n; **~-martial** ⚔ ['kɔ:t'ma:ʃəl] vor ein Kriegs- od. Militärgericht stellen; **~ room** Gerichtssaal m; **~ship** ['kɔ:tʃip] Werbung f; **~yard** Hof m.

cousin ['kʌzn] Vetter m; Base f.

cove [kouv] 1. Bucht f; fig. Obdach n.

covenant ['kʌvinənt] 1. ⚖ Vertrag m; Bund m; 2. v/t. geloben; v/i. übereinkommen.

cover ['kʌvə] 1. Decke f; Deckel m; Umschlag m; Hülle f; Deckung f; Schutz m; Dickicht n; Deckmantel m; Decke f, Mantel m (Bereifung); 2. (be-, zu)decken; einschlagen; einwickeln; verbergen, verdecken; schützen; Weg zurücklegen; ✝ decken; mit e-r Schußwaffe zielen nach; ⚔ Gelände bestreichen; umfassen; fig. erfassen; Zeitung. berichten über (acc.); **~age** [.ərid ʒ]

Berichterstattung f (of über acc.); **~ing** [.riŋ] Decke f; Bett-Bezug m; Überzug m; Bekleidung f; Bedachung f.

covert 1. [['kʌvət] heimlich, versteckt, 2. ['kʌvə] Schutz m; Versteck n; Dickicht n.

covet ['kʌvit] begehren; **~ous** □ [.təs] (be)gierig; habsüchtig.

cow[1] [kau] Kuh f.

cow[2] [.] einschüchtern, ducken.

coward ['kauəd] 1. □ feig; 2. Feigling m. **~ice** [.dis] Feigheit f; **~ly** [.dli] feig(e)

cow|**boy** ['kaubɔi] Cowboy m (berittener Rinderhirt); **~catcher** Am. 🚂 Schienenräumer m.

cower ['kauə] kauern; sich ducken.

cow|**herd** ['kauhə:d] Kuhhirt m; **~hide** 1. Rind(s)leder n; 2. peitschen, **~house** Kuhstall m.

cowl [kaul] Mönchskutte f; Kapuze f; Schornsteinkappe f.

cow|**man** ['kaumən] Melker m; Am. Viehzüchter m; **~puncher** Am. F ['kaupʌntʃə] Rinderhirt m; **~shed** Kuhstall m; **~slip** ⚘ Schlüsselblume f; Am. Sumpfdotterblume f.

coxcomb ['kɔkskoum] Geck m.

coxswain ['kɔkswein, ⚓ mst 'kɔksn] Bootsführer m; Steuermann m.

coy [kɔi] schüchtern; spröde.

crab [kræb] Krabbe f, Taschenkrebs m; ⊕ Winde f; F Querkopf m.

crab-louse ['kræblaus] Filzlaus f.

crack [kræk] 1. Krach m; Riß m, Sprung m; F derber Schlag; Versuch m, Witz m; 2. F erstklassig, 3. v/t. (zer)sprengen; knallen mit et.; (auf)knacken; **~** a joke e-n Witz reißen; v/i platzen, springen; knallen; umschlagen (Stimme); **~ed** geborsten; F verdreht; **~er** ['krækə] Knallbonbon m; n; Schwärmer m; Am. Keks m (ungesüßt); **~le** [.kl] knattern, knistern; **~up** Zs.-stoß m; 🚗 Bruchlandung f.

cradle ['kreidl] 1. Wiege f; Kindheit f (a fig.); 2. (ein)wiegen.

craft [kra:ft] Handwerk n, Gewerbe n; Schiff(e pl.) n; Gerissenheit f; **~sman** ['kra:ftsmən](Hand)werker m; **~y** □ ['kra:fti] gerissen, raffiniert

crag [kræg] Klippe f, Felsspitze f.

cram [kræm] (voll)stopfen; nudeln; mästen; F (ein)pauken.

cramp [kræmp] 1. Krampf m; ⊕ Klammer f; ⊕ Fessel f; 2. verkrampfen; einengen, hemmen.

cranberry ['krænbəri] Preiselbeere f.

crane [krein] 1. Kranich m; ⊕ Kran m; 2. (den Hals) recken; **~fly** zo. ['kreinflai] Schnake f.

crank [kræŋk] 1. Kurbel f; Schwengel m; Wortspiel n; Schrulle f; komischer Kauz; fixe Idee; 2. (an)kurbeln; **~shaft** ⊕ ['kræŋkʃɑ:ft]

Kurbelwelle f; ~y [~ki] wacklig; launisch; verschroben.

cranny ['kræni] Riß m, Ritze f.

crape [kreip] Krepp m, Flor m.

craps Am. [kræps] pl. Würfelspiel.

crash [kræʃ] 1. Krach m (a. ✈); ✈ Absturz m; 2. v/i. krachen; einstürzen; ✈ abstürzen; mot. zs.-stoßen; fahren, fliegen, stürzen (into in, auf acc.); v/t. zerschmettern; 3. Am. F blitzschnell ausgeführt; ~-helmet ['kræʃhelmit] Sturzhelm m; ~-landing Bruchlandung f.

crate [kreit] Lattenkiste f.

crater ['kreitə] Krater m; Trichter m.

crave [kreiv] v/t. dringend bitten od. flehen um; v/i. sich sehnen.

craven ['kreivən] feig.

crawfish ['krɔ:fiʃ] 1. Krebs m; 2. Am. F sich drücken.

crawl [krɔ:l] 1. Kriechen n; 2. kriechen; schleichen; wimmeln; kribbeln; Schwimmen: kraulen; it makes one's flesh ~ man bekommt e-e Gänsehaut davon.

crayfish ['kreifiʃ] Flußkrebs m.

crayon ['kreiən] Zeichenstift m, bsd. Pastellstift m; Pastell(gemälde) n.

craz|e [kreiz] Verrücktheit f; F Fimmel m; be the ~ Mode sein; ~y □ ['kreizi] baufällig; verrückt (for, about nach).

creak [kri:k] knarren.

cream [kri:m] 1. Rahm m, Sahne f; Creme f; Auslese f; das Beste; 2. den Rahm abschöpfen; ~ery ['kri:məri] Molkerei f; Milchgeschäft n; ~y □ [~mi] sahnig.

crease [kri:s] 1. (Bügel)Falte f; 2. (sich) kniffen, (sich) falten.

creat|e [kri(:)'eit] (er)schaffen; thea. e-e Rolle gestalten; verursachen; erzeugen; ernennen; ~ion [~'eiʃən] Schöpfung f; Ernennung f; ~ive [~'eitiv] schöpferisch; ~or [~tə] Schöpfer m; ~ure ['kri:tʃə] Geschöpf n; Kreatur f.

creden|ce ['kri:dəns] Glaube m; ~tials [kri'denʃəlz] pl. Beglaubigungsschreiben n; Unterlagen f/pl.

credible □ ['kredəbl] glaubwürdig; glaubhaft.

credit ['kredit] 1. Glaube(n) m; Ruf m, Ansehen n; Guthaben n; ✝ Kredit m; ✝ Kredit m; Einfluß m; Verdienst n, Ehre f; Am. Schule: (Anrechnungs)Punkt m; 2. j-m glauben; j-m trauen; ✝ gutschreiben; ~ s.o. with s.th. j-m et. zutrauen; ~able □ [~təbl] achtbar; ehrenvoll (to für); ~or [~tə] Gläubiger m.

credulous □ ['kredjuləs] leichtgläubig.

creed [kri:d] Glaubensbekenntnis n.

creek [kri:k] Bucht f; Am. Bach m.

creel [kri:l] Fischkorb m.

creep [kri:p] [irr.] kriechen; fig. (sich ein)schleichen; kribbeln; it makes my flesh ~ ich bekomme e-e Gänsehaut davon; ~er ['kri:pə] Kriecher(in); Kletterpflanze f.

cremator|ium [kremə'tɔ:riəm], bsd. Am. ~y ['kremətəri] Krematorium n.

crept [krept] pret. u. p.p. von creep.

crescent ['kresnt] 1. zunehmend; halbmondförmig; 2. Halbmond m; ♎ City Am. New Orleans.

cress ♧ [kres] Kresse f.

crest [krest] Hahnen-, Berg- etc. Kamm m; Mähne f; Federbusch m; Heraldik: family ~ Familienwappen n; ~-fallen ['krestfɔ:lən] niedergeschlagen.

crevasse [kri'væs] (Gletscher)Spalte f; Am. Deichbruch m.

crevice ['krevis] Riß m, Spalte f.

crew¹ [kru:] Schar f; ⚓, ✈ Mannschaft f.

crew² [~] pret. von crow 2.

crib [krib] 1. Krippe f; Kinderbett (-stelle f) n; F Schule: Klatsche f; bsd. Am. Behälter m; 2. einsperren; F mausen; F abschreiben.

crick [krik] Krampf m; ~ in the neck steifer Hals.

cricket ['krikit] zo. Grille f; Sport: Kricket n; not ~ F nicht fair.

crime [kraim] Verbrechen n.

criminal ['kriminl] 1. verbrecherisch; Kriminal..., Straf...; 2. Verbrecher(in); ~ity [krimi'næliti] Strafbarkeit f; Verbrechertum n.

crimp [krimp] kräuseln.

crimson ['krimzn] karmesin(rot).

cringe [krindʒ] sich ducken.

crinkle ['kriŋkl] 1. Windung f; Falte f; 2. (sich) winden; (sich) kräuseln.

cripple ['kripl] 1. Krüppel m; Lahme(r m) f; 2. verkrüppeln; fig. lähmen.

cris|is ['kraisis], pl. ~es [~si:z] Krisis f, Krise f, Wende-, Höhepunkt m.

crisp [krisp] 1. kraus; knusperig; frisch; klar; steif; 2. (sich) kräuseln; knusperig machen od. werden; 3. ~s pl., a. potato ~s pl. Kartoffelchips pl.

criss-cross ['kriskrɔs] 1. Kreuzzeichen n; 2. (durch)kreuzen.

criteri|on [krai'tiəriən], pl. ~a [~riə] Kennzeichen n, Prüfstein m.

criti|c ['kritik] Kritiker(in); ~cal □ [~kəl] kritisch; bedenklich; ~cism [~isizəm] Kritik f (of an dat.); ~cize [~saiz] kritisieren; beurteilen; tadeln; ~que [kri'ti:k] kritischer Essay; die Kritik.

croak [krouk] krächzen; quaken.

crochet ['krouʃei] 1. Häkelei f; 2. häkeln.

crock [krɔk] irdener Topf; **~ery** ['krɔkəri] Töpferware f.

crocodile zo. ['krɔkədail] Krokodil n.

crone F [kroun] altes Weib.

crony F ['krouni] alter Freund.

crook [kruk] 1. Krümmung f; Haken m; Hirtenstab m; sl. Gauner m; 2. (sich) krümmen; (sich) (ver)biegen; **~ed** ['krukid] krumm; bucklig; unehrlich; [krukt] Krück...

croon [kru:n] schmalzig singen; summen; **~er** ['kru:nə] Schnulzensänger m.

crop [krɔp] 1. Kropf m; Peitschenstiel m; Reitpeitsche f; Ernte f; kurzer Haarschnitt; 2. (ab-, be-) schneiden; (ab)ernten; Acker bebauen; **~ up** fig. auftauchen.

cross [krɔs] 1. Kreuz n (a. fig. Leiden); Kreuzung f; 2. ⎕ sich kreuzend; quer (liegend, laufend etc.); ärgerlich, verdrießlich; entgegengesetzt; Kreuz..., Quer...; 3. v/t. kreuzen; durchstreichen; fig. durchkreuzen; überqueren; in den Weg kommen (dat.); **~** o.s. sich bekreuzigen; keep one's fingers **~ed** den Daumen halten; v/i. sich kreuzen; **~bar** ['krɔsbɑ:] Würfel m; **~breed** (Rassen)Kreuzung f; **~country** querfeldein; **~examination** Kreuzverhör n; **~eyed** schieläugig; **~ing** [~siŋ] Kreuzung f; Übergang m; -fahrt f; **~road** Querstraße f; **~roads** pl. od. sg. Kreuzweg m; **~section** Querschnitt m; **~wise** kreuzweise; **~word (puzzle)** Kreuzworträtsel n.

crotchet ['krɔtʃit] Haken m; ♩ Viertelnote f; wunderlicher Einfall.

crouch [krautʃ] 1. sich ducken; 2. Hockstellung f.

crow [krou] 1. Krähe f; Krähen n; eat **~** Am. F zu Kreuze kriechen; 2. [irr.] krähen; triumphieren; **~bar** ['kroubɑ:] Brecheisen n.

crowd [kraud] 1. Haufen m, Menge f; Gedränge n; F Bande f; 2. (sich) drängen; (über)füllen; wimmeln.

crown [kraun] 1. Krone f; Kranz m; Gipfel m; Scheitel m; 2. krönen; Zahn überkronen; to **~** all zu guter Letzt, zu allem Überfluß.

cruci|al ⎕ ['kru:ʃjəl] entscheidend; kritisch; **~ble** ['kru:sibl] Schmelztiegel m; **~fixion** [kru:si'fikʃən] Kreuzigung f; **~fy** ['kru:sifai] kreuzigen.

crude ⎕ [kru:d] roh; unfertig; unreif; unfein; grob; Roh...; grell.

cruel ⎕ ['kruəl] grausam; hart; fig. blutig; **~ty** [~lti] Grausamkeit f.

cruet ['kru(:)it] (Essig-, Öl)Fläschchen n.

cruise ♣ [kru:z] 1. Kreuzfahrt f, Seereise f; 2. kreuzen; **~r** ['kru:zə]

♣ Kreuzer m; Jacht f; Am. Funkstreifenwagen m.

crumb [krʌm] 1. Krume f; Brocken m; 2. panieren; zerkrümeln; **~le** ['krʌmbl] (zer)bröckeln; fig. zugrunde gehen.

crumple ['krʌmpl] v/t. zerknittern; fig. vernichten; v/i. (sich) knüllen.

crunch [krʌntʃ] (zer)kauen; zermalmen; knirschen.

crusade [kru:'seid] Kreuzzug m (a. fig.); **~r** [~də] Kreuzfahrer m.

crush [krʌʃ] 1. Druck m; Gedränge n; (Frucht)Saft m; Am. sl. Schwarm m; have a **~** on s.o. in j-n verliebt od. verschossen sein; 2. v/t. (zer-, aus)quetschen; zermalmen; fig. vernichten; v/i. sich drängen; **~ barrier** ['krʌʃbæriə] Absperrgitter n.

crust [krʌst] 1. Kruste f; Rinde f; Am. sl. Frechheit f; 2. (sich) be-, überkrusten, verharschen; **~y** ⎕ ['krʌsti] krustig; fig. mürrisch.

crutch [krʌtʃ] Krücke f.

cry [krai] 1. Schrei m; Geschrei n; Ruf m; Weinen n; Gebell n; 2. schreien; (aus)rufen; weinen; **~ for** verlangen nach.

crypt [kript] Gruft f; **~ic** ['kriptik] verborgen, geheim.

crystal ['kristl] Kristall m, n; Am. Uhrglas n; **~line** [~təlain] kristallen; **~lize** [~aiz] kristallisieren.

cub [kʌb] 1. Junge(s) n; Flegel m; Anfänger m; 2. (Junge) werfen.

cub|e ♣ [kju:b] 1. Würfel m; Kubikzahl f; **~ root** Kubikwurzel f; **~ic(al**) ['kju:bik(əl)] würfelförmig; kubisch; Kubik...

cuckoo ['kuku:] Kuckuck m.

cucumber ['kju:kəmbə] Gurke f; as cool as a **~** fig. eiskalt, gelassen.

cud [kʌd] wiedergekäutes Futter; chew the **~** wiederkäuen; fig. überlegen.

cuddle ['kʌdl] v/t. (ver)hätscheln.

cudgel ['kʌdʒəl] 1. Knüttel m; 2. (ver)prügeln.

cue [kju:] Billard-Queue n; Stichwort n; Wink m.

cuff [kʌf] 1. Manschette f; Handschelle f; (Ärmel-, Am. a. Hosen-) Aufschlag m; Faust-Schlag m; 2. puffen, schlagen.

cuisine [kwi(:)'zi:n] Küche f (Art zu kochen).

culminate ['kʌlmineit] gipfeln.

culpable ['kʌlpəbl] strafbar.

culprit ['kʌlprit] Angeklagte(r m) f; Schuldige(r m) f, Missetäter(in).

cultivat|e ['kʌltiveit] kultivieren; an-, bebauen; ausbilden; pflegen; **~ion** [kʌlti'veiʃən] (An-, Acker)Bau m; Ausbildung f; Pflege f, Zucht f; **~or** ['kʌltiveitə] Landwirt m; Züchter m; ♩ Kultivator m (Maschine).

cultural □ ['kʌltʃərəl] kulturell.
culture ['kʌltʃə] Kultur *f*; Pflege *f*; Zucht *f*; ‿d kultiviert.
cumb|er ['kʌmbə] überladen; belasten; ‿ersome [‿əsəm], ‿rous □ [‿brəs] lästig; schwerfällig.
cumulative □ ['kjuːmjulətiv] (an-, auf)häufend; Zusatz...
cunning ['kʌniŋ] **1.** □ schlau, listig; geschickt; *Am.* reizend; **2.** List *f*, Schlauheit *f*; Geschicklichkeit *f*.
cup [kʌp] Becher *m*, Schale *f*, Tasse *f*; Kelch *m*; *Sport*: Pokal *m*; ‿board ['kʌbəd] (Speise- *etc.*)Schrank *m*.
cupidity [kju(ː)'piditi] Habgier *f*.
cupola ['kjuːpələ] Kuppel *f*.
cur [kəː] Köter *m*; Schurke *m*, Halunke *m*.
curable ['kjuərəbl] heilbar.
curate ['kjuərit] Hilfsgeistliche(r) *m*.
curb [kəːb] **1.** Kinnkette *f*; Kandare *f* (*a. fig.*); *a.* ‿stone ['kəːbstoun] Bordschwelle *f*; **2.** an die Kandare nehmen (*a. fig.*); *fig.* zügeln; ‿market *Am. Börse*: Freiverkehr *m*; ‿roof Mansardendach *n*.
curd [kəːd] **1.** Quark *m*; **2.** (*mst* ‿le ['kəːdl]) gerinnen (*laøøen*).
cure [kjuə] **1.** Kur *f*; Heilmittel *n*; Seelsorge *f*; Pfarre *f*; **2.** heilen; pökeln; räuchern; trocknen.
curfew ['kəːfjuː] Abendglocke *f*; *pol.* Ausgehverbot *n*; ‿bell Abendglocke *f*.
curio ['kjuəriou] Rarität *f*; ‿sity [kjuəri'əsiti] Neugier *f*; Rarität *f*; ‿us [‿'kjuəriəs] neugierig; genau; seltsam, merkwürdig.
curl [kəːl] **1.** Locke *f*; **2.** (sich) kräuseln; (sich) locken; (sich) ringeln; ‿y ['kəːli] gekräuselt; lockig.
currant ['kʌrənt] Johannisbeere *f*; *a.* dried ‿ Korinthe *f*.
curren|cy ['kʌrənsi] Umlauf *m*; ✝ Lauffrist *f*; Kurs *m*, Währung *f*; ‿t [‿nt] **1.** □ umlaufend; ✝ kursierend (*Geld*); allgemein (bekannt); laufend (*Jahr etc.*); **2.** Strom *m* (*a. ⚡*); Strömung *f* (*a. fig.*); Luft-Zug *m*.
curricul|um [kə'rikjuləm], *pl.* ‿a [‿lə] Lehr-, Stundenplan *m*; ‿um vitae [‿əm'vaitiː] Lebenslauf *m*.
curry¹ ['kʌri] Curry *m, n*.
curry² [‿] *Leder* zurichten; *Pferd* striegeln.
curse [kəːs] **1.** Fluch *m*; **2.** (ver)fluchen; strafen; ‿d □ ['kəːsid] verflucht.
curt [‿ [kəːt] kurz; knapp; barsch.
curtail [kəː'teil] beschneiden; *fig.* beschränken; kürzen (of um).
curtain ['kəːtn] **1.** Vorhang *m*; Gardine *f*; **2.** verhängen, verschleiern; ‿lecture F Gardinenpredigt *f*.
curts(e)y ['kəːtsi] **1.** Knicks *m*; *m*; **2.** knicksen (to vor).

curvature ['kəːvətʃə] (Ver)Krümmung *f*.
curve [kəːv] **1.** Kurve *f*; Krümmung *f*; **2.** (sich) krümmen; (sich) biegen.
cushion ['kuʃən] **1.** Kissen *n*; Polster *n*; *Billard*-Bande *f*; **2.** polstern.
cuss *Am.* F [kʌs] **1.** Nichtsnutz *m*; **2.** fluchen
custody ['kʌstədi] Haft *f*; (Ob)Hut *f*.
custom ['kʌstəm] Gewohnheit *f*, Brauch *m*; Sitte *f*; Kundschaft *f*; ‿s *pl.* Zoll *m*; ‿ary □ [‿məri] gewöhnlich, üblich; ‿er [‿mə] Kund|e *m*, -in *f*; F Bursche *m*; ‿house Zollamt *n*; ‿made *Am.* maßgearbeitet.
cut [kʌt] **1.** Schnitt *m*; Hieb *m*; Stich *m*, (Schnitt)Wunde *f*; Einschnitt *m*; Graben *m*; Kürzung *f*; Ausschnitt *m*; Wegabkürzung *f* (*mst short-‿*); *Holz*-Schnitt *m*; *Kupfer*-Stich *m*; Schliff *m*; Schnitte *f*, Scheibe *f*, *Karten*-Abheben *n*; *Küche* cold ‿s *pl.* Aufschnitt *m*; give s.o the ‿ (direct) F j. schneiden; **2.** [*irr.*] *v/t.* schneiden; schnitzen; gravieren; ab-, auf-, aus-, be-, durch-, zer-, zuschneiden; *Edelstein etc* schleifen; *Karten* abheben; *j. beim Begegnen* schneiden; ‿ teeth zahnen; ‿ short *j.* unterbrechen; ‿ back einschränken; ‿ down fällen; mähen; beschneiden; *Preis* drücken; ‿ out ausschneiden; *Am. Vieh* aussondern *aus der Herde*; *fig. j.* ausstechen; ⚡ ausschalten; be ‿ out for das Zeug zu e-r S. haben; *v/i.* ‿ in sich einschieben; **3.** *adj.* geschnitten *etc.*, *s. cut 2.*
cute [‿ F [kjuːt] schlau; *Am.* reizend.
cuticle ['kjuːtikl] Oberhaut *f*; ‿ scissors *pl.* Hautschere *f*.
cutlery ['kʌtləri] Messerschmiedearbeit *f*; Stahlwaren *f*/*pl.*; Bestecke *n*/*pl.*
cutlet ['kʌtlit] Kotelett *n*; Schnitzel *n*.
cut|-off *Am.* ['kʌtɔːf] Abkürzung *f* (*Straße, Weg*); ‿out *mot.* Auspuffklappe *f*; ⚡ Sicherung *f*; Ausschalter *m*; *Am.* Ausschneidebogen *m*, -bild *n*; ‿purse Taschendieb *m*; ‿ter ['kʌtə] Schneidende(r *m*) *f*; Schnitzer *m*; Zuschneider(in); *Film*: Cutter *m*; ⊕ Schneidezeug *n*, -maschine *f*; ⚓ Kutter *m*; *Am.* leichter Schlitten; ‿throat Halsabschneider *m*; Meuchelmörder *m*; ‿ting ['kʌtiŋ] **1.** □ schneidend; scharf, ⊕ Schneid..., Fräs...; **2.** Schneiden *n*; 🚂 *etc.* Einschnitt *m*; ♣ Steckling *m*; *Zeitungs*-Ausschnitt *m*; ‿s *pl.* Schnipsel *m*, *n*/*pl.*; ⊕ Späne *m*/*pl.*
cycl|e ['saikl] **1.** Zyklus *m*; Kreis (-lauf) *m*; Periode *f*; ⊕ Arbeitsgang

m; Fahrrad **n; 2.** radfahren; **∼ist** [∼list] Radfahrer(in).
cyclone ['saikloun] Wirbelsturm **m.**
cylinder ['silində] Zylinder **m,** Walze **f;** ⊕ Trommel **f.**
cymbal ♪ ['simbəl] Becken **n.**
cynic ['sinik] **1.** a. **∼al** □ [∼kəl] zynisch; **2.** Zyniker **m.**

cypress ♀ ['saipris] Zypresse **f.**
cyst ✿ [sist] Blase **f;** Sackgeschwulst **f; ∼itis** ✿ [sis'taitis] Blasenentzündung **f.**
Czech [tʃek] **1.** Tschech|e **m,** -in **f; 2.** tschechisch.
Czechoslovak ['tʃekou'slouvæk] **1.** Tschechoslowak|e **m,** -in **f; 2.** tschechoslowakisch.

D

dab [dæb] **1.** Klaps **m;** Tupf(en) **m,** Klecks **m; 2.** klapsen; (be)tupfen.
dabble ['dæbl] bespritzen; plätschern; (hinein)pfuschen.
dad F [dæd], **∼dy** F ['dædi] Papa **m.**
daddy-longlegs F zo. ['dædi'lɔŋlegz] Schnake **f;** Am. Weberknecht **m.**
daffodil ♀ ['dæfədil] gelbe Narzisse.
daft F [dɑːft] blöde, doof.
dagger ['dægə] Dolch **m;** be at **∼s** drawn fig. auf Kriegsfuß stehen.
dago Am. sl. ['deigou] contp. für Spanier, Portugiese, mst Italiener.
daily ['deili] **1.** täglich; **2.** Tageszeitung **f.**
dainty ['deinti] **1.** □ lecker; zart, fein; wählerisch; **2.** Leckerei **f.**
dairy ['dɛəri] Molkerei **f,** Milchwirtschaft **f;** Milchgeschäft **n; ∼ cattle** Milchvieh **n; ∼man** Milchhändler **m.**
daisy ♀ ['deizi] Gänseblümchen **n.**
dale [deil] Tal **n.**
dall|iance ['dæliəns] Trödelei **f;** Liebelei **f; ∼y** ['dæli] vertrödeln; schäkern.
dam [dæm] **1.** Mutter **f** von Tieren; Deich **m,** Damm **m; 2.** (ab)dämmen.
damage ['dæmidʒ] **1.** Schaden **m; ∼s** pl. ⚖ Schadenersatz **m; 2.** (be-)schädigen.
damask ['dæməsk] Damast **m.**
dame [deim] Dame **f;** sl. Weib **n.**
damn [dæm] verdammen; verurteilen; **∼ation** [dæm'neiʃən] Verdammung **f.**
damp [dæmp] **1.** feucht, dunstig; **2.** Feuchtigkeit **f,** Dunst **m;** Gedrücktheit **f; 3.** a. **∼en** ['dæmpən] anfeuchten; dämpfen; niederdrücken; **∼er** [∼pə] Dämpfer **m.**
danc|e [dɑːns] **1.** Tanz **m;** Ball **m; 2.** tanzen (lassen); **∼er** ['dɑːnsə] Tänzer(in); **∼ing** [∼siŋ] Tanzen **n;** attr. Tanz ... [zahn **m.**]
dandelion ♀ [ˈdændilaiən] Löwen-
dandle sl. ['dændl] wiegen, schaukeln.
dandruff ['dændrəf] (Kopf)Schuppen **f/pl.**

dandy ['dændi] **1.** Stutzer **m;** F erstklassige Sache; **2.** Am. F prima.
Dane [dein] Dän|e **m,** -in **f.**
danger ['deindʒə] Gefahr **f; ∼ous** □ [∼dʒrəs] gefährlich; **∼-signal** ▨ Notsignal **n.**
dangle ['dæŋgl] baumeln (lassen); schlenkern (mit); fig. schwanken.
Danish ['deiniʃ] dänisch.
dank [dæŋk] dunstig, feucht.
Danubian [dæ'nju:bjən] Donau...
dapper □ F ['dæpə] nett; behend.
dapple ['dæpl] sprenkeln; **∼d** scheckig; **∼-grey** Apfelschimmel **m.**
dar|e [dɛə] v/i. es wagen; v/t. et. wagen; j-n herausfordern; j-m trotzen; **∼e-devil** ['dɛədevl] Draufgänger **m; ∼ing** □ ['dɛəriŋ] **1.** verwegen; **2.** Verwegenheit **f.**
dark [dɑːk] **1.** □ dunkel; brünett; schwerverständlich; geheim(nisvoll); trüb(selig); **2.** Dunkel(heit **f**) **n;** before (after) **∼** vor (nach) Einbruch der Dunkelheit; 2 Ages pl. das frühe Mittelalter; **∼en** ['dɑːkən] (sich) (ver)dunkeln; (sich) verfinstern; **∼ness** ['dɑːknis] Dunkelheit **f,** Finsternis **f; ∼y** F ['dɑːki] Schwarze(r **m**) **f.**
darling ['dɑːliŋ] **1.** Liebling **m; 2.** Lieblings...; geliebt.
darn [dɑːn] stopfen; ausbessern.
dart [dɑːt] **1.** Wurfspieß **m;** Wurfpfeil **m;** Sprung **m,** Satz **m; ∼s** pl. Wurfpfeilspiel **n; 2.** v/t. schleudern; v/i. fig. schießen, (sich) stürzen.
dash [dæʃ] **1.** Schlag **m,** (Zs.-)Stoß **m;** Klatschen **n;** Schwung **m;** Ansturm **m;** fig. Anflug **m;** Prise **f;** Schuß **m** Rum etc.; Feder-Strich **m;** Gedankenstrich **m; 2.** v/t. schlagen, werfen, schleudern; zerschmettern; vernichten; (be)spritzen; vermengen; verwirren; v/i. stoßen, schlagen; stürzen; stürmen; jagen; **∼-board** mot. ['dæʃbɔːd] Armaturenbrett **n; ∼ing** □ ['dæʃiŋ] schneidig, forsch; flott, F fesch.
dastardly ['dæstədli] heimtückisch; feig.
data ['deitə] pl., Am. a. sg. Angaben

f/pl.; Tatsachen f/pl.; Unterlagen f/pl.; Daten pl.

date [deit] **1.** ♀ Dattel f; Datum n; Zeit f; Termin m; Am. F Verabredung f; Freund(in); out of ~ veraltet, unmodern; up to ~ zeitgemäß, modern; auf dem laufenden; **2.** datieren; Am. F sich verabreden.

dative gr. ['deitiv] a. ~ case Dativ m.

daub [dɔːb] (be)schmieren; (be-) klecksen.

daughter ['dɔːtə] Tochter f; ~-in-law [~ərinlɔː] Schwiegertochter f.

daunt [dɔːnt] entmutigen; ~less ['dɔːntlis] furchtlos, unerschrocken.

daw orn. [dɔː] Dohle f.

dawdle F ['dɔːdl] (ver)trödeln.

dawn [dɔːn] **1.** Dämmerung f; fig. Morgenrot n; **2.** dämmern, tagen; it ~ed upon him fig. es wurde ihm langsam klar.

day [dei] Tag m; oft ~s pl. (Lebens-) Zeit f; ~ off dienst-freier Tag; carry od. win the ~ den Sieg davontragen; the other ~ neulich; this ~ week heute in einer Woche; heute vor einer Woche; let's call it a ~ machen wir Schluß für heute; ~break ['deibreik] Tagesanbruch m; ~-labo(u)rer Tagelöhner m; ~-star Morgenstern m.

daze [deiz] blenden; betäuben.

dazzle ['dæzl] blenden; ✕ tarnen.

dead [ded] **1.** tot; unempfindlich (to für); matt (Farbe etc.); blind (Fenster etc.); erloschen (Feuer); schal (Getränk); tief (Schlaf); ✝ tot (Kapital etc.); ~ bargain Spottpreis m; ~ letter unzustellbarer Brief; ~ loss Totalverlust m; a ~ shot ein Meisterschütze; ~ wall blinde Mauer; ~ wood Reisig n; Am. Plunder m; **2.** adv. gänzlich, völlig, total; durchaus; genau, (haar)scharf; ~ against gerade od. ganz und gar (ent)gegen; **3.** the ~ der Tote; die Toten pl.; Totenstille f; in the ~ of night mitten in der Nacht; ~en ['dedn] abstumpfen; dämpfen; (ab)schwächen; ~-end Sackgasse f (a. fig.); ~-line Am. Sperrlinie f im Gefängnis; Schlußtermin m; Stichtag m; ~-lock Stockung f; fig. toter Punkt; ~ly [~li] tödlich.

deaf [def] taub; ~en ['defn] taub machen; betäuben.

deal [diːl] **1.** Teil m; Menge f; Kartengeben s; F Geschäft n; Abmachung f; a good ~ ziemlich viel; a great ~ sehr viel; **2.** [irr.] v/t. (aus-, ver-, zu)teilen; Karten geben; e-n Schlag versetzen; v/i. handeln (in mit e-r Ware); verfahren, verkehren; ~ with sich befassen mit, behandeln; ~er ['diːlə] Händler m; Kartengeber m; ~ing ['diːliŋ] mst

~s pl. Handlungsweise f; Verfahren n; Verkehr m; ~t [delt] pret. u p.p. von deal 2.

dean [diːn] Dekan m.

dear [diə] **1.** teuer; lieb; **2.** Liebling m; herziges Geschöpf; **3.** o(h) ~!, ~ me! F du liebe Zeit!; ach herrje!

death [deθ] Tod m; Todesfall m; ~-bed ['deθbed] Sterbebett n; ~-duty Erbschaftssteuer f; ~less ['deθlis] unsterblich; ~ly [~li] tödlich; ~-rate Sterblichkeitsziffer f; ~-warrant Todesurteil n.

debar [diˈbɑː] ausschließen; hindern

debarkation [diːbɑːˈkeiʃən] Ausschiffung f

debase [diˈbeis] verschlechtern; erniedrigen, verfälschen.

debat|able [diˈbeitəbl] strittig; umstritten, ~e [diˈbeit] **1.** Debatte f; **2.** debattieren; erörtern; überlegen.

debauch [diˈbɔːtʃ] **1.** Ausschweifung f; **2.** verderben; verführen.

debilitate [diˈbiliteit] schwächen.

debit ✝ [debit] **1.** Debet n, Schuld f; **2.** j-n belasten; debitieren.

debris [ˈdebri:] Trümmer pl.

debt [det] Schuld f; ~or ['detə] Schuldner(in)

debunk [diːˈbʌŋk] den Nimbus nehme (dat.)

début [ˈdeibuː] Debüt n.

decade [ˈdekeid] Jahrzehnt n.

decadence [ˈdekədəns] Verfall m.

decamp [diˈkæmp] aufbrechen; ausreißen, ~ment [~pmənt] Aufbruch m.

decant [diˈkænt] abgießen; umfüllen; ~er [~tə] Karaffe f.

decapitate [diˈkæpiteit] enthaupten; Am ✝ fig. absägen (entlassen).

decay [diˈkei] **1.** Verfall m; Fäulnis f; **2.** verfallen; (ver)faulen.

decease bsd. ✝ [diˈsiːs] **1.** Ableben n; **2.** sterben.

deceit [diˈsiːt] Täuschung f; Betrug m; ~ful [~tful] (be)trügerisch.

deceive [diˈsiːv] betrügen; täuschen, verleiten; ~r [~və] Betrüger(in)

December [diˈsembə] Dezember m.

decen|cy ['diːsnsi] Anstand m; ~t □ [~nt] anständig; F annehmbar, nett.

deception [diˈsepʃən] Täuschung f.

decide [diˈsaid] (sich) entscheiden; bestimmen, ~d □ entschieden; bestimmt, entschlossen.

decimal [ˈdesiməl] Dezimalbruch m; attr. Dezimal...

decipher [diˈsaifə] entziffern.

decisi|on [diˈsiʒən] Entscheidung f; ✖ Urteil n; Entschluß m; Entschlossenheit f; ~ve □ [diˈsaisiv] entscheidend; entschieden.

deck [dek] 1. ⚓ Deck n; Am. Pack m Spielkarten; on ~ Am. F da(bei), bereit; 2. rhet. schmücken; ~-chair ['dek'tʃɛə] Liegestuhl m.

declaim [di'kleim] vortragen; (sich er)eifern.

declar|able [di'klɛərəbl] steuer-, zollpflichtig; ~ation [deklə'reiʃən] Erklärung f; Zoll-Deklaration f; ~e [di'klɛə] (sich) erklären; behaupten; deklarieren.

declension [di'klenʃən] Abfall m (Neigung); Verfall m; gr. Deklination f.

declin|ation [dekli'neiʃən] Neigung f; Abweichung f; ~e [di'klain] 1. Abnahme f; Niedergang m; Verfall m; 2. v/t. neigen, biegen; gr. deklinieren; ablehnen; v/i. sich neigen; abnehmen; verfallen.

declivity [di'kliviti] Abhang m.

declutch mot. ['di:'klʌtʃ] auskuppeln.

decode tel. ['di:'koud] entschlüsseln.

decompose [di:kəm'pouz] zerlegen; (sich) zersetzen; verwesen.

decontrol ['di:kən'troul] Waren, Handel freigeben.

decorat|e ['dekəreit] (ver)zieren; schmücken; ~ion [dekə'reiʃən] Verzierung f; Schmuck m; Orden(sauszeichnung f) m; ♀ Day Am. Heldengedenktag m; ~ive ['dekərətiv] dekorativ; Zier...; ~or [~reitə] Dekorateur m, Maler m.

decor|ous ˩ ['dekərəs] anständig; ~um [di'kɔ:rəm] Anstand m.

decoy [di'kɔi] 1. Lockvogel m (a. fig.); Köder m; 2. ködern; locken.

decrease 1. ['di:kri:s] Abnahme f; 2. [di:'kri:s] (sich) vermindern.

decree [di'kri:] 1. Dekret n, Verordnung f, Erlaß m; ⚖ Entscheid m; 2. beschließen; verordnen, verfügen.

decrepit [di'krepit] altersschwach.

decry [di'krai] in Verruf bringen.

dedicat|e ['dedikeit] widmen; ~ion [dedi'keiʃən] Widmung f.

deduce [di'dju:s] ableiten; folgern.

deduct [di'dʌkt] abziehen; ~ion [~kʃən] Abzug m; ✝ Rabatt m; Schlußfolgerung f.

deed [di:d] 1. Tat f; Heldentat f; Urkunde f; 2. Am. urkundlich übertragen (to auf acc.).

deem [di:m] v/t. halten für; v/i. denken, urteilen (of über acc.).

deep [di:p] 1. ˩ tief; gründlich; schlau; vertieft; dunkel (a. fig.); verborgen; 2. Tiefe f; poet. Meer n; ~en ['di:pən] (sich) vertiefen; (sich) verstärken; ~-freeze 1. tiefkühlen; 2. Tiefkühlfach n, -truhe f; ~ness ['di:pnis] Tiefe f.

deer [diə] Rotwild n; Hirsch m.

deface [di'feis] entstellen; unkenntlich machen; ausstreichen.

defalcation [di:fæl'keiʃən] Unterschlagung f.

defam|ation [defə'meiʃən] Verleumdung f; ~e [di'feim] verleumden; verunglimpfen.

default [di'fɔ:lt] 1. Nichterscheinen n vor Gericht; Säumigkeit f; Verzug m; in ~ of which widrigenfalls; 2. s-n etc. Verbindlichkeiten nicht nachkommen.

defeat [di'fi:t] 1. Niederlage f; Besiegung f; Vereitelung f; 2. ✕ besiegen; vereiteln; vernichten.

defect [di'fekt] Mangel m; Fehler m; ~ive □ [~tiv] mangelhaft; unvollständig; fehlerhaft.

defen|ce, Am. ~se [di'fens] Verteidigung f; Schutzmaßnahme f; witness for the ~ Entlastungszeuge m; ~celess, Am. ~seless [~slis] schutzlos, wehrlos.

defend [di'fend] verteidigen; schützen (from vor dat.); ~ant [~dənt] Angeklagte(r m) f; Beklagte(r m) f; ~er [~də] Verteidiger(in).

defensive [di'fensiv] Defensive f; attr. Verteidigungs...

defer [di'fə:] auf~, verschieben; Am. ✕ zurückstellen; sich fügen; nachgeben; payment on ~red terms Ratenzahlung f; ~ence [di'fərəns] Ehrerbietung f; Nachgiebigkeit f; ~ential □ [defə'renʃəl] ehrerbietig.

defian|ce [di'faiəns] Herausforderung f; Trotz m; ~t □ [~nt] herausfordernd; trotzig.

deficien|cy [di'fiʃənsi] Unzulänglichkeit f; Mangel m; = deficit; ~t □ [~nt] mangelhaft; unzureichend.

deficit ['defisit] Fehlbetrag m.

defile 1. [di'fail] Engpaß m; 2. [di'fail] v/i. vorbeiziehen; v/t. beflekken; schänden.

defin|e [di'fain] definieren; erklären; genau bestimmen; ~ite □ ['definit] bestimmt; deutlich; genau; ~ition [defi'niʃən] (Begriffs-)Bestimmung f; Erklärung f; ~itive □ [di'finitiv] bestimmt; entscheidend; endgültig.

deflect [di'flekt] ablenken; abweichen.

deform [di'fɔ:m] entstellen, verunstalten; ~ed verwachsen; ~ity [~miti] Unförmigkeit f; Mißgestalt f.

defraud [di'frɔ:d] betrügen (of um).

defray [di'frei] Kosten bestreiten.

defroster mot. [di:'frɔstə] Entfroster m.

deft □ [deft] gewandt, flink.

defunct [di'fʌŋkt] verstorben.

defy [di'fai] herausfordern; trotzen.

degenerate 1. [di'dʒenəreit] entarten; 2. □ [~rit] entartet.

degrad|ation [degrə'deiʃən] Absetzung f; ~e [di'greid] v/t. absetzen; erniedrigen; demütigen.

degree [di'gri:] Grad m; fig. Stufe f,

Schritt *m*; Rang *m*, Stand *m*; by ~s allmählich; *in no* ~ in keiner Weise; *in some* ~ einigermaßen; *take one's* ~ sein Abschlußexamen machen.

dehydrated [di:'haidreitid] Trokken...

deify ['di:ifai] vergöttern; vergöttlichen.

deign [dein] geruhen; gewähren.

deity ['di:iti] Gottheit *f*.

deject [di'dʒekt] entmutigen; ~ed ☐ niedergeschlagen; ~ion [~kʃən] Niedergeschlagenheit *f*.

delay [di'lei] 1. Aufschub *m*; Verzögerung *f*; 2. *v/t.* aufschieben; verzögern; *v/i.* zögern; trödeln.

delega|te 1. ['deligeit] abordnen; übertragen; 2. [~git] Abgeordnete(r *m*) *f*; ~tion [deli'geiʃn] Abordnung *f*; *Am. parl. die* Kongreßabgeordneten *m/pl. e-s Staates.*

deliberat|e 1. [di'libəreit] *v/t.* überlegen, erwägen; *v/i.* nachdenken; beraten; 2. ☐ [~rit] bedachtsam; wohlüberlegt; vorsätzlich, ~ion [dilibə'reiʃən] Überlegung *f*; Beratung *f*; Bedächtigkeit *f*.

delica|cy ['delikəsi] Wohlgeschmack *m*; Leckerbissen *m*; Zartheit *f*; Schwächlichkeit *f*; Feinfühligkeit *f*; ~te [~kit] schmackhaft; lecker; zart; fein; schwach; heikel; empfindlich; feinfühlig; wählerisch; ~tessen [delikə'tesn] Feinkost(geschäft *n*) *f*.

delicious [di'liʃəs] köstlich.

delight [di'lait] 1. Lust *f*, Freude *f*, Wonne *f*; 2. entzücken; (sich) erfreuen (*in an dat.*); ~ to *inf.* Freude daran finden, zu *inf.*; ~ful ☐ [~tful] entzückend.   [schildern.]

delineate [di'linieit] entwerfen;|

delinquen|cy [di'liŋkwənsi] Vergehen *n*; Kriminalität *f*; Pflichtvergessenheit *f*; ~t [~nt] 1. straffällig; pflichtvergessen; 2. Verbrecher(in).

deliri|ous ☐ [di'liriəs] wahnsinnig; ~um [~iəm] Fieberwahn *m*.

deliver [di'livə] befreien; über-, aus-, abliefern; *Botschaft* ausrichten; äußern; *Rede etc.* vortragen; halten; 🖈 entbinden; *Schlag* führen; werfen; ~ance [~ərəns] Befreiung *f*; (Meinungs)Äußerung *f*; ~er [~rə] Befreier(in); Überbringer(in); ~y [~ri] 🖈 Entbindung *f*; (Ab)Lieferung *f*; 🏵 Zustellung *f*; Übergabe *f*; Vortrag *m*; Wurf *m*; *special* ~ Lieferung *f* durch Eilboten; ~y-truck, ~y-van Lieferwagen *m*.

dell [del] kleines Tal.

delude [di'lu:d] täuschen; verleiten.

deluge ['delju:dʒ] 1. Überschwemmung *f*, 2. überschwemmen.

delus|ion [di'lu:ʒən] Täuschung *f*, Verblendung *f*; Wahn *m*; ~ive ☐ [~u:siv] (be)trügerisch; täuschend.

demand [di'mɑ:nd] 1. Verlangen *n*; Forderung *f*; Bedarf *m*; ✝ Nachfrage *f*; 👫 Rechtsanspruch *m*; 2. verlangen, fordern; fragen (nach).

demean [di'mi:n] ~ *o.s.* sich benehmen; sich erniedrigen; ~o(u)r [~nə] Benehmen *n*.

demented [di'mentid] wahnsinnig.

demerit [di:'merit] Fehler *m*.

demesne [di'mein] Besitz *m*.

demi... ['demi] Halb..., halb...

demijohn ['demidʒɔn] große Korbflasche, Glasballon *m*.

demilitarize ['di:'militəraiz] entmilitarisieren.

demise [di'maiz] 1. Ableben *n*; 2. vermachen.

demobilize [di:'moubilaiz] demobilisieren

democra|cy [di'mɔkrəsi] Demokratie *f*; ~t ['deməkræt] Demokrat(in); ~tic(al) [demə'krætik(əl)] demokratisch

demolish [di'mɔliʃ] nieder-, abreißen; zerstören.

demon ['di:mən] Dämon *m*; Teufel *m*.

demonstrat|e ['demənstreit] anschaulich darstellen; beweisen; demonstrieren; ~ion [demən'treiʃən] Demonstration *f*; anschauliche Darstellung, Beweis *m*; (Gefühls-)Äußerung *f*, ~ive ☐ [di'mɔnstrətiv] überzeugend; demonstrativ; ausdrucksvoll; auffällig, überschwenglich.

demote [di:'mour] degradieren.

demur [di'mə:] 1. Einwendung *f*; 2. Einwendungen erheben.

demure [di'mjuə] ernst; prüde.

den [den] Höhle *f*; Grube *f*; *sl.* Bude *f.*

denial [di'naiəl] Leugnen *n*; Verneinung *f*, abschlägige Antwort.

denizen [denizn] Bewohner *m*.

denominat|e [di'nɔmineit] (be)nennen; ~ion [dinɔmi'neiʃən] Benennung *f*; Klasse *f*; Sekte *f*, Konfession *f.*

denote [di'nout] bezeichnen; bedeuten

denounce [di'nauns] anzeigen; brandmarken; *Vertrag* kündigen.

dens|e [dens] dicht, dick (*Nebel*); beschränkt, ~ity ['densiti] Dichte *f*; Dichtigkeit *f.*

dent [dent] 1. Kerbe *f*; Beule *f*; 2. ver-, einbeulen.

dent|al ['dentl] Zahn...; ~ surgeon Zahnarzt *m*; ~ist [~tist] Zahnarzt *m.*

denunciat|ion [dinʌnsi'eiʃən] Anzeige *f*; Kündigung *f*; ~or [di-'nʌnsieitə] Denunziant *m.*

deny [di nai] verleugnen; verweigern, abschlagen; *j-n* abweisen.

depart [di'pɑ:t] *v/i.* abreisen, abfahren; abstehen, (ab)weichen;

verscheiden; ~ment [ˌtmənt] Abteilung f; Bezirk m; † Branche f; Am. Ministerium n; State ♀ Am. Außenministerium n; ~ store Warenhaus n; ~ure [ˌtʃə] Abreise f, ⚓, ⚙ Abfahrt f; Abweichung f.

depend [di'pend]: ~ (up)on abhängen von; angewiesen sein auf (acc.); sich verlassen auf (acc.); it ~s F es kommt (ganz) darauf an; ~able [ˌdəbl] zuverlässig; ~ant [ˌənt] Abhängige(r m) f; Angehörige(r m) f; ~ence [ˌdəns] Abhängigkeit f; Vertrauen n; ~ency [ˌsi] Schutzgebiet n; ~ent [ˌnt] 1. ☐ (on) abhängig (von); angewiesen (auf acc.); 2. Am. = dependant.

depict [di'pikt] darstellen; schildern.

deplete [di'pliːt] (ent)leeren; fig. erschöpfen.

deplor|able [di'plɔːrəbl] beklagenswert; kläglich; jämmerlich; ~e [di'plɔː] beklagen, bedauern.

deponent ⚖ [di'pounənt] vereidigter Zeuge. [entvölkern.)

depopulate [diː'pɔpjuleit] (sich))

deport [di'pɔːt] Ausländer abschieben; verbannen; ~ o.s. sich benehmen; ~ment [ˌtmənt] Benehmen n.

depose [di'pouz] absetzen; ⚖ (eidlich) aussagen.

deposit [di'pɔzit] 1. Ablagerung f; Lager n; † Depot n; Bank-Einlage f; Pfand n; Hinterlegung f; 2. (nieder-, ab-, hin)legen; Geld einlegen, einzahlen; hinterlegen; (sich) ablagern; ~ion [depo'ziʃən] Ablagerung f; eidliche Zeugenaussage; Absetzung f; ~or [di'pozitə] Hinterleger m; Einzahler m; Kontoinhaber m.

depot ['depou] Depot n; Lagerhaus n; Am. Bahnhof m.

deprave [di'preiv] sittlich verderben.

deprecate ['deprikeit] ablehnen.

depreciate [di'priːʃieit] herabsetzen; geringschätzen; entwerten.

depredation [depri'deiʃən] Plünderung f.

depress [di'pres] niederdrücken; Preise etc. senken, drücken; bedrücken; ~ed fig. niedergeschlagen; ~ion [ˌeʃən] Senkung f; Niedergeschlagenheit f; † Flaute f, Wirtschaftskrise f; ⚙ Schwäche f; Sinken n.

deprive [di'praiv] berauben; entziehen; ausschließen (of von).

depth [depθ] Tiefe f; attr. Tiefen...

deput|ation [depju(:)'teiʃən] Abordnung f; ~e [di'pjuːt] abordnen; ~y ['depjuti] Abgeordnete(r m) f; Stellvertreter m, Beauftragte(r) m.

derail ⚙ [di'reil] v/i. entgleisen; v/t. zum Entgleisen bringen.

derange [di'reindʒ] in Unordnung bringen; stören; zerrütten; (mentally) ~d geistesgestört; a ~d stomach eine Magenverstimmung.

derelict ['derilikt] 1. verlassen; bsd. Am. nachlässig; 2. herrenloses Gut; Wrack n; ~ion [deri'likʃən] Verlassen n; Vernachlässigung f.

deri|de [di'raid] verlachen, verspotten; ~sion [di'riʒən] Verspottung f; ~sive ☐ [di'raisiv] spöttisch.

deriv|ation [deri'veiʃən] Ableitung f; Herkunft f; ~e [di'raiv] herleiten; Nutzen etc. ziehen (from aus).

derogat|e ['derogeit] schmälern (from acc.); ~ion [derə'geiʃən] Beeinträchtigung f; Herabwürdigung f; ~ory ☐ [di'rogətəri] (to) nachteilig (dat., für); herabwürdigend.

derrick ['derik] ⊕ Drehkran m; ⚓ Ladebaum m; ⚒ Bohrturm m.

descend [di'send] (her-, hin)absteigen, herabkommen; sinken; ⚔ niedergehen; ~ (up)on herfallen über (acc.); einfallen in (acc.); (ab)stammen; ~ant [ˌdənt] Nachkomme m.

descent [di'sent] Herabsteigen n; Abstieg m; Sinken n; Gefälle n; feindlicher Einfall; Landung f; Abstammung f; Abhang m.

describe [dis'kraib] beschreiben.

description [dis'kripʃən] Beschreibung f, Schilderung f; F Art f.

descry [dis'krai] wahrnehmen.

desecrate ['desikreit] entweihen.

desegregate Am. [di'segrigeit] die Rassentrennung aufheben in (dat.).

desert¹ ['dezət] 1. verlassen; wüst, öde; Wüsten...; 2. Wüste f.

desert² [di'zəːt] v/t. verlassen; v/i. ausreißen; desertieren.

desert³ [di'zəːt] Verdienst n.

desert|er [di'zəːtə] Fahnenflüchtige(r) m; ~ion [ˌəːʃən] Verlassen n; Fahnenflucht f.

deserv|e [di'zəːv] verdienen; sich verdient machen (of um); ~ing [ˌviŋ] würdig (of gen.); verdienstvoll.

design [di'zain] 1. Plan m; Entwurf m; Vorhaben n, Absicht f; Zeichnung f, Muster n; 2. ersinnen; zeichnen, entwerfen; planen; bestimmen.

designat|e ['dezigneit] bezeichnen; ernennen, bestimmen; ~ion [dezig'neiʃən] Bezeichnung f; Bestimmung f, Ernennung f.

designer [di'zainə] (Muster)Zeichner(in); Konstrukteur m.

desir|able ☐ [di'zaiərəbl] wünschenswert; angenehm; ~e [di'zaiə] 1. Wunsch m; Verlangen n; 2. verlangen, wünschen; ~ous ☐ [ˌərəs] begierig.

desist [di'zist] abstehen, ablassen.

desk [desk] Pult n; Schreibtisch m.

desolat|e 1. ['desəleit] verwüsten; 2. ☐ [ˌlit] einsam; verlassen; öde; ~ion [desə'leiʃən] Verwüstung f; Einöde f; Verlassenheit f.

despair [dis'pɛə] 1. Verzweiflung f;

2. verzweifeln (of an dat.); **~ing** □ [~ɔriŋ] verzweifelt.

despatch [dis'pætʃ] = *dispatch*.

desperat|e adj Г ['despərit] verzweifelt, hoffnungslos; F schrecklich; **~ion** [despə'reiʃən] Verzweiflung f; Raserei f.

despicable Г ['despikəbl] verächtlich.

despise [dis'paiz] verachten.

despite [dis'pait] **1.** Verachtung f; Trotz m, Bosheit f; in ~ of zum Trotz, trotz; **2.** prp. a. ~ of trotz.

despoil [dis'pɔil] berauben (of gen.).

despond [dis'pɔnd] verzagen, verzweifeln, **~ency** [~dənsi] Verzagtheit f; **~ent** [~nt] verzagt.

despot ['despɔt] Despot m, Tyrann m; **~ism** [~pətizəm] Despotismus m.

dessert [di'zə:t] Nachtisch m, Dessert n; Am Süßspeise f.

destin|ation [desti'neiʃən] Bestimmung(sort m) f; **~e** ['destin] bestimmen, **~y** [~ni] Schicksal n.

destitute ['destitju:t] mittellos, notleidend, entblößt (of von).

destroy [dis'trɔi] zerstören, vernichten, töten; unschädlich machen; **~er** [~ɔiə] Zerstörer(in).

destruct|ion [dis'trakʃən] Zerstörung f; Tötung f; **~ive** [~ktiv] zerstörend; vernichtend (of, to acc.); **~or** [~ɔ] (Müll)Verbrennungsofen m.

desultory Г ['desəltəri] unstet; planlos, oberflächlich.

detach [di'tætʃ] losmachen, (ab-)lösen; absondern; X (ab)kommandieren; **~ed** einzeln (stehend); unbeeinflußt; **~ment** [~ʃmənt] Loslösung f; Trennung f; X Abteilung f.

detail ['di:teil] **1.** Einzelheit f; eingehende Darstellung; X Kommando n, in ~ ausführlich; **2.** genau schildern, X abkommandieren.

detain [di'tein] zurück-, auf-, abhalten, j-n in Haft behalten

detect [di'tekt] entdecken; (auf-)finden, **~ion** [~kʃən] Entdeckung f; **~ive** [~ktiv] Detektiv m; ~ story, ~ novel Kriminalroman m.

detention [di'tenʃən] Vorenthaltung f; Zurück-, Abhaltung f; Haft f [von).]

deter [di'tə:] abschrecken (from)

detergent [di'tə:dʒənt] **1.** reinigend, **2.** Reinigungsmittel n.

deteriorat|e [di'tiəriəreit] (sich) verschlechtern; entarten; **~ion** [ditiəriə reiʃən] Verschlechterung f.

determin|ation [ditə:mi neiʃən] Bestimmung f; Entschlossenheit f; Entscheidung f; Entschluß m; **~e** [di'tə:min] v/t. bestimmen; entscheiden; veranlassen; Strafe festsetzen; beendigen; v/i. sich entschließen; **~ed** entschlossen.

deterrent [di'terənt] **1.** abschreckend; **2.** Abschreckungsmittel n; nuclear ~ pol. atomare Abschreckung.

detest [di'test] verabscheuen; **~able** [~təbl] abscheulich; **~ation** [di:tes'teiʃən] Abscheu m.

dethrone [di'θroun] entthronen.

detonate ['detouneit] explodieren (lassen)

detour, détour ['deituə] **1.** Umweg m, Umleitung f; **2.** e-n Umweg machen

detract [di'trækt]: ~ from s.th. et. beeinträchtigen, schmälern; **~ion** [~kʃən] Verleumdung f; Herabsetzung f

detriment ['detrimənt] Schaden m.

deuce [dju:s] Zwei f im Spiel; Tennis Einstand m; F Teufel m; the ~! zum Teufel!

devalu|ation [di:vælju'eiʃən] Abwertung f; **~e** ['di:'vælju:] abwerten.

devastat|e ['devəsteit] verwüsten; **~ion** [devəs teiʃən] Verwüstung f.

develop [di veləp] (sich) entwickeln; (sich) entfalten, (sich) erweitern; Gelände erschließen; ausbauen; Am. (sich) zeigen, **~ment** [~pmənt] Entwicklung f, Entfaltung f; Erweiterung f, Ausbau m.

deviat|e [di vieit] abweichen; **~ion** [di:vi eiʃən] Abweichung f.

device [di vais] Plan m; Kniff m; Erfindung f, Vorrichtung f; Muster n, Wahlspruch m; leave s.o. to his own s j sich selbst überlassen.

devil [devl] **1.** Teufel m (a. fig.); z/z Hilfsanwalt m; Laufbursche m; **2.** v/t Gericht stark pfeffern; Am. plagen, quälen; **~ish** [~liʃ] teuflisch, **~(t)ry** [l(t)ri] Teufelei f.

devious [di:vjəs] abwegig.

devise [di vaiz] **1.** z/z Vermachen n; Vermächtnis n; **2.** ersinnen; z/z vermachen

devoid [di vɔid] ~ of bar (gen.), ohne.

devot|e [di vout] weihen, widmen; **~ed** ergeben, zärtlich; **~ion** [~ouʃən] Ergebenheit f; Hingebung f; Frömmigkeit f; ~s pl. Andacht f.

devour [di vauə] verschlingen.

devout [di'vaut] andächtig, fromm; innig.

dew [dju] **1.** Tau m; **2.** tauen; **~y** ['dju:i] betaut, taufrisch.

dexter|ity [deks teriti] Gewandtheit f; **~ous** ['dekstərəs] gewandt.

diabolic(al) [daiə'bɔlik(əl)] teuflisch

diagnose ['daiəgnouz] diagnostizieren, erkennen.

diagram [daiəgræm] graphische Darstellung, Schema n, Plan m.

dial [daiəl] **1.** Sonnenuhr f; Zifferblatt n, teleph Wähl(er)scheibe f; Radio Skala f; **2.** teleph. wählen.

dialect ['daiəlekt] Mundart f.

dialo|gue, *Am. a.* **~g** ['daiələg] Dialog *m*, Gespräch *n*.
dial-tone *teleph.* ['daiəltoun] Amtszeichen *n*.
diameter [dai'æmitə] Durchmesser *m*.
diamond ['daiəmənd] Diamant *m*; Rhombus *m*; *Am. Baseball:* Spielfeld *n*; *Karten:* Karo *n*.
diaper ['daiəpə] 1. Windel *f*; 2. *Am. Baby* trockenlegen, wickeln.
diaphragm ['daiəfræm] Zwerchfell *n*; *opt.* Blende *f*; *teleph.* Membran(e) *f*.
diarrh(o)ea ♂ [daiə'riə] Durchfall *m*.
diary ['daiəri] Tagebuch *n*.
dice [dais] 1. *pl. von* die²; 2. würfeln; **~-box** ['daisbɔks] Würfelbecher *m*.
dick *Am. sl.* [dik] Detektiv *m*.
dicker *Am.* F ['dikə] (ver)schachern.
dick(e)y ['diki] 1. *sl.* schlecht, schlimm; 2. F Notsitz *m*; Hemdenbrust *f*; *a.* **~-bird** Piepvögelchen *n*.
dictat|e 1. ['dikteit] Diktat *n*, Vorschrift *f*; Gebot *n*; 2. [dik'teit] diktieren; *fig.* vorschreiben; **~ion** [~'eiʃən] Diktat *n*; Vorschrift *f*; **~orship** [~'eitəʃip] Diktatur *f*.
diction ['dikʃən] Ausdruck(sweise *f*) *m*, Stil *m*; **~ary** [~nri] Wörterbuch *n*.
did [did] *pret. von* do.
die¹ [dai] sterben, umkommen; untergehen; absterben; F schmachten; **~** *away* ersterben; verhallen (*Ton*); **~** sich verlieren (*Farbe*); verlöschen (*Licht*); **~** down hinsiechen; (dahin)schwinden; erlöschen.
die² [~], *pl.* **dice** [dais] Würfel *m*; *pl.* **dies** [daiz] ⊕ Preßform *f*; *Münz*-Stempel *m*; *lower* **~** Matrize *f*.
die-hard ['daiha:d] Reaktionär *m*.
diet ['daiət] 1. Diät *f*; Nahrung *f*, Kost *f*; Landtag *m*; 2. *v/t.* Diät vorschreiben; beköstigen; *v/i.* diät leben.
differ ['difə] sich unterscheiden; anderer Meinung sein (*with, from* als); abweichen; **~ence** ['difrəns] Unterschied *m*; ⅍, ✝ Differenz *f*; Meinungsverschiedenheit *f*; **~ent** □ [~nt] verschieden; anders, andere(r, -s) (*from* als); **~entiate** [difə'renʃieit] (sich) unterscheiden.
difficult □ ['difikəlt] schwierig; **~y** [~ti] Schwierigkeit *f*.
diffiden|ce ['difidəns] Schüchternheit *f*; **~t** □ [~nt] schüchtern.
diffuse 1. *fig.* [di'fju:z] verbreiten; 2. □ [~u:s] weitverbreitet, zerstreut (*bsd. Licht*); weitschweifig; **~ion** [~u:ʒən] Verbreitung *f*.
dig [dig] 1. [*irr.*] (um-, aus)graben; wühlen (*in in dat.*); 2. (Aus)Grabung(sstelle) *f*; **~s** *pl.* F Bude *f*, Einzelzimmer *n*; F Stoß *m*, Puff *m*.
digest 1. [di'dʒest] *v/t.* ordnen; verdauen (*a. fig.* = überdenken); *verwinden*); *v/i.* verdaut werden;

2. ['daidʒest] Abriß *m*; Auslese *f*, Auswahl *f*; ⅍ Gesetzsammlung *f*; **~ible** [di'dʒestəbl] verdaulich; **~ion** [~tʃən] Verdauung *f*; **~ive** [~tiv] Verdauungsmittel *n*.
digg|er ['digə] (*bsd.* Gold)Gräber *m*; *sl.* Australier *m*; **~ings** F ['diginz] *pl.* Bude *f* (*Wohnung*); *Am.* Goldmine(n *pl.*) *f*.
dignif|ied □ ['dignifaid] würdevoll; würdig; **~y** [~fai] Würde verleihen (*dat.*); (be)ehren; *fig.* adeln.
dignit|ary ['dignitəri] Würdenträger *m*; **~y** [~ti] Würde *f*.
digress [dai'gres] abschweifen.
dike [daik] 1. Deich *m*; Damm *m*; Graben *m*; 2. eindeichen; eindämmen. [(lassen).]
dilapidate [di'læpideit] verfallen
dilat|e [dai'leit] (sich) ausdehnen; *Augen* weit öffnen; **~ory** □ ['dilətəri] aufschiebend; saumselig.
diligen|ce ['dilidʒəns] Fleiß *m*; **~t** □ [~nt] fleißig, emsig.
dilute [dai'lju:t] 1. verdünnen; verwässern; 2. verdünnt.
dim [dim] 1. □ trüb; dunkel; matt; 2. (sich) verdunkeln; abblenden; (sich) trüben; matt werden.
dime *Am.* [daim] Zehncentstück *n*.
dimension [di'menʃən] Abmessung *f*; **~s** *pl. a.* Ausmaß *n*.
dimin|ish [di'miniʃ] (sich) vermindern; abnehmen; **~ution** [dimi'nju:ʃən] Verminderung *f*; Abnahme *f*; **~utive** □ [di'minjutiv] winzig.
dimple ['dimpl] 1. Grübchen *n*; 2. Grübchen bekommen.
din [din] Getöse *n*, Lärm *m*.
dine [dain] (zu Mittag) speisen; bewirten; **~r** [~ə] Speisende(r *m*) *f*; (Mittags)Gast *m*; ⊞ *bsd. Am.* Speisewagen *m*; *Am.* Restaurant *n*.
dingle ['diŋgl] Waldschlucht *f*.
dingy □ ['dindʒi] schmutzig.
dining-car ⊞ ['dainiŋka:] Speisewagen *m*; **~-room** Speisezimmer *n*.
dinner ['dinə] (Mittag-, Abend-) Essen *n*; Festessen *n*; **~-jacket** Smoking *m*; **~-pail** *Am.* Essenträger *m* (*Gerät*); **~-party** Tischgesellschaft *f*; **~-service**, **~-set** Tafelgeschirr *n*.
dint [dint] 1. Beule *f*; *by* **~** *of* kraft, vermöge (*gen.*); 2. ver-, einbeulen.
dip [dip] 1. *v/t.* (ein)tauchen; senken; schöpfen; abblenden; *v/i.* (unter)tauchen, untersinken; sich neigen; sich senken; 2. Eintauchen *n* F kurzes Bad; Senkung *f*, Neigung *f*. [rie *f*.]
diphtheria ♂ [dif'θiəriə] Diphthe-
diploma [di'ploumə] Diplom *n*; **~cy** [~əsi] Diplomatie *f*; **~tic(al** □) [diplə'mætik(əl)] diplomatisch; **~tist** [di'ploumətist] Diplomat(in).
dipper ['dipə] Schöpfkelle *f*; *Am. Great od. Big* ♎ *ast. der* Große Bär.

dire ['daiə] gräßlich, schrecklich.

direct [di'rekt] **1.** □ direkt; gerade; unmittelbar; offen, aufrichtig; deutlich; ~ **current** ⚡ Gleichstrom m; ~ **train** durchgehender Zug; **2.** adv. geradeswegs; = ~ly **3.** richten; lenken, steuern; leiten; anordnen; j-n (an)weisen; Brief adressieren; ~ion [~kʃən] Richtung f; Gegend f; Leitung f; Anordnung f; Adresse f; Vorstand m; ~ion-finder [~nfaində] Radio: (Funk)Peiler m; Peil(funk)empfänger m; ~ion-indicator mot. Fahrtrichtungsanzeiger m; ⚓ Kursweiser m; ~ive [~ktiv] richtungweisend; leitend; ~ly [~tli] **1.** adv. sofort; **2.** cj. sobald, als.

director [di'rektə] Direktor m; Film: Regisseur m; board of ~s Aufsichtsrat m; ~ate [~ərit] Direktion f; ~y [~ri] Adreßbuch n; telephone ~ Telephonbuch n.

dirge [də:dʒ] Klage(lied n) f.

dirigible ['diridʒəbl] **1.** lenkbar; **2.** lenkbares Luftschiff.

dirt [də:t] Schmutz m; (lockere) Erde; ~-cheap F ['də:t'tʃi:p] spottbillig; ~y ['də:ti] **1.** □ schmutzig (a. fig.); **2.** beschmutzen; besudeln.

disability [disə'biliti] Unfähigkeit f.

disable [dis'eibl] (dienst-, kampf-)unfähig machen; ~d dienst-, kampfunfähig; körperbehindert; kriegsbeschädigt.

disabuse [disə'bju:z] e-s Besseren belehren (of über acc.).

disadvantage [disəd'va:ntidʒ] Nachteil m; Schaden m; ~ous [disædva:n'teidʒəs] nachteilig, ungünstig.

disagree [disə'gri:] nicht übereinstimmen; uneinig sein; nicht bekommen (with s.o. j-m); ~able □ [~riəbl] unangenehm; ~ment [~ri:mənt] Verschiedenheit f; Unstimmigkeit f; Meinungsverschiedenheit f.

disappear [disə'piə] verschwinden; ~ance [~ərəns] Verschwinden n.

disappoint [disə'pɔint] enttäuschen; vereiteln; j. im Stich lassen; ~ment [~tmənt] Enttäuschung f; Vereitelung f. [Mißbilligung f.\]

disapprobation [disæprou'beiʃən]\

disapprov|al [disə'pru:vəl] Mißbilligung f; ~e ['disə'pru:v] mißbilligen (of et.).

disarm [dis'a:m] v/t. entwaffnen (a. fig.); v/i. abrüsten; ~ament [~məmənt] Entwaffnung f; Abrüstung f.

disarrange ['disə'reindʒ] in Unordnung bringen, verwirren.

disarray ['disə'rei] **1.** Unordnung f; **2.** in Unordnung bringen.

disast|er [di'za:stə] Unglück(sfall m) n, Katastrophe f; ~rous □ [~trəs] unheilvoll; katastrophal.

disband [dis'bænd] entlassen; auflösen.

disbelieve ['disbi'li:v] nicht glauben.

disburse [dis'bə:s] auszahlen.

disc [disk] = disk.

discard 1. [dis'ka:d] Karten, Kleid etc. ablegen; entlassen; **2.** ['diska:d] Karten: Abwerfen n; bsd. Am. Abfall(haufen) m.

discern [di'sə:n] unterscheiden; erkennen; beurteilen; ~ing □ [~niŋ] kritisch, scharfsichtig; ~ment [~nmənt] Einsicht f; Scharfsinn m.

discharge [dis'tʃa:dʒ] **1.** ent-, ab-, ausladen; entlasten, entbinden; abfeuern; Flüssigkeit absondern; Amt versehen; Pflicht etc. erfüllen; Zorn etc. auslassen (on an dat.); Schuld tilgen; quittieren; Wechsel einlösen; entlassen; freisprechen; v/i. sich entladen; eitern; **2.** Entladung f; Abfeuern n; Ausströmen n; Ausfluß m, Eiter(ung f) m; Entlassung f; Entlastung f; Bezahlung f; Quittung f; Erfüllung f e-r Pflicht.

disciple [di'saipl] Schüler m; Jünger m.

discipline ['disiplin] **1.** Disziplin f, Zucht f; Erziehung f; Züchtigung f; **2.** erziehen; schulen; bestrafen.

disclaim [dis'kleim] (ab)leugnen; ablehnen; verzichten auf (acc.).

disclose [dis'klouz] aufdecken; erschließen, offenbaren, enthüllen.

discolo(u)r [dis'kʌlə] (sich) verfärben.

discomfiture [dis'kʌmfitʃə] Niederlage f; Verwirrung f; Vereitelung f.

discomfort [dis'kʌmfət] **1.** Unbehagen n; **2.** j-m Unbehagen verursachen.

discompose [diskəm'pouz] beunruhigen.

disconcert [diskən'sə:t] außer Fassung bringen; vereiteln.

disconnect ['diskə'nekt] trennen (a. ⚡); ⊕ auskuppeln; ⚡ ab-, ausschalten; ~ed □ zs.-hanglos.

disconsolate □ [dis'kɔnsəlit] trostlos.

discontent ['diskən'tent] Unzufriedenheit f; ~ed □ mißvergnügt, unzufrieden.

discontinue ['diskən'tinju(:)] aufgeben, aufhören mit; unterbrechen.

discord ['diskɔ:d], ~ance [dis'kɔ:dəns] Uneinigkeit f; ♪ Mißklang m.

discount ['diskaunt] **1.** † Diskont m; Abzug m, Rabatt m; **2.** † diskontieren; abrechnen; fig. absehen von; Nachricht mit Vorsicht aufnehmen; beeinträchtigen; ~enance [dis'kauntinəns] mißbilligen; entmutigen.

discourage [dis'kʌridʒ] entmutigen;

abschrecken; ~ment [~dʒmənt] Entmutigung f; Schwierigkeit f.

discourse [dis'kɔːs] 1. Rede f; Abhandlung f; Predigt f; 2. reden, sprechen; e-n Vortrag halten.

discourte|ous □ [dis'kɔːtjəs] unhöflich; ~sy [~tisi] Unhöflichkeit f.

discover [dis'kʌvə] entdecken; ausfindig machen; ~y [~əri] Entdeckung f

discredit [dis'kredit] 1. schlechter Ruf; Unglaubwürdigkeit f; 2. nicht glauben; in Mißkredit bringen.

discreet [dis'kriːt] besonnen, vorsichtig; klug; verschwiegen.

discrepancy [dis'krepənsi] Widerspruch m; Unstimmigkeit f.

discretion [dis'kreʃən] Besonnenheit f, Klugheit f; Takt m; Verschwiegenheit f; Belieben n; age (od. years) of ~ Strafmündigkeit f (14 Jahre); surrender at ~ sich auf Gnade und Ungnade ergeben.

discriminat|e [dis'krimineit] unterscheiden; ~ against benachteiligen; ~ing □ [~tiŋ] unterscheidend; scharfsinnig; urteilsfähig; ~ion [diskrimi'neiʃən] Unterscheidung f; unterschiedliche (bsd. nachteilige) Behandlung; Urteilskraft f.

discuss [dis'kʌs] erörtern, besprechen; ~ion [~ʌʃən] Erörterung f.

disdain [dis'dein] 1. Verachtung f; 2. geringschätzen, verachten; verschmähen.

disease [di'ziːz] Krankheit f; ~d krank.

disembark ['disim'baːk] v/t. ausschiffen; v/i. landen, an Land gehen.

disengage ['disin'geidʒ] (sich) freimachen, (sich) lösen; ⊕ loskuppeln.

disentangle ['disin'tæŋgl] entwirren; fig. freimachen (from von).

disfavo(u)r ['dis'feivə] 1. Mißfallen n, Ungnade f; 2. nicht mögen.

disfigure [dis'figə] entstellen.

disgorge [dis'gɔːdʒ] ausspeien.

disgrace [dis'greis] 1. Ungnade f; Schande f; 2. in Ungnade fallen lassen; j-n entehren; ~ful □ [~sful] schimpflich.

disguise [dis'gaiz] 1. verkleiden; Stimme verstellen; verhehlen; 2. Verkleidung f; Verstellung f; Maske f.

disgust [dis'gʌst] 1. Ekel m; 2. anekeln; ~ing □ [~tiŋ] ekelhaft.

dish [diʃ] 1. Schüssel f, Platte f; Gericht n (Speise); the ~es das Geschirr; 2. anrichten; mst ~ up auftischen; ~cloth ['diʃklɔθ] Geschirrspültuch n

dishearten [dis'haːtn] entmutigen.

dishevel(l)ed [di'ʃevəld] zerzaust.

dishonest □ [dis'ɔnist] unehrlich, unredlich; ~y [~ti] Unredlichkeit f.

dishono(u)r [dis'ɔnə] 1. Unehre f,

Schande f; 2. entehren; schänden; Wechsel nicht honorieren; ~able □ [~ərəbl] entehrend; ehrlos.

dish|-pan Am ['diʃpæn] Spülschüssel f; ~rag ~ dish-cloth; ~water Spülwasser n

disillusion [disi'luːʒən] 1. Ernüchterung f, Enttäuschung f; 2. ernüchtern, enttäuschen.

disinclined ['disin'klaind] abgeneigt

disinfect [disin'fekt] desinfizieren; ~ant [~tənt] Desinfektionsmittel n.

disintegrate [dis'intigreit] (sich) auflösen, (sich) zersetzen.

disinterested [dis'intristid] uneigennützig, selbstlos.

disk [disk] Scheibe f; Platte f; Schallplatte f; ~ brake mot. Scheibenbremse f; ~ jockey Ansager m e-r Schallplattensendung.

dislike [dis'laik] 1. Abneigung f, Widerwille m; 2. nicht mögen.

dislocate [dislakeit] aus den Fugen bringen, verrenken; verlagern.

dislodge [dis'lɔdʒ] vertreiben, verjagen; umquartieren.

disloyal ['dis'lɔiəl] treulos.

dismal ['dizməl] trüb(selig); öde; trostlos, elend.

dismantl|e [dis'mæntl] abbrechen, niederreißen; ⊕ abtakeln; ⊕ demontieren; ~ing [~liŋ] Demontage f.

dismay [dis'mei] 1. Schrecken m; Bestürzung f; 2. v/t. erschrecken.

dismember [dis'membə] zerstückeln.

dismiss [dis'mis] v/t. entlassen, wegschicken; ablehnen; Thema etc. fallen lassen; ⅔ abweisen; ~al [~səl] Entlassung f; Aufgabe f; ⅔ Abweichung f.

dismount ['dis'maunt] v/t. aus dem Sattel werfen; demontieren; ⊕ aus-ea.-nehmen; v/i. absteigen.

disobedien|ce [disə'biːdjəns] Ungehorsam m; ~t □ [~nt] ungehorsam.

disobey ['disə'bei] ungehorsam sein.

disoblige ['disə'blaidʒ] ungefällig sein gegen; kränken.

disorder [dis'ɔːdə] 1. Unordnung f; Aufruhr m; ♂ Störung f; 2. in Unordnung bringen; stören; zerrütten; ~ly [~əli] unordentlich; ordnungswidrig; unruhig; aufrührerisch.

disorganize [dis'ɔːgənaiz] zerrütten.

disown [dis'oun] nicht anerkennen, verleugnen; ablehnen.

disparage [dis'pæridʒ] verächtlich machen, herabsetzen.

disparity [dis'pæriti] Ungleichheit f.

dispassionate □ [dis'pæʃnit] leidenschaftslos; unparteiisch.

dispatch [dis'pætʃ] **1.** (schnelle) Erledigung; (schnelle) Absendung; Abfertigung f; Eile f; Depesche f; **2.** (schnell) abmachen, erledigen (a. fig. = töten); abfertigen; (eilig) absenden.

dispel [dis'pel] vertreiben, zerstreuen.

dispensa|ble [dis'pensəbl] entbehrlich; **~ry** [~əri] Apotheke f; **~tion** [dispen'seiʃən] Austeilung f; Befreiung f (with von); göttliche Fügung.

dispense [dis'pens] v/t. austeilen; Gesetze handhaben; Arzneien anfertigen und ausgeben; befreien.

disperse [dis'pə:s] (sich) zerstreuen; auseinandergehen.

dispirit [di'spirit] entmutigen.

displace [dis'pleis] verschieben; absetzen; ersetzen; verdrängen.

display [dis'plei] **1.** Entfaltung f; Aufwand m; Schaustellung f; Schaufenster-Auslage f; **2.** entfalten; zur Schau stellen; zeigen.

displeas|e [dis'pli:z] j-m mißfallen; **~ed** ungehalten; **~ure** [~'leʒə] Mißfallen n; Verdruß m.

dispos|al [dis'pouzəl] Anordnung f; Verfügung(srecht n) f; Beseitigung f; Veräußerung f; Übergabe f; **~e** [~ouz] v/t. (an)ordnen, einrichten; geneigt machen, veranlassen; v/i. **~ of** verfügen über (acc.); erledigen; verwenden; veräußern; unterbringen; beseitigen; **~ed** geneigt; ...gesinnt; **~ition** [dispə'ziʃən] Disposition f; Anordnung f; Neigung f; Sinnesart f; Verfügung f.

dispossess ['dispə'zes] (of) vertreiben (aus od. von); berauben (gen.).

dispraise [dis'preiz] tadeln.

disproof ['dis'pru:f] Widerlegung f.

disproportionate □ [disprə'pɔ:-ʃnit] unverhältnismäßig.

disprove ['dis'pru:v] widerlegen.

dispute [dis'pju:t] **1.** Streit(igkeit f) m; Rechtsstreit m; beyond (all) **~,** past **~** zweifellos; **2.** (be)streiten.

disqualify [dis'kwɔlifai] unfähig od. untauglich machen; für untauglich erklären.

disquiet [dis'kwaiət] beunruhigen.

disregard ['disri'ga:d] **1.** Nicht(be)-achtung f; **2.** unbeachtet lassen.

disreput|able □ [dis'repjutəbl] schimpflich; verrufen; **~e** ['disri-'pju:t] übler Ruf; Schande f.

disrespect ['disris'pekt] Nichtachtung f; Respektlosigkeit f; **~ful** □ [~tful] respektlos; unhöflich.

disroot [dis'ru:t] entwurzeln.

disrupt [dis'rʌpt] zerreißen; spalten.

dissatis|faction ['dissætis'fækʃən] Unzufriedenheit f; **~factory** [~ktə-ri] unbefriedigend; **~fy** ['dis'sætis-fai] nicht befriedigen; j-m mißfallen.

dissect [di'sekt] zerlegen; zergliedern.

dissemble [di'sembl] v/t. verhehlen; v/i. sich verstellen, heucheln.

dissen|sion [di'senʃən] Zwietracht f, Streit m, Uneinigkeit f; **~t** [~nt] **1.** abweichende Meinung; Nichtzugehörigkeit f zur Staatskirche; **2.** andrer Meinung sein (from als).

dissimilar □ ['di'similə] (to) unähnlich (dat.); verschieden (von).

dissimulation [disimju'leiʃən] Verstellung f, Heuchelei f.

dissipat|e ['disipeit] (sich) zerstreuen; verschwenden; **~ion** [disi-'peiʃən] Zerstreuung f; Verschwendung f; ausschweifendes Leben.

dissociate [di'souʃieit] trennen; **~ o.s.** sich distanzieren, abrücken.

dissoluble [di'sɔljubl] (auf)lösbar.

dissolut|e □ ['disəlut] liederlich, ausschweifend; **~ion** [disə'lu:ʃən] Auflösung f; Zerstörung f; Tod m.

dissolve [di'zɔlv] v/t. (auf)lösen; schmelzen; v/i. sich auflösen; vergehen.

dissonant ['disɔnənt] ♪ mißtönend; abweichend; uneinig.

dissuade [di'sweid] j-m abraten.

distan|ce [di'stæns] **1.** Abstand m, Entfernung f, Ferne f; Strecke f; Zurückhaltung f; at a **~** von weitem; in e-r gewissen Entfernung; weit weg; keep s.o. at a **~** j-m gegenüber reserviert sein; **2.** hinter sich lassen; **~t** □ [~nt] entfernt; fern; zurückhaltend; Fern...; **~** control Fernsteuerung f.

distaste [dis'teist] Widerwille m; Abneigung f; **~ful** [~tful] widerwärtig; ärgerlich.

distemper [dis'tempə] Krankheit f (bsd. von Tieren); (Hunde)Staupe f.

distend [dis'tend] (sich) ausdehnen; (auf)blähen; (sich) weiten.

distil [dis'til] herabtröpfeln (lassen); ⚗ destillieren; **~lery** [~ləri] Branntweinbrennerei f.

distinct □ [dis'tiŋkt] verschieden; getrennt; deutlich, klar; **~ion** [~kʃən] Unterscheidung f; Unterschied m; Auszeichnung f; Rang m; **~ive** □ [~ktiv] unterscheidend; apart; kennzeichnend; bezeichnend.

distinguish [dis'tiŋgwiʃ] unterscheiden; auszeichnen; **~ed** berühmt, ausgezeichnet; vornehm.

distort [dis'tɔ:t] verdrehen; verzerren.

distract ['dis'trækt] ablenken, zerstreuen; beunruhigen; verwirren; verrückt machen; **~ion** [~kʃən] Zerstreutheit f; Verwirrung f; Wahnsinn m; Zerstreuung f.

distraught [dis'trɔ:t] verwirrt, bestürzt.

distress [dis'tres] **1.** Qual f; Elend n, Not f; Erschöpfung f; **2.** in Not bringen; quälen; erschöpfen; ~ed in Not befindlich; bekümmert; ~ area Notstandsgebiet n.

distribut|e [dis'tribju(:)t] verteilen; einteilen; verbreiten; ~ion [distri-'bju:ʃən] Verteilung f; Film-Verleih m; Verbreitung f; Einteilung f.

district ['distrikt] Bezirk m; Gegend f.

distrust [dis'trʌst] 1. Mißtrauen n; 2. mißtrauen (dat.); ~ful □ [~tful] mißtrauisch; ~ (of o.s.) schüchtern.

disturb [dis'tə:b] beunruhigen; stören; ~ance [~bəns] Störung f; Unruhe f; Aufruhr m; ~ of the peace ᚦᛏ öffentliche Ruhestörung; ~er [~bə] Störenfried m, Unruhestifter m.

disunite ['disju:'nait] (sich) trennen.

disuse ['dis'ju:z] nicht mehr gebrauchen.

ditch [ditʃ] Graben m.

ditto ['ditou] dito, desgleichen.

divan [di'væn] Diwan m; ~-bed [oft 'daivænbed] Bettcouch f, Liege f.

dive [daiv] 1. (unter)tauchen; vom Sprungbrett springen; e-n Sturzflug machen; eindringen in (acc.); 2. Schwimmen: Springen n; (Kopf-) Sprung m; Sturzflug m; Kellerlokal n; Am. F Kaschemme f; ~r ['daivə] Taucher m.

diverge [dai'və:dʒ] aus-ea.-laufen; abweichen; ~nce [~dʒəns] Abweichung f; ~nt □ [~nt] (von-ea.-)abweichend.

divers ['daivə(:)z] mehrere.

divers|e □ [dai'və:s] verschieden; mannigfaltig; ~ion [~ʃən] Ablenkung f; Zeitvertreib m; ~ity [~siti] Verschiedenheit f; Mannigfaltigkeit f.

divert [dai'və:t] ablenken; j-n zerstreuen; unterhalten; Verkehr umleiten.

divest [dai'vest] entkleiden (a.fig.).

divid|e [di'vaid] 1. v/t. teilen; trennen; einteilen; Ǎ dividieren (by durch); v/i. sich teilen; zerfallen; Ǎ aufgehen; sich trennen od. auflösen; 2. Wasserscheide f; ~end ['dividend] Dividende f.

divine [di'vain] 1. □ göttlich; ~ service Gottesdienst m; 2. Geistliche(r) m; 3. weissagen; ahnen.

diving ['daiviŋ] Kunstspringen n; attr. Taucher...

divinity [di'viniti] Gottheit f; Göttlichkeit f; Theologie f.

divis|ible □ [di'vizəbl] teilbar; ~ion [~iʒən] Teilung f; Trennung f; Abteilung f; ✗; Ǎ Division f.

divorce [di'vɔ:s] 1. (Ehe)Scheidung f; 2. Ehe scheiden; sich scheiden lassen.

divulge [dai'vʌldʒ] ausplaudern; verbreiten; bekanntmachen.

dixie ✗ sl. ['diksi] Kochgeschirr n;

Feldkessel m; ⚲ Am. die Südstaaten pl.; ⚲crat Am. pol. opponierender Südstaatendemokrat.

dizz|iness ['dizinis] Schwindel m; ~y □ ['dizi] schwind(e)lig.

do [du:] [irr.] v/t. tun; machen; (zu)bereiten; Rolle, Stück spielen; ~ London sl. London besichtigen; have done reading fertig sein mit Lesen; ~ in F um die Ecke bringen; ~ into übersetzen in; ~ over überstreifen, -ziehen; ~ up instand setzen; einpacken; v/i. tun; handeln; sich benehmen; sich befinden; genügen; that will ~ das genügt; how ~ you...? guten Tag!, Wie geht's?; ~ well s-e Sache gut machen; gute Geschäfte machen; ~ away with weg-, abschaffen; I could ~ with ... ich könnte ... brauchen od. vertragen; ~ without fertig werden ohne; ~ be quick beeile dich doch; ~ you like London? — I ~ gefällt Ihnen London? — Ja.

docil|e ['dousail] gelehrig; fügsam; ~ity [dou'siliti] Gelehrigkeit f.

dock[1] [dɔk] stutzen; fig. kürzen.

dock[2] [~] 1. ⚓ Dock n; bsd. Am. Kai m, Pier m; ᚦᛏ Anklagebank f; 2. ⚓ docken.

dockyard [dɔk'jɑ:d] Werft f.

doctor ['dɔktə] 1. Doktor m; Arzt m; 2. F verarzten; F fig. (ver)fälschen.

doctrine ['dɔktrin] Lehre f; Dogma n.

document 1. ['dɔkjumənt] Urkunde f; 2. [~ment] beurkunden.

dodge [dɔdʒ] 1. Seitensprung m; Kniff m, Winkelzug m; 2. fig. irreführen; ausweichen; Winkelzüge machen; ~r ['dɔdʒə] Schieber(in); Am. Hand-, Reklamezettel m; Am. Maisbrot n, -kuchen m.

doe [dou] Hirschkuh f; Reh n; Häsin f.

dog [dɔg] 1. Hund m; Haken m, Klammer f; 2. nachspüren (dat.).

dogged □ ['dɔgid] verbissen.

dogma ['dɔgmə] Dogma n; Glaubenslehre f; ~tic(al □) [dɔg'mætik(əl)] dogmatisch; bestimmt; ~tism ['dɔgmətizəm] Selbstherrlichkeit f.

dog's-ear F ['dɔgziə] Eselsohr n im Buch.

dog-tired F ['dɔg'taiəd] hundemüde.

doings ['du(:)iŋz] pl. Dinge n/pl.; Begebenheiten f/pl.; Treiben n; Betragen n.

dole [doul] 1. Spende f; F Erwerbslosenunterstützung f; 2. verteilen.

doleful □ ['doulful] trübselig.

doll [dɔl] Puppe f.

dollar ['dɔlə] Dollar m.

dolly ['dɔli] Püppchen n.

dolorous □ ['dɔlərəs] schmerzhaft; traurig.

dolphin ['dɔlfin] Delphin m.

dolt [doult] Tölpel m.

domain [də'mein] Domäne *f*; *fig.* Gebiet *n*; Bereich *m*.

dome [doum] Kuppel *f*; ⊕ Haube *f*; ~d gewölbt.

Domesday Book ['du:mzdei'buk] Reichsgrundbuch *n Englands.*

domestic [də'mestik] **1.** (~ally) häuslich; inländisch; einheimisch; zahm; ~ *animal* Haustier *n*; **2.** Dienstbote *m*; ~s *pl.* Haushaltsartikel *m/pl.*; ~ate [~keit] zähmen;

domicile ['dɔmisail] Wohnsitz *m*; ~d wohnhaft.

domin|ant ['dɔminənt] (vor)herrschend; ~ate [~neit] (be)herrschen; ~ation [dɔmi'neiʃən] Herrschaft *f*; ~eer [~'niə] (despotisch) herrschen; ~eering [❘] [~'əriŋ] herrisch, tyrannisch; überheblich.

dominion [də'minjən] Herrschaft *f*; Gebiet *n*; ♀ Dominion *n* (*im Brt. Commonwealth*).

don [dɔn] anziehen; *Hut* aufsetzen.

donat|e *Am.* [dou'neit] schenken; stiften; ~ion [~eiʃən] Schenkung *f.*

done [dʌn] **1.** *p.p. von* do; **2.** *adj.* abgemacht; fertig; gar *gekocht.*

donkey ['dɔŋki] *zo.* Esel *m*; *attr.* Hilfs...

donor ['dounə] (🩸 Blut)Spender *m.*

doom [du:m] **1.** Schicksal *n*, Verhängnis *n*; **2.** verurteilen, verdammen.

door [dɔ:] Tür *f*, Tor *n*; *next* ~ nebenan; ~**handle** ['dɔ:hændl] Türgriff *m*; ~**keeper**, *Am.* ~**man** Pförtner *m*; Portier *m*; ~**way** Türöffnung *f*; Torweg *m*; ~**yard** *Am.* Vorhof *m*, Vorgarten *m.*

dope [doup] **1.** Schmiere *f*; *bsd.* 🔧 Lack *m*; Aufputschmittel *n*; Rauschgift *n*; *Am. sl.* Geheimtip *m*; **2.** lackieren; *sl.* betäuben; aufpulvern; *Am. sl.* herauskriegen.

dormant *mst fig.* ['dɔ:mənt] schlafend, ruhend; unbenutzt; † tot.

dormer(-window) ['dɔ:mə(-'windou)] Dachfenster *n.*

dormitory ['dɔ:mitri] Schlafsaal *m*; *bsd. Am.* Studenten(wohn)heim *n.*

dose [dous] **1.** Dosis *f*, Portion *f*; **2.** *j-m* e-e Medizin geben.

dot [dɔt] **1.** Punkt *m*, Fleck *m*; **2.** punktieren, tüpfeln; *fig.* verstreuen.

dot|e [dout]: ~ (*up*)*on* vernarrt sein in (*acc.*); ~**ing** ['doutiŋ] vernarrt.

double ❘ ['dʌbl] **1.** doppelt; zu zweien; gekrümmt; zweideutig; **2.** Doppelte(s) *n*; Doppelgänger(in) *f*; *Tennis.* Doppel(spiel) *n*; **3.** *v/t.* verdoppeln; *a.* ~ *up* zs.-legen; *et.* umfahren, umsegeln; ~d *up* zs.-gekrümmt; *v/i.* sich verdoppeln; *a.* ~ *back* e-n Haken schlagen (*Hase*); ~**breasted** zweireihig (*Jackett*); ~**cross** *sl.* Partner betrügen; ~**dealing** Doppelzüngigkeit *f*; ~**edged** zweischneidig; ~**entry** doppelte Buchführung;

~**feature** *Am.* Doppelprogramm *n im Kino*; ~**header** *Am. Baseball:* Doppelspiel *n*; ~**park** *Am. verboten* in zweiter Reihe parken.

doubt [daut] **1.** *v/i.* zweifeln; *v/t.* bezweifeln; mißtrauen (*dat.*); **2.** Zweifel *m*; no ~ ohne Zweifel; ~**ful** ❒ ['dautful] zweifelhaft; ~**fulness** [~lnis] Zweifelhaftigkeit *f*; ~**less** ['dautlis] ohne Zweifel.

douche [du:ʃ] **1.** Dusche *f*; Irrigator *m*; **2.** duschen; spülen.

dough [dou] Teig *m*; ~**boy** *Am.* F ['doubɔi] Landser *m*; ~**nut** *Schmalzgebackenes.*

dove [dʌv] Taube *f*; *fig.* Täubchen *n.*

dowel ['dauəl] Dübel *m.*

down¹ [daun] Daune *f*; Flaum *m*; Düne *f*; ~s *pl.* Höhenrücken *m.*

down² [~] **1.** *adv.* nieder; her-, hinunter, ab; abwärts; unten; *be* ~ *upon* F über *j-n* herfallen; **2.** *prp.* herab, hinab, her-, hinunter; ~ *the river* flußabwärts; **3.** *adj.* nach unten gerichtet; ~ *platform* Abfahrtsbahnsteig *m* (*London*); ~ *train* Zug *m von* London (fort); **4.** *v/t.* niederwerfen; herunterholen; ~**cast** ['daunka:st] niedergeschlagen; ~**easter** *Am.* Neuengländer *m bsd. von Maine*; ~**fall** Fall *m*, Sturz *m*; Verfall *m*; ~**hearted** niedergeschlagen; ~**hill** bergab; ~**pour** Regenguß *m*; ~**right** ❒ **1.** *adv.* geradezu, durchaus; völlig; **2.** *adj.* ehrlich; plump (*Benehmen*); richtig, glatt (*Lüge etc.*); ~**stairs** die Treppe hinunter, (nach) unten; ~**stream** stromabwärts; ~**town** *bsd. Am.* Hauptgeschäftsviertel *n*; ~**ward(s)** ['daunwəd(z)] abwärts (gerichtet).

downy ['dauni] flaumig; *sl.* gerissen.

dowry ['dauəri] Mitgift *f* (*a. fig.*).

doze [douz] **1.** dösen; **2.** Schläfchen *n.*

dozen ['dʌzn] Dutzend *n.*

drab [dræb] gelblichgrau; eintönig.

draft [dra:ft] **1.** Entwurf *m*; † Tratte *f*; Abhebung *f*; 🔧 (Sonder-) Kommando *n*; Einberufung *f*; = *draught*; **2.** entwerfen; aufsetzen; 🔧 abkommandieren; *Am.* einziehen; ~**ee** *Am.* 🔧 [~'ti:] Dienstpflichtige(r) *m*; ~**sman** ['dra:ftsmən] (technischer) Zeichner; Verfasser *m*, Entwerfer *m.*

drag [dræg] **1.** Schleppnetz *n*; Schleife *f für Lasten*; Egge *f*; **2.** *v/t.* schleppen, ziehen; *v/i.* (sich)schleppen, schleifen; (mit e-m Schleppnetz) fischen; (Libelle *f*.)

dragon ['drægən] Drache *m*; ~**fly**)

drain [drein] **1.** Abfluß(graben *m*, -rohr *n*) *m*; F Schluck *m*; **2.** *v/t.* entwässern; *Glas* leeren; *a.* ~ *off* abziehen; verzehren; *v/i.* ablaufen; ~**age** ['dreinidʒ] Abfluß *m*; Entwässerung(sanlage) *f.*

drake [dreik] Enterich m.
dram [dræm] Schluck m; fig. Schnaps m.
drama ['drɑːmə] Drama n; ~tic [drə'mætik] (~ally) dramatisch; ~tist ['dræmətist] Dramatiker m; ~tize [~taiz] dramatisieren.
drank [dræŋk] pret. von drink 2.
drape [dreip] 1. drapieren; in Falten legen; 2. mst ~s pl. Vorhänge m/pl.; ~ry ['dreipəri] Tuchhandel m; Tuchwaren f/pl.; Faltenwurf m.
drastic ['dræstik] (~ally) drastisch.
draught [drɑːft] Zug m (Ziehen; Fischzug; Zugluft; Schluck); ⚓ Tiefgang m; ~s pl. Damespiel n; s. draft; ~ beer Faßbier n; ~-horse ['drɑːfthɔːs] Zugpferd n; ~sman [~tsmən] Damestein m; = draftsman; ~y [~ti] zugig.
draw [drɔː] 1. [irr.] ziehen; an-, auf-, ein-, zuziehen; (sich) zs.-ziehen; in die Länge ziehen; dehnen; herausziehen, herauslocken; entnehmen; Geld abheben; anlocken, anziehen; abzapfen, ausfischen; Geflügel ausnehmen; zeichnen; entwerfen; Urkunde abfassen; unentschieden spielen; Luft schöpfen; ~ near heranrücken; ~ out in die Länge ziehen; ~ up ab-, verfassen; ~ (up)on + (e-n Wechsel) ziehen auf (acc.); fig. in Anspruch nehmen; 2. Zug m (Ziehen); Lotterie: Ziehung f; Los n; Sport unentschiedenes Spiel; F Zugstück n, -artikel m; ~back ['drɔːbæk] Nachteil m; Hindernis n; ✝ Rückzoll m; Am. Rückzahlung f; ~er ['drɔːə] Ziehende(r m) f; Zeichner m; ✝ Aussteller m, Trassant m; [drɔː] Schublade f; (a pair of) ~s pl. (eine) Unterhose; (ein) Schlüpfer m; mst chest of ~s Kommode f.
drawing ['drɔːiŋ] Ziehen n; Zeichnen n; Zeichnung f; ~account Girokonto n; ~board Reißbrett n; ~room Gesellschaftszimmer n.
drawn [drɔːn] 1. p.p. von draw 1; 2. adj. unentschieden; verzerrt.
dread [dred] 1. Furcht f; Schrecken m; 2. (sich) fürchten; ~ful ['dredful] schrecklich; furchtbar.
dream [driːm] 1. Traum m; 2. [irr.] träumen; ~er ['driːmə] Träumer (-in); ~t [dremt] pret. u. p.p. von dream 2; ~y □ ['driːmi] träumerisch; verträumt.
dreary [['driəri] traurig; öde.
dredge [dredʒ] 1. Schleppnetz n; Bagger(maschine f) m; 2. (aus-) baggern.
dregs [dregz] pl. Bodensatz m, Hefe f.
drench [drentʃ] 1. (Regen)Guß m; 2. durchnässen; fig. baden.
dress [dres] 1. Anzug m; Kleidung f; Kleid n; 2. an-, ein-, zurichten; ✕ (sich) richten; zurechtmachen;

(sich) ankleiden; putzen; ✂ verbinden; frisieren; ~circle thea. ['dres'səːkl] erster Rang; ~er [~sə] Anrichte f, Am. Frisiertoilette f.
dressing [dresiŋ] An-, Zurichten n; Ankleiden n; Verband m; Appretur f; Küche Soße f; Füllung f; ~s pl. ✂ Verbandzeug n; ~ down Standpauke f, ~gown Morgenrock m; ~table Frisiertisch m.
dress|maker ['dresmeikə] Schneiderin f, ~parade Modenschau f.
drew [druː] pret. von draw 1.
dribble [dribl] tröpfeln, träufeln (lassen); geifern; Fußball: dribbeln.
dried [draid] getrocknet; Dörr...
drift [drift] 1. (Dahin)Treiben n; fig. Lauf m, fig. Hang m; Zweck m; (Schnee-, Sand)Wehe f; 2. v/t. (zs.-)treiben, (zs.-)wehen; v/i. (dahin)treiben, sich anhäufen.
drill [dril] 1. Drillbohrer m; Furche f; ✓ Drill-, Sämaschine f; ✕ Exerzieren n (a fig.); 2. bohren; ✕ (ein)exerzieren (a. fig.).
drink [driŋk] 1. Trunk m; (geistiges) Getränk, 2. [irr.] trinken.
drip [drip] 1. Tröpfeln n; Traufe f; 2. tröpfeln (lassen); triefen; ~dry shirt [drip'drai ʃəːt] bügelfreies Hemd, ~ping [ˌpiŋ] Bratenfett n.
drive [draiv] 1. (Spazier)Fahrt f; Auffahrt f, Fahrweg m; ⊕ Antrieb m; fig (Auf)Trieb m; Drang m; Unternehmen n, Feldzug m; Am. Sammelaktion f; 2. [irr.] v/t. (an-, ein)treiben; Geschäft betreiben; fahren; lenken; zwingen; vertreiben; v/i. treiben; fahren; ~ at hinzielen auf
drive-in Am. ['draiv'in] 1. mst attr. Auto..; ~ cinema Autokino n; 2. Autokino n; Autorestaurant n.
drivel [drivl] 1. geifern; faseln; 2. Geifer m; Faselei f.
driven [drivn] p.p. von drive 2.
driver ['draivə] Treiber m; mot. Fahrer m, Chauffeur m; 🚂 Führer m.
driving| licence ['draiviŋ laisəns] Führerschein m; ~ school Fahrschule f
drizzle ['drizl] 1. Sprühregen m; 2. sprühen, nieseln.
drone [droun] 1. zo. Drohne f; fig. Faulenzer m; 2. summen; dröhnen.
droop [druːp] v/t. sinken lassen; v/i. schlaff niederhängen; den Kopf hängen lassen; (ver)welken; schwinden.
drop [drɔp] 1. Tropfen m; Fruchtbonbon m, n; Fall m; Falltür f; thea. Vorhang m; get (have) the ~ on Am. F zuvorkommen; 2. v/t. tropfen (lassen); niederlassen; fallen lassen; Brief einwerfen; Fahrgast absetzen; senken; ~ s.o. a few lines pl. j-m ein paar Zeilen schrei-

ben; v/i. tropfen; (herab)fallen; um-, hinsinken; ~ in unerwartet kommen.

dropsy ✶ ['drɔpsi] Wassersucht f.

drought [draut], **drouth** [drauθ] Trockenheit f, Dürre f.

drove [drouv] **1.** Trift f *Rinder*; Herde f (a. *fig.*); **2.** *pret. von* drive 2.

drown [draun] v/t. ertränken; überschwemmen; *fig.* übertäuben; übertönen; v/i. ertrinken.

drows|e [drauz] schlummern, schläfrig sein *od.* machen; **~y** ['drauzi] schläfrig; einschläfernd.

drudge [drʌdʒ] **1.** *fig.* Sklave m, Packesel m, Kuli m; **2.** sich (ab-) placken.

drug [drʌg] **1.** Droge f, Arzneiware f; Rauschgift n; unverkäufliche Ware; **2.** mit (schädlichen) Zutaten versetzen; Arznei *od.* Rauschgift geben (*dat.*) *od.* nehmen; **~gist** ['drʌgist] Drogist m; Apotheker m; **~store** *Am.* Drugstore m.

drum [drʌm] **1.** Trommel f; Trommelfell n; **2.** trommeln; **⁺~mer** ['drʌmə] Trommler m; *bsd. Am.* F Vertreter m.

drunk [drʌŋk] **1.** *p.p. von* drink 2; **2.** *adj.* (be)trunken; get ~ sich betrinken; **~ard** ['drʌŋkəd] Trinker m, Säufer m; **~en** *adj.* [~kən] (be-) trunken.

dry [drai] **1.** □ trocken; herb (*Wein*); F durstig; F antialkoholisch; ~ *goods pl. Am.* F Kurzwaren f/pl.; **2.** *Am.* F Alkoholgegner m; **3.** trocknen; dörren; ~ *up* austrocknen; verdunsten; **~clean** ['drai'kli:n] chemisch reinigen; **~-nurse** Kinderfrau f.

dual □ ['dju:(:)əl] doppelt; Doppel...

dubious □ ['dju:bjəs] zweifelhaft.

duchess ['dʌtʃis] Herzogin f.

duck [dʌk] **1.** *zo.* Ente f; *Am. sl.* Kerl m; Verbeugung f; Ducken n; (Segel)Leinen n; F Liebling m; **2.** (unter)tauchen; (sich) ducken; *Am. j-m* ausweichen.

duckling ['dʌkliŋ] Entchen n.

dude *Am.* [dju:d] Geck m; ~ *ranch Am.* Vergnügungsfarm f.

dudgeon ['dʌdʒən] Groll m.

due [dju:] **1.** schuldig; gebührend; gehörig; fällig; *in ~ time* zur rechten Zeit; be ~ to *j-m* gebühren; herrühren *od.* kommen von; be ~ to *inf.* sollen, müssen; *Am.* im Begriff sein zu; **2.** *adv.* ✥ gerade; genau; **3.** Schuldigkeit f; Recht n, Anspruch m; Lohn m; *mst ~s pl.* Abgabe(n *pl.*) f, Gebühr(en *pl.*) f; Beitrag m. **2.** sich duellieren.|

duel ['dju(:)əl] **1.** Zweikampf m;|

dug [dʌg] *pret. u. p.p. von* dig 1.

duke [dju:k] Herzog m; **~dom** ['dju:kdəm] Herzogtum n; Herzogswürde f.

dull [dʌl] **1.** □ dumm; träge;

schwerfällig; stumpf(sinnig); matt (*Auge etc.*); schwach (*Gehör*); langweilig; teilnahmslos; dumpf; trüb; ✝ flau; **2.** stumpf machen; *fig.* abstumpfen; (sich) trüben; **~ness** ['dʌlnis] Stumpfsinn m; Dummheit f; Schwerfälligkeit f; Mattheit f; Langweiligkeit f; Teilnahmslosigkeit f; Trübheit f; Flauheit f.

duly *adv.* ['dju:li] gehörig; richtig.

dumb □ [dʌm] stumm; sprachlos; *Am.* F doof, blöd; **~founded** [dʌm'faundid] sprachlos; **~waiter** ['dʌm'weitə] Drehtisch m; *Am.* Speisenaufzug m.

dummy ['dʌmi] Attrappe f; Schein m, Schwindel m; *fig.* Strohmann m; Statist m; *attr.* Schein...; Schwindel...

dump [dʌmp] **1.** v/t. auskippen; *Schutt etc.* abladen; *Waren zu* Schleuderpreisen ausführen; v/i. hinplumpsen; **2.** Klumpen m; Plumps m; Schuttabladestelle f; ✕ Munitionslager n; **~ing** ✝ ['dʌmpiŋ] Schleuderausfuhr f; **~s** *pl.*: (down) in the ~ F niedergeschlagen.

dun [dʌn] mahnen, drängen.

dunce [dʌns] Dummkopf m.

dune [dju:n] Düne f.

dung [dʌŋ] **1.** Dung m; **2.** düngen.

dungeon ['dʌndʒən] Kerker m.

dunk *Am.* F [dʌŋk] (ein)tunken.

dupe [dju:p] anführen, täuschen.

duplex □ ['dju:pleks] *attr.* Doppel...; *Am.* Zweifamilienhaus n.

duplic|ate 1. ['dju:plikit] doppelt; **2.** [~] Duplikat n; **3.** [~keit] doppelt ausfertigen; **~ity** [dju:(:)'plisiti] Doppelzüngigkeit f.

dura|ble □ ['djuərəbl] dauerhaft; **~tion** [djuə'reiʃən] Dauer f.

duress(e) [djuə'res] Zwang m.

during *prp.* ['djuəriŋ] während.

dusk [dʌsk] Halbdunkel n, Dämmerung f; **~y** □ ['dʌski] dämmerig, düster (*a. fig.*); schwärzlich.

dust [dʌst] **1.** Staub m; **2.** abstauben; bestreuen; **~bin** ['dʌstbin] Mülleimer m; **~ bowl** *Am.* Sandstaub-u. Dürregebiet n *im Westen der USA*; **~cart** Müllwagen m; **~er** [~tə] Staublappen m, -wedel m; *Am.* Staubmantel m; **~jacket** *Am.* Schutzumschlag m *e-s Buches*; **~man** Müllabfuhrmann m; **~y** □ [~ti] staubig.

Dutch [dʌtʃ] **1.** holländisch; ~ *treat Am.* F getrennte Rechnung; **2.** Holländisch n; the ~ die Holländer *pl.*

duty ['dju:ti] Pflicht f; Ehrerbietung f; Abgabe f, Zoll m; Dienst m; *off ~* dienstfrei; **~free** zollfrei.

dwarf [dwɔ:f] **1.** Zwerg m; **2.** in der Entwicklung hindern; verkleinern.

dwell [dwel] [*irr.*] wohnen; verweilen (on, upon bei); ~ (up)on bestehen auf (*acc.*); **~ing** ['dweliŋ] Wohnung f.

dwelt [dwelt] *pret. u. p.p. von* dwell.

dwindle ['dwindl] (dahin)schwin-den, abnehmen; (herab)sinken.

dye [dai] **1.** Farbe *f; of deepest ~ fig.* schlimmster Art; **2.** färben.

dying ['daiiŋ] **1.** □ sterbend; Sterbe...; **2.** Sterben *n.*

dynam|ic [dai'næmik] dynamisch, kraftgeladen; **~ics** [~ks] *mst sg.* Dynamik *f;* **~ite** ['dainəmait] **1.** Dynamit *n;* **2.** mit Dynamit sprengen.

dysentery ⚕ ['disntri] Ruhr *f.*

dyspepsia ⚕ [dis'pepsiə] Verdauungsstörung *f.*

E

each [i:tʃ] jede(r, -s); *~ other* einander, sich.

eager □ ['i:gə] (be)gierig; eifrig; **~ness** ['i:gənis] Begierde *f;* Eifer *m.*

eagle ['i:gl] Adler *m; Am.* Zehndollarstück *n;* **~-eyed** scharfsichtig.

ear [iə] Ahre *f;* Ohr *n;* Öhr *n,* Henkel *m; keep an ~ to the ground bsd. Am.* aufpassen, was die Leute sagen *od.* denken; **~-drum** ['iədrʌm] Trommelfell *n.*

earl [ə:l] *englischer* Graf.

early ['ə:li] früh; Früh...; Anfangs-...; erst; bald(ig); *as ~ as* schon in *(dat.).* [nen.]

ear-mark ['iəmɑːk] (kenn)zeich-

earn [ə:n] verdienen; einbringen.

earnest ['ə:nist] **1.** □ ernst(lich, -haft); ernstgemeint; **2.** Ernst *m.*

earnings ['ə:niŋz] Einkommen *n.*

ear|piece *teleph.* ['iəpi:s] Hörmuschel *f;* **~-shot** Hörweite *f.*

earth [ə:θ] **1.** Erde *f;* Land *n;* **2.** *v/t.* ⚡ erden; **~en** ['ə:θən] irden; **~enware** [~nwɛə] **1.** Töpferware *f;* Steingut *n;* **2.** irden; **~ing** ⚡ ['ə:θiŋ] Erdung *f;* **~ly** ['ə:θli] irdisch; **~quake** Erdbeben *n;* **~worm** Regenwurm *m.*

ease [i:z] **1.** Bequemlichkeit *f,* Behagen *n;* Ruhe *f;* Ungezwungenheit *f;* Leichtigkeit *f; at ~* bequem, behaglich; **2.** *v/t.* erleichtern; lindern; beruhigen; bequem(er) machen; *v/i.* sich entspannen *(Lage).*

easel ['i:zl] Staffelei *f.*

easiness ['i:zinis] = ease 1.

east [i:st] **1.** Ost(en *m*); Orient *m; the* ⚋ *Am.* die Oststaaten *der USA;* **2.** Ost...; östlich; ostwärts.

Easter ['i:stə] Ostern *n; attr.* Oster...

easter|ly ['i:stəli] östlich; Ost...; nach Osten; **~n** [~ən] = easterly; orientalisch; **~ner** [~nə] Ostländer (-in); Oriental|e *m,* -in *f;* ⚋ *Am.* Oststaatler(in).

eastward(s) ['i:stwəd(z)] ostwärts.

easy ['i:zi] □ leicht; bequem; frei von Schmerzen; ruhig; willig; ungezwungen; *in ~ circumstances* wohlhabend; *on ~ street Am.* in guten Verhältnissen; *take it ~!* immer mit der Ruhe!; **~ chair** Klubsessel *m;* **~-going** *fig.* bequem.

eat [i:t] **1.** [*irr.*] essen; (zer)fressen; **2.** *~s pl. Am. sl.* Essen *n,* Eßwaren *f/pl.;* **~ables** ['i:təblz] *pl.* Eßwaren *f/pl.;* **~en** ['i:tn] *p.p. von* eat 1.

eaves [i:vz] *pl.* Dachrinne *f,* Traufe *f;* **~drop** ['i:vzdrɔp] (er)lauschen; horchen.

ebb [eb] **1.** Ebbe *f; fig.* Abnahme *f;* Verfall *m;* **2.** verebben; *fig.* abnehmen, sinken; **~-tide** ['eb'taid] Ebbe *f.*

ebony ['ebəni] Ebenholz *n.*

ebullition [ebə'liʃən] Überschäumen *n;* Aufbrausen *n.*

eccentric [ik'sentrik] **1.** exzentrisch; *fig.* überspannt; **2.** Sonderling *m.*

ecclesiastic [ikli:zi'æstik] Geistliche(r) *m;* **~al** □ [~kəl] geistlich, kirchlich.

echo ['ekou] **1.** Echo *n;* **2.** widerhallen; *fig.* echoen, nachsprechen.

eclipse [i'klips] **1.** Finsternis *f;* **2.** (sich) verfinstern, verdunkeln.

econom|ic(al □) [i:kə'nɔmik(əl)] haushälterisch; wirtschaftlich; Wirtschafts...; **~ics** [~ks] *sg.* Volkswirtschaft(slehre) *f;* **~ist** [i(:)'kɔnəmist] Volkswirt *m;* **~ize** [~maiz] sparsam wirtschaften (mit); **~y** [~mi] Wirtschaft *f;* Wirtschaftlichkeit *f;* Einsparung *f; political ~* Volkswirtschaft(slehre) *f.*

ecsta|sy ['ekstəsi] Ekstase *f,* Verzückung *f;* **~tic** [eks'tætik] (~ally) verzückt

eddy ['edi] **1.** Wirbel *m;* **2.** wirbeln.

edge [edʒ] **1.** Schneide *f;* Schärfe *f;* Rand *m;* Kante *f; Tisch-*Ecke *f; be on ~* nervös sein; *have the ~ on s.o. bsd. Am.* F j-m über sein; **2.** schärfen; (um)säumen; (sich) drängen; **~ways, ~wise** ['edʒweiz, 'edʒwaiz] seitwärts; von der Seite.

edging [edʒiŋ] Einfassung *f;* Rand]

edgy [edʒi] scharf; F nervös. [*m.*]

edible [edibl] eßbar.

edict [i:dikt] Edikt *n.*

edifice [edifis] Gebäude *n.*

edifying ['edifaiiŋ] erbaulich.

edit ['edit] *Text* herausgeben, redigieren; *Zeitung* als Herausgeber leiten; **~ion** [i'diʃən] *Buch-*Ausgabe *f;* Auflage *f;* **~or** ['editə] Herausgeber *m;* Redakteur *m;* **~orial**

[edi'tɔ:riəl] Leitartikel *m*; *attr.* Redaktions...; **~orship** ['editəʃip] Schriftleitung *f*, Redaktion *f*.

educat|e ['edju(:)keit] erziehen; unterrichten; **~ion** [edju(:)'keiʃən] Erziehung *f*; (Aus)Bildung *f*; Erziehungs-, Schulwesen *n*; *Ministry of 2* Unterrichtsministerium *n*; **~ional** □ [~nl] erzieherisch; Erziehungs...; Bildungs...; **~or** ['edju:keitə] Erzieher *m*.

eel [i:l] Aal *m*.

efface [i'feis] auslöschen; *fig.* tilgen.

effect [i'fekt] 1. Wirkung *f*; Folge *f*; ⊕ Leistung *f*; **~s** *pl.* Effekten *pl.*; Habseligkeiten *f/pl.*; *be of ~* Wirkung haben; *take ~* in Kraft treten; *in ~* in der Tat; *to the ~ des* Inhalts; 2. bewirken, ausführen; **~ive** □ [~tiv] wirkend; wirksam; eindrucksvoll; wirklich vorhanden; ⊕ nutzbar; *~ date* Tag *m* des Inkrafttretens; **~ual** □ [~tjuəl] wirksam, kräftig.

effeminate □ [i'feminit] verweichlicht; weibisch.

effervesce [efə'ves] (auf)brausen; **~nt** [~snt] sprudelnd, schäumend.

effete [e'fi:t] verbraucht; entkräftet.

efficacy ['efikəsi] Wirksamkeit *f*, Kraft *f*.

efficien|cy [i'fiʃənsi] Leistung(sfähigkeit) *f*; **~** *expert Am.* Rationalisierungsfachmann *m*; **~t** □ [~nt] wirksam; leistungsfähig; tüchtig.

efflorescence [əflɔː'resns] Blütezeit *f*; ♣ Beschlag *m*.

effluence ['efluəns] Ausfluß *m*.

effort ['efət] Anstrengung *f*, Bemühung *f* (*at* um); Mühe *f*.

effrontery [e'frʌntəri] Frechheit *f*.

effulgent □ [e'fʌldʒənt] glänzend.

effus|ion [i'fju:ʒən] Erguß *m*; **~ive** □ [~:siv] überschwenglich.

egg¹ [eg] *mst ~ on* aufreizen.

egg² [~] Ei *n*; *put all one's ~s in one basket* alles auf eine Karte setzen; *as sure as ~s is ~s* F todsicher; **~cup** ['egkʌp] Eierbecher *m*; **~head** *Am. sl.* Intellektuelle(r) *m*.

egotism ['egoutizəm] Selbstgefälligkeit *f*.

egregious iro. □ [i'gri:dʒəs] ungeheuer.

egress ['i:grəs] Ausgang *m*; Ausweg *m*.

Egyptian [i'dʒipʃən] 1. ägyptisch; 2. Ägypter(in).

eider ['aidə]: **~** *down* Eiderdaunen *f/pl.*; Daunendecke *f*.

eight [eit] 1. acht; 2. Acht *f*; *behind the ~ ball Am.* in der (die) Klemme; **~een** ['ei'ti:n] achtzehn; **~eenth** [~nθ] achtzehnt; **~fold** ['eitfould] achtfach; **~h** [eitθ] 1. achte(r, -s); 2. Achtel *n*; **~hly** ['eitθli] achtens; **~ieth** ['eitiiθ] achtzigste(r, -s); **~y** ['eiti] achtzig.

either ['aiðə] 1. *adj. u. pron.* einer

von beiden; beide; 2. *cj.* **~** *... or* entweder oder; *not* (...) **~** auch nicht.

ejaculate [i'dʒækjuleit] *Worte, Flüssigkeit* ausstoßen.

eject [i(:) dʒekt] ausstoßen; vertreiben, ausweisen; entsetzen (*e-s Amtes*).

eke [i:k] **~** *out* ergänzen; verlängern; *sich mit et.* durchhelfen.

el *Am.* F [el] **~** *elevated railroad*.

elaborat|e 1. □ [i'læbərit] sorgfältig ausgearbeitet; kompliziert; 2. [~reit] sorgfältig ausarbeiten; **~eness** [~ritnis], **~ion** [ilæbə'reiʃən] sorgfältige Ausarbeitung.

elapse [i'læps] verfließen, verstreichen

elastic [i'læstik] 1. (**~ally**) dehnbar; spannkräftig; 2. Gummiband *n*; **~ity** [elæs'tisiti] Elastizität *f*, Dehnbarkeit *f*, Spannkraft *f*.

elate [i'leit] (er)heben, ermutigen, froh erregen, stolz machen; **~d** in gehobener Stimmung, freudig erregt (*at* über *acc.*; *with* durch).

elbow ['elbou] 1. Ellbogen *m*; Biegung *f*, ⊕ Knie *n*; *at one's ~* nahe, bei der Hand; *out at ~s fig.* heruntergekommen; 2. mit den Ellbogen (weg)stoßen; **~** *out* verdrängen; **~grease** F Armschmalz *n* (*Kraftanstrengung*).

elder ['eldə] 1. älter; 2. der, die Ältere, (Kirchen)Älteste(r) *m*; ♀ Holunder *m*; **~ly** [~əli] ältlich.

eldest ['eldist] älteste(r, -s).

elect [i'lekt] 1. (aus)gewählt; 2. (aus)er)wählen, aus [~kʃən] Wahl *f*; **~ive** [~ktiv] 1. **~** wählend; gewählt; Wahl...; *Am.* fakultativ; 2. *Am.* Wahlfach *n*; **~or** [~tə] Wähler *m*; *Am.* Wahlmann *m*; Kurfürst *m*; **~oral** [~ərəl] Wahl..., Wähler...; **~** *college Am.* Wahlmänner *m/pl.*; **~orate** [~rit] Wähler(schaft *f*) *m/pl.*

electric|(al □) [i'lektrik(əl)] elektrisch; Elektro...; *fig.* faszinierend; **~al engineer** Elektrotechniker *m*; **~** *blue* stahlblau; **~** *chair* elektrischer Stuhl; **~ian** [ilek'triʃən] Elektriker *m*; **~ity** [~isiti] Elektrizität *f*.

electri|fy [i'lektrifai], **~ze** [~raiz] elektrifizieren; elektrisieren.

electro|cute [i'lektrəkju:t] *auf dem elektrischen Stuhl* hinrichten; *durch elektrischen Strom* töten; **~metallurgy** Elektrometallurgie *f*.

electron [i'lektrɔn] Elektron *n*; **~-ray tube** magisches Auge.

electro|plate [i'lektroupleit] galvanisch versilbern; **~type** galvanischer Druck, Galvano *n*.

elegan|ce ['eligəns] Eleganz *f*; Anmut *f*, **~t** □ [~nt] elegant; geschmackvoll; *Am.* erstklassig.

element ['elimənt] Element *n*; Urstoff *m*; (Grund)Bestandteil *m*; **~s** *pl.* Anfangsgründe *m/pl.*; **~al** □

[eli'mentl] elementar; wesentlich; ~ary [~təri] 1. ☐ elementar; Anfangs...; ~ school Volks-, Grundschule f; 2. elementaries pl. Anfangsgründe m/pl.

elephant ['elifənt] Elefant m.

elevat|e ['eliveit] erhöhen; fig. erheben; ~ed erhaben; ~ (railroad) Am. Hochbahn f; ~ion [eli'veiʃən] Erhebung f, Erhöhung f; Höhe f; Erhabenheit f; ~or ⊕ ['eliveitə] Aufzug m; Am. Fahrstuhl m; ✍ Höhenruder n; (grain) ~ Am. Getreidespeicher m.

eleven [i'levn] 1. elf; 2. Elf f; ~th [~nθ] elfte(r, -s).

elf [elf] Elf(e f) m, Kobold m; Zwerg m.

elicit [i'lisit] hervorlocken, herausholen.

eligible ☐ ['elidʒəbl] geeignet, annehmbar; passend.

eliminat|e [i'limineit] aussondern, ausscheiden; ausmerzen; ~ion [ilimi'neiʃən] Aussonderung f; Ausscheidung f.

élite [ei'liːt] Elite f; Auslese f.

elk zo. [elk] Elch m.

ellipse A [i'lips] Ellipse f.

elm ♀ [elm] Ulme f, Rüster f.

elocution [elə'kjuːʃən] Vortrag(skunst, -sweise f) m.

elongate ['iːlɔŋgeit] verlängern.

elope [i'loup] entlaufen, durchgehen.

eloquen|ce ['eləkwəns] Beredsamkeit f; ~t ☐ [~nt] beredt.

else [els] sonst, andere(r, -s), weiter; ~where ['elsweə] anderswo(hin).

elucidat|e [i'luːsideit] erläutern; ~ion [iluːsi'deiʃən] Aufklärung f.

elude [i'luːd] geschickt umgehen; ausweichen, sich entziehen (dat.).

elus|ive [i'luːsiv] schwer faßbar; ~ory [~səri] trügerisch.

emaciate [i'meiʃieit] abzehren, ausmergeln.

emanat|e ['eməneit] ausströmen; ausgehen (from von); ~ion [emə'neiʃən] Ausströmen n; fig. Ausstrahlung f.

emancipat|e [i'mænsipeit] emanzipieren, befreien; ~ion [imænsi'peiʃən] Emanzipation f; Befreiung f.

embalm [im'baːm] (ein)balsamieren; be ~ed in fortleben in (dat.).

embankment [im'bæŋkmənt] Eindämmung f; Deich m; (Bahn-) Damm m; Uferstraße f, Kai m.

embargo [em'baːgou] (Hafen-, Handels)Sperre f, Beschlagnahme f.

embark [im'baːk] (sich) einschiffen (for nach); Geld anlegen; sich einlassen (in, on, upon in, auf acc.).

embarrass [im'bærəs] (be)hindern; verwirren; in (Geld)Verlegenheit bringen; verwickeln; ~ing ☐ [~siŋ]

unangenehm; unbequem; ~ment [~smənt] (Geld)Verlegenheit f; Schwierigkeit f.

embassy ['embəsi] Botschaft f; Gesandtschaft f.

embed [im'bed] (ein)betten, lagern.

embellish [im'beliʃ] verschönern; ausschmücken. [Asche.\]

embers ['embəz] pl. glühende\

embezzle [im'bezl] unterschlagen; ~ment [~lmənt] Unterschlagung f.

embitter [im'bitə] verbittern.

emblazon [im'bleizən] mit e-m Wappenbild bemalen; fig. verherrlichen.

emblem ['embləm] Sinnbild n; Wahrzeichen n.

embody [im'bɔdi] verkörpern; vereinigen; einverleiben (in dat.).

embolden [im'bouldən] ermutigen.

embolism ✚ ['embəlizəm] Embolie f.

embosom [im'buzəm] ins Herz schließen; ~ed with umgeben von.

emboss [im'bɔs] bossieren; mit dem Hammer treiben.

embrace [im'breis] 1. (sich) umarmen; umfassen; Beruf etc. ergreifen; Angebot annehmen; 2. Umarmung f.

embroider [im'brɔidə] sticken; ausschmücken; ~y [~əri] Stickerei f.

embroil [im'brɔil] (in Streit) verwickeln; verwirren.

emendation [iːmen'deiʃən] Verbesserung f.

emerald ['emərəld] Smaragd m.

emerge [i'məːdʒ] auftauchen; hervorgehen; sich erheben; sich zeigen; ~ncy [~dʒənsi] unerwartetes Ereignis; Notfall m; attr. Not...; ~ brake Notbremse f; ~ call Notruf m; ~ exit Notausgang m; ~ man Sport: Ersatzmann m; ~nt [~nt] auftauchend, entstehend; ~ countries Entwicklungsländer n/pl.

emersion [i(ː)'məːʃən] Auftauchen n.

emigra|nt ['emigrənt] 1. auswandernd; 2. Auswanderer m; ~te [~reit] auswandern; ~tion [emi'greiʃən] Auswanderung f.

eminen|ce ['eminəns] (An)Höhe f; Auszeichnung f; hohe Stellung; Eminenz f (Titel); ☐ [~nt] fig. ausgezeichnet, hervorragend; ~tly [~tli] ganz besonders.

emissary ['emisəri] Emissär m.

emit [i'mit] von sich geben; aussenden, ausströmen; ✝ ausgeben.

emolument [i'mɔljumənt] Vergütung f; ~s pl. Einkünfte pl.

emotion [i'mouʃən] (Gemüts)Bewegung f; Gefühl(sregung f) n; Rührung f; ~al ☐ [~nl] gefühlsmäßig; gefühlvoll, gefühlsbetont; ~less [~nlis] gefühllos, kühl.

emperor ['empərə] Kaiser m.

empha|sis ['emfəsis] Nachdruck *m*; **~size** [~saiz] nachdrücklich betonen; **~tic** [im'fætik] (~ally) nachdrücklich; ausgesprochen.

empire ['empaiə] (Kaiser)Reich *n*; Herrschaft *f*; *the British* ⊆ das britische Weltreich.

empirical ☐ [em'pirikəl] erfahrungsgemäß.

employ [im'plɔi] **1.** beschäftigen, anstellen; an-, verwenden, gebrauchen; **2.** Beschäftigung *f*; *in the ~ of* angestellt bei; **~ee** [emplɔi'i:] Angestellte(r *m*) *f*; Arbeitnehmer(in); **~er** [im'plɔiə] Arbeitgeber *m*; ✝ Auftraggeber *m*; **~ment** [~imənt] Beschäftigung *f*; Arbeit *f*; **~ agency** Stellenvermittlungsbüro *n*; ⊆ *Exchange* Arbeitsamt *n*.

empower [im'pauə] ermächtigen; befähigen.

empress ['empris] Kaiserin *f*.

empt|iness ['emptinis] Leere *f*; Hohlheit *f*; **~y** ☐ ['empti] **1.** leer; *fig.* hohl; **2.** (sich) (aus-, ent)leeren.

emul|ate ['emjuleit] wetteifern mit; nacheifern, es gleichtun (*dat.*); **~ation** [emju'leiʃən] Wetteifer *m*.

enable [i'neibl] befähigen, es *i-m* ermöglichen; ermächtigen.

enact [i'nækt] verfügen, verordnen; *Gesetz* erlassen; *thea.* spielen.

enamel [i'næməl] **1.** Email(le *f*) *n*, (Zahn)Schmelz *m*; Glasur *f*; Lack *m*; **2.** emaillieren; glasieren.

enamo(u)r [i'næmə] verliebt machen; **~ed** *of* verliebt in.

encamp ⚔ [in'kæmp] (sich) lagern.

encase [in'keis] einschließen.

enchain [in'tʃein] anketten; fesseln.

enchant [in'tʃɑint] bezaubern; **~ment** [~tmənt] Bezauberung *f*; Zauber *m*; **~ress** [~tris] Zauberin *f*.

encircle [in'sə:kl] einkreisen.

enclos|e [in'klouz] einzäunen; einschließen; beifügen; **~ure** [~ouʒə] Einzäunung *f*; eingehegtes Grundstück; Bei-, Anlage *f zu e-m Brief*.

encompass [in'kʌmpəs] umgeben.

encore *thea.* [ɔŋ'kɔ:] **1.** um e-e Zugabe bitten; **2.** Zugabe *f*.

encounter [in'kauntə] **1.** Begegnung *f*; Gefecht *n*; **2.** begegnen (*dat.*); auf *Schwierigkeiten etc.* stoßen; mit *j-m* zs.-stoßen.

encourage [in'kʌridʒ] ermutigen; fördern; **~ment** [~idʒmənt] Ermutigung *f*; Unterstützung *f*.

encroach [in'kroutʃ] (*on, upon*) eingreifen, eindringen (in *acc.*); beschränken (*acc.*); mißbrauchen (*acc.*); **~ment** [~ʃmənt] Ein-, Übergriff *m*.

encumb|er [in'kʌmbə] belasten; (be)hindern; **~rance** [~brəns] Last *f*; *fig.* Hindernis *n*; Schuldenlast *f*; *without* ~ ohne (Familien)Anhang.

encyclop(a)edia [ensaiklou'pi:djə]

Enzyklopädie *f*, Konversationslexikon *n*.

end [end] **1.** Ende *n*; Ziel *n*, Zweck *m*; *no* ~ *of* unendlich viel(e), unzählige; *in the* ~ am Ende, auf die Dauer; *on* ~ aufrecht; *stand on* ~ zu Berge stehen; *to no* ~ vergebens; *go off the deep* ~ *fig.* in die Luft gehen; *make both* ~*s meet* gerade auskommen; **2.** enden, beend(ig)en.

endanger [in'deindʒə] gefährden.

endear [in'diə] teuer machen; **~ment** [~mənt] Liebkosung *f*, Zärtlichkeit *f*.

endeavo(u)r [in'devə] **1.** Bestreben *n*, Bemühung *f*; **2.** sich bemühen.

end|ing ['endiŋ] Ende *n*; Schluß *m*; *gr.* Endung *f*; **~less** ☐ ['endlis] endlos, unendlich; ⊕ ohne Ende.

endorse [in'dɔ:s] ✝ indossieren; *et.* vermerken (*on* auf der Rückseite *e-r Urkunde*); gutheißen; **~ment** [~smənt] Aufschrift *f*; ✝ Indossament *n*.

endow [in'dau] ausstatten; **~ment** [~aumənt] Ausstattung *f*; Stiftung *f*.

endue *fig.* [in'dju:] (be)kleiden.

endur|ance [in'djuərəns] (Aus-) Dauer *f*; Ertragen *n*; **~e** [in'djuə] (aus)dauern; ertragen.

enema ⚕ ['enimə] Klistier(spritze *f*) *n*.

enemy ['enimi] **1.** Feind *m*; *the* ⊆ der Teufel; **2.** feindlich.

energ|etic [enə'dʒetik] (~ally) energisch, **~y** ['enədʒi] Energie *f*.

enervate ['enə:veit] entnerven.

enfeeble [in'fi:bl] schwächen.

enfold [in'fould] einhüllen; umfassen.

enforce [in'fɔ:s] erzwingen; aufzwingen (*upon dat.*); bestehen auf (*dat.*); durchführen; **~ment** [~smənt] Erzwingung *f*; Geltendmachung *f*; Durchführung *f*.

enfranchise [in'fræntʃaiz] das Wahlrecht verleihen (*dat.*); *Sklaven* befreien

engage [in'geidʒ] *v/t.* anstellen; verpflichten; mieten; in Anspruch nehmen; ⚔ angreifen; *be ~d* verlobt sein (*to* mit); beschäftigt sein (*in* mit); besetzt sein; ~ *the clutch* einkuppeln; *v/i.* sich verpflichten, versprechen, garantieren; sich beschäftigen (*in* mit); ⚔ angreifen; ⊕ greifen (*Zahnräder*); **~ment** [~dʒmənt] Verpflichtung *f*; Verlobung *f*; Verabredung *f*; Beschäftigung *f*; ⚔ Gefecht *n*; Einrücken *n e-s Ganges etc.*

engaging ☐ [in'geidʒiŋ] einnehmend.

engender *fig.* [in'dʒendə] erzeugen.

engine [in'endʒin] Maschine *f*, Motor *m*; 🚂 Lokomotive *f*; **~driver** Lokomotivführer *m*.

engineer [endʒi'niə] **1.** Ingenieur *m*,

Techniker *m*; Maschinist *m*; *Am.* Lokomotivführer *m*; ✕ Pionier *m*; **2.** Ingenieur sein; bauen; ⁓ing [⁓ɔriŋ] **1.** Maschinenbau *m*; Ingenieurwesen *n*; **2.** technisch; Ingenieur...

English [ˈiŋgliʃ] **1.** englisch; **2.** Englisch *n*; the ⁓ *pl.* die Engländer *pl.*; in plain ⁓ *fig.* unverblümt; ⁓man Engländer *m*.

engrav|e [inˈgreiv] gravieren, stechen; *fig.* einprägen; ⁓er [⁓və] Graveur *m*; ⁓ing [⁓viŋ] (Kupfer-, Stahl)Stich *m*; Holzschnitt *m*.

engross [inˈgrous] an sich ziehen; ganz in Anspruch nehmen.

engulf *fig.* [inˈgʌlf] verschlingen.

enhance [inˈhɑːns] erhöhen.

enigma [iˈnigmə] Rätsel *n*; ⁓tic(al □) [enigˈmætik(əl)] rätselhaft.

enjoin [inˈdʒɔin] auferlegen (*on j-m*).

enjoy [inˈdʒɔi] sich erfreuen an (*dat.*); genießen; *did you ⁓ it?* hat es Ihnen gefallen?; ⁓ *o.s.* sich amüsieren; *I ⁓ my dinner* es schmeckt mir; ⁓able [⁓ɔiəbl] genußreich, erfreulich; ⁓ment [⁓ɔimənt] Genuß *m*, Freude *f*.

enlarge [inˈlɑːdʒ] (sich) erweitern, ausdehnen; vergrößern; ⁓ment [⁓dʒmənt] Erweiterung *f*; Vergrößerung *f*.

enlighten [inˈlaitn] *fig.* erleuchten; *j-n* aufklären; ⁓ment [⁓nmənt] Aufklärung *f*.

enlist [inˈlist] *v/t.* anwerben; gewinnen; ⁓*ed men pl. Am.* ✕ Unteroffiziere *pl.* und Mannschaften *pl.*; *v/i.* sich freiwillig melden.

enliven [inˈlaivn] beleben.

enmity [ˈenmiti] Feindschaft *f*.

ennoble [iˈnoubl] adeln; veredeln.

enorm|ity [iˈnɔːmiti] Ungeheuerlichkeit *f*; ⁓ous □ [⁓məs] ungeheuer.

enough [iˈnʌf] genug.

enquire [inˈkwaiə] = *inquire.*

enrage [inˈreidʒ] wütend machen; ⁓d wütend (*at über acc.*).

enrapture [inˈræptʃə] entzücken.

enrich [inˈritʃ] be-, anreichern.

enrol(l) [inˈroul] *in e-e* Liste eintragen; ✕ anwerben; aufnehmen; ⁓ment [⁓lmənt] Eintragung *f*; *bsd.* ✕ Anwerbung *f*, Einstellung *f*; Aufnahme *f*; Verzeichnis *n*; Schüler-, Studenten-, Teilnehmerzahl *f*.

ensign [ˈensain] Fahne *f*; Flagge *f*; Abzeichen *n*; ⚓ *Am.* [ˈensn] Leutnant *m* zur See.

enslave [inˈsleiv] versklaven; ⁓ment [⁓vmənt] Versklavung *f*.

ensnare *fig.* [inˈsnɛə] verführen.

ensue [inˈsjuː] folgen, sich ergeben.

ensure [inˈʃuə] sichern.

entail [inˈteil] **1.** zur Folge haben; als unveräußerliches Gut vererben; **2.** (Übertragung *f* als) unveräußerliches Gut.

entangle [inˈtæŋgl] verwickeln; ⁓ment [⁓lmənt] Verwicklung *f*; ✕ Draht-Verhau *m*.

enter [ˈentə] *v/t.* (ein)treten in (*acc.*); betreten; einsteigen, einfahren etc. in (*acc.*); eindringen in (*acc.*); eintragen, ✝ buchen; *Protest* einbringen; aufnehmen; melden; ⁓ *s.o. at school* j-n zur Schule anmelden; *v/i.* eintreten; sich einschreiben; *Sport:* sich melden; aufgenommen werden; ⁓ *into fig.* eingehen auf (*acc.*); ⁓ (*up*)*on Amt etc.* antreten; sich einlassen auf (*acc.*).

enterpris|e [ˈentəpraiz] Unternehmen *n*; Unternehmungslust *f*; ⁓ing □ [⁓ziŋ] unternehmungslustig.

entertain [entəˈtein] unterhalten; bewirten; in Erwägung ziehen; *Meinung etc.* hegen; ⁓er [⁓nə] Gastgeber *m*; Unterhaltungskünstler *m*; ⁓ment [⁓nmənt] Unterhaltung *f*; Bewirtung *f*; Fest *n*, Gesellschaft *f*.

enthral(l) *fig.* [inˈθrɔːl] bezaubern.

enthrone [inˈθroun] auf den Thron setzen.

enthusias|m [inˈθjuːziæzəm] Begeisterung *f*; ⁓t [⁓æst] Schwärmer (-in); ⁓tic [inθjuːziˈæstik] (⁓ally) begeistert (*at, about* von).

entice [inˈtais] (ver)locken; ⁓ment [⁓mənt] Verlockung *f*, Reiz *m*.

entire □ [inˈtaiə] ganz; vollständig; ungeteilt; ⁓ly [⁓əli] völlig; lediglich; ⁓ty [⁓əti] Gesamtheit *f*.

entitle [inˈtaitl] betiteln; berechtigen.

entity [ˈentiti] Wesen *n*; Dasein *n*.

entrails [ˈentreilz] *pl.* Eingeweide *n/pl.*; Innere(s) *n*.

entrance [ˈentrəns] Ein-, Zutritt *m*; Einfahrt *f*, Eingang *m*; Einlaß *m*.

entrap [inˈtræp] (ein)fangen; verleiten.

entreat [inˈtriːt] bitten, ersuchen; *et.* erbitten; ⁓y [⁓ti] Bitte *f*, Gesuch *n*.

entrench ✕ [inˈtrentʃ] (mit *od.* in Gräben) verschanzen.

entrust [inˈtrʌst] anvertrauen (*s. th. to s.o.* j-m et.); betrauen.

entry [ˈentri] Eintritt *m*; Eingang *m*; ⚖ Besitzantritt *m* (*on, upon gen.*); Eintragung *f*; *Sport:* Meldung *f*; ⁓ *permit* Einreisegenehmigung *f*; *book-keeping by double (single)* ⁓ doppelte (einfache) Buchführung.

enumerate [iˈnjuːməreit] aufzählen.

enunciate [iˈnʌnsieit] verkünden; *Lehrsatz* aufstellen; aussprechen.

envelop [inˈveləp] einhüllen; einwickeln; umgeben; ✕ einkreisen; ⁓e [ˈenviloup] Briefumschlag *m*; ⁓ment [inˈveləpmənt] Umhüllung *f*.

envi|able □ [ˈenviəbl] beneidenswert; ⁓ous □ [⁓iəs] neidisch.

environ [in'vaiərən] umgeben; ~ment [ʌnmənt] Umgebung f e-r Person; ~s ['environz] pl. Umgebung f e-r Stadt.

envisage [in'vizidʒ] sich et. vorstellen.

envoy ['envɔi] Gesandte(r) m; Bote m.

envy ['envi] 1. Neid m; 2. beneiden.

epic ['epik] 1. episch; 2. Epos n.

epicure ['epikjuə] Feinschmecker m.

epidemic [epi'demik] 1. (~ally) seuchenartig; ~ disease = 2. Seuche f.

epidermis [epi'dɔːmis] Oberhaut f.

epilepsy ['epilepsi] Epilepsie f.

epilogue ['epilog] Nachwort n.

episcopa|cy [i'piskəpəsi] bischöfliche Verfassung; ~l [~əl] bischöflich; ~te [~pit] Bischofswürde f; Bistum n.

epist|le [i'pisl] Epistel f; ~olary [ʌstələri] brieflich; Brief...

epitaph ['epitaːf] Grabschrift f.

epitome [i'pitəmi] Auszug m, Abriß m.

epoch ['iːpɔk] Epoche f.

equable [ː ['ekwəbl] gleichförmig, gleichmäßig; fig. gleichmütig.

equal ['iːkwəl] 1. ☐ gleich, gleichmäßig; ~ to fig. gewachsen (dat.); 2. Gleiche(r) m f; 3. gleichen (dat.); ~ity [i(ː)'kwɔliti] Gleichheit f, ~ization [iːkwəlai'zeiʃən] Gleichstellung f; Ausgleich m; ~ize ['iːkwəlaiz] gleichmachen, gleichstellen; ausgleichen.

equanimity [iːkwə'nimiti] Gleichmut m.

equat|ion [i'kweiʃən] Ausgleich m; A Gleichung f; ~or [~eitə] Äquator m.

equestrian [i'kwestriən] Reiter m.

equilibrium [iːkwi'libriəm] Gleichgewicht n, Ausgleich m.

equip [i'kwip] ausrüsten; ~ment [~pmənt] Ausrüstung f; Einrichtung f.

equipoise ['ekwipɔiz] Gleichgewicht n; Gegengewicht n.

equity ['ekwiti] Billigkeit f; equities pl. ✝ Aktien f/pl.

equivalent [i'kwivələnt] 1. gleichwertig, gleichbedeutend (to mit); 2. Äquivalent n, Gegenwert m.

equivoca|l [ː [i'kwivəkəl] zweideutig, zweifelhaft; ~te [~keit] zweideutig reden.

era ['iərə] Zeitrechnung f; -alter n.

eradicate [i'rædikeit] ausrotten.

eras|e [i'reiz] ausradieren, ausstreichen; auslöschen; ~er [~zə] Radiergummi m; ~ure [i'reizə] Ausradieren n; radierte Stelle.

ere [eə] 1. cj. ehe, bevor; 2. prp. vor.

erect [i'rekt] 1. ☐ aufrecht; 2. aufrichten, Denkmal etc. errichten, aufstellen; ~ion [~kʃən] Auf-, Errichtung f; Gebäude n.

eremite ['erimait] Einsiedler m.

ermine zo ['ɔːmin] Hermelin m.

erosion [i'rouʒən] Zerfressen n; Auswaschung f.

erotic [i rɔtik] 1. erotisch; 2. erotisches Gedicht; ~ism [~isizəm] Erotik f

err [əː] (sich) irren; fehlen, sündigen.

errand ['erənd] Botengang m, Auftrag m ~-boy Laufbursche m.

errant ['erənt] (umher)irrend.

errat|ik [i rætik] (~ally) wandernd; unberechenbar, ~um [e'raːtəm], pl. ~a [~tə] Druckfehler m.

erroneous [i'rouniəs] irrig.

error [erə] Irrtum m, Fehler m; ~s excepted Irrtümer vorbehalten.

erudit|e ['eru(ː)dait] gelehrt; ~ion [eru' diʃən] Gelehrsamkeit f.

erupt [i rʌpt] ausbrechen (Vulkan); durchbrechen (Zähne); ~ion [~pʃən] Vulkan-Ausbruch m; ✍ Hautausschlag m

escala|tion [eskə'leiʃən] Eskalation f (stufenweise Steigerung); ~or ['eskələtə] Rolltreppe f

escap|ade [eskə peid] toller Streich; ~e [is'keip] 1. entschlüpfen, entgehen; entkommen, entrinnen, entweichen; ~ entfallen, 2. Entrinnen n, Entweichen n; Flucht f.

eschew [is tʃuː] (ver)meiden.

escort 1. [eskɔːt] Eskorte f; Geleit n; 2. [is kɔːt] eskortieren, geleiten.

escutcheon [is'kʌtʃən] Wappenschild m; ~ Namenschild n.

especial [i pefəl] besonder; vorzüglich ~ly [~li] besonders.

espionage [espiə'naːʒ] Spionage f.

espresso [es'presou] Espresso m (Kaffee), ~ bar, ~ café Espressobar f

espy [is pai] erspähen.

esquire [is'kwaiə] Landedelmann m, Gutsbesitzer m, auf Briefen: John Smith Esq Herrn J. S.

essay 1. [e sei] versuchen; probieren; 2. [esei] Versuch m; Aufsatz m, kurz Abhandlung, Essay m, n.

essen|ce ['esns] Wesen n e-r Sache; Extrakt m Essenz f, ~tial [i'senʃəl] 1. [ː (to tut) wesentlich; wichtig; 2. Wesentliche(s) n

establish [is tæbliʃ] festsetzen; errichten, gründen; einrichten; einsetzen o.s sich niederlassen; ~ed Church Staatskirche f; ~ment [~ʃmənt] Festsetzung f; Gründung f; Er-, Einrichtung f; (bsd. großer) Haushalt, Anstalt f; Firma f.

estate [is teit] Grundstück n; Grundbesitz m, Gut n; Besitz m; (Konkurs)Masse f, Nachlaß m; Stand m real ~ Liegenschaften pl.; housing ~ Wohnsiedlung f; ~ agent Grundstucksmakler m; ~ car Kombiwagen m, ~ duty Nachlaßsteuer f.

esteem [is'tiːm] 1. Achtung f, Ansehen n (with bei); 2. (hoch)achten, (hoch)schätzen; erachten für.

estimable ['estiməbl] schätzenswert.

estimat|e 1. ['estimeit] (ab)schätzen; veranschlagen; 2. [˷mit] Schätzung f; (Vor)Anschlag m; **˷ion** [esti'meiʃən] Schätzung f; Meinung f; Achtung f.

estrange [is'treindʒ] entfremden.

estuary ['estjuəri] (den Gezeiten ausgesetzte) weite Flußmündung.

etch [etʃ] ätzen, radieren.

etern|al □ [i(:)'tə:nl] immerwährend, ewig; **˷ity** [˷niti] Ewigkeit f.

ether ['i:θə] Äther m; **˷eal** □ [i(:)'θiəriəl] ätherisch (a. fig.).

ethic|al □ ['eθikəl] sittlich, ethisch; **˷s** [˷ks] sg. Sittenlehre f, Ethik f.

etiquette [eti'ket] Etikette f.

etymology [eti'mɔlədʒi] Etymologie f, Wortableitung f.

Eucharist ['ju:kərist] Abendmahl n.

euphemism ['ju:fimizəm] beschönigender Ausdruck.

European [juərə'pi(:)ən] 1. europäisch; 2. Europäer(in).

evacuate [i'vækjueit] entleeren; evakuieren; Land etc. räumen.

evade [i'veid] (geschickt) ausweichen (dat.); umgehen.

evaluate [i'væljueit] zahlenmäßig bestimmen, auswerten; berechnen.

evanescent [i:və'nesnt] (ver)schwindend. [evangelisch.]

evangelic(al □) [i:væn'dʒelik(əl)]\

evaporat|e [i'væpəreit] verdunsten, verdampfen (lassen); **˷ion** [ivæpə'reiʃən] Verdunstung f, Verdampfung f.

evasi|on [i'veiʒən] Umgehung f; Ausflucht f; **˷ve** □ [i'veisiv] ausweichend; **˷ be** ˷ ausweichen.

eve [i:v] Vorabend m; Vortag m; on the ˷ of unmittelbar vor (dat.), am Vorabend (gen.).

even ['i:vən] 1. adj. □ eben, gleich; gleichmäßig; ausgeglichen; glatt; gerade (Zahl); unparteiisch; get ˷ with s.o. fig. mit j-m abrechnen; 2. adv. selbst, sogar, auch; not ˷ nicht einmal; ˷ though, ˷ if wenn auch; 3. ebnen, glätten; gleichstellen; **˷-handed** unparteiisch.

evening ['i:vniŋ] Abend m; ˷ dress Gesellschaftsanzug m; Frack m, Smoking m; Abendkleid n.

evenness ['i:vənnis] Ebenheit f; Geradheit f; Gleichmäßigkeit f; Unparteilichkeit f; Seelenruhe f.

evensong ['i:vənsɔŋ] Abendgottesdienst m.

event [i'vent] Ereignis n; Vorfall m; fig. Ausgang m; sportliche Veranstaltung; athletic ˷s pl. Leichtathletikwettkämpfe m/pl.; at all ˷s auf alle Fälle; in the ˷ of im Falle (gen.); **˷ful** [˷tful] ereignisreich.

eventual □ [i'ventjuəl] etwaig, möglich; schließlich; **˷ly** am Ende; im Laufe der Zeit; gegebenenfalls.

ever ['evə] je, jemals; immer; ˷ so noch so (sehr); as soon as ˷ I can sobald ich nur irgend kann; ˷ after, ˷ since von der Zeit an; ˷ and anon von Zeit zu Zeit; for ˷ für immer, auf ewig; Briefschluß: yours ˷ stets Dein ...; **˷glade** Am. Sumpfsteppe f; **˷green** 1. immergrün; 2. immergrüne Pflanze; **˷lasting** □ [evə-'la:stiŋ] ewig; dauerhaft; **˷more** ['evə'mɔ:] immerfort.

every ['evri] jede(r, -s); alle(s); ˷ now and then dann und wann; ˷ one of them jeder von ihnen; ˷ other day einen Tag um den anderen, jeden zweiten Tag; **˷body** jeder (-mann); **˷day** Alltags...; **˷one** jeder(mann); **˷thing** alles; **˷where** überall.

evict [i(:)'vikt] exmittieren; ausweisen.

eviden|ce [evidəns] 1. Beweis(material n) m; ½½ Zeugnis n; Zeuge m; in ˷ als Beweis; deutlich sichtbar; 2. beweisen; **˷t** □ [˷nt] augenscheinlich, offenbar, klar.

evil ['i:vl] 1. □ übel, schlimm, böse; the ☿ One der Böse (Teufel); 2. Übel n, Böse(s) n; **˷-minded** ['i:vl'maindid] übelgesinnt, boshaft.

evince [i'vins] zeigen, bekunden.

evoke [i'vouk] (herauf)beschwören.

evolution [i:və'lu:ʃən] Entwicklung f; ✕ Entfaltung f e-r Formation.

evolve [i'vɔlv] (sich) entwickeln.

ewe [ju:] Mutterschaf n.

ex [eks] prp. ✝ ab Fabrik etc.; Börse: ohne; aus.

ex-... [˷] ehemalig, früher.

exact [ig'zækt] 1. □ genau; pünktlich; 2. Zahlung eintreiben; fordern; **˷ing** [˷tiŋ] streng, genau; **˷itude** [˷itju:d], **˷ness** [˷tnis] Genauigkeit f; Pünktlichkeit f.

exaggerate [ig'zædʒəreit] übertreiben.

exalt [ig'zɔ:lt] erhöhen, erheben; verherrlichen; **˷ation** [egzɔ:l'teiʃən] Erhöhung f, Erhebung f; Höhe f; Verzückung f.

exam Schul-sl. [ig'zæm] Examen n.

examin|ation [igzæmi'neiʃən] Examen n, Prüfung f; Untersuchung f; Vernehmung f; **˷e** [ig'zæmin] untersuchen; prüfen, verhören.

example [ig'za:mpl] Beispiel n; Vorbild n, Muster n; for ˷ zum Beispiel.

exasperate [ig'za:spəreit] erbittern; ärgern; verschlimmern.

excavate ['ekskəveit] ausgraben, ausheben, ausschachten.

exceed [ik'si:d] überschreiten; übertreffen; zu weit gehen; **˷ing** [˷diŋ] übermäßig; **˷ingly** [˷ŋli] außerordentlich, überaus.

excel [ik'sel] *v/t.* übertreffen; *v/i.* sich auszeichnen; **~lence** ['eksələns] Vortrefflichkeit *f*; hervorragende Leistung; Vorzug *m*; **~lency** [~si] Exzellenz *f*; **~lent** □ [~nt] vortrefflich

except [ik'sept] **1.** ausnehmen; *et.* einwenden; **2.** *prp.* ausgenommen, außer; **~ for** abgesehen von, **~ing** *prp.* [~tiŋ] ausgenommen; **~ion** [~pʃən] Ausnahme *f*; Einwendung *f* (to gegen); *by way of* **~** ausnahmsweise; *take* **~** *to* Anstoß nehmen an (*dat.*); **~ional** [~nl] außergewöhnlich; **~ionally** [~ʃnəli] un-, außergewöhnlich.

excerpt ['eksə:pt] Auszug *m*.

excess [ik'ses] Übermaß *n*; Überschuß *m*; Ausschweifung *f*; *attr.* Mehr...; **~ fare** Zuschlag *m*; **~ luggage** Übergewicht *n* (*Gepäck*); **~ postage** Nachgebühr *f*; **~ive** □ [~siv] übermäßig, übertrieben.

exchange [iks'tʃeindʒ] **1.** (aus-, ein-, um)tauschen (for gegen); wechseln; **2.** (Aus-, Um)Tausch *m*; (*bsd.* Geld)Wechsel *m*; *a. bill of* **~** Wechsel *m*; *a.* ♀ Börse *f*; Fernsprechamt *n*; *foreign* **~s** (*spl.*) Devisen *f/pl.*; (*rate of*) **~** Wechselkurs *m*.

exchequer [iks'tʃekə] Schatzamt *n*; Staatskasse *f*; *Chancellor of the* ♀ (britischer) Schatzkanzler, Finanzminister *m*.

excise¹ [ek'saiz] indirekte Steuer; Verbrauchssteuer *f*.

excise² [~] (her)ausschneiden.

excit|able [ik'saitəbl] reizbar; **~e** [ik'sait] er-, anregen; reizen; **~ement** [~tmənt] Auf-, Erregung *f*; Reizung *f*; **~ing** [~tiŋ] erregend.

exclaim [iks'kleim] ausrufen; eifern.

exclamation [eksklə'meiʃən] Ausruf(ung *f*) *m*; **~s** *pl.* Geschrei *n*; *note of* **~**, *point of* **~**, **~ mark** Ausrufezeichen *n*.

exclude [iks'klu:d] ausschließen.

exclusi|on [iks'klu:ʒən] Ausschließung *f*, Ausschluß *m*; **~ve** □ [~u:siv] ausschließlich; sich abschließend; **~ of** abgesehen von, ohne.

excommunicat|e [ekskə'mju:nikeit] exkommunizieren; **~ion** ['ekskəmju:ni'keiʃən] Kirchenbann *m*.

excrement [ekskrimənt] Kot *m*.

excrete [eks'kri:t] ausscheiden.

excruciat|e [iks'kru:ʃieit] martern; **~ing** [~tiŋ] qualvoll.

exculpate ['ekskʌlpeit] entschuldigen; rechtfertigen; freisprechen (*from* von).

excursion [iks'kə:ʃən] Ausflug *m*; Abstecher *m*.

excursive □ [eks'kə:siv] abschweifend.

excus|able □ [iks'kju:zəbl] entschuldbar; **~e 1.** [iks'kju:z] entschuldigen; **~** *s.o. s.th.* j-m et. erlassen; **2.** [~u:s] Entschuldigung *f*.

exeat ['eksiæt] *Schule etc.*: Urlaub *m.*

execra|ble [['eksikrəbl] abscheulich; **~te** ['eksikreit] verwünschen.

execut|e [eksikju:t] ausführen; vollziehen, ♂ vortragen; hinrichten; *Testament* vollstrecken; **~ion** [eksi-'kju:ʃən] Ausführung *f*; Vollziehung *f*, (Zwangs)Vollstreckung *f*; Hinrichtung *f*, ♪ Vortrag *m*; *put od.* *carry a plan into* **~** e-n Plan ausführen *od* verwirklichen; **~ioner** [~ʃnə] Scharfrichter *m*; **~ive** [ig-'zekjutiv] **1.** vollziehend; **~ committee** Vorstand *m*; **2.** vollziehende Gewalt, *Am* Staats-Präsident *m*; † Geschäftsführer *m*; **~or** [~tə] (Testaments)Vollstrecker *m*.

exemplary [ig'zempləri] vorbildlich

exemplify [ig'zemplifai] durch Beispiele belegen, veranschaulichen.

exempt [ig'zempt] **1.** befreit, frei; **2.** ausnehmen, befreien.

exercise ['eksəsaiz] **1.** Übung *f*; Ausübung *f*, *Schule* Übungsarbeit *f*; Leibesübung *f*, *take* **~** sich Bewegung machen, *Am* **~s** *pl.* Feierlichkeit(er *pl*) *f*; ✗ Manöver *n*; **2.** üben, ausüben; (sich) Bewegung machen, exerzieren

exert [ig'zə:t] *Einfluß etc.* ausüben; **~** *o.s.* sich anstrengen *od.* bemühen; **~ion** [~ə:ʃən] Ausübung *f etc.*

exhale [eks'heil] ausdünsten, ausatmen, aushauchen; *Gefühlen* Luft machen

exhaust [ig'zə:st] **1.** erschöpfen; entleeren, auspumpen; **2.** ⊕ Abgas *n*, Abdampf *m*, Auspuff *m*; **~ box** Auspufftopf *m*, *pipe* Auspuffrohr *n*; **~ed** erschöpft (*a. fig.*); vergriffen (*Auflage*), **~ion** [~tʃən] Erschöpfung *f*, **~ive** □ [~tiv] erschöpfend.

exhibit [ig'zibit] **1.** ausstellen; zeigen, darlegen, aufweisen; **2.** Ausstellungsstück *n*; Beweisstück *n*; **~ion** [eksi'biʃən] Ausstellung *f*; Darlegung *f*, Zurschaustellung *f*; Stipendium *n*

exhilarate [ig ziləreit] erheitern.

exhort [ig zə:t] ermahnen.

exigen|ce, ~cy [eksidʒəns, ~si] dringende Not, Erfordernis *n*; **~t** [~nt] dringlich, anspruchsvoll.

exile ['eksail] **1.** Verbannung *f*, Exil *n*; Verbannte(r *m*) *f*; **2.** verbannen.

exist [ig'zist] existieren, vorhanden sein; leben, **~ence** [~təns] Existenz *f*, Dasein *n*, Vorhandensein *n*; Leben *n*; *in* **~** ...**~ent** [~nt] vorhanden.

exit ['eksit] **1.** Abgang *m*; Tod *m*; Ausgang *m*, **2.** *thea.* (geht) ab.

exodus ['eksədəs] Auszug *m*.

exonerate [ig'zɔnəreit] *fig.* entlasten, entbinden, befreien; rechtfertigen.

exorbitant □ [ig'zɔ:bitənt] maßlos, übermäßig.

exorci|se, **~ze** ['eksɔ:saiz] *Geister* beschwören, austreiben (*from* aus); befreien (*of* von).

exotic [eg'zɔtik] ausländisch, exotisch; fremdländisch.

expan|d [iks'pænd] (sich) ausbreiten; (sich) ausdehnen; (sich) erweitern; *Abkürzungen* (voll) ausschreiben; freundlich *od.* heiter werden; **~se** [~ns], **~sion** [~nʃən] Ausdehnung *f;* Weite *f;* Breite *f;* **~sive** □ [~nsiv] ausdehnungsfähig; ausgedehnt, weit; *fig.* mitteilsam.

expatiate [eks'peiʃieit] sich weitläufig auslassen (*on* über *acc.*).

expatriate [eks'pætrieit] ausbürgern.

expect [iks'pekt] erwarten; F annehmen; *be* **~ing** ein Kind erwarten; **~ant** [~tənt] **1.** erwartend (*of acc.*); **~** *mother* werdende Mutter; **2.** Anwärter *m;* **~ation** [ekspek'teiʃən] Erwartung *f;* Aussicht *f.*

expectorate [eks'pektəreit] *Schleim etc.* aushusten, auswerfen.

expedi|ent [iks'pi:djənt] **1.** □ zweckmäßig; berechnend; **2.** Mittel *n;* (Not)Behelf *m;* **~tion** [ekspi'diʃən] Eile *f;* ✕ Feldzug *m;* (Forschungs)Reise *f;* **~tious** □ [~ʃəs] schnell, eilig, flink.

expel [iks'pel] (hin)ausstoßen; vertreiben, verjagen; ausschließen.

expen|d [iks'pend] *Geld* ausgeben; aufwenden; verbrauchen; **~diture** [~ditʃə] Ausgabe *f;* Aufwand *m;* **~se** [iks'pens] Ausgabe *f;* Kosten *pl.;* **~s** *pl.* Unkosten *pl.;* Auslagen *f/pl.; at the* **~** *of* auf Kosten (*gen.*); *at any* **~** um jeden Preis; *go to the* **~** *of* Geld ausgeben für; **~se account** Spesenrechnung *f;* **~sive** □ [~siv] kostspielig, teuer.

experience [iks'piəriəns] **1.** Erfahrung *f;* Erlebnis *n;* **2.** erfahren, erleben; **~d** erfahren.

experiment 1. [iks'perimənt] Versuch *m;* **2.** [~iment] experimentieren; **~al** □ [eksperi'mentl] Versuchs...; erfahrungsmäßig.

expert ['ekspə:t] **1.** □ [*pred.* eks'pə:t] erfahren, geschickt; fachmännisch; **2.** Fachmann *m;* Sachverständige(r *m*) *f.*

expiate ['ekspieit] büßen, sühnen.

expir|ation [ekspai'reiʃən] Ausatmung *f;* Ablauf *m,* Ende *n;* **~e** [iks'paiə] ausatmen; verscheiden; ablaufen; ✝ verfallen; erlöschen.

explain [iks'plein] erklären, erläutern; *Gründe* auseinandersetzen; **~** *away* wegdiskutieren.

explanat|ion [eksplə'neiʃən] Erklärung *f;* Erläuterung *f;* **~ory** □ [iks'plænətəri] erklärend.

explicable ['eksplikəbl] erklärlich.

explicit □ [iks'plisit] deutlich.

explode [iks'ploud] explodieren (lassen); ausbrechen; platzen (*with* vor).

exploit 1. ['eksplɔit] Heldentat *f;* **2.** [iks'plɔit] ausbeuten; **~ation** [eksplɔi'teiʃən] Ausbeutung *f.*

explor|ation [eksplɔ:'reiʃən] Erforschung *f;* **~e** [iks'plɔ:] erforschen; **~er** [~ɔ:rə] (Er)Forscher *m;* Forschungsreisende(r) *m.*

explosi|on [iks'plouʒən] Explosion *f;* Ausbruch *m;* **~ve** [~ousiv] **1.** □ explosiv; **2.** Sprengstoff *m.*

exponent [eks'pounənt] Exponent *m;* Vertreter *m.*

export 1. [eks'pɔ:t] ausführen; **2.** ['ekspɔ:t] Ausfuhr(artikel *m*) *f;* **~ation** [ekspɔ:'teiʃən] Ausfuhr *f.*

expos|e [iks'pouz] aussetzen; *phot.* belichten; ausstellen; entlarven; bloßstellen; **~ition** [ekspə'ziʃən] Ausstellung *f;* Erklärung *f.*

expostulate [iks'pɔstjuleit] protestieren; **~** *with j-m* Vorhaltungen machen.

exposure [iks'pouʒə] Aussetzen *n;* Ausgesetztsein *n;* Aufdeckung *f;* Enthüllung *f,* Entlarvung *f; phot.* Belichtung *f;* Bild *n;* Lage *f* e-s *Hauses;* **~** *meter* Belichtungsmesser *m.* [legen.]

expound [iks'paund] erklären, auslegen.

express [iks'pres] **1.** □ ausdrücklich, deutlich; Expreß...; Eil...; **~** *company Am.* Transportfirma *f;* **~** *highway* Schnellverkehrsstraße *f;* **2.** Eilbote *m; a.* **~** *train* Schnellzug *m; by* **~** = **3.** *adv.* durch Eilboten; als Eilgut; **4.** äußern, ausdrücken; aussprechen; **~ion** [~ʃən] Ausdruck *m;* **~ive** □ [~siv] ausdrückend (*of acc.*); ausdrucksvoll; **~ly** [~sli] ausdrücklich, eigens; **~way** *Am.* Autobahn *f.* [eignen.]

expropriate [eks'prouprieit] ent-

expulsi|on [iks'pʌlʃən] Vertreibung *f;* **~ve** [~lsiv] (aus)treibend.

expunge [eks'pʌndʒ] streichen.

expurgate ['ekspə:geit] säubern.

exquisite □ ['ekskwizit] auserlesen, vorzüglich; fein; heftig, scharf.

extant [eks'tænt] (noch) vorhanden.

extempor|aneous □ [ekstempə'reinjəs], **~ary** [iks'tempərəri], **~e** [eks'tempəri] aus dem Stegreif (vorgetragen).

extend [iks'tend] *v/t.* ausdehnen; ausstrecken; erweitern; verlängern; *Gunst etc.* erweisen; ✕ (aus)schwärmen lassen; *v/i.* sich erstrecken.

extensi|on [iks'tenʃən] Ausdehnung *f;* Erweiterung *f;* Verlängerung *f;* Aus-, Anbau *m; teleph.* Nebenanschluß *m;* **~** *cord* ✂ Verlängerungsschnur *f; University* ♀ Volkshochschule *f;* **~ve** □ [~nsiv] ausgedehnt, umfassend.

extent [iks'tent] Ausdehnung *f*, Weite *f*, Größe *f*, Umfang *m*; Grad *m*; to the ~ of bis zum Betrage von; to some ~ einigermaßen.

extenuate [eks'tenjueit] abschwächen, mildern, beschönigen.

exterior [eks'tiəriə] 1. äußerlich; Außen...; außerhalb; 2. Äußere(s) *n*; *Film*: Außenaufnahme *f*.

exterminate [eks'tə:mineit] ausrotten, vertilgen.

external [eks'tə:nl] 1. □ äußere(r, -s), äußerlich; Außen...; 2. ~s *pl.* Äußere(s) *n*; *fig.* Äußerlichkeiten *f*/*pl*.

extinct [iks'tiŋkt] erloschen; ausgestorben.

extinguish [iks'tiŋgwiʃ] (aus)löschen; vernichten.

extirpate ['ekstə:peit] ausrotten; ✗ *Organ etc.* entfernen.

extol [iks'tɔl] erheben, preisen.

extort [iks'tɔ:t] erpressen; abnötigen (*from dat.*); ~ion [~ɔ:ʃən] Erpressung *f*.

extra ['ekstrə] 1. Extra...; außer...; Neben...; Sonder...; ~ pay Zulage *f*; 2. *adv.* besonders; außerdem; 3. *et.* Zusätzliches; Zuschlag *m*; Extrablatt *n*; *thea.*, *Film*: Statist(in).

extract 1. ['ekstrækt] Auszug *m*; 2. [iks'trækt] (heraus)ziehen; herauslocken; ab-, herleiten; ~ion [~kʃən] (Heraus)Ziehen *n*; Herkunft *f*.

extradit|e ['ekstrədait] *Verbrecher* ausliefern (lassen); ~ion [ekstrə-'diʃən] Auslieferung *f*.

extraordinary □ [iks'trɔ:dnri]

außerordentlich; Extra...; ungewöhnlich; envoy ~ außerordentlicher Gesandter.

extra student ['ekstrə'stju:dənt] Gasthörer(in).

extravagan|ce [iks'trævigəns] Übertriebenheit *f*; Überspanntheit *f*; Verschwendung *f*, Extravaganz *f*; ~t □ [~nt] übertrieben, überspannt; verschwenderisch; extravagant.

extrem|e [iks'tri:m] 1. □ äußerst, größt, höchst; sehr streng; außergewöhnlich; 2. Äußerste(s) *n*; Extrem *n*; höchster Grad; ~ity [~remiti] Äußerste(s) *n*; höchste Not; äußerste Maßnahme; *extremities pl.* Gliedmaßen *pl.*

extricate ['ekstrikeit] herauswinden, herausziehen; befreien; ⚓ entwickeln.

extrude [eks'tru:d] ausstoßen.

exuberan|ce [ig'zju:bərəns] Überfluß *m*; Überschwenglichkeit *f*; ~t □ [~nt] reichlich; üppig; überschwenglich.

exult [ig'zʌlt] frohlocken.

eye [ai] 1. Auge *n*; Blick *m*; Öhr *n*; Öse *f*; up to the ~s in work bis über die Ohren in Arbeit; with an ~ to mit Rücksicht auf (*acc.*); mit der Absicht zu; 2. ansehen; mustern; ~ball ['aibɔ:l] Augapfel *m*; ~brow Augenbraue *f*; ~d ...äugig; ~glass Augenglas *n*; (*a pair of*) ~es *pl.* (ein) Kneifer; (e-e) Brille; ~lash Augenwimper *f*; ~lid Augenlid *n*; ~sight Augen(licht *n*) *pl.*; Schkraft *f*; ~witness Augenzeug|e *m*, -in *f*.

F

fable ['feibl] Fabel *f*; Mythen *pl.*, Legenden *pl.*; Lüge *f*.

fabric ['fæbrik] Bau *m*, Gebäude *n*; Struktur *f*; Gewebe *n*, Stoff *m*; ~ate [~keit] fabrizieren (*mst fig.* = erdichten, fälschen).

fabulous □ ['fæbjuləs] legendär; sagen-, fabelhaft.

façade △ [fə'sɑ:d] Fassade *f*.

face [feis] 1. Gesicht *n*; Anblick *m*; *fig.* Stirn *f*, Unverschämtheit *f*; (Ober)Fläche *f*; Vorderseite *f*; Zifferblatt *n*; ~ to ~ with Auge in Auge mit; save one's ~ das Gesicht wahren; on the ~ of it auf den ersten Blick; set one's ~ against sich gegen *et.* stemmen; 2. *v/t.* ansehen; gegenüberstehen (*dat.*); (hinaus)gehen auf (*acc.*); die Stirn bieten (*dat.*); einfassen; △ bekleiden; *v/i.* ~ about sich umdrehen; ~cloth ['feisklɔθ] Waschlappen *m*.

facetious □ [fə'si:ʃəs] witzig.

facil|e ['fæsail] leicht; gewandt; ~itate [fə'siliteit] erleichtern; ~ity [~ti] Leichtigkeit *f*; Gewandtheit *f*; *mst facilities pl.* Erleichterung(en *pl.*) *f*, Möglichkeit(en *pl.*) *f*, Gelegenheit(en *pl.*) *f*.

facing ['feisiŋ] ⊕ Verkleidung *f*; ~s *pl. Schneiderei:* Besatz *m*.

fact [fækt] Tatsache *f*; Wirklichkeit *f*; Wahrheit *f*; Tat *f*. [keit *f*.]

faction ['fækʃən] Partei *f*; Uneinig-]

factitious □ [fæk'tiʃəs] künstlich.

factor ['fæktə] *fig.* Umstand *m*, Moment *n*, Faktor *m*; Agent *m*; Verwalter *m*; ~y [~əri] Fabrik *f*.

faculty ['fækəlti] Fähigkeit *f*; Kraft *f*; *fig.* Gabe *f*; *univ.* Fakultät *f*.

fad F *fig.* [fæd] Steckenpferd *n*.

fade [feid] (ver)welken (lassen), verblassen; schwinden; *Radio:* ~ in einblenden.

fag F [fæg] *v/i.* sich placken; *v/t.* erschöpfen, mürbe machen.

fail [feil] 1. *v/i.* versagen, mißlingen, fehlschlagen; versäumen; versiegen; nachlassen; Bankrott machen; durchfallen (*Kandidat*); he ~ed to do es mißlang ihm zu tun; he cannot ~ to er muß (einfach); *v/t.* im Stich lassen, verlassen; versäumen; 2. without ~ unfehlbar; ~ing ['feiliŋ] Fehler *m*, Schwäche *f*; ~ure [~ʃə] Fehlen *n*; Ausbleiben *n*; Fehlschlag *m*; Mißerfolg *m*; Verfall *m*; Versäumnis *n*; Bankrott *m*; Versager *m* (*P.*).

faint [feint] 1. ☐ schwach, matt; 2. schwach werden; in Ohnmacht fallen (*with vor*); 3. Ohnmacht *f*; ~-hearted ☐ ['feint'hɑːtid] verzagt.

fair¹ [fɛə] 1. *adj.* gerecht, ehrlich, anständig, fair; ordentlich; schön (*Wetter*), günstig (*Wind*), reichlich; blond; hellhäutig; freundlich, sauber, in Reinschrift; schön (*Frau*); 2. *adv.* gerecht, ehrlich, anständig, fair; in Reinschrift; direkt.

fair² [~] (Jahr)Markt *m*, Messe *f*. **fair|ly** ['fɛəli] ziemlich; völlig; ~ness ['fɛənis] Schönheit *f*; Blondheit *f*; Gerechtigkeit *f*; Redlichkeit *f*; Billigkeit *f*; ~way ♣ Fahrwasser *n*.

fairy ['fɛəri] Fee *f*; Zauberin *f*; Elf(e *f*) *m*; ~land Feen-, Märchenland *n*; ~tale Märchen *n*.

faith [feiθ] Glaube *m*; Vertrauen *n*; Treue *f*; ~ful ☐ ['feiθful] treu; ehrlich; yours ~ly Ihr ergebener; ~less ☐ ['feiθlis] treulos; ungläubig.

fake *sl.* [feik] 1. Schwindel *m*; Fälschung *f*; Schwindler *m*; 2. *a.* ~ up fälschen.

falcon ['fɔːlkən] Falke *m*.

fall [fɔːl] 1. Fall(en *n*) *m*; Sturz *m*; Verfall *m*; Einsturz *m*; Am. Herbst *m*; Sinken *n der Preise etc.*; Fällen *n*; Wasserfall *m* (*mst pl.*); Senkung *f*, Abhang *m*; 2. [*irr.*] fallen; ab-, einfallen; sinken; sich legen (*Wind*); in e-n Zustand verfallen; ~ back zurückweichen; ~ back (up)on zurückkommen auf; ~ ill *od.* sick krank werden; ~ in love with sich verlieben in (*acc.*); ~ out sich entzweien; sich zutragen; ~ short knapp werden (*of an dat.*); ~ short of zurückbleiben hinter (*dat.*); ~ to sich machen an (*acc.*).

fallacious ☐ [fə'leiʃəs] trügerisch.

fallacy ['fæləsi] Täuschung *f*.

fallen ['fɔːlən] *p.p. von* fall 2.

fall guy *Am. sl.* ['fɔːl'gai] *der* Lackierte, *der* Dumme.

fallible ☐ ['fæləbl] fehlbar.

falling ['fɔːliŋ] Fallen *n*; ~ sickness

Fallsucht *f*; ~ star Sternschnuppe *f*.

fallow ['fælou] *zo.* falb; ⚘ brach (-liegend).

false ☐ [fɔːls] falsch; ~hood ['fɔːlshud], ~ness [~snis] Falschheit *f*.

falsi|fication ['fɔːlsifi'keiʃən] (Ver-) Fälschung *f*; ~fy ['fɔːlsifai] (ver-) fälschen; ~ty [~iti] Falschheit *f*.

falter ['fɔːltə] schwanken; stocken (*Stimme*); stammeln; *fig.* zaudern.

fame [feim] Ruf *m*, Ruhm *m*; ~d [~md] berühmt (*for wegen*).

familiar [fə'miljə] 1. ☐ vertraut; gewohnt; familiär; 2. Vertraute(r *m*) *f*; ~ity [fəmili'æriti] Vertrautheit *f*; (plumpe) Vertraulichkeit; ~ize [fə'miljəraiz] vertraut machen.

family ['fæmili] 1. Familie *f*; 2. Familien..., Haus...; in the ~ way in anderen Umständen; ~ allowance Kinderzulage *f*; ~ tree Stammbaum *m*.

fami|ne ['fæmin] Hungersnot *f*; Mangel *m* (*of an dat.*); ~sh [~iʃ] (aus-, ver)hungern.

famous ☐ ['feiməs] berühmt.

fan¹ [fæn] 1. Fächer *m*; Ventilator *m*; 2. (an)fächeln; an-, *fig.* entfachen.

fan² F [~] *Sport- etc.* Fanatiker *m*, Liebhaber *m*; *Radio:* Bastler *m*; ...narr *m*, ...fex *m*.

fanatic [fə'nætik] 1. *a.* ~al [~kəl] fanatisch; 2. Fanatiker(in).

fanciful ☐ ['fænsiful] phantastisch.

fancy ['fænsi] 1. Phantasie *f*; Einbildung(skraft) *f*; Schrulle *f*; Vorliebe *f*; Liebhaberei *f*; 2. Phantasie...; Liebhaber...; Luxus...; Mode...; ~ ball Maskenball *m*; ~ goods *pl.* Modewaren *f/pl.*; 3. sich einbilden; Gefallen finden an (*dat.*); just ~! denken Sie nur!; ~-work feine Handarbeit, Stickerei *f*.

fang [fæŋ] Fangzahn *m*; Giftzahn *m*.

fantas|tic [fæn'tæstik] (~ally) phantastisch; ~y ['fæntəsi] Phantasie *f*.

far [fɑː] 1. *adj.* fern, entfernt; weit; 2. *adv.* fern; weit; (sehr) viel; as ~ as bis; in so ~ as insofern als; ~-away [fɑːrə'wei] weit entfernt.

fare [fɛə] 1. Fahrgeld *n*; Fahrgast *m*; Verpflegung *f*, Kost *f*; 2. *gut* leben; he ~d well es (er)ging ihm gut; ~well ['fɛə'wel] 1. lebe(n Sie) wohl!; 2. Abschied *m*, Lebewohl *n*.

far|-fetched *fig.* ['fɑː'fetʃt] weit hergeholt, gesucht; ~ gone F fertig (*todkrank, betrunken etc.*).

farm [fɑːm] 1. Bauernhof *m*, -gut *n*, Gehöft *n*, Farm *f*; Züchterei *f*; chicken ~ Hühnerfarm *f*; 2. (ver-) pachten; *Land* bewirtschaften; ~er ['fɑːmə] Landwirt *m*; Pächter *m*; ~hand Landarbeiter(in); ~house Bauern-, Gutshaus *n*; ~ing ['fɑːmiŋ]

1. Acker...; landwirtschaftlich; **2.** Landwirtschaft *f*; ~stead Gehöft *n*; ~yard Wirtschaftshof *m e-s Bauernguts.*

far-off ['fɑːɔːf] entfernt, fern; ~ sighted *fig.* weitblickend.

farthe|r ['fɑːðə] *comp. von far*; ~st ['fɑːðist] *sup. von far.*

fascinat|e ['fæsineit] bezaubern; ~ion [fæsi'neiʃən] Zauber *m*, Reiz *m.*

fashion ['fæʃən] Mode *f*; Art *f*; feine Lebensart; Form *f*; Schnitt *m*; *in (out of)* ~ (un)modern; **2.** gestalten; *Kleid* machen; ~able ['fæʃnəbl] modern, elegant.

fast[1] [fɑːst] schnell; fest; treu; waschecht; flott; *be* ~ vorgehen (*Uhr*).

fast[2] [~] **1.** Fasten *n*; **2.** fasten.

fasten ['fɑːsn] *v/t.* befestigen; anheften; fest (zu)machen; zubinden; *Augen etc.* heften (*on, upon* auf *acc.*); *v/i.* schließen (*Tür*); ~ *upon fig.* sich klammern an (*acc.*); ~er [~nə] Verschluß *m*; Klammer *f.*

fastidious □ [fæs'tidiəs] anspruchsvoll, heikel, wählerisch, verwöhnt.

fat [fæt] **1.** □ fett; dick; fettig; **2.** Fett *n*; **3.** fett machen *od.* werden; mästen.

fatal □ ['feitl] verhängnisvoll (*to* für); Schicksals...; tödlich; ~ity [fə'tæliti] Verhängnis *n*; Unglücks-, Todesfall *m*; Todesopfer *n.*

fate [feit] Schicksal *n*; Verhängnis *n.*

father ['fɑːðə] **1.** Vater *m*; **2.** der Urheber sein von; ~hood [~hud] Vaterschaft *f*; ~-in-law [~rinlɔː] Schwiegervater *m*; ~less [~lis] vaterlos; ~ly [~li] väterlich.

fathom ['fæðəm] **1.** Klafter *f* (*Maß*); ⚓ Faden *m*; **2.** ⚓ loten; *fig.* ergründen; ~less [~mlis] unergründlich.

fatigue [fə'tiːg] **1.** Ermüdung *f*; Strapaze *f*; **2.** ermüden; strapazieren.

fat|ness ['fætnis] Fettigkeit *f*; Fettheit *f*; ~ten ['fætn] fett machen *od.* werden; mästen; *Boden* düngen.

fatuous □ ['fætjuəs] albern.

faucet *Am.* ['fɔːsit] (Zapf)Hahn *m.*

fault [fɔːlt] Fehler *m*; Defekt *m*; Schuld *f*; *find* ~ *with et.* auszusetzen haben an (*dat.*); *be at* ~ auf falscher Fährte sein; ~finder ['fɔːltfaində] Nörgler *m*; ~less □ [~tlis] fehlerfrei, tadellos; ~y [~ti] mangelhaft.

favo(u)r ['feivə] **1.** Gunst(bezeigung) *f*; Gefallen *m*; Begünstigung *f*; *in* ~ *of* zugunsten von *od. gen.*; *do s.o. a* ~ *j-m e-n* Gefallen tun; **2.** begünstigen; beehren; ~able □ [~rəbl] günstig; ~ite [~rit] Günstling *m*; Liebling *m*; *Sport:* Favorit *m*; *attr.* Lieblings...

fawn[1] [fɔːn] **1.** *zo.* (Dam)Kitz *n*; Rehbraun *n*; **2.** (Kitze) setzen.

fawn[2] [~] schwänzeln (*Hund*); kriechen (*upon* vor).

faze *bsd. Am.* F [feiz] durcheinanderbringen.

fear [fiə] **1.** Furcht *f* (*of* vor *dat.*); Befürchtung *f*; Angst *f*; **2.** (be-) fürchten; sich fürchten vor (*dat.*); ~ful □ ['fiəful] furchtsam; furchtbar; ~less □ ['fiəlis] furchtlos.

feasible ['fiːzəbl] ausführbar.

feast [fiːst] **1.** Fest *n*; Feiertag *m*; Festmahl *n*, Schmaus *m*; **2.** *v/t.* festlich bewirten; *v/i.* sich ergötzen; schmausen. [stück *n.*\]

feat [fiːt] (Helden)Tat *f*; Kunst-

feather ['feðə] **1.** Feder *f*; *a.* ~s Gefieder *n*; *show the white* ~ F sich feige zeigen; *in high* ~ in gehobener Stimmung; **2.** mit Federn schmücken; ~bed **1.** *Feder*-Unterbett *n*; **2.** verwöhnen; ~brained, ~headed unbesonnen; albern; ~ed be-, gefiedert; ~y [~əri] feder(art)ig.

feature ['fiːtʃə] **1.** (Gesichts-, Grund-, Haupt-, Charakter)Zug *m*; (charakteristisches) Merkmal; *Radio* Feature *n*; *Am.* Bericht *m*, Artikel *m*; ~s *pl.* Gesicht *n*; Charakter *m*; **2.** kennzeichnen; sich auszeichnen durch; groß aufziehen; *Film* in der Hauptrolle zeigen; ~ film Haupt-, Spielfilm *m.*

February ['februəri] Februar *m.*

fecund ['fiːkənd] fruchtbar.

fed [fed] *pret. u. p.p. von feed* 2.

federa|l ['fedərəl] Bundes...; ~ize [~laiz] (sich) verbünden; ~tion [fedə'reiʃən] Staatenbund *m*; Vereinigung *f*; Verband *m.*

fee [fiː] **1.** Gebühr *f*; Honorar *n*; Trinkgeld *n*; **2.** bezahlen.

feeble ['fiːbl] schwach.

feed [fiːd] **1.** Futter *n*; Nahrung *f*; Fütterung *f*; ⊕ Zuführung *f*, Speisung *f*; **2.** [*irr.*] *v/t.* füttern; speisen (*a.* ⊕), nähren; weiden; *Material etc.* zuführen; *be fed up mit et. od. j-n* satt haben; *well fed* wohlgenährt; *v/i.* (fr)essen; sich nähren; ~er ['fiːdə] Fütterer *m*; *Am.* Viehmäster *m*; Esser(in); ~er road Zubringer(straße *f*) *m*; ~ing-bottle ['fiːdiŋbɔtl] Saugflasche *f.*

feel [fiːl] **1.** [*irr.*] (sich) fühlen; befühlen; empfinden; sich anfühlen; *I* ~ *like doing et.* ich möchte am liebsten tun; **2.** Gefühl *n*; Empfindung *f*; ~er ['fiːlə] Fühler *m*; ~ing ['fiːliŋ] **1.** ~(fühlend; gefühlvoll; **2.** Gefühl *n*; Meinung *f.*

feet [fiːt] *pl. von foot* 1.

feign [fein] heucheln; vorgeben.

feint [feint] Verstellung *f*; Finte *f.*

felicit|ate [fi'lisiteit] beglückwünschen; ~ous □ [~təs] glücklich; ~y [~ti] Glück(seligkeit *f*) *n.*

fell [fel] **1.** *pret. von fall* 2; **2.** niederschlagen; fällen.

felloe ['felou] (Rad)Felge *f*.

fellow ['felou] Gefährt|e *m*, -in *f*, Kamerad(in); Gleiche(r, -s); Gegenstück *n*; *univ*. Fellow *m*, Mitglied *n* e-s *College*; Bursche *m*, Mensch *m*; *attr*. Mit...; *old ~ F* alter Junge; *the ~ of a glove* der andere Handschuh; ~-country-man Landsmann *m*; ~ship [~ouʃip] Gemeinschaft *f*; Kameradschaft *f*; Mitgliedschaft *f*.

felly ['feli] (Rad)Felge *f*.

felon ʒ̣ ['felən] Verbrecher *m*; ~y [~ni] Kapitalverbrechen *n*.

felt¹ [felt] *pret. u. p.p. von feel* 1.

felt² [~] 1. Filz *m*; 2. (be)filzen.

female ['fi:meil] 1. weiblich; 2. Weib *n*; *zo*. Weibchen *n*.

feminine □ ['feminin] weiblich; weibisch.

fen [fen] Fenn *n*, Moor *n*; Marsch *f*.

fence [fens] 1. Zaun *m*; Fechtkunst *f*; *sl*. Hehler(nest *n*) *m*; *sit on the ~* abwarten; 2. *v/t. a. ~ in* ein-, umzäunen; schützen; *v/i*. fechten; *sl*. hehlen.

fencing ['fensiŋ] Einfriedung *f*; Fechten *n*; *attr*. Fecht...

fend [fend]: *~ off* abwehren; ~er ['fendə] Schutzvorrichtung *f*; Schutzblech *n*; Kamingitter *n*, -vorsetzer *m*; Stoßfänger *m*.

fennel ♀ ['fenl] Fenchel *m*.

ferment 1. ['fə:ment] Ferment *n*; Gärung *f*; 2. [fə(:)'ment] gären (lassen); ~ation [fə:men'teiʃən] Gärung *f*.

fern ♀ [fə:n] Farn(kraut *n*) *m*.

feroci|ous □ [fə'rouʃəs] wild; grausam; ~ty [fə'rɔsiti] Wildheit *f*.

ferret ['ferit] 1. *zo*. Frettchen *n*; *fig*. Spürhund *m*; 2. (umher)stöbern; *~ out* aufstöbern.

ferry ['feri] 1. Fähre *f*; 2. übersetzen; ~boat Fährboot *n*, Fähre *f*; ~man Fährmann *m*.

fertil|e ['fə:tail] fruchtbar; reich (*of*, *in* an *dat*.); ~ity [fə:'tiliti] Fruchtbarkeit *f* (*a. fig*.); ~ize ['fə:tilaiz] fruchtbar machen; befruchten; düngen; ~izer [~zə] Düngemittel *n*.

ferven|cy ['fə:vənsi] Glut *f*; Inbrunst *f*; ~t □ [~nt] heiß; inbrünstig, glühend; leidenschaftlich.

fervo(u)r ['fə:və] Glut *f*; Inbrunst *f*.

festal ['festl] festlich.

fester ['festə] eitern; verfaulen.

festiv|al ['festəvəl] Fest *n*; Feier *f*; Festspiele *n*|*pl*.; ~e □ [~tiv] festlich; ~ity [fes'tiviti] Festlichkeit *f*.

festoon [fes'tu:n] Girlande *f*.

fetch [fetʃ] holen; *Preis* erzielen; *Seufzer* ausstoßen; ~ing □ F ['fetʃiŋ] reizend.

fetid ['fetid] stinkend.

fetter ['fetə] 1. Fessel *f*; 2. fesseln.

feud [fju:d] Fehde *f*; Leh(e)n *n*;

~al □ ['fju:dl] lehnbar; Lehns...; ~alism [~dəlizəm] Lehnswesen *n*.

fever ['fi:və] Fieber *n*; ~ish □ [~əriʃ] fieb(e)rig; *fig*. fieberhaft.

few [fju:] wenige; *a ~* ein paar; *quite a ~*, *a good ~* e-e ganze Menge.

fiancé [fi'ã:nsei] Verlobte(r) *m*; ~e [~] Verlobte *f*.

fiat ['faiæt] Befehl *m*; *~ money Am*. Papiergeld *n* (*ohne Deckung*).

fib F [fib] 1. Flunkerei *f*, Schwindelei *f*; 2. schwindeln, flunkern.

fib|re, *Am*. ~er ['faibə] Faser *f*; Charakter *m*; ~rous □ ['faibrəs] faserig.

fickle ['fikl] wankelmütig; unbeständig; ~ness [~lnis] Wankelmut *m*.

fiction ['fikʃən] Erfindung *f*; Roman-, Unterhaltungsliteratur *f*; ~al □ [~nl] erdichtet; Roman...

fictitious □ [fik'tiʃəs] erfunden.

fiddle F ['fidl] 1. Geige *f*, Fiedel *f*; 2. fiedeln; tändeln; ~r [~lə] Geiger (-in); ~stick Fiedelbogen *m*; ~s! *fig*. dummes Zeug!

fidelity [fi'deliti] Treue *f*; Genauigkeit *f*.

fidget F ['fidʒit] 1. nervöse Unruhe; 2. nervös machen *od*. sein; ~y [~ti]) kribbelig.

fie [fai] pfui! [kribbelig.]

field [fi:ld] Feld *n*; (Spiel)Platz *m*; Arbeitsfeld *n*; Gebiet *n*; Bereich *m*; *hold the ~* das Feld behaupten; ~-day ['fi:lddei] ✕ Felddienstübung *f*; Parade *f*; *fig*. großer Tag; *Am*. (Schul)Sportfest *n*; *Am*. Exkursionstag *m*; ~ events *pl*. *Sport*: Sprung- u. Wurfwettkämpfe *m*|*pl*.; ~-glass(es *pl*.) Feldstecher *m*; ~-officer Stabsoffizier *m*; ~-sports *pl*. Jagen *n u*. Fischen *n*.

fiend [fi:nd] böser Feind, Teufel *m*; ~ish □ ['fi:ndiʃ] teuflisch, boshaft.

fierce □ [fiəs] wild; grimmig; ~ness [fiəsnis] Wildheit *f*; Grimm *m*.

fiery □ ['faiəri] feurig; hitzig.

fif|teen ['fif'ti:n] fünfzehn; ~teenth [~nθ] fünfzehnte(r, -s); ~th [fifθ] 1. fünfte(r, -s); 2. Fünftel *n*; ~thly ['fifθli] fünftens; ~tieth ['fiftiiθ] fünfzigste(r, -s); ~ty [~ti] fünfzig; ~ty-fifty F halb und halb.

fig [fig] Feige *f*; F Zustand *m*.

fight [fait] 1. Kampf *m*; Kampflust *f*; *show ~* sich zur Wehr setzen; 2. [*irr*.] *v/t*. bekämpfen; erkämpfen; *v/i*. kämpfen, sich schlagen; ~er ['faitə] Kämpfer *m*, Streiter *m*; ✕ Jagdflugzeug *n*; ~ing ['faitiŋ] Kampf *m*.

figurative □ ['figjurətiv] bildlich.

figure ['figə] 1. Figur *f*; Gestalt *f*; Ziffer *f*; Preis *m*; *be good at ~s* gut im Rechnen sein; 2. *v/t*. abbilden; darstellen; sich *et*. vorstellen; beziffern; *~ up od. out* berechnen; *v/i*. erscheinen; e-e Rolle spielen *as*) als); ~ on *Am. et.* überdenken; ~-skating [~əskeitiŋ] Eiskunstlauf *m*.

filament ['filəmənt] Faden *m*, Faser *f*; ⚡ Staubfaden *m*; ∉ Glüh-, Heizfaden *m*.

filbert ℱ ['filbə(:)t] Haselnuß *f*.

filch [filtʃ] stibitzen (*from dat.*).

file¹ [fail] 1. Akte *f*, Ordner *m*; Ablage *f*; Reihe *f*; ⚔ Rotte *f*; on ~ bei den Akten; 2. *v/t.* aufreihen; *Briefe etc.* einordnen; ablegen; einreichen; *v/i.* hinter-ea. marschieren.

file² [~] 1. Feile *f*; 2. feilen.

filial ['filjəl] kindlich, Kindes...

filibuster ['filibʌstə] 1. *Am.* Obstruktion(spolitiker *m*) *f*; 2. *Am.* Obstruktion treiben.

fill [fil] 1. (sich) füllen; an-, aus-, erfüllen; *Am. Auftrag* ausführen; ~ *in Formular* ausfüllen; 2. Fülle *f*, Genüge *f*; Füllung *f*.

fillet ['filit] Haarband *n*; Lendenbraten *m*; Roulade *f*; *bsd.* △ Band *n*.

filling ['filiŋ] Füllung *f*; ~ station *Am.* Tankstelle *f*.

fillip ['filip] Nasenstüber *m*.

filly ['fili] (Stuten)Füllen *n*; *fig.* wilde Hummel.

film [film] 1. Häutchen *n*; Membran(e) *f*; Film *m*; Trübung *f des Auges*; Nebelschleier *m*; *take od. shoot a ~* e-n Film drehen; 2. (sich) verschleiern; (ver)filmen.

filter ['filtə] 1. Filter *m*; 2. filtern.

filth [filθ] Schmutz *m*; ~y □ ['filθi] schmutzig; *fig.* unflätig.

filtrate ['filtreit] filtrieren.

fin [fin] Flosse *f (a. sl.* = Hand).

final ['fainl] 1. □ letzte(r, -s) endlich; schließlich; End...; endgültig; 2. Schlußprüfung *f*; *Sport:* Schlußrunde *f*, Endspiel *n*.

financ|e [fai'næns] 1. Finanzwesen *n*; ~s *pl.* Finanzen *pl.*; 2. *v/t.* finanzieren; *v/i.* Geldgeschäfte machen; ~ial □ [~nʃəl] finanziell; ~ier [~nsiə] Finanzmann *m*; Geldgeber *m*.

finch *orn.* [fintʃ] Fink *m*.

find [faind] 1. (*irr.*) finden; (an-) treffen; auf-, herausfinden; *schuldig etc.* befinden; beschaffen; versorgen; *all found* freie Station; 2. Fund *m*; ~ings ['faindiŋz] *pl.* Befund *m*; Urteil *n*.

fine¹ □ [fain] 1. schön; fein; verfeinert; rein; spitz, dünn, scharf; geziert; vornehm; 2. *adv.* gut, bestens.

fine² [~] 1. Geldstrafe *f*; 2. zu e-r Geldstrafe verurteilen.

fineness ['fainnis] Fein-, Zart-, Schönheit *f*, Eleganz *f*; Genauigkeit *f*.

finery ['fainəri] Glanz *m*; Putz *m*; Staat *m*.

finger ['fiŋgə] 1. Finger *m*; 2. betasten, (herum)fingern an (*dat.*);

~-language Zeichensprache *f*; ~-nail Fingernagel *m*; ~-print Fingerabdruck *m*.

fini|cal □ ['finikəl], ~cking [~kiŋ], ~kin [~in] geziert; wählerisch.

finish ['finiʃ] 1. *v/t.* beenden, vollenden; fertigstellen; abschließen; vervollkommnen; erledigen; *v/i.* enden; 2. Vollendung *f*, letzter Schliff (*a. fig.*); Schluß *m*.

finite ⅂ ['fainait] endlich, begrenzt.

fink *Am. sl.* [fiŋk] Streikbrecher *m*.

Finn [fin] Finn|e *m*, -in *f*; ~ish ['finiʃ] finnisch.

fir [fə:] (Weiß)Tanne *f*; Fichte *f*; ~-cone ['fə:koun] Tannenzapfen *m*.

fire ['faiə] 1. Feuer *n*; on ~ in Brand, in Flammen; 2. *v/t.* an-, entzünden; *fig.* anfeuern; abfeuern; *Ziegel etc.* brennen; F 'rausschmeißen (*entlassen*); heizen; *v/i.* Feuer fangen (*a. fig.*); feuern; ~-alarm ['faiərəla:m] Feuermelder *m*; ~-brigade Feuerwehr *f*; *bsd. Am.* F Brandstifter *m*; ~-cracker Frosch *m (Feuerwerkskörper)*; ~ department *Am.* Feuerwehr *f*; ~-engine ['faiərendʒin] (Feuer)Spritze *f*; ~-escape [~riskeip] Rettungsgerät *n*; Nottreppe *f*; ~-extinguisher [~rikstiŋgwiʃə] Feuerlöscher *m*; ~-man Feuerwehrmann *m*; Heizer *m*; ~-place Herd *m*; Kamin *m*; ~-plug Hydrant *m*; ~-proof feuerfest; ~-screen Ofenschirm *m*; ~-side Herd *m*; Kamin *m*; ~-station Feuerwache *f*; ~-wood Brennholz *n*; ~-works *pl.* Feuerwerk *n*.

firing ['faiəriŋ] Heizung *f*; Feuerung *f*.

firm [fə:m] 1. □ fest; derb; standhaft; 2. Firma *f*; ~ness ['fə:mnis] Festigkeit *f*.

first [fə:st] 1. *adj.* erste(r, -s); beste(r, -s); 2. *adv.* erstens; zuerst; ~ *of all* an erster Stelle; zu allererst; 3. Erste(r, -s); ~ *of exchange* ✝ Primawechsel *m*; *at* ~ zuerst, anfangs; *from the* ~ von Anfang an; ~-born ['fə:stbɔ:n] erstgeboren; ~ class 1. Klasse (*e-s Verkehrsmittels*); ~-class erstklassig; ~ly [~tli] erstlich; erstens; ~ name Vorname *m*; Beiname *f*; ~-papers *Am.* vorläufige Einbürgerungspapiere; ~-rate ersten Ranges; erstklassig.

firth [fə:θ] Förde *f*; (Flut)Mündung *f*.

fish [fiʃ] 1. Fisch(e *pl.*) *m*; F Kerl *m*; 2. fischen, angeln; haschen; ~-bone ['fiʃboun] Gräte *f*.

fisher ['fiʃə], ~man Fischer *m*; ~y [~əri] Fischerei *f*.

fishing ['fiʃiŋ] Fischen *n*; ~-line Angelschnur *f*; ~-tackle Angelgerät *n*. [händler *m.*]

fishmonger ['fiʃmʌŋgə] Fisch-]

fiss|ion ⑪ ['fiʃən] Spaltung *f*; ~ure ['fiʃə] Spalt *m*; Riß *m*.

fist [fist] Faust f; F Klaue f; ‿icuffs ['fistikʌfs] pl. Faustschläge m/pl.

fit¹ [fit] 1. ☐ geeignet, passend; tauglich; Sport: in (guter) Form; bereit; 2. v/t. passen für od. dat.; anpassen, passend machen; befähigen; geeignet machen (for, to für, zu); a. ‿ on anprobieren; ausstatten; ‿ out ausrüsten; ‿ up einrichten; montieren; v/i. passen; sich schikken; sitzen (Kleid); 3. Sitz m (Kleid).

fit² [‿] Anfall m; ☞ Ausbruch m; Anwandlung f; by ‿s and starts ruckweise; give s.o. a ‿ j-n hochbringen, j-m e-n Schock versetzen.

fit|ful ['fitful] ruckartig, fig. unstet; ‿ness ['fitnis] Schicklichkeit f; Tauglichkeit f; ‿ter ['fitə] Monteur m, Installateur m; ‿ting ['fitiŋ] 1. passend; 2. Montage f; Anprobe f; ‿s pl. Einrichtung f; Armaturen f/pl.

five [faiv] 1. fünf; 2. Fünf f.

fix [fiks] 1. v/t. befestigen, anheften; fixieren, Augen etc. heften, richten; fesseln; aufstellen; bestimmen, festsetzen; bsd. Am. richten, Bett etc. machen; ‿o.s. sich niederlassen; ‿ up in Ordnung bringen, arrangieren; v/i. fest werden; ‿ on sich entschließen für; 2. F Klemme f; Am. Zustand m; ‿ed fest; bestimmt; starr; ‿ing ['fiksiŋ] Befestigen n; Instandsetzen n; Fixieren n; Aufstellen n, Montieren n; Besatz m, Versteifung f; Am. ‿s pl. Zubehör n, Extraausrüstung f; ‿ture [‿stʃə] fest angebrachtes Zubehörteil, feste Anlage; Inventarstück n; lighting ‿ Beleuchtungskörper m.

fizz [fiz] 1. zischen, sprudeln; 2. Zischen n; † Schampus m (Sekt).

flabbergast F ['flæbəgɑːst] verblüffen; be ‿ed baff od. platt sein.

flabby ['flæbi] schlaff, schlapp.

flag [flæg] 1. Flagge f; Fahne f; Fliese f; Schwertlilie f; 2. beflaggen; durch Flaggen signalisieren; mit Fliesen belegen; ermatten, mutlos werden; ‿-day ['flægdei] Opfertag m; Flag Day Am. Tag m des Sternenbanners (14. Juni).

flagitious [‿ [flə'dʒiʃəs] schändlich.

flagrant [['fleigrənt] abscheulich; berüchtigt; offenkundig.

flag|staff ['flægstɑːf] Fahnenstange f; ‿stone Fliese f.

flair [fleə] Spürsinn m, feine Nase.

flake [fleik] 1. Flocke f; Schicht f; 2. (sich) flocken; abblättern.

flame [fleim] 1. Flamme f, Feuer n; fig. Hitze f; 2. flammen, lodern.

flank [flæŋk] 1. Flanke f; Weiche f der Tiere; 2. flankieren.

flannel ['flænl] Flanell m; Waschlappen m; ‿s pl. Flanellhose f.

flap [flæp] 1. (Ohr)Läppchen n;

Rockschoß m; Hut-Krempe f; Klappe f; Klaps m; (Flügel)Schlag m; 2. v/t. klatschen(d schlagen); v/i. lose herabhängen; flattern.

flare [fleə] 1. flackern; sich nach außen erweitern, sich bauschen; ‿ up aufflammen, fig. aufbrausen; 2. flackerndes Licht; Lichtsignal n.

flash [flæʃ] 1. aufgedonnert; unecht; Gauner...; 2. Blitz m; fig. Aufblitzen n; bsd. Am. Zeitung: kurze Meldung; in a ‿ im Nu; ‿ of wit Geistesblitz m; 3. (auf)blitzen; auflodern (lassen); Blick etc. werfen; flitzen, funken, telegraphieren; it ‿ed on me mir kam plötzlich der Gedanke; ‿back ['flæʃbæk] Film Rückblende f; ‿light phot Blitzlicht n; Blinklicht n; Taschenlampe f; ‿y [‿ʃi] auffallend.

flask [flɑːsk] Taschen-, Reiseflasche f.

flat [flæt] 1. ☐ flach, platt; schal; † flau; klar; glatt; ♩ um e-n halben Ton erniedrigt, ‿ price Einheitspreis m; 2. adv. glatt; völlig; fall ‿ danebengehen, sing ‿ zu tief singen; 3. Fläche f, Ebene f; Flachland n, Untiefe f, (Miet)Wohnung f; ♩ B n; F Simpel m; mot. sl. Flachland n od. Untiefe f, (Miet)Wohnung f; Am. sl. Polyp m (Polizist); ‿footed plattfüßig, Am. F fig. stur, eisern; ‿iron Plätteisen n; ‿ness [‿tnis] Flachheit f, Plattheit f; † Flauheit f; ‿ten [‿tn] (sich) ab-, verflachen.

flatter ['flætə] schmeicheln (dat.); ‿er [‿ərə] Schmeichler(in); ‿y [‿ri] Schmeichelei f.

flavo(u)r ['fleivə] 1. Geschmack m; Aroma n, Blume f (Wein); fig. Beigeschmack m, Würze f; 2. würzen; ‿less [‿əlis] geschmacklos, fad.

flaw [flɔː] 1. Sprung m, Riß m; Fehler m, ♣ Bö f; 2. zerbrechen; beschädigen; ‿less ☐ ['flɔːlis] fehlerlos.

flax ♣ [flæks] Flachs m, Lein m.

flay [flei] die Haut abziehen (dat.).

flea [fliː] Floh m.

fled [fled] pret. u. p.p. von flee.

fledg|e [fledʒ] v/i. flügge werden; v/t. befiedern; ‿(e)ling ['fledʒliŋ] Küken n (a. fig.); Grünschnabel m.

flee [fliː] [irr.] fliehen; meiden.

fleec|e [fliːs] 1. Vlies n; 2. scheren; prellen; ‿y ['fliːsi] wollig.

fleer [fliə] höhnen (at über acc.).

fleet [fliːt] 1. ☐ schnell; 2. Flotte f; ♀ Street die (Londoner) Presse.

flesh [fleʃ] 1. lebendiges Fleisch; fig. Fleisch(eslust f) n; 2. hunt. Blut kosten lassen; ‿ly ['fleʃli] fleischlich; irdisch; ‿y [‿ʃi] fleischig; fett.

flew [fluː] pret. von fly 2.

flexib|ility [fleksə'biliti] Biegsamkeit f; ‿le [['fleksəbl] flexibel, biegsam; fig. anpassungsfähig.

flick [flik] schnippen; schnellen.

flicker ['flikə] 1. flackern; flattern; flimmern; 2. Flackern *n*, Flimmern *n*; Flattern *n*; *Am.* Buntspecht *m*.

fier ['flaiə] = flyer.

flight [flait] Flucht *f*; Flug *m* (*a. fig.*); Schwarm *m*; ✈, ✗ Kette *f*; (*∼ of stairs* Treppen)Flucht *f*; *put to ∼* in die Flucht schlagen; *∼y* □ ['flaiti] flüchtig; leichtsinnig.

flimsy ['flimzi] dünn, locker; schwach; *fig.* fadenscheinig.

flinch [flintʃ] zurückweichen; zukken.

fling [fliŋ] 1. Wurf *m*; Schlag *m*; *have one's ∼* sich austoben; 2. [*irr.*] *v/i.* eilen; ausschlagen (*Pferd*); *fig.* toben; *v/t.* werfen, schleudern; *∼ o.s.* sich stürzen; *∼ open* aufreißen.

flint [flint] Kiesel *m*; Feuerstein *m*.

flip [flip] 1. Klaps *m*; Ruck *m*; 2. schnippen; klapsen; (umher-) flitzen.

flippan|cy ['flipənsi] Leichtfertigkeit *f*; *∼t* □ [*∼nt*] leichtfertig; vorlaut.

flirt [flə:t] 1. Kokette *f*; Weiberheld *m*; 2. flirten, kokettieren; = *flip* 2; *∼ation* [flə:'teiʃən] Flirt *m*.

flit [flit] flitzen; wandern; umziehen.

flivver *Am. sl.* ['flivə] 1. Nuckelpinne *f* (*billiges Auto*); 2. mißlingen.

float [flout] 1. Schwimmer *m*; Floß *n*; Plattformwagen *m*; 2. *v/t.* überfluten; flößen; tragen (*Wasser*); ⚓ flott machen, *fig.* in Gang bringen; ✝ gründen; verbreiten; *v/i.* schwimmen, treiben; schweben; umlaufen.

flock [flɔk] 1. Herde *f* (*a. fig.*); Schar *f*; 2. sich scharen; zs.-strömen.

floe [flou] (treibende) Eisscholle.

flog [flɔg] peitschen; prügeln.

flood [flʌd] 1. *a. ∼-tide* Flut *f*; Überschwemmung *f*; 2. überfluten, überschwemmen; *∼gate* ['flʌdgeit] Schleusentor *n*; *∼light* ⚡ Flutlicht *n*.

floor [flɔ:] 1. Fußboden *m*; Stock (-werk *n*) *m*; ✍ Tenne *f*; *∼ leader Am.* Fraktionsvorsitzende(r) *m*; *∼ show* Nachtklubvorstellung *f*; *take the ∼* das Wort ergreifen; 2. dielen; zu Boden schlagen; verblüffen; *∼cloth* ['flɔ:klɔθ] Putzlappen *m*; *∼ing* ['flɔ:riŋ] Dielung *f*; Fußboden *m*; *∼lamp* Stehlampe *f*; *∼walker Am.* ['flɔ:wɔ:kə] = *shopwalker*.

flop [flɔp] 1. schlagen; flattern; (hin)plumpsen (lassen); *Am.* versagen; 2. Plumps *m*; Versager *m*; *∼house Am. sl.* Penne *f*.

florid ⌍ ['flɔrid] blühend.

florin ['flɔrin] Zweischillingstück *n*.

florist ['flɔrist] Blumenhändler *m*.

floss [flɔs] Floretseide *f*.

flounce[1] [flauns] Volant *m*.

flounce[2] [*∼*] stürzen; zappeln.

flounder[1] *ichth.* ['flaundə] Flunder *f*.

flounder[2] [*∼*] sich (ab)mühen.

flour ['flauə] (feines) Mehl.

flourish ['flʌriʃ] 1. Schnörkel *m*; Schwingen *n*; ♪ Tusch *m*; 2. *v/i.* blühen, gedeihen; *v/t.* schwingen.

flout [flaut] (ver)spotten.

flow [flou] 1. Fluß *m*; Flut *f*; 2. fließen, fluten; wallen.

flower ['flauə] 1. Blume *f*; Blüte *f* (*a. fig.*); Zierde *f*; 2. blühen; *∼pot* Blumentopf *m*; *∼y* [*∼əri*] blumig.

flown [floun] *p.p. von* fly 2.

flubdub *Am. sl.* ['flʌbdʌb] Geschwätz *n*.

fluctuat|e ['flʌktjueit] schwanken; *∼ion* [flʌktju'eiʃən] Schwankung *f*.

flu(e)[1] F [flu:] = *influenza*.

flue[2] [flu:] Kaminrohr *n*; Heizrohr *n*.

fluen|cy *fig.* ['flu(:)ənsi] Fluß *m*; *∼t* [*∼nt*] fließend, geläufig (*Rede*).

fluff [flʌf] 1. Flaum *m*; Flocke *f*; *fig.* Schnitzer *m*; 2. *Kissen etc.* aufschütteln; *Federn* aufplustern (*Vogel*); *∼y* ['flʌfi] flaumig; flockig.

fluid ['flu(:)id] 1. flüssig; 2. Flüssigkeit *f*.

flung [flʌŋ] *pret. u. p.p. von* fling 2.

flunk *Am.* F *fig.* [flʌŋk] durchfallen (lassen).

flunk(e)y ['flʌŋki] Lakai *m*.

fluorescent [fluə'resnt] fluoreszierend.

flurry ['flʌri] Nervosität *f*; Bö *f*; *Am. a.* (Regen)Schauer *m*; Schneegestöber *n*.

flush [flʌʃ] 1. ⊕ in gleicher Ebene; reichlich; (über)voll; 2. Erröten *n*; Übermut *m*; Fülle *f*; Wachstum *n*; *fig.* Blüte *f*; Spülung *f*; *Karten:* Flöte *f*; 3. über-, durchfluten; (aus)spülen; strömen; sprießen (lassen); erröten (machen); übermütig machen; aufjagen.

fluster ['flʌstə] 1. Aufregung *f*; 2. *v/t* aufregen.

flute [flu:t] 1. ♪ Flöte *f*; Falte *f*; 2. (auf der) Flöte spielen; riefeln; fälteln.

flutter ['flʌtə] 1. Geflatter *n*; Erregung *f*; F Spekulation *f*; 2. *v/t.* aufregen; *v/i.* flattern.

flux [flʌks] *fig.* Fluß *m*; ✞ Ausfluß *m*.

fly [flai] 1. *zo.* Fliege *f*; Flug *m*; *Am. Baseball:* hochgeschlagener Ball; Droschke *f*; 2. [*irr.*] (*a. fig.*) fliegen (lassen); entfliehen (*Zeit*); ✗ führen; *Flagge* hissen; fliehen; *∼ over* überfliegen; *∼ at* herfallen über; *∼ into a passion od.* rage in Zorn geraten.

flyer ['flaiə] Flieger *m*; Renner *m*; *take a ∼ Am.* F Vermögen riskieren.

fly-flap ['flaiflæp] Fliegenklatsche *f*.

flying ['flaiiŋ] fliegend; Flug...; *∼ squad* Überfallkommando *n*.

fly|-over ['flaiouvə] (Straßen)Überführung *f*; *∼-weight Boxen:* Fliegengewicht n; ~-wheel Schwungrad n.

foal [foul] 1. Fohlen n; 2. fohlen.

foam [foum] 1. Schaum m; 2. schäumen; ~y ['foumi] schaumig.

focus ['foukəs] 1. Brennpunkt m; 2. (sich) im Brennpunkt vereinigen; opt. einstellen (a. fig.); konzentrieren.

fodder ['fɔdə] (Trocken)Futter n.

foe poet [fou] Feind m, Gegner m.

fog [fɔg] 1. (dichter) Nebel; fig. Umnebelung f; phot. Schleier m; 2. mst fig. umnebeln; phot. verschleiern.

fogey F ['fougi]: old ~ komischer alter Kauz.

foggy ['fɔgi] neb(e)lig; fig. nebelhaft.

fogy Am ['fougi] = fogey.

foible fig ['fɔibl] Schwäche f.

foil[1] [fɔil] Folie f; Hintergrund m.

foil[2] [~] 1. vereiteln; 2. Florett n.

fold[1] [fould] 1. Schafhürde f; fig. Herde f; 2. einpferchen.

fold[2] [~] 1. Falte f; Falz m; 2. ...fach, ...fältig; 3. v/t. falten; falzen; Arme kreuzen, ~ (up) einwickeln; v/i. sich falten, Am. F eingehen; ~er ['fouldə] Mappe f, Schnellhefter m; Faltprospekt m.

folding ['fouldiŋ] zs.-legbar; Klapp...; ~bed Feldbett n; ~boat Faltboot n; ~door(s pl.) Flügeltür f; ~-screen spanische Wand; ~seat Klappsitz m.

foliage ['fouliidʒ] Laub(werk) n.

folk [fouk] pl. Leute pl.; ~s pl. Leute pl. (F a Angehörige); ~lore ['fouklɔ:] Volkskunde f; Volkssagen f/pl.; ~song Volkslied n.

follow ['fɔlou] folgen (dat.); folgen auf (acc.); be-, verfolgen; s-m Beruf etc nachgehen; ~er [~ou] Nachfolger(in); Verfolger(in); Anhänger(in), ~ing [~ouiŋ] Anhängerschaft f, Gefolge m.

folly ['fɔli] Torheit f; Narrheit f.

foment [fou'ment] j-m warme Umschläge machen; Unruhe stiften.

fond [fɔnd] zärtlich; vernarrt (of in acc.), be~ of gern haben, lieben; ~le ['fɔndl] liebkosen; streicheln; (ver)hätscheln; ~ness [~dnis] Zärtlichkeit f; Vorliebe f.

font [fɔnt] Taufstein m; Am. Quelle f.

food [fu:d] Speise f, Nahrung f; Futter n; Lebensmittel n/pl.; ~stuff ['fu:dstʌf] Nahrungsmittel n.

fool [fu:l] 1. Narr m, Tor m; Hanswurst m; make a ~ of s.o. j-n zum Narren halten; make a ~ of o.s. sich lächerlich machen; 2. Am. F närrisch, dumm; 3. v/t. narren; prellen (out of um et.); ~ away F vertrödeln; v/i. albern; (herum)spielen; ~ (a)round bsd. Am. Zeit vertrödeln.

fool|ery ['fu:ləri] Torheit f; ~hardy

['fu:lhɑ:di] tollkühn; ~ish □ ['fu:liʃ] töricht; ~ishness [~ʃnis] Torheit f; ~proof kinderleicht.

foot [fut] 1. pl **feet** [fi:t] Fuß m (a. Maß); Fußende n; ⚔ Infanterie f; on ~ zu Fuß; im Gange, in Gang; 2. v/t. mst ~ up addieren; ~ the bill F die Rechnung bezahlen; v/i. ~ it zu Fuß gehen; ~board ['futbɔ:d] Trittbrett n; ~boy Page m; ~fall Tritt m, Schritt m; ~gear Schuhwerk n; ~hold fester Stand; fig. Halt m.

footing ['futiŋ] Halt m, Stand m; Grundlage f, Basis f; Stellung f; fester Fuß, Verhältnis n; ~ Zustand m; Endsumme f; be on a friendly ~ with s.o. ein gutes Verhältnis zu j-m haben; lose one's ~ ausgleiten

foot|lights thea. ['futlaits] pl. Rampenlicht(er pl.) n; Bühne f; ~man Diener m, ~passenger Fußgänger (-in); ~path Fußpfad m; ~print Fußstapfe f, -spur f; ~sore fußkrank; step Fußstapfe f, Spur f; ~stool Fußbank f; ~wear = footgear.

fop [fɔp] Geck m, Fatzke m.

for [fɔ:, fɔr, fə] 1. prp. mst für; Zweck, Ziel, Richtung zu; nach; warten, hoffen etc auf (acc.); sich sehnen etc. nach; Grund, Anlaß aus, vor (dat.), wegen, Zeitdauer: ~ three days drei Tage (lang); seit drei Tagen; Entfernung I walked ~ a mile ich ging eine Meile (weit); Austausch: (an-)statt; in der Eigenschaft als; I ~ one ich zum Beispiel; ~ sure sicher!, gewiß!; 2. cj denn, nämlich.

forage ['fɔridʒ] 1. Futter n; 2. (nach Futter) suchen.

foray ['fɔrei] räuberischer Einfall.

forbear[1] [fɔ:'bɛə] [irr. (bear)] v/t. unterlassen; v/i sich enthalten (from gen.); Geduld haben.

forbear[2] ['fɔ:bɛə] Vorfahr m.

forbid [fə'bid] [irr. (bid)] verbieten; hindern; ~ding [~diŋ] abstoßend.

force [fɔ:s] 1. mst Kraft f, Gewalt f; Nachdruck m; Zwang m; Heer n; Streitmacht f; the ~ die Polizei; armed ~s pl. Streitkräfte f/pl.; come (put) in ~ in Kraft treten (setzen); 2. zwingen, nötigen; erzwingen; aufzwingen; Gewalt antun (dat.); beschleunigen; aufbrechen; künstlich reif machen; ~ open aufbrechen; ~d: ~ landing Notlandung f; ~ loan Zwangsanleihe f; ~ march Eilmarsch m; ~ful □ ['fɔ:sful] kräftig; eindringlich.

forceps 🛠 ['fɔ:seps] Zange f.

forcible □ ['fɔ:səbl] gewaltsam; Zwangs...; eindringlich, wirksam.

ford [fɔ:d] 1. Furt f; 2. durchwaten.

fore [fɔ:] 1. adv. vorn; 2. Vorderteil m, n; bring (come) to the ~ zum

Vorschein bringen (kommen); **3.** *adj.* vorder; Vorder...; **~bode** [fɔ:'boud] vorhersagen; ahnen; **~boding** [~diŋ] (böses) Vorzeichen; Ahnung *f*; **~cast** ['fɔ:ka:st] **1.** Vorhersage *f*; **2.** [*irr.* (cast)] vorhersehen; voraussagen; **~father** Vorfahr *m*; **~finger** Zeigefinger *m*; **~foot** Vorderfuß *m*; **~go** [fɔ:'gou] [*irr.* (go)] vorangehen; **~gone** [fɔ:'gɔn, *adj.* 'fɔ:gɔn] von vornherein feststehend; ~ conclusion Selbstverständlichkeit *f*; **~ground** Vordergrund *m*; **~head** ['fɔrid] Stirn *f*.

foreign ['fɔrin] fremd; ausländisch; auswärtig; **~er** [~nə] Ausländer(in), Fremde(r *m* *f*); ♀ Office Außenministerium *n*; **~ policy** Außenpolitik *f*; ~ trade Außenhandel *m*.

fore|knowledge ['fɔ:'nɔlidʒ] Vorherwissen *n*; **~leg** ['fɔ:leg] Vorderbein *n*; **~lock** Stirnhaar *n*; *fig.* Schopf *m*; **~man** ⚒ Obmann *m*; Vorarbeiter *m*, (Werk)Meister *m*; ⚒ Steiger *m*; **~most** vorderst, erst; **~name** Vorname *m*; **~noon** Vormittag *m*; **~runner** Vorläufer *m*, Vorbote *m*; **~see** [fɔ:'si:] [*irr.* (see)] vorhersehen; **~shadow** ankündigen; **~sight** ['fɔ:sait] Voraussicht *f*; Vorsorge *f*.

forest ['fɔrist] **1.** Wald *m* (*a. fig.*), Forst *m*; **2.** aufforsten.

forestall [fɔ:'stɔ:l] *et.* vereiteln; *j-m* zuvorkommen.

forest|er ['fɔristə] Förster *m*; Waldarbeiter *m*; **~ry** [~tri] Forstwirtschaft *f*; Waldgebiet *n*.

fore|taste ['fɔ:teist] Vorgeschmack *m*; **~tell** [fɔ:'tel] [*irr.* (tell)] vorhersagen; vorbedeuten; **~thought** ['fɔ:θɔ:t] Vorbedacht *m*; **~woman** Aufseherin *f*; Vorarbeiterin *f*; **~word** Vorwort *n*.

forfeit ['fɔ:fit] **1.** Verwirkung *f*; Strafe *f*; Pfand *n*; **2.** verwirken; einbüßen; **~able** [~təbl] verwirkbar.

forge¹ [fɔ:dʒ] *mst* ~ ahead sich vor(wärts)arbeiten.

forge² [~] **1.** Schmiede *f*; **2.** schmieden (*fig. ersinnen*); fälschen; **~ry** ['fɔ:dʒəri] Fälschung *f*.

forget [fə'get] [*irr.*] vergessen; **~ful** □ [~tful] vergeßlich; **~-me-not** ♀ Vergißmeinnicht *n*.

forgiv|e [fə'giv] [*irr.* (give)] vergeben, verzeihen; *Schuld* erlassen; **~eness** [~vnis] Verzeihung *f*; **~ing** □ [~viŋ] versöhnlich; nachsichtig.

forgo [fɔ:'gou] [*irr.* (go)] verzichten auf (*acc.*); aufgeben.

forgot [fə'gɔt] *pret. von* forget; **~ten** [~tn] *p.p. von* forget.

fork [fɔ:k] **1.** Gabel *f*; **2.** (sich) gabeln; **~lift** ['fɔ:klift] Gabelstapler *m*.

forlorn [fə'lɔ:n] verloren, verlassen.

form [fɔ:m] **1.** Form *f*; Gestalt *f*; Formalität *f*; Formular *n*; (Schul-)Bank *f*; *Schul-*Klasse *f*; Kondition

f; geistige Verfassung; **2.** (sich) formen, (sich) bilden, gestalten; ✗ (sich) aufstellen.

formal □ ['fɔ:məl] förmlich; formell; äußerlich; **~ity** [fɔ:'mæliti] Förmlichkeit *f*, Formalität *f*.

formati|on [fɔ:'meiʃən] Bildung *f*; **~ve** ['fɔ:mətiv] bildend; gestaltend; ~ years *pl.* Entwicklungsjahre *n/pl.*

former ['fɔ:mə] vorig, früher; ehemalig, vergangen; erstere(r, -s); jene(r, -s); **~ly** [~əli] ehemals, früher.

formidable □ ['fɔ:midəbl] furchtbar, schrecklich; ungeheuer.

formula ['fɔ:mjulə] Formel *f*; 💊 Rezept *n*; **~te** [~leit] formulieren.

forsake [fə'seik] [*irr.*] aufgeben; verlassen; **~n** [~kən] *p.p. von* forsake.

forsook [fə'suk] *pret. von* forsake.

forsooth *iro.* [fə'su:θ] wahrlich.

forswear [fɔ:'sweə] [*irr.* (swear)] abschwören. [werk *n*) *f*.)

fort ✗ [fɔ:t] Fort *n*, Festungs-)

forth [fɔ:θ] vor(wärts); voran; heraus, hinaus, hervor; weiter, fort(an); **~coming** [fɔ:θ'kʌmiŋ] erscheinend; bereit; bevorstehend; entgegenkommend; **~with** ['fɔ:θ'wiθ] sogleich.

fortieth ['fɔ:tiiθ] **1.** vierzigste(r, -s); Vierzigstel *n*.

forti|fication [fɔ:tifi'keiʃən] Befestigung *f*; **~fy** ['fɔ:tifai] ✗ befestigen; *fig.* (ver)stärken; **~tude** [~itju:d] Seelenstärke *f*; Tapferkeit *f*.

fortnight ['fɔ:tnait] vierzehn Tage.

fortress ['fɔ:tris] Festung *f*.

fortuitous □ [fɔ:'tju(:)itəs] zufällig.

fortunate ['fɔ:tʃnit] glücklich; **~ly** [~tli] glücklicherweise.

fortune ['fɔ:tʃən] Glück *n*; Schicksal *n*; Zufall *m*; Vermögen *n*; **~-teller** Wahrsager(in).

forty ['fɔ:ti] **1.** vierzig; **~-niner** *Am.* kalifornischer Goldsucher von 1849; ~ winks *pl.* F Nickerchen *n*; **2.** Vierzig *f*.

forward ['fɔ:wəd] **1.** *adj.* vorder; bereit(willig); fortschrittlich; vorwitzig, keck; **2.** *adv.* vor(wärts); **3.** *Fußball:* Stürmer *m*; **4.** (be)fördern; (ab-, ver)senden.

forwarding-agent ['fɔ:wədiŋeidʒənt] Spediteur *m*.

foster ['fɔstə] **1.** *fig.* nähren, pflegen; ~ up aufziehen; **2.** Pflege...

fought [fɔ:t] *pret. u. p.p. von* fight **2.**

foul [faul] **1.** ☐ widerwärtig; schmutzig (*a. fig.*); unehrlich; regelwidrig; übelriechend; faul, verdorben; windig; schlecht (*Wetter*); fall ~ of mit *dem Gesetz* in Konflikt kommen; **2.** Zs.-stoß *m*; *Sport:* regelwidriges Spiel; *through fair and ~* durch dick und dünn; **3.** be-, verschmutzen; (sich) verwickeln.

found [faund] 1. *pret. u. p.p. von* find 1; 2. (be)gründen; stiften; ⊕ gießen.

foundation [faun'deiʃən] Gründung *f*; Stiftung *f*; Fundament *n*.

founder ['faundə] 1. (Be)Gründer (-in), Stifter(in); Gießer *m*; 2. *v/i.* scheitern; lahmen.

foundling ['faundliŋ] Findling *m*.

foundry ⊕ ['faundri] Gießerei *f*.

fountain ['fauntin] Quelle *f*; Springbrunnen *m*; **~-pen** Füllfederhalter *m*.

four [fɔ:] 1. vier; 2. Vier *f*; *Sport:* Vierer *m*; **~-flusher** *Am. sl.* ['fɔ:-ˈflʌʃə] Hochstapler *m*; **~-square** viereckig; *fig.* unerschütterlich; **~-stroke** *mot.* Viertakt...; **~teen** ['fɔːˈtin] vierzehn; **~teenth** [~nθ] vierzehnte(r, -s); **~th** [fɔ:θ] 1. vierte(r, -s); 2. Viertel *n*; **~thly** ['fɔːθli] viertens.

fowl [faul] Geflügel *n*; Huhn *n*; Vogel *m*; **~-piece** ['faulinpi:s] Vogelflinte *f*.

fox [fɔks] 1. Fuchs *m*; 2. überlisten; **~-glove** ♀ ['fɔksglʌv] Fingerhut *m*; **~y** ['fɔksi] fuchsartig; schlau.

fraction ['frækʃən] Bruch(teil) *m*.

fracture ['fræktʃə] 1. (*bsd.* Knochen)Bruch *m*; 2. brechen.

fragile ['frædʒail] zerbrechlich.

fragment ['frægmənt] Bruchstück *n*.

fragran|ce ['freigrəns] Wohlgeruch *m*, Duft *m*; **~t** [~nt] wohlriechend.

frail □ [freil] ge-, zerbrechlich; schwach; **~ty** *fig.* ['freilti] Schwäche *f*.

frame [freim] 1. Rahmen *m*; Gerippe *n*; Gerüst *n*; (Brillen)Gestell *n*; Körper *m*; (An)Ordnung *f*; *phot.* (Einzel)Bild *n*; ♀ Frühbeetkasten *m*; **~ of mind** Gemütsverfassung *f*; 2. bilden, formen, bauen; entwerfen; (ein)rahmen; sich entwickeln; **~-house** ['freimhaus] Holzhaus *n*; **~-up** *bsd. Am.* F abgekartetes Spiel; **~work** ⊕ Gerippe *n*; Rahmen *m*; *fig.* Bau *m*.

franchise ⚖ ['fræntʃaiz] Wahlrecht *n*; Bürgerrecht *n*; *bsd. Am.* Konzession *f*.

frank [fræŋk] 1. □ frei(mütig), offen; 2. *Brief* maschinell frankieren.

frankfurter ['fræŋkfətə] Frankfurter Würstchen *n*.

frankness ['fræŋknis] Offenheit *f*.

frantic ['fræntik] (~ally) wahnsinnig.

fratern|al □ [frə'tə:nl] brüderlich; **~ity** [~niti] Brüderlichkeit *f*; Brüderschaft *f*; *Am. univ.* Verbindung *f*.

fraud [frɔ:d] Betrug *m*; F Schwindel *m*; **~ulent** □ ['frɔ:djulənt] betrügerisch.

fray [frei] 1. (sich) abnutzen; (sich) durchscheuern; 2. Schlägerei *f*.

frazzle *bsd. Am.* F ['fræzl] 1. Fetzen *m/pl.*; 2. zerfetzen.

freak [fri:k] Einfall *m*, Laune *f*.

freckle ['frekl] Sommersprosse *f*.

free [fri:] 1. □ *allg.* frei; freigebig (*of* mit); freiwillig; he is ~ *to* inf. es steht ihm frei, zu *inf.*; ~ *and easy* zwanglos; sorglos; *make* ~ sich Freiheiten erlauben; *set* ~ freilassen; 2. befreien; freilassen, *et.* freimachen; **~booter** ['fri:bu:tə] Freibeuter *m*; **~dom** ['fri:dəm] Freiheit *f*; freie Benutzung; Offenheit *f*; Zwanglosigkeit *f*; (plumpe) Vertraulichkeit; ~ *of a city* (Ehren-)Bürgerrecht *n*; **~holder** Grundeigentümer *m*; **~man** freier Mann; Vollbürger *m*; **~mason** Freimaurer *m*; **~wheel** Freilauf *m*.

freez|e [fri:z] [*irr.*] *v/i.* (ge)frieren; erstarren; *v/t.* gefrieren lassen; **~er** ['friːzə] Eismaschine *f*; Gefriermaschine *f*; Gefriertruhe *f*; **~ing** □ [~ziŋ] eisig; **~point** Gefrierpunkt *m*.

freight [freit] 1. Fracht(geld *n*) *f*; *attr. Am.* Güter...; 2. be-, verfrachten; **~-car** *Am.* 🚃 ['freitkɑː: Güterwagen *m*; **~-train** *Am.* Güterzug *m*.

French [frentʃ] 1. französisch; *take* ~ *leave* heimlich weggehen; ~ *window* Balkon-, Verandatür *f*; 2. Französisch *n*; *the* ~ *pl.* die Franzosen *pl.*; **~man** ['frentʃmən] Franzose *m*.

frenz|ied ['frenzid] wahnsinnig; **~y** [~zi] Wahnsinn *m*.

frequen|cy ['fri:kwənsi] Häufigkeit *f*; ⚡ Frequenz *f*; **~t** 1. □ [~nt] häufig; 2. [fri'kwent] (oft) besuchen.

fresh □ [freʃ] frisch; neu; unerfahren; *Am.* F frech; ~ *water* Süßwasser *n*; **~en** ['freʃn] frisch machen *od.* werden; **~et** [~ʃit] Hochwasser *n*; *fig.* Flut *f*; **~man** *univ.* Student *m* im ersten Jahr; **~ness** [~ʃnis] Frische *f*; Neuheit *f*; Unerfahrenheit *f*; **~water** Süßwasser...; ~ *college Am.* drittrangiges College.

fret [fret] 1. Aufregung *f*; Ärger *m*; ♪ Bund *m*, Griffleiste *f*; 2. zerfressen; (sich) ärgern; (sich) grämen; ~ *away*, ~ *out* aufreiben.

fretful □ ['fretful] ärgerlich.

fret-saw ['fretsɔ:] Laubsäge *f*.

fretwork ['fretwə:k] (geschnitztes) Gitterwerk; Laubsägearbeit *f*.

friar ['fraiə] Mönch *m*.

friction ['frikʃən] Reibung *f* (*a. fig.*).

Friday ['fraidi] Freitag *m*.

fridge F [fridʒ] Kühlschrank *m*.

friend [frend] Freund(in); Bekannte(r *m*) *f*; **~ly** ['frendli] freund(schaft)lich; **~ship** [~dʃip] Freundschaft *f*.

frigate ⚓ ['frigit] Fregatte *f*.

frig(e) F [fridʒ] = *fridge*.

fright [frait] Schreck(en) *m*; *fig.* Vogelscheuche *f*; ~en ['fraitn] erschrecken; ~ed *at od.* of bange vor (*dat.*); ~ful [~tful] schrecklich.

frigid [['fridʒid] kalt, frostig.

frill [fril] Krause *f*, Rüsche *f*.

fringe [frindʒ] 1. Franse *f*; Rand *m*; *a.* ~s *pl.* Ponyfrisur *f*; 2. mit Fransen besetzen.

frippery ['fripəri] Flitterkram *m*.

Frisian ['friziən] friesisch.

frisk [frisk] 1. Luftsprung *m*; 2. hüpfen; *sl. nach Waffen etc.* durchsuchen; ~y [['friski] munter.

fritter ['fritə] 1. Pfannkuchen *m*, Krapfen *m*; 2. ~ away verzetteln.

frivol|ity [fri'vɔliti] Frivolität *f*, Leichtfertigkeit *f*; ~ous [['frivələs] nichtig; leichtfertig.

frizzle ['frizl] *a.* ~ up (sich) kräuseln; *Küche* brutzeln.

fro [frou] *to and* ~ hin und her.

frock [frɔk] Kutte *f*; *Frauen-Kleid n*; Kittel *m*; Gehrock *m*.

frog [frɔg] Frosch *m*.

frolic ['frɔlik] 1. Fröhlichkeit *f*; Scherz *m*; 2. scherzen, spaßen; ~some [[~ksəm] lustig, fröhlich.

from [frɔm; frəm] von; aus, von ... her; von ... (an); aus, vor, wegen; nach, gemäß; *defend* ~ schützen vor (*dat.*); ~ amidst mitten aus.

front [frʌnt] 1. Stirn *f*; Vorderseite *f*; ✗ Front *f*; Hemdbrust *f*; Strandpromenade *f*; Kühnheit *f*, Frechheit *f*; *in* ~ vorn; *in* ~ of räumlich vor; 2. Vorder...; 3. *a.* ~ on, ~ towards die Front haben nach; gegenüberstehen, gegenübertreten (*dat.*); ~al ['frʌntl] Stirn...; Front...; Vorder...; ~ door Haustür *f*; ~ier [~tjə] Grenze *f*, *bsd. Am. hist.* Grenze zum Wilden Westen; *attr.* Grenz...; ~iersman [~iersmən] Grenzbewohner *m*; *fig.* Pionier *m*; ~ispiece [~tispiːs] ⚑ Vorderseite *f*; *typ.* Titelbild *n*; ~ man *fig.* Aushängeschild *n*; ~page Zeitung: Titelseite *f*; ~wheel drive *mot.* Vorderradantrieb *m*.

frost [frɔst] 1. Frost *m*; *a.* hoar ~, white ~ Reif *m*; 2. (mit Zucker) bestreuen; glasieren; mattieren; ~ed glass Milchglas *n*; ~bite ⚒ ['frɔstbait] Erfrierung *f*; ~y [[~ti] frostig; bereift.

froth [frɔθ] 1. Schaum *m*; 2. schäumen; zu Schaum schlagen; ~y [['frɔθi] schaumig; *fig.* seicht.

frown [fraun] 1. Stirnrunzeln *n*; finsterer Blick; 2. *v/i.* die Stirn runzeln; finster blicken.

frow|sty [['frausti], ~zy ['frauzi] moderig; schlampig.

froze [frouz] *pret. von* freeze; ~n ['frouzn] 1. *p.p. von* freeze; 2. *adj.* (eis)kalt; (ein)gefroren.

frugal [['fruːgəl] mäßig; sparsam.

fruit [fruːt] 1. Frucht *f*; Früchte *pl.*; Obst *n*; 2. Frucht tragen; ~erer ['fruːtərə] Obsthändler *m*; ~ful [[~tful] fruchtbar; ~less [[~tlis] unfruchtbar.

frustrat|e [frʌs'treit] vereiteln; enttäuschen; ~ion [~eiʃən] Vereitelung *f*; Enttäuschung *f*.

fry [frai] 1. Gebratene(s) *n*; Fischbrut *f*; 2. braten, backen; ~ing-pan ['fraiiŋpæn] Bratpfanne *f*.

fuchsia ⚘ ['fjuːʃə] Fuchsie *f*.

fudge [fʌdʒ] 1. F zurechtpfuschen; 2. Unsinn *m*; Weichkaramelle *f*.

fuel [fjuəl] 1. Brennmaterial *n*; Betriebs-, *mot.* Kraftstoff *m*; 2. *mot.* tanken.

fugitive ['fjuːdʒitiv] 1. flüchtig (*a. fig.*); 2. Flüchtling *m*.

fulfil(l) [ful'fil] erfüllen; vollziehen; ~ment [~lmənt] Erfüllung *f*.

full [ful] 1. ☐ *allg.* voll; Voll...; vollständig, völlig; reichlich; ausführlich; *of* ~ age volljährig; 2. *adv.* völlig, ganz; genau; 3. Ganze(s) *n*; Höhepunkt *m*; *in* ~ völlig; ausführlich; *to the* ~ vollständig; ~blooded ['ful'blʌdid] vollblütig; kräftig; reinrassig; ~dress Gesellschaftsanzug *m*; ~dress ['fuldres] formell, Gala...; *attr.* ausführlich; ~fledged ['ful'fledʒd] flügge; voll ausgewachsen; ~ stop Punkt *m*.

ful(l)ness ['fulnis] Fülle *f*.

full-time ['fultaim] vollbeschäftigt; Voll...

fulminate *fig.* ['fʌlmineit] wettern.

fumble ['fʌmbl] tasten; tummeln.

fume [fjuːm] 1. Dunst *m*, Dampf *m*; 2. rauchen; aufgebracht sein.

fumigate ['fjuːmigeit] ausräuchern, desinfizieren.

fun [fʌn] Scherz *m*, Spaß *m*; *make* ~ of sich lustig machen über (*acc.*).

function ['fʌŋkʃən] 1. Funktion *f*; Beruf *m*; Tätigkeit *f*; Aufgabe *f*; Feierlichkeit *f*; 2. funktionieren; ~ary [~ʃnəri] Beamte(r) *m*; Funktionär *m*.

fund [fʌnd] 1. Fonds *m*; ~s *pl.* Staatspapiere *n/pl.*; Geld(mittel *n/pl.*) *n*; Vorrat *m*; 2. *Schuld* fundieren; *Geld* anlegen.

fundamental ☐ [fʌndə'mentl] 1. grundlegend; Grund...; 2. ~s *pl.* Grundlage *f*, -züge *m/pl.*, -begriffe *m/pl.*

funer|al ['fjuːnərəl] Beerdigung *f*; *attr.* Trauer...; Begräbnis...; ~eal ☐ [fjuː(ː)'niəriəl] traurig, düster.

fun-fair ['fʌnfɛə] Rummelplatz *m*.

funicular [fjuː(ː)'nikjulə] 1. Seil...; 2. *a.* ~ railway (Draht)Seilbahn *f*.

funnel ['fʌnl] Trichter *m*; Rauchfang *m*; ⚓, ⚒ Schornstein *m*.

funnies *Am.* ['fʌniz] *pl.* Comics *pl.* (*primitive Bildserien*).

funny ☐ ['fʌni] spaßig, komisch.

fur [fə:] **1.** Pelz *m*; Belag *m der Zunge*; Kesselstein *m*; ~*s pl.* Pelzwaren *pl.*; **2.** mit Pelz besetzen *od.* füttern.

furbish ['fə:biʃ] putzen, polieren.

furious] ['fjuəriəs] wütend; wild.

furl [fə:l] zs.-rollen; zs.-klappen.

furlough ✕ ['fə:lou] Urlaub *m.*

furnace ['fə:nis] Schmelz-, Hochofen *m*; (Heiz)Kessel *m*; Feuerung *f.*

furnish ['fə:niʃ] versehen (*with* mit); *et.* liefern; möblieren; ausstatten.

furniture ['fə:nitʃə] Möbel *pl.*, Einrichtung *f*; Ausstattung *f*; sectional ~ Anbaumöbel *pl.*

furrier ['fʌriə] Kürschner *m.*

furrow ['fʌrou] **1.** Furche *f*; **2.** furchen.

further ['fə:ðə] **1.** *adj. u. adv.* ferner, weiter; **2.** fördern; ~ance [~ərəns] Förderung *f*; ~more [~ə'mɔ:] ferner, überdies; ~most [~əmoust] weitest.

furthest ['fə:ðist] = *furthermost.*

furtive ☐ ['fə:tiv] verstohlen.

fury ['fjuəri] Raserei *f*, Wut *f*; Furie *f.*

fuse [fju:z] **1.** (ver)schmelzen; ≠ durchbrennen; ausgehen (*Licht*); ✕ mit Zünder versehen; **2.** ≠ (Schmelz)Sicherung *f*; ✕ Zünder *m.*

fuselage ['fju:zilɑ:ʒ] (Flugzeug-) Rumpf *m.*

fusion ['fju:ʒən] Schmelzen *n*; Verschmelzung *f*, Fusion *f*; ~ **bomb** ✕ Wasserstoffbombe *f.*

fuss F [fʌs] **1.** Lärm *m*; Wesen *n*, Getue *n*; **2.** viel Aufhebens machen (*about* um, von); (sich) aufregen.

fusty ['fʌsti] muffig; *fig.* verstaubt.

futile ['fju:tail] nutzlos, nichtig.

future ['fju:tʃə] **1.** (zu)künftig; **2.** Zukunft *f*; *gr.* Futur *n*, Zukunft *f*; ~*s pl.* † Termingeschäfte *n/pl.*

fuzz [fʌz] **1.** feiner Flaum; Fussel *f*; **2.** fusseln, (zer)fasern.

G

gab F [gæb] Geschwätz *n*; *the gift of the* ~ ein gutes Mundwerk.

gabardine ['gæbədi:n] Gabardine *m* (*Wollstoff*).

gabble ['gæbl] **1.** Geschnatter *n*, Geschwätz *n*; **2.** schnattern, schwatzen.

gaberdine ['gæbədi:n] Kaftan *m*; = *gabardine.*

gable ['geibl] Giebel *m.*

gad F [gæd]: ~ *about* sich herumtreiben.

gadfly *zo.* ['gædflai] Bremse *f.*

gadget *sl.* ['gædʒit] Dings *n*, Apparat *m*; Kniff *m*, Pfiff *m.*

gag [gæg] **1.** Knebel *m*; Witz *m*; **2.** knebeln; *pol.* mundtot machen.

gage¹ [geidʒ] Pfand *n.*

gage² [~] = *gauge.*

gaiety ['geiəti] Fröhlichkeit *f.*

gaily ['geili] *adv. von* gay.

gain [gein] **1.** Gewinn *m*; Vorteil *m*; **2.** *v/t.* gewinnen; erreichen; bekommen; *v/i.* vorgehen (*Uhr*); ~ *in* zunehmen an (*acc.*); ~**ful** ['geinful] einträglich.

gait [geit] Gang(art *f*) *m*; Schritt *m.*

gaiter ['geitə] Gamasche *f.*

gal *Am. sl.* [gæl] Mädel *n.*

gale [geil] Sturm *m*; steife Brise.

gall [gɔ:l] **1.** Galle *f*; ⚕ Wolf *m*; Pein *f*; *bsd. Am. sl.* Frechheit *f*; **2.** wundreiben; ärgern.

gallant ['gælənt] **1.** ☐ stattlich; tapfer; galant, höflich; **2.** Kavalier *m*; **3.** galant sein; ~**ry** [~tri] Tapferkeit *f*; Galanterie *f.*

gallery ['gæləri] Galerie *f*; Empore *f.*

galley ['gæli] ⚓ Galeere *f*; ⚓ Kombüse *f*; ~**proof** Korrekturfahne *f.*

gallon ['gælən] Gallone *f* (*4,54 Liter, Am. 3,78 Liter*).

gallop ['gæləp] **1.** Galopp *m*; **2.** galoppieren (lassen).

gallows ['gælouz] *sg.* Galgen *m.*

galore [gə'lɔ:] in Menge.

gamble ['gæmbl] **1.** (um Geld) spielen; **2.** F Glücksspiel *n*; ~**r** [~lə] Spieler(in).

gambol ['gæmbəl] **1.** Luftsprung *m*; **2.** (fröhlich) hüpfen, tanzen.

game [geim] **1.** Spiel *n*; Scherz *m*; Wild *n*; **2.** F entschlossen; furchtlos; **3.** spielen; ~**keeper** f 'geimki:pə] Wildhüter *m*; ~**licence** Jagdschein *m*; ~**ster** ['geimstə] Spieler(in).

gander ['gændə] Gänserich *m.*

gang [gæŋ] **1.** Trupp *m*; Bande *f*; **2.** ~ *up* sich zs.-rotten *od.* zs.-tun; ~**board** ⚓ ['gæŋbɔ:d] Laufplanke *f.*

gangster *Am.* ['gæŋstə] Gangster *m.*

gangway ['gæŋwei] (Durch)Gang *m*; ⚓ Fallreep *n*; ⚓ Laufplanke *f.*

gaol [dʒeil], ~**bird** ['dʒeilbə:d], ~**er** ['dʒeilə] *s. jail etc.*

gap [gæp] Lücke *f*; Kluft *f*; Spalte *f.*

gape [geip] gähnen; klaffen; gaffen.

garage ['gærɑ:ʒ] **1.** Garage *f*; Autowerkstatt *f*; **2.** Auto einstellen.

garb [gɑ:b] Gewand *n*, Tracht *f.*

garbage ['gɑ:bidʒ] Abfall *m*;

Schund *m*; ~ can *Am.* Mülltonne *f*; ~ pail Mülleimer *m*.

garden ['gɑːdn] 1. Garten *m*; 2. Gartenbau treiben; ~er [~nə] Gärtner(in); ~ing [~niŋ] Gartenarbeit *f*.

gargle ['gɑːgl] 1. gurgeln; 2. Gurgelwasser *n*.

garish [, 'geəriʃ] grell, auffallend.

garland ['gɑːlənd] Girlande *f*.

garlic ♀ ['gɑːlik] Knoblauch *m*.

garment ['gɑːmənt] Gewand *n*.

garnish ['gɑːniʃ] garnieren; zieren.

garret ['gærət] Dachstube *f*.

garrison ⚔ ['gærisn] 1. Besatzung *f*; Garnison *f*; 2. mit e-r Besatzung belegen. [haft.〉

garrulous ☐ ['gærʊləs] schwatz-〉

garter ['gɑːtə] Strumpfband *n*; *Am.* Socken-, Strumpfhalter *m*.

gas [gæs] 1. Gas *n*; *Am.* = *gasoline*; 2. *v/t.* vergasen; *v/i.* F faseln; ~eous ['geizjəs] gasförmig.

gash [gæʃ] 1. klaffende Wunde; Hieb *m*; Riß *m*; 2. tief (ein)schneiden in (*acc.*).

gas|-light ['gæslait] Gasbeleuchtung *f*; ~-meter Gasuhr *f*; ~o-lene, ~oline *Am.* mot. ['gæsəliːn] Benzin *n*.

gasp [gɑːsp] 1. Keuchen *n*; 2. keuchen; nach Luft schnappen.

gas|sed [gæst] gasvergiftet; ~-stove ['gæs'stouv] Gasofen *m*, -herd *m*; ~-works ['gæswəːks] *sg.* Gaswerk *n*, -anstalt *f*.

gat *Am. sl.* [gæt] Revolver *m*.

gate [geit] Tor *n*; Pforte *f*; Sperre *f*; ~man ['geitmən] Schrankenwärter *m*; ~way Tor(weg *m*) *n*, Einfahrt *f*.

gather ['gæðə] 1. *v/t.* (ein-, ver-)sammeln; ernten; pflücken; schließen (*from* aus); *zs.* ziehen; kräuseln; ~ speed schneller werden; *v/i.* sich (ver)sammeln; sich vergrößern; ♂ *u. fig.* reifen; 2. Falte *f*; ~ing [~riŋ] Versammlung *f*; Zs.-kunft *f*.

gaudy ☐ ['gɔːdi] grell; protzig.

gauge [geidʒ] 1. (Normal)Maß *n*; Maßstab *m*; ⊕ Lehre *f*; ⊕ Spurweite *f*; Meßgerät *n*; 2. eichen; (aus)messen; *fig.* abschätzen.

gaunt ☐ [gɔːnt] hager; finster.

gauntlet ['gɔːntlit] *fig.* Fehdehandschuh *m*; *run the ~* Spießruten laufen.

gauze [gɔːz] Gaze *f*.

gave [geiv] *pret. von* give.

gavel *Am.* ['gævl] Hammer *m* des Versammlungsleiters *od. Auktionators*.

gawk F [gɔːk] Tölpel *m*; ~y [gɔːki] tölpisch.

gay ☐ [gei] lustig, heiter; bunt, lebhaft, glänzend.

gaze [geiz] 1. starrer *od.* aufmerksamer Blick; 2. starren.

gazette [gə'zet] 1. Amtsblatt *n*; 2. amtlich bekanntgeben.

gear [giə] 1. ⊕ Getriebe *n*; *mot.* Gang *m*; Mechanismus *m*; Gerät *n*; *in ~* mit eingelegtem Gang; in Betrieb; *out of ~* im Leerlauf; außer Betrieb; *landing ~* ✈ Fahrgestell *n*; *steering ~* ⚓ Ruderanlage *f*; *mot.* Lenkung *f*; 2. einschalten; ⊕ greifen; ~ing ['giəriŋ] (Zahnrad-)Getriebe *n*; Übersetzung *f*; ~lever, *bsd. Am.* ~-shift Schalthebel *m*.

gee [dʒiː] 1. *Kindersprache:* Hottehü *n* (*Pferd*); 2. *Fuhrmannsruf:* hü! hott!; *Am.* nanu!, so was!

geese [giːs] *pl. von* goose.

gem [dʒem] Edelstein *m*; Gemme *f*; *fig.* Glanzstück *n*.

gender *gr.* ['dʒendə] Genus *n*, Geschlecht *n*.

general ['dʒenərəl] 1. ☐ allgemein; gewöhnlich; Haupt..., General...; *~ election* allgemeine Wahlen; 2. ⚔ General *m*; Feldherr *m*; ~ity [dʒenə'ræliti] Allgemeinheit *f*; *die* große Masse; ~ize ['dʒenərəlaiz] verallgemeinern; ~ly [~li] im allgemeinen, überhaupt; gewöhnlich.

generat|e ['dʒenəreit] erzeugen; ~ion [dʒenə'reiʃən] (Er)Zeugung *f*; Generation *f*; Menschenalter *n*; ~or ['dʒenəreitə] Erzeuger *m*; ⊕ Generator *m*; *bsd. Am. mot.* Lichtmaschine *f*.

gener|osity [dʒenə'rositi] Großmut *f*; Großzügigkeit *f*; ~ous ☐ ['dʒenərəs] großmütig, großzügig.

genial [, 'dʒiːnjəl] freundlich; anregend; gemütlich (*Person*); heiter.

genitive *gr.* ['dʒenitiv] *a. ~ case* Genitiv *m*.

genius ['dʒiːnjəs] Geist *m*; Genie *n*.

gent F [dʒent] Herr *m*.

genteel ☐ [dʒen'tiːl] vornehm; elegant.

gentile ['dʒentail] 1. heidnisch, nichtjüdisch; 2. Heid|e *m*, -in *f*.

gentle ☐ ['dʒentl] sanft, mild; zahm; leise, sacht; vornehm; ~man Herr *m*; Gentleman *m*; ~manlike, ~manly [~li] gebildet; vornehm; ~ness [~nis] Sanftheit *f*; Milde *f*; Güte *f*, Sanftmut *f*.

gentry ['dʒentri] niederer Adel; gebildete Stände *m/pl.*

genuine ☐ ['dʒenjuin] echt; aufrichtig.

geography [dʒi'ɔgrəfi] Geographie *f*.

geology [dʒi'ɔlədʒi] Geologie *f*.

geometry [dʒi'ɔmitri] Geometrie *f*.

germ [dʒəːm] 1. Keim *m*; 2. keimen.

German[1] ['dʒəːmən] 1. deutsch; 2. Deutsche(r *m*) *f*; Deutsch *n*.

german[2] [~] *brother ~* leiblicher Bruder; *~e* [dʒəː'mein] (*to*) verwandt (mit); entsprechend (*dat.*).

germinate ['dʒəːmineit] keimen.

gesticulat|e [dʒes'tikjuleit] gestikulieren; **~ion** [dʒestikju'leiʃən] Gebärdenspiel n.

gesture ['dʒestʃə] Geste f, Gebärde f.

get [get] [irr.] v/t. erhalten, bekommen, F kriegen; besorgen; holen; bringen; erwerben; verdienen; ergreifen, fassen; (veran)lassen; mit adv. mst bringen, machen; have got haben; ~ one's hair cut sich das Haar schneiden lassen; ~ by heart auswendig lernen; v/i. gelangen, geraten, kommen; gehen; werden; ~ ready sich fertig machen; ~ about auf den Beinen sein; ~ abroad bekannt werden; ~ ahead vorwärtskommen; ~ at (heran-) kommen an ... (acc.); zu et. kommen; ~ away wegkommen; sich fortmachen; ~ in einsteigen; ~ on with s.o. mit j-m auskommen; ~ out aussteigen; ~ to hear (know, learn) erfahren; ~ up aufstehen; **~-up** ['getʌp] Aufmachung f; Am. F Unternehmungsgeist m.

ghastly ['gɑːstli] gräßlich; schrecklich; (toten)bleich; gespenstisch.

gherkin ['gəːkin] Gewürzgurke f.

ghost [goust] Geist m, Gespenst n; fig. Spur f; **~like** ['goustlaik], **~ly** [~li] geisterhaft.

giant ['dʒaiənt] 1. riesig; 2. Riese m.

gibber ['dʒibə] kauderwelschen; **~ish** ['gibəriʃ] Kauderwelsch n.

gibbet ['dʒibit] 1. Galgen m; 2. hängen.

gibe [dʒaib] verspotten, aufziehen.

giblets ['dʒiblits] pl. Gänseklein n.

gidd|iness ['gidinis] ♣ Schwindel m; Unbeständigkeit f; Leichtsinn m; **~y** ['gidi] schwind(e)lig; leichtfertig; unbeständig; albern.

gift [gift] Gabe f; Geschenk n; Talent n; **~ed** ['giftid] begabt.

gigantic [dʒai'gæntik] (~ally) riesenhaft, riesig, gigantisch.

giggle ['gigl] 1. kichern; 2. Gekicher n.

gild [gild] [irr.] vergolden; verschönen; **~ed youth** Jeunesse f dorée.

gill [gil] ichth. Kieme f; ♣ Lamelle f.

gilt [gilt] 1. pret. u. p.p. von gild; 2. Vergoldung f.

gimmick Am. sl. ['gimik] Trick m.

gin [dʒin] Gin m (Wacholderschnaps); Schlinge f; ⊕ Entkörnungsmaschine f.

ginger ['dʒindʒə] 1. Ingwer m; Lebhaftigkeit f; 2. ~ up in Schwung bringen; 3. hellrot, rötlich-gelb; **~bread** Pfefferkuchen m; **~ly** [~əli] zimperlich; sachte.

gipsy ['dʒipsi] Zigeuner(in).

gird [gəːd] sticheln; [irr.] (um)gürten; umgeben.

girder ⊕ ['gəːdə] Tragbalken m.

girdle ['gəːdl] 1. Gürtel m; Hüfthalter m, -gürtel m; 2. umgürten.

girl [gəːl] Mädchen n; ♀ **Guide** ['gəːlgaid] Pfadfinderin f; **~hood** ['gəːlhud] Mädchenzeit f; Mädchenjahre n/pl.; **~ish** [ˈgəːliʃ] mädchenhaft; **~y** Am. F ['gəːli] mit spärlich bekleideten Mädchen (Magazin, Varieté etc.).

girt [gəːt] pret. u. p.p. von gird.

girth [gəːθ] (Sattel)Gurt m; Umfang m.

gist [dʒist] das Wesentliche.

give [giv] [irr.] v/t. geben; ab-, übergeben; her-, hingeben; überlassen; zum besten geben; schenken; gewähren; von sich geben; ergeben; ~ birth to zur Welt bringen; ~ away verschenken; F verraten; ~ forth von sich geben; herausgeben; ~ in einreichen; ~ up Geschäft etc. aufgeben; j-n ausliefern; v/i. mst ~ in nachgeben; weichen; ~ into, ~ (up)on hinausgehen auf (acc.) (Fenster etc.); ~ out aufhören; versagen; **~ and take** [givn'teik] (Meinungs)Austausch m; Kompromiß m, n; **~-away** Preisgabe f; ~ show od. program bsd. Am. Radio, Fernsehen: öffentliche Preisraten; **~n** ['givn] 1. p.p. von give; 2. ~ to ergeben (dat.).

glaci|al ☐ [gleisjəl] eisig; Eis...; Gletscher...; **~er** ['glæsjə] Gletscher m.

glad ☐ [glæd] froh, erfreut; erfreulich; **~ly** gern; **~den** ['glædn] erfreuen.

glade [gleid] Lichtung f; Am. sumpfige Niederung.

gladness ['glædnis] Freude f.

glair [glɛə] Eiweiß n.

glamo|rous ['glæmərəs] bezaubernd; **~(u)r** ['glæmə] 1. Zauber m, Glanz m, Reiz m; 2. bezaubern.

glance [glɑːns] 1. Schimmer m, Blitz m; flüchtiger Blick; 2. hinweggleiten; mst ~ off abprallen; blitzen; glänzen; ~ at flüchtig ansehen; anspielen auf (acc.).

gland anat. [glænd] Drüse f.

glare [glɛə] 1. grelles Licht; wilder, starrer Blick; 2. grell leuchten; wild blicken; (at an)starren.

glass [glɑːs] 1. Glas n; Spiegel m; Opern-, Fernglas n; Barometer n; (a pair of) ~es pl. (eine) Brille; 2. gläsern; Glas...; 3. verglasen; **~-case** ['glɑːskeis] Vitrine f; Schaukasten m; **~-house** Treibhaus n; ✕ sl. Bau m; **~y** [~si] gläsern; glasig.

glaz|e [gleiz] 1. Glasur f; 2. v/t. verglasen; glasieren; polieren; v/i. trüb(e) od. glasig werden (Auge); **~ier** ['gleizjə] Glaser m.

gleam [gliːm] 1. Schimmer m, Schein m; 2. schimmern.

glean [gli:n] *v/t.* sammeln; *v/i.* Ähren lesen.

glee [gli:] Fröhlichkeit *f;* mehrstimmiges Lied; ~ **club** Gesangverein *m.*

glen [glen] Bergschlucht *f.*

glib [glib] glatt, zungenfertig.

glid|e [glaid] 1. Gleiten *n;* ✗ Gleitflug *m;* 2. (dahin)gleiten (lassen); e-n Gleitflug machen; ~**er** ['glaidə] Segelflugzeug *n.*

glimmer ['glimə] 1. Schimmer *m; min.* Glimmer *m;* 2. schimmern.

glimpse [glimps] 1. flüchtiger Blick (of auf *acc.*); Schimmer *m;* flüchtiger Eindruck; 2. flüchtig (er)blicken.

glint [glint] 1. blitzen, glitzern; 2. Lichtschein *m.*

glisten ['glisn], **glitter** ['glitə] glitzern, glänzen.

gloat [glout]: ~ (up)on od. over sich weiden an (*dat.*).

globe [gloub] (Erd)Kugel *f;* Globus *m.*

gloom [glu:m], ~**iness** ['glu:minis] Düsterkeit *f,* Dunkelheit *f;* Schwermut *f;* ~**y** □ ['glu:mi] dunkel, düster; schwermütig; verdrießlich.

glori|fy ['glɔ:rifai] verherrlichen; ~**ous** □ [~iəs] herrlich; glorreich.

glory ['glɔ:ri] 1. Ruhm *m;* Herrlichkeit *f,* Pracht *f;* Glorienschein *m;* 2. frohlocken; stolz sein.

gloss [glɔs] 1. Glosse *f,* Bemerkung *f;* Glanz *m;* 2. Glossen machen (zu); Glanz geben (*dat.*); ~ over beschönigen.

glossary ['glɔsəri] Wörterverzeichnis *n.*

glossy ['glɔsi] glänzend, blank.

glove [glʌv] Handschuh *m.*

glow [glou] 1. Glühen *n;* Glut *f;* 2. glühen.

glower ['glauə] finster blicken.

glow-worm ['glouwə:m] Glühwürmchen *n.*

glucose ['glu:kous] Traubenzucker *m.*

glue [glu:] 1. Leim *m;* 2. leimen.

glum [glʌm] mürrisch.

glut [glʌt] überfüllen.

glutinous ['glu:tinəs] klebrig.

glutton ['glʌtn] Unersättliche(r *m) f;* Vielfraß *m;* ~**ous** □ [~nəs] gefräßig; ~**y** [~ni] Gefräßigkeit *f.*

G-man *Am.* F ['dʒi:mæn] FBI-Agent *m.*

gnarl [nɑ:l] Knorren *m,* Ast *m.*

gnash [næʃ] knirschen (mit).

gnat [næt] (Stech)Mücke *f.*

gnaw [nɔ:] (zer)nagen; (zer)fressen.

gnome [noum] Erdgeist *m,* Gnom *m.*

go [gou] 1. [*irr.*] *allg.* gehen, fahren; vergehen (*Zeit*); werden; führen (to nach); sich wenden (to an); funktionieren, arbeiten; passen; kaputtgehen; let ~ loslassen; ~

shares teilen; ~ to od. and see besuchen; ~ at losgehen auf (*acc.*); ~ between vermitteln (zwischen); ~ by sich richten nach; ~ for gehen nach, holen; ~ for a walk, etc. einen Spaziergang etc. machen; ~ in for an examination e-e Prüfung machen; ~ on weitergehen; fortfahren; ~ through durchgehen; durchmachen; ~ without sich behelfen ohne; 2. F Mode *f;* Schwung *m,* Schneid *m;* on the ~ auf den Beinen; im Gange; it is no ~ es geht nicht; in one ~ auf Anhieb; have a ~ at es versuchen mit.

goad [goud] 1. Stachelstock *m; fig.* Ansporn *m;* 2. *fig.* anstacheln.

go-ahead F ['gouəhed] 1. zielstrebig; unternehmungslustig; 2. *bsd. Am.* F Erlaubnis *f* zum Weitermachen.

goal [goul] Mal *n;* Ziel *n; Fußball:* Tor *n;* ~**keeper** ['goulki:pə] Torwart *m.*

goat [gout] Ziege *f,* Geiß *f.*

gob [gɔb] V Schleimklumpen *m;* F Maul *n; Am.* F Blaujacke *f (Matrose)*

gobble ['gɔbl] *gierig* verschlingen; ~**dygook** *Am. sl.* [~ldiguk] Amts-, Berufsjargon *m;* Geschwafel *n;* ~**r** [~lə] Vielfraß *m;* Truthahn *m.*

go-between ['goubitwi:n] Vermittler(in).

goblet ['gɔblit] Kelchglas *n;* Pokal *m.*

goblin ['gɔblin] Kobold *m,* Gnom *m.*

god, *eccl.* 2 [gɔd] Gott *m; fig.* Abgott *m;* ~**child** ['gɔdtʃaild] Patenkind *n;* ~**dess** ['gɔdis] Göttin *f;* ~**father** Pate *m;* ~**head** Gottheit *f;* ~**less** ['gɔdlis] gottlos; ~**like** gottähnlich; göttlich; ~**ly** [~li] gottesfürchtig; fromm; ~**mother** Patin *f.*

go-getter *Am. sl.* ['gou'getə] Draufgänger *m.*

goggle ['gɔgl] 1. glotzen; 2. ~s *pl.* Schutzbrille *f.*

going ['gouiŋ] 1. gehend; im Gange (befindlich); be ~ to *inf.* im Begriff sein zu *inf.,* gleich *tun* wollen od. werden; 2. Gehen *n;* Vorwärtskommen *n;* Straßenzustand *m;* Geschwindigkeit *f,* Leistung *f;* ~**s-on** F [~ŋz'ɔn] *pl.* Treiben *n.*

gold [gould] 1. Gold *n;* 2. golden; ~**-digger** *Am.* ['goulddigə] Goldgräber *m;* ~**en** *mst fig.* [~dən] golden, goldgelb; ~**finch** *zo.* Stieglitz *m;* ~**smith** Goldschmied *m.*

golf [gɔlf] 1. Golf(spiel) *n;* 2. Golf spielen; ~**course** ['gɔlfkɔ:s], ~**links** *pl.* Golfplatz *m.*

gondola ['gɔndələ] Gondel *f.*

gone [gɔn] 1. *p.p. von* go 1; 2. *adj.* fort; F futsch; vergangen; tot; F hoffnungslos.

good [gud] 1. *allg.* gut; artig; gütig;

† zahlungsfähig; gründlich; ~ at geschickt in (dat.); 2. Gute(s) n; Wohl n, Beste(s) n; ~s pl. Waren f/pl.; Güter n/pl.; that's no ~ das nützt nichts; for ~ für immer; ~by(e) 1. [gud'bai] Lebewohl n; 2. ['gud'bai] (auf) Wiedersehen!; ♀ Friday Karfreitag m; ~ly [gudli] anmutig, hübsch; fig unsehnlich; ~natured gutmütig; ~ness [nis] Güte f; das Beste; thank ~! Gott sei Dank!; ~will Wohlwollen n; † Kundschaft f; † Firmenwert m.

goody ['gudi] Bonbon m, n.

goon Am. sl [gu:n] bestellter Schläger bsd. für Streik, Dummkopf m.

goose [gu:s], pl geese [gi:s] Gans f (a. fig.); Bügeleisen n.

gooseberry ['guzbəri] Stachelbeere f.

goose|-flesh ['gu:sfleʃ], Am. ~pimples pl. fig. Gänsehaut f.

gopher bsd. Am. ['goufə] Erdeichhörnchen n.

gore [gɔ:] 1. (geronnenes) Blut; Schneiderei Keil m; 2. durchbohren, aufspießen.

gorge [gɔ:dʒ] 1. Kehle f, Schlund m; enge (Fels)Schlucht; 2. (ver-)schlingen; (sich) vollstopfen.

gorgeous ['gɔ:dʒəs] prächtig.

gory ['gɔ:ri] blutig.

gospel [gɔspəl] Evangelium n.

gossip ['gɔsip] 1. Geschwätz n; Klatschbase f; 2. schwatzen.

got [gɔt] pret. u. p.p. von get.

Gothic ['gɔθik] gotisch; fig. barbarisch.

gotten Am. ['gɔtn] p.p. von get.

gouge [gaudʒ] 1. ⊕ Hohlmeißel m; 2. ausmeißeln; Am. F betrügen.

gourd ♀ [guəd] Kürbis m.

gout ♂ [gaut] Gicht f.

govern ['gʌvən] v/t regieren, beherrschen; lenken, leiten; v/i. herrschen; ~ess [nis] Erzieherin f; ~ment ['gʌvnmənt] Regierung(s-form) f; Leitung f; Herrschaft f (of über acc.); Ministerium n; Statthalterschaft f; attr Staats...; ~mental [gʌvən mentl] Regierungs...; ~or ['gʌvənə] Gouverneur m; Direktor m, Präsident m; F Alte(r) m (Vater, Chef).

gown [gaun] 1. (Frauen)Kleid n; Robe f, Talar m; 2. kleiden.

grab F [græb] 1. grapsen; an sich reißen, packen; 2. plötzlicher Griff; ⊕ Greifer m; ~bag bsd. Am. Glückstopf m.

grace [greis] 1. Gnade f; Gunst f; (Gnaden)Frist f; Grazie f, Anmut f; Anstand m; Zier(de) f; Reiz m; Tischgebet n; Your ~ Euer Gnaden; 2. zieren, schmücken, begünstigen, auszeichnen; ~ful [greisful] anmutig; ~fulness [nis] Anmut f.

gracious ['greiʃəs] gnädig.

gradation [grə'deiʃən] Abstufung f.

grade [greid] 1. Grad m, Rang m; Stufe f; Qualität f; bsd. Am. = gradient; Am. Schule: Klasse f, Note f; make the ~ Am. Erfolg haben; ~ crossing bsd. Am. schienengleicher Bahnübergang; ~(d) school bsd. Am. Grundschule f; 2. abstufen; einstufen; ⊕ planieren.

gradient ⊕ etc. ['greidjənt] Steigung f.

gradua|l □ ['grædjuəl] stufenweise, allmählich; ~te 1. [ueit] graduieren; (sich) abstufen; die Abschlußprüfung machen; promovieren; 2. univ. [uit] Graduierte(r m) f; ~tion [grædju'eiʃən] Gradeinteilung f; Abschlußprüfung f; Promotion f.

graft [grɑ:ft] 1. ♂ Pfropfreis n; Am. Schiebung f; 2. ♂ pfropfen; ♂ verpflanzen; Am. fig. schieben.

grain [grein] (Samen)Korn n; Getreide n; Gefüge n; fig. Natur f; Gran n (Gewicht).

gram [græm] = gramme.

gramma|r ['græmə] Grammatik f; ~r-school höhere Schule, Gymnasium n; Am. a. Mittelschule f; ~tical □ [grə'mætikəl] grammati(kali)sch.

gramme [græm] Gramm n.

granary ['grænəri] Kornspeicher m.

grand [grænd] 1. fig großartig; erhaben; groß; Groß...; Haupt...; ♀ Old Party Am. Republikanische Partei; ~ stand Sport (Haupt-)Tribüne f; 2. ♪ a. ~ piano Flügel m; Am. sl. tausend Dollar pl.; ~child ['græntʃaild] Enkel(in); ~eur [ndʒə] Größe f, Hoheit f; Erhabenheit f; ~father Großvater m.

grandiose □ ['grændious] großartig.

grand|mother ['grænmʌðə] Großmutter f; ~parents [npeərənts] pl. Großeltern pl.

grange [greindʒ] Gehöft n; Gut n; Am. Name für Farmerorganisation f.

granny F ['græni] Oma f.

grant [grɑ:nt] 1. Gewährung f; Unterstützung f; Stipendium n; 2. gewähren; bewilligen; verleihen; zugestehen; ♂ übertragen; take for ~ed als selbstverständlich annehmen.

granul|ate ['grænjuleit] (sich) körnen; ~e [ə] Körnchen n.

grape [greip] Weinbeere f, -traube f; ~fruit ♀ ['greipfru:t] Pampelmuse f.

graph [græf] graphische Darstellung; ~ic(al □) ['græfik(əl)] graphisch; anschaulich; graphic arts pl. Graphik f; ~ite min. [fait] Graphit m.

grapple ['græpl] entern; packen; ringen.

grasp [grɑːsp] 1. Griff m; Bereich m; Beherrschung f; Fassungskraft f; 2. (er)greifen, packen; begreifen.

grass [grɑːs] Gras n; Rasen m; send to ~ auf die Weide schicken; ~hopper ['grɑːshɔpə] Heuschrecke f; ~ roots pl Am pol die landwirtschaftlichen Bezirke, die Landbevölkerung; ~widow(er) F Strohwitwe(r m) f; ~y [~si] grasig; Gras...

grate [greit] 1. (Kamin)Gitter n; (Feuer)Rost m; 2. (zer)reiben; mit et. knirschen; fig. verletzen.

grateful ['greitful] dankbar.

grater ['greitə] Reibeisen n.

grati|fication [grætifi'keiʃən] Befriedigung f; Freude f; ~fy ['grætifai] erfreuen; befriedigen.

grating ['greitiŋ] 1. ⸗ schrill; unangenehm; 2. Gitter(werk) n.

gratitude ['grætitjuːd] Dankbarkeit f.

gratuit|ous □ [grə'tjuː(ː)itəs] unentgeltlich; freiwillig; ~y [~ti] Abfindung f; Gratifikation f; Trinkgeld n.

grave [greiv] 1. □ ernst; (ge)wichtig; gemessen; 2. Grab n; 3. [irr.] mst fig. (ein)graben; ~digger ['greivdigə] Totengräber m.

gravel ['grævəl] 1. Kies m; ⚕ Harngrieß m; 2. mit Kies bedecken.

graven ['greivən] p.p. von grave 3.

graveyard ['greivjɑːd] Kirchhof m.

gravitation [grævi'teiʃən] Schwerkraft f; fig. Hang m.

gravity ['græviti] Schwere f; Wichtigkeit f; Ernst m; Schwerkraft f

gravy ['greivi] Fleischsaft m, Bratensoße f.

gray bsd. Am. [grei] grau.

graze [greiz] (ab)weiden; (ab)grasen; streifen, schrammen.

grease 1. [griːs] Fett n; Schmiere f; 2. [griːz] (be)schmieren.

greasy □ ['griːzi] fettig; schmierig.

great □ [greit] allg. groß; Groß...; F großartig; ~coat ['greit'kout] Überzieher m; ~grandchild Urenkel(in); ~grandfather Urgroßvater m; ~ly [~tli] sehr; ~ness [~tnis] Größe f; Stärke f.

greed [griːd] Gier f; ~y □ ['griːdi] (be)gierig (of, for nach); habgierig.

Greek [griːk] 1. griechisch; 2. Griech|e m, -in f; Griechisch n.

green [griːn] 1. □ grün (a. fig.); frisch (Fisch etc.); neu; Grün...; 2. Grün n; Rasen m; Wiese f; ~s pl. frisches Gemüse; ~back Am. ['griːnbæk] Dollarnote f, ~grocer Gemüsehändler(in); ~grocery Gemüsehandlung f; ~horn Grünschnabel m; ~house Gewächshaus n; ~ish [~niʃ] grünlich; ~sickness Bleichsucht f.

greet [griːt] (be)grüßen; ~ing ['griːtiŋ] Begrüßung f; Gruß m.

grenade ⚔ [gri'neid] Granate f.

grew [gruː] pret. von grow.

grey [grei] 1. □ grau; 2. Grau n; 3. grau machen od. werden; ~hound ['greihaund] Windhund m.

grid [grid] Gitter n; ✇, ⚡ Netz n; Am. Fußball. Spielfeld n; ~iron ['gridaiən] (Brat)Rost m.

grief [griːf] Gram m, Kummer m; come to ~ zu Schaden kommen.

griev|ance ['griːvəns] Beschwerde f; Mißstand m; ~e [griːv] kränken; (sich) grämen; ~ous □ ['griːvəs] kränkend, schmerzlich; schlimm.

grill [gril] 1. (er)grillen; braten (a. fig.); 2. Bratrost m, Grill m; gegrilltes Fleisch; a. ~room Grillroom m.

grim □ [grim] grimmig; schrecklich.

grimace [gri'meis] 1. Fratze f, Grimasse f; 2. Grimassen schneiden.

grim|e [graim] Schmutz m; Ruß m; ~y □ ['graimi] schmutzig; rußig.

grin [grin] 1. Grinsen n; 2. grinsen.

grind [graind] 1. [irr.] (zer)reiben; mahlen; schleifen; Leierkasten etc. drehen; fig. schinden; mit den Zähnen knirschen; 2. Schinderei f; ~stone ['graindstoun] Schleif-, Mühlstein m.

grip [grip] 1. packen, fassen (a. fig.); 2. Griff m; Gewalt f; Herrschaft f; Am. = gripsack.

gripe [graip] Griff m; ~s pl. Kolik f; bsd. Am. Beschwerden f/pl.

gripsack Am. ['gripsæk] Handtasche f, Köfferchen n.

grisly ['grizli] gräßlich, schrecklich.

gristle ['grisl] Knorpel m.

grit [grit] 1. Kies m; Sand(stein) m; fig. Mut m; 2. knirschen (mit).

grizzly ['grizli] 1. grau; 2. Graubär m.

groan [groun] seufzen, stöhnen.

grocer ['grousə] Lebensmittelhändler m; ~ies [~əriz] pl. Lebensmittel n/pl.; ~y [~ri] Lebensmittelgeschäft n.

groceteria Am. ['grousi'tiəriə] Selbstbedienungsladen m.

groggy ['grɔgi] taumelig; wackelig.

groin anat. [grɔin] Leistengegend f.

groom [grum] 1. Reit-, Stallknecht m; Bräutigam m; 2. pflegen; Am. pol. Kandidaten lancieren.

groove [gruːv] 1. Rinne f, Nut f; fig. Gewohnheit f; 2. nuten, falzen.

grope [group] (be)tasten, tappen.

gross [grous] 1. □ dick; grob; derb; ✝ Brutto...; 2. Gros n (12 Dutzend); in the ~ im ganzen.

grotto ['grɔtou] Grotte f.

grouch Am. F [grautʃ] 1. quengeln, meckern; 2. Griesgram m; schlechte Laune; ~y ['grautʃi] quenglig.

ground[1] [graund] 1. *pret. u. p.p. von* **grind** 1; 2. ~ **glass** Mattglas *n*.

ground[2] [graund] 1. *mst* Grund *m*; Boden *m*; Gebiet *n*; *Spiel- etc.* Platz *m*; *Beweg- etc.* Grund *m*; ⚡ Erde *f*; ~**s** *pl.* Grundstück *n*, Park(s *pl.*) *m*, Gärten *m/pl.*; *Kaffee-* Satz *m*; *on the* ~(*s*) *of* auf Grund (*gen.*); *stand od.* hold *od.* keep one's ~ sich behaupten; 2. niederlegen; (be)gründen, *j-m* die Anfangsgründe beibringen; ⚡ erden; ~**floor** ['graund'flɔ:] Erdgeschoß *n*; ~**hog** [~dhɔg] *bsd. Am.* Murmeltier *n*; ~**less** [~dlis] grundlos; ~**staff** ⚡ Bodenpersonal *n*; ~**work** Grundlage *f*.

group [gru:p] 1. Gruppe *f*; 2. (sich) gruppieren.

grove [grouv] Hain *m*; Gehölz *n*.

grovel *mst fig.* ['grɔvl] kriechen.

grow [grou] [*irr.*] *v/i.* wachsen; werden; *v/t.* ⚘ anpflanzen, anbauen; ~**er** ['grouə] Bauer *m*, Züchter *m*.

growl [graul] knurren, brummen; ~**er** ['graulə] *fig.* Brummbär *m*; *Am. sl.* Bierkrug *m*.

grow|n [groun] 1. *p.p. von* **grow**; 2. *adj.* erwachsen; bewachsen; ~**n-up** ['grounʌp] 1. erwachsen; 2. Erwachsene(r *m*) *f*; ~**th** [grouθ] Wachstum *n*; (An)Wachsen *n*; Entwicklung *f*; Wuchs *m*; Gewächs *n*, Erzeugnis *n*.

grub [grʌb] 1. Raupe *f*, Larve *f*, Made *f*; *contp.* Prolet *m*; 2. graben; sich abmühen; ~**by** [grʌbi] schmierig.

grudge [grʌdʒ] 1. Groll *m*; 2. mißgönnen, ungern geben *od.* tun *etc.*

gruel [gruəl] Haferschleim *m*.

gruff [grʌf] grob, schroff, barsch.

grumble ['grʌmbl] murren, (g)rollen; ~**r** *fig* [~lə] Brummbär *m*.

grunt [grʌnt] grunzen.

guarant|ee [gærən'ti:] 1. Bürge *m*; = **guaranty**; 2. bürgen für; ~**or** [~'tɔ:] Bürge *m*; ~**y** ['gærənti] Bürgschaft *f*, Garantie *f*; Gewähr *f*.

guard [ga:d] 1. Wacht *f*; ⚔ Wache *f*; Wächter *m*, Wärter *m*; 🚆 Schaffner *m*; Schutz(vorrichtung *f*) *m*; 2s *pl.* Garde *f*; *be on* (*off*) one's ~ (nicht) auf der Hut sein; 2. *v/t.* bewachen, (be)schützen (*from* vor *dat.*); *v/i.* sich hüten (*against* vor *dat.*); ~**ian** ['ga:djən] Hüter *m*, Wächter *m*; 🜨 Vormund *m*; *attr.* Schutz…; ~**ianship** [~ʃip] Obhut *f*; Vormundschaft *f*.

guess [ges] 1. Vermutung *f*; 2. vermuten; (er)raten; *Am.* denken.

guest [gest] Gast *m*; ~**house** ['gesthaus] (Hotel)Pension *f*, Fremdenheim *n*; ~**room** Gast-, Fremdenzimmer *n*.

guffaw [gʌ'fɔ:] schallendes Gelächter.

guidance ['gaidəns] Führung *f*; (An)Leitung *f*.

guide [gaid] 1. Führer *m*; ⊕ Führung *f*; *attr.* Führungs…; 2. leiten; führen; lenken; ~**book** ['gaidbuk] Reiseführer *m*; ~**post** Wegweiser *m*.

guild [gild] Gilde *f*, Innung *f*; 2**hall** ['gild'hɔ:l] Rathaus *n* (*London*).

guile [gail] Arglist *f*; ~**ful** □ ['gailful] arglistig; ~**less** □ ['gaillis] arglos.

guilt [gilt] Schuld *f*; Strafbarkeit *f*; ~**less** □ ['giltlis] schuldlos; unkundig; ~**y** □ [~ti] schuldig; strafbar.

guinea ['gini] Guinee *f* (*21 Schilling*); ~**pig** Meerschweinchen *n*.

guise [gaiz] Erscheinung *f*, Gestalt *f*; Maske *f*

guitar ♪ [gi'ta:] Gitarre *f*.

gulch *Am.* [gʌlʃ] tiefe Schlucht.

gulf [gʌlf] Meerbusen *m*, Golf *m*; Abgrund *m*; Strudel *m*.

gull [gʌl] 1. Möwe *f*; Tölpel *m*; 2. übertölpeln; verleiten (*into* zu).

gullet ['gʌlit] Speiseröhre *f*; Gurgel *f*.

gulp [gʌlp] Schluck *m*; Schlucken *n*.

gum [gʌm] 1. *a.* ~**s** *pl.* Zahnfleisch *n*; Gummi *n*; Klebstoff *m*; ~**s** *pl. Am.* Gummischuhe *m/pl.*; 2. gummieren; zukleben.

gun [gʌn] 1. Gewehr *n*; Flinte *f*; Geschütz *n*, Kanone *f*; *Am.* Revolver *m*; *big* ~ F *fig.* hohes Tier; 2. *Am.* auf die Jagd gehen; ~**boat** ['gʌnbout] Kanonenboot *n*; ~**licence** Waffenschein *m*; ~**man** *Am.* Gangster *m*; ~**ner** ⚔ 🜨 ['gʌnə] Kanonier *m*; ~**powder** Schießpulver *n*; ~**smith** Büchsenmacher *m*.

gurgle ['gə:gl] gluckern, gurgeln.

gush [gʌʃ] 1. Guß *m*; *fig.* Erguß *m*; 2. (sich) ergießen, schießen (*from* aus); *fig* schwärmen; ~**er** ['gʌʃə] *fig.* Schwärmer(in); Ölquelle *f*.

gust [gʌst] Windstoß *m*, Bö *f*.

gut [gʌt] Darm *m*; ♪ Darmsaite *f*; ~**s** *pl.* Eingeweide *n/pl.*; *das* Innere; *fig.* Mut *m*.

gutter ['gʌtə] Dachrinne *f*; Gosse *f* (*a. fig.*), Rinnstein *m*.

guy [gai] 1. Halteseil *n*; F Vogelscheuche *f*; *Am.* F Kerl *m*; 2. verulken.

guzzle ['gʌzl] saufen; fressen.

gymnas|ium [dʒim'neizjəm] Turnhalle *f*, -platz *m*; ~**tics** [~'næstiks] *pl.* Turnen *n*; Gymnastik *f*.

gypsy *bsd. Am.* ['dʒipsi] = **gipsy**.

gyrate [dʒaiə'reit] kreisen; wirbeln.

gyroplane ['dʒaiərəplein] Hubschrauber *m*.

H

haberdasher ['hæbədæʃə] Kurzwarenhändler m; Am. Herrenartikelhändler m; ~y [~əri] Kurzwaren (-geschäft n) f/pl.; Am. Herrenartikel m/pl.

habit ['hæbit] 1. (An)Gewohnheit f; Verfassung f; Kleid(ung f) n; fall od. get into bad ~s schlechte Gewohnheiten annehmen, 2. (an-) kleiden; ~able [~təbl] bewohnbar; ~ation [hæbi'teiʃən] Wohnung f.

habitual ['hə'bitjuəl] gewohnt, gewöhnlich; Gewohnheits...

hack [hæk] 1. Hieb m; Einkerbung f; Miet-, Arbeitspferd n (a. fig.); a. ~ writer literarischer Lohnschreiber m; 2. (zer)hacken.

hackneyed fig. ['hæknid] abgedroschen.

had [hæd] pret. u. p.p. von have.

haddock ['hædək] Schellfisch m.

h(a)emorrhage ['heməridʒ] Blutsturz m.

hag [hæg] (mst fig. alte) Hexe.

haggard □ ['hægəd] verstört; hager.

haggle ['hægl] feilschen, schachern.

hail [heil] 1. Hagel m; Anruf m; 2. (nieder)hageln (lassen); anrufen; (be)grüßen; ~ from stammen aus; ~stone ['heilstoun] Hagelkorn n; ~storm Hagelschauer m.

hair [hɛə] Haar n; ~-breadth ['hɛəbredθ] Haaresbreite f; ~cut Haarschnitt m; ~-do Am. Frisur f; ~dresser (bsd. Damen)Friseur m; ~-drier [~draiə] Trockenhaube f; Fön m; ~less ['hɛəlis] ohne Haare, kahl; ~pin Haarnadel f; ~-raising ['hɛəreiziŋ] haarsträubend; ~-splitting Haarspalterei f; ~y ['hɛəri] haarig.

hale [heil] gesund, frisch, rüstig.

half [hɑːf] 1. pl. halves [hɑːvz] Hälfte f; by halves nur halb; go halves halbpart machen, teilen 2. halb; ~ a crown eine halbe Krone; ~back ['hɑːf'bæk] Fußball: Läufer m; ~breed ['hɑːf-briːd] Halbblut n; ~caste Halbblut n; ~hearted ['hɑːf'hɑːtid] lustlos, lau; ~length Brustbild n; ~penny ['heipni] halber Penny; ~time ['hɑːf'taim] Sport Halbzeit f; ~way halbwegs; ~witted einfältig, idiotisch.

halibut ichth. ['hælibət] Heilbutt m.

hall [hɔːl] Halle f; Saal m; Vorraum m; Flur m; Diele f; Herren-, Gutshaus n; univ. Speisesaal m; ~ of residence Studentenwohnheim n.

halloo [hə'luː] (hallo) rufen.

hallow ['hælou] heiligen, weihen; 2mas [~oumæs] Allerheiligenfest n.

halo ['heilou] ast. Hof m; Heiligenschein m.

halt [hɔːlt] 1. Halt(estelle f) m; Stillstand m; 2. (an)halten; mst fig. hinken; schwanken.

halter ['hɔːltə] Halfter f; Strick m.

halve [hɑːv] halbieren; ~s [hɑːvz] pl. von half 1.

ham [hæm] Schenkel m; Schinken m.

hamburger Am. ['hæmbəːgə] Frikadelle f; mit Frikadelle belegtes Brötchen.

hamlet ['hæmlit] Weiler m.

hammer ['hæmə] 1. Hammer m; 2. (be)hämmern.

hammock ['hæmək] Hängematte f.

hamper ['hæmpə] 1. Geschenk-, Eßkorb m; 2. verstricken; behindern.

hamster zo. ['hæmstə] Hamster m.

hand [hænd] 1. Hand f (a. fig.); Handschrift f; Handbreite f; (Uhr)Zeiger m; Mann m, Arbeiter m; Karten: Blatt n; at ~ bei der Hand; nahe bevorstehend; at first ~ aus erster Hand; a good (poor) ~ at (un)geschickt in (dat.); ~ and glove ein Herz und eine Seele; change ~s den Besitzer wechseln; lend a ~ (mit) anfassen; off ~ aus dem Handgelenk od. Stegreif; on ~ ✝ vorrätig, auf Lager; bsd. Am. zur Stelle, bereit; on one's ~s auf dem Halse; on the one ~ einerseits; on the other ~ andererseits; ~ to ~ Mann gegen Mann; come to ~ sich bieten; einlaufen (Briefe); 2. reichen; ~ about herumreichen; ~ down vererben; ~ in einhändigen; einreichen; ~ over aushändigen; ~bag ['hændbæg] Handtasche f; ~bill Hand-, Reklamezettel m; ~brake ⊕ Handbremse f; ~cuff Handfessel f; ~ful [~dful] Handvoll f; F Plage f; ~glass Handspiegel m; Leselupe f.

handicap ['hændikæp] 1. Handikap n; Vorgaberennen n, Vorgabespiel n; (Extra)Belastung f; 2. (extra) belasten; beeinträchtigen.

handi|craft ['hændikrɑːft] Handwerk n; Handfertigkeit f; ~crafts-man Handwerker m; ~work Handarbeit f; Werk n.

handkerchief ['hæŋkətʃi(ː)f] Taschentuch n; Halstuch n.

handle ['hændl] 1. Griff m; Stiel m; Henkel m; Pumpen- etc. Schwengel m; fig. Handhabe f; fly off the ~ F platzen vor Wut; 2. anfassen; handhaben; behandeln; ~bar Lenkstange f e-s Fahrrades.

hand|-luggage ['hændlʌgidʒ] Handgepäck n; ~made handgearbeitet; ~me-downs Am. F pl. Fertigkleidung f; getragene Kleider pl.; ~rail Geländer n; ~shake Händedruck m; ~some □ ['hænsəm] ansehnlich; hübsch; anständig; ~work Handarbeit f; ~writing Handschrift f; ~y □ ['hændi] geschickt; handlich; zur Hand.

hang [hæŋ] 1. [irr.] v/t. hängen; auf-, einhängen; verhängen; (pret. u. p.p. mst ~ed) (er)hängen; hängen lassen; Tapete ankleben; v/i. hängen; schweben; sich neigen; ~ about (Am. around) herumlungern; sich an j-n hängen; ~ back sich zurückhalten; ~ on sich klammern an (acc.); fig. hängen an (dat.); 2. Hang m; Fall m e-r Gardine etc.; F Wesen n; F fig. Kniff m; Dreh m.

hangar ['hæŋə] Flugzeughalle f.

hang-dog ['hæŋdɔg] Armesünder...

hanger ['hæŋə] Aufhänger m; Hirschfänger m; ~-on fig. [ˌər'ɔn] Klette f.

hanging ['hæŋiŋ] 1. Hänge...; 2. ~s pl. Behang m; Tapeten f/pl.

hangman ['hæŋmən] Henker m.

hang-nail ♫ ['hæŋneil] Niednagel m.

hang-over sl. ['hæŋouvə] Katzenjammer m, Kater m.

hanker ['hæŋkə] sich sehnen.

hap|hazard ['hæp'hæzəd] 1. Zufall m; at ~ aufs Geratewohl; 2. zufällig; ~less □ ['hæplis] unglücklich.

happen ['hæpən] sich ereignen, geschehen; he ~ed to be at home er war zufällig zu Hause; ~ (up)on zufällig treffen auf (acc.); ~ in Am. F hereinschneien; ~ing ['hæpniŋ] Breignis n.

happi|ly ['hæpili] glücklicherweise; ~ness [ˌinis] Glück(seligkeit f) n.

happy □ ['hæpi] allg. glücklich; beglückt; erfreut; erfreulich; geschickt; treffend; F angeheitert; ~-go-lucky F unbekümmert.

harangue [hə'ræŋ] 1. Ansprache f, Rede f; 2. v/t. feierlich anreden.

harass ['hærəs] belästigen, quälen.

harbo(u)r ['haːbə] 1. Hafen m; Zufluchtsort m; 2. (be)herbergen; Rache etc. hegen; ankern; ~age [ˌəridʒ] Herberge f; Zuflucht f.

hard [haːd] 1. adj. allg. hart; schwer; mühselig; streng; ausdauernd; fleißig; heftig; Am. stark (Spirituosen); ~ of hearing schwerhörig; 2. adv. stark; tüchtig; mit Mühe; ~ by nahe bei; ~ up in Not; ~-boiled ['haːd'bɔild] hartgesotten; Am. gerissen; ~ cash Bargeld n; klingende Münze; ~en ['haːdn] härten; hart machen od. werden; (sich) abhärten; fig. (sich) verhärten; † sich festigen (Preise); ~-headed nüchtern denkend; ~-hearted □ hartherzig; ~ihood ['haːdihud] Kühnheit f; ~iness [ˌinis] Widerstandsfähigkeit f, Härte f; ~ly ['haːdli] kaum; streng;

mit Mühe; ~ness ['haːdnis] Härte f; Schwierigkeit f; Not f; ~pan Am. harter Boden, fig. Grundlage f; ~ship ['haːdʃip] Bedrängnis f, Not f; Härte f; ~ware Eisenwaren f/pl.; ~y □ ['haːdi] kühn; widerstandsfähig, hart; abgehärtet; winterfest (Pflanze).

hare [hɛə] Hase m; ~bell ♀ ['hɛəbel] Glockenblume f; ~-brained zerfahren; ~lip anat. ['hɛə'lip] Hasenscharte f.

hark [haːk] horchen (to auf acc.).

harlot ['haːlət] Hure f.

harm [haːm] 1. Schaden m; Unrecht n, Böse(s) n; 2. beschädigen, verletzen; schaden, Leid zufügen (dat.); ~ful □ ['haːmful] schädlich; ~less □ ['haːmlis] harmlos; unschädlich.

harmon|ic [haː'mɔnik] (~ally), ~ious □ [haː'mounjəs] harmonisch; ~ize ['haːmənaiz] v/t. in Einklang bringen; v/i. harmonieren; ~y [ˌni] Harmonie f.

harness ['haːnis] 1. Harnisch m; Zug-Geschirr n; die in ~ in den Sielen sterben; 2. anschirren; bändigen; Wasserkraft nutzbar machen.

harp [haːp] 1. Harfe f; 2. Harfe spielen; ~ (up)on herumreiten auf (dat.). [2. harpunieren.)

harpoon [haː'puːn] 1. Harpune f;)

harrow ♪ ['hærou] 1. Egge f; 2. eggen; fig. quälen, martern.

harry ['hæri] plündern; quälen.

harsh [haːʃ] rauh; herb; grell; streng; schroff; barsch.

hart zo. [haːt] Hirsch m.

harvest ['haːvist] 1. Ernte(zeit) f; Ertrag m; 2. ernten; einbringen.

has [hæz] 3. sg. pres. von have.

hash [hæʃ] 1. gehacktes Fleisch; Am. F Essen n, Fraß m; fig. Mischmasch m; 2. (zer)hacken.

hast|e [heist] Eile f; Hast f; make ~ (sich be)eilen; ~en ['heisn] (sich be)eilen; j-n antreiben; et. beschleunigen; ~y □ ['heisti] (vor)eilig; hastig; hitzig, heftig.

hat [hæt] Hut m.

hatch [hætʃ] 1. Brut f, Hecke f; ♫, ⚓ Luke f; serving ~ Durchreiche f; 2. (aus)brüten (a. fig.).

hatchet ['hætʃit] Beil n.

hatchway ⚓ ['hætʃwei] Luke f.

hat|e [heit] 1. Haß m; 2. hassen; ~eful □ ['heitful] verhaßt; abscheulich; ~red ['heitrid] Haß m.

haught|iness ['hɔːtinis] Stolz m; Hochmut m; ~y □ ['hɔːti] stolz; hochmütig.

haul [hɔːl] 1. Ziehen n; (Fisch-) Zug m; Am. Transport(weg) m; 2. ziehen; schleppen; transportieren; ⚒ fördern; ⚓ abdrehen; ~ down one's flag die Flagge streichen; fig. sich geschlagen geben.

haunch [hɔ:ntʃ] Hüfte *f*; Keule *f von Wild*.

haunt [hɔ:nt] 1. Aufenthaltsort *m*; Schlupfwinkel *m*; 2. oft besuchen; heimsuchen; verfolgen; spuken in (*dat.*).

have [hæv] [*irr.*] *v/t.* haben; bekommen; *Mahlzeit* einnehmen; lassen; ~ to do tun müssen; I ~ my hair cut ich lasse mir das Haar schneiden; he will ~ it that ... er behauptet, daß ...; I had better go es wäre besser, wenn ich ginge; I had rather go ich möchte lieber gehen; ~ about one bei *od.* an sich haben; ~ on anhaben; ~ it out with sich auseinandersetzen mit; *v/aux.* haben; *bei v/i.* oft sein; ~ come gekommen sein.

haven ['heivn] Hafen *m* (*a. fig.*).

havoc ['hævɔk] Verwüstung *f*; make ~ of, play ~ with *od.* among verwüsten; übel zurichten.

haw ♀ [hɔ:] Hagebutte *f*.

Hawaiian [hɑ:'waiiən] 1. hawaiisch; 2. Hawaiier(in).

hawk [hɔ:k] 1. Habicht *m*; Falke *m*; 2. sich räuspern; hausieren mit.

hawthorn ♀ ['hɔ:θɔ:n] Weißdorn *m*.

hay [hei] 1. Heu *n*; 2. heuen; ~**cock** ['heikɔk] Heuhaufen *m*; ~**fever** Heuschnupfen *m*; ~**loft** Heuboden *m*; ~**maker** *bsd. Am.* K.o.-Schlag *m*; ~**rick** = haycock; ~**seed** *bsd. Am.* F Bauerntölpel *m*; ~**stack** = haycock.

hazard ['hæzəd] 1. Zufall *m*; Gefahr *f*, Wagnis *n*; Hasard(spiel) *n*; 2. wagen; ~**ous** ⫯ [~dəs] gewagt.

haze [heiz] 1. Dunst *m*; ⫯ ♣ *u. Am.* schinden; F schurigeln.

hazel ['heizl] 1. ♀ Hasel(staude) *f*; 2. nußbraun; ~**nut** Haselnuß *f*.

hazy ⫯ ['heizi] dunstig; *fig.* unklar.

H-bomb ⚔ ['eitʃbɔm] H-Bombe *f*, Wasserstoffbombe *f*.

he [hi:] 1. er; ~ who derjenige, welcher; 2. Mann *m*; *zo.* Männchen *n*; 3. *adj. in Zssgn*: männlich, ...männchen *n*; ~**goat** Ziegenbock *m*.

head [hed] 1. *allg.* Kopf *m* (*a. fig.*); Haupt *n* (*a. fig.*); *nach Zahlwort*: Mann *m* (*a. pl.*); Stück *n* (*a. pl.*); Leiter(in); Chef *m*; Kopfende *n e-s Bettes etc.*; Kopfseite *f e-r Münze*; Gipfel *m*; Quelle *f*; *Schiffs*-Vorderteil *n*; Hauptpunkt *m*, Abschnitt *m*; Überschrift *f*; come to a ~ eitern (*Geschwür*); *fig.* sich zuspitzen, zur Entscheidung kommen; get it into one's ~ that ... es sich in den Kopf setzen, daß; ~ over heels Hals über Kopf; 2. erst; Ober...; Haupt...; 3. *v/t.* (an)führen; an der Spitze von *et.* stehen; vorausgehen (*dat.*); mit e-r Überschrift versehen; ~ off ablenken; *v/i.* ~ zusteuern (for auf *acc.*); *Am.* entspringen (*Fluß*). ~**ache** ['hedeik] Kopfweh *n*; ~

dress Kopfputz *m*; Frisur *f*; ~**gear** Kopfbedeckung *f*; Zaumzeug *n*; ~**ing** ['hediŋ] Brief-, Titelkopf *m*, Rubrik *f*; Überschrift *f*, Titel *m*; *Sport*: Kopfball *m*; ~**land** ['hedlənd] Vorgebirge *n*; ~**light** *mot.* Scheinwerfer(licht *n*) *m*; ~**line** Überschrift *f*; Schlagzeile *f*; ~s *pl. Radio*: das Wichtigste in Kürze; ~**long** 1. *adj.* ungestüm; 2. *adv.* kopfüber; ~**master** Direktor *m e-r Schule*; ~**phone** *Radio*: Hörer *m*; ~**quarters** *pl.* ✕ Hauptquartier *n*; Zentral(stell)e *f*; ~**strong** halsstarrig; ~**waters** *pl.* Quellgebiet *n*; ~**way** Fortschritt(e *pl.*) *m*; make ~ vorwärtskommen; ~**word** Stichwort *n e-s Wörterbuchs*; ~**y** ⫯ ['hedi] ungestüm; voreilig; zu Kopfe steigend.

heal [hi:l] heilen; ~ up zuheilen.

health [helθ] Gesundheit *f*; ~**ful** ⫯ ['helθful] gesund; heilsam; ~**resort** Kurort *m*; ~**y** ⫯ ['helθi] gesund.

heap [hi:p] 1. Haufe(n) *m*; 2. *a.* ~ up (auf)häufen; überhäufen.

hear [hiə] [*irr.*] hören; erfahren; anhören, *j-m* zuhören; erhören; *Zeugen* verhören; *Lektion* abhören; ~**d** [hə:d] *pret. u. p.p. von* hear; ~**er** ['hiərə] (Zu)Hörer(in); ~**ing** [~riŋ] Gehör *n*; Audienz *f*; ♣✕ Verhör *n*; Hörweite *f*; ~**say** Hörensagen *n*.

hearse [hə:s] Leichenwagen *m*.

heart [hɑ:t] *allg.* Herz *n* (*a. fig.*); Innere(s) *n*; Kern *m*; *fig.* Schatz *m*; by ~ auswendig; out of ~ mutlos; lay to ~ sich zu Herzen nehmen; lose ~ den Mut verlieren; take ~ sich ein Herz fassen; ~**ache** ['hɑ:teik] Kummer *m*; ~**break** Herzeleid *n*; ~**breaking** ⫯ [~kiŋ] herzzerbrechend; ~**broken** gebrochenen Herzens; ~**burn** Sodbrennen *n*; ~**en** ['hɑ:tn] ermutigen; ~**failure** ✕ Herzversagen *n*; ~**felt** innig, tief empfunden.

hearth [hɑ:θ] Herd *m* (*a. fig.*).

heart|less ⫯ ['hɑ:tlis] herzlos; ~**rending** ['hɑ:trendiŋ] herzzerreißend; ~ **transplant** Herzverpflanzung *f*; ~**y** ['hɑ:ti] ⫯ herzlich; aufrichtig; gesund; herzhaft.

heat [hi:t] 1. *allg.* Hitze *f*; Wärme *f*; Eifer *m*; *Sport*: Gang *m*, einzelner Lauf *m*; *zo.* Läufigkeit *f*; 2. heizen; (sich) erhitzen (*a. fig.*); ~**er** ⊕ ['hi:tə] Heizer *m*; Ofen *m*.

heath [hi:θ] Heide *f*; ♀ Heidekraut *n*.

heathen ['hi:ðən] 1. Heid|e *m*, -in *f*; 2. heidnisch.

heather ♀ ['heðə] Heide(kraut *n*) *f*.

heat|ing ['hi:tiŋ] Heizung *f*; *attr.* Heiz...; ~ **lightning** *Am.* Wetterleuchten *n*.

heave [hi:v] 1. Heben *n*; Übelkeit *f*;

2. [*irr.*] *v/t.* heben; schwellen; *Seufzer* ausstoßen; *Anker* lichten; *v/i.* sich heben, wogen, schwellen.

heaven ['hevn] Himmel *m*; **~ly** [~nli] himmlisch.

heaviness ['hevinis] Schwere *f*, Druck *m*; Schwerfälligkeit *f*; Schwermut *f*.

heavy [~ ['hevi] *allg.* schwer; schwermütig; schwerfällig; trüb; drückend; heftig (*Regen etc.*); unwegsam (*Straße*); Schwer...; **~current** *ɇ* Starkstrom *m*; **~handed** ungeschickt; **~hearted** niedergeschlagen; **~weight** *Boxen:* Schwergewicht *n*.

heckle ['hekl] durch Zwischenfragen in die Enge treiben.

hectic *⚕* ['hektik] hektisch (*auszehrend; sl. fieberhaft erregt*).

hedge [hedʒ] **1.** Hecke *f*; **2.** *v/t.* einhegen, einzäunen; umgeben; **~** up sperren; *v/i.* sich decken; sich nicht festlegen; **~hog** *zo.* ['hedʒhɔg] Igel *m*; *Am.* Stachelschwein *n*; **~row** Hecke *f*.

heed [hi:d] **1.** Beachtung *f*, Aufmerksamkeit *f*; take **~** of, give **~** to, pay **~** to achtgeben auf (*acc.*), beachten; **2.** beachten, achten auf (*acc.*); **~less** [~ ['hi:dlis] unachtsam; unbekümmert (*of* um).

heel [hi:l] **1.** Ferse *f*; Absatz *m*; *Am. sl.* Lump *m*; head over **~s** Hals über Kopf; down at **~** mit schiefen Absätzen; *fig.* abgerissen; schlampig; **2.** mit e-m Absatz versehen; **~ed** *Am.* F finanzstark; **~er** *Am. sl. pol.* ['hi:lə] Befehlsempfänger *m*.

heft [heft] Gewicht *n*; *Am.* F Hauptteil *m*.

heifer ['hefə] Färse *f* (*junge Kuh*).

height [hait] Höhe *f*; Höhepunkt *m*; **~en** [~ ['haitn] erhöhen; vergrößern.

heinous ['heinəs] abscheulich.

heir [ɛə] Erbe *m*; **~** apparent rechtmäßiger Erbe; **~ess** ['ɛəris] Erbin *f*; **~loom** [~'ɛəlu:m] Erbstück *n*.

held [held] *pret. u. p.p. von* hold 2.

helibus *Am.* F ['helibʌs] Lufttaxi *n*.

helicopter *⚒* ['helikɔptə] Hubschrauber *m*.

hell [hel] Hölle *f*; *attr.* Höllen...; what the **~** ...? F was zum Teufel ...?; raise **~** Krach machen; **~bent** ['helbent] *Am. sl.* unweigerlich entschlossen; **~ish** [~ ['heliʃ] höllisch.

hello ['he'lou] hallo!

helm *⚓* [helm] (Steuer)Ruder *n*.

helmet ['helmit] Helm *m*.

helmsman *⚓* ['helmzmən] Steuermann *m*.

help [help] **1.** *allg.* Hilfe *f*; (Hilfs-) Mittel *n*; (Dienst)Mädchen *n*; **2.** *v/t.* (ab)helfen (*dat.*); unterlassen; *bei Tisch* geben, reichen;

~ *o.s.* sich bedienen, zulangen; I could not **~** laughing ich konnte nicht umhin zu lachen; *v/i.* helfen, dienen; **~er** ['helpə] Helfer(in), Gehilf|e *m*, -in *f*; **~ful** [~ [~pful] hilfreich; nützlich; **~ing** [~piŋ] Portion *f*; **~less** [~ [~plis] hilflos; **~lessness** [~snis] Hilflosigkeit *f*; **~mate**, **~meet** Gehilf|e *m*, -in *f*; Gattin *f*.

helter-skelter ['heltə'skeltə] holterdiepolter.

helve [helv] Stiel *m*, Griff *m*.

Helvetian [hel'vi:ʃjən] Helvetier (-in); *attr.* Schweizer...

hem [hem] **1.** Saum *m*; **2.** *v/t.* säumen; **~** in einschließen; *v/i.* sich räuspern.

hemisphere ['hemisfiə] Halbkugel *f*.

hem-line ['hemlain] *Kleid:* Saum *m*.

hemlock *♀* ['hemlɔk] Schierling *m*; **~tree** Schierlingstanne *f*.

hemp [hemp] Hanf *m*.

hemstitch ['hemstitʃ] Hohlsaum *m*.

hen [hen] Henne *f*; *Vogel*-Weibchen *n*.

hence [hens] weg; hieraus; daher; von jetzt an; *a year* **~** heute übers Jahr; **~forth** ['hens'fɔ:θ], **~forward** [~'ɔ:wəd] von nun an.

hen|-coop ['henku:p] Hühnerstall *m*; **~pecked** unter dem Pantoffel (stehend).

hep *Am. sl.* [hep]: to be **~** to kennen; **~cat** *Am. sl.* ['hepkæt] Eingeweihte(r *m*) *f*; Jazzfanatiker(in).

her [hə:, hə] sie; ihr; ihr(e).

herald ['herəld] **1.** Herold *m*; **2.** (sich) ankündigen; **~** in einführen; **~ry** [~dri] Wappenkunde *f*, Heraldik *f*.

herb [hə:b] Kraut *n*; **~age** ['hə:bidʒ] Gras *n*; Weide *f*; **~ivorous** [hə:'bivərəs] pflanzenfressend.

herd [hə:d] **1.** Herde *f* (*a. fig.*); **2.** *v/t.* Vieh hüten; *v/i.* a. **~** together in e-r Herde leben; zs.-hausen; **~er** ['hə:də], **~sman** ['hə:dzmən] Hirt *m*.

here [hiə] hier; hierher; **~'s** to ...! auf das Wohl von ...!

here|after [hiər'ɑ:ftə] **1.** künftig; **2.** Zukunft *f*; **~by** [~'hiə'bai] hierdurch.

heredit|ary [hi'reditəri] erblich; Erb...; **~y** [~ti] Erblichkeit *f*.

here|in ['hiər'in] hierin; **~of** [hiər-'ɔv] hiervon.

heresy ['herəsi] Ketzerei *f*.

heretic ['herətik] Ketzer(in).

here|tofore ['hiətu'fɔ:] bis jetzt; ehemals; **~upon** ['hiərə'pɔn] hierauf; **~with** hiermit.

heritage ['heritidʒ] Erbschaft *f*.

hermit ['hə:mit] Einsiedler *m*.

hero ['hiərou] Held *m*; **~ic(al** [~ []) [hi'rouik(əl)] heroisch; heldenhaft;

Helden...; **~ine** ['herouin] Heldin *f*; **~ism** [~izəm] Heldenmut *m*, -tum *n*.

heron *zo.* ['herən] Reiher *m*.

herring *ichth.* ['heriŋ] Hering *m*.

hers [hə:z] der (die, das) ihrige; ihr.

herself [hə:'self] (sie, ihr, sich) selbst; sich; *of* ~ von selbst; *by* ~ allein.

hesitat|e ['heziteit] zögern, unschlüssig sein; Bedenken tragen; **~ion** [hezi'teifən] Zögern *n*; Unschlüssigkeit *f*; Bedenken *n*.

hew [hju:] [*irr.*] hauen, hacken; **~n** [hju:n] *p.p. von* hew.

hey [hei] ei!; hei!; he!, heda!

heyday ['heidei] **1.** heisa!; oho!; **2.** *fig.* Höhepunkt *m*, Blüte *f*.

hi [hai] he!, heda!; hallo!

hicc|ough, ~up ['hikʌp] **1** Schlukken *m*; **2.** schlucken; den Schlukken haben.

hid [hid] *pret. u. p.p. von* hide 2; **~den** ['hidn] *p.p. von* hide 2.

hide [haid] **1.** Haut *f*; **2.** [*irr.*] (sich) verbergen, verstecken; **~-and-seek** ['haidənd'si:k] Versteckspiel *n*.

hidebound *fig.* ['haidbaund] engherzig.

hideous □ ['hidiəs] scheußlich.

hiding ['haidiŋ] **1** Tracht *f* Prügel; Verbergen *n*; **~-place** Versteck *n*.

hi-fi *Am.* ['hai'fai] = high-fidelity.

high [hai] **1.** *adj.* □ *allg.* hoch; vornehm; gut, edel (*Charakter*); stolz; hochtrabend; angegangen (*Fleisch*); extrem; stark; üppig, flott (*Leben*); Hoch...; Ober...; *with a ~ hand* arrogant, anmaßend; *in ~ spirits* in gehobener Stimmung, guter Laune; ~ *life die* vornehme Welt; ~ *time* höchste Zeit; ~ *words* heftige Worte; **2.** *meteor.* Hoch *n*; *bsd. Am. für Zssgn wie high school, etc.*; **3.** *adv.* hoch; sehr, mächtig; **~ball** *Am.* ['haibɔ:l] Whisky *m* mit Soda; **~bred** vornehm erzogen; **~brow** F **1.** Intellektuelle(r *m*) *f*; **2.** betont intellektuell; **~class** erstklassig; **~fidelity** mit höchster Wiedergabetreue, Hi-Fi; **~grade** hochwertig; **~handed** anmaßend; **~land** ['hailənd] Hochland *n*; **~ lights** *pl. fig.* Höhepunkte *m/pl.*; **~ly** ['haili] hoch; sehr; *speak ~ of s.o.* j-n loben; **~minded** hochherzig; **~ness** ['hainis] Höhe *f*; *fig.* Hoheit *f*; **~pitched** schrill (*Ton*); steil (*Dach*); **~power**; ~ *station* Großkraftwerk *n*; **~road** Landstraße *f*; ~ **school** höhere Schule; **~strung** überempfindlich; ~ **tea** frühes Abendessen *mit Tee u. Fleisch etc.*; **~water** Hochwasser *n*; **~way** Landstraße *f*; *fig.* Weg *m*; ~ *code* Straßenverkehrsordnung *f*; **~wayman** Straßenräuber *m*.

hike F [haik] **1.** wandern; **2.** Wan-

derung *f*; *bsd. Am.* F Erhöhung *f* (*Preis etc.*); **~r** ['haikə] Wanderer *m*.

hilarious □ [hi'lɛəriəs] ausgelassen.

hill [hil] Hügel *m*, Berg *m*; **~billy** *Am.* F ['hilbili] Hinterwäldler *m*; **~ock** ['hilək] kleiner Hügel; **~side** ['hil'said] Hang *m*; **~y** ['hili] hügelig.

hilt [hilt] Griff *m* (*bsd. am Degen*).

him [him] ihn; ihm; den, der(jenigen); **~self** [him'self] (er, ihm, ihn, sich) selbst; sich; *of* ~ von selbst; *by* ~ allein.

hind[1] *zo.* [haind] Hirschkuh *f*.

hind[2] [~] Hinter...; **~er 1.** ['haində] hintere(r, -s); Hinter...; **2.** ['hində] *v/t.* hindern (*from an dat.*); hemmen; **~most** ['haindmoust] hinterst, letzt.

hindrance ['hindrəns] Hindernis *n*.

hinge [hindʒ] **1.** Türangel *f*; Scharnier *n*; *fig.* Angelpunkt *m*; **2.** ~ *upon fig.* abhängen von.

hint [hint] **1.** Wink *m*; Anspielung *f*; **2.** andeuten; anspielen (*at auf acc.*).

hinterland ['hintəlænd] Hinterland *n*. [(*butte f.*\]

hip [hip] *anat.* Hüfte *f*; ♃ Hage-)

hippopotamus *zo.* [hipə'potəməs] Flußpferd *n*.

hire ['haiə] **1.** Miete *f*; Entgelt *m, n*, Lohn *m*; **2.** mieten; *j-n* anstellen; ~ *out* vermieten.

his [hiz] sein(e); der (die, das) seinige.

hiss [his] *v/i.* zischen; zischeln; *v/t. a.* ~ *off* auszischen, auspfeifen.

histor|ian [his'tɔ:riən] Historiker *m*; **~ic(al** □) [his'tɔrik(əl)] historisch, geschichtlich; Geschichts...; **~y** ['histəri] Geschichte *f*.

hit [hit] **1.** Schlag *m*, Stoß *m*; *fig.* (Seiten)Hieb *m*; (Glücks)Treffer *m*; *thea.*, ♪ Schlager *m*; **2.** [*irr.*] schlagen, stoßen; treffen; auf *et.* stoßen; *gen.* Am. F eintreffen in (*dat.*) ~ *s.o. a blow* j-m e-n Schlag versetzen; ~ *it off with* F sich vertragen mit; ~ (*up)on* (zufällig) kommen *od.* stoßen *od.* verfallen auf (*acc.*).

hitch [hitʃ] **1.** Ruck *m*; ♃ Knoten *m*; *fig.* Haken *m*, Hindernis *n*; **2.** rükken; (sich) festmachen, festhaken; hängenbleiben; rutschen; **~hike** F ['hitʃhaik] per Anhalter fahren.

hither *lit.* ['hiðə] hierher; **~to** bisher.

hive [haiv] **1.** Bienenstock *m*; Bienenschwarm *m*; *fig.* Schwarm *m*; **2.** ~ *up* aufspeichern; zs.-wohnen.

hoard [hɔ:d] **1.** Vorrat *m*, Schatz *m*; **2.** *a.* ~ *up* aufhäufen; horten.

hoarfrost [hɔ:'frost] (Rauh)Reif *m*.

hoarse □ [hɔ:s] heiser, rauh.

hoary ['hɔ:ri] (alters)grau.

hoax [houks] **1.** Täuschung *f*; Falschmeldung *f*; **2.** foppen.

hob [hɔb] = hobgoblin; *raise* ~ *bsd. Am.* F Krach schlagen.

hobble ['hɔbl] 1. Hinken n, Humpeln n; F Klemme f, Patsche f; 2. v/i. humpeln, hinken (a. fig.); v/t. an den Füßen fesseln.

hobby ['hɔbi] fig Steckenpferd n, Hobby n; ~horse Steckenpferd n; Schaukelpferd n.

hobgoblin ['hɔbgɔblin] Kobold m.

hobo Am. sl. ['houbou] Landstreicher m.

hock[1] [hɔk] Rheinwein m.

hock[2] zo. [~] Sprunggelenk n.

hod [hɔd] Mörteltrog m.

hoe ✓ [hou] 1. Hacke f; 2. hacken.

hog [hɔg] 1. Schwein n (a. fig.); 2. Mähne stutzen; mot. drauflos rasen; ~gish □ ['hɔgiʃ] schweinisch; gefräßig.

hoist [hoist] 1. Aufzug m; 2. hochziehen, hissen.

hokum sl. ['houkəm] Mätzchen n/pl.; Kitsch m; Humbug m.

hold [hould] 1. Halten n; Halt m, Griff m; Gewalt f, Einfluß m; ⊕ Lade-, Frachtraum m; catch (od. get, lay, take, seize) ~ of erfassen, ergreifen; sich aneignen; keep ~ of festhalten; 2. [irr.] v/t. allg. halten; fest-, aufhalten; enthalten; fig. behalten; Versammlung etc. abhalten; (inne)haben; Ansicht vertreten; Gedanken etc. hegen; halten für; glauben; behaupten; ~ one's ground, ~ one's own sich behaupten; ~ the line teleph. am Apparat bleiben; ~ on et. (an s-m Platz fest)halten; ~ over aufschieben; ~ up aufrecht halten; (unter)stützen; aufhalten; (räuberisch) überfallen; v/i. (fest)halten; gelten; sich bewähren; standhalten; ~ forth Reden halten; ~ good od. true gelten; sich bestätigen; ~ off sich fernhalten; ~ on ausharren; fortdauern; sich festhalten; teleph. am Apparat bleiben; ~ to festhalten an (dat.); ~ up sich (aufrecht) halten; ~er ['houldə] Pächter m; Halter m (Gerät); Inhaber(in) (bsd. ✝); ~ing ['~diŋ] halten n; Halt m; Pachtgut n; Besitz m; ~ company Dachgesellschaft f; ~over Am. Rest m; ~up Raubüberfall m; Stauung f, Stockung f.

hole [houl] 1. Loch n; Höhle f; F fig. Klemme f; pick ~s in bekritteln; 2. aushöhlen; durchlöchern.

holiday ['hɔlidi] Feiertag m; freier Tag; ~s pl. Ferien pl , Urlaub m; ~maker Urlauber(in)

holler Am F ['hɔlə] laut rufen.

hollow ['hɔlou] 1. □ hohl; leer; falsch; 2. Höhle f, (Aus)Höhlung f; Land-Senke f; 3. aushöhlen.

holly ♀ ['hɔli] Stechpalme f.

holster ['houlstə] Pistolentasche f.

holy ['houli] heilig; ♀ Thursday Gründonnerstag m; ~ water Weihwasser n; ♀ Week Karwoche f.

homage ['hɔmidʒ] Huldigung f; do od. pay od. render ~ huldigen (to dat.).

home [houm] 1. Heim n; Haus n, Wohnung f; Heimat f; Mal n; at ~ zu Hause; 2. adj. (ein)heimisch, inländisch; wirkungsvoll; tüchtig (Schlag etc.); ♀ Office Innenministerium n; ~ rule Selbstregierung f; ♀ Secretary Innenminister m; ~ trade Binnenhandel m; 3. adv. heim, nach Hause; an die richtige Stelle; gründlich; hit od. strike ~ den rechten Fleck treffen; ♀ Counties die Grafschaften um London; ~ economics Am. Hauswirtschaftslehre f; ~felt ['houmfelt] tief empfunden; ~less ['houmlis] heimatlos; ~like anheimelnd, gemütlich; ~ly [~li] anheimelnd, häuslich; fig. hausbacken; schlicht; anspruchslos; reizlos; ~made selbstgemacht, Hausmacher...; ~sickness Heimweh n; ~stead Anwesen n; ~ team Sport Gastgeber m/pl.; ~ward(s) ['houmwəd(z)] heimwärts (gerichtet); Heim...; ~work Hausaufgabe(n pl.) f, Schularbeiten f/pl.

homicide ['hɔmisaid] Totschlag m; Mord m; Totschläger(in).

homogeneous □ [hɔmə'dʒi:njəs] homogen, gleichartig.

hone ⊕ [houn] 1. Abziehstein m; 2. Rasiermesser abziehen.

honest □ ['ɔnist] ehrlich, rechtschaffen; aufrichtig; echt; ~y [~ti] Ehrlichkeit f, Rechtschaffenheit f; Aufrichtigkeit f.

honey ['hʌni] Honig m; fig. Liebling m; ~comb [~koum] (Honig-) Wabe f; ~ed ['hʌnid] honigsüß; ~moon 1. Flitterwochen f/pl.; 2. die Flitterwochen verleben.

honk mot. [hɔŋk] hupen, tuten.

honky-tonk Am. sl. ['hɔŋkitɔŋk] Spelunke f.

honorary ['ɔnərəri] Ehren...; ehrenamtlich.

hono(u)r ['ɔnə] 1. Ehre f; Achtung f; Würde f; fig. Zierde f; Your ♀ Euer Gnaden; 2. (be)ehren; ✝ honorieren; ~able □ ['ɔnərəbl] ehrenvoll; redlich; ehrbar; ehrenwert.

hood [hud] 1. Kapuze f; mot. Verdeck n; Am. (Motor)Haube f; ⊕ Kappe f; 2. mit e-r Kappe etc. bekleiden; ein-, verhüllen.

hoodlum Am. F ['hu:dləm] Strolch m.

hoodoo bsd. Am. ['hu:du:] Unglücksbringer m; Pech n (Unglück).

hoodwink ['hudwiŋk] täuschen.

hooey Am. sl. ['hu:i] Quatsch m.

hoof [hu:f] Huf m; Klaue f.

hook [huk] 1. (bsd. Angel)Haken m; Sichel f; by ~ or by crook so oder so;

2. (sich) (zu-, fest)haken; angeln (*a. fig.*); ~y ['huki] **1.** hakig; **2.**: *play* ~ *Am. sl.* (die Schule) schwänzen.

hoop [hu:p] **1.** *Faß- etc.* Reif(en) *m*; ⊕ Ring *m*; **2.** Fässer binden.

hooping-cough ✻ ['hu:piŋkɒf] Keuchhusten *m*.

hoot [hu:t] **1.** Geschrei *n*; **2.** *v/i.* heulen; johlen; *mot.* hupen; *v/t.* auspfeifen, auszischen.

Hoover ['hu:və] **1.** Staubsauger *m*; **2.** (mit e-m Staubsauger) saugen.

hop [hɒp] **1.** ♀ Hopfen *m*; Sprung *m*; F Tanzerei *f*; **2.** hüpfen, springen (über *acc.*).

hope [houp] **1.** Hoffnung *f*; **2.** hoffen (*for* auf *acc.*); ~ *in* vertrauen auf (*acc.*); ~ful □ ['houpful] hoffnungsvoll; ~less □ ['houplis] hoffnungslos; verzweifelt.

horde [hɔ:d] Horde *f*.

horizon [hə'raizn] Horizont *m*.

horn [hɔ:n] Horn *n*; Schalltrichter *m*; *mot.* Hupe *f*; ~s *pl.* Geweih *n*; ~ *of plenty* Füllhorn *n*.

hornet *zo.* ['hɔ:nit] Hornisse *f*.

horn|swoggle *Am. sl.* ['hɔ:nswɒgl] *j-n* 'reinlegen; ~y ['hɔ:ni] hornig; schwielig.

horr|ible □ ['hɒrəbl] entsetzlich; scheußlich; ~id □ ['hɒrid] gräßlich, abscheulich; schrecklich; ~ify [~ifai] erschrecken; entsetzen; ~or ['hɒrə] Entsetzen *n*, Schauder *m*; Schrecken *m*; Greuel *m*.

horse [hɔ:s] *zo.* Pferd *n*; Reiterei *f*; Bock *m*, Gestell *n*; ~back ['hɔ:sbæk]: *on* ~ zu Pferde; ~hair Roßhaar *n*; ~laugh f wieherndes Lachen; ~man Reiter *m*; ~manship [~ʃip] Reitkunst *f*; ~opera *Am. drittklassiger* Wildwestfilm; ~power Pferdestärke *f*; ~radish Meerrettich *m*; ~shoe Hufeisen *n*.

horticulture ['hɔ:tikʌltʃə] Gartenbau *m*.

hose [houz] Schlauch *m*; Strumpfhose *f*; *coll.* Strümpfe *m/pl.*

hosiery ['houʒəri] Strumpfwaren *f/pl.*

hospitable □ ['hɒspitəbl] gastfrei.

hospital ['hɒspitl] Krankenhaus *n*; ✗ Lazarett *n*; ~ity [hɒspi'tæliti] Gastfreundschaft *f*, Gastlichkeit *f*.

host [houst] Wirt *m*; Gastgeber *m*; Gastwirt *m*; *fig.* Heer *n*; Schwarm *m*; *eccl.* Hostie *f*.

hostage ['hɒstidʒ] Geisel *m, f*.

hostel ['hɒstl] Herberge *f*; *univ.* Studenten(wohn)heim *n*.

hostess ['houstis] Wirtin *f*; Gastgeberin *f*; *= air* ~.

hostil|e ['hɒstail] feindlich (gesinnt); ~ity [hɒs'tiliti] Feindseligkeit *f* (*to* gegen).

hot [hɒt] heiß; scharf; beißend; hitzig, heftig; eifrig; warm (*Speise, Fährte*); *Am. sl.* falsch (*Scheck*); gestohlen; radioaktiv; ~bed ['hɒtbed] Mistbeet *n*; *fig.* Brutstätte *f*.

hotchpotch ['hɒtʃpɒtʃ] Mischmasch *m*; Gemüsesuppe *f*.   [chen.]

hot dog F ['hɒt 'dɒg] heißes Würst-]

hotel [hou'tel] Hotel *n*.

hot|head ['hɒthed] Hitzkopf *m*; ~house Treibhaus *n*; ~pot Irish Stew *n*; ~rod *Am. sl. mot.* frisiertes altes Auto; ~spur Hitzkopf *m*.

hound [haund] **1.** Jagd-, Spürhund *m*; *fig.* Hund *m*; **2.** jagen, hetzen

hour ['auə] Stunde *f*; Zeit *f*, Uhr *f*; ~ly ['auəli] stündlich.

house 1. [haus] *allg.* Haus *n*; *the* ♀ das Unterhaus; die Börse; **2.** [hauz] *v/t.* unterbringen; *v/i.* hausen; ~agent ['hauseidʒənt] Häusermakler *m*; ~breaker ['hausbreikə] Abbrucharbeiter *m*; ~hold Haushalt *m*; *attr.* Haushalts...; Haus...; ~holder Hausherr *m*; ~keeper Haushälterin *f*; ~keeping Haushaltung *f*; ~maid Hausmädchen *n*; ~warming ['hauswɔ:miŋ] Einzugsfeier *f*; ~wife ['hauswaif] Hausfrau *f*; ['hʌzif] Nähtäschchen *n*; ~wifery ['hauswifəri] Haushaltung *f*; ~work Haus(halts)arbeit *f/pl.*

housing ['hauziŋ] Unterbringung *f*; Wohnung *f*; ~ estate Wohnsiedlung *f*.

hove [houv] *pret. u. p.p. von heave* 2.

hovel ['hɒvl] Schuppen *m*; Hütte *f*.

hover ['hɒvə] schweben; lungern; *fig.* schwanken; ~craft Luftkissenfahrzeug *n*.

how [hau] wie; ~ *do you do?* Begrüßungsformel *bei der Vorstellung*; ~ *about* ...? wie steht's mit ...? ~ever [hau'evə] **1.** *adv.* wie auch (immer); wenn auch noch so ...; **2.** *cj.* jedoch.

howl [haul] **1.** heulen, brüllen; **2.** Geheul *n*; ~er ['haulə] Heuler *m*; *sl.* grober Fehler.

hub [hʌb] (Rad)Nabe *f*; *fig.* Mittel-, Angelpunkt *m*.

hubbub ['hʌbʌb] Tumult *m*, Lärm *m*.

hub(by) F ['hʌb(i)] (Ehe)Mann *m*.

huckleberry ♀ ['hʌklberi] amerikanische Heidelbeere.

huckster ['hʌkstə] Hausierer(in).

huddle ['hʌdl] **1.** *a.* ~ *together* (sich) zs.-drängen, zs.-pressen; ~ (*o.s.*) *up* sich zs.-kauern; **2.** Gewirr *n*, Wirrwarr *m*.   [cry Zetergeschrei *n*.]

hue [hju:] Farbe *f*; Hetze *f*; ~ *and*]

huff [hʌf] **1.** üble Laune; **2.** *v/t.* grob anfahren; beleidigen; *v/i.* wütend werden; schmollen.

hug [hʌg] **1.** Umarmung *f*; **2.** an sich drücken, umarmen; *fig.* festhalten an (*dat.*); sich dicht am Weg *etc.* halten.

huge □ ['hju:dʒ] ungeheuer, riesig; ~ness ['hju:dʒnis] ungeheure Größe.

hulk *fig.* ['hʌlk] Klotz *m*.

hull [hʌl] 1. ♀ Schale *f*; Hülse *f*; ⚓ Rumpf *m*; 2. enthülsen; schälen.

hullabaloo [hʌləbə'luː] Lärm *m*.

hullo ['hʌ'lou] hallo (*bsd. teleph.*).

hum [hʌm] summen; brumme(l)n; *make things* ~ F Schwung in die Sache bringen.

human ['hjuːmən] 1. □ menschlich; ~ly nach menschlichem Ermessen; 2. F Mensch *m*; ~e □ [hju(ː)'mein] human, menschenfreundlich; ~itarian [hju(ː)mæni'tɛəriən] 1. Menschenfreund *m*; 2. menschenfreundlich; ~ity [hju(ː)'mæniti] menschliche Natur; Menschheit *f*; Humanität *f*; ~kind ['hjuːmən'kaind] Menschengeschlecht *n*.

humble ['hʌmbl] 1. □ demütig; bescheiden; 2. erniedrigen; demütigen.

humble-bee ['hʌmblbiː] Hummel *f*.

humbleness ['hʌmblnis] Demut *f*.

humbug ['hʌmbʌg] 1. (be)schwindeln; 2. Schwindel *m*.

humdinger *Am. sl.* [hʌm'diŋə] Mordskerl *m*, -sache *f*.

humdrum ['hʌmdrʌm] eintönig.

humid ['hjuːmid] feucht, naß; ~ity [hju(ː)'miditi] Feuchtigkeit *f*.

humiliat|e [hju(ː)'milieit] erniedrigen, demütigen; ~ion [hju(ː)mili'eiʃən] Erniedrigung *f*, Demütigung *f*.

humility [hju(ː)'militi] Demut *f*.

humming F ['hʌmiŋ] mächtig, gewaltig; ~bird zo. Kolibri *m*.

humorous □ ['hjuːmərəs] humoristisch, humorvoll; spaßig.

humo(u)r ['hjuːmə] 1. Laune *f*, Stimmung *f*; Humor *m*; *das* Spaßige; ✲ *hist.* Körpersaft *m*; *out of* ~ schlecht gelaunt; 2. *j-m* s-n Willen lassen; eingehen auf (*acc.*).

hump [hʌmp] 1. Höcker *m*, Buckel *m*; 2. krümmen; ärgern, verdrießen; ~ *o.s. Am. sl.* sich dranhalten; ~back ['hʌmpbæk] = *hunchback*.

hunch [hʌntʃ] 1. Höcker *m*; großes Stück; *Am.* F Ahnung *f*; 2. *a.* ~ *out,* ~ *up* krümmen; ~back ['hʌntʃbæk] Bucklige(r *m*) *f*.

hundred ['hʌndrəd] 1. hundert; 2. Hundert *n*; ~th [~dθ] 1. hundertste; 2. Hundertstel *n*; ~weight englischer Zentner (*50,8 kg*).

hung [hʌŋ] 1. *pret. u. p.p. von* *hang* 1; 2. *adj.* abgehangen (*Fleisch*).

Hungarian [hʌŋ'gɛəriən] 1. ungarisch; 2. Ungar(in); Ungarisch *n*.

hunger ['hʌŋgə] 1. Hunger *m* (*a. fig.*; *for* nach); 2. *v/i.* hungern (*for, after* nach); *v/t.* durch Hunger zwingen (*into* zu).

hungry □ ['hʌŋgri] hungrig.

hunk F [hʌŋk] dickes Stück.

hunt [hʌnt] 1. Jagd *f* (*for* nach); Jagd(revier *n*) *f*; Jagd(gesellschaft) *f*; 2. jagen; *Revier* bejagen; hetzen; ~ *out od.* *up* aufspüren; ~ *for,* ~ *after*

Jagd machen auf (*acc.*); ~er ['hʌntə] Jäger *m*; Jagdpferd *n*; ~ing [~tiŋ] Jagen *n*; Verfolgung *f*; *attr.* Jagd...; ~ing-ground Jagdrevier *n*; ~sman [~tsmən] Jäger *m*; Rüdemann *m* (*Meutenführer*).

hurdle ['həːdl] Hürde *f* (*a. fig.*); ~r [~lə] Hürdenläufer(in); ~race Hürdenrennen *n*.

hurl [həːl] 1. Schleudern *n*; 2. schleudern; *Worte* ausstoßen.

hurricane ['hʌrikən] Orkan *m*.

hurried □ ['hʌrid] eilig; übereilt.

hurry ['hʌri] 1. (große) Eile, Hast *f*; *be in a* ~ es eilig haben; *not ... in a* ~ F nicht so bald, nicht so leicht; 2. *v/t.* (an)treiben; drängen; *et.* beschleunigen; eilig schicken *od.* bringen; *v/i.* eilen, hasten; ~ *up* sich beeilen.

hurt [həːt] 1. Verletzung *f*; Schaden *m*; 2. [*irr.*] verletzen (*a. fig.*); weh tun (*dat.*); schaden (*dat.*).

husband ['hʌzbənd] 1. (Ehe)Mann *m*; 2. haushalten mit; verwalten; ~man Landwirt *m*; ~ry [~dri] Landwirtschaft *f*, Ackerbau *m*.

hush [hʌʃ] 1. still!; 2. Stille *f*; 3. *v/t.* zum Schweigen bringen; beruhigen; *Stimme* dämpfen; ~ *up* vertuschen; still sein; ~money ['hʌʃmʌni] Schweigegeld *n*.

husk [hʌsk] 1. ♀ Hülse *f*, Schote *f*; Schale *f* (*a. fig.*); 2. enthülsen; ~y ['hʌski] 1. □ hülsig; trocken; heiser; F stramm, stämmig; 2. F stämmiger Kerl.

hussy ['hʌsi] Flittchen *n*; Range *f*.

hustle ['hʌsl] 1. *v/t.* (an)rempeln; stoßen; drängen; *v/i.* (sich) drängen; eilen; *bsd. Am.* mit Hochdruck arbeiten; 2. Hochbetrieb *m*; Rührigkeit *f*; ~ *and bustle* Gedränge und Gehetze *n*.

hut [hʌt] Hütte *f*; ✕ Baracke *f*.

hutch [hʌtʃ] Kasten *m*; *bsd.* Kaninchen-Stall *m* (*a. fig.*); Trog *m*.

hyacinth ♀ ['haiəsinθ] Hyazinthe *f*.

hyaena zo. [hai'iːnə] Hyäne *f*.

hybrid ⛔ ['haibrid] Bastard *m*, Mischling *m*; Kreuzung *f*; *attr.* Bastard...; Zwitter...; ~ize [~daiz] kreuzen.

hydrant ['haidrənt] Hydrant *m*.

hydro| ⛔ ['haidrou] Wasser...; ~carbon Kohlenwasserstoff *m*; ~chloric acid [~rə'klɔrikæsid] Salzsäure *f*; ~gen [~ridʒən] Wasserstoff *m*; ~gen bomb Wasserstoffbombe *f*; ~pathy [hai'drɔpəθi] Wasserheilkunde *f*, Wasserkur *f*; ~phobia [haidrə'foubjə] Wasserscheu *f*; ✕ Tollwut *f*; ~plane ['haidrouplein] Wasserflugzeug *n*; (Motor)Gleitboot *n*, Rennboot *m*.

hyena zo. [hai'iːnə] Hyäne *f*.

hygiene ['haidʒiːn] Hygiene *f*.

hymn [him] 1. Hymne *f*; Lobgesang *m*; Kirchenlied *n*; 2. preisen.

hyphen ['haifən] 1. Bindestrich m; 2. mit Bindestrich schreiben od. verbinden; **~ated** [~neitid] mit Bindestrich geschrieben; **~** Americans pl. Halb-Amerikaner m/pl. (z. B. German-Americans). [ren.\
hypnotize ['hipnətaiz] hypnotisie-/
hypo|chondriac [haipou'kondriæk] Hypochonder m; **~crisy** [hi'po-

krəsi] Heuchelei f; **~crite** ['hipə-krit] Heuchler(in); Scheinheilige(r m) f; **~critical** □ [hipə'kritikəl] heuchlerisch; **~thesis** [hai'poθisis] Hypothese f.
hyster|ia [his'tiəriə] Hysterie f; **~ical** □ [~'terikəl] hysterisch; **~ics** [~ks] pl. hysterischer Anfall; go into **~** hysterisch werden.

I

I [ai] ich.
ice [ais] 1. Eis n; 2. gefrieren lassen; a. **~** up vereisen; Kuchen mit Zuckerguß überziehen; in Eis kühlen; **~age** [~'aiseidʒ] Eiszeit f; **~berg** ['aisbə:g] Eisberg m (a. fig.); **~bound** eingefroren; **~box** Eisschrank m; Am. a. Kühlschrank m; **~cream** Speiseeis n; **~floe** Eisscholle f.
icicle ['aisikl] Eiszapfen m.
icing ['aisin] Zuckerguß m; Vereisung f.
icy □ ['aisi] eisig (a. fig.); vereist.
idea [ai'diə] Idee f; Begriff m; Vorstellung f; Gedanke m; Meinung f; Ahnung f; Plan m; **~l** [~'əl] 1. □ ideell; eingebildet; ideal; 2. Ideal n.
identi|cal □ [ai'dentikəl] identisch, gleich(bedeutend); **~fication** [aidentifi'keiʃən] Identifizierung f; Ausweis m; **~fy** [ai'dentifai] identifizieren; ausweisen; erkennen; **~ty** [~iti] Identität f; Persönlichkeit f; Eigenart f; **~** card Personalausweis m, Kennkarte f; **~** disk ⚔ Erkennungsmarke f.
ideological □ [aidiə'lɔdʒikəl] ideologisch.
idiom ['idiəm] Idiom n; Mundart f; Redewendung f.
idiot ['idiət] Idiot(in), Schwachsinnige(r m) f; **~ic** [idi'ɔtik] (~ally) blödsinnig.
idle ['aidl] 1. □ müßig, untätig; träg, faul; unnütz; nichtig; **~** hours pl. Mußestunden f/pl.; 2. v/t. mst **~** away vertrödeln; v/i. faulenzen; ⊕ leer laufen; **~ness** ['aidlnis] Muße f; Trägheit f; Nichtigkeit f; **~r** ['aidlə] Müßiggänger(in).
idol ['aidl] Idol n, Götzenbild n; fig. Abgott m; **~atrous** [ai'dɔlətrəs] abgöttisch; **~atry** [~ri] Abgötterei f; Vergötterung f; **~ize** ['aidəlaiz] vergöttern.
dyl(l) ['idil] Idyll(e f) n.
if [if] 1. wenn, falls; ob; 2. Wenn n; **~fy** Am. F ['ifi] zweifelhaft.
ignite [ig'nait] (sich) entzünden; zünden; **~ion** [ig'niʃən] ⚛ Entzündung f; mot. Zündung f.

ignoble □ [ig'noubl] unedel; niedrig, gemein.
ignominious □ [ignə'miniəs] schändlich, schimpflich.
ignor|ance ['ignərəns] Unwissenheit f; **~ant** [~nt] unwissend; unkundig; **~e** [ig'nɔ:] ignorieren, nicht beachten; ⚖ verwerfen.
ill [il] 1. adj. u. adv. übel, böse; schlimm, schlecht; krank; adv. kaum; fall **~**, be taken **~** krank werden; 2. Übel n; Übel(s) n, Böse(s)n.
ill|-advised □ ['iləd'vaizd] schlecht beraten; unbesonnen, unklug; **~bred** ungebildet, ungezogen; **~** breeding schlechtes Benehmen.
illegal □ [i'li:gəl] ungesetzlich.
illegible □ [i'ledʒəbl] unleserlich.
illegitimate □ [ili'dʒitimit] illegitim; unrechtmäßig; unehelich.
ill|-favo(u)red [il'feivəd] häßlich; **~humo(u)red** übellaunig.
illiberal □ [i'libərəl] engstirnig; intolerant; knauserig.
illicit □ [i'lisit] unerlaubt.
illiterate [i'litərit] 1. ungelehrt, ungebildet; 2. Analphabet(in).
ill|-judged ['il'dʒʌdʒd] unklug, unvernünftig; **~mannered** ungezogen; mit schlechten Umgangsformen; **~natured** □ boshaft, bösartig.
illness ['ilnis] Krankheit f.
illogical □ [i'lɔdʒikəl] unlogisch.
ill|-starred ['il'sta:d] unglücklich; **~tempered** schlecht gelaunt; **~timed** ungelegen; **~treat** mißhandeln.
illuminat|e [i'lju:mineit] be-, erleuchten (a. fig.); erläutern; aufklären; **~ing** [~tin] Leucht…; fig. aufschlußreich; **~ion** [ilju:mi'neiʃən] Er-, Beleuchtung f; Erläuterung f; Aufklärung f.
ill-use ['il'ju:z] mißhandeln.
illus|ion [i'lu:ʒən] Illusion f, Täuschung f; **~ive** [i'lu:siv], **~ory** □ [~səri] illusorisch, täuschend.
illustrat|e ['iləstreit] illustrieren; erläutern; bebildern; **~ion** ['iləs'treiʃən] Erläuterung f; Illustration f; **~ive** □ ['iləstreitiv] erläuternd.

illustrious □ [i'lʌstriəs] berühmt.
ill will ['il'wil] Feindschaft f.
image ['imidʒ] Bild n; Standbild n;
Ebenbild n; Vorstellung f; ~ry
[~dʒəri] Bilder n/pl.; Bildersprache
f, Metaphorik f.
imagin|able □ [i'mædʒinəbl] denk-
bar; ~ary [~əri] eingebildet; ~ation
[imædʒi'neiʃən] Einbildung(skraft)
f; ~ative □ [i'mædʒinətiv] ideen-,
einfallsreich; ~e [i'mædʒin] sich et.
einbilden od. vorstellen od. denken.
imbecile □ ['imbisi:l] 1. geistes-
schwach; 2. Schwachsinnige(r m) f.
imbibe [im'baib] einsaugen; fig.
sich zu eigen machen.
imbue [im'bju:] (durch)tränken;
tief färben; fig. erfüllen.
imitat|e ['imiteit] nachahmen; imi-
tieren; ~ion [imi'teiʃən] 1. Nachahmung f; 2. künstlich, Kunst...
immaculate □ [i'mækjulit] unbefleckt, rein; fehlerlos.
immaterial □ [imə'tiəriəl] un-
körperlich; unwesentlich (to für).
immature [imə'tjuə] unreif.
immeasurable □ [i'meʒərəbl] unermeßlich.
immediate □ [i'mi:djət] unmittelbar; unverzüglich, sofortig; ~ly
[~tli] 1. adv. sofort; 2. cj. gleich
nachdem.
immense □ [i'mens] ungeheuer.
immerse [i'mə:s] (ein-, unter)tau-
chen; fig. ~ o.s. in sich versenken
od. vertiefen in (acc.).
immigra|nt ['imigrənt] Einwan-
derer(in); ~te [~greit] v/i. einwan-
dern; v/t. ansiedeln (into in dat.);
~tion [imi'greiʃən] Einwanderung f.
imminent □ ['iminənt] bevorstehend, drohend.
immobile [i'moubail] unbeweglich.
immoderate □ [i'mɔdərit] maßlos.
immodest □ [i'mɔdist] unbeschei-
den; unanständig.
immoral □ [i'mɔrəl] unmoralisch.
immortal □ [i'mɔ:tl] 1. □ unsterblich; 2. Unsterbliche(r m) f; ~ity
[imɔ:'tæliti] Unsterblichkeit f.
immovable [i'mu:vəbl] 1. □ unbeweglich; unerschütterlich; 2. ~s
pl. Immobilien pl.
immun|e ♂ u. fig. [i'mju:n] immun,
gefeit (from gegen); ~ity [~niti]
Immunität f, Freiheit f (from von);
Unempfänglichkeit f (für).
immutable □ [i'mju:təbl] unveränderlich.
imp [imp] Teufelchen n; Schelm m.
impact ['impækt] (Zs.-)Stoß m;
Anprall m; Einwirkung f.
impair [im'peə] schwächen; (ver-)
mindern; beeinträchtigen.
impart [im'pɑ:t] verleihen; weiter-
geben.
impartial □ [im'pɑ:ʃəl] unparteiisch;
~ity ['impɑ:ʃi'æliti] Unparteilichkeit f, Objektivität f.

impassable □ [im'pɑ:səbl] ungang-
bar, unpassierbar.
impassible □ [im'pæsibl] unempfindlich; gefühllos (to gegen).
impassioned [im'pæʃənd] leidenschaftlich.
impassive □ [im'pæsiv] unempfindlich; teilnahmslos; heiter.
impatien|ce [im'peiʃəns] Ungeduld
f; ~t □ [~nt] ungeduldig.
impeach [im'pi:tʃ] anklagen (of,
with gen.); anfechten, anzweifeln.
impeccable □ [im'pekəbl] sündlos;
makellos, einwandfrei.
impede [im'pi:d] (ver)hindern.
impediment [im'pedimənt] Hindernis n.
impel [im'pel] (an)treiben.
impend [im'pend] hängen, schweben; bevorstehen, drohen.
impenetrable □ [im'penitrəbl] un-
durchdringlich; fig. unergründlich;
fig. unzugänglich (to dat.).
impenitent □ [im'penitənt] un-
bußfertig, verstockt.
imperative □ [im'perətiv] 1. □ notwendig, dringend, unbedingt er-
forderlich; befehlend; gebieterisch;
gr. imperativisch; 2. Befehl m; a.
~ mood gr. Imperativ m, Befehls-
form f.   [unmerklich.)
imperceptible □ [impə'septəbl]]
imperfect □ [im'pə:fikt] 1. □ unvollkommen; unvollendet; 2. a. ~ tense
gr. Imperfekt n.
imperial □ [im'piəriəl] kaiserlich;
Reichs...; majestätisch; großartig;
~ism [~lizəm] Imperialismus m,
Weltmachtpolitik f.
imperil [im'peril] gefährden.
imperious □ [im'piəriəs] gebieterisch, anmaßend; dringend.
imperishable □ [im'periʃəbl] unvergänglich.
impermeable □ [im'pə:mjəbl] un-
durchdringlich, undurchlässig.
impersonal □ [im'pə:snl] unpersönlich.
impersonate [im'pə:səneit] verkörpern; thea. darstellen.
impertinen|ce [im'pə:tinəns] Un-
verschämtheit f; Nebensächlich-
keit f; ~t □ [~nt] unverschämt; ungehörig; nebensächlich.
imperturbable □ [impə(:)'tə:bəbl]
unerschütterlich.
impervious □ [im'pə:vjəs] unzugänglich (to für); undurchlässig.
impetu|ous □ [im'petjuəs] unge-
stüm, heftig; ~s ['impitəs] Antrieb
m.
impiety [im'paiəti] Gottlosigkeit f.
impinge [im'pindʒ] v/i. (ver)stoßen
(on, upon, against gegen).
impious □ ['impiəs] gottlos; pietät-
los; frevelhaft.
implacable □ [im'plækəbl] unversöhnlich, unerbittlich.
implant [im'plɑ:nt] einpflanzen.

implement 1. ['implimənt] Werkzeug *n*; Gerät *n*; **2.** [⌣iment] ausführen.

implicat|e ['implikeit] verwickeln; in sich schließen; ⌣ion [impli'keiʃən] Verwick(e)lung *f*; Folgerung *f*.

implicit ☐ [im'plisir] mit eingeschlossen; blind (*Glaube etc.*).

implore [im'plɔ:] (an-, er)flehen.

imply [im'plai] mit einbegreifen, enthalten; bedeuten; andeuten.

impolite ☐ [impə'lait] unhöflich.

impolitic ☐ [im'pɔlitik] unklug.

import 1. ['impɔ:t] Bedeutung *f*; Wichtigkeit *f*; Einfuhr *f*; ⌣s *pl*. Einfuhrwaren *f*/*pl*.; **2.** [im'pɔ:t] einführen; bedeuten; ⌣ance [⌣təns] Wichtigkeit *f*; ⌣ant ☐ [⌣ənt] wichtig; wichtigtuerisch; ⌣ation [impɔ:'teiʃən] Einfuhr(waren *f*/*pl*.) *f*.

importun|ate ☐ [im'pɔ:tjunit] lästig; zudringlich; ⌣e [im'pɔ:tju:n] dringend bitten; belästigen.

impos|e [im'pouz] *v*/*t*. auf(er)legen, aufbürden (*on, upon dat.*); *v*/*i*. ⌣ *upon j-m* imponieren; *j-n* täuschen; ⌣ition [impə'ziʃən] Auf(er)legung *f*; Steuer *f*; Strafarbeit *f*; Betrügerei *f*.

impossib|ility [impɔsə'biliti] Unmöglichkeit *f*; ⌣le ☐ [im'pɔsəbl] unmöglich.

impost|or [im'pɔstə] Betrüger *m*; ⌣ure [⌣tʃə] Betrug *m*.

impoten|ce ['impətəns] Unfähigkeit *f*; Machtlosigkeit *f*; ⌣t [⌣nt] unvermögend, machtlos, schwach.

impoverish [im'pɔvəriʃ] arm machen; *Boden* auslaugen.

impracticable ☐ [im'præktikəbl] undurchführbar; unwegsam.

impractical [im'præktikəl] unpraktisch; theoretisch; unnütz.

imprecate ['imprikeit] *Böses* herabwünschen (*upon auf acc.*).

impregn|able ☐ [im'pregnəbl] uneinnehmbar; unüberwindlich; ⌣ate ['impregneit] schwängern; ⚥ sättigen; ⊕ imprägnieren.

impress 1. ['impres] (Ab-, Ein-)Druck *m*; *fig.* Stempel *m*; **2.** [im'pres] eindrücken, prägen; *Kraft etc.* übertragen; *Gedanken etc.* einprägen (*on dat.*); *j-n* beeindrucken; *j-n* mit *et.* erfüllen; ⌣ion [⌣eʃən] Eindruck *m*; *typ.* Abdruck *m*; Abzug *m*; Auflage *f*; *be under the* ⌣ *that* den Eindruck haben, daß; ⌣ive [⌣esiv] eindrucksvoll.

imprint 1. ['imprint] aufdrücken, prägen; *fig.* einprägen (*on, in dat.*); **2.** ['imprint] Eindruck *m*; Stempel *m* (*a. fig.*); *typ.* Druckvermerk *m*.

imprison [im'prizn] inhaftieren; ⌣ment [⌣mənt] Haft *f*; Gefängnis (-strafe *f*) *n*.

improbable ☐ [im'prɔbəbl] unwahrscheinlich.

improper ☐ [im'prɔpə] ungeeignet, unpassend; falsch; unanständig.

impropriety [imprə'praiəti] Ungehörigkeit *f*; Unanständigkeit *f*.

improve [im'pru:v] *v*/*t*. verbessern; veredeln; aus-, benutzen; *v*/*i*. sich (ver)bessern; ⌣ *upon* vervollkommnen; ⌣ment [⌣vmənt] Verbesserung *f*, Vervollkommnung *f*; Fortschritt *m* (*on, upon gegenüber dat.*).

improvise ['imprəvaiz] improvisieren.

imprudent ☐ [im'pru:dənt] unklug.

impuden|ce ['impjudəns] Unverschämtheit *f*, Frechheit *f*; ⌣t ☐ [⌣nt] unverschämt, frech.

impuls|e ['impʌls], ⌣ion [im'pʌlʃən] Impuls *m*, (An)Stoß *m*; *fig.* (An)Trieb *m*; ⌣ive ☐ [⌣lsiv] (an-)treibend; *fig.* impulsiv; rasch (handelnd).

impunity [im'pju:niti] Straflosigkeit *f*; *with* ⌣ ungestraft.

impure ☐ [im'pjuə] unrein (*a. fig.*); unkeusch.

imput|ation [impju(:)'teiʃən] Beschuldigung *f*; ⌣e [im'pju:t] zurechnen, beimessen; zur Last legen.

in [in] **1.** *prp.* *allg.* in (*dat.*); *engS.*: (⌣ *the morning,* ⌣ *number,* ⌣ *itself, professor* ⌣ *the university*) an (*dat.*); (⌣ *the street,* ⌣ *English*) auf (*dat.*); (⌣ *this manner*) auf (*acc.*); (*coat* ⌣ *velvet*) aus; (⌣ *Shakespeare,* ⌣ *the daytime,* ⌣ *crossing the road*) bei; (*engaged* ⌣ *reading,* ⌣ *a word*) mit; (⌣ *my opinion*) nach; (*rejoice* ⌣ *s.th.*) über (*acc.*); (⌣ *the circumstances,* ⌣ *the reign of, one* ⌣ *ten*) unter (*dat.*); (*cry out* ⌣ *alarm*) vor (*dat.*); (*grouped* ⌣ *tens, speak* ⌣ *reply,* ⌣ *excuse,* ⌣ *honour of*) zu; ⌣ *1949 im Jahre 1949;* ⌣ *that ... insofern als, weil;* **2.** *adv.* drin(nen); herein; hinein; *be* ⌣ *for et.* zu erwarten haben; *e-e Prüfung etc.* vor sich haben; F *be well* ⌣ *with sich gut mit j-m* stehen; **3.** *adj.* hereinkommend; Innen...

inability [inə'biliti] Unfähigkeit *f*.

inaccessible ☐ [inæk'sesəbl] unzugänglich. [unrichtig.]

inaccurate ☐ [in'ækjurit] ungenau;

inactiv|e ☐ [in'æktiv] untätig, ⚥ lustlos; ⚥ unwirksam; ⌣ity [inæk-'tiviti] Untätig-, Lustlosigkeit *f*.

inadequate ☐ [in'ædikwit] unangemessen; unzulänglich.

inadmissible ☐ [inəd'misəbl] unzulässig.

inadvertent ☐ [inəd'və:tənt] unachtsam; unbeabsichtigt, versehentlich.

inalienable ☐ [in'eiljənəbl] unveräußerlich.

inane ☐ [i'nein] *fig.* leer; albern.

inanimate ☐ [in'ænimit] leblos; *fig.* unbelebt; geistlos, langweilig.

inapproachable [inə'proutʃəbl] unnahbar, unzugänglich.

inappropriate ☐ [inə'proupriit] unangebracht, unpassend.

inapt ☐ [in'æpt] ungeeignet, untauglich; ungeschickt; unpassend.

inarticulate ☐ [ina:'tikjulit] undeutlich; schwer zu verstehen(d); undeutlich sprechend.

inasmuch [inəz'mʌtʃ]: ~ *as* insofern als.   [merksam.]

inattentive ☐ [inə'tentiv] unauf-]

inaudible ☐ [in'ɔ:dəbl] unhörbar.

inaugura|l [i'nɔ:gjurəl] Antrittsrede *f; attr.* Antritts...; ~**te** [~reit] (feierlich) einführen, einweihen; beginnen; ~**tion** [inɔ:gju reiʃən] Einführung *f,* Einweihung *f;* ~ *Day Am.* Amtseinführung *f* des neugewählten Präsidenten der USA.

inborn ['in'bɔ:n] angeboren.

incalculable ☐ [in'kælkjuləbl] unberechenbar; unzählig.

incandescent [inkæn'desnt] weiß glühend; Glüh...

incapa|ble ☐ [in'keipəbl] unfähig, ungeeignet (*of* zu); ~**citate** [inkə-'pæsiteit] unfähig machen; ~**city** [~ti] Unfähigkeit *f.*

incarnate [in'ka:nit] Fleisch geworden; *fig.* verkörpert.

incautious ☐ [in'kɔ:ʃəs] unvorsichtig.

incendiary [in'sendjəri] **1.** brandstifterisch; *fig.* aufwieglerisch; **2.** Brandstifter *m;* Aufwiegler *m.*

incense[1] ['insens] Weihrauch *m.*

incense[2] [in'sens] in Wut bringen.

incentive [in'sentiv] Antrieb *m.*

incessant ☐ [in'sesnt] unaufhörlich.

incest ['insest] Blutschande *f.*

inch [intʃ] Zoll *m (2,54 cm); fig.* ein bißchen; *by* ~*es* allmählich; *every* ~ ganz (*u.* gar).

inciden|ce ['insidəns] Vorkommen *n;* Wirkung *f;* ~**t** [~nt] **1.** (to) vorkommend (bei), eigen (*dat.*); **2.** Zu-, Vor-, Zwischenfall *m;* Nebenumstand *m;* ~**tal** ☐ [insi'dentl] zufällig, gelegentlich; Neben...; *be* ~ *to* gehören zu; ~*ly* nebenbei.

incinerate [in'sinəreit] einäschern; Müll verbrennen.

incis|e [in'saiz] einschneiden; ~**ion** [in'siʒən] Einschnitt *m;* ~**ive** ☐ [in'saisiv] (ein)schneidend, scharf; ~**or** [~aizə] Schneidezahn *m.*

incite [in'sait] anspornen, anregen; anstiften; ~**ment** [~tmənt] Anregung *f;* Ansporn *m;* Anstiftung *f.*

inclement [in'klemənt] rauh.

inclin|ation [inkli'neiʃən] Neigung *f (a. fig.);* ~**e** [in'klain] **1.** *v/i.* sich neigen (*a. fig.*); ~ *to fig.* zu *et.* neigen; *v/t.* neigen; geneigt machen; **2.** Neigung *f,* Abhang *m.*

inclos|e [in'klouz], ~**ure** [~ouʒə] *s.* enclose, enclosure.

inclu|de [in'klu:d] einschließen; enthalten; ~**sive** ☐ [~u:siv] einschließlich; alles einbegriffen; *be* ~ *of* einschließen; ~ *terms pl.* Pauschalpreis *m.*

incoheren|ce, ~**cy** [inkou'hiərəns, ~si] Zs.-hangslosigkeit *f;* Inkonsequenz *f;* ~**t** ☐ [~nt] unzs.-hängend; inkonsequent.

income ['inkəm] Einkommen *n;* ~**-tax** Einkommensteuer *f.*

incommode [inkə'moud] belästigen.

incommunica|do *bsd. Am.* [inkəmju:ni'ka:dou] ohne Verbindung mit der Außenwelt; ~**tive** ☐ [inkə'mju:nikətiv] nicht mitteilsam, verschlossen.

incomparable ☐ [in'kɔmpərəbl] unvergleichlich.

incompatible ☐ [inkəm'pætəbl] unvereinbar; unverträglich.

incompetent [in'kɔmpitənt] unfähig; unzuständig, unbefugt.

incomplete ☐ [inkəm'pli:t] unvollständig; unvollkommen.

incomprehensible ☐ [inkɔmpri-'hensəbl] unbegreiflich.

inconceivable ☐ [inkən'si:vəbl] unbegreiflich, unfaßbar.

incongruous ☐ [in'kɔŋgruəs] nicht übereinstimmend; unpassend.

inconsequent ☐ [in'kɔnsikwənt] inkonsequent, folgewidrig; ~**ial** [inkɔnsi'kwenʃəl] unbedeutend; = inconsequent.

inconsidera|ble ☐ [inkən'sidərəbl] unbedeutend; ~**te** ☐ [~rit] unüberlegt; rücksichtslos.

inconsisten|cy [inkən'sistənsi] Unvereinbarkeit *f;* Inkonsequenz *f;* ~**t** ☐ [~nt] unvereinbar; widerspruchsvoll; inkonsequent.

inconsolable ☐ [inkən'souləbl] untröstlich.

inconstant ☐ [in'kɔnstənt] unbeständig; veränderlich.

incontinent ☐ [in'kɔntinənt] unmäßig; ausschweifend.

inconvenien|ce [inkən'vi:njəns] **1.** Unbequemlichkeit *f;* Unannehmlichkeit *f;* **2.** belästigen; ~**t** ☐ [~nt] unbequem; ungelegen; lästig.

incorporat|e **1.** [in'kɔ:pəreit] einverleiben (*into dat.*); (sich) vereinigen; *als Mitglied* aufnehmen; *als Körperschaft* eintragen; **2.** [~rit] einverleibt; vereinigt; ~**ed** (amtlich) eingetragen; ~**ion** [inkɔ:-pə'reiʃən] Einverleibung *f;* Verbindung *f.*   [fehlerhaft; ungehörig.]

incorrect ☐ [inkə'rekt] unrichtig;]

incorrigible ☐ [in'kɔridʒəbl] unverbesserlich.

increas|e **1.** [in'kri:s] *v/i.* zunehmen; sich vergrößern *od.* vermehren; *v/t.* vermehren, vergrößern; erhöhen; **2.** ['inkri:s] Zunahme *f;* Vergrößerung *f;* Zuwachs *m;* ~**ingly** [in'kri:siŋli] zunehmend, immer (*mit folgendem comp.*); ~ *difficult* immer schwieriger.

incredible ☐ [in'kredəbl] unglaublich.

incredul|ity [inkri'dju:liti] Unglaube *m*; **~ous** □ [in'kredjuləs] ungläubig, skeptisch.

incriminate [in'krimineit] beschuldigen; belasten.

incrustation [inkrʌs'teiʃən] Verkrustung *f*; Kruste *f*; ⊕ Belag *m*.

incub|ate ['inkjubeit] (aus)brüten; **~ator** [~tə] Brutapparat *m*.

inculcate ['inkʌlkeit] einschärfen (*upon dat.*).

incumbent [in'kʌmbənt] obliegend; *be ~ on s.o.* j-m obliegen.

incur [in'kə:] sich *et.* zuziehen; geraten in (*acc.*); *Verpflichtung* eingehen; *Verlust* erleiden.

incurable [in'kjuərəbl] **1.** □ unheilbar; **2.** Unheilbare(r *m f*) *f*.

incurious □ [in'kjuəriəs] gleichgültig, uninteressiert.

incursion [in'kə:ʃən] *feindlicher* Einfall.

indebted [in'detid] verschuldet; *fig.* (zu Dank) verpflichtet.

indecen|cy [in'di:snsi] Unanständigkeit *f*; **~t** □ [~t] unanständig.

indecisi|on [indi'siʒən] Unentschlossenheit *f*; **~ve** □ [~'saisiv] nicht entscheidend; unbestimmt.

indecorous □ [in'dekərəs] unpassend; ungehörig.

indeed [in'di:d] **1.** *adv.* in der Tat, tatsächlich; wirklich; allerdings; **2.** *int.* so?; nicht möglich!

indefatigable □ [indi'fætigəbl] unermüdlich.

indefensible □ [indi'fensəbl] unhaltbar.

indefinite □ [in'definit] unbestimmt; unbeschränkt; ungenau.

indelible □ [in'delibl] untilgbar.

indelicate [in'delikit] unfein; taktlos.

indemni|fy [in'demnifai] sicherstellen; j-m Straflosigkeit zusichern; entschädigen; **~ty** [~iti] Sicherstellung *f*; Straflosigkeit *f*; Entschädigung *f*.

indent 1. [in'dent] einkerben, auszacken; eindrücken; ⅜ *Vertrag* mit Doppel ausfertigen; *~ upon s.o. for s.th.* ✝ *et.* bei j-m bestellen; **2.** [']indent] Kerbe *f*; Vertiefung *f*; ✝ Auslandsauftrag *m*; = *indenture*; **~ation** [inden'teiʃən] Einkerbung *f*; Einschnitt *m*; **~ure** [in'dentʃə] **1.** Vertrag *m*; Lehrbrief *m*; **2.** vertraglich verpflichten.

independen|ce [indi'pendəns] Unabhängigkeit *f*; Selbständigkeit *f*; Auskommen *n*; ♀ *Day Am.* Unabhängigkeitstag *m* (*4. Juli*); **~t** □ [~nt] unabhängig; selbständig.

indescribable □ [indis'kraibəbl] unbeschreiblich.

indestructible □ [indis'trʌktəbl] unzerstörbar.

indeterminate □ [indi'tə:minit] unbestimmt.

index ['indeks] **1.** (An)Zeiger *m*; Anzeichen *n*; Zeigefinger *m*; Index *m*; (Inhalts-, Namen-, Sach)Verzeichnis *n*; **2.** *Buch* mit e-m Index versehen.

Indian ['indjən] **1.** indisch; indianisch; **2.** Inder(in); *a. Red ~* Indianer(in); **~ corn** Mais *m*; **~ file:** *in ~* im Gänsemarsch; **~ pudding** *Am.* Maismehlpudding *m*; **~ summer** Altweiber-, Nachsommer *m*.

Indiarubber ['indjə'rʌbə] Radiergummi *m*.

indicat|e ['indikeit] (an)zeigen; hinweisen auf (*acc.*); andeuten; **~ion** [indi'keiʃən] Anzeige *f*; Anzeichen *n*; Andeutung *f*; **~ive** [in'dikətiv] *a. ~ mood gr.* Indikativ *m*; **~or** ['indikeitə] Anzeiger *m* (*a.* ⊕); *mot.* Blinker *m*.

indict [in'dait] anklagen (*for wegen*); **~ment** [~tmənt] Anklage *f*.

indifferen|ce [in'difrəns] Gleichgültigkeit *f*; **~t** □ [~nt] gleichgültig (*to gegen*); unparteiisch; (nur) mäßig; unwesentlich; unbedeutend.

indigenous [in'didʒinəs] eingeboren, einheimisch.

indigent □ ['indidʒənt] arm.

indigest|ible □ [indi'dʒestəbl] unverdaulich; **~ion** [~tʃən] Verdauungsstörung *f*, Magenverstimmung *f*.

indign|ant □ [in'dignənt] entrüstet, empört, ungehalten; **~ation** [indig'neiʃən] Entrüstung *f*; **~ity** [in'digniti] Beleidigung *f*.

indirect □ [indi'rekt] indirekt; nicht direkt; *gr. a.* abhängig.

indiscre|et □ [indis'kri:t] unbesonnen; unachtsam; indiskret; **~tion** [~reʃən] Unachtsamkeit *f*; Unbesonnenheit *f*; Indiskretion *f*.

indiscriminate □ [indis'kriminit] unterschieds-, wahllos.

indispensable □ [indis'pensəbl] unentbehrlich, unerläßlich.

indispos|ed [indis'pouzd] unpäßlich; abgeneigt; **~ition** [indispo-'ziʃən] Abneigung *f* (*to gegen*); Unpäßlichkeit *f*.

indisputable □ [indis'pju:təbl] unbestreitbar, unstreitig.

indistinct □ [indis'tiŋkt] undeutlich; unklar.

indistinguishable □ [indis'tiŋgwiʃəbl] nicht zu unterscheiden(d).

indite [in'dait] ab-, verfassen.

individual [indi'vidjuəl] **1.** □ persönlich, individuell; besondere(r, -s); einzeln; Einzel...; **2.** Individuum *n*; **~ism** [~lizəm] Individualismus *m*; **~ist** [~list] Individualist *m*; **~ity** [individju'æliti] Individualität *f*.

indivisible □ [indi'vizəbl] unteilbar.

indolen|ce ['indələns] Trägheit *f*;

~t □ [~nt] indolent, träge, lässig; *ℱ* schmerzlos.

indomitable □ [in'dɔmitəbl] unbezähmbar.

indoor ['indɔ:] im Hause (befindlich); Haus..., Zimmer..., *Sport*: Hallen...; ~s ['in'dɔ:z] zu Hause; im *od.* ins Haus.

indorse [in'dɔ:s] = *endorse etc.*

induce [in'dju:s] veranlassen; ~ment [~smənt] Anlaß *m*, Antrieb *m*.

induct [in'dʌkt] einführen; ~ion [~kʃən] Einführung *f*, Einsetzung *f in Amt, Pfründe*; *ℰ* Induktion *f*.

indulge [in'dʌldʒ] nachsichtig sein gegen *j-n*; *j-m* nachgeben; ~ *with j-n* erfreuen mit; ~ (*o.s.*) *in s.th.* sich et. gönnen; sich *e-r* S. hin- *od.* ergeben; ~nce [~dʒəns] Nachsicht *f*; Nachgiebigkeit *f*; Sichgehenlassen *n*; Vergünstigung *f*; ~nt □ [~nt] nachsichtig.

industri|al □ [in'dʌstriəl] gewerbetreibend, gewerblich; industriell; Gewerbe...; Industrie...; ~ *area* Industriebezirk *m*; ~ *estate* Industriegebiet *n e-r Stadt*; ~ *school* Gewerbeschule *f*; ~alist [~list] Industrielle(r) *m*; ~alize [~laiz] industrialisieren; ~ous □ [~əs] fleißig.

industry ['indəstri] Fleiß *m*; Gewerbe *n*; Industrie *f*.

inebriate 1. [i'ni:brieit] betrunken machen; **2.** [~iit] Trunkenbold *m*.

ineffable □ [in'efəbl] unaussprechlich.

ineffect|ive [ini'fektiv], ~ual □ [~tjuəl] unwirksam, fruchtlos.

inefficient □ [ini'fiʃənt] wirkungslos; (leistungs)unfähig.

inelegant □ [in'eligənt] unelegant, geschmacklos.

ineligible □ [in'elidʒəbl] nicht wählbar; ungeeignet; *bsd.* ✕ untauglich.

inept □ [i'nept] unpassend; albern.

inequality [ini(:)'kwɔliti] Ungleichheit *f*; Ungleichmäßigkeit *f*; Unebenheit *f*.

inequitable □ [in'ekwitəbl] unbillig.

inert □ [i'nə:t] träge; ~ia [i'nə:ʃjə], ~ness [i'nə:tnis] Trägheit *f*.

inescapable [inis'keipəbl] unentrinnbar.

inessential ['ini'senʃəl] unwesentlich (*to* für).

inestimable □ [in'estiməbl] unschätzbar.

inevitab|le □ [in'evitəbl] unvermeidlich; ~ly [~li] unweigerlich.

inexact □ [inig'zækt] ungenau.

inexcusable □ [iniks'kju:zəbl] unentschuldbar.

inexhaustible □ [inig'zɔ:stəbl] unerschöpflich; unermüdlich.

inexorable □ [in'eksərəbl] unerbittlich.

inexpedient □ [iniks'pi:djənt] unzweckmäßig, unpassend.

inexpensive □ [iniks'pensiv] nicht teuer, billig, preiswert.

inexperience [iniks'piəriəns] Unerfahrenheit *f*; ~d [~st] unerfahren.

inexpert □ [ineks'pə:t] unerfahren.

inexplicable □ [in'eksplikəbl] unerklärlich.

inexpressi|ble □ [iniks'presəbl] unaussprechlich; ~ve [~siv] ausdruckslos.

inextinguishable □ [iniks'tiŋgwiʃəbl] unauslöschlich.

inextricable □ [in'ekstrikəbl] unentwirrbar.

infallible □ [in'fæləbl] unfehlbar.

infam|ous □ ['infəməs] ehrlos; schändlich; verrufen; ~y [~mi] Ehrlosigkeit *f*; Schande *f*; Niedertracht *f*.

infan|cy ['infənsi] Kindheit *f*; *ℱℱ* Minderjährigkeit *f*; ~t [~nt] Säugling *m*; (kleines) Kind; Minderjährige(r *m*) *f*.

infanti|le ['infəntail], ~ne [~ain] kindlich; Kindes..., Kinder...; kindisch.

infantry ✕ ['infəntri] Infanterie *f*.

infatuate [in'fætjueit] betören; ~d vernarrt (*with in acc.*).

infect [in'fekt] anstecken (*a. fig.*); infizieren, verseuchen, verpesten; ~ion [~kʃən] Ansteckung *f*; ~ious □ [~əs], ~ive [~ktiv] ansteckend; Ansteckungs...

infer [in'fə:] folgern, schließen; ~ence ['infərəns] Folgerung *f*.

inferior [in'fiəriə] **1.** untere(r, -s); minderwertig; ~ *to* niedriger *od.* geringer als; untergeordnet (*dat.*); unterlegen (*dat.*); **2.** Geringere(r *m*) *f*; Untergebene(r *m*) *f*; ~ity [infiəri'ɔriti] geringerer Wert *od.* Stand; Unterlegenheit *f*; Minderwertigkeit *f*.

infern|al □ [in'fə:nl] höllisch; ~o [~nou] Inferno *n*, Hölle *f*.

infertile [in'fə:tail] unfruchtbar.

infest [in'fest] heimsuchen; verseuchen; *fig.* überschwemmen.

infidelity [infi'deliti] Unglaube *m*; Untreue *f* (*to* gegen).

infiltrate ['infiltreit] *v/t.* durchdringen; *v/i.* durchsickern, eindringen.

infinite □ ['infinit] unendlich.

infinitive [in'finitiv] *a.* ~ *mood gr.* Infinitiv *m*, Nennform *f*.

infinity [in'finiti] Unendlichkeit *f*.

infirm □ [in'fə:m] kraftlos, schwach; ~ary [~məri] Krankenhaus *n*; ~ity [~miti] Schwäche *f* (*a. fig.*); Gebrechen *n*.

inflame [in'fleim] entflammen (*mst fig.*); (sich) entzünden (*a. fig. u. ℱ*).

inflamma|ble □ [in'flæməbl] entzündlich; feuergefährlich; ~tion [inflə'meiʃən] Entzündung *f*; ~tory [in'flæmətəri] entzündlich; *fig.* aufrührerisch; hetzerisch; Hetz...

inflat|e [in'fleit] aufblasen, aufblähen (*a. fig.*); **~ion** [~eifən] Aufblähung *f*; **✝** Inflation *f*; *fig.* Aufgeblasenheit *f*.

inflect [in'flekt] biegen; *gr.* flektieren, beugen.

inflexi|ble] [in'fleksəbl] unbiegsam; *fig.* unbeugsam; **~on** [~kʃən] Biegung *f*; *gr.* Flexion *f*, Beugung *f*; Modulation *f*.

inflict [in'flikt] auferlegen; zufügen; *Hieb* versetzen; *Strafe* verhängen; **~ion** [~kʃən] Auferlegung *f*; Zufügung *f*; Plage *f*.

influen|ce ['influəns] 1. Einfluß *m*; 2. beeinflussen; **~tial** □ [influ-'enʃəl] einflußreich.

influenza ✿ [influ'enzə] Grippe *f*.

influx ['inflʌks] Einströmen *n*; *fig.* Zufluß *m*, (Zu)Strom *m*.

inform [in'fɔ:m] *v/t.* benachrichtigen, unterrichten (*of* von); *v/i.* anzeigen (*against* s.o. j.); **~al**] [~ml] formlos, zwanglos; **~ality** [~'mæliti] Formlosigkeit *f*; Formfehler *m*; **~ation** [infə'meiʃən] Auskunft *f*; Nachricht *f*, Information *f*; **~ative** [in'fɔ:mətiv] informatorisch; lehrreich; mitteilsam; **~er** [in'fɔ:mə] Denunziant *m*; Spitzel *m*.

infrequent [in'fri:kwənt] selten.

infringe [in'frindʒ] *a.* **~ upon** *Vertrag etc.* verletzen; übertreten.

infuriate [in'fjuərieit] wütend machen.

infuse [in'fju:z] einflößen; aufgießen.

ingen|ious □ [in'dʒi:njəs] geist-, sinnreich; erfinderisch; raffiniert; genial; **~uity** [indʒi'nju(:)iti] Genialität *f*; **~uous**] [in'dʒenjuəs] freimütig; unbefangen, naiv.

ingot ['iŋgət] *Gold- etc.* Barren *m*.

ingrati|ate [in'greiʃieit]: **~ o.s.** sich beliebt machen (*with* bei); **~tude** [~rætitju:d] Undankbarkeit *f*.

ingredient [in'gri:djənt] Bestandteil *m*.

ingrowing ['ingrouiŋ] nach innen wachsend; eingewachsen.

inhabit [in'hæbit] bewohnen; **~able** [~təbl] bewohnbar; **~ant** [~ənt] Bewohner(in), Einwohner(in).

inhal|ation [inhə'leiʃən] Einatmung *f*; **~e** [in'heil] einatmen.

inherent] [in'hiərənt] anhaftend; innewohnend, angeboren (*in dat.*).

inherit [in'herit] (er)erben; **~ance** [~təns] Erbteil *n*, Erbe *n*; Erbschaft *f*; *biol.* Vererbung *f*.

inhibit [in'hibit] (ver)hindern; verbieten; zurückhalten; **~ion** [inhi'biʃən] Hemmung *f*; Verbot *n*.

inhospitable □ [in'hɔspitəbl] ungastlich, unwirtlich.

inhuman □ [in'hju:mən] unmenschlich.

inimical □ [i'nimikəl] feindlich; schädlich.

inimitable □ [i'nimitəbl] unnachahmlich.

iniquity [i'nikwiti] Ungerechtigkeit *f*; Schlechtigkeit *f*.

initia|l [i'niʃəl] 1. □ Anfangs...; anfänglich; 2. Anfangsbuchstabe *m*; **~te** 1. [~ʃiit] Eingeweihte(r *m*) *f*; 2. [~ʃieit] beginnen; anbahnen; einführen, einweihen; **~tion** [iniʃi-'eiʃən] Einleitung *f*; Einführung *f*, Einweihung *f*; **~ fee** *bsd. Am.* Aufnahmegebühr *f* (*Vereinigung*); **~tive** [i'niʃiətiv] Initiative *f*; einleitender Schritt; Entschlußkraft *f*; Unternehmungsgeist *m*; Volksbegehren *n*; **~tor** [~ieitə] Initiator *m*, Urheber *m*.

inject [in'dʒekt] einspritzen; **~ion** [~kʃən] Injektion *f*, Spritze *f*.

injudicious □ [indʒu(:)'diʃəs] unverständig, unklug, unüberlegt.

injunction [in'dʒʌŋkʃən] gerichtliche Verfügung; ausdrücklicher Befehl.

injur|e [in'dʒə] (be)schädigen; schaden (*dat.*); verletzen; beleidigen; **~ious** [in'dʒuəriəs] schädlich; ungerecht; beleidigend; **~y** ['indʒəri] Unrecht *n*; Schaden *m*; Verletzung *f*; Beleidigung *f*.

injustice [in'dʒʌstis] Ungerechtigkeit *f*; Unrecht *n*.

ink [iŋk] 1. Tinte *f*; *mst printer's* **~** Druckerschwärze *f*; *attr.* Tinten...; 2. (mit Tinte) schwärzen; beklecksen.

inkling ['iŋkliŋ] Andeutung *f*; dunkle *od.* leise Ahnung.

ink|pot ['iŋkpɔt] Tintenfaß *n*; **~stand** Schreibzeug *n*; **~y** ['iŋki] tintig; Tinten...; tintenschwarz.

inland 1. ['inlənd] inländisch; Binnen...; 2. [~] Landesinnere(s) *n*, Binnenland *n*; 3. [in'lænd] landeinwärts.

inlay 1. [in'lei] (*irr.* (*lay*)) einlegen; 2. ['inlei] Einlage *f*; Einlegearbeit *f*.

inlet ['inlet] Bucht *f*; Einlaß *m*.

inmate [in'meit] Insass|e *m*, -in *f*; Hausgenoss|e *m*, -in *f*.

inmost ['inmoust] innerst.

inn [in] Gasthof *m*, Wirtshaus *n*.

innate] [i'neit] angeboren.

inner [in'ə] inner, inwendig; geheim; **~most** innerst; geheimst.

innervate ['inə:veit] Nervenkraft geben (*dat.*); kräftigen.

innings ['ininz] *Sport:* Dransein *n*.

innkeeper ['inki:pə] Gastwirt(in).

innocen|ce ['inəsns] Unschuld *f*; Harmlosigkeit *f*; Einfalt *f*; **~t** [~nt] 1. □ unschuldig; harmlos; 2. Unschuldige(r *m*) *f*; Einfältige(r *m*) *f*.

innocuous □ [i'nɔkjuəs] harmlos.

innovation [inou'veiʃən] Neuerung *f*.

innoxious □ [i'nɔkʃəs] unschädlich.

innuendo [inju(:)'endou] Andeutung *f*.

innumerable ☐ [i'nju:mərəbl] unzählbar, unzählig.

inoccupation ['inɔkju'peiʃən] Beschäftigungslosigkeit *f*.

inoculate [i'nɔkjuleit] (ein)impfen.

inoffensive [inə'fensiv] harmlos.

inofficial [inə'fiʃəl] inoffiziell.

inoperative [in'ɔpərətiv] unwirksam.

inopportune [in'ɔpətju:n] unangebracht, zur Unzeit.

inordinate [in'ɔ:dinit] unmäßig.

in-patient ['inpeiʃənt] Krankenhauspatient *m*, stationärer Patient.

inquest *&* [inkwest] Untersuchung *f*; *coroner's* ~ Leichenschau *f*.

inquir|e [in'kwaiə] fragen, sich erkundigen (*of* bei *j-m*); ~ *into* untersuchen; ~**ing** [~əriŋ] forschend; ~**y** [~ri] Erkundigung *f*, Nachfrage *f*; Untersuchung *f*; Ermittlung *f*.

inquisit|ion [inkwi'ziʃən] Untersuchung *f*; ~**ive** [in'kwizitiv] neugierig, wißbegierig.

inroad ['inroud] *feindlicher* Einfall; Ein-, Übergriff *m*.

insan|e ☐ [in'sein] wahnsinnig; ~**ity** [in'sæniti] Wahnsinn *m*.

insatia|ble ☐ [in'seiʃəbl], ~**te** [~ʃiit] unersättlich (*of* nach).

inscribe [in'skraib] ein-, auf-, beschreiben; beschriften; *fig.* einprägen (*in, on dat.*); *Buch* widmen.

inscription [in'skripʃən] In-, Aufschrift *f*; ✦ Eintragung *f*.

inscrutable ☐ [in'skru:təbl] unerforschlich, unergründlich

insect ['insekt] Insekt *n*; ~**icide** [in'sektisaid] Insektengift *n*.

insecure [insi'kjuə] unsicher.

insens|ate [in'senseit] gefühllos; unvernünftig; ~**ible** [~səbl] unempfindlich; bewußtlos; unmerklich; gleichgültig; ~**itive** [~sitiv] unempfindlich.

inseparable ☐ [in'separəbl] untrennbar; unzertrennlich.

insert 1. [in'sə:t] einsetzen, einschalten, einfügen; (hinein)stecken; *Münze* einwerfen; inserieren; 2. ['insə:t] Bei-, Einlage *f*; ~**ion** [in'sə:ʃən] Einsetzung *f*, Einfügung *f*, Eintragung *f*; Einwurf *m* *e-r Münze*; Anzeige *f*, Inserat *n*.

inshore ⚓ ['in'ʃɔ:] an *od.* nahe der Küste (befindlich); Küsten...

inside [in'said] 1. Innenseite *f*; Innere(s) *n*; *turn* ~ *out* umkrempeln; auf den Kopf stellen; 2. *adj.* inner, inwendig; Innen...; 3. *adv.* im Innern; 4. *prp.* innerhalb.

insidious ☐ [in'sidiəs] heimtückisch.

insight ['insait] Einsicht *f*, Einblick *m*.

insignia [in'signiə] *pl.* Abzeichen *n/pl.*, Insignien *pl.*

insignificant [insig'nifikənt] bedeutungslos; unbedeutend.

insincere [insin'siə] unaufrichtig.

insinuat|e [in'sinjueit] unbemerkt hineinbringen; zu verstehen geben; andeuten; ~**ion** [insinju'eiʃən] Einschmeichelung *f*; Anspielung *f*, Andeutung *f*; Wink *m*.

insipid [in'sipid] geschmacklos, fad.

insist [in'sist] ~ (*up*)*on* bestehen auf (*dat.*); dringen auf (*acc.*); ~**ence** [~təns] Bestehen *n*; Beharrlichkeit *f*; Drängen *n*; ~**ent** ☐ [~nt] beharrlich; eindringlich.

insolent ['insələnt] unverschämt.

insoluble ☐ [in'sɔljubl] unlöslich.

insolvent [in'sɔlvənt] zahlungsunfähig [keit *f*.]

insomnia [in'sɔmniə] Schlaflosig-)

insomuch [insou'mʌtʃ]: ~ *that* dermaßen *od* so sehr, daß.

inspect [in'spekt] untersuchen, prüfen, nachsehen; ~**ion** [~kʃən] Prüfung *f*, Untersuchung *f*; Inspektion *f*; ~**or** [~ktə] Aufsichtsbeamte(r) *m*.

inspir|ation [inspə'reiʃən] Einatmung *f*; Eingebung *f*; Begeisterung *f*; ~**e** [in'spaiə] einatmen; *fig.* eingeben, erfüllen; *j-n* begeistern.

install [in'stɔ:l] einsetzen, (sich) niederlassen; ⊕ installieren; ~**ation** [instə'leiʃən] Einsetzung *f*; ⊕ Installation *f*, Einrichtung *f*; ⊄ *etc.* Anlage *f*.

instal(l)ment [in'stɔ:lmənt] Rate *f*; Teil-, Ratenzahlung *f*; (Teil)Lieferung *f*; Fortsetzung *f*.

instance ['instəns] Ersuchen *n*; Beispiel *n*; (besonderer) Fall; *&* Instanz *f*; *for* ~ zum Beispiel.

instant ['instənt] 1. dringend; sofortig; *on the 10th* ~ am 10. dieses Monats; 2. Augenblick *m*; ~**aneous** ☐ [instən'teinjəs] augenblicklich; Moment...; ~**ly** ['instəntli] sogleich.

instead [in'sted] dafür; ~ *of* anstatt.

instep ['instep] Spann *m*.

instigat|e [in'stigeit] anstiften; aufhetzen; ~**or** [~tə] Anstifter *m*, Hetzer *m*.

instil(l) [in'stil] einträufeln; *fig.* einflößen (*into dat.*).

instinct ['instiŋkt] Instinkt *m*; ~**ive** ☐ [in'stiŋktiv] instinktiv.

institut|e [in'stitjut] 1. Institut *n*; 2. einsetzen, stiften, einrichten; an-, verordnen; ~**ion** [insti'tju:ʃən] Einsetzung *f*; Satzung *f*; Einrichtung *f*; An-, Verordnung *f*; Institut(ion *f*) *n*; Gesellschaft *f*; Anstalt *f*; ~**ional** [~nl] Instituts..., Anstalts...

instruct [in'strʌkt] unterrichten; belehren; *j-n* anweisen; ~**ion** [~kʃən] Vorschrift *f*; Unterweisung *f*; Anweisung *f*; ~**ive** ☐ [~ktiv] lehrreich; ~**or** [~tə] Lehrer *m*; Ausbilder *m*; *Am. univ.* Dozent *m*.

instrument ['instrumənt] Instru-

ment *n*, Werkzeug *n* (*a. fig.*); ɪ̵ɪ̵
Urkunde *f*; **~al** ☐ [instru'mentl]
als Werkzeug dienend; dienlich; *♪*
Instrumental...; **~ality** [instrumen-
'tæliti] Mitwirkung *f*, Mittel *n*.
insubordinat|e [insə'bɔ:dnit] auf-
sässig; **~ion** ['insəbɔ:di'neiʃən] Auf-
lehnung *f*.
insubstantial [insəb'stænʃəl] unwirklich; gebrechlich.
insufferable ☐ [in'sAfərəbl] unerträglich, unausstehlich.
insufficient ☐ [insə'fiʃənt] unzulänglich, ungenügend.
insula|r ☐ ['insjulə] Insel...; *fig.*
engstirnig; **~te** [~leit] isolieren;
~tion [insju'leiʃən] Isolierung *f*.
insult 1. ['insAlt] Beleidigung *f*;
2. [in'sAlt] beleidigen.
insupportable ☐ [insə'pɔ:təbl] unerträglich, unausstehlich.
insur|ance [in'ʃuərəns] Versiche-
rung *f*; *attr.* Versicherungs...;
~ance policy Versicherungspolice
f, -schein *m*; **~e** [in'ʃuə] versichern.
insurgent [in'sə:dʒənt] 1. aufrührerisch; 2. Aufrührer *m*.
insurmountable ☐ [insə(:)'maun-
təbl] unübersteigbar, *fig.* unüberwindlich.
insurrection [insə'rekʃən] Aufstand
m, Empörung *f*.
intact [in'tækt] unberührt; unversehrt.
intangible ☐ [in'tændʒəbl] unfühl-
bar; unfaßbar; unantastbar.
integ|ral ☐ ['intigrəl] ganz, voll-
ständig; wesentlich; **~rate** [~reit]
ergänzen; zs.-tun; einfügen; **~rity**
[in'tegriti] Vollständigkeit *f*; Redlichkeit *f*, Integrität *f*.
intellect ['intilekt] Verstand *m*;
konkr. die Intelligenz; **~ual** [inti-
'lektjuəl] 1. ☐ intellektuell; Verstandes...; geistig; verständig; 2. In-
tellektuelle(r *m*) *f*.
intelligence [in'telidʒəns] Intelligenz *f*; Verstand *m*; Verständnis *n*;
Nachricht *f*, Auskunft *f*; **~ department** Nachrichtendienst *m*.
intellig|ent ☐ [in'telidʒənt] intelli-
gent; klug; **~ible** ☐ [~dʒəbl] verständlich (*to* für).
intempera|nce [in'tempərəns] Un-
mäßigkeit *f*; Trunksucht *f*; **~te** ☐
[~rit] unmäßig; zügellos; unbe-
herrscht; trunksüchtig.
intend [in'tend] beabsichtigen, wollen; **~ for** bestimmen für *od.* zu;
~ed 1. absichtlich; beabsichtigt, *a.*
zukünftig; 2. F Verlobte(r *m*) *f*.
intense ☐ [in'tens] intensiv; ange-
strengt; heftig; kräftig (*Farbe*).
intensify [in'tensifai] (sich) verstärken *od.* steigern.
intensity [in'tensiti] Intensität *f*.
intent [in'tent] 1. ☐ gespannt; bedacht; beschäftigt (*on* mit); 2. Absicht *f*; Vorhaben *n*; *to all* **~s and**

purposes in jeder Hinsicht; **~ion**
[~nʃən] Absicht *f*; Zweck *m*; **~ional**
☐ [~nl] absichtlich; **~ness** [~ntnis]
gespannte Aufmerksamkeit; Eifer
m.
inter [in'tə:] beerdigen, begraben.
inter... ['intə(:)] zwischen; Zwischen...; gegenseitig, einander.
interact [intər'ækt] sich gegenseitig
beeinflussen.
intercede [intə(:)'si:d] vermitteln.
intercept [intə(:)'sept] ab-, auffangen; abhören; aufhalten; unterbrechen; **~ion** [~pʃən] Ab-, Auffangen *n*; Ab-, Mithören *n*; Unterbrechung *f*; Aufhalten *n*.
intercess|ion [intə'seʃən] Fürbitte
f; **~or** [~esə] Fürsprecher *m*.
interchange 1. [intə(:)'tʃeindʒ] *v/t.*
austauschen, auswechseln; *v/i.* abwechseln; 2. ['intə(:)'tʃeindʒ] Austausch *m*; Abwechs(e)lung *f*.
intercourse ['intə(:)kɔ:s] Verkehr *m*.
interdict 1. [intə(:)'dikt] untersagen,
verbieten (*s.th. to s.o.* j-m et.; *s.o.
from doing* j-m zu tun); 2. ['intə(:)-
dikt], **~ion** [intə(:)'dikʃən] Verbot
n; Interdikt *n*.
interest ['intrist] 1. Interesse *n*;
Anziehungskraft *f*; Bedeutung *f*;
Nutzen *m*; ✝ Anteil *m*, Beteiligung
f, Kapital *n*; Zins(en *pl.*) *m*; **~s** *pl.*
Interessenten *m/pl.*, Kreise *m/pl.*;
take an ~ in sich interessieren für;
return a blow with ~ noch heftiger
zurückschlagen; *banking* **~s** *pl.*
Bankkreise *m/pl.*; 2. *allg.* interessieren (*in* für *et.*); **~ing** ☐ [~tiŋ]
interessant.
interfere [intə'fiə] sich einmischen
(*with in acc.*); vermitteln; (ea.)
stören; **~nce** [~ərəns] Einmischung
f; Beeinträchtigung *f*; Störung *f*.
interim ['intərim] 1. Zwischenzeit
f; 2. vorläufig; Interims...
interior [in'tiəriə] 1. ☐ inner; inner-
lich; Innen...; **~ decorator** Innen-
architekt *m*; Maler *m*, Tapezierer
m; 2. Innere(s) *n*; Interieur *n*; *pol.*
innere Angelegenheiten; *Depart-
ment of the* ♀ *Am.* Innenministerium *n*.
interjection [intə(:)'dʒekʃən] Ausruf *m*.
interlace [intə(:)'leis] *v/t.* durch-
flechten, -weben; *v/i.* sich kreuzen.
interlock [intə(:)'lɔk] in-ea.-greifen;
in-ea.-schlingen; in-ea.-haken.
interlocut|ion [intə(:)lou'kju:ʃən]
Unterredung *f*; **~or** [~ə(:)'lɔkjutə]
Gesprächspartner *m*.
interlope [intə(:)'loup] sich ein-
drängen; **~r** ['intə(:)loupə] Eindringling *m*.
interlude ['intə(:)lu:d] Zwischen-
spiel *n*; Zwischenzeit *f*; **~s of bright
weather** zeitweilig schön.
intermarriage [intə(:)'mæridʒ]
Mischehe *f*.

intermeddle [intə(:)'medl] sich einmischen (*with*, *in* in *acc.*).

intermedia|ry [intə(:)'mi:djəri] **1.** = *intermediate*; vermittelnd; **2.** Vermittler *m*; **~te** ☐ [**~ət**] in der Mitte liegend; Mittel..., Zwischen...; **~range ballistic missile** Mittelstreckenrakete *f*; **~ school** *Am.* Mittelschule *f*.

interment [in'tə:mənt] Beerdigung *f*.

interminable ☐ [in'tə:minəbl] endlos, unendlich.

intermingle [intə(:)'miŋgl] (sich) vermischen

intermission [intə(:)'miʃən] Aussetzen *n*, Unterbrechung *f*; Pause *f*.

intermit [intə(:)'mit] unterbrechen, aussetzen; **~tent** ☐ [**~ənt**] aussetzend; **~ fever** 𝔰 Wechselfieber *n*.

intermix [intə(:)'miks] (sich) vermischen.

intern[1] [in'tə:n] internieren.

intern[2] ['intə:n] Assistenzarzt *m*.

internal ☐ [in'tə:nl] inner(lich); inländisch.

international ☐ [intə(:)'næʃənl] international; **~ law** Völkerrecht *n*.

interphone ['intəfoun] Haustelephon *n*; *Am.* 𝔰 Bordsprechanlage *f*.

interpolate [in'tə:pouleit] einschieben.

interpose [intə(:)'pouz] *v/t.* Veto einlegen; Wort einwerfen; *v/i.* dazwischentreten; vermitteln.

interpret [in'tə:prit] auslegen, erklären, interpretieren; (ver)dolmetschen; darstellen; **~ation** [intəpri'teiʃən] Auslegung *f*; Darstellung *f*; **~er** [in'tə:pritə] Ausleger (-in); Dolmetscher(in); Interpret (-in).

interrogat|e [in'terəgeit] (be-, aus-) fragen; verhören; **~ion** [intero'geiʃən] (Be-, Aus)Fragen *n*, Verhör(en) *n*; Frage *f*; *note od. mark od. point of* **~** Fragezeichen *n*; **~ive** ☐ [intə'rɔgətiv] fragend; Frage...

interrupt [intə'rʌpt] unterbrechen; **~ion** [**~pʃən**] Unterbrechung *f*.

intersect [intə(:)'sekt] (sich) schneiden; **~ion** [**~kʃən**] Durchschnitt *m*; Schnittpunkt *m*; *Straßen- etc.* Kreuzung *f*.

intersperse [intə(:)'spə:s] einstreuen; untermengen, durchsetzen.

interstate *Am.* [intə(:)'steit] zwischenstaatlich.

intertwine [intə(:)'twain] verflechten.

interval ['intəvəl] Zwischenraum *m*; Pause *f*; (Zeit)Abstand *m*.

interven|e [intə(:)'vi:n] dazwischenkommen; sich einmischen; einschreiten; dazwischenliegen; **~tion** [**~'venʃən**] Dazwischenkommen *n*; Einmischung *f*; Vermitt(e)lung *f*.

interview ['intəvju:] **1.** Zusammenkunft *f*, Unterredung *f*; Interview *n*; **2.** interviewen.

intestine [in'testin] **1.** inner; **2.** Darm *m*; **~s** *pl.* Eingeweide *n*/*pl.*

intima|cy ['intiməsi] Intimität *f*, Vertraulichkeit *f*; **~te** **1.** [**~meit**] bekanntgeben; zu verstehen geben; **2.** ☐ [**~mit**] intim; **3.** [**~**] Vertraute(r *m*) *f*; **~tion** [inti'meiʃən] Andeutung *f*, Wink *m*; Ankündigung *f*.

intimidate [in'timideit] einschüchtern.

into *prp.* ['intu, *vor Konsonant* 'intə] in (*acc.*), in ... hinein.

intolera|ble ☐ [in'tɔlərəbl] unerträglich; **~nt** ☐ [**~ənt**] unduldsam, intolerant.

intonation [intou'neiʃən] Anstimmen *n*; *gr* Intonation *f*, Tonfall *m*.

intoxica|nt [in'tɔksikənt] **1.** berauschend; **2.** berauschendes Getränk; **~te** [**~keit**] berauschen (*a. fig.*); **~tion** [intɔksi'keiʃən] Rausch *m* (*a. fig.*).

intractable ☐ [in'træktəbl] unlenksam, störrisch; schwer zu bändigen(d).

intransitive ☐ *gr.* [in'trænsitiv] intransitiv.

intrastate *Am.* [intrə'steit] innerstaatlich.

intrench [in'trentʃ] = *entrench*.

intrepid [in'trepid] unerschrocken.

intricate ['intrikit] verwickelt.

intrigue [in'tri:g] **1.** Ränkespiel *n*, Intrige *f*; (Liebes)Verhältnis *n*; **2.** *v/i.* Ränke schmieden, intrigieren; ein (Liebes)Verhältnis haben; *v/t.* neugierig machen; **~r** [**~gə**] Intrigant(in).

intrinsic|al [in'trinsik(əl)] inner(lich); wirklich, wahr.

introduc|e [intrə'dju:s] einführen (*a. fig.*); bekannt machen (*to* mit), vorstellen (*to j-m*); einleiten; **~tion** [**~'dʌkʃən**] Einführung *f*; Einleitung *f*; Vorstellung *f*; *letter of* **~** Empfehlungsschreiben *n*; **~tory** [**~ktəri**] einleitend, einführend.

introspection [introu'spekʃən] Selbstprüfung *f*; Selbstbetrachtung *f*.

introvert 1. [introu'və:t] einwärtskehren; **2.** *psych.* [introuvə:t] nach innen gekehrter Mensch.

intru|de [in'tru:d] hineinzwängen; (sich) ein- od. aufdrängen; **~der** [**~də**] Eindringling *m*; **~sion** [**~u:**ʒən] Eindringen *n*; Auf-, Zudringlichkeit *f*; **~sive** ☐ [**~u:siv**] zudringlich.

intrust [in'trʌst] = *entrust*.

intuition [intju(:)'iʃən] unmittelbare Erkenntnis, Intuition *f*.

inundate ['inʌndeit] überschwemmen.

inure [i'njuə] gewöhnen (*to an acc.*).

invade [in'veid] eindringen in, ein-

fallen in (acc.); fig. befallen; ~r [~də] Angreifer m; Eindringling m.
invalid¹ ['invəli:d] 1. dienstunfähig; kränklich; 2. Invalide m.
invalid² [in'vælid] (rechts)ungültig; ~ate [~deit] entkräften; g̃ ungültig machen. [schätzbar.)
invaluable □ [in'væljuəbl] un-)
invariab|le □ [in'vєəriəbl] unveränderlich; ~ly [~li] ausnahmslos.
invasion [in'veiʒən] Einfall m, Angriff m, Invasion f; Eingriff m; ⚔ Anfall m.
invective [in'vektiv] Schmähung f, Schimpfrede f, Schimpfwort n.
inveigh [in'vei] schimpfen (against über, auf acc.).
inveigle [in'vi:gl] verleiten.
invent [in'vent] erfinden; ~ion [~nʃən] Erfindung(sgabe) f; ~ive □ [~ntiv] erfinderisch; ~or [~tə] Erfinder(in); ~ory ['invəntri] 1. Inventar n; Inventur f; 2. inventarisieren.
invers|e □ ['in'və:s] umgekehrt; ~ion [in'və:ʃən] Umkehrung f; gr. Inversion f.
invert [in'və:t] umkehren; umstellen; ~ed commas pl. Anführungszeichen n/pl.
invest [in'vest] investieren, anlegen; bekleiden; ausstatten; umgeben (with von); ⚔ belagern.
investigat|e [in'vestigeit] erforschen; untersuchen; nachforschen; ~ion [investi'geiʃən] Erforschung f; Untersuchung f; Nachforschung f; ~or [in'vestigeitə] Untersuchende(r m) f.
invest|ment ✝ [in'vestmənt] Kapitalanlage f; Investition f; ~or [~tə] Geldgeber m.
inveterate [in'vetərit] eingewurzelt.
invidious □ [in'vidiəs] verhaßt; gehässig; beneidenswert.
invigorate [in'vigəreit] kräftigen.
invincible □ [in'vinsəbl] unbesiegbar; unüberwindlich.
inviola|ble □ [in'vaiələbl] unverletzlich; ~te [~lit] unverletzt.
invisible □ [in'vizəbl] unsichtbar.
invit|ation [invi'teiʃən] Einladung f, Aufforderung f; ~e [in'vait] einladen; auffordern; (an)locken.
invoice ✝ ['invɔis] Faktura f, Warenrechnung f.
invoke [in'vouk] anrufen; zu Hilfe rufen (acc.); sich berufen auf (acc.); Geist heraufbeschwören.
involuntary □ [in'vɔləntəri] unfreiwillig; unwillkürlich.
involve [in'vɔlv] verwickeln, hineinziehen; in sich schließen, enthalten; mit sich bringen; ~ment [~vmənt] Verwicklung f; (bsd. Geld)Schwierigkeit f.
invulnerable □ [in'vʌlnərəbl] unverwundbar; fig. unanfechtbar.

inward ['inwəd] 1. □ inner(lich); 2. adv. mst ~s einwärts; nach innen; 3. ~s pl. Eingeweide n/pl.
iodine ['aiədi:n] Jod n.
IOU ['aiou'ju:] (= I owe you) Schuldschein m.
irascible □ [i'ræsibl] jähzornig.
irate [ai'reit] zornig, wütend.
iridescent [iri'desnt] schillernd.
iris ['aiəris] anat. Regenbogenhaut f, Iris f; ♀ Schwertlilie f.
Irish ['aiəriʃ] 1. irisch; 2. Irisch n; the ~ pl. die Iren pl.; ~man Ire m.
irksome ['ə:ksəm] lästig, ermüdend.
iron ['aiən] 1. Eisen n; a. flat-~ Bügeleisen n; ~s pl. Fesseln f/pl.; strike while the ~ is hot fig. das Eisen schmieden, solange es heiß ist; 2. eisern (a. fig.); Eisen...; 3. bügeln; in Eisen legen; ~bound eisenbeschlagen; felsig; unbeugsam; ~clad 1. gepanzert; 2. Panzerschiff n; ~ curtain pol. eiserner Vorhang; ~-hearted fig. hartherzig.
ironic(al □) [ai'rɔnik(əl)] ironisch, spöttisch.
iron|ing ['aiəniŋ] Plätten n, Bügeln n; attr. Plätt..., Bügel...; ~ lung ⚔ eiserne Lunge; ~monger Eisenhändler m; ~mongery [~ri] Eisenwaren f/pl.; ~mo(u)ld Rostfleck m; ~work schmiedeeiserne Arbeit; ~works mst sg. Eisenhütte f.
irony¹ ['aiəni] eisenartig, -haltig.
irony² ['aiərəni] Ironie f.
irradiant [i'reidjənt] strahlend (with vor Freude etc.).
irradiate [i'reidieit] bestrahlen (a. ⚔); fig. aufklären; strahlen lassen.
irrational [i'ræʃənl] unvernünftig.
irreclaimable □ [iri'kleiməbl] unverbesserlich.
irrecognizable □ [i'rekəgnaizəbl] nicht (wieder)erkennbar.
irreconcilable □ [i'rekənsailəbl] unversöhnlich; unvereinbar.
irrecoverable □ [iri'kʌvərəbl] unersetzlich; unwiederbringlich.
irredeemable □ [iri'di:məbl] unkündbar; nicht einlösbar; unersetzlich.
irrefutable □ [i'refjutəbl] unwiderleglich, unwiderlegbar.
irregular □ [i'regjulə] unregelmäßig, regelwidrig; ungleichmäßig.
irrelevant □ [i'relivənt] nicht zur Sache gehörig; unzutreffend; unerheblich, belanglos (to für).
irreligious □ [iri'lidʒəs] gottlos.
irremediable □ [iri'mi:djəbl] unheilbar; unersetzlich.
irremovable □ [iri'mu:vəbl] nicht entfernbar; unabsetzbar.
irreparable □ [i'repərəbl] nicht wieder gutzumachen(d).
irreplaceable [iri'pleisəbl] unersetzlich.
irrepressible □ [iri'presəbl] ununterdrückbar; unbezähmbar.

irreproachable □ [iri'prout∫əbl] einwandfrei, untadelig.
irresistible [:] [iri'zistəbl] unwiderstehlich.
irresolute □ [i'rezəlu:t] unentschlossen
irrespective □ [iris'pektiv] (of) rücksichtslos (gegen); ohne Rücksicht (auf acc.); unabhängig (von).
irresponsible [iris'pɔnsəbl] unverantwortlich; verantwortungslos.
irretrievable [iri'tri:vəbl] unwiederbringlich, unersetzlich; nicht wieder gutzumachen(d).
irreverent [i'revərənt] respektlos, ehrfurchtslos
irrevocable [i'revəkəbl] unwiderruflich, unabänderlich, endgültig.
irrigate [i'irigeit] bewässern.
irrita|ble [i'iritəbl] reizbar; **~nt** [~ənt] Reizmittel n; **~te** [~teit] reizen, ärgern, aufreizend, ärgerlich (Sache); **~tion** [iri'teiʃən] Reizung f; Gereiztheit f, Ärger m
irrupt|ion [i'rʌpʃən] Einbruch m (mst fig.); **~ive** [~ptiv] (her)einbrechend
is [iz] 3 sg pres. von be.
island ['ailənd] Insel f; Verkehrsinsel f, **~er** [~də] Inselbewohner(in).
isle [ail] Insel f; **~t** ['ailit] Inselchen n.
isolat|e ['aisəleit] absondern; isolieren; **~ed** abgeschieden; **~ion** [aisə'leiʃən] Isolierung f, Absonderung f; **~ ward** f Isolierstation f; **~ionist** Am. pol. [~ʃnist] Isolationist m.
issue ['isju:, Am. 'iʃu:] 1. Heraus-

kommen n, Herausfließen n; Abfluß m; Ausgang m; Nachkommen (-schaft f) m/pl.; fig. Ausgang m, Ergebnis n; Streitfrage f; Ausgabe f v. Material etc., Erlaß m v. Befehlen; Ausgabe f, Exemplar n; Nummer f e-r Zeitung; ~ in law Rechtsfrage f; be at ~ uneinig sein; point at ~ strittiger Punkt; 2. v/i. herauskommen; herkommen, entspringen; endigen (in in acc.); v/t. von sich geben; Material etc. ausgeben; Befehl erlassen; Buch herausgeben.
isthmus ['isməs] Landenge f.
it [it] 1. es; nach prp. da...(z.B. by ~ dadurch, for ~ dafür); 2. das gewisse Etwas
Italian [i'tæljən] 1. italienisch; 2. Italiener(in); Italienisch n.
italics typ [i'tæliks] Kursivschrift f.
itch [itʃ] 1. ♣ Krätze f; Jucken n; Verlangen n; 2. jucken; be ~ing to inf. darauf brennen, zu inf.; have an ~ing palm raffgierig sein; **~ing** ['itʃiŋ] Jucken n; fig Gelüste n.
item [aitem] 1. desgleichen; 2. Einzelheit f, Punkt m; Posten m; (Zeitungs)Artikel m; **~ize** [~maiz] einzeln angeben od. aufführen.
iterate ['itəreit] wiederholen.
itiner|ant [i'tinərənt] reisend; umherziehend; Reise...; **~ary** [ai'tinərəri] Reiseroute f, -plan m; Reisebericht m; after. Reise...
its [its] sein(e); dessen, deren.
itself [it self] (es, sich) selbst; sich; of ~ von selbst; in ~ in sich, an sich; by ~ für sich allein, besonders.
ivory ['aivəri] Elfenbein n.
ivy ♣ ['aivi] Efeu m.

J

jab F [dʒæb] 1. stechen; stoßen; 2. Stich m, Stoß m.
jabber ['dʒæbə] plappern.
jack [dʒæk] 1. Hebevorrichtung f, bsd. Wagenheber m; Malkugel f beim Bowlspiel; ♣ Gösch f, kleine Flagge; Karten: Bube m; 2. a. ~ up aufbocken [Handlanger m.\]
jackal ['dʒækɔ:l] zo. Schakal m; fig.)
jack|ass ['dʒækæs] Esel m (a. fig.); **~boots** Reitstiefel m/pl.; hohe Wasserstiefel m/pl.; **~daw** orn. Dohle f.
jacket ['dʒækit] Jacke f; ⊕ Mantel m; Schutzumschlag m e-s Buches.
jack|-knife ['dʒæknaif] (großes) Klappmesser n; 2 of all trades Hansdampf in allen Gassen; 2 of all work Faktotum n; **~pot** Poker: Einsatz m; hit the ~ Am. F großes Glück haben.
jade [dʒeid] (Schind)Mähre f, Klepper m; contp. Frauenzimmer n.

jag [dʒæg] Zacken m; sl. Sauferei f; **~ged** ['dʒægid] zackig; gekerbt; bsd. Am. sl. voll (betrunken).
jaguar zo. ['dʒægjuə] Jaguar m.
jail [dʒeil] 1. Kerker m; 2. einkerkern; **~bird** ['dʒeilbə:d] F Knastbruder m; Galgenvogel m; **~er** ['dʒeilə] Kerkermeister m.
jalop(p)y bsd. Am. F mot., ✖ [dʒə-'lɔpi] Kiste f.
jam¹ [dʒæm] Marmelade f.
jam² [~] 1. Gedränge n; ⊕ Hemmung f; Radio Störung f; traffic ~ Verkehrsstockung f; be in a ~ sl. in der Klemme sein; 2. (sich) (fest-, ver)klemmen; pressen, quetschen; versperren; Radio: stören; ~ the brakes mit aller Kraft bremsen.
jamboree [dʒæmbə'ri:] (bsd. Pfadfinder)Treffen n; sl. Vergnügen n, Fez m.

jangle ['dʒæŋgl] schrillen (lassen); laut streiten, keifen.

janitor ['dʒænitə] Portier *m*.

January ['dʒænjuəri] Januar *m*.

Japanese [dʒæpə'niːz] 1. japanisch; 2. Japaner(in); Japanisch *n*; the ~ *pl.* die Japaner *pl.*

jar [dʒɑː] 1. Krug *m*; Topf *m*; Glas *n*; Knarren *n*, Mißton *m*; Streit *m*; mißliche Lage; 2. knarren; unangenehm berühren; erzittern (lassen); streiten.

jaundice ['dʒɔːndis] Gelbsucht *f*; ~d [~st] ⚓ gelbsüchtig; *fig.* neidisch.

jaunt [dʒɔːnt] 1. Ausflug *m*, Spritztour *f*; 2. e-n Ausflug machen; ~y □ ['dʒɔːnti] munter; flott.

javelin ['dʒævlin] Wurfspeer *m*.

jaw [dʒɔː] Kinnbacken *m*, Kiefer *m*; ~s *pl.* Rachen *m*; Maul *n*; Schlund *m*; ⊕ Backen *f/pl.*; ~bone ['dʒɔːboun] Kieferknochen *m*.

jay *orn.* [dʒei] Eichelhäher *m*; ~walker *Am.* F ['dʒeiwɔːkə] achtlos die Straße überquerender Fußgänger.

jazz [dʒæz] 1. Jazz *m*; 2. F grell.

jealous ['dʒeləs] eifersüchtig; besorgt (of um); neidisch; ~y [~si] Eifersucht *f*; Neid *m*.

jeans [dʒiːnz] *pl.* Jeans *pl.*, Nict(en)-hose *f*.

jeep [dʒiːp] Jeep *m*.

jeer [dʒiə] 1. Spott *m*, Spötterei *f*; 2. spotten (at über *acc.*); (ver-)höhnen.

jejune □ [dʒi'dʒuːn] nüchtern, fad.

jelly ['dʒeli] 1. Gallert(e *f*) *n*; Gelee *n*; 2. gelieren; ~fish *zo.* Qualle *f*.

jeopardize ['dʒepədaiz] gefährden.

jerk [dʒɔːk] 1. Ruck *m*; (Muskel-)Krampf *m*; 2. rucken *od.* zerren (an *dat.*); schnellen; schleudern; ~water *Am.* ['dʒɔːkwɔːtə] 1. 🚂 Nebenbahn *f*; 2. F klein, unbedeutend; ~y ['dʒɔːki] 1. □ ruckartig; holperig; 2. *Am.* luftgetrocknetes Rindfleisch.

jersey ['dʒɔːzi] Wollpullover *m*; wollenes Unterhemd.

jest [dʒest] 1. Spaß *m*; 2. scherzen; ~er ['dʒestə] Spaßmacher *m*.

jet [dʒet] 1. (Wasser-, Gas)Strahl *m*; Strahlrohr *n*; ⊕ Düse *f*; Düsenflugzeug *n*; Düsenmotor *m*; 2. hervorsprudeln; ~propelled ['dʒetprəpeld] mit Düsenantrieb.

jetty ⚓ ['dʒeti] Mole *f*; Pier *m*.

Jew [dʒuː] Jude *m*; *attr.* Juden...

jewel ['dʒuːəl] Juwel *m*, *n*; ~(l)er [~lə] Juwelier *m*; ~(le)ry [~lri] Juwelen *pl.*, Schmuck *m*.

Jew|ess ['dʒu(ː)is] Jüdin *f*; ~ish ['dʒu(ː)iʃ] jüdisch.

jib ⚓ [dʒib] Klüver *m*.

jibe *Am.* F [dʒaib] zustimmen.

jiffy F ['dʒifi] Augenblick *m*.

jig-saw ['dʒigsɔː] Laubsägema-

schine *f*; ~ puzzle Zusammensetzspiel *n*.

jilt [dʒilt] 1. Kokette *f*; 2. *Liebhaber* versetzen.

Jim [dʒim]: ~ Crow *Am.* Neger *m*; *Am.* Rassentrennung *f*.

jingle ['dʒiŋgl] 1. Geklingel *n*; 2. klingeln, klimpern (mit).

jitney *Am. sl.* ['dʒitni] 5-Cent-Stück *n*; billiger Omnibus.

jive *Am. sl.* [dʒaiv] *heiße* Jazzmusik; Jazzjargon *m*.

job [dʒɔb] 1. (Stück *n*) Arbeit *f*; Sache *f*, Aufgabe *f*; Beruf *m*; Stellung *f*; by the ~ stückweise; im Akkord; ~ lot F Ramschware *f*; ~ work Akkordarbeit *f*; 2. *v/t.* Pferd *etc.* (ver)mieten; ⚓ vermitteln; *v/i.* im Akkord arbeiten; Maklergeschäfte machen; ~ber ['dʒɔbə] Akkordarbeiter *m*; Makler *m*; Schieber *m*.

jockey ['dʒɔki] 1. Jockei *m*; 2. prellen.

jocose □ [dʒə'kous] scherzhaft, spaßig.

jocular □ ['dʒɔkjulə] lustig; spaßig.

jocund □ ['dʒɔkənd] lustig, fröhlich.

jog [dʒɔg] 1. Stoß(en *n*) *m*; Rütteln *n*; Trott *m*; 2. *v/t.* an)stoßen, (auf-)rütteln; *v/i. mst* ~ along, ~ on dahintrotten, dahinschlendern.

John [dʒɔn]: ~ Bull John Bull (*der Engländer*); ~ Hancock *Am.* F Friedrich Wilhelm *m* (*Unterschrift*).

join [dʒɔin] 1. *v/t.* verbinden, zs.-fügen (to mit); sich vereinigen mit, sich gesellen zu; eintreten in (*acc.*); ~ battle den Kampf beginnen; ~ hands die Hände falten; sich die Hände reichen (*a. fig.*); *v/i.* sich verbinden, sich vereinigen; ~ in mitmachen bei; ~ up Soldat werden; 2. Verbindung(sstelle) *f*.

joiner ['dʒɔinə] Tischler *m*; ~y [~əri] Tischlerhandwerk *n*; Tischlerarbeit *f*.

joint [dʒɔint] 1. Verbindung(sstelle) *f*; Scharnier *n*; *anat.* Gelenk *n*; ⚓ Knoten *m*; Braten *m*; *Am. sl.* Spelunke *f*; put out of ~ verrenken; 2. □ gemeinsam; Mit...; ~ heir Miterbe *m*; ~ stock ⚓ Aktienkapital *n*; 3. zs.-fügen; zerlegen; ~ed ['dʒɔintid] gegliedert; Glieder...; ~stock ⚓ Aktien...; ~ company Aktiengesellschaft *f*.

jok|e [dʒouk] 1. Scherz *m*, Spaß *m*; practical ~ Streich *m*; 2. *v/i.* scherzen; schäkern; *v/t.* necken (about mit); ~er ['dʒoukə] Spaßvogel *m*; *Karten:* Joker *m*; *Am.* versteckte Klausel; ~y □ ['dʒouki] spaßig.

jolly ['dʒɔli] lustig, fidel; F nett.

jolt [dʒoult] 1. stoßen, rütteln; holpern; 2. Stoß *m*; Rütteln *n*.

Jonathan ['dʒɔnəθən]: *Brother* ~ der Amerikaner.

josh *Am. sl.* [dʒɔʃ] **1.** Ulk *m*; **2.** aufziehen, auf die Schippe nehmen.

jostle ['dʒɔsl] **1.** anrennen; zs.-stoßen; **2.** Stoß *m*; Zs.-Stoß *m*.

jot [dʒɔt] **1.** Jota *n*, Pünktchen *n*; **2.** ~ *down* notieren.

journal ['dʒɔːnl] Journal *n*; Tagebuch *n*; Tageszeitung *f*; Zeitschrift *f*; ⊕ Wellenzapfen *m*; ~ism ['dʒɔː-nəlizəm] Journalismus *m*.

journey ['dʒɔːni] **1.** Reise *f*; Fahrt *f*; **2.** reisen; ~man Geselle *m*.

jovial [['dʒouvjəl] heiter; gemütlich.

joy [dʒɔi] Freude *f*; Fröhlichkeit *f*; ~ful ['dʒɔiful] freudig; erfreut; fröhlich; ~less [['dʒɔilis] freudlos; unerfreulich; ~ous □ ['dʒɔiəs] freudig, fröhlich.

jubil|ant ['dʒuːbilənt] jubilierend, frohlockend; ~ate [~leit] jubeln; ~ee [~liː] Jubiläum *n*.

judge [dʒʌdʒ] **1.** Richter *m*; Schiedsrichter *m*; Beurteiler(in), Kenner(in); **2.** *v/i.* urteilen (*of* über *acc.*); *v/t.* richten; aburteilen; beurteilen (*by* nach); ansehen als.

judg(e)ment ['dʒʌdʒmənt] Urteil *n*; Urteilsspruch *m*; Urteilskraft *f*; Einsicht *f*; Meinung *f*; *göttliches* (Straf)Gericht; *Day of* ♀, ♀ *Day* Jüngstes Gericht.

judicature ['dʒuːdikətʃə] Gerichtshof *m*; Rechtspflege *f*.

judicial [dʒuː(ː)'diʃəl] gerichtlich; Gerichts...; kritisch; unparteiisch.

judicious [dʒuː(ː)'diʃəs] verständig, klug; ~ness [~snis] Einsicht *f*.

jug [dʒʌg] Krug *m*, Kanne *f*.

juggle ['dʒʌgl] **1.** Trick *m*; Schwindel *m*; **2.** jonglieren (*a. fig.*); verfälschen; betrügen; ~r [~lə] Jongleur *m*; Taschenspieler(in).

Jugoslav ['juːgouˈslaːv] **1.** Jugoslaw|e *m*, -in *f*; **2.** jugoslawisch.

juic|e [dʒuːs] Saft *m*; *sl. mot.* Sprit *m*, Gas *n*; ~y □ ['dʒuːsi] saftig; F interessant. [sikautomat *m.*]

juke-box *Am.* F ['dʒuːkbɔks] Mu-]

julep ['dʒuːlep] *süßes* (Arznei)Getränk; *bsd. Am.* alkoholisches Eisgetränk.

July [dʒuː(ː)'lai] Juli *m*.

jumble ['dʒʌmbl] **1.** Durcheinander *n*; **2.** *v/t.* durch-ea.-werfen; ~-sale Wohltätigkeitsbasar *m*.

jump [dʒʌmp] **1.** Sprung *m*; ~s *pl.* nervöses Zs.-fahren; *high* (*long*) ~ Hoch- (Weit)Sprung *m*; *get* (*have*) *the* ~ *on Am.* F zuvorkommen; **2.** *v/i.* (auf)springen; ~ *at* sich stürzen auf (*acc.*); ~ *to conclusions* übereilte Schlüsse ziehen; *v/t.* hinwegspringen über (*acc.*); überspringen; springen lassen; ~er ['dʒʌmpə] Springer *m*; Jumper *m*; ~y [~pi] nervös

junct|ion ['dʒʌŋkʃən] Verbindung *f*; Kreuzung *f*; ⊕ Knotenpunkt *m*; ~ure [~ktʃə] Verbindungspunkt *m*, -stelle *f*; (kritischer) Zeitpunkt; *at this* ~ bei diesem Stand der Dinge.

June [dʒuːn] Juni *m*.

jungle ['dʒʌŋgl] Dschungel *m, n, f*.

junior ['dʒuːnjə] **1.** jünger (*to* als); *Am. univ* der Unterstufe (angehörend); ~ *high school Am.* Oberschule *f* mit Klassen 7, 8, 9; **2.** Jüngere(r *m*) *f*; *Am.* (Ober)Schüler *m od.* Student *m* im 3. Jahr; F Kleine(r) *m*.

junk [dʒʌŋk] ⊕ Dschunke *f*; Plunder *m*, alter Kram.

junket ['dʒʌŋkit] Quarkspeise *f*; *Am.* Party *f*; Vergnügungsfahrt *f*.

juris|diction [dʒuəris'dikʃən] Rechtsprechung *f*; Gerichtsbarkeit *f*; Gerichtsbezirk *m*; ~prudence ['dʒuərispruːdəns] Rechtswissenschaft *f*.

juror ['dʒuərə] Geschworene(r) *m*.

jury ['dʒuəri] *die* Geschworenen *pl.*; Jury *f*, Preisgericht *n*; ~man Geschworene(r) *m*.

just [dʒʌst] **1.** *adj.* gerecht; rechtschaffen; **2.** *adv.* richtig; genau; (so)eben; nur; ~ *now* eben *od.* gerade jetzt.

justice ['dʒʌstis] Gerechtigkeit *f*; Richter *m*; Recht *n*; Rechtsverfahren *n*; *court of* ~ Gericht(shof *m*) *n*.

justification [dʒʌstifi'keiʃən] Rechtfertigung *f*.

justify ['dʒʌstifai] rechtfertigen.

justly ['dʒʌstli] mit Recht.

justness ['dʒʌstnis] Gerechtigkeit *f*, Billigkeit *f*; Rechtmäßigkeit *f*; Richtigkeit *f*.

jut [dʒʌt] *a.* ~ *out* hervorragen.

juvenile ['dʒuːvinail] **1.** jung, jugendlich; Jugend...; **2.** junger Mensch.

K

kale [keil] (*bsd.* Kraus-, Grün)Kohl *m*; *Am. sl.* Moos *n* (*Geld*).

kangaroo [kæŋgə'ru:] Känguruh *n*.

keel ⚓ [ki:l] 1. Kiel *m*; 2. ~ *over* kieloben legen *od.* liegen; umschlagen.

keen [ki:n] scharf (*a. fig.*); eifrig, heftig; stark, groß (*Appetit etc.*); ~ *on* F scharf *od.* erpicht auf *acc.*; *be* ~ *on hunting* ein leidenschaftlicher Jäger sein; **~-edged** ['ki:nedʒd] scharfgeschliffen; **~ness** ['ki:nnis] Schärfe *f*; Heftigkeit *f*; Scharfsinn *m*.

keep [ki:p] 1. (Lebens)Unterhalt *m*; *for* ~ F für immer; 2. [*irr.*] *v/t. allg.* halten; behalten; unterhalten; (er-)halten; einhalten; (ab)halten; *Buch, Ware etc* führen; *Bett etc.* hüten; fest-, aufhalten; (bei)behalten; (auf)bewahren; ~ *s.o. company* j-m Gesellschaft leisten; ~ *company with* verkehren mit; ~ *one's temper* sich beherrschen; ~ *time* richtig gehen (*Uhr*); ♪, ✕ Takt, Schritt halten; ~ *s.o. waiting* j-n warten lassen; ~ *away* fernhalten; ~ *s.th. from s.o.* j-m *etc.* vorenthalten; ~ *in* zurückhalten; *Schüler* nachsitzen lassen; ~ *on Kleid* anbehalten, *Hut* aufbehalten; ~ *up* aufrechterhalten; (*Mut*) bewahren; in Ordnung halten; hindern, zu Bett gehen; aufbleiben lassen; ~ *it up* (es) durchhalten; *v/i.* sich halten, bleiben; F sich aufhalten; ~ *doing* immer wieder tun; ~ *away* sich fernhalten; ~ *from* sich enthalten (*gen.*); ~ *off* sich fernhalten; ~ *on talking* fortfahren zu sprechen; ~ *to* sich halten an (*acc.*); ~ *up* sich aufrecht halten; sich aufrechterhalten; ~ *up with* Schritt halten mit; ~ *up with the Joneses* es den Nachbarn gleichtun.

keep|er ['ki:pə] Wärter *m*, Wächter *m*, Aufseher *m*; Verwalter *m*; Inhaber *m*; **~ing** ['ki:piŋ] Verwahrung *f*; Obhut *f*; Gewahrsam *m*, *n*; Unterhalt *m*; *be in (out of)* ~ *with* ... (nicht) übereinstimmen mit ...; **~sake** ['ki:pseik] Andenken *n*.

keg [keg] Fäßchen *n*.

kennel ['kenl] Gosse *f*, Rinnstein *m*; Hundehütte *f*, -zwinger *m*.

kept [kept] *pret. u. p.p. von* **keep** 2.

kerb [kə:b], **~stone** ['kə:bstoun] = curb *etc.*

kerchief ['kə:tʃif] (Kopf)Tuch *n*.

kernel ['kə:nl] Kern *m* (*a. fig.*); Hafer-, Mais- *etc.* Korn *n*.

kettle ['ketl] Kessel *m*; **~drum** ♪ Kesselpauke *f*.

key [ki:] 1. Schlüssel *m* (*a. fig.*); △ Schlußstein *m*; ⊕ Keil *m*; Schraubenschlüssel *m*; *Klavieretc.* Taste *f*; ∮ Taste *f*, Druck-

knopf *m*; ♪ Tonart *f*; *fig.* Ton *m*; 2. ~ *up* ♪ stimmen; erhöhen; *fig.* in erhöhte Spannung versetzen; **~board** ['ki:bɔ:d] Klaviatur *f*, Tastatur *f*; **~hole** Schlüsselloch *n*; **~man** Schlüsselfigur *f*; **~ money** Ablösung *f* (*für e-e Wohnung*); **~note** ♪ Grundton *m*; **~stone** Schlußstein *m*; *fig.* Grundlage *f*.

kibitzer *Am.* F ['kibitsə] Kiebitz *m*, Besserwisser *m*.

kick [kik] 1. (Fuß)Tritt *m*; Stoß *m*; Schwung *m*; F Nervenkitzel *m*; *get a* ~ *out of* F Spaß finden an (*dat.*); 2. *v/t.* (mit dem Fuß) stoßen *od.* treten; *Fußball:* schießen; ~ *out* F hinauswerfen; *v/i.* (hinten) ausschlagen, stoßen (*Gewehr*); sich auflehnen; ~ *in with Am. sl.* Geld 'reinbuttern; ~ *off Fußball:* anstoßen; **~back** *bsd. Am.* F ['kikbæk] Rückzahlung *f*; **~er** ['kikə] Fußballspieler *m*.

kid [kid] 1. Zicklein *n*; *sl.* Kind *n*; Ziegenleder *n*; 2. *sl.* foppen; **~dy** *sl.* ['kidi] Kind *n*; ~ *glove* Glacéhandschuh *m* (*a. fig.*); **~glove** sanft, zart.

kidnap ['kidnæp] entführen; **~(p)er** [~pə] Kindesentführer *m*, Kidnapper *m*.

kidney ['kidni] *anat.* Niere *f*; F Art *f*; ~ *bean* ♀ weiße Bohne.

kill [kil] 1. töten (*a. fig.*); *fig.* vernichten; *parl.* zu Fall bringen; ~ *off* abschlachten; ~ *time* die Zeit totschlagen; 2. Tötung *f*; Jagdbeute *f*; **~er** ['kilə] Totschläger *m*; **~ing** ['kiliŋ] 1. mörderisch; F komisch; 2. *Am.* F *finanzieller* Volltreffer.

kiln [kiln] Brenn-, Darrofen *m*.

kilo|gram(me) ['kilogræm] Kilogramm *n*; **~metre**, *Am.* **~meter** Kilometer *m*.

kilt [kilt] Kilt *m*, Schottenrock *m*.

kin [kin] (Bluts)Verwandtschaft *f*.

kind [kaind] 1. gütig, freundlich; 2. Art *f*, Gattung *f*, Geschlecht *n*; Art und Weise *f*; *pay in* ~ in Naturalien zahlen; *fig.* mit gleicher Münze heimzahlen.

kindergarten ['kindəga:tn] Kindergarten *m*

kind-hearted ['kaind'ha:tid] gütig.

kindle ['kindl] anzünden; (sich) entzünden (*a. fig.*).

kindling ['kindliŋ] Kleinholz *n*.

kind|ly ['kaindli] freundlich; günstig; **~ness** [~dnis] Güte *f*, Freundlichkeit *f*; Gefälligkeit *f*.

kindred ['kindrid] 1. verwandt, gleichartig; 2. Verwandtschaft *f*.

king [kiŋ] König *m* (*a. fig. u. Schach, Kartenspiel*); **~dom** ['kiŋdəm] Königreich *n*; *bsd.* ♀, *zo.* Reich *n*, Gebiet *n*; *eccl.* Reich *n* Gottes; **~like**

['kiŋlaik], ~ly [~li] königlich; ~-size F ['kiŋsaiz] überlang, übergroß.

kink [kiŋk] Schlinge f, Knoten m; fig. Schrulle f, Fimmel m.

kin|ship ['kinʃip] Verwandtschaft f; ~sman ['kinzmən] Verwandte(r) m.

kipper ['kipə] Räucherhering m Bückling m; sl. Kerl m.

kiss [kis] 1. Kuß m; 2. (sich) küssen.

kit [kit] Ausrüstung f (a. ⚔ u. Sport); Handwerkszeug n, Werkzeug n; ~-bag ['kitbæg] ⚔ Tornister m; Seesack m; Reisetasche f.

kitchen ['kitʃin] Küche f; ~ette [kitʃi'net] Kochnische f; ~-garden ['kitʃin'gɑːdn] Gemüsegarten m.

kite [kait] Papier-Drachen m.

kitten ['kitn] Kätzchen n.

Klan Am. [klæn] Ku-Klux-Klan m; ~sman ['klænzmən] Mitglied n des Ku-Klux-Klan.

knack [næk] Kniff m, Dreh m; Geschicklichkeit f. [Rucksack m.\

knapsack ['næpsæk] Tornister m;\

knave [neiv] Schurke m; Kartenspiel: Bube m; ~ry ['neivəri] Gaunerei f.

knead [ni:d] kneten; massieren.

knee [ni:] Knie n; ⊕ Kniestück n; ~-cap ['ni:kæp] Kniescheibe f; ~-deep bis an die Knie (reichend); ~-joint Kniegelenk n; ~l [ni:l] [irr.] knien (to vor dat.).

knell [nel] Totenglocke f.

knelt [nelt] pret. u. p.p. von kneel.

knew [nju:] pret. von know.

knicker|bockers ['nikəbəkəz] pl. Knickerbocker pl., Kniehosen f/pl.; ~s F ['nikəz] pl. Schlüpfer m; = knickerbockers.

knick-knack ['niknæk] Spielerei f; Nippsache f.

knife [naif] 1. pl. knives [naivz] Messer n; 2. schneiden; (er)stechen.

knight [nait] 1. Ritter m; Springer m im Schach; 2. zum Ritter schlagen; ~-errant ['nait'erənt] fahrender Ritter; ~hood ['naithud] Rittertum n; Ritterschaft f; ~ly ['naitli] ritterlich.

knit [nit] [irr.] stricken; (ver)knüp-

fen; (sich) eng verbinden; ~ the brows die Stirn runzeln; ~ting ['nitiŋ] Stricken n; Strickzeug n; attr. Strick...

knives [naivz] pl. von knife 1.

knob [nɔb] Knopf m; Buckel m; Brocken m.

knock [nɔk] 1. Schlag m; Anklopfen n; mot. Klopfen n; 2. v/i. klopfen; pochen; stoßen; schlagen; ~ about F sich herumtreiben; v/t. klopfen, stoßen, schlagen; Am. sl. bekritteln, schlechtmachen; ~ about herumstoßen, übel zurichten; ~ down niederschlagen; Auktion: zuschlagen; ⊕ aus-ea.-nehmen; be ~ed down überfahren werden; ~ off aufhören mit; F zs.-hauen (schnell erledigen); Summe abziehen; ~ out Boxen: k.o. schlagen; ~er ['nɔkə] Klopfende(r) m; Türklopfer m; Am. sl. Kritikaster m; ~-kneed ['nɔkni:d] x-beinig; fig. hinkend; ~-out Boxen: Knockout m, K.o. m; sl. tolle Sache od. Person.

knoll¹ [noul] kleiner Erdhügel.

knoll² [~] (bsd. zu Grabe) läuten.

knot [nɔt] 1. Knoten m; Knorren m; Seemeile f; Schleife f, Band n (a. fig.); Schwierigkeit f; 2. (ver)knoten, (ver)knüpfen (a. fig.); Stirn runzeln; verwickeln; ~ty ['nɔti] knotig; knorrig; fig. verwickelt.

know [nou] [irr.] wissen; (er)kennen; erfahren; ~ French Französisch können; come to ~ erfahren; get to ~ kennenlernen; ~ one's business, ~ the ropes, ~ a thing or two, ~ what's what sich auskennen, Erfahrung haben; you ~ (am Ende des Satzes) nämlich; ~ing : ['nouiŋ] erfahren; klug; schlau; verständnisvoll; wissentlich; ~ledge ['nɔlidʒ] Kenntnis(se pl.) f; Wissen n; to my ~ meines Wissens; ~n [noun] p.p. von know; come to be ~ bekannt werden; make ~ bekanntmachen.

knuckle ['nʌkl] 1. Knöchel m; 2. ~ down, under nachgeben.

Kremlin ['kremlin] der Kremı.

Ku-Klux-Klan Am. ['kju:klʌks-'klæn] Geheimbund in den USA.

L

label ['leibl] 1. Zettel m, Etikett n; Aufschrift f; Schildchen n; Bezeichnung f; 2. etikettieren, beschriften; fig. abstempeln (as als).

laboratory [lə'bɔrətəri] Laboratorium n; ~ assistant Laborant(in).

laborious [lə'bɔːriəs] mühsam; arbeitsam; schwerfällig (Stil).

labo(u)r ['leibə] 1. Arbeit f; Mühe

f; (Geburts)Wehen f/pl.; Arbeiter m/pl.; Ministry of 2 Arbeitsministerium n; hard ~ Zwangsarbeit f; 2. Arbeiter...; Arbeits...; 3. v/i. arbeiten; sich abmühen; ~ under leiden unter (dat.), zu kämpfen haben mit; v/t. ausarbeiten; ~ed schwerfällig (Stil); mühsam (Atem etc.); ~er [~ərə] ungelernter Arbeiter; 2 Exchange Arbeitsamt n; Labour

Party *pol.* Labour Party *f;* **labor union** *Am.* Gewerkschaft *f.*

lace [leis] **1.** Spitze *f;* Borte *f;* Schnur *f;* **2.** (zu)schnüren; mit Spitze *etc.* besetzen; *Schnur* durch-, einziehen; ~ (*into*) *s.o.* j-n verprügeln.

lacerate ['læsəreit] zerreißen; *fig.* quälen.

lack [læk] **1.** Fehlen *n,* Mangel *m;* **2.** *v/t.* ermangeln (*gen.*); he ~s money es fehlt ihm an Geld; *v/i.* be ~ing fehlen, mangeln; ~lustre ['lækləstə] glanzlos, matt.

laconic [lə'kɔnik] (~ally) lakonisch, wortkarg, kurz und prägnant.

lacquer ['lækə] **1.** Lack *m;* **2.** lakkieren.

lad [læd] Bursche *m,* Junge *m.*

ladder ['lædə] Leiter *f;* Laufmasche *f;* ~proof maschenfest (*Strumpf etc.*).

laden ['leidn] beladen.

lading ['leidiŋ] Ladung *f,* Fracht *f.*

ladle ['leidl] **1.** Schöpflöffel *m,* Kelle *f;* **2.** ~ out *Suppe* austeilen.

lady ['leidi] Dame *f;* Lady *f;* Herrin *f;* ~ doctor Ärztin *f;* ~bird Marienkäfer *m;* ~like damenhaft; ~love Geliebte *f;* ~ship [~ʃip]: her ~ die gnädige Frau; *Your* ♀ gnädige Frau, Euer Gnaden.

lag [læg] **1.** zögern; *a.* ~ behind zurückbleiben; **2.** Verzögerung *f.*

lager (beer) ['lɑːɡə(biə)] Lagerbier *n.*

laggard ['lægəd] Nachzügler *m.*

lagoon [lə'ɡuːn] Lagune *f.*

laid [leid] *pret. u. p.p. von lay[2];* ~ up bettlägerig (*with* mit, wegen).

lain [lein] *p.p. von lie[2] 2.*

lair [lɛə] Lager *n* e-s *wilden Tieres.*

laity ['leiiti] Laien *m/pl.*

lake [leik] See *m;* rote Pigmentfarbe.

lamb [læm] **1.** Lamm *n;* **2.** lammen.

lambent ['læmbənt] leckend; züngelnd (*Flamme*); funkelnd.

lamb|kin ['læmkin] Lämmchen *n;* ~like lammfromm.

lame [leim] **1.** □ lahm (*a. fig.* = mangelhaft); **2.** lähmen.

lament [lə'ment] **1.** Wehklage *f;* **2.** (be)klagen; trauern; ~able □ ['læməntəbl] beklagenswert; kläglich; ~ation [læmən'teiʃən] Wehklage *f.*

lamp [læmp] Lampe *f; fig.* Leuchte *f.*

lampoon [læm'puːn] **1.** Schmähschrift *f;* **2.** schmähen.

lamp-post ['læmppoust] Laternenpfahl *m.*

lampshade ['læmpʃeid] Lampenschirm *m.*

lance [lɑːns] **1.** Lanze *f;* Speer *m;* **2.** ✄ aufschneiden; ~corporal ✖ ['lɑːns'kɔːpərəl] Gefreite(r) *m.*

land [lænd] **1.** Land *n;* Grundstück *n;* *by* ~ auf dem Landweg; ~s *pl.*

Ländereien *f/pl.;* **2.** landen; ⚓ löschen; *Preis* gewinnen; ~agent ['lændeidʒənt] Grundstücksmakler *m;* Gutsverwalter *m;* ~ed grundbesitzend; Land..., Grund...; ~holder Grundbesitzer(in).

landing ['lændiŋ] Landung *f;* Treppenabsatz *m;* Anlegestelle *f;* ~field ✠ Landebahn *f;* ~gear Fahrgestell *n;* ~stage Landungsbrücke *f.*

land|lady ['lænleidi] Vermieterin *f,* Wirtin *f;* ~lord [~lɔːd] Vermieter *m;* Wirt *m;* Haus-, Grundbesitzer *m;* ~lubber ⚓ *contp.* Landratte *f;* ~mark Grenz-, Markstein *m* (*a. fig.*); Wahrzeichen *n;* ~owner Grundbesitzer(in); ~scape ['lænskeip] Landschaft *f;* ~slide Erdrutsch *m* (*a. pol.*); *a Democratic* ~ ein Erdrutsch zugunsten der Demokraten; ~slip *konkr.* Erdrutsch *m.*

lane [lein] Feldweg *m;* Gasse *f;* Spalier *n; mot.* Fahrbahn *f,* Spur *f.*

language ['læŋgwidʒ] Sprache *f;* *strong* ~ Kraftausdrücke *m/pl.*

languid □ ['læŋgwid] matt; träg.

languish ['læŋgwiʃ] matt werden; schmachten; dahinsiechen.

languor ['læŋgə] Mattigkeit *f;* Schmachten *n;* Stille *f.*

lank [læŋk] schmächtig, dünn; schlicht; ~y □ ['læŋki] schlaksig.

lantern ['læntən] Laterne *f;* ~slide Dia(positiv) *n,* Lichtbild *n.*

lap [læp] **1.** Schoß *m;* ⊕ Vorstoß *m;* Runde *f;* **2.** über-ea.-legen; (ein-) hüllen; (auf)lecken; schlürfen; plätschern (gegen) (*Wellen*).

lapel [lə'pel] Aufschlag *m am Rock.*

lapse [læps] **1.** Verlauf *m der Zeit;* Verfallen *n;* Versehen *n;* **2.** (ver-) fallen; verfließen; fehlen.

larceny 🎗 ['lɑːsni] Diebstahl *m.*

larch ♦ [lɑːtʃ] Lärche *f.*

lard [lɑːd] **1.** (Schweine)Schmalz *n;* **2.** spicken (*a. fig.*); ~er ['lɑːdə] Speisekammer *f.*

large □ [lɑːdʒ] groß; weit; reichlich; weitherzig; flott; Groß...; *at* ~ auf freiem Fuß; ausführlich; als Ganzes; ~ly ['lɑːdʒli] zum großen Teil, weitgehend; ~minded weitherzig; ~ness ['lɑːdʒnis] Größe *f;* Weite *f;* ~sized groß(formatig).

lariat *Am.* ['læriət] Lasso *n, m.*

lark [lɑːk] *orn.* Lerche *f; fig.* Streich *m.*

larkspur ♦ ['lɑːkspəː] Rittersporn *m.*

larva *zo.* ['lɑːvə] Larve *f,* Puppe *f.*

larynx *anat.* ['læriŋks] Kehlkopf *m.*

lascivious □ [lə'siviəs] lüstern.

lash [læʃ] **1.** Peitsche(nschnur) *f;* Hieb *m;* Wimper *f;* **2.** peitschen; *fig.* geißeln; schlagen; anbinden.

lass, ~ie [læs, 'læsi] Mädchen *n.*

lassitude ['læsitjuːd] Mattigkeit *f,* Abgespanntheit *f;* Desinteresse *n.*

last[1] [lɑ:st] **1.** *adj.* letzt; vorig; äußerst; geringst; ~ *but one* vorletzt; ~ *night* gestern abend; **2.** Letzte(r *m*, -s *n*) *f*; Ende *n*; *at* ~ zuletzt, endlich; **3.** *adv.* zuletzt; ~, *but not least* nicht zuletzt.

last[2] [~] dauern; halten (*Farbe*); ausreichen; ausdauern.

last[3] [~] (Schuhmacher)Leisten *m*.

lasting □ ['lɑ:stiŋ] dauerhaft; beständig.

lastly ['lɑ:stli] zuletzt, schließlich.

latch [lætʃ] **1.** Klinke *f*, Drücker *m*; Druckschloß *n*; **2.** ein-, zuklinken.

late [leit] spät; (kürzlich) verstorben; ehemalig; jüngst; *at* (*the*) ~*st* spätestens; *as* ~ *as* noch (in *dat.*); *of* ~ letzthin; ~*r on* später; *be* ~ (zu) spät kommen; ~*ly* ['leitli] kürzlich.

latent ['leitənt] verborgen, latent; gebunden (*Wärme etc.*).

lateral □ ['lætərəl] seitlich; Seiten...

lath [lɑ:θ] **1.** Latte *f*; **2.** belatten.

lathe ⊕ [leið] Drehbank *f*; Lade *f*.

lather ['lɑ:ðə] **1.** (Seifen)Schaum *m*; **2.** *v/t.* einseifen; *v/i.* schäumen.

Latin ['lætin] **1.** lateinisch; **2.** Latein *n*.

latitude ['lætitju:d] Breite *f*; *fig.* Umfang *m*, Weite *f*; Spielraum *m*.

latter ['lætə] neuer; *der* (*die, das*) letztere; ~*ly* [~əli] neuerdings.

lattice ['lætis] *a.* ~*work* Gitter *n*.

laud [lɔ:d] loben, preisen; ~**able** □ ['lɔ:dəbl] lobenswert, löblich.

laugh [lɑ:f] **1.** Gelächter *n*, Lachen *n*; **2.** lachen; ~ *at j-n* auslachen; *he* ~*s best who* ~*s last* wer zuletzt lacht, lacht am besten; ~**able** □ ['lɑ:fəbl] lächerlich; ~**ter** ['lɑ:ftə] Gelächter *n*, Lachen *n*.

launch [lɔ:ntʃ] **1.** ⚓ Stapellauf *m*; Barkasse *f*; **2.** vom Stapel laufen lassen; *Boot* aussetzen; schleudern (*a. fig.*); *Schläge* versetzen; *Rakete* starten, abschießen; *fig.* in Gang bringen; ~**ing-pad** ['lɔ:ntʃiŋpæd] (Raketen)Abschußrampe *f*.

launderette [lɔ:ndə'ret] Selbstbedienungswaschsalon *m*.

laund|ress ['lɔ:ndris] Wäscherin *f*; ~**ry** [~ri] Waschanstalt *f*; Wäsche *f*.

laurel ⚘ ['lɔrəl] Lorbeer *m* (*a. fig.*).

lavatory ['lævətəri] Waschraum *m*; Toilette *f*; *public* ~ Bedürfnisanstalt *f*.

lavender ⚘ ['lævində] Lavendel *m*.

lavish ['læviʃ] **1.** □ freigebig, verschwenderisch; **2.** verschwenden.

law [lɔ:] Gesetz *n*; (Spiel)Regel *f*; Recht(swissenschaft *f*) *n*; Gericht(sverfahren) *n*; *go to* ~ vor Gericht gehen; *lay down the* ~ den Ton angeben; ~**abiding** ['lɔ:əbaidiŋ] friedlich; ~**court** Gericht(shof *m*) *n*; ~**ful** □ ['lɔ:ful] gesetzlich; gültig; ~**less** □ ['lɔ:lis] gesetzlos; ungesetzlich; zügellos.

lawn [lɔ:n] Rasen(platz) *m*; Batist *m*.

law|suit ['lɔ:sju:t] Prozeß *m*; ~**yer** ['lɔ:jə] Jurist *m*; (Rechts)Anwalt *m*.

lax □ [læks] locker; schlaff (*a. fig.*); lasch; ~**ative** ⚕ ['læksətiv] **1.** abführend; **2.** Abführmittel *n*.

lay[1] [lei] *pret. von lie*[2] **2.**

lay[2] [~] weltlich; Laien...

lay[3] [~] **1.** Lage *f*, Richtung *f*; **2.** [*irr.*] *v/t.* legen; umlegen; *Plan etc.* ersinnen; stellen, setzen; *Tisch* decken; lindern; besänftigen; auferlegen; *Summe* wetten; ~ *before s.o.* j-m vorlegen; ~ *in* einlagern, sich eindecken mit; ~ *low* niederwerfen; ~ *open* darlegen; ~ *out* auslegen; *Garten etc.* anlegen; ~ *up* *Vorräte* hinlegen, sammeln; *be laid up* ans Bett gefesselt sein; ~ *with* belegen mit; *v/i.* (*Eier*) legen; *a.* ~ *a wager* wetten.

lay-by ['leibai] Park-, Rastplatz *m* an e-r Fernstraße.

layer ['leiə] Lage *f*, Schicht *f*.

layman ['leimən] Laie *m*.

lay|off ['lei:ɔf] Arbeitsunterbrechung *f*; ~**out** Anlage *f*; Plan *m*.

lazy □ ['leizi] faul.

lead[1] [led] Blei *n*; ⚓ Lot *n*, Senkblei *n*; *typ.* Durchschuß *m*.

lead[2] [li:d] **1.** Führung *f*; Leitung *f*; Beispiel *n*; *thea.* Hauptrolle *f*; *Kartenspiel:* Vorhand *f*; ⚡ Leitung *f*; *Hunde*-Leine *f*; **2.** [*irr.*] *v/t.* (an-)führen, leiten; bewegen (*to zu*); *Karte* ausspielen; ~ *on* (ver)locken; *v/i.* vorangehen; ~ *off* den Anfang machen; ~ *up to* überleiten zu.

leaden ['ledn] bleiern (*a. fig.*); Blei...

leader ['li:də] (An)Führer(in), Leiter(in); Erste(r) *m*; Leitartikel *m*; ~**ship** [~ʃip] Führerschaft *f*.

leading ['li:diŋ] **1.** leitend; Leit...; Haupt...; **2.** Leitung *f*, Führung *f*.

leaf [li:f], *pl.* **leaves** [li:vz] Blatt *n*; *Tür*- etc. Flügel *m*; *Tisch*-Platte *f*; ~**let** ['li:flit] Blättchen *n*; Flug-, Merkblatt *n*; ~**y** ['li:fi] belaubt.

league [li:g] **1.** Liga *f* (*a. hist. u. Sport*); Bund *m*; *mst poet.* Meile *f*; **2.** (sich) verbünden.

leak [li:k] **1.** Leck *n*; **2.** leck sein; tropfen; ~ *out* durchsickern; ~**age** ['li:kidʒ] Lecken *n*; ⚓ Leckage *f*; Verlust *m* (*a. fig.*), Schwund *m*; Durchsickern *n*; ~**y** ['li:ki] leck; undicht.

lean [li:n] **1.** [*irr.*] (sich) (an)lehnen; (sich) stützen; (sich) (hin)neigen; **2.** mager; **3.** mageres Fleisch.

leant [lent] *pret. u. p.p. von lean* **1.**

leap [li:p] **1.** Sprung *m*; **2.** [*irr.*] (über)springen; ~*t* [lept] *pret. u. p.p. von leap* **2;** ~**year** ['li:pjə:] Schaltjahr *n*.

learn [lə:n] [*irr.*] lernen; erfahren, hören; ~ *from* ersehen aus; ~**ed** ['lə:nid] gelehrt; ~**er** ['lə:nə] Anfänger(in); ~ing ['lə:niŋ] Lernen n; Gelehrsamkeit f; ~t [lə:nt] pret. u. p.p. von learn.

lease [li:s] 1. Verpachtung f, Vermietung f; Pacht f, Miete f; Pacht-, Mietvertrag m; 2. (ver-)pachten, (ver)mieten.

leash [li:ʃ] 1. Koppelleine f; Koppel f (3 Hunde etc.); 2. koppeln.

least [li:st] 1. adj. kleinst, geringst; wenigst, mindest; 2. adv. a. ~ of all am wenigsten; at ~ wenigstens; 3. das Mindeste, das Wenigste; to say the ~ gelinde gesagt.

leather ['leðə] 1. Leder n (fig.Haut); 2. a. ~n ledern; Leder...

leave [li:v] 1. Erlaubnis f; a. ~ of absence Urlaub m; Abschied m; 2. [irr.] v/t. (ver)lassen; zurück-, hinterlassen; übriglassen; überlassen; ~ off aufhören (mit); Kleid ablegen; v/i. ablassen; weggehen, abreisen (for nach).

leaven ['levn] Sauerteig m; Hefe f.

leaves [li:vz] pl. von leaf; Laub n.

leavings ['li:viŋz] pl. Überbleibsel n/pl.

lecherous ['letʃərəs] wollüstig.

lecture ['lektʃə] 1. Vorlesung f, Vortrag m; Strafpredigt f; 2. v/i. Vorlesungen od. Vorträge halten; v/t. abkanzeln; ~r [~.ərə] Vortragende(r m) f; univ. Dozent(in).

led [led] pret. u. p.p. von lead² 2.

ledge [ledʒ] Leiste f; Sims m, n; Riff n.

ledger † ['ledʒə] Hauptbuch n.

leech zo. [li:tʃ] Blutegel m; fig. Schmarotzer m.

leek ♀ [li:k] Lauch m, Porree m.

leer [liə] 1. (lüsterner od. finsterer) Seitenblick m; 2. schielen (at nach).

lees [li:z] pl. Bodensatz m, Hefe f.

lee|ward ♎ ['li:wəd] leewärts; ~way ['li:wei] ♎ Abtrift f; make up ~ fig. Versäumtes nachholen.

left¹ [left] pret. u. p.p. von leave 2.

left² [~] 1. link(s); 2. Linke f; ~handed ['left'hændid] linkshändig; linkisch.

left|-luggage office ['left'lʌgidʒ-ɔfis] Gepäckaufbewahrung(sstelle) f; ~overs pl Speisereste m/pl.

leg [leg] Bein n; Keule f; (Stiefel-)Schaft m; ⚓ Schenkel m; pull s.o.'s ~ j-n am Arm nehmen (hänseln).

legacy ['legəsi] Vermächtnis n.

legal ['li:gəl] gesetzlich; rechtsgültig; juristisch; Rechts...; ~ize [~.laiz] rechtskräftig machen; beurkunden.

legation [li'geiʃən] Gesandtschaft f.

legend ['ledʒənd] Legende f; ~ary [~.dəri] legendär, sagenhaft.

leggings ['leginz] pl. Gamaschen f/pl.

legible □ ['ledʒəbl] leserlich.

legionary ['li:dʒənəri] Legionär m.

legislat|ion [ledʒis'leiʃən] Gesetz-

gebung f; ~ive ['ledʒislətiv] gesetzgebend; ~or [~.leitə] Gesetzgeber m.

legitima|cy [li'dʒitiməsi] Rechtmäßigkeit f; ~te 1. [~.meit] legitimieren; 2. [~.mit] rechtmäßig.

leisure ['leʒə] Muße f; at your ~ wenn es Ihnen paßt; ~ly [~.əli] gemächlich.

lemon ['lemən] Zitrone f; ~ade [lemə'neid] Limonade f; ~ squash Zitronenwasser n.

lend [lend] [irr.] (ver-, aus)leihen; Hilfe leisten, gewähren.

length [leŋθ] Länge f; Strecke f; (Zeit)Dauer f; at ~ endlich, zuletzt; go all ~s aufs Ganze gehen; ~en ['leŋθən] (sich) verlängern, (sich) ausdehnen; ~wise [~.θwaiz] der Länge nach; ~y □ [~.θi] sehr lang.

lenient □ ['li:njənt] mild, nachsichtig.

lens opt. [lenz] Linse f.

lent¹ [lent] pret. u. p.p. von lend.

Lent² [~] Fasten pl., Fastenzeit f.

leopard ['lepəd] Leopard m.

lepr|osy ♎ ['leprəsi] Aussatz m, Lepra f; ~ous [~.əs] aussätzig.

less [les] 1. adj. u. adv. kleiner, geringer; weniger; 2. prp. minus.

lessen ['lesn] v/t. vermindern, schmälern; v/i. abnehmen.

lesser ['lesə] kleiner; geringer.

lesson ['lesn] Lektion f; Aufgabe f; (Unterrichts)Stunde f; Lehre f; ~s pl. Unterricht m.

lest [lest] damit nicht, daß nicht.

let [let] [irr.] lassen; vermieten, verpachten; ~ alone in Ruhe lassen; geschweige denn; ~ down j-n im Stich lassen; ~ go loslassen; ~ into einweihen in (acc.); ~ off abschießen; j-n laufen lassen; ~ out hinauslassen; ausplaudern; vermieten; ~ up aufhören.

lethal ['li:θəl] tödlich; Todes...

lethargy ['leθədʒi] Lethargie f.

letter ['letə] 1. Buchstabe m; Type f; Brief m; ~s pl. Literatur f, Wissenschaft f; attr. Brief...; to the ~ buchstäblich; 2. beschriften, betiteln; ~box Briefkasten m; ~card Kartenbrief m; ~carrier Am. Briefträger m; ~case Brieftasche f; ~cover Briefumschlag m; ~ed (literarisch) gebildet; ~file Briefordner m; ~ing [~.əriŋ] Beschriftung f; ~press Kopierpresse f.

lettuce ♀ ['letis] Lattich m, Salat m.

leuk(a)emia ♎ [lju:'ki:miə] Leukämie f.

levee¹ ['levi] Morgenempfang m.

levee² Am. [~] Uferdamm m.

level ['levl] 1. waag(e)recht; eben; gleich; ausgeglichen; my ~ best mein möglichstes; ~ crossing ♎ schienengleicher Übergang m; 2. ebene Fläche; (gleiche) Höhe, Niveau n, Stand m; fig. Maßstab m; Wasserwaage f; sea ~ Meeresspiegel m; on the ~ F offen, aufrichtig; 3. v/t. gleichmachen, ebnen; fig. anpassen; richten, zielen mit; ~ up erhöhen; v/i. ~ at, against zielen auf (acc.); ~-headed vernünftig, nüchtern.

lever ['li:və] Hebel m; Hebestange f; ~age [~ridʒ] Hebelkraft f.

levity ['leviti] Leichtfertigkeit f.

levy ['levi] 1. Erhebung f von Steuern; ⚔ Aushebung f; Aufgebot n; 2. Steuern erheben; ⚔ ausheben.

lewd ☐ [lu:d] liederlich, unzüchtig.

liability [laiə'biliti] Verantwortlichkeit f; ⚖ Haftpflicht f; Verpflichtung f; fig. Hang m; liabilities pl. Verbindlichkeiten f/pl., ✝ Passiva pl.

liable ☐ ['laiəbl] verantwortlich; haftpflichtig; verpflichtet; ausgesetzt (to dat.); be ~ to neigen zu.

liar ['laiə] Lügner(in).

libel ['laibl] 1. Schmähschrift f; Verleumdung f; 2. schmähen; verunglimpfen.

liberal ['libərəl] 1. ☐ liberal (a. pol.); freigebig; reichlich; freisinnig; 2. Liberale(r) m; ~ity [libə-'ræliti] Freigebigkeit f; Freisinnigkeit f.

liberat|e ['libəreit] befreien; freilassen; ~ion [libə'reiʃən] Befreiung f; ~or ['libəreitə] Befreier m.

libertine ['libə(:)tain] Wüstling m.

liberty ['libəti] Freiheit f; take liberties sich Freiheiten erlauben; be at ~ frei sein.

librar|ian [lai'brɛəriən] Bibliothekar(in); ~y ['laibrəri] Bibliothek f.

lice [lais] pl. von louse.

licen|ce, Am. ~se ['laisəns] 1. Lizenz f; Erlaubnis f; Konzession f; Freiheit f; Zügellosigkeit f; driving ~ Führerschein m; 2. lizenzieren, berechtigen; et. genehmigen; ~see [laisən'si:] Lizenznehmer m.

licentious ☐ [lai'senʃəs] unzüchtig; ausschweifend.

lichen ⚘, ✱ ['laikən] Flechte f.

lick [lik] 1. Lecken n; Salzlecke f; F Schlag m; 2. (be)lecken; F verdreschen; übertreffen; ~ the dust im Staub kriechen; fallen; geschlagen werden; ~ into shape zurechtstutzen.

licorice ['likəris] Lakritze f.

lid [lid] Deckel m; (Augen)Lid n.

lie¹ [lai] Lüge f; give s.o. the ~ j-n Lügen strafen; 2. lügen.

lie² [~] 1. Lage f; 2. [irr.] liegen; ~ by still-, brachliegen; ~ down sich niederlegen; ~ in wait for j-m auflauern; let sleeping dogs ~ fig. daran rühren wir lieber nicht; ~-down [lai'daun] Nickerchen n; ~-in: have a ~ sich gründlich ausschlafen.

lien ⚖ ['liən] Pfandrecht n.

lieu [lju:]: in ~ of (an)statt.

lieutenant [lef'tenənt; ⚓ le'tenənt; Am. lu:'tenənt] Leutnant m; Statthalter m; ~-commander ⚓ Korvettenkapitän m.

life [laif], pl. lives [laivz] Leben n; Menschenleben n; Lebensbeschreibung f; for ~ auf Lebenszeit; for one's ~, for dear ~ ums (liebe) Leben; to the ~ naturgetreu; ~ sentence lebenslängliche Zuchthausstrafe; ~ assurance Lebensversicherung f; ~belt ['laifbelt] Rettungsgürtel m; ~boat Rettungsboot n; ~-guard Leibwache f; Badewärter m am Strand; ~ insurance Lebensversicherung f; ~-jacket ⚓ Schwimmweste f; ~less ☐ ['laiflis] leblos; matt (a. fig.); ~-like lebenswahr; ~-long lebenslänglich; ~-preserver m. ['laif-prizə:və] Schwimmgürtel m; Totschläger m (Stock mit Bleikopf); ~time Lebenszeit f.

lift [lift] 1. Heben n; phys., ✈ Auftrieb m; fig. Erhebung f; Fahrstuhl m; give s.o. a ~ j-m helfen; j-n (im Auto) mitnehmen; 2. v/t. (auf)heben; erheben; beseitigen; sl. klauen, stehlen; v/i. sich heben.

ligature ['ligətʃuə] Binde f; ✱ Verband m.

light¹ [lait] 1. Licht n (a. fig.); Fenster n; Aspekt m, Gesichtspunkt m; Feuer n; Glanz m; fig. Leuchte f; ~s pl. Fähigkeiten f/pl.; will you give me a ~ darf ich Sie um Feuer bitten; put a ~ to anzünden; 2. licht, hell; blond; 3. [irr.] v/t. oft ~ up be-, erleuchten; anzünden; v/i. mst ~ up aufleuchten; ~ out Am. sl. schnell losziehen, abhauen.

light² [~] 1. adj. ☐ u. adv. leicht (a. fig.); ~ current ⚡ Schwachstrom m; make ~ of et. leicht nehmen; 2. ~ (up)on stoßen od. fallen auf (acc.), geraten an (acc.); sich niederlassen auf (dat.).

lighten ['laitn] blitzen; (sich) erhellen; leichter machen; (sich) erleichtern.

lighter ['laitə] Anzünder m; (Taschen)Feuerzeug n; ⚓ L(e)ichter m.

light|-headed ['lait'hedid] wirr im Kopf, irr; ~-hearted ☐ ['~'ha:tid] leichtherzig; fröhlich; ~house ['laithaus] Leuchtturm m.

lighting ['laitiŋ] Beleuchtung f; Anzünden n.

light|-minded ['lait'maindid] leichtsinnig; ~ness ['laitnis] Leichtigkeit f; Leichtsinn m.

lightning ['laitniŋ] Blitz m; ~ bug Am. zo. Leuchtkäfer m; ~-conductor, ~-rod ⚡ Blitzableiter m.

light-weight ['laitweit] Sport: Leichtgewicht n.

like [laik] 1. gleich; ähnlich; wie; such ~ dergleichen; feel ~ F sich aufgelegt fühlen zu *et.*; ~ *that so; what is he* ~*?* wie sieht er aus?; wie ist er?; **2.** Gleiche *m, f, n*; ~*s pl.* Neigungen *f/pl.*; *his* ~ seinesgleichen; *the* ~ der-, desgleichen; **3.** mögen, gern haben; *how do you* ~ *London?* wie gefällt Ihnen L.?; *I should* ~ *to know* ich möchte wissen.

like|lihood ['laiklihud] Wahrscheinlichkeit *f*; ~**ly** ['laikli] wahrscheinlich; geeignet; *he is* ~ *to die* er wird wahrscheinlich sterben.

like|n ['laikən] vergleichen (*to* mit); ~**ness** ['laiknis] Ähnlichkeit *f*; (Ab-) Bild *n*; Gestalt *f*; ~**wise** ['laikwaiz] gleich-, ebenfalls.

liking ['laikiŋ] (*for*) Neigung *f* (für, zu), Gefallen *n* (an *dat.*).

lilac ['lailək] **1.** lila; **2.** ♀ Flieder *m*.

lily ♀ ['lili] Lilie *f*; ~ *of the valley* Maiglöckchen *n*; ~**white** schneeweiß.

limb [lim] *Körper*-Glied *n*; Ast *m*.

limber ['limbə] **1.** biegsam, geschmeidig; **2.**: ~ *up* (sich) lockern.

lime [laim] Kalk *m*; Vogelleim *m*; ♀ Limone *f*; ♀ Linde *f*; ~**light** ['laimlait] Kalklicht *n*; *thea.* Scheinwerfer(licht *n*) *m*; *fig.* Mittelpunkt *m* des öffentlichen Interesses.

limit ['limit] **1.** Grenze *f*; *in* (*off*) ~*s* Zutritt gestattet (verboten) (*to* für); *that is the* ~*!* F das ist der Gipfel!; das ist (doch) die Höhe!; *go the* ~ *Am.* F bis zum Äußersten gehen; **2.** begrenzen; beschränken (*to* auf *acc.*); ~**ation** [limi'teiʃən] Begrenzung *f*, Beschränkung *f*; *fig.* Grenze *f*; *th* Verjährung *f*; ~**ed:** ~ (*liability*) *company* Gesellschaft *f* mit beschränkter Haftung; ~ *in time* befristet; ~**less** □ [~tlis] grenzenlos.

limp [limp] **1.** hinken; **2.** Hinken *n*; **3.** schlaff; weich.

limpid □ ['limpid] klar, durchsichtig.

line [lain] **1.** Linie *f*; Reihe *f*, Zeile *f*; Vers *m*; Strich *m*; Falte *f*; Furche *f*; (Menschen)Schlange *f*; Folge *f*; Verkehrsgesellschaft *f*; Eisenbahnlinie *f*; Strecke *f*; *tel.* Leitung *f*; Branche *f*, Fach *n*; Leine *f*, Schnur *f*; Äquator *m*; Richtung *f*; ☒ Linie(ntruppe) *f*; Front *f*; ~*s pl.* Richtlinien *f/pl.*; Grundlage *f*; ~ *of conduct* Lebensweise *f*; *hard* ~*s pl.* hartes Los, Pech *n*; *in* ~ *with* in Übereinstimmung mit; *stand in* ~ Schlange stehen; *draw the* ~ *fig.* nicht mehr mitmachen; *hold the* ~ *teleph.* am Apparat bleiben; **2.** *v/t.* liniieren; aufstellen; *Weg etc.* säumen, einfassen; *Kleid* füttern; ~ *out* entwerfen; *v/i.* ~ *up* sich auf-, anstellen.

linea|ge ['liniidʒ] Abstammung *f*; Familie *f*; Stammbaum *m*; ~**l** □ [~iəl] gerade, direkt (*Nachkomme*

etc.); ~**ment** [~əmənt] (Gesichts-) Zug *m*; ~**r** ['liniə] geradlinig.

linen ['linin] **1.** Leinen *n*, Leinwand *f*; Wäsche *f*; **2.** leinen; ~**closet**, ~**cupboard** Wäscheschrank *m*; ~**draper** [~ndreipə] Weißwarenhändler *m*, Wäschegeschäft *n*.

liner ['lainə] Linienschiff *n*, Passagierdampfer *m*; Verkehrsflugzeug *n*.

linger ['liŋgə] zögern; (ver)weilen; sich aufhalten; sich hinziehen; dahinsiechen; ~ *at*, ~ *about* sich herumdrücken an *od.* bei (*dat.*).

lingerie ['lɛ̃:nʒəri:] Damenunterwäsche *f*. [Einreibemittel *n.*\]

liniment ☾ ['linimənt] Liniment *n,*\]

lining ['lainiŋ] *Kleider- etc.* Futter *n*; Besatz *m*; ⊕ Verkleidung *f*.

link [liŋk] **1.** *Ketten*-Glied *n*, Gelenk *n*, Manschettenknopf *m*; *fig.* Bindeglied *n*; **2.** (sich) verbinden.

links [liŋks] *pl.* Dünen *f/pl.*; *a. golf*-~ Golf(spiel)platz *m*.

linseed ['linsi:d] Leinsame(n) *m*; ~ *oil* Leinöl *n*.

lion ['laiən] Löwe *m*; *fig.* Größe *f*, Berühmtheit *f*; ~**ess** [~nis] Löwin *f*.

lip [lip] Lippe *f*; Rand *m*; *sl.* Unverschämtheit *f*; ~**stick** ['lipstik] Lippenstift *m*.

liquefy ['likwifai] schmelzen.

liquid ['likwid] **1.** flüssig; † liquid; klar (*Luft etc.*); **2.** Flüssigkeit *f*.

liquidat|e ['likwideit] † liquidieren; bezahlen; ~**ion** [likwi'deiʃən] Abwicklung *f*, Liquidation *f*.

liquor ['likə] Flüssigkeit *f*; Alkohol *m*, alkoholisches Getränk.

liquorice ['likəris] Lakritze *f*.

lisp [lisp] **1.** Lispeln *n*; **2.** lispeln.

list [list] **1.** Liste *f*, Verzeichnis *n*; Leiste *f*; Webkante *f*; **2.** (*in e-e* Liste) eintragen; verzeichnen.

listen ['lisn] (*to*) lauschen, horchen (auf *acc.*); anhören (*acc.*), zuhören (*dat.*); hören (auf *acc.*); ~ *in teleph.*, *Radio* (mit)hören (*to acc.*); ~**er** [~nə] Zuhörer(in); *a.* ~*in* (Rundfunk)Hörer(in).

listless □ ['listlis] gleichgültig; lustlos.

lists [lists] *pl.* Schranken *f/pl.*

lit [lit] *pret. u. p.p. von light*[1] 3.

literal □ ['litərəl] buchstäblich; am Buchstaben klebend; wörtlich.

litera|ry □ ['litərəri] literarisch; *Literatur...*; *Schrift...*; ~**ture** [~ritʃə] Literatur *f*.

lithe [laið] geschmeidig, wendig.

lithography [li'θɔgrəfi] Lithographie *f*, Steindruck *m*.

litigation [liti'geiʃən] Prozeß *m*.

lit|re, *Am. -er* ['li:tə] Liter *n, m*.

litter ['litə] **1.** Sänfte *f*; Tragbahre *f*; Streu *f*; Abfall *m*; Unordnung *f*; Wurf *m junger Tiere*; **2.** ~ *down* mit Streu versehen; ~ *up* in Unordnung bringen; *Junge* werfen; ~**basket**, ~**bin** Abfallkorb *m*.

little ['litl] **1.** adj. klein; gering(fügig); wenig; a ~ one ein Kleines (Kind); **2.** adv. wenig; **3.** Kleinigkeit f; a ~ ein bißchen; ~ by ~ nach und nach; not a ~ nicht wenig.

live 1. [liv] allg. leben; wohnen; ~ to see erleben; ~ s.th. down el. durch guten Lebenswandel vergessen machen; ~ through durchmachen, durchstehen, überleben; ~ up to s-m Ruf gerecht werden, s-n Grundsätzen gemäß leben; Versprechen halten; **2.** [laiv] lebendig; richtig; aktuell; glühend; ✗ scharf (Munition); ⚡ stromführend; Radio Direkt..., Original...; ~lihood ['laivlihud] Unterhalt m; ~liness [~inis] Lebhaftigkeit f; ~ly ['laivli] lebhaft; lebendig; aufregend; schnell; bewegt.

liver anat. ['livə] Leber f.

livery ['livəri] Livree f; (Amts-) Tracht f; at ~ in Futter (stehen etc.).

live|s [laivz] pl. von life; ~-stock ['laivstɔk] Vieh(bestand m) n.

livid ['livid] bläulich; fahl; F wild.

living ['liviŋ] **1.** ~ lebend(ig); the ~ image of das genaue Ebenbild gen.; **2.** Leben n; Lebensweise f; Lebensunterhalt m; eccl. Pfründe f; ~-room Wohnzimmer n.

lizard zo. ['lizəd] Eidechse f.

load [loud] **1.** Last f; Ladung f; **2.** (be)laden; fig. überhäufen; überladen; ~ing ['loudiŋ] Laden n; Ladung f, Fracht f; attr. Lade...

loaf [louf] **1.** pl. **loaves** [louvz] Brot-Laib m; (Zucker)Hut m; **2.** herumlungern.

loafer ['loufə] Bummler m.

loam [loum] Lehm m, Ackerkrume f.

loan [loun] **1.** Anleihe f, Darlehen n; Leihen n; Leihgabe f; on ~ leihweise; **2.** bsd. Am. ausleihen.

loath □ [louθ] abgeneigt; ~e [louð] sich ekeln vor (dat.); verabscheuen; ~ing ['louðiŋ] Ekel m; ~some □ ['louðsəm] ekelhaft; verhaßt.

loaves [louvz] pl. von loaf 1.

lobby ['lɔbi] **1.** Vorhalle f; parl. Wandelgang m; thea. Foyer n; **2.** parl. s-n Einfluß geltend machen.

lobe anat., ⚘ [loub] Lappen m.

lobster ['lɔbstə] Hummer m.

local □ ['loukəl] **1.** örtlich, Orts...; lokal; ~ government Gemeindeverwaltung f; **2.** Zeitung Lokalnachricht f; 🚃 a. ~ train Vorortzug m; F Wirtshaus n (am Ort); ~ity [lou'kæliti] Örtlichkeit f; Lage f; ~ize ['loukəlaiz] lokalisieren.

locat|e [lou'keit] v/t. versetzen, verlegen, unterbringen; ausfindig machen; Am. an-, festlegen; be ~d gelegen sein; wohnen; v/i. sich niederlassen; ~ion [~ʃən] Lage f; Niederlassung f; Am. Anweisung f von Land; angewiesenes Land; Ort

m; Film: Gelände n für Außenaufnahmen.

loch schott. [lɔk] See m; Bucht f.

lock [lɔk] **1.** Tür-, Gewehr- etc. Schloß n; Schleuse(nkammer) f; ⊕ Sperrvorrichtung f; Stauung f; Locke f; Wollflocke f; **2.** (ver-) schließen (a. fig.), absperren; sich verschließen lassen; ⊕ blockieren, sperren, greifen; umschließen; ~ s.o. in j-n einsperren; ~ up weg-schließen; abschließen; einsperren; Geld fest anlegen.

lock|er ['lɔkə] Schrank m, Kasten m; ~et ['lɔkit] Medaillon n; ~-out Aussperrung f von Arbeitern; ~smith Schlosser m; ~-up **1.** Haftzelle f; ✝ zinslose Kapitalanlage; **2.** verschließbar.

loco Am. sl. ['loukou] verrückt.

locomot|ion [loukə'mouʃən] Fortbewegung(sfähigkeit) f; ~ive ['loukəmoutiv] **1.** sich fortbewegend; beweglich; **2.** a. ~ engine Lokomotive f.

locust ['loukəst] zo. Heuschrecke f; ⚘ unechte Akazie.

lode|star ['loudsta:] Leitstern m (a. fig.); ~stone Magnet(eisenstein) m.

lodg|e [lɔdʒ] **1.** Häus-chen n; (Forst-, Park-, Pförtner)Haus n; Portierloge f; Freimaurer-Loge f; **2.** v/t. beherbergen, aufnehmen; Geld hinterlegen; Klage einreichen; Hieb versetzen; v/i. (bsd. zur Miete) wohnen; logieren; ~er ['lɔdʒə] (Unter)Mieter(in); ~ing ['lɔdʒiŋ] Unterkunft f; ~s pl. möbliertes Zimmer; Wohnung f.

loft [lɔft] (Dach)Boden m; Empore f; ~y □ ['lɔfti] hoch; erhaben; stolz.

log [lɔg] Klotz m; Block m; gefällter Baumstamm; ⚓ Log n; ~-cabin ['lɔgkæbin] Blockhaus n; ~-gerhead ['lɔgəhed]: be at ~s sich in den Haaren liegen; ~-house, ~-hut Blockhaus m.

logic ['lɔdʒik] Logik f; ~al □ [~kəl] logisch.

logroll bsd. Am. pol. ['lɔgroul] (sich gegenseitig) in die Hände arbeiten.

loin [lɔin] Lende(nstück n) f.

loiter ['lɔitə] trödeln, schlendern.

loll [lɔl] (sich) strecken; (sich) rekeln; ~ about herumlungern.

lone|liness ['lounlinis] Einsamkeit f; ~ly □ ['lounli], ~some □ ['lounsəm] einsam.

long[1] [lɔŋ] **1.** Länge f; before ~ binnen kurzem; for ~ lange; take ~ lange brauchen od. dauern; **2.** adj. lang; langfristig; langsam; in the ~ run am Ende; auf die Dauer; be ~ lange dauern od. brauchen; **3.** adv. lang(e); so ~! bis dann! (auf Wiedersehen); (no) ~er (nicht) länger od. mehr.

long² [~] sich sehnen (for nach).
long|-distance['lɔŋ'distəns]Fern...,
Weit...; ~evity [lɔn'dʒeviti] Langlebigkeit f; langes Leben; ~hand
['lɔŋhænd] Langschrift f.
longing ['lɔŋiŋ] 1. ⁊ sehnsüchtig;
2. Sehnsucht f; Verlangen n.
longitude geogr. ['lɔndʒitjuːd] Länge f.
long|-shore-man ['lɔŋʃɔːmən] Hafenarbeiterm;~-sighted['lɔŋ'saitid]
weitsichtig; ~-standing seit langer
Zeit bestehend, alt; ~-suffering 1.
langmütig; 2. Langmut f; ~-term
['lɔŋtɔːm] langfristig; ~-winded □
['lɔŋ'windid] langatmig.
look [luk] 1. Blick m; Anblick m;
oft ~s pl. Aussehen n; have a ~ at
s.th. sich et. ansehen; I don't like
the ~ of it es gefällt mir nicht; 2. v/i.
sehen, blicken (at, on auf acc.,
nach); zusehen, daß od. wie...; nachsehen, wer etc. ...; krank etc. aussehen; nach e-r Richtung sehen;
~ after sehen nach, sich kümmern
um; versorgen; nachsehen, nachblicken (dat.); ~ at ansehen; ~ for
erwarten; suchen; ~ forward to sich
freuen auf (acc.); ~ in als Besucher
hereinschauen (on bei); ~ into prüfen; erforschen; ~ on zuschauen
(dat.); betrachten (as als); liegen zu,
gehen auf (acc.) (Fenster); ~ out
vorsehen; ~ (up)on fig. ansehen (as
als); v/t. ~ disdain verächtlich
blicken; ~ over und durchsehen; j-n
mustern; ~ up et. nachschlagen.
looker-on ['lukər'ɔn] Zuschauer(in).
looking-glass ['lukiŋglɑːs] Spiegel
m.
look-out ['luk'aut] Ausguck m,
Ausblick m, Aussicht f (a. fig.);
that is my ~ F das ist meine Sache.
loom [luːm] 1. Webstuhl m; 2. undeutlich zu sehen sein, sich abzeichnen.
loop [luːp] 1. Schlinge f, Schleife f,
Öse f; 2. v/t. in Schleifen legen;
schlingen; v/i. e-e Schleife machen;
sich winden; ~hole ['luːphoul]
Guck-, Schlupfloch n; ⚔ Schießscharte f.
loose [luːs] 1. □ allg. lose, locker;
schlaff; weit; frei; un-zs.-hängend;
ungenau; liederlich; 2. lösen; aufbinden; lockern; ~n ['luːsn] (sich)
lösen, (sich) lockern.
loot [luːt] 1. plündern; 2. Beute f.
lop [lɔp] Baum beschneiden; stutzen; schlaff herunterhängen (lassen); ~-sided ['lɔp'saidid] schief,
einseitig.
loquacious □ [lou'kweiʃəs] geschwätzig.
lord [lɔːd] Herr m; Gebieter m;
Magnat m; Lord m; the ♀ der Herr
(Gott); my ~ [mi'lɔːd] Mylord,
Euer Gnaden; the ♀'s Prayer das
Vaterunser; the ♀'s Supper das

Abendmahl; ~ly ['lɔːdli] vornehm,
edel; großartig; hochmütig; ~ship
['lɔːdʃip] Lordschaft f (Titel).
lore [lɔː] Lehre f, Kunde f.
lorry ['lɔri] Last(kraft)wagen m,
LKW m; ⛟ Lore f.
lose [luːz] [irr.] v/t. verlieren; vergeuden; verpassen; abnehmen; ~
o.s. sich verirren; v/i. verlieren; ~
nachgehen (Uhr).
loss [lɔs] Verlust m; Schaden m;
at a ~ in Verlegenheit; außerstande.
lost [lɔst] pret. u. p.p. von lose; be ~
verlorengehen; verschwunden sein;
fig. versunken sein; ~-property office
Fundbüro n.
lot [lɔt] Los n (a. fig.); Anteil m;
† Partie f; Posten m; F Menge f;
Parzelle f; Am. Film Ateliergelände n; a ~ of people F eine Menge
Leute; draw ~s losen; fall to s.o.'s ~
j-m zufallen.
loth [louθ] s. loath.
lotion ['louʃən] (Haut)Wasser n.
lottery ['lɔtəri] Lotterie f.
loud [laud] laut (a. adv.); fig.
schreiend, grell; ~-speaker ['laud'spiːkə] Lautsprecher m.
lounge [laundʒ] 1. sich rekeln; faulenzen; 2. Bummel m; Wohnzimmer n, -diele f; Gesellschaftsraum
m e-s Hotels; thea. Foyer n; Chaiselongue f; ~-chair ['laundʒ'tʃɛə]
Klubsessel m; ~-suit Straßenanzug
m.
lour ['lauə] finster blicken od. aussehen; die Stirn runzeln.
louse [laus], pl. lice [lais] Laus f;
~y ['lauzi] verlaust; lausig; Lause...
lout [laut] Tölpel m, Lümmel m.
lovable □ ['lʌvəbl] liebenswürdig,
liebenswert.
love [lʌv] 1. Liebe f (of, a. for, to,
towards zu); Liebschaft f; Angebetete f; Liebling m (als Anrede);
liebe Grüße m/pl.; Sport: nichts,null;
attr. Liebes...; give od. send one's
~ to s.o. j-n freundlichst grüßen
(lassen); in ~ with verliebt in (acc.);
fall in ~ with sich verlieben in (acc.);
make ~ to werben um; 2. lieben;
gern haben; ~ to do gern tun;
~-affair ['lʌvəfɛə] Liebschaft f;
~ly ['lʌvli] lieblich; entzückend,
reizend; ~r ['lʌvə] Verehrer(in),
Liebhaber(in).
loving □ ['lʌviŋ] liebevoll.
low¹ [lou] 1. niedrig; tief; gering;
leise; fig. niedergeschlagen;
schwach; gemein; ~est bid Mindestgebot n; 2. meteor. Tief(druckgebiet) n; bsd. Am. Tiefstand m,
-punkt m.
low² [~] brüllen, muhen (Rind).
low-brow F ['loubrau] 1. geistig anspruchslos, spießig; 2. Spießer m,
Banause m.
lower¹ ['louə] 1. niedriger; tiefer;
geringer; leiser; untere(r, -s); Un-

ter...; 2. v/t. nieder-, herunterlassen; senken; erniedrigen; abschwächen; Preis etc herabsetzen; v/i. fallen, sinken.

lower[2] ['lauə] s. lour.

low|land ['louland] Tiefland n; ~liness [·loulinis] Demut f; ~ly ['louli] demütig; bescheiden; ~-necked (tief) ausgeschnitten (Kleid); ~-spirited niedergeschlagen. [Treue f.]

loyal [['lɔiəl] treu; ~ty [~lti])

lozenge ['bzindʒ] Pastille f.

lubber ['lʌbə] Tölpel m, Stoffel m.

lubric|ant ['lu:brikənt] Schmiermittel n, ~ate [~keit] schmieren; ~ation [lu:bri'keiʃən] Schmieren n, ⊕ Ölung f

lucid ['lu:sid] leuchtend, klar.

luck [lʌk] Glück(sfall m) n; Geschick n, good ~ Glück n; bad ~, hard ~, ill ~ Unglück n, Pech n; worse unglücklicherweise, ~ily ['lʌkili] glücklicherweise, zum Glück; ~y [['lʌki] glücklich; Glücks. ; be ~ Glück haben.

lucr|ative [['lu:krətiv] einträglich; ~e ['lu:kə] Gewinn(sucht f) m.

ludicrous [['lu:dikrəs] lächerlich.

lug [lʌg] zerren, schleppen.

luge [lu:ʒ] 1. Rodelschlitten m; 2. rodeln.

luggage ['lʌgidʒ] Gepäck n; ~-carrier Gepäckträger m am Fahrrad; ~-office ⑤ Gepäckschalter m; ~-rack Gepäcknetz n; ~-ticket Gepäckschein m.

lugubrious [[lu:'gju:briəs] traurig.

lukewarm ['lu:kwɔ:m] lau (a. fig.).

lull [lʌl] 1. einlullen; (sich) beruhigen; 2. (Wind)Stille f; Ruhepause f.

lullaby ['lʌləbai] Wiegenlied n.

lumbago [lʌm'beigou] Hexenschuß m

lumber ['lʌmbə] 1. Bau-, Nutzholz n; Gerümpel n; 2. v/t. a. ~ up vollstopfen; v/i rumpeln, poltern; sich (dahin)schleppen; ~er [~ərə], ~jack, ~man Holzfäller m, -arbeiter m; ~mill Sägewerk n; ~-room Rumpelkammer f; ~-yard Holzplatz m, -lager n

lumin|ary ['lu:minəri] Himmelskörper m; Leuchtkörper m; fig. Leuchte f; ~ous [['~nəs] leuchtend; Licht...; Leucht...; fig. lichtvoll.

lump [lʌmp] 1. Klumpen m; fig. Klotz m; Beule f; Stück n Zucker etc.; in the ~ in Bausch und Bogen; ~ sugar Würfelzucker m; ~ sum

Pauschalsumme f; 2. v/t. zs.-werfen, zs.-fassen; v/i. Klumpen bilden; ~ish ['lʌmpiʃ] schwerfällig; ~y [[~pi] klumpig.

lunacy ['lu:nəsi] Wahnsinn m.

lunar ['lu:nə] Mond...

lunatic ['lu:nətik] 1. irr-, wahnsinnig; 2. Irre(r m) f; Wahnsinnige(r m) f; Geistesgestörte(r m) f; ~ asylum Irrenhaus n, -anstalt f.

lunch|(eon) [lʌntʃ, 'lʌntʃən] 1. Lunch m, Mittagessen n; zweites Frühstück; 2. zu Mittag essen; j-m ein Mittagessen geben; ~-hour Mittagszeit f, -pause f.

lung anat [lʌŋ] Lunge(nflügel m) f; the ~s pl die Lunge.

lunge [lʌndʒ] 1. Fechten: Ausfall m; 2. v/i. ausfallen (at gegen); (dahin-)stürmen; v/t. stoßen.

lupin(e) ♀ ['lu:pin] Lupine f.

lurch [lə:tʃ] 1. taumeln, torkeln; 2.: leave in the ~ im Stich lassen.

lure [ljuə] 1. Köder m; fig. Lockung f; 2. ködern, (an)locken.

lurid ['ljuərid] unheimlich; erschreckend, schockierend; düster, finster.

lurk [lə:k] lauern; versteckt liegen.

luscious [['lʌʃəs] köstlich; üppig; süß(lich), widerlich.

lust [lʌst] (sinnliche) Begierde; fig. Gier f, Sucht f.

lust|re, Am. ~er ['lʌstə] Glanz m; Kronleuchter m; ~rous [[~trəs] glänzend.

lusty [['lʌsti] rüstig; fig. lebhaft, kräftig.

lute[1] ♪ [lu:t] Laute f.

lute[2] [~] 1. Kitt m; 2. (ver)kitten.

Lutheran ['lu:θərən] lutherisch.

luxate ⚕ ['lʌkseit] verrenken.

luxur|iant [lʌg'zjuəriənt] üppig; ~ious [[~iəs] luxuriös, üppig; ~y ['lʌkʃəri] Luxus m, Üppigkeit f; Luxusartikel m; Genußmittel n.

lyceum [lai'siəm] Vortragsraum m; bsd. Am. Volkshochschule f.

lye [lai] Lauge f.

lying ['laiiŋ] 1. p.pr. von lie[1] 2 u. lie[2] 2; 2. adj. lügnerisch; ~-in [~ŋ'in] Wochenbett n; ~ hospital Entbindungsheim n.

lymph ⚕ [limf] Lymphe f.

lynch [lintʃ] lynchen; ~-law ['lintʃlɔ:] Lynchjustiz f.

lynx zo. [liŋks] Luchs m.

lyric ['lirik] 1. lyrisch; 2. lyrisches Gedicht; ~s pl. (Lied)Text m (bsd. e-s Musicals); Lyrik f; ~al [[~kəl] lyrisch, gefühlvoll; schwärmerisch, begeistert.

M

ma'am [mæm] Majestät *f* (*Anrede
für die Königin*); Hoheit *f* (*Anrede
für Prinzessinnen*); F [məm] gnä'
Frau *f* (*von Dienstboten verwendete
Anrede*).

macaroni [mækə'rouni] Makkaroni
pl.

macaroon [mækə'ru:n] Makrone
f.

machin|ation [mæki'neiʃən] An-
schlag *m*; ~s *pl.* Ränke *pl.*; ~e
[mə'ʃi:n] 1. Maschine *f*; Mechanismus *m* (*a. fig.*); 2. maschinell herstellen *od.* (be)arbeiten; ~e-made
maschinell hergestellt; ~ery [~nəri]
Maschinen *f/pl.*; Maschinerie *f*;
~ist [~nist] Maschinist *m*; Ma-
schinennäherin *f.*

mackerel *ichth.* ['mækrəl] Makrele
f.

mackinow *Am.* ['mækinɔ:] Stutzer
m (*Kleidungsstück*).

mackintosh ['mækintɔʃ] Regenmantel *m.*

mad □ [mæd] wahnsinnig; toll
(-wütig); *fig.* wild; F wütend; go ~
verrückt werden; *drive* ~ verrückt
machen.

madam ['mædəm] gnädige Frau,
gnädiges Fräulein (*Anrede*).

mad|cap ['mædkæp] 1. toll; 2. Toll-
kopf *m*; Wildfang *m*; ~den ['mædn]
toll *od.* rasend machen.

made [meid] *pret. u. p.p. von
make* 1.

made-up ['meid'ʌp] zurechtgemacht; erfunden; fertig; ~ *clothes
pl.* Konfektion *f.*

mad|house ['mædhaus] Irrenhaus
n; ~man Wahnsinnige(r) *m*; ~ness
['mædnis] Wahnsinn *m*; (Toll)Wut
f.

magazine [mægə'zi:n] Magazin *n*;
(Munitions)Lager *n*; Zeitschrift *f.*

maggot *zo.* ['mægət] Made *f.*

magic ['mædʒik] 1. *a.* ~al [~kəl]
magisch; Zauber...; 2. Zauberei *f*;
fig. Zauber *m*; ~ian [me'dʒiʃən]
Zauberer *m.*

magistra|cy ['mædʒistrəsi] Rich-
teramt *n*; *die* Richter *m/pl.*; ~te
[~rit] (Polizei-, Friedens)Richter *m.*

magnanimous □ [mæg'næniməs]
großmütig.

magnet ['mægnit] Magnet *m*; ~ic
[mæg'netik] (~ally) magnetisch.

magni|ficence [mæg'nifisns] Pracht
f, Herrlichkeit *f*; ~ficent [~nt]
prächtig, herrlich; ~fy ['mægnifai]
vergrößern; ~tude [~itju:d] Größe
f, Wichtigkeit *f.*

magpie *orn.* ['mægpai] Elster *f.*

mahagony [mə'hɔgəni] Mahagoni
(-holz) *n.*

maid [meid] *lit.* Mädchen *n*;
(Dienst)Mädchen *n*; *old* ~ alte

Jungfer; ~ *of all work* Mädchen *n*
für alles; ~ *of honour* Ehren-, Hof-
dame *f.*

maiden ['meidn] 1. = *maid*;
2. jungfräulich; unverheiratet; *fig.*
Jungfern..., Erstlings...; ~ *name*
Mädchenname *m* e-r Frau; ~head
Jungfräulichkeit *f*; ~hood [~hud]
Mädchenjahre *n/pl.*; ~ly [~nli]
jungfräulich, mädchenhaft.

mail[1] [meil] (Ketten)Panzer *m.*

mail[2] [~] 1. Post(dienst *m*) *f*;
Post(sendung) *f*; 2. *Am.* mit der
Post schicken, aufgeben; ~able
Am. ['meiləb] postversandfähig;
~-bag Briefträger-, Posttasche *f*;
Postsack *m*; ~box *bsd. Am.* Briefkasten *m*; ~ carrier *Am.* Briefträger *m*; ~man *Am.* Briefträger *m*;
~-order firm, *bsd. Am.* ~-order
house (Post)Versandgeschäft *n.*

maim [meim] verstümmeln.

main [mein] 1. Haupt..., hauptsächlich; *by* ~ *force* mit voller
Kraft; 2. Hauptrohr *n*, -leitung *f*;
~s *pl.* ∮ (Strom)Netz *n*; *in the* ~ in
der Hauptsache, im wesentlichen;
~land ['meinlənd] Festland *n*; ~ly
[~li] hauptsächlich; ~spring Uhr-
feder *f*, *fig.* Haupttriebfeder *f*;
~stay *♣* Großstag *n*; *fig.* Haupt-
stütze *f* ♀ **Street** *Am.* Hauptstraße
f; ♂ **Streeter** *Am.* Kleinstadt-
bewohner *m.*

maintain [mən'tein] (aufrecht)er-
halten; beibehalten; (unter)stützen;
unterhalten; behaupten.

maintenance ['meintinəns] Erhal-
tung *f*; Unterhalt *m*; ⊕ Wartung *f.*

maize *♀* [meiz] Mais *m.*

majest|ic [mə'dʒestik] (~ally) ma-
jestätisch; ~y ['mædʒisti] Majestät
f; Würde *f*, Hoheit *f.*

major ['meidʒə] 1. größer; wich-
tig(er); mündig; *♪* Dur *n*; ~ *key*
Dur-Tonart *f*; ~ *league Am. Baseball:* Oberliga *f*; 2. ⚔ Major *m*;
Mündige(r *m*) *f*; *Am. univ.* Haupt-
fach *n*; ~general ⚔ Generalmajor
m; ~ity [mə'dʒɔriti] Mehrheit *f*;
Mündigkeit *f*; Majorsrang *m.*

make [meik] 1. [*irr.*] *v/t. allg.* machen; verfertigen, fabrizieren; bilden; (aus)machen; ergeben; (veran)lassen; gewinnen, verdienen;
sich erweisen als, abgeben; *Regel
etc.* aufstellen; *Frieden etc.* schließen; *e-e Rede* halten; ~ *good* wieder
gutmachen; wahr machen; *do you* ~
one of us? machen Sie mit?; ~ *port
♣* den Hafen anlaufen; ~ *way* vorwärtskommen; ~ *into* verarbeiten
zu; ~ *out* ausfindig machen; erkennen; verstehen; entziffern; *Rechnung etc.* ausstellen; ~ *over* übertragen; ~ *up* ergänzen; vervoll-

ständigen; zs.-stellen; bilden, aus-machen; *Streit* beilegen; zurecht-machen, schminken; = ~ *up for (v/i.)*; ~ *up one's mind* sich ent-schließen; *v/i.* sich begeben; gehen; ~ *away with* beseitigen; *Geld* vertun; ~ *for* zugehen auf *(acc.)*; sich aufmachen nach; ~ *off* sich fortmachen; ~ *up* sich zurecht-machen; sich schminken; ~ *up for* nach-, aufholen; für *et.* entschädi-gen; **2.** Mach-, Bauart *f*; Bau *m des Körpers*; Form *f*; Fabrikat *n*, Er-zeugnis *n*; ~**believe** ['meikbili:v] Schein *m*, Vorwand *m*, Verstellung *f*; ~**r** ['meikə] Hersteller *m*; 2̃ Schöpfer *m (Gott)*; ~**shift 1.** Not-behelf *m*; **2.** behelfsmäßig; ~**up** *typ.* Umbruch *m*; *fig.* Charakter *m*; Schminke *f*, Make-up *n*.

maladjustment ['mælə'dʒʌstmənt] mangelhafte Anpassung.

maladministration ['mælədmi-nis'treiʃən] schlechte Verwaltung.

malady ['mælədi] Krankheit *f*.

malcontent ['mælkəntent] **1.** un-zufrieden; **2.** Unzufriedene(r) *m*.

male [meil] **1.** männlich; **2.** Mann *m*; *zo.* Männchen *n*.

malediction [mæli'dikʃən] Fluch *m*.

malefactor ['mælifæktə] Übeltäter *m*.

malevolen|ce [mə'levələns] Bös-willigkeit *f*; ~**t** □ [~nt] böswillig.

malice ['mælis] Bosheit *f*; Groll *m*.

malicious □ [mə'liʃəs] boshaft; böswillig; ~**ness** [~snis] Bosheit *f*.

malign [mə'lain] **1.** □ schädlich; **2.** verleumden; ~**ant** □ [mə-'lignənt] böswillig; ☞ bösartig; ~**ity** [~niti] Bosheit *f*; Schaden-freude *f*; *bsd.* ☞ Bösartigkeit *f*.

malleable ['mæliəbl] hämmerbar; *fig.* geschmeidig.

mallet ['mælit] Schlegel *m*.

malnutrition ['mælnju(:)'triʃən] Unterernährung *f*.

malodorous □ [mæ'loudərəs] übel-riechend.

malpractice ['mæl'præktis] Übel-tat *f*; ☞ falsche Behandlung.

malt [mɔ:lt] Malz *n*.

maltreat [mæl'tri:t] schlecht be-handeln; mißhandeln.

mam(m)a [mə'mɑ:] Mama *f*.

mammal ['mæməl] Säugetier *n*.

mammoth ['mæməθ] riesig.

mammy F ['mæmi] Mami *f*; *Am.* farbiges Kindermädchen.

man [mæn, *in Zssgn* ...mən] **1.** *pl.* **men** [men] Mann *m*; Mensch(en *pl.*) *m*; Menschheit *f*; Diener *m*; *Schach:* Figur *f*; Damestein *m*; **2.** männlich; **3.** ⚔, ☞ bemannen; ~ *o.s.* sich ermannen.

manage ['mænidʒ] *v/t.* handhaben; verwalten, leiten; *Menschen, Tiere* lenken; mit *j-m* fertig werden; *et.*

fertigbringen; ~ *to inf.* es fertig-bringen, zu *inf.*; *v/i.* die Aufsicht haben, die Geschäfte führen; aus-kommen; F es schaffen; ~**able** □ [~dʒəbl] handlich; lenksam; ~**ment** [~dʒmənt] Verwaltung *f*, Leitung *f*, Direktion *f*, Geschäftsführung *f*; geschickte Behandlung; ~**r** [~dʒə] Leiter *m*, Direktor *m*; Regisseur *m*; Manager *m*; ~**ress** [~əres] Leiterin *f*, Direktorin *f*.

managing ['mænidʒiŋ] geschäfts-führend; *Betriebs*...; ~ *clerk* Ge-schäftsführer *m*, Prokurist *m*.

mandat|e ['mændeit] Mandat *n*; Befehl *m*; Auftrag *m*; Vollmacht *f*; ~**ory** [~dətəri] befehlend.

mane [mein] Mähne *f*.

maneuver [mə'nu:və] = ma-noeuvre.

manful □ ['mænful] mannhaft.

mange *vet.* [meindʒ] Räude *f*.

manger ['meindʒə] Krippe *f*.

mangle ['mæŋgl] **1.** Wringmaschine *f*; Wäschemangel *f*; **2.** mangeln; wringen; zerstückeln; *fig.* ver-stümmeln.

mangy ['meindʒi] räudig; *fig.* schäbig.

manhood ['mænhud] Mannesalter *n*; Männlichkeit *f*; die Männer *m/pl.*

mania ['meinjə] Wahnsinn *m*; Sucht *f*, Manie *f*; ~**c** ['meiniæk] **1.** Wahnsinnige(r *m*) *f*; **2.** wahnsin-nig.

manicure ['mænikjuə] **1.** Maniküre *f*; **2.** maniküren.

manifest ['mænifest] **1.** □ offenbar; **2.** ⚓ Ladungsverzeichnis *n*; **3.** *v/t.* offenbaren; kundtun; ~**ation** [mænifes'teiʃən] Offenbarung *f*; Kundgebung *f*; ~**o** [mæni'festou] Manifest *n*.

manifold □ ['mænifould] **1.** man-nigfaltig; **2.** vervielfältigen.

manipulat|e [mə'nipjuleit] (ge-schickt) handhaben; ~**ion** [mənipju'leiʃən] Handhabung *f*, Behand-lung *f*, Verfahren *n*; Kniff *m*.

man|kind [mæn'kaind] die Mensch-heit; ['mænkaind] die Männer *pl.*; ~**ly** ['mænli] männlich; mannhaft.

manner ['mænə] Art *f*, Weise *f*; Stil(art *f*) *m*; Manier *f*; ~**s** *pl.* Ma-nieren *f/pl.*, Sitten *f/pl.*; *in a* ~ gewissermaßen; ~**ed** [~əd] ...gear-tet; gekünstelt; ~**ly** [~əli] manier-lich, gesittet.

manoeuvre, *Am. a.* **maneuver** [mə'nu:və] **1.** Manöver *n* (*a. fig.*); **2.** manövrieren (lassen).

man-of-war ⚓ ['mænəv'wɔ:] Kriegsschiff *n*.

manor ['mænə] Rittergut *n*; *lord of the* ~ Gutsherr *m*; ~**house** Herr-schaftshaus *n*, Herrensitz *m*; Schloß *n*.

manpower ['mænpauə] Men-schenpotential *n*; Arbeitskräfte *f/pl.*

man-servant ['mænsə:vənt] Diener *m*.

mansion ['mænʃən] (herrschaftliches) Wohnhaus.

manslaughter ½ ['mænslɔ:tə] Totschlag *m*, fahrlässige Tötung.

mantel|piece ['mæntlpi:s], **~shelf** Kaminsims *m*, -platte *f*.

mantle ['mæntl] 1. Mantel *m*; *fig.* Hülle *f*; Glühstrumpf *m*; 2. *v/t.* verhüllen; *v/i.* sich röten (*Gesicht*).

manual ['mænjuəl] 1. Hand...; mit der Hand (gemacht); 2. Handbuch *n*. [brik *f*.]

manufactory [mænju'fæktəri] Fa-)

manufactur|e [mænju'fæktʃə] 1. Fabrikation *f*; Fabrikat *n*; 2. fabrizieren; verarbeiten; **~er** [~ərə] Fabrikant *m*; **~ing** [~riŋ] Fabrik...; Gewerbe...; Industrie...

manure [mə'njuə] 1. Dünger *m*; 2. düngen.

manuscript ['mænjuskript] Manuskript *n*; Handschrift *f*.

many ['meni] 1. viele; **~ a** manche(r, -s); *be one too ~ for s.o.* j-m überlegen sein; 2. Menge *f*; *a good ~*, *a great ~* ziemlich viele, sehr viele.

map [mæp] 1. (Land)Karte *f*; 2. aufzeichnen; **~ out** planen; einteilen.

maple ♀ ['meipl] Ahorn *m*.

mar [ma:] schädigen; verderben.

maraud [mə'rɔ:d] plündern.

marble ['ma:bl] 1. Marmor *m*; Murmel *f*; 2. marmorn.

March¹ [ma:tʃ] März *m*.

march² [~] 1. Marsch *m*; Fortschritt *m*; Gang *m der Ereignisse etc.*; 2. marschieren (lassen); *fig.* vorwärtsschreiten.

marchioness ['ma:ʃənis] Marquise *f*.

mare [mɛə] Stute *f*; **~'s nest** *fig.* Schwindel *m*; (Zeitungs)Ente *f*.

marg|arine [ma:dʒə'ri:n], *a.* **~e** F [ma:dʒ] Margarine *f*.

margin ['ma:dʒin] Rand *m*; Grenze *f*; Spielraum *m*; Verdienst-, Gewinn-, Handelsspanne *f*; **~al** [~nl] am Rande (befindlich); Rand...; **~ note** Randbemerkung *f*.

marine [mə'ri:n] Marineinfanterist *m*; Marine *f*; *paint.* Seestück *n*; *attr.* See...; Marine...; Schiffs...; **~r** ['mærinə] Seemann *m*.

marital ['mæritl] ehelich, Ehe...

maritime ['mæritaim] an der See liegend *od.* lebend; See...; Küsten-...; Schiffahrt(s)...

mark¹ [ma:k] Mark *f* (*Geldstück*).

mark² [~] 1. Marke *f*, Merkmal *n*, Zeichen *n*; ✝ Preiszettel *m*; Fabrik-, Schutzmarke *f*; (Körper)Mal *n*; Norm *f*; *Schule:* Zensur *f*, Note *f*, Punkt *m*; *Sport:* Startlinie *f*; Ziel *n*; *a man of ~* ein Mann von Bedeutung; *fig. up to the ~* auf der Höhe; *beside the ~*, *wide of the ~* den Kern der Sache verfehlend; unrichtig; 2. *v/t.* (be)zeichnen, markieren; *Sport:* anschreiben; kennzeichnen; be(ob)achten; sich *et.* merken; **~ off** abtrennen; **~ out** bezeichnen; abstecken; **~ time** auf der Stelle treten; *v/i.* achtgeben; **~ed**] auffallend; merklich; ausgeprägt.

market ['ma:kit] 1. Markt(platz) *m*; Handel *m*; ✝ Absatz *m*; *in the ~* auf dem Markt; *play the ~* an der Börse spekulieren; 2. *v/t.* auf den Markt bringen, verkaufen; *v/i.* einkaufen gehen; **~able** □ [~təbl] marktfähig, -gängig; **~ing** [~tiŋ] ✝ Marketing *n*, Absatzpolitik *f*; Marktbesuch *m*.

marksman ['ma:ksmən] (guter) Schütze.

marmalade ['ma:məleid] Orangenmarmelade *f*.

maroon [mə'ru:n] 1. kastanienbraun; 2. *auf e-r einsamen Insel* aussetzen; 3. Leuchtrakete *f*.

marquee [ma:'ki] (großes) Zelt.

marquis ['ma:kwis] Marquis *m*.

marriage ['mærid3] Heirat *f*, Ehe (*-stand m*) *f*; Hochzeit *f*; *civil ~* standesamtliche Trauung; **~able** [~dʒəbl] heiratsfähig; **~ articles** *pl.* Ehevertrag *m*; **~ lines** *pl.* Trauschein *m*; **~ portion** Mitgift *f*.

married ['mærid] verheiratet; ehelich; Ehe...; **~ couple** Ehepaar *n*.

marrow ['mærou] Mark *n*; *fig.* Kern *m*, Beste(s) *n*; **~y** [~oui] markig.

marry ['mæri] *v/t.* (ver)heiraten; *eccl.* trauen; *v/i.* (sich ver)heiraten.

marsh [ma:ʃ] Sumpf *m*, Morast *m*.

marshal ['ma:ʃəl] 1. Marschall *m*; *hist.* Hofmarschall *m*; Zeremonienmeister *m*; *Am.* Bezirkspolizeichef *m*; Leiter *m* der Feuerwehr; 2. ordnen; führen; zs.-stellen.

marshy ['ma:ʃi] sumpfig.

mart [ma:t] Markt *m*; Auktionsraum *m*.

marten zo. ['ma:tin] Marder *m*.

martial □ ['ma:ʃəl] kriegerisch; Kriegs...; **~ law** Stand-, Kriegsrecht *n*.

martyr ['ma:tə] 1. Märtyrer(in) (*to gen.*); 2. (zu Tode) martern.

marvel ['ma:vel] 1. Wunder *n*; 2. sich wundern; **~lous**] ['ma:viləs] wunderbar, erstaunlich.

mascot ['mæskət] Maskottchen *n*.

masculine ['ma:skjulin] männlich.

mash [mæʃ] 1. Gemisch *n*; Maische *f*; Mengfutter *n*; 2. mischen; zerdrücken; (ein)maischen; **~ed** potatoes *pl.* Kartoffelbrei *m*.

mask [ma:sk] 1. Maske *f*; 2. maskieren; *fig.* verbergen; tarnen; **~ed** *ball* Maskenball *m*.

mason ['meisn] Steinmetz *m*; Maurer *m*; Freimaurer *m*; **~ry** [~nri] Mauerwerk *n*.

masque [maːsk] Maskenspiel *n*.
masquerade [mæskə'reid] 1. Maskenball *m*; Verkleidung *f*; 2. *fig.* sich maskieren.
mass [mæs] 1. *eccl.* Messe *f*; Masse *f*; Menge *f*; ~ meeting Massenversammlung *f*; 2. (sich) (an)sammeln.
massacre ['mæsəkə] 1. Blutbad *n*; 2. niedermetzeln.
massage ['mæsɑːʒ] 1. Massage *f*; 2. massieren.
massif ['mæsiːf] (Gebirgs)Massiv *n*.
massive ['mæsiv] massiv; schwer.
mast ⚓ [maːst] Mast *m*.
master ['maːstə] 1. Meister *m*; Herr *m* (*a. fig.*); Gebieter *m*; Lehrer *m*; Kapitän *m e-s Handelsschiffs*; *Anrede:* (junger) Herr; *univ* Rektor *m e-s College*; ⌐ of Arts Magister *m* Artium; ⌐ of Ceremonies Conférencier *m*; 2. Meister ~; *fig.* führend; 3. Herr sein *od.* werden über (*acc.*); Sprache *etc* meistern, beherrschen; **~builder** Baumeister *m*; **~ful** □ [~ful] herrisch; meisterhaft; **~key** Hauptschlüssel *f*; **~ly** [~əli] meisterhaft; **~piece** Meisterstück *n*; **~ship** [~ʃip] Meisterschaft *f*; Herrschaft *f*; Lehramt *n*; **~y** [~əri] Herrschaft *f*; Vorrang *m*; Oberhand *f*; Meisterschaft *f*; Beherrschung *f*.
masticate ['mæstikeit] kauen.
mastiff ['mæstif] englische Dogge.
mat [mæt] 1. Matte *f*; Deckchen *n*; Unterlage *f*, 2. *fig* bedecken; (sich) verflechten, 3. mattiert, matt.
match¹ [mætʃ] Streichholz *n*.
match² [~] 1. Gleiche(r *m*, -s *n*) *f*; Partie *f*; Wettspiel *n*, -kampf *m*; Heirat *f*; be a ~ for *j-m* gewachsen sein; meet one's ~ s-n Meister finden; 2. *v/t* anpassen; passen zu; *et.* Passendes finden *od.* geben zu; es aufnehmen mit (*dat.*); well ~ed zs.-passend; *v/i.* zs.-passen; to ~ dazu passend; **~less** □ ['mætʃlis] unvergleichlich, ohnegleichen; **~maker** Ehestifter(in).
mate¹ [meit] *Schach* matt (setzen).
mate² [~] 1. Gefährt|e *m*, -in *f*; Kamerad(in); Gatt|e *m*, -in *f*; Männchen *n*, Weibchen *n von Tieren*; Gehilf|e *m*, -in *f*; ⚓ Maat *m*; 2. (sich) verheiraten; (sich) paaren.
material [~ [mə'tiəriəl] 1. materiell; körperlich; materialistisch; wesentlich; 2. Material *n*, Stoff *m*; Werkstoff *m*; writing ~s *pl*. Schreibmaterial(ien *pl*.) *m*.
matern|al [mə'təːnl] mütterlich; Mutter...; mütterlicherseits; **~ity** [~niti] Mutterschaft *f*; Mütterlichkeit *f*; *mst* ~ hospital Entbindungsanstalt *f*.
mathematic|ian [mæθimə'tiʃən] Mathematiker *m*; **~s** [~'mætiks] *mst sg.* Mathematik *f*.

matriculate [mə'trikjuleit] (sich) immatrikulieren (lassen).
matrimon|ial □ [mætri'mounjəl] ehelich; Ehe...; **~y** ['mætriməni] Ehe(stand *m*) *f*.
matrix ['meitriks] Matrize *f*.
matron ['meitrən] Matrone *f*; Hausmutter *f*; Oberin *f*.
matter ['mætə] 1. Materie *f*, Stoff *m*; ⚕ Eiter *m*; Gegenstand *m*; Ursache *f*; Sache *f*; Angelegenheit *f*, Geschäft *n*; printed ~ 📖 Drucksache *f*; what's the ~? was gibt es?; what's the ~ with you? was fehlt Ihnen?; no ~ es hat nichts zu sagen; no ~ who gleichgültig wer; ~ of course Selbstverständlichkeit *f*; for that ~, for the ~ of that was dies betrifft; ~ of fact Tatsache *f*; 2. von Bedeutung sein; it does not ~ es macht nichts; **~-of-fact** tatsächlich; sachlich.
mattress ['mætris] Matratze *f*.
matur|e [mə'tjuə] 1. □ reif; reiflich; ♦ fällig; 2. reifen; zur Reife bringen; ♦ fällig werden; **~ity** [~əriti] Reife *f*; ♦ Fälligkeit *f*.
maudlin ['mɔːdlin] rührselig.
maul [mɔːl] beschädigen; *fig.* heruntermachen; roh umgehen mit.
Maundy Thursday *eccl.* ['mɔːndi 'θəːzdi] Gründonnerstag *m*.
mauve [mouv] 1. Malvenfarbe *f*; 2. hellviolett.
maw [mɔː] *Tier-Magen *m*; Rachen *m*.
mawkish □ ['mɔːkiʃ] rührselig, sentimental.
maxim ['mæksim] Grundsatz *m*; **~um** [~məm] Höchstmaß *n*, -stand *m*, -betrag *m*; *attr.* Höchst...
May¹ [mei] Mai *m*.
may² [~] (*irr.*] mag, kann, darf.
maybe *Am.* ['meibi] vielleicht.
may|-beetle *zo.* ['meibi:tl], **~bug** Maikäfer *m*.
May Day ['meidei] der 1. Mai.
mayor [mεə] Bürgermeister *m*.
maypole ['meipoul] Maibaum *m*.
maz|e [meiz] Irrgarten *m*, Labyrinth *n*; *fig.* Wirrnis *f*; in a ~ = **~ed** [meizd] bestürzt, verwirrt; **~y** □ ['meizi] labyrinthisch; wirr.
me [miː, mi] mich; mir; F ich.
mead [miːd] Met *m*; *poet.* = meadow.
meadow ['medou] Wiese *f*.
meag|re, *Am.* **~er** □ ['miːgə] mager, dürr; dürftig.
meal [miːl] Mahl(zeit *f*) *n*; Mehl *n*.
mean¹ □ [miːn] gemein, niedrig; gering; armselig; knauserig.
mean² [~] 1. mittler, mittelmäßig; Durchschnitts...; in the ~ time inzwischen; 2. Mitte *f*; ~s *pl.* (Geld-)Mittel *n*/*pl.*; (*a. sg.*) Mittel *n*; by all ~s jedenfalls; by no ~s keineswegs; by ~s of mittels (*gen.*).
mean³ [~] [*irr.*] meinen; beabsich-

tigen; bestimmen; bedeuten; ~ well (*ill*) es gut (schlecht) meinen.

meaning ['mi:niŋ] 1. ☐ bedeutsam; 2. Sinn *m*, Bedeutung *f*; **~less** [~nlis] bedeutungslos; sinnlos.

meant [ment] *pret. u. p.p.* von *mean*[3].

mean|time ['mi:n'taim], **~while** mittlerweile, inzwischen.

measles ☸ ['mi:zlz] *sg.* Masern *pl.*

measure ['meʒə] 1. Maß *n*; ♪ Takt *m*; Maßregel *f*; ~ of *capacity* Hohlmaß *n*; beyond ~ über alle Maßen; in a great großenteils; *made to* ~ nach Maß gemacht; 2. (ab-, aus-, ver)messen; *j-m* Maß nehmen; ~ up *Am.* heranreichen; **~less** ☐ [~lis] unermeßlich; **~ment** [~əmənt] Messung *f*; Maß *m*.

meat [mi:t] Fleisch *n*; *fig.* Gehalt *m*; ~ tea frühes Abendessen mit Tee; **~y** ['mi:ti] fleischig; *fig.* gehaltvoll.

mechanic [mi'kænik] Handwerker *m*; Mechaniker *m*; **~al** ☐ [~kəl] mechanisch; Maschinen...; **~ian** [mekə'niʃən] Mechaniker *m*; **~s** [mi'kæniks] *mst sg.* Mechanik *f*.

mechan|ism ['mekənizəm] Mechanismus *m*; **~ize** [~naiz] mechanisieren; ✗ motorisieren.

medal ['medl] Medaille *f*; Orden *m*.

meddle ['medl] sich einmischen (*with*, *in* in *acc.*); **~some** [~lsəm] zu-, aufdringlich.

mediaeval ☐ [medi'i:vəl] mittelalterlich.

media|l ☐ ['mi:djəl], **~n** [~ən] Mittel.., *in der Mitte* (befindlich).

mediat|e ['mi:dieit] vermitteln; **~ion** [mi:di'eiʃən] Vermittlung *f*; **~or** ['mi:dieitə] Vermittler *m*.

medical . ['medikəl] medizinisch, ärztlich; ~ *certificate* Krankenschein *m*, Attest *n*; ~ *evidence* ärztliches Gutachten; ~ *man* Arzt *m*, Mediziner *m*; ~ *supervision* ärztliche Aufsicht.

medicate ['medikeit] medizinisch behandeln, mit Arzneistoff versehen; **~d** *bath* medizinisches Bad.

medicin|al ☐ [me'disinl] medizinisch; heilend, heilsam; **~e** ['medsin] Medizin *f*.

medieval ☐ [medi'i:vəl] = *mediaeval*.

mediocre ['mi:dioukə] mittelmäßig.

meditat|e ['mediteit] *v/i.* nachdenken, überlegen; *v/t.* sinnen auf (*acc.*); erwägen; **~ion** [medi'teiʃən] Nachdenken *n*; innere Betrachtung; **~ive** ['mediteitiv] nachdenklich, meditativ.

Mediterranean [meditə'reinjən] Mittelmeer *n*; *attr.* Mittelmeer...

medium ['mi:djəm] 1. Mitte *f*; Mittel *n*; Vermittlung *f*; Medium *n*; *Lebens*-Element *n*; 2. mittler; Mittel..., Durchschnitts...

medley ['medli] Gemisch *n*; ♪ Potpourri *n*.

meek ☐ [mi:k] sanft-, demütig; **~ness** ['mi:knis] Sanft-, Demut *f*.

meerschaum ['miəʃəm] Meerschaum(pfeife *f*) *m*.

meet[1] [mi:t] passend; schicklich.

meet[2] [~] [*irr.*] *v/t.* treffen; begegnen (*dat.*); abholen; stoßen auf *den Gegner*; *Wunsch etc* befriedigen; *e-r Verpflichtung* nachkommen; *Am.* *j-m* vorgestellt werden; go to ~ *s.o.* j-m entgegengehen; *v/i.* sich treffen; zs.-stoßen; sich versammeln; ~ *with* stoßen auf (*acc.*); erleiden; **~ing** ['mi:tiŋ] Begegnung *f*; (Zs.-)Treffen *n*, Versammlung *f*; Tagung *f*.

melancholy ['melənkəli] 1. Schwermut *f*; 2. melancholisch.

meliorate ['mi:ljəreit] (sich) verbessern.

mellow ['melou] 1. ☐ mürbe; reif; weich; mild; 2. reifen (lassen); weich machen *od.* werden; (sich) mildern.

melo|dious ☐ [mi'loudjəs] melodisch; **~dramatic** [meloudrə'mætik] melodramatisch; **~dy** ['melədi] Melodie *f*; Lied *n*.

melon ♀ ['melən] Melone *f*.

melt [melt] (zer)schmelzen; *fig.* zerfließen; *Gefühl* erweichen.

member ['membə] (Mit)Glied *n*; *parl.* Abgeordnete(r *m*) *f*; **~ship** [~ʃip] Mitgliedschaft *f*; Mitgliederzahl *f*.

membrane ['membrein] Membran(e) *f*, Häutchen *n*. [*n*.]

memento [mi'mentou] Andenken]

memo ['mi:mou] = *memorandum*.

memo|ir ['memwa:] Denkschrift *f*; **~s** *pl.* Memoiren *pl.*

memorable ☐ ['memərəbl] denkwürdig.

memorandum [memə'rændəm] Notiz *f*; *pol.* Note *f*; Schriftsatz *m*.

memorial [mi'mo:riəl] Denkmal *n*; Gedenkzeichen *n*; Denkschrift *f*, Eingabe *f*; *attr.* Gedächtnis..., Gedenk...

memorize ['meməraiz] auswendig lernen, memorieren.

memory ['meməri] Gedächtnis *n*; Erinnerung *f*; Andenken *n*; *commit* to ~ dem Gedächtnis einprägen; *in* ~ *of* zum Andenken an (*acc.*).

men [men] *pl.* von *man* 1; Mannschaft *f*.

menace ['menəs] 1. (be)drohen; 2. Gefahr *f*; Drohung *f*.

mend [mend] 1. *v/t.* (ver)bessern; ausbessern, flicken; besser machen; ~ *one's ways* sich bessern; *v/i.* sich bessern; 2. Flicken *m*; *on the* ~ auf dem Wege der Besserung.

mendacious ☐ [men'deiʃəs] lügnerisch, verlogen.

mendicant ['mendikənt] 1. bet-

telnd; Bettel...; 2. Bettler *m*; Bettel-
mönch *m*.

menial *contp.* ['mi:njəl] 1. □ knecht-
tisch; niedrig; 2. Knecht *m*; Lakai *m*.

meningitis ♂ [menin'dʒaitis] Hirn-
hautentzündung *f*, Meningitis *f*.

mental ['mentl] geistig; Geistes...; ⚢ *arithmetic* Kopfrechnen *n*;
~ity [men'tæliti] Mentalität *f*.

mention ['menʃən] 1. Erwähnung *f*;
2. erwähnen; *don't* ~ *it!* bitte!

menu ['menju:] Speisenfolge *f*,
Menü *n*; Speisekarte *f*.

mercantile ['mə:kəntail] kaufmännisch; Handels...

mercenary ['mə:sinəri] 1. □ feil,
käuflich, gedungen; gewinnsüch-
tig; 2. ✕ Söldner *m*.

mercer ['mə:sə] Seidenwaren-,
Stoffhändler *m*.

merchandise ['mə:tʃəndaiz] Wa-
re(n *pl.*) *f*

merchant ['mə:tʃənt] 1. Kaufmann
m; *Am.* (Klein)Händler *m*; 2. Handels..., Kaufmanns...; *law* ~ Han-
delsrecht *n*; ~**man** Handelsschiff *n*.

merci|ful ['mə:siful] barmher-
zig; ~**less** [~ilis] unbarmherzig.

mercury ['mə:kjuri] Quecksilber *n*.

mercy ['mə:si] Barmherzigkeit *f*;
Gnade *f*; *be at s.o.'s* ~ in j-s Gewalt sein.

mere [miə] rein, lauter; bloß;
~ly ['miəli] bloß, lediglich, allein.

meretricious [meri'triʃəs] aufdringlich; kitschig.

merge [mə:dʒ] verschmelzen (*in*
mit); ~r ['mə:dʒə] Verschmelzung *f*.

meridian [mə'ridiən] *geogr.* Meridian *m*; *fig.* Gipfel *m*; *attr.* Mittags...

merit ['merit] 1. Verdienst *n*; Wert
m; Vorzug *m*; *bsd.* ⚢ ~s *pl.* Haupt-
punkte *m/pl.*, Wesen *n* e-r *Sache*;
make a ~ *of* als Verdienst ansehen;
2. *fig.* verdienen; ~**orious** □
[meri'tɔ:riəs] verdienstvoll.

mermaid ['mə:meid] Nixe *f*.

merriment ['merimənt] Lustigkeit
f; Belustigung *f*.

merry ['meri] lustig, fröhlich;
make ~ lustig sein; ~ **andrew**
Hanswurst *m*; ~**-go-round** Karussell *n*; ~**-making** [~imeikiŋ] Lustbarkeit *f*.

mesh [meʃ] 1. Masche *f*; *fig. oft* ~es
pl. Netz *n*; *be in* ~ ⊕ (in-ea.-)grei-
fen; 2. in e-m Netz fangen.

mess[1] [mes] 1. Unordnung *f*;
Schmutz *m*, F Schweinerei *f*; F Patsche *f*; *make a* ~ *of* verpfuschen; 2.
v/t. in Unordnung bringen; verpfuschen; *v/i.* *about* F herummurksen.

mess[2] [~] Kasino *n*, Messe *f*.

message ['mesidʒ] Botschaft *f*; *go
on a* ~ e-e Besorgung machen.

messenger ['mesindʒə] Bote *m*.

Messieurs, *mst* **Messrs.** ['mesəz]
(die) Herren *m/pl.*; Firma *f*.

met [met] *pret. u. p.p. von* meet[2].

metal ['metl] 1. Metall *n*; Schotter
m; 2. beschottern; ~**lic** [mi'tælik]
(~ally) metallisch; Metall...; ~**lurgy**
[me'tælədʒi] Hüttenkunde *f*.

metamorphose [metə'mɔ:fouz] verwandeln, umgestalten.

metaphor ['metəfə] Metapher *f*.

meteor ['mi:tjə] Meteor *m* (*a. fig.*);
~**ology** [mi:tjə'rɔlədʒi] Meteorologie *f*, Wetterkunde *f*.

meter ['mi:tə] Messer *m*, Zähler *m*;
Am. = metre.

methinks † [mi'θiŋks] mich dünkt.

method ['meθəd] Methode *f*; Art
u. Weise *f*; Verfahren *n*; Ordnung
f, System *n*; ~**ic(al** □) [mi'θɔ-
dik(əl)] methodisch.

methought [mi'θɔ:t] *pret. von*
methinks.

meticulous □ [mi'tikjuləs] peinlich
genau.

met|re, *Am.* ~**er** ['mi:tə] Meter *n*,
m; Versmaß *n*.

metric ['metrik] (~ally) metrisch;
~ *system* Dezimalsystem *n*.

metropoli|s [mi'trɔpəlis] Haupt-
stadt *f*, Metropole *f*; ~**tan** [metrə-
'pɔlitən] hauptstädtisch.

mettle ['metl] Feuereifer *m*, Mut *m*;
be on one's ~ sein Bestes tun.

mews [mju:z] Stallung *f*; *daraus
entstandene* Garagen *f/pl. od.* Wohn-
häuser *n/pl.*

Mexican ['meksikən] 1. mexika-
nisch; 2. Mexikaner(in).

miaow [mi(:)'au] miauen; mauzen.

mice [mais] *pl. von* mouse.

Michaelmas ['miklməs] Michaelis
(-tag *m*) *n* (*29. September*).

micro... ['maikrou] klein..., Klein...

micro|phone ['maikrəfoun] Mikro-
phon *n*; ~**scope** Mikroskop *n*.

mid [mid] mittler, Mitt(el)...; *in* ~
air mitten in der Luft; *in* ~ *winter*
mitten im Winter, ~**day** ['middei]
1. Mittag *m*; 2. mittägig; Mittags...

middle ['midl] 1. Mitte *f*; Hüften
f/pl.; 2. mittler; Mittel...; ⚢ *Ages
pl.* Mittelalter *n*; ~**-aged** von mittlerem Alter; ~**-class** Mittelstands-
...; ~ *class*(es *pl.*) Mittelstand *m*;
~**man** Mittelsmann *m*; ~ **name**
zweiter Vorname *m*; ~**-sized** mittel-
groß; ~**-weight** *Boxen:* Mittelge-
wicht *n*.

middling ['midliŋ] mittelmäßig;
leidlich; Mittel...

middy F ['midi] = midshipman.

midge [midʒ] Mücke *f*; ~**t** ['midʒit]
Zwerg *m*, Knirps *m*.

mid|land ['midlənd] 1. binnenlän-
disch; 2. *the* ⚢s *Am.* Mittelengland *n*;
~**most** mittelste(r, -s); ~**night**
Mitternacht *f*; ~**riff** ['midrif]
Zwerchfell *n*; ~**shipman** Leutnant
m zur See; *Am.* Oberfähnrich *m*
zur See; ~**st** [midst] Mitte *f*; *in the*
~ *of* inmitten (*gen.*); ~**summer**

Sommersonnenwende f; Hochsommer m; ~way 1. halber Weg; Am. Schaubudenstraße f; 2. adj. in der Mitte befindlich; 3. adv. auf halbem Wege; ~wife Hebamme f; ~wifery ['midwifəri] Geburtshilfe f; ~winter Wintersonnenwende f; Mitte f des Winters.

mien [mi:n] Miene f.

might [mait] 1. Macht f, Gewalt f, Kraft f; with ~ and main mit aller Gewalt; 2. pret. von may²; ~y □ ['maiti] mächtig, gewaltig.

migrat|e [mai'greit] (aus)wandern; ~ion [~'eiʃən] Wanderung f; ~ory ['maigrətəri] wandernd; Zug ..

mild [maild] mild, sanft, gelind.

mildew ♀ ['mildju:] Mehltau m.

mildness ['maildnis] Milde f.

mile [mail] Meile f (1609.33 m).

mil|eage ['mailidʒ] Laufzeit f in Meilen, Meilenstand m e-s Autos; Kilometergeld n.

milestone ['mailstoun] Meilenstein m.

milit|ary ['militəri] 1. □ militärisch; Kriegs...; ♀ Government Militärregierung f; 2. das Militär; ~ia [mi'liʃə] Land-, Bürgerwehr f.

milk [milk] 1. Milch f; it's no use crying over spilt ~ geschehen ist geschehen, 2. v/t. melken; v/i. Milch geben; ~maid ['milkmeid] Melkerin f; Milchmädchen n, ~man Milchmann m; ~-powder Milchpulver n; ~-shake Milchmischgetränk n; ~sop Weichling m; ~y ['milki] milchig; Milch...; ♀ Way Milchstraße f.

mill¹ [mil] 1. Mühle f; Fabrik f, Spinnerei f; 2. mahlen; ⊕ fräsen; Geld prägen; Münze rändeln.

mill² Am. [~] ¹/₁₀₀₀ Dollar m.

millepede zo. ['milipi:d] Tausendfüß(l)er m.

miller ['milə] Müller m; ⊕ Fräsmaschine f.

millet ♀ ['milit] Hirse f.

milliner ['milinə] Putzmacherin f, Modistin f; ~y [~əri] Putz-, Modewaren(geschäft n) f.

million ['miljən] Million f; ~aire [miljə'nɛə] Millionär(in); ~th ['miljənθ] 1. millionste(r, -s); 2. Millionstel n.

mill|-pond ['milpɔnd] Mühlteich m; ~stone Mühlstein m.

milt [milt] Milch f der Fische.

mimic ['mimik] 1. mimisch; Schein...; 2. Mime m; 3. nachahmen, nachäffen; ~ry [~kri] Nachahmung f; zo. Angleichung f.

mince [mins] 1. v/t. zerhacken; he does not ~ matters er nimmt kein Blatt vor den Mund; v/i. sich zieren; 2. a. ~d meat Hackfleisch n; ~meat ['minsmi:t] e-e Tortenfüllung; ~-pie Torte f aus mincemeat; ~r [~sə] Fleischwolf m.

mincing-machine ['minsiŋməʃi:n] = mincer.

mind [maind] 1. Sinn m, Gemüt n; Geist m, Verstand m; Meinung f; Absicht f; Neigung f, Lust f; Gedächtnis n; Sorge f; to my ~ meiner Ansicht nach; out of one's ~, not in one's right ~ von Sinnen; change one's ~ sich anders besinnen; bear s.th. in ~ (immer) an et. denken; have (half) a ~ to (beinahe) Lust haben zu; have s.th. on one's ~ et. auf dem Herzen haben; make up one's ~ sich entschließen; 2. merken od. achten auf (acc.); sich kümmern um; etwas (einzuwenden) haben gegen; ~! gib acht!; never ~! macht nichts!; ~ the step! Achtung, Stufe!; I don't ~ (it) ich habe nichts dagegen; do you ~ if I smoke? stört es Sie, wenn ich rauche?; would you ~ taking off your hat? würden Sie bitte den Hut abnehmen?; ~ your own business! kümmern Sie sich um Ihre Angelegenheiten!; ~ful ['maindful] (of) eingedenk (gen.); achtsam (auf acc.).

mine¹ [main] 1. der (die, das) meinige; mein; 2. die Mein(ig)en pl.

mine² [~] 1. Bergwerk n, Grube f; fig. Fundgrube f; ⚒ Mine f; 2. v/i. graben, minieren; v/t. graben; ⚒ fördern; ✕ unterminieren; ✕ verminen; ~r ['mainə] Bergmann m.

mineral ['minərəl] 1. Mineral n; ~s pl. Mineralwasser n; 2. mineralisch.

mingle ['miŋgl] (ver)mischen; sich mischen od. mengen (with unter).

miniature ['minjətʃə] 1. Miniatur (-gemälde n) f; 2. in Miniatur; Miniatur...; Klein...; ~ camera Kleinbildkamera f.

minikin ['minikin] 1. winzig; geziert; 2. Knirps m.

minim|ize ['minimaiz] möglichst klein machen; fig. verringern; ~um [~məm] Minimum n; Mindestmaß n; Mindestbetrag m; attr. Mindest...

mining ['mainiŋ] Bergbau m; attr. Berg(bau)...; Gruben...

minion ['minjən] Günstling m; fig. Lakai m.

miniskirt ['miniskə:t] Minirock m.

minister ['ministə] 1. Diener m; fig. Werkzeug n; Geistliche(r) m; Minister m; Gesandte(r) m; 2. v/t. darreichen; v/i. dienen; Gottesdienst halten.

ministry ['ministri] geistliches Amt; Ministerium n; Regierung f.

mink zo. [miŋk] Nerz m.

minor ['mainə] 1. kleiner, geringer, weniger bedeutend; ♪ Moll n; A ~ A-moll n; 2. Minderjährige(r m) f; Am. univ. Nebenfach n; ~ity [mai'nɔriti] Minderheit f; Unmündigkeit f.

minster ['minstə] Münster n.

minstrel ['minstrəl] Minnesänger m; ~s pl. Negersänger m/pl.

mint [mint] 1. ♀ Minze f; Münze f; fig. Goldgrube f; a ~ of money e-e Menge Geld; 2. münzen, prägen.

minuet ♪ [minju'et] Menuett n.

minus ['mainəs] 1. prp. weniger; F ohne; 2. adj. negativ.

minute 1. ☐ [mai'nju:t] sehr klein, winzig; unbedeutend; sehr genau; 2. ['minit] Minute f; Augenblick m; ~s pl. Protokoll n; ~ness [mai'nju:tnis] Kleinheit f; Genauigkeit f.

mirac|le ['mirəkl] Wunder n; ~ulous ☐ [mi'rækjuləs] wunderbar.

mirage ['mira:ʒ] Luftspiegelung f.

mire ['maiə] 1. Sumpf m; Kot m, Schlamm m; 2. mit Schlamm od. Schmutz bedecken.

mirror ['mirə] 1. Spiegel m; 2. (wider)spiegeln (a. fig.).

mirth [mə:θ] Fröhlichkeit f; ~ful ☐ ['mə:θful] fröhlich; ~less ☐ ['mə:θlis] freudlos.

miry ['maiəri] kotig.

mis... [mis] miß..., übel, falsch.

misadventure ['misəd'ventʃə] Mißgeschick n, Unfall m.

misanthrop|e ['mizənθroup], ~ist [mi'zænθrəpist] Menschenfeind m.

misapply ['misə'plai] falsch anwenden.   [mißverstehen.]

misapprehend ['misæpri'hend]

misappropriate ['misə'prouprieit] unterschlagen, veruntreuen.

misbehave ['misbi'heiv] sich schlecht benehmen.

misbelief ['misbi'li:f] Irrglaube m.

miscalculate ['miskælkjuleit] falsch (be)rechnen.

miscarr|iage [mis'kæridʒ] Mißlingen n; Verlust m v. Briefen; Fehlgeburt f; ~ of justice Fehlspruch m; ~y [~ri] mißlingen; verlorengehen (Brief); fehlgebären.

miscellan|eous ☐ [misi'leinjəs] ge-, vermischt; vielseitig; ~y [mi'seləni] Gemisch n; Sammelband n.

mischief ['mistʃif] Schaden m, Unfug m; Mutwille m, Übermut m; ~-maker Unheilstifter(in).

mischievous ☐ ['mistʃivəs] schädlich; boshaft, mutwillig.

misconceive ['miskən'si:v] falsch auffassen od. verstehen.

misconduct 1. [mis'kɔndəkt] schlechtes Benehmen; Ehebruch m; schlechte Verwaltung; 2. ['miskən'dʌkt] schlecht verwalten; ~ o.s. sich schlecht benehmen; e-n Fehltritt begehen.

misconstrue ['miskən'stru:] mißdeuten.

miscreant ['miskriənt] Schurke m.

misdeed ['mis'di:d] Missetat f.

misdemeano(u)r ɀʰ [misdi'mi:nə] Vergehen n.

misdirect ['misdi'rekt] irreleiten; an die falsche Adresse richten.

misdoing ['misdu(:)iŋ] Vergehen n (mst pl.).

mise en scène thea. ['mi:zã:n'sein] Inszenierung f.

miser ['maizə] Geizhals m.

miserable ☐ ['mizərəbl] elend; unglücklich, erbärmlich.

miserly ['maizəli] geizig, filzig.

misery ['mizəri] Elend n, Not f.

misfit ['misfit] schlecht passendes Stück (Kleid, Stiefel etc.); Einzelgänger m, Eigenbrötler m.

misfortune [mis'fɔ:tʃən] Unglück(sfall m) n; Mißgeschick n.

misgiving [mis'giviŋ] böse Ahnung, Befürchtung f.

misguide ['mis'gaid] irreleiten.

mishap ['mishæp] Unfall m; mot. Panne f.

misinform ['misin'fɔ:m] falsch unterrichten.   [deuten.]

misinterpret ['misin'tə:prit] miß-]

mislay [mis'lei] [irr. (lay)] verlegen.

mislead [mis'li:d] [irr. (lead)] irreführen; verleiten.

mismanage ['mis'mænidʒ] schlecht verwalten.

misplace ['mis'pleis] falsch stellen, verstellen; verlegen; falsch anbringen.

misprint 1. [mis'print] verdrucken; 2. ['mis'print] Druckfehler m.

misread [mis'ri:d] [irr. (read)] falsch lesen od. deuten.

misrepresent['misrepri'zent]falsch darstellen, verdrehen.

miss¹ [mis] mst ♀ Fräulein n.

miss² [~] 1. Verlust m; Fehlschuß m, -stoß m, -wurf m; 2. v/t. (ver)missen; verfehlen; verpassen; auslassen; übersehen; überhören; v/i. fehlen (nicht treffen); fehlgehen.

misshapen ['mis'ʃeipən] verunstaltet; mißgestaltet.

missile ['misail] (Wurf)Geschoß n; Rakete f.

missing ['misiŋ] fehlend; ✕ vermißt; be ~ fehlen; vermißt werden.

mission ['miʃən] Sendung f; Auftrag m; Berufung f, Lebensziel n; Gesandtschaft f; eccl., pol. Mission f; ~ary ['miʃnəri] Missionar m; attr. Missions...

missive ['misiv] Sendschreiben n.

mis-spell ['mis'spel] [irr. (spell)] falsch buchstabieren od. schreiben.

mis-spend ['mis'spend] [irr. (spend)] falsch verwenden; vergeuden.

mist [mist] 1. Nebel m; 2. (um)nebeln; sich trüben; beschlagen.

mistake [mis'teik] 1. [irr. (take)] sich irren in (dat.), verkennen; mißverstehen; verwechseln (for mit); be ~n sich irren; 2. Irrtum m; Versehen n; Fehler m; ~n ☐ [~kən] irrig, falsch (verstanden).

mister ['mistə] Herr *m* (*abbr.* **Mr.**).
mistletoe ♀ ['misltou] Mistel *f*.
mistress ['mistris] Herrin *f*; Hausfrau *f*; Lehrerin *f*; Geliebte *f*; Meisterin *f*.
mistrust ['mis'trʌst] **1.** mißtrauen (*dat.*); **2.** Mißtrauen *n*; ⁓**ful** ☐ [⁓tful] mißtrauisch.
misty ['misti] neb(e)lig; unklar.
misunderstand ['misʌndə'stænd] [*irr.* (*stand*)] mißverstehen; ⁓**ing** [⁓diŋ] Mißverständnis *n*.
misus|age [mis'juːzidʒ] Mißbrauch *m*; Mißhandlung *f*; ⁓**e 1.** ['mis'juːz] mißbrauchen, mißhandeln; **2.** [⁓uːs] Mißbrauch *m*.
mite [mait] *zo.* Milbe *f*; Heller *m*; *fig.* Scherflein *n*; Knirps *m*.
mitigate ['mitigeit] mildern, lindern (*a. fig.*).
mit|re, *Am.* ⁓**er** ['maitə] Bischofsmütze *f*.
mitt [mit] *Baseball*-Handschuh *m*; F Boxhandschuh *m*; ⁓ **mitten**.
mitten ['mitn] Fausthandschuh *m*; Halbhandschuh *m* (*ohne Finger*); *Am. sl.* Tatze *f* (*Hand*).
mix [miks] (sich) (ver)mischen; verkehren (*with mit*); ⁓**ed** gemischt; *fig.* zweifelhaft; ⁓ **up** durch-ea.-bringen; *be* ⁓*ed up with* in *e-e* S. verwickelt sein; ⁓**ture** ['mikstʃə] Mischung *f*.
moan [moun] **1.** Stöhnen *n*; **2.** stöhnen.
moat [mout] Burg-, Stadtgraben *m*.
mob [mɔb] **1.** Pöbel *m*; **2.** anpöbeln.
mobil|e ['moubail] beweglich; ✕ mobil; ⁓**ization**✕ [moubilai'zeiʃn] Mobilmachung *f*; ⁓**ize** ✕ ['moubilaiz] mobil machen.
moccasin ['mɔkəsin] weiches Leder; Mokassin *m* (*Schuh*).
mock [mɔk] **1.** Spott *m*; **2.** Schein...; falsch, nachgemacht; **3.** *v/t.* verspotten; nachmachen; täuschen; *v/i.* spotten (*at* über *acc.*); ⁓**ery** ['mɔkəri] Spötterei *f*, Gespött *n*; Äfferei *f*.
mocking-bird *orn.* ['mɔkiŋbəːd] Spottdrossel *f*.
mode [moud] Art und Weise *f*; (Erscheinungs)Form *f*; Sitte *f*, Mode *f*.
model ['mɔdl] **1.** Modell *n*; Muster *n*; *fig.* Vorbild *n*; Vorführdame *f*; *attr.* Muster...; **2.** modellieren; (ab)formen; *fig.* modeln, bilden.
moderat|e 1. ☐ ['mɔdərit] (mittel-) mäßig; **2.** [⁓reit] (sich) mäßigen; ⁓**ion** [mɔdə'reiʃən] Mäßigung *f*; Mäßigkeit *f*.
modern ['mɔdən] modern, neu; ⁓**ize** [⁓ə(ː)naiz] (sich) modernisieren.
modest ☐ ['mɔdist] bescheiden, anständig; ⁓**y** [⁓ti] Bescheidenheit *f*.
modi|fication [mɔdifi'keiʃən] Ab-,

Veränderung *f*; Einschränkung *f*; ⁓**fy** ['mɔdifai] (ab)ändern; mildern.
mods [mɔdz] *pl.* Halbstarke *m/pl.*
modulate ['mɔdjuleit] modulieren.
moiety ['mɔiəti] Hälfte *f*; Teil *m*.
moist [mɔist] feucht, naß; ⁓**en** ['mɔisn] be-, anfeuchten; ⁓**ure** ['mɔistʃə] Feuchtigkeit *f*.
molar ['moulə] Backenzahn *m*.
molasses [mə'læsiz] Melasse *f*; Sirup *m*.
mole[1] *zo.* [moul] Maulwurf *m*.
mole[2] [⁓] Muttermal *n*.
mole[3] [⁓] Mole *f*, Hafendamm *m*.
molecule ['mɔlikjuːl] Molekül *n*.
molehill ['moulhil] Maulwurfshügel *m*; *make a mountain out of a* ⁓ aus e-r Mücke e-n Elefanten machen.
molest [mou'lest] belästigen.
mollify ['mɔlifai] besänftigen.
mollycoddle ['mɔlikɔdl] **1.** Weichling *m*, Muttersöhnchen *n*; **2.** verzärteln
molten ['moultən] geschmolzen.
moment ['moumənt] Augenblick *m*; Bedeutung *f*; ⁓ *momentum*; ⁓**ary** ☐ [⁓təri] augenblicklich; vorübergehend; ⁓**ous** ☐ [mou'mentəs] (ge)wichtig, bedeutend; ⁓**um** *phys.* [⁓təm] Moment *n*; Triebkraft *f*.
monarch ['mɔnək] Monarch(in); ⁓**y** [⁓ki] Monarchie *f*.
monastery ['mɔnəstəri] (Mönchs-) Kloster *n*.
Monday ['mʌndi] Montag *m*.
monetary ['mʌnitəri] Geld...
money ['mʌni] Geld *n*; *ready* ⁓ Bargeld *n*; ⁓**-box** Sparbüchse *f*; ⁓**-changer** [⁓itʃeindʒə] (Geld-) Wechsler *m*; ⁓**-order** Postanweisung *f*.
monger ['mʌŋgə] ...händler *m*, ...krämer *m*.
mongrel ['mʌŋgrəl] Mischling *m*, Bastard *m*; *attr.* Bastard...
monitor ['mɔnitə] ⊕ Monitor *m*; (Klassen)Ordner *m*.
monk [mʌŋk] Mönch *m*.
monkey ['mʌŋki] **1.** *zo.* Affe *m* (*a. fig.*); ⊕ Rammblock *m*; *put s.o.'s* ⁓ *up* F j-n auf die Palme bringen; ⁓ *business Am. sl.* fauler Zauber; **2.** F (herum)albern; ⁓ *with* herummurksen an (*dat.*); ⁓**-wrench** ⊕ Engländer *m* (*Schraubenschlüssel*); *throw a* ⁓ *in s.th. Am. sl.* et. über den Haufen werfen.
monkish ['mʌŋkiʃ] mönchisch.
mono|... ['mɔnou] ein(fach)...; ⁓**cle** ['mɔnɔkl] Monokel *n*; ⁓**gamy** [mɔ'nɔgəmi] Einehe *f*; ⁓**logue**, *Am. a.* ⁓**log** ['mɔnələg] Monolog *m*; ⁓**polist** [mə'nɔpəlist] Monopolist *m*; ⁓**polize** [⁓laiz] monopolisieren; *fig.* an sich reißen; ⁓**poly** [⁓li] Monopol *n* (*of auf acc.*); ⁓**tonous** ☐ [⁓ɔtnəs] monoton, eintönig; ⁓**tony** [⁓ni] Monotonie *f*.

monsoon [mɔn'su:n] Monsun *m*.

monster ['mɔnstə] Ungeheuer *n* (*a. fig.*); Monstrum *n*; *attr*. Riesen...

monstro|sity [mɔns'trɔsiti] Ungeheuer(lichkeit *f*) *n*; **~us** □ ['mɔnstrəs] ungeheuer(lich); gräßlich.

month [mʌnθ] Monat *m*; *this day* ~ heute in e-m Monat; **~ly** ['mʌnθli] 1. monatlich; Monats...; 2. Monatsschrift *f*.

monument ['mɔnjumənt] Denkmal *n*; **~al** □ [mɔnju'mentl] monumental; Gedenk...; großartig.

mood [mu:d] Stimmung *f*, Laune *f*; **~y** □ ['mu:di] launisch; schwermütig; übellaunig.

moon [mu:n] 1. Mond *m*; *once in a blue* ~ F alle Jubeljahre einmal; 2. *mst* ~ *about* F herumdösen; **~light** ['mu:nlait] Mondlicht *n*, -schein *m*; **~lit** mondhell; **~struck** mondsüchtig.

Moor[1] [muə] Maure *m*; Mohr *m*.

moor[2] [~] Ödland *n*, Heideland *n*.

moor[3] ♧ [~] (sich) vertäuen; **~ings** ♧ ['muəriŋz] *pl*. Vertäuungen *f/pl*.

moose *zo.* [mu:z] *a.* **~-deer** *amerikanischer* Elch.

moot [mu:t] ~ *point* Streitpunkt *m*.

mop [mɔp] 1. Mop *m*; (Haar)Wust *m*; 2. auf-, abwischen.

mope [moup] den Kopf hängen lassen.

moral ['mɔrəl] 1. □ Moral...; moralisch; 2. Moral *f*; Nutzanwendung *f*; **~s** *pl*. Sitten *f/pl*.; **~e** [mɔ'rɑ:l] *bsd.* ✕ Moral *f*, Haltung *f*; **~ity** [mə'ræliti] Moralität *f*; Sittlichkeit *f*, Moral *f*; **~ize** ['mɔrəlaiz] moralisieren.

morass [mə'ræs] Morast *m*, Sumpf *m*.

morbid □ ['mɔ:bid] krankhaft.

more [mɔ:] mehr; *once* ~ noch einmal, wieder; *so much od. all the* ~ um so mehr; *no* ~ nicht mehr.

morel ♧ [mɔ'rel] Morchel *f*.

moreover [mɔ:'rouvə] überdies, weiter, ferner.

morgue [mɔ:g] Leichenschauhaus *n*; Archiv *n*.

moribund ['mɔribʌnd] im Sterben (liegend), dem Tode geweiht.

morning ['mɔ:niŋ] Morgen *m*; Vormittag *m*; *tomorrow* ~ morgen früh; ~ **dress** Tagesgesellschaftsanzug *m*. [*m*) *f*.\

moron ['mɔ:rɔn] Schwachsinnige(r)

morose ☐ [mə'rous] mürrisch.

morph|ia ['mɔ:fjə], **~ine** ['mɔ:fi:n] Morphium *n*.

morsel ['mɔ:səl] Bissen *m*; Stückchen *n*, *das* bißchen.

mortal ['mɔ:tl] 1. □ sterblich; tödlich; Tod(es)...; 2. Sterbliche(r *m*) *f*; **~ity** [mɔ:'tæliti] Sterblichkeit *f*.

mortar ['mɔ:tə] Mörser *m*; Mörtel *m*.

mortgag|e ['mɔ:gidʒ] 1. Pfandgut *n*; Hypothek *f*; 2. verpfänden; **~ee** [mɔ:gə'dʒi:] Hypothekengläubiger *m*; **~er** ['mɔ:gidʒə], **~or** [mɔ:gə'dʒɔ:] Hypothekenschuldner *m*.

mortician *Am.* [mɔ:'tiʃən] Leichenbestatter *m*.

morti|fication [mɔ:tifi'keiʃən] Kasteiung *f*; Kränkung *f*; **~fy** ['mɔ:tifai] kasteien; kränken.

morti|se, ~ce ⊕ ['mɔ:tis] Zapfenloch *n*.

mortuary ['mɔ:tjuəri] Leichenhalle *f*.

mosaic [mə'zeiik] Mosaik *n*.

mosque [mɔsk] Moschee *f*.

mosquito *zo.* [məs'ki:tou] Moskito *m*. [moosig.\

moss [mɔs] Moos *n*; **~y** ['mɔsi]

most [moust] 1. *adj.* □ meist; 2. *adv.* meist, am meisten; höchst; 3. das meiste; die meisten; Höchste(s) *n*; *at* (*the*) ~ höchstens; *make the* ~ *of* möglichst ausnutzen; **~ly** ['moustli] meistens.

moth [mɔθ] Motte *f*; **~-eaten** ['mɔθi:tn] mottenzerfressen.

mother ['mʌðə] 1. Mutter *f*; 2. bemuttern; **~ country** Vaterland *n*; Mutterland *n*; **~hood** [~hud] Mutterschaft *f*; **~-in-law** [~rinlɔ:] Schwiegermutter *f*; **~ly** [~əli] mütterlich; **~-of-pearl** [~rəv'pə:l] Perlmutter *f*; **~-tongue** Muttersprache *f*.

motif [mou'ti:f] (Leit)Motiv *n*.

motion ['mouʃən] 1. Bewegung *f*; Gang *m* (*a.* ⊕); *parl.* Antrag *m*; 2. *v/t.* durch Gebärden auffordern *od.* andeuten; *v/i.* winken; **~less** [~nlis] bewegungslos; ~ **picture** Film *m*.

motivate ['moutiveit] motivieren, begründen.

motive ['moutiv] 1. bewegend; 2. Motiv *n*, Beweggrund *m*; 3. veranlassen; **~less** [~vlis] grundlos.

motley ['mɔtli] (bunt)scheckig.

motor ['moutə] 1. Motor *m*; treibende Kraft; Automobil *n*; ✿ Muskel *m*; 2. motorisch, bewegend; Motor...; Kraft...; Auto...; 3. (im) Auto fahren; **~-assisted** [~ərə-'sistid] mit Hilfsmotor; ~ **bicycle**, **~bike** = *motor cycle*; ~ **boat** Motorboot *n*; ~ **bus** Autobus *m*; **~cade** *Am.* [~əkeid] Autokolonne *f*; **~car** Auto(mobil) *n*; ~ **coach** Reisebus *m*; ~ **cycle** Motorrad *n*; **~ing** [~əriŋ] Autofahren *n*; **~ist** [~rist] Kraftfahrer(in); **~ize** [~raiz] motorisieren; ~ **launch** Motorbarkasse *f*; **~road**, **~way** Autobahn *f*.

mottled ['mɔtld] gefleckt.

mo(u)ld [mould] 1. Gartenerde *f*; Schimmel *m*, Moder *m*; (Guß-) Form *f* (*a. fig.*); Abdruck *m*; Art *f*; 2. formen, gießen (*on*, *upon* nach).

mo(u)lder ['mouldə] zerfallen.
mo(u)lding ⚠ ['mouldin] Fries *m*.
mo(u)ldy ['mouldi] schimm(e)lig, dumpfig, mod(e)rig.
mo(u)lt [moult] (*fig.* sich) mausern.
mound [maund] Erdhügel *m*, -wall *m*.
mount [maunt] **1.** Berg *m*; Reitpferd *n*; **2.** *v/i.* (empor)steigen; aufsteigen (*Reiter*); *v/t.* be-, ersteigen; beritten machen; montieren; aufziehen, aufkleben; *Edelstein* fassen.
mountain ['mauntin] **1.** Berg *m*; ~s *pl.* Gebirge *n*; **2.** Berg..., Gebirgs...; ~eer [maunti'niə] Bergbewohner(in); Bergsteiger(in); ~ous ['mauntinəs] bergig, gebirgig
mountebank ['mauntibæŋk] Marktschreier *m*, Scharlatan *m*.
mourn [mɔ:n] (be)trauern; ~er ['mɔ:nə] Leidtragende(r *m*) *f*; ~ful ['mɔ:nful] Trauer...; traurig, ~ing ['mɔ:nin] Trauer *f*; *attr.* Trauer...   [Maus *f*.)
mouse [maus], *pl.* **mice** [mais])
moustache [məs'tɑ:ʃ] Schnurrbart *m*.
mouth [mauθ], *pl.* ~s [mauðz] Mund *m*; Maul *n*; Mündung *f*; Öffnung *f*; ~ful ['mauθful] Mundvoll *m*; ~ organ Mundharmonika *f*, ~piece Mundstück *n*; *fig.* Sprachrohr *n*.
move [mu:v] **1.** *v/t. allg.* bewegen; in Bewegung setzen; (weg)rücken; (an)treiben; *Leidenschaft* erregen; *seelisch* rühren; beantragen; ~ *heaven and earth* Himmel und Hölle in Bewegung setzen; *v/i.* (fort)bewegen; sich rühren; *Schach*: ziehen; (um)ziehen (*Mieter*); ~ *for s.th. et.* beantragen; ~ *in* einziehen; ~ *on* weitergehen; ~ *out* ausziehen; **2.** Bewegung *f*; *Schach* Zug *m*; *fig.* Schritt *m*; *on the* ~ in Bewegung; *make a* ~ die Tafel aufheben; ~ment ['mu:vmənt] Bewegung *f*; ♩ Tempo *n*; ♩ Satz *m*; ⊕ (Geh-)Werk *n*.
movies F ['mu:viz] *pl.* Kino *n*.
moving [['mu:vin] bewegend; beweglich; ~ *staircase* Rolltreppe *f*.
mow [mou] [*irr.*] mähen; ~er ['mouə] Mäher(in); Mähmaschine *f*; ~ing machine ['mouinməʃi:n] Mähmaschine *f*; ~n [moun] *p.p. von* mow.
much [mʌtʃ] **1.** *adj.* viel; **2.** *adv.* sehr; viel; bei weitem; fast; ~ *as I would like* so gern ich möchte; *I thought as* ~ das dachte ich mir; *make* ~ *of* viel Wesens machen von; *I am not* ~ *of a dancer* ich bin kein großer Tänzer.
muck [mʌk] Mist *m* (F *a. fig.*); ~rake ['mʌkreik] **1.** Mistgabel *f*; ~ *f*; **2.** im Schmutz wühlen; ~raker [~kə] *Am.* Korruptionsschnüffler *m*.
mucus ['mju:kəs] (Nasen)Schleim *m*.

mud [mʌd] Schlamm *m*; Kot *m*; ~dle ['mʌdl] **1.** *v/t.* verwirren; *a.* ~ *up*, ~ *together* durcheinanderbringen; F benebeln; *v/i.* stümpern; ~ *through* F sich durchwursteln; **2.** Wirrwarr *m*; F Wurstelei *f*; ~dy ['mʌdi] schlammig; trüb; ~guard Kotflügel *m*.
muff [mʌf] Muff *m*.
muffin ['mʌfin] Muffin *n* (*heißes Teegebäck*).
muffle ['mʌfl] *oft* ~ *up* ein-, umhüllen, umwickeln; *Stimme etc.* dämpfen; ~r [~lə] Halstuch *n*; Boxhandschuh *m*; *mot.* Auspufftopf *m*.
mug [mʌg] Krug *m*; Becher *m*.
muggy ['mʌgi] schwül.
mugwump *Am. iro.* ['mʌgwʌmp] großes Tier (*Person*); *pol.* Unabhängige(r) *m*.
mulatto [mju(:)'lætou] Mulatt|e *m*, -in *f*.
mulberry ['mʌlbəri] Maulbeere *f*.
mule [mju:l] Maultier *n*, ~esel *m*; störrischer Mensch; ~teer [mju:li-'tiə] Maultiertreiber *m*.
mull[1] [mʌl] ~ *over* überdenken.
mull[2] [~] ~ over überdenken.
mulled [mʌld]: ~ *wine* Glühwein *m*.
mulligan *Am.* F ['mʌligən] Eintopf *m aus Resten*.
mullion ['mʌliən] Fensterpfosten *m*.
multi|farious ☐ [mʌlti'fɛəriəs] mannigfaltig; ~form ['mʌltifɔ:m] vielförmig; ~ple [~ipl] **1.** vielfach; **2.** Vielfache(s) *n*; ~plication [mʌltipli'keiʃən] Vervielfältigung *f*, Vermehrung *f*; Multiplikation *f*; ~compound (*simple*) ~ Großes (Kleines) Einmaleins; ~ table Einmaleins *n*; ~plicity [~i'plisiti] Vielfalt *f*; ~ply ['mʌltiplai] (sich) vervielfältigen; multiplizieren; ~tude [~itju:d] Vielheit *f*, Menge *f*; ~tudinous [mʌlti-'tju:dinəs] zahlreich.
mum [mʌm] still.
mumble ['mʌmbl] murmeln, nuscheln; mummeln (*mühsam essen*).
mummery *contp.* ['mʌməri] Mummenschanz *m*.
mummify ['mʌmifai] mumifizieren.
mummy[1] ['mʌmi] Mumie *f*.
mummy[2] F [~] Mami *f*, Mutti *f*.
mumps ⚕ [mʌmps] *sg.* Ziegenpeter *m*, Mumps *m*.
munch [mʌntʃ] mit vollen Backen (fr)essen, mampfen.
mundane [['mʌndein] weltlich.
municipal [[mju(:)'nisipəl] städtisch, Gemeinde..., Stadt...; ~ity [mju(:)nisi'pæliti] Stadtbezirk *m*; Stadtverwaltung *f*.
munificen|ce [mju(:)'nifisns] Freigebigkeit *f*; ~t [~nt] freigebig.
munitions [mju(:)'niʃənz] *pl.* Munition *f*.
mural ['mjuərəl] Mauer...
murder ['mə:də] **1.** Mord *m*; **2.** (er-)

morden; *fig.* verhunzen; ~er [~ərə] Mörder *m*; ~ess [~ris] Mörderin *f*; ~ous □ [~rəs] mörderisch.

murky □ ['mə:ki] dunkel, finster.

murmur ['mə:mə] 1. Gemurmel *n*; Murren *n*; 2. murmeln; murren.

murrain ['mʌrin] Viehseuche *f*.

musc|le ['mʌsl] 1. Muskel *m*; 2. ~ *in Am. sl.* sich rücksichtslos eindrängen; ~le-bound mit Muskelkater; be ~ Muskelkater haben; ~ular ['mʌskjulə] Muskel...; muskulös.

Muse¹ [mju:z] Muse *f*.

muse² [~] (nach)sinnen, grübeln.

museum [mju(:)'ziəm] Museum *n*.

mush [mʌʃ] Brei *m*, Mus *n*; *Am.* Polenta *f*, Maisbrei *m*.

mushroom ['mʌʃrum] 1. Pilz *m*, *bsd.* Champignon *m*; 2. rasch wachsen; ~ *up* in die Höhe schießen.

music ['mju:zik] Musik *f*; Musikstück *n*; Noten *f/pl.*; set to ~ vertonen; ~al □ [~kəl] musikalisch; Musik...; wohlklingend; ~ box Spieldose *f*; ~ box *Am.* Spieldose *f*; ~-hall Varieté(theater) *n*; ~ian [mju(:)'ziʃən] Musiker(in); ~stand Notenständer *m*; ~stool Klavierstuhl *m*.

musk [mʌsk] Moschus *m*, Bisam *m*; ~-deer *zo.* ['mʌsk'diə] Moschustier *n*.

musket ['mʌskit] Muskete *f*.

musk-rat *zo.* ['mʌskræt] Bisamratte *f*.

muslin ['mʌzlin] Musselin *m*.

musquash ['mʌskwɔʃ] Bisamratte *f*; Bisampelz *m*.

muss *bsd. Am.* F [mʌs] Durcheinander *n*.

mussel ['mʌsl] (Mies)Muschel *f*.

must¹ [mʌst] 1. muß(te); darf; durfte; *I* ~ *not* ich darf nicht; 2. Muß *n*.

must² [~] Schimmel *m*, Moder *m*.

must³ [~] Most *m*.

mustach|e *Am.* [məs'tæʃ], ~io *Am.* [məs'ta:ʃou] = moustache.

mustard ['mʌstəd] Senf *m*.

muster ['mʌstə] 1. ✕ Musterung *f*; *fig.* Heerschau *f*; 2. ✕ mustern; aufbieten, aufbringen.

musty ['mʌsti] mod(e)rig, muffig.

muta|ble □ ['mju:təbl] veränderlich; wankelmütig; ~tion [mju(:)-'teiʃən] Veränderung *f*.

mute [mju:t] 1. □ stumm; 2. Stumme(r *m*) *f*; Statist(in); 3. dämpfen.

mutilate ['mju:tileit] verstümmeln.

mutin|eer [mju:ti'niə] Meuterer *m*; ~ous □ ['mju:tinəs] meuterisch; ~y [~ni] 1. Meuterei *f*; 2. meutern.

mutter ['mʌtə] 1. Gemurmel *n*; Gemurre *n*; 2. murmeln; murren.

mutton ['mʌtn] Hammelfleisch *n*; leg of ~ Hammelkeule *f*; ~ chop Hammelkotelett *n*.

mutual □ ['mju:tjuəl] gegenseitig; gemeinsam.

muzzle ['mʌzl] 1. Maul *n*, Schnauze *f*; Mündung *f* e-r *Feuerwaffe*; Maulkorb *m*; 2. e-n Maulkorb anlegen (*dat.*); *fig.* den Mund stopfen (*dat.*).

my [mai] mein(e).

myrrh ♀ [mə:] Myrrhe *f*.

myrtle ♀ ['mə:tl] Myrte *f*.

myself [mai'self] (ich) selbst; mir; mich; *by* ~ allein.

myster|ious □ [mis'tiəriəs] geheimnisvoll, mysteriös; ~y [~'mistəri] Mysterium *n*; Geheimnis *n*; Rätsel *n*.

mysti|c ['mistik] 1. *a.* ~cal □ [~kəl] mystisch, geheimnisvoll; 2. Mystiker *m*; ~fy [~ifai] mystifizieren, täuschen.

myth [miθ] Mythe *f*, Mythos *m*, Sage *f*.

N

nab *sl.* [næb] schnappen, erwischen.

nacre ['neikə] Perlmutter *f*.

nadir ['neidiə] *ast.* Nadir *m* (*Fußpunkt*); *fig.* tiefster Stand.

nag [næg] 1. F Klepper *m*; 2. *v/i.* nörgeln, quengeln; *v/t.* bekritteln.

nail [neil] 1. (Finger-, Zehen)Nagel *m*; ⊕ Nagel *m*; *zo.* Kralle *f*, Klaue *f*; 2. (an-, fest)nageln; *Augen etc.* heften (*to auf acc.*); ~scissors ['neilsizəz] *pl.* Nagelschere *f*; ~varnish Nagellack *m*.

naïve [na:'i:v], naive □ [neiv] naiv; ungekünstelt.

naked □ ['neikid] nackt, bloß; kahl; *fig.* unverhüllt; *poet.* schutzlos;

~ness [~dnis] Nacktheit *f*, Blöße *f*; Kahlheit *f*; Schutzlosigkeit *f*; *fig.* Unverhülltheit *f*.

name [neim] 1. Name *m*; Ruf *m*; *of od. by the* ~ *of* ... namens ...; *call s.o.* ~s j-n beschimpfen; 2. (be-) nennen; erwähnen; ernennen; ~less □ ['neimlis] namenlos; unbekannt; ~ly [~li] nämlich; ~plate Namens-, Tür-, Firmenschild *n*; ~sake ['neimseik] Namensvetter *m*.

nanny ['næni] Kindermädchen *n*; ~goat Ziege *f*.

nap [næp] 1. *Tuch*-Noppe *f*; Schläfchen *n*; have od. take a ~ ein Nickerchen machen; 2. schlummern.

nape [neip] *mst* ~ *of the neck* Genick *n.*

nap|kin ['næpkin] Serviette *f*; Windel *f*; *mst sanitary* ~ *Am.* Monatsbinde *f*; ~**py** F ['næpi] Windel *f.*

narcosis ~ [nɑː'kousis] Narkose *f.*

narcotic [nɑː'kɔtik] 1. (~*ally*) narkotisch; 2. Betäubungsmittel *n.*

narrat|e [næ'reit] erzählen; ~**ion** [~eiʃən] Erzählung *f*; ~**ive** ['nærətiv] 1. [erzählend; 2. Erzählung *f*; ~**or** [næ'reitə] Erzähler *m.*

narrow ['nærou] 1. eng, schmal; beschränkt; knapp (*Mehrheit, Entkommen*); engherzig; 2. ~*s pl.* Engpaß *m*; Meerenge *f*; 3. (sich) verengen; beschränken; einengen; *Maschen* abnehmen; ~**chested** schmalbrüstig; ~**minded** engherzig; ~**ness** [~ounis] Enge *f*; Beschränktheit *f (a. fig.)*; Engherzigkeit *f.*

nary *Am.* F ['nɛəri] kein.

nasal [['neizəl] nasal; Nasen...

nasty [['nɑːsti] schmutzig; garstig; eklig, widerlich; häßlich; unflätig; ungemütlich

natal ['neitl] Geburts...

nation ['neiʃən] Nation *f*, Volk *n.*

national ['næʃənl] 1. ☐ national; Volks..., Staats...; 2. Staatsangehörige(r *m*) *f*; ~**ity** [næʃə'næliti] Nationalität *f*; ~**ize** ['næʃnəlaiz] naturalisieren, einbürgern; verstaatlichen.

nation-wide ['neiʃənwaid] die ganze Nation umfassend.

native ['neitiv] 1. ☐ angeboren; heimatlich, Heimat...; eingeboren; einheimisch; ~ *language* Muttersprache *f*; 2. Eingeborene(r *m*) *f*; ~**born** (im Lande) geboren, einheimisch.

nativity [nə'tiviti] Geburt *f.*

natter F ['nætə] plaudern.

natural ☐ ['nætʃrəl] natürlich; *engS...* angeboren; ungezwungen; unehelich (*Kind*); ~ *science* Naturwissenschaft *f*; ~**ist** [~list] Naturalist *m*; Naturforscher *m*; Tierhändler *m*; ~**ize** [~laiz] einbürgern; ~**ness** [~lnis] Natürlichkeit *f.*

nature ['neitʃə] Natur *f.*

naught [nɔːt] Null *f*; *set at* ~ für nichts achten; ~**y** ☐ ['nɔːti] unartig.

nause|a ['nɔːsjə] Übelkeit *f*; Ekel *m*; ~**ate** ['nɔːsieit] *v/i.* Ekel empfinden; *v/t.* verabscheuen; *be* ~*d* sich ekeln; ~**ous** [['nɔːsjəs] ekelhaft.

nautical ['nɔːtikəl] nautisch; See...

naval ☓ ['neivəl] See..., Marine...; ~ *base* Flottenstützpunkt *m.*

nave[1] ☓ [neiv] (Kirchen)Schiff *n.*

nave[2] [~] Rad-Nabe *f.*

navel ['neivəl] Nabel *m*; Mitte *f.*

naviga|ble ☐ ['nævigəbl] schiffbar; fahrbar; lenkbar; ~**te** [~geit] *v/i.* schiffen, fahren; *v/t. See etc.* befahren; steuern; ~**tion** [nævi'geiʃən]

Schiffahrt *f*; Navigation *f*; ~**tor** ['nævigeitə] Seefahrer *m.*

navy ['neivi] (Kriegs)Marine *f.*

nay † [nei] nein; nein vielmehr.

near [niə] 1. *adj.* nahe; gerade (*Weg*); nahe verwandt; verwandt; vertraut; genau; knapp; knauserig; ~ *at hand* dicht dabei; 2. *adv.* nahe; 3. *prp.* nahe (*dat.*), nahe bei *od.* an; 4. sich nähern (*dat.*); ~**by** ['niəbai] in der Nähe (gelegen); nah; ~**ly** [~nli] nahe; fast, beinahe; genau; ~**ness** ['niənis] Nähe *f*; ~**sighted** kurzsichtig.

neat [[niːt] nett; niedlich; geschickt; ordentlich; sauber; rein; ~**ness** ['niːtnis] Nettigkeit *f*; Sauberkeit *f*; Zierlichkeit *f.*

nebulous [['nebjuləs] neblig.

necess|ary [['nesisəri] 1. notwendig; unvermeidlich; 2. *mst necessaries pl.* Bedürfnisse *n/pl.*; ~**itate** [ni'sesiteit] *et.* erfordern; zwingen; ~**ity** [~ti] Notwendigkeit *f*; Zwang *m*; Not *f.*

neck [nek] 1. (*a. Flaschen*)Hals *m*; Nacken *m*, Genick *n*; Ausschnitt *m* (*Kleid*); ~ *and* ~ Kopf an Kopf; ~ *or nothing* F alles oder nichts; 2. *sl.* sich abknutschen; ~**band** ['nekbænd] Halsbund *m*; ~**erchief** ['nekətʃif] Halstuch *m*; ~**lace** ['neklis], ~**let** [~lit] Halskette *f*; ~**tie** Krawatte *f.*

necromancy ['nekroumænsi] Zauberei *f.*

née [nei] *bei Frauennamen:* geborene.

need [niːd] 1. Not *f*; Notwendigkeit *f*; Bedürfnis *n*; Mangel *m*, Bedarf *m*; *be od. stand in* ~ *of* brauchen; 2. nötig haben, brauchen; bedürfen (*gen.*); müssen; ~**ful** ['niːdful] notwendig.

needle ['niːdl] 1. Nadel *f*; Zeiger *m*; 2. nähen; *bsd. Am.* irritieren; anstacheln.

needless [['niːdlis] unnötig.

needle|woman ['niːdlwumən] Näherin *f*; ~**work** Handarbeit *f.*

needy [['niːdi] bedürftig, arm.

nefarious [[ni'fɛəriəs] schändlich.

negat|e [ni'geit] verneinen; ~**ion** [~eiʃən] Verneinung *f*; Nichts *n*; ~**ive** ['negətiv] 1. ☐ negativ; verneinend; 2. Verneinung *f*; *phot.* Negativ *n*; 3. ablehnen.

neglect [ni'glekt] 1. Vernachlässigung *f*; Nachlässigkeit *f*; 2. vernachlässigen; ~**ful** ☐ [~tful] nachlässig.

negligen|ce ['neglidʒəns] Nachlässigkeit *f*; ~**t** [[~nt] nachlässig.

negligible ['neglidʒəbl] nebensächlich; unbedeutend.

negotia|te [ni'gouʃieit] verhandeln (über *acc.*); zustande bringen; bewältigen; *Wechsel* begeben; ~**tion** [nigouʃi'eiʃən] Begebung *f e-s Wechsels etc.*; Ver-, Unterhandlung *f*; Bewältigung *f*; ~tor [ni'gouʃieitə] Unterhändler *m*.

negr|ess ['ni:gris] Negerin *f*; ~o [~rou], *pl.* ~oes Neger *m*.

neigh [nei] 1. Wiehern *n*; 2. wiehern.

neighbo(u)r ['neibə] Nachbar(in); Nächste(r *m*) *f*); ~hood [~ʃhud] Nachbarschaft *f*; ~ing [~əriŋ] benachbart; ~ly [~əli] nachbarlich, freundlich; ~ship [~əʃip] Nachbarschaft *f*.

neither ['naiðə] 1. keiner (von beiden); 2. ~ ... nor ... weder ... noch ...; not ... ~ auch nicht.

nephew ['nevju:(:)] Neffe *m*.

nerve [nə:v] 1. Nerv *m*; Sehne *f*; Blatt-Rippe *f*; Kraft *f*, Mut *m*; Dreistigkeit *f*; get on one's ~s e-m auf die Nerven gehen; 2. kräftigen; ermutigen; ~less [] ['nə:vlis] kraftlos.

nervous [] ['nə:vəs] Nerven...; nervig, kräftig; nervös; ~ness [~snis] Nervigkeit *f*; Nervosität *f*.

nest [nest] 1. Nest *n* (*a. fig.*); 2. nisten; ~le [~nesl] *v/i.* (sich ein-) nisten; sich (an)schmiegen; *v/t.* schmiegen.

net¹ [net] 1. Netz *n*; 2. mit e-m Netz fangen *od.* umgeben.

net² [~] 1. netto; Rein...; 2. netto einbringen.

nether ['neðə] nieder; Unter...

nettle ['netl] 1. ⚘ Nessel *f*; 2. ärgern.

network ['netwə:k] (Straßen-, Kanal- *etc.*)Netz *n*; Sendergruppe *f*.

neurosis ⚘ [njuə'rousis] Neurose *f*.

neuter ['nju:tə] 1. geschlechtslos; 2. geschlechtsloses Tier; *gr.* Neutrum *n*.

neutral ['nju:trəl] 1. neutral; unparteiisch; 2. Neutrale(r *m*) *f*); Null(punkt *m*) *f*); Leerlauf(stellung *f*) *m*; ~ity [nju(:)'træliti] Neutralität *f*; ~ize ['nju:trəlaiz] neutralisieren.

neutron *phys.* ['nju:trɔn] Neutron *n*.

never ['nevə] nie(mals); gar nicht; ~more [~'mɔ:] nie wieder; ~theless [nevəðə'les] nichtsdestoweniger.

new [nju:] neu; frisch; unerfahren; ~comer ['nju:'kʌmə] Ankömmling *m*; ~ly ['nju:li] neulich; neu.

news [nju:z] *mst. sg.* Neuigkeit(en *pl.*) *f*, Nachricht(en *pl.*) *f*; ~agent ['nju:zeidʒənt] Zeitungshändler *m*; ~boy Zeitungsausträger *m*; ~butcher *Am. sl.* Zeitungsverkäufer *m*; ~cast Radio: Nachrichten *f/pl.*; ~monger Neuigkeitskrämer *m*; ~paper Zeitung *f*; *attr.* Zeitungs...; ~print Zeitungspapier *n*; ~reel Film: Wochenschau *f*; ~room Lesezimmer *n*; *Am. Zeitung*: Nachrichtenredaktion *f*; ~stall, *Am.* ~stand Zeitungskiosk *m*.

new year ['nju:'jə:] *das* neue Jahr; New Year's Day Neujahr(stag *m*) *n*; New Year's Eve Silvester *n*.

next [nekst] 1. *adj.* nächst; ~ *but one der* übernächste; ~ door to *fig.* beinahe; ~ to nächst (*dat.*); 2. *adv.* zunächst, gleich darauf; nächstens.

nibble ['nibl] *v/t.* knabbern an (*dat.*); *v/i.* ~ at nagen *od.* knabbern an (*dat.*); (herum)kritteln an (*dat.*).

nice [nais] fein; wählerisch; peinlich (genau); heikel; nett; niedlich; hübsch; ~ly ['naisli] F (sehr) gut; ~ty ['naisiti] Feinheit *f*; Genauigkeit *f*; Spitzfindigkeit *f*.

niche [nitʃ] Nische *f*.

nick [nik] 1. Kerbe *f*; *in the* ~ *of time* gerade zur rechten Zeit; 2. (ein)kerben; *sl.* j-n schnappen.

nickel ['nikl] 1. *min.* Nickel *m* (*Am. a. Fünfcentstück*); 2. vernickeln.

nick-nack ['niknæk] = *knickknack*.

nickname ['nikneim] 1. Spitzname *m*; 2. e-n Spitznamen geben (*dat.*).

niece [ni:s] Nichte *f*.

nifty *Am. sl.* ['nifti] elegant; stinkend.

niggard ['nigəd] Geizhals *m*; ~ly [~dli] geizig, knauserig; karg.

nigger F *mst contp.* ['nigə] Nigger *m* (*Neger*); ~ *in the woodpile Am. sl.* der Haken an der Sache.

night [nait] Nacht *f*; Abend *m*; *by* ~, *in the* ~, *at* ~ nachts; ~cap ['nait-kæp] Nachtmütze *f*; Nachttrunk *m*; ~club Nachtlokal *n*; ~dress (Damen)Nachthemd *n*; ~fall Einbruch *m* der Nacht; ~gown = *night-dress*; ~ingale *orn.*['naitiŋgeil] Nachtigall *f*; ~ly ['naitli] nächtlich; jede Nacht; ~mare Alptraum *m*; ~shirt (Herren)Nachthemd *n*; ~spot *Am.* Nachtlokal *n*; ~y ['naiti] F(Damen- *od.* Kinder)Nachthemd *n*.

nil [nil] *bsd. Sport:* nichts, null.

nimble [] ['nimbl] flink, behend.

nimbus ['nimbəs] Nimbus *m*, Heiligenschein *m*; Regenwolke *f*.

nine [nain] 1. neun; 2. Neun *f*; ~pins ['nainpinz] *pl.* Kegel(spiel *n*) *m/pl.*; ~teen ['nain'ti:n] neunzehn; ~ty ['nainti] neunzig.

ninny F ['nini] Dummkopf *m*.

ninth [nainθ] 1. neunte(r, -s); 2. Neuntel *n*; ~ly ['nainθli] neuntens.

nip [nip] 1. Kniff *m*; scharfer Frost; Schlückchen *n*; 2. zwicken; schneiden (*Kälte*); *sl.* flitzen; nippen; ~ *in the bud* im Keime ersticken.

nipper ['nipə] Krebsschere *f*; (*a pair of*) ~s *pl.* (eine) (Kneif)Zange.

nipple ['nipl] Brustwarze *f*.

Nisei *Am.* ['ni:'sei] (*a. pl.*) Japaner *m, geboren in den USA.*

nit|re, *Am.* **~er** ⚘ ['naitə] Salpeter *m.*

nitrogen ['naitridʒən] Stickstoff *m.*

no [nou] 1. *adj.* kein; *in ~ time* im Nu; *~ one* keiner; 2. *adv.* nein; nicht; 3. Nein *n*.

nobility [nou'biliti] Adel *m* (*a. fig.*).

noble ['noubl] 1. ☐ adlig; edel, vornehm; vortrefflich; 2. Adlige(r *m*) *f*; **~man** Adlige(r) *m*; **~minded** edelmütig; **~ness** [␣lnis] Adel *m*; Würde *f*.

nobody ['noubədi] niemand.

nocturnal [nɔk'tə:nl] Nacht...

nod [nɔd] 1. nicken; schlafen; (sich) neigen; **~ding acquaintance** oberflächliche Bekanntschaft; 2. Nicken *n*; Wink *m*.

node [noud] Knoten *m* (*a. ♀ u. ast.*); ♂ Überbein *n*.

noise [nɔiz] 1. Lärm *m*; Geräusch *n*; Geschrei *n*; *big ~ bsd. Am.* F großes Tier (*Person*); 2. *~ abroad* ausschreien; **~less** ☐ ['nɔizlis] geräuschlos.

noisome ['nɔisəm] schädlich; widerlich.

noisy ☐ ['nɔizi] geräuschvoll, lärmend; aufdringlich (*Farbe*).

nomin|al ☐ ['nɔminl] nominell; (nur) dem Namen nach (vorhanden); namentlich; *~ value* Nennwert *m*; **~ate** [␣neit] ernennen; zur Wahl vorschlagen; **~ation** [nɔmi'neiʃən] Ernennung *f*; Vorschlagsrecht *n*.

nominative ['nɔminətiv] *a. ~ case gr.* Nominativ *m*.

non [nɔn] *in Zssgn*: nicht, un..., Nicht...

nonage ['nounidʒ] Minderjährigkeit *f*.

non-alcoholic ['nɔnælkə'hɔlik] alkoholfrei.

nonce [nɔns]: *for the ~* nur für diesen Fall.

non-commissioned ['nɔnkə'miʃənd] nicht bevollmächtigt; *~ officer* ✗ Unteroffizier *m*.

non-committal ['nɔnkə'mitl] unverbindlich.

non-compliance ['nɔnkəm'plaiəns] Zuwiderhandlung *f*, Verstoß *m*.

non-conductor ✗ ['nɔnkəndʌktə] Nichtleiter *m*.

nonconformist ['nɔnkən'fɔ:mist] Dissident(in), Freikirchler(in).

nondescript ['nɔndiskript] unbestimmbar; schwer zu beschreiben(d).

none [nʌn] 1. keine(r, -s); nichts; 2. keineswegs, gar nicht; *~ the less* nichtsdestoweniger.

nonentity [nɔ'nentiti] Nichtsein *n*; Unding *n*; Nichts *n*; *fig.* Null *f*.

non-existence ['nɔnig'zistəns] Nicht(da)sein *n*.

non-fiction ['nɔn'fikʃən] Sachbücher *n/pl*.

nonpareil ['nɔnpərəl] Unvergleichliche(r *m*, -s *n*) *f*.

non-party ['nɔn'pɑ:ti] parteilos.

non-performance ✗ ['nɔnpə-'fɔ:məns] Nichterfüllung *f*.

nonplus ['nɔn'plʌs] 1. Verlegenheit *f*; 2. in Verlegenheit bringen.

non-resident ['nɔn'rezidənt] nicht im Haus *od.* am Ort wohnend.

nonsens|e ['nɔnsəns] Unsinn *m*; **~ical** ☐ [nɔn'sensikəl] unsinnig.

non-skid ['nɔn'skid] rutschfest.

non-smoker ['nɔn'smoukə] Nichtraucher *m*.

non-stop ❤, ✗ ['nɔn'stɔp] durchgehend; Ohnehalt...

non-union ['nɔn'ju:njən] nicht organisiert (*Arbeiter*).

non-violence ['nɔn'vaiələns] (Politik *f* der) Gewaltlosigkeit *f*.

noodle ['nu:dl] Nudel *f*.

nook [nuk] Ecke *f*, Winkel *m*.

noon [nu:n] Mittag *m*; *attr.* Mittags...; **~day** ['nu:ndei], **~tide**, **~time** = *noon.*

noose [nu:s] 1. Schlinge *f*; 2. (mit der Schlinge) fangen; schlingen.

nope *Am.* F [noup] nein.

nor [nɔ:] noch; auch nicht.

norm [nɔ:m] Norm *f*, Regel *f*; Muster *n*; Maßstab *m*; **~al** ☐ ['nɔ:məl] normal; **~alize** [␣laiz] normalisieren; normen.

north [nɔ:θ] 1. Nord(en *m*); 2. nördlich; Nord...; **~east** [nɔ:θ'i:st] 1. Nordost *m*; 2. *a.* **~eastern** [␣tən] nordöstlich; **~erly** ['nɔ:ðəli], **~ern** [␣ən] nördlich; Nord...; **~erner** [␣nə] Nordländer(in); *Am.* ♀ Nordstaatler(in); **~ward(s)** ['nɔ:θwəd(z)] *adv.* nördlich; nordwärts; **~west** ['nɔ:θ'west] 1. Nordwest *m*; 2. *a.* **~western** [␣tən] nordwestlich.

Norwegian [nɔ:'wi:dʒən] 1. norwegisch; 2. Norweger(in); Norwegisch *n*.

nose [nouz] 1. Nase *f*; Spitze *f*; Schnauze *f*; 2. *v/t.* riechen; *~ one's way* vorsichtig fahren; *v/i.* schnüffeln; **~dive** ✗ ['nouzdaiv] Sturzflug *m*; **~gay** ['nouzgei] Blumenstrauß *m*.

nostalgia [nɔs'tældʒiə] Heimweh *n*, Sehnsucht *f*.

nostril ['nɔstril] Nasenloch *n*, Nüster *f*.

nostrum ['nɔstrəm] Geheimmittel *n*; Patentlosung *f*.

nosy F ['nouzi] neugierig.

not [nɔt] nicht.

notable ['noutəbl] 1. ☐ bemerkenswert; 2. angesehene Person.

notary ['noutəri] *oft ~ public* Notar *m*. [*f*.]

notation [nou'teiʃən] Bezeichnung

notch [nɔtʃ] 1. Kerbe *f*, Einschnitt *m*; Scharte *f*; *Am.* Engpaß *m*, Hohlweg *m*; 2. einkerben.

note [nout] 1. Zeichen *n*; Notiz *f*; Anmerkung *f*; Briefchen *n*; (*bsd.* Schuld)Schein *m*; Note *f*; Ton *m*; Ruf *m*; Beachtung *f*; *take ~s* sich

Notizen machen; **2.** be(ob)achten; besonders erwähnen; *a.* ~ *down* notieren; mit Anmerkungen versehen; **~book** ['noutbuk] Notizbuch *n*; **~d** bekannt; berüchtigt; **~paper** Briefpapier *n*; **~worthy** beachtenswert.

nothing ['nʌθiŋ] **1.** nichts; **2.** Nichts *n*; Null *f*; *for* ~ umsonst; *good for* ~ untauglich; *bring (come) to* ~ zunichte machen (werden).

notice ['noutis] **1.** Notiz *f*; Nachricht *f*, Bekanntmachung *f*; Kündigung *f*; Warnung *f*; Beachtung *f*; *at short* ~ kurzfristig; *give* ~ *that* bekanntgeben, daß; *give a week's* ~ acht Tage vorher kündigen; *take* ~ *of* Notiz nehmen von; *without* ~ fristlos; **2.** bemerken; be(ob)achten; **~able** □ [~əbl] wahrnehmbar; bemerkenswert.

noti|fication [noutifi'keiʃən] Anzeige *f*; Meldung *f*; Bekanntmachung *f*; **~fy** ['noutifai] *et.* anzeigen, melden; bekanntmachen.

notion ['nouʃən] Begriff *m*, Vorstellung *f*; Absicht *f*, **~s** *pl. Am.* Kurzwaren *f/pl.*

notorious □ [nou'tɔ:riəs] all-, weltbekannt; notorisch; berüchtigt.

notwithstanding *prp.* [nɔtwiθ-'stændiŋ] ungeachtet, trotz (*gen.*).

nought [nɔ:t] Null *f*, Nichts *n*.

noun *gr.* [naun] Hauptwort *n*.

nourish ['nʌriʃ] (er)nähren; *fig.* hegen; **~ing** [~ʃiŋ] nahrhaft; **~ment** [~ʃmənt] Nahrung(smittel *n*) *f*.

novel ['nɔvəl] **1.** neu; ungewöhnlich; **2.** Roman *m*; **~ist** [~list] Romanschriftsteller(in), Romancier *m*; **~ty** [~lti] Neuheit *f*.

November [nou'vembə] November *m*.

novice ['nɔvis] Neuling *m*; *eccl.* Novize *m, f.*

now [nau] **1.** nun, jetzt; eben; *just* ~ soeben; ~ *and again od.* then dann u. wann; **2.** *cj. a.* ~ *that* nun da.

nowadays ['nauədeiz] heutzutage.

nowhere ['nouwɛə] nirgends.

noxious □ ['nɔkʃəs] schädlich.

nozzle ['nɔzl] ⊕ Düse *f*; Tülle *f.*

nuance [nju(:)'ã:ns] Nuance *f*, Schattierung *f.*

nub [nʌb] Knubbe(n *m*) *f*; *Am.* F springende Punkt *in e-r Sache.*

nucle|ar ['nju:kliə] Kern...; ~ *reactor* Kernreaktor *m*; ~ *research* (Atom-) Kernforschung *f*; **~us** [~əs] Kern *m.*

nude [nju:d] **1.** nackt; **2.** *paint.* Akt *m.*

nudge F [nʌdʒ] **1.** *j-n* heimlich anstoßen; **2.** Rippenstoß *m.*

nugget ['nʌgit] (*bsd.* Gold)Klumpen *m.*

nuisance ['nju:sns] Mißstand *m*;

Ärgernis *n*; Unfug *m*; *fig.* Plage *f*; *what a* ~*l* wie ärgerlich!; *make o.s. od. be a* ~ lästig fallen.

null [nʌl] nichtig; nichtssagend; ~ *and void* null u. nichtig; **~ify** ['nʌlifai] zunichte machen; aufheben, ungültig machen; **~ity** [~iti] Nichtigkeit *f*, Ungültigkeit *f.*

numb [nʌm] **1.** starr; taub (*empfindungslos*); **2.** starr *od.* taub machen; **~ed** erstarrt.

number ['nʌmbə] **1.** Nummer *f*; (An)Zahl *f*; Heft *n*, Lieferung *f*, Nummer *f e-s Werkes*; *without* ~ zahllos; *in* ~ an der Zahl; **2.** zählen; numerieren; **~less** [~əlis] zahllos; **~-plate** *mot.* Nummernschild *n.*

numera|l ['nju:mərəl] **1.** Zahl...; **2.** Ziffer *f*; **~tion** [nju:mə'reiʃən] Zählung *f*; Numerierung *f.*

numerical □ [nju(:)'merikəl] zahlenmäßig; Zahl...

numerous □ ['nju:mərəs] zahlreich.

numskull F ['nʌmskʌl] Dummkopf *m.*

nun [nʌn] Nonne *f*; *orn.* Blaumeise *f.*

nunnery ['nʌnəri] Nonnenkloster *n.*

nuptial ['nʌpʃəl] **1.** Hochzeits..., Ehe...; **2.** ~**s** *pl.* Hochzeit *f.*

nurse [nə:s] **1.** Kindermädchen *n*, Säuglingsschwester *f*; *a.* wet-~ Amme *f*; (Kranken)Pflegerin *f*, (Kranken)Schwester *f*; *at* ~ in Pflege; *put out to* ~ in Pflege geben; **2.** stillen, nähren; großziehen; pflegen; hätscheln; **~ling** ['nə:sliŋ] Säugling *m*; Pflegling *m*; **~maid** ['nə:smeid] Kindermädchen *n*; **~ry** ['nə:sri] Kinderzimmer *n*; ⚹ Pflanzschule *f*; ~ *rhymes* *pl.* Kinderlieder *n/pl.*, -reime *m/pl.*; ~ *school* Kindergarten *m*; ~ *slopes* *pl.* Ski: Idiotenhügel *m/pl.*

nursing ['nə:siŋ] Stillen *n*; (Kranken)Pflege *f*; ~ *bottle* Saugflasche *f*; ~ *home* Privatklinik *f.*

nursling ['nə:sliŋ] = *nurseling.*

nurture ['nə:tʃə] **1.** Pflege *f*; Erziehung *f*; **2.** aufziehen; nähren.

nut [nʌt] Nuß *f*; ⊕ (Schrauben-) Mutter *f*; *sl.* verrückter Kerl; **~s** *pl.* Nußkohle *f*; **~cracker** ['nʌtkrækə] Nußknacker *m*; **~meg** ['nʌtmeg] Muskatnuß *f.*

nutriment ['nju:trimənt] Nahrung *f.*

nutri|tion [nju(:)'triʃən] Ernährung *f*; Nahrung *f*; **~tious** [~əs], **~tive** □ ['nju:tritiv] nahrhaft; Ernährungs...

nut|shell ['nʌtʃel] Nußschale *f*; *in a* ~ in aller Kürze; **~ty** ['nʌti] nußreich; nußartig; *sl.* verrückt.

nylon ['nailən] Nylon *n*; **~s** *pl.* Nylonstrümpfe *m/pl.*

nymph [nimf] Nymphe *f.*

O

o [ou] **1.** oh!; ach!; **2.** (*in Telefon-nummern*) Null *f.*

oaf [ouf] Dummkopf *m*; Tölpel *m.*

oak [ouk] Eiche *f.*

oar [ɔ:] **1.** Ruder *n*; **2.** rudern; **~sman** ['ɔːzmən] Ruderer *m.*

oas|is [ou'eisis], *pl.* **~es** [ou'eisi:z] Oase *f* (*a. fig.*).

oat [out] *mst* **~s** *pl.* Hafer *m*; *feel one's* **~s** *Am.* F groß in Form sein; sich wichtig vorkommen; *sow one's wild* **~s** sich austoben.

oath [ouθ], *pl.* **~s** [ouðz] Eid *m*; Schwur *m*; Fluch *m*; *take* (*make, swear*) *an* **~** e-n Eid leisten, schwören.

oatmeal ['outmi:l] Haferflocken *f/pl.*

obdurate □ ['ɔbdjurit] verstockt.

obedien|ce [ə'bi:djəns] Gehorsam *m*; **~t** □ [**~**nt] gehorsam.

obeisance [ou'beisəns] Ehrerbietung *f*; Verbeugung *f*; *do* **~** huldigen.

obesity [ou'bi:siti] Fettleibigkeit *f.*

obey [ə'bei] gehorchen (*dat.*); *Befehl etc.* befolgen, Folge leisten (*dat.*).

obituary [ə'bitjuəri] Totenliste *f*; Todesanzeige *f*; Nachruf *m*; *attr.* Todes..., Toten...

object 1. ['ɔbdʒikt] Gegenstand *m*; Ziel *n*, *fig.* Zweck *m*; Objekt *n* (*a. gr.*); **2.** [əb'dʒekt] *v/t.* einwenden (*to gegen*); *v/i. et.* dagegen haben (*to ger.* daß).

objection [əb'dʒekʃən] Einwand *m*; **~able** □ [**~**ʃnəbl] nicht einwandfrei; unangenehm.

objective [əb'dʒektiv] **1.** □ objektiv, sachlich; **2.** ✕ Ziel *n.*

object-lens *opt.* ['ɔbdʒiktlenz] Objektiv *n.*

obligat|ion [ɔbli'geiʃən] Verpflichtung *f*; ♣ Schuldverschreibung *f*; *be under* (*an*) **~** *to inf.* j-m zu Dank verpflichtet sein; *be under* **~** *to inf.* die Verpflichtung haben, zu *inf.*; **~ory** □ [ɔ'bligətəri] verpflichtend; verbindlich.

oblig|e [ə'blaidʒ] (zu Dank) verpflichten; nötigen; **~** *s.o.* j-m e-n Gefallen tun; *much* **~d** sehr verbunden; danke bestens; **~ing** □ [**~**dʒiŋ] verbindlich, hilfsbereit, gefällig.

oblique □ [ə'bli:k] schief, schräg.

obliterate [ə'blitəreit] auslöschen, tilgen (*a. fig.*); *Schrift* ausstreichen; *Briefmarken* entwerten.

obliv|ion [ə'bliviən] Vergessen(heit *f*) *n*; **~ous** [**~**iəs] vergeßlich.

oblong ['ɔblɔŋ] länglich; rechteckig.

obnoxious □ [əb'nɔkʃəs] anstößig; widerwärtig, verhaßt.

obscene □ [əb'si:n] unanständig.

obscur|e [əb'skjuə] **1.** □ dunkel (*a. fig.*); unbekannt; **2.** verdunkeln; **~ity** [**~**riti] Dunkelheit *f* (*a. fig.*); Unbekanntheit *f*; Niedrigkeit *f der Geburt.*

obsequies ['ɔbsikwiz] *pl.* Leichenbegängnis *n*, Trauerfeier *f.*

obsequious □ [əb'si:kwiəs] unterwürfig (*to gegen*).

observ|able □ [əb'zə:vəbl] bemerkbar; bemerkenswert; **~ance** [**~**əns] Befolgung *f*; Brauch *m*; **~ant** ⌐ [**~**nt] beobachtend; achtsam; **~ation** [ɔbzə(:)'veiʃən] Beobachtung *f*; Bemerkung *f*; *attr.* Beobachtungs...; Aussichts...; **~atory** [əb'zə:vətri] Sternwarte *f*; **~e** [əb'zə:v] *v/t.* be(ob)achten; acht(geb)en auf (*acc.*); bemerken; *v/i.* sich äußern.

obsess [əb'ses] heimsuchen, quälen; **~ed by** *od.* **with** besessen von; **~ion** [**~**eʃən] Besessenheit *f.*

obsolete ['ɔbsəlit] veraltet.

obstacle ['ɔbstəkl] Hindernis *n.*

obstina|cy ['ɔbstinəsi] Hartnäckigkeit *f*; **~te** □ [**~**nit] halsstarrig; eigensinnig; hartnäckig.

obstruct [əb'strʌkt] verstopfen, versperren; hindern; **~ion** [**~**kʃən] Verstopfung *f*; Hemmung *f*; Hindernis *n*; **~ive** □ [**~**ktiv] hinderlich.

obtain [əb'tein] *v/t.* erlangen, erhalten, erreichen, bekommen; *v/i.* sich erhalten (haben); **~able** ✝ [**~**nəbl] erhältlich.

obtru|de [əb'tru:d] (sich) aufdrängen (*on dat.*); **~sive** □ [**~**u:siv] aufdringlich. [schwerfällig.\]

obtuse ⌐ [əb'tju:s] stumpf(sinnig);\]

obviate ['ɔbvieit] vorbeugen (*dat.*).

obvious ⌐ ['ɔbviəs] offensichtlich, augenfällig, einleuchtend.

occasion [ə'keiʒən] **1.** Gelegenheit *f*; Anlaß *m*; Veranlassung *f*; F (festliches) Ereignis; *on the* **~** *of* anläßlich (*gen.*); **2.** veranlassen; **~al** □ [**~**nl] gelegentlich; Gelegenheits...

occident ['ɔksidənt] Westen *m*; Okzident *m*, Abendland *n*; **~al** □ [ɔksi'dentl] abendländisch, westlich.

occult [ɔ'kʌlt] geheim, verborgen; magisch, okkult.

occup|ant ['ɔkjupənt] Besitzergreifer(in); Bewohner(in); **~ation** [ɔkju'peiʃən] Besitz(ergreifung *f*) *m*; ✕ Besetzung *f*; Beruf *m*; Beschäftigung *f*; **~y** ['ɔkjupai] einnehmen, in Besitz nehmen; ✕ besetzen; besitzen; innehaben; in Anspruch nehmen; beschäftigen.

occur [ə'kə:] vorkommen; sich ereignen; *it* **~red** *to me* es fiel mir ein; **~rence** [ə'kʌrəns] Vorkommen *n*; Vorfall *m*, Ereignis *n.*

ocean ['ouʃən] Ozean m, Meer n.
o'clock [ə'klɔk] Uhr (bei Zeitangaben); five ~ fünf Uhr.
October [ɔk'toubə] Oktober m.
ocul|ar □ ['ɔkjulə] Augen...; ~ist [~list] Augenarzt m.
odd □ [ɔd] ungerade (Zahl); einzeln; und einige od. etwas darüber; überzählig; gelegentlich; sonderbar, merkwürdig; ~ity ['ɔditi] Seltsamkeit f; ~s [ɔdz] oft sg. (Gewinn)Chancen f/pl.; Wahrscheinlichkeit f; Vorteil m; Vorgabe f, Handikap n; Verschiedenheit f; Unterschied m; Streit m; be at ~ with s.o. mit j-m im Streit sein; nicht übereinstimmen mit j-m; ~ and ends Reste m/pl.; Krimskrams m.
ode [oud] Ode f (Gedicht).
odious □ ['oudjəs] verhaßt; ekelhaft.
odo(u)r ['oudə] Geruch m; Duft m.
of prp. [ɔv, əv] allg. von; Ort: bei (the battle ~ Quebec); um (cheat s.o. ~ s.th.); aus (~ charity); vor (dat.) (afraid ~); auf (acc.) (proud ~); über (acc.) (ashamed ~); nach (smell ~ roses; desirous ~); an (acc.) (think ~ s.th.); nimble ~ foot leichtfüßig.
off [ɔːf, ɔf] 1. adv. weg; ab; herunter; aus (vorbei); Zeit: hin (3 months ~); ~ and on ab und an; hin und her; be ~ fort sein, weg sein; engS.: (weg)gehen; zu sein (Hahn etc.); aus sein; well etc. ~ gut etc. daran; 2. prp. von ... (weg, ab, herunter); frei von, ohne; unweit(gen.), neben; ⊕ auf der Höhe von; 3. adj. entfernt(er); abseitsliegend; Neben...; arbeits-, dienstfrei; † ~ shade Fehlfarbe f; 4. int. weg!, fort!, raus!
offal ['ɔfəl] Abfall m; Schund m; ~s pl. Fleischerei: Innereien f/pl.
offen|ce, Am. ~se [ə'fens] Angriff m; Beleidigung f, Kränkung f; Argernis n, Anstoß m; Vergehen n.
offend [ə'fend] v/t. beleidigen, verletzen; ärgern; v/i. sich vergehen; ~er [~də] Übel-, Missetäter(in); Straffällige(r m) f; first ~ noch nicht Vorbestrafte(r m) f.
offensive [ə'fensiv] 1. □ beleidigend; anstößig; ekelhaft; Offensiv..., Angriffs...; 2. Offensive f.
offer ['ɔfə] 1. Angebot n, Anerbieten n; ~ of marriage Heiratsantrag m; 2. v/t. anbieten; Preis, Möglichkeit etc. bieten; Gebet, Opfer darbringen; versuchen; zeigen; Widerstand leisten; v/i. sich bieten; ~ing ['ɔfəriŋ] Opfer n; Anerbieten n, Angebot n.
off-hand ['ɔːf'hænd] aus dem Handgelenk od. Stegreif, unvorbereitet; ungezwungen, frei.
office ['ɔfis] Büro n; Geschäftsstelle

f; Ministerium n; Amt n, Pflicht f; ~s pl. Hilfe f; booking-~ Schalter m; box-~ (Theater- etc.)Kasse f; Divine ♀ Gottesdienst m; ~r [~sə] Beamt|e(r) m, -in f; ✕ Offizier m.
official [ə'fiʃəl] 1. □ offiziell, amtlich; Amts...; 2. Beamte(r) m.
officiate [ə'fiʃieit] amtieren.
officious □ [ə'fiʃəs] aufdring.ich, übereifrig; offiziös, halbamtlich.
off|-licence ['ɔːflaisəns] Schankrecht n über die Straße; ~-print Sonderdruck m; ~set ausgleichen; ~shoot Sproß m; Ausläufer m; ~side ['ɔːf'said] Sport: abseits; ~spring ['ɔːfspriŋ] Nachkomme(nschaft f) m; Ergebnis n.
often ['ɔːfn] oft(mals), häufig.
ogle ['ougl] liebäugeln (mit).
ogre ['ougə] Menschenfresser m.
oh [ou] oh!; ach!
oil [ɔil] 1. Öl n; Erdöl n, Petroleum n; 2. ölen; (a. fig.) schmieren; ~cloth ['ɔilklɔθ] Wachstuch n; ~skin Ölleinwand f; ~s pl. Ölzeug n; ~y □ ['ɔili] ölig (a. fig.); fettig; schmierig (a. fig.).
ointment ['ɔintmənt] Salbe f.
O.K., okay F ['ou'kei] 1. richtig, stimmt!; gut, in Ordnung; 2. annehmen, gutheißen.
old [ould] alt; altbekannt; althergebracht; erfahren; ~ age (das) Alter; days of ~ alte Zeiten f/pl.; ~-age ['ouldeidʒ] Alters...; ~-fashioned ['ould'fæʃənd] altmodisch; altväterlich; ♀ Glory Sternenbanner n; ~ish ['ouldiʃ] ältlich.
olfactory anat. [ɔl'fæktəri] Geruchs...
olive ['ɔliv] ♀ Olive f; Olivgrün n.
Olympic Games [ou'limpik 'geimz] Olympische Spiele pl.
ominous □ ['ɔminəs] unheilvoll.
omission [ou'miʃən] Unterlassung f; Auslassung f.
omit [ou'mit] unterlassen; auslassen.
omnipoten|ce [ɔm'nipətəns] Allmacht f; ~t □ [~nt] allmächtig.
omniscient □ [ɔm'nisiənt] allwissend.
on [ɔn] 1. prp. mst auf; engS.: an (~ the wall, ~ the Thames); auf ... (los), nach ... (hin)(march ~ London); auf ... (hin) (~ his authority); Zeit: an (~ the 1st of April); (gleich) nach, bei (~ his arrival); über (acc.) (talk ~ a subject); nach (~ this model); get ~ a train bsd. Am. in e-n Zug einsteigen; ~ hearing it als ich etc. es hörte; 2. adv. darauf; auf (keep one's hat ~), an (have a coat ~); voraus, vorwärts; weiter (and so ~); be ~ im Gange sein; auf sein (Hahn etc.); an sein (Licht etc.); 3. int. drauf!, ran!
once [wʌns] 1. adv. einmal; einst (-mals); at ~ (so)gleich, sofort; zu-

gleich; ~ *for all* ein für allemal; ~ *in a while* dann und wann; *this* ~ dieses eine Mal; 2. *cj. a.* ~ *that* sobald.

one [wʌn] **1.** ein; einzig; eine(r), ein; eins; man; ~ *day* eines Tages; **2.** Eine(r) *m;* Eins *f; the little* ~*s pl.* die Kleinen *pl.;* ~ *another* einander; *at* ~ einig; ~ *by* ~ einzeln; *I for* ~ ich für meinen Teil.

onerous ⬜ ['ɔnərəs] lästig.

one|self [wʌn'self] (man) selbst, sich; ~**-sided** ⬜ ['wʌn'saidid] einseitig; ~**-way** ['wʌnwei]: ~ *street* Einbahnstraße *f.*

onion ['ʌnjən] Zwiebel *f.*

onlooker ['ɔnlukə] Zuschauer(in).

only ['ounli] **1.** *adj.* einzig; **2.** *adv.* nur; bloß; erst; ~ *yesterday* erst gestern; **3.** *cj.* ~ (*that*) nur daß.

onrush ['ɔnrʌʃ] Ansturm *m.*

onset ['ɔnset], **onslaught** ['ɔnslɔːt] Angriff *m; bsd. fig.* Anfall *m;* Anfang *m.*

onward ['ɔnwəd] **1.** *adj.* fortschreitend; **2.** *a.* ~*s adv.* vorwärts, weiter.

ooze [uːz] **1.** Schlamm *m;* **2.** *v/i.* (durch)sickern; ~ *away* schwinden; *v/t.* ausströmen, ausschwitzen.

opaque ⬜ [ou'peik] undurchsichtig.

open ['oupən] **1.** *allg* offen; geöffnet, auf; frei (*Feld etc.*); öffentlich; offenstehend, unentschieden; aufrichtig; zugänglich (*to dat.*); aufgeschlossen (*to gegenüber*); mild (*Wetter*); **2.** *in the* ~ (*air*) im Freien; *come out into the* ~ *fig.* an die Öffentlichkeit treten; **3.** *v/t.* öffnen; eröffnen (*a. fig.*); *v/i.* (sich) öffnen; anfangen; ~ *into* führen in (*acc.*) (*Tür etc.*); ~ *on to* hinausgehen auf (*acc.*) (*Fenster etc.*); ~ *out* sich ausbreiten; ~**-air** ['oupn'ɛə] im Freien (stattfindend), Freilicht...; Frei-(luft)...; ~**-armed** ['oupn'ɑːmd] herzlich, warm; ~**er** ['oupnə] (Er-)Öffner(in); (Dosen)Öffner *m;* ~**-eyed** ['oupn'aid] wach; mit offenen Augen; aufmerksam; ~**-handed** ['oupn'hændid] freigebig, großzügig; ~**-hearted** ['oupnhɑːtid] offen(herzig), aufrichtig; ~**ing** ['oupniŋ] (Er)Öffnung *f;* Gelegenheit *f; attr.* Eröffnungs...; ~**-minded** *fig.* ['oupn'maindid] aufgeschlossen. (*pl.*) Opernglas *n.*)

opera ['ɔpərə] Oper *f;* ~**-glass**(**se**

operat|e ['ɔpəreit] *v/t.* ⚙ operieren; *bsd. Am.* in Gang bringen; *Maschine* bedienen; *Unternehmen* leiten; *v/i.* (ein)wirken; sich auswirken; arbeiten; ✝, ⚙, ✕ operieren; ~**ion** [ɔpə-'reiʃən] Wirkung *f;* Tätigkeit *f;* ⚙, ✕, ✝ Operation *f; be in* ~ in Betrieb sein; in Kraft sein; ~**ive** ['ɔpərətiv] **1.** ⬜ wirksam, tätig; praktisch; ⚙ operativ; **2.** Arbeiter *m;* ~**or** [~reitə] Operateur *m;* Telephonist(in); ⊕ Maschinist *m.*

opin|e [ou'pain] meinen; ~**ion** [ə'pinjən] Meinung *f;* Ansicht *f;* Stellungnahme *f;* Gutachten *n; in my* ~ meines Erachtens.

opponent [ə'pounənt] Gegner *m.*

opportun|e ⬜ ['ɔpətjuːn] passend; rechtzeitig; günstig; ~**ity** [ɔpə'tjuːniti] (*günstige*) Gelegenheit.

oppos|e [ə'pouz] entgegen-, gegenüberstellen; bekämpfen; ~**ed** entgegengesetzt; *be* ~ *to* gegen ... sein; ~**ite** ['ɔpəzit] **1.** ⬜ gegenüberliegend; entgegengesetzt; **2.** *prp. u. adv.* gegenüber; **3.** Gegenteil *n;* ~**ition** [ɔpə'ziʃən] Gegenüberstehen *n,* Widerstand *m;* Gegensatz *m;* Widerspruch *m,* -streit *m;* ✝ Konkurrenz *f;* Opposition *f.*

oppress [ə'pres] be-, unterdrücken; ~**ion** [~ʃən] Unterdrückung *f;* Druck *m;* Bedrängnis *f;* Bedrücktheit *f;* ~**ive** ⬜ [~esiv] (be)drückend; gewaltsam.

optic ['ɔptik] Augen..., Seh...; ~**-al** [~kəl] optisch; ~**ian** [ɔp'tiʃən] Optiker *m.*

optimism ['ɔptimizəm] Optimismus *m.*

option ['ɔpʃən] Wahl(freiheit) *f;* ✝ Vorkaufsrecht *n,* Option *f;* ~**al** ⬜ [~nl] freigestellt, wahlfrei.

opulence ['ɔpjuləns] Reichtum *m.*

or [ɔː] oder; ~ *else* sonst, wo nicht.

oracular ⬜ [ɔ'rækjulə] orakelhaft.

oral ⬜ ['ɔːrəl] mündlich; Mund...

orange ['ɔrindʒ] **1.** Orange(farbe) *f;* Apfelsine *f;* **2.** orangefarben; ~**ade** ['ɔrindʒ'eid] Orangenlimonade *f.*

orat|ion [ɔ'reiʃən] Rede *f;* ~**or** ['ɔrətə] Redner *m;* ~**ory** [~əri] Redekunst *f,* Rhetorik *f;* Kapelle *f.*

orb [ɔːb] Ball *m; fig.* Himmelskörper *m; poet.* Augapfel *m;* ~**it** ['ɔːbit] **1.** Planetenbahn *f;* Kreis-, Umlaufbahn *f;* Auge(nhöhle *f*) *n;* **2.** sich in e-r Umlaufbahn bewegen.

orchard ['ɔːtʃəd] Obstgarten *m.*

orchestra ♩ ['ɔːkistrə] Orchester *n.*

orchid ⚘ ['ɔːkid] Orchidee *f.*

ordain [ɔː'dein] an-, verordnen; bestimmen; *Priester* ordinieren.

ordeal *fig.* [ɔː'diːl] schwere Prüfung.

order ['ɔːdə] **1.** Ordnung *f;* Anordnung *f;* Befehl *m;* Regel *f;* ✝ Auftrag *m;* Zahlungsanweisung *f;* Klasse *f,* Rang *m;* Orden *m* (*a. eccl.*); *take* (*holy*) ~*s* in den geistlichen Stand treten; *in* ~ *to inf.* um zu *inf.; in* ~ *that* damit; *make to* ~ auf Bestellung anfertigen; *standing* ~*s pol. parl.* Geschäftsordnung *f;* **2.** (an)ordnen; befehlen; ✝ bestellen; *j-n* beordern; ~**ly** ['ɔːdəli] **1.** ordentlich; ruhig; regelmäßig; **2.** ✕ Ordonnanz *f;* ✕ Bursche *m;* Krankenpfleger *m.*

ordinal ['ɔːdinl] **1.** Ordnungs...; **2.** *a.* ~ *number* Ordnungszahl *f.*

ordinance ['ɔːdinəns] Verordnung *f.*

ordinary □ ['ɔːdnri] gewöhnlich.

ordnance ✕, ⚓ ['ɔːdnəns] Artillerie f, Geschütze n/pl.; Feldzeugwesen n.

ordure ['ɔːdjuə] Kot m, Schmutz m.

ore [ɔː] Erz n.

organ ['ɔːgən] ♪ Orgel f; Organ n; ~grinder [~ŋgraində] Leierkastenmann m; ~ic [ɔː'gænik] (~ally) organisch; ~ization [ɔːgənai'zeiʃən] Organisation f; ~ize ['ɔːgənaiz] organisieren; ~izer [~zə] Organisator(in).

orgy ['ɔːdʒi] Ausschweifung f.

orient ['ɔːriənt] 1. Osten m; Orient m, Morgenland n; 2. orientieren; ~al [ɔːri'entl] 1. □ östlich; orientalisch; 2. Oriental|e m, -in f; ~ate ['ɔːrienteit] orientieren.

orifice ['ɔrifis] Mündung f; Öffnung f.

origin ['ɔridʒin] Ursprung m; Anfang m; Herkunft f.

original [ə'ridʒənl] 1. □ ursprünglich; originell; Original...; † Stamm...; 2. Original n; ~ity [ɔridʒi'næliti] Originalität f; ~ly [ə'ridʒnəli] originell; ursprünglich, zuerst, anfangs, anfänglich.

originat|e [ə'ridʒineit] v/t. hervorbringen, schaffen; v/i. entstehen; ~or [~tə] Urheber m.

ornament 1. ['ɔːnəmənt] Verzierung f; fig. Zierde f; 2. [~ment] verzieren; schmücken; ~al [ɔːnə'mentl] zierend; schmückend.

ornate [ɔː'neit] reich verziert; überladen.

orphan ['ɔːfən] 1. Waise f; 2. a. ~ed verwaist; ~age [~nidʒ] Waisenhaus n.

orthodox □ ['ɔːθədɔks] rechtgläubig; üblich; anerkannt.

oscillate ['ɔsileit] schwingen f; fig. schwanken.

osier ⚘ ['ouʒə] Korbweide f.

osprey orn. ['ɔspri] Fischadle· m.

ossify ['ɔsifai] verknöchern.

ostensible □ [ɔs'tensibl] angeblich.

ostentatio|n [ɔsten'teiʃən] Zurschaustellung f; Protzerei f; ~us [~ʃəs] prahlend, prahlerisch.

ostler ['ɔslə] Stallknecht m.

ostracize ['ɔstrəsaiz] verbannen; ächten.

ostrich orn. ['ɔstritʃ] Strauß m.

other ['ʌðə] andere(r, -s); the ~ day neulich; the ~ morning neulich morgens; every ~ day einen Ta; um den anderen, jeden zweiten Tag; ~wise ['ʌðəwaiz] anders; sonst.

otter zo. ['ɔtə] Otter(pelz) m.

ought [ɔːt] sollte; you ~ to have done it Sie hätten es tun sollen.

ounce [auns] Unze f (= 28,35 g).

our ['auə] unser; ~s [auəz] der (die, das) unsrige; unsere(r, -s); pred. unser; ~selves [auə'selvz] wir selbst; uns (selbst).

oust [aust] verdrängen, vertreiben; hinauswerfen; e-s Amtes entheben.

out [aut] 1. adv. aus; hinaus, heraus; draußen; außerhalb; (bis) zu Ende; be ~ with böse sein mit; ~ and ~ durch und durch; ~ and about wieder auf den Beinen; way ~ Ausgang m; 2. Am. F Ausweg m; the ~s pl. parl. die Opposition; 3. † übernormal, Über... (Größe); 4. prp. ~ of aus, aus ... heraus; außerhalb; außer; aus, von.

out|balance [aut'bæləns] schwerer wiegen als; ~bid [~'bid] [irr. (bid)] überbieten; ~board [~'bɔːd] Außenbord...; ~break [~breik] Ausbruch m; ~building [~bildiŋ] Nebengebäude n; ~burst [~bəːst] Ausbruch m; ~cast [~kɑːst] 1. ausgestoßen; 2. Ausgestoßene(r m) f; ~come [~kʌm] Ergebnis n; ~cry [~krai] Aufschrei m, Schrei m der Entrüstung; ~dated [aut'deitid] zeitlich überholt; ~distance [~'distəns] überholen; ~do [~'duː] [irr. (do)] übertreffen; ~door [~'aut-dɔː], ~doors adv. [~'dɔːz] Außen...; draußen, außer dem Hause; im Freien.

outer ['autə] äußer; Außen...; ~most ['autəmoust] äußerst.

out|fit ['autfit] Ausrüstung f, Ausstattung f; Am. Haufen m, Trupp m, (Arbeits)Gruppe f; ~going [~gouiŋ] 1. weg-, abgehend; 2. Ausgehen n; ~s pl. Ausgaben f/pl.; ~grow [aut'grou] [irr. (grow)] herauswachsen aus; hinauswachsen über (acc.); ~house ['authaus] Nebengebäude n; Am. Außenabort m.

outing ['autiŋ] Ausflug m, Tour f.

out|last [aut'lɑːst] überdauern; ~law ['autlɔː] 1. Geächtete(r m) f; 2. ächten; ~lay [~lei] Geld-Auslage(n pl.) f; ~let [~let] Auslaß m; Ausgang m; Abfluß m; ~line [~lain] 1. Umriß m; Überblick m; Skizze f; 2. umreißen; skizzieren; ~live [aut'liv] überleben; ~look ['autluk] Ausblick m (a. fig.); Auffassung f; ~lying [~laiiŋ] entlegen; ~match [aut'mætʃ] weit übertreffen; ~number [~'nʌmbə] an Zahl übertreffen; ~patient ⚕ ['autpei-ʃənt] ambulanter Patient; ~post [~poust] Vorposten m; ~pouring [~pɔːriŋ] Erguß m (a. fig.); ~put [~put] Produktion f, Ertrag m.

outrage ['autreidʒ] 1. Gewalttätigkeit f; Attentat n; Beleidigung f; 2. gröblich verletzen; Gewalt antun (dat.); ~ous [aut'reidʒəs] abscheulich; empörend; gewalttätig.

out|reach [aut'riːtʃ] weiter reichen als; ~right [adj. 'autrait, adv. aut-'rait] gerade heraus; völlig; ~run [~'rʌn] [irr. (run)] schneller laufen als; hinausgehen über (acc.); ~set ['autset] Anfang *m*; Aufbruch *m*; **~shine** [aut'ʃain] [*irr. (shine)*] überstrahlen; **~side** ['aut'said] 1. Außenseite *f*; *fig.* Äußerste(s) *n*; *at the* ~ höchstens; 2. Außen...; außenstehend; äußerst (*Preis*); 3. (nach) (dr)außen; 4. *prp.* außerhalb; **~sider** [~ə] Außenseiter(in), -stehende(r *m*) *f*; **~size** [~saiz] Übergröße *f*; **~skirts** [~skə:ts] *pl.* Außenbezirke *m*/*pl.*, (Stadt)Rand *m*; **~smart** *Am.* F [aut'sma:t] übervorteilen; **~spoken** [~'spoukən] freimütig; **~spread** ['aut'spred] ausgestreckt, ausgebreitet, **~standing** [aut'stændiŋ] hervorragend (*a. fig.*); ausstehend (*Schuld*); offenstehend (*Frage*); **~stretched** ['autstretʃt] = *outspread*; **~strip** [aut'strip] überholen (*a. fig.*).

outward ['autwəd] 1. äußer(lich); nach (dr)außen gerichtet; 2. *adv.* *mst* **~s** auswärts, nach (dr)außen; **~ly** [~dli] äußerlich; an der Oberfläche.

out|weigh [aut'wei] überwiegen; **~wit** [~'wit] überlisten; **~worn** ['autwɔːn] erschöpft; *fig.* abgegriffen; überholt.

oval ['ouvəl] 1. oval; 2. Oval *n*.

oven ['ʌvn] Backofen *m*.

over ['ouvə] 1. *adv.* über; hin-, herüber; drüben; vorbei; übermäßig; darüber; von Anfang bis zu Ende; noch einmal; ~ *and above* neben, zusätzlich zu; *(all)* ~ *again* noch einmal (von vorn); ~ *against* gegenüber (*dat.*); *all* ~ ganz und gar; ~ *and* ~ *again* immer wieder; *read* ~ durchlesen; 2. *prp.* über; *all* ~ *the town* durch die ganze *od.* in der ganzen Stadt.

over|act ['ouvər'ækt] übertreiben; **~all** [~ɔːl] 1. Arbeitsanzug *m*, -kittel *m*; Kittel(schürze *f*) *m*; 2. gesamt, Gesamt...; **~awe** [ouvər'ɔː] einschüchtern; **~balance** [ouvə'bæləns] 1. Übergewicht *n*; 2. umkippen; überwiegen; **~bearing** □ [~'bɛəriŋ] anmaßend; **~board** ⊕ ['ouvəbɔːd] über Bord; **~cast** [~ka:st] bewölkt; **~charge** [~'tʃa:dʒ] 1. überladen; überfordern; 2. Überladung *f*; Überforderung *f*; **~coat** [~kout] Mantel *m*; **~come** [ouvə'kʌm][*irr.(come)*]überwinden, überwältigen; **~crowd** [~'kraud] überfüllen; **~do** [~'du:] [*irr. (do)*] zu viel tun; übertreiben; zu sehr kochen; überanstrengen; **~draw** ['ouvə'drɔː] [*irr. (draw)*] übertreiben; ✝ *Konto* überziehen; **~dress** [~'dres] (sich) übertrieben anziehen; **~due** [~'dju:] (über)fällig; *Eat* [~'iːt] [*irr. (eat)*]: ~ *o.s.* sich übereressen; **~flow** 1. ['ouvə'flou] [*irr. (flow)*] *v/t.* überfluten; *v/i.* überfließen; 2. ['ouvəflou] Überschwemmung *f*; Überfüllung *f*; **~grow**

[~'grou] [*irr. (grow)*] *v/t.* überwuchern; *v/i.* zu sehr wachsen; **~hang** 1. [~'hæŋ] [*irr. (hang)*] *v/t.* über (*acc.*) hängen; *v/i.* überhängen; 2. [~hæŋ] Überhang *m*; **~haul** [ouvə'hɔːl] überholen; **~head** 1. *adv.* ['ouvə'hed] (dr)oben; 2. *adj.* [~hed] Ober...; ↑ allgemein (*Unkosten*); 3. **~s** *pl.* ↑ allgemeine Unkosten *pl.*; **~hear** [ouvə'hiə] [*irr. (hear)*] belauschen; **~joyed** [~'dʒɔid] überglücklich; **~lap** [~'læp] *v/t.* übergreifen auf (*acc.*); überschneiden; *v/i.* ineinandergreifen, überlappen; **~lay** [~'lei] [*irr. (lay)*] belegen; ⊕ überlagern; **~leaf** ['ouvə'liːf] umseitig; **~load** [~'loud] überladen; **~look** [ouvə'luk] übersehen; beaufsichtigen; **~master** [~'ma:stə] überwältigen; **~much** ['ouvə'mʌtʃ] zu viel; **~night** [~'nait] 1. am Vorabend; über Nacht; 2. Nacht...; nächtlich; Übernachtungs...; **~pay** [~'pei] [*irr. (pay)*] zu viel bezahlen für; **~peopled** [ouvə'piːpld] übervölkert; **~plus** ['ouvəplʌs] Überschuß *m*; **~power** [ouvə'pauə] überwältigen; **~rate** ['ouvə'reit] überschätzen; **~reach** [ouvə'riːtʃ] übervorteilen; ~ *o.s.* sich übernehmen; **~ride** *fig.* [~'raid] [*irr. (ride)*] sich hinwegsetzen über (*acc.*); umstoßen; **~rule** [~'ruːl] überstimmen; ✝✝ verwerfen; **~run** [~'rʌn] [*irr. (run)*] überrennen; überziehen; überlaufen; bedecken; **~sea** ['ouvə'siː] 1. *a.* ~**s** überseeisch; Übersee...; 2. ~**s** *in od.* nach Übersee; **~see** [~'siː] [*irr. (see)*] beaufsichtigen; **~seer** [~siə] Aufseher *m*; **~shadow** [ouvə'ʃædou] überschatten; **~sight** ['ouvəsait] Versehen *n*; **~sleep** [~'sliːp] [*irr. (sleep)*] verschlafen; **~state** [~'steit] übertreiben; **~statement** [~'steit-mənt] Übertreibung *f*; **~strain** 1. [~'strein] (sich) überanstrengen; *fig.* übertreiben; 2. [~'strein] Überanstrengung *f*.

overt ['ouvəːt] offen(kundig).

over|take [ouvə'teik] [*irr. (take)*] einholen; *j-n* überraschen; **~tax** ['ouvə'tæks] zu hoch besteuern; *fig.* überschätzen; übermäßig in Anspruch nehmen; **~throw** 1. [ouvə-'θrou] [*irr. (throw)*] (um)stürzen (*a. fig.*); vernichten; 2. ['ouvəθrou] Sturz *m*; Vernichtung *f*; **~time** [~taim] Überstunden *f*/*pl.*

overture ['ouvətjuə] ♪ Ouvertüre *f*; Vorspiel *n*; Vorschlag *m*, Antrag *m*.

over|turn [ouvə'təːn] (um)stürzen; **~value** ['ouvə'væljuː] zu hoch einschätzen; **~weening** [ouvə'wiːniŋ] eingebildet; **~weight** ['ouvəweit] Übergewicht *n*; **~whelm** [ouvə-'welm] überschütten (*a. fig.*); überwältigen; **~work** ['ouvə'wəːk] 1.

Überarbeitung f; 2. [irr. (work)]
sich überarbeiten; ~wrought [~
'rɔːt] überarbeitet; überreizt.
owe [ou] Geld, Dank etc. schulden,
schuldig sein; verdanken.
owing ['ouiŋ] schuldig; ~ to in-
folge
owl orn. [aul] Eule f.
own [oun] 1. eigen; richtig; einzig,
innig geliebt; 2. my ~ mein Eigentum; a house of one's ~ ein eigenes
Haus; hold one's ~ standhalten;

3. besitzen; zugeben; anerkennen;
sich bekennen (to zu).
owner ['ounə] Eigentümer(in); ~ship
['ounəʃip] Eigentum(srecht) n.
ox [ɔks], pl. oxen ['ɔksən] Ochse m;
Rind n.
oxid|ation ⚗ [ɔksi'deiʃən] Oxyda-
tion f, Oxydierung f; ~e ['ɔksaid]
Oxyd n; ~ize ['ɔksidaiz] oxydieren.
oxygen ⚗ ['ɔksidʒən] Sauerstoff m.
oyster ['ɔistə] Auster f.
ozone ⚗ ['ouzoun] Ozon n.

P

pace [peis] 1. Schritt m; Gang m;
Tempo n; 2. v/t. abschreiten; v/i.
(einher)schreiten; (im) Paß gehen.
pacific [pə'sifik] (~ally) friedlich;
the ♀ (Ocean) der Pazifik, der Pazi-
fische od Stille Ozean; ~ation
[pæsifi'keiʃən] Beruhigung f.
pacify ['pæsifai] beruhigen.
pack [pæk] 1. Pack(en) m; Paket n;
Ballen m; Spiel n Karten; Meute f;
Rotte f, Bande f; Packung f; 2. v/t.
oft ~ up (zs.-, ver-, ein)packen; a.
~ off fortjagen; Am F (bei sich)
tragen (als Gepäck etc.); bepacken,
vollstopfen; ⊕ dichten, v/i. oft ~
up packen, sich packen (lassen);
~age ['pækidʒ] Pack m, Ballen m;
bsd. Am Paket n; Packung f;
Frachtstück n; ~er ['pækə] Pak-
ker(in), Am Konservenfabrikant
m; ~et ['pækit] Paket n; Päckchen n;
a. ~boat Postschiff n
packing ['pækiŋ] Packen n; Verpackung f; ~ house Am. (bsd.
Fleisch)Konservenfabrik f.
packthread ['pækθred] Bindfaden
m.
pact [pækt] Vertrag m, Pakt m.
pad [pæd] 1. Polster n; Sport: Bein-
schutz m, Schreibblock m, Stem-
pelkissen n; (Abschuß)Rampe f;
2. (aus)polstern, ~ding ['pædiŋ]
Polsterung f; fig Lückenbüßer m.
paddle ['pædl] 1. Paddel(ruder) n;
⚓ (Rad)Schaufel f, 2. paddeln;
planschen, ~wheel Schaufelrad n.
paddock ['pædək] (Pferde)Koppel
f; Sport Sattelplatz m
padlock ['pædlɔk] Vorhängeschloß
n.
pagan ['peigən] 1. heidnisch;
2. Heid|e m, -in f.
page¹ [peidʒ] 1. Buch-Seite f; fig.
Buch n, 2. paginieren
page² [~] 1. (Hotel)Page m; Am.
Amtsdiener m; 2. Am. (durch e-n
Pagen) holen lassen
pageant ['pædʒənt] historisches
Festspiel; festlicher Umzug.

paid [peid] pret. u. p.p. von pay 2.
pail [peil] Eimer m.
pain [pein] 1. Pein f, Schmerz m;
Strafe f; ~s pl. Leiden n/pl.; Mühe
f; on od. under ~ of death bei
Todesstrafe; be in ~ leiden; take ~s
sich Mühe geben; 2. j-m weh tun;
~ful □ ['peinful] schmerzhaft,
schmerzlich; peinlich; mühevoll;
~less □ ['peinlis] schmerzlos;
~staking □ ['peinzteikiŋ] fleißig.
paint [peint] 1. Farbe f; Schminke f;
Anstrich m; 2. (be)malen; anstreichen; (sich) schminken; ~brush
['peintbrʌʃ] Malerpinsel m; ~er
[~tə] Maler(in); ~ing ['peintiŋ] Malen
n; Malerei f; Gemälde n.
pair [pɛə] 1. Paar n; a ~ of scissors
eine Schere; 2. (sich) paaren; zs.-
passen; a. ~ off paarweise weggehen.
pal sl. [pæl] Kumpel m, Kamerad m.
palace ['pælis] Palast m.
palatable □ ['pælətəbl] schmackhaft. [schmack m (a. fig.).]
palate ['pælit] Gaumen m; Ge-
pale¹ [peil] 1. blaß, bleich; fahl;
~ ale helles Bier; 2. (er)bleichen.
pale² [~] Pfahl m; fig. Grenzen f/pl.
paleness ['peilnis] Blässe f.
palisade [pæli'seid] 1. Palisade f;
Staket n; ~s pl. Am. Steilufer n;
2. umpfählen.
pall [pɔːl] schal werden; ~ (up)on j-n
langweilen.
pallet ['pælit] Strohsack m.
palliat|e ['pælieit] bemänteln; lin-
dern; ~ive [~iətiv] Linderungs-
mittel n.
pall|id □ ['pælid] blaß; ~idness
[~dnis], ~or ['pælə] Blässe f.
palm [paːm] 1. Handfläche f; ♀
Palme f; 2. in der Hand verbergen;
~ s.th. off upon j-m et. andrehen;
~tree ['paːmtriː] Palme f
palpable □ ['pælpəbl] fühlbar; fig.
handgreiflich, klar, eindeutig.
palpitat|e ['pælpiteit] klopfen
(Herz); ~ion [pælpi'teiʃən] Herz-
klopfen n.

palsy ['pɔ:lzi] 1. Lähmung f; fig. Ohnmacht f; 2. fig. lähmen.

palter ['pɔ:ltə] sein Spiel treiben.

paltry □ ['pɔ:ltri] erbärmlich.

pamper ['pæmpə] verzärteln.

pamphlet ['pæmflit] Flugschrift f.

pan [pæn] Pfanne f; Tiegel m.

pan... [~] all..., gesamt...; pan..., Pan...

panacea [pænə'siə] Allheilmittel n.

pancake ['pænkeik] Pfannkuchen m; ~ landing ✠ Bumslandung f.

pandemonium fig. [pændi'mounjəm] Hölle(nlärm m) f.

pander ['pændə] 1. Vorschub leisten (to dat.); kuppeln; 2. Kuppler m.

pane [pein] (Fenster)Scheibe f.

panegyric [pæni'dʒirik] Lobrede f.

panel ['pænl] 1. ⚿ Fach n; Tür-Füllung f; ⚖ Geschworenen(liste f) m/pl.; Diskussionsteilnehmer m/pl.; Kassenarztliste f, 2. täfeln.

pang [pæŋ] plötzlicher Schmerz, Weh n; fig. Angst f, Qual f.

panhandle ['pænhændl] 1. Pfannenstiel m; Am. schmaler Fortsatz e-s Staatsgebiets; 2. Am. F betteln.

panic ['pænik] 1. panisch; 2. Panik f.

pansy ⚘ ['pænzi] Stiefmütterchen n.

pant [pænt] nach Luft schnappen; keuchen; klopfen (Herz); lechzen (for, after nach).

panther zo. ['pænθə] Panther m.

panties F ['pæntiz] (Damen)Schlüpfer m; (Kinder)Hös-chen n.

pantry ['pæntri] Vorratskammer f.

pants [pænts] pl. Hose f; ✝ lange)

pap [pæp] Brei m. [Unterhose.)

papa [pə'pa:] Papa m.

papal □ ['peipəl] päpstlich.

paper ['peipə] 1. Papier n; Zeitung f; Prüfungsaufgabe f; Vortrag m, Aufsatz m; ~s pl. (Ausweis)Papiere n/pl.; 2. tapezieren, ~back Taschenbuch n, Paperback n, ~bag Tüte f; ~clip Büroklammer f; ~fastener Musterklammer f; ~hanger Tapezierer m; ~mill Papierfabrik f; ~weight Briefbeschwerer m.

pappy ['pæpi] breiig.

par [pa:] ✝ Nennwert m, Pari n; at ~ zum Nennwert; be on a ~ with gleich od. ebenbürtig sein (dat.).

parable ['pærəbl] Gleichnis n.

parachut|e ['pærəʃu:t] Fallschirm m; ~ist [~tist] Fallschirmspringer(in).

parade [pə'reid] 1. ✕ (Truppen-) Parade f; Zurschaustellung f; Promenade f; (Um)Zug m, programme ~ Radio: Programmvorschau f; make a ~ of et. zur Schau stellen; 2. ✕ antreten (lassen); ~ vorbeimarschieren (lassen); zur Schau stellen; ~ground ✕ Exerzier-, Paradeplatz m.

paradise ['pærədais] Paradies n.

paragon ['pærəgən] Vorbild n; Muster n.

paragraph ['pærəgra:f] Absatz m; Paragraph(zeichen n) m; kurze Zeitungsnotiz.

parallel ['pærəlel] 1. parallel; 2. Parallele f (a. fig.); Gegenstück n; Vergleich m; without (a) ~ ohnegleichen; 3. vergleichen; entsprechen; gleichen; parallel laufen (mit).

paraly|se ['pærəlaiz] lähmen; fig. unwirksam machen; ~sis ✗ [pə'rælisis] Paralyse f, Lähmung f.

paramount ['pærəmaunt] oberst, höchst, hervorragend; größer, höher stehend (to als).

parapet ['pærəpit] ✕ Brustwehr f; Brüstung f; Geländer n.

paraphernalia [pærəfə'neiljə] pl. Ausrüstung f; Zubehör n, m.

parasite ['pærəsait] Schmarotzer m.

parasol [pærə'sɔl] Sonnenschirm m.

paratroops ✕ ['pærətru:ps] Luftlandetruppen f/pl.

parboil ['pa:bɔil] ankochen.

parcel ['pa:sl] 1. Paket n; Parzelle f; 2. ~ out aus-, aufteilen.

parch [pa:tʃ] rösten, (aus)dörren.

parchment ['pa:tʃmənt] Pergament n.

pard Am. sl. [pa:d] Partner m.

pardon ['pa:dn] 1. Verzeihung f; ⚖ Begnadigung f; 2. verzeihen; ⚖ begnadigen; ~able □ [~nəbl] verzeihlich.

pare [pɛə] (be)schneiden (a. fig.); schälen.

parent ['pɛərənt] Vater m, Mutter f; fig. Ursache f; ~s pl. Eltern pl.; ~age ['~ridʒ] Herkunft f; ~al [pə'rentl] elterlich.

parenthe|sis [pə'renθisis], pl. ~ses [~si:z] Einschaltung f; typ. (runde) Klammer.

paring ['pɛəriŋ] Schälen n, Abschneiden n; ~s pl. Schalen f/pl., Schnipsel m/pl.

parish ['pæriʃ] 1. Kirchspiel n, Gemeinde f; 2. Pfarr...; Gemeinde...; ~ council Gemeinderat m; ~ioner [pə'riʃənə] Pfarrkind n, Gemeindemitglied n.

parity ['pæriti] Gleichheit f.

park [pa:k] 1. Park m, Anlagen f/pl.; Naturschutzgebiet n; mst car~ Parkplatz m; 2. mot. parken; ~ing mot. ['pa:kiŋ] Parken n; ~ing lot Parkplatz m; ~ing meter Parkuhr f.

parlance ['pa:ləns] Ausdrucksweise f.

parley ['pa:li] 1. Unterhandlung f; 2. unterhandeln; sich besprechen.

parliament ['pa:ləmənt] Parlament n; ~arian [pa:ləmen'tɛəriən] Parlamentarier(in) m; ~ary □ [pa:lə'mentəri] parlamentarisch; Parlaments...

parlo(u)r ['pɑːlə] Wohnzimmer n; Empfangs-, Sprechzimmer n; *beauty* ~ *bsd. Am.* Schönheitssalon m; ~ *car* 🚂 *Am.* Salonwagen m; ~maid Stubenmädchen n.

parochial [pə'roukjəl] Pfarr...; Gemeinde...; *fig.* engstirnig, beschränkt.

parole [pə'roul] 1. 🏛 mündlich; 2. ✕ Parole f; Ehrenwort n; *put on* ~ = 3. 🏛 *bsd. Am.* bedingt freilassen.

parquet ['pɑːkei] Parkett(fußboden m) n; *Am. thea.* Parkett n.

parrot ['pærət] 1. *orn.* Papagei m (*a. fig.*); 2. (nach)plappern.

parry [' pæri] abwehren, parieren.

parsimonious [pɑːsi'mounjəs] sparsam, karg, knauserig.

parsley 🌿 ['pɑːsli] Petersilie f.

parson ['pɑːsn] Pfarrer m; ~age [~nidʒ] Pfarrei f; Pfarrhaus n.

part [pɑːt] 1. *mst* Teil m; Anteil m; Partei f; *thea.*, *fig.* Rolle f; ♪ Einzel-Stimme f. Gegend f; *a man of* ~*s* ein fähiger Mensch; *take* ~ *in s.th.* an e-r Sache teilnehmen; *take in good (bad)* gut (übel) aufnehmen; *for my (own)* meinerseits; *in* ~ teilweise; *on the* ~ *of* von seiten (*gen.*); *on my* ~ meinerseits; 2. *adv.* teils; 3. *v/t.* (ab-, ein-, zer)teilen; *Haar* scheiteln; ~ *company* sich trennen (*with von*); *v/i.* sich trennen (*with von*); scheiden.

partake [pɑː'teik] [*irr. (take)*] teilnehmen, teilhaben; ~ *of Mahlzeit* einnehmen; grenzen an (*acc.*).

partial ['pɑːʃəl] Teil... ; teilweise; partiell, parteiisch; eingenommen (*to von, für*), ~ity [pɑːʃi'æliti] Parteilichkeit f; Vorliebe f.

particip|ant [pɑː tisipənt] Teilnehmer(in); ~ate [~peit] teilnehmen; ~ation [pɑːtisi'peiʃən] Teilnahme f.

participle *gr.* ['pɑːtsipl] Partizip n, Mittelwort n.

particle ['pɑːtikl] Teilchen n.

particular [pə'tikjulə] 1. ☐ *mst* besonder, einzeln, Sonder...; genau; eigen, wählerisch; 2. Einzelheit f; Umstand m, *in* insbesondere; ~ity [pətikju'læriti] Besonderheit f; Ausführlichkeit f; Eigenheit f; ~ly [pə tikjuləli] besonders.

parting ['pɑːtiŋ] 1. Trennung f; Teilung f; Abschied m; Haar-Scheitel m; ~ *of the ways bsd. fig.* Scheideweg m; 2. Abschieds...

partisan [pɑːti'zæn] Parteigänger (-in); ✕ Partisan m; *attr.* Partei...

partition [pɑː'tiʃən] 1. Teilung f; Scheidewand f; Verschlag m, Fach n; 2. *mst* ~ *off* (ab)teilen.

partly ['pɑːtli] teilweise, zum Teil.

partner ['pɑːtnə] 1. Partner(in); 2. (sich) zs.-tun mit, zs.-arbeiten mit; ~ship [~əʃip] Teilhaber-, Part-

nerschaft f; ✝ Handelsgesellschaft f.

part-owner ['pɑːtounə] Miteigentümer(in).

partridge *orn.* ['pɑːtridʒ] Rebhuhn n.

part-time ['pɑːtaim] 1. *adj.* Teilzeit. ., Halbtags...; 2. *adv.* halbtags.

party ['pɑːti] Partei f; ✕ Trupp m, Kommando n; Party f, Gesellschaft f; Beteiligte(r) m; *co.* Type f, Individuum n; ~ *line pol.* Parteilinie f, -direktive f.

pass [pɑːs] 1. Paß m, Ausweis m; Passierschein m; Bestehen n e-s *Examens*; *univ.* gewöhnlicher Grad; (kritische) Lage; *Fußball* Paß m; Bestreichung f, Strich m; (Gebirgs-) Paß m, Durchgang m; *Karten:* Passen n; *free* ~ Freikarte f; 2. *v/i.* passieren, geschehen; hingenommen werden; *Karten* passen; (vorbei)gehen, (vorbei)kommen, (vorbei)fahren; vergehen (*Zeit*); sich verwandeln; angenommen werden (*Banknoten*); bekannt sein; vergehen; aussterben; *a.* ~ *away* sterben; durchkommen (*Gesetz*; *Prüfling*); *for* gelten als; ~ *off* vonstatten gehen; ~ *out* F ohnmächtig werden; *come to* ~ geschehen; *bring to* ~ bewirken; *v/t.* vorbeikommen *od.* vorbeifahren an (*dat.*); passieren; kommen *od.* fahren durch; verbringen; reichen, geben; *Bemerkung* machen, von sich geben; *Banknoten* in Umlauf bringen; *Gesetz* durchbringen, annehmen; *Prüfling* durchkommen lassen; *Prüfung* bestehen; (hinaus-) gehen über (*acc.*), *Urteil* abgeben; *Meinung* äußern; bewegen; streichen mit; *Ball* zuspielen; *Truppen* vorbeimaschieren lassen; ~able ☐ ['pɑːsəbl] passierbar; gangbar, gültig (*Geld*), leidlich.

passage ['pæsidʒ] Durchgang m, Durchfahrt f; Überfahrt f; Durchreise f; Korridor m, Gang m; Weg m; Annahme f e-s *Gesetzes*; ♪ Passage f; *Text*-Stelle f; *bird of* ~ Zugvogel m.

passbook ✝ ['pɑːsbuk] Sparbuch n.

passenger ['pæsindʒə] Passagier m, Fahr-, Fluggast m, Reisende(r m) f.

passer-by ['pɑːsə'bai] Vorübergehende(r m) f, Passant(in).

passion ['pæʃən] Leidenschaft f; (Gefühls)Ausbruch m; Zorn m; ♀ *eccl.* Passion f; *be in a* ~ zornig sein; *in* ~ im Affekt; ♀ *Week eccl.* Karwoche f; ~ate ☐ [~nit] leidenschaftlich.

passive ['pæsiv] passiv (*a. gr.*); teilnahmslos; untätig.

passport ['pɑːspɔːt] (Reise)Paß m.

password ✕ ['pɑːswɔːd] Losung f.

past [pɑːst] 1. *adj.* vergangen; *gr.* Vergangenheits...; früher; *for some*

time ~ seit einiger Zeit; ~ *tense* gr.
Vergangenheit f; 2. *adv.* vorbei;
3. *prp.* nach, über; über ... (*acc.*)
hinaus; an ... (*dat.*) vorbei; *half* ~
two halb drei; ~ *endurance* unerträglich; ~ *hope* hoffnungslos;
4. Vergangenheit f (*a. gr.*)

paste [peist] 1. Teig m; Kleister m;
Paste f; 2. (be)kleben; **~board**
['peistbo:d] Pappe f; *attr* Papp...

pastel [pæs'tel] Pastell(bild) n.

pasteurize ['pæstəraiz] pasteurisieren, keimfrei machen

pastime ['pɑ:staim] Zeitvertreib m.

pastor ['pɑ:stə] Pastor m; Seelsorger m; **~al** □ [~ərəl] Hirten...;
pastoral.

pastry ['peistri] Tortengebäck n,
Konditorwaren f/pl.; Pasteten f/pl.;
~cook Pastetenbäcker m, Konditor m.

pasture ['pɑ:stʃə] 1. *Vieh*-Weide f;
Futter n; 2. (ab)weiden

pat [pæt] 1. Klaps m; Portion f
Butter; 2. tätscheln; klopfen; 3. gelegen, gerade recht; bereit.

patch [pætʃ] 1. Fleck m; Flicken m;
Stück n Land; ✞ Pflaster n; 2. flikken; **~work** ['pætʃwə:k] Flickwerk
n.

pate F [peit] Schädel m.

patent ['peitənt, *Am.* 'pætənt] 1. offenkundig; patentiert, Patent...;
letters ~ ['pætənt] *pl* Freibrief m;
~ *leather* Lackleder n; 2. Patent n;
Privileg n, Freibrief m; ~ *agent*
Patentanwalt m; 3. patentieren;
~ee [peitən'ti:] Patentinhaber m.

patern|al □ [pə'tə:nl] väterlich;
~ity [~niti] Vaterschaft f.

path [pɑ:θ], *pl.* ~s [pɑ:ðz] Pfad m;
Weg m.

pathetic [pə'θetik] (**~ally**) pathetisch; rührend, ergreifend.

pathos ['peiθɔs] Pathos n.

patien|ce ['peiʃəns] Geduld f; Ausdauer f; Patience f (*Kartenspiel*);
~t [~nt] 1. □ geduldig; 2. Patient(in).

patio *Am.* ['pætiou] Innenhof m,
Patio m.

patrimony ['pætriməni] väterliches
Erbteil.

patriot ['peitriət] Patriot(in).

patrol ✗ [pə'troul] 1. Patrouille f,
Streife f; ~ *wagon Am* Polizeigefangenenwagen m; 2. (ab)patrouillieren; **~man** [~lmæn] patrouillierender Polizist; Pannenhelfer m *e-s Automobilclubs.*

patron ['peitrən] (Schutz)Patron m;
Gönner m; Kunde m; **~age** ['pætrənidʒ] Gönnerschaft f; Kundschaft f;
Schutz m; **~ize** [~naiz] beschützen;
begünstigen; Kunde sein bei; gönnerhaft behandeln.

patter ['pætə] v/i. platschen; trappeln; v/t. (her)plappern.

pattern ['pætən] 1. Muster n (*a.*

fig.); Modell n; 2. formen (*after, on*
nach).

paunch ['pɔ:ntʃ] Wanst m.

pauper ['pɔ:pə] Fürsorgeempfänger(in); **~ize** [~əraiz] arm machen.

pause [pɔ:z] 1. Pause f; 2. pausieren.

pave [peiv] pflastern; *fig.* Weg bahnen; **~ment** ['peivmənt] Bürgersteig m, Gehweg m; Pflaster n.

paw [pɔ:] 1. Pfote f, Tatze f; 2. scharren; F befingern; rauh behandeln.

pawn [pɔ:n] 1. Bauer m *im Schach*;
Pfand n; *in od.* at ~ verpfändet; 2.
verpfänden; **~broker** ['pɔ:nbroukə]
Pfandleiher m; **~shop** Leihhaus n.

pay [pei] 1. (Be)Zahlung f; Sold m,
Lohn m; 2. [*irr.*] *v/t.* (be)zahlen;
(be)lohnen; sich lohnen für; *Ehre
etc.* erweisen; *Besuch* abstatten; ~
attention od. heed to achtgeben auf
(*acc.*); ~ *down* bar bezahlen; ~ *off j-n*
bezahlen u. entlassen; *j-n* voll
auszahlen; *v/i.* zahlen; sich lohnen;
~ *for* (für) *et.* bezahlen; **~able**
['peiəbl] zahlbar; fällig; **~day**
Zahltag m; **~ee** ✞ [pei'i:] Zahlungsempfänger m; **~ing** ['peiiŋ] lohnend; **~master** Zahlmeister m;
~ment ['peimənt] (Be)Zahlung f;
Lohn m, Sold m; **~off** Abrechnung
f (*a. fig.*); *Am.* F Höhepunkt m;
~roll Lohnliste f.

pea ♀ [pi:] Erbse f.

peace [pi:s] Frieden m, Ruhe f; *at* ~
friedlich; **~able** □ ['pi:səbl] friedliebend, friedlich; **~ful** □ ['pi:sful]
friedlich; **~maker** Friedensstifter(in).

peach ♀ [pi:tʃ] Pfirsich(baum) m.

pea|cock *orn.* ['pi:kɔk] Pfau(hahn)
m; **~hen** *orn.* [~] Pfauhenne f.

peak [pi:k] Spitze f; Gipfel m;
Mützen-Schirm m; *attr.* Spitzen...,
Höchst...; **~ed** [pi:kt] spitz.

peal [pi:l] 1. Geläut n; Glockenspiel n; Dröhnen n; ~s *of laughter*
dröhnendes Gelächter; 2. erschallen (lassen); laut verkünden; dröhnen.

peanut ['pi:nʌt] Erdnuß f.

pear ♀ [pɛə] Birne f.

pearl [pə:l] 1. Perle f (*a. fig.*); *attr.*
Perl(en)...; 2. tropfen, perlen; **~y**
['pə:li] perlenartig.

peasant ['pezənt] 1. Bauer m;
2. bäuerlich; **~ry** [~tri] Landvolk n.

peat [pi:t] Torf m.

pebble ['pebl] Kiesel(stein) m.

peck [pek] 1. Viertelscheffel m
(9,087 *Liter*); *fig.* Menge f; 2. pikken, hacken (*at* nach).

peculate ['pekjuleit] unterschlagen.

peculiar □ [pi'kju:ljə] eigen(tümlich); besonder; seltsam; **~ity**
[pikju:li'æriti] Eigenheit f; Eigentümlichkeit f.

pecuniary [pi'kju:njəri] Geld...

pedagog|ics [pedə'gɔdʒiks] *mst sg.*

Pädagogik *f*; ~ue ['pedəgɔg] Pädagoge *m*; Lehrer *m*.

pedal ['pedl] 1. Pedal *n*; 2. Fuß...; 3. *Radfahren*: fahren, treten.

pedantic [pi'dæntik] (~ally) pedantisch.

peddle ['pedl] hausieren (mit); ~r *Am.* [~lə] = *pedlar*.

pedestal ['pedistl] Sockel *m* (*a. fig.*).

pedestrian [pi'destriən] 1. zu Fuß; nüchtern; 2. Fußgänger(in); ~ *crossing* Fußgängerübergang *m*.

pedigree ['pedigri:] Stammbaum *m*.

pedlar ['pedlə] Hausierer *m*.

peek [pi:k] 1. spähen, gucken, lugen; 2. flüchtiger Blick.

peel [pi:l] 1. Schale *f*; Rinde *f*; 2. *a.* ~ *off v/t.* (ab)schälen; *Kleid* abstreifen; *v/i.* sich (ab)schälen.

peep [pi:p] 1. verstohlener Blick; Piepen *n*; 2. (verstohlen) gucken; *a.* ~ *out* (hervor)gucken (*a. fig.*); piepen; ~**hole** ['pi:phoul] Guckloch *n*.

peer [piə] 1. spähen, lugen; ~ *at* angucken; 2. Gleiche(r *m*) *f*; Pair *m*; ~**less** ☐ ['piəlis] unvergleichlich.

peevish ☐ ['pi:viʃ] verdrießlich.

peg [peg] 1. Stöpsel *m*, Dübel *m*, Pflock *m*; *Kleider*-Haken *m*; *♪* Wirbel *m*; *Wäsche*-Klammer *f*; *fig.* Aufhänger *m*; *take s.o. down a* ~ *or two j-n* demütigen; 2. festpflöcken; *Grenze* abstecken; ~ *away* od. *along* F daraufloarbeiten; ~**top** ['pegtɔp] Kreisel *m*.

pelican *orn.* ['pelikən] Pelikan *m*.

pellet ['pelit] Kügelchen *n*; Pille *f*; Schrotkorn *n*.

pell-mell ['pel'mel] durcheinander.

pelt [pelt] 1. Fell *n*; † *rohe* Haut; 2. *v/t.* bewerfen; *v/i.* niederprasseln.

pelvis *anat.* ['pelvis] Becken *n*.

pen [pen] 1. (Schreib)Feder *f*; Hürde *f*; 2. schreiben; [*irr.*] einpferchen.

penal ☐ ['pi:nl] Straf...; strafbar; ~ *code* Strafgesetzbuch *n*; ~ *servitude* Zuchthausstrafe *f*; ~**ize** ['pi:nəlaiz] bestrafen; ~**ty** ['penlti] Strafe *f*; *Sport:* Strafpunkt *m*; ~ *area Fußball* Strafraum *m*; ~ *kick Fußball:* Freistoß *m*.

penance ['penəns] Buße *f*.

pence [pens] *pl. von penny*.

pencil ['pensl] 1. Bleistift *m*; 2. zeichnen; (mit Bleistift) anzeichnen od. anstreichen; *Augenbrauen* nachziehen; ~**sharpener** Bleistiftspitzer *m*.

pendant ['pendənt] Anhänger *m*.

pending ['pendiŋ] 1. *♫* schwebend; 2. *prp.* während; bis zu.

pendulum ['pendjuləm] Pendel *n*.

penetra|ble ['penitrəbl] durchdringbar; ~**te** [~reit] durchdringen; ergründen; eindringen (*in acc.*); vordringen (*to* bis zu); ~**tion** [peni'treiʃən] Durch-, Eindringen *n*; Scharfsinn *m*; ~**tive** ☐ ['penitrətiv] durchdringend (*a. fig.*); eindringlich; scharfsinnig.

pen-friend ['penfrend] Brieffreund (-in).

penguin *orn.* ['peŋgwin] Pinguin *m*.

penholder ['penhouldə] Federhalter *m*.

peninsula [pi'ninsjulə] Halbinsel *f*.

peniten|ce ['penitəns] Buße *f*, Reue *f*; ~**t** 1. ☐ reuig, bußfertig; 2. Büßer(in); ~**tiary** [peni'tenʃəri] Besserungsanstalt *f*; *Am.* Zuchthaus *n*.

pen|knife ['pennaif] Taschenmesser *n*; ~**man** Schönschreiber *m*; Schriftsteller *m*; ~**name** Schriftstellername *m*, Pseudonym *n*.

pennant ⚓ ['penənt] Wimpel *m*.

penniless ☐ ['penilis] ohne Geld.

penny ['peni], *pl. mst* **pence** [pens] (englischer) Penny (*¹/₁₂ Schilling*); *Am.* Cent *m*; Kleinigkeit *f*; ~**weight** *englisches* Pennygewicht (*1¹/₂ Gramm*).

pension ['penʃən] 1. Pension *f*, Ruhegehalt *n*; 2. *oft* ~ *off* pensionieren; ~**ary**, ~**er** [~nəri, ~nə] Pensionär(in).

pensive ☐ ['pensiv] gedankenvoll.

pent [pent] *pret. u. p.p. von* pen 2; ~**up** aufgestaut (*Zorn etc.*).

Pentecost ['pentikɔst] Pfingsten *n*.

penthouse ['penthaus] Schutzdach *n*; Dachwohnung *f auf e-m Hochhaus.*

penu|rious ☐ [pi'njuəriəs] geizig; ~**ry** ['penjuri] Armut *f*; Mangel *m*.

people ['pi:pl] 1. Volk *n*, Nation *f*; *coll.* die Leute *pl.*; man; 2. bevölkern.

pepper ['pepə] 1. Pfeffer *m*; 2. pfeffern; ~**mint** ♀ Pfefferminze *f*; ~**y** ☐ [~əri] pfefferig; *fig.* hitzig.

per [pə:] per, durch, für; laut; je.

perambulat|e [pə'ræmbjuleit] (durch)wandern; bereisen; ~**or** ['præmbjuleitə] Kinderwagen *m*.

perceive [pə'si:v] (be)merken, wahrnehmen; empfinden; erkennen.

per cent [pə'sent] Prozent *n*.

percentage [pə'sentidʒ] Prozentsatz *m*; Prozente *n/pl.*; *fig.* Teil *m*.

percept|ible ☐ [pə'septəbl] wahrnehmbar; ~**ion** [~pʃən] Wahrnehmung(svermögen *n*) *f*; Erkenntnis *f*; Auffassung(skraft) *f*.

perch [pə:tʃ] 1. *ichth.* Barsch *m*; Rute *f* (*5,029 m*); (Sitz)Stange *f für Vögel*; 2. (sich) setzen; sitzen.

perchance [pə'tʃɑ:ns] zufällig; vielleicht.

percolate ['pə:kəleit] durchtropfen, durchsickern (lassen); sickern.

percussion [pə:'kʌʃən] Schlag *m*; Erschütterung *f*; ❦ Abklopfen *n*.

perdition [pə:'diʃən] Verderben *n*.

peregrination [perigri'neiʃən] Wanderschaft *f*; Wanderung *f*.

peremptory ☐ [pə'remptəri] bestimmt; zwingend; rechthaberisch.

perennial ☐ [pə'renjəl] dauernd; immerwährend; ⚥ perennierend.

perfect 1. ['pə:fikt] ☐ vollkommen; vollendet; gänzlich, völlig; 2. [␣] a. ~ tense gr. Perfekt n; 3. [pə'fekt] vervollkommnen; vollenden; ~ion [␣kʃən] Vollendung f; Vollkommenheit f; fig. Gipfel m.

perfidious ☐ [pə:'fidiəs] treulos (to gegen), verräterisch.

perfidy ['pə:fidi] Treulosigkeit f.

perforate ['pə:fəreit] durchlöchern.

perforce [pə'fɔ:s] notgedrungen.

perform [pə'fɔ:m] verrichten; ausführen; tun; Pflicht etc. erfüllen; thea., ♪ aufführen, spielen, vortragen (a. v/i.); ~ance [␣məns] Verrichtung f; thea. Aufführung f; Vortrag m; Leistung f; ~er [␣mə] Vortragende(r m) f.

perfume 1. ['pə:fju:m] Wohlgeruch m; Parfüm n; 2. [pə'fju:m] parfümieren; ~ry [␣məri] Parfümerie(n pl.) f.

perfunctory ☐ [pə'fʌŋktəri] mechanisch; oberflächlich.

perhaps [pə'hæps, præps] vielleicht.

peril ['peril] 1. Gefahr f; 2. gefährden; ~ous ☐ [␣ləs] gefährlich.

period ['piəriəd] Periode f; Zeitraum m; gr. Punkt m; langer Satz; (Unterrichts)Stunde f; mst ~s pl. ♀ Periode f; [o [piəri'ɔdik] periodisch; ~ical [␣kəl] 1. ☐ periodisch; 2. Zeitschrift f.

perish ['periʃ] umkommen, zugrunde gehen; ~able ☐ [␣ʃəbl] vergänglich; leicht verderblich; ~ing ☐ [␣ʃiŋ] vernichtend, tödlich.

periwig ['periwig] Perücke f.

perjur|e ['pə:dʒə]: ~ o.s. falsch schwören; ~y [␣ri] Meineid m.

perk F [pə:k] v/i. mst ~ up selbstbewußt auftreten; sich wieder erholen; v/t. recken; ~ o.s. (up) sich putzen.

perky ☐ ['pə:ki] keck, dreist; flott.

perm F [pə:m] 1. Dauerwelle f; 2. j-m Dauerwellen machen.

permanen|ce ['pə:mənəns] Dauer f; ~t ☐ [␣nt] dauernd, ständig; dauerhaft; Dauer...; ~ wave Dauerwelle f.

permea|ble ☐ ['pə:mjəbl] durchlässig; ~te ['pə:mieit] durchdringen; eindringen.

permissi|ble ☐ [pə'misəbl] zulässig; ~on [␣ʃən] Erlaubnis f.

permit 1. [pə'mit] erlauben, gestatten; 2. [pə'mit] Erlaubnis f, Genehmigung f; Passierschein m.

pernicious ☐ [pə:'niʃəs] verderblich; ♪ bösartig.

perpendicular ☐ [pə:pən'dikjulə] senkrecht; aufrecht; steil.

perpetrate ['pə:pitreit] verüben.

perpetu|al ☐ [pə'petjuəl] fort-

während, ewig; ~ate [␣ueit] verewigen.

perplex [pə'pleks] verwirren; ~ity [␣siti] Verwirrung f.

perquisites ['pə:kwizits] pl. Nebeneinkünfte pl.

persecut|e ['pə:sikju:t] verfolgen; ~ion [pə:si'kju:ʃən] Verfolgung f; ~or ['pə:sikju:tə] Verfolger m.

persever|ance [pə:si'viərəns] Beharrlichkeit f, Ausdauer f; ~e [pə:si'viə] beharren; aushalten.

persist [pə'sist] beharren (in auf dat.); ~ence, ~ency [␣təns, ␣si] Beharrlichkeit f; ~ent ☐ [␣nt] beharrlich.

person ['pə:sn] Person f (a. gr.); Persönlichkeit f; Rolle f; ~age [␣nidʒ] Persönlichkeit f; thea. Charakter m; ~al ☐ [␣nl] persönlich (a. gr.); attr. Personal...; Privat...; eigen; ~ality [pə:sə'næliti] Persönlichkeit f; personalities pl. persönliche Bemerkungen f/pl.; ~ate ['pə:səneit] darstellen; sich ausgeben für; ~ify [pə:'sonifai] verkörpern; ~nel [pə:sə'nel] Personal n.

perspective [pə'spektiv] Perspektive f; Ausblick m, Fernsicht f.

perspex ['pə:speks] Plexiglas n.

perspicuous ☐ [pə'spikjuəs] klar.

perspir|ation [pə:spə'reiʃən] Schwitzen n; Schweiß m; ~e [pəs'paiə] (aus)schwitzen.

persua|de [pə'sweid] überreden; überzeugen; ~sion [␣eiʒən] Überredung f; Überzeugung f; Glaube m; ~sive ☐ [␣eisiv] überredend, überzeugend. [weis.\

pert ☐ [pə:t] keck, vorlaut, nase-\

pertain [pə:'tein] (to) gehören (dat. od. zu); betreffen (acc.).

pertinacious ☐ [pə:ti'neiʃəs] hartnäckig, zäh.

pertinent ☐ ['pə:tinənt] sachdienlich, -gemäß; zur Sache gehörig.

perturb [pə'tə:b] beunruhigen; stören.

perus|al [pə'ru:zəl] sorgfältige Durchsicht; ~e [␣u:z] durchlesen; prüfen.

pervade [pə:'veid] durchdringen.

pervers|e ☐ [pə'və:s] verkehrt; pervers; eigensinnig; vertrackt (Sache); ~ion [␣ə:ʃən] Verdrehung f; Abkehr f; ~ity [␣ə:siti] Verkehrtheit f; ♪ Perversität f; Eigensinn m.

pervert 1. [pə'və:t] verdrehen; verführen; 2. ['pə:və:t] perverser Mensch.

pessimism ['pesimizəm] Pessimismus m.

pest [pest] Pest f; Plage f; Schädling m; ~er ['pestə] belästigen.

pesti|ferous ☐ [pes'tifərəs] krankheiterregend; ~lence ['pestiləns] Seuche f, bsd. Pest f; ~lent [␣nt] gefährlich; co. verdammt; ~lential

□ [pesti'lenʃəl] pestartig; verderbenbringend.

pet [pet] **1.** üble Laune; zahmes Tier; Liebling *m*; **2.** Lieblings...; ~ **dog** Schoßhund *m*; ~ **name** Kosename *m*; **3.** (ver)hätscheln; knutschen.

petal ♀ ['petl] Blütenblatt *n*.

petition [pi'tiʃən] **1.** Bitte *f*; Bittschrift *f*, Eingabe *f*; **2.** bitten, ersuchen; e-e Eingabe machen.

petrify ['petrifai] versteinern.

petrol *mot.* ['petrəl] Benzin *n*; ~ **station** Tankstelle *f*.

petticoat ['petikout] Unterrock *m*.

pettish □ ['petiʃ] launisch.

petty □ ['peti] klein, geringfügig.

petulant ['petjulənt] gereizt.

pew [pju:] Kirchensitz *m*, -bank *f*.

pewter ['pju:tə] Zinn (gefäße *n*/*pl.*) *n*.

phantasm ['fæntæzəm] Trugbild *n*.

phantom ['fæntəm] Phantom *n*, Trugbild *n*; Gespenst *n*.

Pharisee ['færisi:] Pharisäer *m*.

pharmacy ['fɑ:məsi] Pharmazie *f*; Apotheke *f*. [Phasen.\]

phase [feiz] Phase *f*; ~d [feizd] in]

pheasant *orn.* ['feznt] Fasan *m*.

phenomen|on [fi'nɔminən], *pl.* ~**a** [~nə] Phänomen *n*, Erscheinung *f*.

phial ['faiəl] Phiole *f*, Fläschchen *n*.

philander [fi'lændə] flirten.

philanthropist [fi'lænθrəpist] Menschenfreund(in).

philolog|ist [fi'lɔlədʒist] Philolog|e *m*, -in *f*; ~**y** [~dʒi] Philologie *f*.

philosoph|er [fi'lɔsəfə] Philosoph *m*; ~**ize** [~faiz] philosophieren; ~**y** [~fi] Philosophie *f*.

phlegm [flem] Schleim *m*; Phlegma *n*.

phone F [foun] *s.* telephone.

phonetics [fou'netiks] *pl.* Phonetik *f*, Lautbildungslehre *f*.

phon(e)y *Am. sl.* ['founi] **1.** Fälschung *f*; Schwindler *m*; **2.** unecht.

phosphorus ['fɔsfərəs] Phosphor *m*.

photograph ['foutəgrɑ:f] **1.** Photographie *f* (*Bild*); **2.** photographieren; ~**er** [fə'tɔgrəfə] Photograph (-in); ~**y** [~fi] Photographie *f*.

phrase [freiz] **1.** (Rede)Wendung *f*, Redensart *f*, Ausdruck *m*; **2.** ausdrücken.

physic|al □ ['fizikəl] physisch; körperlich; physikalisch; ~ *education*, ~ *training* Leibeserziehung *f*; ~**ian** [fi'ziʃən] Arzt *m*; ~**ist** ['fizisist] Physiker *m*; ~**s** [~iks] *sg.* Physik *f*.

physique [fi'zi:k] Körperbau *m*.

piano ['pjænou] Klavier *n*.

piazza [pi'ætsə] Piazza *f*, (Markt-) Platz *m*; *Am.* große Veranda.

pick [pik] Auswahl *f*; = *pickaxe*; **2.** auf-, wegnehmen; pflücken; (herum)stochern; in *der Nase* bohren; abnagen; *Schloß* knacken; *Streit* suchen; auswählen; (auf-) picken; bestehlen; ~ *out* auswählen;

herausssuchen; ~ *up* aufreißen, aufbrechen; aufnehmen, auflesen; sich *e-e Fremdsprache* aneignen; erfassen; (*im Auto*) mitnehmen, abholen; *Täter* ergreifen; gesund werden; ~**-a-back** ['pikəbæk] huckepack; ~**axe** Spitzhacke *f*.

picket ['pikit] **1.** Pfahl *m*; ✗ Feldwache *f*; Streikposten *m*; **2.** einpfählen; an e-n Pfahl binden; mit Streikposten besetzen.

picking ['pikiŋ] Picken *n*, Pflücken *n*; Abfall *m*; *mst* ~**s** *pl.* Nebengewinn *m*.

pickle ['pikl] **1.** Pökel *m*; Eingepökelte(s) *n*, Pickles *pl.*; F mißliche Lage; **2.** (ein)pökeln; ~**d** *herring* Salzhering *m*.

pick|lock ['piklɔk] Dietrich *m*; ~**pocket** Taschendieb *m*; ~**up** Ansteigen *n*; Tonabnehmer *m*; Kleinlieferwagen *m*; *sl.* Straßenbekanntschaft *f*.

picnic ['piknik] Picknick *n*.

pictorial [pik'tɔ:riəl] **1.** □ malerisch; illustriert; **2.** Illustrierte *f*.

picture ['piktʃə] **1.** Bild *n*, Gemälde *n*; *et.* Bildschönes; ~**s** *pl.* F Kino *n*; *attr.* Bilder...; *put s.o. in the* ~ j. ins Bild setzen, j. informieren; **2.** (aus-) malen; sich *et.* ausmalen; ~ *post-card* Ansichtskarte *f*; ~**sque** [piktʃə'resk] malerisch.

pie [pai] Pastete *f*; Obsttorte *f*.

piebald ['paibɔ:ld] (bunt)scheckig.

piece [pi:s] **1.** Stück *n*; Geschütz *n*; Gewehr *n*; Teil *n* e-s *Services*; *Schach- etc.* Figur *f*; *a* ~ *of advice* ein Rat; *a* ~ *of news* e-e Neuigkeit; *of a* ~ gleichmäßig; *give s.o. a* ~ *of one's mind* j-m gründlich die Meinung sagen; *take to* ~ zerlegen; **2.** *a.* ~ *up* flicken, ausbessern; ~ *together* zs.-stellen, -setzen, -stücken, -flicken; ~ *out* ausfüllen; ~**meal** ['pi:smi:l] stückweise; ~**work** Akkordarbeit *f*.

pieplant *Am.* ['paiplɑ:nt] Rhabarber *m*.

pier [piə] Pfeiler *m*; Wellenbrecher *m*; Pier *m*, *f*; Hafendamm *m*, Mole *f*, Landungsbrücke *f*.

pierce [piəs] durchbohren; durchdringen; eindringen (in *acc.*).

piety ['paiəti] Frömmigkeit *f*; Pietät *f*.

pig [pig] Ferkel *n*; Schwein *n*.

pigeon ['pidʒin] Taube *f*; ~**-hole 1.** Fach *n*; **2.** in ein Fach legen.

pig|headed ['pig'hedid] dickköpfig; ~**-iron** ['pigaiən] Roheisen *n*; ~**skin** Schweinsleder *n*; ~**sty** Schweinestall *m*; ~**tail** (Haar)Zopf *m*.

pike [paik] ✗ Pike *f*; Spitze *f*; *ichth.* Hecht *m*; Schlagbaum *m*; gebührenpflichtige Straße.

pile [pail] **1.** (Scheiter)Haufen *m*; Stoß *m* (*Holz*); großes Gebäude; ≰ Batterie *f*; Pfahl *m*; Haar *n*;

Noppe *f*; ~*s pl.* ⚶ Hämorrhoiden *f*|*pl.*; *(atomic)* ~ *phys.* Atommeiler *m*, Reaktor *m*; 2. *oft* ~ *up*, ~ *on* auf~, anhäufen, aufschichten.

pilfer ['pilfə] mausen, stibitzen.

pilgrim ['pilgrim] Pilger *m*; ~**age** [~midʒ] Pilgerfahrt *f*.

pill [pil] Pille *f*.

pillage ['pilidʒ] 1. Plünderung *f*; 2. plündern.

pillar ['pilə] Pfeiler *m*, Ständer *m*; Säule *f*; ~**box** Briefkasten *m*.

pillion *mot.* ['piljən] Soziussitz *m*.

pillory ['piləri] 1. Pranger *m*; 2. an den Pranger stellen; anprangern.

pillow ['pilou] (Kopf)Kissen *n*; ~**case**, ~**slip** (Kissen)Bezug *m*.

pilot ['pailət] 1. ✈ Pilot *m*; ⚓ Lotse *m*; *fig.* Führer *m*; 2. lotsen, steuern; ~**balloon** Versuchsballon *m*.

pimp [pimp] 1. Kuppler(in); 2. kuppeln.

pin [pin] 1. (Steck-, Krawatten-, Hut- *etc.*)Nadel *f*; Reißnagel *m*; Pflock *m*; ⚙ Wirbel *m*; Kegel *m*; 2. (an)heften; befestigen; *fig.* festnageln.

pinafore ['pinəfɔ:] Schürze *f*.

pincers ['pinsəz] *pl.* Kneifzange *f*.

pinch [pintʃ] 1. Kniff *m*; Prise *f* (*Tabak etc.*); Druck *m*, Not *f*; 2. *v*|*t.* kneifen, zwicken; F klauen; *v*|*i.* drücken; in Not sein; knausern.

pinch-hit *Am.* ['pintʃhit] einspringen (*for* für).

pincushion ['pinkuʃin] Nadelkissen *n*.

pine [pain] 1. ⚘ Kiefer *f*, Föhre *f*; 2. sich abhärmen; sich sehnen, schmachten; ~**apple** ⚘ ['painæpl] Ananas *f*; ~**cone** Kiefernzapfen *m*.

pinion ['pinjən] 1. Flügel(spitze *f*) *m*; Schwungfeder *f*; ⊕ Ritzel *n* (*Antriebsrad*); 2. die Flügel beschneiden (*dat.*); *fig.* fesseln.

pink [piŋk] 1. ⚘ Nelke *f*; Rosa *n*; *fig.* Gipfel *m*; 2. rosa(farben).

pin-money ['pinmʌni] Nadelgeld *n*.

pinnacle ['pinəkl] △ Zinne *f*, Spitztürmchen *n*; (Berg)Spitze *f*; *fig.* Gipfel *m*.

pint [paint] Pinte *f* (*0,57 od. Am. 0,47 Liter*).

pioneer [paiə'niə] 1. Pionier *m* (*a.* ✕); 2. den Weg bahnen (für).

pious □ ['paiəs] fromm, religiös; pflichtgetreu.

pip [pip] *vet.* Pips *m*; *sl.* miese Laune; Obstkern *m*; Auge *n* auf Würfeln *etc.*; ✕ Stern *m* (*Rangabzeichen*).

pipe [paip] 1. Rohr *n*, Röhre *f*; Pfeife *f* (*a.* ♪); Flöte *f*; Lied *n e-s Vogels*; Luftröhre *f*; Pipe *f* (*Weinfaß* = 477,3 *Liter*); 2. pfeifen; quieken; ~**layer** ['paipleiə] Rohrleger *m*; *Am. pol.* Drahtzieher *m*;

~**line** Ölleitung *f*, Pipeline *f*; ~**r** ['paipə] Pfeifer *m*.

piping ['paipiŋ] 1. pfeifend; schrill (*Stimme*); ~ *hot* siedend heiß; 2. Rohrnetz *n*; *Schneiderei:* Paspel *f*.

piquant □ ['pi:kənt] pikant.

pique [pi:k] 1. Groll *m*; 2. *j-n* reizen; ~ *o.s. on* sich brüsten mit.

piracy ['paiərəsi] Seeräuberei *f*; Raubdruck *m von Büchern*; ~**te** [~rit] 1. Seeräuber(schiff *n*) *m*; Raubdrucker *m*; 2. unerlaubt nachdrucken.

pistol ['pistl] Pistole *f*.

piston ⊕ ['pistən] Kolben *m*; ~**rod** Kolbenstange *f*; ~**stroke** Kolbenhub *m*.

pit [pit] 1. Grube *f* (*a.* ⚒, *anat.*); ♪ Miete *f*; *thea.* Parterre *n*; Pockennarbe *f*; (*Tier*)Falle *f*; *Am. Börse:* Maklerstand *m*; *Am. Obst-*Stein *m*; 2. ♪ einmieten; mit Narben bedecken.

pitch [pitʃ] 1. Pech *n*; Stand(platz) *m*; Tonhöhe *f*; Grad *m*, Stufe *f*; Steigung *f*, Neigung *f*; Wurf *m*; ⚓ Stampfen *n*; 2. *v*|*t.* werfen; schleudern; *Zelt etc.* aufschlagen; ♪ stimmen (*a. fig.*); ~ *too high fig.* Ziel etc. zu hoch stecken; *v*|*i.* ✕ (sich) lagern; fallen; ⚓ stampfen; ~ *into* F herfallen über (*acc.*).

pitcher ['pitʃə] Krug *m*.

pitchfork ['pitʃfɔ:k] Heu-, Mistgabel *f*; ♪ Stimmgabel *f*.

piteous □ ['pitiəs] kläglich.

pitfall ['pitfɔ:l] Fallgrube *f*, Falle *f*.

pith [piθ] Mark *n*; *fig.* Kern *m*; Kraft *f*; ~**y** □ ['piθi] markig, kernig.

pitiable □ ['pitiəbl] erbärmlich.

pitiful □ ['pitiful] mitleidig; erbärmlich, jämmerlich (*a. contp.*).

pitiless □ ['pitilis] unbarmherzig.

pittance ['pitəns] Hungerlohn *m*.

pity ['piti] 1. Mitleid *n* (*on* mit); *it is a* ~ es ist schade; 2. bemitleiden.

pivot ['pivət] 1. ⊕ Zapfen *m*; (Tür-) Angel *f*; *fig.* Drehpunkt *m*; 2. sich drehen (*on, upon* um). (verrückt.)

pixilated *Am.* F ['piksileitid] leicht

placable □ ['plækəbl] versöhnlich.

placard ['plæka:d] 1. Plakat *n*; 2. anschlagen; mit e-m Plakat bekleben.

place [pleis] 1. Platz *m*; Ort *m*; Stadt *f*; Stelle *f*; Stätte *f*; Stellung *f*; Aufgabe *f*; Anwesen *n*, Haus *n*, Wohnung *f*; ~ *of delivery* ✝ Erfüllungsort *m*; *give* ~ *to j-m* Platz machen; *in* ~ *of* an Stelle (*gen.*); *out of* ~ fehl am Platz; 2. stellen, legen, setzen; *j-n* anstellen; *Auftrag* erteilen; *I can't place him fig.* ich weiß nicht, wo ich ihn hintun soll (*identifizieren*).

placid □ ['plæsid] sanft; ruhig.

plagiar|ism ['pleidʒjərizəm] Plagiat *n*; ~**ize** [~raiz] abschreiben.

plague [pleig] 1. Plage *f*; Seuche *f*; Pest *f*; 2. plagen, quälen.

plaice *ichth.* [pleis] Scholle *f*.

plaid [plæd] *schottisches* Plaid.

plain [plein] 1. □ flach, eben; klar; deutlich; rein; einfach, schlicht; unscheinbar; offen, ehrlich; einfarbig; 2. *adv.* klar, deutlich; 3. Ebene *f*, Fläche *f*; *bsd. Am.* Prärie *f*; ~**clothes man** ['plein-klouðz mən] Geheimpolizist *m*; ~ **dealing** ehrliche Handlungsweise; ~**dealing** ehrlich.

plainsman ['pleinzmən] Flachlandbewohner *m*; *Am.* Präriebewohner *m*.

plaint|iff *ᵗᵗ* ['pleintif] Kläger(in); ~**ive** □ [~iv] traurig, klagend.

plait [plæt, *Am.* pleit] 1. Haar- *etc.* Flechte *f*; Zopf *m*; 2. flechten.

plan [plæn] 1. Plan *m*; 2. e-n Plan machen von *od.* zu; *fig.* planen.

plane [plein] 1. flach, eben; 2. Ebene *f*, Fläche *f*; ✈ Tragfläche *f*; Flugzeug *n*; *fig.* Stufe *f*; ⊕ Hobel *m*; 3. ebnen; (ab)hobeln; ✈ fliegen.

plank [plæŋk] 1. Planke *f*, Bohle *f*, Diele *f*; *Am. pol.* Programmpunkt *m*; 2. dielen; verschalen; ~ **down** *sl.*, *Am.* F Geld auf den Tisch legen.

plant [plɑ:nt] 1. Pflanze *f*; ⊕ Anlage *f*; Fabrik *f*; 2. (an-, ein)pflanzen (*a. fig.*); (auf)stellen; anlegen; *Schlag* verpassen; bepflanzen; besiedeln; ~**ation** [plæn'teiʃən] Pflanzung *f* (*a. fig.*); Plantage *f*; Besiedelung *f*; ~**er** ['plɑ:ntə] Pflanzer *m*.

plaque [plɑ:k] Platte *f*; Gedenktafel *f*.

plash [plæʃ] platschen.

plaster ['plɑ:stə] 1. *pharm.* Pflaster *n*; ⊕ Putz *m*; *mst* ~ *of Paris* Gips *m*, Stuck *m*; 2. bepflastern; verputzen.

plastic ['plæstik] 1. (~ally) plastisch; Plastik...; 2. *oft* ~*s pl.* Plastik(material) *n*, Kunststoff *m*.

plat [plæt] *s.* plait; *s.* plot 1.

plate [pleit] 1. *allg.* Platte *f*; Bild-Tafel *f*; Schild *n*; *Kupfer*-Stich *m*; Tafelsilber *n*; Teller *m*; *Am. Baseball:* (Schlag)Mal *n*; ⊕ Grobblech *n*; 2. plattieren; ✕, ⚓ panzern.

platform ['plætfɔ:m] Plattform *f*; *geogr.* Hochebene *f*; ⊞ Bahnsteig *m*; *Am. bsd.* Plattform *f am Wagenende*; Rednerbühne *f*; *pol.* Parteiprogramm *n*; *bsd. Am. pol.* Aktionsprogramm *n im Wahlkampf*.

platinum *min.* ['plætinəm] Platin *n*.

platitude *fig.* ['plætitju:d] Plattheit *f*.

platoon ✕ [plə'tu:n] Zug *m*.

plat(t)en ['plætən] (Schreibmaschinen)Walze *f*.

platter ['plætə] (Servier)Platte *f*.

plaudit ['plɔ:dit] Beifall *m*.

plausible □ ['plɔ:zəbl] glaubhaft.

play [plei] 1. Spiel *n*; Schauspiel *n*; ⊕ Spiel *n*, Gang *m*; Spielraum *m*; 2. spielen; ⊕ laufen; ~ *upon* einwirken auf (*acc.*); ~ *off fig.* ausspielen (*against* gegen); ~*ed out* erledigt; ~**bill** ['pleibil] Theaterzettel *m*; ~**book** *thea.* Textbuch *n*; ~**boy** Playboy *m*; ~**er** ['pleiə] (Schau)Spieler(in); ~*piano* elektrisches Klavier; ~**fellow** Spielgefährt|e *m*, -in *f*; ~**ful** □ [~ful] spielerisch, scherzhaft; ~**goer** ['pleigouə] Theaterbesucher(in); ~**ground** Spielplatz *m*; Schulhof *m*; ~**house** Schauspielhaus *n*; *Am.* Miniaturhaus *n für Kinder*; ~**mate** *s. playfellow*; ~**thing** Spielzeug *n*; ~**wright** Bühnenautor *m*, Dramatiker *m*.

plea [pli:] *ᵗᵗ* Einspruch *m*; Ausrede *f*; Gesuch *n*; *on the* ~ *of od. that* unter dem Vorwand (*gen.*) *od.* daß.

plead [pli:d] *v/i.* plädieren; ~ *for* für *j-n* sprechen; sich einsetzen für; ~ *guilty* sich schuldig bekennen; *v/t. Sache* vertreten; als Beweis anführen; ~**er** *ᵗᵗ* [pli:də] Verteidiger *m*; ~**ing** *ᵗᵗ* [~diŋ] Schriftsatz *m*.

pleasant □ ['pleznt] angenehm; erfreulich; ~**ry** [~tri] Scherz *m*, Spaß *m*.

please [pli:z] *v/i.* gefallen; belieben; *if you* ~ *iro.* stellen Sie sich vor; ~ *come in!* bitte, treten Sie ein!; *v/t. j-m* gefallen, angenehm sein; befriedigen; ~ *yourself* tun Sie, was Ihnen gefällt; *be* ~*d to do et.* gerne tun; *be* ~*d with* Vergnügen haben an (*dat.*); ~*d* erfreut; zufrieden.

pleasing □ ['pli:ziŋ] angenehm.

pleasure ['pleʒə] Vergnügen *n*, Freude *f*; Belieben *n*; *attr.* Vergnügungs...; *at* ~ nach Belieben; ~**ground** (Vergnügungs)Park *m*.

pleat [pli:t] 1. (Plissee)Falte *f*; 2. fälteln, plissieren.

pledge [pledʒ] 1. Pfand *n*; Zutrinken *n*; Gelöbnis *n*; 2. verpfänden; *j-m* zutrinken; *he* ~*d himself* er gelobte.

plenary ['pli:nəri] Voll...

plenipotentiary [plenipə'tenʃəri] Bevollmächtigte(r *m*) *f* [reichlich.)

plenteous □ *poet.* ['plentjəs] voll.)

plentiful □ ['plentiful] reichlich.

plenty ['plenti] 1. Fülle *f*, Überfluß *m*; ~ *of* reichlich; 2. F reichlich.

pliable □ ['plaiəbl] biegsam; *fig.* geschmeidig, nachgiebig.

pliancy ['plaiənsi] Biegsamkeit *f*.

pliers ['plaiəz] *pl.* (*a. pair of* ~ *pl.* eine) (Draht-, Kombi)Zange.

plight [plait] 1. Ehre, Wort verpfänden; verloben; 2. Gelöbnis *n*; Zustand *m*, (Not)Lage *f*.

plod [plɔd] *a.* ~ *along*, ~ *on* sich dahinschleppen; sich plagen, schuften.

plot [plɔt] **1.** Platz *m*; Parzelle *f*; Plan *m*; Komplott *n*, Anschlag *m*; Intrige *f*; Handlung *f* e-s Dramas etc.; **2.** *v/t.* aufzeichnen; planen, anzetteln; *v/i.* intrigieren.

plough, *Am. mst.* **plow** [plau] **1.** Pflug *m*; **2.** pflügen; (*a. fig.*) furchen; **~man** ['plaumən] Pflüger *m*; **~share** ['plauʃɛə] Pflugschar *f*.

pluck [plʌk] **1.** Mut *m*, Schneid *m*, *f*; Innereien *f/pl.*; Zug *m*, Ruck *m*; **2.** pflücken; *Vogel* rupfen (*a. fig.*); reißen; ~ *at* zerren an; ~ *up courage* Mut fassen; **~y** [□ ['plʌki] mutig.

plug [plʌg] **1.** Pflock *m*; Dübel *m*; Stöpsel *m*; ⚡ Stecker *m*; Zahn-Plombe *f*; Priem *m* (*Tabak*); *Am. Radio:* Reklamehinweis *m*; alter Gaul; ~ *socket* Steckdose *f*; *v/t.* zu-, verstopfen; *Zahn* plombieren; stöpseln; *Am.* F im Rundfunk etc. Reklame machen für *et.*

plum [plʌm] Pflaume *f*; Rosine *f* (*a. fig.*).

plumage ['plu:midʒ] Gefieder *n*.

plumb [plʌm] **1.** lotrecht; gerade; richtig; **2.** (Blei)Lot *n*; **3.** *v/t.* lotrecht machen; loten; sondieren (*a. fig.*); F *Wasser-od.* Gasleitungen legen in; *v/i.* F als Rohrleger arbeiten; **~er** ['plʌmə] Klempner *m*, Installateur *m*; **~ing** [.miŋ] Klempnerarbeit *f*; Rohrleitungen *f/pl.*

plume [plu:m] **1.** Feder *f*; Federbusch *m*; **2.** mit Federn schmücken; *die Federn* putzen; ~ *o.s. on* sich brüsten mit.

plummet ['plʌmit] Senkblei *n*.

plump [plʌmp] **1.** *adj.* drall, prall, mollig; F □ glatt (*Absage etc.*); **2.**(hin)plumpsen (lassen); **3.** Plumps *m*; **4.** F *adv.* geradeswegs.

plum pudding ['plʌm'pudiŋ] Plumpudding *m*.

plunder ['plʌndə] **1.** Plünderung *f*; Raub *m*, Beute *f*; **2.** plündern.

plunge [plʌndʒ] **1.** (Unter)Tauchen *n*; (Kopf)Sprung *m*; Sturz *m*; *make od. take the* ~ den entscheidenden Schritt tun; **2.** (unter-) tauchen; (sich) stürzen (*into in acc.*); *Schwert etc.* stoßen; ⚓ stampfen.

plunk [plʌŋk] *v/t.* *Saite* zupfen; *et.* hinplumpsen lassen, hinwerfen; *v/i.* (hin)plumpsen, fallen.

pluperfect *gr.* F ['plu:'pə:fikt] Plusquamperfekt *n*.

plural *gr.* ['pluərəl] Plural *m*, Mehrzahl *f*; **~ity** [pluə'ræliti] Vielheit *f*, Mehrheit *f*; Mehrzahl *f*.

plus [plʌs] **1.** *prp.* plus; **2.** *adj.* positiv; **3.** Plus *n*; Mehr *n*.

plush [plʌʃ] Plüsch *m*.

ply [plai] **1.** Lage *f Tuch etc.*; Strähne *f*; *fig.* Neigung *f*; **2.** *v/t.* fleißig anwenden; *j-m* zusetzen, *j-n* überhäufen; *v/i.* regelmäßig fahren; **~wood** ['plaiwud] Sperrholz *n*.

pneumatic [nju(:)'mætik] **1.** (~*ally*) Luft...; pneumatisch; **2.** Luftreifen *m*.

pneumonia ⚚ [nju(:)'mounjə] Lungenentzündung *f*.

poach [poutʃ] wildern; *Erde* zertreten; ~*ed eggs pl.* verlorene Eier *n/pl.*

poacher ['poutʃə] Wilddieb *m*.

pock ⚚ [pɔk] Pocke *f*, Blatter *f*.

pocket ['pɔkit] **1.** Tasche *f*; ⚡ Luft-Loch *n*; **2.** einstecken (*a. fig.*); *Am. pol. Gesetzesvorlage* nicht unterschreiben; *fig.* Gefühl unterdrücken; **3.** Taschen...; **~book** Notizbuch *n*; Brieftasche *f*; *Am.* Geldbeutel *m*; Taschenbuch *n*.

pod ♀ [pɔd] Hülse *f*, Schale *f*, Schote *f*.

poem ['pouim] Gedicht *n*.

poet ['pouit] Dichter *m*; **~ess** [.tis] Dichterin *f*; **~ic(al** □) [pou'etik(əl)] dichterisch; **~ics** [.ks] *sg.* Poetik *f*; **~ry** ['pouitri] Dichtkunst *f*; Dichtung *f*, *coll.* Dichtungen *f/pl.*

poignan|cy ['pɔinənsi] Schärfe *f*; **~t** [.nt] scharf; *fig.* eindringlich.

point [pɔint] **1.** Spitze *f*; Pointe *f*; Landspitze *f*; *gr.*, ♫, *phys. etc.* Punkt *m*; Fleck *m*, Stelle *f*; ⚡ Kompaßstrich *m*; Auge *n auf Karten etc.*; Grad *m*; (springender) Punkt; Zweck *m*; *fig.* Eigenschaft *f*; **~s** *pl.* ⚙ Weichen *f/pl.*; ~ *of view* Stand-, Gesichtspunkt *m*; *the* ~ *is that* ... die Sache ist die, daß ...; *make a* ~ *of s.th.* auf *et.* bestehen; *in* ~ *of* in Hinsicht auf (*acc.*); *off od. beside the* ~ nicht zur Sache (gehörig); *on the* ~ *of ger.* im Begriff zu *inf.*; *win on* ~ nach Punkten siegen; *to the* ~ zur Sache (gehörig); **2.** *v/t.* (zu)spitzen; *off* od. *out* zeigen, hinweisen auf (*acc.*); punktieren; *at Waffe etc.* richten auf (*acc.*); *v/i.* ~ *at* weisen auf (*acc.*); ~ *to* nach e-r *Richtung* weisen; **~ed** [□ ['pɔintid] spitz(ig), Spitz...; *fig.* scharf; **~er** [.tə] Zeiger *m*; Zeigestock *m*; Hühnerhund *m*; **~less** [.tlis] stumpf; witzlos; zwecklos.

poise [pɔiz] **1.** Gleichgewicht *n*; Haltung *f*; **2.** *v/t.* im Gleichgewicht erhalten; *Kopf etc.* tragen, halten; *v/i.* schweben.

poison ['pɔizn] **1.** Gift *n*; **2.** vergiften; **~ous** □ [.nəs] giftig (*a. fig.*).

poke [pouk] **1.** Stoß *m*, Puff *m*; **2.** *v/t.* stoßen; schüren; *Nase etc. in et.* stecken; *~ fun at* sich über *j-n* lustig machen; *v/i.* stoßen; stochern.

poker ['poukə] Feuerhaken *m*.

poky ['pouki] eng; schäbig; erbärmlich. [*m.*]

polar ['poulə] polar; ~ *bear* Eisbär

Pole¹ [poul] Pole *m*, Polin *f*.

pole² [.] Pol *m*; Stange *f*, Mast *m*; Deichsel *f*; (Sprung)Stab *m*.

polecat zo. ['poulkæt] Iltis m; Am. Skunk m.
polemic [pɔ'lemik], a. ~al □ [~kəl] polemisch; feindselig.
pole-star ['poulsta:] Polarstern m; fig. Leitstern m.
police [pə'li:s] 1. Polizei f; 2. überwachen; ~man Polizist m; ~office Polizeipräsidium n; ~officer Polizeibeamte(r) m, Polizist m; ~station Polizeiwache f.
policy ['polisi] Politik f; (Welt)Klugheit f; Police f; Am. Zahlenlotto n.
polio(myelitis) ✠ ['pouliou(maiə'laitis)] spinale Kinderlähmung.
Polish[1] ['pouliʃ] polnisch.
polish[a] ['poliʃ] 1. Politur f; fig. Schliff m; 2. polieren; fig. verfeinern.
polite □ [pə'lait] artig, höflich; fein; ~ness [~tnis] Höflichkeit f.
politic □ ['politik] politisch; schlau; ~al [pə'litikəl] politisch; staatlich; Staats..; ~ian [poli'tiʃən] Politiker m; ~s ['politiks] oft sg. Staatswissenschaft f, Politik f.
polka ['polkə] Polka f; ~ dot Am. Punktmuster n auf Stoff.
poll [poul] 1. Wählerliste f; Stimmenzählung f; Wahl f; Stimmenzahl f; Umfrage f; co. Kopf m; 2. v/t. Stimmen erhalten; v/i. wählen; ~book ['poulbuk] Wählerliste f.
pollen ✠ ['polin] Blütenstaub m.
polling-district ['poulindistrikt] Wahlbezirk m.
poll-tax ['poultæks] Kopfsteuer f.
pollute [pə'lu:t] beschmutzen, beflecken; entweihen.
polyp|(e) zo. ['polip], ~us ✠ [~pəs] Polyp m.
pommel ['pʌml] 1. Degen-, Sattel-Knopf m; 2. knuffen, schlagen.
pomp [pomp] Pomp m, Gepränge n.
pompous □ ['pompəs] prunkvoll; hochtrabend; pompös.
pond [pond] Teich m, Weiher m.
ponder ['pondə] v/t. erwägen; v/i. nachdenken; ~able [~ərəbl] wägbar; ~ous □ [~rəs] schwer(fällig).
pontiff ['pontif] Hohepriester m; Papst m.
pontoon ✕ [pon'tu:n] Ponton m; ~bridge Schiffsbrücke f.
pony ['pouni] Pony n, Pferdchen n.
poodle ['pu:dl] Pudel m.
pool [pu:l] 1. Teich m; Pfütze f, Lache f (Schwimm)Becken n; (Spiel)Einsatz m; ♣ Ring m, Kartell n; ~ room Am. Billardspielhalle f; Wettannahmestelle f; 2. ♦ zu e-m Ring vereinigen; Gelder zs.-werfen.
poop ♣ [pu:p] Heck n; Achterhütte f.
poor □ [puə] arm(selig); dürftig; schlecht; ~house ['puəhaus] Armenhaus n; ~law ⚖ Armenrecht

n; ~ly [~li] 1. adj. unpäßlich; 2. adv. dürftig; ~ness ['puənis] Armut f.
pop[1] [pop] 1. Knall m; F Sprudel m; F Schampus m; 2. v/t. knallen lassen; Am. Mais rösten; schnell wohin tun, stecken; v/i. puffen, knallen; mit adv. huschen; ~ in hereinplatzen.
pop[2] F [~] 1. populär, beliebt; 2. Schlager m; volkstümliche Musik.
pop[3] Am. F [~] Papa m, alter Herr.
popcorn Am. ['popkɔ:n] Puffmais m.
pope [poup] Papst m.
poplar ✠ ['poplə] Pappel f.
poppy ✠ ['popi] Mohn m; ~cock Am. F Quatsch m.
popu|lace ['popjuləs] Pöbel m; ~lar □ [~lə] Volks...; volkstümlich, populär; ~larity [popju'læriti] Popularität f.
populat|e ['popjuleit] bevölkern; ~ion [popju'leiʃən] Bevölkerung f; ~ous □ ['popjuləs] volkreich.
porcelain ['pɔ:slin] Porzellan n.
porch [pɔ:tʃ] Vorhalle f, Portal n; Am. Veranda f.
porcupine zo. ['pɔ:kjupain] Stachelschwein n.
pore [pɔ:] 1. Pore f; 2. fig. brüten.
pork [pɔ:k] Schweinefleisch n; ~barrel Am. sl. ['pɔ:kbærəl] politisch berechnete Geldzuwendung der Regierung; ~y F [pɔ:ki] 1. fett, dick; 2. Am. = porcupine.
porous □ ['pɔ:rəs] porös.
porpoise ichth. ['pɔ:pəs] Tümmler m.
porridge ['pɔridʒ] Haferbrei m.
port [pɔ:t] 1. Hafen m; ♣ (Pfort-, Lade)Luke f; ♣ Backbord n; Portwein m; 2. ♣ das Ruder nach der Backbordseite umlegen.
portable ['pɔ:təbl] transportabel.
portal ['pɔ:tl] Portal n, Tor n.
portend [pɔ:'tend] vorbedeuten.
portent ['pɔ:tent] (bsd. üble) Vorbedeutung; Wunder n; ~ous □ [pɔ:'tentəs] unheilvoll; wunderbar.
porter ['pɔ:tə] Pförtner m; (Gepäck)Träger m; Porterbier n.
portion ['pɔ:ʃən] 1. (An)Teil m; Portion f Essen; Erbteil n; Aussteuer f; fig. Los n; 2. teilen; ausstatten.
portly ['pɔ:tli] stattlich.
portmanteau [pɔ:t'mæntou] Handkoffer m. [nis n.]
portrait ['pɔ:trit] Porträt n, Bild-]
portray [pɔ:'trei] (ab)malen, porträtieren; schildern; ~al [~eiəl] Porträtieren n; Schilderung f.
pose [pouz] 1. Pose f; 2. (sich) in Positur setzen; F sich hinstellen (as als); Frage aufwerfen.
posh sl. [poʃ] schick, erstklassig.
position [pə'ziʃən] Lage f, Stellung f (a. fig.); Stand m; fig. Standpunkt m.

positive ['pozətiv] 1. □ bestimmt, ausdrücklich; feststehend, sicher; unbedingt; positiv; überzeugt; rechthaberisch; 2. *das* Bestimmte; *gr.* Positiv *m*; *phot.* Positiv *n*.

possess [pə'zes] besitzen; beherrschen; *fig.* erfüllen; ~ *o.s. of et.* in Besitz nehmen; ~ed besessen; ~ion [~eʃən] Besitz *m*; *fig.* Besessenheit *f*; ~ive *gr.* [~esiv] 1. □ besitzanzeigend; ~ *case* Genitiv *m*; 2. Possessivpronomen *n*, besitzanzeigendes Fürwort; Genitiv *m*; ~or [~sə] Besitzer *m*.

possib|lity [posə'biliti] Möglichkeit *f*; ~le ['posəbl] möglich; ~ly [~li] möglicherweise, vielleicht; *if I* ~ *can* wenn ich irgend kann.

post [poust] 1. Pfosten *m*; Posten *m*; Stelle *f*, Amt *n*; Post *f*; ~ *exchange Am.* ✗ Einkaufsstelle *f*; 2. *v/t.* Plakat etc. anschlagen; postieren; eintragen; zur Post geben; per Post senden; ~ *up j-n* informieren; *v/i.* (dahin)eilen.

postage ['poustidʒ] Porto *n*; ~-stamp Briefmarke *f*.

postal □ ['poustəl] 1. postalisch; Post...; ~ *order* Postanweisung *f*; 2. *a.* ~ **card** *Am.* Postkarte *f*.

postcard ['poustkɑːd] Postkarte *f*.

poster ['poustə] Plakat *n*, Anschlag *m*.

posterior [pos'tiəriə] 1. □ später (to als); hinter; 2. Hinterteil *n*.

posterity [pos'teriti] Nachwelt *f*; Nachkommenschaft *f*.

post-free ['poust'friː] portofrei.

post-graduate ['poust'grædjuit] 1. nach beendigter Studienzeit; 2. Doktorand *m*.

post-haste ['poust'heist] eilig(st).

posthumous □ ['postjuməs] nachgeboren; hinterlassen.

post|man ['poustmən] Briefträger *m*; ~mark 1. Poststempel *m*; 2. abstempeln; ~master Postamtsvorsteher *m*.

post-mortem ['poust'mɔːtem] 1. nach dem Tode; 2. Leichenschau *f*.

post|(-)office ['poustɔfis] Postamt *n*; ~ *box* Post(schließ)fach *n*; ~-paid frankiert.

postpone [poust'poun] ver-, aufschieben; ~ment [~mənt] Aufschub *m*. [tum *n*.]

postscript ['pousskript] Postskrip-/

postulate 1. ['postjulit] Forderung *f*; 2. [~leit] fordern; (als gegeben) voraussetzen.

posture ['postʃə] 1. Stellung *f*, Haltung *f des Körpers*; 2. (sich) zurechtstellen; posieren.

post-war ['poust'wɔː] Nachkriegs...

posy ['pouzi] Blumenstrauß *m*.

pot [pot] 1. Topf *m*; Kanne *f*; Tiegel *m*; 2. in e-n Topf tun; einlegen.

potation [pou'teiʃən] *mst* ~*s pl.* Trinken *n*, Zecherei *f*; Trunk *m*.

potato [pə'teitou], *pl.* ~es Kartoffel *f*.

pot-belly ['potbeli] Schmerbauch *m*.

poten|cy ['poutənsi] Macht *f*; Stärke *f*; ~t [~nt] mächtig; stark; ~tial [pə'tenʃəl] 1. potentiell; möglich; 2. Leistungsfähigkeit *f*.

pother ['poðə] Aufregung *f*.

pot|-herb ['pothəːb] Küchenkraut *n*; ~-house Kneipe *f*.

potion ['pouʃən] (Arznei)Trank *m*.

potter[1] ['potə]: ~ *about* herumwerkeln.

potter[2] [~] Töpfer *m*; ~y [~əri] Töpferei *f*; Töpferware(n *pl.*) *f*.

pouch [pautʃ] 1. Tasche *f*; Beutel *m*; 2. einstecken; (sich) beuteln.

poulterer ['poultərə] Geflügelhändler *m*.

poultice ['poultis] Packung *f*.

poultry ['poultri] Geflügel *n*.

pounce [pauns] 1. Stoß *m*, Sprung *m*; 2. sich stürzen (on, upon auf *acc.*).

pound [paund] 1. Pfund *n*; ~ (sterling) Pfund *n* Sterling (*abbr.* £ = 20 shillings); Pfandstall *m*; Tierasyl *n*; 2. (zer)stoßen; stampfen; schlagen.

pounder ['paundə] ...pfünder *m*.

pour [pɔː] *v/t.* gießen, schütten; ~ *out Getränk* eingießen; *v/i.* sich ergießen, strömen; *it never rains but it* ~*s fig.* ein Unglück kommt selten allein.

pout [paut] 1. Schmollen *n*; 2. *v/t.* Lippen aufwerfen; *v/i.* schmollen.

poverty ['povəti] Armut *f*.

powder ['paudə] 1. Pulver *n*; Puder *m*; 2. pulverisieren; (sich) pudern; bestreuen; ~-box Puderdose *f*.

power ['pauə] Kraft *f*; Macht *f*, Gewalt *f*; ✗ Vollmacht *f*; ⚡ Potenz *f*; *in* ~ an der Macht, im Amt; ~-current Starkstrom *m*; ~ful ['pauəful] mächtig, kräftig, wirksam; ~less ['pauəlis] macht-, kraftlos; ~plant *s.* power-station; **politics** *oft sg.* Machtpolitik *f*; ~-station Kraftwerk *n*.

powwow ['pauwau] Medizinmann *m*; *Am.* F Versammlung *f*.

practica|ble □ ['præktikəbl] ausführbar; gangbar (*Weg*); brauchbar; ~l [~l] praktisch; tatsächlich; eigentlich; sachlich; ~ *joke* Schabernack *m*; ~lly [~li] so gut wie.

practice ['præktis] 1. Praxis *f*; Übung *f*; Gewohnheit *f*; Brauch *m*; Praktik *f*; *put into* ~ in die Praxis umsetzen; 2. *Am.* = practise.

practise [~] *v/t.* in die Praxis umsetzen; ausüben; betreiben; üben; *v/i.* (sich) üben; praktizieren; ~ *upon j-s Schwäche* ausnutzen; ~d geübt (*P.*).

practitioner [præk'tiʃnə] a. general ~ praktischer Arzt; Rechtsanwalt m.

prairie Am. ['prɛəri] Grasebene f; Prärie f; ~schooner Am. Planwagen m.

praise [preiz] 1. Preis m, Lob n; 2. loben, preisen.

praiseworthy □ ['preizwə:ði] lobenswert.

pram F [præm] Kinderwagen m.

prance [prɑːns] sich bäumen; paradieren; einherstolzieren.

prank [præŋk] Possen m, Streich m.

prate [preit] 1. Geschwätz n; 2. schwatzen, plappern.

prattle ['prætl] s. prate.

pray [prei] beten; (er)bitten; bitte! **prayer** [prɛə] Gebet n; Bitte f; oft ~s pl. Andacht f; Lord's ♀ Vaterunser n; ~book ['prɛəbuk] Gebetbuch n.

pre... [priː; pri] vor(her)...; Vor...; früher.

preach [priːtʃ] predigen; ~er ['priːtʃə] Prediger(in).

preamble [priː'æmbl] Einleitung f.

precarious □ [pri'kɛəriəs] unsicher.

precaution [pri'kɔːʃən] Vorsicht(smaßregel) f; ~ary [~ʃnəri] vorbeugend.

precede [priː'siːd] voraus-, vorangehen (dat.); ~nce, ~ncy [~dəns, ~si] Vortritt m, Vorrang m; ~nt ['presidənt] Präzedenzfall m.

precept ['priːsept] Vorschrift f, Regel f; ~or [pri'septə] Lehrer m.

precinct ['priːsiŋkt] Bezirk m, bsd. Am. Wahlbezirk m, -kreis m; ~s pl. Umgebung f; Bereich m; Grenze f; pedestrian ~ Fußgängerzone f.

precious □ ['preʃəs] 1. □ kostbar; edel; F arg, gewaltig, schön; 2. F adv. recht, äußerst.

precipi|ce ['presipis] Abgrund m; ~tate 1. [pri'sipiteit] (hinab)stürzen; ⚗ fällen; überstürzen; 2. □ [~tit] übereilt, hastig; 3. [~] ⚗ Niederschlag m; ~tation [prisipi'teiʃən] Sturz m; Überstürzung f, Hast f; ⚗ Niederschlag(en n) m; ~tous □ [pri'sipitəs] steil, jäh.

précis [pri'siː] gedrängte Übersicht, Zs.-fassung f.

precis|e □ [pri'sais] genau; ~ion [~'siʒən] Genauigkeit f; Präzision f.

preclude [pri'kluːd] ausschließen; vorbeugen (dat.); j-n hindern.

precocious □ [pri'kouʃəs] frühreif; altklug.

preconceive ['priːkən'siːv] vorher ausdenken; ~d vorgefaßt (Meinung).

preconception ['priːkən'sepʃən] vorgefaßte Meinung. [m.\

precursor [priː'kəːsə] Vorläufer\ **predatory** ['predətəri] räuberisch.

predecessor ['priːdisesə] Vorgänger m.

predestin|ate [priː'destineit]

vorherbestimmen; ~ed [~nd] auserkoren.

predetermine ['priːdi'təːmin] vorher festsetzen; vorherbestimmen.

predicament [pri'dikəmənt] (mißliche) Lage.

predicate 1. ['predikeit] aussagen; 2. gr. [~kit] Prädikat n, Satzaussage f.

predict [pri'dikt] vorhersagen; ~ion [~kʃən] Prophezeiung f.

predilection [priːdi'lekʃən] Vorliebe f.

predispos|e ['priːdis'pouz] vorher geneigt od. empfänglich machen (to für); ~ition [~spə'ziʃən] Geneigtheit f; bsd. ⚕ Anfälligkeit f (to für).

predomina|nce [pri'dominəns] Vorherrschaft f; Übergewicht n; Vormacht(stellung) f; ~nt □ [~nt] vorherrschend; ~te [~neit] die Oberhand haben; vorherrschen.

pre-eminent □ [priː'eminənt] hervorragend.

pre-emption [priː'empʃən] Vorkauf(srecht n) m.

pre-exist [priːig'zist] vorher dasein.

prefabricate ['priː'fæbrikeit] vorfabrizieren.

preface ['prefis] 1. Vorrede f, Vorwort n, Einleitung f; 2. einleiten.

prefect ['priːfekt] Präfekt m; Schule: Vertrauensschüler m, Klassensprecher m.

prefer [pri'fəː] vorziehen; Gesuch etc. vorbringen; Klage einreichen; befördern; ~able □ ['prefərəbl] (to) vorzuziehen(d) (dat.); vorzüglicher (als); ~ably [~li] vorzugsweise; besser; ~ence [~rəns] Vorliebe f; Vorzug m; ~ential □ [prefə'renʃəl] bevorzugt; Vorzugs-...; ~ment [pri'fəːmənt] Beförderung f.

prefix ['priːfiks] Präfix n, Vorsilbe f.

pregnan|cy ['pregnənsi] Schwangerschaft f; fig. Fruchtbarkeit f; Bedeutungsreichtum m; ~t □ [~nt] schwanger; fig. fruchtbar, inhaltsvoll.

prejud|ge ['priː'dʒʌdʒ] vorher (ver-) urteilen; ~ice ['predʒudis] 1. Voreingenommenheit f; Vorurteil n; Schaden m; 2. voreinnehmen; benachteiligen; e-r S. Abbruch tun; ~d (vor)eingenommen; ~icial □ [predʒu'diʃəl] nachteilig.

prelate ['prelit] Prälat m.

preliminary [pri'liminəri] 1. □ vorläufig; einleitend; Vor...; 2. Einleitung f.

prelude ♪ ['preljuːd] Vorspiel n.

premature □ [premə'tjuə] fig. frühreif; vorzeitig; vorschnell.

premeditat|e [priː'mediteit] vorher überlegen; ~ion [priː'medi'teiʃən] Vorbedacht m.

premier ['premjə] **1.** erst; **2.** Premierminister *m*.

premises ['premisiz] *pl.* (Gebäude *pl.* mit) Grundstück *n*, Anwesen *n*; Lokal *n*.

premium ['pri:mjəm] Prämie *f*; Anzahlung *f*; ✝ Agio *n*; Versicherungsprämie *f*; Lehrgeld *n*; at a ~ über pari; sehr gesucht.

premonition [pri:mə'nifən] Warnung *f*; (Vor)Ahnung *f*.

preoccup|ied [pri(:)'ɔkjupaid] in Gedanken verloren; ~y [~pai] vorher in Besitz nehmen; ausschließlich beschäftigen; in Anspruch nehmen.

prep F [prep] = *preparation*, *preparatory school*.

preparat|ion [prepə'reifən] Vorbereitung *f*; Zubereitung *f*; ~ory □ [pri'pærətəri] vorbereitend; (*school*) Vorschule *f*.

prepare [pri'pɛə] *v/t.* vorbereiten; zurechtmachen; (zu)bereiten; (aus-)rüsten; *v/i.* sich vorbereiten; sich anschicken; ~d bereit.

prepay ['pri:'pei] [*irr.* (*pay*)] vorausbezahlen; frankieren.

preponderla|nce [pri'pɔndərəns] Übergewicht *n*; ~nt □ [~nt] überwiegend; ~te [~reit] überwiegen.

preposition *gr.* [prepə'zifən] Präposition *f*, Verhältniswort *n*.

prepossess [pri:pə'zes] günstig stimmen; ~ing [~siŋ] einnehmend.

preposterous [pri'pɔstərəs] widersinnig, albern; grotesk.

prerequisite ['pri:'rekwizit] Vorbedingung *f*, Voraussetzung *f*.

prerogative [pri'rɔgətiv] Vorrecht *n*.

presage ['presidʒ] **1.** Vorbedeutung *f*; Ahnung *f*; **2.** vorbedeuten; ahnen; prophezeien.

prescribe [pris'kraib] vorschreiben; ✍ verschreiben.

prescription [pris'kripfən] Vorschrift *f*, Verordnung *f*; ✍ Rezept *n*.

presence ['prezns] Gegenwart *f*; Anwesenheit *f*; Erscheinung *f*; ~ of mind Geistesgegenwart *f*.

present[1] ['preznt] **1.**] gegenwärtig; anwesend, vorhanden; jetzig; laufend (*Jahr etc.*); vorliegend (*Fall etc.*); ~ tense *gr.* Präsens *n*; **2.** Gegenwart *f*, *gr. a.* Präsens *n*; Geschenk *n*; at ~ jetzt; for the ~ einstweilen.

present[2] [pri'zent] präsentieren; (dar)bieten; (vor)zeigen; *j-n* vorstellen; vorschlagen; (über)reichen; (be)schenken.

presentation [prezen'teifən] Dar-, Vorstellung *f*; Ein-, Überreichung *f*; Schenkung *f*; Vorzeigen *n*, Vorlage *f*.

presentiment [pri'zentimənt] Vorgefühl *n*, Ahnung *f*.

presently ['prezntli] sogleich, bald (darauf), alsbald; *Am.* zur Zeit.

preservati|on [prezə(:)'veifən] Bewahrung *f*, Erhaltung *f*; ~ve [pri-'zə:vətiv] **1.** bewahrend; **2.** Schutz-, Konservierungsmittel *n*.

preserve [pri'zə:v] **1.** bewahren, behüten; erhalten; einmachen; *Wild* hegen; **2.** *hunt.* Gehege *n* (*a. fig.*); *mst* ~s *pl.* Eingemachte(s) *n*.   [ren (over bei).\
preside [pri'zaid] den Vorsitz füh-/

presiden|cy ['prezidənsi] Vorsitz *m*; Präsidentschaft *f*; ~t [~nt] Präsident *m*, Vorsitzende(r) *m*; *Am.* ✝ Direktor *m*.

press [pres] **1.** Druck *m der Hand*; (Wein- *etc.*)Presse *f*; *die* Presse (*Zeitungen*); Druckerei *f*; Verlag *m*; Druck(en *n*) *m*; *a. printing-*, Druckerpresse *f*; Menge *f*; *fig.* Druck *m*, Last *f*, Andrang *m*; Schrank *m*; **2.** *v/t.* (aus)pressen; drücken; lasten auf (*dat.*); (be)drängen; dringen auf (*acc.*); aufdrängen (on *dat.*); bügeln; be ~ed for time es eilig haben; *v/i.* drücken; (sich) drängen; ~ for sich eifrig bemühen um; ~ on weitereilen; ~ (up)on eindringen auf (*acc.*); ~ agency Nachrichtenbüro *n*; ~ agent Reklameagent *m*; ~ button Druckknopf *m*; ~ing □ ['presiŋ] dringend; ~ure ['prefə] Druck *m* (*a. fig.*); Drang(sal *f*) *m*.

prestige [pres'ti:ʒ] Prestige *n*.

presum|able □ [pri'zju:məbl] vermutlich; ~e [pri'zju:m] *v/t.* annehmen; vermuten; voraussetzen; *v/i.* vermuten; sich erdreisten; anmaßend sein; ~ (up)on pochen auf (*acc.*); ausnutzen, mißbrauchen.

presumpt|ion [pri'zAmpfən] Mutmaßung *f*; Wahrscheinlichkeit *f*; Anmaßung *f*; ~ive □ [~ptiv] mutmaßlich; ~uous □ [~tjuəs] überheblich; vermessen.

presuppos|e [pri:sə'pouz] voraussetzen; ~ition [pri:sApə'zifən] Voraussetzung *f*.

preten|ce, *Am.* ~se [pri'tens] Vortäuschung *f*; Vorwand *m*; Schein *m*, Verstellung *f*.

pretend [pri'tend] vorgeben; vortäuschen; heucheln; Anspruch erheben (to auf *acc.*); ~ed □ angeblich.

pretension [pri'tenfən] Anspruch *m* (to auf *acc.*); Anmaßung *f*.

preterit(e) *gr.* ['pretərit] Präteritum *n*, Vergangenheitsform *f*.

pretext [pri'tekst] Vorwand *m*.

pretty ['priti] **1.**] hübsch, niedlich; nett; **2.** *adv.* ziemlich.

prevail [pri'veil] die Oberhand haben *od.* gewinnen; (vor)herrschen; maßgebend *od.* ausschlaggebend sein; ~ (up)on s.o. *j-n* dazu bewegen, *et.* zu tun; ~ing □ [~liŋ] (vor)herrschend.

prevalent □ ['prevələnt] vorherrschend, weit verbreitet.

prevaricate [pri'værikeit] Ausflüchte machen.

prevent [pri'vent] verhüten, *e-r S.* vorbeugen; *j-n* hindern; ~ion [~n-ʃən] Verhinderung *f*; Verhütung *f*; ~ive [~ntiv] **1.** □ vorbeugend; **2.** Schutzmittel *n*.

preview ['pri:vju:] Vorschau *f*; Vorbesichtigung *f*.

previous □ ['pri:vjəs] vorhergehend; vorläufig; Vor...; ~ to vor *(dat.)*; ~ly [~sli] vorher, früher.

pre-war ['pri:'wɔ:] Vorkriegs...

prey [prei] **1.** Raub *m*, Beute *f*; *beast of* ~ Raubtier *n*; *bird of* ~ Raubvogel *m*; *be a* ~ *to* geplagt werden von; **2.** ~ *(up)on* rauben, plündern; fressen; *fig.* nagen an *(dat.)*.

price [prais] **1.** Preis *m*; Lohn *m*; **2.** *Waren* auszeichnen; die Preise festsetzen für; (ab)schätzen; ~less ['praislis] unschätzbar; unbezahlbar.

prick [prik] **1.** Stich *m*; Stachel *m* *(a. fig.)*; **2.** *v/t.* (durch)stechen; *fig.* peinigen; *a.* ~ *out* Muster punktieren; ~ *up one's ears* die Ohren spitzen; *v/i.* stechen; ~le ['prikl] Stachel *m*, Dorn *m*; ~ly [~li] stachelig.

pride [praid] **1.** Stolz *m*; Hochmut *m*; *take* ~ *in* stolz sein auf *(acc.)*; **2.** ~ *o.s.* sich brüsten *(on, upon* mit).

priest [pri:st] Priester *m*.

prig [prig] Tugendbold *m*, selbstgerechter Mensch; Pedant *m*.

prim □ [prim] steif; zimperlich.

prima|cy ['praiməsi] Vorrang *m*; ~rily [~ərili] in erster Linie; ~ry □ [~ri] **1.** ursprünglich; hauptsächlich; Ur..., Anfangs..., Haupt...; Elementar...; höchst; *ʒ̓, ⚥* Primär...; **2.** *a.* ~ *meeting Am.* Wahlversammlung *f*; ~ry school Elementar-, Grundschule *f*.

prime [praim] **1.** □ erst; wichtigst; Haupt...; vorzüglich(st); ~ *cost* ⚥ Selbstkosten *pl.*; ~ *minister* Ministerpräsident *m*; ~ *number* Primzahl *f*; **2.** *fig.* Blüte(zeit) *f*; Beste(s) *n*; höchste Vollkommenheit; **3.** *v/t.* vorbereiten; *Pumpe* anlassen; instruieren; F vollaufen lassen *(betrunken machen)*; *paint.* grundieren.

primer ['praimə] Fibel *f*, Elementarbuch *n*. [lich; Ur...]

primeval [prai'mi:vəl] uranfäng-]

primitive ['primitiv] **1.** □ erst, ursprünglich; Stamm...; primitiv; **2.** *gr.* Stammwort *n*.

primrose ⚘ ['primrouz] Primel *f*.

prince [prins] Fürst *m*; Prinz *m*; ~ss [prin'ses, *vor npr.* 'prinses] Fürstin *f*; Prinzessin *f*.

principal ['prinsəpəl] **1.** □ erst, hauptsächlich(st); Haupt...; ~ *parts pl. gr.* Stammformen *f/pl. des vb.*;

2. Hauptperson *f*; Vorsteher *m*; *bsd. Am.* (Schul)Direktor *m*, Rektor *m*; ✝ Chef *m*; ⚥ Hauptschuldige(r) *m*; ✝ Kapital *n*; ~ity [prinsi'pæliti] Fürstentum *n*.

principle ['prinsəpl] Prinzip *n*; Grund(satz) *m*; Ursprung *m*; *on* ~ grundsätzlich, aus Prinzip.

print [print] **1.** Druck *m*; (Finger-*etc.*)Abdruck *m*; bedruckter Kattun, Druckstoff *m*; Stich *m*; *phot.* Abzug *m*; *Am.* Zeitungsdrucksache *f*; *out of* ~ vergriffen; **2.** (ab-, auf-, be)drucken; *phot.* kopieren; *fig.* einprägen *(on dat.)*; in Druckbuchstaben schreiben; ~er ['printə] (Buch)Drucker *m*.

printing ['printiŋ] Druck *m*; Drucken *n*; *phot.* Abziehen *n*, Kopieren *n*; ~ink Druckerschwärze *f*; ~-office (Buch)Druckerei *f*; ~-press Druckerpresse *f*.

prior ['praiə] **1.** früher, älter *(to* als); **2.** *adv.* ~ *to* vor *(dat.)*; **3.** *eccl.* Prior *m*; ~ity [prai'ɔriti] Priorität *f*; Vorrang *m*; Vorfahrtsrecht *n*.

prism ['prizəm] Prisma *n*.

prison ['prizn] Gefängnis *n*; ~er [~nə] Gefangene(r *m*) *f*, Häftling *m*; *take s.o.* ~ j-n gefangennehmen.

privacy ['praivəsi] Zurückgezogenheit *f*; Geheimhaltung *f*.

private ['praivit] **1.** □ privat; Privat...; persönlich; vertraulich; geheim; **2.** ⚔ (gewöhnlicher) Soldat; *in* ~ privatim; im geheimen.

privation [prai'veiʃən] Mangel *m*, Entbehrung *f*.

privilege ['privilidʒ] **1.** Privileg *n*; Vorrecht *n*; **2.** bevorrechten.

privy ['privi] **1.** □ ~ *to* eingeweiht in *(acc.)*; ⚥ *Council* Staatsrat *m*; ⚥ *Councillor* Geheimer Rat; ⚥ *Seal* Geheimsiegel *n*; ⚥ ⚙ Mitinteressent *m* *(to an dat.)*; Abort *m*.

prize [praiz] **1.** Preis *m*, Prämie *f*; ⚓ Beute *f*; (Lotterie)Gewinn *m*; **2.** preisgekrönt, Preis...; **3.** (hoch-) schätzen; aufbrechen *(öffnen)*; ~-fighter ['praizfaitə] Berufsboxer *m*.

pro [prou] für.

probab|ility [prɔbə'biliti] Wahrscheinlichkeit *f*; ~le □ ['prɔbəbl] wahrscheinlich.

probation [prə'beiʃən] Probe *f*, Probezeit *f*; ⚖ Bewährungsfrist *f*; ~ *officer* Bewährungshelfer *m*.

probe [proub] **1.** ⚕ Sonde *f*; *fig.* Untersuchung *f*; *lunar* ~ Mondsonde *f*; **2.** *a.* ~ *into* sondieren; untersuchen.

probity ['proubiti] Redlichkeit *f*.

problem ['prɔbləm] Problem *n*; ⚥ Aufgabe *f*; ~atic(al □) [prɔbli'mætik(əl)] problematisch, zweifelhaft. [*n*; Handlungsweise *f*.]

procedure [prə'si:dʒə] Verfahren]

proceed [prə'si:d] weitergehen; fortfahren; vor sich gehen; vorgehen; *univ.* promovieren; ~ *from* von *od.* aus *et.* kommen; ausgehen von; ~ *to* zu *et.* übergehen; ~ing [~diŋ] Vorgehen *n*; Handlung *f*; ~s *pl.* ⚖ Verfahren *n*; Verhandlungen *f/pl.*, (Tätigkeits)Bericht *m*; ~s ['prousi:dz] *pl.* Ertrag *m*, Gewinn *m*.

process ['prouses] 1. Fortschreiten *n*, Fortgang *m*; Vorgang *m*; Verlauf *m der Zeit*; Prozeß *m*, Verfahren *n*; *in* ~ im Gange; *in* ~ *of construction* im Bau (befindlich); 2. gerichtlich belangen; ⊕ bearbeiten; ~ion [prə'seʃən] Prozession *f*.

proclaim [prə'kleim] proklamieren; erklären; ausrufen.

proclamation [prɔklə'meiʃən] Proklamation *f*; Bekanntmachung *f*; Erklärung *f*.

proclivity [prə'kliviti] Neigung *f*.

procrastinate [prou'kræstineit] zaudern.

procreate ['proukrieit] (er)zeugen.

procuration [prɔkjuə'reiʃən] Vollmacht *f*; ✦ Prokura *f*; ~or ['prɔkjuəreitə] Bevollmächtigte(r) *m*.

procure [prə'kjuə] *v/t.* be-, verschaffen; *v/i.* Kuppelei treiben.

prod [prɔd] 1. Stich *m*; Stoß *m*; *fig.* Ansporn *m*; 2. stechen; stoßen; *fig.* anstacheln.

prodigal ['prɔdigəl] 1. ☐ verschwenderisch; *the* ~ *son* der verlorene Sohn; 2. Verschwender(in).

prodigious [prə'didʒəs] erstaunlich, ungeheuer; ~y ['prɔdidʒi] Wunder *n* (*a. fig.*), Ungeheuer *n*; *oft infant* Wunderkind *n*.

produce 1. [prə'dju:s] vorbringen, vorführen, vorlegen; beibringen; hervorbringen; produzieren, erzeugen, *Zinsen etc* (ein)bringen; ⅋ verlängern; *Film etc.* herausbringen; 2. ['prɔdju:s] (Natur)Erzeugnis(se *pl.*) *n*, Produkt *n*, Ertrag *m*; ~r [prə'dju:sə] Erzeuger *m*, Hersteller *m*; *Film* Produzent *m*; *thea.* Regisseur *m*.

product ['prɔdʌkt] Produkt *n*, Erzeugnis *n*; ~ion [prə'dʌkʃən] Hervorbringung *f*; Vorlegung *f*, Beibringung *f*; Produktion *f*, Erzeugung *f*; *thea.* Herausbringen *n*; Erzeugnis *n*; ~ive [~ktiv] schöpferisch; produktiv, erzeugend; ertragreich; fruchtbar; ~iveness [~vnis], ~ivity [prɔdʌk'tiviti] Produktivität *f*.

prof *Am.* F [prɔf] Professor *m*.

profanation [prɔfə'neiʃən] Entweihung *f*; ~e [prə'fein] 1. ☐ profan; weltlich; uneingeweiht; gottlos; 2. entweihen; ~ity [~'fæniti] Gottlosigkeit *f*; Fluchen *n*.

profess [prə'fes] (sich) bekennen (zu); erklären; *Reue etc.* bekunden; *Beruf* ausüben; lehren; ~ed ☐ erklärt; angeblich; Berufs...; ~ion

[~eʃən] Bekenntnis *n*; Erklärung *f*; Beruf *m*; ~ional [~nl] 1. Berufs...; Amts...; berufsmäßig; freiberuflich; ~ *men* Akademiker *m/pl.*; 2. Fachmann *m*; *Sport* Berufsspieler *m*; Berufskünstler *m*; ~or [~esə] Professor *m*.

proffer ['prɔfə] 1. anbieten; 2. Anerbieten *n*.

proficiency [prə'fiʃənsi] Tüchtigkeit *f*; ~t [~nt] 1. ☐ tüchtig; bewandert; 2. Meister *m*.

profile ['proufail] Profil *n*.

profit ['prɔfit] 1. Vorteil *m*, Nutzen *m*, Gewinn *m*; 2. *v/t.* j-m Nutzen bringen; *v/i.* ~ *by* Nutzen ziehen aus; ausnutzen; ~able ☐ [~təbl] nützlich, vorteilhaft, einträglich; ~eer [prɔfi'tiə] 1. Schiebergeschäfte machen; 2. Profitmacher *m*, Schieber *m*; ~-sharing ['prɔfitʃeəriŋ] Gewinnbeteiligung *f*.

profligate ['prɔfligət] 1. ☐ liederlich; 2. liederlicher Mensch.

profound ☐ [prə'faund] tief; tiefgründig; gründlich; *fig.* dunkel.

profundity [prə'fʌnditi] Tiefe *f*.

profuse [prə'fju:s] verschwenderisch; übermäßig, überreich; ~ion *fig.* [~u:ʒən] Überfluß *m*.

progenitor [prou'dʒenitə] Vorfahr *m*, Ahn *m*; ~y ['prɔdʒini] Nachkommen(schaft *f*) *m/pl.*; Brut *f*.

prognosis ☞ [prɔg'nousis], *pl.* ~es [~si:z] Prognose *f*.

prognostication [prəgnɔsti'keiʃən] Vorhersage *f*.

program(me) ['prougræm] Programm *n*.

progress 1. ['prougres] Fortschritt(e *pl.*) *m*; Vorrücken *n* (*a.* ⚔); Fortgang *m*; *in* ~ im Gang; 2. [prə'gres] fortschreiten; ~ion [prə'greʃən] Fortschreiten *n*; ⅋ Reihe *f*; ~ive [~esiv] 1. ☐ fortschreitend; fortschrittlich; 2. *pol.* Fortschrittler *m*.

prohibit [prə'hibit] verbieten; verhindern; ~ion [proui'biʃən] Verbot *n*; Prohibition *f*; ~ionist [~ʃnist] *bsd. Am.* Prohibitionist *m*; ~ive ☐ [prə'hibitiv] verbietend; Sperr...; unerschwinglich.

project 1. ['prɔdʒekt] Projekt *n*; Vorhaben *n*, Plan *m*; 2. [prə'dʒekt] *v/t.* planen; (ent)werfen; ⅋ projizieren; *v/i.* vorspringen; ~ile ['prɔdʒiktail] Projektil *n*, Geschoß *n*; ~ion [prə'dʒekʃən] Werfen *n*; Entwurf *m*; Vorsprung *m*; ⅋, *ast.*, *phot.* Projektion *f*; ~or [~ktə] ✦ Gründer *m*; *opt.* Projektor *m*.

proletarian [proule'tɛəriən] 1. proletarisch; 2. Proletarier(in).

prolific [prə'lifik] (~ally) fruchtbar.

prolix ['prɔuliks] weitschweifig.

prologue, *Am. a.* ~g ['proulɔg] Prolog *m*.

prolong [prə'lɔŋ] verlängern.

promenade [prɔmi'nɑːd] **1.** Promenade *f*; **2.** promenieren.

prominent □ ['prɔminənt] hervorragend (*a. fig.*); *fig.* prominent.

promiscuous □ [prə'miskjuəs] unordentlich, verworren; gemeinsam; unterschiedslos.

promis|e ['prɔmis] **1.** Versprechen *n*; *fig.* Aussicht *f*; **2.** versprechen; **~ing** □ [~siŋ] vielversprechend; **~sory** [~səri] versprechend; **~ note** ✝ Eigenwechsel *m*.

promontory ['prɔməntri] Vorgebirge *n*.

promot|e [prə'mout] *et.* fördern; *j-n* befördern; *bsd. Am. Schule:* versetzen; *parl.* unterstützen; ✝ gründen; *bsd. Am. Verkauf durch Werbung* steigern; **~ion** [~ou∫ən] Förderung *f*; Beförderung *f*; ✝ Gründung *f*.

prompt [prɔmpt] **1.** [schnell; bereit(willig); sofortig, pünktlich; **2.** *j-n* veranlassen; *Gedanken* eingeben; *j-m* vorsagen, soufflieren; **~er** ['prɔmptə] Souffleu|r *m*, -se *f*; **~ness** [~tnis] Schnelligkeit *f*; Bereitschaft *f*.

promulgate ['prɔməlgeit] verkünden, verbreiten.

prone □ [proun] mit dem Gesicht nach unten (liegend); hingestreckt; **~ to** *fig.* geneigt od neigend zu.

prong [prɔŋ] Zinke *f*; Spitze *f*.

pronoun *gr.* ['prounaun] Pronomen *n*, Fürwort *n*.

pronounce [prə'nauns] aussprechen; verkünden; erklären (für).

pronto *Am.* F ['prɔntou] sofort.

pronunciation [prənʌnsi'ei∫ən] Aussprache *f*.

proof [pruːf] **1.** Beweis *m*; Probe *f*, Versuch *m*; *typ.* Korrekturbogen *m*; *typ.,phot.* Probeabzug *m*; **2.** fest; *in Zssgn:* ...fest, ...dicht, ...sicher; **~reader** *typ.* ['pruːfriːdə] Korrektor *m*.

prop [prɔp] **1.** Stütze *f* (*a. fig.*); **2.** *a.* **~ up** (unter)stützen.

propaga|te ['prɔpəgeit] (sich) fortpflanzen; verbreiten; **~tion** [prɔpə'gei∫ən] Fortpflanzung *f*; Verbreitung *f*.

propel [prə'pel] (vorwärts-, an-)treiben; **~ler** [~lə] Propeller *m*, (Schiffs-, Luft)Schraube *f*.

propensity [prə'pensiti] Neigung *f*.

proper □ ['prɔpə] eigen(tümlich); eigentlich; passend, richtig; anständig; **~ty** [~ti] Eigentum *n*, Besitz *m*; Vermögen *n*; Eigenschaft *f*.

prophe|cy ['prɔfisi] Prophezeiung *f*; **~sy** [~sai] prophezeien.

prophet ['prɔfit] Prophet *m*.

propi|tiate [prə'pi∫ieit] günstig stimmen, versöhnen; **~tious** □ [~∫əs] gnädig; günstig.

proportion [prə'pɔ:∫ən] **1.** Verhältnis *n*; Gleichmaß *n*; (An)Teil *m*;

~s *pl.* (Aus)Maße *n/pl.*; **2.** in ein Verhältnis bringen; **~al** □ [~nl] im Verhältnis (*to zu*); **~ate** □ [~∫nit] angemessen.

propos|al [prə'pouzəl] Vorschlag *m*, (*a.* Heirats)Antrag *m*; Angebot *n*; Plan *m*; **~e** [~ouz] *v/t.* vorschlagen; *e-n* Toast ausbringen auf (*acc.*); **~** *to o.s.* sich vornehmen; *v/i.* beabsichtigen; anhalten (*to um*); **~ition** [prɔpə'zi∫ən] Vorschlag *m*, Antrag *m*; Behauptung *f*; Problem *n*.

propound [prə'paund] *Frage etc.* vorlegen; vorschlagen.

propriet|ary [prə'praiətəri] Eigentümer..., Eigentums...; Besitz(er)...; gesetzlich geschützt (*bsd. Arzneimittel*); **~or** [~tə] Eigentümer *m*; **~y** [~ti] Richtigkeit *f*; Schicklichkeit *f*; **the proprieties** *pl.* die Anstandsformen *f/pl.* [*m.*\

propulsion ⊕ [prə'pʌl∫ən] Antrieb\

prorate *Am.* [prou'reit] anteilmäßig verteilen.

prosaic [prou'zeiik] *fig.* prosaisch (*nüchtern, trocken*).

proscribe [prous'kraib] ächten.

proscription [prous'krip∫ən] Achtung *f*; Acht *f*; Verbannung *f*.

prose [prouz] **1.** Prosa *f*; **2.** prosaisch.

prosecut|e ['prɔsikjuːt] (*a.* gerichtlich) verfolgen; *Gewerbe etc.* betreiben; verklagen; **~ion** [prɔsi'kju:∫ən] Verfolgung *f* *e-s Plans etc.*; Betreiben *n* *e-s Gewerbes etc.*; gerichtliche Verfolgung; **~or** 🔒 [~sikju:tə] Kläger *m*; Anklagevertreter *m*; *public* **~** Staatsanwalt *m*.

prospect 1. ['prɔspekt] Aussicht *f* (*a. fig.*); Anblick *m*; ✝ Interessent *m*; **2.** [prəs'pekt] 🔨 schürfen; bohren (*for nach Öl*); **~ive** [~tiv] vorausblickend; voraussichtlich; **~us** [~təs] (Werbe)Prospekt *m*.

prosper ['prɔspə] *v/i.* Erfolg haben, gedeihen, blühen; *v/t.* begünstigen, segnen; **~ity** [prɔs'periti] Gedeihen *n*; Wohlstand *m*; Glück *n*; *fig.* Blüte *f*; **~ous** □ ['prɔspərəs] glücklich, gedeihlich; *fig.* blühend; günstig.

prostitute ['prɔstitjuːt] **1.** Dirne *f*; **2.** zur Dirne machen; (der Schande) preisgeben, feilbieten (*a. fig.*).

prostrat|e 1. ['prɔstreit] hingestreckt; erschöpft; daniederliegend; demütig; gebrochen; **2.** [prɔs'treit] niederwerfen; *fig.* niederschmettern; entkräften; **~ion** [~ei∫ən] Niederwerfung *f*; Fußfall *m*; *fig.* Demütigung *f*; Entkräftung *f*.

prosy *fig.* ['prouzi] prosaisch; langweilig.

protagonist [prou'tægənist] *thea.* Hauptfigur *f*; *fig.* Vorkämpfer(in).

protect [prə'tekt] (be)schützen; **~ion** [~k∫ən] Schutz *m*; Wirtschaftsschutz *m*, Schutzzoll *m*; **~ive**

[˴ktiv] schützend; Schutz...; ~ duty Schutzzoll m; ˴or [˴tə] (Be)Schützer m; Schutz-, Schirmherr m; ˴orate [˴ərit] Protektorat n.

protest 1. ['proutest] Protest m; Einspruch m; **2.** [prə'test] beteuern; protestieren; reklamieren.

Protestant ['prɔtistənt] **1.** protestantisch; **2.** Protestant(in).

protestation [proutes'teiʃən] Beteuerung f; Verwahrung f.

protocol ['proutəkɔl] **1.** Protokoll n; **2.** protokollieren.

prototype ['proutətaip] Urbild n; Prototyp m, Modell n.

protract [prə'trækt] in die Länge ziehen, hinziehen.

protru|de [prə'truːd] (sich) (her-)vorstrecken; (her)vorstehen, (her-)vortreten (lassen); ˴sion [˴uːʒən] Vorstrecken n; (Her)Vorstehen n, (Her)Vortreten n.

protuberance [prə'tjuːbərəns] Hervortreten n; Auswuchs m, Höcker m.

proud □ [praud] stolz (of auf acc.).

prove [pruːv] v/t. be-, er-, nachweisen; prüfen; erleben, erfahren; v/i. sich herausstellen od. erweisen (als); ausfallen; ˴n ['pruːvən] erwiesen; bewährt.

provenance ['prɔvinəns] Herkunft f.

provender ['prɔvində] Futter n.

proverb ['prɔvəb] Sprichwort n.

provide [prə'vaid] v/t. besorgen, beschaffen, liefern; bereitstellen; versehen, versorgen; ½ vorsehen, festsetzen; v/i. (vor)sorgen; ˴d (that) vorausgesetzt, daß, sofern.

providen|ce ['prɔvidəns] Vorsehung f; Voraussicht f; Vorsorge f; ˴t □ [˴nt] vorausblickend; vorsorglich; haushälterisch; ˴tial [prɔvi'denʃəl] durch die göttliche Vorsehung bewirkt; glücklich.

provider [prə'vaidə] Ernährer m der Familie; Lieferant m.

provinc|e ['prɔvins] Provinz f; fig. Gebiet n; Aufgabe f; ˴ial [prə'vinʃəl] **1.** provinziell; kleinstädtisch; **2.** Provinzbewohner(in).

provision [prə'viʒən] Beschaffung f; Vorsorge f; ½ Bestimmung f; Vorkehrung f, Maßnahme f; Vorrat m; ˴s pl. Proviant m, Lebensmittel pl.; ˴al □ [˴nl] provisorisch.

proviso [prə'vaizou] Vorbehalt m.

provocat|ion [prɔvə'keiʃən] Herausforderung f; ˴ive [prə'vɔktiv] herausfordernd; (auf)reizend.

provoke [prə'vouk] auf-, anreizen; herausfordern.

provost ['prɔvəst] Leiter m e-s College; schott. Bürgermeister m; ✕ [prə'vou]: ~ marshal Kommandeur m der Militärpolizei.

prow ⚓ [prau] Bug m, Vorschiff n.

prowess ['prauis] Tapferkeit f.

prowl [praul] **1.** v/i. umherstreifen; v/t. durchstreifen; **2.** Umherstreifen n; ~ car Am. ['praulkɑː] Streifenwagen m der Polizei.

proximity [prɔk'simiti] Nähe f.

proxy ['prɔksi] Stellvertreter m; Stellvertretung f; Vollmacht f; by ~ in Vertretung.

prude [pruːd] Prüde f, Spröde f; Zimperliese f.

pruden|ce ['pruːdəns] Klugheit f, Vorsicht f; ˴t □ [˴nt] klug, vorsichtig.

prud|ery ['pruːdəri] Prüderie f, Sprödigkeit f, Zimperlichkeit f; ˴ish □ [˴diʃ] prüde, zimperlich, spröde.

prune [pruːn] **1.** Backpflaume f; **2.** ✗ beschneiden (a. fig.); a. ~ away, ~ off wegschneiden.

prurient □ ['pruəriənt] geil, lüstern.

pry [prai] **1.** neugierig gucken; ~ into s-e Nase stecken in (acc.); open aufbrechen; ~ up hochheben; **2.** Hebel(bewegung f) m.

psalm [sɑːm] Psalm m.

pseudo|... ['psjuːdou] Pseudo..., falsch; ˴nym [˴dənim] Deckname m.

psychiatr|ist [sai'kaiətrist] Psychiater m (Nervenarzt); ˴y [˴ri] Psychiatrie f.

psychic(al □) ['saikik(əl)] psychisch, seelisch.

psycholog|ical □ [saikə'lɔdʒikəl] psychologisch; ˴ist [sai'kɔlədʒist] Psycholog|e m, -in f; ˴y [˴dʒi] Psychologie f (Seelenkunde).

pub F [pʌb] Kneipe f, Wirtschaft f.

puberty ['pjuːbəti] Pubertät f.

public ['pʌblik] **1.** □ öffentlich; staatlich, Staats...; allbekannt; ~ spirit Gemeinsinn m; **2.** Publikum n; Öffentlichkeit f; ˴an [˴kən] Gastwirt m; ˴ation [pʌbli'keiʃən] Bekanntmachung f; Veröffentlichung f; Verlagswerk n; monthly ~ Monatsschrift f; ~ house Wirtshaus n; ˴ity [pʌb'lisiti] Öffentlichkeit f; Propaganda f, Reklame f, Werbung f; ~ library Volksbücherei f; ~ relations pl. Verhältnis n zur Öffentlichkeit; Public Relations pl.; ~ school Public School f, Internatsschule f.

publish ['pʌbliʃ] bekanntmachen, veröffentlichen; Buch etc. herausgeben, verlegen; ˴ing house Verlag m; ˴er [˴ə] Herausgeber m, Verleger m; ˴s pl. Verlag(sanstalt f) m.

pucker ['pʌkə] **1.** Falte f; **2.** falten; Falten werfen; runzeln.

pudding ['pudiŋ] Pudding m; Süßspeise f; Auflauf m; Wurst f; black ~ Blutwurst f.

puddle ['pʌdl] Pfütze f.

pudent ['pjuːdənt] verschämt.

puerile □ ['pjuərail] kindisch.

puff [pʌf] **1.** Hauch m; Zug m beim

Rauchen; (Dampf-, Rauch)Wölk-chen *n*; Puderquaste *f*; (aufdring-liche) Reklame; **2.** *v/t.* (auf)blasen, pusten; paffen; anpreisen; ~ *out* sich (auf)blähen; ~ *up Preise* hoch-treiben; ~*ed up fig.* aufgeblasen; ~*ed eyes* geschwollene Augen; *v/i.* paffen; pusten; ~**-paste** ['pʌfpeist] Blätterteig *m*; ~**y** ['pʌfi] böig; kurzatmig; geschwollen; dick; bau-schig.

pug [pʌg], ~**-dog** ['pʌgdɔg] Mops *m*.

pugnacious [pʌg'neiʃəs] kämpfe-risch; kampflustig; streitsüchtig.

pug-nose ['pʌgnouz] Stupsnase *f*.

puissant ['pju(ː)isnt] mächtig.

puke [pjuːk] (sich) erbrechen.

pull [pul] **1.** Zug *m*; Ruck *m*; *typ.* Abzug *m*; Ruderpartie *f*; Griff *m*; Vorteil *m*; **2.** ziehen; zerren; rei-ßen; zupfen; pflücken; rudern; ~ *about* hin- u. herzerren; ~ *down* niederreißen; ~ *in* einfahren (*Zug*); ~ *off* zustande bringen; *Preis* errin-gen; ~ *out* heraus-, hinausfahren; ausscheren; ~ *round* wiederher-stellen; ~ *through j-n* durchbringen; ~ *o.s. together* sich zs.-nehmen; ~ *up Wagen* anhalten; halten; ~ *up with*, ~ *up to* einholen.

pulley ⊕ ['puli] Rolle *f*; Flaschen-zug *m*; Riemenscheibe *f*.

pull|-over ['pulouvə] Pullover *m*; ~**up** Halteplatz *m*, Raststätte *f*.

pulp [pʌlp] Brei *m*; *Frucht-, Zahn*-Mark *n*; ⊕ Papierbrei *m*; *a.* ~ *maga-zine Am.* Schundillustrierte *f*.

pulpit ['pulpit] Kanzel *f*.

pulpy ☐ ['pʌlpi] breiig; fleischig.

puls|ate ['pʌl'seit] pulsieren; schla-gen; ~**e** [pʌls] Puls(schlag) *m*.

pulverize ['pʌlvəraiz] *v/t.* pulveri-sieren; *v/i.* zu Staub werden.

pumice ['pʌmis] Bimsstein *m*.

pump [pʌmp] **1.** Pumpe *f*; Pumps *m*; **2.** pumpen; F *j-n* aushorchen.

pumpkin ♀ ['pʌmpkin] Kürbis *m*.

pun [pʌn] **1.** Wortspiel *n*; **2.** ein Wortspiel machen.

Punch[1] [pʌntʃ] Kasperle *n*, *m*.

punch[2] [~] **1.** ⊕ Punze(n *m*) *f*, Locheisen *n*, Locher *m*; Lochzange *f*; (Faust)Schlag *m*; Punsch *m*; **2.** punzen, durchbohren; lochen; knuffen, puffen; *Am.* Vieh treiben, hüten.

puncher ['pʌntʃə] Locheisen *n*; Locher *m*; F Schläger *m*; *Am.* Cowboy *m*.

punctilious [pʌŋk'tiliəs] peinlich (genau), spitzfindig; förmlich.

punctual ☐ ['pʌŋktjuəl] pünktlich; ~**ity** [pʌŋktju'æliti] Pünktlichkeit *f*.

punctuat|e ['pʌŋktjueit] (inter-)punktieren; *fig.* unterbrechen; ~**ion** *gr.* [pʌŋktju'eiʃən] Interpunktion *f*.

puncture ['pʌŋktʃə] **1.** Punktur *f*,

Stich *m*; Reifenpanne *f*; **2.** (durch-)stechen; platzen (*Luftreifen*).

pungen|cy ['pʌndʒənsi] Schärfe *f*; ~**t** [~nt] stechend, beißend, scharf.

punish ['pʌniʃ] (be)strafen; ~**able** ☐ [~ʃəbl] strafbar; ~**ment** [~ʃmənt] Strafe *f*, Bestrafung *f*.

punk *Am.* [pʌŋk] Zunderholz *n*; Zündmasse *f*; F *fig.* Mist *m*, Käse *m*.

puny ☐ ['pjuːni] winzig; schwäch-lich.

pupa *zo.* ['pjuːpə] Puppe *f*.

pupil ['pjuːpl] *anat.* Pupille *f*; Schüler(in); Mündel *m*, *n*.

puppet ['pʌpit] Marionette*f* (*a. fig.*); ~**-show** Puppenspiel *n*.

pup(py) [pʌp, 'pʌpi] Welpe *m*, jun-ger Hund; *fig.* Laffe *m*, Schnösel *m*.

purchase ['pəːtʃəs] **1.** (An-, Ein-) Kauf *m*; Erwerb(ung *f*) *m*; An-schaffung *f*; ⊕ Hebevorrichtung *f*; *fig.* Ansatzpunkt *m*; make ~*s* Ein-käufe machen; **2.** kaufen; *fig.* er-kaufen; anschaffen; ⊕ aufwinden; ~**r** [~sə] Käufer(in).

pure [pjuə] *allg.* rein; *eng S.*: lauter; echt; gediegen; theoretisch; ~**bred** *Am.* ['pjuəbred] reinrassig.

purgat|ive ['pəːgətiv] **1.** abfüh-rend; **2.** Abführmittel *n*; ~**ory** [~təri] Fegefeuer *n*.

purge [pəːdʒ] **1.** ☞ Abführmittel *n*; *pol.* Säuberung *f*; **2.** *mst fig.* reini-gen; *pol.* säubern; ☞ abführen.

purify ['pjuərifai] reinigen; läutern.

Puritan ['pjuəritən] **1.** Puritaner (-in); **2.** puritanisch.

purity ['pjuəriti] Reinheit *f* (*a. fig.*).

purl [pəːl] murmeln (*Bach*).

purlieus ['pəːljuːz] *pl.* Umgebung*f*.

purloin [pəːˈlɔin] entwenden.

purple ['pəːpl] **1.** purpurn, purpur-rot; **2.** Purpur *m*; **3.** (sich) purpurn färben.

purport ['pəːpət] **1.** Sinn *m*; Inhalt *m*; **2.** besagen; beabsichtigen; vor-geben.

purpose ['pəːpəs] **1.** Vorsatz *m*; Absicht *f*, Zweck *m*; Entschluß-kraft *f*; *for the* ~ *of ger.* um zu *inf.*; *on* ~ absichtlich; *to the* ~ zweck-dienlich; *to no* ~ vergebens; **2.** vor-haben, bezwecken; ~**ful** ☐ [~sful] zweckmäßig; absichtlich; zielbe-wußt; ~**less** ☐ [~slis] zwecklos; ziellos; ~**ly** [~li] vorsätzlich.

purr [pəː] schnurren (*Katze*).

purse [pəːs] **1.** Börse *f*, Geldbeutel *m*; Geld(preis) *n*; *public* ~ Staats-säckel *m*; **2.** *oft* ~ *up Mund* spitzen; *Stirn* runzeln; *Augen* zs.-kneifen.

pursuan|ce [pəˈsjuː(ː)ns] Verfol-gung *f*; *in* ~ *of* zufolge (*dat.*); ~**t** ☐ [~nt]: ~ *to* zufolge, gemäß, ent-sprechend (*dat.*).

pursu|e [pəˈsjuː] verfolgen (*a. fig.*); streben nach; *e-m Beruf etc.* nach-gehen; fortsetzen, fortfahren; ~**er**

[~ju(:)ə] Verfolger(in); ~it [~ju:t] Verfolgung *f*; *mst* ~s *pl.* Beschäftigung *f*.

purvey [pə'vei] *Lebensmittel* liefern; ~or [~eiə] Lieferant *m*.

pus [pʌs] Eiter *m*.

push [puʃ] 1. (An-, Vor)Stoß *m*; Schub *m*; Druck *m*; Notfall *m*; Energie *f*; Unternehmungsgeist *m*; Elan *m*; 2. stoßen; schieben; drängen; *Knopf* drücken; (an)treiben; *a.* ~ *through* durchführen; *Anspruch etc.* durchdrücken; ~ *s.th. on s.o.* j-m et. aufdrängen; ~ *one's way* sich durch- *od.* vordrängen; ~ *along*, ~ *on*, ~ *forward* weitermachen, ⚓ -gehen, -fahren *etc.*; ~-button ⚡ ['puʃbʌtn] Druckknopf *m*; ~over *Am. fig.* Kinderspiel *n*; leicht zu beeinflussender Mensch.

pusillanimous ☐ [pju:si'læniməs] kleinmütig.

puss [pus] Kätzchen *n*, Katze *f* (*a. fig.* = *Mädchen*); ~y ['pusi], *a.* ~-cat Mieze *f*, Kätzchen *n*; ~yfoot *Am.* F leisetreten, sich zurückhalten.

put [put] (*irr.*) *v/t.* setzen, legen, stellen, stecken, tun, machen; *Frage* stellen, vorlegen; werfen; ausdrücken, sagen; ~ *about Gerüchte etc.* verbreiten; ⚓ wenden; ~ *across sl.* drehen, schaukeln; ~ *back* zurückstellen; ~ *by Geld* zurücklegen; ~ *down* niederlegen, -setzen, -werfen; aussteigen lassen; notieren; zuschreiben (*to dat.*); unterdrücken; ~ *forth Kräfte* aufbieten; *Knospen etc.* treiben; ~ *forward Meinung etc.* vorbringen; ~ *o.s. forward* sich hervortun; ~ *in* hinein-, hereinst(r)ecken; *Anspruch* erheben; *Gesuch* einreichen; *Urkunde* vorlegen; anstellen; ~ *off* auf-, verschieben; vertrösten; abbringen; hindern; *fig.* ablegen; ~ *on Kleid* anziehen, *Hut* aufsetzen; *fig.* annehmen; an-, einschalten;

vergrößern; ~ *on airs* sich aufspielen; ~ *on weight* zunehmen; ~ *out* ausmachen, (aus)löschen; verrenken; (her)ausstrecken; verwirren; *j-m* Ungelegenheiten bereiten; *Kraft* aufbieten; *Geld* ausleihen; ~ *right* in Ordnung bringen; ~ *through teleph.* verbinden (*to* mit); ~ *to* hinzufügen; ~ *to death* hinrichten; ~ *to the rack od.* torture auf die Folter spannen; ~ *up* aufstellen *etc.*; errichten, bauen; *Waren* anbieten; *Miete* erhöhen; ver-, wegpacken; *Widerstand* leisten; *Kampf* liefern; *Gäste* unterbringen; *Bekanntmachung* anschlagen; *v/i.* ~ *off*, ~ *out*, ~ *to sea* ⚓ auslaufen; ~ *in* ⚓ einlaufen; ~ *up at* einkehren *od.* absteigen in (*dat.*); ~ *up for* sich bewerben um; ~ *up with* sich gefallen lassen; sich abfinden mit.

putrefy ['pju:trifai] (ver)faulen.

putrid ☐ ['pju:trid] faul, verdorben; *sl.* scheußlich, saumäßig; ~ity [pju:'triditi] Fäulnis *f*.

putty ['pʌti] 1. Kitt *m*; 2. kitten.

puzzle ['pʌzl] 1. schwierige Aufgabe, Rätsel *n*; Verwirrung *f*; Geduldspiel *n*; 2. *v/t.* irremachen; *j-m* Kopfzerbrechen machen; ~ *out* austüfteln; *v/i.* sich den Kopf zerbrechen; ~-headed konfus.

pygm|(a)ean [pig'mi:ən] zwerghaft; ~y ['pigmi] Zwerg *m*; *attr.* zwerghaft.

pyjamas [pə'dʒɑ:məz] *pl.* Schlafanzug *m*.

pyramid ['pirəmid] Pyramide *f*; ~al ☐ [pi'ræmidl] pyramidal.

pyre ['paiə] Scheiterhaufen *m*.

pyrotechnic|(al ☐) [pairou'teknik(əl)] pyrotechnisch, Feuerwerks...; ~s *pl.* Feuerwerk *n* (*a. fig.*).

Pythagorean [paiθægə'ri(:)ən] 1.pythagoreisch; 2. Pythagoreer *m*.

pyx *eccl.* [piks] Monstranz *f*.

Q

quack [kwæk] 1. Quaken *n*; Scharlatan *m*; Quacksalber *m*, Kurpfuscher *m*; Marktschreier *m*; 2. quacksalberisch; 3. quaken; quacksalben (an *dat.*); ~ery ['kwækəri] Quacksalberei *f*.

quadrangle ['kwɔdræŋgl] Viereck *n*; Innenhof *m* *es College*.

quadrennial ☐ [kwɔ'dreniəl] vierjährig; vierjährlich.

quadru|ped ['kwɔdruped] Vierfüßer *m*; ~ple [~pl] 1. ☐ vierfach; 2. (sich) vervierfachen; ~plets [~lits] *pl.* Vierlinge *m/pl.*

quagmire ['kwægmaiə] Sumpf (-land *n*) *m*, Moor *n*.

quail¹ *orn.* [kweil] Wachtel *f*.

quail² [~] verzagen; beben.

quaint ☐ [kweint] anheimelnd, malerisch; putzig; seltsam.

quake [kweik] 1. beben, zittern (*with, for vor dat.*); 2. Erdbeben *n*.

Quaker ['kweikə] Quäker *m*.

quali|fication [kwɔlifi'keiʃən] (erforderliche) Befähigung; Einschränkung *f*; *gr.* nähere Bestimmung; ~fy ['kwɔlifai] *v/t.* befähigen; (be-) nennen; *gr.* näher bestimmen; einschränken, mäßigen; mildern; v/i. seine Befähigung nachweisen; ~ty [,iti] Eigenschaft f, Beschaffenheit f; ✝ Qualität f; vornehmer Stand.

qualm [kwɔːm] plötzliche Übelkeit; Zweifel m; Bedenken n.

quandary ['kwɔndəri] verzwickte Lage, Verlegenheit f.

quantity ['kwɔntiti] Quantität f, Menge f; großer Teil.

quantum ['kwɔntəm] Menge f, Größe f, Quantum n; Anteil m.

quarantine ['kwɔrəntiːn] 1. Quarantäne f; 2. unter Quarantäne stellen.

quarrel ['kwɔrəl] 1. Zank m, Streit m; 2. (sich) zanken, streiten; ~some □ [,səm] zänkisch; streitsüchtig.

quarry ['kwɔri] 1. Steinbruch m; fig. Fundgrube f; (Jagd)Beute f; 2. Steine brechen; fig. stöbern.

quart [kwɔːt] Quart n (1,136 l).

quarter ['kwɔːtə] 1. Viertel n, vierter Teil; bsd. Viertelstunde f; Vierteljahr n, Quartal n; Viertelzentner m; Am. 25 Cent; Keule f, Viertel n e-s geschlachteten Tieres; Stadtviertel n; (Himmels)Richtung f, Gegend f; ⚔ Gnade f, Pardon m; ~s pl. Quartier n (a. ⚔), Unterkunft f; fig. Kreise m/pl.; live in close ~s beengt wohnen; at close ~s dicht aufeinander; come to close ~s handgemein werden; 2. vierteln, vierteilen; beherbergen; ⚔ einquartieren; ~back Am. Sport Abwehrspieler m; ~day Quartalstag m; ~deck Achterdeck n; ~ly [,li] 1. vierteljährlich; 2. Vierteljahresschrift f; ~master ⚔ Quartiermeister m. [n.]

quartet(te) ♩ [kwɔːˈtet] Quartett

quarto ['kwɔːtou] Quart(format) n.

quash ♟ [kwɔʃ] aufheben, verwerfen; unterdrücken.

quasi ['kwɑːzi(ː)] gleichsam, sozusagen; Quasi..., Schein...

quaver ['kweivə] 1. Zittern n; ♩ Triller m; 2. mit zitternder Stimme sprechen od. singen; trillern.

quay [kiː] Kai m; Uferstraße f.

queasy □ ['kwiːzi] empfindlich (Magen, Gewissen); heikel, mäkelig; ekelhaft.

queen [kwiːn] Königin f; ~ bee Bienenkönigin f; ~like ['kwiːnlaik], ~ly [,li] wie eine Königin, königlich.

queer [kwiə] sonderbar, seltsam; wunderlich; komisch; homosexuell.

quench [kwentʃ] fig. Durst etc. löschen, stillen; kühlen; Aufruhr unterdrücken.

querulous □ ['kwerʊləs] quengelig, mürrisch, verdrossen.

query ['kwiəri] 1. Frage(zeichen n) f; 2. (be)fragen; (be-, an)zweifeln.

quest [kwest] 1. Suche(n n) f, Nachforschen n; 2. suchen, forschen.

question ['kwestʃən] 1. Frage f; Problem n; Untersuchung f; Streitfrage f; Zweifel m; Sache f, Angelegenheit f; beyond (all) ~ ohne Frage; in ~ fraglich; call in ~ anzweifeln; that is out of the ~ das steht außer od. kommt nicht in Frage; 2. befragen; bezweifeln; ~able □ [,nəbl] fraglich; fragwürdig; ~er Fragende(r m) f; ~mark Fragezeichen n; ~naire [kwestiaˈnɛə] Fragebogen m.

queue [kjuː] 1. Reihe f v. Personen etc., Schlange f; Zopf m; 2. mst ~ up (in e-r Reihe) anstehen, Schlange stehen.

quibble ['kwibl] 1. Wortspiel n; Spitzfindigkeit f; Ausflucht f; 2. fig. ausweichen; witzeln.

quick [kwik] 1. schnell, rasch; voreilig; lebhaft; gescheit; beweglich; lebendig; scharf (Gehör etc.); 2. lebendes Fleisch; the ~ die Lebenden; to the ~ (bis) ins Fleisch; fig. (bis) ins Herz, tief; cut s.o. to the ~ j-n aufs empfindlichste kränken; ~en ['kwikən] v/t. beleben; beschleunigen; v/i. aufleben; sich regen; ~ly [,kli] schnell, rasch; ~ness [,knis] Lebhaftigkeit f; Schnelligkeit f; Voreiligkeit f; Schärfe f des Verstandes etc.; ~sand Triebsand m; ~set ✿ Setzling m, bsd. Hagedorn m; a. ~ hedge lebende Hecke; ~sighted scharfsichtig; ~silver min. Quecksilber n; ~witted schlagfertig.

quid¹ [kwid] Priem m (Kautabak).

quid² sl. [,] Pfund n Sterling.

quiescen|ce [kwaiˈesns] Ruhe f, Stille f; ~t □ [,nt] ruhend; fig. ruhig, still.

quiet ['kwaiət] 1. □ ruhig, still; 2. Ruhe f; on the ~ (sl. on the q.t.) unter der Hand, im stillen; 3. a. ~ down (sich) beruhigen; ~ness [,tnis], ~ude [ˈkwaiitjuːd] Ruhe f, Stille f.

quill [kwil] 1. Federkiel m; fig. Feder f; Stachel m des Igels etc.; 2. rund fälteln; ~ing ['kwiliŋ] Rüsche f, Krause f; ~pen Gänsefeder f zum Schreiben.

quilt [kwilt] 1. Steppdecke f; 2. steppen; wattieren.

quince ♀ [kwins] Quitte f.

quinine pharm. [kwiˈniːn, Am. ˈkwainain] Chinin n.

quinquennial □ [kwiŋˈkweniəl] fünfjährig; fünfjährlich.

quinsy ♟ ['kwinzi] Mandelentzündung f.

quintal ['kwintl] (Doppel)Zentner m.

quintessence [kwinˈtesns] Quintessenz f, Kern m, Inbegriff m.

quintuple ['kwintjupl] 1. □ fünffach; 2. (sich) verfünffachen; ~ts [~lits] pl. Fünflinge m/pl.

quip [kwip] Stich(elei f) m; Witz (-wort n) m; Spitzfindigkeit f.

quirk [kwə:k] Spitzfindigkeit f; Witz(elei f) m; Kniff m; Schnörkel m; Eigentümlichkeit f; ⚠ Hohlkehle f.

quisling ['kwizliŋ] Quisling m, Kollaborateur m.

quit [kwit] 1. v/t. verlassen; aufgeben; Am. aufhören (mit); vergelten; Schuld tilgen; v/i. aufhören; ausziehen (Mieter); give notice to ~ kündigen; 2. quitt; frei, los.

quite [kwait] ganz, gänzlich; recht; durchaus; ~ a hero ein wirklicher Held; ~ (so)!, ~ that! ganz recht; ~ the thing F große Mode.

quittance ['kwitəns] Quittung f.

quitter Am. F ['kwitə] Drückeberger m.

quiver[1] ['kwivə] zittern, beben.

quiver[2] [~] Köcher m.

quiz [kwiz] 1. Prüfung f, Test m; Quiz n; belustigter Blick; 2. (aus-) fragen; prüfen; necken, foppen; anstarren, beäugen; ~zical □ ['kwizikəl] spöttisch; komisch.

quoit [kɔit] Wurfring m; ~s pl. Wurfringspiel n.

Quonset Am. ['kwɔnsit] a. ~ hut Wellblechbaracke f.

quorum parl. ['kwɔ:rəm] beschlußfähige Mitgliederzahl.

quota ['kwoutə] Quote f, Anteil m, Kontingent n.

quotation [kwou'teiʃən] Anführung f, Zitat n; ✝ Preisnotierung f; Kostenvoranschlag m; ~marks pl. Anführungszeichen n/pl.

quote [kwout] anführen, zitieren; ✝ berechnen, notieren (at mit).

quotient ⅍ ['kwouʃənt] Quotient m.

quoth † [kwouθ]: ~ I sagte ich; ~ he sagte er.

quotidian [kwɔ'tidiən] (all)täglich.

R

rabbi ['ræbai] Rabbiner m.

rabbit ['ræbit] Kaninchen n.

rabble ['ræbl] Pöbel(haufen) m.

rabid □ ['ræbid] tollwütig (Tier); fig. wild, wütend.

rabies vet. ['reibi:z] Tollwut f.

raccoon [rə'ku:n] = racoon.

race [reis] 1. Geschlecht n, Stamm m; Rasse f, Schlag m; Lauf m (a. fig.); Wettrennen n; Strömung f; ~s pl. Pferderennen n; 2. rennen; rasen; um die Wette laufen (mit); ⊕ leer laufen; ~course ['reiskɔ:s] Rennbahn f, ~strecke f; ~horse Rennpferd n; ~r ['reisə] Rennpferd n; Rennboot n; Rennwagen m.

racial ['reiʃəl] Rassen... [m.]

racing ['reisiŋ] Rennsport m; attr. Renn...

rack [ræk] 1. Gestell n; Kleiderständer m; Gepäcknetz n; Raufe f, Futtergestell n; Folter(bank) f; go to ~ and ruin völlig zugrunde gehen; 2. strecken; foltern, quälen (a. fig.); ~ one's brains sich den Kopf zermartern.

racket ['rækit] 1. Tennis-Schläger m; Lärm m; Trubel m; Am. F Schwindel(geschäft n) m; Strapaze f; 2. lärmen; sich amüsieren; ~eer Am. [ræki'tiə] Erpresser m; ~eering Am. [~əriŋ] Erpresserwesen n; ~y ['rækiti] ausgelassen.

racoon zo. [rə'ku:n] Waschbär m.

racy □ ['reisi] kraftvoll, lebendig; stark; würzig; urwüchsig.

radar ['reidə] Radar(gerät) n.

radian|ce, ~cy ['reidjəns, ~si] Strahlen n; ~t □ [~nt] strahlend, leuchtend.

radiat|e ['reidieit] (aus)strahlen; strahlenförmig ausgehen; ~ion [reidi'eiʃən] (Aus)Strahlung f; ~or ['reidieitə] Heizkörper m; mot. Kühler m.

radical ['rædikəl] 1. □ Wurzel..., Grund...; gründlich; eingewurzelt; pol. radikal; 2. pol. Radikale(r m) f.

radio ['reidiou] 1. Radio n; Funk (-spruch) m; ~ drama, ~ play Hörspiel n; ~ set Radiogerät n; 2. funken; ~(-)active radioaktiv; ~graph [~ougra:f] 1. Röntgenbild n; 2. ein Röntgenbild machen von; ~tele-gram Funktelegramm n; ~thera-py Strahlen-, Röntgentherapie f.

radish ⚘ ['rædiʃ] Rettich m; (red) ~ Radieschen n.

radius ['reidjəs] Radius m.

raffle ['ræfl] 1. Tombola f, Verlosung f; 2. verlosen.

raft [ra:ft] 1. Floß n; 2. flößen; ~er ['ra:ftə] ⊕ (Dach)Sparren m.

rag[1] [ræg] Lumpen m; Fetzen m; Lappen m.

rag[2] sl. [~] 1. Unfug m; Radau m; 2. Unfug treiben (mit); j-n aufziehen; j-n beschimpfen; herumtollen, Radau machen.

ragamuffin ['rægəmʌfin] Lumpenkerl m; Gassenjunge m.

rage [reidʒ] 1. Wut f, Zorn m, Raserei f; Sucht f, Gier f (for nach); Manie f; Ekstase f; it is all the ~ es ist allgemein Mode; 2. wüten, rasen.

rag-fair ['rægfɛə] Trödelmarkt m.

ragged ☐ ['rægid] rauh; zottig; zackig; zerlumpt.

ragman ['rægmən] Lumpensammler m.

raid [reid] 1. (feindlicher) Überfall, Streifzug m; (Luft)Angriff m; Razzia f; 2. einbrechen in (acc.); überfallen.

rail¹ [reil] schimpfen.

rail² [⎵] 1. Geländer n; Stange f; 🚂 Schiene f; off the ⎵s entgleist; fig. in Unordnung; by ⎵ per Bahn; 2. a. ⎵ in, ⎵ off mit e-m Geländer umgeben.

railing ['reiliŋ], a. ⎵s pl. Geländer n; Staket n.

raillery ['reiləri] Spötterei f.

railroad Am. ['reilroud] Eisenbahn f. [⎵man Eisenbahner m.\]

railway ['reilwei] Eisenbahn f;|

rain [rein] 1. Regen m; 2. regnen; ⎵bow ['reinbou] Regenbogen m; ⎵coat Regenmantel m; ⎵fall Regenmenge f; ⎵-proof 1. regendicht; 2. Regenmantel m; ⎵y ☐ ['reini] regnerisch; Regen...; a ⎵ day fig. Notzeiten f/pl.

raise [reiz] oft ⎵ up heben; (oft fig.) erheben; errichten; erhöhen (a. fig.); Geld etc. aufbringen; Anleihe aufnehmen; verursachen; fig. erwecken; anstiften; züchten, ziehen; Belagerung etc. aufheben.

raisin ['reizn] Rosine f.

rake [reik] 1. Rechen m, Harke f; Wüstling m; Lebemann m; 2. v/t (zs.-)harken; ⎵s.-scharren; fig. (durch)stöbern; ⎵-off Am. sl. ['reikɔf] Schwindelprofit m.

rakish ☐ ['reikif] schnittig; liederlich, ausschweifend; verwegen; salopp.

rally ['ræli] 1. Sammeln n; Treffen n; Am. Massenversammlung f; Erholung f; mot. Rallye f; 2. (sich ver)sammeln; sich erholen, necken.

ram [ræm] 1. zo., ast. Widder m; ⊕, ⚓ Ramme f; 2. (fest)rammen; ⚓ rammen.

ramble ['ræmbl] 1. Streifzug m; 2. umherstreifen; abschweifen; ⎵er [⎵lə] Wanderer m; 🌿 Kletterrose f; ⎵ing [⎵liŋ] weitläufig.

ramify ['ræmifai] (sich) verzweigen.

ramp [ræmp] Rampe f; ⎵ant ☐ ['ræmpənt] wuchernd; fig. zügellos.

rampart ['ræmpɑːt] Wall m.

ramshackle ['ræmʃækl] wack(e)lig.

ran [ræn] pret. von run 1.

ranch [rɑːntʃ], Am. rænt∫] Ranch f, Viehfarm f; ⎵er ['rɑːntʃə, Am. 'ræntʃə], ⎵man Rancher m, Viehzüchter m; Farmer m.

rancid ☐ ['rænsid] ranzig.

ranco(u)r ['ræŋkə] Groll m, Haß m.

random ['rændəm] 1. at ⎵ aufs Geratewohl, blindlings; 2. ziel-, wahllos; zufällig.

rang [ræŋ] pret. von ring 2.

range [reind3] 1. Reihe f; (Berg-) Kette f; † Kollektion f, Sortiment n; Herd m; Raum m; Umfang m, Bereich m; Reichweite f; Schußweite f; (ausgedehnte) Fläche; Schießstand m; 2. v/t. (ein)reihen, ordnen; Gebiet etc. durchstreifen; ⚓ längs et. fahren; v/i. in e-r Reihe od. Linie stehen; (umher-) streifen; sich erstrecken, reichen; ⎵r ['reind3ə] Förster m; Aufseher m e-s Parks; Am. Förster m; ⚔ Nahkampfspezialist m.

rank [ræŋk] 1. Reihe f, Linie f; ⚔ Glied n; Klasse f; Rang m, Stand m; the ⎵s pl., the ⎵ and file die Mannschaften f/pl.; fig. die große Masse; 2. v/t. (ein)reihen, (ein-) ordnen; v/i. sich reihen, sich ordnen; gehören (with zu); e-e Stelle einnehmen (above über dat.); ⎵ as gelten als; 3. üppig; ranzig; stinkend.

rankle fig. ['ræŋkl] nagen.

ransack ['rænsæk] durchwühlen, durchstöbern, durchsuchen; ausrauben.

ransom ['rænsəm] 1. Lösegeld n; Auslösung f; 2. loskaufen; erlösen.

rant [rænt] 1. Schwulst m; 2. Phrasen dreschen; mit Pathos vortragen.

rap [ræp] 1. Klaps m; Klopfen n; fig. Heller m; 2. schlagen, klopfen.

rapacious ☐ [rə'peiʃəs] raubgierig; ⎵ty [rə'pæsiti] Raubgier f.

rape [reip] 1. Raub m; Entführung f; Notzucht f, Vergewaltigung f; 🌿 Raps m; 2. rauben; vergewaltigen.

rapid ['ræpid] 1. ☐ schnell, reißend, rapid(e); steil; 2. ⎵s pl. Stromschnelle(n pl.) f; ⎵ity [rə'piditi] Schnelligkeit f.

rapprochement pol. [ræ'prɔʃmɑːŋ] Wiederannäherung f.

rapt [ræpt] entzückt; versunken; ⎵ure ['ræptʃə] Entzücken n; go into ⎵s in Entzücken geraten.

rare [rɛə] selten; phys. dünn.

rarebit ['rɛəbit]: Welsh ⎵ geröstete Käseschnitte.

rarefy ['rɛərifai] (sich) verdünnen.

rarity ['rɛəriti] Seltenheit f; Dünnheit f.

rascal ['rɑːskəl] Schuft m; co. Gauner m; ⎵ity [rɑːs'kæliti] Schurkerei f; ⎵ly ['rɑːskəli] schuftig; erbärmlich.

rash¹ ☐ [ræʃ] hastig, vorschnell; übereilt; unbesonnen; waghalsig.

rash² 🎇 [⎵] Hautausschlag m.

rasher ['ræʃə] Speckschnitte f.

rasp [rɑːsp] 1. Raspel f; 2. raspeln; j-m weh(e) tun; kratzen; krächzen.

raspberry ['rɑːzbəri] Himbeere f.

rat [ræt] zo. Ratte f; pol. Überläufer m; smell a ⎵ Lunte od. den Braten riechen; ⎵s! Quatsch!

rate [reit] 1. Verhältnis n, Maß n,

Satz *m*; Rate *f*; Preis *m*, Gebühr *f*;
Taxe *f*; (Gemeinde)Abgabe *f*;
Steuer *f*; Grad *m*, Rang *m*; *bsd.* ⚓
Klasse *f*; Geschwindigkeit *f*; *at
any ~* auf jeden Fall; *~ of exchange*
(Umrechnungs)Kurs *m*; *~ of interest*
Zinsfuß *m*; **2.** (ein)schätzen; besteuern; *~ among* rechnen, zählen
zu (*dat.*); ausschelten.
rather ['rɑ:ðə] eher, lieber; vielmehr; besser gesagt; ziemlich; *~!* F
und ob!; *I had od.* would *~* do ich
möchte lieber tun.
ratify ['rætifai] ratifizieren.
rating ['reitiŋ] Schätzung *f*; Steuer-
satz *m*; ⚓ Dienstgrad *m*; ⚓ (Segel-)
Klasse *f*; Matrose *m*; Schelte(n
n) *f*.
ratio ℞ *etc.* ['reiʃiou] Verhältnis *n*.
ration ['ræʃən] **1.** Ration *f*, Zuteilung *f*; **2.** rationieren.
rational □ ['ræʃənl] vernunftge-
mäß; vernünftig, (*a.* ℞) rational;
~ity [ræʃə'næliti] Vernunft(mäßigkeit) *f*; *~ize* ['ræʃnəlaiz] rationali-
sieren; wirtschaftlich gestalten.
rat race ['ræt 'reis] sinnlose Hetze;
rücksichtsloses Aufstiegsstreben.
ratten ['rætn] sabotieren.
rattle ['rætl] **1.** Gerassel *n*; Geklapper *n*; Geplapper *n*; Klapper *f*;
(Todes)Röcheln *n*; **2.** rasseln (mit);
klappern; plappern; röcheln, *~ off*
herunterrasseln, *~brain*, *~pate*
Hohl-, Wirrkopf *m*; *~snake* Klap-
perschlange *f*; *~trap* *fig.* Klapper-
kasten *m* (*Fahrzeug*).
rattling ['rætliŋ] **1.** *adj.* rasselnd;
fig. scharf (*Tempo*); **2.** *adv.* sehr,
äußerst.
raucous □ ['rɔ:kəs] heiser, rauh.
ravage ['rævidʒ] **1.** Verwüstung *f*;
2. verwüsten; plündern.
rave [reiv] rasen, toben; schwärmen
(*about, of* von).
ravel ['rævəl] *v/t.* verwickeln; *~
(out)* auftrennen; *fig.* entwirren;
v/i. a. ~ out ausfasern, aufgehen.
raven *orn.* ['reivn] Rabe *m*.
raven|ing ['rævniŋ], *~ous* □
['rævinəs] gefräßig; heißhungrig;
raubgierig.
ravine [rə'vi:n] Hohlweg *m*;
Schlucht *f*.
ravings ['reiviŋz] *pl.* Delirien *n/pl.*
ravish ['ræviʃ] entzücken; vergewaltigen; rauben; *~ing* [‿ʃiŋ]
hinreißend, entzückend; *~ment*
[‿ʃmənt] Schändung *f*; Entzücken
n.
raw □ [rɔ:] roh; Roh...; wund; rauh
(*Wetter*); ungeführ, unerfahren;
~boned ['rɔ:bound] knochig, hager; *~hide* Rohleder *n*.
ray [rei] Strahl *m*; *fig.* Schimmer *m*.
rayon ['reiɔn] Kunstseide *f*.
raze [reiz] Haus *etc.* abreißen;
Festung schleifen; tilgen.
razor ['reizə] Rasiermesser *n*; Ra-

sierapparat *m*; *~blade* Rasier-
klinge *f*; *~edge* *fig. des* Messers
Schneide *f*, kritische Lage.
razz *Am. sl.* [ræz] aufziehen.
re... [ri:] wieder...; zurück...; neu...;
um...
reach [ri:tʃ] **1.** Ausstrecken *n*; Griff
m; Reichweite *f*; Fassungskraft *f*,
Horizont *m*; Flußstrecke *f*; *beyond
~, out of ~* unerreichbar; *within
easy ~* leicht erreichbar; **2.** *v/i.*
reichen; langen; greifen; sich erstrecken; *v/t.* (hin-, her)reichen,
(hin-, her)langen; ausstrecken; erreichen.
react [ri(:)'ækt] reagieren (*to* auf
acc.); (ein)wirken (*on, upon* auf
acc.); sich auflehnen (*against* gegen).
reaction [ri(:)'ækʃən] Reaktion *f*
(*a. pol.*); *~ary* [‿ʃnəri] **1.** reaktionär;
2. Reaktionär(in).
reactor *phys.* [ri(:)'æktə] Reaktor *m*.
read 1. [ri:d] (*irr.*] lesen; deuten;
(an)zeigen (*Thermometer*); studieren; sich *gut etc.* lesen; lauten; *~ to
s.o.* j-m vorlesen; **2.** [red] *pret. u.
p.p. von* 1; **3.** [‿] *adj.* belesen; *~able*
□ ['ri:dəbl] lesbar; leserlich; lesenswert; *~er* ['ri:də] (Vor)Leser(in);
typ. Korrektor *m*; Lektor *m*; *univ.*
Dozent *m*; Lesebuch *n*.
readi|ly ['redili] *adv.* gleich, leicht;
gern; *~ness* [‿inis] Bereitschaft *f*;
Bereitwilligkeit *f*; Schnelligkeit *f*.
reading ['ri:diŋ] Lesen *n*; Lesung *f*
(*a. parl.*); Stand *m des Thermome-
ters*; Belesenheit *f*; Lektüre *f*; Lesart *f*; Auffassung *f*; *attr.* Lese...
readjust ['ri:ə'dʒʌst] wieder in Ordnung bringen; wieder anpassen;
~ment [‿tmənt] Wiederanpassung
f; Neuordnung *f*.
ready □ ['redi] bereit, fertig; be-
reitwillig; im Begriff (*to do zu*
tun); schnell; gewandt; leicht; zur
Hand; 🕈 bar; *~ for use* gebrauchs-
fertig; *make od. get ~* (sich) fertig
machen; *~made* fertig, Konfek-
tions...
reagent ℞ [ri(:)'eidʒənt] Reagens *n*.
real □ [riəl] wirklich, tatsächlich,
real; echt; *~ estate* Grundbesitz *m*,
Immobilien *pl.*; *~ism* [‿riəlizəm]
Realismus *m*; *~istic* [riə'listik]
(*~ally*) realistisch; sachlich; wirk-
lichkeitsnah; *~ity* [ri(:)'æliti] Wirklichkeit *f*; *~ization* [riəlai'zeiʃən]
Verwirklichung *f*; Erkenntnis *f*;
🕈 Realisierung *f*; *~ize* ['riəlaiz]
sich klarmachen; erkennen; ver-
wirklichen; realisieren, zu Geld
machen; *~ly* [‿li] wirklich, in der
Tat.
realm [relm] Königreich *n*; Reich *n*.
realt|or *Am.* ['riəltə] Grundstücks-
makler *m*; *~y* ⚜ [‿ti] Grundeigen-
tum *n*.
reap [ri:p] *Korn* schneiden; *Feld*

mähen; *fig.* ernten; ~er ['ri:pə]
Schnitter(in); Mähmaschine *f.*

reappear ['ri:ə'piə] wieder erscheinen.

rear [riə] 1. *v/t.* auf-, großziehen;
züchten; *v/i.* sich aufrichten;
2. Rück-, Hinterseite *f*; *mot.*, ⚓
Heck *n*; ✕ Nachhut *f*; *at the* ~ *of,*
in (*the*) ~ *of* hinter (*dat.*); 3. Hinter...,
Nach...; ~ *wheel drive* Hinterradantrieb *m*; ~**-admiral** ⚓ ['riə-
'ædmərəl] Konteradmiral *m*;
~**-guard** ✕ Nachhut *f*; ~**-lamp**
mot. Schlußlicht *n.*

rearm ['ri:'a:m] (wieder)aufrüsten;
~**ament** [~'məmənt] Aufrüstung *f.*

rearmost ['riəmoust] hinterst.

rearward ['riəwəd] 1. *adj.* rückwärtig; 2. *adv. a.* ~s rückwärts.

reason ['ri:zn] 1. Vernunft *f*; Verstand *m*; Recht *n*, Billigkeit *f*; Ursache *f*, Grund *m*; *by* ~ *of* wegen;
for this ~ aus diesem Grund; *listen
to* ~ Vernunft annehmen; *it stands
to* ~ *that* es leuchtet ein, daß; 2.
v/i. vernünftig denken; schließen;
urteilen; argumentieren; *v/t. a.*
~ *out* durchdenken; ~ *away* fortdisputieren; ~ *s.o. into* (*out of*)
s.th. j-m et. ein- (aus)reden;
~**able** ⎕ [~nəbl] vernünftig; billig;
angemessen; leidlich.

reassure ['ri:ə'ʃuə] wieder versichern; (wieder) beruhigen.

rebate ['ri:beit] ✝ Rabatt *m*, Abzug
m; Rückzahlung *f.*

rebel 1. ['rebl] Rebell *m*; Aufrührer
m; 2. [~] rebellisch; 3. [ri'bel] sich
auflehnen; ~**lion** [~ljən] Empörung
f; ~**lious** [~ljəs] → *rebel* 2.

rebirth ['ri:'bə:θ] Wiedergeburt *f.*

rebound [ri'baund] 1. zurückprallen; 2. Rückprall *m*, Rückschlag *m.*

rebuff [ri'bʌf] 1. Zurück-, Abweisung *f*; 2. zurück-, abweisen.

rebuild [ri:'bild] (*irr.* (*build*)) wieder (auf)bauen.

rebuke [ri'bju:k] 1. Tadel *m*;
2. tadeln.

rebut [ri'bʌt] zurückweisen.

recall [ri'kɔ:l] 1. Zurückrufung *f*;
Abberufung *f*; Widerruf *m*; *beyond*
~, *past* ~ unwiderruflich; 2. zurückrufen; ab(be)rufen; (sich) erinnern an (*acc.*); widerrufen; ✝
Kapital kündigen.

recapitulate [ri:kə'pitjuleit] kurz
wiederholen, zs.-fassen.

recapture ['ri:'kæptʃə] wieder (gefangen)nehmen; ✕ zurückerobern.

recast ['ri:'ka:st] [*irr* (*cast*)] ⊕ umgießen; umformen, neu gestalten.

recede [ri(:)'si:d] zurücktreten.

receipt [ri'si:t] 1. Empfang *m*;
Eingang *m v. Waren*; Quittung *f*;
(Koch)Rezept *n*; ~*s pl.* Einnahmen
f/pl.; 2. quittieren.

receiv|able [ri'si:vəbl] annehmbar;
✝ noch zu fordern(d), ausstehend;

~**e** [ri'si:v] empfangen; erhalten,
bekommen; aufnehmen; annehmen; anerkennen; ~**ed** anerkannt;
~**er** [~və] Empfänger *m*; *teleph.*
Hörer *m*; Hehler *m*; *Steuer- etc.*
Einnehmer *m*; *official* ~ ɜ⁄ᵴ Masseverwalter *m.*

recent ⎕ ['ri:snt] neu; frisch; modern; ~ *events pl. die* jüngsten Ereignisse *n/pl.*; ~**ly** [~tli] neulich,
vor kurzem.

receptacle [ri'septəkl] Behälter *m.*

reception [ri'sepʃən] Aufnahme *f*
(*a. fig.*), (*a.* Radio)Empfang *m*;
Annahme *f*; ~**ist** [~nist] Empfangsdame *f*, -herr *m*; ~**-room** Empfangszimmer *n.*

receptive ⎕ [ri'septiv] empfänglich, aufnahmefähig (*of* für).

recess [ri'ses] Pause *f*; *bsd. parl.*
Ferien *pl.*; (entlegener) Winkel;
Nische *f*; ~*es pl. fig.* Tiefe(n *pl.*) *f*;
~**ion** [~eʃən] Zurückziehen *n*, Zurücktreten *n*; ✝ Konjunkturrückgang *m*, rückläufige Bewegung.

recipe ['resipi] Rezept *n.*

recipient [ri'sipiənt] Empfänger(in).

reciproc|al [ri'siprəkəl] wechsel-,
gegenseitig; ~**ate** [~keit] *v/i.* sich
erkenntlich zeigen; ⊕ sich hin- und
herbewegen; *v/t.* Glückwünsche *etc.*
erwidern; ~**ity** [resi'prɔsiti] Gegenseitigkeit *f.*

recit|al [ri'saitl] Bericht *m*; Erzählung *f*; ♪ (Solo)Vortrag *m*, Konzert *n*; ~**ation** [resi'teiʃən] Hersagen *n*; Vortrag *m*; ~**e** [ri'sait] vortragen; aufsagen; berichten.

reckless ⎕ ['reklis] unbekümmert;
rücksichtslos; leichtsinnig.

reckon ['rekən] *v/t.* rechnen; *a.* ~
for, ~ *as* schätzen als, halten für; ~
up zs.-zählen; *v/i.* rechnen; denken,
vermuten; ~ (*up*)*on* sich verlassen
auf (*acc.*); ~**ing** ['rekniŋ] Rechnen
n; (Ab-, Be)Rechnung *f.*

reclaim [ri'kleim] wiedergewinnen;
j-n bessern; zivilisieren; urbar
machen.

recline [ri'klain] (sich) (zurück-)
lehnen; ~ *upon fig.* sich stützen auf.

recluse [ri'klu:s] Einsiedler(in).

recogni|tion [rekəg'niʃən] Anerkennung *f*; Wiedererkennen *n*; ~**ze**
['rekəgnaiz] anerkennen; (wieder-)
erkennen.

recoil [ri'kɔil] 1. zurückprallen;
2. Rückstoß *m*, -lauf *m.*

recollect[1] [rekə'lekt] sich erinnern
an (*acc.*).

re-collect[2] ['ri:kə'lekt] wieder sammeln; ~ *o.s.* sich fassen.

recollection [rekə'lekʃən] Erinnerung *f* (*of an acc.*); Gedächtnis *n.*

recommend [rekə'mend] empfehlen; ~**ation** [rekəmen'deiʃən] Empfehlung *f*; Vorschlag *m.*

recompense ['rekəmpens] 1. Belohnung *f*, Vergeltung *f*; Ersatz *m*;

2. belohnen, vergelten; entschädigen; ersetzen.

reconcil|e ['rekənsail] aus-, versöhnen; in Einklang bringen; schlichten; **~iation** [rekənsili'eiʃən] Ver-, Aussöhnung f.

recondition ['ri:kən'diʃən] wieder herrichten; ⊕ überholen.

reconn|aissance ✕ [ri'kɔnisəns] Aufklärung f, Erkundung f; fig. Übersicht f; **~oitre**, Am. **~oiter** [rekə'nɔitə] erkunden, auskundschaften.

reconsider ['ri:kən'sidə] wieder erwägen; nochmals überlegen.

reconstitute ['ri:'kɔnstitju:t] wiederherstellen.

reconstruct ['ri:kəns'trʌkt] wiederaufbauen; **~ion** [**~**'kʃən] Wiederaufbau m, Wiederherstellung f.

reconvert ['ri:kən'vɜ:t] umstellen.

record **1.** ['rekɔ:d] Aufzeichnung f; ♃ Protokoll n; schriftlicher Bericht; Ruf m, Leumund m; Wiedergabe f; Schallplatte f; Sport Rekord m; place on **~** schriftlich niederlegen; ♧ Office Staatsarchiv n; off the **~** Am. inoffiziell; **2.** [ri'kɔ:d] auf-, verzeichnen; auf Schallplatte etc. aufnehmen; **~er** [**~**də] Registrator m; Stadtrichter m; Aufnahmegerät n, bsd. Tonbandgerät n; ♪ Blockflöte f; **~ing** [**~**diŋ] Radio: Aufzeichnung f, Aufnahme f; **~player** Plattenspieler m.

recount [ri'kaunt] erzählen.

recoup [ri'ku:p] j-n entschädigen (for für); et. wieder einbringen.

recourse [ri'kɔ:s] Zuflucht f; have **~** to s-e Zuflucht nehmen zu.

recover [ri'kʌvə] v/t. wiedererlangen, wiederfinden; wieder einbringen, wiedergutmachen; Schulden etc. eintreiben; be **~ed** wiederhergestellt sein; v/i. sich erholen; genesen; **~y** [**~**əri] Wiedererlangung f; Wiederherstellung f; Genesung f; Erholung f.

recreat|e ['rekrieit] v/t. erfrischen; v/i. a. **~ o.s.** sich erholen; **~ion** [rekri'eiʃən] Erholung(spause) f.

recrimination [rikrimi'neiʃən] Gegenbeschuldigung f; Gegenklage f.

recruit [ri'kru:t] **1.** Rekrut m; fig. Neuling m; **2.** erneuern, ergänzen; Truppe rekrutieren; ✕ Rekruten ausheben; sich erholen.

rectangle ⅍ ['rektæŋgl] Rechteck n.

recti|fy ['rektifai] berichtigen; verbessern; ⚡, Radio: gleichrichten; **~tude** [**~**itju:d] Geradheit f.

rector ['rektə] Pfarrer m; Rektor m; **~y** [**~**əri] Pfarre(i) f; Pfarrhaus n.

recumbent ⃞ [ri'kʌmbənt] liegend.

recuperate [ri'kju:pəreit] wiederherstellen; sich erholen.

recur [ri'kə:] zurück-, wiederkehren (to zu); zurückkommen (to auf acc.); **~ to j-m** wieder einfallen; **~rence**

[ri'kʌrəns] Wieder-, Rückkehr f; **~rent** ⃞ [**~**nt] wiederkehrend.

red [red] **1.** rot; **~ heat** Rotglut f; **~ herring** Bückling m; **~ tape** Amtsschimmel m; **2.** Rot n; (bsd. pol.) Rote(r m) f; be in the **~** Am. F in Schulden stecken.

red|breast ['redbrest] a. robin **~** Rotkehlchen n; **~cap** Militärpolizist m; Am. Gepäckträger m; **~den** ['redn] (sich) röten; erröten; **~dish** ['rediʃ] rötlich.

redecorate ['ri:'dekəreit] Zimmer renovieren (lassen).

redeem [ri'di:m] zurück-, loskaufen; ablösen; Versprechen einlösen; büßen, entschädigen für; erlösen; **2er eccl.** [**~**mə] Erlöser m, Heiland m.

redemption [ri'dempʃən] Rückkauf m; Auslösung f; Erlösung f.

red|-handed ['red'hændid] catch od. take s.o. **~** j-n auf frischer Tat ertappen; **~head** Rotschopf m; Hitzkopf m; **~-headed** rothaarig; **~hot** rotglühend; fig. hitzig; **2 Indian** Indianer(in) f; **~-letter day** Festtag m; fig Freuden-, Glückstag m; **~ness** [rednis] Röte f.

redolent ['redoulənt] duftend.

redouble [ri'dʌbl] (sich) verdoppeln.

redoubt ✕ [ri'daut] Redoute f; **~able** rhet. [**~**təbl] fürchterlich.

redound [ri'daund]: **~ to** beitragen od. gereichen od. führen zu.

redress [ri'dres] **1.** Abhilfe f; Wiedergutmachung f; ♃ Entschädigung f; **2.** abhelfen (dat.); wiedergutmachen.

red|-tapism ['red'teipizəm] Bürokratismus m; **~tapist** [**~**ist] Bürokrat m.

reduc|e [ri'dju:s] fig. zurückführen, bringen (to auf, in acc., zu); verwandeln (to in acc.); verringern, vermindern; einschränken; Preise herabsetzen; (be)zwingen; A, **~** reduzieren; ⚡ einrenken; **~ to writing** schriftlich niederlegen; **~tion** [ri'dʌkʃən] Reduktion f; Verwandlung f; Herabsetzung f, (Preis)Nachlaß m, Rabatt m; Verminderung f; Verkleinerung f; ⚡ Einrenkung f.

redundant ⃞ [ri'dʌndənt] überflüssig; übermäßig; weitschweifig.

reed [ri:d] Schilfrohr n; Rohrflöte f.

re-education ['ri:edju(:)'keiʃən] Umschulung f, Umerziehung f.

reef [ri:f] (Felsen)Riff n; ♧ Reff n.

reefer ['ri:fə] Seemannsjacke f; Am. sl. Marihuana-Zigarette f.

reek [ri:k] **1.** Rauch m, Dampf m; Dunst m; **2.** rauchen, dampfen (with von); unangenehm riechen.

reel [ri:l] **1.** Haspel f; (Garn-, Film)Rolle f, Spule f; **2.** v/t. haspeln; wickeln, spulen; v/i. wirbeln; schwanken; taumeln.

32 SW E

re-elect ['ri:i'lekt] wiederwählen.
re-enter [ri:'entə] wieder eintreten (in acc.).
re-establish ['ri:is'tæbliʃ] wiederherstellen.
refection [ri'fekʃən] Erfrischung f.
refer [ri'fə:]: ~ to ver-, überweisen an (acc.); sich beziehen auf (acc.); erwähnen (acc.); zuordnen (dat.); befragen (acc.), nachschlagen in (dat.); zurückführen auf (acc.), zuschreiben (dat.); ~ee [refə'ri:] Schiedsrichter m; Boxen Ringrichter m; ~ence [refrəns] Referenz f, Empfehlung f, Zeugnis n; Verweisung f; Bezugnahme f; Anspielung f; Beziehung f, Auskunft (-geber m) f; in od with ~ to in betreff (gen.), in bezug auf (acc.); ~ book Nachschlagewerk n; ~ library Handbibliothek f; ~ number Aktenzeichen n; make ~ to et. erwähnen.
referendum [refə'rendəm] Volksentscheid m.
refill 1. ['ri:fil] Nachfüllung f; Ersatzfüllung f; 2. ['ri:'fil] (sich) wieder füllen, auffüllen
refine [ri'fain] (sich) verfeinern od. veredeln; ⊕ raffinieren, (sich) läutern (a. fig.); klügeln; (up)on et. verfeinern, verbessern, ~ment [~nmənt] Verfeinerung f, Vered(e)-lung f; Läuterung f; Feinheit f, Bildung f; Spitzfindigkeit f; ~ry [~nəri] ⊕ Raffinerie f; metall. (Eisen)Hütte f.
refit ⊕ ['ri:'fit] v/t. ausbessern; neu ausrüsten; v/i. ausgebessert werden.
reflect [ri'flekt] v/t zurückwerfen, reflektieren; zurückstrahlen, widerspiegeln (a. fig.); zum Ausdruck bringen; v/i ~ (up)on nachdenken über (acc.); sich abfällig äußern über (acc.); ein schlechte Licht werfen auf (acc.); ~ion [~kʃən] Zurückstrahlung f, Widerspiegelung f; Reflex m; Spiegelbild n, Überlegung f; Gedanke m, abfällige Bemerkung; Makel m, ~ive □ [~ktiv] zurückstrahlend; nachdenklich.
reflex ['ri:fleks] 1. Reflex..., 2.Widerschein m, Reflex m (a physiol.).
reflexive □ [ri'fleksiv] zurückwirkend; gr. reflexiv, rückbezüglich.
reforest ['ri:'fɔrist] aufforsten
reform[1] [ri'fɔ:m] 1. Verbesserung f, Reform f; 2. verbessern, reformieren; (sich) bessern
re-form[2] ['ri:'fɔ:m] (sich) neu bilden; ⚔ sich wieder formieren.
reform|ation [refə'meiʃən] Umgestaltung f; Besserung f, eccl. 2 Reformation f; ~atory [ri'fɔ:mətəri] 1. bessernd, 2. Besserungsanstalt f; ~er [ri'fɔ:mə] eccl. Reformator m; bsd. pol. Reformer m.

refract|ion [ri'frækʃən] Strahlenbrechung f; ~ory □ [~ktəri] widerspenstig; hartnäckig; ⊕ feuerfest.
refrain [ri'frein] 1. sich enthalten (from gen.), unterlassen (from acc.); 2. Kehrreim m, Refrain m.
refresh [ri'freʃ] (sich) erfrischen; auffrischen; ~ment [~ʃmənt] Erfrischung f (a. Getränk etc.).
refrigerat|e [ri'fridʒəreit] kühlen; ~or [~tə] Kühlschrank m, -raum m; ~ car Kühlwagen m
refuel ['ri:'fjuəl] tanken.
refuge ['refju:dʒ] Zuflucht(sstätte) f; a. street-~ Verkehrsinsel f; ~e [refju(:)'dʒi:] Flüchtling m; ~ camp Flüchtlingslager n.
refulgent □ [ri'fʌldʒənt] strahlend.
refund [ri'fʌnd] zurückzahlen.
refurbish ['ri:'fə:biʃ] aufpolieren.
refusal [ri'fju:zəl] abschlägige Antwort; (Ver)Weigerung f; Vorkaufsrecht n (of auf acc.).
refuse[1] [ri'fju:z] v/t. verweigern; abweisen, ablehnen; scheuen vor (dat.); v/i. sich weigern; scheuen (Pferd); ~ [fall m, Müll m.]
refuse[2] ['refju:s] Abschuß m; Ab-
refute [ri'fju:t] widerlegen.
regain [ri'gein] wiedergewinnen.
regal □ [ri'gəl] königlich; Königs...
regale [ri'geil] v/t. festlich bewirten; v/i. schwelgen (on in dat.).
regard [ri'gɑ:d] 1. fester Blick; (Hoch)Achtung f, Rücksicht f, Beziehung f; with ~ to im Hinblick auf (acc.); kind ~s herzliche Grüße; 2. ansehen; (be)achten; betrachten; betreffen; as ~s ... was ... anbetrifft; ~ing [~diŋ] hinsichtlich (gen.); ~less □ [~dlis]: ~ of ohne Rücksicht auf (acc.).
regenerate 1. [ri'dʒenəreit] (sich) erneuern; (sich) regenerieren; (sich) neu bilden; 2. [~rit] wiedergeboren.
regent ['ri:dʒənt] 1. herrschend; 2. Regent m.
regiment ⚔ ['redʒimənt] 1. Regiment n; 2. [~ment] organisieren; ~als ⚔ [redʒi'mentlz] pl. Uniformf.
region ['ri:dʒən] Gegend f, Gebiet n; fig. Bereich m; ~al □ [~nl] örtlich; Orts...
register ['redʒistə] 1. Register n, Verzeichnis n; ⊕ Schieber m, Ventil n; ♪ Register n; Zählwerk n; cash ~ Registrierkasse f; 2. registrieren od. eintragen (lassen); (an-)zeigen, auf-, verzeichnen; Postsache einschreiben (lassen), Gepäck aufgeben; sich polizeilich melden.
registr|ar [redʒis'trɑ:] Registrator m; Standesbeamte(r) m; ~ation [~reiʃən] Eintragung f; ~ fee Anmeldegebühr f; ~y ['redʒistri] Eintragung f; Registratur f; Register n; ~ office Standesamt n.
regress, ~ion ['ri:gres, ri'greʃən] Rückkehr f; fig. Rückgang m.

regret [ri'gret] **1.** Bedauern *n*; Schmerz *m*; **2.** bedauern; *Verlust* beklagen; **~ful** □ [**~**tful] bedauernd; **~fully** [**~**li] mit Bedauern; **~table** □ [**~**təbl] bedauerlich.

regular □ ['regjulə] regelmäßig; regelrecht, richtig; ordentlich; pünktlich; ✕ regulär; **~ity** [regju-'læriti] Regelmäßigkeit *f*; Richtigkeit *f*, Ordnung *f*.

regulat|e ['regjuleit] regeln, ordnen; regulieren; **~ion** [regju'leiʃən] **1.** Regulierung *f*; Vorschrift *f*, Bestimmung *f*; **2.** vorschriftsmäßig.

rehash *fig.* ['riː'hæʃ] **1.** wieder durchkauen *od.* aufwärmen; **2.** Aufguß *m.*

rehears|al [ri'həːsəl] *thea.*, ♪ Probe *f*; Wiederholung *f*; **~e** [ri'həːs] *thea.* proben; wiederholen; aufsagen.

reign [rein] **1.** Regierung *f*; *fig.* Herrschaft *f*; **2.** herrschen, regieren.

reimburse [riːim'bəːs] *j-n* entschädigen; *Kosten* wiedererstatten.

rein [rein] **1.** Zügel *m*; **2.** zügeln.

reindeer *zo.* ['reindiə] Ren(tier)*n.*

reinforce [riːin'fɔːs] verstärken; **~ment** [**~**smənt] Verstärkung *f.*

reinstate [riːin'steit] wieder einsetzen; wieder instand setzen.

reinsure ['riːin'ʃuə] rückversichern.

reiterate [riː'itəreit] (dauernd) wiederholen.

reject [ri'dʒekt] ver-, wegwerfen; ablehnen, ausschlagen; zurückweisen; **~ion** [**~**kʃən] Verwerfung *f*; Ablehnung *f*; Zurückweisung *f.*

rejoic|e [ri'dʒɔis] *v/t.* erfreuen; *v/i.* sich freuen (*at*, *in* über *acc.*); **~ing** [**~**siŋ] **1.** □ freudig; **2.** *oft* **~s** *pl.* Freude(nfest *n*) *f.*

rejoin ['riː'dʒɔin] (sich) wieder vereinigen (mit); wieder zurückkehren zu; [ri'dʒɔin] erwidern.

rejuvenate [ri'dʒuːvineit] verjüngen. [entzünden.\

rekindle ['riː'kindl] (sich) wieder\

relapse [ri'læps] **1.** Rückfall *m*; **2.** zurückfallen, rückfällig werden.

relate [ri'leit] *v/t.* erzählen; in Beziehung bringen; *v/i.* sich beziehen (*to* auf *acc.*); **~d** verwandt (*to* mit).

relation [ri'leiʃən] Erzählung *f*; Beziehung *f*; Verhältnis *n*; Verwandtschaft *f*; Verwandte(r *m*) *f*; *in* **~** *to* in bezug auf (*acc.*); **~ship** [**~**nʃip] Verwandtschaft *f*; Beziehung *f.*

relative ['relətiv] **1.** □ bezüglich (*to gen.*); *gr.* relativ; verhältnismäßig; entsprechend; **2.** *gr.* Relativpronomen *n*; Verwandte(r *m*) *f.*

relax [ri'læks] (sich) lockern; mildern; nachlassen (*in dat.*); (sich) entspannen, ausspannen; milder werden; **~ation** [riːlæk'seiʃən] Lockerung *f*; Nachlassen *n*; Entspannung *f*, Erholung *f.*

relay[1] **1.** [ri'lei] frisches Gespann; Ablösung *f*; ['riː'lei] ≠ Relais *n*; *Radio:* Übertragung *f*; **2.** [**~**] *Radio:* übertragen.

re-lay[2] ['riː'lei] *Kabel etc.* neu verlegen.

relay-race ['riːleireis] *Sport:* Staffellauf *m.*

release [ri'liːs] **1.** Freilassung *f*; *fig.* Befreiung *f*; Freigabe *f*; *Film: oft first* **~** Uraufführung *f*; ⊕, *phot.* Auslöser *m*; **2.** freilassen; erlösen; freigeben; *Recht* aufgeben, übertragen; *Film* uraufführen; ⊕ auslösen.

relegate ['religeit] verbannen; verweisen (*to an acc.*).

relent [ri'lent] sich erweichen lassen; **~less** □ [**~**tlis] unbarmherzig.

relevant ['relivənt] sachdienlich; zutreffend; wichtig, erheblich.

reliab|ility [rilaiə'biliti] Zuverlässigkeit *f*; **~le** □ [ri'laiəbl] zuverlässig.

reliance [ri'laiəns] Ver-, Zutrauen *n*; Verlaß *m.*

relic ['relik] Überrest *m*; Reliquie *f*; **~t** [**~**kt] Witwe *f.*

relief [ri'liːf] Erleichterung *f*; (angenehme) Unterbrechung; Unterstützung *f*; ✕ Ablösung *f*; ✕ Entsatz *m*; Hilfe *f*; △ *etc.* Relief *n*; **~ works** *pl.* Notstandsarbeiten *f/pl.*

relieve [ri'liːv] erleichtern; mildern, lindern; *Arme etc.* unterstützen; ✕ ablösen; ✕ entsetzen; ₪ (ab)helfen (*dat.*); befreien; hervortreten lassen; (angenehm) unterbrechen.

religion [ri'lidʒən] Religion *f*; Ordensleben *n*; *fig.* Ehrensache *f.*

religious □ [ri'lidʒəs] Religions...; religiös; *eccl.* Ordens...; gewissenhaft.

relinquish [ri'liŋkwiʃ] aufgeben; verzichten auf (*acc.*); loslassen.

relish ['reliʃ] **1.** (Bei)Geschmack *m*; Würze *f*; Genuß *m*; **2.** gern essen; Geschmack finden an (*dat.*); schmackhaft machen.

reluctan|ce [ri'lʌktəns] Widerstreben *n*; *bsd. phys.* Widerstand *m*; **~t** □ [**~**nt] widerstrebend, widerwillig.

rely [ri'lai] **~** (*up*)*on* sich verlassen (auf *acc.*), bauen auf (*acc.*).

remain [ri'mein] **1.** (ver)bleiben; übrigbleiben; **2.** **~s** *pl.* Überbleibsel *n/pl.*; Überreste *m/pl.*; sterbliche Reste *m/pl.*; **~der** [**~**ndə] Rest *m.*

remand [ri'mɑːnd] **1.** (ɹ₂ in die Untersuchungshaft) zurückschicken; **2.** (Zurücksendung *f* in die) Untersuchungshaft *f*; *prisoner on* **~** Untersuchungsgefangene(r *m*) *f*; **~ home** Jugendstrafanstalt *f.*

remark [ri'mɑːk] **1.** Beachtung *f*; Bemerkung *f*; **2.** *v/t.* bemerken; *v/i.* sich äußern; **~able** □ [**~**kəbl] bemerkenswert; merkwürdig.

remedy ['remidi] 1. (Heil-, Hilfs-, Gegen-, Rechts)Mittel *n*; (Ab-) Hilfe *f*; 2. heilen; abhelfen (*dat.*).

rememb|er [ri'membə] sich erinnern an (*acc.*); denken an (*acc.*); beherzigen; ~ me to her grüße sie von mir; ~rance [~brəns] Erinnerung *f*; Gedächtnis *n*; Andenken *n*; ~s *pl.* Empfehlungen *f/pl.*, Grüße *m/pl.*

remind [ri'maind] erinnern (*of* an *acc.*); ~er [~də] Mahnung *f*.

reminiscen|ce [remi'nisns] Erinnerung *f*; ~t □ [~nt] (sich) erinnernd.

remiss □ [ri'mis] schlaff, (nach-) lässig; ~ion [~iʃən] Sünden-Vergebung *f*; Erlassung *f v. Strafe etc.*; Nachlassen *n*.

remit [ri'mit] Sünden vergeben; Schuld etc. erlassen; nachlassen in (*dat.*); überweisen; ~tance [~təns] (Geld)Sendung *f*; ✝ Rimesse *f*.

remnant ['remnənt] (Über)Rest *m*.

remodel ['ri:'mɔdl] umbilden.

remonstra|nce [ri'mɔnstrəns] Vorstellung *f*, Einwendung *f*; ~te [~treit] Vorstellungen machen (*on* über *acc.*; *with* s.o. j-m); einwenden.

remorse [ri'mɔ:s] Gewissensbisse *m/pl.*; ~less □ [~slis] hart(herzig).

remote □ [ri'mout] entfernt, entlegen; ~ness [~tnis] Entfernung *f*.

remov|al [ri'mu:vəl] Entfernen *n*; Beseitigung *f*; Umzug *m*; Entlassung *f*; ~ van Möbelwagen *m*; ~e [~u:v] 1. *v/t.* entfernen; wegräumen, wegziehen; beseitigen; entlassen; *v/i.* (aus-, um-, ver)ziehen; 2. Entfernung *f*; Grad *m*; Schule: Versetzung *f*; Abteilung *f e-r Klasse*; ~er [~və] (Möbel)Spediteur *m*.

remunerat|e [ri'mju:nəreit] (be-) lohnen; entschädigen; ~ive □ [~rətiv] lohnend.

Renaissance [rə'neisəns] Renaissance *f*.

renascen|ce [ri'næsns] Wiedergeburt *f*; Renaissance *f*; ~t □ [~nt] wieder wachsend.

rend [rend] [*irr.*] (zer)reißen.

render ['rendə] wieder-, zurückgeben; Dienst etc. leisten; Ehre etc. erweisen; Dank abstatten; übersetzen; ♪ vortragen; darstellen, interpretieren; Grund angeben; ✝ Rechnung überreichen; übergeben; machen (zu); Fett auslassen; ~ing [~əriŋ] Wiedergabe *f*; Interpretation *f*; Übersetzung *f*, Wiedergabe *f*; △ Rohbewurf *m*.

rendition [ren'diʃən] Wiedergabe *f*.

renegade ['renigeid] Abtrünnige(r *m*) *f*.

renew [ri'nju:] erneuern; ~al [~u(:)əl] Erneuerung *f*.

renounce [ri'nauns] entsagen (*dat.*); verzichten auf (*acc.*); verleugnen.

renovate ['renouveit] erneuern.

renown [ri'naun] Ruhm *m*, Ansehen *n*; ~ed [~nd] berühmt, namhaft.

rent¹ [rent] 1. *pret. u. p.p. von* rend; 2. Riß *m*; Spalte *f*.

rent² [~] 1. Miete *f*; Pacht *f*; 2. (ver)mieten, (ver)pachten; ~al ['rentl] (Einkommen *n* aus) Miete *f od.* Pacht *f*.

renunciation [rinʌnsi'eiʃən] Entsagung *f*; Verzicht *m* (*of* auf *acc.*).

repair¹ [ri'pɛə] 1. Ausbesserung *f*, Reparatur *f*; ~s *pl.* Instandsetzungsarbeiten *f/pl.*; ~ shop Reparaturwerkstatt *f*; *in good* ~ in gutem (baulichen) Zustand, gut erhalten; *out of* ~ baufällig; 2. reparieren, ausbessern; erneuern; wiedergutmachen.

repair² [~] ~ *to* sich begeben nach.

reparation [repə'reiʃən] Ersatz *m*; Entschädigung *f*; make ~s *pol.* Reparationen leisten.

repartee [repa:'ti:] schlagfertige Antwort; Schlagfertigkeit *f*.

repast [ri'pa:st] Mahl(zeit *f*) *n*.

repay [ri:'pei] [*irr.* (*pay*)] *et.* zurückzahlen; *fig.* erwidern; *et.* vergelten; *j-n* entschädigen; ~ment [~eimənt] Rückzahlung *f*.

repeal [ri'pi:l] 1. Aufhebung *f von Gesetzen*; 2. aufheben, widerrufen.

repeat [ri'pi:t] 1. (sich) wiederholen; aufsagen; nachliefern; aufstoßen (Essen); 2. Wiederholung *f*; oft ~ order Nachbestellung *f*; ♪ Wiederholungszeichen *n*.

repel [ri'pel] zurückstoßen, zurücktreiben, zurückweisen; *fig.* abstoßen.

repent [ri'pent] bereuen; ~ance [~təns] Reue *f*; ~ant [~nt] reuig.

repercussion [ri:pə'kʌʃən] Rückprall *m*; *fig.* Rückwirkung *f*.

repertory ['repətəri] *thea.* Repertoire *n*; *fig.* Fundgrube *f*.

repetition [repi'tiʃən] Wiederholung *f*; Aufsagen *n*; Nachbildung *f*.

replace [ri'pleis] wieder hinstellen *od.* einsetzen; ersetzen; an *j-s* Stelle treten; ~ment [~smənt] Ersatz *m*.

replant ['ri:'pla:nt] umpflanzen.

replenish [ri'pleniʃ] wieder auffüllen; ~ment [~ʃmənt] Auffüllung *f*; Ergänzung *f*.

replete [ri'pli:t] angefüllt, voll.

replica ['replikə] Nachbildung *f*.

reply [ri'plai] 1. antworten, erwidern (*to* auf *acc.*); 2. Erwiderung *f*.

report [ri'pɔ:t] 1. Bericht *m*; Gerücht *n*; guter Ruf; Knall *m*; school ~ (Schul)Zeugnis *n*; 2. berichten (über *acc.*); (sich) melden; anzeigen; ~er [~tə] Berichterstatter(in).

repos|e [ri'pouz] 1. *allg.* Ruhe *f*; 2. *v/t.* ausruhen; (aus)ruhen lassen; ~ trust etc. in Vertrauen etc. setzen auf (*acc.*); *v/i. a.* ~ *o.s.* (sich) ausruhen; ruhen; beruhen (*on* auf *dat.*); ~**itory** [ri'pozitəri] Verwahrungsort *m*; Warenlager *n*; *fig.* Fundgrube *f*.

reprehend [repri'hend] tadeln.

represent [repri'zent] darstellen; verkörpern; *thea.* aufführen; schildern; bezeichnen (*as* als); vertreten; ~**ation** [reprizən'teiʃən] Darstellung *f*; *thea.* Aufführung *f*; Vorstellung *f*; Vertretung *f*; ~**ative** ☐ [repri'zentətiv] 1. dar-, vorstellend (*of acc.*); vorbildlich; (stell)vertretend; *parl.* repräsentativ; typisch; 2. Vertreter(in); *House of* ~s *Am. parl.* Repräsentantenhaus *n*.

repress [ri'pres] unterdrücken; ~**ion** [~eʃən] Unterdrückung *f*.

reprieve [ri'pri:v] 1. (Gnaden)Frist *f*; Aufschub *m*; 2. *j-m* Aufschub *od.* eine Gnadenfrist gewähren.

reprimand ['reprimɑːnd] 1. Verweis *m*; 2. *j-m* e-n Verweis geben.

reprisal [ri'praizəl] Repressalie *f*.

reproach [ri'proutʃ] 1. Vorwurf *m*; Schande *f*; 2. vorwerfen (*s.o. with s.th.* j-m et.); Vorwürfe machen; ~**ful** ☐ [~sful] vorwurfsvoll.

reprobate ['reproubeit] 1. verkommen, verderbt; 2. verkommenes Subjekt; 3. mißbilligen; verdammen.

reproduc|e [ri:prə'dju:s] wiedererzeugen; (sich) fortpflanzen; wiedergeben, reproduzieren; ~**tion** [~'dʌkʃən] Wiedererzeugung *f*; Fortpflanzung *f*; Reproduktion *f*.

reproof [ri'pru:f] Vorwurf *m*, Tadel *m*.

reprov|al [ri'pru:vəl] Tadel *m*, Rüge *f*; ~**e** [~u:v] tadeln, rügen.

reptile *zo.* ['reptail] Reptil *n*.

republic [ri'pʌblik] Republik *f*; ~**an** [~kən] 1. republikanisch; 2. Republikaner(in).

repudiate [ri'pju:dieit] nicht anerkennen; ab-, zurückweisen.

repugnan|ce [ri'pʌgnəns] Abneigung *f*, Widerwille *m*; ~**t** ☐ [~nt] abstoßend; widerwärtig.

repuls|e [ri'pʌls] 1. Zurück-, Abweisung *f*; 2. zurück-, abweisen; ~**ive** ☐ [~siv] abstoßend; widerwärtig.

reput|able ☐ ['repjutəbl] achtbar; ehrbar, anständig; ~**ation** [repju(:)-'teiʃən] (*bsd. guter*) Ruf, Ansehen *n*; ~**e** [ri'pju:t] 1. Ruf *m*; 2. halten für; ~**ed** vermeintlich; angeblich.

request [ri'kwest] 1. Gesuch *n*, Bitte *f*; Ersuchen *n*; † Nachfrage *f*; *by* ~, *on* ~ auf Wunsch; *in* (*great*) ~ (sehr) gesucht, begehrt; ~ *stop* Bedarfshaltestelle *f*; 2. um et. bitten *od.* ersuchen; *j-n* bitten; et. erbitten.

require [ri'kwaiə] verlangen, fordern; brauchen, erfordern; ~**d** er

forderlich; ~**ment** [~əmənt] (An-)Forderung *f*; Erfordernis *n*.

requisit|e ['rekwizit] 1. erforderlich; 2. Erfordernis *n*; Bedarfs-, Gebrauchsartikel *m*; *toilet* ~s *pl.* Toilettenartikel *m/pl.*; ~**ion** [rekwi-'ziʃən] 1. Anforderung *f*; ✗ Requisition *f*; 2. anfordern; ✗ requirieren.

requital [ri'kwaitl] Vergeltung *f*.

requite [ri'kwait] *j-m et.* vergelten.

rescind [ri'sind] aufheben.

rescission [ri'siʒən] Aufhebung *f*.

rescue ['reskju:] 1. Rettung *f*; (✗✗ gewaltsame) Befreiung; 2. retten; (✗✗ gewaltsam) befreien.

research [ri'sə:tʃ] Forschung *f*; Untersuchung *f*; Nachforschung *f*; ~**er** [~ʃə] Forscher *m*.

resembl|ance [ri'zembləns] Ähnlichkeit *f* (*to* mit); ~**e** [ri'zembl] gleichen, ähnlich sein (*dat.*).

resent [ri'zent] übelnehmen; ~**ful** ☐ [~tful] übelnehmerisch; ärgerlich; ~**ment** [~tmənt] Ärger *m*; Groll *m*.

reservation [rezə'veiʃən] Vorbehalt *m*; *Am* Indianerreservation *f*; Vorbestellung *f von Zimmern etc.*

reserve [ri'zə:v] 1. Vorrat *m*; ↑ Rücklage *f*; Reserve *f* (*u. fig.*, ✗✗); Zurückhaltung *f*, Verschlossenheit *f*; Vorsicht *f*; Vorbehalt *m*; *Sport:* Ersatzmann *m*; 2. aufbewahren, aufsparen; vorbehalten; zurücklegen; *Platz etc.* reservieren; ~**d** ☐ *fig.* zurückhaltend, reserviert.

reservoir ['rezəvwɑ:] Behälter *m* *für Wasser etc.*; Sammel-, Staubekken *n*; *fig.* Reservoir *n*.

reside [ri'zaid] wohnen; (orts)ansässig sein; ~ *in* innewohnen (*dat.*); ~**nce** ['rezidəns] Wohnen *n*; Ortsansässigkeit *f* (Wohn)Sitz *m*; Residenz *f*; ~ *permit* Aufenthaltsgenehmigung *f*; ~**nt** [~nt] 1. wohnhaft; ortsansässig; 2. Ortsansässige(r *m*) *f*, Einwohner(in).

residu|al [ri'zidjuəl] übrigbleibend; ~**e** ['rezidju:] Rest *m*; Rückstand *m*; ✗✗ Reinnachlaß *m*.

resign [ri'zain] *v/t.* aufgeben; *Amt* niederlegen; überlassen; ~ *o.s. to* sich ergeben in (*acc.*), sich abfinden mit; *v/i.* zurücktreten; ~**ation** [re-zig'neiʃən] Rücktritt *m*; Ergebung *f*; Entlassungsgesuch *n*; ~**ed** ☐ ergeben, resigniert.

resilien|ce [ri'ziliəns] Elastizität *f*; ~**t** [~nt] elastisch, *fig.* spannkräftig.

resin ['rezin] 1. Harz *n*; 2. harzen.

resist [ri'zist] widerstehen (*dat.*); sich widersetzen (*dat.*); ~**ance** [~təns] Widerstand *m*; *attr.* Widerstands...; *line of least* ~ Weg *m* des geringsten Widerstands; ~**ant** [~nt] widerstehend; widerstandsfähig.

resolut|e ☐ ['rezəlu:t] entschlossen; ~**ion** [rezə'lu:ʃən] (Auf)Lösung *f*;

Entschluß *m*; Entschlossenheit *f*; Resolution *f*.

resolve [ri'zɔlv] **1.** *v/t.* auflösen; *fig.* lösen; *Zweifel etc.* beheben; entscheiden; *v/i. a.* ~ *o.s.* sich auflösen; beschließen; ~ (*up*)*on* sich entschließen zu; **2.** Entschluß *m*; *Am.* Beschluß *m*; ~d □ entschlossen.

resonan|ce ['reznəns] Resonanz *f*; ~t □ [~nt] nach-, widerhallend.

resort [ri'zɔːt] **1.** Zuflucht *f*; Besuch *m*; Aufenthalt(sort) *m*; Erholungsort *m*; *health* ~ Kurort *m*; *seaside* ~ Seebad *n*; *summer* ~ Sommerfrische *f*; **2.** ~ *to* oft besuchen; seine Zuflucht nehmen zu. [sen).\
resound [ri'zaund] widerhallen(las-)\
resource [ri'sɔːs] natürlicher Reichtum; Hilfsquelle *f*, -mittel *n*, Zuflucht *f*; Findigkeit *f*; Zeitvertreib *m*, Entspannung *f*; ~**ful** □ [~sful] findig.

respect [ris'pekt] **1.** Rücksicht *f* (*to, of* auf *acc.*); Beziehung *f*; Achtung *f*; ~*s pl.* Empfehlungen *f*/*pl.*; **2.** *v/t.* (hoch)achten; Rücksicht nehmen auf (*acc.*); betreffen; ~**able** □ [~təbl] achtbar; ansehnlich; anständig; *bsd.* ♀ solid; ~**ful** □ [~tful] ehrerbietig; *may* ~ *yours* ~ly hochachtungsvoll; ~**ing** [~tiŋ] hinsichtlich (*gen.*); ~**ive** □ [~tiv] jeweilig; *we went to our* ~ *places* wir gingen jeder an seinen Platz; ~**ively** [~vli] beziehungsweise; je.

respirat|ion [respə'reiʃən] Atmen *n*; Atemzug *m*; ~**or** [r'respəreitə] Atemfilter *m*; ♂ Atemgerät *n*; Gasmaske *f*.

respire [ris'paiə] atmen; aufatmen.

respite ['respait] Frist *f*; Stundung *f*.

resplendent □ [ris'plendənt] glänzend.

respond [ris'pɔnd] antworten, erwidern; ~ *to* reagieren auf (*acc.*).

response [ris'pɔns] Antwort *f*, Erwiderung *f*; *fig.* Reaktion *f*.

responsi|bility [risponsə'biliti] Verantwortlichkeit *f*; Verantwortung *f*; ♀ Zahlungsfähigkeit *f*; ~**ble** [ris-'pɔnsəbl] verantwortlich; verantwortungsvoll; ♀ zahlungsfähig.

rest [rest] **1.** Rest *m*; Ruhe *f*; Rast *f*; Schlaf *m*; *fig.* Tod *m*; Stütze *f*; Pause *f*; **2.** *v/i.* ruhen; rasten; schlafen; (sich) lehnen, sich stützen (*on* auf *acc.*); ~ (*up*)*on fig.* beruhen auf (*dat.*); *in e-m Zustand* bleiben; *v/t.* (aus)ruhen lassen; stützen.

restaurant ['restərɔːŋ, ~rɔnt] Gaststätte *f*.

rest-cure ♂ ['restkjuə] Liegekur *f*.

restful ['restful] ruhig, geruhsam.

resting-place ['restiŋpleis] Ruheplatz *m*, -stätte *f*.

restitution [resti'tjuːʃən] Wiederherstellung *f*; Rückerstattung *f*.

restive □ ['restiv] widerspenstig.

restless ['restlis] ruhelos; rastlos; unruhig; ~**ness** [~snis] Ruhelosigkeit *f*; Rastlosigkeit *f*; Unruhe *f*.

restorat|ion [restə'reiʃən] Wiederherstellung *f*; Wiedereinsetzung *f*; Rekonstruktion *f*, Nachbildung *f*; ~**ive** [ris'tɔrətiv] **1.** stärkend; **2.** Stärkungsmittel *n*.

restore [ris'tɔː] wiederherstellen; wiedereinsetzen (*to in acc.*); wiedergeben; ~ *to health* wieder gesund machen.

restrain [ris'trein] zurückhalten (*from* von); in Schranken halten; unterdrücken; einsperren; ~**t** [~nt] Zurückhaltung *f*; Beschränkung *f*, Zwang *m*; Zwangshaft *f*.

restrict [ris'trikt] be-, einschränken; ~**ion** [~kʃən] Be-, Einschränkung *f*; Vorbehalt *m*.

result [ri'zʌlt] **1.** Ergebnis *n*, Folge *f*, Resultat *n*; **2.** folgen, sich ergeben (*from* aus); ~ *in* hinauslaufen auf (*acc.*), zur Folge haben.

resum|e [ri'zjuːm] wiedernehmen, -erlangen; wiederaufnehmen; zs.-fassen; ~**ption** [ri'zʌmpʃən] Zurücknahme *f*; Wiederaufnahme *f*.

resurgent [ri'səːdʒənt] sich wiedererhebend, wieder aufkommend.

resurrection [rezə'rekʃən] Wiederaufleben *n*; ♀ *eccl.* (Wieder)Auferstehung *f*.

resuscitate [ri'sʌsiteit] wiedererwecken, wiederbeleben.

retail 1. ['riːteil] Einzelhandel *m*; *by* ~ im Einzelverkauf; **2.** [~] Einzelhandels..., Detail...; **3.** [riː'teil] im kleinen verkaufen; ~**er** [~lə] Einzelhändler(in).

retain [ri'tein] behalten (*a. fig.*); zurück-, festhalten; beibehalten; *Anwalt* nehmen.

retaliat|e [ri'tælieit] *v/t. Unrecht* vergelten; *v/i.* sich rächen; ~**ion** [ritæli'eiʃən] Vergeltung *f*.

retard [ri'tɑːd] verzögern; aufhalten; verspäten.

retention [ri'tenʃən] Zurück-, Behalten *n*; Beibehaltung *f*.

reticent ['retisənt] verschwiegen; schweigsam; zurückhaltend.

retinue ['retinjuː] Gefolge *n*.

retir|e [ri'taiə] *v/t.* zurückziehen; pensionieren; *v/i.* sich zurückziehen; zurück-, abtreten; in den Ruhestand treten; ~**ed** □ zurückgezogen; im Ruhestand (lebend); entlegen; ~ *pay* Pension *f*; ~**ement** [~əmənt] Sichzurückziehen *n*; Aus-, Rücktritt *m*; Ruhestand *m*; Zurückgezogenheit *f*; ~**ing** [~riŋ] zurückhaltend; schüchtern; ~ *pension* Ruhegehalt *n*.

retort [ri'tɔːt] **1.** Erwiderung *f*; ⚗ Retorte *f*; **2.** erwidern.

retouch ['riː'tʌtʃ] *et.* überarbeiten; *phot.* retuschieren.

retrace [ri'treis] zurückverfolgen; ~ one's steps zurückgehen.

retract [ri'trækt] (sich) zurückziehen; ⊕ einziehen; widerrufen.

retread ['ri:tred] **1.** Reifen runderneuern; **2.** runderneuerter Reifen.

retreat [ri'tri:t] **1.** Rückzug m; Zurückgezogenheit f; Zuflucht(sort m) f; ✕ Zapfenstreich m; beat a ~ fig. es aufgeben; **2.** sich zurückziehen; fig. zurücktreten.

retrench [ri'trentʃ] (sich) einschränken; kürzen; Wort etc. streichen; ✕ verschanzen.

retribution [retri'bju:ʃən] Vergeltung f.

retrieve [ri'tri:v] wiederbekommen; wiederherstellen; wiedergutmachen; hunt. apportieren.

retro|... ['retrou] (zu)rück...; **~active** [retrou'æktiv] rückwirkend; **~grade** ['retrougreid] **1.** rückläufig; **2.** zurückgehen; **~gression** [retrou'greʃən] Rück-, Niedergang m; **~spect** ['retrouspekt] Rückblick m; **~spective** [retrou'spektiv] zurückblickend; rückwirkend.

retry ✕ ['ri:'trai] Prozeß wiederaufnehmen.

return [ri'tə:n] **1.** Rückkehr f; Wiederkehr f; parl. Wiederwahl f; oft ~s pl. ✝ Gewinn m, Ertrag m; Umsatz m; ✝ Rückfall m; Rückgabe f, Rückzahlung f; Vergeltung f; Erwiderung f; Gegenleistung f; Dank m; amtlicher Bericht; Wahlergebnis n; Steuererklärung f; ✝ Rückfahrkarte f; attr. Rück...; many happy ~s of the day herzliche Glückwünsche zum Geburtstag; in ~ dafür; als Ersatz (for für); by ~ (of post) postwendend; ~ ticket Rückfahrkarte f; **2.** v/i. zurückkehren; wiederkehren; v/t. zurückgeben; zurücktun; zurückzahlen; zurücksenden; Dank abstatten; erwidern; berichten, angeben; parl. wählen; Gewinn abwerfen.

reunification pol. ['ri:ju:nifi'keiʃən] Wiedervereinigung f.

reunion ['ri:'ju:njən] Wiedervereinigung f; Treffen n, Zs.-kunft f.

reval|**orization** ✝ [ri:vælərai'zeiʃən] Aufwertung f; **~uation** [~lju-'eiʃən] Neubewertung f.

revamp ⊕ ['ri:'væmp] vorschuhen; Am. F aufmöbeln; erneuern.

reveal [ri'vi:l] enthüllen; offenbaren; **~ing** [~liŋ] aufschlußreich.

revel ['revl] **1.** Lustbarkeit f; Gelage n; **2.** ausgelassen sein; schwelgen; zechen.

revelation [revi'leiʃən] Enthüllung f; Offenbarung f.

revel|**(l)er** ['revlə] Feiernde(r m) f; Zecher m; **~ry** [~lri] Gelage n; Lustbarkeit f, Rummel m; Orgie f.

revenge [ri'vendʒ] **1.** Rache f;

Sport: Revanche f; **2.** rächen; **~ful** □ [~dʒful] rachsüchtig; **~r** [~dʒə] Rächer(in).

revenue ['revinju:] Einkommen n; **~s** pl. Einkünfte pl.; ~ board, ~ office Finanzamt n.

reverberate [ri'və:bəreit] zurückwerfen; zurückstrahlen; widerhallen.

revere [ri'viə] (ver)ehren; **~nce** ['revərəns] **1.** Verehrung f; Ehrfurcht f; **2.** (ver)ehren; **~nd** [~nd] **1.** ehrwürdig; **2.** Geistliche(r) m.

reverent(ial) □ ['revərənt, revə'renʃəl] ehrerbietig, ehrfurchtsvoll.

reverie ['revəri] Träumerei f.

revers|**al** [ri'və:səl] Umkehrung f; Umschwung m; ✝ Umstoßung f; ⊕ Umsteuerung f; **~e** [~ə:s] **1.** Gegenteil n; Kehrseite f; Rückschlag m; **2.** umgekehrt; Rück(wärts)...; ~ (gear) mot Rückwärtsgang m; ~ side linke Stoff-Seite; **3.** umkehren, umdrehen; Urteil umstoßen; ⊕ umsteuern; **~ion** [~ə:ʃən] Umkehrung f; Rückkehr f; ✝ Heimfall m; biol. Ruckartung f.

revert [ri'və:t] um-, zurückkehren; biol. zurückkarten; Blick wenden.

review [ri'vju:] **1.** Nachprüfung f; ✕ Revision f; ✕ Parade f; Rückblick m; Überblick m; Rezension f; Zeitschrift f; pass s.th. in ~ et. Revue passieren lassen; **2.** (über-, nach)prüfen; zurückblicken auf (acc.); überblicken; ✕, ♣ besichtigen; rezensieren; **~er** [~u(:)ə] Rezensent m. [fen.]

revile [ri'vail] schmähen, beschimp-]

revis|**e** [ri'vaiz] überarbeiten, durchsehen, revidieren; **~ion** [ri'viʒən] Revision f; Überarbeitung f.

reviv|**al** [ri'vaivəl] Wiederbelebung f; Wiederaufleben n, Wiederaufblühen n; Erneuerung f; fig. Erweckung f; **~e** [~aiv] wiederbeleben; wieder aufleben (lassen); erneuern; wieder aufblühen.

revocation [revə'keiʃən] Widerruf m; Aufhebung f.

revoke [ri'vouk] v/t. widerrufen; v/i. Karten nicht bedienen.

revolt [ri'voult] **1.** Revolte f, Empörung f, Aufruhr m; **2.** v/i. sich empören; abfallen; v/t. fig. abstoßen.

revolution [revə'lu:ʃən] Umwälzung f, Umdrehung f; pol Revolution f; **~ary** [~ʃnəri] **1.** revolutionär; **2.** a. **~ist** [~ʃnist] Revolutionär(in); **~ize** [~ʃnaiz] aufwiegeln; umgestalten.

revolve [ri'vɔlv] v/i. sich drehen (about, round um); v/t. umdrehen; fig. erwägen; **~ing** [~viŋ] sich drehend; Dreh...

revue thea. [ri'vju:] Revue f; Kabarett n.

revulsion [ri'vʌlʃən] fig. Umschwung m; ✕ Ableitung f.

reward [ri'wɔːd] **1.** Belohnung *f*; Vergeltung *f*; **2.** belohnen; vergelten.

rewrite ['riː'rait] [*irr. (write)*] neu (*od.* um)schreiben.

rhapsody ['ræpsədi] Rhapsodie *f*; *fig.* Schwärmerei *f*; Wortschwall *m*.

rhetoric ['retərik] Rhetorik *f*.

rheumatism ♣ ['ruːmətizəm] Rheumatismus *m*.

rhubarb ♣ ['ruːbɑːb] Rhabarber *m*.

rhyme [raim] **1.** Reim *m* (to auf *acc.*); Vers *m*; *without ~ or reason* ohne Sinn u. Verstand; **2.** (sich) reimen.

rhythm ['riðəm] Rhythmus *m*; **~ic(al** □) ['riðmik(əl)] rhythmisch.

Rialto *Am.* [ri'æltou] Theaterviertel *n e-r Stadt, bsd. in New York*.

rib [rib] **1.** Rippe *f*; **2.** rippen; *sl.* aufziehen, necken.

ribald ['ribəld] lästerlich; unflätig; **~ry** [~dri] Zoten *f/pl.*; derbe Späße *m/pl.*

ribbon ['ribən] Band *n*; Streifen *m*; **~s** *pl.* Fetzen *m/pl.*; Zügel *m/pl.*; *~ building, ~ development* Reihenbau *m*.

rice [rais] Reis *m*.

rich □ [ritʃ] reich (*in an dat.*); reichlich; prächtig, kostbar; ergiebig, fruchtbar; voll (*Ton*); schwer (*Speise, Wein, Duft*); satt (*Farbe*); **~es** ['ritʃiz] *pl.* Reichtum *m*, Reichtümer *m/pl.*; **~ness** [~ʃnis] Reichtum *m*; Fülle *f*.

rick ⚶ [rik] (Heu)Schober *m*.

ricket|s ['rikits] *sg. od. pl.* Rachitis *f*; **~y** [~ti] rachitisch; wack(e)lig (*Möbel*).

rid [rid] [*irr.*] befreien, frei machen (*of von*); *get ~ of* loswerden.

ridden ['ridn] **1.** *p.p. von* ride 2; **2.** *in Zssgn*: bedrückt *od.* geplagt von ...

riddle ['ridl] **1.** Rätsel *n*; grobes Sieb; **2.** sieben; durchlöchern.

ride [raid] **1.** Ritt *m*; Fahrt *f*; Reitweg *m*; **2.** [*irr.*] *v/i.* reiten; rittlings sitzen; fahren; treiben; schweben; liegen; *v/t.* Pferd *etc.* reiten; *Land* durchreiten; **~r** ['raidə] Reiter(in); Fahrende(r *m*) *f*.

ridge [ridʒ] **1.** (Gebirgs)Kamm *m*, Grat *m*; ♣ First *m*; ⚶ Rain *m*; **2.** (sich) furchen.

ridicul|e ['ridikjuːl] **1.** Hohn *m*, Spott *m*; **2.** lächerlich machen; **~ous** □ [ri'dikjuləs] lächerlich.

riding ['raidiŋ] Reiten *n*; *attr.* Reit... [~ with voll von.]

rife □ [raif] häufig; vorherrschend;}

riff-raff ['rifræf] Gesindel *n*.

rifle ['raifl] **1.** Gewehr *n*; **2.** (aus-) plündern; **~man** ♣ Schütze *m*.

rift [rift] Riß *m*, Sprung *m*; Spalte *f*.

rig¹ [rig] **1.** Markt *etc.* manipulieren; **2.** Schwindelmanöver *n*.

rig² [~] **1.** ♣ Takelung *f*; F Aufma-

chung *f*; **2.** auftakeln; **~ s.o. out** j-n versorgen *od.* ausrüsten; j-n herausputzen *od.* herrichten; **~ging** ♣ ['rigiŋ] Takelage *f*.

right [rait] **1.** □ recht; richtig; recht (*Ggs. left*); be *~* recht haben; *all ~!* alles in Ordnung!; ganz recht!; *put od. set ~* in Ordnung bringen; berichtigen; **2.** *adv.* recht, richtig; gerade; direkt; ganz (und gar); *~ away* sogleich; *~ on* geradeaus; **3.** Recht *n*; Rechte *f*, rechte Seite *od.* Hand; *the ~s and wrongs* der wahre Sachverhalt; *by ~ of* auf Grund (*gen.*); *on od. to the ~* rechts; *~ of way* Wegerecht *n*; Vorfahrt(srecht *n*) *f*; **4.** *j-m* Recht verschaffen; *et.* in Ordnung bringen; ♣ (sich) aufrichten; **~-down** ['rait'daun] regelrecht; ausgemacht; wirklich; **~eous** □ ['raitʃəs] rechtschaffen; **~ful** □ ['raitful] recht(mäßig); gerecht.

rigid □ ['ridʒid] starr; *fig. a.* streng, hart; **~ity** [ri'dʒiditi] Starrheit *f*; Strenge *f*, Härte *f*.

rigmarole ['rigməroul] Geschwätz *n*.

rigor ♣ ['raigɔː] Fieberfrost *m*.

rigo(u)r ['rigə] Strenge *f*, Härte *f*.

rigorous □ ['rigərəs] streng, rigoros.

rim [rim] **1.** Felge *f*; Radkranz *m*; Rand *m*; **2.** rändern; einfassen.

rime [raim] Reim *m*; Rauhreif *m*.

rind [raind] Rinde *f*, Schale *f*; *Speck-*Schwarte *f*.

ring¹ [riŋ] **1.** Klang *m*; Geläut(e) *n*; Klingeln *n*; Rufzeichen *n*; Anruf *m*; *give s.o. a ~* j-n anrufen; **2.** [*irr.*] läuten; klingen (lassen); erschallen (with *mit*); *~ again* widerhallen; *~ off teleph.* das Gespräch beenden; *~ the bell* klingeln; *~ s.o. up* j-n *od.* bei j-m anrufen.

ring² [~] **1.** Ring *m*; Kreis *m*; **2.** beringen; *mst ~ in, ~ round, ~ about* umringen; **~leader** ['riŋliːdə] Rädelsführer *m*; **~let** [~lit] (Ringel)Locke *f*.

rink [riŋk] Eisbahn *f*; Rollschuhbahn *f*.

rinse [rins] *oft ~ out* (aus)spülen.

riot ['raiət] **1.** Tumult *m*; Aufruhr *m*; Orgie *f* (*a. fig.*); *run ~* durchgehen; (sich aus)toben; **2.** Krawall machen, im Aufruhr sein; toben; schwelgen; **~er** [~tə] Aufrührer(in); Randalierer *m*; **~ous** □ [~təs] aufrührerisch; lärmend; liederlich (*Leben*).

rip [rip] **1.** Riß *m*; **2.** (auf)trennen; (auf-, zer)reißen; (dahin)sausen.

ripe □ [raip] reif; **~n** ['raipən] reifen; **~ness** ['raipnis] Reife *f*.

ripple ['ripl] **1.** kleine Welle; Kräuselung *f*; Geriesel *n*; **2.** (sich) kräuseln; rieseln.

rise [raiz] **1.** (An-, Auf)Steigen *n*;

Anschwellen *n*; (Preis-, Gehalts-) Erhöhung *f*; *fig.* Aufstieg *m*; Steigung *f*; Anhöhe *f*; Ursprung *m*; *take (one's)* ~ entstehen; entspringen; 2. [*irr.*] sich erheben, aufstehen; die Sitzung schließen; steigen; aufsteigen (*a. fig.*); auferstehen; aufgehen (*Sonne, Samen*); anschwellen; sich empören; entspringen (*Fluß*); ~ *to* sich *e-r* Lage gewachsen zeigen; ~*n* ['rizn] *p.p. von* rise 2; ~*r* ['raizə]: early ~ Frühaufsteher(in).

rising ['raiziŋ] 1. (Auf)Steigen *n*; Steigung *f*; *ast.* Aufgang *m*; Aufstand *m*; 2. heranwachsend (*Generation*).

risk [risk] 1. Gefahr *f*, Wagnis *n*; ✝ Risiko *n*; *run the* ~ Gefahr laufen; 2. wagen, riskieren; ~*y* ['riski] gefährlich, gewagt.

rit|e [rait] Ritus *m*, Brauch *m*; ~*ual* ['ritjuəl] 1. rituell; 2. Ritual *n*.

rival ['raivəl] 1. Nebenbuhler(in); Rivale *m*; 2. rivalisierend; ✝ Konkurrenz...; 3. wetteifern (mit); ~*ry* [~lri] Rivalität *f*; Wetteifer *m*.

rive [raiv] [*irr.*] (sich) spalten; ~*n* ['rivən] *p.p. von* rive.

river ['rivə] Fluß *m*; Strom *m* (*a. fig.*); ~*side* 1. Flußufer *n*; 2. am Wasser (gelegen).

rivet ['rivit] 1. ⊕ Niet(e *f*) *m*; 2. (ver)nieten; *fig.* heften (*to an acc.*; *on, upon auf acc.*); fesseln.

rivulet ['rivjulit] Bach *m*, Flüßchen *n*.

road [roud] Straße *f* (*a. fig.*), Weg *m*; *Am.* = *railroad*; *mst* ~*s pl.* ⚓ Reede *f*; ~*stead* ⚓ ['roudsted] Reede *f*; ~*ster* [~tə] Roadster *m*, offener Sportwagen; ~*way* Fahrbahn *f*.

roam [roum] *v/i.* umherstreifen, wandern; *v/t.* durchstreifen.

roar [rɔ:] 1. brüllen; brausen, tosen, donnern; 2. Gebrüll *n*; Brausen *n*; Krachen *n*, Getöse *n*; brüllendes Gelächter.

roast [roust] 1. rösten, braten; 2. geröstet; gebraten; ~ *meat* Braten *m*.

rob [rɔb] (be)rauben; ~*ber* ['rɔbə] Räuber *m*; ~*bery* [~əri] Raub (-überfall) *m*; Raub *m*.

robe [roub] (Amts)Robe *f*, Talar *m*; (Staats)Kleid *n*; *Am.* Morgenrock *m*.

robin *orn.* ['rɔbin] Rotkehlchen *n*.

robust □ [rə'bʌst] robust, kräftig.

rock [rɔk] 1. Felsen *m*; Klippe *f*; Gestein *n*; Zuckerstange *f*; ~ *crystal* Bergkristall *m*; 2. schaukeln; (ein)wiegen.

rocker ['rɔkə] Kufe *f*; *Am.* Schaukelstuhl *m*; Rocker *m*, Halbstarke(r) *m*.

rocket ['rɔkit] Rakete *f*; *attr.* Ra-

keten...; ~*powered* mit Raketenantrieb; ~*ry* [~tri] Raketentechnik *f*.

rocking-chair ['rɔkiŋtʃeə] Schaukelstuhl *m*.

rocky ['rɔki] felsig; Felsen...

rod [rɔd] Rute *f*; Stab *m*; ⊕ Stange *f*; Meßrute *f* (5½ *yards*); *Am. sl.* Pistole *f*.

rode [roud] *pret. von* ride 2.

rodent ['roudənt] Nagetier *n*.

rodeo *Am.* [rou'deiou] Rodeo *n*; Zusammentreiben *n*; Cowboyturnier *n*.

roe[1] [rou] Reh *n*.

roe[2] *ichth.* [~] *a.* hard ~ Rogen *m*; soft ~ Milch *f*.

rogu|e [roug] Schurke *m*; Schelm *m*; ~*ish* ['rougiʃ] schurkisch; schelmisch.

roister ['rɔistə] krakeelen.

role, rôle *thea.* [roul] Rolle *f* (*a. fig.*).

roll [roul] 1. Rolle *f*; ⊕ Walze *f*; Brötchen *n*, Semmel *f*; Verzeichnis *n*; Urkunde *f*; (Donner)Rollen *n*; (Trommel)Wirbel *m*; ⚓ Schlingern *n*; 2. *v/t.* rollen; wälzen; walzen; *Zigarette* drehen; ~ *up* zs.-rollen; einwickeln; *v/i.* rollen; sich wälzen; wirbeln (*Trommel*); ⚓ schlingern; ~*call* ⚔ ['roulkɔ:l] Appell *m*; ~*er* ['roulə] Rolle *f*, Walze *f*; Sturzwelle *f*; ~ *coaster Am.* Achterbahn *f*; ~ *skate* Rollschuh *m*.

rol|king ['rɔlikiŋ] übermütig.

rolling ['rouliŋ] rollend; Roll..., Walz...; ~ *mill* ⊕ Walzwerk *n*.

Roman ['roumən] 1. römisch; 2. Römer(in); *mst* ♀ *typ.* Antiqua *f*.

romance[1] [rə'mæns] 1. (Ritter-, Vers)Roman *m*; Abenteuer-, Liebesroman *m*; Romanze *f* (*a. fig.*); *fig.* Märchen *n*; Romantik *f*; 2. *fig.* aufschneiden.

Romance[2] *ling.* [~]: ~ *languages* romanische Sprachen *f/pl.*

romancer [rə'mænsə] Romanschreiber(in); Aufschneider(in).

Romanesque [roumə'nesk] 1. romanisch; 2. romanischer Baustil.

romantic [rə'mæntik] (~*ally*) romantisch; ~*ism* [~isizəm] Romantik *f*; ~*ist* [~ist] Romantiker(in).

romp [rɔmp] 1. Range *f*, Wildfang *m*; Balgerei *f*; 2. sich balgen, toben; ~*er(s)* ['rɔmpə(z)] Spielanzug *m*.

rood [ru:d] Kruzifix *n*; Viertelmorgen *m* (10,117 *Ar*).

roof [ru:f] 1. Dach *n*; ~ *of the mouth* Gaumen *m*; 2. *a.* ~ *over* überdachen; ~*ing* ['ru:fiŋ] 1. Bedachung *f*; 2. Dach...; ~ *felt* Dachpappe *f*.

rook [ruk] 1. *Schach:* Turm *m*; *fig.* Gauner *m*; *orn.* Saatkrähe *f*; 2. betrügen.

room [rum] 1. Raum *m*; Platz *m*; Zimmer *n*; Möglichkeit *f*; ~*s pl.* Wohnung *f*; *in my* ~ an meiner Stelle; 2. *Am.* wohnen; ~*er* ['rumə] *bsd. Am.* Untermieter(in); ~ing-house ['ruminhaus] *bsd. Am.* Miets-, Logierhaus *n*; ~mate Stubenkamerad *m*; ~y □ ['rumi] geräumig.

roost [ru:st] **1.** Schlafplatz *m e-s Vogels*; Hühnerstange *f*; Hühnerstall *m*; **2.** sich (zum Schlaf) niederhocken; *fig.* übernachten; ~er ['ru:stə] Haushahn *m*.

root [ru:t] **1.** Wurzel *f*; **2.** (ein)wurzeln; (auf)wühlen; ~ for *Am. sl.* Stimmung machen für; ~ out ausrotten; ~ out *od. up* ausgraben; ~ed ['ru:tid] eingewurzelt; ~er *Am. sl.* ['ru:tə] Fanatiker *m für et.*

rope [roup] **1.** Tau *n*, Seil *n*; Strick *m*; Schnur *f Perlen etc.*; *be at the end of one's* ~ F mit s-m Latein zu Ende sein; *know the* ~s sich auskennen; *fig.* mit e-m Seil befestigen *od.* (*mst* ~ *in od.* off *od.* out) absperren; anseilen; ~way ['roupwei] Seilbahn *f*.

ropy ['roupi] klebrig, zähflüssig.

rosary *eccl.* ['rouzəri] Rosenkranz *m*.

rose¹ [rouz] ⚘ Rose *f*; (Gießkannen)Brause *f*; Rosenrot *n*.

rose² [~] *pret. von* rise 2.

rosebud ['rouzbʌd] Rosenknospe *f*; *Am.* hübsches Mädchen; Debütantin *f*.

rosin ['rozin] (Geigen)Harz *n*.

rostrum ['rostrəm] Rednertribüne *f*.

rosy □ ['rouzi] rosig.

rot [rot] **1.** Fäulnis *f*; *sl.* Quatsch *m*; **2.** *v/t.* faulen lassen; Quatsch machen mit *j-m*; *v/i.* verfaulen, vermodern.

rota|ry ['routəri] drehend; Rotations...; ~te [rou'teit] (sich) drehen, (ab)wechseln; ~tion [~'eiʃən] Umdrehung *f*; Kreislauf *m*; Abwechs(e)lung *f*; ~tory ['routətəri] *s.* rotary; abwechselnd.

rote [rout]: *by* ~ auswendig.

rotten □ ['rotn] verfault, faul(ig); mod(e)rig; morsch (*alle a. fig.*); *sl.* saumäßig, dreckig.

rotund □ [rou'tʌnd] rund; voll (*Stimme*); hochtrabend.

rouge [ru:ʒ] **1.** Rouge *n*; Silberputzmittel *n*; **2.** Rouge auflegen (auf *acc.*).

rough [rʌf] **1.** □ rauh; roh; grob; *fig.* ungehobelt; ungefähr (*Schätzung*); ~ *and ready* grob (gearbeitet); Not..., Behelfs...; ~ *copy* roher Entwurf; **2.** Rauhe *n*, Grobe *n*; Lümmel *m*; **3.** (an-, auf)rauhen; ~ *it* sich mühsam durchschlagen; ~cast ['rʌfkɑ:st] **1.** ⊕ Rohputz *m*; **2.** unfertig; **3.** ⊕ roh verputzen; roh entwerfen; ~en ['rʌfən] rauh machen *od.* werden; ~neck *Am. sl.* Rabauke *m*; ~ness [~nis] Rauheit *f*; Roheit *f*; Grobheit *f*; ~shod: *ride* ~ *over* rücksichtslos behandeln.

round [raund] **1.** □ rund; voll (*Stimme etc.*); flott (*Gangart*); abgerundet (*Stil*); unverblümt; ~ *game* Gesellschaftsspiel *n*; ~ *trip* Rundreise *f*; **2.** *adv.* rund-, ringsum(her); *a.* ~ *about* in der Runde; *all* ~ ringsum; *fig.* ohne Unterschied; *all the year* ~ das ganze Jahr hindurch; **3.** *prp.* um ... herum; **4.** Rund *n*, Kreis *m*; Runde *f*; Kreislauf *m*; (Leiter)Sprosse *f*; Rundgesang *m*; *Lach- etc.*Salve *f*; *100* ~*s* ✕ 100 Schuß; **5.** *v/t.* runden; herumgehen *od.* herumfahren um; ~ *off* abrunden; ~ *up* einkreisen; *v/i.* sich runden; sich umdrehen; ~ *about* ['raundəbaut] **1.** umschweifig; **2.** Umweg *m*; Karussell *n*; Kreisverkehr *m*; ~ish [~diʃ] rundlich; ~up Einkreisung *f*; Razzia *f*.

rous|e [rauz] *v/t.* wecken, ermuntern; aufjagen; (auf)reizen; ~ *o.s.* sich aufraffen; *v/i.* aufwachen; ~ing ['rauziŋ] brausend (*Beifall etc.*).

roustabout *Am.* ['raustəbaut] ungelernter (*mst* Hafen)Arbeiter.

rout [raut] **1.** Rotte *f*; wilde Flucht; *a. put to* ~ vernichtend schlagen; **2.** aufwühlen.

route [ru:t, ✕ *a.* raut] Weg *m*; ✕ Marschroute *f*.

routine [ru:'ti:n] **1.** Routine *f*; **2.** üblich; Routine...

rove [rouv] umherstreifen, umherwandern.

row¹ [rou] **1.** Reihe *f*; Ruderfahrt *f*; **2.** rudern.

row² F [rau] **1.** Spektakel *m*; Krach *m*; Schlägerei *f*; **2.** ausschimpfen.

row-boat ['roubout] Ruderboot *n*.

rower ['rouə] Ruder|er *m*, -in *f*.

royal □ ['rɔiəl] königlich; prächtig; ~ty [~lti] Königtum *n*, -reich *n*; Königswürde *f*; königliche Persönlichkeit; Tantieme *f*.

rub [rʌb] **1.** Reiben *n*; Schwierigkeit *f*; *fig.* Stichelei *f*; Unannehmlichkeit *f*; **2.** *v/t.* reiben; (ab)wischen; (wund)scheuern; schleifen; ~ *down* abreiben; ~ *in* einreiben; *fig.* betonen; ~ *off* abreiben; ~ *out* auslöschen; ~ *up* auffrischen; verreiben; *v/i.* sich reiben; *fig.* ~ *along od. on od.* through sich durchschlagen.

rubber ['rʌbə] **1.** Gummi *m*, *n*; Radiergummi *m*; Masseur *m*; Wischtuch *n*; *Whist:* Robber *m*; ~*s pl. Am.* Gummischuhe *m/pl.*; **2.** Gummi...; ~ *check Am. sl.* geplatzter Scheck; ~neck *Am. sl.* **1.** Gaffer(in); **2.** sich den Hals verrenken; mithören; ~ *stamp* Gummistempel *m*; *Am.* F *fig.* Nachbeter *m*; ~stamp automatisch gutheißen.

rubbish ['rʌbiʃ] Schutt *m*; Abfall *m*; Kehricht *m*; *fig.* Schund *m*; Unsinn *m*.

rubble ['rʌbl] Schutt *m*.

rube *Am.sl.* [ru:b] Bauernlümmel *m.*

ruby ['ru:bi] Rubin(rot *n*) *m.*

rucksack ['ruksæk] Rucksack *m.*

rudder ['rʌdə] ♣ (Steuer)Ruder *n*; ✈ Seitenruder *n.*

rudd|iness ['rʌdinis] Röte *f*; ~y ['rʌdi] rot; rotbäckig.

rude □ [ru:d] unhöflich; unanständig; heftig, unsanft; ungebildet; einfach, kunstlos; robust; roh.

rudiment *biol.* ['ru:dimənt] Ansatz *m*; ~s *pl.* Anfangsgründe *m/pl.*

rueful □ ['ru:ful] reuig; traurig.

ruff [rʌf] Halskrause *f.*

ruffian ['rʌfjən] Rohling *m*; Raufbold *m*; Schurke *m.*

ruffle ['rʌfl] 1. Krause *f*, Rüsche *f*; Kräuseln *n*; *fig.* Unruhe *f*; 2. kräuseln; zerdrücken; zerknüllen; *fig.* aus der Ruhe bringen; stören.

rug [rʌg] (Reise-, Woll)Decke *f*; Vorleger *m*, Brücke *f*; ~ged □ ['rʌgid] rauh (*a. fig.*); uneben; gefurcht.

ruin [ruin] 1. Ruin *m*, Zs.-bruch *m*; Untergang *m*; *mst* ~s *pl.* Ruine(n *pl.*) *f*, Trümmer *pl.*; 2. ruinieren; zugrunde richten; zerstören; verderben; ~ous □ ['ruinəs] ruinenhaft, verfallen; verderblich, ruinös.

rul|e [ru:l] 1. Regel *f*; Vorschrift *f*; Ordnung *f*; Satzung *f*; Herrschaft *f*; Lineal *n*; *as a* ~ in der Regel; ~(s) *of the road* Straßenverkehrsordnung *f*; 2. *v/t.* regeln; leiten; beherrschen; verfügen; liniieren; ~ *out* ausschließen; *v/i.* herrschen; ~er ['ru:lə] Herrscher(in); Lineal *n.*

rum [rʌm] Rum *m*; *Am.* Alkohol *m.*

Rumanian [ru(:)'meinjən] 1. rumänisch; 2. Rumän|e *m*, -in *f*; Rumänisch *n.*

rumble ['rʌmbl] 1. Rumpeln *n*; *a.* ~-seat *Am. mot.* Notsitz *m*; *Am.* F Fehde *f* zwischen Gangsterbanden; 2. rumpeln, rasseln; grollen (*Donner*).

rumina|nt ['ru:minənt] 1. wiederkäuend; 2. Wiederkäuer *m*; ~te [~neit] wiederkäuen; *fig.* nachsinnen.

rummage ['rʌmidʒ] 1. Durchsuchung *f*; Ramsch *m*, Restwaren *f/pl.*; 2. *v/t.* durchsuchen, durchstöbern, durchwühlen; *v/i.* wühlen.

rumo(u)r ['ru:mə] 1. Gerücht *n*; 2. (als Gerücht) verbreiten; *it is* ~ed *es geht das Gerücht.* [*m.*]

rump *anat.* [rʌmp] Steiß *m*; Rumpf

rumple ['rʌmpl] zerknittern; zerren, (zer)zausen.

rum-runner *Am.* ['rʌmrʌnə] Alkoholschmuggler *m.*

run [rʌn] 1. [*irr.*] *v/i. allg.* laufen; rennen (*Mensch, Tier*); eilen; zerlaufen (*Farbe etc.*); umgehen (*Gerücht etc.*); lauten (*Text*); gehen (*Melodie*); ✈ sich stellen (*Preis*); ~ *across s.o.* j-m in die Arme laufen;

~ *away* davonlaufen; ~ *down* ablaufen (*Uhr etc.*); *fig.* herunterkommen; ~ *dry* aus-, vertrocknen; ~ *for parl.* kandidieren für; ~ *into* geraten in (*acc.*); werden zu; *j-m* in die Arme laufen; ~ *low* zur Neige gehen; ~ *mad* verrückt werden; ~ *off* weglaufen; ~ *on* fortfahren; ~ *out*, ~ *short* zu Ende gehen; ~ *through* durchmachen; durchlesen; ~ *to* sich belaufen auf (*acc.*); sich entwickeln zu; ~ *up* to sich belaufen auf (*acc.*); *v/t. Strecke* durchlaufen; *Weg* einschlagen; laufen lassen; *Hand etc.* gleiten lassen; stecken, stoßen; transportieren; *Flut* ergießen; *Geschäft* betreiben, leiten; *hunt.* verfolgen, hetzen; um die Wette rennen mit; schmuggeln; heften; ~ *the blockade* die Blockade brechen; ~ *down* umrennen; zur *Strecke* bringen; *fig.* schlecht machen; heruntermachen; ~ *be down* abgearbeitet sein; ~ *errands* Botengänge machen; ~ *in mot.* einfahren; F *Verbrecher* einbuchten; ~ *off* ablaufen lassen; ~ *out* hinausjagen; ~ *over* überfahren; *Text* überfliegen; ~ *s.o. through* j-n durchbohren; ~ *up Preis, Neubau etc.* emportreiben; *Rechnung etc.* auflaufen lassen; 2. Laufen *n*, Rennen *n*, Lauf *m*; Verlauf *m*; Fahrt *f e-s Schiffes*; Reihe *f*; Folge *f*; Serie *f*; Reise *f*, Ausflug *m*; ✈ Andrang *m*; Ansturm *m*; *Am.* Bach *m*; *Am.* Laufmasche *f*; *Vieh-Trift f*; freie Benutzung *f*; Art *f*, Schlag *m*; the *common* ~ die große Masse; *have a* ~ *of 20 nights thea.* 20mal nacheinander gegeben werden; *in the long* ~ auf die Dauer, am Ende; *in the short* ~ fürs nächste.

run|about *mot.* ['rʌnəbaut] kleiner (Sport)Wagen; ~away Ausreißer *m.*

rune [ru:n] Rune *f.*

rung[1] [rʌŋ] *p.p. von* ring 2.

rung[2] [~] (Leiter)Sprosse *f* (*a. fig.*).

run-in ['rʌn'in] *Sport:* Einlauf *m*; *Am.* F Krach *m*, Zs.-stoß *m* (*Streit*).

run|let ['rʌnlit], ~nel ['rʌnl] Rinnsal *n*; Rinnstein *m.*

runner ['rʌnə] Läufer *m*; Bote *m*; (Schlitten)Kufe *f*; Schieber *m am Schirm*; ⚘ Ausläufer *m*; ~-up [~ər'ʌp] *Sport:* Zweitbeste(r *m*) *f*, Zweite(r *m*) *f.*

running ['rʌniŋ] 1. laufend; *two days* ~ zwei Tage nacheinander; ~ *hand* Kurrentschrift *f*; 2. Rennen *n*; ~board Trittbrett *n.*

runt [rʌnt] *zo.* Zwergrind *n*; *fig.* Zwerg *m*; *attr.* Zwerg...

runway ['rʌnwei] ✈ Rollbahn *f*; *hunt.* Wechsel *m*; Holzrutsche *f*; ~ *watching* Ansitzjagd *f.*

rupture ['rʌptʃə] 1. Bruch *m* (*a.* 🩺); 2. brechen; sprengen.

rural □ ['ruərəl] ländlich; Land...

ruse [ru:z] List *f*, Kniff *m*.

rush [rʌʃ] **1.** ♀ Binse *f*; Jagen *n*, Hetzen *n*, Stürmen *n*; (An)Sturm *m*; Andrang *m*; ✝ stürmische Nachfrage; ~ *hour(s pl.*) Hauptverkehrszeit *f*; **2.** *v/i.* stürzen, jagen, hetzen, stürmen; ~ *at* sich stürzen auf (*acc.*); ~ *into print et.* überstürzt veröffentlichen; *v/t.* jagen, hetzen; drängen; ✕ *u. fig.* stürmen; *sl.* neppen.

russet ['rʌsit] braunrot; grob.

Russian ['rʌʃən] **1.** russisch; **2.** Russe *m*, -in *f*; Russisch *n*.

rust [rʌst] **1.** Rost *m*; **2.** (ver-, ein-) rosten (lassen) (*a. fig.*).

ustic ['rʌstik] **1.** (~*ally*) ländlich; bäurisch; Bauern...; **2.** Bauer *m*.

rustle ['rʌsl] **1.** rascheln (mit *od.* in *dat.*); rauschen; *Am.* F sich ranhalten; *Vieh* stehlen; **2.** Rascheln *n*.

rust|less ['rʌstlis] rostfrei; ~**y** [~ti] rostig; eingerostet (*a. fig.*); verschossen (*Stoff*); rostfarben.

rut [rʌt] Wagenspur *f*; *bsd. fig.* ausgefahrenes Geleise; *hunt.* Brunst *f*, Brunft *f*.

ruthless ⌐ ['ru:θlis] unbarmherzig; rücksichts~, skrupellos.

rutted ['rʌtid] ausgefahren (*Weg*).

rutty ['rʌti] ausgefahren (*Weg*).

rye ♀ [rai] Roggen *m*.

S

sable ['seibl] Zobel(pelz) *m*; Schwarz *n*.

sabotage ['sæbətɑ:ʒ] **1.** Sabotage*f*; **2.** sabotieren.

sabre ['seibə] Säbel *m*.

sack [sæk] **1.** Plünderung *f*; Sack *m*; *Am.* Tüte *f*; Sackkleid *n*; Sakko *m*, *n*; *give* (*get*) *the* ~ F entlassen (werden); den Laufpaß geben (bekommen); **2.** plündern; einsacken; F rausschmeißen; *j-m* den Laufpaß geben; ~**cloth** ['sæklɔθ], ~**ing** ['sækiŋ] Sackleinwand *f*.

sacrament *eccl.* ['sækrəmənt] Sakrament *n*.

sacred ⌐ ['seikrid] heilig; geistlich.

sacrifice ['sækrifais] **1.** Opfer *n*; *at a* ~ ✝ mit Verlust; **2.** opfern; ✝ mit Verlust verkaufen.

sacrilege ['sækrilidʒ] Kirchenraub *m*, -schändung *f*; Sakrileg *n*; ~**ious** ⌐ [sækri'lidʒəs] frevelhaft.

sad ⌐ [sæd] traurig; jämmerlich, kläglich; schlimm, arg; dunkel.

sadden ['sædn] (sich) betrüben.

saddle ['sædl] **1.** Sattel *m*; **2.** satteln; *fig.* belasten; ~**r** [~lə] Sattler *m*.

sadism ['sædizəm] Sadismus *m*.

sadness ['sædnis] Traurigkeit *f*, Trauer *f*, Schwermut *f*.

safe [seif] **1.** ⌐ *allg.* sicher; unversehrt; zuverlässig; **2.** Safe *m*, Geldschrank *m*; Speiseschrank *m*; ~**blower** *Am.* ['seifblouə] Geldschrankknacker *m*; ~ **conduct** freies Geleit; Geleitbrief *m*; ~**guard 1.** Schutz *m*; **2.** sichern, schützen.

safety ['seifti] Sicherheit *f*; ~**belt** *mot.* Sicherheitsgurt *m*; ~ **island** Verkehrsinsel *f*; ~**lock** Sicherheitsschloß *n*; ~**pin** Sicherheitsnadel *f*; ~ **razor** Rasierapparat *m*.

saffron ['sæfrən] Safran(gelb *n*) *m*.

sag [sæg] durchsacken; ⊕ durchhängen; ⊕ (ab)sacken (*a. fig.*).

sagaci|ous ⌐ [sə'geiʃəs] scharfsinnig; ~**ty** [sə'gæsiti] Scharfsinn *m*.

sage [seidʒ] **1.** ⌐ klug, weise; **2.** Weise(r) *m*; ♀ Salbei *m*, *f*.

said [sed] *pret. u. p.p. von* say 1.

sail [seil] **1.** Segel *n*; Fahrt *f*; Windmühlenflügel *m*; (Segel-) Schiff(*e pl.*) *n*; *set* ~ in See stechen; **2.** *v/i.* (ab)segeln, fahren; *fig.* schweben; *v/t.* befahren; *Schiff* führen; ~**boat** *Am.* ['seilbout] Segelboot *n*; ~**er** ['seilə] Segler *m* (*Schiff*); ~**ing-ship** ['seiliŋʃip], ~**ing-vessel** [~ŋvesl] Segelschiff *n*; ~**or** ['seilə] Seemann *m*, Matrose *m*; *be a good* (*bad*) ~ (nicht) seefest sein; ~**plane** Segelflugzeug *n*.

saint [seint] **1.** Heilige(r *m*) *f*; [*vor npr. snt*] Sankt...; **2.** heiligsprechen; ~**ly** [seintli] *adj.* heilig, fromm.

saith † *od. poet.* [seθ] *3. sg. pres. von* say 1.

sake [seik]: *for the* ~ *of* um ... (*gen.*) willen; *for my* ~ meinetwegen; *for God's* ~ um Gottes willen.

salad ['sæləd] Salat *m*.

salary ['sæləri] **1.** Besoldung *f*; Gehalt *n*; **2.** besolden; ~**earner** [~iə:nə] Gehaltsempfänger(in).

sale [seil] (Aus)Verkauf *m*; Absatz *m*; Auktion *f*; *for* ~, *on* ~ zum Verkauf, zu verkaufen, verkäuflich.

sal(e)able ['seiləbl] verkäuflich.

sales|man ['seilzmən] Verkäufer *m*; ~**woman** Verkäuferin *f*.

salient ⌐ ['seiljənt] vorspringend; *fig.* hervorragend, hervortretend; Haupt...

saline ['seilain] salzig; Salz...

saliva [sə'laivə] Speichel *m*.

sallow ['sælou] blaß; gelblich.

sally ['sæli] **1.** ✕ Ausbruch *m*; witziger Einfall; **2.** *a.* ~ *out* ✕ ausbrechen; ~ *forth*, ~ *out* sich aufmachen.

salmon *ichth.* ['sæmən] Lachs *m*, Salm *m*.

saloon [sə'lu:n] Salon *m*; (Gesellschafts)Saal *m*; erste Klasse *auf Schiffen*; *Am.* Kneipe *f*.

salt [sɔ:lt] 1. Salz *n*; *fig.* Würze *f*; *old* ~ alter Seebär; 2. salzig; gesalzen; Salz...; Pökel...; 3. (ein)salzen; pökeln; ~**cellar** ['sɔ:ltselə] Salzfäßchen *n*; ~**petre**, *Am.* ~**peter** [ˌtpi:tə] Salpeter *m*; ~**water** Salzwasser...; ~**y** [ˌti] salzig.

salubrious □ [sə'lu:briəs], **salutary** □ ['sæljutəri] heilsam, gesund.

salut|ation [sælju(:)'teiʃən] Gruß *m*, Begrüßung *f*; Anrede *f*; ~**e** [sə'lu:t] 1. Gruß *m*; *co.* Kuß *m*; ✗ Salut *m*; 2. (be)grüßen; ✗ salutieren.

salvage ['sælvidʒ] 1. Bergung(sgut *n*) *f*; Bergegeld *n*; 2. bergen.

salvation [sæl'veiʃən] Erlösung *f*; (Seelen)Heil *n*; *fig.* Rettung *f*; ♀ *Army* Heilsarmee *f*.

salve¹ [sælv] retten, bergen.

salve² [sɑ:v] 1. Salbe *f*; *fig.* Balsam *m*; 2. *mst fig.* (ein)salben; beruhigen.

salvo ['sælvou] Vorbehalt *m*; ✗ Salve *f* (*fig. Beifall*).

same [seim]: *the* ~ der-, die-, dasselbe; *all the* ~ trotzdem; *it is all the* ~ *to me* es ist mir (ganz) gleich.

samp *Am.* [sæmp] grobgemahlener Mais.

sample ['sɑ:mpl] 1. Probe *f*, Muster *n*; 2. bemustern; (aus)probieren.

sanatorium [sænə'tɔ:riəm] (*bsd.* Lungen)Sanatorium *n*; Luftkurort *m*.

sanct|ify ['sæŋktifai] heiligen; weihen; ~**imonious** □ [ˌsæŋkti'mounjəs] scheinheilig; ~**ion** ['sæŋkʃən] 1. Sanktion *f*; Bestätigung *f*; Genehmigung *f*; Zwangsmaßnahme *f*; 2. bestätigen, genehmigen; ~**ity** [ˌktiti] Heiligkeit *f*; ~**uary** [ˌtjuəri] Heiligtum *n*; *das* Allerheiligste; Asyl *n*, Freistätte *f*.

sand [sænd] 1. Sand *m*; ~*s pl.* Sand (-massen *f/pl.*) *m*; Sandwüste *f*; Sandbank *f*; 2. mit Sand bestreuen.

sandal ['sændl] Sandale *f*.

sand|-glass ['sændglɑ:s] Sanduhr*f*; ~**hill** Sanddüne *f*; ~**piper** *orn.* Flußuferläufer *m*.

sandwich ['sænwidʒ] 1. Sandwich *n*; 2. *a.* ~ *in* einlegen, einklemmen.

sandy ['sændi] sandig; sandfarben.

sane [sein] geistig gesund; vernünftig (*Antwort etc.*).

sang [sæŋ] *pret. von* sing.

sanguin|ary □ ['sæŋgwinəri] blutdürstig; blutig; ~**e** [ˌwin] leichtblütig; zuversichtlich; vollblütig.

sanitarium *Am.* [sæni'tɛəriəm] = *sanatorium*.

sanitary □ ['sænitəri] Gesundheits...; gesundheitlich; ⊕ Sanitär...; ~ *towel* Damenbinde *f*.

sanit|ation [sæni'teiʃən] Gesund-heitspflege *f*; sanitäre Einrichtung; ~**y** ['sæniti] gesunder Verstand.

sank [sæŋk] *pret. von* sink 1.

Santa Claus [ˌsæntə'klɔ:z] Nikolaus *m*.

sap [sæp] 1. ♀ Saft *m*; *fig.* Lebenskraft *f*; ✗ Sappe *f*; 2. untergraben (*a. fig.*); *sl.* büffeln; ~**less** ['sæplis] saft-, kraftlos; ~**ling** [ˌliŋ] junger Baum; *fig.* Grünschnabel *m*.

sapphire *min.* ['sæfaiə] Saphir *m*.

sappy ['sæpi] saftig; *fig.* kraftvoll.

sarcasm ['sɑ:kæzəm] bitterer Spott.

sardine *ichth.* [sɑ:'di:n] Sardine *f*.

sash [sæʃ] Schärpe *f*; Fensterrahmen *m*. [befenster *n.*⟩

sash-window ['sæʃwindou] Schie-⟩

sat [sæt] *pret. u. p.p. von* sit.

Satan ['seitən] Satan *m*.

satchel ['sætʃəl] Schulmappe *f*.

sate [seit] (über)sättigen.

sateen [sæ'ti:n] Satin *m*.

satellite ['sætəlait] Satellit(enstaat) *m*.

satiate ['seiʃieit] (über)sättigen.

satin ['sætin] Seidensatin *m*.

satir|e ['sætaiə] Satire *f*; ~**ist** ['sætərist] Satiriker *m*; ~**ize** [ˌraiz] verspotten.

satisfaction [sætis'fækʃən] Befriedigung *f*; Genugtuung *f*; Zufriedenheit *f*; Sühne *f*; Gewißheit *f*.

satisfactory □ [sætis'fæktəri] befriedigend, zufriedenstellend.

satisfy ['sætisfai] befriedigen; genügen (*dat.*); zufriedenstellen; überzeugen; *Zweifel* beheben.

saturate ⛏ *u. fig.* ['sætʃəreit] sättigen.

Saturday ['sætədi] Sonnabend *m*, Samstag *m*.

saturnine ['sætə:nain] düster, finster.

sauce [sɔ:s] 1. (*oft kalte*) Soße; *Am.* Kompott *n*; *fig.* Würze *f*; F Frechheit *f*; 2. würzen; F frech werden zu *j-m*; ~**boat** ['sɔ:sbout] Soßenschüssel *f*; ~**pan** Kochtopf *m*; Kasserolle *f*; ~**r** ['sɔ:sə] Untertasse *f*.

saucy □ F ['sɔ:si] frech; dreist.

saunter ['sɔ:ntə] 1. Schlendern *n*; Bummel *m*; 2. (umher)schlendern; bummeln.

sausage ['sɔsidʒ] Wurst *f*.

savage ['sævidʒ] 1. □ wild; roh, grausam; 2. Wilde(r *m*) *f*; *fig.* Barbar *m*; ~**ry** [ˌdʒəri] Wildheit *f*; Barbarei *f*.

savant ['sævənt] Gelehrte(r) *m*.

save [seiv] 1. retten; erlösen; bewahren; (er)sparen; schonen; 2. *rhet. prp. u. cj.* außer; ~ *for* bis auf (*acc.*); ~ *that* nur daß.

saver ['seivə] Retter(in); Sparer(in).

saving ['seiviŋ] 1. □ sparsam; 2. Rettung *f*; ~*s pl.* Ersparnisse *f/pl.*

savings|-bank ['seiviŋzbæŋk] Sparkasse *f*; ~**deposit** Spareinlage *f*.

savio(u)r ['seivjə] Retter m; *Saviour eccl.* Heiland m.

savo(u)r ['seivə] 1. Geschmack m; *fig.* Beigeschmack m; 2. *fig.* schmecken, riechen (*of* nach).

savo(u)ry[1] ☐ ['seivəri] schmackhaft; appetitlich; pikant.

savo(u)ry[2] ♣ [↓] Bohnenkraut n.

saw[1] [sɔː] *pret. von* see.

saw[2] [↓] Spruch m.

saw[3] [↓] 1. [*irr.*] sägen; 2. Säge f; ↓dust ['sɔːdʌst] Sägespäne m/pl.; ↓mill Sägewerk n; ↓n [sɔːn] *p.p. von* saw[3] 1.

Saxon ['sæksn] 1. sächsisch; *ling.* oft germanisch; 2. Sachse m, Sächsin f.

say [sei] 1. [*irr.*] sagen; hersagen; berichten; ~ grace das Tischgebet sprechen; *that is to* ~ das heißt; *you don't* ~ *so!* was Sie nicht sagen!; *I* ~ sag(en Sie) mal; ich muß schon sagen; *he is said to be* er soll ... sein; *no sooner said than done* gesagt, getan; 2. Rede f, Wort n; *it is my* ~ *now* jetzt ist die Reihe zu reden an mir; *have a od. some* (*no*) ~ *in s.th.* et. (nichts) zu sagen haben bei et.; ↓ing ['seiiŋ] Rede f; Redensart f; Ausspruch m; *it goes without* ~ es versteht sich von selbst.

scab [skæb] ♣[...], ♣ Schorf m; *vet.* Räude f; *sl.* Streikbrecher m.

scabbard ['skæbəd] *Säbel-*Scheide f.

scabrous ['skeibrəs] heikel.

scaffold ['skæfold] (Bau)Gerüst n; Schafott n; ↓ing [↓diŋ] (Bau)Gerüst n.

scald [skɔːld] 1. Verbrühung f; 2. verbrühen; *Milch* abkochen.

scale[1] [skeil] 1. Schuppe f; Kesselstein m; ♣ Zahnstein m; Waagschale f; (*a pair of*) ↓s *pl.* (eine) Waage; 2. (sich) abschuppen, ablösen; ⊕ *Kesselstein* abklopfen; ♣ *Zähne* vom Zahnstein reinigen; wiegen.

scale[2] [↓] 1. Stufenleiter f; ♪ Tonleiter f; Skala f; Maßstab m; *fig.* Ausmaß n; 2. ersteigen; ~ *up* (*down*) maßstabsgetreu vergrößern (verkleinern).

scallop ['skɔləp] 1. *zo.* Kammuschel f; ⊕ Langette f; 2. ausbogen.

scalp [skælp] 1. Kopfhaut f; Skalp m; 2. skalpieren.

scaly ['skeili] schuppig; voll Kesselstein.

scamp [skæmp] 1. Taugenichts m; 2. pfuschen; ↓er ['skæmpə] 1. (umher)tollen; hetzen; 2. *fig.* Hetzjagd f.

scan [skæn] *Verse* skandieren; absuchen; *fig.* überfliegen.

scandal ['skændl] Skandal m; Ärgernis n; Schande f; Klatsch m; ↓ize [↓dəlaiz] Anstoß erregen bei j-m; ↓ous ☐ [↓əs] skandalös, anstößig; schimpflich; klatschhaft.

Scandinavian [skændi'neivjən]

1. skandinavisch; 2. Skandinavier (-in).

scant *lit.* [skænt] 1. knapp, kärglich; 2. knausern mit, sparen an (*dat.*); ↓y ☐ ['skænti] knapp, spärlich, kärglich, dürftig.

scape|goat ['skeipgout] Sündenbock m; ↓grace [↓greis] Taugenichts m.

scar [skɑː] 1. Narbe f; *fig.* (Schand-)Fleck m, Makel m; Klippe f; 2. *v/t.* schrammen; *v/i.* vernarben.

scarc|e [skeəs] knapp; rar; selten; ↓ely ['skeəsli] kaum; ↓ity [↓siti] Mangel m; Knappheit f; Teuerung f.

scare [skeə] 1. er~, aufschrecken; verscheuchen; ↓d verstört; ängstlich; 2. Panik f; ↓crow ['skeəkrou] Vogelscheuche f (*a. fig.*); ↓head (-*ing*) Riesenschlagzeile f.

scarf [skɑːf], *pl.* ↓s, scarves [↓fs, skɑːvz] Schal m; Hals-, Kopftuch n; Krawatte f; ✕ Schärpe f.

scarlet ['skɑːlit] 1. Scharlach(rot n) m; 2. scharlachrot; ~ *fever* ♣ Scharlach m; ~ *runner* ♣ Feuerbohne f.

scarred [skɑːd] narbig.

scarves [skɑːvz] *pl. von* scarf.

scathing *fig.* ['skeiðiŋ] vernichtend.

scatter ['skætə] (sich) zerstreuen; aus-, verstreuen; (sich) verbreiten.

scavenger ['skævindʒə] Straßenkehrer m.

scenario [si'nɑːriou] *Film:* Drehbuch n.

scene [siːn] Szene f; Bühne(nbild n) f; Schauplatz m; ↓s *pl.* Kulissen f/pl.; ↓ry [si'nəri] Szenerie f; Bühnenausstattung f; Landschaft f.

scent [sent] 1. (Wohl)Geruch m; Duft m; Parfüm n; *hunt.* Witterung(svermögen n) f; Fährte f; 2. wittern; parfümieren; ↓less ['sentlis] geruchlos.

sceptic ['skeptik] Skeptiker(in); ↓al ☐ [↓kəl] skeptisch.

scept|re, *Am.* ~er ['septə] Zepter n.

schedule ['ʃedjuːl, *Am.* 'skedjuːl] 1. Verzeichnis n; Tabelle f; *Am.* Fahrplan m; *on* ~ fahrplanmäßig; 2. auf-, verzeichnen; festsetzen.

scheme [skiːm] 1. Schema n; Zs.-stellung f; Plan m; 2. *v/t.* planen; *v/i.* Pläne machen; Ränke schmieden.

schism ['sizəm] (Kirchen)Spaltung f.

scholar ['skɔlə] Gelehrte(r) m; *univ.* Stipendiat m; † Schüler(in); ↓ly *adj.* [↓li] gelehrt; ↓ship [↓ʃip] Gelehrsamkeit f; Wissenschaftlichkeit f; *univ.* Stipendium n.

scholastic [skə'læstik] 1. (~*ally*) *phls.* scholastisch; schulmäßig; Schul...; 2. *phls.* Scholastiker m.

school [skuːl] 1. Schwarm m; Schule f (*a. fig.*); *univ.* Fakultät f;

Disziplin *f*; Hochschule *f*; *at* ~ *auf od.* in der Schule; 2. schulen, erziehen; ~boy ['sku:lbɔi] Schüler *m*; ~fellow Mitschüler(in); ~girl Schülerin *f*; ~ing [~liŋ] (Schul-)Ausbildung *f*; ~master Lehrer *m* (*bsd. e-r höheren Schule*); ~mate Mitschüler(in); ~mistress Lehrerin *f* (*bsd. e-r höheren Schule*); ~teacher (*bsd.* Volksschul)Lehrer (-in).

schooner ['sku:nə] ⚓ Schoner *m*; *Am.* großes Bierglas; = *prairie-schooner*.

science ['saiəns] Wissenschaft *f*; Naturwissenschaft(en *pl.*) *f*; Technik *f*.

scientific [saiən'tifik] (~ally) (*eng S.* natur)wissenschaftlich; kunstgerecht.

scientist ['saiəntist] (*bsd.* Natur-)Wissenschaftler *m*.

scintillate ['sintileit] funkeln.

scion ['saiən] Sproß *m*, Sprößling *m*.

scissors ['sizəz] *pl.* (*a pair of* ~ *pl.* eine) Schere.

scoff [skɔf] 1. Spott *m*; 2. spotten.

scold [skould] 1. zänkisches Weib; 2. (aus)schelten, schimpfen.

scon(e) [skɔn] weiches Teegebäck.

scoop [sku:p] 1. Schaufel *f*, Schippe *f*; Schöpfeimer *m*, -kelle *f*; F Coup *m*, gutes Geschäft; F Exklusivmeldung *f*; 2. (aus)schaufeln; einscheffeln.

scooter ['sku:tə] (Kinder)Roller *m*; Motorroller *m*.

scope [skoup] Bereich *m*; *geistiger* Gesichtskreis; Spielraum *m*.

scorch [skɔ:tʃ] *v/t.* versengen, verbrennen; *v/i.* F (dahin)rasen.

score [skɔ:] 1. Kerbe *f*; Zeche *f*, Rechnung *f*; 20 Stück; *Sport:* Punktzahl *f*; (Tor)Stand *m*; Grund *m*; ♪ Partitur *f*; ~s *of viele*; *four* ~ achtzig; *run up* ~s Schulden machen; *on the* ~ *of wegen* (*gen.*); 2. (ein)kerben; anschreiben; *Sport:* (Punkte) machen; *Fußball:* ein Tor schießen; gewinnen; instrumentieren; *Am.* F scharfe Kritik üben an (*dat.*).

scorn [skɔ:n] 1. Verachtung *f*; Spott *m*; 2. verachten, verschmähen; ~ful ☐ ['skɔ:nful] verächtlich.

Scotch [skɔtʃ] 1. schottisch; 2. Schottisch *n*; *the* ~ *die* Schotten *pl.*; ~man ['skɔtʃmən] Schotte *m*.

scot-free ['skɔt'fri:] straflos.

Scots [skɔts], ~man ['skɔtsmən] = *Scotch(man).*

scoundrel ['skaundrəl] Schurke *m*.

scour ['skauə] *v/t.* scheuern; reinigen; durchstreifen, absuchen; *v/i.* eilen.

scourge [skə:dʒ] 1. Geißel *f*; 2. geißeln.

scout [skaut] 1. Späher *m*, Kundschafter *m*; ⚓ Aufklärungsfahrzeug

n; ✈ Aufklärer *m*; *mot.* Mitglied *n* der Straßenwacht; (*Boy*) ♀ Pfadfinder *m*; ~ *party* ⚔ Spähtrupp *m*; 2. (aus)kundschaften, spähen; verächtlich zurückweisen.

scowl [skaul] 1. finsteres Gesicht; 2. finster blicken.

scrabble ['skræbl] (be)kritzeln; scharren; krabbeln.

scrag *fig* [skræg] Gerippe *n* (*dürrer Mensch etc.*).

scramble ['skræmbl] 1. klettern; sich balgen (*for um*); ~d *eggs pl.* Rührei *n*; 2. Kletterei *f*; Balgerei *f*.

scrap [skræp] 1. Stückchen *n*; (Zeitungs)Ausschnitt *m*, Bild *n* *zum Einkleben*; Altmaterial *n*; Schrott *m*; ~s *pl* Reste *m/pl.*; 2. ausrangieren; verschrotten; ~book ['skræpbuk] Sammelalbum *n*.

scrap|e [skreip] 1. Kratzen *n*, Scharren *n*; Kratzfuß *m*; Not *f*, Klemme *f*; 2. schrap(p)en; (ab-)schaben; (ab)kratzen; scharren; (entlang)streifen; ~er ['skreipə] Kratzeisen *n*.

scrap|-heap ['skræphi:p] Abfall-, Schrotthaufen *m*; ~iron Alteisen *n*, Schrott *m*.

scratch [skrætʃ] 1. Schramme *f*; *Sport* Startlinie *f*; 2. zs.-gewürfelt; Zufalls...; *Sport:* ohne Vorgabe; 3. (zer)kratzen; (zer)schrammen; *parl. u. Sport:* streichen; ~ *out* ausstreichen.

scrawl [skrɔ:l] 1. kritzeln; 2. Gekritzel *n*.

scrawny *Am.* F ['skrɔ:ni] dürr.

scream [skri:m] 1. Schrei *m*; Gekreisch *n*; *he is a* ~ F er ist zum Schreien komisch; 2. schreien, kreischen.

screech [skri:tʃ] *s. scream*; ~owl *orn.* ['skri:tʃaul] Käuzchen *n*.

screen [skri:n] 1. Wand-, Ofen-, Schutzschirm *m*; *fig.* Schleier *m*; (Film)Leinwand *f*; *der* Film; Sandsieb *n*; (Fliegen)Gitter *n*; 2. (ab-)schirmen; (be)schützen; ⚔ tarnen; auf die Leinwand zeigen; verfilmen; (durch)sieben; ~ *play* Drehbuch *n*; Fernsehfilm *m*.

screw [skru:] 1. Schraube *f*; ✈ Propeller *m*; 2. (fest)schrauben; *fig.* bedrängen; ver-, umdrehen; ~ *up* festschrauben; ~ *up one's courage* Mut fassen; ~ball *Am. sl.* ['skru:bɔ:l] komischer Kauz; ~driver Schraubenzieher *m*; ~jack Wagenheber *m*; ~propeller Schiffs-, Flugzeugschraube *f*.

scribble ['skribl] 1. Gekritzel *n*; 2. kritzeln. [*skimp etc.*]

scrimp [skrimp], ~y ['skrimpi] =]

scrip ✝ [skrip] Interimsschein(e *pl.*) *m*.

script [skript] Schrift *f*; Schreibschrift *f*; Manuskript *n*; *Film:* Drehbuch *n*.

Scripture ['skriptʃə] *mst the Holy* ~ *s pl.* die Heilige Schrift.

scroll [skroul] Schriftrolle *f*, Liste*f*; △ Schnecke *f*; Schnörkel *m*.

scrub [skrʌb] 1. Gestrüpp *n*; Zwerg *m*; *Am. Sport*: zweite Spieler-) Garnitur; 2. schrubben, scheuern.

scrubby ['skrʌbi] struppig, schäbig.

scrup|le ['skru:pl] 1. Skrupel *m*, Zweifel *m*, Bedenken *s*; 2. Bedenken haben; ~ulous ◻ [~pjuləs] (allzu) bedenklich; gewissenhaft; ängstlich.

scrutin|ize ['skru:tinaiz] (genau) prüfen; ~y [~ni] forschender Blick; genaue (*bsd.* Wahl)Prüfung.

scud [skʌd] 1. (Dahin)Jagen *n*; (dahintreibende) Wolkenfetzen *m/pl.*; Bö *f*; 2. eilen, jagen, gleiten.

scuff [skʌf] schlurfen, schlorren.

scuffle ['skʌfl] 1. Balgerei *f*, Rauferei *f*; 2. sich balgen, raufen.

scull ♉ [skʌl] 1. kurzes Ruder; 2. rudern, skullen.

scullery ['skʌləri] Spülküche *f*.

sculptor ['skʌlptə] Bildhauer *m*.

sculpture ['skʌlptʃə] 1. Plastik *f*; Bildhauerkunst *f*, Skulptur *f*; 2. (heraus)meißeln, formen.

scum *fig.* [skʌm] (Ab)Schaum *m*.

scurf [skəːf] (Haut)Schuppen *f/pl.*

scurrilous ['skʌriləs] gemein.

scurry ['skʌri] hasten, rennen.

scurvy[1] ♉ ['skəːvi] Skorbut *m*.

scurvy[2] [~] (hunds)gemein.

scuttle ['skʌtl] 1. Kohlenbehälter *m*; 2. eilen; *fig.* sich drücken.

scythe ♉ [saið] Sense *f*.

sea [siː] See *f*, Meer *n* (*a. fig.*); hohe Welle; *at* ~ auf See; *fig.* ratlos; ~**board** ['siːbɔːd] Küste(ngebiet *n*) *f*; ~**coast** Küste *f*; ~**faring** ['siːfɛəriŋ] seefahrend; ~**food** eßbare Seefische *m/pl.*; Meeresfrüchte *pl.*; ~**going** Hochsee...; ~**gull** (See)Möwe *f*.

seal[1] [siːl] 1. *zo.* Seehund *m*, Robbe *f*; Siegel *n*; Stempel *m*; Bestätigung *f*; 2. versiegeln; *fig.* besiegeln; ~ *up* (fest) verschließen; ⊕ abdichten.

sea-level ['siːlevl] Meeresspiegel *m*.

sealing-wax ['siːliŋwæks] Siegellack *m*.

seam [siːm] 1. Saum *m*; (*a.* ⊕) Naht *f*; ⊕ Fuge *f*; *geol.* Flöz *n*; Narbe *f*; 2. schrammen; furchen.

seaman ['siːmən] Seemann *m*, Matrose *m*.

seamstress ['semstris] Näherin *f*.

sea|-plane ['siːplein] Wasserflugzeug *n*; ~**power** Seemacht *f*.

sear [siə] 1. dürr, welk; 2. austrocknen, versengen; ✕ brennen; *fig.* verhärten.

search [səːtʃ] 1. Suchen *n*, Forschen *n*; Unter-, Durchsuchung *f*; *in* ~ *of* auf der Suche nach; 2. *v/t.* durch-, untersuchen; ✕ sondieren; erfor-

schen; durchdringen; *v/i.* suchen, forschen (*for* nach); ~ *into* ergründen; ~**ing** ↑ ['səːtʃiŋ] forschend, prüfend; eingehend (*Prüfung etc.*); ~**light** (Such)Scheinwerfer *m*; ~**warrant** ✍ Haussuchungsbefehl *m*.

sea|-shore ['siːʃɔː] Seeküste *f*; ~**sick** seekrank; ~**side** Strand *m*, Küste *f*; ~ *place*, ~ *resort* Seebad *n*; *go to the* ~ an die See gehen.

season ['siːzn] 1. Jahreszeit *f*; (rechte) Zeit; Saison *f*; F *für* ~*-ticket*; *cherries are in* ~ jetzt ist Kirschenzeit; *out of* ~ zur Unzeit; *with the compliments of the* ~ mit den besten Wünschen zum Fest; 2. *v/t.* reifen (lassen); würzen; abhärten (*to* gegen); *v/i.* ablagern; ~**able** ◻ [~nəbl] zeitgemäß; rechtzeitig; ~**al** ◻ ['siːznəl] Saison...; periodisch; ~**ing** ['siːzniŋ] Würze *f*; ~*-ticket* ⊞ Zeitkarte *f*; *thea.* Abonnement *n*.

seat [siːt] 1. Sitz *m* (*a. fig.*); Sessel *m*, Stuhl *m*, Bank *f*; (Sitz)Platz *m*; Landsitz *m*; Gesäß *n*; Schauplatz *m*; 2. (hin)setzen; *e-n* Hosenboden einsetzen in (*acc.*); fassen, Sitzplätze haben für; ~*ed* sitzend; *...sitzig*; *be* ~*ed* sitzen; sich setzen; ~*-belt* ✈ ['siːtbelt] Sicherheitsgurt *m*.

sea|-urchin *zo.* ['siːəːtʃin] Seeigel *m*; ~**ward** ['siːwəd] 1. *adj.* seewärts gerichtet; 2. *adv. a.* ~*s* seewärts; ~**weed** ♉ (See)Tang *m*; ~**worthy** seetüchtig.

secede [siˈsiːd] sich trennen.

secession [siˈseʃən] Lossagung *f*; Abfall *m*; ~**ist** [~ʃnist] Abtrünnige(r *m*) *f*.

seclu|de [siˈkluːd] abschließen, absondern; ~**ded** einsam; zurückgezogen; abgelegen; ~**sion** [~uːʒən] Abgeschlossen-, Abgeschiedenheit *f*.

second ['sekənd] 1. ◻ zweite(r, -s) nächste(r, -s); geringer (*to* als); *on* ~ *thoughts* bei genauerer Überlegung; 2. Zweite(r, -s); Sekundant *m*; Beistand *m*; Sekunde *f*; ♩ *a*. *s pl.* Waren *pl.* zweiter Wahl; 3. sekundieren (*dat.*); unterstützen; ~**ary** ◻ [~dəri] sekundär; untergeordnet; Neben...; Hilfs...; Sekundär...; ~**ary school** höhere Schule; weiterführende Schule; ~**-hand** aus zweiter Hand; gebraucht; antiquarisch; ~**ly** [~dli] zweitens; ~**-rate** zweiten Ranges; zweitklassig.

secre|cy ['siːkrisi] Heimlichkeit *f*; Verschwiegenheit *f*; ~**t** [~it] 1. ◻ geheim; Geheim...; verschwiegen, verborgen; 2. Geheimnis *n*; *in* ~ insgeheim; *be in the* ~, *be taken into the* ~ eingeweiht sein.

secretary ['sekrətri] Schriftführer *m*; Sekretär(in); ♀ *of State* Staats-

sekretär *m*, Minister *m*; *Am.* Außenminister *m*.

secret|e [si'kri:t] verbergen; absondern; **~ion** [~i:ʃən] Absonderung *f*; **~ive** [~i:tiv] *fig.* verschlossen; geheimtuerisch.

section ['sekʃən] *⚓* Sektion *f*; (Durch)Schnitt *m*; Teil *m*; Abschnitt *m*, Paragraph *m*; *typ.* Absatz *m*; Abteilung *f*; Gruppe *f*.

secular ⊐ ['sekjulə] weltlich.

secur|e [si'kjuə] 1. ⊐ sicher; 2. (sich *et.*) sichern; schützen; festmachen; **~ity** [~ɔriti] Sicherheit *f*; Sorglosigkeit *f*; Gewißheit *f*; Schutz *m*; Kaution *f*; **securities** *pl.* Wertpapiere *n/pl.*

sedan [si'dæn] Limousine *f*; *a.* **~-chair** Sänfte *f*.

sedate ⊐ [si'deit] gesetzt; ruhig.

sedative *mst* *⚓* ['sedətiv] 1. beruhigend; 2. Beruhigungsmittel *n*.

sedentary ⊐ ['sedntəri] sitzend; seßhaft.

sediment ['sedimənt] (Boden)Satz *m*; *geol.* Ablagerung *f*.

sediti|on [si'diʃən] Aufruhr *m*; **~ous** ⊐ [~ʃəs] aufrührerisch.

seduc|e [si'dju:s] verführen; **~tion** [si'dʌkʃən] Verführung *f*; **~tive** ⊐ [~ktiv] verführerisch.

sedulous ⊐ ['sedjuləs] emsig.

see[1] [si:] [*irr.*] *v/i.* sehen; *fig.* einsehen; *I* ~ ich verstehe; *fig.* ~ *about s.th.* sich um et. kümmern; ~ *through s.o. od. s.th.* j-n *od.* et. durchschauen; ~ *to* achten auf (*acc.*); *v/t.* sehen; beobachten; einsehen; sorgen (*daß et. geschieht*); besuchen; *Arzt* aufsuchen; ~ *s.o. home* j-n nach Hause begleiten; ~ *off Besuch et.* wegbringen; ~ *out Besuch* hinausbegleiten; *et.* zu Ende erleben; ~ *s.th. through et.* durchhalten; ~ *s.o. through* j-m durchhelfen; *live to* ~ erleben.

see[2] [~] (erz)bischöflicher Stuhl.

seed [si:d] 1. Same(n) *m*, Saat(gut *n*) *f*; (Obst)Kern *m*; Keim *m* (*a. fig.*); *go od. run to* ~ in Samen schießen; *fig.* herunterkommen; 2. *v/t.* (be)säen; entkernen; *v/i.* in Samen schießen; **~less** ['si:dlis] kernlos (*Obst*); **~ling** *♂* [~ling] Sämling *m*; **~y** ['si:di] schäbig; F elend.

seek [si:k] [*irr.*] suchen (nach); begehren; trachten nach.

seem [si:m] (er)scheinen; **~ing** ⊐ ['si:miŋ] anscheinend; scheinbar; **~ly** ['si:mli] schicklich.

seen [si:n] *p.p. von* see[1].

seep [si:p] durchsickern, tropfen.

seer ['si(:)ə] Seher(in), Prophet(in).

seesaw ['si:sɔ:] 1. Wippen *n*; Wippe *f*, Wippschaukel *f*; 2. wippen; *fig.* schwanken.

seethe [si:ð] sieden, kochen.

segment ['segmənt] Abschnitt *m*.

segregat|e ['segrigeit] absondern,

trennen; **~ion** [segri'geiʃən] Absonderung *f*; Rassentrennung *f*.

seiz|e [si:z] ergreifen, fassen; mit Beschlag belegen; *fig.* erfassen; *a.* ~ *upon sich et* S. *od. j-s* bemächtigen; **~ure** ['si:ʒə] Ergreifung *f*; *tₜₕ* Beschlagnahme *f*; *⚓* plötzlicher Anfall.

seldom *adv.* ['seldəm] selten.

select [si'lekt] 1. auswählen, auslesen, aussuchen; 2. auserwählt; erlesen; exklusiv; **~ion** [~kʃən] Auswahl *f*, Auslese *f*; **~man** *Am.* Stadtrat *m in den Neuenglandstaaten.*

self [self] 1. *pl.* **selves** [selvz] Selbst *n*, Ich *n*; Persönlichkeit *f*; 2. *pron.* selbst; *♦ od.* F = *myself etc.*; 3. *adj.* *⚓* einfarbig; **~-centered** ['self-'sentəd] egozentrisch; **~-command** Selbstbeherrschung *f*; **~-conceit** Eigendünkel *m*; **~-conceited** dünkelhaft; **~-confidence** Selbstvertrauen *n*; **~-conscious** befangen, gehemmt; **~-contained** (in sich) abgeschlossen; *fig.* verschlossen; **~-control** Selbstbeherrschung *f*; **~-defence**, *Am.* **~-defense** Selbstverteidigung *f*; *in* ~ in (der) Notwehr; **~-denial** Selbstverleugnung *f*; **~-employed** selbständig (*Handwerker etc.*); **~-evident** selbstverständlich; **~-government** Selbstverwaltung *f*, Autonomie *f*; **~-indulgent** bequem; zügellos; **~-interest** Eigennutz *m*; **~ish** ⊐ [~iʃ] selbstsüchtig; **~-possession** Selbstbeherrschung *f*; **~-reliant** [~ri-'laiənt] selbstsicher; **~-righteous** selbstgerecht; **~-seeking** [~'si:kiŋ] eigennützig; **~-willed** eigenwillig.

sell [sel] [*irr.*] *v/t.* verkaufen (*a. fig.*); *Am.* aufschwatzen; *v/i.* handeln; gehen (*Ware*); ~ *off*, ~ *out* ausverkaufen; **~er** ['selə] Verkäufer *m*; *good etc.* ~ *♦* gut *etc.* gehende Ware.

selves [selvz] *pl. von* self 1.

semblance ['sembləns] Anschein *m*; Gestalt *f*.

semi|... ['semi] halb...; Halb...; **~colon** Strichpunkt *m*; **~-detached house** Doppelhaus(hälfte *f*) *n*; **~-final** *Sport.* Vorschlußrunde *f*.

seminary ['seminəri] (Priester)Seminar *n*; *fig.* Schule *f*.

sempstress ['sempstris] Näherin *f*.

senate ['senit] Senat *m*.

senator ['senətə] Senator *m*.

send [send] [*irr.*] senden, schicken; (*mit adj. od. p.pr.*) machen; ~ *for* kommen lassen, holen (lassen); ~ *forth* aussenden; veröffentlichen; ~ *in* einsenden; einreichen; ~ *up* in die Höhe treiben; ~ *word* mitteilen.

senil|e ['si:nail] greisenhaft, senil; **~ity** [si'niliti] Greisenalter *n*.

senior ['si:njə] 1. älter; dienstälter; Ober...; ~ *partner* *♦* Chef *m*; 2. Ältere(r) *m*; Dienstältere(r) *m*;

Senior *m; he is my ~ by a year er ist ein Jahr älter als ich; ~ity [si:ni-'ɔriti] höheres Alter *od.* Dienstalter.

sensation [sen'seiʃən] (Sinnes-) Empfindung *f,* Gefühl *n;* Eindruck *m;* Sensation *f;* ~al □ [~nl] Empfindungs...; sensationell.

sense [sens] 1. *allg.* Sinn *m* (of für); Empfindung *f,* Gefühl *n;* Verstand *m;* Bedeutung *f;* Ansicht *f; in* (out *of*) one's ~s bei (von) Sinnen; *bring* s.o to his ~s j-n zur Vernunft bringen; *make* ~ Sinn haben (*S.*); *talk* ~ vernünftig reden; 2. spüren. **senseless** □ ['senslis] sinnlos; bewußtlos; gefühllos; ~ness [~snis] Sinnlosigkeit *f;* Bewußt-, Gefühllosigkeit *f*

sensibility [sensi'biliti] Sensibilität *f,* Empfindungsvermögen *n;* Empfindlichkeit *f; sensibilities pl.* Empfindsamkeit *f,* Zartgefühl *n.*

sensible □ ['sensəbl] verständig, vernünftig; empfänglich (of für); fühlbar; *be* ~ of sich e-r *S.* bewußt sein; *et.* empfinden.

sensitiv|e □ ['sensitiv] empfindlich (to für); Empfindungs...; feinfühlig; ~eness [~vnis], ~ity [sensi'tiviti] Empfindlichkeit *f* (to für).

sensual □ ['sensjuəl] sinnlich. **sensuous** □ ['sensjuəs] sinnlich; Sinnes...; sinnenfreudig.

sent [sent] *pret. u. p.p. von* send.

sentence ['sentəns] 1. ✠ Urteil *n; gr.* Satz *m; serve* one's ~ s-e Strafe absitzen; 2. verurteilen.

sententious □ [sen'tenʃəs] sentenziös; salbungsvoll; salbaderisch.

sentient ['senʃənt] empfindend.

sentiment ['sentimənt] (seelische) Empfindung, Gefühl *n;* Meinung *f; s. sentimentality;* ~al □ [senti'mentl] empfindsam; sentimental; ~ality [sentimen'tæliti] Sentimentalität *f.*

sentinel ✗ ['sentinl], ~ry ✗ [~tri] Schildwache *f,* Posten *m.*

separa|ble □ ['sepərəbl] trennbar; ~te 1. ['seprit] (ab)getrennt, gesondert, besonder, separat, für sich; 2. ['sepəreit] (sich) trennen; (sich) absondern; (sich) scheiden; ~tion [sepə'reiʃən] Trennung *f,* Scheidung *f.*

sepsis ✗ ['sepsis] Sepsis *f,* Blutvergiftung *f* [*m.*]

September [səp'tembə] September] **septic** ✗ ['septik] septisch.

sepul|chral [si'pʌlkrəl] Grab...; Toten..., *fig.* düster; ~chre, *Am.* ~cher ['sepəlkə] Grab(stätte *f*) *n;* ~ture [~ltʃə] Begräbnis *n.*

sequel ['si:kwəl] Folge *f;* Nachspiel *n,* (Roman)Fortsetzung *f.*

sequen|ce ['si:kwəns] Aufeinander-, Reihenfolge *f; Film.* Szene *f;* ~ of tenses *gr.* Zeitenfolge *f;* ~t [~nt] aufeinanderfolgend.

sequestrate ✠ [si'kwestreit] *Eigentum* einziehen; beschlagnahmen.

serenade [seri'neid] 1. ♪ Serenade *f,* Ständchen *n;* 2. *j-m* ein Ständchen bringen.

seren|e □ [si'ri:n] klar, heiter; ruhig; ~ity [si'reniti] Heiterkeit *f;* Ruhe *f.*

serf [sə:f] Leibeigene(r *m*) *f,* Hörige(r *m*) *f; fig.* Sklave *m.*

sergeant ['sa:dʒənt] ✗ Feldwebel *m,* Wachtmeister *m;* (Polizei)Wachtmeister *m.*

serial □ ['siəriəl] 1. fortlaufend, reihenweise, Serien...; Fortsetzungs...; 2. Fortsetzungsroman *m.*

series ['siəri:z] *sg. u. pl.* Reihe *f,* Serie *f,* Folge *f; biol.* Gruppe *f.*

serious □ ['siəriəs] *allg.* ernst; ernsthaft, ernstlich; *be* ~ es im Ernst meinen; ~ness [~snis] Ernst (-haftigkeit *f*) *m.*

sermon ['sə:mən] (*iro.* Straf)Predigt *f.*

serpent ['sə:pənt] Schlange *f;* ~ine [~tain] schlangengleich, -förmig; Serpentinen...

serum ['siərəm] Serum *n.*

servant ['sə:vənt] Diener(in); *a. domestic* ~ Dienstbote *m,* Bedienstete(r *m*) *f;* Dienstmädchen *n.*

serve [sə:v] 1. *v/t.* dienen (*dat.*); *Zeit* abdienen; bedienen; *Speisen* reichen; *Speisen* auftragen; behandeln; nützen, dienlich sein (*dat.*); *Zweck* erfüllen; *Tennis:* angeben; (*it*) ~s him right (das) geschieht ihm recht; *s. sentence;* ~ out *et.* austeilen; *v/i.* dienen (*a.* ✗; *as,* for als, zu); bedienen; nützen, zweckmäßig sein; ~ *at table* servieren; 2. *Tennis:* Aufschlag *m.*

service ['sə:vis] 1. Dienst *m;* Bedienung *f;* Gefälligkeit *f; a. divine* ~ Gottesdienst *m;* Betrieb *m;* Verkehr *m;* Nutzen *m;* Gang *m* von *Speisen;* Service *n;* ✠ Zustellung *f; Tennis:* Aufschlag *m; be at* s.o.'s ~ j-m zu Diensten stehen; 2. ⊕ warten, pflegen; ~able □ [~səbl] dienlich, nützlich; benutzbar; strapazierfähig; ~ **station** Tankstelle *f;* Werkstatt *f.*

servil|e □ ['sə:vail] sklavisch (*a. fig.*); unterwürfig; kriecherisch; ~ity [sə:'viliti] Unterwürfigkeit *f;* Kriecherei *f.*

serving ['sə:viɳ] Portion *f.*

servitude ['sə:vitju:d] Knechtschaft *f;* Sklaverei *f.*

session ['seʃən] (*a.* Gerichts)Sitzung *f; be in* ~ tagen.

set [set] 1. [*irr.*] *v/t.* setzen; stellen; legen; zurückstellen, (ein)richten, ordnen; *Aufgabe, Wecker* stellen; *Messer* abziehen; *Edelstein* fassen; festsetzen; erstarren lassen; *Haar* legen; ✗ *Knochenbruch* einrichten; ~ s.o. laughing j-n zum Lachen bringen; ~ an example ein Beispiel geben; ~ sail Segel setzen; ~ one's teeth die Zähne zs.-beißen; ~ aside beiseite stellen od. legen; fig. verwerfen; ~ at ease beruhigen; ~ at rest beruhigen; Frage entscheiden; ~ store by Wert legen auf (acc.); ~ forth darlegen; ~ off hervorheben; anrechnen; ~ up auf-, er-, einrichten; aufstellen; j-n etablieren; v/i. ast. untergehen; gerinnen, fest werden; laufen (Flut etc.); sitzen (Kleid etc.); ~ about s.th. sich an et. machen; ~ about s.o. F über j-n herfallen; ~ forth aufbrechen; ~ off aufbrechen; ~ (up)on anfangen; angreifen; ~ out aufbrechen; ~ to sich daran machen; ~ up sich niederlassen; ~ up for sich aufspielen als; 2. fest; starr; festgesetzt, bestimmt; vorgeschrieben; ~ (up)on versessen auf (acc.); ~ with besetzt mit; Barometer: ~ fair beständig; hard ~ in großer Not; ~ speech wohlüberlegte Rede; 3. Reihe f, Folge f, Serie f, Sammlung f, Satz m; Garnitur f; Service n; Radio-Gerät n; ✝ Kollektion f; Gesellschaft f; Sippschaft f; ♂ Setzling m; Tennis: Satz m; Neigung f; Richtung f; Sitz m e-s Kleides etc.; poet. Untergang m der Sonne; thea. Bühnenausstattung f.

set|-back ['setbæk] fig. Rückschlag m; ~-down fig. Dämpfer m; ~-off Kontrast m; fig. Ausgleich m.

settee [se'ti:] kleines Sofa.

setting ['setiŋ] Setzen n; Einrichten n; Fassung f e-s Edelsteins; Lage f; Schauplatz m; Umgebung f; thea. Ausstattung f; fig. Umrahmung f; ♩ Komposition f; (Sonnen- etc.) Untergang m; ⊕ Einstellung f.

settle ['setl] 1. Sitzbank f; 2. v/t. (fest)setzen; Kind etc. versorgen, ausstatten; j-n etablieren; regeln; Geschäft abschließen, abmachen, erledigen; Frage entscheiden; Rechnung begleichen; ordnen, beruhigen; Streit beilegen; Rente aussetzen; ansiedeln; Land besiedeln; v/i. sich senken (Haus); oft ~ down sich niederlassen; a. ~ in sich einrichten; sich legen (Wut etc.); beständig werden (Wetter); sich entschließen; ~ down to sich widmen (dat.); ~d fest; beständig; auf Rechnungen: bezahlt; ~ment [~lmənt] Erledigung f; Übereinkunft f; (Be)Siedlung f; ⚄ (Eigentums)Übertragung f; ~r [~lə] Siedler m.

set|-to F ['set'tu:] Kampf m; Schlägerei f; ~-up F Aufbau m; Am. sl. abgekartete Sache.

seven ['sevn] 1. sieben; 2. Sieben f; ~teen(th) [~n'ti:n(θ)] siebzehn (-te[r, -s]); ~th [~nθ] 1. ⬜ sieb(en)te(r, -s); 2. Sieb(en)tel n; ~thly [~θli] sieb(en)tens; ~tieth [~ntiiθ] siebzigste(r, -s); ~ty [~ti] 1. siebzig; 2. Siebzig f.

sever ['sevə] (sich) trennen; (auf-)lösen; zerreißen.

several ⬚ ['sevrəl] mehrere, verschiedene; einige; einzeln; besonder; getrennt; ~ly [~li] besonders, einzeln.

severance ['sevərəns] Trennung f.

sever|e ⬜ [si'viə] streng; rauh (Wetter); hart (Winter); scharf (Tadel); ernst (Mühe); heftig (Schmerz etc.); schlimm, schwer (Unfall etc.); ~ity [si'veriti] Strenge f, Härte f; Schwere f; Ernst m.

sew [sou] [irr.] nähen; heften.

sewage ['sju(:)idʒ] Abwasser n.

sewer[1] ['souə] Näherin f.

sewer[2] ['sjuə] Abwasserkanal m; ~age [~əridʒ] Kanalisation f.

sew|ing ['souiŋ] Nähen n; Näherei f; attr. Näh...; ~n [soun] p.p. von sew.

sex [seks] Geschlecht n.

sexton ['sekstən] Küster m, Totengräber m.

sexual ⬚ ['seksjuəl] geschlechtlich; Geschlechts...; sexuell; Sexual...

shabby ⬜ ['ʃæbi] schäbig; gemein.

shack Am. [ʃæk] Hütte f, Bude f.

shackle ['ʃækl] 1. Fessel f (fig. mst pl.); 2. fesseln.

shade [ʃeid] 1. Schatten m, Dunkel n (a. fig.); Lampen- etc. Schirm m; Schattierung f; Am. Rouleau n; fig. Spur f, Kleinigkeit f; 2. beschatten; verdunkeln (a. fig.); abschirmen; schützen; schattieren; ~ away, ~ off allmählich übergehen (lassen) (into in acc.).

shadow ['ʃædou] 1. Schatten m (a. fig.); Phantom n; Spur f, Kleinigkeit f; 2. beschatten (mst ~ forth od. out) andeuten; versinnbildlichen; j-n beschatten, überwachen; ~y [~oui] schattig, dunkel; schattenhaft; wesenlos.

shady ['ʃeidi] schattenspendend; schattig; dunkel; F zweifelhaft.

shaft [ʃa:ft] Schaft m; Stiel m; Pfeil m (a. fig.); poet. Strahl m; ⊕ Welle f; Deichsel f; ⚒ Schacht m.

shaggy ['ʃægi] zottig.

shake [ʃeik] 1. [irr.] v/t. schütteln, rütteln; erschüttern; ~ down herunterschütteln; Stroh etc. hinschütten; ~ hands sich die Hände geben od. schütteln; ~ up Bett aufschütteln; fig. aufrütteln; v/i. zittern, beben, wackeln, wanken (with vor dat.); ♩ trillern; 2. Schütteln n; Erschütterung f; Beben n; ♩ Triller m; ~-down ['ʃeik'daun] 1. Notlager n; Am. sl. Erpressung f; 2. adj.: ~ cruise ⚓ Probefahrt f; ~-hands m; Händedruck m; ~n ['ʃeikən] 1. p.p. von shake 1; 2. adj. erschüttert.

shaky □ ['ʃeiki] wack(e)lig (*a. fig.*); (sch)wankend; zitternd, zitterig.

shall [ʃæl] [*irr.*] *v/aux.* soll; werde.

shallow ['ʃælou] **1.** seicht; flach; *fig.* oberflächlich; **2.** Untiefe *f*; **3.** (sich) verflachen.

sham [ʃæm] **1.** falsch; Schein...; **2.** Trug *m*; Täuschung *f*; Schwindler(in); **3.** *v/t.* vortäuschen; *v/i.* sich verstellen; simulieren; ~ ill (-ness) sich krank stellen.

shamble ['ʃæmbl] watscheln; ~s *pl. od. sg.* Schlachthaus *n*; *fig.* Schlachtfeld *n*.

shame [ʃeim] **1.** Scham *f*; Schande *f*; *for* ~!, ~ *on you!* pfui!, schäm dich!; *put to* ~ beschämen; **2.** beschämen; *j-m* Schande machen; ~faced □ ['ʃeimfeist] schamhaft, schüchtern; ~ful □ [~ful] schändlich, beschämend; ~less □ ['ʃeimlis] schamlos.

shampoo [ʃæm'pu:] **1.** Shampoo *n*; Haarwäsche *f*; **2.** *Haare* waschen.

shamrock ['ʃæmrɔk] Kleeblatt *n*.

shank [ʃæŋk] (Unter)Schenkel *m*; ♀ Stiel *m*; (⚓ Anker)Schaft *m*.

shanty ['ʃænti] Hütte *f*, Bude *f*.

shape [ʃeip] **1.** (An)Teil *m*; Beitrag *m*; ♦ Aktie *f*; ⚔ Kux *m*; *have a* ~ *in* teilhaben an (*dat.*); *go* ~s teilen; **2.** *v/t.* teilen; *v/i.* teilhaben (*in an dat.*); ~cropper *Am.* ['ʃeəkrɔpə] *kleiner* Farmpächter; ~holder ♦ Aktionär(in).

shark [ʃɑ:k] *ichth.* Hai(fisch) *m*; Gauner *m*; *Am. sl.* Kanone *f* (*Experte*).

sharp [ʃɑ:p] **1.** □ *allg.* scharf (*a. fig.*); spitz; schneidend, stechend; schrill; hitzig; schnell; pfiffig, schlau, gerissen; *C* ~ ♩ *Cis n*; **2.** *adv.* ♩ zu hoch; F pünktlich; *look* ~! (mach) schnell!; **3.** ♩ Kreuz *n*; durch ein Kreuz erhöhte Note; F Gauner *m*; ~en ['ʃɑ:pən] (ver-)schärfen; spitzen; ~ener ['ʃɑ:pnə] *Messer*-Schärfer *m*; *Bleistift*-Spitzer *m*; ~er ['ʃɑ:pə] Gauner *m*; ~ness ['ʃɑ:pnis] Schärfe *f* (*a. fig.*); ~set ['ʃɑ:p'set] hungrig; erpicht; ~sighted scharfsichtig; ~witted scharfsinnig.

shatter ['ʃætə] zerschmettern, zerschlagen; *Nerven etc.* zerrütten.

shave [ʃeiv] **1.** [*irr.*] (sich) rasieren; (ab)schälen; haarscharf vorbeigehen *od.* vorbeifahren *od.* vorbeikommen an (*dat.*); **2.** Rasieren *n*, Rasur *f*; *have a* ~ sich rasieren (lassen); *a close* ~ ein Entkommen mit knapper Not; ~n ['ʃeivn] *p.p. von* shave 1.

shaving ['ʃeiviŋ] **1.** Rasieren *n*; ~s *pl.* (*bsd.* Hobel)Späne *m/pl.*; **2.** Rasier...

shawl [ʃɔ:l] Schal *m*, Kopftuch *n*.

she [ʃi:] **1.** sie; **2.** Sie *f*; *zo.* Weibchen *n*; **3.** *adj. in Zssgn*: weiblich, ...weibchen *n*; ~dog Hündin *f*.

sheaf [ʃi:f], *pl.* **sheaves** [ʃi:vz] Garbe *f*; Bündel *n*.

shear [ʃiə] **1.** [*irr.*] scheren; *fig.* rupfen; **2.** ~s *pl.* große Schere.

sheath [ʃi:θ] Scheide *f*; ~e [ʃi:ð] (in die Scheide) stecken; einhüllen; ⊕ bekleiden, beschlagen.

sheaves [ʃi:vz] *pl. von* sheaf.

shebang *Am. sl.* [ʃə'bæŋ] Bude *f*, Laden *m*.

shed[1] [ʃed] [*irr.*] aus-, vergießen; verbreiten; *Blätter etc.* abwerfen.

shed[2] [~] Schuppen *m*; Stall *m*.

sheen [ʃi:n] Glanz *m* (*bsd. Stoff*).

sheep [ʃi:p] Schaf(e *pl.*) *n*; Schafleder *n*; ~cot □ ['ʃi:pkɔt] = sheepfold; ~dog Schäferhund *m*; ~fold Schafhürde *f*; ~ish □ ['ʃi:pʃ] blöd(e), einfältig; ~man *Am.* Schafzüchter *m*; ~skin Schaffell *n*; Schafleder *n*; F Diplom *n*.

sheer [ʃiə] rein; glatt; *Am.* hauchdünn; steil; senkrecht; direkt.

sheet [ʃi:t] Bett-, Leintuch *n*, Laken *n*; (*Glas- etc.*)Platte *f*; ⊕ ...blech *n*; Blatt *n*, Bogen *m Papier*; weite Fläche (*Wasser etc.*); ⚓ Schot(e) *f*; *the rain came down in* ~s es regnete in Strömen; ~ *iron* Eisenblech *n*; ~ *lightning* ['ʃi:tlaitniŋ] Wetterleuchten *n*.

shelf [ʃelf], *pl.* **shelves** [ʃelvz] Brett *n*, Regal *n*, Fach *n*; Riff *n*; *on the* ~ *fig.* ausrangiert.

shell [ʃel] **1.** Schale *f*, Hülse *f*, Muschel *f*; Gehäuse *n*; Gerippe *n* *e-s Hauses*; ⚔ Granate *f*; **2.** schälen, enthülsen; ⚔ bombardieren; ~fire ['ʃelfaiə] Granatfeuer *n*; ~fish *zo.* Schalentier *n*; ~proof bombensicher.

shelter ['ʃeltə] **1.** Schuppen *m*; Schutz-, Obdach *n*; *fig.* Schutz *m*, Schirm *m*; **2.** *v/t.* (be)schützen; (be)schirmen; Zuflucht gewähren (*dat.*); *v/i. a. take* ~ Schutz suchen.

shelve [ʃelv] mit Brettern *od.* Regalen versehen; auf ein Brett stellen; *fig.* zu den Akten legen; *fig.* beiseite legen; sich allmählich neigen.

shelves [ʃelvz] *pl. von* shelf.

shenanigan *Am.* F [ʃi'næniɡən] Gaunerei *f*; Humbug *m*.

shepherd ['ʃepəd] **1.** Schäfer *m*, Hirt *m*; **2.** (be)hüten; leiten.

sherbet ['ʃə:bət] Brauselimonade *f*; (*Art*) (Speise)Eis *n*.

shield [ʃi:ld] **1.** (Schutz)Schild *m*; Wappenschild *m*, *n*; **2.** (be)schirmen (*from vor dat.*, *gegen*).

shift [ʃift] **1.** Veränderung *f*, Verschiebung f, Wechsel m; Notbehelf m; List f, Kniff m; Ausflucht f; (Arbeits)Schicht f; make ~ es möglich machen (to inf zu inf.); sich behelfen; sich durchschlagen; 2. v/t. (ver-, weg)schieben; (ab)wechseln; verändern; Platz, Szene verlegen, verlagern; v/i. wechseln; sich verlagern; sich behelfen; ~ for o.s. sich selbst helfen; **~less** □ ['ʃiftlis] hilflos; faul; **~y** □ [~ti] fig. gerissen; unzuverlässig.

shilling ['ʃiliŋ] englischer Schilling.

shin [ʃin] 1. a. **~bone** Schienbein n; 2. ~ up hinaufklettern.

shine [ʃain] 1. Schein m; Glanz m; 2. [irr.] v/i. scheinen; leuchten; fig. glänzen, strahlen; v/t. blank putzen.

shingle ['ʃiŋgl] Schindel f; Am. F (Aushänge)Schild n; Strandkiesel m/pl.; **~s** pl. ♣ Gürtelrose f.

shiny □ ['ʃaini] blank, glänzend.

ship [ʃip] 1. Schiff n; Am. F Flugzeug n; 2. an Bord nehmen od. bringen; verschiffen, versenden; ♣ heuern; **~board** ['ʃipbɔːd]: on ~ ♣ an Bord; **~ment** ['ʃipmənt] Verschiffung f; Versand m, Schiffsladung f; **~owner** Reeder m; **~ping** ['ʃipiŋ] Verschiffung f; Schiffe n/pl., Flotte f; attr Schiffs...; Verschiffungs..., Verlade...; **~wreck** 1. Schiffbruch m; 2. scheitern (lassen); **~wrecked** schiffbrüchig; **~yard** Schiffswerft f.   [schaft f.]

shire ['ʃaiə, in Zssgn ...ʃiə] Grafschaft f.]

shirk [ʃəːk] sich drücken (um et.); **~er** ['ʃəːkə] Drückeberger m.

shirt [ʃəːt] Herrenhemd n; a. **~waist** Am. Hemdbluse f; **~sleeve** ['ʃəːtsliːv] 1. Hemdsärmel m; 2. hemdsärmelig; informell; ~ diplomacy bsd. Am. offene Diplomatie.

shiver ['ʃivə] 1. Splitter m; Schauer m; 2. zersplittern; schau(d)ern; (er)zittern; frösteln; **~y** [~əri] fröstelnd.

shoal [ʃoul] 1. Schwarm m, Schar f; Untiefe f; 2. flacher werden; 3. seicht.

shock [ʃɔk] 1. Garbenhaufen m; (Haar)Schopf m; Stoß m; Anstoß m; Erschütterung f, Schlag m; ♣ (Nerven)Schock m; 2. fig. verletzen; empören, Anstoß erregen bei; erschüttern; **~ing** □ ['ʃɔkiŋ] anstößig; empörend; haarsträubend.

shod [ʃɔd] pret. u. p.p. von shoe 2.

shoddy ['ʃɔdi] 1. Reißwolle f; fig. Schund m; Am. Protz m; 2. falsch; minderwertig; Am. protzig.

shoe [ʃuː] 1. Schuh m; Hufeisen n; 2. [irr.] beschuhen; beschlagen; **~black** ['ʃuːblæk] Schuhputzer m; **~blacking** Schuhwichse f; **~horn** Schuhanzieher m; **~lace** Schnürsenkel m; **~maker** Schuhmacher m; **~string** Schnürsenkel m.

shone [ʃɔn] pret. u. p.p. von shine 2.

shook [ʃuk] pret. von shake 1.

shoot [ʃuːt] 1. fig. Schuß m; ♣ Schößling m; 2. [irr.] v/t. (ab-)schießen; erschießen; werfen, stoßen; Film aufnehmen, drehen; fig. unter ~er Brücke etc. hindurchschießen, über et. hinwegschießen; ♣ treiben; ♣ (ein)spritzen; v/i. schießen; stechen (Schmerz); daherschießen; stürzen; a ~ forth ♣ ausschlagen; ~ ahead vorwärtsschießen; **~er** ['ʃuːtə] Schütze m.

shooting ['ʃuːtiŋ] 1. Schießen n; Schießerei f; Jagd f; Film Dreharbeiten f/pl.; 2. stechend (Schmerz); **~gallery** Schießstand m, -bude f; **~range** Schießplatz m; ~ star Sternschnuppe f.

shop [ʃɔp] 1. Laden m, Geschäft n; Werkstatt f, Betrieb m; talk ~ fachsimpeln; 2. mst go ~ping einkaufen gehen; **~assistant** ['ʃɔpəsistənt] Verkäufer(in); **~keeper** Ladeninhaber(in); **~lifter** ['ʃɔpliftə] Ladendieb m; **~man** Ladengehilfe m; **~per** ['ʃɔpə] Käufer(in); **~ping** ['ʃɔpiŋ] Einkaufen n; attr Einkaufs...; ~ centre Einkaufszentrum n; **~steward** Betriebsrat m; **~walker** ['ʃɔpwɔːkə] Aufsichtsherr m, -dame f; **~window** Schaufenster n.

shore [ʃɔː] 1. Küste f, Ufer n; Strand m; Stütze f; on ~ an Land; 2. ~ up abstützen.

shorn [ʃɔːn] p.p. von shear 1.

short [ʃɔːt] 1. adj. kurz (a. fig.); klein; knapp; mürbe (Gebäck); wortkarg; in ~ kurz(um); ~ of knapp an (dat.); 2. adv. ~ of abgesehen von; come od. fall ~ of nicht erreichen; cut ~ plötzlich unterbrechen; run ~ (of) ausgehen (Vorräte); stop ~ of zurückschrecken vor (dat.); **~age** ['ʃɔːtidʒ] Fehlbetrag m; Gewichtsverlust m; Knappheit f; **~coming** Unzulänglichkeit f; Fehler m; Mangel m; ~ cut Abkürzungsweg m; **~dated** † auf kurze Sicht; **~en** ['ʃɔːtn] v/t. ab-, verkürzen; v/i. kürzer werden; **~ening** [~iŋ] Backfett n; **~hand** Kurzschrift f; ~ typist Stenotypistin f; **~ly** ['ʃɔːtli] adv. kurz; bald; **~ness** ['ʃɔːtnis] Kürze f; Mangel m; **~sighted** kurzsichtig; **~term** kurzfristig; **~winded** kurzatmig.

shot [ʃɔt] 1. pret. u. p.p. von shoot 2; 2. Schuß m; Geschoß n, Kugel f; Schrot(korn) n; Schußweite f; Schütze m; Sport Stoß m, Schlag m, Wurf m; phot., Film Aufnahme f; ♣ Spritze f; have a ~ at et. versuchen; not by a long ~ F noch lange nicht; big ~ F großes Tier; **~gun** ['ʃɔtgʌn] Schrotflinte f; ~ marriage Am. F Mußheirat f.

should [ʃud, ʃəd] pret. von shall.

shoulder ['ʃouldə] **1.** Schulter *f* (*a. v. Tieren*; *fig Vorsprung*); Achsel *f*; **2.** auf die Schulter *od. fig.* auf sich nehmen, ⚒ schultern; drängen; **~-blade** *anat* Schulterblatt *n*; **~strap** Träger *m am Kleid*; ⚔ Schulter-, Achselstück *n*.

shout [ʃaut] **1.** lauter Schrei *od.* Ruf; Geschrei *n*, **2.** laut schreien.

shove [ʃʌv] **1.** Schub *m*, Stoß *m*; **2.** schieben, stoßen.

shovel ['ʃʌvl] **1.** Schaufel *f*; **2.** schaufeln.

show [ʃou] **1.** [*irr.*] *v/t.* zeigen; ausstellen, erweisen; beweisen; **~** *in* hereinführen; **~** *off* zur Geltung bringen; **~** *out* hinausgeleiten; **~** *round* herumführen; **~** *up* hinaufführen, entlarven, *v/i. a* **~** *up* sich zeigen, zu sehen sein; **~** *off* angeben, prahlen, sich aufspielen; **2.** Schau(stellung) *f*; Ausstellung *f*; Auf-, Vorführung *f*, Anschein *m*; on **~** zu besichtigen, **~ business** ['ʃoubiznis] Unterhaltungsindustrie *f*; Schaugeschäft *n*, **~-case** Schaukasten *m*, Vitrine *f*, **~-down** Aufdecken *n* der Karten (*bsd. Am. a. fig.*); *fig.* Kraftprobe *f*.

shower ['ʃauə] **1.** (Regen)Schauer *m*; Dusche *f*; *fig* Fülle *f*; **2.** *v/t.* herabschütten (*a. fig.*); überschütten; *v/i* sich ergießen (*a.*); **~y** ['ʃauəri] regnerisch.

show|n [ʃoun] *p.p. von show* 1; **~room** ['ʃourum] Ausstellungsraum *m*; **~window** Schaufenster *n*; **~y** ▢ ['ʃoui] prächtig, protzig.

shrank [ʃræŋk] *pret von shrink.*

shred [ʃred] **1.** Stückchen *n*; Schnitz(el *n*) *m*; Fetzen *m* (*a. fig.*); **2.** [*irr.*] (zer)schnitzeln, zerfetzen.

shrew [ʃru:] zänkisches Weib.

shrewd ▢ [ʃru:d] scharfsinnig schlau

shriek [ʃri:k] **1.** (Angst)Schrei *m*; Gekreisch *n*; **2.** kreischen, schreien.

shrill [ʃril] **1.** ▢ schrill, gellend; **2.** schrillen, gellen; schreien.

shrimp [ʃrimp] *zo.* Krabbe *f*; *fig.* Knirps *m.* [*m.*]

shrine [ʃrain] Schrein *m*; Altar]

shrink [ʃriŋk] [*irr.*] (ein-, zs.-) schrumpfen (lassen); einlaufen; sich zurückziehen; zurückschrecken (*from, at* vor *dat.*); **~age** ['ʃriŋkidʒ] Einlaufen *n*, Zs.-schrumpfen *n*; Schrumpfung *f*; *fig.* Verminderung *f*.

shrivel ['ʃrivl] einschrumpfen (lassen).

shroud [ʃraud] **1.** Leichentuch *n*; *fig.* Gewand *n*; **2.** in ein Leichentuch einhüllen; *fig.* hüllen.

Shrove|tide ['ʃrouvtaid] Fastnachtszeit *f*; **~ Tuesday** Fastnachtsdienstag *m.*

shrub [ʃrʌb] Strauch *m*; Busch *m*; **~bery** ['ʃrʌbəri] Gebüsch *n.*

shrug [ʃrʌg] **1.** (die Achseln) zucken; **2.** Achselzucken *n.*

shrunk [ʃrʌŋk] *p.p. von shrink*; **~en** ['ʃrʌŋkən] *adj.* (ein)geschrumpft.

shuck *bsd. Am.* [ʃʌk] **1.** Hülse *f*, Schote *f*; **~s!** F Quatsch!; **2.** enthülsen.

shudder ['ʃʌdə] **1.** schaudern; (er-) beben; **2.** Schauder *m.*

shuffle ['ʃʌfl] **1.** schieben; *Karten*: mischen; schlurfen; Ausflüchte machen; **~** *off* von sich schieben, abstreifen; **2.** Schieben *n*; Mischen *n*; Schlurfen *n*; Ausflucht *f*; Schiebung *f*.

shun [ʃʌn] (ver)meiden.

shunt [ʃʌnt] **1.** ⚙ Rangieren *n*; ⚡ Weiche *f*; ⚡ Nebenschluß *m*; **2.** ⚙ rangieren; ⚡ nebenschließen; *fig.* verschieben.

shut [ʃʌt] [*irr.*] (sich) schließen; zumachen; **~** *down Betrieb* schließen; **~** *up* ein-, verschließen; einsperren; **~** *up!* F halt den Mund!; **~ter** ['ʃʌtə] Fensterladen *m*; *phot.* Verschluß *m.*

shuttle ['ʃʌtl] **1.** ⊕ Schiffchen *n*; Pendelverkehr *m*; **2.** pendeln.

shy [ʃai] **1.** ▢ scheu; schüchtern; **2.** (zurück)scheuen (*at* vor *dat.*).

shyness ['ʃainis] Schüchternheit *f*; Scheu *f.*

shyster *sl., bsd. Am.* ['ʃaistə] gerissener Kerl; Winkeladvokat *m.*

Siberian [sai'biəriən] **1.** sibirisch; **2.** Sibirier(in).

sick [sik] krank (*of an dat.*; *with vor dat.*); übel; überdrüssig; be **~** *for* sich sehnen nach; be **~** *of* genug haben von; *go* **~** *report* **~** sich krank melden; **~-benefit** ['sikbenifit] Krankengeld *n*; **~en** ['sikn] *v/i.* krank werden; kränkeln; **~** *at* sich ekeln vor (*dat.*); *v/t.* krank machen; anekeln.

sickle ['sikl] Sichel *f.*

sick|-leave ['sikli:v] Krankheitsurlaub *m*; **~ly** [~li] kränklich; schwächlich; bleich, blaß; ungesund (*Klima*); ekelhaft; matt (*Lächeln*); **~ness** ['siknis] Krankheit *f*; Übelkeit *f.*

side [said] **1.** *allg.* Seite *f*; **~** *by* **~** Seite an Seite; *take* **~** *with* Partei ergreifen für; **2.** Seiten...; Neben...; **3.** Partei ergreifen (*with* für); **~board** ['saidbɔ:d] Anrichte(tisch *m*) *f*, Sideboard *n*; **~car** *mot.* Beiwagen *m*; **~d** ...seitig; **~light** Streiflicht *n*; **~long 1.** *adv.* seitwärts; **2.** *adj.* seitlich; Seiten...; **~-stroke** Seitenschwimmen *n*; **~-track 1.** ⚙ Nebengleis *n*; **2.** auf ein Nebengleis schieben; *bsd. Am. fig.* aufschieben; beiseite schieben; **~walk** *bsd. Am.* Bürgersteig *m*; **~ward(s)** [~wəd(z)], **~ways** seitlich; seitwärts.

siding ⚙ ['saidiŋ] Nebengleis *n.*

sidle ['saidl] seitwärts gehen.

siege [si:dʒ] Belagerung f; *lay ~ to* belagern.

sieve [siv] 1. Sieb n; 2. (durch-) sieben.

sift [sift] sieben; *fig.* sichten; prüfen.

sigh [sai] 1. Seufzer m; 2. seufzen; sich sehnen (*after, for* nach).

sight [sait] 1. Sehvermögen n, Sehkraft f; *fig.* Auge n; Anblick m; Visier n; Sicht f; *~s pl.* Sehenswürdigkeiten f/pl.; *at ~, a. on ~* beim Anblick; *f* vom Blatt; *↑* nach Sicht; *catch ~ of* erblicken, zu Gesicht bekommen; *lose ~ of* aus den Augen verlieren; *within ~* in Sicht; *know by ~* vom Sehen kennen; 2. sichten; (an)visieren; *~ed* ['saitid] ...sichtig; *~ly* ['saitli] ansehnlich, stattlich; *~seeing* ['saitsi:iŋ] Besichtigung f von Sehenswürdigkeiten; *~seer* Tourist(in).

sign [sain] 1. Zeichen n; Wink m; Schild n; *in ~ of* zum Zeichen (*gen.*); 2. *v/i.* winken, Zeichen geben; *v/t.* (unter)zeichnen, unterschreiben.

signal ['signl] 1. Signal n; Zeichen n; 2. □ bemerkenswert, außerordentlich; 3. signalisieren; *~ize* [~nəlaiz] auszeichnen; *~ = signal 3.*

signat|ory ['signətəri] 1. Unterzeichner m; 2. unterzeichnend; *~ powers pl.* Signatarmächte f/pl.; *~ure* [~nitʃə] Signatur f; Unterschrift f; *~ tune Radio:* Kennmelodie f.

sign|board ['sainbɔːd] (Aushänge-) Schild n; *~er* ['sainə] Unterzeichner(in).

signet ['signit] Siegel n.

signific|ance [sig'nifikəns] Bedeutung f; *~ant* □ [~nt] bedeutsam; bezeichnend (*of* für); *~ation* [signifi'keiʃən] Bedeutung f.

signify ['signifai] bezeichnen, andeuten; kundgeben; bedeuten.

signpost ['sainpoust] Wegweiser m.

silence ['sailəns] 1. (Still)Schweigen n; Stille f, Ruhe f; *~!* Ruhe! put od. reduce to ~ = 2. zum Schweigen bringen; *~r* [~sə] ⊕ Schalldämpfer m; *mot.* Auspufftopf m.

silent □ ['sailənt] still; schweigend; schweigsam; stumm; *~ partner ↑* stiller Teilhaber.

silk [silk] Seide f; *attr.* Seiden...; *~en* □ ['silkən] seiden; *~-stocking Am.* □ vornehm; *~worm* Seidenraupe f; *~y* □ [~ki] seid(en)artig.

sill [sil] Schwelle f; Fensterbrett n.

silly □ ['sili] albern, töricht.

silt [silt] 1. Schlamm m; 2. *mst ~ up* verschlammen.

silver ['silvə] 1. Silber n; 2. silbern; Silber...; 3. versilbern; silberig od. silberweiß werden (lassen); *~ware Am.* Tafelsilber n; *~y* [~əri] silberglänzend; silberhell.

---

similar □ ['similə] ähnlich, gleich; *~ity* [simi'læriti] Ähnlichkeit f.

simile ['simili] Gleichnis n.

similitude [si'militjuːd] Gestalt f; Ebenbild n; Gleichnis n.

simmer ['simə] sieden *od.* brodeln (lassen); *fig.* kochen, gären (*Gefühl, Aufstand*); *~ down* ruhig(er) werden.

simper ['simpə] 1. einfältiges Lächeln; 2. einfältig lächeln.

simple □ ['simpl] einfach; schlicht; einfältig, arglos; *~-hearted, ~-minded* arglos, naiv; *~ton* [~ltən] Einfaltspinsel m.

simpli|city [sim'plisiti] Einfachheit f; Klarheit f; Schlichtheit f; Einfalt f; *~fication* [simplifi'keiʃən] Vereinfachung f; *~fy* ['simplifai] vereinfachen.

simply ['simpli] einfach; bloß.

simulate ['simjuleit] vortäuschen; (er)heucheln; sich tarnen als.

simultaneous □ [siməl'teinjəs] gleichzeitig.

sin [sin] 1. Sünde f; 2. sündigen.

since [sins] 1. *prp.* seit; 2. *adv.* seitdem; 3. *cj.* seit(dem); da (ja).

sincer|e □ [sin'siə] aufrichtig; *Yours ~ly* Ihr ergebener; *~ity* [~'seriti] Aufrichtigkeit f.

sinew ['sinju:] Sehne f; *fig. mst. ~s pl.* Nerven(kraft f) m/pl.; Seele f; *~y* [~ju(:)i] sehnig; nervig, stark.

sinful □ ['sinful] sündig, sündhaft, böse.

sing [siŋ] [*irr.*] singen; besingen; *~ to s.o.* j-m vorsingen.

singe [sindʒ] (ver)sengen.

singer ['siŋə] Sänger(in).

singing ['siŋiŋ] Gesang m, Singen n; *~ bird* Singvogel m.

single ['siŋgl] 1. □ einzig; einzeln; Einzel...; einfach; ledig, unverheiratet; *book-keeping by ~ entry* einfache Buchführung; *~ file* Gänsemarsch m; 2. einfache Fahrkarte; *mst ~s pl. Tennis:* Einzel n; 3. *~ out* auswählen, aussuchen; *~-breasted* einreihig (*Jacke etc.*); *~-engined* ✈ einmotorig; *~-handed* eigenhändig, allein; *~-hearted* □, *~-minded* □ aufrichtig; zielstrebig; *~t* [~lit] Unterhemd n; *~-track* eingleisig.

singular ['siŋgjulə] 1. □ einzigartig; eigenartig; sonderbar; 2. *a. ~ number gr.* Singular m, Einzahl f; *~ity* [siŋgju'læriti] Einzigartigkeit f; Sonderbarkeit f.

sinister □ ['sinistə] unheilvoll; böse.

sink [siŋk] 1. [*irr.*] *v/i.* sinken; nieder-, unter-, versinken; sich senken; eindringen; erliegen; *v/t.* (ver)senken; *Brunnen* bohren; *Geld* festlegen; *Namen etc.* aufgeben; 2. Ausguß m; *~ing* ['siŋkiŋ] (Ver-)Sinken n; Versenken n; ⚓ Schwäche(gefühl n) f; Senkung f; *↑*

Tilgung *f*; ~ fund (Schulden)Tilgungsfonds *m*.

sinless ['sinlis] sündenlos, -frei.

sinner ['sinə] Sünder(in)

sinuous ☐ ['sinjuəs] gewunden.

sip [sip] **1.** Schlückchen *n*; **2.** schlürfen; nippen, langsam trinken.

sir [sə:] Herr *m*; ~ Sir (*Titel*).

sire ['saiə] *mst poet* Vater *m*; Vorfahr *m*; *zo.* Vater(tier *n*) *m*.

siren ['saiərin] Sirene *f*.

sirloin ['sə:lɔin] Lendenstück *n*.

sissy *Am.* ['sisi] Weichling *m*.

sister ['sistə] (*a.* Ordens-, Ober-) Schwester *f*; ~hood [~hud] Schwesternschaft *f*; ~in-law [~ərinlɔ:] Schwägerin *f*; ~ly [~əli] schwesterlich

sit [sit] [*irr.*] *v/i.* sitzen; Sitzung halten, tagen; *fig.* liegen; ~ down sich setzen; ~ up aufrecht sitzen; aufbleiben; *v/t.* setzen; sitzen auf (*dat.*).

site [sait] Lage *f*; (Bau)Platz *m*.

sitting ['sitiŋ] Sitzung *f*; ~-room Wohnzimmer *n*.

situat|ed ['sitjueitid] gelegen; be ~ liegen, gelegen sein; ~ion [sitju-'eiʃən] Lage *f*; Stellung *f*.

six [siks] **1.** sechs; **2.** Sechs *f*, ~teen ['siks'ti:n] sechzehn; ~teenth [~nθ] sechzehnte(r, -s); ~th [siksθ] **1.** sechste(r, -s); **2.** Sechstel *n*; ~thly ['siksθli] sechstens; ~tieth [~stiiθ] sechzigste(r, -s); ~ty [~ti] **1.** sechzig; **2.** Sechzig *f*.

size [saiz] **1.** Größe *f*; Format *n*; **2.** nach der Größe ordnen; ~ up *F j-n* abschätzen; ~d von Größe.

siz(e)able ☐ ['saizəbl] ziemlich groß.

sizzle ['sizl] zischen, knistern, brutzeln; *sizzling hot* glühend heiß.

skat|e [skeit] **1.** Schlittschuh *m*; *roller-*~ Rollschuh *m*; **2.** Schlittod. Rollschuh laufen; ~er ['skeitə] Schlittschuh-, Rollschuhläufer(in).

skedaddle F [ski'dædl] abhauen.

skeesicks *Am.* F ['ski:ziks] Nichtsnutz *m*.

skein [skein] Strähne *f*, Docke *f*.

skeleton ['skelitn] Skelett *n*; Gerippe *n*; Gestell *n*; *attr.* Skelett...; ✗ Stamm..., ~ key Nachschlüssel *m*.

skeptic ['skeptik] *s.* sceptic.

sketch [sketʃ] **1.** Skizze *f*; Entwurf *m*; Umriß *m*; **2.** skizzieren, entwerfen.

ski [ski:] **1.** *pl. a.* ski Schi *m*, Ski *m*; **2.** Schi od. Ski laufen.

skid [skid] **1.** Hemmschuh *m*, Bremsklotz *m*; ✗ (Gleit)Kufe *f*; Rutschen *n*; *mot.* Schleudern *n*; **2.** *v/t.* hemmen; *v/i.* (aus)rutschen.

skiddoo *Am. sl.* [ski'du:] abhauen.

ski|er ['ski:ə] Schi-, Skiläufer(in); ~ing ['ski:iŋ] Schi-, Skilauf(en *n*) *m*.

skilful ☐ ['skilful] geschickt; kundig.

~kill [skil] Geschicklichkeit *f*, Fertigkeit *f*; ~ed [skild] geschickt; gelernt; ~ worker Facharbeiter *m*.

skillful *Am.* ['skilful] *s.* skilful.

skim [skim] **1.** abschöpfen; abrahmen; dahingleiten über (*acc.*); *Buch* überfliegen; ~ through durchblättern; **2.** ~ milk Magermilch *f*.

skimp [skimp] *j-n* knapp halten; sparen (mit *et.*); ~y ☐ ['skimpi] knapp, dürftig.

skin [skin] **1.** Haut *f*; Fell *n*; Schale *f*; **2.** *v/t.* (ent)häuten; abbalgen; schälen; ~ off F abstreifen; *v/i. a.* ~ over zuheilen; ~-deep ['skin'di:p] (nur) oberflächlich; ~flint Knicker *m*; ~ny [~ni] mager.

skip [skip] **1.** Sprung *m*; **2.** *v/i.* hüpfen, springen; seilhüpfen; *v/t.* überspringen.

skipper ['skipə] ⚓ Schiffer *m*; ⚓, ✗, *Sport:* Kapitän *m*.

skirmish ['skə:miʃ] **1.** ✗ Scharmützel *n*; **2.** plänkeln.

skirt [skə:t] **1.** (Damen)Rock *m*; (Rock)Schoß *m*; *oft* ~s *pl.* Rand *m*, Saum *m*; **2.** umsäumen; (sich) entlangziehen (an *dat.*); entlangfahren; ~ing-board ['skə:tiŋbɔ:d] Scheuerleiste *f*.

skit [skit] Stichelei *f*; Satire *f*; ~tish ☐ ['skitiʃ] ungebärdig.

skittle ['skitl] Kegel *m*; *play (at)* ~s Kegel schieben; ~alley Kegelbahn *f*. [Gemeinheit *f*.]

skulduggery *Am.* F [skʌl'dʌgəri]]

skulk [skʌlk] schleichen; sich verstecken; lauern; sich drücken; ~er ['skʌlkə] Drückeberger *m*.

skull [skʌl] Schädel *m*.

sky [skai] *oft skies pl.* Himmel *m*; ~lark ['skaila:k] **1.** *orn.* Feldlerche *f*; **2.** Ulk treiben; ~light Oberlicht *n*; Dachfenster *n*; ~line Horizont *m*; Silhouette *f*; ~rocket F emporschnellen; ~scraper Wolkenkratzer *m*; ~ward(s) ['skaiwəd(z)] himmelwärts.

slab [slæb] Platte *f*; Scheibe *f*; Fliese *f*.

slack [slæk] **1.** schlaff; locker; (nach)lässig; ✝ flau; **2.** ⚓ Lose *n* (*loses Tauende*); ✝ Flaute *f*; Kohlengrus *m*; **3.** = slacken; = slake; ~en ['slækən] schlaff machen *od.* werden; verringern; nachlassen; (sich) lockern; (sich) entspannen; (sich) verlangsamen; ~s *pl.* (lange) Hose.

slag [slæg] Schlacke *f*.

slain [slein] *p.p. von* slay.

slake [sleik] *Durst, Kalk* löschen; *fig.* stillen.

slam [slæm] **1.** Zuschlagen *n*; Knall *m*; **2.** *Tür etc.* zuschlagen, zuknallen; *et. auf den Tisch etc.* knallen.

slander ['sla:ndə] **1.** Verleumdung *f*; **2.** verleumden; ~ous ☐ [~rəs] verleumderisch.

slang [slæŋ] **1.** Slang *m*; Berufssprache *f*; lässige Umgangssprache; **2.** *j-n* wüst beschimpfen.

slant [slɑ:nt] **1.** schräge Fläche; Abhang *m*; Neigung *f*; *Am.* Standpunkt *m*; **2.** schräg legen *od.* liegen; sich neigen; ~**ing** *adj.*, □ ['slɑ:ntiŋ], ~**wise** *adv.* [~twaiz] schief, schräg.

slap [slæp] **1.** Klaps *m*, Schlag *m*; **2.** klapsen; schlagen; klatschen; ~**jack** *Am.* ['slæpdʒæk] *Art* Pfannkuchen *m*; ~**stick** (Narren)Pritsche *f*; *a.* ~ comedy *thea.* Posse *f*, Burleske *f*.

slash [slæʃ] **1.** Hieb *m*; Schnitt *m*; Schlitz *m*; **2.** (auf)schlitzen; schlagen, hauen; verreißen (*Kritiker*).

slate [sleit] **1.** Schiefer *m*; Schiefertafel *f*; *bsd. Am.* Kandidatenliste *f*; **2.** mit Schiefer decken; heftig kritisieren; *Am.* F *für e-n* Posten vorschlagen; ~**pencil** ['sleit'pensl] Griffel *m*.

slattern ['slætə(:)n] Schlampe *f*.

slaughter ['slɔ:tə] **1.** Schlachten *n*; Gemetzel *n*; **2.** schlachten; niedermetzeln; ~**house** Schlachthaus *n*.

Slav [slɑ:v] **1.** Slaw|e *m*, -in *f*; **2.** slawisch.

slave [sleiv] **1.** Sklav|e *m*, -in *f* (*a. fig.*); **2.** F sich placken, schuften.

slaver ['sleivə] **1.** Geifer *m*, Sabber *m*; **2.** (be)geifern, F (be)sabbern.

slav|ery ['sleivəri] Sklaverei *f*; F Plackerei *f*; ~**ish** □ [~viʃ] sklavisch.

slay *rhet.* [slei] [*irr.*] erschlagen; töten.

sled [sled] = *sledge* 1.

sledge[1] [sledʒ] **1.** Schlitten *m*; **2.** Schlitten fahren.

sledge[2] [~] *a.* ~**hammer** Schmiedehammer *m*.

sleek [sli:k] **1.** □ glatt, geschmeidig; **2.** glätten; ~**ness** ['sli:knis] Glätte *f*.

sleep [sli:p] **1.** [*irr.*] *v/i.* schlafen; ~ (up)on *od.* over *et.* beschlafen; *v/t.* *j-n* für die Nacht unterbringen; ~ away *Zeit* verschlafen; **2.** Schlaf *m*; go to ~ einschlafen; ~**er** ['sli:pə] Schläfer(in); ⚏ Schwelle *f*; Schlafwagen *m*; ~**ing** [~piŋ] schlafend; Schlaf...; **⚏ing Beauty** Dornröschen *n*; ~**ing-car(riage)** ⚏ Schlafwagen *m*; ~**ing partner** † stiller Teilhaber; ~**less** □ [~plis] schlaflos; ~ **walker** Schlafwandler(in); ~**y** □ [~pi] schläfrig; verschlafen.

sleet [sli:t] **1.** Graupelregen *m*; **2.** graupeln; ~**y** ['sli:ti] graupelig.

sleeve [sli:v] Ärmel *m*; ⊕ Muffe *f*; ~**link** ['sli:vliŋk] Manschettenknopf *m*.

sleigh [slei] **1.** (*bsd.* Pferde)Schlitten *m*; **2.** (im) Schlitten fahren.

sleight [slait]: ~**of-hand** Taschenspielerei *f*; Kunststück *n*.

slender □ ['slendə] schlank; schmächtig; schwach; dürftig.

slept [slept] *pret. u. p.p. von sleep* 1.

sleuth [slu:θ], ~**hound** ['slu:θhaund] Blut-, Spürhund *m* (*a. fig.*).

slew [slu:] *pret. von slay.*

slice [slais] **1.** Schnitte *f*, Scheibe *f*, Stück *n*; Teil *m, n*; **2.** (in) Scheiben schneiden; aufschneiden.

slick F [slik] **1.** *adj.* glatt; *fig.* raffiniert; **2.** *adv.* direkt; **3.** *a.* ~ *paper Am. sl.* vornehme Zeitschrift; ~**er** *Am.* F ['slikə] Regenmantel *m*; gerissener Kerl.

slid [slid] *pret. u. p.p. von slide* 1.

slide [slaid] **1.** [*irr.*] gleiten (lassen); rutschen; schlittern; ausgleiten; geraten (*into* in *acc.*); let things ~ die Dinge laufen lassen; **2.** Gleiten *n*; Rutsche *f*; ⊕ Schieber *m*; Diapositiv *n*; *a.* land. Erdrutsch *m*; ~**rule** ['slaidru:l] Rechenschieber *m*.

slight [slait] **1.** □ schmächtig; schwach; gering, unbedeutend; **2.** Geringschätzung *f*; **3.** geringschätzig behandeln; unbeachtet lassen.

slim [slim] **1.** □ schlank; dünn; schmächtig; dürftig; *sl.* schlau, gerissen; **2.** e-e Schlankheitskur machen.

slim|e [slaim] Schlamm *m*; Schleim *m*; ~**y** ['slaimi] schlammig; schleimig.

sling [sliŋ] **1.** Schleuder *f*; Tragriemen *m*; ✠ Schlinge *f*, Binde *f*; Wurf *m*; **2.** [*irr.*] schleudern; auf~, umhängen; *a.* ~ up hochziehen.

slink [sliŋk] [*irr.*] schleichen.

slip [slip] **1.** [*irr.*] *v/i.* schlüpfen, gleiten, rutschen; ausgleiten; ausrutschen; *oft* ~ away entschlüpfen; sich versehen; *v/t.* schlüpfen *od.* gleiten lassen; loslassen; entschlüpfen, entgleiten (*dat.*); ~ in Bemerkung dazwischenwerfen; ~ into hineinstecken *od.* hineinschieben in (*acc.*); ~ on (off) *Kleid* über-, (ab)streifen; have ~ped *s.o.'s* memory *j-m* entfallen sein; **2.** (Aus)Gleiten *n*; Fehltritt *m* (*a. fig.*); Versehen *n*; (Flüchtigkeits)Fehler *m*; Verstoß *m*; Streifen *m*; Zettel *m*; Unterkleid *n*; *a.* ~**way** ⚓ Helling *f*; (Kissen)Überzug *m*; ~**s** *pl.* Badehose *f*; give s.o. the ~ j-m entwischen; ~**per** ['slipə] Pantoffel *m*, Hausschuh *m*; ~**pery** □ [~əri] schlüpfrig; ~**shod** [~ʃɔd] schlampig, nachlässig; ~**t** [slipt] *pret. u. p.p. von slip* 1.

slit [slit] **1.** Schlitz *m*; Spalte *f*; **2.** [*irr.*] (auf-, zer)schlitzen.

sliver ['slivə] Splitter *m*.

slobber ['slɔbə] **1.** Sabber *m*; Gesabber *n*; **2.** F (be)sabbern.

slogan ['slougən] Schlagwort *n*, Losung *f*; (Werbe)Slogan *m*.

sloop ⚓ [slu:p] Schaluppe *f*.

slop [slɔp] 1. Pfütze f; ~s pl. Spül-, Schmutzwasser n; Krankenspeise f; 2. v/t. verschütten; v/i. überlaufen.

slope [sloup] 1. (Ab)Hang m; Neigung f; 2. schräg legen; ⊕ abschrägen; abfallen; schräg verlaufen; (sich) neigen.

sloppy ☐ ['slɔpi] naß, schmutzig; schlampig; F labb(e)rig; rührselig.

slops [slɔps] pl. billige Konfektionskleidung; ⚓ Kleidung f u. Bettzeug n.

slot [slɔt] Schlitz m.

sloth [slouθ] Faulheit f; zo. Faultier n.

slot-machine ['slɔtməʃiːn] (Warenod. Spiel)Automat m.

slouch [slautʃ] 1. faul herumhängen; F herumlatschen; 2. schlaffe Haltung; ~ hat Schlapphut m.

slough[1] [slau] Sumpf(loch n) m.

slough[2] [slʌf] Haut abwerfen.

sloven ['slʌvn] unordentlicher Mensch; F Schlampe f; ~ly [~nli] liederlich.

slow [slou] 1. ☐ langsam (of in dat.); schwerfällig; lässig; be ~ nachgehen (Uhr); 2. adv. langsam; 3. oft ~ down od. up od. off v/t. verlangsamen; v/i. langsam(er) werden od. gehen od. fahren; ~coach ['sloukoutʃ] Langweiler m; altmodischer Mensch; ~motion picture Zeitlupenaufnahme f; ~worm zo. Blindschleiche f.

sludge [slʌdʒ] Schlamm m; Matsch m.

slug [slʌg] 1. Stück n Rohmetall; zo. Wegschnecke f; Am. F (Faust-)Schlag m; 2. Am. F hauen.

slugg|ard ['slʌgəd] Faulenzer(in); ~ish ☐ [~giʃ] träge, faul.

sluice [sluːs] 1. Schleuse f; 2. ausströmen (lassen); ausspülen; waschen.

slum [slʌm] schmutzige Gasse; ~s pl. Elendsviertel n, Slums pl.

slumber ['slʌmbə] 1. a. ~s pl. Schlummer m; 2. schlummern.

slump [slʌmp] Börse: 1. fallen, stürzen; 2. (Kurs-, Preis)Sturz m.

slung [slʌŋ] pret. u. p.p. von sling 2.

slunk [slʌŋk] pret. u. p.p. von slink.

slur [slə:] 1. Fleck m; fig. Tadel m; ♩ Bindebogen m; 2. v/t. oft ~ over übergehen; ♩ Töne binden.

slush [slʌʃ] Schlamm m; Matsch m; F Kitsch m.

slut [slʌt] F Schlampe f; Nutte f.

sly ☐ [slai] schlau, verschmitzt; hinterlistig; on the ~ heimlich.

smack [smæk] 1. (Bei)Geschmack m; Prise f Salz etc.; fig. Spur f; Schmatz m; Schlag m, Klatsch m, Klaps m; 2. schmecken (of nach); e-n Beigeschmack haben; klatschen, knallen (mit); schmatzen (mit); j-m e-n Klaps geben.

small [smɔːl] 1. allg. klein; unbedeutend; fig. kleinlich; niedrig; wenig; feel ~, look ~ sich gedemütigt fühlen; the ~ hours die frühen Morgenstunden f/pl.; in a ~ way bescheiden; 2. dünner Teil; ~s pl. F Leibwäsche f; ~ of the back anat. Kreuz n; ~arms ['smɔːlɑːmz] pl. Handfeuerwaffen f/pl.; ~ change Kleingeld n; fig. triviale Bemerkungen f/pl.; ~ish [~liʃ] ziemlich klein; ~pox ⚕ [~pɔks] Pocken f/pl.; ~ talk Plauderei f; ~time Am. F unbedeutend.

smart [smɑːt] 1. ☐ scharf; gewandt; geschickt; gescheit; gerissen; schmuck, elegant, adrett; forsch; ~ aleck Am. F Neunmalkluge(r) m; 2. Schmerz m; 3. schmerzen; leiden; ~money ['smɑːtmʌni] Schmerzensgeld n; ~ness [~tnis] Klugheit f; Schärfe f; Gewandtheit f; Gerissenheit f; Eleganz f.

smash [smæʃ] 1. v/t. zertrümmern; fig. vernichten; (zer)schmettern; v/i. zerschellen; zs.-stoßen; fig. zs.-brechen; 2. Zerschmettern n; Krach m; Zs.-bruch m (a. ♱); Tennis: Schmetterball m; ~up ['smæʃʌp] Zs.-stoß m; Zs.-bruch m.

smattering ['smætəriŋ] oberflächliche Kenntnis.

smear [smiə] 1. (be)schmieren; fig. beschmutzen; 2. Schmiere f; Fleck m.

smell [smel] 1. Geruch m; 2. [irr.] riechen (of nach et.); a. ~ at riechen an (dat.); ~y ['smeli] übelriechend.

smelt[1] [smelt] pret. u. p.p. von smell 2.

smelt[2] [~] schmelzen.

smile [smail] 1. Lächeln n; 2. lächeln.

smirch [smə:tʃ] besudeln.

smirk [smə:k] grinsen.

smite [smait] [irr.] schlagen; heimsuchen; schwer treffen; quälen.

smith [smiθ] Schmied m.

smithereens ['smiðə'riːnz] pl. Stücke n/pl., Splitter m/pl, Fetzen m/pl.

smithy ['smiði] Schmiede f.

smitten ['smitn] 1. p.p. von smite; 2. adj. ergriffen; betroffen; fig. hingerissen (with von).

smock [smɔk] 1. fälteln; 2. Kittel m; ~frock ['smɔk'frɔk] Bauernkittel m.

smog [smɔg] Smog m, Gemisch n von Nebel und Rauch.

smoke [smouk] 1. Rauch m; have a ~ (eine) rauchen; 2. rauchen; dampfen; (aus)räuchern; ~dried ['smoukdraid] geräuchert; ~r [~kə] Raucher m; ⚓ F Raucherwagen m, -abteil n; ~stack [~], ⚓ Schornstein m.

smoking ['smoukiŋ] Rauchen n; attr. Rauch(er)...; ~compartment 🚃 Raucherabteil n.

smoky □ ['smouki] rauchig; verräuchert. [der.\]

smolder Am. ['smouldə] = smoul-\]

smooth [smu:ð] 1. □ glatt; fig. fließend; mild; schmeichlerisch; 2. glätten; ebnen (a. fig.); plätten; mildern; a. ~ over, ~ away fig. wegräumen; ~ness ['smu:ðnis] Glätte f.

smote [smout] pret. von smite.

smother ['smʌðə] ersticken.

smoulder ['smouldə] schwelen.

smudge [smʌdʒ] 1. (be)schmutzen; (be)schmieren; 2. Schmutzfleck m.

smug [smʌg] selbstzufrieden.

smuggle ['smʌgl] schmuggeln; ~r [~lə] Schmuggler(in).

smut [smʌt] Schmutz m; Ruß(fleck) m; Zoten f/pl.; 2. beschmutzen.

smutty ['smʌti] schmutzig.

snack [snæk] Imbiß m; ~-bar ['snækba:], ~-counter Snackbar f, Imbißstube f.

snaffle ['snæfl] Trense f.

snag [snæg] (Ast-, Zahn)Stumpf m; fig. Haken m; Am. Baumstumpf m (bsd. unter Wasser).

snail zo. [sneil] Schnecke f.

snake zo. [sneik] Schlange f.

snap [snæp] 1. Schnappen n, Biß m; Knack(s) m; Knall m; fig. Schwung m, Schmiß m; Schnappschloß n; phot. Schnappschuß m; cold ~ Kältewelle f; 2. v/i. schnappen (at nach); zuschnappen (Schloß); krachen; knacken; (zer)brechen; knallen; schnauzen; ~ at s.o. j-n anschnauzen; ~ into it! Am. sl. mach schnell!, Tempo!; ~ out of it! Am. sl. hör auf damit! komm, komm!; v/t. (er)schnappen; (zu)schnappen lassen; phot. knipsen; zerbrechen; ~ out Wort hervorstoßen; ~ up wegschnappen; ~-fastener ['snæpfa:snə] Druckknopf m; ~pish [~piʃ] bissig; schnippisch; ~py [~pi] bissig; F flott; ~shot Schnappschuß m, Photo n, Momentaufnahme f.

snare [snɛə] 1. Schlinge f; 2. fangen; fig. umgarnen.

snarl [sna:l] 1. knurren; murren; 2. Knurren n; Gewirr n.

snatch [snætʃ] 1. schneller Griff; Ruck m; Stückchen n; 2. schnappen; ergreifen; an sich reißen; nehmen; ~ at greifen nach.

sneak [sni:k] 1. v/i. schleichen; F petzen; v/t. F stibitzen; 2. Schleicher m; F Petzer m; ~ers ['sni:kəz] pl. F leichte Segeltuchschuhe m/pl.

sneer [sniə] 1. Hohnlächeln n; Spott m; 2. hohnlächeln; spotten; spötteln.

sneeze [sni:z] 1. niesen; 2. Niesen n.

snicker ['snikə] kichern; wiehern.

sniff [snif] schnüffeln, schnuppern; riechen; die Nase rümpfen.

snigger ['snigə] kichern.

snip [snip] 1. Schnitt m; Schnipsel m, n; 2. schnippeln, schnipseln; knipsen.

snipe [snaip] 1. orn. (Sumpf-) Schnepfe f; 2. ✗ aus dem Hinterhalt (ab)schießen; ~r ✗ ['snaipə] Scharf-, Heckenschütze m.

snivel ['snivl] schniefen; schluchzen; plärren.

snob [snɔb] Großtuer m; Snob m; ~bish □ ['snɔbiʃ] snobistisch.

snoop Am. [snu:p] 1. fig. (herum-) schnüffeln; 2. Schnüffler(in).

snooze F [snu:z] 1. Schläfchen n; 2. dösen.

snore [snɔ:] schnarchen.

snort [snɔ:t] schnauben, schnaufen.

snout [snaut] Schnauze f; Rüssel m.

snow [snou] 1. Schnee m; 2. (be-) schneien; be ~ed under fig. erdrückt werden; ~-bound ['snoubaund] eingeschneit; ~-capped, ~-clad, ~-covered schneebedeckt; ~-drift Schneewehe f; ~-drop ♀ Schneeglöckchen n; ~y □ ['snoui] schneeig; schneebedeckt, verschneit; schneeweiß.

snub [snʌb] 1. schelten, anfahren; 2. Verweis m; ~-nosed ['snʌbnouzd] stupsnasig.

snuff [snʌf] 1. Schnuppe f e-r Kerze; Schnupftabak m; 2. a. take ~ schnupfen; Licht putzen; ~le ['snʌfl] schnauben; näseln.

snug □ [snʌg] geborgen; behaglich; eng anliegend; ~gle ['snʌgl] (sich) schmiegen od. kuscheln (to an acc.).

so [sou] so; deshalb; also; I hope ~ ich hoffe es; are you tired? — I am bist du müde? Ja; you are tired, ~ am I du bist müde, ich auch; ~ far bisher.

soak [souk] v/t. einweichen; durchnässen; (durch)tränken; auf-, einsaugen; v/i. weichen; durchsickern.

soap [soup] 1. Seife f; soft ~ Schmierseife f; 2. (ein)seifen; ~-box ['soupbɔks] Seifenkiste f; improvisierte Rednertribüne; ~y □ ['soupi] seifig; fig. unterwürfig.

soar [sɔ:] sich erheben, sich aufschwingen; schweben; ⚡ segelfliegen.

sob [sɔb] 1. Schluchzen n; 2. schluchzen.

sober ['soubə] 1. □ nüchtern; 2. (sich) ernüchtern; ~ness [~nis], **sobriety** [sou'braiəti] Nüchternheit f.

so-called ['sou'kɔ:ld] sogenannt.

soccer F ['sɔkə] (Verbands)Fußball m (Spiel).

sociable ['souʃəbl] 1. □ gesellig; gemütlich; 2. geselliges Beisammensein.

social ['souʃəl] 1. □ gesellschaftlich; gesellig; sozial(istisch), Sozial...; ~ insurance Sozialversicherung f; ~ services pl. Sozialeinrichtungen f/pl.; 2. geselliges Beisammensein;

~ism [ˌʌlizəm] Sozialismus m; ~ist [ʌist] 1. Sozialist(in); 2. a. ~istic [souʃə'listik] (ʌally) sozialistisch; ~ize ['souʃəlaiz] sozialisieren; verstaatlichen.

society [sə'saiəti] Gesellschaft f; Verein m, Klub m.

sociology [sousi'ɔlədʒi] Sozialwissenschaft f.

sock [sɔk] Socke f; Einlegesohle f.

socket ['sɔkit] (Augen-, Zahn)Höhle f; (Gelenk)Pfanne f; ⊕ Muffe f; ⚡ Fassung f; ⚡ Steckdose f.

sod [sɔd] 1. Grasnarbe f; Rasen (-stück n) m; 2. mit Rasen bedecken.

soda ['soudə] Soda f, n; ~fountain Siphon m; Am. Erfrischungshalle f, Eisdiele f.

sodden ['sɔdn] durchweicht; teigig.

soft [sɔft] 1. □ allg. weich; eng S.: mild; sanft; sacht, leise; zart, zärtlich; weichlich; F einfältig; ~ drink F alkoholfreies Getränk; 2. adv. weich; 3. F Trottel m; ~en ['sɔfn] weich machen; (sich) erweichen; mildern; ~headed schwachsinnig; ~hearted gutmütig.

soggy ['sɔgi] durchnäßt; feucht.

soil [sɔil] 1. Boden m, Erde f; Fleck m; Schmutz m; 2. (be)schmutzen; beflecken.

sojourn ['sɔdʒəːn] 1. Aufenthalt m; 2. sich aufhalten.

solace ['sɔləs] 1. Trost m; 2. trösten.

solar ['soulə] Sonnen...

sold [sould] pret. u. p.p. von sell.

solder ['sɔldə] 1. Lot n; 2. löten.

soldier ['souldʒə] Soldat m; ~like, ~ly [ʌli] soldatisch; ~y [ʌri] Militär n.

sole¹ □ [soul] alleinig, einzig; ~ agent Alleinvertreter m.

sole² [ʌ] 1. Sohle f; 2. besohlen.

solemn □ ['sɔləm] feierlich; ernst; ~ity [sə'lemniti] Feierlichkeit f; Steifheit f; ~ize ['sɔləmnaiz] feiern; feierlich vollziehen.

solicit [sə'lisit] (dringend) bitten; ansprechen, belästigen; ~ation [sɔlisi'teiʃən] dringende Bitte; ~or [sə'lisitə] ⚖ Anwalt m; Am. Agent m, Werber m; ~ous □ [ʌtəs] besorgt; ~ of begierig nach; ~ to inf. bestrebt zu inf.; ~ude [ʌtjuːd] Sorge f, Besorgnis f; Bemühung f.

solid ['sɔlid] 1. □ fest; dauerhaft, haltbar; derb; massiv; ⚛ körperlich, Raum...; fig. gediegen; solid; triftig; solidarisch; a ~ hour e-e volle Stunde; 2. (fester) Körper; ~arity [sɔli'dæriti] Solidarität f; ~ify [sə'lidifai] (sich) verdichten; ~ity [ʌiti] Solidität f; Gediegenheit f.

soliloquy [sə'liləkwi] Selbstgespräch n, Monolog m.

solit|ary □ ['sɔlitəri] einsam; einzeln; einsiedlerisch; ~ude [ʌtjuːd] Einsamkeit f; Verlassenheit f; Öde f.

solo ['soulou] Solo n; ✈ Alleinflug m; ~ist [ʌouist] Solist(in).

solu|ble ['sɔljubl] löslich; (auf)lösbar; ~tion [sə'luːʃən] (Auf)Lösung f; ⊕ Gummilösung f.

solve [sɔlv] lösen; ~nt ['sɔlvənt] 1. (auf)lösend; ✝ zahlungsfähig; 2. Lösungsmittel n.

somb|re, Am. ~er □ ['sɔmbə] düster.

some [sʌm, səm] irgendein; etwas; einige, manche pl.; Am. F prima; ~ 20 miles etwa 20 Meilen; in ~ degree, to ~ extent einigermaßen; ~body ['sʌmbədi] jemand; ~ day eines Tages; ~how irgendwie; ~ or other so oder so; ~one jemand.

somersault ['sʌməsɔːlt] Salto m; Rolle f, Purzelbaum m; turn a ~ e-n Purzelbaum schlagen.

some|thing ['sʌmθiŋ] (irgend) etwas; ~ like so etwas wie, so ungefähr; ~time 1. einmal, dereinst; 2. ehemalig; ~times manchmal; ~what etwas, ziemlich; ~where irgendwo(hin).

somniferous □ [sɔm'nifərəs] einschläfernd.

son [sʌn] Sohn m.

song [sɔŋ] Gesang m; Lied n; Gedicht n; for a mere od. an old ~ für e-n Pappenstiel; ~bird ['sɔŋbəːd] Singvogel m; ~ster ['sɔŋstə] Singvogel m; Sänger m.

sonic ['sɔnik] Schall...

son-in-law ['sʌninlɔː] Schwiegersohn m.

sonnet ['sɔnit] Sonett n.

sonorous □ [sə'nɔːrəs] klangvoll.

soon [suːn] bald; früh; gern; as od. so ~ as sobald als od. wie; ~er ['suːnə] eher; früher; lieber; no ~ ... than kaum ... als; no ~ said than done gesagt, getan.

soot [sut] 1. Ruß m; 2. verrußen.

sooth [suːθ]: in ~ in Wahrheit, fürwahr; ~e [suːð] beruhigen; mildern; ~sayer ['suːθseiə] Wahrsager(in).

sooty □ ['suti] rußig.

sop [sɔp] 1. eingeweichter Brocken; fig. Bestechung f; 2. eintunken.

sophist|icate [sə'fistikeit] verdrehen; verfälschen; ~icated kultiviert, raffiniert; intellektuell; blasiert; hochentwickelt, kompliziert; ~ry ['sɔfistri] Spitzfindigkeit f.

sophomore Am. ['sɔfəmɔː] Student m im zweiten Jahr.

soporific [sɔupə'rifik] 1. (ʌally) einschläfernd; 2. Schlafmittel n.

sorcer|er ['sɔːsərə] Zauberer m; ~ess [ʌris] Zauberin f; Hexe f; ~y [ʌri] Zauberei f.

sordid □ ['sɔːdid] schmutzig, schäbig (bsd. fig.).

sore [sɔː] 1. □ schlimm, entzündet;

wund; weh; empfindlich; ~ throat
Halsweh m; 2. wunde Stelle; ~head
Am. F ['sɔːhed] 1. mürrischer
Mensch; 2. enttäuscht.
sorrel ['sɔrəl] 1. rötlichbraun (bsd.
Pferd); 2. Fuchs m (Pferd).
sorrow ['sɔrou] 1. Sorge f; Kummer m, Leid n; Trauer f; 2. trauern; sich grämen; ~ful □ ['sɔrəful]
traurig, betrübt; elend.
sorry □ ['sɔri] betrübt, bekümmert;
traurig; (I am) (so) ~! es tut mir
(sehr) leid; Verzeihung!; I am ~
for him er tut mir leid; we are ~ to
say wir müssen leider sagen.
sort [sɔːt] 1. Sorte f, Art f; what ~
of was für; of a ~, of ~s F so was
wie; ~ of F gewissermaßen; out of
~s F unpäßlich; verdrießlich; 2.
sortieren; ~ out (aus)sondern.
sot [sɔt] Trunkenbold m.
sough [sau] 1. Sausen n; 2. rauschen.
sought [sɔːt] pret. u. p.p. von seek.
soul [soul] Seele f (a. fig.).
sound [saund] 1. ⌐ allg. gesund;
ganz; vernünftig; gründlich; fest;
✝ sicher; ⚖ gültig; 2. Ton m,
Schall m, Laut m, Klang m; ♪
Sonde f; Meerenge f; Fischblase f;
3. (er)tönen, (er)klingen; erschallen
(lassen); sich gut etc. anhören; sondieren; ⚓ loten; ⌐ abhorchen;
~film ['saundfilm] Tonfilm m;
~ing [‿diŋ] Lotung f; ~s pl.
lotbare Wassertiefe; ~less ⌐ [‿dlis]
lautlos; ~ness [‿dnis] Gesundheit
f; ~proof schalldicht; ~track
Film: Tonspur f; ~wave Schallwelle f.
soup[1] [suːp] Suppe f.
soup[2] Am. sl. mot. [‿] 1. Stärke f;
2. ~ up Motor frisieren.
sour ['sauə] 1. ⌐ sauer; fig. bitter;
mürrisch; 2. v/t. säuern; fig. ver-,
erbittern; v/i. sauer (fig. bitter)
werden.
source [sɔːs] Quelle f; Ursprung m.
sour|ish ⌐ ['sauəriʃ] säuerlich; ~ness ['sauənis] Säure f; fig. Bitterkeit f.
souse [saus] eintauchen; (mit Wasser) begießen; Fisch etc. einlegen,
einpökeln.
south [sauθ] 1. Süd(en m); 2. Süd...;
südlich; ~east ['sauθ'iːst] 1. Südosten m; 2. a. ~eastern [sauθ-
'iːstən] südöstlich.
souther|ly ['sʌðəli], ~n [‿ən] südlich; Süd...; ~ner [‿nə] Südländer(in), Am. Südstaatler(in).
southernmost ['sʌðənmoust] südlichst.
southpaw Am. ['sauθpɔː] Baseball:
Linkshänder m.
southward(s) adv. ['sauθwəd(z)]
südwärts, nach Süden.
south|-west ['sauθ'west] 1. Südwesten m; 2. südwestlich; ~wester [sauθ'westə] Südwestwind

m; ⚓ Südwester m; ~westerly,
~western südwestlich.
souvenir ['suːvəniə] Andenken n.
sovereign ['sɔvrin] 1. □ höchst;
unübertrefflich; unumschränkt;
2. Herrscher(in); Sovereign m (20-
Schilling-Stück); ~ty [‿rənti] Oberherrschaft f, Landeshoheit f.
soviet ['souviet] Sowjet m; attr.
Sowjet...
sow[1] [sau] zo. Sau f, (Mutter-)
Schwein n; ⊕ Sau f, Massel f.
sow[2] [sou] [irr.] (aus)säen, ausstreuen; besäen; ~n [soun] p.p. von
sow[2].

spa [spaː] Heilbad n; Kurort m.
space [speis] 1. (Welt)Raum m;
Zwischenraum m; Zeitraum m;
2. typ. sperren; ~craft [speiskraːft], ~ship Raumschiff n; ~suit Raumanzug m.
spacious □ ['speiʃəs] geräumig;
weit, umfassend.
spade [speid] Spaten m; Kartenspiel: Pik n.
span[1] [spæn] 1. Spanne f; Spannweite f; Am. Gespann f; 2. (um-,
über)spannen; (aus)messen.
span[2] [‿] pret. von spin 1.
spangle ['spæŋgl] 1. Flitter m;
2. (mit Flitter) besetzen; fig. übersäen.
Spaniard ['spænjəd] Spanier(in).
Spanish ['spæniʃ] 1. spanisch; 2.
Spanisch n.
spank F [spæŋk] 1. verhauen;
2. Klaps m; ~ing ['spæŋkiŋ] 1. □
schnell, scharf; 2. F Haue f, Tracht
f Prügel.
spanner ⊕ ['spænə] Schraubenschlüssel m.
spar [spaː] 1. ⚓ Spiere f; 🥊 Holm
m; 2. boxen; fig. sich streiten.
spare [spɛə] 1. □ spärlich, sparsam;
mager; überzählig; überschüssig;
Ersatz...; Reserve...; ~ hours Mußestunden f/pl.; ~ room Gastzimmer
n; ~ time Freizeit f; 2. ⊕ Ersatzteil m, n; 3. (ver)schonen; erübrigen; entbehren; (übrig)haben für;
(er)sparen; sparen mit.
sparing □ ['spɛəriŋ] sparsam.
spark [spaːk] 1. Funke(n) m; fig.
flotter Kerl; Galan m; 2. Funken
sprühen; ~(ing)-plug mot. ['spaːk-
(iŋ)plʌg] Zündkerze f.
sparkle ['spaːkl] 1. Funke(n) m;
Funkeln n; fig. sprühendes Wesen;
2. funkeln; blitzen; schäumen;
sparkling wine Schaumwein m.
sparrow orn. ['spærou] Sperling m,
Spatz m; ~hawk orn. Sperber m.
sparse □ [spaːs] spärlich, dünn.
spasm 💊 ['spæzəm] Krampf m;
~odic(al □) [‿'mɔdik(əl)]
krampfhaft, ~artig; fig. sprunghaft.
spat[1] [spæt] (Schuh)Gamasche f.
spat[3] [‿] pret. u. p.p. von spit[2] 2.
spatter ['spætə] (be)spritzen;

spawn [spɔːn] 1. Laich *m*; *fig.*
contp. Brut *f*; 2. laichen; *fig.* aus-
hecken.

speak [spiːk] [*irr.*] *v/i.* sprechen;
reden; ~ out, ~ up laut sprechen;
offen reden; ~ to j-n *od.* mit *j-m*
sprechen; ~ (aus)sprechen; äußern; ~easy *Am. sl.* ['spiːkiːzi]
Flüsterkneipe *f* (*ohne Konzession*);
~er [~kə] Sprecher(in), Redner(in);
parl. Vorsitzende(r) *m*; ~ing-
trumpet [~kintrʌmpit] Sprachrohr *n*.

spear [spiə] 1. Speer *m*, Spieß *m*;
Lanze *f*; 2. (auf)spießen.

special ['speʃəl] 1. □ besonder;
Sonder...; speziell; Spezial...;
2. Hilfspolizist *m*; Sonderausgabe *f*;
Sonderzug *m*; *Am.* Sonderangebot
n; *Am.* (Tages)Spezialität *f*; ~ist
[~list] Spezialist *m*; ~ity [speʃi'æliti]
Besonderheit *f*; Spezialfach *n*; †
Spezialität *f*; ~ize ['speʃəlaiz] besonders anführen; (sich) speziali-
sieren; ~ty [~lti] *s.* speciality.

specie ['spiːʃiː] Metall-, Hartgeld *n*;
~s [~iːz] *pl. u. sg.* Art *f*, Spezies *f*.
spec|ific [spi'sifik] (~ally) spezi-
fisch; besonder; bestimmt; ~fy
['spesifai] spezifizieren, einzeln angeben; ~men [~imin] Probe *f*,
Exemplar *n*.

specious □ ['spiːʃəs] blendend, be-
stechend; trügerisch; Schein...

speck [spek] 1. Fleck *m*; Stückchen
n; 2. flecken; ~le ['spekl] 1. Fleck-
chen *n*; 2. flecken, sprenkeln.

spectacle ['spektəkl] Schauspiel *n*;
Anblick *m*; (*a pair of*) ~s *pl.* (eine)
Brille.

spectacular [spek'tækjulə] 1. □
eindrucksvoll; auffallend, spekta-
kulär; 2. *Am.* F Galarevue *f*.

spectator [spek'teitə] Zuschauer *m*.
spect|ral □ ['spektrəl] gespenstisch;
~re, *Am.* ~er [~tə] Gespenst *n*.

speculat|e ['spekjuleit] grübeln,
nachsinnen; † spekulieren; ~ion
[spekju'leiʃən] theoretische Betrachtung; Grübelei *f*; † Spekulation *f*; ~ive ['spekjulətiv] grüb-
lerisch; theoretisch; † spekulie-
rend; ~or [~leitə] Denker *m*; †
Spekulant *m*.

sped [sped] *pret. u. p.p. von* speed 2.
speech [spiːtʃ] Sprache *f*; Rede *f*,
Ansprache *f*; *make a* ~ *e-e* Rede
halten; ~day ['spiːtʃdei] *Schule*:
(Jahres)Schlußfeier *f*; ~less □
[~ʃlis] sprachlos.

speed [spiːd] 1. Geschwindigkeit *f*;
Schnelligkeit *f*; Eile *f*; ⊕ Drehzahl
f; 2. [*irr.*] *v/i.* schnell fahren, rasen;
~ up (*pret. u. p.p. ~ed*) die Geschwindigkeit erhöhen; *v/t.* j-m
Glück verleihen; befördern; ~ up
(*pret. u. p.p. ~ed*) beschleunigen;
~limit ['spiːdlimit] Geschwindig-
keitsbegrenzung *f*; ~ometer *mot.*

[spiˈdɔmitə] Geschwindigkeitsmes-
ser *m*, Tachometer *n*; ~way Motor-
radrennbahn *f*; *bsd. Am.* Schnellstraße *f*; ~y □ [~di] schnell.

spell [spel] 1. (Arbeits)Zeit *f*, ⊕
Schicht *f*; Weilchen *n*; Zauber
(-spruch) *m*; 2. abwechseln mit *j-m*;
[*irr.*] buchstabieren; richtig schreiben; bedeuten; ~binder *Am.*
['spelbaində] fesselnder Redner;
~bound *fig.* (fest)gebannt; ~er
bsd. Am. [~lə] Fibel *f*; ~ing
Rechtschreibung *f*; ~ing-book
Fibel *f*.

spelt [spelt] *pret. u. p.p. von*
spell 2.

spend [spend] [*irr.*] verwenden;
(*Geld*) ausgeben; verbrauchen;
verschwenden; verbringen; ~ *o.s.*
sich erschöpfen; ~thrift ['spend-
θrift] Verschwender *m*.

spent [spent] 1. *pret. u. p.p. von*
spend; 2. *adj.* erschöpft, matt.

sperm [spəːm] Same(n) *m*.

spher|e [sfiə] Kugel *f*; Erd-, Him-
melskugel *f*; *fig.* Sphäre *f*; (Wir-
kungs)Kreis *m*; Bereich *m*; *fig.*
Gebiet *n*; ~ical □ ['sferikəl] sphä-
risch; kugelförmig.

spice [spais] 1. Gewürz(e *pl.*) *n*; *fig.*
Würze *f*; Anflug *m*; 2. würzen.

spick and span ['spikən'spæn]
frisch u. sauber; schmuck; funkel-
nagelneu.

spicy ['spaisi] würzig; pikant.

spider *zo.* ['spaidə] Spinne *f*.

spiel *Am. sl.* [spiːl] Gequassel *n*.

spigot ['spigət] (Faß)Zapfen *m*.

spike [spaik] 1. Stift *m*; Spitze *f*;
Dorn *m*; Stachel *m*; *Sport*: Lauf-
dorn *m*; *mot.* Spike *m*; ♀ Ähre *f*;
2. festnageln; mit *eisernen* Stacheln
versehen.

spill [spil] 1. [*irr.*] *v/t.* verschütten;
vergießen; F *Reiter etc.* abwerfen;
schleudern; *v/i.* überlaufen; 2. F
Sturz *m*.

spilt [spilt] *pret. u. p.p. von* spill 1;
cry over ~ *milk* über et. jammern,
was doch nicht zu ändern ist.

spin [spin] 1. [*irr.*] spinnen (*a. fig.*);
wirbeln; sich drehen; *Münze* hochwerfen; sich *et.* ausdenken; erzählen; ≱ trudeln; ~ *along* dahinsau-
sen; ~ *s.th. out* et. in die Länge
ziehen; 2. Drehung *f*; Spritztour *f*;
≱ Trudeln *n*.

spinach ♀ ['spinidʒ] Spinat *m*.

spinal *anat.* ['spainl] Rückgrat...; ~
column Wirbelsäule *f*; ~ *cord*, ~
marrow Rückenmark *n*.

spindle ['spindl] Spindel *f*.

spin-drier ['spindraiə] Wäsche-
schleuder *f*.

spine [spain] *anat.* Rückgrat *n*;
Dorn *m*; (Gebirgs)Grat *m*; (Buch-)
Rücken *m*.

spinning|-mill ['spiniŋmil] Spin-
nerei *f*; ~wheel Spinnrad *n*.

spinster ['spinstə] unverheiratete Frau; (alte) Jungfer.

spiny ['spaini] dornig.

spiral ['spaiərəl] 1. ⎿ spiralig; ~ staircase Wendeltreppe f; 2. Spirale f; fig. Wirbel m.

spire ['spaiə] Turm-, Berg- etc. Spitze f; Kirchturm(spitze f) m.

spirit ['spirit] 1. allg. Geist m; Sinn m; Temperament n, Leben n; Mut m; Gesinnung f; Spiritus m; Sprit m, Benzin n; ~s pl. Spirituosen pl.; high (low) ~s pl. gehobene (gedrückte) Stimmung; 2. ~ away od. off wegzaubern; ~ed geistvoll; temperamentvoll; mutig; ~less □ [~tlis] geistlos; temperamentlos; mutlos.

spiritual □ ['spiritjuəl] geistig; geistlich; geistvoll; ~ism [~lizəm] Spiritismus m.

spirituous ['spiritjuəs] alkoholisch.

spirt [spə:t] (hervor)spritzen.

spit¹ [spit] 1. Bratspieß m; Landzunge f; 2. aufspießen.

spit² [~] 1. Speichel m; F Ebenbild n; 2. [irr.] (aus)spucken; fauchen; sprühen (fein regnen).

spite [spait] 1. Bosheit f; Groll m; in ~ of trotz (gen.); 2. ärgern; kränken; ~ful □ ['spaitful] boshaft, gehässig.

spitfire ['spitfaiə] Hitzkopf m.

spittle ['spitl] Speichel m, Spucke f.

spittoon [spi'tu:n] Spucknapf m.

splash [splæʃ] 1. Spritzfleck m; P(l)atschen n; 2. (be)spritzen; p(l)atschen; planschen; (hin)klecksen.

splay [splei] 1. Ausschrägung f; 2. auswärts gebogen; 3. v/t. ausschrägen; v/i. ausgeschrägt sein; ~foot ['spleifu] Spreizfuß m.

spleen [spli:n] anat. Milz f; üble Laune, Ärger m.

splend|id ⎿ ['splendid] glänzend, prächtig, herrlich; ~o(u)r [~də] Glanz m, Pracht f, Herrlichkeit f.

splice [splais] (ver)spleißen.

splint ⚡ [splint] 1. Schiene f; 2. schienen; ~er ['splintə] 1. Splitter m; 2. (zer)splittern.

split [split] 1. Spalt m, Riß m; fig. Spaltung f; 2. gespalten; 3. [irr.] v/t. (zer)spalten; zerreißen; (sich) et. teilen; ~ hairs Haarspalterei treiben; ~ one's sides with laughter sich totlachen; v/i. sich spalten; platzen; ~ting ['splitiŋ] heftig, rasend (Kopfschmerz).

splutter ['splʌtə] s. sputter.

spoil [spoil] 1. off ~s pl. Beute f, Raub m; fig. Ausbeute f; Schutt m; ~s pl. pol. bsd. Am. Futterkrippe f; 2. [irr.] (be)rauben; plündern; verderben; verwöhnen; Kind verziehen; ~sman Am. pol. ['spɔilzmən] Postenjäger m; ~-sport Spielver-

derber(in); ~s system Am. pol. Futterkrippensystem n.

spoilt [spoilt] pret. u. p.p. von spoil 2.

spoke [spouk] 1. pret. von speak; 2. Speiche f; (Leiter)Sprosse f; ~n ['spoukən] p.p. von speak; ~sman [~ksmən] Wortführer m.

sponge [spʌndʒ] 1. Schwamm m; 2. v/t. mit e-m Schwamm (ab)wischen; ~ up aufsaugen; v/i. schmarotzen; ~cake ['spʌndʒ'keik] Biskuitkuchen m; ~r F fig. [~dʒə] Schmarotzer(in).

spongy ['spʌndʒi] schwammig.

sponsor ['sponsə] 1. Pate m; Bürge m; Förderer m; Auftraggeber m für Werbesendungen; 2. Pate stehen bei; fördern; ~ship [~ʃip] Patenschaft f; Gönnerschaft f.

spontane|ity [spontə'ni:iti] Freiwilligkeit f; eigener Antrieb; ~ous □ [spon'teinjəs] freiwillig, von selbst (entstanden); Selbst...; spontan; unwillkürlich; unvermittelt.

spook [spu:k] Spuk m; ~y ['spu:ki] geisterhaft, Spuk...

spool [spu:l] 1. Spule f; 2. spulen.

spoon [spu:n] 1. Löffel m; 2. löffeln; ~ful ['spu:nful] Löffelvoll m.

sporadic [spə'rædik] (~ally) sporadisch, verstreut.

spore ♀ [spɔ:] Spore f, Keimkorn n.

sport [spɔ:t] 1. Sport m; Spiel n; fig. Spielball m; Scherz m; sl. feiner Kerl; ~s pl. allg. Sport m; Sportfest n; 2. v/i. sich belustigen; spielen; v/t. F protzen mit; ~ive □ ['spɔ:tiv] lustig; scherzhaft; ~sman [~tsmən] Sportler m.

spot [spot] 1. allg. Fleck m; Tupfen m; Makel m; Stelle f; ⚡ Leberfleck m; ⚡ Pickel m; Tropfen m; a ~ of F etwas; on the ~ auf der Stelle; sofort; 2. sofort liefer- od. zahlbar; 3. (be)flecken; ausfindig machen; erkennen; ~less □ ['spotlis] fleckenlos; ~light thea. Scheinwerfer(-licht n) m; ~ter [~tə] Beobachter m; Am. Kontrolleur m; ~ty [~ti] fleckig.

spouse [spauz] Gatte m; Gattin f.

spout [spaut] 1. Tülle f; Strahlrohr n; (Wasser)Strahl m; 2. (aus)spritzen; F salbadern.

sprain ⚡ [sprein] 1. Verstauchung f; 2. verstauchen.

sprang [spræŋ] pret. von spring 2.

sprat ichth. [spræt] Sprotte f.

sprawl [sprɔ:l] sich rekeln, ausgestreckt daliegen; ♀ wuchern.

spray [sprei] 1. zerstäubte Flüssigkeit; Sprühregen m; Gischt m; Spray m, n; = sprayer; 2. zerstäuben; et. besprühen; ~er [~sprei] Zerstäuber m.

spread [spred] 1. [irr.] v/t. a. ~ out ausbreiten; (aus)dehnen; verbreiten; belegen; Butter etc. aufstreichen; Brot etc. bestreichen; ~ the *table* den Tisch decken; *v/i.* sich aus- *od.* verbreiten; **2.** Aus-, Verbreitung *f;* Spannweite *f;* Fläche *f; Am. Bett- etc.* Decke *f; Brot-*Aufstrich *m;* F Festschmaus *m.*

spree F [spri:] Spaß *m,* Jux *m;* Zechgelage *n;* Orgie *f; Kauf- etc.* Welle *f.*

sprig [sprig] Sproß *m,* Reis *n* (*a. fig.*); ⊕ Zwecke *f,* Stift *m.*

sprightly ['spraitli] lebhaft, munter.

spring [spriŋ] **1.** Sprung *m,* Satz *m;* (Sprung)Feder *f;* Federkraft *f,* Elastizität *f;* Triebfeder *f;* Quelle *f; fig.* Ursprung *m;* Frühling *m;* **2.** [*irr.*] *v/t.* springen lassen; (zer-)sprengen; *Wild* aufjagen; *~ a leak* ⚓ leck werden; *~ a surprise on s.o.* j-n überraschen; *v/i.* springen; entspringen; ⚘ sprießen; *~ up* aufkommen (*Ideen etc.*); **~-board** ['spriŋbɔ:d] Sprungbrett *n;* **~ tide** Springflut *f;* **~tide, ~time** Frühling(szeit *f*) *m;* **~y** □ [~ŋi] federnd.

sprinkl|e ['spriŋkl] (be)streuen; (be)sprengen; **~er** [~lə] Berieselungsanlage *f;* Rasensprenger *m;* **~ing** [~liŋ] Sprühregen *m; a ~ of* ein wenig, ein paar.

sprint [sprint] *Sport:* **1.** sprinten; spurten; **2.** Sprint *m;* Kurzstreckenlauf *m;* Endspurt *m;* **~er** ['sprintə] Sprinter *m,* Kurzstreckenläufer *m.*

sprite [sprait] Geist *m,* Kobold *m.*

sprout [spraut] **1.** sprießen, wachsen (lassen); **2.** ⚘ Sproß *m;* (*Brussels*) *~s pl.* Rosenkohl *m.*

spruce¹ □ [~] schmuck, nett.

spruce² ⚘ [~] *a. ~ fir* Fichte *f,* Rottanne *f.*

sprung [sprʌŋ] *pret.* (✎) *u. p.p. von* spring 2.

spry [sprai] munter, flink.

spun [spʌn] *pret. u. p.p. von* spin 1.

spur [spə:] **1.** Sporn *m* (*a. zo.,* ⚘); *fig.* Ansporn *m;* Vorsprung *m,* Ausläufer *m e-s Berges; on the ~ of the moment* der Eingebung des Augenblicks folgend; spornstreichs; **2.** (an)spornen.

spurious □ ['spjuəriəs] unecht, gefälscht.

spurn [spə:n] verschmähen, verächtlich zurückweisen.

spurt [spə:t] **1.** alle s-e Kräfte zs.-nehmen; *Sport:* spurten; *s. spirt;* **2.** plötzliche Anstrengung, Ruck *m; Sport* Spurt *m.*

sputter ['spʌtə] **1.** Gesprudel *n;* **2.** (hervor)sprudeln; spritzen.

spy [spai] **1.** Späher(in); Spion(in); **2.** (er)spähen; erblicken; spionieren; **~glass** ['spaiglɑ:s] Fernglas *n;* **~hole** Guckloch *n.*

squabble ['skwɔbl] **1.** Zank *m,* Kabbelei *f;* **2.** (sich) zanken.

squad [skwɔd] Rotte *f,* Trupp *m;* **~ron** ['skwɔdrən] ⚔ Schwadron *f;* ✈ Staffel *f;* ⚓ Geschwader *n.*

squalid □] ['skwɔlid] schmutzig, armselig.

squall [skwɔ:l] **1.** ⚓ Bö *f;* Schrei *m;* **~s** *pl.* Geschrei *n;* **2.** schreien.

squalor ['skwɔlə] Schmutz *m.*

squander ['skwɔndə] verschwenden.

square [skwɛə] **1.** □ viereckig; quadratisch; rechtwinklig; eckig; passend, stimmend; in Ordnung; direkt; quitt, gleich; ehrlich, offen; F altmodisch, spießig; *~ measure* Flächenmaß *n; ~ mile* Quadratmeile *f;* **2.** Quadrat *n;* Viereck *n; Schach-*Feld *n; öffentlicher Platz;* Winkelmaß *n;* F altmodischer Spießer; **3.** *v/t.* viereckig machen; einrichten (*with nach*), anpassen (*dat.*); ✝ be-, ausgleichen; *v/i.* passen (*with zu*); übereinstimmen; **~-built** ['skwɛə'bilt] vierschrötig; **~ dance** Quadrille *f;* **~-toes** *sg.* F Pedant *m.*

squash¹ [skwɔʃ] **1.** Gedränge *n;* Fruchtsaft *m;* Platsch(en *n*) *m;* Rakettspiel *n;* **2.** (zer-, zs.-)quetschen; drücken.

squash² ⚘ [~] Kürbis *m.*

squat [skwɔt] **1.** kauernd; untersetzt; **2.** hocken, kauern; **~ter** ['skwɔtə] *Am.* Schwarzsiedler *m; Australien* ⚘ Schafzüchter *m.*

squawk [skwɔ:k] **1.** kreischen, schreien; **2.** Gekreisch *n,* Geschrei *n.*

squeak [skwi:k] quieken, quietschen.

squeal [skwi:l] quäken; gell schreien; quieken.

squeamish □ ['ski:miʃ] empfindlich; mäkelig; heikel; penibel.

squeeze [skwi:z] **1.** (sich) drücken, (sich) quetschen; auspressen; *fig.* (be)drängen; **2.** Druck *m;* Gedränge *n;* **~r** ['skwi:zə] Presse *f.*

squelch F [skweltʃ] zermalmen.

squid *zo.* [skwid] Tintenfisch *m.*

squint [skwint] schielen; blinzeln.

squire ['skwaiə] **1.** Gutsbesitzer *m;* (Land)Junker *m; Am.* F (Friedens-)Richter *m;* **2.** *e-e Dame* begleiten.

squirm F [skwə:m] sich winden.

squirrel *zo.* ['skwirəl, *Am.* 'skwə:rəl] Eichhörnchen *n.*

squirt [skwə:t] **1.** Spritze *f;* Strahl *m;* F Wichtigtuer *m;* **2.** spritzen.

stab [stæb] **1.** Stich *m;* **2.** *v/t.* (er-)stechen; *v/i.* stechen (*at nach*).

stabili|ty [stə'biliti] Stabilität *f;* Standfestig-, Beständigkeit *f;* **~ze** ['steibilaiz] stabilisieren (*a.* ✈).

stable¹ ['steibl] stabil, fest.

stable² [~] **1.** Stall *m;* **2.** einstallen.

stack [stæk] **1.** ✴ (Heu-, Stroh-, Getreide)Schober *m;* Stapel *m;* Schornstein(reihe *f*) *m;* Regal *n;* **~s** *pl. Am.* Hauptmagazin *n e-r*

Bibliothek; F Haufen *m;* 2. auf-stapeln.

stadium ['steidjəm] *Sport:* Stadion *n,* Sportplatz *m,* Kampfbahn *f.*

staff [stɑ:f] 1. Stab *m* (*a.* ✕), Stock *m;* Stütze *f;* ♪ Notensystem *n;* Personal *n;* Belegschaft *f;* Beam-ten-, Lehrkörper *m;* 2. (mit Perso-nal, Beamten *od.* Lehrern) besetzen.

stag *zo.* [stæg] Hirsch *m.*

stage [steidʒ] 1. Bühne *f,* Theater *n;* *fig.* Schauplatz *m;* Stufe *f,* Stadium *n;* Teilstrecke *f,* Etappe *f;* Halte-stelle *f;* Gerüst *n,* Gestell *n;* 2. in-szenieren; **~coach** ['steidʒkoutʃ] Postkutsche *f;* **~craft** dramatisches Talent; Theatererfahrung *f;* **~ di-rection** Bühnenanweisung *f;* **~fright** Lampenfieber *n;* **~manag-er** Regisseur *m.*

stagger ['stægə] 1. *v/i.* (sch)wanken, taumeln; *fig.* stutzen; *v/t.* ins Wan-ken bringen; staffeln; 2. Schwan-ken *n;* Staffelung *f.*

stagna|nt □ ['stægnənt] stehend (*Wasser*); stagnierend; stockend; träg; ♱ still; **~te** [‗neit] stocken.

staid □ [steid] gesetzt, ruhig.

stain [stein] 1. Fleck(en) *m* (*a. fig.*); Reize *f;* 2. fleckig machen; *fig.* be-flecken; beizen, färben; **~ed glass** buntes Glas; **~less** □ ['steinlis] un-gefleckt; *fig.* fleckenlos; rostfrei.

stair [stɛə] Stufe *f;* **~s** *pl.* Treppe *f,* Stiege *f;* **~case**, **~way** Treppe(nhaus *n*) *f.*

stake [steik] 1. Pfahl *m;* Marter-pfahl *m;* (Spiel)Einsatz *m* (*a. fig.*); **~s** *pl. Pferderennen:* Preis *m;* Ren-nen *n; pull up* **~s** *Am.* F abhauen; *be at* **~** auf dem Spiel stehen; 2. (um)pfählen; aufs Spiel setzen; **~ out**, **~ off** abstecken.

stale □ [steil] alt; schal, abgestan-den; verbraucht (*Luft*); fad.

stalk [stɔ:k] 1. Stengel *m,* Stiel *m;* Halm *m;* *hunt.* Pirsch *f;* 2. *v/i.* einherstolzieren; heranschleichen; *hunt.* pirschen; *v/t.* beschleichen.

stall [stɔ:l] 1. (Pferde)Box *f;* (Ver-kaufs)Stand *m,* Marktbude *f; thea.* Sperrsitz *m;* 2. *v/t.* einstallen; *Motor* abwürgen; *v/i. mot.* aussetzen.

stallion ['stæljən] Hengst *m.*

stalwart □ ['stɔ:lwət] stramm, stark.

stamina ['stæminə] Ausdauer *f.*

stammer ['stæmə] 1. stottern, stammeln; 2. Stottern *n.*

stamp [stæmp] 1. (Auf)Stampfen *n;* ⊕ Stampfe(r *m*) *f;* Stempel *m* (*a. fig.*); (Brief)Marke *f;* Gepräge *n;* Art *f;* 2. (auf)stampfen; prägen; stanzen; (ab)stempeln (*a. fig.*); frankieren.

stampede [stæm'pi:d] 1. Panik *f,* wilde Flucht; 2. *v/i.* durchgehen; *v/t.* in Panik versetzen.

stanch [stɑ:ntʃ] 1. hemmen; stillen; 2. □ fest; zuverlässig; treu.

stand [stænd] 1. [*irr.*] *v/i. allg.* stehen; sich befinden; beharren; *mst* **~** *still* stillstehen, stehenbleiben; bestehen (bleiben); **~** *against j-m* widerstehen; **~** *aside* beiseite treten; **~** *back* zurücktreten; **~** *by* dabei-stehen; *fig.* (fest) stehen zu; helfen; bereitstehen; **~** *for* kandidieren für; bedeuten; eintreten für; F sich *et.* gefallen lassen; **~** *in* einspringen; **~** *in with* sich gut stellen mit; **~** *off* zurücktreten (von); **~** *off!* weg da!; **~** *on* (*fig.* be)stehen auf; **~** *out* her-vorstehen; sich abheben (*against* gegen); standhalten (*dat.*); **~** *over* stehen *od.* liegen bleiben; **~** *pat Am.* F stur bleiben; **~** *to bleiben bei;* **~** *up* aufstehen; sich erheben; **~** *up for* eintreten für; **~** *up to* sich zur Wehr setzen gegen; standhalten (*dat.*); **~** *upon* (*fig.* be)stehen auf (*dat.*); *v/t.* (hin)stellen; aushalten, (v)ertragen; über sich ergehen lassen; F spen-dieren; 2. Stand *m;* Standplatz *m;* Bude *f;* Standpunkt *m;* Stillstand *m;* Ständer *m;* Tribüne *f; bsd. Am.* Zeugenstand *m; make a od.* one's **~** *against* standhalten (*dat.*).

standard ['stændəd] 1. Standarte *f,* Fahne *f;* Standard *m,* Norm *f,* Regel *f;* Maßstab *m;* Niveau *n;* Stufe *f;* Münzfuß *m;* Währung *f;* Ständer *m,* Mast *m;* 2. maßgebend; Normal...; **~ize** [‗daiz] norm(ie-r)en.

stand-by ['stændbai] Beistand *m.*

standee [stæn'di:] Stehende(r) *m;* *Am.* Stehplatzinhaber *m.*

standing ['stændiŋ] 1. □ stehend; fest; (be)ständig; **~** *orders pl. parl.* Geschäftsordnung *f;* 2. Stellung *f,* Rang *m,* Ruf *m;* Dauer *f; of long* **~** *alt;* **~room** Stehplatz *m.*

stand|off *Am.* ['stændɔ:f] Unent-schieden *n;* Dünkel *m;* **~offish** [‗d'ɔ:fiʃ] zurückhaltend; **~patter** *Am. pol.* [stænd'pætə] sturer Kon-servativer; **~point** ['stændpɔint] Standpunkt *m;* **~still** Stillstand *m;* **~up:** **~** *collar* Stehkragen *m.*

stank [stæŋk] *pret. von* stink 2.

stanza ['stænzə] Stanze *f;* Strophe *f.*

staple¹ ['steipl] Haupterzeugnis *n;* Hauptgegenstand *m; attr.* Haupt...

staple² [‗] Krampe *f;* Heftklam-mer *f.*

star [stɑ:] 1. Stern *m; thea.* Star *m;* ♀s *and Stripes pl. Am.* Sternen-banner *n;* 2. mit Sternen schmücken; *thea., fig.* die Hauptrolle spielen.

starboard ⚓ ['stɑ:bəd] 1. Steuer-bord *n;* 2. *Ruder* steuerbord legen.

starch [stɑ:tʃ] 1. (Wäsche)Stärke *f;* *fig.* Steifheit *f;* 2. stärken.

stare [stɛə] 1. Starren *n;* Staunen *n;* starrer Blick; 2. starren, staunen.

stark [stɑːk] **1.** *adj.* starr; bar, völlig (*Unsinn*); **2.** *adv.* völlig.

starlight ['stɑːlait] Sternenlicht *n.*

starling *orn.* ['stɑːliŋ] Star *m.*

starlit ['stɑːlit] sternenklar.

star|ry ['stɑːri] Stern(en)...; gestirnt; **~-spangled** ['stɑːspæŋgld] sternenbesät; ♀ *Banner Am.* Sternenbanner *n.*

start [stɑːt] **1.** Auffahren *n,* Stutzen *n;* Ruck *m; Sport:* Start *m;* Aufbruch *m;* Anfang *m; fig.* Vorsprung *m; get the* ~ *of s.o.* j-m zuvorkommen; **2.** *v/i.* aufspringen, auffahren; stutzen; *Sport:* starten; abfahren; aufbrechen; *mot.* anspringen; anfangen (*on* mit; *doing* zu tun); *v/t.* in Gang bringen; *mot.* anlassen; *Sport:* starten (lassen); aufjagen; *fig.* anfangen; veranlassen (*doing* zu tun); **~er** ['stɑːtə] *Sport:* Starter *m;* Läufer *m; mot.* Anlasser *m.*

startl|e ['stɑːtl] (er-, auf)schrecken; **~ing** [.liŋ] bestürzend, überraschend, aufsehenerregend.

starv|ation [stɑːˈveiʃən] (Ver)Hungern *n,* Hungertod *m; attr.* Hunger...; **~e** [stɑːv] verhungern (lassen); *fig.* verkümmern (lassen).

state [steit] **1.** Zustand *m;* Stand *m;* Staat *m; pol. mst* ♀ Staat *m; attr.* Staats...; *in* ~ feierlich; **2.** angeben; darlegen, darstellen; feststellen; melden; *Regel etc.* aufstellen; ♀ **Department** *Am. pol.* Außenministerium *n;* **~ly** ['steitli] stattlich; würdevoll; erhaben; **~ment** [.tmənt] Angabe *f;* Aussage *f;* Darstellung *f;* Feststellung *f;* Aufstellung *f;* ♦ (~ *of account* Konto-) Auszug *m;* **~room** Staatszimmer *n;* ♦ Einzelkabine *f;* **~side** *Am.* F **1.** *adj.* USA-...; Heimat...; **2.** *adv.:* *go* ~ heimkehren; **~sman** [.smən] Staatsmann *m.*

static ['stætik] statisch, Ruhe...

station ['steiʃən] **1.** Stand(ort) *m;* Stelle *f;* Stellung *f;* ⚔, ♦, 🚂 Station *f;* Bahnhof *m;* Rang *m,* Stand *m;* **2.** aufstellen, postieren, stationieren; **~ary** [.ʃnəri] stillstehend; feststehend; **~ery** [.] Schreibwaren *f/pl.;* **~master** 🚂 Stationsvorsteher *m;* **~ wagon** *Am. mot.* Kombiwagen *m.*

statistics [stəˈtistiks] *pl.* Statistik *f.*

statu|ary ['stætjuəri] Bildhauer(-kunst *f*) *m;* **~e** [.juː] Standbild *n,* Plastik *f,* Statue *f.*

stature ['stætʃə] Statur *f,* Wuchs *m.*

status ['steitəs] Zustand *m;* Stand *m.*

statute ['stætjuːt] Statut *n,* Satzung *f;* (Landes)Gesetz *n.*

staunch [stɔːntʃ] *s.* stanch.

stave [steiv] **1.** Faßdaube *f;* Strophe *f;* **2.** [*irr.*] *mst* ~ *in* ein Loch schlagen in (*acc.*); ~ *off* abwehren.

stay [stei] **1.** ♦ Stag *n;* ⊕ Strebe *f;* Stütze *f;* Aufschub *m;* Aufenthalt *m;* ~*s pl.* Korsett *n;* **2.** bleiben; wohnen; (sich) aufhalten; Ausdauer haben; hemmen; aufschieben; *Hunger* vorläufig stillen; stützen; **~er** ['steiə] *Sport:* Steher *m.*

stead [sted] Stelle *f,* Statt *f;* **~fast** □ ['stedfəst] fest, unerschütterlich; standhaft; unverwandt (*Blick*).

steady ['stedi] **1.** □ (be)ständig; stetig; sicher; fest; ruhig; gleichmäßig; unerschütterlich; zuverlässig; **2.** stetig *od.* sicher machen *od.* werden; (sich) festigen; stützen; (sich) beruhigen; **3.** *Am.* F feste Freundin, fester Freund.

steal [stiːl] **1.** [*irr.*] *v/t.* stehlen (*a. fig.*); *v/i.* sich stehlen *od.* schleichen; **2.** *Am.* Diebstahl *m.*

stealth [stelθ] Heimlichkeit *f; by* ~ heimlich; **~y** □ ['stelθi] verstohlen.

steam [stiːm] **1.** Dampf *m;* Dunst *m; attr.* Dampf...; **2.** *v/i.* dampfen; ~ *up* beschlagen (*Glas*); *v/t.* ausdünsten; dämpfen; **~er** ⚓ ['stiːmə] Dampfer *m;* **~y** □ [.mi] dampfig; dampfend; dunstig.

steel [stiːl] **1.** Stahl *m;* **2.** stählern; Stahl...; **3.** (ver)stählen.

steep [stiːp] **1.** steil, jäh; F toll; **2.** einweichen; einlegen; eintauchen; tränken; *fig.* versenken.

steeple ['stiːpl] Kirchturm *m;* **~-chase** *Sport:* Hindernisrennen *n.*

steer¹ [stiə] junger Ochse.

steer² [.] steuern; **~age** ⚓ ['stiəridʒ] Steuerung *f;* Zwischendeck *n;* **~ing-wheel** [.riŋwiːl] Steuerrad *f; mot.* Lenkrad *n;* **~sman** ⚓ [.zmən] Rudergänger *m.*

stem [stem] **1.** (Baum-, Wort-) Stamm *m;* Stiel *m;* Stengel *m;* ♦ Vordersteven *m;* **2.** *Am.* (ab)stammen (*from* von); sich stemmen gegen, ankämpfen gegen.

stench [stentʃ] Gestank *m.*

stencil ['stensl] Schablone *f; typ.* Matrize *f.* [graph(in).\

stenographer [steˈnɔgrəfə] Steno-\

step¹ [step] **1.** Schritt *m,* Tritt *m; fig.* Strecke *f;* Fußstapfe *f;* (Treppen)Stufe *f;* Trittbrett *m;* ~*s pl.* Trittleiter *f;* **2.** *v/i.* schreiten; treten, gehen; ~ *out* ausschreiten; *v/t.* ~ *off,* ~ *out* abschreiten; ~ *up* ankurbeln.

step² [.] *in Zssgn* Stief...; **~father** ['stepfɑːðə] Stiefvater *m;* **~mother** Stiefmutter *f.*

steppe [step] Steppe *f.*

stepping-stone *fig.* ['stepiŋstoun] Sprungbrett *n.*

steril|e ['sterail] unfruchtbar; steril; **~ity** [steˈriliti] Sterilität *f;* **~ize** ['sterilaiz] sterilisieren.

sterling ['stəːliŋ] vollwertig, echt; gediegen; ♦ Sterling *m* (*Währung*).

stern [stəːn] **1.** □ ernst; finster, streng, hart; **2.** ♦ Heck *n;* **~ness**

['stə:nnis] Ernst *m*; Strenge *f*; **~-post** ⚓ Hintersteven *m*.
stevedore ⚓ ['sti:vidɔ:] Stauer *m*.
stew [stju:] **1.** schmoren, dämpfen; **2.** Schmorgericht *n*; F Aufregung *f*.
steward [stjuəd] Verwalter *m*; ⚓, ✈ Steward *m*; (Fest)Ordner *m*; **~ess** ⚓, ✈ ['stjuədis] Stewardeß *f*.
stick [stik] **1.** Stock *m*; Stecken *m*; Stab *m*; (Besen- *etc.*)Stiel *m*; Stange *f*; F Klotz *m* (*unbeholfener Mensch*); **~s** *pl.* Kleinholz *n*; the **~s** *pl. Am.* F die hinterste Provinz; **2.** [*irr.*] *v/i.* stecken (bleiben); haften; kleben (*to* an *dat.*); **~** *at nothing* vor nichts zurückscheuen; **~** *out*, **~** *up* hervorstehen; F standhalten; **~** *to* bleiben bei; *v/t.* (ab)stechen; (an)stecken, (an)heften; (an)kleben; F ertragen; **~ing-plaster** ['stikiŋpla:stə] Heftpflaster *n*.
sticky □ ['stiki] kleb(e)rig; zäh.
stiff □ [stif] steif; starr; hart; fest; mühsam; stark (*Getränk*); *be bored* **~** F zu Tode gelangweilt sein; *keep a* **~** *upper lip* die Ohren steifhalten; **~en** ['stifn] (sich) (ver)steifen; **~-necked** [~'nekt] halsstarrig.
stifle ['staifl] ersticken (*a. fig.*).
stigma ['stigmə] (Brand-, Schand-) Mal *n*; Stigma *n*; **~tize** [~ətaiz] brandmarken.
stile [stail] Zauntritt *m*, Zaunübergang *m*.
still [stil] **1.** *adj.* still; **2.** *adv.* noch (immer); **3.** *cj.* doch, dennoch; **4.** stillen; beruhigen; **5.** Destillierapparat *m*; **~-born** ['stilbɔ:n] totgeboren; **~ life** Stilleben *n*; **~ness** Stille *f*, Ruhe *f*.
stilt [stilt] Stelze *f*; **~ed** ['stiltid] gespreizt, hochtrabend, geschraubt.
stimul|ant ['stimjulənt] **1.** ⚕ stimulierend; **2.** ⚕ Reizmittel *n*; Genußmittel *n*; Anreiz *m*; **~ate** [~leit] (an)reizen; anregen; **~ation** [stimju'leiʃən] Reizung *f*, Antrieb *m*; **~us** ['stimjuləs] Antrieb *m*; Reizmittel *n*.
sting [stiŋ] **1.** Stachel *m*; Stich *m*, Biß *m*; *fig.* Schärfe *f*; Antrieb *m*; **2.** [*irr.*] stechen; brennen; schmerzen; (an)treiben.
sting|iness ['stindʒinis] Geiz *m*; **~y** □ ['stindʒi] geizig; knapp, karg.
stink [stiŋk] **1.** Gestank *m*; **2.** [*irr.*] *v/i.* stinken; *v/t.* verstänkern.
stint [stint] **1.** Einschränkung *f*; Arbeit *f*; **2.** knausern mit; einschränken; *j-n* knapp halten.
stipend ['staipend] Gehalt *n*.
stipulat|e ['stipjuleit] *a.* **~** *for* ausbedingen, ausmachen, vereinbaren; **~ion** [stipju'leiʃən] Abmachung *f*; Klausel *f*, Bedingung *f*.
stir [stə:] **1.** Regung *f*; Bewegung *f*; Rühren *n*; Aufregung *f*; Aufsehen *n*; **2.** (sich) rühren; umrühren, bewegen; aufregen; **~** *up* aufrühren; aufrütteln.
stirrup ['stirəp] Steigbügel *m*.
stitch [stitʃ] **1.** Stich *m*; Masche *f*; Seitenstechen *n*; **2.** nähen; heften.
stock [stɔk] **1.** (Baum)Strunk *m*; Pfropfunterlage *f*; Griff *m*, Kolben *m e-s Gewehrs*; Stamm *m*, Herkunft *f*; Rohstoff *m*; (Fleisch-, Gemüse)Brühe *f*; Vorrat *m*, (Waren)Lager *n*; (Wissens)Schatz *m*; *a. live***~** Vieh(bestand *m*) *n*; ✝ Stammkapital *n*; Anleihekapital *n*; **~s** *pl.* Effekten *pl.*; Aktien *f/pl.*; Staatspapiere *n/pl.*; **~s** *pl.* ⚓ Stapel *m*; *in* (*out of*) **~** (nicht) vorrätig; *take* **~** ✝ Inventur machen; *take* **~** *of fig.* sich klarwerden über (*acc.*); **2.** vorrätig; ständig; gängig; Standard...; **3.** versorgen; *Waren* führen; ✝ vorrätig haben.
stockade [stɔ'keid] Staket *n*.
stock|-breeder ['stɔkbri:də] Viehzüchter *m*; **~broker** ✝ Börsenmakler *m*; **~ exchange** ✝ Börse *f*; **~-farmer** Viehzüchter *m*; **~holder** ✝ Aktionär(in).
stockinet [stɔki'net] Trikot *n*.
stocking ['stɔkiŋ] Strumpf *m*.
stock|jobber ✝ ['stɔkdʒɔbə] Börsenmakler *m*; **~-market** ✝ Börse *f*; **~-still** unbeweglich; **~-taking** Inventur *f*; **~y** ['stɔki] stämmig.
stog|ie, ~y *Am.* ['stougi] billige Zigarre.
stoic ['stouik] **1.** stoisch; **2.** Stoiker *m*.
stoker ['stoukə] Heizer *m*.
stole [stoul] *pret. von steal 1*; **~n** ['stoulən] *p.p. von steal 1*.
stolid □ ['stɔlid] schwerfällig; gleichmütig; stur.
stomach ['stʌmək] **1.** Magen *m*; Leib *m*, Bauch *m*; *fig.* Lust *f*; **2.** verdauen, vertragen; *fig.* ertragen.
stomp *Am.* [stɔmp] (auf)stampfen.
stone [stoun] **1.** Stein *m*; (Obst-) Kern *m*; *Gewichtseinheit von 6,35 kg*; **2.** steinern; Stein...; **3.** steinigen; entsteinen; **~-blind** ['stoun'blaind] stockblind; **~-dead** mausetot; **~ware** [~nweə] Steingut *n*.
stony ['stouni] steinig; *fig.* steinern.
stood [stud] *pret. u. p.p. von stand 1*.
stool [stu:l] Schemel *m*; ⚕ Stuhlgang *m*; **~-pigeon** *Am.* ['stu:lpidʒin] Lockvogel *m*; Spitzel *m*.
stoop [stu:p] **1.** *v/i.* sich bücken; sich erniedrigen *od.* herablassen; krumm gehen; *v/t.* neigen; **2.** gebeugte Haltung; *Am.* Veranda *f*.
stop [stɔp] **1.** *v/t.* anhalten; hindern; aufhören; *a.* **~** *up* (ver)stopfen; *Zahn* plombieren; (ver)sperren; *Zahlung* einstellen; *Lohn* einbehalten; *v/i.* stehenbleiben; aufhören; halten; F bleiben; **~** *dead*, **~** *short* plötzlich anhalten; **~** *over* haltmachen; **2.** (Ein)Halt *m*; Pause *f*; Hemmung *f*; ⊕ Anschlag *m*; Aufhören *n*, Ende *n*; Haltestelle *f*; *mst*

full ~ gr. Punkt m; ~gap ['stɔpgæp]
Notbehelf m; ~page [~pidʒ] Verstopfung f; (Zahlungs- etc.)Ein-
stellung f; Sperrung f; (Lohn)Ab-
zug m; Aufenthalt m; ⊕ Hemmung
f; Betriebsstörung f; (Verkehrs-)
Stockung f; ~per [~pə] Stöpsel m;
~ping ⚓ [~piŋ] Plombe f.
storage ['stɔːridʒ] Lagerung f,
Aufbewahrung f; Lagergeld n.
store [stɔː] 1. Vorrat m; fig. Fülle f;
Lagerhaus n; Am. Laden m; ~s pl.
Kauf-, Warenhaus n; in ~ vorrätig,
auf Lager; 2. a. ~ up (auf)speichern;
(ein)lagern; versorgen; ~house
Lagerhaus n; fig. Schatzkammer f;
~keeper Lagerverwalter m; Am.
Ladenbesitzer m.
stor(e)y ['stɔːri] Stockwerk n) m.
storeyed ['stɔːrid] mit ... Stock-
werken, ...stöckig.
storied [~] s. storeyed.
stork [stɔːk] Storch m.
storm [stɔːm] 1. Sturm m; Gewitter n; 2. stürmen; toben; ~y ['stɔː-
mi] stürmisch.
story ['stɔːri] Geschichte f; Erzählung f; Märchen n; thea. Handlung
f; F Lüge f; short ~ Kurzgeschich-
te f.
stout [staut] 1. ☐ stark, kräftig;
derb; dick; tapfer; 2. Starkbier n.
stove [stouv] 1. Ofen m; Herd m;
2. pret. u. p.p. von stave 2.
stow [stou] (ver)stauen, packen;
~away ⚓ ['stouəwei] blinder Passagier.
straddle ['strædl] (die Beine) spreizen; rittlings sitzen auf (dat.); Am.
fig. es mit beiden Parteien halten;
schwanken.
straggl|e ['strægl] verstreut od. ein-
zeln liegen; umherstreifen; bummeln; fig. abschweifen; ⚘ wuchern;
~ing ◇ [~liŋ] weitläufig, lose.
straight [streit] 1. adj. gerade; fig.
aufrichtig, ehrlich; glatt (Haar);
Am. pur, unverdünnt; Am. pol.
hundertprozentig; put ~ in Ordnung bringen; 2. adv. gerade(wegs);
geradeaus; direkt; sofort; ~ away
sofort; ~ out rundheraus; ~en
['streitn] gerade machen od. werden; ~ out in Ordnung bringen;
~forward ☐ [streit'fɔːwəd] gerade;
ehrlich, redlich.
strain [strein] 1. Abstammung f;
Art f; ⊕ Spannung f; (Über)An-
strengung f; starke Inanspruchnahme (on gen.); Druck m; ♂ Zerrung f; Ton m; mst ~s pl. ♩ Weise f;
Hang m (of zu); 2. v/t. (an)spannen;
(über)anstrengen; überspannen; ⊕
beanspruchen; ♂ zerren; durch-
seihen; v/i. sich spannen; sich anstrengen; sich abmühen (after um);
zerren (at an dat.); ~er ['streinə]
Durchschlag m; Filter m; Sieb n.
strait [streit] (in Eigennamen 2s pl.)

Meerenge f, Straße f; ~s pl. Not
(-lage) f; ~ jacket Zwangsjacke f;
~ened ['streitnd] dürftig; in Not.
strand [strænd] 1. Strand m;
Strähne f (a. fig.); 2. auf den Strand
setzen; fig. stranden (lassen).
strange [streindʒ] fremd (a. fig.);
seltsam; ~r ['streindʒə] Fremde(r)
m.
strangle ['stræŋgl] erwürgen.
strap [stræp] 1. Riemen m; Gurt m;
Band n; 2. an-, festschnallen; mit
Riemen peitschen.   [List f.)
stratagem ['strætidʒəm] (Kriegs-))
strateg|ic [strə'tiːdʒik] (~ally) stra-
tegisch; ~y ['strætidʒi] Kriegs-
kunst f, Strategie f.
strat|um geol. ['strɑːtəm], pl. ~a
[~tə] Schicht f (a. fig.), Lage f.
straw [strɔː] 1. Stroh(halm m) n;
2. Stroh...; ~ vote Am. Probeab-
stimmung f; ~berry ['strɔːbəri]
Erdbeere f.
stray [strei] 1. irregehen; sich verirren; abirren; umherschweifen;
2. a. ~ed verirrt; vereinzelt; 3. ver-
irrtes Tier.
streak [striːk] 1. Strich m, Streifen
m; fig. Ader f, Spur f; kurze
Periode; ~ of lightning Blitzstrahl m;
2. streifen; jagen, F flitzen.
stream [striːm] 1. Bach m; Strom
m; Strömung f, 2. v/i. strömen;
triefen; flattern; v/t. strömen lassen; ausströmen; ~er ['striːmə]
Wimpel m; (fliegendes) Band;
Lichtstrahl m; typ. Schlagzeile f.
street [striːt] Straße f; ~car Am.
['striːtkɑː] Straßenbahn(wagen m) f.
strength [streŋθ] Stärke f, Kraft f;
on the ~ of auf ... hin, auf Grund
(gen.); ~en ['streŋθən] v/t. stärken,
kräftigen; bestärken; v/i. erstarken.
strenuous ☐ ['strenjuəs] rührig,
emsig; eifrig; anstrengend.
stress [stres] 1. Druck m; Nachdruck m; Betonung f (a. gr.);
fig. Schwergewicht n; Ton m; psych.
Stress m; 2. betonen.
stretch [stretʃ] 1. v/t. strecken;
(aus)dehnen; mst ~ out ausstrecken;
(an)spannen; fig. überspannen; Gesetz zu weit auslegen; v/i. sich (er-)
strecken; sich dehnen (lassen);
2. Strecken n; Dehnung f; (An-)
Spannung f; Übertreibung f,
Überschreitung f; Strecke f, Fläche
f; ~er ['stretʃə] Tragbahre f;
Streckvorrichtung f.
strew [struː] [irr.] (be)streuen; ~n
[~uːn] p.p. von strew.
stricken ['strikən] 1. p.p. von strike
2; 2. adj. ge-, betroffen.
strict [strikt] streng; genau; ~ly
speaking strenggenommen; ~ness
['striktnis] Genauigkeit f; Strenge f.
stridden ['stridn] p.p. von stride 1.
stride [straid] 1. [irr.] v/t. über-,
durchschreiten; 2. (weiter) Schritt.

strident □ ['straidnt] kreischend.

strife [straif] Streit *m*, Hader *m*.

strike [straik] **1.** Streik *m*; (Öl-, Erz)Fund *m*; *fig.* Treffer *m*; ✗ (Luft)Angriff *m auf ein Einzelziel*; *Am. Baseball*: Verlustpunkt *m*; be on ~ streiken; **2.** [*irr.*] *v/t.* treffen, stoßen; schlagen; gegen *od.* auf (*acc.*) schlagen *od.* stoßen; stoßen *od.* treffen auf (*acc.*); *Flagge etc.* streichen; *Ton* anschlagen; auffallen (*dat.*); ergreifen; *Handel* abschließen; *Streichholz, Licht* anzünden; *Wurzel* schlagen; *Pose* annehmen; *Bilanz* ziehen; ~ up ♪ anstimmen; *Freundschaft* schließen; *v/i.* schlagen; ⚓ auf Grund stoßen; streiken; ~ home (richtig) treffen; ~r ['straikə] Streikende(r) *m*.

striking □ ['straikiŋ] Schlag...; auffallend; eindrucksvoll; treffend.

string [striŋ] **1.** Schnur *f*; Bindfaden *m*; Band *n*; *Am.* F Bedingung *f*; (Bogen)Sehne *f*; ♪ Faser *f*; ♪ Saite *f*; Reihe *f*, Kette *f*; ~s *pl.* ♪ Saiteninstrumente *n/pl.*, Streicher *m/pl.*; *pull the ~s* der Drahtzieher sein; **2.** [*irr.*] spannen; aufreihen; besaiten (*a. fig.*), bespannen; (ver-, zu)schnüren; *Bohnen* abziehen; *Am. sl. j-n* verkohlen; be strung up angespannt *od.* erregt sein; ~band♪ ['striŋbænd] Streichorchester *n*.

stringent □ ['strindʒənt] streng, scharf; bindend; zwingend; knapp.

stringy ['striŋi] faserig; zäh.

strip [strip] **1.** entkleiden (*a. fig.*); (sich) ausziehen; abziehen; *fig.* entblößen, berauben; ⊕ auseinandernehmen; ⚓ abtakeln; *a.* ~ off ausziehen, abstreifen; **2.** Streifen *m*.

stripe [straip] Streifen *m*; ✗ Tresse *f*.

stripling ['stripliŋ] Bürschchen *n*.

strive [straiv] [*irr.*] streben; sich bemühen; ringen (*for* um); ~n ['strivn] *p.p. von* strive.

strode [stroud] *pret. von* stride 1.

stroke [strouk] **1.** Schlag *m* (*a.* ✗); Streich *m*; Stoß *m*; Strich *m*; ~ of luck Glücksfall *m*; **2.** streiche(l)n.

stroll [stroul] **1.** schlendern; umherziehen; **2.** Bummel *m*; Spaziergang *m*; ~er ['stroulə] Bummler(in), Spaziergänger(in); *Am.* (Falt)Sportwagen *m*.

strong □ [stroŋ] *allg.* stark; kräftig; energisch, eifrig; fest; schwer (*Speise etc.*); ~box ['stroŋbɔks] Stahlkassette *f*; ~hold Festung *f*; *fig.* Bollwerk *n*; ~room Stahlkammer *f*; ~willed eigenwillig.

strop [strop] **1.** Streichriemen *m*; **2.** *Messer* abziehen.

strove [strouv] *pret. von* strive.

struck [strʌk] *pret. u. p.p. von* strike 2.

structure ['strʌktʃə] Bau(werk *n*) *m*; Struktur *f*, Gefüge *n*; Gebilde *n*.

struggle ['strʌgl] **1.** sich (ab)mühen; kämpfen, ringen; sich sträuben; **2.** Kampf *m*; Ringen *n*; Anstrengung *f*.

strung [strʌŋ] *pret. u. p.p. von* string 2.

strut [strʌt] **1.** *v/i.* stolzieren; *v/t.* ⊕ abstützen; **2.** Stolzieren *n*; ⊕ Strebe(balken *m*) *f*; Stütze *f*.

stub [stʌb] **1.** (Baum)Stumpf *m*; Stummel *m*; *Am.* Kontrollabschnitt *m*; **2.** (aus)roden; sich *den Fuß* stoßen.

stubble ['stʌbl] Stoppel(n *pl.*) *f*.

stubborn □ ['stʌbən] eigensinnig; widerspenstig; stur; hartnäckig.

stuck [stʌk] *pret. u. p.p. von* stick 2; ~up ['stʌk'ʌp] F hochnäsig.

stud [stʌd] **1.** (Wand)Pfosten *m*; Ziernagel *m*; Knauf *m*; Manschetten-, Kragenknopf *m*; Gestüt *n*; **2.** beschlagen; besetzen; ~book ['stʌdbuk] Gestütbuch *n*.

student ['stju:dənt] Student(in).

studied □ ['stʌdid] einstudiert; gesucht; gewollt.

studio ['stju:diou] Atelier *n*; Studio *n*; *Radio*: Aufnahme-, Senderaum *m*.

studious □ ['stju:djəs] fleißig; bedacht; beflissentlich.

study ['stʌdi] **1.** Studium *n*; Studier-, Arbeitszimmer *n*; *paint. etc.* Studie *f*; be in a brown ~ versunken sein; **2.** (ein)studieren; sich *et.* genau ansehen; sich bemühen um.

stuff [stʌf] **1.** Stoff *m*; Zeug *n*; *fig.* Unsinn *m*; **2.** *v/t.* (voll-, aus)stopfen; ~ed shirt *Am. sl.* Fatzke *m*; *v/i.* sich vollstopfen; ~ing ['stʌfiŋ] Füllung *f*; ~y □ [~fi] dumpf(ig), muffig; stickig; *fig.* verärgert.

stultify ['stʌltifai] lächerlich machen, blamieren; *et.* hinfällig machen.

stumble ['stʌmbl] **1.** Stolpern *n*; Fehltritt *m*; **2.** stolpern; straucheln; ~ upon stoßen auf (*acc.*).

stump [stʌmp] **1.** Stumpf *m*, Stummel *m*; **2.** *v/t.* F verblüffen; *Am.* F herausfordern; ~ the country als Wahlredner im Land umherziehen; *v/i.* (daher)stapfen; ~y □ ['stʌmpi] gedrungen; plump.

stun [stʌn] betäuben (*a. fig.*).

stung [stʌŋ] *pret. u. p.p. von* sting 2.

stunk [stʌŋk] *pret. u. p.p. von* stink 2.

stunning □ F ['stʌniŋ] toll, famos.

stunt[1] F [stʌnt] Kraft-, Kunststück *n*; (Reklame)Trick *m*; Sensation *f*.

stunt[2] [~] im Wachstum hindern; ~ed ['stʌntid] verkümmert.

stupefy ['stju:pifai] *fig.* betäuben; verblüffen; verdummen; ~endous □ [stju:(:)'pendəs] erstaunlich; ~id □ ['stju:pid] dumm, einfältig, stumpfsinnig; blöd; ~idity [stju:(:)-'piditi] Dummheit *f*; Stumpfsinn *m*; ~or ['stju:(:)pə] Erstarrung *f*, Betäubung *f*.

sturdy ['stə:di] derb, kräftig, stark; stämmig; stramm; handfest.

stutter ['stʌtə] 1. stottern; 2. Stottern n.

sty[1] [stai] Schweinestall m, Koben m.

sty[2], **stye** ❀ [~] Gerstenkorn n am Auge.

style [stail] 1. Stil m; Mode f; Betitelung f; 2. (be)nennen, betiteln.

stylish □ ['stailiʃ] stilvoll; elegant; **~ness** [~nis] Eleganz f.

stylo F ['stailou], **~graph** [~ləgrɑ:f] Tintenkuli m.

suave □ [swɑːv] verbindlich; mild.

sub... [sʌb] mst Unter..., unter...; Neben...; Hilfs...; fast ...

subdeb Am. F [sʌb'deb] Backfisch m, junges Mädchen.

subdivision ['sʌbdiviʒn] Unterteilung f; Unterabteilung f.

subdue [səb'djuː] unterwerfen; bezwingen; bändigen; unterdrücken; verdrängen; dämpfen.

subject ['sʌbdʒikt] 1. unterworfen; untergeben, abhängig; untertan; unterliegend (to dat.); be ~ to neigen zu; 2. adv. ~ to vorbehaltlich (gen.); 3. Untertan m, Staatsangehörige(r m) f; phls., gr. Subjekt n; a. ~ matter Thema n, Gegenstand m; 4. [səb'dʒekt] unterwerfen; fig. aussetzen; **~ion** [~kʃən] Unterwerfung f.   [chen.]

subjugate ['sʌbdʒugeit] unterjo-]

subjunctive gr. [səb'dʒʌŋktiv] a. ~ mood Konjunktiv m.

sub|lease [sʌb'liːs], **~let** [irr. (let)] untervermieten.

sublime □ [sə'blaim] erhaben.

submachine-gun ['sʌbmə'ʃiːŋgʌn] Maschinenpistole f.

submarine ['sʌbməriːn] 1. unterseeisch; 2. ⚓ Unterseeboot n.

submerge [səb'məːdʒ] untertauchen; überschwemmen.

submiss|ion [səb'miʃən] Unterwerfung f; Unterbreitung f; **~ive** □ [~isiv] unterwürfig.

submit [səb'mit] (sich) unterwerfen; anheimstellen; unterbreiten, einreichen; sich fügen od. ergeben (to in acc.).

subordinate 1. □ [sə'bɔːdnit] untergeordnet; untergeben; ~ clause gr. Nebensatz m; 2. [~] Untergebene(r m) f; 3. [~dineit] unterordnen.

suborn ⚖ [sʌ'bɔːn] verleiten.

subscribe [səb'skraib] v/t. Geld stiften (to für); Summe zeichnen; s-n Namen setzen (to unter acc.); unterschreiben mit; v/i. ~ to Zeitung etc. abonnieren; e-r Meinung zustimmen, et. unterschreiben; **~r** [~bə] (Unter)Zeichner(in); Abonnent(in); teleph. Teilnehmer(in).

subscription [səb'skripʃən] (Unter-)Zeichnung f; Abonnement n.

subsequent □ ['sʌbsikwent] folgend; später; **~ly** hinterher.

subservient □ [səb'səːvjənt] dienlich; dienstbar; unterwürfig.

subsid|e [səb'said] sinken, sich senken; fig. sich setzen; sich legen (Wind); **~ into** verfallen in (acc.); **~iary** [~'sidjəri] 1. □ Hilfs...; Neben...; untergeordnet; 2. Tochtergesellschaft f; Filiale f; **~ize** ['sʌbsidaiz] mit Geld unterstützen; subventionieren; **~y** [~di] Beihilfe f; Subvention f.

subsist [səb'sist] bestehen; leben (on, by von); **~ence** [~təns] Dasein n; (Lebens)Unterhalt m.

substance ['sʌbstəns] Substanz f; Wesen n; fig. Hauptsache f; Inhalt m; Wirklichkeit f; Vermögen n.

substantial □ [səb'stænʃəl] wesentlich; wirklich; kräftig; stark; solid; vermögend; namhaft (Summe).

substantiate [səb'stænʃieit] beweisen, begründen, dartun.

substantive gr. ['sʌbstəntiv] Substantiv n, Hauptwort n.

substitut|e ['sʌbstitjuːt] 1. an die Stelle setzen od. treten (for von); unterschieben (for statt); 2. Stellvertreter m; Ersatz m; **~ion** [sʌbsti'tjuːʃən] Stellvertretung f; Ersatz m.

subterfuge ['sʌbtəfjuːdʒ] Ausflucht f.

subterranean □ [sʌbtə'reinjən] unterirdisch.

sub-title ['sʌbtaitl] Untertitel m.

subtle □ ['sʌtl] fein(sinnig); subtil; spitzfindig; **~ty** [~lti] Feinheit f.

subtract ⚖ [səb'trækt] abziehen, subtrahieren.

subtropical ['sʌb'trɔpikəl] subtropisch.

suburb ['sʌbəːb] Vorstadt f, Vorort m; **~an** [sə'bəːbən] vorstädtisch.

subvention [səb'venʃən] 1. Subvention f; 2. subventionieren.

subver|sion [sʌb'vəːʃən] Umsturz m; **~sive** [~siv] zerstörend (of acc.); subversiv; **~t** [~ː t] (um-)stürzen; untergraben.

subway ['sʌbwei] (bsd. Fußgänger-) Unterführung f; Am. Untergrundbahn f.

succeed [sək'siːd] Erfolg haben; glücken, gelingen; (nach)folgen (dat.); ~ to übernehmen; erben.

success [sək'ses] Erfolg m; **~ful** □ [~sful] erfolgreich; **~ion** [~ʃən] (Nach-, Erb-, Reihen)Folge f; Nachkommenschaft f; in ~ nacheinander; **~ive** □ [~siv] aufeinanderfolgend; **~or** [~sə] Nachfolger(in).   [fe.]

succo(u)r ['sʌkə] 1. Hilfe f; 2. hel-]

succulent □ ['sʌkjulənt] saftig.

succumb [sə'kʌm] unter-, erliegen.

such [sʌtʃ] solch(er, -e, -es); derartig; so groß; ~ a man ein solcher Mann; ~ as die, welche.

suck [sʌk] 1. (ein)saugen; saugen an (dat.); aussaugen; lutschen; 2. Saugen n; ⁓er ['sʌkə] Saugorgan n; ⚕ Wurzelsproß m; Am. Einfaltspinsel m; ⁓le ['sʌkl] säugen, stillen; ⁓ling [⁓liŋ] Säugling m.

suction ['sʌkʃən] (An)Saugen n; Sog m; attr. Saug...

sudden □ ['sʌdn] plötzlich; all of a ⁓ ganz plötzlich.

suds [sʌdz] pl. Seifenlauge f; Seifenschaum m; ⁓y Am. ['sʌdzi] schaumig, seifig.

sue [sju:] v/t. verklagen; ⁓ out erwirken; v/i. nachsuchen (for um); klagen.

suède [sweid] Wildleder.

suet [sjuit] Nierenfett n; Talg m.

suffer ['sʌfə] v/i. leiden (from an dat.); v/t. erleiden, erdulden, (zu-)lassen; ⁓ance [⁓rəns] Duldung f; ⁓er [⁓rə] Leidende(r m) f; Dulder(in); ⁓ing [⁓riŋ] Leiden n.

suffice [sə'fais] genügen; ⁓ it to say es sei nur gesagt.

sufficien|cy [sə'fiʃənsi] genügende Menge; Auskommen n; ⁓t [⁓nt] genügend, ausreichend.

suffix gr. ['sʌfiks] 1. anhängen; 2. Nachsilbe f, Suffix n.

suffocate ['sʌfəkeit] ersticken.

suffrage ['sʌfridʒ] (Wahl)Stimmef; Wahl-, Stimmrecht n.

suffuse [sə'fju:z] übergießen; überziehen.

sugar ['ʃugə] 1. Zucker m; 2. zuckern; ⁓-basin, Am. ⁓-bowl Zuckerdose f; ⁓-cane ⚕ Zuckerrohr n; ⁓-coat überzuckern, versüßen; ⁓y [⁓ri] zuckerig; zuckersüß.

suggest [sə'dʒest] vorschlagen, anregen; nahelegen; vorbringen; Gedanken eingeben; andeuten; denken lassen an (acc.); ⁓ion [⁓tʃən] Anregung f; Rat m, Vorschlag m; Suggestion f; Eingebung f; Andeutung f; ⁓ive [⁓tiv] anregend; andeutend (of acc.); gehaltvoll; zweideutig.

suicide ['sjuisaid] 1. Selbstmord m; Selbstmörder(in); 2. Am. Selbstmord begehen.

suit [sju:t] 1. (Herren)Anzug m; (Damen)Kostüm n; Anliegen n; (Heirats)Antrag m; Karten: Farbe f; ⁓ Prozeß m; 2. v/t. j-m passen, zusagen, bekommen; j-n kleiden, j-m stehen, passen zu (Kleidungsstück etc.); ⁓ oneself tun, was e-m beliebt; ⁓ s.th. to et. anpassen (dat.); be ⁓ed geeignet sein (for für), passen (to zu); v/i. passen; ⁓able □ ['sju:təbl] passend, geeignet; entsprechend; ⁓case (Hand)Koffer m; ⁓e [swi:t] Gefolge n; (Reihen)Folge f; ♪ Suite f; a. ⁓ of rooms Zimmerflucht f; Garnitur f, (Zimmer)Einrichtung f; ⁓or ['sju:tə] Freier m; ⚖ Kläger(in).

sulk [sʌlk] schmollen, bocken; ⁓iness ['sʌlkinis] üble Laune; ⁓s pl. = sulkiness; ⁓y ['sʌlki] 1. verdrießlich; launisch; schmollend; 2. Sport: Traberwagen m, Sulky m.

sullen □ ['sʌlən] verdrossen, mürrisch.

sully ['sʌli] mst fig. beflecken.

sulphur ⚗ ['sʌlfə] Schwefel m; ⁓ic [sʌl'fjuərik] Schwefel...

sultriness ['sʌltrinis] Schwüle f.

sultry □ ['sʌltri] schwül; fig. heftig, hitzig.

sum [sʌm] 1. Summe f; Betrag m; fig. Inbegriff m, Inhalt m; Rechenaufgabe f; do ⁓s rechnen; 2. mst ⁓ up zs.-rechnen; zs.-fassen.

summar|ize ['sʌməraiz] (kurz) zs.-fassen; ⁓y [⁓ri] 1. □ kurz (zs.-gefaßt); ⚖ Schnell...; 2. (kurze) Inhaltsangabe, Auszug m.

summer ['sʌmə] Sommer m; ⁓ resort Sommerfrische f; ⁓ school Ferienkurs m; ⁓ly [⁓li], ⁓y [⁓ri] sommerlich.

summit ['sʌmit] Gipfel m (a. fig.).

summon ['sʌmən] auffordern; (be-)rufen; ⚖ vorladen; Mut etc. aufbieten; ⁓s Aufforderung f; ⚖ Vorladung f.

sumptuous □ ['sʌmptjuəs] kostbar.

sun [sʌn] 1. Sonne f; attr. Sonnen...; 2. (sich) sonnen; ⁓-bath ['sʌnbɑ:θ] Sonnenbad n; ⁓-beam Sonnenstrahl m; ⁓-burn Sonnenbräune f; Sonnenbrand m.

Sunday ['sʌndi] Sonntag m.

sun|-dial ['sʌndaiəl] Sonnenuhr f; ⁓down Sonnenuntergang m.

sundr|ies ['sʌndriz] pl. bsd. † Verschiedene(s) n; Extraausgabenf/pl.; ⁓y [⁓ri] verschiedene.

sung [sʌŋ] pret. u. p.p. von sing.

sun-glasses ['sʌnglɑ:siz] pl. (a pair of ⁓ pl. eine) Sonnenbrille f.

sunk [sʌŋk] pret. u. p.p. von sink 1.

sunken ['sʌŋkən] 1. p.p. von sink 1; 2. adj. versunken; fig. eingefallen.

sun|ny □ ['sʌni] sonnig; ⁓rise Sonnenaufgang m; ⁓set Sonnenuntergang m; ⁓shade Sonnenschirm m; ⁓shine Sonnenschein m; ⁓stroke ⚕ Sonnenstich m.

sup [sʌp] zu Abend essen.

super F ['sju:pə] erstklassig, prima, super.

super|... ['sju:pə] Über..., über...; Ober..., ober...; Groß...; ⁓abundant □ [sju:pərə'bʌndənt] überreichlich; überschwenglich; ⁓annuate [⁓'rænjueit] pensionieren; ⁓d ausgedient; veraltet (S.).

superb □ [sju(:)'pə:b] prächtig; herrlich.

super|charger mot. ['sju:pətʃɑ:dʒə] Kompressor m; ⁓cilious [sju:pə-

'silias] hochmütig; ~ficial □ [~ə'fiʃəl] oberflächlich; ~fine ['sju:pə'fain] extrafein; ~fluity [sju:pə-flu(:)iti] Überfluß m; ~fluous □ [sju(:)'pə:fluəs] überflüssig; ~heat ⊕ [sju:pə'hi:t] überhitzen; ~human □ [ˌ'hju:mən] übermenschlich; ~impose ['sju:pərim'pouz] darauf-, darüberlegen; ~induce [ˌrin'dju:s] noch hinzufügen; ~intend [sju:prin'tend] die Oberaufsicht haben über (acc.); überwachen; ~intendent [ˌdənt] 1. Leiter m, Direktor m; (Ober)Aufseher m, Inspektor m; 2. aufsichtführend.

superior [sju(:)'piəriə] 1. □ ober; höher(stehend); vorgesetzt; besser, hochwertiger; überlegen (to dat.); vorzüglich; 2. Höherstehende(r m) f, bsd. Vorgesetzte(r m) f; eccl. Obere(r) m; mst Lady ♀, Mother ♀ eccl. Oberin f; ~ity [sju(:)piəri'ɔriti] Überlegenheit f.

super|lative [sju(:)'pə:lətiv] 1. □ höchst; überragend; 2. a. ~ degree gr. Superlativ m; ~market Supermarkt m; ~natural [sju:pə'nætʃ-rəl] übernatürlich; ~numerary [ˌ'nju:mərəri] 1. überzählig; 2. Überzählige(r m) f; thea. Statist (-in); ~scription [ˌ'skripʃən] Über-, Aufschrift f; ~sede [ˌ'si:d] ersetzen; verdrängen; absetzen; fig. überholen; ~sonic phys. ['sju:pə'sɔnik] Überschall...; ~stition [sju:pə'stiʃən] Aberglaube m; ~stitious [ˌʃəs] abergläubisch; ~vene [ˌ'vi:n] noch hinzukommen; unerwartet eintreten; ~vise ['sju:pəvaiz] beaufsichtigen, überwachen; ~vision [sju:pə'viʒən] (Ober)Aufsicht f; Beaufsichtigung f; ~visor f 'sju:pəvaizə] Aufseher m, Inspektor m.

supper ['sʌpə] Abendessen n; the (Lord's) ♀ das Heilige Abendmahl.

supplant [sə'plɑ:nt] verdrängen.

supple ['sʌpl] geschmeidig (machen).

supplement 1. ['sʌplimənt] Ergänzung f; Nachtrag m; (Zeitungsetc.)Beilage f; 2. [ˌment] ergänzen; ~al □ [sʌpli'mentl], ~ary [ˌtəri] Ergänzungs...; nachträglich; Nachtrags...

suppliant ['sʌpliənt] 1. □ demütig bittend, flehend; 2. Bittsteller(in).

supplicat|e ['sʌplikeit] demütig bitten, anflehen; ~ion [sʌpli'keiʃən] demütige Bitte.

supplier [sə'plaiə] Lieferant(in).

supply [sə'plai] 1. liefern; e-m Mangel abhelfen; e-e Stelle ausfüllen; vertreten; ausstatten, versorgen; ergänzen; 2. Lieferung f; Versorgung f; Zufuhr f; Vorrat m; Bedarf m; Angebot n; (Stell)Vertretung f; mst supplies pl. parl. Etat m.

support [sə'pɔ:t] 1. Stütze f; Hilfe f; ⊕ Träger m; Unterstützung f; Lebensunterhalt m; 2. (unter)stützen; unterhalten, sorgen für (Familie etc.); aufrechterhalten; (v)ertragen.

suppose [sə'pouz] annehmen; voraussetzen; vermuten; he is ~d to do er soll tun; ~ we go gehen wir; wie wär's, wenn wir gingen.

supposed □ [sə'pouzd] vermeintlich; ~ly [ˌzidli] vermutlich.

supposition [sʌpə'ziʃən] Voraussetzung f; Annahme f; Vermutung f.

suppress [sə'pres] unterdrücken; ~ion [ˌeʃən] Unterdrückung f.

suppurate ['sʌpjuəreit] eitern.

suprem|acy [sju'preməsi] Oberhoheit f; Vorherrschaft f; Überlegenheit f; Vorrang m; ~e □ [sju(:)'pri:m] höchst; oberst; Ober...; größt.

surcharge [sə:'tʃɑ:dʒ] 1. überladen; Zuschlag od. Nachgebühr erheben von j-m; 2. ['sə:'tʃɑ:dʒ] Überladung f; (Straf)Zuschlag m; Nachgebühr f; Überdruck m auf Briefmarken.

sure □ [ʃuə] allg. sicher; to be ~!, ~ enough!, Am. ~! F sicher(lich)!; ~ly ['ʃuəli] sicherlich; ~ty ['ʃuəti] Bürge m.

surf [sə:f] Brandung f.

surface ['sə:fis] 1. (Ober)Fläche f; ✈ Tragfläche f; 2. ⚓ auftauchen (U-Boot).

surf|-board ['sə:fbɔ:d] Wellenreiterbrett n; ~-boat Brandungsboot n.

surfeit ['sə:fit] 1. Übersättigung f; Ekel m; 2. (sich) überladen.

surf-riding ['sə:fraidiŋ] Sport: Wellenreiten n.

surge [sə:dʒ] 1. Woge f; 2. wogen.

surg|eon ['sə:dʒən] Chirurg m; ~ery [ˌəri] Chirurgie f; Sprechzimmer n; ~ hours pl. Sprechstunde(n pl.) f.

surgical □ ['sə:dʒikəl] chirurgisch.

surly □ ['sə:li] mürrisch; grob.

surmise 1. ['sə:maiz] Vermutung f; Argwohn m; 2. [sə:'maiz] vermuten; argwöhnen.

surmount [sə:'maunt] übersteigen; überragen; fig. überwinden.

surname ['sə:neim] Zu-, Nachname m.

surpass [sə:'pɑ:s] übersteigen; übertreffen; ~ing [ˌsiŋ] überragend.

surplus ['sə:pləs] 1. Überschuß m, Mehr n; 2. überschüssig; Über...

surpr|ise [sə'praiz] 1. Überraschung f; ✗ Überrump(e)lung f; 2. überraschen; ✗ überrumpeln.

surrender [sə'rendə] 1. Übergabe f, Ergebung f; Kapitulation f; Aufgeben n; 2. v/t. übergeben; aufgeben; v/i. a. ~ o.s. sich ergeben.

surround [sə'raund] umgeben; ✗

umzingeln; **~ing** [~diŋ] umliegend; **~ings** pl. Umgebung f.

surtax ['sɔːtæks] Steuerzuschlag m.

survey 1. [səˈvei] überblicken; mustern; begutachten; surv. vermessen; 2. ['sɔːvei] Überblick m (a. fig.); Besichtigung f; Gutachten n; surv. Vermessung f; **~or** [sə(ː)-ˈvei] Land-, Feldmesser m.

surviv|al [səˈvaivəl] Über-, Fortleben n; Überbleibsel n; **~e** [~aiv] überleben; noch leben; fortleben; am Leben bleiben; bestehen bleiben; **~or** [~və] Überlebende(r m) f.

suscept|ible □ [səˈseptəbl], **~ive** [~tiv] empfänglich (of, to für); empfindlich (gegen); be ~ of et. zulassen.

suspect 1. [səsˈpekt] (be)argwöhnen; in Verdacht haben, verdächtigen; vermuten, befürchten; 2. ['sʌspekt] Verdächtige(r m) f; 3. [~] = **~ed** [səsˈpektid] verdächtig.

suspend [səsˈpend] (auf)hängen; aufschieben, in der Schwebe lassen; Zahlung einstellen; aussetzen; suspendieren, sperren; **~ed** schwebend; **~er** [~də] Strumpf-, Sockenhalter m; **~s** pl. Am. Hosenträger m/pl.

suspens|e [səsˈpens] Ungewißheit f; Unentschiedenheit f; Spannung f; **~ion** [~nʃən] Aufhängung f; Aufschub m; Einstellung f; Suspendierung f, Amtsenthebung f; Sperre f; **~ion bridge** Hängebrücke f; **~ive** □ [~nsiv] aufschiebend.

suspici|on [səsˈpiʃən] Verdacht m; Argwohn m; fig. Spur f; **~ous** □ [~ʃəs] argwöhnisch; verdächtig.

sustain [səsˈtein] stützen; fig. aufrechterhalten; aushalten; erleiden; ⅟ anerkennen; **~ed** anhaltend; ununterbrochen.

sustenance ['sʌstinəns] (Lebens-) Unterhalt m; Nahrung f.

svelte [svelt] schlank (Frau).

swab [swɔb] 1. Aufwischmop m; ✶ Tupfer m; ✶ Abstrich m; 2. aufwischen.

swaddl|e ['swɔdl] Baby wickeln; **~ing-clothes** mst fig. [~liŋkloudz] pl. Windeln f/pl.

swagger ['swægə] 1. stolzieren; prahlen, renommieren; 2. F elegant.

swale Am. [sweil] Mulde f, Niederung f.

swallow ['swɔlou] 1. orn. Schwalbe f; Schlund m; Schluck m; 2. (hinunter-, ver)schlucken; fig. Ansicht etc. begierig aufnehmen.

swam [swæm] pret. von swim 1.

swamp [swɔmp] 1. Sumpf m; 2. überschwemmen (a. fig.); versenken; **~y** ['swɔmpi] sumpfig.

swan [swɔn] Schwan m.

swank sl. [swæŋk] 1. Angabe f,

Protzerei f; 2. angeben, protzen; **~y** ['swæŋki] protzig, angeberisch.

swap F [swɔp] 1. Tausch m; 2. (ver-, aus)tauschen.

sward [swɔːd] Rasen m.

swarm [swɔːm] 1. Schwarm m; Haufe(n) m, Gewimmel n; 2. schwärmen; wimmeln (with von).

swarthy □ ['swɔːði] dunkelfarbig.

swash [swɔʃ] plan(t)schen.

swat [swɔt] klatschen.

swath ✶ [swɔːθ] Schwade(n m) f.

swathe [sweið] (ein)wickeln.

sway [swei] 1. Schaukeln n; Einfluß m; Herrschaft f; 2. schaukeln; beeinflussen; beherrschen.

swear [swɛə] [irr.] (be)schwören; fluchen; ~ s.o. in j-n vereidigen.

sweat [swet] 1. Schweiß m; by the ~ of one's brow im Schweiße seines Angesichts; all of a ~ F in Schweiß gebadet (a. fig.); 2. [irr.] v/i. schwitzen; v/t. (aus)schwitzen; in Schweiß bringen; Arbeiter ausbeuten; **~er** ['swetə] Sweater m, Pullover m; Trainingsjacke f; fig. Ausbeuter m; **~y** [~ti] schweißig; verschwitzt.

Swede [swiːd] Schwed|e m, -in f.

Swedish ['swiːdiʃ] 1. schwedisch; 2. Schwedisch n.

sweep [swiːp] 1. [irr.] fegen (a.fig.), kehren; fig. streifen; bestreichen (a. ✕); 2. (majestätisch) (dahin)rauschen; 2. (fig. Dahin)Fegen n; Kehren n; Schwung m; Biegung f; Spielraum m, Bereich m; Schornsteinfeger m; make a clean ~ reinen Tisch machen (of mit); **~er** ['swiːpə] (Straßen)Feger m; Kehrmaschine f; **~ing** □ [~piŋ] weitgehend; schwungvoll; **~ings** pl. Kehricht m, Müll m.

sweet [swiːt] 1. □ süß; lieblich; freundlich; frisch; duftend; have a ~ tooth ein Leckermaul sein; 2. Liebling m; Süßigkeit f, Bonbon m, n; Nachtisch m; **~en** ['swiːtn] (ver)süßen; **~heart** Liebling m, Liebste(r m) f; **~ish** [~tiʃ] süßlich; **~meat** Bonbon m, n; kandierte Frucht; **~ness** [~tnis] Süßigkeit f; Lieblichkeit f; ~ **pea** ♀ Gartenwicke f.

swell [swel] 1. [irr.] v/i. (an)schwellen; sich blähen; sich (aus)bauchen; v/t. (an)schwellen lassen; aufblähen; 2. F fein; sl. prima; 3. Anschwellen n; Schwellung f; ♫ Dünung f; F feiner Herr; **~ing** ['sweliŋ] Geschwulst f.

swelter ['sweltə] vor Hitze umkommen.

swept [swept] pret. u. p.p. von sweep 1.

swerve [swəːv] 1. (plötzlich) abbiegen; 2. (plötzliche) Wendung f.

swift □ [swift] schnell, eilig, flink; **~ness** ['swiftnis] Schnelligkeit f.

swill [swil] 1. Spülicht n; Schweine-trank m; 2. spülen; saufen.

swim [swim] 1. [irr.] (durch-)schwimmen; schweben; my head ~s mir schwindelt; 2. Schwimmen n; be in the ~ auf dem laufenden sein; ~ming ['swimiŋ] 1. Schwimmen n; 2. Schwimm...; ~bath (bsd. Hallen)Schwimmbad n; ~pool Schwimmbecken n; ~suit Badeanzug m.

swindle ['swindl] 1. (be)schwindeln; 2. Schwindel m.

swine [swain] Schwein(e pl.) n.

swing [swiŋ] 1. [irr.] schwingen, schwanken; F baumeln; (sich) schaukeln; schwenken; sich drehen; 2. Schwingen n; Schwung m; Schaukel f; Spielraum m; in full ~ in vollem Gange; ~door ['swindɔ:] Drehtür f.

swinish ['swainiʃ] schweinisch.

swipe [swaip] 1. aus vollem Arm schlagen; 2. starker Schlag.

swirl [swə:l] 1. (herum)wirbeln, strudeln; 2. Wirbel m, Strudel m.

Swiss [swis] 1. schweizerisch, Schweizer...; 2. Schweizer(in); the ~ pl. die Schweizer m/pl.

switch [switʃ] 1. Gerte f; ⚡ Weiche f; ⚡ Schalter m; falscher Zopf; 2. peitschen; ⚡ rangieren; ⚡ (um-)schalten; fig. wechseln, überleiten; ~ on (off) ⚡ ein- (aus)schalten; ~board ⚡ ['switʃbɔ:d] Schaltbrett n, -tafel f.

swivel ⊕ ['swivl] Drehring m; attr. Dreh...

swollen ['swoulən] p.p. von swell 1.

swoon [swu:n] 1. Ohnmacht f; 2. in Ohnmacht fallen.

swoop [swu:p] 1. ~ down on od. upon (herab)stoßen auf (acc.) (Raubvogel); überfallen; 2. Stoß m.

swop F [swɔp] s. swap.

sword [sɔ:d] Schwert n, Degen m.

swordsman ['sɔ:dzmən] Fechter m.

swore [swɔ:] pret. von swear.

sworn [swɔ:n] p.p. von swear.

swum [swʌm] p.p. von swim 1.

swung [swʌŋ] pret. u. p.p. von swing 1.

sycamore ♣ ['sikəmɔ:] Bergahorn m; Am. Platane f.

sycophant ['sikəfənt] Kriecher m.

syllable ['siləbl] Silbe f.

syllabus ['siləbəs] (bsd. Vorlesungs-)Verzeichnis n; (bsd. Lehr)Plan m.

sylvan ['silvən] waldig, Wald...

symbol ['simbəl] Symbol n, Sinnbild n; ~ic(al □ [sim'bɔlik(əl)] sinnbildlich; ~ism ['simbəlizəm] Symbolik f.

symmetr|ical □ [si'metrikəl] ebenmäßig; ~y ['simitri] Ebenmaß n.

sympath|etic [simpə'θetik] (~ally) mitfühlend; sympathisch; ~ strike Sympathiestreik m; ~ize ['simpəθaiz] sympathisieren, mitfühlen; ~y [~θi] Sympathie f, Mitgefühl n.

symphony ♪ ['simfəni] Symphonie f.

symptom ['simptəm] Symptom n.

synchron|ize ['siŋkrənaiz] v/t. gleichzeitig sein; v/t. als gleichzeitig zs.-stellen; Uhren auf-ea. abstimmen; Tonfilm: synchronisieren; ~ous □ [~nəs] gleichzeitig.

syndicate 1. ['sindikit] Syndikat n; 2. [~keit] zu e-m Syndikat verbinden.

synonym ['sinənim] Synonym n; ~ous □ [si'nɔniməs] sinnverwandt.

synop|sis [si'nɔpsis], pl. ~ses [~si:z] zs.-fassende Übersicht.

syntax gr. ['sintæks] Syntax f.

synthe|sis [sin'θisis], pl. ~ses [~si:z] Synthese f, Verbindung f; ~tic(al □) [sin'θetik(əl)] synthetisch.

syringe ['sirindʒ] 1. Spritze f; 2. (be-, ein-, aus)spritzen.

syrup ['sirəp] Sirup m.

system ['sistim] System n; Organismus m, Körper m; Plan m, Ordnung f; ~atic [sisti'mætik] (~ally) systematisch.

T

tab [tæb] Streifen m; Schildchen n; Anhänger m; Schlaufe f, Aufhänger m; F Rechnung f, Konto n.

table ['teibl] 1. Tisch m, Tafel f; Tisch-, Tafelrunde f; Tabelle f, Verzeichnis n; Bibel: Gesetzestafel f; s. ~land; at ~ bei Tisch; turn the ~s den Spieß umdrehen (on gegen); 2. auf den Tisch legen; tabellarisch anordnen.

tableau ['tæblou], pl. ~x [~ouz] lebendes Bild.

table|-cloth ['teiblklɔθ] Tischtuch n; ~land Tafelland n, Plateau n,

Hochebene f; ~linen Tischwäsche f; ~spoon Eßlöffel m.

tablet ['tæblit] Täfelchen n; (Gedenk)Tafel f; (Schreib- etc.)Block m; Stück n Seife; Tablette f.

table-top ['teibltɔp] Tischplatte f.

taboo [tə'bu:] 1. tabu, unantastbar; verboten; 2. Tabu n; Verbot n; 3. verbieten.

tabulate ['tæbjuleit] tabellarisch ordnen.

tacit □ ['tæsit] stillschweigend; ~urn □ [~tə:n] schweigsam.

tack [tæk] 1. Stift m, Zwecke f;

Heftstich *m*; ⚓ Halse *f*; ⚓ Gang *m* beim Lavieren; *fig.* Weg *m*; **2.** *v/t.* (an)heften; *fig.* (an)hängen; *v/i.* ⚓ wenden; *fig.* lavieren.

tackle ['tækl] **1.** Gerät *n*; ⚓ Takel-, Tauwerk *n*; ⊕ Flaschenzug *m*; **2.** (an)packen; in Angriff nehmen; fertig werden mit; *j-n* angehen (for um).

tacky ['tæki] klebrig; *Am.* F schäbig.

tact [tækt] Takt *m*, Feingefühl *n*; **ful** ☐ ['tæktful] taktvoll.

tactics ['tæktiks] Taktik *f*.

tactless ☐ ['tæktlis] taktlos.

tadpole *zo.* ['tædpoul] Kaulquappe*f*.

taffeta ['tæfitə] Taft *m*.

taffy *Am.* ['tæfi] = *toffee*; F Schmus *m*, Schmeichelei *f*.

tag [tæg] **1.** (Schnürsenkel)Stift *m*; Schildchen *n*, Etikett *n*; Redensart *f*, Zitat *n*; Zusatz *m*; loses Ende; Fangen *n* (*Kinderspiel*); **2.** etikettieren, auszeichnen; anhängen (to, onto an *acc.*); ~ *after* herlaufen hinter (*dat.*); ~ *together* an-ea.-reihen.

tail [teil] **1.** Schwanz *m*; Schweif *m*; hinteres Ende, Schluß *m*; ~*s pl.* Rückseite *f* e-r Münze; F Frack *m*; *turn* ~ davonlaufen; ~*s up* in Hochstimmung; **2.** ~ *after s.o.* j-m nachlaufen; ~ *s.o. Am.* j-n beschatten; ~ *away*, ~ *off* abflauen, sich verlieren; zögernd enden; ~**coat** ['teil'kout] Frack *m*; ~**light** *mot. etc.* ['teillait] Rück-, Schlußlicht *n*.

tailor ['teilə] **1.** Schneider *m*; **2.** schneidern; ~**made** Schneider..., Maß...

taint [teint] **1.** Flecken *m*, Makel *m*; 🎗 Ansteckung *f*; *fig.* krankhafter Zug; Verderbnis *f*; **2.** beflecken; verderben; 🎗 anstecken.

take [teik] **1.** [*irr.*] *v/t.* nehmen; an-, ab-, auf-, ein-, fest-, hin-, wegnehmen; (weg)bringen; *Speise* (zu sich) nehmen; *Maßnahme, Gelegenheit* ergreifen; *Eid, Gelübde, Examen* ablegen; *phot.* aufnehmen; *et. gut etc.* aufnehmen; *Beleidigung* hinnehmen; fassen, ergreifen, fangen; *fig.* fesseln; sich *e-e Krankheit* holen; erfordern; brauchen; *Zeit* dauern; auffassen; halten, ansehen (for für); *I* ~ *it that* ich nehme an, daß; ~ *breath* verschnaufen; ~ *comfort* sich trösten; ~ *compassion* on Mitleid empfinden mit; sich erbarmen (*gen.*); ~ *counsel* beraten; ~ *a drive* e-e Fahrt machen; ~ *fire* Feuer fangen; ~ *in hand* unternehmen; ~ *hold of* ergreifen; ~ *pity on* Mitleid haben mit; ~ *place* stattfinden; spielen (*Handlung*); ~ *a seat* Platz nehmen; ~ *a walk* e-n Spaziergang machen; ~ *my word for it* verlaß dich drauf; ~ *about* herumführen; ~ *along* mitnehmen; ~ *down* herunternehmen; notieren; ~ *for* halten für; ~ *from j-m* wegnehmen;

abziehen von; ~ *in* enger machen; *Zeitung* halten; aufnehmen (*als Gast etc.*); einschließen; verstehen; erfassen; F *j-n* reinlegen; ~ *off* ab-, wegnehmen; *Kleid* ausziehen, *Hut* abnehmen; ~ *on* an-, übernehmen; *Arbeiter etc.* einstellen; *Fahrgäste* zusteigen lassen; ~ *out* heraus-, entnehmen; *Fleck* entfernen; *j-n* ausführen; *Versicherung* abschließen; ~ *to pieces* auseinandernehmen; ~ *up* aufnehmen; sich *e-r S.* annehmen; *Raum, Zeit* in Anspruch nehmen; *v/i.* wirken, ein-, anschlagen; gefallen, ziehen; ~ *after j-m* nachschlagen; ~ *off* abspringen; 🎗 aufsteigen, starten; ~ *on F* Anklang finden; ~ *over* die Amtsgewalt übernehmen; ~ *to* liebgewinnen; *fig.* sich verlegen auf (*acc.*); Zuflucht nehmen zu; sich ergeben (*dat.*); ~ *up F* sich bessern (*Wetter*); ~ *up with* sich anfreunden mit; *that won't* ~ *with me* das verfängt bei mir nicht; **2.** Fang *m*; *Geld*-Einnahme *f*; *Film:* Szene(naufnahme) *f*; ~**in** F ['teik'in] Reinfall *m*; ~**n** ['teikən] *p.p. von take 1*; be ~ besetzt sein; be ~ *with* entzückt sein von; be ~ *ill* krank werden; ~**off** ['teikɔf] Karikatur *f*; Absprung *m*; 🎗 Start *m*.

taking ['teikiŋ] **1.** ☐ F anziehend, fesselnd, einnehmend; ansteckend; **2.** (An-, Ab-, Auf-, Ein-, Ent-, Hin-, Weg- *etc.*)Nehmen *n*; Inbesitznahme *f*; 🎗 Einnahme *f*; F Aufregung *f*; ~*s pl.* ♥ Einnahmen *f/pl.*

tale [teil] Erzählung *f*, Geschichte *f*; Märchen *n*, Sage *f*; *it tells its own* ~ es spricht für sich selbst; ~**bearer** ['teilbɛərə] Zuträger(in).

talent ['tælənt] Talent *n*, Begabung *f*, Anlage *f*; ~**ed** [‿tid] talentvoll, begabt.

talk [tɔ:k] **1.** Gespräch *n*; Unterredung *f*; Plauderei *f*; Vortrag *m*; Geschwätz *n*; **2.** sprechen, reden (*von et.*); plaudern; ~**ative** ☐ ['tɔ:kətiv] gesprächig, geschwätzig; ~**er** ['tɔ:kə] Schwätzer(in); Sprechende(r *m*) *f*.

tall [tɔ:l] groß, lang, hoch; F übertrieben, unglaublich; *that's a* ~ *order* F das ist ein bißchen viel verlangt.

tallow ['tælou] ausgelassener Talg.

tally ['tæli] **1.** Kerbholz *n*; Gegenstück *n* (of zu); Kennzeichen *n*; **2.** übereinstimmen.

talon *orn.* ['tælən] Kralle *f*, Klaue *f*.

tame [teim] **1.** ☐ zahm; folgsam; harmlos; lahm, fad(e); **2.** (be)zähmen, bändigen.

Tammany *Am.* ['tæməni] New Yorker Demokraten-Vereinigung.

tamper ['tæmpə]: ~ *with* sich (unbefugt) zu schaffen machen mit;

j-n zu bestechen suchen; *Urkunde* fälschen.

tan [tæn] **1.** Lohe *f;* Lohfarbe *f;* (Sonnen)Bräune *f;* **2.** lohfarben; **3.** gerben; bräunen.

tang [tæŋ] Beigeschmack *m; scharfer* Klang; ♣ Seetang *m.*

tangent ['tændʒənt] ⅄ Tangente *f; fly od.* go off at a ~ vom Gegenstand abspringen.

tangerine ♣ [tændʒə'ri:n] Mandarine *f.*

tangible ☐ ['tændʒəbl] fühlbar, greifbar *(a. fig.);* klar.

tangle ['tæŋgl] **1.** Gewirr *n;* Verwicklung *f;* **2.** (sich) verwirren, verwickeln.

tank [tæŋk] **1.** Zisterne *f,* Wasserbehälter *m;* ⊕, ⚔ Tank *m;* **2.** tanken. [(Bier)Krug *m.*⟩

tankard ['tæŋkəd] Kanne *f, bsd.*⟩

tanner ['tænə] Gerber *m;* ~y [~əri] Gerberei *f.*

tantalize ['tæntəlaiz] quälen.

tantamount ['tæntəmaunt] gleichbedeutend (mit).

tantrum F ['tæntrəm] Koller *m.*

tap [tæp] **1.** leichtes Klopfen; (Wasser-, Gas-, Zapf)Hahn *m;* Zapfen *m;* Schankstube *f;* F Sorte *f;* ~s *pl. Am.* ⚔ Zapfenstreich *m;* **2.** pochen, klopfen, tippen (auf, **an,** gegen *acc.);* an-, abzapfen; **~dance** ['tæpda:ns] Stepptanz *m.*

tape [teip] schmales Band; *Sport:* Zielband *n; tel.* Papierstreifen *m;* Tonband *n; red* ~ Bürokratismus *m;* **~-measure** ['teipmeʒə] Bandmaß *n.*

taper ['teipə] **1.** dünne Wachskerze; **2.** *adj.* spitz (zulaufend); schlank; **3.** *v/i.* spitz zulaufen; *v/t.* zuspitzen.

tape| recorder ['teiprikɔ:də] Tonbandgerät *n;* ~ **recording** Tonbandaufnahme *f.*

tapestry ['tæpistri] Gobelin *m.*

tapeworm ['teipwə:m] Bandwurm*m.*

tap-room ['tæprum] Schankstube*f.*

tar [ta:] **1.** Teer *m;* **2.** teeren.

tardy ☐ ['ta:di] langsam; spät.

tare ✝ [tɛə] Tara *f.*

target ['ta:git] (Schieß)Scheibe *f; fig.* Ziel(scheibe *f) n;* Ziel(leistung *f) n;* Soll *n;* ~ **practice** Scheibenschießen *n.*

tariff ['tærif] *(bsd.* Zoll)Tarif *m.*

tarnish ['ta:niʃ] **1.** *v/t.* ⊕ trüb *od.* blind machen; *fig.* trüben; *v/i.* trüb werden, anlaufen; **2.** Trübung *f;* Belag *m.*

tarry¹ *lit.* ['tæri] säumen, zögern; verweilen.

tarry² ['ta:ri] teerig.

tart [ta:t] **1.** ☐ sauer, herb; *fig.* scharf, schroff; **2.** (Obst)Torte *f; sl.* Dirne *f.*

tartan ['ta:tən] Tartan *m;* Schottentuch *n;* Schottenmuster *n.*

task [ta:sk] **1.** Aufgabe *f;* Arbeit *f; take to* ~ zur Rede stellen; **2.** beschäftigen; in Anspruch nehmen.

tassel ['tæsəl] Troddel *f,* Quaste *f.*

taste [teist] **1.** Geschmack *m;* (Kost)Probe *f;* Lust *f (for* zu); **2.** kosten, schmecken; versuchen; genießen; **~ful** ☐ ['teistful] geschmackvoll; **~less** ☐ [~tlis] geschmacklos.

tasty ☐ F ['teisti] schmackhaft.

ta-ta ['tæ'ta:] auf Wiedersehen!

tatter ['tætə] **1.** zerfetzen; **2.** ~s *pl.* Fetzen *m/pl.*

tattle ['tætl] **1.** schwatzen; tratschen; **2.** Geschwätz *n;* Tratsch *m.*

tattoo [tə'tu:] **1.** ⚔ Zapfenstreich *m;* Tätowierung *f;* **2.** *fig.* trommeln; tätowieren.

taught [tɔ:t] *pret. u. p.p. von* teach.

taunt [tɔ:nt] **1.** Stichelei *f,* Spott *m;* **2.** verhöhnen, verspotten.

taut ⚓ [tɔ:t] steif, straff; schmuck.

tavern ['tævən] Schenke *f.*

tawdry ☐ ['tɔ:dri] billig; kitschig.

tawny ['tɔ:ni] lohfarben.

tax [tæks] **1.** Steuer *f,* Abgabe *f; fig.* Inanspruchnahme *f (on, upon gen.);* **2.** besteuern; *fig.* stark in Anspruch nehmen; *tt Kosten* schätzen; auf e-e harte Probe stellen; *j-n* zur Rede stellen; ~ *s.o.* with *s.th.* j-n e-r S. beschuldigen; **~ation** [tæk'seiʃən] Besteuerung *f;* Steuer(n *pl.) f; bsd. tt* Schätzung *f.*

taxi F ['tæksi] **1.** = ~*cab;* **2.** mit e-m Taxi fahren; ⚔ rollen; **~cab** Taxi *n,* (Auto)Droschke *f.*

taxpayer ['tækspeiə] Steuerzahler *m.*

tea [ti:] Tee *m; high* ~, *meat* ~ frühes Abendbrot mit Tee.

teach [ti:tʃ] *[irr.]* lehren, unterrichten, *j-m et.* beibringen; **~able** ☐ ['ti:tʃəbl] gelehrig; lehrbar; **~er** [~ʃə] Lehrer(in); **~-in** [~ʃ'in] (politische) Diskussion *als Großveranstaltung.*

tea|-cosy ['ti:kouzi] Teewärmer *m;* **~cup** Teetasse *f; storm in a* ~ *fig.* Sturm *m* im Wasserglas; **~-kettle** Wasserkessel *m.*

team [ti:m] Team *n,* Arbeitsgruppe *f;* Gespann *n; bsd. Sport:* Mannschaft *f;* **~ster** ['ti:mstə] Gespannführer *m; Am.* LKW-Fahrer *m;* **~-work** Zusammenarbeit *f,* Teamwork *n;* Zusammenspiel *n.*

teapot ['ti:pot] Teekanne *f.*

tear¹ [tɛə] **1.** *[irr.]* zerren, (zer)reißen; rasen, stürmen; **2.** Riß *m.*

tear² [tiə] Träne *f.*

tearful ☐ ['tiəful] tränenreich.

tea-room ['ti:rum] Tearoom *m.* Teestube *f,* Café *n.*

tease [ti:z] **1.** necken, hänseln; quälen; **2.** Necker *m;* Quälgeist *m.*

teat [ti:t] Zitze *f;* Brustwarze *f;* (Gummi)Sauger *m.*

technic|al □ ['teknikəl] technisch; gewerblich, Gewerbe...; fachlich, Fach...; **~ality** [tekni'kæliti] technische Eigentümlichkeit *od.* Einzelheit; Fachausdruck *m*; **~ian** [tek-'niʃən] Techniker(in).

technique [tek'niːk] Technik *f*, Verfahren *n*.

technology [tek'nɔlədʒi] Gewerbekunde *f*; *school of* ~ Technische Hochschule.

teddy boy F ['tedibɔi] Halbstarke(r) *m*.

tedious □ ['tiːdjəs] langweilig, ermüdend; weitschweifig.

tee [tiː] *Sport:* Mal *n*, Ziel *n*; *Golf:* Abschlagmal *n*.

teem [tiːm] wimmeln, strotzen (*with* von).

teens [tiːnz] *pl.* Lebensjahre *n/pl.* von 13—19.

teeny F ['tiːni] winzig.

teeth [tiːθ] *pl. von* tooth; **~e** [tiːð] zahnen.

teetotal(l)er [tiː'toutlə] Abstinenzler(in).

telecast ['telikɑːst] 1. Fernsehsendung *f*; 2. [*irr.* (*cast*)] im Fernsehen übertragen.

telecourse *Am.* F ['telikɔːs] Fernsehlehrgang *m*.

telegram ['teligræm] Telegramm *n*.

telegraph ['teligrɑːf] 1. Telegraph *m*; 2. Telegraphen...; 3. telegraphieren; **~ic** [teli'græfik] (**~ally**) telegraphisch; telegrammmäßig (*Stil*); **~y** [ti'legrəfi] Telegraphie *f*.

telephon|e ['telifoun] 1. Telephon *n*, Fernsprecher *m*; 2. telephonieren; anrufen; **~e booth** Telephonzelle *f*; **~ic** [teli'fɔnik] (**~ally**) telephonisch; **~y** [ti'lefəni] Fernsprechwesen *n*.

telephoto *phot.* ['teli'foutou] *a.* ~ lens Teleobjektiv *n*.

teleprinter ['teliprintə] Fernschreiber *m*.

telescope ['teliskoup] 1. *opt.* Fernrohr *n*; 2. (sich) ineinanderschieben.

teletype ['telitaip] Fernschreiber *m*.

televis|e ['telivaiz] im Fernsehen übertragen; **~ion** [~viʒən] Fernsehen *n*; *watch* ~ fernsehen; **~ion set**, **~or** [~vaizə] Fernsehapparat *m*.

tell [tel] [*irr.*] *v/t.* zählen; sagen, erzählen; erkennen; ~ *s.o. to do s.th.* j-m sagen, er solle et. tun; ~ *off* abzählen; auswählen; F abkanzeln; *v/i.* erzählen (*of, about* von); (aus)plaudern; sich auswirken; sitzen (*Hieb etc.*); **~er** ['telə] (Er)Zähler *m*; **~ing** ['teliŋ] wirkungsvoll, **~tale** ['telteil] 1. Klatschbase *f*; ⊕ Anzeiger *m*; 2. *fig.* verräterisch.

temerity [ti'meriti] Unbesonnenheit *f*, Verwegenheit *f*.

temper ['tempə] 1. mäßigen, mildern; *Kalk etc.* anrühren; *Stahl* anlassen; 2. ⊕ Härte(grad *m*) *f*;

(Gemüts)Ruhe *f*, Gleichmut *m*; Temperament *n*, Wesen *n*; Stimmung *f*; Wut *f*; *lose one's* ~ in Wut geraten; **~ament** [~rəmənt] Temperament *n*; **~amental** □ [temperə'mentl] anlagebedingt; launisch; **~ance** ['tempərəns] Mäßigkeit *f*; Enthaltsamkeit *f*; **~ate** □ [~rit] gemäßigt; zurückhaltend; maßvoll; mäßig; **~ature** [~pritʃə] Temperatur *f*.

tempest ['tempist] Sturm *m*; Gewitter *n*; **~uous** □ [tem'pestjəs] stürmisch; ungestüm.

temple ['templ] Tempel *m*; *anat.* Schläfe *f*.

tempor|al □ ['tempərəl] zeitlich; weltlich; **~ary** □ [~əri] zeitweilig; vorläufig; vorübergehend; Not..., (Aus)Hilfs...; Behelfs...; **~ize** [~raiz] Zeit zu gewinnen suchen.

tempt [tempt] *j-n* versuchen; verleiten; verlocken; **~ation** [temp'teiʃən] Versuchung *f*; Reiz *m*; **~ing** □ ['temptiŋ] verführerisch.

ten [ten] 1. zehn; 2. Zehn *f*.

tenable ['tenəbl] haltbar (*Theorie etc.*); verliehen (*Amt*).

tenaci|ous □ [ti'neiʃəs] zäh; festhaltend (*of an dat.*); gut (*Gedächtnis*); **~ty** [ti'næsiti] Zähigkeit *f*; Festhalten *n*; Verläßlichkeit *f des Gedächtnisses*.

tenant ['tenənt] Pächter *m*; Mieter *m*.

tend [tend] *v/i.* (*to*) gerichtet sein (auf *acc.*); hinstreben (zu); abzielen (auf *acc.*); neigen (zu); *v/t.* pflegen; hüten; ⊕ bedienen; **~ance** ['tendəns] Pflege *f*; Bedienung *f*; **~ency** [~si] Richtung *f*; Neigung *f*; Zweck *m*.

tender ['tendə] 1. □ zart; weich; empfindlich; heikel (*Thema*); zärtlich; 2. Angebot *n*; Kostenanschlag *m*; ⛟, ⊕ Tender *m*; *legal* ~ gesetzliches Zahlungsmittel; 3. anbieten; *Entlassung* einreichen; **~foot** *Am.* F Neuling *m*, Anfänger *m*; **~loin** *bsd. Am.* Filet *n*; *Am.* berüchtigtes Viertel; **~ness** [~nis] Zartheit *f*; Zärtlichkeit *f*.

tendon *anat.* ['tendən] Sehne *f*.

tendril ♣ ['tendril] Ranke *f*.

tenement ['tenimənt] Wohnhaus *n*; (*bsd.* Miet)Wohnung *f*; ~ *house* Mietshaus *n*.

tennis ['tenis] Tennis(spiel) *n*; **~ court** Tennisplatz *m*.

tenor ['tenə] Fortgang *m*, Verlauf *m*; Inhalt *m*; ♪ Tenor *m*.

tens|e [tens] 1. *gr.* Zeit(form) *f*, Tempus *n*; 2. □ gespannt (*a. fig.*); straff; **~ion** [~ʃən] Spannung *f*.

tent [tent] 1. Zelt *n*; 2. zelten.

tentacle *zo.* ['tentəkl] Fühler *m*; Fangarm *m e-s* Polypen.

tentative □ ['tentətiv] versuchend; Versuchs...; **~ly** versuchsweise.

tenth [tenθ] **1.** zehnte(r, -s); **2.** Zehntel *n*; ~ly ['tenθli] zehntens.

tenuous □ ['tenjuəs] dünn; zart, fein; dürftig.

tenure ['tenjuə] Besitz(art *f*, -dauer *f*) *m*.

tepid □ ['tepid] lau(warm).

term [tə:m] **1.** (bestimmte) Zeit, Frist *f*, Termin *m*; Zahltag *m*; Amtszeit *f*; ⚜ Sitzungsperiode *f*; Semester *n*, Quartal *n*, Trimester *n*, Tertial *n*; ⚕, *phls.* Glied *n*; (Fach-)Ausdruck *m*, Wort *n*, Bezeichnung *f*; Begriff *m*; ~s *pl.* Bedingungen *f/pl.*; Beziehungen *f/pl.*; be on good (bad) ~s with gut (schlecht) stehen mit; come to ~s, make ~s sich einigen; **2.** (be)nennen; bezeichnen (als).

termagant ['tə:məgənt] **1.** □ zanksüchtig; **2.** Zankteufel *m* (*Weib*).

termina|l ['tə:minl] **1.** □ End...; letzt; ~ly terminweise; **2.** Endstück *n*; ⚡ Pol *m*; *Am.* 🚂 Endstation *f*; ~te [~neit] begrenzen; (be)endigen; ~tion [tə:mi'neiʃən] Beendigung *f*; Ende *n*; *gr.* Endung *f*.

terminus ['tə:minəs] Endstation *f*.

terrace ['terəs] Terrasse *f*; Häuserreihe *f*; ~-house Reihenhaus *n*; ~d [~st] terrassenförmig.

terrestrial □ [ti'restriəl] irdisch; Erd...; *bsd. zo.*, ⚘ Land...

terrible □ ['terəbl] schrecklich.

terri|fic [tə'rifik] (~ally) fürchterlich, schrecklich; F ungeheuer, großartig; ~fy ['terifai] *v/t.* erschrecken.

territor|ial [teri'tɔ:riəl] **1.** □ territorial; Land...; Bezirks...; ♀ *Army*, ♀ *Force* Territorialarmee *f*; **2.** ✕ Angehörige(r) *m* der Territorialarmee; ~y ['teritori] Territorium *n*, (Hoheits-, Staats)Gebiet *n*.

terror ['terə] Schrecken *m*, Entsetzen *n*; ~ize [~əraiz] terrorisieren.

terse □ [tə:s] knapp; kurz u. bündig.

test [test] **1.** Probe *f*; Untersuchung *f*; (Eignungs)Prüfung *f*; Test *m*; 🜍 Reagens *n*; **2.** probieren, prüfen, testen.

testament ['testəmənt] Testament *n*.

testicle *anat.* ['testikl] Hode(n *m*) [*m*, *f*.]

testify ['testifai] (be)zeugen; (als Zeuge) aussagen (*on über acc.*).

testimon|ial [testi'mounjəl] (Führungs)Zeugnis *n*; Zeichen *n* der Anerkennung; ~y ['testiməni] Zeugnis *n*; Beweis *m*.

test-tube 🜍 ['testtju:b] Reagenzglas *n*.

testy □ ['testi] reizbar, kribbelig.

tether ['teðə] **1.** Halterstrick *m*; *fig.* Spielraum *m*; *at the end of one's fig.* am Ende s-r Kraft; **2.** anbinden.

text [tekst] Text *m*; Bibelstelle *f*;

~book ['tekstbuk] Leitfaden *m*, Lehrbuch *n*.

textile ['tekstail] **1.** Textil..., Web...; **2.** ~s *pl.* Webwaren *f/pl.*, Textilien *pl.*

texture ['tekstʃə] Gewebe *n*; Gefüge *n*.

than [ðæn, ðən] als.

thank [θæŋk] **1.** danken (*dat.*); ~ you, bei Ablehnung no, ~ you danke; **2.** ~s *pl.* Dank *m*; ~s! vielen Dank!; danke (schön)!; ~s to dank (*dat.*); ~ful □ ['θæŋkful] dankbar; ~less □ [~klis] undankbar; ~sgiving [~ksgivin] Danksagung *f*; Dankfest *n*; ♀ (*Day*) *bsd. Am.* (Ernte)Dankfest *n*.

that [ðæt, ðət] **1.** *pl.* those [ðouz] *pron.* jene(r, -s); der, die, das; der-, die-, das(jenige); welche(r, -s) **2.** *cj.* daß; damit.

thatch [θætʃ] **1.** Dachstroh *n*; Strohdach *n*; **2.** mit Stroh decken.

thaw [θɔ:] **1.** Tauwetter *n*; (Auf-) Tauen *n*; **2.** (auf)tauen.

the [ði: *vor Vokalen* ði; *vor Konsonanten* ðə] **1.** *art.* der, die, das; **2.** *adv.* desto, um so; ~ ... ~ ... je ... desto ...

theat|re, *Am.* ~er ['θiətə] Theater *n*; *fig.* (Kriegs)Schauplatz *m*; ~ric(al □) [θi'ætrik(əl)] Theater...; theatralisch.

thee *Bibel, poet.* [ði:] dich; dir.

theft [θeft] Diebstahl *m*.

their [ðɛə] ihr(e); ~s [~z] der (die, das) ihrige *od.* ihre.

them [ðem, ðəm] sie (*acc. pl.*); ihnen.

theme [θi:m] Thema *n*; Aufgabe *f*.

themselves [ðem'selvz] sie (*acc. pl.*) selbst; sich selbst.

then [ðen] **1.** *adv.* dann; damals; da; by ~ bis dahin; inzwischen; every now and ~ alle Augenblicke; there and ~ sogleich; now ~ nun denn; **2.** *cj.* denn, also, folglich; **3.** *adj.* damalig.

thence *lit.* [ðens] daher; von da.

theolog|ian [θiə'loudʒjən] Theologe *m*; ~y [θi'ɔlədʒi] Theologie *f*.

theor|etic(al □) [θiə'retik(əl)] theoretisch; ~ist ['θiərist] Theoretiker *m*; ~y [~ri] Theorie *f*.

therap|eutic [θerə'pju:tik] **1.** (~ally) therapeutisch; **2.** ~s *mst. sg.* Therapeutik *f*; ~y ['θerəpi] Therapie *f*, Heilbehandlung *f*.

there [ðɛə] da, dort; darin; dorthin; na!; ~ is, ~ are es gibt, es ist, es sind; ~about(s) ['ðɛərəbaut(s)] da herum; so ungefähr...; ~after [ðɛər'a:ftə] danach; ~by ['ðɛə'bai] dadurch, damit; ~fore ['ðɛəfɔ:] darum, deswegen; deshalb, daher; ~upon ['ðɛərə'pɔn] darauf(hin); ~with [ðɛə'wið] damit.

thermal ['θə:məl] **1.** □ Thermal...; *phys.* Wärme...; **2.** Aufwind *m*.

thermo|meter [θəˈmɔmitə] Thermometer n; 2s [ˈθəːmɔs] a. ~ flask, ~ bottle Thermosflasche f.

these [ðiːz] pl. von this.

thes|is [ˈθiːsis], pl. ~es [ˈθiːsiːz] These f; Dissertation f.

they [ðei] sie (pl.).

thick [θik] 1. □ allg. dick; dicht; trüb; legiert (Suppe); heiser; dumm; pred. F dick befreundet; ~ with dicht besetzt mit; 2. dickster Teil; fig. Brennpunkt m; in the ~ of mitten in (dat.); ~en [ˈθikən] (sich) verdicken; (sich) verstärken; legieren; (sich) verdichten; ~et [ˈθikit] Dickicht n; ~-headed dumm; ~ness [ˈθiknis] Dicke f, Stärke f; Dichte f; ~-set dicht (gepflanzt); untersetzt; ~-skinned fig. dickfellig.

thief [θiːf], pl. thieves [θiːvz] Dieb(in); thieve [θiːv] stehlen.

thigh [θai] (Ober)Schenkel m.

thimble [ˈθimbl] Fingerhut m.

thin [θin] 1. □ allg. dünn; leicht; mager; spärlich; dürftig; schwach; fadenscheinig (bsd. fig.); 2. verdünnen; (sich) lichten; abnehmen.

thine Bibel, poet. [ðain] dein; der (die, das) deinige od. deine.

thing [θiŋ] Ding n; Sache f; Geschöpf n; ~s pl. Sachen f/pl.; die Dinge n/pl. (Umstände); the ~ F das Richtige; richtig; die Hauptsache; ~s are going better es geht jetzt besser.

think [θiŋk] [irr.] v/i. denken (of an acc.); nachdenken; sich besinnen; meinen, glauben, gedenken (to inf. zu inf.); v/t. (sich) et. denken; halten für; ~ much etc. of viel etc. halten von; ~ s.th. over (sich) et. überlegen, über et. nachdenken.

third [θəːd] 1. □ dritte(r, -s); 2. Drittel n; ~ly [ˈθəːdli] drittens; ~-rate [ˈθəːdˈreit] drittklassig.

thirst [θəːst] 1. Durst m; 2. dürsten; ~y □ [ˈθəːsti] durstig; dürr (Boden).

thirt|een [ˈθəːˈtiːn] dreizehn; ~eenth [ˌθəːtiːnθ] dreizehnte(r, -s); ~ieth [ˈθəːtiiθ] dreißigste(r, -s); ~y [ˈθəːti] dreißig.

this [ðis], pl. these [ðiːz] diese(r, -s); ~ morning heute morgen.

thistle [ˈθisl] Distel f.

thong [θɔŋ] (Leder-, Peitschen-) Riemen m.

thorn ♀ [θɔːn] Dorn m; ~y [ˈθɔːni] dornig, stach(e)lig; beschwerlich.

thorough □ [ˈθʌrə] vollkommen; vollständig; vollendet; gründlich; ~ly a. durchaus; ~bred Vollblüter m; attr. Vollblut...; ~fare Durchgang m, Durchfahrt f; Hauptverkehrsstraße f; ~going gründlich; tatkräftig.

those [ðouz] pl. von that 1.

thou Bibel, poet. [ðau] du.

though [ðou] obgleich, obwohl, wenn auch; zwar; aber, doch; freilich; as ~ als ob.

thought [θɔːt] 1. pret. u. p.p. von think; 2. Gedanke m; (Nach)Denken n; on second ~s nach nochmaliger Überlegung; ~ful □ [ˈθɔːtful] gedankenvoll, nachdenklich; rücksichtsvoll (of gegen); ~less □ [ˈθɔːtlis] gedankenlos; unbesonnen; rücksichtslos (of gegen).

thousand [ˈθauzənd] 1. tausend; 2. Tausend n; ~th [ˌntθ] 1. tausendste(r, -s); 2. Tausendstel n.

thrash [θræʃ] (ver)dreschen, (ver-) prügeln; (hin und her) schlagen; s. thresh; ~ing [ˈθræʃiŋ] Dresche f, Tracht f Prügel; s. threshing.

thread [θred] 1. Faden m (a. fig.); Zwirn m, Garn n; ⊕ (Schrauben-) Gewinde n; 2. einfädeln; sich durchwinden (durch); durchziehen; ~bare [ˈθredbɛə] fadenscheinig.

threat [θret] Drohung f; ~en [ˈθretn] (be-, an)drohen; ~ening □ [ˌniŋ] bedrohlich.

three [θriː] 1. drei; 2. Drei f; ~fold [ˈθriːfould] dreifach; ~pence [ˈθrepəns] Dreipence(stück n) m/pl.; ~score [ˈθriːˈskɔː] sechzig.

thresh [θreʃ] ⚹ (aus)dreschen; s. thrash; ~ out fig. durchdreschen; ~er [ˈθreʃə] Drescher m; Dreschmaschine f; ~ing [ˈʃiŋ] Dreschen n; ~ing-machine Dreschmaschine f.

threshold [ˈθreʃhould] Schwelle f.

threw [θruː] pret. von throw 1.

thrice [θrais] dreimal.

thrift [θrift] Sparsamkeit f, Wirtschaftlichkeit f; ~less □ [ˈθriftlis] verschwenderisch; ~y □ [ˌti] sparsam; poet. gedeihend.

thrill [θril] 1. v/t. durchdringen, durchschauern; fig. packen, aufwühlen; aufregen; v/i. (er)beben; 2. Schauer m; Beben n; aufregendes Erlebnis; Sensation f; ~er F [ˈθrilə] Reißer m, Thriller m, Schauerroman m, Schauerstück n; ~ing [ˌʃiŋ] spannend.

thrive [θraiv] [irr.] gedeihen; fig. blühen; Glück haben; ~n [ˈθrivn] p.p. von thrive.

throat [θrout] Kehle f; Hals m; Gurgel f; Schlund m; clear one's ~ sich räuspern.

throb [θrɔb] 1. pochen, klopfen, schlagen; pulsieren; 2. Pochen n; Schlagen n; Pulsschlag m.

throes [θrouz] pl. Geburtswehen f/pl. [Thrombose f.]

thrombosis ⚹ [θrɔmˈbousis]

throne [θroun] Thron m.

throng [θrɔŋ] 1. Gedränge n; Menge f, Schar f; 2. sich drängen (in dat.); anfüllen mit.

throstle orn. [ˈθrɔsl] Drossel f.

throttle [ˈθrɔtl] 1. erdrosseln; ⊕ (ab)drosseln; 2. ⊕ Drosselklappe f.

through [θru:] 1. durch; 2. Durchgangs...; durchgehend; **~out** [θru(:)'aut] 1. *prp.* überall in (*dat.*); 2. *adv.* durch u. durch, ganz und gar, durchweg.

throve [θrouv] *pret. von* thrive.

throw [θrou] 1. [*irr.*] (ab)werfen, schleudern; *Am.* F *Wettkampf etc.* betrügerisch verlieren; würfeln; ⊕ schalten; **~ off** (die Jagd) beginnen; **~ over** aufgeben; **~ up** in die Höhe werfen; erbrechen; *fig.* hinwerfen; 2. Wurf *m*; **~n** [θroun] *p.p. von* throw 1.

thru *Am.* [θru:] = through.

thrum [θrʌm] klimpern (auf *dat.*).

thrush *orn.* [θrʌʃ] Drossel *f*.

thrust [θrʌst] 1. Stoß *m*; Vorstoß *m*; ⊕ Druck *m*, Schub *m*; 2. [*irr.*] stoßen; **~** *o.s.* into sich drängen in (*acc.*); **~** upon *s.o.* j-m aufdrängen.

thud [θʌd] 1. dumpf aufschlagen, F bumsen; 2. dumpfer (Auf)Schlag, F Bums *m*.

thug [θʌg] Strolch *m*.

thumb [θʌm] 1. Daumen *m*; Tom ♀ Däumling *m im Märchen*; 2. *Buch etc.* abgreifen; **~** a lift per Anhalter fahren; **~tack** *Am.* ['θʌmtæk] Reißzwecke *f*.

thump [θʌmp] 1. F Bums *m*; F Puff *m*; 2. *v/t.* F bumsen *od.* pochen auf (*acc.*) *od.* gegen; F knuffen, puffen; *v/i.* F (auf)bumsen.

thunder ['θʌndə] 1. Donner *m*; 2. donnern; **~bolt** Blitz *m* (*u.* Donner *m*); **~clap** Donnerschlag *m*; **~ous** □ [~ərəs] donnernd; **~storm** Gewitter *n*; **~struck** wie vom Donner gerührt.

Thursday ['θə:zdi] Donnerstag *m*.

thus [ðʌs] so; also, somit.

thwart [θwɔ:t] 1. durchkreuzen; hintertreiben; 2. Ruderbank *f*.

thy *Bibel, poet.* [ðai] dein(e).

tick[1] *zo.* [tik] Zecke *f*.

tick[2] [~] 1. Ticken *n*; (Vermerk-)Häkchen *n*; 2. *v/i.* ticken *v/t.* anhaken; **~ off** abhaken.

tick[3] [~] Inlett *n*; Matratzenbezug *m*.

ticket ['tikit] 1. Fahrkarte *f*, -schein *m*; Flugkarte *f*; Eintrittskarte *f*; (Straf)Zettel *m*; (Preis- *etc.*)Schildchen *n*; *pol.* (Wahl-, Kandidaten-) Liste *f*; 2. etikettieren, *Ware* auszeichnen; **~-machine** Fahrkartenautomat *m*; **~ office**, **~ window** *bsd. Am.* Fahrkartenschalter *m*.

tickl|e ['tikl] kitzeln (*a. fig.*); **~ish** □ [~liʃ] kitzlig; heikel.

tidal ['taidl]: **~ wave** Flutwelle *f*.

tide [taid] 1. Gezeit(en *pl.*) *f*; Ebbe *f* und Flut *f*; *fig.* Strom *m*, Flut *f*; *in Zssgn*: rechte Zeit; high **~** Flut *f*; low **~** Ebbe *f*; 2. **~ over** *fig.* hinwegkommen *od.* j-m hinweghelfen über (*acc.*).

tidings ['taidiŋz] *pl. od. sg.* Neuigkeiten *f/pl.*, Nachrichten *f/pl.*

tidy ['taidi] 1. ordentlich, sauber, reinlich; F ganz schön, beträchtlich (*Summe*); 2. Behälter *m*; Abfallkorb *m*; 3. *a.* **~ up** zurechtmachen; ordnen; aufräumen.

tie [tai] 1. Band *n* (*a. fig.*); Schleife *f*; Krawatte *f*, Schlips *m*; Bindung *f*; *fig.* Fessel *f*, Verpflichtung *f*; *Sport*: Punkt-, *parl.* Stimmengleichheit *f*; *Sport*: Entscheidungsspiel *n*; 🚄 *Am.* Schwelle *f*; 2. *v/t.* (ver)binden; **~ down** *fig.* binden (to an *acc.*); **~ up** zu-, an-, ver-, zs.-binden; *v/i.* *Sport*: punktgleich sein.

tier [tiə] Reihe *f*; Rang *m*.

tie-up ['taiʌp] (Ver)Bindung *f*; ✚ Fusion *f*; Stockung *f*; *bsd. Am.* Streik *m*.

tiffin ['tifin] Mittagessen *n*.

tiger ['taigə] *zo.* Tiger *m*; *Am.* F Beifallsgebrüll *n*.

tight [tait] 1. □ dicht; fest; eng; knapp (sitzend); straff, prall, knapp; F beschwipst; *be in a* **~** *place od. corner* F in der Klemme sein; 2. *adv.* fest; *hold* **~** festhalten; **~en** ['taitn] *a.* **~ up** (sich) zs.-ziehen; *Gürtel* enger schnallen; **~-fisted** knick(e)rig; **~ness** ['taitnis] Festigkeit *f*, Dichtigkeit *f*; Straffheit *f*; Knappheit *f*; Enge *f*; Geiz *m*; **~s** [taits] *pl.* Trikot *n*.

tigress ['taigris] Tigerin *f*.

tile [tail] 1. (Dach)Ziegel *m*; Kachel *f*; Fliese *f*; 2. mit Ziegeln *etc.* decken; kacheln; fliesen.

till[1] [til] Laden(tisch)kasse *f*.

till[2] [~] 1. *prp.* bis (zu); 2. *cj.* bis.

till[3] ✒ [~] bestellen, bebauen; **~age** ['tilidʒ] (Land)Bestellung *f*; Ackerbau *m*; Ackerland *n*.

tilt [tilt] 1. Plane *f*; Neigung *f*, Kippe *f*; Stoß *m*; Lanzenbrechen *n* (*a. fig.*); 2. kippen; **~** against anrennen gegen.

timber ['timbə] 1. (Bau-, Nutz-) Holz *n*; Balken *m*; Baumbestand *m*, Bäume *m/pl.*; 2. zimmern.

time [taim] 1. Zeit *f*; Mal *n*; Takt *m*; Tempo *n*; **~** and again immer wieder; *at a* **~** zugleich; *for the* **~** *being* einstweilen; *have a good* **~** es gut haben; sich amüsieren; *in* **~**, *on* **~** zur rechten Zeit, rechtzeitig; 2. zeitlich festsetzen; zeitlich abpassen; die Zeitdauer messen; **~-hono(u)red** ['taimɔnəd] altehrwürdig; **~ly** ['taimli] (recht)zeitig; **~piece** Uhr *f*; **~-sheet** Anwesenheitsliste *f*; **~-table** Terminkalender *m*; Fahr-, Stundenplan *m*.

tim|id ['timid], **~orous** □ ['timərəs] furchtsam; schüchtern.

tin [tin] 1. Zinn *n*; Weißblech *n*; (Konserven)Büchse *f*; 2. verzinnen; in Büchsen einmachen, eindosen.

tincture ['tiŋktʃə] 1. Farbe *f*; Tinktur *f*; *fig.* Anstrich *m*; 2. färben.

tinfoil ['tin'fɔil] Stanniol *n*.

tinge [tindʒ] **1.** Färbung *f*; *fig.* Anflug *m*, Spur *f*; **2.** färben; *fig.* e-n Anstrich geben (*dat.*).

tingle ['tiŋgl] klingen; prickeln.

tinker ['tiŋkə] basteln (*at an dat.*).

tinkle ['tiŋkl] klingeln (mit).

tin-opener ['tinoupnə] Dosenöffner *m*; ~**plate** Weißblech *n*.

tinsel ['tinsəl] Flitter(werk *n*) *m*; Lametta *n*.

tin-smith ['tinsmiθ] Klempner *m*.

tint [tint] **1.** Farbe *f*; (Farb)Ton *m*, Schattierung *f*; **2.** färben; (ab-)tönen.

tiny ['taini] winzig, klein.

tip [tip] **1.** Spitze *f*; Mundstück *n*; Trinkgeld *n*; Tip *m*, Wink *m*; leichter Stoß; Schuttabladeplatz *m*; **2.** mit e-r Spitze versehen; (um-)kippen; *j-m* ein Trinkgeld geben; *a.* ~ off *j-m* e-n Wink geben.

tipple ['tipl] zechen, picheln.

tipsy ['tipsi] angeheitert.

tiptoe ['tiptou] **1.** auf Zehenspitzen gehen; **2.** on ~ auf Zehenspitzen.

tire[1] ['taiə] (Rad-, Auto)Reifen *m*.

tire[2] [~] ermüden, müde machen *od.* werden; ~**d** □ müde; ~**less** □ ['taiəlis] unermüdlich; ~**some** □ ['taiəsəm] ermüdend; lästig.

tiro ['taiərou] Anfänger *m*.

tissue ['tisju:, *Am.* 'tiʃu:] Gewebe *n*; ~**paper** Seidenpapier *n*.

tit[1] [tit] = *teat*.

tit[2] *orn.* [~] Meise *f*.

titbit ['titbit] Leckerbissen *m*.

titillate ['titileit] kitzeln.

title ['taitl] **1.** (Buch-, Ehren)Titel *m*; Überschrift *f*; ♂ Anspruch *m*; **2.** betiteln; ~**d** adel *od* d(e)lig.

titmouse *orn.* ['titmaus] Meise *f*.

titter ['titə] **1.** kichern; **2.** Kichern *n*.

tittle ['titl] Pünktchen *n*; *fig.* Tütelchen *n*; ~**tattle** [~ltætl] Schnickschnack *m*.

to [tu:, tu, tə] *prp.* zu (*a. adv.*); gegen, nach, an, in, auf; bis zu, bis an (*acc.*); um zu; für; ~ me etc. mir etc.; I weep ~ think of it ich weine, wenn ich daran denke; here's ~ you! auf Ihr Wohl!, Prosit!

toad *zo.* [toud] Kröte *f*; ~**stool** ['toudstu:l] (größerer Blätter)Pilz; Giftpilz *m*; ~**y** ['toudi] **1.** Speichellecker *m*; **2.** *fig.* vor *j-m* kriechen.

toast [toust] **1.** Toast *m*, geröstetes Brot; Trinkspruch *m*; **2.** toasten, rösten; *fig.* wärmen; trinken auf (*acc.*).

tobacco [tə'bækou] Tabak *m*; ~**nist** [~kənist] Tabakhändler *m*.

toboggan [tə'bɔgən] **1.** Toboggan *m*; Rodelschlitten *m*; **2.** rodeln.

today [tə'dei] heute. [teln.)

toddle ['tɔdl] unsicher gehen; zot-)

toddy ['tɔdi] Art Grog *m*.

to-do F [tə'du:] Lärm *m*, Aufheben *n*.

toe [tou] **1.** Zehe *f*; Spitze *f*; **2.** mit den Zehen berühren.

toffee, ~y ['tɔfi] Sahnebonbon *m*, *n*, Toffee *n*.

together [tə'geðə] zusammen; zugleich; nacheinander.

toil [tɔil] **1.** schwere Arbeit; Mühe *f*, F Plackerei *f*; **2.** sich plagen.

toilet ['tɔilit] Toilette *f*; ~**paper** Toilettenpapier *n*; ~**table** Frisiertoilette *f*. [*n*.)

toils [tɔilz] *pl.* Schlingen *f*/*pl.*, Netz)

toilsome □ ['tɔilsəm] mühsam.

token ['toukən] Zeichen *n*; Andenken *n*, Geschenk *n*; ~ money Notgeld *n*; in ~ of zum Zeichen (*gen.*).

told [tould] *pret. u. p.p. von* tell.

tolerable □ ['tɔlərəbl] erträglich; ~**nce** [~əns] Duldsamkeit *f*; ~**nt** □ [~ənt] duldsam (of gegen); ~**te** [~reit] dulden; ertragen; ~**tion** [tɔlə'reiʃən] Duldung *f*.

toll [toul] **1.** Zoll *m* (*a. fig.*); Wege-, Brücken-, Marktgeld *n*; *fig.* Tribut *m*; ~ of the road die Verkehrsopfer *n*/*pl.*; **2.** läuten; ~**bar** ['toulba:], ~**gate** Schlagbaum *m*.

tomato ♀ [tə'ma:tou, *Am.* tə'meitou], *pl.* ~**es** Tomate *f*.

tomb [tu:m] Grab(mal) *n*.

tomboy ['tɔmbɔi] Range *f*.

tombstone ['tu:mstoun] Grabstein *m*.

tom-cat ['tɔm'kæt] Kater *m*.

tomfool ['tɔm'fu:l] Hansnarr *m*.

tomorrow [tə'mɔrou] morgen.

ton [tʌn] Tonne *f* (*Gewichtseinheit*).

tone [toun] **1.** Ton *m*; Klang *m*; Laut *m*; out of ~ verstimmt; **2.** e-n Ton geben (*dat.*); stimmen; *paint.* abtönen; ~ down (sich) abschwächen, mildern.

tongs [tɔŋz] *pl.* (a pair of ~ *pl.* eine) Zange.

tongue [tʌŋ] Zunge *f*; Sprache *f*; Landzunge *f*; (Schuh)Lasche *f*; hold one's ~ den Mund halten; ~**tied** ['tʌŋtaid] sprachlos; schweigsam; stumm.

tonic ['tɔnik] **1.** (~ally) tonisch; stärkend; **2.** ♪ Grundton *m*; ♀ Stärkungsmittel *n*, Tonikum *n*.

tonight [tə'nait] heute abend *od.* nacht.

tonnage ⚓ ['tʌnidʒ] Tonnengehalt *m*; Lastigkeit *f*; Tonnengeld *n*.

tonsil *anat.* ['tɔnsl] Mandel *f*; ~**litis** ⚕ [tɔnsi'laitis] Mandelentzündung *f*.

too [tu:] zu, allzu; auch, noch dazu.

took [tuk] *pret. von* take 1.

tool [tu:l] Werkzeug *n*, Gerät *n*; ~**bag** ['tu:lbæg], ~**kit** Werkzeugtasche *f*.

toot [tu:t] **1.** blasen, tuten; **2.** Tuten *n*.

tooth [tu:θ] *pl.* teeth [ti:θ] Zahn *m*; ~**ache** ['tu:θeik] Zahnschmerzen *pl.*; ~**brush** Zahnbürste *f*; ~**less** □

['tu:θlis] zahnlos; ~-paste Zahn-
pasta f; ~pick Zahnstocher m;
~some □ ['tu:θsəm] schmackhaft.

top [tɔp] 1. oberstes Ende; Ober-
teil n; Gipfel m (a. fig.); Wipfel m;
Kopf m e-r Seite; mot. Am. Verdeck n; fig. Haupt n, Erste(r) m;
Stiefel-Stulpe f; Kreisel m; at the
~ of one's voice aus voller Kehle;
on ~ obenauf; obendrein; 2. ober(er,
-e, -es); oberst; höchst; 3. oben
bedecken; fig. überragen; vorangehen in (dat.); als erste(r) stehen
auf e-r Liste; ~boots ['tɔp'bu:ts]
pl. Stulpenstiefel m/pl.

toper ['toupə] Zecher m.

tophat F ['tɔp'hæt] Zylinderhut m.

topic ['tɔpik] Gegenstand m, Thema
n; ~al □ [‿kəl] lokal; aktuell.

topmost ['tɔpmoust] höchst, oberst.

topple ['tɔpl] (um)kippen.

topsyturvy □ ['tɔpsi'tə:vi] auf den
Kopf gestellt; das Oberste zuunterst; drunter und drüber.

torch [tɔ:tʃ] Fackel f; electric ~
Taschenlampe f; ~light ['tɔ:tʃlait]
Fackelschein m; ~ procession Fak-
kelzug m.

tore [tɔ:] pret. von tear[1] 1.

torment 1. ['tɔ:ment] Qual f,
Marter f; 2. [tɔ:'ment] martern,
quälen.

torn [tɔ:n] p.p. von tear[1] 1.

tornado [tɔ:'neidou], pl. ~es Wirbelsturm m, Tornado m.

torpedo [tɔ:'pi:dou], pl. ~es 1. Torpedo m; 2. ⊕ torpedieren (a. fig.).

torpid □ ['tɔ:pid] starr; apathisch;
träg; ~idity [tɔ:'piditi], ~or ['tɔ:pə]
Erstarrung f, Betäubung f.

torrent ['tɔrənt] Sturz-, Gießbach
m; (reißender) Strom; ~ial □
[tɔ'renʃəl] gießbachartig; strömend;
fig. ungestüm.

torrid □ ['tɔrid] brennend heiß.

tortoise zo. ['tɔ:təs] Schildkröte f.

tortuous □ ['tɔ:tjuəs] gewunden.

torture ['tɔ:tʃə] 1. Folter f, Marter f,
Tortur f; 2. foltern, martern.

toss [tɔs] 1. Werfen n, Wurf m;
Zurückwerfen n (Kopf); 2. a.
~ about (sich) hin und her werfen;
schütteln; (mit adv.) werfen; a. ~
up hochwerfen; ~ off Getränk hin-
unterstürzen; Arbeit hinhauen; a.
~ up losen (for um); ~up ['tɔsʌp]
Losen n; fig. etwas Zweifelhaftes.

tot F [tɔt] Knirps m (kleines Kind).

total ['toutl] 1. □ ganz, gänzlich;
total; gesamt; 2. Gesamtbetrag m;
3. sich belaufen auf (acc.); sum-
mieren; ~itarian [toutæli'tɛəriən]
totalitär; ~ity [tou'tæliti] Gesamtheit f.

totter ['tɔtə] wanken, wackeln.

touch [tʌtʃ] 1. (sich) berühren; anrühren, anfassen; stoßen an (acc.);
betreffen; fig. rühren; erreichen; ♪
anschlagen; a bit ~ed fig. ein biß-

chen verrückt; ~ at ⚓ anlegen in
(dat.); ~ up auffrischen; retuschieren; 2. Berührung f; Gefühl(s-
sinn m) n; Anflug m, Zug m; Fertigkeit f; ♪ Anschlag m; (Pinsel-)
Strich m; ~and-go ['tʌtʃən'gou]
gewagte Sache; it is ~ es steht auf
des Messers Schneide; ~ing [‿ʃin]
rührend; ~stone Prüfstein m;
~y [‿ʃi] empfindlich; heikel.

tough [tʌf] zäh (a. fig.); schwer,
hart; grob, brutal; übel; ~en ['tʌfn]
zäh machen od. werden; ~ness
[‿nis] Zähigkeit f.

tour [tuə] 1. (Rund)Reise f, Tour
(-nee) f; conducted ~ Führung f;
Gesellschaftsreise f; 2. (be)reisen;
~ist ['tuərist] Tourist(in); ~ agency,
~ bureau, ~ office Reisebüro n; ~
season Reisezeit f.   [n.]

tournament ['tuənəmənt] Turnier

tousle ['tauzl] (zer)zausen.

tow [tou] 1. Schleppen n; take in
~ ins Schlepptau nehmen; 2. (ab-)
schleppen; treideln; ziehen.

toward(s) [tə'wɔ:d(z)] gegen; nach
... zu, auf ... (acc.) zu; (als Beitrag)
zu.

towel ['tauəl] 1. Handtuch n; 2. abreiben; ~rack Handtuchhalter m.

tower ['tauə] 1. Turm m; fig. Hort
m, Bollwerk n; 2. sich erheben;
~ing □ ['tauəriŋ] (turm)hoch; rasend (Wut).

town [taun] 1. Stadt f; 2. Stadt...;
städtisch; ~ clerk Stadtsyndikus m;
~ council Stadtrat m (Versammlung); ~ councillor Stadtrat m
(Person); ~ hall Rathaus n; ~sfolk
['taunzfouk] pl. Städter pl.; ~ship
['taunʃip] Stadtgemeinde f; Stadt-
gebiet n; ~sman ['taunzmən]
(Mit)Bürger m; ~speople [‿zpi:pl]
pl. = townsfolk.

toxic|al □ ['tɔksik(əl)] giftig;
Gift...; ~n [‿in] Giftstoff m.

toy [tɔi] 1. Spielzeug n; Tand m;
~s pl. Spielwaren f/pl.; 2. Spiel-
(zeug)...; Miniatur...; Zwerg...;
3. spielen; ~book ['tɔibuk] Bilder-
buch n.

trace [treis] 1. Spur f (a. fig.);
Strang m; 2. nachspüren (dat.); fig.
verfolgen; herausfinden; (auf-)
zeichnen; (durch)pausen.

tracing ['treisiŋ] Pauszeichnung f.

track [træk] 1. Spur f; Sport: Bahn
f; Rennstrecke f; Pfad m; Gleis
n; ~ events pl. Laufdisziplinen f/pl.;
2. nachspüren (dat.); verfolgen; ~
down, ~ out aufspüren.

tract [trækt] Fläche f, Strecke f,
Gegend f; Traktat n, Abhandlung f.

tractable □ ['træktəbl] lenk-, füg-
sam.

tract|ion ['trækʃən] Ziehen n, Zug
m; ~ engine Zugmaschine f; ~or ⊕
[‿ktə] Trecker m, Traktor m.

trade [treid] **1.** Handel *m*; Gewerbe *n*; Handwerk *n*; *Am.* Kompensationsgeschäft *n*; **2.** Handel treiben; handeln; ~ *on* ausnutzen; ~ **mark** ♣ Warenzeichen *n*, Schutzmarke *f*; ~ **price** Händlerpreis *m*; ~**r** ['treidə] Händler *m*; ~**sman** [,dʒmən] Geschäftsmann *m*; ~ **union** Gewerkschaft *f*; ~ **wind** ⚓ Passatwind *m*.

tradition [trə'diʃən] Tradition *f*, Überlieferung *f*; ~**al** □ [,nl] traditionell.

traffic ['træfik] **1.** Verkehr *m*; Handel *m*; **2.** handeln (*in* mit); ~ **jam** Verkehrsstauung *f*; ~ **light** Verkehrsampel *f*.

traged|ian [trə'dʒi:djən] Tragiker *m*; *thea.* Tragöd|e *m*, -in *f*; ~**y** ['trædʒidi] Tragödie *f*.

tragic(al □) ['trædʒik(əl)] tragisch.

trail [treil] **1.** *fig.* Schweif *m*; Schleppe *f*; Spur *f*; Pfad *m*; **2.** *v/t.* hinter sich (her)ziehen; verfolgen; *v/i.* (sich) schleppen; ⚘ kriechen; ~ **blazer** *Am.* Bahnbrecher *m*; ~**er** ['treilə] (Wohnwagen)Anhänger *m*; ⚘ Kriechpflanze *f*; *Film:* Vorschau *f*.

train [trein] **1.** (Eisenbahn)Zug *m*; *allg.* Zug *m*; Gefolge *n*; Reihe *f*, Folge *f*, Kette *f*; Schleppe *f* *am Kleid*; **2.** erziehen; schulen; abrichten; ausbilden; trainieren; (sich) üben; ~**ee** [trei'ni:] in der Ausbildung Begriffene(r) *m*; ~**er** ['treinə] Ausbilder *m*; Trainer *m*.

trait [trei] (Charakter)Zug *m*.

traitor ['treitə] Verräter *m*.

tram [træm] *s.* ~*-car*, ~*way*; ~*-car* ['træmka:] Straßenbahnwagen *m*.

tramp [træmp] **1.** Getrampel *n*; Wanderung *f*; Tramp *m*, Landstreicher *m*; **2.** trampeln, treten; (durch)wandern; ~**le** ['træmpl] (zer)trampeln.

tramway ['træmwei] Straßenbahn *f*.

trance [trɑ:ns] Trance *f*.

tranquil □ ['træŋkwil] ruhig; gelassen; ~**(l)ity** [træŋ'kwiliti] Ruhe *f*; Gelassenheit *f*; ~**(l)ize** ['træŋkwilaiz] beruhigen; ~**(l)izer** [,zə] Beruhigungsmittel *n*.

transact [træn'zækt] abwickeln, abmachen; ~**ion** [,kʃən] Verrichtung *f*; Geschäft *n*, Transaktion *f*; ~**s** *pl.* (Tätigkeits)Bericht(e *pl.*) *m*.

transalpine ['trænz'ælpain] transalpin(isch).

transatlantic ['trænzət'læntik] transatlantisch, Transatlantik...

transcend [træn'send] überschreiten, übertreffen; hinausgehen über (*acc.*); ~**ence**, ~**ency** [,dəns, ,si] Überlegenheit *f*; *phls.* Transzendenz *f*.

transcribe [træns'kraib] abschreiben; *Kurzschrift* übertragen.

transcript ['trænskript], ~**ion**

[træns'kripʃən] Abschrift *f*; Umschrift *f*.

transfer 1. [træns'fə:] *v/t.* übertragen; versetzen, verlegen; *v/i.* übertreten; *Am.* umsteigen; **2.** ['trænsfə(:)] Übertragung *f*; ♣ Transfer *m*; Versetzung *f*, Verlegung *f*; *Am.* Umsteigefahrschein *m*; ~**able** [træns'fə:rəbl] übertragbar.

transfigure [træns'figə] umgestalten; verklären.

transfix [træns'fiks] durchstechen; ~**ed** *fig.* versteinert, starr (*with* vor *dat.*).

transform [træns'fɔ:m] umformen; um-, verwandeln; ~**ation** [trænsfə'meiʃən] Umformung *f*; Umwandlung *f*.

transfus|e [træns'fju:z] ⚕ Blut etc. übertragen; *fig.* einflößen; *fig.* durchtränken; ~**ion** [,u:ʒən] (*bsd.* ⚕ Blut)Übertragung *f*, Transfusion *f*.

transgress [træns'gres] *v/t.* überschreiten; übertreten, verletzen; *v/i.* sich vergehen; ~**ion** [,eʃən] Überschreitung *f*; Übertretung *f*; Vergehen *n*; ~**or** [,esə] Übertreter *m*.

transient ['trænziənt] **1.** = *transitory*; **2.** *Am.* Durchreisende(r *m*) *f*.

transit ['trænsit] Durchgang *m*; Durchgangsverkehr *m*.

transition [træn'siʒən] Übergang *m*.

transitive □ *gr.* ['trænsitiv] transitiv.

transitory □ ['trænsitəri] vorübergehend; vergänglich, flüchtig.

translat|e [træns'leit] übersetzen, übertragen; überführen; *fig.* umsetzen; ~**ion** [,eiʃən] Übersetzung *f*, Übertragung *f*; *fig.* Auslegung *f*; ~**or** [,eitə] Übersetzer(in).

translucent [trænz'lu:snt] durchscheinend; *fig.* hell.

transmigration [trænzmai'greiʃən] (Aus)Wanderung *f*; Seelenwanderung *f*.

transmission [trænz'miʃən] Übermittlung *f*; *biol.* Vererbung *f*; *phys.* Fortpflanzung *f*; *mot.* Getriebe *n*; *Radio:* Sendung *f*.

transmit [trænz'mit] übermitteln, übersenden; übertragen; senden; *biol.* vererben; *phys.* fortpflanzen; ~**ter** [,tə] Übermittler(in); *tel. etc.* Sender *m*.

transmute [trænz'mju:t] um-, verwandeln.

transparent □ [træns'pɛərənt] durchsichtig (*a. fig.*).

transpire [træns'paiə] ausdünsten, ausschwitzen; *fig.* durchsickern.

transplant [træns'plɑ:nt] um-, verpflanzen; ~**ation** [trænsplɑ:n'teiʃən] Verpflanzung *f*.

transport 1. [træns'pɔ:t] fortschaffen, befördern, transportieren; *fig.* hinreißen; **2.** ['trænspɔ:t] Fortschaffen *n*; Beförderung *f*; Transport *m*; Verkehr *m*; Beförderungsmittel *n*; Transportschiff *n*; Verzückung *f*; *be in* ~*s* außer sich sein; ~**ation** [trænspɔː'teiʃən] Beförderung *f*, Transport *m*.

transpose [træns'pouz] versetzen, umstellen; ♪ transponieren.

transverse □ ['trænzvəːs] quer laufend; Quer...

trap [træp] 1. Falle *f* (*a. fig.*); Klappe *f*; 2. (in e-r Falle) fangen, in die Falle locken; *fig.* ertappen; ~**door** ['træpdɔː] Falltür *f*; *thea.* Versenkung *f*.

trapeze [trə'piːz] *Zirkus:* Trapez *n*.

trapper ['træpə] Trapper *m*, Fallensteller *m*, Pelzjäger *m*.

trappings *fig.* ['træpiŋz] *pl.* Schmuck *m*, Putz *m*.

traps F [træps] *pl.* Siebensachen *pl.*

trash [træʃ] Abfall *m*; *fig.* Plunder *m*; Unsinn *m*, F Blech *n*; Kitsch *m*; ~**y** ['træʃi] wertlos, kitschig.

travel ['trævl] 1. *v/i.* reisen; sich bewegen; wandern; *v/t.* bereisen; 2. *das* Reisen; ⊕ Lauf *m*; ~*s pl.* Reisen *f/pl.*; ~(l)**er** [-lə] Reisende(r) *m*; ~'*s cheque* (*Am. check*) Reisescheck *m.*

traverse ['trævə(ː)s] 1. Durchquerung *f*; 2. (über)queren; durchqueren; *fig.* durchkreuzen.

travesty ['trævisti] 1. Travestie *f*; Karikatur *f*; 2. travestieren; verulken.

trawl [trɔːl] 1. (Grund)Schleppnetz *n*; 2. mit dem Schleppnetz fischen; ~**er** ['trɔːlə] Trawler *m.*

tray [trei] (Servier)Brett *n*, Tablett *n*; Ablage *f*; *pen*-~ Federschale *f.*

treacher|ous □ ['tretʃərəs] verräterisch, treulos; (heim)tückisch; trügerisch; ~**y** [~ri] Verrat *m*, Verräterei *f*, Treulosigkeit *f*; Tücke *f.*

treacle ['triːkl] Sirup *m.*

tread [tred] 1. [*irr.*] treten; schreiten; 2. Tritt *m*, Schritt *m*; Lauffläche *f*; ~*le* [e 'tredl] Pedal *n*; Tritt *m*; ~**mill** Tretmühle *f.*

treason ['triːzn] Verrat *m*; ~**able** □ [~nəbl] verräterisch.

treasure ['treʒə] 1. Schatz *m*, Reichtum *m*; ~ *trove* Schatzfund *m*; 2. *Schätze* sammeln, aufhäufen; ~**r** [~ərə] Schatzmeister *m*, Kassenwart *m.*

treasury ['treʒəri] Schatzkammer *f*; (*bsd.* Staats)Schatz *m*; *parl.* Ministerbank *f*; ♀ **Bench** *parl.* Ministerbank *f*; ♀ **Board**, *Am.* ♀ **Department** Finanzministerium *m.*

treat [triːt] 1. *v/t.* behandeln; betrachten; ~ *s.o. to s.th.* j-m et. spendieren; *v/i.* ~ *of* handeln von; ~ *with* unterhandeln mit; 2. Vergnügen *n*; *school* ~ Schulausflug *m*; *it is my* ~ F es geht auf meine Rechnung; ~**ise** ['triːtiz] Abhandlung *f*;

~**ment** [~tmənt] Behandlung *f*; ♂ Kur *f*; *follow-up* ~ ♂ Nachkur *f*; ~**y** [~ti] Vertrag *m.*

treble ['trebl] 1. ♪ dreifach; 2. Dreifache(s) *n*; ♪ Diskant *m*, Sopran *m*; 3. (sich) verdreifachen.

tree [triː] Baum *m.*

trefoil ♀ ['triːfoil] Klee *m.*

trellis ['trelis] 1. ♂ Spalier *n*; 2. vergittern; ♂ am Spalier ziehen.

tremble ['trembl] zittern.

tremendous □ [tri'mendəs] schrecklich, furchtbar; F kolossal, riesig.

tremor ['tremə] Zittern *n*, Beben *n.*

tremulous □ ['tremjuləs] zitternd, bebend.

trench [trentʃ] 1. (Schützen)Graben *m*; Furche *f*; 2. *v/t.* mit Gräben durchziehen; ♂ umgraben; (*up*)*on* eingreifen in (*acc.*); ~**ant** □ ['trentʃənt] scharf.

trend [trend] 1. Richtung *f*; *fig.* Lauf *m*; *fig.* Strömung *f*; Tendenz *f*; 2. sich erstrecken, laufen.

trepidation [trepi'deiʃən] Zittern *n*, Beben *n*; Bestürzung *f.*

trespass ['trespəs] 1. Übertretung *f*; 2. unbefugt eindringen (*on, upon* in *acc.*); über Gebühr in Anspruch nehmen; ~**er** ☆ [~sə] Rechtsverletzer *m*; Unbefugte(r *m*) *f.*

tress [tres] Haarlocke *f*, -flechte *f.*

trestle ['tresl] Gestell *n*, Bock *m.*

trial ['traiəl] Versuch *m*, Probe *f*, Prüfung *f* (*a. fig.*); Plage *f*; ☆ Verhandlung *f*, Prozeß *m*; *on* ~ auf Probe; vor Gericht; *give s.o. a* ~ es mit j-m versuchen; ~ *run* Probefahrt *f.*

triang|le ['traiæŋgl] Dreieck *n*; ~**ular** □ [trai'æŋgjulə] dreieckig.

tribe [traib] Stamm *m*; Geschlecht *n*; *contp.* Sippe *f*; ♀, *zo.* Klasse *f.*

tribun|al [trai'bjuːnl] Richterstuhl *m*; Gericht(shof *m*) *n*; ~**e** ['tribjuːn] Tribun *m*; Tribüne *f.*

tribut|ary ['tribjutəri] 1. □ zinspflichtig; *fig.* helfend; Neben...; 2. Nebenfluß *m*; ~**e** [~juːt] Tribut *m* (*a. fig.*), Zins *m*; Anerkennung *f.*

trice [trais]: *in a* ~ im Nu.

trick [trik] 1. Kniff *m*, List *f*, Trick *m*; Kunstgriff *m*, -stück *n*; Streich *m*; Eigenheit *f*; 2. betrügen; herausputzen; ~**ery** ['trikəri] Betrügerei *f.*

trickle ['trikl] tröpfeln, rieseln.

trick|ster ['trikstə] Gauner *m*; ~**y** □ [~ki] verschlagen; F heikel; verzwickt, verwickelt, schwierig.

tricycle ['traisikl] Dreirad *n.*

trident ['traidənt] Dreizack *m.*

trifl|e ['traifl] 1. Kleinigkeit *f*; Lappalie *f*; *a* ~ ein bißchen, ein wenig, etwas; 2. *v/i.* spielen, spaßen; *v/t.* ~ *away* verschwenden; ~**ing** □ [~liŋ] geringfügig; unbedeutend.

trig [trig] 1. hemmen; 2. schmuck,

trigger ['trigə] Abzug *m am Gewehr*; *phot.* Auslöser *m*.
trill [tril] 1. Triller *m*; gerolltes R; 2. trillern; *bsd.* das R rollen.
trillion ['triljən] Trillion *f*; *Am.* Billion *f*.
trim [trim] 1. ☐ ordentlich; schmuck; gepflegt; 2. (richtiger) Zustand; Ordnung *f*; 3. zurechtmachen; (~ *up* aus)putzen, schmükken; besetzen; stutzen; beschneiden; ♥, ♦ trimmen; ~**ming** ['trimiŋ] *mst* ~*s pl.* Besatz *m*, Garnierung *f*.
Trinity *eccl.* ['triniti] Dreieinigkeit *f*.
trinket ['triŋkit] wertloses Schmuckstück; ~*s pl.* F Kinkerlitzchen *pl.*
trip [trip] 1. Reise *f*, Fahrt *f*; Ausflug *m*, Spritztour *f*; Stolpern *n*, Fallen *n*; Fehltritt *m* (*a. fig.*); *fig.* Versehen *n*, Fehler *m*; 2. *v/i.* trippeln; stolpern; e-n Fehltritt tun (*a. fig.*); *fig.* e-n Fehler machen; *v/t. a.* ~ *up j-m* ein Bein stellen (*a. fig.*).
tripartite ['trai'pɑːtait] dreiteilig.
tripe [traip] Kaldaunen *f/pl.*
triple ☐ ['tripl] dreifach; ~**ts** [~lits] *pl.* Drillinge *m/pl.*
triplicate 1. ['triplikit] dreifach; 2. [~keit] verdreifachen.
tripod ['traipɔd] Dreifuß *m*; *phot.* Stativ *n*.
tripper F ['tripə] Ausflügler(in).
trite ☐ [trait] abgedroschen, platt.
triturate ['tritjureit] zerreiben.
triumph ['traiəmf] 1. Triumph *m*, Sieg *m*; 2. triumphieren; ~**al** [trai-'ʌmfəl] Sieges..., Triumph...; ~**ant** ☐ [~ənt] triumphierend.
trivial ☐ ['triviəl] bedeutungslos; unbedeutend; trivial; alltäglich.
trod [trɔd] *pret. von* tread 1; ~**den** ['trɔdn] *p.p. von tread* 1.
troll [troul] (vor sich hin)trällern.
troll(e)y ['trɔli] Karren *m*; Draisine *f*; Servierwagen *m*; ⊕ Kontaktrolle *f* e-s Oberleitungsfahrzeugs; *Am.* Straßenbahnwagen *m*; ~ **bus** O(berleitungs)bus *m*. [Hure.\
trollop ['trɔləp] F Schlampe *f*;\
trombone [trɔm'boun] Posaune *f*.
troop [truːp] 1. Truppe *f*; Schar *f*; ✗ (Reiter)Zug *m*; 2. sich scharen, sich sammeln; ~ *away*, ~ *off* abziehen; ~*ing the colour(s)* ✗ Fahnenparade *f*; ~**er** ✗ ['truːpə] Kavallerist *m*.
trophy ['troufi] Trophäe *f*.
tropic ['trɔpik] Wendekreis *m*; ~*s pl.* Tropen *pl.*; ~**al** (☐) [~k(əl)] tropisch.
trot [trɔt] 1. Trott *m*, Trab *m*; 2. traben (lassen).
trouble ['trʌbl] 1. Unruhe *f*; Störung *f*; Kummer *m*, Not *f*; Mühe *f*; Plage *f*; Unannehmlichkeiten *f/pl.*; *ask od. look for* ~ sich (selbst) Schwierigkeiten machen; das

Schicksal herausfordern; *take* (*the*) ~ sich (die) Mühe machen; 2. stören, beunruhigen, belästigen; quälen, plagen; Mühe machen (*dat.*); (sich) bemühen; ~ *s.o.* for *j-n* bemühen um; ~**man**, ~**shooter** *Am.* F Störungssucher *m*; ~**some** ☐ [~ləsəm] beschwerlich, lästig.
trough [trɔf] (Futter)Trog *m*; Backtrog *m*, Mulde *f*.
trounce F [trauns] *j-n* verhauen.
troupe *thea.* [truːp] Truppe *f*.
trousers ['trauzəz] *pl.* (*a pair of* ~ *pl.* eine) (lange) Hose; Hosen *f/pl.*
trousseau ['truːsou] Aussteuer *f*.
trout *ichth.* [traut] Forelle(n *pl.*) *f*.
trowel ['trauəl] Maurerkelle *f*.
truant ['truː(:)ənt] 1. müßig; 2. Schulschwänzer *m*; *fig.* Bummler *m*.
truce [truːs] Waffenstillstand *m*.
truck [trʌk] 1. (offener) Güterwagen; Last(kraft)wagen *m*, Lkw *m*; Transportkarren *m*; Tausch (-handel) *m*; Verkehr *m*; Naturallohnsystem *n*; *Am.* Gemüse *n*; 2. (ver)tauschen; ~**farm** *Am.* ['trʌkfɑːm] Gemüsegärtnerei *f*.
truckle ['trʌkl] zu Kreuze kriechen.
truculent ☐ ['trʌkjulənt] wild, roh.
trudge [trʌdʒ] wandern; sich (dahin)schleppen, mühsam gehen.
true [truː] wahr; echt, wirklich; treu; genau; richtig; *it is* ~ gewiß, freilich, zwar; *come* ~ sich bewahrheiten; in Erfüllung gehen; ~ *to nature* naturgetreu.
truism ['truː(:)izəm] Binsenwahrheit *f*.
truly ['truːli] wirklich; wahrhaft; aufrichtig; genau; treu; *Yours* ~ Hochachtungsvoll.
trump [trʌmp] 1. Trumpf *m*; 2. (über)trumpfen; ~ *up* erdichten; ~**ery** ['trʌmpəri] Plunder *m*.
trumpet ['trʌmpit] 1. Trompete *f*; 2. trompeten; *fig.* ausposaunen.
truncheon ['trʌntʃən] (Polizei-) Knüppel *m*; Kommandostab *m*.
trundle ['trʌndl] rollen.
trunk [trʌŋk] (Baum)Stamm *m*; Rumpf *m*; Rüssel *m*; *großer* Koffer; ~**call** *teleph.* ['trʌŋkɔːl] Ferngespräch *n*; ~**exchange** *teleph.* Fernamt *n*; ~**line** 🚂 Hauptlinie *f*; *teleph.* Fernleitung *f*; ~**s** [trʌŋks] *pl.* Turnhose *f*; Badehose *f*; Herrenunterhose *f*.
trunnion ⊕ ['trʌnjən] Zapfen *m*.
truss [trʌs] 1. Bündel *n*, Bund *n*; ⚕ Bruchband *n*; △ Binder *m*, Gerüst *n*; 2. (zs.-)binden; △ stützen.
trust [trʌst] 1. Vertrauen *n*; Glaube *m*; Kredit *m*; Pfand *n*; Verwahrung *f*; ⚖ Treuhand *f*; ✝ Ring *m*, Trust *m*; ~ *company* Treuhandgesellschaft *f*; *in* ~ zu treuen Händen; 2. *v/t.* (ver)trauen (*dat.*); anvertrauen, übergeben (*s.o. with s.th., s.th. to s.o.* j-m et.); zuversichtlich hoffen;

v/i. vertrauen (*in, to* auf *acc.*); ~ee [trʌs'tiː] Sach-, Verwalter *m*; ɮɮ Treuhänder *m*; ~ful □ ['trʌstful], ~ing □ [~tiŋ] vertrauensvoll; ~worthy [~twəːði] vertrauenswürdig; zuverlässig.

truth [truːθ], *pl.* ~s [truːðz] Wahrheit *f*; Wirklichkeit *f*; Wahrhaftigkeit *f*; Genauigkeit *f*; ~ful □ ['truːθful] wahrhaft(ig).

try [trai] **1.** versuchen; probieren; prüfen; ɮɮ verhandeln über *et. od.* gegen *j-n*; vor Gericht stellen; aburteilen; *die Augen etc.* angreifen; sich bemühen od. bewerben; ~ on *Kleid* anprobieren; **2.** Versuch *m*; ~ing □ ['traiiŋ] anstrengend; kritisch.

Tsar [zaː] Zar *m*.

T-shirt ['tiːʃəːt] kurzärmeliges Sporthemd.

tub [tʌb] **1.** Faß *n*, Zuber *m*; Kübel *m*; Badewanne *f*; F (Wannen)Bad *n*.

tube [tjuːb] Rohr *n*; (*Am. bsd.* Radio)Röhre *f*; Tube *f*; (Luft-) Schlauch *m*; Tunnel *m*; F (Londoner) Untergrundbahn *f*.

tuber ⚕ ['tjuːbə] Knolle *f*; ~culosis [tjuˌbəˑkjuˈlousis] Tuberkulose *f*.

tubular □ ['tjuːbjulə] röhrenförmig.

tuck [tʌk] **1.** Falte *f*; Abnäher *m*; **2.** ab-, aufnähen; packen, stecken; ~ up hochschürzen, aufkrempeln; *in e-e Decke etc.* einwickeln.

Tuesday ['tjuːzdi] Dienstag *m*.

tuft [tʌft] Büschel *n*, Busch *m*; (Haar)Schopf *m*.

tug [tʌg] **1.** Zug *m*, Ruck *m*; ⚓ Schlepper *m*; *fig.* Anstrengung *f*; **2.** ziehen, zerren; ⚓ schleppen; sich mühen.

tuition [tjuˌ(ː)'iʃən] Unterricht *m*; Schulgeld *n*.

tulip ⚕ ['tjuːlip] Tulpe *f*.

tumble ['tʌmbl] **1.** *v/i.* fallen, purzeln; taumeln; sich wälzen; *v/t.* werfen; zerknüllen; **2.** Sturz *m*; Wirrwarr *m*; ~down baufällig; ~r [~lə] Becher *m*; *orn.* Tümmler *m*.

tumid □ ['tjuːmid] geschwollen.

tummy F ['tʌmi] Bäuchlein *n*, Magen *m*.

tumo(u)r ⚕ ['tjuːmə] Tumor *m*.

tumult ['tjuːmʌlt] Tumult *m*; ~uous □ [tjuˌ(ː)'mʌltjuəs] stürmisch.

tun [tʌn] Tonne *f*, Faß *n*.

tuna *ichth.* ['tuːnə] Thunfisch *m*.

tune [tjuːn] **1.** Melodie *f*, Weise *f*; ♪ Stimmung *f* (*a. fig.*); in ~ (gut-) gestimmt; out of ~ verstimmt; **2.** stimmen (*a. fig.*); ~ in *Radio*: einstellen; ~ out *Radio*: ausschalten; ~ up die Instrumente stimmen; *fig. Befinden etc.* heben; *mot.* die Leistung erhöhen; ~ful □ ['tjuːnful] melodisch; ~less □ [~nlis] unmelodisch.

tunnel ['tʌnl] **1.** Tunnel *m*; ✂

Stollen *m*; **2.** e-n Tunnel bohren (durch).

tunny *ichth.* ['tʌni] Thunfisch *m*.

turbid ['təːbid] trüb; dick.

turb|ine ⊕ ['təːbin] Turbine *f*; ~o-jet ['təːbouˈdʒet] Strahlturbine *f*; ~o-prop [~ouˈprɔp] Propellerturbine *f*.

turbot *ichth.* ['təːbət] Steinbutt *m*.

turbulent □ ['təːbjulənt] unruhig; ungestüm; stürmisch, turbulent.

tureen [təˈriːn] Terrine *f*.

turf [təːf] **1.** Rasen *m*; Torf *m*; Rennbahn *f*; Rennsport *m*; **2.** mit Rasen bedecken; ~y ['təːfi] rasenbedeckt.

turgid □ ['təːdʒid] geschwollen.

Turk [təːk] Türk|e *m*, -in *f*.

turkey ['təːki] *orn.* Truthahn *m*, -henne *f*, Pute(r *m*) *f*; *Am. sl. thea.*, *Film* Pleite *f*, Versager *m*.

Turkish ['təːkiʃ] türkisch.

turmoil ['təːmɔil] Aufruhr *m*, Unruhe *f*; Durcheinander *n*.

turn [təːn] **1.** *v/t.* drehen; (um)wenden, umkehren; lenken; verwandeln; abbringen; abwehren; übertragen; bilden; drechseln; verrückt machen; ~ a corner um eine Ecke biegen; ~ *s.o. against* j-n aufhetzen gegen; ~ aside abwenden; ~ away abwenden; abweisen; ~ down umbiegen; *Gas etc.* kleinstellen; *Decke etc.* zurückschlagen; ablehnen; ~ off ableiten (*a. fig.*); hinauswerfen; wegjagen; ~ off (on) ab- (an)drehen, ab- (ein)schalten; ~ out hinauswerfen; *Fabrikat* herausbringen; *Gas etc.* ausdrehen; ~ over umwenden; *fig.* übertragen; ✝ umsetzen; überlegen; ~ up nach oben richten; hochklappen; umwenden; *Hose etc.* auf-, umschlagen; *Gas etc.* aufdrehen; *v/i.* sich (um)drehen; sich wenden; sich verwandeln; umschlagen (*Wetter etc.*); *Christ, grau etc.* werden; *a.* ~ sour sauer werden (*Milch*); ~ about sich umdrehen; ⚔ kehrtmachen; ~ back zurückkehren; ~ in einkehren; F zu Bett gehen; ~ off abbiegen; ~ on sich drehen um; ~ out ausfallen, ausgehen; sich herausstellen als; ~ to sich zuwenden (*dat.*), sich wenden an (*acc.*); werden zu; ~ up auftauchen; ~ upon sich wenden gegen; **2.** (Um)Drehung *f*; Biegung *f*; Wendung *f*; Neigung *f*; Wechsel *m*; Gestalt *f*, Form *f*; Spaziergang *m*; Reihe(nfolge) *f*; Dienst(leistung *f*) *m*; F Schreck *m*; *at every* ~ auf Schritt und Tritt; *by od. in* ~s der Reihe nach, abwechselnd; *it is my* ~ ich bin an der Reihe; *take* ~s mit-ea. abwechseln; *does it serve your* ~? entspricht das Ihren Zwecken?; ~coat ['təːnkout] Abtrünnige(r) *m*; ~er ['təːnə] Drechs-

ler *m*; ~ery [~əri] Drechslerei *f*;
Drechslerarbeit *f*.

turning ['tə:niŋ] Drechseln *n*;
Wendung *f*; Biegung *f*; Straßen-
ecke *f*; (Weg)Abzweigung *f*; Querstraße *f*; ~point *fig.* Wendepunkt
m.

turnip ⚕ ['tə:nip] (*bsd.* weiße) Rübe.

turn|key ['tə:nki:] Schließer *m*; ~
out ['tə:n'aut] Ausstaffierung *f*;
Arbeitseinstellung *f*; ✝ Gesamt-
produktion *f*; ~over ['tə:nouvə] ✝
Umsatz *m*; Verschiebung *f*; ~pike
Schlagbaum *m*; (gebührenpflichtige) Schnellstraße; ~stile Dreh-
kreuz *n*.   [pentin.\
turpentine 🜛 ['tə:pəntain] Ter-/
turpitude ['tə:pitju:d] Schändlich-
keit *f*.

turret ['tʌrit] Türmchen *n*; ✂, ⚓
Panzerturm *m*; ⚔ Kanzel *f*.

turtle ['tə:tl] *zo.* Schildkröte *f*; *orn.*
mst ~dove Turteltaube *f*.

tusk [tʌsk] Fangzahn *m*; Stoßzahn
m; Hauer *m*.

tussle ['tʌsl] 1. Rauferei *f*, Balgerei
f; 2. raufen, sich balgen.

tussock ['tʌsək] Büschel *n*.

tut [tʌt] ach was!; Unsinn!

tutelage ['tju:tilidʒ] ✝ Vormundschaft *f*; Bevormundung *f*.

tutor ['tju:tə] 1. (Privat-, Haus-)
Lehrer *m*; *univ.* Tutor *m*; *Am.univ.*
Assistent *m mit Lehrauftrag*; ⚖
Vormund *m*; 2. unterrichten; schu-
len, erziehen; *fig.* beherrschen;
~ial [tju(:)'tɔ:riəl] *univ.* Unterrichts-
stunde *f o-s Tutors*; *attr.* Lehrer...;
Tutoren...

tuxedo *Am.* [tʌk'si:dou] Smoking *m*.

TV ['ti:'vi:] Fernsehen *n*; Fernseh-
apparat *m*; *attr.* Fernseh...

twaddle ['twɔdl] 1. Geschwätz *n*;
2. schwatzen, quatschen.

twang [twæŋ] 1. Schwirren *n*; *mst*
nasal ~ näselnde Aussprache;
2. schwirren (lassen); klimpern;
näseln.

tweak [twi:k] zwicken.

tweet [twi:t] zwitschern.

tweezers ['twi:zəz] *pl.* (*a pair of* ~
pl. eine) Pinzette.

twelfth [twelfθ] 1. zwölfte(r, -s)
2. Zwölftel *n*; Ջ~night ['twelfθnait]
Dreikönigsabend *m*.

twelve [twelv] zwölf.

twent|ieth ['twentiiθ] 1. zwanzig-
ste(r, -s); 2. Zwanzigstel *n*; ~y [~ti]
zwanzig.

twice [twais] zweimal.

twiddle ['twidl] (sich) drehen; mit
et. spielen.

twig [twig] Zweig *m*, Rute *f*.

twilight ['twailait] Zwielicht *n*;
Dämmerung *f* (*a. fig.*).

twin [twin] 1. Zwillings...; doppelt;
2. Zwilling *m*; ~engined ⚔
['twindʒind] zweimotorig.

twine [twain] 1. Bindfaden *m*,

Schnur *f*; Zwirn *m*; 2. zs.-drehen;
verflechten; (sich) schlingen *od.*
winden; umschlingen, umranken.

twinge [twindʒ] Zwicken *n*; Stich
m; bohrender Schmerz.

twinkle ['twiŋkl] 1. funkeln, blitzen;
huschen; zwinkern; 2. Funkeln *n*,
Blitzen *n*; (Augen)Zwinkern *n*,
Blinzeln *n*.

twirl [twə:l] 1. Wirbel *m*; 2. wirbeln.

twist [twist] 1. Drehung *f*; Windung
f; Verdrehung *f*; Verdrehtheit *f*;
Neigung *f*; (Gesichts)Verzerrung *f*;
Garn *n*; Kringel *m*, Zopf *m* (*Back-
waren*); 2. (sich) drehen *od.* winden;
zs.-drehen; verdrehen, verziehen,
verzerren.

twit *fig.* [twit] *j-n* aufziehen.

twitch [twitʃ] 1. zupfen (an *dat.*);
zucken; 2. Zupfen *n*; Zuckung *f*.

twitter ['twitə] 1. zwitschern; 2. Gezwitscher *n*; be in a ~ zittern.

two [tu:] 1. zwei; in ~ entzwei; *put*
~ *and* ~ *together* sich *et.* zs.-reimen;
2. Zwei *f*; in ~s zu zweien; ~bit
Am. F ['tu:bit] 25-Cent...; *fig.* unbedeutend, Klein...; ~edged ['tu:-
'edʒd] zweischneidig; ~fold ['tu:-
fould] zweifach; ~pence ['tʌpəns]
zwei Pence; ~penny ['tʌpni] zwei
Pence wert; ~piece ['tu:pi:s]
zweiteilig; ~seater mot. ['tu:'si:tə]
Zweisitzer *m*; ~storey ['tu:stɔ:ri],
~storied zweistöckig; ~stroke
mot. Zweitakt...; ~way Doppel...;
~ adapter ⚡ Doppelstecker *m*; ~
traffic Gegenverkehr *m*.

tycoon *Am.* F [tai'ku:n] Industrie-
kapitän *m*, Industriemagnat *m*.

tyke [taik] Köter *m*; Kerl *m*.

type [taip] Typ *m*; Urbild *n*; Vorbild *n*; Muster *n*; Art *f*; Sinnbild *n*;
typ. Type *f*, Buchstabe *m*; *true to* ~
artecht; *set in* ~ setzen; ~write
['taiprait] [*irr.* (write)] (mit der)
Schreibmaschine schreiben; ~
writer Schreibmaschine *f*; ~ ribbon
Farbband *n*.

typhoid 🜍 ['taifoid] 1. typhös; ~
fever = 2. (Unterleibs)Typhus
m.

typhoon [tai'fu:n] Taifun *m*.

typhus 🜍 ['taifəs] Flecktyphus
m.

typi|cal □ ['tipikəl] typisch; rich-
tig; bezeichnend, kennzeichnend;
~fy [~ifai] typisch sein für; versinnbildlichen; ~st ['taipist] *a.* shorthand ~ Stenotypistin *f*.

tyrann|ic(al □) [ti'rænik(əl)] ty-
rannisch; ~ize ['tirənaiz] tyrannisieren; ~y [~ni] Tyrannei *f*.

tyrant ['taiərənt] Tyrann(in).

tyre ['taiə] *s.* tire 1.

tyro ['taiərou] *s.* tiro.

Tyrolese [tirə'li:z] 1. Tiroler(in);
2. tirolisch, Tiroler...

Tzar [zɑ:] Zar *m*.

U

ubiquitous □ [ju(:)'bikwitəs] allgegenwärtig, überall zu finden(d).

udder ['Adə] Euter n.

ugly □ ['Agli] häßlich; schlimm.

ulcer ⚕ ['Alsə] Geschwür n; (Eiter-)Beule f; ~ate ⚕ [~əreit] eitern (lassen); ~ous ⚕ [~rəs] geschwürig.

ulterior □ [Al'tiəriə] jenseitig; fig. weiter; tiefer liegend, versteckt.

ultimate □ ['Altimit] letzt; endlich; End...; ~ly [~tli] zu guter Letzt.

ultimat|um [Alti'meitəm], pl. a. ~a [~tə] Ultimatum n.

ultimo ✝ ['Altimou] vorigen Monats.

ultra ['Altrə] übermäßig; Ultra..., ultra...; ~fashionable ['Altrə'fæʃənəbl] hypermodern; ~modern hypermodern.

umbel ♣ ['Ambəl] Dolde f.

umbrage ['Ambridʒ] Anstoß m (Ärger); Schatten m.

umbrella [Am'brelə] Regenschirm m; fig. Schirm m, Schutz m; ✕ Abschirmung f.

umpire ['Ampaiə] 1. Schiedsrichter m; 2. Schiedsrichter sein.

un... [An] un...; Un...; ent...; nicht...

unabashed ['Anə'bæʃt] unverfroren; unerschrocken.

unabated ['Anə'beitid] unvermindert. [stande.]

unable ['An'eibl] unfähig, außer-/

unaccommodating ['Anə'kɔmədeitiŋ] unnachgiebig.

unaccountable □ ['Anə'kauntəbl] unerklärlich, seltsam; nicht zur Rechenschaft verpflichtet.

unaccustomed ['Anə'kAstəmd] ungewohnt, ungewöhnlich.

unacquainted ['Anə'kweintid]: ~ with unbekannt mit, e-r S unkundig.

unadvised □ ['Anəd'vaizd] unbedacht; unberaten.

unaffected [['Anə'fektid] unberührt, ungerührt; ungekünstelt.

unaided ['An'eidid] ohne Unterstützung; (ganz) allein; bloß (Auge).

unalter|able □ ['An'ɔ:ltərəbl] unveränderlich; ~ed ['An'ɔ:ltəd] unverändert

unanim|ity [ju:nə'nimiti] Einmütigkeit f; ~ous □ [ju(:)'næniməs] einmütig, einstimmig.

unanswer|able □ [An'ɑ:nsərəbl] unwiderleglich; ~ed ['An'ɑ:nsəd] unbeantwortet.

unapproachable [[Anə'proutʃəbl] unzugänglich.

unapt □ ['An'æpt] ungeeignet.

unashamed □ ['Anə'ʃeimd] schamlos.

unasked ['An'ɑ:skt] unverlangt; ungebeten.

unassisted □ ['Anə'sistid] ohne Hilfe od. Unterstützung.

unassuming □ ['Anə'sju:miŋ] anspruchslos, bescheiden.

unattached ['Anə'tætʃt] nicht gebunden; ungebunden, ledig, frei.

unattractive □ [Anə'træktiv] wenig anziehend, reizlos; uninteressant.

unauthorized ['An'ɔ:θəraizd] unberechtigt, unbefugt.

unavail|able ['Anə'veiləbl] nicht verfügbar; ~ing [~liŋ] vergeblich.

unavoidable □ [Anə'vɔidəbl] unvermeidlich.

unaware ['Anə'wɛə] ohne Kenntnis; be ~ of et. nicht merken; ~s [~əz] unversehens, unvermutet; versehentlich.

unbacked ['An'bækt] ohne Unterstützung, ungedeckt (Scheck).

unbag ['An'bæg] aus dem Sack holen od. lassen.

unbalanced ['An'bælənst] nicht im Gleichgewicht befindlich; unausgeglichen; geistesgestört.

unbearable □ [An'bɛərəbl] unerträglich

unbeaten ['An'bi:tn] ungeschlagen; unbetreten (Weg).

unbecoming [['Anbi'kAmiŋ] unkleidsam; unziemlich, unschicklich.

unbeknown F [Anbi'noun] unbekannt.

unbelie|f [Anbi'li:f] Unglaube m; ~vable [[Anbi'li:vəbl] unglaublich; ~ving □ ['Anbi'li:viŋ] ungläubig.

unbend ['An'bend] [irr. (bend)] (sich) entspannen; freundlich werden, auftauen; ~ing [~diŋ] unbiegsam; fig. unbeugsam.

unbias(s)ed [['An'baiəst] vorurteilsfrei, unbefangen, unbeeinflußt.

unbid(den) ['An'bid(n)] ungeheißen, unaufgefordert; ungebeten.

unbind ['An'baind] [irr. (bind)] losbinden, befreien; lösen.

unblushing □ [An'blAʃiŋ] schamlos. [boren.]

unborn ['An'bɔ:n] (noch) unge-/

unbosom [An'buzəm] offenbaren.

unbounded [[An'baundid] unbegrenzt; schrankenlos.

unbroken [['An'broukən] ungebrochen; unversehrt; ununterbrochen.

unbutton ['An'bAtn] aufknöpfen.

uncalled-for [An'kɔ:ldfɔ:] ungerufen; unverlangt (S.); unpassend.

uncanny □ [An'kæni] unheimlich.

uncared-for ['An'kɛədfɔ:] unbeachtet, vernachlässigt.

unceasing □ [An'si:siŋ] unaufhörlich.

unceremonious □ ['Anseri'mounjəs] ungezwungen; formlos.

uncertain □ [ʌn'səːtn] unsicher; ungewiß; unbestimmt; unzuverlässig; **~ty** [~nti] Unsicherheit f.

unchallenged ['ʌn'tʃælindʒd] unangefochten

unchang|eable [ʌn'tʃeindʒəbl] unveränderlich, unwandelbar; **~ed** ['ʌn'tʃeindʒd] unverändert; **~ing** □ [ʌn'tʃeindʒiŋ] unveränderlich

uncharitable [ʌn'tʃæritəbl] lieblos; unbarmherzig, unfreundlich.

unchecked [ʌn'tʃekt] ungehindert.

uncivil ['ʌn'sivl] unhöflich; **~ized** [~vilaizd] unzivilisiert

unclaimed ['ʌn'kleimd] nicht beansprucht, unzustellbar (bsd. Brief).

unclasp [ʌn'klaːsp] auf-, loshaken, auf-, losschnallen, aufmachen.

uncle ['ʌŋkl] Onkel m.

unclean ['ʌn'kliːn] unrein.

unclose ['ʌn'klouz] (sich) öffnen.

uncomely ['ʌn'kʌmli] reizlos; unpassend

uncomfortable □ [ʌn'kʌmfətəbl] unbehaglich, ungemütlich; unangenehm

uncommon □ [ʌn'kɔmən] ungewöhnlich

uncommunicative □ ['ʌnkə'mjuːnikətiv] wortkarg, schweigsam.

uncomplaining ['ʌnkəm'pleiniŋ] klaglos, ohne Murren; geduldig.

uncompromising [ʌn'kɔmprəmaiziŋ] kompromißlos

unconcern ['ʌnkən'səːn] Unbekümmertheit f; Gleichgültigkeit f; **~ed** □ [~nd] unbekümmert; unbeteiligt.

unconditional □ ['ʌnkən'diʃənl] unbedingt, bedingungslos.

unconfirmed ['ʌnkən'fəːmd] unbestätigt, eccl nicht konfirmiert.

unconnected [['ʌnkə'nektid] unverbunden

unconquer|able □ [ʌn'kɔnkərəbl] unüberwindlich; **~ed** [ʌn'kɔnkəd] unbesiegt

unconscionable □ [ʌn'kɔnʃnəbl] gewissenlos, F unverschämt, übermäßig.

unconscious □ [ʌn'kɔnʃəs] unbewußt; bewußtlos; **~ness** [~snis] Bewußtlosigkeit f

unconstitutional □ ['ʌnkɔnsti'tjuːʃənl] verfassungswidrig.

uncontroll|able □ [ʌnkən'trouləbl] unkontrollierbar, unbändig; **~ed** ['ʌnkən'trould] unbeaufsichtigt; fig. unbeherrscht

unconventional [['ʌnkən'venʃənl] unkonventionell; ungezwungen.

unconvinc|ed ['ʌnkən'vinst] nicht überzeugt, **~ing** [~siŋ] nicht überzeugend

uncork ['ʌn'kɔːk] entkorken.

uncount|able ['ʌn'kauntəbl] unzählbar, **~ed** [~tid] ungezählt.

uncouple ['ʌn'kʌpl] loskoppeln.

uncouth □ [ʌn'kuːθ] ungeschlacht.

uncover [ʌn'kʌvə] aufdecken, freilegen; entblößen.

unct|ion ['ʌŋkʃən] Salbung f (a. fig.); Salbe f; **~uous** [['ʌŋktjuəs] fettig, ölig, fig salbungsvoll.

uncult|ivated ['ʌn'kʌltiveitid], **~ured** [~tʃəd] unkultiviert.

undamaged ['ʌn'dæmidʒd] unbeschädigt

undaunted □ [ʌn'dɔːntid] unerschrocken

undeceive ['ʌndi'siːv] j-n aufklären.

undecided ['ʌndi'saidid] unentschieden, unentschlossen.

undefined [ʌndi'faind] unbestimmt, unbegrenzt

undemonstrative [['ʌndi'mɔnstrətiv] zurückhaltend.

undeniable [ʌndi'naiəbl] unleugbar; unbestreitbar.

under ['ʌndə] 1. adv. unten; darunter; 2. prp unter; 3. adj. unter; in Zssgn unter , Unter , mangelhaft ...; **~bid** [~'bid] [irr (bid)] unterbieten; **~brush** [~brʌʃ] Unterholz n, **~carriage** & (Flugzeug)Fahrwerk n, mot Fahrgestell n, **~clothes**, **~clothing** Unterkleidung f, Unterwäsche f; **~cut** [~'kʌt] Preise unterbieten; **~dog** [~dɔg] Unterlegene(r) m; Unterdrückte(r) m; **~done** [~'dʌn] nicht gar . **~estimate** [~r'estimeit] unterschätzen; **~fed** [~'fed] unterernährt, **~go** [ʌndə'gou] [irr (go)] erdulden, sich unterziehen (dat.); **~graduate** [~'grædjuit] Student (-in); **~ground** ['ʌndəgraund] 1. unterirdisch, Untergrund...; 2. Untergrundbahn f, **~growth** Unterholz n, **~hand** unter der Hand; heimlich, **~lie** [ʌndə'lai] [irr (lie)] zugrunde liegen (dat.); **~line** [~'lain] unterstreichen, **~ling** ['ʌndəliŋ] Untergeordnete(r) m; **~mine** [ʌndə'main] unterminieren; fig. untergraben, schwächen; **~most** ['ʌndəmoust] unterst; **~neath** [ʌndə'niːθ] 1. prp. unter (-halb), 2. adv unten, darunter; **~pin** [~'pin] untermauern, **~plot** ['ʌndəplɔt] Nebenhandlung f; **~privileged** [~'prividʒd] benachteiligt, **~rate** [ʌndə'reit] unterschätzen, **~secretary** [ʌndə'sekrətəri] Unterstaatssekretär m; **~sell** ✝ [~'sel] [irr (sell)] j-n unterbieten; Ware verschleudern; **~signed** [~'saind] Unterzeichnete(r) m; **~sized** [~'saizd] zu klein; **~staffed** [ʌndə'staːft] unterbesetzt; **~stand** [~ stænd] [irr (stand)] allg. verstehen, sich verstehen auf (acc.); (als sicher) annehmen, auffassen; (sinngemäß) ergänzen, make o.s. understood sich verständlich machen; an understood thing e-e abgemachte Sache, **~standable** [~dəbl] verständlich; **~standing** [~diŋ]

Verstand m; Einvernehmen n; Verständigung f; Abmachung f; Voraussetzung f; ~state ['ʌndə'steit] zu gering angeben; abschwächen; ~statement Unterbewertung f; Understatement n, Untertreibung f; ~take [ʌndə'teik] irr. (take) unternehmen; übernehmen; sich verpflichten; ~taker ['ʌndəteikə] Bestattungsinstitut n; ~taking [ʌndə'teikiŋ] Unternehmung f; Verpflichtung f; ['ʌndəteikiŋ] Leichenbestattung f; ~tone leiser Ton; ~value [ʌ'vælju:] unterschätzen; ~wear [ʌ'weə] Unterkleidung f, Unterwäsche f; ~wood Unterholz n; ~write [irr. (write)] Versicherung abschließen; ~writer Versicherer m.

undeserv|ed □ ['ʌndi'zə:vd] unverdient; ~ing [ʌ'viŋ] unwürdig.

undesigned □ [ʌndi'zaind] unabsichtlich, absichtslos.

undesirable □ [ʌndi'zairəbl] 1. □ unerwünscht; 2. unerwünschte Person.

undeviating □ [ʌn'di:vieitiŋ] unentwegt.

undignified □ [ʌn'dignifaid] würdelos.

undisciplined □ [ʌn'disiplind] zuchtlos, undiszipliniert; ungeschult.

undisguised □ ['ʌndis'gaizd] unverkleidet; unverhohlen.

undisputed □ ['ʌndis'pju:tid] unbestritten.

undo ['ʌn'du:] [irr. (do)] aufmachen; (auf)lösen; ungeschehen machen, aufheben; vernichten; ~ing [ʌ'u(:)iŋ] Aufmachen n; Ungeschehenmachen n; Vernichtung f; Verderben n; ~ne ['ʌn'dʌn] erledigt, vernichtet.

undoubted □ [ʌn'dautid] unzweifelhaft, zweifellos.

undreamt [ʌn'dremt]: ~of ungeahnt.

undress ['ʌn'dres] 1. (sich) entkleiden od. ausziehen; 2. Hauskleid n; ~ed unbekleidet; unangezogen; nicht zurechtgemacht.

undue □ ['ʌn'dju:] ungebührlich; übermäßig; ✝ noch nicht fällig.

undulat|e ['ʌndjuleit] wogen; wallen; wellig sein; ~ion [ʌndju'leiʃən] wellenförmige Bewegung.

undutiful □ ['ʌn'dju:tiful] ungehorsam, pflichtvergessen.

unearth ['ʌn'ə:θ] ausgraben; fig. aufstöbern; ~ly [ʌn'ə:θli] überirdisch.

uneas|iness [ʌn'i:zinis] Unruhe f; Unbehagen n; ~y □ [ʌn'i:zi] unbehaglich; unruhig; unsicher.

uneducated □ ['ʌn'edjukeitid] unerzogen; ungebildet.

unemotional □ ['ʌni'mouʃənl] leidenschaftslos; passiv; nüchtern.

unemploy|ed ['ʌnim'plɔid] 1. unbeschäftigt; arbeitslos; unbenutzt; 2.: the ~ pl. die Arbeitslosen pl.; ~ment [ʌ'mɔimənt] Arbeitslosigkeit f.

unending □ [ʌn'endiŋ] endlos.

unendurable □ [ʌnin'djuərəbl] unerträglich.

unengaged ['ʌnin'geidʒd] frei.

unequal □ ['ʌn'i:kwəl] ungleich; nicht gewachsen (to dat.); ~(l)ed [ʌ'ld] unvergleichlich, unerreicht.

unerring □ ['ʌn'ə:riŋ] unfehlbar.

unessential □ ['ʌni'senʃəl] unwesentlich, unwichtig (to für).

uneven □ ['ʌn'i:vən] uneben; ungleich(mäßig); ungerade (Zahl).

uneventful □ ['ʌni'ventful] ereignislos; ohne Zwischenfälle.

unexampled □ [ʌnig'za:mpld] beispiellos.

unexceptionable □ [ʌnik'sepʃnəbl] untadelig; einwandfrei.

unexpected □ ['ʌniks'pektid] unerwartet.

unexplained ['ʌniks'pleind] unerklärt.

unfading □ [ʌn'feidiŋ] nicht welkend; unvergänglich; echt (Farbe).

unfailing □ [ʌn'feiliŋ] unfehlbar; nie versagend; unerschöpflich; fig. treu.

unfair □ ['ʌn'feə] unehrlich; unfair; ungerecht.

unfaithful □ ['ʌn'feiθful] un(ge)treu, treulos; nicht wortgetreu.

unfamiliar □ ['ʌnfə'miljə] unbekannt; ungewohnt.

unfasten ['ʌn'fɑ:sn] aufmachen; lösen; ~ed unbefestigt, lose.

unfathomable □ [ʌn'fæðəməbl] unergründlich.

unfavo(u)rable □ ['ʌn'feivərəbl] ungünstig.

unfeeling □ [ʌn'fi:liŋ] gefühllos.

unfilial □ ['ʌn'filjəl] respektlos, pflichtvergessen (Kind).

unfinished □ ['ʌn'finiʃt] unvollendet; unfertig.

unfit 1. □ ['ʌn'fit] ungeeignet, unpassend; 2. ['ʌn'fit] untauglich machen.

unfix ['ʌn'fiks] losmachen, lösen.

unfledged ['ʌn'fledʒd] ungefiedert; (noch) nicht flügge; fig. unreif.

unflinching □ [ʌn'flintʃiŋ] fest entschlossen, unnachgiebig.

unfold ['ʌn'fould] (sich) entfalten od. öffnen; [ʌn'fould] klarlegen; enthüllen.

unforced □ ['ʌn'fɔ:st] ungezwungen.

unforeseen ['ʌnfɔ:'si:n] unvorhergesehen.

unforgettable □ ['ʌnfə'getəbl] unvergeßlich.

unforgiving ['ʌnfə'giviŋ] unversöhnlich.

unforgotten ['ʌnfə'gɔtn] unvergessen.

unfortunate [ʌn'fɔ:tʃnit] 1. □ un-

glücklich; 2. Unglückliche(r m) f; ~ly [~tli] unglücklicherweise, leider.
unfounded ['ʌn'faundid] unbegründet; grundlos.
unfriendly ['ʌn'frendli] unfreundlich; ungünstig.
unfurl [ʌn'fəːl] entfalten, aufrollen.
unfurnished ['ʌn'fəːniʃt] unmöbliert.
ungainly [ʌn'geinli] unbeholfen, plump.
ungenerous □ ['ʌn'dʒenərəs] unedelmütig; nicht freigebig.
ungentle ['ʌn'dʒentl] unsanft.
ungodly [[ʌn'gɔdli] gottlos.
ungovernable [[ʌn'gʌvənəbl] unlenksam, zügellos, unbändig.
ungraceful ['ʌn'greisful] ungraziös, ohne Anmut; unbeholfen.
ungracious : ['ʌn'greiʃəs] ungnädig; unfreundlich.
ungrateful [[ʌn'greitful] undankbar.
unguarded □ ['ʌn'gɑːdid] unbewacht, unvorsichtig; ungeschützt.
unguent ['ʌŋgwənt] Salbe f.
unhampered ['ʌn'hæmpəd] ungehindert [schön.]
unhandsome □ [ʌn'hænsəm] un-]
unhandy [[ʌn'hændi] unhandlich; ungeschickt, unbeholfen
unhappy [[ʌn'hæpi] unglücklich.
unharmed ['ʌn'hɑːmd] unversehrt.
unhealthy [ʌn'helθi] ungesund.
unheard-of [ʌn'həːdɔv] unerhört.
unheed|ed ['ʌn'hiːdid] unbeachtet, unbewacht, ~ing [~diŋ] sorglos.
unhesitating [[ʌn'heziteitiŋ] ohne Zögern, unbedenklich.
unholy [ʌn'houli] unheilig; gottlos.
unhono(u)red ['ʌn'ɔnəd] ungeehrt; uneingelöst (Pfand, Scheck).
unhook ['ʌn'huk] auf-, aushaken.
unhoped-for [ʌn'houptfɔː] unverhofft.
unhurt ['ʌn'həːt] unverletzt.
unicorn ['juːnikɔːn] Einhorn n.
unification [juːnifi'keiʃən] Vereinigung f, Vereinheitlichung f.
uniform ['juːnifɔːm] 1. [gleichförmig, gleichmäßig; einheitlich; 2. Dienstkleidung f; Uniform f; 3. uniformieren; ~ity [juːni'fɔːmiti] Gleichförmigkeit f, Gleichmäßigkeit f.
unify ['juːnifai] verein(ig)en; vereinheitlichen.
unilateral □ ['juːni'lætərəl] einseitig.
unimagina|ble □ [ʌni'mædʒinəbl] undenkbar; ~tive □ ['ʌni'mædʒinətiv] einfallslos.
unimportant □ ['ʌnim'pɔːtənt] unwichtig.
unimproved ['ʌnim'pruːvd] nicht kultiviert, unbebaut (Land); unverbessert.
uninformed ['ʌnin'fɔːmd] nicht unterrichtet.

uninhabit|able ['ʌnin'hæbitəbl] unbewohnbar; ~ed [~tid] unbewohnt.
uninjured ['ʌn'indʒəd] unbeschädigt, unverletzt.
unintelligible [['ʌnin'telidʒəbl] unverständlich.
unintentional [['ʌnin'tenʃənl] unabsichtlich
uninteresting □ ['ʌn'intristiŋ] uninteressant
uninterrupted □ ['ʌnintə'rʌptid] ununterbrochen.
union ['juːnjən] Vereinigung f; Verbindung f, Union f, Verband m; Einigung f, Einigkeit f; Verein m, Bund m, univ (Debattier)Klub m; Gewerkschaft f; ~ist [~nist] Gewerkschaftler m; 2 Jack Union Jack m (britische Nationalflagge); ~ suit Am Hemdhose f.
unique [[juː'niːk] einzigartig, einmalig.
unison ♪ u. fig. ['juːnizn] Einklang m.
unit ['juːnit] Einheit f; ⚡ Einer m; ~e [juː'nait] (sich) vereinigen, verbinden; ~ed vereinigt, vereint; ~y ['juːniti] Einheit f; Einigkeit f.
univers|al □ [juːni'vəːsl] allgemein; allumfassend, Universal..., Welt..., ~ality [juːnivəː'sæliti] Allgemeinheit f, umfassende Bildung, Vielseitigkeit f; ~e ['juːnivəːs] Weltall n, Universum n; ~ity [juːni'vəːsiti] Universität f
unjust ['ʌn'dʒʌst] ungerecht; ~ifiable [[ʌn'dʒʌstifaiəbl] nicht zu rechtfertigen(d), unverantwortlich.
unkempt ['ʌn'kempt] ungepflegt.
unkind □ [ʌn'kaind] unfreundlich.
unknow|ing □ ['ʌn'nouiŋ] unwissend; unbewußt; ~n [~oun] 1. unbekannt; unbewußt; ~ to me wider mein Wissen; 2. Unbekannte(r m, -s n) f.
unlace ['ʌn'leis] aufschnüren.
unlatch ['ʌn'lætʃ] aufklinken.
unlawful [['ʌn'lɔːful] ungesetzlich; weitS unrechtmäßig.
unlearn ['ʌn'ləːn] [irr. (learn)] verlernen.
unless [ən'les] wenn nicht, außer wenn; es sei denn, daß.
unlike ['ʌn'laik] 1. adj. □ ungleich; 2. prp. anders als; ~ly [ʌn'laikli] unwahrscheinlich.
unlimited □ [ʌn'limitid] unbegrenzt.
unload ['ʌn'loud] ent-, ab-, ausladen; Ladung löschen.
unlock ['ʌn'lɔk] aufschließen; Waffe entsichern; ~ed unverschlossen.
unlooked-for [ʌn'luktfɔː] unerwartet.
unloose, ~n ['ʌn'luːs, ʌn'luːsn] lösen, losmachen.
unlov|ely ['ʌn'lʌvli] reizlos, unschön; ~ing [~viŋ] lieblos.
unlucky □ [ʌn'lʌki] unglücklich.

unmake ['ʌn'meik] [irr. (make)] vernichten; rückgängig machen; umbilden; Herrscher absetzen.

unman ['ʌn'mæn] entmannen.

unmanageable □ [ʌn'mænidʒəbl] unlenksam, widerspenstig.

unmarried ['ʌn'mærid] unverheiratet, ledig.

unmask ['ʌn'mɑːsk] (sich) demaskieren; fig. entlarven.

unmatched ['ʌn'mætʃt] unerreicht; unvergleichlich.

unmeaning □ [ʌn'miːniŋ] nichtssagend.

unmeasured [ʌn'meʒəd] ungemessen; unermeßlich.

unmeet ['ʌn'miːt] ungeeignet.

unmentionable [ʌn'menʃnəbl] nicht zu erwähnen(d), unnennbar.

unmerited ['ʌn'meritid] unverdient.

unmindful □ [ʌn'maindful] unbedacht; sorglos; ohne Rücksicht.

unmistakable □ ['ʌnmis'teikəbl] unverkennbar; unmißverständlich.

unmitigated [ʌn'mitigeitid] ungemildert; richtig; fig. Erz...

unmolested ['ʌnmou'lestid] unbelästigt.

unmounted ['ʌn'mauntid] unberitten; nicht gefaßt (Stein); unaufgezogen (Bild); unmontiert.

unmoved □ ['ʌn'muːvd] unbewegt, ungerührt.

unnamed ['ʌn'neimd] ungenannt.

unnatural □ [ʌn'nætʃrəl] unnatürlich.

unnecessary □ [ʌn'nesisəri] unneighbo(u)rly ['ʌn'neibəli] nicht gutnachbarlich.

unnerve ['ʌn'nəːv] entnerven.

unnoticed ['ʌn'noutist] unbemerkt.

unobjectionable □ ['ʌnəb'dʒekʃnəbl] einwandfrei.

unobservant □ ['ʌnəb'zəːvənt] unachtsam; ~ed [~vd] unbemerkt.

unobtainable ['ʌnəb'teinəbl] unerreichbar.

unobtrusive □ ['ʌnəb'truːsiv] unaufdringlich, bescheiden.

unoccupied ['ʌn'ɔkjupaid] unbesetzt; unbewohnt; unbeschäftigt.

unoffending ['ʌnə'fendiŋ] harmlos.

unofficial □ ['ʌnə'fiʃəl] nichtamtlich, inoffiziell.

unopposed ['ʌnə'pouzd] ungehindert.

unostentatious □ ['ʌnɔstən'teiʃəs] anspruchslos; unauffällig; schlicht.

unowned ['ʌn'ound] herrenlos.

unpack ['ʌn'pæk] auspacken.

unpaid ['ʌn'peid] unbezahlt; unbelohnt; & unfrankiert.

unparalleled [ʌn'pærəleld] beispiellos, ohnegleichen.

unperceived □ ['ʌnpə'siːvd] unbemerkt.

unperturbed ['ʌnpə(ː)'təːbd] ruhig, gelassen.

unpleasant □ [ʌn'pleznt] unangenehm; unerfreulich; ~ness [~tnis] Unannehmlichkeit f.

unpolished ['ʌn'pɔliʃt] unpoliert; fig. ungebildet.

unpolluted ['ʌnpə'luːtid] unbefleckt.

unpopular □ ['ʌn'pɔpjulə] unpopulär, unbeliebt; ~ity ['ʌnpɔpju'læriti] Unbeliebtheit f.

unpractical □ ['ʌn'præktikəl] unpraktisch; ~sed, Am. ~ced [ʌn'præktist] ungeübt.

unprecedented □ [ʌn'presidəntid] beispiellos; noch nie dagewesen.

unprejudiced □ [ʌn'predʒudist] unbefangen, unvoreingenommen.

unpremeditated □ ['ʌnpri'mediteitid] unbeabsichtigt.

unprepared □ ['ʌnpri'pɛəd] unvorbereitet.

unpretending [ʌn'pritendiŋ], ~tious □ [~nʃəs] anspruchslos.

unprincipled [ʌn'prinsəpld] ohne Grundsätze; gewissenlos.

unprivileged [ʌn'privilidʒd] sozial benachteiligt; arm.

unprofitable □ [ʌn'prɔfitəbl] unnütz.

unproved ['ʌn'pruːvd] unerwiesen.

unprovided ['ʌnprə'vaidid] nicht versehen (with mit); ~ for unversorgt, mittellos.

unprovoked □ ['ʌnprə'voukt] ohne Grund.

unqualified □ ['ʌn'kwɔlifaid] ungeeignet; unberechtigt; [ʌn'kwɔlifaid] unbeschränkt.

unquestionable □ [ʌn'kwestʃənəbl] unzweifelhaft, fraglos; ~ed [~nd] ungefragt; unbestritten.

unquote ['ʌn'kwout] Zitat beenden.

unravel [ʌn'rævəl] (sich) entwirren; enträtseln.

unready □ ['ʌn'redi] nicht bereit od. fertig; unlustig, zögernd.

unreal □ ['ʌn'riəl] unwirklich; ~istic ['ʌnriə'listik] (~ally) wirklichkeitsfremd, unrealistisch.

unreasonable □ [ʌn'riːznəbl] unvernünftig; grundlos; unmäßig.

unrecognizable □ ['ʌn'rekəgnaizəbl] nicht wiederzuerkennen(d).

unredeemed □ ['ʌnri'diːmd] unerlöst; uneingelöst; ungemildert.

unrefined ['ʌnri'faind] ungeläutert; fig. ungebildet. [dankenlos.]

unreflecting □ ['ʌnri'flektiŋ] ge-]

unregarded ['ʌnri'gɑːdid] unbeachtet; unberücksichtigt.

unrelated ['ʌnri'leitid] ohne Beziehung (to zu).

unrelenting □ ['ʌnri'lentiŋ] erbarmungslos; unerbittlich.

unreliable ['ʌnri'laiəbl] unzuverlässig.

unrelieved □ ['ʌnri'liːvd] ungelindert; ununterbrochen.

unremitting □ [ʌnri'mitiŋ] unablässig, unaufhörlich; unermüdlich.

unrepining □ ['ʌnri'painiŋ] klaglos; unverdrossen.

unrequited □ ['ʌnri'kwaitid] unerwidert; unbelohnt.

unreserved □ ['ʌnri'zəːvd] rückhaltlos; unbeschränkt; ohne Vorbehalt.

unresisting □ ['ʌnri'zistiŋ] widerstandslos.

unresponsive ['ʌnris'ponsiv] unempfänglich (to für).

unrest ['ʌn'rest] Unruhe f.

unrestrained ['ʌnris'treind] ungehemmt; unbeschränkt.

unrestricted ['ʌnris'triktid] uneingeschränkt.

unriddle ['ʌn'ridl] enträtseln.

unrighteous □ ['ʌn'raitʃəs] ungerecht; unredlich.

unripe ['ʌn'raip] unreif.

unrival(l)ed [ʌn'raivəld] unvergleichlich, unerreicht, einzigartig.

unroll ['ʌn'roul] ent-, aufrollen.

unruffled ['ʌn'rʌfld] glatt; ruhig.

unruly [ʌn'ruːli] ungebärdig.

unsafe □, ['ʌn'seif] unsicher.

unsal(e)able ['ʌn'seiləbl] unverkäuflich.

unsanitary ['ʌn'sænitəri] unhygienisch.

unsatis|factory □ ['ʌnsætis'fæktəri] unbefriedigend; unzulänglich; **~ied** ['ʌn'sætisfaid] unbefriedigt; **~ying** [,~iiŋ] = unsatisfactory.

unsavo(u)ry □ ['ʌn'seivəri] unappetitlich (a. fig.), widerwärtig.

unsay ['ʌn'sei] [irr. (say)] zurücknehmen, widerrufen.

unscathed ['ʌn'skeiðd] unversehrt.

unschooled ['ʌn'skuːld] ungeschult; unverbildet.

unscrew ['ʌn'skruː] v/t. ab-, los-, aufschrauben; v/i. sich abschrauben lassen.

unscrupulous □ [ʌn'skruːpjuləs] bedenkenlos; gewissenlos; skrupellos.

unsearchable □ [ʌn'səːtʃəbl] unerforschlich; unergründlich.

unseason|able □ [ʌn'siːznəbl] unzeitig; fig. ungelegen; **~ed** ['ʌn'siːznd] nicht abgelagert (Holz); fig. nicht abgehärtet; ungewürzt.

unseat ['ʌn'siːt] des Amtes entheben; abwerfen.

unseemly [ʌn'siːmli] unziemlich.

unseen ['ʌn'siːn] ungesehen; unsichtbar.

unselfish □ ['ʌn'selfiʃ] selbstlos, uneigennützig; **~ness** [,~nis] Selbstlosigkeit f.

unsettle ['ʌn'setl] in Unordnung

bringen; verwirren; erschüttern; **~d** nicht festgesetzt; unbeständig; ✝ unbezahlt; unerledigt; ohne festen Wohnsitz; unbesiedelt.

unshaken ['ʌn'ʃeikən] unerschüttert; unerschütterlich.

unshaven ['ʌn'ʃeivn] unrasiert.

unship ['ʌn'ʃip] ausschiffen.

unshrink|able ['ʌn'ʃriŋkəbl] nicht einlaufend (Stoff); **~ing** □ [ʌn'ʃriŋkiŋ] unverzagt.

unsightly [ʌn'saitli] häßlich.

unskil(l)ful □ ['ʌn'skilful] ungeschickt; **~led** [,~ld] ungelernt.

unsoci|able [ʌn'souʃəbl] ungesellig; **~al** [,~əl] ungesellig; unsozial.

unsolder [ʌn'soldə] los-, ablöten.

unsolicited [ʌnsə'lisitid] nicht gefragt (S.); unaufgefordert (P.).

unsolv|able [ʌn'solvəbl] unlösbar; **~ed** [,~vd] ungelöst.

unsophisticated [ʌnsə'fistikeitid] unverfälscht, ungekünstelt; unverdorben, unverbildet.

unsound □ ['ʌn'saund] ungesund; verdorben; wurmstichig; morsch; nicht stichhaltig (Beweis); verkehrt.

unsparing □ [ʌn'spɛəriŋ] freigebig; schonungslos, unbarmherzig.

unspeakable □ [ʌn'spiːkəbl] unsagbar, unsäglich.

unspent ['ʌn'spent] unverbraucht; unerschöpft.

unspoil|ed, **~t** ['ʌn'spoilt] unverdorben; unbeschädigt; nicht verzogen (Kind).

unspoken ['ʌn'spouken] ungesagt; **~of** unerwähnt.

unstable □ ['ʌn'steibl] nicht (stand)fest; unbeständig; unstet(ig); labil.

unsteady □ ['ʌn'stedi] unstet(ig), unsicher; schwankend; unbeständig; unsolid; unregelmäßig.

unstrained ['ʌn'streind] unfiltriert; fig. ungezwungen.

unstrap ['ʌn'stræp] los-, abschnallen.

unstressed ['ʌn'strest] unbetont.

unstring ['ʌn'striŋ] [irr. (string)] Saite entspannen.

unstudied ['ʌn'stʌdid] ungesucht, ungekünstelt, natürlich.

unsubstantial □ ['ʌnsəb'stænʃəl] wesenlos, gegenstandslos; inhaltlos; gehaltlos, dürftig.

unsuccessful □ ['ʌnsək'sesful] erfolglos, ohne Erfolg.

unsuitable □ ['ʌn'sjuːtəbl] unpassend; unangemessen.

unsurpassed ['ʌnsə(ː)'pɑːst] unübertroffen.

unsuspect|ed ['ʌnsəs'pektid] unverdächtig; unvermutet; **~ing** [,~tiŋ] nichts ahnend; arglos.

unsuspicious □ ['ʌnsəs'piʃəs] nicht argwöhnisch, arglos.

unswerving ☐ [ʌn'swəːviŋ] unentwegt.

untangle ['ʌn'tæŋgl] entwirren.

untarnished ['ʌn'tɑːniʃt] unbefleckt; ungetrübt.

unteachable ['ʌn'tiːtʃəbl] unbelehrbar (P.); unlehrbar (S.).

untenanted ['ʌn'tənəntid] unvermietet, unbewohnt.

unthankful ☐ ['ʌn'θæŋkful] undankbar.

unthink|able ['ʌn'θiŋkəbl] undenkbar; **~ing** ['ʌn'θiŋkiŋ] gedankenlos.

unthought ['ʌn'θɔːt] unbedacht; **~of** unvermutet.

unthrifty ☐ ['ʌn'θrifti] verschwenderisch; nicht gedeihend.

untidy ☐ [ʌn'taidi] unordentlich.

untie ['ʌn'tai] aufbinden, aufknüpfen; *Knoten etc.* lösen; *j-n* losbinden.

until [ən'til] 1. *prp.* bis; 2. *cj.* bis (daß); *not* ~ erst wenn *od.* als.

untimely [ʌn'taimli] unzeitig; vorzeitig; ungelegen. [lich.)

untiring ☐ [ʌn'taiəriŋ] unermüd-)

unto ['ʌntu] = to.

untold ['ʌn'tould] unerzählt; ungezählt; unermeßlich, unsäglich.

untouched ['ʌn'tʌtʃt] unberührt; *fig.* ungerührt; *phot.* unretuschiert.

untried ['ʌn'traid] unversucht; unerprobt; ⚖ noch nicht verhört.

untrod, ~den ['ʌn'trɔd, ~dn] unbetreten.

untroubled ['ʌn'trʌbld] ungestört.

untrue ☐ ['ʌn'truː] unwahr; untreu.

untrustworthy ☐ ['ʌn'trʌstwəːði] unzuverlässig, nicht vertrauenswürdig.

unus|ed ['ʌn'juːzd] ungebraucht; [~uːst] nicht gewöhnt (*to* an *acc.*; *zu inf.*); **~ual** ☐ [ʌn'juːʒuəl] ungewöhnlich; ungewohnt.

unutterable ☐ [ʌn'ʌtərəbl] unaussprechlich.

unvarnished *fig.* ['ʌn'vɑːniʃt] ungeschminkt.

unvarying ☐ [ʌn'veəriiŋ] unveränderlich.

unveil [ʌn'veil] entschleiern, enthüllen.

unversed ['ʌn'vəːst] unbewandert, unerfahren (*in* in *dat.*).

unvouched ['ʌn'vautʃt] *a.* **~for** unverbürgt, unbezeugt.

unwanted ['ʌn'wɔntid] unerwünscht.

unwarrant|able ☐ [ʌn'wɔrəntəbl] unverantwortlich; **~ed** [~tid] unberechtigt; ['ʌn'wɔrəntid] unverbürgt.

unwary ☐ [ʌn'weəri] unbedachtsam.

unwelcome [ʌn'welkəm] unwillkommen.

unwholesome ['ʌn'houlsəm] ungesund; schädlich.

unwieldy ☐ [ʌn'wiːldi] unhandlich; ungefüge; sperrig.

unwilling ☐ ['ʌn'wiliŋ] un-, widerwillig, abgeneigt.

unwind ['ʌn'waind] [*irr.* (*wind*)] auf-, loswickeln; (sich) abwickeln.

unwise ☐ ['ʌn'waiz] unklug.

unwitting ☐ [ʌn'witiŋ] unwissentlich; unbeabsichtigt.

unworkable ['ʌn'wəːkəbl] undurchführbar; ⊕ nicht betriebsfähig.

unworthy ☐ [ʌn'wəːði] unwürdig.

unwrap ['ʌn'ræp] auswickeln, auspacken, aufwickeln.

unwrought ['ʌn'rɔːt] unbearbeitet; roh; Roh...

unyielding ☐ [ʌn'jiːldiŋ] unnachgiebig.

up [ʌp] 1. *adv.* (her-, hin)auf; aufwärts, empor; oben; auf(gestanden); aufgegangen (*Sonne*); hoch; abgelaufen, um (*Zeit*); *Am. Baseball*: am Schlag; *and about* wieder auf den Beinen; *be hard* ~ in Geldschwierigkeiten sein; ~ *against a task* e-r Aufgabe gegenüber; ~ *to* bis (zu); *it is* ~ *to me to do es ist* an mir, zu tun; *what are you* ~ *to there?* was macht ihr da? *what's* ~? *sl.* was ist los? 2. *prp.* hinauf; ~ *the river* flußaufwärts; 3. *adj.*: ~ *train* Zug *m* nach der Stadt; 4.: *the* ~*s and downs* das Auf und Ab, die Höhen und Tiefen *des Lebens*; 5. F (sich) erheben; hochfahren; hochtreiben.

up|-and-coming *Am.* F ['ʌpən'kʌmiŋ] unternehmungslustig; **~braid** [ʌp'breid] schelten; **~bringing** ['ʌpbriŋiŋ] Erziehung *f*; **~country** ['ʌp'kʌntri] landeinwärts (gelegen); **~heaval** [ʌp'hiːvl] Umbruch *m*; **~hill** ['ʌp'hil] bergan; mühsam; **~hold** [ʌp'hould] [*irr.* (*hold*)] aufrecht(er)halten; stützen; **~holster** [ʌp'houlstə] (auf)polstern; *Zimmer* dekorieren; **~holsterer** [~rə] Tapezierer *m*, Dekorateur *m*, Polsterer *m*; **~holstery** [~ri] Polstermöbel *n/pl.*; Möbelstoffe *m/pl.*; Tapeziererarbeit *f*.

up|keep ['ʌpkiːp] Instandhaltung(skosten *pl.*) *f*; Unterhalt *m*; **~land** ['ʌplənd] Hoch-, Oberland *n*; **~lift** 1. [ʌp'lift] (empor-, er)heben; 2. ['ʌplift] Erhebung *f*; *fig.* Aufschwung *m*.

upon [ə'pɔn] = on.

upper ['ʌpə] ober; Ober...; **~most** oberst, höchst.

up|raise [ʌp'reiz] erheben; **~rear** [ʌp'riə] aufrichten; **~right** 1. ☐ ['ʌp'rait] aufrecht; ~ *piano ♪* Klavier *n*; *fig.* ['ʌprait] rechtschaffen; 2. Pfosten *m*; Ständer *m*; **~rising** [ʌp'raiziŋ] Erhebung *f*, Aufstand *m*.

uproar ['ʌprɔː] Aufruhr *m*; **~ious** ☐ [ʌp'rɔːriəs] tobend; tosend.

up|root [ʌp'ru:t] entwurzeln; (her-) ausreißen; ~set [ʌp'set] [irr. (set)] umwerfen; (um)stürzen; außer Fassung od. in Unordnung bringen; stören; verwirren; be ~ außer sich sein; ~shot ['ʌpʃɔt] Ausgang m; ~side ['ʌpsaid] adv.: ~ down das Oberste zuunterst; verkehrt; ~stairs ['ʌp'steəz] die Treppe hinauf, (nach) oben; ~start ['ʌpstɑːt] Emporkömmling m; ~state Am. ['ʌp'steit] Hinterland n e-s Staates; ~stream ['ʌp'striːm] fluß-, stromaufwärts; ~-to-date ['ʌptə'deit] modern, neuzeitlich; ~town ['ʌp'taun] im od. in den oberen Stadtteil; Am. im Wohn- od. Villenviertel; ~turn [ʌp'təːn] nach oben kehren; ~ward(s) ['ʌpwəd(z)] aufwärts (gerichtet).

uranium ⚛ [juə'reinjəm] Uran n.
urban ['əːbən] städtisch; Stadt...; ~e □ [əː'bein] höflich; gebildet.
urchin ['əːtʃin] Bengel m.
urge [əːdʒ] 1. oft ~ on j-n drängen, (an)treiben; dringen in j-n; dringen auf et.; Recht geltend machen; 2. Drang m; ~ncy ['əːdʒənsi] Dringlichkeit f; Drängen n; ~nt □ [~nt] dringend; dringlich; eilig.
urin|al ['juərinl] Harnglas n; Bedürfnisanstalt f; ~ate [~neit] urinieren; ~e [~in] Urin m, Harn m.
urn [əːn] Urne f; Tee- etc. Maschine f.
us [ʌs, əs] uns; of ~ unser.
usage ['juːzidʒ] Brauch m, Gepflogenheit f; Sprachgebrauch m; Behandlung f, Verwendung f, Gebrauch m.
usance ⚓ ['juːzəns] Wechselfrist f.
use 1. [juːs] Gebrauch m; Benutzung f; Verwendung f; Gewohnheit f, Übung f; Brauch m; Nutzen m; (of) no ~ unnütz, zwecklos; have no ~ for keine Verwendung haben

für; Am. F nicht mögen; 2. [juːz] gebrauchen; benutzen, ver-, anwenden; behandeln; ~ up ver-, aufbrauchen; I ~d to do ich pflegte zu tun, früher tat ich; ~d [juːzd] ge-, verbraucht; [juːst] gewöhnt (to an acc.); gewohnt (to zu od. acc.); ~ful □ ['juːsful] brauchbar; nützlich; Nutz...; ~less □ ['juːslis] nutz-, zwecklos, unnütz.
usher ['ʌʃə] 1. Türhüter m, Pförtner m; Gerichtsdiener m; Platzanweiser m; 2. mst. ~ in (hin)einführen, anmelden; ~ette [ʌʃə'ret] Platzanweiserin f.
usual □ ['juːʒuəl] gewöhnlich; üblich; gebräuchlich.
usurer □ ['juːʒərə] Wucherer m.
usurp [juː'zəːp] sich et. widerrechtlich aneignen, an sich reißen; ~er [~pə] Usurpator m.
usury ['juːʒuri] Wucher(zinsen pl.) m.
utensil [ju(ː)'tensl] Gerät n; Geschirr n.
uterus anat. ['juːtərəs] Gebärmutter f.
utility [ju(ː)'tiliti] 1. Nützlichkeit f, Nutzen m; public ~ öffentlicher Versorgungsbetrieb; 2. Gebrauchs..., Einheits...
utiliz|ation [juːtilai'zeiʃən] Nutzbarmachung f; Nutzanwendung f; ~e ['juːtilaiz] sich et. zunutze machen.
utmost ['ʌtmoust] äußerst.
Utopian [juː'toupjən] 1. utopisch; 2. Utopist(in), Schwärmer(in).
utter ['ʌtə] 1. □ fig. äußerst; völlig, gänzlich; 2. äußern; Seufzer etc. ausstoßen, von sich geben; Falschgeld etc. in Umlauf setzen; ~ance ['ʌtərəns] Äußerung f, Ausdruck m; Aussprache f; ~most ['ʌtəmoust] äußerst.
uvula anat. ['juːvjulə] Zäpfchen n.

V

vacan|cy ['veikənsi] Leere f; leerer od. freier Platz; Lücke f; offene Stelle; ~t □ [~nt] leer (a. fig.); frei (Zeit, Zimmer); offen (Stelle); unbesetzt, vakant (Amt).
vacat|e [və'keit, Am. 'veikeit] räumen; Stelle aufgeben, aus e-m Amt scheiden; ~ion [və'keiʃən, Am. vei'keiʃən] 1. (Schul)Ferien pl.; bsd. Am. Urlaub m; Räumung f; Niederlegung f e-s Amtes; 2. Am. Urlaub machen; ~ionist Am. [~nist] Ferienreisende(r m) f.
vaccin|ate ['væksineit] impfen;

~ation [væksi'neiʃən] Impfung f; ~e ['væksiːn] Impfstoff m.
vacillate ['væsileit] schwanken.
vacu|ous □ ['vækjuəs] fig. leer, geistlos; ~um phys. [~uəm] Vakuum n; ~ cleaner Staubsauger m; ~ flask, ~ bottle Thermosflasche f.
vagabond ['vægəbɔnd] 1. vagabundierend; 2. Landstreicher m.
vagary ['veigəri] wunderlicher Einfall, Laune f, Schrulle f.
vagrant ['veigrənt] 1. wandernd; fig. unstet; 2. Landstreicher m, Vagabund m; Strolch m.
vague □ [veig] unbestimmt; unklar.

vain ☐ [vein] eitel, eingebildet; leer; nichtig; vergeblich; *in* ~ vergebens, umsonst; **~glorious** ☐ [vein'glɔːriəs] prahlerisch.

vale [veil] *poet. od. in Namen*: Tal *n*.

valediction [væli'dikʃən] Abschied(sworte *n/pl.*) *m*.

valentine ['vælɔntain] Valentinsschatz *m*, -gruß *m* (*am Valentinstag, 14. Februar, erwählt, gesandt.*).

valerian ♀ [və'liəriən] Baldrian *m*.

valet ['vælit] 1. (Kammer)Diener *m*; 2. Diener sein bei *j-m*; *j-n* bedienen.

valetudinarian ['vælitjuːdi'nɛəriən] 1. kränklich; 2. kränklicher Mensch; Hypochonder *m*.

valiant ☐ ['væljənt] tapfer.

valid ☐ ['vælid] triftig, richtig, stichhaltig; (rechts)gültig; *be* ~ gelten; **~ity** [və'liditi] Gültigkeit *f*; Triftig-, Richtigkeit *f*.

valise [və'liːz] Reisetasche *f*; ✕ Tornister *m*.

valley ['væli] Tal *n*.

valo(u)r ['vælə] Tapferkeit *f*.

valuable ['væljuəbl] 1. ☐ wertvoll; 2. **~s** *pl*. Wertsachen *f/pl*.

valuation [vælju'eiʃən] Abschätzung *f*; Taxwert *m*.

value ['væljuː] 1. Wert *m*; Währung *f*; *give (get) good* ~ (*for one's money*) ✝ reell bedienen (bedient werden); 2. (ab)schätzen; *fig.* schätzen; **~less** [~julis] wertlos.

valve [vælv] Klappe *f*; Ventil *n*; *Radio*: Röhre *f*.

vamoose *Am. sl.* [və'muːs] *v/i.* abhauen; *v/t.* räumen (*verlassen*).

vamp F [væmp] 1. Vamp *m* (*verführerische Frau*); 2. neppen.

vampire ['væmpaiə] Vampir *m*.

van [væn] Möbelwagen *m*; Lieferwagen *m*; 🚃 Pack-, Güterwagen *m*; ✕ Vorhut *f*.

vane [vein] Wetterfahne *f*; (Windmühlen-, Propeller)Flügel *m*.

vanguard ✕ ['vængɑːd] Vorhut *f*.

vanilla ♀ [və'nilə] Vanille *f*.

vanish ['væniʃ] (ver)schwinden.

vanity ['væniti] Eitelkeit *f*, Einbildung *f*; Nichtigkeit *f*; ~ *bag* Kosmetiktäschchen *n*.

vanquish ['væŋkwiʃ] besiegen.

vantage ['vɑːntidʒ] *Tennis*: Vorteil *m*; **~ground** günstige Stellung.

vapid ☐ ['væpid] schal; fad(e).

vapor|ize ['veipəraiz] verdampfen, verdunsten (lassen); **~ous** ☐ [~rəs] dunstig; nebelhaft.

vapo(u)r ['veipə] Dunst *m*; Dampf *m*.

varia|ble ['vɛəriəbl] veränderlich; **~nce** [~əns] Veränderung *f*; Uneinigkeit *f*; *be at* ~ uneinig sein; (sich) widersprechen; *set at* ~ entzweien; **~nt** [~nt] 1. abweichend; 2. Variante *f*; **~tion** [vɛəri'eiʃən]

Abänderung *f*; Schwankung *f*; Abweichung *f*; ♪ Variation *f*.

varicose ♂ ['værikous] Krampfader(n)...; ~ *vein* Krampfader *f*.

varie|d ☐ ['vɛərid] verschieden, verändert, mannigfaltig, **~gate** [~igeit] bunt gestalten; **~ty** [və'raiəti] Mannigfaltigkeit *f*, Vielzahl *f*; *biol*. Abart *f*; ✝ Auswahl *f*; Menge *f*; ~ *show* Varietévorstellung *f*; ~ *theatre* Varieté(theater) *n*.

various ☐ ['vɛəriəs] verschiedene, mehrere; mannigfaltig; verschiedenartig. [Racker.]

varmint *sl.* ['vɑːmint] *kleiner*

varnish ['vɑːniʃ] 1. Firnis *m*, Lack *m*; *fig.* (äußerer) Anstrich; 2. firnissen, lackieren; *fig.* beschönigen.

vary ['vɛəri] (sich) (ver)ändern; wechseln (mit *et.*); abweichen.

vase [vɑːz] Vase *f*.

vassal ['væsəl] Vasall *m*; *attr.* Vasallen...

vast ☐ [vɑːst] ungeheuer, gewaltig, riesig, umfassend, weit.

vat [væt] Faß *n*; Bottich *m*; Kufe *f*.

vaudeville *Am.* ['voudəvil] Varieté *n*.

vault [vɔːlt] 1. Gewölbe *n*; Wölbung *f*; Stahlkammer *f*; Gruft *f*; *bsd. Sport*: Sprung *m*; *wine-*~ Weinkeller *m*; 2. (über)wölben; *bsd. Sport*: springen (über *acc.*).

vaulting-horse ['vɔːltiŋhɔːs] *Turnen*: Pferd *n*.

vaunt *lit.* [vɔːnt] (sich) rühmen.

veal [viːl] Kalbfleisch *n*; *roast* ~ Kalbsbraten *m*.

veer [viə] (sich) drehen.

vegeta|ble ['vedʒitəbl] 1. Pflanzen..., pflanzlich; 2. Pflanze *f*; *mst* ~*s pl*. Gemüse *n*; **~rian** [vedʒi'tɛəriən] 1. Vegetarier(in); 2. vegetarisch; **~te** ['vedʒiteit] vegetieren; **~tive** [~tətiv] vegetativ; wachstumsfördernd.

vehemen|ce ['viːiməns] Heftigkeit *f*; Gewalt *f*; **~t** ☐ [~nt] heftig; ungestüm.

vehicle ['viːikl] Fahrzeug *n*, Beförderungsmittel *n*; *fig.* Vermittler *m*, Träger *m*; Ausdrucksmittel *n*.

veil [veil] 1. Schleier *m*; Hülle *f*; 2. (sich) verschleiern (a. fig.).

vein [vein] Ader *f* (a. fig.); Anlage *f*; Neigung *f*; Stimmung *f*.

velocipede [vi'lɔsipiːd] *Am.* (Kinder)Dreirad *n*; *hist.* Veloziped *n*.

velocity [vi'lɔsiti] Geschwindigkeit *f*.

velvet ['velvit] 1. Samt *m*; *hunt.* Bast *m*; 2. Samt...; samten; **~y** [~ti] samtig.

venal ['viːnl] käuflich, feil.

vend [vend] verkaufen; **~er**, **~or** ['vendə, ~dɔː] Verkäufer *m*, Händler *m*.

veneer [vi'niə] 1. Furnier *n*; 2. furnieren; *fig.* bemänteln.

venera|ble □ ['venərəbl] ehrwür-
dig; **~te** [~reit] (ver)ehren; **~tion**
[venə'reiʃən] Verehrung f.
venereal [vi'niəriəl] Geschlechts...
Venetian [vi'ni:ʃən] 1. venetianisch;
~ blind (Stab)Jalousie f; 2. Vene-
tianer(in).

vengeance ['vendʒəns] Rache f;
with a ~ F und wie, ganz gehörig.
venial □ ['vi:njəl] verzeihlich.
venison ['venzn] Wildbret n.
venom ['venəm] (bsd. Schlangen-)
Gift n; fig. Gift n; Gehässigkeit f;
~ous □ [~məs] giftig.
venous ['vi:nəs] Venen...; venös.
vent [vent] 1. Öffnung f; Luft-,
Spundloch n; Auslaß m; Schlitz
m; **give ~ to s-m Zorn etc.** Luft
machen; 2. fig. Luft machen (dat.).
ventilat|e ['ventileit] ventilieren,
(be-, ent-, durch)lüften; fig. erörtern; **~ion** [venti'leiʃən] Ventilation f, Lüftung f; fig. Erörterung f;
~or ['ventileitə] Ventilator m.
ventral anat. ['ventrəl] Bauch...
ventriloquist [ven'trilɔkwist]
Bauchredner m.
ventur|e ['ventʃə] 1. Wagnis n;
Risiko n; Abenteuer n; Spekulation f; **at a ~** auf gut Glück;
2. (sich) wagen; riskieren; **~esome**
□ [~əsəm], **~ous** □ [~ərəs] verwegen, kühn.
veracious □ [ve'reiʃəs] wahrhaft.
verb gr. [və:b] Verb(um) n, Zeit-
wort n; **~al** □ ['və:bəl] wörtlich;
mündlich; **~iage** [~biidʒ] Wortschwall m; **~ose** □ [və:'bous] wortreich. [reif.\]
verdant □ ['və:dənt] grün; fig. un-\
verdict ['və:dikt] 醋 (Urteils-)
Spruch m der Geschworenen; fig.
Urteil n; **bring in od. return a ~ of
guilty** auf schuldig erkennen.
verdigris ['və:digris] Grünspan m.
verdure ['və:dʒə] Grün n.
verge [və:dʒ] 1. Rand m, Grenze f;
on the ~ of am Rande (gen.); dicht
vor (dat.); 2. sich (hin)neigen;
~ (up)on grenzen an (acc.).
veri|fy ['verifai] (nach)prüfen; be-
weisen; bestätigen; **~similitude**
[verisi'militju:d] Wahrscheinlichkeit f; **~table** □ ['veritəbl] wahr
(-haftig).
vermic|elli [və:mi'seli] Faden-
nudeln f/pl.; **~ular** [və:'mikjulə]
wurmartig.
vermilion [və'miljən] 1. Zinnoberrot n; 2. zinnoberrot.
vermin ['və:min] Ungeziefer n;
hunt. Raubzeug n; fig. Gesindel n;
~ous □ [~nəs] voller Ungeziefer.
vernacular [və'nækjulə] 1. □ einheimisch; Volks...; 2. Landes-,
Muttersprache f; Jargon m.
versatile □ ['və:sətail] wendig.
verse [və:s] Vers(e pl.) m; Strophe f;
Dichtung f; **~d** [və:st] bewandert.

versify ['və:sifai] v/t. in Verse bringen; v/i. Verse machen.
version ['və:ʃən] Übersetzung f;
Fassung f, Darstellung f; Lesart f.
versus bsd. 醋 ['və:səs] gegen.
vertebra anat. ['və:tibrə], pl. **~e**
[~ri:] Wirbel m.
vertical □ ['və:tikəl] vertikal, senkrecht.
vertig|inous [və:'tidʒinəs]
schwindlig; schwindelnd (Höhe);
~o ['və:tigou] Schwindel(anfall) m.
verve [vəʌv] Schwung m, Verve f.
very ['veri] 1. adv. sehr; **the ~ best**
das allerbeste; 2. adj. wirklich;
eben; bloß; **the ~ same** ebenderse-
be; **in the ~ act** auf frischer Tat;
gerade dabei; **the ~ thing** gerade
das; **the ~ thought** der bloße Gedanke; **the ~ stones** sogar die Steine;
the veriest rascal der größte Schuft.
vesicle ['vesikl] Bläs-chen n.
vessel ['vesl] Gefäß n (a. anat., ⚘,
fig.); ⊕ Fahrzeug n, Schiff n.
vest [vest] 1. Unterhemd n; Weste f;
2. v/t. bekleiden (with mit); j-n einsetzen (in in acc.); et. übertragen
(in s.o. j-m); v/i. verliehen werden.
vestibule ['vestibju:l] Vorhof m
(a. anat.); Vorhalle f; Hausflur m;
bsd. Am. 🚃 Korridor m zwischen
zwei D-Zug-Wagen; **~ train** D-Zug
m.
vestige ['vestidʒ] Spur f.
vestment ['vestmənt] Gewand n.
vestry ['vestri] eccl. Sakristei f;
Gemeindevertretung f; Gemeinde-
saal m; **~man** Gemeindevertreter m.
vet F [vet] 1. Tierarzt m; Am. ✗
Veteran m; 2. co. verarzten; gründlich prüfen.
veteran ['vetərən] 1. ausgedient;
erfahren; 2. Veteran m.
veterinary ['vetərinəri] 1. tierärzt-
lich; 2. a. **~ surgeon** Tierarzt m.
veto ['vi:tou] 1. pl. **~es** Veto n;
2. sein Veto einlegen gegen.
vex [veks] ärgern; schikanieren;
~ation [vek'seiʃən] Verdruß m;
Ärger(nis n) m; **~atious** [~ʃəs]
ärgerlich.
via [vaiə] über, via.
viaduct ['vaiədʌkt] Viadukt m,
Überführung f.
vial ['vaiəl] Phiole f, Fläschchen n.
viand ['vaiənd] mst. **~s** pl. Lebensmittel n/pl.
vibrat|e [vai'breit] vibrieren; zit-
tern; **~ion** [~eiʃən] Schwingung f,
Zittern n, Vibrieren n, Erschütterung f.
vicar eccl. ['vikə] Vikar m; **~age**
[~əridʒ] Pfarrhaus n.
vice¹ [vais] Laster n; Fehler m;
Unart f; ⊕ Schraubstock m.
vice² prp. ['vaisi] an Stelle von.
vice³ [vais] F Stellvertreter m; attr.
Vize..., Unter...; **~roy** ['vaisrɔi]
Vizekönig m.

vice versa ['vaisi'vəːsə] umgekehrt.
vicinity [vi'siniti] Nachbarschaft *f*; Nähe *f*.
vicious □ ['viʃəs] lasterhaft; bösartig; boshaft; fehlerhaft.
vicissitude [vi'sisitjuːd] Wandel *m*, Wechsel *m*; ~s *pl.* Wechselfälle *m/pl.*
victim ['viktim] Opfer *n*; ~ize [~maiz] (hin)opfern; *fig. j-n* hereinlegen.
victor ['viktə] Sieger *m*; 2ian *hist.* [vik'tɔːriən] Viktorianisch; ~ious □ [~iəs] siegreich; Sieges...; ~y ['viktəri] Sieg *m*.
victual ['vitl] 1. (sich) verpflegen *od.* verproviantieren; 2. *mst* ~s *pl.* Lebensmittel *n/pl.*, Proviant *m*; ~(l)er [~lə] Lebensmittellieferant *m*.
video ['vidiou] Fernseh...
vie [vai] wetteifern.
Viennese [vie'niːz] 1. Wiener(in); 2. Wiener...
view [vjuː] 1. Sicht *f*, Blick *m*; Besichtigung *f*; Aussicht *f* (of auf *acc.*); Anblick *m*; Ansicht *f* (a. *fig.*); Absicht *f*; at first ~ auf den ersten Blick; in ~ sichtbar, zu sehen; in ~ of im Hinblick auf (*acc.*); *fig.* angesichts (*gen.*); on ~ zu besichtigen; with a ~ to *inf. od.* of *ger.* in der Absicht zu *inf.*; have (keep) in ~ im Auge haben (behalten); 2. ansehen, besichtigen; *fig.* betrachten; ~er ['vjuːə] Betrachter(in), Zuschauer (-in); ~less ['vjuːlis] ohne eigene Meinung; *poet.* unsichtbar; ~point Gesichts-, Standpunkt *m*.
vigil ['vidʒil] Nachtwache *f*; ~ance [~ləns] Wachsamkeit *f*; ~ant □ [~nt] wachsam.
vigo|rous □ ['vigərəs] kräftig; energisch; nachdrücklich; ~(u)r ['vigə] Kraft *f*; Vitalität *f*; Nachdruck *m*.
viking ['vaikiŋ] 1. Wiking(er) *m*; 2. wikingisch, Wikinger...
vile [vail] gemein; abscheulich.
vilify ['vilifai] verunglimpfen.
village ['vilidʒ] Dorf *n*; ~ green Dorfanger *m*, -wiese *f*; ~r [~dʒə] Dorfbewohner(in).
villain ['vilən] Schurke *m*, Schuft *m*, Bösewicht *m*; ~ous □ [~nəs] schurkisch; F scheußlich; ~y [~ni] Schurkerei *f*.
vim F [vim] Schwung *m*, Schneid *m*.
vindicat|e ['vindikeit] rechtfertigen (from gegen); verteidigen; ~ion [vindi'keiʃən] Rechtfertigung *f*.
vindictive □ [vin'diktiv] rachsüchtig.
vine ♀ [vain] Wein(stock) *m*, Rebe *f*; ~gar ['vinigə] (Wein)Essig *m*; ~growing ['vaingrouiŋ] Weinbau *m*; ~yard ['vinjəd] Weinberg *m*.
vintage ['vintidʒ] 1. Weinlese *f*; (Wein)Jahrgang *m*; 2. klassisch; erlesen; altmodisch; ~ car *mot.* Veteran *m*; ~r [~dʒə] Winzer *m*.

viola ♪ [vi'oulə] Bratsche *f*.
violat|e ['vaiəleit] verletzen; Eid etc. brechen; vergewaltigen, schänden; ~ion [vaiə'leiʃən] Verletzung *f*; (Eid- etc.)Bruch *m*; Vergewaltigung *f*, Schändung *f*.
violen|ce ['vaiələns] Gewalt(samkeit, -tätigkeit) *f*; Heftigkeit *f*; ~t [~nt] gewaltsam; gewalttätig; heftig.
violet ♀ ['vaiəlit] Veilchen *n*.
violin ♪ [vaiə'lin] Violine *f*, Geige *f*.
V.I.P., VIP ['viːai'piː] F hohes Tier.
viper *zo.* ['vaipə] Viper *f*, Natter *f*.
virago [vi'raːgou] Zankteufel *m*.
virgin ['vəːdʒin] 1. Jungfrau *f*; 2. *a.* ~al □ [~nl] jungfräulich; Jungfern...; ~ity [vəː'dʒiniti] Jungfräulichkeit *f*.
viril|e ['virail] männlich; Mannes...; ~ity [vi'riliti] Männlichkeit *f*.
virtu [vəː'tuː]: article of ~ Kunstgegenstand *m*; ~al □ ['vəːtjuəl] eigentlich; ~ally [~li] praktisch; ~e ['vəːtjuː] Tugend *f*; Wirksamkeit *f*; Vorzug *m*, Wert *m*; in *od.* by ~ of kraft, vermöge (*gen.*); make a ~ of necessity aus der Not e-e Tugend machen; ~osity [vəːtju'ɔsiti] Virtuosität *f*; ~ous □ ['vəːtjuəs] tugendhaft.
virulent □ ['virulənt] giftig; ♣ virulent; *fig.* bösartig.
virus ♣ ['vaiərəs] Virus *n*; *fig.* Gift *n*.
visa ['viːzə] Visum *n*, Sichtvermerk *m*; ~ed [~əd] mit e-m Sichtvermerk *od.* Visum versehen.
viscose ♠ ['viskous] Viskose *f*; ~ silk Zellstoffseide *f*.
viscount ['vaikaunt] Vicomte *m*; ~ess [~tis] Vicomtesse *f*.
viscous □ ['viskəs] zähflüssig.
vise *Am.* [vais] Schraubstock *m*.
visé ['viːzei] = visa.
visib|ility [vizi'biliti] Sichtbarkeit *f*; Sichtweite *f*; ~le □ ['vizəbl] sichtbar; *fig.* (er)sichtlich; *pred.* zu sehen (*S.*); zu sprechen (*P.*).
vision ['viʒən] Sehvermögen *n*, Sehkraft *f*; *fig.* Seherblick *m*; Vision *f*, Erscheinung *f*; ~ary ['viʒnəri] 1. phantastisch; 2. Geisterseher(in); Phantast(in).
visit ['vizit] 1. *v/t.* besuchen; besichtigen; *fig.* heimsuchen; *et.* vergelten, *v/i.* Besuche machen; *Am.* sich unterhalten, plaudern (with mit); 2. Besuch *m*; ~ation [vizi'teiʃən] Besuch *m*; Besichtigung *f*; *fig.* Heimsuchung *f*; ~or ['vizitə] Besucher(in), Gast *m*; Inspektor *m*.
vista ['vistə] Durchblick *m*; Rückod. Ausblick *m*.
visual □ ['vizjuəl] Seh...; Gesichts-...; ~ize [~laiz] (sich) vor Augen stellen, sich ein Bild machen von.
vital □ ['vaitl] 1. Lebens...; lebenswichtig, wesentlich; lebensgefähr-

lich; ~ parts pl. = 2. ~s pl. lebenswichtige Organe n/pl.; ~ edle Teile m/pl.; ~ity [vai'tæliti] Lebenskraft f; Vitalität f; ~ize ['vaitəlaiz] beleben.

vitamin(e) ['vitəmin] Vitamin n.

vitiate ['viʃieit] verderben; beeinträchtigen; hinfällig (s⅟₂ ungültig) machen.

vitreous □ ['vitriəs] Glas...; gläsern.

vituperate [vi'tju:pəreit] schelten; schmähen, beschimpfen.

vivaci|ous □ [vi'veiʃəs] lebhaft; ~ty [vi'væsiti] Lebhaftigkeit f.

vivid □ ['vivid] lebhaft, lebendig.

vivify ['vivifai] (sich) beleben.

vixen ['viksn] Füchsin f; zänkisches Weib.

vocabulary [və'kæbjuləri] Wörterverzeichnis n; Wortschatz m.

vocal □ ['voukəl] stimmlich; Stimm...; gesprochen; laut; ♪ Vokal..., Gesang...; klingend; gr. stimmhaft; ~ist [~list] Sänger(in); ~ize [~laiz] (gr. stimmhaft) aussprechen; singen.

vocation [vou'keiʃən] Berufung f; Beruf m; ~al □ [~nl] beruflich; Berufs...

vociferate [vou'sifəreit] schreien.

vogue [voug] Beliebtheit f; Mode f.

voice [vois] 1. Stimme f; active (passive) ~ gr. Aktiv n (Passiv n); give ~ to Ausdruck geben (dat.); 2. äußern, ausdrücken; gr. stimmhaft aussprechen.

void [void] 1. leer; s⅟₂ ungültig; ~ of frei von; aren an (dat.); ohne; 2. Leere f; Lücke f; 3. entleeren; ungültig machen, aufheben.

volatile ['volətail] 🜍 flüchtig (a. fig.); flatterhaft.

volcano [vol'keinou], pl. ~es Vulkan m.

volition [vou'liʃən] Wollen n; Wille(nskraft f) m.

volley ['voli] 1. Salve f; (Geschoß-etc.)Hagel m; fig. Schwall m; Tennis: Flugball m; 2. mst ~ out e-n Schwall von Worten etc. von sich geben; Salven abgeben; fig. hageln; dröhnen; ~-ball Sport: Volleyball m, Flugball m.

volt [voult] Volt n; ~age ƒ ['voultidʒ] Spannung f; ~meter ƒ Volt-, Spannungsmesser m.

volub|ility [volju'biliti] Redegewandtheit f; ~le □ ['voljubl] (rede-)gewandt.

volum|e ['voljum] Band m e-s Buches; Volumen n; fig. Masse f,

große Menge; (bsd. Stimm)Umfang m; ~ of sound Radio: Lautstärke f; ~inous □ [və'lju:minəs] vielbändig; umfangreich, voluminös.

volunt|ary □ ['voləntəri] freiwillig; willkürlich; ~eer [volən'tiə] 1. Freiwillige(r m) f; attr. Freiwilligen...; 2. v/i. freiwillig dienen; sich freiwillig melden; sich erbieten; v/t. anbieten; sich e-e Bemerkung erlauben.

voluptu|ary [və'lʌptjuəri] Wollüstling m; ~ous □ [~uəs] wollüstig; üppig.

vomit ['vomit] 1. (sich) erbrechen; fig. (aus)speien, ausstoßen; 2. Erbrochene(s) n; Erbrechen n.

voraci|ous □ [və'reiʃəs] gefräßig; gierig; ~ty [və'ræsiti] Gefräßigkeit f; Gier f.

vort|ex ['vo:teks], pl. mst ~ices ['vo:tisi:z] Wirbel m, Strudel m (mst fig.).

vote [vout] 1. (Wahl)Stimme f; Abstimmung f; Stimmrecht n; Beschluß m, Votum n; ~ of no confidence Mißtrauensvotum n; cast a ~ (s)eine Stimme abgeben; take a ~ on s.th. über et. abstimmen; 2. v/t. stimmen für; v/i. (ab)stimmen; wählen; ~ for stimmen für; F für et. sein; et. vorschlagen; ~r ['voutə] Wähler(in).

voting ['voutiŋ] Abstimmung f; attr. Wahl...; ~ machine Stimmenzählmaschine f; ~-paper Stimmzettel m; ~-power Stimmrecht n.

vouch [vautʃ] verbürgen; ~ for bürgen für; ~er ['vautʃə] Beleg m, Unterlage f; Gutschein m; Zeuge m; ~safe [vautʃ'seif] gewähren; geruhen.

vow [vau] 1. Gelübde n; (Treu-)Schwur m; 2. v/t. geloben.

vowel gr. ['vauəl] Vokal m, Selbstlaut m.

voyage ['voidʒ] 1. längere (See-, Flug)Reise; 2. reisen, fahren, ~r ['voidʒə] (See)Reisende(r m) f.

vulgar ['vʌlgə] 1. □ gewöhnlich, gemein, vulgär, pöbelhaft; ~ tongue Volkssprache f; 2.: the ~ der Pöbel; ~ism [~rizəm] vulgärer Ausdruck; ~ity [vʌl'gæriti] Gemeinheit f; ~ize ['vʌlgəraiz] gemein machen; erniedrigen; populär machen.

vulnerable □ ['vʌlnərəbl] verwundbar; fig. angreifbar.

vulpine ['vʌlpain] Fuchs...; fuchsartig; schlau, listig.

vulture orn. ['vʌltʃə] Geier m.

vying ['vaiiŋ] wetteifernd.

W

wacky *Am. sl.* ['wæki] verrückt.
wad [wɔd] **1.** (Watte)Bausch *m*; Polster *n*; Pfropf(en) *m*; Banknotenbündel *n*; **2.** wattieren; polstern; zs.-pressen; zustopfen; **~ding** ['wɔdiŋ] Wattierung *f*; Watte *f*.
waddle ['wɔdl] watscheln, wackeln.
wade [weid] *v/i.* waten; *fig.* sich hindurcharbeiten; *v/t.* durchwaten.
wafer ['weifə] Waffel *f*; Oblate *f*; *eccl.* Hostie *f*.
waffle ['wɔfl] **1.** Waffel *f*; **2.** F quasseln.
waft [wɑːft] **1.** wehen, tragen; **2.** Hauch *m*.
wag [wæg] **1.** wackeln (mit); wedeln (mit); **2.** Schütteln *n*; Wedeln *n*; Spaßvogel *m*.
wage¹ [weidʒ] *Krieg* führen.
wage² [~] *mst* **~s** *pl.* Lohn *m*; **~-earner** ['weidʒəːnə] Lohnempfänger *m*.
wager ['weidʒə] **1.** Wette *f*; **2.** wetten.
waggish □ ['wægiʃ] schelmisch.
waggle F ['wægl] wackeln (mit).
wag(g)on ['wægən] (Roll-, Güter-) Wagen *m*; **~er** [~nə] Fuhrmann *m*.
wagtail *orn.* ['wægteil] Bachstelze *f*.
waif [weif] herrenloses Gut; Strandgut *n*; Heimatlose(r *m*) *f*.
wail [weil] **1.** (Weh)Klagen *n*; **2.** (weh)klagen.
wainscot ['weinskət] (Holz)Täfelung *f*.
waist [weist] Taille *f*; schmalste Stelle; ⚓ Mitteldeck *n*; **~coat** ['weiskout] Weste *f*; **~-line** ['weistlain] *Schneiderei*: Taille *f*.
wait [weit] **1.** *v/i.* warten (*for* auf *acc.*); *a. ~ at* (*Am. on*) *table* bedienen, servieren; **~** (*up*)*on j-n* bedienen; *j-n* besuchen; *~ and see* abwarten; *v/t.* abwarten; mit *dem Essen* warten (*for* auf *j-n*); **2.** Warten *n*, Aufenthalt *m*; *lie in ~ for* s.o. *j-m* auflauern; **~er** ['weitə] Kellner *m*; Tablett *n*.
waiting ['weitiŋ] Warten *n*; Dienst *m*; *in ~* diensttuend; **~-room** Wartezimmer *n*; ⇔ *etc.* Wartesaal *m*.
waitress ['weitris] Kellnerin *f*.
waive [weiv] verzichten auf (*acc.*), aufgeben; **~r** ʒⱬ ['weivə] Verzicht *m*.
wake [weik] **1.** ⚓ Kielwasser *n* (*a. fig.*); Totenwache *f*; Kirmes *f*; **2.** [*irr.*] *v/i. a. ~ up* aufwachen; *v/t. a. ~ up* (auf)wecken; erwecken; *fig.* wachrufen; **~ful** □ ['weikful] wachsam; schlaflos; **~n** ['weikən] *s.* wake **2.**
wale *bsd. Am.* [weil] Strieme *f*.
walk [wɔːk] **1.** *v/i.* (zu Fuß) gehen; spazierengehen; wandern; Schritt gehen; **~** *out* F streiken; **~** *out on sl.*

im Stich lassen; *v/t.* führen; *Pferd* Schritt gehen lassen; begleiten; (durch)wandern; umhergehen auf *od.* in (*dat.*); **2.** (Spazier)Gang *m*; Spazierweg *m*; **~** *of life* Lebensstellung *f*, Beruf *m*; **~er** ['wɔːkə] Fuß-, Spaziergänger(in).
walkie-talkie ⚔ ['wɔːkiˈtɔːki] tragbares Sprechfunkgerät.
walking ['wɔːkiŋ] Spazierengehen *n*, Wandern *n*; *attr.* Spazier...; Wander...; **~** *papers* *pl. Am.* F Entlassung(spapiere *n/pl.*) *f*; Laufpaß *m*; **~-stick** Spazierstock *m*; **~-tour** (Fuß)Wanderung *f*.
walk|-out *Am.* ['wɔːkaut] Ausstand *m*; **~over** F Kinderspiel *n*, leichter Sieg.
wall [wɔːl] **1.** Wand *f*; Mauer *f*; **2.** mit Mauern umgeben; **~** *up* zumauern.
wallet ['wɔlit] Ränzel *n*; Brieftasche *f*.
wallflower *fig.* ['wɔːlflauə] Mauerblümchen *n*.
wallop F ['wɔləp] *j-n* verdreschen.
wallow ['wɔlou] sich wälzen.
wall|-paper ['wɔːlpeipə] Tapete *f*; **~-socket** ⚡ Steckdose *f*.
walnut ⚘ ['wɔːlnʌt] Walnuß(baum *m*) *f*.
walrus *zo.* ['wɔːlrəs] Walroß *n*.
waltz [wɔːls] **1.** Walzer *m*; **2.** Walzer tanzen.
wan □ [wɔn] blaß, bleich, fahl.
wand [wɔnd] (Zauber)Stab *m*.
wander ['wɔndə] wandern; umherschweifen, umherwandern; *fig.* abschweifen; irregehen; phantasieren.
wane [wein] **1.** abnehmen (*Mond*); *fig.* schwinden; **2.** Abnehmen *n*.
wangle *sl.* ['wæŋgl] *v/t.* deichseln, hinkriegen; *v/i.* mogeln.
want [wɔnt] **1.** Mangel *m* (*of* an *dat.*); Bedürfnis *n*; Not *f*; **2.** *v/i.:* *be* *~ing* fehlen; *es* fehlen lassen (*in* an *dat.*); unzulänglich sein; **~** *for* Not leiden an (*dat.*); *it ~s* of *es* fehlt an (*dat.*); *v/t.* bedürfen (*gen.*), brauchen; nicht haben; wünschen, (haben) wollen; *it* ~*s* *s.th.* es fehlt an et. (*dat.*); *he ~s energy* es fehlt ihm an Energie; **~ed** gesucht; **~-ad** F ['wɔntæd] Kleinanzeige *f*; Stellenangebot *n*, -gesuch *n*.
wanton ['wɔntən] **1.** □ geil; üppig; mutwillig; **2.** Dirne *f*; **3.** umhertollen.
war [wɔː] **1.** Krieg *m*; *attr.* Kriegs...; *make ~* Krieg führen (*upon* gegen); **2.** (ea. wider)streiten.
warble ['wɔːbl] trillern, singen.
ward [wɔːd] **1.** Gewahrsam *m*; Vormundschaft *f*; Mündel *n*; Schützling *m*; Gefängniszelle *f*; Abteilung *f*, Station *f*, Krankenzimmer *n*;

(Stadt)Bezirk *m*; ⊕ Einschnitt *m im Schlüsselbart*; 2. ~ *off* abwehren; ~en ['wɔːdn] Aufseher *m*; (Luftschutz)Wart *m*; *univ.* Rektor *m*; ~er ['wɔːdə] (Gefangenen)Wärter *m*; ~robe ['wɔːdroub] Garderobe *f*; Kleiderschrank *m*; ~ *trunk* Schrankkoffer *m*.

ware [wɛə] Ware *f*; Geschirr *n*.

warehouse 1. ['wɛəhaus] (Waren-) Lager *n*; Speicher *m*; 2. [~auz] auf Lager bringen, einlagern.

war|fare ['wɔːfɛə] Krieg(führung*f*) *m*; ~head ⚔ Sprengkopf *m e-r Rakete etc.*

wariness ['wɛərinis] Vorsicht *f*.

warlike ['wɔːlaik] kriegerisch.

warm [wɔːm] 1. □ warm (*a. fig.*); heiß; *fig.* hitzig; 2. F Erwärmung *f*; 3. *v/t. a.* ~ *up* (auf-, an-, er)wärmen; *v/i. a.* ~ *up* warm werden, sich erwärmen; ~th [wɔːmθ] Wärme *f*.

warn [wɔːn] warnen (*of, against* vor *dat.*); verwarnen; ermahnen; verständigen; ~ing ['wɔːniŋ] (Ver-) Warnung *f*; Mahnung *f*; Kündigung *f*.

warp [wɔːp] *v/i.* sich verziehen (*Holz*); *v/t. fig.* verdrehen, verzerren; beeinflussen; *j-n* abbringen (*from* von).

warrant ['wɔrənt] 1. Vollmacht *f*; Rechtfertigung *f*; Berechtigung *f*; ⅍ (Vollziehungs)Befehl *m*; Berechtigungsschein *m*; ~ *of arrest* ⅍ Haftbefehl *m*; 2. bevollmächtigen; *j-n* berechtigen; et. rechtfertigen; verbürgen; † garantieren; ~y [~ti] Garantie *f*; Berechtigung *f*.

warrior ['wɔriə] Krieger *m*.

wart [wɔːt] Warze *f*; Auswuchs *m*.

wary □ ['wɛəri] vorsichtig, behutsam; wachsam.

was [wɔz, wəz] *1. und 3. sg. pret. von be; pret. pass. von be; he* ~ *to have come* er hätte kommen sollen.

wash [wɔʃ] 1. *v/t.* waschen; (um-) spülen; ~ *up* abwaschen, spülen; *v/i.* sich waschen (lassen); wasch-echt sein (*a. fig.*); spülen, schlagen (*Wellen*); 2. Waschen *n*; Wäsche *f*; Wellenschlag *m*; Spülwasser *n*; *contp.* Gewäsch *n*; mouth-~ Mundwasser *n*; ~able ['wɔʃəbl] waschbar; ~basin Waschbecken *n*; ~cloth Waschlappen *m*; ~er ['wɔʃə] Wäscher*in f*; Waschmaschine *f*; ⊕ Unterlagscheibe *f*; ~erwoman Waschfrau *f*; ~ing ['wɔʃiŋ] 1. Waschen *n*; Wäsche *f*; ~s *pl.* Spülicht *n*; 2. Wasch...; ~ing-up Abwaschen *n*; ~rag *bsd. Am.* Waschlappen *m*; ~y ['wɔʃi] wässerig.

wasp [wɔsp] Wespe *f*.

wastage ['weistidʒ] Abgang *m*, Verlust *m*; Vergeudung *f*.

waste [weist] 1. wüst, öde; unbebaut; überflüssig; Abfall...; *lay* ~ verwüsten; ~ *paper* Altpapier *n*;

2. Verschwendung *f*, Vergeudung *f*; Abfall *m*; Einöde *f*, Wüste *f*; 3. *v/t.* verwüsten; verschwenden; verzehren; *v/i.* verschwendet werden; ~ful □ ['weistful] verschwenderisch; ~paper-basket [weist'peipəbɑːskit] Papierkorb *m*; ~pipe ['weistpaip] Abflußrohr *n*.

watch [wɔtʃ] 1. Wache *f*; Taschenuhr *f*; 2. *v/i.* wachen; ~ *for* warten auf (*acc.*); ~ *out* F aufpassen; *v/t.* bewachen; beobachten; achtgeben auf (*acc.*); *Gelegenheit* abwarten; ~dog ['wɔtʃdɔg] Wachhund *m*; ~ful □ [~ʃful] wachsam, achtsam; ~maker Uhrmacher *m*; ~man (Nacht)Wächter *m*; ~word Losung *f*.

water ['wɔːtə] 1. Wasser *n*; Gewässer *n*; *drink the* ~s Brunnen trinken; 2. *v/t.* bewässern; (be-) sprengen; (be)gießen; mit Wasser versorgen; tränken; verwässern (*a. fig.*); *v/i.* wässern (*Mund*) tränen (*Augen*); Wasser einnehmen; ~closet (Wasser)Klosett *n*; ~colo(u)r Aquarell(malerei *f*) *n*; ~course Wasserlauf *m*; ~cress ♣ Brunnenkresse *f*; ~fall Wasserfall *m*; ~front Ufer *n*, *bsd. Am.* städtisches Hafengebiet; ~ga(u)ge ⊕ Wasserstands(an)zeiger *m*; Pegel *m*.

watering ['wɔːtəriŋ]: ~can Gießkanne *f*; ~place Wasserloch *n*; Tränke *f*; Bad(eort *m*) *n*; Seebad *n*; ~pot Gießkanne *f*.

water|-level ['wɔːtəlevl] Wasserspiegel *m*; Wasserstand(slinie *f*) *m*; ⊕ Wasserwaage *f*; ~man Fährmann *m*; Bootsführer *m*; Ruderer *m*; ~proof 1. wasserdicht; 2. Regenmantel *m*; 3. imprägnieren; ~shed Wasserscheide *f*; Stromgebiet *n*; ~side 1. Fluß-, Seeufer *n*; 2. am Wasser (gelegen); ~tight wasserdicht; *fig.* unangreifbar; ~way Wasserstraße *f*; ~works *oft sg.* Wasserwerk *n*; ~y [~əri] wässerig.

watt ⚡ [wɔt] Watt *n*.

wattle ['wɔtl] 1. Flechtwerk *n*; 2. aus Flechtwerk herstellen.

wave [weiv] 1. Welle *f*; Woge *f*; Winken *n*; 2. *v/t.* wellig machen, wellen; schwingen; schwenken; ~ *s.o. aside j-n* beiseite winken; *v/i.* wogen; wehen, flattern; winken; ~length *phys.* ['weivleŋθ] Wellenlänge *f*.

waver ['weivə] (sch)wanken; flakkern.

wavy ['weivi] wellig; wogend.

wax[1] [wæks] 1. Wachs *n*; Siegellack *m*; Ohrenschmalz *n*; 2. wachsen; bohnern.

wax[2] [~] [*irr.*] zunehmen (*Mond*).

wax|en *fig.* ['wæksən] wächsern; ~y □ [~si] wachsartig; weich.

way [wei] 1. *mst* Weg *m*; Straße *f*;

Art u. Weise *f*; *eigene* Art; Strecke *f*; Richtung *f*; F Gegend *f*; ⚓ Fahrt *f*; *fig.* Hinsicht *f*; Zustand *m*; ⚓ Helling *f*; ~ *in* Eingang *m*; ~ *out* Ausgang *m*; *fig.* Ausweg *m*; *right of* ~ ⚓ Wegerecht *n*; *bsd. mot.* Vorfahrt(srecht *n*) *f*; *this* ~ hierher, hier entlang; *by the* ~ übrigens; *by* ~ *of* durch; *on the* ~, *on one's* ~ unterwegs; *out of the* ~ ungewöhnlich; *under* ~ in Fahrt; *give* ~ zurückgehen; *mot.* die Vorfahrt lassen (*to dat.*); nachgeben; abgelöst werden (*to von*); sich hingeben (*to dat.*); *have one's* ~ s-n Willen haben; *lead the* ~ vorangehen; **2.** *adv.* weit; ~**bill** ['weibil] Frachtbrief *m*; ~**farer** ['weifɛərə] Wanderer *m*; ~**lay** [wei'lei] (*irr.* (*lay*)) *j-m* auflauern; ~**side** **1.** Wegrand *m*; **2.** am Wege; ~ **station** *Am.* Zwischenstation *f*; ~ **train** *Am.* Bummelzug *m*; ~**ward** □ ['weiwəd] starrköpfig, eigensinnig.

we [wi:, wi] wir.

weak □ [wi:k] schwach; schwächlich; dünn (*Getränk*); ~**en** ['wi:kən] *v/t.* schwächen; *v/i.* schwach werden; ~**ling** ['wi:kliŋ] Schwächling *m*; ~**ly** [~li] schwächlich; ~**minded** ['wi:k'maindid] schwachsinnig; ~**ness** ['wi:knis] Schwäche *f*.

weal [wi:l] Wohl *n*, Strieme *f*.

wealth [welθ] Wohlstand *m*; Reichtum *m*; *fig.* Fülle *f*; ~**y** □ ['welθi] reich; wohlhabend.

wean [wi:n] entwöhnen; ~ *s.o. from s.th.* j-m et. abgewöhnen.

weapon ['wepən] Waffe *f*.

wear [wɛə] **1.** (*irr.*) *v/t.* am Körper tragen; zur Schau tragen; *a.* ~ *away*, ~ *down*, ~ *off*, ~ *out* abnutzen, abtragen, verbrauchen; erschöpfen; ermüden; zermürben; *v/i.* sich *gut etc.* tragen *od.* halten; *a.* ~ *off* *od.* *out* sich abnutzen *od.* abtragen; *fig.* sich verlieren; *a.* ~ *on* vergehen; **2.** Tragen *n*; (Be)Kleidung *f*; Abnutzung *f*; *for hard* ~ strapazierfähig; *the worse for* ~ abgetragen; ~ *and tear* Verschleiß *m*.

wear|iness ['wiərinis] Müdigkeit *f*; Ermüdung *f*; *fig.* Überdruß *m*; ~**some** □ [~isəm] ermüdend; langweilig; ~**y** ['wiəri] **1.** □ müde; *fig.* überdrüssig; ermüdend; anstrengend; **2.** ermüden.

weasel *zo.* ['wi:zl] Wiesel *n*.

weather ['weðə] **1.** Wetter *n*, Witterung *f*; **2.** *v/t.* dem Wetter aussetzen; ⚓ *Sturm* abwettern; *fig.* überstehen; *v/i.* verwittern; ~**beaten** vom Wetter mitgenommen; ~**bureau** Wetteramt *n*; ~**chart** Wetterkarte *f*; ~**forecast** Wetterbericht *m*, -vorhersage *f*; ~**worn** verwittert.

weav|e [wi:v] (*irr.*) weben; wirken; flechten; *fig.* ersinnen, erfinden;

sich schlängeln; ~**er** ['wi:və] Weber *m*.

weazen ['wi:zn] verhutzelt.

web [web] Gewebe *n*; *orn.* Schwimmhaut *f*; ~**bing** ['webiŋ] Gurtband *n*.

wed [wed] heiraten; *fig.* verbinden (*to* mit); ~**ding** ['wediŋ] **1.** Hochzeit *f*; **2.** Hochzeits...; Braut...; Trau...; ~**ring** Ehe-, Trauring *m*.

wedge [wedʒ] **1.** Keil *m*; **2.** (ver-) keilen; *a.* ~ *in* (hin)einzwängen.

wedlock ['wedlɔk] Ehe *f*.

Wednesday ['wenzdi] Mittwoch *m*.

wee [wi:] klein, winzig; *a* ~ *bit* ein klein wenig.

weed [wi:d] **1.** Unkraut *n*; **2.** jäten; säubern (*of* von); ~ *out* ausmerzen; ~**killer** ['wi:dkilə] Unkrautvertilgungsmittel *n*; ~**s** *pl.* *mst* widow's Witwenkleidung *f*; ~**y** ['wi:di] voll Unkraut, verkrautet; *fig.* lang aufgeschossen.

week [wi:k] Woche *f*; *this day* ~ heute in *od.* vor e-r Woche; ~**day** ['wi:kdei] Wochentag *m*; ~**end** ['wi:k'end] Wochenende *n*; ~**ly** ['wi:kli] **1.** wöchentlich; **2.** *a.* ~ *paper* Wochenblatt *n*, Wochen(zeit)-schrift *f*.

weep [wi:p] (*irr.*) weinen; tropfen; ~**ing** ['wi:piŋ] Trauer...; ~ *willow* ♣ Trauerweide *f*.

weigh [wei] *v/t.* (ab)wiegen, *fig.* ab-, erwägen; ~ *anchor* ⚓ den Anker lichten; ~*ed down* niedergebeugt; *v/i.* wiegen (*a. fig.*); ausschlaggebend sein; ~ (*up*)*on* lasten auf (*dat.*).

weight [weit] **1.** Gewicht *n* (*a.fig.*); Last *f* (*a. fig.*); *fig.* Bedeutung *f*; ⚓ Wucht *f*; **2.** beschweren; *fig.* belasten; ~**y** □ ['weiti] (ge)wichtig; wuchtig.

weir [wiə] Wehr *n*; Fischreuse *f*.

weird [wiəd] Schicksals...; unheimlich; F sonderbar, seltsam.

welcome ['welkəm] **1.** willkommen; *you are* ~ *to inf.* es steht Ihnen frei, zu *inf.*; (*you are*) ~*!* gern geschehen!, bitte sehr!; **2.** Willkomm(en *n*) *m*; **3.** willkommen heißen; *fig.* begrüßen.

weld ⊕ [weld] (zs.-)schweißen.

welfare ['welfɛə] Wohlfahrt *f*; ~ **centre** Fürsorgeamt *n*; ~ **state** Wohlfahrtsstaat *m*; ~ **work** Fürsorge *f*, Wohlfahrtspflege *f*; ~ **worker** Fürsorger(in).

well¹ [wel] **1.** Brunnen *m*; *fig.* Quelle *f*; ⊕ Bohrloch *n*; Treppen-, Aufzugs-, Licht-, Luftschacht *m*; **2.** quellen.

well² [~] **1.** wohl; gut; ordentlich, gründlich; gesund; ~ *off* in guten Verhältnissen, wohlhabend; *I am not* ~ mir ist nicht wohl; **2.** *int.* nun!, F na!; ~**being** ['wel'bi:iŋ] Wohl(sein) *n*; ~**born** von guter

Herkunft; ~-bred wohlerzogen; ~-defined deutlich, klar umrissen; ~-favo(u)red gut aussehend; ~intentioned wohlmeinend; gut gemeint; ~ known, ~-known bekannt; ~mannered mit guten Manieren; ~nigh ['welnai] beinahe; ~ timed rechtzeitig; ~-to-do ['weltə'du:] wohlhabend; ~-wisher Gönner m, Freund m; ~-worn abgetragen; fig. abgedroschen.

Welsh [welʃ] 1. walisisch; 2. Walisisch n; the ~ pl. die Waliser pl.; ~ **rabbit** überbackene Käseschnitte.

welt [welt] ⊕ Rahmen m, Schuh-Rahmen m; Einfassung f; Strieme f.

welter ['weltə] 1. rollen, sich wälzen; 2. Wirrwarr m, Durcheinander n.

wench [wentʃ] Mädchen n; Dirne f.

went [went] pret. von go 1.

wept [wept] pret. u. p.p. von weep.

were [wɔː, wə] 1. pret. pl. u. 2. sg. von be; 2. pret. pass. von be; 3. subj. pret. von be.

west [west] 1. West(en m); 2. West...; westlich; westwärts; ~erly ['westəli], ~ern [~ən] westlich; ~erner [~nə] Am. Weststaatler(in); Abendländer(in); ~ward(s) [~twəd(z)] westwärts.

wet [wet] 1. naß, feucht; Am. den Alkoholhandel gestattend; 2. Nässe f; Feuchtigkeit f; 3. [irr.] naß machen, anfeuchten.

wetback Am. sl. ['wetbæk] illegaler Einwanderer aus Mexiko.

wether ['weðə] Hammel m.

wet-nurse ['wetnɔːs] Amme f.

whack F [wæk] 1. verhauen; 2. Hieb m.

whale [weil] Wal m; ~bone ['weilboun] Fischbein n; ~-oil Tran m; ~r ['weilə] Walfischfänger m.

whaling ['weiliŋ] Walfischfang m.

wharf [wɔːf], pl. a. **wharves** [wɔːvz] Kai m, Anlegeplatz m.

what [wɔt] 1. was; das, was; know ~'s ~ Bescheid wissen; 2. was?; wie?; wieviel?; welch(er, -e, -es)?; was für ein(e)?; ~ about ...? wie steht's mit ...?; ~ for? wozu?; ~ of it? was ist denn dabei?; ~ next? was sonst noch?; iro. was denn noch alles?; ~ a blessing! was für ein Segen!; 3. ~ with ... ~ with ... teils durch ... teils durch ...; ~-(so)ever [wɔt(sou)'evə] was od. welcher auch (immer).

wheat ⊕ [wiːt] Weizen m.

wheedle ['wiːdl] beschwatzen; ~ s.th. out of s.o. j-m et. abschwatzen.

wheel [wiːl] 1. Rad n; Steuer n; bsd. Am. F Fahrrad n; Töpferscheibe f; Drehung f; ⚔ Schwenkung f; 2. rollen, fahren, schieben; sich drehen; sich umwenden; ⚔ schwenken; F radeln; ~barrow

['wiːlbærou] Schubkarren m; ~ **chair** Rollstuhl m; ~ed mit Rädern; fahrbar; ...räd(e)rig.

wheeze [wiːz] schnaufen, keuchen.

whelp [welp] 1. zo. Welpe m; allg. Junge(s) n; F Balg m, n (ungezogenes Kind); 2. (Junge) werfen.

when [wen] 1. wann?; 2. wenn; als; während od. da doch; und da.

whence [wens] woher, von wo.

when(so)ever [wen(sou)'evə] immer od. jedesmal wenn; sooft (als).

where [wɛə] wo; wohin; ~about(s) 1. ['wɛərə'bauts] wo herum; 2. [~əbauts] Aufenthalt m; ~as [~r'æz] wohingegen, während (doch); ~at [~'æt] wobei, worüber, worauf; ~by [wɛə'bai] wodurch; ~fore ['wɛəfɔː] weshalb; ~in [wɛər'in] worin; ~of [~r'ɔv] wovon; ~upon [~rə'pɔn] worauf(hin); ~ver [~r'evə] wo(hin) (auch) immer; ~withal ['wɛəwiðɔːl] Erforderliche(s) n; Mittel n/pl.

whet [wet] wetzen, schärfen; anstacheln.

whether ['weðə] ob; ~ or no so oder so.

whetstone ['wetstoun] Schleifstein m.

whey [wei] Molke f.

which [witʃ] 1. welche(r, -s)?; 2. der, die, das; was; ~ever [~ʃ'evə] welche(r, -s) (auch) immer.

whiff [wif] 1. Hauch m; Zug m beim Rauchen; Zigarillo n; 2. paffen.

while [wail] 1. Weile f; Zeit f; for a ~ e-e Zeitlang; worth ~ der Mühe wert; 2. mst ~ away Zeit verbringen; 3. a. **whilst** [wailst] während.

whim [wim] Schrulle f, Laune f.

whimper ['wimpə] wimmern.

whim|sical □ ['wimzikəl] wunderlich; ~sy ['wimzi] Grille f, Laune f.

whine [wain] winseln; wimmern.

whinny ['wini] wiehern.

whip [wip] 1. v/t. peitschen; geißeln (a. fig.); j-n verprügeln; schlagen (F a. fig.); umsäumen; werfen; reißen; ~ in parl. zs.-trommeln; ~ on Kleidungsstück überwerfen; ~ up antreiben; aufraffen; v/i. springen, flitzen; 2. Peitsche f; Geißel f.

whippet zo. ['wipit] Whippet m (kleiner englischer Rennhund).

whipping ['wipiŋ] Prügel pl.; ~-top Kreisel m.

whippoorwill orn. ['wippuəwil] Ziegenmelker m.

whirl [wəːl] 1. wirbeln; (sich) drehen; 2. Wirbel m, Strudel m; ~pool ['wəːlpuːl] Strudel m; ~wind Wirbelwind m.

whir(r) [wəː] schwirren.

whisk [wisk] 1. Wisch m; Staubwedel m; Küche: Schneebesen m; Schwung m; 2. v/t. (ab-, weg)wischen, (ab-, weg)fegen; wirbeln (mit); schlagen; v/i. huschen,

flitzen; **~er** ['wiskə] Barthaar *n*; *mst* *~s pl.* Backenbart *m*.
whisper ['wispə] **1.** flüstern; **2.** Geflüster *n*.
whistle ['wisl] **1.** pfeifen; **2.** Pfeife *f*; Pfiff *m*; F Kehle *f*; **~-stop** *Am.* 🚂 Haltepunkt *m*; *fig.* Kaff *n*; *pol.* kurzes Auftreten *e-s Kandidaten im Wahlkampf.*
Whit [wit] *in Zssgn*: Pfingst...
white [wait] **1.** *allg.* weiß; rein; F anständig; Weiß...; **2.** Weiß(e) *n*; Weiße(r *m*) *f* (*Rasse*); **~-collar** ['wait'kɔlə] geistig, Kopf..., Büro...; *~ workers pl.* Angestellte *pl.*; **~ heat** Weißglut *f*; **~ lie** fromme Lüge; **~n** ['waitn] weiß machen *od.* werden; bleichen; **~ness** [~nis] Weiße *f*; Blässe *f*; **~wash 1.** Tünche *f*; **2.** weißen; *fig* rein waschen.
whither *lit* ['wiðə] wohin.
whitish ['waitiʃ] weißlich.
Whitsun ['witsn] Pfingst...; **~tide** Pfingsten *pl.*
whittle ['witl] schnitze(l)n; *~ away* verkleinern, schwächen.
whiz(z) [wiz] zischen, sausen.
who [hu:, hu] **1.** welche(r, -s); der, die, das; **2.** wer?
whodun(n)it *sl.* [hu:'dʌnit] Krimi (-nalroman, -nalfilm) *m*.
whoever [hu(:)'evə] wer auch immer.
whole [houl] **1.** □ ganz; heil, unversehrt; *made out of ~ cloth Am.* F frei erfunden; **2.** Ganze(s) *n*; *(up)on the ~* im ganzen; im allgemeinen; **~-hearted** □ ['houl'ha:tid] aufrichtig; **~-meal bread** ['houlmi:l bred] Vollkorn-, Schrotbrot *n*; **~sale 1.** *mst ~ trade* Großhandel *m*; **2.** Großhandels...; Engros...; *fig* Massen...; *~ dealer* = **~saler** [~lə] Großhändler *m*; **~some** □ [~səm] gesund.
wholly *adv.* ['houlli] ganz, gänzlich.
whom [hu:m, hum] *acc. von who.*
whoop [hu:p] **1.** Schrei *m*, Geschrei *n*; **2.** laut schreien; *~ it up Am. sl.* laut feiern; **~ee** *Am.* F ['wupi:] Freudenfest *n*; *make ~* auf die Pauke hauen; **~ing-cough** ⚕ ['hu:piŋkɔf] Keuchhusten *m*.
whore [hɔ:] Hure *f*.
whose [hu:z] *gen. von who.*
why [wai] **1.** warum, weshalb; *~ so?* wieso?; **2.** ei!, ja!; (je) nun.
wick [wik] Docht *m*.
wicked □ ['wikid] *moralisch* böse, schlimm; **~ness** [~dnis] Bosheit *f*.
wicker ['wikə] aus Weide geflochten; Weiden...; Korb...; *~ basket* Weidenkorb *m*; *~ chair* Korbstuhl *m*.
wicket ['wikit] Pförtchen *n*; *Kricket*: Dreistab *m*, Tor *n*; **~-keeper** Torhüter *m*.
wide [waid] *a.* □ *u. adv.* weit; ausgedehnt; weitgehend; großzügig; breit; weitab; *~ awake* völlig (*od.* hell)wach; aufgeweckt (*schlau*); *3 feet ~* 3 Fuß breit; **~n** ['waidn] (sich) erweitern; **~-open** ['waid'oupən] weit geöffnet; *Am. sl.* großzügig *in der Gesetzesdurchführung*; **~-spread** weitverbreitet, ausgedehnt.
widow ['widou] Witwe *f*; *attr.* Witwen...; **~er** [~ouə] Witwer *m*.
width [widθ] Breite *f*, Weite *f*.
wield *lit.* [wi:ld] handhaben.
wife [waif], *pl.* **wives** [waivz] (Ehe-) Frau *f*; Gattin *f*; Weib *n*; **~ly** ['waifli] fraulich.
wig [wig] Perücke *f*.
wigging F ['wigiŋ] Schelte *f*.
wild [waild] **1.** □ wild; toll; unbändig; abenteuerlich; planlos; *run ~* wild (auf)wachsen; *talk ~* (wild) darauflos reden; *~ for od. about* (ganz) verrückt nach; **2.** *mst* *~s pl.* Wildnis *f*; **~-cat** ['waildkæt] **1.** *zo.* Wildkatze *f*; *Am.* Schwindelunternehmen *n*; *bsd. Am* wilde Ölbohrung; **2.** wild (*Streik*); Schwindel...; **~erness** ['wildənis] Wildnis *f*, Wüste *f*; Einöde *f*; **~fire**: *like ~* wie ein Lauffeuer.
wile [wail] List *f*; *mst ~s pl.* Tücke *f*.
wil(l)ful □ ['wilful] eigensinnig; vorsätzlich.
will [wil] **1.** Wille *m*; Wunsch *m*; Testament *n*; *of one's own free ~* aus freien Stücken; **2.** [*irr.*] *v/aux.*: *he ~ come* er wird kommen; er kommt gewöhnlich; *I ~ do it* ich will es tun; **3.** wollen; durch Willenskraft zwingen; entscheiden; ⚖ vermachen.
willing □ ['wiliŋ] willig, bereit (-willig); *pred.* gewillt (*to inf.* zu); **~ness** [~ŋnis] (Bereit)Willigkeit *f*.
will-o'-the-wisp ['wiləðwisp] Irrlicht *n*.
willow ⚘ ['wilou] Weide *f*.
willy-nilly ['wili'nili] wohl oder übel.
wilt [wilt] (ver)welken.
wily □ ['waili] schlau, verschmitzt.
win [win] **1.** [*irr.*] *v/t.* gewinnen; erringen; erlangen, erreichen; *j-n* dazu bringen (*to do* zu tun); *~ s.o. over* *j-n* für sich gewinnen; *v/i.* gewinnen; siegen; **2.** *Sport*: Sieg *m*.
wince [wins] (zs.-)zucken.
winch [wintʃ] Winde *f*; Kurbel *f*.
wind¹ [wind, *poet. a.* waind] **1.** Wind *m*; Atem *m*, Luft *f*; ⚕ Blähung *f*; ♪ Blasinstrumente *n/pl.*; **2.** wittern; außer Atem bringen; verschnaufen lassen.
wind² [waind] [*irr.*] *v/t.* winden; wickeln; *Horn* blasen; *~ up Uhr* aufziehen; *Geschäft* abwickeln; † liquidieren; *v/i.* sich winden; sich schlängeln.
wind|bag ['windbæg] Schwätzer *m*; **~fall** Fallobst *n*; Glücksfall *m*.

winding ['waindiŋ] 1. Windung f; 2. □ sich windend; ~ stairs pl. Wendeltreppe f; ~-sheet Leichentuch n.

wind-instrument ♪ ['windinstrumənt] Blasinstrument n.

windlass ⊕ ['windləs] Winde f.

windmill ['winmil] Windmühle f.

window ['windou] Fenster n; Schaufenster n; ~dressing Schaufensterdekoration f; fig. Aufmachung f, Mache f; ~shade Am. Rouleau n; ~shopping Schaufensterbummel m.

wind|pipe ['windpaip] Luftröhre f; ~screen, Am. ~shield mot. Windschutzscheibe f; ~ wiper Scheibenwischer m.

windy [['windi] windig (a. fig. inhaltlos); geschwätzig.

wine [wain] Wein m; ~press ['wainpres] Kelter f.

wing [wiŋ] 1. Flügel m (a. ✕ u. ⚓); Schwinge f; F co. Arm m; mot. Kotflügel m; ✕ Tragfläche f; ✕, ✕ Geschwader n; ~s pl. Kulissen f/pl.; take ~ weg-, auffliegen; on the ~ im Fluge; 2. fig. beflügeln; fliegen.

wink [wiŋk] 1. Blinzeln n, Zwinkern n; not get a ~ of sleep kein Auge zutun; s. forty; 2. blinzeln, zwinkern (mit); ~ at ein Auge zudrücken bei s.; j-m zublinzeln.

winn|er ['winə] Gewinner(in); Sieger(in); ~ing ['winiŋ] 1. □ einnehmend, gewinnend; 2. ~s pl. Gewinn m.

winsome ['winsəm] gefällig, einnehmend.

wint|er ['wintə] 1. Winter m; 2. überwintern; ~ry [~tri] winterlich; fig. frostig.

wipe [waip] (ab-, auf)wischen; reinigen; (ab)trocknen; ~ out wegwischen; (aus)löschen; fig. vernichten; tilgen.

wire ['waiə] 1. Draht m; Leitung f; F Telegramm n; pull the ~s der Drahtzieher sein; s-e Beziehungen spielen lassen; 2. (ver)drahten; telegraphieren; ~drawn ['waiədrɔːn] spitzfindig; ~less ['waiəlis] 1. □ drahtlos; Funk...; 2. a. ~ set Radio (-apparat m) n; on the ~ im Rundfunk; 3. funken; ~netting ['waiə-'netiŋ] Drahtgeflecht n.

wiry □ ['waiəri] drahtig, sehnig.

wisdom ['wizdəm] Weisheit f; Klugheit f; ~ tooth Weisheitszahn m.

wise [waiz] 1. □ weise, verständig; klug; erfahren; ~ guy Am. sl. Schlauberger m; 2. Weise f, Art f.

wise-crack F ['waizkræk] 1. witzige Bemerkung, 2. witzeln.

wish [wiʃ] 1. wünschen; wollen; ~ for (sich) et. wünschen; ~ well (ill) wohl- (übel)wollen; 2. Wunsch m;

~ful □ ['wiʃful] sehnsüchtig; ~ thinking Wunschdenken n.

wisp [wisp] Wisch m; Strähne f.

wistful [['wistful] sehnsüchtig.

wit [wit] 1. Witz m; a. ~s pl. Verstand m; witziger Kopf; be at one's ~'s end mit s-r Weisheit zu Ende sein; keep one's ~s about one e-n klaren Kopf behalten; 2.: to ~ nämlich, das heißt.

witch [witʃ] Hexe f, Zauberin f; ~craft ['witʃkrɑːft], ~ery [~ʃəri] Hexerei f; ~hunt pol. Hexenjagd f (Verfolgung politisch verdächtiger Personen).

with [wið] mit; nebst; bei; von; durch; vor (dat.); ~ it sl. schwer auf der Höhe.

withdraw [wið'drɔː] [irr. (draw)] v/t. ab-, ent-, zurückziehen; zurücknehmen; Geld abheben; v/i. sich zurückziehen; abtreten; ~al [~əl] Zurückziehung f; Rückzug m.

wither ['wiðə] v/i. (ver)welken; verdorren; austrocknen; v/t. welk machen.

with|hold [wið'hould] [irr. (hold)] zurückhalten; et. vorenthalten; ~in [wið'in] 1. adv. lit. im Innern, drin(nen); zu Hause; 2. prp. in(nerhalb); ~ doors im Hause; ~ call in Rufweite; ~out [wið'aut] 1. adv. lit. (dr)außen; äußerlich; 2. prp. ohne; lit. außerhalb, sonst [wið'stænd] [irr. (stand)] widerstehen (dat.).

witness ['witnis] 1. Zeug|e m, -in f; bear ~ Zeugnis ablegen (to für; of von); in ~ of zum Zeugnis (gen.); 2. (be)zeugen; Zeuge sein von et.; ~box, Am. ~stand Zeugenstand m.

wit|ticism ['witisizəm] Witz m; ~ty [['witi] witzig; geistreich.

wives [waivz] pl. von wife.

wiz Am. sl. [wiz] Genie n; ~ard ['wizəd] Zauberer m; Genie n.

wizen(ed) ['wizn(d)] schrump(e)lig.

wobble ['wobl] schwanken; wackeln.

woe [wou] Weh n, Leid n; ~ is me! wehe mir!; ~begone ['woubigon] jammervoll, ~ful [['wouful] jammervoll, traurig, elend.

woke [wouk] pret u. p.p. von wake 2; ~n ['woukən] p.p. von wake 2.

wold [would] (hügeliges) Heideland.

wolf [wulf] 1. zo. pl wolves [wulvz] Wolf m; 2. verschlingen; ~ish [['wulfiʃ] wölfisch; Wolfs...

woman ['wumən], pl. women ['wimin] 1. Frau f; Weib n; 2. weiblich; ~ doctor Ärztin f; ~ student Studentin f; ~hood [~nhud] die Frauen f/pl.; Weiblichkeit f; ~ish □ [~niʃ] weibisch; ~kind [~'kaind] Frauen(welt f) f/pl.; ~like [~nlaik] fraulich; ~ly [~li] weiblich.

womb [wuːm] anat. Gebärmutter f; Mutterleib m; fig. Schoß m.

women ['wimin] *pl. von* woman; **~folk(s)**, **~kind** die Frauen *f/pl.*; F Weibervolk *n*.

won [wʌn] *pret. u. p.p. von* win 1.

wonder ['wʌndə] 1. Wunder *n*; Verwunderung *f*; 2. sich wundern; gern wissen mögen, sich fragen; **~ful** □ [~əful] wunderbar, -voll; **~ing** □ [~əriŋ] staunend, verwundert.

won't [wount] = will not.

wont [~] 1. *pred.* gewohnt; *be* ~ *to inf.* pflegen zu *inf.*; 2. Gewohnheit *f*; *ed* ['wountid] gewohnt.

woo [wuː] werben um; locken.

wood [wud] Wald *m*, Gehölz *n*; Holz *n*; Faß *n*; ♪ Holzblasinstrument (-e *pl.*) *n*; *touch ~!* unberufen!; **~chuck** zo. ['wudtʃʌk] Waldmurmeltier *n*; **~cut** Holzschnitt *m*; **~cutter** Holzfäller *m*; *Kunst* Holzschneider *m*; *ed* ['wudid] bewaldet; **~en** ['wudn] hölzern (*a. fig.*); Holz...; **~man** Förster *m*; Holzfäller *m*; **~pecker** orn. ['wudpekə] Specht *m*; **~sman** ['wudzmən] *s.* woodman; **~wind** ♪ Holzblasinstrument *n*; *oft* **~s** *pl.* ♪ Holzbläser *m/pl.*; **~work** Holzwerk *n*; **~y** ['wudi] waldig; holzig.

wool [wul] Wolle *f*; **~gathering** ['wulgæðəriŋ] Geistesabwesenheit *f*; **~(l)en** ['wulin] 1. wollen; Woll-...; 2. **~s** *pl.* Wollsachen *f/pl.*; **~(l)y** ['wuli] 1. wollig; Woll-...; *be-* legt (*Stimme*); verschwommen; 2. **woollies** *pl.* F Wollsachen *f/pl.*

word [wəːd] 1. *mst* Wort *n*; *eng* S.: Vokabel *f*; Nachricht *f*; ✗ Losung(swort *n*) *f*; Versprechen *n*; Befehl *m*; Spruch *m*; **~s** *pl.* Wörter *n/pl.*; Worte *n/pl.*; *fig.* Wortwechsel *m*; Text *m e-s Liedes*; *have a* ~ *with* mit *j-m* sprechen; 2. (in Worten) ausdrücken, (ab-) fassen; **~ing** ['wəːdiŋ] Wortlaut *m*, Fassung *f*; **~splitting** Wortklauberei *f*.

wordy □ ['wəːdi] wortreich; Wort...

wore [wɔː] *pret. von* wear 1.

work [wəːk] 1. Arbeit *f*; Werk *n*; *attr.* Arbeits...; **~s** *pl.* ⊕ (Uhr-, Feder)Werk *n*; ✗ Befestigungen *pl.*; **~s** *sg.* Werk *n*, Fabrik *f*; ~ *of art* Kunstwerk *n*; *at* ~ bei der Arbeit; *be in* ~ Arbeit haben; *be out of* ~ arbeitslos sein; *set to* ~, *set od. go about one's* ~ an die Arbeit gehen; **~s council** Betriebsrat *m*; 2. [*a. irr.*] *v/i.* arbeiten (*a. fig.*); wirken, gären; sich *hindurch- etc.* arbeiten; ~ *at* arbeiten an (*dat.*); ~ *out* herauskommen (*Summe*); *v/t.* (be)arbeiten; arbeiten lassen; betreiben; *Maschine etc* bedienen; (be)wirken; ausrechnen, *Aufgabe* lösen; ~ *one's way* sich durcharbeiten; ~ *off* abarbeiten; *Gefühl* abreagieren; ✝ abstoßen; ~ *out* ausarbeiten; lösen;

ausrechnen; ~ *up* hochbringen; aufregen; verarbeiten (*into* zu).

work|able □ ['wəːkəbl] bearbeitungs-, betriebsfähig; ausführbar; **~aday** [~ədei] Alltags...; **~day** Werktag *m*; **~er** ['wəːkə] Arbeiter (-in); **~house** Armenhaus *n*; *Am.* Besserungsanstalt *f*, Arbeitshaus *n*.

working ['wəːkiŋ] 1. Bergwerk *n*; Steinbruch *m*; Arbeits-, Wirkungsweise *f*; 2. arbeitend; Arbeits...; Betriebs...; **~class** Arbeiter...; **~day** Werk-, Arbeitstag *m*; **~ hours** *pl.* Arbeitszeit *f*.

workman ['wəːkmən] Arbeiter *m*; Handwerker *m*; **~like** [~nlaik] kunstgerecht; **~ship** [~nʃip] Kunstfertigkeit *f*.

work|out *Am.* F ['wəːkaut] *mst Sport* (Konditions-)Training *n*; Erprobung *f*; **~shop** Werkstatt *f*; **~woman** Arbeiterin *f*.

world [wəːld] *allg.* Welt *f*; *a* ~ *of* e-e Unmenge (von); *bring* (*come*) *into the* ~ zur Welt bringen (kommen); *think the* ~ *of* alles halten von; **~ling** ['wəːldliŋ] Weltkind *n*.

worldly ['wəːldli] weltlich; Welt...; **~wise** [~i'waiz] weltklug.

world|-power *pol.* ['wəːldpauə] Weltmacht *f*; **~wide** weltweit; weltumspannend; Welt...

worm [wəːm] 1. Wurm *m* (*a. fig.*); 2. *ein Geheimnis* entlocken (*out of* dat.); ~ *o.s.* sich schlängeln; *fig.* sich einschleichen (*into* in *acc.*); **~eaten** ['wəːmiːtn] wurmstichig.

worn [wɔːn] *p.p. von* wear 1; **~out** ['wɔːn'aut] abgenutzt; abgetragen; verbraucht (*a. fig.*); müde, erschöpft; abgezehrt; verhärmt.

worry ['wʌri] 1. (sich) beunruhigen; (sich) ärgern; sich sorgen; sich aufregen; bedrücken, zerren, (ab-) würgen; plagen, quälen; 2. Unruhe *f*; Sorge *f*; Ärger *m*; Qual *f*, Plage *f*; Quälgeist *m*.

worse [wəːs] schlechter; schlimmer; ~ *luck!* leider!; um so schlimmer!; *from bad to* ~ vom Regen in die Traufe; **~n** ['wəːsn] (sich) verschlechtern.

worship ['wəːʃip] 1. Verehrung *f*; Gottesdienst *m*; Kult *m*; 2. verehren; anbeten; den Gottesdienst besuchen; **~(p)er** [~pə] Verehrer (-in); Kirchgänger(in).

worst [wəːst] 1. schlechtest; ärgst; schlimmst; 2. überwältigen.

worsted ['wustid] Kammgarn *n*.

worth [wəːθ] 1. wert; ~ *reading* lesenswert; 2. Wert *m*; Würde *f*; **~less** □ ['wəːθlis] wertlos; unwürdig; **~while** ['wəːθ'wail] der Mühe wert; **~y** [~ði] würdig.

would [wud] [*pret. von* will 2] wollte; würde; möchte; pflegte; **~be** ['wudbiː] angeblich, soge-

nannt; möglich, potentiell; Pseu-
do...

wound[1] [wu:nd] **1.** Wunde *f*, Ver-
wundung *f*, Verletzung *f*; *fig.*
Kränkung *f*; **2.** verwunden, verletzen (*a. fig.*).

wound[2] [waund] *pret. u. p.p. von*
wind 2.

wove [wouv] *pret. von* weave; **~n**
['wouvən] *p.p. von* weave.

wow *Am.* [wau] **1.** *int.* Mensch!;
toll!; **2.** *sl.* Bombenerfolg *m.*

wrangle ['ræŋgl] **1.** streiten, (sich)
zanken; **2.** Streit *m*, Zank *m.*

wrap [ræp] **1.** *v/t.* (ein)wickeln; *fig.*
einhüllen; *be ~ped up in* gehüllt sein
in (*acc.*); ganz aufgehen in (*dat.*);
v/i. ~ up sich einhüllen; **2.** Hülle *f*;
engS.: Decke *f*; Schal *m*; Mantel
m; **~per** ['ræpə] Hülle *f*, Umschlag
m; *a. postal ~* Streifband *n*; **~ping**
['ræpiŋ] Verpackung *f.*

wrath *lit.* [rɔ:θ] Zorn *m*, Grimm *m.*

wreak [ri:k] *Rache* üben, *Zorn* auslassen (*upon* an *j-m*).

wreath [ri:θ], *pl.* **~s** [ri:ðz] (Blu-
men)Gewinde *n*; Kranz *m*; Girlande *f*; Ring *m*, Kreis *m*; Schneewehe *f*; **~e** [ri:ð] [*irr.*] *v/t.* (um-)
winden; *v/i.* sich ringeln.

wreck [rek] **1.** ⚓ Wrack *n*; Trümmer *pl.*; Schiffbruch *m*; *fig.* Untergang *m*; **2.** zum Scheitern (⚓ Entgleisen) bringen; zertrümmern;
vernichten; *be ~ed* ⚓ scheitern;
Schiffbruch erleiden; **~age** ['rekidʒ]
Trümmer *pl.*; Wrackteile *n*/*pl.*; **~ed**
schiffbrüchig; ruiniert; **~er** ['rekə]
⚓ Bergungsschiff *n*, -arbeiter *m*;
Strandräuber *m*; Abbrucharbeiter
m; *Am. mot.* Abschleppwagen *m*;
~ing ['rekiŋ] Strandraub *m*; *~ com-*
pany Am. Abbruchfirma *f*; *~ ser-*
vice Am. mot. Abschlepp-, Hilfs-
dienst *m.*

wren *orn.* [ren] Zaunkönig *m.*

wrench [rentʃ] **1.** drehen; reißen;
entwinden (*from s.o.* j-m); verdrehen (*a. fig.*); verrenken; *~ open* aufreißen; **2.** Ruck *m*; Verrenkung *f*;
fig. Schmerz *m*; ⊕ Schraubenschlüssel *m.*

wrest [rest] reißen; verdrehen; ent-
reißen; **~le** ['resl] ringen (mit);
~ling [~liŋ] Ringkampf *m*, Ringen
n.

wretch [retʃ] Elende(r *m*) *f*; Kerl *m.*

wretched ☐ ['retʃid] elend.

wriggle ['rigl] sich winden *od.*
schlängeln; *~ out of* sich drücken
von *et.*

wright [rait]...macher *m*,...bauer *m.*

wring [riŋ] [*irr.*] *Hände* ringen;
(aus)wringen; pressen; *Hals* umdrehen; abringen (*from s.o.* j-m);
~ s.o.'s heart j-m zu Herzen gehen.

wrinkle ['riŋkl] **1.** Runzel *f*; Falte *f*;
Wink *m*; Trick *m*; **2.** (sich) runzeln.

wrist [rist] Handgelenk *n*; *~ watch*
Armbanduhr *f*; **~band** ['ristbænd]
Bündchen *n*, (Hemd)Manschette *f.*

writ [rit] Erlaß *m*; (gerichtlicher)
Befehl; *Holy* 2 Heilige Schrift.

write [rait] [*irr.*] schreiben; *~ down*
auf-, niederschreiben; ausarbeiten;
hervorheben; **~r** ['raitə] Schreiber
(-in); Verfasser(in); Schriftsteller
(-in).

writhe [raið] sich krümmen.

writing ['raitiŋ] Schreiben *n*; Aufsatz *m*; Werk *n*; Schrift *f*; Schrift-
stück *n*; Urkunde *f*; Stil *m*; *attr.*
Schreib...; *in ~* schriftlich; **~-case**
Schreibmappe *f*; **~-desk** Schreibtisch *m*; **~-paper** Schreibpapier *n.*

written ['ritn] **1.** *p.p. von* write;
2. *adj.* schriftlich.

wrong [rɔŋ] **1.** ☐ unrecht; verkehrt,
falsch; *be ~* unrecht haben; *in* Unordnung sein; *falsch gehen* (*Uhr*);
go ~ schiefgehen; *on the ~ side of*
sixty über die 60 hinaus; **2.** Unrecht *n*; Beleidigung *f*; **3.** unrecht
tun (*dat.*); ungerecht behandeln;
~doer ['rɔŋ'duə] Übeltäter(in); **~-**
ful ☐ ['rɔŋful] ungerecht; unrechtmäßig.

wrote [rout] *pret. von* write.

wrought [rɔ:t] *pret. u. p.p. von*
work 2; *~ iron* Schmiedeeisen *n*;
~-iron ['rɔ:t'aiən] schmiedeeisern;
~-up erregt.

wrung [rʌŋ] *pret. u. p.p. von* wring.

wry ☐ [rai] schief, krumm, verzerrt.

X, Y

Xmas ['krisməs] = *Christmas.*

X-ray ['eks'rei] **1.** *~s pl.* Röntgen-
strahlen *m*/*pl.*; **2.** Röntgen...;
3. durchleuchten, röntgen.

xylophone ♪ ['zailəfoun] Xylophon
n.

yacht ⚓ [jɔt] **1.** (Motor)Jacht *f*;
Segelboot *n*; **2.** auf e-r Jacht fah-

ren; segeln; **~-club** ['jɔtklʌb]
Segel-, Jachtklub *m*; **~ing** ['jɔtiŋ]
Segelsport *m*; *attr.* Segel...

Yankee F ['jæŋki] Yankee *m* (*Ameri-*
kaner, bsd. der Nordstaaten).

yap [jæp] kläffen; F quasseln.

yard [ja:d] Yard *n*, *englische* Elle
(*= 0,914 m*); ⚓ Rah(e) *f*; Hof *m*;
(Bau-, Stapel)Platz *m*; *Am.* Garten
m (*um das Haus*); **~measure**

['jɑːdmeʒə], **~stick** Yardstock *m*, -maß *n*.

yarn [jɑːn] **1.** Garn *n*; F Seemannsgarn *n*; abenteuerliche Geschichte; **2.** F erzählen.

yawl ⚓ [jɔːl] Jolle *f*.

yawn [jɔːn] **1.** gähnen; **2.** Gähnen *n*.

ye †, *poet.*, *co.* [jiː] ihr.

yea †, *prov.* [jei] **1.** ja; **2.** Ja *n*.

year [jəː] Jahr *n*; **~ly** ['jəːli] jährlich.

yearn [jəːn] sich sehnen, verlangen; **~ing** ['jəːniŋ] **1.** Sehnen *n*, Sehnsucht *f*; **2.** □ sehnsüchtig.

yeast [jiːst] Hefe *f*; Schaum *m*.

yegg(man) *Am. sl.* ['jeg(mən)] Stromer *m*; Einbrecher *m*.

yell [jel] **1.** (gellend) schreien; aufschreien; **2.** (gellender) Schrei; anfeuernder Ruf.

yellow ['jelou] **1.** gelb; F hasenfüßig (*feig*); Sensations...; Hetz...; **2.** Gelb *n*; **3.** (sich) gelb färben; **~ed** vergilbt; **~ fever** 🗲 Gelbfieber *n*; **~ish** [~ouiʃ] gelblich.

yelp [jelp] **1.** Gekläff *n*; **2.** kläffen.

yen *Am. sl.* [jen] brennendes Verlangen.

yeoman ['joumən] freier Bauer.

yep *Am.* F [jep] ja.

yes [jes] **1.** ja; doch; **2.** Ja *n*.

yesterday ['jestədi] gestern.

yet [jet] **1.** *adv.* noch; bis jetzt; schon; sogar; *as ~* bis jetzt; *not ~* noch nicht; **2.** *cj.* (je)doch, dennoch, trotzdem.

yew ♣ [juː] Eibe *f*, Taxus *m*.

yield [jiːld] **1.** *v/t.* hervorbringen, liefern; ergeben; *Gewinn* (ein)bringen; gewähren; übergeben; zugestehen; *v/i.* 🗲 tragen; sich fügen; nachgeben; **2.** Ertrag *m*; **~ing** □ ['jiːldiŋ] nachgebend; *fig.* nachgiebig.

yip *Am.* F [jip] jaulen.

yod|el, **~le** ['joudl] **1.** Jodler *m*; **2.** jodeln.

yoke [jouk] **1.** Joch *n* (*a. fig.*); Paar *n* (Ochsen); Schultertrage *f*; **2.** an-, zs.-spannen; *fig.* paaren (*to* mit).

yolk [jouk] (Ei)Dotter *m*, *n*, Eigelb *n*.

yon [jɔn], **~der** *lit.* ['jɔndə] **1.** jene(r, -s) jenseitig; **2.** dort drüben.

yore [jɔː]: *of ~* ehemals, ehedem.

you [juː, ju] ihr; du, Sie; man.

young [jʌŋ] **1.** □ jung; *von Kindern a.* klein; **2.** (Tier)Junge(s) *n*; (Tier)Junge *pl.*; *with ~* trächtig; **~ster** ['jʌŋstə] Junge *m*.

your [jɔː] euer(e); dein(e), Ihr(e); **~s** [jɔːz] der (die, das) eurige, deinige, Ihrige; euer; dein, Ihr; **~self** [jɔː'self], *pl.* **~selves** [~lvz] (du, ihr, Sie) selbst; dich, euch, Sie (selbst), sich (selbst); *by ~* allein.

youth [juːθ], *pl.* **~s** [juːðz] Jugend *f*; Jüngling *m*; **~ hostel** Jugendherberge *f*; **~ful** □ ['juːθful] jugendlich.

yule *lit.* [juːl] Weihnacht *f*.

Z

zeal [ziːl] Eifer *m*; **~ot** ['zelət] Eiferer *m*; **~ous** □ [~əs] eifrig; eifrig bedacht (*for* auf *acc.*); innig, heiß.

zebra *zo.* ['ziːbrə] Zebra *n*; **~ crossing** Fußgängerüberweg *m*.

zenith ['zeniθ] Zenit *m*; *fig.* Höhepunkt *m*.

zero ['ziərou] Null *f*; Nullpunkt *m*.

zest [zest] **1.** Würze *f* (*a. fig.*); Lust *f*, Freude *f*; Genuß *m*; **2.** würzen.

zigzag ['zigzæg] Zickzack *m*.

zinc [ziŋk] **1.** *min.* Zink *n*; **2.** verzinken.

zip [zip] Schwirren *n*; F Schwung *m*; **~-fastener** ['zipfɑːsnə], **~per** ['zipə] Reißverschluß *m*.

zodiac *ast.* ['zoudiæk] Tierkreis *m*.

zone [zoun] Zone *f*; *fig.* Gebiet *n*.

Zoo F [zuː] Zoo *m*.

zoolog|ical □ [zouə'lɔdʒikəl] zoologisch; **~y** [zou'ɔlədʒi] Zoologie *f*.

Alphabetical List of the German Irregular Verbs

Infinitive — Preterite — Past Participle

backen - backte (buk) - gebacken
bedingen - bedang (bedingte) - bedungen (*conditional*: bedingt)
befehlen - befahl - befohlen
beginnen - begann - begonnen
beißen - biß - gebissen
bergen - barg - geborgen
bersten - barst - geborsten
bewegen - bewog - bewogen
biegen - bog - gebogen
bieten - bot - geboten
binden - band - gebunden
bitten - bat - gebeten
blasen - blies - geblasen
bleiben - blieb - geblieben
bleichen - blich - geblichen
braten - briet - gebraten
brauchen - brauchte - gebraucht (*v/aux.* brauchen)
brechen - brach - gebrochen
brennen - brannte - gebrannt
bringen - brachte - gebracht
denken - dachte - gedacht
dreschen - drosch - gedroschen
dringen - drang - gedrungen
dürfen - durfte - gedurft (*v/aux.* dürfen)
empfehlen - empfahl - empfohlen
erlöschen - erlosch - erloschen
erschrecken - erschrak - erschrocken
essen - aß - gegessen
fahren - fuhr - gefahren
fallen - fiel - gefallen
fangen - fing - gefangen
fechten - focht - gefochten
finden - fand - gefunden
flechten - flocht - geflochten
fliegen - flog - geflogen
fliehen - floh - geflohen
fließen - floß - geflossen
fressen - fraß - gefressen
frieren - fror - gefroren
gären - gor (*esp. fig.* gärte) - gegoren (*esp. fig.* gegärt)
gebären - gebar - geboren
geben - gab - gegeben
gedeihen - gedieh - gediehen
gehen - ging - gegangen
gelingen - gelang - gelungen
gelten - galt - gegolten
genesen - genas - genesen
genießen - genoß - genossen
geschehen - geschah - geschehen
gewinnen - gewann - gewonnen

gießen - goß - gegossen
gleichen - glich - geglichen
gleiten - glitt - geglitten
glimmen - glomm - geglommen
graben - grub - gegraben
greifen - griff - gegriffen
haben - hatte - gehabt
halten - hielt - gehalten
hängen - hing - gehangen
hauen - haute (hieb) - gehauen
heben - hob - gehoben
heißen - hieß - geheißen
helfen - half - geholfen
kennen - kannte - gekannt
klingen - klang - geklungen
kneifen - kniff - gekniffen
kommen - kam - gekommen
können - konnte - gekonnt (*v/aux.* können)
kriechen - kroch - gekrochen
laden - lud - geladen
lassen - ließ - gelassen (*v/aux.* lassen)
laufen - lief - gelaufen
leiden - litt - gelitten
leihen - lieh - geliehen
lesen - las - gelesen
liegen - lag - gelegen
lügen - log - gelogen
mahlen - mahlte - gemahlen
meiden - mied - gemieden
melken - melkte (molk) - gemolken (gemelkt)
messen - maß - gemessen
mißlingen - mißlang - mißlungen
mögen - mochte - gemocht (*v/aux.* mögen)
müssen - mußte - gemußt (*v/aux.* müssen)
nehmen - nahm - genommen
nennen - nannte - genannt
pfeifen - pfiff - gepfiffen
preisen - pries - gepriesen
quellen - quoll - gequollen
raten - riet - geraten
reiben - rieb - gerieben
reißen - riß - gerissen
reiten - ritt - geritten
rennen - rannte - gerannt
riechen - roch - gerochen
ringen - rang - gerungen
rinnen - rann - geronnen
rufen - rief - gerufen
salzen - salzte - gesalzen (gesalzt)
saufen - soff - gesoffen

saugen - sog - gesogen
schaffen - schuf - geschaffen
schallen - schallte (scholl) - ge-
schallt (for erschallen a. erschol-
len)
scheiden - schied - geschieden
scheinen - schien - geschienen
schelten - schalt - gescholten
scheren - schor - geschoren
schieben - schob - geschoben
schießen - schoß - geschossen
schinden - schund - geschunden
schlafen - schlief - geschlafen
schlagen - schlug - geschlagen
schleichen - schlich - geschlichen
schleifen - schliff - geschliffen
schließen - schloß - geschlossen
schlingen - schlang - geschlungen
schmeißen - schmiß - geschmissen
schmelzen - schmolz - geschmolzen
schneiden - schnitt - geschnitten
schrecken - schrak - † geschrocken
schreiben - schrieb - geschrieben
schreien - schrie - geschrie(e)n
schreiten - schritt - geschritten
schweigen - schwieg - geschwiegen
schwellen - schwoll - geschwollen
schwimmen - schwamm - ge-
schwommen
schwinden - schwand - geschwun-
den
schwingen - schwang - geschwun-
gen
schwören - schwor - geschworen
sehen - sah - gesehen
sein - war - gewesen
senden - sandte - gesandt
sieden - sott - gesotten
singen - sang - gesungen
sinken - sank - gesunken
sinnen - sann - gesonnen
sitzen - saß - gesessen
sollen - sollte - gesollt (v/aux. sollen)
spalten - spaltete - gespalten (ge-
spaltet)
speien - spie - gespie(e)n
spinnen - spann - gesponnen
sprechen - sprach - gesprochen

sprießen - sproß - gesprossen
springen - sprang - gesprungen
stechen - stach - gestochen
stecken - steckte (stak) - gesteckt
stehen - stand - gestanden
stehlen - stahl - gestohlen
steigen - stieg - gestiegen
sterben - starb - gestorben
stieben - stob - gestoben
stinken - stank - gestunken
stoßen - stieß - gestoßen
streichen - strich - gestrichen
streiten - stritt - gestritten
tragen - trug - getragen
treffen - traf - getroffen
treiben - trieb - getrieben
treten - trat - getreten
triefen - triefte (troff) - getrieft
trinken - trank - getrunken
trügen - trog - getrogen
tun - tat - getan
verderben - verdarb - verdorben
verdrießen - verdroß - verdrossen
vergessen - vergaß - vergessen
verlieren - verlor - verloren
verschleißen - verschliß - ver-
schlissen
verzeihen - verzieh - verziehen
wachsen - wuchs - gewachsen
wägen - wog (⚡ wägte) - gewogen
(⚡ gewägt)
waschen - wusch - gewaschen
weben - wob - gewoben
weichen - wich - gewichen
weisen - wies - gewiesen
wenden - wandte - gewandt
werben - warb - geworben
werden - wurde - geworden (worden*)
werfen - warf - geworfen
wiegen - wog - gewogen
winden - wand - gewunden
wissen - wußte - gewußt
wollen - wollte - gewollt (v/aux.
wollen)
wringen - wrang - gewrungen
ziehen - zog - gezogen
zwingen - zwang - gezwungen

* only in connexion with the past participles of other verbs, e.g. er ist gesehen
worden he has been seen.

Alphabetical List of the English Irregular Verbs

Infinitive — Preterite — Past Participle

Irregular forms marked with asterisks (*) can be exchanged for the regular forms.

abide (*bleiben*) - abode* - abode*
arise (*sich erheben*) - arose - arisen
awake (*erwachen*) - awoke - awoke*
be (*sein*) - was - been
bear (*tragen; gebären*) - bore - getragen: borne - *geboren:* born
beat (*schlagen*) - beat - beat(en)
become (*werden*) - became - become
beget (*zeugen*) - begot - begotten
begin (*anfangen*) - began - begun
bend (*beugen*) - bent - bent
bereave (*berauben*) - bereft* - bereft*
beseech (*ersuchen*) - besought -
  besought
bet (*wetten*) - bet* - bet*
bid ([*ge*]*bieten*) - bade, bid - bid(den)
bide (*abwarten*) - bode* - bided
bind (*binden*) - bound - bound
bite (*beißen*) - bit - bitten
bleed (*bluten*) - bled - bled
blend (*mischen*) - blent* - blent*
blow (*blasen; blühen*) - blew - blown
break (*brechen*) - broke - broken
breed (*aufziehen*) - bred - bred
bring (*bringen*) - brought - brought
build (*bauen*) - built - built
burn (*brennen*) - burnt* - burnt*
burst (*bersten*) - burst - burst
buy (*kaufen*) - bought - bought
cast (*werfen*) - cast - cast
catch (*fangen*) - caught - caught
chide (*schelten*) - chid - chid(den)*
choose (*wählen*) - chose - chosen
cleave ([*sich*] *spalten*) cleft, clove* -
  cleft, cloven*
cling (*sich* [*an*]*klammern*) - clung -
  clung
clothe ([*an-, be*]*kleiden*) - clad* -
  clad*
come (*kommen*) - came - come
cost (*kosten*) - cost - cost
creep (*kriechen*) - crept - crept
crow (*krähen*) - crew* - crowed
cut (*schneiden*) - cut - cut
deal (*handeln*) - dealt - dealt
dig (*graben*) - dug - dug
do (*tun*) - did - done
draw (*ziehen*) - drew - drawn
dream (*träumen*) - dreamt* - dreamt*
drink (*trinken*) - drank - drunk
drive (*treiben; fahren*) - drove -
  driven
dwell (*wohnen*) - dwelt - dwelt

eat (*essen*) - ate, eat - eaten
fall (*fallen*) - fell - fallen
feed (*füttern*) - fed - fed
feel (*fühlen*) - felt - felt
fight (*kämpfen*) - fought - fought
find (*finden*) - found - found
flee (*fliehen*) - fled - fled
fling (*schleudern*) - flung - flung
fly (*fliegen*) - flew - flown
forbid (*verbieten*) - forbade - forbidden
forget (*vergessen*) - forgot - forgotten
forsake (*aufgeben; verlassen*) - forsook - forsaken
freeze ([*ge*]*frieren*) - froze - frozen
get (*bekommen*) - got - got, *Am.*
  gotten
gild (*vergolden*) - gilt* - gilt*
gird ([*um*]*gürten*) - girt* - girt*
give (*geben*) - gave - given
go (*gehen*) - went - gone
grave ([*ein*]*graben*) - graved - graven*
grind (*mahlen*) - ground - ground
grow (*wachsen*) - grew - grown
hang (*hängen*) - hung - hung
have (*haben*) - had - had
hear (*hören*) - heard - heard
heave (*heben*) - hove* - hove*
hew (*hauen, hacken*) - hewed - hewn*
hide (*verbergen*) - hid - hid(den)
hit (*treffen*) - hit - hit
hold (*halten*) - held - held
hurt (*verletzen*) - hurt - hurt
keep (*halten*) - kept - kept
kneel (*knien*) - knelt* - knelt*
knit (*stricken*) - knit* - knit*
know (*wissen*) - knew - known
lay (*legen*) - laid - laid
lead (*führen*) - led - led
lean ([*sich*] [*an*]*lehnen*) - leant* -
  leant*
leap ([*über*]*springen*) - leapt* - leapt*
learn (*lernen*) - learnt* - learnt*
leave (*verlassen*) - left - left
lend (*leihen*) - lent - lent
let (*lassen*) - let - let
lie (*liegen*) - lay - lain
light (*anzünden*) - lit* - lit*
lose (*verlieren*) - lost - lost
make (*machen*) - made - made
mean (*meinen*) - meant - meant
meet (*begegnen*) - met - met
mow (*mähen*) - mowed - mown*

pay (*zahlen*) - paid - paid
pen (*einpferchen*) - pent - pent
put (*setzen, stellen*) - put - put
read (*lesen*) - read - read
rend ([*zer*]*reißen*) - rent - rent
rid (*befreien*) - rid* - rid*
ride (*reiten*) - rode - ridden
ring (*läuten*) - rang - rung
rise (*aufstehen*) - rose - risen
rive ([*sich*] *spalten*) - rived - riven*
run (*laufen*) - ran - run
saw (*sägen*) - sawed - sawn*
say (*sagen*) - said - said
see (*sehen*) - saw - seen
seek (*suchen*) - sought - sought
sell (*verkaufen*) - sold - sold
send (*senden*) - sent - sent
set (*setzen*) - set - set
sew (*nähen*) - sewed - sewn*
shake (*schütteln*) - shook - shaken
shave ([*sich*] *rasieren*) - shaved -
shaven*
shear (*scheren*) - sheared - shorn
shed (*ausgießen*) - shed - shed
shine (*scheinen*) - shone - shone
shoe (*beschuhen*) - shod - shod
shoot (*schießen*) - shot - shot
show (*zeigen*) - showed - shown*
shred ([*zer*]*schnitzeln, zerfetzen*) -
shred* - shred*
shrink (*einschrumpfen*) - shrank -
shrunk
shut (*schließen*) - shut - shut
sing (*singen*) - sang - sung
sink (*sinken*) - sank - sunk
sit (*sitzen*) - sat - sat
slay (*erschlagen*) - slew - slain
sleep (*schlafen*) - slept - slept
slide (*gleiten*) - slid - slid
sling (*schleudern*) - slung - slung
slink (*schleichen*) - slunk - slunk
slip (*schlüpfen, gleiten*) - slipt* -
slipt*
slit (*schlitzen*) - slit - slit
smell (*riechen*) - smelt* - smelt*
smite (*schlagen*) - smote - smitten,
smote
sow ([*aus*]*säen*) - sowed - sown*
speak (*sprechen*) - spoke - spoken
speed (*eilen*) - sped* - sped*
spell (*buchstabieren*) - spelt* - spelt*
spend (*ausgeben*) - spent - spent

spill (*verschütten*) - spilt* - spilt*
spin (*spinnen*) - spun - spun
spit ([*aus*]*spucken*) - spat - spat
split (*spalten*) - split - split
spoil (*verderben*) - spoilt* - spoilt*
spread (*verbreiten*) - spread - spread
spring (*springen*) - sprang - sprung
stand (*stehen*) - stood - stood
stave (*den Boden einschlagen*) -
stove* - stove*
steal (*stehlen*) - stole - stolen
stick (*stecken*) - stuck - stuck
sting (*stechen*) - stung - stung
stink (*stinken*) - stank - stunk
strew ([*be*]*streuen*) - strewed -
strewn*
stride (*über-, durchschreiten*) - strode
- stridden
strike (*schlagen*) - struck - struck
string (*spannen*) - strung - strung
strive (*streben*) - strove - striven
swear (*schwören*) - swore - sworn
sweat (*schwitzen*) - sweat* - sweat*
sweep (*fegen*) - swept - swept
swell ([*an*]*schwellen*) - swelled -
swollen
swim (*schwimmen*) - swam - swum
swing (*schwingen*) - swung - swung
take (*nehmen*) - took - taken
teach (*lehren*) - taught - taught
tear (*ziehen*) - tore - torn
tell (*sagen*) - told - told
think (*denken*) - thought - thought
thrive (*gedeihen*) - throve* - thriven*
throw (*werfen*) - threw - thrown
thrust (*stoßen*) - thrust - thrust
tread (*treten*) - trod - trodden
wake (*wachen*) - woke* - woke(n)*
wax (*zunehmen*) - waxed - waxen*
wear ([*Kleider*] *tragen*) - wore - worn
weave (*weben*) - wove - woven
weep (*weinen*) - wept - wept
wet (*nässen*) - wet* - wet*
win (*gewinnen*) - won - won
wind (*winden*) - wound - wound
work (*arbeiten*) - wrought* -
wrought*
wreathe (*[um]winden*) - wreathed -
wreathen*
wring ([*aus*]*wringen*) - wrung -
wrung
write (*schreiben*) - wrote - written

German Proper Names

Aachen ['ɑːxən] n Aachen, Aix-la-Chapelle.

Adenauer ['ɑːdənauər] first chancellor of the German Federal Republic.

Adler ['ɑːdlər] Austrian psychologist.

Adria ['ɑːdria] f Adriatic Sea.

Afrika ['ɑːfrika] n Africa.

Ägypten [ɛ'ɡyptən] n Egypt.

Albanien [al'bɑːnjən] n Albania.

Algerien [al'ɡeːrjən] n Algeria.

Algier ['alʒiːr] n Algiers.

Allgäu ['alɡɔy] n Al(l)gäu (region of Bavaria).

Alpen ['alpən] pl. Alps pl.

Amerika [a'meːrika] n America.

Anden ['andən] pl. the Andes pl.

Antillen [an'tilən] f/pl. Antilles pl.

Antwerpen [ant'verpən] n Antwerp.

Apenninen [ape'niːnən] m/pl. the Apennines pl.

Argentinien [arɡen'tiːnjən] n Argentina, the Argentine.

Ärmelkanal ['ɛrməlkanaːl] m English Channel.

Asien ['ɑːzjən] n Asia.

Athen [a'teːn] n Athens.

Äthiopien [ɛti'oːpjən] n Ethiopia.

Atlantik [at'lantik] m Atlantic.

Australien [au'strɑːljən] n Australia.

Bach [bax] German composer.

Baden-Württemberg ['bɑːdən'vyrtəmberk] n Land of the German Federal Republic.

Barlach ['barlax] German sculptor.

Basel ['bɑːzəl] n Bâle, Basle.

Bayern ['baiərn] n Bavaria (Land of the German Federal Republic).

Becher ['beçər] German poet.

Beckmann ['bekman] German painter.

Beethoven ['beːthoːfən] German composer.

Belgien ['belɡjən] n Belgium.

Belgrad ['belɡrɑːt] n Belgrade.

Berg [berk] Austrian composer.

Berlin [ber'liːn] n Berlin.

Bermuda-Inseln [ber'muːda⁹inzəln] f/pl. Bermudas pl.

Bern [bern] n Bern(e).

Bismarck ['bismark] German statesman.

Bloch [blɔx] German philosopher.

Böcklin ['bœkliːn] German painter.

Bodensee ['boːdənzeː] m Lake of Constance.

Böhm [bøːm] Austrian conductor.

Böhmen ['bøːmən] n Bohemia.

Böll [bœl] German author.

Bonn [bɔn] n capital of the German Federal Republic.

Brahms [brɑːms] German composer.

Brandt [brant] German politician.

Brasilien [bra'ziːljən] n Brazil.

Braunschweig ['braunʃvaik] n Brunswick.

Brecht [breçt] German dramatist.

Bremen ['breːmən] n Land of the German Federal Republic.

Bruckner ['bruknər] Austrian composer.

Brüssel ['brysəl] n Brussels.

Budapest ['buːdapest] n Budapest.

Bukarest ['buːkarest] n Bucharest.

Bulgarien [bul'ɡɑːrjən] n Bulgaria.

Calais [ka'lɛ] n: Straße von ~ Straits of Dover.

Calvin [kal'viːn] Swiss religious reformer.

Chile ['tʃiːlə] n Chile.

China ['çiːna] n China.

Christus ['kristus] m Christ.

Daimler ['daimlər] German inventor.

Dänemark ['dɛːnəmark] n Denmark.

Deutschland ['dɔytʃlant] n Germany.

Diesel ['diːzəl] German inventor.

Döblin [dø'bliːn] German author.

Dolomiten [dolo'miːtən] pl. the Dolomites pl.

Donau ['doːnau] f Danube.

Dortmund ['dɔrtmunt] n industrial city in West Germany.

Dresden ['dreːsdən] n capital of Saxony.

Dublin ['dʌblin] n Dublin.

Dünkirchen ['dynːkirçən] n Dunkirk.

Dürer ['dyːrər] German painter.

Dürrenmatt ['dyrənmat] Swiss dramatist.

Düsseldorf ['dysəldorf] n capital of North Rhine-Westphalia.

Ebert ['eːbərt] first president of the Weimar Republic.

Egk [ɛk] German composer.

Eichendorff ['aiçəndorf] German poet.

Eiger ['aiɡər] Swiss mountain.

Einstein ['ainʃtain] German physicist.

Elbe ['ɛlbə] f German river.

Elsaß ['ɛlzas] n Alsace.

Engels ['ɛŋəls] German philosopher.

England ['eŋlant] n England.
Essen ['esən] n industrial city in West Germany.
Europa [ɔɪ'roːpa] n Europe.

Feldberg ['feltbɛrk] German mountain.
Finnland ['finlant] n Finland.
Florenz [flo'rɛnts] n Florence.
Fontane [fɔn'taːnə] German author.
Franken ['fraŋkən] n Franconia.
Frankfurt ['fraŋkfurt] n Frankfort.
Frankreich ['fraŋkraiç] n France.
Freud [frɔɪt] Austrian psychologist.
Frisch [friʃ] Swiss author.

Garmisch ['garmiʃ] n health resort in Bavaria.
Genf [gɛnf] n Geneva; ~er See m Lake of Geneva.
Genua ['geːnua] n Genoa.
Gibraltar [gi'braltar] n Gibraltar.
Goethe ['gøːtə] German poet.
Grass [gras] German author.
Graubünden [grau'byndən] n the Grisons.
Griechenland ['griːçənlant] n Greece.
Grillparzer ['grilpartsər] Austrian dramatist.
Grönland ['grøːnlant] n Greenland.
Gropius ['groːpjus] German architect. [Great Britain.]
Großbritannien [groːsbri'tanjən] n
Großglockner [groːs'glɔknər] Austrian mountain.
Grünewald ['gryːnəvalt] German painter.

Haag [haːk]: Den ~ The Hague.
Habsburg hist. ['haːpsburk] n Hapsburg (German dynasty).
Hahn [haːn] German chemist.
Hamburg ['hamburk] n Land of the German Federal Republic.
Händel ['hɛndəl] Handel (German composer).
Hannover [ha'noːfər] n Hanover (capital of Lower Saxony).
Hartmann ['hartman] German composer.
Harz [haːrts] m Harz Mountains pl.
Hauptmann ['hauptman] German dramatist.
Haydn ['haidən] Austrian composer.
Hegel ['heːgəl] German philosopher.
Heidegger ['haidegər] German philosopher.
Heidelberg ['haidəlbɛrk] n university town in West Germany.
Heine ['hainə] German poet.
Heinemann ['hainəman] president of the German Federal Republic.
Heisenberg ['haizənbɛrk] German physicist.
Heißenbüttel ['haisənbytəl] German poet.
Helgoland ['hɛlgolant] n Heligoland.

Helsinki ['hɛlziŋki] n Helsinki.
Henze ['hɛntsə] German composer.
Hesse ['hɛsə] German poet.
Hessen ['hɛsən] n Hesse (Land of the German Federal Republic).
Heuß [hɔɪs] first president of the German Federal Republic.
Hindemith ['hindəmit] German composer.
Hohenzollern hist. [hoːən'tsɔlərn] n German dynasty.
Hölderlin ['hœldərliːn] German poet.
Holland ['hɔlant] n Holland.

Indien ['indjən] n India.
Inn [in] m affluent of the Danube.
Innsbruck ['insbruk] n capital of the Tyrol.
Irak [i'raːk] m Iraq, a. Irak.
Irland ['irlant] n Ireland.
Island ['iːslant] n Iceland.
Israel ['israɛl] n Israel.
Italien [i'taːljən] n Italy.

Japan ['jaːpan] n Japan.
Jaspers ['jaspərs] German philosopher.
Jesus ['jeːzus] m Jesus.
Jordanien [jɔr'daːnjən] n Jordan.
Jugoslawien [jugo'slaːvjən] n Yugoslavia.
Jung [juŋ] Swiss psychologist.
Jungfrau ['juŋfrau] f Swiss mountain.

Kafka ['kafka] Czech poet.
Kanada ['kanada] n Canada.
Kant [kant] German philosopher.
Karajan ['kaːrajan] Austrian conductor.
Karlsruhe [karls'ruːə] n city in South-Western Germany.
Kärnten ['kɛrntən] n Carinthia.
Kassel ['kasəl] n Cassel.
Kästner ['kɛstnər] German author.
Kiel [kiːl] n capital of Schleswig-Holstein.
Kiesinger ['kiːziŋər] German politician.
Klee [kleː] German painter.
Kleist [klaist] German poet.
Klemperer ['klɛmpərər] German conductor.
Koblenz ['koːblɛnts] n Coblenz, Koblenz.
Kokoschka [ko'kɔʃka] German painter.
Köln [kœln] n Cologne.
Kolumbien [ko'lumbjən] n Columbia.
Kolumbus [ko'lumbus] m Columbus.
Königsberg ['køːniçsbɛrk] n capital of East Prussia.
Konstanz ['kɔnstants] n Constance.
Kopenhagen [kopən'haːgən] n Copenhagen.
Kordilleren [kɔrdil'jeːrən] f/pl. the Cordilleras pl.

Kreml ['kre:məl] *m the* Kremlin.

Leibniz ['laibnits] *German philosopher.*
Leipzig ['laiptsiç] *n* Leipsic.
Lessing ['lɛsiŋ] *German poet.*
Libanon ['li:banon] *m* Lebanon.
Liebig ['li:biç] *German chemist.*
Lissabon ['lisabon] *n* Lisbon.
London ['lɔndɔn] *n* London.
Lothringen ['lo:triŋən] *n* Lorraine.
Lübeck ['ly:bɛk] *n city in West Germany.*
Luther ['lutər] *German religious reformer.*
Luxemburg ['luksəmburk] *n* Luxemb(o)urg.
Luzern [lu'tsɛrn] *n* Lucerne.

Maas [mɑ:s] *f* Meuse.
Madrid [ma'drit] *n* Madrid.
Mahler ['mɑ:lər] *Austrian composer.*
Mailand ['mailant] *n* Milan.
Main [main] *m German river.*
Mainz [maints] *n* Mayence *(capital of Rhineland-Palatinate).*
Mann [man] *name of three German authors.*
Marokko [ma'rɔko] *n* Morocco.
Marx [marks] *German philosopher.*
Matterhorn ['matərhɔrn] *Swiss mountain.*
Meißen ['maisən] *n* Meissen.
Meitner ['maitnər] *German female physicist.*
Memel ['me:məl] *f frontier river in East Prussia.*
Menzel ['mɛntsəl] *German painter.*
Mexiko ['mɛksiko] *n* Mexico.
Mies van der Rohe ['mi:sfandər-'ro:ə] *German architect.*
Mittelamerika ['mitəlʔa'me:rika] *n* Central America.
Mitteleuropa ['mitəlʔɔʏ'ro:pa] *n* Central Europe.
Mittelmeer ['mitəlme:r] *n* Mediterranean (Sea).
Moldau ['mɔldau] *f Bohemian river.*
Mörike ['mø:rikə] *German poet.*
Mosel ['mo:zəl] *f* Moselle.
Mössbauer ['mœsbauər] *German physicist.*
Moskau ['mɔskau] *n* Moscow.
Mozart ['mo:tsart] *Austrian composer.*
München ['mynçən] *n* Munich *(capital of Bavaria).*

Neapel [ne'ɑ:pəl] *n* Naples.
Neisse ['naisə] *f German river.*
Neufundland [nɔʏ'funtlant] *n* Newfoundland.
Neuseeland [nɔʏ'ze:lant] *n* New Zealand.
Niederlande ['ni:dərlandə] *n/pl. the* Netherlands *pl.*
Niedersachsen ['ni:dərzaksən] *n* Lower Saxony *(Land of the German Federal Republic).*

Nietzsche ['ni:tʃə] *German philosopher.*
Nil [ni:l] *m* Nile.
Nordamerika ['nɔrtʔa'me:rika] *n* North America.
Nordrhein-Westfalen ['nɔrtrain-vest'fa:lən] *n* North Rhine-Westphalia *(Land of the German Federal Republic).*
Nordsee ['nɔrtze:] *f* German Ocean, North Sea.
Norwegen ['nɔrve:gən] *n* Norway.
Nürnberg ['nyrnbɛrk] *n* Nuremberg.

Oder ['o:dər] *f German river.*
Orff [ɔrf] *German composer.*
Oslo ['ɔslo] *n* Oslo.
Ostasien ['ɔst'ɑ:zjən] *n* Eastern Asia.
Ostende [ɔst'endə] *n* Ostend.
Österreich ['ø:stəraiç] *n* Austria.
Ostsee ['ɔstze:] *f* Baltic.

Palästina [pale'sti:na] *n* Palestine.
Paris [pa'ri:s] *n* Paris.
Persien ['pɛrzjən] *n* Persia.
Pfalz [pfalts] *f* Palatinate.
Philippinen [fili'pi:nən] *f/pl.* Philippines *pl.,* Philippine Islands *pl.*
Planck [plaŋk] *German physicist.*
Polen ['po:lən] *n* Poland.
Pommern ['pɔmərn] *n* Pomerania.
Portugal ['pɔrtugal] *n* Portugal.
Prag [prɑ:g] *n* Prague.
Preußen *hist.* ['prɔʏsən] *n* Prussia.
Pyrenäen [pyre'nɛ:ən] *pl.* Pyrenees *pl.*

Regensburg ['re:gənsburk] *n* Ratisbon.
Reykjavik ['raikjavi:k] *n* Reykjavik.
Rhein [rain] *m* Rhine.
Rheinland-Pfalz ['rainlant'pfalts] *n* Rhineland-Palatinate *(Land of the German Federal Republic).*
Rilke ['rilkə] *Austrian poet.*
Rom [ro:m] *n* Rome.
Röntgen ['rœntgən] *German physicist.*
Ruhr [ru:r] *f German river;* Ruhrgebiet ['ru:rgəbi:t] *n industrial centre of West Germany.*
Rumänien [ru'mɛ:njən] *n* Ro(u)mania.
Rußland ['ruslant] *n* Russia.

Saale ['zɑ:lə] *f German river.*
Saar [zɑ:r] *f affluent of the Moselle;* Saarbrücken [zɑ:r'brykən] *n capital of the Saar;* Saarland ['zɑ:rlant] *n* Saar *(Land of the German Federal Republic).*
Sachsen ['zaksən] *n* Saxony.
Scherchen ['ʃɛrçən] *Swiss conductor.*
Schiller ['ʃilər] *German poet.*
Schlesien ['ʃle:zjən] *n* Silesia.
Schleswig-Holstein ['ʃle:sviç'hɔl-

ʃtaɪn] n Land of the German Federal Republic.

Schönberg ['ʃøːnberk] Austrian composer.

Schottland ['ʃɔtlant] n Scotland.

Schubert ['ʃuːbərt] Austrian composer.

Schumann ['ʃuːman] German composer.

Schwaben ['ʃvaːbən] n Swabia.

Schwarzwald ['ʃvartsvalt] m Black Forest.

Schweden ['ʃveːdən] n Sweden.

Schweiz [ʃvaɪts] f: die ~ Switzerland.

Sibirien [ziʹbiːrjən] n Siberia.

Siemens ['ziːmɜns] German inventor.

Sizilien [ziʹtsiːljən] n Sicily.

Skandinavien [skandiʹnaːvjən] n Scandinavia.

Sofia ['zɔfja] n Sofia.

Sowjetunion [zɔʹvjetʔunjoːn] f the Soviet Union.

Spanien ['ʃpaːnjən] n Spain.

Spitzweg ['ʃpitsveːk] German painter.

Spranger ['ʃpraŋər] German philosopher.

Steiermark ['ʃtaɪərmark] f Styria.

Stifter ['ʃtiftər] Austrian author.

Stockholm ['ʃtɔkhɔlm] n Stockholm.

Storm [ʃtɔrm] German poet.

Strauß [ʃtraus] Austrian composer.

Strauss [ʃtraus] German composer.

Stresemann ['ʃtreːzəman] German statesman.

Stuttgart ['ʃtutgart] n capital of Baden-Württemberg.

Südamerika ['zyːtʔaʹmeːrika] n South America.

Sudan [zuʹdaːn] m S(o)udan.

Syrien ['zyːrjən] n Syria.

Themse ['temzə] f Thames.

Thoma ['toːma] German author.

Thüringen ['tyːriŋən] n Thuringia.

Tirana [tiʹraːna] n Tirana.

Tirol [tiʹroːl] n the Tyrol.

Trakl ['traːkəl] Austrian poet.

Tschechoslowakei [tʃeçoslovaʹkaɪ] f: die ~ Czechoslovakia.

Türkei [tyrʹkaɪ] f: die ~ Turkey.

Ungarn ['uŋgarn] n Hungary.

Ural [uʹraːl] m Ural (Mountains pl.).

Vatikan [vatiʹkaːn] m the Vatican.

Venedig [veʹneːdiç] n Venice.

Vereinigte Staaten [vərʹainiçtə 'ʃtaːtən] m/pl. the United States pl.

Vierwaldstätter See [fiːrʹvaltʃtɛtər 'zeː] m Lake of Lucerne.

Wagner ['vaːgnər] German composer.

Wankel ['vaŋkəl] German inventor.

Warschau ['varʃau] n Warsaw.

Weichsel ['vaɪksəl] f Vistula.

Weiß [vaɪs] German dramatist.

Weizsäcker ['vartszekər] German physicist.

Werfel ['verfəl] Austrian author.

Weser ['veːzər] f German river.

Westdeutschland pol. ['vestdɔytʃlant] n West Germany.

Wien [viːn] n Vienna.

Wiesbaden ['viːsbaːdən] n capital of Hesse.

Zeppelin ['tsepəliːn] German inventor.

Zuckmayer ['tsukmaɪər] German dramatist.

Zweig [tsvaɪg] Austrian author.

Zürich ['tsyːriç] n Zurich.

Zypern ['tsyːpərn] n Cyprus.

German Abbreviations

a. a. O. *am angeführten Ort* in the place cited, *abbr.* loc. cit., l. c.
Abb. *Abbildung* illustration.
Abf. *Abfahrt* departure, *abbr.* dep.
Abg. *Abgeordnete* Member of Parliament, *etc.*
Abk. *Abkürzung* abbreviation.
Abs. *Absatz* paragraph; *Absender* sender.
Abschn. *Abschnitt* paragraph, chapter. [dept.]
Abt. *Abteilung* department, *abbr.*
a. D. *außer Dienst* retired.
Adr. *Adresse* address.
AG *Aktiengesellschaft* joint-stock company, *Am.* (stock) corporation.
allg. *allgemein* general.
a. M. *am Main* on the Main.
Ank. *Ankunft* arrival.
Anm. *Anmerkung* note.
a. O. *an der Oder* on the Oder.
a. Rh. *am Rhein* on the Rhine.
Art. *Artikel* article.
atü *Atmosphärenüberdruck* atmospheric excess pressure.
Aufl. *Auflage* edition.

b. *bei* at; with; *with place names:* near, *abbr.* nr; care of, *abbr.* c/o.
Bd. *Band* volume, *abbr.* vol.; **Bde.** *Bände* volumes, *abbr.* vols.
bell. *belllegend* enclosed.
Bem. *Bemerkung* note, comment, observation.
bes. *besonders* especially.
betr. *betreffend, betrifft, betreffs* concerning, respecting, regarding.
Betr. *Betreff, betrifft letter:* subject, re. [reference to.]
bez. *bezahlt* paid; *bezüglich* with)
Bez. *Bezirk* district.
Bhf. *Bahnhof* station.
bisw. *bisweilen* sometimes, occasionally.
BIZ *Bank für Internationalen Zahlungsausgleich* Bank for International Settlements.
Bln. *Berlin* Berlin.
BRD *Bundesrepublik Deutschland* Federal Republic of Germany.
BRT *Bruttoregistertonnen* gross register tons.
b. w. *bitte wenden* please turn over, *abbr.* P.T.O.
bzw. *beziehungsweise* respectively.

C *Celsius* Celsius, *abbr.* C.
ca. *circa, ungefähr, etwa* about, approximately, *abbr.* c.
cbm *Kubikmeter* cubic met|re, *Am.* -er.

ccm *Kubikzentimeter* cubic centimet|re, *Am.* -er, *abbr.* c.c.
CDU *Christlich-Demokratische Union* Christian Democratic Union.
cm *Zentimeter* centimet|re, *Am.* -er.
Co. *Kompagnon* partner; *Kompanie* Company.
CSU *Christlich-Soziale Union* Christian Social Union.

d. Ä. *der Ältere* senior, *abbr.* sen.
DB *Deutsche Bundesbahn* German Federal Railway.
DDR *Deutsche Demokratische Republik* German Democratic Republic.
DGB *Deutscher Gewerkschaftsbund* Federation of German Trade Unions.
dgl. *dergleichen, desgleichen* the like.
d. Gr. *der Große* the Great.
d. h. *das heißt* that is, *abbr.* i. e.
d. i. *das ist that is, abbr.* i. e.
DIN, Din *Deutsche Industrie-Norm (-en)* German Industrial Standards.
Dipl. *Diplom* diploma.
d. J. *dieses Jahres* of this year; *der Jüngere* junior, *abbr.* jr, jun.
DM *Deutsche Mark* German Mark.
d. M. *dieses Monats* instant, *abbr.* inst.
do. *dito ditto, abbr.* do.
d. O. *der (die, das) Obige* the abovementioned.
dpa, DPA *Deutsche Presse-Agentur* German Press Agency.
Dr. *Doktor* Doctor, *abbr.* Dr; **~ jur.** *Doktor der Rechte* Doctor of Laws (LL.D.); **~ med.** *Doktor der Medizin* Doctor of Medicine (M.D.); **~ phil.** *Doktor der Philosophie* Doctor of Philosophy (D. ph[il]., Ph. D.); **~ theol.** *Doktor der Theologie* Doctor of Divinity (D. D.).
DRK *Deutsches Rotes Kreuz* German Red Cross.
dt(sch). *deutsch* German.
Dtz., Dtzd. *Dutzend* dozen.
d. Verf. *der Verfasser* the author.

ebd. *ebenda* in the same place.
ed. edidit — hat (es) herausgegeben.
eig., eigtl. *eigentlich* properly.
einschl. *einschließlich* including, inclusive, *abbr.* incl.
entspr. *entsprechend* corresponding.
Erl. *Erläuterung* explanation, (explanatory) note.
ev. *evangelisch* Protestant.
e. V. *eingetragener Verein* registered association, incorporated, *abbr.* inc.

evtl. *eventuell* perhaps, possibly.
EWG *Europäische Wirtschaftsgemeinschaft* European Economic Community, *abbr.* EEC.
exkl. *exklusive* except(ed), not included.
Expl. *Exemplar* copy.

Fa. *Firma* firm; *letter*: Messrs.
FDGB *Freier Deutscher Gewerkschaftsbund* Free Federation of German Trade Unions.
FDP *Freie Demokratische Partei* Liberal Democratic Party.
FD(-Zug) *Fernschnellzug* long-distance express.
ff. *sehr fein* extra fine; *folgende Seiten* following pages.
Forts. *Fortsetzung* continuation.
Fr. *Frau* Mrs.
frdl. *freundlich* kind.
Frl. *Fräulein* Miss.

g *Gramm* gram(me).
geb. *geboren* born; *geborene* ... née; *gebunden* bound.
Gebr. *Gebrüder* Brothers.
gef. *gefällig(st)* kind(ly).
gegr. *gegründet* founded.
geh. *geheftet* stitched.
gek. *gekürzt* abbreviated.
Ges. *Gesellschaft* association, company; society. [registered.]
ges. gesch. *gesetzlich geschützt* registered.
gest. *gestorben* deceased.
gez. *gezeichnet* signed, *abbr.* sgd.
GmbH *Gesellschaft mit beschränkter Haftung* limited liability company, *abbr.* Ltd., *Am.* closed corporation under German law.

ha *Hektar* hectare.
Hbf. *Hauptbahnhof* central *or* main station.
Hbg. *Hamburg* Hamburg.
h. c. *honoris causa* ━ *ehrenhalber academic title*: honorary.
Hr., Hrn. *Herr(n)* Mr.
hrsg. *herausgegeben* edited, *abbr.* ed.
Hrsg. *Herausgeber* editor, *abbr.* ed.

i. *im, in* in.
i. A. *im Auftrage* for, by order, under instruction.
i. allg. *im allgemeinen* in general, generally speaking.
i. Durchschn. *im Durchschnitt* on an average.
inkl. *inklusive, einschließlich* inclusive.
i. J. *im Jahre* in the year.
Ing. *Ingenieur* engineer.
Inh. *Inhaber* proprietor.
'Interpol *Internationale Kriminalpolizei-Kommission* International Criminal Police Commission, *abbr.* ICPC.
i. V. *in Vertretung* by proxy, as a substitute.

Jb. *Jahrbuch* annual.
jr., jun. *junior, der Jüngere* junior *abbr.* jr, jun.

Kap. *Kapitel* chapter.
kath. *katholisch* Catholic.
Kfm. *Kaufmann* merchant.
kfm. *kaufmännisch* commercial.
Kfz. *Kraftfahrzeug* motor vehicle.
kg *Kilogramm* kilogram(me).
KG *Kommanditgesellschaft* limited partnership.
Kl. *Klasse* class; *school*: form.
km *Kilometer* kilomet|re, *Am.* -er.
'Kripo *Kriminalpolizei* Criminal Investigation Department, *abbr.* CID.
Kto. *Konto* account, *abbr.* a/c.
kW *Kilowatt* kilowatt, *abbr.* kw.
kWh *Kilowattstunde* kilowatt hour.

l *Liter* lit|re, *Am.* -er.
LDP *Liberal-Demokratische Partei* Liberal Democratic Party.
lfd. *laufend* current, running.
lfde. Nr. *laufende Nummer* consecutive number.
Lfg., Lfrg. *Lieferung* delivery; instalment, part.
Lit. *Literatur* literature.
Lkw. *Lastkraftwagen* lorry, truck.
lt. *laut* according to.

m *Meter* met|re, *Am.* -er.
m. A. n. *meiner Ansicht nach* in my opinion.
M. d. B. *Mitglied des Bundestages* Member of the Bundestag.
m. E. *meines Erachtens* in my opinion.
MEZ *mitteleuropäische Zeit* Central European Time.
mg *Milligramm* milligram(me[s]), *abbr.* mg.
Mill. *Million(en)* million(s).
mm *Millimeter* millimet|re, *Am.* -er.
möbl. *möbliert* furnished.
MP *Militärpolizei* Military Police.
mtl. *monatlich* monthly.
m. W. *meines Wissens* as far as I know.

N *Nord(en)* north.
nachm. *nachmittags* in the afternoon, *abbr.* p. m.
n. Chr. *nach Christus* after Christ, *abbr.* A. D.
n. J. *nächsten Jahres* of next year.
n. M. *nächsten Monats* of next month.
No., Nr. *Numero, Nummer* number, *abbr.* N°.
NS *Nachschrift* postscript, *abbr.* P. S.

O *Ost(en)* east.
o. B. *ohne Befund* ⚕ without findings.
od. *oder* or.

OEZ *osteuropäische Zeit* time of the East European zone.

OHG *Offene Handelsgesellschaft* ordinary partnership.

o. J. *ohne Jahr* no date.

p. Adr. *per Adresse* care of, *abbr.* c/o.

Pf *Pfennig* German *coin:* pfennig.

Pfd. *Pfund* German *weight:* pound.

PKW, Pkw. *Personenkraftwagen* (motor) car.

P. P. *praemissis praemittendis* omitting titles, to whom it may concern.

p.p., p.pa., ppa. *per procura* per proxy, *abbr.* per pro.

Prof. *Professor* professor.

PS *Pferdestärke(n)* horse-power, *abbr.* H.P., h.p.; *postscriptum, Nachschrift* postscript, *abbr.* P.S.

qkm *Quadratkilometer* square kilomet|re, *Am.* -er.   [*Am.* -er.]
qm *Quadratmeter* square met|re,]

Reg. Bez. *Regierungsbezirk* administrative district.

Rel. *Religion* religion.

resp. *respektive* respectively.

S *Süd(en)* south.

S. *Seite* page.

s. *siehe* see, *abbr.* v., vid. (= vide).

s. a. *siehe auch* see also.

Sa. *Summa, Summe* sum, total.

s. d. *siehe dies* see this.

SED *Sozialistische Einheitspartei Deutschlands* United Socialist Party of Germany.

sen. *senior, der Ältere* senior.

sm *Seemeile* nautical mile.

s. o. *siehe oben* see above.

sog. *sogenannt* so-called.

SPD *Sozialdemokratische Partei Deutschlands* Social Democratic Party of Germany.

St. *Stück* piece; *Sankt* Saint.

St(d).. Stde. *Stunde* hour, *abbr.* h.

Str. *Straße* street, *abbr.* St.

s. u. *siehe unten* see below.

s. Z. *seinerzeit* at that time.

t *Tonne* ton.

tägl. *täglich* daily, per day.

Tel. *Telephon* telephone; *Telegramm* wire, cable.

TH *Technische Hochschule* technical university *or* college.

u. *und* and.

u. a. *und andere(s)* and others; *unter anderem or anderen* among other things, *inter alia.*

u. ä. *und ähnliche(s)* and the like.

U.A.w.g. *Um Antwort wird gebeten* an answer is requested, *répondez s'il vous plaît, abbr.* R.S.V.P.

u. dgl. (m.) *und dergleichen (mehr)* and the like.

u. d. M. *unter dem Meeresspiegel* below sea level; **ü. d. M.** *über dem Meeresspiegel* above sea level.

UdSSR *Union der Sozialistischen Sowjetrepubliken* Union of Soviet Socialist Republics.

u. E. *unseres Erachtens* in our opinion.   [following.]

u. f., u. ff. *und folgende* and the]

UKW *Ultrakurzwelle* ultra-short wave, very high frequency, *abbr.* VHF.

U/min. *Umdrehungen in der Minute* revolutions per minute, *abbr.* r.p.m.

urspr. *ursprünglich* original(ly).

US(A) *Vereinigte Staaten (von Amerika)* United States (of America).

usw. *und so weiter* and so on, *abbr.* etc.   [stances permitting.]

u. U. *unter Umständen* circum-]

v. *von, vom* of; from; by.

V *Volt* volt; *Volumen* volume.

V. *Vers* line, verse.

v. Chr. *vor Christus* before Christ, *abbr* B.C.

VEB *Volkseigener Betrieb* People's Own Undertaking.

Verf., Vf. *Verfasser* author.

Vcrl. *Verlag* publishing firm; *Verleger* publisher.

vgl. *vergleiche* confer, *abbr.* cf.

v.g.u. *vorgelesen, genehmigt, unterschrieben* read, confirmed signed.

v. H. *vom Hundert* per cent.

v. J. *vorigen Jahres* of last year.

v. M. *vorigen Monats* of last month.

vorm. *vormittags* in the morning, *abbr.* a. m.; *vormals* formerly.

Vors. *Vorsitzender* chairman.

v. T. *vom Tausend* per thousand.

VW *Volkswagen* Volkswagen, People's Car.

W *West(en)* west; *Watt* watt(s).

WE *Wärmeeinheit* thermal unit.

WEZ *westeuropäische Zeit* Western European time (Greenwich time).

WGB *Weltgewerkschaftsbund* World Federation of Trade Unions, *abbr.* WFTU.

Wwe. *Witwe* widow.

Z. *Zahl* number; *Zeile* line.

z. *zu, zum, zur* at; to.

z. B. *zum Beispiel* for instance, *abbr.* e. g.

z. H(d). *zu Händen* attention of, to be delivered to, care of, *abbr.* c/o.

z. S. *zur See* of the navy.

z. T. *zum Teil* partly.

Ztg. *Zeitung* newspaper.

Ztr. *Zentner* centner.

Ztschr. *Zeitschrift* periodical.

zus. *zusammen* together.

zw. *zwischen* between; among.

z. Z(t). *zur Zeit* at the time, at present, for the time being.

American and British Proper Names

Aberdeen [æbə'di:n] *Stadt in Schottland.*
Africa ['æfrikə] Afrika *n.* [U.S.A.]
Alabama [ælə'bæmə] *Staat der* Alaska [ə'læskə] *Staat der U.S.A.*
Albania [æl'beinjə] Albanien *n.*
Alberta [æl'bə:tə] *Provinz in Kanada.* [U.S.A.]
Alleghany ['æligeini] *Gebirge in* Alsace ['ælsæs] Elsaß *n.*
America [ə'merikə] Amerika *n.*
Antilles [æn'tiliz] *die* Antillen.
Appalachians [æpə'leitʃjənz] *die* Appalachen (*Gebirge in U.S.A.*).
Arizona [æri'zounə] *Staat der U.S.A.* [U.S.A.]
Arkansas ['ɑ:kənsɔ:] *Staat der* Arlington ['ɑ:liŋtən] *Nationalfriedhof bei Washington.*
Ascot ['æskət] *Stadt in England.*
Asia ['eiʃə] Asien *n.*
Athens ['æθinz] Athen *n.*
Australia [ɔs'treiljə] Australien *n.*
Austria ['ɔstriə] Österreich *n.*
Avon ['eivən] *Fluß in England.*
Azores [ə'zɔ:z] *die* Azoren.

Bacon ['beikən] *engl. Philosoph.*
Bahamas [bə'hɑ:məz] *die* Bahama-inseln.
Balmoral [bæl'mɔrəl] *Königsschloß in Schottland.*
Bedford(shire) ['bedfəd(ʃiə)] *Grafschaft in England.*
Belfast [bel'fɑ:st] *Hauptstadt von Nordirland.*
Belgium ['beldʒəm] Belgien *n.*
Belgrade [bel'greid] Belgrad *n.*
Ben Nevis [ben'nevis] *höchster Berg in Großbritannien.*
Berkshire ['bɑ:kʃiə] *Grafschaft in England*
Bermudas [bə:'mju:dəz] *die* Bermudainseln.
Bern(e) [bə:n] Bern *n.*
Birmingham ['bə:miŋəm] *Industriestadt in England* [Biskaya.]
Biscay ['biskei] *Bay of ~ Golf m von*
Boston ['bɔstən] *Stadt in U.S.A.*
Bournemouth ['bɔ:nməθ] *Seebad in England.* [land.]
Brighton ['braitn] *Seebad in England.*
Bristol ['bristl] *Hafenstadt in England*
Britten ['britn] *engl. Komponist.*
Brooklyn ['bruklin] *Stadtteil von New York*
Brussels ['brʌslz] Brüssel *n.*
Bucharest ['bju:kərest] Bukarest *n.*
Buckingham(shire) ['bʌkiŋəm(ʃiə)] *Grafschaft in England.*

Budapest ['bju:də'pest] Budapest *n.*
Bulgaria [bʌl'gɛəriə] Bulgarien *n.*
Burns [bə:nz] *schott. Dichter.*
Byron ['baiərən] *engl. Dichter.*

California [kæli'fɔ.njə] Kalifornien *n* (*Staat der U.S.A.*).
Cambridge ['keimbridʒ] *engl. Universitätsstadt; Stadt in U.S.A.; a.* ~shire ['~ʃiə] *Grafschaft in England.*
Canada ['kænədə] Kanada *n.*
Canary Islands [kə'nɛəri 'ailəndz] *die* Kanarischen Inseln.
Canberra ['kænbərə] *Hauptstadt von Australien.* [England.]
Canterbury ['kæntəbəri] *Stadt in*
Capetown ['keiptaun] Kapstadt *n.*
Cardiff ['kɑ:dif] *Hauptstadt von Wales.*
Carinthia [kə'rinθiə] Kärnten *n.*
Carlyle [kɑ:'lail] *engl. Autor.*
Carolina [kærə'lainə]: North ~ Nordkarolina *n* (*Staat der U.S.A.*); South ~ Südkarolina *n* (*Staat der U.S.A.*).
Ceylon [si'lɔn] Ceylon *n.*
Chamberlain ['tʃeimbəlin, ~lein] *Name mehrerer brit. Staatsmänner.*
Cheshire ['tʃeʃə] *Grafschaft in England.*
Chicago [ʃi'kɑ:gou, Am. ʃi'kɔ:gou] *Industriestadt in U.S.A.*
China ['tʃainə] China *n.* [mann.]
Churchill ['tʃə:tʃil] *brit. Staats-*
Cleveland ['kli:vlənd] *Industrie- und Hafenstadt in U.S.A.*
Clyde [klaid] *Fluß in Schottland.*
Coleridge ['koulridʒ] *engl. Dichter.*
Colorado [kɔlə'rɑ:dou] *Staat der U.S.A.*
Columbia [kə'lʌmbiə] *Fluß in U.S.A.; Bundesdistrikt der U.S.A.*
Connecticut [kə'netikət] *Staat der U.S.A.*
Constance ['kɔnstəns]: *Lake of ~* Bodensee *m.*
Cooper ['ku:pə] *amer. Autor.*
Copenhagen [koupn'heigən] Kopenhagen *n.* [dilleren.]
Cordilleras [kɔ:di'ljɛərəz] *die* Kor-
Cornwall ['kɔ:nwəl] *Grafschaft in England.*
Coventry ['kɔvəntri] *Industriestadt in England.* [mann.]
Cromwell ['krɔmwəl] *engl. Staats-*
Cumberland ['kʌmbələnd] *Grafschaft in England.*
Cyprus ['saiprəs] Zypern *n.*
Czecho-Slovakia ['tʃekouslou'væ-kiə] *die* Tschechoslowakei.

Dakota [dǝ'koutǝ]: North ~ Norddakota n (Staat der U.S.A.); South ~ Süddakota n (Staat der U.S.A.).

Defoe [dǝ'fou] engl. Autor.

Delaware ['delǝwɛǝ] Staat der U.S.A.

Denmark ['denmɑːk] Dänemark n.

Derby(shire) ['dɑːbi(ʃǝ)] Grafschaft in England.

Detroit [dǝ'trɔit] Industriestadt in U.S.A.

Devon(shire) ['devn(ʃiǝ)] Grafschaft in England.

Dickens ['dikinz] engl. Autor.

Dorset(shire) ['dɔːsit(ʃiǝ)] Grafschaft in England [land.\

Dover ['douvǝ] Hafenstadt in Eng-)

Downing Street ['dauniŋ 'striːt] Straße in London mit der Amtswohnung des Prime Minister.

Dublin ['dablin] Hauptstadt von Irland.

Dunkirk [dʌn'kǝːk] Dünkirchen n.

Durham ['dʌrǝm] Grafschaft in England.

Edinburgh ['edinbǝrǝ] Edinburg n.

Edison ['edisn] amer Erfinder.

Egypt ['iːdʒipt] Ägypten n.

Eire ['ɛǝrǝ] Republik Irland.

Eisenhower ['aizǝnhauǝ] Präsident der U.S.A

Eliot ['eljǝt] engl Dichter.

Emerson ['emǝsn] amer Philosoph.

England ['iŋglǝnd] England n.

Epsom ['epsǝm] Stadt in England.

Erie ['iǝri] Lake ~ Eriesee m.

Essex ['esiks] Grafschaft in England.

Eton ['iːtʌn] berühmte Public School.

Europe ['juǝrǝp] Europa n.

Falkland Islands ['fɔːlklǝnd 'ailǝndz] die Falklandinseln.

Faulkner ['fɔːknǝ] amer Autor.

Finland ['finlǝnd] Finnland n.

Florida ['flɔridǝ] Staat der U.S.A.

Flushing ['flaʃiŋ] Vlissingen n.

France [frɑːns] Frankreich n.

Franklin ['fræŋklin] amer. Staatsmann und Physiker.

Galsworthy ['gɔːlzwǝːði] engl. Autor.

Geneva [dʒi'niːvǝ] Genf n; Lake of ~ Genfer See m.

Georgia ['dʒɔːdʒǝ] Staat der U.S.A.

Germany ['dʒǝːmǝni] Deutschland n. [nist.\

Gershwin ['gǝːʃwin] amer. Kompo-)

Gibraltar [dʒi'brɔːltǝ] Gibraltar n.

Glasgow ['glɑːsgou] Hafenstadt in Schottland

Gloucester ['glɔstǝ] Stadt in England; a. ~shire ['~ʃiǝ] Grafschaft in England.

Great Britain ['greit 'britn] Großbritannien n.

Greece [griːs] Griechenland n.

Greene [griːn] engl. Autor.

Greenland ['griːnlǝnd] Grönland n.

Greenwich ['grinidʒ] Vorort von London.

Guernsey ['gǝːnzi] Kanalinsel.

Hague [heig]: The ~ Den Haag.

Hampshire ['hæmpʃiǝ] Grafschaft in England.

Harlem ['hɑːlem] Stadtteil von New York.

Harrow ['hærou] berühmte Public School.

Harvard University ['hɑːvǝd juːniˈvǝːsiti] amer. Universität.

Harwich ['hæridʒ] Hafenstadt in England

Hawaii [hɑ'waiiː] Staat der U.S.A.

Hebrides ['hebridiːz] die Hebriden.

Helsinki ['helsiŋki] Helsinki n.

Hemingway ['hemiŋwei] amer. Autor.

Hereford(shire) ['herifǝd(ʃiǝ)] Grafschaft in England

Hertford(shire) ['hɑːtfǝd(ʃiǝ)] Grafschaft in England.

Hollywood ['hɔliwud] Filmstadt in Kalifornien, U.S.A.

Houston ['juːstǝn] Stadt in U.S.A.

Hudson ['hadsn] Fluß in U.S.A.

Hull [hal] Hafenstadt in England.

Hume [hjuːm] engl Philosoph.

Hungary ['haŋgǝri] Ungarn n.

Huntingdon(shire) ['hantiŋdǝn (-ʃiǝ)] Grafschaft in England [m.\

Huron ['hjuǝrǝn]: Lake ~ Huronsee)

Huxley ['haksli] engl. Autor.

Iceland ['aislǝnd] Island n.

Idaho ['aidǝhou] Staat der U.S.A.

Illinois [ili'nɔi] Staat der U.S.A.

India ['indjǝ] Indien n.

Indiana [indi'ænǝ] Staat der U.S.A.

Iowa ['aiouǝ] Staat der U.S.A.

Irak, Iraq [i'rɑːk] Irak m.

Iran [i'rɑːn] Iran m

Ireland ['aiǝlǝnd] Irland n.

Irving ['ǝːviŋ] amer. Autor.

Italy ['itǝli] Italien n.

Jefferson ['dʒefǝsn] Präsident der U.S.A., Verfasser der Unabhängigkeitserklärung von 1776.

Johnson ['dʒɔnsn] 1. engl. Autor; 2. Präsident der U.S.A.

Kansas ['kænzǝs] Staat der U.S.A.

Kashmir [kæʃ'miǝ] Kaschmir n.

Keats [kiːts] engl Dichter.

Kennedy ['kenidi] Präsident der U.S.A.; ~ Airport Flughafen von New York.

Kent [kent] Grafschaft in England.

Kentucky [ken'taki] Staat der U.S.A.

Kipling ['kipliŋ] engl. Dichter.

Klondike ['klɔndaik] Fluß und Landschaft in Kanada und Alaska.

Kremlin ['kremlin] der Kreml.

Labrador ['læbrədɔ:] *Halbinsel Nordamerikas.*

Lancashire ['læŋkəʃiə] *Grafschaft in England.*

Lancaster ['læŋkəstə] *Name zweier Städte in England und U.S.A.; s. Lancashire.* [*land.*]

Leeds [li:dz] *Industriestadt in Eng-*]

Leicester ['lestə] *Stadt in England; a. ~shire ['~ʃiə] Grafschaft in England.*

Lincoln ['liŋkən] 1. *Präsident der U.S.A ; 2. a. ~shire ['~ʃiə] Grafschaft in England.*

Lisbon ['lizbən] Lissabon *n.*

Liverpool ['livəpu:l] *Hafen- und Industriestadt in England.*

Locke [lɔk] *engl Philosoph.*

London ['lʌndən] London *n.*

Los Angeles [lɔs 'ændʒili:z] *Stadt in U.S.A.* [*U.S.A.*]

Louisiana [lu:izi'ænə] *Staat der*]

Lucerne [lu:'sə:n]: *Lake of ~ Vierwaldstätter See m.*

Luxemburg ['lʌksəmbə:g] Luxemburg *n.*

Madrid [mə'drid] Madrid *n.*

Maine [mein] *Staat der U.S.A.*

Malta ['mɔ:ltə] Malta *n.*

Manchester ['mæntʃistə] *Industriestadt in England.*

Manhattan [mæn'hætən] *Stadtteil von New York.* [*Kanada.*]

Manitoba [mæni'toubə] *Provinz in*]

Maryland ['mɛərilənd, Am. 'merilənd] *Staat der U.S.A.*

Massachusetts [mæsə'tʃu:sits] *Staat der U.S.A.*

Melbourne ['melbən] *Stadt in Australien.*

Miami [mai'æmi] *Badeort in Florida, U.S.A.*

Michigan ['miʃigən] *Staat der U.S.A.; Lake ~ Michigansee m.*

Middlesex ['midlseks] *Grafschaft in England.*

Miller ['milə] *amer. Dramatiker.*

Milton ['miltən] *engl. Dichter.*

Milwaukee [mil'wɔ:ki:] *Stadt in U.S.A.*

Minneapolis [mini'æpəlis] *Stadt in U.S.A.* [*U.S.A.*]

Minnesota [mini'soutə] *Staat der*]

Mississippi [misi'sipi] *Strom und Staat der U.S.A.*

Missouri [mi'zuəri] *Fluß und Staat der U S.A.*

Monmouth(shire) ['mɔnməθ(ʃiə)] *Grafschaft in England.*

Monroe [mən'rou] *Präsident der U.S.A.* [*U.S.A.*]

Montana [mɔn'tænə] *Staat der*]

Montgomery [mənt'gɔməri] *brit. Feldmarschall.*

Montreal [mɔntri'ɔ:l] *Stadt in Kanada.*

Moore [muə] *engl. Bildhauer.*

Moscow ['mɔskou] Moskau *n.*

Nebraska [ni'bræskə] *Staat der U.S.A.*

Nelson ['nelsn] *engl. Admiral.*

Netherlands ['neðələndz] *die Niederlande.*

Nevada [ne'vɑ:də] *Staat der U.S.A.*

New Brunswick [nju: 'brʌnzwik] *Provinz in Kanada.*

Newcastle ['nju:kɑ:sl] *Hafenstadt in England.* [*von Indien.*]

New Delhi [nju: 'deli] *Hauptstadt*]

New England [nju: 'iŋglənd] Neuengland *n.* [*Neufundland n.*]

Newfoundland [nju:fənd'lænd]]

New Hampshire [nju: 'hæmpʃiə] *Staat der U.S.A.*

New Jersey [nju: 'dʒə:si] *Staat der U.S.A.*

New Mexico [nju: 'meksikou] Neumexiko *n (Staat der U.S.A.).*

New Orleans [nju: 'ɔ:liəns] *Hafenstadt in U.S.A.*

Newton ['nju:tn] *engl. Physiker.*

New York ['nju: 'jɔ:k] *Stadt und Staat der U.S.A.*

New Zealand [nju: 'zi:lənd] Neuseeland *n.*

Niagara [nai'ægərə] Niagara *m.*

Nixon ['niksn] *Präsident der U.S.A.*

Norfolk ['nɔ:fək] *Grafschaft in England.*

Northampton [nɔ:'θæmptən] *Stadt in England; a. ~shire ['~ʃiə] Grafschaft in England.*

Northumberland [nɔ:'θʌmbələnd] *Grafschaft in England.*

Norway ['nɔ:wei] Norwegen *n.*

Nottingham ['nɔtiŋəm] *Stadt in England; a. ~shire ['~ʃiə] Grafschaft in England.*

Nova Scotia ['nouvə 'skouʃə] *Provinz in Kanada.*

Ohio [ou'haiou] *Staat der U.S.A.*

O'Neill [ou'ni:l] *amer. Dramatiker.*

Ontario [ɔn'tɛəriou] *Provinz in Kanada; Lake ~ Ontariosee m.*

Oregon ['ɔrigən] *Staat der U.S.A.*

Orkney Islands ['ɔ:kni 'ailəndz] *die Orkneyinseln.*

Osborne ['ɔzbən] *engl. Dramatiker.*

Oslo ['ɔzlou] Oslo *n.*

Ostend [ɔs'tend] Ostende *n.*

Ottawa ['ɔtəwə] *Hauptstadt von Kanada.*

Oxford ['ɔksfəd] *engl. Universitätsstadt; a. ~shire ['~ʃiə] Grafschaft in England.*

Pakistan [pɑ:kis'tɑ:n] Pakistan *n.*

Paris ['pæris] Paris *n.*

Pearl Harbour ['pə:l 'hɑ:bə] *Hafenstadt auf Hawaii.*

Pennsylvania [pensil'veinjə] Pennsylvanien *n (Staat der U.S.A.).*

Philadelphia [filə'delfjə] *Stadt in U.S.A.*

Philippines ['filipi:nz] *die Philippinen.*

Pittsburg(h) ['pitsbə:g] *Stadt in U.S.A.*

Plymouth ['pliməθ] *Hafenstadt in England.*

Poe [pou] *amer. Autor.*

Poland ['pouland] Polen *n.*

Portsmouth ['po:tsməθ] *Hafenstadt in England.*

Portugal ['po:tjugəl] Portugal *n.*

Prague [pra:g] Prag *n.*

Purcell ['pə:sl] *engl. Komponist.*

Quebec [kwi'bek] *Provinz und Stadt in Kanada.*

Reykjavik ['reikjəvi:k] Reykjavik *n.*

Rhode Island [roud 'ailənd] *Staat der U.S.A.*

Rocky Mountains ['rɔki 'mauntinz] *Gebirge in U.S.A.*

Rome [roum] Rom *n.*

Roosevelt ['rouzəvelt] *Name zweier Präsidenten der U.S.A.* [*School.*]

Rugby ['rʌgbi] *berühmte Public*

Rumania [ru:'meinjə] Rumänien *n.*

Russell ['rʌsl] *engl. Philosoph.*

Russia ['rʌʃə] Rußland *n.*

Rutland(shire) ['rʌtlənd(ʃiə)] *Grafschaft in England.*

San Francisco [sænfrən'siskou] *Hafenstadt in U.S.A.*

Saskatchewan [səs'kætʃiwən] *Provinz von Kanada.*

Scandinavia [skændi'neivjə] Skandinavien *n.*

Scotland ['skɔtlənd] Schottland *n.*

Shakespeare ['ʃeikspiə] *engl. Dichter.*

Shaw [ʃɔ:] *engl. Dramatiker.*

Shelley ['ʃeli] *engl. Dichter.*

Shetland Islands ['ʃetlənd 'ailəndz] *die Shetlandinseln.*

Shropshire ['ʃrɔpʃiə] *Grafschaft in England.*

Snowdon ['snoudn] *Berg in Wales.*

Sofia ['soufjə] Sofia *n.*

Somerset(shire) ['sʌməsit(ʃiə)] *Grafschaft in England.*

Southhampton [sauθ'æmptən] *Hafenstadt in England.*

Spain [spein] Spanien *n.*

Stafford(shire) ['stæfəd(ʃiə)] *Grafschaft in England.*

Stevenson ['sti:vnsn] *engl. Autor.*

St. Lawrence [snt'brɔns] *der St. Lorenz-Strom.*

St. Louis [snt'luis] *Industriestadt in U.S.A.* [*n.*]

Stockholm ['stɔkhoum] Stockholm

Stratford ['strætfəd]: ~*on-Avon Geburtsort Shakespeares.*

Suffolk ['sʌfək] *Grafschaft in England.* [rer See *m.*]

Superior [sju:'piəriə]: *Lake ~ Obe-*

Surrey ['sʌri] *Grafschaft in England.*

Sussex ['sʌsiks] *Grafschaft in England.*

Sweden ['swi:dn] Schweden *n.*

Swift [swift] *engl. Autor*

Switzerland ['switsələnd] *die Schweiz.* [*tralien.*]

Sydney ['sidni] *Hafenstadt in Aus-*

Tennessee [tene'si] *Staat der U.S.A.*

Tennyson ['tenisn] *engl. Dichter.*

Texas ['teksəs] *Staat der U.S.A.*

Thackeray ['θækəri] *engl. Autor.*

Thames [temz] Themse *f.*

Tirana [ti'ra:nə] Tirana *n.* [*nada.*]

Toronto [tə'rɔntou] *Stadt in Ka-*

Toynbee ['tɔinbi] *engl. Historiker.*

Trafalgar [trə'fælgə] *Vorgebirge bei Gibraltar.* [*U.S.A.*]

Truman ['tru:mən] *Präsident der*

Turkey ['tə:ki] *die Türkei.*

Twain [twein] *amer. Autor.*

Tyrol ['tirəl] Tirol *n.*

United States of America [ju:'naitid 'steitsəvə'merikə] *die* Vereinigten Staaten von Amerika.

Utah ['ju:ta:] *Staat der U.S.A.*

Vancouver [væn'ku:və] *Stadt in Kanada.*

Vermont [və:'mɔnt] *Staat der* Vienna [vi'enə] Wien *n.* [*U.S.A.*]

Virginia [və'dʒinjə] Virginien *n (Staat der U.S.A.)*; West ~ *Staat der U.S.A.*

Wales [weilz] Wales *n.*

Warsaw ['wɔ:sɔ:] Warschau *n.*

Warwick(shire) ['wɔrik(ʃiə)] *Grafschaft in England.*

Washington ['wɔʃiŋtən] 1. *Präsident der U.S.A.*; 2. *Staat der U.S.A.*; 3. *Bundeshauptstadt der U.S.A.*

Wellington ['weliŋtən] *Hauptstadt von Neuseeland.*

Westmorcland ['westmələnd] *Grafschaft in England.*

White House ['wait 'haus] *das* Weiße Haus.

Whitman ['witmən] *amer. Dichter.*

Wilson ['wilsn] 1. *Präsident der U.S.A.*; 2. *brit. Premier.*

Wiltshire ['wiltʃiə] *Grafschaft in England.*

Wimbledon ['wimbldən] *Vorort von London.* [*Kanada.*]

Winnipeg ['winipeg] *Stadt in*

Wisconsin [wis'kɔnsin] *Staat der U.S.A.*

Worcester ['wustə] *Industriestadt in England*; a. ~*shire* ['-ʃiə] *Grafschaft in England.*

Wordsworth ['wə:dzwə:θ] *engl. Dichter.*

Yale University ['jeil ju:ni'və:siti] *amer. Universität.*

York [jɔ:k] *Stadt in England*; a. ~*shire* ['-ʃiə] *Grafschaft in England.*

Yugoslavia ['ju:gou'sla:vjə] Jugoslawien *n.*

American and British Abbreviations

abbr. *abbreviated* abgekürzt; *abbreviation* Abk., Abkürzung *f.*

A.B.C. *American Broadcasting Company* Amer. Rundfunkgesellschaft *f.*

A.C. *alternating current* Wechselstrom *m.*

A.E.C. *Atomic Energy Commission* Atomenergie-Kommission *f.*

AFL-CIO *American Federation of Labor & Congress of Industrial Organizations* (größter amer. Gewerkschaftsverband).

A.F.N. *American Forces Network* (Rundfunkanstalt der amer. Streitkräfte).

Ala. *Alabama.*

Alas. *Alaska.*

a.m. *ante meridiem* (lateinisch = before noon) vormittags.

A.P. *Associated Press* (amer. Nachrichtenbüro).

A.R.C. *American Red Cross* Amer. Rotes Kreuz.

Ariz. *Arizona.*

Ark. *Arkansas.*

arr. *arrival* Ank., Ankunft *f.*

B.A. *Bachelor of Arts* Bakkalaureus *m* der Philosophie.

B.B.C. *British Broadcasting Corporation* Brit. Rundfunkgesellschaft *f.*

B.E.A. *British European Airways* Brit.-Europäische Luftfahrtgesellschaft.

Beds. *Bedfordshire.*

Benelux *Belgium, Netherlands, Luxemburg* (Zollunion).

Berks. *Berkshire.*

B.F.N. *British Forces Network* (Sender der brit. Streitkräfte in Deutschland).

B.L. *Bachelor of Law* Bakkalaureus *m* des Rechts.

B.M. *Bachelor of Medicine* Bakkalaureus *m* der Medizin.

B.O.A.C. *British Overseas Airways Corporation* Brit. Übersee-Luftfahrtgesellschaft *f.*

B.R. *British Railways.*

Br(it). *Britain* Großbritannien *n*; *British* britisch.

B.S. *Bachelor of Science* Bakkalaureus *m* der Naturwissenschaften.

Bucks. *Buckinghamshire.*

C. *Celsius, centigrade.*

c. *cent(s)* Cent *m*; *circa* ca., ungefähr, zirka; *cubic* Kubik...

Cal(if). *California.*

Cambs. *Cambridgeshire.*

Can. *Canada* Kanada *n*; *Canadian* kanadisch.

cf. *confer* vgl., vergleiche.

Ches. *Cheshire.*

C.I.C. *Counter Intelligence Corps* (Spionageabwehrdienst der U.S.A.).

C.I.D. *Criminal Investigation Department* (brit. Kriminalpolizei).

Co. *Company* Gesellschaft *f*; *County* Grafschaft *f*, Kreis *m.*

c/o *care of* p.A., per Adresse, bei.

Col(o). *Colorado.*

Conn. *Connecticut.*

cp. *compare* vgl., vergleiche.

Cumb. *Cumberland.*

cwt. *hundredweight* (etwa 1) Zentner *m.*

d. *penny, pence.*

D.C. *direct current* Gleichstrom *m*; *District of Columbia* (mit der amer. Hauptstadt Washington).

Del. *Delaware.*

dep. *departure* Abf., Abfahrt *f.*

Dept. *Department* Abt., Abteilung *f.*

Derby. *Derbyshire.*

Devon. *Devonshire.*

Dors. *Dorsetshire.*

Dur(h). *Durham.*

dz. *dozen* Dutzend *n od. pl.*

E. *east* Ost(en *m*); *eastern* östlich; *English* englisch.

E.C. *East Central* (London) Mitte-Ost (Postbezirk).

ECOSOC *Economic and Social Council* Wirtschafts- und Sozialrat *m* (U.N.).

Ed., ed. *edition* Auflage *f*; *edited* hrsg., herausgegeben; *editor* Hrsg., Herausgeber *m.*

E.E.C. *European Economic Community* EWG, Europäische Wirtschaftsgemeinschaft.

E.F.T.A. *European Free Trade Association* EFTA, Europäische Freihandelsgemeinschaft od. -zone.

e.g. *exempli gratia* (lateinisch = for instance) z.B., zum Beispiel.

Enc. *enclosure(s)* Anlage(n *pl.*) *f.*

Ess. *Essex.*

F. *Fahrenheit.*

f. *fathom(s)* Faden *m*, Klafter *f, m, n*; *feminine* weiblich; *foot, pl.* feet Fuß *m od. pl.*; *following* folgend.

F.A.O. *Food and Agricultural Organization* Organisation *f* für Ernährung und Landwirtschaft (U.N.).

FBI *Federal Bureau of Investigation* (Bundeskriminalamt der U.S.A.).

fig. *figure(s)* Abb., Abbildung(en).

Fla. *Florida.* [pl.) f.]

F.O. *Foreign Office* brit. Auswärtiges Amt.

fr. *franc(s)* Frank(en *pl.*) *m.*

ft. *foot, pl.* feet Fuß *m od. pl.*

g. *gramme* g, Gramm *n*; *guinea* Guinee *f* (*21 Schilling*).
Ga. *Georgia.*
gal. *gallon* Gallone *f.*
G.A.T.T. *General Agreement on Tariffs and Trade* Allgemeines Zoll- und Handelsabkommen.
G.B. *Great Britain* Großbritannien *n.*
G.I. *government issue* von der Regierung ausgegeben; Staatseigentum *n; fig. der* amer. Soldat.
Glos. *Gloucestershire.*
G.P.O. *General Post Office* Haupt-⌉
gr. *gross* brutto. [postamt *n.*⌋
Gt.Br. *Great Britain* Großbritannien *n.*

h. *hour(s)* Std., Stunde(n *pl.*) *f.*
Hants. *Hampshire.*
H.C. *House of Commons* Unterhaus *n.*
Heref. *Herefordshire.*
Herts. *Hertfordshire.*
hf. *half* halb.
H.I. *Hawaiian Islands.*
H.L. *House of Lords* Oberhaus *n.*
H.M. *His* (*Her*) *Majesty* Seine (Ihre) Majestät.
H.M.S. *His* (*Her*) *Majesty's Service* Dienst *m*, ⅋ Dienstsache *f*; *His* (*Her*) *Majesty's Ship* Seiner (Ihrer) Majestät Schiff *n.*
H.O. *Home Office brit.* Innenministerium *n.* [stärke *f.*⌋
H.P., h.p. *horse-power* PS, Pferde-⌋
H.Q., Hq. *Headquarters* Stab(squartier *n*) *m*, Hauptquartier *n.*
H.R. *House of Representatives* Repräsentantenhaus *n* (*der U.S.A.*).
H.R.H. *His* (*Her*) *Royal Highness* Seine (Ihre) Königliche Hoheit *f.*
Hunts. *Huntingdonshire.*

Ia. *Iowa.*
I.C.B.M. *intercontinental ballistic missile* interkontinentaler ballistischer Flugkörper.
I.D. *Intelligence Department* Nachrichtenamt *n.*
Id(a). *Idaho.* [d.h., das heißt.⌋
i.e. *id est* (*lateinisch = that is to say*)⌋
Ill. *Illinois.*
I.M.F. *International Monetary Fund* Weltwährungsfonds *m.*
in. *inch(es)* Zoll *m od. pl.* [gen.⌋
Inc. *Incorporated* (amtlich) eingetra-⌋
Ind. *Indiana.*
I.O.C. *International Olympic Committee* Internationales Olympisches Komitee.
Ir. *Ireland* Irland *n*; *Irish* irisch.
I.R.C. *International Red Cross* Internationales Rotes Kreuz.

J.P. *Justice of the Peace* Friedensrichter *m.*

Kan(s). *Kansas.*
k.o. *knock(ed) out* Boxen: k.o. (ge-) schlagen; *fig.* erledigen (erledigt).
Ky. *Kentucky.*

£ *pound sterling* Pfund *n* Sterling.
La. *Louisiana.*
Lancs. *Lancashire.* [wicht).⌋
lb. *pound(s)* Pfund *n od. pl.* (Ge-⌋
L.C. *letter of credit* Kreditbrief [*m.*⌋
Leics. *Leicestershire.*
Lincs. *Lincolnshire.*
LP *long-playing* Langspiel...(*Platte*).
L.P. *Labour Party* (*brit. Arbeiterpartei*). [tung.⌋
Ltd. *limited* mit beschränkter Haf-⌋

m. *male* männlich; *metre* m, Meter *n*, m; *mile* Meile *f*; *minute* Min., Minute *f.* [Philosophie.⌋
M.A. *Master of Arts* Magister *m* der⌋
Mass. *Massachusetts.*
M.D. *Medicinae Doctor* (*lateinisch = Doctor of Medicine*) Dr. med., Doktor *m* der Medizin.
Md. *Maryland.*
Me. *Maine.*
mi. *mile* Meile *f.*
Mich. *Michigan.*
Middx. *Middlesex.*
Minn. *Minnesota.*
Miss. *Mississippi.*
Mo. *Missouri.*
M.O. *money order* Postanweisung *f.*
Mon. *Monmouthshire.*
Mont. *Montana.*
MP, M.P. *Member of Parliament* Parlamentsabgeordnete *m*; *Military Police* Militärpolizei *f.*
m.p.h. *miles per hour* Stundenmei-⌋
Mr *Mister* Herr *m.* [len *pl.*⌋
Mrs *Mistress* Frau *f.*
Mt. *Mount* Berg *m.*

N. *north* Nord(en *m*); *northern* nörd-⌉
n. *noon* Mittag *m.* lich.⌋
NASA *National Aeronautics and Space Administration* (*amer. Luftfahrt- und Raumforschungsbehörde*).
NATO *North Atlantic Treaty Organization* Nordatlantikpakt-Organisation *f.*
N.C. *North Carolina.*
N.D(ak). *North Dakota.*
Neb(r). *Nebraska.*
Nev. *Nevada.*
N.H. *New Hampshire.*
N.H.S. *National Health Service* Nationaler Gesundheitsdienst (*brit. Krankenversicherung*).
N.J. *New Jersey.*
N.M(ex). *New Mexico.*
Norf. *Norfolk.*
Northants. *Northamptonshire.*
Northumb. *Northumberland.*
Notts. *Nottinghamshire.*
nt. *net* netto.
N.Y. *New York.* [York.⌋
N.Y.C. *New York City* Stadt *f* New⌋

O. *Ohio*; *order* Auftrag *m.*
O.A.S. *Organization of American States* Organisation *f* amerikanischer Staaten.

O.E.E.C. *Organization of European Economic Co-operation* Organisation *f* für europäische wirtschaftliche Zusammenarbeit.
Okla. *Oklahoma.*
Ore(g). *Oregon.*
Oxon. *Oxfordshire.*

Pa. *Pennsylvania.*
P.A.A. *Pan-American Airways* Panamer. Luftfahrtgesellschaft *f.*
P.C. *police constable* Schutzmann *m.*
p.c. *per cent* %, Prozent *n od. pl.*
pd. *paid* bezahlt.
P.E.N., *mst* **PEN Club** *Poets, Playwrights, Editors, Essayists, and Novelists* Pen-Club *m, (Internationale Vereinigung von Dichtern, Dramatikern, Redakteuren, Essayisten und Romanschriftstellern).*
Penn(a). *Pennsylvania.*
Ph.D. *Philosophiae Doctor (lateinisch = Doctor of Philosophy)* Dr. phil., Doktor *m* der Philosophie.
p.m. *post meridiem (lateinisch = after noon)* nachmittags, abends.
P.O. *Post Office* Postamt *n; postal order* Postanweisung *f.*
P.O.B. *Post Office Box* Postschließfach *n.*
P.S. *Postscript* P.S., Nachschrift *f.*
P.T.O., **p.t.o.** *please turn over* b.w., bitte wenden.
PX *Post Exchange (Verkaufsläden der amer. Streitkräfte).*

R.A.F. *Royal Air Force* Königlich-Brit. Luftwaffe *f.*
Rd. *Road* Straße *f.*
ref(c). *(In) reference (to)* (in) Bezug *m* (auf); Empfehlung *f.*
regd. *registered* eingetragen; & eingeschrieben. [tonne *f.*)
reg. tn. *register ton* RT, Register-)
resp. *respective(ly)* bzw., beziehungsweise.
ret. *retired* i.R., im Ruhestand.
Rev. *Reverend* Ehrwürden.
R.I. *Rhode Island.* Marine *f.*)
R.N. *Royal Navy* Königlich-Brit.)
R.R. *Railroad Am.* Eisenbahn *f.*
Rutland. *Rutlandshire.*
Ry. *Railway* Eisenbahn *f.*

S. *south* Süd(en *m*); *southern* südlich.
s. *second(s)* Sek., Sekunde(n *pl.*) *f*; *shilling(s)* Schilling *m od. pl.*
$ *dollar* Dollar *m.*
S.A. *South Africa* Südafrika *n; South America* Südamerika *n.*
Salop *Shropshire.*
S.C. *South Carolina; Security Council* Sicherheitsrat *m (U.N.).*
S.D(ak). *South Dakota.*
SEATO *South East Asia Treaty Organization* Südostasienpakt-Organisation *f.*
sh. *shilling(s)* Schilling *m od. pl.*
Soc. *society* Gesellschaft *f*; Verein *m.*

Som. *Somersetshire.*
Sq. *Square* Platz *m.*
sq. *square* ... Quadrat...
Staffs. *Staffordshire.*
St(.) *Saint* ... Sankt ...; *Station* Bahnhof *m; Street* Straße *f.*
Suff. *Suffolk.*
suppl. *supplement* Nachtrag *m.*
Sur. *Surrey.*
Suss. *Sussex.*

t. *ton(s)* Tonne(n *pl.*) *f.*
Tenn. *Tennessee.*
Tex. *Texas.*
T.M.O. *telegraph money order* telegraphische Geldanweisung.
T.O. *Telegraph (Telephone) Office* Telegraphen- (Fernsprech)amt *n*
T.U. *Trade(s) Union(s)* Gewerkschaft(en *pl.*) *f.*
T.U.C. *Trade(s) Union Congress* brit. Gewerkschaftsverband *m.*

U.K. *United Kingdom* Vereinigtes Königreich *(England, Schottland, Wales und Nordirland).*
U.N. *United Nations* Vereinte Nationen *pl.*
UNESCO *United Nations Educational, Scientific, and Cultural Organization* Organisation *f* der Vereinten Nationen für Wissenschaft, Erziehung und Kultur.
U.N.S.C. *United Nations Security Council* Sicherheitsrat *m* der Vereinten Nationen.
U.P.I. *United Press International (amer. Nachrichtenagentur).*
U.S.(A.) *United States (of America)* Vereinigte Staaten *pl.* (von Ame-)
Ut. *Utah.* [rika.))

Va. *Virginia.*
vol(s). *volume(s)* Band *m* (Bände)
Vt. *Vermont.* [*pl.*).)
V.T.O.(L.) *vertical take-off (and landing) (aircraft)* Senkrechtstart(er) *m.*

W. *west* West(en *m*); *western* west-)
War. *Warwickshire.* [lich.)
Wash. *Washington.*
W.C. *West Central* (London) Mitte-West *(Postbezirk).*
W.F.T.U. *World Federation of Trade Unions* Weltgewerkschaftsbund *m.*
W.H.O. *World Health Organization* Weltgesundheitsorganisation *f (U.N.).*
W.I. *West Indies* Westindien *n.*
Wilts. *Wiltshire.*
Wis. *Wisconsin.*
Worcs. *Worcestershire.*
wt. *weight* Gewicht *n.*
W.Va. *West Virginia.*
Wyo. *Wyoming.*

yd. *yard(s)* Elle(n *pl.*) *f.*
Yorks. *Yorkshire.*

German Weights and Measures

I. Linear Measure

1 mm   *Millimeter* millimet|re, *Am.* -er = 0.039 inch

1 cm   *Zentimeter* centimet|re, *Am.* -er = 10 mm = 0.394 inch

1 m   *Meter* met|re, *Am.* -er = 100 cm = 1.094 yards = 3.281 feet

1 km   *Kilometer* kilomet|re, *Am.* -er = 1000 m = 0.621 mile

1 sm   *Seemeile* nautical mile = 1852 m

II. Square Measure

1 mm²   *Quadratmillimeter* square millimet|re, *Am.* -er = 0.002 square inch

1 cm²   *Quadratzentimeter* square centimet|re, *Am.* -er = 100 mm² = 0.155 square inch

1 m²   *Quadratmeter* square met|re, *Am.* -er = 10000 cm² = 1.196 square yards = 10.764 square feet

1 a   *Ar* are = 100 m² = 119.599 square yards

1 ha   *Hektar* hectare = 100 a = 2.471 acres

1 km²   *Quadratkilometer* square kilomet|re, *Am.* -er = 100 ha = 247.11 acres = 0.386 square mile

III. Cubic Measure

1 cm³   *Kubikzentimeter* cubic centimet|re, *Am.* -er = 1000 mm³ = 0.061 cubic inch

1 m³   *Kubikmeter* cubic met|re, *Am.* -er = 1000000 cm³ = 35.315 cubic feet = 1.308 cubic yards

1 RT   *Registertonne* register ton = 2,832 m³ = 100 cubic feet

IV. Measure of Capacity

1 l   *Liter* lit|re, *Am.* -er = 1.760 pints = *U.S.* 1.057 liquid quarts *or* 0.906 dry quart

1 hl   *Hektoliter* hectolit|re, *Am.* -er = 100 l = 2.75 bushels = *U.S.* 26.418 gallons

V. Weight

1 g   *Gramm* gram(me) = 15.432 grains

1 Pfd.   *Pfund* pound (German) = 500 g = 1.102 pounds avdp.

1 kg   *Kilogramm* kilogram(me) = 1000 g = 2.205 pounds avdp. = 2.679 pounds troy

1 Ztr.   *Zentner* centner = 100 Pfd. = 0.984 hundredweight = 1.102 *U.S.* hundredweights

1 dz   *Doppelzentner* = 100 kg = 1.968 hundredweights = 2.204 *U.S.* hundredweights

1 t   *Tonne* ton = 1000 kg = 0.984 long ton = *U.S.* 1.102 short tons

American and British Weights and Measures

1. Linear Measure

1 inch (in.) = 2,54 cm
1 foot (ft)
  = 12 inches = 30,48 cm
1 yard (yd)
  = 3 feet = 91,439 cm
1 perch (p.)
  = 5½ yards = 5,029 m
1 mile (m.)
  = 1,760 yards = 1,609 km

2. Nautical Measure

1 fathom (f., fm)
  = 6 feet = 1,829 m
1 nautical mile
  = 6,080 feet = 1853,18 m

3. Square Measure

1 square inch (sq. in.)
  = 6,452 cm²
1 square foot (sq. ft)
  = 144 square inches
  = 929,029 cm²
1 square yard (sq. yd)
  = 9 square feet = 8361,26 cm²
1 square perch (sq. p.)
  = 30¼ square yards = 25,293 m²
1 rood
  = 40 square perches = 10,117 a
1 acre (a.) = 4 roods = 40,47 a
1 square mile
  = 640 acres = 258,998 ha

4. Cubic Measure

1 cubic inch (cu. in.)
  = 16,387 cm³
1 cubic foot (cu. ft)
  = 1,728 cubic inches = 0,028 m³
1 cubic yard (cu. yd)
  = 27 cubic feet = 0,765 m³
1 register ton (reg. ton)
  = 100 cubic feet = 2,832 m³

5. Measure of Capacity
Dry and Liquid Measure

1 British or imperial gill (gl, gi.)
  = 0,142 l
1 British or imperial pint (pt)
  = 4 gills = 0,568 l
1 British or imperial quart (qt)
  = 2 pints = 1,136 l
1 British or imp. gallon (imp. gal.)
  = 4 imperial quarts = 4,546 l

Dry Measure

1 British or imperial peck (pk)
  = 2 imperial gallons = 9,092 l
1 Brit. or imp. bushel (bu., bus.)
  = 8 imperial gallons = 36,366 l

1 Brit. or imp. quarter (qr)
  = 8 imperial bushels = 290,935 l

Liquid Measure

1 Brit. or imp. barrel (bbl, bl)
  = 36 imperial gallons = 163,656 l

      *

1 U.S. dry pint = 0,551 l
1 U.S. dry quart
  = 2 dry pints = 1,101 l
1 U.S. dry gallon
  = 4 dry quarts = 4,405 l
1 U.S. peck
  = 2 dry gallons = 8,809 l
1 U.S. bushel
  = 8 dry gallons = 35,238 l
1 U.S. gill = 0,118 l
1 U.S. liquid pint
  = 4 gills = 0,473 l
1 U.S. liquid quart
  = 2 liquid pints = 0,946 l
1 U.S. liquid gallon
  = 8 liquid pints = 3,785 l
1 U.S. barrel
  = 3½ liquid gallons = 119,228 l
1 U.S. barrel petroleum
  = 42 liquid gallons = 158,97 l

6. Avoirdupois Weight

1 grain (gr.) = 0,065 g
1 dram (dr.)
  = 27.344 grains = 1,772 g
1 ounce (oz.)
  = 16 drams = 28,35 g
1 pound (lb.)
  = 16 ounces = 453,592 g
1 quarter (qr)
  = 28 pounds = 12,701 kg
  (U.S.A. 25 pounds)
  = 11,339 kg)
1 hundredweight (cwt.)
  = 112 pounds
  = 50,802 kg (U.S.A. 100 pounds
  = 45,359 kg)
1 ton (t.)
  (a. long ton) = 20 hundredweights = 1016,05 kg (U.S.A.,
  a. short ton, = 907,185 kg)
1 stone (st.) = 14 pounds = 6,35 kg

7. Troy Weight

1 grain = 0,065 g
1 pennyweight (dwt.)
  = 24 grains = 1,555 g
1 ounce
  = 20 pennyweights = 31,103 g
1 pound = 12 ounces = 373,242 g